Lt. Lyle Raymond Rhodes, Jr.
Room 309
Alpha Company
W. M. A.
Lexington, Mo.

FOURTH EDITION

THE LITERATURE OF ENGLAND

AN ANTHOLOGY AND A HISTORY

VOLUME TWO, from the Dawn of the Romantic Movement to the Present Day

GEORGE B. WOODS, American University

HOMER A. WATT, New York University

GEORGE K. ANDERSON, Brown University

KARL J. HOLZKNECHT, New York University

SCOTT, FORESMAN AND COMPANY, Chicago, Atlanta, Dallas, Palo Alto, Fair Lawn, N. J.

Copyright © 1958 by Scott, Foresman and Company
Previous copyright 1936, 1941, 1948 by Scott, Foresman and Company

PRINTED IN THE UNITED STATES OF AMERICA

Permission for the reprinting of selections in copyright has been secured from the respective publishers. Specific acknowledgment of the courtesy of these publishers is given on the pages where the selections appear.

Contents OF THE FOURTH EDITION

CHAPTER 6 REVOLUTION AND ROMANCE
Romanticism in the Ascendant, 1760-1832

Introductory Essay 1	Sonnet to Mrs. Unwin 82
	The Castaway 82
The Approach to Romanticism	Robert Burns (1759-1796) 83
	Mary Morison 85
James Thomson (1700-1748) 32	To Davie (SECOND EPISTLE) 85
from *The Seasons* 33	Epistle to J. Lapraik, an Old Scottish Bard . 86
from *Winter* 33	Holy Willie's Prayer 88
Rule, Britannia! 39	The Jolly Beggars 89
from *The Castle of Indolence* 39	The Cotter's Saturday Night 95
from CANTO I 39	To a Mouse 98
Thomas Gray (1716-1771) 46	Address to the Deil 99
Ode on a Distant Prospect of Eton College . 48	To a Mountain Daisy 100
Sonnet (ON THE DEATH OF RICHARD WEST) . 49	To a Louse 101
Ode on the Death of a Favorite Cat . . . 49	Of A' the Airts 102
Elegy Written in a Country Churchyard . 50	Auld Lang Syne 102
The Progress of Poesy 52	John Anderson, My Jo 102
The Bard 55	Sweet Afton 102
The Fatal Sisters 58	Willie Brew'd a Peck o' Maut 103
Sketch of His Own Character 59	To Mary in Heaven 103
Letters 59	Tam o' Shanter 104
TO HIS MOTHER 59	Bonie Doon 107
TO RICHARD WEST 60	Ae Fond Kiss 107
TO HIS MOTHER 61	Highland Mary 108
TO HORACE WALPOLE 62	Duncan Gray 108
TO MR. STONHEWER 63	Scots, Wha Hae 109
TO DR. WHARTON 64	A Red, Red Rose 109
William Collins (1721-1759) 66	A Man's a Man for A' That 110
Dirge in *Cymbeline* 68	O, Wert Thou in the Cauld Blast . . 110
Ode (WRITTEN IN THE BEGINNING OF THE YEAR	William Blake (1757-1827) 111
1746) 68	from *Poetical Sketches* 112
Ode to Simplicity 68	TO THE EVENING STAR 112
Ode to Evening 69	MY SILKS AND FINE ARRAY 112
The Passions 70	from *Songs of Innocence* 113
Ode on the Death of Mr. Thomson . . . 72	INTRODUCTION 113
William Cowper (1731-1800) 73	THE LAMB 114
from *Olney Hymns* 75	THE LITTLE BLACK BOY 114
WALKING WITH GOD 75	HOLY THURSDAY 114
PRAISE FOR THE FOUNTAIN OPENED . 75	A CRADLE SONG 115
On the Loss of the *Royal George* . . . 75	THE DIVINE IMAGE 115
from *The Task* 76	A DREAM 115
from BOOK I. THE SOFA 76	from *Songs of Experience* 116
from BOOK II. THE TIME-PIECE . . . 78	THE FLY 116
from BOOK III. THE GARDEN 79	THE TIGER 116
On the Receipt of My Mother's Picture . 79	THE CLOD AND THE PEBBLE 116
To Mary 81	HOLY THURSDAY 116
	A POISON TREE 117

THE GARDEN OF LOVE	117
A LITTLE BOY LOST	117
LONDON	117
THE CHIMNEY-SWEEPER	117
Stanza from *Auguries of Innocence*	118
Thel's Motto	118

The Romantic Triumph in Poetry

William Wordsworth (1770-1850)	118
Lines Written in Early Spring	121
Lines (COMPOSED A FEW MILES ABOVE TINTERN ABBEY)	121
Strange Fits of Passion Have I Known	123
She Dwelt Among the Untrodden Ways	124
I Traveled Among Unknown Men	124
Three Years She Grew in Sun and Shower	124
A Slumber Did My Spirit Seal	125
from *The Prelude*	125
BOOK 1. INTRODUCTION—CHILDHOOD AND SCHOOL-TIME	125
BOOK 5. BOOKS	134
Michael	142
My Heart Leaps Up When I Behold	148
Resolution and Independence	148
Composed upon Westminster Bridge	151
Composed by the Seaside, Near Calais	151
It Is a Beauteous Evening, Calm and Free	151
On the Extinction of the Venetian Republic	151
London, 1802	152
To the Daisy (With little here to do or see)	152
To the Daisy (Bright Flower!)	153
To a Highland Girl	153
The Solitary Reaper	154
To the Cuckoo	154
She Was a Phantom of Delight	155
I Wandered Lonely as a Cloud	155
Ode to Duty	155
To a Skylark (Up with me!)	156
Elegiac Stanzas	157
Character of the Happy Warrior	158
Nuns Fret Not	159
The World Is Too Much with Us	159
Ode on Intimations of Immortality	160
Thought of a Briton on the Subjugation of Switzerland	162
Scorn Not the Sonnet	163
If Thou Indeed Derive Thy Light from Heaven	163
Most Sweet It Is with Unuplifted Eyes	163
Samuel Taylor Coleridge (1772-1834)	163
The Rime of the Ancient Mariner	166
Christabel	175
Kubla Khan; or, a Vision in a Dream	184
France: an Ode	185
Dejection: an Ode	187
Youth and Age	189
Work without Hope	189
Epitaph	190
Sir Walter Scott (1771-1832)	190
from *The Lay of the Last Minstrel*	192
ROSABELLE	192
from *Marmion*	192
WHERE SHALL THE LOVER REST	192
LOCHINVAR	193
Hunting Song	194
from *The Lady of the Lake*	194
HARP OF THE NORTH	194
SOLDIER, REST! THY WARFARE O'ER	195
BOAT SONG	196
CORONACH	196
SOLDIER'S SONG	197
HARP OF THE NORTH, FAREWELL!	197
Proud Maisie	198
Bonny Dundee	198
Glee for King Charles	199
George Noel Gordon, Lord Byron (1788-1824)	200
When We Two Parted	202
from *English Bards and Scotch Reviewers*	203
Maid of Athens, Ere We Part	205
She Walks in Beauty	205
The Destruction of Sennacherib	205
Stanzas for Music (There's not a joy)	206
Stanzas for Music (There be none of Beauty's daughters)	207
Sonnet on Chillon	207
The Prisoner of Chillon	207
Childe Harold's Pilgrimage	212
from CANTO III	212
from CANTO IV	219
To Thomas Moore	224
So We'll Go No More A-Roving	224
from *Don Juan*	224
DEDICATION	225
from CANTO I	227
from CANTO II	228
from CANTO III. THE ISLES OF GREECE	235
from CANTO IV	239
When a Man Hath No Freedom	247
The World Is a Bundle of Hay	247
Who Killed John Keats?	247
Stanzas Written on the Road Between Florence and Pisa	247
On This Day I Complete My Thirty-Sixth Year	247
Percy Bysshe Shelley (1792-1822)	248
Mutability (We are as clouds)	251
Hymn to Intellectual Beauty	251
Ozymandias	253
Stanzas (WRITTEN IN DEJECTION, NEAR NAPLES)	253
Song to the Men of England	254
England in 1819	254
Ode to the West Wind	255
The Indian Serenade	256
Songs from *Prometheus Unbound*	256
ASIA	256
DEMOGORGON	257
The Cloud	257
To a Skylark (Hail to thee)	258
Time Long Past	260
Song (Rarely, rarely, comest thou)	260
To Night	261
To— (Music, when soft voices die)	261
Time	261

CONTENTS

Mutability (The flower that smiles today) . 261
A Lament 262
Adonais 262
Songs from *Hellas* 270
    WORLDS ON WORLDS ARE ROLLING EVER . 270
    FINAL CHORUS FROM *Hellas* 271
Remembrance 272
To— (One word is too often profaned) . 272
Lines (When the lamp is shattered) . . 272
A Dirge (Rough wind) 273
John Keats (1795-1821) 273
  On First Looking into Chapman's Homer . 275
  To One Who Has Been Long in City Pent . 275
  Addressed to Haydon 275
  On Seeing the Elgin Marbles 275
  On the Sea 276
  When I Have Fears That I May Cease to Be . 276
  Lines on the Mermaid Tavern 276
  Robin Hood 276
  In a Drear-Nighted December 277
  Proem from *Endymion* 278
  Fancy 279
  Ode (Bards of Passion and of Mirth) . 280
  Ode on Melancholy 280
  Ode on a Grecian Urn 281
  La Belle Dame sans Merci 282
  On Fame 282
  Another on Fame 283
  Ode to Psyche 283
  Ode to a Nightingale 284
  The Eve of St. Agnes 285
  To Autumn 291
  Bright Star! Would I Were Steadfast as Thou Art 292
  Letters 292
    TO JOHN HAMILTON REYNOLDS . . . 292
    TO JAMES AUGUSTUS HESSEY . . . 294
    TO JOHN HAMILTON REYNOLDS . . . 294
    TO CHARLES BROWN 295

Minor Romantic Poets

Robert Southey (1774-1843) 300
  The Battle of Blenheim 300
  The Old Man's Comforts 301
  The Inchcape Rock 301
Thomas Moore (1779-1852) 302
  Oh, Breathe Not His Name! 302
  The Harp That Once Through Tara's Halls . 303
  'Tis the Last Rose of Summer 303
  The Minstrel Boy 303
  Believe Me, If All Those Endearing Young Charms 303
James Henry Leigh Hunt (1784-1859) . . 304
  Abou Ben Adhem and the Angel . . . 304
  The Glove and the Lions 304
  Rondeau 305
  The Fish, the Man, and the Spirit . . . 305
Thomas Hood (1799-1845) 306
  Silence 306
  Ruth 306
  The Song of the Shirt 306
  The Bridge of Sighs 307
Thomas Lovell Beddoes (1803-1849) . . . 309
  Poor Old Pilgrim Misery 309
  Song (How many times do I love thee, dear?) 309
  To Sea, To Sea! 309
  Dirge (If thou wilt ease thine heart) . . 309
  Lady, Was It Fair of Thee? 309
  Song (Old Adam, the carrion crow) . . 310
  Dream-Pedlary 310
Walter Savage Landor (1775-1864) . . . 311
  Rose Aylmer 311
  Lyrics to Ianthe 311
    Away my verse; and never fear . . 311
    When Helen first saw wrinkles in her face 311
    Past ruined Ilion Helen lives . . . 311
    Ianthe! you are called to cross the sea! . 311
    Pleasure! why thus desert the heart . 312
    Mild is the parting year, and sweet . 312
    It often comes into my head . . . 312
    Why, why repine, my pensive friend . 312
    Years, many parti-colored years . . 312
    Well I remember how you smiled . 312
  Dirce 312
  One Year Ago 312
  Yes, I Write Verses Now and Then . . 313
  The Leaves Are Falling; So Am I . . 313
  Is It Not Better 313
  I Know Not Whether I Am Proud . . 313
  Iphigeneia and Agamemnon 313
  To Youth 314
  To Age 315
  Death Stands Above Me 315
  On His Seventy-Fifth Birthday . . . 315
  To My Ninth Decade 315

Romantic Prose: Revolutionary, Critical, and Imaginative

Percy Bysshe Shelley (1792-1822) . . . 315
  Declaration of Rights 315
William Wordsworth (1770-1850) . . . 318
  from *Preface* to *Lyrical Ballads* . . . 318
Samuel Taylor Coleridge (1772-1834) . . 328
  from *Biographia Literaria* 328
  Characteristics of Shakespeare's Dramas . 332
Charles Lamb (1775-1834) 337
  Dream-Children: A Reverie 338
  The Praise of Chimney-Sweepers . . . 341
  Poor Relations 345
  The Superannuated Man 349
  The Two Races of Men 353
  Letters 357
    TO SAMUEL TAYLOR COLERIDGE . . 357
    TO WILLIAM WORDSWORTH 358
    TO CHARLES COWDEN CLARKE . . . 358
    TO THOMAS MANNING 359
William Hazlitt (1778-1830) 360
  On Going a Journey 361
  from *My First Acquaintance with Poets* . 367
    MEETING WITH COLERIDGE **367**

CONTENTS

Thomas De Quincey (1785-1859) 374
   Confessions of an English Opium Eater . . 375
     from PRELIMINARY CONFESSIONS . . . 375
     On the Knocking at the Gate in *Macbeth* . 387
   from *Suspiria de Profundis* 389
   LEVANA AND OUR LADIES OF SORROW . . . 390
   from *The Poetry of Pope* 394
   LITERATURE OF KNOWLEDGE AND LITERATURE OF POWER 394

CHAPTER 7   DEMOCRACY, SCIENCE, AND INDUSTRIALISM   *The Victorian Age, 1832-1880*

INTRODUCTORY ESSAY 399

Prose Critics of Art and Life

Thomas Babington Macaulay (1800-1859) . . 427
   from *History* 428
   The Revolt Against Classicism 439
John Henry Newman (1801-1890) 445
   from *The Idea of a University* 446
     DISCOURSE V. KNOWLEDGE ITS OWN END . 447
     FROM DISCOURSE VIII. THE DEFINITION OF A GENTLEMAN 458
   from *Apologia pro Vita Sua* 460
     [VISIT TO ITALY] 460
Thomas Carlyle (1795-1881) 464
   from *Sartor Resartus* 465
     THE EVERLASTING NO 466
     CENTER OF INDIFFERENCE 470
     THE EVERLASTING YEA 476
   from *The French Revolution* 482
     THE WHIFF OF GRAPESHOT 482
   from *Past and Present* 485
     THE ENGLISH 486
     LABOR 491
     ARISTOCRACIES 493
John Ruskin (1819-1900) 501
   from *Modern Painters* 503
     EFFECT OF THE SEA AFTER A STORM . . 503
     THE GRAND STYLE 505
     THE PATHETIC FALLACY 507
   from *Unto This Last* 515
     ESSAY I. THE ROOTS OF HONOR . . . 515
   from *The Relation of Art to Morals* . . . 524
Matthew Arnold (1822-1888) 527
   The Function of Criticism at the Present Time 529
   from *Culture and Anarchy* 544
     HEBRAISM AND HELLENISM 544
   from *The Study of Poetry* 552
   Milton 558
Thomas Henry Huxley (1825-1895) 561
   On the Advisableness of Improving Natural Knowledge 562
   Science and Culture 571
Walter Horatio Pater (1839-1894) 580
   from *Leonardo da Vinci* 581
     LA GIOCONDA 581
   from *Studies in the History of the Renaissance* 583
     CONCLUSION 583
   Romanticism 585

Poets of Faith and Doubt

Alfred, Lord Tennyson (1809-1892) 593
   The Poet 596
   The Lady of Shalott 597
   Oenone 599
   The Palace of Art 603
   The Lotos-Eaters 608
   You Ask Me, Why, Though Ill at Ease . . 611
   Of Old Sat Freedom on the Heights . . . 611
   Ulysses 611
   Locksley Hall 613
   Locksley Hall Sixty Years After 618
   Break, Break, Break 626
   Songs from *The Princess* 626
     SWEET AND LOW 626
     THE SPLENDOR FALLS ON CASTLE WALLS . 627
     TEARS, IDLE TEARS 627
     HOME THEY BROUGHT HER WARRIOR DEAD . 627
     ASK ME NO MORE 627
     NOW SLEEPS THE CRIMSON PETAL . . . 628
     COME DOWN, O MAID 628
   from *In Memoriam* 628
     PROLOGUE, Sections 1, 11, 15, 19, 27, 28, 30, 54, 55, 56, 64, 73, 78, 87, 95, 96, 104, 105, 106, 126, 130, 131 629
   The Eagle 637
   The Charge of the Light Brigade 637
   The Song of the Brook 637
   Lyrics from *Maud* 638
     COME INTO THE GARDEN, MAUD . . . 638
     O THAT 'TWERE POSSIBLE 639
     OH, LET THE SOLID GROUND 640
   In the Valley of Cauteretz 641
   The Flower 641
   Northern Farmer, OLD STYLE 641
   Northern Farmer, NEW STYLE 643
   Wages 645
   The Higher Pantheism 645
   Flower in the Crannied Wall 646
   from *The Idylls of the King* 646
     THE COMING OF ARTHUR 646
   By an Evolutionist 654
   Crossing the Bar 654
Robert Browning (1812-1889) 655
   Songs from *Pippa Passes* 657
     All service ranks the same with God . . 657
     The year's at the spring 657

CONTENTS

Overhead the tree-tops meet 658
Cavalier Tunes 658
   1. MARCHING ALONG 658
   2. GIVE A ROUSE 658
   3. BOOT AND SADDLE 659
My Last Duchess 659
In a Gondola 660
The Laboratory 663
"How They Brought the Good News from
    Ghent to Aix" 664
The Lost Leader 666
Meeting at Night 666
Parting at Morning 667
Home-Thoughts, from Abroad 667
Home-Thoughts, from the Sea 667
The Glove 667
The Bishop Orders His Tomb at Saint
    Praxed's Church 670
Saul 672
A Toccata of Galuppi's 679
"De Gustibus—" 681
My Star 681
Respectability 681
Memorabilia 682
A Grammarian's Funeral 682
"Childe Roland to the Dark Tower Came" . 684
Fra Lippo Lippi 688
Andrea Del Sarto 694
Rabbi Ben Ezra 698
Caliban upon Setebos 701
Confessions 705
Prospice 706
Apparent Failure 706
Proem to The Ring and the Book . . . 707
House 707
Why I am a Liberal 708
Epilogue to Asolando 708
Elizabeth Barrett Browning (1806-1861) . . 709
   The Cry of the Children 710
   from Sonnets from the Portuguese . . . 713
   Sonnets 1, 3, 7, 8, 14, 26, 35, 41, 43 . . 713
John Henry Newman (1801-1890) 715
   The Sign of the Cross 715
   The Pillar of the Cloud 715
   from The Dream of Gerontius 715
     SOUL 716
     ANGEL 716
Emily Brontë (1818-1848) 716
   Remembrance 717
   Song 718
   To Imagination 718
   Sympathy 718
   The Night Is Darkening 719
   Fall, Leaves 719
   A Little While 719
   The Old Stoic 720
   Often Rebuked, Yet Always Back Returning . 720
   No Coward Soul Is Mine 720
Arthur Hugh Clough (1819-1861) . . . 721
   Qua Cursum Ventus 721

from Dipsychus 722
   "THERE IS NO GOD," THE WICKED SAITH . . 722
   THIS WORLD IS VERY ODD WE SEE . . . 722
   Say Not the Struggle Naught Availeth . . 723
   "What Went Ye Out for to See?" . . . 723
   Qui Laborat, Orat 723
   Hope Evermore and Believe! 724
   The Latest Decalogue 724
   Ite Domum Saturae, Venit Hesperus . . 725
   In a London Square 725
   All Is Well 726
Matthew Arnold (1822-1888) 726
   Quiet Work 726
   To a Friend 726
   Shakespeare 726
   In Harmony with Nature 727
   The Forsaken Merman 727
   Memorial Verses 729
   Isolation. To Marguerite 730
   Self-Dependence 731
   The Buried Life 731
   Lines (WRITTEN IN KENSINGTON GARDENS) . 732
   Morality 733
   Philomela 733
   Requiescat 734
   The Scholar-Gypsy 734
   Thyrsis 739
   Austerity of Poetry 743
   Dover Beach 744
   The Last Word 744
   Pis-Aller 744
   Rugby Chapel 745
   Geist's Grave 747
Christina Rossetti (1830-1894) 748
   Song (When I am dead) 749
   The Three Enemies 749
   The Heart Knoweth Its Own Bitterness . 750
   A Better Resurrection 751
   An Apple Gathering 751
   Advent 751
   Uphill 752
   Goblin Market 752
   from Sing-Song 759
     "If I were a queen" 759
     Mother shake the cherry-tree . . . 759
     The wind has such a rainy sound . . 759
     Fly away, fly away over the sea . . . 759
     Who has seen the wind? 759
     Boats sail on the rivers 759
   from Monna Innominata 760
James Thomson (1834-1882) 760
   Once in a Saintly Passion 761
   For I Must Sing of All I Feel and Know . 761
   Two Sonnets 762
   The Fire That Filled My Heart of Old . 762
   Give a Man a Horse He Can Ride . . 762
   Let My Voice Ring Out and Over the Earth . 763
   from The City of Dreadful Night (1, 4, 14, 21) 763
George Meredith (1828-1909) 768
   Juggling Jerry 769

viii CONTENTS

from *Modern Love* (Poems 1,16,29,47,48,50) 771
The Lark Ascending 772
Lucifer in Starlight 773
On the Danger of War 774
Meditation under Stars 774
Song in the Songless 775
Youth in Age 775

Poets Aesthetic and Pagan

Edward Fitzgerald (1809-1883) 775
  The Rubáiyát of Omar Khayyám 776
Dante Gabriel Rossetti (1828-1882) . . . 783
  The Blessed Damozel 784
  My Sister's Sleep 786
  The Sea-Limits 787
  Sister Helen 787
  The Song of the Bower 791
  The Ballad of Dead Ladies 792
  Troy Town 792
  Autumn Song 794
  from *The House of Life* 794
    THE SONNET 794
    18. GENIUS IN BEAUTY 794
    19. SILENT NOON 794
    24. PRIDE OF YOUTH 795
    48. DEATH-IN-LOVE 795
    53. WITHOUT HER 795
    55. STILLBORN LOVE 795
    69. AUTUMN IDLENESS 796
    77. SOUL'S BEAUTY 796
    78. BODY'S BEAUTY 796
    86. LOST DAYS 796
  Three Shadows 797
William Morris (1834-1896) 797
  The Defense of Guenevere 798
  Shameful Death 804
  A Garden by the Sea 804
  from *The Earthly Paradise* 805
    AN APOLOGY 805
  The Day Is Coming 806
  A Death Song 807
Algernon Charles Swinburne (1837-1909) . 808

from *Atalanta in Calydon* 810
  WHEN THE HOUNDS OF SPRING . . . 810
  BEFORE THE BEGINNING OF YEARS . . 811
A Match 811
A Ballad of Burdens 812
The Garden of Proserpine 813
Dedication to *Poems and Ballads* 814
Hertha 816
A Forsaken Garden 819
A Jacobite's Farewell 820
A Ballad of François Villon 821
The Higher Pantheism in a Nutshell . . 821
Nephelidia 822
A Child's Laughter 823

Laughing Critics in Verse

Edward Lear (1812-1888) 826
  The Owl and the Pussy-Cat 826
  Incidents in the Life of My Uncle Arly . 826
Charles Stuart Calverley (1831-1884) . . . 827
  Ballad 827
Charles Lutwidge Dodgson ("Lewis Carroll")
  (1832-1898) 828
  The Crocodile 828
  The Voice of the Lobster 828
  Father William 828
  The Mock Turtle's Song 829
  Jabberwocky 829
    GLOSSARY TO *Jabberwocky* 830
  The Walrus and the Carpenter 830
  The White Knight's Ballad 831
  The Baker's Tale 832
William Schwenck Gilbert (1836-1911) . . 833
  The Yarn of the "Nancy Bell" 833
  The Aesthete 835
  Said I to Myself, Said I 835
  They'll None of 'Em Be Missed 836
  Let the Punishment Fit the Crime . . . 837
  Willow, Titwillow 838
James Kenneth Stephen (1859-1892) . . . 838
  Of Lord B. 838
  A Sonnet 839

CHAPTER 8 THE BREAK WITH VICTORIANISM

Fading Traditions and New Patterns, 1880-1914

INTRODUCTORY ESSAY 841

Poetry

William Ernest Henley (1849-1903) . . . 863
  from *In Hospital* 864
    ENTER PATIENT 864
    WAITING 864
    BEFORE 864
    STAFF-NURSE: OLD STYLE 865

    STAFF-NURSE: NEW STYLE 865
    MUSIC 865
    APPARITION 865
    DISCHARGED 866
  Invictus 866
  I. M.: Margaritae Sorori 866
  On the Way to Kew 867
  Ballade of a Toyokuni Color-Print . . . 867
  What Is to Come 867

CONTENTS

    Where Forlorn Sunsets Flare and Fade . . 868
    Space and Dread and the Dark 868
    England, My England 868
Gerard Manley Hopkins (1844-1889) . . . 869
    Heaven—Haven 870
    The Habit of Perfection 870
    God's Grandeur 871
    The Starlight Night 871
    The Sea and the Skylark 871
    The Windhover 871
    Pied Beauty 872
    Peace 872
    Felix Randal 872
    Spring and Fall 873
    Inversnaid 873
    Carrion Comfort 873
    I Wake and Feel the Fell of Dark . . . 873
    To R. B. 874
Robert Louis Stevenson (1850-1894) . . . 874
    A Song of the Road 876
    A Camp 877
    In the States 877
    The Celestial Surgeon 877
    To Alison Cunningham 877
    Bed in Summer 877
    Pirate Story 877
    Foreign Lands 878
    Looking Forward 878
    The Land of Counterpane 878
    System 878
    Happy Thought 878
    The Cow 879
    A Mile an' a Bittock 879
    A Portrait 879
    I Will Make You Brooches 879
    Mater Triumphans 880
    My Wife 880
    Bright Is the Ring of Words 880
    Sing Me a Song 880
    Evensong 881
    Requiem 881
Francis Thompson (1859-1907) 881
    The Hound of Heaven 882
    To a Snowflake 884
    Envoy 885
    The Kingdom of God 885
Rudyard Kipling (1865-1936) 885
    Tommy 887
    Danny Deever 888
    "Fuzzy-Wuzzy" 888
    Gunga Din 889
    Mandalay 890
    The King 891
    The "Mary Gloster" 892
    Recessional 896
    The White Man's Burden 897
    A Smuggler's Song 898
Alfred Edward Housman (1859-1936) . . . 898
    from *A Shropshire Lad* (2, 4, 5, 7, 8, 9, 13, 18,
        19, 21, 26, 27, 40, 44, 45, 48, 49, 54, 63) . 899

    from *Last Poems* (2, 7, 10, 11, 32) 904
    from *More Poems* (They say my verse, etc.,
        7, 8, 9, 15, 22, 27, 37, 38) 905
Thomas Hardy (1840-1928) 907
    A Beauty's Soliloquy During Her Honey-
        moon 908
    Drummer Hodge 908
    The Darkling Thrush 908
    Autumn in King's Hintock Park . . . 909
    God-Forgotten 909
    The To-Be-Forgotten 910
    At Casterbridge Fair 911
        1. THE BALLAD-SINGER 911
        2. FORMER BEAUTIES 911
        3. AFTER THE CLUB-DANCE 911
        4. THE MARKET-GIRL 911
        5. THE INQUIRY 911
        6. A WIFE WAITS 912
        7. AFTER THE FAIR 912
    The Man He Killed 912
    The Curate's Kindness 913
    from *Satires of Circumstance* 913
        1. AT TEA 913
        3. BY HER AUNT'S GRAVE 914
        9. AT THE ALTAR-RAIL 914
    "Ah, Are You Digging on My Grave?" . . 914
    In Time of "The Breaking of Nations" . . 915
    The Oxen 915
    For Life I Had Never Cared Greatly . . . 915
John Masefield (1878-   ) 916
    A Consecration 916
    The Turn of the Tide 917
    Sea-Fever 917
    The West Wind 918
    Cargoes 918
    London Town 919
    St. Mary's Bells 919
    The Seekers 920
    Laugh and Be Merry 920
    Roadways 920
    C. L. M. 921
    Sonnets (1, 2, 3) 921
    On Growing Old 922

Prose

Robert Louis Stevenson (1850-1894) 922
    Aes Triplex 922
    Pan's Pipes 927
    Pulvis et Umbra 929
Rudyard Kipling (1865-1936) 933
    The Man Who Was 933
Joseph Conrad (1857-1924) 942
    The Lagoon 944

Drama

Oscar Wilde (1856-1900) 951
    The Importance of Being Earnest . . . 953
John Millington Synge (1871-1909) 985
    Riders to the Sea 986

CONTENTS

CHAPTER 9 THE STRUGGLE ON THE DARKLING PLAIN *A Time of Conflict and Change, 1914-1957*

INTRODUCTORY ESSAY	995
William Butler Yeats (1865-1939)	1025
The Stolen Child	1026
The White Birds	1026
The Rose of the World	1027
The Lake Isle of Innisfree	1027
When You Are Old	1027
Song (from *The Land of Heart's Desire*)	1027
The Host of the Air	1028
Into the Twilight	1028
He Remembers Forgotten Beauty	1028
The Song of Wandering Aengus	1029
The Fiddler of Dooney	1029
An Irish Airman Foresees His Death	1029
The Second Coming	1030
Leda and the Swan	1030
Sailing to Byzantium	1031
Among School Children	1031
Winston Churchill (1874-)	1032
Prime Minister	1033
Dunkirk	1035
Unconditional Surrender	1040
James Joyce (1882-1941)	1041
from *Ulysses*	1042
Virginia Woolf (1882-1941)	1061
from *The Waves*	1062
Katherine Mansfield (1888-1923)	1069
The Garden Party	1070
Thomas Stearns Eliot (1888-)	1078
from *The Sacred Wood*	1080
• TRADITION AND THE INDIVIDUAL TALENT	1080
The Love Song of J. Alfred Prufrock	1085
Ash Wednesday	1087
Journey of the Magi	1092
Animula	1093
Wilfred Owen (1893-1918)	1093
Greater Love	1094
Apologia pro Poemate Meo	1094
Dulce et Decorum Est	1095
Disabled	1095
The End	1096
Anthem for Doomed Youth	1096
Aldous Huxley (1894-)	1097
Young Archimedes	1098
Noel Coward (1899-)	1117
Cavalcade	1118
Wystan Hugh Auden (1907-)	1145
Watch Any Day His Nonchalant Pauses	1145
There Are Some Birds in These Valleys	1146
Epilogue	1146
Doom Is Dark and Deeper Than Any Sea-Dingle	1146
from *On This Island*	1147
[HERE ON THE CROPPED GRASS]	1147
from *Letter to Lord Byron: IV*	1149
from *In Time of War* (So from the years, etc., II, IV, V, VI, VII, X, XVIII, XXVII)	1154
Musée des Beaux Arts	1156
In Memory of W. B. Yeats	1157
from *The Age of Anxiety*	1158
PART VI, EPILOGUE	1158
Stephen Spender (1909-)	1159
Rolled Over on Europe	1160
Your Body Is Stars	1160
Without That Once Clear Aim	1160
I Think Continually of Those	1160
The Pylons	1161
Not Palaces, an Era's Crown	1161
What I Expected	1162
The Bombed Happiness	1162
George Barker (1913-)	1162
Vision of England '38	1163
Dylan Marlais Thomas (1914-1953)	1169
To-day, This Insect	1170
The Hand That Signed the Paper	1170
And Death Shall Have No Dominion	1170
When All My Five and Country Senses See	1171
Among Those Killed in the Dawn Raid Was a Man Aged a Hundred	1171
Holy Spring	1171
Fern Hill	1172
General Index	1175
Index of First Lines	1193

A Note on the Maps and Illustrations

by KARL J. HOLZKNECHT, *New York University*

More and more in scholarly research and in teaching, the art of literature is being studied, not by itself alone, but in relation to other arts. For literature, in so far as it not only reflects the individual author but also "holds, as 'twere, the mirror up to nature," is but one expression of the thought and the taste of the world which produces it. Architecture, painting, music, and, in humbler ways, even dress and decoration, all reveal "the very age and body of the time his form and pressure." Hence in a book of this kind, which interprets through literature the culture and the life of a people, any illustration must be more than a decorative addition; it must assist the student in peopling the pages of old books with men and women in their habits as they lived and in realizing how colorful and many-sided has been the humanity of every age —especially when it differs most widely from our own.

To this end, in the following pages, an attempt has been made to select from contemporaneous sources graphic illustrations of the life of each period of English history as it was seen by the eyes of artists of the time. What appear to be elaborate and sentimental conventions of romantic literature will, it is hoped, become more enjoyable and understandable when the life which that literature reflects is viewed through other artistic media; so will the complexity of modern literature when it is seen to be an enlightening commentary upon the growing complexity of modern life. A series of parallels running from chapter to chapter—the costume plates, the occupational scenes, the illustrations of sports and pastimes, the architectural sketches, to point out only a few—should make the development of taste and the shifting emphases apparent to the student who in imagination wishes to make the acquaintance of his forefathers.

In selecting the pictorial materials for the new Chapter 9 the same principles have been adhered to. Broadly speaking, the added illustrations are documentary, elucidating the life of the age, rather than merely the literary selections, and attempting within limited space to crystallize that which seems hardly to be history as yet. Inevitably, in a chapter on two wars and an interwar period, some emphasis had to be placed upon war activities and change, but an effort has deliberately been made to suggest more normal interests—sport, the world of fashion, housing and furnishings, transportation, and the advance of comfort and taste. Hence, it is hoped that taken as a whole, in contrasting pairs, or singly, these illustrations will bring an exciting era back to life, and symbolize a great deal more than immediately meets the eye.

Selection has been the principal difficulty; modern life is so many-sided and there is so much material to choose from, that anything like a completely representative survey is impossible. Some things also—like the hopeful Armistice Day enthusiasm of 1918, the garish disillusionment of the "lost generation," Mayfair sophistication, Chelsea Bohemianism and radicalism, the glamor of Jubilee and Coronation, the general lapse from Victorian gentility to neo-Georgian unrestraint or from snobbish social consciousness to an easy democracy—can hardly be suggested pictorially in a book like this. But it is hopeless to try to illustrate everything. Finally, every precaution has been taken to prevent an illustrative program from being transformed into social criticism, in whatever direction it may be biased.

The interchapter maps, too, have been made to serve a useful and an interpretive purpose. As indicated in the list below, each is executed in a style which is characteristic of the period it represents, and each is based upon an actual map of the time. Further, each symbolizes as far as possible some essential in the world outlook of that period. For example, within the circular shape of a medieval *mappamundi* the map for Chapter 1 depicts, not the whole world, but the world as the Anglo-Saxons knew it; that of Chapter 3, with its seas full of galleons and whales and serpents, brings to mind the deeds of Elizabethan seadogs and the tales of Elizabethan voyagers; that for Chapter 5 is a map of London because much Restoration and eighteenth-century literature is literature of the town. The map for Chapter 8—modern and streamlined in style—shows the far-flung Empire and

xii   A NOTE ON THE MAPS AND ILLUSTRATIONS

fits the imperialistic spirit of much late nineteenth and early twentieth-century literature, while that for Chapter 9 is based on the type of war-map with which this generation of readers has become only too familiar. For the most part the places shown on each map are those which have prominence in the chapter—or, in the case of Chapter 9, in the period—to which it is attached; other places will be found on the front end-sheet, the back end-sheet serving as a comprehensive index to all of the maps in the volume.

Except for a few which are necessarily conjectural, all of the cuts have been faithfully adapted from authentic contemporaneous sources, as indicated in the list which follows. The illustrations have all been drawn by Miss Helen Noel, and the maps by Mr. Raymond E. Craig. The skill of both these artists and the pains they have taken in translating photographic copy into the practical medium of line speaks eloquently for itself. Their patience throughout an exacting task has been most worthy of praise.

CHAPTER 6

The Romantic. A French engraving by T. Johannot (early 19th c.)	1
"Ruins after the Roman Manner, for the Termination of Walks, Avenues, etc." Batty Langley's *New Principles of Gardening* (1728)	2
Primitivism. *The English Hermit, or the Surprising Adventures of Philip Quarll*, n.d. (early 19th c.)	3
Spinning in the Home. *Recueil des Planches* in Diderot's *Encyclopédie* (1762-1772)	4
Hargreaves' Spinning-Jenny. A contemporary print	5
Dr. Syntax Meditating among the Tombs. A print by Thomas Rowlandson for William Combe's *Tour of Dr. Syntax in Search of the Picturesque* (1815)	6
The Departure from the Village. A wood-engraving by Thomas Bewick for *Poems by Goldsmith and Parnell* (1804)	7
The Return of the Plowman. An engraving in a French edition of Gray's *Elegy* (c. 1800)	8
Girl and Pigs. A painting by Thomas Gainsborough (1782)	9
A Classical Landscape. R. P. Knight's *The Landscape, a Didactic Poem* (1794)	10
The Same after Romantic Treatment. R. P. Knight's *The Landscape, a Didactic Poem* (1794)	11
Dr. Syntax Sketching a Lake. A print by Thomas Rowlandson for William Combe's *Tour of Dr. Syntax in Search of the Picturesque* (1815)	12
"The Lone Enthusiast, Listening with Pleasing Dread to the Wild Welter of the Waves." An early edition of James Beattie's *The Minstrel*	13
Furnishings in the Revived Greek Style. Thomas Hope's *Household Furniture and Interior Decoration* (1807)	14
Costumes in the Revived Greek Style. Henry Moses's *Series of Designs of Modern Costume* (1823)	15
House in Tavistock Square, Bloomsbury, 1809. A photograph	16
The Prince of Wales Going to Ascot Races. A contemporary print	18
Count D'Orsay Driving. An engraving by George Standfast for John Mills's *D'Horsay, or the Follies of the Day* (1844)	19
A Lady of Fashion. *The Ladies' Magazine* (1816)	20
A Man of Fashion: Count Alfred D'Orsay. A drawing by Daniel Maclise (c. 1830)	21
View of Strawberry Hill. *A Description of Mr. Horace Walpole's Villa at Strawberry Hill* (1784)	22
The Library at Strawberry Hill. *A Description of Mr. Horace Walpole's Villa at Strawberry Hill* (1784)	23
Conventions of the Gothic Romances. *Villeroy, or the Horrors of Zindorf Castle*, n.d. (before 1849)	24
Silhouettes by August Edouart (c. 1828-1830)	25
Shop Scenes. Engravings by Belch (1804)	26-27
Portrait of Congreve, 1700. A painting by Sir Godfrey Kneller	28
Portrait of Scott, 1825. A painting by Sir Edwin Landseer	29
The Waltz. A cartoon (1812)	30
At Mother's Knee. *Pretty Lessons in Verse for Good Children* by Sara Coleridge (1839)	31
Title Page and *The Piper* from *Songs of Innocence* (1789), engraved by William Blake	113
The Tiger from *Songs of Innocence and Experience* (1794), engraved by William Blake	116

CHAPTER 7

An Industrial District. A photograph	399
The Bath Steam Carriage. A print (1828)	400
Early Train on the Liverpool and Manchester Railway. A print (1833)	401
Prince Albert's Model Dwellings, 1851. From a contemporary print	402
The Penny Black, 1840: The first adhesive postage stamp	403
The Crystal Palace: Great Exhibition of 1851. Engraving for *Mighty London Illustrated* (1851)	404
Interior of the Great Exhibition. Engraving for *Mighty London Illustrated* (1851)	405
Dandies. *Modes de Paris* (1838)	406
Belles. A fashion paper (c. 1840)	407
A Victorian House. An architect's drawing of Carlyle House, Chelsea Embankment (c. 1875)	408
A Victorian Interior. Based on photographs	409
Three Generations. *The Gentlemen's Magazine of Fashion* (1857)	410
The Crossing Sweeper. A painting by W. P. Frith	411
Hairdressing in 1863. A contemporary fashion plate	412
Young Ladies. *Le Journal des Demoiselles* (1860)	413
Parlor Music. A drawing by John Leech (c. 1860)	414
The Cry of the Children: Child Labor. From a contemporary print	415
Croquet. An illustrated paper (1870)	415
The Englishman in India, 1860. From a photograph	416
The Lady with the Lamp: Florence Nightingale, in the hospital at Scutari. From a contemporary print	417

A NOTE ON THE MAPS AND ILLUSTRATIONS xiii

Walking Dresses. *Le Courrier de la Mode* (1866-1867) 418
A Victorian Swell. A contemporary cartoon . . 419
Victorian Taste: Exhibits at the Great Exhibition of 1851. Engravings in the official illustrated catalogue 420-421
The Waltz. A cartoon by John Leech (c. 1860) . 422
Tête-à-Tête. A cartoon by John Leech (c. 1860) . 423
Mr. Pickwick. A drawing by Robert Seymour for the original wrappers for *The Pickwick Papers* (1836) 424
Christmas Carolers. A wood engraving in R. Chambers's *Book of Days* (1863) 425
Full Evening Dress. A fashion magazine (1870) . 426
Father William. A drawing by Lewis Carroll in the MS. of *Alice's Adventures Under Ground*, the original version of *Alice in Wonderland* (facsimile, 1886) 828

Chapter 8

An Airplane of 1910. Based upon a photograph of the monoplane in which Louis Blériot crossed the English Channel, July 25, 1909 841
Middle Class, 1870. From a photograph . . . 841
A Late Victorian House. A photograph . . . 842
A Late Victorian Interior. A contemporary sketch 843
Sunday Visitors at Oxford. An illustrated paper (1877) 844
The Hansom Cab: "The Gondola of London." From a contemporary photograph 844
Victorian Sports Costumes. *The Queen* (1870) . 845
Ladies' Golf. An illustrated paper (1873) . . 846
A Man's Game. An illustrated paper (1894) . . 847
The Old: Riding on Horseback. An illustrated paper (1896) 848
The New: The Safety Bicycle. An illustrated paper (1894) 849
The Penny Farthing, 1884. From a contemporary sketch 849
A Tourist Party Abroad. An illustrated paper (1882) 850
A Musicale. An illustrated paper (1877) . . . 851
Kate Greenaway Types. *Kate Greenaway's Birthday Book* (1880) 852
Kate Greenaway Types. *Kate Greenaway's Book of Games* (c. 1885) 853
Archery, 1870. An illustrated paper of the time . 854
Ladies' and Gentlemen's Doubles. An illustrated paper (1888) 855
Fashions, 1889-1914. Fashion magazines of the time 856-857
Motor Car, 1895. An illustrated paper of the time 858
Motor Car, 1903. A photograph 859
Ladies' Hats. *The Queen* (1889) 860
A la Mode. A drawing by Charles Dana Gibson (1901) 861
Ladies' Costumes, 1910: "The Albemarle" and "The Grosvenor." From a fashion magazine . 862
Ladies' Costumes, 1912: Australian Opossum, a popular fur. From a fashion magazine . . . 862

Chapter 9

St. Paul's, 1940. From a photograph 995
Militant Suffragettes. From a photograph of a suffragist riot at Buckingham Palace, 1914 . . . 995
Battleship and Aircraft Carrier. From photographs 996
Artillery and Tanks. From photographs . . . 997
Casualty, 1941. From a photograph 998
El Alamein, 1942. From a photograph . . . 999
The *Queen Elizabeth*, returned to civilian service, 1946. Based on a sketch 1000
A Tram (1929). From a photograph . . . 1001
An Underground Train (1929). From a photograph 1001
A Covered Bus (1929). From a photograph . . 1001
The Dole Queue: unemployed in 1923. From a photograph 1003
Dunkirk, 1940. Based on photographs and sketches 1004
Normandy, 1944. Based on news photographs . 1005
St. Bride's Church, designed by Sir Christopher Wren, 1670-1684. From a photograph . . 1006
St. Bride's Church, 1940. From a photograph . 1007
Fumed Oak, 1911. From a photograph . . . 1008
Automobile, 1920; Rolls-Royce, 1935. From contemporary photographs 1008
Modern Interior. From a photograph of flats at Pullman Court, Streatham (Frederick Gibberd, architect) 1009
Sir Malcolm Campbell's "Bluebird," 1935; Jaguar, 1957. From contemporary photographs . . . 1009
Cricket at Lord's. From a photograph . . . 1010
Riding to Hounds. From a photograph . . . 1010
Steeplechasing. Based on photographs of the Grand National, Aintree, Liverpool 1011
Polo. From a sketch 1011
A Lyons Corner House: luxury and exclusiveness for the masses. Based on a photograph of The Strand Corner House. Courtesy of J. Lyons and Co., Ltd. London 1012
The Flying Scotsman, England's most famous train. From photographs 1013
Lower Middle Class Housing, Tooting. From a photograph 1014
A Street in Whitechapel. From a photograph . . 1014
Upper Middle Class Housing, Wimbledon. From a photograph 1015
Efficiency Flats, 1933. "Highpoint," Highgate (Tecton Architects). From a photograph 1015
Ballroom Dancing, 1920: The Tango. From a contemporary illustration 1016
The Lambeth Walk, 1938. From a photograph . 1017
Fashions, 1914-1957. Based on contemporary fashion drawings, advertisements, and photographs 1018-1019
Bathing costumes, 1925. From a photograph . . 1020
Tennis, 1923. From a photograph 1020
Bathing costume, 1935. From a fashion drawing . 1021
Tennis, 1943. From a photograph 1021
The Commonwealth on the March. Reading counterclockwise: Mechanized Transport Corps, 1940; Malayan; Guard; Royal Navy; Officer of the Wrens (Women's Royal Naval Service); A. T. S. (Auxiliary Territorial Service); Anzacs (Australian and New Zealand Army Corps); South Africans; Dog Patrol; Red Cross Nurse; Gordon Highlander; Army Nurse (St. John Ambulance Brigade); Cyprian; Wren; Scottish Canadian; Army Nurse Corps. From photographs . 1022-1023

MAPS

The British Isles. Decorations from Robert Vaugondy's *Atlas Universal* (1757) xvi

London. Decorations from Tallis's *Illustrated Plan of London and Its Environs* (In Commemoration of The Great Exhibition of Industry of All Nations, 1851) 398

The British Empire, 1914 840
Two Wars in Europe, 1914-1918, 1939-1945 . . 994

For the use of photographs, we give grateful acknowledgment to the following:

Bill Brandt, photo of moors near Haworth, Yorkshire.
British Information Services, photos of Trafalgar Square and Tintern Abbey.
British Travel Association, photo of London.
British Travel and Holidays Association, photos of H.M.S. *Victory* and Radnorshire hills.
J. Allan Cash, Rapho Guillumette Pictures, photo of White Cliffs of Dover.
Free Lance Photographers Guild, photo of St. Paul's Cathedral.
Ewing Galloway, photo of farms in Sussex.
Helmut Gernsheim, photo of Newcastle taken by Lyddell Sawyer in 1888.
Dmitri Kessel, *Life* Magazine, photo of Bannockburn.
Edwin Smith, photo of farmhouse near Bradwell, Derbyshire.
The Times, London, photo of Thames near Hammersmith Bridge.

The Literature of England

VOLUME TWO

The Land and Its Writers

"This City now doth like a garment wear
The beauty of the morning; silent, bare,
Ships, towers, domes, theaters, and temples lie
Open unto the fields, and to the sky . . ."
        Wordsworth, *Composed upon
        Westminster Bridge*

Trafalgar Square, London.

"... Once again
Do I behold these steep and lofty cliffs,
That on a wild secluded scene impress
Thoughts of more deep seclusion ..."
                Wordsworth, *Lines,
Composed a Few Miles above Tintern Abbey*

Tintern Abbey, built in the twelfth century in Wales.

"Is this a holy thing to see
In a rich and fruitful land—
Babes reduced to misery,
Fed with cold and usurous hand?"
            Blake, *Holy Thursday*

A street scene in Newcastle in the late nineteenth century.

Scene of the Battle of Bannockburn (1314), in which Robert Bruce defeated the forces of Edward II of England (see page 109).

"Scots, wha hae wi' Wallace bled,
Scots, wham Bruce has aften led,
Welcome to your gory bed
 Or to victorie!"

Burns, *Scots, Wha Hae*

"Rule, Britannia, rule the waves;
Britons never will be slaves."

Thomson, *Rule, Britannia*

H.M.S. *Victory*, Admiral Lord Nelson's flagship at the Battle of Trafalgar (1805), now in dry-dock at Portsmouth, Hampshire.

". . . the cliffs of England stand,
Glimmering and vast, out in the tranquil bay."
Arnold, *Dover Beach*

The White Cliffs of Dover.

The countryside of Sussex.

"And whoever wakes in England
Sees, some morning, unaware,
That the lowest boughs and the brushwood sheaf
Round the elm-tree bole are in tiny leaf,
While the chaffinch sings on the orchard bough
In England—now!"
    Robert Browning,
        Home-Thoughts, from Abroad

"The house is old, the trees are bare,
    Moonless above bends twilight's dome . . ."
        Emily Brontë, *A Little While*

The moors near Haworth, York (see page 716).

"In the sun that is young once only,
   Time let me play and be
Golden in the mercy of his means..."
                      Thomas, *Fern Hill*

The Welsh hills of Radnorshire.

"The secret of these hills was stone,
   and cottages
Of that stone made,
And crumbling roads
That turned on sudden hidden
   villages."
                      Spender, *The Pylons*

An old stone farmhouse near Bradwell, Derbyshire, built in the fifteenth century.

St. Paul's during an air raid, 1940.

"... we shall fight on the beaches, we shall fight on the landing grounds, we shall fight in the fields and in the streets, we shall fight in the hills; we shall never surrender."
   Churchill, speech on Dunkirk,
   House of Commons, 1940

"Unreal City,
Under the brown fog of a winter dawn..."
   Eliot, *The Wasteland*

Fog on the Thames near Hammersmith Bridge.

"What is to come we know not. But we know
That what has been was good . . ."
                Henley, *What Is to Come*

An aerial view of London showing Westminster Bridge and Parliament.

Chapter 6

Revolution and Romance

Romanticism in the Ascendant, 1760-1832

The Age of Revolution

THERE are two important ways of looking at life. One way is to be guided by reason and a sense of fact; this is the path which leads in art and literature to the rational and the realistic. Such a path the neo-classicist preferred to follow. The other way of looking at life is in terms of the emotions and the imagination; this is the road to what in literature and art is called the romantic. Obviously, the romantic is inimical to the severely rational; it has warmth where the rational has not; it is not restrained by bare fact; it has largeness and sweep and passion, and is as necessary a part of a well-rounded human being's experience as is the purely rational; but it is of the heart rather than of the head.

Definition of "romantic"

Specifically, the romantic urges with intensity that mankind is a vast brotherhood; it stands in awe of man's immense possibilities for both good and evil; it sees the essential beauty as well as the savagery of nature. It praises beauty in all forms; it delights in the comeliness of the body and of the soul alike; it demands the sensuous and the sensitive. It can feel an unrestrained joy in living, or it can grow melancholy at the thought of the inevitable decay and death that await all beauty and life. It honors the glories of the past, but it looks to the future with hope and enthusiasm. It resents anything that stands in its way; it resists what it considers arbitrary restraint and tyranny; it rebels against the unfriendly and remorseless logic of facts that oppose it. It brings softness, color, and warmth to life, and a freedom in the range of human feelings, imagination, and expression. It represents, in a word, the triumph of what man would like to be; it can be mankind's escape from unpleasant reality, but it can be also his inspiration to mighty deeds.

The "romantic" the common trend of English literature

In English literature the romantic "movement," which began about 1740 and triumphed at the end of the eighteenth century, is in reality but a return to normal English currents of thought and expression. The neo-classical[1] literature of eighteenth-century England was, in fact, unusual for English literature as a whole. The mind of the Englishman, from the time of the Anglo-Saxon invasions of Britain to the present, has always been given more to emotion and imagination, and less to intellectual balance, logical neatness, and mannered convention, than the arbiters of eighteenth-century taste would have allowed. It is true that for the space of almost a century and a half certain artistic and literary fashions were imposed upon the Englishman, and a distinctive literary style was produced for him to follow, in some cases whole-heartedly, in some cases reluctantly. For almost the first time, he was enabled to write a prose consistently clear, simple, and straightforward; and if his natural predilection for emotional lyrical utterance was temporarily stifled during this period, still he could find compensation in his strengthened grasp upon realities in his writing—in his novel, in his drama of manners, in his penetrating satire, in his discursive essay.

The results of the neo-classical movement in English literature

The neo-classical period unquestionably contributed much to the mind of the Englishman. But given the introspective quality of the Anglo-Saxon, his energy and adventurousness, plus the quick audacity of the Norman and the wit and fancy of the Celt—it is inconceivable that the literary formalities of the neo-classical age could have prevailed for long. A reaction was inevitable. The seeds of that reaction are to be found implanted within the soil of the neo-classical age itself, in the importance attached by that age to reason and demonstrable truth. *Cogito, ergo sum* ("I think, therefore I exist"), the dictum of the great French philosopher and mathematician Descartes (1596-1650), stands as the keystone of neo-classical thought. The most important English writer influenced by Descartes, John Locke (1632-1704), had preached in his *Essay Concerning Human Understanding* that truth was to be found "in the contemplation of things themselves"—that is, by actual rational insight on the part of each individual, for "the light of reason . . . the candle of

[1] The term "neo-classical" must not be confused with the terms "classical" and "classic." "Classical" and "classic" can be used in either one of two senses: they may be used merely as referring to ancient Greece and Rome, or they may be used—as in Matthew Arnold's work—to refer to "the best." "Neo-classical," as used throughout the present chapter, has reference to the imitation of ancient Greek and Roman standards of art practiced during the seventeenth and eighteenth centuries—an imitation which was arbitrarily hedged in by contemporary European conventions and was usually very far from the truly "classical" standard. To give a specific illustration, Keats's romantic *Ode on a Grecian Urn* is far closer to the spirit of ancient Greece than all the eighteenth-century English Pindaric odes combined.

Ruins after the Roman Manner

the Lord, that is set up within us, shines bright enough for all our purposes." The result, however, of much of this "contemplation of things themselves" was a gradual drift toward a position antithetically opposed to what the neo-classical age represented. Reason came soon to search out the inherent absurdities of the belief in the divine right of kings or in the pretended superiority of the nobility over the common man. In the field of art, the assertions of a Pope or an Addison, when subjected to the light of reason, failed to convince the liberal man that they represented the only possible road to high achievement. The fashions of the neo-classical age became outworn; a change in politics as well as in art was inevitable. Changes of this sort, however, are always attended by violence on the part of enthusiasts.

The coming of revolution to the neo-classical world

Such an enthusiast could assert flatly that all kings were tyrants, or that all men were born equal, or—to descend from the wide and general to the narrow and specific—that art and literature should be free of all formal rules and privileged to take whatever subject-matter they might choose and treat that subject-matter as they saw fit. These enthusiasts had their way in the Western world, at least for a time, and their endeavors resulted in revolution, political, artistic, social, and industrial. An unwise colonial policy practiced by the British government in the 1760's and 1770's, based upon the theory that all colonies existed for the good of the mother country, led to the American Revolution (1775-1783). The short-sighted domineering of the French aristocracy in the eighteenth century brought about the French Revolution. Although the American Revolution was ultimately a more complete example of political overturning, the French Revolution of the 1790's was far more spectacular and violent; it began as the outburst of a disorderly, blindly rebellious mob, and passed through many shapes of blood and fire, with a distinct tendency throughout to the rule of an unscrupulous oligarchy. It had come from a more primitive source—class-hatred engendered by a tactless and often brutal aristocracy; it had a deeper emotional effect on the age and was more turbulent.

Rousseau and his ideas

Back of both the American and the French revolutionists stands the figure of Jean Jacques Rousseau (1712-1778), at various times churchman, vagabond, musician, social theorist, essayist, and novelist. Through the influence of his ideas, Rousseau became one of the most important men of the last three centuries. An erratic and emotional thinker, he convinced millions of the soundness of his religious, political, and social doctrines. He bred revolution in the state, and he gave a powerful impulse to lyrical poetry; but these two apparently unrelated products of Rousseau's genius are not difficult to reconcile if one examines carefully the theories behind all of Rousseau's writings. In his religion, Rousseau is what can be called technically a sentimental deist. To him, God is a spirit working ever for good—not a supernatural being in the image of man, but a beneficent, paternal force

Primitivism

that has created the world and man. Any contemplation of this spirit must necessarily be inspiring, emotionally stimulating, and exalting. Since this creating spirit is manifest in nature and in man, it must follow that man in a natural setting, as free as possible from artificial restraints imposed by the demands of society, is in his happiest possible state. Hence the contemplation of nature, of natural landscape and natural phenomena, was the surest way in which man could approach God; the more primitive man's environment, the closer he was to perfection, which was by no means impossible of attainment on earth, because man was essentially good.

In politics, Rousseau was clearly a republican—a republican by instinct. He was naturally predisposed to insistence on political equality, and although the logic of his anti-monarchical tract, *Du Contrat Social* (1762), was weak, his appeal to the masses of emotional mankind was compelling and for the moment irresistible. Rousseau was not a great writer as regards form or execution of design. His novels, *La Nouvelle Héloïse* (1760) and *Émile* (1762), are valuable only for their primitivistic ideas. But he was supreme as a portrayer of the passions of the human heart and of the beauties of nature. No European of the era was a more influential spokesman for the emotional forces underlying the Age of Revolution.

The Encyclopedists

One cannot say how much of the content of Rousseau's work was really original and how much was derived from the ideas of others. It is seldom that one can have such a good subject for the ancient dispute as to whether the man produces the age or the age the man. The nature-worship which Rousseau made famous was widespread among the intelligentsia of Europe. Moreover, other intellectual forces besides those of Rousseau were behind the theories of revolution. There was a group of philosophers, natural scientists, and mathematicians, known as the Encyclopedists (from their part in the production of the great French *Encyclopédie ou Dictionnaire Universel des Arts et des Sciences*, 1742-1759), which included such men as the versatile Diderot (1713-1784), the critic, philosopher, and man of letters Voltaire (1694-1778), and the mathematician d'Alembert (1717-1783). There was also the German philosopher Immanuel Kant (1724-1804), who, in his *Critique of Pure Reason* (1781), taught that reason had its limitations; when it failed, one must fall back on intuition and instinct. Such men as the Encyclopedists typified the very spirit of the eighteenth century in their preoccupation with natural science and with deistic philosophy, and in their essential grasp upon material things. But by their very hold upon realities they encouraged the feeling against royalty, against the social order then existing, against the narrowness of city life; they stimulated the conception of vastness in the cosmic order, and all this helped to produce a new era in thought and feeling.

Along with political revolution and its antecedent philosophical upheaval, another chain of events created a second revolution, purely social and

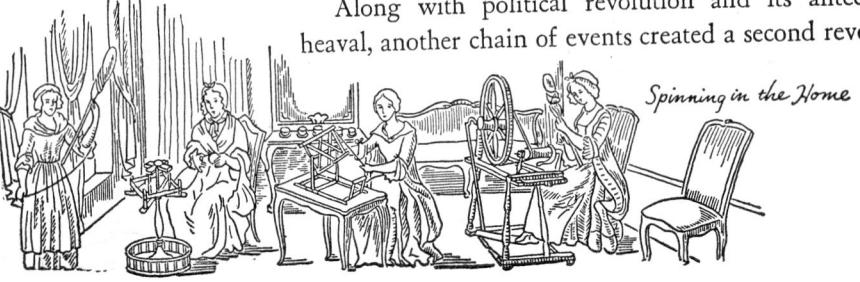

Spinning in the Home

economic, known generally as the Industrial Revolution. Its net effect was to change England from a primarily agricultural nation to one that was primarily industrial and mercantile. During the eighteenth century one man invented the steam-engine; another man, the spinning-jenny; still another, the power-loom. Machines replaced hand-labor, and there came the usual problem of unemployment. The factory system was introduced—in itself a complete revolution—and in the hands of self-seeking employers this system brought evils such as excessive woman- and child-labor, starvation wages, sweat-shops. Ultimately legislation began to catch up with the abuses, but for a long time the lot of the submerged portion of society was the business of every political economist or critic of society. Although the aristocracy and the middle class as a whole remained inert, if not indifferent, still the agitation for legislative reform to take care of the vast and depressing social problems brought in by the Industrial Revolution was so much fuel for the fire of political dispute. The cry for equality, for the rights of man, for human brotherhood arose in the land; many reformers worked long and hard to bring to reality their desire for the betterment of the condition of mankind. The slave-trade in the English colonies was abolished (1807); the penal code was reformed; a more just parliamentary representation was debated and finally enacted (1832). So came the manifestation of the humanitarian instinct. Of all the revolutions to be observed in these years, the Industrial Revolution was ultimately the most important. Its effects are still to be felt, and many of the problems it raised have not yet been solved.

The Industrial Revolution

In spite of all the political agitation, England herself experienced rather quiet years between 1760 and 1830. There was, of course, Napoleon and his constant threat to England from 1800 to 1815. But the country was prosperous, worldly, still ruled by the masculine portion of the landed gentry. Among the upper and middle classes women were sheltered; they were politically negligible everywhere. Education for the majority was poor, but business was good; England was well on her way to becoming a "nation of shopkeepers." Yet the Englishman, for all his native political conservatism, could not avoid the revolutionary ideas that were in the air. These ideas might be repellent to the majority, but there were always some to listen and to break the way to a new order. Excluding the more militant advocates of reform, there still remained the critics of society, both in prose and verse, the political and economic theorists, and the occasional revolutionary journalists to keep the broth boiling. It is an extremely complicated literary and intellectual product that this age of revolution ultimately brought forth, with many paradoxes and cross-currents of thought and emotion, but the general trend of ideas is toward the liberal and the experimental. The enthusiasm, the emotionalism, and the imaginative vigor shown in the literature of the age, if not necessarily in its life, bespeak the dominance of the romantic.

England in this age

Hargreaves' Spinning-Jenny

The Approach to Romanticism in Eighteenth-Century England

THE LAST of the several revolutions produced by the eighteenth century was a revolution in literature. For nearly half a century, between 1740 and 1780, neo-classicism in England was dying a lingering death, while romanticism grew stronger and stronger. To be sure, the full force of the romantic, as it manifests itself in the splendid blooming of the great romantic writers of the early nineteenth century, did not make itself felt at once; nevertheless, the seeds of the romantic, which had lain dormant in English earth during the Restoration, took root and burgeoned slowly but surely during the middle of the eighteenth century.

Thomson and Collins

Shortly after the appearance of characteristically neo-classical works like the important comedies of the Restoration or the works of Dryden, Swift, and Pope, there can be seen the inception of revolts against the prevailing standards of the neo-classical age, in regard to both the subject-matter of literature and its forms. The revolt affecting the subject-matter was for the time being the more considerable. Where the neo-classicists spoke mostly of city life and, if they mentioned country life at all, dwelt on it but feebly and artificially, the Scotchman James Thomson (p. 32) attempted in *The Seasons* (1726-1730) to describe nature, the outdoors, in its grand, impressive aspects. Thomson's break with neo-classical standards is rather timid; he resorts to many neo-classical *clichés* like "youthful swains" for "young men," "household feathery people" for "poultry," "ethereal force" for "wind"; he moralizes at length; but his spirit is that of a man seeking inspiration of soul in Nature the goddess, not as one in city pent, but as one who can ramble in the fields for delight and worship. So began again the long procession of nature poets that is still passing before us. Thomson's other important contribution was *The Castle of Indolence*, the most famous of many contemporary imitations of the manner of Spenser, imaginative, full of nature-consciousness, and with an appreciable amount of the sensuous. This tendency to sensuousness—a direct appeal to any one of the five senses—deepens in the work of such a man as William Collins (p. 66), whose beautiful *Ode to Evening* is a delight not only to the imagination but to the ear as well.

Thomson had tried to represent in his poetry the more general and spectacular side of nature; Collins turned to the gentle, the idyllic, the fleeting mood evoked by a sylvan scene at sunset. During the 1740's and 1750's this cultivation of the pensive grew into a cult of the melancholy in nature which contemplated death, the inevitable end, and brooded upon the grave, the final home. The quality of melancholy, one of the most frequent moods entertained by the romantic mind, is found in the work of Collins; it is darkened

Dr. Syntax Meditating among the Tombs

REVOLUTION AND ROMANCE

and heightened into the characteristic "graveyard" poetry of the period in works like the *Night Thoughts* of Edward Young (1683-1765) and Gray's *Elegy Written in a Country Churchyard* (1751); it reached the macabre in *The Grave* by Robert Blair (1699-1746). Grim Nature and Melancholy soon came to walk hand in hand. At the same time there appeared another cult, that of the supernatural in literature; its chief effect, however, was restricted to the novel (cf. p. 23) until the time of Coleridge.

The "graveyard" school

Thomson's *Castle of Indolence* indicates still another trend of the romantic mind—a reaching out for the glories, either real or imagined, of a past other than that of Greece and Rome, and a clothing of the past in the rosy colors of a mystical glamour. Anything old came to have emotional and imaginative appeal. Spenser and Milton were imitated, and soon the Middle Ages in their pomp and panoply became a favorite interest, with the result that many literary monuments of the past were uncovered. Bishop Thomas Percy (1729-1811) made the first important collection of popular ballads and medieval romances in his noted *Reliques of Ancient English Poetry*, which appeared in 1765. Percy was a scholar, however, rather than a creative writer. Another antiquarian, Thomas Warton (1728-1790), combined research with poems on Arthurian romance-material, aided by his brother Joseph (1722-1800). One who wrote copiously in the manner of ancient Celtic legendry was James Macpherson (1736-1796), whose poems came to have a vogue all over the Western world for their mysterious, veiled narrative of forgotten, far-off deeds by an exotic, passionate folk, who, nevertheless, were remembered as the ancestors of English-speaking people. Similar to Macpherson and more gifted as a poet was Thomas Chatterton (1752-1770), a tragic and precocious youth who wrote in the manner of the medieval romance and ballad. Both Macpherson (who used the name of Ossian as a guise) and Chatterton pretended that their work was but the restoring of lost treasures of the people; both, in short, were literary frauds, but they cannot be idly dismissed. The romantic return to the past, next to appear after the nature poetry and the brooding melancholy, had become a definite literary fashion by 1765; indeed, Collins had foreshadowed it in his *Ode on Popular Superstitions*, as had Thomson in the late 1740's.

The antiquarian group

The Departure from the Village

Still another manifestation of the romantic in the subject-matter of eighteenth-century English literature was the appearance of an interest in individual man, particularly in the down-trodden. This humanitarian interest, with occasional sentimental and idyllic tones, appears in Oliver Goldsmith's *Deserted Village* (Vol. I, p. 1114); the sincere and realistic George Crabbe (1754-1832), who, in his heroic couplets and occasional formal phrases, seems the last outpost of neo-classicism, had an interest in humble life which was romantic in its depth and intensity. But the truly significant humanitarian literature of the age appears in the novel, which will be discussed later (p. 23).

The humanitarian spirit

Love poetry and religious verse

Although love is one of the most important of emotions, there are no great love poets in the eighteenth century until we get to Robert Burns; but both the verse of friendship—the easy table-chat of an intimate—and the poetry of an emotionally religious soul are represented in the work of William Cowper (p. 73), with *The Task* (1785), and the famous *Olney Hymns* (1779). As for religious poetry, there was a steady trickle of hymns from the days of Nahum Tate in the Restoration down to the days of the unhappy Cowper, the "stricken deer" who was driven by his religious frenzy from the ordinary course of life. Indeed, hymn-writing had come to stay throughout the nineteenth century. Its appearance and its rapid development in the middle of the eighteenth century can be traced to the inevitable reaction against the intellectual and comfortless concept of God as a spirit detached and indifferent—the deism of the neo-classical philosophy (Vol. I, p. 822). The movement known as Methodism originated at Oxford in 1729, under the inspiration of John Wesley (1703-1791) and his brother Charles (1708-1788), and developed after 1738 into an emotional evangelical type of religion which demanded that every believer be converted to a new life. The influence of the Wesleys upon English religious verse cannot be overestimated; their lyrics stand in sharp contrast to both the sacred verse of the Middle Ages and the metaphysical verse of the seventeenth century, chiefly because the Wesleyan hymn is a direct appeal to the feelings, not too mystical on the one hand and not too full of conceits on the other.

The Return of the Plowman

Thomas Gray

Probably the most considerable talent among all the writers of mid-eighteenth-century romantic literature was that of Thomas Gray (p. 46). He was schooled in the tradition of the neo-classical, and his early work shows neo-classical phrasing and poetic forms, although he tended to break away from the tradition later. He is not only a poet of real inspiration and a careful workman; he combines an eye for nature with an eye for the past; he suffuses the scene of his poetry with the glamour of melancholy and the color of the medieval. His *Elegy Written in a Country Churchyard* (1751), easily the best-known poem of the eighteenth century, is also the finest poem of the "graveyard" vogue. In it, too, is a notice of the lot of humble men—the humanitarian interest that becomes a favorite theme of most of the later great romantic poets. *To Spring* is chiefly nature poetry; *The Bard* (p. 55) is the transcription of a piece of Welsh legendry; *The Fatal Sisters* (p. 58) turns for subject-matter to the Germanic epic sagas. Strict, formal, and transitional as Gray may be, he stands out, "the scantiest and frailest of classics in our poetry," according to Matthew Arnold, "but ... a classic." In his journals and his letters (p. 59) Gray reveals a romantic appreciation of the wonder and the beauty of nature, especially in her wild and spectacular aspects.

Near the close of the century two remarkable poets appear. The first, Robert Burns (p. 83), is in some respects a transitional figure. A peasant,

Robert Burns

and the son of a peasant, he lived a hard life; but his self-tutored genius, expressing itself in a lyrical love for humanity and for life, triumphed over every obstacle except the short-sightedness of his own generation. Intense in his feeling, Burns has the true artist's instinct which prevents him from being over-emotional; his sentimentality is strictly legitimate. He can weep over the lot of mankind while he himself evokes our pity for his own human failings. No greater love-poet is to be found in English literature, if to be a love-poet means to pour out sincere devotion to the beloved, devoid of all straining effect, artificiality, or pretense. *Sweet Afton, Bonie Doon, Of A' the Airts, Ae Fond Kiss,* and many others are in their own right immortal. *Auld Lang Syne* is still an epitome of friendship. A true Scotch patriot and a lover of liberty for all, Burns is in one sense the pure romanticist. But there is another side to his literary achievement. He is a bitter castigator of hypocrisy; in *The Jolly Beggars* and *Holy Willie's Prayer* he is the almost pitiless realist and satirist. Here, no doubt, is something of the tradition of the neo-classicist. But Burns's satire, fierce though it may be, is actuated by an intense love of humanity; his ugliest pictures of mankind are drawn, as it were, with tears in his eyes. The combination of romanticism and satire exhibits the essentially sane balance in Burns, a wholesome earthiness enveloping a lovable and poignant idealism, now pathetic, now humorous, now quaintly antiquarian, now stirringly libertarian. No matter what the type, the stamp of remarkable originality is upon nearly every poem Burns wrote, especially when he is writing in his own Scottish dialect close to the soil of Scotland. In these dialect poems he seems to attain what Wordsworth later set as an objective of romantic poetry—the language of common man. Burns's immense popularity has been thoroughly earned; in him was the "spark of nature's fire," which is the essential ingredient of a great poet.

William Blake

The second figure, William Blake (p. 111), had an originality of genius equal to that of Burns, but he is far more difficult to analyze. He is the thorough-going mystic; for him God and all the angels are immediate realities; he seems to live at times in another world and to speak in an unearthly voice. Although neglected in his day, he has grown steadily in stature since that time, and many place him among the greatest of English poets. He is, in addition, one of the finest of English engravers; his illustrations for *The Book of Job* and Blair's *The Grave* are impressive, unforgettable. The same epithets can easily be applied to his poetry. The innocent and sinister forces of nature alike are set before us in inspired symbolic poetry, often of transparent simplicity, and again of bewildering obscurity. *Songs of Innocence* has all the lucid freshness of outlook that belongs to a child; *Songs of Experience* pictures the "shades of the prison-house" in which man lives; the various prophetic poems, half-mad as they are, incomprehensible to most readers, have no precise counterpart in English literature. All of Blake's poems have

Girl and Pigs

about them a singular suggestiveness; they lead one to search constantly for new meanings to be found hidden deep within them. Romantic in his subject-matter, particularly in his deep-seated humanitarian instincts, romantic even in his literary approach, Blake nevertheless defies a strict label. He gives instead the impression that he would have written as he did, no matter what his age or his environment, and he is perhaps the most individual writer that England has produced. The appearance of Blake and of Burns is unmistakable evidence that the romantic flowers of the eighteenth century were ready to bloom.

Estimate of the early poetry of the romantic age

To read with understanding the romantically inclined poets of the eighteenth century from Thomson to Burns is to appreciate at once the fact that they had at least touched all the important themes dear to the heart of the English romanticist and had freely developed many of them. They had expressed, with varying emphasis, the love of nature in all her aspects; the love of mankind and of country; the yearning for the remote in space and time, with particular reference to the medieval and the primitive; the passion of the poet's own inmost thoughts and feelings—restless, unsatisfied, ever changing; the contemplation of death and the awesome terror inspired by the thoughts of eventual dissolution, complicated by the revival of the age-old interest in the supernatural. This varied and spectacular subject-matter had been treated with imaginative warmth and fire, and with different degrees of emotional intensity. But all the writers except Burns were intent—sporadically in the case of men like Thomson, permanently in the case of men like Blake—on creating a new kind of reality, a reality that neglected superficial fact for underlying truth. Such is the very essence of the romantic. All but Blake had been more or less hampered by the fraying bonds of neo-classicism, which were tending to slip away entirely with the passing of time, and none except Blake was completely free. Burns came the nearest to ridding himself of the neo-classical tradition in form; but others, who were romantic at heart, were enslaved by neo-classical style.

The Romantic Triumph in Poetry

IN OTHER WORDS, a Declaration of Independence of the romantic writer in this age still remained to be written; and there had been as yet no important body of poetry deliberately flying in the face of the immediate past, unless we again except Blake and a few poems by Burns. William Wordsworth and Samuel Taylor Coleridge (pp. 118 and 163) are responsible for both of these necessary achievements. Their work, at the beginning of their respective careers, is largely complementary; they are to be thought of almost as one. Their little volume of poems done in collaboration, the famous *Lyrical Ballads* (1798), is one of the most important landmarks in the history of Eng-

A Classical Landscape

lish literature. Wordsworth's portion of the first edition was a group of ballad-like poems, simple in diction, plain in style, given to rustic scenes and rustic characters, preaching the kindness of Nature; and, in addition, the sublime nature poem *Tintern Abbey*, proclaiming in magnificent blank verse the pantheism of the true romantic. Coleridge's contribution was the supernatural imaginative literary ballad *The Rime of the Ancient Mariner*, notable for its weird, unearthly atmosphere, and its inspired aptness of phrasing—a poem in its way unmatched in English literature. The *Lyrical Ballads* caused laughter in some quarters and indifference in others, but the authors' purpose justified a second edition in 1800, to which Wordsworth wrote a long preface (p. 318), the reading of which is indispensable for a knowledge of the work of the two men and for an appreciation of the distance which poetry had traveled since the days of Alexander Pope.

The Lyrical Ballads

This *Preface* to the *Lyrical Ballads* contains two extremely important passages. One describes the characteristically romantic conception of the nature and origin of poetry. To quote Wordsworth, ". . . poetry is the spontaneous overflow of powerful feelings; it takes its origin from emotion recollected in tranquility; the emotion is contemplated till, by a species of reaction, the tranquility gradually disappears, and an emotion, kindred to that which was before the subject of contemplation, is gradually produced, and does actually exist in the mind." The author then explains that the mind of the poet, whatever the emotion, will be "on the whole, in a state of enjoyment." The second passage of importance is the statement of the ideals underlying the composition of the *Lyrical Ballads:* "The principal object, then, proposed in these poems was to choose incidents and situations from common life, and to relate or describe them throughout, as far as was possible, in a selection of language really used by men, and, at the same time, to throw over them a certain coloring of the imagination, whereby ordinary things should be presented to the mind in an unusual aspect; and, further, and above all, to make these incidents and situations interesting by tracing in them, truly though not ostentatiously, the primary laws of our nature. . . . Humble and rustic life was generally chosen, because, in that condition, the essential passions of the heart find a better soil in which they can attain their maturity, are less under restraint, and speak a plainer and more emphatic language." The truth of the language of common man and the life of that common man were to Wordsworth "more philosophical" matters than "that which is frequently substituted for it by poets," that is, the neo-classical poets.

Wordsworth's theories of poetry

Wordsworth was sincerely convinced that his theory would make for greater truth and would hence develop greater art. He therefore wrote a multitude of poems in conformity to the theory—some of them angular, homely, fatally unhumorous, even ridiculous. His many failures should deservedly be allowed to die. On the other hand, some of his simple poems, such as *The*

The Same after Romantic Treatment

Solitary Reaper, I Wandered Lonely as a Cloud, and *My Heart Leaps Up,* are not likely soon to pass away. Yet fully as striking are his longer poems—*Tintern Abbey, Ode on Intimations of Immortality,* and parts of his autobiographical poems, *The Prelude* and *The Excursion;* these, together with his many fine sonnets, are magnificent departures from his theory, for in them his poetic flights, unusual in their loftiness and strength, demand—and receive—an utterance beyond the ordinary.

Wordsworth's achievements

Wordsworth is the supreme poet of nature in English literature. He is also a great poet of humanity. He is not, however, a primarily intellectual writer, for in him the spontaneous overflow of powerful feelings, colored by the imagination, outweighs all else. Like all young men of his age, he was profoundly stirred by the French Revolution and wrote much libertarian verse; but, largely for personal reasons which need not be discussed here (cf. p. 119), he turned conservative in 1802. The influence of his powerful though restricted genius has been felt continuously from his day to ours. Many have regarded him as the greatest English poet since Milton, whom, in his seriousness, essential dignity, lack of humor, and consummate poetic insight, Wordsworth strongly resembles.

Wordsworth and Coleridge had, as friends in Somersetshire, in Germany, and later in the Lake Country (cf. pp. 118 and 119), been students of the German philosopher Immanuel Kant (1724-1804), whose *Critique of Pure Reason* has already been mentioned (p. 4). Both were familiar with Plato and his doctrine of the ideal, which has many direct appeals to the emotions and the instincts (cf. pp. 159-160). The effect of Plato can be seen primarily in Wordsworth. Coleridge, who had much the better reasoning mind, was an insatiable student of philosophy, and his brain teemed with ideas on philosophical and religious questions. It was a remarkable intellect—this mind of Coleridge—and a highly poetic one. In sheer poetic imagination, Coleridge was the superior of Wordsworth; one can but deplore the unsteadiness and indolence of his temperament, which could, however, almost in spite of itself, produce fitful flashes of the highest kind of poetry, such as *Kubla Khan, Christabel,* and *The Rime of the Ancient Mariner* (pp. 166 ff.), one of the finest of literary ballads. Romantic English literature owes Coleridge much for his achievements in supernatural and exotic poetry, fragmentary as those achievements too often are.

Samuel Taylor Coleridge as poet

Both Wordsworth and Coleridge began as revolutionists, not only in literature but in their philosophy of life. Coleridge at one time was even so carried away by the idea of a natural community free from restraints that he and Robert Southey conceived the idea of a "pantisocracy," or group of individuals based upon a communistic and primitivistic foundation (p. 164). But later he, like Wordsworth and the great mass of English citizenry, gradually became opposed to revolutionism because of the excesses of the French Revolution and its complete disavowal of God and the state. Wordsworth

Dr. Syntax Sketching a Lake

became virtually a recluse; Coleridge, the springs of his poetry dried up early through indolence and an unfortunate addiction to opium, settled in London, talked incessantly, and planned vast projects. These two men, and other lesser lights of poetry like Southey, the poet laureate, withdrew within themselves. Having sounded the battle-cry of new forms, new standards in poetry, they left the active warfare to younger men.

To that elder generation of romantic poets belongs also Sir Walter Scott (p. 190). It is not customary now to think of Scott as a great poet; his reputation rests more upon his novels (p. 27) than upon his poetry. And yet in his day he did a great service to romanticism in verse. He could write excellent songs, but his greatest poetic talent was for narrative verse; his interest in that form coincided with his interest in the history and folklore of his native Scotland. The ensuing product from Scott's pen is of two kinds—his original narrative poems and his revivals of ancient traditional Scottish songs and ballads. To the first class belong such poems as *The Lay of the Last Minstrel* (1805), *Marmion* (1808), and *The Lady of the Lake* (1810). To the second belongs his exceedingly important collection of popular ballads and songs, *The Minstrelsy of the Scottish Border* (1802-1803). From these two sorts of achievement Scott's position among the romantic writers is clear. He creates in easy-flowing, vigorous, crisp lines of narrative verse a scene remote in time; "creative treatment of the past" best describes his most important work. He is the most scholarly and searching of the antiquarians among the romantics; he continues, more elaborately than his predecessors, the work of Bishop Percy (p. 7) and Robert Burns (p. 84) in assembling the many pieces of the Scottish legendary past. His original poetic narratives had—and still have—a strong appeal to the lovers of adventure. Robert Louis Stevenson thought the first few lines of *The Lady of the Lake* an ideal romantic opening. And though Scott did not reach the poetic heights of some of his contemporaries, on the whole his output is remarkably even and of a generally high level—a credit to the romantic age of which he was so integral a part.

It was the misfortune of the older group of romantic poets—Wordsworth, Coleridge, and Scott—to be separated from the younger group of Byron, Shelley, and Keats by a yawning chasm, the chasm of the misunderstanding of older men by younger. Byron, in his first important work, the satirical *English Bards and Scotch Reviewers* (p. 203), pays his disrespects to all three. Wordsworth is to him a "mild apostate from poetic rule," simple, and inclined to the idiotic; Coleridge is obscure and "to turgid ode and tumid stanza dear"; Scott is a writer "of stale romance." These unflattering sentiments Byron repeated in his last work, *Don Juan*, with equal vehemence; it cannot, therefore, be urged that the insults hurled at the older romantics in *English Bards and Scotch Reviewers* spring from callow, impudent intolerance. Indeed, Byron expressed himself privately as dissatisfied with this new scheme of poetry on which the romantics were busy; he said that it "was not worth

Sir Walter Scott as poet

The Lone Enthusiast

The gulf between the older and the younger romantic poets

a damn in itself." It is easy to see that Byron is at least half a neo-classicist; his whip-lash satire and his avowed admiration of Pope and Dryden make that clear. *Don Juan*, when viewed as a whole, is one of the great satires in English literature. Moreover, there is in Byron an eminently practical streak, earthy and coarse, that may lead at times to pedestrian poetry, but may also bring balance and critical acumen.

George Noel Gordon, Lord Byron

Nevertheless, the glamorous personality that is Byron can be almost wholly romantic. In his *Childe Harold* and in the series of Oriental tales, he created a type of hero, the "Byronic hero," who is moody, melodramatic, violent, tender, sinister, passionate, but restless and unsatisfied—a portrait of Byron himself. Furthermore, many of Byron's early poems are redolent of the sheer perfume of romanticism; such lines as

> She walks in beauty, like the night
> Of cloudless climes and starry skies

need no special interpreter to transmit their sensuous imagery and the emotional force of the pictures which they conjure up. As Byron developed, the satirical outlook in his poems becomes more and more prominent, but there is one romantic trait in his character that does not fade, a trait which is sincere to the very core—his love of human liberty, for which he never ceased to fight in his dashing, spectacular, half-posing manner. This love of liberty is the obverse of his hatred of tyranny, which he exaggerated into utter contempt for the English government of his day and into exceedingly faint praise for Napoleon, the terror of Europe. Even a casual reading of *Childe Harold* and *Don Juan*, the two great Byronic documents, will reveal the true revolutionism of Byron, which is a moderate republicanism. To put the matter in a different way, Byron greatly admired Washington and the type of revolution which he represented; he was suspicious of Rousseau, referring to him very accurately as a "self-torturing sophist," whose ardent frenzy against tyranny had made of France "a fearful monument." How much of this revolutionism of Byron was caused by his own personal misfortunes (p. 200) will never be known; undoubtedly a great deal of it. For Byron was a tremendous egoist. He was the greatest individualist of the age, a world figure, whose influence outside England was greater than that of any other poet of his time. This influence originated partly from the magnetism of his personality and partly from the boldness of his strokes, his impetuousness, his emotional drive. The world might not learn much from Byron but could not fail to feel his presence. The careful critic might point out that Byron's workmanship left much to be desired, that his sense of the delicate in phrase and imagery was often sadly deficient, that he was earthy in spite of all his romance; but such criticism had no effect then and is not a great deterrent now. He is still admired because he possessed a tumultuous force, a sense of humor, and a devastating worldliness that the other great poets of the age lacked, even while they might surpass him in sheer poetic insight and technique.

Furnishings in the Revived Greek Style

Shelley, who loved Byron, is his opposite in almost every point except rebelliousness. No more passionate, sincere visionary exists in English literature; and it is more than doubtful that Shelley could be matched exactly in any other literature. Like every true Platonist, he had seen, once upon a time, Heaven open up before him; and the radiant vision was at once his ideal, the objective of his life and art—and his torment when he saw how far humanity fell short of Heaven. His childlike outlook, pathetically naïve, sublimely contemptuous of harsh realities, led Shelley to writhe at the mere suggestion of discipline, restraint, or law, which he considered tyrannous. This completely anti-social attitude came in part from his bringing up, in part from his school-days, and in part from his association with Rousseauistic doctrines, particularly with those preached by William Godwin. Shelley's life was wrecked by the subversive forces in his philosophy, by his flouting of civil obligations, and most of all by his inability to let two and two equal four and live at peace with his neighbors.

Percy Bysshe Shelley

Nevertheless, the doctrines of Shelley, however tragic their effect upon his personal life, gave him the vision sublime; it was in recapturing that vision, in seeking for the broken lights of that radiance and implanting it in man's soul that Shelley spent his life as a poet. No considerable piece of his poetry can fail to show his haunting, wistful quest. The *Hymn to Intellectual Beauty, The Sensitive Plant, The Cloud, To a Skylark* illustrate his refined sensitivity to beauty in nature, a beauty which in his presentation of it transcends physical limitations and soars into the spiritual. Shelley, like every Platonist, regards spiritual beauty, which is permanent and true, as the only beauty. Only its shadow falls upon earth; the love of it is the light which illumines all worth-while existence. His longer poems like *The Witch of Atlas, Prometheus Unbound,* or *Hellas* bring a violent revolutionary spirit, which demands political and social upheaval, into contact with this Platonic system of beauty; the harmonizing element here is poetically demonstrated in *Prometheus Unbound* to be love—the love of humanity, the New Testament conception of "charity." And so Shelley, to his generation a loathsome atheist, was in his teachings often more akin to Christ than was any other poet in his time.

Shelley's poetry

In Shelley's shorter poems, the characteristic stamp of Platonic philosophy is evident, but here the poet's supreme lyric gifts are the important things. Few English poets have been able to approach Shelley in melody, in finished harmony and sound-effect, in fluency, fire, and intensity. A good reading of his *To Night* is virtually a demonstration of all the possibilities of the lyric. In all his poetry, Shelley is speaking directly for his poetic generation; nowhere could a better distillation of the essence of the romantic be found than in

> The desire of the moth for the star,
> Of the night for the morrow,
> The devotion to something afar
> From the sphere of our sorrow.

Costumes in the Revived Greek Style

If this desire was too hopelessly visionary, and if he sank into moments of the most intense melancholy, still Shelley could rejoice, as in *Adonais*, that the soul seeking beauty could find it in the loveliness of nature, in the contemplation of poetry, and in the thought that

> Life, like a dome of many-colored glass,
> Stains the white radiance of Eternity.

John Keats

A third member of the younger generation of romantic poets, and in some ways the greatest poet of the three, was John Keats (p. 273). Keats, like Shelley, had a profound love of abstract beauty, but he could also worship the warm pulsing beauty of the earthly; and the physical charm of landscape and of humanity alike could inspire him to rare bursts of poetic passion. It is idle to seek in Keats for the element of revolt seen in Byron and Shelley. It is, of course, true that he was in complete opposition to the neo-classical stiffness of form and preciseness of thought that had characterized the preceding century. If he took the heroic couplet as a medium, he would unclose it, as in *Endymion* (p. 278); if he chose a classical subject, as he frequently did (cf. *Hyperion*, *Endymion*, and the *Ode on a Grecian Urn*), he would pour upon it a luxuriant sensuousness that the neo-classical poet would scarcely have comprehended and would certainly not have accepted. That this delight in color and sense-appeal, in the frankly physical, was far more Greek than anything the neo-classical age produced is merely another in the long list of ironies in literary history.

Keats's poetry

An avowed admirer of Spenser, Keats is one of the greatest pictorial poets in world literature; a rich tapestry-weaver whose sense of color and imagery, of light and shade, and of sight and sound is almost unerringly right. Allowances must be made for his earlier work, such as *Endymion*, which exhibits a lack of restraint in the exercise of his almost prodigal powers of sensuous appeal, a fault which he himself recognized and sought successfully to rectify. Keats is the great exemplar of the pensive and the passive in English romanticism; he has no banner to unfurl, no foes to crush; all he demands is the opportunity to worship the beautiful, which is to him the ultimate reality. In the worship thus granted him he comes to a philosophy of life both deep and fragile—fragile to the skeptic and the practical-minded; deep to the sympathetic lover of beauty. Logic and cold reason have no place in the appraisal of Keats; instead there must be a surrender to the emotion and the imagination—what Coleridge once called "the willing suspension of disbelief."

Keats, indeed, has much in common with Coleridge. He has the same interest in the medieval, as *The Eve of St. Agnes* demonstrates; he has also the same witchery in ballad-technique, as *La Belle Dame sans Merci* so brilliantly shows. His magnificent odes (*Ode on Melancholy*, *Ode on a Grecian Urn*, *Ode to a Nightingale*, *To Autumn*), like the short poems of Shelley and of Wordsworth, capture in masterful fashion the soul of romanticism.

House in Tavistock Square, Bloomsbury

The song of the nightingale, the melancholy autumn days (touched here with a wholesomeness quite outside the traditional), the domain of unreality "in faery lands forlorn"—all are more significant to one seeking a definition of the romantic than many paragraphs of objective exposition. One of the most convincing proofs of Keats's genius is the fact that his works can bear repeated reading; his finest poems do not lead to surfeit or exhaustion, for they have an inevitableness of expression which only great poetry can possess. And so Keats, the youngest of the three younger romantic poets of importance, and the first of the three to die a premature and tragic death, comes in his last years to represent a culmination of the English romantic poetry in the early nineteenth century. It is his influence that dominates the early days of the first great poet of the coming Victorian era, Alfred, Lord Tennyson (p. 593); it is Keats's decorativeness and sensuous artistry and Wordsworth's nature poetry that serve as the bridge between the romantic age and the next generation.

Dramatic poetry of the period

The entire period from the publication of the *Lyrical Ballads* (1798) until the appearance of Tennyson's first poems in 1832—the year that saw the death of Sir Walter Scott—was one of great poetic activity, especially in the field of lyric poetry. The drama in this period is on the whole negligible; the professional drama is beneath contempt. Yet many of the great poets of the period—Wordsworth, Coleridge, Byron, Shelley, and Keats—tried their hand at dramatic poetry. The many closet-plays that resulted were often beautiful in their poetry but technically unactable. Two brilliant exceptions should be noted: Byron's *Manfred* (1817) and Shelley's *Cenci* (1820). *The Cenci*, done in the manner of an Elizabethan tragedy, has only its plot, a story of incest, to stand in its way, for it is powerful, dramatically tense, and poetically effective.

Many of the minor poets of the period deserve special mention (p. 296). Many whose tastes were predominantly romantic and whose abilities were better than average lived well into the Victorian age. But none of these does anything that had not been done better by the six great poets just discussed, a band of poetic giants who in spite of garrulity, over-seriousness, and diffuseness are not likely soon to be equaled for passion and power.

Romantic Prose—Imaginative, Critical, Revolutionary

ALTHOUGH IT COULD hardly be expected that an age which was preëminent in lyric poetry would excel in prose-writing, some remarkable prose-writers flourished between 1795 and 1832, and several prose types came to maturity during this period. Excluding for the moment writers of the novel, one can find a body of prose essays impressive in bulk and often impressive in quality.

The periodicals

The background of these essays can be better understood if one pauses to consider briefly the fate of the periodical in the later years of the eighteenth century. The development of periodical writing was one of the great contributions of the neo-classical age. The appearance of newspaper-like periodicals, of which *The Tatler* and *The Spectator* were examples, was followed by the beginning of a few more varied and more casual prose collections that could be called magazines, such as *The Gentleman's Magazine,* starting in 1731. But it is rather difficult to think of these periodicals as magazines in the modern sense, for they usually were strongly political in their interests and hence catered to certain groups. As the eighteenth century rolled along, the newspapers increased in importance, while the "magazines" languished. With the first of the nineteenth century, however, came a group of periodicals which gave a real impetus to literature; they served as a means of publishing not only essays on all sorts of subjects, but a considerable amount of poetry, and even some fiction. In a word, they approach the general conception of a modern magazine.

The social-minded William Cobbett (1762-1835) headed the list of such enterprises with *The Political Register,* beginning in 1802; this periodical was dedicated chiefly to economic and social problems and is valuable as an opening wedge for the later more important periodicals. Next came the famous *Edinburgh Review* in 1802, a publication directed by Sidney Smith (1771-1845) and Francis Jeffrey (1773-1850), an aggressive, hard-hitting periodical, which contained literary reviews that have become noted. The policy of the editors in literary matters was, indeed, very conservative; they could hardly be expected to hail with delight such a radical change in poetry as Wordsworth and Coleridge introduced; and so it is not to be wondered at that the reception accorded Wordsworth's poetry by this review was almost uniformly harsh—often, it may be conceded, with eminent justice. Next in time and fully the equal of the *Edinburgh Review* in importance came the *Quarterly Review* in 1809, the editor of which was William Gifford (1756-1826), a literary Tory and a vigorous opponent of romanticism. Gifford's hand was strengthened by the somewhat paradoxical presence among his contributors of Sir Walter Scott (p. 191) and Robert Southey (p. 296). Leigh Hunt (p. 297) started a periodical, *The Examiner* (1808), of pronounced radical tendencies; but he himself trod upon the toes of royalty and was imprisoned for a time. A fifth periodical, *Blackwood's Magazine* (1817), directed by John Wilson, or "Christopher North," as he preferred to be known (1785-1854), was the very stronghold of Tory conservatism in literature; its attacks upon Keats, in virulent poor taste although with considerable justice, have become notorious and have been ridiculously blamed by sentimentalists for Keats's death from tuberculosis. *Blackwood's Magazine* had a greater variety of offerings than its predecessors; it even began to include fiction.

The Prince of Wales Going to Ascot Races

Thus far, with the exception of Hunt's abortive *Examiner*, all the magazines of the early 1800's had been conservative to the point of actually clinging to neo-classical standards—at least, they decried the brave attempts of younger poets to break away from the older tastes and literary habits. *The London Magazine* (1820), however, gave real encouragement to the finest romantic prose-writers in the age. In the light of subsequent literary history, it is *The London Magazine* that came to bear the burden of developing a new creative spirit, a burden that was later shared by *Fraser's Magazine* (1830). The older magazines, on the other hand, upheld critical standards at the expense of creative vitality. Both types of periodicals, however, had their definite functions. The controversial material in the earlier magazines was the foundation on which was built the finished product that characterized the three prose-writers who stand out conspicuous among the crowd.

These three prose-writers who developed their talents through the periodical essay were Lamb (p. 337), Hazlitt (p. 360), and De Quincey (p. 374). Each of these men had two sides to his work; each was a critic of life as well as a critic of literature. Lamb, the book-lover, the city-dweller by preference, wrote as a kind of avocation, for he earned his living in business. The casual nature of his literary activity does much to explain the abiding charm of his writings. The *Essays of Elia*, which appeared in *The London Magazine* between 1820 and 1823, to be published in book form later, are among the finest of English personal essays—whimsical, quaint, humorous, tender, dreamy, and sad. Comment on their romantic quality is perhaps superfluous; one need only perceive their subjective nature to understand how thoroughly Lamb is a product of his romantic age. The very titles of his better known essays are suggestive: *The Two Races of Men* (borrowers and lenders); *Old China; A Chapter on Ears; Valentine's Day; Poor Relations; Dream-Children*. Here is none of the formal preciseness, even primness, of an Addison; or the pithy penetration of a Lord Bacon. In his sentimentality, Lamb most nearly approaches Steele, but Steele was equipped with a neo-classical style. Lamb was not; he was a free, almost erratic writer of prose which can pause, leap, or linger at will. His content, viewed as a whole, is never so important as the way in which he treats his subject-matter; he lends everlasting conviction to the statement that romance is never so much a material thing as an attitude or an approach.

The informal, personal essay in the hands of Hazlitt reveals the harsher, more acrid character of its writer. There is nothing of a lovable quality in Hazlitt; he is a vigorous and direct speaker, and one of varied interests. In his informal moments, Hazlitt is fully as self-revealing as Lamb; the difference between the two, apart from their personal divergences, is that Hazlitt is more bookish, more satirical, less ingratiating. His style is more formal than Lamb's; it could be called at times pedantic. Yet it shows strength and

Three leading essayists: Charles Lamb

Count D'Orsay Driving

William Hazlitt

finish and a great deal of feeling. Once more, it is an interesting task merely to con the titles of Hazlitt's better essays: *On Going a Journey; On the Fear of Death; On Reading New Books; On the Feeling of Immortality in Youth; The Fight.* There is more love of adventure in Hazlitt than in most of his prose contemporaries outside of the novel; he is a lean, wiry kind of writer with intellectual and artistic sensibilities and acquisitiveness.

Thomas De Quincey

De Quincey's personal essays are markedly different from those of either Lamb or Hazlitt. He is, in effect, a poet in prose—he called himself a writer of "impassioned prose'"—who must necessarily be romantic in his approach. Like Coleridge, De Quincey was for a time addicted to opium; he writes of the effect of the drug in his brilliant *Confessions of an English Opium Eater* (1820-56). The sequel to the *Confessions,* the elaborate *Suspiria de Profundis,* is the very height of De Quincey's magnificent organ-style; it shows how strikingly artificial distinctions of form are in setting up boundaries between prose and poetry. De Quincey's work here is manifestly poetry, and poetry of a high order, encased in a prose mold.

It is extremely difficult to make a synthesis of the creative work of these three fine writers; each is highly individualistic and must be read for his own sake to be fully appreciated. If one turns to the literary criticism that was written by these three, the task is easier, for there is common agreement among them as to their literary idols. They all owe much to Coleridge's able work in the fields of both literary criticism and philosophical writing.

Coleridge as a writer of prose

Coleridge is a prose-writer of great importance. He was the most distinguished literary critic of his day; he was interested not only in the practice of criticism but in its theory as well. He might be called a philosophical critic. He was opposed to the rational, mechanistic, and materialistic philosophy of Locke, which lay at the root of neo-classicism; he was under the general spell of Kant in professing an idealistic philosophy in ethics, politics, and literature. Hence his criticism would stress naturally the spirituality and idealism of a work even more than its material content. Poetry, therefore, came to mean to Coleridge an inspiration, as it meant to Wordsworth a spontaneous overflow of feelings; the didactic was secondary to the inspirational. Specifically, Coleridge was a reviver of Shakespearean criticism; he was more responsible than any other single person for the change in Shakespeare's reputation. The object of the rather condescending approval of the neo-classical age, the great Elizabethan poet and dramatist became the recipient of the whole-souled admiration of the nineteenth century. Coleridge's analysis of *Hamlet* marks the high-water level of his Shakespearean criticism. He was also a frank critic of his friend and associate Wordsworth; his *Biographia Literaria* (1817), his most important prose work, explains the genesis of the *Lyrical Ballads;* it describes the aims of the two poets and illustrates how Coleridge later tended to drift away from the particular

A Lady of Fashion

literary objectives that were Wordsworth's. His lectures and his *Table Talk* of his later years show the brilliance of his mind and his attractive loquaciousness; in those days his personality was even more striking than his actual writing; but then, as earlier, he was doing most capable pioneer work in the field of subjective and philosophical literary criticism. He set a fashion in criticism opposed to the severe, occasionally mean, appraisals in which the neo-classical critics had often indulged.

Coleridge's work was supplemented and expanded by the brilliant three— Lamb, Hazlitt, and De Quincey. Lamb, in his *Tales from Shakespeare* (1807), written in collaboration with his sister Mary, popularized the plays of the great dramatist; his annotated collection, *Specimens of English Dramatic Poets* (1808), did much for the fame of Marlowe, Heywood, Ben Jonson, and others from the spacious times of great Elizabeth. Furthermore, Lamb conceived a literary passion for the seventeenth-century prose-writers like Thomas Browne, Thomas Fuller, and Jeremy Taylor; no doubt it was through his efforts that the elaborate, often strained, effects of these writers came to earn such exalted and even exaggerated praise during the rest of the century. Hazlitt's contributions in the Shakespearean field comprise *Characters of Shakespeare's Plays* (1817), notable for his fine study of Hamlet, and many lectures on Elizabethan literature, terse, salty, though often rather pedantic. His interests throughout the whole range of English literature were considerable; he was a remarkably well-read man, and not in the least backward about parading his command of his reading. In an essay like *On Familiar Style* (1821), he pleads for a freedom and informality of style which is at the same time to be kept free from vulgarity. As for De Quincey, his Shakespearean criticism is rather informal; the best known piece is *On the Knocking at the Gate in Macbeth* (1823). A kind of critical writing of a more general sort is illustrated in his *The Poetry of Pope,* published in the *North British Review* as late as 1848; is contains the section, "The Literature of Knowledge and the Literature of Power," which sums up most convincingly the essential differences between the classical and the romantic minds. All three of these lieutenants of Coleridge in the army of literary critics had penetration, a persuasive style, and that most helpful asset for the convincing writer—entire sympathy with their subject.

Other literary criticism

It would be possible to continue the list of successful literary critics further. The editors of the periodicals described already (p. 18) would swell the throng in considerable fashion; and such men as Leigh Hunt, the champion of romantic rebels (p. 297), and Walter Savage Landor (p. 299), whose felicitous *Imaginary Conversations* and *Pericles and Aspasia* belong in point of time to the Victorian era, may well be mentioned here. Landor, the arch-classicist, urging a balanced view of the great figures of classical life and art, stands out in lonely relief in an age that was preoccupied with the

A Man of Fashion

medieval, the Elizabethan, and the contemporary. Yet even Landor, in his *Citation and Examination of William Shakespeare* (1834), did not escape the common infection. In literary criticism the occasional prose work of the great poets of the period is of abiding significance, particularly (in addition to Coleridge's work just mentioned) Wordsworth's *Preface* to the second edition of the *Lyrical Ballads* (p. 318), Byron's many tonic letters on literary questions and personalities, and Shelley's *Defense of Poetry*, written in 1821, which is a superb statement of the Platonic attitude in poetry, characteristic of the more spiritual work in Shelley himself, in Keats, and in Wordsworth.

Social commentators

The social critics are also numerous. Early in the era (1776) came Adam Smith's *Wealth of Nations*, a landmark in the history of economic thought, a kind of masterwork in the analysis of the capitalistic system of society. Thomas Malthus (1766-1834) believed that the population of the world would increase to the saturation point unless natural forces tending to check the spread of population, such as wars and disease, should be allowed to operate toward that end. But most of the writers of the time were not of such hardy stuff. Jeremy Bentham (1748-1832), with his doctrine of "the greatest good for the greatest number" and his constant testing of an idea or invention by the simple question, "What's the use of it?" (the "utilitarian" viewpoint), was perhaps the most practically democratic theorist of his time. William Cobbett (1762-1835) was the champion of the working-man and of Parliamentary reform. Beside the work of Smith stands that of William Godwin and of his wife Mary Wollstonecraft (1759-1797). They were pioneer radicals, imbued with Rousseauism, intellectual and philosophical anarchists, who attacked all government and restraints upon human beings and advocated complete revolution, not by violence, but by the application of reason to all social problems. Their influence upon Wordsworth and Coleridge was profound, particularly through Godwin's *Enquiry Concerning Political Justice* (1793) and his *Caleb Williams*. As for Shelley, later Godwin's son-in-law, some critics estimate that two-thirds of his ideas, revolutionary and socialistic, were derived from the Godwins.

Estimate of the prose of the romantic age

The prose of this romantic age will probably never have the popular appeal of the poetry, notwithstanding the attractiveness to the general public of such a man as Lamb. The things that romanticism represents, the usually unspoken cravings of the human soul, are from their very nature more adapted to poetry than to prose. But it is well to remember that even the prose-writers of the age have remarkable poetic insight; they have enthusiasm and charm, and, when read in comfortable amounts, a considerable power of inspiration. Obviously, they are more basically intellectual than the poets, but they can often speak with the tongues of angels; even when philosophical, their language always has warmth and human feeling.

View of Strawberry Hill

The Romantic Novel

UNTIL SOME MENTION of the romantic novel has been made, the story of the romantic prose-writers is still half-told. Like all other types of literature written during this romantic age, the novel of emotional and imaginative appeal must be traced back to the middle of the eighteenth century. Richardson, in his *Pamela* and other novels, had set in motion the novel of character-analysis; Fielding had brought the novel of incident and of character into equipoise; Smollett had given to the novel of incident a maritime and an international flavor; Sterne had introduced the whimsical and developed the sentimental. The work of these four men was imitated through the years from 1760 to 1800, and their individual contributions came to be merged into various combinations; a few new novel-types were created. Some of the types of the eighteenth-century novel, such as the sentimental and the picaresque, on the other hand, continued in the main unchanged. It is usual to divide the novels written after 1760 into the Gothic romance, the novel of purpose, the novel of manners, and the historical novel—always with the understanding that one type might touch any other at certain points.

The eighteenth-century background of the romantic novel

The kind of fiction which most clearly portrays the drift toward the romantic, and the earliest to appear unmistakably, was the Gothic romance. The term "Gothic" suggested in the neo-classical environment that gave it special meaning, the wild, the barbaric, and the primitive; specifically, it had reference to the medievalism of a Gothic cathedral, and so to the superstition of the Middle Ages, the mysterious, and the unknown. The Gothic novel represents the romantic return to the medieval, colored with the lurid hues of terror, the horror of the supernatural, the vaguely but monstrously sensational. Like the "graveyard" poetry of the period (p. 7), it is the result of a reaction against neo-classical rationalism. Probably the first striking instance of the Gothic element in an English novel occurs in Smollett's *Ferdinand Count Fathom* (1753), in one scene of which there is a visit to a graveyard in the blackness of midnight as the owls hoot and white figures appear. Smollett, indeed, had often made good use in his novels of the element of terror. A greater impetus was given to the Gothic romance by the appearance of *The Castle of Otranto* (1764) by Horace Walpole (1717-1797). Walpole, like a good many other neo-classicists of the mid-eighteenth century, had a large country-home near London, known as Strawberry Hill. Chiefly because of his personal eccentricity he had equipped the mansion with secret passages, grottoes, and dark staircases. In keeping with the atmosphere of

The Gothic romance

The Library at Strawberry Hill

the house he wrote *The Castle of Otranto* as much for a joke as anything; but joke or not, the work had great influence. The age was ready for this romance and took it hungrily. The novel was a mad tale of a tyrant, Manfred, beautiful young women and a handsome prince, a haunted room, and ghosts.

Although the influence of Walpole is traceable in many minor writers, not until 1787 was there another similar success, and that was *Vathek*, by William Beckford (1759-1844). It happens that *Vathek*, in addition to being a Gothic romance of the supernatural and the terrifying, is also an example of the pseudo-Oriental in fiction. This Orientalism had run riot in France during the early years of the century—even the brilliant Voltaire had been touched by it—and is derived in large measure from the translation into French of the *Tales of the Arabian Nights* by Antoine Galland in the years from 1704 to 1717. There is a considerable amount of the farcical in *Vathek*, but Beckford delights in the orgies of crime sponsored by the wicked Caliph and his monstrous demons, who commit dastardly deeds for the sheer fun of them and suffer agonizing punishment in payment.

The weight was thrown in favor of the Gothic over the Oriental type of romance by Mrs. Anne Radcliffe (1764-1823), who was probably the best writer of the type; her most popular works were *The Mysteries of Udolpho* (1794) and *The Italian* (1797). Although the explanation of her horrors is always made rational, her devices are none the less romantic— all the elements that can be associated with melodrama are dragged in —haunted castles, terrible storms at night, secret footsteps, chastity in peril but eventually preserved, lost wills, forged documents, clanking chains, low moans, and piercing shrieks. There is the same moral justice that is to be found in most penny-dreadfuls. But, in spite of her complete failure at characterization, Mrs. Radcliffe wrote vigorously and at the same time carefully; and her stories, when finished, were complete and satisfying as narratives. Her imagination has been praised, yet candor admits that she, like all other writers of the Gothic romance, was writing a badly-overstrained, far-fetched kind of story, too sensational in treatment to carry the conviction that the lurid subject-matter might have possessed had it been treated by a Scott, a Poe, or a Stevenson. Too frequently the writers of Gothic romance committed serious breaches of good taste, as did Matthew ("Monk") Lewis (1775-1818) in his fantastic *The Monk* (1795). Judged by the artistic element of suggestiveness, the two most vivid specimens of the *genre* are *Melmoth the Wanderer* (1820) by Charles Maturin (1782-1824) and *Frankenstein* (1816) by Mary Godwin Shelley (1797-1851; cf. p. 249), the second of which has had a considerable revival in recent years because its

Conventions of the Gothic Romances

terror is based upon monstrous possibilities of science—the artificial creation of human life.

The Gothic romance, with its blood-and-thunder claptrap, might lead to the impression that romanticism had scored an early and sweeping victory over neo-classicism in the field of the novel. Such was not the case. There was a definite continuation of the eighteenth-century novel of manners— the satirical picture, often picaresque in structure (Vol. I, p. 837), of English life and social customs. But where Defoe and Fielding and Smollett had been forthright, even brutal, in their portraiture, the later writers of the novel of manners were deft, rapier-like in their thrusts, with a sly, gentle little malice that bespoke an amused detachment and a cool appraisal. This distinctly lighter touch may be explained by the fact that the most interesting writers of the *genre* were women. There was Frances Burney (Madam d'Arblay; 1752-1840), the friend of Dr. Johnson, who shows charm, narrative power, and shrewd portraiture in *Evelina* (1778), "the history of a young lady's entrance into the world," and *Cecelia* (1782), to mention but two of her works. There was Maria Edgeworth (1767-1849), a most capable novelist, whose specialties were the delineation of life among the Irish tenants of absentee landlords and the exposition of Irish folk-manners. In *Castle Rackrent* (1800) and *The Absentee* (1809) she suggests many phases of the Irish problem that had plagued England for centuries; in her interest in Irish peasants she foreshadows the similar interest of Sir Walter Scott in the Scotch. Her scope is broad, for she can write well of English "society," as in *Belinda* (1801); indeed, she can be called with all fairness an international novelist. She has taste, vivacity, and often considerable power of character-delineation and of narrative.

The novel of manners

The greatest writer, however, among the novelists of manners in this age was Jane Austen (1775-1817). It is a mistake to attempt to make Miss Austen in any way a romantic. She has all the instincts of the neo-classicist for the satirical; she is anti-enthusiastic, anti-extravagant, anti-sentimental. The remarkable clarity, the good sense, the humor, combined with the unusual detachment which she shows in all her works, belong to the preceding age—they are not to be matched again until the time of Thackeray, almost a half-century later—and even then there will be a difference (p. 424). Her purpose is clearly that of Fielding, and she accomplishes in feminine fashion what he did in his masculine muscularity and directness. Her life was placid and uneventful and cut off prematurely, shortly after she was forty. Most of her days were spent in a quiet town in Hampshire, where her father was rector; later she lived at Southampton, with visits from time to time in Bath. The narrow geographical limits within which she lived have no relation to the obvious universality of her writing. *Pride and Prejudice* (1813) is one of the greatest of English novels. It is the account

Jane Austen

of the conflict of pride in the person of young Darcy with prejudice in the person of young Elizabeth Bennet, the most impressive of Jane Austen's many successful character-portrayals. It is the story of a small-town family and its reactions to people from the outside, of the gossipings and schemings of the women and the futile defenses of the men. *Sense and Sensibility* (1811) is an attack, delivered from the stronghold of common-sense, upon the sentimentality of many contemporary novels; in two sisters is embodied the essential warfare between the two divergent outlooks upon life. *Northanger Abbey*, published posthumously in 1818, is a short but amusing burlesque of the Gothic romance. *Mansfield Park* (1814) is an able piece of realistic observation, but is looser in structure and not so crisp in style as its predecessors. The same defects are apparent in *Emma* (1816), but the satire on village life is so effective as to counterbalance any technical weaknesses. Much of the same can be said for *Persuasion,* published, like *Northanger Abbey*, after the author's death.

Jane Austen's brilliant achievement transmitted the novel of manners to subsequent writers like Thackeray (p. 424), Mrs. Gaskell (p. 422), and George Eliot (p. 425), who owe her much. Posterity has come to award her a place in the first rank of novelists coming between Sterne and Dickens —a position which she shares, for wholly different reasons, with Sir Walter Scott. Many modern critics consider her unmatched by Scott, and certainly superior to Sterne and Dickens.

The novel of purpose

In addition to the Gothic novel and the novel of manners, the age produced a number of characteristic works which clothed revolutionary ideas with the garments of fiction. This type, the so-called novel of purpose, was akin to the novel of manners; it was chiefly in the hands of second-rate writers, however, and consequently exhibited many of the weaknesses of the age—extreme sentimentality, turgidness, prolix characterizations and descriptions. None the less, it is an interesting reflection of the ideas prevalent during the time; it illustrates one side of the romantic temperament that is often overlooked—the missionary spirit, which attained its finest expression in Shelley. The novel of purpose falls roughly into two kinds— that which had a pedagogic aim, and that which advocated reform or revolution of social, political, or economic nature. Of the first kind, not one is of the first rank. All stemmed in some way from Rousseau's *Émile* or *La Nouvelle Héloïse;* they preached the ideal of a natural environment for the growing child, and the inculcation of moral principles based upon the beneficent power of Nature herself. Henry Brooke's *The Fool of Quality* (1766-1770) and Thomas Day's *Sanford and Merton* (1783-1789) are perhaps the best known today. The social revolutionary novel received better treatment; William Godwin was responsible for at least two good narratives, *Caleb Williams* (1794) and *St. Leon* (1799). Godwin's novels

preach the essential features of the author's social philosophy, but they contain also large elements of the Gothic romance, skilfully handled. *Caleb Williams* has been called the first English detective novel. The other writers of this group, such as Thomas Holcroft and Robert Bage and Elizabeth Inchbald, have been deservedly forgotten. The simple fact is that there was no high art among these writers of propagandistic novels; what they advocated was said in much more enduring words by Shelley in his *Revolt of Islam*, *Prometheus Unbound*, and *Hellas*.

Still one more important kind of romantic novel remains to be considered—the historical novel. The tendency to use real people as pegs on which to hang a story was strong in Defoe. With the growth of the antiquarian spirit during the eighteenth century and the inevitable subjective coloring given to fact by the romantic mind, the appearance of the historical novel would be only a question of time; but there was no great writer to blaze the trail. The first novel commonly regarded as romantically historical was *Longsword* (1762), a novel of thirteenth-century feudalism by the Reverend Thomas Leland. As history it is inferior, and yet, in its blend of fact and Gothic romance, it is characteristic of the age which produced it. The historical type having made its beginning, a long list of mediocre writers kept it alive during the remainder of the eighteenth century. Clara Reeve (1729-1807) sticks her head momentarily above the throng with her *Old English Baron* (1777), but it is not until the days of Jane Porter (1776-1850) that we find any appreciable literary talent in the historical novel. Her *Thaddeus of Warsaw* (1803) and *The Scottish Chiefs* (1809) achieved a great success in their time; they showed the usual sentimentalism, the usual mixture of history and romantic plot, but the first-named, at least, departed somewhat from the formula which decreed that every historical novel must treat of the feudal and the medieval. The second of Mrs. Porter's books opens the way, in title and in subject-matter, for a consideration of the greatest figure in English historical fiction and one of the most important of English novelists at any time, Sir Walter Scott.

The historical novel

As has been observed (p. 13), Scott began his career as a poet; he was a great champion of romantic poetry, and he never lost the poetic touch, even in his novels. He had been brought up on tales of border warfare, particularly those which inspired Scottish patriotism. His earliest work was the building up of the ballad as a sophisticated literary form and the applying of free verse-molds and poetic devices to stirring tales of old Scotland. He had long cherished the idea of becoming a writer of historical novels, but his early success as a narrative poet and his need for money to meet his social aspirations deferred the beginning of his career as a novelist. He apparently wrote himself out as a narrative poet with *The Lady of the Lake* (1810)—none of his later poems came up to his former

Sir Walter Scott as novelist

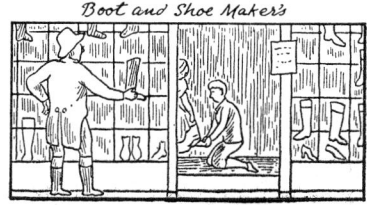

The Waverley novels

high standards—and the coincidental appearance of the fiery Byron in this field brought about his withdrawal. *Waverley*, written in part some years before, was published in 1814, the first of the long line of nearly thirty novels (the Waverley novels) written between 1814 and Scott's death in 1832.

It is impossible to discuss the Waverley novels in detail within the confines of the present chapter. The last half-dozen or so were written at fever haste in an effort to clear the immense debt imposed upon Scott by the failure of his publishers, the Ballantynes (p. 191). In consequence the artistry of Scott is completely inefficient toward the end of his life; his sense of structure, indeed, had never been too good. But his excellent feeling for a good story, his occasional brilliant characterization, and his dramatic as well as his lyric instincts earned for him in his day and later an immense popularity—he became "the wizard of the North." At least nine excellent novels by him are conspicuous. The total list of Waverley novels falls conveniently into three groups: the novels of Scotland, the novels of England, and the later novels, the scenes of which are laid chiefly on the Continent. In the first of these groups come *Guy Mannering* (1815), a story of mid-eighteenth-century England and Scotland, with two fine characters—Meg Merrilies and Dominie Sampson; *The Antiquary* (1816), the scene of which is virtually contemporary with Scott—an unusual thing for a characteristic Scott novel; *Old Mortality* (1816), the epic of the Scottish Covenanters of the seventeenth century; *Rob Roy* (1818), a typical Scott novel of Jacobite rebellion in the reign of King George I of England; *The Heart of Midlothian* (1818), the scene laid in the reign of George II, an affecting story of the one whom many regard as Scott's finest character—Jeanie Deans; *The Bride of Lammermoor* (1819), Scott's most dramatic love story, a tragic tale of Scotland about 1700, the source of one of the most popular of modern operas, Donizetti's *Lucia di Lammermoor*. These six novels are probably the best of Scott's work dealing with Scottish history between the Puritan rebellion and the author's own day. The second group of novels deals with the England of the past. In *Ivanhoe* (1820), the most popular of his works, he turns to the medieval days of Richard the Lion Heart (d. 1199); it is a brilliant piece of romantic history, particularly in its striking contrast of Norman and Anglo-Saxon. *Kenilworth* (1821), although it does some violence to history, is undoubtedly the best literary romance about the Elizabethan age. In the third group, belonging to Scott's later years, the author turns chiefly to the Continent. The most renowned of these novels is *Quentin Durward* (1823), a fine dashing love-story of a Scotchman at the court of the colorful King Louis XI of France (fl. 1470).

Scott is unquestionably the greatest romantic novelist of his age. He has a splendid energy and manliness, a firm command of his characters, particularly of those from the middle class and the peasantry, and a vivid

Portrait of Congreve, 1700

descriptive style shot through with brilliant poetic touches. It is not easy to be unmoved by the account of the murder of Amy Robsart in *Kenilworth*, by the pilgrimage of Jeanie Deans in *The Heart of Midlothian*, by the sight of the Highlanders marching to the battle-field of Preston in *Waverley*, by the fanatical Habakkuk Mucklewrath in *Old Mortality*, or by a dozen other striking scenes and personalities. Scott's pace in his novels is to the modern reader over-leisurely; his language seems at times stilted, his lords and ladies are often pallid individuals—these are undoubtedly faults, perhaps concessions to the taste of his generation, but faults nevertheless. His haste often led to careless errors, as when his sun sinks into the sea off the eastern coast—probably his most famous blunder; and his cavalier adjusting of historical facts to suit his fancy may cause the judicious to grieve. He falls below Jane Austen in intellectuality and humor; nor has he her ruthlessness. He fails, often lamentably, in his attempts to apply the delicate touch—something of which Jane Austen was mistress supreme. On the other hand, he excels in his varied subject-matter, his breadth of interest, the warmth and sweep of his imagination, and in his ready acceptance of the noble possibilities in human kind. Perhaps it is enough to say that he is a romanticist and that Jane Austen is not; his realism, effective though it often may be, does not seem to be so integral a part of Scott's character as his accounts of

Scott's qualities as novelist

> . . . old, unhappy, far-off things,
> And battles long ago.

Portrait of Scott, 1825

Many writers all over Europe imitated Scott during his own lifetime and in the generation immediately following—de Vigny and Dumas in France; Freytag and Ebers in Germany; Manzoni in Italy; Cooper in America. But there is a certain grandeur and solidity in Scott that his disciples did not fully possess; he remains the massive achievement in the history of early nineteenth-century romantic fiction, and his work is an impressive summation of the romantic mind.

The Romantic Age in Review

IT IS EXTREMELY DIFFICULT to give the years from 1760 to 1832 an accurate characterizing title. The early decades of this period witnessed the gradual death of neo-classicism, it is true, but they witnessed also, even near the end of the period, an occasional resurrection of the neo-classical spirit in such a writer as Jane Austen or as Lord Byron in his satirical mood. Nevertheless the drift of the period is strikingly in a direction opposed to neo-classicism. It is the period of the freeing of western civilization from certain habits of thought and action which had prevailed for more than a century—a liberation which expressed itself not only in all the arts but also in politics

Liberal trends

and economics, where it culminated on the one hand in the French Revolution and on the other in the Industrial Revolution.

Such a liberation could be brought about only by a strong reaction against the conservatism, the complacence, and the static but orderly quality of eighteenth-century neo-classicism. As we have seen, the thoughts and actions of men in the latter half of the eighteenth century were increasingly the products of the emotions and the imagination—of what has been termed the romantic. This is not to imply that the whole world suddenly lost all sense of fact and built up a cloud cuckooland of speculation, in which a new heaven and a new earth were to be established immediately upon the ruins of the old. The extreme, the fanatical, and the short-sighted dreamed such dreams, of course, and actually brought some of them to pass in certain parts of Europe, as the French Revolution illustrates. But these people reckoned without the innate conservatism of human nature; they went too fast and produced a general reaction against themselves, which was particularly manifest in England, by nature a reactionary nation. For that matter, the average Englishman of 1820 seems to have been as materialistic as the man of 1770.

An age of political and social revolution

Yet the work of the political revolutionists had not been all in vain. "Liberty, equality, and fraternity," once uttered, was never again to be completely silenced. It was a phrase that was to serve, if only indirectly, as the means by which mankind was best able to adjust itself to the new industrial world that came during the latter half of the eighteenth century. The adjustment was slow and painful and discouraging; it has not yet been completed, and under the influence of the years from 1914 to 1941 the democratic beliefs created in the nineteenth century are now somewhat in eclipse. But the history of these efforts at adjustment is largely the history of the nineteenth century; it makes this age of revolution one with our present-day age—the second fascinating chapter in the story of the modern era, of which the Renaissance and the neo-classical period together formed the first.

Romanticism in the arts

The artistic expression of the period—its literature, art, and music—was highly charged with romanticism; it is represented by fine creators working in dissimilar media—Schumann, Schubert, Chopin, Corot, Turner, Keats, and Goethe. The list might be extended almost indefinitely, so rich was the profuse romantic product. Much of this romantic expression was intended by its originators as a practical remedy for the ills of humanity. So it was with those preaching human brotherhood, the beneficent force of nature, the hatred of tyranny and oppression. Part of the romanticism of the period, on the other hand, was a means of escape from reality. Such was the effect of the vague and yearning quest after the beautiful, the good, and the sublime; the emotional intoxication coming from the glamour

The Waltz

of the past or of the remote in space; the welcoming of melancholy as readily as joy; the anesthetic absorption in an other-worldly religion—all this was the result of a pathetic desire to build an ivory tower for habitation, where only the agreeable and entrancing could enter. It is incorrect to assume that such literature of escape has but a negative value, that it made no effort to advance the fortunes of man. It was in effect a facing away from reality to live in a new world equally real to the romanticist. Grant its occasional futility, but observe that it was idealistic. Many a philosopher has gone to his death maintaining that idealism will outlast all the material achievements of man. If we can dare assume that reality is something more than a mere amassing of facts, then romanticism is a warming, broadening, liberalizing force, as necessary to life as air and water.

The literature of escape

Furthermore, it is difficult to say where, in the mind of the romanticist, practicality ends and romanticism begins. A Rousseau and a Shelley can be regarded as cloudy visionaries; nevertheless, they thought themselves leaders, and many have followed them. Wordsworth prided himself on his desire to speak the language of common man and to share his inmost soul. Byron, the scoffer against the trend of his time in literature, usually the practical man, could dream of helping an enslaved people. The essential lesson to be learned here is the fact that the romantic mind, a highly individualized, subjective kind of mind, calls enticingly to its affinity and repels its opposite. To him who is severely rational and realistic, the romantic is either foolish or incomprehensible; to him who would be romantic, the romantic is the greatest of all forms of art. The true romanticist would make an even stronger statement; he would feel that this age, or any age approaching it (such as the Renaissance), was the only kind of literary age worth while. Let two great romanticists state their case. "The understanding heart," said De Quincey, "is the interchangeable formula for man in his highest state of capacity for the infinite. Tragedy, romance, fairy tale . . . all alike restore to man's mind the ideals of justice, of hope, of truth, of mercy, of retribution, which else (left to the support of daily life in its realities) would languish for want of sufficient illustration." One other element should be added to De Quincey's fine summary of truly romantic literature; that is the element of elusive beauty wedded to wonder, which, as Shelley expresses it in incomparable fashion,

The enduring quality of romanticism

> . . . visits with inconstant glance
> Each human heart and countenance;
> Like hues and harmonies of evening—
> Like clouds in starlight widely spread—
> Like memory of music fled—
> Like aught that for its grace may be
> Dear, and yet dearer for its mystery.

At Mother's Knee

THE APPROACH TO ROMANTICISM

James Thomson
1700-1748

In September on the eve of the eighteenth century, so prolific in English literature, James Thomson was born in the little parish of Ednam, Roxburghshire, Scotland. His youth was uneventful; he went to Edinburgh University, and scribbled verses at an early age. Like most literary fledglings of the day, he went up to London, where he shifted his interest from things ecclesiastic—an interest in which his minister father had encouraged him—to things poetic. According to Samuel Johnson, some letters of recommendation tied in a handkerchief were stolen from Thomson on the street very soon after his arrival in London. But this mishap gave him little worry. He seemed always to have enough self-assurance to keep himself afloat, yet not so much as would tempt him to curry favor with the great men of his day with too much haste. Akin to this self-esteem was a native indolence, which Thomson was not timid in acknowledging.

Winter, his first important work, was brought to successful publication within a year after his introduction to London (1726). During the two years following he wrote *Summer, Spring,* and other poems, and produced *Sophonisba*, a very inadequate tragedy. The play was favorably received, but there is much in it to ridicule. Nevertheless, Thomson's reputation was running high at that time. *Autumn*, completing *The Seasons* in 1730, was followed in 1734 by his bulky poem *Liberty*. Thomson himself considered this last work as his best effort. But it has been judged by posterity to be of no significance and strongly lacking in imagination.

The office of Secretary of the Briefs, an obvious sinecure, fell to Thomson in 1733, and only pampered his indolence. In 1737, the Prince of Wales, professing his state of affairs to be "in a more poetic posture than formerly," granted Thomson a pension of one hundred pounds a year. He was now "obliged to write." During the years from 1738 to 1744 came the world-famous *Rule, Britannia* (p. 39) and four plays. None of the dramas received more than lukewarm approval. *The Castle of Indolence*, Thomson's last work, had its beginnings in a little piece by Thomson joking at his own laziness; it became, in the writing, a very extensive piece of poetry, and the finest of the many imitations of Spenser which were in fashion at the time.

The significance of James Thomson in the history of English literature is plain. Writing in an age that saw the publication of such thoroughly typical neo-classical works as those of Pope, Addison, and Steele, he turned in *The Seasons* to nature in her various moods, and described her in pictorially striking blank verse—not necessarily as a background against which moved that interesting creature man, but largely for her own sake. These descriptions of nature Thomson often made rather timidly, relying upon many of the accepted neo-classical conventions of style and vocabulary, but nevertheless with much poetical enjoyment of the spectacle and with a sincere appreciation for nature's wildness and beauty. Occasionally there is in his works a sympathy for the luckless human—what was to be called later humanitarianism—that is out of the ordinary for the age. In *The Castle of Indolence*, Thomson returned to

from *The Seasons*

(from *Winter*)

The four parts of *The Seasons* were first published separately in this order: *Winter* (1726), *Summer* (1727), *Spring* (1728), and *Autumn* (1730). They were later combined in logical order and republished several times with many additions and revisions. Thomson evidently was conscious that he was making an effort toward "the revival of poetry," as he shows in his Preface to the second edition of *Winter*.

Though written in a neo-classical period and reflecting the neo-classical modes of thought, as shown in the regularity and orderliness of the verse, the moral observations, compliments to patrons, conventional diction, and stock elements of scenery, the poem nevertheless breaks with the temper of the day and marks the real beginning of the nature-worship so characteristic of later romantic poetry (p. 10). Thomson was a keen and sympathetic observer of the various aspects of nature, particularly the sights and sounds associated with the progress of the year, and he writes with much poetic fervor. In his pictures of nature he follows the practice of late seventeenth-century landscape painters in grouping "details in broad masses of color and striking contrasts of light and shadow" (cf. *The Castle of Indolence*, ll. 334 ff., p. 45).

Thomson chose to write *The Seasons* in blank verse modeled after that of Milton rather than in the closed couplets of Pope. He thus helped to reintroduce blank verse as a favorite poetic medium, and in deliberately imitating Milton in both style and vocabulary, he set the fashion of a genuine Miltonic tradition in English poetry.

See, winter comes to rule the varied year,
Sullen and sad, with all his rising train—
Vapors, and clouds, and storms. Be these my theme;
These, that exalt the soul to solemn thought
And heavenly musing. Welcome, kindred glooms!   5
Cogenial horrors, hail! With frequent foot,
Pleased have I, in my cheerful morn of life,
When nursed by careless solitude I lived
And sung of nature with unceasing joy,
Pleased have I wandered through your rough domain;   10
Trod the pure virgin-snows, myself as pure;
Heard the winds roar, and the big torrent burst;
Or seen the deep-fermenting tempest brewed
In the grim evening-sky. Thus passed the time,
Till through the lucid chambers of the south
Looked out the joyous Spring—looked out and smiled.   16

To thee, the patron of this first essay,
The muse, O Wilmington! renews her song.
Since has she rounded the revolving year:
Skimmed the gay spring; on eagle-pinions borne,   20
Attempted through the summer-blaze to rise;
Then swept o'er autumn with the shadowy gale.
And now among the wintry clouds again,
Rolled in the doubling storm, she tries to soar,
To swell her note with all the rushing winds,
To suit her sounding cadence to the floods;   26
As is her theme, her numbers wildly great.
Thrice happy, could she fill thy judging ear
With bold description and with manly thought!
Nor art thou skilled in awful schemes alone,   30

---

6. **Cogenial**, familiar from birth; some modern editors have amended this to "congenial." The original reading, however, makes much better sense.

18. **Wilmington.** *Winter* was dedicated to Sir Spencer Compton (1673?-1743), Speaker of the House of Commons, and made Earl of Wilmington in 1730.

And how to make a mighty people thrive;
But equal goodness, sound integrity,
A firm, unshaken, uncorrupted soul
Amid a sliding age, and burning strong,
Not vainly blazing, for thy country's weal, 35
A steady spirit, regularly free—
These, each exalting each, the statesman light
Into the patriot; these, the public hope
And eye to thee converting, bid the Muse
Record what envy dares not flattery call. 40

Now, when the cheerless empire of the sky
To Capricorn the Centaur-Archer yields,
And fierce Aquarius stains the inverted year—
Hung o'er that farthest verge of heaven, the sun
Scarce spreads o'er ether the dejected day. 45
Faint are his gleams, and ineffectual shoot
His struggling rays in horizontal lines
Through the thick air; as clothed in cloudy storm,
Weak, wan, and broad, he skirts the southern sky; 49
And, soon descending, to the long dark night,
Wide-shading all, the prostrate world resigns.
Nor is the night unwished; while vital heat,
Light, life, and joy the dubious day forsake.
Meantime, in sable cincture, shadows vast,
Deep-tinged and damp, and congregated clouds, 55
And all the vapory turbulence of heaven
Involve the face of things. Thus winter falls,
A heavy gloom oppressive o'er the world,
Through nature shedding influence malign,
And rouses up the seeds of dark disease. 60
The soul of man dies in him, loathing life,
And black with more than melancholy views.
The cattle droop; and o'er the furrowed land,
Fresh from the plow, the dun discolored flocks,
Untended spreading, crop the wholesome root.
Along the woods, along the moorish fens, 66
Sighs the sad genius of the coming storm;
And up among the loose disjointed cliffs

And fractured mountains wild, the brawling brook
And cave, presageful, send a hollow moan, 70
Resounding long in listening fancy's ear.

Then comes the father of the tempest forth,
Wrapped in black glooms. First, joyless rains obscure
Drive through the mingling skies with vapor foul,
Dash on the mountain's brow, and shake the woods 75
That grumbling wave below. The unsightly plain
Lies a brown deluge; as the low-bent clouds
Pour flood on flood, yet unexhausted still
Combine, and, deepening into night, shut up
The day's fair face. The wanderers of heaven,
Each to his home, retire; save those that love
To take their pastime in the troubled air, 82
Or skimming flutter round the dimply pool.
The cattle from the untasted fields return
And ask, with meaning low, their wonted stalls, 85
Or ruminate in the contiguous shade.
Thither the household feathery people crowd,
The crested cock, with all his female train,
Pensive and dripping; while the cottage-hind
Hangs o'er the enlivening blaze, and taleful there 90
Recounts his simple frolic: much he talks,
And much he laughs, nor recks the storm that blows
Without, and rattles on his humble roof.

Wide o'er the brim, with many a torrent swelled,
And the mixed ruin of its banks o'erspread, 95
At last the roused-up river pours along;
Resistless, roaring, dreadful, down it comes,
From the rude mountain and the mossy wild,
Tumbling through rocks abrupt, and sounding far; 99
Then o'er the sanded valley floating spreads,
Calm, sluggish, silent; till again, constrained
Between two meeting hills, it bursts a way

---

42. **Capricorn . . . Centaur-Archer,** two constellations of the zodiac. When the sun passes from one constellation to the next, the first is said to "yield" to the second. Centaur-Archer is the constellation of Sagittarius. The sun leaves the constellation of Sagittarius about December 21, entering then the sign of Capricorn (the Goat); a month later it enters the sign of Aquarius (the Water-bearer). 43. **inverted year,** probably in the figurative sense of "upset" or "overthrown"; possibly in the sense of "changed to the new (year)." 45. **ether,** in the general sense of "the heavens."

89. **cottage-hind,** peasant in a cottage; *hind,* from the Old English *hyne,* "servant," "retainer." Note *Hind Horn* (Vol. 1, p. 118).

Where rocks and woods o'erhang the turbid
    stream;
There, gathering triple force, rapid and deep,
It boils, and wheels, and foams, and thunders
    through.   105

  Nature! great parent! whose unceasing hand
Rolls round the seasons of the changeful year,
How mighty, how majestic are thy works!
With what a pleasing dread they swell the
    soul,
That sees astonished, and astonished sings! 110
Ye too, ye winds! that now begin to blow
With boisterous sweep, I raise my voice to
    you.
Where are your stores, ye powerful beings!
    say,
Where your aërial magazines reserved
To swell the brooding terrors of the storm? 115
In what far-distant region of the sky,
Hushed in deep silence, sleep you when 'tis
    calm?

  When from the pallid sky the sun descends,
With many a spot, that o'er his glaring orb
Uncertain wanders, stained; red fiery streaks
Begin to flush around. The reeling clouds 121
Stagger with dizzy poise, as doubting yet
Which master to obey; while, rising slow,
Blank in the leaden-colored east, the moon
Wears a wan circle round her blunted horns.
Seen through the turbid, fluctuating air,   126
The stars obtuse emit a shivering ray;
Or frequent seem to shoot athwart the gloom,
And long behind them trail the whitening
    blaze.
Snatched in short eddies, plays the withered
    leaf;   130
And on the flood the dancing feather floats.
With broadened nostrils to the sky upturned,
The conscious heifer snuffs the stormy gale.
E'en as the matron, at her nightly task,
With pensive labor draws the flaxen thread,
The wasted taper and the crackling flame 136
Foretell the blast. But chief the plumy race,
The tenants of the sky, its changes speak.

Retiring from the downs, where all day long
They picked their scanty fare, a blackening
    train   140
Of clamorous rooks thick-urge their weary
    flight,
And seek the closing shelter of the grove.
Assiduous, in his bower, the wailing owl
Plies his sad song. The cormorant on high
Wheels from the deep, and screams along the
    land.   145
Loud shrieks the soaring hern; and with wild
    wing
The circling sea-fowl cleave the flaky clouds.
Ocean, unequal pressed, with broken tide
And blind commotion heaves; while from the
    shore,
Eat into caverns by the restless wave,   150
And forest-rustling mountain comes a voice
That, solemn-sounding, bids the world pre-
    pare.
Then issues forth the storm with sudden burst,
And hurls the whole precipitated air
Down in a torrent. On the passive main 155
Descends the ethereal force, and with strong
    gust
Turns from its bottom the discolored deep.
Through the black night that sits immense
    around,
Lashed into foam, the fierce-conflicting brine
Seems o'er a thousand raging waves to burn.
Meantime the mountain-billows, to the clouds
In dreadful tumult swelled, surge above surge,
Burst into chaos with tremendous roar,   163
And anchored navies from their stations drive
Wild as the winds, across the howling waste
Of mighty waters; now the inflated wave
Straining they scale, and now impetuous shoot
Into the secret chambers of the deep,
The wintry Baltic thundering o'er their head.
Emerging thence again, before the breath 170
Of full-exerted heaven they wing their course,
And dart on distant coasts—if some sharp
    rock
Or shoal insidious break not their career,

---

114. **magazines.** As in the case of *stores* (l. 113), *magazines* indicates a place for keeping something; specifically, a storehouse for the storms and thunders of heaven. This meaning of *magazine* is retained in "powder magazine." 127. **obtuse**, blunted, dulled in light.

139. **downs**, treeless chalk uplands, such as those along the southern coast of England. 146. **hern**, heron. 156. **ethereal**, from the heavens, from the sky. The phrase "ethereal force" for "wind" is a good illustration of Thomson's devotion to the neo-classical trick of style which demands an abstract noun of vague force and of Latin derivations, qualified by a usually vague adjective or epithet. "Plumy race" (l. 137) for "birds" is another example. 173. **career**, wild flight.

And in loose fragments fling them floating
    round. 174

Nor less at land the loosened tempest reigns.
The mountain thunders, and its sturdy sons
Stoop to the bottom of the rocks they shade.
Lone on the midnight steep, and all aghast,
The dark wayfaring stranger breathless toils,
And, often falling, climbs against the blast. 180
Low waves the rooted forest, vexed, and
    sheds
What of its tarnished honors yet remain—
Dashed down and scattered, by the tearing
    wind's
Assiduous fury, its gigantic limbs. 184
Thus struggling through the dissipated grove,
The whirling tempest raves along the plain;
And, on the cottage thatched or lordly roof
Keen-fastening, shakes them to the solid base.
Sleep frighted flies; and round the rocking
    dome,
For entrance eager, howls the savage blast. 190
Then too, they say, through all the burdened
    air
Long groans are heard, shrill sounds, and distant sighs,
That, uttered by the demon of the night,
Warn the devoted wretch of woe and death.

    Huge uproar lords it wide. The clouds,
        commixed 195
With stars swift-gliding, sweep along the sky.
All nature reels: till nature's king, who oft
Amid tempestuous darkness dwells alone,
And on the wings of the careering wind
Walks dreadfully serene, commands a calm;
Then straight air, sea, and earth are hushed at
    once. 201

    As yet 'tis midnight deep. The weary clouds,
Slow-meeting, mingle into solid gloom.
Now, while the drowsy world lies lost in
    sleep,
Let me associate with the serious night, 205
And contemplation, her sedate compeer;
Let me shake off the intrusive cares of day,
And lay the meddling senses all aside.

    Where now, ye lying vanities of life!
Ye ever-tempting, ever-cheating train! 210
Where are you now? and what is your
    amount?
Vexation, disappointment, and remorse.
Sad, sickening thought! and yet deluded man,
A scene of crude disjointed visions past,
And broken slumbers, rises still resolved, 215
With new-flushed hopes, to run the giddy
    round.

    Father of light and life! thou Good Supreme!
O teach me what is good! teach me Thyself!
Save me from folly, vanity, and vice,
From every low pursuit; and feed my soul 220
With knowledge, conscious peace, and virtue
    pure—
Sacred, substantial, never-fading bliss!

    The keener tempests come; and, fuming
        dun
From all the livid east or piercing north,
Thick clouds ascend, in whose capacious
    womb 225
A vapory deluge lies, to snow congealed.
Heavy they roll their fleecy world along,
And the sky saddens with the gathered storm.
Through the hushed air the whitening shower
    descends,
At first thin-wavering; till at last the flakes 230
Fall broad and wide and fast, dimming the
    day
With a continual flow. The cherished fields
Put on their winter-robe of purest white.
'Tis brightness all; save where the new snow
    melts
Along the mazy current. Low the woods 235
Bow their hoar head; and, ere the languid sun
Faint from the west emits his evening ray,
Earth's universal face, deep-hid and chill,
Is one wild dazzling waste, that buries wide
The works of man. Drooping, the laborer-
    ox 240
Stands covered o'er with snow, and then demands
The fruit of all his toil. The fowls of heaven,
Tamed by the cruel season, crowd around
The winnowing store, and claim the little
    boon 244

228. **saddens,** grows dark and heavy.

Which Providence assigns them. One alone,
The redbreast, sacred to the household gods,
Wisely regardful of the embroiling sky,
In joyless fields and thorny thickets leaves
His shivering mates, and pays to trusted man
His annual visit. Half afraid, he first   250
Against the window beats; then brisk alights
On the warm hearth; then, hopping o'er the floor,
Eyes all the smiling family askance,
And pecks, and starts, and wonders where he is—   254
Till, more familiar grown, the table-crumbs
Attract his slender feet. The foodless wilds
Pour forth their brown inhabitants. The hare,
Though timorous of heart, and hard beset
By death in various forms, dark snares, and dogs,   259
And more unpitying men, the garden seeks,
Urged on by fearless want. The bleating kind
Eye the bleak heaven, and next the glistening earth,
With looks of dumb despair; then, sad-dispersed,
Dig for the withered herb through heaps of snow.

   Now, shepherds, to your helpless charge be kind;   265
Baffle the raging year, and fill their pens
With food at will; lodge them below the storm,
And watch them strict; for, from the bellowing east,
In this dire season, oft the whirlwind's wing
Sweeps up the burden of whole wintry plains
In one wide waft, and o'er the hapless flocks,
Hid in the hollow of two neighboring hills,   272
The billowy tempest whelms; till, upward urged,
The valley to a shining mountain swells,
Tipped with a wreath high-curling in the sky.   275

   As thus the snows arise, and, foul and fierce,
All winter drives along the darkened air,
In his own loose-revolving fields the swain
Disastered stands; sees other hills ascend,   279
Of unknown joyless brow; and other scenes,
Of horrid prospect, shag the trackless plain;
Nor finds the river nor the forest hid
Beneath the formless wild; but wanders on
From hill to dale, still more and more astray—
Impatient flouncing through the drifted heaps,
Stung with the thoughts of home: the thoughts of home   286
Rush on his nerves and call their vigor forth
In many a vain attempt. How sinks his soul!
What black despair, what horror fills his heart,
When, for the dusky spot which fancy feigned
His tufted cottage rising through the snow,   291
He meets the roughness of the middle waste,
Far from the track and blest abode of man;
While round him night resistless closes fast,
And every tempest, howling o'er his head,   295
Renders the savage wilderness more wild.
Then throng the busy shapes into his mind
Of covered pits, unfathomably deep,
A dire descent! beyond the power of frost;
Of faithless bogs; of precipices huge,   300
Smoothed up with snow; and (what is land unknown,
What water) of the still unfrozen spring,
In the loose marsh or solitary lake,
Where the fresh fountain from the bottom boils.
These check his fearful steps; and down he sinks   305
Beneath the shelter of the shapeless drift,
Thinking o'er all the bitterness of death,
Mixed with the tender anguish nature shoots
Through the wrung bosom of the dying man—
His wife, his children, and his friends unseen.
In vain for him the officious wife prepares   311
The fire fair-blazing and the vestment warm;
In vain his little children, peeping out
Into the mingling storm, demand their sire
With tears of artless innocence. Alas!   315
Nor wife nor children more shall he behold,
Nor friends, nor sacred home. On every nerve
The deadly winter seizes, shuts up sense,
And, o'er his inmost vitals creeping cold,
Lays him along the snows a stiffened corse,

---

261. **bleating kind,** sheep; cf. "plumy race" (l. 137) and "ethereal force" (l. 156 and note).

311. **officious,** busy with duties.

Stretched out, and bleaching in the northern
    blast. 321

Ah! little think the gay licentious proud,
Whom pleasure, power, and affluence surround—
They, who their thoughtless hours in giddy
    mirth,
And wanton, often cruel, riot waste— 325
Ah! little think they, while they dance along,
How many feel, this very moment, death
And all the sad variety of pain;
How many sink in the devouring flood, 329
Or more devouring flame; how many bleed,
By shameful variance betwixt man and man;
How many pine in want, and dungeon-glooms,
Shut from the common air and common use
Of their own limbs; how many drink the cup
Of baleful grief, or eat the bitter bread 335
Of misery; sore pierced by wintry winds,
How many shrink into the sordid hut
Of cheerless poverty; how many shake
With all the fiercer tortures of the mind,
Unbounded passion, madness, guilt, remorse—
Whence, tumbled headlong from the height
    of life, 341
They furnish matter for the tragic muse;
Even in the vale, where wisdom loves to dwell,
With friendship, peace, and contemplation
    joined,
How many, racked with honest passions,
    droop 345
In deep retired distress; how many stand
Around the death-bed of their dearest friends,
And point the parting anguish! Thought fond
    man
Of these, and all the thousand nameless ills
That one incessant struggle render life, 350
One scene of toil, of suffering, and of fate,
Vice in his high career would stand appalled,
And heedless rambling impulse learn to
    think;
The conscious heart of charity would warm,
And her wide wish benevolence dilate; 355
The social tear would rise, the social sigh;
And, into clear perfection, gradual bliss,
Refining still, the social passions work.

And here can I forget the generous band
Who, touched with human woe, redressive
    searched 360
Into the horrors of the gloomy jail?
Unpitied and unheard where misery moans,
Where sickness pines, where thirst and hunger
    burn,
And poor misfortune feels the lash of vice;
While in the land of liberty—the land 365
Whose every street and public meeting glow
With open freedom—little tyrants raged,
Snatched the lean morsel from the starving
    mouth,
Tore from cold wintry limbs the tattered
    weed,
E'en robbed them of the last of comforts,
    sleep, 370
The free-born Briton to the dungeon chained
Or, as the lust of cruelty prevailed,
At pleasure marked him with inglorious
    stripes,
And crushed out lives, by secret barbarous
    ways,
That for their country would have toiled or
    bled. 375
O great design! if executed well,
With patient care and wisdom-tempered
    zeal.
Ye sons of mercy! yet resume the search;
Drag forth the legal monsters into light,
Wrench from their hands oppression's iron
    rod, 380
And bid the cruel feel the pains they give.
Much still untouched remains; in this rank
    age,
Much is the patriot's weeding hand required.
The toils of law—what dark insidious men
Have cumbrous added to perplex the truth
And lengthen simple justice into trade— 386
How glorious were the day that saw these
    broke,
And every man within the reach of right!

*   *   *   *   *

(*1726; 1730*)

359. **generous band**, a committee appointed in 1729 to investigate the conditions of jails and prisons. It discovered that the wardenships of prisons were bought by men who were accustomed to exact heavy fees from prisoners, on the penalty of severe treatment.

Rule, Britannia!

This poem, first published in 1740 in *Alfred: A Masque*, neatly expresses Thomson's patriotism and devotion to national liberty.

When Britain first, at Heaven's command,
  Arose from out the azure main,
This was the charter of the land,
  And guardian angels sung this strain—
    "Rule, Britannia, rule the waves;   5
    Britons never will be slaves."

The nations, not so blessed as thee,
  Must in their turns to tyrants fall;
While thou shalt flourish great and free,
  The dread and envy of them all.   10
    "Rule, Britannia, rule the waves;
    Britons never will be slaves."

Still more majestic shalt thou rise,
  More dreadful from each foreign stroke;
As the loud blast that tears the skies   15
  Serves but to root thy native oak.
    "Rule," *etc.*

Thee haughty tyrants ne'er shall tame;
  All their attempts to bend thee down
Will but arouse thy generous flame,   20
  But work their woe and thy renown.
    "Rule," *etc.*

To thee belongs the rural reign;
  Thy cities shall with commerce shine;
All thine shall be the subject main,   25
  And every shore it circles thine.
    "Rule," *etc.*

The Muses, still with freedom found,
  Shall to thy happy coast repair;
Blessed isle! with matchless beauty crowned,
  And manly hearts to guard the fair.   31
    "Rule, Britannia, rule the waves;
    Britons never will be slaves."   (1740)

16, **oak.** The oak was the material from which were built the famous British men-of-war of the eighteenth century, and the wood was made also the symbol for the bravery of the English seamen; cf. the phrase "hearts and ships of oak."

from *The Castle of Indolence*

(from CANTO I)

The Castle of Indolence is a romantic allegory written in imitation of Spenser. It shows not only a deep admiration for that great poet's work but also some understanding of the qualities of his verse, his phrasing, and his methods of description. A prefatory Advertisement by Thomson states that the "obsolete words and a simplicity of diction" were necessary to perfect the imitation. In the form and in the melody of the stanza; in the intermingling of color, sound, and perfume; and in the presentation of abstract qualities by means of individuals like the "full-spread porter" (Laziness) and his "little roguish page" (Idle Play) of lines 208 ff., the poem ranks as the best of the eighteenth-century imitations of Spenser. In thus harking back to the Elizabethan period for material and for method, *The Castle of Indolence* takes its place alongside *The Seasons* (p. 33) as an influential force in establishing freer poetic traditions. Thomson's highest achievement is shown in the landscape with which the poem opens.

The castle hight* of Indolence,
  And its false luxury;
Where for a little time, alas!
  We lived right jollily.

1

O mortal man! who livest here by toil,
Do not complain of this thy hard estate;

*hight, was called.

That like an emmet thou must ever moil,
Is a sad sentence of an ancient date;
And, certes, there is for it reason great;   5
For, though sometimes it makes thee weep
    and wail,
And curse thy star, and early drudge and late,
Withouten that would come an heavier bale,
Loose life, unruly passions, and diseases pale.

3. **emmet**, ant. 5. **certes**, surely, certainly.

2

In lowly dale, fast by a river's side, 10
With woody hill o'er hill encompassed round,
A most enchanting wizard did abide,
Than whom a fiend more fell is nowhere found.
It was, I ween, a lovely spot of ground;
And there a season atween June and May, 15
Half prankt with spring, with summer half embrowned,
A listless climate made, where, sooth to say,
No living wight could work, ne caréd even for play.

3

Was nought around but images of rest:
Sleep-soothing groves, and quiet lawns between; 20
And flowery beds that slumbrous influence kest
From poppies breathed; and beds of pleasant green,
Where never yet was creeping creature seen.
Meantime unnumbered glittering streamlets played,
And hurléd everywhere their waters sheen; 25
That, as they bickered through the sunny glade,
Though restless still themselves, a lulling murmur made.

4

Joined to the prattle of the purling rills,
Were heard the lowing herds along the vale,
And flocks loud-bleating from the distant hills,
And vacant shepherds piping in the dale: 31
And now and then sweet Philomel would wail,
Or stock-doves plain amid the forest deep,
That drowsy rustled to the sighing gale;
And still a coil the grasshopper did keep; 35
Yet all these sounds yblent inclinéd all to sleep.

5

Full in the passage of the vale, above,
A sable, silent, solemn forest stood;
Where nought but shadowy forms was seen to move,
As Idless fancied in her dreaming mood; 40
And up the hills, or either side, a wood
Of blackening pines, ay waving to and fro,
Sent forth a sleepy horror through the blood;
And where this valley winded out, below,
The murmuring main was heard, and scarcely heard, to flow. 45

6

A pleasing land of drowsyhed it was:
Of dreams that wave before the half-shut eye;
And of gay castles in the clouds that pass,
Forever flushing round a summer sky;
There eke the soft delights, that witchingly 50
Instil a wanton sweetness through the breast,
And the calm pleasures, always hovered nigh;
But whate'er smacked of noyance, or unrest,
Was far, far off expelled from this delicious nest.

7

The landskip such, inspiring perfect ease, 55
Where Indolence (for so the wizard hight)
Close hid his castle mid embowering trees,
That half shut out the beams of Phoebus bright,
And made a kind of checkered day and night;
Meanwhile, unceasing at the massy gate, 60
Beneath a spacious palm, the wicked wight
Was placed; and to his lute, of cruel fate,
And labor harsh, complained, lamenting man's estate.

8

Thither continual pilgrims crowded still,
From all the roads of earth that pass there by;
For, as they chaunced to breathe on neighboring hill, 66
The freshness of this valley smote their eye,
And drew them ever and anon more nigh;

---

16. **prankt**, dressed, decked. 18. **ne**, not. 32. **Philomel**. In classical legend, Philomela, daughter of King Pandion of Athens, was changed into a nightingale; hence, a nightingale. Cf. Matthew Arnold's *Philomela*, p. 733. 35. **coil**, noise, tumult.

50. **eke**, also. 56. **wizard**; cf. Archimago in Spenser's *Faerie Queene* (Vol. I, p. 407, ll. 73 ff.). Stanzas 2, 6, 22, and 29, among others, should be carefully compared with a characteristic stanza or two from *The Faerie Queene*.

'Til clustering round th'enchanter false they hung,
Ymolten with his syren melody; 70
While o'er th'enfeebling lute his hand he flung,
And to the trembling chords these tempting verses sung:

9

"Behold! ye pilgrims of this earth, behold!
See all but man with unearned pleasure gay.
See her bright robes the butterfly unfold, 75
Broke from her wintry tomb in prime of May!
What youthful bride can equal her array?
Who can with her for easy pleasure vie?
From mead to mead with gentle wing to stray,
From flower to flower on balmy gales to fly, 80
Is all she has to do beneath the radiant sky.

10

"Behold the merry minstrels of the morn,
The swarming songsters of the careless grove,
Ten thousand throats! that, from the flowering thorn,
Hymn their good God, and carol sweet of love, 85
Such grateful kindly raptures them emove;
They neither plow, nor sow; ne, fit for flail,
E'er to the barn the nodding sheaves they drove;
Yet theirs each harvest dancing in the gale,
Whatever crowns the hill, or smiles along the vale. 90

11

"Outcast of Nature, man! the wretched thrall
Of bitter-dropping sweat, of sweltry pain,
Of cares that eat away thy heart with gall,
And of the vices, an inhuman train,
That all proceed from savage thirst of gain: 95
For when hard-hearted interest first began
To poison earth, Astraea left the plain;
Guile, violence, and murder seized on man,

87. ne, nor. 97. Astraea, in classical mythology, the goddess of justice.

And, for soft milky streams, with blood the rivers ran.

12

"Come, ye, who still the cumbrous load of life 100
Push hard up hill; but as the farthest steep
You trust to gain, and put an end to strife,
Down thunders back the stone with mighty sweep,
And hurls your labors to the valley deep,
Forever vain; come, and, withouten fee, 105
I in oblivion will your sorrows steep,
Your cares, your toils, will steep you in a sea
Of full delight; O come, ye weary wights, to me!

13

"With me, you need not rise at early dawn,
To pass the joyless day in various stounds; 110
Or, louting low, on upstart fortune fawn,
And sell fair honor for some paltry pounds;
Or through the city take your dirty rounds,
To cheat, and dun, and lie, and visit pay,
Now flattering base, now giving secret wounds; 115
Or prowl in courts of law for human prey,
In venal senate thieve, or rob on broad highway.

14

"No cocks, with me, to rustic labor call,
From village on to village sounding clear;
To tardy swain no shrill-voiced matrons squall; 120
No dogs, no babes, no wives, to stun your ear;
No hammers thump; no horrid blacksmiths sear,
Ne noisy tradesmen your sweet slumbers start,
With sounds that are a misery to hear;
But all is calm, as would delight the heart 125
Of Sybarite of old, all nature, and all art.

99. **milky streams**, an echo of the verse describing the Promised Land: "Unto whom the Lord sware that he would not show them the land which the Lord sware unto their fathers that he would give us, a land that floweth with milk and honey." (*Joshua*, 5:6; cf. also *Isaiah*, 55:1: "Ho, every one that thirsteth, come ye to the waters, and he that hath no money; come ye, buy, and eat; yea, come, buy wine and milk without money and without price.") 110. **stounds**, aches and sorrows. 126. **Sybarite**, an inhabitant of Sybaris, Italy, a city noted in ancient times for its luxurious living.

15

"Here nought but candor reigns, indulgent ease,
Good-natured lounging, sauntering up and down:
They who are pleased themselves must always please;
On others' ways they never squint a frown, 130
Nor heed what haps in hamlet or in town.
Thus, from the source of tender indolence,
With milky blood the heart is overflown,
Is soothed and sweetened by the social sense;
For interest, envy, pride, and strife, are banished hence. 135

16

"What, what, is virtue, but repose of mind,
A pure ethereal calm, that knows no storm;
Above the reach of wild ambition's wind,
Above those passions that this world deform,
And torture man, a proud malignant worm!
But here, instead, soft gales of passion play 141
And gently stir the heart, thereby to form,
A quicker sense of joy; as breezes stray
Across th'enlivened skies, and make them still more gay.

17

"The best of men have ever loved repose: 145
They hate to mingle in the filthy fray,
Where the soul sours, and gradual rancor grows,
Imbittered more from peevish day to day.
Even those whom fame has lent her fairest ray, 149
The most renowned of worthy wights of yore,
From a base world at last have stolen away:
So Scipio, to the soft Cumaean shore
Retiring, tasted joy he never knew before.

18

"But if a little exercise you choose,
Some zest for ease, 'tis not forbidden here. 155
Amid the groves you may indulge the muse,
Or tend the blooms, and deck the vernal year;
Or, softly stealing, with your watery gear,
Along the brooks, the crimson-spotted fry
You may delude: the whilst, amused, you hear
Now the hoarse stream, and now the zephyr's sigh, 161
Attunéd to the birds, and woodland melody.

19

"O grievous folly! to heap up estate,
Losing the days you see beneath the sun; 164
When, sudden, comes blind unrelenting fate,
And gives th'untasted portion you have won,
With ruthless toil, and many a wretch undone,
To those who mock you gone to Pluto's reign,
There with sad ghosts to pine, and shadows dun:
But sure it is of vanities most vain, 170
To toil for what you here untoiling may obtain."

20

He ceased. But still their trembling ears retained
The deep vibrations of his witching song;
That, by a kind of magic power, constrained
To enter in, pell-mell, the listening throng. 175
Heaps poured on heaps, and yet they slipped along,
In silent ease: as when beneath the beam
Of summer-moons, the distant woods among,
Or by some flood all silvered with the gleam,
The soft-embodied fays through airy portal stream. 180

21

By the smooth demon so it ordered was,
And here his baneful bounty first began;
Though some there were who would not further pass,
And his alluring baits suspected han.
The wise distrust the too fair-spoken man. 185
Yet through the gate they cast a wishful eye;
Not to move on, perdie, is all they can;
For, do their very best, they cannot fly,
But often each way look, and often sorely sigh.

152. **Scipio**, Publius Scipio Africanus Major (234?-183 B.C.), famous Roman general, who after a life of warfare retired in 185 B.C. to his native seat near Cumaea, a city in Campania, Italy. 159. **fry**, young fishes. 168. **Pluto**, in classical mythology, the god of the infernal regions. 184. **han**, have (cf. Chaucer's use of the infinitive of the verb "to have," Vol. I, p. 220, l. 490). 187. **perdie**, an oath formed from the French *par Dieu*, "by God!"

22

When this the watchful, wicked wizard saw,
With sudden spring he leaped upon them strait;   191
And soon as touched by his unhallowed paw,
They found themselves within the curséd gate;
Full hard to be repassed, like that of fate.
Not stronger were of old the giant-crew,   195
Who sought to pull high Jove from regal state;
Though feeble wretch he seemed, of sallow hue.
Certes, who bides his grasp, will that encounter rue.

23

For whomsoe'er the villain takes in hand,
Their joints unknit, their sinews melt apace;
As lithe they grow as any willow-wand,   201
And of their vanished force remains no trace;
So when a maiden fair, of modest grace,
In all her buxom, blooming May of charms,
Is seizéd in some losel's hot embrace,   205
She waxeth very weakly as she warms,
Then, sighing, yields her up to love's delicious harms.

24

Waked by the crowd, slow from his bench arose
A comely full-spread porter, swoln with sleep:
His calm, broad, thoughtless aspect breathed repose,   210
And in sweet torpor he was plungéd deep,
Ne could himself from ceaseless yawning keep;
While o'er his eyes the drowsy liquor ran,
Through which his half-waked soul would faintly peep.
Then taking his black staff, he called his man,
And roused himself as much as rouse himself he can.   216

25

The lad leaped lightly at his master's call;
He was, to weet, a little roguish page,
Save sleep and play who minded nought at all,
Like most the untaught striplings of his age.
This boy he kept each band to disengage,   221
Garters and buckles, task for him unfit,
But ill-becoming his grave personage,
And which his portly paunch would not permit,
So this same limber page to all performéd it.   225

26

Meantime the master-porter wide displayed
Great store of caps, of slippers, and of gowns,
Wherewith he those who entered in, arrayed,
Loose, as the breeze that plays along the downs,
And waves the summer-woods when evening frowns.   230
O fair undress, best dress! it checks no vein,
But every flowing limb in pleasure drowns,
And heightens ease with grace. This done, right fain
Sir Porter sat him down, and turned to sleep again.

27

Thus easy robed, they to the fountain sped,
That in the middle of the court up-threw   236
A stream, high-spouting from its liquid bed,
And falling back again in drizzly dew;
There each deep draughts, as deep he thirsted, drew.
It was a fountain of Nepenthe rare;   240
Whence, as Dan Homer sings, huge pleasaunce grew,
And sweet oblivion of vile earthly care,
Fair gladsome waking thoughts, and joyous dreams more fair.

28

This rite performed, all inly pleased and still,
Withouten trump was proclamation made;   245
"Ye sons of indolence, do what you will;
And wander where you list, through hall or glade!
Be no man's pleasure for another's stayed;

---

195. **giant-crew,** in classical mythology, the Titans, who rebelled against Zeus (Jove) and were defeated. 205. **losel,** rascal, worthless person. 218. **to weet,** as far as one could tell. 240. **Nepenthe,** in classical lore, a drug that caused forgetfulness of sorrow and pain. 241. **Dan Homer,** Lord Homer. The reference here is to the *Odyssey,* IV, 220 ff.

Let each as likes him best his hours employ,
And cursed be he who minds his neighbor's trade! 250
Here dwells kind ease and unreproving joy:
He little merits bliss who others can annoy."

29

Strait of these endless numbers, swarming round
As thick as idle motes in sunny ray,
Not one eftsoons in view was to be found, 255
But every man strolled off his own glad way.
Wide o'er this ample court's blank area,
With all the lodges that thereto pertained,
No living creature could be seen to stray;
While solitude and perfect silence reigned; 260
So that to think you dreamt you almost was constrained.

30

As when a shepherd of the Hebrid Isles,
Placed far amid the melancholy main,
(Whether it be lone fancy him beguiles,
Or that aërial beings sometimes deign 265
To stand, embodied, to our senses plain)
Sees on the naked hill, or valley low,
The whilst in ocean Phoebus dips his wain,
A vast assembly moving to and fro;
Then all at once in air dissolves the wondrous show. 270

31

Ye gods of quiet, and of sleep profound!
Whose soft dominion o'er this castle sways,
And all the widely-silent places round,
Forgive me, if my trembling pen displays
What never yet was sung in mortal lays. 275
But how shall I attempt such arduous string,
I who have spent my nights and nightly days
In this soul-deadening place, loose-loitering?
Ah! how shall I for this uprear my molted wing?

32

Come on, my muse, nor stoop to low despair, 280

255. **eftsoons**, immediately. 261. **was**. Singular verbs with plural subjects were not uncommon in earlier English literature. 262. **Hebrid Isles**, the Hebrides, a group of islands to the west of Scotland.

Thou imp of Jove, touched by celestial fire!
Thou yet shalt sing of war, and actions fair,
Which the bold sons of Britain will inspire;
Of ancient bards thou yet shalt sweep the lyre; 284
Thou yet shalt tread in tragic pall the stage,
Paint love's enchanting woes, the hero's ire,
The sage's calm, the patriot's noble rage,
Dashing corruption down through every worthless age.

33

The doors, that knew no shrill alarming bell,
Ne cursèd knocker plied by villain's hand, 290
Self-opened into halls, where who can tell
What elegance and grandeur wide expand,
The pride of Turkey and of Persia land?
Soft quilts on quilts, on carpets carpets spread,
And couches stretch around in seemly band;
And endless pillows rise to prop the head, 296
So that each spacious room was one full-swelling bed.

34

And everywhere huge covered tables stood,
With wines high-flavored and rich viands crowned;
Whatever sprightly juice or tasteful food 300
On the green bosom of this earth are found,
And all old ocean genders in his round;
Some hand unseen these silently displayed,
Even undemanded by a sigh or sound;
You need but wish, and, instantly obeyed, 305
Fair-ranged the dishes rose, and thick the glasses played.

35

Here freedom reigned without the least alloy;
Nor gossip's tale, nor ancient maiden's gall,
Nor saintly spleen durst murmur at our joy,
And with envenomed tongue our pleasures pall. 310
For why? there was but one great rule for all;
To wit, that each should work his own desire,
And eat, drink, study, sleep, as it may fall,
Or melt the time in love, or wake the lyre,
And carol what, unbid, the Muses might inspire. 315

36

The rooms with costly tapestry were hung,
Where was inwoven many a gentle tale;
Such as of old the rural poets sung,
Or of Arcadian or Sicilian vale:
Reclining lovers, in the lonely dale,   320
Poured forth at large the sweetly-tortured heart;
Or, sighing tender passion, swelled the gale,
And taught charmed echo to resound their smart;
While flocks, woods, streams around, repose and peace impart.

37

Those pleased the most, where, by a cunning hand,   325
Depeinten was the patriarchal age;
What time Dan Abraham left the Chaldee land,
And pastured on from verdant stage to stage,
Where fields and fountains fresh could best engage.   329
Toil was not then. Of nothing they took heed,
But with wild beasts the silvan war to wage,
And o'er vast plains their herds and flocks to feed;
Blest sons of nature they! true golden age indeed!

38

Sometimes the pencil, in cool airy halls,
Bade the gay gloom of vernal landskips rise,
Or autumn's varied shades imbrown the walls;   336
Now the black tempest strikes the astonished eyes;
Now down the steep the flashing torrent flies;
The trembling sun now plays o'er ocean blue,
And now rude mountains frown amid the skies;   340
Whate'er Lorrain light-touched with softening hue,
Or savage Rosa dashed, or learnéd Poussin drew.

39

Each sound, too, here to languishment inclined,
Lulled the weak bosom, and inducéd ease.
Aërial music in the warbling wind,   345
At distance rising oft, by small degrees,
Nearer and nearer came, till o'er the trees
It hung, and breathed such soul-dissolving airs
As did, alas! with soft perdition please;
Entangled deep in its enchanting snares,   350
The listening heart forgot all duties and all cares.

40

A certain music, never known before,
Here lulled the pensive melancholy mind;
Full easily obtained. Behooves no more,
But sidelong, to the gently-waving wind,   355
To lay the well-tuned instrument reclined;
From which with airy flying fingers light,
Beyond each mortal touch the most refined,
The god of winds drew sounds of deep delight;
Whence, with just cause, *The Harp of Aeolus* it hight.   360

41

Ah me! what hand can touch the string so fine?
Who up the lofty diapason roll
Such sweet, such sad, such solemn airs divine,
Then let them down again into the soul?
Now rising love they fanned; now pleasing dole   365
They breathed, in tender musings, through the heart;
And now a graver sacred strain they stole,
As when seraphic hands an hymn impart;

---

318. **rural poets,** those who wrote about pastoral subjects; notably Theocritus, Greek poet of the third century B.C. and Virgil (70-19 B.C.), one of the great poets of ancient Rome. 326. **Depeinten,** painted, depicted. 327. **Dan Abraham . . . Chaldee land.** "Lord" Abraham's departure from Chaldea is told in *Genesis,* 11. 331. **silvan war,** combat in the woods. 333. **golden age.** In classical mythology, under the reign of Saturn, one-time king of the gods, all nature was kindly; man knew no want of any kind. This was the Golden Age, to be destroyed when Zeus overcame his father Saturn and inaugurated the reign of the gods of Olympus.

341. **Lorrain,** Claude Lorrain (1600-1682), a famous French landscape painter. 342. **Rosa,** Salvator Rosa (1615-1673), a famous Italian painter of historical scenes, battles, and landscapes. **Poussin,** Nicolas Poussin (1594-1665), noted French landscape and historical painter. 360. **The Harp of Aeolus.** Aeolus was in classical mythology the god of winds. The instrument referred to is the Aeolian harp, consisting of a wooden frame strung with wires; the vibration of the wires caused by the passing wind produces the tone.

Wild warbling nature all, above the reach of art!

42

Such the gay splendor, the luxurious state,
Of Caliphs old, who on the Tygris' shore, 371
In mighty Bagdat, populous and great,
Held their bright court, where was of ladies store;
And verse, love, music still the garland wore;
When sleep was coy, the bard, in waiting there, 375
Cheered the lone midnight with the muse's lore;
Composing music bade his dreams be fair,
And music lent new gladness to the morning air.

43

Near the pavilions where we slept, still ran
Soft-tinkling streams, and dashing waters fell,
And sobbing breezes sighed, and oft began 381
(So worked the wizard) wintry storms to swell,
As heaven and earth they would together mell;
At doors and windows, threatening, seemed to call
The demons of the tempest, growling fell; 385
Yet the least entrance found they none at all;
Whence sweeter grew our sleep, secure in massy hall.

* * * * *

(1748)

372. **Bagdat,** Bagdad, the famous capital of the eastern division of the Mohammedan empire, called the Eastern Caliphate (the *caliphs* were the successors of Mohammed). The city was located on the Tigris River; it was claimed by the Sultan of Turkey until 1924, and is now in the possession of Iran.

383. **mell,** mingle.

Thomas Gray

1716-1771

The only one of a family of twelve children to survive infancy, Thomas Gray was born in Cornhill, London, in 1716. His father was a scrivener by profession and a ne'er-do-well by temperament; from that father Gray received nothing but neglect. But his mother gave him infinite care and a schooling at Eton, for which she herself paid by keeping a shop. It was at Eton that there arose an extraordinary friendship between young Thomas Gray and Horace Walpole, another lad of genteel and fastidious interests who was to become the great letter-writer of the century and the inaugurator in England of the Gothic romance (p. 23). Another great friend at Eton was Richard West, son of the Lord Chancellor of Ireland. The association with West was broken off early by West's untimely death at the age of twenty-six; that with Walpole lasted in the main through the lifetime of Gray.

After Eton came Cambridge, where Gray matriculated in 1734. He spent five years there, steeping himself in the classics, walking excessively, and causing some comment by drinking tea instead of beer for breakfast. At Walpole's suggestion he and Gray left college and set out upon a "grand tour" of the Continent. Their travels are described extensively in the letters of the two men; they were particularly enamored of southern France, of Italy, and of the Alpine regions, which evidently appealed to the sensitiveness that both men had for the beauties and grandeur of nature. There was a rupture in their friendship near the end of their travels; the affair has been garbled by literary gossip-mongers; truth compels the admission that the reasons for the quarrel are still obscure. The break, as it happened, was ultimately mended after their return. Both had received on the Continent a certain new spirit from their recreation and from their broadened horizons.

Gray now retired to Cambridge and became a bachelor of civil law. In the year following he gave poetry his serious attention and wrote the *Ode to Spring*, the *Hymn to Adversity*, and *Ode on a Distant Prospect of Eton College* (1742). The universality of appeal of his Eton ode charmed most of the critics of the day, but displeased Samuel Johnson, who regarded it as commonplace. Gray was, at this time, a real neo-classicist, a true follower of the school of Pope, although he practiced considerable liberty of form—he departed from the closed couplet, using stanzaic structure and reviving the sonnet. He was also a fairly agile writer of Latin verse, but he neglected to pursue the art to any great length. His *Ode on the Death of a Favorite Cat*, a piece of light "society-verse," was published in 1748, and three years later came the famous *Elegy in a Country Churchyard*, which gave the poet his first taste of widespread reputation. A few more poems of importance appeared from Gray's hand during the next dozen years, *The Progress of Poesy* and *The Bard* in 1757, *The Fatal Sisters* and *The Descent of Odin* in 1761. In the last three of these poems, Gray was motivated by a strong interest in Norse and Celtic legendry.

Gray's health had always been fragile, and so in 1765 he made a journey into Scotland, keeping a lively account of his impressions. He came back to Cambridge to accept a professorship in modern history, a post which he had solicited in vain a few years before. But in 1769 he was advised, again as a health measure, to go off to the seashore in the south of England. He visited London once more, and then returned to Cambridge in a state of complete physical and mental dejection. Attacks of gout which he had long suffered in a milder form now tortured him beyond endurance, and he died a painful death on July 3, 1771.

The scanty amount of verse which Gray left us is reflective and somewhat passive; but it is highly important as one of the steps in the growth of the English romantic school. By training Gray was academic and a classicist; it is no wonder, therefore, that he should first enroll under the banner of Pope and the neo-classical group. But he was emotionally responsive to nature, given to a rather melancholy brooding inspired by a love of the mysterious past. These traits of temperament were fatal to the integrity of Gray's neo-classicism, but on the other hand they enhanced his position as a romantic writer. By comparing Gray with Thomson (p. 32) it is easy to see wherein Gray has advanced the literature of emotion and imagination at the expense of the literature of reason and intellect. Gray is more gifted than the majority of his contemporaries as a poet and interpreter of nature.

Mason, Gray's friend and biographer, drew the Eton poet in almost gaudy colors; Johnson, a colder and sharper critic and, be it noted, a thoroughgoing neo-classicist, painted a very drab portrait of him, but one that is hard to efface. On the canvas of the modern, who should be without personal bias, the two interpretations of Gray are merged, leaving a picture that provokes neither amazement nor indifference but rather a quiet interest. The *Elegy*, his most noted poem, can be regarded as a string of platitudes, in the approved neo-classical manner; a sounder attitude would regard the poem as an instance of

> What oft was thought, but ne'er so well expressed;

the enthusiast can point out that there is a finely chiseled beauty and finish in Gray's lines, a poetic harmony of sound and sense, never very deep, but frequently impressive and arresting.

Ode on a Distant Prospect of Eton College

Eton College, founded by King Henry VI in 1440, is situated in the valley of the Thames River, about twenty miles west of London. The royal castle of Windsor stands on an eminence in the city of Windsor on the opposite side of the river. The College is also near the village of Stoke Poges, where Gray was living when he wrote this poem. The poem was written shortly after the death of Richard West, Gray's most intimate friend. Two other friends of college days, Ashton and Walpole, were estranged from Gray at the time.

An example of Gray's early verse, the ode is conventional in its use of neo-classical poetic diction, personification, and moralizing; but it shows a few tendencies toward romanticism in its sensitiveness to nature and in its tone of melancholy.

Ye distant spires, ye antique towers,
   That crown the watery glade,
Where grateful Science still adores
   Her Henry's holy shade;
And ye, that from the stately brow   5
Of Windsor's heights the expanse below
   Of grove, of lawn, of mead survey,
Whose turf, whose shade, whose flowers among
Wanders the hoary Thames along
   His silver-winding way.   10

Ah, happy hills, ah, pleasing shade,
   Ah, fields beloved in vain,
Where once my careless childhood strayed.
   A stranger yet to pain!
I feel the gales, that from ye blow,   15
A momentary bliss bestow,
   As waving fresh their gladsome wing
My weary soul they seem to soothe,
And, redolent of joy and youth,
   To breathe a second spring.   20

Say, Father Thames, for thou hast seen
   Full many a sprightly race
Disporting on thy margent green
   The paths of pleasure trace,
Who foremost now delight to cleave   25
With pliant arm thy glassy wave?
   The captive linnet which enthral?
What idle progeny succeed
To chase the rolling circle's speed,
   Or urge the flying ball?   30

While some on earnest business bent
   Their murmuring labors ply
'Gainst graver hours, that bring constraint
   To sweeten liberty;
Some bold adventurers disdain   35
The limits of their little reign,
   And unknown regions dare descry;
Still as they run they look behind,
They hear a voice in every wind,
   And snatch a fearful joy.   40

Gay hope is theirs by fancy fed,
   Less pleasing when possessed;
The tear forgot as soon as shed,
   The sunshine of the breast;
Theirs buxom health of rosy hue,   45
Wild wit, invention ever-new,
   And lively cheer of vigor born;
The thoughtless day, the easy night,
The spirits pure, the slumbers light,
   That fly the approach of morn.   50

Alas, regardless of their doom,
   The little victims play!
No sense have they of ills to come,
   Nor care beyond today;
Yet see how all around 'em wait   55
The ministers of human Fate,
   And black Misfortune's baleful train!
Ah, show them where in ambush stand,
To seize their prey, the murtherous band!
   Ah, tell them they are men!   60

These shall the fury Passions tear,
   The vultures of the mind,
Disdainful Anger, pallid Fear,
   And Shame that skulks behind;

---

4. **Her Henry**, Henry VI, who founded Eton College in 1440.
23. **margent**, margin, bank.

29. **rolling circle**, etc. The rolling circle is the hoop used in the game of rolling hoops. The *flying ball* in the next line refers to the cricket-ball.

Or pining Love shall waste their youth, 65
Or Jealousy with rankling tooth,
  That inly gnaws the secret heart,
And Envy wan, and faded Care,
Grim-visaged comfortless Despair,
  And Sorrow's piercing dart. 70

Ambition this shall tempt to rise,
  Then whirl the wretch from high,
To bitter Scorn a sacrifice,
  And grinning Infamy.
The stings of Falsehood those shall try, 75
And hard Unkindness' altered eye,
  That mocks the tear it forced to flow;
And keen Remorse with blood defiled,
And moody Madness laughing wild
  Amid severest woe. 80

Lo! in the vale of years beneath
  A grisly troop are seen,
The painful family of Death,
  More hideous than their queen.
This racks the joints, this fires the veins, 85
That every laboring sinew strains,
  Those in the deeper vitals rage;
Lo, Poverty, to fill the band,
That numbs the soul with icy hand,
  And slow-consuming Age. 90

To each his sufferings; all are men,
  Condemned alike to groan,
The tender for another's pain,
  The unfeeling for his own.
Yet ah! why should they know their fate? 95
Since sorrow never comes too late,
  And happiness too swiftly flies,
Thought would destroy their paradise.
No more; where ignorance is bliss,
  'Tis folly to be wise. 100

                (*1742;* 1747)

Sonnet

ON THE DEATH OF RICHARD WEST

In vain to me the smiling mornings shine,
And reddening Phoebus lifts his golden fire;
The birds in vain their amorous descant join;

Richard West (1716-1742) had been Gray's closest friend at Eton. 3. **descant**, melody, song.

Or cheerful fields resume their green attire;
These ears, alas! for other notes repine, 5
A different object do these eyes require;
My lonely anguish melts no heart but mine;
And in my breast the imperfect joys expire.
Yet morning smiles the busy race to cheer,
And new-born pleasure brings to happier men; 10
The fields to all their wonted tribute bear;
To warm their little loves the birds complain;
I fruitless mourn to him that cannot hear,
And weep the more because I weep in vain.

                (*1742;* 1775)

Ode on the Death of a Favorite Cat

DROWNED IN A TUB OF GOLD FISHES

  Written with playful solemnity, this poem shows Gray in one of his lighter moods. The cat was a pet of Horace Walpole, Gray's friend (see p. 46).

'Twas on a lofty vase's side,
Where China's gayest art had dyed
  The azure flowers, that blow;
Demurest of the tabby kind,
The pensive Selima reclined, 5
  Gazed on the lake below.

Her conscious tail her joy declared;
The fair round face, the snowy beard,
  The velvet of her paws,
Her coat, that with the tortoise vies, 10
Her ears of jet, and emerald eyes,
  She saw; and purred applause.

Still had she gazed; but 'midst the tide
Two angel forms were seen to glide,
  The genii of the stream; 15
Their scaly armor's Tyrian hue
Through richest purple to the view
  Betrayed a golden gleam.

The hapless nymph with wonder saw:
A whisker first and then a claw, 20
  With many an ardent wish,
She stretched in vain to reach the prize.

16. **Tyrian hue,** the so-called Tyrian purple, made by the ancient inhabitants of Tyre from the juice of a shell-fish.

What female heart can gold despise?
  What cat's averse to fish?

Presumptuous maid! with looks intent
Again she stretched, again she bent,
  Nor knew the gulf between.
(Malignant Fate sat by, and smiled)
The slippery verge her feet beguiled,
  She tumbled headlong in.   30

Eight times emerging from the flood
She mewed to every watery god,
  Some speedy aid to send.
No dolphin came, no nereid stirred:
Nor cruel Tom, nor Susan heard.   35
  A favorite has no friend!

From hence, ye beauties, undeceived,
Know, one false step is ne'er retrieved,
  And be with caution bold.
Not all that tempts your wandering eyes   40
And heedless hearts, is lawful prize;
  Nor all, that glisters, gold.   (1747; 1748)

Elegy Written in a Country Churchyard

Gray's *Elegy* has long been one of the best known and most popular pieces in the English language. As Dr. Johnson says, it "abounds with images which find a mirror in every mind, and with sentiments to which every bosom returns an echo." The universality of its appeal—thoughts on the ever-present facts of life, death, and the transiency of human labor—combined with beauty and melody of phrase, explain the enduring currency of the poem.

In its form, in the neatness and quotability of its utterance, and in its aphoristic sentiments, Gray's *Elegy* continues the neo-classical tradition; but it points forward to the romantic movement in its delicate feeling for nature, its mood of reflective melancholy, and its exaltation of lowly folk. It is the supreme example of the multitude of so-called "graveyard" poems (p. 7), that in the eighteenth century followed Milton's *Il Penseroso* in expressing a somber and thoughtful view of life (cf. Collins's *Ode to Evening*, p. 69).

If a definite scene for the *Elegy* was in Gray's mind, it was doubtless that of the church and graveyard at Stoke Poges, where the poet now lies buried.

The curfew tolls the knell of parting day,
  The lowing herd wind slowly o'er the lea,
The plowman homeward plods his weary way,
  And leaves the world to darkness and to me.

Now fades the glimmering landscape on the sight,   5
  And all the air a solemn stillness holds,
Save where the beetle wheels his droning flight,
  And drowsy tinklings lull the distant folds;

Save that from yonder ivy-mantled tower
  The moping owl does to the moon complain   10
Of such as, wandering near her secret bower,
  Molest her ancient solitary reign.

Beneath those rugged elms, that yew-tree's shade,
  Where heaves the turf in many a moldering heap,
Each in his narrow cell forever laid,   15
  The rude forefathers of the hamlet sleep.

The breezy call of incense-breathing Morn,
  The swallow twittering from the straw-built shed,
The cock's shrill clarion, or the echoing horn,
  No more shall rouse them from their lowly bed. 20

For them no more the blazing hearth shall burn,
  Or busy housewife ply her evening care;
No children run to lisp their sire's return,
  Or climb his knees the envied kiss to share.

Oft did the harvest to their sickle yield,   25
  Their furrow oft the stubborn glebe has broke;

---

34. **dolphin,** an allusion to the legend that Arion, famous Greek musician, when forced from a ship into the sea, was carried to shore on the back of a dolphin that had been charmed by his music. **nereid,** in Greek mythology, a daughter of Nereus, the Old Man of the Sea; hence, a nymph or water-sprite.

19. **horn,** the huntsman's horn. 26. **glebe,** the sod in cultivated ground.

How jocund did they drive their team afield!
How bowed the woods beneath their sturdy
    stroke!

Let not Ambition mock their useful toil,
    Their homely joys, and destiny obscure;   30
Nor Grandeur hear, with a disdainful smile,
    The short and simple annals of the poor.

The boast of heraldry, the pomp of power,
    And all that beauty, all that wealth e'er
        gave,
Awaits alike the inevitable hour: 35
    The paths of glory lead but to the grave.

Nor you, ye proud, impute to these the fault,
    If Memory o'er their tomb no trophies raise,
Where through the long-drawn aisle and
        fretted vault
    The pealing anthem swells the note of
        praise.   40

Can storied urn or animated bust
    Back to its mansion call the fleeting breath?
Can Honor's voice provoke the silent dust,
    Or Flattery soothe the dull cold ear of
        Death?

Perhaps in this neglected spot is laid   45
    Some heart once pregnant with celestial
        fire;
Hands that the rod of empire might have
        swayed,
    Or waked to ecstasy the living lyre.

But Knowledge to their eyes her ample page
    Rich with the spoils of time did ne'er un-
        roll;   50
Chill Penury repressed their noble rage,
    And froze the genial current of the soul.

Full many a gem of purest ray serene
    The dark unfathomed caves of ocean
        bear;
Full many a flower is born to blush unseen,   55
    And waste its sweetness on the desert air.

Some village Hampden that with dauntless
        breast
    The little tyrant of his fields withstood;
Some mute inglorious Milton here may rest,
    Some Cromwell guiltless of his country's
        blood.   60

The applause of listening senates to com-
        mand,
    The threats of pain and ruin to despise,
To scatter plenty o'er a smiling land,
    And read their history in a nation's eyes,

Their lot forbade; nor circumscribed alone   65
    Their growing virtues, but their crimes con-
        fined;
Forbade to wade through slaughter to a
        throne,
    And shut the gates of mercy on mankind,

The struggling pangs of conscious truth to
        hide,
    To quench the blushes of ingenuous shame,
Or heap the shrine of Luxury and Pride   71
    With incense kindled at the Muse's flame.

Far from the madding crowd's ignoble strife,
    Their sober wishes never learned to stray;
Along the cool sequestered vale of life   75
    They kept the noiseless tenor of their way.

Yet ev'n these bones from insult to protect
    Some frail memorial still erected nigh,
With uncouth rimes and shapeless sculpture
        decked,
    Implores the passing tribute of a sigh.   80

Their name, their years, spelt by the unlettered
        Muse,

---

41. **storied urn,** an urn inscribed with pictures that tell a story; cf. Keats's *Ode on a Grecian Urn,* p. 281. *Animated* in the same line means "lifelike."

57. **Some ... Hampden,** some patriot who would oppose unjust taxes as did John Hampden (1594-1643), noted English statesman and member of the Puritan or Roundhead party, who resisted the unjust levies of King Charles I in the years 1637 and 1638. 59. **Some ... Milton,** some great poet sprung from the lowly classes without technical training who could nevertheless, like Milton, lead a cause with poetic and prophetic power. 60. **Some Cromwell,** someone as great as Cromwell, and as much of a leader, without his faults. Oliver Cromwell (1599-1658), the victorious leader of the Roundheads against the Royalists in the Civil War. and the Lord Protector of the Commonwealth (cf. Vol. 1, p. 639), was regarded throughout the eighteenth century as one who had sacrificed his country to his ambition. In the original draft of this stanza, one of the most famous in the entire poem, Gray had Cato for Hampden, Tully (Cicero) for Milton, and Caesar for Cromwell. The substitution of English names for classical illustrates Gray's tendency toward romanticism, more fully expressed in his later poems. 79. **uncouth,** strange, odd.

The place of fame and elegy supply;
And many a holy text around she strews,
That teach the rustic moralist to die.

For who, to dumb Forgetfulness a prey, 85
  This pleasing anxious being e'er resigned,
Left the warm precincts of the cheerful day,
  Nor cast one longing, lingering look behind?

On some fond breast the parting soul relies,
  Some pious drops the closing eye requires; 90
Ev'n from the tomb the voice of Nature cries,
  Ev'n in our ashes live their wonted fires.

For thee, who mindful of the unhonored dead
  Dost in these lines their artless tale relate;
If chance, by lonely Contemplation led, 95
  Some kindred spirit shall inquire thy fate,

Haply some hoary-headed swain may say,
  "Oft have we seen him at the peep of dawn
Brushing with hasty steps the dews away
  To meet the sun upon the upland lawn. 100

"There at the foot of yonder nodding beech,
  That wreathes its old fantastic roots so high,
His listless length at noontide would he stretch,
  And pore upon the brook that babbles by.

"Hard by yon wood, now smiling as in scorn,
  Muttering his wayward fancies he would rove, 106
Now drooping, woeful wan, like one forlorn,
  Or crazed with care, or crossed in hopeless love.

"One morn I missed him on the customed hill,
  Along the heath, and near his favorite tree;
Another came; nor yet beside the rill, 111
  Nor up the lawn, nor at the wood was he;

"The next with dirges due in sad array
  Slow through the church-way path we saw him borne.
Approach and read (for thou canst read) the lay, 115

Graved on the stone beneath yon aged thorn."

THE EPITAPH

Here rests his head upon the lap of Earth
  A youth to Fortune and to Fame unknown.
Fair Science frowned not on his humble birth,
  And Melancholy marked him for her own.

Large was his bounty, and his soul sincere, 121
  Heaven did a recompense as largely send;
He gave to Misery all he had, a tear,
  He gained from Heaven ('twas all he wished) a friend.

No farther seek his merits to disclose, 125
Or draw his frailties from their dread abode,
(There they alike in trembling hope repose),
  The bosom of his Father and his God.
                        (1750; 1751)

The Progress of Poesy

This and the following poem are known as Gray's Pindaric odes, closely imitative in structure and manner of the odes of the famous Greek lyric poet Pindar (fifth century B. C.). Gray, following Pindar's form, composes his poem in three divisions, each of which consists of three sections corresponding to the strophe, the antistrophe, and the epode of the Greek model.

The Progress of Poesy shows stateliness of poetic measure, dignity and precision of expression, and restraint of thought and feeling, qualities of verse imposed both by the Greek form and by neo-classical standards. And yet the poem is farther from neo-classical ideals than Gray's earlier verse; it stands midway in the poet's progress from classicism to romanticism. The poem shows decided romantic leanings in its spontaneity, its imaginative fervor, its faith in individual genius, and its glorification of older English poetry.

Gray announced this poem in a letter to Walpole, in which he said that he might send very soon to his publisher "an ode to his own tooth, a high Pindaric upon stilts, which one must be a better scholar than he is to understand a line of, and the very best scholars will

---

93. **thee,** Gray himself.

116. **thorn,** hawthorn tree.

understand but a little matter here and there."
When this poem and *The Bard* were published, few persons read them with appreciation. In a letter to his friend Mason, Gray wrote: "I would not have put another note to save the souls of all the owls in London. It is extremely well as it is—nobody understands me, and I am perfectly satisfied."

I. 1*

Awake, Aeolian lyre, awake,
And give to rapture all thy trembling strings.
From Helicon's harmonious springs
A thousand rills their mazy progress take;
The laughing flowers, that round them blow, 5
Drink life and fragrance as they flow.
Now the rich stream of music winds along,
Deep, majestic, smooth, and strong,
Through verdant vales, and Ceres' golden reign;
Now rolling down the steep amain, 10
Headlong, impetuous, see it pour;
The rocks and nodding groves rebellow to the roar.

I. 2

O! Sovereign of the willing soul,
Parent of sweet and solemn-breathing airs,
Enchanting shell! the sullen Cares 15
And frantic Passions hear thy soft control.
On Thracia's hills the Lord of War
Has curbed the fury of his car,
And dropped his thirsty lance at thy command.
Perching on the sceptered hand 20
Of Jove, thy magic lulls the feathered king
With ruffled plumes and flagging wing;
Quenched in dark clouds of slumber lie
The terror of his beak, and lightings of his eye.

I. 3

Thee the voice, the dance, obey, 25
Tempered to thy warbled lay.
O'er Idalia's velvet-green
The rosy-crownéd Loves are seen,
  On Cytherea's day
With antic Sports and blue-eyed Pleasures, 30
Frisking light in frolic measures;
Now pursuing, now retreating,
  Now in circling troops they meet;
To brisk notes in cadence beating
  Glance their many-twinkling feet. 35
Slow melting strains their Queen's approach declare;
Where'er she turns the Graces homage pay.
With arms sublime, that float upon the air,
In gliding state she wins her easy way;
O'er her warm cheek, and rising bosom, move 40
The bloom of young Desire, and purple light of Love.

II. 1

Man's feeble race what ills await!
Labor, and Penury, the racks of Pain,
  Disease, and Sorrow's weeping train,
And Death, sad refuge from the storms of Fate! 45
  The fond complaint, my song, disprove,
  And justify the laws of Jove.
Say, has he given in vain the heavenly Muse?
  Night, and all her sickly dews,
Her specters wan, and birds of boding cry, 50
  He gives to range the dreary sky;
  Till down the eastern cliffs afar
Hyperion's march they spy, and glittering shafts of war.

---

*"The various sources of poetry, which gives life and luster to all it touches, are here described."—Gray's note. **1. Aeolian lyre**, the lyre of Pindar (fifth century B.C.), perhaps the greatest of Greek lyric poets, who came from Aeolia, Asia Minor. **3. Helicon's . . . springs**, the fountain of the Muses on Mt. Helicon, central Greece, from which, so the legend went, the streams of the world's poetry flowed. **9. Ceres' . . . reign**, fields of grain ruled by Ceres (Demeter), the classical goddess of the fields and harvest. **I. 2.** "The power of harmony to calm the turbulent sallies of the soul."—Gray's note. **15. shell**, lyre. The first lyre was said to have been made from a tortoise shell.

I. 3. "The power of harmony to produce all the graces of motion in the body."—Gray's note. **27. Idalia**, a town in Cyprus containing a temple to Venus (Cytherea of l. 29). **29. Cytherea's day**, the day for the worship of Venus, goddess of love. **II. 1.** "To compensate the real and imaginary ills of life, the Muse was given to mankind by the same Providence that sends day by its cheerful presence to disel the gloom and terrors of the night."—Gray's note. **53. Hyperion**, in classical mythology, a sun-god. *Hyperion's march* refers to the rising of the sun.

II. 2

In climes beyond the solar road,
 Where shaggy forms o'er ice-built moun-
  tains roam, 55
 The Muse has broke the twilight gloom
 To cheer the shivering native's dull abode.
And oft, beneath the odorous shade
Of Chili's boundless forest laid,
 She deigns to hear the savage youth repeat,
  In loose numbers wildly sweet, 61
 Their feather-cinctured chiefs and dusky
  loves.
 Her track, where'er the goddess roves,
 Glory pursue, and generous Shame,
Th' unconquerable Mind, and Freedom's holy
  flame. 65

II. 3

Woods, that wave o'er Delphi's steep,
Isles, that crown the Aegean deep,
Fields, that cool Ilissus laves,
Or where Maeander's amber waves
 In lingering labyrinths creep, 70
 How do your tuneful echoes languish,
 Mute, but to the voice of Anguish!
 Where each old poetic mountain
  Inspiration breathed around;
 Every shade and hallowed fountain 75
  Murmured deep a solemn sound;
Till the sad Nine in Greece's evil hour
Left their Parnassus for the Latian plains.
Alike they scorn the pomp of tyrant Power,
 And coward Vice, that revels in her
  chains. 80
When Latium had her lofty spirit lost,
They sought, oh Albion! next thy sea-encir-
 cled coast.

III. 1

Far from the sun and summer-gale,
In thy green lap was Nature's darling laid,
 What time, where lucid Avon strayed, 85
 To him the mighty Mother did unveil
 Her awful face. The dauntless child
 Stretched forth his little arms, and smiled.
This pencil take (she said) whose colors clear
 Richly paint the vernal year; 90
 Thine too these golden keys, immortal boy!
 This can unlock the gates of Joy,
 Of Horror that, and thrilling Fears,
Or ope the sacred source of sympathetic tears.

III. 2

Nor second he, that rode sublime 95
Upon the seraph-wings of Ecstasy,
 The secrets of the Abyss to spy.
He passed the flaming bounds of Place and
 Time;
 The living throne, the sapphire blaze,
 Where angels tremble, while they gaze, 100
 He saw; but, blasted with excess of light,
  Closed his eyes in endless night.
Behold, where Dryden's less presumptuous
 car
 Wide o'er the fields of Glory bear
 Two coursers of ethereal race, 105
With necks in thunder clothed, and long-
 resounding pace.

III. 3

Hark, his hands the lyre explore!
Bright-eyed Fancy hovering o'er
Scattered from her pictured urn
Thoughts that breathe, and words that
 burn. 110
 But, ah! 'tis heard no more—
 Oh! Lyre divine, what daring spirit
 Wakes thee now? Though he inherit
 Nor the pride, nor ample pinion,
 That the Theban Eagle bear 115
 Sailing with supreme dominion
  Through the azure deep of air;

II. 2. "Extensive influence of poetic genius over the remotest and most uncivilized nations; its connection with liberty, and the virtues that naturally attend on it."—Gray's note. 59. **Chili.** Here, as elsewhere in the eighteenth-century poetic tradition, references to places in the Americas are always intended to convey the idea of barbarism or lack of civilization. **II. 3.** "Progress of poetry from Greece to Italy, and from Italy to England."—Gray's note. 66. **Delphi,** the seat of the Greek oracle. 68. **Ilissus,** a small stream flowing through Athens. 69. **Maeander,** a winding river in Asia Minor famous in Greek heroic tradition. So rambling is its course that it has given us the verb "to meander," meaning "to wander aimlessly and in leisurely fashion." 77. **Nine,** the nine Muses. They, according to tradition, left Greece for Rome when Greek civilization declined before the rising power of Rome, during the second century B.C. When Rome fell they moved to Albion (the poetic name for England). 78. **Latian,** Roman. 82. **Albion;** cf. l. 77 and note. The poetic name was probably suggested by the white chalk-cliffs near Dover (from Latin *albus,* "white").

85. **Avon,** the name of several rivers in Britain, but here unquestionably referring to the river flowing through Stratford, the home of Shakespeare, the "Nature's darling" of l. 84. 95. **he . . . sublime,** Milton, the great Puritan poet (1603-1674). 101. **blasted . . . night,** an allusion to Milton's blindness. 115. **Theban Eagle,** Pindar (cf. note to l. 1, p. 53), who compares himself to an eagle in his *Olympian Odes,* II, 159.

Yet oft before his infant eyes would run
  Such forms as glitter in the Muse's ray,
With orient hues unborrowed of the sun; 120
  Yet shall he mount, and keep his distant way
Beyond the limits of a vulgar fate,
Beneath the good how far—but far above the great.   (*1754;* 1757)

The Bard

The Bard is based upon a vague tradition that when King Edward I of England conquered Wales in 1276-84 he ordered all the Welsh bards that fell into his hands to be put to death. Gray gives the following plan of the poem: "The army of Edward I, as they march through a deep valley, and approach Mount Snowdon, are suddenly stopped by the appearance of a venerable figure seated on the summit of an inaccessible rock, who, with a voice more than human, reproaches the king with all the desolation and misery which he had brought on his country; foretells the misfortunes of the Norman race, and with prophetic spirit declares that all his cruelty shall never extinguish the noble ardor of poetic genius in this island; and that men shall never be wanting to celebrate true virtue and valor in immortal strains, to expose vice and infamous pleasure, and boldly censure tyranny and oppression. His song ended, he precipitates himself from the mountain, and is swallowed up in the river that rolls at its foot."

As a piece of imaginative writing, this poem is both original and romantic. Thrilled by the picturesqueness of the medieval theme and of the wild mountain scenery of Wales, Gray writes with dramatic intensity free from all literary restrictions save those imposed by the structure and the manner of the Pindaric ode that he imitates. See note on *The Progress of Poesy* (p. 52).

I. 1

"Ruin seize thee, ruthless King!
Confusion on thy banners wait,
  Though fanned by Conquest's crimson wing
They mock the air with idle state.
Helm, nor hauberk's twisted mail,   5
Nor even thy virtues, Tyrant, shall avail
To save thy secret soul from nightly fears,
  From Cambria's curse, from Cambria's tears!"
Such were the sounds, that o'er the crested pride
Of the first Edward scattered wild dismay,   10
As down the steep of Snowdon's shaggy side
  He wound with toilsome march his long array.
Stout Glo'ster stood aghast in speechless trance;
"To arms!" cried Mortimer, and couched his quivering lance.

I. 2

  On a rock, whose haughty brow   15
Frowns o'er old Conway's foaming flood,
  Robed in the sable garb of woe,
With haggard eyes the Poet stood;
(Loose his beard, and hoary hair
Streamed, like a meteor, to the troubled air)   20
And with a master's hand and prophet's fire,
Struck the deep sorrows of his lyre.
"Hark, how each giant oak, and desert cave,
Sighs to the torrent's awful voice beneath!
O'er thee, oh King! their hundred arms they wave,   25
  Revenge on thee in hoarser murmurs breathe;
Vocal no more, since Cambria's fatal day,
To high-born Hoel's harp, or soft Llewellyn's lay.

I. 3

"Cold is Cadwallo's tongue,
  That hushed the stormy main;   30
Brave Urien sleeps upon his craggy bed;
  Mountains, ye mourn in vain

---

8. **Cambria,** the old name for Wales. 11. **Snowdon,** a high mountain range and peak in northern Wales. 13. **Glo'ster,** the Earl of Gloucester, who was a leader in the army of King Edward I. 14. **Mortimer,** another important lieutenant of King Edward. 16. **Conway,** a small river in northern Wales, dividing Carnarvonshire from Denbighshire and emptying into the Irish Sea. 18. **Poet stood,** etc. Gray represents the old Welsh bard as composing spontaneously under the stress of great emotion. 28. **Hoel,** a prince and poet of North Wales in ancient days. **Llewellyn,** the leader of the Welsh revolt which Edward I was putting down. 29. **Cadwallo,** a common Welsh bardic name; as is also *Urien* (l. 31); but no bard by the name of *Modred* (l. 33) is known.

Modred, whose magic song
Made huge Plinlimmon bow his cloud-topped head.
    On dreary Arvon's shore they lie, 35
  Smeared with gore, and ghastly pale;
Far, far aloof the affrighted ravens sail;
  The famished eagle screams, and passes by.
Dear lost companions of my tuneful art,
  Dear, as the light that visits these sad eyes, 40
Dear, as the ruddy drops that warm my heart,
  Ye died amidst your dying country's cries—
No more I weep. They do not sleep.
  On yonder cliffs, a grisly band,
  I see them sit, they linger yet, 45
  Avengers of their native land;
With me in dreadful harmony they join,
And weave with bloody hands the tissue of thy line.

II. 1

"Weave the warp, and weave the woof,
  The winding-sheet of Edward's race. 50
  Give ample room, and verge enough
  The characters of Hell to trace.
Mark the year, and mark the night,
When Severn shall re-echo with affright
The shrieks of death, through Berkley's roofs that ring, 55
  Shrieks of an agonizing King!
She-wolf of France, with unrelenting fangs,
  That tear'st the bowels of thy mangled mate,
From thee be born, who o'er thy country hangs

The scourge of Heaven. What terrors round him wait! 60
Amazement in his van, with Flight combined,
And Sorrow's faded form, and Solitude behind.

II. 2

"Mighty victor, mighty lord!
Low on his funeral couch he lies!
  No pitying heart, no eye, afford 65
  A tear to grace his obsequies.
Is the sable Warrior fled?
Thy son is gone. He rests among the dead.
The swarm, that in thy noon-tide beam were born?
Gone to salute the rising morn. 70
Fair laughs the morn, and soft the zephyr blows,
  While proudly riding o'er the azure realm
In gallant trim the gilded vessel goes;
  Youth on the prow, and Pleasure at the helm;
Regardless of the sweeping whirlwind's sway, 75
That, hushed in grim repose, expects his evening prey.

II. 3

"Fill high the sparkling bowl,
  The rich repast prepare,
Reft of a crown, he yet may share the feast;
  Close by the regal chair 80
  Fell Thirst and Famine scowl
A baleful smile upon their baffled guest.
  Heard ye the din of battle bray,
  Lance to lance, and horse to horse?
Long years of havoc urge their destined course, 85
And through the kindred squadrons mow their way.

---

34. **Plinlimmon**, a mountain in Wales. 35. **Arvon's shore**, "the shores of Carnarvonshire opposite to the isle of Anglesey." —Gray's note. 38. **famished eagle screams**, a detail which will remind the reader of a common picture in Old English battle-poetry (cf. *Beowulf*, Vol. I, p. 56, l. 2422). 44. **grisly band**, the whole band of murdered bards, who join the sole survivor in prophesying the future of Edward's race. 49. **warp ... woof.** The *warp* is the threads extended lengthwise in the loom in weaving; the *woof* is the threads that cross the warp. 51. **verge**, space. 54. **Severn ... King.** The son of Edward I, later King Edward II, who reigned from 1307 to 1327, was cruelly murdered in Berkeley Castle, near the Severn River, in 1327. It has always been a legend that his wife Queen Isabella was present at the murder and perhaps participated (cf. l. 58). 57. **She-wolf of France.** Isabella, a French princess and Queen of England, wife of Edward II, notorious even during her husband's reign for her adulterous intrigue with Roger Mortimer, son of the leader mentioned in the note to l. 14.

63. **Mighty victor ... lies**; King Edward III, grandson of Edward I, and son of Edward II, who reigned from 1327 to 1377. His death followed that of his popular eldest son Edward, the Black Prince, hero of the early years of the Hundred Years' War. 67. **sable Warrior fled**, an allusion to the death of Prince Edward before his father. The prince was called "Black" from the color of his armor. 71. **Fair laughs, etc.** The next dozen lines (71-82) describe the reign of young Richard II (from 1377 to 1399), and his traditional death by starvation after he had been deposed in favor of Henry of Lancaster, who became Henry IV. 86. **kindred squadrons**, an allusion to the civil war of the fifteenth century between the two royal houses of York and Lancaster, known to history as the Wars of the Roses. The two houses were, of course, related in many ways by marriage and blood-ties.

Ye towers of Julius, London's lasting shame,
With many a foul and midnight murther fed,
Revere his consort's faith, his father's fame,
And spare the meek usurper's holy head.
    Above, below, the rose of snow,   91
Twined with her blushing foe, we spread;
    The bristled boar in infant gore
Wallows beneath the thorny shade.
Now, brothers, bending o'er the accursed loom   95
Stamp we our vengeance deep, and ratify his doom.

III. 1

"Edward, lo! to sudden fate
(Weave we the woof. The thread is spun.)
    Half of thy heart we consecrate.
(The web is wove. The work is done.) 100
    Stay, oh stay! nor thus forlorn,
Leave me unblessed, unpitied, here to mourn;
    In yon bright track, that fires the western skies,
They melt, they vanish from my eyes.
But oh! what solemn scenes on Snowdon's height   105
    Descending slow their glittering skirts unroll?
Visions of glory, spare my aching sight,
    Ye unborn ages, crowd not on my soul!

No more our long-lost Arthur we bewail.
All hail, ye genuine kings, Britannia's issue, hail!   110

III. 2

"Girt with many a baron bold
Sublime their starry fronts they rear;
    And gorgeous dames, and statesmen old
In bearded majesty, appear.
    In the midst a form divine!   115
Her eye proclaims her of the Briton line;
Her lion-port, her awe commanding face,
    Attempered sweet to virgin-grace.
What strings symphonious tremble in the air,
What strains of vocal transport round her play!   120
    Hear from the grave, great Taliessin, hear;
They breathe a soul to animate thy clay.
    Bright Rapture calls, and soaring, as she sings,
Waves in the eye of Heaven her many-colored wings.

III. 3

    "The verse adorn again   125
Fierce War, and faithful Love,
And Truth severe, by fairy fiction drest.
    In buskined measures move
Pale Grief and pleasing Pain,
With Horror, tyrant of the throbbing breast.
    A voice, as of the cherub-choir,   131
Gales from blooming Eden bear;
And distant warblings lessen on my ear,
    That lost in long futurity expire.
Fond impious man, think'st thou, yon sanguine cloud,   135
    Raised by thy breath, has quenched the orb of day?

---

87. **towers of Julius,** the Tower of London, part of which was said to have been built by Julius Caesar. 88. **midnight murther.** Many dignitaries of England were murdered in the Tower of London, notably George, Duke of Clarence, King Edward V, and Richard, Duke of York—all during the troubled period of the Wars of the Roses. But in this line Gray is undoubtedly thinking of King Henry VI, King of England from 1422 to 1471, who died under mysterious circumstances. 89. **Revere . . . fame.** Henry VI's wife, Margaret of Anjou, tried valiantly to save her husband; the father of Henry VI was the brilliant and dashing King Henry V (d. 1422), the Prince Hal of Shakespeare's *Henry IV* plays, the hero of Shakespeare's *Henry V*, and the victor for the English over the French at the great battle of Agincourt (1415). 90. **meek . . . head.** Henry VI was noted for his piety. As a Lancastrian, and grandson of the "usurping" Henry IV, he is here labeled "usurper." 91. **rose of snow.** The white rose was the emblem of the York family; the red rose, of the Lancaster family; hence the "Wars of the Roses." 93. **boar.** The silver boar was the emblem of King Richard III, who was one of the York dynasty, and King of England from 1483 until the fatal battle of Bosworth Field in 1485. His death marks the accession of the Tudor dynasty under Henry VII. Richard was responsible for the death of the two young sons of Edward IV (one of them the boy king Edward V) in the Tower of London in 1483. The two boys stood between Richard and the throne. 99. **Half . . . consecrate.** The queen of Edward I, Eleanor of Castile, lost her life in 1290, after saving her husband's by sucking out the poison from a dagger-wound. 104. **They . . . they,** the "grisly band" of murdered bards mentioned in l. 44.

109. **Arthur.** It was predicted and confidently believed by the Welsh people that King Arthur was still alive and that he would return to rule again over Britain. 110. **genuine kings,** the House of Tudor, whose rule dated from the accession of Henry VII in 1485 to the death of Elizabeth in 1603, and which was descended from Owen Tudor the Welshman. Tudor was the second husband of Catharine, the widowed queen of King Henry V. 115. **form divine,** Elizabeth, Queen of England from 1558 to 1603. 118. **virgin-grace.** Elizabeth is sometimes referred to as the Virgin Queen. The American colony of Virginia was so named in her honor. 121. **Taliessin,** a famous Welsh bard of the sixth century. 125. **The verse . . . again,** an allusion to Spenser's *Faerie Queene* and its allegory; cf. Vol. I, p. 396. 128. **buskined.** The buskin was the high shoe worn by actors of tragedy in the Greek theater; hence "buskined" is the equivalent of "tragic." 131. **A voice,** that of Milton. 133. **distant warblings,** of poets following Milton. 135. **Fond . . . man,** foolish man.

Tomorrow he repairs the golden flood,
    And warms the nations with redoubled
        ray.
    Enough for me. With joy I see
    The different doom our fates assign.   140
      Be thine Despair and sceptered Care;
    To triumph, and to die, are mine."
He spoke, and headlong from the mountain's height
Deep in the roaring tide he plunged to endless
        night.   (*1754;* 1757)

The Fatal Sisters

AN ODE FROM THE NORSE TONGUE

The Fatal Sisters is based upon a Latin translation of an Old Norse poem celebrating an invasion of Ireland by the Norse hero Sictryg.

Thoroughly romantic in content, in form, and in spirit, the poem is especially noteworthy in that it marks an awakened interest in Scandinavian tradition.

Preface

In the eleventh century Sigurd, Earl of the Orkney Islands, went with a fleet of ships and a considerable body of troops into Ireland, to the assistance of Sictryg with the silken beard, who was then making war on his father-in-law Brian, King of Dublin: the Earl and all his forces were cut to pieces, and Sictryg was in danger of a total defeat; but the enemy had a greater loss by the death of Brian, their king, who fell in action. On Christmas day (the day of the battle), a native of Caithness in Scotland, of the name of Darrud, saw at a distance a number of persons on horseback riding full speed towards a hill, and seeming to enter into it. Curiosity led him to follow them, till looking through an opening in the rocks he saw twelve gigantic figures resembling women: they were all employed about a loom; and as they wove, they sang the following dreadful song; which when they had finished, they tore the web into twelve pieces, and (each taking her portion) galloped six to the north and as many to the south.

Now the storm begins to lower,
    (Haste, the loom of Hell prepare!)
Iron-sleet of arrowy shower
    Hurtles in the darkened air.

Glittering lances are the loom,   5
    Where the dusky warp we strain,
Weaving many a soldier's doom,
    Orkney's woe, and Randver's bane.

See the grisly texture grow!
    ('Tis of human entrails made)   10
And the weights, that play below,
    Each a gasping warrior's head.

Shafts for shuttles, dipt in gore,
    Shoot the trembling cords along.
Sword, that once a monarch bore,   15
    Keep the tissue close and strong.

Mista black, terrific maid,
    Sangrida, and Hilda see,
Join the wayward work to aid;
    'Tis the woof of victory.   20

Ere the ruddy sun be set,
    Pikes must shiver, javelins sing,
Blade with clattering buckler meet,
    Hauberk crash, and helmet ring.

(Weave the crimson web of war!)   25
    Let us go, and let us fly,
Where our friends the conflict share,
    Where they triumph, where they die.

As the paths of fate we tread,
    Wading through the ensanguined field,   30

---

141. **Be thine Despair.** Edward I, what with his wars against the Welsh and the Scots, had a very troubled reign.
  The Fatal Sisters. These were the Valkyries, female divinities, servants of Odin (or Woden) in the Germanic mythology. Their name signifies *Choosers of the Slain.* They were mounted on swift horses, with drawn swords in their hands; and in the throng of battle selected such as were destined to slaughter, and conducted them to Valhalla, the hall of Odin, or paradise of the brave; there they attended the banquet, and served the departed heroes with horns of mead and ale. Their numbers are not agreed upon, some authors representing them as six, some as four. (For the function of women at a banquet cf. *Beowulf,* Vol. I, p. 29, ll. 547 ff.)

8. Orkney, Sigurd, the Earl of Orkney. **bane,** destruction.
17. Mista . . . Sangrida . . . Hilda, names of three Valkyries.

Gondula, and Geira, spread
  O'er the youthful king your shield.

We the reins to slaughter give;
  Ours to kill, and ours to spare;
Spite of danger he shall live.   35
  (Weave the crimson web of war!)

They, whom once the desert-beach
  Pent within its bleak domain,
Soon their ample sway shall stretch
  O'er the plenty of the plain.   40

Low the dauntless earl is laid,
  Gored with many a gaping wound;
Fate demands a nobler head;
  Soon a king shall bite the ground.

Long his loss shall Eirin weep,   45
  Ne'er again his likeness see;
Long her strains in sorrow steep,
  Strains of immortality!

Horror covers all the heath,
  Clouds of carnage blot the sun.   50
Sisters, weave the web of death!
  Sisters, cease, the work is done.

Hail the task, and hail the hands!
  Songs of joy and triumph sing!
Joy to the victorious bands;   55
  Triumph to the younger king.

Mortal, thou that hear'st the tale,
  Learn the tenor of our song.
Scotland, through each winding vale
  Far and wide the notes prolong.   60

Sisters, hence with spurs of speed!
  Each her thundering falchion wield;
Each bestride her sable steed.
  Hurry, hurry to the field!   (*1761; 1768*)

Sketch of His Own Character

Too poor for a bribe, and too proud to importune;
He had not the method of making a fortune;
Could love, and could hate, so was thought somewhat odd;
No very great wit, he believed in a God.
A Post or a Pension he did not desire,   5
But left Church and State to Charles Townshend and Squire.   (*1761; 1775*)

31. **Gondula, and Geira,** two Valkyries. 37. **They,** the Norsemen. 41. **the dauntless earl,** Sigurd. 44. **a king,** Brian. 45. **Eirin,** Erin, Ireland. The Norse Vikings had many settlements in Ireland during the Viking Age (cf. Vol. I, p. 5).

56. **younger king,** Sictryg. 62. **falchion,** a short sword. **Sketch of His Own Character.** 6. **Townshend and Squire.** Charles Townshend (1725-1767) was a brilliant young statesman of Gray's time. It was he who passed through Parliament a tax on the American colonies for various commodities, notably tea, which precipitated the Boston Tea Party. Samuel Squire became Bishop of St. David's in 1761.

Letters

1. To His Mother*

Amiens, April 1, N. S. 1739

As we made but a very short journey today, and came to our inn early, I sit down to give you some account of our expedition. On the 29th (according to the style here) we left Dover at twelve at noon, and with a pretty brisk gale, which pleased everybody mighty well, except myself, who was extremely sick the whole time, we reached Calais by five. The weather changed, and it began to snow hard the minute we got into the harbor, where we took the boat and soon landed. Calais is an exceeding old, but very pretty town, and we hardly saw anything there that was not so new and so different from England that it surprised us agreeably. We went the next morning to the great church and were at high Mass (it being Easter Monday). We saw also the convents of the Capuchins, and the nuns of St. Dominic; with these last we held much conversation, especially with an English nun, a Mrs. Davis, of whose work I sent you, by the return of the pacquet, a

*The first three letters given here were written by Gray while he was on a tour of France and Italy with Horace Walpole the novelist (p. 23). 1. **N. S.** During the first few letters of this trip Gray refers to the fact that France was using the new Gregorian calendar, which was about twelve days later than the Old Style (Julian) Calendar used in England until 1752.

letter-case to remember her by. In the afternoon we took a post-chaise (it still snowing very hard) for Boulogne, which was only eighteen miles further. This chaise is a strange sort of conveyance, of much greater use than beauty, resembling an ill-shaped chariot, only with the door opening before instead of the side; three horses draw it, one between the shafts, and the other two on each side, on one of which the postillion rides, and drives too. This vehicle will, upon occasion, go fourscore miles a-day, but Mr. Walpole, being in no hurry, chooses to make easy journeys of it, and they are easy ones indeed, for the motion is much like that of a sedan; we go about six miles an hour, and commonly change horses at the end of it. It is true they are no very graceful steeds, but they go well, and through roads which they say are bad for France, but to me they seem gravel walks and bowling greens; in short it would be the finest traveling in the world were it not for the inns, which are mostly terrible places indeed. But to describe our progress somewhat more regularly, we came into Boulogne when it was almost dark, and went out pretty early on Tuesday morning; so that all I can say about it is that it is a large, old, fortified town, with more English in it than French. On Tuesday we were to go to Abbéville, seventeen leagues, or fifty-one short English miles; but by the way we dined at Montreuil, much to our hearts' content, on stinking mutton cutlets, addled eggs, and ditch water. Madam the hostess made her appearance in long lappets of bone-lace and a sack of linsey-woolsey. We supped and lodged pretty well at Abbéville, and had time to see a little of it before we came out this morning. There are seventeen convents in it, out of which we saw the chapels of Minims and the Carmelite nuns. We are now come further thirty miles to Amiens, the chief city of the province of Picardy. We have seen the cathedral, which is just what that of Canterbury must have been before the Reformation. It is about the same size, a huge Gothic building, beset on the outside with thousands of small statues, and within adorned with beautiful painted windows, and a vast number of chapels dressed out in all their finery of altar-pieces, embroidery, gilding, and marble. Over the high altar are preserved, in a very large wrought shrine of massy gold, the relics of St. Firmin, their patron saint. We went also to the chapels of the Jesuits and Ursuline nuns, the latter of which is very richly adorned. Tomorrow we shall lie at Clermont, and next day reach Paris. The country we have passed through hitherto has been flat, open, but agreeably diversified with villages, fields well-cultivated, and little rivers. On every hillock is a windmill, a crucifix, or a Virgin Mary dressed in flowers, and a sarcenet robe; one sees not many people or carriages on the road; now and then indeed you meet a strolling friar, a countryman with his great muff, or a woman riding astride on a little ass, with short petticoats, and a great head-dress of blue wool.

2. To RICHARD WEST*

Turin, November 16, N. S., 1739

After eight days journey through Greenland, we arrived at Turin. You approach it by a handsome avenue of nine miles long, and quite straight. The entrance is guarded by certain vigilant dragons, called Douaniers, who mumbled us for some time. The city is not large, as being a place of strength, and consequently confined within its fortifications; it has many beauties and some faults; among the first are streets all laid out by the line, regular uniform buildings, fine walks that surround the whole, and in general a good lively clean appearance; but the houses are of brick plastered, which is apt to want repairing; the windows of oiled paper, which is apt to be torn; and everything very slight, which is apt to tumble down. There is an excellent opera, but it is only in the carnival; masquerades, too, but only in the carnival. This carnival lasts only from Christmas to Lent; one half of the remaining part of the year is passed in remembering the last, the other in expecting the future carnival. We cannot well subsist upon such slender diet,

---

15. **sedan,** sedan-chair. 36. **lappet,** a small lap or flap used to ornament a garment. 37. **linsey-woolsey,** coarse cloth of mixed materials.

64. **sarcenet,** a fine, thin silk used for linings.
***West.** See p. 49, and note. 76. **Douaniers,** customs-officers. 77. **mumbled,** worried, as a hound worries the quarry.

no more than upon an execrable Italian comedy, and a puppet-show, called *Rappresentazione d'un' anima dannata*, which, I think, are all the present diversions of the place; except the Marquise de Cavaillac's *Conversazione*, where one goes to see people play at ombre and taroc, a game with 72 cards all painted with suns, and moons, and devils and monks. Mr. Walpole has been at court; the family are at present at a country palace called La Venerie. The palace here in town is the very quintessence of gilding and looking-glass; inlaid floors, carved panels, and painting, wherever they could stick a brush. I own I have not, as yet, anywhere met with those grand and simple works of art, that are to amaze one, and whose sight one is to be the better for: but those of Nature have astonished me beyond expression. In our little journey up to the Grande Chartreuse, I do not remember to have gone ten paces without an exclamation, that there was no restraining: not a precipice, not a torrent, not a cliff, but is pregnant with religion and poetry. There are certain scenes that would awe an atheist into belief, without the help of other argument. One need not have a very fantastic imagination to see spirits there at noonday. You have Death perpetually before your eyes, only so far removed, as to compose the mind without frighting it. I am well persuaded St. Bruno was a man of no common genius to choose such a situation for his retirement; and perhaps should have been a disciple of his, had I been born in his time. You may believe Abélard and Héloïse were not forgot upon this occasion; if I do not mistake, I saw you too every now and then at a distance among the trees; *il me semble, que j'ai vu ce chien de visage là quelque part*. You seemed to call to me from the other side of the precipice, but the noise of the river below was so great, that I really could not distinguish what you said; it seemed to have a cadence like verse. In your next you will be so good to let me know what it was. The week we have since passed among the Alps has not equaled the single day upon that mountain, because the winter was rather too far advanced, and the weather a little foggy. However, it did not want its beauties; the savage rudeness of the view is inconceivable without seeing it. I reckoned in one day, thirteen cascades, the least of which was, I dare say, one hundred feet in height. I had Livy in the chaise with me, and beheld his *Nives coelo prope immistae, tecta informia imposita rupibus, pecora iumentaque torrida frigore, homines intonsi et inculti, animalia inanimaque omnia rigentia gelu; omnia confragosa, praeruptaque*. The creatures that inhabit them are, in all respects, below humanity; and most of them, especially women, have the *tumidum guttur*, which they call *goscia*. Mont Cenis, I confess, carries the permission mountains have of being frightful rather too far; and its horrors were accompanied with too much danger to give one time to reflect upon their beauties. There is a family of the Alpine monsters I have mentioned, upon its very top, that in the middle of winter calmly lay in their stock of provisions and firing, and so are buried in their hut for a month or two under the snow. When we were down it, and got a little way into Piedmont, we began to find *apricos quosdam colles, rivosque prope sylvas, et iam humano cultu digniora loca*. I read Silius Italicus too, for the first time; and wished for you according to custom. We set out for Genoa in two days time.

3. To His Mother

Naples, June 14, 1740

Our journey hither was through the most beautiful part of the finest country in the

---

2. *Rappresentazione . . . dannata*, the representation of a damned soul. 7. **ombre**, a card game usually played by three people. See Pope's *Rape of the Lock*, Canto I, l. 56, and Canto III, ll. 25 ff. (Vol. I, pp. 1074 ff.). *Taroc* is defined by Gray (ll. 7-9). 20. **Grande Chartreuse**, a Carthusian monastery situated about a dozen miles northeast of Grenoble in extreme southeastern France. It was founded in 1084 by St. Bruno (l. 32). 36. **Abélard and Héloïse**. The story of these two lovers was probably suggested to Gray by the monastic and yet romantic surroundings of the Grande Chartreuse. Abélard and Héloïse fell in love and married; but the harsh uncle of Héloïse separated the lovers and had Abélard mutilated. Abélard and Héloïse then took monastic and conventual vows. 39. *il . . . part*, it seemed to me that I saw your dog of a face somewhere.

56. *Nives . . . praeruptaque*. The quotations here and below are from the comprehensive *History of Rome* by the Roman Titus Livius (59 B.C.-A.D. 17), Book xxi. The first quotation can be roughly translated: "Snows intermingled with the heavens, shapeless edifices piled upon crags, cattle and beasts of burden shriveled with cold, men unshaved and uncultivated, all things animate and inanimate stiffened with ice, all things harsh and rugged." 64. *tumidum guttur*, the "wet" goiter. Apparently the incidence of goiter in Alpine regions had been noted as far back as the time of Imperial Rome. 76. *apricos . . . loca*, some sunny hills, streams near the woods, and now places more worthy of human cultivation. 78. **Silius Italicus**, a Roman poet (c. 25-100), whose great work was an epic on Carthage.

world; and every spot of it, on some account or other, famous for these three thousand years past. The season has hitherto been just as warm as one would wish it; no unwholesome airs, or violent heats, yet heard of; the people call it a backward year, and are in pain about their corn, wine, and oil; but we, who are neither corn, wine, nor oil, find it very agreeable. Our road was through Velletri, Cisterna, Terracina, Capua, and Aversa, and so to Naples. The minute one leaves his Holiness's dominions, the face of things begins to change from wide uncultivated plains to olive groves and well-tilled fields of corn, intermixed with ranks of elms, every one of which has its vine twining about it, and hanging in festoons between the rows from one tree to another. The great old fig-trees, the oranges in full bloom, and myrtles in every hedge make one of the delightfulest scenes you can conceive; besides that, the roads are wide, well-kept, and full of passengers, a sight I have not beheld this long time. My wonder still increased upon entering the city, which I think, for number of people, outdoes both Paris and London. The streets are one continued market, and thronged with populace so much that a coach can hardly pass. The common sort are a jolly lively kind of animals, more industrious than Italians usually are; they work till evening; then take their lute or guitar (for they all play) and walk about the city, or upon the seashore with it, to enjoy the fresco. One sees their little brown children jumping about stark-naked, and the bigger ones dancing with castanets, while others play on the cymbal to them. Your maps will show you the situation of Naples; it is on the most lovely bay in the world, and one of the calmest seas; it has many other beauties besides those of Nature. We have spent two days in visiting the remarkable places in the country round it, such as the bay of Baiae, and its remains of antiquity; the lake Avernus, and the Solfatara, Charon's grotto, etc. We have been in the Sybils' Cave and many other strange holes underground (I only name them, because you may consult Sandys' travels); but the strangest hole I ever was in has been today at a place called Portici, where his Sicilian Majesty has a country-seat. About a year ago, as they were digging, they discovered some parts of ancient buildings above thirty feet deep in the ground; curiosity led them on, and they have been digging ever since; the passage they have made, with all its turnings and windings, is now more than a mile long. As you walk you see parts of an amphitheater, many houses adorned with marble columns, and incrusted with the same; the front of a temple, several arched vaults of rooms painted in fresco. Some pieces of painting have been taken out from hence, finer than anything of the kind before discovered, and with these the King has adorned his palace; also a number of statues, medals, and gems; and more are dug out every day. This is known to be a Roman town, that in the Emperor Titus's time was overwhelmed by a furious eruption of Mount Vesuvius, which is hard by. The wood and beams remain so perfect that you may see the grain; but burnt to a coal, and dropping into dust upon the least touch. We were today at the foot of that mountain, which at present smokes only a little, where we saw the materials that fed the stream of fire, which about four years since ran down its side. We have but a few days longer to stay here; too little in conscience for such a place.

4. To Horace Walpole*

Cambridge, February 11, 1751

My dear Sir:

As you have brought me into a little sort of distress, you must assist me, I believe, to get out of it, as well as I can. Yesterday I had the misfortune of receiving a letter from certain gentlemen (as their bookseller ex-

---

10. **Velletri . . . Naples.** The places in this list are all towns on the road from Rome to Naples. Other places named in this letter are in the vicinity of Naples, and many of them are still visited by tourists.

49. **Sandys' travels,** the *Travels* by George Sandys (1578-1644), the famous Elizabethan traveler and miscellaneous writer. 51. **Sicilian Majesty,** Charles of Bourbon, who was King of the two Sicilies from 1735 to 1759; later King Charles III of Spain (1759-1788). 53. **discovered . . . buildings.** Herculaneum was destroyed in A.D. 79; excavations were begun there in 1738.
*This letter concerns the publication of Gray's famous *Elegy* (p. 50). It was actually published by Dodsley four days later (Feb. 15, 1751).

presses it) who have taken the *Magazine of Magazines* into their hands. They tell me that an ingenious poem, called *Reflections in a Country-Churchyard*, has been communicated to them, which they are printing forthwith; that they are informed, that the excellent author of it is I by name, and that they beg not only his indulgence, but the honor of his correspondence, etc.: as I am not at all disposed to be either so indulgent or so correspondent, as they desire; I have but one bad way left to escape the honor they would inflict upon me. And therefore am obliged to desire you would make Dodsley print it immediately (which may be done in less than a week's time) from your copy, but without my name, in what form is most convenient for him, but in his best paper and character. He must correct the press himself, and print it without any interval between the stanzas, because the sense is in some places continued beyond them; and the title must be, *Elegy, wrote in a Country Church-yard*. If he would add a line or two to say it came into his hands by accident, I should like it better. If you think fit, the 102nd line may be read

Awake, and faithful to her wonted fires.

but if this be worse than before; it must go, as it was. In the 126th, for *ancient* thorn, read *aged*.

If you behold the *Magazine of Magazines* in the light that I do, you will not refuse to give yourself this trouble on my account, which you have taken of your own accord before now. Adieu, sir, I am

Yours ever,
T. G.

If Dodsley don't do this immediately, he may as well let it alone.

5. TO MR. STONHEWER*

Stoke, August 18, 1758

I am as sorry as you seem to be, that our acquaintance harped so much on the subject of materialism, when I saw him with you in town, because it was plain to which side of the long-debated question he inclined. That we are indeed mechanical and dependent beings, I need no other proof than my own feelings; and from the same feelings I learn, with equal conviction, that we are not *merely* such: that there is a power within that struggles against the force and bias of that mechanism, that ready obedience which we call *habit;* and all this in conformity to a preconceived opinion (no matter whether right or wrong) to that least material of all agents, a thought. I have known many in his case who, while they thought they were conquering an old prejudice, did not perceive they were under the influence of one far more dangerous; one that furnishes us with a ready apology for all our worst actions, and opens to us a full license for doing whatever we please; and yet these very people were not at all the more indulgent to other men (as they naturally should have been), their indignation to such as offended them, their desire of revenge on anybody that hurt them was nothing mitigated; in short, the truth is, they wished to be persuaded of that opinion for the sake of its convenience, but were not so in their heart; and they would have been glad (as they ought in common prudence) that nobody else should think the same, for fear of the mischief that might ensue to themselves. His French author I never saw, but have read fifty in the same strain, and shall read no more. I can be wretched enough without them. They put me in mind of the Greek sophist that got immortal honor by discoursing so feelingly on the miseries of our condition, that fifty of his audience went home and hanged themselves; yet he lived

---

1. *Magazine of Magazines*, a periodical first published in 1750; its editor was a William Owen. 24. **If . . . accident.** The "advertisement" prefixed to the first edition was written by Walpole: "The following poem came into my hands by accident, if the general approbation with which this little piece has been spread may be called by so slight a term as accident. It is this approbation which makes it unnecessary for me to make any apology but to the author; as he cannot but feel some satisfaction in having pleased so many readers already, I flatter myself he will forgive my communicating that pleasure to many more." But the *Magazine of Magazines* appeared on Feb. 16, 1751, the day after Dodsley's edition, and announced the author as Mr. Gray of Peterhouse, Cambridge, so that Gray's authorship was known from the first.

*Richard Stonhewer (c.1728-1809) was a Fellow at Peterhouse College, Cambridge, a historiographer, and a great friend of Gray. It is believed that his later position as private secretary to the Duke of Grafton (later prime minister) had much to do with the appointment of Gray as Regius Professor of Modern History at Cambridge. 80. **Greek sophist**, Hegesias the Cyrenaic, who encouraged suicide.

himself (I suppose) many years after in very good plight.

You say you cannot conceive how Lord Shaftesbury came to be a philosopher in vogue; I will tell you: first, he was a lord; secondly, he was as vain as any of his readers; thirdly, men are very prone to believe what they do not understand; fourthly, they will believe anything at all, provided they are under no obligation to believe it; fifthly, they love to take a new road, even when that road leads nowhere; sixthly, he was reckoned a fine writer, and seemed always to mean more than he said. Would you have any more reasons? An interval of above forty years has pretty well destroyed the charm. A dead lord ranks but with commoners. Vanity is no longer interested in the matter, for the new road has become an old one. The mode of free-thinking is like that of ruffs and farthingales, and has given place to the mode of not thinking at all; once it was reckoned graceful, half to discover and half conceal the mind, but now we have been long accustomed to see it quite naked; primness and affectation of style, like the good breeding of Queen Anne's court, has turned to hoydening and rude familiarity.

6. To Dr. Wharton*

ca. June 20, 1760

Dear Doctor:

I heard yesterday from your old friend Mr. Field, that Mrs. Wharton had brought you a son, and as I sincerely hope this may be some addition to your happiness, I heartily congratulate you both on the occasion. Another thing I rejoice in is, to know, that you not only grow reconciled to your scene, but discover beauties around you, that once were deformities. I am persuaded the whole matter is to have always something going forward; happy they, that can create a rose-tree, or erect a honeysuckle, that can watch the brood of a hen, or see a fleet of their own ducklings launch into the water! It is with a sentiment of envy I speak it, who never shall have even a thatched roof of my own, nor gather a strawberry but in Covent Garden. I will not believe in the vocality of Old Park till next summer, when perhaps I may trust my own ears.

I remain (bating some few little excursions, that I have made) still in town, though for these three weeks I have been going into Oxfordshire with Madam Speed; but her affairs, as she says, or her vagaries, as I say, have obliged her to alter her mind ten times within that space; no wonder, for she has got at least £30,000 with a house in town, plate, jewels, china, and old-japan infinite, so that indeed, it would be ridiculous for her to know her own mind. I, who know mine, do intend to go to Cambridge, but that Owl Fobus is going thither to the Commencement, so that I am forced to stay till his nonsense is at an end. Chapman, you see, is dead at last, which signifies not much, I take it, to anybody, for his family (they say) are left in good circumstances. I am neither sorry, nor glad, for M. (I doubt) will scarce succeed to his prebend. The old creature is down at Aston, where my Lord has paid him a visit lately, as the town says, in a miff, about the garter, and other frumps he has met with of late. I believe, this at least is certain, that he has deserted his old attachments, and worships another idol, who receives his incense with a good deal of coldness and negligence.

I can tell you but little of St. Germain. He saw Mons. d'Affry at The Hague, who in a day or two (on receiving a courier from his own court) asked the State's leave to apprehend him, but he was gone, and arrived safe in St. Mary-Ax, where he had lodgings (I

---

3. **Lord Shaftesbury,** an English moralistic philosopher (1671-1713) of considerable influence in the eighteenth century.
*__Dr. Wharton,__ Thomas Wharton (1717-1794), not to be confused with Thomas Warton, the antiquarian poet of the same period. Thomas Wharton of Old Park, Durham, was an intimate friend of Gray. 31. **Mr. Field,** Thomas Field, a friend occasionally referred to in the *Letters.*

47. **Covent Garden,** the most famous market in London. 48. **vocality,** the noise of the birds and animals in the country. 51. **bating,** except for. 54. **Madam Speed,** Henrietta Speed (1728-1783), a rich heiress and friend of Gray; it was rumored for a time that they were in love. 62. **Owl Fobus,** old Fobus, a term of contempt derived from Wycherly's Restoration comedy, *The Plain Dealer* (Vol. I, p. 825). Gray and his friend Mason apply it constantly in their letters to the then Duke of Newcastle. 65. **Chapman,** Thomas Chapman, Master of Magdalene College, Cambridge, and prebendary of Durham. 68. **M,** William Mason (1724-1797), the biographer and intimate friend of Gray, also a clergyman and miscellaneous writer. 69. **doubt,** fear. 72. **miff,** fit of ill-humor. **garter . . . frumps.** Mason's patron, Lord Holdernesse, had hoped to receive the Order of the Garter but was disappointed. A *frump* is here "sneer," "mocking action." 78. **St. Germain,** a noted charlatan and adventurer of the time. 79. **Mons. d'Affry,** the then French ambassador at The Hague. 83. **St. Mary-Ax,** a street in London which was part of the Jewish quarter.

fancy) at his old friend La-Cour's, the Jew-physician. After some days a messenger took charge of him, and he was examined (I believe), before Mr. Pitt. They however dismissed him, but with orders to leave England directly, yet I know care was taken, that he should be furnished with proper passports to go safe through Holland to Hamb'rough, which gives some reason to believe, what at first many imagined, that he was charged with some proposal from the French court. He is a likely person enough to make them believe at Paris that he could somehow serve them on such an occasion.

We are in great alarms about Quebec. The force in the town was not 3000 men, sufficient to defend the place (naturally strong) against any attack of the French forces, unfurnished as they must be for a formal siege; but by no means to meet them in the field. This however is what Murray has chose to do, whether from rashness, or deceived by false intelligence, I cannot tell. The returns of our loss are undoubtedly false, for we have above 100 officers killed or taken. All depends upon the arrival of our garrison from Louisbourg, which was daily expected, but even that (unless they bring provisions with them) may increase the distress, for at the time, when we were told of the plenty and cheapness of all things at Quebec, I am assured, a piece of fresh meat could not be had for 20 guineas.

If you have seen Stonhewer he has probably told you of my old Scotch (or rather Irish) poetry. I am gone mad about them. They are said to be translations (literal and in prose) from the Erse tongue, done by one Macpherson, a young clergyman in the Highlands. He means to publish a collection he has of these specimens of antiquity, if it be antiquity; but what plagues me is, I cannot come at any certainty on that head. I was so struck, so *extasié* with their infinite beauty, that I writ into Scotland to make a thousand inquiries. The letters I have in return are ill-wrote, ill-reasoned, unsatisfactory, calculated (one would imagine) to deceive one, and yet not cunning enough to do it cleverly. In short, the whole external evidence would make one believe these fragments (for so he calls them, tho' nothing can be more entire) counterfeit; but the internal is so strong on the other side that I am resolved to believe them genuine, spite of the Devil and the Kirk. It is impossible to convince me that they were invented by the same man that writes me these letters. On the other hand it is almost as hard to suppose, if they are original, that he should be able to translate them so admirably. What can one do? Since Stonhewer went, I have received another of a very different and inferior kind (being merely descriptive) much more modern than the former (he says) yet very old too; this too in its way is extremely fine. In short this man is the very demon of poetry, or he has lighted on a treasure hid for ages. The Welsh poets are also coming to light; I have seen a discourse in mss. about them (by one Mr. Evans, a clergyman) with specimens of their writings. This is in Latin, and, tho' it don't approach the other, there are fine scraps among it.

You will think I am grown mighty poetical of a sudden; you would think so still more, if you knew there was a satire printed against me and Mason jointly. It is called *Two Odes;* the one is inscribed to Obscurity (that is me), the other to Oblivion. It tells me what I never heard before, for (speaking of himself), the author says, tho' he has

Nor the pride, nor self-opinion,
That possess the happy pair,
Each of taste the favorite minion,
Prancing thro' the desert air:
Yet shall he mount, with classic housings graced,
By help mechanic of equestrian block;
And all unheedful of the critic mock
Spur his light courser o'er the bounds of taste.

The writer is a Mr. Coleman, who pub-

---

2. **messenger,** policeman. 8. **Hamb'rough,** Hamburg, Germany. 15. **Quebec.** After the capture of Quebec by Wolfe (Sept., 1759), the French under Levis, Montcalm's successor, attempted to recapture it. General James Murray (later Governor of Canada) was defeated outside the city and besieged by Levis, but he was saved by the arrival of an English naval squadron in the St. Lawrence. 26. **Louisbourg,** a fortress on Cape Breton, Nova Scotia; it had been recaptured by Lord Amherst in 1758. 37. **Erse,** a name for *Gaelic,* particularly Scottish Gaelic. 38. **Macpherson.** See p. 7. 43. *extasié,* in ecstasy. 69. **Mr. Evans.** Evan Evans (1731-1789) was a noted Welsh antiquarian who did much to revive interest in, and knowledge of, early Welsh literature. 76. **Mason.** See p. 64, l. 68, and note. 89. **Mr. Coleman.** Actually the poem was written jointly by George Colman the Elder and Robert Lloyd (1733-1764). George Colman (1732-1794) began to publish the periodical *The Connoisseur* while still an undergraduate at Oxford. He was for a time a lawyer, but through his friendship for the actor Garrick he became enamored of the stage and devoted the rest of his life to the theater, both as playwright and as manager.

lished *The Connoisseur*, nephew to the late Lady Bath, and a friend of Garrick's. I believe his odes sell no more than mine did, for I saw a heap of them lie in a bookseller's window, who recommended them to me as a very pretty thing.

If I did not mention Tristram to you, it was because I thought I had done so before. There is much good fun in it, and humor sometimes hit and sometimes missed. I agree with your opinion of it, and shall see the two future volumes with pleasure. Have you read his sermons (with his own comic figure at the head of them)? They are in the style I think most proper for the pulpit, and show a very strong imagination and a sensible heart; but you see him often tottering on the verge of laughter, and ready to throw his periwig in the face of his audience. Now for my season.

April 10. I observed the elm putting out.
12. That, and the pear looked green. Thermometer at 62.
13. Very fine. White-poplar and willow put out.
15. Standard-pear (sheltered) in full bloom.
18. Lime and horn-beam green.
19. Swallows flying.
20. Thermometer at 60. Wind southwest: sky-lark, chaffinch, thrush, wren and robin singing. Horse-chestnut, wild-briar, bramble, and sallow had spread their leaves. Hawthorn and lilac had formed their blossoms. Blackthorn, double-flowered peach, and pears in full bloom. Double-jonquils, hyacinths, anemones, single-wallflowers and auriculas in flower, in the fields dog-violets, daisies, dandelion, buttercups, red-archangel, and shepherd's purse.
21. Almond out of bloom, and spreading its leaves.
26. Lilacs flowering.

May 1. Gentianella in flower.
2. Pear goes off. Apple blooms. Thermometer at 63. Wind northeast still fair and dry.
3. Evening and all night hard rain.
4. Thermometer at 40, wind northeast, rain.
11. Very fine. Wind northeast. Horse-chestnut in full bloom. Walnut and vine spread. Lilacs, Persian jasmine, tulips, wall-flowers, pheasant-eye, lily-in-the-valley in flower. In the fields, furze, cowslips, hare-bells, and cow-parsnip.

May 13. Jasmine and acacia spread. Fine weather.
18. Showery. Wind high.
19. Same. Thermometer at 56.
20. Thunder, rain. Thermometer at 54.
21. Rain. Wind northeast. at 52.
31. Green peas 15d a quart.

June 1. . . . at 78.
2. Scarlet strawberries, duke-cherries; hay-making here.
3. Wind south-southeast, thermometer at 84 (the highest I ever saw it); it was at noon.
since which, till last week, we had hot dry weather. Now it rains like mad. Cherries and strawberries in bushels.

I believe, there is no fear of war with Spain.

2. **Garrick.** See Vol. I, p. 1124, l. 93, and note. 7. **Tristram**, Laurence Sterne's *The Life and Opinions of Tristram Shandy, Gent.* (cf. Vol. I, p. 841). 13. **his**, Sterne's.

78. **war . . . Spain.** But a new Spanish King, Charles III, coming to the throne in 1759, gradually drifted into an alliance with France, at that time engaged with England in the Seven Years' War. Hostilities between England and Spain, however, did not actually break out until 1762.

William Collins

1721-1759

The sleepy old cathedral town of Chichester, Sussex, was the birthplace of William Collins. He had, it seems, an early aptitude for verse. As a twelve-year-old student at Winchester he wrote a poem on *The Royal Nuptials*, which has been lost. The *Persian Eclogues*, to which Collins later referred contemptuously as "The Irish Eclogues," was written when he was only seventeen. He matriculated at Magdalen College, Oxford, but he nursed a genuine contempt for pedantry and discipline, lapsed into dissipation, and left college when he received his bachelor's degree.

Young Collins was considered by his guardian uncle to be too indolent for the army, and so the Church was recommended to the lad, and the title of a curacy was secured him. But we are told that a tobacconist named Hardman succeeded in turning Collins's mind against taking holy orders. Instead, he went up to London in 1744, a "literary adventurer," with only a few pennies in his pocket but with grandiose literary projects in his mind. Of his projects few materialized; he planned—"and only planned"—tragedies; and he contemplated writing a history of the revival of learning, but this too remained in the speculative stage. Several poems, however, came to publication—the *Ode to Evening, How Sleep the Brave,* and *Dirge in Cymbeline*, all appearing in 1744 and 1746, have become his most famous works. But in his lifetime such favor as Collins was ever able to win was usually bestowed upon a group of poems published at other times: on his *Ode to Fear, Ode to Simplicity, On the Poetical Character*, and *On the Popular Superstitions of the Highlands*. All these poems were written between 1742 and 1752, although a few were not published until after Collins's death. A bookseller allowed Collins, on the credit of a projected translation of Aristotle's *Poetics*, enough money to escape into the country. Soon afterwards, however, at the death of Collins's uncle, the poet was left two thousand pounds; the guineas were promptly repaid the bookseller and the translation was abandoned. Collins was not old, yet he was failing mentally and physically. Following a journey into France, he is said to have been kept for some time in a mad-house in Chelsea, from which he was removed only shortly before his death in 1759.

Had Collins lived beyond his thirty-eighth year, it is conceivable that he would have achieved some supreme poetic creations; all the evidence for such a theory is before us, although the quantity of his verse is small. But this slender amount of verse sprang in the main from a rare imaginative energy which can be powerful but not always sustained. The fitfulness of his talent can be accounted for partly by his unstable, nervous temperament and by his improvident ways. "A man doubtful of his dinner or trembling at a creditor is not much disposed to abstracted meditations or remote inquiries . . . " Such was one of Johnson's observations in his apology for Collins, and it contains a truth which too few critics acknowledge.

Collins never knew a feeling of real security. While he had vigor of mind, he suffered from actual hunger, and the inheritance came after his mind was diseased. Irresolution became out-and-out powerlessness. It is easy to stress the biographical facts in Collins's brief existence and thereby lose sight of the poet's artistic aims and actual performance. Johnson accused Collins of a diction that was "often harsh and unskilfully labored" and of lines that were "slow of motion, clogged, impeded with clusters of consonants." Yet at the same time Johnson, for all his neo-classical bias, perceived the splendor of Collins's creative imagination. To review Collins's less than fifteen hundred lines of poetry is to feel a definite unfairness in Johnson's strictures. As a matter of fact, it is rare to find a poet with a more delicately attuned ear for the niceties of sound-effects than William Collins; his *Ode to Evening* has been hailed by critics as a most skilful and musical use of assonance and onomatopoeia. In his gentle melancholy, in his sensitive patriotism, in his quick perceiving of the more mysterious overtones of nature, and in his protest against the ornateness and artificiality of neo-classical poetry, Collins is, like Gray and Thomson, a landmark in English romantic poetry.

Dirge in Cymbeline

SUNG BY GUIDERUS AND ARVIRAGUS OVER FIDELE, SUPPOSED TO BE DEAD

Shakespeare's *Cymbeline*, IV, ii, 215-258, furnished the inspiration for this song. The brothers there mourn for their sister Imogen, who is disguised as Fidele, and who they think is dead. Cf. Shakespeare's song *Fear No More*, Vol. I, p. 498.

To fair Fidele's grassy tomb
  Soft maids and village hinds shall bring
Each opening sweet, of earliest bloom,
  And rifle all the breathing spring.

No wailing ghost shall dare appear,   5
  To vex with shrieks this quiet grove;
But shepherd lads assemble here,
  And melting virgins own their love.

No withered witch shall here be seen,
  No goblins lead their nightly crew;   10
The female fays shall haunt the green,
  And dress thy grave with pearly dew.

The red-breast oft at evening hours
  Shall kindly lend his little aid,
With hoary moss, and gathered flowers,   15
  To deck the ground where thou art laid.

When howling winds, and beating rain,
  In tempests shake the sylvan cell,
Or 'midst the chase on every plain,
  The tender thought on thee shall dwell.   20

Each lonely scene shall thee restore,
  For thee the tear be duly shed;
Beloved till life can charm no more,
  And mourned, till pity's self be dead.
(1744)

Ode

WRITTEN IN THE BEGINNING OF THE YEAR 1746

This ode commemorates the many English soldiers who had fallen in battle in 1745 both on the Continent, in the War of the Austrian Succession, and in Scotland, in the second Jacobite rebellion under Charles Edward Stuart, the Young Pretender. The poem is notable for its delicate restraint.

How sleep the brave who sink to rest
By all their country's wishes blest!
When Spring, with dewy fingers cold,
Returns to deck their hallowed mold,
She there shall dress a sweeter sod   5
Than Fancy's feet have ever trod.

By fairy hands their knell is rung,
By forms unseen their dirge is sung;
There Honor comes, a pilgrim gray,
To bless the turf that wraps their clay;   10
And Freedom shall awhile repair,
To dwell a weeping hermit there!   (1746)

Ode to Simplicity

To be observed in this poem is the protest against the ornateness and the artificiality of eighteenth-century poetry. In the emphasis upon simplicity and naturalness can be seen the essence of the growing romantic spirit.

O thou, by Nature taught
  To breathe her genuine thought,
In numbers warmly pure, and sweetly strong;
  Who first, on mountains wild,
  In Fancy, loveliest child,   5
Thy babe, or Pleasure's, nursed the powers of song!

  Thou, who, with hermit heart,
  Disdain'st the wealth of art,
And gauds, and pageant weeds, and trailing pall;
  But com'st a decent maid,   10
  In Attic robe arrayed,
O chaste, unboastful nymph, to thee I call;

  By all the honeyed store
  On Hybla's thymy shore;
By all her blooms, and mingled murmurs dear;   15

---

1. **Fidele**; cf. introductory headnote. 2. **hinds**, rustics, peasants. 18. **sylvan**, wooded, in the forest.

9. **gauds**, ornaments of dress. 11. **Attic robe**, a robe marked by its simplicity, characteristic of Athenian life and art. 14. **Hybla's . . . shore**. Mt. Hybla in Sicily was celebrated in ancient poetry for the sweetness of its honey. "Thymy" is "grown with thyme," an aromatic plant.

By her whose lovelorn woe
In evening musings slow
Soothed sweetly sad Electra's poet's ear:

By old Cephisus deep,
Who spread his wavy sweep, 20
In warbled wanderings, round thy green retreat;
On whose enameled side,
When holy Freedom died,
No equal haunt allured thy future feet.

O sister meek of Truth, 25
To my admiring youth,
Thy sober aid and native charms infuse!
The flowers that sweetest breathe,
Though Beauty culled the wreath,
Still ask thy hand to range their ordered hues. 30

While Rome could none esteem
But virtue's patriot theme,
You loved her hills, and led her laureat band:
But stayed to sing alone
To one distinguished throne; 35
And turned thy face, and fled her altered land.

No more, in hall or bower,
The passions own thy power;
Love, only love, her forceless numbers mean;
For thou hast left her shrine; 40
Nor olive more, nor vine,
Shall gain thy feet to bless the servile scene.

Though taste, though genius, bless
To some divine excess,
Faints the cold work till thou inspire the whole; 45
What each, what all supply,

May court, may charm, our eye;
Thou, only thou, canst raise the meeting soul!

Of these let others ask,
To aid some mighty task, 50
I only seek to find thy temperate vale;
Where oft my reed might sound
To maids and shepherds round,
And all thy sons, O Nature, learn my tale.

(1746)

Ode to Evening

This ode, written in unrimed stanzas, is one of the really great poems of the eighteenth century—perfect in form, exquisite in phrasing, and subtle in its power of suggestion. It belongs to the group of romantic poems that express enjoyment of nature in solitude and in the twilight hour (see essay, p. 6, and Gray's *Elegy Written in a Country Churchyard*, p. 50).

If aught of oaten stop, or pastoral song,
May hope, chaste Eve, to soothe thy modest ear,
Like thy own solemn springs,
Thy springs, and dying gales,

O nymph reserved, while now the bright-haired sun 5
Sits in yon western tent, whose cloudy skirts,
With brede ethereal wove,
O'erhang his wavy bed:

Now air is hushed, save where the weak-eyed bat
With short, shrill shriek, flits by on leathern wing; 10
Or where the beetle winds
His small but sullen horn,

As oft he rises 'midst the twilight path,
Against the pilgrim borne in heedless hum:
Now teach me, maid composed, 15
To breathe some softened strain,

Whose numbers, stealing through thy darkening vale,

18. **Electra's poet**, Sophocles, the great Greek tragedian of the fifth century B.C., author of *Electra*. The story of *Electra* is that of a daughter striving against the curse of a family; her brother Orestes had killed his adulterous mother Clytemnestra, wife and slayer of Agamemnon, the Greek leader against Troy. In the play Electra is comforted in her sorrow by the voice of the nightingale. 19. **Cephisus**, a river in Greece, near Athens. 23. **When ... died**, when Greece was conquered by Alexander the Great in 335 B.C. Cf. Gray's *Progress of Poesy*, p. 54, ll. 66 ff. 35. **one ... throne**, that of Augustus Caesar (first emperor of Rome, 27 B.C.-14 A.D.), patron of the famous Latin poets Virgil and Horace. 39. **forceless ... mean**, an allusion to the artificial love poetry of the days of chivalry (cf. "Knight, Priest, and Commoner," Vol. I, pp. 78 ff.).

52. **reed**, the symbol of pastoral poetry.
Ode to Evening. 1. **If ... stop.** If anything played upon the shepherd's oat, or pipe. 7. **brede**, embroidery.

May, not unseemly, with its stillness suit,
   As, musing slow, I hail
   Thy genial loved return!   20

For when thy folding star arising shows
His paly circlet, at his warning lamp
   The fragrant Hours, and elves
   Who slept in flowers the day,

And many a nymph who wreathes her brows
     with sedge,   25
And sheds the freshening dew, and, lovelier
     still,
   The pensive Pleasures sweet
   Prepare thy shadowy car.

Then lead, calm votaress, where some sheety
     lake
Cheers the lone heath, or some time-hallowed
     pile,   30
   Or upland fallows gray
   Reflect its last cool gleam.

But when chill blustering winds, or driving
     rain,
Forbid my willing feet, be mine the hut,
   That from the mountain's side,   35
   Views wilds, and swelling floods,

And hamlets brown, and dim-discovered
     spires;
And hears their simple bell, and marks o'er all
   Thy dewy fingers draw
   The gradual dusky veil.   40

While Spring shall pour his showers, as oft he
     wont,
And bathe thy breathing tresses, meekest Eve!
   While Summer loves to sport
   Beneath thy lingering light;   44

While sallow Autumn fills thy lap with leaves;
Or Winter, yelling through the troublous air,
   Affrights thy shrinking train,
   And rudely rends thy robes;

So long, sure-found beneath the sylvan shed,
Shall Fancy, Friendship, Science, rose-lipped
     Health,   50
   Thy gentlest influence own,
   And hymn thy favorite name!   (1746)

The Passions

AN ODE FOR MUSIC

   This poem pleads for the return of music to its preëminent place in poetry. Although neo-classical echoes are still audible in the poem, Collins regrets that neo-classical verse has grown harsh in sound and has given expression to too much personal opinion at the sacrifice of melody and beauty. Collins attempts to make the sound of his verse harmonize with the sense. (Cf. Dryden's *Song for St. Cecilia's Day* and *Alexander's Feast*, Vol. I, pp. 868 and 869.)

When Music, heavenly maid, was young,
While yet in early Greece she sung,
The Passions oft, to hear her shell,
Thronged around her magic cell,
Exulting, trembling, raging, fainting,   5
Possessed beyond the Muse's painting:
By turns they felt the glowing mind
Disturbed, delighted, raised, refined;
Till once, 'tis said, when all were fired,
Filled with fury, rapt, inspired,   10
From the supporting myrtles round
They snatched her instruments of sound;
And, as they oft had heard apart
Sweet lessons of her forceful art,
Each (for madness ruled the hour)   15
Would prove his own expressive power.

First Fear, his hand, its skill to try,
   Amid the chords bewildered laid,
And back recoiled, he knew not why,
   Even at the sound himself had made.   20

Next Anger rushed; his eyes on fire,
   In lightnings owned his secret stings:
In one rude clash he struck the lyre,
   And swept, with hurried hand, the strings.

---

21. **folding star**, the evening star, which indicated that it was time for the sheep to be put into the fold. 30. **pile**, large building; here, a church. 47. **Affrights . . . train**, that is, "shortens the evening." Compare the remarks on winter here with those in Thomson's *Winter* (p. 33).

3. **shell**, lyre. The first lyre is said to have been made from a tortoise shell. See Gray's *Progress of Poesy*, p. 53, l. 15.

With woeful measures wan Despair 25
  Low, sullen sounds his grief beguiled;
A solemn, strange, and mingled air;
  'Twas sad by fits, by starts 'twas wild.

But thou, O Hope, with eyes so fair,
  What was thy delightful measure? 30
  Still it whispered promised pleasure,
And bade the lovely scenes at distance hail!
Still would her touch the strain prolong;
  And from the rocks, the woods, the vale,
  She called on Echo still, through all the song; 35
  And, where her sweetest theme she chose,
A soft responsive voice was heard at every close,
And Hope enchanted smiled, and waved her golden hair.

And longer had she sung;—but, with a frown,
  Revenge impatient rose: 40
He threw his blood-stained sword, in thunder, down;
  And with a withering look,
  The war-denouncing trumpet took,
And blew a blast so loud and dread,
Were ne'er prophetic sounds so full of woe! 45
  And, ever and anon, he beat
  The doubling drum, with furious heat;
And though sometimes, each dreary pause between,
  Dejected Pity, at his side,

Her soul-subduing voice applied, 50
Yet still he kept his wild unaltered mien,
While each strained ball of sight seemed bursting from his head.
  Thy numbers, Jealousy, to naught were fixed;
  Sad proof of thy distressful state;
Of differing themes the veering song was mixed; 55
And now it courted love, now raving called on hate.

With eyes upraised, as one inspired,
Pale Melancholy sat retired;
And, from her wild sequestered seat,

In notes by distance made more sweet, 60
Poured through the mellow horn her pensive soul:
  And, dashing soft from rocks around,
  Bubbling runnels joined the sound;
Through glades and glooms the mingled measure stole,
Or, o'er some haunted stream, with fond delay, 65
  Round an holy calm diffusing,
  Love of peace, and lonely musing,
In hollow murmurs died away.

But O! how altered was its sprightlier tone,
When Cheerfulness, a nymph of healthiest hue, 70
  Her bow across her shoulder flung,
  Her buskins gemmed with morning dew,
Blew an inspiring air, that dale and thicket rung,
The hunter's call, to faun and dryad known!
The oak-crowned sisters, and their chaste-eyed queen, 75
  Satyrs and sylvan boys, were seen,
  Peeping from forth their alleys green:
Brown Exercise rejoiced to hear;
And Sport leaped up, and seized his beechen spear.

Last came Joy's ecstatic trial: 80
  He, with viny crown advancing,
  First to the lively pipe his hand addressed;
But soon he saw the brisk awakening viol,
  Whose sweet entrancing voice he loved the best;
They would have thought who heard the strain 85
They saw, in Tempe's vale, her native maids,
  Amidst the festal sounding shades,
  To some unwearied minstrel dancing,
While, as his flying fingers kissed the strings,
Love framed with Mirth a gay fantastic round; 90
Loose were her tresses seen, her zone unbound;

---

43. **war-denouncing,** war-announcing. 63. **runnels,** small streams or brooks, rivulets. 75. **oak-crowned sisters,** wood nymphs. 86. **Tempe's vale,** a valley in Thessaly, Greece, noted for its beauty.

And he, amidst his frolic play,
As if he would the charming air repay,
Shook thousand odors from his dewy wings.

O Music! sphere-descended maid!   95
Friend of Pleasure, Wisdom's aid!
Why, goddess! why, to us denied,
Lay'st thou thy ancient lyre aside?
As, in that loved Athenian bower,
You learned an all-commanding power,   100
Thy mimic soul, O nymph endeared,
Can well recall what then it heard;
Where is thy native simple heart,
Devote to virtue, fancy, art?
Arise, as in that elder time,   105
Warm, energetic, chaste, sublime!
Thy wonders, in that godlike age,
Fill thy recording sister's page—
'Tis said, and I believe the tale,
Thy humblest reed could more prevail,   110
Had more of strength, diviner rage,
Than all which charms this laggard age;
E'en all at once together found,
Cecilia's mingled world of sound—
O bid our vain endeavors cease;   115
Revive the just designs of Greece:
Return in all thy simple state!
Confirm the tales her sons relate!

(1746)

Ode on the Death of Mr. Thomson

In yonder grave a druid lies,
  Where slowly winds the stealing wave;
The year's best sweets shall duteous rise
  To deck its poet's sylvan grave.

In yon deep bed of whispering reeds   5
  His airy harp shall now be laid,
That he, whose heart in sorrow bleeds,
  May love through life the soothing shade.

114. **Cecilia's . . . sound.** St. Cecilia was said to have invented the organ. See Dryden's *Song for St. Cecilia's Day* (Vol. I, p. 868).
Ode on the Death of Mr. Thomson. 1. **druid**, James Thomson (1700-1748); cf. p. 32. A druid was a priest of the ancient Celtic religion observed by the Britons before, and during the early years of, the Roman conquest. Thomson, a Scotchman, was considered to be of Celtic race. 6. **airy harp**, the harp of Aeolus, god of the winds; cf. Thomson's *Castle of Indolence*, p. 45, l. 360.

Then maids and youths shall linger here,
  And while its sounds at distance swell,   10
Shall sadly seem in pity's ear
  To hear the woodland pilgrim's knell.

Remembrance oft shall haunt the shore
  When Thames in summer wreaths is dressed,
And oft suspend the dashing oar,   15
  To bid his gentle spirit rest!

And oft, as ease and health retire
  To breezy lawn, or forest deep,
The friend shall view yon whitening spire,
  And 'mid the varied landscape weep.   20

But thou, who own'st that earthy bed,
  Ah! what will every dirge avail;
Or tears, which love and pity shed,
  That mourn beneath the gliding sail?

Yet lives there one whose heedless eye   25
  Shall scorn thy pale shrine glimmering near?
With him, sweet bard, may fancy die,
  And joy desert the blooming year.

But thou, lorn stream, whose sullen tide
  No sedge-crowned sisters now attend,   30
Now waft me from the green hill's side,
  Whose cold turf hides the buried friend!

And see—the fairy valleys fade;
  Dun night has veiled the solemn view!
Yet once again, dear parted shade,   35
  Meek nature's child, again adieu!

The genial meads, assigned to bless
  Thy life, shall mourn thy early doom:
Their hinds and shepherd-girls shall dress,
  With simple hands, thy rural tomb.   40

Long, long, thy stone and pointed clay
  Shall melt the musing Briton's eyes:
O vales and wild woods! shall he say,
  In yonder grave your druid lies!

(1749)

19. **yon . . . spire**, Richmond Church, where Thomson was buried.

William Cowper
1731-1800

The father of Cowper was rector at Great Berkhampstead in Hertfordshire; in that village William Cowper was born. His mother, Anne Donne Cowper, could trace a relationship to John Donne, the seventeenth-century poet; she left an indelible impression upon the memory of her young son William, although she died when he was only six years of age. The motherless boy evinced very early an abnormal sensitiveness and timidity; when he went to his first school, he was easy prey for the bullying of older boys, and the spiritual mark of this suffering was to stay with Cowper for the rest of his life. At the age of fourteen he went to the famous Westminster School and distinguished himself as a scholar. He entered the legal profession, received a small government appointment and chambers in the Inner Temple, one of the important law institutions of London, and was admitted to the bar in 1755. He never showed any desire to practice law, however, and was apparently content to live in expectation of some sort of legal sinecure, basing his expectation upon the influence of his uncle Ashley Cowper, a London citizen of considerable wealth. Indeed, Cowper not only hoped to be a protégé of his uncle but his son-in-law as well; he had fallen in love with Ashley Cowper's elder daughter Theodora. The match was frustrated by the girl's father, however, ostensibly because of the consanguinity of the young couple, but probably because of the potential ineptness of his prospective son-in-law. Theodora was faithful to her lover in true romantic fashion; at the time of her death in 1824, a generation after Cowper's, she entrusted to a friend a packet of Cowper's letters and some early verses which saw publication the next year under the title of *Early Poems*.

When Cowper was about twenty-four, he showed for the first time symptoms of a melancholy disorder which was to increase both in intensity and frequency until a black cloud of insanity settled upon him permanently. As Cowper tells us: "I was struck [at that time] with such a dejection of spirit as none but they who have felt the same can have the least conception of. Day and night I was upon the rack, lying down in horror and rising up in despair." This depressing mental illness took the form of an overwhelming consciousness of sin, a morbid belief that he had transgressed all divine laws, and that because he had committed the unforgivable crime, nothing lay before him but the terrors of damnation. At the time of his first attack, his illness lasted only a few months. The sudden death of his father in 1756 left Cowper in want. He had an opportunity to take over two minor clerical positions, and chose that of Clerk of the Journals of the House of Lords, less lucrative than the other possibility, but insuring greater privacy. The news that he had to take an examination to qualify for this position left him thunderstruck, and his worry over the possible ordeal snapped his delicate hold upon sanity. He tried three times to kill himself, and was committed in 1763 to a private asylum at St. Albans, where he remained until the attack had passed. Two years later he emerged and took up residence at Huntingdon, in order to be near his younger brother, who was a fellow at Cambridge.

Cowper was fortunate to make the acquaintance at Huntingdon of the Unwins. Mr. Unwin was a clergyman and tutor; Cowper boarded at his house; and upon the death of Unwin in 1767 remained as a boarder with Mrs. Unwin. For financial reasons Mrs. Unwin was forced to move to a smaller home in the near-by parish of

Olney, where the energetic John Newton was curate. Cowper, feeling the necessity for some kind of occupation, became an assistant of Newton, visiting the sick and dying in Olney, making parish-calls, and even at times conducting services. The religious environment at Olney, however, was the very worst kind of environment for the sick-minded Cowper. Another disastrous attack of insanity, lasting this time until 1769, meant the end of all his activity in the parish. But he had projected a collection of hymns—the famous *Olney Hymns*—over eighty in number, which, in 1779, became his first considerable publication.

This third attack of madness was followed by the most peaceful years of Cowper's life. He occupied himself with gardening and carpentering and raising domestic animals; the friendship of Mrs. Unwin, his landlady, and of Lady Austen, a rich widow of the vicinity, brightened his social life. Now, at the age of fifty, he began a sudden streak of literary activity. In 1782 appeared a volume comprising *Truth, Table Talk, The Progress of Error, Expostulation, Hope, Charity, Conversation*, and *Retirement*, all moral and didactic poems that do not show Cowper at his best. Lady Austen was chiefly responsible for *The Task* (1785); the part she played in the production resulted in the end of her friendship with Cowper. Sixty-year-old Mrs. Unwin was absurdly jealous of this friendship between a sophisticated society woman and a pathological poet, the least worldly of men.

The Task, in Miltonic blank verse, describes homely folk and working people; it is dedicated to the theme "God made the country and man made the town." It began as a kind of mock-heroic description of the sofa in Cowper's country home; it ended as a piece of spiritual autobiography that reminds one of the later work of Wordsworth like *The Prelude* (p. 125) or *The Excursion*. Included in the volume are the light-hearted *The Diverting History of John Gilpin*, a ballad of semi-farcical nature, and his affecting poem *On the Receipt of My Mother's Picture*. There was now but little left to Cowper's literary activity. In 1791 he published a translation of Homer, and of Milton's Latin and Italian poetry. With the death of Mrs. Unwin in 1796 his mania returned, never to leave him until his death in 1800.

"I was a stricken deer that left the herd long since," wrote Cowper in one of those moments of frank self-revelation that showed his peculiar talents. No fair reader can possibly ignore the fragile personality of the poet, his moments of rare companionability, his shrinking timidity, and his morbid religiosity. His writings are uneven; he is never a great poet expressing great ideas in a grand manner, but rather a modest bard of nature and of rural village society, always with real devotion to the implacable figure that is his God. Like Blake (p. 111), Cowper is something of an isolated phenomenon, and a psychopathic one; but in that very individualism can be seen the strong current of the romantic which runs through his works. His talents as a nature poet are not inconsiderable. He makes an important contribution to emotionally religious poetry; he is one of the most distinguished hymn-writers of the century. Above all, he is a personality as much as a poet, for his letters and autobiographical writings are almost unapproached in their frank and fascinating revelation of a tortured human soul.

from *Olney Hymns*

WALKING WITH GOD

Oh! for a closer walk with God,
   A calm and heavenly frame;
A light to shine upon the road
   That leads me to the Lamb!

Where is the blessedness I knew   5
   When first I saw the Lord?
Where is the soul-refreshing view
   Of Jesus and His word?

What peaceful hours I once enjoyed!
   How sweet their memory still!   10
But they have left an aching void
   The world can never fill.

Return, O holy Dove, return,
   Sweet messenger of rest!
I hate the sins that made Thee mourn,   15
   And drove Thee from my breast.

The dearest idol I have known,
   Whate'er that idol be,
Help me to tear it from Thy throne,
   And worship only Thee.   20

So shall my walk be close with God,
   Calm and serene my frame;
So purer light shall mark the road
   That leads me to the Lamb.   (1779)

PRAISE FOR THE FOUNTAIN OPENED

There is a fountain filled with blood
   Drawn from Emmanuel's veins;
And sinners, plunged beneath that flood,
   Lose all their guilty stains.

The dying thief rejoiced to see   5
   That fountain in his day;
And there have I, as vile as he,
   Washed all my sins away.

Dear dying Lamb, Thy precious blood
   Shall never lose its power,   10

Till all the ransomed church of God
   Be saved, to sin no more.

E'er since, by faith, I saw the stream
   Thy flowing wounds supply,
Redeeming love has been my theme,   15
   And shall be till I die.

Then in a nobler, sweeter song,
   I'll sing Thy power to save;
When this poor lisping stammering tongue
   Lies silent in the grave.   20

Lord, I believe Thou hast prepared
   (Unworthy though I be)
For me a blood-bought free reward,
   A golden harp for me!

'Tis strung, and tuned, for endless years,   25
   And formed by power divine,
To sound in God the Father's ears
   No other name but Thine.   (1779)

On the Loss of the Royal George

On August 29, 1782, the English man-of-war *Royal George*, under the command of Admiral Kempenfelt, capsized and sank while anchored for repairs at Portsmouth, carrying to their doom more than eight hundred visitors and crew. Cowper's poem on the subject was written at the instance of Lady Austen, who wanted some appropriate words that could be sung to the music of the Dead March in Handel's *Scipio*.

Toll for the brave!
   The brave that are no more!
All sunk beneath the wave,
   Fast by their native shore!

Eight hundred of the brave,   5
   Whose courage well was tried,
Had made the vessel heel,
   And laid her on her side.

A land-breeze shook the shrouds,
   And she was overset;   10
Down went the *Royal George*,
   With all her crew complete.

---

15. **I hate . . . breast.** The autobiographical detail in these lines—Cowper's obsession with the Unpardonable Sin—should be compared with that in his *The Castaway*, p. 82.

5. **Eight hundred,** inaccurate: the victims included many tradesmen and visitors aboard the ship.

Toll for the brave!
  Brave Kempenfelt is gone;
His last sea-fight is fought;   15
  His work of glory done.

It was not in the battle;
  No tempest gave the shock;
She sprang no fatal leak;
  She ran upon no rock.   20

His sword was in its sheath;
  His fingers held the pen,
When Kempenfelt went down
  With twice four hundred men.

Weigh the vessel up,   25
  Once dreaded by our foes!
And mingle with our cup
  The tears that England owes.

Her timbers yet are sound,
  And she may float again   30
Full charged with England's thunder,
  And plow the distant main.

But Kempenfelt is gone,
  His victories are o'er;
And he and his eight hundred   35
  Shall plow the wave no more.

(1782; 1803)

from *The Task*

   The Task has been considered by many as Cowper's masterpiece. It takes its title from the fact that Cowper's friend, Lady Austen, asked the poet to write a poem in blank verse on the subject of the parlor sofa. The outcome of this harmless suggestion, in the blight that it brought upon Cowper's friendship with Lady Austen, through the curious jealousy of Mrs. Unwin, has already been noted (p. 74).
   In the "Advertisement" to the poem, Cowper says that he obeyed; "and, having much leisure, connected another subject with it; and, pursuing the train of thought to which my situation and turn of mind led me, brought forth at length, instead of the trifle which I at first intended, a serious affair—a volume!"
   The purpose of the poem, as stated by Cowper in a letter to William Unwin (October 10, 1784), was "to discountenance the modern enthusiasm after a London life, and to recommend rural ease and leisure as friendly to the cause of piety and virtue." Burns calls the religion of *The Task* "the religion of God and nature, the religion that exalts, that ennobles man." And Coleridge, in speaking of "the divine chitchat" of Cowper, pays tribute to his lofty purpose and gracious manner.
   In the six books of this poem is included a variety of themes—an interest in nature, in country life, in lowly people, in animals, and in social reform. A forerunner of Wordsworth (p. 118), Cowper recollects his earlier contacts with nature and gratefully records its healing influences upon his wounded and sensitive spirit. His scenes have actuality, and his minute descriptions, done with keen and sympathetic eye, confirm his faith in the poetic value of simple truth.

from Book I, The Sofa

*   *   *   *   *

For I have loved the rural walk through lanes
Of grassy swarth, close cropped by nibbling
   sheep,   110
And skirted thick with intertexture firm
Of thorny boughs; have loved the rural walk
O'er hills, through valleys, and by rivers' brink,
E'er since a truant boy I passed my bounds
To enjoy a ramble on the banks of Thames;   115
And still remember, nor without regret
Of hours that sorrow since has much endeared,
How oft, my slice of pocket store consumed,
Still hungering, penniless and far from home,
I fed on scarlet hips and stony haws,   120
Or blushing crabs, or berries, that emboss
The bramble, black as jet, or sloes austere.
Hard fare! but such as boyish appetite

120. **hips . . . haws.** *Hips* are the ripe fruit of the rosebush; *haws,* of the hawthorn. 121. **crabs,** crabapples. 122. **sloes austere.** The *sloe* is the fruit of the blackthorn; *austere* is used here in the sense of "sour."

Disdains not; nor the palate, undepraved
By culinary arts, unsavory deems.   125
No Sofa then awaited my return;
Nor Sofa then I needed. Youth repairs
His wasted spirits quickly, by long toil
Incurring short fatigue; and, though our years
As life declines speed rapidly away,   130
And not a year but pilfers as he goes
Some youthful grace that age would gladly keep;
A tooth or auburn lock, and by degrees
Their length and color from the locks they spare;
The elastic spring of an unwearied foot   135
That mounts the stile with ease, or leaps the fence,
That play of lungs, inhaling and again
Respiring freely the fresh air, that makes
Swift pace or steep ascent no toil to me,   139
Mine have not pilfered yet; nor yet impaired
My relish of fair prospect; scenes that soothed
Or charmed me young, no longer young, I find
Still soothing and of power to charm me still.
And witness, dear companion of my walks,
Whose arm this twentieth winter I perceive 145
Fast locked in mine, with pleasure such as love,
Confirmed by long experience of thy worth
And well-tried virtues, could alone inspire—
Witness a joy that thou hast doubled long.
Thou knowest my praise of nature most sincere,   150
And that my raptures are not conjured up
To serve occasions of poetic pomp,
But genuine, and art partner of them all.
How oft upon yon eminence our pace
Has slackened to a pause, and we have borne
The ruffling wind, scarce conscious that it blew,   155
While admiration, feeding at the eye,
And still unsated, dwelt upon the scene.
Thence with what pleasure have we just discerned
The distant plow slow moving, and beside 160
His laboring team, that swerved not from the track,
The sturdy swain diminished to a boy!
Here Ouse, slow winding through a level plain
Of spacious meads with cattle sprinkled o'er,
Conducts the eye along its sinuous course 165
Delighted. There, fast rooted in his bank,
Stand, never overlooked, our favorite elms,
That screen the herdsman's solitary hut;
While far beyond, and overthwart the stream
That, as with molten glass, inlays the vale, 170
The sloping land recedes into the clouds;
Displaying on its varied side the grace
Of hedge-row beauties numberless, square tower,
Tall spire, from which the sound of cheerful bells
Just undulates upon the listening ear,   175
Groves, heaths, and smoking villages remote.
Scenes must be beautiful, which daily viewed,
Please daily, and whose novelty survives
Long knowledge and the scrutiny of years—
Praise justly due to those that I describe.   180

Nor rural sights alone, but rural sounds
Exhilarate the spirit and restore
The tone of languid nature. Mighty winds,
That sweep the skirt of some far-spreading wood
Of ancient growth, make music not unlike 185
The wash of ocean on his winding shore,
And lull the spirit while they fill the mind;
Unnumbered branches waving in the blast,
And all their leaves fast fluttering, all at once.
Nor less composure waits upon the roar   190
Of distant floods, or on the softer voice
Of neighboring fountain, or of rills that slip
Through the cleft rock, and, chiming as they fall
Upon loose pebbles, lose themselves at length
In matted grass, that with a livelier green 195
Betrays the secret of their silent course.
Nature inanimate employs sweet sounds,
But animated nature sweeter still,
To soothe and satisfy the human ear.
Ten thousand warblers cheer the day, and one

---

126. **Sofa.** See the title of this book of *The Task.* 144. **companion . . . walks,** Mary Unwin, from whom Cowper was never separated from 1765 until her death in 1796. See *Sonnet to Mrs. Unwin,* and introductory headnote to Cowper, p. 74.

163. **Ouse,** a small river in Sussex. 180. **those . . . describe,** familiar scenes in the vicinity of Olney, Cowper's home. In a letter to the Reverend William Unwin, dated October 10, 1784, Cowper wrote: "My descriptions are all from nature; not one of them second-hand. My delineations of the heart are from my own experience; not one of them borrowed from books, or in the least degree conjectural."

The livelong night: nor these alone, whose
    notes   201
Nice-fingered art must emulate in vain,
But cawing rooks, and kites that swim sublime
In still repeated circles, screaming loud,
The jay, the pie, and e'en the boding owl   205
That hails the rising moon, have charms for me.
Sounds inharmonious in themselves and harsh,
Yet heard in scenes where peace forever reigns,
And only there, please highly for their sake.

        *   *   *   *   *

Where finds philosophy her eagle eye,
With which she gazes at yon burning disk
Undazzled, and detects and counts his spots?
In London. Where her implements exact,   715
With which she calculates, computes, and
    scans,
All distance, motion, magnitude, and now
Measures an atom, and now girds a world?
In London. Where has commerce such a mart,
So rich, so thronged, so drained, and so supplied,   720
As London—opulent, enlarged, and still
Increasing London? Babylon of old
Not more the glory of the earth than she,
A more accomplished world's chief glory now.

    She has her praise. Now mark a spot or
        two,   725
That so much beauty would do well to purge;
And show this queen of cities that so fair
May yet be foul; so witty, yet not wise.
It is not seemly, nor of good report,
That she is slack in discipline; more prompt   730
To avenge than to prevent the breach of law:
That she is rigid in denouncing death
On petty robbers, and indulges life
And liberty, and oft-times honor too,
To peculators of the public gold: 735
That thieves at home must hang, but he that
    puts
Into his overgorged and bloated purse

The wealth of Indian provinces escapes.
Nor is it well, nor can it come to good,
That, through profane and infidel contempt
Of holy writ, she has presumed to annul   741
And abrogate, as roundly as she may,
The total ordinance and will of God;
Advancing fashion to the post of truth,
And centering all authority in modes   745
And customs of her own, till sabbath rites
Have dwindled into unrespected forms,
And knees and hassocks are well-nigh divorced.

God made the country, and man made the
    town.   749
What wonder then that health and virtue, gifts
That can alone make sweet the bitter draught
That life holds out to all, should most abound
And least be threatened in the fields and
    groves?
Possess ye, therefore, ye who, borne about
In chariots and sedans, know no fatigue   755
But that of idleness, and taste no scenes
But such as art contrives, possess ye still
Your element; there only can ye shine,
There only minds like yours can do no harm.
Our groves were planted to console at noon   760
The pensive wanderer in their shades. At eve
The moonbeam, sliding softly in between
The sleeping leaves, is all the light they wish,
Birds warbling all the music. We can spare
The splendor of your lamps; they but eclipse
Our softer satellite. Your songs confound   766
Our more harmonious notes; the thrush departs
Scared, and the offended nightingale is mute.
There is a public mischief in your mirth;
It plagues your country. Folly such as yours,
Graced with a sword, and worthier of a fan,   771
Has made, what enemies could ne'er have
    done,
Our arch of empire, steadfast but for you,
A mutilated structure, soon to fall.

    from BOOK II. THE TIME-PIECE

Oh, for a lodge in some vast wilderness,
Some boundless contiguity of shade,

---

727. **fair . . . foul;** cf. Shakespeare's *Macbeth*, I, iii, 38: "So foul and fair a day I have not seen." 732. **denouncing,** pronouncing. Petty crimes like shoplifting were at that time punishable in England by death. 735. **peculator,** embezzler. 736. **he . . . escapes.** An allusion to the British policy in India, carried out by Robert Clive (1725-1774) and Warren Hastings (1732-1818) by acts of conquest and pitiless extortion through the period from 1751 to 1785. Clive made a fortune for himself, and Hastings greatly increased the revenue for the British East India Company.

755. **sedans,** sedan-chairs.
    Book II. 1. lodge . . . wilderness; cf. *Jeremiah*, 9:2: "Oh that I had in the wilderness a lodging place of wayfaring men; that I might leave my people, and go from them!"

Where rumor of oppression and deceit,
Of unsuccessful or successful war,
Might never reach me more! My ear is pained,
My soul is sick, with every day's report   6
Of wrong and outrage with which earth is filled.
There is no flesh in man's obdurate heart,
It does not feel for man; the natural bond
Of brotherhood is severed as the flax   10
That falls asunder at the touch of fire.
He finds his fellow guilty of a skin
Not colored like his own; and, having power
To enforce the wrong, for such a worthy cause
Dooms and devotes him as his lawful prey.   15
Lands intersected by a narrow frith
Abhor each other. Mountains interposed
Make enemies of nations, who had else,
Like kindred drops, been mingled into one.
Thus man devotes his brother, and destroys;   20
And, worse than all, and most to be deplored,
As human nature's broadest, foulest blot,
Chains him, and tasks him, and exacts his sweat
With stripes, that Mercy, with a bleeding heart,
Weeps when she sees inflicted on a beast.   25
Then what is man? And what man, seeing this,
And having human feelings, does not blush,
And hang his head, to think himself a man?
I would not have a slave to till my ground,
To carry me, to fan me while I sleep,   30
And tremble when I wake, for all the wealth
That sinews bought and sold have ever earned.
No: dear as freedom is, and in my heart's
Just estimation prized above all price,
I had much rather be myself the slave,   35
And wear the bonds, than fasten them on him.
We have no slaves at home.—Then why abroad?
And they themselves, once ferried o'er the wave
That parts us, are emancipate and loosed.
Slaves cannot breathe in England; if their lungs   40
Receive our air, that moment they are free;
They touch our country, and their shackles fall.
That's noble, and bespeaks a nation proud
And jealous of the blessing. Spread it then,
And let it circulate through every vein   45
Of all your empire; that where Britain's power
Is felt, mankind may feel her mercy too.

* * * * *

from Book III. The Garden

I was a stricken deer that left the herd
Long since; with many an arrow deep infixed
My panting side was charged, when I withdrew   110
To seek a tranquil death in distant shades.
There was I found by One Who had Himself
Been hurt by the archers. In His side He bore,
And in His hands and feet, the cruel scars.
With gentle force soliciting the darts,   115
He drew them forth, and healed, and bade me live.
Since then, with few associates, in remote
And silent woods I wander, far from those
My former partners of the peopled scene,
With few associates, and not wishing more.   120
Here much I ruminate, as much I may,
With other views of men and manners now
Than once, and others of a life to come.
I see that all are wanderers, gone astray
Each in his own delusions; they are lost   125
In chase of fancied happiness, still wooed
And never won; dream after dream ensues,
And still they dream that they shall still succeed,
And still are disappointed: rings the world
With the vain stir. I sum up half mankind,   130
And add two-thirds of the remainder half,
And find the total of their hopes and fears
Dreams, empty dreams. . . .   (1785)

On the Receipt of My Mother's Picture Out of Norfolk

THE GIFT OF MY COUSIN ANN BODHAM

Oh, that those lips had language! Life has passed
With me but roughly since I heard thee last.
Those lips are thine—thy own sweet smile I see,

---

16. **frith**, a narrow arm of the sea. 20. **devotes**, gives over to destruction. 40. **Slaves . . . England.** The court decision that "slaves cannot breathe in England" was given by Lord Mansfield in 1772. The slave trade was not abolished until 1807. Slavery in the British Colonies was abolished in 1833.

109. **Long since.** Cowper's first breakdown came in 1763. See headnote, pp. 73-74.
On the Receipt of My Mother's Picture. 2. **heard thee last.** Cowper was only six years old when his mother died in 1737.

The same that oft in childhood solaced me;
Voice only fails, else how distinct they say, 5
"Grieve not, my child, chase all thy fears
   away!"
The meek intelligence of those dear eyes
(Blest be the art that can immortalize,
The art that baffles Time's tyrannic claim
To quench it) here shines on me still the
   same. 10
  Faithful remembrancer of one so dear,
O welcome guest, though unexpected here!
Who bidd'st me honor with an artless song,
Affectionate, a mother lost so long,
I will obey, not willingly alone, 15
But gladly, as the precept were her own:
And, while that face renews my filial grief,
Fancy shall weave a charm for my relief—
Shall steep me in Elysian reverie,
A momentary dream that thou art she. 20
  My mother! when I learned that thou wast
   dead,
Say, wast thou conscious of the tears I shed?
Hovered thy spirit o'er thy sorrowing son,
Wretch even then, life's journey just begun?
Perhaps thou gavest me, though unfelt, a kiss,
Perhaps a tear, if souls can weep in bliss— 26
Ah, that maternal smile! It answers—Yes.
I heard the bell tolled on thy burial day,
I saw the hearse that bore thee slow away,
And turning from my nursery window, drew
A long, long sigh, and wept a last adieu! 31
But was it such?—It was.—Where thou art
   gone
Adieus and farewells are a sound unknown.
May I but meet thee on that peaceful shore,
The parting word shall pass my lips no more!
Thy maidens, grieved themselves at my con-
   cern, 36
Oft gave me promise of thy quick return.
What ardently I wished, I long believed,
And, disappointed still, was still deceived.
By expectation every day beguiled, 40
Dupe of *tomorrow* even from a child.
Thus many a sad tomorrow came and went,
Till, all my stock of infant sorrow spent,
I learned at last submission to my lot;
But, though I less deplored thee, ne'er forgot.
  Where once we dwelt our name is heard no
   more, 46
Children not thine have trod my nursery
   floor;

And where the gardener Robin, day by day,
Drew me to school along the public way,
Delighted with my bauble coach, and
   wrapped 50
In scarlet mantle warm, and velvet capped,
'Tis now become a history little known,
That once we called the pastoral house our
   own.
Short-lived possession! but the record fair
That memory keeps of all thy kindness there,
Still outlives many a storm that has effaced 55
A thousand other themes less deeply traced.
Thy nightly visits to my chamber made,
That thou mightst know me safe and warmly
   laid;
Thy morning bounties ere I left my home, 60
The biscuit, or confectionary plum;
The fragrant waters on my cheeks bestowed
By thy own hand, till fresh they shone and
   glowed;
All this, and more endearing still than all,
Thy constant flow of love, that knew no fall,
Ne'er roughened by those cataracts and
   brakes 66
That humor interposed too often makes;
All this still legible in memory's page,
And still to be so to my latest age,
Adds joy to duty, makes me glad to pay 70
Such honors to thee as my numbers may;
Perhaps a frail memorial, but sincere,
Not scorned in heaven, though little noticed
   here.
  Could Time, his flight reversed, restore the
   hours,
When, playing with thy vesture's tissued
   flowers, 75
The violet, the pink, and jessamine,
I pricked them into paper with a pin
(And thou wast happier than myself the
   while,
Would softly speak, and stroke my head and
   smile),
Could those few pleasant days again appear,
Might one wish bring them, would I wish
   them here? 81
I would not trust my heart—the dear delight
Seems so to be desired, perhaps I might.—
But no—what here we call our life is such,

53. **pastoral house,** the rectory of Great Berkhampstead, Hertfordshire, where Cowper was born.   67. **humor,** fancy, whim.

So little to be loved, and thou so much,   85
That I should ill requite thee to constrain
Thy unbound spirit into bonds again.

   Thou, as a gallant bark from Albion's coast
(The storms all weathered and the ocean
    crossed)
Shoots into port at some well-havened isle,   90
Where spices breathe, and brighter seasons
    smile,
There sits quiescent on the floods that show
Her beauteous form reflected clear below,
While airs impregnated with incense play
Around her, fanning light her streamers gay;
So thou, with sails how swift! hast reached
    the shore,   96
"Where tempests never beat nor billows
    roar."
And thy loved consort on the dangerous tide
Of life long since has anchored by thy side.
But me, scarce hoping to attain that rest,   100
Always from port withheld, always dis-
    tressed—
Me howling blasts drive devious, tempest
    tossed,
Sails ripped, seams opening wide, and com-
    pass lost,
And day by day some current's thwarting
    force
Sets me more distant from a prosperous
    course.   105
Yet, oh, the thought that thou art safe, and
    he!
That thought is joy, arrive what may to me.
My boast is not that I deduce my birth
From loins enthroned and rulers of the earth;
But higher far my proud pretensions rise—   110
The son of parents passed into the skies!
And now, farewell—Time unrevoked has run
His wonted course, yet what I wished is done.
By contemplation's help, not sought in vain,
I seem to have lived my childhood o'er again;
To have renewed the joys that once were
    mine,   116
Without the sin of violating thine:
And, while the wings of Fancy still are free,
And I can view this mimic show of thee,
Time has but half succeeded in his theft—   120
Thyself removed, thy power to soothe me left.
                (*1790;* 1798)

To Mary

   This poignant poem and the sonnet following pay a debt of gratitude to Mrs. Mary Unwin, who with her husband, the Rev. Morley Unwin, gave Cowper a home and cared for him tenderly for many years. After the death of Mr. Unwin in 1767, Cowper and Mrs. Unwin became engaged, but the engagement was broken in 1773 because of Cowper's recurring attacks of insanity. The opening stanzas of *To Mary* refer to the pathetic incidents of 1773. Mrs. Unwin died in 1796.

The twentieth year is well-nigh past,
Since first our sky was overcast;
Ah, would that this might be the last!
    My Mary!

Thy spirits have a fainter flow,   5
I see thee daily weaker grow;
'Twas my distress that brought thee low,
    My Mary!

Thy needles, once a shining store,
For my sake restless heretofore,   10
Now rust disused, and shine no more,
    My Mary!

For though thou gladly wouldst fulfil
The same kind office for me still,
Thy sight now seconds not thy will,   15
    My Mary!

But well thou playedst the housewife's part,
And all thy threads with magic art
Have wound themselves about this heart,
    My Mary!   20

Thy indistinct expressions seem
Like language uttered in a dream;
Yet me they charm, whate'er the theme,
    My Mary!

---

88. **Albion**, poetic for England. 97. "**Where . . . roar**," incorrectly quoted from Garth's *Dispensary*, 3,226: "Where billows never break, nor tempests roar." 99. **long since**. Cowper's father died in 1756. 109. **rulers of the earth**. On his mother's side Cowper was descended from Henry III.

1. **The twentieth year**, etc., a reference to Cowper's violent attack of insanity in 1773, when his engagement to Mrs. Unwin was broken.

Thy silver locks, once auburn bright, 25
Are still more lovely in my sight
Than golden beams of orient light,
    My Mary!

For, could I view nor them nor thee,
What sight worth seeing could I see? 30
The sun would rise in vain for me,
    My Mary!

Partakers of thy sad decline,
Thy hands their little force resign,
Yet, gently pressed, press gently mine, 35
    My Mary!

And then I feel that still I hold
A richer store ten thousandfold
Than misers fancy in their gold,
    My Mary! 40

Such feebleness of limbs thou provest,
That now at every step thou movest
Upheld by two, yet still thou lovest,
    My Mary!

And still to love, though pressed with ill, 45
In wintry age to feel no chill,
With me is to be lovely still,
    My Mary!

But ah! by constant heed I know,
How oft the sadness that I show 50
Transforms thy smiles to looks of woe,
    My Mary!

And should my future lot be cast
With much resemblance of the past,
Thy worn-out heart will break at last, 55
    My Mary!
        (*1793;* 1803)

Sonnet to Mrs. Unwin

Mary! I want a lyre with other strings;
Such aid from Heaven as some have feigned
    they drew!
An eloquence scarce given to mortals, new,
And undebased by praise of meaner things!
That, ere through age or woe I shed my wings,
I may record thy worth, with honor due, 6
In verse as musical as thou art true—
Verse, that immortalizes whom it sings!
But thou hast little need: there is a book,
By seraphs writ with beams of heavenly light,
On which the eyes of God not rarely look; 11
A chronicle of actions just and bright!
There all thy deeds, my faithful Mary, shine,
And since thou own'st that praise, I spare thee
    mine.   (*1793;* 1803)

The Castaway

Admiral George Anson (1697-1762), the most distinguished British seaman of his time, made an expedition to the South Seas and circumnavigated the globe in 1740-1744. These voyages were described in his *A Voyage Round the World* (1748). In one of the incidents of this book Cowper saw the germ of *The Castaway*, the last of his poems, a deeply personal lyric, in that it gives utterance to the religious despair that haunted the poet for over thirty years of his tragic life. It serves as a good companion-piece to his hymns (p. 75).

Obscurest night involved the sky,
    The Atlantic billows roared,
When such a destined wretch as I,
    Washed headlong from on board,
Of friends, of hope, of all bereft, 5
His floating home forever left.

No braver chief could Albion boast
    Than he with whom he went,
Nor ever ship left Albion's coast
    With warmer wishes sent. 10
He loved them both, but both in vain,
Nor him beheld, nor her again.

Not long beneath the whelming brine,
    Expert to swim, he lay;
Nor soon he felt his strength decline, 15
    Or courage die away;
But waged with death a lasting strife,
Supported by despair of life.

He shouted: nor his friends had failed
    To check the vessel's course, 20
But so the furious blast prevailed,
    That, pitiless perforce,
They left their outcast mate behind,
And scudded still before the wind.

Some succor yet they could afford,
  And such as storms allow,
The cask, the coop, the floated cord,
  Delayed not to bestow.
But he (they knew) nor ship nor shore,
Whate'er they gave, should visit more.

Nor, cruel as it seemed, could he
  Their haste himself condemn,
Aware that flight, in such a sea,
  Alone could rescue them;
Yet bitter felt it still to die
Deserted, and his friends so nigh.

He long survives, who lives an hour
  In ocean, self-upheld;
And so long he, with unspent power,
  His destiny repelled;
And ever, as the minutes flew,
Entreated help, or cried "Adieu!"

At length, his transient respite past,
  His comrades, who before
Had heard his voice in every blast,
  Could catch the sound no more;
For then, by toil subdued, he drank
The stifling wave, and then he sank.

No poet wept him; but the page
  Of narrative sincere,
That tells his name, his worth, his age,
  Is wet with Anson's tear;
And tears by bards or heroes shed
Alike immortalize the dead.

I therefore purpose not, or dream,
  Descanting on his fate,
To give the melancholy theme
  A more enduring date;
But misery still delights to trace
Its semblance in another's case.

No voice divine the storm allayed,
  No light propitious shone,
When, snatched from all effectual aid,
  We perished, each alone:
But I beneath a rougher sea,
And whelmed in deeper gulfs than he.

(1799; 1803)

Robert Burns

1759-1796

    The greatest poet that Scotland has produced was born in Ayrshire, the son of a hard-working farmer whose ambitious hopes for the upbringing of his children were blighted by poverty and discouragement. The childhood and boyhood of the poet consisted largely of a series of transient settlings and sudden uprootings on various unsuccessful farms—at Alloway, at Mt. Oliphant, at Lochlea, all little hamlets in the Lowlands of Scotland. On all of them young Burns labored as a hard-worked plowboy. "This kind of life," he himself said, "the cheerless gloom of a hermit and the unceasing toil of a galley-slave, brought me to my sixteenth year." It is probable that much of Burns's later fragile health and his untimely end before he was forty can both be traced to this arduous life of the plow, the spade, and the flail.

    He went to school for a time at Kirkoswald, not far south of Ayr; his uncertain and unformed ambitions now became more definite. He learned something of the great works of literature, became fired with an enthusiasm for the songs and traditions of his native Scotland, and grew more and more sensitive to the beauties of nature as he saw them all about him in both graceful and severe guises. His immediate problem, however, was existence; he eked out a living with difficulty from the soil. In 1781 he became a flax-dresser at Irvine, Ayrshire; here he became familiar with the life of man in a town, with its sins and joys alike. Here he fell in and out of love—there is more than one such episode in Burns's life—and found himself hailed as a pleasant boon-companion.

In 1784 the poet's father died, and Robert Burns, with his brother Gilbert, resumed the life of a poor farmer on land previously leased at Mossgiel. While at Mossgiel he entered on a liaison with Jean Armour, the daughter of a mason in the vicinity. This affair lasted intermittently for years, but the girl's father raised objections to their marriage, and Burns as a despised suitor was at one time about to sail away to America to try his fortunes. But the publication of his first volume of poems at Kilmarnock in 1786, a collection comprising some of his most famous poems, changed his plans completely. For the obscure young peasant became the literary rage; he was introduced to Edinburgh, the Athens of Scotland, where he was dined and wined but regarded as a rustic prodigy. Burns in the city was something of an anomaly; and his writing of verse in the manner of polite urban society has well been likened to a man's trying to dance the minuet with hobnailed shoes.

The second edition of the *Poems* (1787) brought him enough money for two brief tours: one through the northern counties of England and the other into the Highlands. In the next year Burns took another farm in Dumfriesshire, lost money, wrote more poems, and married Jean Armour. In 1789 he became the exciseman of the district and later took a similar position in the town of Dumfries.

Burns's last year of literary activity (1792) was spent largely in collecting and editing traditional songs and ballads of ancient Scotland; he was responsible for the publication not only of the traditional text of these ballads but of their melodies as well. Much of this editing resulted in virtually original compositions and added to his reputation as a great national poet. His growing sympathy with the ideas underlying the French Revolution (p. 3) lost him many friends; his health declined, and with that decline in health came irritability of temperament and defiance of conventions which led him to occasional excesses and ruined his good name for many decades to come.

His end came in July, 1796. The melancholy pulpiteers of the nineteenth century attributed his premature passing to dissipation, but the more considered view would account for his death as the result of heart disease incurred by his overwork in his early years and somewhat aggravated by his occasionally reckless living. But Burns was neither a sot nor a confirmed libertine; he is the poet of good fellowship, no doubt, and a stout-hearted and tender singer of the passion of love; yet the evidence does not show that he was an habitué of the tavern, and his involvement with three women—Mary Campbell, Elizabeth Paton, and Jean Armour—while scarcely Puritanical, seems in each instance to have been based on sincere feeling. Perhaps the worst that can be said of Burns and his poetry is that both are earthy.

No doubt that very earthiness is one source of Burns's great popularity. But he has other and more spiritual achievements to his credit. He is sincere to the core, tender-hearted and impulsive as well, with the customary romantic individual's instinct to love and shelter the helpless. He is the romantic poet of nature and the sentimentalist at one and the same time; and it would be easy to quote the titles of a dozen poems by Burns—*To a Mouse, To a Mountain Daisy, Sweet Afton* are but three of the most famous—that would serve to illustrate these two cardinal traits of the romanticist. There is in Burns the national and the patriotic; he sings the glory of "auld Scotia," not only by the revival of old ballads, but also by the flaming expression of Scotch independence, as in *Scots, Wha Hae*. He is the poet of domestic felicity and the solid virtues of the humble folk in such poems as *The Cotter's Saturday Night;* he proclaims a triumphant democracy, even revolutionism, in *A Man's a Man for A' That;* he can play on the stops of young romantic love in *To Jeanie* or *Bonnie Wee Thing* and of tried and true devotion in *John Anderson;* he has touched the note of enduring friendship once and for all in *Auld Lang Syne*.

There is, however, another side to Burns which many have come to consider his greater talent, the expression of his satirical instinct. Burns was a lover of humanity —in its most erring as well as in its most endearing aspects. He has no patience with pretensions or hypocrisy; he rebels against the unyielding censoriousness of the "unco guid." When that satirical instinct coincides with his humanitarian promptings, the product is revolutionary poetry of a violent sort with raucous tone and sardonic wit, like *Holy Willie's Prayer* and *The Jolly Beggars*. Both poems, and particularly the latter, are harsh indictments of society which society must reject in self-defense.

There are times when Burns lapses into the didactic tone of the eighteenth-century moralist. Usually when he does so, he writes in a manner strongly suggestive of the English neo-classical poets. His satire, too, belongs by tradition to the foregoing age. But the great body of his poems, with their sweetness, warmth of emotion, lyric lilt, and spontaneous fervor, belong to Burns the Scotch romanticist. He is a transitional figure between the neo-classical and the romantic, but he has almost reached the romanticists' encampment. He belongs not to the scented atmosphere of the drawing-room but to the heaths and moorlands of his native Scotland.

Mary Morison

The subject of this poem may have been either Mary Campbell, Elison Begbie, or the Mary Morison, said to have been "as beautiful as amiable," who lived at Mauchline from 1784 till her death in 1791.

O Mary, at thy window be,
  It is the wish'd, the trysted hour!
Those smiles and glances let me see,
  That make the miser's treasure poor:
How blythely wad I bide the stoure,   5
  A weary slave frae sun to sun,
Could I the rich reward secure,
  The lovely Mary Morison.

Yestreen when to the trembling string
  The dance gaed thro' the lighted ha',   10
To thee my fancy took its wing,
  I sat, but neither heard nor saw:
Tho' this was fair, and that was braw,
  And yon the toast of a' the town,
I sigh'd, and said amang them a',   15
  "Ye are na Mary Morison."

O Mary, canst thou wreck his peace,
  Wha for thy sake wad gladly die?
Or canst thou break that heart of his,
  Whase only faut is loving thee?   20
If love for love thou wilt na gie
  At least be pity to me shown;

5. **bide the stoure**, endure the struggle. 9. **Yestreen**, last night. 10. **gaed**, went. 13. **braw**, fine, handsome. 20. **faut**, fault. 21. **na gie**, not give.

A thought ungentle canna be
  The thought o' Mary Morison. (*1781; 1800*)

To Davie

David Sillar (1760-1830), to whom this poem was addressed, was the son of a farmer near Tarbolton, and a teacher in the parish school. He published a volume of poems in 1789 in imitation of Burns; he had skill both as a poet and as a fiddler.

SECOND EPISTLE

A<small>ULD</small> N<small>EEBOR</small>,
I'm three times doubly o'er your debtor,
For your auld-farrant frien'ly letter:
Tho' I maun say 't, I doubt ye flatter,
    Ye speak sae fair,
For my puir, silly, rhymin clatter   5
    Some less maun sair.

Hale be your heart, hale be your fiddle;
Lang may your elbuck jink an' diddle,
To cheer you thro' the weary widdle
    O' war'ly cares,   10
Till bairns' bairns kindly cuddle
    Your auld gray hairs!

But Davie, lad, I'm red ye 're glaikit;
I'm tauld the Muse ye hae negleckit;

2. **auld-farrant**, old-favoring, i.e., wise, shrewd. 3. **maun**, must, doubt, suspect. 6. **Some . . . sair**, somewhat less must serve. 8. **elbuck . . . diddle**, elbow dance and shake (in fiddling). 9. **widdle**, struggle. 13. **I'm . . . glaikit**, I fear that you are giddy, foolish. 14. **hae negleckit**, have neglected.

An' gif it's sae, ye sud be licket　　　15
　　　Until ye fyke;
Sic han's as you sud ne'er be faiket,
　　　Be hain't wha like.

For me, I'm on Parnassus' brink,
Rivin the words to gar them clink;　　20
Whyles daez't wi' love, whyles daez't wi'
　　　drink,
　　　Wi' jads or Masons;
An' whyles, but ay owre late, I think
　　　Braw sober lessons.

Of a' the thoughtless sons o' man,　　25
Commen' me to the Bardie clan;
Except it be some idle plan
　　　O' rhymin clink—
The devil-haet that I sud ban!—
　　　They never think.　　30

Nae thought, nae view, nae scheme o' living,
Nae cares to gie us joy or grievin;
But just the pouchie put the nieve in,
　　　An' while ought's there
Then hiltie-skiltie, we gae scrievin,　　35
　　　An' fash nae mair.

Leeze me on rhyme! it's aye a treasure,
My chief, amaist my only pleasure;
At hame, a-fiel', at wark or leisure,
　　　The Muse, poor hizzie!　　40
Tho' rough an' raploch be her measure,
　　　She's seldom lazy.

Haud to the Muse, my dainty Davie:
The warl' may play you monie a shavie;
But for the Muse, she'll never leave ye,　　45
　　　Tho' e'er sae puir,
Na, even tho' limpin wi the spavie
　　　Frae door to door!

　　　　　　　　(*1784;* 1789)

15. **gif it's sae**, if it's true. **sud be licket**, should be beaten. 16. **fyke**, fuss, fidget. 17. **Sic han's**, such hands. **faiket**, let off. 18. **Be ... like**, be spared whoever may. 19. **Parnassus**, a mountain range in Greece celebrated as the haunt of the Muses of poetry and music. Burns was preparing his poems for publication. 20. **Rivin**, splitting. **gar them clink**, make them jingle or rime. 21. **Whyles daez't**, sometimes dazed. 22. **jads**, jades, wenches. **Masons**, members of an old and extensive secret society dating from the Middle Ages. 23. **ay owre**, ever too. 24. **Braw**, fine, handsome. 29. **devil-haet ... ban**, the devil have my soul that I should curse them. 33. **pouchie**, pocket. **nieve**, fist. 35. **gae scrievin**, go moving fast. 36. **fash nae mair**, worry no more. 37. **Leeze me on**, commend me to, dear is to me. 40. **hizzie**, hussy. 41. **raploch**, homespun; a coarse undyed woolen. 43. **Haud**, hold. 44. **shavie**, trick, bad turn. 47. **limpin ... spavie**, limping with the spavin (a disease of a horse's hock).

Epistle to J. Lapraik, an Old Scottish Bard

John Lapraik (1727-1807) was an Ayrshire poet. Burns addressed two Epistles to him, both written in 1785.

While briers an' woodbines budding green,
And paitricks scraichin loud at e'en,
An' morning poussie whiddin seen,
　　　Inspire my Muse,
This freedom, in an unknown frien'　　5
　　　I pray excuse.

On Fasten-e'en we had a rockin,
To ca' the crack and weave our stockin;
And there was muckle fun and jokin,
　　　Ye need na doubt;　　10
At length we had a hearty yokin,
　　　At "sang about."

There was ae sang, amang the rest,
Aboon them a' it pleased me best,
That some kind husband had address　　15
　　　To some sweet wife:
It thirl'd the heart-strings thro' the breast,
　　　A' to the life.

I've scarce heard ought describ'd sae weel,
What gen'rous, manly bosoms feel;　　20
Thought I, "Can this be Pope or Steele,
　　　Or Beattie's wark?"
They tauld me 't was an odd kind chiel
　　　About Muirkirk.

It pat me fidgin-fain to hear't,　　25
An' sae about him there I spier't;
Then a' that ken't him round declar'd
　　　He had ingine;
That nane excell'd it, few cam near't,
　　　It was sae fine:　　30

2. **paitricks scraichin**, partridges calling hoarsely. 3. **poussie whiddin**, hare scudding. 7. **Fasten-e'en**, the evening before Lent. **rockin**, social meeting. 8. **ca' the crack**, have a chat. 9. **muckle**, much. 11. **yokin**, turn, set-to. 12. **"sang about,"** a game in which each participant sings a song. 13. **ae sang**, one song, Lapraik's *When I upon Thy Bosom Lean*. 14. **Aboon**, above. 17. **thirl'd**, thrilled. 22. **Beattie**, James Beattie (1735-1803), a Scottish poet, author of *The Minstrel*. 23. **chiel**, fellow. 24. **Muirkirk**, a manufacturing town in East Ayrshire, Scotland. 25. **pat ... fain**, made me tingle with pleasure. 26. **spier't**, asked. 27. **ken't**, knew. 28. **ingine**, genius.

That, set him to a pint of ale,
An' either douce or merry tale,
Or rimes an' sangs he'd made himsel,
    Or witty catches,
'Tween Inverness an' Teviotdale,   35
    He had few matches.

Then up I gat, an' swoor an aith,
Tho' I should pawn my pleugh an' graith,
Or die a cadger pownie's death,
    At some dyke-back,   40
A pint an' gill I'd gie them baith,
    To hear your crack.

But, first an' foremost, I should tell,
Amaist as soon as I could spell,
I to the crambo-jingle fell;   45
    Tho' rude an' rough—
Yet crooning to a body's sel,
    Does weel eneugh.

I am nae poet, in a sense,
But just a rimer like by chance,   50
An' hae to learning nae pretence;
    Yet, what the matter?
Whene'er my Muse does on me glance,
    I jingle at her.

Your critic-folk may cock their nose,   55
And say, "How can you e'er propose,
You, wha ken hardly verse frae prose,
    To mak a sang?"
But, by your leaves, my learned foes,
    Ye're maybe wrang.   60

What's a' your jargon o' your schools,
Your Latin names for horns an' stools?
If honest Nature made you fools,
    What sairs your grammars?
Ye'd better taen up spades and shools,   65
    Or knappin-hammers.

A set o' dull, conceited hashes
Confuse their brains in college-classes;
They gang in stirks, and come out asses,
    Plain truth to speak;   70
An' syne they think to climb Parnassus
    By dint o' Greek!

Gie me ae spark o' Nature's fire!
That's a' the learning I desire;
Then, tho' I drudge thro' dub an' mire   75
    At pleugh or cart,
My Muse, tho' hamely in attire,
    May touch the heart.

O for a spunk o' Allan's glee,
Or Fergusson's, the bauld an' slee,   80
Or bright Lapraik's, my friend to be,
    If I can hit it!
That would be lear eneugh for me,
    If I could get it!

Now, sir, if ye hae friends enow,   85
Tho' real friends, I b'lieve, are few;
Yet, if your catalogue be fow,
    I' se no insist;
But, gif ye want ae friend that's true,
    I'm on your list.   90

I winna blaw about mysel,
As ill I like my fauts to tell;
But friends, an' folks that wish me well,
    They sometimes roose me;
Tho', I maun own, as monie still   95
    As far abuse me.

There's ae wee faut they whyles lay to me—
I like the lasses—Gude forgie me!
For monie a plack they wheedle frae me
    At dance or fair;   100
Maybe some ither thing they gie me,
    They weel can spare.

But Mauchline Race or Mauchline Fair,
I should be proud to meet you there;

---

32. **douce**, serious. 34. **catches**, three-part songs, each sung in turn. 35. **Inverness**, a county in north-central Scotland. **Teviotdale**, Roxburghshire, in southeastern Scotland, so called from the river Teviot, which flows through it. 37. **aith**, oath. 38. **pleugh an' graith**, plow and tools. 39. **cadger pownie's**, peddler's pony's. 40. **dyke-back**, back of a turf fence. 42. **crack**, chat. 45. **crambo-jingle**, riming. Crambo is a game in which one supplies a rime to a word given by another. 57. **ken**, knows. 62. **horns**, ink-horns. 64. **sairs**, serves. 65. **shools**, shovels. 66. **knappin-hammers**, hammers for breaking stone. 67. **hashes**, fools.

69. **gang in stirks**, go in young bullocks. 71. **syne**, afterwards. **climb . . . Greek**, become poets by rule or work. **Parnassus**, a mountain range in Greece, celebrated as the haunt of the Muses of poetry and music. 75. **dub**, puddle. 79. **spunk**, spark. **Allan**, Allan Ramsay (1686-1758), a Scottish poet. 80. **Fergusson**, Robert Fergusson (1750-1774), a Scottish poet. **bauld an' slee**, bold and clever. 83. **lear**, learning. 87. **fow**, full. 88. **I'se no**, I shall not. 91. **winna blaw**, will not brag. 92. **fauts**, faults. 94. **roose**, praise, flatter. 95. **maun**, must. 97. **whyles**, sometimes. 99. **plack**, Scotch coin worth about one cent. **frae**, from. 103. **Mauchline**, a town near Burns's Mossgiel farm.

We'se gie ae night's discharge to care, 105
    If we forgather;
And hae a swap o' rhymin-ware
    Wi' ane anither.

The four-gill chap, we'se gar him clatter,
An' kirsen him wi' reekin' water; 110
Syne we'll sit down an' tak our whitter,
    To cheer our heart;
An' faith, we'se be acquainted better
    Before we part.

Awa, ye selfish, warly race, 115
What think that havins, sense, an' grace,
Ev'n love an' friendship should give place
    To Catch-the-Plack!
I dinna like to see your face,
    Nor hear your crack. 120

But ye whom social pleasure charms,
Whose hearts the tide of kindness warms,
Who hold your being on the terms,
    "Each aid the others,"
Come to my bowl, come to my arms, 125
    My friends, my brothers!

But, to conclude my lang epistle,
As my auld pen's worn to the grissle,
Twa lines frae you wad gar me fissle,
    Who am most fervent, 130
While I can either sing or whistle,
    Your friend and servant.

(*1785; 1786*)

Holy Willie's Prayer

"Holy Willie," the subject of this poem, was William Fisher, an elder in the parish church at Mauchline, in Ayrshire. He was later accused of embezzling church funds and ended in the gutter. The best introduction to the poem is to be found in Burns's own "Argument":

"Holy Willie was a rather oldish bachelor elder, in the parish of Mauchline, and much and justly famed for that polemical chattering which ends in tippling orthodoxy, and for that spiritualized bawdry which refines to liquorish devotion. In a sessional process* with a gentleman in Mauchline—a Mr. Gavin Hamilton—Holy Willie and his priest, Father Auld, after full hearing in the Presbytery of Ayr, came off but second best, owing partly to the oratorical powers of Mr. Robert Aiken, Mr. Hamilton's counsel; but chiefly to Mr. Hamilton's being one of the most irreproachable and truly respected characters in the country. On losing his process, the muse overheard him at his devotions as follows—" The poem then proceeds thus:

O Thou, wha in the Heavens dost dwell,
Wha, as it pleases best Thysel',
Sends ane to heaven an' ten to hell
    A' for Thy glory,
And no for onie guid or ill 5
    They've done bafore Thee!

I bless and praise Thy matchless might,
Whan thousands Thou hast left in night,
That I am here before Thy sight,
    For gifts an' grace, 10
A burning an' a shining light,
    To a' this place.

What was I, or my generation,
That I should get sic exaltation?
I' wha deserv'd sic just damnation 15
    For broken laws,
Five thousand years 'fore my creation,
    Thro' Adam's cause!

When frae my mither's womb I fell,
Thou might hae plung'd me deep in hell, 20
To gnash my gums, to weep and wail,
    In burnin' lake,
Where damnéd devils roar and yell,
    Chain'd to a stake.

Yet I am here, a chosen sample, 25
To show Thy grace is great and ample;
I'm here a pillar in Thy temple,
    Strong as a rock,
A guide, a buckler, an example
    To a' Thy flock. 30

---

105. **We'se**, we shall. 109. **we'se gar him**, we shall make him. 110. **kirsen**, christen. **reekin**, dirty. 111. **whitter**, hearty draught. 115. **warly**, worldly. 116. **havins**, manners. 118. **Catch-the-Plack**, hunt the coin, a game. 119. **dinna**, do not. 129. **gar me fissle**, make me tingle.

*_sessional process_, a trial conducted before an ecclesiastical court that reproved evildoers.

O Lord, Thou kens what zeal I bear,
When drinkers drink, and swearers swear,
And singin there and dancin here,
    Wi' great an' sma':
For I am keepit by Thy fear,   35
    Free frae them a'.

But yet, O Lord! confess I must:
At times I'm fash'd wi' fleshly lust;
An' sometimes, too, wi' warldly trust,
    Vile self gets in;   40
But Thou remembers we are dust,
    Defil'd in sin.

O Lord! yestreen, Thou kens, wi' Meg—
Thy pardon I sincerely beg,
O! may it ne'er be a livin plague   45
    To my dishonor!
An' I'll ne'er lift a lawless leg
    Again upon her.

Besides, I farther maun allow,
Wi' Lizzie's lass, three times, I trow;   50
But, Lord, that Friday I was fou,
    When I came near her,
Or else, Thou kens, Thy servant true
    Wad ne'er hae steered her.

May be Thou lets this fleshly thorn   55
Beset Thy servant e'en and morn,
Lest he owre high and proud should turn,
    'Cause he's sae gifted;
If sae, Thy hand maun e'en be borne,
    Until Thou lift it.   60

Lord, bless Thy chosen in this place,
For here Thou hast a chosen race;
But God confound their stubborn face,
    And blast their name,
Wha bring Thy elders to disgrace,   65
    An' public shame!

Lord, mind Gau'n Hamilton's deserts:
He drinks, an' swears, an' plays at cartes,
Yet has sae monie takin arts
    Wi' grit and sma',   70
Frae God's ain Priest the people's hearts
    He steals awa'.

An' whan we chasten'd him therefore,
Thou kens how he bred sic a splore,
As set the warld in a roar   75
    O' laughin at us;
Curse Thou his basket and his store,
    Kail and potatoes!

Lord, hear my earnest cry an' pray'r
Against that Presbyt'ry o' Ayr!   80
Thy strong right hand, Lord, make it bare
    Upo' their heads;
Lord, weigh it down, an' dinna spare,
    For their misdeeds!

O Lord my God! that glib-tongu'd Aiken,   85
My very heart and flesh are quakin,
To think how we stood sweatin, shakin,
    An' pish'd wi' dread,
While he, wi' hingin lip an' snakin,
    Held up his head.   90

Lord, in the day of vengeance try him;
Lord, visit him wha did employ him,
And pass not in Thy mercy by 'em,
    Nor hear their pray'r:
But, for Thy people's sake, destroy 'em,   95
    An' dinna spare.

But, Lord, remember me and mine
Wi' mercies temp'ral and divine,
That I for gear and grace may shine,
    Excelled by nane;   100
And a' the glory shall be Thine,
    Amen, Amen.   (*1785;* 1808)

38. **fash'd**, beset. 39. **warldly**, worldly. 49. **maun**, must. 51. **fou**, full, drunk. 54. **steered**, meddled with. 67. **Gau'n Hamilton**, Gavin Hamilton. See headnote. 68. **cartes**, cards. Card-playing was against the rule of the church. 74. **sic a splore**, such a fuss. 89. **snakin**, sneering. 99. **gear**, wealth. 100. **nane**, none.

The Jolly Beggars

    This, the most satirical, the most dramatic, and perhaps the most thoroughly revolutionary of Burns's poems, was not regarded highly by the family of the poet. It was not published until after his death; he himself in later years remarked to a friend who had heard of the existence of the poem: "I have forgot the cantata you allude to, as I kept no copy, and, indeed, did not know of its existence; however, I remember that none of the songs pleased myself except the last, something about

>Courts for cowards were erected,
>Churches built to please the priest."

The scene of *The Jolly Beggars* is Mauchline, Ayrshire; it is said that the poet actually visited the resort of Poosie Nansie. Such actual identification of place is doubtless interesting, but the piece has so much vigor and humanity that it transcends geographical limits. It portrays mankind in its most vagrant, vulgar, and earthy state, "wringing from Fate," as Carlyle has said, "another hour of wassail and good cheer." Perhaps the final criticism of *The Jolly Beggars* has been written by Matthew Arnold in his *Study of Poetry* (p. 552): "When the largeness and freedom of Burns get full sweep, as in . . . that puissant and splendid production, *The Jolly Beggars*, his world may be what it will, his poetic genius triumphs over it. In the world of *The Jolly Beggars* there is more than hideousness and squalor, there is bestiality; yet the piece is a superb poetic success. It has a breadth, truth, and power which make the famous scene in Auerbach's Cellar, of Goethe's *Faust*, seem artificial and tame beside it, and which are only matched by Shakespeare and Aristophanes."

A CANTATA

Recitativo

When lyart leaves bestrow the yird,
Or, wavering like the bauckie-bird,
  Bedim cauld Boreas' blast;
When hailstanes drive wi' bitter skyte,
And infant frosts begin to bite,   5
  In hoary cranreuch drest;
Ae night at e'en a merry core
O' randie, gangrel bodies
In Poosie-Nansie's held the splore,
  To drink their orra duddies: 10
    Wi' quaffing and laughing,
      They ranted an' they sang;
    Wi' jumping an' thumping,
      The vera girdle rang.

First, niest the fire, in auld red rags,   15
Ane sat, weel brac'd wi' mealy bags,
  And knapsack a' in order;
His doxy lay within his arm;
Wi' usquebae an' blankets warm,
  She blinket on her sodger.   20
An' ay he gies the tozie drab
  The tither skelpin' kiss,
While she held up her greedy gab,
  Just like an aumous dish:
Ilk smack still, did crack still,   25
  Just like a cadger's whup;
Then, staggering and swaggering,
  He roar'd this ditty up—

Air

tune: *Soldier's Joy*

I am a son of Mars, who have been in many wars,
  And show my cuts and scars wherever I come: 30
This here was for a wench, and that other in a trench
  When welcoming the French at the sound of the drum.

My 'prenticeship I past, where my leader breath'd his last,
  When the bloody die was cast on the heights of Abram;
And I serv'd out my trade when the gallant game was play'd,   35
  And the Moro low was laid at the sound of the drum.

I lastly was with Curtis among the floating batt'ries,

---

1. **lyart**, faded, gray. **yird**, earth. 2. **bauckie-bird**, bat. 3. **Boreas**, the north wind. 4. **skyte**, dash. 6. **cranreuch**, hoarfrost. 7. **core**, company. 8. **randie**, lawless. **gangrel**, vagrant. 9. **splore**, carousal. 10. **orra duddies**, spare rags or clothes. 12. **ranted**, whooped. 14. **girdle**, a round metal plate used as a frying pan. 15. **niest**, next. 16. **mealy bags**, bags that usually contained oatmeal, which could be used for food by the beggar or traded or sold as need might arise. 18. **doxy**, wench. 19. **usquebae**, whisky. 20. **blinket**, smirked. **sodger**, soldier. 21. **gies . . . drab**, gives the tipsy wench. 22. **tither skelpin'**, another smacking.

24. **aumous**, alms. 25. **Ilk**, each. 26. **cadger's whup**, hawker's whip.

Tune: *Soldier's Joy*. All the tunes mentioned in the poem were popular airs of the day. 34. **heights of Abram**, at Quebec, in 1759, where Wolfe defeated Montcalm and made certain the British possession of Canada. 36. **Moro . . . laid**, at Santiago, Cuba, where the British attacked the fortress of El Moro in 1762. 37. **with Curtis**, at Gibraltar in 1782.

And there I left for witness an arm and a limb:
Yet let my country need me, with Eliott to head me,
I'd clatter on my stumps at the sound of the drum. 40

And now, tho' I must beg, with a wooden arm and leg,
And many a tatter'd rag hanging over my bum,
I'm as happy with my wallet, my bottle, and my callet,
As when I us'd in scarlet to follow a drum.

What tho' with hoary locks I must stand the winter shocks, 45
Beneath the woods and rocks oftentimes for a home?
When the tother bag I sell, and the tother bottle tell,
I could meet a troop of hell at the sound of a drum.

RECITATIVO

He ended; and the kebars sheuk
  Aboon the chorus roar; 50
While frighted rattons backward leuk,
  And seek the benmost bore:
A fairy fiddler frae the neuk,
  He skirled out *Encore!*
But up arose the martial chuck, 55
  And laid the loud uproar.

AIR

TUNE: *Soldier Laddie*

I once was a maid, tho' I cannot tell when,
And still my delight is in proper young men.
Some one of a troop of dragoons was my daddie:
No wonder I'm fond of a sodger laddie! 60

The first of my loves was a swaggering blade:
To rattle the thundering drum was his trade;
His leg was so tight, and his cheek was so ruddy,
Transported I was with my sodger laddie.

But the godly old chaplain left him in the lurch; 65
The sword I forsook for the sake of the church;
He ventur'd the soul, and I risked the body:
'Twas then I prov'd false to my sodger laddie.

Full soon I grew sick of my sanctified sot;
The regiment at large for a husband I got; 70
From the gilded spontoon to the fife I was ready:
I asked no more but a sodger laddie.

But the peace it reduc'd me to beg in despair,
Till I met my old boy at Cunningham fair;
His rags regimental they flutter'd so gaudy: 75
My heart it rejoic'd at a sodger laddie.

And now I have liv'd—I know not how long!
But still I can join in a cup or a song;
But whilst with both hands I can hold the glass steady,
Here's to thee, my hero, my sodger laddie! 80

RECITATIVO

Poor Merry Andrew in the neuk
  Sat guzzling wi' a tinkler hizzie;
They mind't na wha the chorus teuk,
  Between themselves they were sae busy;
At length, wi' drink and courting dizzy, 85
He stoitered up an' made a face;
  Then turn'd an' laid a smack on Grizzy,
Syne tun'd his pipes wi' grave grimace.

AIR

TUNE: *Auld Syr Symon*

Sir Wisdom's a fool when he's fou;
  Sir Knave is a fool in a session: 90
He's there but a 'prentice I trow,
  But I am a fool by profession.

---

39. **Eliott**, Sir George Eliott, defender of Gibraltar against the French and the Spanish, 1779-1783. 43. **callet**, wench. 47. **tell**, count. 49. **kebars sheuk**, rafters shook. 50. **Aboon**, above. 51. **rattons**, rats. 52. **benmost bore**, inmost hole. 53. **neuk**, nook, corner. 54. **skirled**, yelled. 55. **chuck**, hen.

63. **tight**, trim, comely. 71. **spontoon**, a weapon carried by officers. 82. **tinkler hizzie**, tinker wench. 86. **stoitered**, staggered. 88. **Syne**, then. 89. **fou**, full, drunk. 90. **session**, court or church session.

My grannie she bought me a beuk,
    And I held awa to the school;
I fear I my talent misteuk,   95
    But what will ye hae of a fool?

For drink I wad venture my neck;
    A hizzie's the half o' my craft:
But what could ye other expect
    Of ane that's avowedly daft?   100

I ance was ty'd up like a stirk
    For civilly swearing and quaffing;
I ance was abus'd i' the kirk
    For towzling a lass i' my daffin.

Poor Andrew that tumbles for sport   105
    Let naebody name wi' a jeer:
There's ev'n, I'm tauld, i' the Court
    A tumbler ca'd the Premier.

Observ'd ye yon reverend lad
    Maks faces to tickle the mob?   110
He rails at our mountebank squad—
    It's rivalship just i' the job!

And now my conclusion I'll tell,
    For faith! I'm confoundedly dry:
The chiel that's a fool for himsel',   115
    Guid Lord! he's far dafter than I.

Recitativo

Then niest outspak a raucle carlin,
What kent fu' weel to cleek the sterlin,
For monie a pursie she had hooked,
And had in monie a well been douked.   120
Her love had been a Highland laddie,
But weary fa' the waefu' woodie!
Wi' sighs an' sabs she thus began
To wail her braw John Highlandman:

Air

TUNE: *O, An' Ye Were Dead, Guidman*

A Highland lad my love was born,   125
The Lawlan' laws he held in scorn:
But he still was faithfu' to his clan,
My gallant braw John Highlandman.

Chorus

Sing hey, my braw John Highlandman!
Sing ho, my braw John Highlandman!   130
There's not a lad in a' the lan'
Was match for my John Highlandman!

With his philabeg, an' tartan plaid,
An' gude claymore down by his side,
The ladies' hearts he did trepan,   135
My gallant braw John Highlandman.

We rangéd a' from Tweed to Spey,
And liv'd like lords and ladies gay;
For a Lawlan' face he feared nane,
My gallant braw John Highlandman.   140

They banish'd him beyond the sea,
But ere the bud was on the tree,
Adown my cheeks the pearls ran,
Embracing my John Highlandman.

But, Oh! they catch'd him at the last,   145
And bound him in a dungeon fast.
My curse upon them every ane,
They've hang'd my braw John Highlandman!

And now a widow I must mourn
The pleasures that will ne'er return;   150
No comfort but a hearty can,
When I think on John Highlandman.

Chorus

Sing hey, my braw John Highlandman!
Sing ho, my braw John Highlandman!
There's not a lad in a' the lan'   155
Was match for my John Highlandman!

Recitativo

A pigmy scraper wi' his fiddle,
Wha us'd at trystes and fairs to driddle,
Her strappin limb an' gausy middle
    (He reach'd nae higher),   160
Had hol't his heartie like a riddle,
    An' blawn 't on fire.

---

101. **stirk**, young bull, i.e., he was made to wear a kind of iron collar. 104. **daffin**, fun. 115. **chiel**, young chap. 117. **raucle carlin**, a sturdy old woman. 118. **cleek the sterlin**, snatch the cash. 122. **woodie**, gallows, on which her lover had been hanged. 124. **braw**, handsome. 126. **Lawlan'**, Lowland. 133. **philabeg**, a short plaited skirt, or kilt. **tartan plaid**, shawl or scarf. 134. **claymore**, broadsword. 135. **trepan**, ensnare. 137. **Tweed, Spey**, rivers at opposite ends of Scotland; the *Tweed* is in the south, the *Spey* in the north. 158. **trystes**, cattle-markets. **fairs**, markets for hiring servants and farm laborers. **driddle**, toddle. 159. **gausy**, buxom. 161. **hol't** pierced. **riddle**, sieve.

Wi' hand on haunch and upward ee,
He crooned his gamut, one, two, three,
Then, in an *arioso* key
    The wee Apollo
Set off wi' *allegretto* glee
    His *giga* solo.

Air
tune: *Whistle Owre the Lave O't*

Let me ryke up to dight that tear;
An' go wi' me an' be my dear,
An' then your every care an' fear
    May whistle owre the lave o't.

Chorus
I am a fiddler to my trade,
And a' the tunes that e'er I played,
The sweetest still to wife or maid
    Was *Whistle Owre the Lave O't*.

At kirns an' weddings we'se be there,
And O, sae nicely 's we will fare!
We'll bowse about till Daddie Care
    Sing *Whistle Owre the Lave O't*.

Sae merrily the banes we'll pyke,
And sun oursels about the dyke;
And at our leisure, when ye like,
    We'll whistle owre the lave o't!

But bless me wi' your heav'n o' charms,
An' while I kittle hair on thairms,
Hunger, cauld, and a' sic harms
    May whistle owre the lave o't.

Chorus
I am a fiddler to my trade,
And a' the tunes that e'er I played,
The sweetest still to wife or maid
    Was *Whistle Owre the Lave O't*.

Recitativo
Her charms had struck a sturdy Caird
As weel as poor Gut-scraper;
He taks the fiddler by the beard,
    An' draws a roosty rapier—
He swoor, by a' was swearing worth,
    To spit him like a pliver,
Unless he would from that time forth
    Relinquish her for ever.

Wi' ghastly ee poor Tweedle-Dee
    Upon his hunkers bended,
And pray'd for grace wi' ruefu' face,
    And sae the quarrel ended.
But tho' his little heart did grieve
    When round the tinkler prest her,
He feigned to snirtle in his sleeve
    When thus the Caird address'd her:

Air
tune: *Clout the Cauldron*

My bonie lass, I work in brass,
    A tinkler is my station;
I've travell'd round all Christian ground
    In this my occupation;
I've ta'en the gold, I've been enrolled
    In many a noble squadron;
But vain they search'd when off I march'd
    To go and clout the cauldron.

Despise that shrimp, that wither'd imp,
    With a' his noise an' cap'rin',
And take a share wi' those that bear
    The budget and the apron!
And by that stoup, my faith and houp!
    And by that dear Kilbagie!
If e'er ye want, or meet wi' scant,
    May I ne'er weet my craigie!

Recitativo
The Caird prevailed: th' unblushing fair
    In his embraces sunk,
Partly wi' love o'ercome sae sair,
    And partly she was drunk.
Sir Violino, with an air
    That show'd a man o' spunk,
Wish'd unison between the pair,
    An' made the bottle clunk
        To their health that night.

---

164. **crooned**, hummed. 165. **arioso**, smooth, melodious. 166. **Apollo**, god of music and poetry; here, songster. 167. **allegretto**, quick, light. 168. **giga**, a lively dance. **Tune**: *Lave*, remainder, rest. 169. **ryke . . . dight**, reach up to wipe. 177. **kirns**, harvest homes. 179. **bowse**, booze. 181. **banes**, bones. **pyke**, pick. 182. **dyke**, stone or turf fence. 186. **kittle . . . thairms**, tickle hair on guts, i.e., play on the fiddle. 193. **Caird**, tinker.

198. **pliver**, plover. 202. **hunkers**, hams. 207. **snirtle**, snicker. **Tune**: *Clout*, mend. 220. **budget**, a tinker's bag of tools. 221. **stoup**, jug. 222. **Kilbagie**, a brand of whisky, named from a noted distillery. 224. **weet my craigie**, wet my throat. 227. **sae sair**, so sorely. 232. **clunk**, gurgle.

But hurchin Cupid shot a shaft,
    That play'd a dame a shavie:
The fiddler rak'd her fore and aft
    Behint the chicken cavie.
Her lord, a wight o' Homer's craft,
    Tho' limpin' wi' the spavie,
He hirpled up, and lap like daft,
    And shored them "Dainty Davie,"
        O'boot that night.

He was a care-defying blade
    As ever Bacchus listed!
Tho' Fortune sair upon him laid,
    His heart, she ever miss'd it.
He had no wish but—to be glad,
    Nor want but—when he thirsted,
He hated nought but—to be sad;
    And thus the Muse suggested
        His sang that night.

AIR

TUNE: *For A' That, An' A' That*

I am a Bard, of no regard
    Wi' gentlefolks, an' a' that,
But Homer-like, the glowrin byke,
    Frae town to town I draw that.

Chorus

For a' that, an' a' that,
    And twice as meickle's a' that;
I've lost but ane, I've twa behin',
    I've wife eneugh for a' that.

I never drank the Muses' stank,
    Castalia's burn, an' a' that;
But there it streams, an' richly reams,
    My Helicon I ca' that.

Great love I bear to a' the fair,
    Their humble slave, an' a' that;
But lordly will, I hold it still
    A mortal sin to thraw that.

In raptures sweet this hour we meet
    Wi' mutual love, an' a' that;
But for how lang the flie may stang,
    Let inclination law that!

Their tricks an' craft hae put me daft,
    They've taen me in, an' a' that;
But clear your decks, an' here's the Sex!
    I like the jads for a' that.

Chorus

For a' that, an' a' that,
    An' twice as meickle's a' that,
My dearest bluid, to do them guid,
    They're welcome till 't, for a' that!

RECITATIVO

So sung the Bard—and Nansie's wa's
    Shook with a thunder of applause,
        Re-echo'd from each mouth!
They toom'd their pocks, and pawn'd their duds,
    They scarcely left to co'er their fuds,
        To quench their lowan drouth.
Then owre again the jovial thrang
    The poet did request
To lowse his pack, an' wale a sang,
    A ballad o' the best:
        He rising, rejoicing
            Between his twa Deborahs,
        Looks round him, an' found them
            Impatient for the chorus.

AIR

TUNE: *Jolly Mortals, Fill Your Glasses*

See the smoking bowl before us!
    Mark our jovial, ragged ring!
Round and round take up the chorus,
    And in raptures let us sing:

Chorus

A fig for those by law protected!
    Liberty's a glorious feast!
Courts for cowards were erected,
    Churches built to please the priest!

---

234. **hurchin**, urchin. 235. **shavie**, trick. 237. **cavie**, coop. 238. **Homer's craft**, the poet's profession. Burns spoke of Homer as "the oldest ballad singer on record." 239. **spavie**, spavin (a disease). 240. **hirpled**, hobbled. **lap like daft**, leaped like mad. 241. **shored**, offered. "**Dainty Davie**," name of a popular love song. 242. **O'boot**, to boot, gratis. 244. **Bacchus**, god of wine. **listed**, enrolled as a follower. 254. **glowrin byke**, staring crowd. 257. **meickle**, much. 260. **stank**, pool, ditch. 261. **Castalia**, a fountain on Mt. Parnassus, Greece, supposed to give inspiration to those who drank of it. **burn**, brook. 262. **reams**, foams; ale is his source of inspiration. 263. **Helicon**, a mountain range in Greece; it had two springs, sacred to the Muses. 267. **thraw**, thwart.

270. **stang**, sting, bite. 271. **law**, rule. 272. **hae put me daft**, have made me foolish. 279. **till't**, to it. 283. **toom'd their pocks**, emptied their wallets. 284. **co'er their fuds**, cover their shirt-tails. 285. **lowan drouth**, raging thirst. 288. **lowse**, open. **wale**, choose. 291. **Deborah**, Hebrew prophetess who celebrated the victory of the Israelites over the Canaanites in a famous song of triumph. See *Judges*, 4-5.

What is title? what is treasure?
  What is reputation's care?
If we lead a life of pleasure,
  'Tis no matter, how or where!   305

With the ready trick and fable
  Round we wander all the day;
And at night, in barn or stable,
  Hug our doxies on the hay.

Does the train-attended carriage   310
  Thro' the country lighter rove?
Does the sober bed of marriage
  Witness brighter scenes of love?

Life is all a variorum,
  We regard not how it goes;   315
Let them cant about decorum,
  Who have characters to lose.

Here's to budgets, bags, and wallets!
  Here's to all the wandering train!
Here's our ragged brats and callets!   320
  One and all, cry out, Amen!

Chorus

A fig for those by law protected!
  Liberty's a glorious feast,
Courts for cowards were erected,
  Churches built to please the priest!

(*1785; 1799*)

The Cotter's Saturday Night

INSCRIBED TO ROBERT AIKEN, ESQ.

    In this poem Burns draws upon his own experience to pay tribute to the simple home life of Scotch peasantry. It was the practice of the poet when moralizing, as here, to use English more freely than Scotch. The poem is written in Spenserian stanzas, but as Burns had not yet read Spenser, he must have borrowed the stanza-form from Spenserian imitators—Shenstone, Thomson (p. 39), and Beattie—with whom he was familiar. The plan and the title of the poem were suggested by Robert Fergusson's *The Farmer's Ingle*.
    Robert Aiken (1739-1807), to whom the poem is inscribed, was an old friend of the Burns family; see the headnote to *Holy Willie's Prayer*, p. 88. He frequently read Burns's poems in public.

Let not Ambition mock their useful toil,
  Their homely joys, and destiny obscure;
Nor Grandeur hear, with a disdainful smile,
  The short and simple annals of the poor.
                —GRAY's *Elegy*.

My lov'd, my honor'd, much respected friend!
No mercenary bard his homage pays;
With honest pride, I scorn each selfish end:
My dearest meed a friend's esteem and praise.
To you I sing, in simple Scottish lays,   5
The lowly train in life's sequester'd scene;
The native feelings strong, the guileless ways;
What Aiken in a cottage would have been;
Ah! tho' his worth unknown, far happier
    there, I ween!

November chill blaws loud wi' angry sugh,   10
The short'ning winter day is near a close;
The miry beasts retreating frae the pleugh,
The black'ning trains o' craws to their repose;
The toil-worn cotter frae his labor goes—
This night his weekly moil is at an end—   15
Collects his spades, his mattocks, and his
    hoes,
Hoping the morn in ease and rest to spend,
And weary, o'er the moor, his course does
    hameward bend.

At length his lonely cot appears in view,
Beneath the shelter of an aged tree;   20
Th' expectant wee-things, toddlin, stacher
    through
To meet their dad, wi' flichterin' noise and
    glee.
His wee bit ingle, blinkin bonilie,
His clean hearth-stane, his thrifty wifie's
    smile,
The lisping infant, prattling on his knee,   25
Does a' his weary kiaugh and care beguile,
An' makes him quite forget his labor and his
    toil.

---

10 ff. This stanza bears a striking resemblance to the opening lines of Gray's *Elegy*, p. 50. 10. **sugh**, sound. 13. **craws**, crows.

21. **stacher**, totter. 22. **flichterin'**, fluttering. 23. **ingle . . . bonilie**, fireplace shining prettily. 26. **kiaugh**, worry.

Belyve, the elder bairns come drapping in,
At service out, amang the farmers roun';
Some ca the pleugh, some herd, some tentie rin 30
A cannie errand to a neebor town:
Their eldest hope, their Jenny, woman grown,
In youthfu' bloom, love sparkling in her e'e,
Comes hame; perhaps, to shew a braw new gown,
Or deposite her sair-won penny-fee, 35
To help her parents dear, if they in hardship be.

With joy unfeign'd, brothers and sisters meet,
And each for other's weelfare kindly spiers:
The social hours, swift-wing'd, unnotic'd fleet;
Each tells the uncos that he sees or hears. 40
The parents, partial, eye their hopeful years;
Anticipation forward points the view;
The mother, wi' her needle and her sheers,
Gars auld claes look amaist as weel's the new;
The father mixes a' wi' admonition due. 45

Their master's and their mistress's command
The younkers a' are warnéd to obey;
And mind their labors wi' an eydent hand,
And ne'er, tho' out o' sight, to jauk or play:
"And O! be sure to fear the Lord alway, 50
And mind your duty, duly, morn and night!
Lest in temptation's path ye gang astray,
Implore His counsel and assisting might:
They never sought in vain that sought the Lord aright!"

But hark! a rap comes gently to the door; 55
Jenny, wha kens the meaning o' the same,
Tells how a neebor lad came o'er the moor,
To do some errands, and convoy her hame.
The wily mother sees the conscious flame
Sparkle in Jenny's e'e, and flush her cheek; 60
With heart-struck, anxious care, enquires his name,
While Jenny hafflins is afraid to speak;
Weel-pleas'd the mother hears it's na wild, worthless rake.

With kindly welcome, Jenny brings him ben;
A strappin' youth, he takes the mother's eye;
Blithe Jenny sees the visit's no ill taen; 66
The father cracks of horses, pleughs, and kye.
The youngster's artless heart o'erflows wi' joy,
But, blate and laithfu', scarce can weel behave;
The mother, wi' a woman's wiles, can spy 70
What makes the youth sae bashfu' and sae grave,
Weel-pleas'd to think her bairn's respected like the lave.

O happy love! where love like this is found!
O heart-felt raptures! bliss beyond compare!
I've pacéd much this weary, mortal round, 75
And sage experience bids me this declare:—
"If Heaven a draught of heavenly pleasure spare,
One cordial in this melancholy vale,
'Tis when a youthful, loving, modest pair,
In other's arms, breathe out the tender tale 80
Beneath the milk-white thorn that scents the ev'ning gale."

Is there, in human form, that bears a heart,
A wretch! a villain! lost to love and truth!
That can, with studied, sly, ensnaring art,
Betray sweet Jenny's unsuspecting youth? 85
Curse on his perjur'd arts! dissembling, smooth!
Are honor, virtue, conscience, all exil'd?
Is there no pity, no relenting ruth,
Points to the parents fondling o'er their child?
Then paints the ruin'd maid, and their distraction wild? 90

But now the supper crowns their simple board,
The healsome parritch, chief of Scotia's food;
The soupe their only hawkie does afford,
That 'yont the hallan snugly chows her cood;
The dame brings forth, in complimental mood, 95
To grace the lad, her weel-hain'd kebbuck, fell;
And aft he's prest, and aft he ca's it guid;

28. **Belyve**, presently. 30. **ca**, drive. **tentie rin**, heedful run. 31. **cannie**, careful. **town**, farm with its buildings. 34. **braw**, fine. 35. **sair** . . . **fee**, hard-won wages. 38. **spiers**, asks. 40. **uncos**, news. 44. **Gars**, makes. **claes**, clothes. 48. **eydent**, diligent. 49. **jauk**, trifle. 56. **wha kens**, who knows. 62. **hafflins**, partly.

64. **ben**, into the inner room. 67. **cracks**, talks. **kye**, cows. 69. **blate and laithfu'**, shy and bashful. 72. **lave**, rest, others. 92. **healsome parritch**, wholesome porridge, i.e., oatmeal. 93. **soupe**, milk. **hawkie**, white-faced cow. 94. **'yont the hallan**, beyond the partition. 96. **weel-hain'd kebbuck**, well-saved cheese. **fell**, ripe, strong. 97. **aft**, often.

The frugal wifie, garrulous, will tell,
How 'twas a towmond auld, sin' lint was i'
  the bell.

The cheerfu' supper done, wi' serious face, 100
They, round the ingle, form a circle wide;
The sire turns o'er, with patriarchal grace,
The big ha'-Bible, ance his father's pride.
His bonnet rev'rently is laid aside,
His lyart haffets wearing thin and bare; 105
Those strains that once did sweet in Zion
  glide,
He wales a portion with judicious care,
And, "Let us worship God!" he says, with
  solemn air.

They chant their artless notes in simple guise;
They tune their hearts, by far the noblest aim;
Perhaps *Dundee's* wild-warbling measures
  rise, 111
Or plaintive *Martyrs*, worthy of the name,
Or noble *Elgin* beets the heavenward flame,
The sweetest far of Scotia's holy lays.
Compar'd with these, Italian trills are tame;
The tickl'd ear no heart-felt raptures raise; 116
Nae unison hae they with our Creator's
  praise.

The priest-like father reads the sacred page—
How Abram was the friend of God on high;
Or Moses bade eternal warfare wage 120
With Amalek's ungracious progeny;
Or how the royal bard did groaning lie
Beneath the stroke of Heaven's avenging ire;
Or Job's pathetic plaint, and wailing cry;
Or rapt Isaiah's wild, seraphic fire; 125
Or other holy seers that tune the sacred lyre.

Perhaps the Christian volume is the theme:
How guiltless blood for guilty man was shed;
How He, who bore in Heaven the second
  name,
Had not on earth whereon to lay His head;
How His first followers and servants sped; 131

The precepts sage they wrote to many a land:
How he, who lone in Patmos banishéd,
Saw in the sun a mighty angel stand,
And heard great Bab'lon's doom pronounc'd
  by Heaven's command. 135

Then kneeling down to Heaven's Eternal King
The saint, the father, and the husband prays:
Hope "springs exulting on triumphant wing,"
That thus they all shall meet in future days;
There, ever bask in uncreated rays, 140
No more to sigh, or shed the bitter tear,
Together hymning their Creator's praise,
In such society, yet still more dear,
While circling Time moves round in an
  eternal sphere.

Compar'd with this, how poor Religion's
  pride, 145
In all the pomp of method and of art;
When men display to congregations wide
Devotion's ev'ry grace, except the heart!
The Power, incens'd, the pageant will desert,
The pompous strain, the sacerdotal stole; 150
But haply, in some cottage far apart,
May hear, well pleas'd, the language of the
  soul,
And in His Book of Life the inmates poor en-
  roll.

Then homeward all take off their sev'ral way;
The youngling cottagers retire to rest; 155
The parent-pair their secret homage pay,
And proffer up to Heaven the warm request,
That He who stills the raven's clamorous nest,
And decks the lily fair in flow'ry pride,
Would, in the way His wisdom sees the best,
For them and for their little ones provide; 161
But chiefly in their hearts with grace divine
  preside.

From scenes like these old Scotia's grandeur
  springs,
That makes her lov'd at home, rever'd
  abroad: 164

---

99. **towmond**, twelve-month. **sin'** ... **bell**, since flax was in blossom. 103. **ha'-Bible**, one originally used in the noble's hall for services for the household. 105. **lyart haffets**, gray locks or temples. 107. **wales**, chooses. 111 ff. ***Dundee*** ... ***Martyrs*** ... ***Elgin***, names of well-known sacred melodies. 113. **beets**, kindles. 121. **Amalek**, a grandson of Esau. When the Amalekites attacked the Israelites in the desert, they were driven off by Joshua and doomed to extermination. 122. **royal bard**, King David; see *2 Samuel*, 12:16. 127. **Christian volume**, the New Testament.

133. **he**, St. John, on the Isle of Patmos. 138. **"springs ... wing."** From Pope's *Windsor Forest*, 112. 150. **sacerdotal stole**, priestly vestment. 158. **stills ... nest**. Cf. *Psalms*, 147, 9: "He giveth to the beast his food, and to the young ravens which cry." 159. **lily ... pride.** Cf. *Matthew*, 6:28-29: "Consider the lilies of the field, how they grow: they toil not, neither do they spin: And yet I say unto you, That even Solomon in all his glory was not arrayed like one of these."

Princes and lords are but the breath of kings,
"An honest man's the noblest work of God";
And certes, in fair virtue's heavenly road,
The cottage leaves the palace far behind;
What is a lordling's pomp? a cumbrous load, 170
Disguising oft the wretch of human kind,
Studied in arts of hell, in wickedness refin'd!

O Scotia! my dear, my native soil!
For whom my warmest wish to Heaven is
    sent!
Long may thy hardy sons of rustic toil
Be blest with health, and peace, and sweet
    content! 175
And O! may Heaven their simple lives prevent
From Luxury's contagion, weak and vile!
Then, howe'er crowns and coronets be rent,
A virtuous populace may rise the while,
And stand a wall of fire around their much-
    lov'd Isle. 180

O Thou! who pour'd the patriotic tide
That stream'd thro' Wallace's undaunted
    heart,
Who dar'd to nobly stem tyrannic pride,
Or nobly die—the second glorious part,
(The Patriot's God, peculiarly thou art, 185
His friend, inspirer, guardian, and reward!)
O never, never, Scotia's realm desert;
But still the patriot, and the patriot-bard,
In bright succession raise, her ornament and
    guard!   (*1785;* 1786)

To a Mouse

ON TURNING UP HER NEST WITH THE PLOW,
NOVEMBER, 1785

Wee, sleekit, cowrin, tim'rous beastie,
O, what a panic's in thy breastie!
Thou need na start awa sae hasty
    Wi' bickering brattle!
I wad be laith to rin an' chase thee, 5
    Wi' murdering pattle!

I'm truly sorry man's dominion
Has broken Nature's social union,
An' justifies that ill opinion
    Which makes thee startle 10
At me, thy poor, earth-born companion
    An' fellow-mortal!

I doubt na, whyles, but thou may thieve;
What then? poor beastie, thou maun live:
A daimen icker in a thrave 15
    'S a sma' request;
I'll get a blessin wi' the lave,
    An' never miss 't!

Thy wee-bit housie, too, in ruin!
Its silly wa's the win's are strewin! 20
An' naething, now, to big a new ane,
    O' foggage green!
An' bleak December's win's ensuin,
    Baith snell an' keen!

Thou saw the fields laid bare an' waste, 25
An' weary winter comin' fast,
An' cozie here, beneath the blast,
    Thou thought to dwell,
Till, crash! the cruel coulter passed
    Out through thy cell. 30

That wee bit heap o' leaves an' stibble,
Has cost thee monie a weary nibble!
Now thou's turned out, for a' thy trouble,
    But house or hald,
To thole the winter's sleety dribble, 35
    An' cranreuch cauld!

But Mousie, thou art no thy lane,
In proving foresight may be vain:
The best-laid schemes o' mice an' men
    Gang aft agley, 40
An' lea'e us naught but grief an' pain,
    For promised joy!

Still thou art blest, compared wi' me!
The present only toucheth thee:
But och! I backward cast my e'e, 45
    On prospects drear!
An' forward, though I canna see,
    I guess an' fear!   (*1785;* 1786)

166. **"An . . . God."** From Pope's *Essay on Man,* 4, 248.
182. **Wallace,** William Wallace (d. 1305), a Scottish national hero. See *Scots, Wha Hae,* p. 109.
    To a Mouse. 1. **sleekit,** sleek. 4. **Wi . . . brattle,** with sudden scamper.
    5. **wad be laith,** would be loath. 6. **pattle,** paddle, used for cleaning the plow.

13. **whyles,** sometimes. 15. **daimen . . . thrave,** an occasional ear or head of grain in a shock (of twenty-four sheaves). 17. **lave,** rest. 21. **big,** build. 22. **foggage,** coarse grass. 24. **snell,** sharp, bitter. 29. **coulter,** cutter attached to the beam of a plow to cut the sward. 34. **But,** without. **hald,** abode. 35. **thole,** endure. 36. **cranreuch,** hoar-frost. 37. **no thy lane,** not alone. 40. **Gang aft agley,** often go awry.

Address to the Deil

> O Prince, O Chief of many thronèd Powers
> That led the embattled Seraphim to war!
> —MILTON.

O thou! whatever title suit thee—
Auld Hornie, Satan, Nick, or Clootie—
Wha in yon cavern grim an' sootie,
    Clos'd under hatches,
Spairges about the brunstane cootie,   5
    To scaud poor wretches!

Hear me, Auld Hangie, for a wee,
An' let poor damnèd bodies be;
I'm sure sma' pleasure it can gie,
    Ev'n to a deil,   10
To skelp an' scaud poor dogs like me
    An' hear us squeel.

Great is thy pow'r an' great thy fame;
Far kend an' noted is thy name;
An' tho' yon lowin heugh's thy hame,   15
    Thou travels far;
An' faith! thou's neither lag, nor lame,
    Nor blate, nor scaur.

Whyles, ranging like a roarin lion,
For prey, a' holes an' corners trying;   20
Whyles, on the strong-wing'd tempest flyin,
    Tirlin the kirks;
Whyles, in the human bosom pryin,
    Unseen thou lurks.

I've heard my rev'rend graunie say,   25
In lanely glens ye like to stray;
Or, where auld ruin'd castles gray
    Nod to the moon,
Ye fright the nightly wand'rer's way
    Wi' eldritch croon.   30

When twilight did my graunie summon,
To say her pray'rs, douce, honest woman!
Aft yont the dyke she's heard you bummin,
    Wi' eerie drone;
Or, rustlin, thro' the boortrees comin,   35
    Wi' heavy groan.

Ae dreary, windy, winter night,
The stars shot down wi' sklentin light,
Wi' you mysel, I gat a fright:
    Ayont the lough,   40
Ye, like a rash-buss, stood in sight,
    Wi' waving sugh.

The cudgel in my nieve did shake,
Each bristl'd hair stood like a stake;
When wi' an eldritch, stoor "quaick, quaick,"
    Amang the springs,   46
Awa ye squatter'd like a drake,
    On whistling wings.

Let warlocks grim, an' wither'd hags,
Tell how wi' you, on ragweed nags,   50
They skim the muirs an' dizzy crags,
    Wi' wicked speed;
And in kirk-yards renew their leagues,
    Owre howkit dead.

Thence, countra wives, wi' toil an' pain,   55
May plunge an' plunge the kirn in vain;
For O! the yellow treasure's taen
    By witching skill;
An' dawtit, twal-pint hawkie 's gaen
    As yell's the bill.   60

Thence, mystic knots mak great abuse
On young guidmen, fond, keen an' croose;
When the best wark-lume i' the house,
    By cantraip wit,
Is instant made no worth a louse,   65
    Just at the bit.

When thowes dissolve the snawy hoord,
An' float the jinglin icy-boord,
Then, water-kelpies haunt the foord,
    By your direction,   70
An' nighted trav'llers are allur'd
    To their destruction.

O Prince, etc. From *Paradise Lost*, I, 128-129 (Vol. I, p. 719). The poem is, in part, a good-natured burlesque of the Miltonic conception of Satan. The first two lines of Burns's poem are imitated from Pope's *Dunciad*. 2 **Clootie,** little hoof. 5. **Spairges,** splashes. **brunstane cootie,** brimstone ladle. 6. **scaud,** scald. 7. **Auld Hangie,** old hangman. **wee,** moment. 11. **skelp,** slap, smack. 15. **lowin heugh,** flaming cavern. 17. **lag,** slow. 18. **blate, nor scaur,** shy nor timid. 19. **Whyles,** sometimes. 22. **Tirlin the kirks,** unroofing the churches. 26. **lanely,** lonely. 30. **eldritch croon,** unearthly moan. 32. **douce,** grave, sober. 33. **Aft yont,** often beyond. **dyke,** wall. **bummin,** humming. 34. **eerie drone,** ghostly sound. 35. **boortrees,** elder bushes. 38. **sklentin,** slanting. 40. **Ayont the lough,** beyond the lake. 41. **rash-buss,** clump of rushes. 42. **sugh,** moan. 43. **nieve,** fist. 45. **eldritch,** unearthly. **stoor,** harsh. 47. **squatter'd,** fluttered on the water. 49. **warlocks,** wizards. 50. **ragweed nags,** ragweed stems used instead of broomsticks for horses. 51. **muirs,** moors. 53. **leagues,** covenants. 54. **Owre howkit,** over dug-up. 56. **kirn,** churn. 57. **yellow . . . skill,** witchcraft prevents the butter from coming. 59. **dawtit . . . bill,** petted twelve-pint white-face has gone as dry as the bull. Ayrshire cattle have white markings. 62. **young guidmen,** newly-married men. **croose,** bold. 63. **wark-lume,** work-loom, tool. 64. **cantraip,** magic. 66. **at the bit,** at the time most needed. 67. **thowes,** thaws. 68. **icy-boord,** surface of ice. 69. **water-kelpies,** river-demons, usually in the form of horses.

And aft your moss-traversing spunkies
Decoy the wight that late an' drunk is:
The bleezin, curst, mischievous monkies 75
    Delude his eyes,
Till in some miry slough he sunk is,
    Ne'er mair to rise.

When Masons' mystic word an' grip
In storms an' tempests raise you up, 80
Some cock or cat your rage maun stop,
    Or, strange to tell!
The youngest brother ye wad whip
    Aff straught to hell.

Lang syne in Eden's bonie yard, 85
When youthfu' lovers first were pair'd,
An' all the soul of love they shar'd,
    The raptur'd hour,
Sweet on the fragrant flow'ry swaird,
    In shady bow'r: 90

Then you, ye auld, snick-drawing dog!
Ye cam to Paradise incog,
An' play'd on man a cursed brogue
    (Black be your fa'!),
An' gied the infant warld a shog, 95
    'Maist ruin'd a'.

D' ye mind that day when in a bizz
Wi' reekit duds, an' reestit gizz,
Ye did present your smoutie phiz
    'Mang better folk; 100
An' sklented on the man of Uzz
    Your spitefu' joke?

An' how ye gat him i' your thrall,
An' brak him out o' house an' hal',
While scabs an' botches did him gall, 105
    Wi' bitter claw;
An' lowsed his ill-tongu'd wicked scaul—
    Was warst ava?

But a' your doings to rehearse,
Your wily snares an' fechtin fierce, 110
Sin' that day Michael did you pierce

Down to this time,
Wad ding a Lallan tongue, or Erse,
    In prose or rhyme.

An' now, Auld Cloots, I ken ye're thinkin, 115
A certain Bardie's rantin, drinkin,
Some luckless hour will send him linkin,
    To your black Pit;
But, faith! he'll turn a corner jinkin,
    An' cheat you yet. 120

But fare-you-weel, Auld Nickie-Ben!
O, wad ye tak a thought an' men'!
Ye aiblins might—I dinna ken—
    Still hae a stake:
I'm wae to think upo' yon den, 125
    Ev'n for your sake!   (*1785; 1786*)

To a Mountain Daisy

ON TURNING ONE DOWN WITH THE PLOW
IN APRIL, 1786

Wee, modest, crimson-tippéd flow'r,
Thou's met me in an evil hour;
For I maun crush amang the stoure
    Thy slender stem:
To spare thee now is past my pow'r, 5
    Thou bonie gem.

Alas! it's no thy neebor sweet,
The bonie lark, companion meet,
Bending thee 'mang the dewy weet,
    Wi' spreckled breast! 10
When upward-springing, blythe, to greet
    The purpling east.

Cauld blew the bitter-biting north
Upon thy early, humble birth;
Yet cheerfully thou glinted forth 15
    Amid the storm,
Scarce reared above the parent-earth
    Thy tender form.

The flaunting flow'rs our gardens yield,
High shelt'ring woods and wa's maun shield:
But thou, beneath the random bield 21

73. **aft**, often. **spunkies**, will-o'-the-wisps. 75. **bleezin**, blazing. 81. **your rage maun stop**, may stop your rage, by being offered as a sacrifice. 85. **Lang syne**, long since. 91. **snick-drawing**, latch-lifting, intruding. 93. **brogue**, trick. 94. **fa'**, lot. 95. **shog**, shock. 97. **bizz**, flurry. 98. **reekit**, smoky. **reestit gizz**, singed wig. 101 **sklented**, directed, turned. **man of Uzz**, Job. See *Job*, 1:1. 107. **lowsed**, let loose. **scaul**, scold; Job's wife. 108. **warst ava**, worst of all. 110. **fechtin**, fighting. 111. **Michael . . . pierce**, as told in *Paradise Lost*, VI, 325 ff.; see also *Revelation*, 12:7-10.

113. **ding**, outdo. **Lallan**, Lowland. **Erse**, Gaelic—the form spoken in the Scottish Highlands. 117. **linkin**, skipping. 119. **jinkin**, dodging. 123. **aiblins**, perhaps. 124. **hae a stake**, have a chance to gain something. 125. **wae**, sad.
To a Mountain Daisy. 3. **maun**, must. **stoure**, dust. 20. **wa's**, walls. 21. **bield**, shelter.

O' clod or stane,
Adorns the histie stibble-field,
　　　Unseen, alane.

There, in thy scanty mantle clad, 25
Thy snawie bosom sunward spread,
Thou lifts thy unassuming head
　　　In humble guise;
But now the share uptears thy bed,
　　　And low thou lies! 30

Such is the fate of artless maid,
Sweet flow'ret of the rural shade!
By love's simplicity betrayed,
　　　And guileless trust;
Till she, like thee, all soiled, is laid 35
　　　Low i' the dust.

Such is the fate of simple Bard,
On Life's rough ocean luckless starred!
Unskilful he to note the card
　　　Of prudent lore, 40
Till billows rage, and gales blow hard,
　　　And whelm him o'er!

Such fate to suffering Worth is giv'n,
Who long with wants and woes has striv'n,
By human pride or cunning driv'n 45
　　　To mis'ry's brink;
Till, wrenched of ev'ry stay but Heav'n,
　　　He, ruined, sink!

Ev'n thou who mourn'st the Daisy's fate,
That fate is thine—no distant date; 50
Stern Ruin's plowshare drives elate,
　　　Full on thy bloom,
Till crushed beneath the furrow's weight
　　　Shall be thy doom! (1786)

To a Louse

ON SEEING ONE ON A LADY'S BONNET AT CHURCH

Ha! wh'are ye gaun, ye crowlin ferlie?
Your impudence protects you sairly;
I canna say but ye strunt rarely,
　　　Owre gauze and lace,
Tho' faith! I fear ye dine but sparely 5
　　　On sic a place.

Ye ugly, creepin, blastit wonner,
Detested, shunned by saunt an' sinner,
How dare ye set your fit upon her,
　　　Sae fine a lady? 10
Gae somewhere else, and seek your dinner
　　　On some poor body.

Swith, in some beggar's hauffet squattle;
There ye may creep, and sprawl, and sprattle
Wi' ither kindred jumping cattle, 15
　　　In shoals and nations;
Whare horn nor bane ne'er dare unsettle
　　　Your thick plantations.

Now haud you there! ye're out o' sight,
Below the fatt'rils, snug an' tight; 20
Na, faith ye yet! ye'll no be right
　　　Till ye've got on it,
The very tapmost tow'ring height
　　　O' Miss's bonnet.

My sooth! right bauld ye set your nose out, 25
As plump an' gray as onie grozet;
O for some rank mercurial rozet,
　　　Or fell red smeddum!
I'd gie you sic a hearty dose o't,
　　　Wad dress your droddum! 30

I wad na been surprised to spy
You on an auld wife's flainen toy;
Or aiblins some bit duddie boy,
　　　On's wyliecoat;
But Miss's fine Lunardi! fie, 35
　　　How daur ye do't?

O Jenny, dinna toss your head,
An' set your beauties a' abread!
Ye little ken what curséd speed
　　　The blastie's makin! 40
Thae winks and finger-ends, I dread,
　　　Are notice takin!

O wad some Power the giftie gie us
To see oursels as ithers see us!

23. **histie**, dry, bare. 39. **card**, compass-card.
To a Louse. 1. **crowlin ferlie**, crawling wonder. 2. **sairly**, greatly. 3. **strunt**, strut.

7. **blastit wonner**, blasted wonder. 9. **fit**, feet. 13. **Swith**, quick. **hauffet**, temple, side of the head. **squattle**, settle, sprawl. 14. **sprattle**, scramble. 17. **horn nor bane**, horn-comb, bone-comb. 19. **haud**, hold. 20. **fatt'rils**, ribbon-ends. 25. **bauld**, bold. 26. **grozet**, gooseberry. 27. **rozet**, rosin. 28. **smeddum**, powder. 30. **droddum**, breech. 32. **flainen toy**, flannel cap. 33. **aiblins**, perhaps. **bit duddie**, small, ragged. 34. **wyliecoat**, undervest. 35. **Lunardi**, balloon bonnet, named after Lunardi (1759-1806), a noted balloonist. 38. **abread**, abroad. 40. **blastie**, blasted creature. 43. **giftie**, small gift.

It wad frae monie a blunder free us, 45
    An' foolish notion:
What airs in dress an' gait wad lea'e us,
    An' ev'n devotion!
                                    (1786)

Of A' the Airts

Of a' the airts the wind can blaw
    I dearly like the west,
For there the bonie lassie lives,
    The lassie I lo'e best.
There wild woods grow, and rivers row, 5
    And monie a hill between,
But day and night my fancy's flight
    Is ever wi' my Jean.

I see her in the dewy flowers—
    I see her sweet and fair. 10
I hear her in the tunefu' birds—
    I hear her charm the air:
There's not a bonie flower that springs
    By fountain, shaw, or green,
There's not a bonie bird that sings, 15
    But minds me o' my Jean.
                              (1788; 1790)

Auld Lang Syne

Should auld acquaintance be forgot,
    And never brought to min'?
Should auld acquaintance be forgot,
    And auld lang syne?

Chorus
    For auld lang syne, my dear, 5
    For auld lang syne,
    We'll tak a cup o' kindness yet
    For auld lang syne.

And surely ye'll be your pint-stowp,
    And surely I'll be mine! 10
And we'll tak a cup o' kindness yet
    For auld lang syne.

We twa hae run about the braes,
    And pu'd the gowans fine;
But we've wandered monie a weary fit 15
    Sin' auld lang syne.

We twa hae paidled i' the burn,
    From mornin' sun till dine;
But seas between us braid hae roared
    Sin' auld lang syne. 20

And there's a hand, my trusty fiere,
    And gie's a hand o' thine;
And we'll tak a right guid-willie waught
    For auld lang syne.   (*1788*; 1796)

John Anderson, My Jo

John Anderson, my jo, John,
    When we were first acquent,
Your locks were like the raven,
    Your bonie brow was brent;
But now your brow is beld, John, 5
    Your locks are like the snaw,
But blessings on your frosty pow,
    John Anderson, my jo!

John Anderson, my jo, John,
    We clamb the hill thegither, 10
And monie a cantie day, John,
    We've had wi' ane anither;
Now we maun totter down, John,
    And hand in hand we'll go,
And sleep thegither at the foot, 15
    John Anderson, my jo!   (1789; 1790)

Sweet Afton

Flow gently, sweet Afton, among thy green
    braes!
Flow gently, I'll sing thee a song in thy praise!
My Mary's asleep by thy murmuring stream—
Flow gently, sweet Afton, disturb not her
    dream!

Of A' the Airts. 1. **airts**, directions. Burns had recently married Jean Armour and had taken a farm at Ellisland. When he wrote this lyric, his wife was in Ayrshire, a few miles to the west. 3. **bonie**, winsome. 5. **row**, roll. 14. **shaw**, wood.
    Auld Lang Syne, Old Long Since, i.e., Old Times. 9. **ye'll . . . pint-stowp**, you will pay for your pint measure of drink.

13. **braes**, hillsides. 14. **pu'd**, pulled. **gowans**, daisies. 15. **fit**, foot, step. 17. **paidled**, paddled, dabbled. **burn**, brook. 18. **dine**, dinner time. 19. **braid**, broad. 21. **fiere**, friend, comrade. 23. **right . . . waught**, hearty good-will draught.
    John Anderson, My Jo. 1. **jo**, sweetheart. 4. **brent**, smooth. 5. **beld**, bald. 7. **pow**, head. 11. **cantie**, happy.
    Sweet Afton. The Afton is a small stream that flows into the River Nith, in Dumfriesshire, Scotland. 1. **braes**, hills.

Thou stock-dove whose echo resounds through
    the glen,   5
Ye wild whistling blackbirds in yon thorny
    den,
Thou green-crested lapwing, thy screaming
    forbear—
I charge you disturb not my slumbering fair!

How lofty, sweet Afton, thy neighboring
    hills,
Far marked with the courses of clear, winding
    rills!   10
There daily I wander, as noon rises high,
My flocks and my Mary's sweet cot in my eye.

How pleasant thy banks and green valleys
    below,
Where wild in the woodlands the primroses
    blow!
There oft, as mild Evening weeps over the lea,
The sweet-scented birk shades my Mary and
    me.   16

Thy crystal stream, Afton, how lovely it glides,
And winds by the cot where my Mary resides!
How wanton thy waters her snowy feet lave,
As, gathering sweet flowerets, she stems thy
    clear wave!   20

Flow gently, sweet Afton, among thy green
    braes!
Flow gently, sweet river, the theme of my lays!
My Mary's asleep by thy murmuring stream—
Flow gently, sweet Afton, disturb not her
    dream!   (1789)

Willie Brew'd a Peck o' Maut

Burns has this to say of the following poem: "The air is Masterton's; the song mine. The occasion of it was this: Mr. William Nicol of the High School, Edinburgh, during the autumn vacation being at Moffat, honest Allan (who was at that time on a visit to Dalswinton) and I went to pay Nicol a visit. We had such a joyous visit, Mr. Masterton and I agreed, each in our own way, that we should celebrate the business." The Allan Masterton

16. **birk,** birch.

referred to was a teacher in the Edinburgh High School from 1789 to 1799.

O, Willie brew'd a peck o' maut,
And Rob an' Allan cam to see:
Three blyther hearts that lee-lang night
Ye wad na found in Christendie.

Chorus

    We are na fou, we're nae that fou,   5
    But just a drappie in our ee;
    The cock may craw, the day may daw,
    And ay we'll taste the barley bree.

Here are we met, three merry boys,
Three merry boys, I trow, are we;   10
And monie a night we've merry been,
And monie mae we hope to be!

It is the moon, I ken her horn,
That's blinkin in the lift sae hie;
She shines sae bright to wyle us hame,   15
But, by my sooth, she'll wait a wee!

Wha first shall rise to gang awa',
A cuckold, coward loun is he!
Wha first beside his chair shall fa',
He is the king amang us three!   20

Chorus

    We are na fou, we're nae that fou,
    But just a drappie in our ee;
    The cock may craw, the day may daw,
    And ay we'll taste the barley bree.
                                     (*1789;* 1790)

To Mary in Heaven

The subject of the poem was Mary Campbell, one of the three women whose names have been most closely linked with that of Burns. "My 'Highland Lassie'," says the poet, "was as warm-hearted, charming a young creature as ever blessed a man with generous love. After a pretty long tract of the most ardent reciprocal attachment, we met by appointment

1. **Maut,** ale. 3. **lee-lang,** live-long. 5. **fou,** full, drunk. 6. **drappie,** small drop. 8. **bree,** brew. 12. **mae,** more. 14. **lift,** sky. 15. **wyle,** entice. 16. **wee,** while.

on the second Sunday of May, in a sequestered spot by the banks of the Ayr, where we spent the day in taking farewell, before she should embark for the West Highlands to arrange matters for our projected change of life. At the close of the autumn following, she crossed the sea to meet me at Greenock, where she had scarce landed when she was seized with a malignant fever, which hurried my dear girl to the grave in a few days, before I could even hear of her illness." The poem was written on the anniversary of her death.

Thou ling'ring star, with less'ning ray,
  That lov'st to greet the early morn,
Again thou usher'st in the day
  My Mary from my soul was torn.
O Mary! dear departed shade!   5
  Where is thy place of blissful rest?
See'st thou thy lover lowly laid?
  Hear'st thou the groans that rend his breast?

That sacred hour can I forget,
  Can I forget the hallowed grove,   10
Where by the winding Ayr we met

To live one day of parting love?
Eternity will not efface
  Those records dear of transports past,
Thy image at our last embrace—   15
  Ah! little thought we 'twas our last!

Ayr, gurgling, kiss'd his pebbl'd shore,
  O'erhung with wild woods, thick'ning green;
The fragrant birch and hawthorn hoar
  Twin'd amorous round the raptur'd scene:
The flow'rs sprang wanton to be prest,   21
  The birds sang love on every spray,
Till too, too soon the glowing west
  Proclaim'd the speed of winged day.

Still o'er these scenes my mem'ry wakes,   25
  And fondly broods with miser care!
Time but th' impression stronger makes,
  As streams their channels deeper wear.
My Mary, dear departed shade!
  Where is thy place of blissful rest?   30
See'st thou thy lover lowly laid?
  Hear'st thou the groans that rend his breast?
                (*1789;* 1790)

Tam o' Shanter

Burns's father was buried in the churchyard of Alloway Kirk. Burns asked an antiquarian friend of his to make a drawing of the church, partly because it was the burial place of his father and partly because Burns himself expected to be buried there. The request was accompanied by the statement that many witch-legends had grown up about the vicinity of the kirk. The antiquarian friend, Francis Grose, agreed to supply the drawing provided Burns would write a witch-tale to go with it. The narrative poem resulting was *Tam o' Shanter*, a fine example of a tale from Scotch folklore, with its hero drawn from real life in the person of Douglas Graham, a convivial soul of Alloway and adjacent parts. Burns himself always liked the poem for its energy and "roguish waggery."

A TALE

Of Brownyis and of Bogillis full is this Buke.
                —GAWIN DOUGLAS.

When chapman billies leave the street,
And drouthy neebors neebors meet,
As market-days are wearing late,
An' folk begin to take the gate;
While we sit bousing at the nappy,   5

An' gettin fou and unco happy,
We think na on the lang Scots miles,
The mosses, waters, slaps, and stiles,
That lie between us and our hame,
Whare sits our sulky, sullen dame,   10
Gathering her brows like gathering storm,
Nursing her wrath to keep it warm.

  This truth fand honest Tam o' Shanter,
As he frae Ayr ae night did canter:

Tam o' Shanter. **Brownyis ... Bogillis,** brownies and hobgoblins. The line is quoted from Douglas's Prologue to a translation of Virgil's *Aeneid.* 1. **chapman billies,** peddler comrades. 2. **drouthy,** thirsty. 4. **take the gate,** take the way, i.e., go home. 5. **bousing at the nappy,** drinking ale.

6. **fou,** full, drunk. **unco,** very. 7. **lang ... miles.** The old Scotch mile was 216 yards longer than the English mile. 8. **mosses,** bogs. **slaps,** fence-gaps or gates. 13. **fand,** found.

(Auld Ayr, wham ne'er a town surpasses,　15
For honest men and bonie lasses.)

O Tam! had'st thou but been sae wise
As taen thy ain wife Kate's advice!
She tauld thee weel thou was a skellum,
A bletherin, blusterin, drunken blellum;　20
That frae November till October,
Ae market-day thou was na sober;
That ilka melder wi' the miller,
Thou sat as lang as thou had siller;
That ev'ry naig was ca'd a shoe on,　25
The smith and thee gat roaring fou on;
That at the Lord's house, even on Sunday,
Thou drank wi' Kirkton Jean till Monday.
She prophesied, that, late or soon,
Thou would be found deep drowned in Doon;
Or catched wi' warlocks in the mirk,　31
By Alloway's auld haunted kirk.

Ah, gentle dames! it gars me greet,
To think how monie counsels sweet,
How monie lengthened sage advices,　35
The husband frae the wife despises!

But to our tale:—Ae market night,
Tam had got planted unco right,
Fast by an ingle, bleezing finely,
Wi' reaming swats that drank divinely;　40
And at his elbow, Souter Johnie,
His ancient, trusty, drouthy cronie:
Tam loe'd him like a very brither;
They had been fou for weeks thegither.
The night drave on wi' sangs and clatter;　45
And ay the ale was growing better:
The landlady and Tam grew gracious
Wi' secret favors, sweet and precious:
The souter tauld his queerest stories;
The landlord's laugh was ready chorus:　50
The storm without might rair and rustle,
Tam did na mind the storm a whistle.

Care, mad to see a man sae happy,
E'en drowned himsel amang the nappy:
As bees flee hame wi' lades o' treasure,　55
The minutes winged their way wi' pleasure;
Kings may be blest, but Tam was glorious,
O'er a' the ills o' life victorious!

But pleasures are like poppies spread,
You seize the flow'r, its bloom is shed;　60
Or like the snow falls in the river,
A moment white—then melts forever;
Or like the borealis race,
That flit ere you can point their place;
Or like the rainbow's lovely form　65
Evanishing amid the storm.
Nae man can tether time nor tide:
The hour approaches Tam maun ride—
That hour, o' night's black arch the keystane,
That dreary hour Tam mounts his beast in;　70
And sic a night he taks the road in,
As ne'er poor sinner was abroad in.

The wind blew as 'twad blawn its last;
The rattling showers rose on the blast;
The speedy gleams the darkness swallowed;　75
Loud, deep, and lang the thunder bellowed:
That night, a child might understand,
The Deil had business on his hand.

Weel mounted on his gray mare, Meg—
A better never lifted leg—　80
Tam skelpit on thro' dub and mire,
Despising wind and rain and fire;
Whiles holding fast his guid blue bonnet,
Whiles crooning o'er some auld Scots sonnet,
Whiles glow'ring round wi' prudent cares,　85
Lest bogles catch him unawares.
Kirk-Alloway was drawing nigh,
Whare ghaists and houlets nightly cry.

By this time he was cross the ford,
Whare in the snaw the chapman smoored;　90
And past the birks and meikle stane,
Whare drunken Charlie brak's neck-bane;
And thro' the whins, and by the cairn,
Whare hunters fand the murdered bairn;
And near the thorn, aboon the well,　95
Whare Mungo's mither hanged hersel.

---

16. **bonie**, winsome. 19. **skellum**, good-for-nothing. 20. **bletherin**, idly talking. **blellum**, babbler, blow-hard. 23. **ilka melder**, every grinding. 24. **siller**, silver, money. 25. **ca'd**, nailed. 28. **Kirkton**, any village near a church. 30. **Doon**, a small stream near Burns's birthplace. See *Bonie Doon*, p. 107. 31. **warlocks**, wizards or witches. **mirk**, dark. 33. **gars me greet**, makes me weep. 38. **unco**, very, exactly. 39. **ingle**, fireplace. **bleezing**, blazing. 40. **reaming swats**, foaming new ale. 41. **Souter**, cobbler. 42. **drouthy**, thirsty.

68. **maun**, must. 69. **hour . . . keystane**, midnight. 81. **skelpit**, clattered. **dub**, puddle. 83. **whiles**, sometimes. 84. **crooning**, humming. **sonnet**, song. 86. **bogles**, hobgoblins. 88. **houlets**, owls. 90 **smoored**, smothered. 91. **birks**, birches. **meikle stane**, great stone. 93. **whins**, furze. **cairn**, pile of stones. 94. **bairn**, child.

Before him Doon pours all his floods;
The doubling storm roars thro' the woods;
The lightnings flash from pole to pole,
Near and more near the thunders roll;   100
When, glimmering thro' the groaning trees
Kirk-Alloway seemed in a bleeze:
Thro' ilka bore the beams were glancing,
And loud resounded mirth and dancing.

    Inspiring bold John Barleycorn!   105
What dangers thou canst make us scorn!
Wi' tippenny we fear nae evil;
Wi' usquebae we'll face the devil!
The swats sae reamed in Tammie's noddle,
Fair play, he cared na deils a boddle.   110
But Maggie stood right sair astonished,
Till, by the heel and hand admonished,
She ventured forward on the light;
And, wow! Tam saw an unco sight!

    Warlocks and witches in a dance;   115
Nae cotillion brent-new frae France,
But hornpipes, jigs, strathspeys, and reels
Put life and mettle in their heels:
A winnock bunker in the east,
There sat Auld Nick in shape o' beast;   120
A towsie tyke, black, grim, and large,
To gie them music was his charge;
He screwed the pipes and gart them skirl,
Till roof and rafters a' did dirl.
Coffins stood round like open presses,   125
That shawed the dead in their last dresses;
And by some devilish cantraip sleight
Each in its cauld hand held a light,
By which heroic Tam was able
To note upon the haly table   130
A murderer's banes in gibbet airns;
Twa span-lang, wee, unchristened bairns;
A thief, new-cutted frae a rape—
Wi' his last gasp his gab did gape;
Five tomahawks, wi' bluid red-rusted;   135
Five scymitars, wi' murder crusted;
A garter, which a babe had strangled;
A knife, a father's throat had mangled,

Whom his ain son o' life bereft—
The gray hairs yet stack to the heft;   140
Wi' mair o' horrible and awfu',
Which even to name wad be unlawfu'.

    As Tammie glowered, amazed and curious,
The mirth and fun grew fast and furious:
The piper loud and louder blew,   145
The dancers quick and quicker flew;
They reeled, they set, they crossed, they cleekit,
Till ilka carlin swat and reekit,
And coost her duddies to the wark
And linket at it in her sark!   150

    Now Tam, O Tam! had thae been queans,
A' plump and strapping in their teens!
Their sarks, instead o' creeshie flannen,
Been snaw-white seventeen hunder linen!—
Thir breeks o' mine, my only pair,   155
That ance were plush, o' guid blue hair,
I wad hae gien them aff my hurdies,
For ae blink o' the bonie burdies!

    But wither'd beldams, auld and droll,
Rigwoodie hags wad spean a foal,   160
Louping and flinging on a crummock,
I wonder didna turn thy stomach.

    But Tam kend what was what fu' brawlie;
There was ae winsome wench and wawlie,
That night enlisted in the core   165
Lang after kend on Carrick shore
(For monie a beast to dead she shot,
An' perished monie a bonie boat,
And shook baith meikle corn and bear,
And kept the countryside in fear).   170
Her cutty sark, o' Paisley harn,
That while a lassie she had worn,
In longitude tho' sorely scanty,
It was her best, and she was vauntie.
Ah! little kend thy reverend grannie,   175
That sark she coft for her wee Nannie,

102. **bleeze**, blaze. 103. **ilka bore**, every crevice. 107. **tippenny**, two-penny ale. 108. **usquebae**, whisky. 109. **swats sae reamed**, ale so foamed. 110. **deils a boddle**, devil a farthing. 114. **unco**, strange. 116. **brent-new**, brand-new. 117. **hornpipes**, etc., names of lively Scottish dances. 119. **winnock bunker**, window seat. 121. **towsie tyke**, shaggy cur. 123. **gart them skirl**, made them scream. 124. **dirl**, ring, tingle. 127. **cantraip sleight**, magic trick. 130. **haly**, holy. 131. **banes in gibbet airns**, bones in gibbet irons. 132. **unchristened**, unbaptized, and therefore lost. 133. **rape**, rope. 134. **gab**, mouth.

143. **glowered**, stared. 147. **cleekit**, caught hold of each other. 148. **ilka . . . reekit**, each hag sweat and steamed. 149. **coost . . . wark**, threw off her clothes for the work. 150. **linket . . . sark**, went at it in her shirt. 151. **queans**, young wenches. 153. **creeshie flannen**, greasy flannel. 154. **seventeen . . . linen**, fine linen, with 1700 threads to a width. 155. **Thir breeks**, these breeches. 157. **hurdies**, hips. 158. **burdies**, lasses. 160. **Rigwoodie**, lean, withered. **spean**, wean (out of disgust). 161. **Louping . . . crummock**, leaping and capering on a crooked staff. 163. **kend**, knew. **fu' brawlie**, full well. 164. **wawlie**, buxom. 165. **core**, company. 166. **Carrick**, the southern district of Ayrshire. 169. **corn and bear**, wheat and barley. 171. **cutty sark**, short shirt. **Paisley harn**, coarse linen made in the town of Paisley. 174. **vauntie**, proud. 176. **coft**, bought.

Wi' twa pund Scots ('twas a' her riches),
Wad ever graced a dance o' witches!

But here my Muse her wing maun cour,
Sic flights are far beyond her power; 180
To sing how Nannie lap and flang,
(A souple jade she was and strang,)
And how Tam stood like ane bewitched,
And thought his very een enriched;
Even Satan glowered and fidged fu' fain, 185
And hotched and blew wi' might and main:
Till first ae caper, syne anither,
Tam tint his reason a' thegither,
And roars out, "Weel done, Cutty-sark!"
And in an instant all was dark: 190
And scarcely had he Maggie rallied,
When out the hellish legion sallied.

As bees bizz out wi' angry fyke,
When plundering herds assail their byke;
As open pussie's mortal foes, 195
When, pop! she starts before their nose;
As eager runs the market-crowd,
When "Catch the thief!" resounds aloud;
So Maggie runs, the witches follow,
Wi' monie an eldritch skriech and hollo. 200

Ah, Tam! ah, Tam! thou'll get thy fairin!
In hell they'll roast thee like a herrin!
In vain thy Kate awaits thy comin!
Kate soon will be a woefu' woman!
Now, do thy speedy utmost, Meg, 205
And win the keystane of the brig:
There at them thou thy tail may toss,
A running stream they dare na cross.
But ere the keystane she could make,
The fient a tail she had to shake! 210
For Nannie, far before the rest,
Hard upon noble Maggie prest,
And flew at Tam wi' furious ettle;
But little wist she Maggie's mettle—
Ae spring brought aff her master hale, 215
But left behind her ain gray tail:
The carlin claught her by the rump,
And left poor Maggie scarce a stump.

Now, wha this tale o' truth shall read,
Ilk man and mother's son, take heed, 220
Whene'er to drink you are inclined,
Or cutty-sarks run in your mind,
Think, ye may buy the joys o'er dear,
Remember Tam o' Shanter's Mare.

(*1789;* 1791)

Bonie Doon

Ye flowery banks o' bonie Doon,
 How can ye blume sae fair?
How can ye chant, ye little birds,
 And I sae fu' o' care?

Thou'll break my heart, thou bonie bird, 5
 That sings upon the bough;
Thou minds me o' the happy days,
 When my fause luve was true.

Thou'll break my heart, thou bonie bird,
 That sings beside thy mate; 10
For sae I sat, and sae I sang,
 And wist na o' my fate.

Aft hae I roved by bonie Doon
 To see the woodbine twine,
And ilka bird sang o' its luve, 15
 And sae did I o' mine.

Wi' lightsome heart I pu'd a rose
 Frae aff its thorny tree;
And my fause luver staw my rose
 But left the thorn wi' me. 20

(*1791;* 1808)

Ae Fond Kiss

The inspiration of this poem was a Mrs. Maclehose, of Edinburgh, with whom Burns had a love affair before he married Jean Armour. Scott said of lines 13 to 16 that they contained "the essence of a thousand love tales."

Ae fond kiss, and then we sever!
Ae farewell, and then forever!
Deep in heart-wrung tears I'll pledge thee,
Warring sighs and groans I'll wage thee.

---

177. **twa pund Scots.** A pound Scots was worth about forty cents. 179. **maun cour,** must lower. 181. **lap and flang,** jumped and kicked. 185. **fidged fu' fain,** fidgeted with pleasure. 186. **hotched,** jerked. 188. **tint,** lost. 193. **fyke,** fuss. 194. **herds,** herdsmen. **byke,** hive. 195. **open,** begin to bark. **pussie's,** the hare's. 200. **eldritch,** unearthly. 201. **fairin,** reward, deserts; literally, a present from a fair. 206. **brig,** bridge. 210. **fient,** devil. 213. **ettle,** aim, intent. 214. **wist,** knew. 217. **claught,** seized.

Bonie Doon. The Doon is a delightful small river near Burns's birthplace. 12. **wist na,** knew not. 15. **ilka,** every. 19. **staw,** stole.
Ae Fond Kiss. 4. **wage,** pledge.

Who shall say that Fortune grieves him, 5
While the star of hope she leaves him?
Me, nae cheerfu' twinkle lights me,
Dark despair around benights me.

I'll ne'er blame my partial fancy:
Naething could resist my Nancy! 10
But to see her was to love her,
Love but her, and love for ever.
Had we never loved sae kindly,
Had we never loved sae blindly,
Never met—or never parted— 15
We had ne'er been broken-hearted.

Fare-the-weel, thou first and fairest!
Fare-the-weel, thou best and dearest!
Thine be ilka joy and treasure,
Peace, Enjoyment, Love, and Pleasure! 20
Ae fond kiss, and then we sever!
Ae farewell, alas, for ever!
Deep in heart-wrung tears I'll pledge thee,
Warring sighs and groans I'll wage thee.

(*1791;* 1792)

Highland Mary

This song concerns Mary Campbell; Burns said that it was in his happiest manner. See *To Mary in Heaven*, p. 103.

Ye banks, and braes, and streams around
  The castle o' Montgomery,
Green be your woods and fair your flowers,
  Your waters never drumlie!
There simmer first unfald her robes, 5
  And there the langest tarry;
For there I took the last fareweel,
  O' my sweet Highland Mary.

How sweetly bloom'd the gay green birk,
  How rich the hawthorn's blossom, 10
As underneath their fragrant shade
  I clasp'd her to my bosom!
The golden hours on angel wings
  Flew o'er me and my dearie;
For dear to me as light and life, 15
  Was my sweet Highland Mary.

19. **ilka**, every.
Highland Mary. 1. **braes**, hillsides. 2. **castle o' Montgomery**, Coilsfield House, near Tarbolton. 4. **drumlie**, muddy. 9. **birk**, birch.

Wi' monie a vow and lock'd embrace
  Our parting was fu' tender;
And, pledging aft to meet again,
  We tore oursels asunder; 20
But O! fell Death's untimely frost,
  That nipt my flower sae early!
Now green's the sod, and cauld's the clay,
  That wraps my Highland Mary!

O pale, pale now, those rosy lips, 25
  I aft hae kiss'd sae fondly!
And clos'd for ay the sparkling glance,
  That dwalt on me sae kindly!
And moldering now in silent dust,
  That heart that lo'ed me dearly! 30
But still within my bosom's core
  Shall live my Highland Mary.

(*1792;* 1799)

Duncan Gray

The tune of this poem, says Burns, "is that kind of lighthorse gallop of an air which precludes sentiment. The ludicrous is its ruling feature."

Duncan Gray came here to woo,
  (Ha, ha, the wooin o't!)
On blythe Yule night when we were fou,
  (Ha, ha, the wooin o't!)
Maggie coost her head fu high, 5
Looked asklent and unco skeigh,
Gart poor Duncan stand abeigh;
  Ha, ha, the wooin o't!

Duncan fleech'd, and Duncan prayed;
  (Ha, ha, the wooin o't!) 10
Meg was deaf as Ailsa Craig,
  (Ha, ha, the wooin o't!)
Duncan sighed baith out and in,
Grat his een baith bleer't and blin',
Spak o' lowpin o'er a linn; 15
  Ha, ha, the wooin o't!

Time and chance are but a tide,
  (Ha, ha, the wooin o't!)

19. **aft**, often.
Duncan Gray. 3. **Yule night**, Christmas Eve. **fou**, full, drunk. 5. **coost**, cast, tossed. 6. **asklent . . . skeigh**, askance and very haughty. 7. **Gart**, made. **abeigh**, aside. 9. **fleech'd**, flattered. 11. **Ailsa Craig**, a small rocky island on the coast of Ayrshire. 14. **Grat**, wept. 15. **lowpin . . . linn**, leaping over a waterfall. 17. **but a tide**. They ebb and flow, like the tides.

Slighted love is sair to bide,
    (Ha, ha, the wooin o't!)   20
"Shall I, like a fool," quoth he,
"For a haughty hizzie die?
She may gae to—France for me!"
    Ha, ha, the wooin o't!

How it comes let doctors tell,   25
    (Ha, ha, the wooin o't!)
Meg grew sick as he grew hale,
    (Ha, ha, the wooin o't!)
Something in her bosom wrings,
For relief a sigh she brings;   30
And O! her een, they spak sic things!
    Ha, ha, the wooin o't!

Duncan was a lad o' grace,
    (Ha, ha, the wooin o't!)
Maggie's was a piteous case,   35
    (Ha, ha, the wooin o't!)
Duncan could na be her death,
Swelling pity smoored his wrath;
Now they're crouse and cantie baith;
    Ha, ha, the wooin o't!   40
                   (1792)

Scots, Wha Hae

In September, 1793, Burns wrote to a friend: "There is in many places of Scotland a tradition . . . that it [the old air *Hey tuttie taitie*] was Robert Bruce's march at the battle of Bannockburn. This thought in my yesternight's evening walk warmed me to a pitch of enthusiasm on the theme of Liberty and Independence, which I threw into a kind of Scottish ode, fitted to the air, that one might suppose to be the gallant royal Scot's address to his heroic followers on that heroic morning. So may God ever defend the cause of truth and liberty as He did that day. Amen."

This victory of Bruce over Edward II at Bannockburn (1314) made Scotland independent of England until the two kingdoms were merged *de facto* in 1603 and *de iure* in 1707 (cf. Vol. I, p. 815). The poem is an expression of Burns's patriotism; but it is impossible to avoid the conclusion that he was powerfully affected in his patriotic libertarianism by the French Revolution, then at its most violent height.

Scots, wha hae wi' Wallace bled,
Scots, wham Bruce has aften led,
Welcome to your gory bed
    Or to victorie!

Now's the day, and now's the hour: 5
See the front o' battle lour,
See approach proud Edward's power—
    Chains and slaverie!

Wha will be a traitor knave?
Wha can fill a coward's grave?   10
Wha sae base as be a slave?—
    Let him turn, and flee!

Wha for Scotland's King and Law
Freedom's sword will strongly draw,
Freeman stand or freeman fa',   15
    Let him follow me!

By Oppression's woes and pains,
By your sons in servile chains,
We will drain our dearest veins.
    But they shall be free!   20

Lay the proud usurpers low!
Tyrants fall in every foe!
Liberty's in every blow!
    Let us do, or die!   *(1793; 1794)*

A Red, Red Rose

O, my luve is like a red, red rose,
    That's newly sprung in June.
O, my luve is like the melodie,
    That's sweetly played in tune.

As fair art thou, my bonie lass,   5
    So deep in luve am I,
And I will luve thee still, my dear,
    Till a' the seas gang dry.

Till a' the seas gang dry, my dear,
    And the rocks melt wi' the sun!   10
And I will luve thee still, my dear,
    While the sands o' life shall run.

---

19. **sair to bide**, hard to bear. 22. **hizzie**, lass. 31. **sic**, such. 38. **smoored**, smothered. 39. **crouse and cantie**, brisk and cheerful.

And fare thee weel, my only luve,
  And fare thee weel a while!
And I will come again, my luve,   15
  Tho' it were ten thousand mile!
                    (*1794;* 1796)

A Man's a Man for A' That

Is there, for honest poverty,
  That hings his head, an' a' that?
The coward slave, we pass him by,
  We dare be poor for a' that!
    For a' that, an' a' that,   5
      Our toils obscure, an' a' that;
    The rank is but the guinea's stamp;
    The man's the gowd for a' that.

What tho' on hamely fare we dine,
  Wear hodden-gray, an' a' that;   10
Gie fools their silks, and knaves their wine,
  A man's a man for a' that.
    For a' that, an' a' that,
      Their tinsel show, an' a' that;
    The honest man, tho' e'er sae poor,   15
    Is king o' men for a' that.

Ye see yon birkie, ca'd a lord,
  Wha struts, an' stares, an' a' that;
Tho' hundreds worship at his word,
  He's but a coof for a' that.   20
    For a' that, an' a' that,
      His riband, star, an' a' that
    The man o' independent mind,
    He looks and laughs at a' that.

A prince can mak a belted knight,   25
  A marquis, duke, an' a' that;
But an honest man's aboon his might,

Guid faith he mauna fa' that!
  For a' that, an' a' that,
    Their dignities, an' a' that,   30
  The pith o' sense, an' pride o' worth,
  Are higher rank than a' that.

Then let us pray that come it may,
  As come it will for a' that,
That sense and worth, o'er a' the earth,   35
  May bear the gree, an' a' that.
    For a' that, an' a' that,
      It's coming yet, for a' that,
    That man to man, the warld o'er,
    Shall brothers be for a' that.   40
                    (*1794;* 1795)

O, Wert Thou in the Cauld Blast

    The young woman honored in this lyric was Jessie Lewars, who nursed Burns during his last illness.

O, wert thou in the cauld blast
  On yonder lea, on yonder lea,
My plaidie to the angry airt,
  I'd shelter thee, I'd shelter thee.
Or did misfortune's bitter storms   5
  Around thee blaw, around thee blaw,
Thy bield should be my bosom,
  To share it a', to share it a'.

Or were I in the wildest waste,
  Sae black and bare, sae black and bare,   10
The desert were a paradise,
  If thou wert there, if thou wert there.
Or were I monarch o' the globe,
  Wi' thee to reign, wi' thee to reign,
The brightest jewel in my crown   15
  Wad be my queen, wad be my queen.
                    (*1796;* 1800)

---

7. **guinea's stamp**, the imprint of the King's head on a coin as a statement of its value. 8. **gowd**, gold. 10. **hodden-gray**, coarse gray woolen cloth, undyed. 17. **birkie**, young fellow. 20. **coof**, fool. 27. **aboon**, above.

28. **mauna fa'**, must not claim or get. 36. **bear the gree**, have the prize.
O, Wert Thou in the Cauld Blast. 3. **airt**, direction, quarter of the wind. 7. **bield**, shelter.

William Blake

1757-1827

There are some writers—poets of the imagination and seers of mystic vision—who can tread with conviction and certainty the misty borderland between fact and fancy, who can behold God sitting in a tree with all his angels, and who can in the next moment turn to something as humble and human as a little lost child. Such a writer was William Blake. His life was in the main placid and uneventful. He was born in London in November, 1757; his father, a hosier of limited means, could do little for the boy's education. But it was soon apparent that young Blake had an unusual eye for design, and the wise father sent the lad to a drawing-school and encouraged his visits to art exhibitions and sales-rooms. In 1771 Blake was apprenticed to an engraver; the practice of engraving later became one of his most successful fields of artistic expression. At the end of this apprenticeship Blake went to school at the Royal Academy.

He cultivated his own talents assiduously, but his training does not appear to have been very academic. Nevertheless he met many of the prominent artists of his day, and with their help he embarked upon a career as an artist; his first picture was exhibited in 1780, and he continued to produce water colors until 1808. In the meantime he had married (1782) Catharine Boucher, who was an extremely wholesome and steadying influence upon his erratic genius, and he had published a few poems under the title of *Poetical Sketches* (1783)—delicate, highly individual little works that showed unmistakable promise.

Blake next set himself up as a print-seller and engraver (1784), first in partnership, and then alone (1787). It was while he was thus occupied that he produced *Songs of Innocence* (1789), a group of poems noteworthy for many reasons—first, because they show us a tender, romantic, thoroughly humanitarian poet in a complex but fascinating blend of the direct and simple with the symbolic; again, because the poems are completely divorced in matter and manner from the neo-classical tradition; and finally, because the production is a masterly combination of the two great arts of poetry and engraving. By a process all Blake's own, he had engraved upon copper both the text and the decorative designs of his poems and had tinted the whole by his own hand after printing. The entire performance bespoke genius.

In the same year (1789) appeared *The Book of Thel*, produced in the same manner as *Songs of Innocence*, but much more mystical and much less attuned to sense. This work was the first of a series of writings that have come to be called Blake's "Prophetic Books," which include among others *The Marriage of Heaven and Hell* (1790), *The Gates of Paradise* (1793), *The Vision of the Daughters of Albion* (1793), *Jerusalem* (1804), *The Emanation of the Giant Albion* (1804), and *Milton* (1804). Little in these books will interest the general reader; one must be a connoisseur of engraving and illustration, a zealot of Blake, and a devotee of ultra-symbolic poetry to understand and appreciate them. They become increasingly obscure in text and thought, and increasingly clear and beautiful as specimens of the engraver's art.

Aside from the works already mentioned, the only other important contribution by Blake to literature was *Songs of Experience* (1794), richly symbolic, to be sure, but without the half-crazed atmosphere of the Prophetic Books. *Songs of Experience* and *Songs of Innocence* treat of similar subjects from the contrasting viewpoints of a mature man and of a child, as the titles of the two collections imply. They are short, arresting lyrics of clarity, skilled technique, impressive power and depth, and unforgettable phrase.

For a time Blake lived in the village of Felpham, Sussex (1801-1804), in the company of the obscure poet Hayley, who was writing a life of William Cowper (p. 73) and who wished Blake to illustrate his work. The enterprise was not successful, and Blake returned to London, where he spent the remaining years of his life until his death in 1827. He wrote nothing of any importance after his return, but his artistic work perhaps reached its peak in these later years. Particularly famous are his illustrations to an edition (1804-1805) of *The Grave*, a well-known "graveyard" poem by the eighteenth-century precursor of the romantic, Robert Blair (1699-1746); his representation of the Canterbury Pilgrims (1809); and his magnificent illustrations to the Book of Job (c. 1825), in which his wild and untrammeled imagination had free play.

Blake has an unusual position in literature. In his towering, mystically imaginative achievements in both poetry and art and in the arresting emotional power of his lyric poetry, he can be classed as romantic, as befitted the time in which he wrote. But somehow his performance transcends ordinary academic limitations. He could see the angels of God about him; he could walk out on the heath and touch God with his finger; he could stand in awe of both the beneficent and the baleful forces of nature, as shown in *The Lamb* on the one hand and in the famous *The Tiger* on the other. He could paint the beauty of the twilight in sheerest poetry in *To the Evening Star;* he could touch all the poignancy of human experience in such a tiny poem as *The Fly*. The romantic envelops him; but the same could be said in some degree of every great poet. It is safest, perhaps, to think of him as an extraordinarily gifted combination of poet, painter, and visionary, who seized the pictorial element of an idea, whether simple or sublime, and translated it into the sensuous language of his deeply religious though unorthodox mystical genius.

from *Poetical Sketches*

TO THE EVENING STAR

Thou fair-haired angel of the evening,
Now, whilst the sun rests on the mountains, light
Thy bright torch of love; thy radiant crown
Put on, and smile upon our evening bed!
Smile on our loves, and while thou drawest the 5
Blue curtains of the sky, scatter thy silver dew
On every flower that shuts its sweet eyes
In timely sleep. Let thy west wind sleep on
The lake; speak silence with thy glimmering eyes,
And wash the dusk with silver. Soon, full soon, 10
Dost thou withdraw; then the wolf rages wide,
And the lion glares through the dun forest:
The fleeces of our flocks are covered with
Thy sacred dew; protect them with thine influence. (1783)

MY SILKS AND FINE ARRAY

My silks and fine array,
My smiles and languished air,
By love are driven away;
And mournful lean Despair
Brings me yew to deck my grave; 5
Such end true lovers have.

His face is fair as heaven
When springing buds unfold;
O why to him was't given
Whose heart is wintry cold? 10
His breast is love's all-worshiped tomb,
Where all love's pilgrims come.

Bring me an ax and spade,
Bring me a winding-sheet;
When I my grave have made 15
Let winds and tempests beat;
Then down I'll lie as cold as clay.
True love doth pass away! (1783)

WILLIAM BLAKE

The Author & Printer W.Blake

from *Songs of Innocence*
INTRODUCTION

Piping down the valleys wild,
Piping songs of pleasant glee,
On a cloud I saw a child,
And he laughing said to me:

"Pipe a song about a Lamb!" 5
So I piped with merry cheer.
"Piper, pipe that song again";
So I piped: he wept to hear.

"Drop thy pipe, thy happy pipe;
Sing thy songs of happy cheer": 10

So I sang the same again,
While he wept with joy to hear.

"Piper, sit thee down and write
In a book, that all may read."
So he vanished from my sight, 15
And I plucked a hollow reed,

And I made a rural pen,
And I stained the water clear,
And I wrote my happy songs
Every child may joy to hear. 20

THE LAMB

Little Lamb, who made thee?
Dost thou know who made thee?
Gave thee life, and bid thee feed,
By the stream and o'er the mead;
Gave thee clothing of delight,   5
Softest clothing, woolly, bright;
Gave thee such a tender voice,
Making all the vales rejoice?
    Little Lamb, who made thee?
    Dost thou know who made thee?   10

Little Lamb, I'll tell thee,
Little Lamb, I'll tell thee:
He is callèd by thy name,
For He calls Himself a Lamb,
He is meek, and He is mild;   15
He became a little child.
I a child, and thou a lamb,
We are callèd by His name.
    Little Lamb, God bless thee!
    Little Lamb, God bless thee!   20

THE LITTLE BLACK BOY

My mother bore me in the southern wild,
And I am black, but O! my soul is white;
White as an angel is the English child,
But I am black, as if bereaved of light.

My mother taught me underneath a tree,   5
And, sitting down before the heat of day,
She took me on her lap and kissèd me,
And, pointing to the east, began to say:

"Look on the rising sun—there God does live,
And gives His light, and gives His heat away; 10
And flowers and trees and beasts and men receive
Comfort in morning, joy in the noonday.

"And we are put on earth a little space,
That we may learn to bear the beams of love;
And these black bodies and this sunburnt face   15
Is but a cloud, and like a shady grove.

"For when our souls have learned the heat to bear,
The cloud will vanish; we shall hear His voice,
Saying: 'Come out from the grove, My love and care,
And round My golden tent like lambs rejoice.'"   20

Thus did my mother say, and kissèd me;
And thus I say to little English boy.
When I from black and he from white cloud free,
And round the tent of God like lambs we joy,

I'll shade him from the heat, till he can bear   25
To lean in joy upon our Father's knee;
And then I'll stand and stroke his silver hair,
And be like him, and he will then love me.

HOLY THURSDAY

'Twas on a Holy Thursday, their innocent faces clean,
The children walking two and two, in red and blue and green;
Gray-headed beadles walked before, with wands as white as snow;
Till into the high dome of Paul's they like Thames' waters flow.

Oh, what a multitude they seemed, these flowers of London town!   5
Seated in companies, they sit with radiance all their own.
The hum of multitudes was there, but multitudes of lambs,
Thousands of little boys and girls raising their innocent hands.

Now like a mighty wind they raise to Heaven the voice of song,
Or like harmonious thunderings the seats of Heaven among.   10
Beneath them sit the agèd men, wise guardians of the poor;
Then cherish pity, lest you drive an angel from your door.

Holy Thursday. Holy Thursday is the Thursday of Holy Week, i.e., the week before Easter. 4. **Paul's**, St. Paul's Cathedral, London.

A CRADLE SONG

Sweet dreams, form a shade
O'er my lovely infant's head!
Sweet dreams of pleasant streams
By happy, silent, moony beams!

Sweet sleep, with soft down
Weave thy brows an infant crown.
Sweet sleep, Angel mild,
Hover o'er my happy child!

Sweet smiles, in the night
Hover over my delight;
Sweet smiles, mother's smile,
All the livelong night beguile.

Sweet moans, dovelike sighs,
Chase not slumber from thy eyes.
Sweet moans, sweeter smile,
All the dovelike moans beguile.

Sleep, sleep, happy child,
All creation slept and smiled;
Sleep, sleep, happy sleep,
While o'er thee thy mother weep.

Sweet babe, in thy face
Holy image I can trace.
Sweet babe, once like thee,
Thy Maker lay and wept for me:

Wept for me, for thee, for all,
When He was an infant small.
Thou His image ever see,
Heavenly face that smiles on thee!

Smiles on thee, on me, on all;
Who became an infant small.
Infant smiles are His own smiles;
Heaven and earth to peace beguiles.

THE DIVINE IMAGE

To Mercy, Pity, Peace, and Love
All pray in their distress;
And to these virtues of delight
Return their thankfulness.

For Mercy, Pity, Peace, and Love
Is God, our Father dear,
And Mercy, Pity, Peace, and Love
Is man, His child and care.

For Mercy has a human heart,
Pity a human face,
And Love, the human form divine,
And Peace, the human dress.

Then every man, of every clime,
That prays in his distress,
Prays to the human form divine,
Love, Mercy, Pity, Peace.

And all must love the human form,
In heathen, Turk, or Jew;
Where Mercy, Love, and Pity dwell
There God is dwelling too.

A DREAM

Once a dream did weave a shade
O'er my angel-guarded bed,
That an emmet lost its way
Where on grass methought I lay.

Troubled, 'wildered, and forlorn,
Dark, benighted, travel-worn,
Over many a tangled spray,
All heart-broke, I heard her say:

"Oh, my children! do they cry,
Do they hear their father sigh?
Now they look abroad to see;
Now return and weep for me."

Pitying, I dropped a tear;
But I saw a glow-worm near,
Who replied, "What wailing wight
Calls the watchman of the night?

"I am set to light the ground,
While the beetle goes his round;
Follow now the beetle's hum;
Little wanderer, hie thee home!"

(1789)

3. emmet, ant.

from *Songs of Experience*

THE FLY

Little Fly,
Thy summer's play
My thoughtless hand
Has brushed away.

Am not I   5
A fly like thee?
Or art not thou
A man like me?

For I dance,
And drink, and sing,   10
Till some blind hand
Shall brush my wing.

If thought is life
And strength and breath,
And the want   15
Of thought is death;

Then am I
A happy fly,
If I live
Or if I die.   20

THE TIGER

Tiger! Tiger! burning bright
In the forests of the night,
What immortal hand or eye
Could frame thy fearful symmetry?

In what distant deeps or skies   5
Burnt the fire of thine eyes?
On what wings dare he aspire?
What the hand dare seize the fire?

And what shoulder, and what art,
Could twist the sinews of thy heart?   10
And when thy heart began to beat,
What dread hand? and what dread feet?

What the hammer? what the chain?
In what furnace was thy brain?
What the anvil? what dread grasp   15
Dare its deadly terrors clasp?

When the stars threw down their spears,
And watered heaven with their tears,
Did he smile his work to see?
Did he who made the Lamb make thee?   20

Tiger! Tiger! burning bright
In the forests of the night,
What immortal hand or eye
Dare frame thy fearful symmetry?

THE CLOD AND THE PEBBLE

"Love seeketh not itself to please,
Nor for itself hath any care,
But for another gives its ease,
And builds a Heaven in Hell's despair."

So sung a little Clod of Clay,   5
Trodden with the cattle's feet,
But a Pebble of the brook
Warbled out these meters meet:

"Love seeketh only Self to please,
To bind another to its delight,   10
Joys in another's loss of ease,
And builds a Hell in Heaven's despite."

HOLY THURSDAY

Is this a holy thing to see
In a rich and fruitful land—
Babes reduced to misery,
Fed with cold and usurous hand?

Is that trembling cry a song?   5
Can it be a song of joy?
And so many children poor?
It is a land of poverty!

And their sun does never shine,
And their fields are bleak and bare,   10
And their ways are filled with thorns:
It is eternal winter there.

For where'er the sun does shine,
And where'er the rain does fall,
Babe can never hunger there,   15
Nor poverty the mind appall.

Holy Thursday. Cf. this poem with one by the same title in *Songs of Innocence*, p. 114.

A POISON TREE

I was angry with my friend:
I told my wrath, my wrath did end.
I was angry with my foe:
I told it not, my wrath did grow.

And I watered it in fears 5
Night and morning with my tears,
And I sunnéd it with smiles
And with soft deceitful wiles.

And it grew both day and night,
Till it bore an apple bright, 10
And my foe beheld it shine,
And he knew that it was mine—

And into my garden stole
When the night had veiled the pole;
In the morning, glad, I see 15
My foe outstretched beneath the tree.

THE GARDEN OF LOVE

I went to the Garden of Love,
And saw what I never had seen:
A chapel was built in the midst,
Where I used to play on the green.

And the gates of this chapel were shut, 5
And "Thou shalt not" writ over the door;
So I turned to the Garden of Love,
That so many sweet flowers bore:

And I saw it was filléd with graves,
And tombstones where flowers should be; 10
And priests in black gowns were walking
 their rounds,
And binding with briars my joys and desires.

A LITTLE BOY LOST

"Nought loves another as itself,
Nor venerates another so,
Nor is it possible to Thought
A greater than itself to know:

"And, Father, how can I love you 5
Or any of my brothers more?
I love you like the little bird
That picks up crumbs around the door."

The Priest sat by and heard the child,
In trembling zeal he seized his hair: 10
He led him by his little coat,
And all admired the priestly care.

And standing on the altar high,
"Lo! what a fiend is here," said he,
"One who sets reason up for judge 15
Of our most holy Mystery."

The weeping child could not be heard,
The weeping parents wept in vain;
They stripped him to his little shirt,
And bound him in an iron chain; 20

And burned him in a holy place,
Where many had been burned before:
The weeping parents wept in vain.
Are such things done on Albion's shore?

LONDON

I wander through each chartered street,
Near where the chartered Thames does flow,
And mark in every face I meet
Marks of weakness, marks of woe.

In every cry of every man, 5
In every infant's cry of fear,
In every voice, in every ban,
The mind-forged manacles I hear:

How the chimney-sweeper's cry
Every blackening church appalls, 10
And the hapless soldier's sigh
Runs in blood down palace walls.

But most, through midnight streets I hear
How the youthful harlot's curse
Blasts the new-born infant's tear, 15
And blights with plagues the marriage hearse.

THE CHIMNEY-SWEEPER

A little black thing among the snow,
Crying "weep! weep!" in notes of woe!
"Where are thy father and mother?
 Say!"—
"They are both gone up to church to pray.

"Because I was happy upon the heath, 5
And smiled among the winter's snow,

They clothed me in the clothes of death,
And taught me to sing the notes of woe.

"And because I am happy, and dance and
  sing,
They think they have done me no injury, 10
And are gone to praise God and His priest
  and king,
Who make up a heaven of our misery."

(1794)

Stanza from *Auguries of Innocence*

To see a World in a grain of sand,
And a Heaven in a wild flower;
Hold Infinity in the palm of your hand,
And eternity in an hour.

(*1801-3;* 1863)

Thel's Motto

Does the eagle know what is in the pit,
  Or wilt thou go ask the mole?
Can wisdom be put in a silver rod,
  Or love in a golden bowl?

(1789)

Thel's Motto. These lines are prefixed to *The Book of Thel,* one of the so-called Prophetic Books, in which Blake presents his ideas on ethics, morality, religion, etc.

THE ROMANTIC TRIUMPH IN POETRY

William Wordsworth
1770-1850

William Wordsworth was born April 7, 1770, in the village of Cockermouth, Cumberland. His father was an attorney who belonged to the class of landed gentry; Wordsworth was therefore able to secure a university education, and entered Cambridge in 1787. His course at the university was interrupted briefly by a tour of Switzerland and northern Italy. France was at that time in revolution, and to that country the young and enthusiastic Wordsworth departed after his graduation in 1791. His stay in France during the year 1792 coincided with some of the most turbulent days of the French Revolution; a new nation was in process of birth; law and order were secondary considerations. The whole picture left an impression upon the young Wordsworth that was years in the effacing; not the least important of his experiences was his affair with Annette Vallon and the birth of a child, Caroline—something that was to color his poetry through the next two decades.

Wordsworth returned to England shortly before the climax of the French Revolution—the execution of King Louis XVI in 1793—and his return found him still under the influence of the great Frenchman Rousseau (p. 3) and of Rousseau's English disciple William Godwin, whose *Enquiry Concerning Political Justice* (1793) was the authoritative work for the little group of English revolutionists with which Wordsworth affiliated himself. The years immediately following 1793 were restless years for the poet; he wandered about England in the absence of his devoted sister Dorothy, settling eventually at Racedown, Dorsetshire, in 1795, where he met Samuel Taylor Coleridge (p. 163) and developed into Coleridge's great friend and constant companion. When Coleridge moved into Somersetshire (1797), Wordsworth followed him, and in the next year the two men published jointly a collection of poems, known simply as *Lyrical Ballads* (1798). The importance of this work—a milestone in the history of English literature—has already been discussed (p. 10); it is sufficient here to repeat that the poems illustrate completely the revolutionary theories of Wordsworth and Coleridge as applied to English poetry; their break with neoclassical ideals, to some of which Wordsworth had faintly subscribed in his very early verse like *An Evening Walk* (1793) or *Descriptive Sketches* (1793), was based in part upon Wordsworth's democratic and humanitarian leanings. The *Lyrical Ballads* was condemned by many as inadequate poetry, by others as revolutionary, a term which by 1798 had become anathema to the English. Even Coleridge himself was bothered by the whole-souled nature-worship of Wordsworth's work in this collection, many of the poems seeming to him pagan and atheistical.

In spite of all the adverse judgments, however, the *Lyrical Ballads* survived; a second edition appeared in 1800, to which Wordsworth added a preface which stated formally the new ideals of sincerity, democracy, nature-worship, and simple, unaffected diction to which he and Coleridge had dedicated themselves. This preface (p. 318) should be read by all who wish to understand thoroughly Wordsworth's contribution to the romantic movement and the romantic movement itself. Between the first and second editions of *Lyrical Ballads*, Wordsworth, his sister, and Coleridge took a trip to Germany; Coleridge to study at the University of Göttingen; Wordsworth to contemplate the new land and to wax nostalgic for the glories of his English countryside. Upon their return, Wordsworth and his sister settled in the superb Lake Country of northern England, taking a small cottage at Grasmere, which became their home for the next few years.

Wordsworth's ideas about the French Revolution, like those of many of the young English revolutionists, underwent a considerable change with the advent of Napoleon and the manifestation of the great Corsican's imperialistic ambitions. At first, however, Wordsworth remained sympathetic toward France. It is known that he had a meeting in France with Annette Vallon; but the decision of the two seems to have been to close the chapter, for shortly thereafter (1802) Wordsworth began to write sonnets against Napoleon, and married Mary Hutchinson, a friend of his sister. The final step in his conservative progress came in 1813, when he became distributor of stamps—an employee of the government—and so turned away from the young romantic and revolutionary group to become the "lost leader" (see Browning's poem of that name, p. 666). He remained by choice in the Lake Country, moving to Rydal Mount near Lake Windermere, where he spent the remainder of his long and peacefully idyllic life. In his seventies he became poet laureate (1843) in succession to Robert Southey (cf. pp. 12 and 296), but his only important piece of laureate verse, addressed to Prince Albert, the consort of Queen Victoria, was completely uninspired and had better be forgotten. His death in 1850 came long after the ideas for which he labored had been not only accepted but in many ways superseded. He lived for a score of years after Byron, the most turbulent of the younger romantics who had scorned him, had passed away.

Wordsworth's significant work was all produced within a span of twenty-five years. In respect to subject-matter, this work is a mixture of realistic humanitarianism, democratic liberalism, "the short and simple annals of the poor," and a pagan and thoroughly pantheistic worship of nature. These ingredients are to be found in *Lyrical Ballads,* particularly exemplified by such poems as *Alice Fell, Michael* (p. 142), the Lucy poems, and *Tintern Abbey* (p. 121). Indeed, they can be found generally throughout most of Wordsworth's verse for the twenty-five years between 1798 and 1823; but whereas Wordsworth was a fairly complete radical in religion and politics about 1793-1795, as his letter to the Bishop of Llandaff will show, he seems to be striving more and more toward an orthodox religious outlook in his later work. That he ever achieves orthodoxy is questionable. But there is clearly discernible a somberer tone in his poetry after 1802, as can be seen in his *Ode to Duty* (p. 155), his *Resolution and Independence* (p. 148), or his *Elegiac Stanzas,* sometimes known as *Peele Castle* (p. 157). Certainly in his great *Ode on Intimations of Immortality* (p. 160), although it preaches the superiority of a child-like and instinctive perception over the more mature reflections prompted by experience, he is groping toward the accepted orthodox faith. On the other hand, there is always in Wordsworth a strong pagan love of natural beauty which no orthodoxy can quench.

Fully as interesting to the student of literature as Wordsworth's philosophical change is his shifting treatment of his theory of poetic diction. In his famous *Preface* to the *Lyrical Ballads* (p. 318), Wordsworth proposed to write his poems "in a selection of language really used by men," which, so far as the type of mankind shown in the *Lyrical Ballads* is concerned, meant the language of humble and perhaps rustic men. In any case, it is clear that Wordsworth cherished the ideal of simple words to express great and essential truths. He wrote many of his best poems, such as *I Wandered Lonely as a Cloud* (p. 155) and *The Solitary Reaper* (p. 154), with just such simplicity of vocabulary. Nevertheless, he could depart from his principles and use elevated language, as in *Tintern Abbey* and in many of the sonnets, with magnificent results; indeed, there are many who would affirm that Wordsworth's important poetry was always that in which he departed from bare simplicity. It seems likely that Wordsworth came to regard these fits of apostasy as inevitable, for most of his later work flies directly in the face of his announced theory in the *Lyrical Ballads*.

The poetry of Wordsworth, like that of every other great romanticist, is self-centered. He wrote two long autobiographical poems: *The Prelude* (p. 125), which is invaluable as a picture of Wordsworth in the days of his youth; and *The Excursion*, more philosophical yet less inspired, although certainly not deserving of Byron's judgment that it was both drowsy and frowsy. Both were to be included in a longer autobiographical work, *The Recluse*, which was never completed. Except for *Laodamia* (1814), the standard of style in his longer work falls off perceptibly after 1813. But his shorter poems, particularly his magnificent sonnets—Wordsworth is one of the most distinguished of English sonneteers—maintain a high standard of excellence until after 1820.

Comment upon Wordsworth's work as a whole is difficult, for no other poet in English literature went in more startling fashion from the poetic sublime to the ridiculous inept. Of the failures in his work due to the too rigid application of his theory of simple diction, to his blind lack of self-criticism, and to his fundamentally deficient sense of humor, it is idle to speak here. These failures were many, particularly in his earlier work. *Peter Bell* and *The Idiot Boy* have written their own epitaphs in some of their absurd bathetic lines. On the other hand, there are even more works from Wordsworth's pen that bear the unmistakable stamp of genius and embody all the great traditions of the romantic movement. Such poems as *To a Highland Girl* (p. 153) and *The Solitary Reaper* (p. 154) hold in suspension almost all the elements, both of subject-matter and of poetic atmosphere, that the romantic poets held dear. The sacred calling of the poet, in *If Thou Indeed Derive Thy Light from Heaven* (p. 163); the intuitive yearnings for the beautiful and undying in the "Immortality Ode" (p. 160); the affection for the gracious and enchanting in nature in *To the Daisy* (p. 152) or *I Wandered Lonely as a Cloud* (p. 155)—all are there for the romanticist to enjoy both for sheer emotional pleasure and for spiritual profit. It is, indeed, as a poet of nature that Wordsworth is greatest; his influence upon subsequent romantic writers has been enormous; it is not too much to say that the whole attitude of English poetry toward nature since his day has been colored by the Wordsworthian outlook. Whether the setting is the city at sunrise, as in the Westminster Bridge sonnet (p. 151), or "the sea that bares her bosom to the moon" (p. 159), or the hills, meadows, and brooksides about Tintern Abbey (below), Wordsworth's message is the same: Nature eternal, vast, and comforting is a mighty panorama into which the human being can sink himself and by so doing achieve solace and peace. Around this tonic message of spiritual comfort and beauty Wordsworth has thrown the mantle of dignity and loftiness; not without reason has he been considered by many the greatest English poet since John Milton. Like Milton, he can, for all his faults of heaviness, lack of humor, and occasional pedestrianism, soar into

>   The light that never was, on sea or land,
>   The consecration and the poet's dream.

Lines Written in Early Spring

I heard a thousand blended notes,
While in a grove I sate reclined,
In that sweet mood when pleasant thoughts
Bring sad thoughts to the mind.

To her fair works did Nature link   5
The human soul that through me ran;
And much it grieved my heart to think
What man has made of man.

Through primrose tufts, in that green bower,
The periwinkle trailed its wreaths;   10
And 'tis my faith that every flower
Enjoys the air it breathes.

The birds around me hopped and played,
Their thoughts I cannot measure—
But the least motion which they made,   15
It seemed a thrill of pleasure.

The budding twigs spread out their fan,
To catch the breezy air;
And I must think, do all I can,
That there was pleasure there.   20

If this belief from heaven be sent,
If such be Nature's holy plan,
Have I not reason to lament
What man has made of man?   (1798)

Lines

COMPOSED A FEW MILES ABOVE TINTERN ABBEY

Five years have past; five summers, with the length
Of five long winters! and again I hear
These waters, rolling from their mountain-springs
With a soft inland murmur.—Once again
Do I behold these steep and lofty cliffs,   5
That on a wild secluded scene impress
Thoughts of more deep seclusion; and connect
The landscape with the quiet of the sky.
The day is come when I again repose
Here, under this dark sycamore, and view   10
These plots of cottage-ground, these orchard-tufts,
Which at this season, with their unripe fruits,
Are clad in one green hue, and lose themselves
Mid groves and copses. Once again I see
These hedgerows, hardly hedgerows, little lines   15
Of sportive wood run wild: these pastoral farms,
Green to the very door; and wreaths of smoke
Sent up, in silence, from among the trees!
With some uncertain notice, as might seem
Of vagrant dwellers in the houseless woods,   20
Or of some Hermit's cave, where by his fire

Tintern Abbey. Tintern Abbey is a famous ruin in Monmouthshire. Wordsworth had visited the place in 1793.

The Hermit sits alone.
      These beauteous forms,
Through a long absence, have not been to me
As is a landscape to a blind man's eye:
But oft, in lonely rooms, and 'mid the din 25
Of towns and cities, I have owed to them,
In hours of weariness, sensations sweet,
Felt in the blood, and felt along the heart;
And passing even into my purer mind,
With tranquil restoration—feelings too 30
Of unremembered pleasure: such, perhaps,
As have no slight or trivial influence
On that best portion of a good man's life,
His little, nameless, unremembered acts
Of kindness and of love. Nor less, I trust, 35
To them I may have owed another gift,
Of aspect more sublime; that blessèd mood,
In which the burthen of the mystery,
In which the heavy and the weary weight
Of all this unintelligible world, 40
Is lightened—that serene and blessèd mood,
In which the affections gently lead us on—
Until, the breath of this corporeal frame
And even the motion of our human blood
Almost suspended, we are laid asleep 45
In body, and become a living soul:
While with an eye made quiet by the power
Of harmony, and the deep power of joy,
We see into the life of things.
       If this
Be but a vain belief, yet, oh! how oft— 50
In darkness and amid the many shapes
Of joyless daylight; when the fretful stir
Unprofitable, and the fever of the world,
Have hung upon the beatings of my heart—
How oft, in spirit, have I turned to thee, 55
O sylvan Wye! thou wanderer through the
  woods,
How often has my spirit turned to thee!
 And now, with gleams of half-extinguished
  thought,
With many recognitions dim and faint,
And somewhat of a sad perplexity, 60
The picture of the mind revives again:
While here I stand, not only with the sense
Of present pleasure, but with pleasing thoughts
That in this moment there is life and food
For future years. And so I dare to hope, 65
Though changed, no doubt, from what I was
  when first
I came among these hills; when like a roe
I bounded o'er the mountains, by the sides
Of the deep rivers, and the lonely streams,
Wherever nature led: more like a man 70
Flying from something that he dreads than
  one
Who sought the thing he loved. For nature
  then
(The coarser pleasures of my boyish days,
And their glad animal movements all gone
  by)
To me was all in all.—I cannot paint 75
What then I was. The sounding cataract
Haunted me like a passion: the tall rock,
The mountain, and the deep and gloomy
  wood,
Their colors and their forms, were then to me
An appetite; a feeling and a love, 80
That had no need of a remoter charm,
By thought supplied, nor any interest
Unborrowed from the eye.—That time is past,
And all its aching joys are now no more,
And all its dizzy raptures. Not for this 85
Faint I, nor mourn nor murmur; other gifts
Have followed; for such loss, I would believe,
Abundant recompense. For I have learned
To look on nature, not as in the hour
Of thoughtless youth; but hearing often-
  times 90
The still, sad music of humanity,
Nor harsh nor grating, though of ample
  power
To chasten and subdue. And I have felt
A presence that disturbs me with the joy
Of elevated thoughts; a sense sublime 95
Of something far more deeply interfused,
Whose dwelling is the light of setting suns,
And the round ocean and the living air,
And the blue sky, and in the mind of man:
A motion and a spirit, that impels 100
All thinking things, all objects of all thought,
And rolls through all things. Therefore am
  I still
A lover of the meadows and the woods,
And mountains; and of all that we behold
From this green earth; of all the mighty
  world 105

72-111. **For nature,** etc. With this passage, compare ll. 175-203 of *Ode or Intimations of Immortality*, p. 162. **97. Whose ... suns,** etc. Tennyson spoke of this line as giving the sense of "the permanent in the transitory."

Of eye, and ear—both what they half create,
And what perceive; well pleased to recognize
In nature and the language of the sense
The anchor of my purest thoughts, the nurse,
The guide, the guardian of my heart, and
    soul   110
Of all my moral being.
                        Nor perchance,
If I were not thus taught, should I the more
Suffer my genial spirits to decay:
For thou art with me here upon the banks
Of this fair river; thou my dearest Friend, 115
My dear, dear Friend; and in thy voice I
    catch
The language of my former heart, and read
My former pleasures in the shooting lights
Of thy wild eyes. Oh! yet a little while
May I behold in thee what I was once,   120
My dear, dear Sister! and this prayer I make,
Knowing that Nature never did betray
The heart that loved her; 'tis her privilege,
Through all the years of this our life, to lead
From joy to joy: for she can so inform   125
The mind that is within us, so impress
With quietness and beauty, and so feed
With lofty thoughts, that neither evil tongues,
Rash judgments, nor the sneers of selfish men,
Nor greetings where no kindness is, nor all 130
The dreary intercourse of daily life,
Shall e'er prevail against us, or disturb
Our cheerful faith, that all which we behold
Is full of blessings. Therefore let the moon
Shine on thee in thy solitary walk;   135
And let the misty mountain-winds be free
To blow against thee: and, in after years,
When these wild ecstasies shall be matured
Into a sober pleasure; when thy mind
Shall be a mansion for all lovely forms,   140
Thy memory be as a dwelling-place
For all sweet sounds and harmonies; oh! then,
If solitude, or fear, or pain, or grief,
Should be thy portion, with what healing
    thoughts
Of tender joy wilt thou remember me,   145
And these my exhortations! Nor, perchance—
If I should be where I no more can hear
Thy voice, nor catch from thy wild eyes these
    gleams

Of past existence—wilt thou then forget
That on the banks of this delightful stream 150
We stood together; and that I, so long
A worshiper of Nature, hither came
Unwearied in that service: rather say
With warmer love—oh! with far deeper zeal
Of holier love. Nor wilt thou then forget 155
That after many wanderings, many years
Of absence, these steep woods and lofty cliffs,
And this green pastoral landscape, were to me
More dear, both for themselves and for thy
    sake!
                          (1798)

Strange Fits of Passion Have I Known

This and the four following poems belong to the so-called "Lucy Poems," written in Germany in 1799. Who Lucy was is unknown.

Strange fits of passion have I known:
And I will dare to tell,
But in the Lover's ear alone,
What once to me befell.

When she I loved looked every day   5
Fresh as a rose in June,
I to her cottage bent my way,
Beneath an evening-moon.

Upon the moon I fixed my eye,
All over the wide lea;   10
With quickening pace my horse drew nigh
Those paths so dear to me.

And now we reached the orchard-plot;
And, as we climbed the hill,
The sinking moon to Lucy's cot   15
Came near, and nearer still.

In one of those sweet dreams I slept,
Kind Nature's gentlest boon!
And all the while my eyes I kept
On the descending moon.   20

My horse moved on; hoof after hoof
He raised, and never stopped:

---

115. **Friend,** Wordsworth's sister Dorothy. 125. **inform,** inspire.

149. **past existence,** the poet's past life.

When down behind the cottage roof,
  At once, the bright moon dropped.

What fond and wayward thoughts will slide 25
Into a Lover's head!
"O mercy!" to myself I cried,
"If Lucy should be dead!"

                        (*1799*; 1800)

She Dwelt Among the Untrodden Ways

She dwelt among the untrodden ways
  Beside the springs of Dove,
A Maid whom there were none to praise
  And very few to love:

A violet by a mossy stone   5
  Half hidden from the eye!
—Fair as a star, when only one
  Is shining in the sky.

She lived unknown, and few could know
  When Lucy ceased to be;   10
But she is in her grave, and, oh,
  The difference to me!

                        (*1799*; 1800)

I Traveled Among Unknown Men

I traveled among unknown men,
  In lands beyond the sea;
Nor, England! did I know till then
  What love I bore to thee.

'Tis past, that melancholy dream!   5
  Nor will I quit thy shore
A second time; for still I seem
  To love thee more and more.

Among thy mountains did I feel
  The joy of my desire;   10
And she I cherished turned her wheel
  Beside an English fire.

She Dwelt Among the Untrodden Ways. 2. **Dove**, a river forming part of the boundary between the counties of Derby and Stafford.

Thy mornings showed, thy nights concealed
  The bowers where Lucy played;
And thine too is the last green field   15
  That Lucy's eyes surveyed.

                        (*1799*; 1807)

Three Years She Grew in Sun and Shower

Three years she grew in sun and shower,
Then Nature said, "A lovelier flower
On earth was never sown;
This Child I to myself will take;
She shall be mine, and I will make   5
A Lady of my own.

"Myself will to my darling be
Both law and impulse: and with me
The Girl, in rock and plain,
In earth and heaven, in glade and bower,   10
Shall feel an overseeing power
To kindle or restrain.

"She shall be sportive as the fawn
That wild with glee across the lawn,
Or up the mountain springs;   15
And hers shall be the breathing balm,
And hers the silence and the calm
Of mute insensate things.

"The floating clouds their state shall lend
To her; for her the willow bend;   20
Nor shall she fail to see
Even in the motions of the Storm
Grace that shall mold the Maiden's form
By silent sympathy.

"The stars of midnight shall be dear   25
To her; and she shall lean her ear
In many a secret place
Where rivulets dance their wayward round,
And beauty born of murmuring sound
Shall pass into her face.   30

"And vital feelings of delight
Shall rear her form to stately height,
Her virgin bosom swell;

Such thoughts to Lucy I will give
While she and I together live
Here in this happy dell." 35

Thus Nature spake.—The work was done.—
How soon my Lucy's race was run!
She died, and left to me
This heath, this calm, and quiet scene; 40
The memory of what has been,
And never more will be.

(*1799;* 1800)

A Slumber Did My Spirit Seal

A slumber did my spirit seal;
  I had no human fears:
She seemed a thing that could not feel
  The touch of earthly years.

No motion has she now, no force; 5
  She neither hears nor sees;
Rolled round in earth's diurnal course,
  With rocks, and stones, and trees.

(*1799;* 1800)

from *The Prelude*

Wordsworth thus describes the occasion and the plan of *The Prelude* in the preface to *The Excursion:*

"Several years ago, when the author retired to his native mountains with the hope of being enabled to construct a literary work that might live, it was a reasonable thing that he should take a review of his own mind, and examine how far nature and education had qualified him for such an employment. As subsidiary to this preparation, he undertook to record, in verse, the origin and progress of his own powers, as far as he was acquainted with them. That work, addressed to a dear friend, most distinguished for his knowledge and genius, and to whom the author's intellect is deeply indebted, has been long finished; and the result of the investigation which gave rise to it, was a determination to compose a philosophical poem, containing views of man, nature, and society, and to be entitled *The Recluse*, as having for its principal subject the sensations and opinions of a poet living in retirement.

"The preparatory poem [*The Prelude*] is biographical, and conducts the history of the author's mind to the point when he was emboldened to hope that his faculties were sufficiently matured for entering upon the arduous labor which he had proposed to himself; and the two works [*The Prelude* and *The Recluse*] have the same kind of relation to each other, if he may so express himself, as the ante-chapel has to the body of a Gothic church. Continuing this allusion, he may be permitted to add, that his minor pieces, which have been long before the public, when they shall be properly arranged, will be found by the attentive reader to have such connection with the main work as may give them claim to be likened to the little cells, oratories, and sepulchral recesses, ordinarily included in those edifices."

The Prelude was to be the introduction to a larger work called *The Recluse;* in this larger work *The Excursion* was to be the second part. The project was not completed, but *The Prelude* and *The Excursion* remain as highly significant autobiographical poems. The "dear friend" to whom *The Prelude* was addressed was Coleridge. The poem was not published until 1850, the year of Wordsworth's death.

BOOK 1. INTRODUCTION — CHILDHOOD AND SCHOOL-TIME

Oh, there is blessing in this gentle breeze,
A visitant that while it fans my cheek
Doth seem half-conscious of the joy it brings
From the green fields, and from yon azure sky.
Whate'er its mission, the soft breeze can come
To none more grateful than to me; escaped 6
From the vast city, where I long had pined
A discontented sojourner: now free,
Free as a bird to settle where I will.

1-45. These lines were written in September, 1795, on the way from Bristol to Racedown, two and one-half years before the idea of *The Prelude* was conceived.

7. **vast city**, London, where Wordsworth had lived from January to September, 1795.

What dwelling shall receive me? in what
    vale   10
Shall be my harbor? underneath what grove
Shall I take up my home? and what clear
    stream
Shall with its murmur lull me into rest?
The earth is all before me. With a heart
Joyous, nor scared at its own liberty,   15
I look about; and should the chosen guide
Be nothing better than a wandering cloud,
I cannot miss my way. I breathe again!
Trances of thought and mountings of the
    mind
Come fast upon me: it is shaken off,   20
That burthen of my own unnatural self,
The heavy weight of many a weary day
Not mine, and such as were not made for
    me.
Long months of peace (if such bold word
    accord
With any promises of human life),   25
Long months of ease and undisturbed de-
    light
Are mine in prospect; whither shall I turn,
By road or pathway, or through trackless
    field,
Up-hill or down, or shall some floating thing
Upon the river point me out my course?   30

    Dear Liberty! Yet what would it avail
But for a gift that consecrates the joy?
For I, methought, while the sweet breath of
    heaven
Was blowing on my body, felt within
A correspondent breeze, that gently moved   35
With quickening virtue, but is now become
A tempest, a redundant energy,
Vexing its own creation. Thanks to both,
And their congenial powers, that, while they
    join
In breaking up a long-continued frost,   40
Bring with them vernal promises, the hope
Of active days urged on by flying hours—
Days of sweet leisure, taxed with patient
    thought
Abstruse, nor wanting punctual service high,
Matins and vespers of harmonious verse!   45

Thus far, O Friend! did I, not used to
    make
A present joy the matter of a song,
Pour forth that day my soul in measured
    strains
That would not be forgotten, and are here
Recorded: to the open fields I told   50
A prophecy: poetic numbers came
Spontaneously to clothe in priestly robe
A renovated spirit singled out,
Such hope was mine, for holy services.
My own voice cheered me, and, far more, the
    mind's   55
Internal echo of the imperfect sound;
To both I listened, drawing from them both
A cheerful confidence in things to come.

    Content and not unwilling now to give
A respite to this passion, I paced on   60
With brisk and eager steps; and came, at
    length,
To a green shady place, where down I sate
Beneath a tree, slackening my thoughts by
    choice,
And settling into gentler happiness.
'Twas autumn, and a clear and placid day,   65
With warmth, as much as needed, from a sun
Two hours declined toward the west; a day
With silver clouds, and sunshine on the grass,
And in the sheltered and the sheltering grove
A perfect stillness. Many were the thoughts
Encouraged and dismissed, till choice was
    made   71
Of a known Vale, whither my feet should
    turn,
Nor rest till they had reached the very door
Of the one cottage which methought I saw.
No picture of mere memory ever looked   75
So fair; and while upon the fancied scene
I gazed with growing love, a higher power
Than Fancy gave assurance of some work
Of glory there forthwith to be begun,
Perhaps too there performed. Thus long I
    mused,   80
Nor e'er lost sight of what I mused upon,
Save when, amid the stately grove of oaks,
Now here, now there, an acorn, from its cup
Dislodged, through sere leaves rustled, or at
    once

---

14. **earth ... me,** one of the many echoes of Milton in the poem. Cf. *Paradise Lost,* XII, 646 (Vol. I, p. 766): "The world was all before them, where to choose." 21-23. Cf. *Lines Composed a Few Miles Above Tintern Abbey,* 37-41, p. 122.

46. **Friend,** Samuel Taylor Coleridge. 72. **Vale,** Racedown.

To the bare earth dropped with a startling
    sound.   85
From that soft couch I rose not, till the sun
Had almost touched the horizon; casting then
A backward glance upon the curling cloud
Of city smoke, by distance ruralized;
Keen as a Truant or a Fugitive,   90
But as a Pilgrim resolute, I took,
Even with the chance equipment of that hour,
The road that pointed toward the chosen
    Vale.
It was a splendid evening, and my soul
Once more made trial of her strength, nor
    lacked   95
Aeolian visitations; but the harp
Was soon defrauded, and the banded host
Of harmony dispersed in straggling sounds,
And lastly utter silence! "Be it so;
Why think of anything but present good?"
So, like a home-bound laborer, I pursued   101
My way beneath the mellowing sun, that shed
Mild influence; nor left in me one wish
Again to bend the Sabbath of that time
To a servile yoke. What need of many
    words?   105
A pleasant loitering journey, through three
    days
Continued, brought me to my hermitage.
I spare to tell of what ensued, the life
In common things—the endless store of
    things,
Rare, or at least so seeming, every day   110
Found all about me in one neighborhood—
The self-congratulation, and, from morn
To night, unbroken cheerfulness serene.
But speedily an earnest longing rose
To brace myself to some determined aim,   115
Reading or thinking; either to lay up
New stores, or rescue from decay the old
By timely interference: and therewith
Came hopes still higher, that with outward life
I might endue some airy phantasies   120
That had been floating loose about for years,
And to such beings temperately deal forth
The many feelings that oppressed my heart.
That hope hath been discouraged; welcome
    light

Dawns from the east, but dawns to disap-
    pear   125
And mock me with a sky that ripens not
Into a steady morning: if my mind,
Remembering the bold promise of the past,
Would gladly grapple with some noble
    theme,
Vain is her wish; where'er she turns she finds
Impediments from day to day renewed.   131

And now it would content me to yield up
Those lofty hopes awhile, for present gifts
Of humbler industry. But, oh, dear Friend!
The Poet, gentle creature as he is,   135
Hath, like the Lover, his unruly times;
His fits when he is neither sick nor well,
Though no distress be near him but his own
Unmanageable thoughts: his mind, best
    pleased
While she as duteous as the mother dove   140
Sits brooding, lives not always to that end,
But like the innocent bird hath goadings on
That drive her as in trouble through the
    groves;
With me is now such passion to be blamed
No otherwise than as it lasts too long.   145

When, as becomes a man who would pre-
    pare
For such an arduous work, I through myself
Make rigorous inquisition, the report
Is often cheering; for I neither seem
To lack that first great gift, the vital soul,   150
Nor general Truths, which are themselves
    a sort
Of Elements and Agents, Under-powers,
Subordinate helpers of the living mind:
Nor am I naked of external things,
Forms, images, nor numerous other aids   155
Of less regard, though won perhaps with toil
And needful to build up a Poet's praise.
Time, place, and manners do I seek, and these
Are found in plenteous store, but nowhere
    such
As may be singled out with steady choice;   160
No little band of yet remembered names
Whom I, in perfect confidence, might hope
To summon back from lonesome banishment,
And make them dwellers in the hearts of men
Now living, or to live in future years.   165

89. **city smoke,** from Bristol. 96. **Aeolian visitations,** thoughts that come and go with the breeze, as sounds are produced when the wind strikes the Aeolian harp, named after Aeolus, god of winds. 104. **Sabbath,** calm, restfulness.

Sometimes the ambitious Power of choice, mistaking
Proud spring-tide swellings for a regular sea,
Will settle on some British theme, some old
Romantic tale by Milton left unsung;
More often turning to some gentle place 170
Within the groves of Chivalry, I pipe
To shepherd swains, or seated harp in hand,
Amid reposing knights by a river side
Or fountain, listen to the grave reports
Of dire enchantments faced and overcome 175
By the strong mind, and tales of warlike feats,
Where spear encountered spear, and sword with sword
Fought, as if conscious of the blazonry
That the shield bore, so glorious was the strife;
Whence inspiration for a song that winds 180
Through ever-changing scenes of votive quest
Wrongs to redress, harmonious tribute paid
To patient courage and unblemished truth,
To firm devotion, zeal unquenchable,
And Christian meekness hallowing faithful loves. 185
Sometimes, more sternly moved, I would relate
How vanquished Mithridates northward passed,
And, hidden in the cloud of years, became
Odin, the Father of a race by whom
Perished the Roman Empire: how the friends 190
And followers of Sertorius, out of Spain
Flying, found shelter in the Fortunate Isles,
And left their usages, their arts and laws,
To disappear by a slow gradual death,
To dwindle and to perish one by one, 195
Starved in those narrow bounds: but not the soul
Of Liberty, which fifteen hundred years
Survived, and, when the European came
With skill and power that might not be withstood,
Did, like a pestilence, maintain its hold 200
And wasted down by glorious death that race
Of natural heroes: or I would record
How, in tyrannic times, some high-souled man,
Unnamed among the chronicles of kings,
Suffered in silence for Truth's sake; or tell, 205
How that one Frenchman, through continued force
Of meditation on the inhuman deeds
Of those who conquered first the Indian Isles,
Went single in his ministry across
The Ocean; not to comfort the oppressed, 210
But, like a thirsty wind, to roam about
Withering the Oppressor: how Gustavus sought
Help at his need in Dalecarlia's mines:
How Wallace fought for Scotland; left the name 214
Of Wallace to be found, like a wild flower,
All over his dear Country; left the deeds
Of Wallace, like a family of Ghosts,
To people the steep rocks and river banks,
Her natural sanctuaries, with a local soul
Of independence and stern liberty. 220
Sometimes it suits me better to invent
A tale from my own heart, more near akin
To my own passions and habitual thoughts;
Some variegated story, in the main
Lofty, but the unsubstantial structure melts
Before the very sun that brightens it, 226
Mist into air dissolving! Then a wish,
My last and favorite aspiration, mounts
With yearning toward some philosophic song
Of Truth that cherishes our daily life; 230
With meditations passionate from deep
Recesses in man's heart, immortal verse
Thoughtfully fitted to the Orphean lyre;
But from this awful burthen I full soon

168. **British theme . . . unsung.** Milton seriously considered writing an epic on the history of Britain before the Conquest and also a poem on King Arthur. 171. **groves of Chivalry,** an allusion to Spenser's *Faerie Queene*, VI. 187. **Mithridates,** King of Pontus, Asia Minor (120-63 B.C.); he was defeated by Pompey in 66 B.C. His identification with Odin, the supreme deity of Scandinavian mythology, was suggested to Wordsworth by a passage in Gibbon's *Decline and Fall of the Roman Empire* (Chap. 10). Gibbon mentions Odin as chief of a tribe of barbarians who retreated to Sweden and laid the foundations for the overthrow of the Roman Empire by the Goths in the 3rd and 4th centuries. 191. **Sertorius,** a famous Roman general who resisted tyrannical rule for eight years, until he was assassinated in 72 B.C. On one of his journeys he landed in Spain, where he learned from sailors about the Fortunate Islands in the Atlantic, supposed to be the Canaries. Wordsworth read about him in Plutarch's *Lives.*

206. **Frenchman,** Dominique de Gourges, who sailed to Florida in 1568 to avenge the massacre of French colonists by the Spaniards. 212. **Gustavus,** Gustavus I of Sweden (1496-1560), who freed his country from the tyranny of Denmark. He worked out his plans in Dalecarlia, a mining district in the west midlands of Sweden, where he often disguised himself as a peasant or a miner to escape capture by the Danes. 215. **Wallace,** William Wallace (d. 1305), celebrated Scottish hero and patriot. 233. **Orphean lyre,** an allusion to the famous lyre of Orpheus, mythological poet and musician, whose music could charm beasts and move trees and stones.

Take refuge and beguile myself with trust 235
That mellower years will bring a riper mind
And clearer insight. Thus my days are passed
In contradiction; with no skill to part
Vague longing, haply bred by want of power,
From paramount impulse not to be withstood, 240
A timorous capacity from prudence,
From circumspection, infinite delay.
Humility and modest awe themselves
Betray me, serving often for a cloak
To a more subtle selfishness; that now 245
Locks every function up in blank reserve,
Now dupes me, trusting to an anxious eye
That with intrusive restlessness beats off
Simplicity and self-presented truth.
Ah! better far than this, to stray about 250
Voluptuously through fields and rural walks,
And ask no record of the hours, resigned
To vacant musing, unreproved neglect
Of all things, and deliberate holiday.
Far better never to have heard the name 255
Of zeal and just ambition, than to live
Baffled and plagued by a mind that every hour
Turns recreant to her task; takes heart again,
Then feels immediately some hollow thought
Hang like an interdict upon her hopes. 260
This is my lot; for either still I find
Some imperfection in the chosen theme,
Or see of absolute accomplishment
Much wanting, so much wanting, in myself,
That I recoil and droop, and seek repose 265
In listlessness from vain perplexity,
Unprofitably traveling toward the grave,
Like a false steward who hath much received
And renders nothing back.
      Was it for this
That one, the fairest of all rivers, loved 270
To blend his murmurs with my nurse's song,
And, from his alder shades and rocky falls,
And from his fords and shallows, sent a voice
That flowed along my dreams? For this, didst thou,
O Derwent! winding among grassy holms 275
Where I was looking on, a babe in arms,
Make ceaseless music that composed my thoughts
To more than infant softness, giving me
Amid the fretful dwellings of mankind
A foretaste, a dim earnest, of the calm 280
That Nature breathes among the hills and groves.

When he had left the mountains and received
On his smooth breast the shadow of those towers
That yet survive, a shattered monument
Of feudal sway, the bright blue river passed
Along the margin of our terrace walk; 286
A tempting playmate whom we dearly loved.
Oh, many a time have I, a five years' child,
In a small mill-race severed from his stream,
Made one long bathing of a summer's day;
Basked in the sun, and plunged and basked again 291
Alternate, all a summer's day, or scoured
The sandy fields, leaping through flowery groves
Of yellow ragwort; or when rock and hill,
The woods, and distant Skiddaw's lofty height, 295
Were bronzed with deepest radiance, stood alone
Beneath the sky, as if I had been born
On Indian plains, and from my mother's hut
Had run abroad in wantonness, to sport,
A naked savage, in the thunder-shower. 300

Fair seed-time had my soul, and I grew up
Fostered alike by beauty and by fear:
Much favored in my birthplace, and no less
In that belovéd Vale to which erelong
We were transplanted—there were we let loose 305
For sports of wider range. Ere I had told
Ten birthdays, when among the mountain-slopes
Frost, and the breath of frosty wind, had snapped
The last autumnal crocus, 'twas my joy
With store of springes o'er my shoulder hung

---

268. **false steward**, an allusion to the parable of the talents. Two of the three stewards were faithful to their trust, but the third was false. See *Matthew*, 25:14-30. 270. **fairest of all rivers**, Derwent. Wordsworth was born at Cockermouth situated at the junction of two rivers—Cocker and Derwent. 275. **holms**, low flat lands.

283. **those towers**, of Cockermouth Castle. 294. **ragwort**, a common European weed. 295. **Skiddaw**, a mountain in Cumberlandshire. 304. **Vale**, Esthwaite, Lancashire, in which the village of Hawkshead, where Wordsworth attended school, is situated. 310. **springes**, snares, traps.

To range the open heights where woodcocks
    run 311
Among the smooth green turf. Through half
    the night,
Scudding away from snare to snare, I plied
That anxious visitation;—moon and stars
Were shining o'er my head. I was alone, 315
And seemed to be a trouble to the peace
That dwelt among them. Sometimes it befell
In these night wanderings, that a strong de-
    sire
O'erpowered my better reason, and the bird
Which was the captive of another's toil 320
Became my prey; and when the deed was
    done,
I heard among the solitary hills
Low breathings coming after me, and sounds
Of undistinguishable motion, steps
Almost as silent as the turf they trod. 325

Nor less when spring had warmed the cul-
    tured Vale,
Roved we as plunderers where the mother-
    bird
Had in high places built her lodge; though
    mean
Our object and inglorious, yet the end
Was not ignoble. Oh! when I have hung 330
Above the raven's nest, by knots of grass
And half-inch fissures in the slippery rock
But ill sustained, and almost (so it seemed)
Suspended by the blast that blew amain,
Shouldering the naked crag, oh, at that time
While on the perilous ridge I hung alone, 336
With what strange utterance did the loud dry
    wind
Blow through my ear! the sky seemed not
    a sky
Of earth—and with what motion moved the
    clouds!

Dust as we are, the immortal spirit grows
Like harmony in music; there is a dark 341
Inscrutable workmanship that reconciles
Discordant elements, makes them cling to-
    gether
In one society. How strange that all
The terrors, pains, and early miseries, 345
Regrets, vexations, lassitudes interfused

326. **Vale**, Yewdale, a valley near Hawkshead.

Within my mind, should e'er have borne a
    part,
And that a needful part, in making up
The calm existence that is mine when I
Am worthy of myself! Praise to the end! 350
Thanks to the means which Nature deigned
    to employ;
Whether her fearless visitings, or those
That came with soft alarm, like hurtless light
Opening the peaceful clouds; or she may use
Severer interventions, ministry 355
More palpable, as best might suit her aim.

One summer evening (led by her) I found
A little boat tied to a willow tree
Within a rocky cave, its usual home.
Straight I unloosed her chain, and stepping
    in 360
Pushed from the shore. It was an act of
    stealth
And troubled pleasure, nor without the voice
Of mountain-echoes did my boat move on;
Leaving behind her still, on either side,
Small circles glittering idly in the moon, 365
Until they melted all into one track
Of sparkling light. But now, like one who
    rows,
Proud of his skill, to reach a chosen point
With an unswerving line, I fixed my view
Upon the summit of a craggy ridge, 370
The horizon's utmost boundary; for above
Was nothing but the stars and the gray sky.
She was an elfin pinnace; lustily
I dipped my oars into the silent lake,
And, as I rose upon the stroke, my boat 375
Went heaving through the water like a swan;
When, from behind that craggy steep till then
The horizon's bound, a huge peak, black and
    huge,
As if with voluntary power instinct 379
Upreared its head. I struck and struck again,
And growing still in stature the grim shape
Towered up between me and the stars, and
    still,
For so it seemed, with purpose of its own
And measured motion like a living thing,
Strode after me. With trembling oars I
    turned, 385
And through the silent water stole my way

357. **her**, Nature. 373. **pinnace**, a light sailing vessel.

Back to the covert of the willow tree;
There in her mooring-place I left my bark—
And through the meadows homeward went, in grave
And serious mood; but after I had seen   390
That spectacle, for many days, my brain
Worked with a dim and undetermined sense
Of unknown modes of being; o'er my thoughts
There hung a darkness, call it solitude
Or blank desertion. No familiar shapes   395
Remained, no pleasant images of trees,
Of sea or sky, no colors of green fields;
But huge and mighty forms, that do not live
Like living men, moved slowly through the mind
By day, and were a trouble to my dreams.   400

 Wisdom and Spirit of the universe!
Thou Soul that art the eternity of thought,
That givest to forms and images a breath
And everlasting motion, not in vain
By day or star-light thus from my first dawn
Of childhood didst thou intertwine for me   406
The passions that build up our human soul;
Not with the mean and vulgar works of man,
But with high objects, with enduring things—
With life and nature—purifying thus   410
The elements of feeling and of thought,
And sanctifying, by such discipline,
Both pain and fear, until we recognize
A grandeur in the beatings of the heart.
Nor was this fellowship vouchsafed to me   415
With stinted kindness. In November days,
When vapors rolling down the valley made
A lonely scene more lonesome, among woods,
At noon and 'mid the calm of summer nights,
When, by the margin of the trembling lake,   420
Beneath the gloomy hills homeward I went
In solitude, such intercourse was mine;
Mine was it in the fields both day and night,
And by the waters, all the summer long.

 And in the frosty season, when the sun   425
Was set, and visible for many a mile
The cottage windows blazed through twilight gloom,
I heeded not their summons: happy time
It was indeed for all of us—for me
It was a time of rapture! Clear and loud   430
The village clock tolled six—I wheeled about,
Proud and exulting like an untired horse
That cares not for his home. All shod with steel,
We hissed along the polished ice in games
Confederate, imitative of the chase   435
And woodland pleasures—the resounding horn,
The pack loud chiming, and the hunted hare.
So through the darkness and the cold we flew,
And not a voice was idle; with the din
Smitten, the precipices rang aloud;   440
The leafless trees and every icy crag
Tinkled like iron; while far distant hills
Into the tumult sent an alien sound
Of melancholy not unnoticed, while the stars
Eastward were sparkling clear, and in the west   445
The orange sky of evening died away.
Not seldom from the uproar I retired
Into a silent bay, or sportively
Glanced sideway, leaving the tumultuous throng,
To cut across the reflex of a star   450
That fled, and, flying still before me, gleamed
Upon the glassy plain; and oftentimes,
When we had given our bodies to the wind,
And all the shadowy banks on either side
Came sweeping through the darkness, spinning still   455
The rapid line of motion, then at once
Have I, reclining back upon my heels,
Stopped short; yet still the solitary cliffs
Wheeled by me—even as if the earth had rolled
With visible motion her diurnal round!   460
Behind me did they stretch in solemn train,
Feebler and feebler, and I stood and watched
Till all was tranquil as a dreamless sleep.

 Ye Presences of Nature in the sky
And on the earth! Ye Visions of the hills!   465
And Souls of lonely places! can I think
A vulgar hope was yours when ye employed
Such ministry, when ye through many a year
Haunting me thus among my boyish sports,
On caves and trees, upon the woods and hills,   470

Impressed upon all forms the characters
Of danger or desire; and thus did make
The surface of the universal earth
With triumph and delight, with hope and fear,
Work like a sea?
     Not uselessly employed,
Might I pursue this theme through every change 476
Of exercise and play, to which the year
Did summon us in his delightful round.

 We were a noisy crew; the sun in heaven
Beheld not vales more beautiful than ours; 480
Nor saw a band in happiness and joy
Richer, or worthier of the ground they trod.
I could record with no reluctant voice
The woods of autumn, and their hazel bowers
With milk-white clusters hung; the rod and line, 485
True symbol of hope's foolishness, whose strong
And unreproved enchantment led us on
By rocks and pools shut out from every star,
All the green summer, to forlorn cascades
Among the windings hid of mountain brooks.
—Unfading recollections! at this hour 491
The heart is almost mine with which I felt,
From some hill-top on sunny afternoons,
The paper kite high among fleecy clouds
Pull at her rein like an impetuous courser; 495
Or, from the meadows sent on gusty days,
Beheld her breast the wind, then suddenly
Dashed headlong, and rejected by the storm.

 Ye lowly cottages wherein we dwelt,
A ministration of your own was yours; 500
Can I forget you, being as you were
So beautiful among the pleasant fields
In which ye stood? or can I here forget
The plain and seemly countenance with which
Ye dealt out your plain comforts? Yet had ye
Delights and exultations of your own. 506
Eager and never weary we pursued
Our home-amusements by the warm peat-fire
At evening, when with pencil, and smooth slate
In square divisions parceled out and all 510
With crosses and with ciphers scribbled o'er,
We schemed and puzzled, head opposed to head
In strife too humble to be named in verse;
Or round the naked table, snow-white deal,
Cherry or maple, sate in close array, 515
And to the combat, Loo or Whist, led on
A thick-ribbed army; not, as in the world,
Neglected and ungratefully thrown by
Even for the very service they had wrought,
But husbanded through many a long campaign. 520
Uncouth assemblage was it, where no few
Had changed their functions; some, plebeian cards
Which Fate, beyond the promise of their birth,
Had dignified, and called to represent
The persons of departed potentates. 525
Oh, with what echoes on the board they fell!
Ironic diamonds—clubs, hearts, diamonds, spades,
A congregation piteously akin!
Cheap matter offered they to boyish wit,
Those sooty knaves, precipitated down 530
With scoffs and taunts, like Vulcan out of heaven:
The paramount ace, a moon in her eclipse,
Queens gleaming through their splendor's last decay,
And monarchs surly at the wrongs sustained
By royal visages. Meanwhile abroad 535
Incessant rain was falling, or the frost
Raged bitterly, with keen and silent tooth;
And, interrupting oft that eager game,
From under Esthwaite's splitting fields of ice
The pent-up air, struggling to free itself, 540
Gave out to meadow-grounds and hills a loud
Protracted yelling, like the noise of wolves
Howling in troops along the Bothnic Main.

 Nor, sedulous as I have been to trace
How Nature by extrinsic passion first 545
Peopled the mind with forms sublime or fair,
And made me love them, may I here omit
How other pleasures have been mine, and joys

---

514. **deal**, pine or fir wood. 516. **Loo**, a card game played for stakes. Cf. the card game described in Pope's *The Rape of the Lock*, 3, 25 ff. (Vol. I, p. 10777). 531. **Vulcan**, the blacksmith of the Gods. 543. **Bothnic Main**, the Baltic Sea, between Sweden and Finland.

Of subtler origin; how I have felt,
Not seldom even in that tempestuous time, 550
Those hallowed and pure emotions of the sense
Which seem, in their simplicity, to own
An intellectual charm; that calm delight
Which, if I err not, surely must belong
To those first-born affinities that fit 555
Our new existence to existing things,
And, in our dawn of being, constitute
The bond of union between life and joy.

Yes, I remember when the changeful earth,
And twice five summers on my mind had stamped 560
The faces of the moving year, even then
I held unconscious intercourse with beauty
Old as creation, drinking in a pure
Organic pleasure from the silver wreaths
Of curling mist, or from the level plain 565
Of waters colored by impending clouds.

The sands of Westmoreland, the creeks and bays
Of Cumbria's rocky limits, they can tell
How, when the Sea threw off his evening shade
And to the shepherd's hut on distant hills 570
Sent welcome notice of the rising moon,
How I have stood, to fancies such as these
A stranger, linking with the spectacle
No conscious memory of a kindred sight,
And bringing with me no peculiar sense 575
Of quietness or peace; yet have I stood,
Even while mine eye hath moved o'er many a league
Of shining water, gathering as it seemed,
Through every hair-breadth in that field of light,
New pleasure like a bee among the flowers.

Thus oft amid those fits of vulgar joy 581
Which, through all seasons, on a child's pursuits
Are prompt attendants, 'mid that giddy bliss
Which, like a tempest, works along the blood
And is forgotten; even then I felt 585

556. new . . . things. Cf. *Ode on Intimations of Immortality*, p. 160. 568. **Cumbria**, Cumberlandshire, most of which made up the ancient British Kingdom of Cumbria.

Gleams like the flashing of a shield; the earth
And common face of Nature spake to me
Rememberable things; sometimes, 'tis true,
By chance collisions and quaint accidents
(Like those ill-sorted unions, work supposed
Of evil-minded fairies), yet not vain 591
Nor profitless, if haply they impressed
Collateral objects and appearances,
Albeit lifeless then, and doomed to sleep
Until maturer seasons called them forth 595
To impregnate and to elevate the mind.
—And if the vulgar joy by its own weight
Wearied itself out of the memory,
The scenes which were a witness of that joy
Remained in their substantial lineaments 600
Depicted on the brain, and to the eye
Were visible, a daily sight; and thus
By the impressive discipline of fear,
By pleasure and repeated happiness,
So frequently repeated, and by force 605
Of obscure feelings representative
Of things forgotten, these same scenes so bright,
So beautiful, so majestic in themselves,
Though yet the day was distant, did become
Habitually dear, and all their forms 610
And changeful colors by invisible links
Were fastened to the affections.
                                    I began
My story early—not misled, I trust,
By an infirmity of love for days
Disowned by memory—ere the birth of spring 615
Planting my snowdrops among winter snows:
Nor will it seem to thee, O Friend! so prompt
In sympathy, that I have lengthened out
With fond and feeble tongue a tedious tale.
Meanwhile, my hope has been that I might fetch 620
Invigorating thoughts from former years;
Might fix the wavering balance of my mind,
And haply meet reproaches too, whose power
May spur me on, in manhood now mature,
To honorable toil. Yet should these hopes 625
Prove vain, and thus should neither I be taught
To understand myself, nor thou to know
With better knowledge how the heart was framed

Of him thou lovest; need I dread from thee
Harsh judgments, if the song be loath to
  quit   630
Those recollected hours that have the charm
Of visionary things, those lovely forms
And sweet sensations that throw back our
  life,
And almost make remotest infancy
A visible scene, on which the sun is shining?

    One end at least hath been attained; my
  mind   636
Hath been revived, and if this genial mood
Desert me not, forthwith shall be brought
  down
Through later years the story of my life. 639
The road lies plain before me;—'tis a theme
Single and of determined bounds; and hence
I choose it rather at this time, than work
Of ampler or more varied argument,
Where I might be discomfited and lost: 644
And certain hopes are with me, that to
  thee
This labor will be welcome, honored Friend!

BOOK 5. BOOKS

When Contemplation, like the night-calm felt
Through earth and sky, spreads widely, and
  sends deep
Into the soul its tranquillizing power,
Even then I sometimes grieve for thee, O
  Man,
Earth's paramount Creature! not so much for
  woes   5
That thou endurest; heavy though that
  weight be,
Cloud-like it mounts, or touched with light
  divine
Doth melt away; but for those palms
  achieved,
Through length of time, by patient exercise
Of study and hard thought; there, there, it is
That sadness finds its fuel. Hitherto,   11
In progress through this Verse, my mind hath
  looked
Upon the speaking face of earth and heaven
As her prime teacher, intercourse with man
Established by the sovereign Intellect,   15
Who through that bodily image hath dif-
  fused,
As might appear to the eye of fleeting time,
A deathless spirit. Thou also, man! hast
  wrought,
For commerce of thy nature with herself,
Things that aspire to unconquerable life;   20
And yet we feel—we cannot choose but feel—
That they must perish. Tremblings of the
  heart
It gives, to think that our immortal being
No more shall need such garments; and yet
  man,
As long as he shall be the child of earth, 25
Might almost "weep to have" what he may
  lose,
Nor be himself extinguished, but survive,
Abject, depressed, forlorn, disconsolate.
A thought is with me sometimes, and I say—
Should the whole frame of earth by inward
  throes   30
Be wrenched, or fire come down from far to
  scorch
Her pleasant habitations, and dry up
Old Ocean, in his bed left singed and bare,
Yet would the living Presence still subsist
Victorious, and composure would ensue,   35
And kindlings like the morning—presage sure
Of day returning and of life revived.
But all the meditations of mankind,
Yea, all the adamantine holds of truth
By reason built, or passion, which itself 40
Is highest reason in a soul sublime;
The consecrated works of Bard and Sage,
Sensuous or intellectual, wrought by men,
Twin laborers and heirs of the same hopes;
Where would they be? Oh! why hath not
  the Mind   45
Some element to stamp her image on
In nature somewhat nearer to her own?
Why, gifted with such powers to send abroad
Her spirit, must it lodge in shrines so frail?

    One day, when from my lips a like com-
  plaint   50
Had fallen in presence of a studious friend,
He with a smile made answer, that in truth
'Twas going far to seek disquietude;

26. **"weep to have,"** from Shakespeare's *Sonnet* 64, l. 14 (Vol I, p. 493).

But on the front of his reproof confessed
That he himself had oftentimes given way 55
To kindred hauntings. Whereupon I told,
That once in the stillness of a summer's noon,
While I was seated in a rocky cave
By the sea-side, perusing, so it chanced,
The famous history of the errant knight 60
Recorded by Cervantes, these same thoughts
Beset me, and to height unusual rose,
While listlessly I sate, and, having closed
The book, had turned my eyes toward the wide sea.
On poetry and geometric truth, 65
And their high privilege of lasting life,
From all internal injury exempt,
I mused; upon these chiefly: and at length,
My senses yielding to the sultry air,
Sleep seized me, and I passed into a dream. 70
I saw before me stretched a boundless plain
Of sandy wilderness, all black and void,
And as I looked around, distress and fear
Came creeping over me, when at my side,
Close at my side, an uncouth shape appeared
Upon a dromedary, mounted high, 76
He seemed an Arab of the Bedouin tribes:
A lance he bore, and underneath one arm
A stone, and in the opposite hand a shell
Of a surpassing brightness. At the sight 80
Much I rejoiced, not doubting but a guide
Was present, one who with unerring skill
Would through the desert lead me; and while yet
I looked and looked, self-questioned what this freight
Which the new-comer carried through the waste 85
Could mean, the Arab told me that the stone
(To give it in the language of the dream)
Was "Euclid's Elements"; and "This," said he,
"Is something of more worth"; and at the word
Stretched forth the shell, so beautiful in shape, 90
In color so resplendent, with command
That I should hold it to my ear. I did so,
And heard that instant in an unknown tongue,
Which yet I understood, articulate sounds,
A loud prophetic blast of harmony; 95
An Ode, in passion uttered, which foretold
Destruction to the children of the earth
By deluge, now at hand. No sooner ceased
The song, than the Arab with calm look declared
That all would come to pass of which the voice 100
Had given forewarning, and that he himself
Was going then to bury those two books:
The one that held acquaintance with the stars,
And wedded soul to soul in purest bond
Of reason, undisturbed by space or time; 105
The other that was a god, yea many gods,
Had voices more than all the winds, with power
To exhilarate the spirit, and to soothe,
Through every clime, the heart of human kind.
While this was uttering, strange as it may seem, 110
I wondered not, although I plainly saw
The one to be a stone, the other a shell;
Nor doubted once but that they both were books,
Having a perfect faith in all that passed.
Far stronger, now, grew the desire I felt 115
To cleave unto this man; but when I prayed
To share his enterprise, he hurried on
Reckless of me; I followed, not unseen,
For oftentimes he cast a backward look, 119
Grasping his twofold treasure.—Lance in rest,
He rode, I keeping pace with him; and now
He, to my fancy, had become the knight
Whose tale Cervantes tells; yet not the knight,
But was an Arab of the desert too;
Of these was neither, and was both at once.
His countenance, meanwhile, grew more disturbed; 126
And, looking backwards when he looked, mine eyes
Saw, over half the wilderness diffused,
A bed of glittering light. I asked the cause:
"It is," said he, "the waters of the deep 130
Gathering upon us"; quickening then the pace

---

60. **errant knight,** wandering knight, Don Quixote, the gaunt hero of *Don Quixote*, a Spanish romance by Cervantes (1547-1616). 77. **Bedouin tribes,** nomadic Arabs of Syria, Arabia, and northern Africa. 88. **"Euclid's Elements,"** a book of mathematics, derived from Euclid, famous Greek geometrician (c. 300 B.C.).

Of the unwieldy creature he bestrode,
He left me: I called after him aloud;
He heeded not; but, with his twofold charge
Still in his grasp, before me, full in view, 135
Went hurrying o'er the illimitable waste,
With the fleet waters of a drowning world
In chase of him; whereat I waked in terror,
And saw the sea before me, and the book,
In which I had been reading, at my side. 140

Full often, taking from the world of sleep
This Arab phantom, which I thus beheld,
This semi-Quixote, I to him have given
A substance, fancied him a living man,
A gentle dweller in the desert, crazed 145
By love and feeling, and internal thought
Protracted among endless solitudes;
Have shaped him wandering upon this quest!
Nor have I pitied him; but rather felt
Reverence was due to a being thus employed; 150
And thought that, in the blind and awful lair
Of such a madness, reason did lie couched.
Enow there are on earth to take in charge
Their wives, their children, and their virgin loves,
Or whatsoever else the heart holds dear; 155
Enow to stir for these; yea, will I say,
Contemplating in soberness the approach
Of an event so dire, by signs in earth
Or heaven made manifest, that I could share
That maniac's fond anxiety, and go 160
Upon like errand. Oftentimes at least
Me hath such strong entrancement overcome,
When I have held a volume in my hand,
Poor earthly casket of immortal verse,
Shakespeare, or Milton, laborers divine! 165

Great and benign, indeed, must be the power
Of living nature, which could thus so long
Detain me from the best of other guides
And dearest helpers, left unthanked, unpraised.
Even in the time of lisping infancy, 170
And later down, in prattling childhood, even
While I was traveling back among those days,
How could I ever play an ingrate's part?
Once more should I have made those bowers resound,
By intermingling strains of thankfulness 175
With their own thoughtless melodies; at least
It might have well beseemed me to repeat
Some simply fashioned tale, to tell again,
In slender accents of sweet verse, some tale
That did bewitch me then, and soothes me now. 180
O Friend! O Poet! brother of my soul,
Think not that I could pass along untouched
By these remembrances. Yet wherefore speak?
Why call upon a few weak words to say
What is already written in the hearts 185
Of all that breathe?—what in the path of all
Drops daily from the tongue of every child,
Wherever man is found? The trickling tear
Upon the cheek of listening Infancy
Proclaims it, and the insuperable look 190
That drinks as if it never could be full.

That portion of my story I shall leave
There registered: whatever else of power
Or pleasure sown, or fostered thus, may be
Peculiar to myself, let that remain 195
Where still it works, though hidden from all search
Among the depths of time. Yet is it just
That here, in memory of all books which lay
Their sure foundations in the heart of man,
Whether by native prose, or numerous verse,
That in the name of all inspiréd souls— 201
From Homer the great Thunderer, from the voice
That roars along the bed of Jewish song,
And that more varied and elaborate,
Those trumpet-tones of harmony that shake
Our shores in England—from those loftiest notes 206
Down to the low and wren-like warblings, made
For cottagers and spinners at the wheel,
And sun-burnt travelers resting their tired limbs,
Stretched under wayside hedge-rows, ballad tones, 210
Food for the hungry ears of little ones,

179. some tale. Cf. ll. 341-425 and 477-534. 200. Whether ... verse, from *Paradise Lost*, V, 150. 205. trumpet-tones, i.e., of Milton.

And of old men who have survived their joys—
'Tis just that in behalf of these, the works,
And of the men that framed them, whether known,
Or sleeping nameless in their scattered graves,
That I should here assert their rights, attest 216
Their honors, and should, once for all, pronounce
Their benediction; speak of them as Powers
Forever to be hallowed; only less,
For what we are and what we may become,
Than Nature's self, which is the breath of God, 221
Or His pure Word by miracle revealed.

Rarely and with reluctance would I stoop
To transitory themes, yet I rejoice,
And, by these thoughts admonished, will pour out 225
Thanks with uplifted heart, that I was reared
Safe from an evil which these days have laid
Upon the children of the land, a pest
That might have dried me up, body and soul.
This verse is dedicate to Nature's self, 230
And things that teach as Nature teaches: then,
Oh! where had been the Man, the Poet where,
Where had we been, we two, belovéd Friend!
If in the season of unperilous choice,
In lieu of wandering, as we did, through vales 235
Rich with indigenous produce, open ground
Of Fancy, happy pastures ranged at will,
We had been followed, hourly watched, and noosed,
Each in his several melancholy walk 239
Stringed like a poor man's heifer at its feed,
Led through the lanes in forlorn servitude;
Or rather like a stalléd ox debarred
From touch of growing grass, that may not taste
A flower till it have yielded up its sweets
A prelibation to the mower's scythe. 245

Behold the parent hen amid her brood,

227. **an evil, etc.**, the system of education that inculcated scientific truth and morality through the use of edifying tales and that prematurely appealed to reason rather than stimulating the imagination.

Though fledged and feathered, and well pleased to part
And straggle from her presence, still a brood,
And she herself from the maternal bond
Still undischarged; yet doth she little more 250
Than move with them in tenderness and love,
A center to the circle which they make;
And now and then, alike from need of theirs
And call of her own natural appetites, 254
She scratches, ransacks up the earth for food,
Which they partake at pleasure. Early died
My honored Mother, she who was the heart
And hinge of all our learnings and our loves:
She left us destitute, and, as we might,
Trooping together. Little suits it me 260
To break upon the sabbath of her rest
With any thought that looks at others' blame;
Nor would I praise her but in perfect love.
Hence am I checked: but let me boldly say,
In gratitude, and for the sake of truth, 265
Unheard by her, that she, not falsely taught,
Fetching her goodness rather from times past,
Than shaping novelties for times to come,
Had no presumption, no such jealousy,
Nor did by habit of her thoughts mistrust 270
Our nature, but had virtual faith that He
Who fills the mother's breast with innocent milk
Doth also for our nobler part provide,
Under His great correction and control, 274
As innocent instincts, and as innocent food;
Or draws for minds that are left free to trust
In the simplicities of opening life
Sweet honey out of spurned or dreaded weeds.
This was her creed, and therefore she was pure
From anxious fear of error or mishap, 280
And evil, overweeningly so called;
Was not puffed up by false unnatural hopes,
Nor selfish with unnecessary cares,
Nor with impatience from the season asked
More than its timely produce; rather loved 285
The hours for what they are, than from regard
Glanced on their promises in restless pride.
Such was she—not from faculties more strong

256. **died . . . Mother.** Wordsworth was eight years old when his mother died in March, 1778.

Than others have, but from the times, per-
  haps,
And spot in which she lived, and through a
  grace   290
Of modest meekness, simple-mindedness,
A heart that found benignity and hope,
Being itself benign.

               My drift I fear
Is scarcely obvious; but, that common sense
May try this modern system by its fruits,   295
Leave let me take to place before her sight
A specimen portrayed with faithful hand.
Full early trained to worship seemliness,
This model of a child is never known
To mix in quarrels; that were far beneath   300
Its dignity; with gifts he bubbles o'er
As generous as a fountain; selfishness
May not come near him, nor the little throng
Of fitting pleasures tempt him from his path;
The wandering beggars propagate his name.
Dumb creatures find him tender as a nun, 306
And natural or supernatural fear,
Unless it leap upon him in a dream,
Touches him not. To enhance the wonder,
  see
How arch his notices, how nice his sense   310
Of the ridiculous; not blind is he
To the broad follies of the licensed world,
Yet innocent himself withal, though shrewd,
And can read lectures upon innocence;
A miracle of scientific lore,   315
Ships he can guide across the pathless sea,
And tell you all their cunning; he can read
The inside of the earth, and spell the stars;
He knows the policies of foreign lands;
Can string you names of districts, cities,
  towns,   320
The whole world over, tight as beads of dew
Upon a gossamer thread; he sifts, he weighs:
All things are put to question; he must live
Knowing that he grows wiser every day
Or else not live at all, and seeing too   325
Each little drop of wisdom as it falls
Into the dimpling cistern of his heart:
For this unnatural growth the trainer blame,
Pity the tree.—Poor human vanity,   329
Wert thou extinguished, little would be left
Which he could truly love; but how escape?
For, ever as a thought of purer birth
Rises to lead him toward a better clime,
Some intermeddler still is on the watch
To drive him back, and pound him, like a
  stray,   335
Within the pinfold of his own conceit.
Meanwhile old grandame earth is grieved to
  find
The playthings, which her love designed for
  him,
Unthought of: in their woodland beds the
  flowers
Weep, and the river sides are all forlorn. 340
Oh! give us once again the wishing-cap
Of Fortunatus, and the invisible coat
Of Jack the Giant-killer, Robin Hood,
And Sabra in the forest with St. George!
The child, whose love is here, at least, doth
  reap   345
One precious gain, that he forgets himself.

    These mighty workmen of our later age,
Who, with a broad highway, have over-
  bridged
The froward chaos of futurity,
Tamed to their bidding; they who have the
  skill   350
To manage books, and things, and make
  them act
On infant minds as surely as the sun
Deals with a flower; the keepers of our time,
The guides and wardens of our faculties,
Sages who in their prescience would control
All accidents, and to the very road   356
Which they have fashioned would confine us
  down,
Like engines; when will their presumption
  learn
That in the unreasoning progress of the
  world
A wiser spirit is at work for us,   360
A better eye than theirs, most prodigal
Of blessings, and most studious of our good,
Even in what seem our most unfruitful
  hours?

---

307. **fear . . . not.** Cf. Book 1, ll. 321-414, pp. 130-131.
322. **gossamer**, cobwebs seen on grass and low bushes, especially in the autumn.

342. **Fortunatus,** the hero of a popular European tale; he
received from Fortune an inexhaustible purse and from the
Sultan a wishing cap that transported him to any desired place.
343. **Robin Hood,** a legendary medieval hero in England, celebrated as a bold and chivalrous outlaw. 344. **Sabra,** in old
ballads the king's daughter rescued from the Dragon by St.
George (c. 310), who since the Crusades has been the patron
saint of England.

There was a Boy: ye knew him well, ye cliffs
And islands of Winander!—many a time   365
At evening, when the earliest stars began
To move along the edges of the hills,
Rising or setting, would he stand alone
Beneath the trees or by the glimmering lake,
And there, with fingers interwoven, both hands   370
Pressed closely palm to palm, and to his mouth
Uplifted, he, as through an instrument,
Blew mimic hootings to the silent owls,
That they might answer him; and they would shout
Across the watery vale, and shout again,   375
Responsive to his call, with quivering peals,
And long halloos and screams, and echoes loud,
Redoubled and redoubled, concourse wild
Of jocund din; and, when a lengthened pause
Of silence came and baffled his best skill,   380
Then sometimes, in that silence while he hung
Listening, a gentle shock of mild surprise
Has carried far into his heart the voice
Of mountain torrents; or the visible scene
Would enter unawares into his mind,   385
With all its solemn imagery, its rocks,
Its woods, and that uncertain heaven, received
Into the bosom of the steady lake.

This Boy was taken from his mates, and died
In childhood, ere he was full twelve years old.   390
Fair is the spot, most beautiful the vale
Where he was born; the grassy churchyard hangs
Upon a slope above the village school,
And through that churchyard when my way has led
On summer evenings, I believe that there
A long half hour together I have stood   395
Mute, looking at the grave in which he lies!
Even now appears before the mind's clear eye
That self-same village church; I see her sit
(The thronéd Lady whom erewhile we hailed)   400
On her green hill, forgetful of this Boy
Who slumbers at her feet—forgetful, too,
Of all her silent neighborhood of graves,
And listening only to the gladsome sounds
That, from the rural school ascending, play
Beneath her and about her. May she long   405
Behold a race of young ones like to those
With whom I herded!—(easily, indeed,
We might have fed upon a fatter soil
Of arts and letters—but be that forgiven)—
A race of real children; not too wise,   411
Too learnéd, or too good; but wanton, fresh,
And bandied up and down by love and hate;
Not unresentful where self-justified;
Fierce, moody, patient, venturous, modest, shy;   415
Mad at their sports like withered leaves in winds;
Though doing wrong and suffering, and full oft
Bending beneath our life's mysterious weight
Of pain, and doubt, and fear, yet yielding not
In happiness to the happiest upon earth.   420
Simplicity in habit, truth in speech,
Be these the daily strengtheners of their minds;
May books and Nature be their early joy!
And knowledge, rightly honored with that name—
Knowledge not purchased by the loss of power!   425

Well do I call to mind the very week
When I was first intrusted to the care
Of that sweet Valley; when its paths, its shores,
And brooks were like a dream of novelty
To my half-infant thoughts; that very week,
While I was roving up and down alone,   431
Seeking I knew not what, I chanced to cross
One of those open fields, which, shaped like ears,
Make green peninsulas on Esthwaite's Lake:
Twilight was coming on, yet through the gloom   435
Appeared distinctly on the opposite shore

364-97. This passage was written in Germany in 1798 and published in 1800. The boy may have been John Vickars, who died in 1782. 365. **Winander**, Windermere, a large lake bordering the counties of Westmoreland and Lancaster. 391. **vale**, Esthwaite. 393. **school**, at Hawkshead.

412. **wanton**, carefree, unrestrained.

A heap of garments, as if left by one
Who might have there been bathing. Long I
    watched,
But no one owned them; meanwhile the calm
    lake   439
Grew dark with all the shadows on its breast,
And, now and then, a fish up-leaping snapped
The breathless stillness. The succeeding day,
Those unclaimed garments telling a plain tale
Drew to the spot an anxious crowd; some
    looked
In passive expectation from the shore,   445
While from a boat others hung o'er the deep,
Sounding with grappling irons and long
    poles.
At last, the dead man, 'mid that beauteous
    scene
Of trees and hills and water, bolt upright
Rose, with his ghastly face, a specter shape 450
Of terror; yet no soul-debasing fear,
Young as I was, a child not nine years old,
Possessed me, for my inner eye had seen
Such sights before, among the shining
    streams
Of faery land, the forest of romance.   455
Their spirit hallowed the sad spectacle
With decoration of ideal grace;
A dignity, a smoothness, like the works
Of Grecian art, and purest poesy.

   A precious treasure had I long possessed, 460
A little yellow, canvas-covered book,
A slender abstract of the Arabian tales;
And, from companions in a new abode,
When first I learnt, that this dear prize of
    mine
Was but a block hewn from a mighty
    quarry—   465
That there were four large volumes, laden all
With kindred matter, 'twas to me, in truth,
A promise scarcely earthly. Instantly,
With one not richer than myself, I made
A covenant that each should lay aside   470
The moneys he possessed, and hoard up
    more,
Till our joint savings had amassed enough
To make this book our own. Through several
    months,
In spite of all temptation, we preserved
Religiously that vow; but firmness failed, 475
Nor were we ever masters of our wish.

And when thereafter to my father's house
The holidays returned me there to find
That golden store of books which I had left,
What joy was mine! How often in the
    course   480
Of those glad respites, though a soft west
    wind
Ruffled the waters to the angler's wish,
For a whole day together, have I lain
Down by thy side, O Derwent! murmuring
    stream,
On the hot stones, and in the glaring sun, 485
And there have read, devouring as I read,
Defrauding the day's glory, desperate!
Till with a sudden bound of smart reproach,
Such as an idler deals with in his shame,
I to the sport betook myself again.   490

   A gracious spirit o'er this earth presides,
And o'er the heart of man: invisibly
It comes, to works of unreproved delight,
And tendency benign, directing those
Who care not, know not, think not what they
    do.   495
The tales that charm away the wakeful night
In Araby, romances; legends penned
For solace by dim light of monkish lamps;
Fictions, for ladies of their love, devised
By youthful squires; adventures endless, spun
By the dismantled warrior in old age,   501
Out of the bowels of those very schemes
In which his youth did first extravagate;
These spread like day, and something in the
    shape
Of these will live till man shall be no more. 505
Dumb yearnings, hidden appetites, are ours,
And *they must* have their food. Our child-
    hood sits,
Our simple childhood, sits upon a throne
That hath more power than all the elements.
I guess not what this tells of Being past, 510
Nor what it augurs of the life to come;
But so it is, and, in that dubious hour,
That twilight when we first begin to see
This dawning earth, to recognize, expect,
And, in the long probation that ensues,   515
The time of trial, ere we learn to live
In reconcilement with our stinted powers;
To endure this state of meager vassalage,

---

503. **extravagate**, wander aimlessly. 507-511. Cf. *Ode on Intimations of Immortality*, p. 160.

Unwilling to forego, confess, submit,
Uneasy and unsettled, yoke-fellows 520
To custom, mettlesome, and not yet tamed
And humbled down—oh! then we feel, we feel,
We know where we have friends. Ye dreamers, then,
Forgers of daring tales! we bless you then,
Impostors, drivelers, dotards, as the ape 525
Philosophy will call you: *then* we feel
With what and how great might ye are in league,
Who make our wish our power, our thought a deed,
An empire, a possession—ye whom time 529
And seasons serve; all Faculties—to whom
Earth crouches, the elements are potter's clay,
Space like a heaven filled up with northern lights,
Here, nowhere, there, and everywhere at once.

   Relinquishing this lofty eminence
For ground, though humbler, not the less a tract 535
Of the same isthmus, which our spirits cross
In progress from their native continent
To earth and human life, the Song might dwell
On that delightful time of growing youth
When craving for the marvelous gives way 540
To strengthening love for things that we have seen;
When sober truth and steady sympathies,
Offered to notice by less daring pens,
Take firmer hold of us, and words themselves
Move us with conscious pleasure.
                  I am sad
At thought of raptures now forever flown;
Almost to tears I sometimes could be sad 547
To think of, to read over, many a page,
Poems withal of name, which at that time
Did never fail to entrance me, and are now
Dead in my eyes, dead as a theater 551
Fresh emptied of spectators. Twice five years
Or less I might have seen, when first my mind
With conscious pleasure opened to the charm
Of words in tuneful order, found them sweet 555
For their own *sakes*, a passion, and a power;
And phrases pleased me chosen for delight,
For pomp, or love. Oft, in the public roads
Yet unfrequented, while the morning light
Was yellowing the hill-tops, I went abroad 560
With a dear friend, and for the better part
Of two delightful hours we strolled along
By the still borders of the misty lake,
Repeating favorite verses with one voice,
Or conning more, as happy as the birds 565
That round us chaunted. Well might we be glad,
Lifted above the ground by airy fancies,
More bright than madness or the dreams of wine;
And, though full oft the objects of our love
Were false, and in their splendor overwrought, 570
Yet was there surely then no vulgar power
Working within us—nothing less, in truth,
Than that most noble attribute of man,
Though yet untutored and inordinate,
That wish for something loftier, more adorned,
Than is the common aspect, daily garb, 576
Of human life. What wonder, then, if sounds
Of exultation echoed through the groves!
For, images, and sentiments, and words,
And everything encountered or pursued 580
In that delicious world of poesy,
Kept holiday, a never-ending show,
With music, incense, festival, and flowers!

   Here must we pause: this only let me add,
From heart-experience, and in humblest sense
Of modesty, that he, who in his youth 586
A daily wanderer among woods and fields
With living Nature hath been intimate,
Not only in that raw unpracticed time
Is stirred to ecstasy, as others are, 590
By glittering verse; but further doth receive,
In measure only dealt out to himself,
Knowledge and increase of enduring joy
From the great Nature that exists in works
Of mighty Poets. Visionary power 595
Attends the motions of the viewless winds,
Embodied in the mystery of words:
There, darkness makes abode, and all the host
Of shadowy things work endless changes—there,
As in a mansion like their proper home, 600

561. **dear friend**, John Fleming, of Rayrigg, Windermere. See Book 2, ll. 329-338. 563. **lake**, Esthwaite.

Even forms and substances are circumfused
By that transparent veil with light divine,
And, through the turnings intricate of verse,
Present themselves as objects recognized,
In flashes, and with glory not their own.

(1795-1805; 1850)

Michael

In a letter to his friend Thomas Poole (1801) Wordsworth says that in this poem he "attempted to give a picture of a man, of strong mind and lively sensibility, agitated by two of the most powerful affections of the human heart: the parental affection and the love of property (*landed* property), including the feelings of inheritance, home, and personal and family independence." In a letter to Charles James Fox (Jan. 14, 1801) he states that the poem was "written with a view to show that men who do not wear fine clothes can feel deeply."

"The character and circumstances of Luke," says Wordsworth in a note, "were taken from a family to whom had belonged, many years before, the house we lived in at Town-end, along with some fields and woodlands on the eastern shore of Grasmere."

The style of *Michael* is notable for its unadorned simplicity.

If from the public way you turn your steps
Up the tumultuous brook of Green-head Ghyll,
You will suppose that with an upright path
Your feet must struggle; in such bold ascent
The pastoral mountains front you, face to face. 5
But, courage! for around that boisterous brook
The mountains have all opened out themselves,
And made a hidden valley of their own.
No habitation can be seen; but they
Who journey thither find themselves alone 10
With a few sheep, with rocks and stones, and kites
That overhead are sailing in the sky.
It is in truth an utter solitude;
Nor should I have made mention of this Dell
But for one object which you might pass by,
Might see and notice not. Beside the brook 15
Appears a straggling heap of unhewn stones!
And to that simple object appertains
A story—unenriched with strange events,
Yet not unfit, I deem, for the fireside, 20
Or for the summer shade. It was the first
Of those domestic tales that spake to me
Of Shepherds, dwellers in the valleys, men
Whom I already loved—not verily
For their own sakes, but for the fields and hills 25
Where was their occupation and abode.
And hence this Tale, while I was yet a Boy
Careless of books, yet having felt the power
Of Nature, by the gentle agency
Of natural objects, led me on to feel 30
For passions that were not my own, and think
(At random and imperfectly indeed)
On man, the heart of man, and human life.
Therefore, although it be a history
Homely and rude, I will relate the same 35
For the delight of a few natural hearts;
And, with yet fonder feeling, for the sake
Of youthful Poets, who among these hills
Will be my second self when I am gone.

Upon the forest-side in Grasmere Vale 40
There dwelt a Shepherd, Michael was his name;
An old man, stout of heart, and strong of limb.
His bodily frame had been from youth to age
Of an unusual strength: his mind was keen,
Intense, and frugal, apt for all affairs, 45
And in his shepherd's calling he was prompt
And watchful more than ordinary men.
Hence had he learned the meaning of all winds,
Of blasts of every tone; and oftentimes,
When others heeded not, he heard the South 50
Make subterraneous music, like the noise
Of bagpipers on distant Highland hills.

---

2. **Ghyll**, a local name for a short, steep, narrow valley with a stream running through it.

The Shepherd, at such warning, of his flock
Bethought him, and he to himself would say,
"The winds are now devising work for
    me!"   55
And, truly, at all times, the storm, that drives
The traveler to a shelter, summoned him
Up to the mountains: he had been alone
Amid the heart of many thousand mists,
That came to him, and left him, on the
    heights.   60
So lived he till his eightieth year was past.
And grossly that man errs, who should sup-
    pose
That the green valleys, and the streams and
    rocks,
Were things indifferent to the Shepherd's
    thoughts.
Fields, where with cheerful spirits he had
    breathed   65
The common air; hills, which with vigorous
    step
He had so often climbed; which had im-
    pressed
So many incidents upon his mind
Of hardship, skill or courage, joy or fear;
Which, like a book, preserved the memory 70
Of the dumb animals, whom he had saved,
Had fed or sheltered, linking to such acts
The certainty of honorable gain;
Those fields, those hills—what could they
    less? had laid
Strong hold on his affections, were to him 75
A pleasurable feeling of blind love,
The pleasure which there is in life itself.

His days had not been passed in singleness.
His Helpmate was a comely matron, old—
Though younger than himself full twenty
    years.   80
She was a woman of a stirring life,
Whose heart was in her house: two wheels
    she had
Of antique form; this large, for spinning
    wool;
That small, for flax; and, if one wheel had
    rest,
It was because the other was at work.   85
The Pair had but one inmate in their house,
An only Child, who had been born to them
When Michael, telling o'er his years, began
To deem that he was old—in shepherd's
    phrase,
With one foot in the grave. This only Son, 90
With two brave sheep-dogs tried in many a
    storm,
The one of an inestimable worth,
Made all their household. I may truly say,
That they were as a proverb in the vale
For endless industry. When day was gone, 95
And from their occupations out of doors
The Son and Father were come home, even
    then,
Their labor did not cease; unless when all
Turned to the cleanly supper-board, and
    there,
Each with a mess of pottage and skimmed
    milk   100
Sat round the basket piled with oaten cakes,
And their plain home-made cheese. Yet when
    the meal
Was ended, Luke (for so the Son was named)
And his old Father both betook themselves
To such convenient work as might employ 105
Their hands by the fireside; perhaps to card
Wool for the Housewife's spindle, or repair
Some injury done to sickle, flail, or scythe,
Or other implement of house or field.

Down from the ceiling, by the chimney's
    edge,   110
That in our ancient uncouth country style
With huge and black projection overbrowed
Large space beneath, as duly as the light
Of day grew dim the Housewife hung a
    lamp;
An aged utensil, which had performed   115
Service beyond all others of its kind.
Early at evening did it burn—and late,
Surviving comrade of uncounted hours,
Which, going by from year to year, had
    found,
And left, the couple neither gay perhaps   120
Nor cheerful, yet with objects and with
    hopes,
Living a life of eager industry.
And now, when Luke had reached his eight-
    eenth year,
There by the light of this old lamp they sate,
Father and Son, while far into the night   125
The Housewife plied her own peculiar work,

Making the cottage through the silent hours
Murmur as with the sound of summer flies.
This light was famous in its neighborhood,
And was a public symbol of the life   130
That thrifty Pair had lived. For, as it chanced,
Their cottage on a plot of rising ground
Stood single, with large prospect, north and south,
High into Easedale, up to Dunmail-Raise,
And westward to the village near the lake;   135
And from this constant light, so regular,
And so far seen, the House itself, by all
Who dwelt within the limits of the vale,
Both old and young, was named THE EVE-
NING STAR.

Thus living on through such a length of years,   140
The Shepherd, if he loved himself, must needs
Have loved his Helpmate; but to Michael's heart
This son of his old age was yet more dear—
Less from instinctive tenderness, the same
Fond spirit that blindly works in the blood of all—   145
Than that a child, more than all other gifts
That earth can offer to declining man,
Brings hope with it, and forward-looking thoughts,
And stirrings of inquietude, when they
By tendency of nature needs must fail.   150
Exceeding was the love he bare to him,
His heart and his heart's joy! For often-times
Old Michael, while he was a babe in arms,
Had done him female service, not alone
For pastime and delight, as is the use   155
Of fathers, but with patient mind enforced
To acts of tenderness; and he had rocked
His cradle, as with a woman's gentle hand.

And in a later time, ere yet the Boy
Had put on boy's attire, did Michael love,   160
Albeit of a stern unbending mind,
To have the Young-one in his sight, when he
Wrought in the field, or on his shepherd's stool
Sate with a fettered sheep before him stretched

Under the large old oak, that near his door
Stood single, and, from matchless depth of shade,   166
Chosen for the Shearer's covert from the sun,
Thence in our rustic dialect was called
The CLIPPING TREE, a name which yet it bears.
There, while they two were sitting in the shade,   170
With others round them. earnest all and blithe,
Would Michael exercise his heart with looks
Of fond correction and reproof bestowed
Upon the Child, if he disturbed the sheep
By catching at their legs, or with his shouts
Scared them, while they lay still beneath the shears.   176

And when by Heaven's good grace the boy grew up
A healthy Lad, and carried in his cheek
Two steady roses that were five years old;
Then Michael from a winter coppice cut   180
With his own hand a sapling, which he hooped
With iron, making it throughout in all
Due requisites a perfect shepherd's staff,
And gave it to the Boy; wherewith equipped
He as a watchman oftentimes was placed   185
At gate or gap, to stem or turn the flock;
And, to his office prematurely called,
There stood the urchin, as you will divine,
Something between a hindrance and a help;
And for this cause not always, I believe,   190
Receiving from his Father hire of praise;
Though naught was left undone which staff, or voice,
Or looks, or threatening gestures could perform.

But soon as Luke, full ten years old, could stand
Against the mountain blasts; and to the heights,   195
Not fearing toil, nor length of weary ways,
He with his Father daily went, and they
Were as companions, why should I relate
That objects which the Shepherd loved before

---

134. **Easedale,** near Grasmere. **Dunmail-Raise,** a pass about three miles from Grasmere.

169. **Clipping,** used in the north of England for "shearing."

Were dearer now? that from the Boy there
    came   200
Feelings and emanations—things which were
Light to the sun and music to the wind;
And that the old Man's heart seemed born
    again?

   Thus in his Father's sight the Boy grew
    up:
And now, when he had reached his eight-
    eenth year,   205
He was his comfort and his daily hope.

   While in this sort the simple household
    lived
From day to day, to Michael's ear there
    came
Distressful tidings. Long before the time
Of which I speak, the Shepherd had been
    bound   210
In surety for his brother's son, a man
Of an industrious life, and ample means;
But unforeseen misfortunes suddenly
Had pressed upon him; and old Michael now
Was summoned to discharge the forfeiture,
A grievous penalty, but little less   216
Than half his substance. This unlooked-for
    claim,
At the first hearing, for a moment took
More hope out of his life than he supposed
That any old man ever could have lost.   220
As soon as he had armed himself with
    strength
To look his trouble in the face, it seemed
The Shepherd's sole resource to sell at once
A portion of his patrimonial fields.   224
Such was his first resolve; he thought again,
And his heart failed him. "Isabel," said he,
Two evenings after he had heard the news,
"I have been toiling more than seventy years,
And in the open sunshine of God's love
Have we all lived; yet, if these fields of ours
Should pass into a stranger's hand, I think   231
That I could not lie quiet in my grave.
Our lot is a hard lot; the sun himself
Has scarcely been more diligent than I;
And I have lived to be a fool at last   235
To my own family. An evil man
That was, and made an evil choice, if he
Were false to us; and, if he were not false,
There are ten thousand to whom loss like this
Had been no sorrow. I forgive him—but   240
'T were better to be dumb than to talk thus.

   "When I began, my purpose was to speak
Of remedies and of a cheerful hope.
Our Luke shall leave us, Isabel; the land
Shall not go from us, and it shall be free;   245
He shall possess it, free as is the wind
That passes over it. We have, thou know'st,
Another kinsman—he will be our friend
In this distress. He is a prosperous man,
Thriving in trade—and Luke to him shall go,
And with his kinsman's help and his own
    thrift   251
He quickly will repair this loss, and then
He may return to us. If here he stay,
What can be done? Where everyone is poor,
What can be gained?"
                  At this the old Man paused,
And Isabel sat silent, for her mind   256
Was busy, looking back into past times.
There's Richard Bateman, thought she to
    herself,
He was a parish-boy—at the church-door
They made a gathering for him, shillings,
    pence,   260
And halfpennies, wherewith the neighbors
    bought
A basket, which they filled with pedlar's
    wares;
And, with this basket on his arm, the lad
Went up to London, found a master there,
Who, out of many, chose the trusty boy   265
To go and overlook his merchandise
Beyond the seas; where he grew wondrous
    rich,
And left estates and monies to the poor,
And, at his birthplace, built a chapel floored
With marble, which he sent from foreign
    lands.   270
These thoughts, and many others of like sort,
Passed quickly through the mind of Isabel,
And her face brightened. The old Man was
    glad,
And thus resumed:—"Well, Isabel! this
    scheme
These two days has been meat and drink to
    me.   275
Far more than we have lost is left us yet.

   "We have enough—I wish indeed that I

Were younger—but this hope is a good hope.
Make ready Luke's best garments, of the best
Buy for him more, and let us send him forth
Tomorrow, or the next day, or tonight: 281
If he *could* go, the Boy should go tonight."

Here Michael ceased, and to the fields went forth
With a light heart. The Housewife for five days 284
Was restless morn and night, and all day long
Wrought on with her best fingers to prepare
Things needful for the journey of her son.
But Isabel was glad when Sunday came
To stop her in her work: for, when she lay
By Michael's side, she through the last two nights 290
Heard him, how he was troubled in his sleep:
And when they rose at morning she could see
That all his hopes were gone. That day at noon
She said to Luke, while they two by themselves 294
Were sitting at the door, "Thou must not go:
We have no other Child but thee to lose,
None to remember—do not go away,
For if thou leave thy Father he will die."
The Youth made answer with a jocund voice;
And Isabel, when she had told her fears, 300
Recovered heart. That evening her best fare
Did she bring forth, and all together sat
Like happy people round a Christmas fire.

With daylight Isabel resumed her work;
And all the ensuing week the house appeared
As cheerful as a grove in spring: at length 306
The expected letter from their kinsman came,
With kind assurances that he would do
His utmost for the welfare of the Boy; 309
To which, requests were added that forthwith
He might be sent to him. Ten times or more
The letter was read over; Isabel
Went forth to show it to the neighbors round;
Nor was there at that time on English land
A prouder heart than Luke's. When Isabel 315
Had to her house returned, the old Man said,
"He shall depart tomorrow." To this word
The Housewife answered, talking much of things
Which, if at such short notice he should go,
Would surely be forgotten. But at length
She gave consent, and Michael was at ease. 321

Near the tumultuous brook of Green-head Ghyll,
In that deep valley, Michael had designed
To build a Sheep-fold; and, before he heard
The tidings of his melancholy loss, 325
For this same purpose he had gathered up
A heap of stones, which by the streamlet's edge
Lay thrown together, ready for the work.
With Luke that evening thitherward he walked:
And soon as they had reached the place he stopped, 330
And thus the old Man spake to him—"My son,
Tomorrow thou wilt leave me: with full heart
I look upon thee, for thou art the same
That wert a promise to me ere thy birth,
And all thy life hath been my daily joy. 335
I will relate to thee some little part
Of our two histories; 't will do thee good
When thou art from me, even if I should touch
On things thou canst not know of.—After thou
First cam'st into the world—as oft befalls 340
To new-born infants—thou didst sleep away
Two days, and blessings from thy Father's tongue
Then fell upon thee. Day by day passed on,
And still I loved thee with increasing love.
Never to living ear came sweeter sounds 345
Than when I heard thee by our own fireside
First uttering, without words, a natural tune;
While thou, a feeding babe, didst in thy joy
Sing at thy Mother's breast. Month followed month,
And in the open fields my life was passed 350
And on the mountains; else I think that thou
Hadst been brought up upon thy Father's knees.
But we were playmates, Luke: among these hills,
As well thou knowest, in us the old and young 354
Have played together, nor with me didst thou

Lack any pleasure which a boy can know."
Luke had a manly heart; but at these words
He sobbed aloud. The old Man grasped his hand,
And said, "Nay, do not take it so—I see
That these are things of which I need not speak. 360
—Even to the utmost I have been to thee
A kind and a good Father: and herein
I but repay a gift which I myself
Received at others' hands; for, though now old
Beyond the common life of man, I still 365
Remember them who loved me in my youth.
Both of them sleep together: here they lived,
As all their Forefathers had done; and, when
At length their time was come, they were not loth
To give their bodies to the family mould. 370
I wished that thou shouldst live the life they lived,
But 't is a long time to look back, my Son,
And see so little gain from threescore years.
These fields were burthened when they came to me;
Till I was forty years of age, not more 375
Than half of my inheritance was mine.
I toiled and toiled; God blessed me in my work,
And till these three weeks past the land was free.
—It looks as if it never could endure
Another Master. Heaven forgive me, Luke,
If I judge ill for thee, but it seems good 381
That thou shouldst go."
     At this the old Man paused;
Then, pointing to the stones near which they stood,
Thus, after a short silence, he resumed:
"This was a work for us; and now, my Son,
It is a work for me. But, lay one stone— 386
Here, lay it for me, Luke, with thine own hands.
Nay, Boy, be of good hope—we both may live
To see a better day. At eighty-four
I still am strong and hale—do thou thy part;
I will do mine.—I will begin again 391
With many tasks that were resigned to thee:
Up to the heights, and in among the storms,
Will I without thee go again, and do

All works which I was wont to do alone, 395
Before I knew thy face.—Heaven bless thee, Boy!
Thy heart these two weeks has been beating fast
With many hopes; it should be so—yes—yes—
I knew that thou couldst never have a wish
To leave me, Luke: thou hast been bound to me 400
Only by links of love: when thou art gone,
What will be left to us!—But I forget
My purposes. Lay now the corner-stone,
As I requested; and hereafter, Luke,
When thou art gone away, should evil men
Be thy companions, think of me, my Son, 405
And of this moment; hither turn thy thoughts,
And God will strengthen thee: amid all fear
And all temptation, Luke, I pray that thou
May'st bear in mind the life thy Fathers lived, 410
Who, being innocent, did for that cause
Bestir them in good deeds. Now, fare thee well—
When thou return'st, thou in this place wilt see
A work which is not here: a covenant
'T will be between us; but, whatever fate 415
Befall thee, I shall love thee to that last,
And bear thy memory with me to the grave."

  The Shepherd ended here; and Luke stooped down,
And, as his Father had requested, laid
The first stone of the Sheep-fold. At the sight 420
The old Man's grief broke from him; to his heart
He pressed his Son, he kisséd him and wept;
And to the house together they returned.
—Hushed was that House in peace, or seeming peace,
Ere the night fell—with morrow's dawn the Boy 425
Began his journey, and, when he had reached
The public way, he put on a bold face;
And all the neighbors, as he passed their doors,
Came forth with wishes and with farewell prayers,
That followed him till he was out of sight. 430

A good report did from their kinsman
    come,
Of Luke and his well-doing: and the Boy
Wrote loving letters, full of wondrous news,
Which, as the Housewife phrased it, were
    throughout
"The prettiest letters that were ever seen." 435
Both parents read them with rejoicing hearts.
So, many months passed on: and once again
The Shepherd went about his daily work
With confident and cheerful thoughts; and
    now
Sometimes when he could find a leisure hour
He to that valley took his way, and there 441
Wrought at the Sheep-fold. Meantime Luke
    began
To slacken in his duty; and, at length,
He in the dissolute city gave himself
To evil courses: ignominy and shame 445
Fell on him, so that he was driven at last
To seek a hiding-place beyond the seas.

There is a comfort in the strength of love;
'T will make a thing endurable, which else
Would overset the brain, or break the heart:
I have conversed with more than one who
    well 451
Remember the old Man, and what he was
Years after he had heard this heavy news.
His bodily frame had been from youth to age
Of an unusual strength. Among the rocks 455
He went, and still looked up to sun and cloud,
And listened to the wind; and, as before,
Performed all kinds of labor for his sheep,
And for the land, his small inheritance.
And to that hollow dell from time to time 460
Did he repair, to build the Fold of which
His flock had need. 'T is not forgotten yet
The pity which was then in every heart
For the old Man—and 'tis believed by all
That many and many a day he thither went,
And never lifted up a single stone. 466

There, by the Sheep-fold, sometimes was
    he seen
Sitting alone, or with his faithful Dog,
Then old, beside him, lying at his feet.
The length of full seven years, from time to
    time, 470
He at the building of this Sheep-fold
    wrought,
And left the work unfinished when he died.
Three years, or little more, did Isabel
Survive her Husband: at her death the estate
Was sold, and went into a stranger's hand.
The Cottage which was named the EVENING
    STAR 476
Is gone—the plowshare has been through the
    ground
On which it stood; great changes have been
    wrought
In all the neighborhood—Yet the oak is left
That grew beside their door; and the remains
Of the unfinished Sheep-fold may be seen 481
Beside the boisterous brook of Green-head
    Ghyll.   (*1800; 1800*)

My Heart Leaps Up When I Behold

My heart leaps up when I behold
  A rainbow in the sky:
So was it when my life began;
So is it now I am a man:
So be it when I shall grow old,   5
  Or let me die!
The Child is father of the Man;
And I could wish my days to be
Bound each to each by natural piety.
                                      (*1802; 1807*)

My Heart Leaps Up. 9. **piety**, reverence, affection.

Resolution and Independence

This poem is also known as *The Leech-Gatherer*. Dorothy Wordsworth tells us that the subject of the poem was an old man that she and her brother met in the course of one of their walks—a man pinched by poverty and crippled. "He had been hurt in driving a cart, his leg broken, his body driven over, his skull fractured." Wordsworth evidently saw in him some of the effects of the maleficent forces of nature; the poem is therefore interesting as showing the attention given by the poet to the possibility that nature was not always kindly. The note of disillusionment appears occasionally in his poems after 1800. Wordsworth himself said, in a letter to some friends (June 14, 1802) speaking of *Resolution and Independence:* "I describe myself as having been exalted to the highest pitch of delight by the joyousness and beauty of nature; and then as depressed, even in the midst of those beautiful objects, to the lowest dejection and despair. A young poet in the midst of the happiness of nature is described as overwhelmed by the thoughts of the miserable reverses which have befallen the happiest of all men . . ." Significant also is the last sentence in the passage: "I cannot conceive a figure more impressive than that of an old man like this . . . traveling alone among the mountains and all lonely places, carrying with him his own fortitude, and the necessities which an unjust state of society has laid upon him."

The sentimentalism of this poem made it an easy subject of ridicule. See the parodies of Edward Lear, *Incidents in the Life of My Uncle Arly* (p. 826), and Lewis Carroll, *The White Knight's Ballad* (p. 831).

There was a roaring in the wind all night;
The rain came heavily and fell in floods;
But now the sun is rising calm and bright;
The birds are singing in the distant woods:
Over his own sweet voice the stock-dove broods;   5
The jay makes answer as the magpie chatters;
And all the air is filled with pleasant noise of waters.

All things that love the sun are out of doors;
The sky rejoices in the morning's birth;
The grass is bright with raindrops;—on the moors   10
The hare is running races in her mirth;
And with her feet she from the plashy earth
Raises a mist, that, glittering in the sun,
Runs with her all the way wherever she doth run.

I was a traveler then upon the moor;   15
I saw the hare that raced about with joy;
I heard the woods and distant waters roar,
Or heard them not, as happy as a boy:
The pleasant season did my heart employ:
My old remembrances went from me wholly;
And all the ways of men so vain and melancholy.   21

But, as it sometimes chanceth, from the might
Of joy in minds that can no further go,
As high as we have mounted in delight
In our dejection do we sink as low,   25
To me that morning did it happen so;
And fears, and fancies, thick upon me came;

Dim sadness—and blind thoughts, I knew not, nor could name.

I heard the skylark warbling in the sky;
And I bethought me of the playful hare: 30
Even such a happy child of earth am I;
Even as these blissful creatures do I fare;
Far from the world I walk, and from all care;
But there may come another day to me—   34
Solitude, pain of heart, distress, and poverty.

My whole life I have lived in pleasant thought,
As if life's business were a summer mood;
As if all needful things would come unsought
To genial faith, still rich in genial good;
But how can he expect that others should   40
Build for him, sow for him, and at his call
Love him, who for himself will take no heed at all?

I thought of Chatterton, the marvelous boy,
The sleepless soul that perished in his pride;
Of him who walked in glory and in joy   45
Following his plow, along the mountain side:
By our own spirits are we deified:
We poets in our youth begin in gladness;
But thereof come in the end despondency and madness.

Now, whether it were by peculiar grace,   50
A leading from above, a something given,
Yet it befell, that, in this lonely place,
When I with these untoward thoughts had striven,

12. **plashy,** swampy, marshy.

43. **Chatterton,** Thomas Chatterton (1752-1770), the youthful poet who in despair and poverty took his own life. See p. 7. 45. **him . . . joy,** Robert Burns. See p. 83.

Beside a pool bare to the eye of heaven
I saw a man before me unawares: 55
The oldest man he seemed that ever wore gray
  hairs.

As a huge stone is sometimes seen to lie
Couched on the bald top of an eminence;
Wonder to all who do the same espy,
By what means it could thither come, and
  whence; 60
So that it seems a thing endued with sense:
Like a sea-beast crawled forth, that on a shelf
Of rock or sand reposeth, there to sun itself;

Such seemed this man, not all alive nor dead,
Nor all asleep—in his extreme old age: 65
His body was bent double, feet and head
Coming together in life's pilgrimage;
As if some dire constraint of pain, or rage
Of sickness felt by him in times long past,
A more than human weight upon his frame
  had cast. 70

Himself he propped, limbs, body, and pale
  face,
Upon a long gray staff of shaven wood:
And, still as I drew near with gentle pace,
Upon the margin of that moorish flood
Motionless as a cloud the old man stood; 75
That heareth not the loud winds when they
  call,
And moveth altogether, if it move at all.

At length, himself unsettling, he the pond
Stirred with his staff and fixedly did look
Upon the muddy water, which he conned, 80
As if he had been reading in a book:
And now a stranger's privilege I took;
And, drawing to his side, to him did say,
"This morning gives us promise of a glorious
  day."

A gentle answer did the old man make, 85
In courteous speech which forth he slowly
  drew;
And him with further words I thus bespake:
"What occupation do you there pursue?
This is a lonesome place for one like you."

<small>74. **moorish**, marshy.</small>

Ere he replied, a flash of mild surprise 90
Broke from the sable orbs of his yet vivid eyes.

His words came feebly, from a feeble chest,
But each in solemn order followed each,
With something of a lofty utterance dressed;
Choice word, and measured phrase, above the
  reach 95
Of ordinary men; a stately speech;
Such as grave Livers do in Scotland use,
Religious men, who give to God and man
  their dues.

He told, that to these waters he had come
To gather leeches, being old and poor: 100
Employment hazardous and wearisome!
And he had many hardships to endure:
From pond to pond he roamed, from moor to
  moor;
Housing, with God's good help, by choice or
  chance;
And in this way he gained an honest main-
  tenance. 105

The old man still stood talking by my side;
But now his voice to me was like a stream
Scarce heard; nor word from word could I
  divide;
And the whole body of the man did seem
Like one whom I had met with in a dream; 110
Or like a man from some far region sent,
To give me human strength, by apt admonish-
  ment.

My former thoughts returned: the fear that
  kills;
And hope that is unwilling to be fed;
Cold, pain and labor, and all fleshly ills; 115
And mighty poets in their misery dead.
Perplexed, and longing to be comforted,
My question eagerly did I renew,
"How is it that you live, and what is it you
  do?"

He with a smile did then his words repeat; 120
And said that, gathering leeches, far and wide
He traveled; stirring thus about his feet
The waters of the pools where they abide.
"Once I could meet with them on every side;
But they have dwindled long by slow decay;

Yet still I persevere, and find them where I
    may." 126

While he was talking thus, the lonely place,
The old man's shape, and speech, all troubled
    me:
In my mind's eye I seemed to see him pace
About the weary moors continually, 130
Wandering about alone and silently.
While I these thoughts within myself pursued,
He, having made a pause, the same discourse
    renewed.

And soon with this he other matter blended,
Cheerfully uttered, with demeanor kind, 135
But stately in the main; and when he ended,
I could have laughed myself to scorn to find
In that decrepit man so firm a mind.
"God," said I, "be my help and stay secure;
I'll think of the leech-gatherer on the lonely
    moor!" 140

(1802; 1807)

Composed upon Westminster Bridge

Earth has not anything to show more fair:
Dull would he be of soul who could pass by
A sight so touching in its majesty:
This City now doth like a garment wear
The beauty of the morning; silent, bare, 5
Ships, towers, domes, theaters, and temples lie
Open unto the fields, and to the sky;
All bright and glittering in the smokeless air.
Never did sun more beautifully steep
In his first splendor valley, rock, or hill; 10
Ne'er saw I, never felt, a calm so deep!
The river glideth at his own sweet will:
Dear God! the very houses seem asleep;
And all that mighty heart is lying still!

(1802; 1807)

Composed by the Seaside, Near Calais

Fair Star of evening, Splendor of the west,
Star of my Country!—on the horizon's brink
Thou hangest, stooping, as might seem, to sink
On England's bosom, yet well pleased to rest,
Meanwhile, and be to her a glorious crest 5
Conspicuous to the Nations. Thou, I think,
Shouldst be my Country's emblem; and
    shouldst wink,
Bright Star! with laughter on her banners,
    dressed
In thy fresh beauty. There! that dusky spot
Beneath thee, that is England; there she lies. 10
Blessings be on you both! one hope, one lot,
One life, one glory!—I, with many a fear
For my dear Country, many heartfelt sighs,
Among men who do not love her, linger here.

(1802; 1807)

It Is a Beauteous Evening, Calm and Free

It is a beauteous evening, calm and free.
The holy time is quiet as a Nun,
Breathless with adoration: the broad sun
Is sinking down in its tranquillity;
The gentleness of heaven broods o'er the sea; 5
Listen! the mighty Being is awake,
And doth with his eternal motion make
A sound like thunder—everlastingly.
Dear Child! dear Girl! that walkest with me
    here,
If thou appear untouched by solemn thought,
Thy nature is not therefore less divine: 11
Thou liest in Abraham's bosom all the year,
And worship'st at the Temple's inner shrine,
God being with thee when we know it not.

(1802; 1807)

On the Extinction of the Venetian Republic

Venice was founded in the fifth century by refugees fleeing before the Huns under Attila. After conquering Constantinople in 1202, the new republic gained extensive possessions in the East and became a bulwark of Western Europe against the Turks. In the sixteenth century her glory declined as the commercial power of England and Holland advanced.

It Is a Beauteous Evening. 9. **Dear Child**, Caroline, the daughter of Wordsworth and Annette Vallon. **here,** on Calais beach, where the sonnet was composed. 12. **in Abraham's bosom,** in the presence or favor of God. See *Luke,* 16:22.

When Venice was conquered by Napoleon in 1797, her territory was divided between France and Austria.

Once did she hold the gorgeous east in fee;
And was the safeguard of the west: the worth
Of Venice did not fall below her birth,
Venice, the eldest Child of liberty.
She was a maiden City, bright and free; 5
No guile seduced, no force could violate;
And when she took unto herself a Mate,
She must espouse the everlasting Sea!
And what if she had seen those glories fade,
Those titles vanish, and that strength decay; 10
Yet shall some tribute of regret be paid
When her long life hath reached its final day:
Men are we, and must grieve when even the Shade
Of that which once was great is passed away.
(*1802;* 1807)

London, 1802

Milton! thou shouldst be living at this hour:
England hath need of thee: she is a fen
Of stagnant waters: altar, sword, and pen,
Fireside, the heroic wealth of hall and bower,
Have forfeited their ancient English dower 5
Of inward happiness. We are selfish men:
Oh! raise us up, return to us again;
And give us manners, virtue, freedom, power.
Thy soul was like a Star, and dwelt apart:
Thou hadst a voice whose sound was like the sea, 10
Pure as the naked heavens, majestic, free;
So didst thou travel on life's common way
In cheerful godliness; and yet thy heart
The lowliest duties on herself did lay.
(*1802;* 1807)

To the Daisy

With little here to do or see
Of things that in the great world be,
Sweet Daisy! oft I talk to thee

8. **She ... Sea!** When the Venetians defeated the Germans in 1177 in defense of Pope Alexander III, the Doge received from the Pope a ring with which he was commanded to wed the Adriatic as a sign of the maritime power of Venice. As a ceremony in token of this espousal, a ring was dropped annually into the Adriatic by the Doge.
London, 1802. 4. **hall and bower.** The hall was the public dwelling of the Teutonic chieftain, and the bower the private apartments.

For thou art worthy,
Thou unassuming Commonplace 5
Of Nature, with that homely face,
And yet with something of a grace
Which Love makes for thee!

Oft on the dappled turf at ease
I sit and play with similes, 10
Loose types of things through all degrees,
Thoughts of thy raising;
And many a fond and idle name
I give to thee, for praise or blame
As is the humor of the game, 15
While I am gazing.

A nun demure, of lowly port;
Or sprightly maiden, of Love's court,
In thy simplicity the sport
Of all temptations; 20
A queen in crown of rubies drest;
A starveling in a scanty vest;
Are all, as seems to suit thee best,
Thy appellations.

A little Cyclops, with one eye 25
Staring to threaten and defy,
That thought comes next—and instantly
The freak is over,
The shape will vanish, and behold!
A silver shield with boss of gold 30
That spreads itself, some faery bold
In fight to cover.

I see thee glittering from afar—
And then thou art a pretty star,
Not quite so fair as many are 35
In heaven above thee!
Yet like a star, with glittering crest,
Self-poised in air thou seem'st to rest;—
May peace come never to his nest
Who shall reprove thee! 40

Sweet Flower! for by that name at last
When all my reveries are past
I call thee, and to that cleave fast,
Sweet silent Creature!
That breath'st with me in sun and air, 45
Do thou, as thou art wont, repair

25. **Cyclops**, in classical legend, one of a race of mythical giants having but one eye.

My heart with gladness, and a share
    Of thy meek nature!
                      (*1802;* 1807)

To the Daisy

Bright Flower! whose home is everywhere,
Bold in maternal Nature's care,
And all the long year through the heir
    Of joy and sorrow;
Methinks that there abides in thee   5
Some concord with humanity,
Given to no other flower I see
    The forest thorough!

Is it that Man is soon deprest?
A thoughtless Thing! who, once unblest,   10
Does little on his memory rest,
    Or on his reason,
And Thou wouldst teach him how to find
A shelter under every wind,
A hope for times that are unkind   15
    And every season?

Thou wander'st the wide world about,
Unchecked by pride or scrupulous doubt,
With friends to greet thee, or without,
    Yet pleased and willing;   20
Meek, yielding to the occasion's call,
And all things suffering from all,
Thy function apostolical
    In peace fulfilling.
                      (*1802;* 1807)

To a Highland Girl

AT INVERSNEYDE, UPON LOCH LOMOND

Sweet Highland Girl, a very shower
Of beauty is thy earthly dower!
Twice seven consenting years have shed
Their utmost bounty on thy head:
And these gray rocks; that household lawn;   5
Those trees, a veil just half withdrawn;
This fall of water that doth make
A murmur near the silent lake;
This little bay; a quiet road

To a Highland Girl. **Loch Lomond,** the largest lake in Scotland, situated in the counties of Stirling and Dumbarton, noted for its beautiful scenery.

That holds in shelter thy Abode—   10
In truth together do ye seem
Like something fashioned in a dream;
Such Forms as from their covert peep
When earthly cares are laid asleep!
But, O fair Creature! in the light   15
Of common day, so heavenly bright,
I bless thee, Vision as thou art,
I bless thee with a human heart;
God shield thee to thy latest years!
Thee, neither know I, nor thy peers;   20
And yet my eyes are filled with tears.
    With earnest feeling I shall pray
For thee when I am far away:
For never saw I mien, or face,
In which more plainly I could trace   25
Benignity and home-bred sense
Ripening in perfect innocence.
Here scattered, like a random seed,
Remote from men, thou dost not need
The embarrassed look of shy distress,   30
And maidenly shamefacédness:
Thou wear'st upon thy forehead clear
The freedom of a Mountaineer:
A face with gladness overspread!
Soft smiles, by human kindness bred!   35
And seemliness complete, that sways
Thy courtesies, about thee plays;
With no restraint, but such as springs
From quick and eager visitings
Of thoughts that lie beyond the reach   40
Of thy few words of English speech:
A bondage sweetly brooked, a strife
That gives thy gestures grace and life!
So have I, not unmoved in mind,
Seen birds of tempest-loving kind—   45
Thus beating up against the wind.
    What hand but would a garland cull
For thee who art so beautiful?
O happy pleasure! here to dwell
Beside thee in some heathy dell;   50
Adopt your homely ways, and dress,
A Shepherd, thou a Shepherdess!
But I could frame a wish for thee
More like a grave reality:
Thou art to me but as a wave   55
Of the wild sea; and I would have
Some claim upon thee, if I could,
Though but of common neighborhood.
What joy to hear thee, and to see!

Thy elder Brother I would be, 60
Thy Father—anything to thee!
   Now thanks to Heaven! that of its grace
Hath led me to this lovely place.
Joy have I had; and going hence
I bear away my recompense. 65
In spots like these it is we prize
Our memory, feel that she hath eyes:
Then, why should I be loath to stir?
I feel this place was made for her;
To give new pleasure like the past, 70
Continued long as life shall last.
Nor am I loath, though pleased at heart,
Sweet Highland Girl! from thee to part:
For I, methinks, till I grow old,
As fair before me shall behold, 75
As I do now, the cabin small,
The lake, the bay, the waterfall;
And thee, the Spirit of them all!

(*1803;* 1807)

The Solitary Reaper

This poem was suggested to Wordsworth by an actual experience in the Scottish Highlands, which he and his sister Dorothy visited in 1803, and also, as recorded in Dorothy Wordsworth's *Recollections*, by the following entry in Thomas Wilkinson's *Tour in Scotland:* "Passed a female who was reaping alone; she sung in Erse, as she bended over her sickle; the sweetest human voice I ever heard: her strains were tenderly melancholy, and felt delicious, long after she was heard no more."

Behold her, single in the field,
Yon solitary Highland lass!
Reaping and singing by herself;
Stop here, or gently pass!
Alone she cuts and binds the grain, 5
And sings a melancholy strain;
O listen! for the vale profound
Is overflowing with the sound.

No nightingale did ever chaunt
More welcome notes to weary bands 10
Of travelers in some shady haunt,
Among Arabian sands:
A voice so thrilling ne'er was heard
In springtime from the cuckoo-bird,
Breaking the silence of the seas 15
Among the farthest Hebrides.

Will no one tell me what she sings?—
Perhaps the plaintive numbers flow
For old, unhappy, far-off things,
And battles long ago: 20
Or is it some more humble lay,
Familiar matter of today?
Some natural sorrow, loss, or pain,
That has been, and may be again?

Whate'er the theme, the maiden sang 25
As if her song could have no ending;
I saw her singing at her work,
And o'er the sickle bending;—
I listened, motionless and still;
And, as I mounted up the hill, 30
The music in my heart I bore,
Long after it was heard no more.

(*1803;* 1807)

To the Cuckoo

O blithe Newcomer! I have heard,
I hear thee and rejoice.
O Cuckoo! shall I call thee Bird,
Or but a wandering Voice?

While I am lying on the grass, 5
Thy twofold shout I hear;
From hill to hill it seems to pass,
At once far off, and near.

Though babbling only to the Vale,
Of sunshine and of flowers, 10
Thou bringest unto me a tale
Of visionary hours.

Thrice welcome, darling of the Spring!
Even yet thou art to me
No bird, but an invisible thing, 15
A voice, a mystery;

The same when in my schoolboy days
I listened to; that Cry

The Solitary Reaper. 16. Hebrides, a group of islands on the west coast of Scotland. **17. what she sings.** She is singing in Gaelic (Erse), which the poet does not understand.

Which made me look a thousand ways
In bush, and tree, and sky.   20

To seek thee did I often rove
Through woods and on the green;
And thou wert still a hope, a love;
Still longed for, never seen.

And I can listen to thee yet;   25
Can lie upon the plain
And listen, till I do beget
That golden time again.

O blessèd Bird! the earth we pace
Again appears to be   30
An unsubstantial, faery place;
That is fit home for thee!   (*1804;* 1807)

She Was a Phantom of Delight

   This poem is a tribute to Mary Hutchinson, whom Wordsworth married in 1802.

She was a phantom of delight
When first she gleamed upon my sight;
A lovely apparition, sent
To be a moment's ornament;
Her eyes as stars of twilight fair;   5
Like twilight's too, her dusky hair;
But all things else about her drawn
From May-time and the cheerful dawn;
A dancing shape, an Image gay,
To haunt, to startle, and waylay.   10

I saw her upon nearer view,
A spirit, yet a woman too!
Her household motions light and free,
And steps of virgin liberty;
A countenance in which did meet   15
Sweet records, promises as sweet;
A creature not too bright or good
For human nature's daily food:
For transient sorrows, simple wiles,
Praise, blame, love, kisses, tears, and smiles.   20

And now I see with eye serene
The very pulse of the machine;

She Was a Phantom of Delight. 22. **machine,** body. The use of this word may have been inspired by the Industrial Revolution. See p. 5. In any case, *machine* had greater poetic value in Wordsworth's day than in our own.

A being breathing thoughtful breath,
A Traveler between life and death;
The reason firm, the temperate will,   25
Endurance, foresight, strength, and skill,
A perfect woman, nobly planned,
To warn, to comfort, and command;
And yet a spirit still, and bright
With something of angelic light.   (*1804;* 1807)

I Wandered Lonely as a Cloud

I wandered lonely as a cloud
That floats on high o'er vales and hills,
When all at once I saw a crowd,
A host, of golden daffodils;
Beside the lake, beneath the trees,   5
Fluttering and dancing in the breeze.

Continuous as the stars that shine
And twinkle on the Milky Way,
They stretched in never-ending line
Along the margin of a bay: 10
Ten thousand saw I at a glance,
Tossing their heads in sprightly dance.

The waves beside them danced; but they
Outdid the sparkling waves in glee:
A poet could not but be gay,   15
In such a jocund company:
I gazed—and gazed—but little thought
What wealth the show to me had brought:

For oft, when on my couch I lie
In vacant or in pensive mood,   20
They flash upon that inward eye
Which is the bliss of solitude;
And then my heart with pleasure fills,
And dances with the daffodils.   (*1804;* 1807)

Ode to Duty

Stern Daughter of the Voice of God!
O Duty! if that name thou love
Who art a light to guide, a rod
To check the erring, and reprove;
Thou, who art victory and law   5

Ode to Duty. Cf. Carlyle's *Sartor Resartus,* p. 465, and Arnold's *Hebraism and Hellenism,* p. 544.

When empty terrors overawe;
From vain temptations dost set free;
And calm'st the weary strife of frail humanity!

There are who ask not if thine eye
Be on them; who, in love and truth,   10
Where no misgiving is, rely
Upon the genial sense of youth:
Glad Hearts! without reproach or blot;
Who do thy work, and know it not:
Oh! if through confidence misplaced   15
They fail, thy saving arms, dread Power!
    around them cast.

Serene will be our days and bright,
And happy will our nature be,
When love is an unerring light,
And joy its own security.   20
And they a blissful course may hold
Even now, who, not unwisely bold,
Live in the spirit of this creed;
Yet seek thy firm support, according to their
    need.

I, loving freedom, and untried;   25
No sport of every random gust,
Yet being to myself a guide,
Too blindly have reposed my trust:
And oft, when in my heart was heard
Thy timely mandate, I deferred   30
The task, in smoother walks to stray;
But thee I now would serve more strictly, if
    I may.

Through no disturbance of my soul,
Or strong compunction in me wrought,
I supplicate for thy control;   35
But in the quietness of thought:
Me this unchartered freedom tires;
I feel the weight of chance desires:
My hopes no more must change their name,
I long for a repose that ever is the same.   40

Stern Lawgiver! yet thou dost wear
The Godhead's most benignant grace;
Nor know we anything so fair
As is the smile upon thy face:
Flowers laugh before thee on their beds   45
And fragrance in thy footing treads;

Thou dost preserve the stars from wrong;
And the most ancient heavens, through Thee,
    are fresh and strong.

To humbler functions, awful Power!
I call thee: I myself commend   50
Unto Thy guidance from this hour;
Oh, let my weakness have an end!
Give unto me, made lowly wise,
The spirit of self-sacrifice;
The confidence of reason give;   55
And in the light of truth Thy Bondman let
    me live!   *(1805; 1807)*

To a Skylark

Up with me! up with me into the clouds!
    For thy song, Lark, is strong;
Up with me, up with me into the clouds!
    Singing, singing,
With clouds and sky about thee ringing,   5
    Lift me, guide me till I find
That spot which seems so to thy mind.

I have walked through wildernesses dreary,
And today my heart is weary;
Had I now the wings of a Faery   10
Up to thee would I fly.
There is madness about thee, and joy divine
In that song of thine;
Lift me, guide me, high and high
To thy banqueting-place in the sky!   15

    Joyous as morning,
Thou art laughing and scorning;
Thou hast a nest for thy love and thy rest,
And, though little troubled with sloth,
Drunken Lark! thou wouldst be loath   20
To be such a traveler as I.
Happy, happy Liver,
With a soul as strong as a mountain river
Pouring out praise to the almighty Giver,
    Joy and jollity be with us both!   25

    Alas! my journey, rugged and uneven,
Through prickly moors or dusty ways must
    wind;

To a Skylark. Cf. Shelley's *To a Skylark,* p. 258.

But hearing thee, or others of thy kind,
  As full of gladness and as free of heaven,
I, with my fate contented, will plod on,   30
And hope for higher raptures, when life's day
    is done.   (*1805;* 1807)

Elegiac Stanzas

SUGGESTED BY A PICTURE OF PEELE CASTLE, IN A STORM, PAINTED BY SIR GEORGE BEAUMONT

    Peele Castle is on the coast of Lancashire. Wordsworth visited a cousin near there. Beaumont, a friend of the poet, painted two pictures of it, one intended for Mrs. Wordsworth; but when Lady Beaumont interfered, it was given to Sir Uvedale Price.

I was thy neighbor once, thou rugged Pile!
Four summer weeks I dwelt in sight of thee:
I saw thee every day; and all the while
Thy Form was sleeping on a glassy sea.

So pure the sky, so quiet was the air!   5
So like, so very like, was day to day!
Whene'er I looked, thy Image still was there;
It trembled, but it never passed away.

How perfect was the calm! it seemed no sleep;
No mood, which season takes away, or brings:
I could have fancied that the mighty Deep   11
Was even the gentlest of all gentle Things.

Ah! then, if mine had been the painter's hand,
To express what then I saw; and add the
    gleam,
The light that never was, on sea or land,   15
The consecration, and the poet's dream;

I would have planted thee, thou hoary Pile,
Amid a world how different from this!
Beside a sea that could not cease to smile;
On tranquil land, beneath a sky of bliss.   20

Thou shouldst have seemed a treasure-house
    divine
Of peaceful years; a chronicle of heaven;—
Of all the sunbeams that did ever shine
The very sweetest had to thee been given.

A picture had it been of lasting ease,   25
Elysian quiet, without toil or strife;
No motion but the moving tide, a breeze,
Or merely silent Nature's breathing life.

Such, in the fond illusion of my heart,
Such picture would I at that time have made:
And seen the soul of truth in every part,   31
A steadfast peace that might not be betrayed.

So once it would have been—'tis so no more;
I have submitted to a new control:
A power is gone, which nothing can restore;   35
A deep distress hath humanized my Soul.

Not for a moment could I now behold
A smiling sea, and be what I have been:
The feeling of my loss will ne'er be old;
This, which I know, I speak with mind serene.

Then, Beaumont, friend! who would have
    been the friend,   41
If he had lived, of him whom I deplore,
This work of thine I blame not, but commend;
This sea in anger, and that dismal shore.

O 'tis a passionate Work!—yet wise and well,
Well chosen is the spirit that is here;   46
That Hulk which labors in the deadly swell,
This rueful sky, this pageantry of fear!

And this huge Castle, standing here sublime,
I love to see the look with which it braves,   50
Cased in the unfeeling armor of old time,
The lightning, the fierce wind, and trampling
    waves.

Farewell, farewell the heart that lives alone,
Housed in a dream, at distance from the Kind!
Such happiness, wherever it be known,   55
Is to be pitied; for 'tis surely blind.

But welcome fortitude, and patient cheer,
And frequent sights of what is to be borne!
Such sights, or worse, as are before me here.—
Not without hope we suffer and we mourn.
                        (*1805;* 1807)

---

18. **different from this,** different from the world of storm as shown in the picture.

26. **Elysian quiet,** the quiet of Elysium, the abode of the blessed after death. 36. **deep distress.** Wordsworth's brother John, a sea captain, was lost with his vessel in February, 1805.

Character of the Happy Warrior

This poem was written shortly after the death of Lord Nelson, England's greatest naval commander, who was killed on board his ship in the Battle of Trafalgar, 1805. The following is Wordsworth's note on the poem:

"The course of the great war with the French naturally fixed one's attention upon the military character, and, to the honor of our country, there were many illustrious instances of the qualities that constitute its highest excellence. Lord Nelson carried most of the virtues that the trials he was exposed to in his department of the service necessarily call forth and sustain, if they do not produce the contrary vices. But his public life was stained with one great crime, so that, though many passages of these lines were suggested by what was generally known as excellent in his conduct, I have not been able to connect his name with the poem as I could wish or even to think of him with satisfaction in reference to the idea of what a warrior ought to be. For the sake of such of my friends as may happen to read this note, I will add that many elements of the character here portrayed were found in my brother John, who perished by shipwreck as mentioned elsewhere. His messmates used to call him the Philosopher, from which it must be inferred that the qualities and dispositions I allude to had not escaped their notice. He often expressed his regret, after the war had continued some time, that he had not chosen the naval, instead of the East India Company's, service, to which his family connection had led him. He greatly valued moral and religious instruction for youth, as tending to make good sailors. The best, he used to say, came from Scotland; the next to them, from the North of England, especially from Westmoreland and Cumberland, where, thanks to the piety and local attachments of our ancestors, endowed, or, as they are commonly called, free, schools abound."

The "crime" of Nelson was his connection with Lady Hamilton, a noted adventuress.

Who is the happy Warrior? Who is he
That every man in arms should wish to be?
—It is the generous Spirit, who, when brought
Among the tasks of real life, hath wrought
Upon the plan that pleased his boyish thought:
Whose high endeavors are an inward light   6
That makes the path before him always bright:
Who, with a natural instinct to discern
What knowledge can perform, is diligent to
    learn;
Abides by this resolve, and stops not there,   10
But makes his moral being his prime care;
Who, doomed to go in company with Pain,
And Fear, and Bloodshed, miserable train!
Turns his necessity to glorious gain;
In face of these doth exercise a power   15
Which is our human nature's highest dower;
Controls them and subdues, transmutes, be-
    reaves
Of their bad influence, and their good receives:
By objects, which might force the soul to abate
Her feeling, rendered more compassionate;   20
Is placable—because occasions rise
So often that demand such sacrifice;
More skilful in self-knowledge, even more pure,
As tempted more; more able to endure,
As more exposed to suffering and distress;   25
Thence, also, more alive to tenderness.
—'Tis he whose law is reason; who depends
Upon that law as on the best of friends;
Whence, in a state where men are tempted still
To evil for a guard against worse ill,   30
And what in quality or act is best
Doth seldom on a right foundation rest,
He labors good on good to fix, and owes
To virtue every triumph that he knows:
—Who, if he rise to station of command,   35
Rises by open means; and there will stand
On honorable terms, or else retire,
And in himself possess his own desire;
Who comprehends his trust, and to the same
Keeps faithful with a singleness of aim;   40
And therefore does not stoop, nor lie in wait
For wealth, or honors, or for worldly state;
Whom they must follow; on whose head
    must fall,
Like showers of manna, if they come at all:
Whose powers shed round him in the com-
    mon strife,   45
Or mild concerns of ordinary life,
A constant influence, a peculiar grace;
But who, if he be called upon to face

Some awful moment to which Heaven has joined
Great issues, good or bad for human kind 50
Is happy as a Lover; and attired
With sudden brightness, like a Man inspired;
And, through the heat of conflict, keeps the law
In calmness made, and sees what he foresaw;
Or if an unexpected call succeed, 55
Come when it will, is equal to the need:
—He who, though thus endued as with a sense
And faculty for storm and turbulence,
Is yet a Soul whose master-bias leans
To home-felt pleasures and to gentle scenes; 60
Sweet images! which, wheresoe'er he be,
Are at his heart; and such fidelity
It is his darling passion to approve;
More brave for this, that he hath much to love—
'Tis, finally, the Man, who, lifted high, 65
Conspicuous object in a Nation's eye,
Or left unthought-of in obscurity—
Who, with a toward or untoward lot,
Prosperous or adverse, to his wish or not—
Plays, in the many games of life, that one 70
Where what he most doth value must be won:
Whom neither shape of danger can dismay,
Nor thought of tender happiness betray;
Who, not content that former worth stand fast,
Looks forward, persevering to the last, 75
From well to better, daily self-surpassed:
Who, whether praise of him must walk the earth
Forever, and to noble deeds give birth,
Or he must fall, to sleep without his fame,
And leave a dead unprofitable name— 80
Finds comfort in himself and in his cause;
And, while the mortal mist is gathering, draws
His breath in confidence of Heaven's applause:
This is the happy Warrior; this is He
That every Man in arms should wish to be.
(*1806;* 1807)

Nuns Fret Not at Their Convent's Narrow Room

Nuns fret not at their convent's narrow room;
And hermits are contented with their cells;
And students with their pensive citadels;
Maids at the wheel, the weaver at his loom,
Sit blithe and happy; bees that soar for bloom,
High as the highest Peak of Furness-fells, 6
Will murmur by the hour in foxglove bells:
In truth the prison, into which we doom
Ourselves, no prison is: and hence for me,
In sundry moods, 'twas pastime to be bound 10
Within the Sonnet's scanty plot of ground;
Pleased if some Souls (for such there needs must be)
Who have felt the weight of too much liberty,
Should find brief solace there, as I have found.
(*1806;* 1807)

The World Is Too Much with Us

The world is too much with us; late and soon,
Getting and spending, we lay waste our powers:
Little we see in Nature that is ours;
We have given our hearts away, a sordid boon!
The sea that bares her bosom to the moon; 5
The winds that will be howling at all hours,
And are up-gathered now like sleeping flowers;
For this, for everything, we are out of tune;
It moves us not.—Great God! I'd rather be
A Pagan suckled in a creed outworn; 10
So might I, standing on this pleasant lea,
Have glimpses that would make me less forlorn;
Have sight of Proteus rising from the sea;
Or hear old Triton blow his wreathéd horn. (*1806;* 1807)

3. **pensive citadels,** retreats suitable for quiet thought. 6. **Furness-fells,** upland tracts of Furness, on the coast of Lancashire. 9. **prison.** Cf. Lovelace's *To Althea, from Prison* (Vol. I, p. 663). 13. **weight . . . liberty.** Writing sonnets was especially helpful to Wordsworth in overcoming his early discursive style.
The World Is Too Much with Us. 13. **Proteus,** a sea god in the service of Neptune, god of the sea. *Triton* (l. 14) is another sea god.

Ode on Intimations of Immortality from Recollections of Early Childhood

This ode is based upon the Platonic doctrine that all knowledge is simply recollection. The arguments for the theory are too delicate and lengthy to be given here, but the following excerpts from Plato's *Phaedo* (in Jowett's translation) may be helpful: "Your favorite doctrine, Socrates, that knowledge is simply recollection, if true, also necessarily implies a previous time in which we learned that which we now recollect. But this would be impossible unless our soul was in some place before existing in the human form; here then is another argument of the soul's immortality. . . . And if we acquired this knowledge before we were born and were born having it, then we also knew before we were born and at the instant of birth. . . . If, after having acquired, we have not forgotten that which we acquired, then we must always have been born with knowledge and shall always continue to know as long as life lasts—for knowledge is the acquiring and retaining knowledge and not forgetting. . . . But if the knowledge which we acquired before birth was lost by us at birth, and if afterwards by the use of the senses we recovered that which we previously knew, will not that which we call learning be a process of recovering our knowledge, and may not this be rightly termed recollection by us?" As Wordsworth says, the child knew the glory of his origin; the man has forgotten, but his vague instincts, based upon his knowledge as a child, can reassure him of his immortal beginnings.

> The Child is father of the man;
> And I could wish my days to be
> Bound each to each by natural piety.

1

There was a time when meadow, grove, and stream,
    The earth, and every common sight,
      To me did seem
    Appareled in celestial light,
The glory and the freshness of a dream.   5
It is not now as it hath been of yore;—
    Turn wheresoe'er I may,
      By night or day,
The things which I have seen I now can see no more.

2

    The Rainbow comes and goes,   10
    And lovely is the Rose;
    The Moon doth with delight
Look round her when the heavens are bare;
    Waters on a starry night
    Are beautiful and fair;   15
    The sunshine is a glorious birth;
But yet I know, where'er I go,
That there hath passed away a glory from the earth.

3

Now, while the birds thus sing a joyous song,
    And while the young lambs bound   20
      As to the tabor's sound,
To me alone there came a thought of grief:
A timely utterance gave that thought relief,
    And I again am strong:
The cataracts blow their trumpets from the steep;   25
No more shall grief of mine the season wrong;
I hear the Echoes through the mountains throng,
The Winds come to me from the fields of sleep,
    And all the earth is gay;
    Land and sea   30
    Give themselves up to jollity,
    And with the heart of May
    Doth every Beast keep holiday;—
    Thou Child of Joy,
Shout round me, let me hear thy shouts, thou happy Shepherd-boy!   35

4

Ye blessèd Creatures, I have heard the call
    Ye to each other make; I see
The heavens laugh with you in your jubilee;
    My heart is at your festival,
    My head hath its coronal,   40

The Child . . . piety, quoted from *My Heart Leaps Up*, p. 148.

21. **tabor**, a small drum. 26. **No . . . wrong**, because of lack of sympathy. 40. **coronal**, garland.

The fulness of your bliss, I feel—I feel it all.
    Oh, evil day! if I were sullen
    While Earth herself is adorning,
      This sweet May-morning,
    And the Children are culling   45
      On every side,
In a thousand valleys far and wide,
Fresh flowers; while the sun shines warm,
And the Babe leaps up on his Mother's arm—
    I hear, I hear, with joy I hear!   50
    —But there's a Tree, of many, one,
A single Field which I have looked upon,
Both of them speak of something that is
    gone:
    The Pansy at my feet
    Doth the same tale repeat: 55
Whither is fled the visionary gleam?
Where is it now, the glory and the dream?

5

Our birth is but a sleep and a forgetting:
The Soul that rises with us, our life's Star,
    Hath had elsewhere its setting,   60
    And cometh from afar:
    Not in entire forgetfulness,
    And not in utter nakedness,
But trailing clouds of glory do we come
    From God, who is our home: 65
Heaven lies about us in our infancy!
Shades of the prison-house begin to close
    Upon the growing Boy,
But he beholds the light, and whence it flows
    He sees it in his joy;   70
The Youth, who daily farther from the east
    Must travel, still is Nature's priest,
    And by the vision splendid
    Is on his way attended;
At length the Man perceives it die away,   75
And fade into the light of common day.

6

Earth fills her lap with pleasures of her own;
Yearnings she hath in her own natural kind,
And even with something of a Mother's mind,
    And no unworthy aim,   80
    The homely Nurse doth all she can
To make her Foster-child, her Inmate Man,
    Forget the glories he hath known,
And that imperial palace whence he came.

7

Behold the Child among his new-born blisses,
A six years' Darling of a pigmy size!   86
See, where 'mid work of his own hand he lies,
Fretted by sallies of his mother's kisses,
With light upon him from his father's eyes!
See, at his feet, some little plan or chart,   90
Some fragment from his dream of human life,
Shaped by himself with newly-learnèd art;
    A wedding or a festival,
    A mourning or a funeral,
    And this hath now his heart,   95
    And unto this he frames his song:
    Then will he fit his tongue
To dialogues of business, love, or strife;
    But it will not be long
    Ere this be thrown aside,   100
    And with new joy and pride
The little Actor cons another part;
Filling from time to time his "humorous stage"
With all the Persons, down to palsied Age,
That Life brings with her in her equipage;   105
    As if his whole vocation
    Were endless imitation.

8

Thou, whose exterior semblance doth belie
    Thy Soul's immensity;
Thou best Philosopher, who yet dost keep   110
Thy heritage, thou Eye among the blind,
That, deaf and silent, read'st the eternal deep,
Haunted forever by the eternal mind—
    Mighty Prophet! Seer blest!
    On whom those truths do rest,   115
Which we are toiling all our lives to find,
In darkness lost, the darkness of the grave;
Thou, over whom thy Immortality
Broods like the Day, a Master o'er a Slave,
A Presence which is not to be put by;   120
Thou little Child, yet glorious in the might
Of heaven-born freedom on thy being's height,
Why with such earnest pains dost thou provoke
The years to bring the inevitable yoke,
Thus blindly with thy blessedness at strife?   125
Full soon thy Soul shall have her earthly
    freight,
And custom lie upon thee with a weight,
Heavy as frost, and deep almost as life!

---

58. **Our birth**, etc. Cf. Vaughan's *Retreat* (Vol. I, p. 678).
64. **trailing**, bringing with us.
102. **Actor . . . part**, an allusion to Jaques' speech in *As You Like It*, II, vii, 139 ff.—"All the world's a stage," etc.
103. **humorous**, changeable, moody. 112. **eternal deep**, deep mysteries of eternity.

9

Oh, joy! that in our embers
    Is something that doth live,   130
    That nature yet remembers
    What was so fugitive!
The thought of our past years in me doth breed
Perpetual benediction: not indeed
For that which is most worthy to be blest; 135
Delight and liberty, the simple creed
Of Childhood, whether busy or at rest,
With new-fledged hope still fluttering in his breast—
    Not for these I raise
    The song of thanks and praise;   140
    But for those obstinate questionings
    Of sense and outward things,
    Fallings from us, vanishings;
    Blank misgivings of a Creature
Moving about in worlds not realized,   145
High instincts before which our mortal nature
Did tremble like a guilty thing surprised:
    But for those first affections,
    Those shadowy recollections,
    Which, be they what they may,   150
Are yet the fountain light of all our day,
Are yet a master light of all our seeing;
    Uphold us, cherish, and have power to make
Our noisy years seem moments in the being
Of the eternal Silence: truths that wake,   155
    To perish never;
Which neither listlessness, nor mad endeavor,
    Nor Man nor Boy,
Nor all that is at enmity with joy,
Can utterly abolish or destroy!   160
    Hence in a season of calm weather
    Though inland far we be,
Our Souls have sight of that immortal sea
    Which brought us hither,
    Can in a moment travel thither,   165
And see the Children sport upon the shore,
And hear the mighty waters rolling evermore.

10

Then sing, ye Birds, sing, sing a joyous song!
    And let the young Lambs bound
    As to the tabor's sound!   170
We in thought will join your throng,
    Ye that pipe and ye that play,
    Ye that through your hearts today
    Feel the gladness of the May!
What though the radiance which was once so bright   175
Be now forever taken from my sight,
    Though nothing can bring back the hour
Of splendor in the grass, of glory in the flower;
    We will grieve not, rather find
    Strength in what remains behind;   180
    In the primal sympathy
    Which having been must ever be;
    In the soothing thoughts that spring
    Out of human suffering;
    In the faith that looks through death,   185
In years that bring the philosophic mind.

11

And O, ye Fountains, Meadows, Hills, and Groves,
Forebode not any severing of our loves!
Yet in my heart of hearts I feel your might;
I only have relinquished one delight   190
To live beneath your more habitual sway.
I love the Brooks which down their channels fret,
Even more than when I tripped lightly as they;
The innocent brightness of a new-born Day
    Is lovely yet;   195
The Clouds that gather round the setting sun
Do take a sober coloring from an eye
That hath kept watch o'er man's mortality.
Another race hath been, and other palms are won.
Thanks to the human heart by which we live,
Thanks to its tenderness, its joys, and fears,   201
To me the meanest flower that blows can give
Thoughts that do often lie too deep for tears.
(1803-06; 1807)

Thought of a Briton on the Subjugation of Switzerland

Switzerland was conquered by the French in 1798. By 1807, when this sonnet was written, Napoleon had made himself master of Europe.

Two Voices are there; one is of the sea,
One of the mountains; each a mighty Voice:
In both from age to age thou didst rejoice,
They were thy chosen music, Liberty!
There came a Tyrant, and with holy glee   5

175-203. **What though,** etc. With this passage compare ll. 72-111 of *Lines Composed a Few Miles above Tintern Abbey*, pp. 122-123. 1. **Two Voices.** The voice of the sea is England; that of the mountains is Switzerland.

Thou fought'st against him; but hast vainly
    striven:
Thou from thy Alpine holds at length art
    driven,
Where not a torrent murmurs heard by thee.
Of one deep bliss thine ear hath been bereft:
Then cleave, O cleave to that which still is
    left;   10
For, high-souled Maid, what sorrow would
    it be
That Mountain floods should thunder as be-
    fore,
And Ocean bellow from his rocky shore,
And neither awful Voice be heard by thee!
                                (1807)

Scorn Not the Sonnet

Scorn not the Sonnet; Critic, you have
    frowned,
Mindless of its just honors; with this key
Shakespeare unlocked his heart; the melody
Of this small lute gave ease to Petrarch's
    wound;
A thousand times this pipe did Tasso sound; 5
With it Camoëns soothed an exile's grief;
The Sonnet glittered a gay myrtle leaf
Amid the cypress with which Dante crowned
His visionary brow; a glowworm lamp,
It cheered mild Spenser, called from Faery-
    land   10
To struggle through dark ways; and when a
    damp
Fell round the path of Milton, in his hand
The Thing became a trumpet; whence he blew
Soul-animating strains—alas, too few!   (1827)

<small>3. **Shakespeare . . . heart.** This is poetic exaggeration; many of Shakespeare's sonnets are conventional in subject-matter and in style. See Vol. I, p. 490. 4. **wound.** love for Laura, the inspiration of many sonnets of the Italian Petrarch (1304-1374). 5. **Tasso,** an Italian poet (1544-1595). 6. **Camoëns . . . grief.** Luís de Camoëns (1524-1580) was a noted Portuguese poet who was banished from Lisbon partly because of his passion for Donna Caterina. After her death he lamented her in his *Rimas.* 7. **myrtle,** a symbol of love; the cypress (l. 8) was a symbol of mourning. The reference is to Dante's love sonnets, inspired by Beatrice. 10. **Spenser,** author of a series of love sonnets entitled *Amoretti.* See Vol. I, p. 461. 12. **Milton.** For Milton's sonnets, see Vol. I, p. 713.</small>

If Thou Indeed Derive Thy Light from Heaven

If thou indeed derive thy light from Heaven,
Then, to the measure of that heaven-born light,
Shine, Poet! in thy place, and be content—
The stars pre-eminent in magnitude,
And they that from the zenith dart their
    beams   5
(Visible though they be to half the earth,
Though half a sphere be conscious of their
    brightness)
Are yet of no diviner origin,
No purer essence, than the one that burns,
Like an untended watch-fire, on the ridge   10
Of some dark mountain; or than those which
    seem
Humbly to hang, like twinkling winter lamps,
Among the branches of the leafless trees;
All are the undying offspring of one sire: 14
Then, to the measure of the light vouchsafed,
Shine, Poet, in thy place, and be content.
                              (*1832;* 1836)

Most Sweet It Is with Unuplifted Eyes

Most sweet it is with unuplifted eyes
To pace the ground, if path be there or none,
While a fair region round the traveler lies
Which he forbears again to look upon;
Pleased rather with some soft ideal scene,   5
The work of Fancy, or some happy tone
Of meditation, slipping in between
The beauty coming and the beauty gone.
If Thought and Love desert us, from that day
Let us break off all commerce with the Muse:
With Thought and Love companions of our
    way,   11
Whate'er the senses take or may refuse,
The Mind's internal heaven shall shed her
    dews
Of inspiration on the humblest lay.
                              (*1833;* 1835)

Samuel Taylor Coleridge
1772-1834

A man who does not make the most of his potentialities is always a tantalizing, provocative subject for discussion; but as far as Coleridge is concerned, any discussion must assume that he was a poet of the first rank, however incomplete his achievement. He was born at Ottery St. Mary, Devonshire, on October 21, 1772; his father, the village vicar, was a lovable and an utterly unworldly person. His death, when Samuel was only nine years of age, threw the boy very much on his own; but he was fortunate enough to secure an opportunity to enter Christ's Hospital, one of the best schools in England at the time. His stay at Christ's Hospital has been attractively described by Charles Lamb (p. 337) in one of his essays, *Christ's Hospital Five-and-Thirty Years Ago*. Lamb pictured the young Coleridge as lonely and friendless; Coleridge himself has told us the same in his *Frost at Midnight*. But his days at Christ's Hospital were not all drab; he fell in love and wrote juvenile poetry and showed great potential imaginative powers in his versifying, although none of his early verses deserved to survive.

In 1791 he matriculated at Jesus College, Cambridge, was a good student at first, but incurred some debts and, frightened, ran away to join the Light Dragoons under the incongruous name of Silas Tomkyn Comberbacke. It was with some difficulty that his friends purchased his discharge from the Dragoons. He returned to Cambridge, but left the university in 1794 without a degree, filled with revolutionary doctrines and a new religious radicalism called Unitarianism—spiritual possessions which he had apparently been nursing throughout his stay at Cambridge. About this time (1794) he met Robert Southey (p. 296), and the two of them hatched the scheme of Pantisocracy. On the banks of the Susquehanna River in Pennsylvania the two, in company with some kindred spirits both male and female, intended to found an ideal community organized along lines suggested by Rousseau and Godwin. The scheme fell through, largely for financial reasons, but in the meantime Southey had married Edith Fricker, and Coleridge, fresh from a rejection by one young woman, had married Mrs. Southey's sister Sarah. The Fricker sisters, it may be interpolated, were the "two milliners of Bath" over whom Byron waxed superciliously merry in *Don Juan* (p. 237, l. 744). The truth of the matter is that the marriage of Coleridge and Sarah Fricker was not made in Heaven.

The rather ill-mated couple finally settled at Nether Stowey, Somersetshire; here it was that Coleridge met the Wordsworths, brother and sister (p. 118). He was at that time trying to breathe a newspaper, *The Watchman*, into life, and was lecturing and preaching Unitarianism the while. The meeting of the two poets in 1797 came a year after Coleridge had published his first poems, the *Juvenile Poems*. These early efforts were of negligible value, but the contact of Coleridge and Wordsworth resulted in a splendid burgeoning of both as poets. Indeed, the year 1797 was something of an *Annus Mirabilis* for Coleridge. *The Rime of the Ancient Mariner* (p. 166), that fine literary ballad of the supernatural; and *Christabel* (p. 175), that "magnificent torso," an uncompleted fragment that caught, even in its fragmentary state, all the magical glamour of medieval romance—these were both composed in 1797. In the next year were written the other great fragment looking out from "magic casements" and romantic witchery, *Kubla Khan* (p. 184), and the stirring *France: an Ode* (p. 185), powerful in its highly charged emotion evoked by the beauties of nature and the tyrannies of governments. In 1798 came the *Lyrical Ballads*, the joint product of Coleridge and Wordsworth; the significance of this work has already been described (pp. 10 and 119). Coleridge's chief contribution to the collection was *The Rime of the Ancient Mariner*, published here for the first time. It might be added that the dates of the composition and the printing of Coleridge's poetry have no special relation to each other, such was the poet's procrastinating tendency.

Coleridge and the Wordsworths now took a trip to Germany, at the time a hotbed of romantic endeavor. Coleridge's purpose was to soak himself in this German romanticism, and with this end in view he attended the University of Göttingen, absorbed large doses of the philosophy of Immanuel Kant (pp. 12 and 20), and mastered the German language so readily that he was able to translate Schiller's drama, *Wallenstein*, within six weeks of his arrival in Germany. The Wordsworths had meanwhile returned and settled at Grasmere (p. 119). Thither Coleridge followed them in 1800 and settled down at Greta Hall, Keswick, twelve miles away, after a few desultory attempts to establish himself as a journalist with the London *Morning Post*. The coming of Coleridge to Keswick coincided with the ebbing of his creative power. By nature neurotically inclined, he had become the victim of opium, and although he was able eventually to free himself from the habit, his abilities were nevertheless stunted and his ambitions dissipated; he still retained his angelic potentialities, but as Lamb observed, his was the look of an "archangel a little damaged." His *Dejection, an Ode* (1802) and *Youth and Age* (1828-1832; p. 189) reflect the disillusionment and bitterness which the realization of his waning abilities brought him.

In 1804, he became for a brief time secretary to the governor of Malta. Eventually he drifted back to London, where, at the home of Mr. Gilman at Highgate, he fought his opium habit and triumphed, to spend the remaining years of his life in a state of creative exhaustion. He lectured extensively; to the very end of his days he was an accomplished conversationalist; and his interests were wide and varied. He did much to build up the present romantic conception of Shakespeare (p. 20); he gave his theories on education to all who would hear him; he planned a monumental work on Christianity; he dabbled in drama with passing success, as his tragedy *Remorse* (1813) shows. He supervised the publication of some of his ancient monuments of glory like *Kubla Khan* and added to the torso of *Christabel;* he gave vent to his political and social urgings, which were liberal views slowly congealing in a shell of growing conservatism, in his *Lay Sermons* (1816). And he constantly scattered little fragments of verse and began occasional longer projects in poetry, some of them personal, some melodramatic in the vein of the ballad or romance, some translations or adaptations, like his famous *Hymn before Sunrise in the Vale of Chamouni*. A very few satirical specimens can be found in Coleridge's work, but for the most part it is highly romantic, and all of the longer attempts, save one, unfinished; *The Rime of the Ancient Mariner* was the only long poem that Coleridge ever completed.

Coleridge had great poetic powers; it has been observed that he had every qualification of the great poet except the utterly commonplace virtues of perseverance and diligence. Had he possessed but a fraction of the industry of his friend Southey, he would have been one of the most noted figures in world literature. His great contribution is in the realm of the supernatural. He speaks with the voice of beauty wedded to imagination; no other poet has so thoroughly imbued his work with the spirit of mystery. It is easy enough to see that he owes something to the Gothic novel (p. 23) and the German tale of terror, but his originality challenges admiration in spite of his known obligations to other works and other poets' minds. As a prose critic of the romantic period, he is virtually supreme; his *Biographia Literaria* (1817; p. 328) is not only a most revealing description of his relations with Wordsworth; it is also an extremely penetrating exposition of the romantic ideals of art and life, and a spiritual autobiography to be ranked among the world's greatest. His studies of Shakespeare set a vogue that is still vital; his *Table Talk* of his last years ranks with the conversations of his great German contemporary Goethe. It is possible to view him as the pathetic man who fails to make the most of his capabilities; it is perhaps fairer to accept Shelley's glowing eulogy:

> You will see Coleridge; he who sits obscure
> In the exceeding luster and the pure

Intense irradiation of a mind
Which, with its own internal lightning blind,
Flags wearily through darkness and despair;
A cloud-encircled meteor of the air,
A hooded eagle among blinking owls.

The Rime of the Ancient Mariner

The first edition of *Lyrical Ballads* (1798) contained this poem anonymously; the second edition made some changes to eliminate a few archaisms which Coleridge had written in the original. It was not published separately under Coleridge's name until 1817; the marginal gloss first appeared at this time. The genesis of the poem has been described thoroughly by Coleridge in *Biographia Literaria* (Chapter XIV; page 328). Wordsworth states that it was he who suggested the shooting of the albatross, but the inspiration of the poem as a whole was probably given Coleridge by a pair of seventeenth-century voyage-narratives, the *Letters of Saint Paulinus to Macarius* (1618) and Capt. T. James's *Strange and Dangerous Voyage* (1633). The idea of the albatross as a bird of good luck belongs to the folklore of the sea. The poem is Coleridge's most famous achievement and perhaps the greatest of all English literary ballads.

In Seven Parts

ARGUMENT

How a Ship having passed the Line was driven by storms to the cold Country towards the South Pole; and how from thence she made her course to the tropical Latitude of the Great Pacific Ocean; and of the strange things that befell: and in what manner the Ancyent Marinere came back to his own Country.

Part I

It is an ancient Mariner, *An ancient Mariner*
And he stoppeth one of three. *meeteth three*
"By thy long gray beard and *Gallants bidden to a wedding-feast,*
    glittering eye, *and detaineth*
Now wherefore stopp'st thou *one.*
    me?

"The Bridegroom's doors are opened wide,   5
And I am next of kin,
The guests are met, the feast is set:
May'st hear the merry din."

He holds him with his skinny hand;
"There was a ship," quoth he.   10
"Hold off! unhand me, gray-beard loon!"
Eftsoons his hand dropt he.

He holds him with his glittering eye—
The Wedding-Guest stood still,
And listens like a three years' child. 15
The Mariner hath his will.

The Wedding-Guest sat on a stone: *The Wedding-Guest is spellbound by the eye of the old seafaring man and constrained to hear his tale.*
He cannot choose but hear;
And thus spake on that ancient man,
The bright-eyed Mariner. 20

"The ship was cheered, the harbor cleared,
Merrily did we drop
Below the kirk, below the hill,
Below the light-house top.

"The sun came up upon the left, *The Mariner tells how the ship sailed southward with a good wind and fair weather, till it reached the Line.*
Out of the sea came he!
And he shone bright, and on the right
Went down into the sea.

"Higher and higher every day,
Till over the mast at noon—" 30
The Wedding-Guest here beat his breast,
For he heard the loud bassoon.

---

12. **Eftsoons**, at once. By the use of such archaic words as this, Coleridge reproduces something of the atmosphere of the old ballads. See Vol. I, pp. 114 ff.

13-16. **He . . . will.** Wordsworth states that he wrote this stanza. 30. **over . . . noon.** The ship is near the equator.

The bride hath paced into the hall,
Red as a rose is she; *The Wedding-Guest heareth the bridal music; but the Mariner continueth his tale.*
Nodding their heads before her goes
The merry minstrelsy.

The Wedding-Guest he beat his breast,
Yet he cannot choose but hear;
And thus spake on that ancient man,
The bright-eyed Mariner.   40

"And now the Storm-blast came, and he *The ship driven by a storm toward the south pole.*
Was tyrannous and strong:
He struck with his o'ertaking wings,
And chased us south along.

"With sloping masts and dipping prow,   45
As who pursued with yell and blow
Still treads the shadow of his foe,
And forward bends his head,
The ship drove fast, loud roared the blast,
And southward aye we fled.   50

"And now there came both mist and snow,
And it grew wondrous cold:
And ice, mast-high, came floating by,
As green as emerald.

"And through the drifts the snowy clifts *The land of ice, and of fearful sounds where no living thing was to be seen.*
Did send a dismal sheen:
Nor shapes of men nor beasts we ken—
The ice was all between.

"The ice was here, the ice was there,
The ice was all around: 60
It cracked and growled, and roared and howled,
Like noises in a swound!

"At length did cross an Albatross, *Till a great sea-bird, called the Albatross, came through the snow-fog, and was received with great joy and hospitality.*
Thorough the fog it came;
As if it had been a Christian soul,
We hailed it in God's name.

58. **between**, between the ship and the land. 62. **swound**, swoon, dream. 64. **Thorough**, an old form of *through*.

"It ate the food it ne'er had eat,
And round and round it flew.
The ice did split with a thunder-fit;
The helmsman steered us through!   70

"And a good south wind sprung up behind; *And lo! the Albatross proveth a bird of good omen, and followeth the ship as it returned northward through fog and floating ice.*
The Albatross did follow,
And every day, for food or play,
Came to the mariners' hollo!

"In mist or cloud, on mast or shroud,   75
It perched for vespers nine;
Whiles all the night, through fog-smoke white,
Glimmered the white moon-shine."

"God save thee, ancient Mariner! *The ancient Mariner inhospitably killeth the pious bird of good omen.*
From the fiends, that plague thee thus!—
Why look'st thou so?"—"With my cross-bow
I shot the Albatross!"

Part II

"The Sun now rose upon the right:
Out of the sea came he,
Still hid in mist, and on the left   85
Went down into the sea.

"And the good south wind still blew behind,
But no sweet bird did follow,
Nor any day for food or play
Came to the mariners' hollo!   90

"And I had done a hellish thing, *His shipmates cry out against the ancient Mariner, for killing the bird of good luck.*
And it would work 'em woe:
For all averred, I had killed the bird
That made the breeze to blow.
Ah, wretch! said they, the bird to slay,   95
That made the breeze to blow!

"Nor dim nor red, like God's own head, *But when the fog cleared off they justify the same, and thus make*
The glorious Sun uprist:

75. **shroud**, a rope running from the masthead to the side of the ship. 76. **vespers**, evenings. 83. **Sun now rose.** The ship has now gone around Cape Horn and is headed north into the Pacific.

Then all averred, I had killed *themselves ac-*
   the bird *complices in*
That brought the fog and mist. 100 *the crime.*
'Twas right, said they, such birds to slay,
That bring the fog and mist.

"The fair breeze blew, the white *The fair breeze*
   foam flew, *continues; the*
The furrow followed free; *ship enters the*
We were the first that ever *Pacific Ocean,*
   burst *and sails north-*
Into that silent sea. *ward, even till*
 it reaches the
 Line.

"Down dropt the breeze, the *The ship hath*
   sails dropt down, *been suddenly*
'Twas sad as sad could be; *becalmed.*
And we did speak only to break
   The silence of the sea! 110

"All in a hot and copper sky,
The bloody Sun, at noon,
Right up above the mast did stand,
No bigger than the Moon.

"Day after day, day after day, 115
We stuck, nor breath nor motion;
As idle as a painted ship
Upon a painted ocean.

"Water, water, everywhere, *And the Alba-*
And all the boards did *tross begins to*
   shrink; *be avenged.*
Water, water, everywhere,
Nor any drop to drink.

"The very deep did rot: O Christ!
That ever this should be!
Yea, slimy things did crawl with legs 125
Upon the slimy sea.

"About, about, in reel and rout *A Spirit had*
The death-fires danced at night; *followed them;*
The water, like a witch's oils, *one of the in-*
Burnt green, and blue and white. *visible inhab-*
 itants of this
 planet, neither
 departed souls
nor angels; concerning whom the learned Jew, Josephus, and
the Platonic Constantinopolitan, Michael Psellus, may be con-

128. **death-fires**, phosphorescent lights, considered omens of
disaster. It is possible that Coleridge has in mind the maritime will-o'-the-wisp phenomenon known as "St. Elmo's fire."

"And some in dreams assured *sulted. They*
   were *are very nu-*
Of the Spirit that plagued us so; *merous, and*
Nine fathom deep he had fol- *there is no*
   lowed us *climate or ele-*
From the land of mist and snow. *ment without*
 one or more.

"And every tongue, through utter *The shipmates,*
   drought, *in their sore*
Was withered at the root; *distress, would*
We could not speak, no more *fain throw the*
   than if *whole guilt on*
We had been choked with soot. *the ancient*
 Mariner: in
 sign whereof
 they hang the
 dead sea-bird
 round his
 neck.

"Ah! well-a-day! what evil looks
Had I from old and young! 140
Instead of the cross, the Alba-
   tross
About my neck was hung.

PART III

"There passed a weary time. Each throat
Was parched, and glazed each eye.
A weary time! a weary time! 145
How glazed each weary eye,
When looking westward, I be- *The ancient*
   held *Mariner be-*
A something in the sky. *holdeth a sign*
 in the ele-
 ment afar off.

"At first it seemed a little speck,
And then it seemed a mist; 150
It moved and moved, and took at last
A certain shape, I wist.

"A speck, a mist, a shape, I wist!
And still it neared and neared:
As if it dodged a water-sprite, 155
It plunged and tacked and veered.

"With throats unslaked, with *At its nearer*
   black lips baked, *approach, it*
We could nor laugh nor wail; *seemeth him*
Through utter drought all dumb *to be a ship;*
   we stood! *and at a dear*
I bit my arm, I sucked the *ransom he*
   blood, *freeth his*
And cried, A sail! a sail! *speech from*
 the bonds of
 160 *thirst.*

152. **wist**, thought, knew.

"With throats unslaked, with black lips baked,
Agape they heard me call:
Gramercy! they for joy did grin, *A flash of joy;*
And all at once their breath drew in,   165
As they were drinking all.

"See! see! (I cried) she tacks no more! *And horror follows. For can it be a ship that comes onward without wind or tide?*
Hither to work us weal—
Without a breeze, without a tide,
She steadies with upright keel!   170

"The western wave was all aflame,
The day was well nigh done!
Almost upon the western wave
Rested the broad bright Sun;
When that strange shape drove suddenly   175
Betwixt us and the Sun.

"And straight the Sun was flecked with bars, *It seemeth him but the skeleton of a ship.*
(Heaven's Mother send us grace!)
As if through a dungeon-grate he peered
With broad and burning face.   180

"Alas! (thought I, and my heart beat loud)
How fast she nears and nears!
Are those her sails that glance in the Sun,
Like restless gossameres?

"Are those her ribs through which the Sun *And its ribs are seen as bars on the face of the setting Sun.*
Did peer, as through a grate?
And is that Woman all her crew? *The Specter-Woman and her Death-mate, and no other on board the skeleton-ship.*
Is that a Death? and are there two?
Is Death that woman's mate?

"Her lips were red, her looks were free,   190 *Like vessel, like crew!*
Her locks were yellow as gold:
Her skin was as white as leprosy,
The Night-mare Life-in-Death was she,
Who thicks man's blood with cold.

164. **Gramercy**, great thanks. 184. **gossameres**, fine spiderwebs.

"The naked hulk alongside came, *Death and Life-in-Death have diced for the ship's crew, and she (the latter) winneth the ancient Mariner.*
And the twain were casting dice;
'The game is done! I've won! I've won!'
Quoth she, and whistles thrice.

"The Sun's rim dips; the stars rush out: *No twilight within the courts of the Sun.*
At one stride comes the dark;   200
With far-heard whisper, o'er the sea,
Off shot the specter-bark.

"We listened and looked sideways up! *At the rising of the Moon,*
Fear at my heart, as at a cup,
My life-blood seemed to sip!   205
The stars were dim, and thick the night,
The steersman's face by his lamp gleamed white;
From the sails the dew did drip—
Till clomb above the eastern bar
The hornéd Moon, with one bright star   210
Within the nether tip.

"One after one, by the star-dogged Moon, *One after another,*
Too quick for groan or sigh,
Each turned his face with a ghastly pang,
And cursed me with his eye.   215

"Four times fifty living men, *His shipmates drop down dead.*
(And I heard nor sigh nor groan)
With heavy thump, a lifeless lump,
They dropt down one by one.

"The souls did from their bodies fly— *But Life-in-Death begins her work on the ancient Mariner.*
They fled to bliss or woe!
And every soul, it passed me by
Like the whizz of my cross-bow!"

Part IV

"I fear thee, ancient Mariner! *The Wedding-Guest feareth that a Spirit is talking to him;*
I fear thy skinny hand!

210. **Moon . . . tip.** In a manuscript note Coleridge remarks that "it is a common superstition among sailors that something evil is about to happen whenever a star dogs the moon." It is impossible, however, for any star to appear between the horns of the crescent moon, for the moon is the celestial object that is nearest the earth.

And thou art long, and lank, and brown,
As is the ribbed sea-sand.

"I fear thee and thy glittering eye,
And thy skinny hand, so brown."—
"Fear not, fear not, thou Wed-
   ding-Guest!
This body dropt not down.

"Alone, alone, all, all alone,
Alone on a wide, wide sea!
And never a saint took pity on
My soul in agony.   235

"The many men, so beautiful!
And they all dead did lie:
And a thousand thousand slimy things
Lived on; and so did I.   239

"I looked upon the rotting sea,
And drew my eyes away;
I looked upon the rotting deck,
And there the dead men lay.

"I looked to heaven, and tried to pray;
But or ever a prayer had gusht,   245
A wicked whisper came, and made
My heart as dry as dust.

"I closed my lids, and kept them close,
And the balls like pulses beat;
For the sky and the sea, and the sea and the
   sky   250
Lay like a load on my weary eye,
And the dead were at my feet.

"The cold sweat melted from
   their limbs,
Nor rot nor reek did they:
The look with which they looked on me   255
Had never passed away.

"An orphan's curse would drag to hell
A spirit from on high;

But the ancient Mariner assureth him of his bodily life, and proceedeth to relate his horrible penance.

He despiseth the creatures of the calm.

And envieth that they should live, and so many lie dead.

But the curse liveth for him in the eye of the dead men.

In his loneliness and fixed-

But oh! more horrible than
   that
Is a curse in a dead man's eye!
Seven days, seven nights, I saw
   that curse,
And yet I could not die.

"The moving Moon went up the
   sky,
And nowhere did abide:
Softly she was going up,
And a star or two beside—

"Her beams bemocked the sul-
   try main,
Like April hoar-frost spread;
But where the ship's huge shadow lay,
The charmèd water burnt alway   270
A still and awful red.

"Beyond the shadow of the ship,
I watched the water-snakes:
They moved in tracks of shining
   white,
And when they reared, the elfish light   275
Fell off in hoary flakes.

"Within the shadow of the ship
I watched their rich attire:
Blue, glossy green, and velvet black,
They coiled and swam; and every track   280
Was a flash of golden fire.

"O happy living things! no
   tongue
Their beauty might declare:
A spring of love gushed from my heart,
And I blessed them unaware;
Sure my kind saint took pity on
   me,   286
And I blessed them unaware.

"The selfsame moment I could pray;
And from my neck so free
The Albatross fell off, and sank   290
Like lead into the sea."

ness he yearneth towards the journeying Moon, and the stars that still sojourn, yet still move onward; and everywhere the blue sky belongs to them, and is their appointed rest, and their native country and their own natural homes, which they enter unannounced, as lords that are certainly expected, and yet there is a silent joy at their arrival.

By the light of the Moon he beholdeth God's creatures of the great calm.

Their beauty and their happiness.

He blesseth them in his heart.

The spell begins to break.

226-227. **And . . . sea-sand.** For these two lines Coleridge acknowledges indebtedness to Wordsworth. 228. **glittering eye.** It is a commonplace of European folklore that a person with evil attributes can do harm to another by fixing him with his eye (the "evil eye" *motif*).

263. **The moving Moon, etc.** The atmosphere of this stanza might profitably be compared with that of the old popular ballad, *Sir Patrick Spens* (Vol. I, p. 122).

Part V

"Oh sleep! it is a gentle thing,
Beloved from pole to pole!
To Mary Queen the praise be given!
She sent the gentle sleep from Heaven,   295
That slid into my soul.

"The silly buckets on the deck, *By grace of the holy Mother, the ancient Mariner is refreshed with rain.*
That had so long remained,
I dreamt that they were filled
    with dew;
And when I awoke, it rained.   300

"My lips were wet, my throat was cold,
My garments all were dank;
Sure I had drunken in my dreams,
And still my body drank.

"I moved, and could not feel my limbs: 305
I was so light—almost
I thought that I had died in sleep,
And was a blessed ghost.

"And soon I heard a roaring *He heareth sounds and seeth strange sights and commotions in the sky and the elements.*
    wind:
It did not come anear;
But with its sound it shook the
    sails,
That were so thin and sere.

"The upper air burst into life!
And a hundred fire-flags sheen,
To and fro they were hurried about!   315
And to and fro, and in and out,
The wan stars danced between.

"And the coming wind did roar more loud,
And the sails did sigh like sedge;
And the rain poured down from one black
    cloud;   320
The Moon was at its edge.

"The thick black cloud was cleft, and still
The Moon was at its side:
Like waters shot from some high crag,
The lightning fell with never a jag,   325
A river steep and wide.

297. **silly**, literally, *innocent;* and by a poetic extension, *unused, empty.* 314. **fire-flags**, perhaps the Northern Lights. **sheen**, bright. 319. **sedge**, coarse marsh grass.

"The loud wind never reached *The bodies of the ship's crew are inspired, and the ship moves on;*
    the ship,
Yet now the ship moved on!
Beneath the lightning and the
    Moon
The dead men gave a groan.   330

"They groaned, they stirred, they all uprose,
Nor spake, nor moved their eyes;
It had been strange, even in a dream,
To have seen those dead men rise.

"The helmsman steered, the ship moved
    on;   335
Yet never a breeze up blew;
The mariners all 'gan work the ropes,
Where they were wont to do;
They raised their limbs like lifeless tools—
We were a ghastly crew.   340

"The body of my brother's son
Stood by me, knee to knee:
The body and I pulled at one rope,
But he said nought to me."

"I fear thee, ancient Mariner!" *But not by the souls of the men, nor by demons of earth or middle air, but by a blessed troop of angelic spirits, sent down by the invocation of the guardian saint.*
"Be calm, thou Wedding-
    Guest!
'Twas not those souls that fled
    in pain,
Which to their corses came
    again,
But a troop of spirits blest:

"For when it dawned—they dropped their
    arms,   350
And clustered round the mast;
Sweet sounds rose slowly through their
    mouths,
And from their bodies passed.

"Around, around, flew each sweet sound,
Then darted to the Sun;   355
Slowly the sounds came back again,
Now mixed, now one by one.

"Sometimes a-dropping from the sky
I heard the skylark sing;
Sometimes all little birds that are,   360

How they seemed to fill the sea and air
With their sweet jargoning!

"And now 'twas like all instruments,
Now like a lonely flute;
And now it is an angel's song, 365
That makes the heavens be mute.

"It ceased; yet still the sails made on
A pleasant noise till noon,
A noise like of a hidden brook
In the leafy month of June, 370
That to the sleeping woods all night
Singeth a quiet tune.

"Till noon we quietly sailed on,
Yet never a breeze did breathe:
Slowly and smoothly went the ship, 375
Moved onward from beneath.

"Under the keel nine fathom deep, *The lonesome Spirit from the South Pole carries on the ship as far as the Line, in obedience to the angelic troop, but still requireth vengeance.*
From the land of mist and snow,
The Spirit slid: and it was he
That made the ship to go.
The sails at noon left off their tune,
And the ship stood still also.

"The Sun, right up above the mast,
Had fixed her to the ocean:
But in a minute she 'gan stir, 385
With a short uneasy motion—
Backwards and forwards half her length
With a short uneasy motion.

"Then like a pawing horse let go,
She made a sudden bound: 390
It flung the blood into my head,
And I fell down in a swound.

"How long in that same fit I lay, *The Polar Spirit's fellow demons, the invisible inhabitants of the element, take part in his wrong; and two of them*
I have not to declare;
But ere my living life returned,

394. **have not**, have not the power or knowledge.

I heard, and in my soul discerned, *relate, one to the other, that penance long and heavy for the ancient Mariner hath been accorded to the Polar Spirit, who returneth southward.*
Two voices in the air.

"'Is it he?' quoth one, 'Is this the man?
By Him who died on cross,
With his cruel bow he laid full low 400
The harmless Albatross.

"'The Spirit who bideth by himself
In the land of mist and snow,
He loved the bird that loved the man
Who shot him with his bow.' 405

"The other was a softer voice,
As soft as honey-dew:
Quoth he, 'The man hath penance done,
And penance more will do.'"

Part VI

First Voice

"'But tell me, tell me! speak again, 410
Thy soft response renewing—
What makes that ship drive on so fast?
What is the ocean doing?'

Second Voice

"'Still as a slave before his lord,
The ocean hath no blast; 415
His great bright eye most silently
Up to the Moon is cast—

"'If he may know which way to go;
For she guides him smooth or grim.
See, brother, see! how graciously 420
She looketh down on him.'

First Voice

"'But why drives on that ship so fast, *The Mariner hath been cast into a trance; for the angelic power causeth the vessel to drive northward faster than human life could endure.*
Without or wave or wind?'

Second Voice

"'The air is cut away before,
And closes from behind.' 425

"'Fly, brother, fly! more high, more high!
Or we shall be belated:
For slow and slow that ship will go,
When the Mariner's trance is abated.'

"I woke, and we were sailing on *The supernatural motion is retarded; the Mariner awakes, and his penance begins anew.*
As in a gentle weather:
'Twas night, calm night, the moon was high;
The dead men stood together.

"All stood together on the deck,
For a charnel-dungeon fitter: 435
All fixed on me their stony eyes,
That in the Moon did glitter.

"The pang, the curse, with which they died,
Had never passed away:
I could not draw my eyes from theirs, 440
Nor turn them up to pray.

"And now this spell was snapt: once more *The curse is finally expiated.*
I viewed the ocean green,
And looked far forth, yet little saw
Of what had else been seen— 445

"Like one, that on a lonesome road
Doth walk in fear and dread,
And having once turned round, walks on,
And turns no more his head;
Because he knows, a frightful fiend 450
Doth close behind him tread.

"But soon there breathed a wind on me,
Nor sound nor motion made:
Its path was not upon the sea,
In ripple or in shade. 455

"It raised my hair, it fanned my cheek
Like a meadow-gale of spring—
It mingled strangely with my fears,
Yet it felt like a welcoming.

"Swiftly, swiftly flew the ship, 460
Yet she sailed softly too:
Sweetly, sweetly blew the breeze—
On me alone it blew.

"Oh! dream of joy! is this indeed *And the ancient Mariner beholdeth his native country.*
The light-house top I see?
Is this the hill? is this the kirk?
Is this mine own countree?

"We drifted o'er the harbor-bar,
And I with sobs did pray—
O let me be awake, my God! 470
Or let me sleep alway.

"The harbor-bay was clear as glass,
So smoothly it was strewn!
And on the bay the moonlight lay,
And the shadow of the Moon. 475

"The rock shone bright, the kirk no less,
That stands above the rock:
The moonlight steeped in silentness
The steady weathercock.

"And the bay was white with silent light 480
Till, rising from the same,
Full many shapes, that shadows were, *The angelic spirits leave the dead bodies,*
In crimson colors came.

"A little distance from the prow
Those crimson shadows were: 485
I turned my eyes upon the deck—
Oh, Christ! what saw I there!

"Each corse lay flat, lifeless and flat,
And, by the holy rood!
A man all light, a seraph-man, *And appear in their own forms of light.*
On every corse there stood.

"This seraph-band, each waved his hand:
It was a heavenly sight!
They stood as signals to the land,
Each one a lovely light; 495

"This seraph-band, each waved his hand,
No voice did they impart—
No voice; but oh! the silence sank
Like music on my heart.

---

435. **charnel-dungeon**, a vault for bones of the dead.

489. **rood**, cross.

"But soon I heard the dash of oars,
I heard the Pilot's cheer;
My head was turned perforce away,
And I saw a boat appear.

"The Pilot and the Pilot's boy,
I heard them coming fast:
Dear Lord in Heaven! it was a joy
The dead men could not blast.

"I saw a third—I heard his voice:
It is the Hermit good!
He singeth loud his godly hymns
That he makes in the wood.
He'll shrieve my soul, he'll wash away
The Albatross's blood."

Part VII

"This Hermit good lives in that wood, *The Hermit of the wood,*
Which slopes down to the sea.
How loudly his sweet voice he rears!
He loves to talk with marineres
That come from a far countree.

"He kneels at morn, and noon, and eve—
He hath a cushion plump:
It is the moss that wholly hides
The rotted old oak-stump.

"The skiff-boat neared: I heard them talk,
'Why, this is strange, I trow!
Where are those lights so many and fair,
That signal made but now?'

"'Strange, by my faith!' the Hermit said— *Approacheth the ship with wonder.*
'And they answered not our cheer!
The planks looked warped! and see those sails,
How thin they are and sere!
I never saw aught like to them,
Unless perchance it were

"'Brown skeletons of leaves that lag
My forest-brook along;
When the ivy-tod is heavy with snow,

And the owlet whoops to the wolf below,
That eats the she-wolf's young.'

"'Dear Lord! it hath a fiendish look—
(The Pilot made reply)
I am a-feared'—'Push on, push on!'
Said the Hermit cheerily.

"The boat came closer to the ship,
But I nor spake nor stirred;
The boat came close beneath the ship,
And straight a sound was heard.

"Under the water it rumbled on, *The ship suddenly sinketh.*
Still louder and more dread:
It reached the ship, it split the bay;
The ship went down like lead.

"Stunned by that loud and dreadful sound, *The ancient Mariner is saved in the Pilot's boat.*
Which sky and ocean smote,
Like one that hath been seven days drowned
My body lay afloat;
But swift as dreams, myself I found
Within the Pilot's boat.

"Upon the whirl, where sank the ship,
The boat spun round and round;
And all was still, save that the hill
Was telling of the sound.

"I moved my lips—the Pilot shrieked
And fell down in a fit;
The holy Hermit raised his eyes,
And prayed where he did sit.

"I took the oars: the Pilot's boy,
Who now doth crazy go,
Laughed loud and long, and all the while
His eyes went to and fro.
'Ha! ha!' quoth he, 'full plain I see,
The Devil knows how to row.'

"And now, all in my own countree,
I stood on the firm land!
The Hermit stepped forth from the boat,
And scarcely he could stand.

---

535. **ivy-tod**, ivy-bush.

558. **hill . . . sound**, referring to the echo of the cataclysm.

"'O shrieve me, shrieve me, holy man!"
The Hermit crossed his brow. *The ancient Mariner earnestly entreateth the Hermit to shrieve him; and the penance of life falls on him.*
'Say quick,' quoth he, 'I bid thee say—
What manner of man art thou?'

"Forthwith this frame of mine was wrenched
With a woful agony,
Which forced me to begin my tale;   580
And then it left me free.

"Since then, at an uncertain hour, *And ever and anon throughout his future life an agony constraineth him to travel from land to land,*
That agony returns;
And till my ghastly tale is told,
This heart within me burns.

"I pass, like night, from land to land;
I have strange power of speech;
That moment that his face I see,
I know the man that must hear me:
To him my tale I teach.   590

"What loud uproar bursts from that door!
The wedding-guests are there:
But in the garden-bower the bride
And bride-maids singing are:
And hark the little vesper bell,   595
Which biddeth me to prayer!

"O Wedding-Guest! this soul hath been
Alone on a wide, wide sea:
So lonely 'twas, that God himself
Scarce seemed there to be.   600

"Oh sweeter than the marriage-feast,
'Tis sweeter far to me,
To walk together to the kirk
With a goodly company!—

"To walk together to the kirk,   605
And all together pray,
While each to his great Father bends,
Old men, and babes, and loving friends,
And youths and maidens gay!

"Farewell, farewell! but this I tell *And to teach by his own example love and reverence to all things that God made and loveth.*
To thee, thou Wedding-Guest!
He prayeth well, who loveth well
Both man and bird and beast.

"He prayeth best, who loveth best
All things both great and small;   615
For the dear God who loveth us,
He made and loveth all."

The Mariner, whose eye is bright,
Whose beard with age is hoar,
Is gone: and now the Wedding-Guest   620
Turned from the bridegroom's door.

He went like one that hath been stunned,
And is of sense forlorn:
A sadder and a wiser man,
He rose the morrow morn.

(*1797-98; 1798*)

575. **crossed his brow,** made the sign of the Cross upon his forehead to avert evil.

623. **of sense forlorn,** deprived of his senses.

Christabel

Coleridge never finished this poem, never even carried it much beyond the beginning of the story. The first part was composed as early as 1797; the second part, which has very little relation to the first, not until 1800. Such portions of the poem as were completed were finally published in 1816. The reasons for the unfinished state of *Christabel* are to be found in Coleridge's own indolent and vacillating temperament, as he himself freely admitted as late as 1833: "The reason of my not finishing *Christabel* is not that I don't know how to do it—for I have, as I always had, the whole plan entire from beginning to end in my mind; but I fear I could not carry on with equal success the execution of the idea, an extremely subtle and difficult one."

The meter of *Christabel* is an interesting revival by Coleridge of the free four-stress line, divisible into two half lines of two stresses each, that was an important characteristic of Old English alliterative verse.

Part I

'Tis the middle of night by the castle clock,
And the owls have awakened the crowing cock,
Tu—whit!——Tu—whoo!
And hark, again! the crowing cock,
How drowsily it crew. 5

Sir Leoline, the Baron rich,
Hath a toothless mastiff bitch;
From her kennel beneath the rock
She maketh answer to the clock,
Four for the quarters, and twelve for the hour; 10
Ever and aye, by shine and shower,
Sixteen short howls, not over loud;
Some say, she sees my lady's shroud.

Is the night chilly and dark?
The night is chilly, but not dark. 15
The thin gray cloud is spread on high,
It covers but not hides the sky.
The moon is behind, and at the full;
And yet she looks both small and dull.
The night is chill, the cloud is gray: 20
'Tis a month before the month of May,
And the Spring comes slowly up this way.

The lovely lady, Christabel,
Whom her father loves so well,
What makes her in the wood so late, 25
A furlong from the castle gate?
She had dreams all yesternight
Of her own betrothéd knight;
And she in the midnight wood will pray
For the weal of her lover that's far away. 30

She stole along, she nothing spoke,
The sighs she heaved were soft and low,
And naught was green upon the oak
But moss and rarest mistletoe:
She kneels beneath the huge oak tree 35
And in silence prayeth she.

The lady sprang up suddenly,
The lovely lady, Christabel!
It moaned as near, as near can be,
But what it is she cannot tell.— 40
On the other side it seems to be,
Of the huge, broad-breasted, old oak tree.

The night is chill; the forest bare;
Is it the wind that moaneth bleak?
There is not wind enough in the air 45
To move away the ringlet curl
From the lovely lady's cheek—
There is not wind enough to twirl
The one red leaf, the last of its clan,
That dances as often as dance it can, 50
Hanging so light, and hanging so high,
On the topmost twig that looks up at the sky.

Hush, beating heart of Christabel!
Jesu Maria, shield her well!
She folded her arms beneath her cloak, 55
And stole to the other side of the oak.
What sees she there?

There she sees a damsel bright,
Drest in a silken robe of white,
That shadowy in the moonlight shone: 60
The neck that made that white robe wan,
Her stately neck, and arms were bare;
Her blue-veined feet unsandalled were,
And wildly glittered here and there
The gems entangled in her hair. 65
I guess, 'twas frightful there to see
A lady so richly clad as she—
Beautiful exceedingly!

"Mary mother, save me now!"
(Said Christabel) "And who art thou?" 70

The lady strange made answer meet,
And her voice was faint and sweet:
"Have pity on my sore distress,
I scarce can speak for weariness":
"Stretch forth thy hand, and have no fear!" 75
Said Christabel, "How camest thou here?"
And the lady, whose voice was faint and sweet,
Did thus pursue her answer meet:

"My sire is of a noble line,
And my name is Geraldine: 80
Five warriors seized me yestermorn.

Me, even me, a maid forlorn:
They choked my cries with force and fright,
And tied me on a palfrey white.
The palfrey was as fleet as wind,   85
And they rode furiously behind.
They spurred amain, their steeds were white:
And once we crossed the shade of night.
As sure as Heaven shall rescue me,
I have no thought what men they be;   90
Nor do I know how long it is
(For I have lain entranced, I wis)
Since one, the tallest of the five,
Took me from the palfrey's back,
A weary woman, scarce alive.   95
Some muttered words his comrades spoke:
He placed me underneath this oak;
He swore they would return with haste;
Whither they went I cannot tell—
I thought I heard, some minutes past,   100
Sounds as of a castle bell.
Stretch forth thy hand (thus ended she),
And help a wretched maid to flee."

Then Christabel stretched forth her hand,
And comforted fair Geraldine: 105
"Oh well, bright dame! may you command
The service of Sir Leoline:
And gladly our stout chivalry
Will he send forth, and friends withal,
To guide and guard you safe and free   110
Home to your noble father's hall."

She rose: and forth with steps they passed
That strove to be, and were not, fast.
Her gracious stars the lady blest,
And thus spake on sweet Christabel: 115
"All our household are at rest,
The hall as silent as the cell;
Sir Leoline is weak in health,
And may not well awakened be,
But we will move as if in stealth,   120
And I beseech your courtesy,
This night, to share your couch with me."

They crossed the moat, and Christabel
Took the key that fitted well;
A little door she opened straight,   125
All in the middle of the gate;
The gate that was ironed within and without,
Where an army in battle array had marched
    out.
The lady sank, belike through pain,
And Christabel with might and main   130
Lifted her up, a weary weight,
Over the threshold of the gate:
Then the lady rose again,
And moved, as she were not in pain.

So free from danger, free from fear,   135
They crossed the court: right glad they
    were.
And Christabel devoutly cried
To the lady by her side:
"Praise we the Virgin all divine
Who hath rescued thee from thy distress!"
"Alas, alas!" said Geraldine,   141
"I cannot speak for weariness."
So free from danger, free from fear,
They crossed the court: right glad they
    were.

Outside her kennel the mastiff old   145
Lay fast asleep, in moonshine cold.
The mastiff old did not awake,
Yet she an angry moan did make!
And what can ail the mastiff bitch?
Never till now she uttered yell   150
Beneath the eye of Christabel.
Perhaps it is the owlet's scritch:
For what can ail the mastiff bitch?

They passed the hall, that echoes still,
Pass as lightly as you will!   155
The brands were flat, the brands were dying,
Amid their own white ashes lying;
But when the lady passed, there came
A tongue of light, a fit of flame;
And Christabel saw the lady's eye,   160
And nothing else saw she thereby,
Save the boss of the shield of Sir Leoline tall,
Which hung in a murky old niche in the
    wall.
"O softly tread," said Christabel,
"My father seldom sleepeth well."   165

129-159. **The lady sank,** etc. These lines show Geraldine to be an evil spirit. She was unable, without aid, to cross the threshold, which had been blessed to keep evil spirits away; she refused to praise the Virgin (l. 142); the dog had a premonition of the presence of evil (l. 148); the action of the fire (ll. 156-159) was caused by the nearness of a supernatural being.

Sweet Christabel her feet doth bare,
And jealous of the listening air,
They steal their way from stair to stair,
Now in glimmer, and now in gloom,
And now they pass the Baron's room,   170
As still as death, with stifled breath!
And now have reached her chamber door;
And now doth Geraldine press down
The rushes of the chamber floor.

The moon shines dim in the open air,   175
And not a moonbeam enters here.
But they without its light can see
The chamber carved so curiously,
Carved with figures strange and sweet,
All made out of the carver's brain,   180
For a lady's chamber meet:
The lamp with twofold silver chain
Is fastened to an angel's feet.

The silver lamp burns dead and dim;
But Christabel the lamp will trim.   185
She trimmed the lamp, and made it bright,
And left it swinging to and fro,
While Geraldine, in wretched plight,
Sank down upon the floor below.

"O weary lady, Geraldine,   190
I pray you, drink this cordial wine!
It is a wine of virtuous powers;
My mother made it of wild flowers."

"And will your mother pity me,
Who am a maiden most forlorn?"   195
Christabel answered—"Woe is me!
She died the hour that I was born.
I have heard the gray-haired friar tell,
How on her death-bed she did say,
That she should hear the castle-bell   200
Strike twelve upon my wedding-day.
O mother dear! that thou wert here!"
"I would," said Geraldine, "she were!"

But soon with altered voice, said she—
"Off, wandering mother! Peak and pine!   205
I have power to bid thee flee."
Alas! what ails poor Geraldine?
Why stares she with unsettled eye?

Can she the bodiless dead espy?
And why with hollow voice cries she.   210
"Off, woman, off! this hour is mine—
Though thou her guardian spirit be,
Off, woman, off! 'tis given to me."

Then Christabel knelt by the lady's side,
And raised to heaven her eyes so blue—   215
"Alas!" said she, "this ghastly ride—
Dear lady! it hath wildered you!"
The lady wiped her moist cold brow,
And faintly said, " 'Tis over now!"

Again the wild-flower wine she drank: 220
Her fair large eyes 'gan glitter bright,
And from the floor whereon she sank,
The lofty lady stood upright;
She was most beautiful to see,
Like a lady of a far countree.   225

And thus the lofty lady spake—
"All they, who live in the upper sky,
Do love you, holy Christabel!
And you love them, and for their sake
And for the good which me befell,   230
Even I in my degree will try,
Fair maiden, to requite you well.
But now unrobe yourself; for I
Must pray, ere yet in bed I lie."

Quoth Christabel, "So let it be!"   235
And as the lady bade, did she.
Her gentle limbs did she undress,
And lay down in her loveliness.

But through her brain of weal and woe
So many thoughts moved to and fro,   240
That vain it were her lids to close:
So half-way from the bed she rose,
And on her elbow did recline
To look at the lady Geraldine.

Beneath the lamp the lady bowed,   245
And slowly rolled her eyes around;
Then drawing in her breath aloud,
Like one that shuddered, she unbound
The cincture from beneath her breast:
Her silken robe, and inner vest,   250

205. **Off . . . mother.** Geraldine has power to drive away the beneficent spirit of Christabel's mother.

249. **cincture,** girdle.

Dropt to her feet, and full in view,
Behold! her bosom and half her side—
A sight to dream of, not to tell!
Oh, shield her! shield sweet Christabel!

Yet Geraldine nor speaks nor stirs; 255
Ah! what a stricken look was hers!
Deep from within she seems half-way
To lift some weight with sick assay,
And eyes the maid and seeks delay;
Then suddenly, as one defied, 260
Collects herself in scorn and pride,
And lay down by the maiden's side!—
And in her arms the maid she took,
    Ah, well-a-day!
And with low voice and doleful look 265
    These words did say:
"In the touch of this bosom there worketh a spell,
Which is lord of thy utterance, Christabel!
Thou knowest tonight, and wilt know tomorrow,
This mark of my shame, this seal of my sorrow: 270
    But vainly thou warrest,
      For this is alone in
    Thy power to declare,
      That in the dim forest
    Thou heard'st a low moaning, 275
And found'st a bright lady, surpassingly fair:
And didst bring her home with thee in love and in charity,
To shield her and shelter her from the damp air."

THE CONCLUSION TO PART I

It was a lovely sight to see
The lady Christabel, when she 280
Was praying at the old oak tree.
    Amid the jagged shadows
    Of mossy leafless boughs,
    Kneeling in the moonlight,
    To make her gentle vows; 285
Her slender palms together prest,
Heaving sometimes on her breast;
Her face resigned to bliss or bale—
Her face, oh call it fair not pale,
And both blue eyes more bright than clear, 290
Each about to have a tear.

With open eyes (ah, woe is me!)
Asleep, and dreaming fearfully,
Fearfully dreaming, yet, I wis,
Dreaming that alone, which is— 295
O sorrow and shame! Can this be she,
The lady, who knelt at the old oak tree?
And lo! the worker of these harms,
That holds the maiden in her arms,
Seems to slumber still and mild, 300
As a mother with her child.

A star hath set, a star hath risen,
O Geraldine! since arms of thine
Have been the lovely lady's prison.
O Geraldine! one hour was thine— 305
Thou'st had thy will! By tairn and rill,
The night-birds all that hour were still.
But now they are jubilant anew,
From cliff and tower, tu—whoo! tu—whoo!
Tu—whoo! tu—whoo! from wood and fell!

And see! the lady Christabel 311
Gathers herself from out her trance;
Her limbs relax, her countenance
Grows sad and soft; the smooth thin lids
Close o'er her eyes; and tears she sheds— 315
Large tears that leave the lashes bright!
And oft the while she seems to smile
As infants at a sudden light!

Yea, she doth smile, and she doth weep,
Like a youthful hermitess, 320
Beauteous in a wilderness,
Who, praying always, prays in sleep.
And, if she move unquietly,
Perchance, 'tis but the blood so free
Comes back and tingles in her feet. 325
No doubt she hath a vision sweet.
What if her guardian spirit 'twere?
What if she knew her mother near?
But this she knows, in joys and woes,
That saints will aid if men will call: 330
For the blue sky bends over all!

Part II

Each matin bell, the Baron saith,
Knells us back to a world of death.
These words Sir Leoline first said,

---

294. **wis**, think. 306. **tairn**, tarn, mountain pool.

When he rose and found his lady dead: 335
These words Sir Leoline will say,
Many a morn to his dying day!

And hence the custom and law began,
That still at dawn the sacristan,
Who duly pulls the heavy bell, 340
Five and forty beads must tell
Between each stroke—a warning knell,
Which not a soul can choose but hear
From Bratha Head to Wyndermere.

Saith Bracy the bard, "So let it knell! 345
And let the drowsy sacristan
Still count as slowly as he can!
There is no lack of such, I ween,
As well fill up the space between."
In Langdale Pike and Witch's lair, 350
And Dungeon-ghyll so foully rent,
With ropes of rock and bells of air
Three sinful sextons' ghosts are pent,
Who all give back, one after t' other,
The death-note to their living brother; 355
And oft too, by the knell offended,
Just as their one! two! three! is ended,
The devil mocks the doleful tale
With a merry peal from Borodale.

The air is still! through mist and cloud 360
That merry peal comes ringing loud;
And Geraldine shakes off her dread,
And rises lightly from the bed;
Puts on her silken vestments white,
And tricks her hair in lovely plight, 365
And nothing doubting of her spell
Awakens the lady Christabel.
"Sleep you, sweet lady Christabel?
I trust that you have rested well."

And Christabel awoke and spied 370
The same who lay down by her side—
Oh, rather say, the same whom she
Raised up beneath the old oak tree!
Nay, fairer yet; and yet more fair!
For she belike hath drunken deep 375
Of all the blessedness of sleep!
And while she spake, her looks, her air,
Such gentle thankfulness declare,
That (so it seemed) her girded vests
Grew tight beneath her heaving breasts. 380
"Sure I have sinned!" said Christabel,
"Now heaven be praised if all be well!"
And in low faltering tones, yet sweet,
Did she the lofty lady greet,
With such perplexity of mind 385
As dreams too lively leave behind.

So quickly she rose, and quickly arrayed
Her maiden limbs, and having prayed
That He, who on the cross did groan,
Might wash away her sins unknown, 390
She forthwith led fair Geraldine
To meet her sire, Sir Leoline.

The lovely maid and lady tall
Are pacing both into the hall,
And pacing on through page and groom, 395
Enter the Baron's presence-room.

The Baron rose, and while he prest
His gentle daughter to his breast,
With cheerful wonder in his eyes
The lady Geraldine espies, 400
And gave such welcome to the same,
As might beseem so bright a dame!

But when he heard the lady's tale,
And when she told her father's name,
Why waxed Sir Leoline so pale, 405
Murmuring o'er the name again,
Lord Roland de Vaux of Tryermaine?

Alas! they had been friends in youth;
But whispering tongues can poison truth;
And constancy lives in realms above; 410
And life is thorny; and youth is vain;
And to be wroth with one we love
Doth work like madness in the brain.
And thus it chanced, as I divine,
With Roland and Sir Leoline. 415
Each spake words of high disdain
And insult to his heart's best brother:

---

344. **Bratha Head**, the source of the River Bratha, which flows through the county of Westmoreland into Lake Windermere. The other places named are in the beautiful and romantic Lake District, but the poem is not meant to be thus localized. 350. **Pike**, peak, hill. 351. **ghyll**, valley or ravine with a stream running through it.

408-426. **Alas!** etc. Coleridge regarded these lines as "the best and sweetest passage" he ever wrote. They may refer to his temporary estrangement from Southey.

They parted—ne'er to meet again!
But never either found another
To free the hollow heart from paining—   420
They stood aloof, the scars remaining,
Like cliffs which had been rent asunder;
A dreary sea now flows between—
But neither heat, nor frost, nor thunder,
Shall wholly do away, I ween,   425
The marks of that which once hath been.

Sir Leoline, a moment's space,
Stood gazing on the damsel's face:
And the youthful Lord of Tryermaine
Came back upon his heart again.   430

Oh then the Baron forgot his age,
His noble heart swelled high with rage;
He swore by the wounds in Jesu's side,
He would proclaim it far and wide,
With trump and solemn heraldry,   435
That they who thus had wronged the dame,
Were base as spotted infamy!
"And if they dare deny the same,
My herald shall appoint a week,
And let the recreant traitors seek   440
My tourney court—that there and then
I may dislodge their reptile souls
From the bodies and forms of men!"
He spake: his eye in lightning rolls!
For the lady was ruthlessly seized; and he kenned   445
In the beautiful lady the child of his friend!

And now the tears were on his face,
And fondly in his arms he took
Fair Geraldine, who met the embrace,
Prolonging it with joyous look.   450
Which when she viewed, a vision fell
Upon the soul of Christabel,
The vision of fear, the touch and pain!
She shrunk and shuddered, and saw again—
(Ah, woe is me! Was it for thee,   455
Thou gentle maid! such sights to see?)

Again she saw that bosom old,
Again she felt that bosom cold,
And drew in her breath with a hissing sound:
Whereat the Knight turned wildly round,   460
And nothing saw but his own sweet maid
With eyes upraised, as one that prayed.

The touch, the sight, had passed away,
And in its stead that vision blest,
Which comforted her after-rest   465
While in the lady's arms she lay,
Had put a rapture in her breast,
And on her lips and o'er her eyes
Spread smiles like light!
      With new surprise,
"What ails then my belovéd child?"   470
The Baron said—His daughter mild
Made answer, "All will yet be well!"
I ween, she had no power to tell
Aught else: so mighty was the spell.

Yet he, who saw this Geraldine,   475
Had deemed her sure a thing divine.
Such sorrow with such grace she blended,
As if she feared she had offended
Sweet Christabel, that gentle maid!
And with such lowly tones she prayed,   480
She might be sent without delay
Home to her father's mansion.
        "Nay!
Nay, by my soul!" said Leoline.
"Ho! Bracy, the bard, the charge be thine!
Go thou, with music sweet and loud,   485
And take two steeds with trappings proud,
And take the youth whom thou lov'st best
To bear thy harp, and learn thy song,
And clothe you both in solemn vest,
And over the mountains haste along,   490
Lest wandering folk, that are abroad,
Detain you on the valley road.
And when he has crossed the Irthing flood,
My merry bard! he hastes, he hastes
Up Knorren Moor, through Halegarth Wood,
And reaches soon that castle good   495
Which stands and threatens Scotland's wastes.

"Bard Bracy! bard Bracy! your horses are fleet
Ye must ride up the hall, your music so sweet
More loud than your horses' echoing feet!   500
And loud and loud to Lord Roland call,
Thy daughter is safe in Langdale hall!
Thy beautiful daughter is safe and free—
Sir Leoline greets thee thus through me.
He bids thee come without delay   505

With all thy numerous array;
And take thy lovely daughter home:
And he will meet thee on the way
With all his numerous array
White with their panting palfreys' foam: 510
And by mine honor! I will say,
That I repent me of the day
When I spake words of fierce disdain
To Roland de Vaux of Tryermaine!—
For since that evil hour hath flown, 515
Many a summer's sun hath shone;
Yet ne'er found I a friend again
Like Roland de Vaux of Tryermaine."

The lady fell, and clasped his knees,
Her face upraised, her eyes o'erflowing; 520
And Bracy replied, with faltering voice,
His gracious hail on all bestowing!—
"Thy words, thou sire of Christabel,
Are sweeter than my harp can tell;
Yet might I gain a boon of thee, 525
This day my journey should not be,
So strange a dream hath come to me;
That I had vowed with music loud
To clear yon wood from thing unblest,
Warned by a vision in my rest! 530
For in my sleep I saw that dove,
That gentle bird, whom thou dost love,
And call'st by thy own daughter's name—
Sir Leoline! I saw the same
Fluttering, and uttering fearful moan, 535
Among the green herbs in the forest alone.
Which when I saw and when I heard,
I wondered what might ail the bird
For nothing near it could I see,
Save the grass and green herbs underneath the
  old tree. 540

"And in my dream methought I went
To search out what might there be found;
And what the sweet bird's trouble meant,
That thus lay fluttering on the ground.
I went and peered, and could descry 545
No cause for her distressful cry;
But yet for her dear lady's sake
I stooped, methought, the dove to take,
When lo! I saw a bright green snake
Coiled around its wings and neck. 550
Green as the herbs on which it couched,
Close by the dove's its head it crouched;
And with the dove it heaves and stirs,
Swelling its neck as she swelled hers!
I woke; it was the midnight hour, 555
The clock was echoing in the tower;
But though my slumber was gone by,
This dream it would not pass away—
It seems to live upon my eye!
And thence I vowed this self-same day, 560
With music strong and saintly song
To wander through the forest bare,
Lest aught unholy loiter there."

Thus Bracy said: the Baron, the while
Half-listening heard him with a smile; 565
Then turned to Lady Geraldine,
His eyes made up of wonder and love;
And said in courtly accents fine,
"Sweet maid, Lord Roland's beauteous dove,
With arms more strong than harp or song, 570
Thy sire and I will crush the snake!"
He kissed her forehead as he spake,
And Geraldine, in maiden wise,
Casting down her large bright eyes,
With blushing cheek and courtesy fine 575
She turned her from Sir Leoline;
Softly gathering up her train,
That o'er her right arm fell again;
And folded her arms across her chest,
And couched her head upon her breast, 580
And looked askance at Christabel—
Jesu Maria, shield her well!

A snake's small eye blinks dull and shy,
And the lady's eyes they shrunk in her head,
Each shrunk up to a serpent's eye, 585
And with somewhat of malice, and more of
  dread,
At Christabel she looked askance!—
One moment—and the sight was fled!
But Christabel in dizzy trance
Stumbling on the unsteady ground 590
Shuddered aloud, with a hissing sound;
And Geraldine again turned round,
And like a thing that sought relief,
Full of wonder and full of grief,
She rolled her large bright eyes divine 595
Wildly on Sir Leoline.

The maid, alas! her thoughts are gone,
She nothing sees—no sight but one!

The maid, devoid of guile and sin,
I know not how, in fearful wise   600
So deeply had she drunken in
That look, those shrunken serpent eyes,
That all her features were resigned
To this sole image in her mind;
And passively did imitate   605
That look of dull and treacherous hate!
And thus she stood, in dizzy trance,
Still picturing that look askance
With forced unconscious sympathy
Full before her father's view—   610
As far as such a look could be
In eyes so innocent and blue!

And when the trance was o'er, the maid
Paused awhile, and inly prayed:
Then falling at the Baron's feet,   615
"By my mother's soul do I entreat
That thou this woman send away!"
She said: and more she could not say:
For what she knew she could not tell,
O'ermastered by the mighty spell.   620

Why is thy cheek so wan and wild,
Sir Leoline? Thy only child
Lies at thy feet, thy joy, thy pride,
So fair, so innocent, so mild;
The same, for whom thy lady died!   625
O, by the pangs of her dear mother
Think thou no evil of thy child!
For her, and thee, and for no other,
She prayed the moment ere she died:
Prayed that the babe for whom she died, 630
Might prove her dear lord's joy and pride!
That prayer her deadly pangs beguiled,
    Sir Leoline!
And wouldst thou wrong thy only child,
    Her child and thine?   635

Within the Baron's heart and brain
If thoughts, like these, had any share,
They only swelled his rage and pain,
And did but work confusion there.
His heart was cleft with pain and rage, 640
His cheeks they quivered, his eyes were wild,
Dishonored thus in his old age;
Dishonored by his only child,
And all his hospitality

To the insulted daughter of his friend   645
By more than woman's jealousy
Brought thus to a disgraceful end—
He rolled his eye with stern regard
Upon the gentle minstrel bard,
And said in tones abrupt, austere—   650
"Why, Bracy! dost thou loiter here?
I bade thee hence!" The bard obeyed;
And turning from his own sweet maid,
The aged knight, Sir Leoline,
Led forth the lady Geraldine!   655

THE CONCLUSION TO PART II

A little child, a limber elf,
Singing, dancing to itself,
A fairy thing with red round cheeks,
That always finds, and never seeks,
Makes such a vision to the sight   660
As fills a father's eyes with light;
And pleasures flow in so thick and fast
Upon his heart, that he at last
Must needs express his love's excess
With words of unmeant bitterness.   665
Perhaps 'tis pretty to force together
Thoughts so all unlike each other;
To mutter and mock a broken charm,
To dally with wrong that does no harm.
Perhaps 'tis tender too and pretty   670
At each wild word to feel within
A sweet recoil of love and pity.
And what, if in a world of sin
(O sorrow and shame should this be true!)
Such giddiness of heart and brain   675
Comes seldom save from rage and pain,
So talks as it's most used to do.

             (1797-1800; 1816)

[According to Coleridge's friend Gilman, the outline of the rest of the *Christabel* story is this: "The following relation was to have occupied a third and fourth canto, and to have closed the tale. Over the mountains, the Bard, as directed by Sir Leoline, hastes with his disciple; but in consequence of one of those inundations supposed to be common to this country, the spot only where the castle once stood is discovered—the edifice itself being washed away.

656. **A little child,** etc. These lines have little connection with the rest of the poem, and it is not likely that they were meant originally to be a part of it. They were sent to Southey in a letter dated May 6, 1801. They do not occur in any of the three extant manuscripts of the poem.

He determines to return. Geraldine, being acquainted with all that is passing, like the weird sisters in *Macbeth,* vanishes. Reappearing, however, she awaits the return of the Bard, exciting in the meantime, by her wily arts, all the anger she could rouse in the Baron's breast, as well as that jealousy of which he is described to have been susceptible. The old Bard and the youth at length arrive, and therefore she can no longer personate the character of Geraldine, the daughter of Lord Roland de Vaux, but changes her appearance to that of the accepted though absent lover of Christabel. Now ensues a courtship most distressing to Christabel, who feels, she knows not why, great disgust for her once favored knight. This coldness is very painful to the Baron, who has no more conception than herself of the supernatural transformation. She at last yields to her father's entreaties, and consents to approach the altar with the hated suitor. The real lover, returning, enters at this moment, and produces the ring which she had once given him in sign of her betrothment. Thus defeated, the supernatural being Geraldine disappears. As predicted, the castle bell tolls, the mother's voice is heard, and, to the exceeding great joy of the parties, the rightful marriage takes place, after which follows a reconciliation and explanation between the father and daughter."]

Kubla Khan; or, *a Vision in a Dream*

Kubla Khan, that most notable fragment, which breathes in every word and line the spirit of adventure, unreality, and glamorous escape from reality, bore in its first printing (1816) a rather lengthy preface, of which the following is perhaps the most significant part:

"In the summer of the year 1797, the author, then in ill health, had retired to a lonely farmhouse between Porlock and Lynton, on the Exmoor confines of Somerset and Devonshire. In consequence of a slight indisposition, an anodyne had been prescribed, from the effects of which he fell asleep in his chair at the moment he was reading the following sentence, or words of the same substance, in *Purchas's Pilgrimage:* 'Here the Khan Kubla commanded a palace to be built, and a stately garden thereunto. And thus ten miles of fertile ground were inclosed with a wall.' The author continued for about three hours in a profound sleep, at least of the external senses, during which time he has the most vivid confidence that he could not have composed less than from two to three hundred lines; if that indeed can be called composition in which all the images rose up before him as *things,* with a parallel production of the correspondent expressions, without any sensation or consciousness of effort. On awaking he appeared to himself to have a distinct recollection of the whole, and taking his pen, ink, and paper, instantly and eagerly wrote down the lines that are here preserved. At this moment he was unfortunately called out by a person on business from Porlock, and detained by him above an hour, and on his return to his room, found, to his no small surprise and mortification, that though he still retained some vague and dim recollection of the general purport of the vision, yet, with the exception of some eight or ten scattered lines and images, all the rest had passed away like the images on the surface of a stream into which a stone had been cast, but, alas! without the after restoration of the latter!"

In Xanadu did Kubla Khan
A stately pleasure-dome decree:
Where Alph, the sacred river, ran
Through caverns measureless to man
Down to a sunless sea.   5
So twice five miles of fertile ground
With walls and towers were girdled round:
And here were gardens bright with sinuous
    rills,
Where blossomed many an incense-bearing
    tree;
And here were forests ancient as the hills,   10
Enfolding sunny spots of greenery.
But oh! that deep romantic chasm which
    slanted
Down the green hill athwart a cedarn cover!
A savage place! as holy and enchanted
As e'er beneath a waning moon was haunted
By woman wailing for her demon-lover!   16
And from this chasm, with ceaseless turmoil
    seething,
As if this earth in fast thick pants were breathing,
A mighty fountain momently was forced;
Amid whose swift half-intermitted burst   20
Huge fragments vaulted like rebounding hail,
Or chaffy grain beneath the thresher's flail:

1. **Xanadu**, a region in Tartary. **Kubla Khan**, Cham or Emperor Kubla. He founded the Mogul dynasty in China in the thirteenth century. 14-16. **savage . . . lover.** These are three of the lines referred to by Kipling in his *Wireless:* "Remember that in all the millions permitted there are no more than five—five little lines—of which one can say, 'These are the magic. These are the vision. The rest is only poetry.'" The other two lines are in Keats's *Ode to a Nightingale,* ll. 69-70, p. 285.

And 'mid these dancing rocks at once and
    ever
It flung up momently the sacred river.
Five miles meandering with a mazy motion 25
Through wood and dale the sacred river ran,
Then reached the caverns measureless to man,
And sank in tumult to a lifeless ocean:
And 'mid this tumult Kubla heard from far
Ancestral voices prophesying war!   30

    The shadow of the dome of pleasure
      Floated midway on the waves;
    Where was heard the mingled measure
      From the fountain and the caves.
It was a miracle of rare device,   35
A sunny pleasure-dome with caves of ice!
    A damsel with a dulcimer
      In a vision once I saw:
    It was an Abyssinian maid,
    And on her dulcimer she played,   40
      Singing of Mount Abora.
    Could I revive within me,
      Her symphony and song,
    To such a deep delight 'twould win me,
That with music loud and long,   45
I would build that dome in air,
That sunny dome! those caves of ice!
And all who heard should see them there,
And all should cry, Beware! Beware!
His flashing eyes, his floating hair!   50
Weave a circle round him thrice,
And close your eyes with holy dread,
For he on honey-dew hath fed,
And drunk the milk of Paradise.

                              (*1797;* 1816)

41. **Mount Abora**, a mountain of Coleridge's imagination; or, possibly, Mount Amara, the seat of a terrestrial paradise in Abyssinia. The words suggest romantic remoteness.

France: an Ode

    This poem was inspired by the French invasion of Switzerland in 1798. In the first stanza Coleridge invokes those objects in nature which, he states, created within him a devotional love of liberty. There is an interesting comparison that can be made between this work and Wordsworth's sonnet, *Thought of a Briton on the Subjugation of Switzerland,* p. 162. The two poems, similar in subject-matter and conclusion, are nevertheless quite different in scope, in feeling, and in poetic details.

Ye Clouds! that far above me float and pause,
    Whose pathless march no mortal may control!
    Ye Ocean-Waves! that, wheresoe'er ye roll,
Yield homage only to eternal laws!
Ye Woods! that listen to the night-birds singing,   5
    Midway the smooth and perilous slope reclined,
Save when your own imperious branches swinging,
Have made a solemn music of the wind!
Where, like a man beloved of God,
Through glooms, which never woodman trod,
    How oft, pursuing fancies holy,   11
My moonlight way o'er flowering weeds I wound,
    Inspired, beyond the guess of folly,
By each rude shape and wild unconquerable sound!

O ye loud Waves! and O ye Forests high!   15
    And O ye Clouds that far above me soared!
Thou rising Sun! thou blue rejoicing Sky!
    Yea, every thing that is and will be free!
    Bear witness for me, wheresoe'er ye be,
With what deep worship I have still adored
    The spirit of divinest Liberty.   21

When France in wrath her giant-limbs upreared,
    And with that oath, which smote air, earth, and sea,
    Stamped her strong foot and said she would be free,
Bear witness for me, how I hoped and feared!
With what a joy my lofty gratulation   26
    Unawed I sang, amid a slavish band:
And when to whelm the disenchanted nation,
    Like fiends embattled by a wizard's wand,
      The Monarchs marched in evil day,   30

And Britain joined the dire array;
  Though dear her shores and circling ocean,
  Though many friendships, many youthful loves
  Had swoln the patriot emotion
And flung a magic light o'er all her hills and groves;   35
Yet still my voice, unaltered, sang defeat
  To all that braved the tyrant-quelling lance,
And shame too long delayed and vain retreat!
For ne'er, O Liberty! with partial aim   39
I dimmed thy light or damped thy holy flame;
  But blessed the paeans of delivered France,
And hung my head and wept at Britain's name.

"And what," I said, "though Blasphemy's loud scream
  With that sweet music of deliverance strove!
  Though all the fierce and drunken passions wove   45
A dance more wild than e'er was maniac's dream!
  Ye storms, that round the dawning East assembled,
The Sun was rising, though ye hid his light!"
  And when, to soothe my soul, that hoped and trembled,
The dissonance ceased, and all seemed calm and bright;   50
  When France her front deep-scarred and gory
  Concealed with clustering wreaths of glory;
    When, insupportably advancing,
    Her arm made mockery of the warrior's ramp;
    While timid looks of fury glancing,   55
  Domestic treason, crushed beneath her fatal stamp,
Writhed like a wounded dragon in his gore;
  Then I reproached my fears that would not flee;
"And soon," I said, "shall Wisdom teach her lore

---

31. **Britain . . . array.** France declared war upon Prussia and Austria in April, 1792, and upon Holland and England in February, 1793. 43. **Blasphemy's loud scream.** On November 10, 1793, the "Goddess of Reason" was enthroned in Notre Dame Cathedral, Paris. 46. **dance . . . dream.** A reference to the excesses of the French Revolution. 48. **Sun,** liberty. 54. **ramp,** act of advancing in warlike posture.

In the low huts of them that toil and groan!   60
And, conquering by her happiness alone,
  Shall France compel the nations to be free,
Till Love and Joy look round, and call the Earth their own."

Forgive me, Freedom! O forgive those dreams!
  I hear thy voice, I hear thy loud lament,   65
From bleak Helvetia's icy caverns sent—
I hear thy groans upon her blood-stained streams!
  Heroes, that for your peaceful country perished,
And ye that, fleeing, spot your mountain-snows
  With bleeding wounds; forgive me, that I cherished   70
One thought that ever blessed your cruel foes!
  To scatter rage, and traitorous guilt,
  Where Peace her jealous home had built;
  A patriot-race to disinherit
Of all that made their stormy wilds so dear;   75
  And with inexpiable spirit
To taint the bloodless freedom of the mountaineer—
O France, that mockest Heaven, adulterous, blind,
  And patriot only in pernicious toils!
Are these thy boasts, Champion of human kind?   80
  To mix with Kings in the low lust of sway,
Yell in the hunt, and share the murderous prey;
To insult the shrine of Liberty with spoils
  From freemen torn; to tempt and to betray?

  The Sensual and the Dark rebel in vain,
  Slaves by their own compulsion! In mad game   86
  They burst their manacles and wear the name
    Of Freedom, graven on a heavier chain!
O Liberty! with profitless endeavor
Have I pursued thee, many a weary hour;   90
  But thou nor swell'st the victor's strain, nor ever
Didst breathe thy soul in forms of human power.

  Alike from all, howe'er they praise thee,

(Nor prayer, nor boastful names delays
    thee)
  Alike from Priestcraft's harpy minions, 95
  And factious Blasphemy's obscener slaves,
  Thou speedest on thy subtle pinions,
The guide of homeless winds, and playmate
    of the waves!
And there I felt thee!—on that sea-cliff's verge,
  Whose pines, scarce traveled by the breeze
    above, 100
Had made one murmur with the distant
    surge!
Yes, while I stood and gazed, my temples bare,
And shot my being through earth, sea, and
    air,
Possessing all things with intensest love,
  O Liberty! my spirit felt thee there. (1798)

Dejection: an Ode

This poem was first addressed to Wordsworth and was printed in *The Morning Post* on his wedding-day, Oct. 4, 1802. In this version Wordsworth was referred to as "Edmund," and that name occurred where "Lady" is found in the present text, and where "Otway" appears in 1. 120. A still earlier version contained the name "William" throughout. An estrangement between the two poets was the cause of the later substitutions.

> Late, late yestreen I saw the new Moon
>   With the old Moon in her arms;
> And I fear, I fear, my Master dear!
>   We shall have a deadly storm.
>   *Ballad of Sir Patrick Spence*

I

Well! If the Bard was weather-wise, who
    made
  The grand old ballad of Sir Patrick Spence,
This night, so tranquil now, will not go
    hence
Unroused by winds, that ply a busier trade
Than those which mold yon cloud in lazy
    flakes, 5
Or the dull sobbing draft, that moans and
    rakes
  Upon the strings of this Aeolian lute,

7. **Aeolian lute**, in ancient times a stringed instrument, usually placed where the wind would strike it and produce music. It took its name from Aeolus, god of winds.

  Which better far were mute;
For lo! the new-moon winter bright!
And overspread with phantom light, 10
  (With swimming phantom light o'erspread
  But rimmed and circled by a silver thread)
I see the old moon in her lap, foretelling
  The coming-on of rain and squally blast.
And oh! that even now the gust were swelling, 15
  And the slant night-shower driving loud
    and fast!
Those sounds which oft have raised me,
    whilst they awed,
  And sent my soul abroad,
Might now perhaps their wonted impulse
    give,
Might startle this dull pain, and make it
    move and live! 20

II

A grief without a pang, void, dark, and drear,
  A stifled, drowsy, unimpassioned grief,
  Which finds no natural outlet, no relief,
    In word, or sigh, or tear—
O Lady! in this wan and heartless mood, 25
To other thoughts by yonder throstle wooed,
  All this long eve, so balmy and serene,
Have I been gazing on the western sky,
  And its peculiar tint of yellow green:
And still I gaze—and with how blank an
    eye! 30
And those thin clouds above, in flakes and
    bars,
That give away their motion to the stars;
Those stars, that glide behind them or between,
  Now sparkling, now bedimmed, but always
    seen:
Yon crescent moon, as fixed as if it grew 35
In its own cloudless, starless lake of blue;
I see them all so excellently fair,
I see, not feel, how beautiful they are!

III

  My genial spirits fail;
  And what can these avail 40
To lift the smothering weight from off my
    breast?
    It were a vain endeavor,
    Though I should gaze forever
On that green light that lingers in the west:

I may not hope from outward forms to win 45
The passion and the life, whose fountains are
    within.

IV

O Lady! we receive but what we give,
And in our life alone does Nature live:
Ours is her wedding garment, ours her
    shroud!
    And would we aught behold, of higher
        worth,
Than that inanimate cold world allowed 51
To the poor loveless ever-anxious crowd,
    Ah! from the soul itself must issue forth
A light, a glory, a fair luminous cloud
    Enveloping the earth— 55
And from the soul itself must there be sent
    A sweet and potent voice, of its own birth,
Of all sweet sounds the life and element!

V

O pure of heart! thou need'st not ask of me
What this strong music in the soul may be! 60
What, and wherein it doth exist,
This light, this glory, this fair luminous mist,
This beautiful and beauty-making power.
    Joy, virtuous Lady! Joy that ne'er was
        given,
Save to the pure, and in their purest hour, 65
Life, and Life's effluence, cloud at once and
    shower,
Joy, Lady! is the spirit and the power,
Which wedding Nature to us gives in dower,
    A new earth and new heaven,
Undreamt of by the sensual and the proud—
Joy is the sweet voice, Joy the luminous
    cloud— 71
        We in ourselves rejoice!
And thence flows all that charms or ear or
    sight,
All melodies the echoes of that voice,
All colors a suffusion from that light. 75

VI

There was a time when, though my path was
    rough,
    This joy within me dallied with distress,
And all misfortunes were but as the stuff
    Whence Fancy made me dreams of happi-
        ness:
For Hope grew round me, like the twining
    vine, 80
And fruits, and foliage, not my own, seemed
    mine.
But now afflictions bow me down to earth:
Nor care I that they rob me of my mirth;
    But oh! each visitation
Suspends what nature gave me at my birth,
    My shaping spirit of Imagination. 86
For not to think of what I needs must feel,
    But to be still and patient, all I can;
And haply by abstruse research to steal
    From my own nature all the natural man—
    This was my sole resource, my only plan: 91
Till that which suits a part infects the whole,
And now is almost grown the habit of my
    soul.

VII

Hence, viper thoughts, that coil around my
    mind,
    Reality's dark dream! 95
I turn from you, and listen to the wind,
    Which long has raved unnoticed. What a
        scream
Of agony by torture lengthened out
That lute sent forth! Thou Wind, that rav'st
    without, 99
    Bare crag, or mountain-tairn, or blasted tree,
Or pine-grove whither woodman never
    clomb,
Or lonely house, long held the witches' home,
    Methinks were fitter instruments for thee,
Mad Lutanist! who in this month of showers,
Of dark-brown gardens, and of peeping
    flowers, 105
Mak'st Devils' yule, with worse than wintry
    song,
The blossoms, buds, and timorous leaves
    among.
    Thou actor, perfect in all tragic sounds!
Thou mighty poet, e'en to frenzy bold!
    What tell'st thou now about? 110
    'Tis of the rushing of an host in rout,
    With groans of trampled men, with smart-
        ing wounds—
At once they groan with pain, and shudder
    with the cold!
But hush! there is a pause of deepest silence!
    And all that noise, as of a rushing crowd,
With groans, and tremulous shudderings—
    all is over— 116
    It tells another tale, with sounds less deep
        and loud!

A tale of less affright,
And tempered with delight,
As Otway's self had framed the tender lay—
'Tis of a little child   121
Upon a lonesome wild,
Not far from home, but she hath lost her way:
And now moans low in bitter grief and fear,
And now screams loud, and hopes to make her mother hear.   125

VIII

'Tis midnight, but small thoughts have I of sleep:
Full seldom may my friend such vigils keep!
Visit her, gentle Sleep! with wings of healing,
And may this storm be but a mountain-birth,
May all the stars hang bright above her dwelling,   130
Silent as though they watched the sleeping earth!
With light heart may she rise,
Gay fancy, cheerful eyes,
Joy lift her spirit, joy attune her voice;
To her may all things live, from pole to pole,
Their life the eddying of her living soul!   136
O simple spirit, guided from above,
Dear Lady! friend devoutest of my choice,
Thus mayest thou ever, evermore rejoice.
                                                        (1802)

Youth and Age

Verse, a breeze amid blossoms straying,
Where Hope clung feeding, like a bee—
Both were mine! Life went a-maying
   With Nature, Hope, and Poesy,
        When I was young!   5
When I was young?—Ah, woeful *When!*
Ah! for the change 'twixt Now and Then!
This breathing house not built with hands,
This body that does me grievous wrong,
O'er aery cliffs and glittering sands,   10
How lightly *then* it flashed along—
Like those trim skiffs, unknown of yore,
On winding lakes and rivers wide,
That ask no aid of sail or oar,
That fear no spite of wind or tide!   15
Nought cared this body for wind or weather
When Youth and I lived in 't together.

Flowers are lovely; Love is flower-like;
Friendship is a sheltering tree;
O! the joys, that came down shower-like,   20
Of Friendship, Love, and Liberty,
        Ere I was old!

Ere I was old? Ah, woeful *Ere*,
Which tells me, Youth's no longer here!
O Youth! for years so many and sweet,   25
'Tis known, that Thou and I were one,
I'll think it but a fond conceit—
It cannot be that Thou art gone!
Thy vesper-bell hath not yet tolled:—
And thou wert aye a masker bold!   30
What strange disguise hast now put on,
To *make believe*, that thou art gone?
I see these locks in silvery slips,
This drooping gait, this altered size:
But Spring-tide blossoms on thy lips,   35
And tears take sunshine from thine eyes!
Life is but thought: so think I will
That Youth and I are house-mates still.

Dew-drops are the gems of morning,
But the tears of mournful eve!   40
Where no hope is, life's a warning
That only serves to make us grieve,
        When we are old:
That only serves to make us grieve
With oft and tedious taking-leave,   45
Like some poor nigh-related guest,
That may not rudely be dismissed;
Yet hath outstayed his welcome while,
And tells the jest without the smile.
                                   (*1823-32*, 1828-32)

Work without Hope

All Nature seems at work. Slugs leave their lair—
The bees are stirring—birds are on the wing—
And Winter slumbering in the open air,
Wears on his smiling face a dream of Spring!

---

120. Otway. See headnote, p. 187. 121. a little child, an allusion to Wordsworth's *Lucy Gray*.
   Youth and Age. This poem should be compared with *Crabbed Age and Youth* (Vol. I, p. 470); Bacon's *Of Youth and Age* (Vol. I, p. 623); Landor's *To Youth* and *To Age* (pp. 314, 315); Byron's *Stanzas for Music* (p. 207); and Browning's *Rabbi Ben Ezra* (p. 698). 8. house ... hands. Cf. *2 Corinthians*, 5:1: "For we know, that if our earthly house of this tabernacle were dissolved, we have a building of God, an house not made with hands, eternal in the heavens."

And I the while, the sole unbusy thing, 5
Nor honey make, nor pair, nor build, nor sing.

Yet well I ken the banks where amaranths blow,
Have traced the fount whence streams of nectar flow.
Bloom, O ye amaranths! bloom for whom ye may,
For me ye bloom not! Glide, rich streams, away! 10
With lips unbrightened, wreathless brow, I stroll:
And would you learn the spells that drowse my soul?
Work without Hope draws nectar in a sieve,
And Hope without an object cannot live.
(*1825;* 1828)

Epitaph

Stop, Christian passer-by!—Stop, child of God,
And read with gentle breast. Beneath this sod
A poet lies, or that which once seemed he.
O, lift one thought in prayer for S.T.C.;
That he who many a year with toil of breath 5
Found death in life, may here find life in death!
Mercy for praise—to be forgiven for fame
He asked, and hoped, through Christ. Do thou the same! (*1833;* 1834)

Sir Walter Scott
1771-1832

Walter Scott was born in Edinburgh, Scotland, August 15, 1771, of a family of gentlefolk, "neither distinguished nor sordid," but related to the old and powerful Scottish clan of Buccleuch. Scott's boyhood was marred by ill health, by an attack of infantile paralysis, which left him slightly lame. In consequence he missed much schooling and was thrown upon his own educational resources. But learning of a sort was easy for him—he was insatiable in his eagerness to learn about Scottish history and to read the legends and folklore of his native Scotland; he became thoroughly precocious in his knowledge of these fields. His rich background of border history, ballad lore, and Jacobite fact and fiction was to stand him in good stead later.

He secured a formal education at the High School, Edinburgh, but even here his antiquarian specialties took most of his time. Ostensibly he was to become a lawyer, and he was admitted to the bar in 1792; later he held a few legal offices—deputy sheriff of Selkirkshire (1799) and a court clerkship (1806). But it was soon apparent that law was a secondary matter for Walter Scott; his first and only love was for the muse of literature. He began his career as poet with translations from German ballads similar to the *Lenore* of Gottfried Bürger—tales of medieval knights and barons, supernatural creatures, love and death. Under the direct influence of these German pieces and of the Gothic novel (p. 23), as was his contemporary Coleridge (p. 163), he began his career in English poetry with *Glenfinlas, The Eve of Saint John, William and Helen,* and other ballads, all from 1795 to 1799. His collection of Scotch ballads and poetic legends, known as *The Minstrelsy of the Scottish Border* (begun 1802), remained the finest collection of its sort until the monumental work by Professor Francis Child, which appeared in the 1880's.

Scott's first popular success, however, was a long narrative in verse, a modern metrical romance of old Scottish clan-history, known as *The Lay of the Last Minstrel* (1805). Two other similar works had even greater success—*Marmion* (1806) and *The Lady of the Lake* (1810). All three of these poems became a kind of literary rage; they were simple, clear, not too philosophical, and the narratives were interesting and vigorous—"light-horse" verse, with an engaging element of melodrama. As Scott himself, in one of his typical bursts of self-analysis, remarked to a friend, they were meant to "engraft a modern refinement on ancient simplicity." Scott had also during this period begun a novel, *Waverley*, but had laid it aside to give his attention to his poetry. By 1812 the star of Lord Byron (p. 200) was, unfortunately for Scott, in the ascendant; Byron's Oriental tales had greater recklessness and vigor and audacity; in consequence Scott felt disposed to abandon the field of narrative verse to his brilliant junior. It is somewhat unfair, however, to suggest that Scott was forced to quit. The fragment of *Waverley*, written some years before, shows that he had always held hopes of becoming a great novelist.

Scott was socially extremely ambitious—he wanted to lead the life of a Scotch laird, and with that in mind he had begun to build the mansion of Abbotsford, on the banks of the Tweed. What was even more a weight upon his financial resources was the fact that he had allied himself to the Ballantynes, a pair of brothers in the printing business; his partnership with them, and his growing reputation as a literary figure, led to his becoming a partner in an elaborate publishing business, which published not only the works of Scott, but side-ventures like a magazine, the *Quarterly Review*, in opposition to the famous *Edinburgh Review*, edited by Francis Jeffrey, perhaps the best-known critic of his day. In short, Scott was attempting to keep up a social and a business activity that no one man could well be expected to continue for long.

To supply some of the grist for the Ballantyne mill, Scott returned to the field of the novel. He resurrected *Waverley* and finished it, publishing it anonymously (1814). Many rumors were afloat as to the real author, and Scott derived much amusement from some of the wild guesses, but for twelve years he concealed his identity as the writer of the long and distinguished series of novels that came from his pen (cf. p. 28). They are virtually all historical and call upon the real erudition that Scott possessed in reference to the social and political backgrounds of Scotland and England. These novels have been treated earlier; here it is necessary only to say that it is on these novels, created with astonishing fecundity, that Scott's reputation has come to rest. Not without good reason did the readers of his day—and later—refer to him as "The Wizard of the North."

In 1825 the Ballantynes, always notoriously bad managers, began to stumble. A related firm, the Constables, failed and pulled the Ballantynes into bankruptcy and Scott along with them. There were debts outstanding in excess of a million dollars. Scott could no doubt have ignored his obligations; but to avoid prosecution and disgrace he chose, however, to try to lift this enormous debt through his own efforts. For five years he toiled unremittingly, turning out any kind of literary work that came his way, most of it hurried and below his former standard. He had repaid perhaps a third of the debt when the end came: apoplexy, a stroke of paralysis, a tardy sea-trip at the expense of the government, and then his death in September, 1832.

Posterity has decided that Scott's achievement in poetry is inferior to that of his great contemporaries—Wordsworth, Coleridge, Byron, Keats, Shelley. His mind, it is true, is neither complex nor profound. But he has an eye for antiquity; he can tell a story; he can sing a song more than acceptably. Finally, he possessed an aristocratic calm and courage that manifests itself in good taste and vigor in his writing and in virtue and heroism in his private life. He was the antiquarian and scholar of the past among romantic writers and one of the great missionaries of romanticism. His influence upon the writers of his time was very great—the whole school of historical novelists through the middle of the nineteenth century owed him a great deal, although none of these quite managed to achieve the combination of color, dignity, adventure, and occasional arresting characterization that their master accomplished.

from *The Lay of the Last Minstrel*
ROSABELLE

Harold, the minstrel of the house of St. Clair, sings this song after the espousal of Margaret of Buccleuch to Lord Cranston. It tells of the death of Rosabelle as she was returning from Ravensheuch Castle to Roslin, the family seat of the St. Clairs in Edinburghshire.

O listen, listen, ladies gay!
   No haughty feat of arms I tell;
Soft is the note, and sad the lay,
   That mourns the lovely Rosabelle.

—"Moor, moor the barge, ye gallant crew! 5
   And, gentle ladye, deign to stay!
Rest thee in Castle Ravensheuch,
   Nor tempt the stormy firth today.

"The blackening wave is edged with white:
   To inch and rock the sea-mews fly; 10
The fishers have heard the Water-Sprite,
   Whose screams forebode that wreck is nigh.

"Last night the gifted Seer did view
   A wet shroud swathed round ladye gay;
Then stay thee, Fair, in Ravensheuch: 15
   Why cross the gloomy firth today?"

" 'Tis not because Lord Lindesay's heir
   Tonight at Roslin leads the ball,
But that my ladye-mother there
   Sits lonely in her castle-hall. 20

" 'Tis not because the ring they ride,
   And Lindesay at the ring rides well,
But that my sire the wine will chide,
   If 'tis not filled by Rosabelle."

O'er Roslin all that dreary night 25
   A wondrous blaze was seen to gleam;
'Twas broader than the watch-fire's light,
   And redder than the bright moon-beam.

It glared on Roslin's castled rock,
   It ruddied all the copse-wood glen; 30
'Twas seen from Dryden's groves of oak,
   And seen from caverned Hawthornden.

Seemed all on fire that chapel proud,
   Where Roslin's chiefs uncoffined lie,
Each Baron, for a sable shroud, 35
   Sheathed in his iron panoply.

Seemed all on fire within, around,
   Deep sacristy and altar's pale;
Shone every pillar foliage-bound,
   And glimmered all the dead men's mail. 40

Blazed battlement and pinnet high,
   Blazed every rose-carved buttress fair—
So still they blaze when fate is nigh
   The lordly line of high St. Clair.

There are twenty of Roslin's barons bold 45
   Lie buried within that proud chapelle;
Each one the holy vault doth hold—
   But the sea holds lovely Rosabelle!

And each St. Clair was buried there,
   With candle, with book, and with knell; 50
But the sea-caves rung, and the wild winds sung,
   The dirge of lovely Rosabelle.

                (1802-04; 1805)

from *Marmion*
WHERE SHALL THE LOVER REST

Where shall the lover rest,
   Whom the fates sever
From his true maiden's breast,
   Parted forever?
Where, through groves deep and high, 5
   Sounds the far billow,
Where early violets die,
   Under the willow.

Chorus
Eleu loro, etc. Soft shall be his pillow.

   There, through the summer day, 10
      Cool streams are laving;

Rosabelle. 10. **inch**, island. 21. **ring they ride.** Riding the ring was a favorite sport in which a horseman rode past a suspended ring and tried to carry it off on the point of his lance.

38. **pale**, inclosure. 41. **pinnet**, pinnacle.

There, while the tempests sway,
    Scarce are boughs waving;
There thy rest shalt thou take,
    Parted forever,   15
Never again to wake,
    Never, O never!

Chorus

Eleu loro, etc. Never, O never!

Where shall the traitor rest,
    He the deceiver,   20
Who could win maiden's breast,
    Ruin and leave her?
In the lost battle,
    Borne down by the flying,
Where mingles war's rattle   25
    With groans of the dying.

Chorus

Eleu loro, etc. There shall he be lying.

Her wing shall the eagle flap
    O'er the false-hearted;
His warm blood the wolf shall lap,   30
    Ere life be parted.
Shame and dishonor sit
    By his grave ever;
Blessing shall hallow it—
    Never, O never!   35

Chorus

Eleu loro, etc. Never, O never!

LOCHINVAR

    This familiar ballad from *Marmion* is sung by Lady Heron, who has come to the court of King James of Scotland in behalf of her husband, an English lord, who is held a prisoner. The names in the ballad are traditional.

Oh! young Lochinvar is come out of the west,
Through all the wide Border his steed was the best;
And save his good broadsword he weapons had none.
He rode all unarmed, and he rode all alone.
So faithful in love and so dauntless in war,   5
There never was knight like the young Lochinvar.

He stayed not for brake and he stopped not for stone,
He swam the Eske River where ford there was none,
But ere he alighted at Netherby gate
The bride had consented, the gallant came late: 10
For a laggard in love and a dastard in war
Was to wed the fair Ellen of brave Lochinvar.

So boldly he entered the Netherby Hall,
Among bridesmen, and kinsmen, and brothers, and all:
Then spoke the bride's father, his hand on his sword—   15
For the poor craven bridegroom said never a word—
"Oh! come ye in peace here, or come ye in war,
Or to dance at our bridal, young Lord Lochinvar?"

"I long wooed your daughter, my suit you denied;
Love swells like the Solway, but ebbs like its tide—   20
And now am I come, with this lost love of mine,
To lead but one measure, drink one cup of wine,
There are maidens in Scotland more lovely by far,
That would gladly be bride to the young Lochinvar."

---

28. **Her wing,** etc. Compare the details in these lines with those to be found in *Beowulf* (Vol. I, p. 55, ll. 2340 ff.).

7. **brake,** brushwood, thicket. 8. **Eske River,** in Dumfriesshire, Scotland, near the English border. 16. **poor . . . bridegroom.** Observe that it is a commonplace of romantic fiction for the husband to be painted in unattractive colors and for the unexpected lover to sweep all before him. The explanation for this fact lies in the inherent rebelliousness of the romantic spirit. 20. **Solway,** Solway Firth, a large inlet of the Irish Sea, partly separating England and Scotland.

The bride kissed the goblet; the knight took
    it up,   25
He quaffed off the wine, and he threw down
    the cup.
She looked down to blush, and she looked up
    to sigh,
With a smile on her lips and a tear in her
    eye.
He took her soft hand ere her mother could
    bar—
"Now tread we a measure!" said young Loch-
    invar.   30

So stately his form, and so lovely her face,
That never a hall such a galliard did grace;
While her mother did fret, and her father
    did fume,
And the bridegroom stood dangling his bon-
    net and plume;
And the bride-maidens whispered, " 'Twere
    better by far   35
To have matched our fair cousin with young
    Lochinvar."

One touch to her hand and one word in her
    ear,
When they reached the hall-door, and the
    charger stood near;
So light to the croupe the fair lady he swung,
So light to the saddle before her he sprung! 40
"She is won! we are gone, over bank, bush,
    and scaur;
They'll have fleet steeds that follow," quoth
    young Lochinvar.

There was mounting 'mong Graemes of the
    Netherby clan;
Forsters, Fenwicks, and Musgraves, they rode
    and they ran:
There was racing and chasing on Cannobie
    Lee,   45
But the lost bride of Netherby ne'er did they
    see.
So daring in love and so dauntless in war,
Have ye e'er heard of gallant like young
    Lochinvar?   *(1806; 1808)*

32. **galliard**, a lively dance. 39. **croupe**, place behind the saddle. 41. **scaur**, steep, rocky eminence. 45. **Cannobie Lee.** Canonbie is a village near the Eske River.

Hunting Song

Waken, lords and ladies gay,
On the mountain dawns the day,
All the jolly chase is here,
With hawk, and horse, and hunting-spear!
Hounds are in their couples yelling,   5
Hawks are whistling, horns are knelling;
Merrily, merrily, mingle they,
"Waken, lords and ladies gay."

Waken, lords and ladies gay,
The mist has left the mountain gray,   10
Springlets in the dawn are steaming,
Diamonds on the brake are gleaming:
And foresters have busy been,
To track the buck in thicket green;
Now we come to chant our lay,   15
"Waken, lords and ladies gay."

Waken, lords and ladies gay,
To the greenwood haste away;
We can show you where he lies,
Fleet of foot, and tall of size;   20
We can show the marks he made,
When 'gainst the oak his antlers frayed;
You shall see him brought to bay;
"Waken, lords and ladies gay."

Louder, louder chant the lay,   25
Waken, lords and ladies gay!
Tell them youth, and mirth, and glee,
Run a course as well as we;
Time, stern huntsman! who can balk,
Stanch as hound, and fleet as hawk: 30
Think of this, and rise with day,
Gentle lords and ladies gay.   *(1808)*

from *The Lady of the Lake*

HARP OF THE NORTH

The harp was the Scottish national musical instrument. The poem, an invocation to ancient Scottish minstrelsy, is a prelude to the entire poem.

Harp of the North! that moldering long hast
    hung

5. **couples**, leashes. 12. **brake**, brushwood, thicket.

On the witch-elm that shades Saint Fillan's
    spring,
And down the fitful breeze thy numbers
    flung,
Till envious ivy did around thee cling,
Muffling with verdant ringlet every string—
    O minstrel Harp, still must thine accents
        sleep?   6
'Mid rustling leaves and fountains murmur-
    ing,
    Still must thy sweeter sounds their silence
        keep,
Nor bid a warrior smile, nor teach a maid to
    weep?

Not thus, in ancient days of Caledon,   10
    Was thy voice mute amid the festal crowd,
When lay of hopeless love, or glory
    won,
    Aroused the fearful, or subdued the proud.
At each according pause was heard aloud
    Thine ardent symphony sublime and
        high!   15
Fair dames and crested chiefs attention
    bowed;
For still the burden of thy minstrelsy
Was Knighthood's dauntless deed, and
    Beauty's matchless eye.

O wake once more! how rude soe'er the
    hand
    That ventures o'er thy magic maze to
        stray;   20
O wake once more! though scarce my skill
    command
Some feeble echoing of thine earlier lay;
    Though harsh and faint, and soon to die
        away,
And all unworthy of thy nobler strain,
Yet if one heart throb higher at its sway,   25
    The wizard note has not been touched in
        vain.
Then silent be no more! Enchantress, wake
    again!

SOLDIER, REST! THY WARFARE O'ER

    This song is sung by Ellen, the heroine of *The Lady of the Lake*, to please the stranger Knight of Snowdoun, the disguised King James of Scotland.

Soldier, rest! thy warfare o'er,
    Sleep the sleep that knows not breaking;
Dream of battled fields no more,
    Days of danger, nights of waking.
In our isle's enchanted hall,   5
    Hands unseen thy couch are strewing,
Fairy strains of music fall,
    Every sense in slumber dewing.
Soldier, rest! thy warfare o'er,
Dream of fighting fields no more;   10
Sleep the sleep that knows not breaking,
Morn of toil, nor night of waking.

No rude sound shall reach thine ear,
    Armor's clang, or war-steed champing,
Trump nor pibroch summon here   15
    Mustering clan or squadron tramping.
Yet the lark's shrill fife may come
    At the daybreak from the fallow,
And the bittern sound his drum,
    Booming from the sedgy shallow.   20
Ruder sounds shall none be near,
Guards nor warders challenge here,
Here's no war-steed's neigh and champing,
Shouting clans or squadrons stamping.

Huntsman, rest! thy chase is done;   25
    While our slumbrous spells assail ye,
Dream not, with the rising sun,
    Bugles here shall sound reveille.
Sleep! the deer is in his den;
    Sleep! thy hounds are by thee lying: 30
Sleep! nor dream in yonder glen
    How thy gallant steed lay dying.
Huntsman, rest! thy chase is done;
Think not of the rising sun,
For at dawning to assail ye   35
Here no bugles sound reveille.

---

2. **witch-elm**, broad-leaved elm. **Saint Fillan**, a Scottish abbot of the seventh century. His name was given to several towns and to many chapels and holy fountains in Scotland. 3. **numbers**, verses. 10. **Caledon**, ancient and poetical name for Scotland. 15. **symphony**. This word is used by Scott not in the present sense of a complex musical composition, but as a synonym for "musical harmony."

15. **Trump**, sound of trumpet. **pibroch**, a kind of Highland bagpipe music. 18. **fallow**, uncultivated ground. 24. **squadrons stamping**. In the poem, there is a pause between this stanza and the next; there is a brief statement that Ellen intends to address the last stanza directly to the Knight of Snowdoun. 28. **reveille**, morning trumpet signal calling soldiers to the duties of the day.

BOAT SONG

The boatmen of Roderick Dhu sing this song as they bring their chieftain to shore. Roderick was the Highland suitor of the Lady of the Lake.

Hail to the Chief who in triumph advances!
  Honored and blessed be the ever-green
    Pine!
Long may the tree, in his banner that glances,
  Flourish, the shelter and grace of our line!
    Heaven send it happy dew,   5
    Earth lend it sap anew,
Gayly to bourgeon and broadly to grow,
    While every Highland glen
    Sends our shout back again,
  "Roderigh Vich Alpine dhu, ho! ieroe!" 10

Ours is no sapling, chance-sown by the fountain,
  Blooming at Beltane, in winter to fade;
When the whirlwind has stripped every leaf
  on the mountain,
  The more shall Clan-Alpine exult in her
    shade.
    Moored in the rifted rock,   15
    Proof to the tempest's shock,
Firmer he roots him the ruder it blow;
    Menteith and Breadalbane, then
    Echo his praise again,
  "Roderigh Vich Alpine dhu, ho! ieroe!" 20

Proudly our pibroch has thrilled in Glen
  Fruin,
  And Bannochar's groans to our slogan replied;
Glen-Luss and Ross-dhu, they are smoking
  in ruin,
  And the best of Loch Lomond lie dead on
    her side.
    Widow and Saxon maid   25
    Long shall lament our raid,
Think of Clan-Alpine with fear and with woe;
    Lennox and Leven-glen
    Shake when they hear again,
  "Roderigh Vich Alpine dhu, ho! ieroe!" 30

Row, vassals, row, for the pride of the Highlands!
  Stretch to your oars for the ever-green
    Pine!
O that the rosebud that graces yon islands
  Were wreathed in a garland around him
    to twine!
    O that some seedling gem,   35
    Worthy such noble stem,
Honored and blessed in their shadow might
  grow!
    Loud should Clan-Alpine then
    Ring from her deepmost glen,
  "Roderigh Vich Alpine dhu, ho! ieroe!" 40

CORONACH

The Coronach of the Highlanders was a wild lamentation by mourners over the body of a departed friend. In this song a group of village maids and matrons lament the death of Duncan, the head of a Highland family on the side of Roderick. See the coronach type of popular ballad, Vol. I, p. 130.

He is gone on the mountain,
  He is lost to the forest,
Like a summer-dried fountain,
  When our need was the sorest.
The font, reappearing,   5
  From the raindrops shall borrow,
But to us comes no cheering,
  To Duncan no morrow!

The hand of the reaper
  Takes the ears that are hoary,   10
But the voice of the weeper
  Wails manhood in glory.
The autumn winds rushing
  Waft the leaves that are searest,
But our flower was in flushing,   15
  When blighting was nearest.

Fleet foot on the correi,
  Sage counsel in cumber,
Red hand in the foray,
  How sound is thy slumber!   20
Like the dew on the mountain,
  Like the foam on the river,

---

7. **bourgeon**, put forth buds. 10. **Roderigh . . . dhu**, Black Roderick. the head of the clan Alpine. 12. **Beltane**, May-day. 18-28. **Menteith . . . Leven-glen**. The districts mentioned in these lines are all in the vicinity of Loch Lomond, situated in the counties of Stirling and Dumbarton, Scotland.

17. **correi**, hollow in a hill, the resort of game. 18. **cumber**, trouble. 21. **dew . . . forever**. Cf. Burns's *Tam o' Shanter*, ll. 59-66, p. 105.

Like the bubble on the fountain,
Thou art gone, and forever!

SOLDIER'S SONG

John of Brent, a fearless yeoman outlaw, sings this rollicking song to a boisterous crew of fellow adventurers after a night of revelry. For other drinking songs in various moods see *Back and Side Go Bare* (Vol. I, p. 468) and Burns's *Willie Brew'd a Peck o' Maut*, p. 103.

Our vicar still preaches that Peter and Poule
Laid a swinging long curse on the bonny
    brown bowl,
That there's wrath and despair in the jolly
    black-jack,
And the seven deadly sins in a flagon of
    sack;
Yet whoop, Barnaby! off with thy liquor,   5
Drink upsees out, and a fig for the vicar.

Our vicar he calls it damnation to sip
The ripe ruddy dew of a woman's dear
    lip,
Says that Beelzebub lurks in her kerchief so
    sly,
And Apollyon shoots darts from her merry
    black eye;   10
Yet whoop, Jack! kiss Gillian the quicker,
Till she bloom like a rose, and a fig for the
    vicar!

Our vicar thus preaches—and why should he
    not?
For the dues of his cure are the placket and
    pot;
And 'tis right of his office poor laymen to
    lurch,   15
Who infringe the domains of our good
    Mother Church.
Yet whoop, bully-boys! off with your liquor,
Sweet Marjorie's the word, and a fig for the
    vicar!

3. **black-jack**, black leather pitcher. 4. **seven sins**, pride, idleness, gluttony, lust, avarice, envy, and wrath. See *Piers Plowman*, "The Shriving of the Seven Deadly Sins" (Vol. I, pp. 200 ff.). **sack**, wine. 6. **upsees out**, deeply, to the bottom of the tankard. 9. **Beelzebub**, prince of demons, a devil. See Milton's *Paradise Lost*, I, 81 (Vol. I, p. 718). 10. **Apollyon**, angel of the bottomless pit in *Revelation*. See Bunyan's *Pilgrim's Progress* (Vol. I, p. 797). 14. **placket and pot**, a vulgar phrase for "women and wine." 15. **lurch**, swindle, rob.

HARP OF THE NORTH, FAREWELL!

Harp of the North, farewell! The hills grow
    dark,
  On purple peaks a deeper shade descend-
    ing;
In twilight copse the glowworm lights her
    spark,
  The deer, half-seen, are to the covert wend-
    ing.
Resume thy wizard elm! the fountain lend-
    ing,   5
  And the wild breeze, thy wilder min-
    strelsy;
Thy numbers sweet with nature's vespers
    blending,
  With distant echo from the fold and lea,
And herd-boy's evening pipe, and hum of
    housing bee.

Yet, once again, farewell, thou Minstrel
    Harp!   10
  Yet, once again, forgive my feeble sway,
And little reck I of the censure sharp
  May idly cavil at an idle lay.
Much have I owed thy strains on life's long
    way,
  Through secret woes the world has never
    known,   15
When on the weary night dawned wearier
    day,
  And bitterer was the grief devoured
    alone.—
That I o'erlive such woes, Enchantress! is
    thine own.

Hark! as my lingering footsteps slow retire,
  Some spirit of the Air has waked thy
    string!   20
'Tis now a seraph bold, with touch of fire,
  'Tis now the brush of Fairy's frolic wing.
Receding now, the dying numbers ring
  Fainter and fainter down the rugged dell;
And now the mountain breezes scarcely
    bring   25
  A wandering witch-note of the distant
    spell—
And now, 'tis silent all!—Enchantress, fare
    thee well!

(1809-10; 1810)

Proud Maisie

Insane Madge Wildfire, in the novel *The Heart of Midlothian*, sings this song on her deathbed.

Proud Maisie is in the wood,
    Walking so early;
Sweet Robin sits on the bush,
    Singing so rarely.

"Tell me, thou bonny bird,   5
    When shall I marry me?"
"When six braw gentlemen
    Kirkward shall carry ye."

"Who makes the bridal bed,
    Birdie, say truly?"   10
"The gray-headed sexton
    That delves the grave duly.

"The glowworm o'er grave and stone
    Shall light thee steady;
The owl from the steeple sing,   15
    'Welcome, proud lady.'"   (1818)

Bonny Dundee

Bonny Dundee is from the drama *The Doom of Devorgoil*. Bonny Dundee was John Graham of Claverhouse, Viscount of Dundee (1649-1689), a supporter of Charles II and James II in Scotland and a power against the Covenanters or Dissenters in Scotland. So stern was his enforcement of laws that he won the nickname "Bloody Claver'se." After the revolution of 1688, Claverhouse opposed William III, raised an army against the royal forces, and won a notable victory at Killiecrankie, in the Highlands of Scotland (1689), but was wounded on the battlefield and died the same day.

To the Lords of Convention 'twas Claver'se
    who spoke,
"Ere the King's crown shall fall there are
    crowns to be broke;
So let each Cavalier who loves honor and
    me,
Come follow the bonnet of Bonny Dundee.

    Come fill up my cup, come fill up my
        can,   5
    Come saddle your horses and call up
        your men;
    Come open the West Port and let me
        gang free,
    And it's room for the bonnets of Bonny
        Dundee!"

Dundee he is mounted, he rides up the
    street,
The bells are rung backward, the drums
    they are beat;   10
But the Provost, douce man, said, "Just e'en
    let him be,
The Gude Town is weel quit of that Deil of
    Dundee."

As he rode down the sanctified bends of the
    Bow,
Ilk carline was flyting and shaking her pow;
But the young plants of grace they looked
    couthie and slee,   15
Thinking luck to thy bonnet, thou Bonny
    Dundee!

With sour-featured Whigs the Grassmarket
    was crammed,
As if half the West had set tryst to be hanged;
There was spite in each look, there was fear
    in each e'e,
As they watched for the bonnets of Bonny
    Dundee.   20

These cowls of Kilmarnock had spits and
    had spears,
And lang-hafted gullies to kill cavaliers;
But they shrunk to close-heads and the causeway was free,
At the toss of the bonnet of Bonny Dundee.

He spurred to the foot of the proud Castle
    rock,   25
And with the gay Gordon he gallantly spoke;

10. **bells . . . backward.** Chimes sounded in reverse order served as a general alarm. 11. **Provost,** mayor, **douce,** sedate, prudent. 13. **bends of the Bow,** windings of Bow Street, Edinburgh. It was inhabited chiefly by Covenanters. 14. **Ilk carline,** each old woman. **flyting,** scolding. **pow,** head. 15. **young . . . grace,** young girls. **couthie and slee,** loving and sly. 17. **Grassmarket,** a square in Edinburgh, formerly the place of executions. 21. **cowls of Kilmarnock,** hooded garments made in the town of Kilmarnock, Ayrshire, here used for the Presbyterians who wore them and who were opposed to the Stuarts. **spits,** swords. 22. **lang-hafted gullies,** long-handled knives. 23. **close-heads,** upper ends of narrow passages leading from the street. **causeway,** a raised road across water or marshy ground. 25. **Castle rock,** the site of Edinburgh Castle, then held by the Duke of Gordon, who opposed Graham. See headnote.

"Let Mons Meg and her marrows speak twa
    words or three,
For the love of the bonnet of Bonny Dundee."

The Gordon demands of him which way he
    goes—
"Where'er shall direct me the shade of Mon-
    trose!   30
Your Grace in short space shall hear tidings
    of me.
Or that low lies the bonnet of Bonny Dundee.

"There are hills beyond Pentland and lands
    beyond Forth,
If there's lords in the Lowlands, there's chiefs
    in the North;
There are wild Duniewassals three thousand
    times three,   35
Will cry *hoigh!* for the bonnet of Bonny
    Dundee.

"There's brass on the target of barkened bull-
    hide;
There's steel in the scabbard that dangles
    beside;
The brass shall be burnished, the steel shall
    flash free,
At a toss of the bonnet of Bonny Dundee. 40

"Away to the hills, to the caves, to the
    rocks—
Ere I own an usurper, I'll couch with the
    fox;
And tremble, false Whigs, in the midst of
    your glee,
You have not seen the last of my bonnet
    and me!"

He waved his proud hand and the trumpets
    were blown,   45
The kettle-drums clashed and the horsemen
    rode on,
Till on Ravelston's cliffs and on Clermiston's
    lee
Died away the wild war-notes of Bonny
    Dundee.

    Come fill up my cup, come fill up my
        can,
    Come saddle the horses and call up the
        men,   50
    Come open your gates and let me gae
        free,
    For it's up with the bonnets of Bonny
        Dundee!   (*1825;* 1830)

Glee for King Charles

A glee is an unaccompanied song for several solo voices, and usually in contrasted movements. This song, from the novel *Woodstock*, is sung by a merry group, just before they separate for the night, in honor of Charles I, King of England (1625-1649).

Bring the bowl which you boast,
    Fill it up to the brim;
'Tis to him we love most,
    And to all who love him.
Brave gallants, stand up,   5
    And avaunt ye, base carles!
Were there death in the cup,
    Here's a health to King Charles.

Though he wanders through dangers,
    Unaided, unknown,   10
Dependent on strangers,
    Estranged from his own;
Though 'tis under our breath,
    Amidst forfeits and perils,
Here's to honor and faith,   15
    And a health to King Charles!

Let such honors abound
    As the time can afford,
The knee on the ground,
    And the hand on the sword;   20
But the time shall come round
    When, 'mid Lords, Dukes, and Earls,
The loud trumpet shall sound,
    Here's a health to King Charles!   (1826)

27. **Mons Meg,** the nickname of a great cannon, supposed to have been made in Mons, Belgium. **marrows,** mates, companions. 30. **Montrose,** James Graham (1612-1650), Earl and Marquis of Montrose, noted Scottish statesman and soldier; as a royalist supporter he led an attack on Scotland in 1650, was captured, and executed. 33. **Pentland,** a range of hills near Edinburgh. **Forth,** the Firth of Forth, a bay on the east coast of Scotland. 35. **Duniewassals,** Highland gentlemen of a rank just below that of chief of a clan or family. 37. **target,** shield. **barkened,** tanned with bark.

6. **carles,** churls, peasants.

George Noel Gordon, Lord Byron
1788-1824

Of the important English poets of the romantic movement, the one with the greatest international reputation is still Lord Byron, however much his countrymen have deprecated him; and even his countrymen have conceded that he had a more forceful personality than any of his English literary contemporaries. He was born in London, January 22, 1788; his father, "mad Jack Byron," a rake from a decayed aristocratic family; his mother, an Aberdeen heiress and a woman of most erratic temperament. The father passed from the picture while Byron was a mere child; the boy was sent to school in Aberdeen until the age of ten, then to Harrow, and eventually to Cambridge, where he remained from 1805 to 1808.

A moment's glance at Byron's ancestry is sufficient to account for the nervous instability, the rebelliousness, and the maladjustment that Byron showed not only as a schoolboy but as a man. His mother, in whose care he remained until his days at Harrow, was given to temper tantrums and to alternate fits of great tenderness and physical violence toward her son. A congenital lameness, painfully and ineffectively treated by various medical practitioners, rankled in the spirit of a morbidly proud, high-spirited boy. Byron tried to excel in every way; he became a good student, an excellent athlete, and—it must be confessed—a considerable playboy. The picture of Byron as a satyr-like debauchee is perhaps an unfair caricature, but even in his Harrow days we hear of love affairs—some harmless flirtations, some passing infatuations, some distinctly unpuritanical. His mother was upset by her son's wayward habits, and there was something of a break between the two, although Byron was sincerely grief-stricken at her death.

It was during his Cambridge days that Byron's first poems were published, the *Hours of Idleness* (1807). These were not very promising poems, and they were criticized unfavorably, particularly by the *Edinburgh Review*, under the editorship of the redoubtable Jeffrey (p. 18). Byron's retort to the critics, with Jeffrey especially in mind—an inevitable retort, considering Byron's character—was well-considered and highly significant. It was *English Bards and Scotch Reviewers* (1809), a direct continuation of the tradition of neo-classical satire (Vol. I, pp. 830 ff.); it shows Byron's admiration for Pope and Dryden; and it illustrates amply the important satirical side of Byron's nature—one which cannot be ignored at any stage of Byron's career. For it happens that Byron had a dual nature: he was a great romanticist, to be sure, but he was a great satirist as well.

After the commotion caused by *English Bards and Scotch Reviewers,* Byron took an extensive tour of the Continent and returned to tell of it in Cantos I and II of *Childe Harold* (1812). He had nursed some political ambitions, but they were joyously cast aside in the sensational reception of *Childe Harold*, when Byron, to paraphrase himself, awoke and found himself famous. The reasons for the success of *Childe Harold* are not hard to give—it had great vigor and descriptive power and fire; and it was extremely opportune, for it was a poetical guide-book of the Europe of Byron's own day, seen not through medieval lenses or through the imagination of a recluse but by an active full-blooded young man with a soul that loved liberty and revolt and adventure. Moreover, there was an interestingly mysterious unhappiness which breathed through the lines; the hero was a melancholy young man with a melodramatic attitude, over whom hung the cloud of the sinister, perhaps of the evil. The romantic appeal of all this to the age was irresistible. In spite of Byron's denials, public opinion then, as now, insisted that the poem was autobiographical;

the young poet was badly spoiled by society—by the feminine portion in particular—although he gained the reputation of being "mad, bad, and dangerous to know."

Having found a real outlet for his natural powers, Byron proceeded to follow it diligently. He launched upon a series of narrative poems, tales of adventure with scenes laid for the most part in the Near East or Mediterranean regions. They can be best described as excellent scenario-material for a modern exotic motion picture. *The Giaour* (1813), *The Bride of Abydos* (1813), *The Corsair* (1814), *Lara* (1814), *The Siege of Corinth* (1816), *Parisina* (1816) are "Oriental tales"; each is good narrative poetry, although the vein is worked a trifle thin toward the end. Added to *Childe Harold* they made Byron distinctly the rage. Appearing in all these poems is what might be called a Byronic heroine as well as a Byronic hero.

Nothing remained in Byron's quest of worldly bliss, it seemed, but a steadying love and an advantageous marriage. Both were apparently forthcoming when, in January, 1815, Byron married Anne Milbanke, a rich, strict, beautiful, but unresponsive heiress. A daughter, Ada, was born to the couple in December; within a month the Byrons had separated. The controversy over the causes of this separation still rages. The explanation by Byron was that they were simply incompatible, as might well be true. A more sinister rumor was that Lady Byron had become aware of an incestuous relationship between Byron and his half-sister Augusta Leigh. But the two women apparently continued on friendly terms after the separation of Lord and Lady Byron. Whatever the cause, the British public chose to believe the worst; and Byron, virtually ostracized, "shook the dust of England from his feet" in April, 1816, and went to the Continent, never to return.

He traveled through Belgium, thence to Switzerland; the fruit of this journey was the third canto of *Childe Harold* (p. 212). The poetic drama of *Manfred* (1817), which was acted occasionally, paints anew the Byronic hero, this time under the spell of an ill-starred love. But Byron's advent in Italy resolved itself into a parade of the poet from one city to another attended by various light ladies. In Venice (1818-19) he kept a virtual harem. He met Shelley once more, was friendly with him, and indulged in a liaison with a relative of Shelley's wife (p. 249). But all this debauchery did not stop a brilliant flow of poetry. When, at Ravenna, he saw the Countess Teresa Guiccioli, the young wife of an old Italian nobleman with revolutionary tendencies, an amicable arrangement was made with the young woman's family; her attachment for Byron was recognized and condoned, and when her family was forced to evacuate one Italian city, Byron moved along with them to the next. In 1819 he moved thus to Ravenna; in 1821 to Pisa; in 1822 to Genoa.

Teresa Guiccioli gave Byron a steadiness that he had never known before. The output of poetry, from the date of his arrival in Italy, mostly under the influence of the Countess Guiccioli, is astonishing. *Childe Harold* was completed (1817); the brilliant satirical *fabliau*, *Beppo*, appeared the same year; narrative poems like *Mazeppa* and *The Prisoner of Chillon* showed no diminution in his romantic story-telling powers; a few dramas, in the main unactable, like *Cain* (1821) or *Marino Faliero* (1820) were written; and the whip-lash satire, *The Vision of Judgment*, blasted not only the poet laureate Robert Southey (p. 296) but the older school of romantic poets like Wordsworth and Coleridge and all that they represented—not to mention the crazed figure of King George III and his fat unlovely son, George IV. The crowning product of Byron's Italian days was *Don Juan* (p. 224), the various cantos of which were spread over the years from 1818 to Byron's death. *Don Juan* is Byron as a whole, his complex character blended into one romantic, cynical, satirical, amorous, adventurous, melodramatic, liberty-loving person who roams over Europe, tasting the joys of life, but ever searching, and ever unsatisfied. If it is possible to see any one phase of Byron's character uppermost in this poem, it is probably the satirical. Such are the shifting moods of the mad and bad Byron, however, that it is impossible to know in advance what type of poetry any given stanza of *Don Juan* will yield. Hence its enduring charm, for it can be witty as well as sentimental; warm and passionate as well as cold and sneering; farcical as well as tragic; trivial as well as powerful and solemnly impressive.

But Byron, though he may well be called his Don Juan incarnate, was not all theatricality and egotism. Neither was he purely a drawing-room revolutionist. He was asked to aid in the Greek war of liberation from the Turks and accepted. Before he could achieve anything of importance, however, he caught fever and died suddenly at Missolonghi, April 19, 1824. From the standpoint of the purist in morals, nothing so much became Byron's life as his death.

But it is useless to moralize over this great personality, whose name was virtually a legend all over Europe. It is recognized now that Byron owes much of his fame to that same great personality, for his technique as a poet is uneven, as is his poetic taste. He can strike off a titanic line in one moment and lapse into the cheap or commonplace in the next. Some of this unevenness is deliberate, no doubt, and designed primarily to shock his reader in theatrical fashion. There is a coarser streak in Byron than is to be found in his great contemporaries—coarseness both as a man and as an artist. His nature poetry is chiefly a background for his powerful ego; unlike Wordsworth's it is highly dramatized and inclined to the tempestuous. As the trumpet of revolution he shares honors with Shelley. Patriotism is submerged in internationalism in his poetry, but his disgust for monarchy is genuine throughout, as the ill-fated venture in Greece bears witness. He is not so great a humanitarian as Shelley, for his was a more practical outlook on life. In many ways he was a great neo-classicist. But it is as a romanticist that Byron made his most powerful impression on the nineteenth century. Matthew Arnold's youthful reaction was:

> He taught us little, but our soul
> Had *felt* him like the thunder's roll.

When We Two Parted

This poem probably refers to Mary Chaworth, for whom Byron cherished a boyhood affection. She married a Mr. Musters, from whom she was later separated.

When we two parted
  In silence and tears,
Half broken-hearted
  To sever for years,
Pale grew thy cheek and cold,   5
  Colder thy kiss;
Truly that hour foretold
  Sorrow to this.

The dew of the morning
  Sunk chill on my brow—   10
It felt like the warning
  Of what I feel now.
Thy vows are all broken,
  And light is thy fame;
I hear thy name spoken,   15
  And share in its shame.

They name thee before me,
  A knell to mine ear;
A shudder comes o'er me—
  Why wert thou so dear?   20
They know not I knew thee,
  Who knew thee too well—
Long, long shall I rue thee,
  Too deeply to tell.

In secret we met—   25
  In silence I grieve
That thy heart could forget,
  Thy spirit deceive.
If I should meet thee
  After long years,   30
How should I greet thee?—
  With silence and tears. (*1808;* 1816)

from *English Bards and Scotch Reviewers*

The immediate cause for this long satirical poem was a review of Byron's first work, *Hours of Idleness*, published in the *Edinburgh Review* for January, 1808. The review, written not by the editor Francis Jeffrey but by Harry Brougham, was extremely harsh. Byron, however, waited to hear from other reviews before making answer. The significant part of this poem is not the reply to the *Edinburgh Review* but rather the lines on Wordsworth, Scott, Southey, and others. These lines show how distinctly Byron was out of sympathy with the older generation of English romantic poets. The revolt of Byron is also seen in his other satirical poetry—*The Vision of Judgment* and *Don Juan*; it is clear that he did not change his opinions of Wordsworth and the others. As Byron said in a letter to Murray, his publisher (September 15, 1817): "We are upon a wrong revolutionary poetical system, or systems, not worth a damn in itself. . . . I am the more confirmed in this by having lately gone over some of our classics, particularly Pope." So spoke the neo-classical part of Byron.

* * * * *

Behold! in various throngs the scribbling crew,
For notice eager, pass in long review:
Each spurs his jaded Pegasus apace, 145
And rime and blank maintain an equal race;
Sonnets on sonnets crowd, and ode on ode;
And tales of terror jostle on the road;
Immeasurable measures move along;
For simpering folly loves a varied song, 150
To strange mysterious dulness still the friend,
Admires the strain she cannot comprehend.
Thus Lays of Minstrels—may they be the last!—
On half-strung harps whine mournful to the blast.
While mountain spirits prate to river sprites, 155
That dames may listen to the sound at nights;
And goblin brats, of Gilpin Horner's brood,
Decoy young border-nobles through the wood,
And skip at every step, Lord knows how high,
And frighten foolish babes, the Lord knows why; 160
While high-born ladies in their magic cell,
Forbidding knights to read who cannot spell,
Dispatch a courier to a wizard's grave,
And fight with honest men to shield a knave.

Next view in state, proud prancing on his roan, 165
The golden-crested haughty Marmion,
Now forging scrolls, now foremost in the fight,
Not quite a felon, yet but half a knight,
The gibbet or the field prepared to grace;
A mighty mixture of the great and base. 170
And think'st thou, Scott! by vain conceit perchance,
On public taste to foist thy stale romance,
Though Murray with his Miller may combine
To yield thy muse just half-a-crown per line?
No! when the sons of song descend to trade, 175
Their bays are sear, their former laurels fade.
Let such forego the poet's sacred name,
Who rack their brains for lucre, not for fame:
Still for stern Mammon may they toil in vain!
And sadly gaze on gold they cannot gain! 180
Such be their meed, such still the just reward
Of prostituted muse and hireling bard!
For this we spurn Apollo's venal son,
And bid a long "good-night to Marmion."

These are the themes that claim our plaudits now; 185
These are the bards to whom the muse must bow;
While Milton, Dryden, Pope, alike forgot,
Resign their hallowed bays to Walter Scott.

---

145. **Pegasus**, a winged horse associated with poetic inspiration. 148. **tales of terror**, an allusion to Lewis's *Tales of Terror* (1799) and *Tales of Wonder* (1800). 149. **Immeasurable . . . along**, a thrust at the new anapestic meters introduced by Cowper (p. 73), Coleridge (p. 163), Southey (p. 296), Moore (p. 297), and others. 153. **Lays . . . last**, a reference to Scott's *Lay of the Last Minstrel* (p. 192), which grew out of a suggestion for a ballad on the Border legend of Gilpin Horner, a goblin; other allusions to this poem follow.

166. **Marmion**. See p. 192. 173. **Murray . . . Miller**, John Murray and William Miller, contemporary publishers. Murray was active in the *Quarterly Review*. See *Who Killed John Keats?* p. 247. 176. **bays**, wreaths of honor made from leaves of the bay-tree, a kind of laurel. 179. **Mammon**, god of riches, the personification of wealth. 183. **Apollo's venal son**, Scott, who received £1000 for *Marmion*. Apollo was the god of poetry and music.

The time has been, when yet the muse was
    young,
When Homer swept the lyre, and Maro
    sung,   190
An epic scarce ten centuries could claim,
While awe-struck nations hailed the magic
    name:
The work of each immortal bard appears
The single wonder of a thousand years.
Empires have moldered from the face of
    earth,   195
Tongues have expired with those who gave
    them birth,
Without the glory such a strain can give,
As even in ruin bids the language live.
Not so with us, though minor bards, con-
    tent,
On one great work a life of labor spent: 200
With eagle pinion soaring to the skies,
Behold the ballad-monger Southey rise!
To him let Camoëns, Milton, Tasso yield,
Whose annual strains, like armies, take the
    field.
First in the ranks see Joan of Arc advance, 205
The scourge of England and the boast of
    France!
Though burnt by wicked Bedford for a
    witch,
Behold her statue placed in glory's niche;
Her fetters burst, and just released from
    prison,
A virgin phoenix from her ashes risen.   210
Next see tremendous Thalaba come on,
Arabia's monstrous, wild, and wondrous
    son;
Domdaniel's dread destroyer, who o'erthrew
More mad magicians than the world e'er
    knew.
Immortal hero! all thy foes o'ercome,   215
Forever reign—the rival of Tom Thumb!

Since startled meter fled before thy face,
Well wert thou doomed the last of all thy
    race!
Well might triumphant genii bear thee hence,
Illustrious conqueror of common sense!   220
Now, last and greatest, Madoc spreads his
    sails,
Cacique in Mexico, and prince in Wales;
Tells us strange tales, as other travelers do,
More old than Mandeville's, and not so true.
Oh! Southey! Southey! cease thy varied
    song!   225
A bard may chant too often and too long:
As thou art strong in verse, in mercy, spare!
A fourth, alas! were more than we could bear.
But if, in spite of all the world can say,
Thou still wilt verseward plod thy weary way;
If still in Berkley ballads most uncivil,   231
Thou wilt devote old women to the devil,
The babe unborn thy dread intent may rue:
"God help thee," Southey, and thy readers too.

Next comes the dull disciple of thy school,
That mild apostate from poetic rule,   236
The simple Wordsworth, framer of a lay
As soft as evening in his favorite May,
Who warns his friend "to shake off toil and
    trouble,
And quit his books for fear of growing
    double";   240
Who, both by precept and example, shows
That prose is verse, and verse is merely prose;
Convincing all, by demonstration plain,
Poetic souls delight in prose insane;
And Christmas stories tortured into rime   245
Contain the essence of the true sublime.
Thus, when he tells the tale of Betty Foy,
The idiot mother of "an idiot boy";
A moon-struck, silly lad, who lost his way,
And, like his bard, confounded night with
    day;   250
So close on each pathetic part he dwells,

190. **Homer**, Greek epic poet assigned to the ninth century B.C. **Maro**, the family name of Virgil, Latin epic poet (70-19 B.C.). 202. **Southey**, prolific writer of ballads and epics (p. 296). 203. **Camoëns**, noted Portuguese poet (1524-1580), author of the *Lusiad*, the national epic. **Tasso**, celebrated Italian epic poet (1544-1595). 205. **Joan of Arc.** Southey's *Joan of Arc, Thalaba,* and *Madoc*, three ponderous epics, appeared in 1796, 1801, and 1805, respectively. 207. **Bedford**, Duke of Bedford (1389-1435), an English general who abetted the execution of Joan of Arc in 1431. 210. **virgin ... risen,** an allusion to the ancient Oriental legend of the phoenix, an immortal bird that, when consumed in fire, was resurrected from its ashes. 213. **Domdaniel**, in the *Arabian Nights* tales a seminary for evil magicians and a resort of evil spirits. 216. **Tom Thumb**, a legendary diminutive personage celebrated in English literature.

222. **Cacique**, chief, petty king. 224. **Mandeville**, Sir John Mandeville, reputed author of a fourteenth-century book of travels. 230. **verseward ... way.** Cf. Gray's *Elegy*, l. 3, p. 50. 231. **Berkley ballads.** One of Southey's ballads was entitled *The Old Woman of Berkeley;* in this the old woman is carried away by the devil. 234. **"God help thee,"** from a poem written by William Gifford (1756-1826) as a parody on Southey's dactylics. Southey had used the phrase in his *Soldier's Wife,* l. 3. 236. **apostate ... rule.** See Wordsworth's *Preface to the Lyrical Ballads,* p. 318, in which he argues that there is little difference between the language of prose and that of poetry. 239. **"to shake ... double,"** from Wordsworth, *The Tables Turned,* ll. 1-4. 247. **tale of Betty Foy,** in *The Idiot Boy.*

And each adventure so sublimely tells,
That all who view the "idiot in his glory"
Conceive the bard the hero of the story.

  Shall gentle Coleridge pass unnoticed here,
To turgid ode and tumid stanza dear?   256
Though themes of innocence amuse him best,
Yet still obscurity's a welcome guest.
If Inspiration should her aid refuse
To him who takes a pixy for a muse,   260
Yet none in lofty numbers can surpass
The bard who soars to elegize an ass.
So well the subject suits his noble mind,
He brays, the laureate of the long-eared kind.

*   *   *   *   *

Maid of Athens, Ere We Part

Ζωή μου, σᾶς ἀγαπῶ.

  The maiden enshrined in this poem is supposed to be Theresa Macri, who later married an Englishman named Black. The Greek phrase means, "My life, I love you."

Maid of Athens, ere we part,
Give, oh, give me back my heart!
Or, since that has left my breast,
Keep it now, and take the rest!
Hear my vow before I go,   5
Ζωή μου, σᾶς ἀγαπῶ.

By those tresses unconfined,
Wooed by each Aegean wind;
By those lids whose jetty fringe
Kiss thy soft cheeks' blooming tinge;   10
By those wild eyes like the roe,
Ζωή μου, σᾶς ἀγαπῶ.

By that lip I long to taste;
By that zone-encircled waist;
By all the token-flowers that tell   15
What words can never speak so well;
By love's alternate joy and woe,
Ζωή μου, σᾶς ἀγαπῶ.

Maid of Athens! I am gone:
Think of me, sweet! when alone.   20
Though I fly to Istanbul,
Athens holds my heart and soul:
Can I cease to love thee? No!
Ζωή μου, σᾶς ἀγαπῶ.

                        (*1810;* 1812)

She Walks in Beauty

  This poem and the next are from *Hebrew Melodies,* a group of lyrics, many of which deal with incidents from the Old Testament; they were meant to be set to music. *She Walks in Beauty* refers to Lady Wilmot Horton, whom Byron had seen at a ball, attired in mourning with spangles on her dress.

She walks in beauty, like the night
  Of cloudless climes and starry skies;
And all that's best of dark and bright
  Meet in her aspect and her eyes:
Thus mellowed to that tender light   5
  Which heaven to gaudy day denies.

One shade the more, one ray the less,
  Had half impaired the nameless grace
Which waves in every raven tress,
  Or softly lightens o'er her face;   10
Where thoughts serenely sweet express
  How pure, how dear their dwelling-place.

And on that cheek, and o'er that brow,
  So soft, so calm, yet eloquent,
The smiles that win, the tints that glow,   15
  But tell of days in goodness spent,
A mind at peace with all below,
  A heart whose love is innocent!

                        (*1814;* 1815)

The Destruction of Sennacherib

The Assyrian came down like the wolf on
    the fold,
And his cohorts were gleaming in purple and
    gold;

---

256. **turgid . . . dear,** a characterization of some of Coleridge's odes but not of the one given in this book, p. **185.** 260. **pixy for a muse,** an allusion to Coleridge's *Songs of the Pixies* (Devonshire fairies). 262. **an ass,** a reference to Coleridge's inane poem *To a Young Ass.*
  Maid of Athens. 8. **Aegean,** the sea east of Greece. 14. **zone-encircled,** girdle-encircled.

21. **Istanbul,** Constantinople.
  The Destruction of Sennacherib. Sennacherib was a king of Assyria who invaded Palestine in the seventh century B.C. The story is told in *2 Kings,* 18-19.

And the sheen of their spears was like stars on the sea,
When the blue wave rolls nightly on deep Galilee.

Like the leaves of the forest when Summer is green, 5
That host with their banners at sunset were seen:
Like the leaves of the forest when Autumn hath blown,
That host on the morrow lay withered and strown.

For the Angel of Death spread his wings on the blast,
And breathed in the face of the foe as he passed; 10
And the eyes of the sleepers waxed deadly and chill,
And their hearts but once heaved, and forever grew still!

And there lay the steed with his nostril all wide,
But through it there rolled not the breath of his pride;
And the foam of his gasping lay white on the turf, 15
And cold as the spray of the rock-beating surf.

And there lay the rider distorted and pale,
With the dew on his brow, and the rust on his mail:
And the tents were all silent—the banners alone—
The lances unlifted—the trumpet unblown. 20

And the widows of Ashur are loud in their wail,
And the idols are broke in the temple of Baal;
And the might of the Gentile, unsmote by the sword,
Hath melted like snow in the glance of the Lord!

(1815)

21. **Ashur**, the highest god of the Assyrians. 22. **Baal**, the supreme divinity of the ancient Syro-Phoenician nations.

Stanzas for Music

Here is an early but characteristic expression of one of Byron's chief moods—romantic glorification of youth and regret at its passing. See Coleridge's *Youth and Age*, p. 189.

There's not a joy the world can give like that it takes away,
When the glow of early thought declines in feeling's dull decay;
'Tis not on youth's smooth cheek the blush alone, which fades so fast,
But the tender bloom of heart is gone, ere youth itself be past.

Then the few whose spirits float above the wreck of happiness 5
Are driven o'er the shoals of guilt or ocean of excess:
The magnet of their course is gone, or only points in vain
The shore to which their shivered sail shall never stretch again.

Then the mortal coldness of the soul like death itself comes down;
It cannot feel for others' woes, it dare not dream its own; 10
That heavy chill has frozen o'er the fountain of our tears,
And though the eye may sparkle still, 'tis where the ice appears.

Though wit may flash from fluent lips, and mirth distract the breast,
Through midnight hours that yield no more their former hope of rest;
'Tis but as ivy-leaves around the ruined turret wreath, 15
All green and wildly fresh without, but worn and gray beneath.

Oh, could I feel as I have felt—or be what I have been,
Or weep as I could once have wept, o'er many a vanished scene;
As springs, in deserts found, seem sweet, all brackish though they be,
So, midst the withered waste of life, those tears would flow to me. (*1815;* 1816)

Stanzas for Music

There be none of Beauty's daughters
   With a magic like thee;
And like music on the waters
   Is thy sweet voice to me:
When, as if its sound were causing   5
The charmèd ocean's pausing,
The waves lie still and gleaming,
And the lulled winds seem dreaming.

And the midnight moon is weaving
   Her bright chain o'er the deep;   10
Whose breast is gently heaving,
   As an infant's asleep:
So the spirit bows before thee,
To listen and adore thee;
With a full but soft emotion,   15
Like the swell of Summer's ocean.
                    (1816)

Sonnet on Chillon

For an explanation of the Castle of Chillon and of François de Bonnivard's imprisonment there, see the headnote to *The Prisoner of Chillon* below.

Eternal Spirit of the chainless Mind!
   Brightest in dungeons, Liberty! thou art:
For there thy habitation is the heart—
   The heart which love of thee alone can bind;
And when thy sons to fetters are consigned—   5
   To fetters, and the damp vault's dayless gloom,
   Their country conquers with their martyrdom,
And Freedom's fame finds wings on every wind.
Chillon! thy prison is a holy place,
   And thy sad floor an altar—for 'twas trod,   10
Until his very steps have left a trace
   Worn, as if thy cold pavement were a sod,
By Bonnivard!—May none those marks efface!
   For they appeal from tyranny to God.
                    (1816)

The Prisoner of Chillon

The Castle of Chillon is situated at the eastern end of Lake Geneva, Switzerland. The poem was written in two days at a small inn where Byron and Shelley were detained by bad weather during a tour of the lake. François de Bonnivard (1493-1570) was a Swiss patriot and religious reformer. For his participation in an effort to make Geneva a republic, free from the control of Charles III, Duke of Savoy, he was imprisoned in the Castle of Chillon from 1530 until he was released by his own party in 1536. Byron presents a romantic idealization of the few facts at his disposal. The brothers are imaginary.

I

My hair is gray, but not with years,
   Nor grew it white
   In a single night,
As men's have grown from sudden fears:
My limbs are bowed, though not with toil,   5
   But rusted with a vile repose,
For they have been a dungeon's spoil,
   And mine has been the fate of those
To whom the goodly earth and air
Are banned, and barred—forbidden fare: 10
But this was for my father's faith
I suffered chains and courted death;
That father perished at the stake
For tenets he would not forsake;
And for the same his lineal race   15
In darkness found a dwelling-place;
We were seven—who now are one,
   Six in youth, and one in age,
Finished as they had begun,
   Proud of Persecution's rage;   20
One in fire, and two in field,
Their belief with blood have sealed,
Dying as their father died,
For the God their foes denied;
Three were in a dungeon cast,   25
Of whom this wreck is left the last.

---

4. **men's . . . fears.** Byron cites in a note the cases of Ludovico Sforza (1451-1508) and others.

II

There are seven pillars of Gothic mold,
In Chillon's dungeons deep and old,
There are seven columns, massy and gray,
Dim with a dull imprisoned ray, 30
A sunbeam which hath lost its way,
And through the crevice and the cleft
Of the thick wall is fallen and left;
Creeping o'er the floor so damp,
Like a marsh's meteor lamp: 35
And in each pillar there is a ring,
   And in each ring there is a chain;
That iron is a cankering thing,
   For in these limbs its teeth remain,
With marks that will not wear away, 40
Till I have done with this new day,
Which now is painful to these eyes,
Which have not seen the sun so rise
For years—I cannot count them o'er,
I lost their long and heavy score, 45
When my last brother drooped and died,
And I lay living by his side.

III

They chained us each to a column stone,
And we were three—yet, each alone;
We could not move a single pace, 50
We could not see each other's face,
But with that pale and livid light
That made us strangers in our sight:
And thus together—yet apart,
Fettered in hand, but joined in heart, 55
'Twas still some solace, in the dearth
Of the pure elements of earth,
To hearken to each other's speech,
And each turn comforter to each
With some new hope, or legend old, 60
Or song heroically bold;
But even these at length grew cold.
Our voices took a dreary tone,
An echo of the dungeon stone,
   A grating sound, not full and free, 65
   As they of yore were wont to be:
It might be fancy, but to me
They never sounded like our own.

IV

I was the eldest of the three,
   And to uphold and cheer the rest 70
   I ought to do—and did my best;
And each did well in his degree.
   The youngest, whom my father loved,
Because our mother's brow was given
To him, with eyes as blue as heaven— 75
   For him my soul was sorely moved;
And truly might it be distressed
To see such bird in such a nest;
For he was beautiful as day—
   (When day was beautiful to me 80
   As to young eagles, being free)—
A polar day, which will not see
A sunset till its summer's gone,
   Its sleepless summer of long light,
The snow-clad offspring of the sun: 85
   And thus he was as pure and bright,
And in his natural spirit gay,
With tears for naught but others' ills,
And then they flowed like mountain rills,
Unless he could assuage the woe 90
Which he abhorred to view below.

V

The other was as pure of mind,
But formed to combat with his kind;
Strong in his frame, and of a mood
Which 'gainst the world in war had stood, 95
And perished in the foremost rank
   With joy—but not in chains to pine:
His spirit withered with their clank,
   I saw it silently decline—
   And so perchance in sooth did mine: 100
But yet I forced it on to cheer
Those relics of a home so dear.
He was a hunter of the hills,
   Had followed there the deer and wolf;
   To him his dungeon was a gulf, 105
And fettered feet the worst of ills.

VI

   Lake Leman lies by Chillon's walls:
A thousand feet in depth below
Its massy waters meet and flow;
Thus much the fathom-line was sent 110
From Chillon's snow-white battlement,
   Which round about the wave enthralls:
A double dungeon wall and wave
Have made—and like a living grave
Below the surface of the lake 115

---

115. **Below . . . lake.** Actually the dungeon is not below the surface of the lake.

The dark vault lies wherein we lay,
We heard it ripple night and day;
  Sounding o'er our heads it knocked;
And I have felt the winter's spray
Wash through the bars when winds were high   120
And wanton in the happy sky;
  And then the very rock hath rocked,
  And I have felt it shake, unshocked,
Because I could have smiled to see
The death that would have set me free.   125

VII

I said my nearer brother pined,
I said his mighty heart declined,
He loathed and put away his food;
It was not that 'twas coarse and rude,
For we were used to hunter's fare,   130
And for the like had little care:
The milk drawn from the mountain goat
Was changed for water from the moat,
Our bread was such as captives' tears
Have moistened many a thousand years,   135
Since man first pent his fellow men
Like brutes within an iron den;
But what were these to us or him?
These wasted not his heart or limb;
My brother's soul was of that mold   140
Which in a palace had grown cold,
Had his free breathing been denied
The range of the steep mountain's side;
But why delay the truth?—he died.
I saw, and could not hold his head,   145
Nor reach his dying hand—nor dead—
Though hard I strove, but strove in vain,
To rend and gnash my bonds in twain.
He died, and they unlocked his chain,
And scooped for him a shallow grave   150
Even from the cold earth of our cave.
I begged them, as a boon, to lay
His corse in dust whereon the day
Might shine—it was a foolish thought,
But then within my brain it wrought,   155
That even in death his freeborn breast
In such a dungeon could not rest.
I might have spared my idle prayer—
They coldly laughed, and laid him there:
The flat and turfless earth above   160
The being we so much did love;
His empty chain above it leant,
Such murder's fitting monument!

VIII

But he, the favorite and the flower,
Most cherished since his natal hour,   165
His mother's image in fair face,
The infant love of all his race,
His martyred father's dearest thought,
My latest care, for whom I sought
To hoard my life, that his might be   170
Less wretched now, and one day free;
He, too, who yet had held untired
A spirit natural or inspired—
He, too, was struck, and day by day
Was withered on the stalk away.   175
Oh, God! it is a fearful thing
To see the human soul take wing
In any shape, in any mood:
I've seen it rushing forth in blood,
I've seen it on the breaking ocean   180
Strive with a swoll'n convulsive motion,
I've seen the sick and ghastly bed
Of Sin delirious with its dread;
But these were horrors—this was woe
Unmixed with such—but sure and slow: 185
He faded, and so calm and meek,
So softly worn, so sweetly weak,
So tearless, yet so tender, kind,
And grieved for those he left behind;
With all the while a cheek whose bloom   190
Was as a mockery of the tomb,
Whose tints as gently sunk away
As a departing rainbow's ray;
An eye of most transparent light,
That almost made the dungeon bright,   195
And not a word of murmur, not
A groan o'er his untimely lot—
A little talk of better days,
A little hope my own to raise,
For I was sunk in silence—lost   200
In this last loss, of all the most;
And then the sighs he would suppress
Of fainting nature's feebleness,
More slowly drawn, grew less and less:
I listened, but I could not hear;   205
I called, for I was wild with fear;
I knew 'twas hopeless, but my dread
Would not be thus admonishèd;
I called, and thought I heard a sound—
I burst my chain with one strong bound,   210
And rushed to him—I found him not,
I only stirred in this black spot,

I only lived, *I* only drew
The accursèd breath of dungeon-dew;
The last, the sole, the dearest link   215
Between me and the eternal brink,
Which bound me to my failing race,
Was broken in this fatal place.
One on the earth, and one beneath—
My brothers—both had ceased to breathe: 220
I took that hand which lay so still,
Alas! my own was full as chill;
I had not strength to stir, or strive,
But felt that I was still alive—
A frantic feeling, when we know   225
That what we love shall ne'er be so.
    I know not why
    I could not die,
I had no earthly hope—but faith,
And that forbade a selfish death.   230

IX

What next befell me then and there
    I know not well—I never knew—
First came the loss of light, and air,
    And then of darkness too:
I had no thought, no feeling—none;   235
Among the stones I stood a stone,
And was, scarce conscious what I wist,
As shrubless crags within the mist;
For all was blank, and bleak, and gray;
It was not night, it was not day;   240
It was not even the dungeon-light,
So hateful to my heavy sight,
But vacancy absorbing space,
And fixedness without a place;
There were no stars, no earth, no time,   245
No check, no change, no good, no crime—
But silence, and a stirless breath
Which neither was of life nor death;
A sea of stagnant idleness,
Blind, boundless, mute, and motionless!   250

X

A light broke in upon my brain—
    It was the carol of a bird;
It ceased, and then it came again,
    The sweetest song ear ever heard,
And mine was thankful till my eyes   255
Ran over with the glad surprise,
And they that moment could not see
    I was the mate of misery;
But then by dull degrees came back
My senses to their wonted track;   260
I saw the dungeon walls and floor
Close slowly round me as before;
I saw the glimmer of the sun
Creeping as it before had done,
But through the crevice where it came   265
That bird was perched, as fond and tame,
    And tamer than upon the tree;
A lovely bird, with azure wings,
And song that said a thousand things,
    And seemed to say them all for me!   270
I never saw its like before,
I ne'er shall see its likeness more:
It seemed like me to want a mate,
But was not half so desolate,
And it was come to love me when   275
None lived to love me so again,
And cheering from my dungeon's brink,
Had brought me back to feel and think.
I know not if it late were free,
    Or broke its cage to perch on mine, 280
But knowing well captivity,
    Sweet bird! I could not wish for thine!
Or if it were, in wingèd guise,
A visitant from Paradise;
For—Heaven forgive that thought! the while
Which made me both to weep and smile— 286
I sometimes deemed that it might be
My brother's soul come down to me;
But then at last away it flew,
And then 'twas mortal—well I knew,   290
For he would never thus have flown,
And left me twice so doubly lone—
Lone—as the corse within its shroud,
Lone—as a solitary cloud—
    A single cloud on a sunny day,   295
While all the rest of heaven is clear,
A frown upon the atmosphere,
That hath no business to appear
    When skies are blue, and earth is gay.

XI

A kind of change came in my fate,   300
My keepers grew compassionate;
I know not what had made them so,
They were inured to sights of woe,

But so it was—my broken chain
With links unfastened did remain, 305
And it was liberty to stride
Along my cell from side to side,
And up and down, and then athwart,
And tread it over every part;
And round the pillars one by one, 310
Returning where my walk begun,
Avoiding only, as I trod,
My brothers' graves without a sod;
For if I thought with heedless tread
My step profaned their lowly bed, 315
My breath came gaspingly and thick,
And my crushed heart felt blind and sick.

XII

I made a footing in the wall,
  It was not therefrom to escape,
For I had buried one and all 320
  Who loved me in a human shape;
And the whole earth would henceforth be
A wider prison unto me:
No child, no sire, no kin had I,
No partner in my misery; 325
I thought of this, and I was glad,
For thought of them had made me mad;
But I was curious to ascend
To my barred windows, and to bend
Once more, upon the mountains high, 330
The quiet of a loving eye.

XIII

I saw them—and they were the same,
They were not changed like me in frame;
I saw their thousand years of snow
On high—their wide long lake below, 335
And the blue Rhone in fullest flow;
I heard the torrents leap and gush
O'er channeled rock and broken bush;
I saw the white-walled distant town,
And whiter sails go skimming down; 340
And then there was a little isle,
Which in my very face did smile,
  The only one in view;
A small green isle, it seemed no more,
Scarce broader than my dungeon floor, 345
But in it there were three tall trees,

327. **had**, would have.

And o'er it blew the mountain breeze,
And by it there were waters flowing,
And on it there were young flowers growing,
  Of gentle breath and hue. 350
The fish swam by the castle wall,
And they seemed joyous each and all;
The eagle rode the rising blast,
Methought he never flew so fast
As then to me he seemed to fly; 355
And then new tears came in my eye,
And I felt troubled—and would fain
I had not left my recent chain;
And when I did descend again,
The darkness of my dim abode 360
Fell on me as a heavy load;
It was as is a new-dug grave,
Closing o'er one we sought to save—
And yet my glance, too much oppressed,
Had almost need of such a rest. 365

XIV

It might be months, or years, or days—
  I kept no count, I took no note,
I had no hope my eyes to raise,
  And clear them of their dreary mote;
At last men came to set me free; 370
  I asked not why, and recked not where;
It was at length the same to me,
Fettered or fetterless to be,
  I learned to love despair.
And thus when they appeared at last, 375
And all my bonds aside were cast,
These heavy walls to me had grown
A hermitage—and all my own!
And half I felt as they were come
To tear me from a second home: 380
With spiders I had friendship made,
And watched them in their sullen trade,
Had seen the mice by moonlight play,
And why should I feel less than they?
We were all inmates of one place, 385
And I, the monarch of each race,
Had power to kill—yet, strange to tell!
In quiet we had learned to dwell;
My very chains and I grew friends,
So much a long communion tends 390
To make us what we are—even I
Regained my freedom with a sigh.

(*1816;* 1816)

Childe Harold's Pilgrimage

The first two cantos of this poem appeared in 1812; the third and fourth after Byron's departure from England. But Byron's own remarks in the preface to the first two cantos hold good for the poem as a whole. "The following poem was written, for the most part, amidst the scenes which it attempts to describe. It was begun in Albania; and the parts relative to Spain and Portugal were composed from the author's observations in those countries. Thus much it may be necessary to state for the correctness of the descriptions. . . . A fictitious character is introduced for the sake of giving some connection to the piece, which, however, makes no pretension to regularity. It has been suggested to me by friends, . . . that in this fictitious character, Childe Harold, I may incur the suspicion of having intended some real personage: this I beg leave, once for all, to disclaim—Harold is the child of imagination, for the purpose I have stated. In some very trivial particulars, and those merely local, there might be grounds for such a notion; but in the main points, I should hope, none whatever." Posterity, nevertheless, has felt that Childe Harold is Byron the romanticist; certainly in this poem, in *Manfred*, and in certain portions of *Don Juan*, Byron is at his romantic best. The figure of Childe Harold is an epitome of the "Byronic hero." The word *Childe* is used by Byron as in the old ballads and romances, signifying a youth of noble birth, usually one awaiting knighthood.

from CANTO III

Is thy face like thy mother's, my fair child!
Ada! sole daughter of my house and heart?
When last I saw thy young blue eyes they smiled,
And then we parted—not as now we part,
But with a hope.—Awaking with a start,   5
The waters heave around me; and on high
The winds lift up their voices: I depart,
Whither I know not, but the hour's gone by,
When Albion's lessening shores could grieve or glad mine eye.

Once more upon the waters! yet once more!   10
And the waves bound beneath me as a steed
That knows his rider. Welcome to their roar!
Swift be their guidance, wheresoe'er it lead!
Though the strained mast should quiver as a reed,
And the rent canvas fluttering strew the gale,
Still must I on; for I am as a weed,   16
Flung from the rock, on Ocean's foam to sail
Where'er the surge may sweep, the tempest's breath prevail.

In my youth's summer I did sing of One,
The wandering outlaw of his own dark mind;

Again I seize the theme, then but begun,   21
And bear it with me, as the rushing wind
Bears the cloud onwards: in that Tale I find
The furrows of long thought, and dried-up tears,
Which, ebbing, leave a sterile track behind,   25
O'er which all heavily the journeying years
Plod the last sands of life—where not a flower appears.

Since my young days of passion—joy, or pain,
Perchance my heart and harp have lost a string,
And both may jar: it may be, that in vain   30
I would essay as I have sung to sing.
Yet, though a dreary strain, to this I cling,
So that it wean me from the weary dream
Of selfish grief or gladness—so it fling
Forgetfulness around me—it shall seem   35
To me, though to none else, a not ungrateful theme.

He who, grown agéd in this world of woe,
In deeds, not years, piercing the depths of life,
So that no wonder waits him; nor below
Can love or sorrow, fame, ambition, strife,   40
Cut to his heart again with the keen knife
Of silent, sharp endurance: he can tell
Why thought seeks refuge in lone caves, yet rife
With airy images, and shapes which dwell

---

5. **with a hope.** Lady Byron left her husband in January, 1816. Ada was then only five weeks old. Byron never saw her again. 9. **Albion**, a poetic name for England. Byron left the country on April 25, 1816, never to return. 19. **I . . . One.** Byron wrote the first canto of *Childe Harold's Pilgrimage* in 1809 at the age of twenty-one.

Still unimpaired, though old, in the soul's haunted cell. 45

'Tis to create, and in creating live
A being more intense that we endow
With form our fancy, gaining as we give
The life we image, even as I do now.
What am I? Nothing: but not so art thou, 50
Soul of my thought! with whom I traverse earth,
Invisible but gazing, as I glow
Mixed with thy spirit, blended with thy birth,
And feeling still with thee in my crushed feeling's dearth.

Yet must I think less wildly—I *have* thought
Too long and darkly, till my brain became, 56
In its own eddy boiling and o'erwrought,
A whirling gulf of phantasy and flame:
And thus, untaught in youth my heart to tame,
My springs of life were poisoned. 'Tis too late! 60
Yet am I changed; though still enough the same
In strength to bear what time cannot abate,
And feed on bitter fruits without accusing Fate.

Something too much of this—but now 'tis past,
And the spell closes with its silent seal. 65
Long absent HAROLD reappears at last;
He of the breast which fain no more would feel,
Wrung with the wounds which kill not, but ne'er heal;
Yet Time, who changes all, had altered him
In soul and aspect as in age: years steal 70
Fire from the mind as vigor from the limb;
And life's enchanted cup but sparkles near the brim.

His had been quaffed too quickly, and he found
The dregs were wormwood; but he filled again,
And from a purer fount, on holier ground, 75
And deemed its spring perpetual; but in vain!
Still round him clung invisibly a chain
Which galled forever, fettering though unseen,
And heavy though it clanked not; worn with pain,
Which pined although it spoke not, and grew keen, 80
Entering with every step he took through many a scene.

Secure in guarded coldness, he had mixed
Again in fancied safety with his kind,
And deemed his spirit now so firmly fixed
And sheathed with an invulnerable mind, 85
That, if no joy, no sorrow lurked behind;
And he, as one, might 'midst the many stand
Unheeded, searching through the crowd to find
Fit speculation; such as in strange land
He found in wonder-works of God and Nature's hand. 90

But who can view the ripened rose, nor seek
To wear it? who can curiously behold
The smoothness and the sheen of Beauty's cheek,
Nor feel the heart can never all grow old?
Who can contemplate Fame through clouds unfold 95
The star which rises o'er her steep, nor climb?
Harold, once more within the vortex, rolled
On with the giddy circle, chasing Time,
Yet with a nobler aim than in his youth's fond prime.

But soon he knew himself the most unfit 100
Of men to herd with Man; with whom he held
Little in common; untaught to submit
His thoughts to others, though his soul was quelled
In youth by his own thoughts; still uncompelled,
He would not yield dominion of his mind 105
To spirits against whom his own rebelled;
Proud though in desolation; which could find
A life within itself, to breathe without mankind.

64. **Something . . . this.** A phrase from *Hamlet*, III, ii, 79.
65. **spell . . . seal.** The seal of silence is set upon the story of his personal tragedy.

91. **nor**, and not. 99. **fond**, foolish.

Where rose the mountains, there to him were
    friends; 109
Where rolled the ocean, thereon was his home;
Where a blue sky, and glowing clime, extends,
He had the passion and the power to roam;
The desert, forest, cavern, breaker's foam,
Were unto him companionship; they spake
A mutual language, clearer than the tome 115
Of his land's tongue, which he would oft forsake
For Nature's pages glassed by sunbeams on
    the lake.

Like the Chaldean, he could watch the stars,
Till he had peopled them with beings bright
As their own beams; and earth, and earth-
    born jars, 120
And human frailties, were forgotten quite:
Could he have kept his spirit to that flight
He had been happy; but this clay will sink
Its spark immortal, envying it the light
To which it mounts, as if to break the link 125
That keeps us from yon heaven which woos
    us to its brink.

But in Man's dwellings he became a thing
Restless and worn, and stern and wearisome,
Drooped as a wild-born falcon with clipped
    wing, 129
To whom the boundless air alone were home:
Then came his fit again, which to o'ercome,
As eagerly the barred-up bird will beat
His breast and beak against his wiry dome
Till the blood tinge his plumage, so the heat
Of his impeded soul would through his bosom
    eat. 135

Self-exiled Harold wanders forth again,
With nought of hope left, but with less of
    gloom,
The very knowledge that he lived in vain,
That all was over on this side the tomb,
Had made Despair a smilingness assume, 140
Which, though 'twere wild—as on the plundered wreck
When mariners would madly meet their doom
With draughts intemperate on the sinking
    deck—

Did yet inspire a cheer, which he forbore to
    check. 144

Stop!— for thy tread is on an Empire's dust!
An Earthquake's spoil is sepulchered below!
Is the spot marked with no colossal bust?
Nor column trophied for triumphal show?
None; but the moral's truth tells simpler so,
As the ground was before, thus let it be;— 150
How that red rain hath made the harvest
    grow!
And is this all the world has gained by thee,
Thou first and last of fields! king-making
    Victory?

And Harold stands upon this place of skulls,
The grave of France, the deadly Waterloo! 155
How in an hour the power which gave annuls
Its gifts, transferring fame as fleeting too!
In "pride of place" here last the eagle flew,
Then tore with bloody talon the rent plain,
Pierced by the shaft of banded nations
    through; 160
Ambition's life and labors all were vain;
He wears the shattered links of the world's
    broken chain.

Fit retribution! Gaul may champ the bit
And foam in fetters;—but is Earth more free?
Did nations combat to make *One* submit; 165
Or league to teach all kings true sovereignty?
What! shall reviving Thralldom again be
The patched-up idol of enlightened days?
Shall we, who struck the Lion down, shall we
Pay the Wolf homage? proffering lowly gaze
And servile knees to thrones? No; *prove* before ye praise! 171

If not, o'er one fallen despot boast no more!
In vain fair cheeks were furrowed with hot
    tears
For Europe's flowers long rooted up before
The trampler of her vineyards; in vain years
Of death, depopulation, bondage, fears, 176
Have all been borne, and broken by the accord

118. **Chaldean.** The Chaldeans were masters of astrology. 131. **came . . . again.** Cf. *Macbeth*, III, iv, 21: "Then comes my fit again."

153. **king-making.** The Battle of Waterloo gave security to the thrones of European kings. 158. **"pride of place,"** a phrase from *Macbeth*, II, iv, 12; it is a term in falconry meaning the highest point of flight. 168. **idol . . . days.** The Holy Alliance, formed in 1815 by the Emperors of Austria and Russia and the King of Prussia, aimed at the restoration of pre-Revolutionary conditions. 169. **Lion**, Napoleon. 170. **Wolf**, the imitation of imperial strength seen in the Emperor of Austria and others.

Of roused-up millions; all that most endears
Glory, is when the myrtle wreathes a sword
Such as Harmodius drew on Athens' tyrant
    lord.   180

There was a sound of revelry by night,
And Belgium's capital had gathered then
Her Beauty and her Chivalry, and bright
The lamps shone o'er fair women and brave
    men;
A thousand hearts beat happily; and when 185
Music arose with its voluptuous swell,
Soft eyes looked love to eyes which spake
    again,
And all went merry as a marriage bell;
But hush! hark! a deep sound strikes like a
    rising knell!

Did ye not hear it?—No; 'twas but the wind,
Or the car rattling o'er the stony street;   191
On with the dance! let joy be unconfined;
No sleep till morn, when Youth and Pleasure
    meet
To chase the glowing Hours with flying feet—
But hark!—that heavy sound breaks in once
    more,   195
As if the clouds its echo would repeat;
And nearer, clearer, deadlier than before!
Arm! Arm! it is—it is—the cannon's opening
    roar!

Within a windowed niche of that high hall
Sat Brunswick's fated chieftain; he did hear
That sound the first amidst the festival,   201
And caught its tone with Death's prophetic
    ear;
And when they smiled because he deemed it
    near,
His heart more truly knew that peal too well
Which stretched his father on a bloody bier,
And roused the vengeance blood alone could
    quell;   206
He rushed into the field, and, foremost fight-
    ing, fell.

Ah! then and there was hurrying to and fro,
And gathering tears, and tremblings of dis-
    tress,   209
And cheeks all pale, which but an hour ago
Blushed at the praise of their own loveliness;
And there were sudden partings, such as press
The life from out young hearts, and choking
    sighs
Which ne'er might be repeated; who could
    guess
If ever more should meet those mutual eyes,
Since upon night so sweet such awful morn
    could rise!   216

And there was mounting in hot haste: the
    steed,
The mustering squadron, and the clattering
    car,
Went pouring forward with impetuous speed,
And swiftly forming in the ranks of war;   220
And the deep thunder peal on peal afar;
And near, the beat of the alarming drum
Roused up the soldier ere the morning star;
While thronged the citizens with terror dumb,
Or whispering, with white lips—"The foe!
    they come! they come!"   225

And wild and high the "Cameron's gather-
    ing" rose!
The war-note of Lochiel, which Albyn's hills
Have heard, and heard, too, have her Saxon
    foes—
How in the noon of night that pibroch thrills,
Savage and shrill! But with the breath which
    fills   230
Their mountain-pipe, so fill the mountaineers
With the fierce native daring which instills
The stirring memory of a thousand years,
And Evan's, Donald's fame rings in each
    clansman's ears!

And Ardennes waves above them her green
    leaves,   235

---

180. **Harmodius . . . lord.** Harmodius and Aristogeiton were Athenian heroes who hid their swords under myrtle branches to aid in their attack upon Hipparchus, the tyrant of Athens, in 514 B.C. 181. **There . . . night.** A ball was given at Brussels on the evening before the Battle of Quatre-Bras, which occurred two days before the Battle of Waterloo. 200. **Brunswick's . . . chieftain,** Frederick William, Duke of Brunswick. His father was killed in the Battle of Auerstadt in 1806.

226. **"Cameron's gathering,"** the war song that summoned the Cameron clan. 227. **Lochiel,** the Cameron clan, from Lochiel, a district in the counties of Argyll and Inverness, Scotland. **Albyn,** a poetic name for Scotland. 228. **Saxon foes,** the English. 229. **pibroch,** a kind of Highland bagpipe music. 234. **Evan, Donald,** Sir Evan Cameron (1629-1719) and Donald Cameron (1695?-1748), Scottish Highland chieftains; Donald Cameron was known as "Gentle Lochiel." They were supporters of the Stuarts. 235. **Ardennes,** in ancient times a large forest in Gaul, modern France.

Dewy with nature's teardrops as they pass,
Grieving, if aught inanimate e'er grieves,
Over the unreturning brave—alas!
Ere evening to be trodden like the grass
Which now beneath them, but above shall
    grow   240
In its next verdure, when this fiery mass
Of living valor, rolling on the foe
And burning with high hope, shall molder
    cold and low.

Last noon beheld them full of lusty life,
Last eve in Beauty's circle proudly gay;   245
The midnight brought the signal-sound of
    strife,
The morn the marshaling in arms—the day
Battle's magnificently stern array!
The thunder-clouds close o'er it, which when
    rent
The earth is covered thick with other clay, 250
Which her own clay shall cover, heaped and
    pent,
Rider and horse—friend, foe—in one red
    burial blent!

          *   *   *   *   *

Lake Leman woos me with its crystal face,
The mirror where the stars and mountains
    view   605
The stillness of their aspect in each trace
Its clear depth yields of their far height and
    hue:
There is too much of man here, to look
    through
With a fit mind the might which I behold;
But soon in me shall Loneliness renew   610
Thoughts hid, but not less cherished than of
    old,
Ere mingling with the herd had penned me in
    their fold.

To fly from, need not be to hate, mankind:
All are not fit with them to stir and toil,
Nor is it discontent to keep the mind   615
Deep in its fountain, lest it overboil
In the hot throng, where we become the spoil
Of our infection, till too late and long
We may deplore and struggle with the coil,
In wretched interchange of wrong for wrong
Midst a contentious world, striving where
    none are strong.   621

There, in a moment we may plunge our years
In fatal penitence, and in the blight
Of our own soul turn all our blood to tears,
And color things to come with hues of Night;
The race of life becomes a hopeless flight 626
To those that walk in darkness: on the sea
The boldest steer but where their ports invite;
But there are wanderers o'er Eternity
Whose bark drives on and on, and anchored
    ne'er shall be.   630

Is it not better, then, to be alone,
And love Earth only for its earthly sake?
By the blue rushing of the arrowy Rhone,
Or the pure bosom of its nursing lake,
Which feeds it as a mother who doth make   635
A fair but froward infant her own care,
Kissing its cries away as these awake;—
Is it not better thus our lives to wear,
Than join the crushing crowd, doomed to in-
    flict or bear?

I live not in myself, but I become   640
Portion of that around me; and to me
High mountains are a feeling, but the hum
Of human cities torture: I can see
Nothing to loathe in nature, save to be
A link reluctant in a fleshly chain,   645
Classed among creatures, when the soul can
    flee,
And with the sky, the peak, the heaving plain
Of ocean, or the stars, mingle, and not in vain.

And thus I am absorbed, and this is life:
I look upon the peopled desert past,   650
As on a place of agony and strife,
Where, for some sin, to sorrow I was cast,
To act and suffer, but remount at last
With a fresh pinion; which I feel to spring,
Though young, yet waxing vigorous as the
    blast   655
Which it would cope with, on delighted wing,
Spurning the clay-cold bonds which round our
    being cling.

251. **pent,** closely confined. 604. **Lake Leman,** Lake Geneva, Switzerland.

629 **wanderers o'er Eternity.** See Shelley's *Adonais*, l. 264 (p. 267). 631 ff. See Shelley's *Stanzas*, l. 22, and note, p. 253. 642. **High . . . feeling.** Cf. Wordsworth's *Lines Composed above Tintern Abbey*, ll. 76 ff., p. 122. 643. **cities torture.** Cf. Keats's *To One Who Has Been Long in City Pent*, p. 275.

And when, at length, the mind shall be all free
From what it hates in this degraded form,
Reft of its carnal life, save what shall be 660
Existent happier in the fly and worm—
When elements to elements conform,
And dust is as it should be, shall I not
Feel all I see, less dazzling, but more warm?
The bodiless thought? the Spirit of each spot?
Of which, even now, I share at times the immortal lot? 666

Are not the mountains, waves, and skies a part
Of me and of my soul, as I of them?
Is not the love of these deep in my heart
With a pure passion? should I not contemn 670
All objects, if compared with these? and stem
A tide of suffering, rather than forgo
Such feelings for the hard and worldly phlegm
Of those whose eyes are only turned below,
Gazing upon the ground, with thoughts which dare not glow? 675

* * * * *

Clear, placid Leman! thy contrasted lake,
With the wild world I dwelt in, is a thing
Which warns me, with its stillness, to forsake
Earth's troubled waters for a purer spring. 760
This quiet sail is as a noiseless wing
To waft me from distraction; once I loved
Torn ocean's roar, but thy soft murmuring
Sounds sweet as if a Sister's voice reproved,
That I with stern delights should e'er have been so moved. 765

It is the hush of night, and all between
Thy margin and the mountains, dusk, yet clear,
Mellowed and mingling, yet distinctly seen,
Save darkened Jura, whose capped heights appear
Precipitously steep; and drawing near, 770
There breathes a living fragrance from the shore,
Of flowers yet fresh with childhood; on the ear
Drops the light drip of the suspended oar,
Or chirps the grasshopper one good-night carol more.

He is an evening reveler, who makes 775
His life an infancy, and sings his fill;
At intervals, some bird from out the brakes
Starts into voice a moment, then is still.
There seems a floating whisper on the hill,
But that is fancy, for the starlight dews 780
All silently their tears of love instill,
Weeping themselves away, till they infuse
Deep into Nature's breast the spirit of her hues.

Ye stars! which are the poetry of heaven!
If in your bright leaves we would read the fate
Of men and empires—'tis to be forgiven, 786
That in our aspirations to be great,
Our destinies o'erleap their mortal state,
And claim a kindred with you; for ye are
A beauty and a mystery, and create 790
In us such love and reverence from afar,
That fortune, fame, power, life have named themselves a star.

All heaven and earth are still—though not in sleep,
But breathless, as we grow when feeling most;
And silent, as we stand in thoughts too deep—
All heaven and earth are still; from the high host 796
Of stars, to the lulled lake and mountain-coast,
All is concentered in a life intense,
Where not a beam, nor air, nor leaf is lost,
But hath a part of being, and a sense 800
Of that which is of all Creator and defense.

Then stirs the feeling infinite, so felt
In solitude, where we are *least* alone;
A truth, which through our being then doth melt,
And purifies from self: it is a tone, 805
The soul and source of music, which makes known
Eternal harmony, and sheds a charm
Like to the fabled Cytherea's zone,
Binding all things with beauty;—'twould disarm

---

769. **Jura**, a chain of mountains in Switzerland and eastern France.

777. **brakes**, thickets. 793. **All . . . still.** Cf. Wordsworth's *It Is a Beauteous Evening*, p. 151. 808. **Cytherea's zone**, the girdle of Venus, goddess of love; it inspired love.

The specter Death, had he substantial power
    to harm.   810

Not vainly did the early Persian make
His altar the high places, and the peak
Of earth-o'ergazing mountains, and thus take
A fit and unwalled temple, there to seek
The Spirit, in whose honor shrines are weak,
Upreared of human hands. Come, and com-
    pare   816
Columns and idol-dwellings, Goth or Greek,
With Nature's realms of worship, earth and
    air,
Nor fix on fond abodes to circumscribe thy
    prayer!

The sky is changed!—and such a change! Oh
    night,   820
And storm, and darkness, ye are wondrous
    strong,
Yet lovely in your strength, as is the light
Of a dark eye in woman! Far along,
From peak to peak, the rattling crags among
Leaps the live thunder! Not from one lone
    cloud,   825
But every mountain now hath found a tongue
And Jura answers, through her misty shroud,
Back to the joyous Alps, who call to her aloud!

And this is in the night—most glorious night!
Thou wert not sent for slumber! let me be   830
A sharer in thy fierce and far delight—
A portion of the tempest and of thee!
How the lit lake shines, a phosphoric sea,
And the big rain comes dancing to the earth!
And now again 'tis black—and now, the glee
Of the loud hills shakes with its mountain-
    mirth,   836
As if they did rejoice o'er a young earth-
    quake's birth.

    *   *   *   *   *

Thus far have I proceeded in a theme
Renewed with no kind auspices—to feel
We are not what we have been, and to deem
We are not what we should be, and to steel
The heart against itself; and to conceal,   995
With a proud caution, love, or hate, or
    aught—
Passion or feeling, purpose, grief or zeal—
Which is the tyrant spirit of our thought,
Is a stern task of soul—no matter—it is taught.

And for these words, thus woven into song,
It may be that they are a harmless wile—   1001
The coloring of the scenes which fleet along,
Which I would seize, in passing, to beguile
My breast, or that of others, for awhile.
Fame is the thirst of youth, but I am not   1005
So young as to regard men's frown or smile,
As loss or guerdon of a glorious lot;
I stood and stand alone—remembered or for-
    got.

I have not loved the world, nor the world me;
I have not flattered its rank breath, nor bowed
To its idolatries a patient knee,   1011
Nor coined my cheek to smiles, nor cried aloud
In worship of an echo; in the crowd
They could not deem me one of such; I stood
Amongst them, but not of them; in a shroud
Of thoughts which were not their thoughts,
    and still could,   1016
Had I not filed my mind, which thus itself
    subdued.

I have not loved the world, nor the world
    me—
But let us part fair foes; I do believe,
Though I have found them not, that there
    may be   1020
Words which are things, hopes which will not
    deceive,
And virtues which are merciful, nor weave
Snares for the failing; I would also deem
O'er others' griefs that some sincerely grieve;
That two, or one, are almost what they seem,
That goodness is no name, and happiness no
    dream.   1026

My daughter! with thy name this song begun;
My daughter! with thy name thus much shall
    end;
I see thee not, I hear thee not, but none
Can be so wrapt in thee; thou art the friend
To whom the shadows of far years extend: 1031
Albeit my brow thou never shouldst behold,
My voice shall with thy future visions blend,

1017. **filed**, defiled. The phrase is from *Macbeth*, III, i, 64.

And reach into thy heart, when mine is cold,
A token and a tone, even from thy father's
    mold.   1035

To aid thy mind's development, to watch
Thy dawn of little joys, to sit and see
Almost thy very growth, to view thee catch
Knowledge of objects—wonders yet to thee!
To hold thee lightly on a gentle knee,   1040
And print on thy soft cheek a parent's kiss—
This, it should seem, was not reserved for me;
Yet this was in my nature: as it is,
I know not what is there, yet something like
    to this.

Yet, though dull hate as duty should be
    taught,   1045
I know that thou wilt love me, though my
    name
Should be shut from thee, as a spell still
    fraught
With desolation, and a broken claim:
Though the grave closed between us—'twere
    the same,
I know that thou wilt love me; though to
    drain   1050
My blood from out thy being were an aim,
And an attainment—all would be in vain—
Still thou wouldst love me, still that more than
    life retain.

The child of love, though born in bitterness,
And nurtured in convulsion—of thy sire 1055
These were the elements, and thine no less.
As yet such are around thee, but thy fire
Shall be more tempered, and thy hope far
    higher.
Sweet be thy cradled slumbers! O'er the sea
And from the mountains where I now respire,
Fain would I waft such blessing upon thee,
As, with a sigh, I deem thou might'st have
    been to me.   1062

from CANTO IV

O Rome! my country! city of the soul!
The orphans of the heart must turn to thee, 695
Lone mother of dead empires! and control
In their shut breasts their petty misery.
What are our woes and sufferance? Come
    and see
The cypress, hear the owl, and plod your way
O'er steps of broken thrones and temples, Ye!
Whose agonies are evils of a day—   701
A world is at our feet as fragile as our clay.

The Niobe of nations! there she stands,
Childless and crownless, in her voiceless woe;
An empty urn within her withered hands, 705
Whose holy dust was scattered long ago;
The Scipios' tomb contains no ashes now,
The very sepulchers lie tenantless
Of their heroic dwellers: dost thou flow,
Old Tiber! through a marble wilderness? 710
Rise, with thy yellow waves, and mantle her
    distress.

The Goth, the Christian, Time, War, Flood,
    and Fire,
Have dealt upon the seven-hilled city's pride;
She saw her glories star by star expire,
And up the steep barbarian monarchs ride 715
Where the car climbed the Capitol; far and
    wide
Temple and tower went down, nor left a site:
Chaos of ruins! who shall trace the void,
O'er the dim fragments cast a lunar light,
And say, "here was, or is," where all is doubly
    night?   720

* * * * *

Arches on arches! as it were that Rome,
Collecting the chief trophies of her line, 1145
Would build up all her triumphs in one dome,
Her Coliseum stands; the moonbeams shine
As 'twere its natural torches, for divine
Should be the light which streams here to
    illume
This long-explored but still exhaustless mine
Of contemplation; and the azure gloom 1151
Of an Italian night, where the deep skies as-
    sume

---

699. **cypress**, an emblem of mourning; it is a common tree in graveyards. 703. **Niobe**, a mythological character, who in the form of a rock wept continually over the loss of her twelve children. 707. **Scipios' tomb**, a group of ancient Roman tombs situated on the Appian Way, near Rome. The Scipios were famous Roman generals, second century B.C. 710. **Tiber**, a river of central Italy; it flows through Rome. 716. **Capitol**, part of the Capitoline Hill in Rome. 1147. **Coliseum**, the celebrated amphitheater in Rome.

Hues which have words, and speak to ye of
    heaven,
Floats o'er this vast and wondrous monument,
And shadows forth its glory. There is given
Unto the things of earth, which Time hath
    bent,   1156
A spirit's feeling, and where he hath leant
His hand, but broke his scythe, there is a
    power
And magic in the ruined battlement,
For which the palace of the present hour 1160
Must yield its pomp, and wait till ages are its
    dower.

O Time! the beautifier of the dead,
Adorner of the ruin, comforter
And only healer when the heart hath bled;
Time! the corrector where our judgments err,
The test of truth, love—sole philosopher, 1166
For all beside are sophists—from thy thrift,
Which never loses though it doth defer—
Time, the avenger! unto thee I lift
My hands, and eyes, and heart, and crave of
    thee a gift: 1170

Amidst this wreck, where thou hast made a
    shrine
And temple more divinely desolate,
Among thy mightier offerings here are mine,
Ruins of years, though few, yet full of fate:
If thou hast ever seen me too elate,   1175
Hear me not; but if calmly I have borne
Good, and reserved my pride against the hate
Which shall not whelm me, let me not have
    worn
This iron in my soul in vain—shall *they* not
    mourn?

And thou, who never yet of human wrong 1180
Left the unbalanced scale, great Nemesis!
Here, where the ancient paid thee homage
    long—
Thou who didst call the Furies from the abyss,
And round Orestes bade them howl and hiss
For that unnatural retribution—just,   1185

<small>1181. **Nemesis,** the classical goddess of retributive justice.
1184. **Orestes,** son of the Greek king Agamemnon and Clytemnestra; he slew his mother and her lover Aegisthus in revenge for their murder of Agamemnon.</small>

Had it but been from hands less near—in this
Thy former realm, I call thee from the dust!
Dost thou not hear my heart?—Awake! thou
    shalt, and must.

It is not that I may not have incurred
For my ancestral faults or mine the wound
I bleed withal, and, had it been conferred 1191
With a just weapon, it had flowed unbound;
But now my blood shall not sink in the
    ground;
To thee I do devote it—*thou* shalt take
The vengeance, which shall yet be sought and
    found,   1195
Which if *I* have not taken for the sake——
But let that pass—I sleep, but thou shalt yet
    awake.

And if my voice break forth, 'tis not that now
I shrink from what is suffered: let him speak
Who hath beheld decline upon my brow, 1200
Or seen my mind's convulsion leave it weak;
But in this page a record will I seek.
Not in the air shall these my words disperse,
Though I be ashes; a far hour shall wreak
The deep prophetic fullness of this verse, 1205
And pile on human heads the mountain of my
    curse!

That curse shall be Forgiveness.—Have I
    not—
Hear me, my mother Earth! behold it,
    Heaven!
Have I not had to wrestle with my lot?
Have I not suffered things to be forgiven? 1210
Have I not had my brain seared, my heart
    riven,
Hopes sapped, name blighted, Life's life lied
    away?
And only not to desperation driven,
Because not altogether of such clay
As rots into the souls of those whom I sur-
    vey.   1215

From mighty wrongs to petty perfidy
Have I not seen what human things could do?
From the loud roar of foaming calumny
To the small whisper of the as paltry few,
And subtler venom of the reptile crew,   1220

The Janus glance of whose significant eye,
Learning to lie with silence, would *seem* true,
And without utterance, save the shrug or sigh,
Deal round to happy fools its speechless
   obloquy.   1224

But I have lived, and have not lived in vain:
My mind may lose its force, my blood its fire,
And my frame perish even in conquering
   pain;
But there is that within me which shall tire
Torture and Time, and breathe when I expire;
Something unearthly, which they deem not of,
Like the remembered tone of a mute lyre, 1231
Shall on their softened spirits sink, and move
In hearts all rocky now the late remorse of
   love.

The seal is set.—Now welcome, thou dread
   power!   1234
Nameless, yet thus omnipotent, which here
Walk'st in the shadow of the midnight hour
With a deep awe, yet all distinct from fear;
Thy haunts are ever where the dead walls rear
Their ivy mantles, and the solemn scene
Derives from thee a sense so deep and clear
That we become a part of what has been, 1241
And grow unto the spot, all-seeing but unseen.

And here the buzz of eager nations ran,
In murmured pity, or loud-roared applause
As man was slaughtered by his fellow man.
And wherefore slaughtered? wherefore, but
   because   1246
Such were the bloody Circus' genial laws,
And the imperial pleasure.—Wherefore not?
What matters where we fall to fill the maws
Of worms—on battle-plains or listed spot? 1250
Both are but theaters where the chief actors
   rot.

I see before me the Gladiator lie:
He leans upon his hand—his manly brow
Consents to death, but conquers agony,
And his drooped head sinks gradually low—
And through his side the last drops, ebbing
   slow   1256
From the red gash, fall heavy, one by one,
Like the first of a thunder-shower; and now
The arena swims around him—he is gone,
Ere ceased the inhuman shout which hailed
   the wretch who won.   1260

He heard it, but he heeded not—his eyes
Were with his heart, and that was far away;
He recked not of the life he lost nor prize,
But where his rude hut by the Danube lay,
There were his young barbarians all at play,
There was their Dacian mother—he, their
   sire,   1266
Butchered to make a Roman holiday—
All this rushed with his blood—Shall he expire
And unavenged? Arise! ye Goths, and glut
   your ire!

But here, where Murder breathed her bloody
   steam;   1270
And here, where buzzing nations choked the
   ways,
And roared or murmured like a mountain
   stream
Dashing or winding as its torrent strays;
Here, where the Roman million's blame or
   praise
Was death or life, the playthings of a crowd,
My voice sounds much—and fall the stars'
   faint rays   1276
On the arena void—seats crushed—walls
   bowed—
And galleries, where my steps seem echoes
   strangely loud.

A ruin—yet what ruin! from its mass
Walls, palaces, half-cities have been reared;
Yet oft the enormous skeleton ye pass,   1281
And marvel where the spoil could have appeared.
Hath it indeed been plundered, or but cleared?

1221. **Janus**, an ancient Roman deity represented with two faces looking in opposite directions. 1247. **Circus**, a large enclosure used frequently for gladiatorial combats in Roman times. 1250. **listed spot**, field of the list or tournament. 1252. **Gladiator**, a statue formerly called *The Dying Gladiator*, but now thought to represent a wounded warrior, and hence called *The Dying Gaul*. It is in the Museum of the Capitol.

1266. **There . . . holiday.** After Trajan had conquered the region north of the Lower Danube and had made it into the Roman province of Dacia (101 B.C.), he carried 10,000 captives to Rome and exhibited them in combats for the amusement of the people.

Alas! developed, opens the decay,
When the colossal fabric's form is neared: 1285
It will not bear the brightness of the day,
Which streams too much on all years, man,
    have reft away.

But when the rising moon begins to climb
Its topmost arch, and gently pauses there;
When the stars twinkle through the loops of
    time, 1290
And the low night-breeze waves along the air
The garland-forest, which the gray walls wear,
Like laurels on the bald first Caesar's head;
When the light shines serene but doth not
    glare,
Then in this magic circle raise the dead: 1295
Heroes have trod this spot—'tis on their dust
    ye tread.

"While stands the Coliseum, Rome shall
    stand;
When falls the Coliseum, Rome shall fall;
And when Rome falls—the World." From
    our own land
Thus spake the pilgrims o'er this mighty wall
In Saxon times, which we are wont to call 1301
Ancient; and these three mortal things are still
On their foundations, and unaltered all;
Rome and her Ruin past Redemption's skill,
The World, the same wide den—of thieves, or
    what ye will. 1305

    *   *   *   *   *

But I forget.—My Pilgrim's shrine is won,
And he and I must part—so let it be—
His task and mine alike are nearly done;
Yet once more let us look upon the sea; 1570
The midland ocean breaks on him and me,
And from the Alban Mount we now behold
Our friend of youth, that Ocean, which when
    we

Beheld it last by Calpe's rock unfold
Those waves, we followed on till the dark
    Euxine rolled 1575

Upon the blue Symplegades: long years—
Long, though not very many—since have done
Their work on both; some suffering and some
    tears
Have left us nearly where we had begun:
Yet not in vain our mortal race hath run; 1580
We have had our reward, and it is here—
That we can yet feel gladdened by the sun,
And reap from earth, sea, joy almost as dear
As if there were no man to trouble what is
    clear.

Oh! that the Desert were my dwelling-place,
With one fair Spirit for my minister, 1586
That I might all forget the human race,
And, hating no one, love but only her!
Ye elements!—in whose ennobling stir
I feel myself exalted—Can ye not 1590
Accord me such a being? Do I err
In deeming such inhabit many a spot?
Though with them to converse can rarely be
    our lot.

There is a pleasure in the pathless woods,
There is a rapture on the lonely shore, 1595
There is society, where none intrudes,
By the deep Sea, and music in its roar:
I love not Man the less, but Nature more,
From these our interviews, in which I steal
From all I may be, or have been before, 1600
To mingle with the Universe, and feel
What I can ne'er express, yet cannot all con-
    ceal.

Roll on, thou deep and dark blue Ocean—roll!
Ten thousand fleets sweep over thee in vain;
Man marks the earth with ruin—his control
Stops with the shore; upon the watery plain
The wrecks are all thy deed, nor doth re-
    main 1607

1293. **laurels . . . head.** In a note Byron quotes Suetonius, the Roman historian, as saying that "Julius Caesar was particularly gratified by that decree of the senate which enabled him to wear a wreath of laurel on all occasions. He was anxious, not to show that he was the conqueror of the world, but to hide that he was bald." 1297. **"While . . . World."** Byron cites Gibbon (*Decline and Fall of the Roman Empire*) as quoting this passage from Bede's *Glossarium* (see Vol. I, p. 62) to prove that the Coliseum was entire when seen by the Anglo-Saxon pilgrims in the seventh and eighth centuries. 1571. **midland ocean,** the Mediterranean. 1572. **Alban Mount,** a mountain near Rome.

1574. **Calpe's rock,** Gibraltar. Byron had last seen the Mediterranean on his return journey to England in 1811. 1575. **Euxine,** the Black Sea. 1576. **Symplegades,** two island rocks at the entrance of the Bosphorus into the Black Sea. 1585 ff. See Shelley's *Stanzas*, l. 22, and note, p. 253. 1586. **one fair Spirit,** Byron's half-sister Augusta. 1601. **mingle . . . Universe.** Cf. Canto III, 640-648, p. 216.

A shadow of man's ravage, save his own,
When for a moment, like a drop of rain,
He sinks into thy depths with bubbling groan,
Without a grave, unknelled, uncoffined, and
    unknown.   1611

His steps are not upon thy paths—thy fields
Are not a spoil for him—thou dost arise
And shake him from thee; the vile strength he
    wields   1614
For earth's destruction thou dost all despise,
Spurning him from thy bosom to the skies,
And send'st him, shivering in thy playful
    spray
And howling, to his gods, where haply lies
His petty hope in some near port or bay,
And dashest him again to earth—there let
    him lay.   1620

The armaments which thunderstrike the walls
Of rock-built cities, bidding nations quake,
And monarchs tremble in their capitals,
The oak leviathans, whose huge ribs make
Their clay creator the vain title take   1625
Of lord of thee, and arbiter of war—
These are thy toys, and, as the snowy flake,
They melt into thy yeast of waves, which mar
Alike the Armada's pride or spoils of Trafal-
    gar.

Thy shores are empires, changed in all save
    thee—   1630
Assyria, Greece, Rome, Carthage, what are
    they?
Thy waters washed them power while they
    were free,
And many a tyrant since; their shores obey
The stranger, slave, or savage; their decay
Has dried up realms to deserts—not so
    thou;—   1635
Unchangeable, save to thy wild waves' play,
Time writes no wrinkle on thine azure brow:
Such as creation's dawn beheld, thou rollest
    now.

Thou glorious mirror, where the Almighty's
    form
Glasses itself in tempests; in all time—   1640
Calm or convulsed, in breeze, or gale, or storm,
Icing the pole, or in the torrid clime
Dark-heaving—boundless, endless, and sub-
    lime,
The image of eternity, the throne
Of the Invisible; even from out thy slime   1645
The monsters of the deep are made; each zone
Obeys thee; thou goest forth, dread, fathom-
    less, alone.

And I have loved thee, Ocean! and my joy
Of youthful sports was on thy breast to be
Borne, like thy bubbles, onward: from a boy
I wantoned with thy breakers—they to me   1651
Were a delight; and if the freshening sea
Made them a terror—'twas a pleasing fear,
For I was as it were a child of thee,
And trusted to thy billows far and near,   1655
And laid my hand upon thy mane—as I do
    here.

My task is done, my song hath ceased, my
    theme
Has died into an echo; it is fit
The spell should break of this protracted
    dream,   1659
The torch shall be extinguished which hath lit
My midnight lamp—and what is writ, is writ;
Would it were worthier! but I am not now
That which I have been—and my visions flit
Less palpably before me—and the glow
Which in my spirit dwelt is fluttering, faint,
    and low.   1665

Farewell! a word that must be, and hath
    been—
A sound which makes us linger;—yet—fare-
    well!
Ye! who have traced the Pilgrim to the scene
Which is his last, if in your memories dwell
A thought which once was his, if on ye swell
A single recollection, not in vain   1671
He wore his sandal-shoon and scallop-shell;
Farewell! with *him* alone may rest the pain,
If such there were—with *you,* the moral of his
    strain.   (*1817;* 1818)

1611. **unknelled,** etc. Cf. Scott's *The Lay of the Last Min-*
strel, VI, 14-16,
    . . . shall go down
    To the vile dust, from which he sprung,
    Unwept, unhonored, and unsung.
1629. **Alike . . . Trafalgar.** One-half of the Spanish Armada that sailed against England in 1588 were destroyed in a storm, as were also most of the French ships captured by Nelson at Trafalgar, in 1805.

1672. **sandal . . . shell.** The sandals indicated travel by land; the scallop-shell, which was worn in the hat, travel by sea.

To Thomas Moore

The first stanza of this poem was written in 1816 as Byron was leaving England. He and Moore, to whom the next poem was written from Venice, were boon companions.

My boat is on the shore,
   And my bark is on the sea;
But, before I go, Tom Moore,
   Here's a double health to thee!

Here's a sigh to those who love me,   5
   And a smile to those who hate;
And, whatever sky's above me,
   Here's heart for every fate.

Though the Ocean roar around me,
   Yet it still shall bear me on;   10
Though a desert should surround me,
   It hath springs that may be won.

Were't the last drop in the well,
   As I gasped upon the brink,
Ere my fainting spirit fell,   15
   'Tis to thee that I would drink.

With that water, as this wine,
   That libation I would pour
Should be—peace with thine and mine,
   And a health to thee, Tom Moore.

(1817; 1821)

So We'll Go No More A-Roving

So we'll go no more a-roving
   So late into the night,
Though the heart be still as loving,
   And the moon be still as bright.

For the sword outwears its sheath,   5
   And the soul wears out the breast,
And the heart must pause to breathe,
   And love itself have rest.

Though the night was made for loving,
   And the day returns too soon,   10
Yet we'll go no more a-roving
   By the light of the moon.

(1817; 1830)

from Don Juan

The poem *Don Juan* owes its title and certain features of the story to an old Spanish legend, really the folklore theme of the Universal Lover. The legend had been popular in Europe for centuries and had undergone a revival during the neo-classical age; there had been a play by Molière (1622-1673) and an opera, *Don Giovanni*, by Mozart (1756-1791). Byron's version, however, is highly original; it is decidedly autobiographical in spirit; and although fragmentary, it is so wide in its range of subject-matter, incident, and character that its incomplete design is immaterial. Byron said in a letter to his friend Thomas Moore (p. 297), dated September 19, 1818: "I have finished the first Canto (a long one, of about 180 octaves) of a poem in the style and manner of *Beppo*, encouraged by the good success of the same. It is called *Don Juan*, and is meant to be a little quietly facetious about everything. But I doubt whether it is not—at least, as far as it has yet gone—too free for these very modest days. However, I shall try the experiment, anonymously; if it don't take, it will be discontinued. It is dedicated to Southey in good, simple, savage verse, upon the Laureate's politics, and the way he got them." The experiment was successful, and the sixteen cantos appeared in steady succession between 1818 and March, 1824, less than a month before Byron's death. Byron's deliberate facetiousness of attitude and his lack of plan make the whole work most informal in tone; but common consent makes it one of the greatest of English satires. The narrative, which is episodic, is less important than the digressions and the occasionally idyllic scenes, such as the love-passages of Juan and Haidée. The hero wanders over Europe much in the manner of another Childe Harold searching for, and experiencing, exciting adventures; the final canto, leaving him far from his native Spain, concludes with Juan upon the threshold of a new adventure, still unsatisfied.

DEDICATION

Bob Southey! You're a poet—Poet laureate,
   And representative of all the race;
Although 'tis true that you turned out a
    Tory at
Last—yours has lately been a common case;
And now, my Epic Renegade! what are ye
    at?   5
With all the Lakers, in and out of place?
A nest of tuneful persons, to my eye
Like "four and twenty Blackbirds in a pye;

"Which pye being opened they began to sing"
   (This old song and new simile holds good),
"A dainty dish to set before the King,"   11
   Or Regent, who admires such kind of
    food;—
And Coleridge, too, has lately taken wing,
   But like a hawk encumbered with his
    hood—
Explaining metaphysics to the nation—   15
I wish he would explain his Explanation.

You, Bob! are rather insolent, you know,
   At being disappointed in your wish
To supersede all warblers here below,
   And be the only Blackbird in the dish;   20
And then you overstrain yourself, or so,
   And tumble downward like the flying fish
Gasping on deck, because you soar too high,
    Bob,
And fall for lack of moisture quite a-dry,
    Bob!

And Wordsworth, in a rather long "Excur-
    sion"   25
   (I think the quarto holds five hundred
    pages),
Has given a sample from the vasty version
   Of his new system to perplex the sages;
'Tis poetry—at least by his assertion,

And may appear so when the dog-star
    rages—   30
And he who understands it would be able
To add a story to the Tower of Babel.

You—Gentlemen! by dint of long seclusion
   From better company, have kept your own
At Keswick, and through still continued
    fusion   35
   Of one another's minds, at last have grown
To deem as a most logical conclusion,
   That poesy has wreaths for you alone;
There is a narrowness in such a notion,
Which makes me wish you'd change your
    lakes for ocean.   40

I would not imitate the petty thought,
   Nor coin my self-love to so base a vice,
For all the glory your conversion brought,
   Since gold alone should not have been its
    price,
You have your salary; was't for that you
    wrought?   45
   And Wordsworth has his place in the Ex-
    cise.
You're shabby fellows—true—but poets still,
And duly seated on the immortal hill.

Your bays may hide the baldness of your
    brows—
   Perhaps some virtuous blushes;—let them
    go—   50
To you I envy neither fruit nor boughs—
   And for the fame you would engross below,
The field is universal, and allows
   Scope to all such as feel the inherent glow;
Scott, Rogers, Campbell, Moore, and Crabbe
    will try   55
'Gainst you the question with posterity.

For me, who, wandering with pedestrian
    Muses,
Contend not with you on the wingéd steed,

---

1. **Southey.** Southey (p. 296), like Wordsworth and Coleridge, was at one time an ardent Republican, but the excesses and the failures of the French Revolution led him finally to become a Tory. 6. **Lakers,** Wordsworth, Coleridge, and others, so called from their residence in the Lake District. 12. **Regent,** the Prince of Wales, afterwards George IV, who was appointed Regent when his father, George III, became insane in 1811. Southey was made poet laureate in 1813. 13. **Coleridge . . . wing,** a reference to his *Biographia Literaria* (p. 328), which appeared in 1817. 25. "**Excursion,**" the title of a long poem by Wordsworth. 32. **Tower of Babel,** a high tower described in *Genesis*, 11: 1-9. The audacious plan of the builders to make it reach heaven angered the Lord and resulted in the confusion of tongues. 35. **Keswick,** a town in the Lake District, where Southey joined Coleridge in 1803. 46. **the Excise.** Wordsworth was appointed Distributor of Stamps for Westmoreland in 1813, but he never had any connection with the excise. 49. **bays,** wreaths of honor made from leaves of the bay-tree, a kind of laurel. 55. **Scott . . . Crabbe.** See pp. 190, 296, and 297. Samuel Rogers (1763-1855) and George Crabbe (1754-1832) were minor poets of the day. 58. **wingéd steed,** Pegasus, associated with poetic inspiration.

I wish your fate may yield ye, when she
    chooses,
  The fame you envy, and the skill you
    need;   60
And recollect a poet nothing loses
  In giving to his brethren their full meed
Of merit, and complaint of present days
  Is not the certain path to future praise.

He that reserves his laurels for posterity 65
  (Who does not often claim the bright re-
    version)
Has generally no great crop to spare it, he
  Being only injured by his own assertion;
And although here and there some glorious
    rarity   69
  Arise like Titan from the sea's immersion,
The major part of such appellants go
  To—God knows where—for no one else can
    know.

If, fallen in evil days on evil tongues,
  Milton appealed to the Avenger, Time,
If Time, the Avenger, execrates his wrongs, 75
  And makes the word "*Miltonic*" mean
    "*sublime*,"
He deigned not to belie his soul in songs,
  Nor turn his very talent to a crime;
He did not loathe the Sire to laud the Son,
  But closed the tyrant-hater he begun.   80

Think'st thou, could he—the blind Old Man
    —arise,
  Like Samuel from the grave, to freeze once
    more
The blood of monarchs with his prophecies,
  Or be alive again—again all hoar
With time and trials, and those helpless
    eyes,   85
  And heartless daughters—worn—and pale
    —and poor;
Would *he* adore a sultan? *he* obey
  The intellectual eunuch Castlereagh?

Cold-blooded, smooth-faced, placid miscreant!
  Dabbling its sleek young hands in Erin's
    gore   90
And thus for wider carnage taught to pant,
  Transferred to gorge upon a sister shore,
The vulgarest tool that Tyranny could want,
  With just enough of talent, and no more,
To lengthen fetters by another fixed,   95
And offer poison long already mixed.

An orator of such set trash of phrase
  Ineffably—legitimately vile,
That even its grossest flatterers dare not
    praise,
  Nor foes — all nations — condescend to
    smile;   100
Not even a sprightly blunder's spark can
    blaze
  From that Ixion grindstone's ceaseless toil,
That turns and turns to give the world a
    notion
  Of endless torments and perpetual motion.

A bungler even in its disgusting trade, 105
  And botching, patching, leaving still be-
    hind
Something of which its masters are afraid,
  States to be curbed, and thoughts to be con-
    fined,
Conspiracy or Congress to be made—
  Cobbling at manacles for all mankind— 110
A tinkering slave-maker, who mends old
    chains,
  With God and man's abhorrence for its gains.

If we may judge of matter by the mind,
  Emasculated to the marrow, *It*
Hath but two objects, how to serve, and
    bind,   115
  Deeming the chain it wears even men may
    fit,
Eutropius of its many masters—blind
  To worth as freedom, wisdom as to wit.
Fearless—because *no* feeling dwells in ice,
Its very courage stagnates to a vice.   120

---

70. **Titan,** one of a mythological race of giants said to have piled mountain upon mountain to scale heaven. 73. **fallen . . . tongues,** from *Paradise Lost,* 7, 26. 79. **loathe . . . Son,** as Southey did with reference to George III and his son. 82. **Samuel.** See *1 Samuel,* 28. 86. **heartless daughters.** Milton is said to have received shameful treatment from his daughters. 88. **Castlereagh,** Robert Stewart (1769-1822), Viscount Castlereagh, whose administration as Foreign Secretary was noted for his cruelty and his contempt for all persons not of the aristocracy. At the time of the Irish rebellion in 1798, he was charged with encouraging inhuman punishments of the rebels.

102. **Ixion,** a legendary king in Greece who for boasting of the favors of Hera, wife of Zeus, was bound to an endlessly revolving wheel in Hades. 117. **Eutropius,** a Byzantine statesman surnamed "The Eunuch," who served as a chamberlain in the household of Arcadius on his succession to the throne as Emperor of the East in 395 A.D.

Where shall I turn me not to *view* its bonds,
  For I will never *feel* them?—Italy!
Thy late reviving Roman soul desponds
  Beneath the lie this State-thing breathed
      o'er thee—
Thy clanking chain, and Erin's yet green
      wounds,   125
Have voices—tongues to cry aloud for me.
Europe has slaves, allies, kings, armies still,
And Southey lives to sing them very ill.

Meantime, Sir Laureate, I proceed to dedicate,
  In honest simple verse, this song to you. 130
And, if in flattering strains I do not predi-
      cate,
'Tis that I still retain my "buff and blue";
My politics as yet are all to educate:
Apostasy's so fashionable, too,
To keep *one* creed's a task grown quite
      Herculean: 135
Is it not so, my Tory, Ultra-Julian?

       from CANTO I
      *   *   *   *   *

My poem's epic and is meant to be
  Divided in twelve books; each book con-
      taining,
With love, and war, a heavy gale at sea, 1595
  A list of ships, and captains, and kings
      reigning,
New characters; the episodes are three:
  A panoramic view of Hell's in training,
After the style of Virgil and of Homer,
So that my name of Epic's no misnomer. 1600

All these things will be specified in time,
  With strict regard to Aristotle's rules,
The *Vade Mecum* of the true sublime,
  Which makes so many poets, and some
      fools:
Prose poets like blank-verse, I'm fond of
      rime,   1605
Good workmen never quarrel with their
      tools;
I've got new mythological machinery,
And very handsome supernatural scenery.

There's only one slight difference between
  Me and my epic brethren gone before, 1610
And here the advantage is my own, I ween
  (Not that I have not several merits more,
But this will more peculiarly be seen);
  They so embellish, that 'tis quite a bore
Their labyrinth of fables to thread
      through,   1615
Whereas this story's actually true.

If any person doubt it, I appeal
  To history, tradition, and to facts,
To newspapers, whose truth all know and
      feel,
  To plays in five, and operas in three
      acts;   1620
All these confirm my statement a good
      deal,
  But that which more completely faith ex-
      acts
Is, that myself, and several now in Seville,
Saw Juan's last elopement with the devil.

If ever I should condescend to prose,   1625
  I'll write poetical commandments, which
Shall supersede beyond all doubt all those
  That went before; in these I shall enrich
My text with many things that no one knows,
  And carry precept to the highest pitch: 1630
I'll call the work "Longinus o'er a Bottle,
Or, Every Poet his *own* Aristotle."

Thou shalt believe in Milton, Dryden, Pope;
  Thou shalt not set up Wordsworth, Cole-
      ridge, Southey;
Because the first is crazed beyond all hope, 1635
  The second drunk, the third so quaint and
      mouthy:
With Crabbe it may be difficult to cope,
  And Campbell's Hippocrene is somewhat
      drouthy:

---

132. **"buff and blue,"** the colors of the uniform adopted by members of the Whig Club; hence the binding of the *Edinburgh Review*, the Whig Organ. 136. **Ultra-Julian.** "I allude not to our friend Landor's hero, the traitor Count Julian [in Landor's *Count Julian*, p. 299], but to Gibbon's hero vulgarly yclept 'The Apostate.'"—Byron. Julian the Apostate was Roman emperor between 361 and 363.
Canto I. In the stanzas omitted Byron gives an account of the parents of Don Juan and their incompatibilities, of his early training, and of his escapades, one of which results in his being sent abroad to "mend his morals." 1602. **Aristotle's rules,** rules regarding epic and narrative poetry. 1603. **Vade Mecum,** handbook; literally, go with me.

1611. **ween,** think. 1623. **Seville,** a city in southwestern Spain. 1631. **Longinus,** a Greek Platonic philosopher and critic (third century). 1637. **Crabbe.** See p. 7. 1638. **Campbell.** See p. 296. **Hippocrene,** a fountain in Greece sacred to the Muses.

Thou shalt not steal from Samuel Rogers,
    nor
Commit — flirtation with the muse of
    Moore.   1640

Thou shalt not covet Mr. Sotheby's Muse,
    His Pegasus, nor anything that's his;
Thou shalt not bear false witness like "the
    Blues"—
    (There's one, at least, is very fond of this);
Thou shalt not write, in short, but what I
    choose;   1645
    This is true criticism, and you may kiss—
Exactly as you please, or not—the rod;
But if you don't, I'll lay it on, by G—d!

If any person should presume to assert
    This story is not moral, first I pray,   1650
That they will not cry out before they're hurt,
    Then that they'll read it o'er again, and say
(But doubtless, nobody will be so pert),
    That this is not a moral tale, though gay;
Besides, in Canto Twelfth, I mean to show
The very place where wicked people go.   1655

If, after all, there should be some so blind
    To their own good this warning to despise,
Led by some tortuosity of mind,
    Not to believe my verse and their own
        eyes,   1660
And cry that they "the moral cannot find,"
    I tell him, if a clergyman, he lies;
Should captains the remark, or critics, make,
    They also lie too—under a mistake.

The public approbation I expect,   1665
    And beg they'll take my word about the
        moral,
Which I with their amusement will connect
    (So children cutting teeth receive a coral);
Meantime they'll doubtless please to recollect
    My epical pretensions to the laurel: 1670
For fear some prudish readers should grow
    skittish,
I've bribed my grandmother's review—the
    British.

I sent it in a letter to the Editor,
    Who thanked me duly by return of post—
I'm for a handsome article his creditor;   1675
    Yet, if my gentle Muse he please to roast,
And break a promise after having made it
    her,
    Denying the receipt of what it cost,
And smear his page with gall instead of
    honey,
All I can say is—that he had the money.   1680

I think that with this holy new alliance
    I may ensure the public, and defy
All other magazines of art or science,
    Daily, or monthly, or three-monthly; I
Have not essayed to multiply their clients,   1685
    Because they tell me 'twere in vain to try,
And that the *Edinburgh Review* and *Quarterly*
Treat a dissenting author very martyrly.

* * * * *

from CANTO II

Oh ye! who teach the ingenuous youth of
    nations,
    Holland, France, England, Germany, or
        Spain,
I pray ye flog them upon all occasions;
    It mends their morals, never mind the pain:
The best of mothers and of educations   5
    In Juan's case were but employed in vain,
Since, in a way that's rather of the oddest, he
Became divested of his native modesty.

Had he but been placed at a public school,
    In the third form, or even in the fourth, 10
His daily task had kept his fancy cool,
    At least, had he been nurtured in the north;
Spain may prove an exception to the rule,
    But then exceptions always prove its
        worth—
A lad of sixteen causing a divorce   15
Puzzled his tutors very much, of course.

I can't say that it puzzles me at all,
    If all things be considered; first, there was
His lady-mother, mathematical,

1639. **Samuel Rogers,** a contemporary minor poet. 1640. **Moore.** See p. 297. 1641. **Sotheby,** William Sotheby (1757-1833), an English scholar and poet. 1642. **Pegasus,** a winged horse associated with poetic inspiration. 1643. **"the Blues,"** the Bluestockings, a name applied to a society of women affecting an interest in literature and politics,

1673. **I . . . Editor.** See Stephen's *Of Lord B,* a parody of Byron, p. 838. 1687. *Edinburgh Review* and *Quarterly.* Both magazines were hostile to Byron; he attacked them in his *English Bards and Scotch Reviewers* (p. 203).
9. **public school,** in England, a private school like Eton.

A——never mind;—his tutor, an old ass; 20
A pretty woman—(that's quite natural,
  Or else the thing had hardly come to pass)
A husband rather old, not much in unity
With his young wife—a time, and opportunity.

Well—well; the world must turn upon its
    axis, 25
  And all mankind turn with it, heads or tails,
  And live and die, make love and pay our
    taxes,
  And as the veering wind shifts, shift our
    sails;
The king commands us, and the doctor
    quacks us,
  The priest instructs, and so our life exhales,
A little breath, love, wine, ambition, fame, 31
Fighting, devotion, dust—perhaps a name.

I said that Juan had been sent to Cadiz—
  A pretty town, I recollect it well—
'Tis there the mart of the colonial trade is, 35
  (Or was, before Peru learned to rebel)
And such sweet girls—I mean, such graceful
    ladies,
  Their very walk would make your bosom
    swell;
I can't describe it, though so much it strike,
Nor liken it—I never saw the like: 40

An Arab horse, a stately stag, a barb
  New broke, a cameleopard, a gazelle,
No—none of these will do—and then their
    garb,
  Their veil and petticoat—Alas! to dwell
Upon such things would very near absorb 45
  A canto—then their feet and ankles—well,
Thank Heaven I've got no metaphor quite
    ready,
(And so, my sober Muse—come, let's be
    steady—

Chaste Muse!—well, if you must, you must)
    —the veil
  Thrown back a moment with the glancing
    hand, 50
While the o'erpowering eye, that turns you
    pale,
  Flashes into the heart—All sunny land
Of Love! when I forget you, may I fail
  To—say my prayers—but never was there
    planned
A dress through which the eyes give such a
    volley, 55
Excepting the Venetian Fazzioli.

But to our tale: the Donna Inez sent
  Her son to Cadiz only to embark;
To stay there had not answered her intent,
  But why?—we leave the reader in the
    dark— 60
'Twas for a voyage the young man was
    meant,
  As if a Spanish ship were Noah's ark,
To wean him from the wickedness of earth,
And send him like a Dove of Promise forth.

Don Juan bade his valet pack his things 65
  According to directions, then received
A lecture and some money: for four springs
  He was to travel; and though Inez grieved
(As every kind of parting has its stings),
  She hoped he would improve—perhaps believed: 70
A letter, too, she gave (he never read it)
Of good advice—and two or three of credit.

In the meantime, to pass her hours away,
  Brave Inez now set up a Sunday school 74
For naughty children, who would rather play
  (Like truant rogues) the devil, or the fool;
Infants of three years old were taught that
    day,
  Dunces were whipped, or set upon a stool:
The great success of Juan's education
Spurred her to teach another generation. 80

Juan embarked—the ship got under way,
  The wind was fair, the water passing rough;
A devil of a sea rolls in that bay,
  As I, who've crossed it oft, know well
    enough;
And, standing on the deck, the dashing spray
  Flies in one's face, and makes it weathertough: 86

---

33. **Cadiz,** a city on the southwest coast of Spain. 41. **barb,** a Barbary horse, noted for speed and endurance. 56. **Fazzioli,** "Literally, little handkerchiefs—the veils most availing of St. Mark."—Byron. 64. **Dove . . . forth,** a reference to the dove sent by Noah from the ark when he wanted to learn whether the waters were receding. See *Genesis*, 6-8.

And there he stood to take, and take again,
His first—perhaps his last—farewell of Spain.

I can't but say it is an awkward sight
    To see one's native land receding through
The growing waters; it unmans one quite, 91
    Especially when life is rather new:
I recollect Great Britain's coast looks white,
    But almost every other country's blue;
When gazing on them, mystified by distance,
We enter on our nautical existence. 96

So Juan stood, bewildered on the deck:
    The wind sung, cordage strained, and sailors swore,
And the ship creaked, the town became a speck,
    From which away so fair and fast they bore. 100
The best of remedies is a beefsteak
    Against seasickness: try it, Sir, before
You sneer, and I assure you this is true,
For I have found it answer—so may you.

Don Juan stood, and, gazing from the stern,
    Beheld his native Spain receding far: 106
First partings form a lesson hard to learn,
    Even nations feel this when they go to war;
There is a sort of unexpressed concern,
    A kind of shock that sets one's heart ajar,
At leaving even the most unpleasant people
And places—one keeps looking at the steeple. 112

But Juan had got many things to leave,
    His mother, and a mistress, and no wife,
So that he had much better cause to grieve 115
    Than many persons more advanced in life:
And if we now and then a sigh must heave
    At quitting even those we quit in strife,
No doubt we weep for those the heart endears—
That is, till deeper griefs congeal our tears. 120

So Juan wept, as wept the captive Jews
    By Babel's waters, still remembering Sion:
I'd weep—but mine is not a weeping Muse,
    And such light griefs are not a thing to die on;
Young men should travel, if but to amuse 125
    Themselves; and the next time their servants tie on
Behind their carriages their new portmanteau,
Perhaps it may be lined with this my canto.

And Juan wept, and much he sighed and thought,
    While his salt tears dropped into the salt sea, 130
"Sweets to the sweet"; (I like so much to quote;
    You must excuse this extract—'tis where she,
The Queen of Denmark, for Ophelia brought
    Flowers to the grave;) and, sobbing often, he
Reflected on his present situation, 135
And seriously resolved on reformation.

"Farewell, my Spain! a long farewell!" he cried,
    "Perhaps I may revisit thee no more,
But die, as many an exiled heart hath died,
    Of its own thirst to see again thy shore: 140
Farewell, where Guadalquivir's waters glide!
    Farewell, my mother! and, since all is o'er,
Farewell, too, dearest Julia!—(here he drew
Her letter out again, and read it through.)

"And oh! if e'er I should forget, I swear— 145
    But that's impossible, and cannot be—
Sooner shall this blue ocean melt to air,
    Sooner shall earth resolve itself to sea,
Than I resign thine image, oh, my fair!
    Or think of anything, excepting thee; 150
A mind diseased no remedy can physic—
(Here the ship gave a lurch, and he grew seasick.)

"Sooner shall Heaven kiss earth—(here he fell sicker)
    Oh, Julia! what is every other woe?—
(For God's sake let me have a glass of liquor;

---

121. **So . . . Sion,** from *Psalms,* 137:1: "By the rivers of Babylon, there we sat down, yea, we wept, when we remembered Zion." The reference is to the story of the Jews taken into captivity by Nebuchadnezzar, King of Babylon. Cf. *2 Kings,* 24:10-16.

131. **"Sweets to the sweet,"** quoted from Gertrude's speech in *Hamlet* (V. i, 266) at the burial of Ophelia.

Pedro, Battista, help me down below.) 156
  Julia, my love!—(you rascal, Pedro, quicker)—
Oh, Julia!—(this curst vessel pitches so)—
Belovéd Julia, hear me still beseeching!"
(Here he grew inarticulate with retching.) 160

He felt that chilling heaviness of heart,
  Or rather stomach, which, alas! attends,
Beyond the best apothecary's art,
  The loss of Love, the treachery of friends,
Or death of those we dote on, when a part 165
  Of us dies with them as each fond hope ends:
No doubt he would have been much more pathetic,
  But the sea acted as a strong emetic.

Love's a capricious power: I've known it hold
  Out through a fever caused by its own heat, 170
But be much puzzled by a cough and cold,
  And find a quinsy very hard to treat;
Against all noble maladies he's bold,
  But vulgar illnesses don't like to meet,
Nor that a sneeze should interrupt his sigh,
Nor inflammation redden his blind eye. 175

But worst of all is nausea, or a pain
  About the lower region of the bowels;
Love, who heroically breathes a vein,
  Shrinks from the applications of hot towels,
And purgatives are dangerous to his reign, 181
  Seasickness death: his love was perfect, how else
Could Juan's passion, while the billows roar,
Resist his stomach, ne'er at sea before?

The ship, called the most holy "Trinidada,"
  Was steering duly for the port Leghorn; 186
For there the Spanish family Moncada
  Were settled long ere Juan's sire was born:
They were relations, and for them he had a
  Letter of introduction, which the morn 190
Of his departure had been sent him by
  His Spanish friends for those in Italy.

186. **Leghorn**, a city in Tuscany, on the west coast of Italy.

His suite consisted of three servants and
  A tutor, the licentiate Pedrillo,
Who several languages did understand, 195
  But now lay sick and speechless on his pillow,
And, rocking in his hammock, longed for land,
  His headache being increased by every billow;
And the waves oozing through the port-hole made
His berth a little damp, and him afraid. 200

'Twas not without some reason, for the wind
  Increased at night, until it blew a gale;
And though 't was not much to a naval mind,
  Some landsmen would have looked a little pale,
For sailors are, in fact, a different kind: 205
  At sunset they began to take in sail,
For the sky showed it would come on to blow,
And carry away, perhaps, a mast or so.

At one o'clock the wind with sudden shift
  Threw the ship right into the trough of the sea, 210
Which struck her aft, and made an awkward rift,
  Started the stern-post, also shattered the
Whole of her stern-frame, and, ere she could lift
  Herself from out her present jeopardy,
The rudder tore away; 'twas time to sound 215
The pumps, and there were four feet water found.

One gang of people instantly was put
  Upon the pumps, and the remainder set
To get up part of the cargo, and what not;
  But they could not come at the leak as yet; 220
At last they did get at it really, but
  Still their salvation was an even bet:
The water rushed through in a way quite puzzling,
While they thrust sheet, shirts, jackets, bales of muslin,

Into the opening; but all such ingredients 225
  Would have been vain, and they must have gone down,

Despite of all their efforts and expedients,
  But for the pumps; I'm glad to make them known
To all the brother tars who may have need hence,
  For fifty tons of water were upthrown   230
By them per hour, and they had all been undone,
  But for the maker, Mr. Mann, of London.

As day advanced the weather seemed to abate,
  And then the leak they reckoned to reduce,
And keep the ship afloat, though three feet yet
  Kept two hand- and one chain-pump still in use.   236
The wind blew fresh again: as it grew late
  A squall came on, and while some guns broke loose,
A gust—which all descriptive power transcends—
Laid with one blast the ship on her beam ends.   240

There she lay, motionless, and seemed upset;
  The water left the hold, and washed the decks,
And made a scene men do not soon forget;
  For they remember battles, fires, and wrecks,
Or any other thing that brings regret,   245
  Or breaks their hopes, or hearts, or heads, or necks:
Thus drownings are much talked of by the divers,
  And swimmers, who may chance to be survivors.

Immediately the masts were cut away,
  Both main and mizzen; first the mizzen went,   250
The main-mast followed: but the ship still lay
  Like a mere log, and baffled our intent.
Foremast and bowsprit were cut down, and they
  Eased her at last (although we never meant   254

---

250. **mizzen**, the aftermost mast of a three-masted vessel. 253. **bowsprit**, a large spar projecting forward from the stem of a ship to carry sail forward and to support the masts by means of stays.

To part with all till every hope was blighted),
And then with violence the old ship righted.

It may be easily supposed, while this
  Was going on, some people were unquiet,
That passengers would find it much amiss
  To lose their lives, as well as spoil their diet;
That even the able seaman, deeming his   261
  Days nearly o'er, might be disposed to riot,
As upon such occasions tars will ask
For grog, and sometimes drink rum from the cask.

There's naught, no doubt, so much the spirit calms   265
  As rum and true religion: thus it was,
Some plundered, some drank spirits, some sung psalms,
  The high wind made the treble, and as bass
The hoarse harsh waves kept time; fright cured the qualms
  Of all the luckless landsmen's seasick maws: 270
Strange sounds of wailing, blasphemy, devotion,
Clamored in chorus to the roaring Ocean.

Perhaps more mischief had been done, but for
  Our Juan, who, with sense beyond his years,
Got to the spirit-room, and stood before   275
  It with a pair of pistols; and their fears,
As if Death were more dreadful by his door
  Of fire than water, spite of oaths and tears,
Kept still aloof the crew, who, ere they sunk,
Thought it would be becoming to die drunk.

"Give us more grog," they cried, "for it will be   281
  All one an hour hence." Juan answered, "No!
'T is true that death awaits both you and me,
  But let us die like men, not sink below
Like brutes"—and thus his dangerous post kept he,   285
  And none liked to anticipate the blow;
And even Pedrillo, his most reverend tutor,
Was for some rum a disappointed suitor.

The good old gentleman was quite aghast,
  And made a loud and pious lamentation;

Repented all his sins, and made a last 291
  Irrevocable vow of reformation;
Nothing should tempt him more (this peril past)
  To quit his academic occupation,
In cloisters of the classic Salamanca, 295
  To follow Juan's wake, like Sancho Panca.

But now there came a flash of hope once more;
  Day broke, and the wind lulled: the masts were gone;
The leak increased; shoals round her, but no shore,
  The vessel swam, yet still she held her own.
They tried the pumps again, and though, before, 301
  Their desperate efforts seemed all useless grown,
A glimpse of sunshine set some hands to bale—
  The stronger pumped, the weaker thrummed a sail.

Under the vessel's keel the sail was passed, 305
  And for the moment it had some effect;
But with a leak, and not a stick of mast,
  Nor rag of canvas, what could they expect?
But still 'tis best to struggle to the last,
  'Tis never too late to be wholly wrecked:
And though 'tis true that man can only die once, 311
  'Tis not so pleasant in the Gulf of Lyons.

There winds and waves had hurled them, and from thence,
  Without their will, they carried them away;
For they were forced with steering to dispense, 315
  And never had as yet a quiet day
On which they might repose, or even commence
  A jurymast or rudder, or could say
The ship would swim an hour, which, by good luck, 319
  Still swam—though not exactly like a duck.

295. **Salamanca**, a city in western Spain, the seat of a celebrated university. 296. **Sancho Panca**, Sancho Panza, the shrewd squire of the hero in *Don Quixote*, a burlesque Spanish romance by Cervantes (1547-1616). 304. **thrummed**, inserted short pieces of rope yarn in canvas to be wrapped about the rigging to prevent chafing. 312. **Gulf of Lyons**, on the southern coast of France. 318. **jurymast**, a temporary mast.

The wind, in fact, perhaps, was rather less,
  But the ship labored so, they scarce could hope
To weather out much longer; the distress
  Was also great with which they had to cope
For want of water, and their solid mess 325
  Was scant enough: in vain the telescope
Was used—nor sail nor shore appeared in sight,
  Naught but the heavy sea, and coming night.

Again the weather threatened—again blew
  A gale, and in the fore and after-hold 330
Water appeared; yet, though the people knew
  All this, the most were patient, and some bold,
Until the chains and leathers were worn through
  Of all our pumps—a wreck complete she rolled,
At mercy of the waves, whose mercies are 335
  Like human beings during civil war.

Then came the carpenter, at last, with tears
  In his rough eyes, and told the captain he
Could do no more: he was a man in years,
  And long had voyaged through many a stormy sea, 340
And if he wept at length, they were not fears
  That made his eyelids as a woman's be,
But he, poor fellow, had a wife and children,
  Two things for dying people quite bewildering.

The ship was evidently settling now 345
  Fast by the head; and, all distinction gone,
Some went to prayers again, and made a vow
  Of candles to their saints—but there were none
To pay them with; and some looked o'er the bow;
  Some hoisted out the boats; and there was one 350
That begged Pedrillo for an absolution,
  Who told him to be damned—in his confusion.

Some lashed them in their hammocks; some put on
  Their best clothes, as if going to a fair;

Some cursed the day on which they saw the
    sun,   355
    And gnashed their teeth, and howling, tore
        their hair;
And others went on as they had begun,
    Getting the boats out, being well aware
That a tight boat will live in a rough sea,
Unless with breakers close beneath her lee. 360

The worst of all was, that in their condition,
    Having been several days in great distress,
'Twas difficult to get out such provision
    As now might render their long suffering
        less.
Men, even when dying, dislike inanition; 365
    Their stock was damaged by the weather's
        stress.
Two casks of biscuit, and a keg of butter,
Were all that could be thrown into the cutter.

But in the long-boat they contrived to stow
    Some pounds of bread, though injured by
        the wet;   370
Water, a twenty-gallon cask or so;
    Six flasks of wine: and they contrived to
        get
A portion of their beef up from below,
    And with a piece of pork, moreover, met,
But scarce enough to serve them for a
        luncheon—   375
Then there was rum, eight gallons in a
        puncheon.

The other boats, the yawl and pinnace, had
    Been stove in the beginning of the gale;
And the long-boat's condition was but bad,
    As there were but two blankets for a sail, 380
And one oar for a mast, which a young lad
    Threw in by good luck over the ship's rail;
And two boats could not hold, far less be
        stored,
To save one half the people then on board.

'Twas twilight, and the sunless day went
        down   385
    Over the waste of waters; like a veil,
Which, if withdrawn, would but disclose the
        frown
    Of one whose hate is masked but to assail.

Thus to their hopeless eyes the night was
    shown,
    And grimly darkled o'er the faces pale, 390
And the dim desolate deep: twelve days had
    Fear
Been their familiar, and now Death was
    here.

Some trial had been making at a raft,
    With little hope in such a rolling sea,
A sort of thing at which one would have
        laughed,   395
    If any laughter at such times could be,
Unless with people who too much have
        quaffed,
    And have a kind of wild and horrid glee,
Half epileptical, and half hysterical—
Their preservation would have been a miracle.   400

At half-past eight o'clock, booms, hencoops,
    spars,
    And all things, for a chance, had been cast
    loose
That still could keep afloat the struggling
    tars,
    For yet they strove, although of no great
    use:
There was no light in heaven but a few stars,
    The boats put off o'ercrowded with their
        crews;   406
She gave a heel, and then a lurch to port,
And, going down head foremost—sunk, in
    short.

Then rose from sea to sky the wild farewell—
    Then shrieked the timid, and stood still the
        brave—   410
Then some leaped overboard with dreadful
    yell,
    As eager to anticipate their grave;
And the sea yawned around her like a hell,
    And down she sucked with her the whirling wave,
Like one who grapples with his enemy, 415
And strives to strangle him before he die.

And first one universal shriek there rushed,
    Louder than the loud Ocean, like a crash

---

376. **puncheon**, a kind of large cask. 377. **yawl**, a ship's small boat rowed by four to six men. **pinnace**, a light sailing vessel sometimes also using oars.

392. **familiar**, attendant spirit. 401. **boom**, a long pole used to extend the bottom of a sail.

Of echoing thunder; and then all was hushed,
    Save the wild wind and the remorseless dash   420
Of billows; but at intervals there gushed,
    Accompanied by a convulsive splash,
A solitary shriek, the bubbling cry
Of some strong swimmer in his agony.
                  (1818-19; 1821)

from CANTO III
THE ISLES OF GREECE

The isles of Greece, the isles of Greece!
    Where burning Sappho loved and sung,
    Where grew the arts of war and peace,
    Where Delos rose, and Phoebus sprung!
Eternal summer gilds them yet,   5
But all, except their sun, is set.

The Scian and the Teian muse,
    The hero's harp, the lover's lute,
Have found the fame your shores refuse:
    Their place of birth alone is mute   10
To sounds which echo further west
Than your sires' "Islands of the Blest."

The mountains look on Marathon—
    And Marathon looks on the sea;
And musing there an hour alone,   15
    I dreamed that Greece might still be free;
For standing on the Persians' grave,
I could not deem myself a slave.

A king sat on the rocky brow
    Which looks o'er sea-born Salamis;   20
And ships, by thousands, lay below,
    And men in nations;—all were his!
He counted them at break of day—
And when the sun set, where were they?

And where are they? and where art thou,   25
    My country? On thy voiceless shore
The heroic lay is tuneless now—
    The heroic bosom beats no more!
And must thy lyre, so long divine,
Degenerate into hands like mine?   30

'Tis something, in the dearth of fame,
    Though linked among a fettered race,
To feel at least a patriot's shame,
    Even as I sing, suffuse my face;
For what is left the poet here?   35
For Greeks a blush—for Greece a tear.

Must *we* but weep o'er days more blest?
    Must *we* but blush?—Our fathers bled.
Earth! render back from out thy breast
    A remnant of our Spartan dead!   40
Of the three hundred grant but three,
To make a new Thermopylae!

What, silent still? and silent all?
    Ah! no;—the voices of the dead
Sound like a distant torrent's fall,   45
    And answer, "Let one living head,
But one arise—we come, we come!"
'Tis but the living who are dumb.

In vain—in vain: strike other chords;
    Fill high the cup with Samian wine!   50
Leave battles to the Turkish hordes,
    And shed the blood of Scio's vine!
Hark! rising to the ignoble call—
How answers each bold Bacchanal!

You have the Pyrrhic dance as yet;   55
    Where is the Pyrrhic phalanx gone?
Of two such lessons, why forget
    The nobler and the manlier one?
You have the letters Cadmus gave—
Think ye he meant them for a slave?   60

Fill high the bowl with Samian wine!
    We will not think of themes like these!

It made Anacreon's song divine:
  He served—but served Polycrates—
A tyrant; but our masters then   65
Were still, at least, our countrymen.

The tyrant of the Chersonese
  Was freedom's best and bravest friend;
That tyrant was Miltiades!
  Oh! that the present hour would lend   70
Another despot of the kind!
Such chains as his were sure to bind.

Fill high the bowl with Samian wine!
  On Suli's rock, and Parga's shore,
Exists the remnant of a line   75
  Such as the Doric mothers bore;
And there, perhaps, some seed is sown,
The Heracleidan blood might own.

Trust not for freedom to the Franks—
  They have a king who buys and sells;   80
In native swords, and native ranks,
  The only hope of courage dwells:
But Turkish force, and Latin fraud,
Would break your shield, however broad.

Fill high the bowl with Samian wine!   85
  Our virgins dance beneath the shade—
I see their glorious black eyes shine;
  But gazing on each glowing maid,
My own the burning tear-drop laves,
To think such breasts must suckle slaves. 90

Place me on Sunium's marbled steep,
  Where nothing, save the waves and I,
May hear our mutual murmurs sweep;
  There, swan-like, let me sing and die:
A land of slaves shall ne'er be mine—   95
Dash down yon cup of Samian wine!

     *   *   *   *   *

Thus sung, or would, or could, or should have sung,
  The modern Greek, in tolerable verse;   690
If not like Orpheus quite, when Greece was young,
  Yet in these times he might have done much worse:
His strain displayed some feeling—right or wrong;
  And feeling, in a poet, is the source
Of others' feeling; but they are such liars, 695
And take all colors—like the hands of dyers.

But words are things, and a small drop of ink,
  Falling like dew, upon a thought, produces
That which makes thousands, perhaps millions, think;
  'Tis strange, the shortest letter which man uses   700
Instead of speech, may form a lasting link
  Of ages; to what straits old Time reduces
Frail man, when paper—even a rag like this,
Survives himself, his tomb, and all that's his!

And when his bones are dust, his grave a blank,   705
  His station, generation, even his nation,
Become a thing, or nothing, save to rank
  In chronological commemoration,
Some dull MS. oblivion long has sank,   709
  Or graven stone found in a barrack's station
In digging the foundation of a closet,
May turn his name up, as a rare deposit.

And glory long has made the sages smile;
  'Tis something, nothing, words, illusion, wind—
Depending more upon the historian's style 715
  Than on the name a person leaves behind:
Troy owes to Homer what whist owes to Hoyle:
  The present century was growing blind
To the great Marlborough's skill in giving knocks,
Until his late Life by Archdeacon Coxe.   720

---

63. **Anacreon,** a Greek lyric poet (c.563-c.478 B.C.). 64. **Polycrates,** Tyrant of Samos (535-522? B.C.), a patron of literature and art. 67. **Chersonese,** a peninsula of ancient Greece, the present-day Gallipoli. 69. **Miltiades,** a celebrated Athenian general (fifth century B.C.). 74. **Suli,** a mountainous district in European Turkey. **Parga,** a seaport in Turkey. 76. **Doric,** from Doris, an ancient province in northern Greece. 78. **Heracleidan,** tracing back to Hercules, i.e., ancient Greek. 91. **Sunium,** in ancient geography the promontory at the southeastern extremity of Attica, Greece. 94. **swan-like.** The swan was said to sing melodiously when about to die.

691. **Orpheus,** a mythological poet and musician whose lyre could charm beasts and move trees and stones. 717. **Troy . . . Homer.** Troy, an ancient city in Asia Minor, is the scene of Homer's *Iliad*. **Hoyle,** Edmund Hoyle (1672-1769), an English writer on whist and other card games. 719. **Marlborough,** John Churchill (1650-1722), Duke of Marlborough, the famous English general who defeated the French in the Battle of Blenheim, Bavaria, in 1704. See Southey's *Battle of Blenheim,* p. 300. 720. **Coxe,** William Coxe (1747-1832), an English historian. His *Memoirs of the Duke of Marlborough* appeared in 1817-1819.

Milton's the prince of poets—so we say;
   A little heavy, but no less divine:
An independent being in his day—
   Learned, pious, temperate in love and wine;
But his life falling into Johnson's way,   725
   We're told this great high priest of all the Nine
Was whipped at college—a harsh sire—odd spouse,
For the first Mrs. Milton left his house.

All these are, *certes,* entertaining facts,
   Like Shakespeare's stealing deer, Lord Bacon's bribes;   730
Like Titus' youth, and Caesar's earliest acts;
   Like Burns (whom Doctor Currie well describes);
Like Cromwell's pranks;—but although truth exacts
   These amiable descriptions from the scribes,
As most essential to their hero's story,   735
They do not much contribute to his glory.

All are not moralists, like Southey, when
   He prated to the world of "Pantisocrasy";
Or Wordsworth unexcised, unhired, who then
   Seasoned his peddler poems with democracy;   740
Or Coleridge, long before his flighty pen
   Let to the Morning Post its aristocracy;
When he and Southey, following the same path,
Espoused two partners (milliners of Bath).

Such names at present cut a convict figure,   745
   The very Botany Bay in moral geography;
Their loyal treason, renegado rigor,
   Are good manure for their more bare biography;
Wordsworth's last quarto, by the way, is bigger
Than any since the birthday of typography;
A drowsy, frowzy poem, called the "Excursion,"   751
Writ in a manner which is my aversion.

He there builds up a formidable dyke
   Between his own and others' intellect;
But Wordsworth's poem, and his followers, like   755
   Joanna Southcote's Shiloh and her sect,
Are things which in this century don't strike
   The public mind—so few are the elect;
And the new births of both their stale virginities
Have proved but dropsies, taken for divinities.

But let me to my story: I must own,   761
   If I have any fault, it is digression,
Leaving my people to proceed alone,
   While I soliloquize beyond expression:
But these are my addresses from the throne,
   Which put off business to the ensuing session: 766
Forgetting each omission is a loss to
The world, not quite so great as Ariosto.

I know that what our neighbors call *"longueurs,"*
   (We've not so good a *word,* but have the *thing,*   770
In that complete perfection which insures
   An epic from Bob Southey every spring—)
Form not the true temptation which allures
   The reader; but 'twould not be hard to bring
Some fine examples of the *épopée,*   775
To prove its grand ingredient is *ennui.*

---

725. life . . . way. Samuel Johnson wrote a life of Milton, published in his *Lives of the English Poets* (1779, 1781). See Vol. I, p. 1135. **726. the Nine,** the nine Muses. **730. stealing deer,** a fictitious anecdote popularly associated with Shakespeare's youth. **Bacon's bribes.** Bacon was charged with accepting bribes and was therefore excluded from Parliament. See Vol. I, p. 613. **731. Titus' youth.** The youth of Titus Vespasianus, Roman Emperor (79-81), like that of Julius Caesar and that of Burns, p. 83, was noted for its voluptuousness. **732. Currie,** James Currie (1756-1805), a Scottish physician, who wrote a life of Burns for the benefit of the Burns family. **733. Cromwell's pranks.** The youthful Cromwell was noted for robbing orchards. **738. "Pantisocrasy,"** the name given to a scheme for an ideal community that Southey, Coleridge, and others planned in 1794 to establish in America. See p. 164. **739. unexcised.** See note on l. 46, p. 225. **740. peddler poems.** A reference to Wordsworth's *Peter Bell,* the hero of which is a peddler. **742. Morning Post.** Coleridge began his contributions to the *Morning Post* in 1798. **744. two partners.** Coleridge married Sarah Fricker, of Bath; Southey married her sister Edith; they were not milliners at the time of their marriage in 1795.

746. Botany Bay, an inlet on the east coast of Australia, formerly used by the British as a convict station. **756. Joanna Southcote,** a visionary who prophesied that she would give birth to a second Shiloh, or Messiah, on October 19, 1814. When that time came, she fell into a trance and died ten days later. **768. Ariosto,** a famous Italian poet (1474-1533). **769. longueurs,** tedious passages. **775. épopée,** epic. **776. ennui,** languid weariness.

We learn from Horace, "Homer sometimes
    sleeps";
  We feel without him, Wordsworth some-
    times wakes—
To show with what complacency he creeps,
    With his dear "*Wagoners,*" around his
    lakes.   780
He wishes for "a boat" to sail the deeps—
  Of ocean?—No, of air; and then he makes
Another outcry for "a little boat,"
And drivels seas to set it well afloat.   784

If he must fain sweep o'er the ethereal plain,
  And Pegasus runs restive in his "Wagon,"
Could he not beg the loan of Charles's Wain?
  Or pray Medea for a single dragon?
Or if, too classic for his vulgar brain,   789
  He feared his neck to venture such a nag on,
And he must needs mount nearer to the moon,
Could not the blockhead ask for a balloon?

"Peddlers," and "Boats," and "Wagons!" Oh!
    ye shades
  Of Pope and Dryden, are we come to this?
That trash of such sort not alone evades   795
  Contempt, but from the bathos' vast abyss
Floats scumlike uppermost, and these Jack
    Cades
  Of sense and song above your graves may
    hiss—
The "little boatman" and his "Peter Bell"
Can sneer at him who drew "Achitophel"!   800

T' our tale.—The feast was over, the slaves
    gone,
  The dwarfs and dancing girls had all re-
    tired;
The Arab lore and poet's song were done,
  And every sound of revelry expired,
The lady and her lover, left alone,   805
  The rosy flood of twilight's sky admired;—
Ave Maria o'er the earth and sea,
That heavenliest hour of Heaven is worthiest
    thee!

Ave Maria! blessèd be the hour   809
  The time, the clime, the spot, where I so oft
Have felt that moment in its fullest power
  Sink o'er the earth so beautiful and soft,
While swung the deep bell in the distant
    tower,
  Or the faint dying day-hymn stole aloft,
And not a breath crept through the rosy air,
And yet the forest leaves seemed stirred with
    prayer.   816

Ave Maria! 'tis the hour of prayer!
  Ave Maria! 'tis the hour of love!
Ave Maria! may our spirits dare
  Look up to thine and to thy Son's above!   820
Ave Maria! oh that face so fair!
  Those downcast eyes beneath the Almighty
    Dove—
What though 'tis but a pictured image?—
    strike—
That painting is no idol—'tis too like.

Some kinder casuists are pleased to say,   825
  In nameless print—that I have no devo-
    tion;
But set those persons down with me to pray,
  And you shall see who has the properest
    notion
Of getting into heaven the shortest way;
  My altars are the mountains and the ocean,
Earth, air, stars—all that springs from the
    great Whole,   831
Who hath produced, and will receive the soul.

Sweet hour of twilight!—in the solitude
  Of the pine forest, and the silent shore
Which bounds Ravenna's immemorial wood,
  Rooted where once the Adrian wave flowed
    o'er,   836
To where the last Caesarean fortress stood,
  Evergreen forest! which Boccaccio's lore
And Dryden's lay made haunted ground to
    me,
How have I loved the twilight hour and thee!

---

777. **Horace**, the famous Latin poet (first century B.C.). Cf. *Ars Poetica*, l. 359. 780. **Wagoners.** One of Wordsworth's poems is entitled *The Wagoner*. 783. **"a little boat."** From *Peter Bell*, stanza 1. 787. **Charles's Wain,** Charles's Wagon, a constellation known as the Big Dipper. 788. **Medea,** an enchantress, who aided her lover Jason to get the golden fleece. 797. **Jack Cades.** Jack Cade was the leader of "Cade's Rebellion," a political uprising in Kent in 1450. 800. **him,** Dryden, of whom Wordsworth was not fond.

830. **My altars . . . stars.** Cf. *Childe Harold's Pilgrimage,* III, 109 ff. (p. 214); 631 ff. (p. 216); 784 ff. (p. 217); and IV, 1594 ff. (p. 222). 835. **Ravenna,** a city and a province in Italy. 839. **Dryden's lay,** *Theodore and Honoria,* a tale of a specter huntsman who haunted the region of Ravenna; it is adapted from Boccaccio's *Decameron,* 5, 8. Boccaccio was a noted Italian writer of the fourteenth century. See Dryden's *Preface to the Fables* (Vol. I, p. 874).

The shrill cicalas, people of the pine,   841
  Making their summer lives one ceaseless song,
Were the sole echoes, save my steed's and mine,
  And vesper bell's that rose the boughs along;
The specter huntsman of Onesti's line,   845
  His hell-dogs, and their chase, and the fair throng
Which learned from this example not to fly
  From a true lover—shadowed my mind's eye.

Oh, Hesperus! thou bringest all good things—
  Home to the weary, to the hungry cheer,   850
To the young bird the parent's brooding wings,
  The welcome stall to the o'erlabored steer;
Whate'er of peace about our hearthstone clings,
  Whate'er our household gods protect of dear,
Are gathered round us by thy look of rest;   855
  Thou bring'st the child, too, to the mother's breast.

Soft hour! which wakes the wish and melts the heart
  Of those who sail the seas, on the first day
When they from their sweet friends are torn apart;
  Or fills with love the pilgrim on his way   860
As the far bell of vesper makes him start,
  Seeming to weep the dying day's decay;
Is this a fancy which our reason scorns?
  Ah! surely nothing dies but something mourns!   (*1819-20; 1821*)

*   *   *   *   *

from CANTO IV

"Whom the gods love die young" was said of yore,
  And many deaths do they escape by this: 90
The death of friends, and that which slays even more—
  The death of friendship, love, youth, all that is,
Except mere breath; and since the silent shore
  Awaits at last even those who longest miss
The old archer's shafts, perhaps the early grave   95
Which men weep over may be meant to save.

Haidée and Juan thought not of the dead.
  The heavens, and earth, and air, seemed made for them:
They found no fault with Time, save that he fled;
  They saw not in themselves aught to condemn;   100
Each was the other's mirror, and but read
  Joy sparkling in their dark eyes like a gem,
And knew such brightness was but the reflection
Of their exchanging glances of affection.

The gentle pressure, and the thrilling touch,
  The least glance better understood than words,   105
Which still said all, and ne'er could say too much;
  A language, too, but like to that of birds,
Known but to them, at least appearing such
  As but to lovers a true sense affords;   110
Sweet playful phrases, which would seem absurd
To those who have ceased to hear such, or ne'er heard.

All these were theirs, for they were children still,
  And children still they should have ever been;
They were not made in the real world to fill
  A busy character in the dull scene,   115
But like two beings born from out a rill,
  A nymph and her belovéd, all unseen
To pass their lives in fountains and on flowers,
And never know the weight of human hours.

---

841. **cicalas**, locusts. 845. **Onesti**, the hero of Boccaccio's story; he becomes Dryden's Theodore. The specter merely appeared to Onesti; it was not of his line. 849. **Hesperus**, the evening star in Greek mythology.
Canto IV. Before resuming the story Byron gives a brief account of his burlesque poetic method. 89. "**Whom . . . young**," a phrase used by the Greek poet Menander (third century B.C.) in *Dis Exapaton*; by the Roman dramatist Plautus (d. 184 B.C.) in *Bacchides*; and by Wordsworth in *The Excursion*, l. 502.

97. **Haidée**, the beautiful Greek maiden who nursed Juan back to health after his shipwreck and fell in love with him.

Moons changing had rolled on, and change-
    less found   121
  Those their bright rise had lighted to such
    joys
As rarely they beheld throughout their round;
  And these were not of the vain kind which
    cloys,   124
For theirs were buoyant spirits, never bound
  By the mere senses; and that which destroys
Most love, possession, unto them appeared
A thing which each endearment more en-
    deared.

Oh beautiful! and rare as beautiful!
  But theirs was love in which the mind de-
    lights   130
To lose itself, when the old world grows dull,
  And we are sick of its hack sounds and
    sights,
Intrigues, adventures of the common school,
  Its petty passions, marriages, and flights,
Where Hymen's torch but brands one strum-
    pet more,   135
Whose husband only knows her not a whore.

Hard words—harsh truth! a truth which
    many know.
Enough.—The faithful and the fairy pair,
Who never found a single hour too slow,
  What was it made them thus exempt from
    care?   140
Young innate feelings all have felt below,
  Which perish in the rest, but in them were
Inherent—what we mortals call romantic,
  And always envy, though we deem it frantic.

This is in others a factitious state,   145
  An opium dream of too much youth and
    reading,
But was in them their nature or their fate.
  No novels e'er had set their young hearts
    bleeding,
For Haidée's knowledge was by no means
    great,   149
And Juan was a boy of saintly breeding;
So that there was no reason for their loves
More than for those of nightingales or doves.

    135. **Hymen,** god of marriage.

They gazed upon the sunset; 'tis an hour
  Dear unto all, but dearest to *their* eyes,
For it had made them what they were: the
    power   155
  Of love had first o'erwhelmed them from
    such skies,
When happiness had been their only dower,
  And twilight saw them linked in passion's
    ties;
Charmed with each other, all things charmed
    that brought   159
The past still welcome as the present thought.

I know not why, but in that hour tonight,
  Even as they gazed, a sudden tremor came,
And swept, as 'twere, across their hearts' de-
    light,
  Like the wind o'er a harp-string, or a flame,
When one is shook in sound, and one in
    sight.   165
  And thus some boding flashed through
    either frame,
And called from Juan's breast a faint low
    sigh,
While one new tear arose in Haidée's eye.

That large black prophet eye seemed to
    dilate
  And follow far the disappearing sun,   170
As if their last day of a happy date
  With his broad, bright, and dropping orb
    were gone.
Juan gazed on her as to ask his fate—
  He felt a grief, but knowing cause for none,
His glance inquired of hers for some excuse 175
For feelings causeless, or at least abstruse.

She turned to him, and smiled, but in that sort
  Which makes not others smile; then turned
    aside: 178
Whatever feeling shook her, it seemed short,
  And mastered by her wisdom or her pride;
When Juan spoke, too—it might be in sport—
  Of this their mutual feeling, she replied—
"If it should be so—but—it cannot be—
Or I at least shall not survive to see."   184

Juan would question further, but she pressed
  His lips to hers, and silenced him with this,

And then dismissed the omen from her breast,
  Defying augury with that fond kiss;
And no doubt of all methods 'tis the best:
  Some people prefer wine—'tis not amiss; 190
I have tried both; so those who would a part take
May choose between the headache and the heartache.

One of the two, according to your choice,
  Woman or wine, you'll have to undergo;
Both maladies are taxes on our joys: 195
  But which to choose, I really hardly know;
And if I had to give a casting voice,
  For both sides I could many reasons show,
And then decide, without great wrong to either,
It were much better to have both than neither.

Juan and Haidée gazed upon each other 201
  With swimming looks of speechless tenderness,
Which mixed all feelings, friend, child, lover, brother;
All that the best can mingle and express
When two pure hearts are poured in one another, 205
  And love too much, and yet cannot love less;
But almost sanctify the sweet excess
By the immortal wish and power to bless.

Mixed in each other's arms, and heart in heart,
  Why did they not then die?—they had lived too long 210
Should an hour come to bid them breathe apart;
  Years could but bring them cruel things or wrong;
The world was not for them, nor the world's art
For beings passionate as Sappho's song;
Love was born *with* them, *in* them, so intense,
It was their very spirit—not a sense. 216

They should have lived together deep in woods,
  Unseen as sings the nightingale; they were
Unfit to mix in these thick solitudes
  Called social, haunts of hate, and vice, and care; 220
How lonely every freeborn creature broods!
  The sweetest song-birds nestle in a pair;
The eagle soars alone; the gull and crow
Flock o'er their carrion, just like men below.

Now pillowed cheek to cheek, in loving sleep,
  Haidée and Juan their siesta took, 226
A gentle slumber, but it was not deep,
  For ever and anon a something shook
Juan, and shuddering o'er his frame would creep;
  And Haidée's sweet lips murmured like a brook 230
A wordless music, and her face so fair
Stirred with her dream, as rose-leaves with the air.

Or as the stirring of a deep clear stream
  Within an Alpine hollow, when the wind
Walks o'er it, was she shaken by the dream,
  The mystical usurper of the mind— 236
O'erpowering us to be whate'er may seem
  Good to the soul which we no more can bind:
Strange state of being! (for 'tis still to be) 239
Senseless to feel, and with sealed eyes to see.

She dreamed of being alone on the seashore,
  Chained to a rock; she knew not how, but stir
She could not from the spot, and the loud roar
  Grew, and each wave rose roughly, threatening her;
And o'er her upper lip they seemed to pour,
  Until she sobbed for breath, and soon they were 246
Foaming o'er her lone head, so fierce and high—
Each broke to drown her, yet she could not die.

---

214. **Sappho,** a famous Greek poetess (seventh century B.C.) noted for the passion of her verse.

218. **Unseen . . . nightingale.** Cf. *The Two Gentlemen of Verona,* V, iv, 2-6:
  This shadowy desert, unfrequented woods,
  I better brook than flourishing, peopled towns.
  Here can I sit alone, unseen of any,
  And, to the nightingale's complaining notes,
  Tune my distresses, and record my woes.

Anon—she was released, and then she strayed
    O'er the sharp shingles with her bleeding
        feet,   250
And stumbled almost every step she made;
    And something rolled before her in a sheet,
Which she must still pursue howe'er afraid:
    'Twas white and indistinct, nor stopped to
        meet
Her glance nor grasp, for still she gazed and
        grasped,   255
And ran, but it escaped her as she clasped.

The dream changed—in a cave she stood, its
        walls
    Were hung with marble icicles; the work
Of ages on its water-fretted halls,
    Where waves might wash, and seals might
        breed and lurk;   260
Her hair was dripping, and the very balls
    Of her black eyes seemed turned to tears,
        and mirk
The sharp rocks looked below each drop they
        caught,
Which froze to marble as it fell—she thought.

And wet, and cold, and lifeless at her feet, 265
    Pale as the foam that frothed on his dead
        brow,
Which she essayed in vain to clear (how
        sweet
    Were once her cares, how idle seemed they
        now!),
Lay Juan, nor could aught renew the beat
    Of his quenched heart; and the sea dirges
        low   270
Rang in her sad ears like a mermaid's song,
    And that brief dream appeared a life too long.

And gazing on the dead, she thought his face
    Faded, or altered into something new—
Like to her father's features, till each trace   275
    More like and like to Lambro's aspect
        grew—
With all his keen worn look and Grecian grace;
    And starting, she awoke, and what to view?
Oh! Powers of Heaven! what dark eye meets
        she there?
'Tis—'tis her father's—fixed upon the pair!   280

Then shrieking, she arose, and shrieking fell,
    With joy and sorrow, hope and fear, to see
Him whom she deemed a habitant where
        dwell
The ocean-buried, risen from death, to be
Perchance the death of one she loved too well:
    Dear as her father had been to Haidée,   286
It was a moment of that awful kind—
I have seen such—but must not call to mind.

Up Juan sprang to Haidée's bitter shriek,
    And caught her falling, and from off the
        wall   290
Snatched down his saber, in hot haste to wreak
    Vengeance on him who was the cause of all:
Then Lambro, who till now forebore to speak,
    Smiled scornfully, and said, "Within my
        call,
A thousand scimitars await the word;   295
Put up, young man, put up your silly sword."

And Haidée clung around him; "Juan, 'tis—
    'Tis Lambro—'tis my father! Kneel with
        me—
He will forgive us—yes—it must be—yes.
Oh! dearest father, in this agony   300
    Of pleasure and of pain—even while I kiss
    Thy garment's hem with transport, can it be
That doubt should mingle with my filial joy?
Deal with me as thou wilt, but spare this boy."

High and inscrutable the old man stood,   305
    Calm in his voice, and calm within his eye—
Not always signs with him of calmest mood:
He looked upon her, but gave no reply;
Then turned to Juan, in whose cheek the blood
    Oft came and went, as there resolved to die;
In arms, at least, he stood, in act to spring   311
    On the first foe whom Lambro's call might
        bring.

"Young man, your sword"; so Lambro once
        more said:
Juan replied, "Not while this arm is free."
The old man's cheek grew pale, but not with
        dread,   315

---

250. **shingles**, rocks. 276. **Lambro**, Haidée's father.

301. **kiss . . . hem.** To kiss the garments was a means of expressing veneration for the person who wore them. Cf. *Matthew*, 14:36 ff., which tells of the sick being healed by touching the hem of Christ's garment.

And drawing from his belt a pistol, he
Replied, "Your blood be then on your own head."
Then looked close at the flint, as if to see
'Twas fresh—for he had lately used the lock—
And next proceeded quietly to cock.   320

It has a strange quick jar upon the ear,
    That cocking of a pistol, when you know
A moment more will bring the sight to bear
    Upon your person, twelve yards off, or so;
A gentlemanly distance, not too near,   325
    If you have got a former friend for foe;
But after being fired at once or twice,
    The ear becomes more Irish, and less nice.

Lambro presented, and one instant more
    Had stopped this Canto, and Don Juan's breath,   330
When Haidée threw herself her boy before;
    Stern as her sire: "On me," she cried, "let death
Descend—the fault is mine; this fatal shore
    He found—but sought not. I have pledged my faith;
I love him—I will die with him: I knew   335
    Your nature's firmness—know your daughter's too."

A minute past, and she had been all tears,
    And tenderness, and infancy; but now
She stood as one who championed human fears—
    Pale, statue-like, and stern, she wooed the blow;   340
And tall beyond her sex, and their compeers,
    She drew up to her height, as if to show
A fairer mark; and with a fixed eye scanned
    Her father's face—but never stopped his hand.

He gazed on her, and she on him; 'twas strange   345
    How like they looked! the expression was the same;
Serenely savage, with a little change
    In the large dark eye's mutual-darted flame;
For she, too, was as one who could avenge,
    If cause should be—a lioness, though tame.

Her father's blood before her father's face   351
Boiled up, and proved her truly of his race.

I said they were alike, their features and
    Their stature, differing but in sex and years:
Even to the delicacy of their hand   355
    There was resemblance, such as true blood wears;
And now to see them, thus divided, stand
    In fixed ferocity, when joyous tears,
And sweet sensations, should have welcomed both,
Shows what the passions are in their full growth.   360

The father paused a moment, then withdrew
    His weapon, and replaced it; but stood still,
And looking on her, as to look her through,
    "Not *I*," he said, "have sought this stranger's ill;
Not *I* have made this desolation: few   365
    Would bear such outrage, and forbear to kill;
But I must do my duty—how thou hast
Done thine, the present vouches for the past.

"Let him disarm, or, by my father's head,
    His own shall roll before you like a ball!" 370
He raised his whistle as the word he said,
    And blew; another answered to the call,
And rushing in disorderly, though led,
    And armed from boot to turban, one and all,   374
Some twenty of his train came, rank on rank;
He gave the word, "Arrest or slay the Frank."

Then, with a sudden movement, he withdrew
    His daughter; while compressed within his clasp,
'Twixt her and Juan interposed the crew;   379
    In vain she struggled in her father's grasp—
His arms were like a serpent's coil: then flew
    Upon their prey, as darts an angry asp,
The file of pirates—save the foremost, who
Had fallen, with his right shoulder half cut through.

The second had his cheek laid open; but   385
    The third, a wary, cool old sworder, took
The blows upon his cutlass, and then put
    His own well in; so well, ere you could look,

---

328. **more Irish**, more accustomed to disagreeable sounds.

His man was floored, and helpless at his foot,
  With the blood running like a little brook 390
From two smart saber gashes, deep and red—
  One on the arm, the other on the head.

And then they bound him where he fell, and bore
  Juan from the apartment: with a sign
Old Lambro bade them take him to the shore,
  Where lay some ships which were to sail at nine. 396
They laid him in a boat, and plied the oar
  Until they reached some galliots, placed in line;
On board of one of these, and under hatches,
They stowed him, with strict orders to the watches. 400

The world is full of strange vicissitudes,
  And here was one exceedingly unpleasant:
A gentleman so rich in the world's goods,
  Handsome and young, enjoying all the present,
Just at the very time when he least broods 405
  On such a thing, is suddenly to sea sent,
Wounded and chained, so that he cannot move,
  And all because a lady fell in love.

Here I must leave him, for I grow pathetic,
  Moved by the Chinese nymph of tears, green tea! 410
Than whom Cassandra was not more prophetic;
  For if my pure libations exceed three,
I feel my heart become so sympathetic,
  That I must have recourse to black Bohea:
'Tis pity wine should be so deleterious, 415
For tea and coffee leave us much more serious,

Unless when qualified with thee, Cogniac!
  Sweet Naiad of the Phlegethontic rill!
Ah! why the liver wilt thou thus attack, 419
  And make, like other nymphs, thy lovers ill?

I would take refuge in weak punch, but *rack*
  (In each sense of the word), whene'er I fill
My mild and midnight beakers to the brim,
  Wakes me next morning with its synonym.

I leave Don Juan for the present, safe— 425
  Not sound, poor fellow, but severely wounded;
Yet could his corporal pangs amount to half
  Of those with which his Haidée's bosom bounded!
She was not one to weep, and rave, and chafe,
  And then give way, subdued because surrounded; 430
Her mother was a Moorish maid from Fez,
Where all is Eden, or a wilderness.

There the large olive rains its amber store
  In marble fonts; there grain, and flour, and fruit, 434
Gush from the earth until the land runs o'er;
  But there, too, many a poison-tree has root,
And midnight listens to the lion's roar,
  And long, long deserts scorch the camel's foot,
Or heaving whelm the helpless caravan;
And as the soil is, so the heart of man. 440

Afric is all the sun's, and as her earth
  Her human clay is kindled; full of power
For good or evil, burning from its birth,
  The Moorish blood partakes the planet's hour,
And like the soil beneath it will bring forth:
  Beauty and love were Haidée's mother's dower; 446
But her large dark eye showed deep Passion's force,
  Though sleeping like a lion near a source.

Her daughter, tempered with a milder ray,
  Like summer clouds all silvery, smooth, and fair, 450
Till slowly charged with thunder they display
  Terror to earth, and tempest to the air,
Had held till now her soft and milky way;
  But overwrought with passion and despair,

---

398. **galliots**, small, swift galleys moved by sails and oars. 411. **Cassandra**, in Greek legend a prophetess, whose predictions, by command of Apollo (whose advances she had repelled), though true were always discredited. 414. **Bohea**, a kind of black tea. 417. **Cogniac**, cognac, a kind of French brandy. 418. **Naiad**, a water nymph. **Phlegethontic rill**, like Phlegethon, the river of fire in Hades.

422. **each . . . word.** *Rack* means both punch and disorder. 424. **its synonym**, a headache. 431. **Fez**, an ancient province and city in Morocco, North Africa.

The fire burst forth from her Numidian
    veins,   455
Even as the Simoom sweeps the blasted plains.

The last sight which she saw was Juan's gore,
    And he himself o'ermastered and cut down;
His blood was running on the very floor   459
    Where late he trod, her beautiful, her own;
Thus much she viewed an instant and no
    more—
    Her struggles ceased with one convulsive
    groan;
On her sire's arm, which until now scarce held
    Her writhing, fell she like a cedar felled.

A vein had burst, and her sweet lips' pure
    dyes   465
    Were dabbled with the deep blood which
    ran o'er;
And her head drooped, as when the lily lies
    O'ercharged with rain: her summoned
    handmaids bore
Their lady to her couch with gushing eyes;
    Of herbs and cordials they produced their
    store,   470
But she defied all means they could employ,
    Like one life could not hold, nor death destroy.

Days lay she in that state unchanged, though
    chill—
    With nothing livid, still her lips were red;
She had no pulse, but death seemed absent
    still;   475
    No hideous sign proclaimed her surely
    dead;
Corruption came not in each mind to kill
    All hope; to look upon her sweet face bred
New thoughts of life, for it seemed full of
    soul—
She had so much, earth could not claim the
    whole.   480

The ruling passion, such as marble shows
    When exquisitely chiseled, still lay there,
But fixed as marble's unchanged aspect throws
    O'er the fair Venus, but forever fair;

O'er the Laocoön's all eternal throes,   485
    And ever-dying Gladiator's air,
Their energy like life forms all their fame,
    Yet looks not life, for they are still the same.

She woke at length, but not as sleepers wake,
    Rather the dead, for life seemed something
    new,   490
A strange sensation which she must partake
    Perforce, since whatsoever met her view
Struck not on memory, though a heavy ache
    Lay at her heart, whose earliest beat still true
Brought back the sense of pain without the
    cause,   495
For, for a while, the furies made a pause.

She looked on many a face with vacant eye,
    On many a token without knowing what;
She saw them watch her without asking why,
    And recked not who around her pillow sat;
Not speechless, though she spoke not; not a
    sigh   501
    Relieved her thoughts; dull silence and
    quick chat
Were tried in vain by those who served; she
    gave
No sign, save breath, of having left the grave.

Her handmaids tended, but she heeded not;
    Her father watched, she turned her eyes
    away;   506
She recognized no being, and no spot,
    However dear or cherished in their day;
They changed from room to room, but all forgot,
    Gentle, but without memory she lay;   510
At length those eyes, which they would fain
    be weaning
Back to old thoughts, waxed full of fearful
    meaning.

And then a slave bethought her of a harp;
    The harper came, and tuned his instrument;
At the first notes, irregular and sharp,   515
    On him her flashing eyes a moment bent,
Then to the wall she turned as if to warp

---

455. **Numidian,** of Numidia, an ancient country of North Africa. 456. **Simoom,** or *simoon,* a hot dry wind of the desert. 464. **fell . . . felled.** Cf. *Zechariah,* 11:2—"Howl, fir tree; for the cedar is fallen." 484. **Venus,** goddess of love. 485. **Laocoön,** an antique group in marble representing the death of the Trojan priest Laocoön and his two sons being crushed by huge serpents. 486. **Gladiator.** See *Childe Harold's Pilgrimage,* IV, 1252 and note, p. 221. 513. **And . . . harp.** See Browning's *Saul* and note, p. 672.

Her thoughts from sorrow through her
    heart re-sent;
And he began a long low island-song
Of ancient days, ere tyranny grew strong. 520

Anon her thin wan fingers beat the wall
    In time to his old tune; he changed the
      theme,
And sung of love; the fierce name struck
    through all
Her recollection; on her flashed the dream
Of what she was, and is, if ye could call 525
    To be so being; in a gushing stream
The tears rushed forth from her o'erclouded
    brain,
Like mountain mists at length dissolved in
    rain.

Short solace, vain relief!—thought came too
    quick,
    And whirled her brain to madness; she
      arose 530
As one who ne'er had dwelt among the sick,
And flew at all she met, as on her foes;
But no one ever heard her speak or shriek,
    Although her paroxysm drew towards its
      close;—
Hers was a frenzy which disdained to rave,
Even when they smote her, in the hope to
    save. 536

Yet she betrayed at times a gleam of sense;
    Nothing could make her meet her father's
      face,
Though on all other things with looks intense
    She gazed, but none she ever could retrace;
Food she refused, and raiment; no pretense 541
    Availed for either; neither change of place,
Nor time, nor skill, nor remedy, could give her
    Senses to sleep—the power seemed gone for-
      ever.

Twelve days and nights she withered thus; at
    last, 545
    Without a groan, or sigh, or glance, to
      show
A parting pang, the spirit from her passed:
    And they who watched her nearest could
      not know
The very instant, till the change that cast
    Her sweet face into shadow, dull and slow,
Glazed o'er her eyes—the beautiful, the
    black— 551
Oh! to possess such luster—and then lack!

She died, but not alone, she held within
    A second principle of life, which might
Have dawned a fair and sinless child of sin;
    But closed its little being without light, 556
And went down to the grave unborn, wherein
    Blossom and bough lie withered with one
      blight;
In vain the dews of Heaven descend above 559
The bleeding flower and blasted fruit of love.

Thus lived—thus died she; never more on her
    Shall sorrow light, or shame. She was not
      made
Through years or moons the inner weight to
    bear,
    Which colder hearts endure till they are laid
By age in earth: her days and pleasures were
    Brief, but delightful—such as had not stayed
Long with her destiny; but she sleeps well 567
By the sea-shore, whereon she loved to dwell.

That isle is now all desolate and bare,
    Its dwellings down, its tenants passed away;
None but her own and father's grave is
    there, 571
    And nothing outward tells of human clay;
Ye could not know where lies a thing so fair,
    No stone is there to show, no tongue to say,
What was; no dirge, except the hollow sea's,
Mourns o'er the beauty of the Cyclades. 576

But many a Greek maid in a loving song
    Sighs o'er her name; and many an islander
With her sire's story makes the night less long;
    Valor was his, and beauty dwelt with her;
If she loved rashly, her life paid for wrong—
    A heavy price must all pay who thus err, 582
In some shape; let none think to fly the danger,
For soon or late Love is his own avenger.

    *   *   *   *   *

(1819-20; 1821)

567. **she sleeps well.** Cf. *Macbeth*, III, ii, 23—"After life's fitful fever he sleeps well." 576. **Cyclades,** a group of islands in the Aegean Sea, east of Greece. 584. The poem is unfinished. Juan recovers, however, and is sold as a slave to the Sultana of Turkey. After numerous startling experiences he finally escapes.

When a Man Hath No Freedom

Byron sent this poem to Moore in November, 1820, as a memorial chant for anyone who might be killed fighting for the cause of the Italian Revolution.

When a man hath no freedom to fight for at home,
    Let him combat for that of his neighbors;
Let him think of the glories of Greece and of Rome,
    And get knocked on the head for his labors.

To do good to mankind is the chivalrous plan,
    And is always as nobly requited;   6
Then battle for freedom wherever you can,
    And, if not shot or hanged, you'll get knighted.   *(1820; 1824)*

The World Is a Bundle of Hay

The world is a bundle of hay,
    Mankind are the asses who pull;
Each tugs it a different way,
    And the greatest of all is John Bull.
        (1820; 1830)

Who Killed John Keats?

These verses are in reference to the current belief that the death of Keats had been caused by a vitriolic attack on his *Endymion*, published in *The Quarterly Review*, April, 1818. See p. 262. In regard to these hostile attacks, Keats wrote his brother and his sister (Oct., 1818): "This is a mere matter of the moment —I think I shall be among the English poets after my death." Henry Hart Milman, Robert Southey (p. 296), and John Barrow were contemporary writers. Milman was also a clergyman.

Who killed John Keats?
    "I," says the Quarterly,
        So savage and Tartarly;
    " 'Twas one of my feats."

Who shot the arrow?   5
    "The poet-priest Milman
        (So ready to kill man),
    Or Southey, or Barrow."   *(1821; 1830)*

Stanzas Written on the Road Between Florence and Pisa

Oh, talk not to me of a name great in story;
The days of our youth are the days of our glory;
And the myrtle and ivy of sweet two-and-twenty
Are worth all your laurels, though ever so plenty.

What are garlands and crowns to the brow that is wrinkled?   5
'Tis but as a dead-flower with May-dew besprinkled.
Then away with all such from the head that is hoary!
What care I for the wreaths that can *only* give glory!

Oh Fame!—if I e'er took delight in thy praises,
'Twas less for the sake of thy high-sounding phrases,   10
Than to see the bright eyes of the dear one discover,
She thought that I was not unworthy to love her.

There chiefly I sought thee, *there* only I found thee;
Her glance was the best of the rays that surround thee;
When it sparkled o'er aught that was bright in my story,   15
I knew it was love, and I felt it was glory.
        (1821; 1830)

On This Day I Complete My Thirty-Sixth Year

'Tis time this heart should be unmoved,
    Since others it hath ceased to move;
Yet, though I cannot be beloved,
    Still let me love!

The World . . . Hay. 4. **John Bull**, a personification of the typical Englishman.

Stanzas Written . . . Pisa. 3. **myrtle and ivy.** The myrtle was a symbol of love; ivy, of constancy in friendship.

My days are in the yellow leaf;
    The flowers and fruits of love are gone;
The worm, the canker, and the grief
        Are mine alone!

The fire that on my bosom preys
    Is lone as some volcanic isle;
No torch is kindled at its blaze—
        A funeral pile.

The hope, the fear, the jealous care,
    The exalted portion of the pain
And power of love, I cannot share,
        But wear the chain.

But 't is not *thus*—and 't is not *here*—
    Such thoughts should shake my soul, nor *now*,
Where glory decks the hero's bier,
        Or binds his brow.

The sword, the banner, and the field,
    Glory and Greece, around me see!

The Spartan, borne upon his shield,
        Was not more free.

Awake! (not Greece—she *is* awake!)
    Awake, my spirit! Think through *whom*
Thy life-blood tracks its parent lake,
        And then strike home!

Tread those reviving passions down,
    Unworthy manhood!—unto thee
Indifferent should the smile or frown
        Of beauty be.

If thou regrett'st thy youth, *why live?*
    The land of honorable death
Is here—up to the field, and give
        Away thy breath!

Seek out—less often sought than found—
    A soldier's grave, for thee the best;
Then look around, and choose thy ground,
        And take thy rest.   (1824)

5. **My . . . leaf**, from *Macbeth*, V, iii, 22—"my way of life/ Is fall'n into the sear, the yellow leaf." 23. **Spartan . . . shield.** In ancient Sparta it was the custom to carry home a fallen warrior on his shield. 27. **life-blood . . . lake.** Byron's mother was a descendant of James I; his father traced his ancestry to heroes of the days of William the Conqueror. 38. **A soldier's grave.** Byron lost his life on a military expedition undertaken for the independence of Greece.

Percy Bysshe Shelley
1792-1822

    Shelley was born on August 4, 1792, in the little village of Horsham, Sussex, where his father was a country squire of average means, but with expectations of a considerable income. From the beginning Shelley showed three strong traits of temperament that were to remain with him throughout his life and were to determine in great measure his achievement. He exhibited an extreme susceptibility to emotions and feelings both physical and spiritual—if he hurt himself, he would become hysterical; if he suffered any kind of mental anguish, his grief would be paroxysmal. He showed almost too lively an imagination; his soaring but uncertain fancy blotted out the essential importance of facts and blunted his common sense. Finally, the child Shelley—like the man Shelley later—was totally unable to accept any sign of authority, parental, scholastic, or religious.
    With these moral peculiarities, which were fraught with disaster not only to Shelley himself but to those about him, the boy went to Eton at the age of twelve. A shy, sensitive lad, who at the sight of beauty might, as he said, "shriek and clasp my hands with ecstasy," would naturally be fair game for the young barbarians of a thoroughly English school like Eton, particularly as the then headmaster, Dr. Goodall, was not a very good disciplinarian. Shelley was hectored, bullied, and subjected to hazing, or as it was called, "fagging," which made every younger boy the virtual slave

of an older boy. This treatment Shelley received with violent protest; his behavior at Eton was so distinctly non-conformist in so many ways that he became known as "Mad Shelley" and later as "Shelley the Atheist."

Eventually Shelley went up to Oxford, had as particular friend Thomas Jefferson Hogg, a later biographer of the poet, and plunged into the study of poetry, philosophy, and the classics. But Hogg and he got into trouble with the college authorities over a little pamphlet entitled *The Necessity of Atheism,* and the pair were expelled in March, 1811, after Shelley had been at Oxford but a bare five months. The whole incident was quite in keeping with Shelley's character. He refused to answer any questions put to him by the authorities, and was probably dismissed as much for this breach of university discipline as for the moral obliquity of his ideas. He went home to an aggrieved father and met there a friend of his sister's, Harriet Westbrook, daughter of a moderately successful retired hotel-keeper. His missionary zeal for atheism had evidently remained with him, for he tried to convert Harriet. She fell desperately in love with him and finally was able to persuade him to elope with her and free her from the tyranny, as he put it, of her father. A marriage ceremony was actually performed in Edinburgh, which, considering Shelley's publicly stated views on the tyranny of the institution of marriage—an idea which he possessed in common with William Godwin—was quite a concession on Shelley's part. The marriage took place in 1811.

The young couple then led a kind of wandering, semi-missionary existence for the next year and a half; they were supported by their two fathers. They covered most of the British Isles, including a trip to Ireland to convert the good Irish Catholics to atheism. Nothing will show better the quixotic impracticality of Shelley than this incident. They returned to London early in 1813, where Shelley's first child was born and where Shelley's first poem of any importance, *Queen Mab,* was produced. Extremely revolutionary toward church and state, it had to be printed privately. Shelley was not happy with Harriet, who was attractive but superficial; he was also bothered greatly by the constant presence of his sister-in-law, who hovered about with superfluous advice.

It happened that Shelley had begun a correspondence with William Godwin, the English disciple of Rousseau (p. 3). They eventually met in London, and Shelley fell in love immediately with Godwin's daughter Mary. To a man of Shelley's childlike character, the procedure to be followed was simple. He left Harriet and eloped (1814) to the Continent with Mary Godwin, not without much complaint from Godwin, who, in spite of his ideas about natural law and free love, was greatly incensed. Shelley's alliance with Mary Godwin marks the true beginning of his poetic development, although the first-fruit of the new Shelley, *Alastor,* did not appear until 1816. The truant couple were forgiven, after a fashion. In 1816 they took another trip to Switzerland, in company with Claire Clairmont, Mary's step-sister, whose real purpose in accompanying them was to see Byron, for whom she had formed an attachment in London. The Clairmont episode is of no importance except to illustrate the naïve unconventionality of Shelley, who became innocently a kind of go-between. The return to London in the fall of 1816 brought tragedy to Shelley. Harriet, who had found consolation of a sort elsewhere, committed suicide in November; and although the way was thus left open for Shelley and Mary to marry, a court order in March, 1817, took from Shelley his two children by Harriet and gave them into the custody of their grandfather. Crushed by the laws of England which he had flouted both in theory and in practice, Shelley, like Byron before him, left England in March, 1818, for Italy, never to return.

The sojourn of the Shelleys in Italy, where they moved about from city to city, is most important in the intellectual and artistic life of the poet. For Shelley developed amazingly on Italian soil. Virtually all his remarkable poetic output appeared between 1818 and his death in 1822. In Italy he developed a friendship for Byron, whom he admired, and platonic attachments to Emilia Viviani at Pisa and to Mrs. Williams ("Jane") at Leghorn. These associations are important chiefly for their effect upon Shelley's poetry. The death of Shelley on July 8, 1822, was extremely typical. He, a poor sailor and no swimmer at all, went out with his friend Williams in a small boat off the west coast of Italy, and the two were drowned in a storm. There was a rumor that the boat was run down by bandits. In any case, Shelley's body was washed ashore, cremated, and buried in the Protestant cemetery at Rome, under the not inappropriate inscription *Cor Cordium!* ("Heart of Hearts!")

Three qualities permeate Shelley's poetry. The first of these is revolutionism. Shelley had an iconoclastic spirit and a martyr's soul—unquestionably there was in him more than a spark of the fanatic and a great deal of the purely visionary. *Queen Mab* (1813) and *The Revolt of Islam* (1818) preach revolution; the first a violent, the second a bloodless one. *Prometheus Unbound* (1819) is a sequel to the *Prometheus Bound* of Aeschylus; it tells of Prometheus (man) chained to the rock by Zeus (tyranny) and freed by Asia (nature and love) and Demogorgon (the spirit of necessity). *Hellas* is an elaborate allegory of revolution written in the form of a beautiful lyrical poetic drama, inspired by the Greek struggle for independence—the same struggle that cost Byron his life in 1824.

But Shelley's brand of revolutionism would lead to mere anarchy, as even he himself would admit, were it not for another quality, idealism. Shelley is the great lyric poet of the beautiful and the sublime, of the ideals—eventually derived from Plato—of absolute goodness and truth. This idealism is at once Shelley's source of greatness and his most obvious defect. Too often it leads to vagueness, unreality, indistinct imagery, a cloudiness and mistiness, and an excess of the sensuous and the sentimental. So Matthew Arnold could apply to Shelley his noted phrase "a beautiful and ineffectual angel." The vagueness and its attendant evils can be seen in *Alastor* (1815), the epic of a poet's mind, and in *The Witch of Atlas* (1824), a long poem on the powers of the poet's fancy. But one need look only at the multitude of exquisite short lyrics, at the *Hymn to Intellectual Beauty,* at the choruses and lyrics from *Prometheus Unbound,* at *The Sensitive Plant,* and the distinguished *Adonais* (1821) (p. 262) the elegy on John Keats, to see how this idealism, clothed in beauty and spirituality and star-dust, has been in its way unapproached in English literature.

Finally there is in Shelley's poetry the undeniable quality of sheer music. Only Milton, Tennyson, and Swinburne have had such a consummate command of rhythm, harmony, and clear-flowing melody. Again, the short lyrics are the best examples that could be named; *The Indian Serenade* (p. 256), *To Night* (p. 261), *To—* (p. 272); the songs from the plays, and portions of his more ambitious poems are excellent alike in their sensuous imagery and in their musical effect.

Shelley's own time passed a severe moral condemnation on him even though everyone who knew him well spoke of his character as noble; it was impossible to think of him and the earthy Byron in the same way. And yet to the moralist, Shelley was almost as objectionable as Byron, although his spirituality might be conceded. He was generous and kindly and naïve; one cannot call him, in all fairness, immoral, but simply unmoral. And still he was constructive enough in his criticism;

the atheist Shelley could, in *Prometheus Unbound,* preach a Gospel of Love far closer to the teachings of Christ than the utterances of many devotional writers. None the less, he was essentially pagan, and a nature-worshiping pagan at that; for nature, even in its cruel forms, was to him a promise of immortality and beauty. The *Ode to the West Wind* (p. 255) and *Adonais* (p. 262) are sufficient illustration for the point. And physical nature, as seen in *To a Skylark* or the *Stanzas Written in Dejection* (pp. 258 and 253), was merely symbolic of something beyond the physical, some ineffable abstraction which the eye and the ear of man have never perceived, but which, he assures us, in spite of his moments of doubt and despair, most certainly exists.

Of his prose (p. 315) little needs to be said. It is clear, direct, and has an exceedingly finished style. It is usually devoted to a defense of his revolutionary ideas. His powerful drama *The Cenci* (1819), eminently actable except for subject-matter, is a tragedy of Renaissance Italy, founded on blood, incest, and horror, but with a poignant simplicity utterly unlike Shelley's usual cloud-like atmosphere. It has been called "the last great Elizabethan drama." It is, however, virtually isolated among Shelley's work. His satirical verse, like *Peter Bell the Third,* is negligible, for he lacked the requisite sense of humor. But his position as a lyric poet is secure; he is purely romantic, a great visionary, and a great singer of visions both large and small.

Mutability

We are as clouds that veil the midnight moon;
 How restlessly they speed, and gleam, and quiver,
Streaking the darkness radiantly!—yet soon
 Night closes round, and they are lost forever:

Or like forgotten lyres, whose dissonant strings   5
 Give various response to each varying blast,
To whose frail frame no second motion brings
 One mood or modulation like the last.

We rest—a dream has power to poison sleep;
 We rise—one wandering thought pollutes the day;   10
We feel, conceive or reason, laugh or weep;
 Embrace fond woe, or cast our cares away:

It is the same!—For, be it joy or sorrow,
 The path of its departure still is free:
Man's yesterday may ne'er be like his morrow;   15
 Naught may endure but Mutability.

(1815; 1816)

Hymn to Intellectual Beauty

Shelley based this poem upon the Platonic idea of Eternal Beauty—in brief, a conception of absolute and perfect beauty, "simple, pure, uncontaminated with the intermixture of human flesh and colors, and all other idle and unreal shapes attendant upon mortality." This absolute beauty, which is of course immortal, pervades everything, although invisible; it can be perceived by him who has dedicated himself to the contemplation of the beautiful, the good, and the true, for "to him alone is accorded the prerogative of bringing forth, not images and shadows of virtue, for he is in contact not with a shadow, but reality, with virtue itself, in the production and nourishment of which he becomes dear to the gods, and, if such a privilege is conceded to any human being, himself immortal." The quotations are from Shelley's translation of Plato's *Symposium.* It may be added that Shelley takes the word "intellectual" in the general sense of "spiritual"; "intellectual beauty," which is immortal, must be distinguished from mere "physical beauty," the kind of beauty that Keats had in mind in his *Ode on Melancholy* (l. 21, p. 281), which is mortal.

The awful shadow of some unseen Power
 Floats though unseen among us—visiting
 This various world with as inconstant wing

As summer winds that creep from flower to
    flower—
Like moonbeams that behind some piny
    mountain shower,   5
    It visits with inconstant glance
    Each human heart and countenance;
Like hues and harmonies of evening—
    Like clouds in starlight widely spread—
    Like memory of music fled—   10
    Like aught that for its grace may be
Dear, and yet dearer for its mystery.

Spirit of Beauty, that dost consecrate
    With thine own hues all thou dost shine
        upon
    Of human thought or form—where art
        thou gone?   15
Why dost thou pass away and leave our
    state,
This dim vast vale of tears, vacant and des-
    olate?
    Ask why the sunlight not forever
    Weaves rainbows o'er yon mountain-
        river,
Why aught should fail and fade that once is
    shown,   20
    Why fear and dream and death and birth
    Cast on the daylight of this earth
    Such gloom—why man has such a scope
For love and hate, despondency and hope?

No voice from some sublimer world hath
    ever   25
    To sage or poet these responses given—
    Therefore the names of Demon, Ghost, and
        Heaven,
Remain the records of their vain endeavor,
Frail spells—whose uttered charm might not
    avail to sever,
    From all we hear and all we see,   30
    Doubt, chance, and mutability.
Thy light alone—like mist o'er mountains
    driven,
    Or music by the night-wind sent
    Through strings of some still instrument,
    Or moonlight on a midnight stream,   35
Gives grace and truth to life's unquiet dream.

<small>26. **these responses,** responses to these questions. 27. **Demon,** a supernatural being of Greek mythology, conceived as holding a position between gods and men.</small>

Love, Hope, and Self-Esteem, like clouds de-
    part
    And come, for some uncertain moments
    lent.
    Man were immortal, and omnipotent,
Didst thou, unknown and awful as thou art,   40
Keep with thy glorious train firm state within
    his heart.
    Thou messenger of sympathies,
    That wax and wane in lovers' eyes—
Thou—that to human thought art nourish-
    ment,
    Like darkness to a dying flame!   45
    Depart not as thy shadow came,
    Depart not—lest the grave should be,
Like life and fear, a dark reality.

While yet a boy I sought for ghosts, and sped
    Through many a listening chamber, cave
        and ruin,   50
    And starlight wood, with fearful steps pur-
        suing
Hopes of high talk with the departed dead.
I called on poisonous names with which our
    youth is fed;
    I was not heard—I saw them not—
    When musing deeply on the lot   55
Of life, at that sweet time when winds are
    wooing
    All vital things that wake to bring
    News of birds and blossoming—
    Sudden, thy shadow fell on me;
I shrieked, and clasped my hands in ecstasy!   60

I vowed that I would dedicate my powers
    To thee and thine—have I not kept the
        vow?
    With beating heart and streaming eyes,
        even now
I called the phantoms of a thousand hours
Each from his voiceless grave: they have in
    visioned bowers   65
    Of studious zeal or love's delight
    Outwatched with me the envious night—
They know that never joy illumed my brow
    Unlinked with hope that thou wouldst
    free
This world from its dark slavery,   70
    That thou—O awful Loveliness,

Wouldst give whate'er these words cannot
    express.

The day becomes more solemn and serene
    When noon is past—there is a harmony
    In autumn, and a luster in its sky,   75
Which through the summer is not heard or
    seen,
As if it could not be, as if it had not been!
    Thus let thy power, which like the truth
    Of nature on my passive youth
Descended, to my onward life supply   80
    Its calm—to one who worships thee,
    And every form containing thee,
    Whom, Spirit fair, thy spells did bind
To fear himself, and love all human kind.

              (*1816;* 1817)

Ozymandias

According to the statement of the Greek historian Diodorus Siculus (first century B.C.), the statue of Ozymandias was reputed to be the largest in Egypt and to bear the following inscription: "I am Ozymandias, the King of Kings; if any man wishes to know what I am and where I am buried, let him surpass me in some of my achievements."

I met a traveler from an antique land
Who said: "Two vast and trunkless legs of
    stone
Stand in the desert. Near them, on the sand,
Half sunk, a shattered visage lies, whose
    frown,
And wrinkled lip, and sneer of cold command,   5
Tell that its sculptor well those passions read
Which yet survive, stamped on these lifeless
    things,
The hand that mocked them, and the heart
    that fed:
And on the pedestal these words appear:
'My name is Ozymandias, king of kings: 10
Look on my works, ye Mighty, and despair!'
Nothing beside remains. Round the decay
Of that colossal wreck, boundless and bare
The lone and level sands stretch far away."

              (*1817;* 1818)

8. **hand . . . them,** hand of the sculptor who imitated or reproduced them. **heart,** of Ozymandias, who nursed those passions.

Stanzas

WRITTEN IN DEJECTION, NEAR NAPLES

In the first year of Shelley's stay in Italy (1818), he suffered from ill-health; he was convinced that he was a victim of tuberculosis. Singularly prophetic are the final lines of the fourth stanza.

The sun is warm, the sky is clear,
    The waves are dancing fast and bright,
Blue isles and snowy mountains wear
    The purple noon's transparent might,
    The breath of the moist earth is light,   5
Around its unexpanded buds;
    Like many a voice of one delight,
The winds, the birds, the ocean floods,
The City's voice itself, is soft like Solitude's.

I see the Deep's untrampled floor   10
    With green and purple seaweeds strown;
I see the waves upon the shore,
    Like light dissolved in star-showers,
        thrown:
I sit upon the sands alone—
The lightning of the noontide ocean   15
    Is flashing round me, and a tone
Arises from its measured motion,
How sweet! did any heart now share in my
    emotion.

Alas! I have nor hope nor health,
    Nor peace within nor calm around,   20
Nor that content surpassing wealth
    The sage in meditation found,
    And walked with inward glory
        crowned—
Nor fame, nor power, nor love, nor leisure.
    Others I see whom these surround—   25
Smiling they live, and call life pleasure;—
To me that cup has been dealt in another
    measure.

Yet now despair itself is mild,
    Even as the winds and waters are;
I could lie down like a tired child,   30

22. **sage . . . found.** Numerous poets and philosophers have found consolation in solitude, the quest of which was one of the distinguishing marks of the romantic spirit. Cf. Cowper's *Task,* II, 1–7 (p. 78); Byron's *Childe Harold's Pilgrimage,* III, 631 ff. (p. 216) and IV, 1585 ff. (p. 222); and Landor's *I Know Not Whether I Am Proud* (p. 313).

And weep away the life of care
Which I have borne and yet must bear,
Till death like sleep might steal on me,
And I might feel in the warm air
My cheek grow cold, and hear the sea 35
Breathe o'er my dying brain its last monotony.

Some might lament that I were cold,
　As I, when this sweet day is gone,
Which my lost heart, too soon grown old,
　Insults with this untimely moan; 40
They might lament—for I am one
Whom men love not—and yet regret,
Unlike this day, which, when the sun
Shall on its stainless glory set,
Will linger, though enjoyed, like joy in
　memory yet. 45

(*1818;* 1824)

Song to the Men of England

This and the next poem were inspired by Shelley's interest in the Manchester Massacre, an attack by soldiers upon a crowd assembled in St. Peter's Field at Manchester, August 16, 1819, to petition Parliament for a redress of grievances regarding taxation and representation.

Men of England, wherefore plow
For the lords who lay ye low?
Wherefore weave with toil and care
The rich robes your tyrants wear?

Wherefore feed, and clothe, and save, 5
From the cradle to the grave,
Those ungrateful drones who would
Drain your sweat—nay, drink your blood?

Wherefore, bees of England, forge
Many a weapon, chain, and scourge, 10
That these stingless drones may spoil
The forced produce of your toil?

Have ye leisure, comfort, calm,
Shelter, food, love's gentle balm?
Or what is it ye buy so dear 15
With your pain and with your fear?

The seed ye sow, another reaps;
The wealth ye find, another keeps;
The robes ye weave, another wears;
The arms ye forge, another bears. 20

Sow seed—but let no tyrant reap;
Find wealth—let no impostor heap;
Weave robes—let not the idle wear;
Forge arms—in your defense to bear.

Shrink to your cellars, holes, and cells; 25
In halls ye deck another dwells.
Why shake the chains ye wrought? Ye see
The steel ye tempered glance on ye.

With plow and spade, and hoe and loom,
Trace your grave, and build your tomb, 30
And weave your winding-sheet, till fair
England be your sepulcher. (*1819;* 1839)

England in 1819

An old, mad, blind, despised, and dying king—
Princes, the dregs of their dull race, who flow
Through public scorn—mud from a muddy spring—
Rulers who neither see, nor feel, nor know,
But leech-like to their fainting country cling, 5
Till they drop, blind in blood, without a blow—
A people starved and stabbed in the untilled field—
An army, which liberticide and prey
Makes as a two-edged sword to all who wield—
Golden and sanguine laws which tempt and slay; 10
Religion, Christless, Godless—a book sealed;
A Senate—Time's worst statute unrepealed—
Are graves, from which a glorious Phantom may
Burst, to illumine our tempestuous day.

(*1819;* 1839)

1. **king**, George III, King of England (1760-1820). He became hopelessly insane in 1810. 12. **Time's . . . unrepealed**, the law that restricted the civil liberties of Roman Catholics; it was repealed in 1829. 13. **Phantom**, liberty.

Ode to the West Wind

This fine ode illustrates the myth-making faculty of Shelley and his power of identifying himself with the object described. The stanza form is adapted from the Italian *terza rima*.

1

O wild West Wind, thou breath of Autumn's being,
Thou, from whose unseen presence the leaves dead
Are driven, like ghosts from an enchanter fleeing,

Yellow, and black, and pale, and hectic red,
Pestilence-stricken multitudes: O thou,　5
Who chariotest to their dark wintry bed

The wingéd seeds, where they lie cold and low,
Each like a corpse within its grave, until
Thine azure sister of the Spring shall blow

Her clarion o'er the dreaming earth, and fill　10
(Driving sweet buds like flocks to feed in air)
With living hues and odors plain and hill:

Wild Spirit, which art moving everywhere;
Destroyer and preserver; hear, oh, hear!

2

Thou on whose stream, mid the steep sky's commotion,　15
Loose clouds like earth's decaying leaves are shed,
Shook from the tangled boughs of Heaven and Ocean,

Angels of rain and lightning: there are spread
On the blue surface of thine aëry surge,
Like the bright hair uplifted from the head　20

Of some fierce Maenad, even from the dim verge
Of the horizon to the zenith's height,
The locks of the approaching storm. Thou dirge

Of the dying year, to which this closing night
Will be the dome of a vast sepulcher,　25
Vaulted with all thy congregated might

Of vapors, from whose solid atmosphere
Black rain, and fire, and hail will burst: oh, hear!

3

Thou who didst waken from his summer dreams
The blue Mediterranean, where he lay,　30
Lulled by the coil of his crystalline streams,

Beside a pumice isle in Baiae's bay,
And saw in sleep old palaces and towers
Quivering within the wave's intenser day,

All overgrown with azure moss and flowers　35
So sweet, the sense faints picturing them! Thou
For whose path the Atlantic's level powers

Cleave themselves into chasms, while far below
The sea-blooms and the oozy woods which wear
The sapless foliage of the ocean, know　40

Thy voice, and suddenly grow gray with fear,
And tremble and despoil themselves: oh, hear!

4

If I were a dead leaf thou mightest bear,
If I were a swift cloud to fly with thee;
A wave to pant beneath thy power, and share

---

9. **sister of the Spring,** the south wind. 21. **Maenad,** a priestess or female votary of Bacchus, god of wine. 24. **closing night,** night sky closing down over the earth. 32. **pumice,** a light, porous volcanic substance. **Baiae,** a small seaport in Italy near Naples. 39-42. **sea-blooms . . . hear.** In a note on these lines Shelley states that "the vegetation at the bottom of the sea, of rivers, and of lakes, sympathizes with that of the land in the change of seasons, and is consequently influenced by the winds which announce it."

The impulse of thy strength, only less free 46
Than thou, O uncontrollable! If even
I were as in my boyhood, and could be

The comrade of thy wanderings over Heaven,
As then, when to outstrip thy skyey speed 50
Scarce seemed a vision; I would ne'er have
    striven

As thus with thee in prayer in my sore need.
Oh, lift me as a wave, a leaf, a cloud!
I fall upon the thorns of life! I bleed!

A heavy weight of hours has chained and
    bowed 55
One too like thee: tameless, and swift, and
    proud.

Make me thy lyre, even as the forest is:
What if my leaves are falling like its own!
The tumult of thy mighty harmonies

Will take from both a deep, autumnal tone, 60
Sweet though in sadness. Be thou, Spirit
    fierce,
My spirit! Be thou me, impetuous one!

Drive my dead thoughts over the universe
Like withered leaves to quicken a new birth!
And, by the incantation of this verse, 65

Scatter, as from an unextinguished hearth
Ashes and sparks, my words among mankind!
Be through my lips to unawakened earth

The trumpet of a prophecy! O Wind,
If Winter comes, can Spring be far behind? 70
            (*1819;* 1820)

The Indian Serenade

I arise from dreams of Thee
    In the first sweet sleep of night,
When the winds are breathing low
    And the stars are shining bright:
I arise from dreams of thee, 5
    And a spirit in my feet

Hath led me—who knows how?
    To thy chamber-window, Sweet!

The wandering airs, they faint
    On the dark, the silent stream— 10
The champak odors fail
    Like sweet thoughts in a dream;
The nightingale's complaint,
    It dies upon her heart,
As I must die on thine, 15
    O beloved as thou art!

Oh, lift me from the grass!
    I die, I faint, I fail!
Let thy love in kisses rain
    On my lips and eyelids pale. 20
My cheek is cold and white, alas!
    My heart beats loud and fast;
Oh! press it close to thine again,
    Where it will break at last.
            (*1819;* 1822)

Songs from *Prometheus Unbound*

The theme of Shelley's lyrical drama, *Prometheus Unbound,* has already been stated (p. 250). In discussing this work, John Addington Symonds remarked: "A genuine liking for *Prometheus Unbound* may be reckoned the touchstone of a man's capacity for understanding lyric poetry. The world in which the action [of the play] is supposed to move, rings with spirit voices; and what these spirits sing is melody more purged of mortal dross than any other poet's ear has caught, while listening to his own heart's song, or to the rhythms of this world. There are hymns in *Prometheus,* which seem to realize the miracle of making words, detached from meaning, the substance of a new ethereal music; and yet although their verbal harmony is such, they are never devoid of definite significance for those who understand."

ASIA

My soul is an enchanted boat,
    Which, like a sleeping swan, doth float
Upon the silver waves of thy sweet singing;
    And thine doth like an angel sit
    Beside a helm conducting it, 5
Whilst all the winds with melody are ringing.

11. **champak**, an Indian tree of the magnolia family.

It seems to float ever, forever,
  Upon that many-winding river,
  Between mountains, woods, abysses,
  A paradise of wildernesses! 10
Till, like one in slumber bound,
Borne to the ocean, I float down, around,
Into a sea profound, of ever-spreading sound:

  Meanwhile thy spirit lifts its pinions
  In music's most serene dominions; 15
  Catching the winds that fan that happy
      heaven.
  And we sail on, away, afar,
  Without a course, without a star,
But, by the instinct of sweet music driven;
  Till through Elysian garden islets 20
  By thee, most beautiful of pilots,
  Where never mortal pinnace glided,
  The boat of my desire is guided:
Realms where the air we breathe is love,
Which in the winds and on the waves doth
    move, 25
Harmonizing this earth with what we feel
    above.

  We have passed Age's icy caves,
  And Manhood's dark and tossing waves,
And Youth's smooth ocean, smiling to betray:
  Beyond the glassy gulfs we flee 30
  Of shadow-peopled Infancy,
Through Death and Birth, to a diviner day;
  A paradise of vaulted bowers,
  Lit by downward-gazing flowers,
  And watery paths that wind between 35
  Wildernesses calm and green,
Peopled by shapes too bright to see,
And rest, having beheld; somewhat like thee;
Which walk upon the sea, and chant melodi-
    ously!

DEMOGORGON

This is the day, which down the void abysm
At the Earth-born's spell yawns for Heaven's
    despotism,
  And Conquest is dragged captive through
      the deep:

20. **Elysian,** of or pertaining to Elysium, the abode of the blessed after death.
    Demogorgon (cf. p. 250). 2. **Earth-born's spell,** the spell of Prometheus, one of the Titans.

Love, from its awful throne of patient power
In the wise heart, from the last giddy hour 5
  Of dead endurance, from the slippery, steep,
And narrow verge of crag-like agony, springs
And folds over the world its healing wings.

Gentleness, Virtue, Wisdom, and Endurance,
These are the seals of that most firm assurance
  Which bars the pit over Destruction's
      strength; 11
And if, with infirm hand, Eternity,
Mother of many acts and hours, should free
  The serpent that would clasp her with his
      length;
These are the spells by which to reassume 15
An empire o'er the disentangled doom.

To suffer woes which Hope thinks infinite;
To forgive wrongs darker than death or night;
  To defy Power, which seems omnipotent;
To love, and bear; to hope till Hope creates 20
From its own wreck the thing it contemplates;
  Neither to change, nor falter, nor repent;
This, like thy glory, Titan, is to be
Good, great and joyous, beautiful and free;
This is alone Life, Joy, Empire, and Victory.
                                (1818-19; 1820)

The Cloud

I bring fresh showers for the thirsting flowers,
  From the seas and the streams;
I bear light shade for the leaves when laid
  In their noonday dreams.
From my wings are shaken the dews that
    waken 5
  The sweet buds every one,
When rocked to rest on their mother's breast,
  As she dances about the sun.
I wield the flail of the lashing hail,
  And whiten the green plains under, 10
And then again I dissolve it in rain,
  And laugh as I pass in thunder.

I sift the snow on the mountains below,
  And their great pines groan aghast;
And all the night 'tis my pillow white, 15
  While I sleep in the arms of the blast.
Sublime on the towers of my skyey bowers,

Lightning my pilot sits;
In a cavern under is fettered the thunder,
   It struggles and howls at fits; 20
Over earth and ocean, with gentle motion,
   This pilot is guiding me,
Lured by the love of the genii that move
   In the depths of the purple sea;
Over the rills, and the crags, and the hills, 25
   Over the lakes and the plains,
Wherever he dream, under mountain or stream,
   The Spirit he loves remains;
And I all the while bask in Heaven's blue smile,
   Whilst he is dissolving in rains. 30

The sanguine Sunrise, with his meteor eyes,
   And his burning plumes outspread,
Leaps on the back of my sailing rack,
   When the morning star shines dead;
As on the jag of a mountain crag, 35
   Which an earthquake rocks and swings,
An eagle alit one moment may sit
   In the light of its golden wings.
And when Sunset may breathe, from the lit sea beneath,
   Its ardors of rest and of love, 40
And the crimson pall of eve may fall
   From the depth of Heaven above,
With wings folded I rest, on mine airy nest,
   As still as a brooding dove.

That orbèd maiden with white fire laden, 45
   Whom mortals call the Moon,
Glides glimmering o'er my fleece-like floor,
   By the midnight breezes strewn;
And wherever the beat of her unseen feet,
   Which only the angels hear, 50
May have broken the woof of my tent's thin roof,
   The stars peep behind her and peer;
And I laugh to see them whirl and flee,
   Like a swarm of golden bees,
When I widen the rent in my wind-built tent,
   Till the calm rivers, lakes, and seas, 56
Like strips of the sky fallen through me on high,
   Are each paved with the moon and these.

I bind the Sun's throne with a burning zone,
   And the Moon's with a girdle of pearl; 60
The volcanoes are dim, and the stars reel and swim
   When the whirlwinds my banner unfurl.
From cape to cape, with a bridge-like shape,
   Over a torrent sea,
Sunbeam-proof, I hang like a roof— 65
   The mountains its columns be.
The triumphal arch, through which I march,
   With hurricane, fire, and snow,
When the Powers of the air are chained to my chair,
   Is the million-colored bow; 70
The sphere-fire above its soft colors wove,
   While the moist Earth was laughing below.

I am the daughter of Earth and Water,
   And the nursling of the Sky;
I pass through the pores of the ocean and shores, 75
   I change, but I cannot die.
For after the rain when with never a stain
   The pavilion of Heaven is bare,
And the winds and sunbeams with their convex gleams
   Build up the blue dome of air, 80
I silently laugh at my own cenotaph,
   And out of the caverns of rain,
Like a child from the womb, like a ghost from the tomb,
   I arise and unbuild it again.   (1820)

To a Skylark

Hail to thee, blithe Spirit!
   Bird thou never wert,
That from Heaven, or near it,
   Pourest thy full heart
In profuse strains of unpremeditated art. 5

Higher still and higher
   From the earth thou springest
Like a cloud of fire;
   The blue deep thou wingest,
And singing still dost soar, and soaring ever singest. 10

---

33. **rack**, broken portion of cloud. 58. **these**, the stars. 59. **zone**, girdle. 81. **cenotaph**, an empty tomb that honors someone lost or buried elsewhere; here, the blue dome of air. **To a Skylark.** Cf. Wordsworth's *To a Skylark*, p. 156.

In the golden lightning
   Of the sunken sun,
O'er which clouds are bright'ning,
   Thou dost float and run;
Like an unbodied joy whose race is just begun.

The pale purple even 16
   Melts around thy flight;
Like a star of Heaven,
   In the broad daylight
Thou art unseen, but yet I hear thy shrill delight, 20

Keen as are the arrows
   Of that silver sphere,
Whose intense lamp narrows
   In the white dawn clear
Until we hardly see—we feel that it is there. 25

All the earth and air
   With thy voice is loud,
As, when night is bare,
   From one lonely cloud
The moon rains out her beams, and Heaven is overflowed. 30

What thou art we know not;
   What is most like thee?
From rainbow clouds there flow not
   Drops so bright to see
As from thy presence showers a rain of melody. 35

Like a Poet hidden
   In the light of thought,
Singing hymns unbidden,
   Till the world is wrought
To sympathy with hopes and fears it heeded not: 40

Like a high-born maiden
   In a palace-tower,
Soothing her love-laden
   Soul in secret hour
With music sweet as love, which overflows her bower: 45

Like a glowworm golden
   In a dell of dew,
Scattering unbeholden
   Its aëreal hue
Among the flowers and grass, which screen it from the view!

Like a rose embowered
   In its own green leaves,
By warm winds deflowered,
   Till the scent it gives
Makes faint with too much sweet those heavy-wingéd thieves: 55

Sound of vernal showers
   On the twinkling grass,
Rain-awakened flowers,
   All that ever was
Joyous, and clear, and fresh, thy music doth surpass: 60

Teach us, Sprite or Bird,
   What sweet thoughts are thine:
I have never heard
   Praise of love or wine
That panted forth a flood of rapture so divine.

Chorus Hymeneal, 66
   Or triumphal chant,
Matched with thine would be all
   But an empty vaunt,
A thing wherein we feel there is some hidden want. 70

What objects are the fountains
   Of thy happy strain?
What fields, or waves, or mountains?
   What shapes of sky or plain?
What love of thine own kind? what ignorance of pain? 75

With thy clear keen joyance
   Languor cannot be:
Shadow of annoyance
   Never came near thee:
Thou lovest—but ne'er knew love's sad satiety.

Waking or asleep, 81
   Thou of death must deem
Things more true and deep
   Than we mortals dream,
Or how could thy notes flow in such a crystal stream? 85

We look before and after,
    And pine for what is not:
Our sincerest laughter
    With some pain is fraught;
Our sweetest songs are those that tell of sad-
    dest thought.   90

Yet if we could scorn
    Hate, and pride, and fear;
If we were things born
    Not to shed a tear,
I know not how thy joy we ever should come
    near.   95

Better than all measures
    Of delightful sound,
Better than all treasures
    That in books are found,
Thy skill to poet were, thou scorner of the
    ground!   100

Teach me half the gladness
    That thy brain must know,
Such harmonious madness
    From my lips would flow
The world should listen then—as I am listen-
    ing now.   (1820)

Time Long Past

Like the ghost of a dear friend dead
    Is Time long past.
A tone which is now forever fled,
A hope which is now forever past,
A love so sweet it could not last,   5
    Was Time long past.

There were sweet dreams in the night
    Of Time long past:
And, was it sadness or delight,
Each day a shadow onward cast   10
Which made us wish it yet might last—
    That Time long past.

There is regret, almost remorse,
    For Time long past.
'Tis like a child's belovéd corse   15

A father watches, till at last
Beauty is like remembrance, cast
    From Time long past.
        (*1820;* 1870)

Song

Rarely, rarely, comest thou,
    Spirit of Delight!
Wherefore hast thou left me now
    Many a day and night?
Many a weary night and day   5
'Tis since thou art fled away.

How shall ever one like me
    Win thee back again?
With the joyous and the free
    Thou wilt scoff at pain.   10
Spirit false! thou hast forgot
All but those who need thee not.

As a lizard with the shade
    Of a trembling leaf,
Thou with sorrow art dismayed;   15
    Even the sighs of grief
Reproach thee, that thou art not near,
And reproach thou wilt not hear.

Let me set my mournful ditty
    To a merry measure;   20
Thou wilt never come for pity;
    Thou wilt come for pleasure;
Pity then will cut away
Those cruel wings, and thou wilt stay.

I love all that thou lovest,   25
    Spirit of Delight!
The fresh Earth in new leaves dressed,
    And the starry night;
Autumn evening, and the morn
When the golden mists are born.   30

I love snow, and all the forms
    Of the radiant frost;
I love waves, and winds, and storms,
    Everything almost
Which is Nature's, and may be   35
Untainted by man's misery.

I love tranquil solitude,
   And such society
As is quiet, wise, and good;
   Between thee and me   40
What difference? but thou dost possess
The things I seek, not love them less.

I love Love—though he has wings,
   And like light can flee,
But above all other things,   45
   Spirit, I love thee—
Thou art love and life! Oh, come,
Make once more my heart thy home.
                  (*1820;* 1824)

To Night

Swiftly walk o'er the western wave,
      Spirit of Night!
Out of the misty eastern cave,
Where, all the long and lone daylight,
Thou wovest dreams of joy and fear,   5
Which make thee terrible and dear—
      Swift be thy flight!

Wrap thy form in a mantle gray,
      Star-inwrought!
Blind with thine hair the eyes of Day;   10
Kiss her until she be wearied out,
Then wander o'er city, and sea, and land,
Touching all with thine opiate wand—
      Come, long-sought!

When I arose and saw the dawn,   15
      I sighed for thee;
When light rode high, and the dew was gone,
And noon lay heavy on flower and tree,
And the weary Day turned to his rest,
Lingering like an unloved guest,   20
      I sighed for thee.

Thy brother Death came, and cried,
      "Wouldst thou me?"
Thy sweet child Sleep, the filmy-eyed,
Murmured like a noontide bee,   25
"Shall I nestle near thy side?
Wouldst thou me?"—And I replied,
      "No, not thee!"

Death will come when thou art dead,
      Soon, too soon—   30
Sleep will come when thou art fled;
Of neither would I ask the boon
I ask of thee, belovéd Night—
Swift be thine approaching flight,
      Come soon, soon!   35
                  (*1821;* 1824)

To ——

Music, when soft voices die,
Vibrates in the memory—
Odors, when sweet violets sicken,
Live within the sense they quicken.

Rose leaves, when the rose is dead,   5
Are heaped for the belovéd's bed;
And so thy thoughts, when thou art gone,
Love itself shall slumber on.   (*1821;* 1824)

Time

Unfathomable Sea! whose waves are years,
   Ocean of Time, whose waters of deep woe
Are brackish with the salt of human tears!
   Thou shoreless flood, which in thy ebb and flow
Claspest the limits of mortality,   5
   And sick of prey, yet howling on for more,
Vomitest thy wrecks on its inhospitable shore;
   Treacherous in calm, and terrible in storm,
      Who shall put forth on thee,
      Unfathomable Sea?
                  (*1821;* 1824)

Mutability

The flower that smiles today
    Tomorrow dies;
All that we wish to stay
    Tempts and then flies.
What is this world's delight?
Lightning that mocks the night,
    Brief even as bright.

Virtue, how frail it is!
    Friendship how rare!

Love, how it sells poor bliss 10
    For proud despair!
But we, though soon they fall,
Survive their joy, and all
    Which ours we call.

Whilst skies are blue and bright, 15
    Whilst flowers are gay,
Whilst eyes that change ere night
    Make glad the day;
Whilst yet the calm hours creep,
Dream thou—and from thy sleep 20
    Then wake to weep.

          (*1821;* 1824)

A Lament

O world! O life! O time!
    On whose last steps I climb,
        Trembling at that where I had stood before;
When will return the glory of your prime?
        No more—Oh, never more! 5

Out of the day and night
    A joy has taken flight;
        Fresh spring, and summer, and winter hoar,
Move my faint heart with grief, but with delight
        No more—Oh, never more! 10

          (*1821;* 1824)

Adonais
AN ELEGY ON THE DEATH OF JOHN KEATS

    Keats's premature death (p. 274) from tuberculosis stirred many of the younger romantic poets, particularly Byron and Shelley. Some of them believed the melancholy event had been hastened, if not directly caused, by a harsh review of Keats's early poem *Endymion* in the *Quarterly Review* for April, 1818, three years before Keats's death. Such an idea was absurd, for Keats was made of sterner stuff than to allow himself to be killed by criticism. Even Byron admitted this likelihood:

    'Tis very strange the mind, that fiery particle
    Should let itself be snuffed out by an article.
            (*Don Juan,* XI, stanza 60).

But to the emotional Shelley, Keats had been murdered by his critics; and *Adonais,* the beautiful elegy on the death of Keats, is partly an oblique attack upon his "murderers," who, as Shelley saw it, had forced him "to drink poison."

    The title of the poem is an adaptation of the name of Adonis, the beautiful youth loved by Venus and killed by a boar. The immediate sources of the poem, particularly at the beginning, are the *Lament for Adonis* by the Greek poet Bion of uncertain date, and the *Lament for Bion* by the poet Moschus, who lived some time during the Alexandrian period of Greek literature (333-146 B.C.). Both Greek poets and Shelley follow the form of the memorial idyll by the Greek poet Theocritus (fl. 270 B.C.), which is poetry of a definitely pastoral nature. Milton had done the same in his *Lycidas* (Vol. I, p. 710). To be noted especially in Shelley's poem is the identification of the dead Keats with nature and the pantheism which underlies virtually all the treatment of nature by the great romantic poets (cf. ll. 370 ff., p. 268). It should not detract from the beauty and nobility of the poem, which, like every great elegy, transcends the individual who inspired it, to observe that Shelley knew Keats but slightly. The two had met at Leigh Hunt's home in London (1817); they never were intimate, and Keats appears not to have cared for Shelley. It is characteristic of Shelley that he made the principle more important than the mere fact. The poem is written in Spenserian stanzas.

I weep for Adonais—he is dead!
O, weep for Adonais! though our tears
Thaw not the frost which binds so dear a head!
And thou, sad Hour, selected from all years
To mourn our loss, rouse thy obscure compeers, 5
And teach them thine own sorrow, say: "With me
Died Adonais; till the Future dares

5. **thy . . . compeers,** the hours less memorable than the one that marked the death of Keats.

Forget the Past, his fate and fame shall be
An echo and a light unto eternity!"

Where wert thou, mighty Mother, when he
    lay, 10
When thy Son lay, pierced by the shaft which
    flies
In darkness? where was lorn Urania
When Adonais died? With veilèd eyes,
'Mid listening Echoes, in her Paradise
She sate, while one, with soft enamored
    breath, 15
Rekindled all the fading melodies,
With which, like flowers that mock the corse
    beneath,
He had adorned and hid the coming bulk of
    Death.

Oh, weep for Adonais—he is dead!
Wake, melancholy Mother, wake and weep! 20
Yet wherefore? Quench within their burning
    bed
Thy fiery tears, and let thy loud heart keep
Like his, a mute and uncomplaining sleep;
For he is gone, where all things wise and
    fair
Descend;—oh, dream not that the amorous
    Deep 25
Will yet restore him to the vital air;
Death feeds on his mute voice, and laughs at
    our despair.

Most musical of mourners, weep again!
Lament anew, Urania!—He died,
Who was the Sire of an immortal strain, 30
Blind, old, and lonely, when his country's
    pride,
The priest, the slave, and the liberticide,
Trampled and mocked with many a loathèd
    rite
Of lust and blood; he went, unterrified,
Into the gulf of death; but his clear Sprite 35
Yet reigns o'er earth; the third among the
    sons of light.

Most musical of mourners, weep anew!
Not all to that bright station dared to climb;
And happier they their happiness who knew,
Whose tapers yet burn through that night of
    time 40
In which suns perished; others more sublime,
Struck by the envious wrath of man or
    god,
Have sunk, extinct in their refulgent prime;
And some yet live, treading the thorny road,
Which leads, through toil and hate, to Fame's
    serene abode. 45

But now, thy youngest, dearest one, has per-
    ished—
The nursling of thy widowhood, who grew,
Like a pale flower by some sad maiden cher-
    ished,
And fed with true-love tears, instead of dew;
Most musical of mourners, weep anew! 50
Thy extreme hope, the loveliest and the last,
The bloom, whose petals nipped before they
    blew
Died on the promise of the fruit, is waste;
The broken lily lies—the storm is overpast.

To that high Capital, where kingly Death 55
Keeps his pale court in beauty and decay,
He came; and bought, with price of purest
    breath,
A grave among the eternal.—Come away!
Haste, while the vault of blue Italian day
Is yet his fitting charnel-roof! while still 60
He lies, as if in dewy sleep he lay;
Awake him not! surely he takes his fill
Of deep and liquid rest, forgetful of all ill.

He will awake no more, oh, never more!—
Within the twilight chamber spreads apace 65
The shadow of white Death, and at the door
Invisible Corruption waits to trace
His extreme way to her dim dwelling-place;
The eternal Hunger sits, but pity and awe
Soothe her pale rage, nor dares she to deface 70
So fair a prey, till darkness, and the law
Of change, shall o'er his sleep the mortal cur-
    tain draw.

---

10. **Mother**, Urania, the muse of astronomy. Shelley here identifies her with Uranian Aphrodite, the spirit of lyrical poetry and heavenly love. 15. **one**, one echo. 30. **the Sire**, Milton, of whose *Lycidas* (Vol. I, p. 710) Shelley's poem is reminiscent. 31. **when . . . blood**, the Restoration period. See Vol. I, pp. 812 ff. 36. **third . . . light**. According to Shelley's *Defense of Poetry*, Homer and Dante were the first and second epic poets.

44. **some yet live**, such as Wordsworth and Byron. 49. **tears . . . dew**. An allusion to Keats's *Isabella*. 51. **extreme, last**. 55. **Capital**, Rome, where Keats had gone for his health (see p. 274). 69. **Hunger**, the corruption of the grave.

Oh, weep for Adonais!—The quick Dreams,
The passion-wingéd Ministers of thought,
Who were his flocks, whom near the living
    streams   75
Of his young spirit he fed, and whom he
    taught
The love which was its music, wander not—
Wander no more, from kindling brain to
    brain,
But droop there, whence they sprung; and
    mourn their lot
Round the cold heart, where, after their sweet
    pain,   80
They ne'er will gather strength, or find a home
    again.

And one with trembling hands clasps his cold
    head,
And fans him with her moonlight wings, and
    cries;
"Our love, our hope, our sorrow, is not dead;
See, on the silken fringe of his faint eyes,   85
Like dew upon a sleeping flower, there lies
A tear some Dream has loosened from his
    brain."
Lost Angel of a ruined Paradise!
She knew not 'twas her own; as with no stain
She faded, like a cloud which had outwept its
    rain.   90

One from a lucid urn of starry dew
Washed his light limbs as if embalming them;
Another clipped her profuse locks, and threw
The wreath upon him, like an anadem,
Which frozen tears instead of pearls begem;   95
Another in her wilful grief would break
Her bow and wingéd reeds, as if to stem
A greater loss with one which was more
    weak;
And dull the barbéd fire against his frozen
    cheek.

Another Splendor on his mouth alit,   100
That mouth, whence it was wont to draw the
    breath
Which gave it strength to pierce the guarded
    wit,
And pass into the panting heart beneath
With lightning and with music: the damp
    death
Quenched its caress upon his icy lips;   105
And, as a dying meteor stains a wreath
Of moonlight vapor, which the cold night
    clips,
It flushed through his pale limbs, and passed
    to its eclipse.

And others came . . . Desires and Adora-
    tions,
Wingéd Persuasions and veiled Destinies,   110
Splendors, and Glooms, and glimmering In-
    carnations
Of hopes and fears, and twilight Phantasies;
And Sorrow, with her family of Sighs,
And Pleasure, blind with tears, led by the
    gleam
Of her own dying smile instead of eyes,   115
Came in slow pomp;—the moving pomp
    might seem
Like pageantry of mist on an autumnal
    stream.

All he had loved, and molded into thought,
From shape, and hue, and odor, and sweet
    sound,
Lamented Adonais. Morning sought   120
Her eastern watch-tower, and her hair un-
    bound,
Wet with the tears which should adorn the
    ground,
Dimmed the aëreal eyes that kindle day;
Afar the melancholy thunder moaned,
Pale Ocean in unquiet slumber lay,   125
And the wild Winds flew round, sobbing in
    their dismay.

Lost Echo sits amid the voiceless mountains,
And feeds her grief with his remembered
    lay,
And will no more reply to winds or fountains,
Or amorous birds perched on the young green
    spray,   130
Or herdsman's horn, or bell at closing day;
Since she can mimic not his lips, more dear
Than those for whose disdain she pined away

---

80. **sweet pain**, birth pangs. 94. **anadem**, crown, chaplet. 107. **clips**, embraces. 127. **Echo**, in classical legend, a beautiful nymph who for love of Narcissus pined away into a mere voice. 133. **those**, of Narcissus.

Into a shadow of all sounds—a drear
Murmur, between their songs, is all the wood-
    men hear.   135

Grief made the young Spring wild, and she
    threw down
Her kindling buds, as if she Autumn were,
Or they dead leaves; since her delight is
    flown,
For whom should she have waked the sullen
    year?
To Phoebus was not Hyacinth so dear   140
Nor to himself Narcissus, as to both
Thou, Adonais: wan they stand and sere
Amid the faint companions of their youth,
With dew all turned to tears; odor, to sighing
    ruth.

Thy spirit's sister, the lorn nightingale 145
Mourns not her mate with such melodious
    pain;
Not so the eagle, who like thee could scale
Heaven, and could nourish in the sun's do-
    main
Her mighty youth with morning, doth com-
    plain,
Soaring and screaming round her empty nest,
As Albion wails for thee: the curse of Cain 151
Light on his head who pierced thy innocent
    breast,
And scared the angel soul that was its earthly
    guest!

Ah, woe is me! Winter is come and gone,
But grief returns with the revolving year; 155
The airs and streams renew their joyous tone;
The ants, the bees, the swallows reappear;
Fresh leaves and flowers deck the dead Sea-
    sons' bier;
The amorous birds now pair in every brake,
And build their mossy homes in field and
    brere;   160
And the green lizard, and the golden snake,
Like unimprisoned flames, out of their trance
    awake.

Through wood and stream and field and hill
    and Ocean
A quickening life from the Earth's heart has
    burst
As it has ever done, with change and motion,
From the great morning of the world when
    first   166
God dawned on Chaos; in its stream im-
    mersed,
The lamps of Heaven flash with a softer
    light;
All baser things pant with life's sacred thirst;
Diffuse themselves; and spend in love's de-
    light,   170
The beauty and the joy of their renewéd
    might.

The leprous corpse, touched by this spirit
    tender,
Exhales itself in flowers of gentle breath;
Like incarnations of the stars, when splendor
Is changed to fragrance, they illumine death
And mock the merry worm that wakes be-
    neath;   176
Nought we know, dies. Shall that alone which
    knows
Be as a sword consumed before the sheath
By sightless lightning?—the intense atom
    glows
A moment, then is quenched in a most cold
    repose.   180

Alas! that all we loved of him should be,
But for our grief, as if it had not been,
And grief itself be mortal! Woe is me!
Whence are we, and why are we? of what
    scene
The actors or spectators? Great and mean 185
Meet massed in death, who lends what life
    must borrow.
As long as skies are blue, and fields are
    green,

140. **Phoebus**, Apollo, god of music and poetry. He loved a beautiful youth named Hyacinthus, whom he accidentally killed with a quoit. Upon his death Hyacinthus was changed into a flower. 141. **Narcissus.** Narcissus fell in love with his own image as it was reflected in a fountain. Upon his death he was changed into a flower because he refused the love of Echo. 145. **nightingale.** An allusion to Keats's *Ode to a Nightingale*, p. 284, and to the melody of Keats's verse. 151. **Albion**, poetic name for England. **curse of Cain.** For killing his brother Abel (*Genesis*, 4:1-15), Cain was condemned to be a homeless wanderer. 152. **his head**, the head of the critic. Shelley wrongly believed that the death of Keats was caused by hostile attacks upon his poetry. See Byron's *Who Killed John Keats?* and note, p. 247; also p. 274. 159. **brake**, thicket.

160. **brere**, briar. 179. **sightless**, invisible.

Evening must usher night, night urge the morrow,
  Month follow month with woe, and year wake year to sorrow.

He will awake no more, oh, never more! 190
"Wake thou," cried Misery, "childless Mother, rise
Out of thy sleep, and slake, in thy heart's core,
A wound more fierce than his, with tears and sighs."
And all the Dreams that watched Urania's eyes,
And all the Echoes whom their sister's song
Had held in holy silence, cried: "Arise!" 196
Swift as a Thought by the snake Memory stung,
From her ambrosial rest the fading Splendor sprung.

She rose like an autumnal Night, that springs
Out of the East, and follows wild and drear 200
The golden Day, which, on eternal wings,
Even as a ghost abandoning a bier,
Had left the Earth a corpse. Sorrow and fear
So struck, so roused, so rapped Urania;
So saddened round her like an atmosphere 205
Of stormy mist; so swept her on her way
Even to the mournful place where Adonais lay.

Out of her secret Paradise she sped,
Through camps and cities rough with stone, and steel,
And human hearts, which to her aëry tread 210
Yielding not, wounded the invisible
Palms of her tender feet where'er they fell:
And barbéd tongues, and thoughts more sharp than they,
Rent the soft Form they never could repel,
Whose sacred blood, like the young tears of May, 215
Paved with eternal flowers that undeserving way.

In the death-chamber for a moment Death,
Shamed by the presence of that living Might,
Blushed to annihilation, and the breath
Revisited those lips, and Life's pale light 220
Flashed through those limbs, so late her dear delight.
"Leave me not wild and drear and comfortless,
As silent lightning leaves the starless night!
Leave me not!" cried Urania: her distress
Roused Death: Death rose and smiled, and met her vain caress. 225

"Stay yet awhile! speak to me once again;
Kiss me, so long but as a kiss may live;
And in my heartless breast and burning brain
That word, that kiss, shall all thoughts else survive,
With food of saddest memory kept alive, 230
Now thou art dead, as if it were a part
Of thee, my Adonais! I would give
All that I am to be as thou now art!
But I am chained to Time, and cannot thence depart!

"O gentle child, beautiful as thou wert, 235
Why didst thou leave the trodden paths of men
Too soon, and with weak hands though mighty heart
Dare the unpastured dragon in his den?
Defenseless as thou wert, oh, where was then
Wisdom the mirrored shield, or scorn the spear? 240
Or hadst thou waited the full cycle, when
Thy spirit should have filled its crescent sphere,
The monsters of life's waste had fled from thee like deer.

"The herded wolves, bold only to pursue; 244
The obscene ravens, clamorous o'er the dead;
The vultures to the conqueror's banner true
Who feed where Desolation first has fed,
And whose wings rain contagion;—how they fled,
When, like Apollo, from his golden bow
The Pythian of the age one arrow sped 250

228. **heartless breast.** Her breast was heartless because she had given her heart to Adonais. 238. **unpastured dragon,** the harsh and insatiable world. 240. **mirrored shield.** A reference to the shield that protected Perseus, famous mythological hero, from the fatal gaze of the demon Gorgons and that enabled him to cut off Medusa's head as he saw it by reflection. 242. **filled . . . sphere,** attained maturity of power. 244. **herded wolves,** contemporary critics, who catered to the political party in power. 250. **Pythian of the age,** Byron, who had "slain" the critics in his *English Bards and Scotch Reviewers* (see p. 203) as Apollo did the Python.

And smiled!—The spoilers tempt no second
    blow,
They fawn on the proud feet that spurn them
    lying low.

"The sun comes forth, and many reptiles
    spawn;
He sets, and each ephemeral insect then
Is gathered into death without a dawn,   255
And the immortal stars awake again;
So is it in the world of living men:
A godlike mind soars forth, in its delight
Making earth bare and veiling heaven, and
    when
It sinks, the swarms that dimmed or shared its
    light   260
Leave to its kindred lamps the spirit's awful
    night."

Thus ceased she: and the mountain shepherds
    came,
Their garlands sere, their magic mantles rent;
The Pilgrim of Eternity, whose fame
Over his living head like Heaven is bent,   265
An early but enduring monument,
Came, veiling all the lightnings of his song
In sorrow; from her wilds Ierne sent
The sweetest lyrist of her saddest wrong,
And Love taught Grief to fall like music from
    his tongue.   270

Midst others of less note, came one frail Form,
A phantom among men; companionless
As the last cloud of an expiring storm
Whose thunder is its knell; he, as I guess,
Had gazed on Nature's naked loveliness,   275
Actaeon-like, and now he fled astray
With feeble steps o'er the world's wilderness,
And his own thoughts, along that rugged way,
Pursued, like raging hounds, their father and
    their prey.

A pardlike Spirit beautiful and swift—   280
A Love in desolation masked;—a Power

Girt around with weakness;—it can scarce up-
    lift
The weight of the superincumbent hour;
It is a dying lamp, a falling shower,
A breaking billow;—even whilst we speak   285
Is it not broken? On the withering flower
The killing sun smiles brightly: on a cheek
The life can burn in blood, even while the
    heart may break.

His head was bound with pansies overblown,
And faded violets, white, and pied, and blue;
And a light spear topped with a cypress
    cone,   291
Round whose rude shaft dark ivy-tresses grew
Yet dripping with the forest's noonday dew,
Vibrated, as the ever-beating heart
Shook the weak hand that grasped it; of that
    crew   295
He came the last, neglected and apart;
A herd-abandoned deer struck by the hunter's
    dart.

All stood aloof, and at his partial moan
Smiled through their tears; well knew that
    gentle band
Who in another's fate now wept his own,   300
As in the accents of an unknown land
He sung new sorrow; sad Urania scanned
The Stranger's mien, and murmured: "Who
    art thou?"

He answered not, but with a sudden hand
Made bare his branded and ensanguined brow,
Which was like Cain's or Christ's—oh! that it
    should be so!   306

What softer voice is hushed over the dead?
Athwart what brow is that dark mantle
    thrown?
What form leans sadly o'er the white death-
    bed,
In mockery of monumental stone,   310
The heavy heart heaving without a moan?
If it be He, who, gentlest of the wise,

---

264. **Pilgrim of Eternity**, Byron, so called from his *Childe Harold's Pilgrimage*, III, 629, p. 216. 268. **Ierne**, Ireland. The reference is to Thomas Moore, p. 297, and his *Irish Melodies*. He sang the tragic death of the Irish patriot Robert Emmet in *Oh, Breathe Not His Name*, p. 302. 271. **one frail Form**, Shelley himself. 276. **Actaeon-like.** Actaeon, the hunter, looked upon Diana and her nymphs bathing, and for so doing was turned into a stag and killed by his own hounds. 280. **pardlike**, leopardlike.

289. **pansies**, etc. The pansy is a symbol of thought; the violet, of modesty; the cypress, of mourning; the ivy, of constancy in friendship. 298. **partial**, fond, sympathetic. 301. **accents . . . land**, the language of England, a land unknown to the Greek muse Urania. 306. **oh . . . so.** Shelley means that he bore marks of cruel treatment such as the world gave to Cain, an enemy of the race, or to Christ, a benefactor. 307. **softer voice**, that of Leigh Hunt, p. 297, Keats's close friend and mentor.

Taught, soothed, loved, honored the departed
  one,
Let me not vex, with inharmonious sighs,
The silence of that heart's accepted sacrifice. 315

Our Adonais has drunk poison—oh!
What deaf and viperous murderer could
  crown
Life's early cup with such a draught of woe?
The nameless worm would now itself disown:
It felt, yet could escape, the magic tone 320
Whose prelude held all envy, hate, and wrong,
But what was howling in one breast alone,
Silent with expectation of the song,
Whose master's hand is cold, whose silver lyre
  unstrung.

Live thou, whose infamy is not thy fame! 325
Live! fear no heavier chastisement from me,
Thou noteless blot on a remembered name!
But be thyself, and know thyself to be!
And ever at thy season be thou free 329
To spill the venom when thy fangs o'erflow:
Remorse and Self-contempt shall cling to thee;
Hot Shame shall burn upon thy secret brow,
And like a beaten hound tremble thou shalt
  —as now.

Nor let us weep that our delight is fled
Far from these carrion kites that scream be-
  low; 335
He wakes or sleeps with the enduring dead;
Thou canst not soar where he is sitting now—
Dust to the dust! but the pure spirit shall flow
Back to the burning fountain whence it came,
A portion of the Eternal, which must glow 340
Through time and change, unquenchably the
  same,
Whilst thy cold embers choke the sordid
  hearth of shame.

Peace, peace! he is not dead, he doth not
  sleep—
He hath awakened from the dream of life—

'Tis we, who lost in stormy visions, keep 345
With phantoms an unprofitable strife,
And in mad trance, strike with our spirit's
  knife
Invulnerable nothings.—*We* decay
Like corpses in a charnel; fear and grief
Convulse us and consume us day by day, 350
And cold hopes swarm like worms within our
  living clay.

He has outsoared the shadow of our night;
Envy and calumny and hate and pain,
And that unrest which men miscall delight,
Can touch him not and torture not again; 355
From the contagion of the world's slow stain
He is secure, and now can never mourn
A heart grown cold, a head grown gray in
  vain;
Nor, when the spirit's self has ceased to burn,
With sparkless ashes load an unlamented urn.

He lives, he wakes—'tis Death is dead, not
  he; 361
Mourn not for Adonais.—Thou young Dawn,
Turn all thy dew to splendor, for from thee
The spirit thou lamentest is not gone;
Ye caverns and ye forests, cease to moan! 365
Cease, ye faint flowers and fountains, and thou
  Air,
Which like a mourning veil thy scarf hadst
  thrown
O'er the abandoned Earth, now leave it bare
Even to the joyous stars which smile on its
  despair!

He is made one with Nature: there is heard
His voice in all her music, from the moan 371
Of thunder, to the song of night's sweet bird;
He is a presence to be felt and known
In darkness and in light, from herb and stone,
Spreading itself where'er that Power may
  move 375
Which has withdrawn his being to its own;
Which wields the world with never-wearied
  love,
Sustains it from beneath, and kindles it above.

He is a portion of the loveliness
Which once he made more lovely: he doth
  bear 380

---

319. **nameless worm**, unnamed serpent. The harsh criticism of *Endymion* in the *Quarterly Review* was unsigned; it was written by J. W. Croker. 322. **one breast alone**, in the breast of the reviewer just referred to. Harsher criticism, however, had appeared in *Blackwood's Magazine*, August, 1818. 325. **Live thou**, the critic of the *Quarterly Review*. 337. **Thou . . . now**, an echo from *Paradise Lost*, IV, 828-829 (Vol. I, p. 753):
  Ye knew me once no mate
For you, there sitting where ye durst not soar.

His part, while the one Spirit's plastic stress
Sweeps through the dull dense world, compelling there,
All new successions to the forms they wear;
Torturing th' unwilling dross that checks its flight
To its own likeness, as each mass may bear;
And bursting in its beauty and its might   386
From trees and beasts and men into the Heaven's light.

The splendors of the firmament of time
May be eclipsed, but are extinguished not;
Like stars to their appointed height they climb,
And death is a low mist which cannot blot   391
The brightness it may veil. When lofty thought
Lifts a young heart above its mortal lair,
And love and life contend in it, for what
Shall be its earthly doom, the dead live there
And move like winds of light on dark and stormy air.   396

The inheritors of unfulfilled renown
Rose from their thrones, built beyond mortal thought,
Far in the Unapparent. Chatterton
Rose pale—his solemn agony had not   400
Yet faded from him; Sidney, as he fought
And as he fell and as he lived and loved
Sublimely mild, a Spirit without spot,
Arose; and Lucan, by his death approved:
Oblivion as they rose shrank like a thing reproved.   405

And many more, whose names on Earth are dark,
But whose transmitted effluence cannot die
So long as fire outlives the parent spark,
Rose, robed in dazzling immortality.
"Thou art become as one of us," they cry,   410
"It was for thee yon kingless sphere has long
Swung blind in unascended majesty,
Silent alone amid an Heaven of Song.
Assume thy wingéd throne, thou Vesper of our throng!"

Who mourns for Adonais? Oh, come forth,
Fond wretch! and know thyself and him aright.   416
Clasp with thy panting soul the pendulous Earth;
As from a center, dart thy spirit's light
Beyond all worlds, until its spacious might
Satiate the void circumference: then shrink   420
Even to a point within our day and night;
And keep thy heart light lest it make thee sink
When hope has kindled hope, and lured thee to the brink.

Or go to Rome, which is the sepulcher,
Oh, not of him, but of our joy: 'tis nought   425
That ages, empires, and religions there
Lie buried in the ravage they have wrought;
For such as he can lend—they borrow not
Glory from those who made the world their prey;
And he is gathered to the kings of thought   430
Who waged contention with their time's decay,
And of the past are all that cannot pass away.

Go thou to Rome—at once the Paradise,
The grave, the city, and the wilderness;
And where its wrecks like shattered mountains rise,   435
And flowering weeds, and fragrant copses dress
The bones of Desolation's nakedness
Pass, till the spirit of the spot shall lead
Thy footsteps to a slope of green access
Where, like an infant's smile, over the dead   440
A light of laughing flowers along the grass is spread;

And gray walls molder round, on which dull Time
Feeds, like slow fire upon a hoary brand;
And one keen pyramid with wedge sublime,

---

381. **plastic**, shaping, molding. 383. **forms they wear.** The spirit of Love and Beauty is thought of as permeating all matter and as molding everything into its appropriate form. Cf. Wordsworth's *Lines Composed a Few Miles above Tintern Abbey*, ll. 93-102, p. 122. 385. **as**, according as. 399. **Chatterton**, Thomas Chatterton (1752-1770), the youthful poet who in despair and poverty took his own life. Cf. Wordsworth's *Resolution and Independence*, l. 43, p. 149. 401. **Sidney**, Sir Philip Sidney (1554-1586), who died from a battle wound at thirty-two. See Vol. I, p. 341. 404. **Lucan**, a Latin poet (39-65) who killed himself at the age of twenty-six to escape execution for taking part in a political conspiracy.

439. **slope ... access**, the Protestant cemetery, where Keats was buried. Shelley's ashes were buried near Keats a short time after the writing of *Adonais*. 444. **one ... pyramid**, the tomb of Caius Cestius, built in the time of Augustus.

Pavilioning the dust of him who planned 445
This refuge for his memory, doth stand
Like flame transformed to marble; and beneath,
A field is spread, on which a newer band
Have pitched in Heaven's smile their camp of death,
Welcoming him we lose with scarce extinguished breath. 450

Here pause: these graves are all too young as yet
To have outgrown the sorrow which consigned
Its charge to each; and if the seal is set,
Here, on one fountain of a mourning mind,
Break it not thou! too surely shalt thou find 455
Thine own well full, if thou returnest home,
Of tears and gall. From the world's bitter wind
Seek shelter in the shadow of the tomb.
What Adonais is, why fear we to become?

The One remains, the many change and pass;
Heaven's light forever shines, Earth's shadows fly; 461
Life, like a dome of many-colored glass,
Stains the white radiance of Eternity,
Until Death tramples it to fragments.—Die,
If thou wouldst be with that which thou dost seek! 465
Follow where all is fled!—Rome's azure sky,
Flowers, ruins, statues, music, words are weak
The glory they transfuse with fitting truth to speak.

Why linger, why turn back, why shrink, my Heart?
Thy hopes are gone before: from all things here 470
They have departed; thou shouldst now depart!
A light is passed from the revolving year,
And man, and woman; and what still is dear
Attracts to crush, repels to make thee wither.
The soft sky smiles—the low wind whispers near: 475

'Tis Adonais calls! oh, hasten thither,
No more let Life divide what Death can join together.

That Light whose smile kindles the Universe,
That Beauty in which all things work and move, 479
That Benediction which the eclipsing Curse
Of birth can quench not, that sustaining Love
Which through the web of being blindly wove
By man and beast and earth and air and sea,
Burns bright or dim, as each are mirrors of
The fire for which all thirst; now beams on me, 485
Consuming the last clouds of cold mortality.

The breath whose might I have invoked in song
Descends on me; my spirit's bark is driven,
Far from the shore, far from the trembling throng 489
Whose sails were never to the tempest given;
The massy earth and spheréd skies are riven!
I am borne darkly, fearfully, afar;
Whilst, burning through the inmost veil of Heaven,
The soul of Adonais, like a star,
Beacons from the abode where the Eternal are. (1821)

Songs from *Hellas*

Hellas is a lyrical drama inspired by the Greek war for independence from Turkey, fought in 1821. Shelley looked upon this struggle as the herald of a new Golden Age of love and freedom.

WORLDS ON WORLDS ARE ROLLING EVER

Worlds on worlds are rolling ever
   From creation to decay,
Like the bubbles on a river
   Sparkling, bursting, borne away.
   But they are still immortal 5
   Who, through birth's orient portal
And death's dark chasm hurrying to and fro,
   Clothe their unceasing flight
   In the brief dust and light
Gathered around their chariots as they go; 10

---

451. **too young.** Shelley's son William, who died in June, 1819, was buried there. The cemetery was new. 465. **that ... seek,** Absolute Beauty.

New shapes they still may weave,
   New gods, new laws receive,
Bright or dim are they as the robes they last
   On Death's bare ribs had cast.

A power from the unknown God,   15
   A Promethean conqueror, came;
Like a triumphal path he trod
   The thorns of death and shame.
   A mortal shape to him
   Was like the vapor dim   20
Which the orient planet animates with light;
   Hell, Sin, and Slavery came,
   Like bloodhounds mild and tame,
Nor preyed, until their lord had taken flight;
   The moon of Mahomet   25
   Arose, and it shall set:
While blazoned as on Heaven's immortal noon
   The cross leads generations on.

Swift as the radiant shapes of sleep
   From one whose dreams are Paradise,   30
Fly, when the fond wretch wakes to weep,
   And Day peers forth with her blank eyes;
   So fleet, so faint, so fair,
   The Powers of earth and air
Fled from the folding-star of Bethlehem: 35
   Apollo, Pan, and Love,
   And even Olympian Jove
Grew weak, for killing Truth had glared on them;
   Our hills and seas and streams,
   Dispeopled of their dreams,   40
Their waters turned to blood, their dew to tears,
   Wailed for the golden years.

FINAL CHORUS FROM *HELLAS*

The world's great age begins anew,
   The golden years return,

The earth doth like a snake renew
   Her winter weeds outworn;
Heaven smiles, and faiths and empires gleam,
Like wrecks of a dissolving dream.   126

A brighter Hellas rears its mountains
   From waves serener far;
A new Peneus rolls his fountains
   Against the morning star.   130
Where fairer Tempes bloom, there sleep
Young Cyclads on a sunnier deep.

A loftier Argo cleaves the main,
   Fraught with a later prize;
Another Orpheus sings again,   135
   And loves, and weeps, and dies.
A new Ulysses leaves once more
Calypso for his native shore.

Oh, write no more the tale of Troy,
   If earth Death's scroll must be!   140
Nor mix with Laian rage the joy
   Which dawns upon the free;
Although a subtler Sphinx renew
Riddles of death Thebes never knew.

Another Athens shall arise,   145
   And to remoter time
Bequeath, like sunset to the skies,
   The splendor of its prime;
And leave, if nought so bright may live,
All earth can take or Heaven can give. 150

Saturn and Love their long repose
   Shall burst, more bright and good

16. **Promethean,** pertaining to Prometheus, in Greek mythology, the founder of civilization and the benefactor of mankind. 25. **Mahomet,** Mohammed (570-632), founder of the Mohammedan religion. 35. **folding-star,** the evening star, which appears about the time the sheep are put into the fold. 36. **Apollo,** god of music and poetry. **Pan,** god of hills and woods, flocks and herds. 37. **Olympian Jove.** The gods were supposed to inhabit Olympus, a mountain in Thessaly, Greece.
Final Chorus from *Hellas*. 121. **The world's great age.** At the end of the "great age" of the ancients, the sun, moon, and planets were to return to their original positions, and the history of the world would repeat itself; the Golden Age would return and be followed by ages of degradation and evil. Cf. Byron's *Isles of Greece*, p. 235.

124. **weeds,** garments. 127. **Hellas,** Greece. 129. **Peneus,** a river in Thessaly, Greece. 131. **Tempe,** a beautiful valley through which the Peneus River flows. 132. **Cyclads,** the Cyclades, islands in the Aegean Sea. 133. **Argo,** the ship of the Argonauts, who accompanied Jason on his quest for the Golden Fleece. 135. **Orpheus,** mythological poet and musician, who went to the lower world to lead his wife Eurydice back to the upper world. He was given permission to do so on condition that he should not look back at her until they reached the upper air. Orpheus broke the condition, and Eurydice vanished. 137. **Ulysses,** King of Ithaca, one of the Greek heroes in the Trojan War. He is the hero of Homer's *Odyssey*. When shipwrecked, he was detained on an island by the nymph Calypso, who promised him immortal youth if he would remain with her, but he refused. See Tennyson's *Ulysses*, p. 612. 141. **Laian rage.** Laius, King of Thebes, upon learning from the oracle that he would be killed by his son, left the infant Oedipus in an exposed place. The boy was rescued and later slew his father unwittingly. 143. **Sphinx ... knew.** The Sphinx was a winged monster in Thebes that killed all who could not solve her riddle. Oedipus solved it, and she cast herself down from a rock and was killed. 151. **Saturn and Love,** supposed to have ruled in the Golden Age of innocence and happiness.

Than all who fell, than One who rose,
   Than many unsubdued;
Not gold, not blood, their altar dowers,   155
But votive tears and symbol flowers.

Oh, cease! must hate and death return?
   Cease! must men kill and die?
Cease! drain not to its dregs the urn
   Of bitter prophecy.   160
The world is weary of the past,
Oh, might it die or rest at last!

                        (*1821;* 1822)

Remembrance

Swifter far than summer's flight—
Swifter far than youth's delight—
Swifter far than happy night,
   Art thou come and gone—
As the earth when leaves are dead,   5
As the night when sleep is sped,
As the heart when joy is fled,
   I am left lone, alone.

The swallow summer comes again—
The owlet night resumes her reign—   10
But the wild-swan youth is fain
   To fly with thee, false as thou.—
My heart each day desires the morrow;
Sleep itself is turned to sorrow;
Vainly would my winter borrow   15
   Sunny leaves from any bough.

Lilies for a bridal bed—
Roses for a matron's head—
Violets for a maiden dead—
   Pansies let *my* flowers be: 20
On the living grave I bear
Scatter them without a tear—
Let no friend, however dear,
   Waste one hope, one fear for me.

                        (*1821;* 1824)

153. **all who fell,** the gods of Greece, Asia, and Egypt. **One who rose,** Christ. 154. **many unsubdued,** objects of the idolatry of China, India, etc.
Remembrance. 10. **owlet night,** dim, uncanny night. 17. **Lilies,** etc. The lily is a symbol of purity; the rose, of constancy; the violet, of modesty; the pansy, of thought or remembrance. Cf. Shelley's *Adonais,* ll. 289-292, p. 267.

To——

This poem was addressed to Jane Williams, the wife of Edward Williams; both were warm friends of Shelley during his later years in Italy. See p. 250.

One word is too often profaned
   For me to profane it,
One feeling too falsely disdained
   For thee to disdain it;
One hope is too like despair   5
   For prudence to smother,
And pity from thee more dear
   Than that from another.

I can give not what men call love,
   But wilt thou accept not   10
The worship the heart lifts above
   And the Heavens reject not—
The desire of the moth for the star,
   Of the night for the morrow,
The devotion to something afar   15
   From the sphere of our sorrow?

                        (*1821;* 1824)

Lines

   When the lamp is shattered,
The light in the dust lies dead—
   When the cloud is scattered,
The rainbow's glory is shed.
   When the lute is broken,   5
Sweet tones are remembered not;
   When the lips have spoken,
Loved accents are soon forgot.

   As music and splendor
Survive not the lamp and the lute,   10
   The heart's echoes render
No song when the spirit is mute—
   No song but sad dirges,
Like the wind through a ruined cell,
   Or the mournful surges   15
That ring the dead seaman's knell.

When hearts have once mingled
Love first leaves the well-built nest;

The weak one is singled
To endure what it once possessed.
  O Love! who bewailest
The frailty of all things here,
  Why choose you the frailest
For your cradle, your home, and your bier?

  Its passions will rock thee
As the storms rock the ravens on high;
  Bright reason will mock thee,
Like the sun from a wintry sky.
  From thy nest every rafter
Will rot, and thine eagle home

Leave thee naked to laughter,
When leaves fall and cold winds come.

(1822; 1824)

A Dirge

Rough wind, that moanest loud
  Grief too sad for song;
Wild wind, when sullen cloud
  Knells all the night long;
Sad storm, whose tears are vain,
Bare woods, whose branches strain,
Deep caves and dreary main—
  Wail, for the world's wrong!

(1822; 1824)

John Keats
1795-1821

    English literature has no more tragic story to offer than that of John Keats, if by tragedy we mean the death of a great personage before maturity. One of the most interesting subjects for speculation is the question as to what the three great young romantic poets of England—Byron, Shelley, and Keats—would have become if they had been allowed to reach the span of life usually allotted man. Byron, it is possible, would have followed the neo-classical bent that was certainly part of his make-up; concerning Shelley and Keats no answer is forthcoming. Both were young in years and in outlook; both were of the very essence of youth and romance, albeit in somewhat different ways. Both were devotees of beauty, particularly in the abstract. Would they ever have become middle-aged, and if so, how would their advancing years have dealt with them?

    John Keats was born October 29, 1795. His father was a London livery-stable keeper. The boy's parents both died when he was young; the father when Keats was but nine; the mother when he was fifteen. He went to school at Enfield, and in 1810 was apprenticed to a surgeon at Edmonton—both towns near London. In school he was a sturdy, aggressive young fellow, athletically inclined. His friends all testified to his fine character and his general high-mindedness. He was a voracious reader and an honor student in school, but he left school as his uncles wanted to fit him for the medical profession. He finished his apprenticeship in 1815. Far more important than this event, however, was his discovery of Spenser's *Faerie Queene,* for the great Renaissance epic opened to him a field of beauty that he had hitherto suspected but never experienced. Although Keats spent a year or so in London hospitals, he was more prone to see elves in the sunbeams than wounds to be dressed, and he finally abandoned the idea of a medical career to take up literature.

    Through his friend Clarke, who had shown him the *Faerie Queene,* Keats met Leigh Hunt, the tireless worker for revolutionary and romantic literature (p. 297), and through Hunt he met Hazlitt (p. 360) and Shelley (p. 248). He was able to publish a few sonnets in Leigh Hunt's periodical, *The Examiner,* and so make a start as a poet. He drifted into acquaintance with Wordsworth (p. 118), Lamb (p. 337), and Coleridge (p. 163). He published (1817) a volume of poems, dedicated to Hunt, and followed this with *Endymion* in 1818. It happened that Hunt, for a variety of reasons, was *persona non grata* with the conservative critics of London, and Keats's friendship for Hunt doomed *Endymion* to harsh criticism, some of which it unquestionably deserved, for it was oversensuous, with a kind of tropical lushness, and with many poor lines to offset the occasional noble ones. The review in the *Quarterly* criticized the literary efforts of Keats, as did *Blackwood's Magazine;* but the latter also insulted Keats's humble beginnings and surgeon's profession beyond all bounds of good taste.

Keats was depressed by these reviews, of course, and even thought for a time of giving up literature. Yet there is certainly no cause to think that he suffered a broken heart and so laid him down to die, as Shelley had it in *Adonais* (p. 262). Indeed, Keats recognized the immaturity of *Endymion*. Family and personal cares, however, saddened him immeasurably. One brother left for America; another brother died of tuberculosis—apparently a family affliction, for Keats's mother had also died of it; financial troubles worried him; and he himself came to feel the ominous symptoms of the family disease. He took a trip through the north of England, but it yielded him no lasting relief. By the end of the year (1818) the suspicion of tuberculosis was confirmed. And, as a sort of tragic climax, he met and fell in love with Fanny Brawne—a hopeless passion, in view of his poverty and illness. None knew that better than John Keats.

He went to live for a time with a friend, Charles Brown, at a house near Hampstead Heath, London, but his illness progressed remorselessly to its fatal conclusion. As a last resort he tried the softer climate of Italy. But it was too late; in less than six months he was dead (February 23, 1821) and buried in the Protestant cemetery at Rome under his own epitaph: "Here lies one whose name was writ in water."

The brief three years from 1818 to 1821 were depressing years for Keats, tragic years indeed, but they developed his genius amazingly. Not even the tremendous efflorescence of Shelley in Italy is any more remarkable. After *Endymion* there came a year's wait while he wrestled with fate and lost; but in the autumn of 1819 came *The Eve of St. Agnes* (p. 285), one of the chief monuments of the English romantic movement; *La Belle Dame sans Merci* (p. 282), a fine witch-ballad; and most of his splendid odes, which many have considered his finest performances. In the following year (1820) came the three narrative poems, *Lamia,* based upon the classical story of the snake woman; *Isabella, or The Pot of Basil,* a tragedy of the Renaissance suggested by a story from Boccaccio's *Decameron;* and an unfinished version of a classical myth, *Hyperion.* In addition to these excellent achievements must be reckoned a number of sonnets and even some dramatic fragments.

Unlike his turbulent contemporaries Byron and Shelley, Keats is a remarkably tranquil poet. His is the gift of the tapestry-weaver and the picture-painter; his master Spenser, himself a poet of pictorial beauty, stands beside Keats in all his work. He is not interested in revolution or reform; he prefers to contemplate the beauty of a Grecian urn, of a beautiful girl, or of the storied past, to contemplate them and ponder upon them in unforgettable phrase until he achieves a sense of nothingness in the face of vast time and space. It is not possible to consider Keats a philosopher. But the passion for decoration, for the rich luxury of sense-stimulating words, for the evocation of moods and feelings—in a word, for everything that can heighten the emotion and the imagination into a sense of escape from realities—this passion Keats cherishes more than any other poet of his generation. He is the very incarnation of the passive side of the romantic movement. His influence upon the later poets of the nineteenth century, upon Tennyson, upon Rossetti, and others was very great. It is, moreover, a legitimate influence, for Keats's worship of beauty has about it something of the timeless and the deathless.

>When old age shall this generation waste,
> Thou shalt remain, in midst of other woe
> Than ours, a friend to man . . .

On First Looking into Chapman's Homer

A translation of Homer by George Chapman (c. 1559-1634), famous Elizabethan dramatist and translator of classics, which Keats and his friend Charles Cowden Clarke spent a night reading, was the inspiration of this notable sonnet.

Much have I traveled in the realms of gold,
And many goodly states and kingdoms seen;
Round many western islands have I been
Which bards in fealty to Apollo hold.
Oft of one wide expanse had I been told 5
That deep-browed Homer ruled as his demesne;
Yet did I never breathe its pure serene
Till I heard Chapman speak out loud and bold:
Then felt I like some watcher of the skies
When a new planet swims into his ken; 10
Or like stout Cortez when with eagle eyes
He stared at the Pacific—and all his men
Looked at each other with a wild surmise—
Silent, upon a peak in Darien.

(*1815;* 1816)

To One Who Has Been Long in City Pent

To one who has been long in city pent
'Tis very sweet to look into the fair
And open face of heaven—to breathe a prayer
Full in the smile of the blue firmament.
Who is more happy, when, with heart's content, 5
Fatigued he sinks into some pleasant lair
Of wavy grass, and reads a debonair
And gentle tale of love and languishment?
Returning home at evening, with an ear
Catching the notes of Philomel—an eye 10

Watching the sailing cloudlet's bright career,
He mourns that day so soon has glided by:
E'en like the passage of an angel's tear
That falls through the clear ether silently.

(*1816;* 1817)

Addressed to Haydon

Great spirits now on earth are sojourning;
He of the cloud, the cataract, the lake,
Who on Helvellyn's summit, wide awake,
Catches his freshness from Archangel's wing:
He of the rose, the violet, the spring, 5
The social smile, the chain for Freedom's sake:
And lo!—whose steadfastness would never take
A meaner sound than Raphael's whispering.
And other spirits there are standing apart
Upon the forehead of the age to come; 10
These, these will give the world another heart,
And other pulses. Hear ye not the hum
Of mighty workings in the human mart?
Listen awhile ye nations, and be dumb.

(*1816;* 1817)

On Seeing the Elgin Marbles

My spirit is too weak—mortality
Weighs heavily on me like unwilling sleep,
And each imagined pinnacle and steep
Of godlike hardship tells me I must die
Like a sick eagle looking at the sky. 5
Yet 'tis a gentle luxury to weep
That I have not the cloudy winds to keep,
Fresh for the opening of the morning's eye.
Such dim-conceivéd glories of the brain
Bring round the heart an undescribable feud;

On First . . . Homer. 4. **Apollo,** god of poetry and music. 11. **Cortez.** It was Balboa, not Cortez, who discovered the Pacific Ocean, in 1513. 14. **Darien,** a district forming the eastern part of the Isthmus of Panama.
To One . . . Pent. 10. **Philomel,** the nightingale.

Addressed to Haydon. Benjamin Robert Haydon (1786-1846) was a noted English historical painter and one of Keats's close friends. 2. **He . . . wing,** Wordsworth, p. 118. 3. **Helvellyn,** a mountain in Cumberlandshire, near Wordsworth's home. 5. **He . . . sake,** Leigh Hunt (p. 297), to whom Keats dedicated his first volume of poems. 7. **whose . . . whispering,** Haydon. 8. **Raphael,** a noted Italian painter (1483-1520).
On Seeing the Elgin Marbles. Thomas Bruce (1766-1841), Earl of Elgin, was a British diplomat who collected the "Elgin Marbles," ancient Greek sculptures brought from the Parthenon, in Athens, in 1803-1812, and placed them subsequently in the British Museum. Keats derived much of his sympathy with Greek ideas of beauty from these antiquities.

On the Sea

It keeps eternal whisperings around
Desolate shores, and with its mighty swell
Gluts twice ten thousand caverns, till the spell
Of Hecate leaves them their old shadowy
    sound.
Often 'tis in such gentle temper found,   5
That scarcely will the very smallest shell
Be moved for days from whence it sometime
    fell,
When last the winds of heaven were unbound.
Oh ye! who have your eye-balls vexed and
    tired,
Feast them upon the wideness of the sea;   10
Oh ye! whose ears are dinned with uproar
    rude,
Or fed too much with cloying melody—
Sit ye near some old cavern's mouth, and
    brood
Until ye start, as if the sea-nymphs quired!
                            (*1817;* 1848)

When I Have Fears That I May Cease to Be

When I have fears that I may cease to be
Before my pen has gleaned my teeming brain,
Before high pilèd books, in charactry,
Hold like rich garners the full-ripened grain;
When I behold, upon the night's starred face, 5
Huge cloudy symbols of a high romance,
And think that I may never live to trace
Their shadows, with the magic hand of
    chance;
And when I feel, fair creature of an hour!
That I shall never look upon thee more,   10
Never have relish in the faery power
Of unreflecting love!—then on the shore
Of the wide world I stand alone, and think
Till Love and Fame to nothingness do sink.
                                  (*1818;* 1848)

4. **Hecate**, an ancient goddess associated in part with the moon. The reference is to the moon's control of the tides. *When I Have Fears.* 3. **charactry**, characters, letters.

Lines on the Mermaid Tavern

J. H. Reynolds (1796-1825), poet, critic, and lawyer, had sent Keats two sonnets on Robin Hood; this poem and the next were sent to Reynolds by Keats in reply. The Mermaid Tavern was a famous London resort of Shakespeare, Ben Jonson, and other Elizabethan dramatists and men of letters. Keats was in full sympathy with the spirit of the Elizabethans.

Souls of Poets dead and gone,
What Elysium have ye known,
Happy field or mossy cavern,
Choicer than the Mermaid Tavern?
Have ye tippled drink more fine   5
Than mine host's Canary wine?
Or are fruits of Paradise
Sweeter than those dainty pies
Of venison? O generous food!
Drest as though bold Robin Hood   10
Would, with his maid Marian,
Sup and bowse from horn and can.

I have heard that on a day
Mine host's sign-board flew away,
Nobody knew whither, till   15
An astrologer's old quill
To a sheepskin gave the story,
Said he saw you in your glory,
Underneath a new old sign
Sipping beverage divine,   20
And pledging with contented smack
The Mermaid in the Zodiac.

Souls of Poets dead and gone,
What Elysium have ye known,
Happy field or mossy cavern,   25
Choicer than the Mermaid Tavern?
                               (*1818;* 1820)

Robin Hood

No! those days are gone away,
And their hours are old and gray,

2. **Elysium**, abode of the blessed after death. 6. **Canary wine**, wine made in the Canary Islands; this was Elizabethan "sack." 10. **Robin Hood**, noted as a chivalrous and generous outlaw. Maid Marian was one of his associates. Keats was fond of this legendary medieval hero. For ballads of Robin Hood, see Vol. I, p. 126. 12. **bowse**, drink. 22. **Mermaid in the Zodiac**, the sign of the Virgin in the Zodiac.
Robin Hood. See previous poem and notes.

So do these wonders a most dizzy pain,   11
That mingles Grecian grandeur with the rude
Wasting of old Time—with a billowy main—
A sun—a shadow of a magnitude.   (1817)

And their minutes buried all
Under the down-trodden pall
Of the leaves of many years:
Many times have winter's shears,
Frozen North, and chilling East,
Sounded tempests to the feast
Of the forest's whispering fleeces,
Since men knew nor rent nor leases.

No, the bugle sounds no more,
And the twanging bow no more;
Silent is the ivory shrill
Past the heath and up the hill;
There is no mid-forest laugh,
Where lone Echo gives the half
To some wight, amazed to hear
Jesting, deep in forest drear.

On the fairest time of June
You may go, with sun or moon,
Or the seven stars to light you,
Or the polar ray to right you;
But you never may behold
Little John, or Robin bold;
Never one, of all the clan,
Thrumming on an empty can
Some old hunting ditty, while
He doth his green way beguile
To fair hostess Merriment,
Down beside the pasture Trent;
For he left the merry tale
Messenger for spicy ale.

Gone, the merry morris din;
Gone, the song of Gamelyn;
Gone, the tough-belted outlaw
Idling in the "grené shawe";
All are gone away and past!
And if Robin should be cast
Sudden from his turféd grave,
And if Marian should have
Once again her forest days,
She would weep, and he would craze:
He would swear, for all his oaks,
Fallen beneath the dockyard strokes,
Have rotted on the briny seas;
She would weep that her wild bees
Sang not to her—strange! that honey
Can't be got without hard money!

So it is: yet let us sing,
Honor to the old bow-string!
Honor to the bugle-horn!
Honor to the woods unshorn!
Honor to the Lincoln green!
Honor to the archer keen!
Honor to tight Little John,
And the horse he rode upon!
Honor to bold Robin Hood,
Sleeping in the underwood!
Honor to Maid Marian,
And to all the Sherwood-clan!
Though their days have hurried by,
Let us two a burden try. *(1818; 1820)*

In a Drear-Nighted December

In a drear-nighted December,
Too happy, happy tree,
Thy branches ne'er remember
Their green felicity:
The north cannot undo them,
With a sleety whistle through them;
Nor frozen thawings glue them
From budding at the prime.

In a drear-nighted December,
Too happy, happy brook,
Thy bubblings ne'er remember
Apollo's summer look;
But with a sweet forgetting,
They stay their crystal fretting,
Never, never petting
About the frozen time.

Ah! would 'twere so with many
A gentle girl and boy!
But were there ever any
Writhed not at passéd joy?
To know the change and feel it,

---

9. **fleeces**, leaves. 13. **ivory**, whistle. 17. **wight**, person. 21. **seven stars**, the Pleiades, or perhaps the Big Dipper. 22. **polar ray**, the North Star. 24. **Little John**, an associate of Robin Hood. 30. **pasture Trent**, fields near the River Trent in Nottinghamshire. 33. **morris**, a popular dance in which the dancers often impersonated Robin Hood, Maid Marian, and other legendary characters. 34. **Gamelyn**, an outlaw hero of a medieval tale, formerly attributed to Chaucer, one of Keats's favorite English writers. 36. **"grené shawe,"** green wood.

53. **Lincoln green**, a cloth made in Lincoln; it was worn by huntsmen. 55. **tight**, trim, well-formed. 60. **Sherwood**, a forest in Nottinghamshire, principal scene of the legendary exploits of Robin Hood and his band. 62. **burden**, chorus, song.
In a Drear-Nighted December. 12. **Apollo**, god of poetry and music. 15. **petting**, complaining.

When there is none to heal it,
Nor numbéd sense to steal it,
Was never said in rime. (*1818?; 1829*)

Proem from *Endymion*

Endymion was composed during the year 1817. Keats spent some time on the Isle of Wight in the spring of that year, and began the poem there. This, the first ambitious poem that Keats wrote, caused him much anxiety and self-dissatisfaction, for he was still a virtual neophyte in poetry but at the same time had a considerable amount of ability to criticize himself. The reception of the poem confirmed Keats's worst fears; the severe, unfavorable criticism accorded it has already been noted (pp. 262 and 274).

In the poem, Keats follows the general outline of the old classical myth of Endymion, the beautiful youth beloved of the moon goddess Diana. But, as he was to do again in *Hyperion*, he elaborates the story by giving it a luxuriant descriptive background, heightening the emotional effects wherever possible, and coloring it heavily with his own fervent imagination. In other words, he has romanticized the story, in greater degree than Wordsworth did the classical material in *Laodamia*, and in a manner that had a powerful influence upon Tennyson in such poems as *Oenone* and *The Lotos-Eaters* (p. 608). To look at the poem from another point of view, *Endymion* is, along with the sonnet *On First Looking into Chapman's Homer* (p. 275), the first important manifestation by Keats of the interest in classical literature common among romantic writers. It may be remarked in passing that in their worship of beauty, the romantic writers like Keats and Shelley often came much closer to the ideals of ancient Greek art than did the neo-classical writers of the eighteenth century, however much the romantic quality of effusiveness ran against the old classical ideal of moderation. The opening passage in *Endymion* should be compared with the great *Ode on a Grecian Urn* (p. 281) for a complete expression of Keats's love of the classical ideal of beauty.

A thing of beauty is a joy forever:
Its loveliness increases; it will never
Pass into nothingness; but still will keep
A bower quiet for us, and a sleep
Full of sweet dreams, and health, and quiet
    breathing.   5
Therefore, on every morrow, are we wreathing
A flowery band to bind us to the earth,
Spite of despondence, of the inhuman dearth
Of noble natures, of the gloomy days,
Of all the unhealthy and o'er-darkened ways
Made for our searching: yes, in spite of all, 11
Some shape of beauty moves away the pall
From our dark spirits. Such the sun, the
    moon,
Trees old, and young, sprouting a shady boon
For simple sheep; and such are daffodils 15
With the green world they live in; and clear
    rills
That for themselves a cooling covert make
'Gainst the hot season; the mid-forest brake,
Rich with a sprinkling of fair musk-rose
    blooms:
And such too is the grandeur of the dooms 20
We have imagined for the mighty dead;
All lovely tales that we have heard or read:
An endless fountain of immortal drink,
Pouring unto us from the heaven's brink.

Nor do we merely feel these essences 25
For one short hour; no, even as the trees
That whisper round a temple become soon
Dear as the temple's self, so does the moon,
The passion poesy, glories infinite,
Haunt us till they become a cheering light 30
Unto our souls, and bound to us so fast,
That, whether there be shine, or gloom o'ercast,
They always must be with us, or we die.

Therefore, 'tis with full happiness that I
Will trace the story of Endymion. 35
The very music of the name has gone
Into my being, and each pleasant scene
Is growing fresh before me as the green
Of our own valleys: so I will begin
Now while I cannot hear the city's din; 40
Now while the early budders are just new,
And run in mazes of the youngest hue
About old forests; while the willow trails
Its delicate amber; and the dairy pails 44
Bring home increase of milk. And, as the year
Grows lush in juicy stalks, I'll smoothly steer
My little boat, for many quiet hours,

18. **brake**, thicket. 20. **dooms**, destinies.

With streams that deepen freshly into bowers.
Many and many a verse I hope to write,
Before the daisies, vermeil-rimmed and white,
Hide in deep herbage; and ere yet the bees 51
Hum about globes of clover and sweet peas,
I must be near the middle of my story.
O may no wintry season, bare and hoary,
See it half finished: but let Autumn bold, 55
With universal tinge of sober gold,
Be all about me when I make an end.
And now at once, adventuresome, I send
My herald thought into a wilderness:
There let its trumpet blow, and quickly dress
My uncertain path with green, that I may speed 61
Easily onward, thorough flowers and weed.

(1817-18; 1818)

Fancy

Keats here identifies fancy and imagination. Cf. *Ode on a Grecian Urn*, ll. 11-12 (p. 281).

Ever let the Fancy roam,
Pleasure never is at home:
At a touch sweet Pleasure melteth,
Like to bubbles when rain pelteth;
Then let wingéd Fancy wander 5
Through the thought still spread beyond her:
Open wide the mind's cage-door,
She'll dart forth, and cloudward soar.
O sweet Fancy! let her loose;
Summer's joys are spoilt by use, 10
And the enjoying of the Spring
Fades as does its blossoming;
Autumn's red-lipped fruitage too,
Blushing through the mist and dew,
Cloys with tasting: What do then? 15
Sit thee by the ingle, when
The sear fagot blazes bright,
Spirit of a winter's night;
When the soundless earth is muffled,
And the cakéd snow is shuffled 20
From the plowboy's heavy shoon;
When the Night doth meet the Noon
In a dark conspiracy
To banish Even from her sky.
Sit thee there, and send abroad, 25
With a mind self-overawed

Fancy, high-commissioned—send her!
She has vassals to attend her:
She will bring, in spite of frost,
Beauties that the earth hath lost; 30
She will bring thee, all together,
All delights of summer weather;
All the buds and bells of May,
From dewy sward or thorny spray;
All the heapéd Autumn's wealth, 35
With a still, mysterious stealth:
She will mix these pleasures up
Like three fit wines in a cup,
And thou shalt quaff it—thou shalt hear
Distant harvest-carols clear; 40
Rustle of the reapéd corn;
Sweet birds antheming the morn:
And, in the same moment—hark!
'Tis the early April lark,
Or the rooks, with busy caw, 45
Foraging for sticks and straw.
Thou shalt, at one glance, behold
The daisy and the marigold;
White-plumed lilies, and the first
Hedge-grown primrose that hath burst; 50
Shaded hyacinth, alway
Sapphire queen of the mid-May;
And every leaf and every flower
Pearléd with the self-same shower.
Thou shalt see the field mouse peep 55
Meager from its celléd sleep;
And the snake all winter-thin
Cast on sunny bank its skin;
Freckled nest-eggs thou shalt see
Hatching in the hawthorn-tree, 60
When the henbird's wing doth rest
Quiet on her mossy nest;
Then the hurry and alarm
When the bee-hive casts its swarm;
Acorns ripe down-pattering, 65
While the autumn breezes sing.

Oh, sweet Fancy! let her loose;
Every thing is spoiled by use:
Where's the cheek that doth not fade,
Too much gazed at? Where's the maid 70
Whose lip mature is ever new?
Where's the eye, however blue,
Doth not weary? Where's the face
One would meet in every place?

62. **thorough,** through.
Fancy. 16. **ingle,** fireplace. 21. **shoon,** shoes.
41. **corn,** wheat.

Where's the voice, however soft, 75
One would hear so very oft?
At a touch sweet Pleasure melteth
Like to bubbles when rain pelteth.
Let, then, wingèd Fancy find
Thee a mistress to thy mind: 80
Dulcet-eyed as Ceres' daughter,
Ere the God of Torment taught her
How to frown and how to chide;
With a waist and with a side
White as Hebe's, when her zone 85
Slipped its golden clasp, and down
Fell her kirtle to her feet,
While she held the goblet sweet,
And Jove grew languid.—Break the mesh
Of the Fancy's silken leash; 90
Quickly break her prison-string
And such joys as these she'll bring.—
Let the wingèd Fancy roam,
Pleasure never is at home. (*1818;* 1820)

Tales and golden histories 75
Of heaven and its mysteries.

Thus ye live on high, and then
On the earth ye live again;
And the souls ye left behind you 25
Teach us, here, the way to find you,
Where your other souls are joying,
Never slumbered, never cloying.
Here, your earth-born souls still speak
To mortals, of their little week; 30
Of their sorrows and delights;
Of their passions and their spites;
Of their glory and their shame;
What doth strengthen and what maim.
Thus ye teach us, every day, 35
Wisdom, though fled far away.

Bards of Passion and of Mirth,
Ye have left your souls on earth!
Ye have souls in heaven too,
Double-lived in regions new! (*1819;* 1820)

Ode

This poem was addressed to Beaumont and Fletcher, Elizabethan dramatists.

Bards of Passion and of Mirth,
Ye have left your souls on earth!
Have ye souls in heaven too,
Double-lived in regions new?
Yes, and those of heaven commune 5
With the spheres of sun and moon;
With the noise of fountains wond'rous,
And the parle of voices thund'rous;
With the whisper of heaven's trees
And one another, in soft ease 10
Seated on Elysian lawns
Browsed by none but Dian's fawns;
Underneath large blue-bells tented,
Where the daisies are rose-scented,
And the rose herself has got 15
Perfume which on earth is not;
Where the nightingale doth sing
Not a senseless, trancèd thing,
But divine melodious truth;
Philosophic numbers smooth; 20

81. **Ceres' daughter**, Prosperpina, whom Pluto, "the God of Torment," carried away as his bride to his realm in the lower world. 85. **Hebe**, the cup-bearer of the gods. **zone**, girdle.
Ode. 8. **parle**, talk, discourse. 11. **Elysian**, of Elysium, the home of the blessed after death. 12. **Dian's fawns.** The fawn was the favorite animal of Diana, goddess of the moon and the chase.

Ode on Melancholy

The quality of melancholy, so common in romantic literature, has never received more poetic treatment than in this poem. The poem, although not published until 1820, was written in 1819, after the disasters which befell Keats in 1818 (p. 274). Keats wrote this letter to his friend Haydon (p. 275 and note) at the beginning of the year 1819: "I have been writing a little now and then lately: but nothing to speak of—being discontented and as it were moulting. Yet I do not think I shall ever come to the rope or the pistol, for after a day or two's melancholy, although I smoke more and more my own insufficiency—I see by little and little more of what is to be done, and how it is to be done, should I ever be able to do it. On my soul, there should be some reward for that continual *agonie ennuyeuse.*"

No, no! go not to Lethe, neither twist
  Wolf's-bane, tight-rooted, for its poisonous
    wine;
Nor suffer thy pale forehead to be kissed
  By nightshade, ruby grape of Proserpine;
Make not your rosary of yew-berries, 5

1. **Lethe**, the river of forgetfulness in Hades. 2. **Wolf's-bane**, aconite, a poisonous plant. 4. **nightshade**, a poisonous herb. **Proserpine.** See *Fancy*, l. 81 and note, col. 1. 5. **yew-berries.** The yew is an emblem of mourning.

Nor let the beetle, nor the death-moth be
  Your mournful Psyche, nor the downy owl
A partner in your sorrow's mysteries;
  For shade to shade will come too drowsily,
    And drown the wakeful anguish of the soul.   10

But when the melancholy fit shall fall
  Sudden from heaven like a weeping cloud,
That fosters the droop-headed flowers all,
  And hides the green hill in an April shroud;
Then glut thy sorrow on a morning rose,   15
  Or on the rainbow of the salt sand-wave,
  Or on the wealth of globéd peonies;
Or if thy mistress some rich anger shows,
  Emprison her soft hand, and let her rave,
    And feed deep, deep upon her peerless eyes.   20

She dwells with Beauty—Beauty that must die;
  And Joy, whose hand is ever at his lips
  Bidding adieu; and aching Pleasure nigh,
    Turning to poison while the bee-mouth sips:
Ay, in the very temple of Delight   25
  Veiled Melancholy has her sovran shrine,
    Though seen of none save him whose strenuous tongue
  Can burst Joy's grape against his palate fine;
His soul shall taste the sadness of her might,
  And be among her cloudy trophies hung.

(1819; 1820)

Ode on a Grecian Urn

According to tradition, the urn that inspired this famous ode was one still preserved in the garden of Holland House, a noted mansion in Kensington, London. But there were many such treasures in the British Museum, decorated with marble urns carved with figures in low relief (see ll. 41-42). The enduring beauty of any one of them would have been enough to confirm Keats in his characteristic belief that Beauty is the all-important element in human experience. Cf. Masefield's *On Growing Old* (p. 922).

Thou still unravished bride of quietness,
  Thou foster-child of Silence and slow Time,
Sylvan historian, who canst thus express
  A flowery tale more sweetly than our rime:
What leaf-fringed legend haunts about thy shape   5
  Of deities or mortals, or of both,
    In Tempe or the dales of Arcady?
What men or gods are these? What maidens loth?
What mad pursuit? What struggle to escape?
  What pipes and timbrels? What wild ecstasy?   10

Heard melodies are sweet, but those unheard
  Are sweeter; therefore, ye soft pipes, play on;
Not to the sensual ear, but, more endeared,
  Pipe to the spirit ditties of no tone:
Fair youth, beneath the trees, thou canst not leave   15
  Thy song, nor ever can those trees be bare;
    Bold Lover, never, never canst thou kiss,
Though winning near the goal—yet, do not grieve;
  She cannot fade, though thou hast not thy bliss,
    Forever wilt thou love, and she be fair!   20

Ah, happy, happy boughs! that cannot shed
  Your leaves, nor ever bid the Spring adieu;
And, happy melodist, unweariéd,
  Forever piping songs forever new.
More happy love! more happy, happy love!   25
  Forever warm and still to be enjoyed,
    Forever panting, and forever young;
All breathing human passion far above,
  That leaves a heart high-sorrowful and cloyed,
    A burning forehead, and a parching tongue.   30

Who are these coming to the sacrifice?
  To what green altar, O mysterious priest,
Lead'st thou that heifer lowing at the skies,
  And all her silken flanks with garlands dressed?
What little town by river or seashore,   35
  Or mountain-built with peaceful citadel,
    Is emptied of this folk, this pious morn?
And, little town, thy streets forevermore

Will silent be; and not a soul to tell
   Why thou art desolate, can e'er return. 40

O Attic shape! Fair attitude! with brede
   Of marble men and maidens overwrought,
With forest branches and the trodden weed;
   Thou, silent form! dost tease us out of thought
As doth eternity: Cold Pastoral! 45
   When old age shall this generation waste,
   Thou shalt remain, in midst of other woe
Than ours, a friend to man, to whom thou say'st,
"Beauty is truth, truth beauty,"—that is all
   Ye know on earth, and all ye need to know.   (*1819;* 1820)

La Belle Dame sans Merci

The ancient folklore theme of the Fairy Lover was illustrated in the old popular ballad *Thomas Rymer* (Vol. I, p. 121). *La Belle Dame sans Merci* is Keats's highly romantic treatment of the same theme and a very distinguished literary ballad. The poem was printed by Leigh Hunt in *The Indicator* for May 10, 1820; the supposed source was a ballad by the French poet Alain Chartier (1392?-1436?), a translation of which was found by Keats in a volume of Chaucer's poetry.

O what can ail thee, knight-at-arms!
   Alone and palely loitering!
The sedge has withered from the lake,
   And no birds sing.

O what can ail thee, knight-at-arms! 5
   So haggard and so woe-begone?
The squirrel's granary is full,
   And the harvest's done.

I see a lily on thy brow
   With anguish moist and fever dew, 10
And on thy cheeks a fading rose
   Fast withereth too.

"I met a lady in the meads,
   Full beautiful—a faery's child,
Her hair was long, her foot was light, 15
   And her eyes were wild.

"I made a garland for her head,
   And bracelets too, and fragrant zone;
She looked at me as she did love,
   And made sweet moan. 20

"I set her on my pacing steed,
   And nothing else saw all day long.
For sidelong would she bend, and sing
   A faery's song.

"She found me roots of relish sweet, 25
   And honey wild and manna-dew;
And sure in language strange she said,
   'I love thee true.'

"She took me to her elfin grot,
   And there she wept and sighed full sore; 30
And there I shut her wild, wild eyes
   With kisses four.

"And there she lullèd me asleep,
   And there I dreamed—ah! woe betide!—
The latest dream I ever dreamed 35
   On the cold hillside.

"I saw pale kings, and princes too,
   Pale warriors, death-pale were they all:
They cried—'La Belle Dame sans Merci
   Hath thee in thrall!' 40

"I saw their starved lips in the gloam
   With horrid warning gapèd wide,
And I woke, and found me here
   On the cold hillside.

"And this is why I sojourn here 45
   Alone and palely loitering,
Though the sedge is withered from the lake,
   And no birds sing."   (*1819;* 1820)

On Fame

You cannot eat your cake and have it too.
                     Proverb.

How fevered is the man, who cannot look
Upon his mortal days with temperate blood,
Who vexes all the leaves of his life's book,
And robs its fair name of its maidenhood;
It is as if the rose should pluck herself, 5
Or the ripe plum finger its misty bloom,

---

41. **brede,** embroidery. 45. **Cold Pastoral,** pastoral story in marble. 49. **Beauty . . . know.** Cf. *Endymion,* ll. 1-5, p. 278. *La Belle Dame sans Merci,* the beautiful lady without pity. 3. **sedge,** coarse marsh grass. 13. **I met,** etc. The knight begins to speak here.

18. **zone,** girdle.

As if a Naiad, like a meddling elf,
Should darken her pure grot with muddy
    gloom:
But the rose leaves herself upon the briar,
For winds to kiss and grateful bees to feed, 10
And the ripe plum still wears its dim attire,
The undisturbéd lake has crystal space,
Why then should man, teasing the world for
    grace,
Spoil his salvation for a fierce miscreed?
                             (*1819;* 1848)

Another on Fame

Fame, like a wayward girl, will still be coy
To those who woo her with too slavish knees,
But makes surrender to some thoughtless boy,
And dotes the more upon a heart at ease;
She is a Gipsy—will not speak to those   5
Who have not learned to be content without
    her;
A Jilt, whose ear was never whispered close,
Who thinks they scandal her who talk about
    her;
A very Gipsy is she, Nilus-born,
Sister-in-law to jealous Potiphar;   10
Ye love-sick bards, repay her scorn for scorn,
Ye artists lovelorn, madmen that ye are!
Make your best bow to her and bid adieu,
Then, if she likes it, she will follow you.
                             (*1819;* 1848)

Ode to Psyche

    The story of Cupid and Psyche is a late Greek romance of the Christian era. It is the story of the love of a god for a mortal woman; but unlike the older tales based on this theme, the story ends happily, for Psyche, after untold hardships, wins deification and bliss among the gods of Olympus with Cupid.
    The letter which Keats wrote to his brother and sister on the subject of this ode has a certain amount of interest for the light it throws on his methods of writing: "The following poem . . . is the first and the only one with which I have taken even moderate pains. I have for the most part dash'd off my lines in a hurry. This I have done leisurely—I think it reads the more richly for it, and will I hope encourage me to write other things in even a more peaceable and healthy spirit."

O Goddess! hear these tuneless numbers,
    wrung
  By sweet enforcement and remembrance
    dear,
And pardon that thy secrets should be sung
  Even into thine own soft-conchéd ear:
Surely I dreamt today, or did I see   5
  The wingéd Psyche with awakened eyes?
I wandered in a forest thoughtlessly,
  And, on the sudden, fainting with surprise,
Saw two fair creatures, couchéd side by side
  In deepest grass, beneath the whisp'ring
    roof   10
  Of leaves and trembled blossoms, where
    there ran
    A brooklet, scarce espied:
'Mid hushed, cool-rooted flowers, fragrant-
    eyed,
  Blue, silver-white, and budded Tyrian,   14
They lay calm-breathing on the bedded grass;
  Their arms embracéd, and their pinions too;
  Their lips touched not, but had not bade
    adieu,
As if disjoinéd by soft-handed slumber,
And ready still past kisses to outnumber
  At tender eye-dawn of aurorean love: 20
    The wingéd boy I knew;
  But who wast thou, O happy, happy dove?
    His Psyche true!

O latest born and loveliest vision far
  Of all Olympus' faded hierarchy!   25
Fairer than Phoebe's sapphire-regioned star,
  Or Vesper, amorous glowworm of the sky;
Fairer than these, though temple thou hast
    none,
  Nor altar heaped with flowers;

On Fame. **7. Naiad,** one of the nymphs believed to live in lakes, rivers, springs, and fountains, and to give life to them. **14. miscreed,** false creed.
    Another on Fame. **9. Nilus-born.** Gypsies were once supposed to have come from Egypt. **10. Potiphar,** one of the officers of Pharaoh, king of Egypt. His wife tried to seduce Joseph. See *Genesis,* 39. The word *sister-in-law* gives Fame the characteristics of Potiphar's wife.

4. conchéd, shell-shaped. **14. budded Tyrian,** with buds of Tyrian purple. **21. wingéd boy,** Cupid, the god of love. **25. Olympus,** a famous mountain in Thessaly, Greece, the home of the gods. **26. Phoebe's . . . star,** the moon. Phoebe is Diana, goddess of the moon. **27. Vesper,** Venus, when an evening star.

Nor virgin-choir to make delicious moan 30
   Upon the midnight hours;
No voice, no lute, no pipe, no incense sweet
   From chain-swung censer teeming;
No shrine, no grove, no oracle, no heat
   Of pale-mouthed prophet dreaming. 35

O brightest! though too late for antique vows,
   Too, too late for the fond believing lyre,
When holy were the haunted forest boughs,
   Holy the air, the water, and the fire;
Yet even in these days so far retired 40
   From happy pieties, thy lucent fans,
     Fluttering among the faint Olympians,
I see, and sing, by my own eyes inspired.
So let me be thy choir, and make a moan
   Upon the midnight hours; 45
Thy voice, thy lute, thy pipe, thy incense sweet
   From swingéd censer teeming;
Thy shrine, thy grove, thy oracle, thy heat
   Of pale-mouthed prophet dreaming.

Yes, I will be thy priest, and build a fane 50
   In some untrodden region of my mind,
Where branchéd thoughts, new grown with
     pleasant pain,
Instead of pines shall murmur in the wind:
Far, far around shall those dark-clustered trees
   Fledge the wild-ridgéd mountains steep by
     steep; 55
And there by zephyrs, streams, and birds, and
     bees,
   The moss-lain Dryads shall be lulled to
     sleep;
And in the midst of this wide quietness
A rosy sanctuary will I dress
With the wreathéd trellis of a working brain,
   With buds, and bells, and stars without a
     name, 61
With all the gardener Fancy e'er could feign,
   Who, breeding flowers, will never breed the
     same;
And there shall be for thee all soft delight
   That shadowy thought can win, 65
A bright torch, and a casement ope at night,
   To let the warm Love in!   (*1819;* 1820)

41. **lucent fans**, transparent wings. 55. **Fledge . . . steep.** Of this line Ruskin says: "Keats puts nearly all that may be said of the pine into one verse, though they are only figurative pines of which he is speaking."—*Modern Painters*, VI, ix, 9, n. 57. **Dryads**, in Greek mythology, nymphs of the trees. 67. **the warm Love**, Cupid.

Ode to a Nightingale

Many have seen in the last two stanzas of this beautiful poem the very essence of romanticism. These stanzas, added to the little lyric of Shelley's, *To—* (p. 272), and the third stanza of Wordsworth's *Solitary Reaper* (p. 154), make a very complete and very satisfying composite picture of the romantic poet. When Keats wrote this poem, he was already entering the valley of the shadow—a fact that lends a peculiar poignancy to the entire ode.

My heart aches, and a drowsy numbness pains
   My sense, as though of hemlock I had
     drunk,
Or emptied some dull opiate to the drains
   One minute past, and Lethe-wards had
     sunk:
'Tis not through envy of thy happy lot, 5
   But being too happy in thine happiness—
     That thou, light-wingéd Dryad of the
     trees,
       In some melodious plot
   Of beechen green, and shadows number-
     less,
       Singest of summer in full-throated ease. 10

O, for a draught of vintage! that hath been
   Cooled a long age in the deep-delvéd earth,
Tasting of Flora and the country green,
   Dance, and Provençal song, and sunburnt
     mirth!
O for a beaker full of the warm South, 15
   Full of the true, the blushful Hippocrene,
     With beaded bubbles winking at the
     brim,
       And purple-stainéd mouth;
   That I might drink, and leave the world
     unseen,
     And with thee fade away into the forest
     dim: 20

Fade far away, dissolve, and quite forget
   What thou among the leaves hast never
     known,

2. **hemlock**, a drug made from leaves or fruit of the poisonous hemlock plant. 4. **Lethe-wards**, toward Lethe, the river of forgetfulness in Hades. 7. **Dryad**, a tree nymph. 13. **Flora**, goddess of the flowers and the spring. 14. **Provençal song.** The medieval lyric flourished in Provence, the home of the troubadours. 16. **Hippocrene**, a fountain on Mt. Helicon, Greece, sacred to the Muses.

The weariness, the fever, and the fret
  Here, where men sit and hear each other
    groan;
Where palsy shakes a few, sad, last gray hairs,
  Where youth grows pale, and specter-thin,
    and dies;   26
    Where but to think is to be full of sorrow
      And leaden-eyed despairs,
    Where Beauty cannot keep her lustrous
      eyes,
    Or new Love pine at them beyond tomor-
      row.   30

Away! away! for I will fly to thee,
  Not charioted by Bacchus and his pards,
But on the viewless wings of Poesy,
  Though the dull brain perplexes and re-
    tards:
Already with thee! tender is the night,   35
  And haply the Queen-Moon is on her
    throne,
    Clustered around by all her starry Fays;
      But here there is no light,
    Save what from heaven is with the breezes
      blown
    Through verdurous glooms and winding
      mossy ways.   40

I cannot see what flowers are at my feet,
  Nor what soft incense hangs upon the
    boughs,
But, in embalmèd darkness, guess each sweet
  Wherewith the seasonable month endows
The grass, the thicket, and the fruit-tree wild;
  White hawthorn, and the pastoral eglan-
    tine;   46
    Fast fading violets covered up in leaves;
      And mid-May's eldest child.

32. **Bacchus,** god of wine, who was often represented as riding in a car drawn by leopards (pards), tigers, or other wild beasts. 33. **viewless,** invisible. 37. **Fays,** fairies. 43. **embalmèd,** balmy, fragrant.

The coming musk-rose, full of dewy wine,
  The murmurous haunt of flies on summer
    eves.   50
Darkling I listen; and, for many a time,
  I have been half in love with easeful Death,
Called him soft names in many a musèd rime,
  To take into the air my quiet breath;
Now more than ever seems it rich to die,   55
  To cease upon the midnight with no pain,
    While thou art pouring forth thy soul
      abroad
      In such an ecstasy!
Still wouldst thou sing, and I have ears in
  vain—
  To thy high requiem become a sod.   60

Thou wast not born for death, immortal Bird!
  No hungry generations tread thee down;
The voice I hear this passing night was heard
  In ancient days by emperor and clown:
Perhaps the self-same song that found a path
  Through the sad heart of Ruth, when, sick
    for home,   66
    She stood in tears amid the alien corn;
      The same that oft-times hath
    Charmed magic casements, opening on the
      foam
    Of perilous seas, in faery lands forlorn. 70

Forlorn! the very word is like a bell
  To toll me back from thee to my sole self,
Adieu! the fancy cannot cheat so well
  As she is famed to do, deceiving elf.
Adieu! adieu! thy plaintive anthem fades   75
  Past the near meadows, over the still stream,
    Up the hillside; and now 'tis buried deep
      In the next valley glades:
    Was it a vision, or a waking dream?   79
      Fled is that music—Do I wake or sleep?
                                          (1819)

67. **corn,** wheat. See the story of Ruth (Vol. I, p. 597). 69. **Charmed . . . forlorn.** See note on *Kubla Khan*, ll. 14-16, p. 184.

The Eve of St. Agnes

St. Agnes was a saint martyred in Rome about the year 300. In the early days of the Catholic Church, on St. Agnes's Day (January 21), the *Agnus Dei* ("Lamb of God") from the mass was chanted, and two lambs were sacrificed, their wools to be woven later by nuns. In the Middle Ages there grew up the legend that a girl on St. Agnes's Eve (January 20) could find out about her future husband; as she lay on her back, with her hands beneath her head, he would appear before her in a dream, kiss her, and feast with her.

The Eve of St. Agnes is not only Keats's finest achievement in the field of the medieval; it can also demand consideration as an almost perfect specimen of romantic art. Here are the "magic casements," "the far-off things," the rich and fruitful warmth and color to which Keats devoted himself. It is perhaps the only poem by Keats of which the author was in any way vain; he read aloud the supper-picture in ll. 262-270 to Leigh Hunt "with manifest pleasure in his work; the sole instance," says Palgrave in his edition of Keats's *Poetical Works* (1884), "I can recall where the poet—modest in proportion to his greatness —yielded even to so innocent an impulse of vanity."

St. Agnes' Eve—Ah, bitter chill it was!
The owl, for all his feathers, was a-cold;
The hare limped trembling through the frozen grass,
And silent was the flock in woolly fold:
Numb were the Beadsman's fingers, while he told 5
His rosary, and while his frosted breath,
Like pious incense from a censer old,
Seemed taking flight for heaven, without a death,
Past the sweet Virgin's picture, while his prayer he saith.

His prayer, he saith, this patient, holy man; 10
Then takes his lamp, and riseth from his knees,
And back returneth, meager, barefoot, wan,
Along the chapel aisle by slow degrees:
The sculptured dead, on each side, seem to freeze,
Emprisoned in black, purgatorial rails: 15
Knights, ladies, praying in dumb orat'ries,
He passeth by; and his weak spirit fails
To think how they may ache in icy hoods and mails.

Northward he turneth through a little door,
And scarce three steps, ere Music's golden tongue 20
Flattered to tears this aged man and poor;
But no—already had his death-bell rung:
The joys of all his life were said and sung:
His was harsh penance on St. Agnes' Eve:
Another way he went, and soon among 25

Rough ashes sat he for his soul's reprieve,
And all night kept awake, for sinners' sake to grieve.

That ancient Beadsman heard the prelude soft;
And so it chanced, for many a door was wide,
From hurry to and fro. Soon, up aloft, 30
The silver, snarling trumpets 'gan to chide:
The level chambers, ready with their pride,
Were glowing to receive a thousand guests:
The carvéd angels, ever eager-eyed,
Stared, where upon their heads the cornice rests, 35
With hair blown back, and wings put crosswise on their breasts.

At length burst in the argent revelry,
With plume, tiara, and all rich array,
Numerous as shadows haunting faerily
The brain, new-stuffed, in youth, with triumphs gay 40
Of old romance. These let us wish away,
And turn, sole-thoughted, to one Lady there,
Whose heart had brooded, all that wintry day,
On love, and winged St. Agnes' saintly care,
As she had heard old dames full many times declare. 45

They told her how, upon St. Agnes' Eve,
Young virgins might have visions of delight,
And soft adorings from their loves receive
Upon the honeyed middle of the night,
If ceremonies due they did aright; 50
As, supperless to bed they must retire,
And couch supine their beauties, lily white;

---

1. **bitter chill.** St. Agnes's Eve, January 20, is supposed to be the coldest night of the year. 5. **Beadsman,** a poor man supported in an almshouse and required to pray for its founder. **told His rosary,** numbered the beads on his rosary as he recited salutations to the Virgin Mary. 16. **dumb orat'ries,** small chapels for prayer, called "dumb" because they contain statues.

37. **argent,** shining. 38. **tiara,** a crownlike head ornament.

Nor look behind, nor sideways, but require
Of Heaven with upward eyes for all that they
    desire.   54

Full of this whim was thoughtful Madeline:
The music, yearning like a god in pain,
She scarcely heard: her maiden eyes divine,
Fixed on the floor, saw many a sweeping train
Pass by—she heeded not at all: in vain
Came many a tiptoe, amorous cavalier,   60
And back retired; not cooled by high disdain,
But she saw not: her heart was otherwhere;
She sighed for Agnes' dreams, the sweetest of
    the year.

She danced along with vague, regardless eyes,
Anxious her lips, her breathing quick and
    short: 65
The hallowed hour was near at hand: she
    sighs
Amid the timbrels, and the thronged resort
Of whisperers in anger, or in sport;
'Mid looks of love, defiance, hate, and scorn,
Hoodwinked with faery fancy; all amort,   70
Save to St. Agnes and her lambs unshorn,
And all the bliss to be before tomorrow morn.

So, purposing each moment to retire,
She lingered still. Meantime, across the moors,
Had come young Porphyro, with heart on fire
For Madeline. Beside the portal doors,   76
Buttressed from moonlight, stands he, and
    implores
All saints to give him sight of Madeline,
But for one moment in the tedious hours,
That he might gaze and worship all unseen;
Perchance speak, kneel, touch, kiss—in sooth
    such things have been.   81

He ventures in: let no buzzed whisper tell:
All eyes be muffled, or a hundred swords
Will storm his heart, Love's fev'rous citadel:
For him, those chambers held barbarian
    hordes,   85
Hyena foemen, and hot-blooded lords,
Whose very dogs would execrations howl
Against his lineage: not one breast affords
Him any mercy, in that mansion foul,
Save one old beldame, weak in body and in
    soul.   90

Ah, happy chance! the aged creature came,
Shuffling along with ivory-headed wand,
To where he stood, hid from the torch's flame,
Behind a broad hall-pillar, far beyond
The sound of merriment and chorus bland: 95
He startled her; but soon she knew his face,
And grasped his fingers in her palsied hand,
Saying, "Mercy, Porphyro! hie thee from this
    place;
They are all here tonight, the whole blood-
    thirsty race!

"Get hence! get hence! there's dwarfish Hilde-
    brand;   100
He had a fever late, and in the fit
He curséd thee and thine, both house and
    land:
Then there's that old Lord Maurice, not a whit
More tame for his gray hairs—Alas me! flit!
Flit like a ghost away."—"Ah, Gossip dear, 105
We're safe enough; here in this armchair sit,
And tell me how"—"Good Saints! not here,
    not here;
Follow me, child, or else these stones will be
    thy bier."

He followed through a lowly archéd way,
Brushing the cobwebs with his lofty plume;
And as she muttered, "Well-a—well-a-day!" 111
He found him in a little moonlight room,
Pale, latticed, chill, and silent as a tomb.
"Now tell me where is Madeline," said he,
"O tell me, Angela, by the holy loom   115
Which none but secret sisterhood may see,
When they St. Agnes' wool are weaving,
    piously."

"St. Agnes! Ah! it is St. Agnes' Eve—
Yet men will murder upon holy days:
Thou must hold water in a witch's sieve,   120
And be liege-lord of all the Elves and Fays,
To venture so: it fills me with amaze
To see thee, Porphyro!—St. Agnes' Eve!

---

58. **sweeping train**, long trailing dress. 67. **timbrels**, small hand drums, or tambourines. 70. **Hoodwinked**, blinded. **amort**, dead. 71. **lambs**. See headnote.

105. **Gossip**, godmother; here, merely devoted friend. 120. **hold . . . sieve**. This feat was regarded as a sign of supernatural power.

God's help! my lady fair the conjuror plays
This very night: good angels her deceive! 125
But let me laugh awhile, I've mickle time to
    grieve."

Feebly she laugheth in the languid moon,
While Porphyro upon her face doth look,
Like puzzled urchin on an aged crone
Who keepeth closed a wond'rous riddle-book,
As spectacled she sits in chimney nook. 131
But soon his eyes grew brilliant, when she told
His lady's purpose; and he scarce could brook
Tears, at the thought of those enchantments
    cold,
And Madeline asleep in lap of legends old.

Sudden a thought came like a full-blown
    rose, 136
Flushing his brow, and in his painéd heart
Made purple riot: then doth he propose
A stratagem, that makes the beldame start:
"A cruel man and impious thou art: 140
Sweet lady, let her pray, and sleep, and dream
Alone with her good angels, far apart
From wicked men like thee. Go, go! I deem
Thou canst not surely be the same that thou
    didst seem."

"I will not harm her, by all saints I swear," 145
Quoth Porphyro: "O may I ne'er find grace
When my weak voice shall whisper its last
    prayer,
If one of her soft ringlets I displace,
Or look with ruffian passion in her face:
Good Angela, believe me by these tears; 150
Or I will, even in a moment's space,
Awake, with horrid shout, my foemen's ears,
And beard them, though they be more fanged
    than wolves and bears."

"Ah! why wilt thou affright a feeble soul?
A poor, weak, palsy-stricken, churchyard
    thing, 155
Whose passing-bell may ere the midnight toll;
Whose prayers for thee, each morn and eve-
    ning,
Were never missed." Thus plaining, doth she
    bring

126. **mickle**, much, ample. 133. **brook**, restrain.

A gentler speech from burning Porphyro;
So woeful, and of such deep sorrowing, 160
That Angela gives promise she will do
Whatever he shall wish, betide her weal or
    woe.

Which was, to lead him, in close secrecy,
Even to Madeline's chamber, and there hide
Him in a closet, of such privacy 165
That he might see her beauty unespied,
And win perhaps that night a peerless bride,
While legioned faeries paced the coverlet,
And pale enchantment held her sleepy-eyed.
Never on such a night have lovers met, 170
Since Merlin paid his Demon all the mon-
    strous debt.

"It shall be as thou wishest," said the Dame:
"All cates and dainties shall be storéd there
Quickly on this feast-night: by the tambour
    frame
Her own lute thou wilt see: no time to spare,
For I am slow and feeble, and scarce dare 176
On such a catering trust my dizzy head.
Wait here, my child, with patience; kneel in
    prayer
The while: Ah! thou must needs the lady wed,
Or may I never leave my grave among the
    dead." 180

So saying, she hobbled off with busy fear.
The lover's endless minutes slowly passed;
The Dame returned, and whispered in his ear
To follow her—with agéd eyes aghast
From fright of dim espial. Safe at last, 185
Through many a dusky gallery, they gain
The maiden's chamber, silken, hushed, and
    chaste;
Where Porphyro took covert, pleased amain.
His poor guide hurried back with agues in
    her brain.

Her faltering hand upon the balustrade, 190
Old Angela was feeling for the stair,
When Madeline, St. Agnes' charméd maid,

171. **Merlin . . . debt.** According to one legend, Merlin, the magician of Arthurian romance, was the son of a demon. He paid the "debt" for his existence when he was killed by the enchantress Vivien, who used a magic spell that he had taught her. 173. **cates**, delicacies. 174. **tambour frame**, an embroidery frame in the shape of a drum. 188. **amain**, exceedingly.

Rose, like a missioned spirit, unaware:
With silver taper's light, and pious care,
She turned, and down the aged gossip led   195
To a safe level matting. Now prepare,
Young Porphyro, for gazing on that bed;
She comes, she comes again, like ring-dove
    frayed and fled.

Out went the taper as she hurried in;
Its little smoke, in pallid moonshine, died: 200
She closed the door, she panted, all akin
To spirits of the air, and visions wide:
No uttered syllable, or, woe betide!
But to her heart, her heart was voluble,
Paining with eloquence her balmy side;   205
As though a tongueless nightingale should
    swell
Her throat in vain, and die, heart-stifled in
    her dell.

A casement high and triple-arched there was,
All garlanded with carven imag'ries
Of fruits, and flowers, and bunches of knot-
    grass,   210
And diamonded with panes of quaint device,
Innumerable of stains and splendid dyes,
As are the tiger-moth's deep-damasked wings;
And in the midst, 'mong thousand heraldries,
And twilight saints, and dim emblazonings,
A shielded scutcheon blushed with blood of
    queens and kings.   216

Full on this casement shone the wintry moon,
And threw warm gules on Madeline's fair
    breast,
As down she knelt for heaven's grace and
    boon;
Rose-bloom fell on her hands, together pressed,
And on her silver cross soft amethyst,   221
And on her hair a glory, like a saint:
She seemed a splendid angel, newly dressed,
Save wings, for heaven—Porphyro grew faint:
She knelt, so pure a thing, so free from mortal
    taint.   225

Anon his heart revives: her vespers done,
Of all its wreathéd pearls her hair she frees;

Unclasps her warméd jewels one by one;
Loosens her fragrant bodice; by degrees
Her rich attire creeps rustling to her
    knees: 230
Half-hidden, like a mermaid in sea-weed,
Pensive awhile she dreams awake, and sees,
In fancy, fair St. Agnes in her bed,
But dares not look behind, or all the charm
    is fled.

Soon, trembling, in her soft and chilly nest,   235
In sort of wakeful swoon, perplexed she lay,
Until the poppied warmth of sleep oppressed
Her soothéd limbs, and soul fatigued away;
Flown, like a thought, until the morrow-
    day;
Blissfully havened both from joy and pain;   240
Clasped like a missal where swart Paynims
    pray;
Blinded alike from sunshine and from rain,
As though a rose should shut, and be a bud
    again.

Stol'n to this paradise, and so entranced,
Porphyro gazed upon her empty dress,   245
And listened to her breathing, if it chanced
To wake into a slumberous tenderness;
Which when he heard, that minute did he
    bless,
And breathed himself: then from the closet
    crept,
Noiseless as fear in a wide wilderness,   250
And over the hushed carpet, silent, stepped,
And 'tween the curtains peeped, where, lo!—
    how fast she slept.

Then by the bedside, where the faded moon
Made a dim, silver twilight, soft he set
A table, and, half anguished, threw thereon   255
A cloth of woven crimson, gold, and jet—
O for some drowsy Morphean amulet!
The boisterous, midnight, festive clarion,
The kettle-drum, and far-heard clarionet,
Affray his ears, though but in dying tone—
The hall door shuts again, and all the noise
    is gone.   261

198. **frayed**, frightened. 218. **gules**, red tinctures (a term in heraldry). 241. **Clasped . . . pray**, closed like a Christian prayer book, which pagans would have no occasion to use. 250. **as fear**, as a person in fear. 257. **Morphean**, sleep-producing, from Morpheus, the son of Sleep and god of dreams. **amulet**, charm.

And still she slept an azure-lidded sleep,
In blanchéd linen, smooth, and lavendered,
While he from forth the closet brought a heap
Of candied apple, quince, and plum, and
    gourd; 265
With jellies soother than the creamy curd,
And lucent syrups, tinct with cinnamon;
Manna and dates, in argosy transferred
From Fez; and spicéd dainties, every one, 269
From silken Samarcand to cedared Lebanon.

These delicates he heaped with glowing hand
On golden dishes and in baskets bright
Of wreathéd silver: sumptuous they stand
In the retiréd quiet of the night, 274
Filling the chilly room with perfume light.—
"And now, my love, my seraph fair, awake!
Thou art my heaven, and I thine eremite:
Open thine eyes, for meek St. Agnes' sake,
Or I shall drowse beside thee, so my soul doth
    ache."

Thus whispering, his warm, unnervéd arm 280
Sank in her pillow. Shaded was her dream
By the dusk curtains—'twas a midnight charm
Impossible to melt as icéd stream:
The lustrous salvers in the moonlight gleam;
Broad golden fringe upon the carpet lies: 285
It seemed he never, never could redeem
From such a steadfast spell his lady's eyes;
So mused awhile, entoiled in wooféd phan-
    tasies.

Awakening up, he took her hollow lute—
Tumultuous—and, in chords that tenderest
    be, 290
He played an ancient ditty, long since mute,
In Provence called "La belle dame sans
    merci";
Close to her ear touching the melody;—
Wherewith disturbed, she uttered a soft
    moan:

He ceased—she panted quick—and sud-
    denly 295
Her blue affrayéd eyes wide open shone:
Upon his knees he sank, pale as smooth-
    sculptured stone.

Her eyes were open, but she still beheld,
Now wide awake, the vision of her sleep:
There was a painful change, that nigh ex-
    pelled 300
The blisses of her dream so pure and deep
At which fair Madeline began to weep,
And moan forth witless words with many a
    sigh;
While still her gaze on Porphyro would
    keep;
Who knelt, with joinéd hands and piteous
    eye, 305
Fearing to move or speak, she looked so
    dreamingly.

"Ah, Porphyro!" said she, "but even now
Thy voice was at sweet tremble in mine ear,
Made tuneable with every sweetest vow;
And those sad eyes were spiritual and clear: 310
How changed thou art! how pallid, chill, and
    drear!
Give me that voice again, my Porphyro,
Those looks immortal, those complainings
    dear!
Oh, leave me not in this eternal woe,
For if thou diest, my Love, I know not where
    to go." 315

Beyond a mortal man impassioned far
At these voluptuous accents, he arose,
Ethereal, flushed, and like a throbbing star
Seen mid the sapphire heaven's deep repose;
Into her dream he melted, as the rose 320
Blendeth its odor with the violet—
Solution sweet; meantime the frost-wind
    blows
Like Love's alarum pattering the sharp sleet
Against the window-panes; St. Agnes' moon
    hath set.

'Tis dark; quick pattereth the flaw-blown
    sleet; 325
"This is no dream, my bride, my Madeline!"

---

263. **lavendered**, perfumed with lavender, a European mint. 266. **soother**, softer, smoother. 267. **tinct**, flavored. 268. **argosy**, a large merchant vessel. 269. **Fez**, an important commercial city in northern Morocco. 270. **Samarcand**, a city in Turkestan, Asiatic Russia, noted for its silks, pottery, silver and gold wares, etc. **Lebanon**, a mountain range in southern Syria, once famous for its forests of cedar. 277. **eremite**, hermit; here, devoted lover. 288. **wooféd phantasies**, fancies woven together like threads. 292. "**La belle . . . merci,**" the beautiful lady without pity. See Keats's poem of that title, **p. 282.**

'Tis dark; the icéd gusts still rave and beat;
"No dream, alas! alas! and woe is mine!
Porphyro will leave me here to fade and
     pine.—
Cruel! what traitor could thee hither bring?
I curse not, for my heart is lost in thine.   331
Though thou forsakest a deceivéd thing;—
A dove forlorn and lost with sick unprunéd
     wing."

"My Madeline! sweet dreamer! lovely bride!
Say, may I be for aye thy vassal blest?   335
Thy beauty's shield, heart-shaped and vermeil-
     dyed?
Ah, silver shrine, here will I take my rest
After so many hours of toil and quest,
A famished pilgrim—saved by miracle.
Though I have found, I will not rob thy
     nest   340
Saving of thy sweet self; if thou think'st well
To trust, fair Madeline, to no rude infidel.

"Hark! 'tis an elfin storm from faery land,
Of haggard seeming, but a boon indeed:
Arise—arise! the morning is at hand—   345
The bloated wassailers will never heed—
Let us away, my love, with happy speed;
There are no ears to hear, or eyes to see—
Drowned all in Rhenish and the sleepy mead;
Awake! arise! my love, and fearless be,   350
For o'er the southern moors I have a home
     for thee."

She hurried at his words, beset with fears,
For there were sleeping dragons all around,
At glaring watch, perhaps, with ready spears—
Down the wide stairs a darkling way they
     found.—   355
In all the house was heard no human sound.
A chain-drooped lamp was flickering by each
     door;
The arras, rich with horseman, hawk, and
     hound,
Fluttered in the besieging wind's uproar;
And the long carpets rose along the gusty
     floor.   360

344. **haggard seeming**, wild appearance. 349. **Rhenish**, wine from the vineyards of the Rhine. **mead**, a fermented drink, made of honey, water, etc. 358. **arras**, tapestry; the word is derived from Arras, France, which was famous in the Middle Ages for such tapestries.

They glide, like phantoms, into the wide hall;
Like phantoms to the iron porch they glide,
Where lay the Porter, in uneasy sprawl,
With a huge empty flagon by his side;
The wakeful bloodhound rose, and shook
     his hide,   365
But his sagacious eye an inmate owns:
By one, and one, the bolts full easy slide—
The chains lie silent on the footworn stones;—
The key turns, and the door upon its hinges
     groans.

And they are gone: aye, ages long ago   370
These lovers fled away into the storm.
That night the Baron dreamt of many a woe,
And all his warrior-guests, with shade and
     form
Of witch, and demon, and large coffin-worm,
Were long be-nightmared. Angela the old
Died palsy-twitched, with meager face de-
     form;   376
The Beadsman, after thousand aves told,
For aye unsought-for slept among his ashes
     cold.   (1819; 1820)

To Autumn

On September 22, 1819, Keats wrote to his friend Reynolds: "How beautiful the season is now—how fine the air. A temperate sharpness about it. Really, without joking, chaste weather—Dian skies—I never liked stubble-fields so much as now—Aye better than the chilly green of the spring. Somehow, a stubble-field looks warm—in the same way that some pictures look warm. This struck me so much in my Sunday's walk that I composed upon it." The composition referred to is the following magnificent ode.

Season of mists and mellow fruitfulness,
   Close bosom-friend of the maturing sun;
Conspiring with him how to load and bless
   With fruit the vines that round the thatch-
        eaves run;
To bend with apples the mossed cottage-
        trees,   5
   And fill all fruit with ripeness to the core;
      To swell the gourd, and plump the hazel
           shells

377. **aves**, salutations to the Virgin Mary. The beads of a rosary are counted as the Aves are uttered.

With a sweet kernel; to set budding more,
  And still more, later flowers for the bees,
  Until they think warm days will never cease,
    For Summer has o'er-brimmed their
      clammy cells.   11

Who hath not seen thee oft amid thy store?
  Sometimes whoever seeks abroad may find
  Thee sitting careless on a granary floor,
    Thy hair soft-lifted by the winnowing wind;
  Or on a half-reaped furrow sound asleep,   16
    Drowsed with the fume of poppies, while
      thy hook
      Spares the next swath and all its twinèd
        flowers:
  And sometime like a gleaner thou dost keep
    Steady thy laden head across a brook;   20
  Or by a cider-press, with patient look,
    Thou watchest the last oozings, hours by
      hours.

Where are the songs of Spring? Ay, where
    are they?
  Think not of them, thou hast thy music
    too—
  While barrèd clouds bloom the soft-dying
    day,   25
  And touch the stubble-plains with rosy hue;
Then in a wailful choir the small gnats mourn
  Among the river sallows, borne aloft
    Or sinking as the light wind lives or dies;
And full-grown lambs loud bleat from hilly
    bourn;   30

28. **sallows**, willows.

Hedge-crickets sing; and now with treble
    soft
The redbreast whistles from a garden-croft,
  And gathering swallows twitter in the
    skies.   (*1819;* 1820)

Bright Star! Would I Were Steadfast as Thou Art

This sonnet in its final form was composed after Keats embarked for Italy on September 30; a preliminary draft had been made the previous year. The sonnet was written in a copy of Shakespeare's poems and given to his friend and companion Severn. As Keats's death-song, the sonnet should be compared with Tennyson's *Crossing the Bar* (p. 654) and Browning's *Epilogue to Asolando* (p. 708).

Bright star! would I were steadfast as thou
    art—
Not in lone splendor hung aloft the night,
And watching, with eternal lids apart,
Like Nature's patient sleepless Eremite,
The moving waters at their priestlike task   5
Of pure ablution round earth's human shores,
Or gazing on the new soft fallen mask
Of snow upon the mountains and the moors—
No—yet still steadfast, still unchangeable,
Pillowed upon my fair love's ripening breast,
To feel forever its soft fall and swell,   11
Awake forever in a sweet unrest,
Still, still to hear her tender-taken breath,
And so live ever—or else swoon to death.
                                (*1820;* 1846)

31. **Hedge-crickets**, grasshoppers. 32. **garden-croft**, garden enclosure.

Letters

I. To John Hamilton Reynolds*

Hampstead, Tuesday, February 3, 1818

My dear Reynolds:

I thank you for your dish of Filberts—would I could get a basket of them by way of dessert every day for the sum of twopence. Would we were a sort of ethereal Pigs, and turned loose to feed upon spiritual Mast and Acorns—which would be merely being a squirrel and feeding upon filberts, for what is a squirrel but an airy pig, or a filbert but a sort of archangelical acorn? About the nuts being worth cracking, all I can say is, that where there are a throng of delightful Images ready drawn, simplicity is the only thing. The first is the best on account of the first line, and the "arrow, foil'd of its antler'd food," and moreover (and this is the only word or two I find fault with, the more because I have had so

*__Reynolds__, a great friend of Keats, a solicitor, poet, humorist, and critic of parts (1796-1852); his two sisters Jane and Mariane are also addressed in several of Keats's letters. 3. **Filberts**, two sonnets which Reynolds had written on Robin Hood and sent to Keats for criticism.

much reason to shun it as a quicksand) the last has "tender and true." We must cut this, and not be rattlesnaked into any more of the like. It may be said that we ought to read our contemporaries, that Wordsworth, etc., should have their due from us. But, for the sake of a few fine imaginative or domestic passages, are we to be bullied into a certain Philosophy engendered in the whims of an Egotist? Every man has his speculations, but every man does not brood or peacock over them till he makes a false coinage and deceives himself. Many a man can travel to the very bourne of Heaven, and yet want confidence to put down his half-seeing. Sancho will invent a Journey heavenward as well as anybody. We hate poetry that has a palpable design upon us, and, if we do not agree, seems to put its hand into its breeches pocket. Poetry should be great and unobtrusive, a thing which enters into one's soul, and does not startle it or amaze it with itself—but with its subject. How beautiful are the retired flowers!—how would they lose their beauty were they to throng into the highway, crying out, "Admire me, I am a violet! Dote upon me, I am a primrose!" Modern poets differ from the Elizabethans in this: each of the moderns like an Elector of Hanover governs his petty state and knows how many straws are swept daily from the Causeways in all his dominions, and has a continual itching that all the Housewives should have their coppers well scoured; the ancients were Emperors of vast Provinces; they had only heard of the remote ones and scarcely cared to visit them. I will cut all this—I will have no more of Wordsworth or Hunt in particular—Why should we be of the tribe of Manasseh, when we can wander with Esau? Why should we kick against the pricks, when we can walk on roses? Why should we be owls, when we can be eagles? Why be teased with "nice-eyed wagtails," when we have in sight "the Cherub Contemplation?" Why with Wordsworth's "Matthew with a bough of wilding in his hand?" when we can have Jaques "under an oak," etc.? The secret of the Bough of Wilding will run through your head faster than I can write it. Old Matthew spoke to him some years ago on some nothing, and because he happens in an Evening Walk to imagine the figure of the old Man, he must stamp it down in black and white, and it is henceforth sacred. I don't mean to deny Wordsworth's grandeur and Hunt's merit, but I mean to say we need not be teased with grandeur and merit when we can have them uncontaminated and unobtrusive. Let us have the old poets and Robin Hood. Your letter and its sonnets gave me more pleasure than will the Fourth Book of Childe Harold and the whole of anybody's life and opinions. In return for your dish of filberts, I have gathered a few catkins; I hope they'll look pretty. . . .

I hope you will like them—they are at least written in the Spirit of Outlawry. Here are the Mermaid lines, . . .

I will call on you at 4 tomorrow, and we will trudge together, for it is not the thing to be a stranger in the Land of Harpsicols. I hope also to bring you my second book. In the hope that these scribblings will be some amusement for you this evening, I remain, copying on the hill,

Your sincere friend and Co-scribbler,

JOHN KEATS.

---

38. **Hunt,** James Henry Leigh Hunt. Cf. p. 297. 39. **Manasseh . . . Esau.** In the Old Testament Manasseh was the firstborn son of Joseph, son of Jacob. His progeny became a leading tribe of Israel, walking in conventional paths of Hebraic history. Esau, one of the twin sons of Isaac, sold his birthright to his brother Jacob (*Genesis,* 25:29-34) and became something of a domestic outlaw, yet, as his father Isaac prophesied (*Genesis,* 27:39-40): "Behold, thy dwelling shall be the fatness of the earth, and of the dew of heaven from above; and by thy sword shalt thou live, and shalt serve thy brother; and it shall come to pass when thou shalt have the dominion, that thou shalt break his yoke from off thy neck." Keats is, in other words asking why we should stay in a conventional rut when we can adventure as did Esau.

41. **kick . . . pricks,** from *The Acts,* 9:5; the Lord, speaking to Saul of Tarsus (later Paul), observes: "I am Jesus whom thou persecutest: it is hard for thee to kick against the pricks." The prick was a goad. 43. **"nice-eyed wagtails,"** a phrase evidently from Reynolds's submitted poems. 44. **"the Cherub Contemplation,"** quoted from Milton's *Il Penseroso,* 54. 46. **"Matthew . . . hand,"** quoted from Wordsworth's *The Two April Mornings,* 59-60; *wilding* is an uncultivated plant or weed. 47. **"under an oak,"** referring to the melancholy Jaques in Shakespeare's *As You Like It,* II, i, 31. 65. **look pretty, etc.** Here Keats inserts a first draft of his poem *Robin Hood* (p. 276). 69. **the Mermaid lines, etc.** Here follows a first draft of the poem, *Ode* (addressed to Beaumont and Fletcher) (p. 280). 72. **Harpsicols,** harpsichords. Keats implies that it is not safe for a man to be alone in the land of petticoats amid hordes of women.

II. To James Augustus Hessey*

Hampstead, October 9, 1818

My dear Hessey:

You are very good in sending me the letters from the Chronicle—and I am very bad in not acknowledging such a kindness sooner —pray forgive me. It has so chanced that I have had that paper every day—I have seen today's. I cannot but feel indebted to those Gentlemen who have taken my part—As for the rest, I begin to get a little acquainted with my own strength and weakness.—Praise or blame has but a momentary effect on the man whose love of beauty in the abstract makes him a severe critic on his own works. My own domestic criticism has given me pain without comparison beyond what Blackwood or the Quarterly could possibly inflict—and also when I feel I am right, no external praise can give me such a glow as my own solitary reperception and ratification of what is fine. J.S. is perfectly right in regard to the slipshod Endymion. That it is so is no fault of mine. No!—though it may sound a little paradoxical. It is as good as I had power to make it—by myself. Had I been nervous about its being a perfect piece, and with that view asked advice, and trembled over every page, it would not have been written; for it is not in my nature to fumble—I will write independently.—I have written independently *without Judgment*. I may write independently, and *with Judgment*, hereafter. The genius of Poetry must work out its own salvation in a man; it cannot be matured by law and precept, but by sensation and watchfulness in itself—that which is creative must create itself—In Endymion, I leaped headlong into the sea, and thereby have become better acquainted with the Soundings, the quicksands, and the rocks, than if I had stayed upon the green shore, and piped a silly pipe, and took tea and comfortable advice. I was never afraid of failure; for I would sooner fail than not be among the greatest—But I am nigh getting into a rant. So, with remembrances to Taylor and Woodhouse, etc., I am,

Yours very sincerely,

John Keats.

III. To John Hamilton Reynolds

Winchester, August 25, 1819

My dear Reynolds:

By this post I write to Rice, who will tell you why we have left Shanklin; and how we like this place. I have indeed scarcely anything else to say, leading so monotonous a life, except I was to give you a history of sensations and day-nightmares. You would not find me at all unhappy in it, as all my thoughts and feelings which are of the selfish nature, home speculations, every day continue to make me more iron—I am convinced more and more, every day, that fine writing is, next to fine doing, the top thing in the world; the Paradise Lost becomes a greater wonder. The more I know what my diligence may in time probably effect, the more does my heart distend with Pride and Obstinacy— I feel it in my power to become a popular writer—I feel it in my power to refuse the poisonous suffrage of a public. My own being which I know to be becomes of more consequence to me than the crowds of Shadows in the shape of men and women that inhabit a kingdom. The soul is a world of itself and has enough to do in its own home. Those whom I know already, and who have grown as it were a part of myself, I could not do without; but for the rest of mankind, they are as much a dream to me as Milton's Hierarchies. I think if I had a free and

---

*Hessey, the junior partner of the publishing firm of Taylor and Hessey. Taylor is referred to in l. 46 below. 3. **letters . . . Chronicle**, two letters addressed to the editor of *The Morning Chronicle*, a London daily, printed in the issues of October 3 and 8, 1818. 16. **Blackwood . . . Quarterly**, Blackwoods's *Edinburgh Magazine* and *The Quarterly Review*, two periodicals (cf. p. 18) which were both hostile to Keats. See also the reference in Shelley's *Adonais* (p. 262), 151-153, and Byron's *Who Killed John Keats?* (p. 247 and note). 21. **J. S.**, John Scott, author of one of the letters in the *Chronicle*. The reference is in particular to this passage from Scott's letter: "That there are also many, very many passages indicating both haste and carelessness I will not deny; nay, I will go further, and assert that a real friend of the author would have dissuaded him from immediate publication." Nevertheless, Scott on the whole defends Keats's *Endymion*, the subject of the controversy.

46. **Woodhouse**, Richard Woodhouse, a young barrister friend of Keats and transcriber of his letters; he was also in the general confidence of the publishers Taylor and Hessey. 51. **Rice**, James Rice, a young solicitor and bosom friend of Reynolds. 52. **Shanklin**, a small sea-town on the Isle of Wight, where Keats, with his friend Charles Brown, had been summering. 78. **Milton's Hierarchies**, the three divisions into which the nine orders of angels were placed. Milton, in *Paradise Lost*, follows the celestial hierarchy already made famous by Dante: (1) Seraphim, (2) Cherubim, (3) Thrones, (4) Dominions, (5) Virtues, (6) Powers, (7) Principalities, (8) Archangels, (9) Angels.

healthy and lasting organization of heart, and lungs as strong as an ox's so as to be able to bear unhurt the shock of extreme thought and sensation without weariness, I could pass my life very nearly alone though it should last eighty years. But I feel my body too weak to support me to the height; I am obliged continually to check myself, and be nothing. It would be vain for me to endeavor after a more reasonable manner of writing to you. I have nothing to speak of but myself, and what can I say but what I feel? If you should have any reason to regret this state of excitement in me, I will turn the tide of your feelings in the right channel, by mentioning that it is the only state for the best sort of poetry—that is all I care for, all I live for. Forgive me for not filling up the whole sheet; letters become so irksome to me that the next time I leave London I shall petition them all to be spared me. To give me credit for constancy and at the same time waive letter writing will be the highest indulgence I can think of.

Ever your affectionate friend,

JOHN KEATS.

IV. To CHARLES BROWN*

Naples, November 1, 1820

MY DEAREST BROWN:

Yesterday we were let out of quarantine, during which my health suffered more from bad air and the stifled cabin than it had done the whole voyage. The fresh air revived me a little, and I hope I am well enough this morning to write to you a short calm letter—if that can be called one, in which I am afraid to speak of what I would fainest dwell upon. As I have gone thus far into it, I must go on a little;—perhaps it may relieve the load of WRETCHEDNESS which presses upon me. The persuasion that I shall see her no more will kill me. My dear Brown, I should have had her when I was in health, and I should have remained well. I can bear to die—I cannot bear to leave her. Oh, God! God! God! Everything I have in my trunks that reminds me of her goes through me like a spear. The silk lining she put in my traveling cap scalds my head. My imagination is horribly vivid about her—I see her—I hear her. There is nothing in the world of sufficient interest to divert me from her a moment. This was the case when I was in England; I cannot recollect, without shuddering, the time that I was a prisoner at Hunt's, and used to keep my eyes fixed on Hampstead all day. Then there was a good hope of seeing her again—Now!—O that I could be buried near where she lives! I am afraid to write to her—to receive a letter from her—to see her handwriting would break my heart—even to hear of her anyhow, to see her name written, would be more than I can bear. My dear Brown, what am I to do? Where can I look for consolation or ease? If I had any chance of recovery, this passion would kill me. Indeed, through the whole of my illness, both at your home and at Kentish Town, this fever has never ceased wearing me out. When you write to me, which you will do immediately, write to Rome (*poste restante*)—if she is well and happy, put a mark thus +; if—

Remember me to all. I will endeavor to bear my miseries patiently. A person in my state of health should not have such miseries to bear. Write a short note to my sister, saying you have heard from me. Severn is very well. If I were in better health, I would urge your coming to Rome. I fear there is no one can give me any comfort. Is there any news of George? O that something fortunate had ever happened to me or my brothers!—then I might hope,—but despair is forced upon me as a habit. My dear Brown, for my sake be her advocate forever. I cannot say a word about Naples; I do not feel at all concerned

---

*Brown. Charles Brown, who afterwards called himself Charles Armitage Brown (1786-1842), began life as a merchant in St. Petersburg, Russia, failed in this business, returned to England, and became a miscellaneous contributor to the various periodicals edited by Leigh Hunt. He lived in Italy for many years following the death of Keats and died in New Zealand.
40. **her**, here, as elsewhere in this letter, Fanny Brawne.

66. **Kentish Town**, a section of metropolitan London. 69. *poste restante*, general delivery. 76. **Severn**, Joseph Severn (1793-1879), an amateur painter, devoted friend of Keats during the latter's fatal illness. He established himself in Rome following Keats's death, became an earnest devotee of painting, and was for a time British consul in Rome, and one of the most familiar figures in the foreign society of the city. 80. **George**, George Keats (1799-1842), the poet's brother, who, with his wife Georgianna, is frequently the addressee of Keats's letters. He was for years a resident of Louisville, Kentucky.

in the thousand novelties around me. I am afraid to write to her—I should like her to know that I do not forget her. Oh, Brown, I have coals of fire in my breast—It surprises me that the human heart is capable of containing and bearing so much misery. Was I born for this end? God bless her, and her mother, and my sister, and George, and his wife, and you, and all!

Your ever affectionate friend, 10

JOHN KEATS.

8. **my sister,** Frances Mary (Fanny) Keats (1803-1889), addressed in many of the most charming of Keats's letters; she married a Spaniard and lived in Madrid to a great old age.

MINOR ROMANTIC POETS

One cannot understand fully a given period of literature merely by understanding the major writers in that period. The lesser writers, who are more numerous, are usually more bound by the tastes and conventions and prejudices of their age. It is, therefore, always possible to see in a minor author the characteristics of the age heightened and popularized, even exaggerated. On the other hand, the less famous writer may be an individualist, differing from the multitude; a man of eccentricity, even, whose voice has a quality all its own and yet is an essential part of the general chorus. All this makes necessary at least passing attention to the following poets—conventional or unconventional—who were for different reasons highly thought of in their time.

ROBERT SOUTHEY (1774-1843) is the first to command attention; he was poet laureate of England for thirty years. He was also the favorite target for the shafts of ridicule hurled by the younger, more revolutionary romantic poets like Byron at the older, more conservative group. Southey was an Oxford man by education and a conservative sycophant by instinct. He was, in the main, a very mediocre poet but an extremely ambitious one. Along with Coleridge, Southey was interested in the free community of the Pantisocracy (p. 164) and for a brief moment fancied himself as a revolutionist, but he was soon cured. He settled down at Greta Hall, near Keswick, in the Lake Country, and soon fell into a definite bondage to his generation. A few ballads from his early years, like *The Battle of Blenheim* (p. 300), have survived; so have a few didactic poems, pleasantly conventional, such as *The Old Man's Comforts* (p. 301); but the ambitious series of bloated epics that Southey attempted on the subject of the great religions of the world have been deservedly forgotten. Southey's output was enormous, as was his steady reading and collecting of books; but his fame, except for his prose *Life of Nelson* (1813), has passed.

A distinguished maker of literary ballads was THOMAS CAMPBELL (1777-1844). He was a Scotchman, and a friend of Sir Walter Scott and the critic Francis Jeffrey (p. 18). His early work was ornately didactic in the manner of Goldsmith's *Deserted Village* (Vol. I, p. 1114); a fair specimen is *The Pleasures of Hope* (1799). Then he turned to his best work—ballads of strong lyrical quality like *Hohenlinden* (1802), *Lord Ullin's Daughter* (1809), and *The Battle of the Baltic* (1809). The last named illustrates Campbell's peculiar felicity in songs of the sea. From the standpoint of the age, Campbell's masterpiece was *Gertrude of Wyoming* (1809), a long narrative poem, sentimental, florid, and artificial. Like his fellow-countryman of the eighteenth century, James Thomson (p. 32), Campbell was a slow worker of indolent disposition. His last years were spent in lecturing and in administering the duties of Rector of Glasgow University.

THOMAS MOORE (1779-1852), lyrist, musician, and society personality, was, next to Byron, the most popular poet of his age. His personal charm accounted partly for this, but the fact remains that he was an accomplished singer and was able to infuse much of this singing quality into his verse. Born in Dublin, the son of a grocer, he became something of an Irish minstrel and a social butterfly. He studied at Trinity College and developed a considerable amount of curious though superficial scholarship. He published a volume of songs (1806) of a light and evanescent sort, which will remind the reader somewhat of the Cavalier lyrics (Vol. I, pp.662 ff.). A second poetic undertaking involved the fitting of words to traditional Irish folktunes; this project kept him partly occupied for nearly twenty years. The resulting lyrics are, in general, Moore's best work. They are grave as well as gay, plaintive as well as stirring, intensely nationalistic. They are written with grace and sentiment; they are never very deep, but on the other hand are never as mawkish as many of the popular songs of the day. One further contribution of Moore should be mentioned here. He wrote two long narrative poems set in an Oriental background, with considerable exotic quality. But the Orientalism is chiefly in descriptive detail; he failed completely to picture the Oriental mind, for he had never been to the Orient and depended upon the library to compensate for this deficiency. These two poems, *Lalla Rookh* (1817) and *The Loves of the Angels* (1822), were immensely popular in their day and for a generation or two later. Time, however, has shown their artificiality and artistic falsity. It is as a national poet that Moore deserves to survive; his folk-music is of the *salon* variety, but it still maintains a slender hold upon later lovers of the Celtic flavor in literature.

Another folk-poet of considerable talent was James Hogg (1770-1835), who, from his birth at Ettrick, Selkirkshire, and from his ancestral occupation of shepherd, has always been known as the Ettrick Shepherd. Hogg is a poet of rural scenery and rural living; he is a true peasant poet, self-educated but ambitious and adventurous in a literary way. He maintains the tradition of Celtic folklore last seen in Sir Walter Scott (p. 190). His poetic aspirations took him to Edinburgh, where he met Scott and was encouraged by him; he undertook periodical work, and in his later life was long associated with *Blackwood's Magazine*. But it is chiefly as a bard of the Scottish border and lowlands that he is significant.

LEIGH HUNT (1784-1859), the journalist *par excellence* of the romantic movement, was early a dabbler in literature, but was not widely known until he became editor of *The Examiner*, almost the only periodical of the day that had no avowed political affiliations. In *The Examiner* Hunt published an attack upon the Prince Regent, later King George IV; as a result he was imprisoned for two years (1813-1815), and, like Defoe in the eighteenth century, became something of a popular hero in the process. Hunt wrote a few extremely felicitous short narrative poems like *Abou Ben Adhem* (p. 304) and *The Glove and the Lions* (p. 304), and a much longer narrative, *The Story of Rimini* (1816), which is especially interesting historically because it marks a real attempt to substitute the freer iambic pentameter couplet (such as that used by Chaucer in *The Canterbury Tales*) for the tightly closed neo-classical heroic couplet. The remainder of Hunt's career is taken up with his relations with Byron and Shelley, his efforts to found a new revolutionary journal, his *Life of Byron* (1827), written in very poor taste, his attempts at dramatic writing, and his occasional deft and agreeable essays.

Two writers who distinguished themselves in the creation of light, humorous verse and parodies are THOMAS LOVE PEACOCK (1785-1866) and THOMAS HOOD (1799-1845). Peacock was by profession a business man for a long time in the service of the East India Company, but he had a pronounced talent for burlesque romances, particularly illustrated by *Headlong Hall* (1816), *Nightmare Abbey* (1817), and *Crotchet Castle* (1831). In these romances he occasionally burst into song, brilliant and rousing lyrics in keeping with the satirical nature of their setting; Saintsbury has called him the last great writer of drinking-songs. In addition to his romancing and his poetizing, Peacock contributed frequently to periodicals and critical miscellanies; and his contributions were always witty, graceful, and ironical. Hood is a less subtle type of humorist; in fact, he depends for the greater part of his humorous effect upon the play on words. His *Odes and Addresses* and his other verse, composed while he had connections with *The London Magazine*, show, however, considerable variety of subject-matter; there is contained in them fanciful verse, humorous verse, and humanitarian verse. Indeed, it is preferable to think of him as a poet who was more interested in the social ills of his time than in mere clowning. He is, actually, a kind of transition figure to the Victorian period (p. 399). His *Bridge of Sighs* (p. 307) and *Song of the Shirt* (p. 306) are to be considered social documents rather than great or even good poetry. A more pedestrian writer, Ebenezer Elliott (1781-1849), sometimes known as the "corn-law rimester," was a sincere and an ardent preacher of reform, gifted with a most morbid imagination and cursed with a most plebeian style. He and Hood, acutely aware of the evils which the Industrial Revolution had brought to England, faced conditions and cried out, emotionally though somewhat hoarsely, against those evils. As humanitarians, Hood and Elliott, breathing the love of their fellow-men, are romanticists; in their specific complaints, however, they belong to the coming generation of Victorian social critics headed by Carlyle (p. 464) and Ruskin (p. 501).

There are two or three important literary figures in early nineteenth-century England who straddle the fence between the romantic and the Victorian ages. Some of the difficulty in classifying them lies in their chronology. Such a problem is illustrated by Robert Stephen Hawker (1803-1875), whose rousing songs of western England—Cornwall and Devonshire in particular—are thoroughly in keeping with the romantic spirit, but who was writing as late as 1869. Hawker has a terseness and poetic insight that make him a most worth-while poet, although he has been strangely neglected.

THOMAS LOVELL BEDDOES (1803-1849) was born the son of Thomas Beddoes, a physician, a speculative scientist, and an earnest missionary of scientific knowledge among the people. The boy was sent to the Charter House School and later to Oxford. In both institutions he showed an original cast of mind and personality, an eccentric behavior, and an unusual degree of aloofness. Like Shelley, with whom he has certain traits in common, Beddoes was a rebellious student. While still at Oxford he published *The Bride's Tragedy* (1822), a play based on Elizabethan models, a product of the Shakespearean and Elizabethan vogue that swept England as a result of the efforts of Coleridge (p. 163), Lamb (p. 337), Hazlitt (p. 360), and De Quincey (p. 374). The attention accorded this play by a few critics encouraged Beddoes to give himself to a career of play-writing. He produced many promising dramatic fragments, often superb poetry; but he did not possess a sufficiently strong sense of plot or dramatic structure to be an effective playwright. Nevertheless he persevered, and in 1829 brought forth a most unusual dramatic effort, *Death's Jest-Book, or The Fool's Tragedy*. His moody discontent with the finished product kept him from publishing it; it did not appear in print until after his death. The work is uneven as a play, but it contains many passages of unusually fine poetry and some songs, inserted in the tragedy in Elizabethan fashion, which have been called almost perfect lyrics. Beddoes did not attempt much more writing after *Death's*

Jest-Book. He moved to Germany, where he followed his father's profession of scientist. He studied physiology and anatomy, participated in the many liberal and democratic movements on the Continent during the 1840's, and died rather suddenly in 1849, probably by suicide, although the circumstances of his death are still rather mysterious.

WALTER SAVAGE LANDOR (1775-1864) is very much of an isolated figure in his own time. He lived through the entire romantic age and a good many years beyond. He stands as an austere artist devoted to ideals of classical Greece and Rome, paying a kind of intellectual service and offering a real artistic sympathy to Shelley, Byron, and Keats, but on the whole facing toward Tennyson and Browning in the Victorian age. His background is that of intellectual aristocracy. He was born in Warwick, January 30, 1775, and in due time studied at Rugby and at Oxford, where he matriculated in 1793, when revolutionism and republicanism were in the very air he breathed. He was entirely in sympathy with the ideals of liberty being preached, and consequently got into difficulties with the university authorities. He therefore left Oxford without taking a degree, but he had achieved an excellent training in Latin and was to write as fluently in that language as in English. A volume of poems appeared in 1795 and in the same year a *Moral Epistle* in prose, decidedly in the neo-classical manner. In these two productions Landor exhibited a gift for dignified phrase, and an artistic prose style quite beyond the ordinary. But it was not until the publication of *Gebir* (1798), an Oriental tale in the current fashion, that Landor became in any sense well known. This poem in blank verse he soon translated into Latin; indeed, he had originally tried both languages in the composition of the work.

Almost the only truly romantic episode in Landor's life followed shortly afterwards. He raised a regiment and took it off to fight Napoleon in Spain (1808). The affair was eventually unsuccessful, but Landor took on for the moment the aspect of a hero of liberty, and a great patriot to boot. His contact with Spain bore fruit in a tragedy, *Count Julian* (1812), highly praised by many, but veering toward the turgid and tumid. In the meantime (1811) he married and went to live in a kind of baronial estate in Wales, where he remained for three years, making several humanitarian efforts to improve the lot of his tenants, but finally giving up in disgust with their stupidity and the scheming of lawyers and their crew. After a time he set sail for the Continent, passed through France, and wandered about Italy for nearly three years, finally settling in Florence (1821), where he remained until 1835.

In Florence he began writing his *Imaginary Conversations*, which appeared in various series and editions between 1824 and 1853. These are dialogues between important people in history—dialogues approaching debates at times—on all conceivable subjects, but generally on attitudes toward life, birth, death, love, and hate. For the time being, Landor was devoted to prose. He turned to literary criticism in his *Citation and Examination of William Shakespeare* (1834); to a prose work that could almost be called a novel, *Pericles and Aspasia* (1836), a long series of imaginary letters between the great Athenian Pericles, his mistress Aspasia, and their friends; and to a series of dialogues between the fourteenth-century Italian poets Boccaccio (1313-1375) and Petrarch (1304-1374), entitled *The Pentameron*.

The next stage in Landor's productivity can be called his period of Latin poetry. For some time he wrote Latin verse of all types—idyllic, elegiac, lyric, and satiric—in both direct and indirect imitation of the chief writers in Roman literature. These poems followed the tradition of Virgil, Catullus, Horace, Juvenal, and others. In the year 1847 Landor published them under the title of *Poemata et Inscriptiones;* and in the same year he put into English verse a series of poems on Greek topics called *The Hellenics.* A second version of *The Hellenics* appeared twelve years later.

For almost a score of years after this fine fruition of Landor's classical tastes he lingered on. His disposition became more and more aloof and his poetry, if anything, more finished and severe in form and technique. Into this final period he put much of his best poetic work. There was *Last Fruit Off an Old Tree* (1853), notable for a little group of five dramatic scenes on the end of Beatrice Cenci, the heroine of Shelley's masterly poetic drama *The Cenci* (p. 251). A group of twelve dramatic dialogues, called *Antony and Octavius,* appeared in 1856; a miscellany of poetry entitled *Dry Sticks Fagoted by W. S. Landor* in 1858; and finally *Heroic Idyls* in 1863. He returned to Italy in 1858, and remained there until his death on September 17, 1864.

By disposition Landor was a hot-headed youth and a crusty old man. His first departure to Italy was due partly to his inability to get along with his neighbors in Wales; his return to England in 1835 was the result of a quarrel with his family; and his final return to Italy in 1858 was prompted by a libel suit in which one of his satirical epigrams had involved him. In his writings, however, little of that irascibility is apparent, for Landor is usually calm, restrained, polished, and considerate. He never won popular favor as a writer, although his talents were considerable; his personality may have militated against it, but the more likely reason is that he is too intellectual in his work—too basically unemotional to appeal to any but a restricted group. His short poems, however, terse, poised, and beautiful with a hard and rather glittering beauty, are still read with pleasure. His prose is ingenious, rich in melody and suggestive phrase. Landor did not court popularity. Rather he stood aloof saying: "I claim no place in the world of letters; I am alone, and will be alone, as long as I live, and after."

Robert Southey

1774-1843

The Battle of Blenheim

It was a summer evening;
   Old Kaspar's work was done,
And he before his cottage door
   Was sitting in the sun;
And by him sported on the green   5
   His little grandchild Wilhelmine.

She saw her brother Peterkin
   Roll something large and round,
Which he beside the rivulet,
   In playing there had found: 10
He came to ask what he had found,
That was so large and smooth and round.

The Battle of Blenheim. In the battle fought at Blenheim, Bavaria, August 13, 1704, British and German allies under the Duke of Marlborough and the Austrian Prince Eugene inflicted a crushing defeat upon the French and the Bavarians.

Old Kaspar took it from the boy,
   Who stood expectant by;
And then the old man shook his head,   15
   And with a natural sigh,
"'Tis some poor fellow's skull," said he,
"Who fell in the great victory.

"I find them in the garden,
   For there's many here about;   20
And often, when I go to plow,
   The plowshare turns them out;
For many thousand men," said he,
"Were slain in that great victory."

"Now tell us what 'twas all about,"   25
   Young Peterkin he cries;
And little Wilhelmine looks up
   With wonder-waiting eyes;
"Now tell us all about the war,
And what they fought each other for."   30

"It was the English," Kaspar cried,
   "Who put the French to rout;

But what they fought each other for,
  I could not well make out;
But everybody said," quoth he,   35
  "That 'twas a famous victory.

"My father lived at Blenheim then,
  Yon little stream hard by;
They burnt his dwelling to the ground,
  And he was forced to fly;   40
So with his wife and child he fled,
  Nor had he where to rest his head.

"With fire and sword the country round
  Was wasted far and wide,
And many a childing mother then,   45
  And new-born baby, died;
But things like that, you know, must be
  At every famous victory.

"They say it was a shocking sight
  After the field was won;   50
For many thousand bodies here
  Lay rotting in the sun:
But things like that, you know, must be
  After a famous victory.

"Great praise the Duke of Marlborough won,
  And our good Prince Eugene."   56
"Why, 'twas a very wicked thing!"
  Said little Wilhelmine.
"Nay, nay, my little girl," quoth he;
  "It was a famous victory.   60

"And everybody praised the Duke,
  Who this great fight did win."
"But what good came of it at last?"
  Quoth little Peterkin.
"Why, that I cannot tell," said he; 65
  "But 'twas a famous victory."
                           (1798)

The Old Man's Comforts

AND HOW HE GAINED THEM

"You are old, Father William," the young
    man cried,
  "The few locks which are left you are gray;

The Old Man's Comforts. See the brilliant parody of this poem by Lewis Carroll, *Father William,* p. 828.

You are hale, Father William, a hearty old
    man,
  Now tell me the reason, I pray."

"In the days of my youth," Father William
    replied,   5
  "I remembered that youth would fly fast,
And abused not my health, and my vigor at
    first,
  That I never might need them at last."

"You are old, Father William," the young
    man cried,
  "And pleasures with youth pass away; 10
And yet you lament not the days that are
    gone,
  Now tell me the reason, I pray."

"In the days of my youth," Father William
    replied,
  "I remembered that youth could not
    last;
I thought of the future, whatever I did, 15
  That I never might grieve for the past."

"You are old, Father William," the young
    man cried,
  "And life must be hastening away;
You are cheerful, and love to converse upon
    death,
  Now tell me the reason, I pray."   20

"I am cheerful, young man," Father William
    replied,
  "Let the cause thy attention engage;
In the days of my youth I remembered my
    God!
  And He hath not forgotten my age."
                           (1799)

The Inchcape Rock

No stir in the air, no stir in the sea,
The ship was still as she could be;
Her sails from heaven received no motion;
Her keel was steady in the ocean.

The Inchcape Rock. The Inchcape Rock was a great hidden rock twelve miles out in the German Sea; it was dangerous because it was covered at every tide. Southey's poem includes traditional details.

Without either sign or sound of their shock, 5
The waves flowed over the Inchcape Rock;
So little they rose, so little they fell,
They did not move the Inchcape Bell.

The Abbot of Aberbrothok
Had placed that Bell on the Inchcape Rock; 10
On a buoy in the storm it floated and swung,
And over the waves its warning rung.

When the Rock was hid by the surge's swell,
The mariners heard the warning Bell;
And then they knew the perilous Rock, 15
And blessed the Abbot of Aberbrothok.

The sun in heaven was shining gay;
All things were joyful on that day;
The sea-birds screamed as they wheeled round,
And there was joyance in their sound. 20

The buoy of the Inchcape Bell was seen,
A darker speck on the ocean green:
Sir Ralph the Rover walked his deck,
And he fixed his eye on the darker speck.

He felt the cheering power of spring; 25
It made him whistle, it made him sing:
His heart was mirthful to excess,
But the Rover's mirth was wickedness.

His eye was on the Inchcape float;
Quoth he, "My men, put out the boat, 30
And row me to the Inchcape Rock,
And I'll plague the Abbot of Aberbrothok."

The boat is lowered, the boatmen row,
And to the Inchcape Rock they go;
Sir Ralph bent over from the boat, 35
And he cut the Bell from the Inchcape float.

Down sunk the Bell with a gurgling sound;
The bubbles rose and burst around:
Quoth Sir Ralph, "The next who comes to the Rock
Won't bless the Abbot of Aberbrothok." 40

Sir Ralph the Rover sailed away;
He scoured the seas for many a day;
And now, grown rich with plundered store,
He steers his course for Scotland's shore.

So thick a haze o'erspreads the sky, 45
They cannot see the sun on high;
The wind hath blown a gale all day;
At evening it hath died away.

On the deck the Rover takes his stand;
So dark it is, they see no land. 50
Quoth Sir Ralph, "It will be lighter soon,
For there is the dawn of the rising moon."

"Canst hear," said one, "the breakers roar?
For methinks we should be near the shore."
"Now where we are I cannot tell, 55
But I wish I could hear the Inchcape Bell."

They hear no sound; the swell is strong;
Though the wind hath fallen, they drift along,
Till the vessel strikes with a shivering shock;
"O Christ! it is the Inchcape Rock!" 60

Sir Ralph the Rover tore his hair,
He cursed himself in his despair;
The waves rushed in on every side;
The ship is sinking beneath the tide.

But, even in his dying fear, 65
One dreadful sound could the Rover hear—
A sound as if, with the Inchcape Bell,
The Devil below was ringing his knell.

(1802)

Thomas Moore

1779-1852

Oh, Breathe Not His Name!

ROBERT EMMET

This poem is a tribute to Robert Emmet, the famous Irish revolutionist executed in 1803 because of his part in stirring up a rebellion in Dublin. He was the leader of The United Irishmen, a prominent revolutionary society.

Oh, breathe not his name! let it sleep in the shade,
Where cold and unhonored his relics are laid;

Sad, silent, and dark be the tears that we shed,
As the night-dew that falls on the grass o'er
   his head.

But the night-dew that falls, though in silence
   it weeps,
Shall brighten with verdure the grave where
   he sleeps;
And the tear that we shed, though in secret
   it rolls,
Shall long keep his memory green in our souls.
                              (*1807;* 1808)

The Harp That Once Through Tara's Halls

The harp that once through Tara's halls
   The soul of music shed,
Now hangs as mute on Tara's walls
   As if that soul were fled.
So sleeps the pride of former days,
   So glory's thrill is o'er,
And hearts that once beat high for praise
   Now feel that pulse no more!

No more to chiefs and ladies bright
   The harp of Tara swells;
The chord alone that breaks at night
   Its tale of ruin tells.
Thus Freedom now so seldom wakes,
   The only throb she gives
Is when some heart indignant breaks,
   To show that still she lives.   (*1807;* 1808)

'Tis the Last Rose of Summer

'Tis the last rose of summer
   Left blooming alone;
All her lovely companions
   Are faded and gone;
No flower of her kindred,
   No rose-bud is nigh,
To reflect back her blushes,
   Or give sigh for sigh.

I'll not leave thee, thou lone one!
   To pine on the stem;

The Harp . . . Halls. 1. **Tara,** a city near Dublin; it was famous in early history as a residence of Irish kings.

Since the lovely are sleeping,
   Go, sleep thou with them.
Thus kindly I scatter
   Thy leaves o'er the bed,
Where thy mates of the garden
   Lie scentless and dead.

So soon may *I* follow,
   When friendships decay,
And from Love's shining circle
   The gems drop away.
When true hearts lie withered,
   And fond ones are flown,
Oh! who would inhabit
   This bleak world alone?   (*1807;* 1808)

The Minstrel Boy

The Minstrel boy to the war is gone,
   In the ranks of death you'll find him;
His father's sword he has girded on,
   And his wild harp slung behind him.—
"Land of song!" said the warrior-bard,
   "Though all the world betrays thee,
One sword, at least, thy rights shall guard,
   One faithful harp shall praise thee!"

The Minstrel fell!—but the foeman's chain
   Could not bring his proud soul under;
The harp he loved ne'er spoke again,
   For he tore its cords asunder;
And said, "No chains shall sully thee,
   Thou soul of love and bravery!
Thy songs were made for the brave and
   free,
   They shall never sound in slavery!"
                              (*1807;* 1808)

Believe Me, If All Those Endearing Young Charms

Believe me, if all those endearing young
   charms,
   Which I gaze on so fondly today,
Were to change by tomorrow, and fleet in my
   arms,
   Like fairy-gifts fading away,
Thou wouldst still be adored, as this moment
   thou art,

Let thy loveliness fade as it will,
And around the dear ruin each wish of my
    heart
  Would entwine itself verdantly still.

It is not while beauty and youth are thine own,
  And thy cheeks unprofaned by a tear,   10
That the fervor and faith of a soul can be
    known,
  To which time will but make thee more
    dear;
No, the heart that has truly loved never for-
    gets,
  But as truly loves on to the close,
As the sun-flower turns on her god, when he
    sets,   15
  The same look which she turned when he
    rose.   *(1807; 1808)*

James Henry Leigh Hunt
1784-1859

Abou Ben Adhem and the Angel

    This poem is based upon an incident recorded in D'Herbelot's *Bibliothèque Orientale* (1697).

Abou Ben Adhem (may his tribe increase)
Awoke one night from a deep dream of peace,
And saw, within the moonlight in his room,
Making it rich, and like a lily in bloom,
An angel writing in a book of gold—   5
Exceeding peace had made Ben Adhem
    bold,
And to the presence in the room he said,
"What writest thou?"—The vision raised its
    head,
And with a look made of all sweet accord,
Answered, "The names of those who love
    the Lord."   10
"And is mine one?" said Abou. "Nay, not so,"
Replied the angel. Abou spoke more low,
But cheerly still; and said, "I pray thee then,
"Write me as one that loves his fellow
    men."

The angel wrote, and vanished. The next
    night   15
It came again with a great wakening light,
And showed the names whom love of God
    had blessed,
And lo! Ben Adhem's name led all the rest.
                        (1834; 1844)

The Glove and the Lions

King Francis was a hearty king, and loved a
    royal sport,
And one day, as his lions fought, sat looking
    on the court.
The nobles filled the benches, with the ladies
    in their pride,
And 'mongst them sat the Count de Lorge,
    with one for whom he sighed:
And truly 'twas a gallant thing to see that
    crowning show,   5
Valor and love, and a king above, and the
    royal beasts below.

Ramped and roared the lions, with horrid
    laughing jaws;
They bit, they glared, gave blows like beams,
    a wind went with their paws;
With wallowing might and stifled roar they
    rolled on one another,
Till all the pit with sand and mane was in a
    thunderous smother;   10
The bloody foam above the bars came whisk-
    ing through the air;
Said Francis then, "Faith, gentlemen, we're
    better here than there."

De Lorge's love o'erheard the King, a beau-
    teous lively dame,
With smiling lips and sharp bright eyes,
    which always seemed the same;
She thought, "The Count, my lover, is brave
    as brave can be;   15
He surely would do wondrous things to show
    his love of me;
King, ladies, lovers, all look on; the occasion
    is divine;
I'll drop my glove, to prove his love; great
    glory will be mine."

She dropped her glove, to prove his love, then
    looked at him and smiled;

The Glove and the Lions. Cf. Browning's *The Glove*, p. 667. **1. King Francis,** Francis I, King of France (1515-1547).

He bowed, and in a moment leaped among
    the lions wild;   20
The leap was quick, return was quick, he has
    regained his place,
Then threw the glove, but not with love, right
    in the lady's face.
"By Heaven," said Francis, "rightly done!"
    and he rose from where he sat;
"No love," quoth he, "but vanity, sets love a
    task like that."   (1836)

Rondeau

The Jenny of this poem was Jane Welsh, wife of Thomas Carlyle. Hunt visited her in 1838 after he had been ill, and impetuously she jumped up and kissed him.

Jenny kissed me when we met,
    Jumping from the chair she sat in;
Time, you thief, who love to get
    Sweets into your list, put that in;
Say I'm weary, say I'm sad,   5
    Say that health and wealth have missed me,
Say I'm growing old, but add,
    Jenny kissed me.   (1838)

The Fish, the Man, and the Spirit

To Fish

You strange, astonished-looking, angle-faced,
Dreary-mouthed, gaping wretches of the sea,
Gulping salt-water everlastingly,
Cold-blooded, though with red your blood
    be graced,
And mute, though dwellers in the roaring
    waste;   5
And you, all shapes beside, that fishy be—
Some round, some flat, some long, all devilry,
Legless, unloving, infamously chaste—

O scaly, slippery, wet, swift, staring wights,
What is't ye do? what life lead? eh, dull
    goggles?   10
How do ye vary your vile days and nights?
How pass your Sundays? Are ye still but
    joggles
In ceaseless wash? Still nought but gapes
    and bites,
And drinks, and stares, diversified with
    boggles?

A Fish Answers

Amazing monster! that, for aught I know, 15
With the first sight of thee didst make our
    race
Forever stare! O flat and shocking face,
Grimly divided from the breast below!
Thou that on dry land horribly dost go
With a split body and most ridiculous pace, 20
Prong after prong, disgracer of all grace,
Long-useless-finned, haired, upright, unwet,
    slow!

O breather of unbreathable, sword-sharp air,
How canst exist? How bear thyself, thou dry
And dreary sloth? What particle canst share
Of the only blessèd life, the watery?   26
I sometimes see of ye an actual *pair*
Go by! linked fin by fin! most odiously.

The Fish turns into a Man, and then into a Spirit, and again speaks

Indulge thy smiling scorn, if smiling still,
O man! and loathe, but with a sort of
    love: 30
For difference must its use by difference prove,
And, in sweet clang, the spheres with music
    fill.
One of the spirits am I, that at his will
Live in whate'er has life—fish, eagle, dove— 34
No hate, no pride, beneath nought, nor above,
A visitor of the rounds of God's sweet skill.

Man's life is warm, glad, sad, 'twixt loves and
    graves,
Boundless in hope, honored with pangs
    austere,
Heaven-gazing; and his angel-wings he
    craves:
The fish is swift, small-needing, vague yet
    clear,   40
A cold, sweet, silver life, wrapped in round
    waves,
Quickened with touches of transporting fear.
    (1857)

---

9. **wights**, creatures.

14. **boggles**, blotches.

Thomas Hood
1799-1845

Silence

There is a silence where hath been no sound,
  There is a silence where no sound may be,
In the cold grave—under the deep, deep sea,
Or in wide desert where no life is found,
Which hath been mute, and still must sleep
    profound;   5
No voice is hushed—no life treads silently,
  But clouds and cloudy shadows wander
    free,
That never spoke, over the idle ground:
But in green ruins, in the desolate walls
Of antique palaces, where man hath been, 10
Though the dun fox, or wild hyena, calls,
  And owls, that flit continually between,
Shriek to the echo, and the low winds moan,
There the true Silence is, self-conscious and
    alone.   (1823)

Ruth

She stood breast-high amid the corn,
Clasped by the golden light of morn,
Like the sweetheart of the sun,
Who many a glowing kiss had won.

On her cheek an autumn flush,   5
Deeply ripened;—such a blush
In the midst of brown was born,
Like red poppies grown with corn.

Round her eyes her tresses fell;
Which were blackest none could tell,   10
But long lashes veiled a light
That had else been all too bright.

And her hat, with shady brim,
Made her tressy forehead dim;—
Thus she stood amid the stooks,   15
Praising God with sweetest looks—

"Sure," I said, "heav'n did not mean,
Where I reap thou shouldst but glean,

Ruth. For the story of Ruth, see Vol. I, p. 597. Cf. Keats's *Ode to a Nightingale,* ll. 65-70, p. 285. 1. **corn,** grain. 15. **stooks,** shocks of grain.

Lay thy sheaf adown and come,
Share my harvest and my home."
    (1827)

The Song of the Shirt

This humanitarian poem was inspired by the sordid conditions of workers in London. One widow was trying to support herself and family by making trousers at seven shillings a week—"a good living," her employer called it. Hood's monument bears the inscription "He Sang the Song of the Shirt."

With fingers weary and worn,
  With eyelids heavy and red,
A woman sat, in unwomanly rags,
  Plying her needle and thread—
Stitch! stitch! stitch!   5
  In poverty, hunger, and dirt,
And still with a voice of dolorous pitch
  She sang the "Song of the Shirt."

"Work! work! work!
  While the cock is crowing aloof!   10
And work—work—work,
  Till the stars shine through the roof!
It's Oh! to be a slave
  Along with the barbarous Turk,
Where woman has never a soul to save,   15
  If this is Christian work.

"Work—work—work,
  Till the brain begins to swim;
Work—work—work,
  Till the eyes are heavy and dim!   20
Seam, and gusset, and band,
  Band, and gusset, and seam,
Till over the buttons I fall asleep,
  And sew them on in a dream!

"Oh, men, with sisters dear!   25
  Oh, men, with mothers and wives!
It is not linen you're wearing out
  But human creatures' lives!
Stitch—stitch—stitch,
  In poverty, hunger, and dirt,   30
Sewing at once, with a double thread,
  A Shroud as well as a Shirt.

"But why do I talk of Death?
  That phantom of grisly bone,

I hardly fear its terrible shape, 35
  It seems so like my own—
It seems so like my own,
  Because of the fasts I keep;
Oh, God! that bread should be so dear,
  And flesh and blood so cheap! 40

"Work—work—work!
  My labor never flags;
And what are its wages? A bed of straw,
  A crust of bread—and rags.
That shattered roof—this naked floor— 45
  A table—a broken chair—
And a wall so blank, my shadow I thank
  For sometimes falling there!

"Work—work—work!
  From weary chime to chime, 50
Work—work—work,
  As prisoners work for crime!
Band, and gusset, and seam,
  Seam, and gusset, and band,
Till the heart is sick, and the brain benumbed, 55
  As well as the weary hand.

"Work—work—work,
  In the dull December light,
And work—work—work,
  When the weather is warm and bright— 60
While underneath the eaves
  The brooding swallows cling
As if to show me their sunny backs
  And twit me with the spring.

"Oh! but to breathe the breath 65
  Of the cowslip and primrose sweet—
With the sky above my head,
  And the grass beneath my feet;
For only one short hour
  To feel as I used to feel, 70
Before I knew the woes of want
  And the walk that costs a meal.

"Oh! but for one short hour!
  A respite however brief!
No blessèd leisure for love or hope, 75
  But only time for grief!
A little weeping would ease my heart,
  But in their briny bed

My tears must stop, for every drop
  Hinders needle and thread!" 80

Seam, and gusset, and band,
  Band, and gusset, and seam,
Work—work—work,
  Like the engine that works by steam!
A mere machine of iron and wood 85
  That toils for Mammon's sake,
Without a brain to ponder and craze
  Or a heart to feel—and break!

With fingers weary and worn,
  With eyelids heavy and red, 90
A woman sat, in unwomanly rags,
  Plying her needle and thread—
Stitch! stitch! stitch!
  In poverty, hunger, and dirt,
And still with a voice of dolorous pitch— 95
  Would that its tone could reach the rich!—
She sang this "Song of the Shirt"! (1843)

The Bridge of Sighs

"Drown'd, drown'd."—*Hamlet*

One more Unfortunate,
  Weary of breath,
Rashly importunate,
  Gone to her death!

Take her up tenderly, 5
  Lift her with care;
Fashioned so slenderly,
  Young, and so fair!

Look at her garments
Clinging like cerements; 10
  Whilst the wave constantly
  Drips from her clothing;
Take her up instantly,
  Loving, not loathing.

Touch her not scornfully; 15
Think of her mournfully,
  Gently and humanly,
  Not of the stains of her;

---

86. **Mammon**, the god of riches and the personification of wealth; cf. Milton's *Paradise Lost*, I, 678 (Vol. I, p. 726). **The Bridge of Sighs.** The speech from *Hamlet*, IV, vii, 185, is Queen Gertrude's, telling Laertes about Ophelia. 10. **cerements**, waxed cloths used for wrapping dead bodies.

All that remains of her
  Now is pure womanly.

Make no deep scrutiny
Into her mutiny
  Rash and undutiful:
Past all dishonor,
Death has left on her
  Only the beautiful.

Still, for all slips of hers,
  One of Eve's family—
Wipe those poor lips of hers
  Oozing so clammily.

Loop up her tresses
  Escaped from the comb,
Her fair auburn tresses;
Whilst wonderment guesses
  Where was her home?

Who was her father?
  Who was her mother?
Had she a sister?
  Had she a brother?
Or was there a dearer one
Still, and a nearer one
  Yet, than all other?

Alas! for the rarity
Of Christian charity
  Under the sun!
O, it was pitiful!
Near a whole city full,
  Home she had none.

Sisterly, brotherly,
Fatherly, motherly
  Feelings had changed:
Love, by harsh evidence,
Thrown from its eminence;
Even God's providence
  Seeming estranged.

Where the lamps quiver
So far in the river,
  With many a light
From window to casement,
From garret to basement,
She stood with amazement,
  Houseless by night.

The bleak wind of March
  Made her tremble and shiver;
But not the dark arch,
  Or the black flowing river:
Mad from life's history,
Glad to death's mystery,
  Swift to be hurled—
Anywhere, anywhere
  Out of the world!

In she plunged boldly—
No matter how coldly
  The rough river ran—
Over the brink of it,
Picture it—think of it,
  Dissolute Man!
Lave in it, drink of it,
  Then, if you can!

Take her up tenderly,
  Lift her with care;
Fashioned so slenderly,
  Young, and so fair!

Ere her limbs frigidly
Stiffen too rigidly,
  Decently, kindly,
Smooth and compose them;
And her eyes, close them,
  Staring so blindly!

Dreadfully staring
  Through muddy impurity,
As when with the daring
Last look of despairing
  Fixed on futurity.

Perishing gloomily,
Spurred by contumely,
Cold inhumanity,
Burning insanity,
  Into her rest—
Cross her hands humbly,
As if praying dumbly,
  Over her breast!

Owning her weakness,
  Her evil behavior,
And leaving with meekness,
  Her sins to her Savior!   (1844)

Thomas Lovell Beddoes
1803-1849

Poor Old Pilgrim Misery

Poor old pilgrim Misery,
  Beneath the silent moon he sate,
A-listening to the screech owl's cry,
  And the cold wind's goblin prate;
Beside him lay his staff of yew   5
  With withered willow twined,
His scant gray hair all wet with dew,
  His cheeks with grief ybrined;
    And his cry it was ever, alack!
    Alack, and woe is me!   10

Anon a wanton imp astray
  His piteous moaning hears,
And from his bosom steals away
  His rosary of tears:
With his plunder fled that urchin elf,   15
  And hid it in your eyes,
Then tell me back the stolen pelf,
  Give up the lawless prize;
    Or your cry shall be ever, alack!
    Alack, and woe is me!   (1822)

Song

How many times do I love thee, dear?
  Tell me how many thoughts there be
    In the atmosphere
    Of a new-fall'n year,
Whose white and sable hours appear   5
  The latest flake of Eternity:
So many times do I love thee, dear.

How many times do I love again?
  Tell me how many beads there are
    In a silver chain   10
    Of evening rain,
Unraveled from the tumbling main,
  And threading the eye of a yellow star:
So many times do I love again.   (*1825;* 1851)

Song. Cf. Mrs. Browning's *How Do I Love Thee?* (p. 714).

To Sea, To Sea!

To sea, to sea! The calm is o'er;
  The wanton water leaps in sport,
And rattles down the pebbly shore;
  The dolphin wheels, the sea-cows snort,
And unseen Mermaids' pearly song   5
Comes bubbling up, the weeds among.
  Fling broad the sail, dip deep the oar;
  To sea, to sea! the calm is o'er.

To sea, to sea! Our wide-winged bark
  Shall billowy cleave its sunny way,   10
And with its shadow, fleet and dark,
  Break the caved Triton's azure day,
Like mighty eagle soaring light
O'er antelopes on Alpine height.
  The anchor heaves, the ship swings free, 15
  The sails swell full. To sea, to sea!
                (1850)

Dirge

If thou wilt ease thine heart
Of love and all its smart,
    Then sleep, dear, sleep;
And not a sorrow
  Hang any tear on your eye-lashes;   5
    Lie still and deep,
Sad soul, until the sea-wave washes
The rim o' the sun tomorrow,
    In eastern sky.

But wilt thou cure thine heart   10
Of love and all its smart,
    Then die, dear, die;
'Tis deeper, sweeter,
  Than on a rose bank to lie dreaming
    With folded eye;   15
  And then alone, amid the beaming
Of love's stars, thou'lt meet her
    In eastern sky.   (1850)

Lady, Was It Fair of Thee?

Lady, was it fair of thee
To seem so passing fair to me?
  Not every star to every eye

To Sea, To Sea! 12. **Triton,** one of the sea gods.

    Is fair; and why
Art thou another's share?
    Did thine eyes shed brighter glances,
Thine unkissed bosom heave more fair,
    To his than to my fancies?
        But I'll forgive thee still;
        Thou'rt fair without thy will.
    So be: but never know,
    That 'tis the hue of woe.

Lady, was it fair of thee
To be so gentle still to me?
    Not every lip to every eye
      Should let smiles fly.
Why didst thou never frown,
    To frighten from my pillow
Love's head, round which Hope wove a crown,
    And saw not 'twas of willow?
      But I'll forgive thee still,
      Thou knew'st not smiles could kill.
    Smile on: but never know,
    I die, nor of what woe.

                (1825-32; 1850)

Song

Old Adam, the carrion crow,
    The old crow of Cairo;
He sat in the shower, and let it flow
    Under his tail and over his crest;
        And through every feather
        Leaked the wet weather;
    And the bough swung under his nest;
    For his beak it was heavy with marrow,
Is that the wind dying? O no;
It's only two devils, that blow
Through a murderer's bones, to and fro,
    In the ghosts' moonshine.

Ho! Eve, my gray carrion wife,
    When we have supped on king's marrow,
Where shall we drink and make merry our life?
    Our nest it is Queen Cleopatra's skull,
      'Tis cloven and cracked,
      And battered and hacked,
But with tears of blue eyes it is full:
    Let us drink then, my raven of Cairo.
Is that the wind dying? O no;
It's only two devils, that blow
Through a murderer's bones, to and fro,
    In the ghosts' moonshine.

                (1825-32; 1850)

Song. 2. **Cairo**, the capital of Egypt.

Dream-Pedlary

If there were dreams to sell,
    What would you buy?
Some cost a passing bell;
    Some a light sigh,
That shakes from Life's fresh crown
Only a rose-leaf down,
If there were dreams to sell,
Merry and sad to tell,
And the crier rang the bell,
    What would you buy?

A cottage lone and still,
    With bowers nigh,
Shadowy, my woes to still,
    Until I die.
Such pearl from Life's fresh crown
Fain would I shake me down.
Were dreams to have at will,
This would best heal my ill,
    This would I buy.

But there were dreams to sell
    Ill didst thou buy;
Life is a dream, they tell,
    Waking, to die.
Dreaming a dream to prize,
Is wishing ghosts to rise;
And if I had the spell
To call the buried well,
    Which one would I?

If there are ghosts to raise,
    What shall I call,
Out of hell's murky haze,
    Heaven's blue pall?
Raise my loved long-lost boy,
To lead me to his joy.—
There are no ghosts to raise;
Out of death lead no ways;
    Vain is the call.

Know'st thou not ghosts to sue,
  No love thou hast.
Else lie, as I will do,   40
  And breathe thy last.
So out of Life's fresh crown
Fall like a rose-leaf down.
Thus are the ghosts to woo;
Thus are all dreams made true,   45
  Ever to last!   (1851)

Walter Savage Landor
1775-1864

Rose Aylmer

Rose Aylmer, the daughter of Henry, Baron Aylmer, was a devoted friend to Landor during his early years in Wales, 1795-1798. The poem was inspired by news of her death in India in 1800.

Ah, what avails the sceptered race,
  Ah, what the form divine!
What every virtue, every grace!
  Rose Aylmer, all were thine.
Rose Aylmer, whom these wakeful eyes   5
  May weep, but never see,
A night of memories and of sighs
  I consecrate to thee.   (1806)

Lyrics to Ianthe

The subject of these lyrics was Sophia Jane Swift (afterwards Comtesse de Molandé), early sweetheart of Landor for whom he retained a lifelong affection. After her husband's death in Paris, she spent two years in Italy (1829-1831); she died in Paris in 1851.

Away my verse; and never fear,
  As men before such beauty do;
On you she will not look severe.
  She will not turn her eyes from you.
Some happier graces could I lend   5
  That in her memory you should live,
Some little blemishes might blend,
  For it would please her to forgive. (1831)

✦

Rose Aylmer. 1. **sceptered race**, an allusion to the titled Aylmer family.

When Helen first saw wrinkles in her face
('Twas when some fifty long had settled there
And intermarried and branched off awide)
She threw herself upon her couch and wept:
On this side hung her head, and over that   5
Listlessly she let fall the faithless brass
That made the men as faithless.
                    But when you
Found them, or fancied them, and would not hear
That they were only vestiges of smiles,
Or the impression of some amorous hair   10
Astray from cloistered curls and roseate band,
Which had been lying there all night perhaps
Upon a skin so soft, "No, no," you said,
"Sure, they are coming, yes, are come, are here:
Well, and what matters it, while thou art too!"   (1831)

✦

Past ruined Ilion Helen lives,
  Alcestis rises from the shades;
Verse calls them forth; 'tis verse that gives
  Immortal youth to mortal maids.

Soon shall Oblivion's deepening veil   5
  Hide all the peopled hills you see,
The gay, the proud, while lovers hail
  These many summers you and me. (1831)

✦

Ianthe! you are called to cross the sea!
  A path forbidden *me!*
Remember, while the Sun his blessing sheds
  Upon the mountain-heads,
How often we have watched him laying down 5
  His brow, and dropped our own
Against each other's, and how faint and short
  And sliding the support!
What will succeed it now? Mine is unblessed,
  Ianthe! nor will rest   10
But on the very thought that swells with pain.
  O bid me hope again!

1. **Helen.** Helen of Troy, wife of Menelaus, was carried off by Paris because of her great beauty. The incident caused the Trojan War. 6. **brass**, an article serving as a mirror.
1. *Past ruined Ilion.* Ilion is Troy. See preceding poem. 2. **Alcestis**, wife of Admetus, King of Thessaly. She voluntarily died to save her husband's life and was brought back from Hades by Hercules. The legend is the subject of a tragedy by Euripides, Greek dramatist of the fifth century B.C.

O give me back what Earth, what (without
        you)
    Not Heaven itself can do,
One of the golden days that we have passed;
    And let it be my last!   16
Or else the gift would be, however sweet,
    Fragile and incomplete.   (1831)

✦

Pleasure! why thus desert the heart
    In its spring-tide?
I could have seen her, I could part,
    And but have sighed!
O'er every youthful charm to stray,   5
    To gaze, to touch—
Pleasure! why take so much away,
    Or give so much!   (1831)

✦

Mild is the parting year, and sweet
    The odor of the falling spray;
Life passes on more rudely fleet,
    And balmless is its closing day.

I wait its close, I court its bloom,   5
    But mourn that never must there fall
Or on my breast or on my tomb
    The tear that would have soothed it all.
        (1831)

✦

It often comes into my head
That we may dream when we are dead,
    But I am far from sure we do.
O that it were so! then my rest
Would be indeed among the blest;   5
    I should forever dream of you.   (1846)

✦

Why, why repine, my pensive friend,
    At pleasures slipped away?
Some the stern Fates will never lend,
    And all refuse to stay.

I see the rainbow in the sky,   5
    The dew upon the grass—
I see them, and I ask not why
    They glimmer or they pass.

With folded arms I linger not
    To call them back; 'twere vain;   10
In this, or in some other spot,
    I know they'll shine again.   (1846)

Years, many parti-colored years,
    Some have crept on, and some have flown
Since first before me fell those tears
    I never could see fall alone.
Years, not so many, are to come,   5
Years not so varied, when from you
One more will fall: when, carried home,
    I see it not, nor hear *adieu*.   (1853)

✦

Well I remember how you smiled
    To see me write your name upon
The soft sea-sand. "O! *what a child!*
    You think you're writing upon stone!"
I have since written what no tide   5
    Shall ever wash away, what men
Unborn shall read o'er ocean wide
    And find Ianthe's name again.   (1863)

Dirce

In Greek legend Dirce was the second wife of Lycus, King of Thebes. She mistreated Antiope, his first wife, who fled and unknowingly found refuge with her twin sons living with a herdsman. Dirce ordered the young men to tie Antiope to the horns of a wild bull; but discovering that she was their mother, they inflicted that punishment upon Dirce. In the poem she is on the way to Hades and is being ferried across the River Styx by Charon.

Stand close around, ye Stygian set,
    With Dirce in one boat conveyed,
Or Charon, seeing, may forget
    That he is old, and she a shade.   (1836)

One Year Ago

One year ago my path was green,
My footstep light, my brow serene;
Alas! and could it have been so
    One year ago?

There is a love that is to last   5
When the hot days of youth are past:
Such love did a sweet maid bestow
    One year ago.

I took a leaflet from her braid
And gave it to another maid,   10
Love! broken should have been thy bow
    One year ago.   (1846)

Yes, I Write Verses Now and Then

Yes; I write verses now and then,
But blunt and flaccid is my pen,
No longer talked of by young men
    As rather clever:
In the last quarter are my eyes,   5
You see it by their form and size;
Is it not time then to be wise?
    Or now or never.

Fairest that ever sprang from Eve!
While Time allows the short reprieve,   10
Just look at me! would you believe
    'Twas once a lover?
I cannot clear the five-bar gate,
But, trying first its timbers' state,
Climb stiffly up, take breath, and wait   15
    To trundle over.

Thro' gallopade I cannot swing
The entangling blooms of Beauty's spring:
I cannot say the tender thing,
    Be't true or false,   20
And am beginning to opine
Those girls are only half-divine
Whose waists yon wicked boys entwine
    In giddy waltz.

I fear that arm above that shoulder,   25
I wish them wiser, graver, older,
Sedater, and no harm if colder,
    And panting less.
Ah! people were not half so wild
In former days, when, starchly mild,   30
Upon her high-heeled Essex smiled
    The brave Queen Bess.   (1846)

The Leaves Are Falling; So Am I

The leaves are falling; so am I;
The few late flowers have moisture in the
    eye;
    So have I too.
Scarcely on any bough is heard
Joyous, or even unjoyous, bird   5
    The whole wood through.

Winter may come: he brings but nigher
His circle (yearly narrowing) to the fire
    Where old friends meet:
Let him; now heaven is overcast,   10
And spring and summer both are past,
    And all things sweet.   (1846)

Is It Not Better

Is it not better at an early hour
    In its calm cell to rest the weary head,
While birds are singing and while blooms the
    bower,
    Than sit the fire out and go starved to bed?
    (1846)

I Know Not Whether I Am Proud

I know not whether I am proud,
But this I know, I hate the crowd:
Therefore pray let me disengage
My verses from the motley page,
Where others far more sure to please   5
Pour out their choral song with ease.

And yet perhaps, if some should tire
With too much froth or too much fire,
There is an ear that may incline
Even to words so dull as mine.
    (1846)

Iphigeneia and Agamemnon

Agamemnon was the leader of the Greek expedition against Troy; Iphigeneia was his daughter. Because Agamemnon had slain a stag sacred to Artemis (Diana, goddess of the chase), the goddess held the Greek fleet at Aulis, a seaport on the east coast of Greece. The soothsayer Calchas reported that the death of Iphigeneia was the only means of appeasing Artemis. In one form of the legend, Artemis prevented the sacrifice and carried Iphigeneia to Tauris, where she became a priestess.

Iphigeneia, when she heard her doom
At Aulis, and when all beside the king
    Had gone away, took his right hand, and
    said,
"O father! I am young and very happy.

---

17. **gallopade**, a kind of lively dance. 31. **Essex**, Robert Devereaux (1567-1601), second Earl of Essex, a favorite of Queen Elizabeth.

I Know Not Whether. 2. **I . . . crowd.** Cf. Shelley's *Stanzas*, l. 22, and note, p. 253.

I do not think the pious Calchas heard 5
Distinctly what the goddess spake. Old age
Obscures the senses. If my nurse, who knew
My voice so well, sometimes misunderstood
While I was resting on her knee both arms
And hitting it to make her mind my words, 10
And looking in her face, and she in mine,
Might he not also hear one word amiss,
Spoken from so far off, even from Olympus?"
The father placed his cheek upon her head,
And tears dropped down it, but the king of
    men 15
Replied not. Then the maiden spake once
    more.
"O father! sayst thou nothing? Hearest thou
    not
Me, whom thou ever hast, until this hour,
Listened to fondly, and awakened me
To hear my voice amid the voice of birds, 20
When it was inarticulate as theirs,
And the down deadened it within the nest?"
He moved her gently from him, silent still,
And this, and this alone, brought tears from
    her,
Although she saw fate nearer: then with sighs,
"I thought to have laid down my hair before 26
Benignant Artemis, and not have dimmed
Her polished altar with my virgin blood;
I thought to have selected the white flowers
To please the Nymphs, and to have asked of
    each 30
By name, and with no sorrowful regret,
Whether, since both my parents willed the
    change,
I might at Hymen's feet bend my clipped
    brow;
And (after those who mind us girls the most)
Adore our own Athena, that she would 35
Regard me mildly with her azure eyes.
But father! to see you no more, and see
Your love, O father! go ere I am gone—"
Gently he moved her off, and drew her back,
Bending his lofty head far over hers, 40
And the dark depths of nature heaved and
    burst.
He turned away; not far, but silent still.
She now first shuddered; for in him, so nigh,

So long a silence seemed the approach of
    death,
And like it. Once again she raised her voice. 45
"O father! if the ships are now detained,
And all your vows move not the Gods above,
When the knife strikes me, there will be one
    prayer
The less to them: and pure can there be
Any, or more fervent than the daughter's
    prayer 50
For her dear father's safety and success?"
A groan that shook him shook not his resolve.
An aged man now entered, and without
One word, stepped slowly on, and took the
    wrist
Of the pale maiden. She looked up and saw 55
The fillet of the priest and calm cold eyes.
Then turned she where her parent stood, and
    cried,
"O father! grieve no more: the ships can sail."
    (1846)

To Youth

Where art thou gone, light-ankled Youth?
    With wing at either shoulder,
And smile that never left thy mouth
    Until the Hours grew colder:

Then somewhat seemed to whisper near 5
    That thou and I must part;
I doubted it: I felt no fear,
    No weight upon the heart:

If aught befell it, Love was by
    And rolled it off again; 10
So, if there ever was a sigh,
    'Twas not a sigh of pain.

I may not call thee back; but thou
    Returnest when the hand
Of gentle Sleep waves o'er my brow 15
    His poppy-crested wand;

Then smiling eyes bend over mine,
    Then lips once pressed invite;
But Sleep hath given a silent sign,
    And both, alas! take flight.
    (1853)

12. **he,** Calchas. 13. **Olympus,** Mt. Olympus, in Greece, the abode of Artemis and other gods and goddesses. 33. **Hymen,** god of marriage. 35. **Athena,** goddess of wisdom and war; she was the patroness of Argos, the most ancient city in Greece.

56. **fillet,** a narrow band worn around the forehead.
To Youth. Cf. the treatment of age in this and the following poems with that of Coleridge in *Youth and Age.* See p. 189, and note.

To Age

Welcome, old friend! These many years
  Have we lived door by door:
The Fates have laid aside their shears
  Perhaps for some few more.

I was indocile at an age 5
  When better boys were taught,
But thou at length hast made me sage,
  If I am sage in aught.

Little I know from other men,
  Too little they from me, 10
But thou hast pointed well the pen
  That writes these lines to thee.

Thanks for expelling Fear and Hope,
  One vile, the other vain;
One's scourge, the other's telescope, 15
  I shall not see again:

Rather what lies before my feet
  My notice shall engage—
He who hath braved Youth's dizzy heat
  Dreads not the frost of Age. 20

(1853)

3. Fates ... shears. Cf. Milton's *Lycidas*, l. 75 (Vol. I, p. 711).

Death Stands Above Me

Death stands above me, whispering low
  I know not what into my ear:
Of his strange language all I know
  Is, there is not a word of fear.

(1853)

On His Seventy-Fifth Birthday

I strove with none; for none was worth my strife,
  Nature I loved, and next to Nature, Art;
I warmed both hands before the fire of life,
  It sinks, and I am ready to depart.

(*1850;* 1853)

To My Ninth Decade

To my ninth decade I have tottered on,
  And no soft arm bends now my steps to steady;
She, who once led me where she would, is gone,
  So when he calls me, Death shall find me ready.

(1863)

On His Seventy-Fifth Birthday. Cf. Tennyson's *Crossing the Bar*, p. 654, and Browning's *Prospice*, p. 706.

ROMANTIC PROSE: REVOLUTIONARY, CRITICAL, AND IMAGINATIVE

Percy Bysshe Shelley*

1792-1822

Declaration of Rights

    The broadside *Declaration of Rights*, printed in Ireland while the Shelleys were there in 1812, was shipped with other pamphlets to Shelley's friend Elizabeth Hitchener for distribution in England. Customs officials at Holyhead seized the box containing the papers and expressed great concern over the "dangerous tendency" of the *Declaration*. Later, Shelley's servant Daniel Hill was imprisoned for trying to distribute the broadside.

*For the biographical sketch of Shelley, see p. 248; see also p. 15.

1

Government has no rights; it is a delegation from several individuals for the purpose of securing their own. It is therefore just only so far as it exists by their consent, useful only so far as it operates to their wellbeing.

2

If these individuals think that the form of government which they, or their forefathers, constituted is ill adapted to produce their happiness, they have a right to change it.

3

Government is devised for the security of rights. The rights of man are liberty and an equal participation of the commonage of nature.

4

As the benefit of the governed is, or ought to be, the origin of government, no men can have any authority that does not expressly emanate from their will.

5

Though all governments are not so bad as that of Turkey, yet none are so good as they might be; the majority of every country have a right to perfect their government; the minority should not disturb them; they ought to secede and form their own system in their own way.

6

All have a right to an equal share in the benefits and burdens of government. Any disabilities for opinion imply by their existence barefaced tyranny on the side of government, ignorant slavishness on the side of the governed.

7

The rights of man in the present state of society are only to be secured by some degree of coercion to be exercised on their violator. The sufferer has a right that the degree of coercion employed be as slight as possible.

8

It may be considered as a plain proof of the hollowness of any proposition, if power be used to enforce instead of reason to persuade its admission. Government is never supported by fraud until it cannot be supported by reason.

9

No man has a right to disturb the public peace by personally resisting the execution of a law however bad. He ought to acquiesce, using at the same time the utmost powers of his reason to promote its repeal.

10

A man must have a right to act in a certain manner before it can be his duty. He may, before he ought.

11

A man has a right to think as his reason directs; it is a duty he owes to himself to think with freedom, that he may act from conviction.

12

A man has a right to unrestricted liberty of discussion; falsehood is a scorpion that will sting itself to death.

13

A man has not only a right to express his thoughts, but it is his duty to do so.

14

No law has a right to discourage the practice of truth. A man ought to speak the truth on every occasion; a duty can never be criminal; what is not criminal cannot be injurious.

15

Law cannot make what is in its nature virtuous or innocent to be criminal, any more than it can make what is criminal to be innocent. Government cannot make a law; it can only pronounce that which was the law before its organization—viz., the moral result of the imperishable relations of things.

16

The present generation cannot bind their posterity. The few cannot promise for the many.

17

No man has a right to do an evil thing that good may come.

18

Expediency is inadmissible in morals. Politics are only sound when conducted on principles of morality. They are, in fact, the morals of nations.

19

Man has no right to kill his brother; it is no excuse that he does so in uniform. He only adds the infamy of servitude to the crime of murder.

20

Man, whatever be his country, has the same rights in one place as another, the rights of universal citizenship.

21

The government of a country ought to be perfectly indifferent to every opinion. Religious differences, the bloodiest and most rancorous of all, spring from partiality.

22

A delegation of individuals, for the purpose of securing their rights, can have no undelegated power of restraining the expression of their opinion.

23

Belief is involuntary; nothing involuntary is meritorious or reprehensible. A man ought not to be considered worse or better for his belief.

24

A Christian, a Deist, a Turk, and a Jew have equal rights: they are men and brethren.

25

If a person's religious ideas correspond not with your own, love him nevertheless. How different would yours have been, had the chance of birth placed you in Tartary or India!

26

Those who believe that Heaven is, what earth has been, a monopoly in the hands of a favored few, would do well to reconsider their opinion: if they find that it came from their priest or their grandmother, they could not do better than reject it.

27

No man has a right to be respected for any other possessions but those of virtue and talents. Titles are tinsel, power a corruptor, glory a bubble, and excessive wealth a libel on its possessor.

28

No man has a right to monopolize more than he can enjoy; what the rich give to the poor, whilst millions are starving, is not a perfect favor, but an imperfect right.

29

Every man has a right to a certain degree of leisure and liberty, because it is his duty to attain a certain degree of knowledge. He may, before he ought.

30

Sobriety of body and mind is necessary to those who would be free, because without sobriety a high sense of philanthropy cannot actuate the heart, nor cool and determined courage execute its dictates.

31

The only use of government is to repress the vices of man. If man were today sinless, tomorrow he would have a right to demand that government and all its evils should cease.

* * * * *

No. 25. Tartary, the name formerly applied to the middle portion of the Eurasiatic continent; its people were warlike tribes.

Man! thou whose rights are here declared, be no longer forgetful of the loftiness of thy destination. Think of thy rights; of those possessions which will give thee virtue and wisdom, by which thou mayest arrive at happiness and freedom. They are declared to thee by one who knows thy dignity, for every hour does his heart swell with honorable pride in the contemplation of what thou mayest attain, by one who is not forgetful of thy degeneracy, for every moment brings home to him the bitter conviction of what thou art.

Awake!—arise!—or be forever fallen.

William Wordsworth*
1770-1850

from *Preface* to *Lyrical Ballads*

This famous essay was published with the second edition of *Lyrical Ballads* (1800). It should be compared with Chapter XIV of Coleridge's *Biographia Literaria* (p. 328).

* * * * *

The principal object, then, proposed in these poems was to choose incidents and situations from common life, and to relate or describe them, throughout, as far as was possible in a selection of language really used by men, and at the same time to throw over them a certain coloring of imagination, whereby ordinary things should be presented to the mind in an unusual aspect; and, further, and above all, to make these incidents and situations interesting by tracing in them, truly though not ostentatiously, the primary laws of our nature: chiefly, as far as regards the manner in which we associate ideas in a state of excitement. Humble and rustic life was generally chosen, because, in that condition, the essential passions of the heart find a better soil in which they can attain their maturity, are less under restraint, and speak a plainer and more emphatic language; because in that condition of life our elementary feelings coexist in a state of greater simplicity, and, consequently, may be more accurately contemplated, and more forcibly communicated; because the manners of rural life germinate from those elementary feelings, and, from the necessary character of rural occupations, are more easily comprehended, and are more durable; and, lastly, because in that condition the passions of men are incorporated with the beautiful and permanent forms of nature. The language, too, of these men has been adopted (purified indeed from what appear to be its real defects, from all lasting and rational causes of dislike or disgust) because such men hourly communicate with the best objects from which the best part of language is originally derived; and because, from their rank in society and the sameness and narrow circle of their intercourse, being less under the influence of social vanity, they convey their feelings and notions in simple and unelaborated expressions. Accordingly, such a language, arising out of repeated experience and regular feelings, is a more permanent and a far more philosophical language than that which is frequently substituted for it by poets, who think that they are conferring honor upon themselves and their art, in proportion as they separate themselves from the sympathies of men, and indulge in arbitrary and capricious habits of expression, in order to furnish food for fickle tastes and fickle appetites of their own creation.

I cannot, however, be insensible to the present outcry against the triviality and meanness, both of thought and language, which some of my contemporaries have occasionally

---

*For the biographical sketch of Wordsworth see p. 118; see also p. 10.

2. **these poems,** those published in *Lyrical Ballads*.

58. **contemporaries.** Possibly a reference to Southey, p. 296, and Crabbe.

introduced into their metrical compositions; and I acknowledge that this defect, where it exists, is more dishonorable to the writer's own character than false refinement or arbitrary innovation, though I should contend at the same time that it is far less pernicious in the sum of its consequences. From such verses the poems in these volumes will be found distinguished at least by one mark of difference, that each of them has a worthy *purpose*. Not that I always began to write with a distinct purpose formally conceived; but habits of meditation have, I trust, so prompted and regulated my feelings that my descriptions of such objects as strongly excite those feelings will be found to carry along with them a *purpose*. If this opinion be erroneous, I can have little right to the name of a poet. For all good poetry is the spontaneous overflow of powerful feelings: and though this be true, poems to which any value can be attached were never produced on any variety of subjects but by a man who, being possessed of more than usual organic sensibility, had also thought long and deeply. For our continued influxes of feeling are modified and directed by our thoughts, which are indeed the representatives of all our past feelings; and, as by contemplating the relation of these general representatives to each other, we discover what is really important to men, so, by the repetition and continuance of this act, our feelings will be connected with important subjects, till at length, if we be originally possessed of much sensibility, such habits of mind will be produced, that, by obeying blindly and mechanically the impulses of those habits, we shall describe objects and utter sentiments, of such a nature, and in such connection with each other, that the understanding of the reader must necessarily be in some degree enlightened, and his affections strengthened and purified.

It has been said that each of these poems has a purpose. Another circumstance must be mentioned which distinguishes these poems from the popular poetry of the day; it is this, that the feeling therein developed gives importance to the action and situation, and not the action and situation to the feeling.

A sense of false modesty shall not prevent me from asserting that the reader's attention is pointed to this mark of distinction, far less for the sake of these particular poems than from the general importance of the subject. The subject is indeed important! For the human mind is capable of being excited without the application of gross and violent stimulants; and he must have a very faint perception of its beauty and dignity who does not know this, and who does not further know that one being is elevated above another, in proportion as he possesses this capability. It has therefore appeared to me that to endeavor to produce or enlarge this capability is one of the best services in which, at any period, a writer can be engaged; but this service, excellent at all times, is especially so at the present day. For a multitude of causes, unknown to former times, are now acting with a combined force to blunt the discriminating powers of the mind, and, unfitting it for all voluntary exertion, to reduce it to a state of almost savage torpor. The most effective of these causes are the great national events which are daily taking place, and the increasing accumulation of men in cities, where the uniformity of their occupations produces a craving for extraordinary incident, which the rapid communication of intelligence hourly gratifies. To this tendency of life and manners the literature and theatrical exhibitions of the country have conformed themselves. The invaluable works of our elder writers—I had almost said the works of Shakespeare and Milton—are driven into neglect by frantic novels, sickly and stupid German tragedies, and deluges of idle and extravagant stories in verse.—When I think

---

19. **all good poetry,** etc. Cf. Wordsworth's statements regarding poets and poetry with those of Coleridge (p. 331, l. 31, and p. 332, l. 11), Hazlitt (p. 363, l. 50), Arnold (p. 553, l. 43), and Tennyson, *The Poet* (p. 596).

57. **human mind,** etc. Cf. Ruskin's *The Relation of Art to Morals* (p. 524). 75. **national events.** Such as the war with France, the Irish Rebellion, and the passage of important labor laws. 87. **frantic novels.** Like Mrs. Radcliffe's *Mysteries of Udolpho* (1794) and other Gothic romances. See p. 23. **stupid . . . tragedies.** Such as August Kotzebue's *Misanthropy and Repentance* (1790), known in England as *The Stranger.* 88. **idle . . . verse.** A probable reference to such poems as *Maviad* (1795) and *Baviad* (1794), two satires by William Gifford (1756-1826), editor of *Quarterly Review;* Landor's *Gebir* (1798); and Scott's translations of Bürger's *Lenore.*

upon this degrading thirst after outrageous stimulation, I am almost ashamed to have spoken of the feeble endeavor made in these volumes to counteract it; and, reflecting upon the magnitude of the general evil, I should be oppressed with no dishonorable melancholy, had I not a deep impression of certain inherent and indestructible qualities of the human mind, and likewise of certain powers in the great and permanent objects that act upon it, which are equally inherent and indestructible; and were there not added to this impression a belief that the time is approaching when the evil will be systematically opposed, by men of greater powers, and with far more distinguished success.

Having dwelt thus long on the subjects and aim of these poems, I shall request the reader's permission to apprise him of a few circumstances relating to their *style*, in order, among other reasons, that he may not censure me for not having performed what I never attempted. The reader will find that personifications of abstract ideas rarely occur in these volumes; and are utterly rejected, as an ordinary device, to elevate the style and raise it above prose. My purpose was to imitate, and, as far as possible, to adopt the very language of men; and assuredly such personifications do not make any natural or regular part of that language. They are, indeed, a figure of speech occasionally prompted by passion, and I have made use of them as such; but have endeavored utterly to reject them as a mechanical device of style, or as a family language which writers in meter seem to lay claim to by prescription. I have wished to keep the reader in the company of flesh and blood, persuaded that by so doing I shall interest him. Others who pursue a different track will interest him likewise; I do not interfere with their claim, but wish to prefer a claim of my own. There will also be found in these volumes little of what is usually called poetic diction; as much pains has been taken to avoid it as is ordinarily taken to produce it; this has been done for the reason already alleged, to bring my language near to the language of men, and further, because the pleasure which I have proposed to myself to impart, is of a kind very different from that which is supposed by many persons to be the proper object of poetry. Without being culpably particular, I do not know how to give my reader a more exact notion of the style in which it was my wish and intention to write than by informing him that I have at all times endeavored to look steadily at my subject; consequently, there is, I hope, in these poems little falsehood of description, and my ideas are expressed in language fitted to their respective importance. Something must have been gained by this practice, as it is friendly to one property of all good poetry, namely, good sense: but it has necessarily cut me off from a large portion of phrases and figures of speech which from father to son have long been regarded as the common inheritance of poets. I have also thought it expedient to restrict myself still further, having abstained from the use of many expressions, in themselves proper and beautiful, but which have been foolishly repeated by bad poets, till such feelings of disgust are connected with them as it is scarcely possible by any art of association to overpower.

If in a poem there should be found a series of lines, or even a single line, in which the language, though naturally arranged and according to the strict laws of meter, does not differ from that of prose, there is a numerous class of critics, who, when they stumble upon these prosaisms, as they call them, imagine that they have made a notable discovery, and exult over the poet as over a man ignorant of his own profession. Now these men would establish a canon of criticism which the reader will conclude he must utterly reject if he wishes to be pleased with these volumes. And it would be a most easy task to prove to him that not only the language of a large portion of every good poem, even of the most elevated character, must necessarily, except with reference to the meter, in no respect differ from that of good prose, but likewise that some of the most interesting parts of the best poems will be found to be strictly the language of prose when prose is well written. The truth of this assertion might be demonstrated by innumerable passages from almost all the poetical writings, even of Milton himself. To illustrate the subject in a general manner, I will here adduce a short composition of Gray, who was at the head of those who, by their reasonings, have attempted to widen the space of separation betwixt Prose and Metrical composition, and was more than any other man curiously elaborate in the structure of his own poetic diction.

In vain to me the smiling mornings shine,
   And reddening Phoebus lifts his golden fire;
The birds in vain their amorous descant join,
   Or cheerful fields resume their green attire.
These ears, alas! for other notes repine;
A different object do these eyes require;
My lonely anguish melts no heart but mine;
And in my breast the imperfect joys expire;
Yet morning smiles the busy race to cheer,
   And new-born pleasure brings to happier men;
The fields to all their wonted tribute bear;
   To warm their little loves the birds complain.
I fruitless mourn to him that cannot hear,
And weep the more because I weep in vain.

It will easily be perceived, that the only part of this Sonnet which is of any value is the lines printed in Italics; it is equally obvious that, except in the rime and in the use of the single word "fruitless" for "fruitlessly," which is so far a defect, the language of these lines does in no respect differ from that of prose.

By the foregoing quotation it has been shown that the language of Prose may yet be well adapted to Poetry; and it was previously asserted that a large portion of the language of every good poem can in no respect differ from that of good Prose. We will go further. It may be safely affirmed that there neither is, nor can be, any *essential* difference between the language of prose and metrical composition. We are fond of tracing the resemblance between Poetry and Painting, and, accordingly, we call them Sisters; but where shall we find bonds of connection sufficiently strict to typify the affinity betwixt metrical and prose composition? They both speak by and to the same organs; the bodies in which both of them are clothed may be said to be of the same substance, their affections are kindred, and almost identical, not necessarily differing even in degree; Poetry sheds no tears "such as Angels weep," but natural and human tears; she can boast of no celestial ichor that distinguishes her vital juices from those of Prose; the same human blood circulates through the veins of them both.

If it be affirmed that rime and metrical arrangement of themselves constitute a distinction which overturns what has just been said on the strict affinity of metrical language with that of prose, and paves the way for other artificial distinctions which the mind voluntarily admits, I answer that the language of such poetry as is here recommended is, as far as is possible, a selection of the language really spoken by men; that this selection, wherever it is made with true taste and feeling, will of itself form a distinction far greater than would at first be imagined, and will entirely separate the composition from the vulgarity and meanness of ordinary life; and, if meter be superadded thereto, I believe that a dissimilitude will be produced altogether sufficient for the gratification of a rational mind. What other distinction would we have? Whence is it to come? And where is it to exist? Not, surely, where the poet speaks through the mouths of his characters— it cannot be necessary here, either for elevation of style, or any of its supposed ornaments; for, if the poet's subject be judiciously chosen, it will naturally, and upon fit occasion, lead him to passions the language of which, if selected truly and judiciously, must necessarily be dignified and variegated, and alive with metaphors and figures. I forbear

---

10. **In vain,** etc.. Gray's *Sonnet on the Death of Richard West,* p. 49.

51. **Poetry.** "I here use the word 'Poetry' (though against my own judgment) as opposed to the word 'Prose,' and synonymous with metrical composition. But much confusion has been introduced into criticism by this contradistinction of Poetry and Prose, instead of the more philosophical one of Poetry and Matter of Fact, or Science. The only strict antithesis to Prose is Meter; nor is this, in truth, a *strict* antithesis, because lines and passages of meter so naturally occur in writing prose, that it would be scarcely possible to avoid them, even were it desirable."—Wordsworth's note. 53. **ichor,** an ethereal fluid that flowed in the veins of the gods. 55. **same . . . both.** It is precisely this kind of statement that Byron derides in his *English Bards and Scotch Reviewers,* p. 204, l. 242.

to speak of an incongruity which would shock the intelligent reader, should the poet interweave any foreign splendor of his own with that which the passion naturally suggests; it is sufficient to say that such addition is unnecessary. And, surely, it is more probable that those passages, which with propriety abound with metaphors and figures, will have their due effect, if, upon other occasions where the passions are of a milder character, the style also be subdued and temperate.

But, as the pleasure which I hope to give by the poems now presented to the reader must depend entirely on just notions upon this subject, and, as it is in itself of high importance to our taste and moral feelings, I cannot content myself with these detached remarks. And if, in what I am about to say, it shall appear to some that my labor is unnecessary, and that I am like a man fighting a battle without enemies, such persons may be reminded, that, whatever be the language outwardly holden by men, a practical faith in the opinions which I am wishing to establish is almost unknown. If my conclusions are admitted and carried as far as they must be carried if admitted at all, our judgments concerning the works of the greatest poets both ancient and modern will be far different from what they are at present, both when we praise, and when we censure; and our moral feelings influencing and influenced by these judgments will, I believe, be corrected and purified.

Taking up the subject, then, upon general grounds, let me ask, what is meant by the word poet? What is a poet? To whom does he address himself? And what language is to be expected from him?—He is a man speaking to men: a man, it is true, endowed with more lively sensibility, more enthusiasm and tenderness, who has a greater knowledge of human nature, and a more comprehensive soul than are supposed to be common among mankind; a man pleased with his own passions and volitions, and who rejoices more than other men in the spirit of life that is in him; delighting to contemplate similar volitions and passions as manifested in the goings-on of the Universe, and habitually impelled to create them where he does not find them. To these qualities he has added a disposition to be affected more than other men by absent things as if they were present; an ability of conjuring up in himself passions which are indeed far from being the same as those produced by real events, yet (especially in those parts of the general sympathy which are pleasing and delightful) do more nearly resemble the passions produced by real events, than anything which, from the motions of their own minds merely, other men are accustomed to feel in themselves—whence, and from practice, he has acquired a greater readiness and power in expressing what he thinks and feels, and especially those thoughts and feelings which, by his own choice, or from the structure of his own mind, arise in him without immediate external excitement.

But whatever portion of this faculty we may suppose even the greatest poet to possess, there cannot be a doubt that the language which it will suggest to him must often, in liveliness and truth, fall short of that which is uttered by men in real life, under the actual pressure of those passions, certain shadows of which the poet thus produces, or feels to be produced, in himself.

However exalted a notion we would wish to cherish of the character of a poet, it is obvious that while he describes and imitates passions, his employment is in some degree mechanical, compared with the freedom and power of real and substantial action and suffering. So that it will be the wish of the poet to bring his feelings near to those of the persons whose feelings he describes, nay, for short spaces of time, perhaps, to let himself slip into an entire delusion, and even confound and identify his own feelings with theirs; modifying only the language which is thus suggested to him by a consideration that he describes for a particular purpose, that of giving pleasure. Here, then, he will apply the principle of selection which has been already insisted upon. He will depend upon this for removing what would otherwise be painful or disgusting in the passion; he will feel that

---

37. **What is a poet?** Cf. Wordsworth's *If Thou Indeed Derive Thy Light from Heaven*, p. 163.

there is no necessity to trick out or to elevate nature; and, the more industriously he applies this principle, the deeper will be his faith that no words, which *his* fancy or imagination can suggest, will be to be compared with those which are the emanations of reality and truth.

But it may be said by those who do not object to the general spirit of these remarks that, as it is impossible for the poet to produce upon all occasions language as exquisitely fitted for the passion as that which the real passion itself suggests, it is proper that he should consider himself as in the situation of a translator, who does not scruple to substitute excellencies of another kind for those which are unattainable by him; and endeavors occasionally to surpass his original, in order to make some amends for the general inferiority to which he feels that he must submit. But this would be to encourage idleness and unmanly despair. Further, it is the language of men who speak of what they do not understand; who talk of poetry as of a matter of amusement and idle pleasure; who will converse with us as gravely about a *taste* for poetry, as they express it, as if it were a thing as indifferent as a taste for rope-dancing, or Frontiniac or Sherry. Aristotle, I have been told, has said that poetry is the most philosophic of all writing; it is so; its object is truth, not individual and local, but general and operative; not standing upon external testimony, but carried alive into the heart by passion; truth which is its own testimony, which gives competence and confidence to the tribunal to which it appeals, and receives them from the same tribunal. Poetry is the image of man and nature. The obstacles which stand in the way of the fidelity of the biographer and historian, and of their consequent utility, are incalculably greater than those which are to be encountered by the poet who comprehends the dignity of his art. The poet writes under one restriction only, namely, the necessity of giving immediate pleasure to a human being possessed of that information which may be expected from him, not as a lawyer, a physician, a mariner, an astronomer, or a natural philosopher, but as a man. Except this one restriction, there is no object standing between the poet and the image of things; between this, and the biographer and historian, there are a thousand.

Nor let this necessity of producing immediate pleasure be considered as a degradation of the poet's art. It is far otherwise. It is an acknowledgment of the beauty of the universe, an acknowledgment the more sincere, because not formal, but indirect; it is a task light and easy to him who looks at the world in the spirit of love; further, it is a homage paid to the native and naked dignity of man, to the grand elementary principle of pleasure, by which he knows, and feels, and lives, and moves. We have no sympathy but what is propagated by pleasure—I would not be misunderstood; but wherever we sympathize with pain, it will be found that the sympathy is produced and carried on by subtle combinations with pleasure. We have no knowledge, that is, no general principles drawn from the contemplation of particular facts, but what has been built up by pleasure, and exists in us by pleasure alone. The man of science, the chemist and mathematician, whatever difficulties and disgusts they may have had to struggle with, know and feel this. However painful may be the objects with which the anatomist's knowledge is connected, he feels that his knowledge is pleasure; and where he has no pleasure, he has no knowledge. What then does the poet? He considers man and the objects that surround him as acting and reacting upon each other, so as to produce an infinite complexity of pain and pleasure; he considers man in his own nature and in his ordinary life as contemplating this with a certain quantity of immediate knowledge, with certain convictions, intuitions, and deductions, which from habit acquire the quality of intuitions; he considers him as looking upon this complex scene of ideas and sensations, and finding everywhere objects that immediately excite in him sympathies which, from the necessities of his nature, are accompanied by an overbalance of enjoyment.

---

28. **Frontiniac or Sherry**, kinds of wine; one French, the other Spanish. **Aristotle**, the most famous and influential of Greek philosophers (384-322 B.C). In his *Poetics*, 9, 3, he says, "Poetry is more philosophical and more serious than history."

To this knowledge which all men carry about with them, and to these sympathies in which, without any other discipline than that of our daily life, we are fitted to take delight, the poet principally directs his attention. He considers man and nature as essentially adapted to each other, and the mind of man as naturally the mirror of the fairest and most interesting properties of nature. And thus the poet, prompted by this feeling of pleasure, which accompanies him through the whole course of his studies, converses with general nature, with affections akin to those, which, through labor and length of time, the man of science has raised up in himself by conversing with those particular parts of nature which are the objects of his studies. The knowledge both of the poet and the man of science is pleasure; but the knowledge of the one cleaves to us as a necessary part of our existence, our natural and unalienable inheritance; the other is a personal and individual acquisition, slow to come to us, and by no habitual and direct sympathy connecting us with our fellow-beings. The man of science seeks truth as a remote and unknown benefactor; he cherishes and loves it in his solitude; the poet, singing a song in which all human beings join with him, rejoices in the presence of truth as our visible friend and hourly companion. Poetry is the breath and finer spirit of all knowledge; it is the impassioned expression which is in the countenance of all science. Emphatically may it be said of the poet, as Shakespeare hath said of man, "that he looks before and after." He is the rock of defense for human nature; an upholder and preserver, carrying everywhere with him relationship and love. In spite of difference of soil and climate, of language and manners, of laws and customs, in spite of things silently gone out of mind, and things violently destroyed; the poet binds together by passion and knowledge the vast empire of human society, as it is spread over the whole earth and over all time. The objects of the poet's thoughts are everywhere; though the eyes and senses of man are, it is true, his favorite guides, yet he will follow wheresoever he can find an atmosphere of sensation in which to move his wings. Poetry is the first and last of all knowledge—it is as immortal as the heart of man. If the labors of men of science should ever create any material revolution, direct or indirect, in our condition and in the impressions which we habitually receive, the poet will sleep then no more than at present; he will be ready to follow the steps of the man of science, not only in those general indirect effects, but he will be at his side, carrying sensation into the midst of the objects of science itself. The remotest discoveries of the chemist, the botanist, or mineralogist, will be as proper objects of the poet's art as any upon which it can be employed, if the time should ever come when these things shall be familiar to us, and the relations under which they are contemplated by the followers of these respective sciences shall be manifestly and palpably material to us as enjoying and suffering beings. If the time should ever come when what is now called science, thus familiarized to men, shall be ready to put on, as it were, a form of flesh and blood, the poet will lend his divine spirit to aid the transfiguration, and will welcome the being thus produced, as a dear and genuine inmate of the household of man.—It is not, then, to be supposed that anyone, who holds that sublime notion of poetry which I have attempted to convey, will break in upon the sanctity and truth of his pictures by transitory and accidental ornaments, and endeavor to excite admiration of himself by arts, the necessity of which must manifestly depend upon the assumed meanness of his subject.

What has been thus far said applies to poetry in general; but especially to those parts of composition where the poet speaks through the mouths of his characters; and upon this point it appears to authorize the conclusion that there are few persons of good sense, who would not allow that the dramatic parts of composition are defective, in proportion as they deviate from the real language of nature,

---

36. "that . . . after," *Hamlet*, IV, iv, 37.

62. **discoveries of the chemist**, etc. Cf. Huxley's *Science and Culture*, p. 571.

and are colored by a diction of the poet's own, either peculiar to him as an individual poet or belonging simply to poets in general; to a body of men who, from the circumstance of their compositions being in meter, it is expected will employ a particular language.

It is not, then, in the dramatic parts of composition that we look for this distinction of language; but still it may be proper and necessary where the poet speaks to us in his own person and character. To this I answer by referring the reader to the description before given of a poet. Among the qualities there enumerated as principally conducing to form a poet is implied nothing differing in kind from other men, but only in degree. The sum of what was said is, that the poet is chiefly distinguished from other men by a greater promptness to think and feel without immediate external excitement and a greater power in expressing such thoughts and feelings as are produced in him in that manner. But these passions and thoughts and feelings are the general passions and thoughts and feelings of men. And with what are they connected? Undoubtedly with our moral sentiments and animal sensations, and with the causes which excite these; with the operations of the elements and the appearances of the visible universe; with storm and sunshine, with the revolutions of the seasons, with cold and heat, with loss of friends and kindred, with injuries and resentments, gratitude and hope, with fear and sorrow. These, and the like, are the sensations and objects which the poet describes, as they are the sensations of other men, and the objects which interest them. The poet thinks and feels in the spirit of human passions. How, then, can his language differ in any material degree from that of all other men who feel vividly and see clearly? It might be *proved* that it is impossible. But supposing this were not the case, the poet might then be allowed to use a peculiar language when expressing his feelings for his own gratification, or that of men like himself. But poets do not write for poets alone, but for men. Unless therefore we are advocates for that admiration which subsists upon ignorance, and that pleasure which arises from hearing what we do not understand, the poet must descend from this supposed height; and, in order to excite rational sympathy, he must express himself as other men express themselves. To this it may be added, that while he is only selecting from the real language of men, or, which amounts to the same thing, composing accurately in the spirit of such selection, he is treading upon safe ground, and we know what we are to expect from him. Our feelings are the same with respect to meter; for, as it may be proper to remind the reader, the distinction of meter is regular and uniform, and not, like that which is produced by what is usually called POETIC DICTION, arbitrary and subject to infinite caprices upon which no calculation whatever can be made. In the one case, the reader is utterly at the mercy of the poet, respecting what imagery or diction he may choose to connect with the passion; whereas, in the other, the meter obeys certain laws to which the poet and reader both willingly submit because they are certain, and because no interference is made by them with the passion, but such as the concurring testimony of ages has shown to heighten and improve the pleasure which co-exists with it.

It will now be proper to answer an obvious question, namely: Why, professing these opinions, have I written in verse? To this, in addition to such answer as is included in what has been already said, I reply, in the first place: Because, however I may have restricted myself, there is still left open to me what confessedly constitutes the most valuable object of all writing, whether in prose or verse—the great and universal passions of men, the most general and interesting of their occupations, and the entire world of nature before me to supply endless combinations of forms and imagery. Now, supposing for a moment that whatever is interesting in these objects may be as vividly described in prose, why should I be condemned for attempting to superadd to such description the charm which, by the consent of all nations, is acknowledged to exist in metrical language? To this, by such as are yet unconvinced, it may be answered that a very small part of the pleasure given by poetry depends upon the meter, and that it is injudicious to write in meter unless it be accompanied with the other artificial distinctions of style with which meter is usually accompanied, and that, by such deviation, more will be lost from the shock which will thereby be given to the reader's associations than will be counterbalanced by any pleasure which he can derive from the general power of numbers. In answer to those who still contend for the necessity of accompanying meter with certain appropriate colors of style in order to the accomplishment of its appropriate end, and who also, in my opinion, greatly underrate the power of meter in itself, it might, perhaps, as far as relates to these volumes, have been almost sufficient to observe, that poems are extant, written upon more humble subjects, and in a still more naked and simple style, which have continued to give pleasure from generation to generation. Now, if nakedness and simplicity be a defect, the fact here mentioned affords a strong presumption that poems somewhat less naked and simple are capable of affording pleasure at the present day; and, what I wished *chiefly* to attempt, at present, was to justify myself for having written under the impression of this belief. . . .

I have said that poetry is the spontaneous overflow of powerful feelings: it takes its origin from emotion recollected in tranquillity; the emotion is contemplated till, by a species of reaction, the tranquillity gradually disappears, and an emotion, kindred to that which was before the subject of contemplation, is gradually produced, and does itself actually exist in the mind. In this mood successful composition generally begins, and in a mood similar to this it is carried on; but the emotion, of whatever kind and in whatever degree, from various causes, is qualified by various pleasures, so that in describing any passions whatsoever which are voluntarily described, the mind will, upon the whole, be in a state of enjoyment. If nature be thus cautious to preserve in a state of enjoyment a being so employed, the poet ought to profit by the lesson held forth to him and ought especially to take care that, whatever passions he communicates to his reader, those passions, if his reader's mind be sound and vigorous, should always be accompanied with an overbalance of pleasure. Now the music of harmonious metrical language, the sense of difficulty overcome, and the blind association of pleasure which has been previously received from works of rime or meter of the same or similar construction, an indistinct perception perpetually renewed of language closely resembling that of real life, and yet, in the circumstance of meter, differing from it so widely—all these imperceptibly make up a complex feeling of delight which is of the most important use in tempering the painful feeling always found intermingled with powerful descriptions of the deeper passions. This effect is always produced in pathetic and impassioned poetry; while, in lighter compositions, the ease and gracefulness with which the poet manages his numbers are themselves confessedly a principal source of the gratification of the reader. All that it is *necessary* to say, however, upon this subject may be effected by affirming—what few persons will deny—that, of two descriptions, either of passions, manners, or characters, each of them equally well executed, the one in prose and the other in verse, the verse will be read a hundred times where the prose is read once.

Having thus explained a few of my reasons for writing in verse, and why I have chosen subjects from common life, and endeavored to bring my language near to the real language of men, if I have been too minute in pleading my own cause, I have at the same time been treating a subject of general interest; and for this reason a few words shall be added with reference solely to these particular poems and to some defects which will probably be found in them. I am sensible that my associations must have sometimes been particular instead of general, and that, consequently, giving to things a false importance, I may have sometimes written upon unworthy subjects; but I am less apprehensive on this account than that my language may frequently have suffered from those arbitrary

---

10. **numbers**, the mechanics of verse, or verse itself. What Wordsworth says is part of the theory of free verse.

connections of feelings and ideas with particular words and phrases from which no man can altogether protect himself. Hence I have no doubt, that, in some instances, feelings, even of the ludicrous, may be given to my readers by expressions which appeared to me tender and pathetic. Such faulty expressions, were I convinced they were faulty at present and that they must necessarily continue to be so, I would willingly take all reasonable pains to correct. But it is dangerous to make these alterations on the simple authority of a few individuals, or even of certain classes of men; for where the understanding of an author is not convinced, or his feelings altered, this cannot be done without great injury to himself: for his own feelings are his stay and support; and if he set them aside in one instance, he may be induced to repeat this act till his mind shall lose all confidence in itself, and become utterly debilitated. To this it may be added that the critic ought never to forget that he is himself exposed to the same errors as the poet, and, perhaps, in a much greater degree: for there can be no presumption in saying of most readers that it is not probable they will be so well acquainted with the various stages of meaning through which words have passed, or with the fickleness or stability of the relations of particular ideas to each other; and, above all, since they are so much less interested in the subject, they may decide lightly and carelessly.

Long as the reader has been detained, I hope he will permit me to caution him against a mode of false criticism which has been applied to poetry, in which the language closely resembles that of life and nature. Such verses have been triumphed over in parodies, of which Dr. Johnson's stanza is a fair specimen:

> I put my hat upon my head
> And walked into the Strand,
> And there I met another man
> Whose hat was in his hand.

Immediately under these lines let us place one of the most justly-admired stanzas of the *Babes in the Wood*:

> These pretty Babes with hand in hand
> Went wandering up and down;
> But never more they saw the Man
> Approaching from the Town.

In both these stanzas the words and the order of the words in no respect differ from the most unimpassioned conversation. There are words in both, for example, "the Strand," and "the Town," connected with none but the most familiar ideas; yet the one stanza we admit as admirable and the other as a fair example of the superlatively contemptible. Whence arises this difference? Not from the meter, not from the language, not from the order of the words; but the *matter* expressed in Dr. Johnson's stanza is contemptible. The proper method of treating trivial and simple verses, to which Dr. Johnson's stanza would be a fair parallelism, is not to say, this is a bad kind of poetry, or, this is not poetry; but, this wants sense; it is neither interesting in itself nor can *lead* to anything interesting; the images neither originate in that sane state of feeling which arises out of thought nor can excite thought or feeling in the reader. This is the only sensible manner of dealing with such verses. Why trouble yourself about the species till you have previously decided upon the genus? Why take pains to prove that an ape is not a Newton when it is self-evident that he is not a man?

One request I must make of my reader, which is, that in judging these poems he would decide by his own feelings genuinely and not by reflection upon what will probably be the judgment of others. How common is it to hear a person say, I myself do not object to this style of composition, or this or that expression, but, to such and such classes of people it will appear mean or ludicrous! This mode of criticism, so destructive of all sound unadulterated judgment, is almost universal; let the reader then abide, independently, by his own feelings, and, if he finds himself affected, let him not suffer such conjectures to interfere with his pleasure. . . .   (1800)

---

40. **Dr. Johnson**, Samuel Johnson (Vol. I, p. 1125), who had little interest in ballads, the style of which he parodies in the stanza quoted here. 42. **Strand**, a prominent street in London.

77. **Newton**, Sir Isaac Newton (1642-1727), celebrated English mathematician, scientist, and natural philosopher.

Samuel Taylor Coleridge*
1772-1834

from *Biographia Literaria*

CHAPTER XIV

During the first year that Mr. Wordsworth and I were neighbors, our conversations turned frequently on the two cardinal points of poetry: the power of exciting the sympathy of the reader by a faithful adherence to the truth of nature, and the power of giving the interest of novelty by the modifying colors of imagination. The sudden charm, which accidents of light and shade, which moonlight or sunset, diffused over a known and familiar landscape, appeared to represent the practicability of combining both. These are the poetry of nature. The thought suggested itself (to which of us I do not recollect) that a series of poems might be composed of two sorts. In the one, the incidents and agents were to be, in part at least, supernatural; and the excellence aimed at was to consist in the interesting of the affections by the dramatic truth of such emotions as would naturally accompany such situations, supposing them real. And real in this sense they have been to every human being who, from whatever source of delusion, has at any time believed himself under supernatural agency. For the second class, subjects were to be chosen from ordinary life; the characters and incidents were to be such as will be found in every village and its vicinity where there is a meditative and feeling mind to seek after them or to notice them when they present themselves.

In this idea originated the plan of the *Lyrical Ballads;* in which it was agreed that my endeavors should be directed to persons and characters supernatural, or at least romantic; yet so as to transfer from our inward nature a human interest and a semblance of truth sufficient to procure for these shadows of imagination that willing suspension of disbelief for the moment which constitutes poetic faith. Mr. Wordsworth, on the other hand, was to propose to himself as his object, to give the charm of novelty to things of every day, and to excite a feeling analogous to the supernatural by awakening the mind's attention from the lethargy of custom and directing it to the loveliness and the wonders of the world before us; an inexhaustible treasure, but for which, in consequence of the film of familiarity and selfish solicitude, we have eyes, yet see not, ears that hear not, and hearts that neither feel nor understand.

With this view I wrote the *Ancient Mariner,* and was preparing, among other poems, the *Dark Ladie* and the *Christabel,* in which I should have more nearly realized my ideal than I had done in my first attempt. But Mr. Wordsworth's industry had proved so much more successful, and the number of his poems so much greater that my compositions, instead of forming a balance, appeared rather an interpolation of heterogeneous matter. Mr. Wordsworth added two or three poems written in his own character, in the impassioned, lofty, and sustained diction which is characteristic of his genius. In this form the *Lyrical Ballads* were published; and were presented by him, as an experiment, whether subjects, which from their nature rejected the usual ornaments and extracolloquial style of poems in general, might not be so managed in the language of ordinary life as to produce the pleasurable interest which it is the peculiar business of poetry to impart. To the second edition he added a preface of considerable length; in which, notwithstanding some passages of apparently a contrary import, he was understood to contend for the extension of this style to poetry of all kinds, and to reject as vicious and indefensible all phrases and forms

---

*For the biographical sketch of Coleridge see p. 163.
Biographia Literaria. Cf. Wordsworth's *Preface* to *Lyrical Ballads* (p. 318). 1. **first year**, 1797-1798.

50. **eyes ... understand.** Phrases used many times in the Bible. See *Psalms,* 115:5-7; *Isaiah,* 6:9-10; *Matthew,* 13:13.

of style that were not included in what he (unfortunately, I think, adopting an equivocal expression) called the language of real life. From this preface prefixed to poems in which it was impossible to deny the presence of original genius, however mistaken its direction might be deemed, arose the whole long-continued controversy. For from the conjunction of perceived power with supposed heresy I explain the inveteracy and in some instances, I grieve to say, the acrimonious passions, with which the controversy has been conducted by the assailants.

Had Mr. Wordsworth's poems been the silly, the childish things which they were for a long time described as being; had they been really distinguished from the compositions of other poets merely by meanness of language and inanity of thought; had they indeed contained nothing more than what is found in the parodies and pretended imitations of them; they must have sunk at once, a dead weight, into the slough of oblivion, and have dragged the preface along with them. But year after year increased the number of Mr. Wordsworth's admirers. They were found, too, not in the lower classes of the reading public, but chiefly among young men of strong sensibility and meditative minds; and their admiration (inflamed perhaps in some degree by opposition) was distinguished by its intensity, I might almost say, by its religious fervor. These facts and the intellectual energy of the author, which was more or less consciously felt where it was outwardly and even boisterously denied, meeting with sentiments of aversion to his opinions, and of alarm at their consequences, produced an eddy of criticism, which would of itself have borne up the poems by the violence with which it whirled them round and round. With many parts of this preface, in the sense attributed to them, and which the words undoubtedly seem to authorize, I never concurred; but, on the contrary, objected to them as erroneous in principle and as contradictory (in appearance at least) both to other parts of the same preface and to the author's own practice in the greater number of the poems themselves. Mr. Wordsworth, in his recent collection, has, I find, degraded this prefatory disquisition to the end of his second volume, to be read or not at the reader's choice. But he has not, as far as I can discover, announced any change in his poetic creed. At all events, considering it as the source of a controversy, in which I have been honored more than I deserve by the frequent conjunction of my name with his, I think it expedient to declare, once for all, in what points I coincide with his opinions and in what points I altogether differ. But in order to render myself intelligible, I must previously, in as few words as possible, explain my ideas, first, of a poem; and secondly, of poetry itself, in kind and in essence.

The office of philosophical disquisition consists in just distinction; while it is the privilege of the philosopher to preserve himself constantly aware that distinction is not division. In order to obtain adequate notions of any truth, we must intellectually separate its distinguishable parts; and this is the technical process of philosophy. But having so done, we must then restore them in our conceptions to the unity in which they actually co-exist; and this is the result of philosophy. A poem contains the same elements as a prose composition; the difference, therefore, must consist in a different combination of them, in consequence of a different object proposed. According to the difference of the object will be the difference of the combination. It is possible that the object may be merely to facilitate the recollection of any given facts or observations by artificial arrangement; and the composition will be a poem, merely because it is distinguished from prose by meter, or by rime, or by both conjointly. In this, the lowest sense, a man might attribute the name of a poem to the well-known enumeration of the days in the several months:

> Thirty days hath September,
> April, June, and November, etc.

and others of the same class and purpose. And as a particular pleasure is found in anticipating the recurrence of sound and quantities, all compositions that have this charm superadded,

---

7. **whole . . . controversy,** that over Wordsworth's theory and practice of poetic art.

whatever be their contents, *may* be entitled poems.

So much for the superficial form. A difference of object and contents supplies an additional ground of distinction. The immediate purpose may be the communication of truths: either of truth absolute and demonstrable, as in works of science; or of facts experienced and recorded, as in history. Pleasure, and that of the highest and most permanent kind, may result from the attainment of the end; but it is not itself the immediate end. In other works the communication of pleasure may be the immediate purpose; and though truth, either moral or intellectual, ought to be the ultimate end, yet this will distinguish the character of the author, not the class to which the work belongs. Blest indeed is that state of society, in which the immediate purpose would be baffled by the perversion of the proper ultimate end; in which no charm of diction or imagery could exempt the Bathyllus even of an Anacreon, or the Alexis of Virgil, from disgust and aversion!

But the communication of pleasure may be the immediate object of a work not metrically composed; and that object may have been in a high degree attained, as in novels and romances. Would then the mere superaddition of meter, with or without rime, entitle these to the name of poems? The answer is, that nothing can permanently please which does not contain in itself the reason why it is so, and not otherwise. If meter be superadded, all other parts must be made consonant with it. They must be such as to justify the perpetual and distinct attention to each part which an exact correspondent recurrence of accent and sound are calculated to excite. The final definition then, so deduced, may be thus worded. A poem is that species of composition which is opposed to works of science by proposing for its immediate object pleasure, not truth; and from all other species (having this object in common with it) it is discriminated by proposing to itself such delight from the whole as is compatible with a distinct gratification from each component part.

Controversy is not seldom excited in consequence of the disputants' attaching each a different meaning to the same word; and in few instances has this been more striking than in disputes concerning the present subject. If a man chooses to call every composition a poem which is rime, or measure, or both, I must leave his opinion uncontroverted. The distinction is at least competent to characterize the writer's intention. If it were subjoined, that the whole is likewise entertaining or affecting as a tale, or as a series of interesting reflections, I of course admit this as another fit ingredient of a poem and an additional merit. But if the definition sought for be that of a legitimate poem, I answer, it must be one the parts of which mutually support and explain each other; all in their proportion harmonizing with and supporting the purpose and known influences of metrical arrangement. The philosophic critics of all ages coincide with the ultimate judgment of all countries in equally denying the praises of a just poem, on the one hand, to a series of striking lines or distichs, each of which, absorbing the whole attention of the reader to itself, disjoins it from its context and makes it a separate whole, instead of a harmonizing part; and on the other hand, to an unsustained composition from which the reader collects rapidly the general result unattracted by the component parts. The reader should be carried forward, not merely or chiefly by the mechanical impulse of curiosity, or by a restless desire to arrive at the final solution; but by the pleasurable activity of mind excited by the attractions of the journey itself. Like the motion of a serpent, which the Egyptians made the emblem of intellectual power; or like the path of sound through the air, at every step he pauses and half recedes, and from the retrogressive movement collects the force which again carries him onward. *Praecipitandus est liber spiritus,* says Petronius Arbiter most happily. The epithet, *liber,* here balances the preceding verb; and it is not easy to conceive more meaning condensed in fewer words.

But if this should be admitted as a satis-

---

22. **Bathyllus**, a youth of Samos beloved by Anacreon, Greek lyric poet of the sixth century B.C.; *Ode* 17 is addressed to him. 23. **Alexis**, a youth beloved by the shepherd Corydon in the second *Eclogue* of Virgil (70-19 B.C.), famous Roman epic, didactic, and idyllic poet. 40. **A poem, etc.** See Wordsworth's *Preface* and note to l. 19, p. 319.

90. **Praecipitandus**, etc., the free spirit ought to be urged onward (from *Satyricon*, by Petronius Arbiter, a Roman satirist of the first century; he directed the imperial pleasures at the court of Nero).

factory character of a poem, we have still to seek for a definition of poetry. The writings of Plato and Bishop Taylor, and the *Theoria Sacra* of Burnet furnish undeniable proofs that poetry of the highest kind may exist without meter, and even without the contra-distinguishing objects of a poem. The first chapter of *Isaiah* (indeed a very large proportion of the whole book) is poetry in the most emphatic sense; yet it would be not less irrational than strange to assert that pleasure, and not truth, was the immediate object of the prophet. In short, whatever specific import we attach to the word poetry, there will be found involved in it, as a necessary consequence, that a poem of any length neither can be, nor ought to be, all poetry. Yet if a harmonious whole is to be produced, the remaining parts must be preserved in keeping with the poetry; and this can be not otherwise effected than by such a studied selection and artificial arrangement as will partake of one, though not a peculiar property of poetry. And this again can be no other than the property of exciting a more continuous and equal attention than the language of prose aims at, whether colloquial or written.

My own conclusions on the nature of poetry, in the strictest use of the word, have been in part anticipated in the preceding disquisition on the fancy and imagination. What is poetry? is so nearly the same question with, what is a poet? that the answer to the one is involved in the solution of the other. For it is a distinction resulting from the poetic genius itself, which sustains and modifies the images, thoughts, and emotions of the poet's own mind. The poet, described in ideal perfection, brings the whole soul of man into activity, with the subordination of its faculties to each other, according to their relative worth and dignity. He diffuses a tone and spirit of unity that blends and (as it were) fuses each into each, by that synthetic and magical power to which we have exclusively appropriated the name of imagination. This power, first put in action by the will and understanding, and retained under their irremissive, though gentle and unnoticed, control (*laxis effertur habenis*), reveals itself in the balance or reconciliation of opposite or discordant qualities: of sameness, with difference; of the general, with the concrete; the idea, with the image; the individual, with the representative; the sense of novelty and freshness, with old and familiar objects; a more than usual state of emotion, with more than usual order; judgment ever awake and steady self-possession with enthusiasm and feeling profound or vehement; and while it blends and harmonizes the natural and the artificial, still subordinates art to nature; the manner to the matter; and our admiration of the poet to our sympathy with the poetry. "Doubtless," as Sir John Davies observes of the soul (and his words may with slight alteration be applied, and even more appropriately, to the poetic imagination)—

Doubtless this could not be, but that she turns
Bodies to spirit by sublimation strange,
As fire converts to fire, the things it burns,
As we our food into our nature change.

From their gross matter she abstracts their forms,
And draws a kind of quintessence from things;
Which to her proper nature she transforms
To bear them light on her celestial wings.

Thus does she, when from individual states
She doth abstract the universal kinds;
Which then re-clothed in divers names and fates
Steal access through our senses to our minds.

Finally, good sense is the body of poetic genius, fancy its drapery, motion its life, and imagination the soul that is everywhere, and in each; and forms all into one graceful and intelligent whole. *(1815-16; 1817)*

---

3. **Plato**, celebrated Greek philosopher (427-347 B.C.). **Bishop Taylor**, Jeremy Taylor (1613-1667), an English bishop and theological writer. 4. **Burnet**, Thomas Burnet (1635-1715), an English bishop, author of works notable for their vivid imagery and purity of style. In his *Sacred Theory of the Earth* he gives a fanciful hypothesis about the formation of the earth. 16. **poem . . . poetry.** Cf. Poe's *Poetic Principle*, which sets forth the doctrine that there is no such thing as a long poem. 30. **preceding disquisition**, Chapter 4 of *Biographia Literaria*.

49. **laxis, etc.,** is borne along with loose reins. 64. **Sir John Davies**, an English statesman and poet (1569-1626). The stanzas are quoted with slight alterations from his poem *Of the Soul of Man*, 4, 45-56. 74. **proper**, own.

Characteristics of Shakespeare's Dramas

IN LECTURES of which amusement forms a large part of the object, there are some peculiar difficulties. The architect places his foundation out of sight, and the musician tunes his instrument before he makes his appearance; but the lecturer has to try his chords in the presence of the assembly, an operation not likely, indeed, to produce much pleasure, but yet indispensably necessary to a right understanding of the subject to be developed.

Poetry in essence is as familiar to barbarous as to civilized nations. The Laplander and the savage Indian are cheered by it as well as the inhabitants of London and Paris; its spirit takes up and incorporates surrounding materials, as a plant clothes itself with soil and climate, whilst it exhibits the working of a vital principle within, independent of all accidental circumstances. And to judge with fairness of an author's works, we ought to distinguish what is inward and essential from what is outward and circumstantial. It is essential to poetry that it be simple, and appeal to the elements and primary laws of our nature; that it be sensuous, and by its imagery elicit truth at a flash; that it be impassioned, and be able to move our feelings and awaken our affections. In comparing different poets with each other, we should inquire which have brought into the fullest play our imagination and our reason, or have created the greatest excitement and produced the completest harmony. If we consider great exquisiteness of language and sweetness of meter alone, it is impossible to deny to Pope the character of a delightful writer; but whether he be a poet must depend upon our definition of the word; and, doubtless, if everything that pleases be poetry, Pope's satires and epistles must be poetry. This I must say, that poetry, as distinguished from other modes of composition, does not rest in meter, and that it is not poetry if it make no appeal to our passions or our imagination. One character belongs to all true poets, that they write from a principle within, not originating in anything without; and that the true poet's work in its form, its shapings, and its modifications, is distinguished from all other works that assume to belong to the class of poetry, as a natural from an artificial flower, or as the mimic garden of a child from an enameled meadow. In the former the flowers are broken from their stems and stuck into the ground; they are beautiful to the eye and fragrant to the sense, but their colors soon fade, and their odor is transient as the smile of the planter; while the meadow may be visited again and again with renewed delight; its beauty is innate in the soil, and its bloom is of the freshness of nature.

The next ground of critical judgment, and point of comparison, will be as to how far a given poet has been influenced by accidental circumstances. As a living poet must surely write, not for the ages past, but for that in which he lives, and those which are to follow, it is, on the one hand, natural that he should not violate, and on the other, necessary that he should not depend on, the mere manners and modes of his day. See how little does Shakespeare leave us to regret that he was born in his particular age! The great era in modern times was what is called the Restoration of Letters; the ages preceding it are called the dark ages; but it would be more wise, perhaps, to call them the ages in which we were in the dark. It is usually overlooked that the supposed dark period was not universal, but partial and successive, or alternate; that the dark age of England was not the dark age of Italy, but that one country was in its light and vigor, whilst another was in its gloom and bondage. But no sooner had the Reformation sounded through Europe like the blast of an archangel's trumpet, than from king to peasant there arose an enthusiasm for knowledge; the discovery of a manuscript became the subject of an embassy; Erasmus read by moonlight, because he could not afford a torch, and begged a penny, not for the love of charity,

---

Characteristics of Shakespeare's Dramas. Cf. the criticism on Shakespeare by De Quincey, p. 387. 23. **simple . . . impassioned.** Milton defined poetry as "simple, sensuous, passionate." See other definitions, p. 319, l. 19, and note. 39. **Pope's . . . epistles.** See Vol. I, p. 1094.

52. **enameled**, variegated, adorned, as with flowers. 86. **enthusiasm for knowledge.** See Vol. I, pp. 301 ff. 88. **Erasmus**, Dutch classical scholar (1466-1536). See Vol. I, p. 301.

but for the love of learning. The three great points of attention were religion, morals, and taste; men of genius as well as men of learning, who in this age need to be so widely distinguished, then alike became copyists of the ancients; and this, indeed, was the only way by which the taste of mankind could be improved, or their understandings informed. Whilst Dante imagined himself a humble follower of Virgil, and Ariosto of Homer, they were both unconscious of that greater power working within them, which in many points carried them beyond their supposed originals. All great discoveries bear the stamp of the age in which they are made; hence we perceive the effects of the purer religion of the moderns, visible for the most part in their lives; and in reading their works we should not content ourselves with the mere narratives of events long since passed, but should learn to apply their maxims and conduct to ourselves.

Having intimated that times and manners lend their form and pressure to genius, let me once more draw a slight parallel between the ancient and modern stage, the stages of Greece and of England. The Greeks were polytheists; their religion was local; almost the only object of their knowledge, art, and taste was their gods; and, accordingly, their productions were, if the expression may be allowed, statuesque, whilst those of the moderns are picturesque. The Greeks reared a structure which in its parts, and as a whole, filled the mind with the calm and elevated impression of perfect beauty, and symmetrical proportions. The moderns also produced a whole, a more striking whole; but it was by blending materials and fusing the parts together. And as the Pantheon is to York Minster or Westminster Abbey, so is Sophocles compared with Shakespeare; in the one a completeness, a satisfaction, an excellence, on which the mind rests with complacency; in the other a multitude of interlaced materials, great and little, magnificent and mean, accompanied, indeed, with the sense of a falling short of perfection, and yet, at the same time, so promising of our social and individual progression that we would not, if we could, exchange it for that repose of the mind which swells on the forms of symmetry in the acquiescent admiration of grace. This general characteristic of the ancient and modern drama might be illustrated by a parallel of the ancient and modern music, the one consisting of melody arising from a succession only of pleasing sounds, the modern embracing harmony also, the result of combination and the effect of a whole.

I have said, and I say it again, that great as was the genius of Shakespeare, his judgment was at least equal to it. Of this anyone will be convinced, who attentively considers those points in which the dramas of Greece and England differ, from the dissimilitude of circumstances by which each was modified and influenced. The Greek stage had its origin in the ceremonies of a sacrifice, such as of the goat to Bacchus, whom we most erroneously regard as merely the jolly god of wine; for among the ancients he was venerable, as the symbol of that power which acts without our consciousness in the vital energies of nature—the *vinum mundi*—as Apollo was that of the conscious agency of our intellectual being. The heroes of old under the influences of this Bacchic enthusiasm performed more than human actions; hence tales of the favorite champions soon passed into dialogue. On the Greek stage the chorus was always before the audience; the curtain was never dropped, as we should say; and change of place being therefore, in general, impossible, the absurd notion of condemning it merely as improbable in itself was never entertained by anyone. If we can believe ourselves at Thebes in one act, we may believe ourselves at Athens in the next. If a story lasts twenty-four hours or twenty-four years, it is equally improbable. There seems to be no just boundary but what the feelings prescribe.

---

9. **Dante**, the most famous of Italian poets (1265-1321). 10. **Virgil**, celebrated Roman epic, didactic, and idyllic poet (70-19 B.C.). **Ariosto**, a famous Italian poet (1474-1533). **Homer**, ancient Greek poet, reputed author of the *Iliad* and the *Odyssey*. 23. **pressure**, impression. From *Hamlet*, III, ii, 27. 39. **Pantheon**, a circular temple at Rome, built 27 B.C. 40. **Sophocles**, one of the great tragic dramatists of Greece (fifth century B.C.).

69. **goat ... Bacchus.** The goat was a common victim of sacrifice in the wild orgies of the devotees of Bacchus, god of wine and of luxuriant fertility. 74. *vinum mundi*, wine of the world. **Apollo**, god of poetry and music.

But on the Greek stage where the same persons were perpetually before the audience, great judgment was necessary in venturing on any such change. The poets never, therefore, attempted to impose on the senses by bringing places to men, but they did bring men to places, as in the well known instance in the *Eumenides,* where, during an evident retirement of the chorus from the orchestra, the scene is changed to Athens, and Orestes is first introduced in the temple of Minerva, and the chorus of Furies come in afterwards in pursuit of him.

In the Greek drama there were no formal divisions into scenes and acts; there were no means, therefore, of allowing for the necessary lapse of time between one part of the dialogue and another, and unity of time in a strict sense was, of course, impossible. To overcome that difficulty of accounting for time, which is effected on the modern stage by dropping a curtain, the judgment and great genius of the ancients supplied music and measured motion, and with the lyric ode filled up the vacuity. In the story of the *Agamemnon* of Aeschylus, the capture of Troy is supposed to be announced by a fire lighted on the Asiatic shore and the transmission of the signal by successive beacons to Mycenae. The signal is first seen at the 21st line, and the herald from Troy itself enters at the 486th, and Agamemnon himself at the 783rd line. But the practical absurdity of this was not felt by the audience, who, in imagination stretched the minutes into hours, while they listened to the lofty narrative odes of the chorus which almost entirely filled up the interspace. Another fact deserves attention here, namely, that regularly on the Greek stage a drama, or acted story, consisted in reality of three dramas, called together a trilogy, and performed consecutively in the course of one day. Now you may conceive a tragedy of Shakespeare's as a trilogy connected in one single representation. Divide *Lear* into three parts, and each would be a play with the ancients; or take the three Aeschylean dramas of *Agamemnon,* and divide them into, or call them, as many acts, and they together would be one play. The first act would comprise the usurpation of Aegisthus and the murder of Agamemnon; the second, the revenge of Orestes and the murder of his mother; and the third, the penance and absolution of Orestes;—occupying a period of twenty-two years.

The stage in Shakespeare's time was a naked room with a blanket for a curtain; but he made it a field for monarchs. That law of unity, which has its foundations, not in the factitious necessity of custom, but in nature itself, the unity of feeling, is everywhere and at all times observed by Shakespeare in his plays. Read *Romeo and Juliet:* all is youth and spring; youth with its follies, its virtues, its precipitancies; spring with its odors, its flowers, and its transciency. It is one and the same feeling that commences, goes through, and ends the play. The old men, the Capulets and the Montagues, are not common old men; they have an eagerness, a heartiness, a vehemence, the effect of spring; with Romeo, his change of passion, his sudden marriage, and his rash death, are all the effects of youth; whilst in Juliet, love has all that is tender and melancholy in the nightingale, all that is voluptuous in the rose, with whatever is sweet in the freshness of spring; but it ends with a long deep sigh like the last breeze of the Italian evening. This unity of feeling and character pervades every drama of Shakespeare.

It seems to me that his plays are distinguished from those of all other dramatic poets by the following characteristics:

1. Expectation in preference to surprise. It is like the true reading of the passage: "God said, Let there be light, and there was *light*"; not there *was* light. As the feeling with which we startle at a shooting star compared with that of watching the sunrise at the pre-established moment, such and so low is surprise compared with expectation.

2. Signal adherence to the great law of

---

8. **Eumenides,** a tragedy by Aeschylus, great Greek dramatist (fifth century B.C.); the incident mentioned is in Act V, 230-239. The Eumenides are the Furies. 10. **Orestes,** a son of the Greek king Agamemnon and Clytemnestra; he slew his mother and her lover Aegisthus in revenge for their murder of Agamemnon. 11. **Minerva,** goddess of wisdom. 29. **Mycenae,** an ancient city in Greece.

47. **three . . . dramas,** *Agamemnon, Choephorai,* and *Eumenides.* 87. **God . . . light.** Quoted from *Genesis,* 1:3.

nature, that all opposites tend to attract and temper each other. Passion in Shakespeare generally displays libertinism, but involves morality; and if there are exceptions to this, they are, independently of their intrinsic value, all of them indicative of individual character, and, like the farewell admonitions of a parent, have an end beyond the parental relation. Thus the Countess's beautiful precepts to Bertram, by elevating her character, raise that of Helena her favorite, and soften down the point in her which Shakespeare does not mean us not to see, but to see and to forgive, and at length to justify. And so it is in Polonius, who is the personified memory of wisdom no longer actually possessed. This admirable character is always misrepresented on the stage. Shakespeare never intended to exhibit him as a buffoon; for although it was natural that Hamlet (a young man of fire and genius, detesting formality, and disliking Polonius on political grounds, as imagining that he had assisted his uncle in his usurpation) should express himself satirically; yet this must not be taken as exactly the poet's conception of him. In Polonius a certain induration of character had arisen from long habits of business; but take his advice to Laertes, and Ophelia's reverence for his memory, and we shall see that he was meant to be represented as a statesman somewhat past his faculties—his recollections of life all full of wisdom, and showing a knowledge of human nature, whilst what immediately takes place before him and escapes from him is indicative of weakness.

But as in Homer all the deities are in armor, even Venus, so in Shakespeare all the characters are strong. Hence real folly and dullness are made by him the vehicles of wisdom. There is no difficulty for one being a fool to imitate a fool; but to be, remain, and speak like a wise man and a great wit, and yet so as to give a vivid representation of a veritable fool—*hic labor, hoc opus est*. A drunken constable is not uncommon, nor hard to draw; but see and examine what goes to make up a Dogberry.

3. Keeping at all times in the high road of life. Shakespeare has no innocent adulteries, no interesting incests, no virtuous vice; he never renders that amiable which religion and reason alike teach us to detest, or clothe impurity in the garb of virtue, like Beaumont and Fletcher, the Kotzebues of the day. Shakespeare's fathers are roused by ingratitude, his husbands stung by unfaithfulness; in him, in short, the affections are wounded in those points in which all may, nay, must, feel. Let the morality of Shakespeare be contrasted with that of the writers of his own, or the succeeding, age, or of those of the present day, who boast their superiority in this respect. No one can dispute that the result of such a comparison is altogether in favor of Shakespeare; even the letters of women of high rank in his age were often coarser than his writings. If he occasionally disgusts a keen sense of delicacy, he never injures the mind; he neither excites nor flatters passion in order to degrade the subject of it; he does not use the faulty thing for a faulty purpose, nor carries on warfare against virtue by causing wickedness to appear as no wickedness through the medium of a morbid sympathy with the unfortunate. In Shakespeare vice never walks as in twilight; nothing is purposely out of its place; he inverts not the order of nature and propriety, does not make every magistrate a drunkard or glutton, nor every poor man meek, humane, and temperate; he has no benevolent butchers, nor any sentimental rat-catchers.

4. Independence of the dramatic interest on the plot. The interest in the plot is always in fact on account of the characters, not *vice versa,* as in almost all other writers; the plot is a mere canvass and no more. Hence arises the true justification of the same stratagem being used in regard to Benedict and Beatrice, the vanity in each being alike. Take away from the *Much Ado About Nothing* all that which is not indispensable to the plot, either

---

9. **precepts to Bertram.** In *All's Well That Ends Well,* I, i. 14. **Polonius,** the king's chamberlain and the father of Ophelia and Laertes in *Hamlet.* 28. **advice to Laertes.** In Act I, iii, 58-81. 38. **Venus,** goddess of love. 45. **hic . . . est,** this is the labor, this is the work (*Aeneid,* 6, 129). 48. **Dogberry,** a stupid constable in *Much Ado About Nothing.* 54. **Beaumont and Fletcher,** prominent dramatists contemporary with Shakespeare; they did notable work in tragi-comedy and romance. 55. **Kotzebue,** August Kotzebue (1761-1819), prolific German writer of emotional plays for many years popular in England.

as having little to do with it, or, at best, like Dogberry and his comrades, forced into the service when any other less ingeniously absurd watchmen and night-constables would have answered the mere necessities of the action; take away Benedict, Beatrice, Dogberry, and the reaction of the former on the character of Hero, and what will remain? In other writers the main agent of the plot is always the prominent character; in Shakespeare it is so, or is not so, as the character is in itself calculated, or not calculated, to form the plot. Don John is the main-spring of the plot of this play; but he is merely shown and then withdrawn.

5. Independence of the interest on the story as the groundwork of the plot. Hence Shakespeare never took the trouble of inventing stories. It was enough for him to select from those that had been already invented or recorded such as had one or other, or both, of two recommendations, namely, suitableness to his particular purpose, and their being parts of popular tradition—names of which we had often heard, and of their fortunes, and as to which all we wanted was, to see the man himself. So it is just the man himself, the Lear, the Shylock, the Richard, that Shakespeare makes us for the first time acquainted with. Omit the first scene in *Lear,* and yet everything will remain; so the first and second scenes in *The Merchant of Venice.* Indeed it is universally true.

6. Interfusion of the lyrical (that which in its very essence is poetical) not only with the dramatic, as in the plays of Metastasio, where at the end of the scenes comes the *aria* as the *exit* speech of the character, but also in and through the dramatic. Songs in Shakespeare are introduced as songs only, just as songs are in real life, beautifully as some of them are characteristic of the person who has sung or called for them, as Desdemona's "Willow," and Ophelia's wild snatches, and the sweet carollings in *As You Like It.* But the whole of the *Midsummer-Night's Dream* is one continued specimen of the dramatized

36. **Metastasio,** an Italian lyric dramatist (1698-1782). 37. *aria,* an elaborate melody sung by a single voice in operas, cantatas, etc. 44. **"Willow."** In *Othello,* IV, iii, 41-57, a song of forsaken love.

lyrical. And observe how exquisitely the dramatic of Hotspur:

Marry and I'm glad on't with all my heart;
I'd rather be a kitten and cry mew, &c.

melts away into the lyric of Mortimer:

I understand thy looks: that pretty Welsh
Which thou pour'st down from these swelling
    heavens
I am too perfect in, &c.

1 Henry IV, III, i

7. The characters of the *dramatis personae,* like those in real life, are to be inferred by the reader; they are not told to him. And it is well worth remarking that Shakespeare's characters, like those in real life, are very commonly misunderstood, and almost always understood by different persons in different ways. The causes are the same in either case. If you take only what the friends of the character say, you may be deceived, and still more so, if that which his enemies say; nay, even the character himself sees through the medium of his character, and not exactly as he is. Take all together, not omitting a shrewd hint from the clown, or the fool, and perhaps your impression will be right; and you may know whether you have in fact discovered the poet's own idea, by all the speeches receiving light from it, and attesting its reality by reflecting it.

Lastly, in Shakespeare the heterogeneous is united, as it is in nature. You must not suppose a pressure or passion always acting on or in the character. Passion in Shakespeare is that by which the individual is distinguished from others, not that which makes a different kind of him. Shakespeare followed the main march of the human affections. He entered into no analysis of the passions or faiths of men, but assured himself that such and such passions and faiths were grounded in our common nature, and not in the mere accidents of ignorance or disease. This is an important consideration and constitutes our Shakespeare the morning star, the guide and the pioneer, of true philosophy. (*1818;* 1836)

Charles Lamb
1775-1834

Charles Lamb was born in London, February 10, 1775, the son of a scrivener in the service of one of the leading lawyers of the city. The boy's schooling was at Christ's Hospital, the same institution that trained Coleridge; indeed, Coleridge and Lamb were schoolmates, and Lamb has left us an interesting picture of the great poet in several essays written years afterwards. An impediment in Lamb's speech prevented him from taking examinations for honors, and he was therefore excluded from the opportunity of taking a college degree; he quit his schooling at the age of fourteen and began to earn his living. Three years later he entered the service of the East India House, and became a most valuable accountant for the great commercial organization upon which rested the foundations of the British Empire in the Orient. Professionally his life was spent in this accountantship; he was finally pensioned off in 1825, an experience which he described whimsically in *The Superannuated Man* (see p. 349). After nine peaceful years of leisure he died in 1834.

Lamb was distinctly a Londoner. He loved the city in all its aspects—its crowds and its quaint districts alike, its bookshops and its taverns. "I often shed tears in the motley Strand," he once wrote, "for fulness of joy at so much life." Unlike Byron, the hum of cities was not torture to him; he throve upon the opportunity London offered him to meet the great literary men of his time, for his avocation from the very first was literature. He tried drama, with complete lack of success; he published a rather feeble prose tale called *Rosamund Gray;* he "obtruded upon the public," to use his own words, "sundry other poems and light prose matter, collected in two slight crown octavos and pompously christened his works, though in fact they were his recreations." Unfortunately Lamb's deprecatory tone about these literary efforts is near the truth—none of the works he produced in drama or poetry is of any special value. Two poems, *Hester* and *The Old Familiar Faces*, have a sentimental wistfulness that might be considered charming; their success depends upon the fact that some see in them a faint glimpse of the gracious, lovable personality of their author.

It is chiefly when Lamb reveals to us that personality that he becomes a significant writer. In a brief autobiographic sketch he remarks that he is "below the middle stature; cast of face slightly Jewish, with no Judaic tinge in his complexional religion; stammers abominably, and is therefore more apt to discharge his occasional conversation in a quaint aphorism, or a poor quibble, than in set and edifying speeches; has consequently been libeled as a person always aiming at wit, which as he told a dull fellow that charges him with it, is at least as good as aiming at dullness; a small eater but not drinker, confesses a partiality for the product of the juniper berry; was a fiercer smoker of tobacco, but may be resembled to a volcano burnt out, emitting only now and then a casual puff." The light tone that Lamb here uses in speaking of himself is one part of his personality; the whimsical air with which he carries off his sayings is another. But there is another part, deep-seated and pathetic, even tragic, in Lamb's make-up. He was disappointed in love as a youth, probably because he recognized a trace of insanity in his family. He himself spent six weeks in an asylum (1795-1796); and the next year his only sister Mary killed her mother in a fit of mania. Lamb himself fully recovered, but his sister was subject to recurrent attacks, during which she had to be confined. Lamb took tender care of her; she became, during her sane intervals, his constant companion, and collaborated with him in some books for children, notably the *Tales from Shakespeare* (1807) and the *Adventures of Ulysses* (1808). The current of tragedy running throughout Lamb's life, the sadness and frustration which he met most heroically, go far to explain the coupling of pathos and poignant dreaminess with brave laughter to be found in his characteristic work.

That characteristic work is, first of all, the fine series of personal essays entitled the *Essays of Elia,* which appeared in *The London Magazine* (1820-1823) and later in book form (1823). A second series, running from 1824 to 1825, was collected and printed in 1833, a year before his death. *Elia* is Lamb himself. The pseudonym he chose was the name of an Italian previously in the service of the South Sea House, possibly a friend of his brother John—the subject of the first essay—who was at that time a clerk in that institution. The essays are written in an easy-flowing, informal style, now sprightly and whimsical in *A Dissertation upon Roast Pig* or *A Chapter on Ears,* now gently satirical in *Mrs. Battle's Opinions on Whist,* now quietly domestic in *Mackery End,* now delicately nostalgic in the exquisite reverie *Dream-Children.* Seldom has there been a more subtly touched portrait in literature than that of Mary Lamb (Bridget Elia) in *Mackery End* and in *Old China.* It is customary to underestimate Lamb's style; it is not so sharp as that of Hazlitt nor so impassioned as that of De Quincey, but even a first reading of such an essay as *Poor Relations* (p. 345) demonstrates Lamb's skilful incisiveness. The student of English literature can further thank Lamb for an excellent series of essays on Shakespeare, the other important Elizabethan writers, and the prose authors of the seventeenth century. There is not a trace of affectation in Lamb. His *Letters,* like his essays, bring to life a gentle, witty, lovable soul, tender in his sympathy for mankind; a man who, for all the darkness and disaster of life, could see and enjoy the world through the rose-tinted spectacles of courage and equanimity.

Dream-Children: A Reverie

This essay, a masterly combination of wistful melancholy and tender pathos, was prompted by the death of Lamb's brother John on October 26, 1821. The two men had never been very friendly, but the passing of John made Charles perhaps more aware of his loneliness in life. He had but one relative left, his sister Mary, and she was often away from him for months at a time recovering from fits of insanity. It is scarcely to be wondered at that Lamb should turn, in his hours of solitude, to the thoughts of what his life might have been had there been no such cloud over his family, and if he had been able to marry Alice Winterton, his old sweetheart.

CHILDREN love to listen to stories about their elders, when *they* were children; to stretch their imagination to the conception of a traditionary great-uncle, or grandame, whom they never saw. It was in this spirit that my little ones crept about me the other evening to hear about their great-grandmother Field, who lived in a great house in Norfolk (a hundred times bigger than that in which they and papa lived) which had been the scene—so at least it was generally believed in that part of the country—of the tragic incidents which they had lately become familiar with from the ballad of the Children in the Wood. Certain it is that the whole story of the children and their cruel uncle was to be seen fairly carved out in wood upon the chimney-piece of the great hall, the whole story down to the Robin Redbreasts, till a

8. **Norfolk.** Lamb's grandmother lived at Blakesware, Hertfordshire, not Norfolk. The county may have been changed by Lamb because William Plumer, also a resident of Hertfordshire, who had dismantled Blakesware, was still living when *Dream-Children* was published.

19. **Robin Redbreasts.** At the end of the ballad they cover the bodies of the murdered children with leaves.

foolish rich person pulled it down to set up a marble one of modern invention in its stead, with no story upon it. Here Alice put out one of her dear mother's looks, too tender to be called upbraiding. Then I went on to say how religious and how good their great-grandmother Field was, how beloved and respected by everybody, though she was not indeed the mistress of this great house, but had only the charge of it (and yet in some respects she might be said to be the mistress of it too) committed to her by the owner, who preferred living in a newer and more fashionable mansion which he had purchased somewhere in the adjoining county; but still she lived in it in a manner as if it had been her own, and kept up the dignity of the great house in a sort while she lived, which afterwards came to decay, and was nearly pulled down, and all its old ornaments stripped and carried away to the owner's other house, where they were set up, and looked as awkward as if someone were to carry away the old tombs they had seen lately at the Abbey, and stick them up in Lady C.'s tawdry gilt drawing-room. Here John smiled, as much as to say, "that would be foolish, indeed." And then I told how, when she came to die, her funeral was attended by a concourse of all the poor, and some of the gentry too, of the neighborhood for many miles round, to show their respect for her memory, because she had been such a good and religious woman; so good indeed that she knew all the Psaltery by heart, ay, and a great part of the Testament besides. Here little Alice spread her hands. Then I told what a tall, upright, graceful person their great-grandmother Field once was; and how in her youth she was esteemed the best dancer—here Alice's little right foot played an involuntary movement, till upon my looking grave, it desisted—the best dancer, I was saying, in the county, till a cruel disease, called a cancer, came, and bowed her down with pain; but it could never bend her good spirits, or make them stoop, but they were still upright, because she was so good and religious. Then I told how she was used to sleep by herself in a lone chamber of the great lone house; and how she believed that an apparition of two infants was to be seen at midnight gliding up and down the great staircase near where she slept, but she said "those innocents would do her no harm"; and how frightened I used to be, though in those days I had my maid to sleep with me, because I was never half so good or religious as she—and yet I never saw the infants. Here John expanded all his eyebrows and tried to look courageous. Then I told how good she was to all her grandchildren, having us to the great house in the holidays, where I in particular used to spend many hours by myself, in gazing upon the old busts of the twelve Caesars, that had been emperors of Rome, till the old marble heads would seem to live again, or I to be turned into marble with them; how I never could be tired with roaming about that huge mansion, with its vast empty rooms, with their worn-out hangings, fluttering tapestry, and carved oaken panels, with the gilding almost rubbed out—sometimes in the spacious old-fashioned gardens, which I had almost to myself, unless when now and then a solitary gardening man would cross me—and how the nectarines and peaches hung upon the walls without my ever offering to pluck them, because they were forbidden fruit, unless now and then—and because I had more pleasure in strolling about among the old melancholy-looking yew-trees, or the firs, and picking up the red berries, and the fir apples, which were good for nothing but to look at—or in lying about upon the fresh grass, with all the fine garden smells around me—or basking in the orangery, till I could almost fancy myself ripening too along with the oranges and the limes in that grateful warmth—or in watching the dace that darted to and fro in the fishpond, at the bottom of the garden, with here and there a great sulky pike hanging midway down the water in silent

---

34. **Psaltery**, the version of the *Psalms* in the *Book of Common Prayer*. 36. **spread her hands**. A sign of astonishment. 51. **apparition of two infants**. An old legend of the Plumer family. 64. **busts . . . Caesars**, busts of Roman emperors from Julius Caesar to Domitian. These busts were among the things removed from Blakesware by Mr. Plumer. 76. **nectarine**, a kind of peach. 78. **forbidden fruit**. See *Genesis*, 2:16-17; also the opening lines of *Paradise Lost* (Vol. I, p. 716). 83. **fir apples**, fir cones.

state, as if it mocked at their impertinent friskings—I had more pleasure in these busy-idle diversions than in all the sweet flavors of peaches, nectarines, oranges, and such-like common baits of children. Here John slyly deposited back upon the plate a bunch of grapes which, not unobserved by Alice, he had meditated dividing with her, and both seemed willing to relinquish them for the present as irrelevant. Then in somewhat a more heightened tone, I told how, though their great-grandmother Field loved all her grandchildren, yet in an especial manner she might be said to love their uncle, John L—— because he was so handsome and spirited a youth, and a king to the rest of us; and, instead of moping about in solitary corners, like some of us, he would mount the most mettlesome horse he could get, when but an imp no bigger than themselves, and make it carry him half over the county in a morning, and join the hunters when there were any out—and yet he loved the old great house and gardens too, but had too much spirit to be always pent up within their boundaries—and how their uncle grew up to man's estate as brave as he was handsome, to the admiration of everybody, but of their great-grandmother Field most especially; and how he used to carry me upon his back when I was a lame-footed boy—for he was a good bit older than me—many a mile when I could not walk for pain;—and how in after-life he became lame-footed too, and I did not always (I fear) make allowances enough for him when he was impatient, and in pain, nor remember sufficiently how considerate he had been to me when I was lame-footed; and how when he died, though he had not been dead an hour, it seemed as if he had died a great while ago, such a distance there is betwixt life and death; and how I bore his death as I thought pretty well at first, but afterwards it haunted and haunted me; and though I did not cry or take it to heart as some do, and as I think he would have done if I had died, yet I missed him all day long, and knew not till then how much I had loved him. I missed his kindness, and I missed his crossness, and wished him to be alive again, to be quarreling with him (for we quarreled sometimes), rather than not have him again, and was as uneasy without him, as he, their poor uncle, must have been when the doctor took off his limb. Here the children fell a-crying, and asked if their little mourning which they had on was not for Uncle John, and they looked up, and prayed me not to go on about their uncle, but to tell them some stories about their pretty dead mother. Then I told how for seven long years, in hope sometimes, sometimes in despair, yet persisting ever, I courted the fair Alice W——n; and, as much as children could understand, I explained to them what coyness, and difficulty, and denial meant in maidens—when suddenly, turning to Alice, the soul of the first Alice looked out at her eyes with such a reality of representment, that I became in doubt which of them stood there before me, or whose that bright hair was; and while I stood gazing, both the children gradually grew fainter to my view, receding, and still receding till nothing at last but two mournful features were seen in the uttermost distance, which without speech, strangely impressed upon me the effects of speech: "We are not of Alice, nor of thee, nor are we children at all. The children of Alice call Bartrum father. We are nothing; less than nothing, and dreams. We are only what might have been, and must wait upon the tedious shores of Lethe millions of ages before we have existence and a name"—and immediately awaking, I found myself quietly seated in my bachelor armchair, where I had fallen asleep, with the faithful Bridget unchanged by my side—but John L. (or James Elia) was gone forever.

(1822)

1. **impertinent friskings.** The pike feeds upon dace. 14. **John L——**, Lamb's brother John.

54. **doctor . . . limb.** A detail of Lamb's imagination. 63. **Alice W——n.** Winterton, a feigned name. She was probably Ann Simmons, Lamb's boyhood sweetheart; she married a man named Bartrum. 65. **difficulty,** shyness. 68. **representment,** reincarnation. 70. **whose,** the first or the second Alice's. 82. **Lethe,** the river of forgetfulness in Hades. In the *Aeneid* (VI, 703-751) Virgil tells how the soul, after drinking of Lethe, will return after many years to earth in a new body. 86. **Bridget . . . James Elia,** names given by Lamb to his sister Mary and his brother John in *My Relations*.

The Praise of Chimney-Sweepers

I LIKE to meet a sweep—understand me—not a grown sweeper—old chimney-sweepers are by no means attractive—but one of those tender novices, blooming through their first nigritude, the maternal washings not quite effaced from the cheek—such as come forth with the dawn, or somewhat earlier, with their little professional notes sounding like the *peep-peep* of a young sparrow; or liker to the matin lark should I pronounce them, in their aërial ascents not seldom anticipating the sunrise?

I have a kindly yearning toward these dim specks—poor blots—innocent blacknesses—

I reverence these young Africans of our own growth—these almost clergy imps, who sport their cloth without assumption; and from their little pulpits (the tops of chimneys), in the nipping air of a December morning, preach a lesson of patience to mankind.

When a child, what a mysterious pleasure it was to witness their operation! to see a chit no bigger than one's self enter, one knew not by what process, into what seemed the *fauces Averni*—to pursue him in imagination, as he went sounding on through so many dark stifling caverns, horrid shades!—to shudder with the idea that "now, surely, he must be lost forever!"—to revive at hearing his feeble shout of discovered daylight—and then (O fullness of delight) running out of doors, to come just in time to see the sable phenomenon emerge in safety, the brandished weapon of his art victorious like some flag waved over a conquered citadel! I seem to remember having been told that a bad sweep was once left in a stack with his brush, to indicate which way the wind blew. It was an awful spectacle certainly; not much unlike the old stage direction in Macbeth, where the "Apparition of a child crowned with a tree in his hand rises."

Reader, if thou meetest one of these small gentry in thy early rambles, it is good to give him a penny. It is better to give him twopence. If it be starving weather, and to the proper troubles of his hard occupation, a pair of kibed heels (no unusual accompaniment) be superadded, the demand on thy humanity will surely rise to a tester.

There is a composition, the groundwork of which I have understood to be the sweet wood 'yclept sassafras. This wood boiled down to a kind of tea, and tempered with an infusion of milk and sugar, hath to some tastes a delicacy beyond the China luxury. I know not how thy palate may relish it; for myself, with every deference to the judicious Mr. Read, who hath time out of mind kept open a shop (the only one, he avers, in London) for the vending of this "wholesome and pleasant beverage, on the south side of Fleet Street, as thou approachest Bridge Street—*the only Salopian house*,"—I have never yet ventured to dip my own particular lip in a basin of his commended ingredients—a cautious premonition to the olfactories constantly whispering to me that my stomach must infallibly, with all due courtesy, decline it. Yet I have seen palates, otherwise not uninstructed in dietetical elegances, sup it up with avidity.

I know not by what particular conformation of the organ it happens, but I have always found that this composition is surprisingly gratifying to the palate of a young chimney-sweeper—whether the oily particles (sassafras is slightly oleaginous) do attenuate and soften the fuliginous concretions, which are sometimes found (in dissections) to adhere to the roof of the mouth in these unfledged practitioners; or whether Nature, sensible that she had mingled too much of bitter wood in the lot of these raw victims, caused to grow out of the earth her sassafras for a sweet lenitive—but so it is, that no possible taste or odor to

---

8. **peep-peep.** Compare the short lyric by William Blake beginning:
    A little black thing among the snow
      Crying "weep! weep!" in notes of woe . . .
25. *fauces Averni*, jaws of Hades. 40. **"Apparition,"** etc. In *Macbeth*, IV, i.

48. **kibed**, having chilblains. 50. **tester**, sixpence. 53. **'yclept**, called. 62. **Fleet Street**, a continuation of the Strand and one of the busiest streets in the business section of central London; it has long been associated with newspapers and journalism. 64. **Salopian house**, a place where saloop tea is served; it is made from an herb similar to sassafras. 79. **fuliginous concretions**, deposits of soot. 83. **bitter wood**, wormwood. 85. **lenitive**, soothing balm.

the senses of a young chimney-sweeper can convey a delicate excitement comparable to this mixture. Being penniless, they will yet hang their black heads over the ascending steam, to gratify one sense if possible, seemingly no less pleased than those domestic animals—cats—when they purr over a new-found sprig of valerian. There is something more in these sympathies than philosophy can inculcate.

Now albeit Mr. Read boasteth, not without reason, that his is the *only Salopian house;* yet be it known to thee, reader—if thou art one who keepest what are called good hours, thou art haply ignorant of the fact—he hath a race of industrious imitators, who from stalls and under open sky dispense the same savory mess to humbler customers, at that dead time of the dawn, when (as extremes meet) the rake, reeling home from his midnight cups, and the hard-handed artisan leaving his bed to resume the premature labors of the day, jostle, not unfrequently to the manifest disconcerting of the former, for the honors of the pavement. It is the time when, in summer, between the expired and the not yet relumined kitchen-fires, the kennels of our fair metropolis give forth their least satisfactory odors. The rake, who wisheth to dissipate his o'er-night vapors in more grateful coffee, curses the ungenial fume, as he passeth; but the artisan stops to taste, and blesses the fragrant breakfast.

This is *Saloop*—the precocious herb-woman's darling—the delight of the early gardener, who transports his smoking cabbages by break of day from Hammersmith to Covent Garden's famed piazzas—the delight and, oh, I fear, too often the envy of the unpennied sweep. Him shouldest thou haply encounter, with his dim visage pendent over the grateful steam, regale him with a sumptuous basin (it will cost thee but three halfpennies) and a slice of delicate bread and butter (an added halfpenny)—so may thy culinary fires, eased of the o'er-charged secretions from thy worse-placed hospitalities, curl up a lighter volume to the welkin—so may the descending soot never taint thy costly well-ingredienced soups—nor the odious cry, quick-reaching from street to street, of the *fired chimney,* invite the rattling engines from ten adjacent parishes to disturb for a casual scintillation thy peace and pocket!

I am by nature extremely susceptible of street affronts; the jeers and taunts of the populace; the low-bred triumph they display over the casual trip or splashed stocking of a gentleman. Yet can I endure the jocularity of a young sweep with something more than forgiveness.—In the last winter but one, pacing along Cheapside with my accustomed precipitation when I walk westward, a treacherous slide brought me upon my back in an instant. I scrambled up with pain and shame enough—yet outwardly trying to face it down, as if nothing had happened—when the roguish grin of one of these young wits encountered me. There he stood, pointing me out with his dusky finger to the mob, and to a poor woman (I suppose his mother) in particular, till the tears for the exquisiteness of the fun (so he thought it) worked themselves out at the corners of his poor red eyes, red from many a previous weeping, and soot-inflamed, yet twinkling through all with such a joy, snatched out of desolation, that Hogarth—but Hogarth has got him already (how could he miss him?) in the March to Finchley, grinning at the pie-man—there he stood, as he stands in the picture, irremovable, as if the jest was to last forever—with such a maximum of glee and minimum of mischief, in his mirth—for the grin of a genuine sweep hath absolutely no malice in it—that I could have been content, if the honor of a gentleman might endure it, to have remained his butt and his mockery till midnight.

I am by theory obdurate to the seductiveness of what are called a fine set of teeth. Every pair of rosy lips (the ladies must pardon me) is a casket, presumably holding such

---

8. **valerian**, catnip. 37. **Hammersmith**, a section in western London. 38. **Covent Garden**, still one of the most famous of London market-places.

48. **welkin**, sky. 54. **scintillation**, shower of sparks. 62. **Cheapside**, a street in London, formerly noted for its shops. 77. **Hogarth**, William Hogarth (1697-1764), noted engraver and painter of London life. 79. **March to Finchley**, the subject of one of Hogarth's engravings. Finchley is a London suburban district in Middlesex.

jewels; but, methinks, they should take leave to "air" them as frugally as possible. The fine lady, or fine gentleman, who show me their teeth, show me bones. Yet must I confess, that from the mouth of a true sweep a display (even to ostentation) of those white and shining ossifications, strikes me as an agreeable anomaly in manners and an allowable piece of foppery. It is, as when

A sable cloud
Turns forth her silver lining on the night.

It is like some remnant of gentry not quite extinct; a badge of better days; a hint of nobility—and, doubtless, under the obscuring darkness and double night of their forlorn disguisement, oftentimes lurketh good blood and gentle conditions, derived from lost ancestry, and a lapsed pedigree. The premature apprenticements of these tender victims give but too much encouragement, I fear, to clandestine and almost infantile abductions; the seeds of civility and true courtesy, so often discernible in these young grafts (not otherwise to be accounted for), plainly hint at some forced adoptions; many noble Rachels mourning for their children, even in our days, countenance the fact; the tales of fairy-spiriting may shadow a lamentable verity, and the recovery of the young Montagu be but a solitary instance of good fortune, out of many irreparable and hopeless *defiliations*.

In one of the state-beds at Arundel Castle, a few years since—under a ducal canopy—(that seat of the Howards is an object of curiosity to visitors, chiefly for its beds, in which the late duke was especially a connoisseur)—encircled with curtains of delicatest crimson, with starry coronets inwoven—folded between a pair of sheets whiter and softer than the lap where Venus lulled Ascanius—was discovered by chance, after all methods of search had failed, at noon-day, fast asleep, a lost chimney-sweeper. The little creature, having somehow confounded his passage among the intricacies of those lordly chimneys, by some unknown aperture had alighted upon this magnificent chamber; and, tired with his tedious explorations, was unable to resist the delicious invitement to repose which he there saw exhibited; so, creeping between the sheets very quietly, laid his black head upon the pillow, and slept like a young Howard.

Such is the account given to the visitors at the Castle.—But I cannot help seeming to perceive a confirmation of what I have just hinted at in this story. A high instinct was at work in the case, or I am mistaken. Is it probable that a poor child of that description, with whatever weariness he might be visited, would have ventured under such a penalty as he would be taught to expect, to uncover the sheets of a Duke's bed, and deliberately to lay himself down between them, when the rug or the carpet presented an obvious couch, still far above his pretensions—is this probable, I would ask, if the great power of nature, which I contend for, had not been manifested within him, prompting to the adventure? Doubtless this young nobleman (for such my mind misgives me that he must be) was allured by some memory, not amounting to full consciousness, of his condition in infancy, when he was used to be lapped by his mother, or his nurse, in just such sheets as he there found, into which he was but now creeping back as into his proper *incunabula,* and resting-place.—By no other theory than by this sentiment of a pre-existent state (as I may call it), can I explain a deed so venturous, and, indeed, upon any other system, so indecorous, in this tender, but unseasonable, sleeper.

My pleasant friend JEM WHITE was so impressed with a belief of metamorphoses like this frequently taking place, that in some sort to reverse the wrongs of fortune in these poor

---

10. **A . . . night.** From Milton's *Comus,* 221-222. 25. **Rachel.** Cf. *Jeremiah,* 31:15—"A voice was heard in Ramah, lamentation, and bitter weeping; Rachel weeping for her children refused to be comforted for her children, because they were not." 29. **Montagu,** Edward Wortley Montagu (1713-1776), son of the famous Lady Mary Montagu, ran away from school and served for a time as a chimney-sweep. 31. **defiliations,** losses of sons. 32. **Arundel Castle,** the Sussex seat of the Dukes of Norfolk. 34. **Howard,** the family name of the Dukes of Norfolk. 40. **Venus,** goddess of love. **Ascanius,** son of Aeneas; he accompanied his father in his wanderings after the fall of Troy and became the mythical head of the family of the Caesars.

77. *incunabula,* cradle; now used specifically with reference to books printed before 1500. 84. **Jem White,** a school-fellow of Lamb's at Christ's Hospital, a famous charity school for boys, in London.

changelings, he instituted an annual feast of chimney-sweepers, at which it was his pleasure to officiate as host and waiter. It was a solemn supper held in Smithfield, upon the yearly return of the fair of St. Bartholomew. Cards were issued a week before to the master-sweeps in and about the metropolis, confining the invitation to their younger fry. Now and then an elderly stripling would get in among us and be good-naturedly winked at; but our main body were infantry. One unfortunate wight, indeed, who, relying upon his dusky suit, had intruded himself into our party, but by tokens was providentially discovered in time to be no chimney-sweeper (all is not soot which looks so), was quoited out of the presence with universal indignation, as not having on the wedding garment; but in general the greatest harmony prevailed. The place chosen was a convenient spot among the pens, at the north side of the fair, not so far distant as to be impervious to the agreeable hubbub of that vanity; but remote enough not to be obvious to the interruption of every gaping spectator in it. The guests assembled about seven. In those little temporary parlors three tables were spread with napery, not so fine as substantial, and at every board a comely hostess presided with her pan of hissing sausages. The nostrils of the young rogues dilated at the savor. JAMES WHITE, as head waiter, had charge of the first table; and myself with our trusty companion BIGOD ordinarily ministered to the other two. There was clambering and jostling, you may be sure, who should get at the first table—for Rochester in his maddest days could not have done the humors of the scene with more spirit than my friend. After some general expression of thanks for the honor the company had done him, his inaugural ceremony was to clasp the greasy waist of old dame Ursula (the fattest of the three), that stood frying and fretting, half-blessing, half-cursing "the gentleman," and imprint upon her chaste lips a tender salute, whereat the universal host would set up a shout that tore the concave, while hundreds of grinning teeth startled the night with their brightness. O it was a pleasure to see the sable younkers lick in the unctuous meat, with *his* more unctuous sayings—how he would fit the tit-bits to the puny mouths, reserving the lengthier links for the seniors —how he would intercept a morsel even in the jaws of some young desperado, declaring it "must to the pan again to be browned, for it was not fit for a gentleman's eating" —how he would recommend this slice of white bread, or that piece of kissing-crust, to a tender juvenile, advising them all to have a care of cracking their teeth, which were their best patrimony—how genteelly he would deal about the small ale, as if it were wine, naming the brewer, and protesting, if it were not good he should lose their custom; with a special recommendation to wipe the lip before drinking. Then we had our toasts— "The King"—the "Cloth"—which, whether they understood or not, was equally diverting and flattering;—and for a crowning sentiment, which never failed, "May the Brush Supersede the Laurel." All these, and fifty other fancies, which were rather felt than comprehended by his guests, would he utter, standing upon tables, and prefacing every sentiment with a "Gentlemen, give me leave to propose so and so," which was a prodigious comfort to those young orphans; every now and then stuffing into his mouth (for it did not do to be squeamish on these occasions) indiscriminate pieces of those reeking sausages, which pleased them mightily, and was the savoriest part, you may believe, of the entertainment.

---

4. **Smithfield**, a region in London; originally a scene of tournaments, but later a trading mart and a place of executions. 5. **St. Bartholomew**, a September fair held annually at Smithfield from 1133 to 1855. 16. **quoited**, thrown. 18. **wedding garment**, the garb of a sweep. See *Matthew*, 22:11-13—"And when the king came in to see the guests, he saw there a man which had not on a wedding garment . . . Then said the king to the servants, Bind him hand and foot, and take him away, and cast him into outer darkness." 23. **vanity**. See Bunyan's *Pilgrim's Progress* (Vol. I, p. 800). 33. **Bigod**, John Fenwick, an early nineteenth-century editor; a friend of Lamb's. Lamb borrowed the name *Bigod* from the old family name of the Earls of Norfolk. 36. **Rochester**, the Earl of Rochester (1647-1680), a notorious rake.

42. **Ursula**, a name taken from a character in Ben Jonson's *Bartholomew Fair*. 49. **brightness**. See *Paradise Lost*, I, 541-542 (Vol. I, p. 724):
At which the universal host up-sent
A shout that tore Hell's concave, and beyond . . .
50. **younkers**, youngsters. 59. **kissing-crust**, the soft part of the crust, where loaves touched one another in baking. 68. **the "Cloth,"** the profession of chimney-sweepers. 71. **Brush . . . Laurel**. The brush is used as the emblem of chimney-sweepers as the laurel is of the poet.

Golden lads and lasses must,
As chimney-sweepers, come to dust—

JAMES WHITE is extinct, and with him these suppers have long ceased. He carried away with him half the fun of the world when he died—of my world at least. His old clients look for him among the pens; and, missing him, reproach the altered feast of St. Bartholomew and the glory of Smithfield departed forever.

(1822)

1. **Golden . . . dust.** From a song in *Cymbeline*, IV, ii, 262-263:
> Golden lads and girls all must,
> As chimney-sweepers, come to dust.

See the song beginning "Fear no more the heat of the sun" (Vol. I, p. 498).

Poor Relations

A POOR RELATION—is the most irrelevant thing in nature,—a piece of impertinent correspondency,—an odious approximation,—a haunting conscience,—a preposterous shadow, lengthening in the noontide of your prosperity,—an unwelcome remembrancer,—a perpetually recurring mortification,—a drain on your purse,—a more intolerable dun upon your pride,—a drawback upon success,—a rebuke to your rising,—a stain in your blood,—a blot on your scutcheon,—a rent in your garment,—a death's head at your banquet,—Agathocles' pot,—a Mordecai in your gate,—a Lazarus at your door,—a lion in your path,—a frog in your chamber,—a fly in your ointment,—a mote in your eye,—a triumph to your enemy, an apology to your friends,—the one thing not needful,—the hail in harvest,—the ounce of sour in a pound of sweet.

He is known by his knock. Your heart telleth you, "That is Mr. ——." A rap, between familiarity and respect, that demands, and at the same time seems to despair of, entertainment. He entereth smiling and—embarrassed. He holdeth out his hand to you to shake, and—draweth it back again. He casually looketh in about dinner-time—when the table is full. He offereth to go away, seeing you have company—but is induced to stay. He filleth a chair, and your visitor's two children are accommodated at a side table. He never cometh upon open days, when your wife says with some complacency, "My dear, perhaps Mr. —— will drop in today." He remembereth birthdays—and professeth he is fortunate to have stumbled upon one. He declareth against fish, the turbot being small—yet suffereth himself to be importuned into a slice, against his first resolution. He sticketh by the port—yet will be prevailed upon to empty the remainder glass of claret, if a stranger press it upon him. He is a puzzle to the servants, who are fearful of being too obsequious, or not civil enough, to him. The guests think "they have seen him before." Everyone speculateth upon his condition; and the most part take him to be—a tide-waiter. He calleth you by your Christian name, to imply that his other is the same with your own. He is too familiar by half, yet you wish he had less diffidence. With half the familiarity, he might pass for a casual dependent; with more boldness, he would be in no danger of being taken for what he is. He is too humble for a friend; yet taketh on him more state than befits a client. He is a worse guest than a country tenant, inasmuch as he bringeth up no rent—yet 'tis odds, from his garb and demeanor, that your guests take him for one. He is asked to make one at the whist-table; refuseth on the score of poverty, and—resents being left out. When the company

Poor Relations. Cf. the Character Writers, Vol. I, pp. 681 ff. 12. **death's head.** An allusion to the custom of the Egyptians of having a coffin containing a representation of a dead body carried through the banquet hall at the close of a feast to remind the guests of their necessary end, and to suggest that they should drink and be merry. 13. **Agathocles' pot.** Agathocles, tyrant of Sicily (361-289 B.C.), hated the sight of a pot because it reminded him that he was the son of a potter. **Mordecai . . . gate.** A reference to the vigils of Mordecai at the gates of King Ahasuerus to learn what happened to Esther. See *Esther,* 3:1-2; 5:11-13. 14. **Lazarus . . . door.** Lazarus was the beggar who placed himself at the gate of a rich man to get the crumbs from his table. See *Luke,* 16:20. **lion . . . path,** *1 Kings,* 13:24. 15. **frog . . . chamber,** *Exodus,* 8:3-4. **fly . . . ointment,** *Ecclesiastes,* 10:1. 16. **mote . . . eye,** *Matthew,* 7:3-5. 18. **one . . . needful,** *Luke,* 10:42. **hail in harvest,** *Proverbs,* 26:1. 19. **ounce . . . sweet,** Spenser's *Faerie Queene,* I, 3, 30. This phrase was the motto of Hunt's *Indicator,* one of his journalistic ventures.

46. **condition,** social rank. 47. **tide-waiter,** literally, a minor customs official who waits for the arrival of ships and enforces the revenue laws; here, one, like Micawber in *David Copperfield,* who waits for something lucky to turn up. 56. **client,** dependent.

break up, he proffereth to go for a coach—and lets the servant go. He recollects your grandfather; and will thrust in some mean and quite unimportant anecdote of—the family. He knew it when it was not quite so flourishing as "he is blest in seeing it now." He reviveth past situations, to institute what he calleth—favorable comparisons. With a reflecting sort of congratulation, he will inquire the price of your furniture; and insults you with a special commendation of your window-curtains. He is of opinion that the urn is the more elegant shape, but, after all, there was something more comfortable about the old tea-kettle—which you must remember. He dare say you must find a great convenience in having a carriage of your own, and appealeth to your lady if it is not so. Inquireth if you have had your arms done on vellum yet; and did not know, till lately, that such-and-such had been the crest of the family. His memory is unseasonable; his compliments perverse; his talk a trouble; his stay pertinacious; and when he goeth away, you dismiss his chair into a corner, as precipitately as possible, and feel fairly rid of two nuisances.

There is a worse evil under the sun, and that is—a female Poor Relation. You may do something with the other; you may pass him off tolerably well; but your indigent she-relative is hopeless. "He is an old humorist," you may say, "and affects to go threadbare. His circumstances are better than folks would take them to be. You are fond of having a Character at your table, and truly he is one." But in the indications of female poverty there can be no disguise. No woman dresses below herself from caprice. The truth must out without shuffling. "She is plainly related to the L——s; or what does she at their house?" She is, in all probability, your wife's cousin. Nine times out of ten, at least, this is the case. Her garb is something between a gentlewoman and a beggar, yet the former evidently predominates. She is most provokingly humble, and ostentatiously sensible to her inferiority. He may require to be repressed sometimes—*aliquando sufflaminandus erat;*—but there is no raising her. You send her soup at dinner, and she begs to be helped—after the gentlemen. Mr. —— requests the honor of taking wine with her; she hesitates between port and Madeira, and chooses the former—because he does. She calls the servant "Sir"; and insists on not troubling him to hold her plate. The housekeeper patronizes her. The children's governess takes upon her to correct her when she has mistaken the piano for a harpsichord.

Richard Amlet, Esq., in the play, is a notable instance of the disadvantages to which this chimerical notion of *affinity constituting a claim to acquaintance* may subject the spirit of a gentleman. A little foolish blood is all that is betwixt him and a lady of great estate. His stars are perpetually crossed by the malignant maternity of an old woman, who persists in calling him "her son Dick." But she has wherewithal in the end to recompense his indignities, and float him again upon the brilliant surface, under which it had been her seeming business and pleasure all along to sink him. All men, besides, are not of Dick's temperament. I knew an Amlet in real life, who, wanting Dick's buoyancy, sank indeed. Poor W—— was of my own standing at Christ's, a fine classic, and a youth of promise. If he had a blemish, it was too much pride; but its quality was inoffensive; it was not of that sort which hardens the heart, and serves to keep inferiors at a distance; it only sought to ward off derogation from itself. It was the principle of self-respect carried as far as it could go without infringing upon that respect which he would have everyone else equally maintain for himself. He would have you to think alike with him on this topic. Many a quarrel have I had with him, when we were rather older boys and our tallness made us more obnoxious to observation in the blue clothes, because I would not thread the alleys

---

32. **humorist,** an eccentric person. 33. **affects,** chooses.

49. ***aliquando . . . erat,*** sometimes he had to be checked. 54. **Madeira,** a kind of wine from the Portuguese island of Madeira northwest of Africa. 61. **the play,** *The Confederacy,* by Sir John Vanbrugh (1666-1726). See Vol. I, p. 826. 77. **Poor W—.** Lamb says elsewhere that W— was his friend Favell, who "left Cambridge because he was ashamed of his father, who was a house-painter there." See p. 347, ll. 27 ff. 78. **Christ's,** Christ's Hospital. See p. 337. 90. **our tallness.** Lamb was really short of stature. 91. **blue clothes.** Boys at Christ's Hospital wore long blue coats and yellow stockings.

and blind ways of the town with him to elude notice, when we have been out together on a holiday in the streets of this sneering and prying metropolis. W—— went, sore with these notions, to Oxford, where the dignity and sweetness of a scholar's life, meeting with the alloy of a humble introduction, wrought in him a passionate devotion to the place, with a profound aversion from the society. The servitor's gown (worse than his school array) clung to him with Nessian venom. He thought himself ridiculous in a garb under which Latimer must have walked erect, and in which Hooker, in his young days, possibly flaunted in a vein of no discommendable vanity. In the depth of college shades or in his lonely chamber, the poor student shrunk from observation. He found shelter among books, which insult not; and studies, that ask no questions of a youth's finances. He was lord of his library, and seldom cared for looking out beyond his domains. The healing influence of studious pursuits was upon him, to soothe and to abstract. He was almost a healthy man; when the waywardness of his fate broke out against him with a second and worse malignity. The father of W—— had hitherto exercised the humble profession of house-painter at N——, near Oxford. A supposed interest with some of the heads of the colleges had now induced him to take up his abode in that city, with the hope of being employed upon some public works which were talked of. From that moment I read in the countenance of the young man the determination which at length tore him from academical pursuits forever. To a person unacquainted with our universities, the distance between the gownsmen and the townsmen, as they are called—the trading part of the latter especially—is carried to an excess that would appear harsh and incredible. The temperament of W——'s father was diametrically the reverse of his own. Old W—— was a little, busy, cringing tradesman, who, with his son upon his arm, would stand bowing and scraping, cap in hand, to anything that wore the semblance of a gown—insensible to the winks and opener remonstrances of the young man, to whose chamber-fellow or equal in standing, perhaps, he was thus obsequiously and gratuitously ducking. Such a state of things could not last. W—— must change the air of Oxford or be suffocated. He chose the former; and let the sturdy moralist, who strains the point of the filial duties as high as they can bear, censure the dereliction; he cannot estimate the struggle. I stood with W——, the last afternoon I ever saw him, under the eaves of his paternal dwelling. It was in the fine lane leading from the High-street to the back of —— College, where W—— kept his rooms. He seemed thoughtful and more reconciled. I ventured to rally him—finding him in a better mood —upon a representation of the artist Evangelist, which the old man, whose affairs were beginning to flourish, had caused to be set up in a splendid sort of frame over his really handsome shop, either as a token of prosperity or badge of gratitude to his saint. W—— looked up at the Luke, and, like Satan, "knew his mounted sign—and fled." A letter on his father's table the next morning announced that he had accepted a commission in a regiment about to embark for Portugal. He was among the first who perished before the walls of St. Sebastian.

I do not know how, upon a subject which I began with treating half seriously, I should have fallen upon a recital so eminently painful; but this theme of poor relationship is replete with so much matter for tragic as well as comic associations that it is difficult to keep the account distinct without blending. The earliest impressions which I received on this matter are certainly not attended with anything painful or very humiliating in the recalling. At my father's table (no very splendid one) was to be found, every Saturday, the

---

10. **servitor's gown**, the distinguishing dress of an undergraduate who was partly supported by college funds, and who waited on table at the Commons. 11. **Nessian venom.** Hercules slew the centaur Nessus with a poisoned arrow and lost his own life by wearing a shirt dipped in the envenomed blood of Nessus. 12. **Latimer**, Hugh Latimer (1488-1555), famous preacher and reformer, who had been a sizar (servitor) at Christ's College, Cambridge. 14. **Hooker**, Richard Hooker (1553-1600), noted English divine, who had been a servitor at Oxford. 29. **N——**, a substitution for Cambridge. See p. 346, note to l. 77.

65. **artist Evangelist**, St. Luke, who by tradition was a painter as well as a physician. 71. "**knew . . . fled,**" *Paradise Lost,* IV, 1013. 77. **St. Sebastian**, a seaport on the north coast of Spain; it was taken by Wellington in 1813.

mysterious figure of an aged gentleman, clothed in neat black, of a sad yet comely appearance. His deportment was of the essence of gravity; his words few or none; and I was not to make a noise in his presence. I had little inclination to have done so—for my cue was to admire in silence. A particular elbow-chair was appropriated to him, which was in no case to be violated. A peculiar sort of sweet pudding, which appeared on no other occasion, distinguished the days of his coming. I used to think him a prodigiously rich man. All I could make out of him was that he and my father had been schoolfellows a world ago at Lincoln, and that he came from the Mint. The Mint I knew to be a place where all the money was coined—and I thought he was the owner of all that money. Awful ideas of the Tower twined themselves about his presence. He seemed above human infirmities and passions. A sort of melancholy grandeur invested him. From some inexplicable doom I fancied him obliged to go about in an eternal suit of mourning; a captive, a stately being, let out of the Tower on Saturdays. Often have I wondered at the temerity of my father, who, in spite of an habitual general respect which we all in common manifested towards him, would venture now and then to stand up against him in some argument touching their youthful days. The houses of the ancient city of Lincoln are divided (as most of my readers know) between the dwellers on the hill and in the valley. This marked distinction formed an obvious division between the boys who lived above (however brought together in a common school) and the boys whose paternal residence was on the plain; a sufficient cause of hostility in the code of these young Grotiuses. My father had been a leading Mountaineer; and would still maintain the general superiority, in skill and hardihood, of the *Above Boys* (his own faction) over the *Below Boys* (so were they called), of which party his contemporary had been a chieftain. Many and hot were the skirmishes on this topic—the only one upon which the old gentleman was ever brought out—and bad blood bred; even sometimes almost to the recommencement (so I expected) of actual hostilities. But my father, who scorned to insist upon advantages, generally contrived to turn the conversation upon some adroit by-commendation of the old Minster; in the general preference of which before all other cathedrals in the island, the dweller on the hill and the plain-born could meet on a conciliating level, and lay down their less important differences. Once only I saw the old gentleman really ruffled, and I remembered with anguish the thought that came over me: "Perhaps he will never come here again." He had been pressed to take another plate of the viand which I have already mentioned as the indispensable concomitant of his visits. He had refused with a resistance amounting to rigor, when my aunt—an old Lincolnian, but who had something of this in common with my cousin Bridget, that she would sometimes press civility out of season—uttered the following memorable application: "Do take another slice, Mr. Billet, for you do not get pudding every day." The old gentleman said nothing at the time; but he took occasion in the course of the evening, when some argument had intervened between them, to utter with an emphasis which chilled the company, and which chills me now as I write it—"Woman, you are superannuated!" John Billet did not survive long after the digesting of this affront, but he survived long enough to assure me that peace was actually restored; and if I remember aright, another pudding was discreetly substituted in the place of that which had occasioned the offense. He died at the Mint (*anno* 1781), where he had long held what he accounted a comfortable independence; and with five pounds, fourteen shillings, and a penny, which were found in his *escritoire* after his decease, left the world, blessing God that he had enough to bury him and that he had never been obliged to any man for a sixpence. This was—a Poor Relation.

(1823)

16. **the Mint,** located near the *Tower* (l. 19) of London, the historic state prison. 40. **young Grotiuses,** law students. Hugo Grotius (1583-1645) was the great Dutch authority on international law.

70. **Bridget.** See p. 340, note to l. 86.

The Superannuated Man

Lamb was retired with a pension from the East India Company during the last week of March, 1825. On April 6 he wrote his friend Wordsworth as follows: "Here I am then, after thirty-three years' slavery, sitting in my own room at eleven o'clock this finest of all April mornings, a freed man, with £441 a year for the remainder of my life. . . . I came home FOREVER on Tuesday in last week. The incomprehensibleness of my condition overwhelmed me. It was like passing from life into eternity. Every year to be as long as three, i. e., to have three times as much real time—time that is my own, in it! I wandered about thinking I was happy, but feeling I was not. But that tumultuousness is passing off, and I begin to understand the nature of the gift. Holidays, even the annual month, were always uneasy joys; their conscious fugitiveness; the craving after making the most of them. Now, when all is holiday, there are no holidays. I can sit at home, in rain or shine, without a restless impulse for walkings. I am daily steadying, and shall soon find it as natural to me to be my own master, as it has been irksome to have had a master. . . . I eat, drink, and sleep sound as ever. I lay no anxious schemes for going hither and thither, but take things as they occur. Yesterday I excursioned twenty miles; today I write a few letters. Pleasuring was for fugitive playdays; mine are fugitive only in the sense that life is fugitive. Freedom and life coexistent!"

The Superannuated Man is one of the most autobiographically accurate of all Lamb's essays.

If PERADVENTURE, Reader, it has been thy lot to waste the golden years of thy life—thy shining youth—in the irksome confinement of an office; to have thy prison days prolonged through middle age down to decrepitude and silver hairs, without hope of release or respite; to have lived to forget that there are such things as holidays, or to remember them but as the prerogatives of childhood; then, and then only, will you be able to appreciate my deliverance.

It is now six and thirty years since I took my seat at the desk in Mincing Lane. Melancholy was the transition at fourteen from the abundant playtime, and the frequently intervening vacations of school days, to the eight, nine, and sometimes ten hours' a-day attendance at a counting-house. But time partially reconciles us to anything. I gradually became content—doggedly content, as wild animals in cages.

It is true I had my Sundays to myself, but Sundays, admirable as the institution of them is for purposes of worship, are for that very reason the very worst adapted for days of unbending and recreation. In particular, there is a gloom for me attendant upon a city Sunday, a weight in the air. I miss the cheerful cries of London, the music, and the ballad-singers—the buzz and stirring murmur of the streets. Those eternal bells depress me. The closed shops repel me. Prints, pictures, all the glittering and endless succession of knacks and gewgaws, and ostentatiously displayed wares of tradesmen, which make a weekday saunter through the less busy parts of the metropolis so delightful—are shut out. No book-stalls deliciously to idle over. No busy faces to recreate the idle man who contemplates them ever passing by—the very face of business a charm by contrast to his temporary relaxation from it. Nothing to be seen but unhappy countenances—or half-happy at best—of emancipated 'prentices and little tradesfolks, with here and there a servant maid that has got leave to go out, who, slaving all the week, with the habit has lost almost the capacity of enjoying a free hour; and livelily expressing the hollowness of a day's pleasuring. The very strollers in the fields on that day looked anything but comfortable.

But besides Sundays I had a day at Easter, and a day at Christmas, with a full week in the summer to go and air myself in my native fields of Hertfordshire. This last was a great

---

13. **Mincing Lane,** a street in the eastern section of London, the center of colonial trade; it was the location of the East India House, where Lamb worked for thirty-three years. He had previously worked three years in the South Sea Office.

55. **Hertfordshire.** Lamb was born in London; but he spent some of his boyhood days with his grandmother in Hertfordshire. See *Dream-Children* and note to l. 8, p. 338.

indulgence; and the prospect of its recurrence, I believe, alone kept me up through the year, and made my durance tolerable. But when the week came round, did the glittering phantom of the distance keep touch with me? or rather was it not a series of seven uneasy days, spent in restless pursuit of pleasure, and a wearisome anxiety to find out how to make the most of them? Where was the quiet, where the promised rest? Before I had a taste of it, it was vanished. I was at the desk again, counting upon the fifty-one tedious weeks that must intervene before such another snatch would come. Still the prospect of its coming threw something of an illumination upon the darker side of my captivity. Without it, as I have said, I could scarcely have sustained my thraldom.

Independently of the rigors of attendance, I have ever been haunted with a sense (perhaps a mere caprice) of incapacity for business. This, during my latter years, had increased to such a degree that it was visible in all the lines of my countenance. My health and my good spirits flagged. I had perpetually a dread of some crisis, to which I should be found unequal. Besides my daylight servitude, I served over again all night in my sleep, and would awake with terrors of imaginary false entries, errors in my accounts, and the like. I was fifty years of age, and no prospect of emancipation presented itself. I had grown to my desk, as it were; and the wood had entered into my soul.

My fellows in the office would sometimes rally me upon the trouble legible in my countenance; but I did not know that it had raised the suspicions of any of my employers, when on the 5th of last month, a day ever to be remembered by me, L——, the junior partner in the firm, calling me on one side, directly taxed me with my bad looks, and frankly inquired the cause of them. So taxed, I honestly made confession of my infirmity, and added that I was afraid I should eventually be obliged to resign his service. He spoke some words of course to hearten me, and there the matter rested. A whole week I remained laboring under the impression that I had acted imprudently in my disclosure; that I had foolishly given a handle against myself, and had been anticipating my own dismissal. A week passed in this manner, the most anxious one, I verily believe in my whole life, when on the evening of the 12th of April, just as I was about quitting my desk to go home (it might be about eight o'clock) I received an awful summons to attend the presence of the whole assembled firm in the formidable back parlor. I thought, now my time is surely come, I have done for myself, I am going to be told that they have no longer occasion for me. L——, I could see, smiled at the terror I was in, which was a little relief to me, when to my utter astonishment B——, the eldest partner, began a formal harangue to me on the length of my services, my very meritorious conduct during the whole of the time (the deuce, thought I, how did he find out that? I protest I never had the confidence to think as much). He went on to descant on the expediency of retiring at a certain time of life (how my heart panted!) and asking me a few questions as to the amount of my own property, of which I have a little, ended with a proposal, to which his three partners nodded a grave assent, that I should accept from the house, which I had served so well, a pension for life to the amount of two-thirds of my accustomed salary—a magnificent offer! I do not know what I answered between surprise and gratitude, but it was understood that I accepted their proposal, and I was told that I was free from that hour to leave their service. I stammered out a bow, and at just ten minutes after eight I went home—forever. This noble benefit—gratitude forbids me to conceal their names—I owe to the kindness of the most munificent firm in the world—the house of Boldero, Merryweather, Bosanquet, and Lacy.

Esto perpetua!

For the first day or two I felt stunned, over-

---

36. **rally**, banter, ridicule. 40. **L——**, Lacy, a fictitious name (see note to l. 89). 65. **B——**, Boldero, another fictitious name (see note to l. 89). 71. **descant**, speak at length. 89. **Boldero . . . Lacy**, fictitious names for the directors of the East India Company. 91. *Esto perpetua!* Be eternal.

whelmed. I could only apprehend my felicity; I was too confused to taste it sincerely. I wandered about, thinking I was happy, and knowing that I was not. I was in the condition of a prisoner in the Old Bastile, suddenly let loose after a forty years' confinement. I could scarce trust myself with myself. It was like passing out of Time into Eternity—for it is a sort of Eternity for a man to have his Time all to himself. It seemed to me that I had more time on my hands than I could ever manage. From a poor man, poor in Time, I was suddenly lifted up into a vast revenue; I could see no end of my possessions; I wanted some steward, or judicious bailiff, to manage my estates in Time for me. And here let me caution persons grown old in active business, not lightly, nor without weighing their own resources, to forego their customary employment all at once, for there may be danger in it. I feel it by myself, but I know that my resources are sufficient; and now that those first giddy raptures have subsided, I have a quiet home-feeling of the blessedness of my condition. I am in no hurry. Having all holidays, I am as though I had none. If Time hung heavy upon me, I could walk it away; but I do *not* walk all day long, as I used to do in those old transient holidays, thirty miles a day, to make the most of them. If Time were troublesome, I could read it away, but I do *not* read in that violent measure, with which having no Time my own but candlelight Time, I used to weary out my head and eyesight in by-gone winters. I walk, read, or scribble (as now) just when the fit seizes me. I no longer hunt after pleasure; I let it come to me. I am like the man

—That's born, and has his years come to him,
In some green desert.

"Years," you will say; "what is this superannuated simpleton calculating upon? He has already told us he is past fifty."

I have indeed lived nominally fifty years, but deduct out of them the hours which I have lived to other people, and not to myself, and you will find me still a young fellow. For *that* is the only true Time, which a man can properly call his own, that which he has all to himself; the rest, though in some sense he may be said to live it, is other people's time, not his. The remnant of my poor days, long or short, is at least multiplied for me threefold. My ten next years, if I stretch so far, will be as long as any preceding thirty. 'Tis a fair rule-of-three sum.

Among the strange fantasies which beset me at the commencement of my freedom, and of which all traces are not yet gone, one was, that a vast tract of time had intervened since I quitted the Counting House. I could not conceive of it as an affair of yesterday. The partners, and the clerks with whom I had for so many years, and for so many hours in each day of the year, been so closely associated—being suddenly removed from them—they seemed as dead to me. There is a fine passage, which may serve to illustrate this fancy, in a Tragedy by Sir Robert Howard, speaking of a friend's death:

—'Twas but just now he went away;
I have not since had time to shed a tear;
And yet the distance does the same appear
As if he had been a thousand years from me,
Time takes no measure in Eternity.

To dissipate this awkward feeling, I have been fain to go among them once or twice since; to visit my old desk-fellows—my cobrethren of the quill—that I had left below in the state militant. Not all the kindness with which they received me could quite restore to me that pleasant familiarity, which I had heretofore enjoyed among them. We cracked some of our old jokes, but methought they went off but faintly. My old desk; the peg where I hung my hat, were appropriated to another. I knew it must be, but I could not take it kindly. D——l take me if I did not feel some remorse—beast, if I had not—at quitting my

---

5. **Old Bastile**, the notorious prison in Paris, destroyed by a mob at the beginning of the French Revolution; see Carlyle's *Storm and Victory*. 39. **That's ... desert.** From *The Mayor of Quinborough*, I, i, 102-103, a comedy by Thomas Middleton (1570-1627).

69. **a Tragedy**, *The Vestal Virgin, or the Roman Ladies;* Howard was a Restoration dramatist (1626-1698), Dryden's brother-in-law. The lines are quoted from Act **V,** i.

old compeers, the faithful partners of my toils for six and thirty years, that smoothed for me with their jokes and conundrums the ruggedness of my professional road. Had it been so rugged then after all? or was I a coward simply? Well, it is too late to repent; and I also know that these suggestions are a common fallacy of the mind on such occasions. But my heart smote me. I had violently broken the bands betwixt us. It was at least not courteous. I shall be some time before I get quite reconciled to the separation. Farewell, old cronies, yet not for long, for again and again I will come among ye, if I shall have your leave. Farewell, Ch——, dry, sarcastic, and friendly! Do——, mild, slow to move, and gentlemanly! Pl——, officious to do, and to volunteer, good services!—and thou, thou dreary pile, fit mansion for a Gresham or a Whittington of old, stately House of Merchants; with thy labyrinthine passages, and light-excluding, pent-up offices, where candles for one-half the year supplied the place of the sun's light; unhealthy contributor to my weal, stern fosterer of my living, farewell! In thee remain, and not in the obscure collection of some wandering bookseller, my "works"! There let them rest, as I do from my labors, piled on thy massy shelves, more MSS. in folio than ever Aquinas left, and full as useful! My mantle I bequeath among ye.

A fortnight has passed since the date of my first communication. At that period I was approaching to tranquillity, but had not reached it. I boasted of a calm indeed, but it was comparative only. Something of the first flutter was left; an unsettling sense of novelty; the dazzle to weak eyes of unaccustomed light. I missed my old chains, forsooth, as if they had been some necessary part of my apparel. I was a poor Carthusian, from strict cellular discipline suddenly by some revolution returned upon the world. I am now as if I had never been other than my own master. It is natural to me to go where I please, to do what I please. I find myself at eleven o'clock in the day in Bond Street, and it seems to me that I have been sauntering there at that very hour for years past. I digress into Soho, to explore a book-stall. Methinks I have been thirty years a collector. There is nothing strange nor new in it. I find myself before a fine picture in the morning. Was it ever otherwise? What is become of Fish Street Hill? Where is Fenchurch Street? Stones of old Mincing Lane which I have worn with my daily pilgrimage for six and thirty years, to the footsteps of what toil-worn clerk are your everlasting flints now vocal? I indent the gayer flags of Pall Mall. It is 'Change time, and I am strangely among the Elgin marbles. It was no hyperbole when I ventured to compare the change in my condition to a passing into another world. Time stands still in a manner to me. I have lost all distinction of season. I do not know the day of the week, or of the month. Each day used to be individually felt by me in its reference to the foreign post days; in its distance from, or propinquity to the next Sunday. I had my Wednesday feelings, my Saturday nights' sensations. The genius of each day was upon me distinctly during the whole of it, affecting my appetite, spirits, etc. The phantom of the next day, with the dreary five to follow, sat as a load upon my poor Sabbath recreations. What charm has washed the Ethiop white? What is gone of Black Monday? All days are the same. Sunday itself—that unfortunate failure of a holiday as it too often proved, what with my sense of its fugitiveness, and over-care to get the greatest quantity of pleasure out of it—is melted down into a week day. I can spare to go to church now, without grudging the huge cantle which it used to seem to cut out of the holiday. I have Time for everything. I can visit a sick friend. I can interrupt the man of much occupation when he is busiest.

15. **Ch——, Do——, Pl——,** probably John Chambers, Henry Dodwell, and W. D. Plumley. 19. **pile,** building. **Gresham,** Sir Thomas Gresham (1519?-1579), a prominent English financier, founder of the Royal Exchange. 20. **Whittington,** Sir Richard Whittington (d. 1423), the famous mayor of London and the hero of popular legend. 27. **my "works,"** the ledgers that Lamb had kept. 30. **Aquinas,** Saint Thomas Aquinas, a thirteenth-century Italian scholastic philosopher whose writings filled seventeen volumes. 41. **was . . . Carthusian,** was like a Carthusian monk, a member of the strict monastic order founded by St. Bruno about 1085.

50. **Soho,** a square in the west-central part of London; the name is now given to the neighboring district. 60. **Pall Mall,** a prominent street in London, the center of club life. 61. **'Change time,** Exchange time, the time of day when men are most actively engaged in business. 62. **Elgin marbles,** a collection of Greek sculpture in the British Museum. See Keats's sonnet *On Seeing the Elgin Marbles,* p. 275. 85. **cantle,** slice.

I can insult over him with an invitation to take a day's pleasure with me to Windsor this fine May-morning. It is Lucretian pleasure to behold the poor drudges, whom I have left behind in the world, carking and caring; like horses in a mill, drudging on in the same eternal round—and what is it all for? A man can never have too much Time to himself, nor too little to do. Had I a little son, I would christen him NOTHING-TO-DO; he should do nothing. Man, I verily believe, is out of his element as long as he is operative. I am altogether for the life contemplative. Will no kindly earthquake come and swallow up those accursed cotton mills? Take me that lumber of a desk there, and bowl it down

As low as to the fiends.

I am no longer ——, clerk to the firm of, etc. I am Retired Leisure. I am to be met with in trim gardens. I am already come to be known by my vacant face and careless gesture, perambulating at no fixed pace nor with any settled purpose. I walk about; not to and from. They tell me, a certain *cum dignitate* air, that has been buried so long with my other good parts, has begun to shoot forth in my person. I grow into gentility perceptibly. When I take up a newspaper it is to read the state of the opera. *Opus operatum est.* I have done all that I came into this world to do. I have worked taskwork, and have the rest of the day to myself.   (1825)

2. **Windsor,** a town in Berkshire, situated on the Thames, about 20 miles from London, the site of the famous royal castle. Across the river is Eton, known for its boys' school. 3. **Lucretian pleasure,** an allusion to a well-known passage in Book II of *On the Nature of Things,* by Lucretius (first century B.C.), a celebrated Roman poet and philosopher. The passage begins, "It is sweet, when on the great sea the winds trouble its waters, to behold from land another's deep distress." The passage is paraphrased by Bacon in his essay *Of Truth* (Vol. I, p. 615).

18. **As low ... fiends,** from *Hamlet,* II, ii, 518-519:
    And bowl the round nave down the hill of heaven
    As low as to the fiends!
20. **Retired Leisure.** Cf. Milton's *Il Penseroso,* 49-50:
    And add to these retired Leisure
    That in trim gardens takes his pleasure.
25. **cum dignitate,** from Cicero's phrase *otium cum dignitate,* leisure with dignity. 30. **Opus operatum est,** the work has been finished.

The Two Races of Men

THE HUMAN species, according to the best theory I can form of it, is composed of two distinct races, *the men who borrow,* and *the men who lend.* To these two original diversities may be reduced all those impertinent classifications of Gothic and Celtic tribes, white men, black men, red men. All the dwellers upon earth, "Parthians, and Medes, and Elamites," flock hither, and do naturally fall in with one or other of these primary distinctions. The infinite superiority of the former, which I choose to designate as the *great race,* is discernible in their figure, port, and a certain instinctive sovereignty. The latter are born degraded. "He shall serve his brethren." There is something in the air of one of this cast, lean and suspicious; contrasting with the open, trusting, generous manners of the other.

Observe who have been the greatest borrowers of all ages—Alcibiades—Falstaff—Sir Richard Steele—our late incomparable Brinsley—what a family likeness in all four!

What a careless, even deportment hath your borrower! what rosy gills! what a beautiful reliance on Providence doth he manifest—taking no more thought than lilies! What contempt for money—accounting it (yours and mine especially) no better than dross. What a liberal confounding of those pedantic distinctions of *meum* and *tuum!* or rather, what a noble simplification of language (beyond Tooke), resolving these supposed opposites into one clear, intelligible pronoun adjective!—What near approaches doth he

8. **"Parthians ... Elamites,"** quoted from *The Acts,* 2:9. 15. **"He ... brethren."** See *Genesis,* 9:25.

21. **Alcibiades ... Brinsley.** *Alcibiades* was the famous Athenian general and politician (450-404 B.C.), *Falstaff* the earthy character in Shakespeare's plays of *Henry IV* and *The Merry Wives of Windsor;* for Sir Richard Steele, see Vol. I, p. 975; *Brinsley* is Richard Brinsley Sheridan. 27. **taking ... lilies.** See *Matthew,* 6:28-29: "And why take ye thought for raiment? Consider the lilies of the field, how they grow; they toil not, neither do they spin: And yet I say unto you, That even Solomon in all his glory was not arrayed like one of these." 31. **meum and tuum,** mine and thine. 33. **Tooke,** John Horne Tooke (1736-1812), an English politician and philologist.

make to the primitive *community*—to the extent of one half of the principle at least!

He is the true taxer who "calleth all the world up to be taxed"; and the distance is as vast between him and *one of us* as subsisted betwixt the Augustan Majesty and the poorest obolary Jew that paid it tribute-pittance at Jerusalem!—His exactions, too, have such a cheerful, voluntary air! So far removed from your sour parochial or state-gatherers—those ink-horn varlets, who carry their want of welcome in their faces! He cometh to you with a smile, and troubleth you with no receipt; confining himself to no set season. Every day is his Candlemas, or his Feast of Holy Michael. He applieth the *Lene tormentum* of a pleasant look to your purse—which to that gentle warmth expands her silken leaves, as naturally as the cloak of the traveler, for which sun and wind contended! He is the true Propontic which never ebbeth! The sea which taketh handsomely at each man's hand. In vain the victim, whom he delighteth to honor, struggles with destiny; he is in the net. Lend therefore cheerfully, O man ordained to lend—that thou lose not in the end, with thy worldly penny, the reversion promised. Combine not preposterously in thine own person the penalties of Lazarus and of Dives!—but, when thou seest the proper authority coming, meet it smilingly, as it were half-way. Come, a handsome sacrifice! See how light *he* makes of it! Strain not courtesies with a noble enemy.

Reflections like the foregoing were forced upon my mind by the death of my old friend, Ralph Bigod, Esq., who departed this life on Wednesday evening, dying, as he had lived, without much trouble. He boasted himself a descendant from mighty ancestors of that name, who heretofore held ducal dignities in this realm. In his actions and sentiments he belied not the stock to which he pretended. Early in life he found himself invested with ample revenues, which, with that noble disinterestedness which I have noticed as inherent in men of the *great race*, he took almost immediate measures entirely to dissipate and bring to nothing: for there is something revolting in the idea of a king holding a private purse; and the thoughts of Bigod were all regal. Thus furnished, by the very act of disfurnishment; getting rid of the cumbersome luggage of riches, more apt (as one sings)

To slacken virtue, and abate her edge
Than prompt her to do aught may merit praise;

he set forth, like some Alexander, upon his great enterprise, "borrowing and to borrow"!

In his periegesis, or triumphant progress throughout this island, it has been calculated that he laid a tythe part of the inhabitants under contribution. I reject this estimate as greatly exaggerated:—but having had the honor of accompanying my friend, divers times, in his perambulations about this vast city, I own I was greatly struck at first with the prodigious number of faces we met who claimed a sort of respectful acquaintance with us. He was one day so obliging as to explain the phenomenon. It seems these were his tributaries; feeders of his exchequer; gentlemen, his good friends (as he was pleased to express himself), to whom he had occasionally been beholden for a loan. Their multitudes did no way disconcert him. He rather took a pride in numbering them; and, with Comus, seemed pleased to be "stocked with so fair a herd."

With such sources, it was a wonder how he contrived to keep his treasury always empty. He did it by force of an aphorism, which he had often in his mouth, that "money kept longer than three days stinks." So he made

---

3. **"calleth . . . taxed."** Cf. *Luke*, 2:1: "And it came to pass in those days, that there went out a decree from Caesar Augustus, that all the world should be taxed." The quotation should make clear the allusion in the next couple of lines. 7. **obolary**, having only an obolus, a small silver coin of ancient Greece and Asia Minor, of extremely low monetary value. 15. **Candlemas . . . Michael.** Candlemas, or the feast of the candles, celebrates the presentation of Christ in the Temple of Jerusalem, and is observed on Midwinter Day (February 2); the Feast of Holy Michael, or Michaelmas, is celebrated on September 29. 16. **Lene tormentum**, mild torture or gentle stimulus, quoted from Horace, *Odes*, Book III, no. 21, l. 13. 21. **Propontic . . . ebbeth.** See Shakespeare's *Othello*, III, iii, 453. The Propontic, or Pontic Sea, is another name for the Black Sea. 29. **Lazarus . . . Dives.** The parable of Lazarus, the pauper, and Dives, the rich man, is told in *Luke*, 16: 19-31. Dives went to Hell and Lazarus to Heaven. 37. **Ralph Bigod.** It has not been established that Bigod represents any real person.

56. **"To . . . praise,"** quoted from Milton's *Paradise Regained*, Book II, 455-6. 59. **"borrowing . . . borrow,"** adapted from *Revelation*, 6:2: "And I saw, and behold a white horse: and he that sat on him had a bow; and a crown was given unto him: and he went forth conquering, and to conquer." 62. **tythe**, tenth. 78. **"stocked . . . herd,"** quoted from Milton's *Comus*, 152.

use of it while it was fresh. A good part he drank away (for he was an excellent tosspot), some he gave away, the rest he threw away, literally tossing and hurling it violently from him—as boys do burrs, or as if it had been infectious—into ponds, or ditches, or deep holes—inscrutable cavities of the earth; —or he would bury it (where he would never seek it again) by a river's side under some bank, which (he would facetiously observe) paid no interest—but out away from him it must go peremptorily, as Hagar's offspring into the wilderness, while it was sweet. He never missed it. The streams were perennial which fed his fisc. When new supplies became necessary, the first person that had the felicity to fall in with him, friend or stranger, was sure to contribute to the deficiency. For Bigod had an *undeniable* way with him. He had a cheerful, open exterior, a quick jovial eye, a bald forehead, just touched with gray (*cana fides*). He anticipated no excuse, and found none. And, waiving for awhile my theory as to the *great race*, I would put it to the most untheorizing reader, who may at times have disposable coin in his pocket, whether it is not more repugnant to the kindliness of his nature to refuse such a one as I am describing, than to say *no* to a poor petitionary rogue (your bastard borrower) who, by his mumping visnomy, tells you that he expects nothing better, and, therefore, whose preconceived notions and expectations you do in reality so much less shock in the refusal.

When I think of this man; his fiery glow of heart; his swell of feeling; how magnificent, how *ideal* he was; how great at the midnight hour; and when I compare with him the companions with whom I have associated since, I grudge the saving of a few idle ducats, and think that I am fallen into the society of *lenders,* and *little men.*

To one like Elia, whose treasures are rather cased in leather covers than closed in iron coffers, there is a class of alienators more formidable than that which I have touched upon; I mean your *borrowers of books*—those mutilators of collections, spoilers of the symmetry of shelves, and creators of odd volumes. There is Comberbatch, matchless in his depredations!

That foul gap in the bottom shelf facing you, like a great eye-tooth knocked out (you are now with me in my little back study in Bloomsbury, reader!), with the huge Switzer-like tomes on each side (like the Guildhall giants, in their reformed posture, guardant of nothing), once held the tallest of my folios, *Opera Bonaventurae*, choice and massy divinity, to which its two supporters (school divinity also, but of a lesser calibre—Bellarmine, and Holy Thomas), showed but as dwarfs—itself an Ascapart—that Comberbatch abstracted upon the faith of a theory he holds, which is more easy, I confess, for me to suffer by than to refute, namely, that "the title to property in a book (my Bonaventure, for instance) is in exact ratio to the claimant's powers of understanding and appreciating the same." Should he go on acting upon this theory, which of our shelves is safe?

The slight vacuum in the left-hand case—two shelves from the ceiling—scarcely distinguishable but by the quick eye of a loser—was whilom the commodious resting-place of Browne on *Urn Burial.* C. will hardly allege that he knows more about that treatise than I do, who introduced it to him, and was indeed the first (of the moderns) to discover its beauties—but so have I known a foolish lover to praise his mistress in the presence of a rival more qualified to carry her off than himself.—Just below, Dodsley's dramas want

---

12. **Hagar's . . . wilderness.** Hagar was the handmaid of Sarah, the wife of Abraham (cf. *Genesis,* 16). Abraham's relations with Hagar, suggested by Sarah (who was sterile) resulted in the son Ishmael. Sarah, reproved by her conscience, turned upon Hagar, who was banished (with the Lord's approval) into the wilderness, where Ishmael grew to be "a wild man; his hand against every man, and every man's hand against him." 15. **fisc,** treasury. 22. *cana fides,* gray-haired fidelity; quoted from Virgil's *Aeneid,* I, 292. 31. **mumping visnomy,** mumbling physiognomy, or face.

51. **Comberbatch.** As pointed out on p. 164, Coleridge at one time ran away from Cambridge and enlisted in the dragoons under the name of Silas Tomkyn Comberbacke. The reference here is undoubtedly to Coleridge, in spite of the slightly modified form of the pseudonym. 56. **Switzer-like,** huge, like the giant Swiss guards who protect the Pope. 57. **Guildhall giants,** referring to the colossal figures in the council hall at London, known as Gog and Magog. 60. *Opera Bonaventurae,* the works of St. Bonaventure, a famous medieval scholastic philosopher (1221-1274), who was later canonized. 62. **Bellarmine,** Robert Bellarmino, a Jesuit theologian and cardinal (1542-1621). 63. **Holy Thomas,** St. Thomas Aquinas (c. 1225-1274), generally considered the greatest of medieval Catholic theologians and philosophers. 77. **Browne on** *Urn Burial.* See Vol. I, p. 691. C., Comberbatch, or Coleridge. 84. **Dodsley,** Robert Dodsley (1703-1764), an eminent bookseller and editor; his collection of English drama, the most famous of the time, was first printed in 1744.

their fourth volume, where *Vittoria Corrombona* is! The remainder nine are as distasteful as Priam's refuse sons, when the Fates *borrowed Hector*. Here stood *The Anatomy of Melancholy*, in sober state.—There loitered *The Complete Angler*, quiet as in life, by some stream side.—In yonder nook, *John Buncle*, a widower-volume, with "eyes closed," mourns his ravished mate.

One justice I must do my friend, that if he sometimes, like the sea, sweeps away a treasure, at another time, sea-like, he throws up as rich an equivalent to match it. I have a small under-collection of this nature (my friend's gatherings in his various calls), picked up, he has forgotten at what odd places, and deposited with as little memory at mine. I take in these orphans, the twice-deserted. These proselytes of the gate are welcome as the true Hebrews. There they stand in conjunction; natives, and naturalized. The latter seem as little disposed to inquire out their true lineage as I am.—I charge no warehouse-room for these deodands, nor shall ever put myself to the ungentlemanly trouble of advertising a sale of them to pay expenses.

To lose a volume to C. carries some sense and meaning in it. You are sure that he will make one hearty meal on your viands, if he can give no account of the platter after it. But what moved thee, wayward, spiteful K., to be so importunate to carry off with thee, in spite of tears and adjurations to thee to forbear, the *Letters* of that princely woman, the thrice noble Margaret Newcastle?—knowing at the time, and knowing that I knew also, thou most assuredly wouldst never turn over one leaf of the illustrious folio:—what but the mere spirit of contradiction, and childish love of getting the better of thy friend?—Then, worst cut of all! to transport it with thee to the Gallican land—

Unworthy land to harbor such a sweetness,
A virtue in which all ennobling thoughts dwelt,
Pure thoughts, kind thoughts, high thoughts, her
   sex's wonder!

—hadst thou not thy play-books, and books of jests and fancies, about thee, to keep thee merry, even as thou keepest all companies with thy quips and mirthful tales?—Child of the Green-room, it was unkindly done of thee. Thy wife, too, that part-French, better-part Englishwoman!—that *she* could fix upon no other treatise to bear away, in kindly token of remembering us, than the works of Fulke Greville, Lord Brooke—of which no Frenchman, nor woman of France, Italy, or England, was ever by nature constituted to comprehend a tittle! *Was there not Zimmerman on Solitude?*

Reader, if haply thou art blessed with a moderate collection, be shy of showing it; or if thy heart overfloweth to lend them, lend thy books; but let it be to such a one as S.T.C.—he will return them (generally anticipating the time appointed) with usury; enriched with annotations, tripling their value. I have had experience. Many are these precious MSS. of his—(in *matter* oftentimes, and almost in *quantity* not unfrequently vying with the originals)—in no very clerkly hand—legible in my Daniel; in old Burton; in Sir Thomas Browne; and those abstruser cogitations of the Greville, now, alas! wandering in Pagan lands—I counsel thee, shut not thy heart, nor thy library, against S.T.C.

(1820)

---

1. ***Vittoria Corrombona***, or *The White Devil*, now better known by the English title, a grim and bloody tragedy (1612) by the Elizabethan playwright John Webster. 3. **Priam . . . Hector.** In the Trojan War, Hector, the favorite son of King Priam of Troy and the most illustrious of Trojan champions, was slain by the Greek hero Achilles. With nine of his fifty sons still living, Priam begged Achilles for the body of Hector. The incident is told in the *Iliad*, Book XXIV, 486 ff. 4. **The . . . *Melancholy*,** an exhaustive treatise (1621) on the causes, nature, and cure of melancholy by Robert Burton (1577-1640). 6. ***The Complete Angler.*** See Vol. I, p. 704. 7. ***John Buncle***, a novel (1756-66) of the picaresque type by Thomas Amory (1691?-1788). The reference in this line is to the fact that John Buncle, the hero of the book, made the statement that when one of his wives died he remained four days with his eyes shut. In the course of the novel, be it observed, he embarked upon no less than seven matrimonial adventures. 24. **deodands**, in English law, things forfeited to the crown. 32. **wayward, spiteful K.,** James Kenney (1780-1849), a minor dramatist of the time. 36. ***Letters* . . . Newcastle,** the *Sociable Letters* of Margaret Cavendish, Lady Newcastle (c. 1625-1673).

52. **Green-room,** originally the dressing-room of the theater; then applied to the stage as a whole. 56. **Fulke Greville,** first Lord Brooke (1554-1628), an Elizabethan poet, courtier, and statesman, friend of Queen Elizabeth and of Sir Philip Sidney in particular; one of the most famous of Elizabethan gentlemen of the court. 60. ***Zimmerman,*** Johann Georg van Zimmerman (1728-1795), a Swiss physician and philosophical writer, best known for his monograph on solitude, which appeared in 1784-85. 66. **S.T.C.,** Samuel Taylor Coleridge. 73. **Daniel,** Samuel Daniel, the Elizabethan poet (see Vol. I, p. 477).

CHARLES LAMB

Letters

I. To Samuel Taylor Coleridge

August 26, 1814

Let the hungry soul rejoice; there is corn in Egypt. Whatever thou hast been told to the contrary by designing friends, who perhaps inquired carelessly, or did not inquire at all, in hope of saving their money, there is a stock of "Remorse" on hand, enough, as Pople conjectures, for seven years' consumption; judging from experience of the last two years. Methinks it makes for the benefit of sound literature, that the best books do not always go off best. Inquire in seven years' time for the "Rokebys" and the "Laras," and where shall they be found?—fluttering fragmentally in some thread-paper—whereas thy "Wallenstein" and thy "Remorse" are safe on Longman's or Pople's shelves, as in some Bodleian; there they shall remain; no need of a chain to hold them fast—perhaps for ages —tall copies—and people shan't run about hunting for them as in old Ezra's shrievalty they did for a Bible, almost without effect till the great-great-grand-niece (by the mother's side) of Jeremiah or Ezekiel (which was it?) remembered something of a book, with odd reading in it, that used to lie in the green closet in her aunt Judith's bedchamber.

Thy caterer Price was at Hamburgh when last Pople heard of him, laying up for thee, like some miserly old father for his generous-hearted son to squander.

Mr. Charles Aders, whose books also pant for that free circulation which thy custody is sure to give them, is to be heard of at his kinsmen, Messrs. Jameson and Aders, No. 7, Laurence-Pountney-Lane, London, according to the information which Crabius with his parting breath left me. Crabius is gone to Paris. I prophesy he and the Parisians will part with mutual contempt. His head has a twist Alemagne, like thine, dear mystic.

I have been reading Madame Staël on Germany. An impudent clever woman. But if "Faust" be no better than in her abstract of it, I counsel thee to let it alone. How canst thou translate the language of cat-monkeys? Fie on such fantasies! But I will not forget to look for Proclus. It is a kind of book which when one meets with it, one shuts the lid faster than one opened it. Yet I have some bastard kind of recollection that somewhere, some time ago, upon some stall or other, I saw it. It was either that or Plotinus, 205-270 A.D., Neoplatonist, or Saint Augustine's "City of God." So little do some folks value, what to others, sc. to you, "well used," had been the "Pledge of Immortality." Bishop Bruno I never touched upon. Stuffing too good for the brains of such "a Hare" as thou describest. May it burst his pericranium, as the gobbets of fat and turpentine (a nasty thought of the seer) did that old dragon in the Apocrypha! May he go mad in trying to understand his author! May he lend the third volume of him before he has quite translated the second, to a friend who shall lose it, and so spoil the publication; and may his friend find it and send it to him just as thou or some such less dilatory spirit shall have announced the whole for the press; lastly, may he be hunted by Reviewers, and the devil jug him! So I think I have answered all the questions except about Morgan's cos-lettuces. The first per-

---

7. "**Remorse**," *Osorio*, or *Remorse*, a poetic tragedy written by Coleridge between 1798, when the first two acts were composed, and 1813, when the play was published. It was not a successful play, then or later. 8. **Pople**, a London bookseller. 13. "**Rokebys**" . . . "**Laras**." *Rokeby* was a narrative poem written by Sir Walter Scott and published in 1813; *Lara* was a very popular narrative poem by Byron (1814). 16. "**Wallenstein**," a trilogy of historical dramas (1798-99) by the German poet Schiller (1759-1805), translated by Coleridge in part (he completed only two of the three plays—*The Piccolomini* and *The Death of Wallenstein*). 17. **Longman**, a London publisher and bookseller. 18. **Bodleian**, the name of the great library at Oxford. 21. **shrievalty**, term as sheriff. 32. **Charles Aders**, a publisher friend of Lamb's great friend Crabb Robinson (the Crabius of l. 37 below). Lamb often met Aders at Robinson's, where they went to talk and play whist. 41. **twist Alemagne**, a bias or prejudice in favor of Germany and the Germans. 42. **Madame Staël**, Louise Necker, Madame de Staël (1766-1817), a brilliant French woman whose *On Germany* (1808) was not only a notable treatment of that country but also a link between the English and French romantics and Germany. In addition, Madame de Staël wrote two novels, *Delphine* (1806) and *Corinne* (1807), and attracted the enmity of Napoleon. 44. "**Faust**," the masterpiece and life work of the German poet Goethe (1749-1832). 48. **Proclus**, a Byzantine philosopher (412-485), whose writings are characterized by great vagueness—hence Lamb's rather caustic criticism. 54. "**City of God**," probably the greatest mystic work of the church father Augustine, Bishop of Hippo (354-430). 56. *sc.*, abbreviation of the Latin *scilicet*, namely, particularly. 57. **Bishop Bruno**, possibly the Bishop of the Rat-Tower at Bingen, Germany, who, according to legend, was devoured by rats; but E. V. Lucas, the editor of Lamb's letters, observes that this passage is "beyond annotation." 60. **pericranium**, the external surface of the skull. 62. **dragon** . . . **Apocrypha**, as told in *Bel and the Dragon*, one of the more fabulous books of the Old Testament Apocrypha. 73. **Morgan**, John Morgan, the friend and companion of Coleridge, with whom the poet stayed for a long time. **cos-lettuce**, a kind of lettuce introduced into England from the Greek island of Cos, in the Aegean Sea.

sonal peculiarity I ever observed of him (all worthy souls are subject to 'em) was a particular kind of rabbit-like delight in munching salads with oil without vinegar after dinner—a steady contemplative browsing on them—didst ever take note of it? Canst think of any other queries in the solution of which I can give thee satisfaction? Do you want any books that I can procure for you? Old Jimmy Boyer is dead at last. Trollope has got his living, worth £1000 a year net. See, thou sluggard, thou heretic-sluggard, what mightest thou not have arrived at! Lay thy animosity against Jimmy in the grave. Do not *entail* it on thy posterity.

CHARLES LAMB.

II. To WILLIAM WORDSWORTH

July, 1824

DEAR WORDSWORTH:

Mr. Ainsworth of Manchester, whom I believe to be a very estimable man, and know to be an Enthusiast in Poetry, etc., desires to be introduced to you. Have I credit enough with you to effect it? I am almost shy of doing it, because I want to introduce to you in a few weeks my friend Barron Field from Sydney, who has desired such letters, being on his travels northward. You must be often troubled with intruders, but I think I have not added many to the number.

My poor holydays are over. We have sneaked about to Ware, Kingston, etc.—sleeping out a night or two at a time, but have ventured on no more daring excursion—

I hope your eyes are tolerable. I have suffered sadly from one lately. How do you manage about *reading* in that case? There are books, which are good to read out, or hear read, as to read by oneself; but the lighter offal, Mags., Newspapers, etc., it is indispensable to glance over *per se*. I cannot be the auditor of a paragraph.

No news stirring. Coleridge is seen daily trudging on Highgate Hill, and blooming. Mary is in capital health, and I have a hope at bottom that it be better for her that we did not go out of town this summer. I have a conceit, that she has one, that she may escape illness by this moderation. Her thinking so (tho' we say nothing about it) may go a great way.

Do you know Watery Ware? It is redolent in springs and clear brooks; two or three rivers meet there. It is quite far enough for a Gentleman to purge off town air, a snug and safe distance, and shall be my future tether. The trouts in particular are admirable.

The Dyers were with us on Sunday. Mrs. D. amused a lady at our house with an account of her family economy. It seems G.D. shifts every other day, besides night shirts, etc.—He on t'other hand commends her as the most *cleanly creature;* as you would commend a cat. Matrimony I take it is a great cleanser. Everybody says how clean he is now. That is all the idea Frend seems to have of his old college crony! Beasts! not to have discerned G.D. but by the courtesy of a little soap.

My head aches with a dull opera last night. I do not know a flatness comparable to coming home after a play that has not amused—nor a pleasanter thing, than to talk over a contrary one at supper.

N.B. This is no letter, only a letter of recommendation.

God bless you. Love to all.

C. LAMB.

III. To CHARLES COWDEN CLARKE*

Enfield, October, 1828

DEAR CLARKE:

We did expect to see you with Victoria and the Novellos before this, and do not quite

---

9. **Jimmy Boyer,** the Reverend James Boyer, headmaster of Christ's Hospital school during the student days of Coleridge and Lamb. His successor was the Reverend Arthur William Trollope, who was headmaster until 1826. Boyer was a severe taskmaster, and he and Coleridge had had some friction; yet, in spite of Lamb's playful allusion to this in the last line of this letter, Coleridge was in the main kindly disposed toward Boyer.
30. **We,** Lamb and his sister Mary. 31. **Ware,** a town in Hertfordshire, north of London. **Kingston,** a village in Surrey. Both Ware and Kingston are present-day suburbs of London.

43. **Coleridge ... Highgate Hill.** See p. 171.
*Clarke, a well-known literary figure (1787-1877); he was a miscellaneous writer, a noted lecturer on Shakespeare and the Elizabethan drama, and a publisher, in partnership with the noted English musical and literary family, the Novellos. He married Mary Victorio Novello, and at the time of this letter was on his honeymoon.

understand why we have not. Mrs. N. and V. (Vincent) promised us after the York expedition; a day being named before, which failed. 'Tis not too late. The autumn leaves drop gold, and Enfield is beautifuller—to a common eye—than when you lurked at the Greyhound. Benedicks are close, but how I so totally missed you at that time, going for my morning cup of ale daily, is a mystery. 'Twas stealing a match before one's face in earnest. But certainly we had not a dream of your appropinquity. I instantly prepared an epithalamium, in the form of a sonata—which I was sending to Novello to compose—but Mary forbid it me, as too light for the occasion—as if the subject required anything heavy—so in a tiff with her I sent no congratulation at all. Tho' I promise you the wedding was very pleasant news to me indeed. Let your reply name a day this next week, when you will come as many as a coach will hold; such a day as we had at Dulwich. My very kindest love and Mary's to Victoria and the Novellos.

The enclosed is from a friend nameless, but highish in office, and a man whose accuracy of statement may be relied on with implicit confidence. He wants the *exposé* to appear in a newspaper as the "greatest piece of legal and Parliamentary villainy he ever remembered," and he has had experience in both; and thinks it would answer afterwards in a cheap pamphlet printed at Lambeth in 80 sheet, as 16,000 families in that parish are interested. I know not whether the present *Examiner* keeps up the character of exposing abuses, for I scarce see a paper now. If so, you may ascertain Mr. Hunt of the strictest truth of the statement, at the peril of my head. But if this won't do, transmit it me back, I beg, per coach, or better, bring it with you. Yours unaltered,

C. LAMB.

7. **Benedicks**, married men, more properly newly married men. The name is derived from Benedick, the hero of Shakespeare's *Much Ado about Nothing*, who after some futile defensive sparring with the witty Beatrice is finally reduced to subjection and marries. 12. **appropinquity**, nearness. 15. **Mary**, Lamb's sister. 22. **Dulwich**, a borough of South London. 36. **Examiner**, the periodical established by Leigh Hunt; as a result of an attack by Hunt in this crusading journal on the reputation of the Prince Regent, later King George IV, Hunt was imprisoned for a period of two years. The *Examiner*, later revived, followed a much less radical policy.

IV. To Thomas Manning*

May 10, 1834

You made me feel so funny, so happy-like, it was as if I was reading one of your old letters taken out of hazard any time between the last twenty years, 'twas so the same. The Unity of place, a Garden! the old Dramatis Personae, a Landlady and Daughter. The puns the same in mold. Will nothing change you? 'Tis but a short week since honest Ryle and I were lamenting the gone-by days of Manning and whist. How savorily did he remember them! Might some great year but bring them back again! This was my exclaim, and R. did not ask for an explanation.

I have had a scurvy nine years of it, and am now in the sorry fifth act. Twenty weeks nigh has she been now violent, with but a few sound months before, and those in such dejection that her fever might seem a relief to it. I tried to bring her down in the winter once or twice, but it failed. Tuthill led me to expect that this illness would lengthen with her years, and it has cruelly, with that new feature of despondency after. I am with her alone now in a proper house. She is I hope recovering. We play picquet, and it is like the old times awhile, then goes off— I struggle up town rarely, and then to see London with little other motive, for what is left there hardly! The streets and shops entertaining ever, else I feel as in a desert, and get me home to my cave. Save that once a month I pass a day, a gleam in my life, with Cary at the Museum. (He is the flower of clergymen) and breakfast next morn with Robinson. I look to this as a treat. It sustains me. C. is a dear fellow, with but two vices,

*__Manning__, Thomas Manning (1772-1840), a mathematician at Caius College, Cambridge, and one of Lamb's best friends. Much of Manning's time after 1806 was spent in China; but upon his return there are many letters between the two men. The opening paragraph of this letter is a series of reminiscences on the earlier days in the relationship of Lamb and Manning. 52. **Ryle**, Charles Ryle, an associate of Lamb at the East India House and notable as the executor of Lamb's will; he was also a good friend of Manning. 60. **she**, here as elsewhere in so many of Lamb's letters, his sister Mary. 64. **Tuthill**, Mary Lamb's physician. 69. **picquet**, a two-handed game of cards in which the cards below seven are discarded. 77. **Cary**, Henry Francis Cary (1772-1844), a clergyman and noted poet-scholar of the time. His best known work is his translation of Dante's *Divine Comedy*, which he completed in 1812. He also occupied a position at the British Museum, in addition to his regular clerical duties as an ordained clergyman. 79. **Robinson**, Crabb Robinson; see p. 357, note to l. 32. 80. **C.**, Cary.

which in any less good than himself would be crimes, past redemption. He has no relish for Parson Adams—hints that he might not be a very great Greek Scholar after all (does Fielding hint that he was a Porson?) and prefers "Ye Shepherds so cheerful and gay" and "my banks they are furnished with bees" to the "Schoolmistress." I have not seen Wright's—but the faithfulness of C.— Mary and I can attest. For last year in a good interval, I giving some lessons to Emma, now Mrs. Moxon, in the sense part of her Italian (I knew no words) Mary pertinaciously undertook, being 69, to read the Inferno all thro' with the help of his translation, and we got thro' it with dictionaries and grammars of course to our satisfaction. Her perseverance was gigantic, almost painful. Her head was over her task like a sticking bee, morn to night. We were beginning the Purgatory, but got on less rapidly, our great authority for grammar, Emma, being fled, but should have proceeded but for this misfortune. Do not come to town without apprising me. We must all three meet somehow, and drink a cup.

Yours ever,
C. L.

P.S.
Mary strives and struggles to be content, when she *is* well. Last year when we talked of being dull (we had just lost our seven years nearly inmate) and Cary's invitation came, she said, "Did not I say something or other would turn up?" In her first walk *out* of the house, she would read every auction advertisement along the road, and when I would stop her, she said, "These are my playbills." She felt glad to get into the world again, but then follows lowness.—

She is getting about tho,' I very much hope. She is rising, and will claim her morning picquet. I go to put this in the post first.—

I walk nine or ten miles a day alway up the road, dear Londonwards. Fields, flowers, birds, and green lanes I have no heart for. The Ware road is cheerful, and almost good as a street. I saunter to the Red Lion duly, as you used to the Peacock!

3. **Parson Adams,** an amusing and sympathetic clerical character in Fielding's *Joseph Andrews* (Vol. I, p. 839). 5. **Porson,** Richard Porson (1759-1808), a contemporary classical scholar. This is a not too painful sample of Lamb's lamentable habit of punning. 6. "**Ye Shepherds . . . bees,**" titles of two poems by William Shenstone (1714-1763), whose best known poem is the gently satirical and withal sentimental poem of reminiscence, *The Schoolmistress* (1737). 9. **Wright,** Ichabod Charles Wright (1795-1871), who published a metrical translation of Dante's *Inferno* in 1833.

47. **Red Lion . . . Peacock,** social gathering places.

William Hazlitt
1778-1830

It is always ironically amusing to posterity when a man with pretensions in one field of human activity achieves whatever fame is to be his in something different. Such a man was William Hazlitt, the son of a Unitarian minister, born in Maidstone, April 10, 1778. His father lived for a time in America, but returned to England when the boy was nine years of age. Hazlitt was largely privately educated. Although his father would have liked to see his son in the ministry, the son was otherwise inclined. He was interested in philosophy of the speculative sort and in painting. Indeed, he finally decided (1802) not only to undertake painting as a career, but also to continue his study of metaphysics as a kind of second vocation. Hazlitt was neither an important philosopher nor an adequate picture-painter, but the combination of the two interests apparently formed a third, and a very important one. The logical processes of metaphysical thought and the eye for color and form necessary to the art of painting developed in Hazlitt an unusual critical ability; and when he applied this ability to literature and life, he had discovered his appointed path.

Hazlitt's first important piece of writing was the *Essay on Principles of Human Action* (1807), but it is poor metaphysics and interesting now only because of the promise of style apparent in it. Resigned to his failure as a philosopher, Hazlitt turned to general critical writing, contributing to Hunt's *Examiner* (p. 297), and grouping together a collection of essays known as *The Round Table*. His first solid achievement in literary criticism was *The Characters of Shakespeare's Plays* (1817); his most valuable miscellaneous collection of prose writings is *Table Talk* (1821). The years 1807 to 1821, easily the most active period of Hazlitt's life, saw the writing of the three prose collections just mentioned, and a considerable amount of lecturing, much of it on the Elizabethan playwrights, for whom Hazlitt shared the enthusiasm shown by Coleridge (who had first interested him in metaphysics and literature), and by Hunt, Lamb, and De Quincey.

All his life Hazlitt was extremely liberal, not to say radical, in his tendencies. He had a lack of faith in Wordsworth and Southey, whom he regarded as turncoats; and he was constantly in hot water because of his relations with Hunt and the "extremists" of the age. His liberalism usually meant unfavorable criticisms of his work from the reviewers, particularly from those on the *Quarterly Review*. Nor did Hazlitt's private life help his isolated position. His first marriage was a dismal failure, although he put up with it for fourteen years. In 1823, however, he became involved with a servant-girl; his wife and he separated; and he felt impelled to write *Liber Amoris*, an indiscreet account of the rather sordid affair, which won him little sympathy from anyone. He removed to the Continent, having contracted a rather casual second marriage in the meantime. Soon after (1825), he returned and published what may be called his critical farewell, *The Spirit of the Age*. This work still exhibits Hazlitt's critical felicity; yet the complaint was raised that he was more happy in his analysis of writers of the past than in his evaluation of the writers of his own day. Such a complaint, however, is scarcely surprising, for in matters critical it takes a bold man to venture on a prophecy, and a lucky as well as a bold man to be right in his judgment. In the *Life of Napoleon* (1828-1830), Hazlitt clearly showed that he had passed his peak. His death occurred September 18, 1830.

Hazlitt was very much an individualist. He is an impressive combination of intellect and passion; a critic with a prose style vigorous but very bookish in manner and often very careless and inaccurate in details. He has charm, but not the essential warmth of Lamb nor the fine poetic sensibilities of De Quincey; yet he is an extremely good self-depicter, and his interests in life, for all his intellectuality, are clearly romantic. Probably his critical work in the history of English drama will keep him alive long after his personal opinions about life have become obsolete, for he was an honest and outspoken dramatic critic who was none the less keenly appreciative. In his more general criticisms of life, he is prejudiced, somewhat bitter and opinionated; but on the whole he had enough personal magnetism and literary influence to make Robert Louis Stevenson, himself an excellent essayist, remark once in a kind of jesting despair, "We are fine fellows, but we can't write like William Hazlitt."

On Going a Journey

ONE of the pleasantest things in the world is going a journey; but I like to go by myself. I can enjoy society in a room; but out of doors, nature is company enough for me. I am then never less alone than when alone.

The fields his study, nature was his book.

I cannot see the wit of walking and talking at the same time. When I am in the country, I wish to vegetate like the country. I am not for criticizing hedge-rows and black cattle. I go out of town in order to forget the town and all that is in it. There are those who for this purpose go to watering-places, and carry the metropolis with them. I like more elbow-room and fewer incumbrances. I like solitude, when I give myself up to it, for the sake of solitude; nor do I ask for

7. *The . . . book*, Robert Bloomfield (fl. 1800), *Spring*, l. 31.

a friend in my retreat,
Whom I may whisper solitude is sweet.

The soul of a journey is liberty, perfect liberty, to think, feel, do just as one pleases. We go a journey chiefly to be free of all impediments and of all inconveniences; to leave ourselves behind, much more to get rid of others. It is because I want a little breathing-space to muse on indifferent matters, where
10 Contemplation

May plume her feathers and let grow her wings,
That in the various bustle of resort
Were all too ruffled, and sometimes impaired,

that I absent myself from the town for a while, without feeling at a loss the moment I am left by myself. Instead of a friend in a post-chaise or in a Tilbury, to exchange good things with, and vary the same stale topics over again, for once let me have a truce with im-
20 pertinence. Give me the clear blue sky over my head, and the green turf beneath my feet, a winding road before me, and a three-hours' march to dinner—and then to thinking! It is hard if I cannot start some game on these lone heaths. I laugh, I run, I leap, I sing for joy. From the point of yonder rolling cloud I plunge into my past being, and revel there, as the sun-burned Indian plunges headlong into the wave that wafts him to his native
30 shore. Then long-forgotten things, like "sunken wreck and sumless treasuries," burst upon my eager sight, and I begin to feel, think, and be myself again. Instead of an awkward silence, broken by attempts at wit or dull commonplaces, mine is that undisturbed silence of the heart which alone is perfect eloquence. No one likes puns, alliterations, antitheses, argument, and analysis better than I do; but I sometimes had rather be without them.
40 "Leave, oh, leave me to my repose!" I have just now other business in hand, which would seem idle to you, but is with me "very stuff o' the conscience." Is not this wild rose sweet without a comment? Does not this daisy leap to my heart set in its coat of emerald? Yet if I were to explain to you the circumstance that has so endeared it to me, you would only smile. Had I not better then keep it to myself, and let it serve me to brood over, from here to yonder craggy point, and from 50 thence onward to the far-distant horizon? I should be but bad company all that way, and therefore prefer being alone. I have heard it said that you may, when the moody fit comes on, walk or ride on by yourself, and indulge your reveries. But this looks like a breach of manners, a neglect of others, and you are thinking all the time that you ought to rejoin your party. "Out upon this half-faced fellowship," say I. I like to be either 60 entirely to myself, or entirely at the disposal of others; to talk or be silent, to walk or sit still, to be sociable or solitary. I was pleased with an observation of Mr. Cobbett's, that "he thought it a bad French custom to drink our wine with our meals, and that an Englishman ought to do only one thing at a time." So I cannot talk and think, or indulge in melancholy musing and lively conversation by fits and starts. "Let me have a companion 70 of my way," says Sterne, "were it but to remark how the shadows lengthen as the sun declines." It is beautifully said; but in my opinion, this continual comparing of notes interferes with the involuntary impression of things upon the mind, and hurts the sentiment. If you only hint what you feel in a kind of dumb show, it is insipid: if you have to explain it, it is making a toil of a pleasure. You cannot read the book of nature without 80 being perpetually put to the trouble of translating it for the benefit of others. I am for the synthetical method on a journey in preference to the analytical. I am content to lay in a stock of ideas then, and to examine and anatomize them afterwards. I want to see my vague

---

1. **a friend . . . sweet,** Cowper, *Retirement*, ll. 741-742. 11. **May . . . impaired,** Milton, *Comus*, ll. 378-380. 17. **Tilbury,** a light two-wheeled open carriage, named after the inventor, a coach-maker of the early nineteenth century. 30. **"sunken . . . treasuries,"** *Henry V*, I, ii, 165. 40. **"Leave . . . repose,"** Gray, *The Descent of Odin*, l. 50.

42. **"very . . . conscience,"** *Othello*, I, ii, 2. 59. **"Out . . . fellowship,"** *1 Henry IV*, I, iii, 208. 64. **Mr. Cobbett,** William Cobbett (1762-1835), an English essayist and politician. 71. **Sterne,** Laurence Sterne (1713-1768), an English novelist and clergyman. The quotation is from his *Sermons*, 18.

notions float like the down of the thistle before the breeze, and not to have them entangled in the briars and thorns of controversy. For once, I like to have it all my own way; and this is impossible unless you are alone, or in such company as I do not covet. I have no objection to argue a point with anyone for twenty miles of measured road, but not for pleasure. If you remark the scent of a bean-field crossing the road, perhaps your fellow-traveler has no smell. If you point to a distant object, perhaps he is shortsighted, and has to take out his glass to look at it. There is a feeling in the air, a tone in the color of a cloud, which hits your fancy, but the effect of which you are unable to account for. There is then no sympathy, but an uneasy craving after it, and a dissatisfaction which pursues you on the way, and in the end probably produces ill humor. Now I never quarrel with myself, and take all my own conclusions for granted till I find it necessary to defend them against objections. It is not merely that you may not be of accord on the objects and circumstances that present themselves before you—these may recall a number of objects, and lead to associations too delicate and refined to be possibly communicated to others. Yet these I love to cherish, and sometimes still fondly clutch them, when I can escape from the throng to do so. To give way to our feelings before company seems extravagance or affectation; and on the other hand, to have to unravel this mystery of our being at every turn, and to make others take an equal interest in it (otherwise the end is not answered) is a task to which few are competent. We must "give it an understanding, but no tongue." My old friend C——, however, could do both. He could go on in the most delightful explanatory way over hill and dale, a summer's day, and convert a landscape into a didactic poem or a Pindaric ode. "He talked far above singing." If I could so clothe my ideas in sounding and flowing words, I might perhaps wish to have someone with me to admire the swelling theme; or I could be more content, were it possible for me still to hear his echoing voice in the woods of All-Foxden. They had "that fine madness in them which our first poets had"; and if they could have been caught by some rare instrument, would have breathed such strains as the following:

> Here be woods as green
> As any, air likewise as fresh and sweet
> As when smooth Zephyrus plays on the fleet
> Face of the curled stream, with flow'rs as many
> As the young spring gives, and as choice as any;
> Here be all new delights, cool streams, and wells,
> Arbors o'ergrown with woodbine, caves, and dells;
> Choose where thou wilt, whilst I sit by and sing,
> Or gather rushes to make many a ring
> For thy long fingers; tell thee tales of love,
> How the pale Phoebe, hunting in a grove,
> First saw the boy Endymion, from whose eyes
> She took eternal fire that never dies;
> How she conveyed him softly in a sleep,
> His temples bound with poppy, to the steep
> Head of old Latmos, where she stoops each night,
> Gilding the mountain with her brother's light,
> To kiss her sweetest.

(*Faithful Shepherdess*)

Had I the words and images at command like these, I would attempt to wake the thoughts that lie slumbering on golden ridges in the evening clouds; but at the sight of nature my fancy, poor as it is, droops and closes up its leaves, like flowers at sunset. I can make nothing out on the spot: I must have time to collect myself.

In general, a good thing spoils out-of-door prospects: it should be reserved for Table-talk. L—— is for this reason, I take it, the

---

38. "give . . . tongue," *Hamlet*, I, ii, 250. 39. **C——**, Coleridge. 43. **Pindaric ode.** See Gray's *Progress of Poesy* and note, p. 52. "**He . . . singing**," Beaumont and Fletcher, *Philaster*, V, v, 165. 49. **All-Foxden**, the home of Wordsworth near Nether Stowey, in Somersetshire. It was a large country house surrounded by a wooded park. 50. "**that . . . had**," Michael Drayton, *To My Dearly Loved Friend*, l. 109. 54. **Here be woods**, etc., Fletcher, *The Faithful Shepherdess*, I, iii, 27-43. 56. **Zephyrus**, the west wind. 64. **Phoebe**, the moon goddess (Diana), who loved Endymion, the shepherd boy on Mt. Latmos in Asia Minor. See Keats's *Endymion*, p. 278. 82. **L——**, Charles Lamb.

worst company in the world out of doors; because he is the best within. I grant there is one subject on which it is pleasant to talk on a journey, and that is, what one shall have for supper when we get to our inn at night. The open air improves this sort of conversation or friendly altercation by setting a keener edge on appetite. Every mile of the road heightens the flavor of the viands we expect at the end of it. How fine it is to enter some old town, walled and turreted, just at the approach of nightfall, or to come to some straggling village, with the lights streaming through the surrounding gloom; and then after inquiring for the best entertainment that the place affords, to "take one's ease at one's inn!" These eventful moments in our lives' history are too precious, too full of solid, heartfelt happiness to be frittered and dribbled away in imperfect sympathy. I would have them all to myself, and drain them to the last drop; they will do to talk of or to write about afterwards. What a delicate speculation it is, after drinking whole goblets of tea—

The cups that cheer, but not inebriate—

and letting the fumes ascend into the brain, to sit considering what we shall have for supper—eggs and a rasher, a rabbit smothered in onions, or an excellent veal cutlet! Sancho in such a situation once fixed upon cow-heel; and his choice, though he could not help it, is not to be disparaged. Then, in the intervals of pictured scenery and Shandean contemplation, to catch the preparation and the stir in the kitchen.—*Procul, O procul este, profani!* These hours are sacred to silence and to musing, to be treasured up in the memory, and to feed the source of smiling thoughts hereafter. I would not waste them in idle talk; or if I must have the integrity of fancy broken in upon, I would rather it were by a stranger than a friend. A stranger takes his hue and character from the time and place; he is a part of the furniture and costume of an inn. If he is a Quaker, or from the West Riding of Yorkshire, so much the better. I do not even try to sympathize with him, and he breaks no squares. I associate nothing with my traveling companion but present objects and passing events. In his ignorance of me and my affairs I in a manner forget myself. But a friend reminds one of other things, rips up old grievances, and destroys the abstraction of the scene. He comes in ungraciously between us and our imaginary character. Something is dropped in the course of conversation that gives a hint of your profession and pursuits; or from having someone with you that knows the less sublime portions of your history, it seems that other people do. You are no longer a citizen of the world; but your "unhoused free condition is put into circumscription and confine." The *incognito* of an inn is one of its striking privileges—"lord of one's self, uncumbered with a name." Oh! it is great to shake off the trammels of the world and of public opinion—to lose our importunate, tormenting, everlasting personal identity in the elements of nature, and become the creature of the moment, clear of all ties —to hold to the universe only by a dish of sweetbreads, and to owe nothing but the score of the evening—and no longer seeking for applause and meeting with contempt, to be known by no other title than *the Gentleman in the parlor!* One may take one's choice of all characters in this romantic state of uncertainty as to one's real pretensions and become indefinitely respectable and negatively right-worshipful. We baffle prejudice and disappoint conjecture; and from being so to others, begin to be objects of curiosity and wonder even to ourselves. We are no more those hackneyed commonplaces that we appear in the world; an inn restores us to the level of nature and quits scores with society! I have certainly spent some enviable hours at inns—sometimes when I have been left entirely to myself and have tried to solve some

16. **"take . . . inn!"** Paraphrased from *1 Henry IV*, III, iii, 93. 25. **The . . . inebriate,** Cowper, *The Task*, 4, 39. 29. **Sancho,** Don Quixote's squire in Cervantes's burlesque romance *Don Quixote.* 33. **Shandean,** like Walter Shandy in Sterne's novel *Tristram Shandy;* hence, discursive, whimsical. 35. **Procul . . . profani!** Aloof, oh, be aloof, ye profane (*Aeneid*, VI, 258).

45. **West Riding,** one of the three parts of Yorkshire. If from that section, he would be an uncouth provincial. 48. **breaks no squares,** does no harm. 62. **"unhoused . . . confine,"** *Othello,* I, ii, 26. 64. **"lord . . . name,"** Dryden, *To My Honored Kinsman,* l. 18.

metaphysical problem, as once at Witham-Common, where I found out the proof that likeness is not a case of the association of ideas—at other times, when there have been pictures in the room, as at St. Neot's (I think it was) where I first met with Gribelin's engravings of the Cartoons, into which I entered at once, and at a little inn on the borders of Wales, where there happened to be hanging some of Westall's drawings, which I compared triumphantly (for a theory that I had, not for the admired artist) with the figure of a girl who had ferried me over the Severn, standing up in the boat between me and the twilight—at other times I might mention luxuriating in books with a peculiar interest in this way, as I remember sitting up half the night to read *Paul and Virginia,* which I picked up at an inn at Bridgewater, after being drenched in the rain all day; and at the same place I got through two volumes of Madame D'Arblay's *Camilla.* It was on the 10th of April, 1798, that I sat down to a volume of the *New Eloise,* at the inn at Llangollen, over a bottle of sherry and a cold chicken. The letter I chose was that in which St. Preux describes his feelings as he first caught a glimpse from the heights of the Jura of the Pays de Vaud, which I had brought with me as a *bon bouche* to crown the evening with. It was my birthday, and I had for the first time come from a place in the neighborhood to visit this delightful spot. The road to Llangollen turns off between Chirk and Wrexham; and on passing a certain point you come all at once upon the valley, which opens like an amphitheater, broad, barren hills rising in majestic state on either side, with "green upland swells that echo to the bleat of flocks"

below, and the river Dee babbling over its stony bed in the midst of them. The valley at this time "glittered green with sunny showers," and a budding ash-tree dipped its tender branches in the chiding stream. How proud, how glad I was to walk along the high road that overlooks the delicious prospect, repeating the lines which I have just quoted from Mr. Coleridge's poems! But besides the prospect which opened beneath my feet, another also opened to my inward sight, a heavenly vision, on which were written, in letters large as Hope could make them, these four words, LIBERTY, GENIUS, LOVE, VIRTUE; which have since faded into the light of common day, or mock my idle gaze.

The beautiful is vanished and returns not.

Still I would return some time or other to this enchanted spot; but I would return to it alone. What other self could I find to share that influx of thoughts, of regret, and delight, the fragments of which I could hardly conjure up to myself, so much have they been broken and defaced! I could stand on some tall rock and overlook the precipice of years that separates me from what I then was. I was at that time going shortly to visit the poet whom I have above named. Where is he now? Not only I myself have changed; the world, which was then new to me, has become old and incorrigible. Yet will I turn to thee in thought, O sylvan Dee, in joy, in youth and gladness as thou then wert; and thou shalt always be to me the river of Paradise, where I will drink of the waters of life freely!

There is hardly anything that shows the shortsightedness or capriciousness of the imagination more than traveling does. With

---

1, 5. **Witham-Common, St. Neot's,** towns not far from London, now suburban. 6. **Gribelin,** Simon Gribelin (1661-1733), a line engraver. He made a set of seven small plates of the Cartoons, drawings of religious subjects by Raphael (1483-1520), the great Italian painter. 10. **Westall,** Richard Westall (1765-1836), a prominent English historical painter. 13. **Severn,** a river in southwestern England. 18. *Paul and Virginia,* a romantic story by Bernardin de Saint Pierre (1737-1814). 19. **Bridgewater,** a town in Somersetshire. 22. *Camilla,* a novel by Frances Burney (Madame D'Arblay) published 1796. 24. *New Eloise,* a French novel written in the form of letters by Jean Jacques Rousseau (1712-1778). The reference is to Letter 17 of Part IV. **Llangollen,** a town in northern Wales. 28. **Jura,** a chain of mountains on the border of Pays de Vaud, a canton of Switzerland. 30. *bon bouche,* dainty morsel. 34. **Chirk and Wrexham,** towns in northern Wales. 38. "green . . . flocks," Coleridge, *Ode on the Departing Year,* ll. 125-126.

40. **Dee,** a river flowing through Chester to the Irish Sea. 42. "**glittered . . . showers,**" Coleridge, *ibid,* l. 124. 53. **Liberty . . . Virtue.** At the time referred to, 1798, Hazlitt shared with Coleridge and others a hope for the triumph of the principles of the French Revolution. See p. 3. 54. **faded . . . day,** Wordsworth, *Ode on Intimations of Immortality,* l. 76, p. 101. 56. **The . . . not,** Coleridge, Translation of Schiller's *Death of Wallenstein,* V, i, 68. 67. **Where is he now?** When this essay was first published, Coleridge's creative power had waned, and his vigor had been impaired by ill health and the use of drugs; see p. 165. Moreover, like Wordsworth, Coleridge had become a conservative. Hazlitt remained a radical to the end. 70. **Yet . . . Dee.** Cf. Wordsworth's *Lines Composed a Few Miles above Tintern Abbey,* ll. 55-57, p. 122. 73. **river . . . freely.** Cf. *Revelation,* 22:17: "Whosoever will, let him take of the water of life freely."

change of place we change our ideas; nay, our opinions and feelings. We can by an effort indeed transport ourselves to old and long-forgotten scenes, and then the picture of the mind revives again; but we forget those that we have just left. It seems that we can think but of one place at a time. The canvas of the fancy is but of a certain extent, and if we paint one set of objects upon it, they immediately efface every other. We cannot enlarge our conceptions, we only shift our point of view. The landscape bares its bosom to the enraptured eye, we take our fill of it, and seem as if we could form no other image of beauty or grandeur. We pass on, and think no more of it: the horizon that shuts it from our sight also blots it from our memory like a dream. In traveling through a wild barren country I can form no idea of a woody and cultivated one. It appears to me that all the world must be barren, like what I see of it. In the country we forget the town, and in town we despise the country. "Beyond Hyde Park," says Sir Fopling Flutter, "all is a desert." All that part of the map that we do not see before us is a blank. The world in our conceit of it is not much bigger than a nutshell. It is not one prospect expanded into another, county joined to county, kingdom to kingdom, lands to seas, making an image voluminous and vast;—the mind can form no larger idea of space than the eye can take in at a single glance. The rest is a name written in a map, a calculation of arithmetic. For instance, what is the true signification of that immense mass of territory and population known by the name of China to us? An inch of pasteboard on a wooden globe, of no more account than a China orange! Things near us are seen of the size of life; things at a distance are diminished to the size of the understanding. We measure the universe by ourselves, and even comprehend the texture of our own being only piecemeal. In this way, however, we remember an infinity of things and places. The mind is like a mechanical instrument that plays a great variety of tunes, but it must play them in succession.

One idea recalls another, but it at the same time excludes all others. In trying to renew old recollections, we cannot as it were unfold the whole web of our existence; we must pick out the single threads. So in coming to a place where we have formerly lived, and with which we have intimate associations, everyone must have found that the feeling grows more vivid the nearer we approach the spot, from the mere anticipation of the actual impression: we remember circumstances, feelings, persons, faces, names, that we had not thought of for years; but for the time all the rest of the world is forgotten!—To return to the question I have quitted above.

I have no objection to go to see ruins, aqueducts, pictures, in company with a friend or a party, but rather the contrary, for the former reason reversed. They are intelligible matters, and will bear talking about. The sentiment here is not tacit, but communicable and overt. Salisbury Plain is barren of criticism, but Stonehenge will bear a discussion antiquarian, picturesque, and philosophical. In setting out on a party of pleasure, the first consideration always is where we shall go to: in taking a solitary ramble, the question is what we shall meet with by the way. "The mind is its own place"; nor are we anxious to arrive at the end of our journey. I can myself do the honors indifferently well to works of art and curiosity. I once took a party to Oxford with no mean *éclat*—showed them that seat of the Muses at a distance,

> With glistering spires and pinnacles adorned—

descanted on the learned air that breathes from the grassy quadrangles and stone walls of halls and colleges—was at home in the Bodleian; and at Blenheim quite superseded the powdered Cicerone that attended us, and that pointed in vain with his wand to commonplace beauties in matchless pictures.—As

---

23. **"Beyond . . . desert,"** Etherege, *The Man of Mode*, V, ii. The quotation is spoken by Harriet, not by Sir Fopling. 71. **Stonehenge,** a group of prehistoric ruins near the town of Salisbury, Wiltshire. 76. **"The . . place,"** *Paradise Lost,* I, 254 (Vol. I, p. 720). 81. *éclat,* display. Hazlitt accompanied Charles and Mary Lamb through Oxford on their way to London in 1810. 83. **With . . . adorned,** *Paradise Lost,* III, 350. 87. **Bodleian,** the famous Oxford University Library, named after Sir Thomas Bodley, a benefactor. **Blenheim,** the mansion of the Duke of Marlborough, near Oxford. 88. **Cicerone,** guide, so called after Cicero, the Roman orator, because of his talkativeness.

another exception to the above reasoning, I should not feel confident in venturing on a journey in a foreign country without a companion. I should want at intervals to hear the sound of my own language. There is an involuntary antipathy in the mind of an Englishman to foreign manners and notions that requires the assistance of social sympathy to carry it off. As the distance from home increases, this relief, which was at first a luxury, becomes a passion and an appetite. A person would almost feel stifled to find himself in the deserts of Arabia without friends and countrymen: there must be allowed to be something in the view of Athens or old Rome that claims the utterance of speech; and I own that the Pyramids are too mighty for any single contemplation. In such situations, so opposite to all one's ordinary train of ideas, one seems a species by one's self, a limb torn off from society, unless one can meet with instant fellowship and support.—Yet I did not feel this want or craving very pressing once, when I first set my foot on the laughing shores of France. Calais was peopled with novelty and delight. The confused, busy murmur of the place was like oil and wine poured into my ears; nor did the mariners' hymn, which was sung from the top of an old crazy vessel in the harbor, as the sun went down, send an alien sound into my soul. I only breathed the air of general humanity. I walked over "the vine-covered hills and gay regions of France," erect and satisfied; for the image of man was not cast down and chained to the foot of arbitrary thrones: I was at no loss for language, for that of all the great schools of painting was open to me. The whole is vanished like a shade. Pictures, heroes, glory, freedom, all are fled: nothing remains but the Bourbons and the French people!—There is undoubtedly a sensation in traveling into foreign parts that is to be had nowhere else; but it is more pleasing at the time than lasting. It is too remote from our habitual associations to be a common topic of discourse or reference, and, like a dream or another state of existence, does not piece into our daily modes of life. It is an animated but a momentary hallucination. It demands an effort to exchange our actual for our ideal identity; and to feel the pulse of our old transports revive very keenly, we must "jump" all our present comforts and connections. Our romantic and itinerant character is not to be domesticated. Dr. Johnson remarked how little foreign travel added to the facilities of conversation in those who had been abroad. In fact, the time we have spent there is both delightful and in one sense instructive; but it appears to be cut out of our substantial, downright existence, and never to join kindly on to it. We are not the same, but another, and perhaps more enviable individual, all the time we are out of our own country. We are lost to ourselves, as well as our friends. So the poet somewhat quaintly sings:

Out of my country and myself I go.

Those who wish to forget painful thoughts do well to absent themselves for a while from the ties and objects that recall them; but we can be said only to fulfil our destiny in the place that gave us birth. I should on this account like well enough to spend the whole of my life in traveling abroad, if I could anywhere borrow another life to spend afterwards at home! (1822)

---

24. **when . . . France,** in 1802, when he went to Paris to study the masterpieces of art collected there by Napoleon. 33. **"the . . . France,"** William Roscoe (1753-1831), *Song*, 1.

41. **Bourbons,** members of the French royal house that ruled from 1589 to the Revolution, and from the fall of Napoleon to 1830. They were noted for their policies of conservatism and repression. 53. **"jump,"** risk. Quoted from *Macbeth*, I, vii, 7: "We'd jump the life to come." 56. **Dr. Johnson . . . abroad.** Reported by Boswell under the year 1778.

from *My First Acquaintance with Poets* *Coleridge*

MEETING WITH COLERIDGE

My FATHER was a Dissenting Minister at W——m in Shropshire; and in the year 1798 (the figures that compose that date are to me like the "dreaded name of Demogorgon") Mr. Coleridge came to Shrewsbury, to succeed Mr. Rowe in the spiritual charge of a

2. **W——m,** Wem, a village near Shrewsbury.

4. **"dreaded . . . Demogorgon,"** *Paradise Lost*, II, 964 (Vol. I, p. 740). Demogorgon was a mysterious infernal deity who controlled the fates of both gods and men.

Unitarian congregation there. He did not come till late on the Saturday afternoon before he was to preach; and Mr. Rowe, who himself went down to the coach in a state of anxiety and expectation to look for the arrival of his successor, could find no one at all answering the description but a round-faced man in a short black coat (like a shooting jacket) which hardly seemed to have been made for him, but who seemed to be talking at a great rate to his fellow-passengers. Mr. Rowe had scarce returned to give an account of his disappointment, when the round-faced man in black entered, and dissipated all doubts on the subject, by beginning to talk. He did not cease while he stayed; nor has he since, that I know of. He held the good town of Shrewsbury in delightful suspense for three weeks that he remained there, "fluttering the *proud Salopians* like an eagle in dove-cote"; and the Welsh mountains that skirt the horizon with their tempestuous confusion agree to have heard no such mystic sounds since the days of

High-born Hoel's harp or soft Llewellyn's lay!

As we passed along between W——m and Shrewsbury, and I eyed their blue tops seen through the wintry branches, or the red rustling leaves of the sturdy oak-trees by the roadside, a sound was in my ears as of a siren's song; I was stunned, startled with it, as from deep sleep; but I had no notion then that I should ever be able to express my admiration to others in motley imagery or quaint allusion, till the light of his genius shone into my soul, like the sun's rays glittering in the puddles of the road. I was at that time dumb, inarticulate, helpless, like a worm by the wayside, crushed, bleeding, lifeless; but now, bursting from the deadly bands that bound them,

With Styx nine times round them,

my ideas float on winged words, and as they expand their plumes, catch the golden light of other years. My soul has indeed remained in its original bondage, dark, obscure, with longings infinite and unsatisfied; my heart, shut up in the prison-house of this rude clay, has never found, nor will it ever find, a heart to speak to; but that my understanding also did not remain dumb and brutish, or at length found a language to express itself, I owe to Coleridge. But this is not to my purpose.

My father lived ten miles from Shrewsbury, and was in the habit of exchanging visits with Mr. Rowe and with Mr. Jenkins of Whitchurch (nine miles farther on) according to the custom of Dissenting Ministers in each other's neighborhood. A line of communication is thus established, by which the flame of civil and religious liberty is kept alive, and nourishes its smoldering fire unquenchable, like the fires in the *Agamemnon* of Aeschylus, placed at different stations, that waited for ten long years to announce with their blazing pyramids the destruction of Troy. Coleridge had agreed to come over to see my father, according to the courtesy of the country, as Mr. Rowe's probable successor; but in the meantime I had gone to hear him preach the Sunday after his arrival. A poet and a philosopher getting up into a Unitarian pulpit to preach the Gospel was a romance in these degenerate days, a sort of revival of the primitive spirit of Christianity, which was not to be resisted.

It was in January, 1798, that I rose one morning before daylight, to walk ten miles in the mud, and went to hear this celebrated person preach. Never, the longest day I have to live, shall I have such another walk as this cold, raw, comfortless one, in the winter of the year 1798. *Il y a des impressions que ni le temps ni les circonstances peuvent effacer. Dusse-je vivre des siècles entiers, le doux temps de ma jeunesse ne peut renaître pour moi, ni s'effacer jamais dans ma mémoire.* When I got there, the organ was playing the 100th psalm, and,

---

19. "fluttering . . . dove-cote," Shakespeare, *Coriolanus*, V, vi, 115. Salopians are the inhabitants of Shropshire, from its old Latin name *Salopia*. 24. **High-born . . . lay!** Gray, *The Bard*, l. 28, p. 55. 29. **siren**, one of the sea nymphs said to inhabit an island near Italy and by their singing to lure mariners to destruction. The story of their attempts to lure Ulysses and his crew is told in Homer's *Odyssey*, Book XII. 40. **With . . . them**, Pope, *Ode on St. Cecilia's Day*, l. 90.

61. *Agamemnon*, a tragedy by Aeschylus, famous Greek dramatist (fifth century B.C.), in which fires are used to announce the fall of Troy. 80. *Il y a des*, etc., There are impressions which neither times nor circumstances can efface. Were I enabled to live entire ages, the sweet days of my youth could not return for me, nor ever be obliterated from my memory.—Rousseau, *Confessions*, II, 7.

when it was done, Mr. Coleridge rose and gave out his text, "And he went up into the mountain to pray, HIMSELF, ALONE." As he gave out this text, his voice "rose like a steam of rich distilled perfumes," and when he came to the two last words, which he pronounced loud, deep, and distinct, it seemed to me, who was then young, as if the sounds had echoed from the bottom of the human heart, and as if that prayer might have floated in solemn silence through the universe. The idea of St. John came into mind, "of one crying in the wilderness, who had his loins girt about, and whose food was locusts and wild honey." The preacher then launched into his subject, like an eagle dallying with the wind. The sermon was upon peace and war; upon church and state—not their alliance, but their separation—on the spirit of the world and the spirit of Christianity, not as the same, but as opposed to one another. He talked of those who had "inscribed the cross of Christ on banners dripping with human gore." He made a poetical and pastoral excursion—and to show the fatal effects of war, drew a striking contrast between the simple shepherd boy, driving his team afield, or sitting under the hawthorn, piping to his flock, "as though he should never be old," and the same poor country-lad, crimped, kidnaped, brought into town, made drunk at an ale-house, turned into a wretched drummer-boy, with his hair sticking on end with powder and pomatum, a long cue at his back, and tricked out in the loathsome finery of the profession of blood.

Such were the notes our once-loved poet sung.

And for myself, I could not have been more delighted if I had heard the music of the spheres. Poetry and Philosophy had met together. Truth and Genius had embraced, under the eye and with the sanction of Religion. This was even beyond my hopes. I returned home well satisfied. The sun that was still laboring pale and wan through the sky, obscured by thick mists, seemed an emblem of the *good cause;* and the cold dank drops of dew that hung half melted on the beard of the thistle had something genial and refreshing in them; for there was a spirit of hope and youth in all nature that turned everything into good. The face of nature had not then the brand of JUS DIVINUM on it:

Like to that sanguine flower inscribed with
   woe.

On the Tuesday following, the half-inspired speaker came. I was called down into the room where he was, and went half-hoping, half-afraid. He received me very graciously, and I listened for a long time without uttering a word. I did not suffer in his opinion by my silence. "For those two hours," he afterwards was pleased to say, "he was conversing with W. H.'s forehead!" His appearance was different from what I had anticipated from seeing him before. At a distance, and in the dim light of the chapel, there was to me a strange wildness in his aspect, a dusky obscurity, and I thought him pitted with the small-pox. His complexion was at that time clear, and even bright—

As are the children of yon azure sheen.

His forehead was broad and high, light as if built of ivory, with large projecting eyebrows, and his eyes rolling beneath them like the sea with darkened luster. "A certain tender bloom his face o'erspread," a purple tinge as we see it in the pale thoughtful complexions of the Spanish portrait-painters, Murillo and Velasquez. His mouth was gross, voluptuous, open, eloquent; his chin good-humored and

---

2. "**And . . . alone**," *John,* 6:15. 4. "**rose . . . perfumes**," Milton, *Comus,* l. 556. 12. "**of one . . . honey**," *Matthew,* 3:3-4. 28. "**as . . . old**," Sidney, *Arcadia,* l. 2. 33. **pomatum**, perfumed ointment for the hair. 36. **Such . . . sung**, Pope, *Epistle to Robert, Earl of Oxford,* l. 38. **music . . . spheres**. The ancients believed that the movement of the celestial planets produced music. 40. **Truth . . . embraced**. Cf. *Psalms,* 85:10—"Mercy and truth are met together; righteousness and peace have kissed each other." 46. *good cause,* Liberty; the phrase had been popular during the time of the French Revolution. 52. *jus divinum,* divine right, especially the divine right of kings. 53. **Like . . . woe**, *Lycidas,* 106 (Vol. I, p. 712). The petals of the hyacinth (sanguine flower) were supposed to be marked with the exclamation *Ai* (alas), in lamentation for the Greek youth Hyacinthus, from whose blood the flower was said to have sprung. 70. **As . . . sheen**, Thomson, *The Castle of Indolence,* 2, 295. 74. "**A . . . o'erspread**," *ibid,* l. 507. Thomson has *gloom* instead of *bloom.* 77. **Murillo and Velasquez**, Spanish painters of the seventeenth century.

round; but his nose, the rudder of the face, the index of the will, was small, feeble, nothing—like what he has done. It might seem that the genius of his face as from a height surveyed and projected him (with sufficient capacity and huge aspiration) into the world unknown of thought and imagination, with nothing to support or guide his veering purpose, as if Columbus had launched his adventurous course for the New World in a scallop, without oars or compass. So at least I comment on it after the event. Coleridge in his person was rather above the common size, inclining to the corpulent, or like Lord Hamlet, "somewhat fat and pursy." His hair (now, alas! gray) was then black and glossy as the raven's, and fell in smooth masses over his forehead. This long pendulous hair is peculiar to enthusiasts, to those whose minds tend heavenward; and is traditionally inseparable (though of a different color) from the pictures of Christ. It ought to belong, as a character, to all who preach *Christ crucified,* and Coleridge was at that time one of those!

It was curious to observe the contrast between him and my father, who was a veteran in the cause and then declining into the vale of years. He had been a poor Irish lad, carefully brought up by his parents, and sent to the University of Glasgow (where he studied under Adam Smith) to prepare him for his future destination. It was his mother's proudest wish to see her son a Dissenting Minister. So if we look back to past generations (as far as eye can reach) we see the same hopes, fears, wishes, followed by the same disappointments, throbbing in the human heart; and so we may see them (if we look forward) rising up forever, and disappearing, like vaporish bubbles, in the human breast! After being tossed about from congregation to congregation in the heats of the Unitarian controversy and squabbles about the American war, he had been relegated to an obscure village, where he was to spend the last thirty years of his life, far from the only converse that he loved, the talk about disputed texts of Scripture and the cause of civil and religious liberty. Here he passed his days, repining but resigned in the study of the Bible, and the perusal of the Commentators—huge folios, not easily got through, one of which would outlast a winter! Why did he pore on these from morn to night (with the exception of a walk in the fields or a turn in the garden to gather broccoli plants or kidney-beans of his own rearing, with no small degree of pride and pleasure)? Here were "no figures nor no fantasies"—neither poetry nor philosophy—nothing to dazzle, nothing to excite modern curiosity; but to his lack-luster eyes there appeared, within the pages of the ponderous, unwieldy, neglected tomes, the sacred name of JEHOVAH in Hebrew capitals: pressed down by the weight of the style, worn to the last fading thinness of the understanding, there were glimpses, glimmering notions of the patriarchal wanderings, with palm-trees hovering in the horizon, and processions of camels at the distance of three thousand years; there was Moses with the Burning Bush, the number of the Twelve Tribes, types, shadows, glosses on the law and the prophets; there were discussions (dull enough) on the age of Methuselah, a mighty speculation! there were outlines, rude guesses at the shape of Noah's Ark and of the riches of Solomon's Temple; questions as to the date of the creation, predictions of the end of all things; the great lapses of time, the strange mutations of the globe were unfolded with the voluminous leaf, as it turned over; and though the soul might slumber with an hieroglyphic veil of inscrutable mysteries drawn over it, yet it was in a slumber ill-exchanged for all the sharpened realities of sense, wit, fancy, or reason. My father's life was comparatively a dream; but it was a dream of infinity and eternity, of death, the resurrection, and a judgment to come!

No two individuals were ever more unlike than were the host and his guest. A poet was to my father a sort of nondescript: yet what-

---

11. **scallop**, a kind of sea-shell. 15. **pursy**, scant of breath. From *Hamlet*, V, ii, 298. 31. **Adam Smith**, a celebrated Scottish political economist (1723-1790).

57. "**no . . . fantasies**," *Julius Caesar*, II, i, 231. 70. **Moses . . . Bush**, a reference to the angel of the Lord that appeared in a burning bush to Moses. Cf. *Exodus*. 3:1-6. 71. **Twelve Tribes**, of Israel. See *Genesis*, 49. 74. **Methuselah**, a Hebrew patriarch said to have lived 969 years. See *Genesis*, 5:27. 76. **Noah's Ark**, described in *Genesis*, 6:14-16. **riches . . . Temple**, described in *1 Kings*, 6:20-35.

ever added grace to the Unitarian cause was to him welcome. He could hardly have been more surprised or pleased if our visitor had worn wings. Indeed, his thoughts had wings; and as the silken sounds rustled round our little wainscoted parlor, my father threw back his spectacles over his forehead, his white hairs mixing with its sanguine hue; and a smile of delight beamed across his rugged cordial face, to think that Truth had found a new ally in Fancy! Besides, Coleridge seemed to take considerable notice of me, and that of itself was enough. He talked very familiarly, but agreeably, and glanced over a variety of subjects. At dinner-time he grew more animated, and dilated in a very edifying manner on Mary Wollstonecraft and Mackintosh. The last, he said, he considered (on my father's speaking of his *Vindiciae Gallicae* as a capital performance) as a clever scholastic man—a master of the topics—or as the ready warehouseman of letters, who knew exactly where to lay his hand on what he wanted, though the goods were not his own. He thought him no match for Burke, either in style or matter. Burke was a metaphysician, Mackintosh a mere logician. Burke was an orator (almost a poet) who reasoned in figures, because he had an eye for nature: Mackintosh, on the other hand, was a rhetorician, who had only an eye to commonplaces. On this I ventured to say that I had always entertained a great opinion of Burke, and that (as far as I could find) the speaking of him with contempt might be made the test of a vulgar democratical mind. This was the first observation I ever made to Coleridge, and he said it was a very just and striking one. I remember the leg of Welsh mutton and the turnips on the table that day had the finest flavor imaginable. Coleridge added that Mackintosh and Tom Wedgwood (of whom, however, he spoke highly) had expressed a very indifferent opinion of his friend Mr. Wordsworth, on which he remarked to them—"He strides on so far before you that he dwindles in the distance!" Godwin had once boasted to him of having carried on an argument with Mackintosh for three hours with dubious success; Coleridge told him—"If there had been a man of genius in the room, he would have settled the question in five minutes." He asked me if I had ever seen Mary Wollstonecraft, and I said I had once for a few moments, and that she seemed to me to turn off Godwin's objections to something she advanced with quite a playful, easy air. He replied, that "this was only one instance of the ascendancy which people of imagination exercised over those of mere intellect." He did not rate Godwin very high (this was caprice or prejudice, real or affected) but he had a great idea of Mrs. Wollstonecraft's powers of conversation, none at all of her talent for book-making. We talked a little about Holcroft. He had been asked if he was not much struck *with* him, and he said he thought himself in more danger of being struck *by* him. I complained that he would not let me get on at all, for he required a definition of every commonest word, exclaiming, "What do you mean by a *sensation*, Sir? What do you mean by an *idea?*" This, Coleridge said, was barricadoing the road to truth—it was setting up a turnpike-gate at every step we took. I forgot a great number of things, many more than I remember; but the day passed off pleasantly, and the next morning Mr. Coleridge was to return to Shrewsbury. When I came down to breakfast, I found that he had just received a letter from his friend T. Wedgwood, making him an offer of £150 a year if he chose to waive his present pursuit, and devote himself entirely to the study of poetry and philosophy. Coleridge seemed to make up his mind to close with this proposal in the act of tying on one of his shoes. It threw an additional damp on his departure. It took the wayward enthusiast quite from us to cast him into Deva's winding

---

10. **ally in Fancy.** "My father was one of those who mistook his talent after all. He used to be very much dissatisfied that I preferred his Letters to his Sermons. The last were forced and dry; the first came naturally from him. For ease, half-plays on words, and a supine, monkish, indolent pleasantry, I have never seen them equaled."—Hazlitt. 16. **Mary Wollstonecraft,** a radical English author (1759-1797), wife of William Godwin, and mother of the second wife of Shelley. 17. **Mackintosh,** Sir James Mackintosh (1765-1832), a Scottish philosopher and historian in sympathy with the French Revolution; he published *Vindiciae Gallicae* (1791) in answer to Edmund Burke's *Reflections on the Revolution in France* (1790). 41. **Tom Wedgwood.** See ll. 80 ff.

64. **Holcroft,** Thomas Holcroft (1745-1809), an English dramatist, actor, and miscellaneous writer; also a prominent radical. 72. **barricadoing,** barricading. 88. **Deva,** the old Latin name for the River Dee, in North Wales.

vales, or by the shores of old romance. Instead of living at ten miles distance, of being the pastor of a Dissenting congregation at Shrewsbury, he was henceforth to inhabit the Hill of Parnassus, to be a Shepherd on the Delectable Mountains. Alas! I knew not the way thither, and felt very little gratitude for Mr. Wedgwood's bounty. I was presently relieved from the dilemma; for Mr. Coleridge, asking for a pen and ink, and going to a table to write something on a bit of card, advanced towards me with undulating step, and giving me the precious document, said that that was his address, *Mr. Coleridge, Nether Stowey, Somersetshire;* and that he should be glad to see me there in a few weeks' time, and, if I chose, would come half-way to meet me. I was not less surprised than the shepherd-boy (this simile is to be found in *Cassandra*) when he sees a thunder-bolt fall close at his feet. I stammered out my acknowledgments and acceptance of this offer (I thought Mr. Wedgwood's annuity a trifle to it) as well as I could; and this mighty business being settled, the poet-preacher took leave, and I accompanied him six miles on the road. It was a fine morning in the middle of winter, and he talked the whole way. The scholar in Chaucer is described as going

—sounding on his way.

So Coleridge went on his. In digressing, in dilating, in passing from subject to subject, he appeared to me to float in air, to slide on ice. He told me in confidence (going along) that he should have preached two sermons before he accepted the situation at Shrewsbury, one on Infant Baptism, the other on the Lord's supper, showing that he could not administer either, which would have effectually disqualified him for the object in view. I observed that he continually crossed me on the way by shifting from one side of the footpath to the other. This struck me as an odd movement; but I did not at that time connect it with any instability of purpose or involuntary change of principle, as I have done since. He seemed unable to keep on in a straight line. He spoke slightingly of Hume (whose *Essay on Miracles* he said was stolen from an objection started in one of South's sermons —*Credat Judaeus Apella!*) I was not very much pleased at this account of Hume, for I had just been reading, with infinite relish, that completest of all metaphysical *chokepears,* his *Treatise on Human Nature,* to which the *Essays,* in point of scholastic subtlety and close reasoning, are mere elegant trifling, light summer-reading. Coleridge even denied the excellence of Hume's general style, which I think betrayed a want of taste or candor. He however made me amends by the manner in which he spoke of Berkeley. He dwelt particularly on his *Essay on Vision* as a masterpiece of analytical reasoning. So it undoubtedly is. He was exceedingly angry with Dr. Johnson for striking the stone with his foot, in allusion to this author's *Theory of Matter and Spirit,* and saying, "Thus I confute him, Sir." Coleridge drew a parallel (I don't know how he brought about the connection) between Bishop Berkeley and Tom Paine. He said the one was an instance of a subtle, the other of an acute mind, than which no two things could be more distinct. The one was a shop-boy's quality, the other the characteristic of a philosopher. He considered Bishop Butler as a true philosopher, a profound and conscientious thinker, a genuine reader of nature and of his own mind. He did not speak of his *Analogy,* but of his *Sermons at the Rolls' Chapel,* of which I had never heard. Coleridge somehow always contrived to prefer the *unknown* to the *known.* In this instance he was right. The *Analogy*

---

1. **by . . . romance.** Cf. Wordsworth's *A Narrow Girdle of Rough Stones and Crags,* 38: "Sole-sitting by the shores of old romance." 4. **inhabit . . . Parnassus,** become a poet. Parnassus is a mountain range in Greece, celebrated as the haunt of the Muses of poetry and music. 5. **Shepherd . . . Mountains.** In Bunyan's *Pilgrim's Progress,* Christian and Hopeful escape from Giant Despair and come to the Shepherds of the Delectable Mountains. See Vol. I, pp. 801 ff. 19. *Cassandra,* a French historical romance by La Calprenède (1610-1663). 30. **sounding . . . way.** From Chaucer's *Prologue,* l. 307 (Vol. I, p. 216). 48. **Hume,** David Hume (1711-1776), famous Scottish philosopher. His *Essay on Miracles* shocked orthodox theologians of the period. 50. **South,** Robert South (1634-1716), a celebrated English divine. 51. **Credat . . . Apella!** Let the Jew Apella—i.e., a credulous person, believe it; I shall not (Horace, *Satires,* Book I, Satire V, 101). 62. **Berkeley,** George Berkeley (1685-1753), an Irish bishop and idealistic philosopher. 68. "**Thus . . . Sir.**" Related in Boswell's *Life of Johnson* (see Vol. I, p. 1160, ll. 54 ff.). 71. **Tom Paine,** Anglo-American liberal political writer (1737-1809). 77. **Bishop Butler,** Joseph Butler (1692-1752), an English theologian.

is a tissue of sophistry, of wire-drawn, theological special-pleading; the *Sermons* (with the Preface to them) are in a fine vein of deep, matured reflection, a candid appeal to our observation of human nature, without pedantry and without bias. I told Coleridge I had written a few remarks, and was sometimes foolish enough to believe that I had made a discovery on the same subject (the *Natural Disinterestedness of the Human Mind*)—and I tried to explain my view of it to Coleridge, who listened with great willingness, but I did not succeed in making myself understood. I sat down to the task shortly afterwards for the twentieth time, got new pens and paper, determined to make clear work of it, wrote a few meager sentences in the skeleton-style of a mathematical demonstration, stopped half way down the second page; and, after trying in vain to pump up any words, images, notions, apprehensions, facts, or observations, from that gulf of abstraction in which I had plunged myself for four or five years preceding, gave up the attempt as labor in vain, and shed tears of helpless despondency on the blank unfinished paper. I can write fast enough now. Am I better than I was then? Oh, no! One truth discovered, one pang of regret at not being able to express it, is better than all the fluency and flippancy in the world. Would that I could go back to what I then was! Why can we not revive past times as we can revisit old places? If I had the quaint Muse of Sir Philip Sidney to assist me, I would write a *Sonnet to the Road between W——m and Shrewsbury,* and immortalize every step of it by some fond enigmatical conceit. I would swear that the very milestones had ears, and that Harmer-hill stooped with all its pines to listen to a poet as he passed! I remember but one other topic of discourse in this walk. He mentioned Paley, praised the naturalness and clearness of his style, but condemned his sentiments, thought him a mere time-serving casuist, and said that "the fact of his work on *Moral and Political Philosophy* being made a textbook in our Universities was a disgrace to the national character." We parted at the six-mile stone; and I returned homeward, pensive but much pleased. I had met with unexpected notice from a person whom I believed to have been prejudiced against me. "Kind and affable to me had been his condescension, and should be honored ever with suitable regard." He was the first poet I had known, and he certainly answered to that inspired name. I had heard a great deal of his powers of conversation, and was not disappointed. In fact, I never met with anything at all like them, either before or since. I could easily credit the accounts which were circulated of his holding forth to a large party of ladies and gentlemen, an evening or two before, on the Berkeleian Theory, when he made the whole material universe look like a transparency of fine words; and another story (which I believe he has somewhere told himself) of his being asked to a party at Birmingham, of his smoking tobacco and going to sleep after dinner on a sofa, where the company found him to their no small surprise, which was increased to wonder when he started up of a sudden, and rubbing his eyes, looked about him, and launched into a three-hours' description of the third heaven, of which he had had a dream, very different from Mr. Southey's *Vision of Judgment,* and also from that other *Vision of Judgment,* which Mr. Murray, the Secretary of the Bridge-street Junto, has taken into his especial keeping!

On my way back I had a sound in my ears; it was the voice of Fancy—I had a light before me; it was the face of Poetry. The one still lingers there; the other has not quitted my side! Coleridge in truth met me halfway on the ground of philosophy, or I should not have been won over to his imaginative creed. I had an uneasy, pleasurable sensation

---

9. *Natural . . . Mind,* not published until 1805. 34. **Sidney.** See Vol. I, p. 341. 39. **Harmer-hill,** a prominent hill on the road between Wem and Shrewsbury. 42. **Paley,** William Paley (1743-1805), orthodox theologian and philosopher.

53. "Kind . . . regard," *Paradise Lost,* VIII, 648-650. 67. he . . . himself. In *Biographia Literaria,* 10. 69. **Birmingham,** a large manufacturing city in Warwickshire. 77. **Southey's** *Vision.* It describes the entrance of George III into heaven. The "other *Vision*" is Byron's ferocious satire of Southey's poem. 79. **Mr. Murray,** John Murray (1778-1843), Byron's publisher. He was publisher also of the Tory *Quarterly Review.* The Bridge-Street Association (called "Gang" by its enemies) was organized in 1821 to prevent seditious publications and acts.

all the time, till I was to visit him. During those months the chill breath of winter gave me a welcoming; the vernal air was balm and inspiration to me. The golden sunsets, the silver star of evening, lighted me on my way to new hopes and prospects. *I was to visit Coleridge in the spring.* This circumstance was never absent from my thoughts, and mingled with all my feelings. I wrote to him at the time proposed, and received an answer postponing my intended visit for a week or two, but very cordially urging me to complete my promise then. This delay did not damp, but rather increased my ardor. In the meantime I went to Llangollen Vale, by way of initiating myself in the mysteries of natural scenery; and I must say I was enchanted with it. I had been reading Coleridge's description of England, in his fine *Ode on the Departing Year*, and I applied it, *con amore*, to the objects before me. That valley was to me (in a manner) the cradle of a new existence: in the river that winds through it, my spirit was baptized in the waters of Helicon! . . . (1823)

15. **Llangollen Vale.** In Wales, about 35 miles from Wem. 21. **con amore,** with love. 25. **Helicon,** a mountain in Greece; it had two springs sacred to the Muses.

Thomas De Quincey

1785-1859

Thomas De Quincey was born near Manchester, the son of a rich merchant who died when the boy was young but who left a handsome patrimony, which seems to have endured through De Quincey's lifetime. The boy was unusually precocious and was educated in such a way as to encourage that precocity; he could write Greek fluently at the age of thirteen and could talk it with ease at fifteen. One of his teachers remarked that his pupil could have addressed a mob of Athenians with more effect than the teacher could have addressed a mob of Englishmen. In spite of his proficiency, De Quincey abhorred his early schooling, and on one occasion ran away to London, to be brought back and prepared for college only with the greatest difficulty. He went to Oxford, where his career was most irregular; he ran away again, and in the second year of his course became addicted to the opium habit, which was brought on through the use of the drug to alleviate the pain of an annoying illness. He left Oxford in 1808, having studied brilliantly but erratically, without a degree because he could not stand the necessary oral examination.

His interest in literature had been marked from the very first. It was not surprising, therefore, that De Quincey should be attracted to the company of the literary lights of the day, who in 1809 were assuredly Wordsworth and Coleridge. He went to the Lake Country, took a home near Wordsworth at Grasmere (p. 119), and remained there for about ten years, studying the classics and cultivating Coleridge and Wordsworth. From Coleridge he got an interest in the Elizabethans and in German literature, at the time almost an unknown field. He married in 1816 and became the father of a large family. All this time there had been no significant work from his pen. But in 1820 he moved to London, where he renewed the acquaintance with Lamb which he had made in earlier days and learned from him much about the English prose-writers of the seventeenth century, Browne, Fuller, and Taylor.

De Quincey's *Confessions of an English Opium Eater* appeared in 1821. He had taken enormous quantities of opium at one time (1813); but had greatly reduced the daily allowance before his marriage, although there had been some relapses. The book sold very well; it was authentically intimate in a sensational way; it was exciting and romantic in its account of De Quincey's early days when he had fled to London from school and college; and it was written in a beautiful prose style—rich, sensuous, imaginative, and pulsing with a singular driving power. The remainder of De Quincey's output was originally written for periodicals, particularly *Blackwood's Magazine;* it consists of essays on personal, political, social, critical, and historical subjects; some might even be called philosophical essays. Of these essays *The English Mail Coach; Suspiria de Profundis,* a sequel to the *Confessions; The Flight of a Tartar Tribe; Murder Considered as One of the Fine Arts;* and *Joan of Arc* are the best known.

De Quincey moved to Edinburgh in middle age, and remained there until his death on December 8, 1859. He was extremely quiet and secluded in his living, entertaining but rarely, though impressively. All this was in keeping with his gentle, scholarly, eccentric character. The desire for solitude amounted at times almost to a craze, for he would abandon his living quarters and go away to some other place, locking his study-door behind him. Six such apartments, locked and stuffed with papers, were discovered after his death. Yet in spite of his eccentricity, all who met him were impressed by his courtesy, his generosity, his charm, and his tolerance.

De Quincey never became an extremist of any political party, but his drift was toward liberalism. More accurately, he went from liberal conservative to conservative liberal; never by any stretch of the imagination could he be called radical. He rather fancied himself as a political writer, and his historical writings have some permanence. His great contribution, however, lay in his general writings on personal topics; the more subjective De Quincey is, as a rule, the better he writes. That should be expected of the romanticist; and a romanticist De Quincey surely was. Give his imagination sea-room, and his heart and pen would do the rest.

De Quincey's style is his chief monument. Now it can be profuse and discursive; now the writing of a scholar, a wit, a man of the world. Always it is polished, and as De Quincey himself called it, "impassioned" prose. He was proud of his calling as a writer, for he regarded literature as the greatest of the arts. His own classification of his works is significant: *"first,* that class which proposes primarily to amuse the reader; *second,* papers which address themselves purely to the understanding as an insulated faculty, or do so primarily [in this group would fall his historical and political essays]; *third,* in virtue of their aim, as a far higher class of compositions, modes of impassioned prose ranging under no precedents that I am aware of in any literature." To this last group De Quincey's best work belongs. He errs in considering such impassioned prose original with him; but no one else has managed to maintain such a lofty flight in prose for so long a time.

"There is, first," said De Quincey (p. 394), "the literature of knowledge, and, secondly, the literature of power. The function of the first is to teach; the function of the second is to move; the first is a rudder; the second, an oar or a sail." De Quincey's best work, like the best work of any great romanticist, belongs to the literature of power.

Confessions of an English Opium Eater

from PRELIMINARY CONFESSIONS
* * * * *

I HAVE often been asked how I first came to be a regular opium eater; and have suffered, very unjustly, in the opinion of my acquaintance, from being reputed to have brought upon myself all the sufferings which I shall have to record, by a long course of indulgence in this practice purely for the sake of creating an artificial state of pleasurable excitement. This, however, is a misrepresentation of my case. True it is, that for nearly ten years I did occasionally take opium for the sake of the exquisite pleasure it gave me: but, so long as I took it with this view, I was effectually protected from all material bad consequences, by the necessity of interposing long intervals between the several acts of indulgence, in order to renew the pleasurable sensations. It was not for the purpose of creating pleasure, but of mitigating pain in the severest degree, that I first began to use opium as an article of daily diet. In the twenty-eighth year of my age, a most painful affection of the stomach, which I had first experienced about ten years before, attacked me in great strength. This affection had originally been caused by extremities of hunger, suffered in my boyish days. During the season of hope and redundant happiness which succeeded (that is, from eighteen to twenty-four) it had slumbered; for the three following years it had revived at intervals; and now, under unfavorable circumstances, from depression of spirits, it attacked me with a violence that yielded to no remedies but opium. As the youthful sufferings which first produced this derangement of the stomach were interesting in themselves and in the circumstances that attended them, I shall here briefly retrace them.

My father died when I was about seven years old, and left me to the care of four guardians. I was sent to various schools, great and small; and was very early distinguished for my classical attainments, especially for my knowledge of Greek. At thirteen I wrote Greek with ease; and at fifteen my command of that language was so great that I not only composed Greek verses in lyric meters, but could converse in Greek fluently and without embarrassment—an accomplishment which I have not since met with in any scholar of my times, and which, in my case, was owing to the practice of daily reading off the newspapers into the best Greek I could furnish *extempore;* for the necessity of ransacking my memory and invention, for all sorts and combinations of periphrastic expressions, as equivalents for modern ideas, images, relations of things, etc., gave me a compass of diction which would never have been called out by a dull translation of moral essays, etc. "That boy," said one of my masters, pointing the attention of a stranger to me, "that boy could harangue an Athenian mob better than you and I could address an English one." He who honored me with this eulogy was a scholar, "and a ripe and good one"; and of all my tutors was the only one whom I loved or reverenced. Unfortunately for me (and, as I afterwards learned, to this worthy man's great indignation) I was transferred to the care, first of a blockhead, who was in a perpetual panic, lest I should expose his ignorance; and finally to that of a respectable scholar, at the head of a great school on an ancient foundation. This man had been appointed to his situation by [Brasenose] College, Oxford; and was a sound, well-built scholar, but (like most men whom I have known from that college) coarse, clumsy, and inelegant. A miserable contrast he presented, in my eyes, to the Etonian brilliancy of my favorite master; and beside, he could not disguise from my hourly notice the poverty and meagerness of his understanding. It is a bad thing for a boy to be, and to know himself, far beyond his tutors, whether in knowledge or in power of mind. This was the case, so far as regarded knowledge at least, not with myself only, for the two boys who jointly with myself composed the first form were better Grecians than the headmaster, though not more elegant scholars, nor at all more accustomed to sacrifice to the graces. When I first entered, I remember that we read Sophocles; and it was a constant matter of triumph to us, the learned triumvirate of the first form, to see our "Archididascalus" (as he loved to be called) conning our lessons before we went up, and laying

---

31. **My father,** Thomas De Quincey, a merchant of Manchester, who died July 18, 1793. 33. **various schools.** At Bath, at Winkfield, and at Manchester.

53. **one . . . masters,** Mr. Morgan, master of Bath School. 58. **"and . . . one,"** Shakespeare, *Henry VIII*, IV, ii, 51. 63. **blockhead,** Mr. Spencer, master of Winkfield School. 65. **respectable scholar,** Mr. Charles Lawson, master of Manchester School, founded by Hugh Oldham, Bishop of Exeter, in 1519. 68. **[Brasenose.]** The name of the college has been supplied from the 1856 edition of the *Confessions*. 72. **Etonian brilliancy,** an allusion to the emphasis placed upon classical training at Eton. 86. **Sophocles,** one of the greatest tragic poets of Greece (fifth century B.C.). 88. **"Archididascalus,"** a Greek word meaning *head master*.

a regular train, with lexicon and grammar, for blowing up and blasting (as it were) any difficulties he found in the choruses; whilst *we* never condescended to open our books until the moment of going up, and were generally employed in writing epigrams upon his wig, or some such important matter. My two class-fellows were poor and dependent for their future prospects at the university on the recommendation of the head-master; but I, who had a small patrimonial property, the income of which was sufficient to support me at college, wished to be sent thither immediately. I made earnest representations on the subject to my guardians, but all to no purpose. One, who was more reasonable and had more knowledge of the world than the rest, lived at a distance; two of the other three resigned all their authority into the hands of the fourth; and this fourth with whom I had to negotiate was a worthy man, in his way, but haughty, obstinate, and intolerant of all opposition to his will. After a certain number of letters and personal interviews, I found that I had nothing to hope for, not even a compromise of the matter, from my guardian; unconditional submission was what he demanded; and I prepared myself, therefore, for other measures. Summer was now coming on with hasty steps, and my seventeenth birthday was fast approaching; after which day I had sworn within myself that I would no longer be numbered amongst schoolboys. Money being what I chiefly wanted, I wrote to a woman of high rank, who, though young herself, had known me from a child, and had latterly treated me with great distinction, requesting that she would "lend" me five guineas. For upwards of a week no answer came; and I was beginning to despond, when, at length, a servant put into my hands a double letter, with a coronet on the seal. The letter was kind and obliging; the fair writer was on the seacoast, and in that way the delay had arisen; she enclosed double of what I had asked, and good-naturedly hinted that if I should *never* repay her, it would not absolutely ruin her. Now then, I was prepared for my scheme; ten guineas, added to about two which I had remaining from my pocket money, seemed to me sufficient for an indefinite length of time; and at that happy age, if no *definite* boundary can be assigned to one's power, the spirit of hope and pleasure makes it virtually infinite.

It is a just remark of Dr. Johnson's (and what cannot often be said of his remarks, it is a very feeling one), that we never do anything consciously for the last time (of things, that is, which we have long been in the habit of doing) without sadness of heart. This truth I felt deeply, when I came to leave Manchester Grammar School, a place which I did not love, and where I had not been happy. On the evening before I left Manchester forever, I grieved when the ancient and lofty school-room resounded with the evening service, performed for the last time in my hearing and at night, when the muster-roll of names was called over, and mine (as usual) was called first, I stepped forward, and, passing the head-master, who was standing by, I bowed to him, and looked earnestly in his face, thinking to myself, "He is old and infirm, and in this world I shall not see him again." I was right: I never *did* see him again, nor ever shall. He looked at me complacently, smiled good-naturedly, returned my salutation (or rather, my valediction), and we parted (though he knew it not) forever. I could not reverence him intellectually; but he had been uniformly kind to me and had allowed me many indulgences; and I grieved at the thought of the mortification I should inflict upon him.

The morning came which was to launch me into the world, and from which my whole succeeding life has, in many important points, taken its coloring. I lodged in the head-master's house, and had been allowed, from my first entrance, the indulgence of a private room, which I used both as a sleeping room and as a study. At half after three I rose, and gazed with deep emotion at the ancient towers of the College Church, "dressed in earliest light," and be-

---

20. **the fourth**, the Reverend Samuel Hall, curate of Salford, a part of Manchester. 35. **woman . . . rank**, Lady Carbery, a friend of De Quincey's mother. 39. **five guineas**, now more than $25. 56. **remark of Dr. Johnson's**. Found in *The Idler*. No. 103 (the last paper). 94. **towers**. Now the Manchester Cathedral.

ginning to crimson with the radiant luster of a cloudless July morning. I was firm and immovable in my purpose; but yet agitated by anticipation of uncertain danger and troubles; and, if I could have foreseen the hurricane and perfect hailstorm of affliction which soon fell upon me, well might I have been agitated. To this agitation the deep peace of the morning presented an affecting contrast, and in some degree a medicine. The silence was more profound than that of midnight; and to me the silence of a summer morning is more touching than all other silence, because, the light being broad and strong, as that of noon-day at other seasons of the year, it seems to differ from perfect day, chiefly because man is not yet abroad; and thus, the peace of nature, and of the innocent creatures of God, seems to be secure and deep, only so long as the presence of man, and his restless and unquiet spirit, are not there to trouble its sanctity. I dressed myself, took my hat and gloves, and lingered a little in the room. For the last year and a half this room had been my "pensive citadel"; here I had read and studied through all the hours of night; and, though true it was, that for the latter part of this time I, who was framed for love and gentle affections, had lost my gayety and happiness, during the strife and fever of contention with my guardian; yet, on the other hand, as a boy, so passionately fond of books, and dedicated to intellectual pursuits, I could not fail to have enjoyed many happy hours in the midst of general dejection. I wept as I looked round on the chair, hearth, writing-table, and other familiar objects, knowing too certainly, that I looked upon them for the last time. Whilst I write this, it is eighteen years ago; and yet, at this moment, I see distinctly, as if it were yesterday, the lineaments and expression of the object on which I fixed my parting gaze; it was a picture of the lovely ——, which hung over the mantlepiece; the eyes and mouth of which were so beautiful, and the whole countenance so radiant with benignity and divine tranquillity, that I had a thousand times laid down my pen, or my book, to gather consolation from it, as a devotee from his patron saint. Whilst I was yet gazing upon it, the deep tones of Manchester clock proclaimed that it was four o'clock. I went up to the picture, kissed it, and then gently walked out, and closed the door forever!

* * * * *

Meantime, what had become of poor Ann? For her I have reserved my concluding words: according to our agreement, I sought her daily, and waited for her every night, so long as I stayed in London, at the corner of Titchfield Street. I inquired for her of everyone who was likely to know her; and during the last hours of my stay in London I put into activity every means of tracing her that my knowledge of London suggested, and the limited extent of my power made possible. The street where she had lodged I knew, but not the house: and I remembered at last some account which she had given me of ill treatment from her landlord, which made it probable that she had quitted those lodgings before we parted. She had few acquaintance; most people, besides, thought that the earnestness of my inquiries arose from motives which moved their laughter, or their slight regard; and others, thinking I was in chase of a girl who had robbed me of some trifles, were naturally and excusably indisposed to give me any clue to her, if, indeed, they had any to give. Finally, as my despairing resource, on the day I left London I put into the hands of the only person who (I was sure) must know Ann by sight, from having been in company with us once or twice, an address to —— in ——shire, at that time the residence of my family. But, to this hour, I have never heard a syllable about her. This, amongst such troubles as most men meet with in this life, has been my heaviest affliction.—If she lived, doubtless we must have been sometimes in search of each other, at the very same moment, through the mighty labyrinths of London; perhaps even within a few feet of each other—a barrier no wider in

---

12. **silence . . . morning.** Cf. p. 385, ll. 52 ff.; also p. 386, ll. 26 ff. 25. **"pensive citadel,"** Wordsworth, *Nuns Fret Not*, l. 3, p. 159. 43. **the lovely——,** a portrait of an unknown lady. 54. **the door forever.** De Quincey then departed for London. 56. **Ann,** a young street-walker who befriended De Quincey when as a youth he was adrift in London. 84. **to——,** to St. John's Priory in Chester, Cheshire.

a London street often amounting in the end to a separation for eternity! During some years, I hoped that she *did* live; and I suppose that, in the literal and unrhetorical use of the word *myriad,* I may say that on my different visits to London, I have looked into many, many myriads of female faces, in the hope of meeting her. I should know her again amongst a thousand, if I saw her for a moment; for, though not handsome, she had a sweet expression of countenance, and a peculiar and graceful carriage of the head.—I sought her, I have said, in hope. So it was for years; but now I should fear to see her; and her cough, which grieved me when I parted with her, is now my consolation. I now wish to see her no longer; but think of her, more gladly, as one long since laid in the grave; in the grave, I would hope, of a Magdalen; taken away, before injuries and cruelty had blotted out and transfigured her ingenuous nature, or the brutalities of ruffians had completed the ruin they had begun.

So then, Oxford Street, stony-hearted stepmother! thou that listenest to the sighs of orphans, and drinkest the tears of children, at length I was dismissed from thee; the time was come at last that I no more should pace in anguish thy never-ending terraces; no more should dream, and wake in captivity to the pangs of hunger. Successors, too many, to myself and Ann, have, doubtless, since trodden in our footsteps—inheritors of our calamities; other orphans than Ann have sighed; tears have been shed by other children; and thou, Oxford Street, hast since, doubtless, echoed to the groans of innumerable hearts. For myself, however, the storm which I had outlived seemed to have been the pledge of a long fair-weather; the premature sufferings which I had paid down to have been accepted as a ransom for many years to come, as a price of long immunity from sorrow; and if again I walked in London, a solitary and contemplative man (as oftentimes I did), I walked for the most part in serenity and peace of mind. And, although it is true that the calamities of my noviciate in London had struck root so deeply in my bodily constitution that afterwards they shot up and flourished afresh, and grew into a noxious umbrage that has overshadowed and darkened my latter years, yet these second assaults of suffering were met with a fortitude more confirmed, with the resources of a maturer intellect, and with alleviations from sympathizing affection—how deep and tender!

Thus, however, with whatsoever alleviations, years that were far asunder were bound together by subtle links of suffering derived from a common root. And herein I notice an instance of the short-sightedness of human desires, that oftentimes on moonlight nights, during my first mournful abode in London, my consolation was (if such it could be thought) to gaze from Oxford Street up every avenue in succession which pierces through the heart of Marylebone to the fields and the woods; "and *that,*" said I, traveling with my eyes up the long vistas which lay part in light and part in shade, "*that* is the road to the north, and therefore to [Grasmere], and if I had the wings of a dove, *that* way I would fly for comfort." Thus I said, and thus I wished, in my blindness; yet, even in that very northern region it was, even in that very valley, nay, in that very house to which my erronous wishes pointed, that this second birth of my sufferings began; and that they again threatened to besiege the citadel of life and hope. There it was that for years I was persecuted by visions as ugly, and as ghastly phantoms as ever haunted the couch of Orestes; and in this unhappier than he, that sleep which comes to all as a respite and a restoration, and to him especially, as a blessed balm for his wounded heart and his haunted brain, visited me as my bitterest scourge. Thus blind was I in my desires; yet, if a veil interposes between the dimsightedness of man and his future calamities,

---

19. **Magdalen,** Mary Magdalen, traditionally regarded as the repentant sinner forgiven by Christ. See *Luke,* 7:36. 29. **terraces,** ranges, or rows, of houses.

48. **noviciate,** time of probation as a novice. 68. **Marylebone,** a section of London. 72. **Grasmere,** a village in Westmoreland, long the home of Wordsworth (see p. 119). 73. **wings ... comfort.** From *Psalms,* 55:6. 78. **second ... sufferings.** This was in 1817; the first period of De Quincey's sufferings was in 1813-1814. 83. **Orestes,** son of the Greek king Agamemnon and Clytemnestra. After he had slain his mother and her lover in vengeance for their murder of his father, Orestes was pursued by the Furies, called the Eumenides. He is the hero of *Orestes,* a Greek tragedy by Euripides (fifth century B.C.),

the same veil hides from him their alleviations; and a grief which had not been feared is met by consolations which had not been hoped. I, therefore, who participated, as it were, in the troubles of Orestes (excepting only in his agitated conscience), participated no less in all his supports: my Eumenides, like his, were at my bed-feet, and stared in upon me through the curtains: but, watching by my pillow, or defrauding herself of sleep to bear me company through the heavy watches of the night, sat my Electra: for thou, beloved [Margaret], dear companion of my later years, thou wast my Electra! and neither in nobility of mind nor in long-suffering affection wouldst permit that a Grecian sister should excel an English wife. For thou thoughtest not much to stoop to humble offices of kindness, and to servile ministrations of tenderest affection;—to wipe away for years the unwholesome dews upon the forehead, or to refresh the lips when parched and baked with fever; nor, even when thy own peaceful slumbers had by long sympathy become infected with the spectacle of my dread contest with phantoms and shadowy enemies that oftentimes bade me "sleep no more!"—not even then didst thou utter a complaint or any murmur, nor withdraw thy angelic smiles, nor shrink from thy service of love more than Electra did of old. For she too, though she was a Grecian woman, and the daughter of the king of men, yet wept sometimes, and hid her face in her robe.

But these troubles are past; and thou wilt read these records of a period so dolorous to us both as the legend of some hideous dream that can return no more. Meantime, I am again in London; and again I pace the terraces of Oxford Street by night: and oftentimes, when I am oppressed by anxieties that demand all my philosophy and the comfort of thy presence to support, and yet remember that I am separated from thee by three hundred miles, and the length of three dreary months—I look up the streets that run northwards from Oxford Street, upon moonlight nights, and recollect my youthful ejaculation of anguish;—and remembering that thou art sitting alone in that same valley, and mistress of that very house to which my heart turned in its blindness nineteen years ago, I think that, though blind indeed, and scattered to the winds of late, the promptings of my heart may yet have had reference to a remoter time, and may be justified if read in another meaning—and, if I could allow myself to descend again to the impotent wishes of childhood, I should again say to myself, as I look to the north, "Oh, that I had the wings of a dove—" and with how just a confidence in thy good and gracious nature might I add the other half of my early ejaculation—"And *that* way I would fly for comfort." . . .

But now farewell, a long farewell, to happiness, winter or summer! farewell to smiles and laughter! farewell to peace of mind! farewell to hope and to tranquil dreams, and to the blessed consolations of sleep! For more than three years and a half I am summoned away from these, I am now arrived at an Iliad of woes: for I have now to record

THE PAINS OF OPIUM

"—as when some great painter dips
His pencil in the gloom of earthquake and
  eclipse"

* * * * *

I now pass to what is the main subject of these latter confessions, to the history and journal of what took place in my dreams; for these were the immediate and proximate cause of my acutest suffering.

The first notice I had of any important change going on in this part of my physical economy was from the reawakening of a state of eye generally incident to childhood, or exalted states of irritability. I know not whether my reader is aware that many children, perhaps most, have a power of painting, as it were, upon the darkness, all sorts of phantoms:

---

12. **Electra**, the heroine of *Electra*, a Greek tragedy by Sophocles in the fifth century B.C. (see p. 379, l. 83, and note). Margaret was De Quincey's wife; she died in 1837. 26. **"sleep no more!"** From *Macbeth*, II, ii. 35; words that Macbeth heard just after he had killed Duncan. 32. **king of men**, Agamemnon.

70. **Iliad of woes**, unnumbered woes; in allusion to the opening lines of Homer's *Iliad*. 72. **"—as when, etc.,"** from Shelley's *Revolt of Islam*, Canto 5, stanza 23. 74. **I now pass**, after mentioning the intellectual torpor induced by excessive use of opium.

in some that power is simply a mechanic affection of the eye; others have a voluntary or a semi-voluntary power to dismiss or to summon them; or, as a child once said to me when I questioned him on this matter, "I can tell them to go, and they go; but sometimes they come when I don't tell them to come." Whereupon I told him that he had almost as unlimited a command over apparitions as a Roman centurion over his soldiers.—In the middle of 1817, I think it was, that this faculty became positively distressing to me: at night, when I lay awake in bed, vast processions passed along in mournful pomp; friezes of never-ending stories, that to my feelings were as sad and solemn as if they were stories drawn from times before Oedipus or Priam, before Tyre, before Memphis. And, at the same time, a corresponding change took place in my dreams; a theater seemed suddenly opened and lighted up within my brain, which presented, nightly, spectacles of more than earthly splendor. And the four following facts may be mentioned, as noticeable at this time:

1. That, as the creative state of the eye increased, a sympathy seemed to arise between the waking and the dreaming states of the brain in one point—that whatsoever I happened to call up and to trace by a voluntary act upon the darkness was very apt to transfer itself to my dreams; so that I feared to exercise this faculty; for, as Midas turned all things to gold, that yet baffled his hopes and defrauded his human desires, so whatsoever things capable of being visually represented I did but think of in the darkness, immediately shaped themselves into phantoms of the eye; and, by a process apparently no less inevitable, when thus once traced in faint and visionary colors, like writings in sympathetic ink, they were drawn out, by the fierce chemistry of my dreams, into insufferable splendor that fretted my heart.

2. For this and all other changes in my dreams were accompanied by deep-seated anxiety and gloomy melancholy, such as are wholly incommunicable by words. I seemed every night to descend—not metaphorically, but literally to descend—into chasms and sunless abysses, depths below depths, from which it seemed hopeless that I could ever reascend. Nor did I, by waking, feel that I *had* reascended. This I do not dwell upon; because the state of gloom which attended these gorgeous spectacles, amounting at least to utter darkness, as of some suicidal despondency, cannot be approached by words.

3. The sense of space and in the end the sense of time were both powerfully affected. Buildings, landscapes, etc., were exhibited in proportions so vast as the bodily eye is not fitted to receive. Space swelled, and was amplified to an extent of unutterable infinity. This, however, did not disturb me so much as the vast expansion of time. I sometimes seemed to have lived for seventy or one hundred years in one night; nay, sometimes had feelings representative of a millennium, passed in that time, or, however, of a duration far beyond the limits of any human experience.

4. The minutest incidents of childhood, or forgotten scenes of later years, were often revived. I could not be said to recollect them; for if I had been told of them when waking, I should not have been able to acknowledge them as parts of my past experience. But placed as they were before me, in dreams like intuitions, and clothed in all their evanescent circumstances and accompanying feelings, I *recognized* them instantaneously. I was once told by a near relative of mine that having in her childhood fallen into a river, and being on the very verge of death but for the critical assistance which reached her, she saw in a moment her whole life, in its minutest incidents, arrayed before her simultaneously as in a mirror; and she had a faculty developed as suddenly for comprehending the whole and every part. This, from some opium experiences of mine, I can believe; I have, indeed, seen the same thing asserted twice in modern books, and accompanied by a remark which

---

10. **centurion.** In the armies of ancient Rome, the centurion was the captain of a century, or company of a hundred men. 17. **Oedipus, etc.** Oedipus was a legendary king of Thebes; Priam, a legendary king of Troy. Tyre was an ancient city of Phoenicia; Memphis, the ancient capital of Egypt. 32. **Midas,** a mythological king of Phrygia, who was granted the power of changing to gold everything he touched. For favoring Pan rather than Apollo in a musical contest, Apollo changed his ears into ass's ears. 40. **sympathetic ink,** a fluid for invisible writing, which becomes visible when heated.

I am convinced is true, namely, that the dread book of account which the Scriptures speak of is, in fact, the mind itself of each individual. Of this, at least, I feel assured, that there is no such thing as *forgetting* possible to the mind; a thousand accidents may and will interpose a veil between our present consciousness and the secret inscriptions on the mind; accidents of the same sort will also rend away this veil; but alike, whether veiled or unveiled, the inscription remains forever; just as the stars seem to withdraw before the common light of day, whereas, in fact, we all know that it is the light which is drawn over them as a veil, and that they are waiting to be revealed, when the obscuring daylight shall have withdrawn.

Having noticed these four facts as memorably distinguishing my dreams from those of health, I shall now cite a case illustrative of the first fact; and shall then cite any others that I remember, either in their chronological order, or any other that may give them more effect as pictures to the reader.

I had been in youth, and ever since for occasional amusement, a great reader of Livy, whom I confess that I prefer, both for style and matter, to any other of the Roman historians; and I had often felt as most solemn and appalling sounds, and most emphatically representative of the majesty of the Roman people, the two words so often occurring in Livy—*Consul Romanus;* especially when the consul is introduced in his military character. I mean to say, that the words *king, sultan, regent,* etc., or any other titles of those who embody in their own persons the collective majesty of a great people, had less power over my reverential feelings. I had also, though no great reader of history, made myself minutely and critically familiar with one period of English history, namely, the period of the Parliamentary War, having been attracted by the moral grandeur of some who figured in that day, and by the many interesting memoirs which survive those unquiet times. Both these parts of my lighter reading, having furnished me often with matter of reflection, now furnished me with matter for my dreams. Often I used to see, after painting upon the blank darkness a sort of rehearsal whilst waking, a crowd of ladies, and perhaps a festival, and dances. And I heard it said, or I said to myself, "These are English ladies from the unhappy times of Charles I. These are the wives and daughters of those who met in peace, and sat at the same tables, and were allied by marriage or by blood; and yet, after a certain day in August, 1642, never smiled upon each other again, nor met but in the field of battle; and at Marston Moor, at Newbury, or at Naseby, cut asunder all ties of love by the cruel saber, and washed away in blood the memory of ancient friendship." The ladies danced, and looked as lovely as at the court of George IV. Yet I knew, even in my dream, that they had been in the grave for nearly two centuries. This pageant would suddenly dissolve; and, at a clapping of hands, would be heard the heartquaking sound of *Consul Romanus;* and immediately came "sweeping by," in gorgeous paludaments, Paulus, or Marius girt round by a company of centurions, with the crimson tunic hoisted on a spear, and followed by the *alalagmos* of the Roman legions.

Many years ago, when I was looking over Piranesi's *Antiquities of Rome,* Mr. Coleridge, who was standing by, described to me a set of plates by that artist, called his *Dreams,* and which record the scenery of his own visions during the delirium of a fever: some of them (I describe only from memory of Mr. Coleridge's account) representing vast Gothic halls; on the floor of which stood all sorts of engines and machinery, wheels, cables, pulleys, levers, catapults, etc., etc., expressive of enormous power put forth, and resistance overcome. Creeping along the sides of the walls, you perceived a staircase; and upon it, groping his way upwards, was Piranesi himself. Fol-

---

1. **dread . . . account,** the book of life, in which human deeds are recorded. See *Revelation,* 20:12. 25. **Livy,** a famous Roman historian (59 B.C.-17 A.D.). 41. **Parliamentary War,** that between Charles I and the Parliamentary party; it began in 1642. See Vol. I, pp. 631 ff. 60. **Marston Moor,** in Yorkshire, scene of a battle on July 2, 1644. **Newbury,** in Berkshire, scene of two battles—September, 1643. and October, 1644. **Naseby,** in Northamptonshire, scene of a battle in 1645. 64. **George IV,** King of England (1820-1830). 70. **"sweeping by,"** *Il Penseroso,* l. 98. 71. **paludaments,** military cloaks worn by officers. **Paulus, Marius,** Roman generals (second century B.C.). 73. **tunic . . . spear.** A signal for battle. 74. **alalagmos,** the collective Roman war cries; originally the war cry of the Greeks. 76. **Piranesi,** an Italian engraver (1720-1778).

low the stairs a little further, and you perceive it to come to a sudden, abrupt termination, without any balustrade, and allowing no step onwards to him who had reached the extremity, except into the depths below. Whatever is to become of poor Piranesi, you suppose, at least, that his labors must in some way terminate here. But raise your eyes, and behold a second flight of stairs still higher; on which again Piranesi is perceived, by this time standing on the very brink of the abyss. Again elevate your eye, and a still more aërial flight of stairs is beheld; and again is poor Piranesi busy on his aspiring labors; and so on, until the unfinished stairs and Piranesi both are lost in the upper gloom of the hall. With the same power of endless growth and self-reproduction did my architecture proceed in dreams. In the early stage of my malady, the splendors of my dreams were indeed chiefly architectural; and I beheld such pomp of cities and palaces as was never yet beheld by the waking eye, unless in the clouds. From a great modern poet I cite the part of a passage which describes, as an appearance actually beheld in the clouds, what in many of its circumstances I saw frequently in sleep:

> The appearance, instantaneously disclosed,
> Was of a mighty city—boldly say
> A wilderness of building, sinking far
> And self-withdrawn into a wondrous depth,
> Far sinking into splendor—without end!
> Fabric it seemed of diamond, and of gold,
> With alabaster domes and silver spires,
> And blazing terrace upon terrace, high
> Uplifted; here, serene pavilions bright,
> In avenues disposed; there towers begirt
> With battlements that on their restless fronts
> Bore stars—illumination of all gems!
> By earthly nature had the effect been wrought
> Upon the dark materials of the storm
> Now pacified; on them, and on the coves,
> And mountain-steeps and summits, whereunto
> The vapors had receded—taking there
> Their station under a cerulean sky, etc.

The sublime circumstance—"battlements that on their *restless* fronts bore stars"— might have been copied from my architectural dreams, for it often occurred. We hear it reported of Dryden, and of Fuseli in modern times, that they thought proper to eat raw meat for the sake of obtaining splendid dreams: how much better, for such a purpose, to have eaten opium, which yet I do not remember that any poet is recorded to have done, except the dramatist Shadwell; and in ancient days, Homer is, I think, rightly reputed to have known the virtues of opium.

To my architecture succeeded dreams of lakes and silvery expanses of water: these haunted me so much, that I feared (though possibly it will appear ludicrous to a medical man) that some dropsical state or tendency of the brain might thus be making itself (to use a metaphysical word) *objective* and the sentient organ *project* itself as its own object. For two months I suffered greatly in my head—a part of my bodily structure which had hitherto been so clear from all touch or taint of weakness (physically, I mean) that I used to say of it, as the last Lord Orford said of his stomach, that it seemed likely to survive the rest of my person. Till now I had never felt a headache even, or any the slightest pain, except rheumatic pains caused by my own folly. However, I got over this attack, though it must have been verging on something very dangerous.

The waters now changed their character —from translucent lakes, shining like mirrors, they now became seas and oceans. And now came a tremendous change, which, unfolding itself slowly like a scroll, through many months, promised an abiding torment; and, in fact, it never left me until the winding up of my case. Hitherto the human face had

---

28. **The appearance, etc.,** Wordsworth, *The Excursion*, II, 834 ff. 50. **Dryden.** See Vol. I, p. 858. **Fuseli,** John Henry Fuseli (1741-1825), a Swiss painter and art critic, who lived most of his life in England. 56. **Shadwell,** Thomas Shadwell (1640-1692), a Restoration dramatist; he was satirized in Dryden's *MacFlecknoe* (Vol. I, p. 864). 57. **Homer . . . opium.** In the *Odyssey* of Homer (IV, 220-221) Helen gives Telemachus a drug that banishes sorrow. This has been thought to be opium. 71. **last Lord Orford,** Horace Walpole (1717-1797), fourth Earl of Orford. See p. 23.

mixed often in my dreams, but not despotically, nor with any special power of tormenting. But now that which I have called the tyranny of the human face began to unfold itself. Perhaps some part of my London life might be answerable for this. Be that as it may, now it was that upon the rocking waters of the ocean the human face began to appear; the sea appeared paved with innumerable faces, upturned to the heavens; faces imploring, wrathful, despairing, surged upwards by thousands, by myriads, by generations, by centuries: my agitation was infinite, my mind tossed, and surged with the ocean.

May, 1818.—The Malay has been a fearful enemy for months. I have been every night, through his means, transported into Asiatic scenes. I know not whether others share in my feelings on this point; but I have often thought that if I were compelled to forego England, and to live in China, and among Chinese manners and modes of life and scenery, I should go mad. The causes of my horror lie deep, and some of them must be common to others. Southern Asia, in general, is the seat of awful images and associations. As the cradle of the human race, it would alone have a dim and reverential feeling connected with it. But there are other reasons. No man can pretend that the wild, barbarous, and capricious superstitions of Africa, or of savage tribes elsewhere, affect him in the way that he is affected by the ancient, monumental, cruel, and elaborate religions of Indostan, etc. The mere antiquity of Asiatic things, of their institutions, histories, modes of faith, etc., is so impressive, that to me the vast age of the race and name overpowers the sense of youth in the individual. A young Chinese seems to me an antediluvian man renewed. Even Englishmen, though not bred in any knowledge of such institutions, cannot but shudder at the mystic sublimity of *castes* that have flowed apart, and refused to mix, through such immemorial tracts of time; nor can any man fail to be awed by the names of the Ganges, or the Euphrates. It contributes much to these feelings, that Southern Asia is, and has been for thousands of years, the part of the earth most swarming with human life, the great *officina gentium*. Man is a weed in those regions. The vast empires, also, into which the enormous population of Asia has always been cast, give a further sublimity to the feelings associated with all oriental names or images. In China, over and above what it has in common with the rest of Southern Asia, I am terrified by the modes of life, by the manners, and the barrier of utter abhorrence, and want of sympathy, placed between us by feelings deeper than I can analyze. I could sooner live with lunatics, or brute animals. All this, and much more than I can say, or have time to say, the reader must enter into, before he can comprehend the unimaginable horror which these dreams of oriental imagery, and mythological tortures, impressed upon me. Under the connecting feeling of tropical heat and vertical sunlights, I brought together all creatures, birds, beasts, reptiles, all trees and plants, usages and appearances, that are found in all tropical regions, and assembled them together in China or Indostan. From kindred feelings, I soon brought Egypt and all her gods under the same law. I was stared at, hooted at, grinned at, chattered at, by monkeys, by paroquets, by cockatoos. I ran into pagodas, and was fixed, for centuries, at the summit, or in secret rooms: I was the idol; I was the priest; I was worshiped; I was sacrificed. I fled from the wrath of Brama through all the forests of Asia: Vishnu hated me; Seeva laid wait for me. I came suddenly upon Isis and Osiris; I had done a deed, they said, which the ibis and the crocodile trembled at. I was buried for a thousand years in stone coffins, with mummies and sphinxes, in narrow chambers at the heart of eternal pyramids. I was kissed, with cancerous kisses, by crocodiles; and laid, confounded with all unutterable slimy things, amongst reeds and Nilotic mud.

35. **Indostan,** India. 47. **Ganges,** the sacred river in northern India. 48. **Euphrates,** a river in southwestern Asia. 52. *officina gentium,* beehive of nations. 83. **Brama, etc.** Brahma, the creator, Vishnu, the protector, and Siva, the destroyer, constitute the so-called Triad of Hindu mythology. Osiris, the creator, and Isis, his sister and wife, were Egyptian deities. The ibis and the crocodile were sacred animals among the Egyptians. 93. **Nilotic,** belonging to the Nile.

I thus give the reader some slight abstraction of my oriental dreams, which always filled me with such amazement at the monstrous scenery that horror seemed absorbed, for a while, in sheer astonishment. Sooner or later came a reflux of feeling that swallowed up the astonishment, and left me, not so much in terror, as in hatred and abomination of what I saw. Over every form, and threat, and punishment, and dim sightless incarceration, brooded a sense of eternity and infinity that drove me into an oppression as of madness. Into these dreams only, it was, with one or two slight exceptions, that any circumstances of physical horror entered. All before had been moral and spiritual terrors. But here the main agents were ugly birds, or snakes, or crocodiles, especially the last. The cursed crocodile became to me the object of more horror than almost all the rest. I was compelled to live with him; and (as was always the case, almost, in my dreams) for centuries. I escaped sometimes, and found myself in Chinese houses with cane tables, etc. All the feet of the tables, sofas, etc., soon became instinct with life: the abominable head of the crocodile, and his leering eyes, looked out at me, multiplied into a thousand repetitions; and I stood loathing and fascinated. And so often did this hideous reptile haunt my dreams that many times the very same dream was broken up in the very same way: I heard gentle voices speaking to me (I hear everything when I am sleeping), and instantly I awoke: it was broad noon, and my children were standing, hand in hand, at my bedside; come to show me their colored shoes, or new frocks, or to let me see them dressed for going out. I protest that so awful was the transition from the damned crocodile, and the other unutterable monsters and abortions of my dreams, to the sight of innocent *human* natures and of infancy, that, in the mighty and sudden revulsion of mind, I wept, and could not forbear it, as I kissed their faces.

June, 1819.—I have had occasions to remark, at various periods of my life, that the deaths of those whom we love, and, indeed, the contemplation of death generally, is (*caeteris paribus*) more affecting in summer than in any other season of the year. And the reasons are these three, I think: first, that the visible heavens in summer appear far higher, more distant, and (if such a solecism may be excused) more infinite; the clouds by which chiefly the eye expounds the distance of the blue pavilion stretched over our heads are in summer more voluminous, massed, and accumulated in far grander and more towering piles; secondly, the light and the appearances of the declining and the setting sun are much more fitted to be types and characters of the infinite; and, thirdly (which is the main reason), the exuberant and riotous prodigality of life naturally forces the mind more powerfully upon the antagonist thought of death, and the wintry sterility of the grave. For it may be observed generally that, wherever two thoughts stand related to each other by a law of antagonism, and exist, as it were, by mutual repulsion, they are apt to suggest each other. On these accounts it is that I find it impossible to banish the thought of death when I am walking alone in the endless days of summer; and any particular death, if not more affecting, at least haunts my mind more obstinately and besiegingly in that season. Perhaps this cause, and a slight incident which I omit, might have been the immediate occasions of the following dream, to which, however, a predisposition must always have existed in my mind; but, having been once roused, it never left me, and split into a thousand fantastic varieties, which often suddenly reunited, and composed again the original dream.

I thought that it was a Sunday morning in May; that it was Easter Sunday, and as yet very early in the morning. I was standing, as it seemed to me, at the door of my own cottage. Right before me lay the very scene which could really be commanded from that situation, but exalted, as was usual, and solemnized by the power of dreams. There were the same mountains, and the same lovely valley at their feet; but the mountains were raised to more than Alpine height, and there was

---

50. *caeteris paribus,* other conditions being the same.

interspace far larger between them of meadows and forest lawns; the hedges were rich with white roses; and no living creature was to be seen, excepting that in the green churchyard there were cattle tranquilly reposing upon the verdant graves, and particularly round about the grave of a child whom I had tenderly loved, just as I had really beheld them, a little before sunrise in the same summer, when that child died. I gazed upon the well-known scene, and I said aloud (as I thought) to myself, "It yet wants much of sunrise; and it is Easter Sunday; and that is the day on which they celebrate the first-fruits of resurrection. I will walk abroad; old griefs shall be forgotten today; for the air is cool and still, and the hills are high, and stretch away to heaven; and the forest-glades are as quiet as the churchyard; and with the dew I can wash the fever from my forehead, and then I shall be unhappy no longer." And I turned, as if to open my garden gate; and immediately I saw upon the left a scene far different; but which yet the power of dreams had reconciled into harmony with the other. The scene was an Oriental one; and there also it was Easter Sunday, and very early in the morning. And at a vast distance were visible, as a stain upon the horizon, the domes and cupolas of a great city—an image or faint abstraction, caught perhaps in childhood from some picture of Jerusalem. And not a bow-shot from me, upon a stone, and shaded by Judean palms, there sat a woman; and I looked; and it was—Ann! She fixed her eyes upon me earnestly; and I said to her at length: "So then I have found you at last." I waited: but she answered me not a word. Her face was the same as when I saw it last, and yet again how different! Seventeen years ago, when the lamplight fell upon her face, as for the last time I kissed her lips (lips, Ann, that to me were not polluted), her eyes were streaming with tears: the tears were now wiped away; she seemed more beautiful than she was at that time, but in all other points the same, and not older. Her looks were tranquil, but with unusual solemnity of expression; and I now gazed upon her with some awe, but suddenly her countenance grew dim, and, turning to the mountains, I perceived vapors rolling between us; in a moment, all had vanished; thick darkness came on; and, in the twinkling of an eye, I was far away from mountains, and by lamplight in Oxford Street, walking again with Ann—just as we walked seventeen years before, when we were both children.

As a final specimen, I cite one of a different character, from 1820.

The dream commenced with a music which now I often heard in dreams—a music of preparation and of awakening suspense; a music like the opening of the Coronation Anthem, and which, like *that,* gave the feeling of a vast march—of infinite cavalcades filing off—and the tread of innumerable armies. The morning was come of a mighty day—a day of crisis and of final hope for human nature, then suffering some mysterious eclipse, and laboring in some dread extremity. Somewhere, I knew not where—somehow, I knew not how—by some beings, I knew not whom—a battle, a strife, an agony, was conducting—was evolving like a great drama, or piece of music; with which my sympathy was the more insupportable from my confusion as to its place, its cause, its nature, and its possible issue. I, as is usual in dreams (where, of necessity, we make ourselves central to every movement), had the power, and yet had not the power, to decide it. I had the power, if I could raise myself, to will it, and yet again had not the power, for the weight of twenty Atlantics was upon me, or the oppression of inexpiable guilt. "Deeper than ever plummet sounded," I lay inactive. Then, like a chorus, the passion deepened. Some greater interest was at stake; some mightier cause than ever yet the sword had pleaded, or trumpet had proclaimed. Then came sudden alarms: hurryings to and fro: trepidations of innumerable fugitives, I knew not whether from the good cause or the bad: darkness and lights: tempest and human faces: and at last, with the sense that all was lost, female

---

7. **child . . . loved,** Catherine Wordsworth.

86. **"Deeper . . . sounded,"** *The Tempest,* V, i, 56.

forms, and the features that were worth all the world to me, and but a moment allowed —and clasped hands, and heart-breaking partings, and then—everlasting farewells! and with a sigh, such as the caves of hell sighed when the incestuous mother uttered the abhorrent name of death, the sound was reverberated—everlasting farewells! and again, and yet again reverberated—everlasting farewells!

And I awoke in struggles, and cried aloud— "I will sleep no more!"   (*1820-22; 1821-22*)

6. **incestuous mother**, Sin. In *Paradise Lost*, II, 787 ff. (Vol. I, p. 738).

12. "I . . . more!" *Macbeth*, II, ii, 35; words heard by Macbeth just after he had killed Duncan.

On the Knocking at the Gate in Macbeth

FROM my boyish days I had always felt a great perplexity on one point in *Macbeth*. It was this: the knocking at the gate which succeeds to the murder of Duncan produced to my feelings an effect for which I never could account. The effect was that it reflected back upon the murderer a peculiar awfulness and a depth of solemnity; yet, however obstinately I endeavored with my understanding to comprehend this, for many years I never could see *why* it should produce such an effect.

Here I pause for one moment to exhort the reader never to pay any attention to his understanding when it stands in opposition to any other faculty of his mind. The mere understanding, however useful and indispensable, is the meanest faculty in the human mind and the most to be distrusted; and yet the great majority of people trust to nothing else —which may do for ordinary life, but not for philosophical purposes. Of this, out of ten thousand instances that I might produce, I will cite one. Ask of any person whatsoever who is not previously prepared for the demand by a knowledge of perspective, to draw in the rudest way the commonest appearance which depends upon the laws of that science —as, for instance, to represent the effect of two walls standing at right angles to each other, or the appearance of the houses on each side of a street, as seen by a person looking down the street from one extremity. Now, in all cases, unless the person has happened to observe in pictures how it is that artists produce these effects, he will be utterly unable to make the smallest approximation to it. Yet why? For he has actually seen the effect every day of his life. The reason is that he allows his understanding to overrule his eyes. His understanding, which includes no intuitive knowledge of the laws of vision, can furnish him with no reason why a line which is known and can be proved to be a horizontal line should not *appear* a horizontal line: a line that made any angle with the perpendicular less than a right angle would seem to him to indicate that his houses were all tumbling down together. Accordingly he makes the line of his houses a horizontal line, and fails of course to produce the effect demanded. Here then is one instance out of many, in which not only the understanding is allowed to overrule the eyes, but where the understanding is positively allowed to obliterate the eyes, as it were; for not only does the man believe the evidence of his understanding in opposition to that of his eyes, but (what is monstrous) the idiot is not aware that his eyes ever gave such evidence. He does not know that he has seen (and therefore *quoad* his consciousness has *not* seen) that which he *has* seen every day of his life.

But to return from this digression. My understanding could furnish no reason why the knocking at the gate in *Macbeth* should produce any effect, direct or reflected. In fact, my understanding said positively that it could *not* produce any effect. But I knew better; I felt that it did; and I waited and clung to

18. **meanest**, lowest.

61. **quoad his consciousness**, as far as his consciousness is concerned.

the problem until further knowledge should enable me to solve it. At length, in 1812, Mr. Williams made his *début* on the stage of Ratcliffe Highway, and executed those unparalleled murders which have procured for him such a brilliant and undying reputation. On which murders, by the way, I must observe, that in one respect they have had an ill effect, by making the connoisseur in murder very fastidious in his taste, and dissatisfied with anything that has been since done in that line. All other murders look pale by the deep crimson of his; and, as an amateur once said to me in a querulous tone, "There has been absolutely nothing *doing* since his time, or nothing that's worth speaking of." But this is wrong, for it is unreasonable to expect all men to be great artists, and born with the genius of Mr. Williams. Now it will be remembered that in the first of these murders (that of the Marrs) the same incident (of a knocking at the door soon after the work of extermination was complete) did actually occur which the genius of Shakespeare has invented; and all good judges, and the most eminent dilettanti, acknowledged the felicity of Shakespeare's suggestion as soon as it was actually realized. Here, then, was a fresh proof that I had been right in relying on my own feeling in opposition to my understanding; and again I set myself to study the problem. At length I solved it to my own satisfaction; and my solution is this—Murder, in ordinary cases, where the sympathy is wholly directed to the case of the murdered person, is an incident of coarse and vulgar horror; and for this reason—that it flings the interest exclusively upon the natural but ignoble instinct by which we cleave to life: an instinct which, as being indispensable to the primal law of self-preservation, is the same in kind (though different in degree) amongst all living creatures. This instinct, therefore, because it annihilates all distinctions, and degrades the greatest of men to the level of "the poor beetle that we tread on," exhibits human nature in its most abject and humiliating attitude. Such an attitude would little suit the purposes of the poet. What then must he do? He must throw the interest on the murderer. Our sympathy must be with *him* (of course I mean a sympathy of comprehension, a sympathy by which we enter into his feelings, and are made to understand them—not a sympathy of pity or approbation). In the murdered person all strife of thought, all flux and reflux of passion and of purpose, are crushed by one overwhelming panic; the fear of instant death smites him "with its petrific mace." But in the murderer, such a murderer as a poet will condescend to, there must be raging some great storm of passion—jealousy, ambition, vengeance, hatred—which will create a hell within him; and into this hell we are to look.

In *Macbeth,* for the sake of gratifying his now enormous and teeming faculty of creation, Shakespeare has introduced two murderers: and, as usual in his hands, they are remarkably discriminated: but—though in Macbeth the strife of mind is greater than in his wife, the tiger spirit not so awake, and his feelings caught chiefly by contagion from her—yet, as both were finally involved in the guilt of murder, the murderous mind of necessity is finally to be presumed in both. This was to be expressed; and on its own account, as well as to make it a more proportionable antagonist to the unoffending nature of their victim, "the gracious Duncan," and adequately to expound "the deep damnation of his taking off," this was to be expressed with peculiar energy. We were to be made to feel that the human nature—i.e., the divine nature of love and mercy, spread through the

---

2. **in 1812.** It was in December, 1811; two families were murdered—the Marrs and the Williamsons. **Mr. Williams,** John Williams, an English seaman and a notorious murderer of the early nineteenth century. 4. **Ratcliffe Highway,** a public thoroughfare in a disreputable quarter of the eastern wharf-district of London. 13. **amateur,** here, one who makes a study of murders. 22. **knocking at the door.** By the servant of the Marrs, who had been sent out to buy oysters. 26. **dilettanti,** lovers of the art of murder; literally, lovers of art.

45. "**the . . . on,**" Shakespeare, *Measure for Measure,* III, i, 78. 51. **sympathy.** "It seems almost ludicrous to guard and explain my use of a word in a situation where it would naturally explain itself. But it has become necessary to do so, in consequence of the unscholar-like use of the word *sympathy,* at present so general, by which, instead of taking it in its proper sense, as the act of reproducing in our minds the feelings of another, whether for hatred, indignation, love, pity, or approbation, it is made a mere synonym of the word *pity;* and hence, instead of saying 'sympathy *with* another,' many writers adopt the monstrous barbarism of 'sympathy *for* another.' "—De Quincey. 59. **petrific,** petrifying. The phrase is from *Paradise Lost,* X, 293. 80. "**the gracious Duncan,**" *Macbeth,* III, i, 66. 81. "**the deep . . . off,**" *ibid.,* I, vii, 20.

hearts of all creatures, and seldom utterly withdrawn from man—was gone, vanished, extinct, and that the fiendish nature had taken its place. And, as this effect is marvelously accomplished in the *dialogues* and *soliloquies* themselves, so it is finally consummated by the expedient under consideration; and it is to this that I now solicit the reader's attention. If the reader has ever witnessed a wife, daughter, or sister, in a fainting fit, he may chance to have observed that the most affecting moment in such a spectacle is *that* in which a sign and a stirring announce the recommencement of suspended life. Or, if the reader has ever been present in a vast metropolis on the day when some great national idol was carried in funeral pomp to his grave, and, chancing to walk near the course through which it passed, has felt powerfully, in the silence and desertion of the streets and in the stagnation of ordinary business, the deep interest which at that moment was possessing the heart of man—if all at once he should hear the death-like stillness broken up by the sound of wheels rattling away from the scene, and making known that the transitory vision was dissolved, he will be aware that at no moment was his sense of the complete suspension and pause in ordinary human concerns so full and affecting as at that moment when the suspension ceases, and the goings-on of human life are suddenly resumed. All action in any direction is best expounded, measured, and made apprehensible, by reaction. Now apply this to the case in *Macbeth*. Here, as I have said, the retiring of the human heart and the entrance of the fiendish heart was to be expressed and made sensible. Another world has stepped in; and the murderers are taken out of the region of human things, human purposes, human desires. They are transfigured: Lady Macbeth is "unsexed"; Macbeth has forgot that he was born of woman; both are conformed to the image of devils; and the world of devils is suddenly revealed. But how shall this be conveyed and made palpable? In order that a new world may step in, this world must for a time disappear. The murderers, and the murder, must be insulated—cut off by an immeasurable gulf from the ordinary tide and succession of human affairs —locked up and sequestered in some deep recess; we must be made sensible that the world of ordinary life is suddenly arrested—laid asleep—tranced—racked into a dread armistice; time must be annihilated; relation to things without abolished; and all must pass self-withdrawn into a deep syncope and suspension of earthly passion. Hence it is that, when the deed is done, when the work of darkness is perfect, then the world of darkness passes away like a pageantry in the clouds: the knocking at the gate is heard, and it makes known audibly that the reaction has commenced; the human has made its reflux upon the fiendish: the pulses of life are beginning to beat again; and the reestablishment of the goings-on of the world in which we live first makes us profoundly sensible of the awful parenthesis that had suspended them.

O mighty poet! Thy works are not as those of other men, simply and merely great works of art, but are also like the phenomena of nature, like the sun and the sea, the stars and the flowers, like frost and snow, rain and dew, hail-storm and thunder, which are to be studied with entire submission of our own faculties, and in the perfect faith that in them there can be no too much or too little, nothing useless or inert, but that, the farther we press in our discoveries, the more we shall see proofs of design and self-supporting arrangement where the careless eye had seen nothing but accident! (1823)

43. "unsexed," *ibid.*, I, v, 42.

59. syncope, cessation, swoon.

from *Suspiria de Profundis*

De Quincey planned but never finished a series of "dreams and noon-day visions" intended to be a sequel to the *Confessions of an English Opium Eater.* Under the title

Suspiria de Profundis (Sighs from the Depths), he published three of these articles in *Blackwood's Magazine*, the one given here being the third. It is generally regarded as the author's most famous example of prose poetry.

LEVANA AND OUR LADIES OF SORROW

OFTENTIMES at Oxford I saw Levana in my dreams. I knew her by her Roman symbols. Who is Levana? Reader, that do not pretend to have leisure for very much scholarship, you will not be angry with me for telling you. Levana was the Roman goddess that performed for the new-born infant the earliest office of ennobling kindness—typical, by its mode, of that grandeur which belongs to man everywhere, and of that benignity in powers invisible which even in pagan worlds sometimes descends to sustain it. At the very moment of birth, just as the infant tasted for the first time the atmosphere of our troubled planet, it was laid on the ground. *That* might bear different interpretations. But immediately, lest so grand a creature should grovel there for more than one instant, either the paternal hand, as proxy for the goddess Levana, or some near kinsman, as proxy for the father, raised it upright, bade it look erect as the king of all this world, and presented its forehead to the stars, saying, perhaps, in his heart, "Behold what is greater than yourselves!" This symbolic act represented the function of Levana. And that mysterious lady, who never revealed her face (except to me in dreams), but always acted by delegation, had her name from the Latin verb (as still it is the Italian verb) *levare*, to raise aloft.

This is the explanation of Levana. And hence it has arisen that some people have understood by Levana the tutelary power that controls the education of the nursery. She, that would not suffer at his birth even a prefigurative or mimic degradation for her awful ward, far less could be supposed to suffer the real degradation attaching to the non-development of his powers. She therefore watches over human education. Now, the word *edŭco*, with the penultimate short, was derived (by a process often exemplified in the crystallization of languages) from the word *edūco*, with the penultimate long. Whatsoever *educes*, or develops, *educates*. By the education of Levana, therefore, is meant—not the poor machinery that moves by spelling-books and grammars, but that mighty system of central forces hidden in the deep bosom of human life, which by passion, by strife, by temptation, by the energies of resistance, works forever upon children—resting not day or night, any more than the mighty wheel of day and night themselves, whose moments, like restless spokes, are glimmering forever as they revolve.

If, then, *these* are the ministries by which Levana works, how profoundly must she reverence the agencies of grief! But you, reader, think that children generally are not liable to grief such as mine. There are two senses in the word *generally*—the sense of Euclid, where it means *universally* (or in the whole extent of the *genus*), and a foolish sense of this word, where it means *usually*. Now, I am far from saying that children universally are capable of grief like mine. But there are more than you ever heard of who die of grief in this island of ours. I will tell you a common case. The rules of Eton require that a boy on the *foundation* should be there twelve years: he is superannuated at eighteen, consequently he must come at six. Children torn away from mothers and sisters at that age not unfrequently die. I speak of what I know. The complaint is not entered by the registrar

---

56. **restless spokes.** "As I have never allowed myself to covet any man's ox nor his ass, nor anything that is his, still less would it become a philosopher to covet other people's images or metaphors. Here, therefore, I restore to Mr. Wordsworth this fine image of the revolving wheel and the glimmering spokes, as applied by him to the flying successions of day and night. I borrowed it for one moment in order to point my own sentence; which being done, the reader is witness that I now pay it back instantly by a note made for that sole purpose. On the same principle I often borrow their seals from young ladies, when closing my letters, because there is sure to be some tender sentiment upon them about 'memory,' or 'hope,' or 'roses,' or 'reunion,' and my correspondent must be a sad brute who is not touched by the eloquence of the seal, even if his taste is so bad that he remains deaf to mine."—De Quincey. 63. **Euclid,** a famous Greek geometrician (c. 300 B.C.). 71. **Eton,** Eton College. 72. **on the foundation,** holding a scholarship provided for in the original endowments of the College. 76. **of . . . know,** of knowledge gained while attending private schools. See p. 376, ll. 33 ff.

as grief, but *that* it is. Grief of that sort, and at that age, has killed more than ever have been counted amongst its martyrs.

Therefore it is that Levana often communes with the powers that shake a man's heart; therefore it is that she dotes upon grief. "These ladies," said I softly to myself, on seeing the ministers with whom Levana was conversing, "these are the Sorrows, and they are three in number, as the *Graces* are three, who dress man's life with beauty; the *Parcae* are three, who weave the dark arras of man's life in their mysterious loom always with colors sad in part, sometimes angry with tragic crimson and black; the *Furies* are three, who visit with retributions called from the other side of the grave offenses that walk upon this; and once even the *Muses* were but three, who fit the harp, the trumpet, or the lute, to the great burdens of man's impassioned creations. These are the Sorrows, all three of whom I know." The last words I say *now;* but in Oxford I said, "one of whom I know, and the others too surely I *shall* know." For already, in my fervent youth, I saw (dimly relieved upon the dark background of my dreams) the imperfect lineaments of the awful Sisters.

These Sisters—by what name shall we call them? If I say simply, "The Sorrows," there will be a chance of mistaking the term; it might be understood of individual sorrow—separate cases of sorrow—whereas I want a term expressing the mighty abstractions that incarnate themselves in all individual sufferings of man's heart, and I wish to have these abstractions presented as impersonations—that is, as clothed with human attributes of life, and with functions pointing to flesh. Let us call them, therefore, *Our Ladies of Sorrow.*

I know them thoroughly, and have walked in all their kingdoms. Three sisters they are, of one mysterious household; and their paths are wide apart; but of their dominion there is no end. Them I saw often conversing with Levana, and sometimes about myself. Do they talk, then? O no! Mighty phantoms like these disdain the infirmities of language. They may utter voices through the organs of man when they dwell in human hearts, but amongst themselves is no voice nor sound; eternal silence reigns in *their* kingdoms. They spoke not as they talked with Levana; they whispered not; they sang not; though oftentimes methought they *might* have sung: for I upon earth had heard their mysteries oftentimes deciphered by harp and timbrel, by dulcimer and organ. Like God, whose servants they are, they utter their pleasure not by sounds that perish, or by words that go astray, but by signs in heaven, by changes on earth, by pulses in secret rivers, heraldries painted on darkness, and hieroglyphics written on the tablets of the brain. *They* wheeled in mazes; *I* spelled the steps. *They* telegraphed from afar; *I* read the signals. *They* conspired together; and on the mirrors of darkness *my* eye traced the plots. *Theirs* were the symbols; *mine* are the words.

What is it the Sisters are? What is it that they do? Let me describe their form and their presence, if form it were that still fluctuated in its outline, or presence it were that forever advanced to the front or forever receded amongst shades.

The eldest of the three is named *Mater Lachrymarum*, Our Lady of Tears. She it is that night and day raves and moans, calling for vanished faces. She stood in Rama, where a voice was heard of lamentation—Rachel weeping for her children, and refusing to be comforted. She it was that stood in Bethlehem on the night when Herod's sword swept its nurseries of Innocents, and the little feet were stiffened forever which, heard at times as they trotted along floors overhead, woke pulses of love in household hearts that were not unmarked in heaven. Her eyes are sweet and subtle, wild and sleepy, by turns; oftentimes rising to the clouds, oftentimes challenging the heavens. She wears a diadem round her

---

11. **the *Parcae*,** the Fates. 12. **arras,** tapestry, named from Arras, France, the city in which tapestry was first made. 20. **burdens,** choruses.

65. **telegraphed,** signaled. De Quincey knew nothing of the modern telegraph. 79. **Rama.** Cf. *Jeremiah*, 31:15—"A voice was heard in Ramah, lamentation and bitter weeping; Rachel weeping for her children refused to be comforted for her children, because they were not." 83. **Herod's sword.** Hoping to kill the new-born Christ, Herod, King of Judea, ordered all children under two years of age to be slain. See *Matthew*, 2:13-18.

head. And I knew by childish memories that she could go abroad upon the winds, when she heard the sobbing of litanies, or the thundering of organs, and when she beheld the mustering of summer clouds. This Sister, the elder, it is that carries keys more than papal at her girdle, which open every cottage and every palace. She, to my knowledge, sat all last summer by the bedside of the blind beggar, him that so often and so gladly I talked with, whose pious daughter, eight years old, with the sunny countenance, resisted the temptations of play and village mirth, to travel all day long on dusty roads with her afflicted father. For this did God send her a great reward. In the spring-time of the year, and whilst yet her own spring was budding, He recalled her to himself. But her blind father mourns forever over *her;* still he dreams at midnight that the little guiding hand is locked within his own; and still he wakens to a darkness that is *now* within a second and a deeper darkness. This *Mater Lachrymarum* also has been sitting all this winter of 1844-45 within the bedchamber of the Czar, bringing before his eyes a daughter (not less pious) that vanished to God not less suddenly, and left behind her a darkness not less profound. By the power of the keys it is that Our Lady of Tears glides, a ghostly intruder, into the chambers of sleepless men, sleepless women, sleepless children, from Ganges to the Nile, from Nile to Mississippi. And her, because she is the first-born of her house, and has the widest empire, let us honor with the title of "Madonna."

The second Sister is called *Mater Suspiriorum*, Our Lady of Sighs. She never scales the clouds, nor walks abroad upon the winds. She wears no diadem. And her eyes, if they were ever seen, would be neither sweet nor subtle; no man could read their story; they would be found filled with perishing dreams, and with wrecks of forgotten delirium. But she raises not her eyes; her head, on which sits a dilapidated turban, droops forever, forever fastens on the dust. She weeps not. She groans not. But she sighs inaudibly at intervals. Her sister, Madonna, is oftentimes stormy and frantic, raging in the highest against heaven, and demanding back her darlings. But Our Lady of Sighs never clamors, never defies, dreams not of rebellious aspirations. She is humble to abjectness. Hers is the meekness that belongs to the hopeless. Murmur she may, but it is in her sleep. Whisper she may, but it is to herself in the twilight. Mutter she does at times, but it is in solitary places that are desolate as she is desolate, in ruined cities, and when the sun has gone down to his rest. This Sister is the visitor of the Pariah, of the Jew, of the bondsman to the oar in the Mediterranean galleys; of the English criminal in Norfolk Island, blotted out from the books of remembrance in sweet far-off England; of the baffled penitent reverting his eyes forever upon a solitary grave, which to him seems the altar overthrown of some past and bloody sacrifice, on which altar no oblations can now be availing, whether toward pardon that he might implore, or toward reparation that he might attempt. Every slave that at noonday looks up to the tropical sun with timid reproach, as he points with one hand to the earth, our general mother, but for *him* a stepmother, as he points with the other hand to the Bible, our general teacher, but against *him* sealed and sequestered, every woman sitting in darkness, without love to shelter her head, or hope to illumine her solitude, because the heaven-born instincts kindling in her nature germs of holy affections, which God implanted in her womanly bosom, having been stifled by social necessities, now burn sullenly to waste, like sepulchral lamps amongst the ancients; every nun defrauded of her unreturning Maytime by wicked kinsman, whom God will judge; every captive in every dungeon; all that are betrayed, and all that are rejected; outcasts by traditionary law, and children of *hereditary* disgrace—all these walk with Our

---

25. **the Czar,** Nicholas I, of Russia (1825-1858), whose daughter Alexandra died in August, 1844.

61. **Pariah,** an outcast; the Pariahs are low-caste Hindus in India and are shunned by the higher castes. 63. **Norfolk Island,** an island in the South Pacific, formerly used by England as a criminal colony. 72. **Every slave, etc.** "This, the reader will be aware, applies chiefly to the cotton and tobacco States of North America; but not to them only: on which account I have not scrupled to figure the sun, which looks down upon slavery, as *tropical*—no matter if strictly within the tropics, or simply so near to them as to produce a similar climate."—De Quincey.

Lady of Sighs. She also carries a key, but she needs it little. For her kingdom is chiefly amongst the tents of Shem, and the houseless vagrant of every clime. Yet in the very highest ranks of man she finds chapels of her own; and even in glorious England there are some that, to the world, carry their heads as proudly as the reindeer, who yet secretly have received her mark upon their foreheads.

But the third Sister, who is also the youngest——! Hush! whisper whilst we talk of *her!* Her kingdom is not large, or else no flesh should live; but within that kingdom all power is hers. Her head, turreted like that of Cybele, rises almost beyond the reach of sight. She droops not; and her eyes, rising so high, *might* be hidden by distance. But, being what they are, they cannot be hidden; through the treble veil of crape which she wears the fierce light of a blazing misery, that rests not for matins or for vespers, for noon of day or noon of night, for ebbing or for flowing tide, may be read from the very ground. She is the defier of God. She also is the mother of lunacies, and the suggestress of suicides. Deep lie the roots of her power; but narrow is the nation that she rules. For she can approach only those in whom a profound nature has been upheaved by central convulsions; in whom the heart trembles and the brain rocks under conspiracies of tempest from without and tempest from within. Madonna moves with uncertain steps, fast or slow, but still with tragic grace. Our Lady of Sighs creeps timidly and stealthily. But this youngest Sister moves with incalculable motions, bounding, and with a tiger's leaps. She carries no key; for, though coming rarely amongst men, she storms all doors at which she is permitted to enter at all. And *her* name is *Mater Tenebrarum*—Our Lady of Darkness.

These were the *Semnai Theai* or Sublime Goddesses, these were the *Eumenides* or Gracious Ladies (so called by antiquity in shuddering propitiation) of my Oxford dreams. Madonna spoke. She spoke by her mysterious hand. Touching my head, she beckoned to Our Lady of Sighs; and *what* she spoke, translated out of the signs which (except in dreams) no man reads, was this:

"Lo! here is he whom in childhood I dedicated to my altars. This is he that once I made my darling. Him I led astray, him I beguiled; and from heaven I stole away his young heart to mine. Through me did he become idolatrous; and through me it was, by languishing desires, that he worshiped the worm, and prayed to the wormy grave. Holy was the grave to him; lovely was its darkness; saintly its corruption. Him, this young idolator, I have seasoned for thee, dear gentle Sister of Sighs! Do thou take him now to *thy* heart, and season him for our dreadful sister. And thou"—turning to the *Mater Tenebrarum*, she said—"wicked sister, that temptest and hatest, do thou take him from *her*. See that thy scepter lie heavy on his head. Suffer not woman and her tenderness to sit near him in his darkness. Banish the frailties of hope, wither the relenting of love, scorch the fountains of tears, curse him as only *thou* canst curse. So shall he be accomplished in the furnace, so shall he see the things that ought *not* to be seen, sights that are abominable, and secrets that are unutterable. So shall he read elder truths, sad truths, grand truths, fearful truths. So shall he rise again *before* he dies. And so shall our commission be accomplished which from God we had—to plague his heart until we had unfolded the capacities of his spirit."

(1845)

---

3. **amongst . . . Shem,** among outcasts—i.e., among the Arabs and other nomadic tribes said to be descendants of Shem, eldest son of Noah. See *Genesis*, 9:26-27. 15. **Cybele,** in Roman mythology, the mother of the Olympian gods; in art she was represented with a turreted crown. 42. **Sublime Goddesses.** "The word σεμνός is usually rendered *venerable* in dictionaries—not a very flattering epithet for females. But I am disposed to think that it comes nearest to our idea of the *sublime*—as near as a Greek word *could* come."—De Quincey. 43. *Eumenides,* the Fates.

70. **fountain of tears.** Cf. *Jeremiah*, 9:1: "Oh, that my head were waters, and mine eyes a fountain of tears that I might weep day and night for the slain of the daughter of my people!" 80. **spirit.** "The reader who wishes at all to understand the course of these Confessions ought not to pass over this dream-legend. There is no great wonder that a vision which occupied my waking thoughts in those years should reappear in my dreams. It was, in fact, a legend recurring in sleep, most of which I had myself silently written or sculptured in my daylight reveries. But its importance to the present Confessions is this, that it rehearses or prefigures their course. This first part belongs to Madonna. The third belongs to the 'Mater Suspiriorum,' and will be entitled *The Pariah Worlds*. The fourth, which terminates the work, belongs to the 'Mater Tenebrarum,' and will be entitled *The Kingdom of Darkness*. As to the second, it is an interpolation requisite to the effect of the others, and will be explained in its proper place."—De Quincey.

from *The Poetry of Pope*

LITERATURE OF KNOWLEDGE AND LITERATURE OF POWER

What is it that we mean by *literature*? Popularly, and amongst the thoughtless, it is held to include everything that is printed in a book. Little logic is required to disturb *that* definition. The most thoughtless person is easily made aware that in the idea of *literature* one essential element is—some relation to a general and common interest of man, so that what applies only to a local or professional or merely personal interest, even though presenting itself in the shape of a book, will not belong to literature. So far the definition is easily narrowed; and it is as easily expanded. For not only is much that takes a station in books not literature, but, inversely, much that really *is* literature never reaches a station in books. The weekly sermons of Christendom, that vast pulpit literature which acts so extensively upon the popular mind—to warn, to uphold, to renew, to comfort, to alarm—does not attain the sanctuary of libraries in the ten-thousandth part of its extent. The drama, again, as for instance the finest of Shakespeare's plays in England and all leading Athenian plays in the noontide of the Attic stage, operated as a literature on the public mind, and were (according to the strictest letter of that term) *published* through the audiences that witnessed their representation, some time before they were published as things to be read; and they were published in this scenical mode of publication with much more effect than they could have had as books during ages of costly copying or of costly printing.

Books, therefore, do not suggest an idea co-extensive and interchangeable with the idea of literature; since much literature, scenic, forensic, or didactic (as from lecturers and public orators), may never come into books, and much that does come into books may connect itself with no literary interest. But a far more important correction, applicable to the common vague idea of literature, is to be sought not so much in a better definition of literature as in a sharper distinction of the two functions which it fulfils. In that great social organ which, collectively, we call literature, there may be distinguished two separate offices that may blend and often do so, but capable, severally, of a severe insulation, and naturally fitted for reciprocal repulsion. There is, first, the literature of *knowledge*, and secondly, the literature of *power*. The function of the first is to *teach;* the function of the second is to *move;* the first is a rudder, the second an oar or a sail. The first speaks to the mere discursive understanding; the second speaks ultimately, it may happen, to the higher understanding or reason, but always through affections of pleasure and sympathy. Remotely, it may travel towards an object seated in what Lord Bacon calls *dry* light; but, proximately, it does and must operate —else it ceases to be a literature of *power*— on and through that *humid* light which clothes itself in the mists and glittering *iris* of human passions, desires, and genial emotions. Men have so little reflected on the higher functions of literature as to find it a paradox if one should describe it as a mean or subordinate purpose of books to give information. But this is a paradox only in the sense which makes it honorable to be paradoxical. Whenever we talk in ordinary language of seeking information or gaining knowledge, we understand the words as connected with something of absolute novelty. But it is the grandeur of all truth which *can* occupy a very high place in human interests that it is never absolutely novel to the meanest of minds: it exists eternally by way of germ or latent principle in the lowest as in the highest, needing to be developed, but

---

25. **noontide . . . stage,** the time of Aeschylus, Sophocles, and Euripides, famous Greek dramatists of the fifth century B.C. 28. **published . . . audiences.** "Charles I, for example, when Prince of Wales, and many others in his father's court, gained their known familiarity with Shakespeare—not through the original quartos, so slenderly diffused, nor through the first folio of 1623, but through the court representations of his chief dramas at Whitehall."—De Quincey.

63. **Bacon . . . light.** "Heraclitus the Obscure said: *The dry light was the best soul*—meaning, when the faculties intellectual are in vigor, not wet, nor, as it were, blooded by the affections."—Bacon, *Apothegms New and Old,* I. 268. 67. **iris,** rainbow; from Iris, goddess of the rainbow.

never to be planted. To be capable of transplantation is the immediate criterion of a truth that ranges on a lower scale. Besides which, there is a rarer thing than truth—namely, *power,* or deep sympathy with truth. What is the effect, for instance, upon society, of children? By the pity, by the tenderness, and by the peculiar modes of admiration, which connect themselves with the helplessness, with the innocence, and with the simplicity of children, not only are the primal affections strengthened and continually renewed, but the qualities which are dearest in the sight of heaven—the frailty, for instance, which appeals to forbearance, the innocence which symbolizes the heavenly, and the simplicity which is most alien from the worldly—are kept up in perpetual remembrance, and their ideals are continually refreshed. A purpose of the same nature is answered by the higher literature, viz., the literature of power. What do you learn from *Paradise Lost?* Nothing at all. What do you learn from a cookery-book? Something new, something that you did not know before, in every paragraph. But would you therefore put the wretched cookery-book on a higher level of estimation than the divine poem? What you owe to Milton is not any knowledge, of which a million separate items are still but a million of advancing steps on the same earthly level; what you owe is *power*—that is, exercise and expansion to your own latent capacity of sympathy with the infinite, where every pulse and each separate influx is a step upwards, a step ascending as upon a Jacob's ladder from earth to mysterious altitudes above the earth. *All the steps of knowledge, from first to last, carry you further on the same plane, but could never raise you one foot above your ancient level of earth: whereas the very first step in power is a flight—is an ascending movement into another element where earth is forgotten.*

Were it not that human sensibilities are ventilated and continually called out into exercise by the great phenomena of infancy, or of real life as it moves through chance and change, or of literature as it recombines these elements in the mimicries of poetry, romance, etc., it is certain that, like any animal power or muscular energy falling into disuse, all such sensibilities would gradually droop and dwindle. It is in relation to these great *moral* capacities of man that the literature of power, as contradistinguished from that of knowledge, lives and has its field of action. It is concerned with what is highest in man; for the Scriptures themselves never condescended to deal by suggestion or co-operation with the mere discursive understanding: when speaking of man in his intellectual capacity, the Scriptures speak not of the understanding, but of *"the understanding heart"*—making the heart, i.e., the great *intuitive* (or non-discursive) organ, to be the interchangeable formula for man in his highest state of capacity for the infinite. Tragedy, romance, fairy tale, or epopee, all alike restore to man's mind the ideals of justice, of hope, of truth, of mercy, of retribution, which else (left to the support of daily life in its realities) would languish for want of sufficient illustration.

What is meant, for instance, by *poetic justice?* It does not mean a justice that differs by its object from the ordinary justice of human jurisprudence, for then it must be confessedly a very bad kind of justice; but it means a justice that differs from common forensic justice by the degree in which it attains its object—a justice that is more omnipotent over its own ends, as dealing, not with the refractory elements of earthly life, but with the elements of its own creation, and with materials flexible to its own purest preconceptions. It is certain that, were it not for the literature of power, these ideals would often remain amongst us as mere arid notional forms; whereas, by the creative forces of man put forth in literature, they gain a vernal life of restoration, and germinate into vital activities. The commonest novel, by moving in alliance with human fears and hopes, with human instincts of wrong and right, sustains and quickens those affections. Calling them

---

22. *Paradise Lost.* See Vol. I, p. 715. 36. **Jacob's ladder.** In a dream Jacob beheld a ladder that reached from earth to heaven. See *Genesis,* 28:12.

63. **"the . . . heart,"** *1 Kings,* 3:9, 12—"Give therefore thy servant an understanding heart to judge thy people." 68. **epopee,** epic poem.

into action, it rescues them from torpor. And hence the pre-eminency over all authors that merely *teach,* of the meanest that *moves,* or that teaches, if at all, indirectly by moving. The very highest work that has ever existed in the literature of knowledge is but a provisional work—a book upon trial and sufferance, and *quamdiu bene se gesserit.* Let its teaching be even partially revised, let it be but expanded—nay, even let its teaching be but placed in a better order—and instantly it is superseded. Whereas the feeblest works in the literature of power, surviving at all, survive as finished and unalterable amongst men. For instance, the *Principia* of Sir Isaac Newton was a book militant on earth from the first. In all stages of its progress it would have to fight for its existence: first, as regards absolute truth; secondly, when that combat was over, as regards its form or mode of presenting the truth. And as soon as a Laplace, or anybody else, builds higher upon the foundations laid by this book, effectually he throws it out of the sunshine into decay and darkness; by weapons won from this book he superannuates and destroys this book, so that soon the name of Newton remains as a mere *nominis umbra,* but his book, as a living power, has transmigrated into other forms. Now, on the contrary, the *Iliad,* the *Prometheus* of Aeschylus, the *Othello* or *King Lear,* the *Hamlet* or *Macbeth,* and the *Paradise Lost,* are not militant, but triumphant forever, as long as the languages exist in which they speak or can be taught to speak. They never *can* transmigrate into new incarnations. To reproduce these in new forms, or variations, even if in some things they should be improved, would be to plagiarize. A good steam engine is properly superseded by a better. But one lovely pastoral valley is not superseded by another, nor a statue of Praxiteles by a statue of Michael Angelo. These things are separated not by imparity but by disparity. They are not thought of as unequal under the same standard, but as different in *kind,* and, if otherwise equal, as equal under a different standard. Human works of immortal beauty and works of nature in one respect stand on the same footing: they never absolutely repeat each other, never approach so near as not to differ, and they differ not as better and worse, or simply by more and less —they differ by undecipherable and incommunicable differences, that cannot be caught by mimicries, that cannot be reflected in the mirror of copies, that cannot become ponderable in the scales of vulgar comparison.

Applying these principles to Pope as a representative of fine literature in general, we would wish to remark the claim which he has, or which any equal writer has, to the attention and jealous winnowing of those critics in particular who watch over public morals. Clergymen, and all organs of public criticism put in motion by clergymen, are more especially concerned in the just appreciation of such writers, if the two canons are remembered which we have endeavored to illustrate, viz., that all works in this class, as opposed to those in the literature of knowledge, 1st, work by far deeper agencies, and 2dly, are more permanent; in the strictest sense they are κτήματα ἐς ἀεί: and what evil they do, or what good they do, is commensurate with the national language, sometimes long after the nation has departed. At this hour, five hundred years since their creation, the tales of Chaucer, never equaled on this earth for their tenderness, and for life of picturesqueness, are read familiarly by many in the charming language of their natal day, and by others in the modernisations of Dryden, of Pope, and Wordsworth. At this hour, one thousand eight hundred years since their creation, the Pagan tales of Ovid, never equaled on this earth for the gayety of their movement and the capricious graces of their narrative, are read by all Christendom. This man's people and their monuments are dust; but *he* is alive: he has survived them, as he told us that he had it in his commission to

---

8. quamdiu . . . gesserit, as long as it bore itself well. **15. Principia,** *The Mathematical Principles of Natural Philosophy,* published in 1687. **21. Laplace,** a French astronomer and mathematician (1749-1827). **28. nominis umbra,** shadow of a name. **30. Iliad,** the story of the Trojan War, by Homer. **31. Aeschylus.** See note to l. 25, p. 394. **42. Praxiteles . . . Michael Angelo.** The work of the Greek sculptor Praxiteles (fourth centry B.C.) is noted for its grace and naturalness; that of the Italian Michael Angelo (1475-1564) for its power.

73. κτήματα ἐς ἀεί, permanent possessions. **78. tales of Chaucer.** See Vol. I, pp. 225 ff. **85. Ovid,** famous Roman storyteller and poet (43 B.C.-17 A.D.). See Dryden's comparison of Ovid and Chaucer (Vol. I, pp. 874 ff.).

do, by a thousand years "and *shall* a thousand more."

All the literature of knowledge builds only ground-nests, that are swept away by floods, or confounded by the plow; but the literature of power builds nests in aërial altitudes of temples sacred from violation, or of forests inaccessible to fraud. *This* is a great prerogative of the *power* literature; and it is a greater which lies in the mode of its influence. The *knowledge* literature, like the fashion of this world, passeth away. An Encyclopedia is its abstract; and, in this respect, it may be taken for its speaking symbol—that before one generation has passed, an Encyclopedia is superannuated; for it speaks through the dead memory and unimpassioned understanding, which have not the repose of higher faculties, but are continually enlarging and varying their phylacteries. But all literature properly so called—literature κατ' ἐξοχήν —for the very same reason that it is so much more durable than the literature of knowledge, is (and by the very same proportion it is) more intense and electrically searching in its impressions. The directions in which the tragedy of this planet has trained our human feelings to play, and the combinations into which the poetry of this planet has thrown our human passions of love and hatred, of admiration and contempt, exercise a power for bad or good over human life that cannot be contemplated, when stretching through many generations, without a sentiment allied to awe. And of this let everyone be assured—that he owes to the impassioned books which he has read many a thousand more of emotions than he can consciously trace back to them. Dim by their origination, these emotions yet arise in him and mold him through life, like forgotten incidents of his childhood. (1848)

20. **phylacteries**, records; literally, boxes containing slips of parchment on which certain passages of scripture are written. They are bound on forehead and left forearm by Jews at prayer.

21. κατ' ἐξοχήν, *par excellence*, preëminently.

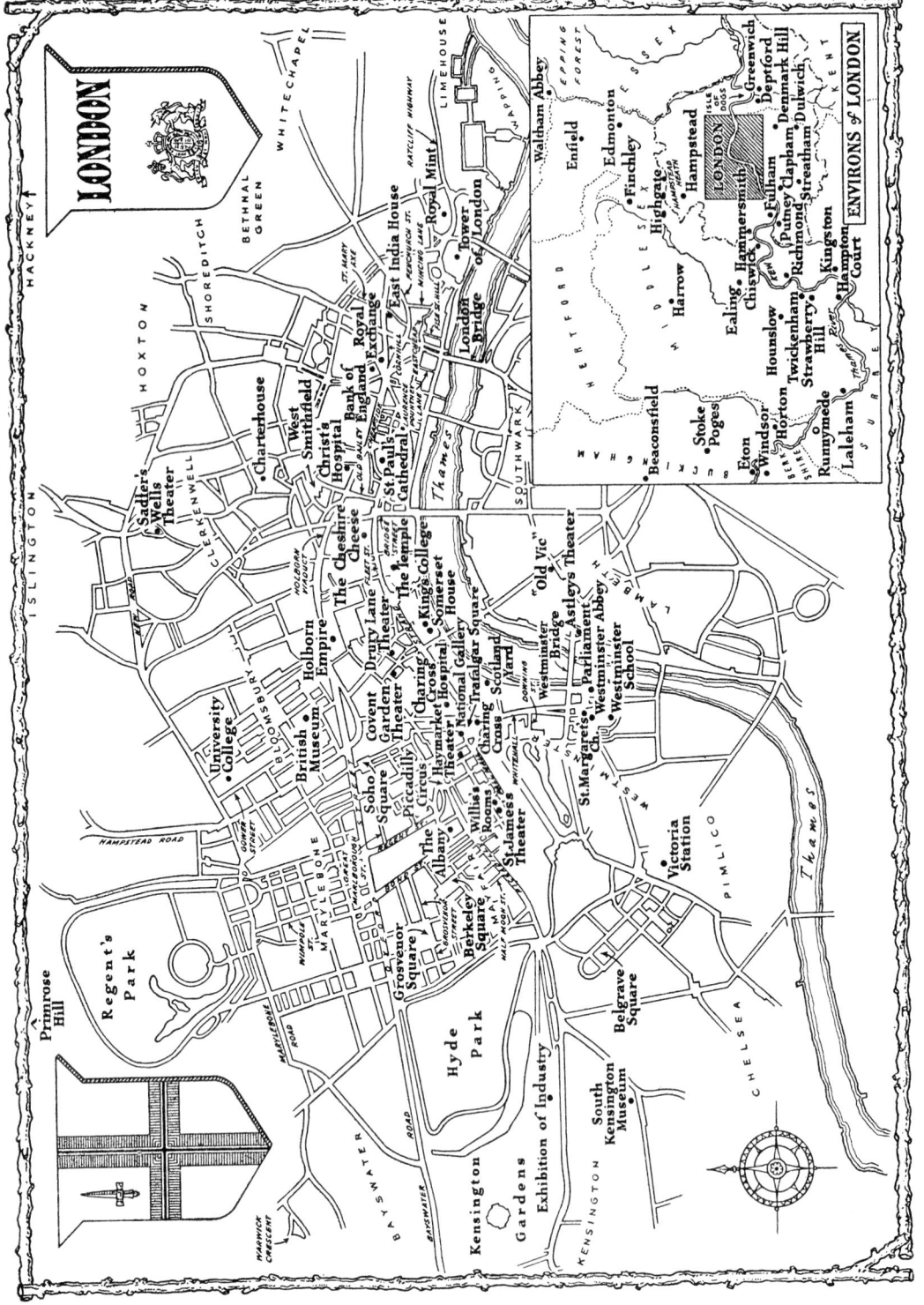

Chapter 7

Democracy, Science, and Industrialism

The Victorian Age, 1832-1880

The Heritage of Revolution

IN EVERY period of revolt are buried the seeds of convention. So the revolutionary spirit which was active in England in the first years of the nineteenth century (see pp. 3-5) was tempered by that natural conservatism of the English which has always led them to prefer slow processes of change and reform to the violence of open revolt. By a slow but steady process the English adjusted themselves in the nineteenth century to the forces of political and social revolution, with the result that the world of George V differed vastly from that of George III. Much of the tumult and the shouting of the continental struggles of the early nineteenth century died away with the defeat and exile of Napoleon in 1815. But the leaven of revolution and reform continued to work, and to its close the century was a period of ferment and adjustment. The age of Victoria was a serious age, a complex era that stamped itself on almost every literary form to which it gave expression. To understand Victorian literature, therefore, it is necessary first to know something of the storm and stress of the times.

Convention and revolt

The progress of these social forces covers many decades. It is not possible to point to any exact date and say, "In this year the changes began." Yet if this must be done, the year 1832 may well be chosen. In this year was

Time limits of the Victorian age

passed the first of the great political reform bills that mark the advance of democracy in nineteenth-century England. In some respects it is a date almost as important as 1215, the year of Magna Charta. In literature, too, the year is notable. In 1832 died Sir Walter Scott, the most completely typical novelist of the romantic movement; and on the Continent the year marks the passing of the German poet Goethe. In 1832 appeared the first collected poems of Alfred Tennyson, in many ways the most Victorian of Victorian poets, the poet laureate, and the bardic voice of his age. It was not until five years later that Victoria, granddaughter of George III, ascended the throne, succeeding her stuffy uncles George IV (1820-1830) and William IV (1830-1837), but 1837 is a less significant date than 1832. What date should be chosen for the end of this era of democracy, science, and industrialism? The period might be carried down to the end of Victoria's long reign in 1901. But again, the date of the queen's death is of no particular significance. She had become in her declining years hardly more than a revered symbol of her empire's power, and at least two decades before her death there were evidences in society and in literature of the beginnings of a break with Victorianism. The year 1880 may therefore be selected as marking the distinct waning though not the definite end of those elements in English life and letters which bear the name *Victorian*. This date marks the end of a half century that is sometimes sneered at by a later generation as too "moral"; but because of its fullness, richness, and complexity, it will take its place as one of the most important periods in English life and letters.

Nationalism and Imperialism

Expansion of the British Empire

THE EXPANSION of a tiny island kingdom into a world empire had its inception in the growth of English commerce in the reign of Queen Elizabeth or earlier. The physical expansion, however, occurred largely in the reign of Queen Victoria, when the British flag was carried by diplomacy and military conquest into almost every part of the habitable world. During the nineteenth century England became definitely Great Britain; she swung her trident over the seven seas, seized the channels and the ports necessary to her expansion, and gradually extended her rule over a territory five times the size of all Europe. She acquired Egypt and the Sudan, the home of Kipling's Fuzzy-Wuzzies. Her control of the Suez Canal (1875) gave her command of the eastern part of the Mediterranean just as her fortifications at Gibraltar gave her command of the western part. In the Crimean War of 1854 she blocked Russia's purpose to establish a fleet on the Black Sea, and in India she guarded the northern passes against possible Russian invasion by land. The repression of the bloody Indian mutiny of

The Bath Steam Carriage

1857 was followed by Victoria's assumption of the title first of Sovereign of India and, twenty years later, of Empress of India. In the later partition of Africa Great Britain gained a dominion at the southern end of that continent. Canada, Australia, and New Zealand provided a new type of colonial connection by becoming the "free nations" of the empire under independent governments. It is doubtful, indeed, whether the British Empire could have expanded so widely under the eighteenth-century theory of colonization. In the reign of George III the political conception that the colony existed solely for the purpose of contributing to the wealth of the mother country was exploded both by the violence of the American Revolution and by the growth of a democratic spirit in England. Colonial policy under Victoria, especially as it was concerned with subjects of English blood, was vastly more liberal and generous. And although certain parts of the British Empire were bought—to use Kipling's vivid phrases—"with the sword and the flame" and "salted down with the bones" of British soldiers, a much vaster area merged happily, peacefully, and democratically into the great empire.

It might seem that this rapid growth of kingdom into empire would have resulted in tempering the English spirit of nationalism and bringing the island into a closer and more friendly association with its continental neighbors. Some connection with them was, of course, inevitable. In the problems incident to the partitioning of Africa, the commercial invasion of China and Japan, and the curbing of Russia's ambitions, the British had not only to sit at the council table but also to engage in armed alliances with the continental powers. On the whole, however, the England of Victoria's reign was self-centered and nationalistic. Wealthy and self-satisfied, she could not believe that any country outside the empire was necessary to her happiness and well-being, and her insularity developed into a national smugness and priggishness which aroused the disgust of her own critics and prophets. Part of this insularity was native to her character. Part, however, grew out of her fear of entangling alliances with the nations of the Continent. Democracy was slowly being forced upon her by industrial changes and political reforms. But democracy acquired as the French had acquired it she did not want, and she watched with troubled and suspicious eye the various political disturbances of her nearest neighbor. In *The Princess* Tennyson represents his typical beef-eating English gentleman as looking across the channel at the "pale shores of France" and praying God's blessing on "the narrow seas that keep her off"; and this sentiment was echoed by most Victorian gentlemen. Finally, the English were so taken up with problems at home that they did not have time to be overmuch concerned with those of other nations. Problems of a growing democratic spirit in politics and problems of social and industrial adjustment needed to be solved,

English nationalism and insularity

Early Train on the Liverpool and Manchester Railway

Science and Society

The effects of science on society

IT IS ALWAYS to be questioned whether science is the servant of man or man the slave of science. In the Victorian age, certainly, it seemed to many as though the Englishman was likely to be destroyed, like Frankenstein, by the monster which he had created. The seeds of the momentous social change attending the Industrial Revolution (see p. 5) were planted in the eighteenth century by inventors who attempted to reduce human bondage to labor by subduing the forces of nature to the service of man. That the fruit of these seeds could be bitter as well as sweet it remained for the Victorians to discover. Two aspects of scientific development gripped and molded Victorian England. The control of natural powers and the applications of mechanical principles to industry affected living and working conditions; new scientific conceptions in biology and geology affected man's attitudes in religion and his methods of thought. It is perhaps difficult to say which form of science was the more significant in its ultimate effects, that which concerned man's physical and social life or that which changed so radically his spiritual attitudes and his intellectual outlook. But the one with which the Victorians had to come to grips first was the application of science to labor.

Development of the "factory system" of industry

As early as the second half of the eighteenth century men began to devise methods for mechanical multiple-production in the industry of weaving. The spinning-jenny of Hargreaves (1764), the improved spinning machines of Arkwright (1779), and finally the power-loom of Cartwright (1784) made it possible for one operator to do the work of many craftsmen. Water power succeeded horse power, steam power followed water power, and at the beginning of the nineteenth century the "factory system" had virtually replaced the older "domestic system" of industry. The change in methods of labor brought about other profound changes. To begin with, it resulted in a redistribution of the population. Workers instead of being scattered more or less evenly over the country were drawn from the rural parts into the factory towns. The factory towns became great cities with belching chimneys, and England came soon to be divided into the industrial north and the conservative south. An admirable depiction of this rapid transformation of rural community into factory town appears incidentally in George Eliot's *Silas Marner;* another may be found in Miss Mulock's *John Halifax, Gentleman.*

Prince Albert's Model Dwellings

Finally, to supply the factories with coal and iron, new industries developed, and new and vastly more intricate systems of transportation were needed. So mining, canal-boating, and—after the middle of the century—railroading assumed positions of immense importance.

But far more significant than the physical changes were those involving human beings. Since the erection and operation of the factories demanded two things, money for building and maintenance and "mill-hands" to operate the power-looms, England soon found herself with two new major classes of society, that representing capital and that representing labor, the employer and the employed. The adjustment of a rational and humane balance between these two groups was to provide England with one of the knottiest and most vexing of problems. Innumerable abuses arose from the "factory system" and continued for a long time. To secure mill-hands at low wages, owners employed more women than men. Worse than that, they employed little children, taking them from the homes of greedy parents or from orphanages and "workhouses." It seems astonishing that a nation which in 1833 freed the Negro slaves in the British colonies should have allowed a worse industrial slavery to develop within its own borders. But these conditions, sordid as they were, combined with the enormous numerical growth of factory workers of all kinds to bring about social and political reforms of very great significance.

Capital and labor

The New Democracy

TWO DOCTRINES which arose in connection with industrialism appeared even before the beginning of the Victorian period. These were *laissez-faire* and legislative reform. The first, as the name implies, was the economic theory of "hands off"; according to this theory economic adjustments follow certain natural laws which can be depended upon to work to the ultimate advantage of humanity; and these laws should be allowed to function without interference. The other was more direct and positive; it required for its operation legislative action and control of industry. It was soon obvious that in spite of the energy and enthusiasm of social and industrial reformers, no adequate industrial control could be effected while parliamentary representation was almost entirely in the hands of a dwindling aristocracy and a set of wealthy mill-owners. Before 1832 members in the House of Commons were often not chosen by any fair method of regional distribution and popular election but nominated by noblemen in the House of Lords. The new industrial cities with their teeming populations were almost unrepresented, whereas rural districts in which few persons lived were over-represented. The First Reform Bill of 1832 abolished fifty-six of these nomination, or rotten, boroughs, as they were called, and the two subsequent Reform Bills of 1867 and 1884-

Laissez-faire and legislative reform

The Reform Bill of 1832

1885 extended the franchise first to the towns and second to the agricultural districts. In this half century of legislation England became a modern democracy, and the workers of England shifted their status from that of clients to that of patrons. The story of the tilt between Victoria and Gladstone in which her assertion that she was "queen of England" was countered by his insistence that he was "the people of England" may be apocryphal, but it is nevertheless illuminating. In the age of Victoria Parliament had come to represent the whole people of England, and the prime minister to be their agent and not the personal representative of the crown, as Strafford had been in the reign of Charles I and Lord North at the time of the American Revolution.

Economic theorists: the Utilitarians

These radical changes were not brought about without the labor of economic theorists and pressure groups. Among the theorists were not only the advocates of *laissez-faire*, who have just been mentioned, but the Utilitarians, who inherited their ideas from Jeremy Bentham (1748-1832). Bentham's social ideas, expressed at their fullest in his *Fragment on Government* (1776) and *Introduction to Principles of Morals and Legislation* (1789), include the philosophical doctrine of Utility, which he defined as "the greatest happiness for the greatest number." Bentham's greatest disciple in England was James Mill (1773-1836), who provided in the *Analysis of the Human Mind* (1829) a psychological basis for Bentham's economic theories. John Stuart Mill (1806-1873), son of James Mill, carried the utilitarian theories into the Victorian period. He founded the Utilitarian Society in 1823 and edited Bentham's *Treatise upon Evidence* in 1825. Later in life, however, he began to modify Bentham's ideas, asserting in his *Utilitarianism* that pleasures differ in quality as well as in quantity, and that the social feelings of mankind, man's desire to be in unity with his fellow creatures, constitute "the ultimate sanction of the greatest happiness, morality." Against the utilitarian doctrine as against that of *laissez-faire* Carlyle inveighed loudly; no human being, he declared, has a *right* to any happiness, and work, not pleasure, should be man's objective in life.

The Chartists

The Chartists were more practically active than the utilitarian theorists; from 1837 to 1848, when they ceased to have an independent existence, they fought vigorously for definite political reforms. They derived their name from a document called the People's Charter, and their program of reform was based upon the "Six Points" of Universal Suffrage, Vote by Ballot, Annual Parliaments, Payment of Members, Abolition of Property Qualifications, and Equal Electoral Districts. Some of their proposals became effective during the period of their activity; others were adopted later. Their long struggle for the ballot and for universal suffrage earned for them from Karl Marx the title of the real democrats of England.

The industrial workers, finally, organized themselves into the Trade

The Crystal Palace

DEMOCRACY, SCIENCE, AND INDUSTRIALISM

Unionists to fight the battles of adequate factory legislation; thus the older trade guilds gave place to the powerful trade unions.

The Trade Unionists

Against all these groups were arrayed the conservatives, who fought a long but losing battle. But the warfare was not between crown and people, as it had been in the days just before the Puritan Interlude (see Vol. I, pp. 633-635), but between factions of the people. The great rival statesmen, Gladstone and Disraeli, were both middle-class—Gladstone the son of a Scotch West Indian merchant, and Disraeli the son of a Jewish man of letters. Even before the period of the influence of these two the voice of Victorian England was literally the voice of the Victorian people, and this fact is in no way better shown than in the extent to which the queen herself embodied the spirit and the character of her subjects. George III had ascended the throne with the words of his autocratic mother ringing in his ears: "George, be a king"; Victoria ascended it in 1837 with a simple promise: "I will be good."

Democracy supreme

The Warfare of Science and Theology

SCIENCE APPLIED to industry did much ultimately to change English political and social philosophy. At the same time scientific thought in the fields of biology and geology created another revolution of a different sort. Against the ancient belief that man was created the center of the universe and was made in the image of God and endowed by his creator with authority over beast, bird, and fish, was advanced a new philosophy shocking beyond measure to many orthodox Victorians. The theory of evolution claimed for man no such central position in the plan of creation; by slow growth and through a process of long development he ascended, rather, from earlier and lowlier forms. Thus his relation to God was not so scientifically demonstrable as was his kinship with the great apes and even with animals lower in the scale.

New scientific thinking

The new doctrine was the work of scientific philosophers. Of these the most notable were Charles Lyell (1797-1875), Alfred Russel Wallace (1823-1913), Charles Darwin (1809-1882), and Thomas Henry Huxley (1825-1895). The seeds of the doctrine lay in the early geological writings of Lyell and Wallace, but the thinker who brought them to fruition was Darwin, and the scientist-educator who battled valiantly against "clerical minds" for their acceptance was Huxley. It was Darwin's *Origin of Species* (1859), based on innumerable data which he had collected while naturalist on H. M. S. *Beagle*, that shocked Bishop Wilberforce and many other adherents of the older beliefs into coming vigorously to their defense. Darwin himself was a scientist too much absorbed in his own researches and thinking to fight for his hypotheses. In Huxley, however, who came to be popularly

Interior of the Great Exhibition.

The scientific philosophers and their opponents

known as "Darwin's bull-dog," he found a tireless, clear-headed, and skilful supporter. The echoes of these battles between science and theology may still be heard. Darwin's *Descent of Man* (1871) provided much ammunition for the scientists, and Huxley's *Man's Place in Nature* (1863) and *Lay Sermons* (1870) are popular and non-technical expositions of both the biological theory and its geological counterpart. On the side of the conservatives were many clergymen and writers, including Bishop Wilberforce, who met Huxley on the debating-platform, and Charles Kingsley, who attacked the biologists scathingly in *The Water Babies* (1863). Matthew Arnold, though characterizing Huxley as "the prince of debaters," could not agree with him that the scientific method of investigation should be made the staple of education. In *Dover Beach* (p. 744), however, the melancholy poet expresses his belief that the "Sea of Faith" was ebbing; in the poems of Tennyson are many echoes of the suggestion that God and Nature are at strife, and that Nature cares not for the individual but only for the type.

Some benefits of the new philosophy

If the new philosophy was disturbing to some minds, it was also stimulating. By removing man from his smug post at the center of the universe, it gave him a sounder view of the physical universe and a better sense of proportion. And the method of scientific investigation stiffened his system of thought; skepticism, as Huxley pointed out, was no longer a sin but a virtue, and knowledge based on human authority was replaced, at least in the empire of physical phenomena, by that rooted strongly in careful investigation, observation, and logical induction. So by seeing the world and by taking thought about it man increased his intellectual independence and his mental stature.

The Oxford Movement

Leaders of the movement

THE VICTORIAN WARFARE between science and theology embraced a long series of skirmishes. To many of the contestants there seemed to be in general two ways out of the difficulties in which Victorian theological thinkers found themselves. One led forward with the scientists into atheism or agnosticism; the other led into the mystical region of divinely revealed truth. Before Darwin's disturbing *Origin of Species* had appeared, a definite change in the Church of England which took this second direction had already occurred. This was the Oxford Movement, named for its origin at Oxford University; it was also called Tractarianism, from the circumstance that the Oxford reformers published their doctrines in a series of *Tracts for the Times*, which began in September, 1833, and ended with the famous Tract XC in 1842. The birthday of the movement was July 14, 1833, the date of a sermon by John Keble on national apostasy, delivered before the judges of assize at Oxford. The saintly author of *The Christian Year* was

thus the founder of the Oxford Movement. The most powerful of the Oxford reformers, however, was John Henry Newman (see p. 445), fellow of Oriel College and vicar of St. Mary's, the university church, as well as that of the parish at Oxford. Associated with him were Richard Hurrell Froude and Edward Bouverie Pusey, professor of Hebrew at Oxford. When the movement flamed into being in 1833, Newman and Froude were traveling in the Mediterranean. Filled with a sense that he had work to do in England, Newman turned back to the battle-line, praying for guidance in his hymn of faith, "Lead, kindly light" (p. 715). On his arrival at Oxford, he preached stirringly from his pulpit at St. Mary's and contributed to the *Tracts for the Times*. The publication of *The Literary Remains of Richard Hurrell Froude* in 1838 with its condemnation of the Protestant Reformation greatly alarmed the supporters of the Oxford Movement, and Matthew Arnold attacked "the Oxford malignants." Tract XC, written by Newman, was regarded as directed so definitely against the Church of England that the author could no longer continue to occupy his pulpit. He resigned in September, 1843, and two years later was received into the Church of Rome. Some few followed him, but most of his disciples did not; and with his conversion the Oxford Movement came to an end as an acute controversy, although in spirit and, sometimes in name, it continued in both the Church of England and the American Episcopal Church.

Belles

The Oxford Movement defined

The cycles of convention and revolt seem to operate in religion as in literature. The theological forms of religious faith tend gradually to imprison the spirit of religion; belief becomes secularized and cold, and worship is conducted in the outer courts of the temple and far from the holy of holies. Religious reform seeks to reëstablish faith, usually by a break with existing theologies and rituals and sometimes by a reactionary return to an earlier form of worship. The leading Oxford reformers, although most of them probably did not realize it, were religious romanticists. Just as in literature the romantic movement included a revolt against strait-jacketing and a return to the Middle Ages, so the Oxford Movement was, in a sense, a return to the more picturesque religious observances of the centuries before the Protestant Reformation. Newman particularly was a romanticist, a mystic, and an artist. Like Carlyle, Arnold, and Ruskin, he believed that the correction of the evils of his times lay in the return to earlier social forms and philosophies. Furthermore, it is impossible to read *The Dream of Gerontius* (see p. 715) or the *Lyra Apostolica* without perceiving that he had a spirit of mysticism curiously alien to the materialism and utilitarianism of Victorian England. In certain parts of his *Apologia pro Vita Sua* (p. 460), finally, there is a marked indication of his leaning toward the colorful and artistic richness of the Roman Catholic service. At the time of his admission to that faith it was said of him that, strangely enough, he alone had failed to perceive earlier the direction in which his philosophy and artistic inclinations were leading him. And since he was the leader, if not the original author, of the Oxford Movement, it may be epitomized, not unfairly, as the romantic movement in religion.

Social Influences on Victorian Literature

Literature for the people

THE STORY of English literature is usually told from the point of view of the English authors. It may be told also, however, from the point of view of English readers, inasmuch as the content and the form of literature are determined as largely by the readers as by the writers. Thus it was that in the age of Elizabeth the patronage of the court had much to do with the characteristics of the literature and particularly of lyric poetry and certain types of drama. In Victorian England the pressure of reader on writer is even more evident. Victorian literature, like all literature that is great enough to survive, contains, to be sure, those universal elements of human interest and literary art which preserve it for posterity. But it is marked also by the mold and pressure of Victorianism. Just as Elizabethan literature was largely written for the court, so most of Victorian literature was written for the people. In the literature as in the social life of the Victorian age it is obvious that the people rule. No longer can the poet address his poem or the dramatist dedicate his play to a patron; his readers are not individuals but the many-headed multitude, sitting about the family lamp at night, or snatching a glance at essay or story in office or workshop. This circumstance accounts, no doubt, for the prominence of the Victorian novel.

A talking age

The popular character of Victorian literature extends to many forms besides the novel. More than in any earlier period it was a talking and a printing age. Virtually all the major prose prophets of the period—Carlyle, Newman, Arnold, Ruskin, and Huxley—were at one time or another platform or pulpit men, delivering their ideas orally and printing them later. Even the novelists could not resist the pressure to meet their readers face to face, and Thackeray, Dickens, Kingsley, and others delivered lectures and gave readings to numerous audiences. Writers were thus audience-conscious, and few wrote without their readers in mind. It was, as Stevenson might have said, an age of talkers.

A Victorian House

Another channel of communication that had a definite effect on Victorian literature was the growing body of magazines which catered to all classes of readers. Early in the century the reviews came into being as quarterlies that had a definite political bias; thus the *Edinburgh Review* (1802) was a Whig organ, and the rival *Quarterly Review* (1808) was Tory. But with the rapid development of great masses of readers the quarterly reviews gave way to monthly magazines, and numerous new periodicals were founded, which provided an outlet for writers—*Blackwood's Magazine* (1817), *The London Magazine* (1820-1829), the *Westminster Review* (1824), *The Athenaeum* (1827), *The Spectator* (1828), a weekly, *Fraser's Magazine* (1830), and the inimitable *Punch* (1841), which has been demonstrating for a century now the capacity of the English to laugh at themselves. Most of these, as the name *magazine* implies, were miscellanies, providing a medium for reviews, political, social, and literary comment, prose fiction, and even poetry. So useful were the magazines to writers that some authors established definite connections with one or more of them, as did Thackeray in assuming the editorship of *The Cornhill Magazine;* and in one or two instances literary groups even created their own magazine (p. 416). The magazines greatly increased the volume of writing by providing ready outlets for literary work. Their effect upon literature, however, was not an altogether unmixed good; by encouraging serial methods of writing novels, for example, they tended to drag creative work to the lower level of mere journalism, and to develop in prose fiction a prolixity and looseness of structure which is the characteristic defect of the Victorian novel. It is not an exaggeration to say, however, that without their service to writers and readers alike, the literature of the Victorian age would hardly have been so full and rich as it is.

The Victorian magazines

Another remarkable element in Victorian writing is the extent to which women appear as authors. Before 1800 it is startling to consider the extent to which women were excluded from literary activity. If a few minor women writers be omitted, the entire history of English literature down to the nineteenth century may be written without mentioning a single woman author. Then, in the realm of prose fiction, women emerged by the side of their brother authors and have maintained their position ever since. Certain forms of literature they have taken over with particular success. Drama and essay they can hardly yet be said to have conquered, but poetry and fiction are literary forms that seem especially fitted to them In the field of the novel, particularly, they have been notably able, and the history of nineteenth-century prose fiction cannot be completely presented without consideration of the genius of Charlotte Brontë, George Eliot, and other women fiction writers of first rank. So one phase of Victorian democracy in literature appears with the opening of the profession of letters to women.

Women as writers

Romance and Realism

So many ingredients went into the making of the complex half century of English literature from 1832 to 1880 that it is difficult to indicate the prevailing elements. Two seem, however, to be highly characteristic of the literature of the period. The first is the extent to which romance and realism

A Victorian Interior.

Romantic elements in Victorian literature

were intermingled, and the second is the recurrence of an insistent note of morality and didacticism. The Victorian age inherited the spirit of romance from the great age of romance which preceded it. Not all of the predominating elements of the romantic movement appear in their full strength, however, in Victorian literature. The nature worship of Wordsworth, for example, is not a striking characteristic of the work of his successors; they tended to be more concerned with men and women than with rocks and rills. The romantic interest in medievalism persisted for a time. This circumstance may be explained, perhaps, not so much by the inherent strength of this particular aspect of romanticism as by the fact that the Middle Ages provided the Victorians not only with an escape from the increasing drabness of contemporary life and a pleasing contrast with it, but also with a realm of artistic beauty. So it was that Thomas Carlyle—romantic peasant-prophet—glorified the Middle Ages and condemned his own times in *Past and Present* (p. 485); that John Ruskin condemned railroads and other scientific innovations; and that William Morris—"the idle singer of an empty day"—filled the vivid pages of *The Earthly Paradise* with medieval legends. Some of the early poetry of the Victorian age has much of the purely romantic quality of John Keats, but the romance of later Victorian poetry was marked by the intrusion of realistic and didactic elements just as marble may become streaked and fretted with other stone as the vein runs out. So it was with Tennyson. The anemic and pallid ladies of his earlier poems—his Isabellas and Marianas—are distinctly, though feebly, romantic in type; the romance of his later poems becomes, however, often the agency of a moral purpose. So it has been said, quite correctly, that the knights and ladies whom he borrowed from Malory for his *Idylls of the King* are really gentlemen and ladies in Prince Alberts and crinolines. Somewhat similarly Arnold's romanticism is hardly pure stuff. Romance there is, to be sure, in *Sohrab and Rustum*, *The Scholar-Gypsy*, and *The Forsaken Merman*, but Arnold was by birth and inclination a teacher, and his verse is permeated with his characteristic melancholy and his constant suggestion of a purpose in everything. The Victorian age cannot be regarded, therefore, as essentially a romantic period, although many Victorian writers made a practice of romanticizing realism, and many romanticists learned, in the course of the period, to write realistically.

Three Generations

The intrusion of realism

The pressure of social problems on the Victorian conscience tended to create an increasing interest in human beings and human relationships, and this interest is reflected in the literature. At no time did realism totally eclipse romanticism, but the tendency was undeniably in that direction—so much so in fact, that a reaction against realism must be listed as one of the aspects of the break with Victorianism that occurred in the eighties (see pp. 846-847). Victorian realism was concerned not so much with individuals as with social groups. Individuals appeared, to be sure, but usually they were types—mouthpieces of the many-headed. So Victorian literature—and especially the Victorian novel—often gives the impression of a crowded stage; it forms a comedy of manners, interpreting society at large rather than the individual, and being concerned—like Nature—with the type rather than with the single life.

The Morality of Victorian Literature

THE POPULAR REACTION against Victorianism in the early decades of the twentieth century is not entirely unlike that against Puritanism after the Restoration of 1660 (see Vol. I, p. 812). To be sure, the reaction was not so violent as the earlier one, but the causes of the revolt were similar. In both instances the reaction was, partly at least, a move for freedom against social restraints and taboos. In the early twentieth century Victorianism was identified popularly with social restrictions in the realm of sex. These particular taboos were, no doubt, characteristic of the period. Socially sex was assumed to be non-existent; the flames of youth were controlled by watchful parents and careful chaperons; marriages were arranged by the elders; and separation and divorce were shocking. But the attitude of society toward the natural impulses was only one, and perhaps not even the most important, among Victorian characteristics. It seems, indeed, to have been only one phase of a much more general tendency, the widespread middle-class agreement to take life seriously, to look for a high purpose in living, and, in general, to "be good." The Victorian age was, on the whole, a Puritan age; social conventions were rather clearly marked out, and any overstepping of the lines was promptly condemned and punished by ostracism. Like most periods of social strait-jacketing, it was a self-righteous, smug, almost priggish age. And it was, quite inevitably, a didactic age replete with sermons and lectures dutifully delivered by those called upon to preach and teach and more or less dutifully listened to by those eager to conform.

Puritan elements in the Victorian age

The bulk of Victorian literature bears the moral stamp of the times. Some of the major prose-writers wrote not so much to entertain as to interpret and to correct. In most of their essays on social and industrial problems the "prophets," Carlyle, Arnold, Newman, and Ruskin, undeniably give the impression of feeling that the "time is out of joint" and that they have been called upon to set it right. This feeling, together with a consistently high spiritual and intellectual quality, is the common bond which unites them. The purposefulness of the period is reflected also in the prose fiction. In the most romantic of George Eliot's novels, *Romola*, the hero exists for the purpose of revealing that the wages of self-indulgence, selfishness, and social sin is death. Many of the novels of Charles Dickens

Moral characteristics of the literature

The Crossing Sweeper

are vehicles for conveying his moral and social ideas. In the poetry there is the same reflection of the morality of the age. Arnold insists that great literature must be characterized by "high seriousness." Although Browning's poems are often more intellectual than emotional, they are almost always "moral" in the Victorian sense of the word. Tennyson, finally, embodies the very essence of the age. In spite of the range and variety of his poetry, the Victorian note predominates. He is the most Victorian of poets, moral to the core, self-conscious to the end. Like the queen, whose laureate he was for more than forty years, he understood the middle-class virtues of his period and took pride in teaching them through the medium of his poems. It was this purpose, no doubt, even more than his high art, which made him the most popular of Victorian poets. It is not entirely unfair to think of him as the Longfellow of Victorian England, for, like the New England poet of his own time, he embodied and expressed the conventional philosophies and moralities of his readers.

The Victorian Drama

The ebb-tide of drama

IN THE VICTORIAN AGE the dominant literary form was probably the novel. It was most certainly not the drama; few periods in English literature have been, in fact, so dramatically arid. For this condition there are two general reasons: first, the stage was strangled to death by legislation; second, the temper of the times was not favorable to dramatic production. So drama in the early Victorian period reached a low-water mark; tragedy became melodrama, and comedy became burlesque and farce.

Government regulation of the stage

The regulation of the theater was under the control of the lord chamberlain. Down to 1843 only three playhouses were licensed to produce dramas; these were Drury Lane, Covent Garden, and the Haymarket. The ratio of theaters to population was, therefore, very low, with the resulting tendency on the part of the controllers of the licensed playhouses to enlarge their structures to such a point that anything like intimate drama became physically impossible, and melodrama and farce, with their unnatural and grossly exaggerated characters and situations, predominated. Furthermore, there was a government control over dramatic themes, and dramatists found themselves closely restricted and far from able to "hold the mirror up to nature." Their dramatic mirror, indeed, was exceedingly narrow, and the reflections were crazed and warped out of all resemblance to normal human life. Certain "illegitimate" playhouses did come into existence and led a precarious life in defiance of regulations, but it was not until the passage of the Theater Regulation Act of 1843 that any real freedom was granted the theaters—and by that time damage had been done from which it took several decades to recover.

Hairdressing in 1863

But, after all, the anemic condition of the Victorian theater was caused not so much by government regulations as by the circumstance that the spirit of the times was not favorable to play production. The Victorian age was clearly not a dramatic age. It was scientific, analytical, and critical—concerned with human affairs in real life and not in the microcosm of the stage. Furthermore, the age was one of careful social restraint. All of these elements have little kinship with drama, which is, in its highest manifestations, emotional, free, unrestrained. In the social conflicts of Victorian life, there were abundant themes for good drama, but the Victorians seldom used the stage as a vehicle for interpreting them. It was an age of reading and reflecting, and the mass of readers looked not to the theater for pictures of current life but to another, more popular form of literature—the novel of manners.

The lack of popular demand for drama

What has just been said of the Victorian drama has been concerned with the popular stage. It should be mentioned that some of the major poets and novelists devoted considerable time to writing plays, but most of these must be regarded as literary and sophisticated rather than in any sense popular. Both Tennyson and Browning essayed dramas, but in spite of the poetic beauty of their productions and of occasional highly dramatic scenes, neither poet can be thought of as a great dramatist. Browning came nearer to the mark than did his brother poet; encouraged by the producer Macready, he wrote *Strafford* in 1837, and for several years thereafter devoted his best efforts to dramatic composition. Elements of dramatic power he certainly possessed, but somehow he could not combine these elements in dramas which could hold the stage. Probably he was too much of an intellectual and too much of a poet to be sufficiently unrestrained in his dramatic work. In actual production his lines were often too subtle, and his situations were so encased in character analysis and rationalizing that the action lacked sweep. But whatever the reason may be, excepting for occasional revivals by the sophisticates, his plays have remained chamber dramas, and critics have generally agreed that Browning's literary powers appear better in his dramatic monologues (see p. 655) than in his dramas.

Chamber dramas

One or two typical Victorian dramatists should be mentioned—for Tennyson and Browning were hardly typical. Bulwer-Lytton, the novelist and miscellaneous writer (see p. 421), wrote half a dozen melodramas, of which *The Lady of Lyons* (1838) and *Richelieu* (1838) were outstanding successes and are still occasionally reproduced. Another novelist, Charles Reade, had a sense for the dramatic but little sense for dramatic structure. By uniting forces, however, with the facile Tom Taylor and borrowing his plots from French drama he managed to score as a dramatist in the popular *Masks and Faces* (1852) and one or two other plays. Taylor alone wrote a popular success, *The Ticket-of-Leave Man* (1863). Charles Reade also collaborated

Popular dramatists: Bulwer-Lytton, Reade, Taylor, and Boucicault

with an even more important dramatist than Taylor—Dion Boucicault (1822-1890). Boucicault was an adept at constructing melodrama—that form seasoned, as in his French models, with sensational incidents, tense situations, and broad humor. Many of his heroic plays are inflated and stagey; but in some of his Irish dramas he comes close to creating natural types, and *The Colleen Bawn*, *Arrah-na-Pogue*, and *The Shaughraun* are almost naturalistic.

Thomas William Robertson

Two dramatists, finally, who wrote near the end of the period, deserve especial mention. Thomas William Robertson (1829-1871) actually did succeed, as earlier dramatists of the period did not, in presenting realistic studies of social groups. As compared with the virile work of the Restoration dramatists (see Vol. I, p. 823) and the twentieth-century dramatic students of social relationships (see p. 859) his plays seem feeble; but though delicate, they are distinct and mark a definite movement in the direction of introducing social manners on the stage. Of his plays which aimed to copy contemporary life naturally three might be mentioned: *Society* (1865), *Ours* (1866), and *Caste* (1867).

William Schwenck Gilbert

The other and even more important figure is William Schwenck Gilbert (1836-1911; see p. 825), who began his dramatic career as a writer of farces and poetical plays and ended it as the eternally popular author of comic operas. The plays of his pre-opera period are, for the most part, satirical phantasies in which airy themes are somewhat cynically reduced to vulgar levels. Among these should be mentioned *Pygmalion and Galatea* (1871) and *Broken Hearts* (1875). The first of his comic operas, *Trial by Jury*, appeared in the same year as *Broken Hearts*, and from that day to this these operas have continued to delight lovers of the whimsical and the clever.

Victorian Poetry

An age of great poetry

A PERIOD SO SOCIALLY RESTRAINED that it could not produce great drama might seem unlikely also to be capable of producing great poetry. This was, in fact, the opinion of some of the early critics in the Victorian age. To Carlyle it seemed that the spiritual and intellectual ideals of the period would have to be expressed in prose; poetry, he thought, was a weak and decadent form. With this point of view Matthew Arnold, who ultimately became professor of poetry at Oxford, did not agree; but Matthew Arnold stopped writing poetry early in his career (see p. 527) that he might have a larger audience through the medium of prose. Neither Carlyle nor Arnold could have foreseen that the Victorian age was destined to be a period of truly great poetry—one of the most significant poetic periods in the history of English literature. Not only did Tennyson, Browning, Arnold, Swinburne, and other great poets arise to replace Wordsworth, Coleridge, Byron, Shelley, and Keats—the giants of the romantic movement—but the period is notable,

Parlor Music

DEMOCRACY, SCIENCE, AND INDUSTRIALISM

like the Elizabethan age, for the number of minor verse-makers of high merit. In variety and range Victorian verse is so rich and varied that it seems futile to attempt to characterize it in general terms. Certain prevailing characteristics, however, the poetry of this half century seems to possess.

Victorian poetry shared with prose the function of interpreting to a large mass of readers the storms, stresses, problems, and philosophies of a complex era. Thus the complexity of Victorian life is stamped visibly on its verse. One note that is often struck is that of the humanitarianism of the times. In certain poems—such as Elizabeth Barrett Browning's *Cry of the Children* (see p. 710)—the springs of the poet's emotion are in his sympathy with human beings submerged or crushed by conditions of life and labor. Usually, however, the poetic themes are not narrowed to a single contemporary situation or set of situations but have to do specifically with the experiences and emotions of human beings. Few of the great poets of the period have escaped this concern with men and women. Browning yielded to the motive most readily of all, perhaps, devoting his genius without stint to the analysis of human action. Tennyson did not analyze the human soul so deeply as did Browning, but most of his themes are directly or indirectly social, and he is seldom as much concerned with the story in his narrative poems as with the human problems involved.

Human interest as a poetic motive

The Cry of the Children

It might be supposed that this primary interest in men and their social problems would have resulted in the creation of realistic poetry dealing with contemporary life. Sometimes it did—as in the poems of Mrs. Browning and Charles Kingsley. For the most part, however, and especially in the earlier part of the period, the pressure toward contemporary realism did not stem entirely the strong current of romanticism which the Victorian era inherited from the preceding age. In poetry the interest in human beings and in contemporary social problems resulted not so much in killing the spirit of romanticism as in changing it. So it was, to illustrate, that Tennyson's *Princess*—a whimsical satire on women's colleges—is rather a romantic and an allegorical treatment of a Victorian problem than a pure romance. Similarly his Arthurian idylls are romances in form rather than in purpose, and his *Ulysses*—a classical theme—shows concern not with the romantic adventures of the hero, but with his decision in a given situation. Browning's counts, ladies, alchemists, monks, and other figures from the Middle Ages, medieval though they are in externals and often in their mental attitudes, interest their creator because of their souls and because of the problems presented by their social relationships. If the romantic narrative poems of William Morris (see p. 797) seem to be woven about figures rather than characters, it is by no means because he lacked social interests but because he took toward his poetry more of an external attitude than did either of the two greater poets just named.

Romance and realism in Victorian poetry

Croquet

The conscious objectivity of Victorian poetry

The purposeful quality of most Victorian poetry gives it a distinctly artful and deliberate direction. In the verse of this era there is very little spontaneous, unpremeditated song. The wine, women, and song element seems, indeed, almost entirely lacking; it is difficult to conceive of a Victorian poem with the "Hey, nonny, nonny" refrain of the Elizabethan outburst, or even the unrestrained love note of Burns's overflowing lyrics. Victorian verse is artistic, but seldom artless; it is careful and controlled rather than free and unrestrained. This characteristic appears in the widespread experiments in meter, in the range and type of subjects, and in the generally intellectual and deliberate quality of the poetry. An indication of these characteristics appears in the early manuscripts of Tennyson's poems which are preserved in the British Museum—carefully written, scratched, corrected, changed with infinite care and almost invariably with marked improvement in the word or line rewritten.

Elements of revolt: the Pre-Raphaelite Brotherhood

Against the purposeful quality of so much of the Victorian poetry there were individual and group rebellions. The largest group of rebels were those who banded themselves together under the name of the Pre-Raphaelite Brotherhood. The leader of the group was Dante Gabriel Rossetti (see p. 783), and his associates were William Holman Hunt, John Everett Millais, Thomas Woolner, and—later—James Collinson, Frederick George Stephens, Walter Deverell, and William Michael Rossetti (brother of Dante Gabriel), all young poets or artists. Several others were at one time or another associated with the Brotherhood or in sympathy with its ideas and objectives; among these were Christina Rossetti (see p. 748)—sister of Dante Gabriel and William—William Morris (see p. 797), and John Ruskin (see p. 501), who came valiantly to their rescue when they were attacked by the conservatives. The P. R. B., as the Brotherhood signed itself, published from January to April, 1850, four numbers of a little magazine called *The Germ: Thoughts towards Nature in Poetry, Literature, and Art*. This journal contained not only a statement of their artistic theories but specimens of their work in poetry and art. Eleven of the finest of D. G. Rossetti's lyrics appeared in *The Germ*.

Artistic theories of the Pre-Raphaelite Brotherhood

The Pre-Raphaelite Brotherhood took its name from its objective, which was fidelity to nature as she was presented by the later medieval Italian painters before Raphael (1483-1520). In this medievalism the Pre-Raphaelite revolt was romantic; in their presentation of nature, however, there was an artistic sophistication which differentiated it sharply from the simple pantheism of Wordsworth. Their work was, indeed, in both painting and poetry, a blending of the romantic, the realistic, and the supernatural. Because there was little in it of the conventionally spiritual and moral qualities of the Victorians, the P. R. B. was vigorously attacked for its sensuousness. The spirit-damsel of D. G. Rossetti's *Blessed Damozel* (see p. 784), who made

The Englishman in India

the golden bar of heaven warm with the pressure of her bosom, seemed to most conservatives to be hardly disembodied and spiritual. This and similar "thoughts towards nature" and "adherences to the simplicity of art" led to the vitriolic attack of the critic Robert Buchanan upon the "fleshly" school of poetry in 1871-1872, in spite of Ruskin's earlier defense of the P. R. B. and its objectives. To most modern readers the poetry of the Brotherhood hardly seems shockingly pagan or even "fleshly"; it seems rather to be exotic, colorful, romantic, and beautiful in its form and in its suggestion of the mystical and the remote from life.

Other rebels: Fitzgerald and Swinburne

Besides the Pre-Raphaelite Brotherhood there were other poets who deviated—not, perhaps, deliberately—from what seem to have been the main philosophical and spiritual currents of Victorian poetry. Of these, two should have special mention, Edward Fitzgerald (see p. 775) and Algernon Charles Swinburne (see p. 808). Fitzgerald's claim to a position among the pagan poets of the period rests in his remarkable paraphrase of the *Rubáiyát* of the Persian poet Omar Khayyám. In a hundred delightfully startling quatrains he expressed the tempting, fatalistic doctrine of enjoying the present and ignoring "the rumble of a distant drum." They shocked conservative believers in immortality and thrilled the bold with their near-eastern frankness and their spiced imagery. Swinburne like Fitzgerald aroused prejudice against himself and his poetry by the unconventional nature of his subjects and the frankly pagan quality of his treatment of them. Although an excellent classical student, who loved the rich beauty of Greek song and story, he was essentially a romanticist, not so much in the injection of his personality—Byron-like—into his poetry, as in his highly aesthetic quality. Of all Victorian poets he was perhaps the most naturally artistic. He possessed an extraordinary capacity for creating lush melody in verse; severe critics, in fact, have condemned what they believe to be a cloying overcharge of richness in his poetry. This distinctly romantic method he applied not only to his medieval themes but also to those which he took from Greek legend; thus, the classical stories underwent at his hands a change into a form that is romantically full, unrestrained, and decorative. In his aesthetic qualities and his love of art for its own sake Swinburne's spiritual kinship is with the Pre-Raphaelites. His craft, however, was more natural and facile than theirs; he was the skilful silversmith of song.

Humorous and satirical verse

One other group of poems should be especially commented on—if only for the reason that critics of Victorian verse so seldom take them into account. This is the satirical group, the nonsense verses, and the parodies. The stolid, phlegmatic character of the English and their capacity for laughing quietly at themselves may have helped save the Victorian age from armed revolt. With the aid of the valuable *Punch* (see p. 409), the satirical poets poked fun at the bugs and humbugs of the times, the manners and morals, the art

The Lady With the Lamp

and the letters. From the pages of *Punch* and other magazines have come down to the twentieth century a flood of excellent comical-satirical verses (see pp. 823-839) that are read too seldom in connection with the sober poetry of the same period. If they were read more and understood better, the Victorian age would be seen to be not altogether heavy, drab, corseted, and moral as a rainy day but brightened with flashes of wit and good fun, which illuminate every corner of Victorian life.

The quality and diversity of Victorian poetry

Victorian poetry is of high quality and of great variety. Probably in no other period of English literature is there such richness and diversity. In subject-matter the range extends from the familiar classical legends down to episodes from Victorian life; in mood classical restraint, romantic freedom, and current realism all appear. The poets of the period were almost all scholars. They had a wide acquaintance with the poetry of all countries and all times, but—on the whole—their art was not smothered by their knowledge. Much of the poetry is permeated with the personalities of the poets. On the other hand, most of it expresses the age rather than the individual literary craftsman. In this particular it differs from the poetry of the romantic movement. In an age of revolution and romance the tendency is ultimately in the direction of highly individualized creation; thus the romantic movement expressed not only clear reflection of the times but also the personal emotions of strongly marked individuals. The Victorian age could hardly have produced a Byron, detached, self-conscious, irrationally rebellious, proud. Tennyson was consciously the poet of his age, as has been said; and Browning, Arnold, Clough, and others, though distinctive enough in craft, were also conscious of the time-pressures. Even the pagan aesthetes, like Swinburne and the Pre-Raphaelites, were aware of the movements of Victorianism and conscious of the extent to which their art diverged from the main drifts. So it was that with all its variety of content and structure the poetry of the Victorian age was characteristically Victorian.

Walking Dresses

Victorian Prose

THE TYPICAL ESSAYIST of the romantic movement was controlled, like the romantic poet, primarily by an interest in himself and a desire to give expression to his own emotions and experiences. It is for this reason that the "personal" essays of Lamb, De Quincey, Hazlitt, and other romanticists contain so much that is autobiographical and almost lyric; their work, to use philosophic terms, tended essentially to be subjective and not objective, internal and not external. They presented the world of their own spirits rather than the world of outside life, or at least colored their opinions rather deliberately with their own emotions. From this group of essayists the Victorian writers of non-fictional prose differ rather sharply. It is true, of course, that they did not detach themselves completely from their personal attitude toward life, and some of them, like Carlyle, stamped their personalities distinctly on their writing. Their essential interest, however, was not avowedly in themselves and their own experiences but in the social problems of Victorian England.

Progressives and reactionaries

The Victorian masters of prose may be divided generally into what might now be called the progressives and the reactionaries. Certain writers had a marked faith in their own times and expressed repeatedly their belief that all was essentially right with the Victorian world and that progress lay forward. To this group belong, among others, Macaulay and Huxley. The reactionaries were not so optimistic; they saw in the social life of their period much to be criticized and corrected. They believed particularly that spiritual values were being eclipsed by materialism, and that faith in culture and art was yielding to faith in "machinery," as Arnold liked to call the wealth, the legislation, the social programs, and, in general, the externals of the period. Of the two groups the hostile critics were, as might be expected, the more explosive; they fulminated and scolded and expressed, on the whole, little satisfaction with a world so confused, complicated, and uncertain as that of Victorian England.

Thomas Babington Macaulay

One of the most buoyant of those who had faith in the times was Thomas Babington Macaulay (see p. 427). Instead of standing on the outside of life and condemning it, he took a very active part in its affairs. He was an ardent Whig member of Parliament, and to him it seemed that the political changes that were giving the government over to the people were natural and desirable. He had, in fact, a firm faith in democracy, a faith which he expressed not only in his political activities but also in his conception of history as the record of a people—not of a few rulers. Macaulay was masculine and direct in his career and in his writings; there was in his work no tinge of the neurotic or the unstable. He never shouted like Carlyle, sneered like Arnold, or scolded like Ruskin. Dramatic he frequently was, but he was seldom vituperative.

Thomas Henry Huxley

Thomas Henry Huxley's interests lay in directions different from those of Macaulay, but he shared the older writer's faith in democracy and progress. His service to Victorian England consisted, indeed, in fighting a lifelong series of skirmishes with those who possessed reactionary spirits and—to use his own phrase—"clerical minds." Primarily he was a scientist, but he was no cold and detached investigator; his objective was to popularize science, and he spent his best years in spreading the gospel of evolution and in attacking non-scientific methods of thought. He was modest enough to decry his own literary ability; actually his writing is direct, clear, non-technical, and seasoned with humor and human interest. And his simple faith in the common man of his time is refreshing.

A Victorian Swell

Social commentators: Carlyle, Newman, Arnold, and Ruskin

One dominating element in Macaulay was his lively interest in the life of people of past centuries; in Huxley the strongest element lay in his vision of a world made new—materially and spiritually—by scientific advancement. The great Victorian prophets, Carlyle, Newman, Arnold, and Ruskin, were imaginative in another way. In the past they saw cultural and spiritual values superior to the materialism of Victorian England, and out of other times they drew the lessons for their own period. To them the complex and feverish nineteenth century seemed socially and economically sick, and each prescribed a panacea for its ills. Carlyle advocated labor, spirituality, submission to a God-given leader. Newman would have led the way to an earlier religious faith. To Arnold culture—knowing the best that has been thought and said in the world—was a cure for materialism. Ruskin, finally, believed that the brutality of the times could be overcome by art. Each man was vigorous in his own manner, and each argued his case tirelessly, if sometimes hopelessly. Of the group Carlyle was the most aggressive; scarcely any one of the current social and economic philosophies escaped his attack. He assailed Chartism, Utilitarianism, and faith in legislation and the ballot. Arnold's assaults on Victorian smugness and "Philistinism," as he called the wealthy, middle-class philosophy of life, earned him the title of the "kid-glove Jeremiah." Ruskin attacked Renaissance architecture and became almost rabid in his mouthings at the extension of the railways and the telegraph lines into the rural districts of England. The conviction of a mission to perform gave to the addresses and writings of these prophets that tincture of confidence and self-righteousness that often pervades the work of earnest reformers. In their aggressiveness the prophets were always earnest; what they lacked most was restraint, balance, and a saving sense of humor.

Critics of art and letters

Another great body of Victorian prose lies in the realm of literary and artistic criticism. Out of this prose came Arnold's striking definition of culture, and many sound suggestions for making critical evaluations in art and letters. And there were, of course, innumerable critical battles. Is the lover of art permitted by his conscience to live in a "palace of art"—an ivory tower—shut off from the vulgar herd and feeding his soul on the delights of a higher epicureanism, or does retribution lie in wait for the selfish one who does not share with the less privileged the opportunities for aesthetic development which come to him? This question William Morris answered in one way, Walter Pater in another. Is art detached from morals, or are ethics and aesthetics interrelated? The question expresses another critical battle which left its scars upon the prose of Ruskin. Again, should literary criticism take the form of appreciation, as Pater argued and practiced, or of condemnation, as Ruskin declared sometimes necessary? Some of the critical arguments were more specific than these, as was the prolonged exchange between Matthew Arnold and Francis Newman—the Cardinal's brother—on the

Victorian Taste

translations of Homer's epics. But whether general or restricted, they were fought with a keenness and high intelligence which have brought to later decades not, to be sure, universal agreement with either point of view but a stimulation of the faculties of literary judgment, which is only one of the notable contributions that Victorian prose has made to English thought.

The Victorian Novel

THE NOVEL IS ONE of the most important types in Victorian literature; and because it presents Victorian life in action rather than in cold analysis and exposition, it is also significant and helpful in revealing the social backgrounds of the period. The Victorian age was a reading age, and the readers were the people—not one special group. The Victorian novel, therefore, is democratic. The popular magazines did a valiant service (see p. 408) in providing an outlet for literary products, and a great many Victorian novels were issued from month to month in sections. Because these installments usually appeared fresh from the pen of the author and often before he had completed his plan for the whole novel, the effect of this method of publication was not entirely good. It increased the natural Victorian tendency toward prolixity, and it had, moreover, a disintegrating effect upon the unity of the whole structure, for not infrequently—as, for example, with Dickens's *Pickwick Papers* (1836)—the plan for the book underwent considerable modification after several installments had been published. Novels published in this way tended, therefore, to be episodic and ill-proportioned with a story that was leisurely in development and with a unity that centered not so much in the plot as in the leading characters. But in spite of such results, the period produced ten or a dozen major novelists and a flock of minor fiction writers whose stories are known now only to scholars.

Some general characteristics of the Victorian novel

The Victorian novel took many forms, some inherited from the earlier decades of the nineteenth century, and some revealing the social pressures of the times. Three traditional forms are significant enough to mention: the sensational tale, the historical romance, and the novel of social life and manners. The first of these can be dismissed with a word, for the tale of terror was by no means as important in the Victorian period as in the preceding era; it appeared in some of the books of Bulwer-Lytton, who had a flair for the supernatural, but the major novelists made little use of it.

Types of the Victorian novel

The historical romance is a more important Victorian form, but there was no Victorian novelist—excepting Thackeray in *Esmond*—who equaled Sir Walter Scott in this field of prose fiction. Edward Bulwer-Lytton— Baron Lytton—(1803-1873) was melodramatic rather than romantic; his historical tales have, moreover, a lumbering, self-conscious manner, quite foreign to the genius of Scott, and are stagey and artificial. *The Last Days of*

The historical romance

Victorian Taste

Pompeii (1834), *Rienzi, the Last of the Tribunes* (1835), *The Last of the Barons* (1843), and *Harold, the Last of the Saxon Kings* (1848) reveal in their very titles this footlight quality, for the adjective *last* is suggestive of the popular-heroic and the melodramatic. Another historical novelist with dramatic leanings was Charles Reade (1814-1884), whose *Cloister and the Hearth* (1861), a beautiful story of the romance of the parents of Erasmus in the Europe of the fifteenth century, is one of the really great historical novels that came out of the period. Charles Kingsley (1819-1875) turned his hand to many types of literature; his historical novels, *Hereward the Wake* (1866) and *Westward Ho!* (1855)—a tale of the days of the Spanish Armada—are entertaining but not so well balanced as Reade's great tale. Finally, some of the major novelists tried their hand at this form of fiction. Thackeray's *Esmond* (1852) is one of the greatest historical novels in English literature. Dicken's two contributions to the genre, *Barnaby Rudge* (1841) and *A Tale of Two Cities* (1859), are more sensational and sentimental than historical. George Eliot's *Romola* (1863) is historically accurate but heavy with morality; it is, in fact, a problem novel (see p. 423) stretched over a historical framework.

The novel of manners

The novel of manners, made popular in the preceding era by Jane Austen (see p. 25), was a type to which the Victorians took eagerly, and many of the best of the Victorian novels belong in this class. In general, two essential elements enter into the making of these stories: first, a realistic copy of contemporary life, and, second, an interpretation of human foibles and human relationships. For some reason this is the type of prose fiction which women writers seem to have done best. Jane Austen was supreme in it, touching off social types with an accuracy and a delicacy that is yet to be surpassed. The great successors of her own sex were Elizabeth Cleghorn Gaskell (1810-1865), whose *Cranford* (1853) is a charming picture of English village life, and Charlotte Brontë (1816-1855), one of the three talented daughters of a vicar of Haworth, who drew out of the narrowness of her own experience materials for *The Professor* (1857), *Villette* (1853), and *Jane Eyre* (1847). A later novelist in the field of simple, democratic realism is Anthony Trollope (1815-1882); his Barsetshire series of tales—*The Warden* (1855), *Barchester Towers* (1857), and *The Three Clerks* (1858)—were so popular in their delightful naturalness as to lead critics to believe that romance in prose fiction had been quite eclipsed by realism. It remained for Robert Louis Stevenson (see p. 874) to explode this belief and to prove that romance can never die.

Not only did the Victorian novelists carry on the earlier fondness for historical and social tales, but they developed to a great height certain other types not so prominent in the preceding age. As might be expected, the novel of purpose made a very frequent appearance in Victorian England;

The Waltz

and so, too, did what would now be called the psychological story. The first of these types was a vehicle which carried to English readers the social ideas of the authors. Such novels were sometimes propagandistic and sometimes merely expository; but since their center of interest was in a missionary purpose and not in either character or plot, they seldom belong among the best of Victorian tales. To this form nearly all Victorian novelists contributed at one time or another. Mrs. Gaskell's *Mary Barton* (1848) and *North and South* (1855) deal respectively with problems of capital and labor and the evils of the factory system. Charles Kingsley used the problems of agricultural labor as the basis for *Yeast* (1848) and those of industrial labor for *Alton Locke* (1850). Cardinal Newman's *Loss and Gain* (1848) is autobiographical in its conversion theme, but it also interprets the Anglo-Catholic movement with which he was so intimately connected (see p. 407). Dickens devoted himself conscientiously and sometimes to the abandonment of plot interest to his theories of reform. *Oliver Twist* (1838) deals with the poor laws, *Nicholas Nickleby* (1839) with school reform, *Bleak House* (1853) with the red tape of the Court of Chancery, and *Hard Times* (1854) with the author's economic theories. But unlike most of the propagandist novelists Dickens did not give up the entire story to the presentation of his ideas of reform, but poured these elements into the complex literary mixture of his novels.

The novel of purpose

The psychological novel is often also the "problem" novel. That is, it frequently presents—even attempts to solve—some problem in human relationship, but in doing so, it must, perforce, analyze human nature. The greatest novelists in this field are George Eliot and George Meredith. As compared with Dickens, George Eliot is solid, profound, accurate in her analyses of human characters. Her successor, George Meredith (1828-1909), was probably not her equal in range and power, but he was one of the best of the Victorians in the realm of the problem novel and the human character study. He was a poet (see p. 768) and an essayist (his *Essay on Comedy*—1877—is one of the best analyses of the subject) as well as a novelist. His first novel, *The Ordeal of Richard Feverel* (1859), is typical of his work. It presents the psychological problem that arises out of a conflict between natural impulses in a youth and the educational system under which his father is trying to bring him up. The characters were taken—like most of Meredith's characters—from the upper classes; in this respect he differs from most of the earlier Victorian novelists. A few of the best of Meredith's other psychological studies are *Rhoda Fleming* (1865), *Beauchamp's Career* (1876), *The Egoist* (1879)—perhaps his most famous novel—*Diana of the Crossways* (1885), and *The Amazing Marriage* (1895).

The psychological, or problem, novel

Three Victorian novelists stand out so distinctly above their fellow fiction writers that—like Tennyson and Browning among the poets—they

Tête-à-Tête

deserve fuller treatment. They are Charles Dickens (1812-1870), William Makepeace Thackeray (1811-1863), and George Eliot (1819-1880).

Charles Dickens

Of the three major novelists Dickens was unquestionably the most popular. This was the natural result of his inclination to bring into his stories types familiar to the mass of readers and to display his men and women in familiar situations in which they were moved by what may be called "popular" emotions. He was essentially a realist in his art, but he romanticized and sentimentalized his realism. To Dickens, moreover, more than to either of the other two more restrained novelists, may be applied the popular *cliché*, "He ran the gamut of human emotions." His great popularity lay partly in his melodramatic fondness for playing deliberately on his readers' feelings. Dickens was a literary caricaturist. His art included a capacity for effective exaggeration. Applied to characters this created unforgettable types so striking that the tag-names he gave them became common for the characteristics represented—Pecksniff for hypocrisy, Micawber for irresponsibility, Uriah Heep for false and vicious humility. Applied to comic situations his flair for exaggeration resulted in broadly humorous episodes. Applied to pathetic situations, however, the result was often tawdry emotionalism. For this he has been criticized in his own time and since. Sorrow, say the critics, is most touching when restrained. But Dickens was a consciously popular writer and exaggerated all situations; and melodrama and sentimentalism are undeniably more popular than drama and sentiment. Dickens, finally, was popular because he was the novelist of the middle and lower classes. The aristocracy he did not know and could not interpret. His Sir Mulberry Hawks and Lady Dedlocks are lay figures, and Sidney Carton was his only successful aristocrat. But among the middle-class and the lowly he was completely at home—understanding, sympathetic, delightful.

William Makepeace Thackeray

Dickens's literary ancestor among the early novelists was Tobias Smollett, the writer of picaresque tales; Thackeray's was Henry Fielding, moralist and satirist. The affinity of Thackeray and Fielding is not difficult to understand; their temperaments were much alike. Like Fielding, Thackeray was a moralist. He hated shams; he hated "man's inhumanity to man." With the essential kindliness in his writing is mingled a strain of cynicism. He disclaimed writing novels of purpose, and his material, indeed, is not always, as is that of Dickens, drawn from contemporary life. Unlike Dickens, again, he depicted the upper and middle classes. He called himself a snob, and perhaps he was one essentially, but he loathed snobs and snobbery and social pretense. The moral character of his works appears not only in his occasional invasion of his story in order to preach a sermon but in the high poetic justice of his climaxes. For example, his two most famous women characters, Becky Sharp (the nearest to a social vampire in Victorian literature) and

Beatrix Esmond (the beauty whose selfishness cost an amorous prince his throne), both appear at the end of the story washed out and finished. In these and similar scenes Thackeray is never melodramatic and stagey; his characters who pay the price of sin are not picturesquely drowned, like Dickens's Quilp and Steerforth, but the effect of the lesson is probably greater because the treatment is more restrained. Thackeray was a critic of life and a good one. Unlike Dickens, however, he did not identify himself with his characters. He was a dissector of life, not an actor in it; he was the showman; his characters—to use his own figure from *Vanity Fair*—were puppets, and when the curtain went down, he put them back into the box.

Christmas Carolers

Thackeray's list of novels is not nearly so long as that of Dickens, for he was a slow worker and a methodical one. But what he did was almost all first class whereas some of Dickens's novels, like some of Scott's, show the pressure that was forcing them to the level of journalistic hack-work. *Vanity Fair* (1847-1848) is probably the best known of Thackeray's tales. Others are *Pendennis* (1848-1850), *The Newcomes* (1853-1855), *The Virginians* (1857-1859), and—in some respects the best of all—*Henry Esmond* (1852), a story built upon the Jacobite plots to restore the Old Pretender to the throne of England.

To classify George Eliot (born Mary Ann Evans), as has sometimes been done, among the "women" novelists of the period is in some respects unfair and—one is tempted to say—Victorian, for it suggests an apology. She needs none; she is one of the absolutely great writers of the period and stands with Dickens and Thackeray secure of a high place in English literature. As a scholar and philosopher, indeed, and in sheer intellectual power she transcends both. In the two decades in which her great novels were written the social-political novel was popular, and she lent her talents first to this type. *Adam Bede, The Mill on the Floss,* and *Silas Marner* are all tales of work and workers into which she has woven her own vital experiences; in Adam there is much of her father, and in Tom and Maggie Tulliver she and her brother appear. In her later novels the trend was somewhat away from the social study and in the direction of problems of human relationships. *Middlemarch*, to illustrate, presents the problem of a young girl who is tricked by her admiration for scholarship into marriage with a desiccated old pedant; and *Romola* is a study in consummate pride and selfishness, as well as a painstakingly complete and accurate historical picture of Italy in the days of Savonarola. The greatness of these and of her other novels lies in their penetration and power. Among Victorian novelists George Eliot is the representative of culture, sound philosophy, keen observation of men and women, and amazing ability in presenting life effectively. She is, it may be said, among Victorian novelists what Browning is among Victorian poets, and her place is as secure as his.

George Eliot

The Age in Retrospect

A characterization of the Victorian age

MATTHEW ARNOLD's characterization of Victorian England as

> . . . a darkling plain
> Swept with confused alarms of struggle and flight,
> Where ignorant armies clash by night

is pessimistic but not entirely devoid of truth. The age, especially in its earlier decades, was a time of storm and stress, and the lines between parties and between principles were not always clearly marked. It is small wonder, therefore, that certain social prophets like Carlyle sought a way out by attacking current philosophies and advocating a return to what they conceived to be the better social and economic practices of earlier centuries. England at large, however, muddled through, feeling that the way out lay forward and not backward. Most of the English saw, indeed, that uncertainty and doubt, courageously faced, are marks of progress, whereas the search for a safe port in a storm must be regarded as a retreat and not an advancement. Courage, then, was a principle of Victorian conduct. Out of this determination and as a result of the labors of the economic reformers the new industrialism of the nineteenth century, which had threatened for a time to submerge and brutalize the English masses, yielded them ultimately better living conditions and a democratic control of the country.

The sweep of Victorian literature

The literature which sought to interpret the Victorian world reflects the strain, the richness, the complexity, the variety, and the democratic spirit of the times. Victorian literature is notable in all modern forms excepting drama. In poetry Tennyson, Browning, Arnold, Swinburne, Morris, Rossetti, Meredith, and many others of less note made of the age a great period for verse of all types. Into the full stream went the currents of classicism, romanticism, realism. Victorian verse is, on the whole, intellectual in mood and makes interpretation of contemporary life its objective; much of it, however, lies in the realm of pure art; and in few periods, moreover, does poetry reveal such metrical variety and such artistic structure. Victorian prose is sometimes progressive in its interpretations of the Victorian spirit, sometimes reactionary in its attacks upon current philosophy and manners. Like poetry its forms are various. The novel was carried to new heights by Dickens, Thackeray, George Eliot, and dozens of less important writers. Most of the subjects and moods of the novel of the preceding period were continued in the Victorian age, and others were added. Realism and romanticism were both prominent in prose fiction with realism and a tendency toward propaganda predominating. The immense industry of Victorian authors, prose writers and poets alike, and the high quality of their work united to make the Victorian age one of the most remarkable periods in the literary history of England.

Full Evening Dress

PROSE CRITICS OF ART AND LIFE

Thomas Babington Macaulay
1800-1859

Thomas Babington Macaulay was fortunate in being born in an era which suited his temperament. Although raised to a peerage in 1857 as Baron Macaulay of Rothley—the place of his birth—he was born a commoner and was politically a Whig and an ardent believer in democracy, election by ballot, reform bills, and most of the popular Victorian ideas which his contemporary Carlyle despised and attacked. He was the eldest child of Zachary Macaulay, anti-slavery philanthropist. After attending school at Clapham, where his parents lived for a while, and at Little Shefford, near Cambridge, he entered Trinity College, Cambridge, and soon gained a reputation for his diligent pursuit of the classical literatures. He was awarded a Cambridge fellowship in 1824, one year before the appearance in the *Edinburgh Review* of his famous essay on Milton (see Vol. I, pp. 635-639) and two years before his admission to the bar. His political career began with his appointment as commissioner of bankruptcy and his election to Parliament in 1830. The first of his many brilliant speeches in the House of Commons was on the Reform Bill of 1832. Two years later, in order to improve his financial situation, he went to India as legal adviser to the Supreme Council. He returned to England in 1838, toured Italy, and in 1839 was elected to represent Edinburgh in Parliament. He served in the cabinet as Secretary of War but was forced out of office in 1841 by the fall of the Melbourne ministry.

The time and freedom which he gained by severing his political ties he devoted to literary work. *The Lays of Ancient Rome* was published in 1842 and was immediately popular. The first two volumes of what he regarded as his life work, a *History of England from the Accession of James II,* appeared in 1848, and volumes three and four came out in 1855. The fifth and last volume, which brought the history down to the death of William III, was issued, in incomplete form, shortly after his death in 1859. To the distinction which he earned by his literary work was added that which came to him in his election to the Lord Rectorship of Glasgow in 1849, his return to Parliament for Edinburgh in 1852, his elevation to the peerage, and his burial in the Poets' Corner of Westminster Abbey.

Macaulay was one of the most industrious of Victorian writers, and there were few types of literature which he did not attempt. Parliamentarian and poet are titles that can be applied to few Englishmen, but Macaulay earned both. His reputation as a poet has suffered a decline in recent years, but in his own time his *Lays of Ancient Rome* rivaled his *History of England* in popularity. Few critics would claim a high position for Macaulay the poet; yet his heroic narratives in verse are undeniably both sweeping and stirring. The most famous ones are the four long lays from Roman legend that constitute his major poetic achievement, but some of his earlier and shorter poems have higher poetic merit. In *The Last Buccaneer,* for example, there is in the story of the ghost ship that fled full-sail through the storm a suggestion of the mystic and the romantic that Macaulay did not often introduce into either his poetry or his prose.

It is as a prose-writer, however, that he has earned his place in literature. Many who are familiar with his five-volume history of England do not know that for a period of twenty years he contributed scores of biographical and critical essays to the *Edinburgh Review*, and that some of the best of the literary and historical biographies in the current edition of the *Encyclopaedia Britannica*—including those of Bunyan, Goldsmith, and Samuel Johnson—came from his active pen. It is an interesting fact, too, that some of his best known biographical essays, including those on Milton, Addison, Dryden, Johnson, and Byron, appeared in the *Edinburgh Review* not as detached essays but as book reviews. Following the practice of the times Macaulay used his book reviews as frames over which he stretched his own ideas and comments; an ironic result of this practice is that many of his reviews are still read whereas the books reviewed have long since been forgotten. A catalogue of these miscellaneous reviews and magazine articles reveals Macaulay's immense range of information, his general preference for history, biography, and literature, and his concern with contemporary political philosophies and problems.

If Macaulay had not been a historian and biographer, it is conceivable that he might have been a novelist. His master in the art of writing history was not Dr. Dryasdust, with his arid documentations, but Sir Walter Scott, who made the dry bones of history live in novels in which historical figures act and speak. This method of reviving the past Macaulay expressed in his theory of history and practiced in his historical writings. History to him was a revival of the past by its re-creation in detailed pageantry. "The talent which is required to write history," he believed, "bears a considerable affinity to the talent of a great dramatist." The statement is significant, for in his historical writing Macaulay not only brought his characters to life but created effects, as a dramatist does, by introducing sharp contrasts and striking oppositions. So it is that his history not only moves but has perspective and light and shade.

These vivid qualities appear in Macaulay's prose style. There is in his writing so much colorful, rich detail that it suggests a verbal pageantry. His fondness for contrasts and dramatic effects resulted, moreover, in a balanced style of writing, with paragraphs and sentences reflecting in their structure the balance and contrast in the thought. His writing is clear and lucid almost to the point of superficiality. There is in his thought nothing of the mystic and spiritual; he is a frank materialist, and his writing reflects his superficial and objective attitude toward life. His style is direct, concrete, perhaps a little hard and brittle. But it is eminently readable and free from artificialities and conscious elaborations. The best tribute to its quality is the fact that the English public awaited eagerly the appearance of every volume of the *History of England* and read history, for the first time in their lives, as they would have read an exciting romance.

from *History*

Macaulay's essay on *History* appeared in the *Edinburgh Review* for May, 1828, ostensibly as a critical review of Henry Neele's *Romance of History* (London, 1828); actually it is an independent monograph that contains not only a keen comment on classical and modern historians but an expression of Macaulay's theory of historical composition. The persistence with which the author clung to his theory is apparent in the circumstance that in his *History of England from the Accession of James II*, the first two volumes of which appeared twenty years after this essay was published, Macaulay plays the rôle of his own "perfect historian . . . in whose work the character and spirit of an age is exhibited in miniature." Macaulay's essay on history should be compared with that of Thomas Carlyle, published in *Fraser's Magazine* in 1830; the essential difference between the two historians is that Macaulay is a Whig—Carlyle a Tory; Macaulay a democrat—Carlyle an aristocrat. In reprinting Macaulay's long essay here two omissions have been made at the points indicated by ellipses. Of these the first is of seven and a half paragraphs, the second of thirty-seven paragraphs; in these omitted portions the author comments on the work of various Greek and Latin historians.

To write history respectably—that is, to abbreviate dispatches, and make extracts from speeches, to intersperse in due proportion epithets of praise and abhorrence, to draw up antithetical characters of great men, setting forth how many contradictory virtues and vices they united, and abounding in *withs* and *withouts*—all this is very easy. But to be a really great historian is perhaps the rarest of intellectual distinctions. Many scientific works are, in their kind, absolutely perfect. There are poems which we should be inclined to designate as faultless, or as disfigured only by blemishes which pass unnoticed in the general blaze of excellence. There are speeches, some speeches of Demosthenes particularly, in which it would be impossible to alter a word without altering it for the worse. But we are acquainted with no history which approaches to our notion of what a history ought to be—with no history which does not widely depart, either on the right hand or on the left, from the exact line.

The cause may easily be assigned. This province of literature is a debatable land. It lies on the confines of two distinct territories. It is under the jurisdiction of two hostile powers; and, like other districts similarly situated, it is ill-defined, ill-cultivated, and ill-regulated. Instead of being equally shared between its two rulers, the Reason and the Imagination, it falls alternately under the sole and absolute dominion of each. It is sometimes fiction. It is sometimes theory.

History, it has been said, is philosophy teaching by examples. Unhappily, what the philosophy gains in soundness and depth the examples generally lose in vividness. A perfect historian must possess an imagination sufficiently powerful to make his narrative affecting and picturesque. Yet he must control it so absolutely as to content himself with the materials which he finds, and to refrain from supplying deficiencies by additions of his own. He must be a profound and ingenious reasoner. Yet he must possess sufficient self-command to abstain from casting his facts in the mold of his hypothesis. Those who can justly estimate these almost insuperable difficulties will not think it strange that every writer should have failed, either in the narrative or in the speculative department of history.

It may be laid down as a general rule, though subject to considerable qualifications and exceptions, that history begins in novel and ends in essay. Of the romantic historians Herodotus is the earliest and the best. His animation, his simple-hearted tenderness, his wonderful talent for description and dialogue, and the pure sweet flow of his language, place him at the head of narrators. He reminds us of a delightful child. There is a grace beyond the reach of affectation in his awkwardness, a malice in his innocence, an intelligence in his nonsense, an insinuating eloquence in his lisp. We know of no writer who makes such interest for himself and his book in the heart of the reader. At the distance of three-and-twenty centuries, we feel for him the same sort of pitying fondness which Fontaine and Gay are said to have inspired in society. He has written an incomparable book. He has written something better perhaps than the best history; but he has not written a good history; he is, from the first to the last chapter, an inventor. We do not here refer merely to those gross fictions with which he has been reproached by the critics of later times. We speak of that coloring which is equally diffused over his whole narrative, and which perpetually leaves the most sagacious reader

---

16. **Demosthenes**, a famous Greek orator (fourth century B.C.). 35. **History . . . examples**, an expression found in Thucydides, I, 2 (see p. 430, note 5); in Dionysius of Halicarnassus, a Greek rhetorician and historian (first century B.C.), *Art of Rhetoric*, 11, 2; and in Henry St. John, an English statesman (1678-1751), *On the Study and Use of History*. Carlyle in his essay *On History* published in *Fraser's Magazine* in 1830, defines history as "Philosophy teaching by Experience."

58. **Herodotus**, a Greek historian (fifth century B.C.), called the Father of History. He was the first significant writer of Greek prose. 71. **Fontaine**, Jean de La Fontaine, a French poet (1621-1695), noted for his absent-mindedness. 72. **Gay**, John Gay (1685-1732), an English poet of Pope's circle (see Vol. I, pp. 832 and 1101). He was shy but received kindly treatment from several patrons.

in doubt what to reject and what to receive. The most authentic parts of his work bear the same relation to his wildest legends which *Henry the Fifth* bears to *The Tempest*. . . .

The history of Thucydides differs from that of Herodotus as a portrait differs from the representation of an imaginary scene; as the Burke or Fox of Reynolds differs from his Ugolino or his Beaufort. In the former case, the archetype is given; in the latter, it is created. The faculties which are required for the latter purpose are of a higher and rarer order than those which suffice for the former, and indeed necessarily comprise them. He who is able to paint what he sees with the eye of the mind will surely be able to paint what he sees with the eye of the body. He who can invent a story, and tell it well, will also be able to tell, in an interesting manner, a story which he has not invented. If, in practice, some of the best writers of fiction have been among the worst writers of history, it has been because one of their talents had merged in another so completely that it could not be severed; because, having long been habituated to invent and narrate at the same time, they found it impossible to narrate without inventing.

Some capricious and discontented artists have affected to consider portrait-painting as unworthy of a man of genius. Some critics have spoken in the same contemptuous manner of history. Johnson puts the case thus: The historian tells either what is false or what is true; in the former case he is no historian; in the latter he has no opportunity for displaying his abilities, for truth is one, and all who tell the truth must tell it alike.

It is not difficult to elude both the horns of this dilemma. We will recur to the analogous art of portrait-painting. Any man with eyes and hands may be taught to take a likeness. The process, up to a certain point, is merely mechanical. If this were all, a man of talents might justly despise the occupation. But we could mention portraits which are resemblances—but not mere resemblances; faithful—but much more than faithful; portraits which condense into one point of time, and exhibit, at a single glance, the whole history of turbid and eventful lives—in which the eye seems to scrutinize us, and the mouth to command us—in which the brow menaces, and the lip almost quivers with scorn—in which every wrinkle is a comment on some important transaction. The account which Thucydides has given of the retreat from Syracuse is, among narratives, what Vandyck's Lord Strafford is among paintings.

Diversity, it is said, implies error; truth is one, and admits of no degrees. We answer, that this principle holds good only in abstract reasonings. When we talk of the truth of imitation in the fine arts, we mean an imperfect and a graduated truth. No picture is exactly like the original; nor is a picture good in proportion as it is like the original. When Sir Thomas Lawrence paints a handsome peeress, he does not contemplate her through a powerful microscope, and transfer to the canvas the pores of the skin, the blood-vessels of the eye, and all the other beauties which Gulliver discovered in the Brobdignaggian maids of honor. If he were to do this, the effect would not merely be unpleasant, but, unless the scale of the picture were proportionably enlarged, would be absolutely *false*. And, after all, a microscope of greater power than that which he had employed would convict him of innumerable omissions. The same may be said of history. Perfectly and absolutely true it cannot be, for, to be perfectly

---

4. **Henry . . . Tempest.** In *Henry V* Shakespeare followed sources with considerable fidelity, but *The Tempest* was a fanciful dream with no historical basis. 5. **Thucydides,** the second famous Greek historian (fifth century B.C.); he wrote the history of the struggle between Athens and Sparta. 8. **Burke,** Edmund Burke (1729-1797), a celebrated British orator and statesman. **Fox,** Charles James Fox (1749-1806), an English orator and statesman. **Reynolds,** Sir Joshua Reynolds (1723-1792), an English portrait painter. His portraits of Burke and Fox are from actual life. Those of Ugolino (see p. 556, note 54) and Henry Beaufort (d. 1447), an English prelate and statesman, are from imagination. 33. **Johnson,** Samuel Johnson. See Vol. I, pp. **833 and 1125.**

57. **retreat from Syracuse.** Syracuse, the chief city of ancient Sicily, was besieged by the Athenians in 415-413 B.C.; but the attack failed, and after heavy sacrifices of ships and men the Athenians retreated. 58. **Vandyck's Lord Strafford.** There are three celebrated portraits of Thomas Wentworth, Earl of Strafford (1593-1641), an English statesman, by Sir Anthony Vandyck (1599-1641), who was a Flemish portrait painter attached to the court of Charles I. 68. **Sir Thomas Lawrence,** a fashionable English portrait painter (1769-1830). 73. **Gulliver . . . honor.** In Part II of Swift's *Gulliver's Travels* (Vol. I, pp. 1019 ff.), Gulliver goes to Brobdingnag, a country of giants sixty feet in height. In Swift's description of these giants physical details are naturally made prominent.

and absolutely true, it ought to record *all* the slightest particulars of the slightest transactions—all the things done and all the words uttered during the time of which it treats. The omission of any circumstance, however insignificant, would be a defect. If history were written thus, the Bodleian library would not contain the occurrences of a week. What is told in the fullest and most accurate annals bears an infinitely small proportion to what is suppressed. The difference between the copious work of Clarendon and the account of the civil wars in the abridgment of Goldsmith vanishes when compared with the immense mass of facts respecting which both are equally silent.

No picture, then, and no history, can present us with the whole truth; but those are the best pictures and the best histories which exhibit such parts of the truth as most nearly produce the effect of the whole. He who is deficient in the art of selection may, by showing nothing but the truth, produce all the effect of the grossest falsehood. It perpetually happens that one writer tells less truth than another, merely because he tells more truths. In the imitative arts we constantly see this. There are lines in the human face, and objects in landscape, which stand in such relations to each other, that they ought either to be all introduced into a painting together or all omitted together. A sketch into which none of them enters may be excellent; but, if some are given and others left out, though there are more points of likeness, there is less likeness. An outline scrawled with a pen, which seizes the marked features of a countenance, will give a much stronger idea of it than a bad painting in oils. Yet the worst painting in oils that ever hung at Somerset House resembles the original in many more particulars. A bust of white marble may give an excellent idea of a blooming face. Color the lips and cheeks of the bust, leaving the hair and eyes unaltered, and the similarity, instead of being more striking, will be less so.

History has its foreground and its background; and it is principally in the management of its perspective that one artist differs from another. Some events must be represented on a large scale, others diminished; the great majority will be lost in the dimness of the horizon; and a general idea of their joint effect will be given by a few slight touches.

In this respect no writer has ever equaled Thucydides. He was a perfect master of the art of gradual diminution. His history is sometimes as concise as a chronological chart; yet it is always perspicuous. It is sometimes as minute as one of Lovelace's letters; yet it is never prolix. He never fails to contract and to expand it in the right place.

Thucydides borrowed from Herodotus the practice of putting speeches of his own into the mouths of his characters. In Herodotus this usage is scarcely censurable. It is of a piece with his whole manner. But it is altogether incongruous in the work of his successor, and violates, not only the accuracy of history, but the decencies of fiction. When once we enter into the spirit of Herodotus, we find no inconsistency. The conventional probability of his drama is preserved from the beginning to the end. The deliberate orations and the familiar dialogues are in strict keeping with each other. But the speeches of Thucydides are neither preceded nor followed by anything with which they harmonize. They give to the whole book something of the grotesque character of those Chinese pleasure-grounds in which perpendicular rocks of granite start up in the midst of a soft green plain. Invention is shocking where truth is in such close juxtaposition.

Thucydides honestly tells us that some of these discourses are purely fictitious. He may have reported the substance of others correctly. But it is clear from the internal evidence that he has preserved no more than the substance. His own peculiar habits of thought and expression are everywhere discernible.

---

7. **Bodleian library**, the famous library of Oxford University.
12. **Clarendon**, Edward Hyde, Earl of Clarendon (1609-1674), an English Royalist statesman and historian. His *History of the Great Rebellion* is full of details and digressions and fills fifteen books in three large volumes; Oliver Goldsmith's *History of England* is a short work with but a brief account of the Civil Wars. 40. **Somerset House**, a palace on the Strand, London, now used for government offices. From 1771 to 1837 it housed the schools of the Royal Academy of Arts.

60. **Lovelace**, the chief male character in Richardson's *Clarissa Harlowe*, noted for his long and detailed letters.

Individual and national peculiarities are seldom to be traced in the sentiments, and never in the diction. The oratory of the Corinthians and Thebans is not less Attic, either in matter or in manner, than that of the Athenians. The style of Cleon is as pure, as austere, as terse, and as significant as that of Pericles.

In spite of this great fault, it must be allowed that Thucydides has surpassed all his rivals in the art of historical narration, in the art of producing an effect on the imagination, by skilful selection and disposition, without indulging in the license of invention. But narration, though an important part of the business of a historian, is not the whole. To append a moral to a work of fiction is either useless or superfluous. A fiction may give a more impressive effect to what is already known; but it can teach nothing new. If it presents to us characters and trains of events to which our experience furnishes us with nothing similar, instead of deriving instructions from it, we pronounce it unnatural. We do not form our opinions from it; but we try it by our preconceived opinions. Fiction, therefore, is essentially imitative. Its merit consists in its resemblance to a model with which we are already familiar, or to which at least we can instantly refer. Hence it is that the anecdotes which interest us most strongly in authentic narrative are offensive when introduced into novels; that what is called the romantic part of history is in fact the least romantic. It is delightful as history, because it contradicts our previous notions of human nature, and of the connection of causes and effects. It is, on that very account, shocking and incongruous in fiction. In fiction, the principles are given, to find the facts; in history, the facts are given, to find the principles; and the writer who does not explain the phenomena as well as state them performs only one half of his office. Facts are the mere dross of history. It is from the abstract truth which interpenetrates them, and lies latent among them like gold in the ore, that the mass derives its whole value; and the precious particles are generally combined with the baser in such a manner that the separation is a task of the utmost difficulty. . . .

The writers of modern times have far surpassed those of antiquity. The historians of our own country are unequaled in depth and precision of reason; and even in the works of our mere compilers, we often meet with speculations beyond the reach of Thucydides or Tacitus.

But it must, at the same time, be admitted that they have characteristic faults, so closely connected with their characteristic merits, and of such magnitude, that it may well be doubted whether, on the whole, this department of literature has gained or lost during the last two-and-twenty centuries.

The best historians of later times have been seduced from truth, not by their imagination, but by their reason. They far excel their predecessors in the art of deducing general principles from facts. But unhappily they have fallen into the error of distorting facts to suit general principles. They arrive at a theory from looking at some of the phenomena; and the remaining phenomena they strain or curtail to suit the theory. For this purpose it is not necessary that they should assert what is absolutely false; for all questions in morals and politics are questions of comparison and degree. Any proposition which does not involve a contradiction in terms may by possibility be true; and if all the circumstances which raise a probability in its favor be stated and enforced, and those which lead to an opposite conclusion be omitted or lightly passed over, it may appear to be demonstrated. In every human character and transaction there is a mixture of good and evil; a little exaggeration, a little suppression, a judicious use of epithets, a watchful and searching skepticism with respect to the evidence on one side, a convenient credulity with respect to every report or tradition on the other, may easily

---

3. **oratory . . . Athenians.** The language and the culture of Corinth and of Thebes were different from those of Athens; yet Thucydides makes the speeches of their leaders conform to the style of Athens. 6. **Cleon,** an Athenian demagogue (d. 422 B.C.), especially good at haranguing a mob; his style would naturally differ widely from that of Pericles, the celebrated Athenian orator and statesman (fifth century B.C.).

57. **Tacitus,** a noted Roman historian and legal orator (55-117?). Macaulay says that Tacitus is "unrivaled among historians in the delineation of character and has very few superiors among dramatists and novelists." 71. **They . . . theory.** This charge has also been laid against Macaulay.

make a saint of Laud, or a tyrant of Henry the Fourth.

This species of misrepresentation abounds in the most valuable works of modern historians. Herodotus tells his story like a slovenly witness, who, heated by partialities and prejudices, unacquainted with the established rules of evidence, and uninstructed as to the obligations of his oath, confounds what he imagines with what he has seen and heard, and brings out facts, reports, conjectures, and fancies, in one mass. Hume is an accomplished advocate. Without positively asserting much more than he can prove, he gives prominence to all the circumstances which support his case; he glides lightly over those which are unfavorable to it; his own witnesses are applauded and encouraged; the statements which seem to throw discredit on them are controverted; the contradictions into which they fall are explained away; a clear and connected abstract of their evidence is given. Everything that is offered on the other side is scrutinized with the utmost severity; every suspicious circumstance is a ground for comment and invective; what cannot be denied is extenuated, or passed by without notice; concessions even are sometimes made; but this insidious candor only increases the effect of the vast mass of sophistry.

We have mentioned Hume as the ablest and most popular writer of his class; but the charge which we have brought against him is one to which all our most distinguished historians are in some degree obnoxious. Gibbon, in particular, deserves very severe censure. Of all the numerous culprits, however, none is more deeply guilty than Mr. Mitford. We willingly acknowledge the obligations which are due to his talents and industry. The modern historians of Greece had been in the habit of writing as if the world had learned nothing new during the last sixteen hundred years. Instead of illustrating the events which they narrated by the philosophy of a more enlightened age, they judged of antiquity by itself alone. They seemed to think that notions, long driven from every other corner of literature, had a prescriptive right to occupy this last fastness. They considered all the ancient historians as equally authentic. They scarcely made any distinction between him who related events at which he had himself been present and him who five hundred years after composed a philosophic romance for a society which had in the interval undergone a complete change. It was all Greek, and all true! The centuries which separated Plutarch from Thucydides seemed as nothing to men who lived in an age so remote. The distance of time produced an error similar to that which is sometimes produced by distance of place. There are many good ladies who think that all the people in India live together, and who charge a friend setting out for Calcutta with kind messages to Bombay. To Rollin and Barthélemy, in the same manner, all the classics were contemporaries.

Mr. Mitford certainly introduced great improvements; he showed us that men who wrote in Greek and Latin sometimes told lies; he showed us that ancient history might be related in such a manner as to furnish not only allusions to schoolboys, but important lessons to statesmen. From that love of theatrical effect and high-flown sentiment which had poisoned almost every other work on the same subject his book is perfectly free. But his passion for a theory as false, and far more ungenerous, led him substantially to violate truth in every page. Statements unfavorable to democracy are made with unhesitating confidence, and with the utmost bitterness of language. Every charge brought against a

---

1. **Laud,** William Laud (1573-1645), Archbishop of Canterbury; he dictated the ecclesiastical policy of Charles I. Macaulay, a Whig, took a partisan attitude toward Laud and his period. **Henry the Fourth.** In 1598 Henry IV of France issued the famous Edict of Nantes, which guaranteed the rights of Protestants. But because of his vigorous efforts to improve conditions in his country, he was frequently called a despot. 12. **Hume,** David Hume (1711-1776), a Scottish philosopher and historian; author of *History of England* (1754-1761), which was still popular in 1828. He wrote from the Tory point of view. 35. **obnoxious,** liable. **Gibbon,** Edward Gibbon (1737-1794), an English historian; author of *The History of the Decline and Fall of the Roman Empire.* 38. **Mr. Mitford,** William Mitford (1744-1827), an English historian, whose *History of Greece* appeared at intervals from 1784 to 1810. As a Tory he stressed the bad effects of democracy. In a caustic review of the *History,* Macaulay says that he tried to "reduce an overpraised writer to his proper level."

58. **Plutarch,** a famous Greek historian, author of *Lives* of forty-six eminent Greeks and Romans. He lived in the first century A.D.; Thucydides in the fifth century B.C. 65. **Calcutta . . . Bombay,** cities in India about 1100 miles apart. 66. **Rollin and Barthélemy,** French historians of the eighteenth century; both were read in Macaulay's time.

monarch or an aristocracy is sifted with the utmost care. If it cannot be denied, some palliating supposition is suggested; or we are at least reminded that some circumstances now unknown *may* have justified what at present appears unjustifiable. Two events are reported by the same author in the same sentence; their truth rests on the same testimony; but the one supports the darling hypothesis, and the other seems inconsistent with it. The one is taken and the other is left.

The practice of distorting narrative into a conformity with theory is a vice not so unfavorable as at first sight it may appear to the interests of political science. We have compared the writers who indulge in it to advocates; and we may add that their conflicting fallacies, like those of advocates, correct each other. It has always been held, in the most enlightened nations, that a tribunal will decide a judicial question most fairly when it has heard two able men argue, as unfairly as possible, on the two opposite sides of it; and we are inclined to think that this opinion is just. Sometimes, it is true, superior eloquence and dexterity will make the worse appear the better reason; but it is at least certain that the judge will be compelled to contemplate the case under two different aspects. It is certain that no important consideration will altogether escape notice.

This is at present the state of history. The Poet Laureate appears for the Church of England, Lingard for the Church of Rome. Brodie has moved to set aside the verdicts obtained by Hume; and the cause in which Mitford succeeded is, we understand, about to be reheard. In the midst of these disputes, however, history proper, if we may use the term, is disappearing. The high, grave, impartial summing up of Thucydides is nowhere to be found.

While our historians are practicing all the arts of controversy, they miserably neglect the art of narration, the art of interesting the affections and presenting pictures to the imagination. That a writer may produce these effects without violating truth is sufficiently proved by many excellent biographical works. The immense popularity which well-written books of this kind have acquired deserves the serious consideration of historians. Voltaire's *Charles the Twelfth*, Marmontel's *Memoirs*, Boswell's *Life of Johnson*, Southey's account of Nelson are perused with delight by the most frivolous and indolent. Whenever any tolerable book of the same description makes its appearance, the circulating libraries are mobbed; the book societies are in commotion; the new novel lies uncut; the magazines and newspapers fill their columns with extracts. In the meantime histories of great empires, written by men of eminent ability, lie unread on the shelves of ostentatious libraries.

The writers of history seem to entertain an aristocratical contempt for the writers of memoirs. They think it beneath the dignity of men who describe the revolutions of nations to dwell on the details which constitute the charm of biography. They have imposed on themselves a code of conventional decencies as absurd as that which has been the bane of the French drama. The most characteristic and interesting circumstances are omitted or softened down, because, as we are told, they are too trivial for the majesty of history. The majesty of history seems to resemble the majesty of the poor King of Spain, who died a

---

10. **one . . . left.** Cf. *Matthew*, 24:40: "Then shall two be in the field; the one shall be taken, and the other left." 26. **make . . . reason.** Said of Belial in *Paradise Lost*, II, 112-114 (Vol. I, p. 729). 33. **Poet Laureate,** Robert Southey (p. 296), who wrote two books in support of the Established Church. 34. **Lingard,** John Lingard (1771-1851), an English Roman Catholic priest and historian, whose *History of England* was highly praised for its scholarly insight. He was attacked by Southey. **Brodie,** George Brodie (1786?-1867), an ardent Whig, who wrote *A History of the British Empire from the Accession of Charles I to the Restoration* (1822). He attacked Hume's work. 36. **cause . . . reheard.** George Grote (1794-1871), who was writing his *History of Greece* at the time, was much more friendly toward democracy than was Mitford. In April, 1826, Grote contributed to the *Westminster Review* a powerful article against Mitford's *History*. 44. **neglect . . . narration.** This was Macaulay's chief criticism against the historians of his time. 52. **Charles the Twelfth,** a history of the famous King of Sweden (1697-1718) by the celebrated French writer Voltaire (1694-1778). 53. **Memoirs,** by Jean François Marmontel (1723-1799), a disciple of Voltaire. 54. **Life of Johnson.** See Vol. I, p. 1125. **Nelson,** Horatio Nelson (1758-1805), the greatest of English naval commanders. His *Life* was written by Robert Southey (p. 296). 55. **perused . . . indolent.** A typical exaggeration of Macaulay. 58. **book societies,** reading circles, or book clubs. 71. **code . . . drama.** The French drama of the seventeenth century, based upon strict adherence to classical theories of tragedy, was cold and formal. The code excluded comic elements and stage representations of murder and insisted upon rigid observance of the unities of time, place, and action. See Vol. I, pp. 817-823. 76. **trivial . . . history.** This is a favorite idea of Macaulay. 78. **King of Spain,** Philip III (1578-1621), who was reported to have died of a fever induced by excessive heat from a fire that attendants refused to diminish because etiquette reserved that function to a certain nobleman who was absent.

martyr to ceremony because the proper dignitaries were not at hand to render him assistance.

That history would be more amusing if this etiquette were relaxed will, we suppose, be acknowledged. But would it be less dignified or less useful? What do we mean when we say that one past event is important and another insignificant? No past event has any intrinsic importance. The knowledge of it is valuable only as it leads us to form just calculations with respect to the future. A history which does not serve this purpose, though it may be filled with battles, treaties, and commotions, is as useless as the series of turnpike tickets collected by Sir Matthew Mite.

Let us suppose that Lord Clarendon, instead of filling hundreds of folio pages with copies of state papers in which the same assertions and contradictions are repeated till the reader is overpowered with weariness, had condescended to be the Boswell of the Long Parliament. Let us suppose that he had exhibited to us the wise and lofty self-government of Hampden, leading while he seemed to follow, and propounding unanswerable arguments in the strongest forms with the modest air of an inquirer anxious for information; the delusions which misled the noble spirit of Vane; the coarse fanaticism which concealed the yet loftier genius of Cromwell, destined to control a mutinous army and a factious people, to abase the flag of Holland, to arrest the victorious arms of Sweden, and to hold the balance firm between the rival monarchies of France and Spain. Let us suppose that he had made his Cavaliers and Roundheads talk in their own style; that he had reported some of the ribaldry of Rupert's pages, and some of the cant of Harrison and Fleetwood. Would not his work in that case have been more interesting? Would it not have been more accurate?

A history in which every particular incident may be true may on the whole be false. The circumstances which have most influence on the happiness of mankind, the changes of manners and morals, the transition of communities from poverty to wealth, from knowledge to ignorance, from ferocity to humanity—these are, for the most part, noiseless revolutions. Their progress is rarely indicated by what historians are pleased to call important events. They are not achieved by armies, or enacted by senates. They are sanctioned by no treaties, and recorded in no archives. They are carried on in every school, in every church, behind ten thousand counters, at ten thousand firesides. The upper current of society presents no certain criterion by which we can judge of the direction in which the undercurrent flows. We read of defeats and victories. But we know that nations may be miserable amidst victories and prosperous amidst defeats. We read of the fall of wise ministers and of the rise of profligate favorites. But we must remember how small a proportion the good or evil effected by a single statesman can bear to the good or evil of a great social system.

Bishop Watson compares a geologist to a gnat mounted on an elephant, and laying down theories as to the whole internal structure of the vast animal, from the phenomena of the hide. The comparison is unjust to the geologists; but is very applicable to those historians who write as if the body politic were homogeneous, who look only on the surface of affairs, and never think of the mighty and various organization which lies deep below.

---

10. **knowledge . . . future.** Cf. Newman's *Knowledge Its Own End*, p. 447. 15. **turnpike,** tollgate. 16. **Sir Matthew Mite,** the chief character in *The Nabob*, a farce by Samuel Foote (1720-1777). Macaulay describes Mite as a dissolute and tyrannical Anglo-Indian chief. 22. **Boswell . . . Parliament,** reporter of everything that was said, as Boswell was a reporter of the conversation of Samuel Johnson. The Long Parliament was in session from November 3, 1640, until it was dissolved by Cromwell on April 20, 1653. See Vol. I, pp. 635 ff. 25. **Hampden,** the great English commoner, greatly admired by Macaulay. See p. 51, note 57. 30. **Vane,** Sir Henry Vane (1613-1662), an English statesman and leader of the extreme Puritans in the Long Parliament. 31. **Cromwell.** See Vol. I, p. 639. 32. **mutinous army and a factious people.** The allusion is to the numerous factions among the Puritans and especially to the rebellion of the new model army against the authority of a Parliament controlled by Presbyterians; this quarrel culminated in Pride's Purge in 1648, by which all members of Parliament opposed to the army were forcibly expelled by Colonel Pride. 33. **abase . . . Holland.** Cromwell was engaged in war with Holland, 1652-1654. 34. **arrest . . . Sweden.** Charles X of Sweden carried on extensive military operations against European nations from 1654 to 1660. Cromwell, however, was not active in restraining Charles.

37. **Cavaliers and Roundheads.** See Vol. I, pp. 635-639. 39. **Rupert,** a German nephew of Charles I and commander of the Royalist cavalry in the Civil War. His followers were often dissolute rakes. 40. **Harrison and Fleetwood.** Thomas Harrison (1606-1660) and Charles Fleetwood (d. 1692), generals on the Parliamentary side during the war, were both noted for their religious zeal. 71. **Bishop Watson,** Richard Watson (1737-1816), Bishop of Llandaff, a staunch defender of inspired religion.

In the works of such writers as these, England, at the close of the Seven Years' War, is in the highest state of prosperity; at the close of the American war she is in a miserable and degraded condition; as if the people were not on the whole as rich, as well governed, and as well educated at the latter period as at the former. We have read books called Histories of England, under the reign of George the Second, in which the rise of Methodism is not even mentioned. A hundred years hence this breed of authors will, we hope, be extinct. If it should still exist, the late ministerial interregnum will be described in terms which will seem to imply that all government was at end; that the social contract was annulled; and that the hand of every man was against his neighbor until the wisdom and virtue of the new cabinet educed order out of the chaos of anarchy. We are quite certain that misconceptions as gross prevail at this moment respecting many important parts of our annals.

The effect of historical reading is analogous, in many respects, to that produced by foreign travel. The student, like the tourist, is transported into a new state of society. He sees new fashions. He hears new modes of expression. His mind is enlarged by contemplating the wide diversities of laws, of morals, and of manners. But men may travel far, and return with minds as contracted as if they had never stirred from their own market-town. In the same manner, men may know the dates of many battles and the genealogies of many royal houses, and yet be no wiser. Most people look at past times as princes look at foreign countries. More than one illustrious stranger has landed on our island amidst the shouts of a mob, has dined with the King, has hunted with the master of the staghounds, has seen the guards reviewed, and a knight of the garter installed, has cantered along Regent Street, has visited Saint Paul's, and noted down its dimensions; and has then departed, thinking that he has seen England. He has, in fact, seen a few public buildings, public men, and public ceremonies. But of the vast and complex system of society, of the fine shades of national character, of the practical operation of government and laws, he knows nothing. He who would understand these things rightly must not confine his observations to palaces and solemn days. He must see ordinary men as they appear in their ordinary business and in their ordinary pleasures. He must mingle in the crowds of the exchange and the coffee-house. He must obtain admittance to the convivial table and the domestic hearth. He must bear with vulgar expression. He must not shrink from exploring even the retreats of misery. He who wishes to understand the condition of mankind in former ages must proceed on the same principle. If he attends only to public transactions, to wars, congresses, and debates, his studies will be as unprofitable as the travels of those imperial, royal, and serene sovereigns who form their judgment of our island from having gone in state to a few fine sights, and from having held formal conferences with a few great officers.

The perfect historian is he in whose work the character and spirit of an age is exhibited in miniature. He relates no fact, he attributes no expression to his characters, which is not authenticated by sufficient testimony. But, by judicious selection, rejection, and arrangement, he gives to truth those attractions which have been usurped by fiction. In his narrative a due subordination is observed: some transactions are prominent; others retire. But the scale on which he represents them is increased or diminished, not according to the dignity of the person concerned in them, but according to the degree in which they elucidate the con-

---

2. **Seven Years' War,** that waged in 1756-1763 with Prussia and Britain against Austria, Russia, Poland, and Sweden. During the same period England was at war with France; at the close of the struggle England was triumphant in both America and India. 4. **American war,** the American Revolution (1775-1783). 9. **George the Second,** King of England (1727-1760). 10. **rise of Methodism.** See p. 8. 13. **late . . . interregnum.** For a period of six weeks in the spring of 1827 legislation was interrupted because George IV was unwilling to appoint William Canning as Prime Minister; he finally yielded. 16. **social contract,** in political science, an expressed or implied agreement for the regulation of affairs among members of a party or between them and their government. 41. **master . . . staghounds,** an officer in the royal household nominally in charge of the hunting dogs. 43. **the garter,** the highest order in England, composed of the sovereign, princes, twenty-five knights-companions, foreign rulers, and others specially chosen. The order was originated about 1344. 44. **Regent Street,** one of the main thoroughfares of London. **Saint Paul's,** a celebrated cathedral in London.

dition of society and the nature of man. He shows us the court, the camp, and the senate. But he shows us also the nation. He considers no anecdote, no peculiarity of manner, no familiar saying, as too insignificant for his notice which is not too insignificant to illustrate the operation of laws, of religion, and of education, and to mark the progress of the human mind. Men will not merely be described, but will be made intimately known to us. The changes of manners will be indicated, not merely by a few general phrases or a few extracts from statistical documents, but by appropriate images presented in every line.

If a man, such as we are supposing, should write the history of England, he would assuredly not omit the battles, the sieges, the negotiations, the seditions, the ministerial changes. But with these he would intersperse the details which are the charm of historical romances. At Lincoln Cathedral there is a beautiful painted window, which was made by an apprentice out of the pieces of glass which had been rejected by his master. It is so far superior to every other in the church, that, according to the tradition, the vanquished artist killed himself from mortification. Sir Walter Scott, in the same manner, has used those fragments of truth which historians have scornfully thrown behind them in a manner which may well excite their envy. He has constructed out of their gleanings works which, even considered as histories, are scarcely less valuable than theirs. But a truly great historian would reclaim those materials which the novelist has appropriated. The history of the government, and the history of the people, would be exhibited in that mode in which alone they can be exhibited justly, in inseparable conjunction and intermixture. We should not then have to look for the wars and votes of the Puritans in Clarendon, and for their phraseology in *Old Mortality*; for one half of *King James* in Hume, and for the other half in *The Fortunes of Nigel*.

The early part of our imaginary history would be rich with coloring from romance, ballad, and chronicle. We should find ourselves in the company of knights, such as those of Froissart, and of pilgrims, such as those who rode with Chaucer from the Tabard. Society would be shown from the highest to the lowest—from the royal cloth of state to the den of the outlaw; from the throne of the Legate to the chimney-corner where the begging friar regaled himself. Palmers, minstrels, crusaders —the stately monastery, with the good cheer in its refectory and the high-mass in its chapel— the manor-house, with its hunting and hawking—the tournament, with the heralds and ladies, the trumpets and the cloth of gold— would give truth and life to the representation. We should perceive, in a thousand slight touches, the importance of the privileged burgher, and the fierce and haughty spirit which swelled under the collar of the degraded villein. The revival of letters would not merely be described in a few magnificent periods. We should discern, in innumerable particulars, the fermentation of mind, the eager appetite for knowledge, which distinguished the sixteenth from the fifteenth century. In the Reformation we should see, not merely a schism which changed the ecclesiastical constitution of England and the mutual relations of the European powers, but a moral war which raged in every family, which set the father against the son, and the son against the father, the mother against the daughter, and the daughter against the mother. Henry would be painted with the skill of Tacitus. We should have the change of his character from his profuse and joyous youth to his savage and imperious old age. We should perceive the gradual progress of selfish and tyrannical passions in a mind not naturally

---

22. **Lincoln Cathedral**, the famous minster in the city of Lincoln; it embodies the earliest purely Gothic work in England. 24. **pieces . . . master.** Cf. *Mark*, 12:10: "The stone which the builders rejected is become the head of the corner." 44. *Old Mortality*, a novel dealing with the time of the rising of the Scottish Covenanters in 1679; *The Fortunes of Nigel* deals with the time of James I (1603-1625). Scott's work presents the spirit of the times but is not authenticated history. See pp. 28 and 190.

51. **Froissart**, a famous French chronicler of contemporary fourteenth-century chivalry. 52. **Tabard**, the inn in Southwark, London, from which Chaucer's pilgrims started on their journey to Canterbury. See Vol. I, pp. 210 ff. 55. **Legate**, the ambassador of the Pope. 57. **Palmers**, pilgrims who wore palm leaves in token that they had visited the Holy Land. 68. **villein**, a member of the serf class in Feudal England; he was subject to the lord of the manor. 71. **fermentation of mind.** See Vol. I, pp. 298 ff. 81. **Henry**, Henry VIII, King of England (1509-1547).

insensible or ungenerous; and to the last we should detect some remains of that open and noble temper which endeared him to a people whom he oppressed, struggling with the hardness of despotism and the irritability of disease. We should see Elizabeth in all her weakness and in all her strength, surrounded by the handsome favorites whom she never trusted, and the wise old statesman whom she never dismissed, uniting in herself the most contradictory qualities of both her parents—the coquetry, the caprice, the petty malice of Anne—the haughty and resolute spirit of Henry. We have no hesitation in saying that a great artist might produce a portrait of this remarkable woman at least as striking as that in the novel of *Kenilworth*, without employing a single trait not authenticated by ample testimony. In the meantime, we should see arts cultivated, wealth accumulated, the conveniences of life improved. We should see the keeps, where nobles, insecure themselves, spread insecurity around them, gradually giving place to the halls of peaceful opulence, to the oriels of Longleat, and the stately pinnacles of Burleigh. We should see towns extended, deserts cultivated, the hamlets of fishermen turned into wealthy havens, the meal of the peasant improved, and his hut more commodiously furnished. We should see those opinions and feelings which produced the great struggle against the House of Stuart slowly growing up in the bosom of private families, before they manifested themselves in parliamentary debates. Then would come the Civil War. Those skirmishes on which Clarendon dwells so minutely would be told, as Thucydides would have told them, with perspicuous conciseness. They are merely connecting links. But the great characteristics of the age, the loyal enthusiasm of the brave English gentry, the fierce licentiousness of the swearing, dicing, drunken reprobates whose excesses disgraced the royal cause—the austerity of the Presbyterian Sabbaths in the city, the extravagance of the independent preachers in the camp, the precise garb, the severe countenance, the petty scruples, the affected accent, the absurd names and phrases which marked the Puritans—the valor, the policy, the public spirit, which lurked beneath these ungraceful disguises—the dreams of the raving Fifth-monarchy-man, the dreams, scarcely less wild, of the philosophic republican—all these would enter into the representation, and render it at once more exact and more striking.

The instruction derived from history thus written would be of a vivid and practical character. It would be received by the imagination as well as by the reason. It would be not merely traced on the mind, but branded into it. Many truths, too, would be learned, which can be learned in no other manner. As the history of states is generally written, the greatest and most momentous revolutions seem to come upon them like supernatural inflictions, without warning or cause. But the fact is, that such revolutions are almost always the consequences of moral changes, which have gradually passed on the mass of the community, and which ordinarily proceed far, before their progress is indicated by any public measure. An intimate knowledge of the domestic history of nations is therefore absolutely necessary to the prognosis of political events. A narrative, defective in this respect, is as useless as a medical treatise which should pass by all the symptoms attendant on the early stage of a disease and mention only what occurs when the patient is beyond the reach of remedies.

A historian such as we have been attempting to describe would indeed be an intellectual prodigy. In his mind, powers scarcely compatible with each other must be tempered into an exquisite harmony. We shall sooner see

---

6. **Elizabeth,** Queen of England (1558-1603). 13. **Anne,** Anne Boleyn, wife of Henry VIII and mother of Elizabeth. 17. **Kenilworth,** a novel by Sir Walter Scott which deals with the times of Elizabeth; chapter 34 contains a famous description of the queen. 22. **keeps,** central towers or strongholds of medieval castles. 25. **oriels,** bay windows. **Longleat,** in Wiltshire, and **Burleigh,** in Northamptonshire, palatial residences built in the late sixteenth century. 32. **struggle . . . Stuart,** that against James I and Charles I, the first members of the royal family of Stuarts. 36. **Civil War,** that between Parliament and the Royalists (1642-1649). See Vol. I, pp. 633 ff.

52. **Fifth-monarchy-man,** a member of the fanatical sect that supported Cromwell's government in the faith that to do so would hasten the establishment of Christ as the ruler of the fifth and last monarchy. The earlier monarchies named by the prophet are Assyria, Persia, Greece, and Rome. 54. **philosophic republican,** a follower of James Harrington (1611-1677), who wrote *Oceana*, a treatise on republican government. Both Royalists and Puritans were opposed to Harrington's theories.

another Shakespeare or another Homer. The highest excellence to which any single faculty can be brought would be less surprising than such a happy and delicate combination of qualities. Yet the contemplation of imaginary models is not an unpleasant or useless employment of the mind. It cannot indeed produce perfection; but it produces improvement, and nourishes that generous and liberal fastidiousness which is not inconsistent with the strongest sensibility to merit, and which, while it exalts our conceptions of the art, does not render us unjust to the artist.

(1828)

The Revolt Against Classicism

This selection is substantially the second quarter of Macaulay's review of *Letters and Journals of Lord Byron: with Notices of His Life,* by Thomas Moore (London, 1830), which appeared in the *Edinburgh Review* for June, 1831. It reveals the author's extensive reading of literature, his remarkable memory, his distaste for artificiality and form for its own sake, his predilection for his own times, and his capacity for dealing sensibly and clearly with problems of literary criticism. His explanation of correctness, classicism, and romanticism in literature should be compared with Pater's definition of classicism and romanticism (p. 585).

* * * * *

THAT poetical dynasty which had dethroned the successors of Shakespeare and Spenser was, in turn, dethroned by a race who represented themselves as heirs of the ancient line, so long dispossessed by usurpers. The real nature of this revolution has not, we think, been comprehended by the great majority of those who concurred in it. Wherein especially does the poetry of our times differ from that of the last century? Ninety-nine persons out of a hundred would answer that the poetry of the last century was correct, but cold and mechanical, and that the poetry of our time, though wild and irregular, presented far more vivid images and excited the passions far more strongly than that of Parnell, of Addison, or of Pope. In the same manner we constantly hear it said that the poets of the age of Elizabeth had far more genius, but far less correctness, than those of the age of Anne. It seems to be taken for granted that there is some incompatibility, some antithesis, between correctness and creative power. We rather suspect that this notion arises merely from an abuse of words, and that it has been the parent of many of the fallacies which perplex the science of criticism.

What is meant by correctness in poetry? If by correctness be meant the conforming to rules which have their foundation in truth and in the principles of human nature, then correctness is only another name for excellence. If by correctness be meant the conforming to rules purely arbitrary, correctness may be another name for dullness and absurdity.

A writer who describes visible objects falsely, and violates the propriety of character, a writer who makes the mountains "nod their drowsy heads" at night, or a dying man take leave of the world with a rant like that of Maximin, may be said, in the high and just sense of the phrase, to write incorrectly. He violates the first great law of his art. His imitation is altogether unlike the thing imitated. The four poets who are most eminently free from incorrectness of this description are Homer, Dante, Shakespeare, and Milton. They are therefore, in one sense, and that the best sense, the most correct of poets.

When it is said that Virgil, though he had less genius than Homer, was a more correct writer, what sense is attached to the word correctness? Is it meant that the story of the *Aeneid* is developed more skillfully than that

---

1. **That poetical dynasty,** the poets of the Puritan period (see Vol. I, pp. 631 ff.). They were in turn overthrown by the Classicists (see Vol. I, pp. 811 ff.). 16. **Parnell,** Thomas Parnell (1679-1718), a scholarly English poet with a slight gift of description. For Addison and Pope see Vol. I, pp. 975 and 1063. 18 ff. **poets . . . Elizabeth . . . Anne.** See Vol. I, pp. 297 ff. and 811 ff.

41. **Maximin,** a ranting Roman emperor in Dryden's play *Tyrannic Love* (1689). 47 ff. **Homer . . . Dante . . . Virgil.** See p. 333, notes 9 and 10.

of the *Odyssey?* that the Roman describes the face of the external world, or the emotions of the mind, more accurately than the Greek? that the characters of Achates and Mnestheus are more nicely discriminated, and more consistently supported, than those of Achilles, of Nestor, and of Ulysses? The fact incontestably is that, for every violation of the fundamental laws of poetry which can be found in Homer, it would be easy to find twenty in Virgil.

Troilus and Cressida is perhaps, of all the plays of Shakespeare, that which is commonly considered as the most incorrect. Yet it seems to us infinitely more correct, in the sound sense of the term, than what are called the most correct plays of the most correct dramatists. Compare it, for example, with the *Iphigénie* of Racine. We are sure that the Greeks of Shakespeare bear a far greater resemblance than the Greeks of Racine to the real Greeks who besieged Troy; and for this reason, that the Greeks of Shakespeare are human beings, and the Greeks of Racine mere names, mere words printed in capitals at the head of paragraphs of declamation. Racine, it is true, would have shuddered at the thought of making a warrior at the siege of Troy quote Aristotle. But of what use is it to avoid a single anachronism, when the whole play is one anachronism, the sentiments and phrases of Versailles in the camp of Aulis?

In the sense in which we are now using the word correctness, we think that Sir Walter Scott, Mr. Wordsworth, Mr. Coleridge, are far more correct poets than those who are commonly extolled as the models of correctness—Pope, for example, and Addison. The single description of a moonlight night in Pope's *Iliad* contains more inaccuracies than can be found in all *The Excursion.* There is not a single scene in *Cato* in which all that conduces to poetical illusion, all the propriety of character, of language, of situation, is not more grossly violated than in any part of *The Lay of the Last Minstrel*. No man can possibly think that the Romans of Addison resemble the real Romans so closely as the moss-troopers of Scott resemble the real moss-troopers. Wat Tinlinn and William of Deloraine are not, it is true, persons of so much dignity as Cato. But the dignity of the persons represented has as little to do with the correctness of poetry as with the correctness of painting. We prefer a gypsy by Reynolds to His Majesty's head on a signpost, and a Borderer by Scott to a senator by Addison.

In what sense, then, is the word correctness used by those who say, with the author of *The Pursuits of Literature*, that Pope was the most correct of English poets, and that next to Pope came the late Mr. Gifford? What is the nature and value of that correctness, the praise of which is denied to *Macbeth*, to *Lear*, and to *Othello*, and given to Hoole's translations and to all the Seatonian prize-poems? We can discover no eternal rule, no rule founded in reason and in the nature of things, which Shakespeare does not observe much more strictly than Pope. But if by correctness be meant the conforming to a narrow legislation which, while lenient to the *mala in se*, multiplies without the shadow of a reason the *mala prohibita*—if by correctness be meant a strict attention to certain ceremonious observances, which are no more essential to poetry than etiquette to good government, or than the washings of a Pharisee to devotion —then, assuredly, Pope may be a more correct poet than Shakespeare; and, if the code were

---

4. **Achates and Mnestheus,** heroes in Virgil's *Aeneid.* Achilles and Nestor are heroes in Homer's *Iliad;* Ulysses is the hero of Homer's *Odyssey.* 19. **Racine,** a famous French tragic dramatist (1639-1699), who followed the rules of the classical school. 29. **Aristotle.** See p. 323, note 28. 31. **phrases . . . Aulis,** phrases of modern France in the camp of ancient Greece. Aulis was in ancient times a town on the eastern coast of Greece. 41. *The Excursion,* a long philosophic poem by Wordsworth (1814). 42. *Cato,* a classical tragedy by Addison (1713). Cato (first century B.C.) was a Roman philosopher and patriot who opposed Caesar.

45. *The Lay . . . Minstrel,* a narrative poem by Scott, intended "to illustrate the customs and manners which anciently prevailed on the Borders of Scotland and England." See p. 190. 50. **Wat Tinlinn and William of Deloraine,** warriors in *The Lay of the Last Minstrel.* 55. **Reynolds,** Sir Joshua Reynolds (1723-1792), a famous English portrait painter. 60. *The Pursuits of Literature,* a vigorous satire on contemporary authors by Thomas James Mathias (1754?-1835). 62. **Mr. Gifford,** William Gifford (1756-1826), the author of the satirical epics *The Baviad* and *The Maviad* and editor of the *Quarterly Review.* He was a rigid adherent of the classical school of poetry. 65. **Hoole,** John Hoole (1727-1803), an English translator and playwright. Because of his insipid translations Scott called Hoole "a transmuter of gold into lead." 66. **Seatonian prize-poems,** poems awarded the Seatonian prize founded at Cambridge by Thomas Seaton (1684-1741), a fellow of Clare College. 72. *mala in se,* offenses that are such from their own nature. 74. *mala prohibita,* offenses that are such because prohibited by law. 78. **washings of a Pharisee.** The Pharisees were ancient Jews who rigidly observed the exact forms of religion. Cf. *Luke,* 11:39: "Now do ye Pharisees make clean the outside of the cup and the platter; but your inward part is full of ravening and wickedness."

a little altered, Colley Cibber might be a more correct poet than Pope. But it may well be doubted whether this kind of correctness be a merit, nay, whether it be not an absolute fault.

It would be amusing to make a digest of the irrational laws which bad critics have framed for the government of poets. First in celebrity and in absurdity stand the dramatic unities of place and time. No human being has ever been able to find anything that could, even by courtesy, be called an argument for these unities, except that they have been deduced from the general practice of the Greeks. It requires no very profound examination to discover that the Greek dramas, often admirable as compositions, are, as exhibitions of human character and human life, far inferior to the English plays of the age of Elizabeth. Every scholar knows that the dramatic part of the Athenian tragedies was at first subordinate to the lyrical part. It would, therefore, have been little less than a miracle if the laws of the Athenian stage had been found to suit plays in which there was no chorus. All the greatest masterpieces of the dramatic art have been composed in direct violation of the unities, and could never have been composed if the unities had not been violated. It is clear, for example, that such a character as that of Hamlet could never have been developed within the limits to which Alfieri confined himself. Yet such was the reverence of literary men during the last century for the unities, that Johnson, who, much to his honor, took the opposite side, was, as he says, "frightened at his own temerity," and "afraid to stand against the authorities which might be produced against him."

There are other rules of the same kind without end. "Shakespeare," says Rymer, "ought not to have made Othello black; for the hero of a tragedy ought always to be white." "Milton," says another critic, "ought not to have taken Adam for his hero; for the hero of an epic poem ought always to be victorious." "Milton," says another, "ought not to have put so many similes into his first book; for the first book of an epic poem ought always to be the most unadorned. There are no similes in the first book of the *Iliad*." "Milton," says another, "ought not to have placed in an epic poem such lines as these:

While thus I called, and strayed I knew not
    whither."

And why not? The critic is ready with a reason—a lady's reason. "Such lines," says he, "are not, it must be allowed, unpleasing to the ear; but the redundant syllable ought to be confined to the drama, and not admitted into epic poetry." As to the redundant syllable in heroic rime on serious subjects, it has been, from the time of Pope downward, proscribed by the general consent of all the correct school. No magazine would have admitted so incorrect a couplet as that of Drayton:

As when we lived untouched with these
    disgraces,
When as our kingdom was our dear embraces.

Another law of heroic rime which, fifty years ago, was considered as fundamental, was that there should be a pause, a comma at least, at the end of every couplet. It was also provided that there should never be a full stop except at the end of a line. Well do we remember to have heard a most correct judge of poetry revile Mr. Rogers for the incorrectness of that most sweet and graceful passage—

Such grief was ours—it seems but yesterday—
When in thy prime, wishing so much to stay,

---

1. **Colley Cibber,** an eighteenth-century playwright who revamped some of Shakespeare's plays to make them conform to contemporary taste. 9. **dramatic unities,** the principles governing the structure of drama derived by French classical writers from Aristotle's *Poetics*. These rules required that a play should consist of one main action and that it should occur at one time and in one place. See Vol. I, p. 819. 16. **Greek dramas,** those written by the great tragic dramatists—Aeschylus, Sophocles, and Euripides (fifth century B.C.). 32. **Alfieri,** an Italian dramatist (1749-1803), the author of a score of tragedies noted for their severe classical form. 35. **Johnson,** Samuel Johnson. See Vol. I, p. 1125. 41. **Rymer,** Thomas Rymer (1641-1713), a hostile critic of Shakespeare and other Elizabethan dramatists. The attack on *Othello* is in his *A Short View of Tragedy* (1692).

44. **another critic.** Macaulay is not alluding to Addison, whose criticism of *Paradise Lost* appeared in the *Spectator* papers from January 5 to May 3, 1712, but to several minor critics, who condemned the epic because it failed to conform to certain arbitrary neo-classical formulas. 54. **While . . . whither.** *Paradise Lost*, VIII, 283. 61. **heroic rime.** Two successive iambic pentameter lines that rhyme. 65. **Drayton,** Michael Drayton. See Vol. I, p. 478. 75. **Mr. Rogers,** Samuel Rogers (1763-1855), an English poet and a friend of literary men. The quotation is from his *Human Life*, ll. 440 ff.

'Twas thine, Maria, thine without a sigh
At midnight in a sister's arms to die.
O thou wert lovely; lovely was thy frame,
And pure thy spirit as from heaven it came;
And when recalled to join the blest above
Thou diedst a victim to exceeding love,
Nursing the young to health. In happier hours,
When idle fancy wove luxuriant flowers,
Once in thy mirth thou badst me write on thee:
And now I write what thou shalt never see.

Sir Roger Newdigate is fairly entitled, we think, to be ranked among the great critics of this school. He made a law that none of the poems written for the prize which he established at Oxford should exceed fifty lines. This law seems to us to have at least as much foundation in reason as any of those which we have mentioned—nay, much more, for the world, we believe, is pretty well agreed in thinking that the shorter a prize poem is, the better. We do not see why we should not make a few more rules of the same kind; why we should not enact that the number of scenes in every act shall be three or some multiple of three, that the number of lines in every scene shall be an exact square, that the *dramatis personae* shall never be more or fewer than sixteen, and that, in heroic rimes, every thirty-sixth line shall have twelve syllables. If we were to lay down these canons, and to call Pope, Goldsmith, and Addison incorrect writers for not having complied with our whims, we should act precisely as those critics act who find incorrectness in the magnificent imagery and the varied music of Coleridge and Shelley.

The correctness which the last century prized so much resembles the correctness of those pictures of the garden of Eden which we see in old Bibles. We have an exact square, enclosed by the rivers Pison, Gihon, Hiddekel, and Euphrates, each with a convenient bridge in the center, rectangular beds of flowers, a long canal, neatly bricked and railed in; the tree of knowledge, clipped like one of the limes behind the Tuileries, standing in the center of the grand alley, the snake twined round it, the man on the right hand, the woman on the left, and the beasts drawn up in an exact circle round them. In one sense the picture is correct enough. That is to say, the squares are correct, the circles are correct; the man and the woman are in a most correct line with the tree; and the snake forms a most correct spiral. But if there were a painter so gifted that he could place on the canvas that glorious paradise seen by the interior eye of him whose outward sight had failed with long watching and laboring for liberty and truth—if there were a painter who could set before us the mazes of the sapphire brook, the lake with its fringe of myrtles, the flowery meadows, the grottoes overhung by vines, the forests shining with Hesperian fruit and with the plumage of gorgeous birds, the massy shade of that nuptial bower which showered down roses on the sleeping lovers—what should we think of a connoisseur who should tell us that this painting, though finer than the absurd picture in the old Bible, was not so correct? Surely we should answer, It is both finer and more correct, and it is finer because it is more correct. It is not made up of correctly drawn diagrams, but it is a correct painting, a worthy representation of that which it is intended to represent.

It is not in the fine arts alone that this false correctness is prized by narrow-minded men, by men who cannot distinguish means from ends, or what is accidental from what is essential. M. Jourdain admired correctness in fencing. "You had no business to hit me then. You must never thrust in quart till you have thrust in tierce." M. Tomès liked correctness in medical practice. "I stand up for Artemius. That he killed his patient is plain enough. But still he acted quite according to rule. A man dead is a man dead, and there is an end

11. **Sir Roger Newdigate**, an English antiquary (1719-1806), the founder of the Newdigate Prize at Oxford for English verse. This prize of twenty-one guineas is open each year for competition among undergraduates; it has been won by a number of distinguished poets since the first award in 1806. 40. **Pison . . . Euphrates**, the four divisions of the river that flowed out of the Garden of Eden (*Genesis*, 2:10-14).

45. **Tuileries**, a royal palace in Paris, built on the site of a *tuilerie*, a brickyard. 63. **Hesperian fruit**, golden apples grown in the mythical garden of Hesperides. 80. **M. Jourdain**, a character in Molière's drama *Le Bourgeois Gentilhomme* who was obsessed with a desire to be known as a perfect gentleman. The quotation is from Act III, sc. iii. 82. **in quart . . . in tierce**, terms in fencing, designating the fourth and the third arm movements. 83. **M. Tomès**, a doctor in Molière's *L'Amour Médecin*. *Artemius* is mentioned in the same play as a contemporary physician. The quotation is from Act II.

of the matter. But if rules are to be broken, there is no saying what consequences may follow." We have heard of an old German officer who was a great admirer of correctness in military operations. He used to revile Bonaparte for spoiling the science of war, which had been carried to such exquisite perfection by Marshal Daun. "In my youth we used to march and countermarch all the summer without gaining or losing a square league, and then we went into winter quarters. And now comes an ignorant, hot-headed young man, who flies about from Bologne to Ulm, and from Ulm to the middle of Moravia, and fights battles in December. The whole system of his tactics is monstrously incorrect." The world is of opinion, in spite of critics like these, that the end of fencing is to hit, that the end of medicine is to cure, that the end of war is to conquer, and that those means are the most correct which best accomplish the ends.

And has poetry no end, no eternal and immutable principles? Is poetry like heraldry, mere matter of arbitrary regulation? The heralds tell us that certain scutcheons and bearings denote certain conditions, and that to put colors on colors, or metals on metals, is false blazonry. If all this were reversed, if every coat of arms in Europe were new fashioned, if it were decreed that *or* should never be placed but on *argent,* or *argent* but on *or,* that illegitimacy should be denoted by a *lozenge,* and widowhood by a *bend,* the new science would be just as good as the old science, because both the new and old would be good for nothing. The mummery of Portecullis and Rouge Dragon, as it has no other value than that which caprice has assigned to it, may well submit to any laws which caprice may impose upon it. But it is not so with that great imitative art, to the power of which all ages, the rudest and the most enlightened, bear witness. Since its first great masterpieces were produced, everything that is changeable in this world has been changed. Civilization has been gained, lost, gained again. Religions, and languages, and forms of government, and usages of private life, and modes of thinking, all have undergone a succession of revolutions. Everything has passed away but the great features of nature and the heart of man, and the miracles of that art of which it is the office to reflect back the heart of man and the features of nature. Those two strange old poems, the wonder of ninety generations, still retain all their freshness. They still command the veneration of minds enriched by the literature of many nations and ages. They are still, even in wretched translations, the delight of schoolboys. Having survived ten thousand capricious fashions, having seen successive codes of criticism become obsolete, they still remain to us, immortal with the immortality of truth, the same when perused in the study of an English scholar as when they were first chanted at the banquets of the Ionian princes.

Poetry is, as was said more than two thousand years ago, imitation. It is an art analogous in many respects to the art of painting, sculpture, and acting. The imitations of the painter, the sculptor, and the actor are indeed, within certain limits, more perfect than those of the poet. The machinery which the poet employs consists merely of words; and words cannot, even when employed by such an artist as Homer or Dante, present to the mind images of visible objects quite so lively and exact as those which we carry away from looking on the works of the brush and the chisel. But, on the other hand, the range of poetry is infinitely wider than that of any other imitative art, or than that of all the other imitative arts together. The sculptor can imitate only form; the painter only form and color; the actor—until the poet supplies him with words—only form, color, and motion. Poetry holds the outer world in common with the other arts; the heart of man is the province of poetry and of poetry alone. The painter, the sculptor, and the actor can exhibit no more of human passion and character than that small portion which overflows

---

8. **Marshal Daun,** Count von Daun (1705-1766), a noted Austrian field marshal. 13. **Bologne . . . Ulm . . . Moravia.** *Boulogne* is a seaport in northern France; *Ulm* is a city in southern Germany; *Moravia* is a province in what is now Czechoslovakia. 30. *or,* gold. 31. *argent,* silver. 33. *lozenge,* a diamond-shaped design. *bend,* a broad band across the shield. 36. **Portecullis,** in heraldry, an officer who has the figure of a portecullis, a drawbridge, as a badge. A *Rouge Dragon* is an officer who wears the figure of a red dragon.

54. **two . . . poems,** the *Iliad* and the *Odyssey,* by the Greek poet Homer. 66. **Ionian,** of Ionia, a province in ancient Greece. 67. **Poetry . . . imitation.** A statement in Aristotle's *Poetics,* 1, 2. Cf. Wordsworth's *Preface* to the *Lyrical Ballads,* p. 319 and note 19.

into the gesture and the face, always an imperfect, often a deceitful, sign of that which is within. The deeper and more complex parts of human nature can be exhibited by means of words alone. Thus the objects of the imitation of poetry are the whole external and the whole internal universe, the face of nature, the vicissitudes of fortune, man as he is in himself, man as he appears in society, all things which really exist, all things of which we can form an image in our minds by combining together parts of things which really exist. The domain of this imperial art is commensurate with the imaginative faculty.

An art essentially imitative ought not, surely, to be subjected to rules which tend to make its imitations less perfect than they otherwise would be; and those who obey such rules ought to be called, not correct, but incorrect, artists. The true way to judge of the rules by which English poetry was governed during the last century is to look at the effects which they produced.

It was in 1780 that Johnson completed his *Lives of the Poets*. He tells us in that work that since the time of Dryden English poetry had shown no tendency to relapse into its original savageness, that its language had been refined, its numbers tuned, and its sentiments improved. It may perhaps be doubted whether the nation had any great reason to exult in the refinements and improvements which gave it *Douglas*, for *Othello*, and *The Triumphs of Temper* for *The Faerie Queene*. It was during the thirty years which preceded the appearance of Johnson's *Lives* that the diction and versification of English poetry were, in the sense in which the word is commonly used, most correct. Those thirty years are, as respects poetry, the most deplorable part of our literary history. They have indeed bequeathed to us scarcely any poetry which deserves to be remembered. Two or three hundred lines of Gray, twice as many of Goldsmith, a few stanzas of Beattie and Collins, a few strophes of Mason, and a few clever prologues and satires were the masterpieces of this age of consummate excellence. They may all be printed in one volume, and that volume would be by no means a volume of extraordinary merit. It would contain no poetry of the very highest class, and little which could be placed very high in the second class. The *Paradise Regained* or *Comus* would outweigh it all.

At last, when poetry had fallen into such utter decay that Mr. Hayley was thought a great poet, it began to appear that the excess of the evil was about to work the cure. Men became tired of an insipid conformity to a standard which derived no authority from nature or reason. A shallow criticism had taught them to ascribe a superstitious value to the spurious correctness of poetasters. A deeper criticism brought them back to the true correctness of the first great masters. The eternal laws of poetry regained their power, and the temporary fashions which had superseded those laws went after the wig of Lovelace and the hoop of Clarissa.

It was in a cold and barren season that the seeds of that rich harvest which we have reaped were first sown. While poetry was every year becoming more feeble and more mechanical, while the monotonous versification which Pope had introduced, no longer redeemed by his brilliant wit and his compactness of expression, palled on the ear of the public, the great works of the old masters were every day attracting more and more of the admiration which they deserved. The plays of Shakespeare were better acted, better edited, and better known than they had ever been. Our fine ancient ballads were again read with pleasure, and it became a fashion to imitate them. Many of the imitations were altogether contemptible. But they showed that men had at least begun to admire the excellence which they could not rival. A literary revolution was at hand. . . . (1831)

34. ***Douglas***, a romantic tragedy by John Home (1722-1808), a Scottish clergyman. ***The Triumphs of Temper***, a poem by William Hayley (1745-1820), an author of a variety of prose and verse. Southey said that everything was good about Hayley except his poetry. 46. **Beattie**, James Beattie (1735-1803), best known as the author of *The Minstrel*, a poem in Spenserian stanzas.

47. **Mason**, William Mason (1725-1797), the author of odes and didactic verse; he was a devoted friend of Gray. For Goldsmith, see Vol. I, p. 1113; for Gray and Collins see pp. 46 and 66. 55. *Paradise . . . Comus*, poems by Milton (see Vol. I, pp. 646 and 715). 70. *Lovelace . . . Clarissa*, characters in Richardson's novel *Clarissa Harlowe* (1747-1748). Wigs with abundant curls were part of the fashionable dress of men of the eighteenth century; the hoop was the fashionable hoopskirt of the time. 86. **fashion . . . them**. See p. 7.

John Henry Newman
1801-1890

John Henry Newman belongs to that group of writers who are thought of always in connection with some great movement in which they participated. Newman was the central figure in that stirring religious revolt in Victorian England which is known as the Oxford Movement. The story of this movement and of Newman's guiding hand in it has already been told in "Democracy, Science, and Industrialism" (p. 407). Quiet and apparently unimpassioned as he was, Newman was, nevertheless, one of the most vigorous and effective of the controversialists of his time, and his life was a series of battles. These began at Oxford—that noble center of lost causes—where Newman held a fellowship at Oriel College and later became vicar of St. Mary's. In 1833 he visited Italy with his friend Hurrell Froude. He returned to England in July, 1833, just before John Keble's sermon at Oxford on national apostasy fired the opening shot of a theological war that was to last for more than a decade. The outlets for the ideas of the Oxford reformers were the pulpits and the *Tracts for the Times*, to which Newman contributed extensively. Gradually he came to believe that "there are but two alternatives, the way to Rome and the way to atheism." He took the way to Rome. After the storm created by the famous Tract XC, he left Oxford, resigned his charge at St. Mary's, and on October 9, 1845, was received into the Church of Rome. The following year his ordination in Rome made him one of the most prominent Catholics in England.

The storms which gradually drove Newman into what he probably hoped would be the quiet harborage of the Catholic faith were succeeded by others that he could not have foreseen. It was perhaps inevitable that he should be subjected to some attack from the Protestant clergy. Of these assaults the sharpest and most inexcusable was that of Charles Kingsley, who accused the Roman Catholic clergy of not making a virtue of truth and went out of his way to bring this charge directly against Newman. The accusation was fortunate in that it drove Newman to the necessity of writing one of the finest spiritual autobiographies in the English language. *Apologia pro Vita Sua* was written in 1864 in reply to Kingsley's charges; it was a total refutation and put Kingsley in a very weak light. The *Apologia* is *not* an apology, for Newman had none to make; it is a defense and a vivid record of the stages by which Newman had been led to embrace Catholicism. The book is simple, direct, moving; it is not only the stirring record of a soul's agony and search for truth but one of the finest pieces of prose in the English language.

Newman's controversy with Kingsley was not so bitter or so prolonged as that with a prominent member of his new faith. In 1858 Cardinal Manning opposed Newman's suggestion for the establishment of a Catholic Hall at Oxford and for thirty years blocked many other efforts that he made, even charging Newman at Rome with an attempt to spread false dogma among English Catholics. Superficially it appeared that Manning was the leader of one Catholic group, Newman the leader of another; actually the controversy had a personal bias, for the two prelates were poles apart in temperament, and Manning had little sympathy for the artistic and mystical quality of his opponent. This prolonged warfare was the most conspicuous of several conflicts in which Newman found himself engaged. Despite these troubles, however, he was immensely admired and respected by English Catholics, and it was largely through their insistence that Pope Leo XIII conferred the red cap upon him in 1879, eleven years before his death.

Because of his connection with the Anglo-Catholic movement, Newman is usually thought of as a writer on religious subjects, even his two novels, *Loss and Gain* and *Callista*, dealing with conversions. These religious writings provided the bulk of his work, but among educators he is also known for a remarkable series of lectures on university education. These were delivered in connection with the establishment in Dublin of a Catholic university which Newman was invited to head. His *Idea of a University* (published in 1873) is really a series of definitions in which he attempted to make clear his conception not only of the general function of a university but also of the relationships of science and knowledge, learning and knowledge, liberal and professional studies, etc. These conceptions are expressed so clearly and vigorously that the lectures have furnished a basis for scores of subsequent lectures on university education. The university soon ceased to exist, but Newman's lectures remain as one of the most substantial educational documents of the times.

Newman's other work includes his *Grammar of Assent* (1870), a solid analysis of the logic of belief, two or three novels in support of the Anglo-Catholic point of view (see preceding paragraph), and a body of fine poems which were composed, for the most part, early in his career. The shorter ones of these, all on religious subjects, were written while he was sojourning in Italy with Hurrell Froude, just prior to the stirring events of 1833. They were contributed first to *The British Magazine* and published in 1836 with hymns of other writers in a collection called *Lyra Apostolica*. Together they form a group of battle-hymns and prayers for guidance toward the light of divine understanding. These early lyrics provide an interesting comparison with his *Dream of Gerontius*, written in 1865. In this great poem all of the mystery and power of Newman appear. The *Dream* is apocalyptic, medieval, mystic, and altogether powerful in its vivid imagery and affecting mood. In this work and in certain of the descriptive and self-analytical chapters of the *Apologia* Newman the literary artist appears at his best.

Newman's prose style is remarkable. It is smooth, supple, and quiet, and in these respects differs radically from that of Carlyle and of Arnold. It is, moreover, clear, lucid, simple, and free from all affectations. It is a style which he developed in the pulpit in the series of sermons delivered faithfully and for many years at St. Mary's, Oxford. These sermons he wrote and rewrote, subjecting his expression to a severe discipline that made it extraordinarily direct and limpid. As a result, his writing offers the finest examples of expository composition in the nineteenth century. In one sense Newman cannot be characterized as either a preacher or a lecturer; he read his sermons and lectures, and their effectiveness resulted from his quiet power and not from his oratory or rhetorical tricks, for he had none. He secured attention by his silences, and not—like Carlyle—by his shouting.

from *The Idea of a University*

In 1854 Newman was appointed rector of the newly established Catholic University of Dublin. Two years before his formal appointment he delivered a series of lectures on *The Scope and Nature of University Education*. In 1859 appeared another series, *Lectures on Universities*. Both series were published in 1873 under the title *The Idea of a University defined and illustrated*. In these "Discourses" Newman opposed the doctrine that university instruction should diffuse useful knowledge and argued, among other things, that the function of the university should be to discipline the mind very much as exercise disciplines the body. He also insisted—quite naturally—that religious training should be a part of this discipline. His educational definitions are so logical and clear that they have been accepted widely by educators who have faith in the value of a training in the liberal arts.

Discourse V

KNOWLEDGE ITS OWN END

A UNIVERSITY may be considered with reference either to its Students or to its Studies; and the principle, that all Knowledge is a whole and the separate Sciences parts of one, which I have hitherto been using in behalf of its studies, is equally important when we direct our attention to its students. Now then I turn to the students, and shall consider the education which, by virtue of this principle, a University will give them; and thus I shall be introduced, Gentlemen, to the second question, which I proposed to discuss, viz., whether and in what sense its teaching, viewed relatively to the taught, carries the attribute of Utility along with it.

I.

I have said that all branches of knowledge are connected together, because the subject-matter of knowledge is intimately united in itself, as being the acts and the work of the Creator. Hence it is that the Sciences, into which our knowledge may be said to be cast, have multiplied bearings one on another, and an internal sympathy, and admit, or rather demand, comparison and adjustment. They complete, correct, balance each other. This consideration, if well-founded, must be taken into account, not only as regards the attainment of truth, which is their common end, but as regards the influence which they exercise upon those whose education consists in the study of them. I have said already, that to give undue prominence to one is to be unjust to another; to neglect or supersede these is to divert those from their proper object. It is to unsettle the boundary lines between science and science, to disturb their action, to destroy the harmony which binds them together. Such a proceeding will have a corresponding effect when introduced into a place of education. There is no science but tells a different tale, when viewed as a portion of a whole, from what it is likely to suggest when taken by itself, without the safeguard, as I may call it, of others.

Let me make use of an illustration. In the combination of colors, very different effects are produced by a difference in their selection and juxtaposition; red, green, and white change their shades, according to the contrast to which they are submitted. And, in like manner, the drift and meaning of a branch of knowledge varies with the company in which it is introduced to the student. If his reading is confined simply to one subject, however such division of labor may favor the advancement of a particular pursuit, a point into which I do not here enter, certainly it has a tendency to contract his mind. If it is incorporated with others, it depends on those others as to the kind of influence which it exerts upon him. Thus the Classics, which in England are the means of refining the taste, have in France subserved the spread of revolutionary and deistical doctrines. In Metaphysics, again, Butler's *Analogy of Religion* which has had so much to do with the conversion of members of the University of Oxford, appeared to Pitt and others, who had received a different training, to operate only

---

5. **hitherto**, in earlier lectures in the series; see headnote. 11. **second question**. The first was whether theology has a place in university teaching.

61. **Classics . . . doctrines.** From the beginning of the Renaissance the classics gave a cultural impetus to English life and thought; but in France, the Catholic University of Paris objected to that type of learning. Greek was regarded as the language of the devil. Hence the study of the classics forced many devotees of learning into the camp at war with Rome. 65. **Butler**, Joseph Butler (1692-1752), an English prelate and theologian. His *Analogy of Religion*, published in 1736, was written to counteract the influence of deists and other freethinkers of the day. As an effective exposition of revealed or supernatural religion, it won many followers. 68. **Pitt**, William Pitt (1708-1778), a famous Whig statesman and orator.

in the direction of infidelity. And so again, Watson, Bishop of Llandaff, as I think he tells us in the narrative of his life, felt the science of Mathematics to indispose the mind to religious belief, while others see in its investigations the best defense of the Christian Mysteries. In like manner, I suppose, Arcesilaus would not have handled logic as Aristotle, nor Aristotle have criticized poets as Plato; yet reasoning and poetry are subject to scientific rules.

It is a great point then to enlarge the range of studies which a University professes, even for the sake of the students; and, though they cannot pursue every subject which is open to them, they will be the gainers by living among those and under those who represent the whole circle. This I conceive to be the advantage of a seat of universal learning, considered as a place of education. An assemblage of learned men, zealous for their own sciences, and rivals of each other, are brought, by familiar intercourse and for the sake of intellectual peace, to adjust together the claims and relations of their respective subjects of investigation. They learn to respect, to consult, to aid each other. Thus is created a pure and clear atmosphere of thought, which the student also breathes, though in his own case he only pursues a few sciences out of the multitude. He profits by an intellectual tradition, which is independent of particular teachers, which guides him in his choice of subjects, and duly interprets for him those which he chooses. He apprehends the great outlines of knowledge, the principles on which it rests, the scale of its parts, its lights and its shades, its great points and its little, as he otherwise cannot apprehend them. Hence it is that his education is called "Liberal." A habit of mind is formed which lasts through life, of which the attributes are, freedom, equitableness, calmness, moderation, and wisdom; or what in a former Discourse I have ventured to call a philosophical habit. This then I would assign as the special fruit of the education furnished at a University, as contrasted with other places of teaching or modes of teaching. This is the main purpose of a University in its treatment of its students.

And now the question is asked me, What is the *use* of it? And my answer will constitute the main subject of the Discourses which are to follow.

II.

Cautious and practical thinkers, I say, will ask of me, what, after all, is the gain of this Philosophy, of which I make such account, and from which I promise so much. Even supposing it to enable us to give the degree of confidence exactly due to every science respectively, and to estimate precisely the value of every truth which is anywhere to be found, how are we better for this master view of things, which I have been extolling? Does it not reverse the principle of the division of labor? will practical objects be obtained better or worse by its cultivation? to what then does it lead? where does it end? what does it do? how does it profit? what does it promise? Particular sciences are respectively the basis of definite arts, which carry on to results tangible and beneficial the truths which are the subjects of the knowledge attained; what is the Art of this science of sciences? what is the fruit of such a Philosophy? what are we proposing to effect, what inducements do we hold out to the Catholic community, when we set about the enterprise of founding a University?

I am asked what is the end of University Education, and of the Liberal or Philosophical Knowledge which I conceive it to impart: I answer, that what I have already said has been sufficient to show that it has a very tangible, real, and sufficient end, though the end cannot be divided from that knowledge itself. Knowledge is capable of being its own end. Such is the constitution of the human mind, that any kind of knowledge, if it be really such, is its own reward. And if this is true of all knowledge, it is true also of that special Philosophy, which I have made to consist in a comprehensive view of truth in all its branches, of the relations of science to science,

---

2. **Watson**, Richard Watson (1737-1816), an English prelate, theological writer, and chemist. 7. **Arcesilaus**, a Greek skeptical philosopher (c. 316-c. 241 B.C.). 8. **Aristotle**. See p. 323, note 28. 9. **Plato**. See p. 331, note 3. 44. **former Discourse**, Discourse IV, 3.

of their mutual bearings, and their respective values. What the worth of such an acquirement is, compared with other objects which we seek—wealth or power or honor or the conveniences and comforts of life—I do not profess here to discuss; but I would maintain, and mean to show, that it is an object, in its own nature so really and undeniably good, as to be the compensation of a great deal of thought in the compassing, and a great deal of trouble in the attaining.

Now, when I say that Knowledge is, not merely a means to something beyond it, or the preliminary of certain arts into which it naturally resolves, but an end sufficient to rest in and to pursue for its own sake, surely I am uttering no paradox, for I am stating what is both intelligible in itself, and has ever been the common judgment of philosophers and the ordinary feeling of mankind. I am saying what at least the public opinion of this day ought to be slow to deny, considering how much we have heard of late years, in opposition to Religion, of entertaining, curious, and various knowledge. I am but saying what whole volumes have been written to illustrate, by a "selection from the records of Philosophy, Literature, and Art, in all ages and countries, of a body of examples, to show how the most unpropitious circumstances have been unable to conquer an ardent desire for the acquisition of knowledge." That further advantages accrue to us and redound to others by its possession, over and above what it is in itself, I am very far indeed from denying; but, independent of these, we are satisfying a direct need of our nature in its very acquisition; and, whereas our nature, unlike that of the inferior creation, does not at once reach its perfection, but depends, in order to it, on a number of external aids and appliances, Knowledge, as one of the principal gifts or accessories by which it is completed, is valuable for what its very presence in us does for us after the manner of a habit, even though it be turned to no further account, nor subserve any direct end.

23. **much . . . knowledge.** This was an age of conflict between science and religion. See p. 405. 27. **"selection from,"** etc. From *The Pursuit of Knowledge under Difficulties*, by George Lillie Craik (1798-1866).

III.

Hence it is that Cicero, in enumerating the various heads of mental excellence, lays down the pursuit of Knowledge for its own sake, as the first of them. "This pertains most of all to human nature," he says, "for we are all of us drawn to the pursuit of Knowledge; in which to excel we consider excellent, whereas to mistake, to err, to be ignorant, to be deceived, is both an evil and a disgrace." And he considers Knowledge the very first object to which we are attracted, after the supply of our physical wants. After the calls and duties of our animal existence, as they may be termed, as regards ourselves, our family, and our neighbors, follows, he tells us, "the search after truth. Accordingly, as soon as we escape from the pressure of necessary cares, forthwith we desire to see, to hear, to learn; and consider the knowledge of what is hidden or is wonderful a condition of our happiness."

This passage, though it is but one of many similar passages in a multitude of authors, I take for the very reason that it is so familiarly known to us; and I wish you to observe, Gentlemen, how distinctly it separates the pursuit of Knowledge from those ulterior objects to which certainly it can be made to conduce, and which are, I suppose, solely contemplated by the persons who would ask of me the use of a University or Liberal Education. So far from dreaming of the cultivation of Knowledge directly and mainly in order to our physical comfort and enjoyment, for the sake of life and person, of health, of the conjugal and family union, of the social tie and civil security, the great Orator implies, that it is only after our physical and political needs are supplied, and when we are "free from necessary duties and cares," that we are in a condition for "desiring to see, to hear, and to learn." Nor does he contemplate in the least degree the reflex or subsequent action of Knowledge, when acquired, upon those material goods which we set out by securing before we seek it; on the contrary, he expressly denies its bearing upon social life altogether,

51. **"This pertains,"** etc. From Cicero's *De Officio, Initium.* See p. 576, note 35.

strange as such a procedure is to those who live after the rise of the Baconian philosophy, and he cautions us against such a cultivation of it as will interfere with our duties to our fellow-creatures. "All these methods," he says, "are engaged in the investigation of truth; by the pursuit of which to be carried off from public occupations is a transgression of duty. For the praise of virtue lies altogether in action; yet intermissions often occur, and then we recur to such pursuits; not to say that the incessant activity of the mind is vigorous enough to carry us on in the pursuit of knowledge, even without any exertion of our own." The idea of benefiting society by means of "the pursuit of science and knowledge," did not enter at all into the motives which he would assign for their cultivation.

This was the ground of the opposition which the elder Cato made to the introduction of Greek Philosophy among his countrymen, when Carneades and his companions, on occasion of their embassy, were charming the Roman youth with their eloquent expositions of it. The fit representative of a practical people, Cato estimated everything by what it produced; whereas the Pursuit of Knowledge promised nothing beyond Knowledge itself. He despised that refinement or enlargement of mind of which he had no experience.

IV.

Things, which can bear to be cut off from everything else and yet persist in living, must have life in themselves; pursuits, which issue in nothing, and still maintain their ground for ages, which are regarded as admirable, though they have not as yet proved themselves to be useful, must have their sufficient end in themselves, whatever it turn out to be. And we are brought to the same conclusion by considering the force of the epithet, by which the knowledge under consideration is popularly designated. It is common to speak of "*liberal* knowledge," of the "*liberal* arts and studies," and of a "*liberal* education," as the especial characteristic or property of a University and of a gentleman; what is really meant by the word? Now, first, in its grammatical sense it is opposed to *servile*; and by "servile work" is understood, as our catechisms inform us, bodily labor, mechanical employment, and the like, in which the mind has little or no part. Parallel to such works are those arts, if they deserve the name of which the poet speaks, which owe their origin and their method to hazard, not to skill; as, for instance, the practice and operations of an empiric. As far as this contrast may be considered as a guide into the meaning of the word, liberal knowledge and liberal pursuits are exercises of mind, of reason, of reflection.

But we want something more for its explanation, for there are bodily exercises which are liberal, and mental exercises which are not so. For instance, in ancient times the practitioners in medicine were commonly slaves; yet it was an art as intellectual in its nature, in spite of the pretense, fraud, and quackery with which it might then, as now, be debased, as it was heavenly in its aim. And so in like manner, we contrast a liberal education with a commercial education or a professional; yet no one can deny that commerce and the professions afford scope for the highest and most diversified powers of mind. There is then a great variety of intellectual exercises, which are not technically called "liberal"; on the other hand, I say, there are exercises of the body which do receive that appellation. Such, for instance, was the palaestra, in ancient times; such the Olympic games, in which strength and dexterity of body as well as of mind gained the prize. In Xenophon we read of the young Persian nobility being taught to ride on horseback and to speak the truth—both being among the accomplishments of a gentleman. War, too, however rough a profession, has ever been accounted liberal, unless in cases when

---

2. **Baconian philosophy.** Francis Bacon (Vol. I, p. 612) believed that man should be supreme over nature because of the practical benefits that would result. 20. **elder Cato,** Marcus Porcius Cato (234-149 B.C.), a Roman patriot. 22. **Carneades . . . companions.** Carneades was a Greek skeptical philosopher and rhetorician (c. 213-129 B.C.). With Diogenes the Stoic and Critolaüs, he was sent as ambassador to Rome in 155 B.C.

53. **name . . . speaks.** In a note Newman cites Aristotle, *Nichomachean Ethics*, 6: "Art loves fate and fate loves art." 57. **empiric,** one who forms judgments upon the basis of practical experience. 80. **palaestra,** a place for athletic exercises, especially wrestling. **Olympic games,** a famous Greek festival held every four years. in which contests were held in various athletic games. 83. **Xenophon,** an Athenian historian and general (434?-355? B.C.).

it becomes heroic, which would introduce us to another subject.

Now comparing these instances together, we shall have no difficulty in determining the principle of this apparent variation in the application of the term which I am examining. Manly games, or games of skill, or military prowess, though bodily, are, it seems, accounted liberal; on the other hand, what is merely professional, though highly intellectual, nay, though liberal in comparison of trade and manual labor, is not simply called liberal, and mercantile occupations are not liberal at all. Why this distinction? because that alone is liberal knowledge, which stands on its own pretentions, which is independent of sequel, expects no complement, refuses to be *informed* (as it is called) by any end, or absorbed into any art, in order duly to present itself to our contemplation. The most ordinary pursuits have this specific character, if they are self-sufficient and complete; the highest lose it, when they minister to something beyond them. It is absurd to balance, in point of worth and importance, a treatise on reducing fractures with a game of cricket or a fox-chase; yet of the two the bodily exercise has that quality which we call "liberal," and the intellectual has it not. And so of the learned professions altogether, considered merely as professions; although one of them be the most popularly beneficial, and another the most politically important, and the third the most intimately divine of all human pursuits, yet the very greatness of their end, the health of the body, or of the commonwealth, or of the soul, diminishes, not increases, their claim to the appellation "liberal," and that still more, if they are cut down to the strict exigencies of that end. If, for instance, Theology, instead of being cultivated as a contemplation, be limited to the purposes of the pulpit or be represented by the catechism, it loses—not its usefulness, not its divine character, not its meritoriousness (rather it increases these qualities by such charitable condescension)—but it does lose the particular attribute which I am illustrating; just as a face worn by tears and fasting loses its beauty, or a laborer's hand loses its delicateness;—for Theology thus exercised is not simple knowledge, but rather is an art or a business making use of Theology. And thus it appears that even what is supernatural need not be liberal, nor need a hero be a gentleman, for the plain reason that one idea is not another idea. And in like manner the Baconian Philosophy, by using its physical sciences in the service of man, does thereby transfer them from the order of Liberal Pursuits to, I do not say the inferior, but the distinct class of the Useful. And, to take a different instance, hence again, as is evident, whenever personal gain is the motive, still more distinctive an effect has it upon the character of a given pursuit; thus racing, which was a liberal exercise in Greece, forfeits its rank in times like these, so far as it is made the occasion of gambling.

All that I have been now saying is summed up in a few characteristic words of the great Philosopher. "Of possessions," he says, "those rather are useful, which bear fruit; those *liberal, which tend to enjoyment.* By fruitful, I mean, which yield revenue; by enjoyable, where *nothing accrues of consequence beyond the use.*"

V.

Do not suppose, Gentlemen, that in thus appealing to the ancients, I am throwing back the world two thousand years, and fettering Philosophy with the reasonings of paganism. While the world lasts, will Aristotle's doctrine on these matters last, for he is the oracle of nature and of truth. While we are men, we cannot help, to a great extent, being Aristotelians, for the great Master does but analyze the thoughts, feelings, views, and opinions of human kind. He has told us the meaning of our own words and ideas, before we were born. In many subject-matters, to think correctly, is to think like Aristotle; and we are his disciples whether we will or no, though we may not know it. Now, as to

18. **informed,** endowed with form. 30. **learned professions,** medicine, law, and theology.

70. **the great Philosopher,** Aristotle. The quotation is from his *Rhetoric*, I, 5. 81. **While . . . truth.** Newman was one of the numerous worshipers of Aristotle; indeed, many of the greatest systems of philosophy owe to Aristotle their chief ideas and methods.

the particular instance before us, the word "liberal" as applied to Knowledge and Education, expresses a specific idea, which ever has been, and ever will be, while the nature of man is the same, just as the idea of the Beautiful is specific, or of the Sublime, or of the Ridiculous, or of the Sordid. It is in the world now, it was in the world then; and, as in the case of the dogmas of faith, it is illustrated by a continuous historical tradition, and never was out of the world, from the time it came into it. There have indeed been differences of opinion from time to time, as to what pursuits and what arts came under that idea, but such differences are but an additional evidence of its reality. That idea must have a substance in it, which has maintained its ground amid these conflicts and changes, which has ever served as a standard to measure things withal, which has passed from mind to mind unchanged, when there was so much to color, so much to influence any notion or thought whatever, which was not founded in our very nature. Were it a mere generalization, it would have varied with the subjects from which it was generalized; but though its subjects vary with the age, it varies not itself. The palaestra may seem a liberal exercise to Lycurgus, and illiberal to Seneca; coach-driving and prize-fighting may be recognized in Elis, and be condemned in England; music may be despicable in the eyes of certain moderns, and be in the highest place with Aristotle and Plato—(and the case is the same in the particular application of the idea of Beauty, or of Goodness, or of Moral Virtue, there is a difference of tastes, a difference of judgments)—still these variations imply, instead of discrediting, the archetypal idea, which is but a previous hypothesis or condition, by means of which issue is joined between contending opinions, and without which there would be nothing to dispute about.

I consider, then, that I am chargeable with no paradox, when I speak of a Knowledge which is its own end, when I call it liberal

29. **Lycurgus**, a Spartan lawgiver (ninth century B.C.). **Seneca**, a Roman Stoic philosopher and author (first century A.D.). 31. **Elis**, an ancient division of Greece. 39. **archetypal**, constituting a model.

knowledge, or a gentleman's knowledge, when I educate for it, and make it the scope of a University. And still less am I incurring such a charge, when I make this acquisition consist, not in Knowledge in a vague and ordinary sense, but in that Knowledge which I have especially called Philosophy or, in an extended sense of the word, Science; for whatever claims Knowledge has to be considered as a good, these it has in a higher degree when it is viewed not vaguely, not popularly, but precisely and transcendently as Philosophy. Knowledge, I say, is then especially liberal, or sufficient for itself, apart from every external and ulterior object, when and so far as it is philosophical, and this I proceed to show.

VI.

Now bear with me, Gentlemen, if what I am about to say, has at first sight a fanciful appearance. Philosophy, then, or Science, is related to Knowledge in this way: Knowledge is called by the name of Science or Philosophy, when it is acted upon, informed, or if I may use a strong figure, impregnated by Reason. Reason is the principle of that intrinsic fecundity of Knowledge, which, to those who possess it, is its especial value, and which dispenses with the necessity of their looking abroad for any end to rest upon external to itself. Knowledge, indeed, when thus exalted into a scientific form, is also power; not only is it excellent in itself, but whatever such excellence may be, it is something more, it has a result beyond itself. Doubtless; but that is a further consideration, with which I am not concerned. I only say that, prior to its being a power, it is a good; that it is, not only an instrument, but an end. I know well it may resolve itself into an art, and terminate in a mechanical process, and in tangible fruit; but it also may fall back upon that Reason, which informs it, and resolve itself into Philosophy. In one case it is called Useful Knowledge, in the other Liberal. The same person may cultivate it in both ways at once; but this again is a matter foreign to my subject; here I do but say that there are two ways of using Knowledge, and in matter of fact those who use it in one way are not likely to use it in the other, or at least in a very limited measure. You see, then, here are two methods of Education; the end of the one is to be philosophical, of the other to be mechanical; the one rises towards general ideas, the other is exhausted upon what is particular and external. Let me not be thought to deny the necessity, or to decry the benefit, of such attention to what is particular and practical, as belongs to the useful or mechanical arts; life could not go on without them; we owe our daily welfare to them; their exercise is the duty of the many, and we owe to the many a debt of gratitude for fulfilling that duty. I only say that Knowledge, in proportion as it tends more and more to be particular, ceases to be Knowledge. It is a question whether Knowledge can in any proper sense be predicated of the brute creation; without pretending to metaphysical exactness of phraseology, which would be unsuitable to an occasion like this, I say, it seems to me improper to call that passive sensation, or perception of things, which brutes seem to possess, by the name of Knowledge. When I speak of Knowledge, I mean something intellectual, something which grasps what it perceives through the senses; something which takes a view of things; which sees more than the senses convey; which reasons upon what it sees, and while it sees; which invests it with an idea. It expresses itself, not in a mere enunciation, but by an enthymeme: it is of the nature of science from the first, and in this consists its dignity. The principle of real dignity in Knowledge, its worth, its desirableness, considered irrespectively of its results, is this germ within it of a scientific or a philosophical process. This is how it comes to be an end in itself; this is why it admits of being called Liberal. Not to know the relative disposition of things is the state of slaves or children; to have mapped out the Universe is the boast, or at least the ambition, of Philosophy.

Moreover, such knowledge is not a mere

36. **enthymeme,** a process of logical reasoning.

extrinsic or accidental advantage, which is ours today and another's tomorrow, which may be got up from a book, and easily forgotten again, which we can command or communicate at our pleasure, which we can borrow for the occasion, carry about in our hand, and take into the market; it is an acquired illumination, it is a habit, a personal possession, and an inward endowment. And this is the reason, why it is more correct, as well as more usual, to speak of a University as a place of education, than of instruction, though, when knowledge is concerned, instruction would at first sight have seemed the more appropriate word. We are instructed, for instance, in manual exercises, in the fine and useful arts, in trades, and in ways of business; for these are methods, which have little or no effect upon the mind itself, are contained in rules committed to memory, to tradition, or to use, and bear upon an end external to themselves. But education is a higher word; it implies an action upon our mental nature, and the formation of a character; it is something individual and permanent, and is commonly spoken of in connection with religion and virtue. When, then, we speak of the communication of Knowledge as being Education, we thereby really imply that that Knowledge is a state or condition of mind; and since cultivation of mind is surely worth seeking for its own sake, we are thus brought once more to the conclusion, which the word "Liberal" and the word "Philosophy" have already suggested, that there is a Knowledge, which is desirable, though nothing come of it, as being of itself a treasure, and a sufficient remuneration of years of labor.

VII.

This, then, is the answer which I am prepared to give to the question with which I opened this Discourse. Before going on to speak of the object of the Church in taking up Philosophy, and the uses to which she puts it, I am prepared to maintain that Philosophy is its own end, and, as I conceive, I have now begun proving it. I am prepared to maintain that there is a knowledge worth possessing for what it is, and not merely for what it does; and what minutes remain to me today I shall devote to the removal of some portion of the indistinctness and confusion with which the subject may in some minds be surrounded.

It may be objected then, that, when we profess to seek Knowledge for some end or other beyond itself, whatever it be, we speak intelligibly; but that, whatever men may have said, however obstinately the idea may have kept its ground from age to age, still it is simply unmeaning to say that we seek Knowledge for its own sake, and for nothing else; for that it ever leads to something beyond itself, which therefore is its end, and the cause why it is desirable;—moreover, that this end is twofold, either of this world or of the next; that all knowledge is cultivated either for secular objects or for eternal; that if it is directed to secular objects, it is called Useful Knowledge, if to eternal, Religious or Christian Knowledge;—in consequence, that if, as I have allowed, this Liberal Knowledge does not benefit the body or estate, it ought to benefit the soul; but if the fact be really so, that it is neither a physical or a secular good on the one hand, nor a moral good on the other, it cannot be a good at all, and is not worth the trouble which is necessary for its acquisition.

And then I may be reminded that the professors of this Liberal or Philosophical Knowledge have themselves, in every age, recognized this exposition of the matter, and have submitted to the issue in which it terminates; for they have ever been attempting to make men virtuous; or, if not, at least have assumed that refinement of mind was virtue, and that they themselves were the virtuous portion of mankind. This they have professed on the one hand; and on the other, they have utterly failed in their professions, so as ever to make themselves a proverb among men, and a laughing-stock both to the grave and the dissipated portion of mankind, in consequence of them. Thus they have furnished against themselves both the ground and the means of their own exposure, without any trouble at all to anyone else. In a word, from the time that Athens was the University of the world, what has Philosophy taught men, but to promise without practicing, and to aspire without attaining? What has the deep and lofty thought of its disciples ended in but eloquent words? Nay, what has its teaching ever meditated, when it was boldest in its remedies for human ill, beyond charming us to sleep by its lessons, that we might feel nothing at all? like some melodious air, or rather like those strong and transporting perfumes, which at first spread their sweetness over everything they touch, but in a little while do but offend in proportion as they once pleased us. Did Philosophy support Cicero under the disfavor of the fickle populace, or nerve Seneca to oppose an imperial tyrant? It abandoned Brutus, as he sorrowfully confessed, in his greatest need, and it forced Cato, as his panegyrist strangely boasts, into the false position of defying heaven. How few can be counted among its professors, who, like Polemo, were thereby converted from a profligate course, or like Anaxagoras, thought the world well lost in exchange for its possession? The philosopher in *Rasselas* taught a superhuman doctrine, and then succumbed without an effort to a trial of human affection.

"He discoursed," we are told, "with great energy on the government of the passions. His look was venerable, his action graceful, his pronunciation clear, and his diction elegant. He showed, with great strength of sentiment and variety of illustration, that human

51. **time . . . world,** the fifth century B.C., the period of the great philosophers, dramatists, and orators. 66. **Cicero.** He was assassinated in 43 B.C. because of his attack upon Antony. 67. **Seneca . . . tyrant.** Because he was charged with having a share in the conspiracy against the tyrant Nero in 65 A.D., Seneca was forced to commit suicide. 68. **Brutus,** Marcus Junius Brutus (85-42 B.C.), one of the assassins of Julius Caesar. Defeated in battle by Octavius, Brutus committed suicide. 70. **Cato,** Marcus Cato, the Younger (93-46 B.C.), who committed suicide at Utica, North Africa, upon hearing of Caesar's victory at Thapsus, rather than be conquered. Cato had several panegyrists. The Roman poet Lucan, in his epic *Pharsalia,* spoke of Cato as "the noblest Roman of them all"; and Addison (Vol. I, p. 975) exalted Cato in his classical tragedy *Cato.* 73. **Polemo,** an Athenian Platonic philosopher, a man of great wealth and political distinction (d. 273 B.C.). In his youth he was extremely profligate, but upon hearing a discourse on temperance in the school of Xenocrates, he reformed, and later became head of the school. 74. **Anaxagoras,** a famous Greek philosopher and teacher (fifth century B.C.); because he advanced new theories of the order of the universe and presented scientific accounts of rainbows, eclipses, etc., he was arrested and exiled on the charge of contravening religious dogma. 76. *Rasselas,* a philosophical romance by Samuel Johnson (Vol. I, p. 1125).

nature is degraded and debased, when the lower faculties predominate over the higher. He communicated the various precepts given, from time to time, for the conquest of passion, and displayed the happiness of those who had obtained the important victory, after which man is no longer the slave of fear, nor the fool of hope. . . . He enumerated many examples of heroes immovable by pain or pleasure, who looked with indifference on those modes or accidents to which the vulgar give the names of good and evil."

Rasselas in a few days found the philosopher in a room half darkened, with his eyes misty, and his face pale. "Sir," said he, "you have come at a time when all human friendship is useless; what I suffer cannot be remedied, what I have lost cannot be supplied. My daughter, my only daughter, from whose tenderness I expected all the comforts of my age, died last night of a fever." "Sir," said the prince, "mortality is an event by which a wise man can never be surprised; we know that death is always near, and it should therefore always be expected." "Young man," answered the philosopher, "you speak like one who has never felt the pangs of separation." "Have you, then, forgot the precept," said Rasselas, "which you so powerfully enforced? . . . consider that external things are naturally variable, but truth and reason are always the same." "What comfort," said the mourner, "can truth and reason afford me? Of what effect are they now, but to tell me that my daughter will not be restored?"

VIII.

Better, far better, to make no professions, you will say, than to cheat others with what we are not, and to scandalize them with what we are. The sensualist, or the man of the world, at any rate is not the victim of fine words, but pursues a reality and gains it. The Philosophy of Utility, you will say, Gentlemen, has at least done its work; and I grant it—it aimed low, but it has fulfilled its aim. If that man of great intellect who has been its Prophet in the conduct of life played false to his own professions, he was not bound by his philosophy to be true to his friend or faithful in his trust. Moral virtue was not the line in which he undertook to instruct men; and though, as the poet calls him, he were the "meanest" of mankind, he was so in what may be called his private capacity, and without any prejudice to the theory of induction. He had a right to be so, if he chose, for anything that the Idols of the den or the theater had to say to the contrary. His mission was the increase of physical enjoyment and social comfort; and most wonderfully, most awfully has he fulfilled his conception and his design. Almost day by day have we fresh and fresh shoots, and buds, and blossoms, which are to ripen into fruit, on that magical tree of Knowledge which he planted, and to which none of us perhaps, except the very poor, but owes, if not his present life, at least his daily food, his health, and general well-being. He was the divinely provided minister of temporal benefits to all of us so great, that, whatever I am forced to think of him as a man, I have not the heart, from mere gratitude, to speak of him severely. And in spite of the tendencies of his philosophy, which are, as we see at this day, to depreciate, or to trample on Theology, he has himself, in his writings, gone out of his way, as if with a prophetic misgiving of those tendencies, to insist on it as the instrument of that beneficent Father, who, when He came on earth in visible form, took on Him first and most prominently the office of assuaging the bodily wounds of human nature. And truly, like the old mediciner in the tale, "he sat diligently at his work, and hummed, with cheerful countenance, a pious song"; and then in turn "went out singing into the meadows so gayly, that those who had seen him from

---

42. **Philosophy of Utility,** the doctrine that the useful is the good, and that any conduct is to be adjudged good if its consequences are useful.

45. **man . . . intellect,** Francis Bacon. He was convicted of bribery in 1621. He proved faithless to his early patron, the Earl of Essex, who was convicted and executed for treason. At the Queen's request Bacon drew up the charges against Essex and conducted the case. 51. **the poet,** Pope, who calls Bacon, "the wisest, brightest, meanest of mankind," in *An Essay on Man*, IV, 282. 56. **Idols . . . theater.** See Bacon's *Novum Organum* (Vol. I, p. 626). 78. **insist . . . Father.** In Bacon's *De Augmentis Scientiarum*, IV, 2. 83. **"he sat,"** etc. From *The Unknown Patient,* by Friedrich Fouqué (1777-1843), a German poet and author.

afar might well have thought it was a youth gathering flowers for his beloved, instead of an old physician gathering healing herbs in the morning dew."

Alas, that men, in the action of life or in their heart of hearts, are not what they seem to be in their moments of excitement, or in their trances or intoxications of genius—so good, so noble, so serene! Alas, that Bacon too in his own way should after all be but the fellow of those heathen philosophers who in their disadvantages had some excuse for their inconsistency, and who surprise us rather in what they did say than in what they did not do! Alas, that he too, like Socrates or Seneca, must be stripped of his holy-day coat, which looks so fair, and should be but a mockery amid his most majestic gravity of phrase; and, for all his vast abilities, should, in the littleness of his own moral being, but typify the intellectual narrowness of his school! However, granting all this, heroism after all was not his philosophy: I cannot deny he has abundantly achieved what he proposed. His is simply a Method whereby bodily discomforts and temporal wants are to be most effectually removed from the greatest number; and already, before it has shown any signs of exhaustion, the gifts of nature, in their most artificial shapes and luxurious profusion and diversity, from all quarters of the earth, are, it is undeniable, by its means brought even to our doors, and we rejoice in them.

IX.

Useful Knowledge then, I grant, has done its work; and Liberal Knowledge as certainly has not done its work—supposing, that is, as the objectors assume, its direct end, like Religious Knowledge, is to make men better; but this I will not for an instant allow, and unless I allow it, those objectors have said nothing to the purpose. I admit, rather I maintain, what they have been urging, for I consider Knowledge to have its end in itself. For all its friends, or its enemies, may say, I insist upon it, that it is as real a mistake to burden it with virtue or religion as with the mechanical arts. Its direct business is not to steel the soul against temptation, or to console it in affliction, any more than to set the loom in motion, or to direct the steam carriage; be it ever so much the means or the condition of both material and moral advancement, still, taken by and in itself, it as little mends our hearts as it improves our temporal circumstances. And if its eulogists claim for it such a power, they commit the very same kind of encroachment on a province not their own as the political economist who should maintain that his science educated him for casuistry or diplomacy. Knowledge is one thing, virtue is another; good sense is not conscience, refinement is not humility, nor is largeness and justness of view faith. Philosophy, however enlightened, however profound, gives no command over the passions, no influential motives, no vivifying principles. Liberal Education makes not the Christian, not the Catholic, but the gentleman. It is well to be a gentleman, it is well to have a cultivated intellect, a delicate taste, a candid, equitable, dispassionate mind, a noble and courteous bearing in the conduct of life;—these are the connatural qualities of a large knowledge; they are the objects of a University; I am advocating, I shall illustrate and insist upon them; but still, I repeat, they are no guarantee for sanctity or even for conscientiousness they may attach to the man of the world, to the profligate, to the heartless —pleasant, alas, and attractive as he shows when decked out in them. Taken by themselves, they do but seem to be what they are not; they look like virtue at a distance, but they are detected by close observers, and on the long run; and hence it is that they are popularly accused of pretense and hypocrisy, not, I repeat, from their own fault, but because their professors and their admirers persist in taking them for what they are not; and are officious in arrogating for them a

---

15. **Socrates**, a famous Greek philosopher (fifth century B.C.); accused of impiety and of corrupting the youth, he drank hemlock rather than compromise with his opinions. In spite of his high-sounding utterances, he was criticized for not adequately supporting his family. 16. **Seneca**, a very wealthy man, voiced high ethical sentiments and spoke against riches; many persons thought that he did not live up to his utterances.

61. **casuistry**, sophistical, equivocal reasoning. 74. **connatural**, inherent, connected by nature.

praise to which they have no claim. Quarry the granite rock with razors, or moor the vessel with a thread of silk; then may you hope with such keen and delicate instruments as human knowledge and human reason to contend against these giants, the passion and the pride of man.

Surely we are not driven to theories of this kind in order to vindicate the value and dignity of Liberal Knowledge. Surely the real grounds on which its pretensions rest are not so very subtle or abstruse, so very strange or improbable. Surely it is very intelligible to say, and that is what I say here, that Liberal Education, viewed in itself, is simply the cultivation of the intellect as such, and its object is nothing more or less than intellectual excellence. Every thing has its own perfection, be it higher or lower in the scale of things; and the perfection of one is not the perfection of another. Things animate, inanimate, visible, invisible, all are good in their kind, and have a *best* of themselves, which is an object of pursuit. Why do you take such pains with your garden or your park? You see to your walks and turf and shrubberies; to your trees and drives; not as if you meant to make an orchard of the one, or corn or pasture land of the other, but because there is a special beauty in all that is goodly in wood, water, plain, and slope, brought all together by art into one shape, and grouped into one whole. Your cities are beautiful, your palaces, your public buildings, your territorial mansions, your churches; and their beauty leads to nothing beyond itself. There is a physical beauty and a moral: there is a beauty of person, there is a beauty of our moral being, which is natural virtue; and in like manner there is a beauty, there is a perfection, of the intellect. There is an ideal perfection in these various subject-matters, towards which individual instances are seen to rise, and which are the standards for all instances whatever. The Greek divinities and demigods, as the statuary has molded them, with their symmetry of figure, and their high forehead and their regular features, are the perfection of physical beauty. The heroes, of whom history tells, Alexander, or Caesar, or Scipio, or Saladin, are the representatives of that magnanimity or self-mastery which is the greatness of human nature. Christianity too has its heroes, and in the supernatural order, and we call them saints. The artist puts before him beauty of feature and form; the poet, beauty of mind; the preacher, the beauty of grace: then intellect too, I repeat, has its beauty, and it has those who aim at it. To open the mind, to correct it, to refine it, to enable it to know, and to digest, master, rule, and use its knowledge, to give it power over its own faculties, application, flexibility, method, critical exactness, sagacity, resource, address, eloquent expression, is an object as intelligible (for here we are inquiring, not what the object of a Liberal Education is worth, nor what use the Church makes of it, but what it is in itself), I say, an object as intelligible as the cultivation of virtue, while, at the same time, it is absolutely distinct from it.

X.

This indeed is but a temporal object, and a transitory possession; but so are other things in themselves which we make much of and pursue. The moralist will tell us that man, in all his functions, is but a flower which blossoms and fades, except so far as a higher principle breathes upon him, and makes him and what he is immortal. Body and mind are carried on into an eternal state of being by the gifts of Divine Munificence; but at first they do but fail in a failing world; and if the powers of intellect decay, the powers of the body have decayed before them, and, as an Hospital or an Almshouse, though its end be ephemeral, may be sanctified to the service of religion, so surely may a University, even were it nothing more than I have as yet described it. We attain to heaven by using this world well, though it is to pass

---

29. **corn,** grain, wheat.

50. **Alexander,** Alexander the Great, King of Macedon (336-323 B.C.). **Caesar,** Julius Caesar (100-44 B.C.), the famous Roman general, statesman, and writer. 51. **Scipio,** the family name of two famous Roman generals who fought against the Carthaginians in the second century B.C. **Saladin,** a famous Sultan of Egypt and Syria (1137-1193).

away; we perfect our nature, not by undoing it, but by adding to it what is more than nature, and directing it towards aims higher than its own.

FROM DISCOURSE VIII

THE DEFINITION OF A GENTLEMAN

...An age like this, not pagan, but professedly Christian, cannot venture to reprobate humility in set terms, or to make a boast of pride. Accordingly, it looks out for some expedient by which it may blind itself to the real state of the case. Humility, with its grave and self-denying attributes, it cannot love; but what is more beautiful, what more winning, than modesty? what virtue, at first sight, simulates humility so well? though what in fact is more radically distinct from it? In truth, great as is its charm, modesty is not the deepest or the most religious of virtues. Rather it is the advanced guard or sentinel of the soul militant, and watches continually over its nascent intercourse with the world about it. It goes the round of the senses; it mounts up into the countenance; it protects the eye and the ear; it reigns in the voice and gesture. Its province is the outward deportment, as other virtues have relation to matters theological, others to society, and others to the mind itself. And being more superficial than other virtues, it is more easily disjoined from their company; it admits of being associated with principles or qualities naturally foreign to it, and is often made the cloak of feelings or ends for which it was never given to us. So little is it the necessary index of humility, that it is even compatible with pride. The better for the purpose of Philosophy; humble it cannot be, so forthwith modesty becomes its humility.

Pride, under such training, instead of running to waste in the education of the mind, is turned to account; it gets a new name, it is called self-respect; and ceases to be the disagreeable, uncompanionable quality which it is in itself. Though it be the motive principle of the soul, it seldom comes to view; and when it shows itself, then delicacy and gentleness are its attire, and good sense and sense of honor direct its motions. It is no longer a restless agent, without definite aim; it has a large field of exertion assigned to it, and it subserves those social interests which it would naturally trouble. It is directed into the channel of industry, frugality, honesty, and obedience; and it becomes the very staple of the religion and morality held in honor in a day like our own. It becomes the safeguard of chastity, the guarantee of veracity, in high and low; it is the very household god of society, as at present constituted, inspiring neatness and decency in the servant girl, propriety of carriage and refined manners in her mistress, uprightness, manliness, and generosity in the head of the family. It diffuses a light over town and country; it covers the soil with handsome edifices and smiling gardens; it tills the fields, it stocks and embellishes the shop. It is the stimulating principle of providence on the one hand, and of free expenditure on the other; of an honorable ambition, and of elegant enjoyment. It breathes upon the face of the community, and the hollow sepulcher is forthwith beautiful to look upon.

Refined by the civilization which has brought it into activity, this self-respect infuses into the mind an intense horror of exposure, and a keen sensitiveness of notoriety and ridicule. It becomes the enemy of extravagances of any kind; it shrinks from what are called scenes; it has no mercy on the mock-heroic, on pretense or egotism, on verbosity in language, or what is called prosiness in conversation. It detests gross adulation; not that it tends at all to the eradication of the appetite to which the flatterer ministers, but it sees the absurdity of indulging it, it understands the annoyance thereby given to others, and if a tribute must be paid to the wealthy or the powerful, it demands greater subtlety and art in the preparation. Thus vanity is changed into a more dangerous self-conceit, as being checked in its natural eruption. It teaches men to suppress their feelings, and to control their tempers, and to mitigate both the severity and the tone of their judgments. As Lord Shaftesbury would desire, it prefers playful wit and satire in putting down what is objectionable, as a more refined and good-natured, as well as a more effectual method, than the expedient which is natural to uneducated minds. It is from this impatience of the tragic and the bombastic that it is now quietly but energetically opposing itself to the unchristian practice of dueling, which it brands as simply out of taste, and as the remnant of a barbarous age; and certainly it seems likely to effect what Religion has aimed at abolishing in vain.

Hence it is that it is almost a definition of a gentleman to say he is one who never inflicts pain. This description is both refined and, as far as it goes, accurate. He is mainly occupied in merely removing the obstacles which hinder the free and unembarrassed action of those about him; and he concurs with their movements rather than takes the initiative himself. His benefits may be considered as parallel to what are called comforts or conveniences in arrangements of a personal nature: like an easy chair or a good fire, which do their part in dispelling cold and fatigue, though nature provides both means of rest and animal heat without them. The true gentleman in like manner carefully avoids whatever may cause a jar or a jolt in the minds of those with whom he is cast;—all clashing of opinion, or collision of feeling, all restraint, or suspicion, or gloom, or resentment; his great concern being to make everyone at their ease and at home. He has his eyes on all his company; he is tender towards the bashful, gentle towards the distant, and merciful towards the absurd; he can recollect to whom he is speaking; he guards against unseasonable allusions, or topics which may irritate; he is seldom prominent in conversation, and never wearisome. He makes light of favors while he does them, and seems to be receiving when he is conferring. He never speaks of himself except when compelled, never defends himself by a mere retort; he has no ears for slander or gossip, is scrupulous in imputing motives to those who interfere with him, and interprets everything for the best. He is never mean or little in his disputes, never takes unfair advantage, never mistakes personalities or sharp sayings for arguments, or insinuates evil which he dare not say out. From a long-sighted prudence, he observes the maxim of the ancient sage, that we should ever conduct ourselves towards our enemy as if he were one day to be our friend. He has too much good sense to be affronted at insults, he is too well employed to remember injuries, and too indolent to bear malice. He is patient, forbearing, and resigned, on philosophical principles; he submits to pain, because it is inevitable, to bereavement, because it is irreparable, and to death, because it is his destiny. If he engages in controversy of any kind, his disciplined intellect preserves him from the blundering discourtesy of better, perhaps, but less educated minds; who, like blunt weapons, tear and hack instead of cutting clean, who mistake the point in argument, waste their strength on trifles, misconceive their adversary, and leave the question more involved than they find it. He may be right or wrong in his opinion, but he is too clear-headed to be unjust; he is as simple as he is forcible, and as brief as he is decisive. Nowhere shall we find greater candor, consideration, indulgence: he throws himself into the minds of his opponents, he accounts for their mistakes. He knows the weakness of human reason as well as its strength, its province and its limits. If he be an unbeliever, he will be too profound and large-minded to ridicule religion or to act against it; he is too wise to be a dogmatist or fanatic in his infidelity. He respects piety and devotion; he even supports institutions as venerable, beautiful, or useful, to which he does not assent; he honors the ministers of religion, and it contents him to decline its mysteries without assailing or denouncing them. He is a friend of religious toleration, and that, not only because his philosophy has taught him to look on all forms of faith with an impartial eye, but also from the gentleness

---

2. **Lord Shaftesbury**, Anthony Ashley Cooper (1671-1713), an eminent skeptical philosopher, who held that the moral sense of man was innate. In the portion omitted at the beginning, Newman had quoted several passages from Shaftesbury's writings. 10. **dueling.** Dueling was forbidden by law by acts of 1844 and 1879. 15. **a gentleman.** Cf. the Character Writers (Vol. I, pp. 681 ff.).

and effeminacy of feeling, which is the attendant on civilization.

Not that he may not hold a religion too, in his own way, even when he is not a Christian. In that case his religion is one of imagination and sentiment; it is the embodiment of those ideas of the sublime, majestic, and beautiful, without which there can be no large philosophy. Sometimes he acknowledges the being of God; sometimes he invests an unknown principle or quality with the attributes of perfection. And this deduction of his reason, or creation of his fancy, he makes the occasion of such excellent thoughts, and the starting-point of so varied and systematic a teaching, that he even seems like a disciple of Christianity itself. From the very accuracy and steadiness of his logical powers, he is able to see what sentiments are consistent in those who hold any religious doctrine at all, and he appears to others to feel and to hold a whole circle of theological truths, which exist in his mind no otherwise than as a number of deductions.

Such are some of the lineaments of the ethical character, which the cultivated intellect will form, apart from religious principle. They are seen within the pale of the Church and without it, in holy men, and in profligate; they form the *beau idéal* of the world; they partly assist and partly distort the development of the Catholic. They may subserve the education of a St. Francis de Sales or a Cardinal Pole; they may be the limits of the contemplation of a Shaftesbury or a Gibbon. Basil and Julian were fellow-students at the schools of Athens; and one became the Saint and Doctor of the Church, the other her scoffing and relentless foe.

(1852)

30. *beau idéal,* perfect model. 33. **St. Francis de Sales,** Bishop of Geneva, noted for his piety and kindness (1567-1622). **Cardinal Pole,** Reginald Pole (1500-1558), Archbishop of Canterbury; he was hostile to the Protestants during the reign of Queen Mary (1553-1558). 35. **Gibbon,** Edward Gibbon (1737-1794), the author of *The History of the Decline and Fall of the Roman Empire,* in which an unsympathetic attitude is expressed toward the early Christians. **Basil,** one of the orthodox fathers of the Greek Church (329-379). 36. **Julian,** Roman Emperor (361-363); he was brought up in the Christian faith, but he renounced it upon his accession to the throne; hence his title "The Apostate."

from *Apologia pro Vita Sua*

Newman's *Apologia pro Vita Sua* was occasioned by the necessity of his defending himself against Kingsley's charge that he did not consider truth a necessary virtue. But it was more than a reply to one man; in it, as he himself said, he aimed to vanquish not his accuser but his judges. He wrote it in seven parts, and it was published serially before appearing in book form in 1864. He composed it in burning eagerness to record his spiritual history. Like Carlyle's *Sartor Resartus* (see p. 465) the book is an account of the storms and stresses which plagued the author. But unlike *Sartor Resartus* with its noise and bustle, it is dignified, simple, lucid, forceful by a quiet sincerity. These qualities it possesses in spite of the speed with which it was composed; in writing the sermons that he delivered at St. Mary's, Newman early acquired a finished prose style. The *Apologia* holds high rank among English autobiographies.

[VISIT TO ITALY]

WHILE I was engaged in writing my work upon the Arians, great events were happening at home and abroad, which brought out into form and passionate expression the various beliefs which had so gradually been winning their way into my mind. Shortly before, there had been a revolution in France; the Bourbons had been dismissed; and I believed that it was unchristian for nations to cast off their governors, and, much more, sovereigns who had the divine right of inheritance. Again, the great Reform agitation was

2. **Arians,** followers of Arius, a famous churchman of Alexandria who held among other doctrines that Christ was not God, and that he was not divine. Newman finished his *History of the Arians* in 1832.

8. **Bourbons . . . dismissed.** Charles X, one of the Bourbon rulers of France (1824-1830) and a staunch supporter of the Catholic Church, was compelled to abdicate by the July Revolution of 1830. The Revolution greatly lessened the power of the clergy in government. 11. **who . . . inheritance.** According to this doctrine rulers were divinely appointed and could not be removed from office. 12. **Reform agitation,** that which culminated in the passage of the Reform Bill of 1832. See p. 403.

going on around me as I wrote. The Whigs had come into power; Lord Grey had told the bishops to set their house in order, and some of the prelates had been insulted and threatened in the streets of London. The vital question was how were we to keep the Church from being liberalized? There was such apathy on the subject in some quarters, such imbecile alarm in others; the true principles of churchmanship seemed so radically decayed, and there was such distraction in the councils of the clergy. The Bishop of London of the day, an active and open-hearted man, had been for years engaged in diluting the high orthodoxy of the Church by the introduction of the Evangelical body into places of influence and trust. He had deeply offended men who agreed in opinion with myself, by an off-hand saying (as it was reported) to the effect that belief in the Apostolical succession had gone out with the non-jurors. "We can count you," he said to some of the gravest and most venerated persons of the old school. And the Evangelical party itself seemed, with their late successes, to have lost their simplicity and unworldliness which I admired so much in Milner and Scott. It was not that I did not venerate such men as the then Bishop of Lichfield, and others of similar sentiments, who were not yet promoted out of the ranks of the clergy, but I thought little of them as a class. I thought they played into the hands of the Liberals. With the Establishment thus divided and threatened, thus ignorant of its true strength, I compared that fresh vigorous power of which I was reading in the first centuries. In her triumphant zeal on behalf of that primeval mystery to which I had had so great a devotion from my youth, I recognized the movement of my Spiritual Mother. "*Incessu patuit Dea.*" The self-conquest of her ascetics, the patience of her martyrs, the irresistible determination of her bishops, the joyous swing of her advance, both exalted and abashed me. I said to myself, "Look on this picture and on that"; I felt affection for my own Church, but not tenderness; I felt dismay at her prospects, anger and scorn at her do-nothing perplexity. I thought that if Liberalism once got a footing within her, it was sure of the victory in the event. I saw that Reformation principles were powerless to rescue her. As to leaving her, the thought never crossed my imagination; still I ever kept before me that there was something greater than the Established Church, and that that was the Church Catholic and Apostolic, set up from the beginning, of which she was but the local presence and organ. She was nothing, unless she was this. She must be dealt with strongly, or she would be lost. There was need of a second Reformation.

At this time I was disengaged from college duties, and my health had suffered from the labor involved in the composition of my volume. It was ready for the press in July, 1832, though not published till the end of 1833. I was easily persuaded to join Hurrell Froude and his father, who were going to the south of Europe for the health of the former.

We set out in December, 1832. It was during this expedition that my verses which are in the *Lyra Apostolica* were written;—a few indeed before it, but not more than one or two of them after it. Exchanging, as I was, definite tutorial labors, and the literary quiet and pleasant friendships of the last six years, for

---

1. **Whigs . . . power.** The Whigs won the election in 1830, and Earl Grey (1764-1845) became Prime Minister in November on the issue of reform. Bills passed brought about a more radical policy in ecclesiastical legislation. Among the abuses attacked was the system that allowed High Church officials to receive large revenues for work they delegated to underpaid curates. 12. **Bishop of London,** Charles James Blomfield (1786-1857). 15. **Evangelical body,** the small party in the Anglican Church that stood for religious zeal and that manifested enthusiasm in prison reform, antislavery legislation, etc. They were descendants of the evangelical revival of the eighteenth century. 20. **Apostolical succession.** It is a belief in the Anglican Church that bishops and priests trace an uninterrupted ecclesiastical descent from the Apostles. 21. **non-jurors,** the four hundred clergymen and nine bishops of the Anglican Church who had refused in 1688 to take the oath of allegiance to William and Mary on the ground that allegiance had already been sworn to the preceding monarch, James II. 26. **Milner and Scott,** Joseph Milner (1744-1797) and Thomas Scott (1747-1821), Anglican divines of the Evangelical party. 28. **Bishop of Lichfield,** Henry Ryder (1777-1836), who at first stood aloof from the rising Evangelical party of which he later became a distinguished adherent. He was appointed Bishop of Lichfield in 1824; but opposition to his liberal views was expressed as early as 1812. 31. **them,** the Evangelicals. 33. **Establishment,** the Established, or Anglican, Church.

37. **primeval mystery,** the mystery of the Holy Incarnation, the doctrine that Christ and God are one. 40. **Spiritual Mother,** the Catholic Church. "*Incessu . . . Dea,*" that she is a goddess is made clear by her step.—Virgil's *Aeneid,* I, 405. 45. "**Look . . . that,**" Hamlet's words to his mother (*Hamlet,* III, iv, 53) when he compares her first husband (his father) with the second (Claudius) 51. **Reformation principles,** mere arguments for reform. 61. **second Reformation.** For the first, see Vol. I, p. 303. 67. **Hurrell Froude,** a clergyman of the Anglican Church (1803-1836), elder brother of James Anthony Froude, a famous historian. 72. **Lyra Apostolica,** a collection of hymns for the Church written by Newman, Hurrell Froude, John Keble (1792-1866), and other Anglican divines.

foreign countries and an unknown future, I naturally was led to think that some inward changes, as well as some larger course of action, were coming upon me. At Whitchurch, while waiting for the down mail to Falmouth, I wrote the verses about my Guardian Angel, which begin with these words: "Are these the tracks of some unearthly Friend?" and go on to speak of "the vision" which haunted me: that vision is more or less brought out in the whole series of those compositions.

I went to various coasts of the Mediterranean, parted with my friends at Rome; went down for the second time to Sicily, at the end of April, and got back to England by Palermo in the early part of July. The strangeness of foreign life threw me back into myself; I found pleasure in historical sites and beautiful scenes, not in men and manners. We kept clear of Catholics throughout our tour. I had a conversation with the Dean of Malta, a most pleasant man, lately dead; but it was about the fathers, and the library of the great church. I knew the Abbate Santini, at Rome, who did no more than copy for me the Gregorian tones. Froude and I made two calls upon Monsignore (now Cardinal) Wiseman at the Collegio Inglese, shortly before we left Rome. I do not recollect being in a room with any other ecclesiastics, except a priest at Castro-Giovanni in Sicily, who called on me when I was ill, and with whom I wished to hold a controversy. As to church services, we attended the Tenebrae, at the Sestine, for the sake of the Miserere; and that was all. My general feeling was, "All, save the spirit of man, is divine." I saw nothing but what was external; of the hidden life of Catholics I knew nothing. I was still more driven back into myself, and felt my isolation. England was in my thoughts solely, and the news from England came rarely and imperfectly. The Bill for the Suppression of the Irish Sees was in progress, and filled my mind. I had fierce thoughts against the Liberals.

It was the success of the Liberal cause which fretted me inwardly. I became fierce against its instruments and its manifestations. A French vessel was at Algiers; I would not even look at the tricolor. On my return, though forced to stop a day in Paris, I kept indoors the whole time, and all that I saw of that beautiful city, was what I saw from the diligence. The Bishop of London had already sounded me as to my filling one of the Whitehall preacherships, which he had just then put on a new footing; but I was indignant at the line which he was taking, and from my steamer I had sent home a letter declining the appointment by anticipation, should it be offered to me. At this time I was specially annoyed with Dr. Arnold, though it did not last into later years. Someone, I think, asked in conversation at Rome, whether a certain interpretation of Scripture was Christian? it was answered that Dr. Arnold took it; I interposed, "But is *he* a Christian?" The subject went out of my head at once; when afterwards I was taxed with it, I could say no more in explanation, than that I thought I must have been alluding to some free views of Dr. Arnold about the *Old Testament*—I thought I must have meant, "But who is to answer for Arnold?" It was at Rome too that we began the *Lyra Apostolica* which appeared monthly in the *British Magazine.* The motto shows the feeling of both Froude and myself at the time: we borrowed from M. Bunsen a Homer, and Froude chose the words in which Achilles, on returning to the battle, says, "You shall know the difference, now that I am back again."

4. **Whitchurch**, a small town in Hampshire. 6. **Falmouth**, a seaport of Cornwall. 22. **Malta**, an island in the Mediterranean Sea, under British control since 1814. 26. **Gregorian tones**, a collection of chants compiled by Pope Gregory I (590-604). 27. **Monsignore . . . Wiseman**, Nicholas Patrick Wiseman (1802-1865), at the time rector of the Catholic English College in Rome. He was made an English Cardinal in 1850. 35. **Tenebrae**, in the Catholic Church, the matins and lauds for the last three days of Holy Week commemorating the suffering and death of Christ. **Sestine**, the Sistine Chapel, the Pope's chapel in the Vatican. 36. **Miserere**, the musical setting of *Psalm* 51, which in Latin begins with this word. 44. **Bill . . . Sees**, the Irish Church Temperalities Act, passed in 1833, which abolished nearly half of the Church of England archbishoprics and bishoprics in Ireland. 51. **tricolor**, the national flag of France consisting of vertical stripes of blue, white, and red. It was adopted after the Revolution, with which Newman was not in sympathy. 54. **diligence**, a public stagecoach. 56. **Whitehall**, a royal chapel near Westminster Abbey; it was the center of missionary activity. 63. **Dr. Arnold**, Thomas Arnold (1795-1842), the famous headmaster of Rugby School and father of Matthew Arnold; he was regarded as very liberal in his religious views. 77. **British Magazine**, a High Church magazine founded in 1832 by Hugh James Rose (1795-1838), an Anglican divine. 79. **a Homer**, a copy of Homer's *Iliad*. The incident occurs in Book XVIII, 187 ff. See p. 333, note 10.

Especially when I was left by myself, the thought came upon me that deliverance is wrought, not by the many but by the few, not by bodies but by persons. Now it was, I think, that I repeated to myself the words, which had ever been dear to me from my school days, *"Exoriare aliquis!"*—now too, that Southey's beautiful poem of *Thalaba*, for which I had an immense liking, came forcibly to my mind. I began to think that I had a mission. There are sentences of my letters to my friends to this effect, if they are not destroyed. When we took leave of Monsignore Wiseman, he had courteously expressed a wish that we might make a second visit to Rome; I said with great gravity, "We have a work to do in England." I went down at once to Sicily, and the presentiment grew stronger. I struck into the middle of the island, and fell ill of a fever at Leonforte. My servant thought I was dying, and begged for my last directions. I gave them, as he wished; but I said, "I shall not die." I repeated, "I shall not die, for I have not sinned against light, I have not sinned against light." I never have been able to make out at all what I meant.

I got to Castro-Giovanni, and was laid up there for nearly three weeks. Towards the end of May I set off for Palermo, taking three days for the journey. Before starting from my inn in the morning of May 26th or 27th, I sat down on my bed and began to sob bitterly. My servant, who had acted as my nurse, asked what ailed me. I could only answer, "I have a work to do in England."

I was aching to get home; yet for want of a vessel I was kept at Palermo for three weeks. I began to visit the churches, and they calmed my impatience, though I did not attend any services. I knew nothing of the presence of the Blessed Sacrament there. At last I got off in an orange boat, bound for Marseilles. We were becalmed a whole week in the Straits of Bonifacio. Then it was that I wrote the lines, "Lead, kindly light," which have since become well-known. I was writing verses the whole time of my passage. At length I got to Marseilles and set off for England. The fatigue of traveling was too much for me, and I was laid up for several days at Lyons. At last I got off again and did not stop night or day till I reached England, and my mother's house. My brother had arrived from Persia only a few hours before. This was on Tuesday. The following Sunday, July 14th, Mr. Keble preached the assize sermon in the University pulpit. It was published under the title of "National Apostasy." I have ever considered and kept the day as the start of the religious movement of 1833.

(1864)

* * * * *

[In its book form the *Apologia pro Vita Sua* is divided into five chapters and a body of notes and supplemental matter. The section reprinted here consists of the last eight paragraphs of Chapter I. This chapter covers the history of Newman's religious opinions up to 1833, the date made famous by Keble's assize sermon and by Newman's return from Italy to take up the battle for reform in the Church of England. The succeeding chapters are planned just as simply as is the first; each one covers a significant period in Newman's spiritual struggle to adjust himself and brings his autobiography up to another crisis. Chapter II begins with his return to England and concludes with a statement of his status in the spring of 1839. Chapter III covers two short but full and highly significant years; it ends with the publication in February, 1841, of Tract 90, which raised such a storm of protest that Newman felt obliged to withdraw from his charge. Chapter IV embraces the period from his withdrawal from his own church to his admission to the Roman Catholic Church in 1845. The fifth and last chapter recounts the position of his mind from 1845 up to the date of his reply in 1864 to the attacks upon him by Charles Kingsley.]

---

40. **presence . . . Sacrament.** In the Roman Catholic Church it is the belief that Christ is actually present in bread and wine during the ceremony of the Mass, and that he remains present in the consecrated host. 43. **Straits of Bonifacio,** in the Mediterranean between Corsica and Sardinia. 45. **"Lead, kindly light."** See p. 715. 55. **Mr. Keble,** John Keble, an Anglican divine, regarded by Newman as the father of the Oxford Movement of 1833. See p. 406. 56. **assize sermon,** that delivered before one of the periodical sessions of the judges of the superior courts. Keble spoke at the opening of the Oxford Assizes. He was disgusted with the conditions in the Anglican Church and denounced the action of the commissioners appointed under recent legislation.

---

7. *"Exoriare aliquis!"* Let someone rise up.—Virgil's *Aeneid,* IV, 625. 8. **Thalaba,** an Oriental epic by Robert Southey (see p. 296), in which the hero destroys a race of magicians through the power of a talisman. 20. **Leonforte,** a town in the province of Catania, Sicily. 29. **Palermo,** a seaport of Sicily.

Thomas Carlyle
1795-1881

The activities of Thomas Carlyle were spiritual rather than physical and social, and the events of his life are few in number. He was born in Ecclefechan, Dumfriesshire (the Entepfuhl of *Sartor Resartus*), December 4, 1795. After completing his elementary studies in the grammar school at Annan, he went to the University of Edinburgh but left in 1814 without a degree. His parents wished him to take a course in divinity and become a minister in the Scottish church, but his independence of spirit made such a life program impossible, and in 1817 he definitely abandoned the idea. Similarly he gave up school-teaching after a year's trial of it. This was in 1816; it was in this year that he fell in love with, and was rejected by, the young woman whom he calls "Blumine" in *Sartor Resartus* (see p. 466, note to l. 36). His love affair was followed by the period of doubt and uncertainty described vividly in *Sartor Resartus*.

Carlyle's first literary work reveals clearly his admiration for German thought and philosophy, and especially for the two great German poets Schiller and Goethe. His *Life of Schiller* appeared in *The London Magazine* in 1823-1824, and was reprinted in book form in 1825, when Carlyle was thirty. This work was followed by a translation of Goethe's *Wilhelm Meister's Lehrjahre* (1824) and by a series of essays on German literature which appeared during 1827 in the *Edinburgh Review, The Foreign Review,* and *The Foreign Quarterly Review.* The style of these early writings is strikingly different from the verbal explosions which characterize his later manner; it is simple, clear, limpid, and relatively free from exaggerated figures.

In 1826 Carlyle married Jane Welsh of Haddington, a brilliant and charming woman, and two years later he retired with her to her farm at Craigenputtock, "the dreariest spot in all the British dominions." Whatever the six years of his burial at Craigenputtock meant to Mrs. Carlyle, it was to him what the Horton period was to Milton. He went to Craigenputtock an obscure writer of essays and translations; he emerged six years later one of the foremost literary figures in England. During the farm period Carlyle wrote his famous essay on Robert Burns and *Sartor Resartus*, the grim account of his spiritual life.

In 1834 the Carlyles emerged from their retirement and took up a residence at 5 Cheyne Row, Chelsea, London. Here "the Sage of Chelsea" lived and wrote for the rest of a long life. From his home there issued a long series of books, the products of prodigious labor. The first was his *History of the French Revolution*. The manuscript of the first volume was completed in 1835, but its accidental destruction delayed the appearance of the three volumes until two years later. It brought him fame but no great wealth. As a result of this comparative poverty he was induced to give four series of public lectures. Of these the most famous were those *On Heroes, Hero-Worship, and the Heroic in History*, delivered in 1840 and published in 1841; they express fully Carlyle's creed of individualism and of the importance of personality. His essays on *Chartism* (1839), *Past and Present* (1843), and *Latter Day Pamphlets* (1850) present his economic and industrial theories. With *The Letters and Speeches of Oliver Cromwell* (1845), *The Life of John Sterling* (1851), and the tremendous *History of Frederick II of Prussia, Called Frederick the Great* (1858-1865) he returned to biography. The long preparation for his *Frederick the Great* took him to Germany to survey the battlefields of the Emperor's campaigns; this was one of the very few journeys that he made from London. Carlyle was seventy when the third and last volume of *Frederick the Great* appeared; it was the last of his major labors; and though he lived until 1881, his work was essentially over. The honor which came to him in being made Lord Rector of Edinburgh in 1865 turned to ashes in his mouth with the sudden death of his wife shortly afterwards.

Carlyle's literary work falls naturally into four major divisions: biography, history, literary comment, economic and social criticism. He has been accused of inconsistencies in his work, and minor inconsistencies no doubt appear, as might be expected in half a century of furious writing. Essentially, however, his creed is a unit and may be traced in all his work. Its roots lie in his insistence on the ascendancy of the spiritual values over the material and on the importance of the individual as compared with the mass of mankind. He has been characterized as a "moral brass-band," and his work has been alluded to derisively as "the doctrine of silence in twenty volumes." His service to the Victorian world was, nevertheless, genuine; he preached, furiously and tirelessly, that principles are superior to rules, that cant is hollow and sincerity sound, that love of labor is to be preferred to love of pleasure, that duty and not indulgence is the true guide of life. In the Revolutionary doctrine of human equality he had no faith whatever. Men, he believed, are created unequal; some are born to be heroes and leaders, and some to be followers. He was, therefore, essentially aristocratic, an interesting fact in view of his peasant birth and heritage. "Big, black democracy" he loathed and feared; and the American Civil War for the freedom of the slaves he alluded to sneeringly. Similarly, the French Revolution was to him far from glorious; it provided simply a horrible example which should serve as a warning to the English. His success as a biographer and his distinction as a historian spring from his faith in the power of the individual. History he believed to be "the essence of innumerable biographies"; and his *French Revolution* thus bristles with personalities. His sermons for his own time were also molded by his creed of individualism. He looked for the strong, just man to slay the dragons of materialism and greed. Political economy was a "dismal science" that he hated; the doctrine of *laissez-faire* was anathema to him, but he had no faith in the value of social and industrial legislation. From all these circumstances it will be apparent that Carlyle stood alone; he subscribed to no current creed, he belonged to no political group. He was an individualist, an advocate of the supreme value of innate nobility, the voice of one crying in the wilderness.

The stormy quality of Carlyle's preaching finds a natural reflection in the style of his writing during and after the Craigenputtock period. He is himself a vitriolic Jeremiah, his ideas are dynamic, and his style is—as John Stuart Mill said—"an insane rhapsody." Some of the obvious typographical characteristics of it come, no doubt, from his familiarity with German. But Carlyle's style goes beyond such superficial characteristics. It has an echo of the utterances of the Old Testament prophets. It is almost, if not entirely, apocalyptic. It abounds in vigorous figures which give it a savage, dour roughness and leave the reader hardly time to come up for air. It is not a restful style; it reflects the writer's savage indignation and passionate love of truth. Like its creator it is profound, harsh, and grim with earnestness.

from *Sartor Resartus*

Sartor Resartus was the product of Carlyle's formative years at Craigenputtock. It is his "spiritual autobiography" and contains the essence of his social philosophy and his prose style. The title means "The Tailor Retailored," and the "clothes philosophy" of the first part Carlyle took from Swift's similar ideas in *A Tale of a Tub*. *Sartor Resartus* is not a narrative in the ordinary sense of the word; it is a philosophical romance. The first part sets forth the idea that the universe is to be considered as "a large suit of clothes which invests everything"; the second is an autobiographical romance in which Carlyle, under the figure of a philosophical German named Diogenes Teufelsdröckh (God-begotten devil's dung), Professor of Things in General at the University of Weissnichtwo (I know not where), sets forth his own spiritual strains and stresses. It is in this second part that the author presents the episode of his denial of kinship with the Devil (the Everlasting No), his theory of The Center of Indifference, and his Everlasting Yea. The material and the style of this astonishing production kept some publishers from considering it; ultimately it appeared in *Fraser's Magazine* in 1833-1834. It nearly wrecked the magazine; subscriptions fell off, and critics damned it, one writer summarizing it as "a heap of clotted nonsense." It survived this storm of adverse criticism, however, and appeared in book form in New York in 1836 and in London in 1838. The "cracked and crazed" style, an "insane rhapsody" of figures, Germanisms, unusual words and phrases, helped to increase its unpopularity. Carlyle declared, however, that the style was natural, that he had, indeed, adapted it from the usual aggressive and chaotic vigor of his father's normal expression. Certainly it fits his personality and his subject-matter as no smoothly bromidic style could possibly do.

THE EVERLASTING NO

UNDER the strange nebulous envelopment, wherein our Professor has now shrouded himself, no doubt but his spiritual nature is nevertheless progressive, and growing for how can the "Son of Time," in any case, stand still? We behold him, through those dim years, in a state of crisis, of transition: his mad Pilgrimings, and general solution into aimless Discontinuity, what is all this but a mad Fermentation; wherefrom, the fiercer it is, the clearer product will one day evolve itself?

Such transitions are ever full of pain: thus the Eagle when he molts is sickly; and, to attain his new beak, must harshly dash-off the old one upon rocks. What Stoicism soever our Wanderer, in his individual acts and motions, may affect, it is clear that there is a hot fever of anarchy and misery raging within; coruscations of which flash out: as, indeed, how could there be other? Have we not seen him disappointed, bemocked of Destiny, through long years? All that the young heart might desire and pray for has been denied; nay, as in the last worst instance, offered and then snatched away. Ever an "excellent Passivity"; but of useful, reasonable Activity, essential to the former as Food to Hunger, nothing granted: till at length, in this wild Pilgrimage, he must forcibly seize for himself an Activity, though useless, unreasonable. Alas, his cup of bitterness, which had been filling drop by drop, ever since that first "ruddy morning" in the Hinterschlag Gymnasium, was at the very lip; and then with that poison-drop, of the Towgood-and-Blumine business, it runs over, and even hisses over in a deluge of foam.

He himself says once, with more justice than originality: "Man is, properly speaking, based upon Hope; he has no other possession but Hope; this world of his is emphatically the 'Place of Hope.'" What, then, was our Professor's possession? We see him, for the present, quite shut-out from Hope; looking not into the golden orient, but vaguely all round into a dim copper firmament, pregnant with earthquake and tornado.

Alas, shut-out from Hope, in a deeper sense than we yet dream of! For, as he wanders

1. **nebulous envelopment.** Frustrated in love and consumed by inward misery, Teufelsdröckh, calling himself a "Son of Time," becomes a despairing wanderer over the earth. 14. **Eagle . . . rocks.** A London book, *Domestic Habits of Birds* (1833), quotes St. Augustine as saying that "when the eagle becomes very old, the upper mandible of the beak grows so long that the bird can no longer feed, in which case it betakes itself to a rock or rough stone, and rubs its beak till the overgrown part is ground down into proper proportion." Carlyle's figure of speech, however, is not sound; the eagle molts its feathers but not its beak.

25. **last worst instance,** the refusal of the young lady, Blumine, to return Teufelsdröckh's love, after first appearing to do so. 28. **former,** passivity. 34. **Hinterschlag Gymnasium,** literally, the Strike-behind Academy; it represents the Annan Grammar School, Dumfries, Scotland, which Carlyle entered at the age of ten. 36. **Towgood . . . business.** Towgood was Teufelsdröckh's most intimate friend: Blumine his lady-love. After his painful last meeting with Blumine and his rejection by her, Teufelsdröckh wandered to the mountains, where he saw Towgood and Blumine drive past him on their wedding journey. (See p. 468, note 74.)

wearisomely through this world, he has now lost all tidings of another and higher. Full of religion, or at least of religiosity, as our Friend has since exhibited himself, he hides not that, in those days, he was wholly irreligious: "Doubt had darkened into Unbelief," says he; "shade after shade goes grimly over your soul, till you have the fixed, starless, Tartarean black." To such readers as have 10 reflected, what can be called reflecting, on man's life, and happily discovered, in contradiction to much Profit-and-Loss Philosophy, speculative and practical, that Soul is *not* synonymous with Stomach; who understands, therefore, in our Friend's words, "that, for man's well-being, Faith is properly the one thing needful; how, with it, Martyrs, otherwise weak, can cheerfully endure the shame and the cross; and without it, Worldlings 20 puke-up their sick existence, by suicide, in the midst of luxury": to such it will be clear that, for a pure moral nature, the loss of his religious Belief was the loss of everything. Unhappy young man! All wounds, the crush of long-continued Destitution, the stab of false Friendship and of false Love, all wounds in thy so genial heart, would have healed again, had not its life-warmth been withdrawn. Well might he exclaim, in his wild way: "Is 30 there no God, then; but at best an absentee God, sitting idle, ever since the first Sabbath, at the outside of his Universe, and *see*ing it go? Has the word Duty no meaning; is what we call Duty no divine Messenger and Guide, but a false earthly Fantasm, made-up of Desire and Fear, of emanations from the Gallows and from Doctor Graham's Celestial-Bed? Happiness of an approving Conscience! Did not Paul of Tarsus, whom admiring men have since named Saint, feel that *he* was 'the chief of sinners'; and Nero of Rome, jocund in spirit (*wohlgemuth*), spend much of his time in fiddling? Foolish Wordmonger and Motive-grinder, who in thy Logic-mill hast an earthly mechanism for the Godlike itself, and wouldst fain grind me out Virtue from the husks of Pleasure—I tell thee, Nay! To the unregenerate Prometheus Vinctus of a man, it is ever the bitterest aggravation of his wretchedness that he is conscious of Virtue, that he feels himself the victim not of suffering only, but of injustice. What then? Is the heroic inspiration we name Virtue but some Passion; some bubble of the blood, bubbling in the direction others *profit* by? I know not: only this I know, If what thou namest Happiness be our true aim, then are we all astray. With Stupidity and sound Digestion man may front much. But what, in these dull unimaginative days, are the terrors of Conscience to the diseases of the Liver! Not on Morality, but on Cookery, let us build our stronghold: there brandishing our frying-pan, as censer, let us offer sweet incense to the Devil, and live at ease on the fat things *he* has provided for his Elect!"

Thus has the bewildered Wanderer to stand, as so many have done, shouting question after question into the Sibyl-cave of Destiny, and receive no Answer but an echo. It is all a grim Desert, this once-fair world of his; wherein is heard only the howling of wild-beasts, or the shrieks of despairing, hate-filled men; and no Pillar of Cloud by day, and no Pillar of Fire by night, any longer guides the Pilgrim. To such length has the spirit of Inquiry carried him. "But what boots it (*was thut's*)?" cries he: "it is but the common lot in this era. Not having come to spiritual majority prior to the *Siècle de Louis Quinze,* and not

---

9. **Tartarean,** of Tartarus, the lowest portion of Hell. 10. **what ... reflecting.** This sentence is a good example of the broken syntax frequently found in Carlyle. 12. **Profit-and-Loss Philosophy,** the doctrine of Utilitarianism (see p. 404), which held that conduct was morally good according as it promoted the greatest good of the greatest number. This doctrine was supported by Jeremy Bentham (1748-1832) and John Stuart Mill (1806-1873); Carlyle and Ruskin were among its vigorous opponents (see p. 501). 16. **one thing needful.** Cf. *Luke,* 10:42: "But one thing is needful: and Mary hath chosen that good part, which shall not be taken away from her." Mary "sat at Jesus' feet, and heard his word" while her sister Martha was "cumbered about much serving." 37. **Doctor ... Bed.** James Graham (1745-1794) was a notorious quack doctor whose famous "Celestial-Bed" was guaranteed, for fifty pounds, to cure sterility in those who slept upon it. Carlyle refers to the bed as a symbol of false hopes.

41. **chief of sinners.** Paul so labels himself in *1 Timothy,* 1:15. **Nero ... fiddling.** The Emperor Nero (37-68 A.D.) is said to have played the fiddle while Rome was burning. 48. **unregenerate ... man,** the man who, like Prometheus, refuses to recognize a supreme being. Because Prometheus stole fire from heaven for man, he was conquered (Vinctus) and chained to a rock by order of Zeus. 69. **Sibyl-cave of Destiny.** An allusion to the visit of Aeneas to the Sibyl, a prophetess, to learn his future (*Aeneid,* VI, 36 ff.). 74. **Pillar ... night.** From *Exodus,* 13:21-22: "And the Lord went before them by day in a pillar of cloud, to lead them the way; and by night in a pillar of fire, to give them light." 80. **Siècle ... Quinze,** the age of Louis XV, the eighteenth century, noted for its rationalism and skepticism. Voltaire (1694-1778) wrote a book with this title.

being born purely a Loghead (*Dummkopf*), thou hadst no other outlook. The whole world is, like thee, sold to Unbelief; their old Temples of the Godhead, which for long have not been rainproof, crumble down; and men ask now: where is the Godhead; our eyes never saw him?"

Pitiful enough were it, for all these wild utterances, to call our Diogenes wicked. Unprofitable servants as we all are, perhaps at no era of his life was he more decisively the Servant of Goodness, the Servant of God, than even now when doubting God's existence. "One circumstance I note," says he: "after all the nameless woe that Inquiry, which for me, what it is not always, was genuine Love of Truth, had wrought me, I nevertheless still loved Truth, and would bate no jot of my allegiance to her. 'Truth!' I cried, 'though the Heavens crush me for following her: no Falsehood! though a whole celestial Lubberland were the price of Apostasy.' In conduct it was the same. Had a divine Messenger from the clouds, or miraculous Handwriting on the wall, convincingly proclaimed to me *This thou shalt do,* with what passionate readiness, as I often thought, would I have done it, had it been leaping into the infernal Fire. Thus, in spite of all Motive-grinders, and Mechanical Profit-and-Loss Philosophies, with the sick ophthalmia and hallucination they had brought on, was the Infinite nature of Duty still dimly present to me: living without God in the world, of God's light I was not utterly bereft; if my as yet sealed eyes with their unspeakable longing, could nowhere see Him, nevertheless in my heart He was present, and His heaven-written Law still stood legible and sacred there."

Meanwhile, under all these tribulations, and temporal and spiritual destitutions, what must the Wanderer, in his silent soul, have endured! "The painfullest feeling," writes he, "is that of your own Feebleness (*Unkraft*); ever, as the English Milton says, to be weak is the true misery. And yet of your Strength there is and can be no clear feeling, save by what you have prospered in, by what you have done. Between vague wavering Capability and fixed indubitable Performance, what a difference! A certain inarticulate Self-consciousness dwells dimly in us; which only our Works can render articulate and decisively discernible. Our Works are the mirror wherein the spirit first sees its natural lineaments. Hence, too, the folly of that impossible Precept, *Know thyself;* till it be translated into this partially possible one, *Know what thou canst work at.*

"But for me, so strangely unprosperous had I been, the net-result of my Workings amounted as yet simply to—Nothing. How then could I believe in my Strength, when there was as yet no mirror to see it in? Ever did this agitating, yet, as I now perceive, quite frivolous question, remain to me insoluble: Hast thou a certain Faculty, a certain Worth, such even as the most have not; or art thou the completest Dullard of these modern times? Alas, the fearful Unbelief is unbelief in yourself; and how could I believe? Had not my first, last Faith in myself, when even to me the Heavens seemed laid open, and I dared to love, been all-too cruelly belied? The speculative Mystery of Life grew ever more mysterious to me: neither in the practical Mystery had I made the slightest progress, but been everywhere buffeted, foiled, and contemptuously cast out. A feeble unit in the middle of a threatening Infinitude, I seemed to have nothing given me but eyes, whereby to discern my own wretchedness. Invisible yet impenetrable walls, as of Enchantment, divided me from all living: was there, in the wide world,

---

9. **Diogenes,** God-begotten, the first name of Teufelsdröckh. 10. **Unprofitable servants,** a phrase from *Luke,* 17:10. 12. **Servant . . . existence.** Cf. Tennyson's *In Memoriam,* 96, 3-4 (p. 635). 25. **Handwriting on the wall.** Daniel interpreted the handwriting on the wall, which appeared to King Belshazzar at a feast, to mean the loss of his kingdom. See *Daniel,* 5.

46. **to be . . . misery.** In Satan's speech to Beelzebub—"To be weak is miserable."—*Paradise Lost,* I, 157 (Vol. I, p. 719). 55. **Our Works.** Here is a suggestion of Carlyle's gospel of work, which he speaks of as noble and sacred. See *Past and Present,* p. 485. 58. **Know thyself,** the famous maxim of the Greek lawgiver Solon (c. 638-559 B.C.); it is inscribed over the entrance to the temple of Apollo at Delphi. 61. "**But for me,**" etc. This passage is highly autobiographical. From 1819 to 1822 Carlyle suffered from insomnia and dyspepsia, which he called "a rat gnawing at the pit of his stomach." He was also sorely perplexed by mental and spiritual conflicts. 74. **I . . . love.** A reference to the love affair with Blumine (see note 36, p. 466); perhaps Carlyle is thinking of his boyhood love for Margaret Gordon, or of his great love for Jane Welsh, which at first was fraught with misunderstanding and many obstacles. 77. **Mystery,** trade, occupation.

any true bosom I could press trustfully to mine? O Heaven, No, there was none! I kept a lock upon my lips: why should I speak much with that shifting variety of so-called Friends, in whose withered, vain and too-hungry souls Friendship was but an incredible tradition? In such cases, your resource is to talk little, and that little mostly from the Newspapers. Now when I look back, it was a strange isolation I then lived in. The men and women around me, even speaking with me, were but Figures; I had, practically, forgotten that they were alive, that they were not merely automatic. In the midst of their crowded streets and assemblages, I walked solitary; and (except as it was my own heart, not another's, that I kept devouring) savage also, as the tiger in his jungle. Some comfort it would have been, could I, like a Faust, have fancied myself tempted and tormented of the Devil; for a Hell, as I imagine, without Life, though only diabolic Life, were more frightful: but in our age of Down-pulling and Disbelief, the very Devil has been pulled down, you cannot so much as believe in a Devil. To me the Universe was all void of Life, of Purpose, of Volition, even of Hostility: it was one huge dead, immeasurable Steam-engine, rolling on, in its dead indifference, to grind me limb from limb. O, the vast, gloomy, solitary Golgotha, and Mill of Death! Why was the Living banished thither companionless, conscious? Why, if there is no Devil; nay, unless the Devil is your God?"

A prey incessantly to such corrosions, might not, moreover, as the worst aggravation to them, the iron constitution even of a Teufelsdröckh threaten to fail? We conjecture that he has known sickness; and, in spite of his locomotive habits, perhaps sickness of the chronic sort. Hear this, for example: "How beautiful to die of broken-heart, on Paper! Quite another thing in practice; every window of your Feeling, even of your intellect, as it were, begrimed and mud-bespattered, so that no pure ray can enter; a whole Drug-shop in your inwards; the fordone soul drowning slowly in quagmires of Disgust!"

Putting all which external and internal miseries together, may we not find in the following sentences, quite in our Professor's still vein, significance enough? "From Suicide a certain aftershine (*Nachschein*) of Christianity withheld me: perhaps also a certain indolence of character; for, was not that a remedy I had at any time within reach? Often, however, was there a question present to me: Should some one now, at the turning of that corner, blow thee suddenly out of Space, into the other World, or other No-world, by pistol-shot—how were it? On which ground, too, I often, in sea-storms and sieged cities and other death-scenes, exhibited an imperturbability, which passed, falsely enough, for courage."

"So had it lasted," concludes the Wanderer, "so had it lasted as in bitter protracted Death-agony, through long years. The heart within me, unvisited by any heavenly dewdrop, was smoldering in sulphurous, slow-consuming fire. Almost since earliest memory I had shed no tear; or once only when I, murmuring half-audibly, recited Faust's Death-song, that wild *Selig der den er im Siegesglanze findet* (Happy whom *he* finds in Battle's splendor), and thought that of this last Friend even I was not forsaken, that Destiny itself could not doom me not to die. Having no hope, neither had I any definite fear, were it of Man or of Devil: nay, I often felt as if it might be solacing, could the Arch-Devil himself, though in Tartarean terrors, but rise to me, that I might tell him a little of my mind. And yet, strangely enough, I lived in a continual, indefinite, pining fear; tremulous, pusillanimous, apprehensive of I knew not what; it seemed as if all things in the Heavens above and the Earth beneath would hurt me; as if the Heavens and the Earth were but boundless jaws of a devouring monster, wherein I, palpitating, waited, to be devoured.

"Full of such humor, and perhaps the miser-

---

19. **Faust,** a medieval scholar and magician, reputed to have sold his soul to the devil. He is the hero of Goethe's *Faust* (1808, 1832), and of Marlowe's *Dr. Faustus* (Vol. I, p. 502). 23. **in our age.** Carlyle's age was a time of vigorous reconstruction and of eager building. See p. 400. 31. **Golgotha,** the place of the crucifixion of Christ; see *Matthew,* 27:33; the word means "the place of the skull."

52. **Suicide.** During his years of misery Carlyle had contemplated suicide. 73. **Faust's Death-song.** In Goethe's *Faust,* IV, 1572-1576.

ablest man in the whole French Capital or Suburbs, was I, one sultry Dogday, after much perambulation, toiling along the dirty little *Rue Saint-Thomas de l'Enfer,* among civic rubbish enough, in a close atmosphere, and over pavements hot as Nebuchadnezzar's Furnace; whereby doubtless my spirits were little cheered; when, all at once, there rose a Thought in me, and I asked myself: 'What *art* thou afraid of? Wherefore, like a coward, dost thou forever pip and whimper, and go cowering and trembling? Despicable biped! what is the sum-total of the worst that lies before thee? Death? Well, Death; and say the pangs of Tophet too, and all that the Devil and Man may, will, or can do against thee! Hast thou not a heart; canst thou not suffer whatsoever it be; and, as a Child of Freedom, though outcast, trample Tophet itself under thy feet, while it consumes thee? Let it come, then; I will meet it and defy it!' And as I so thought, there rushed like a stream of fire over my whole soul; and I shook base Fear away from me forever. I was strong, of unknown strength; a spirit, almost a god. Ever from that time, the temper of my misery was changed: not Fear or whining Sorrow was it, but Indignation and grim fire-eyed Defiance.

"Thus had the EVERLASTING NO (*das ewige Nein*) pealed authoritatively through all the recesses of my Being, of my ME; and then was it that my whole ME stood up, in native God-created majesty, and with emphasis recorded its Protest. Such a Protest, the most important transaction in Life, may that same Indignation and Defiance, in a psychological point of view, be fitly called. The Everlasting No had said: 'Behold, thou art fatherless, outcast, and the Universe is mine (the Devil's)'; to which my whole ME now made answer: '*I am not thine, but Free, and forever hate thee!*'

"It is from this hour that I incline to date my Spiritual New-birth, or Baphometic Firebaptism; perhaps I directly thereupon began to be a Man." (II, 7)

CENTER OF INDIFFERENCE

Though, after this "Baphometic Fire-baptism" of his, our Wanderer signifies that his Unrest was but increased; as, indeed, "Indignation and Defiance," especially against things in general, are not the most peaceable inmates; yet can the Psychologist surmise that it was no longer a quite hopeless Unrest; that henceforth it had at least a fixed center to revolve round. For the fire-baptized soul, long so scathed and thunder-riven, here feels its own Freedom, which feeling is its Baphometic Baptism: the citadel of its whole kingdom it has thus gained by assault, and will keep inexpugnable; outwards from which the remaining dominions, not indeed without hard battling, will doubtless by degrees be conquered and pacificated. Under another figure, we might say, if in that great moment, in the *Rue Saint-Thomas de l'Enfer,* the old inward Satanic School was not yet thrown out of doors, it received peremptory judicial notice to quit;—whereby, for the rest, its howl-chantings, Ernulphus-cursings, and rebellious gnashings of teeth, might, in the meanwhile, become only the more tumultuous, and difficult to keep secret.

Accordingly, if we scrutinize these Pilgrimings well, there is perhaps discernible henceforth a certain incipient method in their madness. Not wholly as a Specter does Teufelsdröckh now storm through the world; at worst as a specter-fighting Man, nay who will one day be a Specter-queller. If pilgriming restlessly to so many "Saints' Wells," and ever without quenching of his thirst, he nevertheless finds little secular wells, whereby from time to time some alleviation is ministered. In a word, he is now, if not ceasing,

2. **one sultry Dogday,** etc. This incident actually happened to Carlyle in Leith Walk, Edinburgh, in June, 1821. The *Rue de l'Enfer* may be translated *Hell Street.* The term *dog days* is applied to the sultry period of July and August when Sirius, the Dog Star, is in the ascendant. 6. **Nebuchadnezzar's Furnace,** the fiery furnace into which King Nebuchadnezzar cast Shadrach, Meshach, and Abednego on their refusal to worship the image that he had set up (*Daniel,* 3). 15. **Tophet,** hell; also the name of a furnace in the Valley of Hinnom, near Jerusalem, where human sacrifices by fire were performed. See *2 Kings,* 23:10.

44. **Baphometic.** Baphomet, a medieval corruption of the word *Mahomet,* was an idol that the Knights Templar were accused of worshiping. In the story of the Fallen Master, Baffometus fails to build a temple at the Lord's command, and the Lord anoints his chin, brow, cheeks, and heart with hot fluid gold and sets a burning crown of gold upon his head, all that remains of him. The entire phrase suggests sudden deliverance through spiritual illumination. 69. **Ernulphus-cursings,** the excommunication curse of Ernulf, Bishop of Rochester (1040-1124), which is repeated by Dr. Slop in Sterne's *Tristram Shandy,* Book III, Ch. xi. 79. **Specter-queller,** specter-killer.

yet intermitting to "eat his own heart"; and clutches round him outwardly on the NOT-ME for wholesomer food. Does not the following glimpse exhibit him in a much more natural state?

"Towns also and Cities, especially the ancient, I failed not to look upon with interest. How beautiful to see thereby, as through a long vista, into the remote Time! to have, as it were, an actual section of almost the earliest Past brought safe into the Present, and set before your eyes! There, in that old City, was a live ember of Culinary Fire put down, say only two thousand years ago; and there, burning more or less triumphantly, with such fuel as the region yielded, it has burnt, and still burns, and thou thyself seest the very smoke thereof. Ah! and the far more mysterious live ember of VITAL FIRE was then also put down there; and still miraculously burns and spreads; and the smoke and ashes thereof (in these Judgment-Halls and Churchyards), and its bellows-engines (in these Churches), thou still seest; and its flame, looking out from every kind countenance, and every hateful one, still warms thee or scorches thee.

"Of Man's Activity and Attainment the chief results are aeriform, mystic, and preserved in Tradition only: such are his Forms of Government, with the Authority they rest on; his Customs, or Fashions both of Cloth-habits and of Soul-habits; much more his collective stock of Handicrafts, the whole Faculty he has acquired of manipulating Nature: all these things, as indispensable and priceless as they are, cannot in any way be fixed under lock and key, but must flit, spiritlike, on impalpable vehicles, from Father to Son; if you demand sight of them, they are nowhere to be met with. Visible Ploughmen and Hammermen there have been, ever from Cain and Tubalcain downwards: but where does your accumulated Agricultural, Metallurgic, and other Manufacturing SKILL lie warehoused? It transmits itself on the atmospheric air, on the sun's rays (by Hearing and by Vision); it is a thing aeriform, impalpable, of quite

42. **Cain and Tubalcain.** See *Genesis*, 4:2, 22; Cain was the first "tiller of the soil," and Tubalcain was "an instructor of every artificer in brass and iron."

spiritual sort. In like manner, ask me not, Where are the LAWS; where is the GOVERNMENT? In vain wilt thou go to Schönbrunn, to Downing Street, to the Palais Bourbon; thou findest nothing there but brick or stone houses, and some bundles of Papers tied with tape. Where, then, is that same cunningly-devised almighty GOVERNMENT of theirs to be laid hands on? Everywhere, yet nowhere: seen only in its works, this too is a thing aeriform, invisible; or if you will, mystic and miraculous. So spiritual (*geistig*) is our whole daily Life: all that we do springs out of Mystery, Spirit, invisible Force; only like a little Cloud-image, or Armida's Palace, air-built, does the Actual body itself forth from the great mystic Deep.

"Visible and tangible products of the Past, again, I reckon-up to the extent of three: Cities, with their Cabinets and Arsenals; then tilled Fields, to either or to both of which divisions Roads with their Bridges may belong; and thirdly——Books. In which third truly, the last invented, lies a worth far surpassing that of the two others. Wondrous indeed is the virtue of a true Book. Not like a dead city of stones, yearly crumbling, yearly needing repair; more like a tilled field, but then a spiritual field: like a spiritual tree, let me rather say, it stands from year to year, and from age to age (we have Books that already number some hundred-and-fifty human ages); and yearly comes its new produce of leaves (Commentaries, Deductions, Philosophical, Political Systems; or were it only Sermons, Pamphlets, Journalistic Essays), every one of which is talismanic and thaumaturgic, for it can persuade men. O thou who art able to write a Book, which once in the two centuries or oftener there is a man gifted to do, envy not him whom they name City-builder, and inexpressibly pity him whom they name Conqueror or City-burner! Thou too art a Conqueror and Victor: but of the true sort, namely over the Devil: thou too hast built what will outlast all marble and

51. **Schönbrunn, Downing Street, Palais Bourbon,** government centers of Germany, England, and France. 63. **Armida's Palace,** in Tasso's *Jerusalem Delivered*, Book 16, the palace with its enchanted garden to which the sorceress Armida lured the Christian knights from their siege of Jerusalem. 85. **thaumaturgic,** magical.

metal, and be a wonder-bringing City of the Mind, a Temple and Seminary and Prophetic Mount, whereto all kindreds of the Earth will pilgrim.—Fool! why journeyest thou wearisomely, in thy antiquarian fervor, to gaze on the stone pyramids of Geeza, or the clay ones of Sacchara? These stand there, as I can tell thee, idle and inert, looking over the Desert, foolishly enough, for the last three-thousand years: but canst thou not open thy Hebrew BIBLE, then, or even Luther's Version thereof?"

No less satisfactory is his sudden appearance not in Battle, yet on some Battle-field; which, we soon gather, must be that of Wagram; so that here, for once, is a certain approximation to distinctness of date. Omitting much, let us impart what follows:

"Horrible enough! A whole Marchfeld strewed with shell-splinters, cannon-shot, ruined tumbrils, and dead men and horses; stragglers still remaining not so much as buried. And those red mould heaps: ay, there lie the Shells of Men, out of which all the Life and Virtue has been blown; and now are they swept together, and crammed-down out of sight, like blown Egg-shells!—Did Nature, when she bade the Donau bring down his mould-cargoes from the Carinthian and Carpathian Heights, and spread them out here into the softest, richest level—intend thee, O Marchfeld, for a corn-bearing Nursery, whereon her children might be nursed; or for a Cockpit, wherein they might the more commodiously be throttled and tattered? Were thy three broad Highways, meeting here from the ends of Europe, made for Ammunition-wagons, then? Were thy Wagrams and Stillfrieds but so many ready-built Casemates, wherein the house of Hapsburg might batter with artillery, and with artillery be battered? König Ottokar, amid yonder hillocks, dies under Rodolf's truncheon; here Kaiser Franz falls a-swoon under Napoleon's: within which five centuries, to omit the others, how has thy breast, fair Plain, been defaced and defiled! The greensward is torn-up and trampled-down; man's fond care of it, his fruit-trees, hedge-rows, and pleasant dwellings, blown away with gunpowder; and the kind seedfield lies a desolate, hideous Place of Skulls.—Nevertheless, Nature is at work; neither shall these Powder-Devilkins with their utmost devilry gainsay her: but all that gore and carnage will be shrouded-in, absorbed into manure; and next year the Marchfeld will be green, nay greener. Thrifty unwearied Nature, ever out of our great waste educing some little profit of thy own—how dost thou, from the very carcass of the Killer, bring Life for the Living!

"What, speaking in quite unofficial language, is the net-purport and upshot of war? To my own knowledge, for example, there dwell and toil, in the British village of Dumdrudge, usually some five-hundred souls. From these, by certain "Natural Enemies" of the French, there are successively selected, during the French war, say thirty able-bodied men. Dumdrudge, at her own expense, has suckled and nursed them: she has, not without difficulty and sorrow, fed them up to manhood, and even trained them to crafts, so that one can weave, another build, another hammer, and the weakest can stand under thirty stone avoirdupois. Nevertheless, amid much weeping and swearing, they are selected; all dressed in red; and shipped away, at the public charges, some two thousand miles, or say only to the south of Spain; and fed there till wanted. And now to that same spot, in the south of Spain, are thirty similar French artisans, from a French Dumdrudge, in like manner wending, till at length, after

---

6. **stone pyramids of Geeza,** the trio of royal monuments at Gizeh near Cairo. 7. **Sacchara,** Saqqara, inferior brick tombs of an earlier dynasty than those at Gizeh. 11. **Luther's Version,** the translation of the Bible into German in 1534 by the Protestant reformer Martin Luther (1483-1546). 16. **Wagram,** an Austrian village in the plain of the Marchfeld (see 1. 19), which gave its name to a battle fought there on July 5 and 6, 1809, between the French army under Napoleon and the Austrian army under the archduke Charles; the Austrians were defeated, but the casualties on both sides were unusually severe. 28. **Donau,** German form of "Danube." 39. **Stillfried,** a battle fought, like Wagram, on the banks of the March River in Austria, August 26, 1278, between Rudolph I (1218-1291) of the House of Hapsburg and Ottokar II, King of Bohemia; Ottokar was defeated and killed. In his earlier allusion to Marchfeld "strewed with shell-splinters, cannon-shot, ruined tumbrils" it is evident that Carlyle had in mind Wagram and not the thirteenth-century battle, in which gunpowder was not, of course, used.

40. **Casemates,** bomb-proof chambers. 44. **Kaiser Franz,** the popular name for Francis I (1768-1835), Emperor of Austria. 52. **Place of Skulls,** an allusion to Calvary, or Golgotha ("the place of a skull"); see *John*, 19:17. 66. **Dumdrudge,** Carlyle's coined name for any typical British village. 77. **stone,** an English measure of weight, fourteen pounds.

infinite effort, the two parties come into actual juxtaposition; and Thirty stands fronting Thirty, each with a gun in his hand. Straightway the word "Fire!" is given, and they blow the souls out of one another; and in place of sixty brisk useful craftsmen, the world has sixty dead carcasses, which it must bury, and anew shed tears for. Had these men any quarrel? Busy as the Devil is, not the smallest! They lived far enough apart; were the entirest strangers; nay, in so wide a Universe, there was even, unconsciously, by Commerce, some mutual helpfulness between them. How then? Simpleton! their Governors had fallen out; and, instead of shooting one another, had the cunning to make these poor blockheads shoot.—Alas, so is it in Deutschland, and hitherto in all other lands; still as of old, 'what devilry soever Kings do, the Greeks must pay the piper!'— In that fiction of the English Smollett, it is true, the final Cessation of War is perhaps prophetically shadowed forth; where the two Natural Enemies, in person, take each a Tobacco-pipe, filled with Brimstone; light the same, and smoke in one another's faces, till the weaker gives in: but from such predicted Peace-Era, what blood-filled trenches, and contentious centuries, may still divide us!"

Thus can the Professor, at least in lucid intervals, look away from his own sorrows, over the many-colored world, and pertinently enough note what is passing there. We may remark, indeed, that for the matter of spiritual culture, if for nothing else, perhaps few periods of his life were richer than this. Internally, there is the most momentous instructive Course of Practical Philosophy, with Experiments, going on; towards the right comprehension of which his Peripatetic habits, favorable to Meditation, might help him rather than hinder. Externally, again, as he wanders to and fro, there are, if for the longing heart little substance, yet for the seeing eye sights enough: in these so boundless Travels of his, granting that the Satanic School was even partially kept down, what an incredible knowledge of our Planet, and its Inhabitants and their Works, that is to say, of all knowable things, might not Teufelsdröckh acquire!

"I have read in most Public Libraries," says he, "including those of Constantinople and Samarcand: in most Colleges, except the Chinese Mandarin ones, I have studied, or seen that there was no studying. Unknown Languages have I oftenest gathered from their natural repertory, the Air, by my organ of Hearing; Statistics, Geographics, Topographics came, through the Eye, almost of their own accord. The ways of Man, how he seeks food, and warmth, and protection for himself, in most regions, are ocularly known to me. Like the great Hadrian, I meted out much of the terraqueous Globe with a pair of Compasses that belonged to myself only.

"Of great Scenes why speak? Three summer days, I lingered reflecting, and even composing (*dichtete*), by the Pine-chasms of Vaucluse; and in that clear Lakelet moistened my bread. I have sat under the Palm-trees of Tadmor; smoked a pipe among the ruins of Babylon. The great Wall of China I have seen; and can testify that it is of gray brick, coped and covered with granite, and shows only second-rate masonry.—Great Events, also, have not I witnessed? Kings sweated-down (*ausgemergelt*) into Berlin-and-Milan Customhouse-Officers; the World well won, and the World well lost; oftener than once a hundred thousand individuals shot (by each other) in one day. All kindreds and peoples and nations dashed together and shifted and shoveled into heaps that they might ferment there, and in time unite. The birth-pangs of Democracy, wherewith convulsed Europe was groaning in cries that reached Heaven, could not escape me.

"For great Men I have ever had the warmest predilection; and can perhaps boast that few such in this era have wholly escaped me. Great Men are the inspired (speaking and acting) Texts of that divine BOOK OF REVELATIONS, whereof a Chapter is completed from epoch to epoch, and by some named HISTORY; to which inspired Texts your numerous talented men, and your innumerable untalented men, are the better or worse exegetic Com-

---

21. **Smollett**, Tobias Smollett (1721-1771), English novelist.

54. **Samarcand**, a city of Russian Turkestan, once a great center of learning. 64. **Hadrian**, Roman emperor (117-138). 70. **Vaucluse**, a village in southeastern France. 72. **Tadmor**, Palmyra, an ancient city in an oasis of the Syrian desert.

mentaries, and wagonload of too-stupid, heretical or orthodox, weekly Sermons. For my study the inspired Texts themselves! Thus did not I, in very early days, having disguised me as tavern-waiter, stand behind the field-chairs, under that shady Tree at Treisnitz by the Jena Highway; waiting upon the great Schiller and greater Goethe; and hearing what I have not forgotten. For——"

——But at this point the Editor recalls his principle of caution, some time ago laid down, and must suppress much. Let not the sacredness of Laureled, still more, of Crowned Heads, be tampered with. Should we, at a future day, find circumstances altered, and the time come for Publication, then may these glimpses into the privacy of the Illustrious be conceded; which for the present were little better than treacherous, perhaps traitorous Eavesdroppings. Of Lord Byron, therefore, of Pope Pius, Emperor Tarakwang, and the "White Water-roses" (Chinese Carbonari) with their mysteries, no notice here! Of Napoleon himself we shall only, glancing from afar, remark that Teufelsdröckh's relation to him seems to have been of very varied character. At first we find our poor Professor on the point of being shot as a spy; then taken into private conversation, even pinched on the ear, yet presented with no money; at last indignantly dismissed, almost thrown out of doors, as an "Ideologist." "He himself," says the Professor, "was among the completest Ideologists, at least Ideopraxists: in the Idea (*in der Idee*) he lived, moved, and fought. The man was a Divine Missionary, though unconscious of it; and preached, through the cannon's throat, that great doctrine, *La carrière ouverte aux talens* (The Tools to him that can handle them), which is our ultimate Political Evangel, wherein alone can liberty lie. Madly enough he preached, it is true, as Enthusiasts and first Missionaries are wont, with imperfect utterance, amid much frothy rant; yet as articulately perhaps as the case admitted. Or call him, if you will, an American Backwoodsman, who had to fell unpenetrated forests, and battle with innumerable wolves, and did not entirely forbear strong liquor, rioting, and even theft; whom, notwithstanding, the peaceful Sower will follow, and, as he cuts the boundless harvest, bless."

More legitimate and decisively authentic is Teufelsdröckh's appearance and emergence (we know not well whence) in the solitude of the North Cape, on that June Midnight. He has "a light-blue Spanish cloak" hanging round him, as his "most commodious, principal, indeed sole upper garment"; and stands there, on the World-promontory, looking over the infinite Brine, like a little blue Belfry (as we figure), now motionless indeed, yet ready, if stirred, to ring quaintest changes.

"Silence as of death," writes he; "for Midnight, even in the Arctic latitudes, has its character: nothing but the granite cliffs ruddy-tinged, the peaceable gurgle of that slow-heaving Polar Ocean, over which in the utmost North the great Sun hangs low and lazy, as if he too were slumbering. Yet is his cloud-couch wrought of crimson and cloth-of-gold; yet does his light stream over the mirror of waters, like a tremulous fire-pillar, shooting downwards to the abyss, and hide itself under my feet. In such moments, Solitude also is invaluable; for who would speak, or be looked on, when behind him lies all Europe and Africa, fast asleep, except the watchmen; and before him the silent Immensity, and Palace of the Eternal, whereof our Sun is but a porch-lamp?

"Nevertheless, in this solemn moment comes a man, or monster, scrambling from among the rock-hollows; and, shaggy, huge as the Hyperborean Bear, hails me in Russian speech: most probably, therefore, a Russian Smuggler. With courteous brevity, I signify my indifference to contraband trade, my humane intentions, yet strong wish to be private. In vain: the monster, counting doubtless on his superior stature, and minded to make sport for himself, or perhaps profit, were it with murder, continues to advance, ever assailing me with his importunate train-oil breath, and now has advanced, till we stand both on the verge of the rock, the deep

---

7. **Jena**, a town in Germany, rich in memories of Goethe and Schiller. 21. **Emperor Tarakwang**, contemporary Emperor of China. 22. **Carbonari**, a secret Italian political association; Carlyle applies the name to a similar group in China. 34. **Ideopraxist**, one who puts ideas into practice.

85. **Hyperborean**, from the extreme north, a region inhabited by a mythological race.

Sea rippling greedily down below. What argument will avail? On the thick Hyperborean, cherubic reasoning, seraphic eloquence were lost. Prepared for such extremity, I, deftly enough, whisk aside one step; draw out, from my interior reservoirs, a sufficient Birmingham Horse-pistol, and say, "Be so obliging as retire, Friend (*Er ziehe sich zurück, Freund*), and with promptitude!" This logic even the Hyperborean understands; fast enough, with apologetic, petitionary growl, he sidles off; and, except for suicidal as well as homicidal purposes, need not return.

"Such I hold to be the genuine use of Gunpowder: that it makes all men alike tall. Nay, if thou be cooler, cleverer than I, if thou have more *Mind*, though all but no Body whatever, then canst thou kill me first, and art the taller. Hereby, at last, is the Goliath powerless, and the David resistless; savage Animalism is nothing, inventive Spiritualism is all.

"With respect to Duels, indeed, I have my own ideas. Few things, in this so surprising world, strike me with more surprise. Two little visual Spectra of men, hovering with insecure enough cohesion in the midst of the Unfathomable, and to dissolve therein, at any rate, very soon—make pause at the distance of twelve paces asunder; whirl round; and, simultaneously by the cunningest mechanism, explode one another into Dissolution; and off-hand become Air, and Non-extant! Deuce on it (*verdammt*), the little spitfires!—Nay, I think with old Hugo von Trimberg: 'God must needs laugh outright, could such a thing be, to see his wondrous Manikins here below.'"

But amid these specialties, let us not forget the great generality, which is our chief quest here: How prospered the inner man of Teufelsdröckh under so much outward shifting? Does Legion still lurk in him, though repressed; or has he exorcised that Devil's Brood? We can answer that the symptoms continue promising. Experience is the grand spiritual Doctor; and with him Teufelsdröckh has now been long a patient, swallowing many a bitter bolus. Unless our poor Friend belong to the numerous class of Incurables, which seems not likely, some cure will doubtless be effected. We should rather say that Legion, or the Satanic School, was now pretty well extirpated and cast out, but next to nothing introduced in its room; whereby the heart remains, for the while, in a quiet but no comfortable state.

"At length, after so much roasting," thus writes our Autobiographer, "I was what you might name calcined. Pray only that it be not rather, as is the more frequent issue, reduced to a *caput mortuum*! But in any case, by mere dint of practice, I had grown familiar with many things. Wretchedness was still wretched; but I could now partly see through it, and despise it. Which highest mortal, in this inane Existence, had I not found a Shadow-hunter, or Shadow-hunted; and, when I looked through his brave garnitures, miserable enough? Thy wishes have all been sniffed aside, thought I: but what, had they even been all granted! Did not the Boy Alexander weep because he had not two Planets to conquer; or a whole Solar System; or after that, a whole Universe? *Ach Gott*, when I gazed into these Stars, have they not looked down on me as if with pity, from their serene spaces, like Eyes glistening with heavenly tears over the little lot of man! Thousands of human generations, all as noisy as our own, have been swallowed-up of Time, and there remains no wreck of them any more; and Arcturus and Orion and Sirius and the Pleiades are still shining in their courses, clear and young, as when the Shepherd first noted them in the plain of Shinar. Pshaw! what is this paltry little Dog-cage of an Earth; what art thou that sittest whining there? Thou art still Nothing, Nobody; true; but who, then, is Something, Somebody? For

---

19. **Goliath.** For the story of David and Goliath, see *I Samuel*, 17. 34. **Hugo von Trimberg**, a German moral writer of the thirteenth century. 42. **Legion.** See *Mark*, 5:9, where the "unclean spirit" replies to Jesus, "My name is Legion: for we are many."

48. **bolus**, pill. 52. **Satanic School.** Carlyle may have had in mind the epithet given by Southey in his *Vision of Judgment* to Byron, Shelley, and other romantic poets of their period. 61. **caput mortuum**, a death's head, or skull; Carlyle's allusions to "roasting" and "calcining" indicate that he may have had in mind the term applied by chemists to the worthless residue after distillation. 82. **Arcturus**, etc., stars and constellations. 84. **Shepherd . . . Shinar.** See *Genesis*, 15:5, where Abraham is told by the Lord to "Look now toward heaven and tell (i.e., count) the stars"; Abraham's ancestral home was in the plain of Shinar in Babylonia.

thee the Family of Man has no use; it rejects thee; thou art wholly as a dissevered limb; so be it; perhaps it is better so!"

Too-heavy-laden Teufelsdröckh! Yet surely his bands are loosening; one day he will hurl the burden far from him, and bound forth free and with a second youth.

"This," says our Professor, "was the CENTER OF INDIFFERENCE I had now reached; through which whoso travels from the Negative Pole to the Positive must necessarily pass." (II, 8)

THE EVERLASTING YEA

"Temptations in the Wilderness!" exclaims Teufelsdröckh. "Have we not all to be tried with such? Not so easily can the old Adam, lodged in us by birth, be dispossessed. Our Life is compassed round with Necessity; yet is the meaning of Life itself no other than Freedom, than Voluntary Force: thus have we a warfare; in the beginning, especially, a hard-fought battle. For the God-given mandate, *Work thou in Welldoing,* lies mysteriously written, in Promethean Prophetic Characters, in our hearts; and leaves us no rest, night or day, till it be deciphered and obeyed; till it burn forth, in our conduct, a visible, acted Gospel of Freedom. And as the clay-given mandate, *Eat thou and be filled,* at the same time persuasively proclaims itself through every nerve—must not there be a confusion, a contest, before the better Influence can become the upper?

"To me nothing seems more natural than that the Son of Man, when such God-given mandate first prophetically stirs within him, and the Clay must now be vanquished, or vanquish—should be carried of the spirit into grim Solitudes, and there fronting the Tempter do grimmest battle with him; defiantly setting him at naught, till he yield and fly. Name it as we choose: with or without visible Devil, whether in the natural Desert of rocks and sands, or in the populous moral Desert of selfishness and baseness—to such Temptation are we all called. Unhappy if we are not! Unhappy if we are but Half-men, in whom that divine handwriting has never blazed forth, all-subduing, in true sun-splendor; but quivers dubiously amid meaner lights or smolders, in dull pain, in darkness, under earthly vapors!—Our Wilderness is the wide World in an Atheistic Century; our Forty Days are long years of suffering and fasting: nevertheless, to these also comes an end. Yes, to me also was given, if not Victory, yet the consciousness of Battle, and the resolve to persevere therein while life or faculty is left. To me also, entangled in the enchanted forests, demon-peopled, doleful of sight and of sound, it was given, after weariest wanderings, to work out my way into the higher sunlit slopes—of that Mountain which has no summit, or whose summit is in Heaven only!"

He says elsewhere, under a less ambitious figure, as figures are, once for all, natural to him: "Has not thy Life been that of most sufficient men (*tüchtigen Männer*) thou hast known in this generation? An outflush of foolish young Enthusiasm, like the first fallow crop, wherein are as many weeds as valuable herbs: this all parched away, under the Droughts of practical and spiritual Unbelief, as Disappointment, in thought and act, often-repeated gave rise to Doubt, and Doubt gradually settled into Denial! If I have had a second-crop, and now see the perennial greensward, and sit under umbrageous cedars, which defy all Drought (and Doubt); herein, too, be the Heavens praised, I am not without examples, and even exemplars."

So that, for Teufelsdröckh also, there has been a "glorious revolution": these mad shadow-hunting and shadow-hunted Pilgrimings of his were but some purifying "Temptation in the Wilderness," before his Apostolic work (such as it was) could begin; which Temptation is now happily over, and the Devil once more worsted! Was "that high moment in the *Rue de l'Enfer,*" then, properly the turning-point of the battle; when the Fiend said, *Worship me or be torn in shreds;*

---

12. **"Temptations in the Wilderness."** See *Matthew*, 4, which contains an account of the forty days of Jesus's fasting, followed by his temptation by Satan. 14. **old Adam,** human frailty inherited by all from Adam. 22. **Promethean.** In Greek myth Prometheus was a Titan who was punished by Zeus for giving to man the gift of fire; Promethean Characters are, therefore, letters written in divine fire. 27. *Eat . . . filled.* See *Matthew*, 4:3; a "clay-given" mandate is an appeal to the flesh.

76. **umbrageous,** shady. 87. **"that . . . l'Enfer."** Cf. pp. 469-470, ll. 92 ff.

and was answered valiantly with an *Apage Satana?*—Singular Teufelsdröckh, would thou hadst told thy singular story in plain words! But it is fruitless to look there, in those Paper-bags, for such. Nothing but innuendoes, figurative crotchets: a typical Shadow, fitfully wavering, prophetico-satiric; no clear logical Picture. "How paint to the sensual eye," asks he once, "what passes in the Holy-of-Holies of Man's Soul; in what words, known to these profane times, speak even afar-off of the unspeakable?" We ask in turn: Why perplex these times, profane as they are, with needless obscurity, by omission and by commission? Not mystical only is our Professor, but whimsical; and involves himself, now more than ever, in eye-bewildering *chiaroscuro*. Successive glimpses, here faithfully imparted, our more gifted readers must endeavor to combine for their own behoof.

He says: "The hot Harmattan wind had raged itself out; its howl went silent within me; and the long-deafened soul could now hear. I paused in my wild wanderings; and sat me down to wait, and consider; for it was as if the hour of change drew nigh. I seemed to surrender, to renounce utterly, and say: Fly, then, false shadows of Hope; I will chase you no more, I will believe you no more. And ye too, haggard specters of Fear, I care not for you; ye too are all shadows and a lie. Let me rest here: for I am way-weary and life-weary; I will rest here, were it but to die: to die or to live is alike to me; alike insignificant."—And again: "Here, then, as I lay in that CENTER OF INDIFFERENCE; cast, doubtless by benignant upper Influence, into a healing sleep, the heavy dreams rolled gradually away, and I awoke to a new Heaven and a new Earth. The first preliminary moral Act, Annihilation of Self (*Selbsttödtung*), had been happily accomplished; and my mind's eyes were now unsealed, and its hands ungyved."

Might we not also conjecture that the following passage refers to his Locality, during this same "healing sleep"; that his Pilgrimstaff lies cast aside here, on "the high table-land"; and indeed that the repose is already taking wholesome effect on him? If it were not that the tone, in some parts, has more of riancy, even of levity, than we could have expected! However, in Teufelsdröckh, there is always the strangest Dualism: light dancing, with guitar-music, will be going on in the fore-court, while by fits from within comes the faint whimpering of woe and wail. We transcribe the piece entire:

"Beautiful it was to sit there, as in my skyey Tent, musing and meditating; on the high table-land, in front of the Mountains; over me, as roof, the azure Dome, and around me, for walls, four azure-flowing curtains—namely, of the Four azure winds, on whose bottom-fringes also I have seen gilding. And then to fancy the fair Castles that stood sheltered in these Mountain hollows; with their green flower-lawns, and white dames and damosels, lovely enough: or better still, the straw-roofed Cottages, wherein stood many a Mother baking bread, with her children round her:—all hidden and protectingly folded-up in the valley-folds; yet there and alive, as sure as if I beheld them. Or to see, as well as fancy, the nine Towns and Villages, that lay round my mountain-seat, which, in still weather, were wont to speak to me (by their steeple-bells) with metal tongue; and, in almost all weather, proclaimed their vitality by repeated Smoke-clouds; whereon, as on a culinary horologe, I might read the hour of the day. For it was the smoke of cookery, as kind housewives at morning, midday, eventide were boiling their husbands' kettles; and ever a blue pillar rose up into the air, successively or simultaneously, from each of the nine, saying, as plainly as smoke could say: Such and such a meal is getting ready here. Not uninteresting! For you have the whole Borough, with all its love-makings and scandal-mongeries, contentions and contentments, as in miniature, and could cover it all with your hat.—If, in my wide Wayfarings, I had learned to look into the business of the World in its details, here perhaps was the place for combining it into general propositions, and deducing inferences therefrom.

---

1. *Apage Satana*. See *Matthew*, 4:10, "Get thee hence, Satan." 18. *chiaroscuro*, pictorial art in black and white. 21. **Harmattan**, a dry wind that blows at certain seasons westward from the interior of Africa toward the Atlantic coast. 39. **new . . . Earth**, from *Revelation*, 21: 1.

52. **riancy**, gayety.

"Often also could I see the black Tempest marching in anger through the Distance: round some Schreckhorn, as yet grim-blue, would the eddying vapor gather, and there tumultuously eddy, and flow down like a mad witch's hair; till, after a space, it vanished, and, in the clear sunbeam, your Schreckhorn stood smiling grim-white, for the vapor had held snow. How thou fermentest and elaboratest, in thy great fermenting-vat and laboratory of an Atmosphere, of a World, O Nature!—Or what is Nature? Ha! why do I not name thee GOD? Art not thou the "Living Garment of God"? O Heavens, is it, in very deed, HE, then, that ever speaks through thee; that lives and loves in thee, that lives and loves in me?

"Fore-shadows, call them rather fore-splendors, of that Truth, and Beginning of Truths, fell mysteriously over my soul. Sweeter than Dayspring to the Shipwrecked in Nova Zembla; ah, like the mother's voice to her little child that strays bewildered, weeping, in unknown tumults; like soft streamings of celestial music to my too-exasperated heart, came that Evangel. The Universe is not dead and demoniacal, a charnel-house with specters; but godlike, and my Father's!

"With other eyes, too, could I now look upon my fellow man; with an infinite Love, an infinite Pity. Poor, wandering, wayward man! Art thou not tired, and beaten with stripes, even as I am? Ever, whether thou bear the royal mantle or the beggar's gabardine, art thou not so weary, so heavy-laden; and thy Bed of Rest is but a Grave. O my Brother, my Brother, why cannot I shelter thee in my bosom, and wipe away all tears from thy eyes! Truly, the din of many-voiced Life, which, in this solitude, with the mind's organ, I could hear, was no longer a maddening discord, but a melting one; like inarticulate cries, and sobbings of a dumb creature, which in the ear of Heaven are prayers. The poor Earth, with her poor joys, was now my needy Mother, not my cruel Stepdame. Man, with his so mad Wants and so mean Endeavors, had become the dearer to me; and even for his sufferings and his sins, I now first named him Brother. Thus was I standing in the porch of that '*Sanctuary of Sorrow*'; by strange, steep ways had I too been guided thither; and ere long its sacred gates would open, and the '*Divine Depth of Sorrow*' lie disclosed to me."

The Professor says he here first got eye on the Knot that had been strangling him, and straightway could unfasten it, and was free. "A vain interminable controversy," writes he, "touching what is at present called Origin of Evil, or some such thing, arises in every soul, since the beginning of the world; and in every soul, that would pass from idle Suffering into actual Endeavoring, must first be put an end to. The most, in our time, have to go content with a simple, incomplete enough Suppression of this controversy; to a few some Solution of it is indispensable. In every new era, too, such Solution comes-out in different terms; and ever the Solution of the last era has become obsolete, and is found unserviceable. For it is man's nature to change his Dialect from century to century; he cannot help it though he would. The authentic *Church-Catechism* of our present century has not yet fallen into my hands: meanwhile, for my own private behoof, I attempt to elucidate the matter so. Man's Unhappiness, as I construe, comes of his Greatness; it is because there is an Infinite in him, which with all his cunning he cannot quite bury under the Finite. Will the whole Finance Ministers and Upholsterers and Confectioners of modern Europe undertake, in jointstock company, to make one Shoeblack HAPPY? They cannot accomplish it, above an hour or two; for the Shoeblack also has a Soul quite other than his Stomach; and would require, if you consider it, for his permanent satisfaction and saturation, simply this allotment, no more, and no less: *God's infinite Universe altogether to himself*, therein to enjoy infinitely, and fill every wish as fast as it rose. Oceans of Hochheimer, a Throat like that of Ophiuchus: speak not of them; to the infinite Shoeblack they are as nothing. No sooner is your ocean filled than he grumbles that it might

---

3. **Schreckhorn,** a high mountain in the Bernese Oberland, Switzerland; the name means "peak of terror."

94. **Hochheimer,** a superior wine from the Rheingau district of Germany. **Ophiuchus,** in ancient astronomy a northern constellation that was represented on charts as a man holding a serpent.

have been of better vintage. Try him with half of a Universe, of an Omnipotence, he sets to quarreling with the proprietor of the other half and declares himself the most maltreated of men.—Always there is a black spot in our sunshine: it is even as I said, the *Shadow of Ourselves.*

"But the whim we have of Happiness is somewhat thus. By certain valuations, and averages, of our own striking, we come upon some sort of average terrestrial lot; this we fancy belongs to us by nature, and of indefeasible right. It is simple payment of our wages, of our deserts; requires neither thanks nor complaint; only such *overplus* as there may be do we account Happiness; any *deficit* again is Misery. Now consider that we have the valuation of our own deserts ourselves, and what a fund of Self-conceit there is in each of us—do you wonder that the balance should so often dip the wrong way, and many a Blockhead cry: See there, what a payment; was ever worthy gentleman so used!—I tell thee, Blockhead, it all comes of thy Vanity; of what thou *fanciest* those same deserts of thine to be. Fancy that thou deservest to be hanged (as is most likely), thou wilt feel it happiness to be only shot: fancy that thou deservest to be hanged in a hair-halter, it will be a luxury to die in hemp.

"So true is it, what I then say, that *the Fraction of Life can be increased in value not so much by increasing your Numerator as by lessening your Denominator.* Nay, unless my Algebra deceive me, *Unity* itself divided by *Zero* will give *Infinity.* Make thy claim of wages a zero, then; thou hast the world under thy feet. Well did the Wisest of our time write: 'It is only with Renunciation (*Entsagen*) that Life, properly speaking, can be said to begin.'

"I asked myself: What is this that, ever since earliest years, thou hast been fretting and fuming, and lamenting and self-tormenting, on account of? Say it in a word: is it not because thou art not HAPPY? Because the THOU (sweet gentleman) is not sufficiently honored, nourished, soft-bedded, and lovingly cared for? Foolish soul! What Act of Legislature was there that *thou* shouldst be Happy? A little while ago thou hadst no right to *be* at all. What if thou wert born and predestined not to be Happy, but to be Unhappy! Art thou nothing other than a Vulture, then, that fliest through the Universe seeking after somewhat to *eat;* and shrieking dolefully because carrion enough is not given thee? Close thy *Byron;* open thy *Goethe.*"

"*Es leuchtet mir ein,* I see a glimpse of it!" cries he elsewhere: "there is in man a HIGHER than Love of Happiness: he can do without Happiness, and instead thereof find Blessedness! Was it not to preach forth this same HIGHER that sages and martyrs, the Poet and the Priest, in all times, have spoken and suffered; bearing testimony, through life and through death, of the Godlike that is in Man, and how in the Godlike only has he Strength and Freedom? Which God-inspired Doctrine art thou also honored to be taught; O Heavens! and broken with manifold merciful Afflictions, even till thou become contrite, and learn it! O, thank thy Destiny for these; thankfully bear what yet remain: thou hadst need of them; the Self in thee needed to be annihilated. By benignant fever-paroxysms is Life rooting out the deep-seated chronic Disease, and triumphs over Death. On the roaring billows of Time, thou art not engulfed, but borne aloft into the azure of Eternity. Love not Pleasure; love God. This is the EVERLASTING YEA, wherein all contradiction is solved: wherein whoso walks and works, it is well with him."

And again: "Small is it that thou canst trample the Earth with its injuries under thy feet, as old Greek Zeno trained thee: thou canst love the Earth while it injures thee, and even because it injures thee; for this a Greater than Zeno was needed, and he too was sent. Knowest thou that '*Worship of Sorrow*'? The Temple thereof, founded some eighteen centuries ago, now lies in ruins, overgrown with jungle, the habitation of doleful crea-

---

29. **hair-halter,** a noose made of hair. 38. **the Wisest . . . time,** Johann Wolfgang von Goethe (1749-1832), German author whom Carlyle admired greatly.

88. **Zeno,** Greek philosopher (336?-264? B.C.), founder of the Stoic school of philosophy. 93. **Temple . . . ago.** The allusion is, of course, to the founding of Christianity.

tures: nevertheless, venture forward; in a low crypt, arched out of falling fragments, thou findest the Altar still there, and its sacred Lamp perennially burning."

Without pretending to comment on which strange utterances, the Editor will only remark that there lies beside them much of a still more questionable character; unsuited to the general apprehension; nay wherein he himself does not see his way. Nebulous disquisitions on Religion, yet not without bursts of splendor; on the "perennial continuance of Inspiration"; on Prophecy; that there are "true Priests, as well as Baal-Priests, in our own day": with more of the like sort. We select some fractions, by way of finish to this farrago.

"Cease, my much-respected Herr von Voltaire," thus apostrophizes the Professor: "shut thy sweet voice; for the task appointed thee seems finished. Sufficiently hast thou demonstrated this proposition, considerable or otherwise: That the Mythus of the Christian Religion looks not in the eighteenth century as it did in the eighth. Alas, were thy six-and-thirty quartos, and the six-and-thirty thousand other quartos and folios, and flying sheets or reams, printed before and since on the same subject, all needed to convince us of so little! But what next? Wilt thou help us to embody the divine Spirit of that Religion in a new Mythus, in a new vehicle and vesture, that our Souls, otherwise too like perishing, may live? What! thou hast no faculty in that kind? Only a torch for burning, no hammer for building? Take our thanks, then, and ——thyself away.

"Meanwhile what are antiquated Mythuses to me? Or is the God present, felt in my own heart, a thing which Herr von Voltaire will dispute out of me; or dispute into me? To the '*Worship of Sorrow*' ascribe what origin and genesis thou pleasest, *has* not that Worship originated, and been generated; is it not *here*? Feel it in thy heart, and then say whether it is of God! This is Belief; all else is Opinion—for which latter whoso will let him worry and be worried."

"Neither," observes he elsewhere, "shall ye tear-out one another's eyes, struggling over 'Plenary Inspiration,' and suchlike: try rather to get a little even Partial Inspiration, each of you for himself. One BIBLE I know, of whose Plenary Inspiration doubt is not so much as possible; nay with my own eyes I saw the God's-Hand writing it: thereof all other Bibles are but leaves—say, in Picture-Writing to assist the weaker faculty."

Or, to give the wearied reader relief, and bring it to an end, let him take the following perhaps more intelligible passage:

"To me, in this our life," says the Professor, "which is an internecine warfare with the Time-spirit, other warfare seems questionable. Hast thou in any way a Contention with thy brother, I advise thee, think well what the meaning thereof is. If thou gauge it to the bottom, it is simply this: 'Fellow, see! thou art taking more than thy share of Happiness in the world, something from *my* share: which, by the Heavens, thou shalt not; nay I will fight thee rather.'—Alas, and the whole lot to be divided is such a beggarly matter, truly a 'feast of shells,' for the substance has been spilled out: not enough to quench one Appetite; and the collective human species clutching at them!—Can we not, in all such cases, rather say: 'Take it, thou too-ravenous individual; take that pitiful additional fraction of a share, which I reckoned mine, but which thou so wantest; take it with a blessing: would to Heaven I had enough for thee!'—If Fichte's *Wissenschaftslehre* be, 'to a certain extent, Applied Christianity,' surely to a still greater extent, so is this. We have here not a Whole Duty of Man, yet a Half Duty, namely the Passive half: could we but do it, as we can demonstrate it!

"But indeed Conviction, were it never so excellent, is worthless till it convert itself into Conduct. Nay properly Conviction is not possible till then; inasmuch as all Speculation is by nature endless, formless, a vortex amid vortices: only by a felt indubitable cer-

---

14. **Baal-Priests**, priests who serve the altars of false gods; cf. *Kings*, 18:17-40. 18. **Voltaire**, French philosopher and author (1694-1778); Carlyle alludes here to his skepticism.

83. Fichte's *Wissenschaftslehre*, the Theory of the Sciences by Johann Gottlieb Fichte (1762-1814), German philosopher. 86. **Whole . . . Man**, an anonymous devotional book published in 1658 and popular; cf. also *Micah*, 6:8.

tainty of Experience does it find any center to revolve round, and so fashion itself into a system. Most true is it, as a wise man teaches us, that 'Doubt of any sort cannot be removed except by Action.' On which ground, too, let him who gropes painfully in darkness or uncertain light, and prays vehemently that the dawn may ripen into day, lay this other precept well to heart, which to me was of invaluable service: '*Do the Duty which lies nearest thee*,' which thou knowest to be a Duty! Thy second Duty will already have become clearer.

"May we not say, however, that the hour of Spiritual Enfranchisement is even this: When your Ideal World, wherein the whole man has been dimly struggling and inexpressibly languishing to work, becomes revealed, and thrown open; and you discover, with amazement enough, like the Lothario in *Wilhelm Meister*, that your 'America is here or nowhere'? The Situation that has not its Duty, its Ideal, was never yet occupied by man. Yes, here, in this poor, miserable, hampered, despicable Actual, wherein thou even now standest, here or nowhere is thy Ideal: work it out therefrom; and working, believe, live, be free. Fool! the Ideal is in thyself, the impediment too is in thyself: thy Condition is but the stuff thou art to shape that same Ideal out of: what matters whether such stuff be of this sort or that, so the Form thou give it be heroic, be poetic? O thou that pinest in the imprisonment of the Actual, and criest bitterly to the gods for a kingdom wherein to rule and create, know this of a truth: the thing thou seekest is already with thee, 'here or nowhere,' couldst thou only see!

"But it is with man's Soul as it was with Nature: the beginning of Creation is—Light. Till the eye have vision, the whole members are in bonds. Divine moment, when over the tempest-tossed Soul, as once over the wild-weltering Chaos, it is spoken: Let there be Light! Ever to the greatest that has felt such moment, is it not miraculous and God-announcing; even as, under simpler figures, to the simplest and least. The mad primeval Discord is hushed; the rudely jumbled conflicting elements bind themselves into separate Firmaments: deep silent rock-foundations are built beneath; and the skyey vault with its everlasting Luminaries above: instead of a dark wasteful Chaos, we have a blooming, fertile, heaven-encompassed World.

"I too could now say to myself: Be no longer a Chaos, but a World, or even Worldkin. Produce! Produce! Were it but the pitifullest infinitesimal fraction of a Product, produce it, in God's name! 'Tis the utmost thou hast in thee: out with it, then. Up, up! Whatsoever thy hand findeth to do, do it with thy whole might. Work while it is called Today; for the Night cometh, wherein no man can work."

(II, 9) (1833-1834)

21. *Wilhelm Meister,* Goethe's *Wilhelm Meister's Travels.* 44. **Let . . . light,** God's first command of creation; cf. *Genesis,* 1:3. 57. **World . . . Worldkin,** i.e., a Macrocosm, or great world, or a microcosm, or man. 64. **Night . . . work,** quoted from *John,* 9:4; this final paragraph expresses in brief Carlyle's doctrine of labor, which he amplified in *Past and Present,* Book III, Chapter XI, (1843).

from *The French Revolution*

"You have not had for a hundred years any book that comes more direct and flaming from the heart of a living man." Thus spoke Carlyle to his wife as he threw down the pen with which he had written, in January, 1837, the last words of *The French Revolution*. He was right; the history was written with a flaming purpose. Carlyle had no faith in democracy, and the book is essentially an argument against government by the masses. He also had no faith in any science or theory of history; to him events are significant because of the human personalities which direct them. For this reason he emphasized personalities throughout his history and made it alive with moving human figures. Furthermore, his purpose was not simply to record events, but to arrange and present them so that out of the dead past there might come living lessons for the present. His *French Revolution* was almost written around a text: those who sow to the wind shall reap the whirlwind. From the dreadful experiences of her neighbor across the channel he would have England learn the terrors of revolution and the dangers of democracy as a form of government. He preached the need of the strong, just man in national affairs.

THE WHIFF OF GRAPESHOT

IN FACT, what can be more natural, one may say inevitable, as a Post-Sansculottic transitionary state, than even this? Confused wreck of a Republic of the Poverties, which ended in Reign of Terror, is arranging itself into such composure as it can. Evangel of Jean-Jacques, and most other Evangels, becoming incredible, what is there for it but return to the old Evangel of Mammon? *Contrat-Social* is true or untrue, Brotherhood is Brotherhood or Death; but money always will buy money's worth: in the wreck of human dubitations, this remains indubitable, that Pleasure is pleasant. Aristocracy of Feudal Parchment has passed away with a mighty rushing; and now, by a natural course, we arrive at Aristocracy of the Moneybag. It is the course through which all European Societies are, at this hour, traveling. Apparently a still baser sort of Aristocracy? An infinitely baser; the basest yet known.

In which, however, there is this advantage, that, like Anarchy itself, it cannot continue. Hast thou considered how Thought is stronger than Artillery-parks, and (were it fifty years after death and martyrdom, or were it two thousand years) writes and unwrites Acts of Parliament, removes mountains; models the World like soft clay? Also how the beginning of all Thought, worth the name, is Love; and the wise head never yet was, without first the generous heart? The Heavens cease not their bounty; they send us generous hearts into every generation. And now what generous heart can pretend to itself, or be hoodwinked into believing, that Loyalty to the Moneybag is a noble Loyalty? Mammon, cries the generous heart out of all ages and countries, is the basest of known Gods, even of known Devils. In him what glory is there, that ye should worship him? No glory discernible; not even terror: at best, detestability, ill-matched with despicability! —Generous hearts, discerning, on this hand, widespread Wretchedness, dark without and within, moistening its ounce-and-half of bread with tears; and, on that hand, mere Balls in flesh-colored drawers, and inane or foul glitter of such sort—cannot but ejaculate, cannot but announce: Too much, O divine Mammon; somewhat too much!—The voice of these, once announcing itself, carries *fiat* and *pereat* in it, for all things here below.

Meanwhile we will hate Anarchy as Death, which it is; and the things worse than Anarchy shall be hated *more*. Surely Peace alone is fruitful. Anarchy is destruction; a burning up, say, of Shams and Insupportabilities; but which leaves Vacancy behind. Know this

---

2. **Post-Sansculottic,** after-revolutionary; the term *sansculotte,* meaning "without breeches," was given by the aristocrats of France to the republicans, who had substituted pantaloons for the short breeches of the upper classes. 7. **Jean-Jacques,** Jean Jacques Rousseau (1712-1778), French philosopher and author, whose social theories helped to stimulate the French Revolution. 9. **Mammon,** the god of riches; cf. Milton's *Paradise Lost,* Vol. I, p. 726, ll. 678-684.

52. *fiat* and *pereat,* let it be created and let it pass away.

also, that out of a world of Unwise nothing but an Unwisdom can be made. Arrange it, constitution-build it, sift it through ballot-boxes as thou wilt, it is and remains an Unwisdom—the new prey of new quacks and unclean things, the latter end of it slightly better than the beginning. Who can bring a wise thing out of men unwise? Not one. And so Vacancy and general Abolition having come for this France, what can Anarchy do more? Let there be Order, were it under the Soldier's Sword; let there be Peace, that the bounty of the Heavens be not split; that what of Wisdom they do send us bring fruit in its season!—It remains to be seen how the quellers of Sansculottism were themselves quelled, and sacred right of Insurrection was blown away by gunpowder; wherewith this singular eventful History called *French Revolution* ends.

The Convention, driven such a course by wild wind, wild tide, and steerage and non-steerage, these three years, has become weary of its own existence, sees all men weary of it; and wishes heartily to finish. To the last, it has to strive with contradictions: it is now getting fast ready with a Constitution, yet knows no peace. Sieyès, we say, is making the Constitution once more; has as good as made it. Warned by experience, the great Architect alters much, admits much. Distinction of Active and Passive Citizen, that is, Money-qualification for Electors: nay, Two Chambers, "Council of Ancients," as well as "Council of Five-hundred"; to that conclusion have we come! In a like spirit, eschewing that fatal self-denying ordinance of your Old Constituents, we enact not only that actual Convention Members are re-eligible, but that Two-thirds of them must be re-elected. The Active Citizen Electors shall for this time have free choice of only One-third of their National Assembly. Such enactment, of Two-thirds to be re-elected, we append to our Constitution; we submit our Constitution to the Townships of France, and say, Accept *both*, or reject both. Unsavory as this appendix may be, the Townships, by overwhelming majority, accept and ratify. With Directory of Five; with Two good Chambers, double-majority of them nominated by ourselves, one hopes this Constitution may prove final. *March* it will; for the legs of it, the re-elected Two-thirds, are already here, able to march. Sieyès looks at his paper-fabric with just pride.

But now see how the contumacious Sections, Lepelletier foremost, kick against the pricks! Is it not manifest infraction of one's Elective Franchise, Rights of Man, and Sovereignty of the People, this appendix of re-electing *your* Two-thirds? Greedy tyrants who would perpetuate yourselves!—For the truth is, victory over Saint-Antoine, and long right of Insurrection, has spoiled these men. Nay, spoiled all men. Consider too how each man was free to hope what he liked; and now there is to be no hope, there is to be fruition, fruition of *this*.

In men spoiled by long right of Insurrection, what confused ferments will rise, tongues once begun wagging! Journalists declaim, your Lacretelles, Laharpes; Orators spout. There is Royalism traceable in it, and Jacobinism. On the West Frontier, in deep secrecy, Pichegru, durst he trust his Army, is treating with Condé: in these Sections, there spout wolves in sheep's clothing, masked Emigrants and Royalists. All men, as we say, had hoped, each that the Election would do something for his own side: and now there is no Election, or only the third of one. Black is united with white against this clause

---

21. **The Convention.** The National Convention replaced the Legislative Assembly in September, 1792, proclaimed a Republic in France, and brought the king, Louis XVI, to the guillotine; in October, 1795, the Convention gave place to the Directory. 28. **Sieyès**, Count Emmanuel Joseph Sieyès (1748-1836), French revolutionist. 37. **self-denying ordinance.** In English history the Self-Denying Ordinance was passed by the Long Parliament April 3, 1645; it provided, in part, that members of the Parliament should bind themselves not to accept certain posts in the army. 57. **Lepelletier**, a municipal district of the city of Paris. **kick . . . pricks**, quoted from *Acts*, 9:5; the figure is that of a draft animal goaded the harder because of its resistance. 63. **Saint-Antoine.** At the battle of Faubourg, St. Antoine (July 2, 1652) French insurrectionists under the Prince of Condé were defeated by royalists under Turenne but were saved by the citizens of Paris, who opened the city gates to the beaten insurgents. 72. **Lacretelles**. Pierre Louis de Lacretelle (1751-1824), French politician and writer, and his brother Jean Charles Dominique (1766-1855) were both active journalists during the revolution and the restoration that followed. **Laharpes**, Jean François de La Harpe (1739-1803), French critic and extremist in his support of the Convention. 75. **Pichegru**, Charles Pichegru (1761-1804), French general; at one time he was commander-in-chief of the army of the Rhine-and-Moselle, but he was later arrested in 1804 for leading a royalist uprising against Napoleon and was strangled in prison. 76. **Condé**, José Antonio Condé (1766-1820), Spanish scholar and politician.

of the Two-thirds; all the Unruly of France, who see their trade thereby near ending.

Section Lepelletier, after Addresses enough, finds that such clause is a manifest infraction; that it, Lepelletier, for one, will simply not conform thereto; and invites all other free Sections to join it, "in central Committee," in resistance to oppression. The Sections join it, nearly all; strong with their Forty-thousand fighting men. The Convention therefore may look to itself! Lepelletier, on this 12th day of Vendémiaire, 4th of October, 1795, is sitting in open contravention, in its Convent of Filles Saint-Thomas, Rue Vivienne, with guns primed. The Convention has some Five-thousand regular troops at hand; Generals in abundance; and a Fifteen-hundred of miscellaneous persecuted Ultra-Jacobins, whom in this crisis it has hastily got together and armed, under the title *Patriots of Eighty-nine*. Strong in Law, it sends its General Menou to disarm Lepelletier.

General Menou marches accordingly, with due summons and demonstration; with no result. General Menou, about eight in the evening, finds that he is standing ranked in the Rue Vivienne, emitting vain summonses; with primed guns pointed out of every window at him; and that he cannot disarm Lepelletier. He has to return with whole skin, but without success; and be thrown into arrest, as "a traitor." Whereupon the whole Forty-thousand join this Lepelletier which cannot be vanquished: to what hand shall a quaking Convention now turn? Our poor Convention, after such voyaging, just entering harbor, so to speak, has *struck on the bar;*—and labors there frightfully, with breakers roaring round it, Forty-thousand of them, like to wash it, and its Sieyès Cargo and the whole future of France, into the deep! Yet one last time, it struggles, ready to perish.

Some call for Barras to be made Commandant; he conquered in Thermidor. Some, what is more to the purpose, bethink them of the Citizen Bonaparte, unemployed Artillery-Officer, who took Toulon. A man of head, a man of action: Barras is named Commandant's-Cloak; this young Artillery-Officer is named Commandant. He was in the Gallery at the moment, and heard it; he withdrew, some half-hour, to consider with himself; after a half-hour of grim compressed considering, to be or not to be, he answers *Yea.*

And now, a man of head being at the center of it, the whole matter gets vital. Swift, to Camp of Sablons; to secure the Artillery, there are not twenty men guarding it! A swift Adjutant, Murat is the name of him, gallops; gets thither some minutes within time, for Lepelletier was also on march that way: the Cannon are ours. And now beset this post, and beset that; rapid and firm: at Wicket of the Louvre, in Cul-de-sac Dauphin, in Rue Saint-Honoré, from Pont-Neuf all along the north Quays, southward to Pont *ci-devant* Royal—rank round the Sanctuary of the Tuileries, a ring of steel discipline; let every gunner have his match burning, and all men stand to their arms!

Thus there is Permanent-session through the night; and thus at sunrise of the morrow, there is seen sacred Insurrection once again: vessel of State laboring on the bar; and tumultuous sea all round her, beating *générale,* arming and sounding—not ringing tocsin, for we have left no tocsin but our own in the Pavilion of Unity. It is an imminence of shipwreck, for the whole world to gaze at. Frightfully she labors, that poor ship, within cable-length of port; huge peril for her. However, she has a man at the helm. Insurgent messages, received and not received; messenger admitted blindfolded; counsel and counter-counsel: the poor ship labors!—Vendémiaire 13th, year 4: curious enough, of all

---

22. **Menou,** J. F. Baron de Menou (1750-1810). French general who assumed command of the French army in Egypt in 1800. 43. **Barras,** Paul François Nicolas, Comte de Barras (1755-1829), a revolutionist who became prominent because of his success in directing the overthrow of the Robespierre faction in the *coup d'etat* of Thermidor 9 by the Revolutionary Calendar (July 29), 1794; he had also been with Bonaparte at the siege of Toulon. 60. **Murat,** Joachim Murat (1767-1815), one of the most prominent figures of the period; after having served under Napoleon as commander of the cavalry of the Grand Army, he was appointed by the emperor to the vacant throne of Naples, but he later broke with Napoleon and plotted against him. 68. **Pont** *ci-devant* **Royal,** the *former* Bridge Royal, the king having been executed. 78. **tocsin,** an alarm; the tocsin was used as the signal in several of the earlier revolutionary gatherings. 86. **Vendémiaire 13th, year 4.** The Revolutionary Calendar was adopted by the National Convention in 1793. In it the year began at midnight of September 21 and was divided into twelve months of thirty days each with extra days for festivals; the new calendar began with the birth of the republic, September 22, 1792. Napoleon abolished it in 1805.

days, it is the fifth day of October, eve of the anniversary of that Menad-march, six years ago; by sacred right of Insurrection we are got thus far.

Lepelletier has seized the Church of Saint-Roch; has seized the Pont-Neuf, our picket there retreating without fire. Stray shots fall from Lepelletier; rattle down on the very Tuileries Staircase. On the other hand, women advance disheveled, shrieking, Peace; Lepelletier behind them waving its hat in sign that we shall fraternize. Steady! The Artillery-Officer is steady as bronze; can, if need were, be quick as lightning. He sends eight-hundred muskets with ball-cartridges to the Convention itself; honorable Members shall act with these in case of extremity: whereat they look grave enough. Four of the afternoon is struck. Lepelletier, making nothing by messengers, by fraternity or hat-waving, bursts out, along the Southern Quai Voltaire, along streets and passages, treble-quick, in huge veritable onslaught! Whereupon, thou bronze Artillery-Officer—? "Fire!" say the bronze lips. And roar and thunder, roar and again roar, continual, volcano-like, goes his great gun, in the Cul-de-sac Dauphin against the Church of Saint-Roch; go his great guns on the Pont-Royal; go all his great guns—blow to air some two-hundred men, mainly about the Church of Saint-Roch! Lepelletier cannot stand such horseplay; no Sectioner can stand it; the Forty-thousand yield on all sides, scour toward covert. "Some hundred or so of them gathered about the Théâtre de la République; but," says he, "a few shells dislodged them. It was all finished at six."

The Ship is *over* the bar, then; free she bounds shoreward—amid shouting and vivats! Citoyen Bonaparte is "named General of the Interior, by acclamation"; quelled Sections have to disarm in such humor as they may; sacred right of Insurrection is gone for ever! The Sieyès Constitution can disembark itself, and begin marching. The miraculous Convention Ship has got to land;—and is there, shall we figuratively say, changed, as Epic Ships are wont, into a kind of *Sea Nymph*, never to sail more; to roam the waste Azure, a Miracle in History!

"It is false," says Napoleon, "that we fired first with blank charge; it had been a waste of life to do that." Most false: the firing was with sharp and sharpest shot: to all men it was plain that here was no sport; the rabbets and plinths of Saint-Roch Church show splintered by it to this hour.—Singular: in old Broglie's time, six years ago, this Whiff of Grapeshot was promised; but it could not be given then; could not have profited then. Now, however, the time is come for it, and the man; and behold, you have it; and the thing we specifically call *French Revolution* is blown into space by it, and become a thing that was! (1837)

2. **Menad-march . . . ago.** In Greek myth the Maenads were women celebrants of the drunken rites of Bacchus; hence the term means any unrestrained, riotous individual. The historical allusion here is to the riotous attack on the palace at Versailles on October 5, 1789. 40. **vivats,** the noun plural from the verb *vivat*, long may it live. 49. **Epic . . . Nymph,** an allusion to the episode in Book IX, ll. 119-124, of Virgil's *Aeneid;* the Trojan ships, attacked with fire by Turnus while they were at anchor, plunged from the shore and were changed into sea-nymphs. 56. **rabbets and plinths,** terms from architecture. 58. **old Broglie,** Victor François Duc de Broglie (1718-1804), marshal of France and an ardent opponent of the Revolution.

from *Past and Present*

Past and Present was first published in 1843. It belongs to the economic-social group of Carlyle's writings, and is remarkable, among other things, for the fact that it was written in seven weeks; such ease of composition the author seldom commanded. As the title implies, Carlyle attempted in this series of essays to gather from the past some good lessons for the present. To personalize the material in his usual manner, he compared Victorian conditions to those recorded in the ancient chronicle written by Jocelyn of Brakelond, English monk of Bury St. Edmunds, at the beginning of the thirteenth century. Jocelyn's Latin narrative of the fortunes of his own monastery contains a glowing account of the work of Abbot Samson, whom Carlyle admired greatly. Carlyle's comparison of past and present is almost entirely in favor of the past, the advantages of which are highly, but very artistically, exaggerated. Carlyle's direct comment on contemporary conditions includes attacks on his radical, legislating friends, and a setting forth of his own theories of duty, responsibility, work, reward, capital, and labor—all presented vigorously in terms of abstract principle rather than concrete practicality.

THE ENGLISH

AND YET, with all thy theoretic platitudes, what a depth of practical sense in thee, great England! A depth of sense, of justice, and courage; in which, under all emergencies and world-bewilderments, and under this most complex of emergencies we now live in, there is still hope, there is still assurance!

The English are a dumb people. They can do great acts, but not describe them. Like the old Romans, and some few others, *their* Epic Poem is written on the Earth's surface: England her Mark! It is complained that they have no artists: one Shakespeare indeed; but for Raphael only a Reynolds; for Mozart nothing but a Mr. Bishop: not a picture, not a song. And yet they did produce one Shakespeare: consider how the element of Shakespearean melody does lie imprisoned in their nature; reduced to unfold itself in mere Cotton-mills, Constitutional Governments, and such like;—all the more interesting when it does become visible, as even in such unexpected shapes it succeeds in doing! Goethe spoke of the Horse, how impressive, almost affecting it was that an animal of such qualities should stand obstructed so; its speech nothing but an inarticulate neighing, its handiness mere *hoof*iness, the fingers all constricted, tied together, the finger-nails coagulated into a mere hoof, shod with iron. The more significant, thinks he, are those eye-flashings of the generous noble quadruped; those prancings, curvings of the neck clothed with thunder.

A Dog of Knowledge has free utterance; but the Warhorse is almost mute, very far from free! It is even so. Truly, your freest utterances are not by any means always the best; they are the worst rather; the feeblest, trivialest; their meaning prompt, but small, ephemeral. Commend me to the silent English, to the silent Romans. Nay, the silent Russians, too, I believe to be worth something: are they not even now drilling, under much obloquy, an immense semi-barbarous half-world from Finland to Kamtschatka, into rule, subordination, civilization—really in the old Roman fashion; speaking no word about it; quietly hearing all manner of vituperative Able Editors speak! While your ever-talking, ever-gesticulating French, for example, what are they at this moment drilling?—Nay, of all animals, the freest of utterance, I should judge, is the genus *Simia:* go into the Indian woods, say all Travelers, and look what a brisk, adroit, unresting Ape-population it is!

The spoken Word, the written Poem, is said to be an epitome of the man; how much more the done work. Whatsoever of morality and of intelligence; what of patience, perseverance, faithfulness, of method, insight, ingenuity, energy; in a word, whatsoever of Strength the man had in him will lie written in the Work he does. To work: why, it is to try himself against Nature, and her everlasting unerring Laws; these will tell a true verdict as to the man. So much of virtue and of faculty did *we* find in him; so much and no more! He had such capacity of harmonizing himself with *me* and my unalterable ever-veracious Laws; of co-operating and working as *I* bade him;—and has prospered, and has not prospered, as you see!—Working as great Nature bade him: does not that mean virtue of a kind; nay of all kinds? Cotton can be spun and sold, Lancashire operatives can be got to spin it, and at length one has the woven webs and sells them, by following Nature's

---

14. **Raphael,** a celebrated Italian painter (1483-1520). **Reynolds,** Sir Joshua Reynolds (1723-1792), an English portrait painter. See Goldsmith's *Retaliation,* 137 ff. (Vol. I, p. 1121). **Mozart,** a famous Austrian composer (1756-1791). 15. **Mr. Bishop,** Sir Henry Rowley Bishop (1786-1855), an English musician, composer of operas, songs, cantatas, etc. 23. **Goethe . . . Horse.** Carlyle quotes with slight changes a passage in Goethe's *General Principles of Natural Science,* Sec. II.

46. **Kamtschatka,** a large peninsula in the Maritime Province of eastern Siberia, of which it became a part in 1855. 54. *Simia,* monkeys. 76. **Lancashire,** an important manufacturing county of England; the chief seat of cotton manufacture in the world.

regulations in that matter: by not following Nature's regulations, you have them not. You have them not;—there is no Cotton-web to sell: Nature finds a bill against you; your "Strength" is not Strength, but Futility! Let faculty be honored, so far as it is faculty. A man that can succeed in working is to me always a man.

How one loves to see the burly figure of him, this thick-skinned, seemingly opaque, perhaps sulky, almost stupid Man of Practice, pitted against some adroit Man of Theory, all equipped with clear logic, and able anywhere to give you Why for Wherefore! The adroit Man of Theory, so light of movement, clear of utterance, with his bow full-bent and quiver full of arrow-arguments—surely he will strike down the game, transfix everywhere the heart of the matter; triumph everywhere, as he proves that he shall and must do? To your astonishment, it turns out oftenest No. The cloudy-browed, thick-soled, opaque Practicality, with no logic utterance, in silence mainly, with here and there a low grunt or growl, has in him what transcends all logic-utterance: a Congruity with the Unuttered. The Speakable, which lies atop, as a superficial film, or outer skin, is his or is not his: but the Doable, which reaches down to the World's center, you find him there!

The rugged Brindley has little to say for himself; the rugged Brindley, when difficulties accumulate on him, retires silent, "generally to his bed"; retires "sometimes for three days together to his bed, that he may be in perfect privacy there," and ascertain in his rough head how the difficulties can be overcome. The ineloquent Brindley, behold he *has* chained seas together; his ships do visibly float over valleys, invisibly through the hearts of mountains; the Mersey and the Thames, the Humber and the Severn have shaken hands; Nature most audibly answers, Yea! The man of Theory twangs his full-bent bow;

Nature's Fact ought to fall stricken, but does not: his logic-arrow glances from it as from a scaly dragon, and the obstinate Fact keeps walking its way. How singular! At bottom, you will have to grapple closer with the dragon; take it home to you, by real faculty, not by seeming faculty; try whether you are stronger, or it is stronger. Close with it, wrestle it—sheer obstinate toughness of muscle; but much more, what we call toughness of heart, which will mean persistence hopeful and even desperate, unsubduable patience, composed, candid openness, clearness of mind: all this shall be "strength" in wrestling your dragon; the whole man's real strength is in this work; we shall get the measure of him here.

Of all the Nations in the world at present the English are the stupidest in speech, the wisest in action. As good as a "dumb" Nation, I say, who cannot speak, and have never yet spoken—spite of the Shakespeares and Miltons who show us what possibilities there are!—O Mr. Bull, I look in that surly face of thine with a mixture of pity and laughter, yet also with wonder and veneration. Thou complainest not, my illustrious friend; and yet I believe the heart of thee is full of sorrow, of unspoken sadness, seriousness—profound melancholy (as some have said) the basis of thy being. Unconsciously, for thou speakest of nothing, this great Universe is great to thee. Not by levity of floating, but by stubborn force of swimming, shalt thou make thy way. The Fates sing of thee that thou shalt many times be thought an ass and a dull ox, and shalt with a godlike indifference believe it. My friend—and it is all untrue, nothing ever falser in point of fact! Thou art of those great ones whose greatness the small passer-by does not discern. Thy very stupidity is wiser than their wisdom. A grand *vis inertiae* is in thee; how many grand qualities unknown to small men! Nature alone knows thee, acknowledges the bulk and strength of thee; thy Epic, unsung in words, is written in huge characters on the face of this Planet—

---

31. **Brindley,** James Brindley (1716-1772), an eccentric English engineer and builder of aqueducts and canals, the most important of which was the Trent and Mersey canal known as the Grand Trunk. Brindley was illiterate and did most of his work in his head without drawings, and when he had a puzzling bit of work to do, he would go to bed and think it out. 41. **Mersey,** a river in Lancashire flowing into the Irish Sea. 42. **Humber,** a river in northeastern England. The Severn is in southwestern England.

67. **Mr. Bull,** John Bull, the typical Englishman; the personification of England. Cf. Byron's *The World Is a Bundle of Hay,* p. 247. 76. **levity of floating,** aimless and unstable floating. 85. *vis inertiae,* tendency to remain inactive.

sea-moles, cotton-trades, railways, fleets and cities, Indian Empires, Americas, New-Hollands; legible throughout the Solar System!

But the dumb Russians too, as I said, they, drilling all wild Asia and wild Europe into military rank and file, a terrible yet hitherto a prospering enterprise, are still dumber. The old Romans also could not *speak,* for many centuries—not till the world was theirs; and so many speaking Greekdoms, their logic-arrows all spent, had been absorbed and abolished. The logic-arrows, how they glanced futile from obdurate thick-skinned Facts; Facts to be wrestled down only by the real vigor of Roman thews!—As for me, I honor, in these loud-babbling days, all the Silent rather. A grand Silence that of Romans;—nay the grandest of all, is it not that of the gods! Even Triviality, Imbecility, that can sit silent, how respectable is it in comparison! The "talent of silence" is our fundamental one. Great honor to him whose Epic is a melodious hexameter Iliad; not a jingling Sham-Iliad, nothing true in it but the hexameters and forms merely. But still greater honor, if his Epic be a mighty Empire slowly built together, a mighty Series of Heroic Deeds—a mighty Conquest over Chaos; *which* Epic the "Eternal Melodies" have, and must have, informed and dwelt in, as *it* sung itself! There is no mistaking that latter Epic. Deeds are greater than Words. Deeds have such a life, mute but undeniable, and grow as living trees and fruit-trees do; they people the vacuity of Time, and make it green and worthy. Why should the oak prove logically that it ought to grow, and will grow? Plant it, try it; what gifts of diligent judicious assimilation and secretion it has, of progress and resistance, of *force* to grow, will then declare themselves. My much-honored, illustrious, extremely inarticulate Mr. Bull!—

Ask Bull his spoken opinion of any matter —oftentimes the force of dullness can no farther go. You stand silent, incredulous, as over a platitude that borders on the Infinite. The man's Churchisms, Dissenterisms, Puseyisms, Benthamisms, College Philosophies, Fashionable Literatures, are unexampled in this world. Fate's prophecy is fulfilled; you call the man an ox and an ass. But set him once to work—respectable man! His spoken sense is next to nothing, nine-tenths of it palpable *non*sense; but his unspoken sense, his inner silent feeling of what is true, what does agree with fact, what is doable and what is not doable—this seeks its fellow in the world. A terrible worker; irresistible against marshes, mountains, impediments, disorder, incivilization; everywhere vanquishing disorder, leaving it behind him as method and order. He "retires to his bed three days" and considers!

Nay withal, stupid as he is, our dear John —ever, after infinite tumblings, and spoken platitudes innumerable from barrel-heads and parliament-benches, he does settle down somewhere about the just conclusion; you are certain that his jumblings and tumblings will end, after years or centuries, in the stable equilibrium. Stable equilibrium, I say; center-of-gravity lowest;—not the unstable, with center-of-gravity highest, as I have known it done by quicker people! For indeed, do but jumble and tumble sufficiently, you avoid that worst fault, of settling with your center-of-gravity highest; your center-of-gravity is certain to come lowest, and to stay there. If slowness, what we in our impatience call "stupidity," be the price of stable equilibrium over unstable, shall we grudge a little slowness? Not the least admirable quality of Bull is, after all, that of remaining insensible to logic; holding out for considerable periods, ten years or more, as in this of the Corn-Laws, after all

---

1. **sea-moles,** large mounds or works of masonry laid in the sea as breakwaters. 2. **New-Hollands,** gains in territory made by England at the close of the Napoleonic Wars at the expense of Holland; these included the Island of Ceylon and the colony of the Cape of Good Hope in South Africa. 9. **world was theirs.** In the first century B.C. 10. **Greekdoms,** small Greek nations speaking different dialects. 21. **"talent of silence."** An allusion to the servant who hid his talent as related in *Matthew,* 25:14-30. 23. **melodious . . . Iliad.** An allusion to the original Greek epics, the *Iliad* and the *Odyssey,* written in hexameter measure.

48. **Puseyism,** a system of principles set forth in *Tracts for the Times* (1833-1843) aimed at growing liberalism in the Church of England (see p. 445); so called from Edward B. Pusey (1800-1882), one of the leaders of the High Church party. He urged a revival of early church doctrine and ritual. **Benthamism,** a phrase of the doctrine of Utilitarianism taught by Jeremy Bentham (1748-1832), an English philosopher and jurist. See p. 404. 85. **Corn-Laws.** In 1815 laws were passed imposing a tariff on the export and import of grain; they worked a hardship on the poor by raising the price of flour, grain, etc. Carlyle was among those who were violently opposed to the laws, which were finally repealed in 1846.

arguments and shadow of arguments have faded away from him, till the very urchins on the street titter at the arguments he brings. Logic—Λογιχὴ, the "Art of Speech"—does indeed speak so and so, clear enough: nevertheless Bull still shakes his head; will see whether nothing else *illogical,* not yet "spoken," not yet able to be "spoken," do not lie in the business, as there so often does!—My firm belief is, that, finding himself now enchanted, hand-shackled, foot-shackled, in Poor-Law Bastilles and elsewhere, he will retire three days to his bed, and *arrive* at a conclusion or two! His three-years' "total stagnation of trade," alas, is not that a painful enough "lying in bed to consider himself"? Poor Bull!

Bull is a born Conservative; for this too I inexpressibly honor him. All great Peoples are conservative; slow to believe in novelties; patient of much error in actualities; deeply and forever certain of the greatness that is in Law, in Custom once solemnly established, and now long recognized as just and final.— True, O Radical Reformer, there is no Custom that can, properly speaking, be final; none. And yet thou seest *Customs* which, in all civilized countries, are accounted final; nay, under the Old-Roman name of *Mores,* are accounted *Morality,* Virtue, Laws of God Himself. Such, I assure thee, not a few of them are; such almost all of them once were. And greatly do I respect the solid character —a blockhead, thou wilt say; yes, but a well-conditioned blockhead, and the best-conditioned—who esteems all "Customs once solemnly acknowledged" to be ultimate, divine, and the rule for a man to walk by, nothing doubting, not inquiring farther. What a time of it had we, were all men's life and trade still, in all parts of it, a problem, a hypothetic seeking, to be settled by painful Logics and Baconian Inductions! The Clerk in Eastcheap cannot spend the day in verifying his Ready-Reckoner; he must take it as verified,

true and indisputable; or his Bookkeeping by Double Entry will stand still. "Where is your Posted Ledger?" asks the master at night.—"Sir," answers the other, "I was verifying my Ready-Reckoner, and find some errors. The Ledger is—!"—Fancy such a thing!

True, all turns on your Ready-Reckoner being moderately correct, being *not* insupportably incorrect! A Ready-Reckoner which has led to distinct entries in your Ledger such as these: "*Creditor* an English People by fifteen hundred years of good Labor; and *Debtor* to lodging in enchanted Poor-Law Bastilles: *Creditor* by conquering the largest empire the Sun ever saw; and *Debtor* to Donothingism and 'Impossible' written on all departments of the government thereof; *Creditor* by mountains of gold ingots earned; and *Debtor* to No Bread purchasable by them" —*such* Ready-Reckoner, methinks, is beginning to be suspect; nay is ceasing, and has ceased to be suspect! Such Ready-Reckoner is a Solecism in Eastcheap; and must, whatever be the press of business, and will and shall be rectified a little. Business can go on no longer with *it.* The most Conservative English People, thickest-skinned, most patient of Peoples, is driven alike by its Logic and its Unlogic, by things "spoken," and by things not yet spoken or very speakable, but only felt and very unendurable, to be wholly a Reforming People. Their life, as it is, has ceased to be longer possible for them.

Urge not this noble silent People; rouse not the Berserkir-rage that lies in them! Do you know their Cromwells, Hampdens, their Pyms and Bradshaws? Men very peaceable, but men that can be made very terrible! Men who like their old Teutsch Fathers in Agrippa's days, "have a soul that despises death";

---

11. **Poor-Law Bastilles,** poorhouses. Laws relating to the poor sent the destitute to poorhouses, or workhouses, where the inmates were subjected to injustice, deprivation, and cruelty. 12. **retire . . . bed.** See p. 487, note 31. 42. **Baconian Inductions.** Francis Bacon (Vol. I, p. 612) was regarded as the father of the inductive process of reasoning, based upon scientific observation of occurrences. **Eastcheap,** a famous marketplace in the eastern section of London; the scene of many of Falstaff's exploits in Shakespeare's *Henry IV.* 44. **Ready-Reckoner,** a book of tables used in rapid computations.

58. **largest . . . saw,** India. 67. **Solecism,** something absurdly incongruous. 79. **Berserkir-rage.** In Norse tradition and folklore, the berserker was one of a class of wild warriors of the heathen age, possessed of a savage frenzy. 80. **Cromwell.** See Vol. I, p. 639. **Hampden.** See p. 51, note 57. 81. **Pym,** John Pym (1584-1643), an English statesman and influential Parliamentary leader against Charles I. **Bradshaw,** John Bradshaw (1602-1659), an English judge and politician, famous as a regicide. He was President of the High Court of Justice that tried Charles I, January, 1649. 83. **Teutsch . . . days,** German ancestors in the days of Marcus Vipsanius Agrippa (63-12 B.C.), celebrated Roman statesman and general and minister of Emperor Augustus. Agrippa was a writer on geography and was well known for his map of the world. Roman writers of the time, including Tacitus (c. 55-c. 120 A.D.), have much to say about the character of the ancient German peoples and their fierce and independent spirit.

to whom "death," compared with falsehoods and injustices, is light;—"in whom there is a rage unconquerable by the immortal gods!" Before this, the English People have taken very preternatural-looking Specters by the beard, saying virtually: "And if thou *wert* 'preternatural?' Thou with thy 'divine-rights' grown diabolic wrongs? Thou—not even 'natural'; decapitable; totally extinguishable!"—Yes, just so godlike as this People's patience was, even so godlike will and must its impatience be. Away, ye scandalous Practical Solecisms, children actually of the Prince of Darkness; ye have near broken our hearts; we can and will endure you no longer. Begone, we say; depart, while the play is good! By the Most High God, whose sons and born missionaries true men are, ye shall not continue here! You and we have become incompatible; can inhabit one house no longer. Either you must go, or we. Are ye ambitious to try *which* it shall be?

O my Conservative friends, who still specially name and struggle to approve yourselves "Conservative," would to Heaven I could persuade you of this world-old fact, than which Fate is not surer, That Truth and Justice alone are *capable* of being "conserved" and preserved! The thing which is unjust, which is *not* according to God's Law, will you, in a God's Universe, try to conserve that? It is so old, say you? Yes, and the hotter haste ought *you*, of all others, to be in to let it grow no older! If but the faintest whisper in your hearts intimate to you that it is not fair—hasten, for the sake of Conservatism itself, to probe it rigorously, to cast it forth at once and forever if guilty. How will or can you preserve *it*, the thing that is not fair? "Impossibility" a thousandfold is marked on that. And ye call yourselves Conservatives, Aristocracies—ought not honor and nobleness of mind, if they had departed from all the Earth elsewhere, to find their last refuge with you? Ye unfortunate!

The bough that is dead shall be cut away, for the sake of the tree itself. Old? Yes, it is too old. Many a weary winter has it swung and creaked there, and gnawed and fretted, with its dead wood, the organic substance and still living fiber of this good tree; many a long summer has its ugly naked brown defaced the fair green umbrage; every day it has done mischief, and that only: off with it, for the tree's sake, if for nothing more; let the Conservatism that would preserve cut *it* away. Did no wood-forester apprise you that a dead bough with its dead root left sticking there is extraneous, poisonous; is as a dead iron spike, some horrid rusty plowshare driven into the living substance;—nay is far worse; for in every wind-storm ("commercial crisis" or the like), it frets and creaks, jolts itself to and fro, and cannot lie quiet as your dead iron spike would.

If I were the Conservative Party of England (which is another bold figure of speech), I would not for a hundred thousand pounds an hour allow those Corn-Laws to continue! Potosi and Golconda put together would not purchase my assent to them. Do you count what treasuries of bitter indignation they are laying up for you in every just English heart? Do you know what questions, not as to Corn-prices and Sliding-scales alone, they are *forcing* every reflective Englishman to ask himself? Questions insoluble, or hitherto unsolved; deeper than any of our Logic-plummets hitherto will sound—questions deep enough—which it were better that we did not name even in thought! You are forcing us to think of them, to begin uttering them. The utterance of them is begun; and where will it be ended, think you? When two millions of one's brother-men sit in Workhouses, and five millions, as is insolently said, "rejoice in potatoes," there are various things that must be begun, let them end where they can. (III, 5)

7. **'divine-rights' . . . decapitable.** A reference to the English rejection of the doctrine that kings held their position by the authority of God as shown by the execution of Charles I in 1649. 8. **not even 'natural,'** unnatural, inhuman.

48. **bough . . . away.** Cf. *John,* 15:2: "Every branch in me that beareth not fruit he taketh away." 73. **Potosi,** a department in Bolivia once noted for its rich silver mines. **Golconda,** the old name of Hyderabad, India, formerly celebrated for its diamonds. 90. **"rejoice in potatoes,"** equivalent to "have more than they need."

LABOR

For there is a perennial nobleness, and even sacredness, in Work. Were he never so benighted, forgetful of his high calling, there is always hope in a man that actually and earnestly works: in Idleness alone is there perpetual despair. Work, never so Mammonish, mean, *is* in communication with Nature; the real desire to get Work done will itself lead one more and more to truth, to Nature's appointments and regulations, which are truth.

The latest Gospel in this world is, Know thy work and do it. "Know thyself": long enough has that poor "self" of thine tormented thee; thou wilt never get to "know" it, I believe! Think it not thy business, this of knowing thyself; thou art an unknowable individual: know what thou canst work at; and work at it, like a Hercules! That will be thy better plan.

It has been written, "an endless significance lies in Work"; a man perfects himself by working. Foul jungles are cleared away, fair seedfields rise instead, and stately cities; and withal the man himself first ceases to be a jungle and foul unwholesome desert thereby. Consider how, even in the meanest sorts of Labor, the whole soul of a man is composed into a kind of real harmony, the instant he sets himself to work! Doubt, Desire, Sorrow, Remorse, Indignation, Despair itself, all these like helldogs lie beleaguering the soul of the poor dayworker, as of every man: but he bends himself with free valor against his task, and all these are stilled, all these shrink murmuring far off into their caves. The man is now a man. The blessed glow of Labor in him, is it not as purifying fire, wherein all poison is burnt up, and of sour smoke itself there is made bright blessed flame!

Destiny, on the whole, has no other way of cultivating us. A formless Chaos, once set it *revolving*, grows round and ever rounder; ranges itself, by mere force of gravity, into strata, spherical courses; is no longer a Chaos, but a round compacted World. What would become of the Earth, did she cease to revolve? In the poor old Earth, so long as she revolves, all inequalities, irregularities disperse themselves; all irregularities are incessantly becoming regular. Hast thou looked on the Potter's wheel—one of the venerablest objects; old as the Prophet Ezekiel and far older? Rude lumps of clay, how they spin themselves up, by mere quick whirling, into beautiful circular dishes. And fancy the most assiduous Potter, but without his wheel; reduced to make dishes or rather amorphous botches, by mere kneading and baking! Even such a Potter were Destiny, with a human soul that would rest and lie at ease, that would not work and spin! Of an idle unrevolving man the kindest Destiny, like the most assiduous Potter without wheel, can bake and knead nothing other than a botch; let her spend on him what expensive coloring, what gilding and enameling she will, he is but a botch. Not a dish; no, a bulging, kneaded, crooked, shambling, squint-cornered, amorphous botch—a mere enameled vessel of dishonor! Let the idle think of this.

Blessed is he who has found his work; let him ask no other blessedness. He has a work, a life-purpose; he has found it, and will follow it! How, as a free-flowing channel, dug and torn by noble force through the sour mud-swamp of one's existence, like an ever-deepening river there, it runs and flows;—draining-off the sour festering water, gradually from the root of the remotest grass-blade; making, instead of pestilential swamp, a green fruitful meadow with its clear-flowing stream. How blessed for the

---

7. **Mammonish**, devoted merely to gaining money. Cf. *Matthew*, 6:24: "Ye cannot serve God and mammon." In *Paradise Lost* (Vol. I, p. 716) Mammon is the fallen angel who advocates the getting of wealth. There is an earlier charter on the Gospel of Mammonism in *Past and Present*. 13. "**Know thyself**." See p. 468, note 58. 19. **Hercules**, in classical mythology the son of Jupiter; he was noted for his great strength and for achieving the twelve "impossible labors" imposed upon him as a result of the hatred of Juno, wife of Jupiter. 21. "**an . . . Work.**" Apparently Carlyle is quoting himself. The idea is the center of *Sartor Resartus*. See the chapter on Helotage.

53. **Potter's wheel.** The incident of the potter and the wheel is found in *Jeremiah*, 18:1-6, not in *Ezekiel*. There is a "Vision of the Wheels," however, in *Ezekiel*, 1:15-21. Cf. Browning's *Rabbi Ben Ezra*, ll. 148 ff, p. 700. 71. **squint-cornered**, irregular. 72. **vessel of dishonor.** Cf. *Romans*, 9:21: "Hath not the potter power over the clay, of the same lump to make one vessel unto honor and another unto dishonor?"

meadow itself, let the stream and *its* value be great or small! Labor is Life: from the inmost heart of the Worker rises his god-given Force, the sacred celestial Life-essence breathed into him by Almighty God; from his inmost heart awakens him to all nobleness—to all knowledge, "self-knowledge" and much else, so soon as Work fitly begins. Knowledge? The knowledge that will hold good in working, cleave thou to that; for Nature herself accredits that, says Yea to that. Properly thou hast no other knowledge but what thou hast got by working: the rest is yet all a hypothesis of knowledge; a thing to be argued of in schools, a thing floating in the clouds, in endless logic-vortices, till we try it and fix it. "Doubt, of whatever kind, can be ended by Action alone."

And again, hast thou valued Patience, Courage, Perseverance, Openness to light; readiness to own thyself mistaken, to do better next time? All these, all virtues, in wrestling with the dim brute Powers of Fact, in ordering of thy fellows in such wrestle, there and elsewhere not at all, thou wilt continually learn. Set down a brave Sir Christopher in the middle of black ruined Stone-heaps, of foolish unarchitectural Bishops, redtape Officials, idle Nell-Gwyn Defenders of the Faith; and see whether he will ever raise a Paul's Cathedral out of all that, yea or no! Rough, rude, contradictory are all things and persons, from the mutinous masons and Irish hodmen, up to the idle Nell-Gwyn Defenders, to blustering red-tape Officials, foolish unarchitectural Bishops. All these things and persons are there not for Christopher's sake and his Cathedral's; they are there for their own sake mainly! Christopher will have to conquer and constrain all these—if he be able. All these are against him. Equitable Nature herself, who carries her mathematics and architectonics not on the face of her, but deep in the hidden heart of her—Nature herself is but partially for him; will be wholly against him, if he constrain her not! His very money, where is it to come from? The pious munificence of England lies far-scattered, distant, unable to speak, and say, "I am here";—must be spoken to before it can speak. Pious munificence, and all help, is so silent, invisible like the gods; impediment, contradictions manifold are so loud and near! O brave Sir Christopher, trust thou in those notwithstanding, and front all these; understand all these; by valiant patience, noble effort, insight, by man's-strength, vanquish and compel all these—and, on the whole, strike down victoriously the last topstone of that Paul's Edifice; thy monument for certain centuries, the stamp "Great Man" impressed very legibly on Portland-stone there!—

Yes, all manner of help, and pious response from Men or Nature, is always what we call silent; cannot speak or come to light, till it be seen, till it be spoken to. Every noble work is at first "impossible." In very truth, for every noble work the possibilities will lie diffused through Immensity; inarticulate, undiscoverable except to faith. Like Gideon thou shalt spread out thy fleece at the door of thy tent; see whether under the wide arch of Heaven there be any bounteous moisture, or none. Thy heart and life-purpose shall be as a miraculous Gideon's fleece, spread out in silent appeal to Heaven: and from the kind Immensities, what from the poor unkind Localities and town and country Parishes there never could, blessed dew-moisture to suffice thee shall have fallen!

---

15. **schools**, schools of philosophy. 17. **"Doubt . . . alone."** A profound saying of Goethe. 28. **Sir Christopher**, Sir Christopher Wren (1632-1723), a famous English architect, designer of St. Paul's Cathedral and conspicuous in the rebuilding of London after the Great Fire of 1666. (See Pepys's *Diary*, Vol. I, pp. 854 ff.) 30. **Nell Gwyn**, a popular actress of the Restoration period and a mistress of Charles II. The title "Defender of the Faith" was bestowed by the Pope upon Henry VIII (1491-1547) for his *Defense of the Seven Sacraments* (1521), a book against Martin Luther, and the title has been retained by subsequent English sovereigns.

63. **monument**. Wren's monument in St. Paul's bears the inscription, "If you would seek his monument, look around you." 65. **Portland-stone**, a light-colored building stone from the Isle of Portland, on the coast of Dorset, England. 74. **Gideon . . . tent**. Gideon (*Judges*, 6:36-38) was assured through two miracles that God would favor Israel. In the first, a fleece of wool left on the floor became wet with dew while the ground about it was dry; in the second, the fleece remained dry while the ground was wet.

Work is of a religious nature—work is of a *brave* nature; which it is the aim of all religion to be. All work of man is as the swimmer's: a waste ocean threatens to devour him; if he front it not bravely, it will keep its word. By incessant wise defiance of it, lusty rebuke and buffet of it, behold how it loyally supports him, bears him as its conqueror along. "It is so," says Goethe, "with all things that man undertakes in this world."

Brave Sea-captain, Norse Sea-king—Columbus, my hero, royalest Sea-king of all! it is no friendly environment this of thine, in the waste deep waters; around thee mutinous discouraged souls, behind thee disgrace and ruin, before thee the unpenetrated veil of Night. Brother, these wild water-mountains, bounding from their deep bases (ten miles deep, I am told), are not entirely there on thy behalf! Meseems *they* have other work than floating thee forward—and the huge Winds, that sweep from Ursa Major to the Tropics and Equators, dancing their giant-waltz through the kingdoms of Chaos and Immensity, they care little about filling rightly or filling wrongly the small shoulder-of-mutton sails in this cockle-skiff of thine! Thou art not among articulate-speaking friends, my brother; thou art among immeasurable dumb monsters, tumbling, howling wide as the world here. Secret, far off, invisible to all hearts but thine, there lies a help in them: see how thou wilt get at that. Patiently thou wilt wait till the mad Southwester spend itself, saving thyself by dextrous science of defense, the while: valiantly, with swift decision, wilt thou strike in, when the favoring East, the Possible, springs up. Mutiny of men thou wilt sternly repress; weakness, despondency, thou wilt cheerily encourage: thou wilt swallow down complaint, unreason, weariness, weakness of others and thyself;—how much wilt thou swallow down! There shall be a depth of Silence in thee, deeper than this Sea, which is but ten miles deep: a Silence unsoundable; known to God only. Thou shalt be a Great Man. Yes, my World-Soldier, thou of the World Marine-service—thou wilt have to be *greater* than this tumultuous unmeasured World here round thee is; thou, in thy strong soul, as with wrestler's arms, shalt embrace it, harness it down; and make it bear thee on—to new Americas, or whither God wills! (III, 11)

ARISTOCRACIES

To predict the Future, to manage the Present, would not be so impossible, had not the Past been so sacrilegiously mishandled; effaced, and what is worse, defaced! The Past cannot be seen; the Past, looked at through the medium of "Philosophical History" in these times, cannot even be *not* seen: it is misseen; affirmed to have existed—and to have been a godless impossibility. Your Norman Conquerors, true royal souls, crowned kings as such, were vulturous irrational tyrants: your Becket was a noisy egoist and hypocrite; getting his brains spilt on the floor of Canterbury Cathedral, to secure the main chance—somewhat uncertain how! "Policy, Fanaticism"; or say "Enthusiasm," even "honest-Enthusiasm"—ah yes, of course:

> The Dog, to gain his private ends,
> *Went* mad, and bit the Man!—

For in truth, the eye sees in all things "what it brought with it the means of seeing." A godless century, looking back on centuries that were godly, produces portraitures more miraculous than any other. All was inane discord in the Past; brute Force bore rule everywhere; Stupidity, sav-

---

23. **Ursa Major,** the Great Bear, or Dipper, a constellation over the North Pole. 28. **cockle-skiff,** a flimsy boat.

62. **"Philosophical History."** In his essay *On History* Carlyle denies that history is philosophy teaching by experience. He holds a moral conception of history, in which he sees the laws of God made manifest in fact. He is aiming primarily at David Hume (1711-1776) and William Robertson (1721-1793), both Scottish historians. 68. **Becket,** Thomas à Becket (1118-1170), Archbishop of Canterbury, who defended the Church against King Henry II, and was slain in Canterbury Cathedral by knights who had overheard the King's prayer "to be rid of this turbulent priest." Becket's shrine was the objective of Chaucer's pilgrims (Vol. I, p. 210). 75. **The Dog . . . Man,** Goldsmith, *An Elegy on the Death of a Mad Dog,* ll. 19-20.

age Unreason, fitter for Bedlam than for a human World! Whereby indeed it becomes sufficiently natural that the like qualities, in new sleeker habiliments, should continue in our time to rule. Millions enchanted in Bastille Workhouses; Irish Widows proving their relationship by typhus-fever: what would you have? It was ever so, or worse. Man's History, was it not always even this: the cookery and eating-up of imbecile Dupedom by successful Quackhood; the battle, with various weapons, of vulturous Quack and Tyrant against vulturous Tyrant and Quack? No God was in the Past Time; nothing but Mechanisms and Chaotic Brute-Gods: how shall the poor "Philosophic Historian," to whom his own century is all godless, see any God in other centuries?

Men believe in Bibles, and disbelieve in them: but of all Bibles the frightfulest to disbelieve in is this "Bible of Universal History." This is the Eternal Bible and God's Book, "which every born man," till once the soul and eyesight are extinguished in him, "can and must, with his own eyes, see the God's-Finger writing!" To discredit this, is an *infidelity* like no other. Such infidelity you would punish, if not by fire and faggot, which are difficult to manage in our times, yet by the most peremptory order, To hold its peace till it got something wiser to say. Why should the blessed Silence be broken into noises, to communicate only the like of this? If the Past have no God's-Reason in it, nothing but Devil's-Unreason, let the Past be eternally forgotten: mention *it* no more;—we whose ancestors were all hanged, why should we talk of ropes!

It is, in brief, not true that men ever lived by Delirium, Hypocrisy, Injustice, or any form of Unreason, since they came to inhabit this Planet. It is not true that they ever did, or ever will, live except by the reverse of these. Men will again be taught this. Their acted History will then again be a Heroism; their written History, what it once was, an Epic. Nay, forever it is either such, or else it virtually is—Nothing. Were it written in a thousand volumes, the Unheroic of such volumes hastens incessantly to be forgotten: the net content of an Alexandrian Library of Unheroics is, and will ultimately show itself to be, *zero*. What man is interested to remember *it;* have not all men, at all times, the liveliest interest to forget it?—"Revelations," if not celestial, then infernal, will teach us that God is; we shall then, if needful, discern without difficulty that He has always been! The Dryasdust Philosophisms and enlightened Skepticisms of the Eighteenth Century, historical and other, will have to survive for a while with the Physiologists, as a memorable *Nightmare-Dream*. All this haggard epoch, with its ghastly Doctrines, and death's-head Philosophies "teaching by example" or otherwise, will one day have become, what to our Moslem friends their godless ages are, "the Period of Ignorance."

If the convulsive struggles of the last Half-Century have taught poor struggling convulsed Europe any truth, it may perhaps be this as the essence of innumerable others: That Europe requires a real Aristocracy, a real Priesthood, or it cannot continue to exist. Huge French Revolutions, Napoleonisms, then Bourbonisms with their corollary of Three Days, finishing in very unfinal Louis-Philippisms: all this ought to be didactic! All this may have taught us: That

1. **Bedlam**, a hospital for the insane in London. 5. **Bastille Workhouses**, poorhouses, so called from the Bastille, the infamous French prison in Paris. 6. **Irish . . . typhus-fever**. An allusion to the epidemics in Ireland caused by impoverishment of the people.

51. **Alexandrian Library**. A famous library formed at Alexandria in the third and fourth centuries B.C. and partially destroyed by fire in the siege of the city by Julius Caesar in the first century B.C. 59. **Dryasdust Philosophisms**, subtle sophistries uttered by a type of dreary historian given to mere facts and details. 60. **enlightened . . Century**. A reference to the rationalistic philosophy of such men in France as Rousseau and Voltaire, and in England as William Godwin (see p. 22). 63. **Physiologists**, the new mechanists, who reduced bodily functions to principles of physics and chemistry contrary to the old idea of God-given vitalism. The group included such men as Albrecht von Haller (1708-1777) and Johannes Müller (1801-1858) in Germany and Georges Cuvier (1769-1832), Etienne Geoffroy Saint-Hilaire (1772-1844), and Jean Lamarck (1744-1829) in France. 68. **Moslem friends**, followers of the Mohammedan religion. 77. **Bourbonisms**, obstinate conservatisms, characteristic of the Bourbon dynasty in France. 78. **Three Days**, the revolution of July, 1830, which drove Charles X from the French throne. 79. **Louis-Philippisms**. A reference to the unstable career of Louis Philippe (1773-1850), King of the French (1830-1848). He was in and out of political favor most of his life. He was deposed by the Revolution of 1848.

False Aristocracies are insupportable; that No-Aristocracies, Liberty-and-Equalities are impossible; that True Aristocracies are at once, indispensable and not easily attained.

Aristocracy and Priesthood, a Governing Class and a Teaching Class: these two, sometimes separate, and endeavoring to harmonize themselves, sometimes conjoined as one, and the King a Pontiff-King: there did no Society exist without these two vital elements, there will none exist. It lies in the very nature of man: you will visit no remotest village in the most republican country of the world, where virtually or actually you do not find these two powers at work. Man, little as he may suppose it, is necessitated to obey superiors. He is a social being in virtue of this necessity; nay he could not be gregarious otherwise. He obeys those whom he esteems better than himself, wiser, braver; and will forever obey such; and even be ready and delighted to do it.

The Wiser, Braver: these, a Virtual Aristocracy everywhere and everywhen, do in all Societies that reach any articulate shape, develop themselves in a ruling class, an Actual Aristocracy, with settled modes of operating, what are called laws and even *private-laws* or privileges, and so forth; very notable to look upon in this world.—Aristocracy and Priesthood, we say, are sometimes united. For indeed the Wiser and the Braver are properly but one class; no wise man but needed first of all to be a brave man, or he never had been wise. The noble Priest was always a noble *Aristos* to begin with, and something more to end with. Your Luther, your Knox, your Anselm, Becket, Abbot Samson, Samuel Johnson, if they had not been brave enough, by what possibility could they ever have been wise?—If, from accident or forethought, this your Actual Aristocracy have got discriminated into Two Classes, there can be no doubt but the Priest Class is the more dignified; supreme over the other, as governing head is over active hand. And yet in practice again, it is likeliest the reverse will be found arranged;—a sign that the arrangement is already vitiated; that a split is introduced into it, which will widen and widen till the whole be rent asunder.

In England, in Europe generally, we may say that these two Virtualities have unfolded themselves into Actualities, in by far the noblest and richest manner any region of the world ever saw. A spiritual Guideship, a practical Governorship, fruit of the grand conscious endeavors, say rather of the immeasurable unconscious instincts and necessities of men, have established themselves; very strange to behold. Everywhere, while so much has been forgotten, you find the King's Palace, and the Viceking's Castle, Mansion, Manorhouse; till there is not an inch of ground from sea to sea but has both its King and Viceking, long due series of Vicekings, its Squire, Earl, Duke or whatever the title of him—to whom you have given the land, that he may govern you in it.

More touching still, there is not a hamlet where poor peasants congregate, but, by one means and another, a Church-Apparatus has been got together—roofed edifice, with revenues and belfries; pulpit, reading-desk, with Books and Methods: possibility, in short, and strict prescription: That a man stand there and speak of spiritual things to men. It is beautiful;—even in its great obscuration and decadence, it is among the beautifulest, most touching objects one sees on the Earth. This Speaking Man has indeed, in these times, wandered terribly from the point; has, alas, as it were, totally lost sight of the point: yet, at bottom, whom have we to compare with him? Of all pub-

---

36. *Aristos*, aristocrat; it is a Greek word for "the best." 38. **Luther**, Martin Luther (1483-1546), the leader of the German Reformation. **Knox**, John Knox (1505-1572), a Scottish Protestant reformer and partisan. **Anselm**, Saint Anselm (1033-1109), Archbishop of Canterbury. He was an uncompromising defender of the Church against both William II and Henry I. 39. **Abbot Samson**, Abbot of St. Edmonds (1182-1211), a valiant economic and political reformer interested in the welfare of the people. He rebuffed Richard I while protecting a wealthy ward left in his care. **Samuel Johnson**. See Vol. I, p. 1125.

64. **Viceking**, the governor of a county or province who rules as the representative of his sovereign. Under the feudal system in England the land, which theoretically belonged to the King, was administered in practice by barons, or vicekings. 80. **obscuration**, the act or state of being obscured.

lic functionaries boarded and lodged on the Industry of Modern Europe, is there one worthier of the board he has? A man even professing, and never so languidly making still some endeavor, to save the souls of men: contrast him with a man professing to do little but shoot the partridges of men! I wish he could find the point again, this Speaking One; and stick to it with tenacity, with deadly energy; for there is need of him yet! The Speaking Function, this of Truth coming to us with a living voice, nay in a living shape, and as a concrete practical exemplar: this, with all our Writing and Printing Functions, has a perennial place. Could he but find the point again—take the old spectacles off his nose, and looking up discover, almost in contact with him, what the *real* Satanas, and soul-devouring, world-devouring *Devil*, now is! Original Sin and such-like are bad enough, I doubt not: but distilled Gin, dark Ignorance, Stupidity, dark Corn-Law, Bastille and Company, what are they! *Will* he discover our new real Satan, whom he has to fight; or go on droning through his old nose-spectacles about old extinct Satans; and never see the real one, till he *feel* him at his own throat and ours? That is a question, for the world! Let us not intermeddle with it here.

Sorrowful, phantasmal as this same Double Aristocracy of Teachers and Governors now looks, it is worth all men's while to know that the purport of it is and remains noble and most real. Dryasdust, looking merely at the surface, is greatly in error as to those ancient Kings. William Conqueror, William Rufus or Redbeard, Stephen Curthose himself, much more Henry Beauclerc and our brave Plantagenet Henry: the life of these men was not a vulturous Fighting; it was a valorous Governing—to which occasionally Fighting did, and alas must yet, though far seldomer now, superadd itself as an accident, a distressing impedimental adjunct. The fighting too was indispensable, for ascertaining who had the might over whom, the right over whom. By much hard fighting, as we once said, "the unrealities, beaten into dust, flew gradually off"; and left the plain reality and fact, "Thou stronger than I; thou wiser than I; thou king, and subject I," in a somewhat clearer condition.

Truly we cannot enough admire, in those Abbot-Samson and William Conqueror times, the arrangement they had made of their Governing Classes. Highly interesting to observe how the sincere insight, on their part, into what did, of primary necessity, behove to be accomplished, had led them to the way of accomplishing it, and in the course of time to get it accomplished! No imaginary Aristocracy would serve their turn; and accordingly they attained a real one. The Bravest men, who, it is ever to be repeated and remembered, are also on the whole the Wisest, Strongest, everyway Best, had here, with a respectable degree of accuracy, been got selected; seated each on his piece of territory, which was lent him, then gradually given him, that he might govern it. These Vickings, each on his portion of the common soil of England, with a Head King over all, were a "Virtuality perfected into an Actuality" really to an astonishing extent.

For those were rugged stalwart ages; full of earnestness, of a rude God's-truth—nay, at any rate, their *quilting* was so unspeakably *thinner* than ours; Fact came swiftly on them, if at any time they had yielded to Phantasm! "The Knaves and Dastards" had to be "arrested" in some measure; or the world, almost within year and day, found that it could not live. The Knaves and Dastards accordingly were got arrested. Dastards upon the very throne had to be got arrested, and taken off the throne—by such methods as there were; by the roughest

---

19. *real* Satanas. For the ancient Satan, the incarnation of Sin, the modern man had to resist the other devils which Carlyle enumerates in the next sentence. 20. **Original Sin,** that supposed to have been inherited by all persons from Adam. 23. **Corn-Law.** See p. 488, note 85. 37. **William Conqueror,** King of England (1066-1087). 38. **William Rufus,** King of England (1087-1100). **Stephen Curthose,** King of England (1135-1154); his father Robert was also surnamed *Curthose* (short hose). 39. **Henry Beauclerc,** Henry I, King of England (1100-1135); he gained the surname *Beauclerc* on account of his scholarship. 40. **Plantagenet Henry,** Henry II, King of England (1154-1189).

method, if there chanced to be no smoother one! Doubtless there was much harshness of operation, much severity; as indeed government and surgery are often somewhat severe. Gurth, born thrall of Cedric, it is like, got cuffs as often as pork-parings, if he misdemeaned himself; but Gurth did belong to Cedric: no human creature then went about connected with nobody; left to go his way into Bastilles or worse, under *Laissez-faire;* reduced to prove his relationship by dying of typhus-fever!—Days come when there is no King in Israel, but every man is his own king, doing that which is right in his own eyes;—and tarbarrels are burnt to "Liberty," "Ten-pound Franchise," and the like, with considerable effect in various ways!—

That Feudal Aristocracy, I say, was no imaginary one. To a respectable degree, its *Jarls,* what we now call Earls, were *Strong-Ones* in fact as well as etymology; its Dukes *Leaders;* its Lords *Law-wards.* They did all the Soldiering and Police of the country, all the Judging, Law-making, even the Church-Extension; whatsoever in the way of Governing, of Guiding and Protecting could be done. It was a Land Aristocracy; it managed the Governing of this English People, and had the reaping of the Soil of England in return. It is, in many senses, the Law of Nature, this same Law of Feudalism;—no right Aristocracy but a Land one! The curious are invited to meditate upon it in these days. Soldiering, Police, and Judging, Church-Extension, nay real Government and Guidance, all this was actually *done* by the Holders of the Land in return for their Land. How much of it is now done by them; done by anybody? Good Heavens, "*Laissez-faire*, Do ye nothing, eat your wages and sleep" is everywhere the passionate half-wise cry of this time; and they will not so much as do nothing, but must do mere Corn-Laws! We raise Fifty-two millions, from the general mass of us, to get our Governing done—or, alas, to get ourselves persuaded that it is done: and the "peculiar burden of the Land" is to pay, not all this, but to pay, as I learn, one twenty-fourth part of all this. Our first Chartist Parliament, or Oliver *Redivivus,* you would say, will know where to lay the new taxes of England!—Or, alas, taxes? If we made the Holders of the Land pay every shilling still of the expense of Governing the Land, what were all that? The Land, by mere hired Governors, cannot be got governed. You cannot hire men to govern the Land; it is by mission not contracted for in the Stock-Exchange, but felt in their own hearts as coming out of Heaven, that men can govern a Land. The mission of a Land Aristocracy is a *sacred* one, in both the senses of that old word. The footing it stands on, at present, might give rise to thoughts other than of Corn-Laws!—

But truly a "Splendor of God," as in William Conqueror's rough oath, did dwell in those old rude veracious ages; did inform, more and more, with a heavenly nobleness, all departments of their work and life. Phantasms could not yet walk abroad in mere Cloth Tailorage; they were at least Phantasms "on the rim of the horizon," penciled there by an eternal Lightbeam from within. A most "practical" Hero-worship went on, unconsciously or half-consciously, everywhere. A Monk Samson, with a maximum of two shillings in his pocket, could, without a ballot-box, be made a Viceking of, being seen to be worthy. The difference between a good man and a bad man was as yet felt to be, what it forever is,

---

5. **Gurth,** the swineherd of Cedric the Saxon in Scott's *Ivanhoe;* in the chapter on democracy Carlyle refers to Gurth "with the brass collar round his neck." 11. *Laissez-faire,* a doctrine that favored unrestricted competition and stoutly opposed governmental intervention for regulating conditions of industry and helping the laborer. It became the accepted policy of the English government during the early decades of the nineteenth century (see p. 404). 13. **no King . . . eyes.** Cf. *Judges,* 17:6: "In those days there was no king in Israel, but every man did that which was right in his own eyes." 16. **"Ten-pound Franchise."** In the Reform Bill of 1832 the franchise was limited to persons paying an annual house-rent of ten pounds or more. 21. *Strong-Ones.* Carlyle is not always accurate in his etymologies. Anglo-Saxon *eorl* means nobleman; and *hlaf-weard* means bread-keeper, not law-keeper.

51. **first . . . Parliament,** the one held after the adoption of reforms advocated by the Chartists, political agitators who voiced their demands in what was called "the people's charter." See p. 404. 52. **Oliver** *Redivivus,* Oliver Restored. A reference to Oliver Cromwell, as a symbol of the Chartist movement. 68. **"Splendor of God,"** the favorite oath of William the Conqueror.

an immeasurable one. Who *durst* have elected a Pandarus Dogdraught, in those days, to any office, Carlton Club, Senatorship, or place whatsover? It was felt that the arch Satanas and no other had a clear right of property in Pandarus; that it were better for you to have no hand in Pandarus, to keep out of Pandarus his neighborhood! Which is, to this hour, the mere fact; though for the present, alas, the forgotten fact. I think they were comparatively blessed times those, in their way! "Violence," "war," "disorder": well, what is war, and death itself, to such a perpetual life-in-death, and "peace, peace, where there is no peace"! Unless some Hero-worship, in its new appropriate form, can return, this world does not promise to be very habitable long.

Old Anselm, exiled Archbishop of Canterbury, one of the purest-minded "men of genius," was traveling to make his appeal to Rome against King Rufus—a man of rough ways, in whom the "inner Lightbeam" shone very fitfully. It is beautiful to read, in Monk Eadmer, how the Continental populations welcomed and venerated this Anselm, as no French population now venerates Jean-Jacques or giant-killing Voltaire; as not even an American population now venerates a Schnüspel the distinguished Novelist! They had, by phantasy and true insight, the intensest conviction that a God's-Blessing dwelt in this Anselm—as is my conviction too. They crowded round, with bent knees and enkindled hearts, to receive his blessing, to hear his voice, to see the light of his face. My blessings on them and on him! —But the notablest was a certain necessitous or covetous Duke of Burgundy, in straitened circumstances we shall hope—who reflected that in all likelihood this English Archbishop, going towards Rome to appeal, must have taken store of cash with him to bribe the Cardinals. Wherefore he of Burgundy, for his part, decided to lie in wait and rob him. "In an open space of a wood," some "wood" then green and growing, eight centuries ago, in Burgundian Land—this fierce Duke, with fierce steel followers, shaggy, savage, as the Russian bear, dashes out on the weak old Anselm; who is riding along there, on his small quiet-going pony; escorted only by Eadmer and another poor Monk on ponies; and, except small modicum of roadmoney, not a gold coin in his possession. The steel-clad Russian bear emerges, glaring: the old white-bearded man starts not—paces on unmoved, looking into him with those clear old earnest eyes, with that venerable sorrowful time-worn face; of whom no man or thing need be afraid, and who also is afraid of no created man or thing. The fire-eyes of his Burgundian Grace meet these clear eye-glances, convey them swift to his heart: he bethinks him that probably this feeble, fearless, hoary Figure has in it something of the Most High God; that probably he shall be damned if he meddle with it—that, on the whole, he had better not. He plunges, the rough savage, from his war-horse, down to his knees; embraces the feet of old Anselm: he too begs his blessing; orders men to escort him, guard him from being robbed, and under dread penalties see him safe on his way. *Per os Dei*, as his Majesty was wont to ejaculate!

Neither is this quarrel of Rufus and Anselm, of Henry and Becket uninstructive to us. It was, at bottom, a great quarrel. For, admitting that Anselm was full of divine blessing, he by no means included in him all forms of divine blessing—there were far other forms withal, which he little dreamed of; and William Redbeard was unconsciously the representative and spokesman of

2. **Pandarus Dogdraught.** A name invented by Carlyle to describe the unscrupulous politician who buys his way into office. Pandarus was a go-between for the lovers Troilus and Cressida, in medieval story. 3. **Carlton Club,** a conservative political club established in London in 1832. 8. **Pandarus his.** An old form of the possessive. 15. **"peace . . . peace."** *Jeremiah,* 6:14. 25. **Monk Eadmer,** a twelfth-century monk of Canterbury, companion and friend of Anselm, whose *Life* he wrote. 28. **Jean-Jacques,** Rousseau (1712-1778), the noted French philosopher and writer (see p. 3) who interpreted "Liberty, Fraternity, and Equality" to the French people. **Voltaire,** François Voltaire (1694-1778), a famous French writer noted for his fearless skepticism. 30. **Schnüspel . . . Novelist.** An allusion to Dickens, under a coined German pseudonym; Dickens returned from a popular lecture tour in America shortly before *Past and Present* was composed.

76. ***Per os Dei,*** by the bones of God, an oath of William the Conqueror.

these. In truth, could your divine Anselm, your divine Pope Gregory have had their way, the results had been very notable. Our Western World had all become a European Thibet, with one Grand Lama sitting at Rome; our one honorable business that of singing mass, all day and all night. Which would not in the least have suited us. The Supreme Powers willed it not so.

It was as if King Redbeard unconsciously, addressing Anselm, Becket, and the others, had said: "Right Reverend, your Theory of the Universe is indisputable by man or devil. To the core of our heart we feel that this divine thing, which you call Mother Church, does fill the whole world hitherto known, and is and shall be all our salvation and all our desire. And yet—and yet—Behold, though it is an unspoken secret, the world is *wider* than any of us think, Right Reverend! Behold, there are yet other immeasurable Sacrednesses in this that you call Heathenism, Secularity! On the whole, I, in an obscure but most rooted manner, feel that I cannot comply with you. Western Thibet and perpetual mass-chanting—No. I am, so to speak, in the family-way; with child, of I know not what—certainly of something far different from this! I have —*Per os Dei*, I have Manchester Cotton-trades, Bromwicham Iron-trades, American Commonwealths, Indian Empires, Steam Mechanisms, and Shakespeare Dramas, in my belly; and cannot do it, Right Reverend!"—So accordingly it was decided: and Saxon Becket spilt his life in Canterbury Cathedral, as Scottish Wallace did on Tower-hill, and as generally a noble man and martyr has to do—not for nothing; no, but for a divine something other than *he* had altogether calculated. We will now quit this of the hard, organic, but limited Feudal Ages; and glance timidly into the immense Industrial Ages, as yet all inorganic, and in a quite pulpy condition, requiring desperately to harden themselves into some organism!

Our Epic having now become *Tools and the Man*, it is more than usually impossible to prophesy the Future. The boundless Future does lie there, predestined, nay already extant though unseen; hiding, in its Continents of Darkness, "gladness and sorrow"; but the supremest intelligence of man cannot prefigure much of it—the united intelligence and effort of All Men in all coming generations, this alone will gradually prefigure it, and figure and form it into a seen fact! Straining our eyes hitherto, the utmost effort of intelligence sheds but some most glimmering dawn, a little way into its dark enormous Deeps: only huge outlines loom uncertain on the sight; and the ray of prophecy, at a short distance, expires. But may we not say, here as always, Sufficient for the day is the evil thereof! To shape the whole Future is not our problem; but only to shape faithfully a small part of it, according to rules already known. It is perhaps possible for each of us, who will with due earnestness inquire, to ascertain clearly what he, for his own part, ought to do: this let him, with true heart, do, and continue doing. The general issue will, as it has always done, rest well with a Higher Intelligence than ours.

One grand "outline," or even two, many earnest readers may perhaps, at this stage of the business, be able to prefigure for themselves—and draw some guidance from. One prediction, or even two, are already possible. For the Life-Tree Igdrasil, in all its new developments, is the selfsame world-old Life-Tree: having found an element or ele-

---

2. **Pope Gregory**, Gregory the Great, Pope from 590 to 604. He was a zealous promoter of the Church; in 597 he sent St. Augustine and forty monks to Ethelbert, King of Kent. See Vol. I, p. 7. 5. **Thibet**, a land in central Asia, a dependency of China. The Buddhism of Thibet and Mongolia was directed by two high priests known as Grand Lamas, each supreme in his own sphere. Carlyle means that if Anselm and Gregory had had their way, England would have been over-religious and of course subject to the Pope. 30. **Manchester**, a city noted for its manufactories. See Shelley's *Song to the Men of England*, p. 254. 31. **Bromwicham**, from West Bromwich, a town in Staffordshire. 37. **Wallace**, William Wallace, a famous thirteenth-century Scottish hero and patriot. He was captured by the English and executed for treason. 38. **Tower-hill**, a hill of execution in London.

48. ***Tools and the Man.*** Contrast with *Arms and the Man*, the opening words of the *Aeneid*. 65. **Sufficient . . . thereof!** From *Matthew*, 6:34. 82. **Igdrasil**, in Norse mythology the great ash tree symbolizing the universe.

ments there, running from the very roots of it in Hela's Realms, in the Well of Mimer and of the Three Nornas or TIMES, up to this present hour of it in our own hearts, we conclude that such will have to continue. A man has, in his own soul, an Eternal; can read something of the Eternal there, if he will look! He already knows what will continue; what cannot, by any means or appliance whatsoever, be made to continue!

One wide and widest "outline" ought really, in all ways, to be becoming clear to us; this namely: That a "Splendor of God," in one form or other, will have to unfold itself from the heart of these our Industrial Ages too; or they will never get themselves "organized"; but continue chaotic, distressed, distracted evermore, and have to perish in frantic suicidal dissolution. A second "outline" or prophecy, narrower, but also wide enough, seems not less certain: That there will again *be* a King in Israel; a system of Order and Government; and every man shall, in some measure, see himself constrained to do that which is right in the King's eyes. This too we may call a sure element of the Future; for this too is of the Eternal;—this too is of the Present, though hidden from most; and without it no fiber of the Past ever was. An actual new Sovereignty, Industrial Aristocracy, real not imaginary Aristocracy, is indispensable and indubitable for us.

But what an Aristocracy; on what new, far more complex and cunningly devised conditions than that old Feudal fighting one! For we are to bethink us that the Epic verily is not *Arms and the Man*, but *Tools and the Man*—an infinitely wider kind of Epic. And again we are to bethink us that men cannot now be bound to men by *brass-collars*—not at all: that this brass-collar method, in all figures of it, has vanished out of Europe forevermore! Huge Democracy, walking the streets everywhere in its Sack Coat, has asserted so much; irrevocably, brooking no reply! True enough, man *is* forever the "born thrall" of certain men, born master of certain other men, born equal of certain others, let him acknowledge the fact or not. It is unblessed for him when he cannot acknowledge this fact; he is in the chaotic state, ready to perish, till he do get the fact acknowledged. But no man is, or can henceforth be, the brass-collar thrall of any man; you will have to bind him by other, far nobler and cunninger methods. Once for all, he is to be loose of the brass-collar, to have a scope *as* wide as his faculties now are—will he not be all the usefuler to you in that new state? Let him go abroad as a trusted one, as a free one; and return home to you with rich earnings at night! Gurth could only tend pigs; this one will build cities, conquer waste worlds. —How, in conjunction with inevitable Democracy, indispensable Sovereignty is to exist: certainly it is the hugest question ever heretofore propounded to Mankind! The solution of which is work for long years and centuries. Years and centuries, of one knows not what complexion;—blessed or unblessed, according as they shall, with earnest valiant effort, make progress therein, or, in slothful unveracity and dilettantism, only talk of making progress. For either progress therein, or swift and ever swifter progress towards dissolution, is henceforth a necessity.

It is of importance that this grand reformation were begun; that Corn-Law Debatings and other jargon, little less than delirious in such a time, had fled far away, and left us room to begin! For the evil has grown practical, extremely conspicuous; if it be not seen and provided for, the blindest fool will have to feel it ere long. There is much that can wait; but there is something also that cannot wait. With millions of eager Working Men

---

2. **Hela,** the Norse goddess of earth who presided over Niflheim, the hell of Scandinavian mythology. **Well of Mimer,** a well at the roots of Igdrasil presided over by Mimer, a giant water-demon; it was the source of wisdom. 3. **Nornas,** the Scandinavian Norns or Fates: Urth, Verthandi, and Skuld, representing the past, the present, and the future. 21. **there will . . . Israel.** Cf. *1 Samuel,* 8:19: "Nevertheless, the people refused to obey the voice of Samuel: and they said Nay; but we will have a king over us." See p. 497, note 13. 41. **bound . . . brass-collars.** See p. 497, note 5. Carlyle is speaking ironically.

74. **dilettantism,** superficial dabbling. 87. **millions . . . Men.** "*The Return of the Paupers for England and Wales* at Ladyday, 1842, is 'Indoor, 221,687. Outdoor, 1,207,402; Official Report.'"—Carlyle.

imprisoned in "Impossibility" and Poor-Law Bastilles, it is time that some means of dealing with them were trying to become "possible"! Of the Government of England, of all articulate-speaking functionaries, real and imaginary Aristocracies, of me and of thee, it is imperatively demanded, "How do you mean to manage these men? Where are they to find a supportable existence? What is to become of them—and of you!" (IV, 1.) (1843)

John Ruskin
1819-1900

John Ruskin liked to think of himself as a disciple of Thomas Carlyle, and in certain important aspects their characters are alike. Both were rebels against social and economic conditions in Victorian England and advocates of spiritual values. Both disliked materialism, utilitarianism, sordid and brutalized industry. Both had a marked self-confidence and a persistent ruthlessness in controversy. At most points in their opposition to Victorian ideals they would have been at one.

In *Praeterita*, the story of Ruskin's early life which he published in sections from 1885 to 1889, he attributes much of his adult philosophy to his loneliness as an only child and to the lack of independence that resulted from parental pampering and protection. He was the son of a wealthy London wine merchant, who engaged private tutors for the boy and took him on long coaching trips through the British Isles and Europe. Another influence on Ruskin's impressionable young mind was the training in the Bible which he got at the knee of his Calvinistic mother. She forced him to read the book aloud to her from *Genesis* to *Revelation* not once but many times, and this discipline he characterized later as the one really essential part of his boyhood training. In 1836 he entered Christ Church, Oxford, from which he graduated in 1843. In 1840 he met J. M. W. Turner, the great English landscape painter, who had recently entered upon his third stylistic period. Turner's new water-colors were being severely criticized, and Ruskin, himself keenly interested in painting, was moved to go to his defense. The result was the first volume of *Modern Painters*, published in 1843 under the anonymity of "a Graduate of Oxford." Of these brilliant comments on painters and the art of painting there were ultimately five volumes, the last appearing in 1860.

The first volume of *Modern Painters* was written at Herne Hill, the home of Ruskin's parents outside London. His stern mother seems still to have dominated him, and it is even possible that she forced him into his unhappy marriage with Euphemia Gray in 1849; the union was annulled five years later. On the death of his mother in 1871 Ruskin bought the beautiful property of Brantwood on the hilly shores of Coniston Lake in Westmoreland. For some years he divided his time between Brantwood and Oxford, where, from 1870 to 1879, and again in 1883-1884, he delivered lectures on art as Slade Professor. A mental breakdown forced his resignation, and he spent the last two decades of his long life at Brantwood, doing some writing during his better moments but undergoing a gradual decline in power until his death in 1900.

If Ruskin had died before 1862, the date of the appearance of *Unto This Last*, a series of articles on wealth, his place in literature would be that of a brilliant critic of the fine arts. His writing is divided by that year into work primarily aesthetic and work primarily ethical. Friends who read and disapproved of *Unto This Last* were convinced that the old Ruskin had been eclipsed, somehow, by a new, uncomfortably didactic writer. Actually, however, the trend toward the social and economic criticism which forms the great body of Ruskin's later writing is apparent in his earlier writing on art. His very theory of aesthetics was ethical, for he conceived of art as related to morals, and considered a stone building or a painting largely in terms of the character of its creator. So Gothic architecture was noble and Renaissance architecture ignoble, and a painting of gamblers throwing dice could not be a good painting, because the painter had chosen an immoral subject. Ruskin's philosophy, in fact, though seeming to undergo a change with the appearance of his first publication on economics, was essentially consistent throughout his life.

The books that belong to what may be called the early phase of his work are stylistically the best. The five volumes of *Modern Painters*, published between 1843 and 1860, have already been mentioned. After the second volume of this long series had been published, he issued, in 1849, his *Seven Lamps of Architecture*. The "seven lamps" are what he conceived to be the seven leading principles of the art: Sacrifice, Truth, Power, Beauty, Life, Memory, and Obedience. *The Stones of Venice*, published in three volumes in 1851-1853, was written, as the author said, to glorify Gothic art and attack "the pestilent art of the Renaissance." Here again Ruskin the moralist and socialist and Ruskin the artist labored together. With *Unto This Last* (see p. 515), as has been said, he seemed to his friends completely to have abandoned art for economic theory. When the four essays which comprise the volume appeared in the *Cornhill Magazine*, they aroused such opposition that the projected series was abruptly discontinued by Thackeray, the editor. A similar series in *Fraser's Magazine* in 1862-1863—published ten years later in book form under the title *Munera Pulveris*—suffered a like fate. *Sesame and Lilies* (1865) is—in spite of its name—three lectures on the reading, education and duties of women, and "The Mystery of Life and Its Arts." *The Crown of Wild Olive* (1866) is a collection of four lectures, given at various places, on War, The Future of England, Work, and Traffic; all lean to social and economic interpretation. So also does his *Fors Clavigera,* which appeared between 1871 and 1884 as a series of open letters to the workingmen of England on a great variety of sociological topics.

Ruskin's eagerness to help others was expressed throughout his life. It appeared in 1843 when he broke a lance in defense of Turner, and it appeared again in 1851 when he came to the rescue of the Pre-Raphaelites (see p. 416) in a series of letters to *The Times*. Later in life, when his interest in social problems had grown apace, his mind was alive with schemes for the betterment of mankind. St. George's Guild was the most prominent result of Ruskin's attempts to combine industry, art, and science, but The Hinksey Diggers, the hand-made-linen workers of Langdale, and similar groups derived their inspiration and their resources from him.

Like Carlyle, Ruskin had an earlier and a later literary style, but the distinction between his styles is not so marked as with Carlyle. His essays on art are smooth, ornate, almost over-elaborate; in those on economic theory, however, he seems to have imitated Carlyle, and the richness of his earlier manner disappeared. His earlier style he apparently thought he acquired from his reading of Wordsworth and other English poets and, more especially, from that thorough saturation in the Bible for which his mother was responsible. These influences undoubtedly helped form his style, but to them should be added that which came from his training as a painter. The accuracy, the detail, the color, the ornateness of his language are those of an artist, even if the flow and sweep of his sentences suggest the cadences and melody of the psalms and the prophetical books of the English Bible. There is in Ruskin's writing a romantic, almost rhapsodic, quality. His *Modern Painters* and *The Stones of Venice* contain some of the finest illustrations of the "grand style" in the whole range of Victorian prose.

from *Modern Painters*

The first volume of Ruskin's five-volume treatise on painters and painting was published in 1843 when the author was only twenty-four and had but recently graduated from Oxford. It was inspired by the attack of art critics on Turner, the landscape painter whom Ruskin had already defended in a short reply to *Blackwood's* criticism seven years earlier. Besides praising Turner in the first volume, he set forth there his own views of the principles of art. The second volume appeared in 1846; it continues the exposition of the author's theories of art and especially his ideas concerning the function of the imagination in art. Volume three (1856) deals with the Grand Style and Idealism and outlines the development of appreciation of landscape throughout the history of the civilized world. The fourth volume (1856) contains chapters on color, illumination, and natural landscape—clouds, water, leaves, etc. The fifth and last volume (1860) continues the discussion of natural landscape and then comments on the four orders of landscape painters: Heroic, Classical, Pastoral, and Contemplative. *Modern Painters* and *The Stones of Venice* contain the essence of Ruskin's theories of art.

EFFECT OF THE SEA AFTER A STORM

Few people, comparatively, have ever seen the effect on the sea of a powerful gale continued without intermission for three or four days and nights; and to those who have not, I believe it must be unimaginable, not from the mere force or size of surge, but from the complete annihilation of the limit between sea and air. The water, from its prolonged agitation, is beaten, not into mere creaming foam, but into masses of accumulated yeast, which hang in ropes and wreaths from wave to wave, and, where one curls over to break, form a festoon like a drapery, from its edge; these are taken up by the wind, not in dissipating dust, but bodily, in writhing, hanging, coiling masses, which make the air white and thick as with snow, only the flakes are a foot or two long each; the surges themselves are full of foam in their very bodies, underneath, making them white all through, as the water is under a great cataract; and their masses, being thus half water and half air, are torn to pieces by the wind whenever they rise, and carried away in roaring smoke, which chokes and strangles like actual water. Add to this that when the air has been exhausted of its moisture by long rain, the spray of the sea is caught by it as described above (Section III, Chapter IV, § 13), and covers its surface, not merely with the smoke of finely divided water, but with boiling mist; imagine also the low rain clouds brought down to the very level of the sea, as I have often seen them, whirling and flying in rags and fragments from wave to wave; and finally, conceive the surges themselves in their utmost pitch of power, velocity, vastness, and madness, lifting themselves in precipices and peaks, furrowed with their whirl of ascent, through all this chaos; and you will understand that there is indeed no distinction left between the sea

---

7. **annihilation . . . air.** Cf. Shakespeare's *Winter's Tale*, III, iii, 85. In describing the storm that lashes the sea, the Clown says, "I am not to say it is a sea, for it is now the sky."

and air; that no object, nor horizon, nor any landmark or natural evidence of position is left; that the heaven is all spray, and the ocean all cloud, and that you can see no farther in any direction than you could see through a cataract. Suppose the effect of the first sunbeam sent from above to show this annihilation to itself, and you have the sea picture of the Academy, 1842—*The Snowstorm*, one of the very grandest statements of sea motion, mist, and light that has ever been put on canvas, even by Turner. Of course it was not understood; his finest works never are; but there was some apology for the public's not comprehending this, for few people have had the opportunity of seeing the sea at such a time, and, when they have, cannot face it. To hold by a mast or a rock, and watch it, is a prolonged endurance of drowning which few people have courage to go through. To those who have it is one of the noblest lessons of nature.

But I think the noblest sea that Turner has ever painted, and if so, the noblest certainly ever painted by man, is that of *The Slave Ship*, the chief Academy picture of the exhibition of 1840. It is a sunset on the Atlantic after prolonged storm; but the storm is partially lulled, and the torn and streaming rain clouds are moving in scarlet lines to lose themselves in the hollow of the night. The whole surface of sea included in the picture is divided into two ridges of enormous swell, not high nor local, but a low, broad heaving of the whole ocean, like the lifting of its bosom by deep-drawn breath after the torture of the storm. Between these two ridges the fire of the sunset falls along the trough of the sea, dyeing it with an awful but glorious light, the intense and lurid splendor which burns like gold and bathes like blood. Along this fiery path and valley the tossing waves by which the swell of the sea is restlessly divided lift themselves in dark, indefinite, fantastic forms, each casting a faint and ghastly shadow behind it along the illumined foam. They do not rise everywhere, but three or four together in wild groups, fitfully and furiously, as the under-strength of the swell compels or permits them; leaving between them treacherous spaces of level and whirling water, now lighted with green and lamplike fire, now flashing back the gold of the declining sun, now fearfully dyed from above with the undistinguishable images of the burning clouds, which fall upon them in flakes of crimson and scarlet and give to the reckless waves the added motion of their own fiery flying. Purple and blue, the lurid shadows of the hollow breakers are cast upon the mist of night, which gathers cold and low, advancing like the shadow of death upon the guilty ship as it labors amidst the lightning of the sea, its thin masts written upon the sky in lines of blood, girded with condemnation in that fearful hue which signs the sky with horror, and mixes its flaming flood with the sunlight, and, cast far along the desolate heave of the sepulchral waves, incarnadines the multitudinous sea.

I believe, if I were reduced to rest Turner's immortality upon any single work, I should choose this. Its daring conception—ideal in the highest sense of the word—is based on the purest truth, and wrought out with the concentrated knowledge of a life; its color is absolutely perfect, not one false or morbid hue in any part or line, and so modulated that every square inch of canvas is a perfect composition; its drawing as accurate as fearless; the ship buoyant, bending, and full of motion; its tones as true as they are wonderful; and the whole picture dedicated to the most sublime of subjects and impressions—(completing thus the perfect system of all truth, which we have shown to be formed by Turner's works)—the power, majesty, and deathfulness of the open, deep, illimitable sea.

(II, 5, 3, 38-40)

63. **guilty ship.** So called because it is engaged in the slave trade. 69. **incarnadines . . . sea.** Cf. *Macbeth*, II, ii, 61-63.

No, this my hand will rather
The multitudinous seas incarnadine,
Making the green one red.

9. **the Academy,** the Royal Academy of Arts, London, which holds an annual exhibition of paintings. ***The Snowstorm,*** a painting by J. M. W. Turner; see headnote.

THE GRAND STYLE

... It seems to me, and may seem to the reader, strange that we should need to ask the question, "What is poetry?" Here is a word we have been using all our lives, and I suppose, with a very distinct idea attached to it; and when I am now called upon to give a definition of this idea, I find myself at a pause. What is more singular, I do not at present recollect hearing the question often asked, though surely it is a very natural one; and I never recollect hearing it answered, or even attempted to be answered. In general, people shelter themselves under metaphors, and while we hear poetry described as an utterance of the soul, an effusion of Divinity, or voice of nature, or in other terms equally elevated and obscure, we never attain anything like a definite explanation of the character which actually distinguishes it from prose.

I come, after some embarrassment, to the conclusion, that poetry is "the suggestion by the imagination, of noble grounds for the noble emotions." I mean, by the noble emotions, those four principal sacred passions—Love, Veneration, Admiration, and Joy (this latter especially, if unselfish); and their opposites—Hatred, Indignation (or Scorn), Horror, and Grief, this last when unselfish, becoming Compassion. These passions in their various combinations constitute what is called "poetical feeling" when they are felt on noble grounds, that is, on great and true grounds. Indignation, for instance, is a poetical feeling, if excited by serious injury; but it is not a poetical feeling if entertained on being cheated out of a small sum of money. It is very possible the manner of the cheat may have been such as to justify considerable indignation; but the feeling is nevertheless not poetical unless the grounds of it be large as well as just. In like manner, energetic admiration may be excited in certain minds by a display of fireworks, or a street of handsome shops; but the feeling is not poetical, because the grounds of it are false, and therefore ignoble. There is in reality nothing to deserve admiration either in the firing of packets of gunpowder, or in the display of the stocks of warehouses. But admiration excited by the budding of a flower is a poetical feeling, because it is impossible that this manifestation of spiritual power and vital beauty can ever be enough admired.

Farther, it is necessary to the existence of poetry that the grounds of these feelings should be *furnished by the imagination*. Poetical feeling, that is to say, mere noble emotion, is not poetry. It is happily inherent in all human nature deserving the name, and is found often to be purest in the least sophisticated. But the power of assembling, by *the help of the imagination*, such images as will excite these feelings, is the power of the poet or literally of the "Maker."

Now this power of exciting the emotions depends of course on the richness of the imagination, and on its choice of those images which, in combination, will be most effective, or, for the particular work to be done, most fit. And it is altogether impossible for a writer not endowed with invention to conceive what tools a true poet will make use of, or in what way he will apply them, or what unexpected results he will bring out by them; so that it is vain to say that the details of poetry ought to possess, or ever do possess, any *definite* character. Generally speaking, poetry runs into finer and more delicate details than prose; but the details are not poetical because they are more delicate, but because they are employed so as to bring out an affecting result. For instance, no one but a true poet would have thought of exciting our pity for a bereaved father by describing his way of locking the door of his house:

> Perhaps to himself at that moment he said,
> "The key I must take, for my Ellen is dead";
> But of this in my ears not a word did he speak;
> And he went to the chase with a tear on his cheek.

---

3. **"What is poetry?"** See p. 319, note 19. 21. **"the suggestion . . . emotions."** Ruskin later stated that the definition should include rhythm.

64. **"Maker,"** an old word for poet. 86. **Perhaps . . . cheek,** Wordsworth, *The Childless Father*, ll. 20 ff.

In like manner, in painting, it is altogether impossible to say beforehand what details a great painter may make poetical by his use of them to excite noble emotions; and we shall, therefore, find presently that a painting is to be classed in the great or inferior schools, not according to the kind of details which it represents, but according to the uses for which it employs them.

It is only farther to be noticed, that infinite confusion has been introduced into this subject by the careless and illogical custom of opposing painting to poetry, instead of regarding poetry as consisting in a noble use, whether of colors or words. Painting is properly to be opposed to *speaking or writing*, but not to *poetry*. Both painting and speaking are methods of expression. Poetry is the employment of either for the noblest purposes.

This question being thus far determined, we may proceed with our paper in the *Idler*.

"It is very difficult to determine the exact degree of enthusiasm that the arts of Painting and Poetry may admit. There may, perhaps, be too great indulgence as well as too great a restraint of imagination; if the one produces incoherent monsters, the other produces what is full as bad, lifeless insipidity. An intimate knowledge of the passions, and good sense, but not common sense, must at last determine its limits. It has been thought, and I believe with reason, that Michael Angelo sometimes transgressed those limits; and, I think, I have seen figures of him of which it was very difficult to determine whether they were in the highest degree sublime or extremely ridiculous. Such faults may be said to be the ebullitions of genius; but at least he had this merit, that he never was insipid; and whatever passion his works may excite, they will always escape contempt.

"What I have had under consideration is the sublimest style, particularly that of Michael Angelo, the Homer of painting. Other kinds may admit of this naturalness, which of the lowest kind is the chief merit; but in painting, as in poetry, the highest style has the least of common nature."

From this passage we gather three important indications of the supposed nature of the Great Style. That it is the work of men in a state of enthusiasm. That it is like the writing of Homer; and that it has as little as possible of "common nature" in it.

First, it is produced by men in a state of enthusiasm. That is, by men who feel *strongly* and *nobly;* for we do not call a strong feeling of envy, jealousy, or ambition, enthusiasm. That is, therefore, by men who feel poetically. This much we may admit, I think, with perfect safety. Great art is produced by men who feel acutely and nobly; and it is in some sort an expression of this personal feeling. We can easily conceive that there may be a sufficiently marked distinction between such art, and that which is produced by men who do not feel at all, but who reproduce, though ever so accurately, yet coldly, like human mirrors, the scenes which pass before their eyes.

Secondly, Great Art is like the writing of Homer, and this chiefly because it has little of "common nature" in it. We are not clearly informed what is meant by common nature in this passage. Homer seems to describe a great deal of what is common—cookery, for instance, very carefully in all its processes. I suppose the passage in the *Iliad* which, on the whole, has excited most admiration, is that which describes a wife's sorrow at parting from her husband, and a child's fright at its father's helmet; and I hope, at least, the former feeling may be considered "common nature." But the true greatness of Homer's style is, doubtless, held by our author to consist in his imaginations of things not only uncommon but impossible (such as spirits in brazen armor, or monsters with heads of men and bodies of beasts), and in his occasional delineations of the human character and form in their utmost, or heroic, strength and beauty. We gather then on the whole, that a painter in the Great Style must be enthusiastic, or full of emotion, and must

---

21. **our . . . Idler.** *The Idler* was a publication by Samuel Johnson (Vol. I, p. 1128). Sir Joshua Reynolds (1723-1792), noted English portrait painter, wrote the essay from which Ruskin quotes.   32. **Michael Angelo.** See p. 696, note 130.   44. **Homer of painting.** Michael Angelo is to painting what Homer is to epic poetry, i.e., he is supreme.

75. **cookery.** See the *Iliad*, I, 463 ff.   79. **wife's sorrow . . . helmet.** See the *Iliad*, Book VI, 390-502. The allusion is to the description of Hector's parting with Andromache and his infant son Astyanax.

paint the human form in its utmost strength and beauty, and perhaps certain impossible forms besides, liable by persons not in an equally enthusiastic state of mind to be looked upon as in some degree absurd. This I presume to be Reynolds's meaning, and to be all that he intends us to gather from his comparisons of the Great Style with the writings of Homer. But if that comparison be a just one in all respects, surely two other corollaries ought to be drawn from it, namely, first, that these Heroic or Impossible images are to be mingled with others very unheroic and very possible; and, secondly, that in the representation of the Heroic or Impossible forms, the greatest care must be taken in *finishing the details,* so that a painter must not be satisfied with painting well the countenance and the body of his hero, but ought to spend the greatest part of his time (as Homer the greatest number of verses) in elaborating the sculptured pattern on his shield. (III, 4, 1, 12-18.)

THE PATHETIC FALLACY

German dullness, and English affectation, have of late much multiplied among us the use of two of the most objectionable words that were ever coined by the troublesomeness of metaphysicians—namely, "Objective" and "Subjective."

No words can be more exquisitely, and in all points, useless; and I merely speak of them that I may, at once and forever, get them out of my way, and out of my reader's. But to get that done, they must be explained.

The word "Blue," say certain philosophers, means the sensation of color which the human eye receives in looking at the open sky, or at a bell gentian.

Now, say they farther, as this sensation can only be felt when the eye is turned to the object, and as, therefore, no such sensation is produced by the object when nobody looks at it, therefore the thing, when it is not looked at, is not blue; and thus (say they) there are many qualities of things which depend as much on something else as on themselves. To be sweet, a thing must have a taster; it is only sweet while it is being tasted, and if the tongue had not the capacity of taste, then the sugar would not have the quality of sweetness.

And then they agree that the qualities of things which thus depend upon our perception of them, and upon our human nature as affected by them, shall be called Subjective; and the qualities of things which they always have, irrespective of any other nature, as roundness or squareness, shall be called Objective.

From these ingenious views the step is very easy to a farther opinion, that it does not much matter what things are in themselves, but only what they are to us; and that the only real truth of them is their appearance to, or effect upon, us. From which position, with a hearty desire for mystification, and much egotism, selfishness, shallowness, and impertinence, a philosopher may easily go so far as to believe, and say, that everything in the world depends upon his seeing or thinking of it, and that nothing, therefore, exists, but what he sees or thinks of.

Now, to get rid of all these ambiguities and troublesome words at once, be it observed that the word "Blue" does *not* mean the *sensation* caused by a gentian on the human eye; but it means the *power* of producing that sensation; and this power is always there, in the thing, whether we are there to experience it or not, and would remain there though there were not left a man on the face of the earth. Precisely in the same way gunpowder has a power of exploding. It will not explode if you put no match to it. But it has always the power of so exploding, and is therefore called an explosive compound, which it very positively and assuredly is, whatever philosophy may say to the contrary.

In like manner, a gentian does not produce the sensation of blueness if you don't look at it. But it has always the power of doing so; its particles being everlastingly so arranged by its Maker. And, therefore, the gentian and the sky are always verily blue, whatever philosophy may say to the contrary; and

---

94. **blue . . . yours.** "It is quite true that in all qualities involving sensation there may be a doubt whether different

if you do not see them blue when you look at them, it is not their fault but yours.

Hence I would say to these philosophers: If, instead of using the sonorous phrase, "It is objectively so," you will use the plain old phrase, "It *is* so," and if instead of the sonorous phrase, "It is subjectively so," you will say, in plain old English, "It does so," or "It seems so to me"; you will, on the whole, be more intelligible to your fellow-creatures; and besides, if you find that a thing which generally "does so" to other people (as a gentian looks blue to most men), does *not* so to you, on any particular occasion, you will not fall into the impertinence of saying that the thing is not so, or did not so, but you will say simply (what you will be all the better for speedily finding out) that something is the matter with you. If you find that you cannot explode the gunpowder, you will not declare that all gunpowder is subjective and all explosion imaginary, but you will simply suspect and declare yourself to be an ill-made match. Which, on the whole, though there may be a distant chance of a mistake about it, is, nevertheless, the wisest conclusion you can come to until farther experiment.

Now, therefore, putting these tiresome and absurd words quite out of our way, we may go on at our ease to examine the point in question—namely, the difference between the ordinary, proper, and true appearances of things to us; and the extraordinary, or false appearances, when we are under the influence of emotion, or contemplative fancy; false appearances, I say, as being entirely unconnected with any real power or character in the object, and only imputed to it by us.

For instance—

"The spendthrift crocus, bursting through the mold
Naked and shivering, with his cup of gold."

This is very beautiful, and yet very untrue. The crocus is not a spendthrift, but a hardy plant; its yellow is not gold, but saffron. How is it that we enjoy so much the having it put into our heads that it is anything else than a plain crocus?

It is an important question. For, throughout our past reasonings about art, we have always found that nothing could be good or useful, or ultimately pleasurable, which was untrue. But here is something pleasurable in written poetry which is nevertheless *untrue*. And what is more, if we think over our favorite poetry, we shall find it full of this kind of fallacy, and that we like it all the more for being so.

It will appear also, on consideration of the matter, that this fallacy is of two principal kinds. Either, as in this case of the crocus, it is the fallacy of willful fancy, which involves no real expectation that it will be believed; or else it is a fallacy caused by an excited state of the feelings, making us, for the time, more or less irrational. Of the cheating of the fancy we shall have to speak presently; but, in this chapter, I want to examine the nature of the other error, that which the mind admits when affected strongly by emotion. Thus, for instance, in *Alton Locke*—

"They rowed her in across the rolling foam—
The cruel, crawling foam."

The foam is not cruel, neither does it crawl. The state of mind which attributes to it these characters of a living creature is one in which the reason is unhinged by grief. All violent feelings have the same effect. They produce in us a falseness in all our impressions of external things, which I would generally characterize as the "Pathetic fallacy."

Now we are in the habit of considering this

---

people receive the same sensation from the same thing (compare Part II, Sec. I, Chap. V, 6); but, though this makes such facts not distinctly explicable, it does not alter the facts themselves. I derive a certain sensation, which I call sweetness, from sugar. That is a fact. Another person feels a sensation, which *he* also calls sweetness, from sugar. That is also a fact. The sugar's power to produce these two sensations, which we suppose to be, and which are, in all probability, very nearly the same in both of us, and, on the whole, in the human race, is its sweetness."—Ruskin. 27. **farther experiment.** At this point Ruskin added a footnote on *subness* and *obness*, in which he parodied the metaphysical style of the German philosophers. 36. **contemplative fancy.** A footnote cross-reference of Ruskin's has been omitted here.

42. **The . . . gold.** "Holmes (Oliver Wendell), quoted by Miss Mitford in her *Recollections of a Literary Life.*"—Ruskin. 73. *Alton Locke,* a novel (published 1850) by Charles Kingsley (1819-1875), English novelist.

fallacy as eminently a character of poetical description, and the temper of mind in which we allow it, as one eminently poetical, because passionate. But, I believe, if we look well into the matter, that we shall find the greatest poets do not often admit this kind of falseness—that it is only the second order of poets who much delight in it.

Thus, when Dante describes the spirits falling from the bank of Acheron "as dead leaves flutter from a bough," he gives the most perfect image possible of their utter lightness, feebleness, passiveness, and scattering agony of despair, without, however, for an instant losing his own clear perception that *these* are souls, and *those* are leaves: he makes no confusion of one with the other. But when Coleridge speaks of

"The one red leaf, the last of its clan,
That dances as often as dance it can,"

he has a morbid, that is to say, a so far false, idea about the leaf: he fancies a life in it, and will, which there are not; confuses its powerlessness with choice, its fading death with merriment, and the wind that shakes it with music. Here, however, there is some beauty, even in the morbid passage; but take an instance in Homer and Pope. Without the knowledge of Ulysses, Elpenor, his youngest follower, has fallen from an upper chamber in the Circean palace, and has been left dead, unmissed by his leader, or companions, in the haste of their departure. They cross the sea to the Cimmerian land; and Ulysses summons the shades from Tartarus. The first which appears is that of the lost Elpenor. Ulysses, amazed, and in exactly the spirit of bitter and terrified lightness which is seen in Hamlet, addresses the spirit with the simple, startled words:

"Elpenor? How camest thou under the shadowy darkness? Hast thou come faster on foot than I in my black ship?"

Which Pope renders thus:

"O, say, what angry power Elpenor led
To glide in shades, and wander with the dead?
How could thy soul, by realms and seas disjoined,
Outfly the nimble sail, and leave the lagging wind?"

I sincerely hope the reader finds no pleasure here, either in the nimbleness of the sail, or the laziness of the wind! And yet how is it that these conceits are so painful now, when they have been pleasant to us in the other instances?

For a very simple reason. They are not a *pathetic* fallacy at all, for they are put into the mouth of the wrong passion—a passion which never could possibly have spoken them—agonized curiosity. Ulysses wants to know the facts of the matter; and the very last thing his mind could do at the moment would be to pause, or suggest in anywise what was *not* a fact. The delay in the first three lines, and conceit in the last, jar upon us instantly, like the most frightful discord in music. No poet of true imaginative power could possibly have written the passage.

---

7. **the second . . . it.** "I admit two orders of poets, but no third; and by these two orders I mean the Creative (Shakespeare, Homer, Dante), and Reflective or Perceptive (Wordsworth, Keats, Tennyson). But both of these must be *first-rate in their range*, though their range is different; and with poetry second-rate in *quality* no one ought to be allowed to trouble mankind. There is quite enough of the best—much more than we can ever read or enjoy in the length of a life; and it is a literal wrong or sin in any person to encumber us with inferior work. I have no patience with apologies made by young pseudo-poets, 'that they believe there is *some* good in what they have written: that they hope to do better in time,' etc. *Some* good! If there is not *all* good, there is no good. If they ever hope to do better, why do they trouble us now? Let them rather courageously burn all they have done and wait for the better days. There are few men, ordinarily educated, who in moments of strong feeling could not strike out a poetical thought and afterwards polish it so as to be presentable. But men of sense know better than so to waste their time; and those who sincerely love poetry know the touch of the master's hands on the chords too well to fumble among them after him. Nay, more than this; all inferior poetry is an injury to the good, inasmuch as it takes away the freshness of rimes, blunders upon and gives a wretched commonalty to good thoughts; and, in general, adds to the weight of human weariness in a most woeful and culpable manner. There are few thoughts likely to come across ordinary men, which have not already been expressed by greater men in the best possible way; and it is a wiser, more generous, more noble thing to remember and point out the perfect words than to invent poorer ones wherewith to encumber temporarily the world."—Ruskin. 9. **Dante . . . spirits,** in the *Inferno* of *Divina Commedia*. 18. **Coleridge.** See *Christabel*, ll. 49-50 (p. 176). 28. **Homer,** from *The Odyssey,* beginning of Book XI. 39. **seen in Hamlet.** "Well said, old mole! can'st work i' the ground so fast?"—Ruskin's note, a quotation from *Hamlet*, I, V, 162; Hamlet thus addresses the ghost of his father that moves beneath the platform. 52. **conceit,** an affected conception. 67. **passage.** "It is worth while comparing the way a similar question is put by the exquisite sincerity of Keats:

"'He wept, and his bright tears
Went trickling down the golden bow he held.
Thus, with half-shut, suffused eyes, he stood;
While from beneath some cumb'rous boughs hard by,
With solemn step, an awful goddess came.
And there was purport in her looks for him,
Which he with eager guess began to read:
Perplexed the while, melodiously he said,
"How can'st thou over the unfooted sea?"'
Hyperion, 3, 42."—Ruskin.

Therefore, we see that the spirit of truth must guide us in some sort, even in our enjoyment of fallacy. Coleridge's fallacy has no discord in it, but Pope's has set our teeth on edge. Without farther questioning, I will endeavor to state the main bearings of this matter.

The temperament which admits the pathetic fallacy is, as I said above, that of a mind and body in some sort too weak to deal fully with what is before them or upon them; borne away, or over-clouded, or over-dazzled by emotion; and it is a more or less noble state, according to the force of the emotion which has induced it. For it is no credit to a man that he is not morbid or inaccurate in his perceptions, when he has no strength of feeling to warp them; and it is in general a sign of higher capacity and stand in the ranks of being that the emotions should be strong enough to vanquish, partly, the intellect, and make it believe what they choose. But it is still a grander condition when the intellect also rises, till it is strong enough to assert its rule against, or together with, the utmost efforts of the passions; and the whole man stands in an iron glow, white hot, perhaps, but still strong, and in no wise evaporating; even if he melts, losing none of his weight.

So, then, we have the three ranks: the man who perceives rightly, because he does not feel, and to whom the primrose is very accurately the primrose, because he does not love it. Then, secondly, the man who perceives wrongly, because he feels, and to whom the primrose is anything else than a primrose—a star, or a sun, or a fairy's shield, or a forsaken maiden. And then, lastly, there is the man who perceives rightly in spite of his feelings, and to whom the primrose is forever nothing else than itself— a little flower, apprehended in the very plain and leafy fact of it, whatever and how many soever the associations and passions may be, that crowd around it. And, in general, these three classes may be rated in comparative order, as the men who are not poets at all, and the poets of the second order, and the poets of the first; only however great a man may be, there are always some subjects which *ought* to throw him off his balance; some, by which his poor human capacity of thought should be conquered, and brought into the inaccurate and vague state of perception, so that the language of the highest inspiration becomes broken, obscure, and wild in metaphor, resembling that of the weaker man, overborne by weaker things.

And thus, in full, there are four classes: the men who feel nothing, and therefore see truly; the men who feel strongly, think weakly, and see untruly (second order of poets); the men who feel strongly, think strongly, and see truly (first order of poets); and the men who, strong as human creatures can be, are yet submitted to influences stronger than they, and see in a sort untruly, because what they see is inconceivably above them. This last is the usual condition of prophetic inspiration.

I separate these classes, in order that their character may be clearly understood; but of course they are united each to the other by imperceptible transitions, and the same mind, according to the influences to which it is subjected, passes at different times into the various states. Still, the difference between the great and less man is, on the whole, chiefly in this point of *alterability*. That is to say, the one knows too much, and perceives and feels too much of the past and future, and of all things beside and around that which immediately affects him, to be in anywise shaken by it. His mind is made up; his thoughts have an accustomed current; his ways are steadfast; it is not this or that new sight which will at once unbalance him. He is tender to impression at the surface, like a rock with deep moss upon it; but there is too much mass of him to be moved. The smaller man, with the same degree of sensibility, is at once carried off his feet; he wants to do something he did not want to do before; he views all the universe in a new light through his tears; he is gay or enthusiastic, melancholy or passionate, as things come and

---

33. **to whom the primrose,** etc. The allusion is to Wordsworth's *Peter Bell*, Part I, Stanza 12:
    A primrose by a river's brim
    A yellow primrose was to him,
    And it was nothing more.

go to him. Therefore the high creative poet might even be thought, to a great extent, impassive (as shallow people think Dante stern), receiving indeed all feelings to the full, but having a great center of reflection and knowledge in which he stands serene, and watches the feeling, as it were, from far off.

Dante, in his most intense moods, has entire command of himself, and can look around calmly, at all moments, for the image or the word that will best tell what he sees to the upper or lower world. But Keats and Tennyson, and the poets of the second order are generally themselves subdued by the feelings under which they write, or, at least, write as choosing to be so, and therefore admit certain expressions and modes of thought which are in some sort diseased or false.

Now so long as we see that the *feeling* is true, we pardon, or are even pleased by, the confessed fallacy of sight which it induces: we are pleased, for instance, with those lines of Kingsley's, above quoted, not because they fallaciously describe foam, but because they faithfully describe sorrow. But the moment the mind of the speaker becomes cold, that moment every such expression becomes untrue, as being for ever untrue in the external facts. And there is no greater baseness in literature than the habit of using these metaphorical expressions in cold blood. An inspired writer, in full impetuosity of passion, may speak wisely and truly of "raging waves of the sea, foaming out their own shame"; but it is only the basest writer who cannot speak of the sea without talking of "raging waves," "remorseless floods," "ravenous billows," etc.; and it is one of the signs of the highest power in a writer to check all such habits of thought, and to keep his eyes fixed firmly on the *pure fact*, out of which if any feeling comes to him or his reader, he knows it must be a true one.

To keep to the waves, I forget who it is who represents a man in despair, desiring that his body may be cast into the sea,

"*Whose changing mound, and foam that passed away,*
Might mock the eye that questioned where I lay."

Observe, there is not a single false, or even overcharged, expression. "Mound" of the sea wave is perfectly simple and true; "changing" is as familiar as may be; "foam that passed away," strictly literal; and the whole line descriptive of the reality with a degree of accuracy which I know not any other verse, in the range of poetry, that altogether equals. For most people have not a distinct idea of the clumsiness and massiveness of a large wave. The word "wave" is used too generally of ripples and breakers, and bendings in light drapery or grass: it does not by itself convey a perfect image. But the word "mound" is heavy, large, dark, definite; there is no mistaking the kind of wave meant, nor missing the sight of it. Then the term "changing" has a peculiar force also. Most people think of waves as rising and falling. But if they look at the sea carefully, they will perceive that the waves do not rise and fall. They change. Change both place and form, but they do not fall; one wave goes on, and on, and still on; now lower, now higher, now tossing its mane like a horse, now building itself together like a wall, now shaking, now steady, but still the same wave, till at last it seems struck by something, and changes, one knows not how, —becomes another wave.

The close of the line insists on this image, and paints it still more perfectly—"foam that passed away." Not merely melting, disappearing, but passing on, out of sight, on the career of the wave. Then, having put the absolute ocean fact as far as he may before our eyes, the poet leaves us to feel about it as we may, and to trace for ourselves the opposite fact—the image of the green mounds that do not change, and the white and written stones that do not pass away; and thence to follow out also the associated images of the calm life with the quiet grave, and the despairing life with the fading foam:

"Let no man move his bones."
"As for Samaria, her king is cut off like the foam upon the water."

But nothing of this is actually told or pointed out, and the expressions, as they stand, are perfectly severe and accurate, utterly uninfluenced by the firmly governed emotion of the writer. Even the word "mock" is hardly an exception, as it may stand merely for "deceive" or "defeat," without implying any impersonation of the waves.

It may be well, perhaps, to give one or two more instances to show the peculiar dignity possessed by all passages which thus limit their expression to the pure fact, and leave the hearer to gather what he can from it. Here is a notable one from the *Iliad*. Helen, looking from the Scaean gate of Troy over the Grecian host, and telling Priam the names of its captains, says at last:

"I see all the other dark-eyed Greeks; but two I cannot see—Castor and Pollux—whom one mother bore with me. Have they not followed from fair Lacedaemon, or have they indeed come in their sea-wandering ships, but now will not enter into the battle of men, fearing the shame and the scorn that is in Me?"

Then Homer:

"So she spoke. But them, already, the life-giving earth possessed, there in Lacedaemon, in the dear fatherland."

Note, here, the high poetical truth carried to the extreme. The poet has to speak of the earth in sadness, but he will not let that sadness affect or change his thoughts of it. No; though Castor and Pollux be dead, yet the earth is our mother still, fruitful, life-giving. These are the facts of the thing. I see nothing else than these. Make what you will of them.

Take another very notable instance from Casimir de la Vigne's terrible ballad, "La Toilette de Constance." I must quote a few lines out of it here and there, to enable the reader who has not the book by him to understand its close.

"Vite, Anna, vite; au miroir
Plus vite, Anna. L'heure s'avance

11. *Iliad.* The passage is from Book III. 36. **Casimir de la Vigne,** Jean François Casimir Delavigne (1793-1843), French poet and dramatist, famous for his patriotic poems and very popular in his own time. *Constance's Toilette* is the tragedy of a gay young girl who, having dressed for the ambassador's ball, was burned to death when her robe caught fire; for her it was "farewell ball, pleasure, love"—but at the ambassador's, after a "Poor Constance," the dance went on.

Et je vais au bal ce soir
  Chez l'ambassadeur de France.

Y pensez-vous, ils sont fanés, ces noeuds,
  Ils sont d'hier, mon Dieu, comme tout passe!
Que du réseau qui retient mes cheveux
  Les glands d'azur retombent avec grâce.
Plus haut! Plus bas! Vous ne comprenez rien!
Que sur mon front ce saphir étincelle:
Vous me piquez, mal-adroite. Ah, c'est bien,
  Bien—chère Anna! Je t'aime, je suis belle.

Celui qu'en vain je voudrais oublier
  (Anna, ma robe) il y sera, j'espère.
(Ah, fi, profane, est-ce là mon collier?
  Quoi! ces grains d'or bénits par le Saint-Père!)
Il y sera; Dieu, s'il pressait ma main,
  En y pensant, à peine je respire;
Père Anselmo doit m'entendre demain,
  Comment ferai-je, Anna, pour tout lui dire?

  Vite un coup d'oeil au miroir,
  Le dernier. ——J'ai l'assurance
Qu'on va m'adorer ce soir
  Chez l'ambassadeur de France.

Près du foyer, Constance s'admirait.
  Dieu! sur sa robe il vole une étincelle!
Au feu. Courez; Quand l'espoir l'enivrait,
  Tout perdre ainsi! Quoi! Mourir—et si belle!
L'horrible feu ronge avec volupté
  Ses bras, son sein, et l'entoure, et s'élève,
Et sans pitié dévore sa beauté,
  Ses dix-huit ans, hélas, et son doux rêve!

  Adieu, bal, plaisir, amour!
  On disait, Pauvre Constance!
Et on dansait, jusqu'au jour,
  Chez l'ambassadeur de France."

Yes, that is the fact of it. Right or wrong, the poet does not say. What you may think about it, he does not know. He has nothing to do with that. There lie the ashes of the dead girl in her chamber. There they danced, till the morning, at the Ambassador's of France. Make what you will of it.

If the reader will look through the ballad, of which I have quoted only about the third part, he will find that there is not, from beginning to end of it, a single poetical (so-called) expression, except in one stanza. The girl speaks as simple prose as may be; there is not a word she would not have actually used as she was dressing. The poet stands by, impassive as a statue, recording her words just as they come. At last the doom seizes her, and in the very presence of death, for an instant, his own emotions conquer him. He records no longer the facts only, but the facts as they seem to him. The fire gnaws with *voluptuousness—without pity.* It is soon past. The fate is fixed for ever; and he retires into his pale and crystalline atmosphere of truth. He closes all with the calm veracity,

"They said, 'Poor Constance!'"

Now in this there is the exact type of the consummate poetical temperament. For, be it clearly and constantly remembered that the greatness of a poet depends upon the two faculties, acuteness of feeling and command of it. A poet is great, first in proportion to the strength of his passion, and then, that strength being granted, in proportion to his government of it; there being, however, always a point beyond which it would be inhuman and monstrous if he pushed this government, and, therefore, a point at which all feverish and wild fancy becomes just and true. Thus the destruction of the kingdom of Assyria cannot be contemplated firmly by a prophet of Israel. The fact is too great, too wonderful. It overthrows him, dashes him into a confused element of dreams. All the world is, to his stunned thought, full of strange voices. "Yea, the fir-trees rejoice at thee, and the cedars of Lebanon, saying, 'Since thou art gone down to the grave, no feller is come up against us.'" So, still more, the thought of the presence of Deity cannot be borne without this great astonishment. "The mountains and the hills shall break forth before you into singing, and all the trees of the field shall clap their hands."

But by how much this feeling is noble when it is justified by the strength of its cause, by so much it is ignoble when there is not cause enough for it; and beyond all other ignobleness is the mere affectation of it, in hardness of heart. Simply bad writing may almost always, as above noticed, be known by its adoption of these fanciful metaphorical expressions, as a sort of current coin; yet there is even a worse, at least a more harmful, condition of writing than this, in which such expressions are not ignorantly and feelinglessly caught up, but, by some master, skilful in handling, yet insincere, deliberately wrought out with chill and studied fancy; as if we should try to make an old lava stream look red-hot again, by covering it with dead leaves, or white-hot, with hoar-frost.

When Young is lost in veneration, as he dwells on the character of a truly good and holy man, he permits himself for a moment to be overborne by the feeling so far as to exclaim—

"Where shall I find him? angels, tell me where.
You know him; he is near you; point him out.
Shall I see glories beaming from his brow,
Or trace his footsteps by the rising flowers?"

This emotion has a worthy cause, and is thus true and right. But now hear the cold-hearted Pope say to a shepherd girl—

"Where'er you walk, cool gales shall fan the glade;
Trees, where you sit, shall crowd into a shade;
Your praise the birds shall chant in every grove,
And winds shall waft it to the powers above.
But would you sing, and rival Orpheus' strain,
The wondering forests soon should dance again;
The moving mountains hear the powerful call,

---

36. **a prophet of Israel.** See *Isaiah*, 14:8. 47. **"The mountains, etc."** See *Isaiah*, 55:12. 69. **Young,** Edward Young. See p. 7. 80. **Pope,** Alexander Pope. See Vol. I, p. 1063. 85. **Orpheus,** famous musician of Greek mythology.

And headlong streams hang, listening, in their fall."

This is not, nor could it for a moment be mistaken for, the language of passion. It is simple falsehood, uttered by hypocrisy; definite absurdity, rooted in affectation, and coldly asserted in the teeth of nature and fact. Passion will indeed go far in deceiving itself; but it must be a strong passion, not the simple wish of a lover to tempt his mistress to sing. Compare a very closely parallel passage in Wordsworth, in which the lover has lost his mistress:

"Three years had Barbara in her grave been laid,
When thus his moan he made:

'Oh, move, thou cottage, from behind yon oak,
Or let the ancient tree uprooted lie,
That in some other way yon smoke
  May mount into the sky.
If still behind yon pine-tree's ragged bough,
  Headlong, the waterfall must come,
  Oh, let it, then, be dumb—
Be anything, sweet stream, but that which thou art now.'"

Here is a cottage to be moved, if not a mountain, and a waterfall to be silent, if it is not to hang listening: but with what different relation to the mind that contemplates them! Here, in the extremity of its agony, the soul cries out wildly for relief, which at the same moment it partly knows to be impossible, but partly believes possible, in a vague impression that a miracle *might* be wrought to give relief even to a less sore distress—that nature is kind, and God is kind, and that grief is strong; it knows not well what *is* possible to such grief. To silence a stream, to move a cottage wall—one might think it could do as much as that!

I believe these instances are enough to illustrate the main point I insist upon respecting the pathetic fallacy—that so far as it *is* a fallacy, it is always the sign of a morbid state of mind, and comparatively of a weak one.

13. **"Three years, etc.,"** from *'Tis Said That Some Have Died for Love*, 11-16, 33-36.

Even in the most inspired prophet it is a sign of the incapacity of his human sight or thought to bear what has been revealed to it. In ordinary poetry, if it is found in the thoughts of the poet himself, it is at once a sign of his belonging to the inferior school; if in the thoughts of the characters imagined by him, it is right or wrong according to the genuineness of the emotion from which it springs; always, however, implying necessarily *some* degree of weakness in the character.

Take two most exquisite instances from master hands. The Jessy of Shenstone, and the Ellen of Wordsworth, have both been betrayed and deserted. Jessy, in the course of her most touching complaint, says:

"If through the garden's flowery tribes I stray,
  Where bloom the jasmines that could once allure,
'Hope not to find delight in us,' they say,
'For we are spotless, Jessy; we are pure.'"

Compare with this some of the words of Ellen:

"'Ah, why,' said Ellen, sighing to herself,
'Why do not words, and kiss, and solemn pledge,
And nature, that is kind in woman's breast,
And reason, that is wise and good,
And fear of Him who is a righteous Judge—
Why do not these prevail for human life,
To keep two hearts together, that began
Their springtime with one love, and that have need
Of mutual pity and forgiveness, sweet
To grant, or be received; while that poor bird—
O, come and hear him! Thou who hast to me
Been faithless, hear him;—though a lowly creature,
One of God's simple children, that yet know not
The Universal Parent, *how* he sings!
As if he wished the firmament of heaven
Should listen, and give back to him the voice
Of his triumphant constancy and love.

60. **"If through, etc.,"** from *Describing the Sorrow of an Ingenuous Mind*, 61-64, by William Shenstone (1714-1763), English poet. 66. **"'Ah, why, etc.,"** from *The Excursion*, VI, 869 ff.

The proclamation that he makes, how far
His darkness doth transcend our fickle
  light.'"

The perfection of both these passages, as far as regards truth and tenderness of imagination in the two poets, is quite insuperable. But, of the two characters imagined, Jessy is weaker than Ellen, exactly in so far as something appears to her to be in nature which is not. The flowers do not really reproach her. God meant them to comfort her, not to taunt her; they would do so if she saw them rightly.

Ellen, on the other hand, is quite above the slightest erring emotion. There is not the barest film of fallacy in all her thoughts. She reasons as calmly as if she did not feel. And, although the singing of the bird suggests to her the idea of its desiring to be heard in heaven, she does not for an instant admit any veracity in the thought. "As if," she says,—"I know he means nothing of the kind; but it does verily seem as if." The reader will find, by examining the rest of the poem, that Ellen's character is throughout consistent in this clear though passionate strength.

It then being, I hope, now made clear to the reader in all respects that the pathetic fallacy is powerful only so far as it is pathetic, feeble so far as it is fallacious, and, therefore, that the dominion of Truth is entire, over this, as over every other natural and just state of the human mind, we may go on to the subject for the dealing with which this prefatory inquiry became necessary; and why necessary, we shall see forthwith.

(III, 4, 11, 1-16.) (1843-60)

26. **strength.** "I cannot quit this subject without giving two more instances, both exquisite, of the pathetic fallacy, which I have just come upon, in *Maud*:
  " 'For a great speculation had failed;
  And ever he muttered and maddened, and ever wanned with
    despair;
  And out he walked, when the wind like a broken worldling
    wailed,
  And the *flying gold of the ruined woodlands* drove thro'
    the air.'
  " 'There has fallen a splendid tear
    From the passion-flower at the gate.
  The red rose cries, " ' "She is near, she is near!"
  And the white rose weeps, " ' "She is late."
  The larkspur listens, " ' "I hear, I hear!"
  And the lily whispers, " ' "I wait." '
    From Tennyson's *Maud* (1855), Part I, I, 3 and
    XXII, 10 (with ll. 3 and 4 omitted)."—Ruskin.

from *Unto This Last*

"From 1845 to 1860," wrote Ruskin, "I went on with more or less of public applause; and then in 1860 people saw a change come over me which they highly disapproved, and I went on from 1860 to 1875 under the weight of continuously increasing public recusancy and reprobation." The immediate cause of the shift in popular favor of which Ruskin was so conscious was the publication in 1860-1862 of four essays on economics called *Unto This Last*. These appeared in the *Cornhill Magazine* and were intended as the first of a greater number; such an outcry was raised against the series, however, that it was abruptly discontinued. The four surviving articles deal with employment, wages, legislative control of industry, true wealth, and other economic and social topics. Of all who read these papers at the time only Carlyle praised the author; others regarded him as a warped and impractical visionary and could not foresee that many of the reforms which he advocated would come, in time, to be generally accepted.

Essay I.

THE ROOTS OF HONOR

1. AMONG the delusions which at different periods have possessed themselves of the minds of large masses of the human race, perhaps the most curious—certainly the least creditable—is the modern *soi-disant* science of political economy, based on the idea that an advantageous code of social action may be determined irrespectively of the influence of social affection.

Of course, as in the instances of alchemy, astrology, witchcraft, and other such popular creeds, political economy has a plausible idea at the root of it. "The social affections," says the economist, "are accidental and disturbing elements in human nature; but avarice and

5. *soi-disant*, self-named, so-called.

the desire of progress are constant elements. Let us eliminate the inconstants, and, considering the human being merely as a covetous machine, examine by what laws of labor, purchase, and sale, the greatest accumulative result in wealth is attainable. Those laws once determined, it will be for each individual afterwards to introduce as much of the disturbing affectionate element as he chooses, and to determine for himself the result on the new conditions supposed."

2. This would be a perfectly logical and successful method of analysis, if the accidentals afterwards to be introduced were of the same nature as the powers first examined. Supposing a body in motion to be influenced by constant and inconstant forces, it is usually the simplest way of examining its course to trace it first under the persistent conditions, and afterwards introduce the causes of variation. But the disturbing elements in the social problem are not of the same nature as the constant ones; they alter the essence of the creature under examination the moment they are added; they operate, not mathematically, but chemically, introducing conditions which render all our previous knowledge unavailable. We made learned experiments upon pure nitrogen, and have convinced ourselves that it is a very manageable gas: but behold! the thing which we have practically to deal with is its chloride; and this, the moment we touch it on our established principles, sends us and our apparatus through the ceiling.

3. Observe, I neither impugn nor doubt the conclusions of the science, if its terms are accepted. I am simply uninterested in them, as I should be in those of a science of gymnastics which assumed that men had no skeletons. It might be shown, on that supposition, that it would be advantageous to roll the students up into pellets, flatten them into cakes, or stretch them into cables; and that when these results were effected, the re-insertion of the skeleton would be attended with various inconveniences to their constitution. The reasoning might be admirable, the conclusions true, and the science deficient only in applicability. Modern political economy stands on a precisely similar basis. Assuming, not that the human being has no skeleton, but that it is all skeleton, it founds an ossifiant theory of progress on this negation of a soul; and having shown the utmost that may be made of bones, and constructed a number of interesting geometrical figures with death's-heads and humeri, successfully proves the inconvenience of the reappearance of a soul among these corpuscular structures. I do not deny the truth of this theory: I simply deny its applicability to the present phase of the world.

4. This inapplicability has been curiously manifested during the embarrassment caused by the late strikes of our workmen. Here occurs one of the simplest cases, in a pertinent and positive form, of the first vital problem which political economy has to deal with (the relation between employer and employed); and at a severe crisis, when lives in multitudes, and wealth in masses, are at stake, the political economists are helpless—practically mute; no demonstrable solution of the difficulty can be given by them, such as may convince or calm the opposing parties. Obstinately the masters take one view of the matter; obstinately the operatives another; and no political science can set them at one.

5. It would be strange if it could, it being not by "science" of any kind that men were ever intended to be set at one. Disputant after disputant vainly strives to show that the interests of the masters are, or are not, antagonistic to those of the men: none of the pleaders ever seeming to remember that it does not absolutely or always follow that the persons must be antagonistic because their interests are. If there is only a crust of bread in the house, and mother and children are starving, their interests are not the same. If the mother eats it, the children want it; if the children eat it, the mother must go hungry to her work. Yet it does not necessarily follow that there will be "antagonism" between them, that they will fight for the crust, and that the mother, being strongest, will get it, and eat it. Neither, in any other case, whatever the relations of the persons may be, can it be assumed

52. **ossifiant**, hardening, turning to bone. 56. **death's-heads and humeri**, skulls and crossbones. 64. **late strikes**, the builders' strikes in the fall of 1859.

for certain that, because their interests are diverse, they must necessarily regard each other with hostility, and use violence or cunning to obtain the advantage.

6. Even if this were so, and it were as just as it is convenient to consider men as actuated by no other moral influences than those which affect rats or swine, the logical conditions of the question are still indeterminable. It can never be shown generally either that the interests of master and laborer are alike, or that they are opposed; for, according to circumstances, they may be either. It is, indeed, always the interest of both that the work should be rightly done, and a just price obtained for it; but, in the division of profits, the gain of the one may or may not be the loss of the other. It is not the master's interest to pay wages so low as to leave the men sickly and depressed, nor the workman's interest to be paid high wages if the smallness of the master's profit hinders him from enlarging his business, or conducting it in a safe and liberal way. A stoker ought not to desire high pay if the company is too poor to keep the engine wheels in repair.

7. And the varieties of circumstances which influence these reciprocal interests are so endless, that all endeavor to deduce rules of action from balance of expediency is in vain. And it is meant to be in vain. For no human actions ever were intended by the Maker of men to be guided by balances of expediency, but by balances of justice. He has therefore rendered all endeavors to determine expediency futile for evermore. No man ever knew, or can know, what will be the ultimate result to himself, or to others, of any given line of conduct. But every man may know, and most of us do know, what is a just and unjust act. And all of us may know also, that the consequences of justice will be ultimately the best possible, both to others and ourselves, though we can neither say what *is* best, nor how it is likely to come to pass.

I have said balances of justice, meaning, in the term justice, to include affection—such affection as one man *owes* to another. All right relations between master and operative, and all their best interests, ultimately depend on these.

8. We shall find the best and simplest illustration of the relations of master and operative in the position of domestic servants.

We will suppose that the master of a household desires only to get as much work out of his servants as he can, at the rate of wages he gives. He never allows them to be idle; feeds them as poorly and lodges them as ill as they will endure, and in all things pushes his requirements to the exact point beyond which he cannot go without forcing the servant to leave him. In doing this, there is no violation on his part of what is commonly called "justice." He agrees with the domestic for his whole time and service, and takes them;—the limits of hardship in treatment being fixed by the practice of other masters in his neighborhood; that is to say, by the current rate of wages for domestic labor. If the servant can get a better place, he is free to take one, and the master can only tell what is the real market value of his labor, by requiring as much as he will give.

This is the politico-economical view of the case, according to the doctors of that science; who assert that by this procedure the greatest average of work will be obtained from the servant, and therefore, the greatest benefit to the community, and through the community, by reversion, to the servant himself.

That, however, is not so. It would be so if the servant were an engine of which the motive power was steam, magnetism, gravitation, or any other agent of calculable force. But he being, on the contrary, an engine whose motive power is a Soul, the force of this very peculiar agent, as an unknown quantity, enters into all the political economist's equations, without his knowledge, and falsifies every one of their results. The largest quantity of work will not be done by this curious engine for pay, or under pressure, or by help of any kind of fuel which may be supplied by the chaldron. It will be done only when the motive force, that is to say, the will or spirit of the creature, is brought to its greatest strength by its own proper fuel; namely, by the affections.

9. It may indeed happen, and does happen often, that if the master is a man of sense and energy, a large quantity of material work may

be done under mechanical pressure, enforced by strong will and guided by wise method; also it may happen, and does happen often, that if the master is indolent and weak (however good-natured), a very small quantity of work, and that bad, may be produced by the servant's undirected strength, and contemptuous gratitude. But the universal law of the matter is that, assuming any given quantity of energy and sense in master and servant, the greatest material result obtainable by them will be, not through antagonism to each other, but through affection for each other; and that if the master, instead of endeavoring to get as much work as possible from the servant, seeks rather to render his appointed and necessary work beneficial to him, and to forward his interests in all just and wholesome ways, the real amount of work ultimately done, or of good rendered, by the person so cared for, will indeed be the greatest possible.

Observe, I say, "of good rendered," for a servant's work is not necessarily or always the best thing he can give his master. But good of all kinds, whether in material service, in protective watchfulness of his master's interest and credit, or in joyful readiness to seize unexpected and irregular occasions of help.

Nor is this one whit less generally true because indulgence will be frequently abused, and kindness met with ingratitude. For the servant who, gently treated, is ungrateful, treated ungently, will be revengeful; and the man who is dishonest to a liberal master will be injurious to an unjust one.

10. In any case, and with any person, this unselfish treatment will produce the most effective return. Observe, I am here considering the affections wholly as a motive power; not at all as things in themselves desirable or noble, or in any other way abstractedly good. I look at them simply as an anomalous force, rendering every one of the ordinary political economist's calculations nugatory; while, even if he desired to introduce this new element into his estimates, he has no power of dealing with it; for the affections only become a true motive power when they ignore every other motive and condition of political economy. Treat the servant kindly, with the idea of turning his gratitude to account, and you will get, as you deserve, no gratitude, nor any value for your kindness; but treat him kindly without any economical purpose, and all economical purposes will be answered; in this, as in all other matters, whosoever will save his life shall lose it, whoso loses it shall find it.

11. The next clearest and simplest example of relation between master and operative is that which exists between the commander of a regiment and his men.

Supposing the officer only desires to apply the rules of discipline so as, with least trouble to himself, to make the regiment most effective, he will not be able, by any rules, or administration of rules, on this selfish principle, to develop the full strength of his subordinates. If a man of sense and firmness, he may, as in the former instance, produce a better result than would be obtained by the irregular kindness of a weak officer; but let the sense and firmness be the same in both cases, and assuredly the officer who has the most direct personal relations with his men, the most care for their interests, and the most value for their lives, will develop their effective strength, through their affection for his own person, and trust in his character, to a degree wholly unattainable by other means. The law applies still more stringently as the numbers concerned are larger; a charge may often be successful, though the men dislike their officers;

56. **whosoever . . . it.** From *Matthew*, 16:25. "The difference between the two modes of treatment, and between their effective material results, may be seen very accurately by a comparison of the relations of Esther and Charlie in *Bleak House*, with those of Miss Brass and the Marchioness in *Master Humphrey's Clock*. The essential value and truth of Dickens's writings have been unwisely lost sight of by many thoughtful persons, merely because he presents his truth with some color of caricature. Unwisely, because Dickens's caricature, though often gross, is never mistaken. Allowing for his manner of telling them, the things he tells us are always true. I wish that he could think it right to limit his brilliant exaggeration to works written only for public amusement; and when he takes up a subject of high national importance, such as that which he handled in *Hard Times*, that he would use severer and more accurate analysis. The usefulness of that work (to my mind, in several respects, the greatest he has written) is with many persons seriously diminished because Mr. Bounderby is a dramatic monster, instead of a characteristic example of a worldly master; and Stephen Blackpool a dramatic perfection, instead of a characteristic example of an honest workman. But let us not lose the use of Dickens's wit and insight, because he chooses to speak in a circle of stage fire. He is entirely right in his main drift and purpose in every book he has written; and all of them, but especially *Hard Times*, should be studied with close and earnest care by persons interested in social questions. They will find much that is partial, and, because partial, apparently unjust; but if they examine all the evidence on the other side, which Dickens seems to overlook, it will appear, after all their trouble, that his view was the finally right one, grossly and sharply told."—Ruskin.

a battle has rarely been won, unless they loved their general.

12. Passing from these simple examples to the more complicated relations existing between a manufacturer and his workmen, we are met first by certain curious difficulties, resulting, apparently, from a harder and colder state of moral elements. It is easy to imagine an enthusiastic affection existing among soldiers for the colonel. Not so easy to imagine an enthusiastic affection among cotton-spinners for the proprietor of the mill. A body of men associated for purposes of robbery (as a Highland clan in ancient times) shall be animated by perfect affection, and every member of it be ready to lay down his life for the life of his chief. But a band of men associated for purposes of legal production and accumulation is usually animated, it appears, by no such emotions, and none of them are in anywise willing to give his life for the life of his chief. Not only are we met by this apparent anomaly, in moral matters, but by others connected with it, in administration of system. For a servant or a soldier is engaged at a definite rate of wages, for a definite period; but a workman at a rate of wages variable according to the demand for labor, and with the risk of being at any time thrown out of his situation by chances of trade. Now, as, under these contingencies, no action of the affections can take place, but only an explosive action of *dis*affections, two points offer themselves for consideration in the matter.

The first—How far the rate of wages may be so regulated as not to vary with the demand for labor.

The second—How far it is possible that bodies of workmen may be engaged and maintained at such fixed rate of wages (whatever the state of trade may be), without enlarging or diminishing their number, so as to give them permanent interest in the establishment with which they are connected, like that of the domestic servants in an old family, or an *esprit de corps,* like that of the soldiers in a crack regiment.

13. The first question is, I say, how far it may be possible to fix the rate of wages irrespectively of the demand for labor.

Perhaps one of the most curious facts in the history of human error is the denial by the common political economist of the possibility of thus regulating wages; while, for all the important, and much of the unimportant, labor on the earth, wages are already so regulated.

We do not sell our prime-ministership by Dutch auction; nor, on the decease of a bishop, whatever may be the general advantages of simony, do we (yet) offer his diocese to the clergyman who will take the episcopacy at the lowest contract. We (with exquisite sagacity of political economy!) do indeed sell commissions, but not openly, generalships: sick, we do not inquire for a physician who takes less than a guinea; litigious, we never think of reducing six-and-eightpence to four-and-sixpence; caught in a shower, we do not canvass the cabmen, to find one who values his driving at less than sixpence a mile.

It is true that in all these cases there is, and in every conceivable case there must be, ultimate reference to the presumed difficulty of the work, or number of candidates for the office. If it were thought that the labor necessary to make a good physician would be gone through by a sufficient number of students with the prospect of only half-guinea fees, public consent would soon withdraw the unnecessary half-guinea. In this ultimate sense, the price of labor is indeed always regulated by the demand for it; but so far as the practical and immediate administration of the matter is regarded, the best labor always has been, and is, as *all* labor ought to be, paid by an invariable standard.

14. "What!" the reader perhaps answers amazedly: "pay good and bad workmen alike?"

Certainly. The difference between one prelate's sermons and his successor's—or between one physician's opinion and another's—is far greater, as respects the qualities of mind in-

---

14. **Highland clan.** Cf. the Robin Hood ballads (Vol. I, pp. 126-129).

58. **Dutch auction,** the public offer of property at a price above its value and the subsequent lowering of the price until a purchaser is found. 60. **simony,** buying or selling ecclesiastical preferment. 66. **litigious . . . four-and-sixpence,** if involved in a lawsuit, we do not quibble over the fee asked by a good lawyer. 88. **"pay . . . alike?"** This condition has resulted from the establishment of labor unions.

volved, and far more important in result to you personally, than the difference between good and bad laying of bricks (though that is greater than most people suppose). Yet you pay with equal fee, contentedly, the good and bad workmen upon your soul, and the good and bad workmen upon your body; much more may you pay, contentedly, with equal fees, the good and bad workmen upon your house.

"Nay, but I choose my physician and (?) my clergyman, thus indicating my sense of the quality of their work." By all means, also, choose your bricklayer; that is the proper reward of the good workman, to be "chosen." The natural and right system respecting all labor is, that it should be paid at a fixed rate, but the good workman employed, and the bad workman unemployed. The false, unnatural, and destructive system is when the bad workman is allowed to offer his work at half-price, and either take the place of the good, or force him by his competition to work for an inadequate sum.

15. This equality of wages, then, being the first object towards which we have to discover the directest available road; the second is, as above stated, that of maintaining constant numbers of workmen in employment, whatever may be the accidental demand for the article they produce.

I believe the sudden and extensive inequalities of demand which necessarily arise in the mercantile operations of an active nation, constitute the only essential difficulty which has to be overcome in a just organization of labor. The subject opens into too many branches to admit of being investigated in a paper of this kind; but the following general facts bearing on it may be noted.

The wages which enable any workman to live are necessarily higher, if his work is liable to intermission, than if it is assured and continuous; and however severe the struggle for work may become, the general law will always hold, that men must get more daily pay if, on the average, they can only calculate on work three days a week, than they would require if they were sure of work six days a week. Supposing that a man cannot live on less than a shilling a day, his seven shillings he must get, either for three days' violent work, or six days' deliberate work. The tendency of all modern mercantile operations is to throw both wages and trade into the form of a lottery, and to make the workman's pay depend on intermittent exertion, and the principal's profit on dexterously used chance.

16. In what partial degree, I repeat, this may be necessary, in consequence of the activities of modern trade, I do not here investigate; contenting myself with the fact, that in its fatallest aspects it is assuredly unnecessary, and results merely from love of gambling on the part of the masters, and from ignorance and sensuality in the men. The masters cannot bear to let any opportunity of gain escape them, and frantically rush at every gap and breach in the walls of Fortune, raging to be rich, and affronting, with impatient covetousness, every risk of ruin; while the men prefer three days of violent labor, and three days of drunkenness, to six days of moderate work and wise rest. There is no way in which a principal, who really desires to help his workmen, may do it more effectually than by checking these disorderly habits both in himself and them; keeping his own business operations on a scale which will enable him to pursue them securely, not yielding to temptations of precarious gain; and, at the same time, leading his workmen into regular habits of labor and life, either by inducing them rather to take low wages in the form of a fixed salary, than high wages, subject to the chance of their being thrown out of work; or, if this be impossible, by discouraging the system of violent exertion for nominally high day wages, and leading the men to take lower pay for more regular labor.

In effecting any radical changes of this kind, doubtless there would be great inconvenience and loss incurred by all the originators of movement. That which can be done with perfect convenience and without loss, is not always the thing that most needs to be

---

11. **and (?).** Ruskin isn't quite sure about his choosing his clergyman.

done, or which we are most imperatively required to do.

17. I have already alluded to the difference hitherto existing between regiments of men associated for purposes of violence, and for purposes of manufacture; in that the former appear capable of self-sacrifice—the latter, not; which singular fact is the real reason of the general lowness of estimate in which the profession of commerce is held, as compared with that of arms. Philosophically, it does not, at first sight, appear reasonable (many writers have endeavored to prove it unreasonable) that a peaceable and rational person, whose trade is buying and selling, should be held in less honor than an unpeaceable and often irrational person, whose trade is slaying. Nevertheless, the consent of mankind has always, in spite of the philosophers, given precedence to the soldier.

And this is right.

For the soldier's trade, verily and essentially, is not slaying, but being slain. This, without well knowing its own meaning, the world honors it for. A bravo's trade is slaying; but the world has never respected bravos more than merchants: the reason it honors the soldier is, because he holds his life at the service of the State. Reckless he may be—fond of pleasure or of adventure—all kinds of by-motives and mean impulses may have determined the choice of his profession, and may affect (to all appearance exclusively) his daily conduct in it; but our estimate of him is based on this ultimate fact—of which we are well assured—that, put him in a fortress breach, with all the pleasures of the world behind him, and only death and his duty in front of him, he will keep his face to the front; and he knows that this choice may be put to him at any moment, and has beforehand taken his part—virtually takes such part continually—does, in reality, die daily.

18. Not less is the respect we pay to the lawyer and physician, founded ultimately on their self-sacrifice. Whatever the learning or acuteness of a great lawyer, our chief respect for him depends on our belief that, set in a judge's seat, he will strive to judge justly, come of it what may. Could we suppose that he would take bribes, and use his acuteness and legal knowledge to give plausibility to iniquitous decisions, no degree of intellect would win for him our respect. Nothing will win it, short of our tacit conviction, that in all important acts of his life justice is first with him; his own interest, second.

In the case of a physician, the ground of the honor we render him is clearer still. Whatever his science, we should shrink from him in horror if we found him regard his patients merely as subjects to experiment upon; much more, if we found that, receiving bribes from persons interested in their deaths, he was using his best skill to give poison in the mask of medicine.

Finally, the principle holds with utmost clearness as it respects clergymen. No goodness of disposition will excuse want of science in a physician or of shrewdness in an advocate; but a clergyman, even though his power of intellect be small, is respected on the presumed ground of his unselfishness and serviceableness.

19. Now there can be no question but that the tact, foresight, decision, and other mental powers, required for the successful management of a large mercantile concern, if not such as could be compared with those of a great lawyer, general, or divine, would at least match the general conditions of mind required in the subordinate officers of a ship, or of a regiment, or in the curate of a country parish. If, therefore, all the efficient members of the so-called liberal professions are still, somehow, in public estimate of honor, preferred before the head of a commercial firm, the reason must lie deeper than in the measurement of their several powers of mind.

And the essential reason for such preference will be found to lie in the fact that the merchant is presumed to act always selfishly. His work may be very necessary to the community; but the motive of it is understood to be wholly personal. The merchant's first object in all his dealings must be (the public believe) to get as much for himself, and leave

---

18. **consent . . . soldier.** Ruskin is only partly accurate here. Cf. Kipling's *Tommy*, p. 887. 43. **die daily.** A phrase St. Paul applies to himself in *1 Corinthians*, 15:31.

as little to his neighbor (or customer) as possible. Enforcing this upon him, by political statute, as the necessary principle of his action; recommending it to him on all occasions, and themselves reciprocally adopting it; proclaiming vociferously, for law of the universe, that a buyer's function is to cheapen, and a seller's to cheat—the public, nevertheless, involuntarily condemn the man of commerce for his compliance with their own statement, and stamp him forever as belonging to an inferior grade of human personality.

20. This they will find, eventually, they must give up doing. They must not cease to condemn selfishness; but they will have to discover a kind of commerce which is not exclusively selfish. Or, rather, they will have to discover that there never was, or can be, any other kind of commerce; that this which they have called commerce was not commerce at all, but cozening; and that a true merchant differs as much from a merchant according to laws of modern political economy, as the hero of the *Excursion* from Autolycus. They will find that commerce is an occupation which gentlemen will every day see more need to engage in, rather than in the businesses of talking to men, or slaying them: that, in true commerce, as in true preaching, or true fighting, it is necessary to admit the idea of occasional voluntary loss;—that sixpences have to be lost, as well as lives, under a sense of duty; that the market may have its martyrdoms as well as the pulpit; and trade its heroisms, as well as war.

May have—in the final issue, must have—and only has not had yet, because men of heroic temper have always been misguided in their youth into other fields, not recognizing what is in our days, perhaps, the most important of all fields; so that, while many a zealous person loses his life in trying to teach the form of a gospel, very few will lose a hundred pounds in showing the practice of one.

21. The fact is, that people never have had clearly explained to them the true functions of a merchant with respect to other people. I should like the reader to be very clear about this.

Five great intellectual professions, relating to daily necessities of life, have hitherto existed —three exist necessarily, in every civilized nation:

The Soldier's profession is to *defend* it.
The Pastor's to *teach* it.
The Physician's, to *keep it in health*.
The Lawyer's, to *enforce justice* in it.
The Merchant's, to *provide* for it.

And the duty of all these men is, on due occasion, to *die* for it.

"On due occasion," namely:

The Soldier, rather than leave his post in battle.

The Physician, rather than leave his post in plague.

The Pastor, rather than teach Falsehood.

The Lawyer, rather than countenance Injustice.

The Merchant—What is *his* "due occasion" of death?

22. It is the main question for the merchant, as for all of us. For, truly, the man who does not know when to die, does not know how to live.

Observe, the merchant's function (or manufacturer's, for in the broad sense in which it is here used the word must be understood to include both) is to provide for the nation. It is no more his function to get profit for himself out of that provision than it is a clergyman's function to get his stipend. The stipend is a due and necessary adjunct, but not the object, of his life, if he be a true clergyman, any more than his fee (or *honorarium*) is the object of life to a true physician. Neither is his fee the object of life to a true merchant. All three, if true men, have a work to be done irrespective of fee—to be done even at any cost, or for quite the contrary of fee; the pastor's function being to teach, the physician's to heal, and the merchant's, as I have said, to provide. That is to say, he has to understand to their very root the qualities of the thing he deals in, and the means of obtaining or producing it; and he has to apply all his sagacity and energy to the producing or obtaining it in perfect state, and

---

24. **hero . . . Autolycus.** The hero of Wordsworth's *Excursion* is a mild and pious recluse; Autolycus, in Shakespeare's *Winter's Tale*, is a thieving rogue.

distributing it at the cheapest possible price where it is most needed.

And because the production or obtaining of any commodity involves necessarily the agency of many lives and hands, the merchant becomes in the course of his business the master and governor of large masses of men in a more direct, though less confessed way, than a military officer or pastor; so that on him falls, in great part, the responsibility for the kind of life they lead: and it becomes his duty, not only to be always considering how to produce what he sells in the purest and cheapest forms, but how to make the various employments involved in the production, or transference of it, most beneficial to the men employed.

23. And as into these two functions, requiring for their right exercise the highest intelligence, as well as patience, kindness, and tact, the merchant is bound to put all his energy, so for their just discharge he is bound, as soldier or physician is bound, to give up, if need be, his life, in such way as it may be demanded of him. Two main points he has in his providing function to maintain: first, his engagements (faithfulness to engagements being the real root of all possibilities in commerce); and, secondly, the perfectness and purity of the thing provided; so that, rather than fail in any engagement, or consent to any deterioration, adulteration, or unjust and exorbitant price of that which he provides, he is bound to meet fearlessly any form of distress, poverty, or labor, which may, through maintenance of these points, come upon him.

24. Again: in his office as governor of the men employed by him, the merchant or manufacturer is invested with a distinctly paternal authority and responsibility. In most cases, a youth entering a commercial establishment is withdrawn altogether from home influence; his master must become his father, else he has, for practical and constant help, no father at hand: in all cases the master's authority, together with the general tone and atmosphere of his business, and the character of the men with whom the youth is compelled in the course of it to associate, have more immediate and pressing weight than the home influence, and will usually neutralize it either for good or evil; so that the only means which the master has of doing justice to the men employed by him is to ask himself sternly whether he is dealing with such subordinate as he would with his own son, if compelled by circumstances to take such a position.

Supposing the captain of a frigate saw it right, or were by any chance obliged, to place his own son in the position of a common sailor; as he would then treat his son, he is bound always to treat every one of the men under him. So, also, supposing the master of a manufactory saw it right, or were by any chance obliged, to place his own son in the position of an ordinary workman; as he would then treat his son, he is bound always to treat every one of his men. This is the only effective, true, or practical RULE which can be given on this point of political economy.

And as the captain of a ship is bound to be the last man to leave his ship in case of wreck, and to share his last crust with the sailors in case of famine, so the manufacturer, in any commercial crisis or distress, is bound to take the suffering of it with his men, and even to take more of it for himself than he allows his men to feel; as a father would in a famine, shipwreck, or battle, sacrifice himself for his son.

25. All which sounds very strange: the only real strangeness in the matter being, nevertheless, that it should so sound. For all this is true, and that not partially nor theoretically, but everlastingly and practically: all other doctrine than this respecting matters political being false in premises, absurd in deduction, and impossible in practice, consistently with any progressive state of national life; all the life which we now possess as a nation showing itself in the resolute denial and scorn, by a few strong minds and faithful hearts, of the economic principles taught to our multitudes, which principles, so far as accepted, lead straight to national destruction. Respecting the modes and forms of destruction to which they lead, and, on the other hand, respecting the farther practical working of true polity, I hope to reason further in a following paper. (1860)

from *The Relation of Art to Morals*

> From 1870 until his breakdown in 1879 and for a second period in 1883-1884 Ruskin was at Oxford University as Slade Professor of Art. His lectures were so pungent, informative, and vigorous that great crowds often attended them, and Ruskin was frequently forced to repeat his discourses. In recognition of his notable success he was elected honorary fellow of Corpus Christi College. Out of his appointment at Oxford came eight volumes of lectures, many of which—like the following—contain repetitions or elaborations of theories which he expressed earlier in *Modern Painters, The Stones of Venice,* and other publications. To Ruskin great art was inseparable from a sound life in the individual, nation, and race; and this belief provided the channel that connected his conceptions of art and his theories of economics.

... AND NOW I pass to the arts with which I have special concern, in which, though the facts are exactly the same, I shall have more difficulty in proving my assertion, because very few of us are as cognizant of the merit of painting as we are of that of language; and I can only show you whence that merit springs, after having thoroughly shown you in what it consists. But in the meantime, I have simply to tell you, that the manual arts are as accurate exponents of ethical state, as other modes of expression; first, with absolute precision, of that of the workman; and then with precision, disguised by many distorting influences, of that of the nation to which it belongs.

And, first, they are a perfect exponent of the mind of the workman: but, being so, remember, if the mind be great or complex, the art is not an easy book to read; for we must ourselves possess all the mental characters of which we are to read the signs. No man can read the evidence of labor who is not himself laborious, for he does not know what the work cost: nor can he read the evidence of true passion if he is not passionate; nor of gentleness if he is not gentle: and the most subtle signs of fault and weakness of character he can only judge by having had the same faults to fight with. I myself, for instance, know impatient work, and tired work, better than most critics, because I am myself always impatient, and often tired: so also, the patient and indefatigable touch of a mighty master becomes more wonderful to me than to others.

Yet, wonderful in no mean measure it will be to you all, when I make it manifest;—and as soon as we begin our real work, and you have learned what it is to draw a true line, I shall be able to make manifest to you—and undisputably so—that the day's work of a man like Mantegna or Paul Veronese consists of an unfaltering, uninterrupted, succession of movements of the hand more precise than those of the finest fencer: the pencil leaving one point and arriving at another, not only with unerring precision at the extremity of the line, but with an unerring and yet varied course—sometimes over spaces a foot or more in extent—yet a course so determined everywhere that either of these men could, and Veronese often does, draw a finished profile, or any other portion of the contour of the face with one line, not afterwards changed. Try, first, to realize to yourselves the muscular precision of that action, and the intellectual strain of it; for the movement of a fencer is perfect in practiced monotony; but the movement of the hand of a great painter is at every instant governed by direct and new intention. Then imagine that muscular firmness and subtlety, and the instantaneously selective and ordinant energy of the brain, sustained all day long, not only without fatigue, but with a visible joy in the exertion, like that which an eagle seems to take in the wave of his wings, and this all life long, and through long life, not only without failure of power, but with visible increase of it, until the actu-

---

4. **my assertion.** That fine art has three functions—"the enforcing of the religious sentiments of men, the perfecting of their ethical state, and the doing them material service." 13. **the workman,** the artist.

42. **Mantegna,** Andrea Mantegna (1431-1506), an Italian painter and engraver; his work is noted for its precision of outline. **Paul Veronese** (1530-1588), a well-known painter of the Venetian School. 63. **ordinant,** commanding, placing in order.

ally organic changes of old age. And then consider, so far as you know anything of physiology, what sort of an ethical state of body and mind that means!—ethic through ages past! what fineness of race there must be to get it, what exquisite balance and symmetry of the vital powers! And then, finally, determine for yourselves whether a manhood like that is consistent with any viciousness of soul, with any mean anxiety, any gnawing lust, any wretchedness of spite or remorse, any consciousness of rebellion against law of God or man, or any actual, though unconscious violation of even the least law to which obedience is essential for the glory of life, and the pleasing of its Giver.

It is, of course, true that many of the strong masters had deep faults of character, but their faults always show in their work. It is true that some could not govern their passions; if so, they died young, or they painted ill when old. But the greater part of our misapprehension in the whole matter is from our not having well known who the great painters were, and taking delight in the petty skill that was bred in the fumes of the taverns of the North, instead of theirs who breathed empyreal air, sons of the morning, under the woods of Assisi and the crags of Cadore.

It is true, however, also, as I have pointed out long ago, that the strong masters fall into two great divisions, one leading simple and natural lives, the other restrained in a Puritanism of the worship of beauty; and these two manners of life you may recognize in a moment by their work. Generally the naturalists are the strongest; but there are two of the Puritans, whose work if I can succeed in making clearly understandable to you during my three years here, it is all I need care to do. But of these two Puritans one I cannot name to you, and the other I at present will not. One I cannot, for no one knows his name, except the baptismal one, Bernard, or "dear little Bernard"—Bernardino, called from his birthplace (Luino, on the Lago Magiore), Bernard of Luino. The other is a Venetian, of whom many of you probably have never heard, and of whom, through me, you shall not hear, until I have tried to get some picture by him over to England. . . .

Finally, you must remember that great obscurity has been brought upon the truth in this matter by the want of integrity and simplicity in our modern life. I mean integrity in the Latin sense, wholeness. Everything is broken up, and mingled in confusion, both in our habits and thoughts; besides being in great part imitative: so that you not only cannot tell what a man is, but sometimes you cannot tell whether he *is* at all!—whether you have indeed to do with a spirit, or only with an echo. And thus the same inconsistencies appear now, between the work of artists of merit and their personal characters, as those which you find continually disappointing expectation in the lives of men of modern literary power;— the same conditions of society having obscured or misdirected the best qualities of the imagination, both in our literature and art. Thus there is no serious question with any of us as to the personal character of Dante and Giotto, of Shakespeare and Holbein; but we pause timidly in the attempt to analyze the moral laws of the art skill in recent poets, novelists, and painters.

Let me assure you once for all, that as you grow older, if you enable yourselves to distinguish by the truth of your own lives, what is true in those of other men, you will gradually perceive that all good has its origin in good, never in evil; that the fact of either literature or painting being truly fine of their kind, whatever their mistaken aim, or partial error, is proof of their noble origin: and that, if there is indeed sterling value in the thing done, it has come of a sterling worth in the soul that did it, however alloyed or defiled by conditions of sin which are sometimes more appalling or more strange than those which

---

25. **skill . . . North.** Ruskin refers to Dutch art, for which he had strong dislike; he preferred the art of Italy. 29. **Assisi,** a district in central Italy. **Cadore,** a town in northern Italy. 30. **pointed out.** In *The Stones of Venice*, II, 10 (1853). 40. **three years here,** at Oxford University; see headnote. 45. **Bernardino,** a noted Italian painter of the sixteenth century; a pupil of Leonardo da Vinci. 47. **The other,** Vittorio Carpaccio (c. 1450-c. 1522). The National Gallery, London, purchased one of his pictures in 1865 for £3400. 73. **Dante.** See p. 556, note 54. **Giotto,** a celebrated Florentine painter, sculptor, and architect. When asked by a messenger of the Pope for a specimen of his work, Giotto sent a perfect circle drawn freehand. 74. **Holbein,** Hans Holbein (c. 1460-1524), an eminent German painter.

all may detect in their own hearts, because they are part of a personality altogether larger than ours, and as far beyond our judgment in its darkness as beyond our following in its light. And it is sufficient warning against what some might dread as the probable effect of such a conviction on your own minds, namely, that you might permit yourselves in the weakness which you imagined to be allied to genius, when they took the form of personal temptations;—it is surely, I say, sufficient warning against so mean a folly, to discern, as you may with little pains, that, of all human existences, the lives of men of that distorted and tainted nobility of intellect are probably the most miserable.

I pass to the second, and for us the more practically important question, What is the effect of noble art upon other men; what has it done for national morality in time past: and what effect is the extended knowledge or possession of it likely to have upon us now? And here we are at once met by the facts, which are as gloomy as indisputable, that while many peasant populations, among whom scarcely the rudest practice of art has ever been attempted, have lived in comparative innocence, honor, and happiness, the worst foulness and cruelty of savage tribes have been frequently associated with fine ingenuities of decorative design; also, that no people has ever attained the higher stages of art skill, except at a period of its civilization which was sullied by frequent, violent, and even monstrous crime; and, lastly, that the attaining of perfection in art power, has been hitherto, in every nation, the accurate signal of the beginning of its ruin.

Respecting which phenomena, observe first, that although good never springs out of evil, it is developed to its highest by contention with evil. There are some groups of peasantry, in far-away nooks of Christian countries, who are nearly as innocent as lambs; but the morality which gives power to art is the morality of men, not of cattle.

Secondly, the virtues of the inhabitants of many country districts are apparent, not real; their lives are indeed artless, but not innocent; and it is only the monotony of circumstances, and the absence of temptation, which prevent the exhibition of evil passions not less real because often dormant, nor less foul because shown only in petty faults, or inactive malignities.

But you will observe also that *absolute* artlessness, to men in any kind of moral health, is impossible; they have always, at least, the art by which they live—agriculture or seamanship; and in these industries, skilfully practiced, you will find the law of their moral training; while, whatever the adversity of circumstances, every rightly-minded peasantry, such as that of Sweden, Denmark, Bavaria, or Switzerland, has associated with its needful industry a quite studied school of pleasurable art in dress; and generally also in song, and simple domestic architecture.

Again, I need not repeat to you here what I endeavored to explain in the first lecture in the book I called *The Two Paths*, respecting the arts of savage races: but I may now note briefly that such arts are the result of an intellectual activity which has found no room to expand, and which the tyranny of nature or of man has condemned to disease through arrested growth. And where neither Christianity, nor any other religion conveying some moral help, has reached, the animal energy of such races necessarily flames into ghastly conditions of evil, and the grotesque or frightful forms assumed by their art are precisely indicative of their distorted moral nature.

But the truly great nations nearly always begin from a race possessing this imaginative power; and for some time their progress is very slow, and their state not one of innocence, but of feverish and faultful animal energy. This is gradually subdued and exalted into bright human life; the art instinct purifying itself with the rest of the nature, until social perfectness is nearly reached; and then comes the period when conscience and intellect are so highly developed, that new forms of error begin in the inability to fulfill the demands of the one, or to answer the doubts of the other. Then the wholeness of the people is lost; all kinds of hypocrisies

---

71. *The Two Paths,* two lectures delivered in 1858-1859 and published in 1859.

and oppositions of science develop themselves; their faith is questioned on one side, and compromised with on the other; wealth commonly increases at the same period to a destructive extent; luxury follows; and the ruin of the nation is then certain: while the arts, all this time, are simply, as I said at first, the exponents of each phase of its moral state, and no more control it in its political career than the gleam of the firefly guides its oscillation. It is true that their most splendid results are usually obtained in the swiftness of the power which is hurrying to the precipice; but to lay the charge of the catastrophe to the art by which it is illumined is to find a cause for the cataract in the hues of its iris. It is true that the colossal vices belonging to periods of great national wealth (for wealth, you will find, is the real root of all evil) can turn every good gift and skill of nature or of man to evil purpose. If, in such times, fair pictures have been misused, how much more fair realities? And if Miranda is immoral to Caliban, is that Miranda's fault? . . . (1870)

16. **iris**, rainbow-effect produced by spray from the cataract or waterfall. 18. **wealth . . . evil.** Cf. *1 Timothy*, 6:10: "For the love of money is the root of all evil." 23. **Miranda**, the daughter of Prospero in Shakespeare's *Tempest*. 24. **Caliban**, a brutal and degraded slave of Prospero.

Matthew Arnold

1822-1888

One of the best classical scholars and most brilliant literary critics of the Victorian age was Matthew Arnold. He was born in Laleham in 1822, the eldest son of Thomas Arnold, the famous head master of Rugby. He entered Rugby in 1837, studied there under his father's direction, and proceeded to Oxford four years later. Here he studied hard at the classics, earned the Newdigate poetry prize with a poem called *Cromwell*, refused to be stirred by Newman and the other "Oxford malignants," and won in 1844 a fellowship at Oriel. Leaving Oxford, he became secretary to Lord Lansdowne in 1847, and shortly afterwards accepted a government post as inspector of schools which he was destined to hold for the rest of his active life. Much of the work connected with his new post he found sheer drudgery, but his born instinct for educational work and his stern sense of duty led him to make the most of the position. It enabled him in 1851 to marry Frances Lucy Wightman, to whom he had been long engaged. In 1859 Arnold was made foreign assistant commissioner on education. The new appointment took him to the continent for an extensive study of the school systems. As a result of his investigations he wrote *Popular Education in France* (1861), *A French Eton* (1864), and *Schools and Universities on the Continent* (1868)—reports so accurate and illuminating that they became standard educational treatises. Oxford honored him in 1857 by an appointment to the chair of poetry, and he lectured there for ten years. In 1883 he made what had come by that time to be, for English men of letters, the usual American lecture tour; the lectures appeared under the title *Discourses in America*. Three years later he resigned his school inspectorship and was retired on a state pension. He died at Liverpool on April 15, 1888.

Matthew Arnold was one of the most active and most dissatisfied men of the Victorian age. His morbid conviction that the times were out of joint and the rather aloof austerity with which he set himself to the task of setting them right earned for him the popular and not entirely inaccurate epithet of "the kid-glove Jeremiah."

Arnold's prescription for the "doubts, disputes, distractions, fears" of the Victorians was essentially the medicine of culture. This he defined as being a compound of "sweetness and light" and consisting of a knowledge of "the best that has been thought and said in the world." The materialism of his own time he hated; the "machinery" upon which the Victorians depended so smugly he condemned as utterly futile. His theory of culture led him backward to Greek and Roman civilization, and he sought to "Hellenize" Victorian life by stripping away the emotional elements that were the Hebrew—or Puritan—parts and by bringing everybody to "see life steadily and see it whole." The hope for the future of England lay, he believed—if any hope could be felt at all—not in the aristocrats, whom he called Barbarians, nor with the working classes, whom he called the Populace, but with the great middle class of Philistines. But the Philistine he defined as the "strong, dogged, unenlightened opponent of light." Philistines were crude, vulgar, uncultured; still, what he spoke and wrote for the cure of Victorian England he addressed to them.

Like Newman's, Arnold's lectures and essays were often controversial. He engaged with Huxley in an extended debate on the place of the scientific method in education and defended "cultural" education with intensity and vigor. In the field of social comment his best known books are *Culture and Anarchy* (1869) and *Friendship's Garland* (1871).

The diversity of Arnold's interests led him not only into the fields of social relations and education but also into that of religion. For the Tractarians he had no use whatever, and he cared as little for narrow dogmatism. He may justly be called, in fact, both the prose master and the poet of agnosticism. His conceptions of religion in its relation to society are expressed in language vigorous and direct almost to the point of bigotry in *St. Paul and Protestantism* (1870), *Literature and Dogma* (1873), *God and the Bible* (1875), and *Last Essays on Church and Religion* (1877). His attitude on religion is indicated in his famous definition of it as "morality touched with emotion."

Arnold was not only a critic of life; he was also a brilliant critic of literature. His devotion to Greek culture did not deter him from reading and admiring the work of his Continental contemporaries. He was, indeed, more interested in Continental than in English writers and brought himself eagerly under the influence of Goethe, Sainte-Beuve, and other German and French critics and creators. In Greek literature Homer and Sophocles influenced him most; in English literature he owed most to Wordsworth. Arnold's skill as a critic lies not only in penetrating understanding of literature but in an unexcelled power of stating literary theories in unforgettable words. Scores of stock phrases in criticism were originally Arnold's; "the grand style" in poetry, poetry the "criticism of life," "detachment" the chief requisite in literary criticism, "high seriousness" a requisite of great literature, and many others are his coinages. He had, moreover, the educator's instinct for emphasizing by repetition, and in his lectures and essays his vigorous phrases and sentences recur like the repeated text in a sermon. The best of Arnold's literary criticisms appeared in *Essays in Criticism* (1865-1888), *The Study of Celtic Literature* (1867), and *On Translating Homer* (1861).

Arnold's poetry was almost all written early in his career. He abandoned this form of expression, he said, because prose gave him a wider audience. It is questionable whether his reputation as a poet would have been increased by his continuing to write verse. Many of his poems are so exquisite as to justify his classification if not with the major poets, Tennyson and Browning, at least in a world between majors and minors. But his emotional range is unquestionably narrow. The mood of gray melancholy which tinctures his prose utterances on social and educational problems is present also in his poems. He is the most elegiac of the Victorians and seems at his best in verse that suggests the yew tree and the funeral urn. Even where the subject of his verse is not directly memorial—as it is in *Thyrsis* and *Rugby Chapel*—it still suggests the ebon grief over things that are gone, or things that can never be. This mood appears in *The Strayed Reveler, The Scholar-Gypsy, The Forsaken Merman*, as well as in his longer poems, *Empedocles on Etna, Balder Dead*, and *Sohrab and Rustum*. It is the suicide note of wormwood and gall. The mood suggests that he took literally his later prescription that all great literary art must be characterized by "high seriousness." It is as though cheerfulness were a vulgar note and the light gayety of the lyrics of wine, women, and song unthinkable. Arnold's technical skill in verse is great; but because of the sad monotony of his mood it is impossible to read him as steadily as the more variable Tennyson or the more intellectually stimulating Browning. He was a poet of negation and agnosticism.

The Function of Criticism at the Present Time

This essay appeared first in *The National Review*, November, 1864, and was reissued as the first of the *Essays in Criticism* in 1865. It reveals Arnold's broad scholarship, his interest in the contemporary literature of Europe, and his carping attitude toward the smug politicians and self-satisfied economists of his own time and country.

MANY objections have been made to a proposition which, in some remarks of mine on translating Homer, I ventured to put forth; a proposition about criticism, and its importance at the present day. I said: "Of the literature of France and Germany, as of the intellect of Europe in general, the main effort, for now many years, has been a critical effort; the endeavor, in all branches of knowledge, theology, philosophy, history, art, science, to see the object as in itself it really is." I added, that owing to the operation in English literature of certain causes, "almost the last thing for which one would come to English literature is just that very thing which now Europe most desires—criticism"; and that the power and value of English literature was thereby impaired. More than one rejoinder declared that the importance I here assigned to criticism was excessive, and asserted the inherent superiority of the creative effort of the human spirit over its critical effort. And the other day, having been led by an excellent notice of Wordsworth published in the *North British Review*, to turn again to his biography, I found, in the words of this great man, whom I, for one, must always listen to with the profoundest respect, a sentence passed on the critic's business, which seems to justify every possible disparagement of it. Wordsworth says in one of his letters:

"The writers in these publications [the Reviews], while they prosecute their inglorious employment, can not be supposed to be in a state of mind very favorable for being affected by the finer influences of a thing so pure as genuine poetry."

And a trustworthy reporter of his conversation quotes a more elaborate judgment to the same effect:

"Wordsworth holds the critical power very low, infinitely lower than the inventive; and he said today that if the quantity of time consumed in writing critiques on the works of others were given to original composition, of whatever kind it might be, it would be much better employed; it would make a man find out sooner his own level, and it would do infinitely less mischief. A false or malicious criticism may do much injury to the minds of others; a stupid invention, either in prose or verse, is quite harmless."

It is almost too much to expect of poor human nature, that a man capable of producing some effect in one line of literature, should, for the greater good of society, voluntarily doom himself to impotence and obscurity in another. Still less is this to be expected from men addicted to the composition of the "false or malicious criticism," of which Wordsworth speaks. However, everybody would admit that a false or malicious criticism had better never have been written. Everybody, too, would be willing to admit, as a general proposition, that the critical faculty is lower than the inventive. But is it true that criticism is really, in itself, a baneful and injurious employment; is it true that all time given to writing critiques on the works of others would be much better employed if it were given to original composition, of whatever kind this may be? Is it

---

2. **remarks . . . Homer,** in the conclusion of his second lecture *On Translating Homer* (1861). 23. **notice of Wordsworth,** an article entitled *Wordsworth: the Man and the Poet*, written by John Campbell Shairp, Professor of Poetry at Oxford (1877-1885). 31. **one . . . letters,** one written in 1816 to the Quaker poet Bernard Barton.

true that Johnson had better have gone on producing more *Irenes* instead of writing his *Lives of the Poets;* nay, is it certain that Wordsworth himself was better employed in making his *Ecclesiastical Sonnets,* than when he made his celebrated *Preface,* so full of criticism, and criticism of the works of others? Wordsworth was himself a great critic, and it is to be sincerely regretted that he has not left us more criticism; Goethe was one of the greatest of critics, and we may sincerely congratulate ourselves that he has left us so much criticism. Without wasting time over the exaggeration which Wordsworth's judgment on criticism clearly contains, or over an attempt to trace the causes—not difficult I think to be traced—which may have led Wordsworth to this exaggeration, a critic may with advantage seize an occasion for trying his own conscience, and for asking himself of what real service, at any given moment, the practice of criticism either is, or may be made, to his own mind and spirit, and to the minds and spirits of others.

The critical power is of lower rank than the creative. True; but in assenting to this proposition, one or two things are to be kept in mind. It is undeniable that the exercise of a creative power, that a free creative activity, is the true function of man; it is proved to be so by man's finding in it his true happiness. But it is undeniable, also, that men may have the sense of exercising this free creative activity in other ways than in producing great works of literature or art; if it were not so, all but a very few men would be shut out from the true happiness of all men; they may have it in well-doing, they may have it in learning, they may have it even in criticizing. This is one thing to be kept in mind. Another is, that the exercise of the creative power in the production of great works of literature or art, however high this exercise of it may rank, is not at all epochs and under all conditions possible; and that therefore labor may be vainly spent in attempting it, which might with more fruit be used in preparing for it, in rendering it possible. This creative power works with elements, with materials; what if it has not those materials, those elements, ready for its use? In that case it must surely wait till they are ready. Now in literature —I will limit myself to literature, for it is about literature that the question arises—the elements with which the creative power works are ideas; the best ideas, on every matter which literature touches, current at the time; at any rate we may lay it down as certain that in modern literature no manifestation of the creative power not working with these can be very important or fruitful. And I say *current* at the time, not merely accessible at the time; for creative literary genius does not principally show itself in discovering new ideas; that is rather the business of the philosopher: the grand work of the literary genius is a work of synthesis and exposition, not of analysis and discovery; its gift lies in the faculty of being happily inspired by a certain intellectual and spiritual atmosphere, by a certain order of ideas, when it finds itself in them; of dealing divinely with these ideas, presenting them in the most effective and attractive combination—making beautiful works with them, in short. But it must have the atmosphere, it must find itself amidst the order of ideas, in order to work freely; and these it is not so easy to command. This is why great creative epochs in literature are so rare; this is why there is so much that is unsatisfactory in the productions of many men of real genius; because for the creation of a master-work of literature two powers must concur, the power of the man and the moment, and the man is not enough without the moment, the creative power has, for its happy exercise, appointed elements, and those elements are not in its own control.

Nay, they are more within the control of the critical power. It is the business of the critical power, as I said in the words already quoted, "in all branches of knowledge, theology, philosophy, history, art, science, to see the object as in itself it really is." Thus it tends, at last, to make an intellectual situation of which

---

2. ***Irene***, a heavy classical tragedy by Samuel Johnson (Vol. I, p. 1125). Johnson is really at his best in his *Lives of the English Poets*. 5. ***Ecclesiastical Sonnets***, a series of 132 sonnets (1821-1822) dealing with the history of the Church in England. 6. ***Preface***, the *Preface* to the *Lyrical Ballads* (see p. 318).

84. **power . . . moment.** An illustration is the work of Shakespeare in the Elizabethan period.

the creative power can profitably avail itself. It tends to establish an order of ideas, if not absolutely true, yet true by comparison with that which it displaces; to make the best ideas prevail. Presently these new ideas reach society, the touch of truth is the touch of life, and there is a stir and growth everywhere; out of this stir and growth come the creative epochs of literature.

Or, to narrow our range, and quit these considerations of the general march of genius and of society, considerations which are apt to become too abstract and impalpable—everyone can see that a poet, for instance, ought to know life and the world before dealing with them in poetry; and life and the world being, in modern times, very complex things, the creation of a modern poet, to be worth much, implies a great critical effort behind it; else it must be a comparatively poor, barren, and short-lived affair. This is why *Byron's poetry* had so little endurance in it, and Goethe's so much; both Byron and Goethe had a great productive power, but Goethe's was nourished by a great critical effort providing the true materials for it, and Byron's was not; Goethe knew life and the world, the poet's necessary subjects, much more comprehensively and thoroughly than Byron. He knew a great deal more of them, and he knew them much more as they really are.

It has long seemed to me that the burst of creative activity in our literature, through the first quarter of this century, had about it, in fact, something premature; and that from this cause its productions are doomed, most of them, in spite of the sanguine hopes which accompanied and do still accompany them, to prove hardly more lasting than the productions of far less splendid epochs. And this prematureness comes from its having proceeded without having its proper data, without sufficient materials to work with. In other words, the English poetry of the first quarter of this century, with plenty of energy, plenty of creative force, did not know enough. This makes Byron so empty of matter, Shelley so incoherent, Wordsworth even, profound as he is, yet so wanting in completeness and variety. Wordsworth cared little for books, and disparaged Goethe. I admire Wordsworth, as he is, so much that I cannot wish him different; and it is in vain, no doubt, to imagine such a man different from what he is, to suppose that he could have been different; but surely the one thing wanting to make Wordsworth an even greater poet than he is—his thought richer, and his influence of wider application—was that he should have read more books, among them, no doubt, those of that Goethe whom he disparaged without reading him.

But to speak of books and reading may easily lead to a misunderstanding here. It was not really books and reading that lacked to our poetry, at this epoch; Shelley had plenty of reading, Coleridge had immense reading. Pindar and Sophocles—as we all say so glibly, and often with so little discernment of the real import of what we are saying—had not many books; Shakespeare was no deep reader. True; but in the Greece of Pindar and Sophocles, in the England of Shakespeare, the poet lived in a current of ideas in the highest degree animating and nourishing to the creative power; society was, in the fullest measure, permeated by fresh thought, intelligent and alive; and this state of things is the true basis for the creative power's exercise—in this it finds its data, its materials, truly ready for its hand; all the books and reading in the world are only valuable as they are helps to this. Even when this does not actually exist, books and reading may enable a man to construct a kind of semblance of it in his own mind, a world of knowledge and intelligence in which he may live and work: this is by no means an equivalent, to the artist, for the nationally diffused life and thought of the epochs of Sophocles or Shakespeare, but, besides that it may be a means of preparation for such epochs, it does really constitute, if many share in it, a quickening and sustaining atmosphere of great value. Such an atmosphere the many-sided

21. **Byron's poetry.** See pp. 14 and 200. 32. **burst . . . literature.** See pp. 532 ff. 47. **Shelley.** See pp. 15 and 248.

67. **Coleridge.** See pp. 10, 12, and 163. 68. **Pindar**, a Greek lyric poet (d. c. 443 B.C.), noted especially for his odes. See Gray's Pindaric odes, pp. 52 ff. **Sophocles.** See p. 333, note 40.

learning and the long and widely-combined critical effort of Germany formed for Goethe, when he lived and worked. There was no national glow of life and thought there, as in the Athens of Pericles, or the England of Elizabeth. That was the poet's weakness. But there was a sort of equivalent for it in the complete culture and unfettered thinking of a large body of Germans. That was his strength. In the England of the first quarter of this century, there was neither a national glow of life and thought, such as we had in the age of Elizabeth, nor yet a culture and a force of learning and criticism, such as were to be found in Germany. Therefore the creative power of poetry wanted, for success in the highest sense, materials and a basis; a thorough interpretation of the world was necessarily denied to it.

At first sight it seems strange that out of the immense stir of the French Revolution and its age should not have come a crop of works of genius equal to that which came out of the stir of the great productive time of Greece, or out of that of the Renaissance, with its powerful episode the Reformation. But the truth is that the stir of the French Revolution took a character which essentially distinguished it from such movements as these. These were, in the main, disinterestedly intellectual and spiritual movements; movements in which the human spirit looked for its satisfaction in itself and in the increased play of its own activity: the French Revolution took a political, practical character. The movement which went on in France under the old *régime*, from 1700 to 1789, was far more really akin than that of the Revolution itself to the movement of the Renaissance; the France of Voltaire and Rousseau told far more powerfully upon the mind of Europe than the France of the Revolution. Goethe reproached this last expressly with having "thrown quiet culture back." Nay, and the true key to how much in our Byron, even in our Wordsworth, is this!—that they had their source in a great movement of feeling, not in a great movement of mind. The French Revolution, however— that object of so much blind love and so much blind hatred—found undoubtedly its motive-power in the intelligence of men and not in their practical sense;—this is what distinguishes it from the English Revolution of Charles the First's time; this is what makes it a more spiritual event than our Revolution, an event of much more powerful and world-wide interest, though practically less successful;—it appeals to an order of ideas which are universal, certain, permanent. 1789 asked of a thing, Is it rational? 1642 asked of a thing, Is it legal? or, when it went furthest, Is it according to conscience? This is the English fashion; a fashion to be treated, within its own sphere, with the highest respect; for its success, within its own sphere, has been prodigious. But what is law in one place is not law in another; what is law here today is not law even here tomorrow; and as for conscience, what is binding on one man's conscience is not binding on another's; the old woman who threw her stool at the head of the surpliced minister in St. Giles' Church at Edinburgh obeyed an impulse to which millions of the human race may be permitted to remain strangers. But the prescriptions of reason are absolute, unchanging, of universal validity; *to count by tens is the easiest way of counting*—that is a proposition of which everyone, from here to the Antipodes, feels the force; at least, I should say so, if we did not live in a country where it is not impossible that any morning we may find a letter in the *Times* declaring that a decimal coinage is an absurdity. That a whole nation should have been penetrated with an enthusiasm for pure reason, and with an ardent zeal for making its prescriptions triumph, is a very remarkable thing, when we consider how little of mind, or anything so worthy and quickening as mind, comes into the motives which alone, in general, impel great masses of men. In spite of the extravagant direction given to this enthusiasm, in spite of the crimes and follies in which it lost itself, the

---

5. **Athens of Pericles**, i.e., in the fifth century B.C. **England of Elizabeth.** See Vol. I, pp. 297 ff. 39. **France . . . Rousseau**, the eighteenth century. See p. 589, note 35.

53. **English Revolution.** See Vol. I, pp. 631 ff. 71. **old woman . . . Edinburgh.** According to tradition Jenny Geddes acted thus in the church when the attempt was made to read the new service prescribed by Charles I for Scotland.

French Revolution derives from the force, truth, and universality of the ideas which it took for its law, and from the passion with which it could inspire a multitude for these ideas, a unique and still living power; it is—it will probably long remain—the greatest, the most animating event in history. And, as no sincere passion for the things of the mind, even though it turn out in many respects an unfortunate passion, is ever quite thrown away and quite barren of good, France has reaped from hers one fruit, the natural and legitimate fruit, though not precisely the grand fruit she expected; she is the country in Europe where *the people* is most alive.

But the mania for giving an immediate political and practical application to all these fine ideas of the reason was fatal. Here an Englishman is in his element: on this theme we can all go on for hours. And all we are in the habit of saying on it has undoubtedly a great deal of truth. Ideas cannot be too much prized in and for themselves, cannot be too much lived with; but to transport them abruptly into the world of politics and practice, violently to revolutionize this world to their bidding—that is quite another thing. There is the world of ideas, and there is the world of practice; the French are often for suppressing the one and the English the other; but neither is to be suppressed. A member of the House of Commons said to me the other day: "That a thing is an anomaly, I consider to be no objection to it whatever." I venture to think he was wrong; that a thing is an anomaly *is* an objection to it, but absolutely and in the sphere of ideas; it is not necessarily, under such and such circumstances, or at such and such a moment, an objection to it in the sphere of politics and practice. Joubert has said beautifully: *C'est la force et le droit qui règlent toutes choses dans le monde: la force en attendant le droit.* (Force and right are the governors of this world; force till right is ready.) *Force till right is ready;* and till right is ready, force, the existing order of things, is justified, is the legitimate ruler. But right is something moral, and implies inward recognition, free assent of the will; we are not ready for right—*right, so far as we are concerned, is not ready*—until we have attained this sense of seeing it and willing it. The way in which for us it may change and transform force, the existing order of things, and become, in its turn, the legitimate ruler of the world, will depend on the way in which, when our time comes, we see it and will it. Therefore for other people enamored of their own newly discerned right, to attempt to impose it upon us as ours, and violently to substitute their right for our force, is an act of tyranny, and to be resisted. It sets at naught the second great half of our maxim, *force till right is ready.* This was the grand error of the French Revolution; and its movement of ideas, by quitting the intellectual sphere and rushing furiously into the political sphere, ran, indeed, a prodigious and memorable course, but produced no such intellectual fruit as the movement of ideas of the Renaissance, and created, in opposition to itself, what I may call an *epoch of concentration.* The great force of that epoch of concentration was England; and the great voice of that epoch of concentration was Burke. It is the fashion to treat Burke's writings on the French Revolution as superannuated and conquered by the event; as the eloquent but unphilosophical tirades of bigotry and prejudice. I will not deny that they are often disfigured by the violence and passion of the moment, and that in some directions Burke's view was bounded, and his observation therefore at fault; but on the whole, and for those who can make the needful corrections, what distinguishes these writings is their profound, permanent, fruitful, philosophical truth; they contain the true philosophy of an epoch of concentration, dissipate the heavy atmosphere which its own nature is apt to engender round it, and make its resistance rational instead of mechanical.

But Burke is so great because, almost alone in England, he brings thought to bear upon politics, he saturates politics with thought; it

---

41. **Joubert**, Joseph Joubert (1754-1824), a French essayist and moralist; he is the subject of one of Arnold's essays.

75. **Burke**, Edmund Burke (1729-1797), a famous British statesman, writer, and orator.

is his accident that his ideas were at the service of an epoch of concentration, not of an epoch of expansion; it is his characteristic that he so lived by ideas, and had such a source of them welling up within him, that he could float even an epoch of concentration and English Tory politics with them. It does not hurt him that Dr. Price and the Liberals were enraged with him; it does not even hurt him that George the Third and the Tories were enchanted with him. His greatness is that he lived in a world which neither English Liberalism nor English Toryism is apt to enter;—the world of ideas, not the world of catchwords and party habits. So far is it from being really true of him that he "to party gave up what was meant for mankind," that at the very end of his fierce struggle with the French Revolution, after all his invectives against its false pretensions, hollowness, and madness, with his sincere conviction of its mischievousness, he can close a memorandum on the best means of combating it, some of the last pages he ever wrote—the *Thoughts on French Affairs*, in December, 1791—with these striking words:

"The evil is stated, in my opinion, as it exists. The remedy must be where power, wisdom, and information, I hope, are more united with good intentions than they can be with me. I have done with this subject, I believe, forever. It has given me many anxious moments for the last two years. *If a great change is to be made in human affairs, the minds of men will be fitted to it; the general opinions and feelings will draw that way. Every fear, every hope will forward it; and then they who persist in opposing this mighty current in human affairs will appear rather to resist the decrees of Providence itself, than the mere designs of men. They will not be resolute and firm, but perverse and obstinate.*"

That return of Burke upon himself has always seemed to me one of the finest things in English literature, or indeed in any literature. That is what I call living by ideas; when one side of a question has long had your earnest support, when all your feelings are engaged, when you hear all round you no language but one, when your party talks this language like a steam-engine and can imagine no other—still to be able to think, still to be irresistibly carried, if so it be, by the current of thought to the opposite side of the question, and, like Balaam, to be unable to speak anything *but what the Lord has put in your mouth*. I know nothing more striking, and I must add that I know nothing more un-English.

For the Englishman in general is like my friend the Member of Parliament, and believes, point-blank, that for a thing to be an anomaly is absolutely no objection to it whatever. He is like the Lord Auckland of Burke's day, who, in a memorandum on the French Revolution, talks of "certain miscreants, assuming the name of philosophers, who have presumed themselves capable of establishing a new system of society." The Englishman has been called a political animal, and he values what is political and practical so much that ideas easily become objects of dislike in his eyes, and thinkers "miscreants," because ideas and thinkers have rashly meddled with politics and practice. This would be all very well if the dislike and neglect confined themselves to ideas transported out of their own sphere, and meddling rashly with practice; but they are inevitably extended to ideas as such, and to the whole life of intelligence; practice is everything, a free play of the mind is nothing. The notion of the free play of the mind upon all subjects being a pleasure in itself, being an object of desire, being an essential provider of elements without which a nation's spirit, whatever compensations it may have for them, must, in the long run, die of inanition, hardly enters into an Englishman's thoughts. It is noticeable that the word *curiosity*, which in other languages is used in a good sense, to mean, as a high and

---

8. **Dr. Price,** Richard Price (1723-1791), a Unitarian clergyman and an advocate of civil liberty. 16. **"to party . . . mankind,"** Goldsmith, *Retaliation*, l. 32 (Vol. I, p. 1122). 23. **last . . . wrote.** Arnold is in error; Burke wrote his *Letter to a Noble Lord* and his *Letters on a Regicide Peace* in 1796.

56. **Balaam,** an Old Testament prophet who was requested by Balak, King of Moab, to pronounce a curse upon Israel. Since he was permitted to speak only what the Lord said unto him, his utterance was a blessing instead of a curse. See *Numbers*, 22-24. 64. **Lord Auckland,** William Eden (1744-1814), an English statesman and diplomatist.

fine quality of man's nature, just this disinterested love of a free play of the mind on all subjects, for its own sake—it is noticeable, I say, that this word has in our language no sense of the kind, no sense but a rather bad and disparaging one. But criticism, real criticism, is essentially the exercise of this very quality; it obeys an instinct prompting it to try to know the best that is known and thought in the world, irrespectively of practice, politics, and everything of the kind; and to value knowledge and thought as they approach this best, without the intrusion of any other considerations whatever. This is an instinct for which there is, I think, little original sympathy in the practical English nature, and what there was of it has undergone a long benumbing period of blight and suppression in the epoch of concentration which followed the French Revolution.

But epochs of concentration cannot well endure forever; epochs of expansion, in the due course of things, follow them. Such an epoch of expansion seems to be opening in this country. In the first place all danger of a hostile forcible pressure of foreign ideas upon our practice has long disappeared; like the traveler in the fable, therefore, we begin to wear our cloak a little more loosely. Then, with a long peace, the ideas of Europe steal gradually and amicably in, and mingle, though in infinitesimally small quantities at a time, with our own notions. Then, too, in spite of all that is said about the absorbing and brutalizing influence of our passionate material progress, it seems to me indisputable that this progress is likely, though not certain, to lead in the end to an apparition of intellectual life; and that man, after he has made himself perfectly comfortable and has now to determine what to do with himself next, may begin to remember that he has a mind, and that the mind may be made the source of great pleasure. I grant it is mainly the privilege of faith, at present, to discern this end to our railways, our business, and our fortune-making; but we shall see if, here as elsewhere, faith is not in the end the true prophet. Our ease, our traveling, and our unbounded liberty to hold just as hard and securely as we please to the practice to which our notions have given birth, all tend to beget an inclination to deal a little more freely with these notions themselves, to canvass them a little, to penetrate a little into their real nature. Flutterings of curiosity, in the foreign sense of the word, appear amongst us, and it is in these that criticism must look to find its account. Criticism first; a time of true creative activity, perhaps—which, as I have said, must inevitably be preceded amongst us by a time of criticism—hereafter, when criticism has done its work.

It is of the last importance that English criticism should clearly discern what rule for its course, in order to avail itself of the field now opening to it, and to produce fruit for the future, it ought to take. The rule may be summed up in one word—*disinterestedness.* And how is criticism to show disinterestedness? By keeping aloof from practice; by resolutely following the law of its own nature, which is to be a free play of the mind on all subjects which it touches; by steadily refusing to lend itself to any of those ulterior, political, practical considerations about ideas which plenty of people will be sure to attach to them, which perhaps ought often to be attached to them, which in this country at any rate are certain to be attached to them quite sufficiently, but which criticism has really nothing to do with. Its business is, as I have said, simply to know the best that is known and thought in the world, and by in its turn making this known, to create a current of true and fresh ideas. Its business is to do this with inflexible honesty, with due ability; but its business is to do no more, and to leave alone all questions of practical consequences and applications, questions which will never fail to have due prominence given to them. Else criticism, besides being really false to its own nature, merely continues in the old rut which it has hitherto followed in this country, and will certainly miss the chance now given to it. For what is at present the bane

---

28. **in the fable.** The Greek fabulist Aesop (fifth century B.C.) tells the story of a contest between the wind and the sun as to which could more quickly make a traveler remove his coat. The victory went to the sun.

82. **to know . . . world.** One of Arnold's most famous sayings.

of criticism in this country? It is that practical considerations cling to it and stifle it; it subserves interests not its own; our organs of criticism are organs of men and parties having practical ends to serve, and with them those practical ends are the first thing and the play of mind the second; so much play of mind as is compatible with the prosecution of those practical ends is all that is wanted. An organ like the *Revue des Deux Mondes*, having for its main function to understand and utter the best that is known and thought in the world, existing, it may be said, as just an organ for a free play of the mind, we have not; but we have the *Edinburgh Review*, existing as an organ of the old Whigs, and for as much play of mind as may suit its being that; we have the *Quarterly Review*, existing as an organ of the Tories, and for as much play of mind as may suit its being that; we have the *British Quarterly Review*, existing as an organ of the political Dissenters, and for as much play of mind as may suit its being that; we have the *Times*, existing as an organ of the common, satisfied, well-to-do Englishman, and for as much play of mind as may suit its being that. And so on through all the various fractions, political and religious, of our society; every fraction has, as such, its organ of criticism, but the notion of combining all fractions in the common pleasure of a free disinterested play of mind meets with no favor. Directly this play of mind wants to have more scope, and to forget the pressure of practical considerations a little, it is checked, it is made to feel the chain; we saw this the other day in the extinction, so much to be regretted, of the *Home and Foreign Review;* perhaps in no organ of criticism in this country was there so much knowledge, so much play of mind; but these could not save it; the *Dublin Review* subordinates play of mind to the practical business of English and Irish Catholicism, and lives. It must needs be that men should act in sects and parties, that each of these sects and parties should have its organ, and should make this organ subserve the interests of its action; but it would be well, too, that there should be a criticism, not the minister of these interests, not their enemy, but absolutely and entirely independent of them. No other criticism will ever attain any real authority or make any real way towards its end—the creating a current of true and fresh ideas.

It is because criticism has so little kept in the pure intellectual sphere, has so little detached itself from practice, has been so directly polemical and controversial, that it has so ill accomplished, in this country, its best spiritual work; which is to keep man from a self-satisfaction which is retarding and vulgarizing, to lead him towards perfection, by making his mind dwell upon what is excellent in itself, and the absolute beauty and fitness of things. A polemical practical criticism makes men blind even to the ideal imperfection of their practice, makes them willingly assert its ideal perfection, in order the better to secure it against attack; and clearly this is narrowing and baneful for them. If they were reassured on the practical side, speculative considerations of ideal perfection they might be brought to entertain, and their spiritual horizon would thus gradually widen. Mr. Adderley says to the Warwickshire farmers:

"Talk of the improvement of breed! Why, the race we ourselves represent, the men and women, the old Anglo-Saxon race, are the best breed in the whole world. . . . The absence of a too enervating climate, too unclouded skies, and a too luxurious nature, has produced so vigorous a race of people, and has rendered us so superior to all the world."

Mr. Roebuck says to the Sheffield cutlers:

"I look around me and ask what is the state of England? Is not property safe? Is not every man able to say what he likes? Can you not walk from one end of England to the other in perfect security? I ask you whether, the world over or in past history, there is anything like it? Nothing. I pray that our unrivaled happiness may last."

---

10. **Revue . . . Mondes,** the *Review of Two Worlds,* a French literary, political, and scientific review, founded in 1829. 38. **Home . . . Review.** Published in London from 1862 to 1864.

75. **Mr. Adderley,** Charles Bowyer Adderley (1814-1905), a Tory statesman. 85. **Mr. Roebuck,** John Arthur Roebuck (1802-1879), a British politician and historical writer. He was a typical member of the advanced Liberal party.

Now obviously there is a peril for poor human nature in words and thoughts of such exuberant self-satisfaction, until we find ourselves safe in the streets of the Celestial City.

Das wenige verschwindet leicht dem Blicke
Der vorwärts sieht, wie viel noch übrig bleibt

says Goethe; the little that is done seems nothing when we look forward and see how much we have yet to do. Clearly this is a better line of reflection for weak humanity, so long as it remains on this earthly field of labor and trial. But neither Mr. Adderley nor Mr. Roebuck is by nature inaccessible to considerations of this sort. They only lose sight of them owing to the controversial life we all lead, and the practical form which all speculation takes with us. They have in view opponents whose aim is not ideal, but practical; and in their zeal to uphold their own practice against these innovators, they go so far as even to attribute to this practice an ideal perfection. Somebody has been wanting to introduce a six-pound franchise, or to abolish church-rates, or to collect agricultural statistics by force, or to diminish local self-government. How natural, in reply to such proposals, very likely improper or ill-timed, to go a little beyond the mark, and to say stoutly, "Such a race of people as we stand, so superior to all the world! The old Anglo-Saxon race, the best breed in the whole world! I pray that our unrivaled happiness may last! I ask you whether, the world over or in past history, there is anything like it!" And so long as criticism answers this dithyramb by insisting that the old Anglo-Saxon race would be still more superior to all others if it had no church-rates, or that our unrivaled happiness would last yet longer with a six-pound franchise, so long will the strain, "The best breed in the whole world!" swell louder and louder, everything ideal and refining will be lost out of sight, and both the assailed and their critics will remain in a sphere, to say the truth, perfectly unvital, a sphere in which spiritual progression is impossible. But let criticism leave church-rates and the franchise alone, and in the most candid spirit, without a single lurking thought of practical innovation, confront with our dithyramb this paragraph on which I stumbled in a newspaper soon after reading Mr. Roebuck:

"A shocking child murder has just been committed at Nottingham. A girl named Wragg left the workhouse there on Saturday morning with her young illegitimate child. The child was soon afterwards found dead on Mapperly Hills, having been strangled. Wragg is in custody."

Nothing but that; but, in juxtaposition with the absolute eulogies of Mr. Adderley and Mr. Roebuck, how eloquent, how suggestive are those few lines! "Our old Anglo-Saxon breed, the best in the whole world!"—how much that is harsh and ill-favored there is in this best. *Wragg!* If we are to talk of ideal perfection, of "the best in the whole world," has anyone reflected what a touch of grossness in our race, what an original shortcoming in the more delicate spiritual perceptions, is shown by the natural growth amongst us of such hideous names—Higginbottom, Stiggins, Bugg! In Ionia and Attica they were luckier in this respect than "the best race in the world"; by the Ilissus there was no Wragg, poor thing! And "our unrivaled happiness"; —what an element of grimness, bareness, and hideousness mixes with it and blurs it; the workhouse, the dismal Mapperly Hills —how dismal those who have seen them will remember;—the gloom, the smoke, the cold, the strangled illegitimate child! "I ask you whether the world over, or in past history, there is anything like it? Perhaps not, one is inclined to answer; but at any rate, in that case, the world is very much to be pitied. And the final touch—short, bleak, and inhuman: *Wragg is in custody.* The sex lost

---

6. ***Das . . . bleibt,*** *Iphigenie auf Tauris,* I, ii, 91-92. Arnold gives the translation in the rest of the sentence. 24. **a six-pound franchise.** The franchise at the time was limited to persons who paid an annual house-rent of £10 a year or more. 25. **church-rates,** taxes assessed against property in a parish for the support of the Church. 36. **dithyramb,** an impassioned utterance.

74. **Ionia and Attica,** provinces of Ancient Greece. 76. **Ilissus,** a river of Attica, Greece.

in the confusion of our unrivaled happiness; or (shall I say?) the superfluous Christian name lopped off by the straightforward vigor of our old Anglo-Saxon breed! There is profit for the spirit in such contrasts as this; criticism serves the cause of perfection by establishing them. By eluding sterile conflict, by refusing to remain in the sphere where alone narrow and relative conceptions have any worth and validity, criticism may diminish its momentary importance, but only in this way has it a chance of gaining admittance for those wider and more perfect conceptions to which all its duty is really owed. Mr. Roebuck will have a poor opinion of an adversary who replies to his defiant songs of triumph only by murmuring under his breath, *Wragg is in custody;* but in no other way will these songs of triumph be induced gradually to moderate themselves, to get rid of what in them is excessive and offensive, and to fall into a softer and truer key.

It will be said that it is a very subtle and indirect action which I am thus prescribing for criticism, and that by embracing in this manner the Indian virtue of detachment and abandoning the sphere of practical life, it condemns itself to a slow and obscure work. Slow and obscure it may be, but it is the only proper work of criticism. The mass of mankind will never have any ardent zeal for seeing things as they are; very inadequate ideas will always satisfy them. On these inadequate ideas reposes, and must repose, the general practice of the world. That is as much as saying that whoever sets himself to see things as they are will find himself one of a very small circle; but it is only by this small circle resolutely doing its own work that adequate ideas will ever get current at all. The rush and roar of practical life will always have a dizzying and attracting effect upon the most collected spectator, and tend to draw him into its vortex; most of all will this be the case where that life is so powerful as it is in England. But it is only by remaining collected, and refusing to lend himself to the point of view of the practical man, that the critic can do the practical man any service; and it is only by the greatest sincerity in pursuing his own course, and by at last convincing even the practical man of his sincerity, that he can escape misunderstandings which perpetually threaten him.

For the practical man is not apt for fine distinctions, and yet in these distinctions truth and the highest culture greatly find their account. But it is not easy to lead a practical man—unless you reassure him as to your practical intentions, you have no chance of leading him—to see that a thing which he has always been used to look at from one side only, which he greatly values, and which, looked at from that side, more than deserves, perhaps, all the prizing and admiring which he bestows upon it—that this thing, looked at from another side, may appear much less beneficent and beautiful, and yet retain all its claims to our practical allegiance. Where shall we find language innocent enough, how shall we make the spotless purity of our intentions evident enough, to enable us to say to the political Englishman that the British Constitution itself, which seen from the practical side, looks such a magnificent organ of progress and virtue, seen from the speculative side—with its compromises, its love of facts, its horror of theory, its studied avoidance of clear thoughts—that, seen from this side, our august Constitution sometimes looks—forgive me, shade of Lord Somers!—a colossal machine for the manufacture of Philistines? How is Cobbett to say this and not be misunderstood, blackened as he is with the smoke of a lifelong conflict in the field of political practice? how is Mr. Carlyle to say it and not be misunderstood, after his furious raid—into this field with his *Latter-Day Pamphlets?* how is Mr. Ruskin, after his pugnacious political economy? I say, the critic must keep out of the region of immediate practice in the political, social, humanitarian sphere, if he wants to make a beginning for that more free speculative treatment of things, which may perhaps one day make its benefits felt even in this

---

81. **Lord Somers,** John Somers (1651-1716), Lord Chancellor. He was the great champion of the English Constitution as determined by the Revolution of 1688. 82. **Philistine,** a name used by Arnold to designate a solid, respectable person of the middle class, devoid of culture and enlightenment. **Cobbett,** William Cobbett (1762-1835), an English democratic agitator. 86. **Carlyle.** See p. 464. 89. **Ruskin.** See p. 501.

sphere, but in a natural and thence irresistible manner.

Do what he will, however, the critic will still remain exposed to frequent misunderstandings, and nowhere so much as in this country. For here people are particularly indisposed even to comprehend that without this free disinterested treatment of things, truth and the highest culture are out of the question. So immersed are they in practical life, so accustomed to take all their notions from this life and its processes, that they are apt to think that truth and culture themselves can be reached by the processes of this life, and that it is an impertinent singularity to think of reaching them in any other. "We are all *terrae filii*," cries their eloquent advocate; "all Philistines together. Away with the notion of proceeding by any other course than the course dear to the Philistines; let us have a social movement, let us organize and combine a party to pursue truth and new thought, let us call it *the liberal party*, and let us all stick to each other, and back each other up. Let us have no nonsense about independent criticism, and intellectual delicacy, and the few and the many; don't let us trouble ourselves about foreign thought; we shall invent the whole thing for ourselves as we go along: if one of us speaks well, applaud him; if one of us speaks ill, applaud him too; we are all in the same movement, we are all liberals, we are all in pursuit of truth." In this way the pursuit of truth becomes really a social, practical, pleasurable affair, almost requiring a chairman, a secretary, and advertisements; with the excitement of an occasional scandal, with a little resistance to give the happy sense of difficulty overcome; but, in general, plenty of bustle and very little thought. To act is so easy, as Goethe says; to think is so hard! It is true that the critic has many temptations to go with the stream, to make one of the party of movement, one of these *terrae filii;* it seems ungracious to refuse to be a *terrae filius,* when so many excellent people are; but the critic's duty is to refuse, or, if resistance is vain, at least to cry with Obermann: *Périssons en résistant.*

How serious a matter it is to try and resist, I had ample opportunity of experiencing when I ventured some time ago to criticize the celebrated first volume of Bishop Colenso. The echoes of the storm which was then raised I still, from time to time, hear grumbling round me. That storm arose out of a misunderstanding almost inevitable. It is a result of no little culture to attain to a clear perception that science and religion are two wholly different things; the multitude will forever confuse them, but happily that is of no great real importance, for while the multitude imagines itself to live by its false science, it does really live by its true religion. Dr. Colenso, however, in his first volume did all he could to strengthen the confusion, and to make it dangerous. He did this with the best intentions, I freely admit, and with the most candid ignorance that this was the natural effect of what he was doing; but, says Joubert, "Ignorance, which in matters of morals extenuates the crime, is itself, in intellectual matters, a crime of the first order." I criticized Bishop Colenso's speculative confusion. Immediately there was a cry raised: "What is this? here is a liberal attacking a liberal. Do not you belong to the movement? are not you a friend of truth? Is not Bishop Colenso in pursuit of truth? then speak with proper respect of his book. Dr. Stanley is another friend of truth, and you speak with proper respect of his book; why make these invidious differences? both books are excellent, admirable, liberal; Bishop Colenso's perhaps the most so, because it is the boldest, and will have the best practical consequences for the liberal cause. Do you want to encourage to the attack of a brother liberal his, and your, and our implac-

---

17. **terrae filii**, children of the earth—i.e., nobodies. 48. **Périssons en résistant,** let us perish resisting. Obermann was the hero of a psychological romance of that name in the form of a series of letters, by Etienne Pivert de Sénancour (1770-1846), a French novelist. The quotation is from Letter 90. 53. **Bishop Colenso,** J. W. Colenso (1814-1883), Bishop of Natal. In his *Critical Examination of the Pentateuch* (the first five Books of the Old Testament) he tried to prove that these books were forgeries. Because of his dislike of personal controversy, Arnold regretted having published his attack on the essays (1863). 80. **Dr. Stanley,** Arthur Penrhyn Stanley (1815-1881), Dean of Westminster Abbey, who supported Colenso in a book entitled *The Bible: Its Form and Its Substance* (1863).

able enemies, the *Church and State Review* or the *Record*—the High Church rhinoceros and Evangelical hyena? Be silent, therefore; or rather speak, speak as loud as ever you can, and go into ecstasies over the eighty and odd pigeons."

But criticism cannot follow this coarse and indiscriminate method. It is unfortunately possible for a man in pursuit of truth to write a book which reposes upon a false conception. Even the practical consequences of a book are to genuine criticism no recommendation of it, if the book is, in the highest sense, blundering. I see that a lady who herself, too, is in pursuit of truth, and who writes with great ability, but a little too much, perhaps, under the influence of the practical spirit of the English liberal movement, classes Bishop Colenso's book and M. Renan's together, in her survey of the religious state of Europe, as facts of the same order, works, both of them, of "great importance"; "great ability, power, and skill"; Bishop Colenso's, perhaps the most powerful; at least, Miss Cobbe gives special expression to her gratitude that to Bishop Colenso "has been given the strength to grasp, and the courage to teach, truths of such deep import." In the same way, more than one popular writer has compared him to Luther. Now it is just this kind of false estimate which the critical spirit is, it seems to me, bound to resist. It is really the strongest possible proof of the low ebb at which, in England, the critical spirit is, that while the critical hit in the religious literature of Germany is Dr. Strauss's book, in that of France M. Renan's book, the book of Bishop Colenso is the critical hit in the religious literature of England. Bishop Colenso's book reposes on a total misconception of the essential elements of the religious problem, as that problem is now presented for solution. To criticism, therefore, which seeks to have the best that is known and thought on this problem, it is, however well meant, of no importance whatever. M. Renan's book attempts a new synthesis of the elements furnished to us by the Four Gospels. It attempts, in my opinion, a synthesis, perhaps premature, perhaps impossible, certainly not successful. Up to the present time, at any rate, we must acquiesce in Fleury's sentence on such recastings of the Gospel-story: *Quiconque s'imagine la pouvoir mieux écrire, ne l'entend pas.* M. Renan had himself passed by anticipation a like sentence on his own work, when he said: "If a new presentation of the character of Jesus were offered to me, I would not have it; its very clearness would be, in my opinion, the best proof of its insufficiency." His friends may with perfect justice rejoin that at the sight of the Holy Land, and of the actual scene of the Gospel-story, all the current of M. Renan's thoughts may have naturally changed and a new casting of that story irresistibly suggested itself to him; and that this is just a case for applying Cicero's maxim: Change of mind is not inconsistency—*nemo doctus unquam mutationem consilii inconstantiam dixit esse.* Nevertheless, for criticism, M. Renan's first thought must still be the truer one, as long as his new casting so fails more fully to commend itself, more fully (to use Coleridge's happy phrase about the Bible), to *find* us. Still M. Renan's attempt is, for criticism, of the most real interest and importance, since, with all its difficulty, a fresh synthesis of the New Testament *data* —not a making war on them, in Voltaire's fashion, not a leaving them out of mind, in the world's fashion, but the putting a new construction upon them, the taking them from under the old, adoptive, traditional, unspiritual point of view and placing them under a

3. **Evangelical.** See page 461, note 15. 5. **eighty . . . pigeons.** In commenting on *Leviticus,* 10:16-20, Colenso had said, "The very pigeons to be brought as sin-offerings for the birth of children would have averaged according to the story more than 250 a day; and each priest would have had to eat daily more than 80 for his own portion 'in the most holy place'!" 14. **a lady,** Frances Power Cobbe, a philanthropist and religious writer (1822-1904) who expresses the views mentioned in her *Broken Lights* (1864). 19. **M. Renan,** Ernest Renan (1823-1892), a learned French writer and historian, famous for his *Vie de Jésus* (1863) and other religious books. 36. **Dr. Strauss's book,** *Das Leben Jesu* (1835, 1864), by David Friedrich Strauss, a German rationalistic philosopher (1808-1874).

52. *Quiconque . . . pas,* whoever imagines that he can write it better does not understand it. From the Preface to *Ecclesiastical History* (1691), by Claude Fleury, a French ecclesiastical historian (1640-1723). 68. *nemo . . . esse,* no wise person ever said that change of opinion was inconsistency. The quotation is from Cicero's *Letters to Atticus,* 15, 7, 3. See p. 576, note 35. 74. **to *find* us.** In *Confessions of an Inquiring Spirit,* Letter I.

new one—is the very essence of the religious problem, as now presented; and only by efforts in this direction can it receive a solution.

Again, in the same spirit in which she judges Bishop Colenso, Miss Cobbe, like so many earnest liberals of our practical race, both here and in America, herself sets vigorously about a positive reconstruction of religion, about making a religion of the future out of hand, or at least setting about making it; we must not rest, she and they are always thinking and saying, in negative criticism, we must be creative and constructive; hence we have such works as her recent *Religious Duty*, and works still more considerable, perhaps, by others, which will be in everyone's mind. These works often have much ability; they often spring out of sincere convictions, and a sincere wish to do good; and they sometimes, perhaps, do good. Their fault is (if I may be permitted to say so) one which they have in common with the British College of Health, in the New Road. Everyone knows the British College of Health; it is that building with the lion and the statue of the Goddess Hygeia before it; at least, I am sure about the lion, though I am not absolutely certain about the Goddess Hygeia. This building does credit, perhaps, to the resources of Dr. Morrison and his disciples; but it falls a good deal short of one's idea of what a British College of Health ought to be. In England, where we hate public interference and love individual enterprise, we have a whole crop of places like the British College of Health; the grand name without the grand thing. Unluckily, creditable to individual enterprise as they are, they tend to impair our taste by making us forget what more grandiose, noble, or beautiful character properly belongs to a public institution. The same may be said of the religions of the future of Miss Cobbe and others. Creditable, like the British College of Health, to the resources of their authors, they yet tend to make us forget what more grandiose, noble, or beautiful character properly belongs to religious constructions. The historic religions, with all their faults, have had this; it certainly belongs to the religious sentiment, when it truly flowers, to have this; and we impoverish our spirit if we allow a religion of the future without it. What then is the duty of criticism here? To take the practical point of view, to applaud the liberal movement and all its works—its New Road religions of the future into the bargain—for their general utility's sake? By no means; but to be perpetually dissatisfied with these works, while they perpetually fall short of a high and perfect ideal.

For criticism, these are elementary laws; but they never can be popular, and in this country they have been very little followed, and one meets with immense obstacles in following them. That is a reason for asserting them again and again. Criticism must maintain its independence of the practical spirit and its aims. Even with well-meant efforts of the practical spirit it must express dissatisfaction, if in the sphere of the ideal they seem impoverishing and limiting. It must not hurry on to the goal because of its practical importance. It must be patient, and know how to wait; and flexible, and know how to attach itself to things and how to withdraw from them. It must be apt to study and praise elements that for the fullness of spiritual perfection are wanted, even though they belong to a power which in the practical sphere may be maleficent. It must be apt to discern the spiritual shortcomings or illusions of powers that in the practical sphere may be beneficent. And this without any notion of favoring or injuring, in the practical sphere, one power or the other; without any notion of playing off, in this sphere, one power against the other. When one looks, for instance, at the English Divorce Court—an institution which perhaps has its practical conveniences, but which in the ideal sphere is so hideous; an institution which neither makes divorce impossible nor makes it decent, which allows a man to get rid of his wife, or a wife of her husband, but makes them drag one another first, for the public edification, through a mire of unutterable infamy—when one looks at this charming institution, I say, with its crowded benches, its newspaper-reports, and its money-

---

23. **New Road**, an outlying street in the northwest section of London. 25. **Goddess Hygeia**, the goddess of health. 29. **Dr. Morrison**, James Morrison (1770-1840), the inventor of a "universal cure-all" called Morrison's pills.

compensations, this institution in which the gross unregenerate British Philistine has indeed stamped an image of himself—one may be permitted to find the marriage-theory of Catholicism refreshing and elevating. Or when Protestantism, in virtue of its supposed rational and intellectual origin, gives the law to criticism too magisterially, criticism may and must remind it that its pretensions, in this respect, are illusive and do it harm; that the Reformation was a moral rather than an intellectual event; that Luther's theory of grace no more exactly reflects the mind of the spirit than Bossuet's philosophy of history reflects it; and that there is no more antecedent probability of the Bishop of Durham's stock of ideas being agreeable to perfect reason than of Pope Pius the Ninth's. But criticism will not on that account forget the achievements of Protestantism in the practical and moral sphere; nor that, even in the intellectual sphere, Protestantism, though in a blind and stumbling manner, carried forward the Renaissance, while Catholicism threw itself violently across its path.

I lately heard a man of thought and energy contrasting the want of ardor and movement which he now found amongst young men in this country with what he remembered in his own youth, twenty years ago. "What reformers we were then!" he exclaimed; "what a zeal we had! how we canvassed every institution in Church and State, and were prepared to remodel them all on first principles!" He was inclined to regret, as a spiritual flagging, the lull which he saw. I am disposed rather to regard it as a pause in which the turn to a new mode of spiritual progress is being accomplished. Everything was long seen, by the young and ardent amongst us, in inseparable connection with politics and practical life; we have pretty well exhausted the benefits of seeing things in this connection; we have got all that can be got by so seeing them. Let us try a more disinterested mode of seeing them; let us betake ourselves more to the serener life of the mind and spirit. This life, too, may have its excesses and dangers; but they are not for us at present. Let us think of quietly enlarging our stock of true and fresh ideas, and not, as soon as we get an idea or half an idea, be running out with it into the street, and trying to make it rule there. Our ideas will, in the end, shape the world all the better for maturing a little. Perhaps in fifty years' time it will in the English House of Commons be an objection to an institution that it is an anomaly, and my friend the Member of Parliament will shudder in his grave. But let us in the meanwhile rather endeavor that in twenty years' time it may, in English literature, be an objection to a proposition that it is absurd. That will be a change so vast, that the imagination almost fails to grasp it. *Ab integro saeclorum nascitur ordo.*

If I have insisted so much on the course which criticism must take where politics and religion are concerned, it is because, where these burning matters are in question, it is most likely to go astray. I have wished, above all, to insist on the attitude which criticism should adopt towards everything; on its right tone and temper of mind. Then comes the question as to the subject-matter which criticism should most seek. Here, in general, its course is determined for it by the idea which is the law of its being; the idea of a disinterested endeavor to learn and propagate the best that is known and thought in the world, and thus to establish a current of fresh and true ideas. By the very nature of things, as England is not all the world, much of the best that is known and thought in the world cannot be of English growth, must be foreign; by the nature of things, again, it is just this that we are least likely to know, while English thought is streaming in upon us from all sides and takes excellent care that we shall not be ignorant of its existence; the English critic, therefore, must dwell much on foreign

---

4. **marriage-theory of Catholicism,** that Catholics should marry only Catholics, and that divorce is not recognized. 12. **Luther's . . . grace.** Luther revived the doctrine of justification by the faith of the individual. 14. **Bossuet,** a famous French preacher and dogmatic theologian (1627-1704). It was his belief that divine intervention could be traced in every stage of history. Cf. Carlyle's view, p. 493, note 62. 16. **Bishop of Durham,** Charles Baring (1807-1879), an evangelical preacher noted for his piety and independence. 18. **Pope . . . Ninth.** He served as Pope from 1846 to 1878. Arnold probably has in mind the *Syllabus* of December 8, 1864, in which Pius claimed for the Church the control of all culture, all science, and of the whole educational system.

64. *Ab . . . ordo,* from the renewal of the ages order is born (Virgil, *Eclogue,* IV, 5).

thought, and with particular heed on any part of it, which, while significant and fruitful in itself, is for any reason specially likely to escape him. Again, judging is often spoken of as the critic's one business; and so in some sense it is; but the judgment which almost insensibly forms itself in a fair and clear mind, along with fresh knowledge, is the valuable one; and thus knowledge, and ever fresh knowledge, must be the critic's great concern for himself; and it is by communicating fresh knowledge, and letting his own judgment pass along with it—but insensibly, and in the second place not the first, as a sort of companion and clue, not as an abstract lawgiver—that he will generally do most good to his readers. Sometimes, no doubt, for the sake of establishing an author's place in literature, and his relation to a central standard (and if this is not done, how are we to get at our *best in the world?*), criticism may have to deal with a subject-matter so familiar that fresh knowledge is out of the question, and then it must be all judgment; an enunciation and detailed application of principles. Here the great safeguard is never to let oneself become abstract, always to retain an intimate and lively consciousness of the truth of what one is saying, and, the moment this fails us, to be sure that something is wrong. Still, under all circumstances, this mere judgment and application of principles is, in itself, not the most satisfactory work to the critic; like mathematics, it is tautological, and cannot well give us, like fresh learning, the sense of creative activity.

But stop, some one will say; all this talk is of no practical use to us whatever; this criticism of yours is not what we have in our minds when we speak of criticism; when we speak of critics and criticism, we mean critics and criticism of the current English literature of the day; when you offer to tell criticism its function, it is to this criticism that we expect you to address yourself. I am sorry for it, for I am afraid I must disappoint these expectations. I am bound by my own definition of criticism; *a disinterested endeavor to learn and propagate the best that is known and thought in the world.* How much of current English literature comes into this "best that is known and thought in the world"? Not very much, I fear; certainly less, at this moment, than of the current literature of France or Germany. Well, then, am I to alter my definition of criticism, in order to meet the requirements of a number of practicing English critics, who, after all, are free in their choice of a business? That would be making criticism lend itself just to one of those alien practical considerations, which, I have said, are so fatal to it. One may say, indeed, to those who have to deal with the mass—so much better disregarded—of current English literature, that they may at all events endeavor, in dealing with this, to try it, so far as they can, by the standard of the best that is known and thought in the world; one may say, that to get anywhere near this standard, every critic should try and possess one great literature, at least, besides his own; and the more unlike his own, the better. But, after all, the criticism I am really concerned with—the criticism which alone can much help us for the future, the criticism which, throughout Europe, is at the present day meant, when so much stress is laid on the importance of criticism and the critical spirit—is a criticism which regards Europe as being, for intellectual and spiritual purposes, one great confederation, bound to a joint action and working to a common result; and whose members have, for their proper outfit, a knowledge of Greek, Roman, and Eastern antiquity, and of one another. Special, local, and temporary advantages being put out of account, that modern nation will in the intellectual and spiritual sphere make most progress, which most thoroughly carries out this program. And what is that but saying that we too, all of us, as individuals, the more thoroughly we carry it out, shall make the more progress?

There is so much inviting us!—what are we to take? what will nourish us in growth

---

51. **Not very much.** Arnold was not entirely in sympathy with the work of his great English contemporaries—Tennyson, Browning, Rossetti, Morris, Thackeray, and Eliot. He apparently valued more highly such German writers as Otto Ludwig (1813-1865), Emmanuel Geibel (1815-1884), Gustav Freytag (1816-1895), and Theodor Storm (1817-1888), who reacted against the preceding romantic movement; and French reactionaries like Gustave Flaubert (1821-1880), Alexandre Dumas *fils* (1824-1895), Charles A. Sainte-Beuve (1804-1869), Théophile Gautier (1811-1872), and Leconte de Lisle (1818-1894).

towards perfection? That is the question which, with the immense field of life and of literature lying before him, the critic has to answer; for himself first, and afterwards for others. In this idea of the critic's business the essays brought together in the following pages have had their origin; in this idea, widely different as are their subjects, they have, perhaps, their unity.

I conclude with what I said at the beginning: to have the sense of creative activity is the great happiness and the great proof of being alive, and it is not denied to criticism to have it; but then criticism must be sincere, simple, flexible, ardent, ever widening its knowledge. Then it may have, in no contemptible measure, a joyful sense of creative activity; a sense which a man of insight and conscience will prefer to what he might derive from a poor, starved, fragmentary, inadequate creation. And at some epochs no other creation is possible.

Still, in full measure, the sense of creative activity belongs only to genuine creation; in literature we must never forget that. But what true man of letters ever can forget it? It is no such common matter for a gifted nature to come into possession of a current of true and living ideas, and to produce amidst the inspiration of them, that we are likely to underrate it. The *epochs of Aeschylus* and Shakespeare make us feel their pre-eminence. In an epoch like those is, no doubt, the true life of a literature; there is the promised land, towards which criticism can only beckon. That promised land it will not be ours to enter, and we shall die in the wilderness: but to have desired to enter it, to have saluted it from afar, is already, perhaps, the best distinction among contemporaries; it will certainly be the best title to esteem with posterity.

(1864)

6. **essays . . . pages,** those published under the title *Essays in Criticism* (1865).

31. **epoch of Aeschylus,** that of the fifth century B.C., the period of the highest literary culture in Greece. Aeschylus was one of several famous Greek tragic dramatists. 34. **the promised land.** An allusion to the better country promised by the Lord to the Israelites. See *Genesis,* 12:7 and *Exodus,* 6:8.

from *Culture and Anarchy*

Some of the utterances that earned for Arnold the name of "elegant Jeremiah" appear in the series of essays on political and social conditions and problems which he issued in 1869 under the title *Culture and Anarchy.* Of these *Hebraism and Hellenism,* an analysis of opposing cultures, forms Chapter IV.

HEBRAISM AND HELLENISM

This fundamental ground is our preference of doing to thinking. Now, this preference is a main element in our nature, and as we study it we find ourselves opening up a number of large questions on every side.

Let me go back for a moment to Bishop Wilson, who says, "First, never go against the best light you have; secondly, take care that your light be not darkness." We show, as a nation, laudable energy and persistence in walking according to the best light we have, but are not quite careful enough, perhaps, to see that our light be not darkness. This is only another version of the old story that energy is our strong point and favorable characteristic, rather than intelligence. But we may give to this idea a more general form still, in which it will have a yet larger range of application. We may regard this energy driving at practice, this paramount sense of the obligation of duty, self-control, and work, this earnestness in going manfully with the best light we have, as one force. And we may

1. **This . . . ground.** A reference to the concluding paragraph of the preceding chapter: "We see, then, how indispensable to that human perfection which we seek is, in the opinion of good judges, some public recognition and establishment of our best self, or right reason. We see how our habits and practice oppose themselves to such a recognition, and the many inconveniences which we therefore suffer. But now let us try to go a little deeper, and to find beneath our actual habits and practice, the very ground and cause out of which they spring." 6. **Bishop Wilson,** Thomas Wilson (1663-1755), Bishop of Sodor and Man. His *Maxims* and other writings appealed strongly to Arnold.

regard the intelligence driving at those ideas which are, after all, the basis of right practice, the ardent sense for all the new and changing combinations of them which man's development brings with it, the indomitable impulse to know and adjust them perfectly, as another force. And these two forces we may regard as in some sense rivals—rivals, not by the necessity of their own nature, but as exhibited in man and his history; and rivals dividing the empire of the world between them. And to give these forces names from the two races of men who have supplied the most signal and splendid manifestations of them, we may call them respectively the forces of Hebraism and Hellenism. Hebraism and Hellenism—between these two points of influence moves our world. At one time it feels more powerfully the attraction of one of them, at another time of the other; and it ought to be, though it never is, evenly and happily balanced between them.

The final aim of both Hellenism and Hebraism, as of all great spiritual disciplines, is no doubt the same: man's perfection, or salvation. The very language which they both of them use in schooling us to reach this aim is often identical. Even when their language indicates by variation—sometimes a broad variation, often a but slight and subtle variation —the different courses of thought which are uppermost in each discipline, even then the unity of the final end and aim is still apparent. To employ the actual words of that discipline with which we ourselves are all of us most familiar, and the words of which, therefore, come most home to us, that final end and aim is "that we might be partakers of the divine nature." These are the words of a Hebrew apostle; but of Hellenism and Hebraism alike this is, I say, the aim. When the two are confronted, as they very often are confronted, it is nearly always with what I may call a rhetorical purpose: the speaker's whole design is to exalt and enthrone one of the two, and he uses the other only as a foil and to enable him the better to give effect to his purpose. Obviously, with us, it is usually Hellenism which is thus reduced to minister to the triumph of Hebraism. There is a sermon on Greece and the Greek spirit by a man never to be mentioned without interest and respect, Frederick Robertson, in which this rhetorical use of Greece and the Greek spirit, and the inadequate exhibition of them necessarily consequent upon this, is almost ludicrous, and would be censurable if it were not to be explained by the exigencies of a sermon. On the other hand, Heinrich Heine and other writers of his sort give us the spectacle of the tables completely turned, and of Hebraism brought in just as a foil and contrast to Hellenism and to make the superiority of Hellenism more manifest. In both these cases there is injustice and misrepresentation. The aim and end of both Hebraism and Hellenism is, as I have said, one and the same, and this aim and end is august and admirable.

Still, they pursue this aim by very different courses. The uppermost idea with Hellenism is to see things as they really are; the uppermost idea with Hebraism is conduct and obedience. Nothing can do away with this ineffaceable difference. The Greek quarrel with the body and its desires is that they hinder right thinking; the Hebrew quarrel with them is that they hinder right acting. "He that keepeth the law, happy is he"; "Blessed is the man that feareth the Eternal, that delighteth greatly in His commandments";—that is the Hebrew notion of felicity; and, pursued with passion and tenacity, this notion would not let the Hebrew rest till, as is well known, he had at last got out of the law a network of prescriptions to enwrap his whole life, to govern every moment of it, every impulse, every action. The Greek notion of felicity, on the other hand, is perfectly conveyed in these words of a great French moralist: "*C'est le bonheur des hommes*"—when? when they

---

38. "that . . . nature," words of the Apostle Paul, *2 Peter*, 1:4.

52. **Frederick Robertson**, a brilliant Anglican clergyman (1816-1853), whose sermon "The Grecian" (1849) expressed a rather liberal point of view. 59. **Heine**, Heinrich Heine (1797-1856), a German poet of Hebrew descent. He says, "All men are either Jews or Hellenes, men ascetic in their instincts, hostile to culture, spiritual fanatics, or men of vigorous good cheer, full of the pride of life. Naturalists."—*Über Ludwig Börne*. 72. **conduct and obedience.** Cf. Wordsworth's *Ode to Duty*, p. 155. 77. "**He that . . . he.**" From *Proverbs*, 29:18. 78. "**Blessed . . . commandments.**" From *Psalms*, 112:1. 89. "*C'est . . . hommes*," it is the good fortune of men.

abhor that which is evil? no;—when they exercise themselves in the law of the Lord day and night? no;—when they die daily? no;—when they walk about the New Jerusalem with palms in their hands? no;—but when they think aright, when their thought hits: *"quand ils pensent juste."* At the bottom of both the Greek and the Hebrew notion is the desire, native in man, for reason and the will of God, the feeling after the universal order—in a word, the love of God. But while Hebraism seizes upon certain plain, capital intimations of the universal order, and rivets itself, one may say, with unequaled grandeur of earnestness and intensity on the study and observance of them, the bent of Hellenism is to follow, with flexible activity, the whole play of the universal order, to be apprehensive of missing any part of it, of sacrificing one part to another, to slip away from resting in this or that intimation of it, however capital. An unclouded clearness of mind, an unimpeded play of thought, is what this bent drives at. The governing idea of Hellenism is *spontaneity of consciousness;* that of Hebraism, *strictness of conscience.*

Christianity changed nothing in this essential bent of Hebraism to set doing above knowing. Self-conquest, self-devotion, the following not our own individual will but the will of God, *obedience,* is the fundamental idea of this form, also, of the discipline to which we have attached the general name of Hebraism. Only, as the old law and the network of prescriptions with which it enveloped human life were evidently a motive-power not driving and searching enough to produce the result aimed at—patient continuance in well-doing, self-conquest—Christianity substituted for them boundless devotion to that inspiring and affecting pattern of self-conquest offered by Jesus Christ; and by the new motive-power, of which the essence was this, though the love and admiration of Christian churches have for centuries been employed in varying, amplifying, and adorning the plain description of it, Christianity, as St. Paul truly says, "establishes the law," and, in the strength of the ampler power which she has thus supplied to fulfil it, has accomplished the miracles, which we all see, of her history.

So long as we do not forget that both Hellenism and Hebraism are profound and admirable manifestations of man's life, tendencies, and powers, and that both of them aim at a like final result, we can hardly insist too strongly on the divergence of line and of operation with which they proceed. It is a divergence so great that it most truly, as the prophet Zechariah says, "has raised up thy sons, O Zion, against thy sons, O Greece!" The difference whether it is by doing or by knowing that we set most store, and the practical consequences which follow from this difference, leave their mark on all the history of our race and of its development. Language may be abundantly quoted from both Hellenism and Hebraism to make it seem that one follows the same current as the other towards the same goal. They are, truly, borne towards the same goal; but the currents which bear them are infinitely different. It is true, Solomon will praise knowing: "Understanding is a well-spring of life unto him that hath it." And in the New Testament, again, Jesus Christ is a "light," and "truth makes us free." It is true, Aristotle will undervalue knowing: "In what concerns virtue," says he, "three things are necessary—knowledge, deliberate will, and perseverance; but whereas the two last are all-important, the first is a matter of little importance." It is true that with the same impatience with which St. James enjoins a man to be not a forgetful hearer but a *doer of the word*, Epictetus exhorts us to *do* what we have demonstrated to ourselves we ought to do; or he taunts us with futility, for being armed at all points to prove that lying is wrong, yet all the time continuing to lie. It

---

1. **abhor . . . evil, etc.** Phrases from *Romans*, 12:9; *Psalms*, 1:2; *1 Corinthians*, 15:31; *Revelation*, 3:12; 7:9. 12. **capital**, important (from L. *caput*, head). 38. **patient . . . well-doing.** From *Romans*, 2:7.

48. **"establishes the law."** From *Romans*, 3:31. 60. **"has . . . Greece!"** From *Zechariah*, 9:13. 73. **"Understanding . . . it."** From *Proverbs*, 16:22. 76. **"light . . . free."** Cf. *John*, 8:12, 32: "I am the light of the world." "And ye shall know the truth, and the truth shall make you free." See also *John*, 1:1-12. 77. **Aristotle**, the most famous of the Greek philosophers (384-322 B.C.). The quotation is from his *Nicomachean Ethics*, 2, 3. 83. **St. James.** In *James*, 1:25. 85. **Epictetus**, a noted Stoic philosopher (first century A.D.). The reference is to his *Discourses*, 2, 19.

is true, Plato, in words which are almost the words of the New Testament or the *Imitation*, calls life a learning to die. But underneath the superficial agreement the fundamental divergence still subsists. The "understanding" of Solomon is "the walking in the way of the commandments"; this is "the way of peace," and it is of this that blessedness comes. In the New Testament, the truth which gives us the peace of God and makes us free is the love of Christ constraining us to crucify, as he did, and with a like purpose of moral regeneration, the flesh with its affections and lusts, and thus establishing, as we have seen, the law. The moral virtues, on the other hand, are with Aristotle but the porch and access to the intellectual, and with these last is blessedness. That partaking of the divine life, which both Hellenism and Hebraism, as we have said, fix as their crowning aim, Plato expressly denies to the man of practical virtue merely, of self-conquest with any other motive than that of perfect intellectual vision. He reserves it for the lover of pure knowledge, of seeing things as they really are—the φιλομαθής.

Both Hellenism and Hebraism arise out of the wants of human nature, and address themselves to satisfying those wants. But their methods are so different, they lay stress on such different points, and call into being by their respective disciplines such different activities, that the face which human nature presents when it passes from the hands of one of them to those of the other is no longer the same. To get rid of one's ignorance, to see things as they are, and by seeing them as they are to see them in their beauty, is the simple and attractive ideal which Hellenism holds out before human nature; and from the simplicity and charm of this ideal, Hellenism, and human life in the hands of Hellenism, is invested with a kind of aërial ease, clearness, and radiancy; they are full of what we call sweetness and light. Difficulties are kept out of view, and the beauty and rationalness of the ideal have all our thoughts. "The best man is he who most tries to perfect himself, and the happiest man is he who most feels that he *is* perfecting himself"—this account of the matter by Socrates, the true Socrates of the *Memorabilia*, has something so simple, spontaneous, and unsophisticated about it that it seems to fill us with clearness and hope when we hear it. But there is a saying which I have heard attributed to Mr. Carlyle about Socrates—a very happy saying, whether it is really Mr. Carlyle's or not—which excellently marks the essential point in which Hebraism differs from Hellenism. "Socrates," this saying goes, "is terribly *at ease in Zion*." Hebraism—and here is the source of its wonderful strength—has always been severely pre-occupied with an awful sense of the impossibility of being at ease in Zion; of the difficulties which oppose themselves to man's pursuit or attainment of that perfection of which Socrates talks so hopefully, and, as from this point of view one might almost say, so glibly. It is all very well to talk of getting rid of one's ignorance, of seeing things in their reality, seeing them in their beauty; but how is this to be done when there is something which thwarts and spoils all our efforts?

This something is *sin;* and the space which sin fills in Hebraism, as compared with Hellenism, is indeed prodigious. This obstacle to perfection fills the whole scene, and perfection appears remote and rising away from earth, in the background. Under the name of sin, the difficulties of knowing oneself and conquering oneself which impede man's passage to perfection become, for Hebraism, a positive, active entity hostile to man, a mysterious

---

1. **Plato,** the famous Greek philosopher (427-347 B.C.). The reference is to his *Gorgias.* 2. **the *Imitation,*** *Imitation of Christ,* a famous devotional manual attributed to Thomas à Kempis (c. 1380-1471), a German religious writer. It traces the development of the soul toward Christian perfection through detachment from the world and union with God. 6. **"the walking . . . commandments."** From *Psalms,* 119:32-35. 7. **"the way of peace."** From *Isaiah,* 59:8. 9. **truth . . . law,** phrases from *2 Corinthians,* 5:14 and *Galatians,* 5:24. 25. φιλομαθής, a lover of learning.

44. **sweetness and light,** a phrase that Arnold acknowledged he borrowed from Swift's *Battle of the Books;* it here means beauty and intelligence. In the episode of the Spider and the Bee, Swift summarizes the superiority of the ancient writers over the modern, and says: "Instead of dirt and poison we have rather chose to fill our hives with honey and wax, thus furnishing mankind with the two noblest of things, which are sweetness and light." 50. **Socrates,** a famous Greek philosopher (fifth century B.C.); *the true Socrates* as portrayed by his disciple Xenophon in *Memorabilia of Socrates,* rather than the Socrates of the *Dialogues* of Plato, in which he appears in part as the spokesman for Plato himself. The quotation is from *Memorabilia,* 4, 8. 55. **Mr. Carlyle.** See p. 464. 60. *at ease in Zion.* Cf. *Amos,* 6:1: "Woe to them that are at ease in Zion." 80. **knowing oneself.** See Carlyle's *Everlasting No,* p. 468, note 58.

power which I heard Dr. Pusey the other day, in one of his impressive sermons, compare to a hideous hunchback seated on our shoulders, and which it is the main business of our lives to hate and oppose. The discipline of the Old Testament may be summed up as a discipline teaching us to abhor and flee from sin; the discipline of the New Testament, as a discipline teaching us to die to it. As Hellenism speaks of thinking clearly, seeing things in their essence and beauty, as a grand and precious feat for man to achieve, so Hebraism speaks of becoming conscious of sin, of awakening to a sense of sin, as a feat of this kind. It is obvious to what wide divergence these differing tendencies, actively followed, must lead. As one passes and repasses from Hellenism to Hebraism, from Plato to St. Paul, one feels inclined to rub one's eyes and ask oneself whether man is indeed a gentle and simple being, showing the traces of a noble and divine nature, or an unhappy chained captive, laboring with groanings that cannot be uttered to free himself from the body of this death.

Apparently it was the Hellenic conception of human nature which was unsound, for the world could not live by it. Absolutely to call it unsound, however, is to fall into the common error of its Hebraizing enemies; but it was unsound at that particular moment of man's development, it was premature. The indispensable basis of conduct and self-control, the platform upon which alone the perfection aimed at by Greece can come into bloom, was not to be reached by our race so easily; centuries of probation and discipline were needed to bring us to it. Therefore the bright promise of Hellenism faded, and Hebraism ruled the world. Then was seen that astonishing spectacle, so well marked by the often-quoted words of the prophet Zechariah, when men of all languages and nations took hold of the skirt of him that was a Jew, saying, "We will go with you, for we have heard that God is with you." And the Hebraism which thus received and ruled a world all gone out of the way, and altogether become unprofitable, was and could not but be the later, the more spiritual, the more attractive development of Hebraism. It was Christianity; that is to say, Hebraism aiming at self-conquest and rescue from the thrall of vile affections, not by obedience to the letter of a law, but by conformity to the image of a self-sacrificing example. To a world stricken with moral enervation Christianity offered its spectacle of an inspired self-sacrifice; to men who refused themselves nothing, it showed one who refused himself everything;—"my Savior banished joy!" says George Herbert. When the *alma Venus*, the life-giving and joy-giving power of nature, so fondly cherished by the pagan world, could not save her followers from self-dissatisfaction and *ennui*, the severe words of the apostle came bracingly and refreshingly: "Let no man deceive you with vain words, for because of these things cometh the wrath of God upon the children of disobedience." Through age after age and generation after generation, our race, or all that part of our race which was most living and progressive, was *baptized into a death;* and endeavored, by suffering in the flesh, to cease from sin. Of this endeavor, the animating labors and afflictions of early Christianity, the touching asceticism of medieval Christianity, are the great historical manifestations. Literary monuments of it, each in its own way incomparable, remain in the *Epistles* of St. Paul, in St. Augustine's *Confessions*, and in the two original and simplest books of the *Imitation*.

Of two disciplines laying their main stress, the one on clear intelligence, the other on firm obedience; the one on comprehensively knowing the grounds of one's duty, the other on diligently practicing it; the one on taking all possible care (to use Bishop Wilson's words again) that the light we have be not

---

1. **Dr. Pusey,** Edward B. Pusey (1800-1882), an outstanding scholar of the Anglican Church and a leader, with Newman, in the Tractarian movement at Oxford University; see p. 407. 22. **chained captive,** etc. Cf. *Romans,* 8:26: "The Spirit itself maketh intercession for us with groanings which cannot be uttered"; and 7:24: "O wretched man that I am! who shall deliver me from the body of this death?" 37. **the bright . . . Hellenism.** The flowering time of Greek culture was the fifth century B.C. 43. "**We . . . you.**" From *Zechariah,* 8:23.

60. **George Herbert,** poet and clergyman (1593-1633). See Vol. I. p. 675. The quotation is from his *The Size,* 5. 66. "**Let . . . disobedience,**" words of Paul in *Ephesians,* 5:6. 72. *baptized . . . death.* From *Romans,* 6:3. 80. **St. Augustine,** the most famous of the Fathers of the Roman Church (354-430).

darkness, the other that according to the best light we have we diligently walk, the priority naturally belongs to that discipline which braces all man's moral powers and founds for him an indispensable basis of character. And, therefore, it is justly said of the Jewish people, who were charged with setting powerfully forth that side of the divine order to which the words "conscience" and "self-conquest" point, that they were "entrusted with the oracles of God"; as it is justly said of Christianity, which followed Judaism and which set forth this side with a much deeper effectiveness and a much wider influence, that the wisdom of the old pagan world was foolishness compared to it. No words of devotion and admiration can be too strong to render thanks to these beneficent forces which have so borne forward humanity in its appointed work of coming to the knowledge and possession of itself; above all, in those great moments when their action was the wholesomest and the most necessary.

But the evolution of these forces, separately and in themselves, is not the whole evolution of humanity, their single history is not the whole history of man; whereas their admirers are always apt to make it stand for the whole history. Hebraism and Hellenism are, neither of them, the *law* of human development, as their admirers are prone to make them; they are, each of them, *contributions* to human development, august contributions, invaluable contributions, and each showing itself to us more august, more invaluable, more preponderant over the other, according to the moment in which we take them and the relation in which we stand to them. The nations of our modern world, children of that immense and salutary movement which broke up the pagan world, inevitably stand to Hellenism in a relation which dwarfs it and to Hebraism in a relation which magnifies it. They are inevitably prone to take Hebraism as the law of human development, and not as simply a contribution to it, however precious. And yet the lesson must perforce be learned, that the human spirit is wider than the most priceless of the forces which bear it onward, and that to the whole development of man Hebraism itself is, like Hellenism, but a contribution.

Perhaps we may help ourselves to see this clearer by an illustration drawn from the treatment of a single great idea which has profoundly engaged the human spirit, and has given it eminent opportunities for showing its nobleness and energy. It surely must be perceived that the idea of immortality, as this idea rises in its generality before the human spirit, is something grander, truer, and more satisfying than it is in the particular forms by which St. Paul, in the famous fifteenth chapter of the *Epistle to the Corinthians*, and Plato, in the *Phaedo*, endeavor to develop and establish it. Surely we cannot but feel that the argumentation with which the Hebrew apostle goes about to expound this great idea is, after all, confused and inconclusive; and that the reasoning, drawn from analogies of likeness and equality, which is employed upon it by the Greek philosopher, is over-subtle and sterile. Above and beyond the inadequate solutions which Hebraism and Hellenism here attempt, extends the immense and august problem itself, and the human spirit which gave birth to it. And this single illustration may suggest to us how the same thing happens in other cases also.

But meanwhile, by alternations of Hebraism and Hellenism, of a man's intellectual and moral impulses, of the effort to see things as they really are and the effort to win peace by self-conquest, the human spirit proceeds; and each of these two forces has its appointed hours of culmination and seasons of rule. As the great movement of Christianity was a triumph of Hebraism and man's moral im-

---

10. **"entrusted . . . God."** From *Romans,* 3:2. 15. **wisdom . . . foolishness.** Cf. *1 Corinthians,* 3:19: "For the wisdom of this world is foolishness with God."

63. **forms . . . it.** St. Paul rests his belief in immortality upon the spiritual appearance of Christ after his death, as that appearance was observed by a number of persons including himself. In *Phaedo* (1. 65) Plato argues for a belief in immortality on the assumption of the eternity of mind and knowledge. Opposite states, he says, come from their opposites, and because such a process is reciprocal, it follows that life must succeed death, since death certainly succeeds life. Cf. Wordsworth's *Ode on Immortality,* and headnote, p. 160.

pulses, so the great movement which goes by the name of the Renascence was an uprising and reinstatement of man's intellectual impulses and of Hellenism. We in England, the devoted children of Protestantism, chiefly know the Renascence by its subordinate and secondary side of the Reformation. The Reformation has been often called a Hebraizing revival, a return to the ardor and sincereness of primitive Christianity. No one, however, can study the development of Protestantism and of Protestant churches without feeling that into the Reformation too—Hebraizing child of the Renascence, and offspring of its fervor rather than its intelligence, as it undoubtedly was—the subtle Hellenic leaven of the Renascence found its way, and that the exact respective parts, in the Reformation, of Hebraism and of Hellenism are not easy to separate. But what we may with truth say is that all which Protestantism was to itself clearly conscious of, all which it succeeded in clearly setting forth in words, had the characters of Hebraism rather than of Hellenism. The Reformation was strong in that it was an earnest return to the Bible and to doing from the heart the will of God as there written. It was weak in that it never consciously grasped or applied the central idea of the Renascence —the Hellenic idea of pursuing, in all lines of activity, the law and science, to use Plato's words, of things as they really are. Whatever direct superiority, therefore, Protestantism had over Catholicism was a moral superiority, a superiority arising out of its greater sincerity and earnestness—at the moment of its apparition, at any rate—in dealing with the heart and conscience. Its pretensions to an intellectual superiority are in general quite illusory. For Hellenism, for the thinking side in man as distinguished from the acting side, the attitude of mind of Protestantism towards the Bible in no respect differs from the attitude of mind of Catholicism towards the Church. The mental habit of him who imagines that Balaam's ass spoke in no respect differs from the mental habit of him who imagines that a Madonna of wood or stone winked; and the one, who says that God's Church makes him believe what he believes, and the other, who says that God's Word makes him believe what he believes, are for the philosopher perfectly alike in not really and truly knowing, when they say "God's Church" and "God's Word," what it is they say or whereof they affirm.

In the sixteenth century, therefore, Hellenism reëntered the world, and again stood in presence of Hebraism—a Hebraism renewed and purged. Now, it has not been enough observed, how, in the seventeenth century, a fate befell Hellenism in some respects analogous to that which befell it at the commencement of our era. The Renascence, that great reawakening of Hellenism, that irresistible return of humanity to nature and to seeing things as they are, which in art, in literature, and in physics produced such splendid fruits, had, like the anterior Hellenism of the pagan world, a side of moral weakness and of relaxation or insensibility of the moral fiber, which in Italy showed itself with the most startling plainness, but which in France, England, and other countries was very apparent too. Again this loss of spiritual balance, this exclusive preponderance given to man's perceiving and knowing side, this unnatural defect of his feeling and acting side, provoked a reaction. Let us trace that reaction where it most nearly concerns us.

Science has now made visible to everybody the great and pregnant elements of difference which lie in race, and in how signal a manner they make the genius and history of an Indo-European people vary from those of a Semitic people. Hellenism is of Indo-European growth, Hebraism is of Semitic growth; and we English, a nation of Indo-European stock, seem to belong naturally to the movement of Hellenism. But nothing more strongly marks the essential unity of man than the affinities we can perceive, in this point or that, between members of one family of peoples and members of another. And no affinity of this kind is more strongly marked than that likeness in

---

2. **Renascence.** See Vol. I, p. 301. 7. **Reformation.** See Vol. I, p. 303. 46. **Balaam's ass spoke.** As related in *Numbers*, 22:21-35.

the strength and prominence of the moral fiber, which, notwithstanding immense elements of difference, knits in some special sort the genius and history of us English, and our American descendants across the Atlantic, to the genius and history of the Hebrew people. Puritanism, which has been so great a power in the English nation, and in the strongest part of the English nation, was originally the reaction in the seventeenth century of the conscience and moral sense of our race against the moral indifference and lax rule of conduct which in the sixteenth century came in with the Renascence. It was a reaction of Hebraism against Hellenism; and it powerfully manifested itself, as was natural, in a people with much of what we call a Hebraizing turn, with a signal affinity for the bent which was the master-bent of Hebrew life. Eminently Indo-European by its *humor*, by the power it shows, through this gift, of imaginatively acknowledging the multiform aspects of the problem of life and of thus getting itself unfixed from its own over-certainty, of smiling at its own over-tenacity, our race has yet (and a great part of its strength lies here), in matters of practical life and moral conduct, a strong share of the assuredness, the tenacity, the intensity of the Hebrews. This turn manifested itself in Puritanism, and has had a great part in shaping our history for the last two hundred years. Undoubtedly it checked and changed amongst us that movement of the Renascence which we see producing in the reign of Elizabeth such wonderful fruits. Undoubtedly it stopped the prominent rule and direct development of that order of ideas which we call by the name of Hellenism, and gave the first rank to a different order of ideas. Apparently, too, as we said of the former defeat of Hellenism, if Hellenism was defeated this shows that Hellenism was imperfect and that its ascendency at that moment would not have been for the world's good.

Yet there is a very important difference between the defeat inflicted on Hellenism by Christianity eighteen hundred years ago, and the check given to the Renascence by Puritanism. The greatness of the difference is well measured by the difference in force, beauty, significance, and usefulness between primitive Christianity and Protestantism. Eighteen hundred years ago it was altogether the hour of Hebraism. Primitive Christianity was legitimately and truly the ascendant force in the world at that time, and the way of mankind's progress lay through its full development. Another hour in man's development began in the fifteenth century, and the main road of his progress then lay for a time through Hellenism. Puritanism was no longer the central current of the world's progress; it was a side stream crossing the central current and checking it. The cross and the check may have been necessary and salutary, but that does not do away with the essential difference between the main stream of man's advance and a cross or side stream. For more than two hundred years the main stream of man's advance has moved towards knowing himself and the world, seeing things as they are, spontaneity of consciousness; the main impulse of a great part, and that the strongest part, of our nation has been towards strictness of conscience. They have made the secondary the principal at the wrong moment, and the principal they have at the wrong moment treated as secondary. This contravention of the natural order has produced, as such contravention always must produce, a certain confusion and false movement, of which we are now beginning to feel, in almost every direction, the inconvenience. In all directions our habitual causes of action seem to be losing efficaciousness, credit, and control, both with others and even with ourselves. Everywhere we see the beginnings of confusion, and we want a clue to some sound order and authority. This we can only get by going back upon the actual instincts and forces which rule our life, seeing them as they really are, connecting them with other instincts and forces, and enlarging our whole view and rule of life. (1867-1868)

---

7. **Puritanism.** See Vol. I, p. 631. 20. *humor*, predominating mood or trait.

59. **Another . . . Hellenism.** The allusion to the Renaissance (see Vol. I, pp. 297 ff.). The ultimate source of the Renaissance was Greek culture.

from *The Study of Poetry*

The Study of Poetry appeared as the introductory essay to *The English Poets*, an anthology of poetry edited in 1880 by T. H. Ward. In his introduction Arnold sets forth very clearly his own theory of the meaning and function of poetry, in phrases which are still quoted, gives some very practical suggestions for acquiring a taste for verse, and comments, finally, on the work of great poets in England and elsewhere. He warns the reader who would acquire a true estimate of the best in poetry to avoid the discolorations of his judgment that come from the "historic estimate" and the "personal estimate," and to seek the detachment and freedom from bias that will enable him to secure "a sense for the best, the really excellent" in poetry. The part of this concluding review which concerns English writers has been omitted in the following reprint of the essay. With Arnold's ideas about poetry should be compared those of other critics and poets; see, for example, Wordsworth's *Preface* to the *Lyrical Ballads* (p. 319, l. 19, and note).

The future of poetry is immense, because in poetry, where it *is* worthy of its high destinies, our race, as time goes on, will find an ever surer and surer stay. There is not a creed which is not shaken, not an accredited dogma which is not shown to be questionable, not a received tradition which does not threaten to dissolve. Our religion has materialized itself in the fact, in the supposed fact; it has attached its emotion to the fact, and now the fact is failing it. But for poetry the idea is everything; the rest is a world of illusion, of divine illusion. Poetry attaches its emotion to the idea; the idea *is* the fact. The strongest part of our religion today is its unconscious poetry."

Let me be permitted to quote these words of my own, as uttering the thought which should, in my opinion, go with us and govern us in all our study of poetry. In the present work it is the course of one great contributory stream to the world-river of poetry that we are invited to follow. We are here invited to trace the stream of English poetry. But whether we set ourselves, as here, to follow only one of the several streams that make the mighty river of poetry, or whether we seek to know them all, our governing thought should be the same. We should conceive of poetry worthily, and more highly than it has been the custom to conceive of it. We should conceive of it as capable of higher uses, and called to higher destinies, than those which in general men have assigned to it hitherto. More and more mankind will discover that we have to turn to poetry to interpret life for us, to console us, to sustain us. Without poetry, our science will appear incomplete; and most of what now passes with us for religion and philosophy will be replaced by poetry. Science, I say, will appear incomplete without it. For finely and truly does Wordsworth call poetry "the impassioned expression which is in the countenance of all science"; and what is a countenance without its expression? Again, Wordsworth finely and truly calls poetry "the breath and finer spirit of all knowledge": our religion, parading evidences such as those on which the popular mind relies now; our philosophy, pluming itself on its reasonings about causation and finite and infinite being; what are they but the shadows and dreams and false shows of knowledge? The day will come when we shall wonder at ourselves for having trusted to them, for having taken them seriously; and the more we perceive their hollowness, the more we shall prize "the breath and finer spirit of knowledge" offered to us by poetry.

But if we conceive thus highly of the destinies of poetry, we must also set our standard for poetry high, since poetry, to be capable of fulfilling such high destinies, must be poetry of a high order of excellence. We must ac-

---

8. **religion . . . fact.** An allusion to the growth of scientific knowledge and its influence on religious faith during the nineteenth century. See p. 405. 17. **these words.** Quoted with slight changes from Arnold's Introduction to *The Hundred Greatest Men* (1879).

37. **Without . . . incomplete.** Cf. Huxley's *Science and Culture*, p. 571. 42. **Wordsworth.** The quotations are from the *Preface to the Lyrical Ballads*, p. 324, ll. 31 ff.

custom ourselves to a high standard and to a strict judgment. Sainte-Beuve relates that Napoleon one day said, when somebody was spoken of in his presence as a charlatan: "Charlatan as much as you please; but where is there *not* charlatanism?"—"Yes," answers Sainte-Beuve, "in politics, in the art of governing mankind, that is perhaps true. But in the order of thought, in art, the glory, the eternal honor is that charlatanism shall find no entrance; herein lies the inviolableness of that noble portion of man's being." It is admirably said, and let us hold fast to it. In poetry, which is thought and art in one, it is the glory, the eternal honor, that charlatanism shall find no entrance; that this noble sphere be kept inviolate and inviolable. Charlatanism is for confusing or obliterating the distinctions between excellent and inferior, sound and unsound or only half-sound, true and untrue or only half-true. It is charlatanism, conscious or unconscious, whenever we confuse or obliterate these. And in poetry, more than anywhere else, it is unpermissible to confuse or obliterate them. For in poetry the distinction between excellent and inferior, sound and unsound or only half-sound, true and untrue or only half-true, is of paramount importance. It is of paramount importance because of the high destinies of poetry. In poetry, as a criticism of life under the conditions fixed for such a criticism by the laws of poetic truth and poetic beauty, the spirit of our race will find, we have said, as time goes on and as other helps fail, its consolation and stay. But the consolation and stay will be of power in proportion to the power of the criticism of life. And the criticism of life will be of power in proportion as the poetry conveying it is excellent rather than inferior, sound rather than unsound or half-sound, true rather than untrue or half-true.

The best poetry is what we want; the best poetry will be found to have a power of forming, sustaining, and delighting us, as nothing else can. A clearer, deeper sense of the best in poetry, and of the strength and joy to be drawn from it, is the most precious benefit which we can gather from a poetical collection such as the present. And yet in the very nature and conduct of such a collection there is inevitably something which tends to obscure in us the consciousness of what our benefit should be, and to distract us from the pursuit of it. We should therefore steadily set it before our minds at the outset, and should compel ourselves to revert constantly to the thought of it as we proceed.

Yes; constantly in reading poetry, a sense for the best, the really excellent, and of the strength and joy to be drawn from it, should be present in our minds and should govern our estimate of what we read. But this real estimate, the only true one, is liable to be superseded, if we are not watchful, by two other kinds of estimate, the historic estimate and the personal estimate, both of which are fallacious. A poet or a poem may count to us historically, they may count to us on grounds personal to ourselves, and they may count to us really. They may count to us historically. The course of development of a nation's language, thought, and poetry is profoundly interesting; and by regarding a poet's work as a stage in this course of development we may easily bring ourselves to make it of more importance as poetry than in itself it really is, we may come to use a language of quite exaggerated praise in criticizing it; in short, to overrate it. So arises in our poetic judgments the fallacy caused by the estimate which we may call historic. Then, again, a poet or a poem may count to us on grounds personal to ourselves. Our personal affinities, liking, and circumstances have great power to sway our estimate of this or that poet's work, and to make us attach more importance to it as poetry than in itself it really possesses, because to us it is, or has been, of high importance. Here also we overrate the object of our interest, and apply to it a language of praise which is quite exaggerated. And thus we get the source of a second fallacy in our poetic judgments—the fallacy caused by an estimate which we may call personal.

---

2. **Sainte-Beuve,** Charles Augustin Sainte-Beuve (1804-1869), a distinguished French literary critic, who influenced Arnold's critical theories.

50. **collection . . . present.** See headnote, p. 552.

Both fallacies are natural. It is evident how naturally the study of the history and development of a poetry may incline a man to pause over reputations and works once conspicuous but now obscure, and to quarrel with a careless public for skipping, in obedience to mere tradition and habit, from one famous name or work in its national poetry to another, ignorant of what it misses, and of the reason for keeping what it keeps, and of the whole process of growth in its poetry. The French have become diligent students of their own early poetry, which they long neglected; the study makes many of them dissatisfied with their so-called classical poetry, the court-tragedy of the seventeenth century, a poetry which Pellisson long ago reproached with its want of the true poetic stamp, with its *politesse stérile et rampante*, but which nevertheless has reigned in France as absolutely as if it had been the perfection of classical poetry indeed. The dissatisfaction is natural; yet a lively and accomplished critic, M. Charles d'Héricault, the editor of Clément Marot, goes too far when he says that "the cloud of glory playing round a classic is a mist as dangerous to the future of a literature as it is intolerable for the purposes of history." "It hinders," he goes on, "it hinders us from seeing more than one single point, the culminating and exceptional point; the summary, fictitious and arbitrary, of a thought and of a work. It substitutes a halo for a physiognomy, it puts a statue where there was once a man, and hiding from us all trace of the labor, the attempts, the weaknesses, the failures, it claims not study but veneration; it does not show us how the thing is done, it imposes upon us a model. Above all, for the historian this creation of classic personages is inadmissible; for it withdraws the poet from his time, from his proper life, it breaks historical relationships, it blinds criticism by conventional admiration, and renders the investigation of literary origins unacceptable. It gives us a human personage no longer, but a God seated immovable amidst His perfect work, like Jupiter on Olympus; and hardly will it be possible for the young student, to whom such work is exhibited at such a distance from him, to believe that it did not issue ready made from that divine head."

All this is brilliantly and tellingly said, but we must plead for a distinction. Everything depends on the reality of a poet's classic character. If he is a dubious classic, let us sift him; if he is a false classic, let us explode him. But if he is a real classic, if his work belongs to the class of the very best (for this is the true and right meaning of the word *classic, classical*), then the great thing for us is to feel and enjoy his work as deeply as ever we can, and to appreciate the wide difference between it and all work which has not the same high character. This is what is salutary, this is what is formative; this is the great benefit to be got from the study of poetry. Everything which interferes with it, which hinders it, is injurious. True, we must read our classic with open eyes, and not with eyes blinded with superstition; we must perceive when his work comes short, when it drops out of the class of the very best, and we must rate it, in such cases, at its proper value. But the use of this negative criticism is not in itself, it is entirely in its enabling us to have a clearer sense and a deeper enjoyment of what is truly excellent. To trace the labor, the attempts, the weaknesses, the failures of a genuine classic, to acquaint oneself with his time and his life and his historical relationship, is mere literary dilettantism unless it has that clear sense and deeper enjoyment for its end. It may be said that the more we know about a classic the better we shall enjoy him; and, if we lived as long as Methuselah and had all of us heads of perfect clearness and wills of perfect steadfastness, this might be true in fact as it is plausible in theory. But the case here is much the same as the case with the Greek and Latin studies of our schoolboys. The elaborate philological

12. **their . . . poetry,** that of the Old French period, of the eleventh and twelfth centuries. The "so-called classical poetry" of the seventeenth century was noted for its emphasis upon set rules of form and correctness. 17. **Pellisson,** Paul Pellisson (1624-1693), a French writer and politician. 18. **politesse . . . rampante,** barren and inflated courtesy. 24. **d'Héricault,** a French novelist, critic, and historian of the nineteenth century. **Marot,** a noted French romantic poet (c. 1495-1544), with a decided modern flavor.

48. **Olympus,** a mountain in Greece, the reputed home of Jupiter and the other gods. 86. **Methuselah,** one of the Hebrew patriarchs, who according to *Genesis,* 5:27, lived 969 years.

groundwork which we require them to lay is in theory an admirable preparation for appreciating the Greek and Latin authors worthily. The more thoroughly we lay the groundwork, the better we shall be able, it may be said, to enjoy the authors. True, if time were not so short, and schoolboys' wits not so soon tired and their power of attention exhausted; only, as it is, the elaborate philological preparation goes on, but the authors are little known and less enjoyed. So with the investigator of "historic origins" in poetry. He ought to enjoy the true classic all the better for his investigations; he often is distracted from the enjoyment of the best, and with the less good he overbusies himself, and is prone to overrate it in proportion to the trouble which it has cost him.

The idea of tracing historic origins and historical relationships cannot be absent from a compilation like the present. And naturally the poets to be exhibited in it will be assigned to those persons for exhibition who are known to prize them highly, rather than to those who have no special inclination towards them. Moreover the very occupation with an author, and the business of exhibiting him, disposes us to affirm and amplify his importance. In the present work, therefore, we are sure of frequent temptation to adopt the historic estimate, or the personal estimate, and to forget the real estimate; which latter, nevertheless, we must employ if we are to make poetry yield us its full benefit. So high is that benefit, the benefit of clearly feeling and of deeply enjoying the really excellent, the truly classic in poetry, that we do well, I say, to set it fixedly before our minds as our object in studying poets and poetry, and to make the desire of attaining it the one principle to which, as the *Imitation* says, whatever we may read or come to know, we always return. *Cum multa legeris et cognoveris, ad unum semper oportet redire principium.*

The historic estimate is likely in especial to affect our judgment and our language when we are dealing with ancient poets; the personal estimate when we are dealing with poets our contemporaries, or at any rate modern. The exaggerations due to the historic estimate are not in themselves, perhaps, of very much gravity. Their report hardly enters the general ear; probably they do not always impose even on the literary men who adopt them. But they lead to a dangerous abuse of language. So we hear Caedmon, amongst our own poets, compared to Milton. I have already noticed the enthusiasm of one accomplished French critic for "historic origins." Another eminent French critic, M. Vitet, comments upon that famous document of the early poetry of his nation, the *Chanson de Roland*. It is indeed a most interesting document. The *joculator* or *jongleur* Taillefer, who was with William the Conqueror's army at Hastings, marched before the Norman troops, so said the tradition, singing "of Charlemagne and of Roland and of Oliver, and of the vassals who died at Roncevaux"; and it is suggested that in the *Chanson de Roland* by one Turoldus or Théroulde, a poem preserved in a manuscript of the twelfth century in the Bodleian Library at Oxford, we have certainly the matter, perhaps even some of the words, of the chant which Taillefer sang. The poem has vigor and freshness; it is not without pathos. But M. Vitet is not satisfied with seeing in it a document of some poetic value, and of very high historic and linguistic value; he sees in it a grand and beautiful work, a monument of epic genius. In its general design he finds the grandiose conception, in its details he finds the constant union of simplicity with greatness, which are the marks, he truly says, of the genuine epic, and distinguish it from the artificial epic of literary ages. One thinks of Homer; this is the sort of praise which is

---

40. *Imitation.* See p. 547, note 2. 42. *Cum ... principium*, although you have read and known many things, you must always return to one principle (3, 43, 2).

56. **Caedmon**, an Anglo-Saxon religious poet. See Vol. I, pp. 12 and 65 ff. 60. **Vitet**, Ludovic Vitet (1802-1873), a French critic, dramatist, and politician. 62. **Chanson de Roland**, the *Song of Roland*, French national epic of the eleventh century. Roland, the hero of the poem, is a brave warrior of Charlemagne (742-814), the celebrated King of the Franks. Oliver is Roland's companion in arms. 64. *joculator* or *jongleur*, minstrel. 65. **Hastings**, the Battle of Hastings in 1066. See Vol. I, pp. 73 ff. 67. **Charlemagne**, Charlemagne the Great, Emperor of the West (800-814) and King of the Franks (768-814). 69. **Roncevaux**, a pass in the Pyrenees, between Spain and France, the scene of events narrated in the *Chanson*. 70. **Turoldus.** The Oxford manuscript of the epic closes with the line, "Here ends the geste that Turoldus tells." He may have been the author of the poem, the minstrel who sang it, or the scribe who copied it.

given to Homer, and justly given. Higher praise there cannot well be, and it is the praise due to epic poetry of the highest order only, and to no other. Let us try, then, the *Chanson de Roland* at its best. Roland, mortally wounded, lays himself down under a pine-tree, with his face turned towards Spain and the enemy—

> De plusurs choses à remembrer li prist,
> De tantes teres cume li bers cunquist,
> De dulce France, des humes de sun lign,
> De Carlemagne sun seignor ki l'nurrit.

That is primitive work, I repeat, with an undeniable poetic quality of its own. It deserves such praise, and such praise is sufficient for it. But now turn to Homer—

> Ὣς φάτο, τοὺς δ' ἤδη κατέχεν φυσίζοος αἶα
> ἐν Λακεδαίμονι αὖθι, φίλη ἐν πατρίδι γαίῃ

We are here in another world, another order of poetry altogether; here is rightly due such supreme praise as that which M. Vitet gives to the *Chanson de Roland*. If our words are to have any meaning, if our judgments are to have any solidity, we must not heap that supreme praise upon poetry of an order immeasurably inferior.

Indeed there can be no more useful help for discovering what poetry belongs to the class of the truly excellent, and can therefore do us most good, than to have always in one's mind lines and expressions of the great masters, and to apply them as a touchstone to other poetry. Of course we are not to require this other poetry to resemble them; it may be very dissimilar. But if we have any tact we shall find them, when we have lodged them well in our minds, an infallible touchstone for detecting the presence or absence of high poetic quality, and also the degree of this quality, in all other poetry which we may place beside them. Short passages, even single lines, will serve our turn quite sufficiently. Take the two lines which I have just quoted from Homer, the poet's comment on Helen's mention of her brothers;—or take his

> Ἆ δειλώ, τί σφῶι δόμεν Πηλῆι ἄνακτι
> θνητῷ; ὑμεῖς δ' ἐστὸν ἀγήρω τ' ἀθανάτω τε.
> ἦ ἵνα δυστήνοισι μετ' ἀνδράσιν ἄλγε'
> ἔχητον;

the address of Zeus to the horses of Peleus;—or take finally his

> Καὶ σέ, γέρον, τὸ πρὶν μὲν ἀκούομεν ὄλβιον εἶναι

the words of Achilles to Priam, a suppliant before him. Take that incomparable line and a half of Dante, Ugolino's tremendous words:

> Io no piangeva; sì dentro impietrai.
> Piangevan elli . . .

take the lovely words of Beatrice to Virgil:

> Io son fatta da Dio, sua mercè, tale,
> Che la vostra miseria non mi tange,
> Nè fiamma d'esto incendio non m'assale . . .

take the simple, but perfect, single line:

> In la sua volontade è nostra pace.

---

9. **De plusurs,** etc., Then began he to call many things to remembrance—all the lands which his valor conquered, and pleasant France, and the men of his lineage, and Charlemagne his liege lord who nourished him (*Chanson de Roland*, III, 939-942). 17. Ὣς ϕάτο, etc.,
So said she; they long since in Earth's soft arms
  were reposing.
There in their own dear land, their fatherland,
  Lacedaemon (*Iliad*, III, 243-244. Hawtrey's translation).
22. **If our words,** etc. Cf. Ruskin's *Roots of Honor*, p. 519, ll. 71 ff.

45. **brothers,** the twins, Castor and Pollux, horsemen and patrons of games. 46. Ἆ δειλώ, etc., Ah, unhappy pair, why gave we you to King Peleus, to a mortal? but ye are without old age, and immortal. Was it that with men born to misery ye might have sorrow? (*Iliad*, XVII, 443-445). 49. **Peleus,** King of Thessaly and father of Achilles, a principal character in the *Iliad*. 51. Καὶ σε, etc., Nay, and thou too, old man, in former days wast, as we hear, happy (*Iliad*, XXIV, 543). 52. **Priam,** King of Troy at the time of the Trojan War. 54. **Dante,** the greatest of the Italian poets (1265-1321); author of *The Divine Comedy*, in three parts—Hell, Purgatory, and Paradise. **Ugolino,** an Italian political leader (thirteenth century) who, with his two nephews, was starved to death in prison at Pisa in 1288. Dante represents him as gnawing the head of his enemy in Hell, where both are frozen together in a lake of ice. 55. **Io no piangeva,** etc., I wailed not; so of stone grew I within; they wailed (*Inferno*, XXXIII, 39-40). 57. **Beatrice to Virgil.** Beatrice Portinari (1266-1290) was the beautiful Italian lady celebrated in the poetry of Dante. In *The Divine Comedy*, Virgil guided Dante through Hell and Purgatory, but Beatrice guided him through Paradise. 58. **Io son fatta,** etc., Of such sort hath God, thanked be His mercy, made me, that your misery toucheth me not, neither doth the flame of this fire strike me (*Inferno*, II, 91-93). 62. **In . . . pace,** In His will is our peace (*Paradiso*, III, 85).

Take of Shakespeare a line or two of Henry the Fourth's expostulation with sleep:

> Wilt thou upon the high and giddy mast
> Seal up the ship-boy's eyes, and rock his brains
> In cradle of the rude imperious surge . . .

and take, as well, Hamlet's dying request to Horatio:

> If thou didst ever hold me in thy heart,
> Absent thee from felicity awhile,
> And in this harsh world draw thy breath in pain,
> To tell my story . . .

Take of Milton that Miltonic passage:

> Darkened so, yet shone
> Above them all the archangel; but his face
> Deep scars of thunder had intrenched, and care
> Sat on his faded cheek . . .

add two such lines as:

> And courage never to submit or yield
> And what is else not to be overcome . . .

and finish with the exquisite close to the loss of Proserpine, the loss

> . . . which cost Ceres all that pain
> To seek her through the world.

These few lines, if we have tact and can use them, are enough even of themselves to keep clear and sound our judgments about poetry, to save us from fallacious estimates of it, to conduct us to a real estimate.

The specimens I have quoted differ widely from one another, but they have in common this: the possession of the very highest poetical quality. If we are thoroughly penetrated by their power, we shall find that we have acquired a sense enabling us, whatever poetry may be laid before us, to feel the degree in which a high poetical quality is present or wanting there. Critics give themselves great labor to draw out what in the abstract constitutes the characters of a high quality of poetry. It is much better simply to have recourse to concrete examples;—to take specimens of poetry of the high, the very highest quality, and to say: The characters of a high quality poetry are what is expressed *there*. They are far better recognized by being felt in the verse of the master, than by being perused in the prose of the critic. Nevertheless if we are urgently pressed to give some critical account of them, we may safely, perhaps, venture on laying down, not indeed how and why the characters arise, but where and in what they arise. They are in the matter and substance of the poetry, and they are in its manner and style. Both of these, the substance and matter on the one hand, the style and manner on the other, have a mark, an accent of high beauty, worth, and power. But if we are asked to define this mark and accent in the abstract, our answer must be: No, for we should thereby be darkening the question, not clearing it. The mark and accent are given by the substance and matter of that poetry, by the style and manner of that poetry, and of all other poetry which is akin to it in quality.

Only one thing we may add as to the substance and matter of poetry, guiding ourselves by Aristotle's profound observation that the superiority of poetry over history consists in its possessing a higher truth and a higher seriousness (φιλοσοφώτερον καὶ σπουδαιότερον). Let us add, therefore, to what we have said, this: that the substance and matter of the best poetry acquire their special character from possessing, in an eminent degree, truth and seriousness. We may add yet further, what

---

3. **Wilt thou,** etc. From *2 Henry IV*, III, i, 18-20. 8. **If thou didst,** etc. From *Hamlet*, V, ii, 361-362. 13. **Darkened so,** etc. From *Paradise Lost*, I, 599-602 (Vol. I, p. 725). 18. **And courage,** etc., *ibid.*, I, 108-109. 21. **Proserpine.** See Swinburne's *The Garden of Proserpine* and note, p. 813. 22. **which cost,** etc. From *Paradise Lost*, IV, 271-272 (See Vol. I, p. 746).

67. **Aristotle,** the most famous of the Greek philosophers (384-322 B.C.). 70. φιλοσοφώτερον, etc., more philosophic and more serious (*Poetics*, 9).

is in itself evident, that to the style and manner of the best poetry their special character, their accent, is given by their diction, and, even yet more, by their movement. And though we distinguish between the two characters, the two accents, of superiority, yet they are nevertheless vitally connected one with the other. The superior character of truth and seriousness, in the matter and substance of the best poetry, is inseparable from the superiority of diction and movement marking its style and manner. The two superiorities are closely related, and are in steadfast proportion one to the other. So far as high poetic truth and seriousness are wanting to a poet's matter and substance, so far also, we may be sure, will a high poetic stamp of diction and movement be wanting to his style and manner. In proportion as this high stamp of diction and movement, again, is absent from a poet's style and manner, we shall find, also, that high poetic truth and seriousness are absent from his substance and matter.

[In the rest of the essay Arnold traces the history of poetry in France and in England.]

Milton

This essay was originally an address delivered in St. Margaret's Church, Westminster, on February 13, 1888, on the occasion of the unveiling of a memorial window, which was the gift of Mr. George W. Childs of Philadelphia. It was published the same year in *Essays in Criticism; Second Series.*

THE most eloquent voice of our century uttered, shortly before leaving the world, a warning cry against "the Anglo-Saxon contagion." The tendencies and aims, the view of life and the social economy of the ever-multiplying and spreading Anglo-Saxon race, would be found congenial, this prophet feared, by all the prose, all the vulgarity amongst mankind, and would invade and overpower all nations. The true ideal would be lost, a general sterility of mind and heart would set in.

The prophet had in view, no doubt, in the warning thus given, us and our colonies, but the United States still more. There the Anglo-Saxon race is already most numerous, there it increases fastest; there material interests are most absorbing and pursued with most energy; there the ideal, the saving ideal, of a high and rare excellence, seems perhaps to suffer most danger of being obscured and lost. Whatever one may think of the general danger to the world from the Anglo-Saxon contagion, it appears to me difficult to deny that the growing greatness and influence of the United States does bring with it some danger to the ideal of a high and rare excellence. The *average man* is too much a religion there; his performance is unduly magnified, his shortcomings are not duly seen and admitted. A lady in the State of Ohio sent to me only the other day a volume on American authors; the praise given throughout was of such high pitch that in thanking her I could not forbear saying that for only one or two of the authors named was such a strain of praise admissible, and that we lost all real standard of excellence by praising so uniformly and immoderately. She answered me with charming good temper, that very likely I was quite right, but it was pleasant to her to think that excellence was common and abundant. But excellence is not common and abundant; on the contrary, as the Greek poet long ago said, excellence dwells among rocks hardly accessible, and a man must almost wear his heart out before he can reach her. Whoever talks of excellence as common and abundant, is on the way to lose all right

1. **eloquent voice . . . century.** The allusion has been claimed for Goethe (1749-1832), Victor Hugo (1802-1885), Emerson (1803-1882), Coleridge (1772-1834), and Carlyle (1795-1881). In his lecture on Emerson given in America in 1884 and published in *Macmillan's Magazine* in May of that year and later in *Discourses in America* (1885) Arnold speaks of the "puissant voice of Carlyle," the "clear and pure voice" of Emerson, and "the voice of Goethe" as "the greatest voice of the century." Since it was his practice to repeat his own phrases, it would seem almost certain that the present allusion is to Goethe.

44. **the Greek poet,** Simonides of Ceos (556?-468? B.C.), a Greek lyric poet; the reference is to Fragment 58. Hesiod (fl. 776 B.C.), a Greek epic poet, expresses a similar idea in *Works and Days,* 289 ff. Cf. also the Latin poet Ovid, *Ars Amatoria,* II, 537: "There is no excellence without difficulty."

standard of excellence. And when the right standard of excellence is lost, it is not likely that much which is excellent will be produced.

To habituate ourselves, therefore, to approve, as the Bible says, things that are really excellent, is of the highest importance. And some apprehension may justly be caused by a tendency in Americans to take, or, at any rate, attempt to take, profess to take, the average man and his performances too seriously, to overrate and overpraise what is not really superior.

But we have met here today to witness the unveiling of a gift in Milton's honor, and a gift bestowed by an American, Mr. Childs of Philadelphia; whose cordial hospitality so many Englishmen, I myself among the number, have experienced in America. It was only last autumn that Stratford-upon-Avon celebrated the reception of a gift from the same generous donor in honor of Shakespeare. Shakespeare and Milton—he who wishes to keep his standard of excellence high cannot choose two better objects of regard and honor. And it is an American who has chosen them, and whose beautiful gift in honor of one of them, Milton, with Mr. Whittier's simple and true lines inscribed upon it, is unveiled today. Perhaps this gift in honor of Milton, of which I am asked to speak, is, even more than the gift in honor of Shakespeare, one to suggest edifying reflections to us.

Like Mr. Whittier, I treat the gift of Mr. Childs as a gift in honor of Milton, although the window given is in memory of his second wife, Catherine Woodcock, the "late espoused saint" of the famous sonnet, who died in childbed at the end of the first year of her marriage with Milton, and who lies buried here with her infant. Milton is buried in Cripplegate, but he lived for a good while in this parish of St. Margaret's, Westminster, and here he composed part of *Paradise Lost*, and the whole of *Paradise Regained* and *Samson Agonistes*.

When death deprived him of the Catherine whom the new window commemorates, Milton had still some eighteen years to live, and Cromwell, his "chief of men," was yet ruling England. But the Restoration, with its "Sons of Belial," was not far off; and in the meantime Milton's heavy affliction had laid fast hold upon him, his eyesight had failed totally, he was blind. In what remained to him of life he had the consolation of producing the *Paradise Lost* and the *Samson Agonistes*, and such a consolation we may indeed count as no slight one. But the daily life of happiness in common things and in domestic affections —a life of which, to Milton as to Dante, too small a share was given—he seems to have known most, if not only, in his one married year with the wife who is here buried. Her form "vested all in white," as in his sonnet he relates that after her death she appeared to him, her face veiled, but with "love, sweetness, and goodness" shining in her person—this fair and gentle daughter of the rigid sectarist of Hackney, this lovable companion with whom Milton had rest and happiness one year, is a part of Milton indeed, and in calling up her memory, we call up his.

And in calling up Milton's memory we call up, let me say, a memory upon which, in prospect of the Anglo-Saxon contagion and of its dangers supposed and real, it may be well to lay stress even more than upon Shakespeare's. If to our English race an inadequate sense for perfection of work is a real danger, if the discipline of respect for a high and flawless excellence is peculiarly needed by us, Milton is of all our gifted men the best lesson, the most salutary influence. In the sure and flawless perfection of his rhythm and diction he is as admirable as Virgil or Dante, and in this respect he is unique amongst us. No one else in English literature and art possesses the like distinction.

Thomson, Cowper, Wordsworth, all of

---

5. **the Bible says.** Cf. *Philippians*, 1:10: "That ye may approve things that are excellent." 27. **Whittier's . . . lines,** *Milton*, by John Greenleaf Whittier (1807-1892):
  The new world honors him whose lofty plea
   For England's freedom made her own more sure,
  Whose song, immortal in its theme, shall be
   Their common freehold while both worlds endure.
37. **famous sonnet,** *On His Deceased Wife* (Vol. I, p. 715).
40. **Cripplegate,** a section of London northeast of Westminster.

49. **"Sons of Belial."** Belial was the ancient Hebrew personification of wickedness; hence identified with the devil. The phrase is used several times in the Old Testament (see *1 Samuel*, 2:12), and is also found in Milton's *Paradise Lost*, I, 502 (Vol. I, p. 723). 59. **Dante.** See p. 556, note 54. 67. **rigid . . . Hackney.** Her father was a strict Presbyterian; Hackney is a borough of London. 84. **Virgil.** Roman epic, didactic, and idyllic poet (70-19 B.C.). 88. **Thomson.** See p. 32. **Cowper.** See p. 73. **Wordsworth.** See p. 118.

them good poets who have studied Milton, followed Milton, adopted his form, fail in their diction and rhythm if we try them by that high standard of excellence maintained by Milton constantly. From style really high and pure Milton never departs; their departures from it are frequent.

Shakespeare is divinely strong, rich, and attractive. But sureness of perfect style Shakespeare himself does not possess. I have heard a politician express wonder at the treasures of political wisdom in a certain celebrated scene of *Troilus and Cressida;* for my part I am at least equally moved to wonder at the fantastic and false diction in which Shakespeare has in that scene clothed them. Milton, from one end of *Paradise Lost* to the other, is in his diction and rhythm constantly a great artist in the great style. Whatever may be said as to the subject of his poem, as to the conditions under which he received his subject and treated it, that praise, at any rate, is assured to him.

For the rest, justice is not at present done, in my opinion, to Milton's management of the inevitable matter of a Puritan epic, a matter full of difficulties, for a poet. Justice is not done to the *architectonics*, as Goethe would have called them, of *Paradise Lost;* in these, too, the power of Milton's art is remarkable. But this may be a proposition which requires discussion and development for establishing it, and they are impossible on an occasion like the present.

That Milton, of all our English race, is by his diction and rhythm the one artist of the highest rank in the great style whom we have; this I take as requiring no discussion, this I take as certain.

The mighty power of poetry and art is generally admitted. But where the soul of this power, of this power at its best, chiefly resides, very many of us fail to see. It resides chiefly in the refining and elevation wrought in us by the high and rare excellence of the great style. We may feel the effect without being able to give ourselves clear account of its cause, but the thing is so. Now, no race needs the influences mentioned, the influences of refining and elevation, more than ours; and in poetry and art our grand source for them is Milton.

To what does he owe this supreme distinction? To nature first and foremost, to that bent of nature for inequality which to the worshipers of the average man is so unacceptable; to a gift, a divine favor. "The older one grows," says Goethe, "the more one prizes natural gifts, because by no possibility can they be procured and stuck on." Nature formed Milton to be a great poet. But what other poet has shown so sincere a sense of the grandeur of his vocation, and a moral effort so constant and sublime to make and keep himself worthy of it? The Milton of religious and political controversy, and perhaps of domestic life also, is not seldom disfigured by want of amenity, by acerbity. The Milton of poetry, on the other hand, is one of those great men "who are modest"—to quote a fine remark of Leopardi, that gifted and stricken young Italian, who in his sense for poetic style is worthy to be named with Dante and Milton—"who are modest, because they continually compare themselves, not with other men, but with that idea of the perfect which they have before their mind." The Milton of poetry is the man, in his own magnificent phrase, of "devout prayer to that Eternal Spirit that can enrich with all utterance and knowledge, and sends out his Seraphim with the hallowed fire of his altar, to touch and purify the lips of whom he pleases." And finally, the Milton of poetry is, in his own words again, the man of "industrious and select reading." Continually he lived in companionship with high and rare excellence, with the great Hebrew poets and prophets, with the great poets of Greece and Rome. The Hebrew compositions were not in verse, and can be not inadequately represented by the grand, measured prose of our English Bible. The verse of the poets of Greece and Rome

---

12. **certain . . . scene,** Act I, sc. 3. 19. **the great style.** Arnold places unusual emphasis on this point. Cf. Ruskin's *Grand Style,* p. 505.

70. **Leopardi,** a brilliant Italian poet, essayist, and scholar (1798-1837); he was sickly and deformed from his youth, and was deaf and half-blind before he was thirty. 78. "**devout prayer,**" etc. In *The Reason of Church-Government,* 2. 80. **Seraphim,** one of the highest order of angels, excelling in wisdom and zeal in the service of God.

no translation can adequately reproduce. Prose cannot have the power of verse; verse-translation may give whatever of charm is in the soul and talent of the translator himself, but never the specific charm of the verse and poet translated. In our race are thousands of readers, presently there will be millions, who know not a word of Greek and Latin, and will never learn those languages. If this host of readers are ever to gain any sense of the power and charm of the great poets of antiquity, their way to gain it is not through translations of the ancients, but through the original poetry of Milton, who has the like power and charm, because he has the like great style.

Through Milton they may gain it, for, in conclusion, Milton is English; this master in the great style of the ancients is English. Virgil, whom Milton loved and honored, has at the end of the *Aeneid* a noble passage, where Juno, seeing the defeat of Turnus and the Italians imminent, the victory of the Trojan invaders assured, entreats Jupiter that Italy may nevertheless survive and be herself still, may retain her own mind, manners, and language, and not adopt those of the conqueror.

Sit Latium, sint Albani per secula reges!

Jupiter grants the prayer; he promises perpetuity and the future to Italy—Italy reinforced by whatever virtue the Trojan race has, but Italy, not Troy. This we may take as a sort of parable suiting ourselves. All the Anglo-Saxon contagion, all the flood of Anglo-Saxon commonness, beats vainly against the great style but cannot shake it, and has to accept its triumph. But it triumphs in Milton, in one of our own race, tongue, faith, and morals. Milton has made the great style no longer an exotic here; he has made it an inmate amongst us, a leaven, and a power. Nevertheless he, and his hearers on both sides of the Atlantic, are English, and will remain English—

Sermonem Ausonii patrium moresque tenebunt.

The English race overspreads the world, and at the same time the ideal of an excellence the most high and the most rare abides a possession with it forever.   (1888)

21. **Juno . . . Turnus.** In classical mythology Juno was the wife of Jupiter and queen of the gods. Turnus, King of the Rutuli, fought against Aeneas, to whom Latinus, King of Latium, had offered his daughter Lavinia, although she was betrothed to Turnus.

27. **Sit . . . reges!** "Let Latium exist; let Alban kings flourish forever."—Virgil, *Aeneid,* XII, 826. 44. **Sermonem . . . tenebunt,** "the Ausonians will hold to the language and the customs of their fathers."—*Ibid.,* XII, 834.

Thomas Henry Huxley

1825-1895

The best portrait of Thomas Henry Huxley presents him as standing at a lecture table with a human skull in his hand. The posture suggests his life interests. Huxley was a brilliant biologist and a skilful and an eager teacher. To him, perhaps more than to any other Victorian prose writer, may be applied Chaucer's characterization of the Clerk of Oxenford, ". . . gladly wolde he lerne, and gladly teche." Huxley's life was devoted to the acquiring of biological truth and to its earnest dissemination in language which the layman could understand.

He was the seventh child of George Huxley, master of a school at Ealing. Part of his early education he acquired at this school and part at home. Later he became a medical student at Charing Cross Hospital and took his degree there in 1845. The following year he was given an assignment as assistant surgeon on H.M.S. *Rattlesnake,* and for four years he traveled the seven seas, acquiring immense quantities of data and sending scientific articles by the dozen to technical journals in England without learning until his return whether or not any had been accepted. Some of these had been accepted, however, and—although Huxley did not know it at the time—they had laid a foundation for his reputation as a scientist. In 1855 he was appointed Lecturer on Natural History to the School of Science and Naturalist to the Geographical Survey. The appointment made it possible for him to marry; and he settled down in London to a life of intense scientific and educational activity.

Huxley's own characterization of his career is that it consisted of an endless battle for truth as he understood truth. It was his aim, he declared, "to smite all humbugs, however great; to set an example of abstinence from petty personal controversies, and of toleration for everything but lying; to be indifferent as to whether the work is recognized as mine or not, so long as it is done." His most prolonged and vigorous battle was his defense of Darwin's theory of evolution against the attacks of men with "clerical minds" like Owen and Wilberforce. Huxley was a skilled anatomist; Darwin was not. Huxley was much better able, therefore, actually to demonstrate the soundness of the theory of evolution by making those keen studies in comparative anatomy for which he became famous. He was, moreover, a popularizer of science as well as an industrious scholar. Unlike most scientists, he did not shut himself up in his laboratory, hermit-like. He has asserted very modestly that he was not a natural writer and public speaker, and that he had to discipline himself severely in the art of composition. However true this may be, it is certain that he was for years one of the most brilliant of popular expositors of scientific facts and theories.

The chief literary characteristic of both his oral and written style is its luminosity; whatever he says or writes is clear. His sense of anatomical structure seems to have stood him in good stead in the organization of his lectures and essays. Moreover, he made courteous allowances for audiences not trained in scientific methods. His illustrations, his figures of speech, his sense of humor, his good platform manners all helped to put his listeners at ease and to entertain them at the same time that they were acquiring facts and ideas. He was one of the most skilful and industrious of the Victorian group who had faith in their own times and who were eager to see England advance in the way which seemed to them to be the path of truth and light.

Huxley's collected essays and addresses suggest both his scientific and his educational interests. The books by which he is best known are: *Man's Place in Nature* (1863); *The Physical Basis of Life* (1868); *Lay Sermons, Addresses, and Reviews* (1870); *Science and Morals* (1886); *Essays upon Some Controverted Questions* (1892); *Ethics and Evolution* (1893); and an autobiography. Scattered articles in the contemporary magazines include those which grew out of a fascinating controversy between "Darwin's Bulldog"—as Huxley was often called—and the staunch old Gladstone on the matter of the Gadarene swine, a discussion that seems strangely like the tilts between William Jennings Bryan and the scientists many decades later in America.

On the Advisableness of Improving Natural Knowledge

This essay appeared first as an address delivered in St. Martin's Hall, London, on January 7, 1866. It is one of the numerous contributions which Huxley, as scientist-educator, made to the cause of popular education, especially in the field of the biological sciences.

THIS time two hundred years ago—in the beginning of January, 1666—those of our forefathers who inhabited this great and ancient city, took breath between the shocks of two fearful calamities, one not quite past, although its fury had abated; the other to come.

5. **calamities**, the London plague and the London fire. See Defoe's *Journal of the Plague Year* (Vol. I, p. 972) and Pepys's *Diary* (Vol. I, pp. 853 ff.).

Within a few yards of the very spot on which we are assembled, so the tradition runs, that painful and deadly malady, the plague, appeared in the latter months of 1664; and, though no new visitor, smote the people of England, and especially of her capital, with a violence unknown before, in the course of the following year. The hand of a master has pictured what happened in those dismal months; and in that truest of fictions, *The History of the Plague Year*, Defoe shows death, with every accompaniment of pain and terror, stalking through the narrow streets of old London, and changing their busy hum into a silence broken only by the wailing of the mourners of fifty thousand dead; by the woeful denunciations and mad prayers of fanatics; and by the madder yells of despairing profligates.

But, about this time in 1666, the death rate had sunk to nearly its ordinary amount; a case of plague occurred only here and there, and the richer citizens who had flown from the pest had returned to their dwellings. The remnant of the people began to toil at the accustomed round of duty, or of pleasure; and the stream of city life bid fair to flow back along its old bed, with renewed and uninterrupted vigor.

The newly kindled hope was deceitful. The great plague, indeed, returned no more; but what it had done for the Londoners, the great fire, which broke out in the autumn of 1666, did for London; and, in September of that year, a heap of ashes and the indestructible energy of the people were all that remained of the glory of five-sixths of the city within the walls.

Our forefathers had their own ways of accounting for each of these calamities. They submitted to the plague in humility and in penitence, for they believed it to be the judgment of God. But towards the fire they were furiously indignant, interpreting it as the effect of the malice of man—as the work of the Republicans, or of the Papists, according as their prepossessions ran in favor of loyalty or of Puritanism.

It would, I fancy, have fared but ill with one who, standing where I now stand, in what was then a thickly-peopled and fashionable part of London, should have broached to our ancestors the doctrine which I now propound to you—that all their hypotheses were alike wrong; that the plague was no more, in their sense, a Divine judgment, than the fire was the work of any political, or of any religious, sect; but that they were themselves the authors of both plague and fire, and that they must look to themselves to prevent the recurrence of calamities, to all appearance so peculiarly beyond the reach of human control—so evidently the result of the wrath of God, or of the craft and subtlety of an enemy.

And one may picture to oneself how harmoniously the holy cursing of the Puritan of that day would have chimed in with the unholy cursing and the crackling wit of the Rochesters and Sedleys, and with the revilings of the political fanatics, if my imaginary plain dealer had gone on to say that, if the return of such misfortunes were ever rendered impossible, it would not be in virtue of the victory of the faith of Laud, or of that of Milton; and, as little, by the triumph of republicanism, as by that of monarchy. But that the one thing needful for compassing this end was that the people of England should second the efforts of an insignificant corporation, the establishment of which, a few years before the epoch of the great plague and the great fire, had been as little noticed, as they were conspicuous.

Some twenty years before the outbreak of the plague a few calm and thoughtful students banded themselves together for the purpose, as they phrased it, of "improving natural knowledge." The ends they proposed to attain cannot be stated more clearly than in the words of one of the founders of the organization:

"Our business was (precluding matters of theology and state affairs) to discourse and

---

45. **the Republicans,** the supporters of Cromwell's party and the republican form of government as opposed to the monarchical. 48. **Puritanism.** See The Puritan Interlude (Vol. I, p. 631). 69. **Rochesters and Sedleys.** John Wilmot (1647-1680), Earl of Rochester, and Sir Charles Sedley (1639?-1701) were friends of Charles II. They were court dramatists and poets noted for their sharp wit and dissolute living. 74. **Laud,** William Laud (1573-1645), Archbishop of Canterbury, a violent opponent of Puritanism; he was executed by order of Parliament. 79. **corporation,** the Royal Society for the Improvement of Natural Knowledge; it was founded by Charles II in 1662.

consider of philosophical inquiries, and such as related thereunto: as Physick, Anatomy, Geometry, Astronomy, Navigation, Staticks, Magneticks, Chymicks, Mechanicks, and Natural Experiments; with the state of these studies and their cultivation at home and abroad. We then discoursed of the circulation of the blood, the valves in the veins, the venae lacteae, the lymphatic vessels, the Copernican hypothesis, the nature of comets and new stars, the satellites of Jupiter, the oval shape (as it then appeared) of Saturn, the spots on the sun and its turning on its own axis, the inequalities and selenography of the moon, the several phases of Venus and Mercury, the improvement of telescopes and grinding of glasses for that purpose, the weight of air, the possibility or impossibility of vacuities and nature's abhorrence thereof, the Torricellian experiment in quicksilver, the descent of heavy bodies and the degree of acceleration therein, with divers other things of like nature, some of which were then but new discoveries, and others not so generally known and embraced as now they are; with other things appertaining to what hath been called the New Philosophy, which from the times of Galileo at Florence, and Sir Francis Bacon (Lord Verulam) in England, hath been much cultivated in Italy, France, Germany, and other parts abroad, as well as with us in England."

The learned Dr. Wallis, writing in 1696, narrates in these words, what happened half a century before, or about 1645. The associates met at Oxford, in the rooms of Dr. Wilkins, who was destined to become a bishop; and subsequently coming together in London, they attracted the notice of the king. And it is a strange evidence of the taste for knowledge which the most obviously worthless of the Stuarts shared with his father and grandfather, that Charles the Second was not content with saying witty things about his philosophers, but did wise things with regard to them. For he not only bestowed upon them such attention as he could spare from his poodles and his mistresses, but, being in his usual state of impecuniosity, begged for them of the Duke of Ormond; and, that step being without effect, gave them Chelsea College, a charter, and a mace: crowning his favors in the best way they could be crowned, by burdening them no further with royal patronage or state interference.

Thus it was that the half-dozen young men, studious of the "New Philosophy," who met in one another's lodgings in Oxford or in London, in the middle of the seventeenth century, grew in numerical and in real strength, until, in its latter part, the "Royal Society for the Improvement of Natural Knowledge" had already become famous, and had acquired a claim upon the veneration of Englishmen, which it has ever since retained, as the principal focus of scientific activity in our islands, and the chief champion of the cause it was formed to support.

It was by the aid of the Royal Society that Newton published his *Principia*. If all the books in the world, except the *Philosophical Transactions*, were destroyed, it is safe to say that the foundations of physical science would remain unshaken, and that the vast intellectual progress of the last two centuries would be largely, though incompletely, recorded. Nor have any signs of halting or of decrepitude manifested themselves in our own times. As in Dr. Wallis's days, so in these, "our business is, precluding theology and state affairs, to discourse and consider of philosophical inquiries." But our "Mathematick" is one which

3. **Staticks,** that branch of mechanics which deals with the condition of rest or the equilibrium of forces. 4. **Chymicks,** chemistry. 8. **venae lacteae,** lacteal veins. 9. **Copernican hypothesis,** that established by Copernicus (1473-1543), a famous Polish astronomer—that the earth rotates daily on its axis, and that the planets revolve in orbits around the sun. 14. **selenography,** the science of the physical features of the moon. 19. **Torricellian experiment.** In 1643 Torricelli, an Italian physicist, had discovered the principle of the barometer. 26. **New Philosophy,** the ideas on science and philosophy set forth in the writings of Francis Bacon (Vol. I, p. 612). 27. **Galileo,** a famous Italian astronomer and physicist (1564-1642). His most noted work was the construction of a telescope and a thermometer; he made important discoveries regarding the pendulum, the satellites of Jupiter, the motion of the moon, and the law of gravitation. 32. **Dr. Wallis,** John Wallis (1616-1703), Professor of Mathematics at Oxford. 35. **Dr. Wilkins,** John Wilkins (1614-1672), Warden of Wadham College and Bishop of Chester. 38. **the king,** Charles II (1660-1685).

41. **father and grandfather,** Charles I and James I. 49. **Duke of Ormond,** James Butler (1610-1688), an influential Irish statesman and soldier, who was very active in support of Charles II. After the Restoration in 1660, Ormond regained his enormous estates in Ireland (lost during the war), received large grants of money from the king, and was made Lord High Steward of England. 50. **Chelsea College,** Chelsea Royal Hospital, for invalid soldiers, initiated by Charles II but not opened until 1694. 51. **a mace,** a staff carried as an emblem of authority. 69. **Newton,** Sir Isaac Newton (1642-1727), a famous mathematician and natural philosopher, who published his theory about gravitation in his *Principia* in 1687. 70. **Philosophical Transactions,** one of the regular publications of the Royal Society.

Newton would have to go to school to learn; our "Staticks, Mechanicks, Magneticks, Chymicks, and Natural Experiments" constitute a mass of physical and chemical knowledge, a glimpse at which would compensate Galileo for the doings of a score of inquisitorial cardinals; our "Physick" and "Anatomy" have embraced such infinite varieties of being, have laid open such new worlds in time and space, have grappled, not unsuccessfully, with such complex problems, that the eyes of Vesalius and of Harvey might be dazzled by the sight of the tree that has grown out of their grain of mustard seed.

The fact is perhaps rather too much, than too little, forced upon one's notice, nowadays, that all this marvelous intellectual growth has a no less wonderful expression in practical life; and that, in this respect, if in no other, the movement symbolized by the progress of the Royal Society stands without a parallel in the history of mankind.

A series of volumes as bulky as the *Transactions* of the Royal Society might possibly be filled with the subtle speculations of the schoolmen; not improbably, the obtaining a mastery over the products of medieval thought might necessitate an even greater expenditure of time and of energy than the acquirement of the "New Philosophy"; but though such work engrossed the best intellects of Europe for a longer time than has elapsed since the great fire, its effects were "writ in water," so far as our social state is concerned.

On the other hand, if the noble first President of the Royal Society could revisit the upper air and once more gladden his eyes with a sight of the familiar mace, he would find himself in the midst of a material civilization more different from that of his day than that of the seventeenth was from that of the first century. And if Lord Brouncker's native sagacity had not deserted his ghost, he would need no long reflection to discover that all these ships, these railways, these telegraphs, these factories, these printing presses, without which the whole fabric of modern English society would collapse into a mass of stagnant and starving pauperism—that all these pillars of our State are but the ripples and the bubbles upon the surface of that great spiritual stream, the springs of which, only, he and his fellows were privileged to see; and seeing, to recognize as that which it behoved them above all things to keep pure and undefiled.

It may not be too great a flight of imagination to conceive our noble *revenant* not forgetful of the great troubles of his own day, and anxious to know how often London had been burned down since his time, and how often the plague had carried off its thousands. He would have to learn that, although London contains tenfold the inflammable matter that it did in 1666; though, not content with filling our rooms with woodwork and light draperies, we must needs lead inflammable and explosive gases into every corner of our streets and houses, we never allow even a street to burn down. And if he asked how this had come about, we should have to explain that the improvement of natural knowledge had furnished us with dozens of machines for throwing water upon fires, any one of which would have furnished the ingenious Mr. Hooke, the first "curator and experimenter" of the Royal Society, with ample materials for discourse before half a dozen meetings of that body; and that, to say truth, except for the progress of natural knowledge, we should not have been able to make even the tools by which these machines are constructed. And, further, it would be necessary to add that, although severe fires sometimes occur and inflict great damage, the loss is very generally compensated by societies, the operations of which have been rendered possible only by the progress of natural knowledge in the direction of mathematics, and the accumulation of wealth in virtue of other natural knowledge.

6. **inquisitorial cardinals.** Galileo was forced by the Inquisition in 1633 to renounce the Copernican theory of astronomy. 11. **Vesalius,** Andreas Vesalius (1514-1564), a noted Belgian anatomist. 12. **Harvey,** William Harvey (1578-1657), a celebrated English physician, who discovered the circulation of the blood. 13. **tree . . . seed.** Cf. *Luke,* 13:19: The kingdom of heaven "is like a grain of mustard seed, which a man took and cast into his garden; and it grew, and waxed a great tree." 25. **the schoolmen,** philosophers of the Middle Ages who engaged in fine-spun arguments. 33. **"writ in water,"** a part of the inscription on the tomb of Keats in the Protestant Cemetery at Rome. 35. **first President,** William Viscount Brouncker (1620?-1684).

45. **ships, these railways, etc.** Cf. Ruskin's *Fors Clavigera.* 57. *revenant,* ghost. 74. **Mr. Hooke,** Robert Hooke (1635-1703), an experimental philosopher. 85. **societies,** insurance companies.

But the plague? My Lord Brouncker's observation would not, I fear, lead him to think that Englishmen of the nineteenth century are purer in life, or more fervent in religious faith, than the generation which could produce a Boyle, an Evelyn, and a Milton. He might find the mud of society at the bottom instead of at the top, but I fear that the sum total would be as deserving of swift judgment as at the time of the Restoration. And it would be our duty to explain once more, and this time not without shame, that we have no reason to believe that it is the improvement of our faith, nor that of our morals, which keeps the plague from our city; but, again, that it is the improvement of our natural knowledge.

We have learned that pestilences will only take up their abode among those who have prepared unswept and ungarnished residences for them. Their cities must have narrow, unwatered streets, foul with accumulated garbage. Their houses must be ill-drained, ill-lighted, ill-ventilated. Their subjects must be ill-washed, ill-fed, ill-clothed. The London of 1665 was such a city. The cities of the East, where plague has an enduring dwelling, are such cities. We, in later times, have learned somewhat of nature, and partly obey her. Because of this partial improvement of our natural knowledge and of that fractional obedience, we have no plague; because that knowledge is still very imperfect and that obedience yet incomplete, typhus is our companion and cholera our visitor; but it is not presumptuous to express the belief that, when our knowledge is more complete and our obedience the expression of our knowledge, London will count her centuries of freedom from typhus and cholera, as she now gratefully reckons her two hundred years of ignorance of that plague, which swooped upon her thrice in the first half of the seventeenth century.

Surely, there is nothing in these explanations which is not fully borne out by the facts? Surely, the principles involved in them are now admitted among the fixed beliefs of all thinking men? Surely, it is true that our countrymen are less subject to fire, famine, pestilence, and all the evils which result from a want of command over and due anticipation of the course of nature, than were the countrymen of Milton; and health, wealth, and wellbeing are more abundant with us than with them? But no less certainly is the difference due to the improvement of our knowledge of nature, and the extent to which that improved knowledge has been incorporated with the household words of men, and has supplied the springs of their daily actions.

Granting for a moment, then, the truth of that which the depreciators of natural knowledge are so fond of urging, that its improvement can only add to the resources of our material civilization; admitting it to be possible that the founders of the Royal Society themselves looked for no other reward than this, I cannot confess that I was guilty of exaggeration when I hinted, that to him who had the gift of distinguishing between prominent events and important events, the origin of a combined effort on the part of mankind to improve natural knowledge might have loomed larger than the Plague and have outshone the glare of the Fire; as a something fraught with a wealth of beneficence to mankind, in comparison with which the damage done by those ghastly evils would shrink into insignificance.

It is very certain that for every victim slain by the plague, hundreds of mankind exist and find a fair share of happiness in the world by the aid of the spinning jenny. And the great fire, at its worst, could not have burned the supply of coal, the daily working of which, in the bowels of the earth, made possible by the steam pump, gives rise to an amount of wealth to which the millions lost in old London are but as an old song.

But spinning jenny and steam pump are, after all, but toys, possessing an accidental value; and natural knowledge creates multi-

---

6. **Boyle**, Robert Boyle (1627-1691), an English chemist, the discoverer of the law of the elasticity of the air. He was noted for his piety. See headnote to Swift's *Meditation upon a Broomstick* (Vol. I, p. 1005). **Evelyn**, John Evelyn (1620-1706), a famous English diarist and a man of wide scientific interest. Like Boyle he was unusually pious.

84. **spinning jenny**, a machine for spinning wool and cotton by means of many spindles (see p. 402).

tudes of more subtle contrivances, the praises of which do not happen to be sung because they are not directly convertible into instruments for creating wealth. When I contemplate natural knowledge squandering such gifts among men, the only appropriate comparison I can find for her is, to liken her to such a peasant woman as one sees in the Alps, striding ever upward, heavily burdened, and with mind bent only on her home; but yet, without effort and without thought, knitting for her children. Now stockings are good and comfortable things, and the children will undoubtedly be much the better for them; but surely it would be short-sighted, to say the least of it, to depreciate this toiling mother as a mere stocking-machine—a mere provider of physical comforts?

However, there are blind leaders of the blind, and not a few of them, who take this view of natural knowledge, and can see nothing in the bountiful mother of humanity but a sort of comfort-grinding machine. According to them, the improvement of natural knowledge always has been, and always must be, synonymous with no more than the improvement of the material resources and the increase of the gratifications of men.

Natural knowledge is, in their eyes, no real mother of mankind, bringing them up with kindness, and, if need be, with sternness in the way they should go, and instructing them in all things needful for their welfare; but a sort of fairy godmother, ready to furnish her pets with shoes of swiftness, swords of sharpness, and omnipotent Aladdin's lamps, so that they may have telegraphs to Saturn, and see the other side of the moon, and thank God they are better than their benighted ancestors.

If this talk were true, I, for one, should not greatly care to toil in the service of natural knowledge. I think I would just as soon be quietly chipping my own flint ax, after the manner of my forefathers a few thousand years back, as be troubled with the endless malady of thought which now infests us all, for such reward. But I venture to say that such views are contrary alike to reason and to fact. Those who discourse in such fashion seem to me to be so intent upon trying to see what is above nature, or what is behind her, that they are blind to what stares them in the face, in her.

I should not venture to speak thus strongly if my justification were not to be found in the simplest and most obvious facts—if it needed more than an appeal to the most notorious truths to justify my assertion, that the improvement of natural knowledge, whatever direction it has taken, and however low the aims of those who may have commenced it —has not only conferred practical benefits on men, but, in so doing, has effected a revolution in their conceptions of the universe and of themselves, and has profoundly altered their modes of thinking and their views of right and wrong. I say that natural knowledge, seeking to satisfy natural wants, has found the ideas which can alone still spiritual cravings. I say that natural knowledge, in desiring to ascertain the laws of comfort, has been driven to discover those of conduct, and to lay the foundations of a new morality.

Let us take these points separately; and, first, what great ideas has natural knowledge introduced into men's minds?

I cannot but think that the foundations of all natural knowledge were laid when the reason of man first came face to face with the facts of nature; when the savage first learned that the fingers of one hand are fewer than those of both; that it is shorter to cross a stream than to head it; that a stone stops where it is unless it be moved, and that it drops from the hand which lets it go; that light and heat come and go with the sun; that sticks burn away in a fire; that plants and animals grow and die; that if he struck his fellow savage a blow he would make him angry, and perhaps get a blow in return; while if he offered him a fruit he would please him, and perhaps receive a fish in exchange. When men had acquired this much knowledge, the outlines, rude though they were,

---

19. **blind . . . blind.** Cf. *Matthew*, 15:14: "Let them alone: they be blind leaders of the blind. And if the blind lead the blind, both shall fall into the ditch." 30. **bringing . . . go.** Cf. *Proverbs*, 22:6: "Train up a child in the way he should go; and when he is old, he will not depart from it." 35. **shoes . . . sharpness**, magic objects of folklore. 36. **Aladdin**, a youth in the *Arabian Nights* who possessed a magic lamp and a ring that when rubbed brought genii to do his bidding.

of mathematics, of physics, of chemistry, of biology, of moral, economical, and political science, were sketched. Nor did the germ of religion fail when science began to bud. Listen to words which, though new, are yet three thousand years old:

> ... When in heaven the stars about the moon
> Look beautiful, when all the winds are laid,
> And every height comes out, and jutting peak
> And valley, and the immeasurable heavens
> Break open to their highest, and all the stars
> Shine, and the shepherd gladdens in his heart.

But if the half-savage Greek could share our feelings thus far, it is irrational to doubt that he went further, to find, as we do, that upon that brief gladness there follows a certain sorrow—the little light of awakened human intelligence shines so mere a spark amidst the abyss of the unknown and unknowable; seems so insufficient to do more than illuminate the imperfections that cannot be remedied, the aspirations that cannot be realized, of man's own nature. But in this sadness, this consciousness of the limitation of man, this sense of an open secret which he cannot penetrate, lies the essence of all religion; and the attempt to embody it in the forms furnished by the intellect is the origin of the higher theologies.

Thus it seems impossible to imagine but that the foundations of all knowledge—secular or sacred—were laid when intelligence dawned, though the superstructure remained for long ages so slight and feeble as to be compatible with the existence of almost any general view respecting the mode of governance of the universe. No doubt, from the first, there were certain phenomena which, to the rudest mind, presented a constancy of occurrence, and suggested that a fixed order ruled, among them at any rate. I doubt if the grossest of fetish worshipers ever imagined that a stone must have a god within it to make it fall, or that a fruit had a god within it to make it taste sweet. With regard to such matters as these, it is hardly questionable that mankind from the first took strictly positive and scientific views.

But, with respect to all the less familiar occurrences which present themselves, uncultured man, no doubt, has always taken himself as a standard of comparison, as the center and measure of the world; nor could he well avoid doing so. And finding that his apparently uncaused will has a powerful effect in giving rise to many occurrences, he naturally enough ascribed other and greater events to other and greater volitions, and came to look upon the world and all that therein is, as the product of the volitions of persons like himself, but stronger, and capable of being appeased or angered, as he himself might be soothed or irritated. Through such conceptions of the plan and working of the universe all mankind have passed, or are passing. And we may now consider what has been the effect of the improvement of natural knowledge on the views of men who have reached this stage, and who have begun to cultivate natural knowledge with no desire but that of "increasing God's honor and bettering man's estate."

For example: what could seem wiser, from a mere material point of view, more innocent from a theological one, to an ancient people, than that they should learn the exact succession of the seasons, as warnings for their husbandmen; or the position of the stars, as guides to their rude navigators? But what has grown out of this search for natural knowledge of so merely useful a character? You all know the reply. Astronomy—which of all sciences has filled men's minds with general ideas of a character most foreign to their daily experience, and has, more than any other, rendered it impossible for them to accept the

---

7. **When in,** etc. "Need it be said that this is Tennyson's English for Homer's Greek?"—Huxley. The lines are from Tennyson's *Specimens of a Translation of the Iliad in Blank Verse (Iliad,* VIII, 555-59).

42. **fetish worshipers,** worshipers of charms or objects of supposed magical power. 59. **product . . . himself.** Cf. Browning's *Caliban upon Setebos,* p. 701. 70. "**increasing . . . estate,**" Bacon's statement of his purpose in writing *Of the Advancement of Learning,* I, 5, 11. See Vol. I, p. 625.

beliefs of their fathers. Astronomy—which tells them that this so vast and seemingly solid earth is but an atom among atoms, whirling, no man knows whither, through illimitable space; which demonstrates that what we call the peaceful heaven above us, is but that space, filled by an infinitely subtle matter whose particles are seething and surging, like the waves of an angry sea; which opens up to us infinite regions where nothing is known, or ever seems to have been known, but matter and force, operating according to rigid rules; which leads us to contemplate phenomena the very nature of which demonstrates that they must have had a beginning, and that they must have an end, but the very nature of which also proves that the beginning was, to our conceptions of time, infinitely remote, and that the end is as immeasurably distant.

But it is not alone those who pursue astronomy who ask for bread and receive ideas. What more harmless than the attempt to lift and distribute water by pumping it; what more absolutely and grossly utilitarian? But out of pumps grew the discussions about nature's abhorrence of a vacuum; and then it was discovered that nature does not abhor a vacuum, but that air has weight; and that notion paved the way for the doctrine that all matter has weight, and that the force which produces weight is co-extensive with the universe—in short, to the theory of universal gravitation and endless force. And learning how to handle gases led to the discovery of oxygen and to modern chemistry, and to the notion of the indestructibility of matter.

Again, what simpler, or more absolutely practical, than the attempt to keep the axle of a wheel from heating when the wheel turns round very fast? How useful for carters and gig drivers to know something about this; and how good were it, if any ingenious person would find out the cause of such phenomena, and thence educe a general remedy for them. Such an ingenious person was Count Rumford; and he and his successors have landed us in the theory of the persistence or indestructibility of force. And in the infinitely minute, as in the infinitely great, the seekers after natural knowledge of the kinds called physical and chemical, have everywhere found a definite order and succession of events which seem never to be infringed.

And how has it fared with "Physick" and Anatomy? Have the anatomist, the physiologist, or the physician, whose business it has been to devote themselves assiduously to that eminently practical and direct end, the alleviation of the sufferings of mankind—have they been able to confine their vision more absolutely to the strictly useful? I fear they are the worst offenders of all. For if the astronomer has set before us the infinite magnitude of space, and the practical eternity of the duration of the universe; if the physical and chemical philosophers have demonstrated the infinite minuteness of its constituent parts, and the practical eternity of matter and of force; and if both have alike proclaimed the universality of a definite and predicable order and succession of events, the workers in biology have not only accepted all these, but have added more startling theses of their own. For, as the astronomers discover in the earth no center of the universe, but an eccentric speck, so the naturalists find man to be no center of the living world, but one amidst endless modifications of life; and as the astronomer observes the mark of practically endless time set upon the arrangements of the solar system, so the student of life finds the records of ancient forms of existence peopling the world for ages, which, in relation to human experience, are infinite.

Furthermore, the physiologist finds life to be as dependent for its manifestation on particular molecular arrangements as any physical or chemical phenomenon; and, wherever he extends his researches, fixed order and unchanging causation reveal themselves, as plainly as in the rest of nature.

Nor can I find that any other fate has awaited the germ of Religion. Arising, like all other kinds of knowledge, out of the action and interaction of man's mind, with that

---

21. **ask . . . ideas.** Cf. *Matthew*, 7:9: "Or what man is there of you, whom if his son ask bread, will he give him a stone?" 45. **Count Rumford,** Benjamin Thompson (1753-1814), a scientist and an inventor, American by birth.

75. **eccentric,** not located at the center.

which is not man's mind, it has taken the intellectual coverings of Fetishism or Polytheism; of Theism or Atheism; of Superstition or Rationalism. With these, and their relative merits and demerits, I have nothing to do; but this it is needful for my purpose to say, that if the religion of the present differs from that of the past, it is because the theology of the present has become more scientific than that of the past; because it has not only renounced idols of wood and idols of stone, but begins to see the necessity of breaking in pieces the idols built up of books and traditions and fine-spun ecclesiastical cobwebs: and of cherishing the noblest and most human of man's emotions, by worship "for the most part of the silent sort" at the altar of the Unknown and Unknowable.

Such are a few of the new conceptions implanted in our minds by the improvement of natural knowledge. Men have acquired the ideas of the practically infinite extent of the universe and of its practical eternity; they are familiar with the conception that our earth is but an infinitesimal fragment of that part of the universe which can be seen; and that, nevertheless, its duration is, as compared with our standards of time, infinite. They have further acquired the idea that man is but one of innumerable forms of life now existing on the globe, and that the present existences are but the last of an immeasurable series of predecessors. Furthermore, every step they have made in natural knowledge has tended to extend and rivet in their minds the conception of a definite order of the universe—which is embodied in what are called, by an unhappy metaphor, the laws of nature—and to narrow the range and loosen the force of men's belief in spontaneity, or in changes other than such as arise out of that definite order itself.

Whether these ideas are well or ill founded is not the question. No one can deny that they exist, and have been the inevitable outgrowth of the improvement of natural knowledge. And if so, it cannot be doubted that they are changing the form of men's most cherished and most important convictions.

And as regards the second point—the extent to which the improvement of natural knowledge has remodeled and altered what may be termed the intellectual ethics of men—what are among the moral convictions most fondly held by barbarous and semi-barbarous people?

They are the convictions that authority is the soundest basis of belief; that merit attaches to a readiness to believe; that the doubting disposition is a bad one, and skepticism a sin; that when good authority has pronounced what is to be believed, and faith has accepted it, reason has no further duty. There are many excellent persons who yet hold by these principles, and it is not my present business, or intention, to discuss their views. All I wish to bring clearly before your minds is the unquestionable fact that the improvement of natural knowledge is affected by methods which directly give the lie to all these convictions, and assume the exact reverse of each to be true.

The improver of natural knowledge absolutely refuses to acknowledge authority, as such. For him, skepticism is the highest of duties; blind faith the one unpardonable sin. And it cannot be otherwise, for every great advance in natural knowledge has involved the absolute rejection of authority, the cherishing of the keenest skepticism, the annihilation of the spirit of blind faith; and the most ardent votary of science holds his firmest convictions, not because the men he most venerates hold them; not because their verity is testified by portents and wonders; but because his experience teaches him that whenever he chooses to bring these convictions into contact with their primary source, nature—whenever he thinks fit to test them by appealing to experiment and to observation—nature will confirm them. The man of science has learned to believe in justification, not by faith, but by verification.

Thus, without for a moment pretending to despise the practical results of the improve-

---

16. **"for . . . sort."** From Carlyle. 17. **altar . . . Unknown,** Paul's statement in *Acts*, 17:23: "I found an altar with this inscription, To the Unknown God. Whom therefore ye ignorantly worship, him declare I unto you."

90. **justification, not by faith.** Cf. *Romans*, 3:28: "Therefore we conclude that a man is justified by faith without the deeds of the law."

ment of natural knowledge, and its beneficial influence on material civilization, it must, I think, be admitted that the great ideas, some of which I have indicated, and the ethical spirit which I have endeavored to sketch, in the few moments which remained at my disposal, constitute the real and permanent significance of natural knowledge.

If these ideas be destined, as I believe they are, to be more and more firmly established as the world grows older; if that spirit be fated, as I believe it is, to extend itself into all departments of human thought, and to become co-extensive with the range of knowledge; if, as our race approaches its maturity, it discovers, as I believe it will, that there is but one kind of knowledge and but one method of acquiring it; then we, who are still children, may justly feel it our highest duty to recognize the advisableness of improving natural knowledge, and so to aid ourselves and our successors in our course towards the noble goal which lies before mankind.

(*1866;* 1870)

Science and Culture

At the opening of the new Science College founded by Sir Josiah Mason at Birmingham, an industrial city in the Midlands, October 1, 1880, Huxley gave the principal address. It was published the following year in *Science and Education* (*Collected Essays*, Vol. III). Huxley's ideas of the relationship of science and culture, and particularly his allusions to Arnold's doctrines, were replied to by "our chief apostle of culture" in an essay read at Cambridge University (1882), repeated—with some modifications—in a lecture delivered in America in 1883-1884, and published a year later in *Discourses in America* under the title *Literature and Science*. In this essay Arnold argues for literature, not science, as the staple of education. He attacks "the present movement for ousting letters from their old predominance in education, and transferring the predominance in education to the natural sciences."

SIX years ago, as some of my present hearers may remember, I had the privilege of addressing a large assemblage of the inhabitants of this city, who had gathered together to do honor to the memory of their famous townsman, Joseph Priestley; and, if any satisfaction attaches to posthumous glory, we may hope that the *manes* of the burnt-out philosopher were then finally appeased.

No man, however, who is endowed with a fair share of common sense, and not more than a fair share of vanity, will identify either contemporary or posthumous fame with the highest good; and Priestley's life leaves no doubt that he, at any rate, set a much higher value upon the advancement of knowledge, and the promotion of that freedom of thought which is at once the cause and the consequence of intellectual progress.

Hence I am disposed to think that, if Priestley could be amongst us today, the occasion of our meeting would afford him even greater pleasure than the proceedings which celebrated the centenary of his chief discovery. The kindly heart would be moved, the high sense of social duty would be satisfied, by the spectacle of well-earned wealth neither squandered in tawdry luxury and vainglorious show, nor scattered with the careless charity which blesses neither him that gives nor him that takes, but expended in the execution of a well-considered plan for the aid of present and future generations of those who are willing to help themselves.

We shall all be of one mind thus far. But it is needful to share Priestley's keen interest in physical science; and to have learned, as he had learned, the value of scientific training in

---

6. **Joseph Priestley**, a noted scientist, theologian, and political economist (1733-1804). Because of his sympathy with the French Revolution, mobs attacked him in 1791 and burned his house with all his instruments and manuscripts. 8. **manes**, ancestral spirits.

24. **chief discovery**, oxygen, announced in 1774. 30. **blesses ... takes.** Cf. *The Merchant of Venice*, IV, i, 184-187:
The quality of mercy . . . is twice blest;
It blesseth him that gives and him that takes.

fields of inquiry apparently far remote from physical science; in order to appreciate, as he would have appreciated, the value of the noble gift which Sir Josiah Mason has bestowed upon the inhabitants of the Midland district.

For us children of the nineteenth century, however, the establishment of a college under the conditions of Sir Josiah Mason's Trust, has a significance apart from any which it could have possessed a hundred years ago. It appears to be an indication that we are reaching the crisis of the battle, or rather of the long series of battles, which have been fought over education in a campaign which began long before Priestley's time, and will probably not be finished just yet.

In the last century, the combatants were the champions of ancient literature on the one side, and those of modern literature on the other; but, some thirty years ago, the contest became complicated by the appearance of a third army, ranged round the banner of physical science.

I am not aware that anyone has authority to speak in the name of this new host. For it must be admitted to be somewhat of a guerilla force, composed largely of irregulars, each of whom fights pretty much for his own hand. But the impressions of a full private, who has seen a good deal of service in the ranks, respecting the present position of affairs and the conditions of a permanent peace, may not be devoid of interest; and I do not know that I could make a better use of the present opportunity than by laying them before you.

From the time that the first suggestion to introduce physical science into ordinary education was timidly whispered, until now, the advocates of scientific education have met with opposition of two kinds. On the one hand, they have been pooh-poohed by the men of business who pride themselves on being the representatives of practicality; while, on the other hand, they have been excommunicated by the classical scholars, in their capacity of Levites in charge of the ark of culture and monopolists of liberal education.

The practical men believed that the idol whom they worship—rule of thumb—has been the source of the past prosperity, and will suffice for the future welfare of the arts and manufactures. They were of opinion that science is speculative rubbish; that theory and practice have nothing to do with one another; and that the scientific habit of mind is an impediment, rather than an aid, in the conduct of ordinary affairs.

I have used the past tense in speaking of the practical men—for although they were very formidable thirty years ago, I am not sure that the pure species has not been extirpated. In fact, so far as mere argument goes, they have been subjected to such a *feu d'enfer* that it is a miracle if any have escaped. But I have remarked that your typical practical man has an unexpected resemblance to one of Milton's angels. His spiritual wounds, such as are inflicted by logical weapons, may be as deep as a well and as wide as a church door, but beyond shedding a few drops of ichor, celestial or otherwise, he is no whit the worse. So, if any of these opponents be left, I will not waste time in vain repetition of the demonstrative evidence of the practical value of science; but knowing that a parable will sometimes penetrate where syllogisms fail to effect an entrance, I will offer a story for their consideration.

Once upon a time, a boy, with nothing to depend upon but his own vigorous nature, was thrown into the thick of the struggle for existence in the midst of a great manufacturing population. He seems to have had a hard fight, inasmuch as, by the time he was thirty years of age, his total disposable funds amounted to twenty pounds. Nevertheless, middle life found him giving proof of his

---

18. **ancient . . . literature.** Swift's *Battle of the Books* (1704) is a satire on the controversy that raged over the subject. 20. **thirty years ago.** "The advocacy of the introduction of physical science into general education by George Combe (1788-1858) and others commenced a good deal earlier; but the movement had acquired hardly any practical force before the time to which I refer."—Huxley.

46. **Levites . . . culture.** A reference to the ark of the Lord entrusted to the care of the Levites, as related in *Numbers*, 3:14-32. English universities were hostile to the introduction of scientific studies. 47. **liberal education.** See Newman's *Knowledge Its Own End*, p. 447. 49. **rule of thumb,** judgment and practical experience as distinguished from scientific knowledge. 63. **feu d'enfer,** fire from hell. 66. **one . . . angels,** Satan, who when wounded with a sword shed "a stream of nectarous humor," but was soon healed (*Paradise Lost*, VI, 326 ff.). 68. **deep . . . door,** language used by Mercutio in referring to his wound, in *Romeo and Juliet*, III, i, 99. 70. **ichor,** an ethereal fluid, instead of blood, in the veins of the gods. 79. **a boy,** Sir Josiah Mason (1795-1881).

comprehension of the practical problems he had been roughly called upon to solve, by a career of remarkable prosperity.

Finally, having reached old age with its well-earned surroundings of "honor, troops of friends," the hero of my story bethought himself of those who were making a like start in life, and how he could stretch out a helping hand to them.

After long and anxious reflection this successful practical man of business could devise nothing better than to provide them with the means of obtaining "sound, extensive, and practical scientific knowledge." And he devoted a large part of his wealth and five years of incessant work to this end.

I need not point the moral of a tale which, as the solid and spacious fabric of the Scientific College assures us, is no fable, nor can anything which I could say intensify the force of this practical answer to practical objections.

We may take it for granted then, that, in the opinion of those best qualified to judge, the diffusion of thorough scientific education is an absolutely essential condition of industrial progress; and that the college which has been opened today will confer an inestimable boon upon those whose livelihood is to be gained by the practice of the arts and manufactures of the district.

The only question worth discussion is, whether the conditions, under which the work of the college is to be carried out, are such as to give it the best possible chance of achieving permanent success.

Sir Josiah Mason, without doubt most wisely, has left very large freedom of action to the trustees, to whom he proposes ultimately to commit the administration of the college, so that they may be able to adjust its arrangements in accordance with the changing conditions of the future. But, with respect to three points, he has laid most explicit injunctions upon both administrators and teachers.

Party politics are forbidden to enter into the minds of either, so far as the work of the college is concerned; theology is as sternly banished from its precincts; and finally, it is especially declared that the college shall make no provision for "mere literary instruction and education."

It does not concern me at present to dwell upon the first two injunctions any longer than may be needful to express my full conviction of their wisdom. But the third prohibition brings us face to face with those other opponents of scientific education, who are by no means in the moribund condition of the practical man, but alive, alert, and formidable.

It is not impossible that we shall hear this express exclusion of "literary instruction and education" from a college which, nevertheless, professes to give a high and efficient education, sharply criticized. Certainly the time was that the Levites of culture would have sounded their trumpets against its walls as against an educational Jericho.

How often have we not been told that the study of physical science is incompetent to confer culture; that it touches none of the higher problems of life; and, what is worse, that the continual devotion to scientific studies tends to generate a narrow and bigoted belief in the applicability of scientific methods to the search after truth of all kinds? How frequently one has reason to observe that no reply to a troublesome argument tells so well as calling its author a "mere scientific specialist." And, as I am afraid it is not permissible to speak of this form of opposition to scientific education in the past tense, may we not expect to be told that this, not only omission, but prohibition, of "mere literary instruction and education" is a patent example of scientific narrow-mindedness?

I am not acquainted with Sir Josiah Mason's reasons for the action which he has taken; but if, as I apprehend is the case, he refers to the ordinary classical course of our schools and universities by the name of "mere literary instruction and education," I venture to offer sundry reasons of my own in support of that action.

For I hold very strongly by two convictions.

---

5. **"honor . . . friends."** From *Macbeth*, V, iii, 25. 13. **"sound . . . knowledge."** Quoted from Mason.

66. **Levites . . . Jericho.** A reference to the destruction of the walls of Jericho when the priests of the Levites blew with the trumpets, as related in *Joshua*, 6.

The first is that neither the discipline nor the subject-matter of classical education is of such direct value to the student of physical science as to justify the expenditure of valuable time upon either; and the second is, that for the purpose of attaining real culture, an exclusively scientific education is at least as effectual as an exclusively literary education.

I need hardly point out to you that these opinions, especially the latter, are diametrically opposed to those of the great majority of educated Englishmen, influenced as they are by school and university traditions. In their belief, culture is obtainable only by a liberal education; and a liberal education is synonymous, not merely with education and instruction in literature, but in one particular form of literature, namely, that of Greek and Roman antiquity. They hold that the man who has learned Latin and Greek, however little, is educated; while he who is versed in other branches of knowledge, however deeply, is a more or less respectable specialist, not admissible into the cultured caste. The stamp of the educated man, the university degree, is not for him.

I am too well acquainted with the generous catholicity of spirit, the true sympathy with scientific thought, which pervades the writings of our chief apostle of culture to identify him with these opinions; and yet one may cull from one and another of those epistles to the Philistines, which so much delight all who do not answer to that name, sentences which lend them some support.

Mr. Arnold tells us that the meaning of culture is "to know the best that has been thought and said in the world." It is the criticism of life contained in literature. That criticism regards "Europe as being, for intellectual and spiritual purposes, one great confederation, bound to a joint action and working to a common result; and whose members have, for their common outfit, a knowledge of Greek, Roman, and Eastern antiquity, and of one another. Special, local, and temporary advantages being put out of account, that modern nation will in the intellectual and spiritual sphere make most progress, which most thoroughly carries out this program. And what is that but saying that we too, all of us, as individuals, the more thoroughly we carry it out, shall make the more progress?"

We have here to deal with two distinct propositions. The first, that a criticism of life is the essence of culture; the second, that literature contains the materials which suffice for the construction of such criticism.

I think that we must all assent to the first proposition. For culture certainly means something quite different from learning or technical skill. It implies the possession of an ideal, and the habit of critically estimating the value of things by comparison with a theoretic standard. Perfect culture should supply a complete theory of life, based upon a clear knowledge alike of its possibilities and of its limitations.

But we may agree to all this, and yet strongly dissent from the assumption that literature alone is competent to supply this knowledge. After having learned all that Greek, Roman, and Eastern antiquity have thought and said, and all that modern literatures have to tell us, it is not self-evident that we have laid a sufficiently broad and deep foundation for that criticism of life which constitutes culture.

Indeed, to anyone acquainted with the scope of physical science, it is not at all evident. Considering progress only in the "intellectual and spiritual sphere," I find myself wholly unable to admit that either nations or individuals will really advance, if their common outfit draws nothing from the stores of physical science. I should say that an army, without weapons of precision and with no particular base of operations, might more hopefully enter upon a campaign on the Rhine, than a man, devoid of a knowledge of what physical science has done in the last century, upon a criticism of life.

When a biologist meets with an anomaly, he instinctively turns to the study of develop-

---

30. **chief . . . culture,** Matthew Arnold (p. 527). In the Bible the Philistines were enemies of the Hebrews. Arnold called the English people of the middle class Philistines because he thought they were opposed to cultural enlightenment or were trying to gain it by wrong methods. 37. **"to know . . . world,"** a favorite saying of Arnold, used in many of his writings. See p. 543, l. 48. 40. **"Europe . . . progress."** From Arnold's *Function of Criticism at the Present Time,* p. 543, ll. 78 ff.

63. **habit . . . standard.** See Arnold's *Study of Poetry,* p. 552, ll. 59 ff.

ment to clear it up. The rationale of contradictory opinions may with equal confidence be sought in history.

It is, happily, no new thing that Englishmen should employ their wealth in building and endowing institutions for educational purposes. But, five or six hundred years ago, deeds of foundation expressed or implied conditions as nearly as possible contrary to those which have been thought expedient by Sir Josiah Mason. That is to say, physical science was practically ignored, while a certain literary training was enjoined as a means to the acquirement of knowledge which was essentially theological.

The reason of this singular contradiction between the actions of men alike animated by a strong and disinterested desire to promote the welfare of their fellows, is easily discovered.

At that time, in fact, if anyone desired knowledge beyond such as could be obtained by his own observation, or by common conversation, his first necessity was to learn the Latin language, inasmuch as all the higher knowledge of the western world was contained in works written in that language. Hence, Latin grammar, with logic and rhetoric, studied through Latin, were the fundamentals of education. With respect to the substance of the knowledge imparted through this channel, the Jewish and Christian Scriptures, as interpreted and supplemented by the Romish Church, were held to contain a complete and infallibly true body of information.

Theological dicta were, to the thinkers of those days, that which the axioms and definitions of Euclid are to the geometers of these. The business of the philosophers of the Middle Ages was to deduce from the data furnished by the theologians, conclusions in accordance with ecclesiastical decrees. They were allowed the high privilege of showing, by logical process, how and why that which the Church said was true, must be true. And if their demonstrations fell short of or exceeded this limit, the Church was maternally ready to check their aberrations; if need were by the help of the secular arm.

Between the two, our ancestors were furnished with a compact and complete criticism of life. They were told how the world began and how it would end; they learned that all material existence was but a base and insignificant blot upon the fair face of the spiritual world, and that nature was, to all intents and purposes, the playground of the devil; they learned that the earth is the center of the visible universe, and that man is the cynosure of things terrestrial; and more especially was it inculcated that the course of nature had no fixed order, but that it could be, and constantly was, altered by the agency of innumerable spiritual beings, good and bad, according as they were moved by the deeds and prayers of men. The sum and substance of the whole doctrine was to produce the conviction that the only thing really worth knowing in this world was how to secure that place in a better which, under certain conditions, the Church promised.

Our ancestors had a living belief in this theory of life, and acted upon it in their dealings with education, as in all other matters. Culture meant saintliness—after the fashion of the saints of those days; the education that led to it was, of necessity, theological; and the way to theology lay through Latin.

That the study of nature—further than was requisite for the satisfaction of everyday wants —should have any bearing on human life was far from the thoughts of men thus trained. Indeed, as nature had been cursed for man's sake, it was an obvious conclusion that those who meddled with nature were likely to come into pretty close contact with Satan. And, if any born scientific investigator followed his instincts, he might safely reckon upon earning the reputation, and probably upon suffering the fate, of a sorcerer.

Had the western world been left to itself in Chinese isolation, there is no saying how long this state of things might have endured. But, happily, it was not left to itself. Even earlier than the thirteenth century, the development of Moorish civilization in Spain and

---

37. **Euclid,** a celebrated Greek geometrician of Alexandria, Egypt (third century B.C.).

58. **cynosure,** center of attraction. 82. **nature . . . sake.** After Adam's temptation and fall, God said unto him: "Cursed is the ground for thy sake . . . In the sweat of thy face shalt thou eat bread" (*Genesis*, 3:17-19).

the great movement of the Crusades had introduced the leaven which, from that day to this, has never ceased to work. At first, through the intermediation of Arabic translations, afterwards by the study of the originals, the western nations of Europe became acquainted with the writings of the ancient philosophers and poets, and, in time, with the whole of the vast literature of antiquity.

Whatever there was of high intellectual aspiration or dominant capacity in Italy, France, Germany, and England, spent itself for centuries in taking possession of the rich inheritance left by the dead civilizations of Greece and Rome. Marvelously aided by the invention of printing, classical learning spread and flourished. Those who possessed it prided themselves on having attained the highest culture then within the reach of mankind.

And justly. For, saving Dante on his solitary pinnacle, there was no figure in modern literature at the time of the Renascence to compare with the men of antiquity; there was no art to compete with their sculpture; there was no physical science but that which Greece had created. Above all, there was no other example of perfect intellectual freedom—of the unhesitating acceptance of reason as the sole guide to truth and the supreme arbiter of conduct.

The new learning necessarily soon exerted a profound influence upon education. The language of the monks and schoolmen seemed little better than gibberish to scholars fresh from Virgil and Cicero, and the study of Latin was placed upon a new foundation. Moreover, Latin itself ceased to afford the sole key to knowledge. The student who sought the highest thought of antiquity, found only a second-hand reflection of it in Roman literature, and turned his face to the full light of the Greeks. And after a battle, not altogether dissimilar to that which is at present being fought over the teaching of physical science, the study of Greek was recognized as an essential element of all higher education.

Thus the Humanists, as they were called, won the day; and the great reform which they effected was of incalculable service to mankind. But the Nemesis of all reformers is finality; and the reformers of education, like those of religion, fell into the profound, however common, error of mistaking the beginning for the end of the work of reformation.

The representatives of the Humanists, in the nineteenth century, take their stand upon classical education as the sole avenue to culture, as firmly as if we were still in the age of Renascence. Yet, surely, the present intellectual relations of the modern and the ancient worlds are profoundly different from those which obtained three centuries ago. Leaving aside the existence of a great and characteristically modern literature, of modern painting, and, especially, of modern music, there is one feature of the present state of the civilized world which separates it more widely from the Renascence than the Renascence was separated from the Middle Ages.

This distinctive character of our own times lies in the vast and constantly increasing part which is played by natural knowledge. Not only is our daily life shaped by it, not only does the prosperity of millions of men depend upon it, but our whole theory of life has long been influenced, consciously or unconsciously, by the general conceptions of the universe which have been forced upon us by physical science.

In fact, the most elementary acquaintance with the results of scientific investigation shows us that they offer a broad and striking contradiction to the opinion so implicitly credited and taught in the Middle Ages.

The notions of the beginning and the end of the world entertained by our forefathers are no longer credible. It is very certain that the earth is not the chief body in the material universe, and that the world is not subordinated to man's use. It is even more certain that nature is the expression of a definite order

---

20. **Dante.** See p. 588, note 81. 22. **the Renascence,** the great revival of art and letters, of the fourteenth and fifteenth centuries, as referred to in the preceding paragraph. 33. **schoolmen.** See p. 565, note 25. 35. **Cicero,** Roman orator, statesman, and man of letters (106-43 B.C.).

47. **Humanists,** Renaissance scholars who engaged in the study of the humanities—i.e., polite learning, especially that derived from the Greek and the Roman classics. They expressed faith in individualism, rebelled against established intellectual authorities, and gave themselves to the spirit of sincere inquiry after truth. See Vol. I, pp. 301 ff. 50. **Nemesis,** an ancient goddess of retributive justice.

with which nothing interferes, and that the chief business of mankind is to learn that order and govern themselves accordingly. Moreover this scientific "criticism of life" presents itself to us with different credentials from any other. It appeals not to authority, nor to what anybody may have thought or said, but to nature. It admits that all our interpretations of natural fact are more or less imperfect and symbolic, and bids the learner seek for truth not among words but among things. It warns us that the assertion which outstrips evidence is not only a blunder but a crime.

The purely classical education advocated by the representatives of the Humanists in our day, gives no inkling of all this. A man may be a better scholar than Erasmus, and know no more of the chief causes of the present intellectual fermentation than Erasmus did. Scholarly and pious persons, worthy of all respect, favor us with allocutions upon the sadness of the antagonism of science to their medieval way of thinking, which betray an ignorance of the first principles of scientific investigation, an incapacity for understanding what a man of science means by veracity, and an unconsciousness of the weight of established scientific truths, which is almost comical.

There is no great force in the *tu quoque* argument, or else the advocates of scientific education might fairly enough retort upon the modern Humanists that they may be learned specialists, but that they possess no such sound foundation for a criticism of life as deserves the name of culture. And, indeed, if we were disposed to be cruel, we might urge that the Humanists have brought this reproach upon themselves, not because they are too full of the spirit of the ancient Greek, but because they lack it.

The period of the Renascence is commonly called that of the "Revival of Letters," as if the influences then brought to bear upon the mind of Western Europe had been wholly exhausted in the field of literature. I think it is very commonly forgotten that the revival of science, effected by the same agency, although less conspicuous, was not less momentous.

In fact, the few and scattered students of nature of that day picked up the clue to her secrets exactly as it fell from the hands of the Greeks a thousand years before. The foundations of mathematics were so well laid by them, that our children learn their geometry from a book written for the schools of Alexandria two thousand years ago. Modern astronomy is the natural continuation and development of the work of Hipparchus and of Ptolemy; modern physics of that of Democritus and of Archimedes; it was long before modern biological science outgrew the knowledge bequeathed to us by Aristotle, by Theophrastus, and by Galen.

We cannot know all the best thoughts and sayings of the Greeks unless we know what they thought about natural phenomena. We cannot fully apprehend their criticism of life unless we understand the extent to which that criticism was affected by scientific conceptions. We falsely pretend to be the inheritors of their culture, unless we are penetrated, as the best minds among them were, with an unhesitating faith that the free employment of reason, in accordance with scientific method, is the sole method of reaching truth.

Thus I venture to think that the pretensions of our modern Humanists to the possession of the monopoly of culture and to the exclusive inheritance of the spirit of antiquity must be abated, if not abandoned. But I should be very sorry that anything I have said should be taken to imply a desire on my part to depreciate the value of classical education, as it might be and as it sometimes is. The native capacities of mankind vary no less than their opportunities; and while culture is one, the

---

17. **Erasmus**, Desiderius Erasmus (1466-1536), a famous Dutch classical scholar, the most learned man of his time. 21. **allocutions**, solemn hortatory addresses. 30. *tu quoque*, thou too. 56. **book . . . ago**, the *Elements* of geometry, written by Euclid. See p. 575, note 37. 59. **Hipparchus**, a Greek astronomer (second century B.C.), who founded the science of astronomy. 60. **Ptolemy**, an Alexandrine astronomer, who evolved the theory that the earth is the center of the universe and that the planets revolve around it—the so-called Ptolemaic System. **Democritus**, a celebrated Greek physical philosopher (fifth century B.C.); he was known as "the laughing philosopher" because of his cheerful disposition even after he became blind. 61. **Archimedes**, a noted Greek mathematician (third century B.C.), who invented the water-screw and discovered the principle of the lever. 63. **Aristotle**, the most celebrated of the Greek philosophers (fourth century B.C.), the founder of natural science. **Theophrastus**, a Greek botanist (372-287 B.C.). 64. **Galen**, a Greek physician (130-200 A.D.), the greatest medical authority until the Renaissance.

road by which one man may best reach it is widely different from that which is most advantageous to another. Again, while scientific education is yet inchoate and tentative, classical education is thoroughly well organized upon the practical experience of generations of teachers. So that, given ample time for learning and estimation for ordinary life, or for a literary career, I do not think that a young Englishman in search of culture can do better than follow the course usually marked out for him, supplementing its deficiencies by his own efforts.

But for those who mean to make science their serious occupation; or who intend to follow the profession of medicine; or who have to enter early upon the business of life; for all these, in my opinion, classical education is a mistake; and it is for this reason that I am glad to see "mere literary education and instruction" shut out from the curriculum of Sir Josiah Mason's College, seeing that its inclusion would probably lead to the introduction of the ordinary smattering of Latin and Greek.

Nevertheless, I am the last person to question the importance of genuine literary education, or to suppose that intellectual culture can be complete without it. An exclusively scientific training will bring about a mental twist as surely as an exclusively literary training. The value of the cargo does not compensate for a ship's being out of trim; and I should be very sorry to think that the Scientific College would turn out none but lopsided men.

There is no need, however, that such a catastrophe should happen. Instruction in English, French, and German is provided, and thus the three greatest literatures of the modern world are made accessible to the student.

French and German, and especially the latter language, are absolutely indispensable to those who desire full knowledge in any department of science. But even supposing that the knowledge of these languages acquired is not more than sufficient for purely scientific purposes, every Englishman has, in his native tongue, an almost perfect instrument of literary expression; and, in his own literature, models of every kind of literary excellence. If an Englishman cannot get literary culture out of his Bible, his Shakespeare, his Milton, neither, in my belief, will the profoundest study of Homer and Sophocles, Virgil and Horace, give it to him.

Thus, since the constitution of the college makes sufficient provision for literary as well as for scientific education, and since artistic instruction is also contemplated, it seems to me that a fairly complete culture is offered to all who are willing to take advantage of it.

But I am not sure that at this point the "practical" man, scotched but not slain, may ask what all this talk about culture has to do with an institution, the object of which is defined to be "to promote the prosperity of the manufactures and the industry of the country." He may suggest that what is wanted for this end is not culture, nor even a purely scientific discipline, but simply a knowledge of applied science.

I often wish that this phrase, "applied science," had never been invented. For it suggests that there is a sort of scientific knowledge of direct practical use, which can be studied apart from another sort of scientific knowledge, which is of no practical utility, and which is termed "pure science." But there is no more complete fallacy than this. What people call applied science is nothing but the application of pure science to particular classes of problems. It consists of deductions from those general principles, established by reasoning and observation, which constitute pure science. No one can safely make these deductions until he has a firm grasp of the principles; and he can obtain that grasp only by personal experience of the operations of observation and of reasoning on which they are founded.

Almost all the processes employed in the arts and manufactures fall within the range either of physics or of chemistry. In order to improve them, one must thoroughly understand them; and no one has a chance of really understanding them, unless he has obtained that mastery of principles and that habit of dealing with facts, which is given by long-

65. **scotched,** cut through. Cf. *Macbeth*, III, ii, 13-14:
We have scotch'd the snake, not kill'd it:
She'll close and be herself.

continued and well-directed purely scientific training in the physical and the chemical laboratory. So that there really is no question as to the necessity of purely scientific discipline, even if the work of the college were limited by the narrowest interpretation of its stated aims.

And, as to the desirableness of a wider culture than that yielded by science alone, it is to be recollected that the improvement of manufacturing processes is only one of the conditions which contribute to the prosperity of industry. Industry is a means and not an end; and mankind work only to get something which they want. What that something is depends partly on their innate, and partly on their acquired, desires.

If the wealth resulting from prosperous industry is to be spent upon the gratification of unworthy desires, if the increasing perfection of manufacturing processes is to be accompanied by an increasing debasement of those who carry them on, I do not see the good of industry and prosperity.

Now it is perfectly true that men's views of what is desirable depend upon their characters; and that the innate proclivities to which we give that name are not touched by any amount of instruction. But it does not follow that even mere intellectual education may not, to an indefinite extent, modify the practical manifestation of the characters of men in their actions, by supplying them with motives unknown to the ignorant. A pleasure-loving character will have pleasure of some sort; but, if you give him the choice, he may prefer pleasures which do not degrade him to those which do. And this choice is offered to every man, who possesses in literary or artistic culture a never-failing source of pleasures, which are neither withered by age, nor staled by custom, nor embittered in the recollection by the pangs of self-reproach.

If the institution opened today fulfills the intention of its founder, the picked intelligences among all classes of the population of this district will pass through it. No child born in Birmingham, henceforward, if he have the capacity to profit by the opportunities offered to him, first in the primary and other schools, and afterwards in the Scientific College, need fail to obtain, not merely the instruction, but the culture most appropriate to the conditions of his life.

Within these walls, the future employer and the future artisan may sojourn together for a while, and carry, through all their lives, the stamp of the influences then brought to bear upon them. Hence, it is not beside the mark to remind you, that the prosperity of industry depends not merely upon the improvement of manufacturing processes, not merely upon the ennobling of the individual character, but upon a third condition, namely, a clear understanding of the conditions of social life, on the part of both the capitalist and the operative, and their agreement upon common principles of social action. They must learn that social phenomena are as much the expression of natural laws as any others; that no social arrangements can be permanent unless they harmonize with the requirements of social statics and dynamics; and that, in the nature of things, there is an arbiter whose decisions execute themselves.

But this knowledge is only to be obtained by the application of the methods of investigation adopted in physical researches to the investigation of the phenomena of society. Hence, I confess, I should like to see one addition made to the excellent scheme of education propounded for the college, in the shape of provision for the teaching of sociology. For though we are all agreed that party politics are to have no place in the instruction of the college; yet in this country, practically governed as it is now by universal suffrage, every man who does his duty must exercise political functions. And, if the evils which are inseparable from the good of political liberty are to be checked, if the perpetual oscillation of nations between anarchy and despotism is to be replaced by the steady march of self-restraining freedom; it will be because men will gradually bring themselves to deal with political, as they now deal with scientific questions; to be as ashamed of undue haste and partisan prejudice in the one case as in the other; and to believe that the machinery of

---

72. **social . . . dynamics,** the fixed and the moving moral forces or laws of society. 91. **perpetual . . . despotism.** Cf. the political conditions in France from 1789 to 1815.

society is at least as delicate as that of a spinning-jenny, and as little likely to be improved by the meddling of those who have not taken the trouble to master the principles of its action.

In conclusion, I am sure that I make myself the mouthpiece of all present in offering to the venerable founder of the institution, which now commences its beneficent career, our congratulations on the completion of his work; and in expressing the conviction, that the remotest posterity will point to it as a crucial instance of the wisdom which natural piety[10] leads all men to ascribe to their ancestors.

(1880; 1881)

13. natural piety, affection.

Walter Horatio Pater
1839-1894

Macaulay, Arnold, Ruskin, Huxley, and Morris were active participants in the social, intellectual, and artistic life of Victorian England. Walter Horatio Pater, on the other hand, lived the existence of an aesthetic recluse viewing life shyly through the windows of his palace of art and not desiring closer contact. If, as Huxley said, Arnold was the "apostle of culture," Pater might be characterized as the hermit of art and criticism.

Pater was the second son of Richard Glode Pater, a physician in the East End of London. He was born in Shadwell, but on the early death of his father the family moved to Chase Side, Enfield. He had his elementary schooling at King's School, Canterbury, and entered Queen's College, Oxford, in 1858. Four years later found him a private tutor in Oxford, and six years later a Fellow of Brasenose College. Pater remained in Oxford until 1885; he then moved, with his sisters, who had been keeping house for him, to London, retaining, however, rooms in the university city that was always the center of his intellectual life. He returned to Oxford a year before his death in 1894 and completed his last work in the shadow of its venerable buildings.

Pater's self-absorption and extreme fastidiousness resulted in his being very slow in completing any writing; he was almost a prose Gray. Nothing came from his pen until he was twenty-eight; then, in 1867, the *Westminster Review* published his essay on Winckelmann. After this the stream of essays was fairly steady, and in 1873 they were gathered into his first volume, *Studies in the History of the Renaissance*, discussions of the aesthetic principles of art and literature. Then followed an interval of twelve years before the appearance of *Marius the Epicurean*, a philosophical romance of a young Roman drawn against the background of the early Roman empire. In 1887 was published his *Imaginary Portraits*—four in number—and two years later the collection of critical essays called *Appreciations*, studies of Shakespeare, Wordsworth, and others. *Plato and Platonism*, in some respects a return to his first love, philosophy, was issued in 1893. *The Child in the House* (1894) is an exquisite and imaginative treatment of the sensitive boy who was himself. *Greek Studies* and *Gaston de Latour*—left unfinished—were published after his death.

Pater might well have been the hero of Tennyson's *The Palace of Art* (see p. 603) if it were not for the fact that his withdrawal into the seclusion of his Ivory Tower was deliberate and untinged by any regret or remorse of conscience about serving humanity. His philosophy of life led him to believe that the highest wisdom lay in extracting from literature and art a quickened sense of life, an ecstasy of beauty. This concept was undeniably hedonistic or pleasure-seeking, but the hedonism was of a refined, noble type. His epicurean philosophy was capable of being misunderstood, however, in a world which believed that the highest objective in life lay in direct service to mankind. Epicureanism, moreover, was popularly understood to be the philosophy of physical self-indulgence, and many read Pater's essays with the condescension and disapproval that accompany a suspicion of soft decadence.

Pater's literary style undoubtedly increased the popular misconception of his philosophy of life and art. His love of the beauty of perfect art resulted in increasing his fastidiousness of expression. There was about his writing a phosphorescent beauty that annoyed the Philistines. His writing was subjective and highly artificial and suggested, therefore, an unnaturalness that it did not actually possess, for it was undeniably the expression of the author's own personality. It was, moreover, full, harmonious, and rich with the flavor of creative art. But Pater's essays are "caviar to the general" and are likely to remain literature for the lovers of artistic finish rather than reading for the multitude.

"Pater," says Professor Hugh Walker, "illustrates the complexity of the age, which so deeply impressed him, by the multitude of strands which are twined together in his own work. The Middle Ages and the Italian Renaissance, painting and poetry, classicism and romanticism, all contribute to it. No one carries the suggestion of more numerous and more varied writers. . . And yet through all this he remains highly original and individual. Few writers are more completely non-dramatic than Pater. Whatever the character he depicts, it is always really Pater who appears upon the canvas."

Pater's criticism has its roots in his philosophy of life. He began his intellectual career with philosophy, and Plato and Goethe were probably the greatest literary influences in his life. But from philosophy his interest narrowed down to aesthetics, to a study of the principles of beauty in art and literature. Thus he became, in a sense, a connoisseur of beauty, and a high priest of art. His criticisms took the form of discovering the best in literature and art and of revealing these master strokes in *appreciations* of the craftsmen. His vision was thus upward; he praised the best rather than condemned the worst. And incidentally this continued contemplation of the best gave him a soundness and quickness of judgment that made possible such discriminating definitions as the lucid distinction between the classical and the romantic, where, without prejudice, he penetrates to the core of both moods of expression and makes clear the beauty of each. To Walter Pater the realms of art and literature probably owe more than they have yet been ready to acknowledge.

from *Leonardo da Vinci*

The best of several descriptions of Leonardo da Vinci's masterpiece, the famous *Mona Lisa*, is that of Walter Pater; it appeared in the essay on Leonardo da Vinci which forms one of his *Studies in the History of the Renaissance* (1873). The romantic, subtle, and enigmatic qualities of this portrait inspired in Pater the mood of the painting. Leonardo da Vinci, Italian painter, architect, musician, scientist, engineer, painted the portrait between 1503 and 1506 in Florence. His subject was the beautiful Mona (or Madonna, or Lady) Lisa, "the young third wife of Francesco del Giocondo," a Florentine nobleman. La Gioconda's rapt expression, Leonardo explained, came from the effect of soft music which was played while he painted her. The King of France, François I, bought the portrait not long after it was finished, and took it to Paris, where it became ultimately one of the glories of the Louvre.

LA GIOCONDA

La Gioconda is, in the truest sense, Leonardo's masterpiece, the revealing instance of his mode of thought and work. In suggestiveness, only the *Melancholia* of Dürer is com-

4. **Dürer**, Albrecht Dürer (1471-1582), the greatest artist of the Renaissance in Germany; he was a painter, an engraver, a sculptor, and an architect. His *Melancholia* is a copperplate engraving.

parable to it; and no crude symbolism disturbs the effect of its subdued and graceful mystery. We all know the face and hands of the figure, set in its marble chair, in that circle of fantastic rocks, as in some faint light under sea. Perhaps of all ancient pictures time has chilled it least. As often happens with works in which invention seems to reach its limit, there is an element in it given to, not invented by, the master. In that inestimable folio of drawings, once in the possession of Vasari, were certain designs by Verrocchio, faces of such impressive beauty that Leonardo in his boyhood copied them many times. It is hard not to connect with these designs of the elder, by-past master, as with its germinal principle, the unfathomable smile, always with a touch of something sinister in it, which plays over all Leonardo's work. Besides, the picture is a portrait. From childhood we see this image defining itself on the fabric of his dreams, and but for express historical testimony, we might fancy that this was but his ideal lady, embodied and beheld at last. What was the relationship of a living Florentine to this creature of his thought? By what strange affinities had the dream and the person grown up thus apart, and yet so closely together? Present from the first incorporeally in Leonardo's brain, dimly traced in the designs of Verrocchio, she is found present at last in *Il Gioconda's* house. That there is much of mere portraiture in the picture is attested by the legend that by artificial means, the presence of mimes and fluteplayers, that subtle expression was protracted on the face. Again, was it in four years and by renewed labor never really completed, or in four months and as by stroke of magic, that the image was projected?

The presence that rose so strangely beside the waters, is expressive of what in the ways of a thousand years men had come to desire. Hers is the head upon which all "the ends of the world are come," and the eyelids are a little weary. It is a beauty wrought out from within upon the flesh, the deposit, little cell by cell, of strange thoughts and fantastic reveries and exquisite passions. Set it for a moment beside one of those white Greek goddesses or beautiful women of antiquity, and how would they be troubled by this beauty, into which the soul with all its maladies has passed! All the thoughts and experience of the world have etched and molded there, in that which they have of power to refine and make expressive the outward form, the animalism of Greece, the lust of Rome, the mysticism of the middle age with its spiritual ambition and imaginative loves, the return of the Pagan world, the sins of the Borgias. She is older than the rocks among which she sits; like the vampire, she has been dead many times, and learned the secrets of the grave; and has been a diver in deep seas, and keeps their fallen day about her; and trafficked for strange webs with Eastern merchants, and, as Leda, was the mother of Helen of Troy, and, as Saint Anne, the mother of Mary; and all this has been to her but as the sound of lyres and flutes, and lives only in the delicacy with which it has molded the changing lineaments, and tinged the eyelids and the hands. The fancy of a perpetual life, sweeping together ten thousand experiences, is an old one; and modern philosophy has conceived the idea of humanity as wrought upon by, and summing up in itself, all modes of thought and life. Certainly Lady Lisa might stand as the embodiment of the old fancy, the symbol of the modern idea.

(1873)

---

5. **circle,** a kind of natural amphitheater. 12. **Vasari,** Giorgio Vasari (1511-1574), an Italian architect, painter. and writer on art. Browning's *Fra Lippo Lippi* (see p. 688) and *Andrea Del Sarto* (p. 694) were based on his *Lives of the Most Excellent Italian Painters, Sculptors, and Architects.* **Verrocchio,** Andrea Verrocchio (1435-1488), an Italian sculptor and painter. 35. **mimes,** jesters, clowns.

45. **"the ends . . . come."** From *1 Corinthians*, 10:11. 58. **animalism,** the doctrine that men are animals; the worship of physical form. 61. **the return . . . world.** Near the end of the Middle Ages, Christianity lost much of its influence over the lives of the people. 62. **Borgias,** a fifteenth-century family in Italy notorious for its violence, treachery, vices, and crimes. Leonardo served them in numerous ways. 63. **vampire,** in medieval belief the reanimated body of a dead person, supposed to come from the grave and to wander about at night sucking the blood of persons asleep, thus causing their death and gaining a horrible immortality for itself. 66. **their fallen day,** the gloom that prevails at great depths in the sea. 68. **Leda,** in Greek mythology the wife of the Spartan king Tyndareus and mistress of Zeus. Helen of Troy, regarded as the most beautiful woman of her time, was faithless to her husband Menelaus. Thus, in its relation to Leda and Helen and to St. Anne and Mary, the face of La Gioconda reveals elements of the beautiful wanton wife and the saintly mother.

from *Studies in the History of the Renaissance*

CONCLUSION

This chapter from Pater's *Studies in the History of the Renaissance*, which expresses so much of his theory of life and art, was printed in the first edition of 1873, omitted from the second edition of 1877, and finally restored in 1888 with the following explanation by Pater: "This brief 'Conclusion' was omitted in the second edition of this book, as I conceived it might possibly mislead some of those young men into whose hands it might fall. On the whole, I have thought best to reprint it here, with some slight changes which bring it closer to my original meaning. I have dealt more fully in *Marius the Epicurean* with the thoughts suggested by it."

Λέγει που Ἡράκλειτος ὅτι πάντα Χωρεῖ
καὶ οὐδὲν μένει.

To REGARD all things and principles of things as inconstant modes or fashions has more and more become the tendency of modern thought. Let us begin with that which is without—our physical life. Fix upon it in one of its more exquisite intervals—the moment, for instance, of delicious recoil from the flood of water in summer heat. What is the whole physical life in that moment but a combination of natural elements to which science gives their names? But these elements, phosphorus and lime and delicate fibers, are present not in the human body alone: we detect them in places most remote from it. Our physical life is a perpetual motion of them—the passage of the blood, the wasting and repairing of the lenses of the eye, the modification of the tissues of the brain by every ray of light and sound—processes which science reduces to simpler and more elementary forces. Like the elements of which we are composed, the action of these forces extends beyond us; it rusts iron and ripens corn. Far out on every side of us those elements are broadcast, driven by many forces; and birth and gesture and death and the springing of violets from the grave are but a few out of ten thousand resultant combinations. That clear, perpetual outline of face and limb is but an image of ours, under which we group them—a design in a web, the actual threads of which pass out beyond it. This at least of flame-like our life has, that it is but the concurrence, renewed from moment to moment, of forces parting sooner or later on their ways.

Or if we begin with the inward whirl of thought and feeling, the whirlpool is still more rapid, the flame more eager and devouring. There it is no longer the gradual darkening of the eye and fading of color from the wall—the movement of the shoreside, where the water flows down indeed, though in apparent rest—but the race of the mid-stream, a drift of momentary acts of sight and passion and thought. At first sight experience seems to bury us under a flood of external objects, pressing upon us with a sharp and importunate reality, calling us out of ourselves in a thousand forms of action. But when reflection begins to act upon those objects they are dissipated under its influence; the cohesive force seems suspended like a trick of magic; each object is loosed into a group of impressions—color, odor, texture—in the mind of the observer. And if we continue to dwell in thought on this world, not of objects in the solidity with which language invests them, but of impressions unstable, flickering, inconsistent, which burn and are extinguished with our consciousness of them, it contracts still further; the whole scope of observation is dwarfed to the narrow chamber of the individual mind. Experience, already reduced to a swarm of impressions, is ringed round for each one of us by that thick wall of personality through which no real voice has ever pierced on its way to us, or from us to that which we can only conjecture to be without. Every one of those impressions is the impression of the

---

Λέγει που, etc., Heraclitus says somewhere that everything flows and nothing remains (Plato, *Cratylus*). 23. **corn**, grain, wheat. 26. **gesture**, bearing, behavior.

individual in his isolation, each mind keeping as a solitary prisoner its own dream of a world.

Analysis goes a step farther still, and assures us that those impressions of the individual mind to which, for each one of us, experience dwindles down, are in perpetual flight; that each of them is limited by time, and that as time is infinitely divisible, each of them is infinitely divisible also; all that is actual in it being a single moment, gone while we try to apprehend it, of which it may ever be more truly said that it has ceased to be than that it is. To such a tremulous wisp constantly reforming itself on the stream, to a single sharp impression, with a sense in it —a relic more or less fleeting—of such moments gone by, what is real in our life fines itself down. It is with this movement, with the passage and dissolution of impressions, images, sensations, that analysis leaves off— that continual vanishing away, that strange, perpetual weaving and unweaving of ourselves.

Philosophiren, says Novalis, *ist dephlegmatisiren, vivificiren*. The service of philosophy, of speculative culture, toward the human spirit is to rouse, to startle it into sharp and eager observation. Every moment some form grows perfect in hand or face; some tone on the hills or the sea is choicer than the rest; some mood of passion or insight or intellectual excitement is irresistibly real and attractive for us—but for that moment only. Not the fruit of experience, but experience itself, is the end. A counted number of pulses only is given to us of a variegated, dramatic life. How may we see in them all that is to be seen in them by the finest senses? How shall we pass most swiftly from point to point, and be present always at the focus where the greatest number of vital forces unite in their purest energy?

To burn always with this hard, gemlike flame, to maintain this ecstasy, is success in life. In a sense it might even be said that our failure is to form habits: for, after all, habit is relative to a stereotyped world, and meantime it is only the roughness of the eye that makes any two persons, things, situations, seem alike. While all melts under our feet, we may well catch at any exquisite passion, or any contribution to knowledge that seems by a lifted horizon to set the spirit free for a moment, or any stirring of the senses, strange dyes, strange colors, and curious odors, or work of the artist's hands, or the face of one's friend. Not to discriminate every moment some passionate attitude in those about us, and in the brilliancy of their gifts some tragic dividing of forces on their ways, is, on this short day of frost and sun, to sleep before evening. With this sense of the splendor of our experience and of its awful brevity, gathering all we are into one desperate effort to see and touch, we shall hardly have time to make theories about the things we see and touch. What we have to do is to be forever curiously testing new opinions and courting new impressions, never acquiescing in a facile orthodoxy of Comte, or of Hegel, or of our own. Philosophical theories or ideas, as points of view, instruments of criticism, may help us to gather up what might otherwise pass unregarded by us. "Philosophy is the microscope of thought." The theory or idea or system which requires of us the sacrifice of any part of this experience, in consideration of some interest into which we cannot enter, or some abstract theory we have not identified with ourselves, or what is only conventional, has no real claim upon us.

One of the most beautiful passages in the writings of Rousseau is that in the sixth book of the *Confessions*, where he describes the awakening in him of the literary sense. An undefinable taint of death had always clung about him, and now in early manhood he believed himself smitten by mortal disease. He asked himself how he might make as much as possible of the interval that re-

---

25. *Philosophiren,* etc., to be a philosopher is to rid oneself of apathy, to become alive. **Novalis,** the pseudonym of Friedrich von Hardenberg (1772-1801), a German romantic poet and novelist.

47. **habit . . . world,** habit becomes fixed as man in his world becomes stereotyped. 71. **Comte,** a celebrated French philosopher (1798-1857), who held that science is the key to the temple of truth because it abides rigorously by fact. **Hegel,** a famous German philosopher (1770-1831), in whom idealistic philosophy found its peak of intellectual acceptance. 84. **Rousseau.** See p. 532, note 39 and p. 589, note 35.

mained; and he was not biased by anything in his previous life when he decided that it must be by intellectual excitement, which he found just then in the clear, fresh writings of Voltaire. Well! we are all *condamnés,* as Victor Hugo says: we are all under sentence of death but with a sort of indefinite reprieve —*les hommes sont tous condamnés à mort avec des sursis indéfinis;* we have an interval, and then our place knows us no more. Some spend this interval in listlessness, some in high passions, the wisest—at least among "the children of this world"—in art and song. For our one chance lies in expanding that interval, in getting as many pulsations as possible into the given time. Great passions may give us this quickened sense of life, ecstasy and sorrow of love, the various forms of enthusiastic activity, disinterested or otherwise, which come naturally to many of us. Only be sure it is passion—that it does yield you this fruit of a quickened, multiplied consciousness. Of this wisdom, the poetic passion, the desire of beauty, the love of art for art's sake, has most; for art comes to you professing frankly to give nothing but the highest quality to your moments as they pass, and simply for those moments' sake. (1873)

5. **Voltaire,** French philosopher and skeptic (1694-1778). *condamnés,* condemned. 6. **Victor Hugo,** celebrated French poet and novelist (1802-1885), the recognized leader of the romantic school of the nineteenth century in France. 8. **les hommes,** etc. Pater has just given the translation of the quotation, which is from the scene at the barricade in *Les Misérables.*

Romanticism

The following brilliant definitions of classicism and romanticism, which reveal Pater's power of clear, exact thinking, appeared first in *Macmillan's Magazine* for November, 1876, under the title here given; the essay was republished as the Postscript to *Appreciations,* 1889.

αἰνεῖ δὲ παλαιὸν μὲν οἶνον, ἄνθεα δ' ὕμνων
νεωτέρων

THE words *classical* and *romantic* although, like many other critical expressions, sometimes abused by those who have understood them too vaguely or too absolutely, yet define two real tendencies in the history of art and literature. Used in an exaggerated sense, to express a greater opposition between those tendencies than really exists, they have at times tended to divide people of taste into opposite camps. But in that *House Beautiful,* which the creative minds of all generations—the artists and those who have treated life in the spirit of art—are always building together, for the refreshment of the human spirit, these oppositions cease; and the *Interpreter* of the *House Beautiful,* the true aesthetic critic, uses these divisions, only so far as they enable him to enter into the peculiarities of the objects with which he has to do. The term *classical,* fixed, as it is, to a well-defined literature, and a well-defined group in art, is clear, indeed; but then it has often been used in a hard, and merely scholastic sense, by the praisers of what is old and accustomed, at the expense of what is new, by critics who would never have discovered for themselves the charm of any work, whether new or old, who value what is old, in art or literature, for its accessories, and chiefly for the conventional authority that has gathered about it—people who would never really have been made glad by any Venus fresh-risen from the sea, and who praise the Venus of old Greece and Rome, only because they fancy her grown now into something staid and tame.

And as the term *classical* has been used in a too absolute, and therefore in a misleading sense, so the term *romantic* has been used much too vaguely, in various accidental senses. The sense in which Scott is called a romantic writer is chiefly this: that, in opposition to the literary tradition of the last century, he loved strange adventure, and sought it in the Middle Age. Much later, in a Yorkshire village, the spirit of romanticism bore a more

αἰνεῖ δὲ, etc., in wine it is the age we praise, in poetry the freshness. 11. **House Beautiful . . . Interpreter.** Both terms are from Bunyan's *Pilgrim's Progress,* Chapter 8. 17. **aesthetic critic,** one who judges a work of art with relation to its appeal to the sense of beauty and form. A judicial critic judges according to a set standard. An historical critic judges in relation to backgrounds and development.

32. **Venus,** goddess of love and beauty. In Greek mythology, as Aphrodite, she arose from the foam of the sea and landed at Cythera.

really characteristic fruit in the work of a young girl, Emily Brontë, the romance of *Wuthering Heights;* the figures of Hareton Earnshaw, of Catherine Linton, and of Heathcliffe—tearing open Catherine's grave, removing one side of her coffin, that he may really lie beside her in death—figures so passionate, yet woven on a background of delicately beautiful, moorland scenery, being typical examples of that spirit. In Germany, again, that spirit is shown less in Tieck, its professional representative, than in Meinhold, the author of *Sidonia the Sorceress* and the *Amber-Witch.* In Germany and France, within the last hundred years, the term has been used to describe a particular school of writers; and, consequently, when Heine criticizes the *Romantic School* in Germany—that movement which culminated in Goethe's *Goetz von Berlichingen;* or when Théophile Gautier criticizes the romantic movement in France, where, indeed, it bore its most characteristic fruits, and its play is hardly yet over—where, by a certain audacity, or *bizarrerie* of motive, united with faultless literary execution, it still shows itself in imaginative literature—they use the word, with an exact sense of special artistic qualities, indeed; but use it, nevertheless, with a limited application to the manifestation of those qualities at a particular period. But the romantic spirit is, in reality, an ever-present, an enduring principle, in the artistic temperament; and the qualities of thought and style which that, and other similar uses of the word *romantic* really indicate, are indeed but symptoms of a very continuous and widely working influence.

2. **Emily Brontë,** an English novelist and poet. See p. 716. 11. **Tieck,** Ludwig Tieck (1773-1853), the most prolific of the poets of the romantic school in Germany. 12. **Meinhold,** Johann Wilhelm Meinhold (1797-1851), a German theologian and writer. 17. **Heine,** Heinrich Heine (1797-1856), a celebrated German lyric poet and critic, of Hebrew descent. The romantic school in Germany and that of France correspond to the romantic movement in England. See p. 3. In his *Romantic School* (1836) Heine defines romanticism as "the reproduction in modern art or literature of the life and thought of the Middle Ages." 19. **Goethe,** the celebrated German poet, dramatist, and philosopher (1749-1832). His *Goetz von Berlichingen* is a drama dealing with the story of a robber knight of the German Empire of the sixteenth century. The drama, however, belongs to the "storm and stress" period, with its formlessness and worship of genius, rather than to the later romantic movement. 20. **Gautier,** a French poet, critic, and novelist (1811-1872). He was a leader of a group of young and extravagant enthusiasts of the French romantic movement. His novel *Les Jeunes-France* (1833) shows in a humorous and satirical way the follies of the youthful Romantics. 24. *bizarrerie,* extravagance, oddity.

Though the words *classical* and *romantic,* then, have acquired an almost technical meaning in application to certain developments of German and French taste, yet this is but one variation of an old opposition, which may be traced from the very beginning of the formation of European art and literature. From the first formation of anything like a standard of taste in these things, the restless curiosity of their more eager lovers necessarily made itself felt, in the craving for new motives, new subjects of interest, new modifications of style. Hence, the opposition between the classicists and the romanticists—between the adherents, in the culture of beauty, of the principles of liberty, and authority, respectively—of strength, and order or what the Greeks called κοσμιότης.

Sainte-Beuve, in the third volume of the *Causeries du Lundi,* has discussed the question, *What is meant by a classic?* It was a question he was well fitted to answer, having himself lived through many phases of taste, and having been in earlier life an enthusiastic member of the romantic school: he was also a great master of that sort of "philosophy of literature," which delights in tracing traditions in it, and the way in which various phases of thought and sentiment maintain themselves, through successive modifications, from epoch to epoch. His aim, then, is to give the word *classic* a wider and, as he says, a more generous sense than it commonly bears, to make it expressly *grandiose et flottant;* and, in doing this, he develops, in a masterly manner, those qualities of measure, purity, temperance, of which it is the especial function of classical art and literature, whatever meaning, narrower or wider, we attach to the term, to take care.

The charm, therefore, of what is classical, in art or literature, is that of the well-known tale, to which we can, nevertheless, listen over and over again, because it is told so well. To the absolute beauty of its artistic form, is added the accidental, tranquil charm of

55. κοσμιότης, decorum. 56. **Sainte-Beuve,** Charles Augustin Sainte-Beuve (1804-1869), an eminent French critic and poet. 57. **Causeries du Lundi,** *Gossips of Monday,* a series of literary studies (1851-1862), by Sainte-Beuve. 71. **grandiose et flottant,** large and flowing.

familiarity. There are times, indeed, at which these charms fail to work on our spirits at all, because they fail to excite us. "*Romanticism*," says Stendhal, "is the art of presenting to people the literary works which, in the actual state of their habits and beliefs, are capable of giving them the greatest possible pleasure; *classicism*, on the contrary, of presenting them with that which gave the greatest possible pleasure to their grandfathers." But then, beneath all changes of habits and beliefs, our love of that mere abstract proportion—of music—which what is classical in literature possesses, still maintains itself in the best of us, and what pleased our grandparents may at least tranquilize us. The "classic" comes to us out of the cool and quiet of other times, as the measure of what a long experience has shown will at least never displease us. And in the classical literature of Greece and Rome, as in the classics of the last century, the essentially classical element is that quality of order in beauty, which they possess, indeed, in a preeminent degree, and which impresses some minds to the exclusion of everything else in them.

It is the addition of strangeness to beauty, that constitutes the romantic character in art; and the desire of beauty being a fixed element in every artistic organization, it is the addition of curiosity to this desire of beauty, that constitutes the romantic temper. Curiosity and the desire of beauty, have each their place in art, as in all true criticism. When one's curiosity is deficient, when one is not eager enough for new impressions, and new pleasures, one is liable to value mere academical proprieties too highly, to be satisfied with worn-out or conventional types, with the insipid ornament of Racine, or the prettiness of that later Greek sculpture, which passed so long for true Hellenic work; to miss those places where the handiwork of nature, or of the artist, has been most cunning; to find the most stimulating products of art a mere irritation. And when one's curiosity is in excess, when it overbalances the desire of beauty, then one is liable to value in works of art what is inartistic in them; to be satisfied with what is exaggerated in art, with productions like some of those of the romantic school in Germany; not to distinguish, jealously enough, between what is admirably done, and what is done not quite so well, in the writings, for instance, of Jean Paul. And if I had to give instances of these defects, then I should say, that Pope, in common with the age of literature to which he belonged, had too little curiosity, so that there is always a certain insipidity in the effect of his work, exquisite as it is; and, coming down to our own time, that Balzac had an excess of curiosity—curiosity not duly tempered with the desire of beauty.

But, however falsely those two tendencies may be opposed by critics, or exaggerated by artists themselves, they are tendencies really at work at all times in art, molding it, with the balance sometimes a little on one side, sometimes a little on the other, generating, respectively, as the balance inclines on this side or that, two principles, two traditions, in art, and in literature so far as it partakes of the spirit of art. If there is a great overbalance of curiosity, then, we have the grotesque in art: if the union of strangeness and beauty, under very difficult and complex conditions, be a successful one, if the union be entire, then the resultant beauty is very exquisite, very attractive. With a passionate care for beauty, the romantic spirit refuses to have it, unless the condition of strangeness be first fulfilled. Its desire is for a beauty born of unlikely elements, by a profound alchemy, by a difficult initiation, by the charm which wrings it even out of terrible things; and a trace of distortion, of the grotesque, may perhaps

---

4. **Stendhal**, the pen name of Marie Henri Beyle (1783-1842), a French novelist; he was a pioneer and a devotee of romanticism. The quotation is from his *Racine et Shakespeare* (1823). 21. **classics . . . century**, the neo-classical writings of the eighteenth century. 40. **Racine**, Jean Baptiste Racine (1639-1699), a celebrated French classical dramatist and poet. Although he gave classical names to his characters, as a court poet he depicted the life and manners of the society around him. Pater here expresses the Englishman's opinion of the greatest poet of France. **prettiness . . . work**. Greek art of the Hellenistic period, the third century B.C., was noted for its prettiness in contrast to the beauty and strength of the true Hellenic art of the fifth and sixth centuries B.C.

55. **Jean Paul**, Jean Paul Richter (1763-1825), a German writer noted for his monotonous portrayal of whimsical characters. 57. **Pope**. See Vol. I, pp. 831 and 1063. 62. **Balzac**, Honoré de Balzac (1799-1850), the chief of the realistic school of French novelists. His works give a full and detailed picture of contemporary society, done with unrestrained frankness.

linger, as an additional element of expression, about its ultimate grace. Its eager, excited spirit will have strength, the grotesque, first of all—the trees shrieking as you tear off the leaves; for Jean Valjean, the long years of convict life; for Redgauntlet, the quicksands of Solway Moss; then, incorporate with this strangeness, and intensified by restraint, as much sweetness, as much beauty, as is compatible with that. *Énergique, frais, et dispos*—these, according to Saint-Beuve, are the characteristics of a genuine classic—*les ouvrages anciens ne sont pas classiques parce qu'ils sont vieux, mais parce qu'ils sont énergiques, frais, et dispos.* Energy, freshness, intelligent and masterly disposition:—these are characteristics of Victor Hugo when his alchemy is complete, in certain figures, like Marius and Cosette, in certain scenes, like that in the opening of *Les Travailleurs de la Mer*, where Déruchette writes the name of *Gilliatt* in the snow, on Christmas morning; but always there is a certain note of strangeness discernible there, as well.

The essential elements, then, of the romantic spirit are curiosity and the love of beauty; and it is only as an illustration of these qualities, that it seeks the Middle Age, because, in the overcharged atmosphere of the Middle Age, there are unworked sources of romantic effect, of a strange beauty, to be won, by strong imagination, out of things unlikely or remote.

Few, probably, now read Madame de Staël's *De l'Allemagne*, though it has its interest, the interest which never quite fades out of work really touched with the enthusiasm of the spiritual adventurer, the pioneer in culture. It was published in 1810, to introduce to French readers a new school of writers—the romantic school, from beyond the Rhine; and it was followed, twenty-three years later, by Heine's *Romantische Schule*, as at once a supplement and a correction. Both these books, then, connect romanticism with Germany, with the names especially of Goethe and Tieck; and, to many English readers, the idea of romanticism is still inseparably connected with Germany—that Germany which, in its quaint old towns, under the spire of Strasbourg or the towers of Heidelberg, was always listening in rapt inaction to the melodious, fascinating voices of the Middle Age, and which, now that it has got Strasbourg back again, has, I suppose, almost ceased to exist. But neither Germany, with its Goethe and Tieck, nor England, with its Byron and Scott, is nearly so representative of the romantic temper as France, with Murger, and Gautier, and Victor Hugo. It is in French literature that its most characteristic expression is to be found; and that, as most closely derivative, historically, from such peculiar conditions, as ever reinforce it to the utmost.

For, although temperament has much to do with the generation of the romantic spirit, and although this spirit, with its curiosity, its thirst for a curious beauty, may be always traceable in excellent art (traceable even in Sophocles), yet still, in a limited sense, it may be said to be a product of special epochs. Outbreaks of this spirit, that is, come naturally with particular periods—times, when, in men's approaches toward art and poetry, curiosity may be noticed to take the lead, when men come to art and poetry, with a deep thirst for intellectual excitement, after a long *ennui*, or in reaction against the strain of outward, practical things: in the later Middle Age, for instance; so that medieval poetry, centering in Dante, is often opposed to Greek

---

4. **the trees ... leaves.** See p. 589, note 3. 5. **Jean Valjean,** the hero of Victor Hugo's *Les Misérables* (1862). For stealing a loaf of bread he was sentenced to prison. See p. 585, note 6. 6. **Redgauntlet,** the hero of Scott's novel *Redgauntlet,* who in Letter IV rescues Darsie Latimer from the dangerous quicksands of Solway Moss, a drained area in Cumberlandshire. Redgauntlet was an ardent supporter of Prince Charles Stuart, the Young Pretender to the English throne in the middle of the eighteenth century, who in the novel was captured near Solway Moss. 12. **les ... dispos,** ancient writings are not classics because they are old, but because they are spirited, fresh, and well-ordered. 18. **Marius and Cosette,** in Book 2 of *Les Misérables;* they are the hero and heroine of the romantic part of the story. 20. **Les ... Mer,** *The Toilers of the Sea.* The act of Déruchette, the heroine of the novel, is a prophecy of the early and tragic death of Gilliatt. 34. **Madame de Staël,** Anne Louise Necker (1766-1817), a famous French writer; her book on Germany is her masterpiece. In it she revolts against classical rules and models and exalts native ability, subjectivity, and imagination, all of which she finds in the German writers.

54. **got ... again.** Strasbourg is in the territory of Alsace-Lorraine, taken by Louis XIV of France (1643-1715), regained by Germany in 1871, and restored to France after the World War. 57. **Byron and Scott.** See pp. 200 and 190. 59. **Murger,** Henri Murger (1822-1861), a French writer who was noted for his imaginative treatment of realistic details and for his originality and sensibility. 70. **Sophocles,** the great Greek tragic dramatist (fifth century B.C.), who is a genuine classicist. 81. **Dante,** the most famous of Italian poets (1265-1321); he wrote in Italian, rather than in Latin, and by so doing gave an impulse to the rise of vernacular literature.

and Roman poetry, as romantic poetry to the classical. What the romanticism of Dante is, may be estimated, if we compare the lines in which Virgil describes the hazel-wood, from whose broken twigs flows the blood of Polydorus, not without the expression of a real shudder at the ghastly incident, with the whole canto of the *Inferno*, into which Dante has expanded them, beautifying and softening it, meanwhile, by a sentiment of profound pity. And it is especially in that period of intellectual disturbance, immediately preceding Dante, amid which the romance languages define themselves at last, that this temper is manifested. Here, in the literature of Provence, the very name of *romanticism* is stamped with its true signification: here we have indeed a romantic world, grotesque even, in the strength of its passions, almost insane in its curious expression of them, drawing all things into its sphere, making the birds, nay! lifeless things, its voices and messengers, yet so penetrated with the desire for beauty and sweetness, that it begets a wholly new species of poetry, in which the *Renaissance* may be said to begin. The last century was pre-eminently a classical age, an age in which, for art and literature, the element of a comely order was in the ascendant; which, passing away, left a hard battle to be fought between the classical and the romantic schools. Yet, it is in the heart of this century, of Goldsmith, and Stothard, of Watteau and the *Siècle de Louis XIV*—in one of its central, if not most characteristic figures, in Rousseau—that the modern or French romanticism really originates. But, what in the eighteenth century is but an exceptional phenomenon, breaking through its fair reserve and discretion only at rare intervals, is the habitual guise of the nineteenth, breaking through it perpetually, with a feverishness, an incomprehensible straining and excitement, which all experience to some degree, but yearning also, in the genuine children of the romantic school, to be *énergique, frais, et dispos*—for those qualities of energy, freshness, comely order; and often, in Murger, in Gautier, in Victor Hugo, for instance, with singular felicity attaining them.

It is in the terrible tragedy of Rousseau, in fact, that French romanticism, with much else, begins: reading his *Confessions* we seem actually to assist at the birth of this new, strong spirit in the French mind. The wildness which has shocked so many, and the fascination which has influenced almost everyone, in the squalid, yet eloquent figure, we see and hear so clearly in that book, wandering under the apple-blossoms and among the vines of Neuchâtel or Vevey actually give it the quality of a very successful romantic invention. His strangeness or distortion, his profound subjectivity, his passionateness—the *cor laceratum*—Rousseau makes all men in love with these. *Je ne suis fait comme aucun de ceux que j'ai sus. Mais si je ne vaux pas mieux, au moins je suis autre.*—"I am not made like anyone else I have ever known: yet, if I am not better, at least I am different." These words, from the first page of the *Confessions*, anticipate all the Werthers, Renés, Obermanns, of the last hundred years. For Rousseau did but anticipate a trouble in the spirit of the whole world; and thirty years afterwards, what in him was a peculiarity, became part of the general consciousness. A storm was coming: Rousseau, with others, felt

3. **lines ... hazel-wood**, in the *Aeneid*, III, 23 ff. Polydorus in Greek legend was the youngest son of King Priam of Troy. Dante devotes Canto 13 of the *Inferno* to the episode of the bleeding bush. 11. **period ... Dante**. This was the time when various languages and dialects were fighting against Latin and contending for supremacy as the language of Italy. 32. **Goldsmith**. See Vol. I, p. 1113. 33. **Stothard**, Thomas Stothard (1755-1834), a famous English engraver and painter. Although lacking in force and passion, and accuracy in detail, his works are characterized by exquisite grace and beauty. **Watteau**, Jean Antoine Watteau (1684-1721), a French pastoral painter of Flemish origin; he is said to "incarnate every grace and poetic spirit of the eighteenth century." He revolted against the pompousness of classical art and prepared the soil for the flowering of impressionism. *Siècle de Louis XIV*, the age of Louis XIV, King of France (1643-1715); it was characterized by its emphasis upon form and correctness in writing. 35. **Rousseau**. See p. 532, ll. 39 ff. Rousseau was a remarkable and an unfortunate genius; his life was made up of alternate fits of passion and virtue; he was unstable in love and friendship. Exiled from France because of the daring and the frankness of his writings, he sought refuge in Switzerland, his native country. In his *Confessions* Rousseau makes a candid and passionate revelation of his emotional life.

60. **Neuchâtel**, name borne by a city, a lake, and a canton in Switzerland. **Vevey**, a town on Lake Geneva, Switzerland, noted for its festival of vine-dressers. 64. *cor laceratum*, torn heart. 71. **Werthers**. In Goethe's sentimental romance *The Sorrows of Werther*, the hero falls in love with Lotte, the wife of a friend, and in passionate despair takes his own life. **Renés**. *René* is a romance by François René Chateaubriand (1768-1848), a celebrated French author and statesman. The story abounds in Romantic excesses—insatiable desires, disappointments, melancholy, sentimental memories and affections, and a final plunge into the solitude of an American wilderness. René, the hero, is the author under a thin disguise. 72. **Obermanns**. *Obermann* is a psychological romance by Senancour (1804); it is named from the hero, a dreamer who is striving to escape the actual.

it in the air, and they helped to bring it down: they introduced a disturbing element into French literature, then so trim and formal, like our own literature of the age of Queen Anne.

In 1815 the storm had come and gone, but had left, in the spirit of "young France," the *ennui* of an immense disillusion. In the last chapter of Edgar Quinet's *Révolution Française*, a work itself full of irony, of disillusion, he distinguishes two books, Senancour's *Obermann* and Chateaubriand's *Génie du Christianisme*, as characteristic of the first decade of the present century. In those two books we detect already the disease and the cure—in *Obermann* the irony, refined into a plaintive philosophy of "indifference"—in Chateaubriand's *Génie du Christianisme*, the refuge from a tarnished actual present, a present of disillusion, into a world of strength and beauty in the Middle Age, as at an earlier period—in *René* and *Atala*—into the free play of them in savage life. It is to minds in this spiritual situation, weary of the present, but yearning for the spectacle of beauty and strength, that the works of French romanticism appeal. They set a positive value on the intense, the exceptional; and a certain distortion is sometimes noticeable in them, as in conceptions like Victor Hugo's *Quasimodo*, or *Gwynplaine*, something of a terrible grotesque, of the *macabre*, as the French themselves call it; though always combined with perfect literary execution, as in Gautier's *La Morte Amoureuse*, or the scene of the "maimed" burial-rites of the player, dead of the frost, in his *Capitaine Fracasse*—true "flowers of the yew." It becomes grim humor in Victor Hugo's combat of Gilliatt with the devil-fish, or the incident, with all its ghastly comedy drawn out at length, of the great gun detached from its fastenings on shipboard, in *Quatre-Vingt-Treize* (perhaps the most terrible of all the accidents that can happen by sea) and in the entire episode, in that book, of the *Convention*. Not less surely does it reach a genuine pathos; for the habit of noting and distinguishing one's own intimate passages of sentiment makes one sympathetic, begetting, as it must, the power of entering, by all sorts of finer ways, into the intimate recesses of other minds; so that pity is another quality of romanticism, both Victor Hugo and Gautier being great lovers of animals, and charming writers about them, and Murger being unrivaled in the pathos of his *Scènes de la Vie de Jeunesse*. Penetrating so finely into all situations which appeal to pity, above all, into the special or exceptional phases of such feeling, the romantic humor is not afraid of the quaintness or singularity of its circumstances or expression, pity, indeed, being of the essence of humor; so that Victor Hugo does but turn his romanticism into practice, in his hunger and thirst after practical *Justice!*—a justice which shall no longer wrong children, or animals, for instance, by ignoring in a stupid, mere breadth of view, minute facts about them. Yet the romanticists are antinomian, too, sometimes, because the love of energy and beauty, of distinction in passion, tended naturally to become a little *bizarre*, plunging into the Middle Age, into the secrets of old Italian story. *Are we in the Inferno?*—we are tempted to ask, wondering at something malign in so much beauty. For over all a care for the refreshment of the human spirit by fine art manifests itself, a predominant sense of literary charm, so that, in their search for the secret of exquisite expression, the romantic school went back to the forgotten world of early French poetry, and literature itself became the most delicate of the arts—like "goldsmith's work," says Sainte-Beuve, of Bertrand's *Gaspard de la Nuit*—and that

---

9. **Edgar Quinet**, a French historian and man of letters (1803-1875). In spite of his own republicanism his book on the French Revolution was unfriendly to the acts of the revolutionists. 12. **Génie du Christianisme**, *The Spirit of Christianity* (1802), a defense of the Christian religion on the ground of its emotional appeal to man's deepest instincts. 22. **Atala**, a romance by Chateaubriand, the scene of which is laid in North America. Atala, the heroine, a daughter of an American Indian, has been brought up in Christian faith and vowed to virginity. She rescues her lover, flees with him into the desert, keeps her vow, but finally poisons herself in despairing fanaticism. This story was later incorporated in the *Génie du Christianisme*. 34. **La Morte Amoureuse**, *Amorous Death*, a fantastic story in which a wild love overcomes death. 37. **"flowers of the yew,"** products of sorrow; the yew is an emblem of grief. 39. **combat . . . devil-fish.** In *The Toilers of the Sea*.

42. **Quatre-Vingt-Treize**, *Ninety-Three* (1784), a tragic romance of great power and beauty, dealing with the events of 1793. 45. **the Convention**, the constitutional assembly that ruled France from 1792 to 1795. 56. **Scènes . . . Jeunesse**, *Scenes from the Life of Youth*. 69. **antinomian**, opposed to the doctrine that the moral law is obligatory. 85. **Bertrand**, Jacques-Louis Bertrand (1807-1841), a French poet and journalist. **Gaspard de la Nuit** is a series of short sketches.

peculiarly French gift, the gift of exquisite speech, *argute loqui,* attained in them a perfection which it had never seen before.

Stendhal, a writer whom I have already quoted, and of whom English readers might well know much more than they do, stands between the earlier and later growths of the romantic spirit. His novels are rich in romantic quality and his other writings—partly criticism, partly personal reminiscences—are a very curious and interesting illustration of the needs out of which romanticism arose. In his book on *Racine and Shakespeare,* Stendhal argues that all good art was romantic in its day; and this is perhaps true in Stendhal's sense. That little treatise, full of "dry light" and fertile ideas, was published in the year 1823, and its object is to defend an entire independence and liberty in the choice and treatment of subject, both in art and literature, against those who upheld the exclusive authority of precedent. In pleading the cause of romanticism, therefore, it is the novelty, both of form and of motive, in writings like the *Hernani* of Victor Hugo (which soon followed it, raising a storm of criticism) that he is chiefly concerned to justify. To be interesting and really stimulating, to keep us from yawning even, art and literature must follow the subtle movements of that nimbly-shifting *Time-Spirit,* or *Zeit-Geist,* understood by French not less than by German criticism, which is always modifying men's taste, as it modifies their manners and their pleasures. This, he contends, is what all great workmen had always understood. Dante, Shakespeare, Molière, had exercised an absolute independence in their choice of subject and treatment. To turn always with that ever-changing spirit, yet to retain the flavor of what was admirably done in past generations, in the classics, as we say—is the problem of true romanticism. "Dante," he observes, "was pre-eminently the romantic poet. He adored Virgil, yet he wrote the *Divine Comedy,* with the episode of Ugolino, which is as unlike the *Aeneid* as can possibly be. And those who thus obey the fundamental principle of romanticism, one by one become classical, and are joined to that ever-increasing common league, formed by men of all countries, to approach nearer and nearer to perfection."

Romanticism, then, although it has its epochs, is in its essential characteristics rather a spirit which shows itself at all times, in various degrees, in individual workmen and their work, and the amount of which criticism has to estimate in them taken one by one, than the peculiarity of a time or a school. Depending on the varying proportion of curiosity and the desire of beauty, natural tendencies of the artistic spirit at all times, it must always be partly a matter of individual temperament. The eighteenth century in England has been regarded as almost exclusively a classical period; yet William Blake, a type of so much which breaks through what are conventionally thought the influences of that century, is still a noticeable phenomenon in it, and the reaction in favor of naturalism in poetry begins in that century, early. There are, thus, the born romanticists and the born classicists. There are the born classicists who start with *form,* to whose minds the comeliness of the old, immemorial, well-recognized types in art and literature, have revealed themselves impressively; who will entertain no matter which will not go easily and flexibly into them; whose work aspires only to be a variation upon, or study from, the older masters. " 'Tis art's decline, my son!" they are always saying, to the progressive element in their own generation; to those who care for that which in fifty years' time everyone will be caring for. On the other hand, there are the born romanticists, who start with an original, untried *matter,* still in fusion; who conceive

---

2. *argute loqui,* to speak subtly. 26. *Hernani,* a very romantic play. In its utter disregard of unities, and of set patterns of speech and versification, it was the peak of the romantic movement. 38. **Molière,** the greatest of the French writers of comedy (1622-1673). He ridiculed brilliantly various types of folly and vice in French society.

46. **Ugolino,** a nobleman of Pisa of the thirteenth century, who was imprisoned with his two sons and two nephews in a tower by his political enemy and left to die. Dante represents him in Hell as gnawing the head of his foe while both are frozen together in a lake of ice. Dante's story contains a ghastliness of detail that is foreign to the *Aeneid.* 67. **Blake.** See pp. 9 and 111. 71. **reaction . . . naturalism.** It is seen in the poetry of Thomson (p. 32), Cowper (p. 73), and others. See p. 10. 82. " 'Tis . . . son!" From Browning's *Fra Lippo Lippi,* l. 233, p. 691.

this vividly, and hold by it as the essence of their work; who, by the very vividness and heat of their conception, purge away, sooner or later, all that is not organically appropriate to it, till the whole effect adjusts itself in clear, orderly, proportionate form; which form, after a very little time, becomes classical in its turn.

The romantic or classical character of a picture, a poem, a literary work, depends, then, on the balance of certain qualities in it; and in this sense, a very real distinction may be drawn between good classical and good romantic work. But all critical terms are relative; and there is at least a valuable suggestion in that theory of Stendhal's, that all good art was romantic in its day. In the beauties of Homer and Pheidias, quiet as they now seem, there must have been, for those who confronted them for the first time, excitement and surprise, the sudden, unforeseen satisfaction of the desire of beauty. Yet the *Odyssey*, with its marvelous adventure, is more romantic than the *Iliad*, which nevertheless contains, among many other romantic episodes, that of the immortal horses of Achilles, who weep at the death of Patroclus. Aeschylus is more romantic than Sophocles, whose *Philoctetes*, were it written now, might figure, for the strangeness of its motive and the perfectness of its execution, as typically romantic; while, of Euripides, it may be said, that his method in writing his plays is to sacrifice readily almost everything else, so that he may attain the fullness of a single romantic effect. These two tendencies, indeed, might be applied as a measure or standard, all through Greek and Roman art and poetry, with very illuminating results; and for an analyst of the romantic principle in art, no exercise would be more profitable, than to walk through the collection of classical antiquities at the Louvre, or the British Museum, or to examine some representative collection of Greek coins, and note how the element of curiosity, of the love of strangeness, insinuates itself into classical design, and record the effects of the romantic spirit there, the traces of struggle, of the grotesque even, though over-balanced here by sweetness; as in the sculpture of Chartres and Rheims, the real sweetness of mind in the sculptor is often overbalanced by the grotesque, by the rudeness of his strength.

Classicism, then, means for Stendhal, for that younger enthusiastic band of French writers whose unconscious method he formulated into principles, the reign of what is pedantic, conventional, and narrowly academical in art; for him, all good art is romantic. To Sainte-Beuve, who understands the term in a more liberal sense, it is the characteristic of certain epochs, of certain spirits in every epoch, not given to the exercise of original imagination, but rather to the working out of refinements of manner on some authorized matter; and who bring to their perfection, in this way, the elements of sanity, of order and beauty in manner. In general criticism, again, it means the spirit of Greece and Rome, of some phases in literature and art that may seem of equal authority with Greece and Rome, the age of Louis the Fourteenth, the age of Johnson; though this is at best an uncritical use of the term, because in Greek and Roman work there are typical examples of the romantic spirit. But explain the terms as we may, in application to particular epochs, there are these two elements always recognizable; united in perfect art—in Sophocles, in Dante, in the highest work of Goethe, though not always absolutely balanced there; and these two elements may be not inappropriately termed the classical and romantic tendencies.

Material for the artist, motives of inspiration, are not yet exhausted: our curious, com-

---

18. **Pheidias**, a celebrated Greek sculptor (fifth century B.C.). 26. **horses . . . Patroclus**. In the *Iliad*, 17, 426 ff. Patroclus is the intimate friend of Achilles. When Achilles sulks and withdraws from the fight, he gives his armor to Patroclus, who enters the battle against the Trojans and is killed by Hector. Of the grief of the immortal horses of Achilles, which Patroclus had been driving, the epic says: "And hot tears flowed from their eyes . . . as they mourned in sorrow for their charioteer." 27. **Aeschylus, Sophocles, Euripides**, famous Greek tragic dramatists (fifth century B.C.). Pater's statement is a characteristic exaggeration. Perhaps he finds Aeschylus romantic when he broods over deep questions and the dark mysteries of fate and paints men as they ought to be. Sophocles may be said to be more human than Aeschylus.

42. **Louvre**, the chief royal palace in Paris from the thirteenth century until Louis XIV took up his residence at Versailles in 1682. Since 1793 it has been occupied by a museum of art and public offices. 43. **British Museum**, a national museum in London for the preservation of antiquities, books, etc. It was founded in 1753. 50. **Chartres**, a cathedral in France famous for its sculptures, numbering no fewer than 10,000. 51. **Rheims**, a French cathedral, one of the greatest in the world. It was largely destroyed in the First World War.

plex, aspiring age still abounds in subjects for aesthetic manipulation by the literary as well as by other forms of art. For the literary art, at all events, the problem just now is, to induce order upon the contorted, proportionless accumulation of our knowledge and experience, our science and history, our hopes and disillusion, and, in effecting this, to do consciously what has been done hitherto for the most part too unconsciously, to write our English language as the Latins wrote theirs, as the French write, as scholars should write. Appealing, as he may, to precedent in this matter, the scholar will still remember that if "the style is the man" it is also the age: that the nineteenth century too will be found to have had its style, justified by necessity—a style very different, alike from the baldness of an impossible "Queen Anne" revival, and an incorrect, incondite exuberance, after the mode of Elizabeth: that we can only return to either at the price of an impoverishment of form or matter, or both, although, an intellectually rich age such as ours being necessarily an eclectic one, we may well cultivate some of the excellences of literary types so different as those: that in literature as in other matters it is well to unite as many diverse elements as may be: that the individual writer or artist, certainly, is to be estimated by the number of graces he combines, and his power of interpenetrating them in a given work. To discriminate schools, of art, of literature, is, of course, part of the obvious business of literary criticism: but, in the work of literary production, it is easy to be overmuch occupied concerning them. For, in truth, the legitimate contention is, not of one age or school of literary art against another, but of all successive schools alike, against the stupidity which is dead to the substance, and the vulgarity which is dead to form. (1876)

10. **to write . . . write,** to write with precision. 15. **"the style is the man."** The cryptic saying of Buffon (1707-1788), a celebrated French naturalist, in his *Discourse on Style* delivered when he took his seat in the French Academy, 1753. 20. **incondite,** crude, ill-composed.

25. **eclectic,** selected from what is thought best in doctrines and opinions from various sources.

POETS OF FAITH AND DOUBT

Alfred, Lord Tennyson

1809-1892

The most representative poet of the Victorian age was Alfred, Lord Tennyson. Both for good and for ill he was the voice of Victorian England, and no choice of Poet Laureate was ever more appropriate than his elevation to that position on the death of Wordsworth in 1850. He lived and labored through the whole of the Victorian age, and his name is almost as closely associated with the period as that of Victoria herself.

Tennyson was born into a talented family in the Lincolnshire rectory of Somersby not far from the sea. He was the fourth child in a family of eight sons and four daughters. All were brought up in an atmosphere of high thinking and aspirations, and two of his brothers, Frederick and Charles, had some gift of verse-making. Tennyson's first venture into print was made in a slim volume of poems entitled *Poems by Two Brothers* but containing the work of all three. These early verses appeared a year before he entered Trinity College, Cambridge, in 1828. In college Tennyson led an active life. With the other alert young men of his generation he took a keen interest in politics and was a member of The Apostles, a club of young poets, critics, and thinkers. In this group was Arthur Henry Hallam (1811-1833), Tennyson's closest friend, whose untimely death was to provide Tennyson with the deepest spiritual experience of his life. Tennyson won the Chancellor's prize for a poem called *Timbuctoo* the year after he entered Cambridge, and in 1830, just a year before he left Cambridge, he published *Poems, Chiefly Lyrical*. His second volume of poems was issued in 1832 (under date of 1833), the year of the first Reform Bill (see p. 403), and in spite of some sneering but not altogether unjustified critical reviews, it was favorably received. The volume was highly romantic in manner and revealed the young poet as in no small degree a disciple of Keats. Many critics have felt that a considerable share of Tennyson's best poetry is his work in the romantic spirit and technique.

The year following the publication of Tennyson's second volume occurred an event which penetrated to the very core of his spiritual being, deepened his character, enriched his literary powers, and transformed him, in brief, from a youth into a man. Arthur Henry Hallam, the friend of his college days and the betrothed of his sister Emily, died suddenly in Vienna. The shock to the young poet was so serious as to affect his health and spirits, for he and Hallam had been like David and Jonathan for many years. When his mind grew calmer, he began the long poem of faith and doubt, *In Memoriam;* and through the seventeen years of his labor on the poem he battled his way to a resignation to fate and a richer and deeper understanding of life. In the poem, moreover, he attempted to make the adjustment between religious faith and science that many other Victorian thinkers were also attempting to make. That he succeeded is not certain; Bishop Wilberforce believed that he attained only "a minimum basis of faith"; and Professor Corson called *In Memoriam* "that beautiful poem of nineteenth-century skepticism." While laboring on this memorial to his dead friend, he also worked at times on the *Idylls of the King,* the long series of picturesque narratives which he drew from Malory (see Vol. I, p. 277) and molded into a Victorian pattern. For ten years, however, he published nothing. Then, in 1842, appeared two volumes entitled *Poems*. The public response was immediate, and the book was universally acclaimed. Into it went some of the highly romantic poems of his earlier volumes—most of them greatly improved by the poet's careful emendations; to these were added such maturer and graver poems as *Ulysses* and *Morte D'Arthur*. The popularity of this book did not save him from some bitter experiences during the decade in which it appeared. An unwise speculation left him penniless, and two attacks of nervous prostration threatened to end his career. In spite of these difficulties his highly popular *Princess* (see p. 626), a semi-burlesque satire on woman's place in the world, appeared in 1847.

The middle of the century brought a change for the better in Tennyson's affairs. In 1850 he married Emily Sellwood—a most happy union. In the same year he published *In Memoriam*. And in that year he succeeded Wordsworth as Poet Laureate. After this appointment Tennyson's career was that of a highly popular poet to England and the English people. The queen took pleasure in honoring him, especially after his dedication of an edition of the *Idylls of the King* to the memory of Prince Albert, who died in 1861; and in 1884 he was raised to the peerage. Some few shifts in popular favor did appear to wound his sensitive nature, but he surmounted them, and continued to be for the people of England the venerable incarnation of the soul of poetry. During the last forty years of his life the stream of his literary work continued unstemmed. His rather formal, but nevertheless noble *Ode on the Death of the Duke of Wellington* was published in 1852—just a year before he moved to his farm of Farringford in the Isle of Wight. *Maud,* a long romance of love and tragedy, together with some other poems, came out in 1855. In 1859 the first series of his *Idylls of the King* appeared and obtained an immense popular success. The sentimental *Enoch Arden,* a tale of a self-sacrificing sailor, was issued in 1864, together with his dialect poems *Northern Farmer.* In 1867 he moved to Blackdown in Surrey, where he lived for the rest of his life in a lovely home which he named Aldworth. Shortly afterwards he added the last stories to his *Idylls of the King* and then turned his hand to a series of historical tragedies designed to illustrate the "Making of England." *Queen Mary* (1875), *Harold* (1876), and *Becket* (1884) were more poetic, on the whole, than dramatic; of the three *Becket* was the most vigorous and moving, and it was his only success on the stage. His last years were filled, like his earlier ones, with the writing of poems; *Tiresias and Other Poems* appeared in 1885, *Locksley Hall Sixty Years After* in 1886, *Demeter and Other Poems* in 1889, and *The Death of Oenone* in 1892, just after the poet's own death. He was buried in Westminster Abbey.

Few English poets have enjoyed the almost unbroken success and popularity which came to Tennyson. Of all the Victorian poets he was physically the most like a poet. In a tall, gaunt frame, surmounted by a magnificent head, dwelt a spirit of range and power, sometimes austerely remote and severe, but capable of feeling and expressing the most intense emotions. He took his high calling with an almost religious seriousness and pursued it with amazing tenseness and persistence. Part of his success may be attributed to these facts, for the Victorians loved a display of morality and "high seriousness." His popularity had roots, moreover, in a sympathetic understanding of Victorian life. He knew the whole range of the period; he studied science assiduously; he was aware of the religious unrest of the times; he knew what philosophies were stirring his English contemporaries. He was intensely English. His patriotism was almost narrow, and he had little world outlook on contemporary life and art. This love of England was increased by his sense of obligation as the official bard of England. If those poems and plays of his that glorify England directly or remotely were to be assembled in one book, they would make a large volume. His view of life, if sometimes narrowly national, was always lofty. He lived a noble life, and the art and the man were one.

An estimate of Tennyson's poetic art made nearly half a century after his death is certain to place him among that large group of poets who were more highly regarded by their own generation than by succeeding ones. The reason for this is not difficult to understand: he was too Victorian to be universal. He had the self-consciousness of the Victorian people, their insular point of view, their admiration for the ornate, and their sentimentality; and the revolt against these characteristics which came near the end of the nineteenth century was also a revolt against the art of the man who gave poetic expression to them. Much of his poetry became outmoded with the passing of Victorian manners. English poetry has tended since his death to become rough, rugged, and over-intellectualized. In contrast with these qualities some of Tennyson's poetry seems insipid, over-luscious, flat, "pretty," but lacking fiber. *The Princess,* for example, presents ideas that are as Victorian as lace-caps and hoop-skirts; and the only parts of this long poem that are of permanent poetic value are the incidental lyrics. *Enoch Arden* is almost mawkish in its sentimentality. Not a little of Tennyson's poetry has these qualities and now seems artificial and intellectually narrow.

Yet Tennyson is one of the major poets of the Victorian era, and is unlikely ever to lose this position. In spite of the characteristics that marred large sections of his poetry, he attained high art in scores of his poems. It seems likely that ultimately Tennyson's reputation will come to rest less and less on those long poems to which he attached most importance and more and more on the lovely lyrics written in his romantic manner. In *The Lady of Shalott*, the *Bugle Song* from *The Princess*, *The Lotos-Eaters*, and *Ulysses*, for example, there are golden qualities of beauty and sweetness both in the themes and in the language that appear only in great poetry.

The Poet

This poem expresses Tennyson's early ideas of the high calling; his theory should be compared with that of Wordsworth in the *Preface* to the *Lyrical Ballads*, p. 318.

The poet in a golden clime was born,
    With golden stars above;
Dowered with the hate of hate, the scorn of scorn,
    The love of love.

He saw through life and death, through good and ill,   5
    He saw through his own soul.
The marvel of the everlasting will,
    An open scroll,

Before him lay; with echoing feet he threaded
    The secretest walks of fame: 10
The viewless arrows of his thoughts were headed
    And winged with flame,

Like Indian reeds blown from his silver tongue,
    And of so fierce a flight,
From Calpe unto Caucasus they sung,   15
    Filling with light

And vagrant melodies the winds which bore
    Them earthward till they lit;
Then, like the arrow-seeds of the field flower,
    The fruitful wit   20

Cleaving took root, and springing forth anew
    Where'er they fell, behold,
Like to the mother plant in semblance, grew
    A flower all gold,

And bravely furnished all abroad to fling   25
    The wingéd shafts of truth,
To throng with stately blooms the breathing spring
    Of Hope and Youth.

So many minds did gird their orbs with beams,
    Though one did fling the fire;   30
Heaven flowed upon the soul in many dreams
    Of high desire.

Thus truth was multiplied on truth, the world
    Like one great garden showed,
And through the wreaths of floating dark upcurled,   35
    Rare sunrise flowed.

And Freedom reared in that august sunrise
    Her beautiful bold brow,
When rites and forms before his burning eyes
    Melted like snow.   40

---

1. **The poet ... love.** When he wrote these lines, Tennyson said that he meant that the poet is moved by a hatred for the quality of hate, etc., but later he thought it a finer interpretation to regard "hate of hate," etc., as meaning "the quintessence of hate," etc. 13. **reeds**, arrows shot with the breath from blowpipes. 15. **From ... Caucasus**, from Gibraltar to the Caucasus Mountains, conventional western and eastern limits of Europe; **Calpe** is an early name for Gibraltar.

19. **field flower**, the dandelion, the seeds of which are attached to delicate shafts that the poet likens to arrows.

There was no blood upon her maiden robes
  Sunned by those orient skies;
But round about the circles of the globes
  Of her keen eyes

And in her raiment's hem was traced in
    flame 45
  Wisdom, a name to shake
All evil dreams of power—a sacred name.
  And when she spake,

Her words did gather thunder as they ran,
  And as the lightning to the thunder 50
Which follows it, riving the spirit of man,
  Making earth wonder,

So was their meaning to her words. No
    sword
  Of wrath her right arm whirled, 54
But one poor poet's scroll, and with *his* word
  She shook the world.   (1830)

The Lady of Shalott

  This poem reveals Tennyson's early interest in the stories of King Arthur and the Table Round. The material was more fully developed later in the idyll *Lancelot and Elaine*, where the heroine is called "the fair maid of *Astolat.*" The symbolism of *The Lady of Shalott* is simple. Tennyson explains it as follows: "The new-born love for something, for someone in the wide world from which she has been so long excluded, takes her out of the region of shadows into that of realities." The poem is reminiscent of Keats in substance and in style.

PART 1

On either side the river lie
Long fields of barley and of rye,
That clothe the wold and meet the sky;
And through the field the road runs by
    To many-towered Camelot; 5
And up and down the people go,
Gazing where the lilies blow
Round an island there below,
    The island of Shalott.

Willows whiten, aspens quiver, 10
Little breezes dusk and shiver
Through the wave that runs forever
By the island in the river
    Flowing down to Camelot.
Four gray walls, and four gray towers, 15
Overlook a space of flowers,
And the silent isle embowers
    The Lady of Shalott.

By the margin, willow-veiled,
Slide the heavy barges trailed 20
By slow horses; and unhailed
The shallop flitteth silken-sailed
    Skimming down to Camelot:
But who hath seen her wave her hand?
Or at the casement seen her stand? 25
Or is she known in all the land,
    The Lady of Shalott?

Only reapers, reaping early
In among the bearded barley,
Hear a song that echoes cheerly 30
From the river winding clearly,
    Down to towered Camelot;
And by the moon the reaper weary,
Piling sheaves in uplands airy,
Listening, whispers, " 'Tis the fairy 35
    Lady of Shalott."

PART 2

There she weaves by night and day
A magic web with colors gay.
She has heard a whisper say,
A curse is on her if she stay 40
    To look down to Camelot.
She knows not what the curse may be,
And so she weaveth steadily,
And little other care hath she,
    The Lady of Shalott. 45

---

3. **wold**, a plain. 5. **Camelot**, the city of King Arthur's court, in Cornwall. 7. **blow**, bloom. 10. **Willows whiten.** The wind turns up the white underside of the leaves. 22. **shallop**, a light open boat.

And moving through a mirror clear
That hangs before her all the year,
Shadows of the world appear.
There she sees the highway near
    Winding down to Camelot; 50
There the river eddy whirls,
And there the surly village-churls,
And the red cloaks of market girls,
    Pass onward from Shalott.

Sometimes a troop of damsels glad, 55
An abbot on an ambling pad,
Sometimes a curly shepherd-lad,
Or long-haired page in crimson clad,
    Goes by to towered Camelot;
And sometimes through the mirror blue 60
The knights come riding two and two;
She hath no loyal knight and true,
    The Lady of Shalott.

But in her web she still delights
To weave the mirror's magic sights, 65
For often through the silent nights
A funeral, with plumes and lights
    And music, went to Camelot;
Or when the moon was overhead,
Came two young lovers lately wed; 70
"I am half sick of shadows," said
    The Lady of Shalott.

PART 3

A bow-shot from her bower eaves,
He rode between the barley sheaves;
The sun came dazzling through the leaves, 75
And flamed upon the brazen greaves
    Of bold Sir Lancelot.
A red-cross knight forever kneeled
To a lady in his shield,
That sparkled on the yellow field, 80
    Beside remote Shalott.

The gemmy bridle glittered free,
Like to some branch of stars we see
Hung in the golden Galaxy.
The bridle bells rang merrily 85

As he rode down to Camelot;
And from his blazoned baldric slung
A mighty silver bugle hung,
And as he rode his armor rung,
    Beside remote Shalott. 90

All in the blue unclouded weather
Thick-jeweled shone the saddle-leather,
The helmet and the helmet-feather
Burned like one burning flame together
    As he rode down to Camelot; 95
As often through the purple night,
Below the starry clusters bright,
Some bearded meteor, trailing light,
    Moves over still Shalott.

His broad clear brow in sunlight glowed; 100
On burnished hooves his war horse trode;
From underneath his helmet flowed
His coal-black curls as on he rode,
    As he rode down to Camelot.
From the bank and from the river 105
He flashed into the crystal mirror,
"Tirra lirra," by the river
    Sang Sir Lancelot.

She left the web, she left the loom,
She made three paces through the room, 110
She saw the water lily bloom,
She saw the helmet and the plume,
    She looked down to Camelot.
Out flew the web and floated wide;
The mirror cracked from side to side; 115
"The curse is come upon me," cried
    The Lady of Shalott.

PART 4

In the stormy east wind straining,
The pale yellow woods were waning,
The broad stream in his banks complaining,
Heavily the low sky raining 121
    Over towered Camelot;
Down she came and found a boat
Beneath a willow left afloat,
And round about the prow she wrote 125
    The Lady of Shalott.

---

46. **mirror.** It is used in weaving to reflect the pattern hanging behind her and the finished tapestry on the loom. 56. **pad,** an easy-gaited horse. 76. **greaves,** armor for the legs. 78. **A red-cross knight.** Cf. Spenser's *Faerie Queene,* I (Vol. I, pp. 392 ff.). 84. **Galaxy,** the Milky Way.

87. **baldric,** a belt worn over the shoulder to support a sword or bugle.

And down the river's dim expanse
Like some bold seër in a trance,
Seeing all his own mischance—
    With a glassy countenance 130
        Did she look to Camelot.
And at the closing of the day
She loosed the chain, and down she lay;
The broad stream bore her far away,
        The Lady of Shalott. 135

Lying, robed in snowy white
That loosely flew to left and right—
The leaves upon her falling light—
Through the noises of the night
        She floated down to Camelot; 140
And as the boat-head wound along
The willowy hills and fields among,
They heard her singing her last song,
        The Lady of Shalott.

Heard a carol, mournful, holy, 145
Chanted loudly, chanted lowly,
Till her blood was frozen slowly,
And her eyes were darkened wholly,
        Turned to towered Camelot.

For ere she reached upon the tide 150
The first house by the waterside,
Singing in her song she died,
        The Lady of Shalott.

Under tower and balcony,
By garden wall and gallery, 155
A gleaming shape she floated by,
Dead-pale between the houses high,
        Silent into Camelot.
Out upon the wharfs they came,
Knight and burgher, lord and dame, 160
And round the prow they read her name,
        The Lady of Shalott.

Who is this? And what is here?
And in the lighted palace near
Died the sound of royal cheer; 165
And they crossed themselves for fear,
        All the knights at Camelot.
But Lancelot mused a little space;
He said, "She has a lovely face;
God in his mercy lend her grace, 170
        The Lady of Shalott."

(*1832;* 1842)

Oenone

    This is one of Tennyson's poems on classical themes; others are *The Lotos-Eaters* (p. 608), *Ulysses* (p. 611), and *Tithonus*. In these poems Tennyson shows greater creative power than in his realistic English idylls like *Dora* and *The Gardener's Daughter*. The story of Oenone is found in Ovid, Euripides, and other classical writers. Although the poem is classical in theme and outline, it is modern in sentiment; the speech of Pallas (ll. 142 ff.) expresses Tennyson's own philosophy of life. The descriptions of scenery in the poem belong to the Pyrenees Mountains, visited by the poet in 1830, rather than to Mt. Ida. Part of *Oenone* was written in the valley of Cauteretz, in the Pyrenees; see *In the Valley of Cauteretz*, page 641.
    Oenone was a nymph of Mt. Ida, in Troas, a country in Asia Minor. She was the wife of Paris, son of King Priam of Troy (Ilion), who deserted her for Helen of Troy.

There lies a vale in Ida, lovelier
Than all the valleys of Ionian hills.
The swimming vapor slopes athwart the glen,
Puts forth an arm, and creeps from pine to pine,
And loiters, slowly drawn. On either hand 5
The lawns and meadow-ledges midway down
Hang rich in flowers, and far below them roars

The long brook falling through the cloven ravine
In cataract after cataract to the sea.
Behind the valley topmost Gargarus 10
Stands up and takes the morning; but in front
The gorges, opening wide apart, reveal
Troas and Ilion's columned citadel,
The crown of Troas.

6. **lawns,** open places in the woods. **meadow-ledges,** open flat spaces on the hillsides.

10. **Gargarus,** the highest part of Mt. Ida. 11. **takes,** receives (when the morning sun gilds it).

Hither came at noon
Mournful Oenone, wandering forlorn   15
Of Paris, once her playmate on the hills.
Her cheek had lost the rose, and round her neck
Floated her hair or seemed to float in rest.
She, leaning on a fragment twined with vine,
Sang to the stillness, till the mountain-shade
Sloped downward to her seat from the upper cliff.   21

"O mother Ida, many-fountained Ida,
Dear mother Ida, harken ere I die.
For now the noonday quiet holds the hill;
The grasshopper is silent in the grass;   25
The lizard, with his shadow on the stone,
Rests like a shadow, and the winds are dead.
The purple flower droops, the golden bee
Is lily-cradled; I alone awake.
My eyes are full of tears, my heart of love,   30
My heart is breaking, and my eyes are dim,
And I am all aweary of my life.

"O mother Ida, many-fountained Ida,
Dear mother Ida, harken ere I die.
Hear me, O Earth, hear me, O Hills, O Caves
That house the cold crowned snake! O mountain brooks,   36
I am the daughter of a river-god.
Hear me, for I will speak, and build up all
My sorrow with my song, as yonder walls
Rose slowly to a music slowly breathed,   40
A cloud that gathered shape; for it may be
That, while I speak of it, a little while
My heart may wander from its deeper woe.

"O mother Ida, many-fountained Ida,
Dear mother Ida, harken ere I die.   45
I waited underneath the dawning hills;
Aloft the mountain lawn was dewy-dark,
And dewy-dark aloft the mountain pine.
Beautiful Paris, evil-hearted Paris,
Leading a jet-black goat white-horned, white-hoofed,   50
Came up from reedy Simois all alone.

"O mother Ida, harken ere I die.
Far-off the torrent called me from the cleft;
Far up the solitary morning smote
The streaks of virgin snow. With down-dropped eyes   55
I sat alone; white-breasted like a star
Fronting the dawn he moved; a leopard skin
Drooped from his shoulder, but his sunny hair
Clustered about his temples like a god's;
And his cheek brightened as the foam-bow brightens   60
When the wind blows the foam, and all my heart
Went forth to embrace him coming ere he came.

"Dear mother Ida, harken ere I die.
He smiled, and opening out his milk-white palm,
Disclosed a fruit of pure Hesperian gold,   65
That smelt ambrosially, and while I looked
And listened, the full-flowing river of speech
Came down upon my heart:
            'My own Oenone,
Beautiful-browed Oenone, my own soul,
Behold this fruit, whose gleaming rind ingraven   70
"For the most fair," would seem to award it thine,
As lovelier than whatever oread haunt
The knolls of Ida, loveliest in all grace
Of movement, and the charm of married brows.'

"Dear mother Ida, harken ere I die.   75
He pressed the blossom of his lips to mine,
And added, 'This was cast upon the board,
When all the full-faced presence of the gods
Ranged in the halls of Peleus; whereupon
Rose feud, with question unto whom 'twere due;   80
But light-foot Iris brought it yester-eve,

22. **many-fountained.** Several rivers have their source on Mt. Ida. 36. **snake.** The snake was early recognized as a divinity; it symbolized the power of the underworld. 37. **river-god.** The river referred to is the Kebren, a small stream in Troas. 39. **walls . . . music.** According to Ovid, Troy was built to the music of Apollo's lyre. 51. **Simois,** a small stream in Troas.

65. **fruit . . . gold,** a golden apple from the garden of the Hesperides, daughters of Hesperus, or Night. 72. **oread,** a mountain nymph. 74. **married brows,** meeting eyebrows, regarded as a mark of beauty in the East. 79. **Peleus,** king of Thessaly, who had gathered the gods to witness his marriage to the sea nymph Thetis. 80. **feud.** Eris, the goddess of discord, angered at not being invited, threw among the guests a golden apple marked "for the most beautiful." It was claimed by Juno (Heré), wife of Jupiter and queen of heaven; by Minerva (Pallas), goddess of wisdom; and by Venus (Aphrodite), goddess of love. 81. **Iris,** goddess of the rainbow, the messenger of the gods.

Delivering, that to me, by common voice
Elected umpire, Heré comes today,
Pallas and Aphrodite, claiming each
This meed of fairest. Thou, within the cave
Behind yon whispering tuft of oldest pine, 86
Mayst well behold them unbeheld, unheard
Hear all, and see thy Paris judge of gods.'

"Dear mother Ida, harken ere I die.
It was the deep midnoon; one silvery cloud 90
Had lost his way between the piny sides
Of this long glen. Then to the bower they came,
Naked they came to that smooth-swarded bower,
And at their feet the crocus brake like fire,
Violet, amaracus, and asphodel, 95
Lotos and lilies; and a wind arose,
And overhead the wandering ivy and vine,
This way and that, in many a wild festoon
Ran riot, garlanding the gnarléd boughs
With bunch and berry and flower through and through. 100

"O mother Ida, harken ere I die.
On the tree-tops a crested peacock lit,
And o'er him flowed a golden cloud, and leaned
Upon him, slowly dropping fragrant dew.
Then first I heard the voice of her to whom
Coming through heaven, like a light that grows 106
Larger and clearer, with one mind the gods
Rise up for reverence. She to Paris made
Proffer of royal power, ample rule
Unquestioned, overflowing revenue 110
Wherewith to embellish state, 'from many a vale
And river-sundered champaign clothed with corn,
Or labored mine undrainable of ore.
Honor,' she said, 'and homage, tax and toll,
From many an inland town and haven large,
Mast-thronged beneath her shadowing citadel 116
In glassy bays among her tallest towers.'

"O mother Ida, harken ere I die.
Still she spake on and still she spake of power,
'Which in all action is the end of all; 120
Power fitted to the season; wisdom-bred
And throned of wisdom—from all neighbor crowns
Alliance and allegiance, till thy hand
Fail from the scepter-staff. Such boon from me,
From me, heaven's queen, Paris, to thee king-born, 125
A shepherd all thy life but yet king-born,
Should come most welcome, seeing men, in power
Only, are likest gods, who have attained
Rest in a happy place and quiet seats
Above the thunder, with undying bliss 130
In knowledge of their own supremacy.'

"Dear mother Ida, harken ere I die.
She ceased, and Paris held the costly fruit
Out at arm's-length, so much the thought of power 134
Flattered his spirit; but Pallas where she stood
Somewhat apart, her clear and baréd limbs
O'erthwarted with the brazen-headed spear
Upon her pearly shoulder leaning cold,
The while, above, her full and earnest eye
Over her snow-cold breast and angry cheek
Kept watch, waiting decision, made reply: 141

" 'Self-reverence, self-knowledge, self-control,
These three alone lead life to sovereign power.
Yet not for power (power of herself
Would come uncalled for) but to live by law,
Acting the law we live by without fear; 146
And, because right is right, to follow right
Were wisdom in the scorn of consequence.'

"Dear mother Ida, harken ere I die.
Again she said: 'I woo thee not with gifts. 150
Sequel of guerdon could not alter me
To fairer. Judge thou me by what I am,

95. **amaracus**, the modern marjoram; the asphodel is a lily-shaped plant. 102. **peacock**. The peacock was sacred to Juno. 112. **champaign**, a stretch of flat open country. **corn**, grain, wheat.

122. **throned of wisdom**, put in high place by wisdom. 126. **a shepherd ... king-born**. Because of a prophecy at the birth of Paris that he would ruin his country, he was left to perish on Mt. Ida, but he was found by a peasant and brought up as a shepherd. 136. **limbs ... spear**. The spear was carried across her body and over one shoulder. 151. **Sequel of guerdon**, the giving of a reward for choosing me.

So shalt thou find me fairest.
                              Yet, indeed,
If gazing on divinity disrobed
Thy mortal eyes are frail to judge of fair,   155
Unbiased by self-profit, oh, rest thee sure
That I shall love thee well and cleave to thee,
So that my vigor, wedded to thy blood,
Shall strike within thy pulses, like a god's,
To push thee forward through a life of shocks,   160
Dangers, and deeds, until endurance grow
Sinewed with action, and the full-grown will,
Circled through all experiences, pure law,
Commeasure perfect freedom.'
                              Here she ceased,
And Paris pondered, and I cried, 'O Paris,   165
Give it to Pallas!' but he heard me not,
Or hearing would not hear me, woe is me!

"O mother Ida, many-fountained Ida,
Dear mother Ida, harken ere I die.
Idalian Aphrodite beautiful,   170
Fresh as the foam, new-bathed in Paphian wells,
With rosy slender fingers backward drew
From her warm brows and bosom her deep hair
Ambrosial, golden round her lucid throat   174
And shoulder; from the violets her light foot
Shone rosy-white, and o'er her rounded form
Between the shadows of the vine-bunches
Floated the glowing sunlights, as she moved.

"Dear mother Ida, harken ere I die.
She with a subtle smile in her mild eyes,   180
The herald of her triumph, drawing nigh
Half-whispered in his ear, 'I promise thee
The fairest and most loving wife in Greece.'
She spoke and laughed; I shut my sight for fear;
But when I looked, Paris had raised his arm,
And I beheld great Heré's angry eyes,   186
As she withdrew into the golden cloud,
And I was left alone within the bower;
And from that time to this I am alone,
And I shall be alone until I die.   190

"Yet, mother Ida, harken ere I die.
Fairest—why fairest wife? am I not fair?
My love hath told me so a thousand times.
Methinks I must be fair, for yesterday,   194
When I passed by, a wild and wanton pard,
Eyed like the evening star, with playful tail
Crouched fawning in the weed. Most loving is she?
Ah me, my mountain shepherd, that my arms
Were wound about thee, and my hot lips pressed
Close, close to thine in that quick-falling dew   200
Of fruitful kisses, thick as autumn rains
Flash in the pools of whirling Simois!

"O mother, hear me yet before I die.
They came, they cut away my tallest pines,
My tall dark pines, that plumed the craggy ledge   205
High over the blue gorge, and all between
The snowy peak and snow-white cataract
Fostered the callow eaglet—from beneath
Whose thick mysterious boughs in the dark morn
The panther's roar came muffled, while I sat
Low in the valley. Never, never more   211
Shall lone Oenone see the morning mist
Sweep through them; never see them overlaid
With narrow moonlit slips of silver cloud,
Between the loud stream and the trembling stars.   215

"O mother, hear me yet before I die.
I wish that somewhere in the ruined folds,
Among the fragments tumbled from the glens,
Or the dry thickets, I could meet with her
The Abominable, that uninvited came   220
Into the fair Peleïan banquet-hall,
And cast the golden fruit upon the board,
And bred this change; that I might speak my mind,
And tell her to her face how much I hate
Her presence, hated both of gods and men.

170. **Idalian,** so called from one of her favorite seats, Idalium, a mountain city in Cyprus. 171. **Paphian.** The city of Paphos, in Cyprus, was the center of the worship of Venus. 183. **The fairest,** Helen of Troy.

195. **wanton pard,** sportive leopard. 204. **They,** the Trojan shipbuilders who cut down the pines to build ships for Paris's journey to Sparta. 220. **The Abominable,** Eris. (See note to line 80.)

"O mother, hear me yet before I die.   226
Hath he not sworn his love a thousand
    times,
In this green valley, under this green hill,
Even on this hand, and sitting on this stone?
Sealed it with kisses? watered it with tears?
O happy tears, and how unlike to these!   231
O happy heaven, how canst thou see my
    face?
O happy earth, how canst thou bear my
    weight?
O death, death, death, thou ever-floating cloud,
There are enough unhappy on this earth, 235
Pass by the happy souls, that love to live;
I pray thee, pass before my light of life,
And shadow all my soul, that I may die.
Thou weighest heavy on the heart within,
Weigh heavy on my eyelids; let me die.   240

"O mother, hear me yet before I die.
I will not die alone, for fiery thoughts
Do shape themselves within me, more and
    more,

Whereof I catch the issue, as I hear
Dead sounds at night come from the inmost
    hills,   245
Like footsteps upon wool. I dimly see
My far-off doubtful purpose, as a mother
Conjectures of the features of her child
Ere it is born. Her child!—a shudder comes
Across me; never child be born of me,   250
Unblest, to vex me with his father's eyes!

"O mother, hear me yet before I die.
Hear me, O earth. I will not die alone,
Lest their shrill happy laughter come to me
Walking the cool and starless road of death
Uncomforted, leaving my ancient love   256
With the Greek woman. I will rise and go
Down into Troy, and ere the stars come forth
Talk with the wild Cassandra, for she says
A fire dances before her, and a sound   260
Rings ever in her ears of arméd men.
What this may be I know not, but I know
That, wheresoe'er I am by night and day,
All earth and air seem only burning fire."
                                  (*1832;* 1842)

242. **I . . . alone.** Oenone was gifted with prophecy and the art of healing. She told Paris that he would be wounded and that she alone could cure him. When he came to her later, she avenged herself for his act of desertion by refusing to aid him.

257. **the Greek woman,** Helen of Troy. 259. **Cassandra,** daughter of Priam; she was gifted with prophetic power. She predicted the destruction of Troy but was thought to be mad.

The Palace of Art

Tennyson definitely regarded himself as a teacher. In this poem he expresses his belief that the selfishness that leads a talented, artistic, and privileged individual to withdraw from common duties brings its own retribution. It is an expression of his lack of regard for the artistic recluse and of his high regard for the teacher and the giver; he believes that great qualities become ignoble and base if unshared with others.

I built my soul a lordly pleasure-house,
    Wherein at ease for aye to dwell.
I said, "O Soul, make merry and carouse,
    Dear soul, for all is well."

A huge crag-platform, smooth as burnished
    brass,   5
    I chose. The rangéd ramparts bright
From level meadow-bases of deep grass
    Suddenly scaled the light.

Thereon I built it firm. Of ledge or shelf
    The rock rose clear, or winding stair.   10

My soul would live alone unto herself
    In her high palace there.

And "while the world runs round and round,"
    I said,
"Reign thou apart, a quiet king,   14
Still as, while Saturn whirls, his steadfast shade
    Sleeps on his luminous ring."

To which my soul made answer readily:
    "Trust me, in bliss I shall abide
In this great mansion, that is built for me,
    So royal-rich and wide."   20

3. **"O Soul . . . well."** Cf. *Luke*, 12:19: "And I will say to my soul, Soul, thou hast much goods laid up for many years; take thine ease, eat, drink, and be merry."

16. **Sleeps . . . ring.** As seen through the telescope, the shadow of the planet Saturn, thrown on the luminous ring surrounding the planet, appears to be motionless.

Four courts I made, East, West, and South
    and North,
  In each a squaréd lawn, wherefrom
The golden gorge of dragons spouted forth
    A flood of fountain-foam.

And round the cool green courts there ran a
    row   25
  Of cloisters, branched like mighty woods,
Echoing all night to that sonorous flow
    Of spouted fountain-floods;

And round the roofs a gilded gallery
  That lent broad verge to distant lands,   30
Far as the wild swan wings, to where the sky
    Dipped down to sea and sands.

From those four jets four currents in one
    swell
  Across the mountain streamed below
In misty folds, that floating as they fell   35
    Lit up a torrent-bow.

And high on every peak a statue seemed
  To hang on tiptoe, tossing up
A cloud of incense of all odor steamed
    From out a golden cup.   40

So that she thought, "And who shall gaze
    upon
  My palace with unblinded eyes,
While this great bow will waver in the
    sun,
    And that sweet incense rise?"

For that sweet incense rose and never failed,
  And, while day sank or mounted higher, 46
The light aerial gallery, golden-railed,
    Burnt like a fringe of fire.

Likewise the deep-set windows, stained and
    traced,
  Would seem slow-flaming crimson fires   50
From shadowed grots of arches interlaced,
    And tipped with frost-like spires.
            .   .   .   .   .

Full of long-sounding corridors it was,
  That over-vaulted grateful gloom,
Through which the livelong day my soul did
    pass,   55
    Well-pleased, from room to room.

Full of great rooms and small the palace
    stood,
  All various, each a perfect whole
From living Nature, fit for every mood
    And change of my still soul.   60

For some were hung with arras green and
    blue,
  Showing a gaudy summer-morn,
Where with puffed cheek the belted hunter
    blew
    His wreathéd bugle-horn.

One seemed all dark and red—a tract of sand,
  And someone pacing there alone,   66
Who paced forever in a glimmering land,
    Lit with a low large moon.

One showed an iron coast and angry waves.
  You seemed to hear them climb and fall 70
And roar rock-thwarted under bellowing
    caves,
    Beneath the windy wall.

And one, a full-fed river winding slow
  By herds upon an endless plain,
The ragged rims of thunder brooding low, 75
    With shadow-streaks of rain.

And one, the reapers at their sultry toil.
  In front they bound the sheaves. Behind
Were realms of upland, prodigal in oil,
    And hoary to the wind.   80

And one a foreground black with stones and
    slags;
  Beyond, a line of heights; and higher
All barred with long white cloud the scornful
    crags;
    And highest, snow and fire.

---

23. **gorge,** throat. Lines 23 and 24 are notable for their assonance; perhaps Tennyson meant for the *o*'s to suggest the open mouths of the spouting dragons. 30. **lent . . . lands,** gave a wide view of distant lands. 49. **traced,** ornamented.

61. **arras,** tapestry; from the city of Arras, France, where it was made. 79. **prodigal in oil,** rich in olive oil. 80. **hoary . . . wind.** The wind turned up the whitish-gray underside of the olive leaves.

And one, an English home—gray twilight poured 85
  On dewy pastures, dewy trees,
Softer than sleep—all things in order stored,
  A haunt of ancient Peace.

. . . . .

Nor these alone, but every landscape fair,
  As fit for every mood of mind, 90
Or gay, or grave, or sweet, or stern, was there,
  Not less than truth designed.

. . . . .

Or the maid-mother by a crucifix,
  In tracts of pasture sunny-warm,
Beneath branch-work of costly sardonyx 95
  Sat smiling, babe in arm.

Or in a clear-walled city on the sea,
  Near gilded organ-pipes, her hair
Wound with white roses, slept Saint Cecily;
  An angel looked at her. 100

Or thronging all one porch of Paradise
  A group of Houris bowed to see
The dying Islamite, with hands and eyes
  That said, We wait for thee.

Or mythic Uther's deeply wounded son 105
  In some fair space of sloping greens
Lay, dozing in the vale of Avalon,
  And watched by weeping queens.

Or hollowing one hand against his ear,
  To list a footfall, ere he saw 110
The wood-nymph, stayed the Ausonian king to hear
  Of wisdom and of law.

Or over hills with peaky tops engrailed,
  And many a tract of palm and rice,
The throne of Indian Cama slowly sailed 115
  A summer fanned with spice.

Or sweet Europa's mantle blew unclasped,
  From off her shoulder backward borne;
From one hand drooped a crocus; one hand grasped
  The mild bull's golden horn. 120

Or else flushed Ganymede, his rosy thigh
  Half-buried in the eagle's down,
Sole as a flying star shot through the sky
  Above the pillared town.

Nor these alone; but every legend fair 125
  Which the supreme Caucasian mind
Carved out of Nature for itself was there,
  Not less than life designed.

. . . . .

Then in the towers I placed great bells that swung,
  Moved of themselves, with silver sound; 130
And with choice paintings of wise men I hung
  The royal dais round.

For there was Milton like a seraph strong,
  Beside him Shakespeare bland and mild;
And there the world-worn Dante grasped his song, 135
  And somewhat grimly smiled.

And there the Ionian father of the rest;
  A million wrinkles carved his skin;
A hundred winters snowed upon his breast,
  From cheek and throat and chin. 140

Above, the fair hall-ceiling stately-set
  Many an arch high up did lift,
And angels rising and descending met
  With interchange of gift.

Below was all mosaic choicely planned 145
  With cycles of the human tale
Of this wide world, the times of every land
  So wrought they will not fail.

---

93. **maid-mother**, the Virgin Mary, at a wayside shrine. 99. **Saint Cecily**, St. Cecilia, the patron saint of music and reputed inventor of the organ (third century). Cf. Dryden's *Song for St. Cecilia's Day* (Vol. I, p. 868). 102. **Houris**. According to the Moslems, or Islamites, the Houris are beautiful maidens who will be the companions of the faithful in paradise. 105. **Uther's . . . son**, King Arthur. See Malory's *Morte Darthur* (Vol. I, p. 279); also Tennyson's *Coming of Arthur*, p. 646. 107. **Avalon**, in Celtic mythology, the Land of the Blessed, an earthly paradise in the western seas. 111. **Ausonian king**, Numa Pompilius, the legendary second king of Rome, who is said to have been instructed by the wood nymph Egeria. Ausonia is a poetic name for Italy. 113. **engrailed**, indented in curved lines. 115. **Cama**, the god of love in Hindu mythology, frequently represented as riding on a parrot.

117. **Europa**, a princess of Phoenicia whom Zeus, in the form of a white bull, carried off to Crete. 121. **Ganymede**, a beautiful Trojan boy whom Zeus, in the form of an eagle, carried to Olympus to become cupbearer to the gods. 126. **supreme . . . mind**. An example of Tennyson's worship of his own race. Cf. *Locksley Hall*, l. 184, p. 618. 137. **Ionian father**, Homer.

The people here, a beast of burden slow,
    Toiled onward, pricked with goads and
        stings;   150
Here played a tiger, rolling to and fro
    The heads and crowns of kings;

Here rose an athlete, strong to break or bind
    All force in bonds that might endure,
And here once more like some sick man declined,   155
    And trusted any cure.

But over these she trod; and those great bells
    Began to chime. She took her throne;
She sat betwixt the shining oriels,
    To sing her songs alone.   160

And through the topmost oriels' colored flame
    Two godlike faces gazed below:
Plato the wise, and large-browed Verulam,
    The first of those who know.

And all those names that in their motion
    were   165
    Full-welling fountain-heads of change,
Betwixt the slender shafts were blazoned fair
    In diverse raiment strange;

Through which the lights, rose, amber, emerald, blue,
    Flushed in her temples and her eyes,   170
And from her lips, as morn from Memnon, drew
    Rivers of melodies.

No nightingale delighteth to prolong
    Her low preamble all alone,
More than my soul to hear her echoed song
    Throb through the ribbéd stone;   176

Singing and murmuring in her feastful mirth,
    Joying to feel herself alive,
Lord over Nature, lord of the visible earth,
    Lord of the senses five;   180

Communing with herself: "All these are mine,
    And let the world have peace or wars,
'Tis one to me." She—when young night divine
    Crowned dying day with stars,

Making sweet close of his delicious toils— 185
    Lit light in wreaths and anadems,
And pure quintessences of precious oils
    In hollowed moons of gems,

To mimic heaven; and clapped her hands and cried,
    "I marvel if my still delight   190
In this great house so royal-rich and wide
    Be flattered to the height.

"O all things fair to sate my various eyes!
    O shapes and hues that please me well!
O silent faces of the Great and Wise,   195
    My gods, with whom I dwell!

"O godlike isolation which art mine,
    I can but count thee perfect gain,
What time I watch the darkening droves of swine
    That range on yonder plain.   200

"In filthy sloughs they roll a prurient skin,
    They graze and wallow, breed and sleep;
And oft some brainless devil enters in,
    And drives them to the deep."

Then of the moral instinct would she prate
    And of the rising from the dead,   206
As hers by right of full-accomplished Fate;
    And at the last she said:

"I take possession of man's mind and deed.
    I care not what the sects may brawl.   210
I sit as God holding no form of creed,
    But contemplating all."

    .   .   .   .   .

Full oft the riddle of the painful earth
    Flashed through her as she sat alone,

---

149. **The people, etc.** The people of France before and during the French Revolution. The tiger (l. 151) may represent rebellion, the athlete (l. 153) democracy, and the sick man (l. 155) anarchy. 159. **oriels,** bay-windows. 163. **Plato,** the famous Greek philosopher (427?-347 B.C.). **Verulam,** Francis Bacon (1561-1626), who was made Baron Verulam by King James I in 1618. See Vol. I, p. 612. 171. **Memnon,** a large statue near Thebes, Egypt, said to give forth music when hit by the rays of the morning sun.

186. **anadems,** garlands. 188. **moons of gems,** gems hollowed out for lamps. 203. **devil ... deep.** An allusion to the devils cast out of two men as told in *Matthew*, 8:28-33. The devils went into a herd of swine which "ran violently down a steep place into the sea, and perished in the waters."

Yet not the less held she her solemn mirth, 215
    And intellectual throne.

And so she throve and prospered; so three years
    She prospered; on the fourth she fell,
Like Herod, when the shout was in his ears,
    Struck through with pangs of hell. 220

Lest she should fail and perish utterly,
    God, before whom ever lie bare
The abysmal deeps of personality,
    Plagued her with sore despair.

When she would think, where'er she turned her sight 225
    The airy hand confusion wrought,
Wrote, "Mene, mene," and divided quite
    The kingdom of her thought.

Deep dread and loathing of her solitude
    Fell on her, from which mood was born 230
Scorn of herself; again, from out that mood
    Laughter at her self-scorn.

"What! is not this my place of strength," she said,
    "My spacious mansion built for me,
Whereof the strong foundation stones were laid 235
    Since my first memory?"

But in dark corners of her palace stood
    Uncertain shapes; and unawares
On white-eyed phantasms weeping tears of blood,
    And horrible nightmares, 240

And hollow shades enclosing hearts of flame,
    And, with dim fretted foreheads all,
On corpses three-months-old at noon she came,
    That stood against the wall.

A spot of dull stagnation, without light 245
    Or power of movement, seemed my soul,
'Mid onward-sloping motions infinite
    Making for one sure goal;

A still salt pool, locked in with bars of sand,
    Left on the shore, that hears all night 250
The plunging seas draw backward from the land
    Their moon-led waters white;

A star that with the choral starry dance
    Joined not, but stood, and standing saw
The hollow orb of moving Circumstance 255
    Rolled round by one fixed law.

Back on herself her serpent pride had curled.
    "No voice," she shrieked in that lone hall,
"No voice breaks through the stillness of this world;
    One deep, deep silence all!" 260

She, moldering with the dull earth's moldering sod,
    Inwrapt tenfold in slothful shame,
Lay there exiled from eternal God,
    Lost to her place and name;

And death and life she hated equally, 265
    And nothing saw, for her despair,
But dreadful time, dreadful eternity,
    No comfort anywhere;

Remaining utterly confused with fears,
    And ever worse with growing time, 270
And ever unrelieved by dismal tears,
    And all alone in crime.

Shut up as in a crumbling tomb, girt round
    With blackness as a solid wall,
Far off she seemed to hear the dully sound 275
    Of human footsteps fall:

As in strange lands a traveler walking slow,
    In doubt and great perplexity,
A little before moonrise hears the low
    Moan of an unknown sea; 280

---

219. **Like Herod**, etc. After Herod had spoken to the people from the throne, "the people gave a shout, saying, It is the voice of a god, and not of a man. And immediately the angel of the Lord smote him, because he gave not God the glory" (*Acts*, 12:21-23). 227. **Mene**, the first word of the mysterious writing on the wall of Belshazzar's palace, meaning "God hath numbered thy kingdom and finished it." Daniel interpreted the writing. See *Daniel*, 5:17-31. 242. **fretted**, wrinkled.

253. **star ... law.** The star represents the soul, which stood aloof as the universe swept by; but it saw that life in all its seeming confusion is subject to a controlling law.

And knows not if it be thunder, or a sound
   Of rocks thrown down, or one deep cry
Of great wild beasts; then thinketh, "I have
    found
   A new land, but I die."

She howled aloud, "I am on fire within.   285
   There comes no murmur of reply.
What is it that will take away my sin,
   And save me lest I die?"

So when four years were wholly finished,
   She threw her royal robes away.   290
"Make me a cottage in the vale," she said,
   "Where I may mourn and pray."

"Yet pull not down my palace towers, that are
   So lightly, beautifully built;
Perchance I may return with others there   295
   When I have purged my guilt."

                        (*1832;* 1842)

The Lotos-Eaters

    The story of the Lotos-Eaters Tennyson took from a brief episode in Book IX of the *Odyssey*, which narrated how the sailors who ate of "the lotos' honeyed fruit" wished "never to leave the place but with Lotos-Eaters there to stay, to feed on lotos and forget going home." The poem is rich with the sensuousness of the poet's early Keatsian manner. Especially notable is the skill with which mood and metrical melody have been harmonized.

"Courage!" he said, and pointed toward the
    land,
"This mounting wave will roll us shoreward
    soon."
In the afternoon they came unto a land
In which it seeméd always afternoon.
All round the coast the languid air did swoon,
Breathing like one that hath a weary dream.   6
Full-faced above the valley stood the moon;
And, like a downward smoke, the slender
    stream
Along the cliff to fall and pause and fall did
    seem.

A land of streams! some, like a downward
    smoke,   10
Slow-dropping veils of thinnest lawn, did
    go;
And some through wavering lights and shadows broke,
Rolling a slumbrous sheet of foam below.
They saw the gleaming river seaward flow
From the inner land; far off, three mountain-
    tops,   15
Three silent pinnacles of aged snow,
Stood sunset-flushed; and, dewed with showery drops,
Up-clomb the shadowy pine above the woven
    copse.

The charméd sunset lingered low adown
In the red West; through mountain clefts the
    dale   20
Was seen far inland, and the yellow down
Bordered with palm, and many a winding
    vale
And meadow, set with slender galingale;
A land where all things always seemed the
    same!
And round about the keel with faces pale,   25
Dark faces pale against that rosy flame,
The mild-eyed melancholy Lotos-eaters came.

Branches they bore of that enchanted stem,
Laden with flower and fruit, whereof they
    gave
To each, but whoso did receive of them   30
And taste, to him the gushing of the wave
Far far away did seem to mourn and rave
On alien shores; and if his fellow spake,
His voice was thin, as voices from the grave;
And deep-asleep he seemed, yet all awake,   35
And music in his ears his beating heart did
    make.

They sat them down upon the yellow sand
Between the sun and moon upon the shore;

---

21. **down,** a tract of open upland. See l. 149. 23. **galingale,** a kind of grasslike herb.

And sweet it was to dream of Fatherland,
Of child, and wife, and slave; but evermore 40
Most weary seemed the sea, weary the oar,
Weary the wandering fields of barren foam.
Then someone said, "We will return no more";
And all at once they sang, "Our island home
Is far beyond the wave; we will no longer roam." 45

CHORIC SONG

There is sweet music here that softer falls
Than petals from blown roses on the grass,
Or night-dews on still waters between walls
Of shadowy granite, in a gleaming pass;
Music that gentlier on the spirit lies, 50
Than tired eyelids upon tired eyes;
Music that brings sweet sleep down from the blissful skies.
Here are cool mosses deep,
And through the moss the ivies creep,
And in the stream the long-leaved flowers weep, 55
And from the craggy ledge the poppy hangs in sleep.

Why are we weighed upon with heaviness,
And utterly consumed with sharp distress,
While all things else have rest from weariness?
All things have rest; why should we toil alone, 60
We only toil, who are the first of things,
And make perpetual moan,
Still from one sorrow to another thrown;
Nor ever fold our wings,
And cease from wanderings, 65
Nor steep our brows in slumber's holy balm;
Nor harken what the inner spirit sings,
"There is no joy but calm!"—
Why should we only toil, the roof and crown of things?

Lo! in the middle of the wood, 70
The folded leaf is wooed from out the bud
With winds upon the branch, and there
Grows green and broad, and takes no care,
Sun-steeped at noon, and in the moon

44. **island home,** Ithaca, off the west coast of Greece.

Nightly dew-fed; and turning yellow 75
Falls, and floats adown the air.
Lo! sweetened with the summer light,
The full-juiced apple, waxing over-mellow,
Drops in a silent autumn night.
All its allotted length of days 80
The flower ripens in its place,
Ripens and fades, and falls, and hath no toil,
Fast-rooted in the fruitful soil.

Hateful is the dark-blue sky,
Vaulted o'er the dark-blue sea. 85
Death is the end of life; ah, why
Should life all labor be?
Let us alone. Time driveth onward fast,
And in a little while our lips are dumb.
Let us alone. What is it that will last? 90
All things are taken from us, and become
Portions and parcels of the dreadful past.
Let us alone. What pleasure can we have
To war with evil? Is there any peace
In ever climbing up the climbing wave? 95
All things have rest, and ripen toward the grave
In silence—ripen, fall, and cease;
Give us long rest or death, dark death, or dreamful ease.

How sweet it were, hearing the downward stream
With half-shut eyes ever to seem 100
Falling asleep in a half-dream!
To dream and dream, like yonder amber light,
Which will not leave the myrrh-bush on the height;
To hear each other's whispered speech;
Eating the Lotos day by day, 105
To watch the crisping ripples on the beach,
And tender curving lines of creamy spray;
To lend our hearts and spirits wholly
To the influence of mild-minded melancholy;
To muse and brood and live again in memory, 110
With those old faces of our infancy
Heaped over with a mound of grass,
Two handfuls of white dust, shut in an urn of brass!

Dear is the memory of our wedded lives,
And dear the last embraces of our wives 115

And their warm tears; but all hath suffered change;
For surely now our household hearths are cold,
Our sons inherit us, our looks are strange,
And we should come like ghosts to trouble joy.
Or else the island princes over-bold   120
Have eat our substance, and the minstrel sings
Before them of the ten years' war in Troy,
And our great deeds, as half-forgotten things.
Is there confusion in the little isle?
Let what is broken so remain.   125
The gods are hard to reconcile;
'Tis hard to settle order once again.
There *is* confusion worse than death,
Trouble on trouble, pain on pain,
Long labor unto aged breath,   130
Sore task to hearts worn out by many wars
And eyes grown dim with gazing on the pilot-stars.

But, propped on beds of amaranth and moly,
How sweet—while warm airs lull us, blowing lowly—
With half-dropped eyelid still,   135
Beneath a heaven dark and holy,
To watch the long bright river drawing slowly
His waters from the purple hill—
To hear the dewy echoes calling
From cave to cave through the thick-twined vine—   140
To watch the emerald-colored water falling
Through many a woven acanthus-wreath divine!
Only to hear and see the far-off sparkling brine,
Only to hear were sweet, stretched out beneath the pine.

The Lotos blooms below the barren peak,   145
The Lotos blows by every winding creek;
All day the wind breathes low with mellower tone;
Through every hollow cave and alley lone
Round and round the spicy downs the yellow Lotos-dust is blown.
We have had enough of action, and of motion we,   150
Rolled to starboard, rolled to larboard, when the surge was seething free,
Where the wallowing monster spouted his foam-fountains in the sea.
Let us swear an oath, and keep it with an equal mind,
In the hollow Lotos-land to live and lie reclined
On the hills like gods together, careless of mankind.   155
For they lie beside their nectar, and the bolts are hurled
Far below them in the valleys, and the clouds are lightly curled
Round their golden houses, girdled with the gleaming world;
Where they smile in secret, looking over wasted lands,
Blight and famine, plague and earthquake, roaring deeps and fiery sands,   160
Clanging fights, and flaming towns, and sinking ships, and praying hands.
But they smile, they find a music centered in a doleful song
Steaming up, a lamentation and an ancient tale of wrong,
Like a tale of little meaning though the words are strong;
Chanted from an ill-used race of men that cleave the soil,   165
Sow the seed, and reap the harvest with enduring toil,
Storing yearly little dues of wheat, and wine and oil;
Till they perish and they suffer—some, 'tis whispered—down in hell
Suffer endless anguish, others in Elysian valleys dwell,
Resting weary limbs at last on beds of asphodel.   170

---

120. **island princes,** princes from other islands near Greece; these men were courting Odysseus' wife, Penelope, in his absence, and living in his palace. See *Ulysses,* p. 611. 132. **pilot-stars,** stars used as guides by sailors; they had no compass then. 133. **amaranth,** an imaginary flower supposed never to fade. **moly,** a fabulous herb of magic power. It was given by Hermes, messenger of the gods, to Odysseus as a protection against the enchantress Circe. 142. **acanthus,** a plant sacred to the gods.

156. **bolts,** thunderbolts. 169. **Elysian . . . asphodel.** The Elysian Fields, the paradise of the Greeks, were said by Homer to be covered with asphodels, or daffodils.

Surely, surely, slumber is more sweet than
    toil, the shore
Than labor in the deep mid-ocean, wind and
    wave and oar;
O rest ye, brother mariners, we will not wan-
    der more.   (*1832;* 1842)

You Ask Me, Why, Though Ill at Ease

    Tennyson's interest in current political events and problems is revealed in this poem, written from the point of view of English conservatism. The incident which prompted the poem may have had to do with the rejection of the first Reform Bill of 1832 by the House of Lords (see p. 403).

You ask me, why, though ill at ease,
    Within this region I subsist,
    Whose spirits falter in the mist,
And languish for the purple seas.

It is the land that freemen till,   5
    That sober-suited Freedom chose,
    The land where, girt with friends or foes,
A man may speak the thing he will;

A land of settled government,
    A land of just and old renown,   10
    Where Freedom slowly broadens down
From precedent to precedent;

Where faction seldom gathers head,
    But, by degrees to fullness wrought,
    The strength of some diffusive thought   15
Hath time and space to work and spread.

Should banded unions persecute
    Opinion, and induce a time
    When single thought is civil crime,
And individual freedom mute,   20

Though power should make from land to
    land
    The name of Britain trebly great—
    Though every channel of the State
Should fill and choke with golden sand—

Yet waft me from the harbor-mouth,   25
    Wild wind! I seek a warmer sky,
    And I will see before I die
The palms and temples of the South.
                            (*c. 1833;* 1842)

Of Old Sat Freedom on the Heights

Of old sat Freedom on the heights,
    The thunders breaking at her feet;
Above her shook the starry lights;
    She heard the torrents meet.

There in her place she did rejoice,   5
    Self-gathered in her prophet-mind,
But fragments of her mighty voice
    Came rolling on the wind.

Then stepped she down through town and
    field
    To mingle with the human race,   10
And part by part to men revealed
    The fullness of her face—

Grave mother of majestic works,
    From her isle-altar gazing down,
Who, godlike, grasps the triple forks,   15
    And, king-like, wears the crown.

Her open eyes desire the truth.
    The wisdom of a thousand years
Is in them. May perpetual youth
    Keep dry their light from tears;   20

That her fair form may stand and shine,
    Make bright our days and light our dreams,
Turning to scorn with lips divine
    The falsehood of extremes! (*c. 1833;* 1842)

Ulysses

    Like *The Lotos-Eaters* the idea of this poem was taken from the *Odyssey*. Tennyson modified it considerably, however, on a hint from a passage in Canto 26 of Dante's

---

14. **isle-altar**, England. 15. **Who . . . forks.** Britannia, the female figure symbolizing Great Britain, carries the trident of Neptune, god of the sea, as an indication of Britain's control of the seas.

Inferno which represents the hero as pushing his single ship beyond the Straits of Gibraltar, which in ancient belief marked the end of the world. The Greek epic ends with the return of the hero and his recovery of his home from the "island princes" who had courted his wife and devoured his substance while he was away. Tennyson himself said that the poem, written shortly after the death of Hallam, gave expression to his need of "going forward and braving the struggle of life."

It little profits that an idle king,
By this still hearth, among these barren crags,
Matched with an aged wife, I mete and dole
Unequal laws unto a savage race,
That hoard, and sleep, and feed, and know not me.   5
I cannot rest from travel; I will drink
Life to the lees. All times I have enjoyed
Greatly, have suffered greatly, both with those
That loved me, and alone; on shore, and when
Through scudding drifts the rainy Hyades   10
Vexed the dim sea. I am become a name;
For always roaming with a hungry heart
Much have I seen and known—cities of men
And manners, climates, councils, governments,
Myself not least, but honored of them all—   15
And drunk delight of battle with my peers,
Far on the ringing plains of windy Troy.
I am a part of all that I have met;
Yet all experience is an arch wherethrough
Gleams that untraveled world whose margin fades   20
Forever and forever when I move.
How dull it is to pause, to make an end,
To rust unburnished, not to shine in use!
As though to breathe were life! Life piled on life
Were all too little, and of one to me   25
Little remains; but every hour is saved
From that eternal silence, something more,
A bringer of new things; and vile it were
For some three suns to store and hoard myself,
And this gray spirit yearning in desire   30
To follow knowledge like a sinking star,
Beyond the utmost bound of human thought.
  This is my son, mine own Telemachus,
To whom I leave the scepter and the isle—
Well-loved of me, discerning to fulfill   35
This labor, by slow prudence to make mild
A rugged people, and through soft degrees
Subdue them to the useful and the good.
Most blameless is he, centered in the sphere
Of common duties, decent not to fail   40
In offices of tenderness, and pay
Meet adoration to my household gods,
When I am gone. He works his work, I mine.
  There lies the port; the vessel puffs her sail;
There gloom the dark, broad seas. My mariners,   45
Souls that have toiled, and wrought, and thought with me—
That ever with a frolic welcome took
The thunder and the sunshine, and opposed
Free hearts, free foreheads—you and I are old;
Old age hath yet his honor and his toil.   50
Death closes all; but something ere the end,
Some work of noble note, may yet be done,
Not unbecoming men that strove with gods.
The lights begin to twinkle from the rocks;
The long day wanes; the slow moon climbs; the deep   55
Moans round with many voices. Come, my friends.
'Tis not too late to seek a newer world.
Push off, and sitting well in order smite
The sounding furrows; for my purpose holds
To sail beyond the sunset, and the baths   60
Of all the western stars, until I die.
It may be that the gulfs will wash us down;
It may be we shall touch the Happy Isles,
And see the great Achilles, whom we knew.

---

2. **crags.** On the bleak island of Ithaca, the home of Ulysses. 3. **aged wife,** Penelope. 10. **Hyades,** a group of seven stars in the constellation Taurus. They were associated with the rainy season. 27. **eternal silence,** a pagan view of death.

49. **you,** Ulysses' companions. The attitude expressed here is modern. 63. **Happy Isles,** the Islands of the Blest, identified with the Elysian Fields as the abode of just men after death. 64. **Achilles,** the most famous of the Greek heroes in the Trojan War. After slaying Hector and dragging his body three times around the walls, Achilles was finally killed by Paris, wounded with a poisoned arrow in the heel, his only vulnerable spot. The arms of Achilles were awarded to Ulysses.

Though much is taken, much abides; and though   65
We are not now that strength which in old days

> 65. **Though . . . yield.** These lines express Tennyson's favorite doctrine of the unconquerable will. Cf. Henley's *Invictus*, p. 866.

Moved earth and heaven, that which we are, we are—
One equal temper of heroic hearts,
Made weak by time and fate, but strong in will
To strive, to seek, to find, and not to yield.
(1842)

Locksley Hall

The optimism of the young man in this poem, who, though rejected by the woman he loved, determines to rise superior to the rebuff, forms a contrast with the disillusionment and pessimism of the old man who utters his ripened philosophy in *Locksley Hall Sixty Years After*. Both poems reveal Tennyson's interest in science and his faith in his race; and both have the tendency to romantic sentimentalism which suggests in some of his poems a lack of robustness.

Comrades, leave me here a little, while as yet 'tis early morn;
Leave me here, and when you want me, sound upon the bugle horn.

'Tis the place, and all around it, as of old, the curlews call,
Dreary gleams about the moorland flying over Locksley Hall;

Locksley Hall, that in the distance overlooks the sandy tracts,   5
And the hollow ocean-ridges roaring into cataracts.

Many a night from yonder ivied casement, ere I went to rest,
Did I look on great Orion sloping slowly to the west.

Many a night I saw the Pleiads, rising through the mellow shade,
Glitter like a swarm of fireflies tangled in a silver braid.   10

Here about the beach I wandered, nourishing a youth sublime
With the fairy tales of science, and the long result of time;

When the centuries behind me like a fruitful land reposed;
When I clung to all the present for the promise that it closed;

When I dipped into the future far as human eye could see,   15
Saw the vision of the world and all the wonder that would be.—

In the spring a fuller crimson comes upon the robin's breast;
In the spring the wanton lapwing gets himself another crest;

In the spring a livelier iris changes on the burnished dove;
In the spring a young man's fancy lightly turns to thoughts of love.   20

Then her cheek was pale and thinner than should be for one so young,
And her eyes on all my motions with a mute observance hung.

And I said, "My cousin Amy, speak and speak the truth to me;
Trust me, cousin, all the current of my being sets to thee."

> 4. **gleams.** Probably in apposition to *curlews;* or the entire phrase may be taken as an absolute construction. 8. **Orion,** a conspicuous constellation in the heavens. 9. **Pleiads,** a group of seven stars in the constellation Taurus.
>
> 19. **iris . . . dove.** The rainbow colors on the dove's neck become brighter during the mating season.

On her pallid cheek and forehead came a
    color and a light,   25
As I have seen the rosy red flushing in the
    northern night.

And she turned—her bosom shaken with a
    sudden storm of sighs—
All the spirit deeply dawning in the dark of
    hazel eyes—

Saying, "I have hid my feelings, fearing they
    should do me wrong";
Saying, "Dost thou love me, cousin?" weep-
    ing, "I have loved thee long."   30

Love took up the glass of Time, and turned
    it in his glowing hands;
Every moment, lightly shaken, ran itself in
    golden sands.

Love took up the harp of Life, and smote on
    all the chords with might;
Smote the chord of Self, that, trembling,
    passed in music out of sight.

Many a morning on the moorland did we
    hear the copses ring,   35
And her whisper thronged my pulses with
    the fullness of the spring.

Many an evening by the waters did we watch
    the stately ships,
And our spirits rushed together at the touch-
    ing of the lips.

O my cousin, shallow-hearted! O my Amy,
    mine no more!
O the dreary, dreary moorland! O the barren,
    barren shore!   40

Falser than all fancy fathoms, falser than all
    songs have sung,
Puppet to a father's threat, and servile to a
    shrewish tongue!

Is it well to wish thee happy?—having known
    me—to decline

<small>41. **all fancy fathoms**, everything the imagination comprehends. 42. **Puppet . . . tongue.** Her father and her mother forced her to marry another—a man of coarser nature.</small>

On a range of lower feelings and a narrower
    heart than mine!

Yet it shall be; thou shalt lower to his level
    day by day,   45
What is fine within thee growing coarse to
    sympathize with clay.

As the husband is, the wife is; thou art mated
    with a clown,
And the grossness of his nature will have
    weight to drag thee down.

He will hold thee, when his passion shall have
    spent its novel force,
Something better than his dog, a little dearer
    than his horse.   50

What is this? his eyes are heavy; think not
    they are glazed with wine.
Go to him, it is thy duty; kiss him, take his
    hand in thine.

It may be my lord is weary, that his brain is
    overwrought;
Soothe him with thy finer fancies, touch him
    with thy lighter thought.

He will answer to the purpose, easy things to
    understand—   55
Better thou wert dead before me, though I
    slew thee with my hand!

Better thou and I were lying, hidden from
    the heart's disgrace,
Rolled in one another's arms, and silent in a
    last embrace.

Curséd be the social wants that sin against
    the strength of youth!
Curséd be the social lies that warp us from
    the living truth!   60

Curséd be the sickly forms that err from hon-
    est Nature's rule!
Curséd be the gold that gilds the straitened
    forehead of the fool!

Well—'tis well that I should bluster!—Hadst
    thou less unworthy proved—

Would to God—for I had loved thee more
    than ever wife was loved.

Am I mad, that I should cherish that which
    bears but bitter fruit?   65
I will pluck it from my bosom, though my
    heart be at the root.

Never—though my mortal summers to such
    length of years should come
As the many-wintered crow that leads the
    clanging rookery home.

Where is comfort? in division of the records
    of the mind?
Can I part her from herself, and love her, as I
    knew her, kind?   70

I remember one that perished; sweetly did she
    speak and move;
Such a one do I remember, whom to look at
    was to love.

Can I think of her as dead, and love her for
    the love she bore?
No—she never loved me truly; love is love
    for evermore.

Comfort? comfort scorned of devils! this is
    truth the poet sings,   75
That a sorrow's crown of sorrow is remem-
    bering happier things.

Drug thy memories, lest thou learn it, lest thy
    heart be put to proof,
In the dead unhappy night, and when the rain
    is on the roof.

Like a dog, he hunts in dreams, and thou art
    staring at the wall,
Where the dying night-lamp flickers, and the
    shadows rise and fall.   80

Then a hand shall pass before thee, pointing
    to his drunken sleep,
To thy widowed marriage-pillows, to the tears
    that thou wilt weep.

Thou shalt hear the "Never, never," whis-
    pered by the phantom years,
And a song from out the distance in the ring-
    ing of thine ears;

And an eye shall vex thee looking ancient
    kindness on thy pain.   85
Turn thee, turn thee on thy pillow; get thee
    to thy rest again.

Nay, but Nature brings thee solace; for a
    tender voice will cry.
'Tis a purer life than thine, a lip to drain thy
    trouble dry.

Baby lips will laugh me down; my latest rival
    brings thee rest.
Baby fingers, waxen touches, press me from
    the mother's breast.   90

Oh, the child too clothes the father with a
    dearness not his due.
Half is thine and half is his; it will be worthy
    of the two.

Oh, I see thee old and formal, fitted to thy
    petty part,
With a little hoard of maxims preaching down
    a daughter's heart.

"They were dangerous guides, the feelings—
    she herself was not exempt—   95
Truly, she herself had suffered"—Perish in
    thy self-contempt!

Overlive it—lower yet—be happy! wherefore
    should I care?
I myself must mix with action, lest I wither
    by despair.

What is that which I should turn to, lighting
    upon days like these?
Every door is barred with gold, and opens
    but to golden keys.   100

68. **crow**, rook. 75. **comfort . . . devils**, as in *Paradise Lost*, I and II (Vol. I, pp. 716 ff.). 76. **That . . . things**. A favorite idea of the poets. Dante says in his *Inferno*, V, 121, "There is no greater sorrow than to remember happy times when one is in misery." 79. **he**, Amy's husband, a fox-hunting squire.

Every gate is thronged with suitors, all the markets overflow.
I have but an angry fancy; what is that which I should do?

I had been content to perish, falling on the foeman's ground,
When the ranks are rolled in vapor, and the winds are laid with sound.

But the jingling of the guinea helps the hurt that Honor feels, 105
And the nations do but murmur, snarling at each other's heels.

Can I but relive in sadness? I will turn that earlier page.
Hide me from my deep emotion, O thou wondrous Mother-Age!

Make me feel the wild pulsation that I felt before the strife,
When I heard my days before me, and the tumult of my life; 110

Yearning for the large excitement that the coming years would yield,
Eager-hearted as a boy when first he leaves his father's field,

And at night along the dusky highway near and nearer drawn,
Sees in heaven the light of London flaring like a dreary dawn;

And his spirit leaps within him to be gone before him then, 115
Underneath the light he looks at, in among the throngs of men;

Men, my brothers, men the workers, ever reaping something new;
That which they have done but earnest of the things that they shall do.

For I dipped into the future, far as human eye could see,

Saw the Vision of the world, and all the wonder that would be; 120

Saw the heavens fill with commerce, argosies of magic sails,
Pilots of the purple twilight, dropping down with costly bales;

Heard the heavens fill with shouting, and there rained a ghastly dew
From the nations' airy navies grappling in the central blue;

Far along the world-wide whisper of the south wind rushing warm, 125
With the standards of the peoples plunging through the thunder-storm;

Till the war drum throbbed no longer, and the battle-flags were furled
In the Parliament of man, the Federation of the world.

There the common sense of most shall hold a fretful realm in awe,
And the kindly earth shall slumber, lapped in universal law. 130

So I triumphed ere my passion sweeping through me left me dry,
Left me with the palsied heart, and left me with the jaundiced eye;

Eye, to which all order festers, all things here are out of joint.
Science moves, but slowly, slowly, creeping on from point to point;

Slowly comes a hungry people, as a lion, creeping nigher, 135
Glares at one that nods and winks behind a slowly dying fire.

Yet I doubt not through the ages one increasing purpose runs,

---

104. **winds are laid.** It was an old belief that the discharge of cannon during a battle stilled the winds.

121-128. **Saw ... world.** These lines are a prophetic glimpse of modern aviation and of battles fought in the air. 128. **Parliament ... world.** Cf. the idea of the present United Nations. 132. **jaundiced**, prejudiced. 135. **a hungry people.** An allusion to the "dangerous" advance of democracy felt in the discontent preceding the revolutions in Europe in 1848—in France, in Germany, in Italy, in Austro-Hungary, and in Ireland.

And the thoughts of men are widened with
    the process of the suns.

What is that to him that reaps not harvest
    of his youthful joys,
Though the deep heart of existence beat forever like a boy's?   140

Knowledge comes, but wisdom lingers, and I
    linger on the shore,
And the individual withers, and the world is
    more and more.

Knowledge comes, but wisdom lingers, and
    he bears a laden breast,
Full of sad experience, moving toward the
    stillness of his rest.

Hark, my merry comrades call me, sounding
    on the bugle horn,   145
They to whom my foolish passion were a
    target for their scorn.

Shall it not be scorn to me to harp on such a
    moldered string?
I am shamed through all my nature to have
    loved so slight a thing.

Weakness to be wroth with weakness!
    woman's pleasure, woman's pain—
Nature made them blinder motions bounded
    in a shallower brain.   150

Woman is the lesser man, and all thy passions,
    matched with mine,
Are as moonlight unto sunlight, and as water
    unto wine—

Here at least, where nature sickens, nothing.
    Ah, for some retreat
Deep in yonder shining Orient, where my life
    began to beat,

Where in wild Mahratta-battle fell my father
    evil-starred—   155
I was left a trampled orphan, and a selfish
    uncle's ward.

Or to burst all links of habit—there to wander
    far away,
On from island unto island at the gateways
    of the day—

Larger constellations burning, mellow moons
    and happy skies,
Breadths of tropic shade and palms in cluster,
    knots of Paradise;   160

Never comes the trader, never floats an European flag,
Slides the bird o'er lustrous woodland, swings
    the trailer from the crag;

Droops the heavy-blossomed bower, hangs the
    heavy-fruited tree—
Summer isles of Eden lying in dark-purple
    spheres of sea.

There methinks would be enjoyment more
    than in this march of mind,   165
In the steamship, in the railway, in the
    thoughts that shake mankind.

There the passions cramped no longer shall
    have scope and breathing space;
I will take some savage woman, she shall rear
    my dusky race.

Iron-jointed, supple-sinewed, they shall dive,
    and they shall run,
Catch the wild goat by the hair, and hurl their
    lances in the sun;   170

Whistle back the parrot's call, and leap the
    rainbows of the brooks,
Not with blinded eyesight poring over miserable books—

Fool, again the dream, the fancy! but I *know*
    my words are wild,
But I count the gray barbarian lower than the
    Christian child.

I, to herd with narrow foreheads, vacant of
    our glorious gains,   175

---

138. **process of the suns**, the passing of the years. 141. **Knowledge . . . more**, new facts of life crowd in upon us, but fundamental truths are constant; science and evolution show us that the mass of humanity is more important than the individual. Cf. *In Memoriam*, 55, 7-8, p. 632. 150. **motions**, impulses. 155. **fell my father**. The hero is represented as having been born in India, the son of a British soldier who fell in battle against the Mahrattas, a people living in central and western India.

162. **trailer**, a trailing vine.

Like a beast with lower pleasures, like a beast with lower pains!

Mated with a squalid savage—what to me were sun or clime?
I the heir of all the ages, in the foremost files of time—

I that rather held it better men should perish one by one,
Than that earth should stand at gaze like Joshua's moon in Ajalon! 180

Not in vain the distance beacons. Forward, forward let us range,
Let the great world spin forever down the ringing grooves of change.

Through the shadow of the globe we sweep into the younger day;
Better fifty years of Europe than a cycle of Cathay.

Mother-Age—for mine I knew not—help me as when life begun; 185
Rift the hills, and roll the waters, flash the lightnings, weigh the sun.

Oh, I see the crescent promise of my spirit hath not set.
Ancient founts of inspiration well through all my fancy yet.

Howsoever these things be, a long farewell to Locksley Hall!
Now for me the woods may wither, now for me the roof-tree fall. 190

Comes a vapor from the margin, blackening over heath and holt,
Cramming all the blast before it, in its breast a thunderbolt.

Let it fall on Locksley Hall, with rain or hail, or fire or snow;
For the mighty wind arises, roaring seaward, and I go.

(1842)

180. **Joshua's moon in Ajalon.** From *Joshua*, 10:12-13: "Then spake Joshua . . . in the sight of Israel, Sun, stand thou still upon Gibeon; and thou, Moon, in the valley of Ajalon. And the sun stood still, and the moon stayed, until the people had avenged themselves upon their enemies." 181. **beacons,** lights a signal for advance. 182. **grooves.** When Tennyson first rode on a railroad train in 1830, he thought that the wheels ran in a groove. He states that he composed this line at that time (*Memoir*, I, 195). 184. **a cycle of Cathay,** a very long period spent in China. This is an illustration of Tennyson's somewhat arrogant worship of Western culture.

186. **Rift the hills, etc.** This line probably refers to Francis Baily's experiments (1838-1842) for determining the mean density of the earth and the weight of the sun. 190. **for me,** as far as I am concerned.

Locksley Hall Sixty Years After

This poem is a sequel to *Locksley Hall*. The young lover has become an old man eighty years of age, and England has become a great Empire.

Late, my grandson! half the morning have I paced these sandy tracts,
Watched again the hollow ridges roaring into cataracts,

Wandered back to living boyhood while I heard the curlews call,
I myself so close on death, and death itself in Locksley Hall.

So—your happy suit was blasted—she the faultless, the divine; 5
And you liken—boyish babble—this boy-love of yours with mine.

I myself have often babbled doubtless of a foolish past;
Babble, babble; our old England may go down in babble at last.

"Curse him!" curse your fellow-victim? call him dotard in your rage?
Eyes that lured a doting boyhood well might fool a dotard's age. 10

Jilted for a wealthier! wealthier? yet perhaps she was not wise;
I remember how you kissed the miniature with those sweet eyes.

In the hall there hangs a painting—Amy's
   arms about my neck—
Happy children in a sunbeam sitting on the
   ribs of wreck.

In my life there was a picture, she that clasped
   my neck had flown;   15
I was left within the shadow sitting on the
   wreck alone.

Yours has been a slighter ailment; will you
   sicken for her sake?
You, not you! your modern amorist is of
   easier, earthlier make.

Amy loved me, Amy failed me, Amy was a
   timid child;
But your Judith—but your worldling—*she*
   had never driven me wild.   20

She that holds the diamond necklace dearer
   than the golden ring,
She that finds a winter sunset fairer than a
   morn of spring.

She that in her heart is brooding on his briefer
   lease of life,
While she vows "till death shall part us," she,
   the would-be-widow wife.

She the worldling born of worldlings—father,
   mother—be content,   25
Even the homely farm can teach us there is
   something in descent.

Yonder in that chapel, slowly sinking now
   into the ground,
Lies the warrior, my forefather, with his feet
   upon the hound.

Crossed! for once he sailed the sea to crush
   the Moslem in his pride;
Dead the warrior, dead his glory, dead the
   cause in which he died.   30

Yet how often I and Amy in the moldering
   aisle have stood,
Gazing for one pensive moment on that
   founder of our blood.

29. **Crossed**, with his feet crossed to indicate that he had been a Crusader against the Turk, or Moslem.

There again I stood today, and where of old
   we knelt in prayer,
Close beneath the casement crimson with the
   shield of Locksley—there,

All in white Italian marble, looking still as if
   she smiled,   35
Lies my Amy dead in childbirth, dead the
   mother, dead the child.

Dead—and sixty years ago, and dead her aged
   husband now—
I, this old white-headed dreamer, stooped and
   kissed her marble brow.

Gone the fires of youth, the follies, furies,
   curses, passionate tears,
Gone like fires and floods and earthquakes
   of the planet's dawning years— 40

Fires that shook me once, but now to silent
   ashes fallen away.
Cold upon the dead volcano sleeps the gleam
   of dying day.

Gone the tyrant of my youth, and mute below
   the chancel stones,
All his virtues—I forgive them—black in
   white above his bones.

Gone the comrades of my bivouac, some in
   fight against the foe,   45
Some through age and slow diseases, gone as
   all on earth will go.

Gone with whom for forty years my life in
   golden sequence ran,
She with all the charm of woman, she with all
   the breadth of man,

Strong in will and rich in wisdom, Edith, yet
   so lowly-sweet,
Woman to her inmost heart, and woman to
   her tender feet,   50

Very woman of very woman, nurse of ailing
   body and mind,
She that linked again the broken chain that
   bound me to my kind.

Here today was Amy with me, while I wandered down the coast,
Near us Edith's holy shadow, smiling at the slighter ghost.

Gone our sailor son thy father, Leonard early lost at sea; 55
Thou alone, my boy, of Amy's kin and mine art left to me.

Gone thy tender-natured mother, wearying to be left alone,
Pining for the stronger heart that once had beat beside her own.

Truth, for truth is truth, he worshiped, being true as he was brave;
Good, for good is good, he followed, yet he looked beyond the grave, 60

Wiser there than you, that crowning barren Death as lord of all,
Deem this over-tragic drama's closing curtain is the pall!

Beautiful was death in him, who saw the death, but kept the deck,
Saving women and their babes, and sinking with the sinking wreck,

Gone forever! Ever? No—for since our dying race began, 65
Ever, ever, and forever was the leading light of man.

Those that in barbarian burials killed the slave, and slew the wife,
Felt within themselves the sacred passion of the second life.

Indian warriors dream of ampler hunting grounds beyond the night;
Even the black Australian dying hopes he shall return, a white. 70

Truth for truth, and good for good! The good, the true, the pure, the just—
Take the charm "Forever" from them, and they crumble into dust.

Gone the cry of "Forward, forward," lost within a growing gloom;
Lost, or only heard in silence from the silence of a tomb.

Half the marvels of my morning, triumphs over time and space, 75
Staled by frequence, shrunk by usage into commonest commonplace!

"Forward" rang the voices then, and of the many mine was one.
Let us hush this cry of "Forward" till ten thousand years have gone.

Far among the vanished races, old Assyrian kings would flay
Captives whom they caught in battle—iron-hearted victors they. 80

Ages after, while in Asia, he that led the wild Moguls,
Timur built his ghastly tower of eighty thousand human skulls;

Then, and here in Edward's time, an age of noblest English names,
Christian conquerors took and flung the conquered Christian into flames.

Love your enemy, bless your haters, said the Greatest of the great; 85
Christian love among the Churches looked the twin of heathen hate.

From the golden alms of Blessing man had coined himself a curse:
Rome of Caesar, Rome of Peter, which was crueler? which was worse?

79. **flay Captives.** The Assyrian kings were noted for their cruelty to captives. 82. **Timur,** Tamerlane, the famous Mongolian conqueror, notorious for his atrocities. In 1398 he sacked Delhi, India, and is said to have put to death 100,000 prisoners. 83. **here ... flames.** A reference to the religious persecutions in England perpetrated by the sovereigns immediately following Henry VIII. Edward VI was crowned in 1547. 85. **Love ... great.** A reference to Christ's saying, "But I say unto you, Love your enemies, bless them that curse you, do good to them that hate you, and pray for them that despitefully use you, and persecute you."—*Matthew*, 5:44. 88. **Rome of Caesar.** During the first century pagan Rome. especially under Nero, persecuted and killed great numbers of Christians. **Rome of Peter,** the See of St. Peter, at Rome. Religious persecutions were common among all medieval peoples. Tennyson, the Protestant, here refers to the treatment of heretics by Roman Catholics.

France had shown a light to all men, preached
    a Gospel, all men's good;
Celtic Demos rose a Demon, shrieked and
    slaked the light with blood.   90

Hope was ever on her mountain, watching till
    the day begun—
Crowned with sunlight—over darkness—
    from the still unrisen sun.

Have we grown at last beyond the passions
    of the primal clan?
"Kill your enemy, for you hate him," still,
    "your enemy" was a man.

Have we sunk below them? Peasants maim
    the helpless horse, and drive   95
Innocent cattle under thatch, and burn the
    kindlier brutes alive.

Brutes, the brutes are not your wrongers—
    burned at midnight, found at morn,
Twisted hard in mortal agony with their off-
    spring, born-unborn,

Clinging to the silent mother! Are we devils?
    are we men?
Sweet Saint Francis of Assisi, would that he
    were here again,   100

He that in his Catholic wholeness used to call
    the very flowers
Sisters, brothers—and the beast—whose pains
    are hardly less than ours!

Chaos, Cosmos! Cosmos, Chaos! who can tell
    how all will end?
Read the wide world's annals, you, and take
    their wisdom for your friend.

Hope the best, but hold the Present fatal
    daughter of the Past,   105
Shape your heart to front the hour, but dream
    not that the hour will last.

Aye, if dynamite and revolver leave you cour-
    age to be wise—
When was age so crammed with menace?
    madness? written, spoken lies?

Envy wears the mask of Love, and, laughing
    sober fact to scorn,
Cries to weakest as to strongest, "Ye are
    equals, equal-born."   110

Equal-born? Oh, yes, if yonder hill be level
    with the flat.
Charm us, orator, till the lion look no larger
    than the cat,

Till the cat through that mirage of overheated
    language loom
Larger than the lion—Demos end in working
    its own doom.

Russia bursts our Indian barrier; shall we
    fight her? shall we yield?   115
Pause! before you sound the trumpet, hear
    the voices from the field.

Those three hundred millions under one Im-
    perial scepter now,
Shall we hold them? shall we loose them?
    take the suffrage of the plow.

Nay, but these would feel and follow Truth
    if only you and you,
Rivals of realm-ruining party, when you speak
    were wholly true.   120

Plowmen, shepherds, have I found, and more
    than once, and still could find,
Sons of God, and kings of men in utter noble-
    ness of mind,

---

89. **France . . . blood.** During the French Revolution and the Reign of Terror, 1793-1794, hundreds were sent to the guillotine. The doctrine of the Revolution was "Liberty, Equality, Fraternity." 90. **Demos,** a Greek word meaning people. 95. **Peasants . . . alive.** A reference to incidents of the agricultural disturbances of the time. 100. **Saint Francis,** an Italian friar (1182-1226) noted for his gentleness and nobility of character. 103. **Chaos, Cosmos.** Tennyson refers to the conflict between those who see no meaning in life and those who see an ordered purpose in it.

115. **Russia . . . yield.** A reference to Russia's persistent efforts during the nineteenth century to gain control of Afghanistan, the "Indian barrier." In 1877-1878 Russia sent an expedition through the Balkans to Constantinople, and England promptly sent a fleet in opposition. 116. **voices . . . field,** the votes of the laboring classes.

Truthful, trustful, looking upward to the practiced hustings-liar;
So the higher wields the lower, while the lower is the higher.

Here and there a cotter's babe is royal-born by right divine; 125
Here and there my lord is lower than his oxen or his swine.

Chaos, Cosmos! Cosmos, Chaos! once again the sickening game;
Freedom, free to slay herself, and dying while they shout her name.

Step by step we gained a freedom known to Europe, known to all;
Step by step we rose to greatness—through the tonguesters we may fall. 130

You that woo the Voices—tell them "old experience is a fool,"
Teach your flattered kings that only those who cannot read can rule.

Pluck the mighty from their seat, but set no meek ones in their place;
Pillory Wisdom in your markets, pelt your offal at her face.

Tumble Nature heel o'er head, and, yelling with the yelling street, 135
Set the feet above the brain and swear the brain is in the feet.

Bring the old dark ages back without the faith, without the hope,
Break the State, the Church, the Throne, and roll their ruins down the slope.

Authors—essayist, atheist, novelist, realist, rimester, play your part,
Paint the mortal shame of nature with the living hues of art. 140

Rip your brothers' vices open, strip your own foul passions bare;
Down with Reticence, down with Reverence —forward—naked—let them stare.

Feed the budding rose of boyhood with the drainage of your sewer;
Send the drain into the fountain, lest the stream should issue pure.

Set the maiden fancies wallowing in the troughs of Zolaism— 145
Forward, forward, aye, and backward, downward too into the abysm!

Do your best to charm the worst, to lower the rising race of men;
Have we risen from out the beast, then back into the beast again?

Only "dust to dust" for me that sicken at your lawless din,
Dust in wholesome old-world dust before the newer world begin. 150

Heated am I? you—you wonder—well, it scarce becomes mine age—
Patience! let the dying actor mouth his last upon the stage.

Cries of unprogressive dotage ere the dotard fall asleep?
Noises of a current narrowing, not the music of a deep?

Aye, for doubtless I am old, and think gray thoughts, for I am gray; 155
After all the stormy changes shall we find a changeless May?

After madness, after massacre, Jacobinism and Jacquerie,
Some diviner force to guide us through the days I shall not see?

When the schemes and all the systems, kingdoms and republics fall,

---

123. **hustings,** the platform from which the candidates for Parliament addressed the voters. 131. **the Voices,** the approval of the masses. 139 ff. These lines show Tennyson's dislike of the realistic novels of the period. Émile Zola (l. 145) was a contemporary French realist; see p. 856.

157. **Jacobinism,** mad opposition to regular government. The Jacobins were a society of violent radicals in France during the Revolution of 1789. **Jacquerie,** the French peasant revolt of 1358.

Something kindlier, higher, holier—all for
    each and each for all? 160

All the full-brain, half-brain races, led by
    Justice, Love, and Truth;
All the millions one at length with all the
    visions of my youth?

All diseases quenched by Science, no man
    halt, or deaf, or blind;
Stronger ever born of weaker, lustier body,
    larger mind?

Earth at last a warless world, a single race,
    a single tongue— 165
I have seen her far away—for is not Earth as
    yet so young?—

Every tiger madness muzzled, every serpent
    passion killed,
Every grim ravine a garden, every blazing
    desert tilled,

Robed in universal harvest up to either pole
    she smiles,
Universal ocean softly washing all her warless
    isles. 170

Warless? when her tens are thousands, and
    her thousands millions, then—
All her harvest all too narrow—who can fancy
    warless men?

Warless? war will die out late then. Will it
    ever? late or soon?
Can it, till this outworn earth be dead as yon
    dead world the moon?

Dead the new astronomy calls her.—On this
    day and at this hour, 175
In this gap between the sand hills, whence you
    see the Locksley tower,

Here we met, our latest meeting—Amy—
    sixty years ago—
She and I—the moon was falling greenish
    through a rosy glow,

Just above the gateway tower, and even where
    you see her now—

Here we stood and clasped each other, swore
    the seeming-deathless vow.— 180

Dead, but how her living glory lights the hall,
    the dune, the grass!
Yet the moonlight is the sunlight, and the sun
    himself will pass.

Venus near her! smiling downward at this
    earthlier earth of ours,
Closer on the sun, perhaps a world of never
    fading flowers.

Hesper, whom the poet called the bringer
    home of all good things— 185
All good things may move in Hesper, perfect
    peoples, perfect kings.

Hesper—Venus—were we native to that splendor or in Mars,
We should see the globe we groan in, fairest
    of their evening stars.

Could we dream of wars and carnage, craft
    and madness, lust and spite,
Roaring London, raving Paris, in that point
    of peaceful light? 190

Might we not in glancing heavenward on a
    star so silver-fair,
Yearn, and clasp the hands and murmur,
    "Would to God that we were there"?

Forward, backward, backward, forward, in
    the immeasurable sea,
Swayed by vaster ebbs and flows than can be
    known to you or me.

All the suns—are these but symbols of innumerable man, 195
Man or Mind that sees a shadow of the planner or the plan?

Is there evil but on earth? or pain in every
    peopled sphere?
Well, be grateful for the sounding watchword
    "Evolution" here,

182. **sun . . . pass.** It is believed that the sun is slowly diminishing. 185. **Hesper**, Venus, the evening star. **the poet,** Sappho, a Greek lyric poetess (600 B.C.). The Greek passage is paraphrased by Byron in *Don Juan*, III, 107.

Evolution ever climbing after some ideal
    good,
And Reversion ever dragging Evolution in
    the mud.   200

What are men that He should heed us? cried
    the king of sacred song;
Insects of an hour, that hourly work their
    brother insect wrong,

While the silent heavens roll, and suns along
    their fiery way,
All their planets whirling round them, flash
    a million miles a day.

Many an aeon molded earth before her high-
    est, man, was born,   205
Many an aeon too may pass when earth is
    manless and forlorn,

Earth so huge, and yet so bounded—pools of
    salt, and plots of land—
Shallow skin of green and azure—chains of
    mountain, grains of sand!

Only That which made us meant us to be
    mightier by and by,
Set the sphere of all the boundless heavens
    within the human eye,   210

Sent the shadow of Himself, the boundless,
    through the human soul;
Boundless inward in the atom, boundless out-
    ward in the Whole.

. . . . .

Here is Locksley Hall, my grandson, here the
    lion-guarded gate.
Not tonight in Locksley Hall—tomorrow—
    you, you come so late.

Wrecked—your train—or all but wrecked? a
    shattered wheel? a vicious boy!   215
Good, this forward, you that preach it, is it
    well to wish you joy?

Is it well that while we range with Science,
    glorying in the Time,
City children soak and blacken soul and sense
    in city slime?

There among the glooming alleys Progress
    halts on palsied feet,
Crime and hunger cast our maidens by the
    thousand on the street.   220

There the master scrimps his haggard semp-
    stress of her daily bread,
There a single sordid attic holds the living
    and the dead.

There the smoldering fire of fever creeps
    across the rotted floor,
And the crowded couch of incest in the war-
    rens of the poor.

Nay, your pardon, cry your "Forward," yours
    are hope and youth, but I—   225
Eighty winters leave the dog too lame to fol-
    low with the cry,

Lame and old, and past his time, and passing
    now into the night;
Yet I would the rising race were half as eager
    for the light.

Light the fading gleam of even? light the
    glimmer of the dawn?
Aged eyes may take the growing glimmer for
    the gleam withdrawn.   230

Far away beyond her myriad coming changes
    earth will be
Something other than the wildest modern
    guess of you and me.

Earth may reach her earthly worst, or if she
    gain her earthly best,
Would she find her human offspring this ideal
    man at rest?

Forward then, but still remember how the
    course of Time will swerve,   235
Crook and turn upon itself in many a back-
    ward streaming curve.

201. **What ... us**, from *Psalms*, 8:4: "What is man, that thou art mindful of him?" **king ... song**, David.

221. **master ... bread.** Cf. Hood's *Song of the Shirt*, p. 306.
224. **in ... poor.** A reference to the crowded conditions of poor families. A warren is a protected piece of ground for the breeding of rabbits.

Not the Hall tonight, my grandson! Death and Silence hold their own.
Leave the master in the first dark hour of his last sleep alone.

Worthier soul was he than I am, sound and honest, rustic squire,
Kindly landlord, boon companion—youthful jealousy is a liar. 240

Cast the poison from your bosom, oust the madness from your brain.
Let the trampled serpent show you that you have not lived in vain.

Youthful! youth and age are scholars yet but in the lower school,
Nor is he the wisest man who never proved himself a fool.

Yonder lies our young sea-village—Art and Grace are less and less; 245
Science grows and Beauty dwindles—roofs of slated hideousness!

There is one old hostel left us where they swing the Locksley shield,
Till the peasant cow shall butt the "lion passant" from his field.

Poor old Heraldry, poor old History, poor old Poetry, passing hence,
In the common deluge drowning old political common sense! 250

Poor old voice of eighty crying after voices that have fled!
All I loved are vanished voices, all my steps are on the dead.

All the world is ghost to me, and as the phantom disappears,
Forward far and far from here is all the hope of eighty years.

. . . . .

238. **the master,** Amy's husband, the dead master of Locksley Hall. See l. 37. 248. **"lion passant,"** lion walking, a term in heraldry describing the figure of a lion on a shield. The lion is the national emblem of Great Britain.

In this hostel—I remember—I repent it o'er his grave— 255
Like a clown—by chance he met me—I refused the hand he gave.

From that casement where the trailer mantles all the moldering bricks—
I was then in early boyhood, Edith but a child of six—

While I sheltered in this archway from a day of driving showers—
Peeped the winsome face of Edith like a flower among the flowers. 260

Here tonight! the Hall tomorrow, when they toll the chapel bell!
Shall I hear in one dark room a wailing, "I have loved thee well"?

Then a peal that shakes the portal—one has come to claim his bride,
Her that shrank, and put me from her, shrieked, and started from my side—

Silent echoes! You, my Leonard, use and not abuse your day, 265
Move among your people, know them, follow him who led the way,

Strove for sixty widowed years to help his homelier brother men,
Served the poor, and built the cottage, raised the school, and drained the fen.

Hears he now the voice that wronged him? who shall swear it cannot be?
Earth would never touch her worst, were one in fifty such as he. 270

Ere she gain her heavenly best, a god must mingle with the game.
Nay, there may be those about us whom we neither see nor name,

Felt within us as ourselves, the Powers of Good, the Powers of Ill,

266. **him,** the dead master of Locksley Hall. See l. 238.

Strowing balm, or shedding poison in the
    fountains of the will.

Follow you the star that lights a desert path-
    way, yours or mine.   275
Forward, till you see the Highest Human
    Nature is divine.

Follow Light, and do the Right—for man
    can half-control his doom—
Till you find the deathless Angel seated in the
    vacant tomb.

Forward, let the stormy moment fly and
    mingle with the past.
I that loathed have come to love him. Love
    will conquer at the last.   280

Gone at eighty, mine own age, and I and you
    will bear the pall;
Then I leave thee lord and master, latest lord
    of Locksley Hall.   (1886)

278. **deathless . . . tomb.** An allusion to the angel seated at the tomb of the risen Christ. See *Matthew*, 28.

Break, Break, Break

This is one of the poems inspired by the death of Tennyson's intimate friend, Arthur Hallam. See *In Memoriam* and note, p. 628.

Break, break, break,
    On thy cold gray stones, O Sea!
And I would that my tongue could utter
    The thoughts that arise in me.

O well for the fisherman's boy,   5
    That he shouts with his sister at play!
O well for the sailor lad,
    That he sings in his boat on the bay!

And the stately ships go on
    To their haven under the hill;   10
But O for the touch of a vanished hand,
    And the sound of a voice that is still!

Break, break, break,
    At the foot of thy crags, O Sea!
But the tender grace of a day that is dead   15
    Will never come back to me.   (1842)

11. **vanished hand,** Hallam's.

Songs from *The Princess*

    It was Tennyson's belief that normal human affections should not be repressed by social patterns. *The Princess*, a semi-burlesque narrative poem, recounts the failure of a princess to carry out her plan of establishing a college for women alone. A young prince gains admission to the college, disguised as a girl, but is discovered, and finds himself ultimately fighting in battle against warriors who have come to the aid of the princess. He is defeated, but his very defeat brings him victory, for the sympathy of the princess for the wounded hero leads to her falling in love with him and marrying him. The symbol of the triumph of natural affections over artificial ideas is a child whom the princess loves and fondles even when she seems most adamant in carrying on her plans for the college. The songs in the poem suggest the moods of the action. Some of these were inserted in the second edition of 1850. They are among the finest of Tennyson's lyrics, and some have been set to music.

SWEET AND LOW

Sweet and low, sweet and low,
    Wind of the western sea,
Low, low, breathe and blow,
    Wind of the western sea!
Over the rolling waters go,   5
Come from the dying moon, and blow,
    Blow him again to me;
While my little one, while my pretty one,
    sleeps.

Sleep and rest, sleep and rest,
    Father will come to thee soon;   10
Rest, rest, on mother's breast,
    Father will come to thee soon;
Father will come to his babe in the nest,
Silver sails all out of the west
    Under the silver moon;   15
Sleep, my little one, sleep, my pretty one,
    sleep.

THE SPLENDOR FALLS ON CASTLE WALLS

The splendor falls on castle walls
   And snowy summits old in story;
The long light shakes across the lakes,
   And the wild cataract leaps in glory.
Blow, bugle, blow, set the wild echoes flying,
Blow, bugle; answer, echoes, dying, dying,
   dying.   6

O hark, O hear! how thin and clear,
   And thinner, clearer, farther going!
O sweet and far from cliff and scar
   The horns of Elfland faintly blowing!   10
Blow, let us hear the purple glens replying,
Blow, bugle; answer, echoes, dying, dying,
   dying.

O love, they die in yon rich sky,
   They faint on hill or field or river;
Our echoes roll from soul to soul,   15
   And grow forever and forever.
Blow, bugle, blow, set the wild echoes flying,
And answer, echoes, answer, dying, dying,
   dying.

TEARS, IDLE TEARS

Tears, idle tears, I know not what they mean;
Tears from the depth of some divine despair
Rise in the heart, and gather to the eyes,
In looking on the happy autumn fields,
And thinking of the days that are no more.   5

   Fresh as the first beam glittering on a sail,
That brings our friends up from the underworld,
Sad as the last which reddens over one
That sinks with all we love below the verge;
So sad, so fresh, the days that are no more.   10

   Ah, sad and strange as in dark summer dawns
The earliest pipe of half-awakened birds
To dying ears, when unto dying eyes
The casement slowly grows a glimmering square;
So sad, so strange, the days that are no more.   15

Dear as remembered kisses after death,
And sweet as those by hopeless fancy feigned
On lips that are for others; deep as love,
Deep as first love, and wild with all regret;
O Death in Life, the days that are no more!   20

HOME THEY BROUGHT HER WARRIOR DEAD

Home they brought her warrior dead,
   She nor swooned nor uttered cry.
All her maidens, watching, said,
   "She must weep or she will die."

Then they praised him, soft and low,   5
   Called him worthy to be loved,
Truest friend and noblest foe;
   Yet she neither spoke nor moved.

Stole a maiden from her place,
   Lightly to the warrior stepped,   10
Took the face-cloth from the face;
   Yet she neither moved nor wept.

Rose a nurse of ninety years,
   Set his child upon her knee—
Like summer tempest came her tears—   15
   "Sweet my child, I live for thee."

ASK ME NO MORE

Ask me no more—the moon may draw the sea;
   The cloud may stoop from heaven and take the shape,
   With fold to fold, of mountain or of cape;
But O too fond, when have I answered thee?
   Ask me no more.   5

Ask me no more—what answer should I give?
   I love not hollow cheek or faded eye;
   Yet, O my friend, I will not have thee die!
Ask me no more, lest I should bid thee live;
   Ask me no more.   10

Ask me no more—thy fate and mine are sealed;
   I strove against the stream and all in vain;
   Let the great river take me to the main.
No more, dear love, for at a touch I yield;
   Ask me no more   15

NOW SLEEPS THE CRIMSON PETAL

Now sleeps the crimson petal, now the white;
Nor waves the cypress in the palace walk;
Nor winks the gold fin in the porphyry font.
The firefly wakens; waken thou with me.

Now droops the milk-white peacock like a ghost, 5
And like a ghost she glimmers on to me.

Now lies the Earth all Danaë to the stars,
And all thy heart lies open unto me.

Now slides the silent meteor on, and leaves
A shining furrow, as thy thoughts in me. 10

Now folds the lily all her sweetness up,
And slips into the bosom of the lake.
So fold thyself, my dearest, thou, and slip
Into my bosom and be lost in me.

COME DOWN, O MAID

Come down, O maid, from yonder mountain height.
What pleasure lives in height (the shepherd sang),
In height and cold, the splendor of the hills?
But cease to move so near the heavens, and cease
To glide a sunbeam by the blasted pine. 5
To sit a star upon the sparkling spire;
And come, for Love is of the valley, come,
For Love is of the valley, come thou down
And find him; by the happy threshold, he,
Or hand in hand with Plenty in the maize, 10
Or red with spirted purple of the vats,
Or foxlike in the vine, nor cares to walk
With Death and Morning on the Silver Horns,
Nor wilt thou snare him in the white ravine,
Nor find him dropped upon the firths of ice;
That huddling slant in furrow-cloven falls 15
To roll the torrent out of dusky doors.
But follow; let the torrent dance thee down
To find him in the valley; let the wild
Lean-headed eagles yelp alone, and leave 20
The monstrous ledges there to slope, and spill
Their thousand wreaths of dangling water-smoke,
That like a broken purpose waste in air.
So waste not thou, but come; for all the vales
Await thee; azure pillars of the hearth 25
Arise to thee; the children call, and I,
Thy shepherd, pipe, and sweet is every sound,
Sweeter thy voice, but every sound is sweet;
Myriads of rivulets hurrying through the lawn,
The moan of doves in immemorial elms, 30
And murmuring of innumerable bees. (1850)

7. **Now . . . stars.** The earth is compared to Danaë, the princess whom Zeus in the form of a shower of gold visited in a tower of brass in which her father had imprisoned her. 12. **foxlike in the vine.** Cf. *The Song of Solomon*, 2:15: "Take us the foxes, the little foxes, that spoil the vines: for our vines have tender grapes." 13. **Silver Horns**, peaks of the mountains. The Silverhorn is a spur of the Jungfrau, in the Alps. 15. **firths of ice**, glaciers. 16. **furrow-cloven**, split by crevasses. 17. **dusky doors**, the piled-up mass of refuse through which the stream emerges at the foot of the glacier. 25. **azure . . . hearth**, columns of blue smoke.

from *In Memoriam*

The spiritual upheaval which Tennyson experienced after the death of his dearest friend Arthur Hallam and his struggle to adjust himself to life through the quatrains of *In Memoriam* have already been outlined (see p. 594). Tennyson's own explanation of the purpose of *In Memoriam* throws much light on the poem: "It must be remembered," he wrote in *Memoir*, I, 304-305, "that this is a poem, *not* an actual biography. . . . It was meant to be a kind of *Divina Commedia*, ending with happiness. . . . The different moods of sorrow as in a drama are dramatically given, and my conviction that fear, doubts, and suffering will find answer and relief only through Faith in a God of Love. *I* is not always the author speaking of himself, but the voice of the human race speaking through him." The action of the poem covers less than five years from the death of Hallam in September, 1833, and the bringing of his body back to England, to the spring of 1838. The composition required seventeen years. Tennyson's ultimate conviction after the long agony of sorrow, doubt, and fear was that only faith can discover the eternal purpose of God and solve the problem of immortality. *In Memoriam*, one of the greatest elegies in English literature, should be compared with Milton's *Lycidas* (Vol. I, p. 710), Shelley's *Adonais* (p. 262), and Arnold's *Thyrsis* (p. 739).

IN MEMORIAM A. H. H.
OBIIT 1833

PROLOGUE

Strong Son of God, immortal Love,
  Whom we, that have not seen thy face,
  By faith, and faith alone, embrace,
Believing where we cannot prove;

Thine are these orbs of light and shade;   5
  Thou madest Life in man and brute;
  Thou madest Death; and lo, thy foot
Is on the skull which thou hast made.

Thou wilt not leave us in the dust:
  Thou madest man, he knows not why,   10
  He thinks he was not made to die;
And thou hast made him; thou art just.

Thou seemest human and divine,
  The highest, holiest manhood, thou.
  Our wills are ours, we know not how;   15
Our wills are ours, to make them thine.

Our little systems have their day;
  They have their day and cease to be;
  They are but broken lights of thee,
And thou, O Lord, art more than they.   20

We have but faith; we cannot know,
  For knowledge is of things we see;
  And yet we trust it comes from thee,
A beam in darkness; let it grow.

Let knowledge grow from more to more,   25
  But more of reverence in us dwell;
  That mind and soul, according well,
May make one music as before,

But vaster. We are fools and slight;
  We mock thee when we do not fear.   30
  But help thy foolish ones to bear;
Help thy vain worlds to bear thy light.

Forgive what seemed my sin in me,
  What seemed my worth since I began;
  For merit lives from man to man,   35
And not from man, O Lord, to thee.

Forgive my grief for one removed,
  Thy creature, whom I found so fair.
  I trust he lives in thee, and there
I find him worthier to be loved.   40

Forgive these wild and wandering cries,
  Confusions of a wasted youth;
  Forgive them where they fail in truth,
And in thy wisdom make me wise.

                      (*1849; 1850*)

1

I held it truth, with him who sings
  To one clear harp in divers tones,
  That men may rise on stepping-stones
Of their dead selves to higher things.

But who shall so forecast the years   5
  And find in loss a gain to match?
  Or reach a hand through time to catch
The far-off interest of tears?

Let Love clasp Grief lest both be drowned,
  Let darkness keep her raven gloss.   10
  Ah, sweeter to be drunk with loss,
To dance with Death, to beat the ground,

Than that the victor Hours should scorn
  The long result of love, and boast,
  "Behold the man that loved and lost,   15
But all he was is overworn."

11

Calm is the morn without a sound,
  Calm as to suit a calmer grief,
  And only through the faded leaf
The chestnut pattering to the ground;

Prologue. 5. **orbs ... shade,** the planets, partly in the light of the sun and partly in shadow. 17. **systems,** i.e., of theology and philosophy. 28. **as before,** before mind and soul had become separated by the modern movement of science and skepticism. 32. **thy light,** the light of knowledge.

42. **wasted,** made desolate.
Section 1. 1. **him,** the German poet Goethe, ranked by Tennyson as the greatest among modern lyric poets.

Calm and deep peace on this high wold,   5
   And on these dews that drench the furze,
   And all the silvery gossamers
That twinkle into green and gold;

Calm and still light on yon great plain
   That sweeps with all its autumn bowers, 10
   And crowded farms and lessening towers,
To mingle with the bounding main;

Calm and deep peace in this wide air,
   These leaves that redden to the fall—
   And in my heart, if calm at all,   15
If any calm, a calm despair;

Calm on the seas, and silver sleep,
   And waves that sway themselves in rest,
   And dead calm in that noble breast
Which heaves but with the heaving deep. 20

15

Tonight the winds begin to rise
   And roar from yonder dropping day;
   The last red leaf is whirled away,
The rooks are blown about the skies;

The forest cracked, the waters curled,   5
   The cattle huddled on the lea;
   And wildly dashed on tower and tree
The sunbeam strikes along the world.

And but for fancies, which aver
   That all thy motions gently pass   10
   Athwart a plane of molten glass,
I scarce could brook the strain and stir

That makes the barren branches loud;
   And but for fear it is not so,
   The wild unrest that lives in woe   15
Would dote and pore on yonder cloud

That rises upward always higher,
   And onward drags a laboring breast,
   And topples round the dreary west,
A looming bastion fringed with fire.   20

19

The Danube to the Severn gave
   The darkened heart that beat no more;
   They laid him by the pleasant shore,
And in the hearing of the wave.

There twice a day the Severn fills;   5
   The salt sea-water passes by,
   And hushes half the babbling Wye,
And makes a silence in the hills.

The Wye is hushed nor moved along,
   And hushed my deepest grief of all,   10
   When filled with tears that cannot fall,
I brim with sorrow drowning song.

The tide flows down, the wave again
   Is vocal in its wooded walls;
   My deeper anguish also falls,   15
And I can speak a little then.

27

I envy not in any moods
   The captive void of noble rage
   The linnet born within the cage,
That never knew the summer woods;

I envy not the beast that takes   5
   His license in the field of time,
   Unfettered by the sense of crime,
To whom a conscience never wakes;

Nor, what may count itself as blest,
   The heart that never plighted troth   10
   But stagnates in the weeds of sloth;
Nor any want-begotten rest.

I hold it true, whate'er befall;
   I feel it, when I sorrow most—
   'Tis better to have loved and lost   15
Than never to have loved at all.

28

The time draws near the birth of Christ.
   The moon is hid; the night is still;

Section 11. 7. **gossamers**, fine cobwebs seen on grass and low shrubs. 11. **lessening**, appearing smaller in the distance. 12. **bounding main**, bordering sea. 19. **noble breast**, the body of Hallam being brought by ship to England.
    Section 15. 10. **thy motions**, those of the ship. 20. **bastion**, a part of a fortification projecting outward from the wall like a bay window.

Section 19. 1. **Danube.** Hallam died in Vienna, on the Danube River; he was buried in Clevedon, on the Severn River, in southwestern England. The River Wye (l. 7) joins the Severn near Clevedon. 5. **There . . . fills.** The Severn, flowing into the Bristol Channel, is affected by the tides even above Clevedon.

The Christmas bells from hill to hill
Answer each other in the mist.

Four voices of four hamlets round, 5
  From far and near, on mead and moor,
  Swell out and fail, as if a door
Were shut between me and the sound;

Each voice four changes on the wind,
  That now dilate, and now decrease, 10
  Peace and goodwill, goodwill and peace,
Peace and goodwill, to all mankind.

This year I slept and woke with pain,
  I almost wished no more to wake,
  And that my hold on life would break 15
Before I heard those bells again.

But they my troubled spirit rule,
  For they controlled me when a boy;
  They bring me sorrow touched with joy,
The merry, merry bells of Yule. 20

30

With trembling fingers did we weave
  The holly round the Christmas hearth;
  A rainy cloud possessed the earth,
And sadly fell our Christmas Eve.

At our old pastimes in the hall 5
  We gamboled, making vain pretense
  Of gladness, with an awful sense
Of one mute Shadow watching all.

We paused. The winds were in the beech;
  We heard them sweep the winter land; 10
  And in a circle hand-in-hand
Sat silent, looking each at each.

Then echo-like our voices rang;
  We sung, though every eye was dim,
  A merry song we sang with him 15
Last year; impetuously we sang.

We ceased; a gentler feeling crept
  Upon us: surely rest is meet.

Section 28. 5. **four ... round,** church bells in the four villages near Somersby, Tennyson's home. 9. **four changes.** Each church has four bells. 13. **This year,** 1833, the year of Hallam's death, in September.

"They rest," we said, "their sleep is sweet."
And silence followed, and we wept. 20

Our voices took a higher range;
  Once more we sang: "They do not die
  Nor lose their mortal sympathy,
Nor change to us, although they change;

"Rapt from the fickle and the frail 25
  With gathered power, yet the same,
  Pierces the keen seraphic flame
From orb to orb, from veil to veil."

Rise, happy morn, rise, holy morn,
  Draw forth the cheerful day from night; 30
  O Father, touch the east, and light
The light that shone when Hope was born.

54

O yet we trust that somehow good
  Will be the final goal of ill,
  To pangs of nature, sins of will,
Defects of doubt, and taints of blood;

That nothing walks with aimless feet; 5
  That not one life shall be destroyed,
  Or cast as rubbish to the void,
When God hath made the pile complete;

That not a worm is cloven in vain;
  That not a moth with vain desire 10
  Is shriveled in a fruitless fire,
Or but subserves another's gain.

Behold, we know not anything;
  I can but trust that good shall fall
  At last—far off—at last, to all, 15
And every winter change to spring.

So runs my dream; but what am I?
  An infant crying in the night;
  An infant crying for the light,
And with no language but a cry. 20

55

The wish, that of the living whole
  No life may fail beyond the grave,
  Derives it not from what we have
The likest God within the soul?

Are God and Nature then at strife,
   That Nature lends such evil dreams?
   So careful of the type she seems,
So careless of the single life,

That I, considering everywhere
   Her secret meaning in her deeds,
   And finding that of fifty seeds
She often brings but one to bear,

I falter where I firmly trod,
   And falling with my weight of cares
   Upon the great world's altar-stairs
That slope through darkness up to God,

I stretch lame hands of faith, and grope,
   And gather dust and chaff, and call
   To what I feel is Lord of all,
And faintly trust the larger hope.

56

"So careful of the type?" but no.
   From scarpéd cliff and quarried stone
   She cries, "A thousand types are gone;
I care for nothing, all shall go.

"Thou makest thine appeal to me.
   I bring to life, I bring to death;
   The spirit does but mean the breath.
I know no more." And he, shall he,

Man, her last work, who seemed so fair,
   Such splendid purpose in his eyes,
   Who rolled the psalm to wintry skies,
Who built him fanes of fruitless prayer,

Who trusted God was love indeed
   And love Creation's final law—
   Though Nature, red in tooth and claw
With ravine, shrieked against his creed—

Who loved, who suffered countless ills,
   Who battled for the True, the Just,

Be blown about the desert dust,
Or sealed within the iron hills?

No more? A monster then, a dream,
   A discord. Dragons of the prime,
   That tear each other in their slime,
Were mellow music matched with him.

O life as futile, then, as frail!
   O for thy voice to soothe and bless!
   What hope of answer, or redress?
Behind the veil, behind the veil.

64

Dost thou look back on what hath been,
   As some divinely gifted man,
   Whose life in low estate began
And on a simple village green;

Who breaks his birth's invidious bar,
   And grasps the skirts of happy chance,
   And breasts the blows of circumstance,
And grapples with his evil star;

Who makes by force his merit known
   And lives to clutch the golden keys,
   To mold a mighty state's decrees,
And shape the whisper of the throne;

And moving up from high to higher,
   Becomes on Fortune's crowning slope
   The pillar of a people's hope,
The center of a world's desire;

Yet feels, as in a pensive dream,
   When all his active powers are still,
   A distant dearness in the hill,
A secret sweetness in the stream,

The limit of his narrowed fate,
   While yet beside its vocal springs
   He played at counselors and kings,
With one that was his earliest mate;

Who plows with pain his native lea
   And reaps the labor of his hands,

Section 55. 5. **Are ... strife.** This was an age of conflict between science and religion. See p. 405. 7. **careful ... type.** Cf. *Locksley Hall*, ll. 141-142, p. 617. Tennyson has in mind the doctrine of selection, which in 1859 was explained by Darwin in his *Origin of Species* (p. 405). 20. **larger hope**, faith in the ultimate salvation of all humanity.
Section 56. 2. **cliff ... gone.** Geology gives evidence that countless forms of life have vanished. 16. **ravine**, something seized and devoured as prey.

22. **Dragons ... prime**, prehistoric monsters. 26. **thy voice**, that of Hallam.
Section 64. 10. **golden keys**, symbols of high position.

Or in the furrow musing stands:
"Does my old friend remember me?"

73

So many worlds, so much to do,
  So little done, such things to be,
  How know I what had need of thee,
For thou wert strong as thou wert true?

The fame is quenched that I foresaw,
  The head hath missed an earthly wreath;
  I curse not Nature, no, nor Death,
For nothing is that errs from law.

We pass; the path that each man trod
  Is dim, or will be dim, with weeds.
  What fame is left for human deeds
In endless age? It rests with God.

O hollow wraith of dying fame,
  Fade wholly, while the soul exults,
  And self-infolds the large results
Of force that would have forged a name.

78

Again at Christmas did we weave
  The holly round the Christmas hearth;
  The silent snow possessed the earth;
And calmly fell our Christmas Eve.

The yule-clog sparkled keen with frost,
  No wing of wind the region swept,
  But over all things brooding slept
The quiet sense of something lost.

As in the winters left behind,
  Again our ancient games had place,
  The mimic picture's breathing grace,
And dance and song and hoodman-blind.

Who showed a token of distress?
  No single tear, no mark of pain:
  O sorrow, then can sorrow wane?
O grief, can grief be changed to less?

O last regret, regret can die!
  No—mixed with all this mystic frame,

Her deep relations are the same,
But with long use her tears are dry.

87

I passed beside the reverend walls
  In which of old I wore the gown;
  I roved at random through the town,
And saw the tumult of the halls;

And heard once more in college fanes
  The storm their high-built organs make,
  And thunder-music, rolling, shake
The prophet blazoned on the panes;

And caught once more the distant shout,
  The measured pulse of racing oars
  Among the willows; paced the shores
And many a bridge, and all about

The same gray flats again, and felt
  The same, but not the same; and last
  Up that long walk of limes I passed
To see the rooms in which he dwelt.

Another name was on the door.
  I lingered; all within was noise
  Of songs, and clapping hands, and boys
That crashed the glass and beat the floor;

Where once we held debate, a band
  Of youthful friends, on mind and art,
  And labor, and the changing mart,
And all the framework of the land;

When one would aim an arrow fair,
  But send it slackly from the string;
  And one would pierce an outer ring,
And one an inner, here and there;

And last the master-bowman, he,
  Would cleave the mark. A willing ear
  We lent him. Who but hung to hear
The rapt oration flowing free

From point to point, with power and grace
  And music in the bounds of law,

Section 78. 1. **at Christmas.** The second after Hallam's death. Cf. Sections 30 and 105. 5. **yule-clog,** a large log burned in the fireplace on Christmas Eve. 11. **mimic picture,** the game of charades.

Section 87. 1. **walls,** those of Trinity College, Cambridge. 21. **a band,** called "The Apostles" and also "The Water Club" because the members drank no wine.

To those conclusions when we saw 35
The God within him light his face,

And seem to lift the form, and glow
   In azure orbits heavenly wise;
   And over those ethereal eyes
The bar of Michael Angelo? 40

95

By night we lingered on the lawn,
   For underfoot the herb was dry;
   And genial warmth; and o'er the sky
The silver haze of summer drawn;

And calm that let the tapers burn 5
   Unwavering. Not a cricket chirred;
   The brook alone far-off was heard,
And on the board the fluttering urn.

And bats went round in fragrant skies,
   And wheeled or lit the filmy shapes 10
   That haunt the dusk, with ermine capes
And woolly breasts and beaded eyes;

While now we sang old songs that pealed
   From knoll to knoll, where, couched at ease,
   The white kine glimmered, and the trees 15
Laid their dark arms about the field.

But when those others, one by one,
   Withdrew themselves from me and night,
   And in the house light after light
Went out, and I was all alone, 20

A hunger seized my heart; I read
   Of that glad year which once had been,
   In those fallen leaves which kept their green,
The noble letters of the dead.

And strangely on the silence broke 25
   The silent-speaking words, and strange
   Was love's dumb cry defying change
To test his worth; and strangely spoke

The faith, the vigor, bold to dwell
   On doubts that drive the coward back, 30
   And keen through wordy snares to track
Suggestion to her inmost cell.

So word by word, and line by line,
   The dead man touched me from the past,
   And all at once it seemed at last 35
The living soul was flashed on mine,

And mine in his was wound, and whirled
   About empyreal heights of thought,
   And came on that which is, and caught
The deep pulsations of the world, 40

Aeonian music measuring out
   The steps of Time—the shocks of Chance—
   The blows of Death. At length my trance
Was canceled, stricken through with doubt.

Vague words! but ah, how hard to frame 45
   In matter-molded forms of speech,
   Or even for intellect to reach
Through memory that which I became;

Till now the doubtful dusk revealed
   The knolls once more where, couched at ease, 50
   The white kine glimmered, and the trees
Laid their dark arms about the field;

And sucked from out the distant gloom
   A breeze began to tremble o'er
   The large leaves of the sycamore, 55
And fluctuate all the still perfume,

And gathering freshlier overhead,
   Rocked the full-foliaged elms, and swung
   The heavy-folded rose, and flung
The lilies to and fro, and said, 60

"The dawn, the dawn," and died away;
   And East and West, without a breath,
   Mixed their dim lights, like life and death,
To broaden into boundless day.

---

40. **bar ... Angelo.** Hallam had a ridge above his eyes resembling one that was said to mark Michelangelo (1475-1564), the famous Italian artist.
   Section 95. This Section has been referred to as "the crown of *In Memoriam*." 8. **the ... urn**, the boiling tea-urn. 10. **filmy shapes**, moths.

34. **dead man ... past.** Tennyson, in a trance, gains a vision of the divine purpose in the universe. The poet was subject to such trances from boyhood.

96

You say, but with no touch of scorn,
   Sweet-hearted, you, whose light-blue eyes
   Are tender over drowning flies,
You tell me, doubt is Devil-born.

I know not. One indeed I knew   5
   In many a subtle question versed,
   Who touched a jarring lyre at first,
But ever strove to make it true;

Perplexed in faith, but pure in deeds,
   At last he beat his music out.   10
   There lives more faith in honest doubt,
Believe me, than in half the creeds.

He fought his doubts and gathered strength,
   He would not make his judgment blind,
   He faced the specters of the mind   15
And laid them; thus he came at length

To find a stronger faith his own,
   And Power was with him in the night,
   Which makes the darkness and the light,
And dwells not in the light alone,   20

But in the darkness and the cloud,
   As over Sinaï's peaks of old,
   While Israel made their gods of gold,
Although the trumpet blew so loud.

104

The time draws near the birth of Christ;
   The moon is hid, the night is still;
   A single church below the hill
Is pealing, folded in the mist.

A single peal of bells below,   5
   That wakens at this hour of rest
   A single murmur in the breast,
That these are not the bells I know.

Like strangers' voices here they sound,
   In lands where not a memory strays,   10
   Nor landmark breathes of other days,
But all is new unhallowed ground.

105

Tonight ungathered let us leave
   This laurel, let this holly stand;
   We live within the stranger's land,
And strangely falls our Christmas Eve.

Our father's dust is left alone   5
   And silent under other snows;
   There in due time the woodbine blows,
The violet comes, but we are gone.

No more shall wayward grief abuse
   The genial hour with mask and mime;   10
   For change of place, like growth of time,
Has broke the bond of dying use.

Let cares that petty shadows cast,
   By which our lives are chiefly proved,
   A little spare the night I loved,   15
And hold it solemn to the past.

But let no footstep beat the floor,
   Nor bowl of wassail mantle warm;
   For who would keep an ancient form
Through which the spirit breathes no more?

Be neither song, nor game, nor feast;   21
   Nor harp be touched, nor flute be blown;
   No dance, no motion, save alone
What lightens in the lucid East

Of rising worlds by yonder wood.   25
   Long sleeps the summer in the seed;
   Run out your measured arcs, and lead
The closing cycle rich in good.

106

Ring out, wild bells, to the wild sky,
   The flying cloud, the frosty light;

Section 96. 1. **You,** some woman of simple trust. 5. **One,** Hallam. 11. **There ... creeds.** Honest doubt, Tennyson holds, is a reverent search for truth. 21. **But ... loud.** A reference to the appearance of God before Moses on Mt. Sinai. The people could hear the thunder and see the lightning, but they could not see God because he was hid in a cloud of fire and smoke. The Israelites had made and worshiped a golden calf. See *Exodus,* 19:16-25; 32:1-6.
   Section 104. 1. **The time,** etc., Christmas of 1837. Cf. Sections 28, 30, and 78. 3. **church,** Waltham Abbey Church, near the new home of Tennyson.

Section 105. 7. **blows,** blossoms. 10. **mime,** a dramatic representation imitating scenes from life, usually in ridicule. 18. **wassail mantle,** wine covered with froth. 25. **rising worlds,** the rising stars. 28. **closing cycle,** the final period of perfection.

The year is dying in the night;
Ring out, wild bells, and let him die.

Ring out the old, ring in the new,
   Ring, happy bells, across the snow;
   The year is going, let him go;
Ring out the false, ring in the true.

Ring out the grief that saps the mind,
   For those that here we see no more;
   Ring out the feud of rich and poor,
Ring in redress to all mankind.

Ring out a slowly dying cause,
   And ancient forms of party strife;
   Ring in the nobler modes of life,
With sweeter manners, purer laws.

Ring out the want, the care, the sin,
   The faithless coldness of the times;
   Ring out, ring out my mournful rimes,
But ring the fuller minstrel in.

Ring out false pride in place and blood,
   The civic slander and the spite;
   Ring in the love of truth and right,
Ring in the common love of good.

Ring out old shapes of foul disease;
   Ring out the narrowing lust of gold;
   Ring out the thousand wars of old,
Ring in the thousand years of peace.

Ring in the valiant man and free,
   The larger heart, the kindlier hand;
   Ring out the darkness of the land,
Ring in the Christ that is to be.

126

Love is and was my lord and king,
   And in his presence I attend
   To hear the tidings of my friend,
Which every hour his couriers bring.

Love is and was my king and lord,
   And will be, though as yet I keep

Within the court on earth, and sleep
Encompassed by his faithful guard,

And hear at times a sentinel
   Who moves about from place to place,
   And whispers to the worlds of space,
In the deep night, that all is well.

130

Thy voice is on the rolling air;
   I hear thee where the waters run;
   Thou standest in the rising sun,
And in the setting thou art fair.

What art thou then? I cannot guess;
   But though I seem in star and flower
   To feel thee some diffusive power,
I do not therefore love thee less.

My love involves the love before;
   My love is vaster passion now;
   Though mixed with God and Nature thou,
I seem to love thee more and more.

Far off thou art, but ever nigh;
   I have thee still, and I rejoice;
   I prosper, circled with thy voice;
I shall not lose thee though I die.

131

O living will that shalt endure
   When all that seems shall suffer shock,
   Rise in the spiritual rock,
Flow through our deeds and make them pure,

That we may lift from out of dust
   A voice as unto him that hears,
   A cry above the conquered years
To one that with us works, and trust,

With faith that comes of self-control,
   The truths that never can be proved
   Until we close with all we loved,
And all we flow from, soul in soul.

(1833-50; 1850)

Section 106. 28. **the ... peace.** These are mentioned several times in *Revelation*, 20. 32. **the Christ ... be.** When harmony prevails because of no controversies about creeds.

Section 131. 1. **living will,** "free-will, the higher and enduring part of man."—Tennyson. 3. **spiritual rock.** Cf. *1 Corinthians*, 10:4: "And did all drink the same spiritual drink; for they drank of that spiritual Rock that followed them: and that Rock was Christ." 7. **the ... years,** the victor Hours of Section 1, line 13, overcome by Love and Immortality.

The Eagle

FRAGMENT

He clasps the crag with crooked hands;
Close to the sun in lonely lands,
Ringed with the azure world, he stands.

The wrinkled sea beneath him crawls;
He watches from his mountain walls,   5
And like a thunderbolt he falls.   (1851)

The Charge of the Light Brigade

Tennyson's strong patriotism is revealed in this account of the famous charge of the Light Cavalry under Lord Cardigan at Balaclava near Sebastopol, on September 26, 1854, during the Crimean War. Through an error in orders the intrepid troop was thrown into the teeth of the entire Russian army of twelve thousand, supported by artillery; of 673 officers and men who participated, 247 were either killed or wounded.

Half a league, half a league,
Half a league, onward,
All in the valley of Death
    Rode the six hundred.
"Forward the Light Brigade!   5
Charge for the guns!" he said.
Into the valley of Death
    Rode the six hundred.

"Forward, the Light Brigade!"
Was there a man dismayed?   10
Not though the soldier knew
    Someone had blundered.
Theirs not to make reply,
Theirs not to reason why,
Theirs but to do and die.   15
Into the valley of Death
    Rode the six hundred.

Cannon to right of them,
Cannon to left of them,
Cannon in front of them   20
    Volleyed and thundered;
Stormed at with shot and shell,
Boldly they rode and well,
Into the jaws of Death,
Into the mouth of hell   25
    Rode the six hundred.

Flashed all their sabers bare,
Flashed as they turned in air
Sabering the gunners there,
Charging an army, while   30
    All the world wondered.
Plunged in the battery smoke
Right through the line they broke;
Cossack and Russian
Reeled from the saber stroke   35
    Shattered and sundered.
Then they rode back, but not,
    Not the six hundred.

Cannon to right of them,
Cannon to left of them,   40
Cannon behind them
    Volleyed and thundered;
Stormed at with shot and shell,
While horse and hero fell,
They that had fought so well   45
Came through the jaws of Death,
Back from the mouth of hell,
All that was left of them,
    Left of six hundred.

When can their glory fade?   50
O the wild charge they made!
    All the world wondered.
Honor the charge they made!
Honor the Light Brigade,
    Noble six hundred!   (*1854;* 1854)

The Song of the Brook

This lyric is an incidental part of an English idyll called *The Brook*, which tells of the return home of a man after an absence of twenty years and of his wandering by the brook and recalling scenes of his boyhood. It is one of the poet's most successful descriptions of moving water.

I come from haunts of coot and hern,
    I make a sudden sally,

---

1. **coot**, a kind of ducklike bird. **hern**, the heron.

And sparkle out among the fern,
    To bicker down a valley.

By thirty hills I hurry down,   5
    Or slip between the ridges,
By twenty thorps, a little town,
    And half a hundred bridges.

Till last by Philip's farm I flow
    To join the brimming river,   10
For men may come and men may go,
    But I go on forever.

I chatter over stony ways,
    In little sharps and trebles,
I bubble into eddying bays,   15
    I babble on the pebbles.

With many a curve my banks I fret
    By many a field and fallow,
And many a fairy foreland set
    With willow-weed and mallow.   20

I chatter, chatter, as I flow
    To join the brimming river,
For men may come and men may go,
    But I go on forever.

I wind about, and in and out,   25
    With here a blossom sailing,

*7. **thorps**, hamlets. 9. **Philip**, a character in the idyll.*

And here and there a lusty trout,
    And here and there a grayling,

And here and there a foamy flake
    Upon me, as I travel   30
With many a silvery water-break
    Above the golden gravel,

And draw them all along and flow
    To join the brimming river,
For men may come and men may go,   35
    But I go on forever.

I steal by lawns and grassy plots,
    I slide by hazel covers;
I move the sweet forget-me-nots
    That grow for happy lovers.   40

I slip, I slide, I gloom, I glance
    Among my skimming swallows;
I make the netted sunbeam dance
    Against my sandy shallows.

I murmur under moon and stars   45
    In brambly wildernesses;
I linger by my shingly bars,
    I loiter round my cresses;

And out again I curve and flow
    To join the brimming river,   50
For men may come and men may go,
    But I go on forever.   (1855)

Lyrics from *Maud*

These lyrics were part of a long poetical romance in which a morbid youth tells the story of his tragic love for Maud, the playmate of his youth, of the loss of his reason, and of his restoration under the emotions aroused by the Crimean War. The poem is filled with Tennyson's reflections on the problems of conflict and sorrow.

COME INTO THE GARDEN, MAUD

Come into the garden, Maud,
    For the black bat, night, has flown,
Come into the garden, Maud,
    I am here at the gate alone;
And the woodbine spices are wafted abroad,
    And the musk of the rose is blown.   6

Come into the Garden, Maud. Cf. Now Sleeps the Crimson Petal (p. 628). In that song the flowers sleep in sympathy.

For a breeze of morning moves,
    And the planet of Love is on high,
Beginning to faint in the light that she loves
    On a bed of daffodil sky,   10
To faint in the light of the sun she loves,
    To faint in his light, and to die.

*8. **planet of Love**, Venus.*

All night have the roses heard
    The flute, violin, bassoon;
All night has the casement jessamine stirred
    To the dancers dancing in tune; 16
Till a silence fell with the waking bird,
    And a hush with the setting moon.

I said to the lily, "There is but one,
    With whom she has heart to be gay. 20
When will the dancers leave her alone?
    She is weary of dance and play."
Now half to the setting moon are gone,
    And half to the rising day;
Low on the sand and loud on the stone 25
    The last wheel echoes away.

I said to the rose, "The brief night goes
    In babble and revel and wine.
O young lord-lover, what sighs are those,
    For one that will never be thine? 30
But mine, but mine," so I sware to the rose,
    "Forever and ever, mine."

And the soul of the rose went into my blood,
    As the music clashed in the hall;
And long by the garden lake I stood, 35
    For I heard your rivulet fall
From the lake to the meadow and on to the wood,
    Our wood, that is dearer than all;

From the meadow your walks have left so sweet
    That whenever a March wind sighs 40
He sets the jewel-print of your feet
    In violets blue as your eyes,
To the woody hollows in which we meet
    And the valleys of Paradise.

The slender acacia would not shake 45
    One long milk-bloom on the tree;
The white lake-blossom fell into the lake
    As the pimpernel dozed on the lea;
But the rose was awake all night for your sake,
    Knowing your promise to me; 50
The lilies and roses were all awake,
    They sighed for the dawn and thee.

Queen rose of the rosebud garden of girls,
    Come hither, the dances are done,
In gloss of satin and glimmer of pearls, 55
    Queen lily and rose in one;
Shine out, little head, sunning over with curls,
    To the flowers, and be their sun.

There has fallen a splendid tear
    From the passion-flower at the gate. 60
She is coming, my dove, my dear;
    She is coming, my life, my fate.
The red rose cries, "She is near, she is near";
    And the white rose weeps, "She is late";
The larkspur listens, "I hear, I hear"; 65
    And the lily whispers, "I wait."

She is coming, my own, my sweet;
    Were it ever so airy a tread,
My heart would hear her and beat,
    Were it earth in an earthy bed; 70
My dust would hear her and beat,
    Had I lain for a century dead,
Would start and tremble under her feet,
    And blossom in purple and red.

O THAT 'TWERE POSSIBLE

Tennyson regarded this lyric as "the most touching of his works." Swinburne called it "the poem of deepest charm and fullest delight of pathos and melody ever written by Mr. Tennyson." It suggests his grief for his lost friend Hallam.

O that 'twere possible
After long grief and pain
To find the arms of my true love
Round me once again!

When I was wont to meet her 5
In the silent woody places
By the home that gave me birth,
We stood tranced in long embraces
Mixed with kisses sweeter, sweeter
Than anything on earth. 10

A shadow flits before me,
Not thou, but like to thee.
Ah, Christ, that it were possible
For one short hour to see
The souls we loved, that they might tell us 15
What and where they be!

It leads me forth at evening,
It lightly winds and steals
In a cold white robe before me,
When all my spirit reels   20
At the shouts, the leagues of lights,
And the roaring of the wheels.

Half the night I waste in sighs,
Half in dreams I sorrow after
The delight of early skies;   25
In a wakeful doze I sorrow
For the hand, the lips, the eyes,
For the meeting of the morrow,
The delight of happy laughter,
The delight of low replies.   30

'Tis a morning pure and sweet,
And a dewy splendor falls
On the little flower that clings
To the turrets and the walls;
'Tis a morning pure and sweet,   35
And the light and shadow fleet.
She is walking in the meadow,
And the woodland echo rings;
In a moment we shall meet.
She is singing in the meadow,   40
And the rivulet at her feet
Ripples on in light and shadow
To the ballad that she sings.

Do I hear her sing as of old,
My bird with the shining head,   45
My own dove with the tender eye?
But there rings on a sudden a passionate cry,
There is someone dying or dead,
And a sullen thunder is rolled;
For a tumult shakes the city,   50
And I wake, my dream is fled.
In the shuddering dawn, behold,
Without knowledge, without pity,
By the curtains of my bed
That abiding phantom cold!   55

Get thee hence, nor come again,
Mix not memory with doubt,
Pass, thou deathlike type of pain,
Pass and cease to move about!
'Tis the blot upon the brain   60
That *will* show itself without.

Then I rise, the eave-drops fall,
And the yellow vapors choke
The great city sounding wide;
The day comes, a dull red ball   65
Wrapped in drifts of lurid smoke
On the misty river-tide.

Through the hubbub of the market
I steal, a wasted frame;
It crosses here, it crosses there,   70
Through all that crowd confused and loud,
The shadow still the same;
And on my heavy eyelids
My anguish hangs like shame.

Alas for her that met me,   75
That heard me softly call,
Came glimmering through the laurels
At the quiet evenfall,
In the garden by the turrets
Of the old manorial hall!   80

Would the happy spirit descend
From the realms of light and song,
In the chamber or the street,
As she looks among the blest,
Should I fear to greet my friend   85
Or to say, "Forgive the wrong,"
Or to ask her, "Take me, sweet,
To the regions of thy rest"?

But the broad light glares and beats,
And the shadow flits and fleets   90
And will not let me be;
And I loathe the squares and streets,
And the faces that one meets,
Hearts with no love for me.
Always I long to creep   95
Into some still cavern deep,
There to weep, and weep, and weep
My whole soul out to thee.

OH, LET THE SOLID GROUND

Oh, let the solid ground
   Not fail beneath my feet
Before my life has found
   What some have found so sweet!
Then let come what come may,   5
What matter if I go mad,
I shall have had my day.

Let the sweet heavens endure,
  Not close and darken above me
Before I am quite, quite sure   10
  That there is one to love me!
Then let come what come may
  To a life that has been so sad—
I shall have had my day.

                (*1854;* 1857)

In the Valley of Cauteretz

Cauteretz is a beautiful valley in the Pyrenees Mountains, visited by Tennyson and Arthur Hallam in 1830, and again by Tennyson in 1861.

All along the valley, stream that flashest white,
Deepening thy voice with the deepening of the night,
All along the valley, where thy waters flow,
I walked with one I loved two and thirty years ago.
All along the valley, while I walked today,   5
The two and thirty years were a mist that rolls away;
For all along the valley, down thy rocky bed,
Thy living voice to me was as the voice of the dead,
And all along the valley, by rock and cave and tree,
The voice of the dead was a living voice to me.

                (*1861;* 1864)

The Flower

Although Tennyson states (*Memoir*, II, 10) that this poem is "an universal apologue and parable," it fittingly suggests that his own poetry, little cared for at first, gained in popular approval after it found many imitators.

Once in a golden hour
  I cast to earth a seed.
Up there came a flower,
  The people said, a weed.

To and fro they went   5
  Through my garden-bower,
And muttering discontent
  Cursed me and my flower.

Then it grew so tall
  It wore a crown of light,   10
But thieves from o'er the wall
  Stole the seed by night;

Sowed it far and wide
  By every town and tower,
Till all the people cried,   15
  "Splendid is the flower."

Read my little fable:
  He that runs may read.
Most can raise the flowers now
  For all have got the seed.   20

And some are pretty enough,
  And some are poor indeed;
And now again the people
  Call it but a weed.   (1864)

Northern Farmer

OLD STYLE

Tennyson states that this poem was "founded on the dying words of a farm-bailiff as reported to me by a grand-uncle of mine when verging upon 80—'God A'mighty little knows what He's about a-taking me. An' Squire will be so mad an' all.'" The poet's interest in dialect poems probably resulted from his acquaintance with those of William Barnes (1801-1886), whose *Dorset Poems* (1844-1863) are accurate reproductions of the peculiarities of provincial speech and philosophy. Among other dialect poems by Tennyson are *Northern Farmer: New Style*, *The Spinster's Sweet-Arts*, *Owd Roä*, and *The Church-Warden and the Curate*.

Wheer 'asta beän saw long and meä liggin' 'ere aloän?
Noorse? thoort nowt o' a noorse; whoy, Doctor's abeän an' agoän;

---

1. **'asta beän**, hast thou been. **liggin' 'ere aloän**, lying here alone. 2. **Noorse?** ... **noorse**, Nurse? thou art of no use as a nurse. **abeän an' agoän**, been and gone.

Says that I moänt 'a naw moor aäle, but I
    beänt a fool;
Git ma my aäle, fur I beänt a-gawin' to breäk
    my rule.

Doctors, they knaws nowt, fur a says what's
    nawways true;   5
Naw soort o' koind o' use to saäy the things
    that a do.
I've 'ed my point o' aäle ivry noight sin' I
    beän 'ere.
An' I've 'ed my quart ivry market-noight for
    foorty year.

Parson's a beän loikewoise, an' a sittin' ere o'
    my bed.
"The Amoighty's a taäkin o' you to 'issén,
    my friend," a said,   10
An' a towd ma my sins, an' 's toithe were due,
    an' I gied it in hond;
I done moy duty boy 'um, as I 'a done boy
    the lond.

Larned a ma' beä. I reckons I 'annot sa
    mooch to larn.
But a cast oop, thot a did, 'bout Bessy Marris's
    barne.
Thaw a knaws I hallus voäted wi' Squoire an'
    choorch an' staäte,   15
An' i' the woost o' toimes I wur niver agin
    the raäte.

An' I hallus coomed to 's choorch afoor moy
    Sally wur deäd,
An' 'eärd 'um a bummin' awaäy loike a buz-
    zard-clock ower my 'eäd,
An' I niver knawed whot a meäned but I
    thowt a 'ad summut to saäy,
An' I thowt a said whot a owt to 'a said, an'
    I coomed awaäy.   20

Bessy Marris's barne! tha knaws she laäid it
    to meä.

Mowt a beän, mayhap, for she wur a bad un,
    sheä.
'Siver, I kep 'um, I kep 'um, my lass, tha mun
    understond;
I done moy duty boy 'um, as I 'a done boy
    the lond.

But Parson a cooms an' a goäs, an' a says it
    eäsy an' freeä: 25
"The Amoighty's a taäkin o' you to 'issén, my
    friend," says 'ea.
I weänt saäy men be loiars, thaw summun
    said it in 'aäste;
But 'e reäds wonn sarmin a weeäk, an' I 'a
    stubbed Thurnaby waäste.

D' ya moind the waäste, my lass? naw, naw,
    tha was not born then;
Theer wur a boggle in it, I often 'eärd 'um
    mysén;   30
Moäst loike a butter-bump, fur I 'eärd 'um
    about an' about,
But I stubbed 'um oop wi' the lot, an' raäved
    an' rembled 'um out.

Keäper's it wur; fo' they fun 'um theer
    a-laäid of 'is faäce
Down i' the woild 'enemies afoor I coomed to
    the plaäce.
Noäks or Thimbleby—toäner 'ed shot 'um as
    deäd as a naäil.   35
Noäks wur 'anged for it oop at 'soize—but
    git ma my aäle.

Dubbut looök at the waäste; theer warn't not
    feeäd for a cow;
Nowt at all but bracken an' fuzz, an' looök at
    it now—
Warn't worth nowt a haäcre, an' now theer 's
    lots o' feeäd,
Fourscoor yows upon it, an' some on it down
    i' seeäd.   40

3. **moänt 'a**, may not have. 5. **a**, he. 7 **point**, pint. 10. **you**. *Ou* is pronounced as in *hour*. **'issén**, himself. 11. **towd**, told. **an' 's toithe**, and his tithe. 12. **boy**, by. 13. **Larned a ma' beä**, learned he may be. 14. **a cast oop**, he brought up against me. **barne**, child. 16. **the raäte**, the poor tax. 18. **buzzard-clock**, cockchafer (a kind of buzzing insect). 23. **'Siver, I kep 'um**, however, I supported him. 27. **summun**, someone (David; see *Psalms*, 116:11: "I said in my haste, All men are liars"). 28. **'e**, he (the parson). **'a stubbed**, have cleared the land of trees, roots, etc. 30. **boggle**, bogie, ghost. 31. **butter-bump**, bittern (a bird with a loud, hollow note). 32. **raäved an' rembled 'um out**. plowed him up and threw him out. 33. **Keäper's it wur**, it was the ghost of the gamekeeper. **a-laäid of 'is faäce**, lying on his face. 34. **i' the woild 'enemies**, among the wild anemones. 35. **toäner**, one of the other (Noäks or Thimbleby). 36. **at 'soize**, at the assizes (court hearing) 37. **Dubbut**, do but. 38. **bracken an' fuzz**, fern and furze. 39. **nowt a haäcre**, nothing an acre. 40. **yows**, ewes. **i' seeäd**, seeded to clover.

Nobbut a bit on it's left, an' I meäned to 'a
    stubbed it at fall,
Done it ta-year I meäned, an' runned plow
    thruff it an' all,
If Godamoighty an' parson 'ud nobbut let ma
    aloän—
Meä, wi' haäte hoonderd haäcre o' Squoire's,
    an' lond o' my oän.

Do Godamoighty knaw what a's doing, a-
    taäkin' o' meä?   45
I beänt wonn as saws 'ere a beän an' yonder
    a peä;
An' Squoire 'ull be sa mad an' all—a' dear,
    a' dear!
And I 'a managed for Squoire coom Michael-
    mas thutty year.

A mowt 'a taäen owd Joänes, as 'ant not a
    'aäpoth o' sense,
Or a mowt 'a taäen young Robins—a niver
    mended a fence;   50
But Godamoighty a moost taäke meä an'
    taäke ma now,
Wi' aäf the cows to cauve an' Thurnaby
    hoälms to plow!

Looök 'ow quoloty smoiles when they seeäs
    ma a passin' boy,
Says to thessén, naw doubt, "What a man a
    beä sewer-loy!"
Fur they knaws what I beän to Squoire sin'
    fust a coomed to the 'All;   55
I done moy duty by Squoire an' I done moy
    duty boy hall.

Squoire's i' Lunnon, an' summun I reckons
    'ull 'a to wroite,
For whoä's to howd the lond ater meä thot
    muddles ma quoit;
Sartin-sewer I beä thot a weänt niver give it
    to Joänes,
Naw, nor a moänt to Robins—a niver rembles
    the stoäns.   60

But summun 'ull come ater meä mayhap wi'
    'is kittle o' steäm
Huzzin' an' maäzin' the blessed feälds wi' the
    divil's oän teäm.
Sin' I mun doy I mun doy, thaw loife they
    says is sweet,
But sin' I mun doy I mun doy, for I couldn
    abeär to see it.

What atta stannin' theer fur, an' doesn bring
    ma the aäle?   65
Doctor's a 'toättler, lass, an a's hallus i' the
    owd taäle;
I weänt breäk rules fur Doctor, a knaws naw
    moor nor a floy;
Git ma my aäle, I tell tha, an' if I mun doy
    I mun doy.   (1864)

Northern Farmer

NEW STYLE

In this poem the independent farmer has succeeded the bailiff or Squire's representative of the earlier poem. The poem was suggested by a favorite saying of a rich neighbor of Tennyson: "When I canters my 'erse along the ramper [highway], I 'ears proputty, proputty, proputty" (*Memoirs* II, 9). The farmer and his son are on horseback, and the speaker's remarks are occasionally addressed to his horse.

Dosn't thou 'ear my 'erse's legs, as they canters
    awaäy?
Proputty, proputty, proputty—that's what I
    'ears 'em saäy.
Proputty, proputty, proputty—Sam, thou's an
    ass for thy païns;
Theer's moor sense i' one o' 'is legs nor in all
    thy braïns.

---

41. **Nobbut,** only. 42. **ta-year,** this year. 44. **haäte,** eight. 46. **wonn as saws,** such a one as sows. 48. **Michaelmas,** a church festival celebrated on September 29. **thutty,** thirty. 49. **mowt 'a taäen,** might have taken. **as . . . sense,** who hasn't a half-penny's worth of sense. 52. **cauve,** calve. **hoälms** (low flat lands along the river). 53. **quoloty,** quality; the gentry. 54. **thessén,** themselves. **sewerloy,** surely. 58. **howd,** hold. **muddles . . . quoit,** puzzles me quite. 59. **Sartin-sewer,** certain sure, i.e., dead-sure.

60. **rembles,** removes. 61. **kittle o' steäm,** boiler of steam. The steam thresher was introduced into Lincolnshire in 1848. 62. **Huzzin' an' maäzin,** worrying and frightening. 64. **it,** the presence of the threshing machine. 65. **atta,** art thou. 66. **'toättler,** teetotaler. **a's . . . taäle,** he is always telling the same story. 67. **floy,** fly.
Northern Farmer: New Style. 1. **'erse's,** horse's. 2. **Proputty,** property.

Woä—theer's a craw to pluck wi' tha, Sam;
    yon's parson's 'ouse— 5
Dosn't thou knaw that a man mun be eäther
    a man or a mouse?
Time to think on it then; for thou'll be twenty
    to weeäk.
Proputty, proputty—woä then, woä—let ma
    'ear mysén speäk.

Me an' thy muther, Sammy, 'as beän a-talkin'
    o' thee;
Thou's beän talkin' to muther, an' she beän
    a-tellin' it to me. 10
Thou'll not marry for munny—thou's sweet
    upo' parson's lass—
Noä—thou'll marry for luvv—an' we boäth
    on us thinks tha an ass.

Seeäed her todaäy goä by—Saäint's-daäy—
    they was ringing the bells.
She's a beauty, thou thinks—an' soä is scoors
    o' gells,
Them as 'as munny an' all—wot's a beauty?—
    the flower as blaws. 15
But proputty, proputty sticks, an' proputty,
    proputty graws.

Do'ant be stunt; taäke time. I knaws what
    maäkes tha sa mad.
Warn't I craäzed fur the lasses mysén when
    I wur a lad?
But I knawed a Quaäker feller as often 'as
    towd ma this:
"Doänt thou marry for munny, but goä
    wheer munny is!" 20

An' I went wheer munny war; an' thy muther
    coom to 'and,
Wi' lots o' munny laäid by, an' a nicetish bit
    o' land.
Maäybe she warn't a beauty—I niver giv it a
    thowt—
But warn't she as good to cuddle an' kiss as
    a lass as 'ant nowt?

Parson's lass 'ant nowt, an' she weänt 'a nowt
    when 'e's deäd, 25
Mun be a guvness, lad, or summut, and addle
    her breäd.
Why? fur 'e's nobbut a curate, an' weänt
    niver git hissén clear,
An' 'e maäde the bed as 'e ligs on afoor 'e
    coomed to the shere.

An' thin 'e coomed to the parish wi' lots o'
    Varsity debt,
Stook to his taäil they did, an' 'e 'ant got shut
    on 'em yet. 30
An' 'e ligs on 'is back i' the grip, wi' noän to
    lend 'im a shove,
Woorse nor a far-weltered yowe; fur, Sammy,
    'e married fur luvv.

Luvv? what's luvv? thou can luvv thy lass
    an' 'er munny too,
Maäkin' 'em goä togither, as they've good
    right to do.
Couldn' I luvv thy muther by cause o' 'er
    munny laäid by? 35
Naäy—fur I luvved 'er a vast sight moor fur
    it; reäson why.

Ay, an' thy muther says thou wants to marry
    the lass,
Cooms of a gentleman burn; an' we boäth on
    us thinks tha an ass.
Woä then, proputty, wiltha?—an ass as near
    as mays nowt—
Woä then, wiltha? dangtha!—the bees is as
    fell as owt. 40

Breäk me a bit o' the esh for his 'eäd, lad, out
    o' the fence!
Gentleman burn! what's gentleman burn? is
    it shillins an' pence?

---

5. **craw to pluck**, crow to pick; something disagreeable to take up. 6. **mun**, must. 7. **to weeäk**, this week. 8. **let** . . . **speäk**, let me hear myself speak. 14. **scoors o' gells**, scores of girls. 17. **stunt**, stubborn. 19. **'as** . . . **this**, who often has told me this. 24. **as 'ant nowt**, that has nothing.

25. **weänt 'a**, will not have. 26. **Mun be**, must become. **addle her breäd**, earn her own living. 27. **nobbut**, only. **clear**, out of debt. 28. **ligs**, lies. **shere**, shire, county. 30. **shut on 'em**, rid of them. 31. **ligs on**, lies on. **grip**, draining-ditch or trench. 32. **far-weltered yowe**, ewe lying on its back. (When a sheep gets on its back, it cannot get up without help.) 38. **burn**, born. 39. **Woä then**, addressed to the horse molested by flies. **mays nowt**, makes nothing. 40. **dangtha**, curse you (to the horse). **the bees** . . . **owt**, the flies are as fierce as anything. 41. **esh**, ash.

Proputty, proputty's ivrything 'ere, an',
    Sammy, I'm blest
If it isn't the saäme oop yonder, fur them as
    'as it's the best.

Tis'n them as 'as munny as breäks into 'ouses
    an' steäls,   45
Them as 'as coäts to their backs an' taäkes
    their regular meäls.
Noä, but it's them as niver knaws wheer a
    meäl's to be 'ad.
Taäke my word for it, Sammy, the poor in
    a loomp is bad.

Them or thir feythers, tha sees, mun 'a beän
    a laäzy lot,
Fur work mun 'a gone to the gittin' whiniver
    munny was got.   50
Feyther 'ad ammost nowt; leästways 'is
    munny was 'id.
But 'e tued an' moiled 'issén deäd, an' 'e died
    a good un, 'e did.

Looök thou theer wheer Wrigglesby beck
    cooms out by the 'ill!
Feyther run oop to the farm, an' I runs oop
    to the mill;
An' I'll run oop to the brig, an' that thou'll
    live to see;   55
And if thou marries a good un I'll leäve the
    land to thee.

Thim's my noätions, Sammy, wheerby I
    meäns to stick;
But if thou marries a bad un, I'll leäve the
    land to Dick.—
Coom oop, proputty, proputty—that's what I
    'ears 'im saäy—
Proputty, proputty, proputty—canter an' can-
    ter awaäy.

            (1869)

---

44. **fur . . . best**, for those who have it are the best.
49. **mun 'a beän**, must have been. 51. **ammost nowt**, almost nothing. 52. **tued . . . deäd**, tugged and toiled himself to death. 53. **beck**, brook. 54. **Feyther run oop**, father extended his property to. 55. **brig**, bridge.

Wages

Glory of warrior, glory of orator, glory of
    song,
    Paid with a voice flying by to be lost on
        an endless sea—
Glory of Virtue, to fight, to struggle, to
    right the wrong—
    Nay, but she aimed not at glory, no lover
        of glory she;
Give her the glory of going on, and still
    to be.   5

The wages of sin is death; if the wages of
    Virtue be dust,
    Would she have heart to endure for the
        life of the worm and the fly?
She desires no isles of the blest, no quiet
    seats of the just,
    To rest in a golden grove, or to bask in a
        summer sky;
Give her the wages of going on, and not to
    die.   (1867; 1868)

The Higher Pantheism

Tennyson believed that Pantheism, the doctrine that identifies the world taken as a whole with God, stops short of the higher doctrine that God dwells in the world but transcends it. The poem should be compared with Swinburne's parody of it, *The Higher Pantheism in a Nutshell*, p. 821.

The sun, the moon, the stars, the seas, the
    hills, and the plains—
    Are not these, O Soul, the Vision of Him
        who reigns?

Is not the Vision He, though He be not that
    which He seems?
    Dreams are true while they last, and do we
        not live in dreams?

Earth, these solid stars, this weight of body
    and limb,   5
    Are they not sign and symbol of thy division
        from Him?

Wages. 6. **The . . . death**, quoted from *Romans*, 6:23.

Dark is the world to thee; thyself art the
    reason why,
For is He not all but thou, that hast power to
    feel "I am I"?

Glory about thee, without thee; and thou
    fulfillest thy doom,
Making Him broken gleams and a stifled
    splendor and gloom.   10

Speak to Him, thou, for He hears, and Spirit
    with Spirit can meet—
Closer is He than breathing, and nearer than
    hands and feet.

God is law, say the wise; O Soul, and let us
    rejoice,
For if He thunder by law, the thunder is yet
    His voice.

Law is God, say some; no God at all, says the
    fool,   15
For all we have power to see is a straight staff
    bent in a pool;

And the ear of man cannot hear, and the eye
    of man cannot see;
But if we could see and hear, this Vision—
    were it not He?   (1869)

Flower in the Crannied Wall

Flower in the crannied wall,
I pluck you out of the crannies,
I hold you here, root and all, in my hand,
Little flower—but *if* I could understand
What you are, root and all, and all in all,   5
I should know what God and man is.
    (1869)

8. "I am I." Cf. *Exodus*, 3:14; *John*, 8:58; and *Revelation*, 1:18.

15. **no God . . . fool.** Cf. *Psalms*, 14:1: "The fool hath said in his heart, There is no God." The poem is full of Biblical allusions.

from *The Idylls of the King*

    The most popular of Tennyson's long poems is the series of romances called collectively *The Idylls of the King*. The poem consists of twelve narratives that deal with the history of King Arthur and the Knights of the Table Round: *The Coming of Arthur; Gareth and Lynette; The Marriage of Geraint; Geraint and Enid; Balin and Balan; Merlin and Vivien; Lancelot and Elaine; The Holy Grail; Pelleas and Ettarre; The Last Tournament; Guinevere; The Passing of Arthur.* Most of the material for these *Idylls* Tennyson gathered from Malory's *Morte Darthur* (see Vol. I, p. 279). The first of the *Idylls* was published in 1859, the last in 1885. Earlier poems in the same field include *The Lady of Shalott, Morte D'Arthur, Sir Lancelot and Queen Guinevere,* and *Sir Galahad.* The general moral is the overcoming of virtue and hope by slowly corrupting sin. The sweep and imagery of Tennyson's *Idylls* have made them immensely popular. Many critics believe, however, that his attempt to use the old romantic material for his Victorian morality resulted in stultifying the knights and ladies of Malory and in creating tales that were neither wholly medieval nor wholly Victorian but an incongruous mixture of both moods.

THE COMING OF ARTHUR

Leodogran, the king of Cameliard,
Had one fair daughter, and none other child;
And she was fairest of all flesh on earth,
Guinevere, and in her his one delight.

For many a petty King ere Arthur came   5
Ruled in this isle and, ever waging war
Each upon other, wasted all the land;
And still from time to time the heathen host
Swarmed over-seas, and harried what was left.
And so there grew great tracts of wilderness,
Wherein the beast was ever more and more,   11
But man was less and less, till Arthur came.
For first Aurelius lived and fought and died,
And after him King Uther fought and died,
But either failed to make the kingdom one.   15
And after these King Arthur for a space,
And through the puissance of his Table
    Round,

8. **heathen host,** the Angles and Saxons, who later overcame the Britons.

13. **Aurelius,** a descendant of the last Roman general in Britain. 14. **Uther,** younger brother of Aurelius; he was called Pendragon because he wore a dragon on his helmet.

Drew all their petty princedoms under him,
Their King and head, and made a realm and reigned.

And thus the land of Cameliard was waste,
Thick with wet woods, and many a beast therein, 21
And none or few to scare or chase the beast;
So that wild dog and wolf and boar and bear
Came night and day, and rooted in the fields,
And wallowed in the gardens of the King. 25
And ever and anon the wolf would steal
The children and devour, but now and then,
Her own brood lost or dead, lent her fierce teat
To human sucklings; and the children, housed
In her foul den, there at their meat would growl, 30
And mock their foster-mother on four feet,
Till, straightened, they grew up to wolf-like men,
Worse than the wolves. And King Leodogran
Groaned for the Roman legions here again
And Caesar's eagle: then his brother King, 35
Urien, assailed him: last a heathen horde,
Reddening the sun with smoke and earth with blood,
And on the spike that split the mother's heart
Spitting the child, brake on him, till, amazed,
He knew not whither he should turn for aid. 40

But—for he heard of Arthur newly crowned,
Though not without an uproar made by those
Who cried, "He is not Uther's son"—the King
Sent to him, saying, "Arise, and help us thou!
For here between the man and beast we die." 45

And Arthur yet had done no deed of arms,
But heard the call and came: and Guinevere
Stood by the castle walls to watch him pass;
But since he neither wore on helm or shield
The golden symbol of his kinglihood, 50
But rode a simple knight among his knights,
And many of these in richer arms than he,
She saw him not, or marked not, if she saw,
Once among many, though his face was bare.
But Arthur, looking downward as he passed
Felt the light of her eyes into his life 56
Smite on the sudden, yet rode on, and pitched
His tents beside the forest. Then he drave
The heathen; after, slew the beast, and felled
The forest, letting in the sun, and made 60
Broad pathways for the hunter and the knight,
And so returned.

    For while he lingered there,
A doubt that ever smoldered in the hearts
Of those great lords and barons of his realm 64
Flashed forth and into war; for most of these,
Colleaguing with a score of petty kings,
Made head against him, crying: "Who is he
That he should rule us? who hath proven him
King Uther's son? for lo! we look at him,
And find nor face nor bearing, limbs nor voice, 70
Are like to those of Uther whom we knew.
This is the son of Gorloïs, not the King:
This is the son of Anton, not the King."

And Arthur, passing thence to battle, felt
Travail, and throes and agonies of the life, 75
Desiring to be joined with Guinevere,
And thinking as he rode: "Her father said
That there between the man and beast they die.
Shall I not lift her from this land of beasts
Up to my throne and side by side with me? 80
What happiness to reign a lonely king,
Vexed—O ye stars that shudder over me,
O earth that soundest hollow under me,
Vexed with waste dreams? for saving I be joined
To her that is the fairest under heaven, 85
I seem as nothing in the mighty world,
And cannot will my will nor work my work

---

31. **mock**, imitate. 34. **Roman legions.** These were withdrawn from Britain in 410 (see Vol. I, p. 3). 36. **Urien**, King of North Wales. **heathen horde**, the Scots and Picts from the North, or possibly the Angles and Saxons (see Vol. I, pp. 4 and 5).

50. **golden symbol**, the dragon of his father Uther; it was borne at the head of the army. 72. **Gorloïs**, the Lord of Tintagel, in Cornwall. See ll. 185 ff. 73. **Anton.** See ll. 221 ff.

Wholly, nor make myself in mine own realm
Victor and lord. But were I joined with her,
Then might we live together as one life,   90
And reigning with one will in everything
Have power on this dark land to lighten it,
And power on this dead world to make it
    live."

    Thereafter—as he speaks who tells the
    tale—   94
When Arthur reached a field of battle bright
With pitched pavilions of his foe, the world
Was all so clear about him that he saw
The smallest rock far on the faintest hill,
And even in high day the morning star.   99
So when the King had set his banner broad,
At once from either side, with trumpet-blast,
And shouts, and clarions shrilling unto blood,
The long-lanced battle let their horses run.
And now the barons and the kings prevailed,
And now the King, as here and there that
    war   105
Went swaying; but the Powers who walk the
    world
Made lightnings and great thunders over him,
And dazed all eyes, till Arthur by main
    might,
And mightier of his hands with every blow,
And leading all his knighthood threw the
    kings   110
Carádos, Urien, Cradlemont of Wales,
Claudius, and Clariance of Northumberland,
The King Brandagoras of Latangor,
With Anguisant of Erin, Morganore,
And Lot of Orkney. Then, before a voice   115
As dreadful as the shout of one who sees
To one who sins, and deems himself alone
And all the world asleep, they swerved and
    brake
Flying, and Arthur called to stay the brands
That hacked among the flyers, "Ho! they
    yield!"   120
So like a painted battle the war stood
Silenced, the living quiet as the dead,
And in the heart of Arthur joy was lord.
He laughed upon his warrior whom he loved

And honored most. "Thou dost not doubt me
    King,   125
So well thine arm hath wrought for me to-
    day."
"Sir and my liege," he cried, "the fire of God
Descends upon thee in the battlefield:
I know thee for my King!" Whereat the two,
For each had warded either in the fight,   130
Sware on the field of death a deathless love.
And Arthur said, "Man's word is God in
    man:
Let chance what will, I trust thee to the
    death."

    Then quickly from the foughten field he
    sent
Ulfius, and Brastias, and Bedivere,   135
His new-made knights, to King Leodogran,
Saying, "If I in aught have served thee well,
Give me thy daughter Guinevere to wife."

    Whom when he heard, Leodogran in heart
Debating—"How should I that am a king,   140
However much he holp me at my need,
Give my one daughter saving to a king,
And a king's son?"—lifted his voice, and
    called
A hoary man, his chamberlain, to whom
He trusted all things, and of him required   145
His counsel: "Knowest thou aught of Ar-
    thur's birth?"

    Then spake the hoary chamberlain and said:
"Sir King, there be but two old men that
    know;
And each is twice as old as I: and one
Is Merlin, the wise man that ever served   150
King Uther through his magic art; and one
Is Merlin's master—so they call him—Bleys,
Who taught him magic; but the scholar ran
Before the master, and so far that Bleys   154
Laid magic by, and sat him down, and wrote
All things and whatsoever Merlin did
In one great annal-book, where after-years
Will learn the secret of our Arthur's birth."

    To whom the King Leodogran replied:
"O friend, had I been holpen half as well   160

---

94. **he,** Malory. See Vol. I, p. 277.   99. **high day,** noon.
102. **shrilling unto blood,** calling to battle.   103. **long-lanced
battle,** mounted knights with long lances.   115. **Orkney,** a
group of islands north of Scotland.   124. **warrior . . . loved,**
Lancelot.

150. **Merlin,** the magician of Arthur's court.

By this King Arthur as by thee today,
Then beast and man had had their share of me;
But summon here before us yet once more
Ulfius, and Brastias, and Bedivere."

Then, when they came before him, the King said: 165
"I have seen the cuckoo chased by lesser fowl,
And reason in the chase; but wherefore now
Do these your lords stir up the heat of war,
Some calling Arthur born of Gorloïs,
Others of Anton? Tell me, ye yourselves 170
Hold ye this Arthur for King Uther's son?"

And Ulfius and Brastias answered, "Ay."
Then Bedivere, the first of all his knights
Knighted by Arthur at his crowning, spake—
For bold in heart and act and word was he, 175
Whenever slander breathed against the King—

"Sir, there be many rumors on this head:
For there be those who hate him in their hearts,
Call him baseborn, and since his ways are sweet,
And theirs are bestial, hold him less than man; 180
And there be those who deem him more than man,
And dream he dropped from heaven: but my belief
In all this matter—so ye care to learn—
Sir, for ye know that in King Uther's time 184
The prince and warrior Gorloïs, he that held
Tintagil castle by the Cornish sea,
Was wedded with a winsome wife, Ygerne;
And daughters had she borne him—one whereof,
Lot's wife, the Queen of Orkney, Bellicent,
Hath ever like a loyal sister cleaved 190
To Arthur—but a son she had not borne.
And Uther cast upon her eyes of love;
But she, a stainless wife to Gorloïs,
So loathed the bright dishonor of his love
That Gorloïs and King Uther went to war, 195
And overthrown was Gorloïs and slain.
Then Uther in his wrath and heat besieged
Ygerne within Tintagil, where her men,
Seeing the mighty swarm about their walls,
Left her and fled, and Uther entered in, 200
And there was none to call to but himself.
So, compassed by the power of the King,
Enforced she was to wed him in her tears,
And with a shameful swiftness; afterward, 204
Not many moons, King Uther died himself,
Moaning and wailing for an heir to rule
After him, lest the realm should go to wrack.
And that same night, the night of the new year,
By reason of the bitterness and grief
That vexed his mother, all before his time 210
Was Arthur born, and all as soon as born
Delivered at a secret postern-gate
To Merlin, to be holden far apart
Until his hour should come; because the lords
Of that fierce day were as the lords of this, 215
Wild beasts, and surely would have torn the child
Piecemeal among them, had they known; for each
But sought to rule for his own self and hand,
And many hated Uther for the sake 219
Of Gorloïs. Wherefore Merlin took the child,
And gave him to Sir Anton, an old knight
And ancient friend of Uther; and his wife
Nursed the young prince, and reared him with her own;
And no man knew. And ever since the lords
Have foughten like wild beasts among themselves, 225
So that the realm has gone to wrack; but now,
This year, when Merlin—for his hour had come—
Brought Arthur forth, and set him in the hall,
Proclaiming, 'Here is Uther's heir, your King,'
A hundred voices cried: 'Away with him! 230
No king of ours! a son of Gorloïs he;
Or else the child of Anton, and no king,
Or else baseborn.' Yet Merlin, through his craft,
And while the people clamored for a king,
Had Arthur crowned; but after, the great lords 235
Banded, and so brake out in open war."

---

166. **cuckoo . . . fowl.** The cuckoo destroys eggs of other birds and lays its own eggs in their nests.

Then while the King debated with himself
If Arthur were the child of shamefulness,
Or born the son of Gorloïs after death,
Or Uther's son and born before his time, 240
Or whether there were truth in anything
Said by these three, there came to Cameliard,
With Gawain and young Modred, her two sons,
Lot's wife, the Queen of Orkney, Bellicent; 244
Whom as he could, not as he would, the King
Made feast for, saying, as they sat at meat:
"A doubtful throne is ice on summer seas.
Ye come from Arthur's court. Victor his men
Report him! Yea, but ye—think ye this king— 249
So many those that hate him, and so strong,
So few his knights, however brave they be—
Hath body enow to hold his foemen down?"

"O King," she cried, "and I will tell thee: few,
Few, but all brave, all of one mind with him;
For I was near him when the savage yells 255
Of Uther's peerage died, and Arthur sat
Crowned on the daïs, and his warriors cried,
'Be thou the king, and we will work thy will
Who love thee.' Then the King in low deep tones,
And simple words of great authority, 260
Bound them by so strait vows to his own self
That when they rose, knighted from kneeling, some
Were pale as at the passing of a ghost,
Some flushed, and others dazed, as one who wakes
Half-blinded at the coming of a light. 265

"But when he spake, and cheered his Table Round
With large, divine, and comfortable words,
Beyond my tongue to tell thee—I beheld
From eye to eye through all their Order flash
A momentary likeness of the King; 270
And ere it left their faces, through the cross
And those around it and the Crucified,
Down from the casement over Arthur, smote
Flame-color, vert, and azure, in three rays,
One falling upon each of three fair queens 275
Who stood in silence near his throne, the friends
Of Arthur, gazing on him, tall, with bright
Sweet faces, who will help him at his need.

"And there I saw mage Merlin, whose vast wit
And hundred winters are but as the hands 280
Of loyal vassals toiling for their liege.

"And near him stood the Lady of the Lake,
Who knows a subtler magic than his own—
Clothed in white samite, mystic, wonderful.
She gave the King his huge cross-hilted sword, 285
Whereby to drive the heathen out: a mist
Of incense curled about her, and her face
Wellnigh was hidden in the minster gloom;
But there was heard among the holy hymns
A voice as of the waters, for she dwells 290
Down in a deep—calm, whatsoever storms
May shake the world—and when the surface rolls,
Hath power to walk the waters like our Lord.

"There likewise I beheld Excalibur 294
Before him at his crowning borne, the sword
That rose from out the bosom of the lake,
And Arthur rowed across and took it—rich
With jewels, elfin Urim, on the hilt,
Bewildering heart and eye—the blade so bright
That men are blinded by it—on one side, 300
Graven in the oldest tongue of all this world,
'Take me,' but turn the blade and ye shall see,
And written in the speech ye speak yourself,
'Cast me away!' And sad was Arthur's face
Taking it, but old Merlin counseled him, 305
'Take thou and strike! the time to cast away
Is yet far-off.' So this great brand the King
Took, and by this will beat his foemen down."

Thereat Leodogran rejoiced, but thought
To sift his doubtings to the last, and asked, 310
Fixing full eyes of question on her face,
"The swallow and the swift are near akin,
But thou art closer to this noble prince,

---

274. **vert**, green. 275. **fair queens**. These were fairies.

279. **mage**, magician. 282. **Lady of the Lake**, a fairy, well-known in romances and fairy tales. In the allegory of the *Idylls* she typifies the power of religion. 284. **samite**, a rich silk fabric. 301. **oldest tongue**, Hebrew.

Being his own dear sister"; and she said,
"Daughter of Gorloïs and Ygerne am I"; 315
"And therefore Arthur's sister?" asked the
    King.
She answered, "These be secret things," and
    signed
To those two sons to pass, and let them be.
And Gawain went, and breaking into song
Sprang out, and followed by his flying hair 320
Ran like a colt, and leaped at all he saw;
But Modred laid his ear beside the doors,
And there half-heard—the same that after-
    ward
Struck for the throne, and striking found his
    doom.

    And then the Queen made answer: "What
        know I? 325
For dark my mother was in eyes and hair,
And dark in hair and eyes am I; and dark
Was Gorloïs; yea, and dark was Uther too,
Wellnigh to blackness; but this King is fair
Beyond the race of Britons and of men. 330
Moreover, always in my mind I hear
A cry from out the dawning of my life,
A mother weeping, and I hear her say,
'O that ye had some brother, pretty one,
To guard thee on the rough ways of the
    world.'" 335

    "Ay," said the King, "and hear ye such a
        cry?
But when did Arthur chance upon thee first?"

    "O King!" she cried, "and I will tell thee
        true:
He found me first when yet a little maid:
Beaten I had been for a little fault 340
Whereof I was not guilty; and out I ran
And flung myself down on a bank of heath,
And hated this fair world and all therein,
And wept, and wished that I were dead; and
    he—
I know not whether of himself he came, 345
Or brought by Merlin, who, they say, can
    walk
Unseen at pleasure—he was at my side,
And spake sweet words, and comforted my
    heart,
And dried my tears, being a child with me.

And many a time he came, and evermore 350
As I grew greater grew with me; and sad
At times he seemed, and sad with him was I,
Stern too at times, and then I loved him not,
But sweet again, and then I loved him well.
And now of late I see him less and less, 355
But those first days had golden hours for me,
For then I surely thought he would be king.

    "But let me tell thee now another tale:
For Bleys, our Merlin's master, as they say,
Died but of late, and sent his cry to me, 360
To hear him speak before he left his life.
Shrunk like a fairy changeling lay the mage;
And when I entered told me that himself
And Merlin ever served about the King,
Uther, before he died; and on the night 365
When Uther in Tintagil passed away
Moaning and wailing for an heir, the two
Left the still King, and passing forth to
    breathe,
Then from the castle gateway by the chasm
Descending through the dismal night—a
    night 370
In which the bounds of heaven and earth were
    lost—
Beheld, so high upon the dreary deeps
It seemed in heaven, a ship, the shape thereof
A dragon winged, and all from stem to stern
Bright with a shining people on the decks, 375
And gone as soon as seen. And then the two
Dropped to the cove, and watched the great
    sea fall,
Wave after wave, each mightier than the last,
Till last, a ninth one, gathering half the deep
And full of voices, slowly rose and plunged 380
Roaring, and all the wave was in a flame:
And down the wave and in the flame was
    borne
A naked babe, and rode to Merlin's feet,
Who stooped and caught the babe and cried,
    'The King! 384
Here is an heir for Uther!' And the fringe
Of that great breaker, sweeping up the strand,
Lashed at the wizard as he spake the word,
And all at once all round him rose in fire,
So that the child and he were clothed in fire.

362. **Shrunk . . . changeling.** According to an old superstition healthy children were taken from their cradles by fairies, who left their own weakly children. Cf. Yeats's *Stolen Child*, p. 1026.

And presently thereafter followed calm,   390
Free sky and stars: 'And this same child,' he said,
'Is he who reigns; nor could I part in peace
Till this were told.' And saying this the seer
Went through the strait and dreadful pass of death,
Not ever to be questioned any more   395
Save on the further side; but when I met
Merlin, and asked him if these things were truth—
The shining dragon and the naked child
Descending in the glory of the seas—   399
He laughed as is his wont, and answered me
In riddling triplets of old time, and said—

'Rain, rain, and sun! a rainbow in the sky!
A young man will be wiser by and by;
An old man's wit may wander ere he die.   404

'Rain, rain, and sun! a rainbow on the lea!
And truth is this to me, and that to thee;
And truth or clothed or naked let it be.

'Rain, sun, and rain! and the free blossom blows:
Sun, rain, and sun! and where is he who knows?
From the great deep to the great deep he goes.'   410

"So Merlin riddling angered me; but thou
Fear not to give this King thine only child,
Guinevere: so great bards of him will sing
Hereafter; and dark sayings from of old
Ranging and ringing through the minds of men,   415
And echoed by old folk beside their fires
For comfort after their wage-work is done,
Speak of the King; and Merlin in our time
Hath spoken also, not in jest, and sworn
Though men may wound him that he will not die,   420
But pass, again to come, and then or now
Utterly smite the heathen underfoot,
Till these and all men hail him for their king."

She spake and King Leodogran rejoiced,
But musing "Shall I answer yea or nay?"   425
Doubted, and drowsed, nodded and slept, and saw,
Dreaming, a slope of land that ever grew,
Field after field, up to a height, the peak
Haze-hidden, and thereon a phantom king,
Now looming, and now lost; and on the slope
The sword rose, the hind fell, the herd was driven,   431
Fire glimpsed; and all the land from roof and rick,
In drifts of smoke before a rolling wind,
Streamed to the peak, and mingled with the haze   434
And made it thicker; while the phantom king
Sent out at times a voice; and here or there
Stood one who pointed toward the voice, the rest
Slew on and burnt, crying, "No king of ours,
No son of Uther, and no King of ours";
Till with a wink his dream was changed, the haze   440
Descended, and the solid earth became
As nothing, but the King stood out in heaven,
Crowned. And Leodogran awoke, and sent
Ulfius, and Brastias, and Bedivere,
Back to the court of Arthur answering yea.   445

Then Arthur charged his warrior whom he loved
And honored most, Sir Lancelot, to ride forth
And bring the Queen, and watched him from the gates;
And Lancelot passed away among the flowers—
For then was latter April—and returned   450
Among the flowers, in May, with Guinevere.
To whom arrived, by Dubric the high saint,
Chief of the church in Britain, and before
The stateliest of her altar-shrines, the King
That morn was married, while in stainless white,   455
The fair beginners of a nobler time,
And glorying in their vows and him, his knights
Stood round him, and rejoicing in his joy.

391. **Free,** clear.

431. **hind fell,** peasants were killed. **herd was driven,** cattle were driven away by robbers. 432. **rick,** stack of grain or hay. 452. **Dubric,** the ambassador of the Pope.

Far shone the fields of May through open
    door,   459
The sacred altar blossomed white with May,
The Sun of May descended on their King,
They gazed on all earth's beauty in their
    Queen,
Rolled incense, and there passed along the
    hymns
A voice as of the waters, while the two   464
Sware at the shrine of Christ a deathless
    love:
And Arthur said, "Behold, thy doom is mine.
Let chance what will, I love thee to the
    death!"
To whom the Queen replied with drooping
    eyes,
"King and my lord, I love thee to the death!"
And holy Dubric spread his hands and spake:
"Reign ye, and live and love, and make the
    world   471
Other, and may thy Queen be one with thee,
And all this Order of thy Table Round
Fulfill the boundless purpose of their King!"

    So Dubric said; but when they left the
    shrine,   475
Great lords from Rome before the portal
    stood,
In scornful stillness gazing as they passed;
Then while they paced a city all on fire
With sun and cloth of gold, the trumpets
    blew,
And Arthur's knighthood sang before the
    King—   480

    "Blow trumpet, for the world is white with
    May!
Blow trumpet, the long night hath rolled
    away!
Blow through the living world—'Let the
    King reign!'

    "Shall Rome or Heathen rule in Arthur's
    realm?
Flash brand and lance, fall battle-ax upon
    helm,   485
Fall battle-ax, and flash brand! Let the King
    reign!

    "Strike for the King and live! his knights
    have heard
That God hath told the King a secret word.
Fall battle-ax, and flash brand! Let the King
    reign!

    "Blow trumpet! he will lift us from the
    dust.   490
Blow trumpet! live the strength, and die the
    lust!
Clang battle-ax, and clash brand! Let the
    King reign!

    "Strike for the King and die! and if thou
    diest,
The King is king, and ever wills the highest.
Clang battle-ax, and clash brand! Let the
    King reign!   495

    "Blow, for our Sun is mighty in his May!
Blow, for our Sun is mightier day by day!
Clang battle-ax, and clash brand! Let the
    King reign!

    "The King will follow Christ, and we the
    King,
In whom high God hath breathed a secret
    thing.   500
Fall battle-ax, and clash brand! Let the King
    reign!"

    So sang the knighthood, moving to their
    hall.
There at the banquet those great lords from
    Rome,
The slowly fading mistress of the world,   504
Strode in and claimed their tribute as of yore.
But Arthur spake: "Behold, for these have
    sworn
To wage my wars, and worship me their
    King;
The old order changeth, yielding place to new;
And we that fight for our fair father Christ,
Seeing that ye be grown too weak and old 510
To drive the heathen from your Roman wall,
No tribute will we pay." So those great lords
Drew back in wrath, and Arthur strove with
    Rome.

---

460. **May,** hawthorn.

496. **Sun,** king. **May,** youth.

And Arthur and his knighthood for a
    space
Were all one will, and through that strength
    the King   515
Drew in the petty princedoms under him,
Fought, and in twelve great battles overcame
The heathen hordes, and made a realm and
    reigned.   (1869)

By an Evolutionist

This poem should be compared with Locksley Hall Sixty Years After, *page 618, and with Browning's* Rabbi Ben Ezra, *page 698.*

The Lord let the house of a brute to the soul
    of a man,
  And the man said, "Am I your debtor?"
And the Lord—"Not yet; but make it as
    clean as you can,
  And then I will let you a better."

1

If my body come from brutes, my soul uncertain or a fable,   5
  Why not bask amid the senses while the
    sun of morning shines,
I, the finer brute rejoicing in my hounds,
    and in my stable,
  Youth and health, and birth and wealth,
    and choice of women and of wines?

2

What hast thou done for me, grim Old Age,
    save breaking my bones on the rack?
  Would I had passed in the morning that
    looks so bright from afar!   10

Old Age

Done for thee? starved the wild beast that
    was linked with thee eighty years
    back.
  Less weight now for the ladder-of-heaven
    that hangs on a star.

1

If my body come from brutes, though somewhat finer than their own,
I am heir, and this my kingdom. Shall
    the royal voice be mute?
No, but if the rebel subject seek to drag me
    from the throne,   15
  Hold the scepter, Human Soul, and rule
    thy province of the brute.

2

I have climbed to the snows of Age, and I
    gaze at a field in the Past,
  Where I sank with the body at times in
    the sloughs of a low desire,
But I hear no yelp of the beast, and the Man
    is quiet at last,
  As he stands on the heights of his life with
    a glimpse of a height that is higher.
                                (1889)

Crossing the Bar

A few days before he died, Tennyson gave instructions that this lyric should be put at the end of all editions of his poems. Cf. Keats's Bright Star! Would I Were Steadfast As Thou Art, *p. 292, and Browning's* Epilogue to Asolando, *p. 708.*

Sunset and evening star,
  And one clear call for me!
And may there be no moaning of the bar,
  When I put out to sea,

But such a tide as moving seems asleep,   5
  Too full for sound and foam,
When that which drew from out the boundless deep
  Turns again home.

Twilight and evening bell,
  And after that the dark!   10
And may there be no sadness of farewell,
  When I embark;

For though from out our bourne of Time and
    Place
  The flood may bear me far,
I hope to see my Pilot face to face   15
  When I have crossed the bar.   (1889)

Robert Browning
1812-1889

"Two poets in two different ages born" could hardly have been more unlike than were the Victorian contemporaries, Tennyson and Browning. Tennyson was thoroughly English; Browning was a citizen of the world, or at least of Europe. Tennyson was learned without being erudite; Browning was so erudite that his thoughts often sank to depths from which the ordinary reader could not recover them. Tennyson was popular, and his poetry was, on the whole, so simple that it offered little challenge to the lover of the cryptic and the mystic. No Tennyson Clubs needed to gather their collective brains to understand him. Browning's poetry, on the other hand, was much admired by his contemporaries but not much read and understood by them. His poems did not yield their meaning without much wrestling, for he dealt in sharper analyses of character than were possible to Tennyson, loved out-of-the-way problems and startlingly new deductions from them, cared little for smooth easiness of phrase, used a realism of detail and word that was alien to the prevailing poetic manner, and developed what was in effect a new poetic form—the dramatic monologue, in which background, mood, thought were all revealed through the speech of a single chief character on a significant, or at least self-revealing, occasion in his life. Twentieth-century poetry is, on the whole, more like that of Browning than like that of Tennyson. In comparison, indeed, with some of its cryptic and compressed obscurities, much of the difficulty of Browning's poetry vanishes. And his sharp originality, his trenchant phrasing, have won their way. In his own day, however, readers who preferred to feel rather than to think were repelled by his rough intellectuality and by the challenge which his poetry offered to their minds.

Browning's father was a well-to-do clerk in the Bank of England. He had a large library of classical and modern books and a genuine interest in reading. When his son Robert was born, he was prepared, therefore, to give him more than the usual bringing up. Except for a little schooling at Peckham and a few lectures at the University of London in 1829-1830, Browning got his education entirely from private tutors and from his own reading in his father's library and elsewhere. Thus he became that rare person, an English writer who had not attended an English university, but who was, nevertheless, one of the most learned men of his time.

Save for a little volume of boyish verse privately printed by his father under the title *Incondita*, Browning's first publication was *Pauline*, 1833. The expenses of this publication were paid by a benevolent aunt, and the poem made no stir whatever. The influence that it reveals is that of Shelley—not Keats, who was at the same time undergoing a reincarnation in the early poems of Tennyson. The next year Browning went to St. Petersburg and thence to Italy, the first of a number of sojourns in Europe that kept him out of England for a good part of his life. On his return in 1835 he published *Paracelsus*, a dramatic poem based on the life of the fifteenth-century magician and alchemist. In the selection of this subject and the treatment of it Browning displayed early his fondness for Renaissance subjects and his interest in men and their motives, for nothing, he once remarked, but human beings interested him much. At the request of the producer Macready, Browning next attempted a play. *Strafford*, based on the tragedy of the minister of Charles I (see Vol. I, p. 634), was the first of the poet's dramatic failures; it ran only five nights at Covent Garden in 1836. The long and remarkably obscure and difficult poem of *Sordello* appeared in 1840; its erudition, its detail, its general profundity did a great deal toward giving Browning a reputation for being unintelligible and for limiting at the start his circle of readers. To popularize his work, his publishers issued many of his poems, between 1841 and 1846, in eight cheap pamphlets under the general title of *Bells and Pomegranates;* this series contained among other items *Pippa Passes, A Blot in the 'Scutcheon,* and some of the best of his dramatic monologues (1843).

In 1846 occurred one of the most important events in the poet's life, his marriage to Elizabeth Barrett. She was six years his senior, and her reputation as a poet far exceeded his. He fell in love with her poems, then with her. They were secretly married in September and left almost immediately for Italy, partly because of the state of Mrs. Browning's health and partly that she might get beyond the range of influence of a domineering and possessive Victorian father. In spite of the disparity of their ages, the marriage was ideal. The two poets were developed by their sympathetic companionship and by the idyllic life which they lived at Casa Guidi in Florence from 1848 until Mrs. Browning's death thirteen years later. They became interested in Italian politics and Italian art, and their poetry—that of Browning especially—bears the impress of this long sojourn in a country that became a second fatherland to them. Here Browning wrote *Christmas Eve and Easter Day* (1850) and—most important of all—*Men and Women* (1855).

The death of his wife changed the poet's whole manner of life. He returned almost immediately to England and settled in Warwick Crescent, London. At first he was a recluse, but his own sound philosophy soon drove him from this way of living, and he again traveled and accepted social engagements. He also continued to write. *Dramatis Personae* appeared in 1864, and four years later he issued in four volumes the remarkable many-faceted poem entitled *The Ring and the Book.* It did much to establish his contemporary reputation.

Browning's *Ring and the Book* is based upon a Roman murder case which the poet found related in an old, parchment-covered volume that he picked up from a second-hand bookstall in Florence. This is "the book"; "the ring" is the symbol of the poet's making of the story into a perfect circle of truth by adding, as a jeweler would do to a real ring, some of himself as the alloy. The tale has to do with the trial of a dissolute and impoverished count, Guido Franceschini, for the murder of his base-born wife, Pompilia, on his discovery that he had been tricked into marriage with her by the misrepresentations of her foster parents that she was an heiress. Involved in the trial was a young canon, Giuseppe Caponsacchi, who had interfered in behalf of the girl and had helped her escape from her brutal husband; the count ultimately found and mortally wounded her at the home of her foster parents. Count Guido was pronounced guilty in the papal court and sentenced to be executed. The astonishing character of the poem lies in the fact that Browning repeats the story of the crime and trial ten times, each time from the point of view of a different person or group of persons; thus the stories of the murderer, the murdered girl, and the canon appear as do the arguments of the attorneys, the opinions of the Roman populace, and finally that of the Pope. So skilfully, however, has the whole structure been handled that no monotony from the repetition is evident; on the contrary, each division of the poem is vivid in its revelation of the story through the soul of the character speaking. The poem is, in effect, a brilliant succession of dramatic monologues built around a single series of episodes.

The Ring and the Book was Browning's poetic capstone. In the last two decades of his life he produced some few truly great poems but much that was grotesque and fantastic. He turned, too, to translations and transcriptions from the Greek tragedies; in spite of some powerful passages, these were not highly successful attempts. In 1878, for the first time since his wife's death, the poet revisited Italy. Seven years later he negotiated unsuccessfully for a house in Venice, intending to make it his permanent home. He died in 1889 in the Venetian palazzo owned by his son. His body lies in Westminster Abbey not far from that of Tennyson, who died three years later.

In his own time, as has been said, Browning never achieved the popularity of Tennyson. In the years since his death, however, his reputation has been steadily growing, and it is likely that he has more influence today than Tennyson, who seems "cabined, cribbed, and confined" in the mold of Victorianism. In spite of the difficulty of such poems as *Sordello*, and the fantastic grotesqueness of some of those which came after *The Ring and the Book*, Browning's real power as a poet is becoming increasingly recognized and regarded. He has in all his work a high degree of force. His poetry always marches; it never seems static, like so much of Tennyson's. And as a delineator of the souls of men and women he probably has no equal in Victorian literature; with great directness and power he stripped off the exteriors and exposed the quivering characters beneath, forcing them, indeed, in his dramatic monologues, to reveal their own strength and weakness. But his knowledge that human souls are often leprous did not destroy his love of humanity. There is little of the merely sentimental in Browning's poems, and nothing of the mawkish; on the contrary, there is a great deal of sturdy optimism and faith in humanity which is bracing despite his suggestion of the ills to which all flesh is inevitably subject. Finally, there is in his verse a new realism of phrase, strong, rugged, and often lacking polish. Browning was a good metrist, but he did not have Tennyson's interest in meter for its own sake. That he was a facile craftsman in verse, however, who could secure almost any effect he wished, is revealed in such poems as *The Pied Piper of Hamelin*, the *Songs* from *Pippa Passes*, and *How They Brought the Good News*. His philosophy, his vision, his penetration, and his technique were all those of a potent, idiosyncratic personality, whose power is more highly understood and regarded today than it was in his own time.

Songs from *Pippa Passes*

Pippa Passes is a dramatic poem in which Pippa, the little silk-winder of Asolo, Italy, goes singing through the streets of the village on New Year's Day, her one holiday, and unconsciously influences the lives and actions of others.

All service ranks the same with God:
If now, as formerly he trod
Paradise, his presence fills
Our earth, each only as God wills
Can work—God's puppets, best and worst,   5
Are we; there is no last nor first.

Say not "a small event!" Why "small"?
Costs it more pain that this, ye call
A "great event," should come to pass,
Than that? Untwine me from the mass   10
Of deeds which make up life, one deed
Power shall fall short in or exceed!

———

The year's at the spring
And day's at the morn;
Morning's at seven;
The hillside's dew-pearled;
The lark's on the wing;   5
The snail's on the thorn:
God's in his heaven—
All's right with the world!

Overhead the tree-tops meet,
Flowers and grass spring 'neath one's feet;
There was naught above me, naught below,
My childhood had not learned to know;
For, what are the voices of birds 5
—Aye, and of beasts—but words, our words,
Only so much more sweet?
The knowledge of that with my life begun.
But I had so near made out the sun,
And counted your stars, the seven and one, 10
Like the fingers of my hand.
Nay, I could all but understand
Wherefore through heaven the white moon ranges;
And just when out of her soft fifty changes
No unfamiliar face might overlook me— 15
Suddenly God took me.

(1841)

Cavalier Tunes

The three songs under this title express the loyalty of the Cavaliers to King Charles I of England (1625-1649) and their contempt for his Puritan enemies. (See Vol. I, pp. 634 ff.)

1. MARCHING ALONG

Kentish Sir Byng stood for his King,
Bidding the crop-headed Parliament swing;
And, pressing a troop unable to stoop
And see the rogues flourish and honest folk droop,
Marched them along, fifty-score strong, 5
Great-hearted gentlemen, singing this song:

God for King Charles! Pym and such carles
To the Devil that prompts 'em their treasonous parles!
Cavaliers, up! Lips from the cup,
Hands from the pasty, nor bite take nor sup 10
Till you're—

CHORUS—

Marching along, fifty-score strong,
Great-hearted gentlemen, singing this song.

Hampden to hell, and his obsequies' knell
Serve Hazelrig, Fiennes, and young Harry as well! 15
England, good cheer! Rupert is near!
Kentish and loyalists, keep we not here,

CHORUS—

Marching along, fifty-score strong,
Great-hearted gentlemen, singing this song?

Then, God for King Charles! Pym and his snarls 20
To the Devil that pricks on such pestilent carles!
Hold by the right, you double your might;
So, onward to Nottingham, fresh for the fight,

CHORUS—

Marching along, fifty-score strong,
Great-hearted gentlemen, singing this song.

2. GIVE A ROUSE

King Charles, and who'll do him right now?
King Charles, and who's ripe for fight now?
Give a rouse; here's, in hell's despite now,
King Charles!
Who gave me the goods that went since? 5
Who raised me the house that sank once?
Who helped me to gold I spent since?
Who found me in wine you drank once?

---

10. **seven and one**, the Pleiades (consisting of seven stars) and one other star.
Marching Along. 2. **crop-headed Parliament**, the Parliament of 1640, controlled by the Puritans, who wore their hair short in protest against the fashion of the Cavaliers, who wore theirs long and in curls. 3. **pressing**, pressing into service. 7. **Pym**, John Pym (1584-1643), a leader of Parliament against the King. **carles**, churls. 8. **parles**, debates.

14. **Hampden**, John Hampden (1594-1643), associated with Pym in Parliament. 15. **Hazelrig, Fiennes, and young Harry.** The Puritans were aided by Sir Arthur Hazelrig, Nathaniel Fiennes, and Sir Henry Vane, son of the elder Sir Henry Vane, one of Charles's secretaries. Young Harry was Governor of Massachusetts Bay Colony, 1636-1637. He was executed for treason after the accession of Charles II. 16. **Rupert**, Rupert, Prince of Bavaria (1619-1682), a nephew of Charles I and commander of his cavalry. 23. **Nottingham.** The first stand of the Royalists was made at Nottingham, a city in central England, in August, 1642.
Give a Rouse. A rouse is a shout that accompanies drinking. 8. **found me in**, supplied me with.

CHORUS—
> *King Charles, and who'll do him right now?*
> *King Charles, and who's ripe for fight now?* 10
> *Give a rouse; here's, in hell's despite now, King Charles.*

To whom used my boy George quaff else,
By the old fool's side that begot him?
For whom did he cheer and laugh else, 15
While Noll's damned troopers shot him?

CHORUS—
> *King Charles, and who'll do him right now?*
> *King Charles, and who's ripe for fight now?*
> *Give a rouse; here's, in hell's despite now, King Charles.* 20

3. BOOT AND SADDLE

Boot, saddle, to horse, and away!
Rescue my castle before the hot day
Brightens to blue from its silvery gray.

CHORUS—
> *Boot, saddle, to horse, and away!*

Ride past the suburbs, asleep as you'd say; 5
Many's the friend there, will listen and pray,
"God's luck to gallants that strike up the lay—

CHORUS—
> *Boot, saddle, to horse, and away!"*

Forty miles off, like a roebuck at bay,
Flouts Castle Brancepeth the Roundheads' array; 10
Who laughs, "Good fellows ere this, by my fay,

CHORUS—
> *Boot, saddle, to horse, and away!"*

Who? My wife Gertrude; that, honest and gay,

---

16. **Noll**, a contemptuous nickname for Cromwell, leader of the Puritans.
Boot and Saddle. 10. **Brancepeth**, the castle of the Royalist nobleman who sings the song; it is situated near Durham.

Laughs when you talk of surrendering, "Nay!
I've better counselors; what counsel they? 15

CHORUS—
> *Boot, saddle, to horse, and away!"*

(1842)

My Last Duchess

The speaker is the Duke of Ferrara. Ferrara is an old and proud city in northern Italy. The Duke is negotiating with an envoy for the hand of a Count's daughter.

FERRARA

That's my last Duchess painted on the wall,
Looking as if she were alive. I call
That piece a wonder, now; Frà Pandolf's hands
Worked busily a day, and there she stands.
Will 't please you sit and look at her? I said 5
"Frà Pandolf" by design, for never read
Strangers like you that pictured countenance,
The depth and passion of its earnest glance,
But to myself they turned (since none puts by
The curtain I have drawn for you, but I) 10
And seemed as they would ask me, if they durst,
How such a glance came there; so, not the first
Are you to turn and ask thus. Sir, 'twas not
Her husband's presence only, called that spot
Of joy into the Duchess' cheek; perhaps 15
Frà Pandolf chanced to say, "Her mantle laps
Over my lady's wrist too much," or "Paint
Must never hope to reproduce the faint
Half-flush that dies along her throat." Such stuff
Was courtesy, she thought, and cause enough
For calling up that spot of joy. She had 21
A heart—how shall I say?—too soon made glad,
Too easily impressed; she liked whate'er
She looked on, and her looks went everywhere.
Sir, 'twas all one! My favor at her breast, 25
The dropping of the daylight in the West,
The bough of cherries some officious fool

---

3. **Frà Pandolf**, an imaginary artist-monk.

Broke in the orchard for her, the white mule
She rode with round the terrace—all and each
Would draw from her alike the approving
    speech, 30
Or blush, at least. She thanked men—good!
    but thanked
Somehow—I know not how—as if she ranked
My gift of a nine-hundred-years-old name
With anybody's gift. Who'd stoop to blame
This sort of trifling? Even had you skill 35
In speech—which I have not—to make your
    will
Quite clear to such an one, and say, "Just this
Or that in you disgusts me; here you miss,
Or there exceed the mark"—and if she let
Herself be lessoned so, nor plainly set 40
Her wits to yours, forsooth, and made ex-
    cuse—
E'en then would be some stooping; and I
    choose
Never to stoop. Oh, sir, she smiled, no doubt,
Whene'er I passed her; but who passed with-
    out
Much the same smile? This grew; I gave
    commands; 45
Then all smiles stopped together. There she
    stands
As if alive. Will 't please you rise? We'll
    meet
The company below, then. I repeat,
The Count your master's known munifi-
    cence
Is ample warrant that no just pretense 50
Of mine for dowry will be disallowed;
Though his fair daughter's self, as I avowed
At starting, is my object. Nay, we'll go
Together down, sir. Notice Neptune, though,
Taming a sea-horse, thought a rarity, 55
Which Claus of Innsbruck cast in bronze for
    me! (1842)

45. **commands . . . together.** Browning said that he meant that "the commands were that she should be put to death, or he might have had her shut up in a convent." 54. **Neptune,** god of the sea. 56. **Claus of Innsbruck,** an imaginary sculptor. Innsbruck, the capital of Tyrol in Austria, is noted for its bronze work on the tomb of the Emperor Maximilian (1459-1519).

In a Gondola

    One of Browning's poems descriptive of paintings. The first stanza was written on his hearing of *The Serenade*, a painting by Daniel Maclise (1806-1870); after he had seen the picture, he completed the poem.

He sings:

I send my heart up to thee, all my heart
    In this my singing.
For the stars help me, and the sea bears part;
    The very night is clinging
Closer to Venice' streets to leave one space 5
    Above me, whence thy face
May light my joyous heart to thee its dwelling-
    place.

She speaks:

Say after me, and try to say
    My very words, as if each word
Came from you of your own accord, 10
    In your own voice, in your own way:
"This woman's heart and soul and brain
    Are mine as much as this gold chain
She bids me wear; which" (say again)
    "I choose to make by cherishing 15
A precious thing, or choose to fling
    Over the boat-side, ring by ring."
And yet once more say—no word more!
Since words are only words. Give o'er!

Unless you call me, all the same, 20
    Familiarly by my pet name,
Which if the Three should hear you call,
    And me reply to, would proclaim
At once our secret to them all.
Ask of me, too, command me, blame— 25
    Do, break down the partition-wall
'Twixt us, the daylight world beholds
    Curtained in dusk and splendid folds!
What's left but—all of me to take?
I am the Three's; prevent them, slake 30
    Your thirst! 'Tis said, the Arab sage,
In practicing with gems, can loose

22. **the Three,** her husband and his two friends or relatives, Paul and Gian. See ll. 106-107; *Himself* (l. 107) is her husband.

Their subtle spirit in his cruce
And leave but ashes; so, sweet mage,
Leave them my ashes when thy use   35
Sucks out my soul, thy heritage!

He sings:

Past we glide, and past, and past!
  What's that poor Agnese doing
Where they make the shutters fast?
  Gray Zanobi's just a-wooing   40
To his couch the purchased bride;
  Past we glide!

Past we glide, and past, and past!
  Why's the Pucci Palace flaring
Like a beacon to the blast?   45
  Guests by hundreds, not one caring
If the dear host's neck were wried;
  Past we glide!

She sings:

The moth's kiss, first!
Kiss me as if you made believe   50
You were not sure, this eve,
How my face, your flower, had pursed
Its petals up; so, here and there
You brush it, till I grow aware
Who wants me, and wide ope I burst.   55

The bee's kiss, now!
Kiss me as if you entered gay
My heart at some noonday,
A bud that dares not disallow
The claim, so all is rendered up,   60
And passively its shattered cup
Over your head to sleep I bow.

He sings:

What are we two?
I am a Jew,
And carry thee, farther than friends can
    pursue,   65
To a feast of our tribe;
Where they need thee to bribe
The devil that blasts them unless he imbibe
Thy—Scatter the vision forever! And now,
As of old, I am I, thou art thou!   70

33. **cruce**, crucible. 34. **mage**, magician.

Say again, what we are?
The sprite of a star,
I lure thee above where the destinies bar
My plumes their full play
Till a ruddier ray   75
Than my pale one announce there is wither-
    ing away
Some—Scatter the vision forever! And now,
As of old, I am I, thou art thou!

He muses:

Oh, which were best, to roam or rest?
The land's lap or the water's breast?   80
To sleep on yellow millet-sheaves,
Or swim in lucid shallows just
Eluding water-lily leaves,
An inch from Death's black fingers, thrust
To lock you, whom release he must;   85
Which life were best on summer eves?

He speaks, musing:

Lie back; could thought of mine improve you?
From this shoulder let there spring
A wing; from this, another wing;
Wings, not legs and feet, shall move you!   90
Snow-white must they spring, to blend
With your flesh, but I intend
They shall deepen to the end,

Broader, into burning gold,
Till both wings crescent-wise enfold   95
Your perfect self, from 'neath your feet
To o'er your head, where, lo, they meet
As if a million sword-blades hurled
Defiance from you to the world!

Rescue me thou, the only real!   100
And scare away this mad ideal
That came, nor motions to depart!
Thanks! Now, stay ever as thou art!

Still he muses:

What if the Three should catch at last
Thy serenader? While there's cast   105
Paul's cloak about my head, and fast
Gian pinions me, Himself has past
His stylet through my back; I reel;
And—is it thou I feel?

They trail me, these three godless knaves, 110
Past every church that saints and saves,
Nor stop till, where the cold sea raves
By Lido's wet accursèd graves,
They scoop mine, roll me to its brink,
And—on thy breast I sink! 115

She replies, musing:

Dip your arm o'er the boat-side, elbow-deep,
As I do—thus; were death so unlike sleep,
Caught this way? Death's to fear from flame or steel,
Or poison doubtless; but from water—feel!

Go find the bottom! Would you stay me? There! 120
Now pluck a great blade of that ribbon-grass
To plait in where the foolish jewel was,
I flung away; since you have praised my hair,
'Tis proper to be choice in what I wear.

He speaks:

Row home? must we row home? Too surely
Know I where its front's demurely 126
Over the Giudecca piled;
Window just with window mating,
Door on door exactly waiting,
All's the set face of a child; 130
But behind it, where's a trace
Of the staidness and reserve,
And formal lines without a curve,
In the same child's playing-face?
No two windows look one way 135
O'er the small sea-water thread
Below them. Ah, the autumn day
I, passing, saw you overhead!

First, out a cloud of curtain blew,
Then a sweet cry, and last came you— 140
To catch your lory that must needs
Escape just then, of all times then,
To peck a tall plant's fleecy seeds,
And make me happiest of men.
I scarce could breathe to see you reach 145
So far back o'er the balcony
To catch him ere he climbed too high
Above you in the Smyrna peach,
That quick the round smooth cord of gold,
This coiled hair on your head, unrolled, 150
Fell down you like a gorgeous snake
The Roman girls were wont, of old,
When Rome there was, for coolness' sake
To let lie curling o'er their bosoms.
Dear lory, may his beak retain 155
Ever its delicate rose stain
As if the wounded lotus-blossoms
Had marked their thief to know again!

Stay longer yet, for others' sake
Than mine! What should your chamber do?
—With all its rarities that ache 161
In silence while day lasts, but wake
At nighttime and their life renew,
Suspended just to pleasure you
Who brought against their will together 165
These objects, and, while day lasts, weave
Around them such a magic tether
That dumb they look; your harp, believe,
With all the sensitive tight strings
Which dare not speak, now to itself 170
Breathes slumberously, as if some elf
Went in and out the chords, his wings
Make murmur wheresoe'er they graze,
As an angel may, between the maze
Of midnight palace-pillars, on 175
And on, to sow God's plagues, have gone
Through guilty glorious Babylon.
And while such murmurs flow, the nymph
Bends o'er the harp-top from her shell
As the dry limpet for the lymph 180
Come with a tune he knows so well.
And how your statues' hearts must swell!
And how your pictures must descend
To see each other, friend with friend!
Oh, could you take them by surprise, 185
You'd find Schidone's eager Duke
Doing the quaintest courtesies

113. **Lido's ... graves,** the old Jewish cemetery on the Lido, a chain of sandy islands between the lagoons of Venice and the Adriatic Sea. 127. **the Giudecca,** one of the Venetian canals. 141. **lory,** a kind of parrot.

148. **the Smyrna peach,** a peach tree native to Smyrna, a province of Turkey. 151-154. **snake ... bosoms.** Classical writers—Lucian, Pliny, Cicero, Seneca, and others—tell of snakes being kept as pets in both Greece and Rome. 177. **Babylon,** the ancient capital of Babylonia; it was noted for its wealth and its wickedness. 180. **As ... well,** as the dry limpet on the rock or the shore thrusts himself out from his shell when he hears the familiar sound of the water. 186. **eager Duke,** a painting by Bartolommeo Schidone (1560-1616), an Italian artist.

To that prim saint by Haste-thee-Luke!
And, deeper into her rock den,
Bold Castelfranco's Magdalen 190
You'd find retreated from the ken
Of that robed counsel-keeping Ser—
As if the Tizian thinks of her,
And is not, rather, gravely bent
On seeing for himself what toys 195
Are these, his progeny invent,
What litter now the board employs
Whereon he signed a document
That got him murdered! Each enjoys
Its nights so well, you cannot break 200
The sport up, so, indeed must make
More stay with me, for others' sake.

She speaks:

Tomorrow, if a harp-string, say,
Is used to tie the jasmine back
That overfloods my room with sweets, 205
Contrive your Zorzi somehow meets
My Zanze! If the ribbon's black,
The Three are watching; keep away!

Your gondola—let Zorzi wreathe
A mesh of water-weeds about 210
Its prow, as if he unaware
Had struck some quay or bridge-foot stair!
That I may throw a paper out
As you and he go underneath.

There's Zanze's vigilant taper; safe are we. 215
Only one minute more tonight with me?
Resume your past self of a month ago!
Be you the bashful gallant; I will be
The lady with the colder breast than snow. 219
Now bow you, as becomes, nor touch my hand
More than I touch yours when I step to land,
And say, "All thanks, Siora!"—
                    Heart to heart

And lips to lips! Yet once more, ere we part,
Clasp me and make me thine, as mine thou art!

He is surprised, and stabbed.

It was ordained to be so, sweet!—and best
Comes now, beneath thine eyes, upon thy breast. 226
Still kiss me! Care not for the cowards! Care
Only to put aside thy beauteous hair
My blood will hurt! The Three, I do not scorn
To death, because they never lived; but I 230
Have lived indeed, and so—(yet one more kiss)—can die!   (1842)

The Laboratory

ANCIENT RÉGIME

The phrase *Ancient Régime* (Old Order), originally used to designate the period before the French Revolution, suggests that the incident here recorded is characteristic of former days. During the sixteenth and seventeenth centuries poisoning was a favorite means of getting rid of rivals and other objectionable persons, and regular schools of poisoners for this purpose flourished in Italy. The first water-color painted by D. G. Rossetti (see p. 783) illustrated this poem and was labeled "Which is the poison to poison her, prithee?"

Now that I, tying thy glass mask tightly,
May gaze through these faint smokes curling whitely,
As thou pliest thy trade in this devil's-smithy—
Which is the poison to poison her, prithee?

He is with her, and they know that I know 5
Where they are, what they do; they believe my tears flow
While they laugh, laugh at me, at me fled to the drear
Empty church, to pray God in, for them!—I am here.

Grind away, moisten and mash up thy paste,
Pound at thy powder—I am not in haste! 10

188. **Haste-thee-Luke,** the nickname of Luca Giordana (1632-1705), a painter of Naples. He was so called because his father constantly urged him to hurry. 190. **Castelfranco,** Giorgio Barbarelli (1478-1511), a painter born in the city of Castelfranco, in northern Italy. 192. **Ser,** an Italian title of courtesy, like *sir.* 193. **Tizian,** Tiziano Vecellio (1477-1576) (Titian), a noted Venetian painter called "Il Divino." His most famous paintings are the "Assumption of the Madonna," "The Tribute Money," "Holy Family and St. Catherine," "Ecce Homo," "Diana and Acteon." 206. **Zorzi,** his servant. 207. **Zanze,** her servant. 222. **Siora,** Venetian for Italian *Signora,* Lady.

Better sit thus, and observe thy strange things,
Than go where men wait me and dance at
  the King's.

That in the mortar—you call it a gum?
Ah, the brave tree whence such gold oozings
  come!
And yonder soft phial, the exquisite blue, 15
Sure to taste sweetly—is that poison too?

Had I but all of them, thee and thy treasures,
What a wild crowd of invisible pleasures!
To carry pure death in an earring, a casket,
A signet, a fan-mount, a filigree basket! 20

Soon, at the King's, a mere lozenge to give,
And Pauline should have just thirty minutes
  to live!
But to light a pastile, and Elise, with her head
And her breast and her arms and her hands,
  should drop dead!

Quick—is it finished? The color's too grim!
Why not soft like the phial's, enticing and
  dim? 26
Let it brighten her drink, let her turn it and
  stir,
And try it and taste, ere she fix and prefer!

What a drop! She's not little, no minion like
  me!

That's why she ensnared him; this never will
  free 30
The soul from those masculine eyes—say
  "no!"
To that pulse's magnificent come-and-go.

For only last night, as they whispered, I
  brought
My own eyes to bear on her so, that I thought
Could I keep them one half minute fixed, she
  would fall 35
Shriveled; she fell not; yet this does it all!

Not that I bid you spare her the pain;
Let death be felt and the proof remain;
Brand, burn up, bite into its grace—
He is sure to remember her dying face! 40

Is it done? Take my mask off! Nay, be not
  morose;
It kills her, and this prevents seeing it close:
The delicate droplet, my whole fortune's fee!
If it hurts her, beside, can it ever hurt me?

Now, take all my jewels, gorge gold to your
  fill, 45
You may kiss me, old man, on my mouth if
  you will!
But brush this dust off me, lest horror it brings
Ere I know it—next moment I dance at the
  King's!

(1844)

29. minion, a tiny and dainty person; cf. *minimus*.

"How They Brought the Good News from Ghent to Aix"

Browning declared that there was no historical foundation for this poem. "I wrote it," he said, "under the bulwark of a vessel, off the African coast, after I had been at sea long enough to appreciate even the fancy of a gallop on the back of a certain good horse 'York,' then in my stable at home." The poem is remarkable for its sense of rapid movement and for the skill with which the meter suggests the galloping of the horses. The cities and towns mentioned as lying along the route indicate the distances covered. Lokeren is twelve miles from Ghent; Boom, sixteen miles beyond Lokeren; Düffield, twelve miles further along; Mecheln just beyond Düffield; Aershot, fifteen miles beyond Düffield; Hasselt, twenty-five miles from Aershot and eighty from Ghent. Looz, Tongres, and Dalhem (l. 41) are along the route but not on the main highway.

I sprang to the stirrup, and Joris, and
  he;
I galloped, Dirck galloped, we galloped all
  three;

"Good speed!" cried the watch, as the gate-
  bolts undrew;
"Speed!" echoed the wall to us galloping
  through;

Behind shut the postern, the lights sank to rest,
And into the midnight we galloped abreast. 5

Not a word to each other; we kept the great pace
Neck by neck, stride by stride, never changing our place;
I turned in my saddle and made its girths tight,
Then shortened each stirrup, and set the pique right, 10
Rebuckled the cheek-strap, chained slacker the bit,
Nor galloped less steadily Roland a whit.

'Twas moonset at starting; but while we drew near
Lokeren, the cocks crew and twilight dawned clear;
At Boom, a great yellow star came out to see;
At Düffeld, 'twas morning as plain as could be; 16
And from Mecheln church-steeple we heard the half-chime,
So Joris broke silence with, "Yet there is time!"

At Aershot, up leaped of a sudden the sun,
And against him the cattle stood black every one, 20
To stare through the mist at us galloping past,
And I saw my stout galloper Roland at last,
With resolute shoulders, each butting away
The haze, as some bluff river headland its spray;

And his low head and crest, just one sharp ear bent back 25
For my voice, and the other pricked out on his track;

And one eye's black intelligence—ever that glance
O'er its white edge at me, his own master, askance!
And the thick heavy spume-flakes which aye and anon
His fierce lips shook upwards in galloping on.

By Hasselt, Dirck groaned; and cried Joris, "Stay spur! 31
Your Roos galloped bravely, the fault's not in her,
We'll remember at Aix"—for one heard the quick wheeze
Of her chest, saw the stretched neck and staggering knees,
And sunk tail, and horrible heave of the flank,
As down on her haunches she shuddered and sank. 36

So we were left galloping, Joris and I,
Past Looz and past Tongres, no cloud in the sky;
The broad sun above laughed a pitiless laugh,
'Neath our feet broke the brittle bright stubble like chaff; 40
Till over by Dalhem a dome-spire sprang white,
And "Gallop," gasped Joris, "for Aix is in sight!"

"How they'll greet us!"—and all in a moment his roan
Rolled neck and croup over, lay dead as a stone;
And there was my Roland to bear the whole weight 45
Of the news which alone could save Aix from her fate,
With his nostrils like pits full of blood to the brim,
And with circles of red for his eye-sockets' rim.

Then I cast loose my buffcoat, each holster let fall,
Shook off both my jack-boots, let go belt and all, 50

---

5. **postern,** the rear gate. 9. **girths,** the bands which encircled the body of the horse. 10. **pique,** the pommel of the saddle. 11. **cheek-strap,** the part of the bridle that passed down the side of the horse's head. 14. **twilight,** here the half light between darkness and dawn. 19. **leaped . . . sun.** For a similar vivid action-verb, cf. l. 41; all these words add to the breathlessness of the tempo.

Stood up in the stirrup, leaned, patted his ear,
Called my Roland his pet-name, my horse without peer;
Clapped my hands, laughed and sang, any noise, bad or good,
Till at length into Aix Roland galloped and stood.

And all I remember is—friends flocking round
As I sat with his head 'twixt my knees on the ground; 55
And no voice but was praising this Roland of mine,
As I poured down his throat our last measure of wine,
Which (the burgesses voted by common consent)
Was no more than his due who brought good news from Ghent. (1845)

The Lost Leader

Browning stated that the idea of this poem was suggested by Wordsworth's change of politics from Liberalism to Conservatism, but he emphatically denied that any detailed identification was intended. See p. 119.

Just for a handful of silver he left us,
  Just for a riband to stick in his coat—
Found the one gift of which fortune bereft us,
  Lost all the others she lets us devote;
They, with the gold to give, doled him out silver, 5
  So much was theirs who so little allowed;
How all our copper had gone for his service!
  Rags—were they purple, his heart had been proud!

We that had loved him so, followed him, honored him,
  Lived in his mild and magnificent eye, 10
Learned his great language, caught his clear accents,
  Made him our pattern to live and to die!
Shakespeare was of us, Milton was for us,
  Burns, Shelley, were with us—they watch from their graves!
He alone breaks from the van and the freemen— 15
  He alone sinks to the rear and the slaves!

We shall march prospering—not through his presence;
  Songs may inspirit us—not from his lyre;
Deeds will be done—while he boasts his quiescence,
  Still bidding crouch whom the rest bade aspire; 20
Blot out his name, then, record one lost soul more,
  One task more declined, one more footpath untrod,
One more devils'-triumph and sorrow for angels,
  One wrong more to man, one more insult to God!
Life's night begins; let him never come back to us! 25
  There would be doubt, hesitation, and pain,
Forced praise on our part—the glimmer of twilight,
  Never glad confident morning again!
Best fight on well, for we taught him—strike gallantly,
  Menace our heart ere we master his own; 30
Then let him receive the new knowledge and wait us,
  Pardoned in heaven, the first by the throne! (1845)

Meeting at Night

The gray sea and the long black land;
And the yellow half-moon large and low;
And the startled little waves that leap
In fiery ringlets from their sleep,
As I gain the cove with pushing prow, 5
And quench its speed i' the slushy sand.

Then a mile of warm sea-scented beach;
Three fields to cross till a farm appears;
A tap at the pane, the quick sharp scratch
And blue spurt of a lighted match, 10

---

29. **Best fight,** it were best for him to fight.

And a voice less loud, through its joys and
    fears,
Than the two hearts beating each to each!
                                        (1845)

Parting at Morning

Round the cape of a sudden came the sea,
And the sun looked over the mountain's rim:
And straight was a path of gold for him,
And the need of a world of men for me.
                                        (1845)

Home-Thoughts, from Abroad

Oh, to be in England
Now that April's there,
And whoever wakes in England
Sees, some morning, unaware,
That the lowest boughs and the brushwood
    sheaf   5
Round the elm-tree bole are in tiny leaf,
While the chaffinch sings on the orchard
    bough
In England—now!

And after April, when May follows,
And the whitethroat builds, and all the swal-
    lows!   10
Hark, where my blossomed pear-tree in the
    hedge
Leans to the field and scatters on the clover
Blossoms and dewdrops—at the bent spray's
    edge—
That's the wise thrush; he sings each song
    twice over,

3. **him**, the sun.
Home-Thoughts, from Abroad. 6. **bole**, trunk.

Lest you should think he never could recap-
    ture   15
The first fine careless rapture!
And though the fields look rough with hoary
    dew,
All will be gay when noontide wakes anew
The buttercups, the little children's dower—
Far brighter than this gaudy melon-flower!
                                        (1845)

Home-Thoughts, from the Sea

Browning wrote this poem one evening in April while on shipboard off the northwest coast of Africa on a voyage to Italy, probably his first in 1838; or his second, in 1844.

Nobly, nobly Cape Saint Vincent to the north-
    west died away;
Sunset ran, one glorious blood-red, reeking
    into Cadiz Bay;
Bluish 'mid the burning water, full in face
    Trafalgar lay;
In the dimmest northeast distance dawned
    Gibraltar grand and gray;
"Here and here did England help me; how
    can I help England?"—say,   5
Whoso turns as I, this evening, turn to God
    to praise and pray,
While Jove's planet rises yonder, silent over
    Africa.   (1845)

20. **melon-flower**, blossom on the melon vine.
Home-Thoughts, from the Sea. 1. **Cape Saint Vincent**, the southwestern point of Portugal, near which England won a naval victory over Spain in 1797. 2. **Cadiz Bay**, on the southern coast of Spain, east of Cape St. Vincent, where an English fleet destroyed the second Spanish Armada in 1596. 3. **Trafalgar**, a cape east of Cadiz Bay, off which Lord Nelson won his greatest victory over the French and Spanish fleets in 1805. 4. **Gibraltar**, the famous British stronghold at the entrance to the Mediterranean. It was acquired from Spain by the Peace of Utrecht in 1713. 7. **Jove's planet**, Jupiter.

The Glove

The incident here related is supposed to be told by Pierre de Ronsard, a famous French poet of the sixteenth century. The story has been told also by another French writer, St. Croix (1746-1809), by the German poet Schiller (1759-1805), and by Leigh Hunt, *The Glove and the Lions*, p. 304.

(PETER RONSARD *loquitur*)

"Heigho," yawned one day King Francis,
"Distance all value enhances!

1. **King Francis**, Francis I (1494-1547), King of France.

When a man's busy, why, leisure
Strikes him as wonderful pleasure;
'Faith, and at leisure once is he?   5
Straightway he wants to be busy.
Here we've got peace; and aghast I'm

Caught thinking war the true pastime.
Is there a reason in meter?
Give us your speech, master Peter!"   10
I who, if mortal dare say so,
Ne'er am at loss with my Naso,
"Sire," I replied, "joys prove cloudlets;
Men are the merest Ixions"—
Here the King whistled aloud, "Let's   15
—Heigho—go look at our lions!"
Such are the sorrowful chances
If you talk fine to King Francis.

And so, to the courtyard proceeding
Our company, Francis was leading,   20
Increased by new followers tenfold
Before he arrived at the penfold;
Lords, ladies, like clouds which bedizen
At sunset the western horizon.
And Sir De Lorge pressed 'mid the foremost
With the dame he professed to adore most. 26
Oh, what a face! One by fits eyed
Her, and the horrible pitside;
For the penfold surrounded a hollow
Which led where the eye scarce dared follow,
And shelved to the chamber secluded   31
Where Bluebeard, the great lion, brooded.
The King hailed his keeper, an Arab
As glossy and black as a scarab,
And bade him make sport and at once stir 35
Up and out of his den the old monster.
They opened a hole in the wire-work
Across it, and dropped there a firework,
And fled; one's heart's beating redoubled;
A pause, while the pit's mouth was troubled,
The blackness and silence so utter,   41
By the firework's slow sparkling and sputter;
Then earth in a sudden contortion
Gave out to our gaze her abortion.
Such a brute! Were I friend Clement Marot
(Whose experience of nature's but narrow, 46
And whose faculties move in no small mist
When he versifies David the Psalmist)
I should study that brute to describe you
Illum Juda Leonem de Tribu.   50

12. **Naso**, Ovid (Publius Ovidius Naso), a Roman poet (43 B.C.-17 A.D.). 14. **Ixions.** In Greek mythology Ixion was a king who was bound to an endlessly revolving wheel in Hades for boasting of the love of Hera, wife of Zeus. She deceived him by sending him a cloud in her shape, by which he became father of the race of centaurs. 22. **penfold**, an inclosure for animals, the arena. 34. **scarab**, a large black dung beetle. 45. **Marot**, a noted French court poet (1496-1544), who versified forty-nine of the Psalms, ascribed to David. 50. *Illum . . . Tribu,* that lion of the tribe of Judah.

One's whole blood grew curdling and creepy
To see the black mane, vast and heapy,
The tail in the air stiff and straining,
The wide eyes, nor waxing nor waning,
As over the barrier which bounded   55
His platform, and us who surrounded
The barrier, they reached and they rested
On space that might stand him in best stead;
For who knew, he thought, what the amazement,
The eruption of clatter and blaze meant,   60
And if, in this minute of wonder,
No outlet, 'mid lightning and thunder,
Lay broad, and, his shackles all shivered,
The lion at last was delivered?
Aye, that was the open sky o'er head!   65
And you saw by the flash on his forehead,
By the hope in those eyes wide and steady,
He was leagues in the desert already,
Driving the flocks up the mountain,
Or catlike couched hard by the fountain   70
To waylay the date-gathering negress;
So guarded he entrance or egress.
"How he stands!" quoth the King; "we may well swear
(No novice, we've won our spurs elsewhere
And so can afford the confession)   75
We exercise wholesome discretion
In keeping aloof from his threshold;
Once hold you, those jaws want no fresh hold—
Their first would too pleasantly purloin
The visitor's brisket or surloin;   80
But who's he would prove so foolhardy?
Not the best man of Marignan, pardie!"

The sentence no sooner was uttered,
Than over the rails a glove fluttered,
Fell close to the lion, and rested;   85
The dame 'twas, who flung it and jested
With life so, De Lorge had been wooing
For months past; he sat there pursuing
His suit, weighing out with nonchalance
Fine speeches like gold from a balance.   90

Sound the trumpet, no true knight's a tarrier!
De Lorge made one leap at the barrier,
Walked straight to the glove—while the lion

82. **Marignan,** Melegnano, an Italian town ten miles southeast of Milan. **pardie**, surely; originally an oath, *by God.*

Ne'er moved, kept his far-reaching eye on
The palm-tree-edged desert-spring's sapphire,
And the musky oiled skin of the Kaffir—   96
Picked it up, and as calmly retreated,
Leaped back where the lady was seated,
And full in the face of its owner
Flung the glove.   100

"Your heart's queen, you dethrone her?
So should I!"—cried the King—" 'twas mere vanity,
Not love, set that task to humanity!"
Lords and ladies alike turned with loathing
From such a proved wolf in sheep's clothing.

Not so, I; for I caught an expression   106
In her brow's undisturbed self-possession
Amid the Court's scoffing and merriment—
As if from no pleasing experiment
She rose, yet of pain not much heedful   110
So long as the process was needful—
As if she had tried in a crucible,
To what "speeches like gold" were reducible,
And, finding the finest prove copper,
Felt the smoke in her face was but proper;   115
To know what she had *not* to trust to,
Was worth all the ashes and dust too.
She went out 'mid hooting and laughter;
Clement Marot stayed; I followed after,
And asked, as a grace, what it all meant?   120
If she wished not the rash deed's recallment?
"For I"—so I spoke—"am a poet;
Human nature—behooves that I know it!"

She told me, "Too long had I heard
Of the deed proved alone by the word;   125
For my love—what De Lorge would not dare!
With my scorn—what De Lorge could compare!
And the endless descriptions of death
He would brave when my lip formed a breath
I must reckon as braved, or, of course,   130
Doubt his word—and moreover, perforce,
For such gifts as no lady could spurn,
Must offer my love in return.
When I looked on your lion, it brought
All the dangers at once to my thought,   135
Encountered by all sorts of men,

Before he was lodged in his den—
From the poor slave whose club or bare hands
Dug the trap, set the snare on the sands,
With no King and no Court to applaud,   140
By no shame, should he shrink, overawed,
Yet to capture the creature made shift,
That his rude boys might laugh at the gift
—To the page who last leaped o'er the fence
Of the pit, on no greater pretense   145
Than to get back the bonnet he dropped,
Lest his pay for a week should be stopped.
So, wiser I judged it to make
One trial what 'death for my sake'
Really meant, while the power was yet mine,
Than to wait until time should define   151
Such a phrase not so simply as I,
Who took it to mean just 'to die.'
The blow a glove gives is but weak;
Does the mark yet discolor my cheek?   155
But when the heart suffers a blow,
Will the pain pass so soon, do you know?"

I looked, as away she was sweeping,
And saw a youth eagerly keeping
As close as he dared to the doorway.   160
No doubt that a noble should more weigh
His life than befits a plebeian;
And yet, had our brute been Nemean—
I judge by a certain calm fervor
The youth stepped with, forward to serve her
—He'd have scarce thought you did him the worst turn   166
If you whispered, "Friend, what you'd get, first earn!"
And when, shortly after, she carried
Her shame from the Court, and they married,
To that marriage some happiness, maugre   170
The voice of the Court, I dared augur.

For De Lorge, he made women with men vie,
Those in wonder and praise, these in envy;
And in short stood so plain a head taller
That he wooed and won—how do you call her?   175
The beauty, that rose in the sequel
To the King's love, who loved her a week well.
And 'twas noticed he never would honor

---

96. **Kaffir**, a member of a South African tribe noted as lion hunters.

163. **our ... Nemean.** An allusion to a monstrous lion in the valley of Nemea, in ancient Greece, slain by Hercules.

De Lorge (who looked daggers upon her)
With the easy commission of stretching   180
His legs in the service, and fetching
His wife, from her chamber, those straying
Sad gloves she was always mislaying,
While the King took the closet to chat in—
But of course this adventure came pat in.   185
And never the King told the story,
How bringing a glove brought such glory,
But the wife smiled—"His nerves are grown firmer;
Mine he brings now and utters no murmur."

Venienti occurrite morbo!   190
With which moral I drop my theorbo. (1845)

The Bishop Orders His Tomb at Saint Praxed's Church

Ruskin's high tribute to this dramatic monologue in which Browning has interpreted the spirit of the Renaissance is colored by the critic's dislike of the whole period (see p. 502) but contains, nevertheless, an admirable list of the traits that the Bishop revealed in his last orders. "I know no other piece of modern English, prose or poetry, in which there is so much told, as in these lines of the Renaissance spirit—its worldliness, inconsistency, pride, hypocrisy, ignorance of itself, love of art, of luxury, and of good Latin. It is nearly all that I said of the central Renaissance in thirty pages of *The Stones of Venice*, put into as many lines, Browning's being also the antecedent work." The Bishop is a typical prelate of the sixteenth century, a scholar learned in pagan lore, a priest filled with visions of the saints, mystic, artist, child of the world.

ROME, 15—

Vanity, saith the preacher, vanity!
Draw round my bed; is Anselm keeping back?
Nephews—sons mine ... ah, God, I know not! Well—
She, men would have to be your mother once,
Old Gandolf envied me, so fair she was!   5
What's done is done, and she is dead beside,
Dead long ago, and I am Bishop since,
And as she died so must we die ourselves,
And thence ye may perceive the world's a dream.
Life, how and what is it? As here I lie   10
In this state-chamber, dying by degrees,
Hours and long hours in the dead night, I ask,
"Do I live, am I dead?" Peace, peace seems all.
Saint Praxed's ever was the church for peace;
And so, about this tomb of mine. I fought   15
With tooth and nail to save my niche, ye know—
Old Gandolf cozened me, despite my care;
Shrewd was that snatch from out the corner South
He graced his carrion with, God curse the same!
Yet still my niche is not so cramped but thence   20
One sees the pulpit o' the epistle-side,
And somewhat of the choir, those silent seats,
And up into the aëry dome where live
The angels, and a sunbeam's sure to lurk;
And I shall fill my slab of basalt there,   25
And 'neath my tabernacle take my rest,
With those nine columns round me, two and two,
The odd one at my feet where Anselm stands:
Peach-blossom marble all, the rare, the ripe
As fresh-poured red wine of a mighty pulse.   30
—Old Gandolf with his paltry onion-stone,
Put me where I may look at him! True peach,
Rosy and flawless; how I earned the prize!
Draw close; that conflagration of my church—
What then? So much was saved if aught were missed!   35
My sons, ye would not be my death? Go dig
The white-grape vineyard where the oil-press stood,

---

190. *Venienti ... morbo,* encounter the approaching disease; or, meet trouble as it comes. 191. **theorbo,** a light stringed instrument.
The Bishop Orders His Tomb. The church is named after the virgin St. Praxed, or Praxedes, a Christian saint of the first century. Both the bishop and the tomb are imaginary. 1. **Vanity, etc.** From *Ecclesiastes,* 1:2: "Vanity of vanities, saith the Preacher, vanity of vanities; all is vanity."

5. **Gandolf,** the Bishop's predecessor and rival. 21. **the epistle-side,** the side of an altar from which the Epistle is read; the right-hand side as one faces the altar. The left is the gospel-side. 25. **basalt,** a hard rock of dark color. 26. **tabernacle,** a protecting canopy. 29. **Peach-blossom marble,** exceptionally fine marble of a pinkish hue. 30. **of ... pulse,** of great strength. 31. **onion-stone,** an inferior greenish marble that easily splits into thin layers like those of the onion. It is called *cipollino,* from *cipolla* (onion).

Drop water gently till the surface sink,
And if ye find . . . Ah, God, I know not, I! . . .
Bedded in store of rotten fig-leaves soft,   40
And corded up in a tight olive-frail,
Some lump, ah, God, of *lapis lazuli*,
Big as a Jew's head cut off at the nape,
Blue as a vein o'er the Madonna's breast . . .
Sons, all have I bequeathed you, villas, all,   45
That brave Frascati villa with its bath,
So, let the blue lump poise between my knees,
Like God the Father's globe on both his hands
Ye worship in the Jesu Church so gay,
For Gandolf shall not choose but see and burst!
Swift as a weaver's shuttle fleet our years;   51
Man goeth to the grave, and where is he?
Did I say basalt for my slab, sons? Black—
'Twas ever antique-black I meant! How else
Shall ye contrast my frieze to come beneath?
The bas-relief in bronze ye promised me,   56
Those Pans and Nymphs ye wot of, and perchance
Some tripod, thyrsus, with a vase or so,
The Savior at his sermon on the mount,
Saint Praxed in a glory, and one Pan   60
Ready to twitch the Nymph's last garment off,
And Moses with the tables . . . but I know
Ye mark me not! What do they whisper thee,
Child of my bowels, Anselm? Ah, ye hope
To revel down my villas while I gasp   65
Bricked o'er with beggar's moldy travertine
Which Gandolf from his tomb-top chuckles at!
Nay, boys, ye love me—all of jasper, then!
'Tis jasper ye stand pledged to, lest I grieve
My bath must needs be left behind, alas!   70
One block, pure green as a pistachio-nut,
There's plenty jasper somewhere in the world—

And have I not Saint Praxed's ear to pray
Horses for ye, and brown Greek manuscripts,
And mistresses with great smooth marbly limbs?   75
—That's if ye carve my epitaph aright
Choice Latin, picked phrase, Tully's every word,
No gaudy ware like Gandolf's second line—
Tully, my masters? Ulpian serves his need!
And then how I shall lie through centuries,   80
And hear the blessed mutter of the Mass,
And see God made and eaten all day long,
And feel the steady candle-flame, and taste
Good strong thick stupefying incense-smoke!
For as I lie here, hours of the dead night,   85
Dying in state and by such slow degrees,
I fold my arms as if they clasped a crook,
And stretch my feet forth straight as stone can point,
And let the bedclothes, for a mortcloth, drop
Into great laps and folds of sculptor's work;   90
And as yon tapers dwindle, and strange thoughts
Grow, with a certain humming in my ears
About the life before I lived this life,
And this life too, popes, cardinals, and priests,
Saint Praxed at his sermon on the mount,   95
Your tall pale mother with her talking eyes,
And new-found agate urns as fresh as day,
And marble's language, Latin pure, discreet—
Aha, ELUCESCEBAT quoth our friend?
No Tully, said I, Ulpian at the best!   100
Evil and brief hath been my pilgrimage.
All *lapis*, all, sons! Else I give the Pope
My villas! Will ye ever eat my heart?
Ever your eyes were as a lizard's quick,
They glitter like your mother's for my soul,   105
Or ye would heighten my impoverished frieze,
Piece out its starved design, and fill my vase
With grapes, and add a visor and a term,
And to the tripod ye would tie a lynx
That in his struggle throws the thyrsus down.

---

41. **olive-frail**, a basket for holding olives. 42. *lapis lazuli*, a valuable blue stone, stolen by the Bishop from his own church. 46. **Frascati**, a wealthy resort near Rome. 49. **Jesu Church**, Il Gesu, the church of the Jesuits in Rome; it contains an image of God holding a globe made of lapis lazuli. 51. **Swift . . . years.** From *Job*, 7:6: "My days are swifter than a weaver's shuttle, and are spent without hope." 54. **antique-black**, Nero-antico, a beautiful black marble. 57. **Pans.** Pan was the god of flocks and pastures. The bas-relief was to contain a curious mixture of pagan and Christian symbols. 58. **tripod**, the three-legged stool on which the priestess of Apollo sat when giving responses to persons consulting the oracle at Delphi. **thyrsus**, the staff used by followers of Bacchus, god of wine. 59. **sermon on the mount.** Found in *Matthew*, 5-7 (see Vol. I, p. 610). 62. **Moses . . . tables.** The account is found in *Exodus*, 24-34. 66. **travertine**, a kind of white limestone. 68. **jasper**, a dark green smooth stone.

74. **brown**, brown with age. 77. **Tully's . . . word**, in the style of Cicero (106-43 B.C.), i.e., the purest classic Latin. 79. **Ulpian**, a noted Roman jurist (170-228), whose Latin style was apparently inferior to that of Cicero. 82. **God . . . long**, in the sacrament of the Mass. 87. **crook**, a crozier, the pastoral staff of a bishop; it is the symbol of his office as shepherd of the flock. 89. **mortcloth**, a funeral pall. 95. **his.** The Bishop's mind is confused: St. Praxed was a woman. 99. *elucescebat*, he was famous. The Bishop hates the form of the word, the classic form being *elucebat*. 108. **visor**, mask. **term**, combined bust and pedestal.

To comfort me on my entablature 111
Whereon I am to lie till I must ask,
"Do I live, am I dead?" There, leave me, there!
For ye have stabbed me with ingratitude
To death—ye wish it—God, ye wish it! Stone— 115
Gritstone, a-crumble! Clammy squares which sweat

116. **Gritstone**, a kind of coarse sandstone.

As if the corpse they keep were oozing through—
And no more *lapis* to delight the world!
Well, go! I bless ye. Fewer tapers there,
But in a row; and, going, turn your backs—
Aye, like departing altar-ministrants, 121
And leave me in my church, the church for peace,
That I may watch at leisure if he leers—
Old Gandolf—at me, from his onion-stone,
As still he envied me, so fair she was! (1845)

Saul

The source of this noble religious poem is *1 Samuel*, 16:14-23. King Saul of Israel was troubled with an evil spirit. He was told that he would be cured by music, and hearing that David the shepherd boy could play the harp, Saul sent for him and was cured by the boy's playing. In the poem David is alone with his sheep. He tells the story of his playing before Saul.

1

Said Abner, "At last thou art come! Ere I tell, ere thou speak,
Kiss my cheek, wish me well!" Then I wished it, and did kiss his cheek.
And he: "Since the King, O my friend, for thy countenance sent,
Neither drunken nor eaten have we; nor until from his tent
Thou return with the joyful assurance the King liveth yet, 5
Shall our lip with the honey be bright, with the water be wet.
For out of the black mid-tent's silence, a space of three days,
Not a sound hath escaped to thy servants, of prayer nor of praise,
To betoken that Saul and the Spirit have ended their strife,
And that, faint in his triumph, the monarch sinks back upon life. 10

2

"Yet now my heart leaps, O beloved! God's child with his dew
On thy gracious gold hair, and those lilies still living and blue

1. **Abner**, the cousin of Saul and the commander of his army. **thou**, David.

Just broken to twine round thy harp-strings, as if no wild heat
Were now raging to torture the desert!"

3

Then I, as was meet,
Knelt down to the God of my fathers, and rose on my feet, 15
And ran o'er the sand burnt to powder. The tent was unlooped;
I pulled up the spear that obstructed, and under I stooped;
Hands and knees on the slippery grass-patch, all withered and gone,
That extends to the second enclosure, I groped my way on
Till I felt where the foldskirts fly open. Then once more I prayed, 20
And opened the foldskirts and entered, and was not afraid
But spoke, "Here is David, thy servant!" And no voice replied.
At the first I saw naught but the blackness; but soon I descried
A something more black than the blackness—the vast, the upright
Main prop which sustains the pavilion; and slow into sight 25

Grew a figure against it, gigantic and blackest of all.
Then a sunbeam, that burst through the tent-roof, showed Saul.

4

He stood as erect as that tent-prop, both arms stretched out wide
On the great cross-support in the center, that goes to each side;
He relaxed not a muscle, but hung there as, caught in his pangs 30
And waiting his change, the king-serpent all heavily hangs,
Far away from his kind, in the pine, till deliverance come
With the spring-time—so agonized Saul, drear and stark, blind and dumb.

5

Then I tuned my harp—took off the lilies we twine round its chords
Lest they snap 'neath the stress of the noontide—those sunbeams like swords! 35
And I first played the tune all our sheep know, as, one after one,
So docile they come to the pen-door till folding be done.
They are white and untorn by the bushes, for lo, they have fed
Where the long grasses stifle the water within the stream's bed;
And now one after one seeks its lodging, as star follows star 40
Into eve and the blue far above us—so blue and so far!

6

—Then the tune for which quails on the cornland will each leave his mate
To fly after the player; then, what makes the crickets elate
Till for boldness they fight one another; and then, what has weight
To set the quick jerboa a-musing outside his sand house— 45
There are none such as he for a wonder, half bird and half mouse!
God made all the creatures and gave them our love and our fear,
To give sign, we and they are his children, one family here.

7

Then I played the help-tune of our reapers, their wine-song, when hand
Grasps at hand, eye lights eye in good friendship, and great hearts expand 50
And grow one in the sense of this world's life.
—And then, the last song
When the dead man is praised on his journey—"Bear, bear him along,
With his few faults shut up like dead flowerets! Are balm seeds not here
To console us? The land has none left such as he on the bier.
Oh, would we might keep thee, my brother!"
—And then, the glad chaunt 55
Of the marriage—first go the young maidens; next, she whom we vaunt
As the beauty, the pride of our dwelling.—And then, the great march
Wherein man runs to man to assist him and buttress an arch
Naught can break; who shall harm them, our friends? Then, the chorus intoned
As the Levites go up to the altar in glory enthroned. 60
But I stopped here; for here in the darkness Saul groaned.

8

And I paused, held my breath in such silence, and listened apart;
And the tent shook, for mighty Saul shuddered; and sparkles 'gan dart
From the jewels that woke in his turban, at once with a start,
All its lordly male-sapphires, and rubies courageous at heart. 65
So the head; but the body still moved not, still hung there erect.

---

31. **king-serpent**, probably the boa-constrictor, waiting the change that will come with the sloughing of his skin in the spring. 42. **corn-land**, grain-land. 45. **jerboa**, the jumping hare, a small animal of the rat family.

60. **Levites . . . enthroned.** The sons of Levi were priests. An account of the service required of them appears in 1 Chronicles, 23:24-32. 65. **male-sapphire.** It reveals a star of bright rays. The ruby shows a bright red light at the center.

And I bent once again to my playing, pursued it unchecked,
As I sang:

9

"Oh, our manhood's prime vigor! No spirit feels waste,
Not a muscle is stopped in its playing nor sinew unbraced.
Oh, the wild joys of living! the leaping from rock up to rock, 70
The strong rending of boughs from the fir-tree, the cool silver shock
Of the plunge in a pool's living water, the hunt of the bear,
And the sultriness showing the lion is couched in his lair.
And the meal, the rich dates yellowed over with gold dust divine,
And the locust-flesh steeped in the pitcher, the full draft of wine, 75
And the sleep in the dried river-channel where bulrushes tell
That the water was wont to go warbling so softly and well.
How good is man's life, the mere living! how fit to employ
All the heart and the soul and the senses forever in joy!
Hast thou loved the white locks of thy father, whose sword thou didst guard 80
When he trusted thee forth with the armies, for glorious reward?
Didst thou see the thin hands of thy mother held up as men sung
The low song of the nearly-departed, and hear her faint tongue
Joining in while it could to the witness, 'Let one more attest,
I have lived, seen God's hand through a lifetime, and all was for best'? 85
Then they sung through their tears in strong triumph, not much, but the rest.
And thy brothers, the help and the contest, the working whence grew
Such results, as from seething grape-bundles, the spirit strained true;
And the friends of thy boyhood—that boyhood of wonder and hope,
Present promise and wealth of the future beyond the eye's scope— 90
Till lo, thou art grown to a monarch; a people is thine;
And all gifts, which the world offers singly, on one head combine!
On one head, all the beauty and strength, love and rage (like the throe
That, a-work in the rock, helps its labor and lets the gold go),
High ambition and deeds which surpass it, fame crowning them—all 95
Brought to blaze on the head of one creature —King Saul!"

10

And lo, with that leap of my spirit—heart, hand, harp, and voice,
Each lifting Saul's name out of sorrow, each bidding rejoice
Saul's fame in the light it was made for—as when, dare I say,
The Lord's army, in rapture of service, strains through its array, 100
And upsoareth the cherubim-chariot—"Saul!" cried I, and stopped,
And waited the thing that should follow. Then Saul, who hung propped
By the tent's cross-support in the center, was struck by his name.
Have ye seen when Spring's arrowy summons goes right to the aim,
And some mountain—the last to withstand her, that held (he alone, 105
While the vale laughed in freedom and flowers) on a broad bust of stone
A year's snow bound about for a breastplate —leaves grasp of the sheet?
Fold on fold all at once it crowds thunderously down to his feet,
And there fronts you, stark, black, but alive yet, your mountain of old,
With his rents, the successive bequeathings of ages untold— 110
Yea, each harm got in fighting your battles, each furrow and scar

---

75. **locust-flesh**, in ancient Hebrew times locusts were frequently used as food, especially by nomads.

101. **cherubim-chariot.** The cherubim are mysterious beings described in *Ezekiel*, 1 and 10 as having four faces and four wings; they were the footstool and the chariot of the Almighty, and were appointed to guard the gates of Paradise after the fall of man (*Genesis*, 3:24).

Of his head thrust 'twixt you and the tempest
    —all hail, there they are!
—Now again to be softened with verdure,
    again hold the nest
Of the dove, tempt the goat and its young to
    the green on his crest
For their food in the ardors of summer. One
    long shudder thrilled   115
All the tent till the very air tingled, then sank
    and was stilled
At the King's self left standing before me,
    released and aware.
What was gone, what remained? All to tra-
    verse 'twixt hope and despair,
Death was past, life not come; so he waited.
    Awhile his right hand
Held the brow, helped the eyes left too vacant
    forthwith to remand   120
To their place what new objects should enter;
    'twas Saul as before.
I looked up and dared gaze at those eyes, nor
    was hurt any more
Than by slow pallid sunsets in autumn, ye
    watch from the shore,
At their sad level gaze o'er the ocean—a sun's
    slow decline
Over hills which, resolved in stern silence,
    o'erlap and entwine   125
Base with base to knit strength more intensely;
    so, arm folded arm
O'er the chest whose slow heavings subsided.

11

            What spell or what charm
(For awhile there was trouble within me),
    what next should I urge
To sustain him where song had restored him?
    —Song filled to the verge
His cup with the wine of this life, pressing all
    that it yields   130
Of mere fruitage, the strength and the beauty;
    beyond, on what fields,
Glean a vintage more potent and perfect to
    brighten the eye
And bring blood to the lip, and commend
    them the cup they put by?
He saith, "It is good"; still he drinks not;
    he lets me praise life,
Gives assent, yet would die for his own
    part.

12

            Then fancies grew rife
Which had come long ago on the pasture,
    when round me the sheep   135
Fed in silence—above, the one eagle wheeled
    slow as in sleep;
And I lay in my hollow and mused on the
    world that might lie
'Neath his ken, though I saw but the strip
    'twixt the hill and the sky;
And I laughed—"Since my days are ordained
    to be passed with my flocks,   140
Let me people at least, with my fancies, the
    plains and the rocks,
Dream the life I am never to mix with, and
    image the show
Of mankind as they live in those fashions I
    hardly shall know!
Schemes of life, its best rules and right uses,
    the courage that gains,
And the prudence that keeps what men strive
    for." And now these old trains   145
Of vague thought came again; I grew surer;
    so, once more the string
Of my harp made response to my spirit, as
    thus—

13

            "Yea, my King,"
I began—"thou dost well in rejecting mere
    comforts that spring
From the mere mortal life held in common by
    man and by brute;
In our flesh grows the branch of this life, in
    our soul it bears fruit.   150
Thou hast marked the slow rise of the tree—
    how its stem trembled first
Till it passed the kid's lip, the stag's antler;
    then safely outburst
The fan-branches all round; and thou mindest
    when these too, in turn,
Broke a-bloom and the palm-tree seemed per-
    fect; yet more was to learn,
E'en the good that comes in with the palm-
    fruit. Our dates shall we slight,   155
When their juice brings a cure for all sorrow?
    or care for the plight
Of the palm's self whose slow growth pro-
    duced them? Not so! stem and branch
Shall decay, nor be known in their place,
    while the palm-wine shall stanch

Every wound of man's spirit in winter. I pour
    thee such wine.
Leave the flesh to the fate it was fit for! the
    spirit be thine!   160
By the spirit, when age shall o'ercome thee,
    thou still shalt enjoy
More indeed, than at first when inconscious,
    the life of a boy.
Crush that life, and behold its wine running!
    Each deed thou hast done
Dies, revives, goes to work in the world; until
    e'en as the sun
Looking down on the earth, though clouds
    spoil him, though tempests efface,   165
Can find nothing his own deed produced not,
    must everywhere trace
The results of his past summer-prime—so,
    each ray of thy will,
Every flash of thy passion and prowess, long
    over, shall thrill
Thy whole people, the countless, with ardor,
    till they too give forth
A like cheer to their sons, who, in turn, fill
    the South and the North   170
With the radiance thy deed was the germ of.
    Carouse in the past!
But the license of age has its limit; thou diest
    at last:
As the lion when age dims his eyeball, the rose
    at her height,
So with man—so his power and his beauty
    forever take flight.
No! Again a long draft of my soul-wine!
    Look forth o'er the years!   175
Thou hast done now with eyes for the actual;
    begin with the seer's!
Is Saul dead? In the depth of the vale make
    his tomb—bid arise
A gray mountain of marble heaped four-
    square, till, built to the skies,
Let it mark where the great First King slum-
    bers; whose fame would ye know?
Up above see the rock's naked face, where the
    record shall go   180
In great characters cut by the scribe—Such
    was Saul, so he did;
With the sages directing the work, by the
    populace chid—
For not half, they'll affirm, is comprised there!
    Which fault to amend,

In the grove with his kind grows the cedar,
    whereon they shall spend
(See, in tablets 'tis level before them) their
    praise, and record,   185
With the gold of the graver, Saul's story—
    the statesman's great word
Side by side with the poet's sweet comment.
    The river's a-wave
With smooth paper-reeds grazing each other
    when prophet-winds rave;
So the pen gives unborn generations their due
    and their part
In thy being! Then, first of the mighty, thank
    God that thou art!"   190

14

And behold while I sang . . . but O Thou
    who didst grant me that day,
And before it not seldom hast granted thy
    help to essay,
Carry on and complete an adventure—my
    shield and my sword
In that act where my soul was thy servant,
    thy word was my word—
Still be with me, who then at the summit of
    human endeavor   195
And scaling the highest, man's thought could,
    gazed hopeless as ever
On the new stretch of heaven above me—till,
    mighty to save,
Just one lift of thy hand cleared that distance
    —God's throne from man's grave!
Let me tell out my tale to its ending—my
    voice to my heart
Which can scarce dare believe in what mar-
    vels last night I took part,   200
As this morning I gather the fragments, alone
    with my sheep,
And still fear lest the terrible glory evanish
    like sleep!
For I wake in the gray dewy covert, while
    Hebron upheaves
The dawn struggling with night on his shoul-
    der, and Kidron retrieves
Slow the damage of yesterday's sunshine.

188. **paper-reeds,** papyrus plants, used as paper for writing by the ancient Egyptians, Greeks, and Romans. **prophet-winds,** winds that foretell a storm. 203. **Hebron,** an old city in Palestine, situated on a hill. 204. **Kidron,** a small brook near Jerusalem.

15

I say then—my song
While I sang thus, assuring the monarch, and
    ever more strong   206
Made a proffer of good to console him—he
    slowly resumed
His old motions and habitudes kingly. The
    right hand replumbed
His black locks to their wonted composure,
    adjusted the swathes
Of his turban, and see—the huge sweat that
    his countenance bathes,   210
He wipes off with the robe; and he girds now
    his loins as of yore,
And feels slow for the armlets of price, with
    the clasp set before.
He is Saul ye remember in glory—ere error
    had bent
The broad brow from the daily communion;
    and still, though much spent
Be the life and the bearing that front you, the
    same God did choose   215
To receive what a man may waste, desecrate,
    never quite lose.
So sank he along by the tent-prop till, stayed
    by the pile
Of his armor and war-cloak and garments, he
    leaned there awhile,
And sat out my singing—one arm round the
    tent-prop, to raise
His bent head, and the other hung slack—
    till I touched on the praise   220
I foresaw from all men in all time, to the man
    patient there;
And thus ended, the harp falling forward.
    Then first I was 'ware
That he sat, as I say, with my head just above
    his vast knees,
Which were thrust out on each side around
    me, like oak roots which please
To encircle a lamb when it slumbers. I looked
    up to know   225
If the best I could do had brought solace;
    he spoke not, but slow
Lifted up the hand slack at his side, till he
    laid it with care
Soft and grave, but in mild settled will, on my
    brow; through my hair
The large fingers were pushed, and he bent
    back my head, with kind power—
All my face back, intent to peruse it, as men
    do a flower.   230
Thus held he me there with his great eyes that
    scrutinized mine—
And, oh, all my heart how it loved him! but
    where was the sign?
I yearned—"Could I help thee, my father,
    inventing a bliss,
I would add, to that life of the past, both the
    future and this;
I would give thee new life altogether, as good,
    ages hence,   235
As this moment—had love but the warrant,
    love's heart to dispense!"

16

Then the truth came upon me. No harp more
    —no song more! Outbroke:

17

"I have gone the whole round of creation; I
    saw and I spoke;
I, a work of God's hand for that purpose, re-
    ceived in my brain
And pronounced on the rest of his handwork
    —returned him again   240
His creation's approval or censure; I spoke as
    I saw;
I report, as a man may of God's work—all's
    love, yet all's law.
Now I lay down the judgeship he lent me.
    Each faculty tasked
To perceive him has gained an abyss, where
    a dewdrop was asked.
Have I knowledge? confounded it shrivels at
    Wisdom laid bare.   245
Have I forethought? how purblind, how
    blank, to the Infinite Care!
Do I task any faculty highest, to image suc-
    cess?
I but open my eyes—and perfection, no more
    and no less,

---

213. **ere . . . communion.** A reference to God's rejection of Saul because he disobeyed the command to destroy all the Amalekites and their possessions. See *1 Samuel*, 15.

237. **Outbroke.** David first played on his harp (ll. 36-60); then he sang (ll. 68-190); finally he spoke (ll. 237-312).

In the kind I imagined, full-fronts me, and
    God is seen God
In the star, in the stone, in the flesh, in the
    soul, and the clod.   250
And thus looking within and around me, I
    ever renew
(With that stoop of the soul which in bending
    upraises it too)
The submission of man's nothing-perfect to
    God's all-complete,
As by each new obeisance in spirit, I climb to
    his feet.
Yet with all this abounding experience, this
    deity known,   255
I shall dare to discover some province, some
    gift of my own.
There's a faculty pleasant to exercise, hard to
    hoodwink,
I am fain to keep still in abeyance (I laugh as
    I think),
Lest, insisting to claim and parade in it, wot
    ye, I worst
E'en the Giver in one gift.—Behold, I could
    love if I durst!   260
But I sink the pretension as fearing a man
    may o'ertake
God's own speed in the one way of love; I
    abstain for love's sake.
—What, my soul? see thus far and no farther?
    when doors great and small,
Nine-and-ninety flew ope at our touch, should
    the hundredth appall?
In the least things have faith, yet distrust in
    the greatest of all?   265
Do I find love so full in my nature, God's
    ultimate gift,
That I doubt his own love can compete with
    it? Here, the parts shift?
Here, the creature surpass the Creator—the
    end, what Began?
Would I fain in my impotent yearning do all
    for this man,
And dare doubt he alone shall not help him,
    who yet alone can?   270
Would it ever have entered my mind, the bare
    will, much less power,
To bestow on this Saul what I sang of, the
    marvelous dower
Of the life he was gifted and filled with? to
    make such a soul,
Such a body, and then such an earth for in-
    sphering the whole?
And doth it not enter my mind (as my warm
    tears attest)   275
These good things being given, to go on, and
    give one more, the best?
Aye, to save and redeem and restore him,
    maintain at the height
This perfection—succeed with life's day-
    spring, death's minute of night?
Interpose at the difficult minute, snatch Saul
    the mistake,
Saul the failure, the ruin he seems now—and
    bid him awake   280
From the dream, the probation, the prelude,
    to find himself set
Clear and safe in new light and new life—a
    new harmony yet
To be run, and continued, and ended—who
    knows?—or endure!
The man taught enough by life's dream, of
    the rest to make sure;
By the pain-throb, triumphantly winning in-
    tensified bliss,   285
And the next world's reward and repose, by
    the struggles in this.

18

"I believe it! 'Tis thou, God, that givest, 'tis
    I who receive;
In the first is the last, in thy will is my power
    to believe.
All's one gift; thou canst grant it moreover,
    as prompt to my prayer
As I breathe out this breath, as I open these
    arms to the air.   290
From thy will stream the worlds, life, and
    nature, thy dread Sabaoth;
I will?—the mere atoms despise me! Why am
    I not loath
To look that, even that, in the face too? Why
    is it I dare
Think but lightly of such impuissance? What
    stops my despair?
This—'tis not what man Does which exalts
    him, but what man Would do!   295

291. **Sabaoth,** literally, armies or hosts; it indicates the omnipotence of God. 295. **'tis . . . do!** Cf. *A Grammarian's Funeral,* ll. 113-120, p. 684, *Andrea del Sarto,* ll. 97-98, p. 695, and *Rabbi Ben Ezra,* ll. 40-41, p. 698.

See the King—I would help him but cannot
   —the wishes fall through.
Could I wrestle to raise him from sorrow,
   grow poor to enrich,
To fill up his life, starve my own out, I would
   —knowing which,
I know that my service is perfect. Oh, speak
   through me now!
Would I suffer for him that I love? So wouldst
   thou—so wilt thou!   300
So shall crown thee the topmost, ineffablest,
   uttermost crown—
And thy love fill infinite wholly, nor leave
   up nor down
One spot for the creature to stand in! It is by
   no breath,
Turn of eye, wave of hand, that salvation
   joins issue with death!
As thy love is discovered almighty, almighty
   be proved   305
Thy power, that exists with and for it, of
   being Beloved!
He who did most shall bear most; the strong-
   est shall stand the most weak.
'Tis the weakness in strength that I cry for!
   my flesh, that I seek
In the Godhead! I seek and I find it. O Saul,
   it shall be
A Face like my face that receives thee; a
   Man like to me,   310
Thou shalt love and be loved by, forever; a
   Hand like this hand
Shall throw open the gates of new life to thee!
   See the Christ stand!"

19

I know not too well how I found my way
   home in the night.
There were witnesses, cohorts about me, to
   left and to right,
Angels, powers, the unuttered, unseen, the
   alive, the aware;   315
I repressed, I got through them as hardly, as
   strugglingly there,
As a runner beset by the populace famished
   for news—
Life or death. The whole earth was awakened, hell loosed with her crews;
And the stars of night beat with emotion, and
   tingled and shot
Out in fire the strong pain of pent knowledge; but I fainted not,   320
For the Hand still impelled me at once and
   supported, suppressed
All the tumult, and quenched it with quiet,
   and holy behest,
Till the rapture was shut in itself, and the
   earth sank to rest.
Anon at the dawn, all that trouble had withered from earth—
Not so much, but I saw it die out in the day's
   tender birth;   325
In the gathered intensity brought to the gray
   of the hills;
In the shuddering forests' held breath; in the
   sudden wind-thrills;
In the startled wild beasts that bore off, each
   with eye sidling still
Though averted with wonder and dread; in
   the birds stiff and chill
That rose heavily, as I approached them,
   made stupid with awe;   330
E'en the serpent that slid away silent—he felt
   the new law.
The same stared in the white humid faces
   upturned by the flowers;
The same worked in the heart of the cedar
   and moved the vine-bowers;
And the little brooks, witnessing, murmured,
   persistent and low,
With their obstinate, all but hushed voices—
   "E'en so, it is so!"   *(1845; 1855)*

A Toccata of Galuppi's

   Baldassare Galuppi (1706-1785) was a noted popular Italian musician and composer. During his last years he was organist at St. Mark's Cathedral in Venice. Browning was very fond of playing his music. A toccata (Italian *toccare*, to touch) is a musical composition characterized by lightness of tone and freedom of movement. *A Toccata* is regarded as one of the finest of Browning's music poems.

O Galuppi, Baldassare, this is very sad to
   find!
I can hardly misconceive you; it would prove
   me deaf and blind;

But although I take your meaning, 'tis with
    such a heavy mind!

Here you come with your old music, and
    here's all the good it brings.
What, they lived once thus at Venice where
    the merchants were the kings,   5
Where St. Mark's is, where the Doges used
    to wed the sea with rings?

Aye, because the sea's the street there; and
    'tis arched by—what you call—
Shylock's bridge with houses on it, where
    they kept the carnival.
I was never out of England—it's as if I saw
    it all.

Did young people take their pleasure when
    the sea was warm in May?   10
Balls and masks begun at midnight, burning
    ever to mid-day,
When they made up fresh adventures for the
    morrow, do you say?

Was a lady such a lady, cheeks so round and
    lips so red—
On her neck the small face buoyant, like a
    bell-flower on its bed,
O'er the breast's superb abundance where a
    man might base his head?   15

Well, and it was graceful of them—they'd
    break talk off and afford—
She, to bite her mask's black velvet—he, to
    finger on his sword,
While you sat and played toccatas, stately
    at the clavichord?

What? Those lesser thirds so plaintive, sixths
    diminished, sigh on sigh,
Told them something? Those suspensions,
    those solutions—"Must we die?"   20
Those commiserating sevenths—"Life might
    last! we can but try!"

"Were you happy?"—"Yes."—"And are you
    still as happy?"—"Yes. And you?"
—"Then, more kisses!"—"Did *I* stop them,
    when a million seemed so few?"
Hark, the dominant's persistence till it must
    be answered to!

So, an octave struck the answer. Oh, they
    praised you, I dare say!   25
"Brave Galuppi! that was music! good alike
    at grave and gay!
I can always leave off talking when I hear a
    master play!"

Then they left you for their pleasure; till in
    due time, one by one,
Some with lives that came to nothing, some
    with deeds as well undone,
Death stepped tacitly and took them where
    they never see the sun.   30

But when I sit down to reason, think to take
    my stand nor swerve,
While I triumph o'er a secret wrung from
    nature's close reserve,
In you come with your cold music till I creep
    through every nerve.

Yes, you, like a ghostly cricket, creaking
    where a house was burned:
"Dust and ashes, dead and done with, Venice
    spent what Venice earned.   35
The soul, doubtless, is immortal—where a
    soul can be discerned.

"Yours, for instance: you know physics, some-
    thing of geology,
Mathematics are your pastime; souls shall rise
    in their degree;
Butterflies may dread extinction—you'll not
    die, it cannot be!

"As for Venice and her people, merely born
    to bloom and drop,   40
Here on earth they bore their fruitage, mirth
    and folly were the crop;
What of soul was left, I wonder, when the
    kissing had to stop?

---

6. **Doges.** The Doge was the chief magistrate of the city. **wed . . . rings.** See Wordsworth's *On the Extinction of the Venetian Republic,* and notes, p. 151. 8. **Shylock's bridge,** the Rialto, a bridge over the Grand Canal. Cf. Shakespeare's *Merchant of Venice.* 18. **clavichord,** an old-fashioned instrument with keys and strings, the predecessor of the modern piano. 19-24. The technical musical terms in these lines are made clear by accompanying phrases.

35-43. The quotation is what the music says to the speaker in the monologue concerning the men and the women for whom life meant merely a butterfly pleasure.

"Dust and ashes!" So you creak it, and I
    want the heart to scold.
Dear dead women, with such hair, too—
    what's become of all the gold
Used to hang and brush their bosoms? I feel
    chilly and grown old.   (1855)

"De Gustibus—"

Your ghost will walk, you lover of trees,
    (If our loves remain)
    In an English lane,
By a cornfield-side a-flutter with poppies.
Hark, those two in the hazel coppice—   5
A boy and a girl, if the good fates please,
    Making love, say—
    The happier they!
Draw yourself up from the light of the moon,
And let them pass, as they will too soon,   10
    With the beanflowers' boon,
    And the blackbird's tune,
    And May, and June!

What I love best in all the world
Is a castle, precipice-encurled,   15
In a gash of the wind-grieved Apennine.
Or look for me, old fellow of mine,
(If I get my head from out the mouth
O' the grave, and loose my spirit's bands,
And come again to the land of lands)   20
In a sea-side house to the farther South,
Where the baked cicala dies of drouth,
And one sharp tree—'tis a cypress—stands,
By the many hundred years red-rusted,
Rough iron-spiked, ripe fruit-o'ercrusted,   25
My sentinel to guard the sands
To the water's edge. For, what expands
Before the house, but the great opaque
Blue breadth of sea without a break?
While, in the house, forever crumbles   30
Some fragment of the frescoed walls,
From blisters where a scorpion sprawls.
A girl barefooted brings, and tumbles
Down on the pavement, green-flesh melons,
And says there's news today—the king   35
Was shot at, touched in the liver-wing,
Goes with his Bourbon arm in a sling—
She hopes they have not caught the felons.
Italy, my Italy!
Queen Mary's saying serves for me—   40
    (When fortune's malice
    Lost her, Calais)—
Open my heart and you will see
Graved inside of it, "Italy."
Such lovers old are I and she;   45
So it always was, so shall ever be!   (1855)

My Star

    This lyric is supposed to refer to Mrs. Browning. Cf. *Prospice*, p. 706.

    All that I know
      Of a certain star
    Is, it can throw
      (Like the angled spar)
    Now a dart of red,   5
      Now a dart of blue;
Till my friends have said
    They would fain see, too,
My star that dartles the red and the blue!
Then it stops like a bird; like a flower, hangs
    furled.   10
    They must solace themselves with the
      Saturn above it.
What matter to me if their star is a world?
    Mine has opened its soul to me; therefore
      I love it.   (1855)

Respectability

Dear, had the world in its caprice
    Deigned to proclaim, "I know you both,
    Have recognized your plighted troth,
    Am sponsor for you; live in peace!"—
How many precious months and years   5
    Of youth had passed, that speed so fast,

---

36. **liver-wing**, the right wing (the right arm). 37. **Bourbon**, Ferdinand II, King of the Two Sicilies (1830-1859), a member of the House of Bourbon. Browning is pleased that Italy is active against the Bourbons. 40. **Queen Mary's saying**, that the word *Calais* would be found written upon her heart. Queen Mary of England (1553-1558) made this statement when England lost Calais, her French seaport, in 1558.
    My Star. 4. **Like . . . spar**, like a prism, which reflects different colors from different angles.

    "De Gustibus—" The title is part of a Latin proverb—*De gustibus non disputandum*, there is no disputing about tastes. 2. **If . . . remain**, if we live after death. 4. **cornfield**, grainfield.

Before we found it out at last,
The world, and what it fears!

How much of priceless life were spent
    With men that every virtue decks,   10
    And women models of their sex,
Society's true ornament—
Ere we dared wander, nights like this,
    Through wind and rain, and watch the Seine,
    And feel the Boulevard break again   15
To warmth and light and bliss!

I know! the world proscribes not love;
    Allows my finger to caress
    Your lips' contour and downiness,
Provided it supply a glove.   20
The world's good word!—the Institute!
    Guizot receives Montalembert!
    Eh? Down the court three lampions flare;
Put forward your best foot!   (1855)

Memorabilia

The title means *Things Worth Remembering*. Browning first became acquainted with Shelley's poetry about 1825 and instantly fell under its spell. The poem was inspired by Browning's overhearing a stranger remark one day in a London bookshop that he had seen and talked with Shelley.

Ah, did you once see Shelley plain,
    And did he stop and speak to you,
And did you speak to him again?
    How strange it seems and new!

But you were living before that,   5
    And also you are living after;
And the memory I started at—
    My starting moves your laughter!

14. **Seine**, the Seine River, in Paris. 17. **the world ... glove.** The world will allow the caress if we buy gloves from it, i.e., if we pay the price by being conventional. 21. **the Institute,** the Institute of France, a national society established in 1795 to promote science, literature, and art. 22. **Guizot,** François Guizot (1787-1874), a French statesman and historian and a member of the Constitutional Royalist party. **Montalembert,** Charles Montalembert (1810-1870), a French publicist and historian and a member of the Liberal party. Although Guizot disliked Montalembert, he welcomed him into the Institute as a matter of convention. 23. **lampions,** lamps, which indicate a place where respectables are gathered; hence you must be conventional as you approach, or be condemned.

I crossed a moor, with a name of its own
    And a certain use in the world, no doubt,   10
Yet a hand's-breadth of it shines alone
    'Mid the blank miles round about;

For there I picked up on the heather,
    And there I put inside my breast
A molted feather, an eagle-feather!   15
    Well, I forget the rest.   (1855)

A Grammarian's Funeral

SHORTLY AFTER THE REVIVAL OF LEARNING IN EUROPE

The speaker of the poem is a disciple of a dead scholar of the early Renaissance noted for his inexhaustible passion for knowledge. He leads other disciples as they bear the body of their master to the top of a lofty mountain for burial at sunrise. Cf. Pater's *Renaissance*, p. 583. See Vol. I, pp. 301 ff.

Let us begin and carry up this corpse,
    Singing together.
Leave we the common crofts, the vulgar thorpes,
    Each in its tether
Sleeping safe on the bosom of the plain,   5
    Cared for till cock-crow;
Look out if yonder be not day again
    Rimming the rock-row!
That's the appropriate country; there, man's thought,
    Rarer, intenser,   10
Self-gathered for an outbreak, as it ought,
    Chafes in the censer.
Leave we the unlettered plain its herd and crop;
    Seek we sepulture
On a tall mountain, citied to the top,   15
    Crowded with culture!
All the peaks soar, but one the rest excels;
    Clouds overcome it;
No! yonder sparkle is the citadel's

3. **crofts,** enclosed farm lands. **thorpes,** hamlets. 7. **day ... rock-row.** The sun's rays are just striking the rocky tops of the mountains. 12. **in the censer.** The figure of speech likens man's seething brain to the censer or ecclesiastical vessel which holds the burning incense. 18. **overcome,** conceal.

Circling its summit.   20
Thither our path lies; wind we up the heights;
    Wait ye the warning?
Our low life was the level's and the night's;
    He's for the morning.
Step to a tune, square chests, erect each head,
    'Ware the beholders!   26
This is our master, famous, calm, and dead,
    Borne on our shoulders.

Sleep, crop and herd! sleep, darkling thorpe
        and croft,
    Safe from the weather!   30
He whom we convoy to his grave aloft,
    Singing together,
He was a man born with thy face and throat,
    Lyric Apollo!
Long he lived nameless; how should Spring
        take note   35
    Winter would follow?
Till lo, the little touch, and youth was gone!
    Cramped and diminished,
Moaned he, "New measures, other feet anon!
    My dance is finished"?   40
No, that's the world's way (keep the moun-
        tain-side,
    Make for the city!);
He knew the signal, and stepped on with
        pride
    Over men's pity;
Left play for work, and grappled with the
        world   45
    Bent on escaping;
"What's in the scroll," quoth he, "thou keep-
        est furled?
    Show me their shaping,
Theirs who most studied man, the bard and
        sage—
    Give!"—So, he gowned him,   50
Straight got by heart that book to its last page;
    Learned, we found him.
Yea, but we found him bald too, eyes like lead,
    Accents uncertain;
"Time to taste life," another would have said,

"Up with the curtain!"   55
This man said rather, "Actual life comes
        next?
    Patience a moment!
Grant I have mastered learning's crabbed text,
    Still there's the comment.   60
Let me know all! Prate not of most or least,
    Painful or easy!
Even to the crumbs I'd fain eat up the feast,
    Aye, nor feel queasy."
Oh, such a life as he resolved to live,   65
    When he had learned it,
When he had gathered all books had to give!
    Sooner, he spurned it.
Image the whole, then execute the parts—
    Fancy the fabric   70
Quite, ere you build, ere steel strike fire from
        quartz,
    Ere mortar dab brick!

(Here's the town-gate reached; there's the
        market-place
    Gaping before us.)
Yea, this in him was the peculiar grace   75
    (Hearten our chorus!)
That before living he'd learn how to live—
    No end to learning;
Earn the means first—God surely will contrive
    Use for our earning.   80
Others mistrust and say, "But time escapes;
    Live now or never!"
He said, "What's time? Leave Now for dogs
        and apes!
    Man has Forever."
Back to his book then; deeper drooped his
        head;   85
    Calculus racked him;
Leaden before, his eyes grew dross of lead;
    Tussis attacked him.
"Now, master, take a little rest!"—not he!
    (Caution redoubled,   90
Step two abreast, the way winds narrowly!)
    Not a whit troubled,
Back to his studies, fresher than at first,
    Fierce as a dragon
He (soul-hydroptic with a sacred thirst)   95
    Sucked at the flagon.
Oh, if we draw a circle premature,

25-26. These lines are directions to the bearers, as are also the passages in parentheses in lines 41, 73, 76, 90. 26. **'Ware the beholders**, i.e., reveal our pride to the onlookers. 34. **Apollo**, the Greek god of manly beauty and of music. 47. **scroll**, manuscript; this was before the time of books. 50. **he gowned him**, he put on the scholastic gown.

86. **Calculus**, the disease called the stone. 88. **Tussis**, a bronchial cough. 95. **soul-hydroptic**, soul-thirsty.

Heedless of far gain,
Greedy for quick returns of profit, sure
    Bad is our bargain!   100
Was it not great? did not he throw on God
    (He loves the burthen)—
God's task to make the heavenly period
    Perfect the earthen?
Did not he magnify the mind, show clear 105
    Just what it all meant?
He would not discount life, as fools do here,
    Paid by instalment.
He ventured neck or nothing—heaven's success
    Found, or earth's failure: 110
"Wilt thou trust death or not?" He answered "Yes!
Hence with life's pale lure!"
That low man seeks a little thing to do,
    Sees it and does it;
This high man, with a great thing to pursue,
    Dies ere he knows it.   116
That low man goes on adding one to one,
    His hundred's soon hit;
This high man, aiming at a million,
    Misses an unit.   120
That, has the world here—should he need the next,
    Let the world mind him!
This, throws himself on God, and unperplexed
    Seeking shall find him.
So, with the throttling hands of death at strife,
    Ground he at grammar;   126
Still, through the rattle, parts of speech were rife;
    While he could stammer
He settled *Hoti's* business—let it be!—
    Properly based *Oun*—   130
Gave us the doctrine of the enclitic *De*,
    Dead from the waist down.
Well, here's the platform, here's the proper place;
    Hail to your purlieus,
All ye highfliers of the feathered race,   135
    Swallows and curlews!
Here's the top-peak; the multitude below
    Live, for they can, there;
This man decided not to Live but Know—
    Bury this man there?   140
Here—here's his place, where meteors shoot, clouds form,
    Lightnings are loosened,
Stars come and go! Let joy break with the storm,
    Peace let the dew send!
Lofty designs must close in like effects;   145
    Loftily lying,
Leave him—still loftier than the world suspects,
    Living and dying.   (1855)

113-124. These lines express a favorite doctrine with Browning. Cf. *Saul*, l. 295, p. 678, *Andrea del Sarto*, ll. 97-98, p. 695, and *Rabbi Ben Ezra*, ll. 40-41, p. 698.

127. **the rattle**, the death rattle in his throat. 129-131. *Hoti, Oun,* and *De* are Greek particles meaning respectively *that, therefore,* and *toward;* they provide critical points of syntax. 134. **purlieus**, haunts.

"Childe Roland to the Dark Tower Came"

This poem is based upon Edgar's mad song in *King Lear*, III, iv, 171-173:

> Child Rowland to the dark tower came,
> His word was still—Fie, foh, and fum,
> I smell the blood of a British man.

The title *Childe* was given as an appellation to a youth of noble birth and appears occasionally in the ballads. Browning's statement of the moral of the poem was that it commended the idea that "He that endureth to the end shall be saved."

My first thought was, he lied in every word,
    That hoary cripple, with malicious eye
    Askance to watch the working of his lie
On mine, and mouth scarce able to afford
Suppression of the glee, that pursed and scored   5
    Its edge, at one more victim gained thereby.

What else should he be set for, with his staff?
  What, save to waylay with his lies, ensnare
  All travelers who might find him posted there,
And ask the road? I guessed what skull-like laugh   10
Would break, what crutch 'gin write my epitaph
  For pastime in the dusty thoroughfare,

If at his counsel I should turn aside
  Into that ominous tract which, all agree,
  Hides the Dark Tower. Yet acquiescingly
I did turn as he pointed—neither pride   15
Nor hope rekindling at the end descried,
  So much as gladness that some end might be.

For, what with my whole world-wide wandering,
  What with my search drawn out through years, my hope   20
  Dwindled into a ghost not fit to cope
With that obstreperous joy success would bring—
  I hardly tried now to rebuke the spring
  My heart made, finding failure in its scope.

As when a sick man very near to death   25
  Seems dead indeed, and feels begin and end
  The tears, and takes the farewell of each friend,
And hears one bid the other go, draw breath
Freelier outside ("since all is o'er," he saith,
  "And the blow fallen no grieving can amend"),   30

While some discuss if near the other graves
  Be room enough for this, and when a day
  Suits best for carrying the corpse away,
With care about the banners, scarves, and staves;
And still the man hears all, and only craves   35
  He may not shame such tender love and stay.

Thus, I had so long suffered in this quest,
  Heard failure prophesied so oft, been writ
  So many times among "The Band"—to wit,
The knights who to the Dark Tower's search addressed   40
  Their steps—that just to fail as they, seemed best,
  And all the doubt was now—should I be fit?

So, quiet as despair, I turned from him,
  That hateful cripple, out of his highway
  Into the path he pointed. All the day   45
Had been a dreary one at best, and dim
Was settling to its close, yet shot one grim
  Red leer to see the plain catch its estray.

For mark! no sooner was I fairly found
  Pledged to the plain, after a pace or two,   50
  Than, pausing to throw backward a last view
O'er the safe road, 'twas gone; gray plain all round—
Nothing but plain to the horizon's bound.
  I might go on; naught else remained to do.

So, on I went. I think I never saw   55
  Such starved ignoble nature; nothing throve;
  For flowers—as well expect a cedar grove!
But cockle, spurge, according to their law
Might propagate their kind, with none to awe,
  You'd think; a burr had been a treasure trove.   60

No! penury, inertness, and grimace,
  In some strange sort, were the land's portion. "See
  Or shut your eyes," said Nature peevishly,
"It nothing skills—I cannot help my case;
'Tis the Last Judgment's fire must cure this place,   65
  Calcine its clods, and set my prisoners free."

If there pushed any ragged thistle-stalk
  Above its mates, the head was chopped; the bents
  Were jealous else. What made those holes and rents
In the dock's harsh swarth leaves, bruised as to balk   70

---

48. **estray**, the one who has strayed—namely, Childe Roland. 58. **cockle, spurge**, common wild shrubs. 64. **skills**, matters. 66. **Calcine**, reduce to powder by heat. 68. **bents**, coarse grasses. 70. **dock**, a kind of weed.

All hope of greenness? 'Tis a brute must walk
  Pashing their life out, with a brute's intents.

As for the grass, it grew as scant as hair
  In leprosy; thin dry blades pricked the mud,
  Which underneath looked kneaded up with blood. 75
One stiff blind horse, his every bone a-stare,
Stood stupefied, however he came there—
  Thrust out past service from the devil's stud!

Alive? He might be dead for aught I know,
  With that red gaunt and colloped neck a-strain, 80
  And shut eyes underneath the rusty mane;
Seldom went such grotesqueness with such woe;
I never saw a brute I hated so;
  He must be wicked to deserve such pain.

I shut my eyes and turned them on my heart.
  As a man calls for wine before he fights, 86
  I asked one draft of earlier, happier sights,
Ere fitly I could hope to play my part.
Think first, fight afterwards—the soldier's art;
  One taste of the old time sets all to rights. 90

Not it! I fancied Cuthbert's reddening face
  Beneath its garniture of curly gold,
  Dear fellow, till I almost felt him fold
An arm in mine to fix me to the place,
That way he used. Alas, one night's disgrace!
  Out went my heart's new fire and left it cold. 96

Giles then, the soul of honor—there he stands
  Frank as ten years ago when knighted first.
  What honest man should dare (he said) he durst.
Good—but the scene shifts—faugh! what hangman hands 100
Pin to his breast a parchment? His own bands
  Read it. Poor traitor, spit upon and cursed!

Better this present than a past like that;
  Back therefore to my darkening path again!

No sound, no sight as far as eye could strain. 105
Will the night send a howlet or a bat?
I asked—when something on the dismal flat
  Came to arrest my thoughts and change their train.

A sudden little river crossed my path
  As unexpected as a serpent comes. 110
  No sluggish tide congenial to the glooms;
This, as it frothed by, might have been a bath
For the fiend's glowing hoof—to see the wrath
  Of its black eddy bespate with flakes and spumes.

So petty yet so spiteful! All along, 115
  Low scrubby alders kneeled down over it;
  Drenched willows flung them headlong in a fit
Of mute despair, a suicidal throng;
The river which had done them all the wrong,
  Whate'er that was, rolled by, deterred no whit. 120

Which, while I forded—good saints, how I feared
  To set my foot upon a dead man's cheek,
  Each step, or feel the spear I thrust to seek
For hollows, tangled in his hair or beard!
—It may have been a water rat I speared, 125
  But, ugh! it sounded like a baby's shriek.

Glad was I when I reached the other bank.
  Now for a better country. Vain presage!
  Who were the strugglers, what war did they wage,
Whose savage trample thus could pad the dank 130
Soil to a plash? Toads in a poisoned tank,
  Or wild cats in a red-hot iron cage—

The fight must so have seemed in that fell cirque.
  What penned them there, with all the plain to choose?
  No footprint leading to that horrid mews,
None out of it. Mad brewage set to work 135

---

72. **Pashing**, crushing. 76. **One . . . horse.** The figure of a lean horse in a piece of tapestry in Browning's drawing-room furnished this picture. 80. **colloped**, marked with ridges.

114. **bespate**, spattered. 130. **pad**, tread down. 131. **plash**, puddle. 133. **cirque**, circle. 135. **mews**, enclosure, pen.

Their brains, no doubt, like galley-slaves the Turk
    Pits for his pastime, Christians against Jews.

And more than that—a furlong on—why, there!
    What bad use was that engine for, that wheel,   140
Or brake, not wheel—that harrow fit to reel
Men's bodies out like silk? with all the air
Of Tophet's tool, on earth left unaware,
    Or brought to sharpen its rusty teeth of steel.

Then came a bit of stubbed ground, once a wood,   145
    Next a marsh, it would seem, and now mere earth
    Desperate and done with—so a fool finds mirth,
Makes a thing and then mars it, till his mood
Changes and off he goes!—within a rood,
    Bog, clay, and rubble, sand, and stark black dearth.   150

Now blotches rankling, colored gay and grim,
    Now patches where some leanness of the soil's
    Broke into moss or substances like boils;
Then came some palsied oak, a cleft in him
Like a distorted mouth that splits its rim   155
    Gaping at death, and dies while it recoils.

And just as far as ever from the end!
    Naught in the distance but the evening, naught
    To point my footstep further! At the thought
A great black bird, Apollyon's bosom friend,
Sailed past, nor beat his wide wing dragon-penned   161
    That brushed my cap—perchance the guide I sought.

For, looking up, aware I somehow grew,
    'Spite of the dusk, the plain had given place

All round to mountains—with such name to grace   165
    Mere ugly heights and heaps now stolen in view.
    How thus they had surprised me—solve it, you!
How to get from them was no clearer case.

Yet half I seemed to recognize some trick
    Of mischief happened to me, God knows when—   170
    In a bad dream, perhaps. Here ended, then,
Progress this way. When, in the very nick
Of giving up, one time more, came a click
    As when a trap shuts—you're inside the den!

Burningly it came on me all at once,   175
    This was the place! those two hills on the right,
    Crouched like two bulls locked horn in horn in fight;
While to the left, a tall scalped mountain . . . Dunce,
Dotard, a-dozing at the very nonce,
    After a life spent training for the sight!   180

What in the midst lay but the Tower itself?
    The round squat turret, blind as the fool's heart,
    Built of brown stone, without a counterpart
In the whole world. The tempest's mocking elf
Points to the shipman thus the unseen shelf   185
    He strikes on, only when the timbers start.

Not see? because of night, perhaps?—why, day
    Came back again for that! before it left,
    The dying sunset kindled through a cleft;
The hills, like giants at a hunting, lay   190
Chin upon hand, to see the game at bay—
    "Now stab and end the creature—to the heft!"

Not hear? when noise was everywhere! it tolled
    Increasing like a bell. Names in my ears,
    Of all the lost adventurers my peers—   195

---

143. **Tophet**, an Old Testament name for hell. 150. **rubble**, broken stone. 160. **Apollyon**, the devil; he is "the angel of the bottomless pit" in *Revelation*, 9. 161. **dragon-penned**, furnished with feathers like those in a dragon's wing.

How such a one was strong, and such was
    bold,
And such was fortunate, yet each of old
    Lost, lost! one moment knelled the woe of
    years.

There they stood, ranged along the hillsides,
    met

To view the last of me, a living frame   200
For one more picture! in a sheet of flame
I saw them and I knew them all. And yet
Dauntless the slug-horn to my lips I set,
    And blew. "*Childe Roland to the Dark
    Tower came.*"   (*1852;* 1855)

203. **slug-horn**, a trumpet; an erroneous use of *slughorn*, the early form of *slogan*.

Fra Lippo Lippi

Fra Lippo Lippi (1406-1469)—Filippo Lippi—was a famous Florentine painter. The account upon which Browning based his interpretation of Lippi's life and art was found in Vasari's *Lives of the Painters*. Lippi is talking to Florentine guards who have caught him in a nocturnal frolic.

I am poor brother Lippo, by your leave!
You need not clap your torches to my face.
Zooks, what's to blame? you think you see a
    monk!
What, 'tis past midnight, and you go the
    rounds,
And here you catch me at an alley's end   5
Where sportive ladies leave their doors ajar?
The Carmine's my cloister; hunt it up,
Do—harry out, if you must show your zeal,
Whatever rat, there, haps on his wrong hole,
And nip each softling of a wee white mouse,
Weke, weke, that's crept to keep him com-
    pany!   11
Aha, you know your betters! Then, you'll
    take
Your hand away that's fiddling on my throat,
And please to know me likewise. Who am I?
Why, one, sir, who is lodging with a friend   15
Three streets off—he's a certain . . . how d'
    ye call?
Master—a . . . Cosimo of the Medici,
I' the house that caps the corner. Boh! you
    were best!
Remember and tell me, the day you're hanged,
How you affected such a gullet's gripe!   20
But you, sir, it concerns you that your knaves
Pick up a manner nor discredit you;

Zooks, are we pilchards, that they sweep the
    streets
And count fair prize what comes into their
    net?
He's Judas to a tittle, that man is!   25
Just such a face! Why, sir, you make amends.
Lord, I'm not angry! Bid your hangdogs go
Drink out this quarter-florin to the health
Of the munificent House that harbors me
(And many more beside, lads! more beside!)
And all's come square again! I'd like his
    face—   31
His, elbowing on his comrade in the door
With the pike and lantern—for the slave that
    holds
John Baptist's head a-dangle by the hair
With one hand ("Look you, now," as who
    should say)   35
And his weapon in the other, yet unwiped!
It's not your chance to have a bit of chalk,
A wood-coal or the like? or you should see!
Yes, I'm the painter, since you style me so.
What, brother Lippo's doings, up and down,
You know them and they take you? like
    enough!   41
I saw the proper twinkle in your eye—
'Tell you, I liked your looks at very first.
Let's sit and set things straight now, hip to
    haunch.

3. **Zooks**, an oath shortened from *Gadzooks, Godzooks;* the meaning of the second syllable is not clear. 7. **The Carmine's.** Lippo entered the monastery of the Carmelite friars of the Carmine in Florence in 1420. 17. **Cosimo of the Medici,** Cosimo de' Medici (1389-1464), a rich Florentine banker, statesman, and patron of art and literature; the Medici palace, now known as the Palazzo Riccardi, is on the corner of Via Cavour and Via Gori.

23. **pilchards,** a kind of cheap common fish. 28. **quarter-florin.** The florin was a small gold coin first issued in Florence in 1252. It was probably worth about two dollars. 33. **the slave . . . hair,** an imaginary picture; in Lippo's real picture of the beheading of John the Baptist, the head is carried on a great platter by Salome, the daughter of Herodias. See *Matthew*, 14:1-12.

Here's spring come, and the nights one makes
    up bands   45
To roam the town and sing out carnival,
And I've been three weeks shut within my
    mew,
A-painting for the great man, saints and saints
And saints again. I could not paint all night—
Ouf! I leaned out of window for fresh air. 50
There came a hurry of feet and little feet,
A sweep of lute strings, laughs, and whiffs
    of song—
Flower o' the broom,
Take away love, and our earth is a tomb!
Flower o' the quince, 55
I let Lisa go, and what good in life since?
Flower o' the thyme—and so on. Round they
    went.
Scarce had they turned the corner when a
    titter
Like the skipping of rabbits by moonlight—
    three slim shapes,
And a face that looked up . . . zooks, sir,
    flesh and blood, 60
That's all I'm made of! Into shreds it went,
Curtain and counterpane and coverlet,
All the bed furniture—a dozen knots,
There was a ladder! Down I let myself,
Hands and feet, scrambling somehow, and so
    dropped, 65
And after them. I came up with the fun
Hard by Saint Laurence, hail fellow, well
    met—
Flower o' the rose,
If I've been merry, what matter who knows?
And so as I was stealing back again 70
To get to bed and have a bit of sleep
Ere I rise up tomorrow and go work
On Jerome knocking at his poor old breast
With his great round stone to subdue the
    flesh,
You snap me of a sudden. Ah, I see! 75
Though your eye twinkles still, you shake
    your head—
Mine's shaved—a monk, you say—the sting's
    in that!
If Master Cosimo announced himself,
Mum's the word naturally; but a monk!
Come, what am I a beast for? tell us, now! 80
I was a baby when my mother died
And father died and left me in the street.
I starved there, God knows how, a year or two
On fig skins, melon parings, rinds, and shucks,
Refuse and rubbish. One fine frosty day, 85
My stomach being empty as your hat,
The wind doubled me up, and down I went.
Old Aunt Lapaccia trussed me with one hand
(Its fellow was a stinger as I knew),
And so along the wall, over the bridge, 90
By the straight cut to the convent. Six words
    there,
While I stood munching my first bread that
    month:
"So, boy, you're minded," quoth the good fat
    father,
Wiping his own mouth—'twas refection
    time—
"To quit this very miserable world? 95
Will you renounce" . . . "the mouthful of
    bread?" thought I;
By no means! Brief, they made a monk of me;
I did renounce the world, its pride and greed,
Palace, farm, villa, shop, and banking house,
Trash, such as these poor devils of Medici
Have given their hearts to—all at eight years
    old. 101
Well, sir, I found in time, you may be sure,
'Twas not for nothing—the good bellyful,
The warm serge, and the rope that goes all
    round,
And day-long blessed idleness beside! 105
"Let's see what the urchin's fit for"—that
    came next.
Not overmuch their way, I must confess.
Such a to-do! They tried me with their books;
Lord, they'd have taught me Latin in pure
    waste!
Flower o' the clove, 110
All the Latin I construe is "amo," I love!

---

46. **carnival**, a period of gayety preceding Lent. 47. **mew**, coop, pen. (Lippo had been engaged to paint pictures in the palace and had been locked in a room until the work should be done.) 52. **song**. The song that follows is a *stornello*, a kind of short folksong of the Italians, usually improvised on the name of a flower or some other familiar object. 67. **Saint Laurence**, the Church of San Lorenzo. 73. **Jerome . . . breast.** Saint Jerome (340?-420) was the most learned of the early Fathers of the Latin Church. He lived in the desert for several years as a penance for his youthful sins. Early Christian art depicted him on his knees before a crucifix, beating his breast with a stone.

88. **Aunt Lapaccia**, Mona Lapaccia, his father's sister. **trussed me**, lifted me up. 94. **refection time**, lunch time.

But, mind you, when a boy starves in the streets
Eight years together, as my fortune was,
Watching folk's faces to know who will fling
The bit of half-stripped grape-bunch he desires, 115
And who will curse or kick him for his pains—
Which gentleman processional and fine,
Holding a candle to the Sacrament,
Will wink and let him lift a plate and catch
The droppings of the wax to sell again, 120
Or holla for the Eight and have him whipped—
How say I?—nay, which dog bites, which lets drop
His bone from the heap of offal in the street—
Why, soul and sense of him grow sharp alike;
He learns the look of things, and none the less
For admonition from the hunger pinch. 126
I had a store of such remarks, be sure,
Which, after I found leisure, turned to use.
I drew men's faces on my copy books,
Scrawled them within the antiphonary's marge, 130
Joined legs and arms to the long music-notes,
Found eyes and nose and chin for A's and B's,
And made a string of pictures of the world
Betwixt the ins and outs of verb and noun,
On the wall, the bench, the door. The monks looked black. 135
"Nay," quoth the Prior, "turn him out, d'ye say?
In no wise. Lose a crow and catch a lark.
What if at last we get our man of parts,
We Carmelites, like those Camaldolese
And Preaching Friars, to do our church up fine 140
And put the front on it that ought to be!"
And hereupon he bade me daub away.

117. **gentleman processional**, etc., gentlemen wearing fine robes and walking in the religious procession. 121. **the Eight**, the magistrates who governed Florence. 130. **antiphonary's marge**, the margins of the books used by the choir. 131. **long music-notes**. The medieval music notes were square or oblong with long stems. 139. **Carmelites**, etc. The Carmelites were monks of the Order of Mount Carmel, in Syria; the **Camaldolese** belonged to the convent of Camaldoli, near Florence; the **Preaching Friars** are the Dominicans, named after St. Dominic; they were called Brothers Preachers by Pope Innocent III in 1215. These orders owned various monasteries and churches and were eager to possess the greatest religious paintings. 141. **the front**, etc. The façade of the Church of the Medici in Florence (San Lorenzo), designed by Michaelangelo, has never been finished but presents ragged brickwork, waiting for its marble veneer.

Thank you! my head being crammed, the walls a blank,
Never was such prompt disemburdening.
First, every sort of monk, the black and white,
I drew them, fat and lean; then, folk at church,
From good old gossips waiting to confess 147
Their cribs of barrel droppings, candle ends—
To the breathless fellow at the altar foot,
Fresh from his murder, safe and sitting there
With the little children round him in a row 151
Of admiration, half for his beard and half
For that white anger of his victim's son
Shaking a fist at him with one fierce arm,
Signing himself with the other because of Christ 155
(Whose sad face on the cross sees only this
After the passion of a thousand years),
Till some poor girl, her apron o'er her head
(Which the intense eyes looked through),
came at eve
On tiptoe, said a word, dropped in a loaf, 160
Her pair of earrings, and a bunch of flowers
(The brute took growling), prayed, and so was gone.
I painted all, then cried, "'Tis ask and have;
Choose, for more's ready!"—laid the ladder flat, 164
And showed my covered bit of cloister wall.
The monks closed in a circle and praised loud
Till checked, taught what to see and not to see,
Being simple bodies—"That's the very man!
Look at the boy who stoops to pat the dog!
That woman's like the Prior's niece who comes
To care about his asthma; it's the life!" 171
But there my triumph's straw-fire flared and funked;
Their betters took their turn to see and say;
The Prior and the learned pulled a face
And stopped all that in no time. "How? what's here? 175
Quite from the mark of painting, bless us all!
Faces, arms, legs, and bodies like the true
As much as pea and pea! It's devil's game!
Your business is not to catch men with show,
With homage to the perishable clay, 180

148. **Their cribs**, etc., small thefts of wine, wax, etc. 150. **safe**, because he is in a sacred place, which by the law of the medieval church protected him from arrest. 154. **Shaking . . . Christ**. Revenge and religion are at war in him. 157. **passion** suffering. 172. **funked**, smoked.

But lift them over it, ignore it all,
Make them forget there's such a thing as flesh.
Your business is to paint the souls of men—
Man's soul, and it's a fire, smoke . . . no, it's not . . .
It's vapor done up like a new-born babe   185
(In that shape when you die it leaves your mouth)—
It's . . . well, what matters talking, it's the soul!
Give us no more of body than shows soul!
Here's Giotto, with his Saint a-praising God,
That sets us praising—why not stop with him?   190
Why put all thoughts of praise out of our head
With wonder at lines, colors, and what not?
Paint the soul, never mind the legs and arms!
Rub all out, try at it a second time.
Oh, that white smallish female with the breasts,   195
She's just my niece . . . Herodias, I would say—
Who went and danced and got men's heads cut off!
Have it all out!" Now, is this sense, I ask?
A fine way to paint soul, by painting body
So ill the eye can't stop there, must go further
And can't fare worse! Thus, yellow does for white   201
When what you put for yellow's simply black,
And any sort of meaning looks intense
When all beside itself means and looks naught.
Why can't a painter lift each foot in turn,   205
Left foot and right foot, go a double step,
Make his flesh liker and his soul more like,
Both in their order? Take the prettiest face,
The Prior's niece . . . patron saint—is it so pretty
You can't discover if it means hope, fear,   210
Sorrow, or joy? won't beauty go with these?
Suppose I've made her eyes all right and blue,
Can't I take breath and try to add life's flash,
And then add soul and heighten them threefold?
Or say there's beauty with no soul at all   215
(I never saw it—put the case the same);
If you get simple beauty and naught else,
You get about the best thing God invents—
That's somewhat; and you'll find the soul you have missed,
Within yourself, when you return him thanks.
"Rub all out!" Well, well, there's my life, in short,   221
And so the thing has gone on ever since.
I'm grown a man no doubt, I've broken bounds;
You should not take a fellow eight years old
And make him swear to never kiss the girls.   225
I'm my own master, paint now as I please—
Having a friend, you see, in the Corner-house!
Lord, it's fast holding by the rings in front—
Those great rings serve more purposes than just
To plant a flag in, or tie up a horse!   230
And yet the old schooling sticks, the old grave eyes
Are peeping o'er my shoulder as I work,
The heads shake still—"It's art's decline, my son!
You're not of the true painters, great and old;
Brother Angelico's the man, you'll find;   235
Brother Lorenzo stands his single peer—
Fag on at flesh, you'll never make the third!"
Flower o' the pine,
You keep your mistr . . . manners, and I'll stick to mine!
I'm not the third, then; bless us, they must know!   240
Don't you think they're the likeliest to know,
They with their Latin? So, I swallow my rage,
Clench my teeth, suck my lips in tight, and paint
To please them—sometimes do and sometimes don't;
For, doing most, there's pretty sure to come   245
A turn, some warm eve finds me at my saints—
A laugh, a cry, the business of the world
(*Flower o' the peach,*
Death for us all, and his own life for each!)—

189. **Giotto**, Giotto di Bondone (1267?-1337), a famous Florentine painter, architect, and sculptor. He expressed the soul in his paintings and cared nothing for realistic art. Lippo and Guidi (l. 276) introduced realism, which Lippo here defends. 196. **Herodias**. See note on ll. 33-34, p. 688.

228. **the rings in front**, large iron rings on the front of the palace. Lippo used them in climbing in and out of his window. 235. **Brother Angelico**, Fra Angelico, Giovanni da Fiesole (1387-1455), the greatest of the medieval school of religious artists who "painted souls." 236. **Brother Lorenzo**, Lorenzo Monaco, a painter of the Order of the Camaldolese, who also "painted souls."

And my whole soul revolves, the cup runs
    over,   250
The world and life's too big to pass for a
    dream,
And I do these wild things in sheer despite,
And play the fooleries you catch me at,
In pure rage! The old mill-horse, out at grass
After hard years, throws up his stiff heels so,
Although the miller does not preach to him 256
The only good of grass is to make chaff.
What would men have? Do they like grass
    or no—
May they or mayn't they? All I want's the
    thing
Settled forever one way. As it is,   260
You tell too many lies and hurt yourself;
You don't like what you only like too much,
You do like what, if given you at your word,
You find abundantly detestable.
For me, I think I speak as I was taught;   265
I always see the garden and God there
A-making man's wife; and, my lesson
    learned—
The value and significance of flesh—
I can't unlearn ten minutes afterwards.

    You understand me; I'm a beast, I know. 270
But see, now—why, I see as certainly
As that the morning star's about to shine,
What will hap some day. We've a youngster
    here
Comes to our convent, studies what I do,
Slouches and stares and lets no atom drop. 275
His name is Guidi—he'll not mind the
    monks—
They call him Hulking Tom; he lets them talk;
He picks my practice up—he'll paint apace,
I hope so—though I never live so long,
I know what's sure to follow. You be judge!
You speak no Latin more than I, belike;   281
However, you're my man, you've seen the
    world—
The beauty and the wonder and the power,
The shapes of things, their colors, lights, and
    shades,
Changes, surprises—and God made it all!   285

—For what? Do you feel thankful, aye or no,
For this fair town's face, yonder river's line,
The mountain round it and the sky above,
Much more the figures of man, woman, child,
These are the frame to? What's it all about?
To be passed over, despised? or dwelt upon, 291
Wondered at? Oh, this last of course!—you
    say.
But why not do as well as say—paint these
Just as they are, careless what comes of it?
God's works—paint any one, and count it
    crime   295
To let a truth slip. Don't object, "His works
Are here already; nature is complete:
Suppose you reproduce her—which you can't—
There's no advantage! you must beat her,
    then."
For, don't you mark? we're made so that we
    love   300
First when we see them painted, things we
    have passed
Perhaps a hundred times nor cared to see;
And so they are better, painted—better to us,
Which is the same thing. Art was given for
    that;
God uses us to help each other so,   305
Lending our minds out. Have you noticed,
    now,
Your cullion's hanging face? A bit of chalk,
And trust me but you should, though! How
    much more,
If I drew higher things with the same truth!
That were to take the Prior's pulpit-place, 310
Interpret God to all of you! Oh, oh,
It makes me mad to see what men shall do
And we in our graves! This world's no blot
    for us,
Nor blank; it means intensely, and means
    good—
To find its meaning is my meat and drink. 315
"Aye, but you don't so instigate to prayer!"
Strikes in the Prior; "when your meaning's
    plain,
It does not say to folk—remember matins,
Or, mind you fast next Friday!" Why, for this
What need of art at all? A skull and bones,
Two bits of stick nailed crosswise, or, what's
    best,   321

---

276. **Guidi**, Tommaso Guidi, or Masaccio (1401-1428), nicknamed Hulking Tom. He is said to have been the first Italian artist to paint a nude figure. He was Lippo's master, not his disciple.

307. cullion, a low fellow.

A bell to chime the hour with does as
    well.
I painted a Saint Laurence six months since
At Prato, splashed the fresco in fine style;
"How looks my painting, now the scaffold's
    down?"   325
I ask a brother. "Hugely," he returns—
"Already not one phiz of your three slaves
Who turn the Deacon off his toasted side,
But's scratched and prodded to our heart's
    content,
The pious people have so eased their own   330
With coming to say prayers there in a rage;
We get on fast to see the bricks beneath.
Expect another job this time next year,
For pity and religion grow i' the crowd—
Your painting serves its purpose!" Hang the
    fools!   335

—That is—you'll not mistake an idle word
Spoke in a huff by a poor monk, God wot,
Tasting the air this spicy night, which turns
The unaccustomed head like Chianti wine!
Oh, the church knows! don't misreport me,
    now!   340
It's natural a poor monk out of bounds
Should have his apt word to excuse himself;
And hearken how I plot to make amends.
I have bethought me: I shall paint a piece
. . . There's for you! Give me six months,
    then go, see   345
Something in Sant' Ambrogio's! Bless the
    nuns!
They want a cast o' my office. I shall paint
God in the midst, Madonna and her babe,
Ringed by a bowery, flowery angel brood,
Lilies and vestments and white faces, sweet
As puff on puff of grated orris root   351
When ladies crowd to Church at midsummer.
And then i' the front, of course a saint or
    two—
Saint John, because he saves the Florentines,
Saint Ambrose, who puts down in black and
    white   355
The convent's friends and gives them a long
    day,
And Job, I must have him there past mistake,
The man of Uz (and Us without the z,
Painters who need his patience). Well, all
    these
Secured at their devotion, up shall come   360
Out of a corner when you least expect,
As one by a dark stair into a great light,
Music and talking, who but Lippo! I!—
Mazed, motionless, and moonstruck—I'm the
    man!
Back I shrink—what is this I see and hear?
I, caught up with my monk's-things by mis-
    take,   365
My old serge gown and rope that goes all
    round,
I, in this presence, this pure company!
Where's a hole, where's a corner for escape?
Then steps a sweet angelic slip of a thing 370
Forward, puts out a soft palm: "Not so fast!"
—Addresses the celestial presence, "Nay,
He made you and devised you, after all,
Though he's none of you! Could Saint John
    there draw—
His camel-hair make up a painting-brush?   375
We come to brother Lippo for all that,
Iste perfecit opus!" So, all smile—
I shuffle sideways with my blushing face
Under the cover of a hundred wings
Thrown like a spread of kirtles when you're
    gay   380
And play hot cockles, all the doors being shut,
Till, wholly unexpected, in there pops
The hothead husband! Thus I scuttle off
To some safe bench behind, not letting go
The palm of her, the little lily thing   385
That spoke the good word for me in the nick,
Like the Prior's niece . . . Saint Lucy, I
    would say.
And so all's saved for me, and for the church

---

323. **a Saint Laurence**, a picture of St. Laurence, who was martyred in 258 by being burned to death on a gridiron. 324. **At Prato**. Some of Lippo's most important work is in the Cathedral at Prato, a town near Florence. 339. **Chianti wine**, wine from Chianti, a region south of Florence. 346. **Sant' Ambrogio's**, Saint Ambrose's Church in Florence. St. Ambrose was a famous Church leader during the fourth century. He became Bishop of Milan in 374. 347. **I shall paint, etc.** The picture described is *The Coronation of the Virgin*, now in the Academy of Fine Arts, Florence. The model for the Virgin was Lucrezia Buti, Lippo's mistress. 354. **Saint John**, St. John the Baptist, the patron saint of Florence.

357. **Job**. Cf. *Job*, 1:1: "There was a man in the land of Uz, whose name was Job." 361. **Out of a corner . . . I**. Lippo's head appears in the lower right-hand corner of the picture. 374. **Saint John . . . camel-hair**. Cf. *Mark*, 1:6: "And John was clothed with camel's hair." 377. *Iste . . . opus*, this one did the work. The inscription is on a scroll in the picture. 380. **kirtles**, tunics, coats. 381. **hot cockles**, an old English game in which a blindfolded player tries to guess who strikes him.

A pretty picture gained. Go, six months
    hence!
Your hand, sir, and good-by; no lights, no
    lights!   390
The street's hushed, and I know my own way
    back,
Don't fear me! There's the gray beginning.
    Zooks!   (1855)

Andrea Del Sarto

CALLED "THE FAULTLESS PAINTER"

Andrea d'Angelo di Francesca (1486-1531) was called "del Sarto" because he was the son of a tailor (*sarto*). The perfection of his frescoes in the Church of the Annunziata in Florence won him the title of "The Faultless Painter." In 1512 he married Lucrezia del Fede, whose influence led Andrea to neglect his art work. The poem is based upon the account of Andrea found in Vasari's *Lives of the Painters.*

But do not let us quarrel any more,
No, my Lucrezia; bear with me for once.
Sit down and all shall happen as you wish.
You turn your face, but does it bring your
    heart?
I'll work then for your friend's friend, never
    fear,   5
Treat his own subject after his own way,
Fix his own time, accept too his own price,
And shut the money into this small hand
When next it takes mine. Will it? tenderly?
Oh, I'll content him—but tomorrow, Love!
I often am much wearier than you think,   11
This evening more than usual, and it seems
As if—forgive now—should you let me sit
Here by the window with your hand in mine
And look a half-hour forth on Fiesole,   15
Both of one mind, as married people use,
Quietly, quietly the evening through,
I might get up tomorrow to my work
Cheerful and fresh as ever. Let us try.
Tomorrow, how you shall be glad for this!   20
Your soft hand is a woman of itself,
And mine the man's bared breast she curls
    inside.
Don't count the time lost, neither; you must
    serve
For each of the five pictures we require—
It saves a model. So! keep looking so—   25
My serpentining beauty, rounds on rounds!
—How could you ever prick those perfect ears,
Even to put the pearl there! oh, so sweet—
My face, my moon, my everybody's moon,
Which everybody looks on and calls his,   30
And, I suppose, is looked on by in turn,
While she looks—no one's: very dear, no less.
You smile? why, there's my picture ready
    made,
There's what we painters call our harmony!
A common grayness silvers everything—   35
All in a twilight, you and I alike—
You, at the point of your first pride in me
(That's gone, you know), but I, at every
    point;
My youth, my hope, my art, being all toned
    down
To yonder sober pleasant Fiesole.   40
There's the bell clinking from the chapel-top;
That length of convent-wall across the way
Holds the trees safer, huddled more inside;
The last monk leaves the garden; days de-
    crease,
And autumn grows, autumn in everything.   45
Eh? the whole seems to fall into a shape
As if I saw alike my work and self
And all that I was born to be and do,
A twilight-piece. Love, we are in God's hand.
How strange now looks the life he makes us
    lead;   50
So free we seem, so fettered fast we are!
I feel he laid the fetter; let it lie!
This chamber, for example—turn your head—
All that's behind us! You don't understand,
Nor care to understand, about my art,   55
But you can hear at least when people speak;

15. **Fiesole**, a suburb of Florence. 23. **you . . . model.** Lucrezia is discernible in nearly all the women of Andrea's pictures.

And that cartoon, the second from the door—
It is the thing, Love! so such thing should be—
Behold Madonna!—I am bold to say.
I can do with my pencil what I know, 60
What I see, what at bottom of my heart
I wish for, if I ever wish so deep—
Do easily, too—when I say perfectly,
I do not boast, perhaps; yourself are judge,
Who listened to the Legate's talk last week, 65
And just as much they used to say in France.
At any rate, 'tis easy, all of it!
No sketches first, no studies—that's long past;
I do what many dream of all their lives—
Dream? strive to do, and agonize to do, 70
And fail in doing. I could count twenty such
On twice your fingers, and not leave this town,
Who strive—you don't know how the others strive
To paint a little thing like that you smeared
Carelessly passing with your robes afloat— 75
Yet do much less, so much less, Someone says
(I know his name, no matter)—so much less!
Well, less is more, Lucrezia; I am judged.
There burns a truer light of God in them,
In their vexed, beating, stuffed, and stopped-up brain, 80
Heart, or whate'er else, than goes on to prompt
This low-pulsed forthright craftsman's hand of mine.
Their works drop groundward, but themselves, I know,
Reach many a time a heaven that's shut to me,
Enter and take their place there sure enough,
Though they come back and cannot tell the world. 86
My works are nearer heaven, but I sit here.
The sudden blood of these men! at a word—
Praise them, it boils; or blame them, it boils too.
I, painting from myself and to myself, 90
Know what I do, am unmoved by men's blame
Or their praise either. Somebody remarks
Morello's outline there is wrongly traced,
His hue mistaken; what of that? or else,
Rightly traced and well ordered; what of that? 95
Speak as they please, what does the mountain care?
Ah, but a man's reach should exceed his grasp,
Or what's a heaven for? All is silver-gray,
Placid and perfect with my art: the worse!
I know both what I want and what might gain, 100
And yet how profitless to know, to sigh,
"Had I been two, another and myself,
Our head would have o'erlooked the world!"
No doubt.
Yonder's a work now, of that famous youth,
The Urbinate, who died five years ago. 105
('Tis copied; George Vasari sent it me.)
Well, I can fancy how he did it all,
Pouring his soul, with kings and popes to see,
Reaching, that heaven might so replenish him,
Above and through his art—for it gives way;
That arm is wrongly put—and there again—
A fault to pardon in the drawing's lines, 112
Its body, so to speak: its soul is right,
He means right—that, a child may understand.
Still, what an arm! and I could alter it; 115
But all the play, the insight, and the stretch—
Out of me, out of me! And wherefore out?
Had you enjoined them on me, given me soul,
We might have risen to Rafael, I and you!
Nay, Love, you did give all I asked, I think—
More than I merit, yes, by many times. 121
But had you—oh, with the same perfect brow,
And perfect eyes, and more than perfect mouth,
And the low voice my soul hears, as a bird
The fowler's pipe, and follows to the snare—
Had you, with these the same, but brought a mind! 126
Some women do so. Had the mouth there urged,
"God and the glory! never care for gain.
The present by the future, what is that?

---

65. **the Legate's talk.** The Legate was the representative of the Pope. 82. **forthright,** unswerving. 93. **Morello,** a high peak of the Apennines, north of Florence.

97. **Ah . . . for?** Cf. *Saul,* l. 295, p. 678, *A Grammarian's Funeral,* ll. 113-120, p. 684, and *Rabbi Ben Ezra,* ll. 40-41, p. 698. 105. **The Urbinate,** Raphael Sanzio (1483-1520), one of the greatest of Italian painters; he was born in the city of Urbino. 106. **George Vasari** (1512-1574), a pupil of Andrea and author of *The Lives of the Most Eminent Painters Sculptors, and Architects.*

Live for fame, side by side with Agnolo! 130
Rafael is waiting; up to God, all three!"
I might have done it for you. So it seems;
Perhaps not. All is as God overrules.
Beside, incentives come from the soul's self;
The rest avail not. Why do I need you? 135
What wife had Rafael, or has Agnolo?
In this world, who can do a thing, will not;
And who would do it, cannot, I perceive;
Yet the will's somewhat—somewhat, too, the power—
And thus we half-men struggle. At the end,
God, I conclude, compensates, punishes. 141
'Tis safer for me, if the award be strict,
That I am something underrated here,
Poor this long while, despised, to speak the truth.
I dared not, do you know, leave home all day,
For fear of chancing on the Paris lords. 146
The best is when they pass and look aside;
But they speak sometimes; I must bear it all.
Well may they speak! That Francis, that first time,
And that long festal year at Fontainebleau!
I surely then could sometimes leave the ground, 151
Put on the glory, Rafael's daily wear,
In that humane great monarch's golden look—
One finger in his beard or twisted curl
Over his mouth's good mark that made the smile; 155
One arm about my shoulder, round my neck;
The jingle of his gold chain in my ear—
I painting proudly with his breath on me,
All his Court round him, seeing with his eyes,
Such frank French eyes, and such a fire of souls 160
Profuse, my hand kept plying by those hearts;
And, best of all, this, this, this face beyond,
This in the background, waiting on my work,
To crown the issue with a last reward!
A good time, was it not, my kingly days? 165
And had you not grown restless . . . but I know—
'Tis done and past; 'twas right, my instinct said;
Too live the life grew, golden and not gray,
And I'm the weak-eyed bat no sun should tempt
Out of the grange whose four walls make his world. 170
How could it end in any other way?
You called me, and I came home to your heart.
The triumph was—to reach and stay there; since
I reached it ere the triumph, what is lost?
Let my hands frame your face in your hair's gold, 175
You beautiful Lucrezia that are mine!
"Rafael did this, Andrea painted that;
The Roman's is the better when you pray,
But still the other's Virgin was his wife"—
Men will excuse me. I am glad to judge 180
Both pictures in your presence; clearer grows
My better fortune, I resolve to think.
For, do you know, Lucrezia, as God lives,
Said one day Agnolo, his very self,
To Rafael . . . I have known it all these years . . . 185
(When the young man was flaming out his thoughts
Upon a palace-wall for Rome to see,
Too lifted up in heart because of it),
"Friend, there's a certain sorry little scrub
Goes up and down our Florence, none cares how, 190
Who, were he set to plan and execute
As you are, pricked on by your popes and kings,
Would bring the sweat into that brow of yours!"
To Rafael's!—And indeed the arm is wrong.
I hardly dare . . . yet, only you to see, 195
Give the chalk here—quick, thus the line should go!
Ay, but the soul! he's Rafael! rub it out!

130. **Agnolo**, Michelangelo (1475-1564), celebrated as painter, sculptor, architect, and poet. 149. **That Francis**, Francis I, King of France (1515-1547). He had invited Andrea to come to Fontainebleau, the seat of the richest of the royal palaces. While engaged upon important work there, Andrea was suddenly called home by Lucrezia. He was given money with which to secure works of art for the French king, but he purchased a house with it for Lucrezia.

178. **The Roman's**, Raphael's. 186. **When . . . it**, probably a reference to Raphael's decorations made in certain rooms of the Vatican under Julius II (1443-1513).

Still, all I care for, if he spoke the truth
(What he? why, who but Michel Agnolo?)
Do you forget already words like those?), 200
If really there was such a chance, so lost—
Is, whether you're—not grateful—but more
    pleased.
Well, let me think so. And you smile indeed!
This hour has been an hour! Another smile?
If you would sit thus by me every night, 205
I should work better, do you comprehend?
I mean that I should earn more, give you
    more.
See, it is settled dusk now; there's a star;
Morello's gone, the watch-lights show the wall,
The cue-owls speak the name we call them by.
Come from the window, love—come in, at
    last, 211
Inside the melancholy little house
We built to be so gay with. God is just.
King Francis may forgive me; oft at nights
When I look up from painting, eyes tired
    out, 215
The walls become illumined, brick from brick
Distinct, instead of mortar, fierce bright gold,
That gold of his I did cement them with!
Let us but love each other. Must you go?
That Cousin here again? he waits outside?
Must see you—you, and not with me? Those
    loans? 221
More gaming debts to pay? you smiled for
    that?
Well, let smiles buy me! have you more to
    spend?
While hand and eye and something of a heart
Are left me, work's my ware, and what's it
    worth? 225
I'll pay my fancy. Only let me sit
The gray remainder of the evening out,
Idle, you call it, and muse perfectly
How I could paint, were I but back in France,
One picture, just one more—the Virgin's
    face, 230
Not yours this time! I want you at my side
To hear them—that is, Michel Agnolo—
Judge all I do and tell you of its worth.
Will you? Tomorrow, satisfy your friend.
I take the subjects for his corridor, 235
Finish the portrait out of hand—there, there,
And throw him in another thing or two
If he demurs; the whole should prove enough
To pay for this same Cousin's freak. Beside—
What's better and what's all I care about— 240
Get you the thirteen scudi for the ruff!
Love, does that please you? Ah, but what
    does he,
The Cousin! what does he to please you
    more?

I am grown peaceful as old age tonight.
I regret little, I would change still less. 245
Since there my past life lies, why alter it?
The very wrong to Francis!—it is true
I took his coin, was tempted, and complied,
And built this house and sinned, and all is
    said.
My father and my mother died of want. 250
Well, had I riches of my own? you see
How one gets rich! Let each one bear his lot.
They were born poor, lived poor, and poor
    they died;
And I have labored somewhat in my time
And not been paid profusely. Some good
    son 255
Paint my two hundred pictures—let him try!
No doubt, there's something strikes a balance.
    Yes,
You loved me quite enough, it seems tonight.
This must suffice me here. What would one
    have?
In heaven, perhaps, new chances, one more
    chance— 260
Four great walls in the New Jerusalem,
Meted on each side by the angel's reed,
For Leonard, Rafael, Agnolo, and me
To cover—the three first without a wife, 264
While I have mine! So—still they overcome
Because there's still Lucrezia—as I choose.

    Again the Cousin's whistle! Go, my Love.
                            (1855)

210. **cue-owls**, small European owls. 220. **Cousin**, a euphemism for *lover*. Cf. ll. 29-32. 241. **scudi**, plural of *scudo*, an Italian coin worth about one dollar. 261. **the New Jerusalem**. For a description of the New Jerusalem and its walls, see *Revelation*, 21:10-21. 263. **Leonard**, Leonardo da Vinci (1452-1519), one of the greatest of Italian painters. See Pater's *La Gioconda*, p. 581.

Rabbi Ben Ezra

Rabbi Ben Ezra was a distinguished Jewish philosopher, physician, astronomer, and poet of the twelfth century. Although the ideas in the poem are drawn largely from his writings, the poem is one of the best expressions of Browning's own philosophy of life. See Coleridge's *Youth and Age*, and note (p. 189), Fitzgerald's *Rubáiyát*, p. 776, and Browning's *Saul*, ll. 161-164, p. 676.

Grow old along with me!
The best is yet to be,
The last of life, for which the first was made.
Our times are in his hand
Who saith, "A whole I planned;   5
Youth shows but half. Trust God; see all, nor be afraid!"

Not that, amassing flowers,
Youth sighed, "Which rose make ours,
Which lily leave and then as best recall?"
Not that, admiring stars,   10
It yearned, "Nor Jove, nor Mars;
Mine be some figured flame which blends, transcends them all!"

Not for such hopes and fears
Annulling youth's brief years,
Do I remonstrate—folly wide the mark!   15
Rather I prize the doubt
Low kinds exist without,
Finished and finite clods, untroubled by a spark.

Poor vaunt of life indeed,
Were man but formed to feed   20
On joy, to solely seek and find and feast.
Such feasting ended, then
As sure an end to men;
Irks care the crop-full bird? Frets doubt the maw-crammed beast?

Rejoice we are allied   25
To that which doth provide
And not partake, effect and not receive!
A spark disturbs our clod;
Nearer we hold of God
Who gives, than of his tribes that take, I must believe. 30

Then, welcome each rebuff
That turns earth's smoothness rough,
Each sting that bids nor sit nor stand but go!
Be our joys three parts pain!
Strive, and hold cheap the strain;   35
Learn, nor account the pang; dare, never grudge the throe!

For thence—a paradox
Which comforts while it mocks—
Shall life succeed in that it seems to fail:
What I aspired to be,   40
And was not, comforts me;
A brute I might have been, but would not sink i' the scale.

What is he but a brute
Whose flesh has soul to suit,
Whose spirit works lest arms and legs want play? 45
To man, propose this test—
Thy body at its best,
How far can that project thy soul on its lone way?

Yet gifts should prove their use:
I own the Past profuse   50
Of power each side, perfection every turn;
Eyes, ears took in their dole,
Brain treasured up the whole;
Should not the heart beat once, "How good to live and learn"?

Not once beat, "Praise be thine!   55
I see the whole design,
I, who saw power, see now Love perfect too;
Perfect I call thy plan.
Thanks that I was a man!

7. **Not that.** *Not that* of ll. 7 and 10 and *Not for* of l. 13 go with *Do I remonstrate* of l. 15. 24. **Irks . . . bird**, does care irk the crop-full bird?

40. **What . . . me.** Cf. *A Grammarian's Funeral*, ll. 113-120, p. 684, *Saul*, ll. 295-296, p. 678, and *Andrea del Sarto*, ll. 97-98, p. 695. 57. **I . . . too.** Cf. *Saul*, ll. 242, 305-306, pp. 677, 679.

Maker, remake, complete—I trust what thou
    shalt do!"   60

For pleasant is this flesh;
Our soul, in its rose-mesh
Pulled ever to the earth, still yearns for rest.
Would we some prize might hold
To match those manifold   65
Possessions of the brute—gain most, as we
    did best!

Let us not always say,
"Spite of this flesh today
I strove, made head, gained ground upon the
    whole!"
As the bird wings and sings,   70
Let us cry, "All good things
Are ours, nor soul helps flesh more, now, than
    flesh helps soul!"

Therefore I summon age
To grant youth's heritage,
Life's struggle having so far reached its term.
Thence shall I pass, approved   76
A man, for aye removed
From the developed brute—a god, though in
    the germ.

And I shall thereupon
Take rest, ere I be gone   80
Once more on my adventure brave and new;
Fearless and unperplexed,
When I wage battle next,
What weapons to select, what armor to indue.

Youth ended, I shall try   85
My gain or loss thereby;
Leave the fire ashes, what survives is gold.
And I shall weigh the same,
Give life its praise or blame.
Young, all lay in dispute; I shall know, being
    old.   90

For note, when evening shuts,
A certain moment cuts
The deed off, calls the glory from the gray;
A whisper from the west
Shoots—"Add this to the rest,   95
Take it and try its worth. Here dies another
    day."

So, still within this life,
Though lifted o'er its strife,
Let me discern, compare, pronounce at last,
"This rage was right i' the main,   100
That acquiescence vain;
The Future I may face, now I have proved
    the Past."

For more is not reserved
To man, with soul just nerved
To act tomorrow what he learns today;   105
Here, work enough to watch
The Master work, and catch
Hints of the proper craft, tricks of the tool's
    true play.

As it was better, youth
Should strive, through acts uncouth,   110
Toward making, than repose on aught found
    made;
So, better, age, exempt
From strife, should know, than tempt
Further. Thou waitedst age; wait death nor
    be afraid!

Enough now, if the Right   115
And Good and Infinite
Be named here, as thou callest thy hand thine
    own,
With knowledge absolute,
Subject to no dispute
From fools that crowded youth, nor let thee
    feel alone.   120

Be there, for once and all,
Severed great minds from small,
Announced to each his station in the Past!
Was I, the world arraigned,
Were they, my soul disdained,   125
Right? Let age speak the truth and give us
    peace at last!

Now, who shall arbitrate?
Ten men love what I hate,

61-72. Cf. *Fra Lippo Lippi*, ll. 205-214, p. 691. 81. **adventure . . . new**, the life of an old person after the passions and problems of youth are left behind. 84. **to indue**, to put on. 87. **Leave . . . ashes**, if the fire leaves ashes.

124. **Was I.** Supply *whom* after *I* and also after *they*, l. 125.

Shun what I follow, slight what I receive;
Ten, who in ears and eyes   130
   Match me. We all surmise,
They this thing, and I that; whom shall my
      soul believe?

Not on the vulgar mass
Called "work," must sentence pass—
Things done, that took the eye and had the
      price;   135
O'er which, from level stand,
The low world laid its hand,
Found straightway to its mind, could value in
      a trice:

But all, the world's coarse thumb
And finger failed to plumb,   140
So passed in making up the main account;
All instincts immature,
All purposes unsure,
That weighed not as his work, yet swelled the
      man's amount:

Thoughts hardly to be packed   145
Into a narrow act,
Fancies that broke through language and es-
      caped;
All I could never be,
All, men ignored in me,
This, I was worth to God, whose wheel the
      pitcher shaped.   150

Aye, note that Potter's wheel,
That metaphor! and feel
Why time spins fast, why passive lies our
      clay—
Thou, to whom fools propound,
When the wine makes its round,   155
"Since life fleets, all is change; the Past gone,
      seize today!"

Fool! All that is, at all,
Lasts ever, past recall;
Earth changes, but thy soul and God stand
      sure.

151. **Potter's wheel.** Cf. *Isaiah*, 64:8: "But now, O Lord, thou art our father; we are the clay, and thou our potter; and we all are the work of thy hand." Cf. also Fitzgerald's *Rubáiyát*, ll. 325-360, p. 782.

What entered into thee,   160
That was, is, and shall be.
Time's wheel runs back or stops; Potter and
      clay endure.

He fixed thee 'mid this dance
Of plastic circumstance,
This Present, thou, forsooth, would fain ar-
      rest—   165
Machinery just meant
To give thy soul its bent,
Try thee and turn thee forth, sufficiently im-
      pressed.

What though the earlier grooves,
Which ran the laughing loves   170
Around thy base, no longer pause and
      press?
What though, about thy rim,
Skull-things in order grim
Grow out, in graver mood, obey the sterner
      stress?

Look not thou down but up!   175
To uses of a cup,
The festal board, lamp's flash, and trumpet's
      peal,
The new wine's foaming flow,
The Master's lips aglow!
Thou, heaven's consummate cup, what needst
      thou with earth's wheel?   180

But I need, now as then,
Thee, God, who moldest men;
And since, not even while the whirl was worst,
Did I—to the wheel of life
With shapes and colors rife,   185
Bound dizzily—mistake my end, to slake Thy
      thirst.

So, take and use Thy work;
Amend what flaws may lurk,
What strain o' the stuff, what warpings past
      the aim!
My times be in Thy hand!   190
Perfect the cup as planned!
Let age approve of youth, and death complete
      the same!
                                        (1864)

Caliban upon Setebos

OR, NATURAL THEOLOGY IN THE ISLAND

Caliban is a kind of semi-intelligent monster, one of the servants of Prospero and his daughter Miranda on the island in Shakespeare's *Tempest*. He was the son of the witch Sycorax, who worshiped Setebos, the god of the Patagonians. Caliban sees this god as a capricious and wilful being like himself. The poem is a satire on Calvinism and the anthropomorphic idea of God. The quotation at the head of the poem is from *Psalms*, 50:21; it is spoken by God to the wicked.

"Thou thoughtest that I was altogether such an one as thyself."

['Will sprawl, now that the heat of day is best,
Flat on his belly in the pit's much mire,
With elbows wide, fists clenched to prop his chin.
And, while he kicks both feet in the cool slush,
And feels about his spine small eft-things course,   5
Run in and out each arm, and make him laugh;
And while above his head a pompion-plant,
Coating the cave-top as a brow its eye,
Creeps down to touch and tickle hair and beard,
And now a flower drops with a bee inside, 10
And now a fruit to snap at, catch and crunch—
He looks out o'er yon sea, which sunbeams cross
And recross till they weave a spider-web
(Meshes of fire, some great fish breaks at times),
And talks to his own self, howe'er he please,
Touching that other, whom his dam called God. 16
Because to talk about Him, vexes—ha,
Could He but know! and time to vex is now,
When talk is safer than in winter-time.
Moreover Prosper and Miranda sleep 20
In confidence he drudges at their task;
And it is good to cheat the pair, and gibe,
Letting the rank tongue blossom into speech.]

Setebos, Setebos, and Setebos! 24
'Thinketh He dwelleth i' the cold o' the moon.

'Thinketh He made it, with the sun to match,
But not the stars; the stars came otherwise;
Only made clouds, winds, meteors, such as that;
Also this isle, what lives and grows thereon,
And snaky sea which rounds and ends the same. 30

'Thinketh, it came of being ill at ease;
He hated that He cannot change His cold,
Nor cure its ache. 'Hath spied an icy fish
That longed to 'scape the rock-stream where she lived,
And thaw herself within the lukewarm brine
O' the lazy sea her stream thrusts far amid, 36
A crystal spike 'twixt two warm walls of wave;
Only, she ever sickened, found repulse
At the other kind of water, not her life
(Green-dense and dim-delicious, bred o' the sun), 40
Flounced back from bliss she was not born to breathe,
And in her old bounds buried her despair,
Hating and loving warmth alike: so He.

'Thinketh, He made thereat the sun, this isle,
Trees and the fowls here, beast and creeping thing; 45
Yon otter, sleek-wet, black, lithe as a leech;
Yon auk, one fire-eye in a ball of foam,
That floats and feeds; a certain badger brown
He hath watched hunt with that slant white-wedge eye
By moonlight; and the pie with the long tongue 50

1-23. **'Will . . . speech.** In these lines Caliban describes his physical background and the reason for his theological speculations. In most of the poem he speaks of himself in the third person. 5. **eft-things,** lizard-like animals. 7. **pompion-plant,** a vine of the pumpkin family. 17. **Him.** Pronouns referring to Setebos are capitalized. 18. **time . . . now,** in summer, when Setebos is likely to be away from the island; in winter he would usually be at home, on or near the island.

33. **'Hath,** he (Caliban) hath. 50. **pie,** magpie.

That pricks deep into oakwarts for a worm,
And says a plain word when she finds her prize,
But will not eat the ants; the ants themselves
That build a wall of seeds and settled stalks
About their hole—He made all these and more, 55
Made all we see, and us, in spite; how else?
He could not, Himself, make a second self
To be His mate—as well have made Himself;
He would not make what He mislikes or slights,
An eyesore to Him, or not worth His pains;
But did, in envy, listlessness, or sport, 61
Make what Himself would fain, in a manner, be—
Weaker in most points, stronger in a few,
Worthy, and yet mere playthings all the while,
Things He admires and mocks too—that is it.
Because, so brave, so better though they be, 66
It nothing skills if He begin to plague.
Look now, I melt a gourd-fruit into mash,
Add honeycomb and pods, I have perceived,
Which bite like finches when they bill and kiss— 70
Then, when froth rises bladdery, drink up all,
Quick, quick, till maggots scamper through my brain;
Last, throw me on my back i' the seeded thyme,
And wanton, wishing I were born a bird.
Put case, unable to be what I wish, 75
I yet could make a live bird out of clay;
Would not I take clay, pinch my Caliban
Able to fly?—for, there, see, he hath wings,
And great comb like the hoopoe's to admire,
And there, a sting to do his foes offense; 80
There, and I will that he begin to live,
Fly to yon rock-top, nip me off the horns
Of grigs high up that make the merry din,
Saucy through their veined wings, and mind me not.
In which feat, if his leg snapped, brittle clay,
And he lay stupid-like—why, I should laugh;
And if he, spying me, should fall to weep, 87
Beseech me to be good, repair his wrong,
Bid his poor leg smart less or grow again—
Well, as the chance were, this might take or else 90
Not take my fancy; I might hear his cry,
And give the manikin three sound legs for one,
Or pluck the other off, leave him like an egg,
And lessoned he was mine and merely clay.
Were this no pleasure, lying in the thyme, 95
Drinking the mash, with brain become alive,
Making and marring clay at will? So He.

'Thinketh, such shows nor right nor wrong in Him,
Nor kind, nor cruel; He is strong and Lord.
'Am strong myself compared to yonder crabs
That march now from the mountain to the sea; 101
'Let twenty pass, and stone the twenty-first,
Loving not, hating not, just choosing so.
'Say, the first straggler that boasts purple spots
Shall join the file, one pincer twisted off; 105
'Say, this bruised fellow shall receive a worm,
And two worms he whose nippers end in red;
As it likes me each time, I do. So He.

Well then, 'supposeth He is good i' the main,
Placable if His mind and ways were guessed,
But rougher than His handiwork, be sure! 111
Oh, He hath made things worthier than Himself,
And envieth that, so helped, such things do more
Than He who made them! What consoles but this?
That they, unless through Him, do naught at all, 115
And must submit; what other use in things?
'Hath cut a pipe of pithless elder-joint
That, blown through, gives exact the scream o' the jay
When from her wing you twitch the feathers blue;
Sound this, and little birds that hate the jay
Flock within stone's throw, glad their foe is hurt. 121

---

71. **bladdery**, in bladder-like bubbles. 75. **Put case**, etc. If Caliban were the Creator, he would do things out of spite or envy, or as an exercise of absolute will; so does Setebos. 79. **hoopoe**, a kind of bird with a beautiful crest. 83. **grigs**, crickets.

103. **Loving ... so.** This line and ll. 98-108 correspond with the Calvinistic doctrine of election and reprobation, whereby some persons are predestined to eternal life and others to eternal death.

Put case such pipe could prattle and boast forsooth,
"I catch the birds, I am the crafty thing,
I make the cry my maker cannot make
With his great round mouth; he must blow through mine!" 125
Would not I smash it with my foot? So He.

But wherefore rough, why cold and ill at ease?
Aha, that is a question! Ask, for that,
What knows—the something over Setebos
That made Him, or He, may be, found and fought, 130
Worsted, drove off, and did to nothing, perchance.
There may be something quiet o'er His head,
Out of His reach, that feels nor joy nor grief,
Since both derive from weakness in some way.
I joy because the quails come; would not joy 135
Could I bring quails here when I have a mind;
This Quiet, all it hath a mind to, doth.
'Esteemeth stars the outposts of its couch,
But never spends much thought nor care that way.
It may look up, work up—the worse for those 140
It works on! 'Careth but for Setebos
The many-handed as a cuttle-fish,
Who, making Himself feared through what He does,
Looks up, first, and perceives he cannot soar
To what is quiet and hath happy life; 145
Next looks down here, and out of very spite
Makes this a bauble-world to ape yon real,
These good things to match those as hips do grapes.
'Tis solace making baubles, aye, and sport.
Himself peeped late, eyed Prosper at his books
Careless and lofty, lord now of the isle; 151
Vexed, 'stitched a book of broad leaves, arrow-shaped,
Wrote thereon, he knows what, prodigious words;
Has peeled a wand and called it by a name;
Weareth at whiles for an enchanter's robe 155
The eyed skin of a supple oncelot;
And hath an ounce sleeker than youngling mole,

156. **oncelot**, the ounce, or snow leopard.

A four-legged serpent he makes cower and couch,
Now snarl, now hold its breath and mind his eye,
And saith she is Miranda and my wife. 160
'Keeps for his Ariel a tall pouch-bill crane
He bids go wade for fish and straight disgorge;
Also a sea-beast, lumpish, which he snared,
Blinded the eyes of, and brought somewhat tame,
And split its toe-webs, and now pens the drudge 165
In a hole o' the rock and calls him Caliban—
A bitter heart that bides its time and bites.
'Plays thus at being Prosper in a way,
Taketh his mirth with make-believes. So He.

His dam held that the Quiet made all things
Which Setebos vexed only; 'holds not so. 171
Who made them weak, meant weakness He might vex.
Had He meant other, while His hand was in,
Why not make horny eyes no thorn could prick,
Or plate my scalp with bone against the snow,
Or overscale my flesh 'neath joint and joint,
Like an orc's armor? Aye—so spoil His sport! 177
He is the One now; only He doth all.

'Saith, He may like, perchance, what profits Him.
Aye, himself loves what does him good; but why? 180
'Gets good no otherwise. This blinded beast
Loves whoso places flesh-meat on his nose,
But, had he eyes, would want no help, but hate
Or love, just as it liked him; He hath eyes.
Also it pleaseth Setebos to work, 185
Use all His hands, and exercise much craft,
By no means for the love of what is worked.
'Tasteth, himself, no finer good i' the world
When all goes right, in this safe summer-time,
And he wants little, hungers, aches not much,
Than trying what to do with wit and strength. 191

161. **Ariel**, an airy spirit in the service of Prospero. 177. **orc**, a sea monster.

'Falls to make something; 'piled yon pile of turfs,
And squared and stuck there squares of soft white chalk,
And, with a fish-tooth, scratched a moon on each,
And set up endwise certain spikes of tree, 195
And crowned the whole with a sloth's skull a-top,
Found dead i' the woods, too hard for one to kill.
No use at all i' the work, for work's sole sake;
'Shall some day knock it down again. So He.

'Saith He is terrible; watch His feats in proof!
One hurricane will spoil six good months' hope. 201
He hath a spite against me, that I know,
Just as He favors Prosper, who knows why?
So it is, all the same, as well I find.
'Wove wattles half the winter, fenced them firm 205
With stone and stake to stop she-tortoises
Crawling to lay their eggs here; well, one wave,
Feeling the foot of Him upon its neck,
Gaped as a snake does, lolled out its large tongue,
And licked the whole labor flat—so much for spite. 210
'Saw a ball flame down late (yonder it lies)
Where, half an hour before, I slept i' the shade.
Often they scatter sparkles; there is force!
'Dug up a newt He may have envied once
And turned to stone, shut up inside a stone.
Please Him and hinder this?—What Prosper does? 216
Aha, if He would tell me how! Not He!
There is the sport; discover how or die!
All need not die, for of the things o' the isle
Some flee afar, some dive, some run up trees.
Those at His mercy—why, they please Him most 221
When . . . when . . . well, never try the same way twice!
Repeat what act has pleased, He may grow wroth.

You must not know His ways, and play Him off,
Sure of the issue. 'Doth the like himself: 225
'Spareth a squirrel that it nothing fears
But steals the nut from underneath my thumb,
And when I threat, bites stoutly in defense;
'Spareth an urchin that contrariwise,
Curls up into a ball, pretending death 230
For fright at my approach—the two ways please.
But what would move my choler more than this,
That either creature counted on its life
Tomorrow and next day and all days to come,
Saying, forsooth, in the inmost of its heart, 235
"Because he did so yesterday with me,
And otherwise with such another brute,
So must he do henceforth and always."—Aye?
Would teach the reasoning couple what "must" means!
'Doth as he likes, or wherefore Lord? So He.

'Conceiveth all things will continue thus, 241
And we shall have to live in fear of Him
So long as He lives, keeps His strength; no change,
If He have done His best, make no new world
To please Him more, so leave off watching this— 245
If He surprise not even the Quiet's self
Some strange day—or, suppose, grow into it
As grubs grow butterflies; else, here we are,
And there is He, and nowhere help at all.

'Believeth with the life, the pain shall stop.
His dam held different, that after death 251
He both plagued enemies and feasted friends:
Idly! He doth His worst in this our life,
Giving just respite lest we die through pain,
Saving last pain for worst—with which, an end. 255
Meanwhile, the best way to escape His ire
Is, not to seem too happy. 'Sees, himself,
Yonder two flies, with purple films and pink,
Bask on the pompion-bell above; kills both.
'Sees two black painful beetles roll their ball 260
On head and tail as if to save their lives;
Moves them the stick away they strive to clear.

---

196. **sloth**, a slow-moving animal resembling the anteater.
205. **wattles**, twigs.

Even so, 'would have Him misconceive, suppose
This Caliban strives hard and ails no less,
And always, above all else, envies Him; 265
Wherefore he mainly dances on dark nights,
Moans in the sun, gets under holes to laugh,
And never speaks his mind save housed as now:
Outside, 'groans, curses. If He caught me here,
O'erheard this speech, and asked, "What chucklest at?" 270
'Would, to appease Him, cut a finger off,
Or of my three kid yearlings burn the best,
Or let the toothsome apples rot on tree,
Or push my tame beast for the orc to taste—
While myself lit a fire, and made a song 275
And sung it, *"What I hate, be consecrate*
To celebrate Thee and Thy state, no mate
For Thee; what see for envy in poor me?"
Hoping the while, since evils sometimes mend,
Warts rub away, and sores are cured with slime, 280
That some strange day, will either the Quiet catch
And conquer Setebos, or likelier He
Decrepit may doze, doze, as good as die.

———

[What, what? A curtain o'er the world at once!
Crickets stop hissing; not a bird—or yes, 285
There scuds His raven that has told Him all!
It was fool's play, this prattling! Ha! The wind
Shoulders the pillared dust, death's house o' the move,
And fast invading fires begin! White blaze—
A tree's head snaps—and there, there, there, there, there, 290
His thunder follows! Fool to gibe at Him!
Lo! 'Lieth flat and loveth Setebos!
'Maketh his teeth meet through his upper lip,
Will let those quails fly, will not eat this month
One little mess of whelks, so he may 'scape!]

(1864)

Confessions

What is he buzzing in my ears?
 "Now that I come to die,
Do I view the world as a vale of tears?"
 Ah, reverend sir, not I!

What I viewed there once, what I view again
 Where the physic bottles stand 6
On the table's edge—is a suburb lane,
 With a wall to my bedside hand.

That lane sloped, much as the bottles do,
 From a house you could descry 10
O'er the garden-wall; is the curtain blue
 Or green to a healthy eye?

To mine, it serves for the old June weather
 Blue above lane and wall;
And that farthest bottle labeled "Ether" 15
 Is the house o'ertopping all.

At a terrace, somewhere near the stopper,
 There watched for me, one June,
A girl; I know, sir, it's improper,
 My poor mind's out of tune. 20

Only, there was a way . . . you crept
 Close by the side, to dodge
Eyes in the house, two eyes except;
 They styled their house "The Lodge."

What right had a lounger up their lane? 25
 But, by creeping very close,
With the good wall's help—their eyes might strain
 And stretch themselves to Oes,

Yet never catch her and me together,
 As she left the attic, there, 30
By the rim of the bottle labeled "Ether,"
 And stole from stair to stair,

And stood by the rose-wreathed gate. Alas,
 We loved, sir—used to meet;
How sad and bad and mad it was— 35
 But then, how it was sweet!

(1864)

Prospice

The title means *Look Forward*. The poem was written shortly after the death of Mrs. Browning; it is a triumphant statement of Browning's faith in personal immortality. Cf. *My Star*, p. 681, and Tennyson's *Crossing the Bar*, p. 654.

Fear death?—to feel the fog in my throat,
    The mist in my face,
When the snows begin, and the blasts denote
    I am nearing the place,
The power of the night, the press of the storm,
    The post of the foe;   6
Where he stands, the Arch Fear in a visible form,
    Yet the strong man must go.
For the journey is done and the summit attained,
    And the barriers fall,   10
Though a battle's to fight ere the guerdon be gained,
    The reward of it all.
I was ever a fighter, so—one fight more,
    The best and the last!
I would hate that death bandaged my eyes, and forebore,   15
    And bade me creep past.
No! let me taste the whole of it, fare like my peers,
    The heroes of old,
Bear the brunt, in a minute pay glad life's arrears
    Of pain, darkness, and cold.   20
For sudden the worst turns the best to the brave,
    The black minute's at end,
And the elements' rage, the fiend-voices that rave,
    Shall dwindle, shall blend,
Shall change, shall become first a peace out of pain,   25
    Then a light, then thy breast,
O thou soul of my soul! I shall clasp thee again,
    And with God be the rest!   *(1861; 1864)*

Apparent Failure

Browning wrote this poem in an effort to save from destruction the famous Paris Morgue on the bank of the Seine River. He had visited the Morgue in 1856, when he was first in Paris to see the baptism of Prince Louis Napoleon, son of Emperor Napoleon III, born March 16, 1856.

"We shall soon lose a celebrated building."
    —*Paris Newspaper*

No, for I'll save it! Seven years since,
    I passed through Paris, stopped a day
To see the baptism of your Prince;
    Saw, made my bow, and went my way.
Walking the heat and headache off,   5
    I took the Seine-side, you surmise,
Thought of the Congress, Gortschakoff,
    Cavour's appeal and Buol's replies,
So sauntered till—what met my eyes?

Only the Doric little Morgue!   10
    The dead-house where you show your drowned.
Petrarch's Vaucluse makes proud the Sorgue;
    Your Morgue has made the Seine renowned.
One pays one's debt in such a case;
    I plucked up heart and entered—stalked,
Keeping a tolerable face   16
    Compared with some whose cheeks were chalked.
Let them! No Briton's to be balked!

First came the silent gazers; next,
    A screen of glass, we're thankful for;   20
Last, the sight's self, the sermon's text,
    The three men who did most abhor
Their life in Paris yesterday,
    So killed themselves; and now, enthroned
Each on his copper couch, they lay   25
    Fronting me, waiting to be owned.
I thought, and think, their sin's atoned.

Poor men, God made, and all for that!
    The reverence struck me; o'er each head
Religiously was hung its hat,   30

7. **the Congress.** The Congress of Paris, composed of representatives of several European powers, met in Paris in 1856 to discuss the unity of Italy. Prince Alexander **Gortschakoff** (1798-1883) represented Russia; Count Camillo di **Cavour** (1810-1861), Sardinia; Count von Buol-Schauenstein (1797-1865), Austria. Cavour was the great unifier of Italy. 12. **Vaucluse.** The Fountain of Vaucluse is the source of the Sorgue River in southeastern France. The famous Italian poet Petrarch (1304-1374) once lived in Vaucluse, near Avignon.

Each coat dripped by the owner's bed,
Sacred from touch; each had his berth,
His bounds, his proper place of rest,
Who last night tenanted on earth
Some arch, where twelve such slept abreast—
Unless the plain asphalt seemed best.   36

How did it happen, my poor boy?
You wanted to be Buonaparte
And have the Tuileries for toy,
And could not, so it broke your heart?   40
You, old one by his side, I judge,
Were, red as blood, a socialist,
A leveler! Does the Empire grudge
You've gained what no Republic missed?
Be quiet, and unclench your fist!   45

And this—why he was red in vain,
Or black—poor fellow that is blue!
What fancy was it turned your brain?
Oh, women were the prize for you!
Money gets women, cards and dice   50
Get money, and ill-luck gets just
The copper couch and one clear nice
Cool squirt of water o'er your bust,
The right thing to extinguish lust!

It's wiser being good than bad;   55
It's safer being meek than fierce;
It's fitter being sane than mad.
My own hope is, a sun will pierce
The thickest cloud earth ever stretched;
That, after Last, returns the First,   60
Though a wide compass round be fetched;
That what began best, can't end worst,
Nor what God blessed once, prove accurst.
                                (1864)

Proem to *The Ring and the Book*

Browning's greatest triumph in the dramatic monologue, his *Ring and the Book*, has been already outlined and characterized (see p. 656). The amazing study of human nature which resulted from his imaginative reconstruction of the murder case recounted in *The Old Yellow Book* is his longest and perhaps his greatest poem. The selection given here is the closing passage of Book I; it was intended as a memorial to Mrs. Browning, who died in 1861.

O lyric Love, half angel and half bird,
And all a wonder and a wild desire—
Boldest of hearts that ever braved the sun,
Took sanctuary within the holier blue,
And sang a kindred soul out to his face—   5
Yet human at the red-ripe of the heart—
When the first summons from the darkling earth
Reached thee amid thy chambers, blanched their blue,
And bared them of the glory—to drop down,
To toil for man, to suffer or to die—   10
This is the same voice: can thy soul know change?
Hail then, and hearken from the realms of help!
Never may I commence my song, my due
To God who best taught song by gift of thee,
Except with bent head and beseeching hand—
That still, despite the distance and the dark,   15
What was, again may be; some interchange
Of grace, some splendor once thy very thought,
Some benediction anciently thy smile:
—Never conclude, but raising hand and head
Thither where eyes, that cannot reach, yet yearn   21
For all hope, all sustainment, all reward,
Their utmost up and on—so blessing back
In those thy realms of help, that heaven thy home,
Some whiteness which, I judge, thy face makes proud,   25
Some wanness where, I think, thy foot may fall!

House

Shall I sonnet-sing you about myself?
Do I live in a house you would like to see?
Is it scant of gear, has it store of pelf?
"Unlock my heart with a sonnet-key"?

---

39. **Tuileries,** the royal palace in Paris. 46. **red . . . black,** a reference to the gambling game of rouge-et-noir—red and black—named from colors on the table.

23. **so blessing back, etc.** My eyes yearn for reward from you in heaven—a glimpse of some whiteness glorified by your presence, of some wanness reflected wherever you walk, which will be evidence of your blessing to me. *Blessing* is a participle modifying *whiteness* and *wanness;* both nouns are parallel in construction with *hope* and *reward* (l. 22).

Invite the world, as my betters have done? 5
  "Take notice: this building remains on view,
Its suites of reception every one,
  Its private apartment and bedroom too;

"For a ticket, apply to the Publisher."
  No; thanking the public, I must decline. 10
A peep through my window, if folk prefer;
  But, please you, no foot over threshold of mine!

I have mixed with a crowd and heard free talk
  In a foreign land where an earthquake chanced
And a house stood gaping, naught to balk 15
  Man's eye wherever he gazed or glanced.

The whole of the frontage shaven sheer,
  The inside gaped; exposed to day,
Right and wrong and common and queer,
  Bare, as the palm of your hand, it lay. 20

The owner? Oh, he had been crushed, no doubt!
  "Odd tables and chairs for a man of wealth!
What a parcel of musty old books about!
  He smoked—no wonder he lost his health!

"I doubt if he bathed before he dressed. 25
  A brasier?—the pagan, he burned perfumes!
You see it is proved, what the neighbors guessed:
  His wife and himself had separate rooms."

Friends, the goodman of the house at least
  Kept house to himself till an earthquake came; 30
'Tis the fall of its frontage permits you feast
  On the inside arrangement you praise or blame.

Outside should suffice for evidence;
  And whoso desires to penetrate
Deeper, must dive by the spirit-sense— 35
  No optics like yours, at any rate!

"Hoity-toity! A street to explore,
  Your house the exception! *'With this same key
Shakespeare unlocked his heart,'* once more!"
  Did Shakespeare? If so, the less Shakespeare he!
                          (1876)

Why I am a Liberal

"Why?" Because all I haply can and do,
All that I am now, all I hope to be—
Whence comes it save from fortune setting free
Body and soul the purpose to pursue,
God traced for both? If fetters not a few, 5
Of prejudice, convention, fall from me,
These shall I bid men—each in his degree
Also God-guided—bear, and gayly, too?

But little do or can the best of us;
That little is achieved through Liberty. 10
Who then, dares hold, emancipated thus,
His fellow shall continue bound? Not I,
Who live, love, labor freely, nor discuss
A brother's right to freedom. That is "Why."
                          (1885)

Epilogue to *Asolando*

    This is Browning's last poem; it appears at the end of a collection of miscellaneous poems published under the title *Asolando*, from Asolo, Italy, where Browning lived during his last summer. The poem should be compared with Keats's *Bright Star*, p. 292, and Tennyson's *Crossing the Bar*, p. 654.

At the midnight in the silence of the sleep-time,
  When you set your fancies free,
Will they pass to where—by death, fools think, imprisoned—
Low he lies who once so loved you, whom you loved so,
    —Pity me? 5

38. *'With . . . heart.'* From Wordsworth's *Scorn Not the Sonnet*, 2-3, p. 163. Poets who wrote about themselves in sonnets include Dante, Petrarch, Spenser (Vol. I, p. 461), Milton (Vol. I, p. 713), and Keats, p. 275.
Why I Am a Liberal. Cf. *The Lost Leader*, p. 666.

Oh, to love so, be so loved, yet so mistaken!
  What had I on earth to do
With the slothful, with the mawkish, the unmanly?
Like the aimless, helpless, hopeless, did I drivel—
      Being—who?   10

One who never turned his back but marched breast forward,
  Never doubted clouds would break,
Never dreamed, though right were worsted, wrong would triumph,
  Held we fall to rise, are baffled to fight better,
      Sleep to wake.   15

No! At noonday, in the bustle of man's worktime,
  Greet the unseen with a cheer!
Bid him forward, breast and back as either should be,
  "Strive and thrive!" cry, "Speed—fight on, fare ever
      There as here!"   (1889)

11. **One . . . forward.** With the idea expressed here may be compared the philosophy contained in *Prospice*, p. 706.

Elizabeth Barrett Browning
1806-1861

    The supreme date in the life of Elizabeth Barrett was September 12, 1846. On that day, by a clandestine marriage, she became Mrs. Robert Browning, and a week later she left her dark and unhappy home at 50 Wimpole Street, London, where she had been dominated by an ogre-like father, for the light and happiness of Casa Guidi in sunny Florence; there she was for the rest of her life to be the "Lyric Love, half angel and half bird" of one of the greatest of English poets and the most devoted of lovers.

    Elizabeth Barrett's tragic life up to her forty-first year has become familiar through recent story and drama. An injury to her spine when she was fifteen, the shock of her brother Edward's death by drowning in July, 1840, and the insane insistence of an unbalanced father that none of his daughters should marry, made her life dark indeed. Elizabeth was confined in her gloomy home by her invalidism and even more by the treatment of it. But she read and wrote, and no little volume of verse ever produced a richer return than her *Poems* of 1844; for Robert Browning read the poems, loved them, loved her, and came to her rescue like Prince Charming in the fairy story. And they lived happily ever afterwards. One child—a son—was born in 1849. Mrs. Browning was not always well, but her health was better than it had been, and above all she was happy.

    Browning was attracted to Elizabeth Barrett not only by her poetry but by the quality of her mind. As a recluse invalid she had ample time to study, and she read Greek and Hebrew until—as she said—she got fairly dizzy. The Brownings were not only ideal lovers; they were also intellectual companions, for in her he found one who understood and admired his poetry. Before Browning, then an obscure poet, came to know her, she was already popularly thought of as a rival of Tennyson. Her scholarship had been displayed in her *Essay on Mind; with Other Poems*, published when she was only twenty, and in a translation of the *Prometheus Bound* of Aeschylus in 1833. *The Seraphim and Other Poems*, part obviously written under the influence of Byron, was published in 1838. It was the volume called *Poems* which appeared in 1844 that attracted Browning to her work and to her. In this volume her deep, and almost painful, social sympathy is expressed in *The Cry of the Children* and *Cry of the Human*. In *Lady Geraldine's Courtship* she made an allusion to the work of the little-read Browning which flattered and touched him.

For the first two years after her marriage Mrs. Browning's genius definitely spread its wings. During her engagement days she had written some sonnets to the man she loved; she added to these, and in 1850 she gave him as a gift from poet-wife to poet-husband the *Sonnets from the Portuguese*. The intimate nature of these love poems is revealed in the title, for Browning had playfully called her his "little Portuguese" in allusion to her dark complexion. They form one of the supreme contributions in verse of this type, and represent, in some respects, her highest achievement, for the confinement of the fourteen lines of the sonnet prevented the prolixity that is characteristic of much of her poetry.

Mrs. Browning's human sympathy resulted in an interest in Italian political affairs which her husband shared. This absorption and the delicacy of her health kept her from writing as much in the last years of her life as she had done earlier. *Casa Guidi Windows* (1851) and *Poems before Congress* (1860) are concerned with Italian affairs. *Aurora Leigh* (1857), her longest poem, is a romance in blank verse which, under the guise of an orphan's tale of love and life, gave Mrs. Browning an opportunity not only to introduce many reflections on her own romantic career but also to give expression to her ideas on social, political, and economic subjects. The two volumes on Italy and this long romance were the last books that she saw through the press. Her *Last Poems* was published in 1862, a year after her death. She lies buried in Florence.

Elizabeth Barrett's contemporary popularity was largely due to the presence in her of that humanitarian sentiment which was one of the most marked of Victorian characteristics. Her own suffering and, it may be added, her strongly marked femininity, gave her a capacity for feeling the hardships of others which was at times almost agonizing to her. Some of her social poems seem written in blood, and they could not but move those who felt as she did. When, however, the conditions which gave them birth have been forgotten, and they are read in the cold light of a later day, they sometimes seem convulsive rather than powerful and sentimental rather than moving. Her greatest fault, however, was an inability to write with sufficient compression. If art, as Aristotle says, is the elimination of the superfluous, she never attained high art—excepting, as has been pointed out, in her sonnets, where the restricted form checked her natural inclination to prolixity. But in spite of her faults of taste and her lack of concentration, much of her work is genuine poetry and some is of high quality. It can be seen now that she never was a real rival of Tennyson, and that her husband at all times was a greater poet; her niche in Victorian poetry is, however, secure.

The Cry of the Children

Do ye hear the children weeping, O my brothers,
  Ere the sorrow comes with years?
They are leaning their young heads against their mothers,
  And *that* cannot stop their tears.
The young lambs are bleating in the meadows,   5
  The young birds are chirping in the nest,
The young fawns are playing with the shadows,
  The young flowers are blowing toward the west—
But the young, young children, O my brothers,
  They are weeping bitterly!   10
They are weeping in the playtime of the others,
  In the country of the free.

Do you question the young children in the sorrow
    Why their tears are falling so?
The old man may weep for his tomorrow   15
    Which is lost in Long Ago;
The old tree is leafless in the forest,
    The old year is ending in the frost,
The old wound, if stricken, is the sorest,
    The old hope is hardest to be lost.   20
But the young, young children, O my brothers,
    Do you ask them why they stand
Weeping sore before the bosoms of their mothers,
    In our happy Fatherland?

They look up with their pale and sunken faces,   25
    And their looks are sad to see,
For the man's hoary anguish draws and presses
    Down the cheeks of infancy;
"Your old earth," they say, "is very dreary;
    Our young feet," they say, "are very weak;
Few paces have we taken, yet are weary—   31
    Our grave-rest is very far to seek.
Ask the aged why they weep, and not the children,
    For the outside earth is cold,
And we young ones stand without, in our bewildering,   35
    And the graves are for the old.

"True," say the children, "it may happen
    That we die before our time.
Little Alice died last year; her grave is shapen
    Like a snowball, in the rime.   40
We looked into the pit prepared to take her;
    Was no room for any work in the close clay!
From the sleep wherein she lieth none will wake her,
    Crying, 'Get up, little Alice! it is day.'   44
If you listen by that grave, in sun and shower,
    With your ear down, little Alice never cries;
Could we see her face, be sure we should not know her,
    For the smile has time for growing in her eyes;
And merry go her moments, lulled and stilled in
    The shroud by the kirk-chime.   50
It is good when it happens," say the children,
    "That we die before our time."

Alas, alas, the children! they are seeking
    Death in life, as best to have;
They are binding up their hearts away from breaking,   55
    With a cerement from the grave.
Go out, children, from the mine and from the city,
    Sing out, children, as the little thrushes do;
Pluck your handfuls of the meadow-cowslips pretty.
    Laugh aloud, to feel your fingers let them through!   60
But they answer, "Are your cowslips of the meadows
    Like our weeds anear the mine?
Leave us quiet in the dark of the coal-shadows,
    From your pleasures fair and fine!

"For, oh," say the children, "we are weary,
    And we cannot run or leap;   66
If we cared for any meadows, it were merely
    To drop down in them and sleep.
Our knees tremble sorely in the stooping,
    We fall upon our faces, trying to go;   70
And, underneath our heavy eyelids drooping
    The reddest flower would look as pale as snow.
For, all day, we drag our burden tiring
    Through the coal-dark, underground;
Or, all day, we drive the wheels of iron   75
    In the factories, round and round.

"For all day the wheels are droning, turning;
    Their wind comes in our faces,
Till our hearts turn, our heads with pulses burning,
    And the walls turn in their places.   80
Turns the sky in the high window, blank and reeling,
    Turns the long light that drops adown the wall,

---

40. **rime**, hoarfrost.

56. **cerement**, grave-cloth.

Turn the black flies that crawl along the
    ceiling;
  All are turning, all the day—and we with
    all.
And all day the iron wheels are droning, 85
  And sometimes we could pray,
'O ye wheels' (breaking out in a mad moan-
    ing),
  'Stop! be silent for today!' "

Aye, be silent! Let them hear each other
    breathing
  For a moment, mouth to mouth! 90
Let them touch each other's hands, in a fresh
    wreathing
  Of their tender human youth!
Let them feel that this cold metallic motion
  Is not all the life God fashions or reveals;
Let them prove their living souls against the
    notion 95
  That they live in you, or under you, O
    wheels!
Still, all day, the iron wheels go onward,
  Grinding life down from its mark;
And the children's souls, which God is calling
    sunward,
  Spin on blindly in the dark. 100

Now tell the poor young children, O my
    brothers,
  To look up to Him and pray;
So the blessèd One who blesseth all the others,
  Will bless them another day.
They answer, "Who is God that He should
    hear us, 105
  While the rushing of the iron wheels is
    stirred?
When we sob aloud, the human creatures
    near us
  Pass by, hearing not, or answer not a word.
And *we* hear not (for the wheels in their
    resounding)
  Strangers speaking at the door; 110
Is it likely God, with angels singing round
    Him,
  Hears our weeping any more?

"Two words, indeed, of praying we remember,
  And at midnight's hour of harm,
'Our Father,' looking upward in the chamber,
  We say softly for a charm. 115
We know no other words except 'Our Father,'
  And we think that, in some pause of angels'
    song,
God may pluck them with the silence sweet
    to gather,
  And hold both within his right hand, which
    is strong. 120
'Our Father!' If He heard us, He would
    surely
  (For they call Him good and mild)
Answer, smiling down the steep world very
    purely,
  'Come and rest with me, my child.'

"But, no!" say the children, weeping faster,
  "He is speechless as a stone; 125
And they tell us, of His image is the master
  Who commands us to work on.
Go to!" say the children—"up in Heaven,
  Dark, wheel-like, turning clouds are all we
    find. 130
Do not mock us; grief has made us unbeliev-
    ing:
  We look up for God, but tears have made
    us blind."
Do you hear the children weeping and dis-
    proving,
  O my brothers, what ye preach?
For God's possible is taught by his world's
    loving, 135
  And the children doubt of each.

And well may the children weep before you!
  They are weary ere they run;
They have never seen the sunshine, nor the
    glory
  Which is brighter than the sun. 140
They know the grief of man, without its
    wisdom;
  They sink in man's despair, without its
    calm—
Are slaves, without the liberty in Christdom,
  Are martyrs, by the pang without the palm,
Are worn as if with age, yet unretrievingly 145
  The harvest of its memories cannot reap—
Are orphans of the earthly love and heavenly.
  Let them weep! let them weep!

144. **palm**, palm branch, the symbol of victory, the prize.

They look up with their pale and sunken faces,
    And their look is dread to see, 150
For they mind you of their angels in high places,
    With eyes turned on Deity.
"How long," they say, "how long, O cruel nation,
    Will you stand, to move the world, on a child's heart—
Stifle down with a mailèd heel its palpitation,
    And tread onward to your throne amid the mart? 156
Our blood splashes upward, O gold-heaper,
    And your purple shows your path!
But the child's sob in the silence curses deeper
    Than the strong man in his wrath."

                                           (1843)

from *Sonnets from the Portuguese*

1

I thought once how Theocritus had sung
Of the sweet years, the dear and wished-for years,
Who each one in a gracious hand appears
To bear a gift for mortals, old or young;
And, as I mused it in his antique tongue, 5
I saw, in gradual vision through my tears,
The sweet, sad years, the melancholy years,
Those of my own life, who by turns had flung
A shadow across me. Straightway I was 'ware,
So weeping, how a mystic Shape did move 10
Behind me, and drew me backward by the hair;
And a voice said in mastery, while I strove—
"Guess now who holds thee?"—"Death," I said. But, there,
The silver answer rang—"Not Death, but Love."

3

Unlike are we, unlike, O princely Heart!
Unlike our uses and our destinies.
Our ministering two angels look surprise
On one another, as they strike athwart
Their wings in passing. Thou, bethink thee, art 5
A guest for queens to social pageantries,
With gages from a hundred brighter eyes
Than tears even can make mine, to play thy part
Of chief musician. What hast *thou* to do
With looking from the lattice-lights at me, 10
A poor, tired, wandering singer, singing through
The dark, and leaning up a cypress tree?
The chrism is on thine head—on mine, the dew—
And Death must dig the level where these agree.

7

The face of all the world is changed, I think,
Since first I heard the footsteps of thy soul
Move still, oh, still, beside me, as they stole
Betwixt me and the dreadful outer brink
Of obvious death, where I, who thought to sink, 5
Was caught up into love, and taught the whole
Of life in a new rhythm. The cup of dole
God gave for baptism, I am fain to drink,
And praise its sweetness, Sweet, with thee anear.
The names of country, heaven, are changed away 10
For where thou art or shalt be, there or here;
And this . . . this lute and song . . . loved yesterday
(The singing angels know), are only dear
Because thy name moves right in what they say.

8

What can I give thee back, O liberal
And princely giver, who hast brought the gold

Sonnet 1. 1. **Theocritus**, a famous Greek pastoral poet of the third century B.C. 13. **Death.** Miss Barrett had been an invalid for years.
    Sonnet 3. 7. **gages**, pledges.

12. **cypress tree**, a symbol of death. Cf. Sonnet 1.

And purple of thine heart, unstained, untold,
And laid them on the outside of the wall
For such as I to take or leave withal, 5
In unexpected largesse? Am I cold,
Ungrateful, that for these most manifold
High gifts, I render nothing back at all?
Not so; not cold—but very poor instead.
Ask God, who knows. For frequent tears have run 10
The colors from my life, and left so dead
And pale a stuff, it were not fitly done
To give the same as pillow to thy head.
Go farther! let it serve to trample on.

14

If thou must love me, let it be for naught
Except for love's sake only. Do not say
"I love her for her smile—her look—her way
Of speaking gently—for a trick of thought
That falls in well with mine, and certes brought 5
A sense of pleasant ease on such a day"—
For these things in themselves, Belovéd, may
Be changed, or change for thee—and love, so wrought,
May be unwrought so. Neither love me for
Thine own dear pity's wiping my cheeks dry— 10
A creature might forget to weep, who bore
Thy comfort long, and lose thy love thereby!
But love me for love's sake, that evermore
Thou mayst love on, through love's eternity.

26

I lived with visions for my company
Instead of men and women, years ago,
And found them gentle mates, nor thought to know
A sweeter music than they played to me.
But soon their trailing purple was not free 5
Of this world's dust, their lutes did silent grow,
And I myself grew faint and blind below
Their vanishing eyes. Then THOU didst come —to be,
Belovéd, what they seemed. Their shining fronts,
Their songs, their splendors (better, yet the same, 10
As river-water hallowed into fonts),
Met in thee, and from out thee overcame
My soul with satisfaction of all wants:
Because God's gifts put man's best dreams to shame.

35

If I leave all for thee, wilt thou exchange
And be all to me? Shall I never miss
Home-talk and blessing and the common kiss
That comes to each in turn, nor count it strange,
When I look up, to drop on a new range 5
Of walls and floors, another home than this?
Nay, wilt thou fill that place by me which is
Filled by dead eyes too tender to know change?
That's hardest. If to conquer love, has tried,
To conquer grief, tries more, as all things prove; 10
For grief indeed is love and grief beside.
Alas, I have grieved so I am hard to love.
Yet love me—wilt thou? Open thine heart wide,
And fold within the wet wings of thy dove.

41

I thank all who have loved me in their hearts,
With thanks and love from mine. Deep thanks to all
Who paused a little near the prison wall
To hear my music in its louder parts
Ere they went onward, each one to the mart's 6
Or temple's occupation, beyond call.
But thou, who, in my voice's sink and fall
When the sob took it, thy divinest Art's
Own instrument didst drop down at thy foot
To hearken what I said between my tears . . .
Instruct me how to thank thee! Oh, to shoot 11
My soul's full meaning into future years,
That *they* should lend it utterance, and salute
Love that endures, from Life that disappears!

43

How do I love thee? Let me count the ways.
I love thee to the depth and breadth and height

Sonnet 35. 1. **leave all.** Because of the attitude of the father of Miss Barrett, her marriage meant the severance of all home ties.

My soul can reach, when feeling out of sight
For the ends of Being and ideal Grace.
I love thee to the level of everyday's 5
Most quiet need, by sun and candle-light.
I love thee freely, as men strive for Right;
I love thee purely, as they turn from Praise.
I love thee with the passion put to use
In my old griefs, and with my childhood's
    faith. 10
I love thee with a love I seemed to lose
With my lost saints—I love thee with the
    breath,
Smiles, tears, of all my life!—and, if God
    choose,
I shall but love thee better after death.
                                    (*1845-1846;* 1850)

Sonnet 43. 14. I shall . . . death. Cf. Browning's *Prospice*, p. 706.

John Henry Newman
1801-1890

For the sketch of Newman's life and the story of his connection with the Oxford Movement, see pp. 407 and 445. The two lyrics which follow are from the sacred songs contributed monthly by Keble, Newman, R. H. Froude, Wilberforce, and Williams to the *British Magazine* in the early years of the Oxford Movement and published in 1836 under the title *Lyra Apostolica*. Newman alludes to them in his *Apologia pro Vita Sua* (see p. 462). *The Pillar of the Cloud* became better known as *Lead, Kindly Light;* it was written on shipboard when Newman was returning to England from Italy, sick with doubts and fears, to take up the struggle for reform. The title as here given refers to God's leadership of the children of Israel as recounted in *Exodus,* 13:21: "And the Lord went before them by day in a pillar of a cloud, to lead them the way; and by night in a pillar of fire, to give them light."

The Sign of the Cross

Whene'er across this sinful flesh of mine
    I draw the Holy Sign,
All good thoughts stir within me, and renew
    Their slumbering strength divine;
Till there springs up a courage high and true
    To suffer and to do. 6

And who shall say, but hateful spirits around,
    For their brief hour unbound,
Shudder to see, and wail their overthrow?
    While on far heathen ground 10
Some lonely Saint hails the fresh odor, though
    Its source he cannot know. (*1832;* 1836)

The Pillar of the Cloud

Lead, Kindly Light, amid the encircling
    gloom,
        Lead Thou me on!
The night is dark, and I am far from home—
        Lead Thou me on!
Keep Thou my feet; I do not ask to see 5
    The distant scene—one step enough for me.

I was not ever thus, nor prayed that Thou
        Shouldst lead me on.
I loved to choose and see my path; but now
        Lead Thou me on! 10
I loved the garish day, and, spite of fears,
Pride ruled my will; remember not past years.

So long Thy power hath blessed me, sure it
        still
    Will lead me on,
O'er moor and fen, o'er crag and torrent, till
    The night is gone; 15
And with the morn those angel faces smile
Which I have loved long since, and lost
        awhile. (*1833;* 1836)

from The Dream of Gerontius

The Dream of Gerontius, written twenty years after Newman had embraced the Roman Catholic faith, records—for the most part in dramatic monologue—the thoughts and emotions of a just old man who is dying, and whose soul at death is conducted to Purgatory by his guardian angel.

SOUL

Take me away, and in the lowest deep
    There let me be,
And there in hope the lone night-watches keep,
    Told out for me.
There, motionless and happy in my pain,   5
    Lone, not forlorn—
There will I sing my sad perpetual strain,
    Until the morn.

There will I sing, and soothe my stricken breast,
    Which ne'er can cease   10
To throb and pine, and languish, till possessed
    Of its Sole Peace.
There will I sing my absent Lord and Love—
    Take me away,
That sooner I may rise, and go above,   15
    And see Him in the truth of everlasting day.

ANGEL

Now let the golden prison ope its gates,
Making sweet music, as each fold revolves
Upon its ready hinge. And ye great powers,
Angels of Purgatory, receive from me   20
    My charge, a precious soul, until the day,
When, from all bond and forfeiture released,
    I shall reclaim it for the courts of light.

*   *   *   *   *

Softly and gently, dearly-ransomed soul,
    In my most loving arms I now enfold thee,
And, o'er the penal waters, as they roll,   25
    I poise thee, and I lower thee, and hold thee.

And carefully I dip thee in the lake,
    And thou, without a sob or a resistance,
Dost through the flood thy rapid passage take,   30
    Sinking deep, deeper into the dim distance.

Angels, to whom the willing task is given,
    Shall tend, and nurse, and lull thee, as thou liest;
And Masses on the earth, and prayers in heaven,
    Shall aid thee at the Throne of the Most Highest.   35

Farewell, but not forever! brother dear,
    Be brave and patient on thy bed of sorrow;
Swiftly shall pass thy night of trial here,
    And I will come and wake thee on the morrow.   *(1865;* 1865)

Emily Brontë
1818-1848

    Victorian literature provided numerous examples of literary families in which more than one member was talented. The Tennysons, the Newmans, the Kingsleys, the Rossettis, and the Brontës all reveal the fact that heritage and familiar contacts in the home often create little family communities of writers. Of these the Brontë sisters were striking illustrations. There were three of them, Charlotte (1816-1855), Emily (1818-1848), and Anne (1819-1849). They were the children of an impoverished clergyman of Haworth in Yorkshire, and out of their bleak and meager existence they all spun poetry and prose that have survived. Of the three the most talented and most famous was Charlotte; her sisters died at thirty, while she lived on to add two novels, *Shirley* and *Villette*, to the more famous *Jane Eyre*, which had appeared the year before Emily's death (see p. 422). Anne was the most artistically fragile of the sisters. Neither she nor her much more famous sister Charlotte had the gift of poetry that Emily had.
    The lives of all three sisters were exceedingly uneventful; living at boarding

schools, teaching, losing their health and their spirits under the confinement and irksome grind—it is a dull, commonplace story with no relief except Charlotte's late marriage and the writing of novels and verse. They were unhappy a good deal of the time and wore themselves out in a struggle for independence which never came. Emily seems to have been especially liberty-loving. "Liberty," Charlotte wrote, "was the breath of Emily's nostrils: without it she perished." The one break from the round of duties which fate had imposed upon Emily was her excursion to Brussels with Charlotte in 1842, where the two sisters remained for eight months as pupil-teachers in a *pensionat*. Later all three sisters attempted to make a living by taking private pupils at Haworth, but the enterprise was a gloomy failure. Meanwhile they were bravely writing, and in 1846 they had the courage to publish a thin little volume of *Poems by Currer, Ellis, and Acton Bell*. "Ellis" was Emily; and the other sisters generously admitted that the genuine poetry in the volume was hers. There was in Emily's verse not only good technique but a sturdy, vigorous note that was characteristic of the lover of freedom who had written the poems. It was no idle boast when "Ellis Bell" wrote "no coward soul is mine"; she had subdued a savage bull-dog once with her bare hands. "Currer Bell's" *Jane Eyre* appeared in October of the following year, and made her immediately famous. It preceded by only two months *Wuthering Heights* by Emily and *Agnes Gray* by Anne, which were issued in one volume. *Wuthering Heights* is a somber romance of love and sorrow, in which the central figure and villain is the stormy Heathcliff, a gypsy waif whose love for Catherine Earnshaw, daughter of his foster father, provides the core of the plot. The essential and rebellious vigor that lived in Emily's frail frame appears fully in this novel, as it does, indeed, in the best of her poems. Emily died at Haworth in December, 1848, still at odds with the existence that life had imposed upon her.

Remembrance

Cold in the earth—and the deep snow piled above thee,
Far, far removed, cold in the dreary grave!
Have I forgot, my only Love, to love thee,
Severed at last by Time's all-severing wave?

Now, when alone, do my thoughts no longer hover   5
Over the mountains, on that northern shore,
Resting their wings where heath and fern-leaves cover
Thy noble heart forever, ever more?

Cold in the earth—and fifteen wild Decembers,
From those brown hills, have melted into spring;   10
Faithful, indeed, is the spirit that remembers
After such years of change and suffering!

Sweet Love of youth, forgive, if I forget thee,
While the world's tide is bearing me along;
Other desires and other hopes beset me,   15
Hopes which obscure, but cannot do thee wrong!

No later light has lightened up my heaven,
No second morn has ever shone for me;
All my life's bliss from thy dear life was given,
All my life's bliss is in the grave with thee.   20

But, when the days of golden dreams had perished,
And ev'n Despair was powerless to destroy;
Then did I learn how existence could be cherished,
Strengthened, and fed without the aid of joy.

Then did I check the tears of useless passion— 25
Weaned my young soul from yearning after thine;
Sternly denied its burning wish to hasten
Down to that tomb already more than mine.

And, even yet, I dare not let it languish,
Dare not indulge in memory's rapturous pain; 30
Once drinking deep of that divinest anguish,
How could I seek the empty world again?
(*1845;* 1846)

Song

The linnet in the rocky dells,
  The moor-lark in the air,
The bee among the heather bells
  That hide my lady fair:

The wild deer browse above her breast; 5
  The wild birds raise their brood;
And they, her smiles of love caressed,
  Have left her solitude.

I ween that, when the grave's dark wall
  Did first her form retain, 10
They thought their hearts could ne'er recall
  The light of joy again.

They thought the tide of grief would flow
  Unchecked through future years;
But where is all their anguish now, 15
  And where are all their tears?

Well, let them fight for honor's breath,
  Or pleasure's shade pursue—
The dweller in the land of death
  Is changed and careless too. 20

And, if their eyes should watch and weep
  Till sorrow's source were dry,
She would not, in her tranquil sleep,
  Return a single sigh.

Blow, west wind, by the lonely mound, 25
  And murmur, summer streams!
There is no need of other sound
  To soothe my lady's dreams. (1846)

To Imagination

When weary with the long day's care,
  And earthly change from pain to pain,
And lost, and ready to despair,
  Thy kind voice calls me back again,
Oh, my true friend! I am not lone, 5
While thou canst speak with such a tone!

So hopeless is the world without;
  The world within I doubly prize;
Thy world, where guile, and hate, and doubt,
  And cold suspicion never rise; 10
Where thou, and I, and Liberty,
Have undisputed sovereignty.

What matters it, that all around
  Danger, and guilt, and darkness lie,
If but within our bosom's bound 15
  We hold a bright, untroubled sky,
Warm with ten thousand mingled rays
Of suns that know no winter days?

Reason, indeed, may oft complain
  For Nature's sad reality, 20
And tell the suffering heart how vain
  Its cherished dreams must always be;
And Truth may rudely trample down
The flowers of Fancy, newly-blown:

But thou art ever there, to bring 25
  The hovering vision back, and breathe
New glories o'er the blighted spring,
  And call a lovelier Life from Death,
And whisper, with a voice divine,
Of real worlds, as bright as thine. 30

I trust not to thy phantom bliss,
  Yet, still, in evening's quiet hour,
With never-failing thankfulness,
  I welcome thee, Benignant Power,
Sure solacer of human cares, 35
And sweeter hope, when hope despairs!
(1846)

Sympathy

There should be no despair for you
  While nightly stars are burning,
While evening pours its silent dew,

And sunshine gilds the morning.
There should be no despair—though tears
  May flow down like a river:
Are not the best beloved of years
  Around your heart forever?

They weep, you weep—it must be so;
  Winds sigh as you are sighing,
And Winter sheds its grief in snow
  Where Autumn's leaves are lying:
Yet, these revive, and from their fate
  Your fate cannot be parted:
Then, journey on, if not elate,
  Still *never* broken-hearted!

(1846)

The Night Is Darkening

The night is darkening round me,
  The wild winds coldly blow;
But a tyrant spell has bound me,
  And I cannot, cannot go.

The giant trees are bending
  Their bare boughs weighed with snow;
The storm is fast descending,
  And yet I cannot go.

Clouds beyond clouds above me,
  Wastes beyond wastes below;
But nothing drear can move me:
  I will not, cannot go.

(1846)

Fall, Leaves

Fall, leaves, fall; die, flowers, away;
Lengthen night and shorten day:
Every leaf speaks bliss to me,
Fluttering from the autumn tree;

I shall smile when wreaths of snow
Blossom where the rose should grow:
I shall sing when night's decay
Ushers in the drearier day.

(1846)

A Little While

A little while, a little while,
  The weary task is put away,
And I can sing and I can smile,
  Alike, while I have holiday.

Where wilt thou go, my harassed heart—
  What thought, what scene invites thee now?
What spot, or near or far apart,
  Has rest for thee, my weary brow?

There is a spot, 'mid barren hills,
  Where winter howls, and driving rain;
But, if the dreary tempest chills,
  There is a light that warms again.

The house is old, the trees are bare,
  Moonless above bends twilight's dome;
But what on earth is half so dear—
  So longed for—as the hearth of home?

The mute bird sitting on the stone,
  The dank moss dripping from the wall,
The thorn trees gaunt, the walks o'ergrown,
  I love them—how I love them all!

Still, as I mused, the naked room,
  The alien firelight died away;
And from the midst of cheerless gloom,
  I passed to bright, unclouded day.

A little and a lone green lane
  That opened on a common wide;
A distant, dreamy, dim blue chain
  Of mountains circling every side.

A heaven so clear, an earth so calm,
  So sweet, so soft, so hushed an air;
And, deepening still the dreamlike charm,
  Wild moor-sheep feeding everywhere.

That was the scene, I knew it well;
  I knew the turfy pathway's sweep,
That, winding o'er each billowy swell,
  Marked out the tracks of wandering sheep.

Could I have lingered but an hour,
  It well had paid a week of toil;
But Truth has banished Fancy's power:
  Restraint and heavy task recoil.

Even as I stood with raptured eye,
  Absorbed in bliss so deep and dear,

My hour of rest had fleeted by,
And back came labor, bondage, care.
(1850)

The Old Stoic

Riches I hold in light esteem,
    And Love I laugh to scorn;
And lust of fame was but a dream
    That vanished with the morn;

And if I pray, the only prayer   5
    That moves my lips for me
Is, "Leave the heart that now I bear,
    And give me liberty!"

Yes, as my swift days near their goal,
    'Tis all that I implore: 10
In life and death a chainless soul,
    With courage to endure.
(1846)

Often Rebuked, Yet Always Back Returning

Often rebuked, yet always back returning
    To those first feelings that were born with me,
And leaving busy chase of wealth and learning
    For idle dreams of things which cannot be:

Today, I will seek not the shadowy region;   5
    Its unsustaining vastness waxes drear;
And visions rising, legion after legion,
    Bring the unreal world too strangely near.

I'll walk, but not in old heroic traces,
    And not in paths of high morality,   10
And not among the half-distinguished faces,
    The clouded forms of long-past history.

I'll walk where my own nature would be leading—
    It vexes me to choose another guide—
Where the gray flocks in ferny glens are feeding,   15
    Where the wild wind blows on the mountain-side.

What have those lonely mountains worth revealing?

The Old Stoic. The Stoics were a school of Greek philosophers (second century B.C.) who held that virtue was the highest good and that all feelings should be rigidly subdued.
Often Rebuked, etc. 17. **those lonely mountains**, the moors in Yorkshire, where Emily Brontë lived.

More glory and more grief than I can tell:
The earth that wakes one human heart to feeling
Can center both the worlds of Heaven and Hell.
(1850)

No Coward Soul Is Mine

These are the last lines Emily Brontë ever wrote.

No coward soul is mine,
No trembler in the world's storm-troubled sphere;
    I see Heaven's glories shine,
And faith shines equal, arming me from fear.

    O God within my breast,   5
Almighty, ever-present Deity!
    Life—that in me has rest,
As I—undying Life—have power in Thee!

    Vain are the thousand creeds
That move men's hearts—unutterably vain;   10
    Worthless as withered weeds,
Or idlest froth amid the boundless main,

    To waken doubt in one
Holding so fast by Thine infinity;
    So surely anchored on   15
The steadfast rock of immortality.

    With wide-embracing love
Thy spirit animates eternal years,
    Pervades and broods above,
Changes, sustains, dissolves, creates, and rears.

    Though earth and man were gone,   21
And suns and universes ceased to be,
    And Thou were left alone,
Every existence would exist in Thee.

    There is not room for Death,   25
Nor atom that his might could render void;
    Thou—Thou art Being and Breath,
And what Thou art may never be destroyed.
(1850)

Arthur Hugh Clough
1819-1861

Like Newman and the Tennyson of *In Memoriam* Arthur Hugh Clough (pronounced *klŭf*) displayed in his poetry the spiritual agitation that accompanies religious doubt. Fears and anxieties harassed him during his Oxford days and pursued him thereafter until his death in Florence in 1861. He died in the same year and in the same city as Elizabeth Barrett Browning. His friend and brother poet Arnold commemorated the passing of his perturbed spirit in the elegy *Thyrsis* (see p. 739).

Clough's father was a Liverpool cotton merchant. The boy went to Rugby, where he was a pupil of Arnold's father, the famous headmaster there. He was Balliol Scholar at Oxford in 1837 and after graduation became a fellow and tutor in Oriel College. This post he resigned in 1848. After a year of rest in Italy, where he spent much of his time in Venice, he returned to England to take up the headship of University Hall, a dormitory for students of the University of London. He remained in London only two years; then he accepted a position in Cambridge, Massachusetts. The following year, however, saw him back in London in the Education Office, and this work remained his vocation for the rest of his life. Ill health drove him again to southern Europe, and from this journey he never returned.

Clough's literary work does not form a large body. His first long poem, *The Bothie of Tober-na-Vuolich*, was published in 1848. He wrote the poem in hexameters—not a form which lends itself very flexibly to the English language—and described it as "a Long-Vacation Pastoral." Its simple plot has to do with the love of Philip Hewson, a young Oxford scholar and thinker, for Elspie, the daughter of a Highland farmer. The *bothie*, it should be explained, was the Highland cottage. *Amours de Voyage*, another romance in hexameters, was written in 1849 but remained unpublished until 1858. Two long poems published after Clough's death were *Mari Magno*, a series of verse tales, and *Dipsychus*, a poem which is spiritually autobiographical in its representation of the "conflict between a tender conscience and the world"—as Clough described it—and which was thrown into the rather conventional form of a series of dialogues between the hero and a Satanic spirit who represents the tempter. Some of Clough's fine lyrics are as representative of his spiritual storm and strain as is this longer poem. *Qui Laborat, Orat* (He who works, prays) is, like *Dipsychus*, remotely suggestive of Carlyle; and the even finer *Say Not the Struggle Naught Availeth* is Clough's "everlasting yea" to the devil of pessimism and despair. It is hardly surprising that Arnold gave him a kind of immortality in *Thyrsis*, for the two poets were much alike in their melancholy natures. But Matthew Arnold was robustness itself as compared with the fearful, doubting spirit that was Clough.

Qua Cursum Ventus

The title means *As the Wind Blows (So the Vessel Takes Its Course)*. The words are taken from Virgil's *Aeneid*, III, 269. The poem suggests the break between Clough and W. G. Ward (1812-1882), a religious thinker who became a Roman Catholic in 1845, in the same year that Newman embraced that faith.

As ships, becalmed at eve, that lay
  With canvas drooping, side by side,
Two towers of sail at dawn of day
  And scarce long leagues apart descried;

When fell the night, upsprung the breeze,   5
  And all the darkling hours they plied,
Nor dreamt but each the self-same seas
  By each was cleaving, side by side:

E'en so, but why the tale reveal
  Of those, whom year by year unchanged, 10

Brief absence joined anew to feel,
  Astounded, soul from soul estranged?

At dead of night their sails were filled,
  And onward each rejoicing steered—
Ah, neither blame, for neither willed,   15
  Or wist, what first with dawn appeared!

To veer, how vain! On, onward strain,
  Brave barks! In light, in darkness too,
Through winds and tides one compass guides—
  To that, and your own selves, be true.   20

But O blithe breeze; and O great seas,
  Though ne'er, that earliest parting past,
On your wide plain they join again,
  Together lead them home at last.

One port, methought, alike they sought,   25
  One purpose hold where'er they fare—
O bounding breeze, O rushing seas!
  At last, at last, unite them there!   (1849)

from *Dipsychus*

Dipsychus is a satiric poem presenting in loosely dramatic episodes a modern version of the Faust theme (see Vol. I, p. 502). The speakers are Dipsychus and a Mephistophelian Spirit, who go about together and who stop and converse whenever they come to a well-known place. The scene is mostly in Venice.

"THERE IS NO GOD," THE WICKED SAITH

"There is no God," the wicked saith,
  "And truly it's a blessing,
For what He might have done with us
  It's better only guessing."

"There is no God," a youngster thinks,   5
  "Or really, if there may be,
He surely did not mean a man
  Always to be a baby."

"There is no God, or if there is,"
  The tradesman thinks, "'twere funny   10

"*There is no God*," from *Psalms*, 14:1: "The fool hath said in his heart, There is no God." This poem is spoken by the Spirit to Dipsychus, who had been troubled all night by a dream in which a bell kept tolling out the words, "There is no God."

If He should take it ill in me
  To make a little money."

"Whether there be," the rich man says,
  "It matters very little,
For I and mine, thank somebody,   15
  Are not in want of victual."

Some others, also, to themselves,
  Who scarce so much as doubt it,
Think there is none, when they are well
  And do not think about it.   20

But country folks who live beneath
  The shadow of the steeple;
The parson and the parson's wife,
  And mostly married people;

Youths green and happy in first love,   25
  So thankful for illusion;
And men caught out in what the world
  Calls guilt, in first confusion;

And almost everyone when age,
  Disease, or sorrows strike him,   30
Inclines to think there is a God,
  Or something very like Him.   (1849; 1862)

THIS WORLD IS VERY ODD WE SEE

This world is very odd we see,
  We do not comprehend it;
But in one fact we all agree,
  God won't, and we can't mend it.

Being common sense, it can't be sin   5
  To take it as I find it;
The pleasure to take pleasure in;
  The pain, try not to mind it.

These juicy meats, this flashing wine,
  May be an unreal mere appearance;   10
Only—for my inside, in fine,
  They have a singular coherence.

Oh yes, my pensive youth, abstain;
  And any empty sick sensation,
Remember, anything like pain   15
  Is only your imagination.

Trust me, I've read your German sage
  To far more purpose e'er than you did;
You find it in his wisest page,
  Whom God deludes is well deluded.

Say Not the Struggle Naught Availeth

Say not the struggle naught availeth,
  The labor and the wounds are vain,
The enemy faints not, nor faileth,
  And as things have been they remain.

If hopes were dupes, fears may be liars; 5
  It may be, in yon smoke concealed,
Your comrades chase e'en now the fliers,
  And, but for you, possess the field.

For while the tired waves, vainly breaking,
  Seem here no painful inch to gain, 10
Far back, through creeks and inlets making,
  Comes silent, flooding in, the main.

And not by eastern windows only,
  When daylight comes, comes in the light,
In front, the sun climbs slow, how slowly, 15
  But westward, look, the land is bright.
                              (1849; 1862)

"What Went Ye Out for to See?"

  The title is taken from *Matthew*, 11:7: "What went ye out in the wilderness to see? A reed shaken with the wind?" In the Bible the allusion is to John the Baptist; in the poem it is to Christ.

Across the sea, along the shore,
In numbers more and ever more,
From lonely hut and busy town,
The valley through, the mountain down,
What was it ye went out to see, 5
Ye silly folk of Galilee?
The reed that in the wind doth shake?
The weed that washes in the lake?
The reeds that waver, the weeds that float?—
A young man preaching in a boat. 10

What was it ye went out to hear
By sea and land, from far and near?
A teacher? Rather seek the feet
Of those who sit in Moses' seat.
Go humbly seek, and bow to them, 15
Far off in great Jerusalem.
From them that in her courts ye saw,
Her perfect doctors of the law,
What is it ye came here to note?—
A young man preaching in a boat. 20

A prophet! Boys and women weak!
Declare or cease to rave;
Whence is it he hath learned to speak?
Say, who his doctrine gave?
A prophet? Prophet wherefore he 25
Of all in Israel tribes?—
He teacheth with authority,
  And not as do the Scribes.   (1851; 1862)

Qui Laborat, Orat

O only Source of all our light and life,
  Whom as our truth, our strength, we see and feel,
But whom the hours of mortal moral strife
  Alone aright reveal!

Mine inmost soul, before Thee inly brought, 5
  Thy presence owns ineffable, divine;
Chastised each rebel self-encentered thought,
  My will adoreth Thine.

With eye down-dropped, if then this earthly mind
  Speechless remain, or speechless e'en depart; 10
Nor seek to see—for what of earthly kind
  Can see Thee as Thou art?—

If well-assured 'tis but profanely bold
  In thought's abstractest forms to seem to see,
It dare not dare the dread communion hold 15
  In ways unworthy Thee,

O not unowned, thou shalt unnamed forgive,
  In worldly walks the prayerless heart prepare;

27. *He teacheth,* etc. The people were astonished at Christ's teaching in the synagogue, for "he taught them as one that had authority, and not as the scribes" (*Mark*, 1:22).
  Qui Laborat, Orat. The title means *He Who Labors, Prays.*

And if in work its life it seem to live,
  Shalt make that work be prayer.   20

Nor times shall lack, when while the work it plies,
  Unsummoned powers the blinding film shall part,
And scarce by happy tears made dim, the eyes
  In recognition start.

But, as thou willest, give or e'en forbear   25
  The beatific supersensual sight,
So, with Thy blessing blessed, that humbler prayer
  Approach Thee morn and night.
                                        (1862)

Hope Evermore and Believe!

Hope evermore and believe, O man, for e'en as thy thought
  So are the things that thou see'st; e'en as thy hope and belief.
Cowardly art thou and timid? they rise to provoke thee against them;
  Hast thou courage? enough, see them exulting to yield.
Yea, the rough rock, the dull earth, the wild sea's furying waters   5
  (Violent say'st thou and hard, mighty thou think'st to destroy),
All with ineffable longing are waiting their Invader,

  All with one varying voice, call to him, Come and subdue;
Still for their Conqueror call, and, but for the joy of being conquered
  (Rapture they will not forego), dare to resist and rebel;   10
Still, when resisting and raging, in soft undervoice say unto him,
  Fear not, retire not, O man; hope evermore and believe.
Go from the east to the west, as the sun and the stars direct thee,
  Go with the girdle of man, go and encompass the earth.

Not for the gain of the gold; for the getting, the hoarding, the having,   15
  But for the joy of the deed; but for the Duty to do.
Go with the spiritual life, the higher volition and action,
  With the great girdle of God, go and encompass the earth.

Go; say not in thy heart, And what then were it accomplished,
  Were the wild impulse allayed, what were the use or the good!   20
Go, when the instinct is stilled, and when the deed is accomplished,
  What thou hast done and shalt do, shall be declared to thee then.
Go with the sun and the stars, and yet evermore in thy spirit
  Say to thyself: It is good; yet is there better than it.
This that I see is not all, and this that I do is but little;   25
  Nevertheless it is good, though there is better than it.
                                        (1862)

The Latest Decalogue

Thou shalt have one God only; who
Would be at the expense of two?
No graven images may be
Worshiped, except the currency.
Swear not at all; for, for thy curse   5
Thine enemy is none the worse.
At church on Sunday to attend
Will serve to keep the world thy friend.
Honor thy parents; that is, all
From whom advancement may befall.   10
Thou shalt not kill; but need'st not strive
Officiously to keep alive.
Do not adultery commit;
Advantage rarely comes of it.
Thou shalt not steal; an empty feat,   15
When it's so lucrative to cheat.
Bear not false witness; let the lie
Have time on its own wings to fly.
Thou shalt not covet, but tradition
Approves all forms of competition.   (1862)

The Latest Decalogue. Cf. with Biblical decalogue, *Exodus*, 20:1-17. 24. **good . . . it.** Cf. Browning's *Saul*, l. 295, p. 678.

Ite Domum Saturae, Venit Hesperus

The title means *Go Home Satisfied, Hesperus Comes;* it is taken from the tenth *Eclogue* of Virgil, in which a goatherd is addressing his herd. Hesperus is the evening star. Clough makes the speaker a peasant girl who is driving home her cows named Rose, Provence, and La Palie.

The skies have sunk, and hid the upper snow
(Home, Rose, and home, Provence and La
    Palie),
The rainy clouds are filing fast below,
And wet will be the path, and wet shall we.
Home, Rose, and home, Provence and La
    Palie.   5

Ah dear, and where is he, a year agone,
Who stepped beside and cheered us on and on?
My sweetheart wanders far away from me,
In foreign land or on a foreign sea.
Home, Rose, and home, Provence and La
    Palie.   10

The lightning zigzags shoot across the sky
(Home, Rose, and home, Provence and La
    Palie),
And through the vale the rains go sweeping
    by;
Ah me, and when in shelter shall we be?
Home, Rose, and home, Provence and La
    Palie.   15

Cold, dreary cold, the stormy winds feel they
O'er foreign lands and foreign seas that stray
(Home, Rose, and home, Provence and La
    Palie).
And doth he e'er, I wonder, bring to mind
The pleasant huts and herds he left behind?
And doth he sometimes in his slumbering
    see   21

The feeding kine, and doth he think of me,
My sweetheart wandering wheresoe'er it be?
Home, Rose, and home, Provence and La
    Palie.
The thunder bellows far from snow to snow
(Home, Rose, and home, Provence and La
    Palie),   26
And loud and louder roars the flood below.
Heigho! but soon in shelter shall we be;
Home, Rose, and home, Provence and La
    Palie.

Or shall he find before his term be sped,   30
Some comelier maid that he shall wish to
    wed?
(Home, Rose, and home, Provence and La
    Palie),
For weary is work, and weary day by day
To have your comfort miles on miles away.
Home, Rose, and home, Provence and La
    Palie.   35

Or may it be that I shall find my mate,
And he returning see himself too late?
For work we must, and what we see, we see,
And God, He knows, and what must be,
    must be,
When sweethearts wander far away from me.
Home, Rose, and home, Provence and La
    Palie.   41

The sky behind is brightening up anew
(Home, Rose, and home, Provence and La
    Palie),
The rain is ending, and our journey too;
Heigho! aha! for here at home are we—   45
In, Rose, and in, Provence and La Palie.
    (1862)

In a London Square

Put forth thy leaf, thou lofty plane—
  East wind and frost are safely gone;
With zephyr mild and balmy rain
  The summer comes serenely on;
Earth, air, and sun and skies combine   5
  To promise all that's kind and fair.
But thou, O human heart of mine,
  Be still, contain thyself, and bear.

December days were brief and chill,
  The winds of March were wild and drear,   10
And, nearing and receding still,
  Spring never would, we thought, be here.

The leaves that burst, the suns that shine,
  Had, not the less, their certain date—
And thou, O human heart of mine,
  Be still, refrain thyself, and wait.   (1869)

All Is Well

Whate'er you dream, with doubt possessed,
Keep, keep it snug within your breast,
And lay you down and take your rest;
Forget in sleep the doubt and pain,
And when you wake, to work again.
The wind it blows, the vessel goes,
And where and whither, no one knows.

'Twill all be well—no need of care;
Though how it will, and when, and where,
We cannot see, and can't declare.
In spite of dreams, in spite of thought,
'Tis not in vain, and not for naught,
The wind it blows, the ship it goes,
Though where and whither, no one knows.
                                  (1869)

Matthew Arnold*
1822-1888

Quiet Work

One lesson, Nature, let me learn of thee,
One lesson which in every wind is blown,
One lesson of two duties kept at one
Though the loud world proclaim their enmity—
Of toil unsevered from tranquillity!
Of labor, that in lasting fruit outgrows
Far noisier schemes, accomplished in repose,
Too great for haste, too high for rivalry!
Yes, while on earth a thousand discords ring,
Man's fitful uproar mingling with his toil,
Still do thy sleepless ministers move on,
Their glorious tasks in silence perfecting;
Still working, blaming still our vain turmoil,
Laborers that shall not fail, when man is gone.   (1849)

To a Friend

This sonnet expresses Arnold's characteristic reverence for classical literature and philosophy.

Who prop, thou ask'st, in these bad days, my mind?
He much, the old man, who, clearest-souled of men,
Saw The Wide Prospect, and the Asian Fen,
And Tmolus' hill, and Smyrna bay, though blind.
Much he, whose friendship I not long since won,
That halting slave, who in Nicopolis
Taught Arrian, when Vespasian's brutal son
Cleared Rome of what most shamed him. But be his
My special thanks, whose even-balanced soul,
From first youth tested up to extreme old age,
Business could not make dull, nor Passion wild:
Who saw life steadily, and saw it whole;
The mellow glory of the Attic stage;
Singer of sweet Colonus, and its child.
                                  (1849)

Shakespeare

Others abide our question. Thou art free.
We ask and ask—thou smilest and art still,
Out-topping knowledge. For the loftiest hill,
Who to the stars uncrowns his majesty,
Planting his steadfast footsteps in the sea,
Making the heaven of heavens his dwelling-place,
Spares but the cloudy border of his base

---

* For an account of the life and poetry of Matthew Arnold see p. 527.
  To a Friend. 2. **the old man,** Homer, who was said to be blind. 3. **The Wide Prospect,** Europe (a literal translation of the Greek word Εὐρώπη). **Asian Fens,** the marshy, low-lying districts along the rivers in Asia Minor.

4. **Tmolus' hill,** a mountain in Lydia, Asia Minor. **Smyrna bay.** Smyrna, one of the many towns that claimed to be the birthplace of Homer, is the chief seaport of Asia Minor. 6. **slave,** Epictetus (A.D. c.60-c.120), the Stoic philosopher, who was lame and at one time a slave. He lived at Nicopolos, Greece, after he was banished from Rome by the Emperor Domitian, the brutal son of Vespasian. One of the pupils of Epictetus was Arrian, a famous philosopher and historian. 8. **his,** a reference to Sophocles (497-406 B.C.), the Athenian dramatist whose plays are noted for their serenity. He was born at Colonus (l. 14), a village near Athens.
  Shakespeare. 1. **Others . . . free,** other poets are easily understood. Thou art too deep for our understanding.

To the foiled searching of mortality;
And thou, who didst the stars and sunbeams
    know,
Self-schooled, self-scanned, self-honored, self-
    secure,   10
Didst tread on earth unguessed at.—Better so!
All pains the immortal spirit must endure,
All weakness which impairs, all griefs which
    bow,
Find their sole speech in that victorious brow.
    (1849)

In Harmony with Nature

    The poem is addressed to a preacher who had urged his audience to live in harmony with nature.

TO A PREACHER

"In harmony with Nature?" Restless fool,
Who with such heat dost preach what were
    to thee,
When true, the last impossibility—
To be like Nature strong, like Nature cool!
Know, man hath all which Nature hath, but
    more,   5
And in that *more* lie all his hopes of good.
Nature is cruel, man is sick of blood;
Nature is stubborn, man would fain adore;
Nature is fickle, man hath need of rest;
Nature forgives no debt, and fears no grave;
Man would be mild, and with safe conscience
    blest.   11
Man must begin, know this, where Nature
    ends;
Nature and man can never be fast friends.
Fool, if thou canst not pass her, rest her slave!
    (1849)

The Forsaken Merman

    Tales dealing with relations between mortals and mermen or mermaids are common in folklore. This story belongs to Danish legend.

Come, dear children, let us away;
Down and away below!
Now my brothers call from the bay,
Now the great winds shoreward blow,
Now the salt tides seaward flow;   5
Now the wild white horses play,
Champ and chafe and toss in the spray.
Children dear, let us away!
This way, this way!

Call her once before you go—   10
Call once yet!
In a voice that she will know:
"Margaret! Margaret!"
Children's voices should be dear
(Call once more) to a mother's ear;   15
Children's voices, wild with pain—
Surely she will come again!
Call her once and come away;
This way, this way!
"Mother dear, we cannot stay!   20
The wild white horses foam and fret."
Margaret! Margaret!

Come, dear children, come away down;
Call no more!
One last look at the white-walled town,   25
And the little gray church on the windy shore,
Then come down!
She will not come though you call all day;
Come away, come away!

Children dear, was it yesterday   30
We heard the sweet bells over the bay?
In the caverns where we lay,
Through the surf and through the swell,
The far-off sound of a silver bell?
Sand-strewn caverns, cool and deep,   35
Where the winds are all asleep;
Where the spent lights quiver and gleam,
Where the salt weed sways in the stream,
Where the sea-beasts, ranged all round,
Feed in the ooze of their pasture-ground;   40
Where the sea-snakes coil and twine,
Dry their mail and bask in the brine;
Where great whales come sailing by,
Sail and sail, with unshut eye,
Round the world for ever and aye?   45
When did music come this way?
Children dear, was it yesterday?

Children dear, was it yesterday
(Call yet once) that she went away?

13. **Margaret,** a favorite name with Arnold; it means sea-pearl. See *Isolation,* p. 730.

Once she sate with you and me, 50
On a red gold throne in the heart of the sea,
And the youngest sate on her knee.
She combed its bright hair, and she tended it well,
When down swung the sound of a far-off bell.
She sighed, she looked up through the clear green sea; 55
She said: "I must go, for my kinsfolk pray
In the little gray church on the shore today.
'Twill be Easter-time in the world—ah me!
And I lose my poor soul, Merman! here with thee."
I said: "Go up, dear heart, through the waves;
Say thy prayer, and come back to the kind sea-caves!" 61
She smiled, she went up through the surf in the bay.
Children dear, was it yesterday?

   Children dear, were we long alone? 64
"The sea grows stormy, the little ones moan;
Long prayers," I said, "in the world they say;
Come!" I said; and we rose through the surf in the bay.
We went up the beach, by the sandy down
Where the sea-stocks bloom, to the white-walled town;
Through the narrow paved streets, where all was still, 70
To the little gray church on the windy hill.
From the church came a murmur of folk at their prayers,
But we stood without in the cold blowing airs.
We climbed on the graves, on the stones worn with rains,
And we gazed up the aisle through the small leaded panes. 75
She sate by the pillar; we saw her clear:
"Margaret, hist! come quick, we are here!
Dear heart," I said, "we are long alone;
The sea grows stormy, the little ones moan."
But, ah, she gave me never a look, 80
For her eyes were sealed to the holy book!
Loud prays the priest; shut stands the door.
Come away, children, call no more!
Come away, come down, call no more!

Down, down, down! 85
Down to the depths of the sea!
She sits at her wheel in the humming town,
Singing most joyfully.
Hark what she sings: "O joy, O joy,
For the humming street, and the child with its toy! 90
For the priest, and the bell, and the holy well;
For the wheel where I spun,
And the blessed light of the sun!"
And so she sings her fill,
Singing most joyfully, 95
Till the spindle drops from her hand,
And the whizzing wheel stands still.
She steals to the window, and looks at the sand,
And over the sand at the sea;
And her eyes are set in a stare; 100
And anon there breaks a sigh,
And anon there drops a tear,
From a sorrow-clouded eye,
And a heart sorrow-laden,
A long, long sigh; 105
For the cold strange eyes of a little Mermaiden
And the gleam of her golden hair.

   Come away, away, children;
Come, children, come down!
The hoarse wind blows coldly; 110
Lights shine in the town.
She will start from her slumber
When gusts shake the door;
She will hear the winds howling,
Will hear the waves roar. 115
We shall see, while above us
The waves roar and whirl,
A ceiling of amber,
A pavement of pearl.
Singing: "Here came a mortal, 120
But faithless was she!
And alone dwell forever
The kings of the sea."

But, children, at midnight,
When soft the winds blow, 125
When clear falls the moonlight,
When spring-tides are low;

---

69. **sea-stocks**, sea gillyflowers. 82. **shut . . . door**. According to popular belief, heaven and the benefits of Christianity are denied fairies and certain other supernatural beings.

91. **holy well**, a well or spring venerated for its healing properties. It may be used here, however, for the fount of holy water in the church with which the priest sprinkles the worshipers.

When sweet airs come seaward
From heaths starred with broom,
And high rocks throw mildly   130
On the blanched sands a gloom;
Up the still, glistening beaches,
Up the creeks we will hie,
Over banks of bright seaweed
The ebb-tide leaves dry.   135
We will gaze, from the sand-hills,
At the white, sleeping town;
At the church on the hillside—
And then come back down,
Singing: "There dwells a loved one,   140
But cruel is she!
She left lonely forever
The kings of the sea."   (1849)

Memorial Verses

APRIL, 1850

Goethe died in 1832 and was buried in Weimar, Germany. Byron died in 1824 while aiding the Greeks in their fight for independence. Wordsworth died in 1850. Arnold gave high place to all three poets; he was influenced especially by the poetry of Wordsworth.

Goethe in Weimar sleeps, and Greece,
Long since, saw Byron's struggle cease.
But one such death remained to come;
The last poetic voice is dumb—
We stand today by Wordsworth's tomb.   5

When Byron's eyes were shut in death,
We bowed our head and held our breath.
He taught us little; but our soul
Had *felt* him like the thunder's roll.
With shivering heart the strife we saw   10
Of passion with eternal law;
And yet with reverential awe
We watched the fount of fiery life
Which served for that Titanic strife.

When Goethe's death was told, we said: 15
Sunk, then, is Europe's sagest head.
Physician of the iron age,

14. **Titanic strife.** Byron was noted for his fiery, passionate nature, and the word *Titanic* is fittingly applied to him (see p. 200). The Titans were superhuman beings of great size who rebelled against the gods. 17. **iron age,** so called because of the terrible years of the French Revolution and the period following. To Goethe they seemed to portend the destruction of Europe.

Goethe has done his pilgrimage.
He took the suffering human race,
He read each wound, each weakness clear;   20
And struck his finger on the place,
And said: *Thou ailest here, and here!*
He looked on Europe's dying hour
Of fitful dream and feverish power;
His eye plunged down the weltering strife,   25
The turmoil of expiring life—
He said: *The end is everywhere,*
Art still has truth, take refuge there!
And he was happy, if to know
Causes of things, and far below   30
His feet to see the lurid flow
Of terror, and insane distress,
And headlong fate, be happiness.

And Wordsworth!—Ah, pale ghosts, rejoice!
For never has such soothing voice   35
Been to your shadowy world conveyed,
Since erst, at morn, some wandering shade
Heard the clear song of Orpheus come
Through Hades, and the mournful gloom.
Wordsworth has gone from us—and ye,   40
Ah, may ye feel his voice as we!
He too upon a wintry clime
Had fallen—on this iron time
Of doubts, disputes, distractions, fears.
He found us when the age had bound   45
Our souls in its benumbing round;
He spoke, and loosed our heart in tears.
He laid us, as we lay at birth,
On the cool flowery lap of earth;
Smiles broke from us, and we had ease;   50
The hills were round us, and the breeze
Went o'er the sun-lit fields again;
Our foreheads felt the wind and rain.
Our youth returned; for there was shed
On spirits that had long been dead,   55
Spirits dried up and closely furled,
The freshness of the early world.

Ah! since dark days still bring to light
Man's prudence and man's fiery might,
Time may restore us in his course   60
Goethe's sage mind and Byron's force;
But where will Europe's latter hour
Again find Wordsworth's healing power?

29. **And he . . . happiness.** These lines are translated from Virgil's *Georgics*, II, 490-492. 38. **Orpheus.** See p. 236, note 691.

Others will teach us how to dare,
And against fear our breast to steel; 65
Others will strengthen us to bear—
But who, ah! who, will make us feel?
The cloud of mortal destiny,
Others will front it fearlessly—
But who, like him, will put it by? 70

Keep fresh the grass upon his grave,
O Rotha, with thy living wave!
Sing him thy best! for few or none
Hears thy voice right, now he is gone. (1850)

Isolation. To Marguerite

This poem and the next are from a group of six love poems entitled *Switzerland*. The two poems given here were originally published independently.

We were apart; yet, day by day,
I bade my heart more constant be.
I bade it keep the world away,
And grow a home for only thee;
Nor feared but thy love likewise grew, 5
Like mine, each day, more tried, more true.

The fault was grave! I might have known,
What far too soon, alas! I learned—
The heart can bind itself alone,
And faith may oft be unreturned. 10
Self-swayed our feelings ebb and swell—
Thou lov'st no more;—Farewell! Farewell!

Farewell!—and thou, thou lonely heart,
Which never yet without remorse
Even for a moment didst depart 15
From thy remote and spheréd course
To haunt the place where passions reign—
Back to thy solitude again!

Back! with the conscious thrill of shame
Which Luna felt, that summer-night, 20
Flash through her pure immortal frame,
When she forsook the starry height
To hang over Endymion's sleep
Upon the pine-grown Latmian steep.

Yet she, chaste queen, had never proved 25
How vain a thing is mortal love,
Wandering in heaven, far removed.
But thou hast long had place to prove
This truth—to prove, and make thine own:
"Thou hast been, shalt be, art alone." 30

Or, if not quite alone, yet they
Which touch thee are unmating things—
Ocean and clouds and night and day;
Lorn autumns and triumphant springs;
And life, and others' joy and pain, 35
And love, if love, of happier men.

Of happier men—for they, at least,
Have *dreamed* two human hearts might blend
In one, and were through faith released
From isolation without end 40
Prolonged; nor knew, although not less
Alone than thou, their loneliness. (1855)

72. **Rotha**, a small stream near Grasmere, Westmoreland, where Wordsworth is buried.
Isolation. 20. **Luna**, Diana, goddess of the moon and of chastity. She fell in love with Endymion, the shepherd boy whom she found sleeping on Mt. Latmos, in Asia Minor.

TO MARGUERITE—CONTINUED

Yes! in the sea of life enisled,
With echoing straits between us thrown,
Dotting the shoreless watery wild,
We mortal millions live *alone*.
The islands feel the enclasping flow, 5
And then their endless bounds they know.

But when the moon their hollows lights,
And they are swept by balms of spring,
And in their glens, on starry nights,
The nightingales divinely sing; 10
And lovely notes, from shore to shore,
Across the sounds and channels pour—

Oh! then a longing like despair
Is to their farthest caverns sent;
For surely once, they feel, we were 15
Parts of a single continent!
Now round us spreads the watery plain—
Oh, might our marges meet again!

Who ordered that their longing's fire
Should be, as soon as kindled, cooled? 20
Who renders vain their deep desire?—

A god, a god their severance ruled!
And bade betwixt their shores to be
The unplumbed, salt, estranging sea.   (1852)

Self-Dependence

Weary of myself, and sick of asking
What I am, and what I ought to be,
At this vessel's prow I stand, which bears me
Forwards, forwards, o'er the starlit sea.

And a look of passionate desire   5
O'er the sea and to the stars I send:
"Ye who from my childhood up have calmed me,
Calm me, ah, compose me to the end!

"Ah, once more," I cried, "ye stars, ye waters,
On my heart your mighty charm renew;   10
Still, still let me, as I gaze upon you,
Feel my soul becoming vast like you!"

From the intense, clear, star-sown vault of heaven,
Over the lit sea's unquiet way,
In the rustling night-air came the answer: 15
"Wouldst thou *be* as these are? *Live* as they.

"Unaffrighted by the silence round them,
Undistracted by the sights they see,
These demand not that the things without them
Yield them love, amusement, sympathy.   20

"And with joy the stars perform their shining,
And the sea its long moon-silvered roll;
For self-poised they live, nor pine with noting
All the fever of some differing soul.

"Bounded by themselves, and unregardful   25
In what state God's other works may be,
In their own tasks all their powers pouring,
These attain the mighty life you see."

O air-born voice! long since, severely clear,
A cry like thine in mine own heart I hear: 30
"Resolve to be thyself; and know that he
Who finds himself loses his misery!"
                                           (1852)

The Buried Life

The title of this poem refers to man's hidden self—the source of his thought and his feeling.

Light flows our war of mocking words, and yet,
Behold, with tears mine eyes are wet!
I feel a nameless sadness o'er me roll.
Yes, yes, we know that we can jest,
We know, we know that we can smile!   5
But there's a something in this breast,
To which thy light words bring no rest,
And thy gay smiles no anodyne.
Give me thy hand, and hush awhile,
And turn those limpid eyes on mine,   10
And let me read there, love! thy inmost soul.

Alas! is even love too weak
To unlock the heart, and let it speak?
Are even lovers powerless to reveal
To one another what indeed they feel?   15
I knew the mass of men concealed
Their thoughts, for fear that if revealed
They would by other men be met
With blank indifference, or with blame reproved;
I knew they lived and moved   20
Tricked in disguises, alien to the rest
Of men, and alien to themselves—and yet
The same heart beats in every human breast!

But we, my love!—doth a like spell benumb
Our hearts, our voices?—must we too be dumb?   25
Ah! well for us, if even we,
Even for a moment, can get free
Our heart, and have our lips unchained;
For that which seals them hath been deep-ordained!

Fate, which foresaw   30
How frivolous a baby man would be—
By what distractions he would be possessed,
How he would pour himself in every strife,
And well-nigh change his own identity—
That it might keep from his capricious play
His genuine self, and force him to obey   35
Even in his own despite his being's law,
Bade through the deep recesses of our breast

The unregarded river of our life
Pursue with indiscernible flow its way;　40
And that we should not see
The buried stream, and seem to be
Eddying at large in blind uncertainty,
Though driving on with it eternally.

But often, in the world's most crowded
　　streets,　45
But often, in the din of strife,
There rises an unspeakable desire
After the knowledge of our buried life;
A thirst to spend our fire and restless force
In tracking out our true, original course;　50
A longing to inquire
Into the mystery of this heart which beats
So wild, so deep in us—to know
Whence our lives come and where they go.
And many a man in his own breast then
　　delves,　55
But deep enough, alas! none ever mines.
And we have been on many thousand lines,
And we have shown, on each, spirit and
　　power;
But hardly have we, for one little hour,
Been on our own line, have we been our-
　　selves—　60
Hardly had skill to utter one of all
The nameless feelings that course through
　　our breast,
But they course on forever unexpressed.
And long we try in vain to speak and act
Our hidden self, and what we say and do　65
Is eloquent, is well—but 'tis not true!
And then we will no more be racked
With inward striving, and demand
Of all the thousand nothings of the hour
Their stupefying power;　70
Ah yes, and they benumb us at our call!
Yet still, from time to time, vague and for-
　　lorn,
From the soul's subterranean depth upborne
As from an infinitely distant land,
Come airs, and floating echoes, and convey　75
A melancholy into all our day.
Only—but this is rare—
When a belovéd hand is laid in ours,
When, jaded with the rush and glare
Of the interminable hours,　80
Our eyes can in another's eyes read clear,

77. Only . . . goes. Cf. *Dover Beach*, lines 29-37, p. 744.

When our world-deafened ear
Is by the tones of a loved voice caressed—
A bolt is shot back somewhere in our breast,
And a lost pulse of feeling stirs again;　85
The eye sinks inward, and the heart lies plain,
And what we mean, we say, and what we
　　would, we know.
A man becomes aware of his life's flow,
And hears its winding murmur; and he sees
The meadows where it glides, the sun, the
　　breeze.　90

And there arrives a lull in the hot race
Wherein he doth forever chase
That flying and elusive shadow, rest.
An air of coolness plays upon his face,
And an unwonted calm pervades his breast.
And then he thinks he knows　96
The hills where his life rose,
And the sea where it goes.　　　(1852)

Lines

WRITTEN IN KENSINGTON GARDENS

　　Kensington is a borough in the western part of London; the Gardens are surrounded by busy streets. This poem is regarded as one of the most Wordsworthian that Arnold wrote.

In this lone, open glade I lie,
Screened by deep boughs on either hand;
And at its end, to stay the eye,
Those black-crowned, red-boled pine trees
　　stand!

Birds here make song, each bird has his,　5
Across the girdling city's hum.
How green under the boughs it is!
How thick the tremulous sheep-cries come!

Sometimes a child will cross the glade
To take his nurse his broken toy;　10
Sometimes a thrush flits overhead
Deep in her unknown day's employ.

Here at my feet what wonders pass,
What endless, active life is here!
What blowing daisies, fragrant grass!　15
An air-stirred forest, fresh and clear.

4. **red-boled,** having reddish trunks.

Scarce fresher is the mountain-sod
Where the tired angler lies, stretched out,
And, eased of basket and of rod,
Counts his day's spoil, the spotted trout.   20

In the huge world, which roars hard by,
Be others happy if they can!
But in my helpless cradle I
Was breathed on by the rural Pan.

I, on men's impious uproar hurled,   25
Think often, as I hear them rave,
That peace has left the upper world
And now keeps only in the grave.

Yet here is peace forever new!
When I who watch them am away,   30
Still all things in this glade go through
The changes of their quiet day.

Then to their happy rest they pass!
The flowers upclose, the birds are fed,
The night comes down upon the grass,   35
The child sleeps warmly in his bed.

Calm soul of all things! make it mine
To feel, amid the city's jar,
That there abides a peace of thine,
Man did not make, and cannot mar.   40

The will to neither strive nor cry,
The power to feel with others give!
Calm, calm me more! nor let me die
Before I have begun to live.   (1852)

Morality

We cannot kindle when we will
The fire which in the heart resides;
The spirit bloweth and is still,
In mystery our soul abides.
   But tasks in hours of insight willed   5
   Can be through hours of gloom fulfilled.

With aching hands and bleeding feet
We dig and heap, lay stone on stone;
We bear the burden and the heat

Of the long day, and wish 'twere done.   10
   Not till the hours of light return,
   All we have built do we discern.

Then, when the clouds are off the soul,
When thou dost bask in Nature's eye,
Ask, how *she* viewed thy self-control,   15
Thy struggling, tasked morality—
   Nature, whose free, light, cheerful air,
   Oft made thee, in thy gloom, despair.

And she, whose censure thou dost dread,
Whose eye thou wast afraid to seek,   20
See, on her face a glow is spread,
A strong emotion on her cheek!
   "Ah, child!" she cries, "that strife divine,
   Whence was it, for it is not mine?

"There is no effort on *my* brow—   25
I do not strive, I do not weep;
I rush with the swift spheres and glow
In joy, and when I will, I sleep.
   Yet that severe, that earnest air,
   I saw, I felt it once—but where?   30

"I knew not yet the gauge of time,
Nor wore the manacles of space;
I felt it in some other clime,
I saw it in some other place.
   'Twas when the heavenly house I trod,   35
   And lay upon the breast of God."   (1852)

Philomela

Philomela and Procne were daughters of Pandion, King of Athens. Procne was the wife of Tereus, King of Thrace. Tereus dishonored Philomela and then cut out her tongue that she might not betray him; but Philomela wove the story in a piece of tapestry, which she gave to her sister. Procne then killed her son Itys (Itylus), served him as food to his father, and fled with Philomela. On being pursued by Tereus, the sisters prayed for deliverance and were changed into birds—Philomela into a nightingale and Procne into a swallow. In the poem Arnold has reversed the positions of the sisters (see l. 21).

Hark! ah, the nightingale—
The tawny-throated!

---

18. **angler.** Arnold was an enthusiastic fisherman. 24. **Pan,** god of shepherds and of the country. Arnold was born at Laleham, a country village in Middlesex.

Hark, from that moonlit cedar what a burst!
What triumph! hark!—what pain!

O wanderer from a Grecian shore, 5
Still, after many years, in distant lands,
Still nourishing in thy bewildered brain
That wild, unquenched, deep-sunken, old-
    world pain—
Say, will it never heal?
And can this fragrant lawn 10
With its cool trees, and night,
And the sweet, tranquil Thames,
And moonshine, and the dew,
To thy racked heart and brain
Afford no balm? 15

Dost thou tonight behold,
Here, through the moonlight on this English
    grass,
The unfriendly palace in the Thracian wild?
Dost thou again peruse
With hot cheeks and seared eyes 20
The too clear web, and thy dumb sister's
    shame?
Dost thou once more assay
Thy flight, and feel come over thee,
Poor fugitive, the feathery change
Once more, and once more seem to make
    resound 25
With love and hate, triumph and agony,
Lone Daulis, and the high Cephissian vale?

Listen, Eugenia—
How thick the bursts come crowding through
    the leaves?
Again—thou hearest? 30
Eternal passion!
Eternal pain! (1853)

27. **Daulis**, the scene of the tragedy, in Phocis, Greece. The Cephissus was the chief river of Phocis.
28. **Eugenia**, an imaginary person.

Requiescat

Strew on her roses, roses,
    And never a spray of yew!
In quiet she reposes;
    Ah, would that I did too!

Her mirth the world required; 5
    She bathed it in smiles of glee.
But her heart was tired, tired,
    And now they let her be.

Her life was turning, turning,
    In mazes of heat and sound. 10
But for peace her soul was yearning,
    And now peace laps her round.

Her cabined, ample spirit,
    It fluttered and failed for breath.
Tonight it doth inherit 15
    The vasty hall of death. (1853)

Requiescat. The title means *May She Rest*. 2. **yew**, a common tree in graveyards. 13. **cabined**, confined, shut up as in a cabin.

The Scholar-Gypsy

Arnold drew the story for this poem from *The Vanity of Dogmatizing* (1661), an attack on scholastic philosophy written by Joseph Glanvil (1636-1680). Into the tale Arnold wove a praise of the country life and a condemnation of "the strange disease of modern life."

Go, for they call you, shepherd, from the hill;
    Go, shepherd, and untie the wattled cotes!
    No longer leave thy wistful flock unfed,
    Nor let thy bawling fellows rack their
        throats,
Nor the cropped herbage shoot another
        head. 5
    But when the fields are still,
And the tired men and dogs all gone to
        rest,
    And only the white sheep are sometimes
        seen

2. **wattled cotes**, sheepfolds built of wattles, interwoven twigs.

Cross and recross the strips of moon-blanched green,
Come, shepherd, and again begin the quest!	10

Here, where the reaper was at work of late—
In this high field's dark corner, where he leaves
His coat, his basket, and his earthen cruse,
And in the sun all morning binds the sheaves,
Then here, at noon, comes back his stores to use—	15
Here will I sit and wait,
While to my ear from uplands far away
The bleating of the folded flocks is borne,
With distant cries of reapers in the corn—
All the live murmur of a summer's day.	20

Screened is this nook o'er the high, half-reaped field,
And here till sun-down, shepherd! will I be.
Through the thick corn the scarlet poppies peep
And round green roots and yellowing stalks I see
Pale pink convolvulus in tendrils creep;	25
And air-swept lindens yield
Their scent, and rustle down their perfumed showers
Of bloom on the bent grass where I am laid,
And bower me from the August sun with shade;
And the eye travels down to Oxford's towers.	30

And near me on the grass lies Glanvil's book—
Come let me read the oft-read tale again!
The story of the Oxford scholar poor,
Of pregnant parts and quick inventive brain,
Who, tired of knocking at preferment's door,	35
One summer-morn forsook
His friends, and went to learn the gypsy-lore,
And roamed the world with that wild brotherhood,
And came, as most men deemed, to little good,
But came to Oxford and his friends no more.	40

But once, years after, in the country-lanes,
Two scholars, whom at college erst he knew,
Met him, and of his way of life inquired;
Whereat he answered that the gypsy-crew,
His mates, had arts to rule as they desired
The workings of men's brains,	45
And they can bind them to what thoughts they will.
"And I," he said, "the secret of their art,
When fully learned, will to the world impart;
But it needs heaven-sent moments for this skill."	50

This said, he left them, and returned no more.—
But rumors hung about the country-side,
That the lost scholar long was seen to stray,
Seen by rare glimpses, pensive and tongue-tied,
In hat of antique shape, and cloak of gray,
The same the gypsies wore.	55
Shepherds had met him on the Hurst in spring;
At some lone alehouse in the Berkshire moors,
On the warm ingle-bench, the smock-frocked boors
Had found him seated at their entering.	60
But 'mid their drink and clatter, he would fly.
And I myself seem half to know thy looks,
And put the shepherds, wanderer! on thy trace;

---

10. **the quest**, the search for the Scholar-Gypsy, who is supposed still to haunt the vicinity. 19. **corn**, wheat, grain. 25. **convolvulus**, a kind of morning-glory. 31. **Glanvil's book.** See headnote. 34. **pregnant parts**, inventive faculties.

57. **Hurst**, Cumner Hurst, a prominent hill in the parish of Cumner, southwest of Oxford. 58. **Berkshire**, a county south of Oxford. 59. **ingle-bench**, bench in the chimney-corner.

And boys who in lone wheatfields scare the rooks
  I ask if thou hast passed their quiet place;
    Or in my boat I lie   66
  Moored to the cool bank in the summer-heats,
    'Mid wide grass meadows which the sunshine fills,
    And watch the warm, green-muffled Cumner hills,
  And wonder if thou haunt'st their shy retreats.   70

For most, I know, thou lov'st retired ground!
  Thee at the ferry Oxford riders blithe,
    Returning home on summer nights, have met
  Crossing the stripling Thames at Bab-lock-hithe,
    Trailing in the cool stream thy fingers wet,   75
    As the punt's rope chops round;
  And leaning backward in a pensive dream,
    And fostering in thy lap a heap of flowers
    Plucked in shy fields and distant Wychwood bowers,
  And thine eyes resting on the moonlit stream.   80

And then they land, and thou art seen no more!—
  Maidens, who from the distant hamlets come
    To dance around the Fyfield elm in May,
  Oft through the darkening fields have seen thee roam,
    Or cross a stile into the public way.   85
    Oft thou hast given them store
  Of flowers—the frail-leafed, white anemone,
    Dark bluebells drenched with dews of summer eves,
    And purple orchises with spotted leaves—
  But none hath words she can report of thee.

And, above Godstow Bridge, when hay-time's here   91
  In June, and many a scythe in sunshine flames,
    Men who through those wide fields of breezy grass
  Where black-winged swallows haunt the glittering Thames,
    To bathe in the abandoned lasher pass,   95
    Have often passed thee near
  Sitting upon the river bank o'ergrown;
    Marked thine outlandish garb, thy figure spare,
    Thy dark vague eyes, and soft abstracted air—
  But, when they came from bathing, thou wast gone!   100

At some lone homestead in the Cumner hills,
  Where at her open door the housewife darns,
    Thou hast been seen, or hanging on a gate
  To watch the threshers in the mossy barns.
    Children, who early range these slopes and late   105
    For cresses from the rills,
  Have known thee eying, all an April-day,
    The springing pastures and the feeding kine;
    And marked thee, when the stars come out and shine,
  Through the long dewy grass move slow away.   110

In autumn, on the skirts of Bagley Wood—
  Where most the gypsies by the turf-edged way
    Pitch their smoked tents, and every bush you see
  With scarlet patches tagged and shreds of gray,
    Above the forest-ground called Thessaly—
    The blackbird, picking food,   116
  Sees thee, nor stops his meal, nor fears at all;

---

74. **Bab-lock-hithe,** a ferry over the Thames about two miles west of the village of Cumner. 76. **punt's . . . round.** The Scholar-Gypsy is seen reposing in a boat moored to the bank. The punt, or ferryboat, is pulled across the stream by a rope, and the boat moves in a kind of curve. The rope "chops" or suddenly shifts with the wind or the current. 79. **Wychwood,** a forest ten miles northwest of Oxford. 83. **Fyfield . . . May,** a reference to the maypole dance at Fyfield, a village six miles southwest of Oxford. The large elm was a landmark for all the countryside.

91. **Godstow Bridge,** about two miles up the Thames River from Oxford. 95. **lasher pass,** pool below a dam. 111. **Bagley Wood,** southwest of Oxford; it was a favorite place of Arnold's father. 114. **scarlet patches . . . gray.** The bright-colored tattered garments of the gypsies were hung on the bushes. 115. **Thessaly,** a piece of forest ground near Bagley Wood.

So often has he known thee past him stray,
   Rapt, twirling in thy hand a withered spray,
   And waiting for the spark from heaven to fall.   120

And once, in winter, on the causeway chill
   Where home through flooded fields foot-travelers go,
      Have I not passed thee on the wooden bridge,
      Wrapped in thy cloak and battling with the snow,
      Thy face tow'rd Hinksey and its wintry ridge?   125
      And thou hast climbed the hill,
   And gained the white brow of the Cumner range;
      Turned once to watch, while thick the snowflakes fall,
      The line of festal light in Christ-Church hall—
   Then sought thy straw in some sequestered grange.   130

But what—I dream! Two hundred years are flown
   Since first thy story ran through Oxford halls,
      And the grave Glanvil did the tale inscribe
   That thou wert wandered from the studious walls
      To learn strange arts, and join a gypsy tribe;   135
      And thou from earth art gone
   Long since, and in some quiet churchyard laid—
      Some country-nook, where o'er thy unknown grave
      Tall grasses and white flowering nettles wave,
   Under a dark, red-fruited yew-tree's shade.

—No, no, thou hast not felt the lapse of hours!   141
   For what wears out the life of mortal men?
'Tis that from change to change their being rolls;
'Tis that repeated shocks, again, again,
   Exhaust the energy of strongest souls   145
      And numb the elastic powers,
   Till having used our nerves with bliss and teen,
      And tired upon a thousand schemes our wit,
   To the just-pausing Genius we remit
   Our worn-out life, and are—what we have been.   150

Thou hast not lived, why should'st thou perish, so?
   Thou hadst *one* aim, *one* business, *one* desire;
      Else wert thou long since numbered with the dead!
      Else hadst thou spent, like other men, thy fire!
   The generations of thy peers are fled,   155
      And we ourselves shall go;
   But thou possessest an immortal lot,
      And we imagine thee exempt from age
      And living as thou liv'st on Glanvil's page,
   Because thou hadst—what we, alas! have not.

For early didst thou leave the world, with powers   161
   Fresh undiverted to the world without,
      Firm to their mark, not spent on other things;
   Free from the sick fatigue, the languid doubt,
      Which much to have tried, in much been baffled, brings.   165
      O life unlike to ours!
   Who fluctuate idly without term or scope,
      Of whom each strives nor knows for what he strives,
      And each half lives a hundred different lives;
   Who wait like thee, but not, like thee, in hope.   170

125. **Hinksey**, a village south of Oxford. 129. **Christ-Church hall**, the dining-hall in Christ Church College, Oxford.

147. **teen**, sorrow. 149. **just-pausing Genius.** According to the ancients the Genius of a man was his spirit or guardian angel. The phrase may mean that the Genius pauses just for a moment before departing, or that the even-handed Spirit of the world impartially ends individual lives.

Thou waitest for the spark from heaven! and we,
  Light half-believers of our casual creeds,
    Who never deeply felt, nor clearly willed,
    Whose insight never has borne fruit in deeds,
      Whose vague resolves never have been fulfilled; 175
        For whom each year we see
      Breeds new beginnings, disappointments new;
        Who hesitate and falter life away,
        And lose tomorrow the ground won today—
          Ah! do not we, wanderer! await it too? 180

Yes, we await it!—but it still delays,
    And then we suffer! and amongst us one,
    Who most has suffered, takes dejectedly
  His seat upon the intellectual throne;
      And all his store of sad experience he 185
        Lays bare of wretched days;
  Tells us his misery's birth and growth and signs,
    And how the dying spark of hope was fed,
    And how the breast was soothed, and how the head,
      And all his hourly varied anodynes. 190

This for our wisest! and we others pine,
    And wish the long unhappy dream would end,
    And waive all claim to bliss, and try to bear;
  With close-lipped patience for our only friend,
    Sad patience, too near neighbor to despair— 195
      But none has hope like thine!
  Thou through the fields and through the woods dost stray,
    Roaming the country-side, a truant boy,
    Nursing thy project in unclouded joy,
  And every doubt long blown by time away.

O born in days when wits were fresh and clear, 201
  And life ran gayly as the sparkling Thames;
    Before this strange disease of modern life,
  With its sick hurry, its divided aims,
    Its heads o'ertaxed, its palsied hearts, was rife— 205
      Fly hence, our contact fear!
    Still fly, plunge deeper in the bowering wood!
      Averse, as Dido did with gesture stern
      From her false friend's approach in Hades turn,
  Wave us away, and keep thy solitude! 210

Still nursing the unconquerable hope,
  Still clutching the inviolable shade,
    With a free, onward impulse brushing through,
    By night, the silvered branches of the glade—
      Far on the forest-skirts, where none pursue, 215
        On some mild pastoral slope
    Emerge, and resting on the moonlit pales
      Freshen thy flowers as in former years
      With dew, or listen with enchanted ears,
  From the dark dingles, to the nightingales!

But fly our paths, our feverish contact fly! 221
  For strong the infection of our mental strife,
    Which, though it gives no bliss, yet spoils for rest;
    And we should win thee from thy own fair life,
      Like us distracted, and like us unblest.
        Soon, soon thy cheer would die, 226
    Thy hopes grow timorous, and unfixed thy powers,
      And thy clear aims be cross and shifting made;
      And then thy glad perennial youth would fade,
  Fade, and grow old at last, and die like ours. 230

Then fly our greetings, fly our speech and smiles!
  —As some grave Tyrian trader, from the sea,

182. **one . . . suffered, etc.** These lines have been applied to Carlyle or Tennyson. 190. **anodynes,** pain-soothing drugs. 208. **Dido . . . turn.** Dido, Queen of Carthage, killed herself because she was deserted by Aeneas. On his journey through Hades Aeneas met the shade of Dido, but she turned scornfully away from him (*Aeneid,* VI, 450-471). 220. **dingles,** wooded dells. 232. **Tyrian trader.** The Phoenicians of the city of Tyre were the chief traders in the Mediterranean from 900 to 700 B.C. They were gradually displaced by the Greeks.

Descried at sunrise an emerging prow
Lifting the cool-haired creepers stealthily,
  The fringes of a southward-facing brow
    Among the Aegean isles; 236
And saw the merry Grecian coaster come,
  Freighted with amber grapes, and Chian wine,
  Green, bursting figs, and tunnies steeped in brine—
And knew the intruders on his ancient home, 240
  The young light-hearted masters of the waves—
And snatched his rudder, and shook out more sail;
And day and night held on indignantly
O'er the blue Midland waters with the gale,
  Betwixt the Syrtes and soft Sicily, 245
  To where the Atlantic raves
Outside the western straits; and unbent sails
There, where down cloudy cliffs, through sheets of foam,
  Shy traffickers, the dark Iberians come;
And on the beach undid his corded bales.

(1853)

234. **cool-haired creepers**, foliage overhanging the entrance to some cavern or inlet. 236. **Aegean isles**, islands in the Aegean Sea, between Greece and Asia Minor. 238. **Chian wine**, wine from Chios, an island in the Aegean Sea. 239. **tunnies**, a kind of large fish.

244. **Midland waters**, Mediterranean Sea. 245. **Syrtes**, the Gulf of Sidra, on the northeast coast of Africa. 247. **western straits**, Strait of Gibraltar. 249. **Iberians**, early inhabitants of Spain and Portugal.

Thyrsis

A MONODY, TO COMMEMORATE THE AUTHOR'S FRIEND, ARTHUR HUGH CLOUGH, WHO DIED AT FLORENCE, 1861

Arnold's poetical memorial to his dead friend, Arthur Hugh Clough (see p. 721), is written in the pastoral form and mood employed in such tributes; see Milton's *Lycidas* (Vol. I, p. 710). In the poem Arnold speaks of himself as Corydon and of Clough as Thyrsis. The elegy is filled with reminiscences of the days which Arnold and Clough spent together in Oxford and its neighborhood.

How changed is here each spot man makes or fills!
In the two Hinkseys nothing keeps the same;
  The village street its haunted mansion lacks,
And from the sign is gone Sibylla's name
  And from the roofs the twisted chimney-stacks— 5
    Are ye too changed, ye hills?
See, 'tis no foot of unfamiliar men
  Tonight from Oxford up your pathway strays!
  Here came I often, often, in old days—
Thyrsis and I; we still had Thyrsis then. 10

Runs it not here, the track by Childsworth Farm,
Past the high wood, to where the elm-tree crowns
  The hill behind whose ridge the sunset flames?
The signal-elm, that looks on Ilsley Downs,
  The Vale, the three lone weirs, the youthful Thames?— 15
    This winter's eve is warm,
Humid the air! leafless, yet soft as spring,
  The tender purple spray on copse and briers!
  And that sweet city with her dreaming spires,
She needs not June for beauty's heightening,

Lovely all times she lies, lovely tonight!— 21
  Only, methinks, some loss of habit's power

2. **two Hinkseys**, villages southwest of Oxford across the river. 4. **Sibylla**, the first name of a woman who kept this lodging house near Oxford. 5 **twisted**, set at an angle. 11. **Childsworth Farm**, modern Chilswell Farm, three miles from Oxford.

14. **signal-elm**. This famous tree has frequently been identified with an oak tree standing at the top of the knoll on the Oxford side of the ridge; but a large elm a short distance below the summit of the ridge better fits the description. **Ilsley Downs**. Ilsley is a parish in West Berkshire. 15. **weirs**, dams. **youthful Thames**. The Thames River is about fifty yards wide at Oxford. 19. **sweet city**, Oxford.

Befalls me wandering through this up-
    land dim;
  Once passed I blindfold here, at any hour;
  Now seldom come I, since I came with
    him.   25
    That single elm tree bright
Against the west—I miss it! it is gone?
  We prized it dearly; while it stood, we
    said,
  Our friend, the gypsy-scholar, was not
    dead;
While the tree lived, he in these fields lived
    on.   30

Too rare, too rare, grow now my visits here,
  But once I knew each field, each flower,
    each stick;
    And with the country folk acquaintance
      made
  By barn in threshing-time, by new-built
    rick.
    Here, too, our shepherd-pipes we first
      assayed.   35
    Ah me! this many a year
My pipe is lost, my shepherd's holiday!
  Needs must I lose them, needs with heavy
    heart
  Into the world and wave of men depart;
But Thyrsis of his own will went away.   40

It irked him to be here; he could not rest.
  He loved each simple joy the country yields,
  He loved his mates; but yet he could not
    keep,
  For that a shadow lowered on the fields,
    Here with the shepherds and the silly
      sheep.   45
    Some life of men unblest
He knew, which made him droop, and filled
    his head.
  He went; his piping took a troubled
    sound
  Of storms that rage outside our happy
    ground;
He could not wait their passing, he is dead.

<small>29. **gypsy-scholar.** See *The Scholar-Gypsy* and note, p. 734. 35. **shepherd-pipes,** the usual pastoral symbol for poetry. 36. **many a year ... lost.** Arnold had not published any poetry for nine years. 40. **Thyrsis ... away.** Clough resigned his fellowship in Oriel College, Oxford, in 1848, partly on religious grounds. 45. **silly,** simple. 49. **storms that rage.** Much of the poetry of Clough reflects his spiritual struggles.</small>

So, some tempestuous morn in early June,   51
  When the year's primal burst of bloom is
    o'er,
  Before the roses and the longest day—
  When garden-walks and all the grassy floor
    With blossoms red and white of fallen
      May   55
    And chestnut flowers are strewn—
So have I heard the cuckoo's parting cry,
  From the wet field, through the vexed
    garden-trees,
  Come with the volleying rain and tossing
    breeze:
*The bloom is gone, and with the bloom
    go I!*   60

Too quick despairer, wherefore wilt thou go?
  Soon will the high midsummer pomps come
    on.
  Soon will the musk carnations break and
    swell,
  Soon shall we have gold-dusted snapdragon,
    Sweet-William with his homely cottage-
      smell,   65
    And stocks in fragrant blow;
Roses that down the alleys shine afar,
  And open, jasmine-muffled lattices,
  And groups under the dreaming garden-
    trees,
And the full moon, and the white evening-
    star.   70

He hearkens not! light comer, he is flown!
  What matters it? next year he will return,
  And we shall have him in the sweet
    spring days,
  With whitening hedges, and uncrumpling
    fern,
    And bluebells trembling by the forest-
      ways,   75
    And scent of hay new-mown.
But Thyrsis never more we swains shall see;
  See him come back, and cut a smoother
    reed,
  And blow a strain the world at last shall
    heed—
For Time, not Corydon, hath conquered
    thee!   80

<small>62. **pomps,** shows, displays. 66. **stocks,** gillyflowers.</small>

Alack, for Corydon no rival now! —
  But when Sicilian shepherds lost a mate,
    Some good survivor with his flute would go,
  Piping a ditty sad for Bion's fate;
    And cross the unpermitted ferry's flow,
      And relax Pluto's brow,   86
    And make leap up with joy the beauteous head
      Of Proserpine, among whose crownéd hair
    Are flowers first opened on Sicilian air,
    And flute his friend, like Orpheus, from the dead.   90

O easy access to the hearer's grace
  When Dorian shepherds sang to Proserpine!
    For she herself had trod Sicilian fields,
    She knew the Dorian water's gush divine,
    She knew each lily white which Enna yields,   95
      Each rose with blushing face;
    She loved the Dorian pipe, the Dorian strain.
      But, ah, of our poor Thames she never heard!
      Her foot the Cumner cowslips never stirred;
    And we should tease her with our plaint in vain!   100

Well! wind-dispersed and vain the words will be,
  Yet, Thyrsis, let me give my grief its hour
    In the old haunt, and find our tree-topped hill!
  Who, if not I, for questing here hath power?
    I know the wood which hides the daffodil,
    I know the Fyfield tree,   106
  I know what white, what purple fritillaries
    The grassy harvest of the river-fields,
      Above by Ensham, down by Sandford, yields,
    And what sedged brooks are Thames's tributaries;   110

I know these slopes; who knows them if not I?—
  But many a dingle on the loved hillside,
    With thorns once studded, old, white-blossomed trees,
  Where thick the cowslips grew, and far descried
    High towered the spikes of purple orchises,   115
      Hath since our day put by
    The coronals of that forgotten time;
      Down each green bank hath gone the plowboy's team,
      And only in the hidden brookside gleam
    Primroses, orphans of the flowery prime.   120

Where is the girl, who by the boatman's door,
  Above the locks, above the boating throng,
    Unmoored our skiff when through the Wytham flats,
  Red loosestrife and blond meadow-sweet among
    And darting swallows and light water-gnats,   125
      We tracked the shy Thames shore?
    Where are the mowers, who, as the tiny swell
      Of our boat passing heaved the river-grass,
      Stood with suspended scythe to see us pass?—
    They are all gone, and thou art gone as well!   130

Yes, thou art gone! and round me too the night
  In ever-nearing circle weaves her shade.
    I see her veil draw soft across the day,
    I feel her slowly chilling breath invade
      The cheek grown thin, the brown hair sprent with gray;   135

---

82. **Sicilian shepherds**, pastoral poets of Sicily; a reference to the lament for Bion, a Sicilian pastoral poet, written by his friend Moschus, second century B.C. 85. **unpermitted . . . flow**, the River Styx, over which only the dead were permitted to pass. 86. **Pluto**, the god of the underworld. He is said to have carried off Proserpine to be his wife. He found her in the vale of Enna (l. 95), in Sicily, where she was gathering lilies and violets. 90. **Orpheus.** See p. 236, note 691. 92. **Dorian**, Sicilian. 99. **Cumner**, hills near Oxford. 106. **Fyfield tree**, a giant elm near the village of Fyfield, six miles southwest of Oxford. 107. **fritillaries**, lily-like flowers.

109. **Ensham**, Eynsham, a village northwest of Oxford. Sandford is south of Oxford. 112. **dingle**, wooded dell. 123. **Wytham flats**, about two miles northwest of Oxford, between the village of Wytham and the Thames. 135. **sprent**, sprinkled.

I feel her finger light
　Laid pausefully upon life's headlong train—
　　　The foot less prompt to meet the morn-
　　　　　ing dew,
　　　The heart less bounding at emotion new,
　　　And hope, once crushed, less quick to
　　　　　spring again.   140

And long the way appears, which seemed so
　　　　short
　To the less practiced eye of sanguine youth;
　　　And high the mountain-tops, in cloudy
　　　　air,
　　　The mountain-tops, where is the throne of
　　　　Truth,
　　　　　Tops in life's morning-sun so bright and
　　　　　　bare!   145
　　　Unbreachable the fort
Of the long-battered world uplifts its wall;
　And strange and vain the earthly turmoil
　　　grows,
　And near and real the charm of thy re-
　　　pose,
　And night as welcome as a friend would
　　　fall.   150

But hush! the upland hath a sudden loss
　Of quiet!—Look, adown the dusk hillside,
　　A troop of Oxford hunters going home,
　　As in old days, jovial and talking, ride!
　　　From hunting with the Berkshire hounds
　　　　they come.   155
　　　Quick! let me fly, and cross
Into yon farther field;—'Tis done; and
　　see,
　Backed by the sunset, which doth glorify
　　The orange and pale violet evening sky,
　Bare on its lonely ridge, the Tree! the Tree!

I take the omen! Eve lets down her veil,   161
　The white fog creeps from bush to bush
　　about,
　　　The west unflushes, the high stars grow
　　　　bright,
　　　And in the scattered farms the lights come
　　　　out.

　　I cannot reach the signal-tree tonight,   165
　　Yet, happy omen, hail!
Hear it from thy broad lucent Arno-vale
　(For there thine earth-forgetting eyelids
　　keep
　The morningless and unawakening sleep
Under the flowery oleanders, pale),   170

Hear it, O Thyrsis, still our tree is there!—
　Ah, vain! These English fields, this upland
　　dim,
　　These brambles pale with mist engar-
　　　landed,
　That lone, sky-pointing tree, are not for
　　him;
　To a boon southern country he is fled,   175
　　And now in happier air,
　Wandering with the great Mother's train
　　divine
(And purer or more subtle soul than thee,
　I trow, the mighty Mother doth not see)
Within a folding of the Apennine,   180

Thou hearest the immortal chants of old!—
　Putting his sickle to the perilous grain
　　In the hot cornfield of the Phrygian king,
　For thee the Lityerses-song again
　Young Daphnis with his silver voice doth
　　sing;   185
　　Sings his Sicilian fold,
His sheep, his hapless love, his blinded
　eyes—
　And how a call celestial round him rang,
　And heavenward from the fountain-brink
　　he sprang,
　And all the marvel of the golden skies.   190

There thou art gone, and me thou leavest here
Sole in these fields! yet will I not despair.
　Despair I will not, while I yet descry

---

137. **pausefully**, so as to make it pause. 155. **Berkshire**, a county south of Oxford. 160. **the Tree.** See lines 12-14.

167. **Arno.** Clough died in Italy and was buried in Florence by the Arno River. 175. **boon**, rich, benign. 177. **great Mother**, Cybele, the goddess of nature, and the mother of the gods. 183. **Phrygian king**, Lityerses, who made strangers contest with him in reaping grain; if he defeated them, he put them to death. The Sicilian shepherd Daphnis (l. 185), son of Hermes, messenger of the gods, engaged in such a contest in order to release his mistress, who was in the power of the king. Hercules reaped the grain for Daphnis and killed Lityerses. The Lityerses-song connected with the tradition used to be sung by Greek grain reapers. Another tradition represented Daphnis as having been blinded by a nymph whose love he slighted. Hermes raised Daphnis to Olympus and marked by a fountain the place of his ascent.

'Neath the mild canopy of English air
  That lonely tree against the western sky.
    Still, still these slopes, 'tis clear,   196
  Our gypsy-scholar haunts, outliving thee!
    Fields where soft sheep from cages pull
      the hay,
  Woods with anemones in flower till May,
  Know him a wanderer still; then why not
    me?   200

A fugitive and gracious light he seeks,
  Shy to illumine; and I seek it too.
    This does not come with houses or with
      gold,
    With place, with honor, and a flattering
      crew;
    'Tis not in the world's market bought
      and sold—   205
      But the smooth-slipping weeks
  Drop by, and leave its seeker still untired;
  Out of the heed of mortals he is gone,
  He wends unfollowed, he must house
    alone;
  Yet on he fares, by his own heart inspired.

Thou too, O Thyrsis, on like quest wast
    bound;   211
  Thou wanderedst with me for a little
    hour!
  Men gave thee nothing; but this happy
    quest,
  If men esteemed thee feeble, gave thee
    power,
  If men procured thee trouble, gave thee
    rest.   215
    And this rude Cumner ground,
  Its fir-topped Hurst, its farms, its quiet
    fields,
    Here cam'st thou in thy jocund youthful
      time,
    Here was thine height of strength, thy
      golden prime!   219
  And still the haunt beloved a virtue yields.

What though the music of thy rustic flute
  Kept not for long its happy, country tone;
    Lost it too soon, and learned a stormy
      note

Of men contention-tossed, of men who
    groan,
  Which tasked thy pipe too sore, and tired
    thy throat—   225
    It failed, and thou wast mute!
Yet hadst thou alway visions of our light,
  And long with men of care thou couldst
    not stay,
  And soon thy foot resumed its wandering
    way,
  Left human haunt, and on alone till
    night.   230

Too rare, too rare, grow now my visits here!
  'Mid city-noise, not, as with thee of yore,
    Thyrsis! in reach of sheep-bells is my
      home.
    —Then through the great town's harsh,
      heart-wearying roar,
    Let in thy voice a whisper often come,
      To chase fatigue and fear: 236
  Why faintest thou? I wandered till I died.
  Roam on! The light we sought is shining
    still.
    Dost thou ask proof? Our tree yet crowns
      the hill,
  Our scholar travels yet the loved hillside.
                                                  (1866)

Austerity of Poetry

That son of Italy who tried to blow,
Ere Dante came, the trump of sacred song,
In his light youth amid a festal throng
Sate with his bride to see a public show.
Fair was the bride, and on her front did glow   5
Youth like a star; and what to youth belong—
Gay raiment, sparkling gauds, elation strong.
A prop gave way! crash fell a platform! lo,
'Mid struggling sufferers, hurt to death, she
    lay!
Shuddering, they drew her garments off—
    and found   10
A robe of sackcloth next the smooth, white
    skin.

---

202. **Shy to illumine,** reluctant to shine forth. 217. **Hurst,** a prominent hill in the parish of Cumner.

1. **son of Italy,** Giacopone di Todi, a poet of the thirteenth century. Upon the death of his bride, as related in the poem, he became a Franciscan monk.

Such, poets, is your bride, the Muse! young, gay,
Radiant, adorned outside; a hidden ground
Of thought and of austerity within.   (1867)

Dover Beach

The sea is calm tonight,
The tide is full, the moon lies fair
Upon the straits;—on the French coast the light
Gleams and is gone; the cliffs of England stand,   4
Glimmering and vast, out in the tranquil bay.
Come to the window, sweet is the night-air!

Only, from the long line of spray
Where the sea meets the moon-blanched land,
Listen! you hear the grating roar
Of pebbles which the waves draw back, and fling,   10
At their return, up the high strand,
Begin, and cease, and then again begin,
With tremulous cadence slow, and bring
The eternal note of sadness in.

Sophocles long ago   15
Heard it on the Aegean, and it brought
Into his mind the turbid ebb and flow
Of human misery; we
Find also in the sound a thought,
Hearing it by this distant northern sea.   20

The Sea of Faith
Was once, too, at the full, and round earth's shore
Lay like the folds of a bright girdle furled.
But now I only hear
Its melancholy, long, withdrawing roar,   25
Retreating, to the breath
Of the night-wind, down the vast edges drear
And naked shingles of the world.

Ah, love, let us be true
To one another! for the world, which seems
To lie before us like a land of dreams,   31
So various, so beautiful, so new,
Hath really neither joy, nor love, nor light,
Nor certitude, nor peace, nor help for pain;
And we are here as on a darkling plain   35
Swept with confused alarms of struggle and flight,
Where ignorant armies clash by night.   (1867)

The Last Word

Creep into thy narrow bed,
Creep, and let no more be said!
Vain thy onset! all stands fast.
Thou thyself must break at last.

Let the long contention cease!   5
Geese are swans, and swans are geese.
Let them have it how they will!
Thou art tired; best be still.

They out-talked thee, hissed thee, tore thee?
Better men fared thus before thee;   10
Fired their ringing shot and passed,
Hotly charged—and sank at last.

Charge once more, then, and be dumb!
Let the victors, when they come,
When the forts of folly fall,   15
Find thy body by the wall!   (1867)

Pis-Aller

"Man is blind because of sin;
Revelation makes him sure.
Without that, who looks within
Looks in vain, for all's obscure."

Nay, look closer into man!   5
Tell me, can you find indeed
Nothing sure, no moral plan
Clear prescribed, without your creed?

"No, I nothing can perceive!
Without that, all's dark for men.   10
That, or nothing, I believe."—
For God's sake, believe it then!   (1867)

---

15. **Sophocles,** famous Greek tragic dramatist of the fifth century B.C. The reference is to a passage in *Antigone,* 583 ff. 28. **shingles,** beaches covered with shingles, large stones.

16. **body . . . wall,** where it fell in attacking the forts of folly.
Pis-Aller. The title means *A Last Resource.*

Rugby Chapel

This poem was written in memory of the poet's father, Dr. Thomas Arnold, the celebrated headmaster of Rugby School. He died suddenly in June, 1842, and was buried in the College Chapel.

NOVEMBER, 1857

Coldly, sadly descends
The autumn evening. The field
Strewn with its dank yellow drifts
Of withered leaves, and the elms,
Fade into dimness apace, 5
Silent—hardly a shout
From a few boys late at their play!
The lights come out in the street,
In the schoolroom windows;—but cold,
Solemn, unlighted, austere, 10
Through the gathering darkness, arise
The chapel walls, in whose bound
Thou, my father! art laid.

There thou dost lie, in the gloom
Of the autumn evening. But ah! 15
That word, *gloom,* to my mind
Brings thee back, in the light
Of thy radiant vigor, again;
In the gloom of November we passed
Days not dark at thy side; 20
Seasons impaired not the ray
Of thy buoyant cheerfulness clear.
Such thou wast! and I stand
In the autumn evening, and think
Of by-gone autumns with thee. 25

Fifteen years have gone round
Since thou arosest to tread,
In the summer morning, the road
Of death, at a call unforeseen,
Sudden. For fifteen years, 30
We who till then in thy shade
Rested as under the boughs
Of a mighty oak, have endured
Sunshine and rain as we might,
Bare, unshaded, alone, 35
Lacking the shelter of thee.

O strong soul, by what shore
Tarriest thou now? For that force,
Surely, has not been left vain!
Somewhere, surely, afar, 40
In the sounding labor-house vast
Of being, is practiced that strength,
Zealous, beneficent, firm!

Yes, in some far-shining sphere,
Conscious or not of the past, 45
Still thou performest the word
Of the Spirit in whom thou dost live—
Prompt, unwearied, as here!
Still thou upraisest with zeal
The humble good from the ground, 50
Sternly repressest the bad!
Still, like a trumpet, dost rouse
Those who with half-open eyes
Tread the border-land dim
'Twixt vice and virtue; revivest, 55
Succorest!—this was thy work,
This was thy life upon earth.

What is the course of the life
Of mortal men on the earth?—
Most men eddy about 60
Here and there—eat and drink,
Chatter and love and hate,
Gather and squander, are raised
Aloft, are hurled in the dust,
Striving blindly, achieving 65
Nothing; and then they die—
Perish;—and no one asks
Who or what they have been,
More than he asks what waves,
In the moonlit solitudes mild 70
Of the midmost Ocean, have swelled,
Foamed for a moment, and gone.
And there are some, whom a thirst
Ardent, unquenchable, fires,
Not with the crowd to be spent, 75
Not without aim to go round
In an eddy of purposeless dust,
Effort unmeaning and vain.
Ah, yes! some of us strive
Not without action to die 80
Fruitless, but something to snatch

From dull oblivion, nor all
Glut the devouring grave!
We, we have chosen our path—
Path to a clear-purposed goal,
Path of advance!—but it leads
A long, steep journey, through sunk
Gorges, o'er mountains in snow.
Cheerful, with friends, we set forth—
Then, on the height, comes the storm.
Thunder crashes from rock
To rock, the cataracts reply,
Lightnings dazzle our eyes.
Roaring torrents have breached
The track, the stream-bed descends
In the place where the wayfarer once
Planted his footstep—the spray
Boils o'er its borders! aloft
The unseen snow-beds dislodge
Their hanging ruin; alas,
Havoc is made in our train!
Friends, who set forth at our side,
Falter, are lost in the storm.
We, we only are left!
With frowning foreheads, with lips
Sternly compressed, we strain on,
On—and at nightfall at last
Come to the end of our way,
To the lonely inn 'mid the rocks;
Where the gaunt and taciturn host
Stands on the threshold, the wind
Shaking his thin white hairs—
Holds his lantern to scan
Our storm-beat figures, and asks:
Whom in our party we bring?
Whom we have left in the snow?

Sadly we answer: We bring
Only ourselves! we lost
Sight of the rest in the storm.
Hardly ourselves we fought through,
Stripped, without friends, as we are.
Friends, companions, and train,
The avalanche swept from our side.

But thou would'st not alone
Be saved, my father! alone
Conquer and come to thy goal,
Leaving the rest in the wild.
We were weary, and we
Fearful, and we in our march
Fain to drop down and to die.
Still thou turnedst, and still
Beckonedst the trembler, and still
Gavest the weary thy hand.

If, in the paths of the world,
Stones might have wounded thy feet,
Toil or dejection have tried
Thy spirit, of that we saw
Nothing—to us thou wast still
Cheerful, and helpful, and firm!
Therefore to thee it was given
Many to save with thyself;
And, at the end of thy day,
O faithful shepherd! to come,
Bringing thy sheep in thy hand.

And through thee I believe
In the noble and great who are gone;
Pure souls honored and blessed
By former ages, who else—
Such, so soulless, so poor,
Is the race of men whom I see—
Seemed but a dream of the heart,
Seemed but a cry of desire.
Yes! I believe that there lived
Others like thee in the past,
Not like the men of the crowd
Who all round me today
Bluster or cringe, and make life
Hideous, and arid, and vile;
But souls tempered with fire,
Fervent, heroic, and good,
Helpers and friends of mankind.

Servants of God!—or sons
Shall I not call you? because
Not as servants ye knew
Your Father's innermost mind,
His, who unwillingly sees
One of his little ones lost—
Yours is the praise, if mankind
Hath not as yet in its march
Fainted, and fallen, and died!

---

110. **host,** probably Time, or Death.

148. **who else, etc.,** who, but for what I have known of thee, would have seemed a dream. 162. **Servants . . . sons.** Cf. *John,* 1:12: "But as many as received him, to them gave he power to become the sons of God."

See! In the rocks of the world
Marches the host of mankind,
A feeble, wavering line.
Where are they tending?—A God
Marshaled them, gave them their goal.   175
Ah, but the way is so long!
Years they have been in the wild!
Sore thirst plagues them, the rocks,
Rising all round, overawe;
Factions divide them, their host   180
Threatens to break, to dissolve.
—Ah, keep, keep them combined!
Else, of the myriads who fill
That army, not one shall arrive;
Sole they shall stray; in the rocks   185
Stagger forever in vain,
Die one by one in the waste.

Then, in such hour of need
Of your fainting, dispirited race,
Ye, like angels, appear,   190
Radiant with ardor divine!
Beacons of hope, ye appear!
Languor is not in your heart,
Weakness is not in your word,
Weariness not on your brow.   195
Ye alight in our van! at your voice,
Panic, despair, flee away.
Ye move through the ranks, recall
The stragglers, refresh the outworn,
Praise, re-inspire the brave!   200
Order, courage, return.
Eyes rekindling, and prayers,
Follow your steps as ye go.
Ye fill up the gaps in our files,
Strengthen the wavering line,   205
Stablish, continue our march,
On, to the bound of the waste,
On, to the City of God.   (1867)

Geist's Grave

Geist was a dachshund much loved by the Arnold family.

Four years!—and didst thou stay above
The ground, which hides thee now, but four?

And all that life, and all that love,
Were crowded, Geist! into no more?

Only four years those winning ways,   5
Which make me for thy presence yearn,
Called us to pet thee or to praise,
Dear little friend! at every turn?

That loving heart, that patient soul,
Had they indeed no longer span,   10
To run their course, and reach their goal,
And read their homily to man?

That liquid, melancholy eye,
From whose pathetic, soul-fed springs
Seemed surging the Virgilian cry,   15
The sense of tears in mortal things—

That steadfast, mournful strain, consoled
By spirits gloriously gay,
And temper of heroic mold—
What, was four years their whole short day?

Yes, only four!—and not the course   21
Of all the centuries yet to come,
And not the infinite resource
Of Nature, with her countless sum

Of figures, with her fullness vast   25
Of new creation evermore,
Can ever quite repeat the past,
Or just thy little self restore.

Stern law of every mortal lot!
Which man, proud man, finds hard to bear,   30
And builds himself I know not what
Of second life I know not where.

But thou, when struck thine hour to go,
On us, who stood despondent by,
A meek last glance of love didst throw,   35
And humbly lay thee down to die.

Yet would we keep thee in our heart—
Would fix our favorite on the scene,
Nor let thee utterly depart
And be as if thou ne'er hadst been.   40

---

190. **Ye**, the servants of God of line 162.

15. **Virgilian cry**, *Sunt lacrimae rerum*—There is sadness in human affairs (*Aeneid*, I, 462).

And so there rise these lines of verse
On lips that rarely form them now;
While to each other we rehearse:
Such ways, such arts, such looks hadst thou!

We stroke thy broad brown paws again, 45
We bid thee to thy vacant chair,
We greet thee by the window-pane,
We hear thy scuffle on the stair.

We see the flaps of thy large ears
Quick raised to ask which way we go; 50
Crossing the frozen lake, appears
Thy small black figure on the snow.

Nor to us only art thou dear
Who mourn thee in thine English home;
Thou hast thine absent master's tear, 55
Dropped by the far Australian foam.

Thy memory lasts both here and there,
And thou shalt live as long as we.
And after that—thou dost not care!
In us was all the world to thee. 60

Yet, fondly zealous for thy fame,
Even to a date beyond our own
We strive to carry down thy name,
By mounted turf and graven stone.

We lay thee, close within our reach, 65
Here, where the grass is smooth and warm,
Between the holly and the beech,
Where oft we watched thy couchant form,

Asleep, yet lending half an ear
To travelers on the Portsmouth road— 70
There build we thee, O guardian dear,
Marked with a stone, thy last abode!

Then some, who through this garden pass,
When we too, like thyself, are clay,
Shall see thy grave upon the grass, 75
And stop before the stone, and say:

People who lived here long ago
Did by this stone, it seems, intend
To name for future times to know
The dachshund, Geist, their little friend.

(1881)

55. **absent master,** Arnold's son Richard, who was in Australia when the dog died.

70. **Portsmouth road.** Arnold lived in the parish of Cobham, Surrey, on the road from London to Portsmouth.

Christina Rossetti

1830-1894

The spirit of Italy which influenced so notably the poetry of the Brownings during their long sojourn in Florence was born in the blood of another remarkable couple of English poets, the Rossettis, a brother and a sister who were Italian by parentage and English in environment. Their father, Gabriele Rossetti, was an Italian patriot and scholar who was obliged to flee from Naples in 1822 because of his opposition to Austrian oppression; he settled in London in 1825 and married Frances Polidori; there his four children were born. Dante Gabriel was the eldest and Christina the youngest. Of the first-born and most notable member of the family more will be said later (p. 783). The gentle sister was somewhat eclipsed in her own time by her brilliant brother and the group of painters and poets with whom she associated. But she wrote poetry that has given her a secure place in Victorian literature.

As a child Christina remained quietly at her London home and never received any education beyond what she acquired from her mother and from her own habit of diligent reading. But her girlhood was far from drab; to the home of the noted Italian refugee came Italian painters, musicians, and writers; and the contacts with literature and art thus afforded the Rossetti children were unusual. Furthermore, the friendship which her brother enjoyed with Ford Madox Brown, Holman Hunt, and other painters resulted in her sitting as model to all of these young artists. For these Pre-Raphaelites (see p. 416) she was an excellent model, with the pale, sensitive anaemic features and dark hair that they believed to be needed for ideal female beauty. Most of the group wrote poetry, and this provided for her another link with them. Seven of her early lyrics appeared in the Pre-Raphaelite magazine, *The Germ*, in 1850. After these had appeared she maintained a long silence, shyly permitting her brother and his friends to eclipse her, until in 1862 she issued in one volume the lyrics which she had been writing since 1848. The book was entitled *Goblin Market, and Other Poems* and contains in the goblin story her most famous single poem and some of the best of her lyrics. A journey to Normandy in 1861 and one to Switzerland and Italy in 1865 were her sole excursions to the Continent. The year after her return from Italy, where, she said, "all was music," she published *The Prince's Progress*. In 1871 an almost fatal illness made of her a cloistered invalid, and from then until her death in 1894 she saw few people and scarcely ventured out excepting to attend the Anglican services in a neighboring church. In these trying years her naturally religious spirit deepened in intensity, and much of her work was devotional in subject and mood. *Sing-Song*, a little collection of verse for children, appeared in 1872. *Annus Domini* (1874) was distinctly religious, and *A Pageant* (1881) largely so. *Time Flies* (1885) was a mixture of prose and verse; and her last publication, *The Face of the Deep* (1892), revealed in its curious interpretation of the *Apocalypse* the persistent mysticism of her nature. The religious intensity that is apparent here had already led to her firm rejection of a scholar-suitor with whose more liberal religious views she was not in agreement.

Christina shared her poet-brother's love of beauty. His art was richly sensuous; and in spite of her natural shyness and innate reserve Christina possessed much of the same instinct for the loveliness of outward form, nor did her deep sense of religion ever deprive her of it. Her *Goblin Market*—a fairy tale of how a devoted girl braves the temptations of goblin fruit and rescues her sister from the curse that came upon her for eating it—abounds in color and physical detail; nevertheless, it has a moral basis, for it presents in allegory the necessity of resisting worldly pleasures. This same admixture of vivid detail and abstract mysticism appears also in some of her lyrics. Most of these have a filigree delicacy and reserve that give them a marked flavor and charm.

Song

When I am dead, my dearest,
  Sing no sad songs for me;
Plant thou no roses at my head,
  Nor shady cypress tree.
Be the green grass above me   5
  With showers and dewdrops wet;
And if thou wilt, remember,
  And if thou wilt, forget.

I shall not see the shadows,
  I shall not feel the rain;   10
I shall not hear the nightingale
  Sing on as if in pain.
And dreaming through the twilight
  That doth not rise nor set,
Haply I may remember,   15
  And haply may forget.   (*1848; 1862*)

Song. Cf. Shakespeare's Sonnet 71. 4. **cypress tree.** The cypress is a symbol of mourning; it is a common tree in graveyards.

The Three Enemies

THE FLESH

"Sweet, thou art pale."
                      "More pale to see,
Christ hung upon the cruel tree
And bore His Father's wrath for me."

"Sweet, thou art sad."
          "Beneath a rod
More heavy, Christ for my sake trod   5
The winepress of the wrath of God."

"Sweet, thou art weary."
          "Not so Christ,
Whose mighty love of me sufficed
For Strength, Salvation, Eucharist."

"Sweet, thou art footsore."
          "If I bleed,   10
His feet have bled; yea, in my need
His Heart once bled for mine indeed."

THE WORLD

"Sweet, thou art young."
          "So He was young
Who for my sake in silence hung
Upon the Cross with Passion wrung."   15

"Look, thou art fair."
          "He was more fair
Than men, Who deigned for me to wear
A visage marred beyond compare."

"And thou hast riches."
          "Daily bread;
All else is His—Who, living, dead,   20
For me lacked where to lay His Head."

"And life is sweet."
          "It was not so
To Him, Whose Cup did overflow
With mine unutterable woe."

THE DEVIL

"Thou drinkest deep."
          "When Christ would sup   25
He drained the dregs from out my cup;
So how should I be lifted up?"

6. **winepress . . . God.** Cf. *Isaiah*, 63:2-3: "Wherefore art thou red in thine apparel, and thy garments like him that treadeth in the winefat? I have trodden the winepress alone; and of the people there was none with me; for I will tread them in mine anger, and trample them in my fury; and their blood shall be sprinkled upon my garments, and I will stain all my raiment." 9. **Eucharist**, the Sacrament of the Lord's Supper. 21. **lacked . . . Head.** Cf. *Luke*, 9:58: "And Jesus said unto him, Foxes have holes, and birds of the air have nests; but the Son of man hath not where to lay his head."

"Thou shalt win Glory."
          "In the skies,
Lord Jesus, cover up mine eyes
Lest they should look on vanities."   30

"Thou shalt have Knowledge."
          "Helpless dust!
In thee, O Lord, I put my trust;
Answer Thou for me, Wise and Just."

"And Might."—
          "Get thee behind me. Lord,
Who hast redeemed and not abhorred   35
My soul, oh, keep it by Thy Word."
                              (*1851;* 1862)

The Heart Knoweth Its Own Bitterness

Weep yet awhile—
Weep till that day shall dawn when
     thou shalt smile:
     Watch till the day
When all save only love shall pass away.

     Weep, sick and lonely,   5
     Bow thy heart to tears,
     For none shall guess the secret
     Of thy griefs and fears.
     Weep, till the day dawn,
     Refreshing dew: 10
     Weep till the spring:
     For genial showers
     Bring up the flowers,
     And thou shalt sing
In summertime of blossoming.   15

     Heart-sick and silent,
     Weep and watch in pain.
     Weep for hope perished,
     Not to live again:
     Weep for love's hope and fear   20
     And passion vain.
     Watch till the day
When all save only love shall pass away.

     Then love rejoicing
     Shall forget to weep: 25

34. "**Get . . . me,**" words spoken by Christ to Satan at the time of the temptation, as told in *Luke*, 4:8.

Shall hope or tear no more,
   Or watch, or sleep,
But only love and cease not,
   Deep beyond deep.
Now we sow love in tears,   30
   But then shall reap.
Have patience as the Lord's own flock of sheep:
Have patience with His love
Who died below, who lives for thee above.
                                (*1852*)

A Better Resurrection

I have no wit, no words, no tears;
   My heart within me like a stone
Is numbed too much for hopes or fears.
   Look right, look left, I dwell alone;
I lift mine eyes, but dimmed with grief   5
   No everlasting hills I see.
My life is in the falling leaf;
   O Jesus, quicken me.

My life is like a faded leaf,
   My harvest dwindled to a husk;   10
Truly my life is void and brief
   And tedious in the barren dusk;
My life is like a frozen thing,
   No bud nor greenness can I see;
Yet rise it shall—the sap of Spring;   15
   O Jesus, rise in me.

My life is like a broken bowl,
   A broken bowl that cannot hold
One drop of water for my soul
   Or cordial in the searching cold;   20
Cast in the fire the perished thing;
   Melt and remold it, till it be
A royal cup for Him, my King;
   O Jesus, drink of me.   (*1857; 1862*)

An Apple Gathering

I plucked pink blossoms from mine apple-tree
   And wore them all that evening in my hair;
Then in due season when I went to see,
   I found no apples there.

With dangling basket all along the grass   5
   As I had come I went the self-same track;
My neighbors mocked me while they saw me pass
   So empty-handed back.

Lilian and Lilias smiled in trudging by,
   Their heaped-up basket teased me like a jeer;   10
Sweet-voiced they sang beneath the sunset sky—
   Their mother's home was near.

Plump Gertrude passed me with her basket full,
   A stronger hand than hers helped it along;
A voice talked with her through the shadows cool   15
   More sweet to me than song.

Ah Willie, Willie, was my love less worth
   Than apples with their green leaves piled above?
I counted rosiest apples on the earth
   Of far less worth than love.   20

So once it was with me you stooped to talk,
   Laughing and listening in this very lane;
To think that by this way we used to walk
   We shall not walk again!

I let my neighbors pass me, ones and twos   25
   And groups; the latest said the night grew chill,
And hastened. But I loitered; while the dews
   Fell fast I loitered still.   (*1857; 1862*)

Advent

This Advent moon shines cold and clear,
   These Advent nights are long;
Our lamps have burned year after year,
   And still their flame is strong.
"Watchman, what of the night?" we cry,   5
   Heart-sick with hope deferred;
"No speaking signs are in the sky,"
   Is still the watchman's word.

The Porter watches at the gate,
   The servants watch within;   10

A Better Resurrection. 5. **lift . . . hills.** Cf. *Psalms*, 121:1: "I will lift up mine eyes unto the hills, from whence cometh my help." 7. **life . . . leaf.** Cf. *Macbeth*, V, iii, 22-23: "My way of life / Is fall'n into the *sear*, the yellow leaf."

Advent. Advent is the period including the four Sundays preceding Christmas. 5. **Watchman . . . night,** from *Isaiah*, 21:11. 6. **Heart-sick . . . deferred,** from *Proverbs*, 13:12: "Hope deferred maketh the heart sick."

The watch is long betimes and late,
    The prize is slow to win.
"Watchman, what of the night?" But still
    His answer sounds the same:
"No daybreak tops the utmost hill,   15
    Nor pale our lamps of flame."

One to another hear them speak
    The patient virgins wise:
"Surely He is not far to seek"—
    "All night we watch and rise."   20
"The days are evil looking back,
    The coming days are dim;
Yet count we not His promise slack,
    But watch and wait for Him."

One with another, soul with soul,   25
    They kindle fire from fire:
"Friends watch us who have touched the goal."
    "They urge us, come up higher."
"With them shall rest our waysore feet,
    With them is built our home,   30
With Christ."—"They sweet, but He most sweet,
    Sweeter than honeycomb."

There no more parting, no more pain,
    The distant ones brought near,
The lost so long are found again,   35
    Long lost but longer dear;
Eye hath not seen, ear hath not heard,
    Nor heart conceived that rest,
With them our good things long deferred,
    With Jesus Christ our Best.   40

We weep because the night is long,
    We laugh for day shall rise,
We sing a slow contented song
    And knock at Paradise.
Weeping we hold Him fast Who wept   45
    For us, we hold Him fast;
And will not let Him go except
    He bless us first or last.

Weeping we hold Him fast tonight;
    We will not let Him go   50
Till daybreak smite our wearied sight
    And summer smite the snow.
Then figs shall bud, and dove with dove
    Shall coo the livelong day;
Then He shall say, "Arise, My love,   55
    My fair one, come away."   (1858; 1862)

Uphill

Does the road wind uphill all the way?
    Yes, to the very end.
Will the day's journey take the whole long day?
    From morn to night, my friend.

But is there for the night a resting-place?   5
    A roof for when the slow dark hours begin.
May not the darkness hide it from my face?
    You cannot miss that inn.

Shall I meet other wayfarers at night?
    Those who have gone before.   10
Then must I knock, or call when just in sight?
    They will not keep you standing at that door.

Shall I find comfort, travel-sore and weak?
    Of labor you shall find the sum.
Will there be beds for me and all who seek?   15
    Yea, beds for all who come.   (1858; 1861)

---

18. **virgins, etc.** See the parable of the ten virgins, *Matthew*, 25:1-13. 32. **Sweeter than honeycomb**, from *Psalms*, 19:10. 33. **no . . . pain.** Cf. *Revelation*, 21:4: "And God shall wipe away all tears from their eyes; and there shall be no more death, neither sorrow, nor crying, neither shall there be any more pain." 37. **Eye . . . rest**, from *1 Corinthians*, 2:9: "Eye hath not seen, nor ear heard, neither have entered into the heart of man, the things which God hath prepared for them that love him."

47. **will . . . us.** Cf. *Genesis*, 32:26: "And he said, I will not let thee go, except thou bless me." 55. **"Arise . . . away,"** from *The Song of Solomon*, 2:13.
Uphill. 11. **knock . . . door**, from *Revelation*, 3:20: "Behold, I stand at the door and knock."

Goblin Market

    "I have more than once heard Christina say that she did not mean anything profound by this fairy-tale—it is not a moral apologue consistently carried out in detail. Still the incidents are such as to be at any rate suggestive, and different minds may be likely to read different messages into them. I find at times that people do not see the central point of the story, such as the authoress intended it; and she has expressed it too, but perhaps not with due emphasis. The foundation of the narrative is this: That the goblins tempt women to eat their luscious but uncanny fruits; that a first taste produces a rabid craving for a second taste; but that the second taste is never accorded, and, in default of it, the woman pines away and dies. Then comes the central point: Laura having tasted the fruits once, and being at death's door through inability to get a second taste, her sister Lizzie determines to save her at all hazards; so she goes to the goblins, refuses to eat their fruits, and beguiles them into forcing the fruits upon her with so much insistency that her face is all smeared and steeped with the juices; she gets Laura to kiss and suck these juices off her face, and Laura, having thus obtained the otherwise impossible second taste, rapidly recovers."—W. M. ROSSETTI.

Morning and evening
Maids heard the goblins cry,
"Come buy our orchard fruits,
Come buy, come buy:
Apples and quinces, 5
Lemons and oranges,
Plump unpecked cherries,
Melons and raspberries,
Bloom-down-cheeked peaches,
Swart-headed mulberries, 10
Wild free-born cranberries,
Crab-apples, dewberries,
Pineapples, blackberries,
Apricots, strawberries—
All ripe together 15
In summer weather—
Morns that pass by,
Fair eves that fly;
Come buy, come buy:
Our grapes fresh from the vine, 20
Pomegranates full and fine,
Dates and sharp bullaces,
Rare pears and greengages,
Damsons and bilberries,
Taste them and try; 25
Currants and gooseberries,
Bright-fire-like barberries,
Figs to fill your mouth,
Citrons from the South,
Sweet to tongue and sound to eye; 30
Come buy, come buy."

Evening by evening
Among the brook-side rushes,
Laura bowed her head to hear,
Lizzie veiled her blushes; 35
Crouching close together
In the cooling weather,

With clasping arms and cautioning lips,
With tingling cheeks and finger tips.
"Lie close," Laura said, 40
Pricking up her golden head.
"We must not look at goblin men,
We must not buy their fruits;
Who knows upon what soil they fed
Their hungry thirsty roots?" 45
"Come buy," call the goblins
Hobbling down the glen.
"Oh," cried Lizzie, "Laura, Laura,
You should not peep at goblin men."
Lizzie covered up her eyes, 50
Covered close lest they should look;
Laura reared her glossy head,
And whispered like the restless brook:
"Look, Lizzie, look, Lizzie,
Down the glen tramp little men. 55
One hauls a basket,
One bears a plate,
One lugs a golden dish
Of many pounds' weight.
How fair the vine must grow 60
Whose grapes are so luscious!
How warm the wind must blow
Through those fruit bushes!"
"No," said Lizzie, "No, no, no;
Their offers should not charm us, 65
Their evil gifts would harm us."
She thrust a dimpled finger
In each ear, shut eyes and ran.
Curious Laura chose to linger,
Wondering at each merchant man. 70
One had a cat's face,
One whisked a tail,
One tramped at a rat's pace,
One crawled like a snail, 74
One like a wombat prowled obtuse and furry,

22. **bullaces,** small European plums. 23. **greengages,** greenish-yellow plums. 24. **Damsons,** small dark-purple plums. **bilberries,** whortleberries (similar to blueberries).

75. **wombat,** an animal of Australia that looks like a small bear. It carries its young in a pouch, like the kangaroo.

One like a ratel tumbled hurry-skurry.
She heard a voice like voice of doves
Cooing all together;
They sounded kind and full of loves
In the pleasant weather.   80

Laura stretched her gleaming neck
Like a rush-imbedded swan,
Like a lily from the beck,
Like a moonlit poplar branch,
Like a vessel at the launch   85
When its last restraint is gone.

Backward up the mossy glen
Turned and trooped the goblin men,
With their shrill repeated cry,
"Come buy, come buy."   90
When they reached where Laura was,
They stood stock still upon the moss,
Leering at each other,
Brother with queer brother;
Signaling each other,   95
Brother with sly brother.
One set his basket down,
One reared his plate;
One began to weave a crown
Of tendrils, leaves, and rough nuts brown.
(Men sell not such in any town);   101
One heaved the golden weight
Of dish and fruit to offer her;
"Come buy, come buy" was still their cry.
Laura stared but did not stir,   105
Longed but had no money.
The whisk-tailed merchant bade her taste
In tones as smooth as honey,
The cat-faced purred,
The rat-paced spoke a word   110
Of welcome, and the snail-paced even was heard;
One parrot-voiced and jolly
Cried, "Pretty Goblin" still for "Pretty Polly";
One whistled like a bird.

But sweet-tooth Laura spoke in haste: 115
"Good folk, I have no coin;
To take were to purloin.
I have no copper in my purse,
I have no silver either,
And all my gold is on the furze   120

76. **ratel**, a South African animal, like the badger in size, form, and habits. 83. **beck**, a small brook.

That shakes in windy weather
Above the rusty heather."
"You have much gold upon your head,"
They answered all together;
"Buy from us with a golden curl."   125
She clipped a precious golden lock,
She dropped a tear more rare than pearl,
Then sucked their fruit globes fair or red.
Sweeter than honey from the rock,
Stronger than man-rejoicing wine,   130
Clearer than water flowed that juice;
She never tasted such before,
How should it cloy with length of use?
She sucked and sucked and sucked the more
Fruits which that unknown orchard bore;
She sucked until her lips were sore;   135
Then flung the emptied rinds away,
But gathered up one kernel stone,
And knew not was it night or day
As she turned home alone.   140

Lizzie met her at the gate,
Full of wise upbraidings:
"Dear, you should not stay so late,
Twilight is not good for maidens;
Should not loiter in the glen   145
In the haunts of goblin men.
Do you not remember Jeanie,
How she met them in the moonlight,
Took their gifts both choice and many,
Ate their fruits and wore their flowers   150
Plucked from bowers
Where summer ripens at all hours?
But ever in the moonlight
She pined and pined away;
Sought them by night and day,   155
Found them no more, but dwindled and grew gray;
Then fell with the first snow,
While to this day no grass will grow
Where she lies low;
I planted daisies there a year ago   160
That never blow.
You should not loiter so."
"Nay, hush," said Laura;
"Nay, hush, my sister.
I ate and ate my fill,   165
Yet my mouth waters still.
Tomorrow night I will
Buy more"; and kissed her.
"Have done with sorrow;

I'll bring you plums tomorrow
Fresh on their mother twigs,
Cherries worth getting;
You cannot think what figs
My teeth have met in,
What melons icy-cold
Piled on a dish of gold
Too huge for me to hold,
What peaches with a velvet nap,
Pellucid grapes without one seed.
Odorous indeed must be the mead
Whereon they grow, and pure the wave they drink
With lilies at the brink,
And sugar-sweet their sap."

Golden head by golden head,
Like two pigeons in one nest
Folded in each other's wings,
They lay down in their curtained bed;
Like two blossoms on one stem,
Like two flakes of new-fallen snow,
Like two wands of ivory
Tipped with gold for awful kings.
Moon and stars gazed in at them,
Wind sang to them lullaby,
Lumbering owls forebore to fly,
Not a bat flapped to and fro
Round their nest;
Cheek to cheek and breast to breast
Locked together in one nest.

Early in the morning
When the first cock crowed his warning,
Neat like bees, as sweet and busy,
Laura rose with Lizzie;
Fetched in honey, milked the cows,
Aired and set to rights the house,
Kneaded cakes of whitest wheat,
Cakes for dainty mouths to eat,
Next churned butter, whipped up cream,
Fed their poultry, sat and sewed;
Talked as modest maidens should—
Lizzie with an open heart,
Laura in an absent dream,
One content, one sick in part;
One warbling for the mere bright day's delight,
One longing for the night.

At length slow evening came.

They went with pitchers to the reedy brook;
Lizzie most placid in her look,
Laura most like a leaping flame.
They drew the gurgling water from its deep.
Lizzie plucked purple and rich golden flags,
Then turning homeward said: "The sunset flushes
Those furthest loftiest crags;
Come, Laura, not another maiden lags.
No willful squirrel wags;
The beasts and birds are fast asleep."

But Laura loitered still among the rushes,
And said the bank was steep,
And said the hour was early still,
The dew not fallen, the wind not chill;
Listening ever, but not catching
The customary cry,
"Come buy, come buy,"
With its iterated jingle
Of sugar-baited words;
Not for all her watching
Once discerning even one goblin
Racing, whisking, tumbling, hobbling–
Let alone the herds
That used to tramp along the glen,
In groups or single,
Of brisk fruit-merchant men.

Till Lizzie urged, "O Laura, come;
I hear the fruit-call, but I dare not look.
You should not loiter longer at this brook;
Come with me home.
The stars rise, the moon bends her arc,
Each glowworm winks her spark.
Let us get home before the night grows dark,
For clouds may gather
Though this is summer weather,
Put out the lights and drench us through;
Then if we lost our way what should we do?"

Laura turned cold as stone
To find her sister heard that cry alone,
That goblin cry,
"Come buy our fruits, come buy."
Must she then buy no more such dainty fruit?
Must she no more such succous pasture find,

258. **succous**, juicy.

Gone deaf and blind?
Her tree of life drooped from the root;   260
She said not one word in her heart's sore ache;
But peering through the dimness, naught discerning,
Trudged home, her pitcher dripping all the way;
So crept to bed, and lay
Silent till Lizzie slept;   265
Then sat up in a passionate yearning,
And gnashed her teeth for balked desire, and wept
As if her heart would break.

Day after day, night after night,
Laura kept watch in vain   270
In sullen silence of exceeding pain.
She never caught again the goblin cry,
"Come buy, come buy";
She never spied the goblin men
Hawking their fruits along the glen.   275
But when the noon waxed bright
Her hair grew thin and gray;
She dwindled, as the fair full moon doth turn
To swift decay and burn
Her fire away.   280

One day, remembering her kernel-stone,
She set it by a wall that faced the south;
Dewed it with tears, hoped for a root,
Watched for a waxing shoot,
But there came none.   285
It never saw the sun,
It never felt the trickling moisture run;
While with sunk eyes and faded mouth
She dreamed of melons, as a traveler sees
False waves in desert drouth   290
With shade of leaf-crowned trees,
And burns the thirstier in the sandful breeze.

She no more swept the house,
Tended the fowls or cows,
Fetched honey, kneaded cakes of wheat,   295
Brought water from the brook;
But sat down listless in the chimney-nook
And would not eat.

Tender Lizzie could not bear
To watch her sister's cankerous care,   300
Yet not to share.
She night and morning
Caught the goblins' cry:
"Come buy our orchard fruits,
Come buy, come buy."   305
Beside the brook, along the glen,
She heard the tramp of goblin men,
The voice and stir
Poor Laura could not hear;
Longed to buy fruit to comfort her,   310
But feared to pay too dear.
She thought of Jeanie in her grave,
Who should have been a bride;
But who for joys brides hope to have
Fell sick and died   315
In her gay prime,
In earliest winter time,
With the first glazing rime,
With the first snow-fall of crisp winter time.

Till Laura dwindling   320
Seemed knocking at Death's door.
Then Lizzie weighed no more
Better and worse;
But put a silver penny in her purse,
Kissed Laura, crossed the heath with clumps of furze   325
At twilight, halted by the brook,
And for the first time in her life
Began to listen and look.

Laughed every goblin
When they spied her peeping;   330
Came toward her hobbling,
Flying, running, leaping,
Puffing and blowing,
Chuckling, clapping, crowing,
Clucking and gobbling,   335
Mopping and mowing,
Full of airs and graces,
Pulling wry faces,
Demure grimaces,
Cat-like and rat-like,   340
Ratel- and wombat-like,
Snail-paced in a hurry,
Parrot-voiced and whistler,
Helter-skelter, hurry-skurry,
Chattering like magpies,   345
Fluttering like pigeons,
Gliding like fishes—
Hugged her and kissed her,

Squeezed and caressed her,
Stretched up their dishes, 350
Panniers, and plates:
"Look at our apples
Russet and dun,
Bob at our cherries,
Bite at our peaches, 355
Citrons and dates,
Grapes for the asking,
Pears red with basking
Out in the sun,
Plums on their twigs; 360
Pluck them and suck them—
Pomegranates, figs."

"Good folk," said Lizzie,
Mindful of Jeanie,
"Give me much and many"; 365
Held out her apron,
Tossed them her penny.
"Nay, take a seat with us,
Honor and eat with us,"
They answered, grinning; 370
"Our feast is but beginning.
Night yet is early,
Warm and dew-pearly,
Wakeful and starry.
Such fruits as these 375
No man can carry;
Half their bloom would fly,
Half their dew would dry,
Half their flavor would pass by.
Sit down and feast with us, 380
Be welcome guest with us,
Cheer you and rest with us."—
"Thank you," said Lizzie, "but one waits
At home alone for me;
So without further parleying, 385
If you will not sell me any
Of your fruits though much and many,
Give me back my silver penny
I tossed you for a fee."—
They began to scratch their pates, 390
No longer wagging, purring,
But visibly demurring,
Grunting and snarling.
One called her proud,
Cross-grained, uncivil; 395
Their tones waxed loud,
Their looks were evil.
Lashing their tails,

They trod and hustled her,
Elbowed and jostled her, 400
Clawed with their nails,
Barking, mewing, hissing, mocking,
Tore her gown and soiled her stocking,
Twitched her hair out by the roots,
Stamped upon her tender feet, 405
Held her hands and squeezed their fruits
Against her mouth to make her eat.

White and golden Lizzie stood,
Like a lily in a flood—
Like a rock of blue-veined stone 410
Lashed by tides obstreperously—
Like a beacon left alone
In a hoary, roaring sea,
Sending up a golden fire—
Like a fruit-crowned orange-tree 415
White with blossoms honey-sweet
Sore beset by wasp and bee—
Like a royal virgin town
Topped with gilded dome and spire
Close beleaguered by a fleet 420
Mad to tug her standard down.

One may lead a horse to water;
Twenty cannot make him drink.
Though the goblins cuffed and caught her,
Coaxed and fought her, 425
Bullied and besought her,
Scratched her, pinched her black as ink,
Kicked and knocked her,
Mauled and mocked her,
Lizzie uttered not a word; 430
Would not open lip from lip
Lest they should cram a mouthful in;
But laughed in heart to feel the drip
Of juice that siruped all her face,
And lodged in dimples of her chin, 435
And streaked her neck which quaked like curd.
At last the evil people,
Worn out by her resistance,
Flung back her penny, kicked their fruit
Along whichever road they took, 440
Not leaving root or stone or shoot;
Some writhed into the ground,
Some dived into the brook
With ring and ripple,
Some scudded on the gale without a sound,
Some vanished in the distance. 446

In a smart, ache, tingle,
Lizzie went her way;
Knew not was it night or day;
Sprang up the bank, tore through the furze, 450
Threaded copse and dingle,
And heard her penny jingle
Bouncing in her purse—
Its bounce was music to her ear.
She ran and ran 455
As if she feared some goblin man
Dogged her with gibe or curse
Or something worse;
But not one goblin skurried after,
Nor was she pricked by fear; 460
The kind heart made her windy-paced
That urged her home quite out of breath with haste
And inward laughter.

She cried, "Laura," up the garden,
"Did you miss me? 465
Come and kiss me.
Never mind my bruises,
Hug me, kiss me, suck my juices
Squeezed from goblin fruits for you,
Goblin pulp and goblin dew. 470
Eat me, drink me, love me;
Laura, make much of me;
For your sake I have braved the glen
And had to do with goblin merchant men."

Laura started from her chair, 475
Flung her arms up in the air,
Clutched her hair:
"Lizzie, Lizzie, have you tasted
For my sake the fruit forbidden?
Must your light like mine be hidden, 480
Your young life like mine be wasted,
Undone in mine undoing,
And ruined in my ruin,
Thirsty, cankered, goblin-ridden?"—
She clung about her sister, 485
Kissed and kissed and kissed her;
Tears once again
Refreshed her shrunken eyes,
Dropping like rain
After long sultry drouth; 490
Shaking with aguish fear, and pain,
She kissed and kissed her with a hungry mouth.

Her lips began to scorch,
That juice was wormwood to her tongue,
She loathed the feast. 495
Writhing as one possessed, she leaped and sung,
Rent all her robe, and wrung
Her hands in lamentable haste,
And beat her breast.
Her locks streamed like the torch 500
Borne by a racer at full speed,
Or like the mane of horses in their flight,
Or like an eagle when she stems the light
Straight toward the sun,
Or like a caged thing freed, 505
Or like a flying flag when armies run.

Swift fire spread through her veins, knocked at her heart,
Met the fire smoldering there
And overbore its lesser flame;
She gorged on bitterness without a name—
Ah, fool, to choose such part 511
Of soul-consuming care!
Sense failed in the mortal strife;
Like the watch-tower of a town
Which an earthquake shatters down, 515
Like a lightning-stricken mast,
Like a wind-uprooted tree
Spun about,
Like a foam-topped waterspout
Cast down headlong in the sea, 520
She fell at last;
Pleasure past and anguish past,
Is it death or is it life?

Life out of death.
That night long Lizzie watched by her, 525
Counted her pulse's flagging stir,
Felt for her breath,
Held water to her lips, and cooled her face
With tears and fanning leaves.
But when the first birds chirped about their eaves. 530
And early reapers plodded to the place
Of golden sheaves,
And dew-wet grass
Bowed in the morning winds so brisk to pass,
And new buds with new day 535
Opened of cup-like lilies on the stream,
Laura awoke as from a dream,
Laughed in the innocent old way,

Hugged Lizzie but not twice or thrice;
Her gleaming locks showed not one thread
    of gray,   540
Her breath was sweet as May,
And light danced in her eyes.

Days, weeks, months, years
Afterwards, when both were wives
With children of their own;   545
Their mother-hearts beset with fears,
Their lives bound up in tender lives;
Laura would call the little ones
And tell them of her early prime,
Those pleasant days long gone   550
Of not-returning time;
Would talk about the haunted glen,
The wicked quaint fruit-merchant men,
Their fruits like honey to the throat
But poison in the blood   555
(Men sell not such in any town);
Would tell them how her sister stood
In deadly peril to do her good,
And win the fiery antidote;
Then joining hands to little hands   560
Would bid them cling together—
"For there is no friend like a sister
In calm or stormy weather;
To cheer one on the tedious way,
To fetch one if one goes astray,   565
To lift one if one totters down,
To strengthen whilst one stands."
                      (*1859;* 1862)

from *Sing-Song*

Sing-Song was the happy title given by Christina Rossetti to a collection of lyrics, some of which are suggestive of Mother Goose. Cf. Stevenson's poems, pp. 877 ff.

    "If I were a queen,
        What would I do?
    I'd make you king,
        And I'd wait on you."

    "If I were a king,   5
        What would I do?
    I'd make you queen,
        For I'd marry you."

✦

    Mother shake the cherry-tree,
        Susan catch a cherry;
    Oh, how funny that will be—
        Let's be merry!

    One for brother, one for sister,   5
        Two for mother more,
    Six for father, hot and tired,
        Knocking at the door.

✦

The wind has such a rainy sound
    Moaning through the town,
The sea has such a windy sound—
    Will the ships go down?

The apples in the orchard   5
    Tumble from their tree.
Oh, will the ships go down, go down,
    In the windy sea?

✦

Fly away, fly away over the sea,
    Sun-loving swallow, for summer is done;
Come again, come again, come back to me,
    Bringing the summer and bringing the
        sun.

✦

Who has seen the wind?
    Neither I nor you;
But when the leaves hang trembling
    The wind is passing through.

Who has seen the wind?   5
    Neither you nor I;
But when the trees bow down their heads
    The wind is passing by.

✦

    Boats sail on the rivers,
        And ships sail on the seas;
    But clouds that sail across the sky
        Are prettier far than these.

    There are bridges on the rivers,   5
        As pretty as you please;
    But the bow that bridges heaven,
        And overtops the trees,
    And builds a road from earth to sky,
        Is prettier far than these.   (1872)

from *Monna Innominata*

The title means *Nameless Lady*. Christina Rossetti explained that the fourteen sonnets of this poem were supposed to have been spoken by one of the unnamed ladies exalted by poets before Dante honored Beatrice and before Petrarch honored Laura. Her brother W. M. Rossetti asserted, however, that the "nameless lady" is Christina herself and that in the poem she expresses her love for Charles Cayley, a scholar whom she declined to marry because she could not share his liberal religious views.

The quotation from Dante prefixed to the poem may be translated, "Come after me and let the people talk" (*Purgatory*, V, 13). The second quotation, from Petrarch, means, "Pointing the dangers of this life below" (Sonnet, 244, 12).

2

Vien dietro a me e lascia dir le genti.—DANTE.
Contando i casi della vita nostra.—PETRARCA.

Many in aftertimes will say of you
"He loved her"—while of me what will they
    say?
Not that I loved you more than just in play,
For fashion's sake as idle women do.
Even let them prate; who know not what we
    knew   5
Of love and parting in exceeding pain,
Of parting hopeless here to meet again,
Hopeless on earth, and heaven is out of view.
But by my heart of love laid bare to you,
My love that you can make not void nor vain;
Love that forgoes you but to claim anew   11
Beyond this passage of the gate of death,
I charge you at the Judgment make it plain
My love of you was life and not a breath.

(Before 1882)

James Thomson

1834-1882

No other Victorian writer, perhaps, had such a wretched childhood as did James Thomson. His father was an impecunious sailor who became paralyzed when the boy was six. His mother was religious to the point of profound melancholy, and died while he was still a boy. The poet was born in Port Glasgow, but soon afterwards the family moved to London. There he was admitted as a student to the Royal Caledonian Asylum, where he remained for eight years. On leaving in 1850 he took a one-year course in the military training school in Chelsea to prepare himself as an army teacher, and the next year found him stationed at Ballincollig, near Cork. Two persons whom he met in this new world had a profound effect upon him. The first was a beautiful young girl, Matilda Weller, to whom Thomson became passionately devoted. Her death in 1853—the same year in which he also lost his father—left him pessimistic almost to the point of suicide. This mood helped to open the way for the influence of Charles Bradlaugh, a free-thinking trooper, under whose tutelage Thomson became a professed atheist. Later he joined Bradlaugh in London, becoming one of a group of daring and radical young journalists and contributing many of his poems to his friend's paper, *The National Reformer*. Dismissal from the army in 1862 was followed by miscellaneous activities in various parts of the world. He was a solicitor's clerk in London, secretary to a mining company in America, war correspondent in Spain. But London remained the chief center of his activity, and to London he returned to continue his writing and try to drown in drink the demons of despair who haunted him. A quarrel with his friend and supporter Bradlaugh was followed by "seven songless years"; then in 1880 came his two most important volumes of poems, *The City of Dreadful Night and Other Poems* and *Vane's Story, Weddah, and Om-el-Bonain and Other Poems*. Two years later he died in the University College Hospital, London, of intemperance and exhaustion.

This sketch of Thomson's gloomy life, revealing, as it does, a weak will yielding to a long train of misfortunes, suggests that his nature was compact entirely of morbid pessimism; and his best-known poem, *The City of Dreadful Night*, does nothing to dispel that impression. He had, however, a wider range of moods than is popularly supposed. His intimate friends knew that he could be sunny, gay, even courageous. These occasional elements in his character—for they were only occasional—appear here and there in his poetry, as they do, for example, in the healthy little idylls *Sunday up the River* and *Sunday at Hempstead*. But joy was by no means his prevailing mood; it was rather melancholy, often unrelieved by any lift in the cloud.

Thomson's prose writing took the form usually of penetrating studies of Ben Jonson, Blake, and other English authors. The two writers who influenced him most definitely were Shelley, whose atheism and melancholy he probably recognized as akin to his own, and Novalis, the eighteenth-century German romantic poet and novelist. His admiration for these two writers he signified by signing his poems Bysshe Vanolis, which he frequently abbreviated to B. V. It was thus he was known to the readers of *The National Reformer*, in which most of his best poetry appeared. In this magazine was published his most famous poem, *The City of Dreadful Night*. For sustained gloom this poem probably transcends all others in English literature; it is reminiscent of De Quincey's gloomiest prose and of some of Edgar Allan Poe's nightmarish verses. "It was," Thomson wrote to George Eliot, "the outcome of much sleepless hypochondria," and it is saturated with pathos, pain, and despair. Thomson's *Insomnia* (1882) was drawn from the same well of sickness and terror. From such an existence as is depicted in these two poems, his death could have come only as a welcome release.

Once in a Saintly Passion

Once in a saintly passion
  I cried with desperate grief,
"O Lord, my heart is black with guile,
  Of sinners I am chief."
Then stooped my guardian angel   5
  And whispered from behind,
"Vanity, my little man,
  You're nothing of the kind."

For I Must Sing of All I Feel and Know

For I must sing of all I feel and know,
  Waiting with Memnon passive near the palms,
Until the heavenly light doth dawn and grow
  And thrill my silence into mystic psalms;
From unknown realms the wind streams sad or gay,   5
The trees give voice responsive to its sway.

For I must sing: of mountains, deserts, seas,
  Of rivers ever flowing, ever flowing;
Of beasts and birds, of grass and flowers and trees
  Forever fading and forever growing;   10
Of calm and storm, of night and eve and noon,
Of boundless space, and sun and stars and moon;

And of the secret sympathies that bind
  All beings to their wondrous dwelling-place;
And of the perfect Unity enshrined   15
  In omnipresence throughout time and space,
Alike informing with its full control
The dust, the stars, the worm, the human soul;

And most supremely of my human kin—
  Their thoughts and deeds, their valors and their fears,   20
Their griefs and joys, their virtue and their sin,
  Their feasts and wars, their cradles and their biers,
Their temples, prisons, homes and ships and marts,
The subtlest windings of their brains and hearts.

For I Must . . . Know. 2. **Memnon**, a colossal statue near Thebes, Egypt, that was supposed to give forth a musical sound at daybreak.

17. **informing**, animating, giving form to.

So rich and sweet is Life. And what is Death?—
   The tranquil slumbers dear and strange and
      boon   26
That feed at whiles our waking being's
      breath;
   The solemn midnight of this glorious noon,
With countless distant stars, and each a
      sun,
   Revealed harmonious with our daily one. 30
                 (*1857;* 1859)

Two Sonnets

1

"Why are your songs all wild and bitter sad
As funeral dirges with the orphans' cries?
Each night since first the world was made
      hath had
A sequent day to laugh it down the skies.
Chant us a glee to make our hearts rejoice, 5
Or seal in silence this unmanly moan."
My friend, I have no power to rule my voice—
A spirit lifts me where I lie alone,
And thrills me into song by its own laws;
That which I feel, but seldom know, indeed 10
Tempering the melody it could not cause.
The bleeding heart cannot forever bleed
Inwardly solely; on the wan lips, too,
Dark blood will bubble ghastly into view.

2

Striving to sing glad songs, I but attain
Wild discords sadder than Grief's saddest
      tune;
As if an owl with his harsh screech should
      strain
To over-gratulate a thrush of June.
The nightingale upon its thorny spray 5
Finds inspiration in the sullen dark;
The kindling dawn, the world-wide joyous
      day
Are inspiration to the soaring lark;
The seas are silent in the sunny calm,
Their anthem surges in the tempest boom; 10
The skies outroll no solemn thunder psalm

Sonnet 2. 4. **over-gratulate,** surpass in expressing a feeling of joy. 5. **nightingale . . . spray.** The nightingale was supposed to sing more sweetly when a thorn was piercing its breast.

Till they have clothed themselves with clouds
      of gloom.
My mirth can laugh and talk, but cannot sing;
My grief finds harmonies in everything.
                 (1860)

The Fire That Filled My Heart of Old

The fire that filled my heart of old
   Gave luster while it burned;
Now only ashes gray and cold
   Are in its silence urned.
Ah! better was the furious flame, 5
   The splendor with the smart;
I never cared for the singer's fame,
   But, oh! for the singer's heart
      Once more—
   The burning fulgent heart! 10

No love, no hate, no hope, no fear,
   No anguish and no mirth;
Thus life extends from year to year,
   A flat of sullen dearth.
Ah! life's blood creepeth cold and tame, 15
   Life's thought plays no new part;
I never cared for the singer's fame,
   But, oh! for the singer's heart
      Once more—
   The bleeding passionate heart! 20
                 (1864)

Give a Man a Horse He Can Ride

Give a man a horse he can ride,
   Give a man a boat he can sail;
And his rank and wealth, his strength and
      health,
   On sea nor shore shall fail.

Give a man a pipe he can smoke, 5
   Give a man a book he can read;
And his home is bright with a calm delight,
   Though the room be poor indeed.

Give a man a girl he can love,
   As I, O my Love, love thee; 10
And his heart is great with the pulse of Fate,
   At home, on land, on sea.   (*1865;* 1869)

Let My Voice Ring Out and Over the Earth

Let my voice ring out and over the earth,
  Through all the grief and strife,
With a golden joy in a silver mirth:
  Thank God for Life!

Let my voice swell out through the great
    abyss   5
  To the azure dome above,
With a chord of faith in the harp of bliss:
  Thank God for Love!

Let my voice thrill out beneath and above,
  The whole world through: 10
O my Love and Life, O my Life and Love,
  Thank God for you!   (1865; 1869)

Let ... Earth. This is the seventeenth of the little idylls in *Sunday up the River*.

from *The City of Dreadful Night*

Thomson's torturing attacks of insomnia drove him often to roam the midnight streets of London. From the brain-sick images and ideas which he thus gathered he composed an imaginary City of Despair. See the headnote, p. 760.

1

The City is of Night; perchance of Death,
  But certainly of Night; for never there
Can come the lucid morning's fragrant breath
  After the dewy dawning's cold gray air;   46
The moon and stars may shine with scorn or
    pity;
The sun has never visited that city,
  For it dissolveth in the daylight fair;

Dissolveth like a dream of night away,   50
  Though present in distempered gloom of
    thought
And deadly weariness of heart all day.
  But when a dream night after night is
    brought
Throughout a week, and such weeks few or
    many
Recur each year for several years, can any   55
  Discern that dream from real life in
    aught?

For life is but a dream whose shapes return,
  Some frequently, some seldom, some by
    night
And some by day, some night and day; we
    learn,
  The while all change and many vanish
    quite,   60
In their recurrence with recurrent changes
A certain seeming order; where this ranges
  We count things real; such is memory's
    might.

A river girds the city west and south,   64
  The main north channel of a broad lagoon,
Regurging with the salt tides from the mouth;
    Waste marshes shine and glister to the
    moon
For leagues, then moorland black, then stony
    ridges;
Great piers and causeways, many noble
    bridges,
  Connect the town and islet suburbs strewn.

Upon an easy slope it lies at large,   71
  And scarcely overlaps the long curved crest
Which swells out two leagues from the river
    marge.
A trackless wilderness rolls north and west,
Savannahs, savage woods, enormous moun-
    tains,   75
  Bleak uplands, black ravines with torrent
    fountains;
  And eastward rolls the shipless sea's unrest.

The city is not ruinous, although
  Great ruins of an unremembered past,
With others of a few short years ago,   80

Section 1. 66. **Regurging**, surging back. 75. **Savannahs**, open, level regions.

More sad, are found within its precincts vast.
The street-lamps always burn; but scarce a casement
In house or palace front from roof to basement
Doth glow or gleam athwart the mirk air cast.

The street-lamps burn amidst the baleful glooms, 85
Amidst the soundless solitudes immense
Of rangéd mansions dark and still as tombs.
The silence which benumbs or strains the sense
Fulfills with awe the soul's despair unweeping;
Myriads of habitants are ever sleeping, 90
Or dead, or fled from nameless pestilence!

Yet, as in some necropolis you find
Perchance one mourner to a thousand dead,
So there: worn faces that look deaf and blind
Like tragic masks of stone. With weary tread, 95
Each wrapped in his own doom, they wander, wander,
Or sit foredone and desolately ponder
Through sleepless hours with heavy drooping head.

Mature men chiefly, few in age or youth,
A woman rarely, now and then a child—
A child! If here the heart turns sick with ruth 101
To see a little one from birth defiled,
Or lame or blind, as preordained to languish
Through youthless life, think how it bleeds with anguish 104
To meet one erring in that homeless wild.

They often murmur to themselves, they speak
To one another seldom, for their woe
Broods maddening inwardly and scorns to wreak
Itself abroad; and if at whiles it grow
To frenzy which must rave, none heeds the clamor, 110

Unless there waits some victim of like glamour,
To rave in turn, who lends attentive show.

The City is of Night, but not of Sleep;
There sweet sleep is not for the weary brain;
The pitiless hours like years and ages creep,
A night seems termless hell. This dreadful strain 116
Of thought and consciousness, which never ceases,
Or which some moments' stupor but increases,
This, worse than woe, makes wretches there insane. 119

They leave all hope behind who enter there;
One certitude while sane they cannot leave,
One anodyne for torture and despair—
The certitude of Death, which no reprieve
Can put off long; and which, divinely tender,
But waits the outstretched hand to promptly render 125
That draft whose slumber nothing can bereave.

4

He stood alone within the spacious square,
Declaiming from the central grassy mound,
With head uncovered and with streaming hair, 205
As if large multitudes were gathered round—
A stalwart shape, the gestures full of might,
The glances burning with unnatural light:

"As I came through the desert thus it was,
As I came through the desert: All was black,
In heaven no single star, on earth no track; 211
A brooding hush without a stir or note,
The air so thick it clotted in my throat;
And thus for hours; then some enormous things
Swooped past with savage cries and clanking wings. 215
But I strode on austere;
No hope could have no fear.

92. **necropolis**, a city of the dead. 105. **erring**, wandering. 120. **They . . . there.** Cf. the inscription over the portal to hell in Dante's *Inferno*—"Leave all hope, ye that enter."

"As I came through the desert thus it was,
As I came through the desert: Eyes of fire 219
Glared at me throbbing with a starved desire;
The hoarse and heavy and carnivorous breath
Was hot upon me from deep jaws of death;
Sharp claws, swift talons, fleshless fingers cold
Plucked at me from the bushes, tried to hold.
  But I strode on austere;   225
  No hope could have no fear.

"As I came through the desert thus it was,
As I came through the desert: Lo you, there,
That hillock burning with a brazen glare;
Those myriad dusky flames with points a-glow   230
Which writhed and hissed and darted to and fro;
A Sabbath of the Serpents, heaped pell-mell
For Devil's roll-call and some fête of hell.
  Yet I strode on austere;
  No hope could have no fear.   235

"As I came through the desert thus it was,
As I came through the desert: Meteors ran
And crossed their javelins on the black sky-span;
The zenith opened to a gulf of flame,
The dreadful thunderbolts jarred earth's fixed frame;   240
The ground all heaved in waves of fire that surged
And weltered round me sole there unsubmerged.
  Yet I strode on austere;
  No hope could have no fear.

"As I came through the desert thus it was, 245
As I came through the desert: Air once more,
And I was close upon a wild seashore;
Enormous cliffs arose on either hand,
The deep tide thundered up a league-broad strand;
White foambelts seethed there, wan spray swept and flew;   250
The sky broke, moon and stars and clouds and blue.

Section 4. 232. **Sabbath of the Serpents,** a midnight meeting supposed to be held annually by demons, witches, etc., under the leadership of Satan, for the purpose of indulging in unholy orgies.

And I strode on austere;
No hope could have no fear.

"As I came through the desert thus it was,
As I came through the desert: On the left 255
The sun arose and crowned a broad crag-cleft;
There stopped and burned out black, except a rim,
A bleeding, eyeless socket, red and dim;
Whereon the moon fell suddenly southwest,
And stood above the right-hand cliffs at rest.
  Still I strode on austere;   261
  No hope could have no fear.

"As I came through the desert thus it was,
As I came through the desert: From the right
A shape came slowly with a ruddy light; 265
A woman with a red lamp in her hand,
Bareheaded and barefooted on that strand;
O desolation moving with such grace!
O anguish with such beauty in thy face!
  I fell as on my bier,   270
  Hope travailed with such fear.

"As I came through the desert thus it was,
As I came through the desert: I was twain,
Two selves distinct that cannot join again;
One stood apart and knew but could not stir,
And watched the other stark in swoon and her;   276
And she came on, and never turned aside,
Between such sun and moon and roaring tide.
  And as she came more near
  My soul grew mad with fear.   280

"As I came through the desert thus it was,
As I came through the desert: Hell is mild
And piteous matched with that accursèd wild;
A large black sign was on her breast that bowed,
A broad black band ran down her snow-white shroud;   285
That lamp she held was her own burning heart,
Whose blood-drops trickled step by step apart.
  The mystery was clear;
  Mad rage had swallowed fear.

"As I came through the desert thus it was, 290
As I came through the desert: By the sea
She knelt and bent above that senseless me;

Those lamp-drops fell upon my white brow there,
She tried to cleanse them with her tears and hair;
She murmured words of pity, love, and woe,
She heeded not the level rushing flow. 296
    And mad with rage and fear,
    I stood stonebound so near.

"As I came through the desert thus it was, 299
As I came through the desert: When the tide
Swept up to her there kneeling by my side,
She clasped that corpse-like me, and they were borne
Away, and this vile me was left forlorn;
I know the whole sea cannot quench that heart,
Or cleanse that brow, or wash those two apart.
    They love; their doom is drear, 306
    Yet they nor hope nor fear;
    But I, what do I here?"

14

Large glooms were gathered in the mighty fane,
    With tinted moongleams slanting here and there;
And all was hush—no swelling organ-strain,
    No chant, no voice or murmuring of prayer;
No priests came forth, no tinkling censers fumed, 690
And the high altar space was unillumed.

Around the pillars and against the walls
    Leaned men and shadows; others seemed to brood,
Bent or recumbent, in secluded stalls.
    Perchance they were not a great multitude
Save in that city of so lonely streets 696
Where one may count up every face he meets.

All patiently awaited the event
    Without a stir or sound, as if no less
Self-occupied, doomstricken, while attent. 700
    And then we heard a voice of solemn stress
From the dark pulpit, and our gaze there met
Two eyes which burned as never eyes burned yet—

Two steadfast and intolerable eyes
    Burning beneath a broad and rugged brow;
The head behind it of enormous size. 706
    And as black fir-groves in a large wind bow,
Our rooted congregation, gloom-arrayed,
By that great sad voice deep and full were swayed:

"O melancholy Brothers, dark, dark, dark! 710
O battling in black floods without an ark!
O spectral wanderers of unholy Night!
My soul hath bled for you these sunless years,
With bitter blood-drops running down like tears;
    Oh, dark, dark, dark, withdrawn from joy and light! 715

"My heart is sick with anguish for your bale;
Your woe hath been my anguish; yea, I quail
    And perish in your perishing unblest.
And I have searched the heights and depths, the scope
Of all our universe, with desperate hope 720
    To find some solace for your wild unrest.

"And now at last authentic word I bring,
Witnessed by every dead and living thing;
    Good tidings of great joy for you, for all;
There is no God; no Fiend with names divine
Made us and tortures us; if we must pine, 726
    It is to satiate no Being's gall.

"It was the dark delusion of a dream,
That living Person conscious and supreme,
    Whom we must curse for cursing us with life; 730
Whom we must curse because the life He gave
Could not be buried in the quiet grave,
    Could not be killed by poison or by knife.

"This little life is all we must endure,
The grave's most holy peace is ever sure, 735
    We fall asleep and never wake again;
Nothing is of us but the moldering flesh,
Whose elements dissolve and merge afresh
    In earth, air, water, plants, and other men.

Section 14. 724. *Good . . . joy.* Cf. *Luke,* 2:10: "And the angel said unto them, Fear not: for, behold, I bring you good tidings of great joy, which shall be to all people." 725. **There . . . God.** See *Dipsychus,* p. 722, footnote.

"We finish thus; and all our wretched race
Shall finish with its cycle, and give place
  To other beings, with their own time-doom;
Infinite aeons ere our kind began;
Infinite aeons after the last man
  Has joined the mammoth in earth's tomb
    and womb.

"We bow down to the universal laws,
Which never had for man a special clause
  Of cruelty or kindness, love or hate;
If toads and vultures are obscene to sight,
If tigers burn with beauty and with might,
  Is it by favor or by wrath of fate?

"All substance lives and struggles evermore
Through countless shapes continually at war,
  By countless interactions interknit;
If one is born a certain day on earth,
All times and forces tended to that birth,
  Not all the world could change or hinder it.

"I find no hint throughout the Universe
Of good or ill, of blessing or of curse;
  I find alone Necessity Supreme;
With infinite Mystery, abysmal, dark,
Unlighted ever by the faintest spark
  For us the flitting shadows of a dream.

"O Brothers of sad lives! they are so brief;
A few short years must bring us all relief—
  Can we not bear these years of laboring
    breath?
But if you would not this poor life fulfill,
Lo, you are free to end it when you will,
  Without the fear of waking after death."

The organ-like vibrations of his voice
  Thrilled through the vaulted aisles and died
    away;
The yearning of the tones which bade rejoice
Was sad and tender as a requiem lay;
Our shadowy congregation rested still
As brooding on that "End it when you will."

21

Anear the center of that northern crest
  Stands out a level upland bleak and bare,
From which the city east and south and
    west
Sinks gently in long waves; and thronéd
    there
An Image sits, stupendous, superhuman,
The bronze colossus of a wingéd Woman,
  Upon a graded granite base foursquare.

Low-seated she leans forward massively,
  With cheek on clenched left hand, the fore-
    arm's might
Erect, its elbow on her rounded knee;
  Across a clasped book in her lap the right
Upholds a pair of compasses; she gazes
With full set eyes, but wandering in thick
    mazes
  Of somber thought beholds no outward
    sight.

Words cannot picture her; but all men know
  That solemn sketch the pure sad artist
    wrought
Three centuries and threescore years ago,
  With phantasies of his peculiar thought:
The instruments of carpentry and science
Scattered about her feet, in strange alliance
  With the keen wolf-hound sleeping undis-
    traught;

Scales, hour-glass, bell, and magic-square
    above;
The grave and solid infant perched beside,
With open winglets that might bear a dove,
  Intent upon its tablets, heavy-eyed;
Her folded wings as of a mighty eagle,
But all too impotent to lift the regal
  Robustness of her earth-born strength and
    pride;

And with those wings, and that light wreath
    which seems
  To mock her grand head and the knotted
    frown
Of forehead charged with baleful thoughts
    and dreams,
  The household bunch of keys, the house-
    wife's gown

Section 21. 1055. **sad artist,** Albrecht Dürer (1471-1528), a famous German painter and engraver. His *Melancholia* is one of his most noted engravings. 1061. **bell, and magic-square.** The bell, a symbol of faith, summons people to prayer. The magic-square, a symbol of equality, is a square diagram consisting of several small squares each containing a number. The numbers are so arranged that the sum of those in each of the various rows is the same.

Voluminous, indented, and yet rigid
As if a shell of burnished metal frigid,
   The feet thick-shod to tread all weakness
      down;   1074

The comet hanging o'er the waste dark seas,
   The massy rainbow curved in front of it,
Beyond the village with the masts and trees;
   The snaky imp, dog-headed, from the Pit,
Bearing upon its batlike leathern pinions   1079
Her name unfolded in the sun's dominions,
   The "MELANCOLIA" that transcends all wit.

Thus has the artist copied her, and thus
   Surrounded to expound her form sublime,
Her fate heroic and calamitous;   1084
   Fronting the dreadful mysteries of Time,
Unvanquished in defeat and desolation,
Undaunted in the hopeless conflagration
   Of the day setting on her baffled prime.

Baffled and beaten back she works on still,
   Weary and sick of soul she works the more,
Sustained by her indomitable will;   1091
   The hands shall fashion, and the brain shall
      pore,
And all her sorrow shall be turned to labor,
Till Death, the friend-foe, piercing with his
      saber
   That mighty heart of hearts, ends bitter
      war.   1095

But as if blacker night could dawn on night,
   With tenfold gloom on moonless night un-
      starred,
A sense more tragic than defeat and blight,
   More desperate than strife with hope de-
      barred,

More fatal than the adamantine Never   1100
   Encompassing her passionate endeavor,
      Dawns glooming in her tenebrous regard—

The sense that every struggle brings defeat
   Because Fate holds no prize to crown suc-
      cess;
That all the oracles are dumb or cheat   1105
   Because they have no secret to express;
That none can pierce the vast black veil un-
      certain
Because there is no light beyond the curtain;
   That all is vanity and nothingness.   1109

Titanic from her high throne in the north,
   That City's somber Patroness and Queen,
In bronze sublimity she gazes forth.
   Over her Capital of teen and threne,
Over the river with its isles and bridges,
The marsh and moorland, to the stern rock-
      ridges,   1115
   Confronting them with a coëval mien.

The moving moon and stars from east to
      west
   Circle before her in the sea of air;
Shadows and gleams glide round her solemn
      rest.
   Her subjects often gaze up to her there:
The strong to drink new strength of iron en-
      durance,   1121
   The weak new terrors; all, renewed assurance
      And confirmation of the old despair.

(1870-1874; 1874)

1102. **tenebrous regard,** dusky look. 1109. **all is vanity.** Cf. *Ecclesiastes,* 12:8: "Vanity of vanities, saith the Preacher; all is vanity." 1113. **teen and threne,** sorrow and lamentation.

George Meredith
1828-1909

     Like Matthew Arnold, George Meredith turned from poetry to prose partly because the audience for his verse was so slender as to dishearten him; but unlike the older writer he did not give up his verse-making but continued it while he also wrote novels. His highly significant novels have been already commented on (see p. 423). Here an attempt will be made to determine his importance as a poet.

     Meredith was born in Portsmouth in 1828. His father was a tailor who was apparently not in a position to do much for his son. After one year in a German school in 1843-1844, he was apprenticed to a London lawyer. But the profession of

---

The poems of George Meredith are reprinted from his *Poetical Works* (1928) by permission of Charles Scribner's Sons, New York.

law did not attract him, and in 1848 he took up journalism and began sending his verses to the magazines. A year later he married the daughter of the poet Thomas Love Peacock. His wife proved to be a very difficult, temperamental lady, and after ten years of disagreeing together, they finally separated; this losing struggle toward matrimonial adjustment formed the basis of the fifty connected poems which he called *Modern Love* (1862). If the sequence is a correct reflection of his experience, neither Meredith nor his wife was entirely responsible for the tragedy in their lives:

> In tragic life, God wot,
> No villain need be! Passions spin the plot;
> We are betrayed by what is false within.

Two years later Meredith married Marie Vulliamy. The Merediths settled in Surrey, where the poet-novelist lived and wrote for the rest of his life. His last years were darkened by the serious ill-health of himself and his wife, but his life cannot on the whole be characterized as an unhappy one.

Meredith's poetry has been called difficult and obscure. Its difficulty lies partly in its extraordinary compression of phrase; few poets have been able to pack so much concentrated thinking into so few words. To those who had not his rapidity of thought and his condensed method of expression he seems deliberately obscure—although this he never was. Solid and intellectual would be sounder terms to apply to his poetry. As a novelist he was a penetrating interpreter of human nature and social problems, and as a poet he displayed also his concern for man. But he is also a nature poet, and man's debt to nature for such spiritual blessings as the ecstasy of natural beauty, the calm of the countryside, and the thrill that comes with the lark's song forms much of the subject-matter of his verse. He had a fertile imagination, but he had also an unerring accuracy in descriptive details. For correct reproduction of nature, to take one example, his *Lark Ascending* is superior to the famous lark poems of Wordsworth and of Shelley; neither of these romantic poets, indeed, could have approached Meredith's skilful resinging of the bird's song. The two guiding inspirations in his life and art appear in some of the titles of a long list of publications which extend from his first ventures into verse in *Poems* (1851) to *A Reading of Life, with Other Poems* (1901). Between these dates *Modern Love* was issued with other poems in 1862; *Poems and Lyrics of the Joy of Earth* in 1883, *Ballads and Poems of Tragic Life* in 1887, *A Reading of Earth* the year following; *The Empty Purse, and Other Poems* in 1892, and *Odes in Contribution to the Song of French History* in 1898.

Juggling Jerry

Pitch here the tent, while the old horse grazes;
    By the old hedge-side we'll halt a stage.
It's nigh my last above the daisies;
    My next leaf'll be man's blank page.
Yes, my old girl! and it's no use crying;   5
    Juggler, constable, king, must bow.
One that outjuggles all's been spying
    Long to have me, and has me now.

We've traveled times to this old common;
    Often we've hung our pots in the gorse.   10

10. **gorse**, furze, a kind of spiny evergreen shrub.

We've had a stirring life, old woman!
    You, and I, and the old gray horse.
Races, and fairs, and royal occasions,
    Found us coming to their call;
Now they'll miss us at our stations—   15
    There's a Juggler outjuggles all!

Up goes the lark, as if all were jolly!
    Over the duck-pond the willow shakes;
It's easy to think that grieving's folly,
    When the hand's firm as driven stakes!   20
Aye, when we're strong, and braced, and manful,
    Life's a sweet fiddle, but we're a batch

Born to become the Great Juggler's han'ful:
  Balls he shies up, and is safe to catch.

Here's where the lads of the village cricket—
  I was a lad not wide from here;   26
Couldn't I juggle the bail off the wicket?
  Like an old world those days appear!
Donkey, sheep, geese and thatched alehouse—
    I know them!
  They are old friends of my halts, and seem,
Somehow, as if kind thanks I owe them;   31
  Juggling don't hinder the heart's esteem.

Juggling's no sin, for we must have victual;
  Nature allows us to bait for the fool.   34
Holding one's own makes us juggle no little;
  But, to increase it, hard juggling's the rule.
You that are sneering at my profession,
  Haven't you juggled a vast amount?
There's the Prime Minister, in one Session,
  Juggles more games than my sins'll count.

I've murdered insects with mock thunder;   41
  Conscience, for that, in men don't quail.
I've made bread from the bump of wonder;
  That's my business, and there's my tale.
Fashion and rank all praised the professor; 45
  Aye! and I've had my smile from the Queen—
Bravo, Jerry! she meant; God bless her!
  Ain't this a sermon on that scene?

I've studied men from my topsy-turvy
  Close, and, I reckon, rather true.   50
Some are fine fellows; some, right scurvy;
  Most, a dash between the two.
But it's a woman, old girl, that makes me
  Think more kindly of the race;
And it's a woman, old girl, that shakes me 55
  When the Great Juggler I must face.

We two were married, due and legal;
  Honest we've lived since we've been one.
Lord! I could then jump like an eagle;
  You danced bright as a bit o' the sun.   60
Birds in a May-bush we were! right merry!
  All night we kissed, we juggled all day.
Joy was the heart of Juggling Jerry!
  Now from his old girl he's juggled away.

It's past parsons to console us;   65
  No, nor no doctor fetch for me—
I can die without my bolus;
  Two of a trade, lass, never agree!
Parson and Doctor—don't they love rarely,
  Fighting the devil in other men's fields! 70
Stand up yourself and match him fairly;
  Then see how the rascal yields!

I, lass, have lived no gypsy, flaunting
  Finery while his poor helpmate grubs;   74
Coin I've stored, and you won't be wanting—
  You shan't beg from the troughs and tubs.
Nobly you've stuck to me, though in his kitchen
  Many a marquis would hail you cook!
Palaces you could have ruled and grown rich in,
  But your old Jerry you never forsook.   80

Hand up the chirper! ripe ale winks in it;
  Let's have comfort and be at peace,
Once a stout draft made me light as a linnet.
  Cheer up! the Lord must have his lease. 84
May be—for none see in that black hollow—
  It's just a place where we're held in pawn,
And, when the Great Juggler makes as to swallow,
  It's just the sword-trick—I ain't quite gone.

Yonder came smells of the gorse, so nutty,
  Gold-like and warm; it's the prime of May.
Better than mortar, brick, and putty,   91
  Is God's house on a blowing day.
Lean me more up the mound; now I feel it!
  All the old heath-smells! Ain't it strange?
There's the world laughing, as if to conceal it!
  But He's by us, juggling the change.   96

I mind it well, by the sea-beach lying,
  Once—it's long gone—when two gulls we beheld,
Which, as the moon got up, were flying

25. **cricket**, play cricket. 27. **juggle . . . wicket.** In the game of cricket, when the batsman is not in place, he may be put "out" if the wicket-keeper knocks off the bails (crosspieces) with the ball. 49. **topsy-turvy**, varied points of view. 67. **bolus**, a large pill. 81. **chirper**, a cup that cheers. 95. **it**, the change from life to death.

Down a big wave that sparked and swelled.
Crack went a gun: one fell; the second   101
  Wheeled round him twice, and was off for
    new luck;
There in the dark her white wing beckoned—
Drop me a kiss—I'm the bird dead-struck!
                                        (1859)

from *Modern Love*

This is a series of sixteen-line poems recording the thoughts and feelings of a husband and a wife who loved each other once, but whose love has long been dying. The husband sometimes speaks in his own person as "I." For its probable connection with Meredith's matrimonial experience see biographical sketch, p. 769.

1

By this he knew she wept with waking eyes:
That, at his hand's light quiver by her head,
The strange low sobs that shook their common bed
Were called into her with a sharp surprise,
And strangled mute, like little gaping snakes,
Dreadfully venomous to him. She lay   6
Stone-still, and the long darkness flowed away
With muffled pulses. Then, as midnight makes
Her giant heart of Memory and Tears
Drink the pale drug of silence, and so beat   10
Sleep's heavy measure, they from head to feet
Were moveless, looking through their dead black years,
By vain regret scrawled over the blank wall.
Like sculptured effigies they might be seen
Upon their marriage-tomb, the sword between;   15
Each wishing for the sword that severs all.

16

In our old shipwrecked days there was an hour,
When in the firelight steadily aglow,
Joined slackly, we beheld the red chasm grow
Among the clicking coals. Our library-bower
That eve was left to us; and hushed we sat   5
As lovers to whom Time is whispering.
From sudden-opened doors we heard them sing;
The nodding elders mixed good wine with chat.
Well knew we that Life's greatest treasure lay
With us, and of it was our talk. "Ah, yes!   10
Love dies!" I said (I never thought it less).
She yearned to me that sentence to unsay.
Then when the fire domed blackening, I found
Her cheek was salt against my kiss, and swift
Up the sharp scale of sobs her breast did lift.—   15
Now am I haunted by that taste! that sound!

29

Am I failing? For no longer can I cast
A glory round about this head of gold.
Glory she wears, but springing from the mold;
Not like the consecration of the Past!
Is my soul beggared? Something more than earth   5
I cry for still; I cannot be at peace
In having Love upon a mortal lease.
I cannot take the woman at her worth!
Where is the ancient wealth wherewith I clothed
Our human nakedness, and could endow   10
With spiritual splendor a white brow
That else had grinned at me the fact I loathed?
A kiss is but a kiss now! and no wave
Of a great flood that whirls me to the sea.
But, as you will! we'll sit contentedly,   15
And eat our pot of honey on the grave.

47

We saw the swallows gathering in the sky,
And in the osier-isle we heard them noise.
We had not to look back on summer joys,
Or forward to a summer of bright dye;
But in the largeness of the evening earth   5
Our spirits grew as we went side by side.
The hour became her husband and my bride.
Love, that had robbed us so, thus blessed our dearth!
The pilgrims of the year waxed very loud

Sonnet 47. 2. **osier-isle**, island overgrown with osiers—i.e., willows.

In multitudinous chatterings, as the flood 10
Full brown came from the West, and like pale
    blood
Expanded to the upper crimson cloud.
Love, that had robbed us of immortal things,
This little moment mercifully gave,
Where I have seen across the twilight wave 15
The swan sail with her young beneath her
    wings.

48

Their sense is with their senses all mixed in,
Destroyed by subtleties these women are!
More brain, O Lord, more brain! or we shall
    mar
Utterly this fair garden we might win.
Behold! I looked for peace, and thought it
    near. 5
Our inmost hearts had opened, each to each
We drank the pure daylight of honest speech.
Alas! that was the fatal draft, I fear.
For when of my lost Lady came the word,
This woman, O this agony of flesh! 10
Jealous devotion bade her break the mesh,
That I might seek that other like a bird.
I do adore the nobleness! despise
The act! She has gone forth, I know not
    where.
Will the hard world my sentience of her
    share? 15
I feel the truth; so let the world surmise.

50

Thus piteously Love closed what he begat:
The union of this ever-diverse pair!
These two were rapid falcons in a snare,
Condemned to do the flitting of the bat.
Lovers beneath the singing sky of May, 5
They wandered once, clear as the dew on
    flowers.
But they fed not on the advancing hours;
Their hearts held cravings for the buried day.
Then each applied to each that fatal knife,
Deep questioning, which probes to endless
    dole. 10
Ah, what a dusty answer gets the soul
When hot for certainties in this our life!—
In tragic hints here see what evermore
Moves dark as yonder midnight ocean's force,

Thundering like ramping hosts of warrior
    horse, 15
To throw that faint thin line upon the shore!
    (1862)

The Lark Ascending

He rises and begins to round;
He drops the silver chain of sound,
Of many links without a break,
In chirrup, whistle, slur, and shake—
All intervolved and spreading wide, 5
Like water-dimples down a tide
Where ripple ripple overcurls
And eddy into eddy whirls;
A press of hurried notes that run
So fleet they scarce are more than one, 10
Yet changingly the trills repeat
And linger ringing while they fleet—
Sweet to the quick o' the ear, and dear
To her beyond the handmaid ear,
Who sits beside our inner springs, 15
Too often dry for this he brings,
Which seems the very jet of earth
At sight of sun, her music's mirth,
As up he wings the spiral stair,
A song of light, and pierces air 20
With fountain ardor, fountain play,
To reach the shining tops of day,
And drink in everything discerned,
An ecstasy to music turned—
Impelled by what his happy bill 25
Disperses; drinking, showering still,
Unthinking save that he may give
His voice the outlet, there to live
Renewed in endless notes of glee,
So thirsty of his voice is he, 30
For all to hear and all to know
That he is joy, awake, aglow—
The tumult of the heart to hear
Through pureness filtered crystal-clear—
And know the pleasure sprinkled bright 35
By simple singing of delight,
Shrill, irreflective, unrestrained,
Rapt, ringing, on the jet sustained
Without a break, without a fall,
Sweet-silvery, sheer lyrical, 40
Perennial, quavering up the chord

The Lark Ascending. Cf. the skylark odes of Wordsworth and of Shelley, pp. 156 and 258. 14. **her,** the spirit of earth or nature within us.

Like myriad dews of sunny sward
That trembling into fullness shine,
And sparkle dropping argentine;
Such wooing as the ear receives 45
From zephyr caught in choric leaves
Of aspens when their chattering net
Is flushed to white with shivers wet;
And such the water-spirit's chime
On mountain heights in mornings prime, 50
Too freshly sweet to seem excess,
Too animate to need a stress;
But wider over many heads
The starry voice ascending spreads,
Awakening, as it waxes thin, 55
The best in us to him akin;
And every face to watch him raised
Puts on the light of children praised—
So rich our human pleasure ripes
When sweetness on sincereness pipes, 60
Though naught be promised from the seas—
But only a soft-ruffling breeze
Sweep glittering on a still content,
Serenity in ravishment.

For singing till his heaven fills, 65
'Tis love of earth that he instills,
And ever winging up and up,
Our valley is his golden cup,
And he the wine which overflows
To lift us with him as he goes— 70
But not from earth is he divorced,
He joyfully to fly enforced.
The woods and brooks, the sheep and kine,
He is, the hills, the human line,
The meadows green, the fallows brown, 75
The dreams of labor in the town;
He sings the sap, the quickened veins;
The wedding song of sun and rains
He is, the dance of children, thanks
Of sowers, shout of primrose-banks, 80
And eye of violets while they breathe;
All these the circling song will wreathe,
And you shall hear the herb and tree,
The better heart of men shall see,
Shall feel celestially—as long 85
As you crave nothing save the song.

Was never voice of ours could say
Our inmost in the sweetest way,

Like yonder voice aloft, and link
All hearers in the song they drink. 90
Our wisdom speaks from failing blood,
Our passion is too full in flood;
We want the key of his wild note
Of truthful in a tuneful throat,
The song seraphically free 95
Of taint of personality—
So pure that it salutes the suns,
The voice of one for millions,
In whom the millions rejoice
For giving their one spirit voice. 100

Yet men have we, whom we revere,
Now names—and men still housing here—
Whose lives, by many a battle-dint
Defaced, and grinding wheels on flint,
Yield substance, though they sing not, sweet
For song our highest heaven to greet; 106
Whom heavenly singing gives us new,
Enspheres them brilliant in our blue,
From firmest base to farthest leap,
Because their love of Earth is deep, 110
And they are warriors in accord
With life to serve, and pass reward—
So touching purest and so heard
In the brain's reflex of yon bird.
Wherefore their soul in me—or mine, 115
Through self-forgetfulness divine,
In them—that song aloft maintains,
To fill the sky and thrill the plains
With showerings drawn from human stores,
As he to silence nearer soars, 120
Extends the world at wings and dome,
More spacious making more our home,
Till lost on his aërial rings
In light—and then the fancy sings.

(*1881;* 1881)

Lucifer in Starlight

On a starred night Prince Lucifer uprose.
Tired of his dark dominion, swung the fiend
Above the rolling ball, in cloud part screened,
Where sinners hugged their specter of repose.
Poor prey to his hot fit of pride were those. 5

---

44. **argentine,** silver-like substance.

96. **taint of personality,** egotism. 112. **pass,** do without.
114. **brain's reflex,** mind's reflection or interpretation. 122.
More . . . home, extending our habitat.
Lucifer in Starlight. 2. **his dark dominion,** hell.

And now upon his western wing he leaned,
Now his huge bulk o'er Afric's sands careened,
Now the black planet shadowed Arctic snows.
Soaring through wider zones that pricked his
    scars
With memory of the old revolt from Awe,   10
He reached a middle height, and at the stars,
Which are the brain of heaven, he looked, and
    sank.
Around the ancient track marched, rank on
    rank,
The army of unalterable law.   (1883)

On the Danger of War

Avert, High Wisdom, never vainly wooed,
This threat of War, that shows a land brain-
    sick.
When nations gain the pitch where rhetoric
Seems reason they are ripe for cannon's food.
Dark looms the issue though the cause be
    good,   5
But with the doubt 'tis our old devil's trick.
O now the down-slope of the lunatic
Illumine lest we redden of that brood.
For not since man in his first view of thee
Ascended to the heavens giving sign   10
Within him of deep sky and sounded sea,
Did he unforfeiting thy laws transgress;
In peril of his blood his ears incline
To drums whose loudness is their emptiness.
    (1885)

Meditation under Stars

What links are ours with orbs that are
    So resolutely far?—
The solitary asks, and they
Give radiance as from a shield:
    Still at the death of day,   5
    The seen, the unrevealed.
    Implacable they shine
To us who would of Life obtain
An answer for the life we strain,
    To nourish with one sign.   10
Nor can imagination throw
The penetrative shaft: we pass

9. **scars,** those received in his battle with the angels and in his fall through the regions of air with the rebel hosts. See *Paradise Lost,* II (Vol. I, pp. 728 ff.).

The breath of thought, who would divine
    If haply they may grow
As Earth; have our desire to know;   15
If life comes there to grain from grass,
And flowers like ours of toil and pain;
    Has passion to beat bar,
    Win space from cleaving brain;
    The mystic link attain,   20
    Whereby star holds on star.

Those visible immortals beam
    Allurement to the dream:
Ireful at human hungers brook
    No question in the look.   25
    Forever virgin to our sense,
Remote they wane to gaze intense:
Prolong it, and in ruthlessness they smite
The beating heart behind the ball of sight:
    Till we conceive their heavens hoar,   30
    Those lights they raise but sparkles frore,
And Earth, our blood-warm Earth, a shud-
    dering prey
To that frigidity of brainless ray.
Yet space is given for breath of thought
Beyond our bounds when musing: more   35
When to that musing love is brought,
And love is asked of love's wherefore.
'Tis Earth's, her gift; else have we naught:
Her gift, her secret, here our tie.
And not with her and yonder sky?   40
Bethink you: were it Earth alone
Breeds love, would not her region be
    The sole delight and throne
    Of generous Deity?

    To deeper than this ball of sight   45
Appeal the lustrous people of the night.
Fronting yon shoreless, sown with fiery sails,
    It is our ravenous that quails,
Flesh by its craven thirsts and fears distraught.
    The spirit leaps alight,   50
    Doubts not in them is he,
The binder of his sheaves, the same, the
    right:
Of magnitude to magnitude is wrought,
To feel it large of the great life they hold:
In them to come, or vaster intervolved,   55
The issues known in us, our unsolved solved:

31. **frore,** frozen. 48. **our ravenous,** the ravenous part of us: egoism.

That there with toil Life climbs the selfsame
    Tree,
Whose roots enrichment have from ripeness
    dropped.

So may we read and little find them cold:
Let it but be the lord of Mind to guide   60
Our eyes; no branch of Reason's growing
    lopped;
Nor dreaming on a dream; but fortified
By day to penetrate black midnight; see,
Hear, feel, outside the senses; even that we,
The specks of dust upon a mound of mold,   65
We who reflect those rays, though low our
    place,
    To them are lastingly allied.

So may we read, and little find them cold:
Not frosty lamps illuming dead space,
Not distant aliens, not senseless Powers.   70
The fire is in them whereof we are born;
The music of their motion may be ours.
Spirit shall deem them beckoning Earth and
    voiced
Sisterly to her, in her beams rejoiced.
Of love, the grand impulsion, we behold   75
    The love that lends her grace
    Among the starry fold.
Then at new flood of customary morn,

<small>72. **music . . . ours.** Cf. *Job*, 38:4-7: "Where wast thou . . . When the morning stars sang together, and all the sons of God shouted for joy?" The ancients believed that the stars made music as they revolved in their spheres.</small>

Look at her through her showers,
    Her mists, her streaming gold,   80
A wonder edges the familiar face:
She wears no more that robe of printed hours;
Half strange seems Earth, and sweeter than
    her flowers.   (1888)

Song in the Songless

They have no song, the sedges dry,
    And still they sing.
It is within my breast they sing,
    As I pass by.
Within my breast they touch a string,   5
    They wake a sigh.
There is but sound of sedges dry;
    In me they sing.   (1900)

Youth in Age

Once I was part of the music I heard
    On the boughs or sweet between earth and
        sky;
For joy of the beating of wings on high
My heart shot into the breast of the bird.

I hear it now and I see it fly,   5
    And a life in wrinkles again is stirred;
My heart shoots into the breast of the bird,
As it will for sheer love till the last long sigh.
                                            (1908)

POETS AESTHETIC AND PAGAN

Edward Fitzgerald

1809-1883

It is very seldom that a poet attains immortality by writing a single poem, but that was the fate of Edward Fitzgerald. *The Rubáiyát of Omar Khayyám* stands well toward the top in any list of indispensable Victorian poems; and he wrote nothing else that has brought him popular favor.

Fitzgerald was born Purcell, but his father changed the family name when his son was nine. The boy's childhood home was in Suffolk; he attended school at Bury St. Edmunds, and college at Trinity, Cambridge. Here he came to know Thackeray and Tennyson. On graduating he took up no occupation but settled down in Suffolk as a country gentleman studying Greek, Spanish, and Persian, dabbling and dibbling about his estate, and living, in brief, the epicurean life of a man of leisure. After the appearance of *The Rubáiyát* in 1859 he bought a yacht and spent much of the rest of his shy and easy existence in knocking about the North Sea. He died in 1883.

Fitzgerald's earliest literary activity was his writing and publishing in 1851 of a Platonic dialogue in prose entitled *Euphranor*. In 1856 appeared his *Six Dramas of Calderon*, the fruit of a long and intensive study of Spanish. These dramas were not accurate translations, by any means; they did succeed, however, in transferring into English much of the spirit and flavor of the old Spanish playwright. The same may be said of his later paraphrases—they can hardly be called translations—of the *Agamemnon* of Aeschylus (1865), and the two *Oedipus* tragedies of Sophocles (1880-1881). But it is only his *Rubáiyát* which brought him enduring fame.

When the quatrains appeared on January 15, 1859, Fitzgerald had been studying Persian for six years, and he could have made an entirely accurate translation of the old poem if he had chosen to do so. He preferred, however, to make what may be called a transmutation. It is as though the soul of the old astronomer-poet of the twelfth century had undergone a delightful reincarnation in the body of a Suffolk epicure-scholar, who loved life heartily in all its pleasant aspects of wine, women, song, friends, flowers, music, and verses. Thus the poem became completely English. Fitzgerald made a whimsical comment on it in a letter to his friend Professor E. B. Cowell, who had taught him Persian. "It is," he wrote, "most ingeniously tesselated into a sort of Epicurean Eclogue in a Persian Garden." It is unblushingly and refreshingly pagan, and the author remarked to Bishop Parker that "he might find it rather dangerous among his Divines." On its first appearance it made no stir whatever; then Rossetti, Swinburne, and others discovered and acclaimed it; and now it may be found—in all manner of elegant bindings—in the library of Everyman.

The Rubáiyát of Omar Khayyám

Fitzgerald's study of Persian brought him an acquaintance with Omar Khayyám, the great mathematician, astronomer, free-thinker, and poet. The name *Khayyám* means *tent-maker;* it was probably derived from his father's occupation. The exact date of his birth is not known, but tradition gives 1123 A.D. as that of his death. Supported by an annual stipend from the Seljūk sultan Alp-Arslan, he devoted most of his time to the study of mathematics and astronomy and wrote a standard work on algebra. His poetical renown he owes to his *rubā'īs,* or quatrains, a collection of some five hundred epigrams, not connected by any structural continuity. Each *rubā'ī* consists of four lines of which the first, second, and fourth rime, with the third unrimed. They vary in content but express in general the free-thinker's rebellion against orthodox belief. His praise of wine and love are rhapsodic, and his denunciations of inexorable decay and death are equally passionate. Because of his satire he has been called "the Voltaire of the East," and his irony equals that of the French writer.

Fitzgerald's translation—or rather transcription—of the Persian epigrams appeared first (1859) in seventy-five quatrains; the edition of 1868 had one hundred and ten; and those of 1872 and 1879 one hundred and one. Not only did the poet vary the number of quatrains in these successive editions, but he also made considerable modifications of the content and phrasing, often with the objective of sparing the feelings of his more easily disturbed readers. He was not, it should be added, a dogmatist, and he had no idea of publishing the poem to convert anybody to free-thinking or drinking. His rime scheme in his iambic pentameter lines is that of his original.

Wake! For the Sun, who scattered into flight
The Stars before him from the Field of Night,
   Drives Night along with them from Heav'n
      and strikes
The Sultán's Turret with a Shaft of Light.

Before the phantom of False morning died, 5
Methought a Voice within the Tavern cried,

5. **phantom . . . morning,** "a transient light on the horizon about an hour before the true dawn—a common phenomenon in the East" (Fitzgerald).

"When all the Temple is prepared within,
Why nods the drowsy Worshiper outside?"

And, as the Cock crew, those who stood before
The Tavern shouted—"Open, then, the
    Door!   10
  You know how little while we have to stay,
And, once departed, may return no more."

Now the New Year reviving old Desires,
The thoughtful Soul to Solitude retires,
  Where the WHITE HAND OF MOSES on the
    Bough   15
Puts out, and Jesus from the Ground suspires.

Iram indeed is gone with all his Rose,
And Jamshyd's Sev'n-ringed Cup where no
    one knows;
  But still a Ruby kindles in the Vine,
And many a Garden by the Water blows.   20

And David's lips are locked; but in divine
High-piping Pehleví, with "Wine! Wine!
    Wine!
  Red Wine!"—the Nightingale cries to the
    Rose
That sallow cheek of hers to incarnadine.

Come, fill the Cup, and in the fire of Spring   25
Your Winter-garment of Repentance fling;
  The Bird of Time has but a little way
To flutter—and the Bird is on the Wing.

Whether at Naishápúr or Babylon,
Whether the Cup with sweet or bitter run,   30
  The Wine of Life keeps oozing drop by
    drop,
The Leaves of Life keep falling one by one.

Each Morn a thousand Roses brings, you say;
Yes, but where leaves the Rose of Yesterday?

And this first Summer month that brings
    the Rose   35
Shall take Jamshyd and Kaikobád away.

Well, let it take them! What have we to do
With Kaikobád the Great, or Kaikhosrú?
  Let Zál and Rustum bluster as they will,
Or Hátim call to Supper—heed not you.   40

With me along the strip of Herbage strown
That just divides the desert from the sown,
  Where name of Slave and Sultán is forgot—
And Peace to Mahmúd on his golden Throne!

A Book of Verses underneath the Bough,   45
A Jug of Wine, a Loaf of Bread—and Thou
  Beside me singing in the Wilderness—
Oh, Wilderness were Paradise enow!

Some for the Glories of This World; and
    some
Sigh for the Prophet's Paradise to come;   50
  Ah, take the Cash, and let the Credit go,
Nor heed the rumble of a distant Drum!

Look to the blowing Rose about us—"Lo,
Laughing," she says, "into the world I blow,
  At once the silken tassel of my Purse   55
Tear, and its Treasure on the Garden throw."

And those who husbanded the Golden Grain,
And those who flung it to the winds like Rain,
  Alike to no such aureate Earth are turned
As, buried once, Men want dug up again.   60

The Worldly Hope men set their Hearts upon
Turns Ashes—or it prospers; and anon,
  Like Snow upon the Desert's dusty Face,
Lighting a little hour or two—is gone.

Think, in this battered Caravanserai   65
Whose Portals are alternate Night and Day,

---

13. **New Year.** The Persian year begins with the vernal equinox. 15. **White . . . Bough.** At the command of the Lord, Moses put his hand into his bosom and "when he took it out, behold, his hand was leprous as snow" (*Exodus*, 4:6). The metaphor is applied to the blooming of the flowers. 16. **Jesus . . . suspires.** The Persians believed that the healing power of Jesus resided in his breath. 17. **Iram,** an ancient Persian garden, now obliterated. 18. **Jamshyd,** a legendary king of Persia. His seven-ringed cup symbolized the seven heavens, the seven planets, the seven seas, etc. 21. **David . . . Pehleví.** David's tongue is forgotten, but the nightingale still cries in Pehleví, the ancient literary language of Persia. 29. **Naishápúr,** a village in Persia; Omar's native place.

36. **Kaikobád,** the founder of the most celebrated of the dynasties of ancient Persia. 38. **Kaikhosrú,** a famous Persian hero, identified with Cyrus the Great (sixth century B.C.), founder of the Persian Empire. 39. **Zál and Rustum,** noted Persian heroes; Zál was the father of Rustum. 40. **Hátim,** "a type of Oriental Generosity" (Fitzgerald). 44. **Mahmúd,** the Sultan. Mahmud the Great (c. 970-1030) was the famous Mohammedan conqueror of India; he was sultan of Ghazni, the city of his birth in Afghanistan. 50. **the Prophet,** Mohammed. 57. **Golden Grain,** wealth. 65. **Caravanserai,** an Oriental inn, where caravans rest at night.

How Sultán after Sultán with his Pomp
Abode his destined Hour, and went his way.

They say the Lion and the Lizard keep
The Courts where Jamshyd gloried and drank deep; 70
  And Bahrám, that great hunter—the Wild Ass
Stamps o'er his Head, but cannot break his Sleep.

I sometimes think that never blows so red
The Rose as where some buried Caesar bled;
That every Hyacinth the Garden wears 75
Dropped in her Lap from some once lovely Head.

And this reviving Herb whose tender Green
Fledges the River-Lip on which we lean—
  Ah, lean upon it lightly! for who knows
From what once lovely Lip it springs unseen!

Ah, my Belovéd, fill the Cup that clears 81
Today of past Regrets and future Fears:
  Tomorrow!—Why, Tomorrow I may be
Myself with Yesterday's Sev'n Thousand Years.

For some we loved, the loveliest and the best 85
That from his Vintage rolling Time hath prest,
  Have drunk their Cup a Round or two before,
And one by one crept silently to rest.

And we, that now make merry in the Room
They left, and Summer dresses in new bloom,
  Ourselves must we beneath the Couch of Earth 91
Descend—ourselves to make a Couch—for whom?

Ah, make the most of what we yet may spend,
Before we too into the Dust descend;
  Dust into Dust, and under Dust, to lie, 95
Sans Wine, sans Song, sans Singer, and—sans End!

Alike for those who for TODAY prepare,
And those that after some TOMORROW stare,
  A Muezzín from the Tower of Darkness cries,
"Fools, your Reward is neither Here nor There." 100

Why, all the Saints and Sages who discussed
Of the Two Worlds so wisely—they are thrust
  Like foolish Prophets forth; their Words to Scorn
Are scattered, and their Mouths are stopped with Dust.

Myself when young did eagerly frequent 105
Doctor and Saint, and heard great argument
  About it and about; but evermore
Came out by the same door where in I went.

With them the seed of Wisdom did I sow,
And with mine own hand wrought to make it grow; 110
  And this was all the Harvest that I reaped—
"I came like Water, and like Wind I go."

Into this Universe, and *Why* not knowing
Nor *Whence*, like Water willy-nilly flowing;
  And out of it, as Wind along the Waste, 115
I know not *Whither*, willy-nilly blowing.

What, without asking, hither hurried *Whence?*
And, without asking, *Whither* hurried hence!
  Oh, many a Cup of this forbidden Wine
Must drown the memory of that insolence!

Up from the Earth's Center through the Seventh Gate 121
I rose, and on the Throne of Saturn sate,
  And many a Knot unraveled by the Road;
But not the Master-knot of Human Fate.

---

70. **Courts.** Jamshyd's capital was Persepolis. 71. **Bahrám,** a Persian ruler who lost his life in a swamp while hunting a wild ass. 75. **Hyacinth,** a flower named after Hyacinthus, a youth accidentally killed by his friend, Apollo, god of the sun. The flower sprang up where the blood of Hyacinthus flowed upon the ground. 84. **Sev'n Thousand Years,** a thousand years to each planet.

96. **Sans,** without. 99. **Muezzín,** the officer who summons the faithful to prayer in Mohammedan countries. 119. **forbidden Wine.** Orthodox Mohammedanism regards the use of wine as one of twelve capital sins. 122. **Saturn,** the lord of the seventh heaven, one of the concentric spheres into which, according to the ancients, the space around the earth was divided.

There was the Door to which I found no Key;
There was the Veil through which I might
    not see;   126
  Some little talk awhile of Me and Thee
There was—and then no more of Thee and
    Me.

Earth could not answer; nor the Seas that
    mourn
In flowing Purple, of their Lord forlorn;   130
  Nor rolling Heaven, with all his Signs re-
    vealed
And hidden by the sleeve of Night and Morn.

Then of the Thee in Me who works behind
The Veil, I lifted up my hands to find   134
  A lamp amid the Darkness; and I heard,
As from Without—"The Me within Thee
    blind!"

Then to the Lip of this poor earthen Urn
I leaned, the Secret of my Life to learn;
  And Lip to Lip it murmured—"While you
    live,
Drink!—for, once dead, you never shall re-
    turn."   140

I think the Vessel, that with fugitive
Articulation answered, once did live,
  And drink; and Ah! the passive Lip I
    kissed,
How many Kisses might it take—and give!

For I remember stopping by the way   145
To watch a Potter thumping his wet Clay;
  And with its all-obliterated Tongue
It murmured—"Gently, Brother, gently, pray!"

And has not such a Story from of Old
Down Man's successive generations rolled   150
  Of such a clod of saturated Earth
Cast by the Maker into Human mold?

And not a drop that from our Cups we throw
For Earth to drink of, but may steal below
  To quench the fire of Anguish in some Eye
There hidden—far beneath, and long ago.   156

As then the Tulip, for her morning sup
Of Heav'nly Vintage, from the soil looks up,
  Do you devoutly do the like, till Heav'n
To Earth invert you—like an empty Cup.   160

Perplexed no more with Human or Divine,
Tomorrow's tangle to the winds resign,
  And lose your fingers in the tresses of
The Cypress-slender Minister of Wine.

And if the Wine you drink, the Lip you press,
End in what All begins and ends in—Yes;   166
  Think that you are Today what Yesterday
You were—Tomorrow you shall not be less.

So when that Angel of the darker Drink
At last shall find you by the river-brink,   170
  And offering his Cup, invite your Soul
Forth to your Lips to quaff—you shall not
    shrink.

Why, if the Soul can fling the Dust aside,
And naked on the Air of Heaven ride,
  Were 't not a Shame—were 't not a Shame
    for him   175
In this clay carcass crippled to abide?

'Tis but a Tent where takes his one day's rest
A Sultán to the realm of Death addrest;
  The Sultán rises, and the dark Ferrásh
Strikes, and prepares it for another Guest.   180

And fear not lest Existence closing your
Account, and mine, should know the like no
    more;
  The Eternal Sákí from that Bowl has poured
Millions of Bubbles like us, and will pour.

When You and I behind the Veil are past,   185
Oh, but the long, long while the World shall
    last,
  Which of our Coming and Departure heeds
As the Sea's self should heed a pebble-cast.

A Moment's Halt—a momentary taste   189
Of Being from the Well amid the Waste—

---

131. **Signs**, the signs of the zodiac. 153. **drop . . . Earth.** It was an old custom to throw a little wine on the ground before drinking; it refreshed some wine-drinker who had gone before. 164. **Cypress-slender . . . Wine**, the maiden who passes the wine; she is as slender as a cypress tree. 165. **And if, etc.** This stanza stresses the joy of wine mingled with the joy of love. 179. **Ferrásh**, a servant, a camp-follower. 183. **Sákí**, wine-bearer.

And Lo!—the phantom Caravan has reached
The Nothing it set out from—Oh, make haste!

Would you that spangle of Existence spend
About the secret—quick about it, Friend!
  A Hair perhaps divides the False and True—   195
And upon what, prithee, does life depend?

A Hair perhaps divides the False and True—
Yes; and a single Alif were the clue—
  Could you but find it—to the Treasure-house,
And peradventure to The Master too;   200

Whose secret Presence, through Creation's veins
Running Quicksilver-like, eludes your pains;
  Taking all shapes from Máh to Máhi; and
They change and perish all—but He remains;

A moment guessed—then back behind the Fold
Immersed of Darkness round the Drama rolled   206
  Which, for the Pastime of Eternity,
He doth Himself contrive, enact, behold.

But if in vain, down on the stubborn floor
Of Earth, and up to Heav'n's unopening Door,
  You gaze Today, while You are You—how then   211
Tomorrow, when You shall be You no more?

Waste not your Hour, nor in the vain pursuit
Of This and That endeavor and dispute;
  Better be jocund with the fruitful Grape
Than sadden after none, or bitter, Fruit.   216

You know, my Friends, with what a brave Carouse
I made a Second Marriage in my house;
  Divorced old barren Reason from my Bed,
And took the Daughter of the Vine to Spouse.

For "Is" and "Is-not" though with Rule and Line,   221
And "Up-and-down" by Logic, I define,

198. **Alif**, the first letter of some ancient alphabets. 203. **from Máh to Máhi**, from fish to moon.

Of all that one should care to fathom, I
Was never deep in anything but—Wine.

Ah, but my Computations, People say,   225
Reduced the Year to better reckoning?—Nay,
  'Twas only striking from the Calendar
Unborn Tomorrow, and dead Yesterday.

And lately, by the Tavern Door agape,
Came shining through the Dusk an Angel Shape   230
  Bearing a Vessel on his Shoulder; and
He bid me taste of it; and 'twas—the Grape!

The Grape that can with Logic absolute
The Two-and-Seventy jarring Sects confute;
  The sovereign Alchemist that in a trice   235
Life's leaden metal into Gold transmute;

The mighty Mahmúd, Allah-breathing Lord,
That all the misbelieving and black Horde
  Of fears and Sorrows that infest the Soul
Scatters before him with his whirlwind Sword.

Why, be this Juice the growth of God, who dare   241
Blaspheme the twisted tendril as a Snare?
  A Blessing, we should use it, should we not?
And if a Curse—why, then, Who set it there?

I must abjure the Balm of Life, I must,   245
Scared by some After-reckoning ta'en on trust
  Or lured with Hope of some Diviner Drink,
To fill the Cup—when crumbled into Dust!

Oh threats of Hell and Hopes of Paradise!
One thing at least is certain—*This* Life flies;   250
  One thing is certain and the rest is Lies—
The Flower that once has blown forever dies.

Strange, is it not? that of the myriads who
Before us passed the door of Darkness through,
  Not one returns to tell us of the Road,   255
Which to discover we must travel too.

225. **Computations.** Omar was a learned astronomer, one of eight men employed to reform the calendar. 234. **Two-and-Seventy**, the number of religions supposed to be in the world. 237. **Allah-breathing.** The sultan worshiped Allah, the Mohammedan deity, and forced others to do likewise. 252. **blown**, bloomed.

The Revelations of Devout and Learned
Who rose before us, and as Prophets burned,
  Are all but Stories, which, awoke from Sleep,
They told their comrades, and to Sleep re-
    turned.   260

I sent my Soul through the Invisible,
Some letter of that After-life to spell;
  And by and by my Soul returned to me,
And answered, "I Myself am Heav'n and
    Hell"—

Heav'n but the Vision of fulfilled Desire, 265
And Hell the Shadow from a Soul on fire
  Cast on the Darkness into which Ourselves,
So late emerged from, shall so soon expire.

We are no other than a moving row   269
Of Magic Shadow-shapes that come and go
  Round with the Sun-illumined Lantern
    held
In Midnight by the Master of the Show;

But helpless Pieces of the Game He plays
Upon this Checker-board of Nights and Days;
  Hither and thither moves, and checks, and
    slays,   275
And one by one back in the Closet lays.

The Ball no question makes of Ayes and Noes,
But Here or There as strikes the Player goes;
  And He that tossed you down into the Field,
He knows about it all—HE knows—HE
    knows!   280

The Moving Finger writes, and, having writ,
Moves on; nor all your Piety nor Wit
  Shall lure it back to cancel half a Line,
Nor all your Tears wash out a Word of it.

And that inverted Bowl they call the Sky, 285
Whereunder crawling cooped we live and die,
  Lift not your hands to *It* for help—for It
As impotently moves as you or I.

With Earth's first Clay They did the Last Man
    knead,   289
And there of the Last Harvest sowed the Seed;

And the first Morning of Creation wrote
What the Last Dawn of Reckoning shall read.

YESTERDAY *This* Day's Madness did prepare;
TOMORROW'S Silence, Triumph, or Despair.
  Drink! for you know not whence you came,
    nor why;   295
Drink, for you know not why you go, nor
    where.

I tell you this—When, started from the Goal,
Over the flaming shoulders of the Foal
  Of Heav'n Parwín and Mushtarí they flung,
In my predestined Plot of Dust and Soul 300

The Vine had struck a fiber; which about
If clings my Being—let the Dervish flout;
  Of my Base metal may be filed a Key,
That shall unlock the Door he howls without.

And this I know: whether the one True
    Light   305
Kindle to Love, or Wrath—consume me quite,
  One Flash of It within the Tavern caught
Better than in the Temple lost outright.

What! out of senseless Nothing to provoke
A conscious Something to resent the yoke 310
  Of unpermitted Pleasure, under pain
Of Everlasting Penalties, if broke!

What! from his helpless Creature be repaid
Pure Gold for what he lent him dross-allayed—
  Sue for a Debt he never did contract,   315
And cannot answer—Oh, the sorry trade!

Oh Thou, who didst with pitfall and with gin
Beset the Road I was to wander in,
  Thou wilt not with Predestined Evil round
Enmesh, and then impute my Fall to Sin! 320

Oh Thou, who Man of Baser Earth didst make,
And ev'n with Paradise devise the Snake,
  For all the Sin wherewith the Face of Man
Is blackened—Man's forgiveness give—and
    take!

277. **The Ball**, etc. An allusion to the game of polo, of ancient Persian origin. 298. **Foal Of Heav'n**, an equatorial constellation known as Equuleus (the Little Horse). 299. **Parwín and Mushtarí**, the Pleiades and Jupiter. 302. **Dervish**, a Mohammedan devotee. 317. **gin**, trap.

As under cover of departing Day 325
Slunk hunger-stricken Ramazán away,
  Once more within the Potter's house alone
I stood, surrounded by the Shapes of Clay—

Shapes of all Sorts and Sizes, great and small,
That stood along the floor and by the wall; 330
  And some loquacious Vessels were; and some
Listened perhaps, but never talked at all.

Said one among them—"Surely not in vain
My substance of the common Earth was ta'en
  And to this Figure molded, to be broke, 335
Or trampled back to shapeless Earth again."

Then said a Second—"Ne'er a peevish Boy
Would break the Bowl from which he drank in joy;
  And He that with his hand the Vessel made
Will surely not in after Wrath destroy." 340

After a momentary silence spake
Some Vessel of a more ungainly Make:
  "They sneer at me for leaning all awry;
What! did the Hand, then, of the Potter shake?"

Whereat someone of the loquacious Lot— 345
I think a Súfi pipkin—waxing hot—
  "All this of Pot and Potter—Tell me then,
Who is the Potter, pray, and who the Pot?"

"Why," said another, "Some there are who tell
Of one who threatens he will toss to Hell 350
  The luckless Pots he marred in making—Pish!
He's a Good Fellow, and 'twill all be well."

"Well," murmured one, "Let whoso make or buy,
My Clay with long Oblivion is gone dry;
  But fill me with the old familiar Juice, 355
Methinks I might recover by and by."

So while the Vessels one by one were speaking
The little Moon looked in that all were seeking;
  And then they jogged each other, "Brother! Brother!
Now for the Porter's shoulder-knot a-creaking!" 360

Ah, with the Grape my fading Life provide,
And wash the Body whence the Life has died,
  And lay me, shrouded in the living Leaf,
By some not unfrequented Garden-side—

That ev'n my buried Ashes such a snare 365
Of Vintage shall fling up into the Air
  As not a True-believer passing by
But shall be overtaken unaware.

Indeed the Idols I have loved so long
Have done my credit in this World much wrong, 370
  Have drowned my Glory in a shallow Cup,
And sold my Reputation for a Song.

Indeed, indeed, Repentance oft before
I swore—but was I sober when I swore?
  And then and then came Spring, and Rose-in-hand 375
My thread-bare Penitence apieces tore.

And much as Wine has played the Infidel,
And robbed me of my Robe of Honor—Well,
  I wonder often what the Vintners buy
One-half so precious as the stuff they sell. 380

Yet Ah, that Spring should vanish with the Rose!
That Youth's sweet-scented manuscript should close!
  The Nightingale that in the branches sang,
Ah whence, and whither flown again, who knows!

Would but the Desert of the Fountain yield 385
One glimpse—if dimly, yet indeed, revealed,

---

326. **Ramazán**, the fasting month of the Mohammedans, during which they ate no food between sunrise and sunset. 346. **Súfi**, a member of a Persian sect whose purpose was to gain insight into the Divine Being through contemplation. 358. **Moon . . . seeking**, the new moon, which would mark the end of the fasting period. 360. **shoulder-knot a-creaking**, with the load of wine he was carrying. The shoulder-knot was a strap on which the jars were hung. 369. **Idols**, wine and wine-poetry.

To which the fainting Traveler might spring,
As springs the trampled herbage of the field!

Would but some wingéd Angel ere too late
Arrest the yet unfolded Roll of Fate, 390
And make the stern Recorder otherwise
Enregister, or quite obliterate!

Ah, Love! could you and I with Him conspire
To grasp this sorry Scheme of Things entire,
Would not we shatter it to bits—and then
Remold it nearer to the Heart's Desire! 396

Yon rising Moon that looks for us again—
How oft hereafter will she wax and wane;
How oft hereafter rising look for us
Through this same Garden—and for *one* in vain! 400

And when like her, O Sákí, you shall pass
Among the Guests Star-scattered on the Grass,
And in your joyous errand reach the spot
Where I made One—turn down an empty Glass!

(1859, 1868, 1872, 1879)

Dante Gabriel Rossetti

1828-1882

Some of the facts of Dante Gabriel Rossetti's life and art have already been given in connection with his sister Christina (see p. 748) and the Pre-Raphaelite Brotherhood (see pp. 416 and 749). Something, however, needs to be added here. Dante Gabriel, like Ruskin, was accomplished in two major arts, for he was at the same time a painter and a poet. His expression of himself in words and in pigments was the same; in both forms of art he was a sensitive, sensuous, beauty-loving romanticist, who gave to his poetry a richness and an abundance of physical detail that is Italian and southern rather than English and northern.

Like his sister Christina he was born in London, but unlike her he had a formal education. He attended King's College School from 1837 to 1843; and, finding himself intensely interested in painting, he then studied art at Cary's Art Museum, and became in 1846 a student at the Royal Academy. Subsequently he painted for a short time in the studio of his friend Ford Madox Brown. His association in 1849 with the Pre-Raphaelite Brotherhood has been detailed at some length (p. 416). To the little magazine of that unusual group of painters and poets—*The Germ*— he contributed in 1850 eleven of his finest lyrics including *My Sister's Sleep* and *The Blessed Damozel*. In this year also he became acquainted with Elizabeth Siddall, the lovely daughter of a London tradesman, and three years later they were betrothed. His lack of money made an immediate marriage impossible, however, and they were not married until 1860. In the meantime she sat as the model for his paintings and served as the inspiration for his poetry. Elizabeth Siddall had the pale, lily-like beauty which was the incarnation of the romantic mood as the Pre-Raphaelites conceived it. She was the "blessed damozel" of Rossetti's visions. Her interest in his work was probably increased by the circumstance that she painted in water-colors. But she was too frail to "serve as human nature's daily food," and in 1862 she died of a baffling malady, leaving him disconsolate. His grief was so great that he buried in her coffin a bundle of manuscript poems of which he had kept no copy. Seven years later these were recovered; they were published in 1870 under the title *Poems*. This volume contains his sonnet sequence, *The House of Life*, a record of his love for his wife, and other lyrics. He was neurotic by temperament, and this tendency increased after his wife's death. Failing eyesight cut him off from painting, and he turned to his poetry for what comfort he could get. To cure chronic insomnia he began taking chloral; this treatment brought on hallucinations and depression of spirits, and his last years were spent almost in seclusion. He died in 1882, just a year after the appearance of his last volume, *Ballads and Sonnets*.

Like Ruskin and like the other Pre-Raphaelites, Rossetti was a romanticist whose theory of art carried him back of the Renaissance and into the Middle Ages. There is about his sensuous, beauty-saturated poetry a heady exotic intoxication. Filled with physical details it forms a sharp contrast with the stark realism of some of the Victorian verse which dealt with social problems, and suggests the birth of a new romantic spirit. In spite of the abundance of physical detail, its tone is often remote and mystic; and in texture and technique it is highly sophisticated. It is the work, in brief, of a sensitive, delicately-balanced artist who yielded without restraint to his visions and his emotions and reveled in the luxury of poetic color and melody.

The Blessed Damozel

The poet designed this poem as a complement to Poe's *The Raven* (1845), which represents a lover yearning hopelessly for "a sainted maiden whom the angels name Lenore." "I saw," Rossetti said, "that Poe had done the utmost possible to do with the grief of the lover on earth, and I determined to reverse the conditions, and give utterance to the yearning of the loved one in heaven." Of the two poems, Rossetti's is naturally the more mystic.

The blessed damozel leaned out
  From the gold bar of heaven;
Her eyes were deeper than the depth
  Of waters stilled at even;
She had three lilies in her hand,   5
  And the stars in her hair were seven.

Her robe, ungirt from clasp to hem,
  No wrought flowers did adorn,
But a white rose of Mary's gift,
  For service meetly worn;   10
Her hair that lay along her back
  Was yellow like ripe corn.

Herseemed she scarce had been a day
  One of God's choristers;
The wonder was not yet quite gone   15
  From that still look of hers;

10. **For . . . worn**, fittingly worn in the service of the Virgin Mary. 13. **Herseemed**, it seemed to her.

Albeit, to them she left, her day
  Had counted as ten years.

(To *one* it is ten years of years.
  . . . Yet now, and in this place,   20
Surely she leaned o'er me—her hair
  Fell all about my face. . . .
Nothing: the autumn fall of leaves.
  The whole year sets apace.)

It was the rampart of God's house   25
  That she was standing on;
By God built over the sheer depth
  The which is Space begun;
So high, that looking downward thence
  She scarce could see the sun.   30

It lies in heaven, across the flood
  Of ether, as a bridge.
Beneath, the tides of day and night

With flame and darkness ridge
  The void, as low as where this earth   35
  Spins like a fretful midge.

Around her, lovers, newly met
  'Mid deathless love's acclaims,
Spoke evermore among themselves
  Their heart-remembered names;   40
And the souls mounting up to God
  Went by her like thin flames.

And still she bowed herself and stooped
  Out of the circling charm;
Until her bosom must have made   45
  The bar she leaned on warm,
And the lilies lay as if asleep
  Along her bended arm.

From the fixed place of heaven she saw
  Time like a pulse shake fierce   50
Through all the worlds. Her gaze still strove
  Within the gulf to pierce
Its path; and now she spoke as when
  The stars sang in their spheres.

The sun was gone now; the curled moon   55
  Was like a little feather
Fluttering far down the gulf; and now
  She spoke through the still weather.
Her voice was like the voice the stars
  Had when they sang together.   60

(Ah, sweet! Even now, in that bird's song,
  Strove not her accents there,
Fain to be harkened? When those bells
  Possessed the midday air,
Strove not her steps to reach my side   65
  Down all the echoing stair?)

"I wish that he were come to me,
  For he will come," she said.
"Have I not prayed in heaven?—on earth,
  Lord, Lord, has he not prayed?   70
Are not two prayers a perfect strength?
  And shall I feel afraid?

"When round his head the aureole clings,
  And he is clothed in white,

I'll take his hand and go with him   75
  To the deep wells of light;
As unto a stream we will step down,
  And bathe there in God's sight.

"We two will stand beside that shrine,
  Occult, withheld, untrod,   80
Whose lamps are stirred continually
  With prayers sent up to God;
And see our old prayers, granted, melt
  Each like a little cloud.

"We two will lie i' the shadow of   85
  That living mystic tree
Within whose secret growth the Dove
  Is sometimes felt to be,
While every leaf that His plumes touch
  Saith His Name audibly.   90

"And I myself will teach to him,
  I myself, lying so,
The songs I sing here; which his voice
  Shall pause in, hushed and slow,
And find some knowledge at each pause,   95
  Or some new thing to know."

(Alas! We two, we two, thou say'st!
  Yea, one wast thou with me
That once of old. But shall God lift
  To endless unity   100
The soul whose likeness with thy soul
  Was but its love for thee?)

"We two," she said, "will seek the groves
  Where the lady Mary is,
With her five handmaidens, whose names   105
  Are five sweet symphonies,
Cecily, Gertrude, Magdalen,
  Margaret, and Rosalys.

"Circlewise sit they, with bound locks
  And foreheads garlanded;   110
Into the fine cloth white like flame

---

36. **midge**, a kind of small gnat. 54. **stars . . . spheres.** See p. 775, note 72.

86. **living . . . tree**, the tree of life (see *Revelation*, 22). 87. **Dove**, a symbol of the Holy Spirit, the third member of the Trinity; cf. *Luke*, 3:22. 107. **Cecily . . . Rosalys.** These are names of famous Christian saints. *St. Cecilia* (third century) is the patron saint of the blind and of musicians (see Dryden's *A Song for St. Cecilia's Day*, Vol. I, p. 868); *St. Gertrude* (seventh century) is the patron saint of travelers; *St. Mary Magdalen* is the patron saint of penitents; *St. Margaret* is the chosen type of female innocence and meekness; *St. Rosalie* (twelfth century) is the patron saint of the city of Palermo, Sicily.

Weaving the golden thread,
To fashion the birth-robes for them
Who are just born, being dead.

"He shall fear, haply, and be dumb; 115
Then will I lay my cheek
To his, and tell about our love,
Not once abashed or weak;
And the dear Mother will approve
My pride, and let me speak. 120

"Herself shall bring us, hand in hand,
To Him round whom all souls
Kneel, the clear-ranged unnumbered heads
Bowed with their aureoles;
And angels meeting us shall sing 125
To their citherns and citoles.

"There will I ask of Christ the Lord
Thus much for him and me—
Only to live as once on earth
With Love, only to be, 130
As then awhile, forever now,
Together, I and he."

She gazed and listened and then said,
Less sad of speech than mild—
"All this is when he comes." She ceased. 135
The light thrilled toward her, filled
With angels in strong, level flight.
Her eyes prayed, and she smiled.

(I saw her smile.) But soon their path
Was vague in distant spheres; 140
And then she cast her arms along
The golden barriers,
And laid her face between her hands,
And wept. (I heard her tears.)
(*1847;* 1850, 1856, 1870)

My Sister's Sleep

This is an imaginative poem without basis of fact in Rossetti's life.

She fell asleep on Christmas Eve;
 At length the long-ungranted shade
Of weary eyelids overweighed
 The pain naught else might yet relieve.

Our mother, who had leaned all day 5
 Over the bed from chime to chime,
 Then raised herself for the first time,
And as she sat her down, did pray.

Her little work-table was spread
 With work to finish. For the glare, 10
 Made by her candle, she had care
To work some distance from the bed.

Without, there was a cold moon up,
 Of winter radiance sheer and thin;
 The hollow halo it was in 15
Was like an icy crystal cup.

Through the small room, with subtle sound
 Of flame, by vents the fireshine drove
 And reddened. In its dim alcove
The mirror shed a clearness round. 20

I had been sitting up some nights,
 And my tired mind felt weak and blank;
 Like a sharp strengthening wine it drank
The stillness and the broken lights.

Twelve struck. That sound, by dwindling years 25
 Heard in each hour, crept off; and then
 The ruffled silence spread again,
Like water that a pebble stirs.

Our mother rose from where she sat;
 Her needles, as she laid them down, 30
 Met lightly, and her silken gown
Settled—no other noise than that.

"Glory unto the Newly Born!"
 So, as said angels, she did say;
 Because we were in Christmas Day, 35
Though it would still be long till morn.

Just then in the room over us
 There was a pushing back of chairs,
 As some who had sat unawares
So late, now heard the hour, and rose. 40

126. **citherns and citoles,** medieval stringed musical instruments.

25. **dwindling years,** old persons.

With anxious, softly-stepping haste
  Our mother went where Margaret lay,
    Fearing the sounds o'erhead—should they
Have broken her long-watched-for rest!

She stooped an instant, calm, and turned, 45
  But suddenly turned back again;
    And all her features seemed in pain
With woe, and her eyes gazed and yearned.

For my part, I but hid my face,
  And held my breath, and spoke no word. 50
    There was none spoken; but I heard
The silence for a little space.

Our mother bowed herself and wept;
  And both my arms fell, and I said,
    "God knows I knew that she was dead." 55
And there, all white, my sister slept.

Then kneeling, upon Christmas morn
  A little after twelve o'clock
    We said, ere the first quarter struck,
"Christ's blessing on the newly born!" 60
              (*1847; 1850*)

The Sea-Limits

Consider the sea's listless chime:
  Time's self it is, made audible—
    The murmur of the earth's own shell.
Secret continuance sublime
  Is the sea's end; our sight may pass 5
    No furlong further. Since time was,
This sound hath told the lapse of time.

No quiet, which is death's—it hath
  The mournfulness of ancient life,
    Enduring always at dull strife. 10
As the world's heart of rest and wrath,
  Its painful pulse is in the sands.
    Last utterly, the whole sky stands,
Gray and not known, along its path.

Listen alone beside the sea, 15
  Listen alone among the woods;
    Those voices of twin solitudes
Shall have one sound alike to thee.
  Hark where the murmurs of thronged men
    Surge and sink back and surge again— 20
Still the one voice of wave and tree.

Gather a shell from the strown beach
  And listen at its lips; they sigh
    The same desire and mystery,
The echo of the whole sea's speech. 25
  And all mankind is thus at heart
    Not anything but what thou art;
And Earth, Sea, Man, are all in each.
              (*1849; 1850*)

Sister Helen

    The basis of this poem is the old superstition that melting a waxen image of a person will bring suffering and death upon him. The false lover whom Helen is punishing is Keith of Ewern (l. 87). The refrain is a characteristic of the so-called Pre-Raphaelite ballads of the period. See *Ballad*, the parody by Calverley, p. 827.

"Why did you melt your waxen man,
        Sister Helen?
Today is the third since you began."
"The time was long, yet the time ran,
        Little brother." 5
      (*O Mother, Mary Mother,*
Three days today, between Hell and Heaven!)

"But if you have done your work aright,
        Sister Helen,
You'll let me play, for you said I might." 10
"Be very still in your play tonight,
        Little brother."
      (*O Mother, Mary Mother,*
Third night, tonight, between Hell and Heaven!)

"You said it must melt ere vesper-bell, 15
        Sister Helen;
If now it be molten, all is well."
"Even so—nay, peace! you cannot tell,
        Little brother."
      (*O Mother, Mary Mother,* 20
Oh, what is this, between Hell and Heaven?)

"Oh, the waxen knave was plump today,
        Sister Helen;
How like dead folk he has dropped away!"
"Nay now, of the dead what can you say,   25
        Little brother?"
        (*O Mother, Mary Mother,*
What of the dead, between Hell and Heaven?)

"See, see, the sunken pile of wood,
        Sister Helen,   30
Shines through the thinned wax red as blood!"
"Nay now, when looked you yet on blood,
        Little brother?"
        (*O Mother, Mary Mother,* 34
How pale she is, between Hell and Heaven!)

"Now close your eyes, for they're sick and sore,
        Sister Helen,
And I'll play without the gallery door."
"Aye, let me rest—I'll lie on the floor,
        Little brother."   40
        (*O Mother, Mary Mother,*
What rest tonight, between Hell and Heaven?)

"Here high up in the balcony,
        Sister Helen,
The moon flies face to face with me."   45
"Aye, look and say whatever you see,
        Little brother."
        (*O Mother, Mary Mother,*
What sight tonight, between Hell and Heaven?)

"Outside it's merry in the wind's wake,   50
        Sister Helen;
In the shaken trees the chill stars shake."
"Hush, heard you a horse-tread as you spake,
        Little brother?"
        (*O Mother, Mary Mother,* 55
What sound tonight, between Hell and Heaven?)

"I hear a horse-tread, and I see,
        Sister Helen,
Three horsemen that ride terribly."
"Little brother, whence come the three,   60
       Little brother?"
        (*O Mother, Mary Mother,*
Whence should they come, between Hell and Heaven?)

"They come by the hill-verge from Boyne Bar,
        Sister Helen,   65
And one draws nigh, but two are afar."
"Look, look, do you know them who they are,
        Little brother?"
        (*O Mother, Mary Mother,*
Who should they be, between Hell and Heaven?)   70

"Oh, it's Keith of Eastholm rides so fast,
        Sister Helen,
For I know the white mane on the blast."
"The hour has come, has come at last,
        Little brother!"   75
        (*O Mother, Mary Mother,*
Her hour at last, between Hell and Heaven!)

"He has made a sign and called Halloo!
        Sister Helen,
And he says that he would speak with you."
"Oh, tell him I fear the frozen dew,   81
        Little brother."
        (*O Mother, Mary Mother,*
Why laughs she thus, between Hell and Heaven?)

"The wind is loud, but I hear him cry,   85
        Sister Helen,
That Keith of Ewern's like to die."
"And he and thou, and thou and I,
        Little brother."
        (*O Mother, Mary Mother,* 90
And they and we, between Hell and Heaven!)

"Three days ago, on his marriage-morn,
        Sister Helen,
He sickened, and lies since then forlorn."
"For bridegroom's side is the bride a thorn,   95
        Little brother?"
        (*O Mother, Mary Mother,*
Cold bridal cheer, between Hell and Heaven!)

"Three days and nights now he has lain abed,
        Sister Helen,   100

---

64. **Boyne Bar**, a famous sand bar at the mouth of the Boyne River, Leinster, Ireland.

And he prays in torment to be dead."
"The thing may chance, if he have prayed,
   Little brother!"
  (*O Mother, Mary Mother,*
If he have prayed, between Hell and Heaven!)

"But he has not ceased to cry today,   106
   Sister Helen,
That you should take your curse away."
"*My* prayer was heard—he need but pray,
   Little brother!"   110
  (*O Mother, Mary Mother,*
Shall God not hear, between Hell and Heaven?)

"But he says, till you take back your ban,
   Sister Helen,
His soul would pass, yet never can."   115
"Nay then, shall I slay a living man,
   Little brother?"
  (*O Mother, Mary Mother,*
A living soul, between Hell and Heaven!)

"But he calls forever on your name,   120
   Sister Helen,
And says that he melts before a flame."
"My heart for his pleasure fared the same,
   Little brother."
  (*O Mother, Mary Mother,* 125
Fire at the heart, between Hell and Heaven!)

"Here's Keith of Westholm riding fast,
   Sister Helen,
For I know the white plume on the blast."
"The hour, the sweet hour I forecast,   130
   Little brother!"
  (*O Mother, Mary Mother,*
Is the hour sweet, between Hell and Heaven!)

"He stops to speak, and he stills his horse,
   Sister Helen;   135
But his words are drowned in the wind's course."
"Nay hear, nay hear, you must hear perforce,
   Little brother!"
  (*O Mother, Mary Mother,*
What word now heard, between Hell and Heaven!)   140

"Oh, he says that Keith of Ewern's cry,
   Sister Helen,
Is ever to see you ere he die."
"In all that his soul sees, there am I,
   Little brother!"   145
  (*O Mother, Mary Mother,*
The soul's one sight, between Hell and Heaven!)

"He sends a ring and a broken coin,
   Sister Helen,
And bids you mind the banks of Boyne."   150
"What else he broke will he ever join,
   Little brother?"
  (*O Mother, Mary Mother,*
No, never joined, between Hell and Heaven!)

"He yields you these and craves full fain,   155
   Sister Helen,
You pardon him in his mortal pain."
"What else he took will he give again,
   Little brother?"
  (*O Mother, Mary Mother,* 160
Not twice to give, between Hell and Heaven!)

"He calls your name in an agony,
   Sister Helen,
That even dead Love must weep to see."
"Hate, born of Love, is blind as he,   165
   Little brother!"
  (*O Mother, Mary Mother,*
Love turned to hate, between Hell and Heaven!)

"Oh, it's Keith of Keith now that rides fast,
   Sister Helen,   170
For I know the white hair on the blast."
"The short, short hour will soon be past,
   Little brother!"
  (*O Mother, Mary Mother,*
Will soon be past, between Hell and Heaven!)

"He looks at me and he tries to speak,   176
   Sister Helen,
But oh! his voice is sad and weak!"
"What here should the mighty Baron seek,
   Little brother?"   180

148. **broken coin.** The two had broken a coin, and each had kept half as a pledge.

(O Mother, Mary Mother,
Is this the end, between Hell and Heaven?)

"Oh, his son still cries, if you forgive,
        Sister Helen,
The body dies, but the soul shall live."   185
"Fire shall forgive me as I forgive,
        Little brother!"
(O Mother, Mary Mother,
As she forgives, between Hell and Heaven!)

"Oh, he prays you, as his heart would rive, 190
        Sister Helen,
To save his dear son's soul alive."
"Fire cannot slay it; it shall thrive,
        Little brother!"
(O Mother, Mary Mother, 195
Alas, alas, between Hell and Heaven!)

"He cries to you, kneeling in the road,
        Sister Helen,
To go with him for the love of God!"
"The way is long to his son's abode,   200
        Little brother."
(O Mother, Mary Mother,
The way is long, between Hell and Heaven!)

"A lady's here, by a dark steed brought,
        Sister Helen,   205
So darkly clad, I saw her not."
"See her now or never see aught,
        Little brother!"
(O Mother, Mary Mother,
What more to see, between Hell and Heaven!)

"Her hood falls back, and the moon shines fair,   211
       Sister Helen,
On the Lady of Ewern's golden hair."
"Blest hour of my power and her despair,
        Little brother!"   215
(O Mother, Mary Mother,
Hour blest and banned, between Hell and Heaven!)

"Pale, pale her cheeks, that in pride did glow,
        Sister Helen,
'Neath the bridal-wreath three days ago."   220
"One morn for pride and three days for woe,
        Little brother!"
(O Mother, Mary Mother,
Three days, three nights, between Hell and Heaven!)

"Her clasped hands stretch from her bending head,   225
       Sister Helen;
With the loud wind's wail her sobs are wed."
"What wedding-strains hath her bridal-bed,
        Little brother?"
(O Mother, Mary Mother, 230
What strain but death's, between Hell and Heaven!)

"She may not speak, she sinks in a swoon,
        Sister Helen—
She lifts her lips and gasps on the moon."
"Oh! might I but hear her soul's blithe tune,
        Little brother!"   236
(O Mother, Mary Mother,
Her woe's dumb cry, between Hell and Heaven!)

"They've caught her to Westholm's saddle-bow,
        Sister Helen,   240
And her moonlit hair gleams white in its flow."
"Let it turn whiter than winter snow,
        Little brother!"
(O Mother, Mary Mother,
Woe-withered gold, between Hell and Heaven!)   245

"O Sister Helen, you heard the bell,
        Sister Helen!
More loud than the vesper-chime it fell."
"No vesper-chime, but a dying knell,
        Little brother!"   250
(O Mother, Mary Mother,
His dying knell, between Hell and Heaven!)

"Alas! but I fear the heavy sound,
        Sister Helen;
Is it in the sky or in the ground?"   255
"Say, have they turned their horses round,
        Little brother?"
(O Mother, Mary Mother,
What would she more, between Hell and Heaven?)

"They have raised the old man from his knee,
    Sister Helen, 261
And they ride in silence hastily."
"More fast the naked soul doth flee,
    Little brother!"
    (O Mother, Mary Mother, 265
The naked soul, between Hell and Heaven!)

"Flank to flank are the three steeds gone,
    Sister Helen,
But the lady's dark steed goes alone."
"And lonely her bridegroom's soul hath flown,
    Little brother." 271
    (O Mother, Mary Mother,
The lonely ghost, between Hell and Heaven!)

"Oh, the wind is sad in the iron chill,
    Sister Helen, 275
And weary sad they look by the hill."
"But Keith of Ewern's sadder still,
    Little brother!"
    (O Mother, Mary Mother, 279
Most sad of all, between Hell and Heaven!)

"See, see, the wax has dropped from its place,
    Sister Helen,
And the flames are winning up apace!"
"Yet here they burn but for a space,
    Little brother!" 285
    (O Mother, Mary Mother,
Here for a space, between Hell and Heaven!)

"Ah! what white thing at the door has crossed,
    Sister Helen?
Ah! what is this that sighs in the frost?" 290
"A soul that's lost as mine is lost,
    Little brother!"
    (O Mother, Mary Mother,
Lost, lost, all lost, between Hell and Heaven!)
    (1851-1852; 1853, 1870)

The Song of the Bower

Say, is it day, is it dusk in thy bower,
  Thou whom I long for, who longest for me?
Oh! be it light, be it light, 'tis Love's hour,
  Love's that is fettered as Love's that is free,
Free Love has leaped to that innermost chamber, 5
  Oh! the last time, and the hundred before;
Fettered Love, motionless, can but remember,
  Yet something that sighs from him passes the door.

Nay, but my heart when it flies to thy bower,
  What does it find there that knows it again?
There it must droop like a shower-beaten flower, 11
  Red at the rent core and dark with the rain.
Ah! yet what shelter is still shed above it—
  What waters still image its leaves torn apart?
Thy soul is the shade that clings round it to love it, 15
  And tears are its mirror deep down in thy heart.

What were my prize, could I enter thy bower,
  This day, tomorrow, at eve or at morn?
Large lovely arms and a neck like a tower,
  Bosom then heaving that now lies forlorn.
Kindled with love-breath (the sun's kiss is colder!) 21
  Thy sweetness all near me, so distant today;
My hand round thy neck and thy hand on my shoulder,
  My mouth to thy mouth as the world melts away. 24

What is it keeps me afar from thy bower—
  My spirit, my body, so fain to be there?
Waters engulfing or fires that devour?—
  Earth heaped against me or death in the air?
Nay, but in day-dreams, for terror, for pity,
  The trees wave their heads with an omen to tell; 30
Nay, but in night-dreams, throughout the dark city,
  The hours, clashed together, lose count in the bell.

Shall I not one day remember thy bower,
  One day when all days are one day to me?
Thinking, "I stirred not, and yet had the power"— 35
  Yearning, "Ah, God, if again it might be!"
Peace, peace! such a small lamp illumes, on this highway,
  So dimly so few steps in front of my feet—

Yet shows me that her way is parted from my
    way. . . .
Out of my sight, beyond light, at what goal
    may we meet?   (1870)

The Ballad of Dead Ladies

(FROM FRANÇOIS VILLON)

The Ballad of Dead Ladies is a translation of *Ballade des Dames du Temp Jadis,* by François Villon, the greatest of the French medieval poets. (See Swinburne's *A Ballad of François Villon,* p. 821.)

Tell me now in what hidden way is
    Lady Flora the lovely Roman?
Where's Hipparchia, and where is Thaïs,
    Neither of them the fairer woman?
    Where is Echo, beheld of no man,   5
Only heard on river and mere—
    She whose beauty was more than human? . . .
But where are the snows of yester-year?

Where's Héloïse, the learned nun,
    For whose sake Abeillard, I ween,   10
Lost manhood and put priesthood on?
    (From Love he won such dule and teen!)
And where, I pray you, is the Queen
Who willed that Buridan should steer
    Sewed in a sack's mouth down the Seine? . . .   15
But where are the snows of yester-year?

White Queen Blanche, like a queen of lilies,
    With a voice like any mermaiden—
Bertha Broadfoot, Beatrice, Alice,
    And Ermengarde the lady of Maine—   20
And that good Joan whom Englishmen
At Rouen doomed and burned her there—
    Mother of God, where are they then? . . .
But where are the snows of yester-year?

Nay, never ask this week, fair lord,   25
    Where they are gone, nor yet this year,
Except with this for an overword—
But where are the snows of yester-year?
    (*1869;* 1869)

Troy Town

The basis of the poem is the legend repeated by Pliny (23-79 A.D.), Roman historian and naturalist, that Helen of Troy dedicated to Venus, the goddess of love, a goblet molded in the shape of her breast. Woven into the poem is also the story of the elopement of Helen with Paris, son of Priam, King of Troy. At the wedding of Peleus and Thetis the goddess of discord had thrown among the guests a golden apple inscribed "To the Fairest." Juno, Minerva, and Venus all claimed it, but Paris, called upon to make the award, gave it to Venus. In return Venus gave him Helen, with the ultimate result that Troy was besieged, sacked, and burned by the angry Greeks under the leadership of Helen's husband, Menelaus, King of Sparta.

Heavenborn Helen, Sparta's queen,
    (*O Troy Town!*)
Had two breasts of heavenly sheen,
The sun and moon of the heart's desire:
All Love's lordship lay between.   5
    (*O Troy's down!*
        Tall Troy's on fire.)

---

2. **Lady Flora,** perhaps the Roman goddess of flowers and spring; other identifications made her a wealthy and beautiful woman, or any one of several famous courtesans of Rome, named Flora. 3. **Hipparchia,** the wife of Crates, the famous Cynic philosopher of Thebes, Greece (third century B.C.). **Thaïs,** perhaps the celebrated Athenian courtesan who accompanied Alexander the Great on his expedition into Asia, 331 B.C.; see Dryden's *Alexander's Feast,* 9 (Vol. I, p. 869). Another Thaïs was the famous Egyptian courtesan who became a saint. 5. **Echo,** a beautiful nymph who for love of Narcissus pined away until nothing was left of her but her voice. 9. **Héloïse,** the beautiful niece of Canon Fulbert, of Paris. She fell in love with her teacher, Pierre Abélard (1079-1142), a scholastic philosopher and theologian. After they eloped and were married, she returned to her uncle's house and denied the marriage, in order that her love might not be a hindrance to Abélard's advancement in the church. Fulbert was so enraged at this move that he caused Abélard to be emasculated in order to make him canonically incapable of ecclesiastical preferment. Abélard then became a monk in the abbey of St. Denis, in Paris, and induced Héloïse to become a nun. 10. **ween,** think. 12. **dule and teen,** grief and pain. 13. **the Queen,** Marguerite de Bourgogne, wife of Louis le Hutin (fourteenth century). She is the heroine of the legend of the Tour de Nesle, according to which she had her numerous lovers killed and thrown into the Seine; one of them, *Jean Buridan,* rector of the University of Paris, escaped this fate.

17. **Queen Blanche,** probably Blanche of Castille, mother of Louis IX, king of France (1226-1270). 19. **Bertha Broadfoot,** the mother of Charlemagne (742-814), King of the Franks and Emperor of the West. She is a prominent character in medieval romances dealing with Charlemagne and his court. **Beatrice, Alice.** These were names of various well-known women of the Middle Ages, and it is impossible to tell the exact persons meant. Beatrice might be Dante's Beatrice or Béatrix de Provence, wife of Charles, son of Louis VIII, King of France (1223-1226). Alice may be Aelis, one of the characters in the romance *Aliscans,* or Alix de Champagne, wife of Louis le Jeune (twelfth century). 20. **Ermengarde,** the daughter of d'Helie, Count of Maine, an old province in northwestern France. She was the wife of Foulques V, Count of Anjou. She died in 1126. 21. **Joan,** Joan of Arc (1412-1431), who saved France from conquest, but who later was imprisoned at Rouen, France, by the English, convicted of witchcraft and heresy, and burned at the stake. She was made a saint in 1920.

Helen knelt at Venus' shrine,
          (*O Troy Town!*)
Saying, "A little gift is mine,
A little gift for a heart's desire.
Hear me speak and make me a sign!
          (*O Troy's down,*
          Tall Troy's on fire!)

"Look, I bring thee a carven cup;
          (*O Troy Town!*)
See it here as I hold it up—
Shaped it is to the heart's desire,
Fit to fill when the gods would sup.
          (*O Troy's down,*
          Tall Troy's on fire!)

"It was molded like my breast;
          (*O Troy Town!*)
He that sees it may not rest,
Rest at all for his heart's desire.
O give ear to my heart's behest!
          (*O Troy's down,*
          Tall Troy's on fire!)

See my breast, how like it is;
          (*O Troy Town!*)
See it bare for the air to kiss!
Is the cup to thy heart's desire?
O for the breast, O make it his!
          (*O Troy's down,*
          Tall Troy's on fire!)

"Yea, for my bosom here I sue:
          (*O Troy Town!*)
Thou must give it where 'tis due,
Give it there to the heart's desire.
Whom do I give my bosom to?
          (*O Troy's down,*
          Tall Troy's on fire!)

"Each twin breast is an apple sweet!
          (*O Troy Town!*)
Once an apple stirred the beat
Of thy heart with the heart's desire:
Say, who brought it then to thy feet?
          (*O Troy's down,*
          Tall Troy's on fire!)

"They that claimed it then were three:
          (*O Troy Town!*)
For thy sake two hearts did he
Make forlorn of the heart's desire.
Do for him as he did for thee!
          (*O Troy's down,*
          Tall Troy's on fire!)

"Mine are apples grown to the south,
          (*O Troy Town!*)
Grown to taste in the days of drouth,
Taste and waste to the heart's desire:
Mine are apples meet for his mouth!"
          (*O Troy's down,*
          Tall Troy's on fire!)

Venus looked on Helen's gift,
          (*O Troy Town!*)
Looked and smiled with subtle drift,
Saw the work of her heart's desire—
"There thou kneel'st for Love to lift!"
          (*O Troy's down,*
          Tall Troy's on fire!)

Venus looked in Helen's face,
          (*O Troy Town!*)
Knew far off an hour and place,
And fire lit from the heart's desire;
Laughed and said, "Thy gift hath grace!"
          (*O Troy's down,*
          Tall Troy's on fire!)

Cupid looked on Helen's breast,
          (*O Troy Town!*)
Saw the heart within its nest,
Saw the flame of the heart's desire—
Marked his arrow's burning crest.
          (*O Troy's down,*
          Tall Troy's on fire!)

Cupid took another dart,
          (*O Troy Town!*)
Fledged it for another heart,
Winged the shaft with the heart's desire,
Drew the string and said, "Depart!"
          (*O Troy's down,*
          Tall Troy's on fire!)

Paris turned upon his bed,
          (*O Troy Town!*)

---

45. **apple**, the golden apple of discord.

Turned upon his bed and said,
Dead at heart with the heart's desire— 95
"O to clasp her golden head!"
>   (*O Troy's down,*
>   *Tall Troy's on fire!*)
>   (1870)

Autumn Song

Know'st thou not at the fall of the leaf
How the heart feels a languid grief
   Laid on it for a covering;

Autumn Song. Cf. Keats's *To Autumn,* p. 291.

And how sleep seems a goodly thing
In Autumn at the fall of the leaf? 5

And how the swift beat of the brain
Falters because it is in vain,
   In Autumn at the fall of the leaf
   Knowest thou not? and how the chief
Of joys seems—not to suffer pain? 10

Know'st thou not at the fall of the leaf
How the soul feels like a dried sheaf
   Bound up at length for harvesting,
   And how death seems a comely thing
In Autumn at the fall of the leaf? (*1848;* 1883)

from *The House of Life*

These sonnets were written during a period of thirty-three years—1848-1881. Although they do not form an organic whole, they fulfill the mission indicated in the introductory sonnet. The title came from Rossetti's interest in astrology, according to which the heavens were regarded as divided into "houses," the most important of which was the "house of human life." The sonnets are largely autobiographical. They were mainly inspired by Elizabeth Siddall, with whom Rossetti fell deeply in love in 1850 and whom he married in 1860; see biographical sketch, page 783.

THE SONNET

A sonnet is a moment's monument—
Memorial from the Soul's eternity
To one dead deathless hour. Look that it be,
Whether for lustral rite or dire portent,
Of its own arduous fullness reverent. 5
Carve it in ivory or in ebony,
As Day or Night may rule; and let Time see
Its flowering crest impearled and orient.
A sonnet is a coin; its face reveals
The Soul—its converse, to what Power 'tis
   due:— 10
Whether for tribute to the august appeals
Of Life, or dower in Love's high retinue,
It serve; or 'mid the dark wharf's cavernous
   breath,
In Charon's palm it pay the toll to Death.
                                    (*1880;* 1881)

18. GENIUS IN BEAUTY

Beauty like hers is genius. Not the call
Of Homer's or of Dante's heart sublime—

The Sonnet. 4. *lustral rite,* ceremony of purification. 14. *Charon's . . . Death.* Charon was the boatman who ferried the souls of the dead over the Styx, one of the rivers of Hades. His pay was a coin found in the mouth of the passenger.

Not Michael's hand furrowing the zones of
   time—
Is more with compassed mysteries musical;
Nay, not in Spring's or Summer's sweet foot-
   fall 5
More gathered gifts exuberant Life bequeathes
Than doth this sovereign face, whose love-
   spell breathes
Even from its shadowed contour on the wall.
As many men are poets in their youth,
But for one sweet-strung soul the wires pro-
   long 10
Even through all change the indomitable
   song;
So in like wise the envenomed years, whose
   tooth
Rends shallower grace with ruin void of ruth,
Upon this beauty's power shall wreak no
   wrong.   (1881)

19. SILENT NOON

Your hands lie open in the long, fresh grass—
The finger-points look through like rosy
   blooms;

3. **Michael,** Michelangelo (1475-1564), a celebrated Italian painter, sculptor, and architect. The reference is to his figures of "Day," "Evening," "Night," etc.

Your eyes smile peace. The pasture gleams
    and glooms
'Neath billowing skies that scatter and amass.
All round our nest, far as the eye can pass,   5
Are golden kingcup-fields with silver edge
Where the cow-parsley skirts the hawthorn
    hedge.
'Tis visible silence, still as the hour-glass.
Deep in the sun-searched growths the dragon-
    fly
Hangs like a blue thread loosened from the
    sky—   10
So this winged hour is dropped to us from
    above.
Oh! clasp we to our hearts, for deathless dower,
This close-companioned inarticulate hour
When twofold silence was the song of love.
    (1881)

24. PRIDE OF YOUTH

Even as a child, of sorrow that we give
The dead, but little in his heart can find,
Since without need of thought to his clear
    mind
Their turn it is to die and his to live—
Even so the winged New Love smiles to re-
    ceive   5
Along his eddying plumes the auroral wind,
Nor, forward glorying, casts one look behind
Where night-rack shrouds the Old Love fugi-
    tive.
There is a change in every hour's recall,
And the last cowslip in the fields we see   10
On the same day with the first corn-poppy.
Alas for hourly change! Alas for all
The loves that from his hand proud Youth
    lets fall,
Even as the beads of a told rosary!   (1881)

48. DEATH-IN-LOVE

There came an image in Life's retinue
That had Love's wings and bore his gonfalon;
Fair was the web, and nobly wrought thereon,
O soul-sequestered face, thy form and hue!
Bewildering sounds, such as spring wakens to,
Shook in its folds; and through my heart its
    power   6
Sped trackless as the immemorial hour

<small>Sonnet 24. 14. told, counted.
Sonnet 48. 2. gonfalon, banner.</small>

When birth's dark portal groaned and all was
    new.
But a veiled woman followed, and she caught
The banner round its staff, to furl and cling—
Then plucked a feather from the bearer's
    wing,   11
And held it to his lips that stirred it not,
And said to me, "Behold, there is no breath;
I and this Love are one, and I am Death."
    (1870)

53. WITHOUT HER

What of her glass without her? The blank
    gray
There where the pool is blind of the moon's
    face.
Her dress without her? The tossed empty space
Of cloud-rack whence the moon has passed
    away.   4
Her paths without her? Day's appointed sway
Usurped by desolate night. Her pillowed place
Without her? Tears, ah me! for love's good
    grace,
And cold forgetfulness of night or day.
What of the heart without her? Nay, poor
    heart,
Of thee what word remains ere speech be still?
A wayfarer by barren ways and chill,   11
Steep ways and weary, without her thou art,
Where the long cloud, the long wood's coun-
    terpart,
Sheds doubled darkness up the laboring hill.
    (1881)

55. STILLBORN LOVE

The hour which might have been yet might
    not be,
Which man's and woman's heart conceived
    and bore
Yet whereof life was barren—on what shore
Bides it the breaking of Time's weary sea?
Bondchild of all consummate joys set free,   5
It somewhere sighs and serves, and mute be-
    fore
The house of Love, hears through the echoing
    door
His hours elect in choral consonancy.
But lo! what wedded souls now hand in hand
Together tread at last the immortal strand   10

With eyes where burning memory lights love
    home?
Lo! how the little outcast hour has turned
And leaped to them and in their faces
    yearned—
"I am your child; O parents, ye have come!"
(1869; 1870)

69. AUTUMN IDLENESS

This sunlight shames November where he
    grieves
In dead red leaves, and will not let him shun
The day, though bough with bough be over-
    run.
But with a blessing every glade receives
High salutation; while from hillock-eaves   5
The deer gaze calling, dappled white and dun,
As if, being foresters of old, the sun
Had marked them with the shade of forest-
    leaves.
Here dawn today unveiled her magic glass;
Here noon now gives the thirst and takes the
    dew;   10
Till eve bring rest when other good things
    pass.
And here the lost hours the lost hours renew
While I still lead my shadow o'er the grass,
Nor know, for longing, that which I should
    do.   (1870)

77. SOUL'S BEAUTY
(*Sibylla Palmifera*)

    The original title of this sonnet was *Sibylla Palmifera*, and it was written for a painting so named. In the picture, Sibyl, the ancient prophetess, bears a palm branch and is seated on a throne beneath a canopy of stone overlooking the court of a temple.

Under the arch of Life, where love and death,
Terror and mystery, guard her shrine I saw
Beauty enthroned; and though her gaze
    struck awe,
I drew it in as simply as my breath.
Hers are the eyes which, over and beneath,   5
The sky and sea bend on thee—which can
    draw,
By sea or sky or woman, to one law,
The allotted bondman of her palm and
    wreath.

Sonnet 69. Cf. *Autumn Song,* p. 794.

This is that Lady Beauty, in whose praise
Thy voice and hand shake still;—long known
    to thee   10
By flying hair and fluttering hem—the beat
Following her daily of thy heart and feet,
How passionately and irretrievably,
In what fond flight, how many ways and
    days!   (*1866;* 1870)

78. BODY'S BEAUTY
(*Lilith*)

    Originally called *Lilith,* this sonnet was written for a painting entitled *Lady Lilith.* Lilith was the traditional first wife of Adam. In both the painting and the sonnet she represents fleshly beauty and passion.

Of Adam's first wife, Lilith, it is told
(The witch he loved before the gift of Eve)
That, ere the snake's, her sweet tongue could
    deceive,
And her enchanted hair was the first gold.
And still she sits, young while the earth is old,
And, subtly of herself contemplative,   6
Draws men to watch the bright web she can
    weave,
Till heart and body and life are in its hold.
The rose and poppy are her flowers; for where
Is he not found, O Lilith, whom shed scent   10
And soft-shed kisses and soft sleep shall snare?
Lo! as that youth's eyes burned at thine, so
    went
Thy spell through him, and left his straight
    neck bent
And round his heart one strangling golden
    hair.   (*1864;* 1870)

86. LOST DAYS

The lost days of my life until today,
What were they, could I see them on the street
Lie as they fell? Would they be ears of wheat
Sown once for food but trodden into clay?
Or golden coins squandered and still to
    pay?   5
Or drops of blood dabbling the guilty feet?
Or such spilt water as in dreams must cheat
The undying throats of hell, athirst alway?
I do not see them here; but after death
God knows I know the faces I shall see,   10
Each one a murdered self, with low last breath.

"I am thyself—what hast thou done to me?"
"And I—and I—thyself" (lo! each one saith),
"And thou thyself to all eternity!"
                              (*1858;* 1869)

Three Shadows

I looked and saw your eyes
  In the shadow of your hair,
As a traveler sees the stream
  In the shadow of the wood;
And I said, "My faint heart sighs,   5
  Ah me! to linger there,
To drink deep and to dream
  In that sweet solitude."

I looked and saw your heart
  In the shadow of your eyes,   10
As a seeker sees the gold
  In the shadow of the stream;
And I said, "Ah me! what art
  Should win the immortal prize,
Whose want must make life cold   15
  And heaven a hollow dream?"

I looked and saw your love
  In the shadow of your heart,
As a diver sees the pearl
  In the shadow of the sea;   20
And I murmured, not above
  My breath, but all apart—
"Ah! you can love, true girl,
  And is your love for me?"
                              (*1876;* 1881)

William Morris
1834-1896

The spiritual affinities of William Morris were with the Pre-Raphaelite lovers of pre-Renaissance art. He was one of the most persistent and skilful interpreters of medieval beauty to Victorian England and at the same time one of the most rational. Beneath the shock of thick hair which rose above his smooth, broad forehead was the brain of a visionary and dreamer who could devote himself, nevertheless, to the practical task of giving beauty of design and color to textiles, stained glass, carpets, furniture, and book-bindings. So his gift to England was not alone a philosophy of art; it included an actual transformation of Victorian commonplaceness and stuffy ugliness in the physical setting of life into the rare and beautiful.

Morris was the son of a wealthy broker of Walthamstow. He obtained his formal education at Marlborough and at Exeter College, Oxford. At Oxford his interest in architecture and painting was developed by an acquaintance with Edward Burne-Jones, the famous painter. This influence was so strong that for a time Morris was determined to devote his life to art. He gave up the idea in favor of a more practical career; but his artistic interests brought him an acquaintance with D. G. Rossetti and other painters and poets of the Pre-Raphaelite Brotherhood (see p. 416). With Rossetti, Burne-Jones, Madox Brown, and others as technical advisers, Morris founded a firm that sought to correct English taste by bringing art into English homes. Ultimately the business passed into the able hands of Morris alone, and he became widely known for the quality and beauty of the carpets, tapestries, and furniture which came from his factory. In 1891 he founded the famous Kelmscott Press at his country estate at Hammersmith on the Thames, and in the five-year period before his death he published fifty-three books remarkable for their beauty of print, paper, and binding. The crowning glory of these was the *Kelmscott Chaucer*. Whatever product Morris made—carpet, chair, book—brought into visible being the romance and loveliness of which he dreamed.

Like Ruskin, Morris allowed his hatred of the ugly and unjust in life to express itself in attacks on the existing order, but unlike Ruskin, he espoused the cause of socialism; for several years he was so ardent a socialist that he all but deserted his art and poetry for the cause. He became treasurer of the National Liberal League in 1879; and, seceding with others of the extreme left four years later, he assisted in forming the Social Democrat Federation and soon became the leader of the organization. Disappointed by the sordid lack of idealism of some of his associates, he lost the leadership in 1889 and returned to his poetry and his practical art. His *Dream of John Ball* (1888) and *News from Nowhere* (1891), a Utopian vision, are the important literary products of this episode in Morris's life; he wrote also a number of stirring "marching songs" for his companions in socialism.

Morris's first poems were strongly influenced by the Pre-Raphaelite tendencies in poetic technique (see p. 417). His later technique shows the marked influence of Chaucer, in the prevailing narrative quality and in a certain smooth fluency and factual quality in the details. But Morris does not have Chaucer's racy realism, for he was not the reporter of contemporary life that Chaucer was. In his later narratives particularly he used words as he used threads in his tapestries; with them he wove beautiful designs that suggest drifting, wandering tales rather than direct narratives. The tempo of his stories in verse is slow—almost static; the tone is melancholy; the descriptions are numerous; the characters are medieval and classical types of faint beauty but as little vital as the figures on a vase. Excepting for the propagandist romances of the years of his socialistic activity, his writings had one main purpose—to express in the melody of words the same beauty which he expressed in his woods, glass, and textiles. As a result his verse almost cloys the reader with its high color and profuse richness.

The first of Morris's publications was *The Defense of Guenevere and Other Poems* (1858). It was characterized by the Pre-Raphaelite style of his early manner. His *Life and Death of Jason* (1867), written in heroic couplets, was a romantic treatment of the Greek tale of Jason and Medea. In *The Earthly Paradise* (1868-1870) he combined in a prologue, epilogue, and twenty-four tales an equal number of Greek legends and Norse sagas. His framework in this poem suggests the influence of Chaucer's *Canterbury Tales*, although the scheme by which he divides the stories according to the months of the year with appropriate lyrics for each month has the flavor of the *Shepheardes Calender* plan. Two journeys to Iceland inspired what may be regarded as his greatest long poem, *Sigurd the Volsung* (1876), a retelling of the great Norse saga in four books of anapestic couplets. After his excursion into socialistic writing he undertook an amazing series of light prose romances, adorned with lyrics, that are totally different from any type of writing which appeared elsewhere in Victorian England. To these he gave the poetic titles of *The House of the Wolfings* (1889), *The Story of the Glittering Plain* (1890), *The Roots of the Mountains* (1890), *The Wood Beyond the World* (1894), *Child Christopher* (1895), *The Well at the World's End* (1896), *The Water of the Wondrous Isles* (1897), and *The Story of the Sundering Flood* (1898). These have the same flavor of remote and pensive beauty as have his long poems. The last of them were published after his death; Morris carried to the end of his career the eagerness for expressing beauty with which he began it.

The Defense of Guenevere

An instinct for the picturesque and the dramatic led Morris to select from classical and medieval legends those episodes and situations which are most vivid and tense. In *The Defense of Guenevere* he represents King Arthur's queen as defending herself against the charge of adultery with Sir Launcelot which was brought against her by Sir Gauwaine. This was her second trial on the same charge; at the first she was saved by Launcelot, who slew her accuser, Sir Mellyagraunce, in a trial by combat (see ll. 166-219). In her defense at the second trial she accuses Sir Gauwaine of plotting and of perjury; but her infatuation for Sir Launcelot is so great that she seems more intent on praising him than on attempting to establish her own innocence (ll. 132-141). Morris drew the general material for his poem from Malory's *Morte Darthur* (Vol. I, p. 279 ff.), but changed many of the details. Furthermore, he brings into his account of the relations of Launcelot and Guenevere none of the morality which appears in Tennyson's *Idylls of the King* (p. 646), where the sin of the knight and the queen destroyed the virtue of the Table Round. *The Defense of Guenevere* is written in the *terza rima*, or three-line iambic pentameter stanza.

But, knowing now that they would have her speak,
She threw her wet hair backward from her brow,
Her hand close to her mouth touching her cheek,

As though she had had there a shameful blow,
And feeling it shameful to feel aught but shame
All through her heart, yet felt her cheek burned so,   6

She must a little touch it; like one lame
She walked away from Gauwaine, with her head
Still lifted up; and on her cheek of flame

The tears dried quick; she stopped at last and said: 10
"O knights and lords, it seems but little skill
To talk of well-known things past now and dead.

"God wot I ought to say, I have done ill,
And pray you all forgiveness heartily!
Because you must be right, such great lords; still   15

"Listen—suppose your time were come to die,
And you were quite alone and very weak;
Yea, laid a-dying, while very mightily

"The wind was ruffling up the narrow streak
Of river through your broad lands running well;   20
Suppose a hush should come, then someone speak:

"'One of these cloths is heaven, and one is hell;
Now choose one cloth forever—which they be,
I will not tell you; you must somehow tell

11. **skill**, reason, wisdom. 13. **wot**, knows.

"'Of your own strength and mightiness; here, see!'   25
Yea, yea, my lord, and you to ope your eyes,
At foot of your familiar bed to see

"A great God's angel standing, with such dyes,
Not known on earth, on his great wings, and hands,
Held out two ways, light from the inner skies

"Showing him well, and making his commands   31
Seem to be God's commands, moreover, too,
Holding within his hands the cloths on wands;

"And one of these strange choosing cloths was blue,
Wavy and long, and one cut short and red;   35
No man could tell the better of the two.

"After a shivering half-hour you said:
'God help! heaven's color, the blue'; and he said, 'hell.'
Perhaps you would then roll upon your bed,

"And cry to all good men that loved you well,
'Ah, Christ! if only I had known, known, known';   41
Launcelot went away, then I could tell,

"Like wisest man how all things would be, moan,
And roll and hurt myself, and long to die,
And yet fear much to die for what was sown.

"Nevertheless, you, O Sir Gauwaine, lie;   46
Whatever may have happened through these years,
God knows I speak truth, saying that you lie."

46. **you . . . lie.** Gauwaine is here presented as an accuser. See headnote.

Her voice was low at first, being full of tears,
But as it cleared, it grew full loud and shrill,
Growing a windy shriek in all men's ears, 51

A ringing in their startled brains, until
She said that Gauwaine lied, then her voice sunk,
And her great eyes began again to fill,

Though still she stood right up, and never shrunk, 55
But spoke on bravely, glorious lady fair!
Whatever tears her full lips may have drunk,

She stood, and seemed to think, and wrung her hair,
Spoke out at last with no more trace of shame,
With passionate twisting of her body there: 60

"It chanced upon a day that Launcelot came
To dwell at Arthur's court—at Christmas-time
This happened; when the heralds sung his name,

"Son of King Ban of Benwick, seemed to chime
Along with all the bells that rang that day, 65
O'er the white roofs, with little change of rime.

"Christmas and whitened winter passed away,
And over me the April sunshine came,
Made very awful with black hail-clouds; yea,

"And in the summer I grew white with flame,
And bowed my head down; autumn, and the sick 71
Sure knowledge things would never be the same,

"However often spring might be most thick
Of blossoms and buds, smote on me, and I grew
Careless of most things, let the clock tick, tick,

"To my unhappy pulse, that beat right through 76
My eager body; while I laughed out loud,
And let my lips curl up at false or true,

"Seemed cold and shallow without any cloud.
Behold, my judges, then the cloths were brought; 80
While I was dizzied thus, old thoughts would crowd,

"Belonging to the time ere I was bought
By Arthur's great name and his little love;
Must I give up forever then, I thought,

"That which I deemed would ever round me move 85
Glorifying all things; for a little word,
Scarce ever meant at all, must I now prove

"Stone-cold forever? Pray you, does the Lord
Will that all folks should be quite happy and good?
I love God now a little, if this cord 90

"Were broken, once for all what striving could
Make me love anything in earth or heaven?
So day by day it grew, as if one should

"Slip slowly down some path worn smooth and even,
Down to a cool sea on a summer day; 95
Yet still in slipping there was some small leaven

"Of stretched hands catching small stones by the way,
Until one surely reached the sea at last,
And felt strange new joy as the worn head lay

"Back, with the hair like sea-weed; yea, all past
Sweat of the forehead, dryness of the lips, 101
Washed utterly out by the dear waves o'ercast,

"In the lone sea, far off from any ships!
Do I not know now of a day in spring?
No minute of that wild day ever slips 105

"From out my memory; I hear thrushes sing,
And wheresoever I may be, straightway
Thoughts of it all come up with most fresh sting.

80. **the cloths.** See ll. 21 ff.

"I was half mad with beauty on that day,
And went, without my ladies, all alone,   110
In a quiet garden walled round every way;

"I was right joyful of that wall of stone,
That shut the flowers and trees up with the
    sky,
And trebled all the beauty; to the bone—

"Yea, right through to my heart, grown very
    shy   115
With wary thoughts—it pierced, and made
    me glad,
Exceedingly glad, and I knew verily,

"A little thing just then had made me mad;
I dared not think, as I was wont to do,
Sometimes, upon my beauty; if I had   120

"Held out my long hand up against the blue,
And, looking on the tenderly darkened fingers,
Thought that by rights one ought to see quite
    through,

"There, see you, where the soft still light yet
    lingers,   124
Round by the edges; what should I have done,
If this had joined with yellow spotted singers,

"And startling green drawn upward by the
    sun?
But shouting, loosed out, see now! all my
    hair,
And trancedly stood watching the west wind
    run

"With faintest half-heard breathing sound—
    why there   130
I lose my head e'en now in doing this.
But shortly listen: In that garden fair

"Came Launcelot walking; this is true, the
    kiss
Wherewith we kissed in meeting that spring
    day,
I scarce dare talk of the remembered bliss, 135

"When both our mouths went wandering in
    one way,
And aching sorely, met among the leaves;
Our hands, being left behind, strained far
    away.

"Never within a yard of my bright sleeves
Had Launcelot come before—and now so
    nigh!   140
After that day why is it Guenevere grieves?

"Nevertheless, you, O Sir Gauwaine, lie,
Whatever happened on through all those
    years—
God knows I speak truth, saying that you lie.

"Being such a lady, could I weep these tears 145
If this were true? A great queen such as I,
Having sinned this way, straight her conscience sears;

"And afterwards she liveth hatefully,
Slaying and poisoning—certes never weeps;
Gauwaine, be friends now, speak me lovingly.

"Do I not see how God's dear pity creeps   151
All through your frame, and trembles in your
    mouth?
Remember in what grave your mother sleeps,

"Buried in some place far down in the south,
Men are forgetting as I speak to you;   155
By her head, severed in that awful drouth

"Of pity that drew Agravaine's fell blow,
I pray your pity! let me not scream out
Forever after, when the shrill winds blow

"Through half your castle-locks! let me not
    shout   160
Forever after in the winter night
When you ride out alone! in battle-rout

"Let not my rusting tears make your sword
    light!
Ah! God of mercy, how he turns away!
So, ever must I dress me to the fight,   165

---

126. **yellow ... singers**, thrushes (l. 106).

153. **your mother.** According to Malory she was Morgawse, Arthur's sister. She was slain by her son Sir Gaheris (not Agravaine) when he found her faithless to her husband, King Lot, in Orkney (*Morte Darthur*, X, 24).

"So—let God's justice work! Gauwaine, I say,
See me hew down your proofs; yea, all men
 know,
Even as you said, how Mellyagraunce one day,

"One bitter day in *la Fausse Garde*, for so
All good knights held it after, saw— 170
Yea, sirs, by cursed unknightly outrage,
 though

"You, Gauwaine, held his word without a
 flaw,
This Mellyagraunce saw blood upon my bed—
Whose blood then pray you? is there any law

"To make a queen say why some spots of red
Lie on her coverlet? or will you say, 176
'Your hands are white, lady, as when you wed,

" 'Where did you bleed?' and must I stammer
 out—'Nay,
I blush indeed, fair lord, only to rend 179
My sleeve up to my shoulder, where there lay

" 'A knife-point last night': so must I defend
The honor of the Lady Guenevere?
Not so, fair lords, even if the world should end

"This very day, and you were judges here
Instead of God. Did you see Mellyagraunce
When Launcelot stood by him?—what white
 fear 186

"Curdled his blood, and how his teeth did
 dance,
His side sink in? as my knight cried and said:
'Slayer of unarmed men, here is a chance!

" 'Setter of traps, I pray you guard your head;
By God, I am so glad to fight with you, 191
Stripper of ladies, that my hand feels lead

" 'For driving weight; hurrah now! draw and
 do,
For all my wounds are moving in my breast,
And I am getting mad with waiting so.' 195

"He struck his hands together o'er the beast,
Who fell down flat, and groveled at his feet,
And groaned at being slain so young. 'At
 least,'

"My knight said, 'Rise you, sir, who are so
 fleet
At catching ladies; half-armed will I fight, 200
My left side all uncovered!' Then, I weet,

"Up sprang Sir Mellyagraunce with great
 delight
Upon his knave's face; not until just then
Did I quite hate him, as I saw my knight

"Along the lists look to my stake and pen 205
With such a joyous smile, it made me sigh
From agony beneath my waist-chain, when

"The fight began, and to me they drew nigh;
Ever Sir Launcelot kept him on the right,
And traversed warily, and ever high 210

"And fast leapt caitiff's sword, until my
 knight
Sudden threw up his sword to his left hand,
Caught it, and swung it; that was all the
 fight,

"Except a spout of blood on the hot land;
For it was hottest summer; and I know 215
I wondered how the fire, while I should stand,

"And burn, against the heat, would quiver so,
Yards above my head; thus these matters went;
Which things were only warnings of the woe

"That fell on me. Yet Mellyagraunce was shent,
For Mellyagraunce had fought against the
 Lord; 221
Therefore, my lords, take heed lest you be
 blent

"With all his wickedness—say no rash word
Against me, being so beautiful; my eyes,
Wept all away to gray, may bring some sword

"To drown you in your blood; see my breast
 rise, 226

---

168. **Mellyagraunce.** See headnote. 169. *la Fausse Garde*, the false prison in which Mellyagraunce had held her. 171. **unknightly outrage.** Mellyagraunce had entered the chamber of Guenevere before she was up. 190. **Setter of traps.** Mellyagraunce had trapped Launcelot.

201. **weet**, observed, knew. 216. **while . . . burn.** Upon the testimony of Mellyagraunce she was sentenced to be burned. The appearance and the victory of Launcelot saved her. 220. **shent**, destroyed. 222. **blent**, blinded.

Like waves of purple sea, as here I stand;
And how my arms are moved in wonderful
  wise;

"Yea, also at my full heart's strong command,
See through my long throat how the words
  go up   230
In ripples to my mouth; how in my hand

"The shadow lies like wine within a cup
Of marvelously colored gold; yea, now
This little wind is rising, look you up,

"And wonder how the light is falling so   235
Within my moving tresses. Will you dare
When you have looked a little on my brow,

"To say this thing is vile? or will you care
For any plausible lies of cunning woof,
When you can see my face with no lie there

"Forever? Am I not a gracious proof?—   241
'But in your chamber Launcelot was found'—
Is there a good knight then would stand aloof,

"When a queen says with gentle queenly
  sound,
'O true as steel, come now and talk with me;
I love to see your step upon the ground   246

"'Unwavering; also well I love to see
That gracious smile light up your face, and
  hear
Your wonderful words, that all mean verily

"'The thing they seem to mean. Good friend,
  so dear   250
To me in everything, come here tonight,
Or else the hours will pass most dull and
  drear.

"'If you come not, I fear this time I might
Get thinking overmuch of times gone by,
When I was young, and green hope was in
  sight;   255

"'For no man cares now to know why I sigh;
And no man comes to sing me pleasant songs,
Nor any brings me the sweet flowers that lie

"'So thick in the gardens; therefore one so
  longs
To see you, Launcelot, that we may be   260
Like children once again, free from all wrongs

"'Just for one night.' Did he not come to me?
What thing could keep true Launcelot away
If I said, 'Come'? There was one less than three

"In my quiet room that night, and we were
  gay;   265
Till sudden I rose up, weak, pale, and sick,
Because a bawling broke our dream up; yea,

"I looked at Launcelot's face and could not
  speak,
For he looked helpless, too, for a little while;
Then I remember how I tried to shriek,   270

"And could not, but fell down; from tile to
  tile
The stones they threw up rattled o'er my head
And made me dizzier; till within a while

"My maids were all about me, and my head
On Launcelot's breast was being soothed away
From its white chattering, until Launcelot
  said . . .   276

"By God! I will not tell you more today—
Judge any way you will; what matters it?
You know quite well the story of that fray,

"How Launcelot stilled their bawling, the
  mad fit   280
That caught up Gauwaine, all, all, verily,
But just that which would save me; these
  things flit.

"Nevertheless, you, O Sir Gauwaine, lie;
Whatever may have happened these long
  years,
God knows I speak truth, saying that you lie!

"All I have said is truth, by Christ's dear
  tears."   286
She would not speak another word, but stood
Turned sideways, listening, like a man who
  hears

---

242. 'But . . . found.' For the story of the fight in Guenevere's chamber, see Malory's *Morte Darthur*, XX, 4.

280. **mad fit.** Gauwaine was not present. 282. **that . . . me**, her innocence.

His brother's trumpet sounding through the wood
Of his foes' lances. She leaned eagerly, 290
And gave a slight spring sometimes, as she could

At last hear something really; joyfully
Her cheek grew crimson, as the headlong speed
Of the roan charger drew all men to see
The knight who came was Launcelot at good need. (1858)

Shameful Death

There were four of us about that bed:
    The mass-priest knelt at the side,
I and his mother stood at the head,
    Over his feet lay the bride;
We were quite sure that he was dead, 5
    Though his eyes were open wide.

He did not die in the night,
    He did not die in the day,
But in the morning twilight
    His spirit passed away, 10
When neither sun nor moon was bright,
    And the trees were merely gray.

He was not slain with the sword,
    Knight's ax, or the knightly spear,
Yet spoke he never a word 15
    After he came in here;
I cut away the cord
    From the neck of my brother dear.

He did not strike one blow,
    For the recreants came behind, 20
In a place where the hornbeams grow,
    A path right hard to find,
For the hornbeam boughs swing so
    That the twilight makes it blind.

They lighted a great torch then, 25
    When his arms were pinioned fast,
Sir John the knight of the Fen,
    Sir Guy of the Dolorous Blast,
With knights threescore and ten,
    Hung brave Lord Hugh at last. 30

I am threescore and ten,
    And my hair is all turned gray,
But I met Sir John of the Fen,
    Long ago on a summer day,
And am glad to think of the moment when 35
    I took his life away.

I am threescore and ten,
    And my strength is mostly passed,
But long ago I and my men,
    When the sky was overcast, 40
And the smoke rolled over the reeds of the fen,
    Slew Guy of the Dolorous Blast.

And now, knights all of you,
    I pray you pray for Sir Hugh,
A good knight and a true, 45
    And for Alice, his wife, pray too. (1858)

A Garden by the Sea

A lyric in Book 4 of The Life and Death of Jason, *this is the "sweet song sung not yet to any man" by the water-nymph as she lulls to sleep the Theban youth Hylas. He had wandered away from his companions who had landed on the shore of Mysia, Asia Minor, in search of fresh water. Hylas was left behind by his companions.*

I know a little garden close
Set thick with lily and red rose,
Where I would wander if I might
From dewy dawn to dewy night,
And have one with me wandering. 5

And though within it no birds sing,
And though no pillared house is there,
And though the apple boughs are bare
Of fruit and blossom, would to God,
Her feet upon the green grass trod, 10
And I beheld them as before.

There comes a murmur from the shore,
And in the close two fair streams are,
Drawn from the purple hills afar,

---

291. **as**, as if. 295. **knight . . . need.** Launcelot and his kinsmen rescued the Queen from the fire.
Shameful Death. 2. **mass-priest**, a priest whose special duty was to say mass for the dead. 21. **hornbeams**, trees with smooth gray bark and leaves resembling those of the beech.

1. **close**, enclosure.

Drawn down unto the restless sea: 15
Dark hills whose heath-bloom feeds no bee,
Dark shore no ship has ever seen,
Still beaten by the billows green,
Whose murmur comes unceasingly
Unto the place for which I cry. 20

For which I cry both day and night,
For which I let slip all delight,
That maketh me both deaf and blind,
Careless to win, unskilled to find,
And quick to lose what all men seek. 25

Yet tottering as I am, and weak,
Still have I left a little breath
To seek within the jaws of death
An entrance to that happy place,
To seek the unforgotten face 30
Once seen, once kissed, once reft from me
Anigh the murmuring of the sea. (1867)

from *The Earthly Paradise*

AN APOLOGY

In *The Earthly Paradise* Morris employed the familiar medieval device of a framework to bind together a series of tales. The enveloping action has to do with a band of medieval mariners, who set out from Europe to find a country in which they can be happy. They chance upon an island, the "Earthly Paradise," where live the descendants of Greeks who had colonized the country centuries before. At each of a series of banquets, which occur twice a month, the mariners relate some medieval romance, or the hosts tell an ancient Greek legend. Thus the cycle of tales runs two a month throughout the year —twelve medieval and twelve Greek legends being retold. Each set of two stories is preceded by a lyric appropriate to the month of the year in which the tales are recited. The following *Apology* introduces the whole series.

Of Heaven or Hell I have no power to sing;
I cannot ease the burden of your fears,
Or make quick-coming death a little thing,
Or bring again the pleasure of past years;
Nor for my words shall ye forget your tears, 5

1. **Of Heaven or Hell.** Morris disclaims equality with earlier poets who used these themes—Virgil, Dante, Milton.

Or hope again for aught that I can say—
The idle singer of an empty day.

But rather, when aweary of your mirth,
From full hearts still unsatisfied ye sigh,
And, feeling kindly unto all the earth, 10
Grudge every minute as it passes by,
Made the more mindful that the sweet days die—
Remember me a little then, I pray,
The idle singer of an empty day.

The heavy trouble, the bewildering care 15
That weighs us down who live and earn our bread,
These idle verses have no power to bear;
So let me sing of names remembered,
Because they, living not, can ne'er be dead,
Or long time take their memory quite away 20
From us poor singers of an empty day.

Dreamer of dreams, born out of my due time,
Why should I strive to set the crooked straight?
Let it suffice me that my murmuring rime,
Beats with light wing against the ivory gate, 25
Telling a tale not too importunate
To those who in the sleepy region stay,
Lulled by the singer of an empty day.

Folk say, a wizard to a northern king
At Christmas-tide such wondrous things did show, 30
That through one window men beheld the spring,
And through another saw the summer glow,
And through a third the fruited vines a-row,
While still, unheard, but in its wonted way,
Piped the drear wind of that December day. 35

So with this Earthly Paradise it is,
If ye will read aright, and pardon me,
Who strive to build a shadowy isle of bliss
Midmost the beating of the steely sea,
Where tossed about all hearts of men must be; 40
Whose ravening monsters mighty men shall slay—
Not the poor singer of an empty day.
(1868-1870)

25. **the ivory gate.** The house of Morpheus, god of sleep, had two gates through which dreams issued. True dreams passed through a gate of horn; false dreams, through a gate of ivory.

The Day Is Coming

Late in the seventies Morris became interested in politics and joined the Socialist Party. Virtually all his time in 1883-1885 was given to the cause. This poem expresses his interest in the welfare of the lower classes. It was published with other poems in a pamphlet entitled *Chants for Socialists*.

Come hither, lads, and harken, for a tale there is to tell,
Of the wonderful days a-coming, when all shall be better than well.

And the tale shall be told of a country, a land in the midst of the sea,
And folk shall call it England in the days that are going to be.

There more than one in a thousand in the days that are yet to come, 5
Shall have some hope of the morrow, some joy of the ancient home.

For then—laugh not, but listen to this strange tale of mine—
All folk that are in England shall be better lodged than swine.

Then a man shall work and bethink him, and rejoice in the deeds of his hand,
Nor yet come home in the even too faint and weary to stand. 10

Men in that time a-coming shall work and have no fear
For tomorrow's lack of earning and the hunger-wolf anear.

I tell you this for a wonder, that no man then shall be glad
Of his fellow's fall and mishap to snatch at the work he had,

For that which the worker winneth shall then be his indeed, 15
Nor shall half be reaped for nothing by him that sowed no seed.

O strange new wonderful justice! But for whom shall we gather the gain?
For ourselves and for each of our fellows, and no hand shall labor in vain.

Then all Mine and all Thine shall be Ours, and no more shall any man crave
For riches that serve for nothing but to fetter a friend for a slave. 20

And what wealth then shall be left us when none shall gather gold
To buy his friend in the market, and pinch and pine the sold?

Nay, what save the lovely city, and the little house on the hill,
And the wastes and the woodland beauty, and the happy fields we till;

And the homes of ancient stories, the tombs of the mighty dead; 25
And the wise men seeking out marvels, and the poet's teeming head;

And the painter's hand of wonder; and the marvelous fiddle-bow,
And the banded choirs of music—all those that do and know.

For all these shall be ours and all men's; nor shall any lack a share
Of the toil and the gain of living in the days when the world grows fair. 30

Ah! such are the days that shall be! But what are the deeds of today,
In the days of the years we dwell in, that wear our lives away?

Why, then, and for what are we waiting? There are three words to speak—
WE WILL IT—and what is the foeman but the dream-strong wakened and weak?

O why and for what are we waiting? while our brothers droop and die, 35
And on every wind of the heavens a wasted life goes by.

How long shall they reproach us where crowd
    on crowd they dwell,
Poor ghosts of the wicked city, the gold-
    crushed, hungry hell?

Through squalid life they labored, in sordid
    grief they died,
Those sons of a mighty mother, those props
    of England's pride.   40

They are gone; there is none can undo it, nor
    save our souls from the curse;
But many a million cometh, and shall they be
    better or worse?

It is we must answer and hasten, and open
    wide the door
For the rich man's hurrying terror, and the
    slow-foot hope of the poor.

Yea, the voiceless wrath of the wretched, and
    their unlearned discontent,   45
We must give it voice and wisdom till the
    waiting-tide be spent.

Come, then, since all things call us, the living
    and the dead,
And o'er the weltering tangle a glimmering
    light is shed.

Come, then, let us cast off fooling, and put by
    ease and rest,
For the Cause alone is worthy till the good
    days bring the best.   50

Come, join in the only battle wherein no man
    can fail,
Where whoso fadeth and dieth, yet his deed
    shall still prevail.

Ah! come cast off all fooling, for this, at least,
    we know:
That the Dawn and the Day is coming, and
    forth the Banners go.   (1884)

A Death Song

This poem was written to be sold as a penny pamphlet to aid the children of Morris's friend Alfred Linnell, who died from injuries received when the police attacked marchers in a great Socialist parade in London, November 13, 1887. Morris was one of the marchers.

What cometh here from west to east a-wend-
    ing?
And who are these, the marchers stern and
    slow?
We bear the message that the rich are sending
Aback to those who bade them wake and
    know.
*Not one, not one, nor thousands must they
    slay,*   5
But one and all if they would dusk the day.

We asked them for a life of toilsome earn-
    ing—
They bade us bide their leisure for our
    bread;
We craved to speak to tell our woeful learn-
    ing—
We come back speechless, bearing back our
    dead.   10
*Not one, not one, nor thousands must they
    slay,*
But one and all if they would dusk the day.

They will not learn; they have no ears to
    hearken;
They turn their faces from the eyes of fate;
Their gay-lit halls shut out the skies that
    darken.   15
But, lo! this dead man knocking at the
    gate.
*Not one, not one, nor thousands must they
    slay,*
But one and all if they would dusk the day.

Here lies the sign that we shall break our
    prison;
Amidst the storm he won a prisoner's rest;   20
But in the cloudy dawn the sun arisen
Brings us our day of work to win the best.
*Not one, not one, nor thousands must they
    slay,*
But one and all if they would dusk the day.
    (1891)

Algernon Charles Swinburne

1837-1909

Algernon Charles Swinburne made an early start in his craft. He was born in London but spent most of his youth on the Isle of Wight, where his father, Admiral Charles Henry Swinburne, had an estate, and in Northumberland, where his grandfather, Sir John Edward Swinburne, lived. So there entered into his blood the beat of the sea and the freedom of the heath. To these early passions—among the most important in their influence on his art—he added at Eton and at Balliol College, Oxford, an intense love for poetry. His ties at college and immediately after were with Rossetti and his circle; Swinburne was not a member of the Pre-Raphaelite Brotherhood (see p. 416), but he had a kinship with those lovers of the medieval and of sensuous beauty. He shared with them a love of the rich and varied romance of the Middle Ages; but he was also a brilliant classical scholar, and his interpretations of Greek legend recaptured much of the spirit of the classics. Furthermore, his range of interests included French literature; he wrote French almost as well as English, translated the flippant pagan songs of Villon, and worshiped at the shrine of Victor Hugo, whom he regarded as his master in verse form and romantic feeling. In English literature, moreover, his sympathies were restricted to no one period. He was moved by the old romances, but he knew also the Elizabethan dramatists, and turned often from verse-making to praise their power in studies that are inspiring if too unrestrained and effusive. Of the romantic poets his idol was Shelley—as was natural, for, like Shelley, he was an atheist and an arch-rebel against all restraints of the human spirit. Swinburne's name belongs, indeed, with those of the aristocratic young rebels like Byron and Shelley, whose love of liberty and aggressive resistance to authority fascinated society but alarmed the conservative members of it. Swinburne has sometimes been called "the Victorian Byron." Like all other innate rebels, he disliked organized religions; his rebellion was not alone against the creeds of Victorian England, but took the much broader form of resistance to anything that he conceived to be religious tyranny in any place or age.

Swinburne's first publication revealed his regard for the Pre-Raphaelites, for it was dedicated to D. G. Rossetti. *The Queen Mother, Rosamond—Two Plays* (1860) contains two romantic dramas in blank verse with occasional lyrics in English and French. These plays attracted no attention. The same cannot be said, however, of *Atalanta in Calydon* (1865). This was a drama in the classical Greek form based on the ancient legend of the Calydonian boar hunt. In the amazingly melodious choruses of the play, it was apparent that a master of verse had appeared. It is even probable that Swinburne's *Hymn to Artemis*, sung as the opening chorus by a group of Aetolian maidens, is his most famous poem. Certainly it is one of his most melodious, and it is doubtful whether any other lyric in the English language conveys so perfectly in words the sounds of nature—the "lisp of leaves and ripple of rain" and the "noise of winds and many rivers." The veil between this lyric and the beauty of naked nature is as thin as lawn. If it had not been that the paganism of the drama is in harmony with its remote story, the shock that Swinburne gave to Victorian conventionalities would have come before the publication of *Poems and Ballads* the following year, for not only is the "hoofed heel of a satyr" stamped upon the choruses, but the entire drama is permeated with a rebellion against the tyranny of creeds and against the gods with their instruments of death and decay.

The year of the Hellenic play saw also *Chastelard*, the first of three romantic dramas dealing with the story of Mary Stuart. It was sixteen years before he completed this trilogy; *Bothwell: a Tragedy*, probably the best of the series, was published in 1874, and *Mary Stuart* in 1881. In these plays the swiftness of action, the penetrating delineation of the characters, and the dramatic power suggest that the poet had not studied his Elizabethan tragic playwrights in vain. The *Poems and Ballads* of 1866 has already been mentioned. Few publications in Victorian literature created such an immediate stir. Swinburne suddenly became famous—not to say notorious. The unconventional thoughts and moods of the poems led to their being vehemently attacked by the conservatives. At the same time, however, the lovers of poetry were enchanted by his verses.

The lyrics that first revealed Swinburne as the unblushing pagan poet were followed by a second series in 1878 and a third in 1889. His enthusiasm for the cause of Italian liberty and union he expressed in *A Song of Italy* (1867) and *Songs before Sunrise* (1871). In 1880 appeared two volumes of verse that echo the sound of the sea; these were *Songs of Springtides* and *Studies in Song*. The early influence of the Pre-Raphaelite Brotherhood brought late fruit in *Tristram of Lyonesse* (1882), a romantic poem in rimed couplets which displays Swinburne's warmth, color, and metrical agility, but lacks the structural strength of Morris's medieval tales. This long Arthurian romance was written only a few years after Swinburne's friend Theodore Watts-Dunton, the literary critic, had not only helped the poet through a period of dissipation and sickness but had taken him into his home on Putney Hill, where he continued to live for the rest of his life. The work that came in the last decade and a half of his busy life, when he was by no means well, shows some indications that he had fallen into the "sere and yellow leaf." In the tragedy of *Marino Faliero* (1885) he attempted to outdo Byron, who had used the same heroic material. *Astrophel* (1894), *A Tale of Balen* (1896), and *A Channel Passage* (1904) were followed by *The Duke of Gandia* (1908). The following year Swinburne died of an attack of influenza which developed into pneumonia.

In the field of criticism Swinburne expressed his admiration of writers from whose work he had drawn much of his inspiration. He wrote critical monographs on Shakespeare, Ben Jonson, Chapman, and other Elizabethan dramatists, as well as on his French idol, Victor Hugo. Shorter critical sketches appeared in the *Encyclopaedia Britannica*, and a number of others were gathered together and published in his *Essays and Studies* (1875) and *Miscellanies* (1886). This biographical and critical prose makes, on the whole, stimulating reading. Its chief defect as criticism is that it leans too much in the direction of undiluted appreciation. Swinburne usually wrote with the enthusiastic admiration of a passionate poet, and his comments on the work of poets and dramatists whom he admired are panegyrics rather than balanced critical estimates.

Certainly no other Victorian poet—not even Tennyson when most musical—had Swinburne's sustained power of creating melody in words. Tennyson, indeed, acknowledged this power: "Swinburne," he said, "is a reed through which all things blow into music." He was first and last an artist; he did not aspire to be a philosopher or a prophet but was content to be a singer. And it is as a singer that he made his greatest contribution to English literature. Ideas he did have, but they were neither profound nor numerous, and he had a way of repeating them until they were worn thin. Even in his rebellion against the restraints of conventionality and custom he had no articulated plan. His ideas threatened constantly to melt into mere moods. But as a lyric poet he was a major figure. He has been criticized, indeed, for drawing so much attention to the siren-quality of his verse that his readers forget to look for his thought. Perhaps this fault—if it be one—is not to his discredit, for the very criticism is an admission that Swinburne was the most lyrical of the Victorian poets.

from *Atalanta in Calydon*

In this drama Swinburne attempted, he said, "to do something original in English which might in some degree reproduce for English readers the likeness of a Greek tragedy with something of its true poetic life and charm." The play concerns the famous hunt for the wild boar which was sent, according to legend, by Artemis, revengeful goddess of the moon, to ravage Calydon, a province in ancient Greece. Meleager killed the beast and presented the spoils of victory to Atalanta, a beautiful Arcadian huntress with whom he had fallen in love. When Toxeus and Plexippus, brothers of Queen Althaea, Meleager's mother, attempted to rob the huntress of her prize, their nephew slew them. On hearing of the tragedy, Meleager's mother burned to ashes the fagot upon which her son's life depended, and which she had carefully preserved up to that time. The poem which follows here is the opening chorus of the drama, sung by a group of maidens from Aetolia, an ancient Grecian province.

WHEN THE HOUNDS OF SPRING

When the hounds of spring are on winter's traces,
   The mother of months in meadow or plain
Fills the shadows and windy places
   With lisp of leaves and ripple of rain;
And the brown bright nightingale amorous 5
Is half assuaged for Itylus,
For the Thracian ships and the foreign faces,
   The tongueless vigil, and all the pain.

Come with bows bent and with emptying of quivers,
   Maiden most perfect, lady of light, 10
With a noise of winds and many rivers,
   With a clamor of waters, and with might;
Bind on thy sandals, O thou most fleet,
Over the splendor and speed of thy feet;
For the faint east quickens, the wan west shivers, 15
   Round the feet of the day and the feet of the night.

Where shall we find her, how shall we sing to her,
   Fold our hands round her knees, and cling?
Oh, that man's heart were as fire and could spring to her,
   Fire, or the strength of the streams that spring! 20
For the stars and the winds are unto her
   As raiment, as songs of the harp-player;
For the risen stars and the fallen cling to her,
   And the southwest wind and the west wind sing.

For winter's rains and ruins are over, 25
   And all the season of snows and sins;
The days dividing lover and lover,
   The light that loses, the night that wins;
And time remembered is grief forgotten,
And frosts are slain and flowers begotten, 30
And in green underwood and cover
   Blossom by blossom the spring begins.

The full streams feed on flower of rushes,
   Ripe grasses trammel a traveling foot,
The faint fresh flame of the young year flushes
   From leaf to flower and flower to fruit; 35
And fruit and leaf are as gold and fire,
And the oat is heard above the lyre,
And the hoofèd heel of a satyr crushes
   The chestnut-husk at the chestnut-root. 40

And Pan by noon and Bacchus by night,
   Fleeter of foot than the fleet-foot kid,

2. **mother of months,** Artemis, goddess of the moon. 6. **Itylus.** See Arnold's *Philomela*, and headnote, p. 733. 28. **light . . . wins,** a reference to the short days and long nights of winter. 38. **oat,** the shepherd's pipe of oaten straw. 39. **satyr,** a sylvan demigod, half man and half goat. 41. **Pan,** the god of flocks and pastures. **Bacchus,** the god of wine.

Follows with dancing and fills with delight
   The Maenad and the Bassarid;
And soft as lips that laugh and hide   45
The laughing leaves of the trees divide,
And screen from seeing and leave in sight
   The god pursuing, the maiden hid.

The ivy falls with the Bacchanal's hair
   Over her eyebrows hiding her eyes;   50
The wild vine slipping down leaves bare
   Her bright breast shortening into sighs;
The wild vine slips with the weight of its
   leaves,
But the berried ivy catches and cleaves
To the limbs that glitter, the feet that scare   55
   The wolf that follows, the fawn that flies.
                              (1865)

BEFORE THE BEGINNING OF YEARS

   This song is sung by the Chorus after Althaea had departed to prepare her son Meleager for the hunt, "lest love or some man's anger work him harm."

Before the beginning of years
   There came to the making of man
Time, with a gift of tears;
   Grief, with a glass that ran;
Pleasure, with pain for leaven;   5
   Summer, with flowers that fell;
Remembrance fallen from heaven,
   And madness risen from hell;
Strength without hands to smite;
   Love that endures for a breath;   10
Night, the shadow of light,
   And life, the shadow of death.

And the high gods took in hand
   Fire, and the falling of tears,
And a measure of sliding sand   15
   From under the feet of the years;
And froth and drift of the sea;
   And dust of the laboring earth;
And bodies of things to be
   In the houses of death and of birth;   20

And wrought with weeping and laughter,
   And fashioned with loathing and love,
With life before and after
   And death beneath and above,
For a day and a night and a morrow,   25
   That his strength might endure for a span
With travail and heavy sorrow,
   The holy spirit of man.

From the winds of the north and the south
   They gathered as unto strife;   30
They breathed upon his mouth,
   They filled his body with life;
Eyesight and speech they wrought
   For the veils of the soul therein,
A time for labor and thought,   35
   A time to serve and to sin;
They gave him light in his ways,
   And love, and a space for delight,
And beauty and length of days,
   And night, and sleep in the night.   40
His speech is a burning fire;
   With his lips he travaileth;
In his heart is a blind desire,
   In his eyes foreknowledge of death;
He weaves, and is clothed with derision;   45
   Sows, and he shall not reap;
His life is a watch or a vision
   Between a sleep and a sleep.   (1865)

A Match

If love were what the rose is,
   And I were like the leaf,
Our lives would grow together
In sad or singing weather,
Blown fields or flowerful closes,   5
   Green pleasure or gray grief;
If love were what the rose is,
   And I were like the leaf.

If I were what the words are,
   And love were like the tune,   10
With double sound and single
Delight our lips would mingle,
With kisses glad as birds are
   That get sweet rain at noon;
If I were what the words are,   15
   And love were like the tune.

---

44. **Maenad**, a female worshiper of Bacchus. The name is derived from a Greek word meaning *to be frenzied*. **Bassarid**, a Thracian worshiper of Bacchus. The celebrations of the Bassarids included licentious excesses and a sacrifice of some animal on the altar of the god. The participants ate the flesh raw. 47. **screen . . . hid.** As the god and the maiden slip through the forest, they are alternately concealed and revealed by the wind-swayed foliage.

35. **time . . . sin.** Cf. *Ecclesiastes*, 3:1-8.

If you were life, my darling,
   And I your love were death,
We'd shine and snow together
Ere March made sweet the weather   20
With daffodil and starling
   And hours of fruitful breath;
If you were life, my darling,
   And I your love were death.

If you were thrall to sorrow,   25
   And I were page to joy,
We'd play for lives and seasons
With loving looks and treasons
And tears of night and morrow
   And laughs of maid and boy;   30
If you were thrall to sorrow,
   And I were page to joy.

If you were April's lady,
   And I were lord in May,
We'd throw with leaves for hours   35
And draw for days with flowers,
Till day like night were shady
   And night were bright like day;
If you were April's lady,
   And I were lord in May.   40

If you were queen of pleasure,
   And I were king of pain,
We'd hunt down love together,
Pluck out his flying-feather,
And teach his feet a measure,   45
   And find his mouth a rein;
If you were queen of pleasure,
   And I were king of pain.   (1866)

A Ballad of Burdens

The burden of fair women. Vain delight,
   And love self-slain in some sweet shameful way,
And sorrowful old age that comes by night
   As a thief comes that has no heart by day,
   And change that finds fair cheeks and leaves them gray,   5
And weariness that keeps awake for hire,
   And grief that says what pleasure used to say;
This is the end of every man's desire.

The burden of bought kisses. This is sore
   A burden without fruit in childbearing;   10
Between the nightfall and the dawn threescore,
   Threescore between the dawn and evening.
   The shuddering in thy lips, the shuddering
In thy sad eyelids tremulous like fire,
   Makes love seem shameful and a wretched thing.   15
This is the end of every man's desire.

The burden of sweet speeches. Nay, kneel down,
   Cover thy head, and weep; for verily
These marked-men that buy thy white and brown
   In the last days shall take no thought for thee.   20
   In the last days like earth thy face shall be,
Yea, like sea-marsh made thick with brine and mire,
   Sad with sick leavings of the sterile sea.
This is the end of every man's desire.

The burden of long living. Thou shalt fear   25
   Waking, and sleeping mourn upon thy bed;
And say at night, "Would God the day were here,"
   And say at dawn, "Would God the day were dead."
   With weary days thou shalt be clothed and fed,
And wear remorse of heart for thine attire,   30
   Pain for thy girdle and sorrow upon thine head;
This is the end of every man's desire.

The burden of bright colors. Thou shalt see
   Gold tarnished, and the gray above the green;
And as the thing thou seest thy face shall be,   35
   And no more as the thing beforetime seen.
   And thou shalt say of mercy, "It hath been,"
And living, watch the old lips and loves expire,
   And talking, tears shall take thy breath between;
This is the end of every man's desire.   40

The burden of sad sayings. In that day
   Thou shalt tell all thy days and hours, and tell

Thy times and ways and words of love, and say
How one was dear and one desirable,
And sweet was life to hear and sweet to smell, 45
But now with lights reverse the old hours retire
And the last hour is shod with fire from hell;
This is the end of every man's desire.

The burden of four seasons. Rain in spring,
White rain and wind among the tender trees; 50
A summer of green sorrows gathering,
Rank autumn in a mist of miseries,
With sad face set toward the year, that sees
The charred ash drop out of the dropping pyre,
And winter wan with many maladies; 55
This is the end of every man's desire.

The burden of dead faces. Out of sight
And out of love, beyond the reach of hands,
Changed in the changing of the dark and light,
They walk and weep about the barren lands
Where no seed is nor any garner stands, 61
Where in short breaths the doubtful days respire,
And time's turned glass lets through the sighing sands;
This is the end of every man's desire. 64

The burden of much gladness. Life and lust
Forsake thee, and the face of thy delight;
And underfoot the heavy hour strews dust,
And overhead strange weathers burn and bite;
And where the red was, lo, the bloodless white,
And where truth was, the likeness of a liar, 70
And where day was, the likeness of the night;
This is the end of every man's desire.

L'ENVOI

Princes, and ye whom pleasure quickeneth,
Heed well this rime before your pleasure tire;
For life is sweet, but after life is death. 75
This is the end of every man's desire.

(1866)

The Garden of Proserpine

In Greek mythology Proserpine was the goddess and queen of the lower world. She was the daughter of Zeus and Demeter, or Ceres, goddess of the harvest, and was carried off by Pluto, god of the lower world, while she was gathering flowers in the Vale of Enna in Sicily. Her mother wandered over the whole earth in search of her. On Demeter's prayer to Zeus that Proserpine be allowed to return to the upper world, he permitted her to spend six months of the year on earth; her alternate periods on earth and in Hades symbolize the changes of the seasons.

This poem Swinburne represents as spoken by a Roman pagan.

Here, where the world is quiet;
Here, where all trouble seems
Dead winds' and spent waves' riot
In doubtful dreams of dreams;
I watch the green field growing 5
For reaping folk and sowing,
For harvest-time and mowing,
A sleepy world of streams.

I am tired of tears and laughter,
And men that laugh and weep, 10
Of what may come hereafter
For men that sow to reap;
I am weary of days and hours,
Blown buds of barren flowers,
Desires and dreams and powers 15
And everything but sleep.

Here life has death for neighbor,
And far from eye or ear
Wan waves and wet winds labor,
Weak ships and spirits steer; 20
They drive adrift, and whither
They wot not who make thither;
But no such winds blow hither,
And no such things grow here.

14. Blown . . . flowers, blossoming flowers that will produce no fruit. They are used as a symbol of unfulfilled desires and dreams. 22. wot, know.

No growth of moor or coppice, 25
  No heather-flower or vine,
But bloomless buds of poppies,
  Green grapes of Proserpine,
Pale beds of blowing rushes
Where no leaf blooms or blushes 30
Save this whereout she crushes
  For dead men deadly wine.

Pale, without name or number,
  In fruitless fields of corn,
They bow themselves and slumber 35
  All night till light is born;
And like a soul belated,
In hell and heaven unmated,
By cloud and mist abated
  Comes out of darkness morn. 40

Though one were strong as seven,
  He too with death shall dwell,
Nor wake with wings in heaven,
  Nor weep for pains in hell;
Though one were fair as roses, 45
  His beauty clouds and closes;
And well though love reposes,
  In the end it is not well.

Pale, beyond porch and portal,
  Crowned with calm leaves, she stands 50
Who gathers all things mortal
  With cold immortal hands;
Her languid lips are sweeter
Than love's who fears to greet her
To men that mix and meet her 55
  From many times and lands.

She waits for each and other,
  She waits for all men born;
Forgets the earth her mother,
  The life of fruits and corn; 60

And spring and seed and swallow
Take wing for her and follow
Where summer song rings hollow
  And flowers are put to scorn.

There go the loves that wither, 65
  The old loves with wearier wings;
And all dead years draw thither,
  And all disastrous things;
Dead dreams of days forsaken,
Blind buds that snows have shaken, 70
Wild leaves that winds have taken,
  Red strays of ruined springs.

We are not sure of sorrow,
  And joy was never sure;
Today will die tomorrow; 75
  Time stoops to no man's lure;
And love, grown faint and fretful,
With lips but half regretful
Sighs, and with eyes forgetful
  Weeps that no loves endure. 80

From too much love of living,
  From hope and fear set free,
We thank with brief thanksgiving
  Whatever gods may be
That no life lives forever; 85
That dead men rise up never;
That even the weariest river
  Winds somewhere safe to sea.

Then star nor sun shall waken,
  Nor any change of light; 90
Nor sound of waters shaken,
  Nor any sound or sight;
Nor wintry leaves nor vernal,
Nor days nor things diurnal;
Only the sleep eternal 95
  In an eternal night.   (1866)

27. **poppies**, the flowers of oblivion, sacred to Proserpine, who was often represented with a crown of them on her head (l. 50). 34. **corn**, grain, wheat. 83. **thank . . . may be.** Cf. Henley's *Invictus*, p. 866. 94. **diurnal**, belonging to the daylight.

Dedication to *Poems and Ballads*

Swinburne dedicated the first series of his *Poems and Ballads* (1866) to Sir Edward Burne-Jones (1833-1898), an English painter, who was a member of the Pre-Raphaelite group of artists and poets, a pupil of Rossetti's, and a friend of Swinburne's.

The sea gives her shells to the shingle,
  The earth gives her streams to the sea;
They are many, but my gift is single,
  My verses, the first fruits of me.

Let the wind take the green and the gray leaf,
  Cast forth without fruit upon air; 6
Take rose-leaf and vine-leaf and bay-leaf
  Blown loose from the hair.

1. **shingle**, coarse rounded stones on the seashore. 7. **bay-leaf**, laurel-leaf, sacred to the gods.

The night shakes them round me in legions,
   Dawn drives them before her like dreams;
Time sheds them like snows on strange
     regions,   11
   Swept shoreward on infinite streams;
Leaves pallid and somber and ruddy,
   Dead fruits of the fugitive years;
Some stained as with wine and made bloody,
   And some as with tears.   16

Some scattered in seven years' traces,
   As they fell from the boy that was then;
Long left among idle green places,
   Or gathered but now among men;   20
On seas full of wonder and peril,
   Blown white round the capes of the north;
Or in islands where myrtles are sterile
   And loves bring not forth.

O daughters of dreams and of stories   25
   That life is not wearied of yet,
Faustine, Fragoletta, Dolores,
   Félise and Yolande and Juliette,
Shall I find you not still, shall I miss you,
   When sleep, that is true or that seems,   30
Comes back to me hopeless to kiss you,
   O daughters of dreams?

They are past as a slumber that passes
   As the dew of a dawn of old time;
More frail than the shadows on glasses,   35
   More fleet than a wave or a rime.
As the waves after ebb drawing seaward,
   When their hollows are full of the night,
So the birds that flew singing to me-ward
   Recede out of sight.   40

The songs of dead seasons, that wander
   On wings of articulate words;
Lost leaves that the shore-wind may squander,
   Light flocks of untameable birds;
Some sang to me dreaming in class time   45
   And truant in hand as in tongue;
For the youngest were born of boy's pastime,
   The eldest are young.

Is there shelter while life in them lingers,
   Is there hearing for songs that recede,   50
Tunes touched from a harp with man's fingers
   Or blown with boy's mouth in a reed?
Is there place in the land of your labor,
   Is there room in your world of delight,
Where change has not sorrow for neighbor   55
   And day has not night?

In their wings though the sea-wind yet
     quivers,
   Will you spare not a space for them there
Made green with the running of rivers
   And gracious with temperate air;   60
In the fields and the turreted cities,
   That cover from sunshine and rain
Fair passions and bountiful pities
   And loves without stain?

In a land of clear colors and stories,   65
   In a region of shadowless hours,
Where earth has a garment of glories
   And a murmur of musical flowers;
In woods where the spring half uncovers
   The flush of her amorous face,   70
By the waters that listen for lovers,
   For these is there place?

For the song-birds of sorrow, that muffle
   Their music as clouds do their fire;
For the storm-birds of passion, that ruffle   75
   Wild wings in a wind of desire;
In the stream of the storm as it settles
   Blown seaward, borne far from the sun,
Shaken loose on the darkness like petals
   Dropped one after one?   80

Though the world of your hands be more
     gracious
   And lovelier in lordship of things
Clothed round by sweet art with the spacious
   Warm heaven of her imminent wings,
Let them enter, unfledged and nigh fainting,
   For the love of old loves and lost times;   85
And receive in your palace of painting
   This revel of rimes.

Though the seasons of man full of losses
   Make empty the years full of youth,   90
If but one thing be constant in crosses,
   Change lays not her hand upon truth;

---

17. **seven years' traces.** The poems in the volume were apparently written between 1859 and 1866. 23. **myrtles.** Poets were crowned with wreaths of myrtle, sacred to the gods. 27. **Faustine . . . Juliette,** names of women appearing in the poems of the 1866 volume. 45. **in class time,** while he was at Eton, 1849–1853.

81. **the world . . . hands,** the paintings of Burne-Jones. See headnote.

Hopes die, and their tombs are for token
    That the grief as the joy of them ends
Ere time that breaks all men has broken   95
    The faith between friends.

Though the many lights dwindle to one light,
    There is help if the heaven has one;
Though the skies be discrowned of the sunlight
    And the earth dispossessed of the sun,   100
They have moonlight and sleep for repayment,
    When, refreshed as a bride and set free,
With stars and sea-winds in her raiment,
    Night sinks on the sea.   (1866)

Hertha

In Germanic mythology Hertha was goddess of the earth and of fertility and growth; Swinburne conceived of her as the personification of the world-soul. Of this poem he wrote in a letter to Stedman (February 21, 1875): "Of all I have done I rate *Hertha* highest as a single piece, finding in it the most lyric force and music combined with the most of condensed and clarified thought."

I am that which began;
    Out of me the years roll;
    Out of me God and man;
    I am equal and whole;
God changes, and man, and the form of them bodily; I am the soul.   5

    Before ever land was,
    Before ever the sea,
    Or soft hair of the grass,
    Or fair limbs of the tree,
Or the flesh-colored fruit of my branches, I was, and thy soul was in me.   10

    First life on my sources
    First drifted and swam;
    Out of me are the forces
    That save it or damn;
Out of me man and woman, and wild-beast and bird; before God was, I am.   15

    Beside or above me
    Naught is there to go;
    Love or unlove me,
    Unknow me or know,
I am that which unloves me and loves; I am stricken, and I am the blow.   20

    I the mark that is missed
    And the arrows that miss,
    I the mouth that is kissed
    And the breath in the kiss,
The search, and the sought, and the seeker, the soul and the body that is.   25

    I am that thing which blesses
    My spirit elate;
    That which caresses
    With hands uncreate
My limbs unbegotten that measure the length of the measure of fate.   30

    But what thing dost thou now,
    Looking Godward, to cry,
    "I am I, thou art thou,
    I am low, thou art high"?
I am thou, whom thou seekest to find him; find thou but thyself, thou art I.   35

    I the grain and the furrow,
    The plow-cloven clod
    And the plowshare drawn thorough,
    The germ and the sod,
The deed and the doer, the seed and the sower, the dust which is God.   40

    Hast thou known how I fashioned thee,
    Child, underground?
    Fire that impassioned thee,
    Iron that bound,
Dim changes of water, what thing of all these hast thou known of or found?   45

    Canst thou say in thine heart
    Thou hast seen with thine eyes

---

15. before . . . am. Cf. *Exodus*, 3:14: "And God said unto Moses, I am that I am"; also *John*, 8:58: "Jesus said unto them, Verily, verily, I say unto you, Before Abraham was, I am." **20-40. I am that,** etc. The thought of these lines is suggestive of Emerson's *Brahma*, especially ll. 10-12:

When me they fly, I am the wings;
I am the doubter and the doubt,
And I the hymn the Brahmin sings.

41. Hast thou known, etc. With these questions compare the words spoken to Job by the Lord out of the whirlwind (*Job*, 38-39). See Vol. I, p. 601.

With what cunning of art
    Thou wast wrought in what wise,
By what force of what stuff thou wast shapen,
    and shown on my breast to the skies?   50

    Who hath given, who hath sold it thee,
        Knowledge of me?
    Hath the wilderness told it thee?
        Hast thou learnt of the sea?
Hast thou communed in spirit with night?
    Have the winds taken counsel with thee?

    Have I set such a star   56
        To show light on thy brow
    That thou sawest from afar
        What I show to thee now?
Have ye spoken as brethren together, the sun
    and the mountains and thou?   60

    What is here, dost thou know it?
        What was, hast thou known?
    Prophet nor poet
        Nor tripod nor throne
Nor spirit nor flesh can make answer, but only
    thy mother alone.   65

    Mother, not maker,
        Born, and not made;
    Though her children forsake her,
        Allured or afraid,
Praying prayers to the God of their fashion,
    she stirs not for all that have prayed.   70

    A creed is a rod,
        And a crown is of night;
    But this thing is God,
        To be man with thy might,
To grow straight in the strength of thy spirit,
    and live out thy life as the light.   75

    I am in thee to save thee,
        As my soul in thee saith;
    Give thou as I gave thee,
        Thy life-blood and breath,
Green leaves of thy labor, white flowers of thy
    thought, and red fruit of thy death.   80

    Be the ways of thy giving
        As mine were to thee;
    The free life of thy living,
        Be the gift of it free;
Not as servant to lord, nor as master to slave,
    shalt thou give thee to me.   85

    O children of banishment,
        Souls overcast,
    Were the lights ye see vanish meant
        Alway to last,
Ye would know not the sun overshining the
    shadows and stars overpast.   90

    I that saw where ye trod
        The dim paths of the night
    Set the shadow called God
        In your skies to give light;
But the morning of manhood is risen, and the
    shadowless soul is in sight.   95

    The tree many-rooted
        That swells to the sky
    With frondage red-fruited,
        The life-tree am I;
In the buds of your lives is the sap of my
    leaves; ye shall live and not die.   100

    But the gods of your fashion
        That take and that give,
    In their pity and passion
        That scourge and forgive,
They are worms that are bred in the bark that
    falls off; they shall die and not live.   105

    My own blood is what stanches
        The wounds in my bark;
    Stars caught in my branches
        Make day of the dark,
And are worshiped as suns till the sunrise
    shall tread out their fires as a spark.   110

    Where dead ages hide under
        The live roots of the tree,
    In my darkness the thunder
        Makes utterance of me;

---

64. **Nor . . . throne**, neither priest nor king. The tripod was the altar, supported on three legs, on which the priestesses of Apollo at Delphi sat when they delivered their oracles. 67. **Born . . . made.** These lines are a protest against the idea of a single act of creation. Swinburne conceives nature as a continuous process of evolution.

88. **lights**, religious creeds and dogmas. 96. **The tree many-rooted**, the mighty ash tree Yggdrasil, supposed, in Norse mythology, to support the entire universe. It represents the whole of the universe, for its roots are in hell, it trunk is in earth, and its branches are in heaven.

In the clash of my boughs with each other ye
    hear the waves sound of the sea.   115

    That noise is of Time,
        As his feathers are spread
    And his feet set to climb
        Through the boughs overhead,
And my foliage rings round him and rustles,
    and branches are bent with his tread.   120

    The storm-winds of ages
        Blow through me and cease,
    The war-wind that rages,
        The spring-wind of peace,
Ere the breath of them roughen my tresses,
    ere one of my blossoms increase.   125

    All sounds of all changes,
        All shadows and lights
    On the world's mountain-ranges
        And stream-riven heights,
Whose tongue is the wind's tongue and language of storm-clouds on earth-shaking nights;   130

    All forms of all faces,
        All works of all hands
    In unsearchable places
        Of time-stricken lands,
All death and all life, and all reigns and all
    ruins, drop through me as sands.   135

    Though sore be my burden
        And more than ye know,
    And my growth have no guerdon
        But only to grow,
Yet I fail not of growing for lightnings above
    me or deathworms below.   140

    These too have their part in me,
        As I too in these;
    Such fire is at heart in me,
        Such sap is this tree's,
Which hath in it all sounds and all secrets of
    infinite lands and of seas.   145

    In the spring-colored hours
        When my mind was as May's,
    There brake forth of me flowers
        By centuries of days,
Strong blossoms with perfume of manhood
    shot out from my spirit as rays.   150

    And the sound of them springing
        And smell of their shoots
    Were as warmth and sweet singing
        And strength to my roots;
And the lives of my children made perfect
    with freedom of soul were my fruits.   155

    I bid you but be;
        I have need not of prayer;
    I have need of you free
        As your mouths of mine air;
That my heart may be greater within me,
    beholding the fruits of me fair.   160

    More fair than strange fruit is
        Of faiths ye espouse;
    In me only the root is
        That blooms in your boughs;
Behold now your God that ye made you, to
    feed him with faith of your vows.   165

    In the darkening and whitening
        Abysses adored,
    With dayspring and lightning
        For lamp and for sword,
God thunders in heaven, and his angels are
    red with the wrath of the Lord.   170

    O my sons, O too dutiful
        Toward gods not of me,
    Was not I enough beautiful?
        Was it hard to be free?
For behold, I am with you, am in you and of
    you; look forth now and see.   175

    Lo, winged with world's wonders,
        With miracles shod,
    With the fires of his thunders
        For raiment and rod,
God trembles in heaven, and his angels are
    white with the terror of God.   180

    For his twilight is come on him,
        His anguish is here;

181. **his twilight.** The idea of the twilight of the gods is derived from Norse mythology. This is the period, known as Ragnarok, which involves the destruction of the universe. After this period a new heaven and a new earth will arise out of the sea.

And his spirits gaze dumb on him,
   Grown gray from his fear;
And his hour taketh hold on him stricken, the
   last of his infinite year.   185

   Thought made him and breaks him,
      Truth slays and forgives;
   But to you, as time takes him,
      This new thing it gives,
Even love, the beloved Republic, that feeds
   upon freedom and lives.   190

   For truth only is living,
      Truth only is whole,
   And the love of his giving
      Man's polestar and pole;
Man, pulse of my center, and fruit of my
   body, and seed of my soul;   195

   One birth of my bosom;
      One beam of mine eye;
   One topmost blossom
      That scales the sky;
Man, equal and one with me, man that is
   made of me, man that is I.   (1871)

A Forsaken Garden

The scene is East Dene, on the Isle of Wight, where Swinburne spent much of his youth.

In a coign of the cliff between lowland and
   highland,
   At the sea-down's edge between windward
      and lee,
Walled round with rocks as an inland island,
   The ghost of a garden fronts the sea.
A girdle of brushwood and thorn encloses   5
   The steep square slope of the blossomless
      bed
Where the weeds that grew green from the
   graves of its roses
      Now lie dead.

The fields fall southward, abrupt and broken,
   To the low last edge of the long lone land. 10
If a step should sound or a word be spoken,

1. **coign,** corner, projection.

   Would a ghost not rise at the strange guest's
      hand?
So long have the gray bare walks lain guest-
   less,
   Through branches and briars if a man make
      way,
He shall find no life, but the sea-wind's, rest-
   less   15
      Night and day.

The dense hard passage is blind and stifled
   That crawls by a track none turn to climb
To the strait waste place that the years have
   rifled
   Of all but the thorns that are touched not
      of time.   20
The thorns he spares when the rose is taken;
   The rocks are left when he wastes the plain.
The wind that wanders, the weeds wind-
   shaken,
      These remain.

Not a flower to be pressed of the foot that falls
   not;   25
   As the heart of a dead man the seed-plots
      are dry;
From the thicket of thorns whence the night-
   ingale calls not,
   Could she call, there were never a rose to
      reply.
Over the meadows that blossom and wither
   Wings but the note of a sea-bird's song;   30
Only the sun and the rain come hither
      All year long.

The sun burns sear and the rain dishevels
   One gaunt bleak blossom of scentless breath.
Only the wind here hovers and revels   35
   In a round where life seems barren as death.
Here there was laughing of old, there was
   weeping,
   Haply, of lovers none ever will know,
Whose eyes went seaward a hundred sleeping
      Years ago.   40

Heart handfast in heart as they stood, "Look
   thither,"
   Did he whisper? "look forth from the flow-
      ers to the sea;

For the foam-flowers endure when the rose-
    blossoms wither,
  And men that love lightly may die—but we?"
And the same wind sang and the same waves
    whitened,   45
  And or ever the garden's last petals were
    shed,
In the lips that had whispered, the eyes that
    had lightened,
    Love was dead.

Or they loved their life through, and then
    went whither?
  And were one to the end—but what end
    who knows?   50
Love deep as the sea as a rose must wither,
  As the rose-red seaweed that mocks the rose.
Shall the dead take thought for the dead to
    love them?
  What love was ever as deep as a grave? 54
They are loveless now as the grass above them
    Or the wave.

All are at one now, roses and lovers,
  Not known of the cliffs and the fields and
    the sea.
Not a breath of the time that has been hovers
  In the air now soft with a summer to be. 60
Not a breath shall there sweeten the seasons
    hereafter
  Of the flowers or the lovers that laugh now
    or weep,
When as they that are free now of weeping
    and laughter
    We shall sleep.

Here death may deal not again forever;   65
  Here change may come not till all change
    end.
From the graves they have made they shall
    rise up never,
  Who have left naught living to ravage and
    rend.
Earth, stones, and thorns of the wild ground
    growing,
  While the sun and the rain live, these shall
    be;   70
Till a last wind's breath upon all these blow-
    ing
    Roll the sea.

Till the slow sea rise and the sheer cliff crum-
    ble,
  Till terrace and meadow the deep gulfs
    drink,
Till the strength of the waves of the high tides
    humble   75
  The fields that lessen, the rocks that shrink,
Here now in his triumph where all things
    falter,
  Stretched out on the spoils that his own
    hand spread,
As a god self-slain on his own strange altar,
    Death lies dead.   (1876)

A Jacobite's Farewell
1716

    The Jacobites were the supporters of James II, who was driven from the throne of England by the revolution of 1688, of his son James Stuart, the "Old Pretender," and of his grandson Charles Edward Stuart, the "Young Pretender." They derived their name from *Jacobus,* Late Latin for James. The date 1716 marks the end of the Old Pretender's unsuccessful attempt to secure the throne. Swinburne was descended from an old Northumbrian family noted for its Jacobite sympathies (see p. 808). The speaker in the poem is an old Scottish cavalier who had been loyal to the dethroned Stuarts.

There's nae mair lands to tyne, my dear,
  And nae mair lives to gie;
Though a man think sair to live nae mair,
  There's but one day to die.

For a' things come and a' days gane,   5
  What needs ye rend your hair?
But kiss me till the morn's morrow,
  Then I'll kiss ye nae mair.

O lands are lost and life's losing,
  And what were they to gie?   10
Fu' mony a man gives all he can,
  But nae man else gives ye.

Our king wons ower the sea's water,
  And I in prison sair;

---

1. **to tyne**, to lose.   13. **wons**, dwells. The Pretender lived for a while in France.

But I'll win out the morn's morrow,   15
    And ye'll see me nae mair.   (1877)

A Ballad of François Villon

PRINCE OF ALL BALLAD-MAKERS

François Villon (1431-1463?) was a French poet and vagabond, famous for his *ballades*. See Rossetti's *Ballad of Dead Ladies*, and headnote, p. 792.

Bird of the bitter bright gray golden morn
    Scarce risen upon the dusk of dolorous years,
First of us all and sweetest singer born
    Whose far shrill note the world of new men hears
    Cleave the cold shuddering shade as twilight clears;   5
When song new-born put off the old world's attire
    And felt its tune on her changed lips expire,
Writ foremost on the roll of them that came
Fresh girt for service of the latter lyre,
    Villon, our sad bad glad mad brother's name!   10

Alas the joy, the sorrow, and the scorn,
    That clothed thy life with hopes and sins and fears,
And gave thee stones for bread and tares for corn
    And plume-plucked gaol-birds for thy starveling peers
    Till death clipped close their flight with shameful shears;   15
Till shifts came short and loves were hard to hire,
When lilt of song nor twitch of twangling wire
    Could buy thee bread or kisses; when light fame
Spurned like a ball and haled through brake and briar,
    Villon, our sad bad glad mad brother's name!   20

Poor splendid wings so frayed and soiled and torn!
    Poor kind wild eyes so dashed with light quick tears!
Poor perfect voice, most blithe when most forlorn,
    That rings athwart the sea whence no man steers
    Like joy-bells crossed with death-bells in our ears!   25
What far delight has cooled the fierce desire
That like some ravenous bird was strong to tire
    On that frail flesh and soul consumed with flame,
But left more sweet than roses to respire,
    Villon, our sad bad glad mad brother's name?   30

ENVOI

Prince of sweet songs made out of tears and fire,
A harlot was thy nurse, a god thy sire;
    Shame soiled thy song, and song assoiled thy shame.
But from thy feet now death has washed the mire,   34
Love reads out first at head of all our quire,
    Villon, our sad bad glad mad brother's name.   (1877)

---

1. **golden morn**, the Renaissance, which succeeded the "dusk" of the Middle Ages. 6. **song new-born**. Villon is regarded as the first and as one of the greatest of the French lyric poets of the modern school. His verse, characterized by polish, raciness, and intense subjectivity, had great influence. 13. **stones for bread**. From Christ's Sermon on the Mount, *Matthew*, 7:9: "Or what man is there of you, whom if his son ask bread, will he give him a stone?" **tares for corn**. An allusion to the parable of the tares sown among the wheat (*Matthew*, 13:25-40). 14. **gaol-birds . . . peers**. For a number of years Villon was the leader of a band of vagabonds and thieves that infested the streets of Paris. He was arrested and imprisoned several times for robbery. 16. **shifts came short**, his expedients for a livelihood were exhausted.

29. **respire**, breathe. 32. **harlot . . . sire**. Many poets have sprung from humble origin, but Villon is unique in his startling combination of artistic fineness and baseness of life.

The Higher Pantheism in a Nutshell

This poem is a parody on Tennyson's *Higher Pantheism*, p. 645.

One, who is not, we see; but one, whom we see not, is.
Surely this is not that; but that is assuredly this.

What, and wherefore, and whence? for under
    is over and under;
If thunder could be without lightning, light-
    ning could be without thunder.

Doubt is faith, in the main; but faith, on the
    whole, is doubt.   5
We cannot believe by proof; but could we be-
    lieve without?

Why, and whither, and how? for barley and
    rye are not clover;
Neither are straight lines curves—yet over is
    under and over.

Two and two may be four, but four and four
    are not eight;
Fate and God may be twain, but God is the
    same thing as fate.   10

Ask a man what he thinks, and get from a
    man what he feels;
God, once caught in the fact, shows you a
    fair pair of heels.

Body and spirit are twins; God only knows
    which is which—
The soul squats down in the flesh, like a
    tinker drunk in a ditch.

More is the whole than a part, but half is
    more than the whole;   15
Clearly, the soul is the body—but is not the
    body the soul?

One and two are not one, but one and noth-
    ing is two;
Truth can hardly be false, if falsehood cannot
    be true.

Once the mastodon was; pterodactyls were
    common as cocks.
Then the mammoth was God; now is He a
    prize ox.   20

Parallels all things are—yet many of these are
    askew;
You are certainly I, but certainly I am not you.

    12. **fact**, deed, act.

Springs the rock from the plain, shoots the
    stream from the rock;
Cocks exist for the hen, but hens exist for the
    cock.

God, whom we see not, is; and God, who is
    not, we see.   25
Fiddle, we know, is diddle; and diddle, we
    take it, is dee.   (1880)

Nephelidia

    The title means *Cloudlets*. Swinburne here parodies his own mannerisms of diction and rhythm.

From the depth of the dreamy decline of the
    dawn through a notable nimbus of
    nebulous noonshine,
    Pallid and pink as the palm of the flag-
        flower that flickers with fear of the flies
        as they float,
Are the looks of our lovers that lustrously
    lean from a marvel of mystic, mirac-
    ulous moonshine,
    These that we feel in the blood of our
        blushes that thicken and threaten with
        throbs through the throat?
Thicken and thrill as a theater thronged at
    appeal of an actor's appalled agitation,
    Fainter with fear of the fires of the future
        than pale with the promise of pride in
        the past;   6
Flushed with the famishing fullness of fever
    that reddens with radiance of rathe
    recreation,
    Gaunt as the ghastliest of glimpses that
        gleam through the gloom of the gloam-
        ing when ghosts go aghast?
Nay, for the nick of the tick of the time is
    a tremulous touch on the temples of
    terror,
    Strained as the sinews yet strenuous with
        strife of the dead who is dumb as the
        dust-heaps of death;   10
Surely no soul is it, sweet as the spasm of
    erotic emotional exquisite error,
    Bathed in the balms of beatified bliss, bea-
        tific itself by beatitudes' breath.

    7. **rathe**, quick, fast.

Surely no spirit or sense of a soul that was soft
    to the spirit and soul of our senses
  Sweetens the stress of suspiring suspicion
      that sobs in the semblance and sound
      of a sigh;
Only this oracle opens Olympian, in mystical
      moods and triangular tenses—   15
  "Life is the lust of a lamp for the light that
      is dark till the dawn of the day when
      we die."
Mild is the mirk and monotonous music of
      memory, melodiously mute as it may
      be,
  While the hope in the heart of a hero is
      bruised by the breach of men's rapiers,
      resigned to the rod;
Made meek as a mother whose bosom-beats
      bound with the bliss-bringing bulk of
      a balm-breathing baby,
  As they grope through the graveyard of
      creeds, under skies growing green at a
      groan for the grimness of God.   20
Blank is the book of his bounty beholden of
      old, and its binding is blacker than
      bluer;
  Out of blue into black is the scheme of the
      skies, and their dews are the wine of
      the bloodshed of things;
Till the darkling desire of delight shall be free
      as a fawn that is freed from the fangs
      that pursue her,
  Till the heart-beats of hell shall be hushed
      by a hymn from the hunt that has
      harried the kennel of kings.   (1880)

14. **suspiring**, sighing, desiring. 15. **Olympian**, godlike, after the manner of the gods of Mt. Olympus, in ancient Greece.

A Child's Laughter

All the bells of heaven may ring,
All the birds of heaven may sing,
All the wells on earth may spring,
All the winds on earth may bring
    All sweet sounds together;   5
Sweeter far than all things heard,
Hand of harper, tone of bird,
Sound of woods at sundawn stirred,
Welling water's winsome word,
    Wind in warm wan weather,   10

One thing yet there is, that none
Hearing ere its chime be done
Knows not well the sweetest one
Heard of man beneath the sun,
    Hoped in heaven hereafter;   15
Soft and strong and loud and light,
Very sound of very light
Heard from morning's rosiest height,
When the soul of all delight
    Fills a child's clear laughter.   20

Golden bells of welcome rolled
Never forth such notes, nor told
Hours so blithe in tones so bold,
As the radiant mouth of gold
    Here that rings forth heaven.   25
If the golden-crested wren
Were a nightingale—why, then,
Something seen and heard of men
Might be half as sweet as when
    Laughs a child of seven.   (1882)

LAUGHING CRITICS IN VERSE

The popular conception of the Victorian age is that the period was moral, serious, purposeful, and heavy. These qualities it did possess; the Victorians had more than a dash of the Puritan in them, and they attacked in sober seriousness the critical social problems of their times. This purpose, as has been shown, is amply reflected in their literature. To suppose, however, that the Victorians were devoid of humor and especially that they were incapable of laughing at themselves is far from correct. The period had many humorists in verse who enjoyed laughing at society, and much of the nature of the age can be learned from their satirical and humorous verses.

The laughing verse of the Victorian age took many forms. The best of it, perhaps, was satirical, and it is this satirical verse which provides the student of the period with an easy understanding of the foibles and eccentricities of the times. But much of it was pure nonsense verse, a delightful diversion from the basic seriousness of most Victorian poetry. Such a poem is Edward Lear's *The Owl and the Pussy-Cat*, and only a Dr. DryasDust totally devoid of humor would attempt to read into the nonsense any allegory or criticism of life. This and many other nonsense poems of the period provide vacations in the land of the absurd and the whimsical; they clear the brain of fog and weariness; but they have no critical objective—and need none.

The verse critics helped to correct society by laughing at it or by mocking its foibles. In this poetry there is little that is bitter; it is ironic rather than sarcastic and seasoned rather than sauced with satire. Some of these verses are directed against the solemn pretenses of society; so W. S. Gilbert's delightful *Bab Ballads* and the rollicking songs from the comic operas rub salt into the smug conventions which attend Victorian life in the navy, the church, the bar—everywhere. Art and literature do not escape these attacks. The verse critics knew that parody is the keenest form of ridicule; therefore their verses are often parodies in which flatness, smugness, banality, poor taste in poetry are exhibited in verses which copy the forms and expose the weaknesses of the originals. So sharp and clever are some of these parodies that not infrequently the originals would have been forgotten entirely save for the reflected immortality which they have acquired from parodies greater than themselves. This is true, for example, of the namby-pamby moral poems of Southey, flat and flashy things, which have only the distinction of having inspired sparkling parodies by their very defects. Lewis Carroll put into the mouths of his Alice and the miscellaneous creatures of her dream-worlds several of the best of these parodies.

EDWARD LEAR (1812-1888) was a friend of Tennyson, a painter by profession, and by avocation the writer of some of the most easy and rollicking of the nonsense verses of the period. While painting birds and animals on the estate of the Earl of Derby he amused himself and the Earl's grandson by writing absurd limericks and nonsense verses. From the painting of animals he turned to landscape painting, and traveled to Africa and other little-known parts of the world in search of subject-matter for his brush. His wanderings he recorded with excellent good humor in *Illustrated Journal of a Landscape Painter* (1869). Toward the end of his life he retired to a villa at San Remo in Italy, where, among other things, he made two hundred drawings to illustrate the poetry of his friend Tennyson. It is not for these illustrations, however, that he is so widely known but for the drollery, fantasy, and absurdity of verses that have made him one of the most popular of the Victorian writers of nonsense. Some of his verses, like *The Owl and the Pussy-Cat*, have attained the permanence of nursery classics.

CHARLES STUART CALVERLEY (1831-1884) was the son of a Worcestershire clergyman. At Cambridge he was brilliant but lazy, and his social charm and grace made him popular among his fellows. Even in college he wrote parodies and clever rimes, displaying then the dexterity and mastery of verse forms that distinguished his later work. By profession he was a barrister; verse writing was to him an avocation and a source of amusement. A skating accident in the winter of 1866-1867 in which he struck his head on the ice cut short a brilliant career. Although he lived until 1884, he found it impossible to carry on his profession, and his sparkling verses appeared only at rare intervals. The principal publications by which Calverley is known are *Verses and Translations* (1862), *Translations into English and Latin* (1866), *Theocritus Translated into English Verse* (1869), and *Fly Leaves* (1872).

CHARLES LUTWIDGE DODGSON (1832-1898) is better known by his pen name of Lewis Carroll. He was a lecturer in mathematics at Oxford and the author, under his own name, of *An Elementary Treatise on Determinants* (1867), *Symbolic Logic* (1896), and other scholarly treatises which would hardly have given him a place in English literature. Charles Dodgson, indeed, would have been completely forgotten but for the work of his *alter ego*, Lewis Carroll. Lewis Carroll, shy in the company of adults, loved children and knew and understood the world of the imagination in which the most sensitive of them lived. So he put his little friend Alice Liddell into a dream-story and found himself famous as the author of *Alice in Wonderland* (1865). Alice figures in another story, *Through the Looking-Glass* (1871), in which she has a series of adventures on a giant chessboard. These are Lewis Carroll's best-known classics of childhood, but there are some excellent things in *The Hunting of the Snark* (1876) and *Silvie and Bruno* (1889-1893). His unity of mood, whimsical quality, the accurate but mild satire, and above all the rich fertility of his imagination give Lewis Carroll's stories charm and individuality. The parodies of poems which Alice knew "by heart" or which were recited to her by various odd creatures in her dream-worlds are excellent fun. Dodgson was a mathematician, but Carroll knew poetry as well as he knew children and their world, and was an adept at making absurd metrical caricatures of some of the most moral and didactic of the poems which Victorian children were required to memorize to "make them good."

WILLIAM SCHWENCK GILBERT (1836-1911) is probably the best known of the Victorian nonsense poets, for the whimsical light operas which he wrote in collaboration with Sir Arthur Sullivan still delight thousands because of qualities that are not Victorian but universal. Gilbert was born in London and educated in London University. He was successively an officer in the Gordon Highlanders, a clerk in a government office, and a practicing barrister in London—experiences which gave him the material for his verse satires of these occupations. In 1861 he began writing for the magazine *Fun,* and in his *Bab Ballads* appeared the characteristic humor that made him famous in his comic-opera lyrics. "All humor," he believed, "is based upon a grave and quasi-respectful treatment of the ludicrous." The *Bab Ballads* were issued in two volumes in 1869 and 1873 respectively. Between these dates he took to stage criticism, and this work led to the writing of light dramatic travesties. The first of his light operas was *Trial by Jury* (1875); others that every music lover knows are *H.M.S. Pinafore* (1878), *The Pirates of Penzance* (1879), *Patience* (1881), *Iolanthe* (1882), *The Mikado* (1885), *Ruddigore* (1887), *The Yeoman of the Guard* (1888), and *The Gondoliers* (1889). The music for these was written by Sir Arthur Sullivan, and in light opera the names Gilbert and Sullivan are as inseparable as are those of Beaumont and Fletcher in Elizabethan drama. The success of Gilbert lay in his whimsicality, his solemn and apparently irrefutable illogicalities, his rich variety, his subtlety, and—perhaps most of all—his easy and flexible verse making. He was probably the most facile versifier of the group, and his songs have such excellent sense under the surface of their absurdities that it is perhaps unfair to call him a maker of nonsense verse.

JAMES KENNETH STEPHEN (1859-1892) was a friend of Charles Stuart Calverley and, like Calverley, a student at Cambridge and an undergraduate composer of parodies and light verse. He did not have quite the older poet's facility, but he had, nevertheless, a remarkable control of metrical forms that makes his verses smooth and easy. From head injuries sustained as a boy he gradually sickened, and died in 1892. His work as a parodist and light-verse writer appears in *Lapsus Calami* (1891), *Quo Musa Tendis* (1891), *Lapsus Calami, and Other Verses* (1896).

Edward Lear
1812-1888

The Owl and the Pussy-Cat

The Owl and the Pussy-Cat went to sea
  In a beautiful pea-green boat;
They took some honey, and plenty of money
  Wrapped up in a five-pound note.
The Owl looked up to the stars above,   5
  And sang to a small guitar,
"O lovely Pussy, O Pussy, my love,
  What a beautiful Pussy you are,
      You are,
      You are!   10
What a beautiful Pussy you are!"

Pussy said to the Owl, "You elegant fowl,
  How charmingly sweet you sing!
Oh! let us be married; too long we have tarried;
  But what shall we do for a ring?"   15
They sailed away, for a year and a day,
  To the land where the bong-tree grows;
And there in a wood a Piggy-wig stood,
  With a ring at the end of his nose,
      His nose,   20
      His nose,
With a ring at the end of his nose.

"Dear Pig, are you willing to sell for one shilling
  Your ring?" Said the Piggy, "I will."
So they took it away, and were married next day   25
  By the Turkey who lives on the hill.
They dined on mince and slices of quince,
  Which they ate with a runcible spoon;
And hand in hand, on the edge of the sand,
  They danced by the light of the moon,   30
      The moon,
      The moon,
They danced by the light of the moon.
              (1871)

17. **bong-tree**, a made-up, nonsensical word. 28. **runcible spoon**, a kind of fork with three broad prongs, one with a sharp edge, curved like a spoon.

Incidents in the Life of My Uncle Arly

This is a parody of Wordsworth's *Resolution and Independence*, p. 148. Cf. Lewis Carroll's *White Knight's Ballad*, p. 831, another parody of the same poem.

O my agéd Uncle Arly!
Sitting on a heap of Barley
  Through the silent hours of night—
Close beside a leafy thicket:—
On his nose there was a Cricket,   5
In his hat a Railway-Ticket;—
  (But his shoes were far too tight.)

Long ago, in youth, he squandered
All his goods away, and wandered
  To the Tiniskoop-hills afar.   10
There on golden sunsets blazing,
Every evening found him gazing—
Singing—"Orb! you're quite amazing!
  How I wonder what you are!"

Like the ancient Medes and Persians,   15
Always by his own exertions
  He subsisted on those hills;
Whiles—by teaching children spelling;
Or at times by merely yelling,
Or at intervals by selling   20
  "Propter's Nicodemus Pills."

Later, in his morning rambles
He perceived the moving brambles
  Something square and white disclose;
'Twas a First-class Railway-Ticket;   25
But, on stooping down to pick it
Off the ground, a pea-green Cricket
  Settled on my uncle's Nose.

Never—never more—oh! never
Did that Cricket leave him ever,   30
  Dawn or evening, day or night;—
Clinging as a constant treasure,

10. **Tiniskoop-hills**, a made-up word satirizing the hills in Wordsworth's poetry. 15. **Medes**, people of ancient Media, a kingdom in what is now northwestern Persia; it attained its greatest power in the seventh and sixth centuries before Christ. 21. **"Propter's Nicodemus Pills,"** a ludicrous reference to some contemporary quack medicine.

Chirping with a cheerious measure,
Wholly to my uncle's pleasure;—
    (Though his shoes were far too tight.) 35

So for three-and-forty winters,
Till his shoes were worn to splinters,
    All those hills he wandered o'er—
Sometimes silent, sometimes yelling—
Till he came to Borley-Melling, 40
Near his old ancestral dwelling:—
    (But his shoes were far too tight.)

On a little heap of Barley
Died my agéd Uncle Arly,
    And they buried him one night— 45
Close beside the leafy thicket;
There—his hat and Railway-Ticket;
There—his ever-faithful Cricket;—
    (But his shoes were far too tight.)

Charles Stuart Calverley
1831-1884

Ballad

This is a parody of Pre-Raphaelite ballads like Rossetti's *Sister Helen*, p. 787, and *Troy Town*, p. 792. These ballads are characterized by a refrain that is often inconsequential and meaningless, and therefore most appropriate for parody.

PART 1

The auld wife sat at her ivied door,
    (*Butter and eggs and a pound of cheese*)
A thing she had frequently done before;
    And her spectacles lay on her aproned knees.

The piper he piped on the hilltop high, 5
    (*Butter and eggs and a pound of cheese*)
Till the cow said, "I die," and the goose asked "Why?"
    And the dog said nothing, but searched for fleas.

The farmer he strode through the square farmyard;
    (*Butter and eggs and a pound of cheese*) 10

His last brew of ale was a trifle hard,
    The connection of which with the plot one sees.

The farmer's daughter hath frank blue eyes;
    (*Butter and eggs and a pound of cheese*)
She hears the rooks caw in the windy skies, 15
    As she sits at her lattice and shells her peas.

The farmer's daughter hath ripe red lips;
    (*Butter and eggs and a pound of cheese*)
If you try to approach her away she skips
    Over tables and chairs with apparent ease. 20

The farmer's daughter hath soft brown hair;
    (*Butter and eggs and a pound of cheese*)
And I met with a ballad, I can't say where,
    Which wholly consisted of lines like these.

PART 2

She sat with her hands 'neath her dimpled cheeks, 25
    (*Butter and eggs and a pound of cheese*)
And spake not a word. While a lady speaks
    There is hope, but she didn't even sneeze.

She sat with her hands 'neath her crimson cheeks;
    (*Butter and eggs and a pound of cheese*) 30
She gave up mending her father's breeks,
    And let the cat roll in her best chemise.

She sat with her hands 'neath her burning cheeks,
    (*Butter and eggs and a pound of cheese*)
And gazed at the piper for thirteen weeks; 35
    Then she followed him out o'er the misty leas.

Her sheep followed her, as their tails did them,
    (*Butter and eggs and a pound of cheese*)
And this song is considered a perfect gem; 39
    And as to the meaning, it's what you please.
                         (1872)

40. **Borley-Melling**, a made-up word.

31. **breeks**, breeches.

Charles Lutwidge Dodgson
("Lewis Carroll")
1832-1898

The Crocodile

This poem is a parody of Isaac Watts's *How Doth the Little Busy Bee.*

> How doth the little crocodile
>   Improve his shining tail,
> And pour the waters of the Nile
>   On every shining scale!
>
> How cheerfully he seems to grin, 5
>   How neatly spreads his claws,
> And welcomes little fishes in
>   With gently smiling jaws.   (1865)

The Voice of the Lobster

> "Tis the voice of the Lobster: I heard him declare
> 'You have baked me too brown, I must sugar my hair.'
> As a duck with its eyelids, so he with his nose
> Trims his belt and his buttons, and turns out his toes.
> When the sands are all dry, he is gay as a lark,
> And will talk in contemptuous tones of the Shark;   6
> But, when the tide rises and sharks are around,
> His voice has a timid and tremulous sound.
>
> "I passed by his garden and marked, with one eye,
> How the Owl and the Panther were sharing a pie;   10
> The Panther tock pie-crust, and gravy, and meat,
> While the Owl had the dish as its share of the treat.
> When the pie was finished, the Owl, as a boon,
> Was kindly permitted to pocket the spoon;
> While the Panther received knife and fork with a growl,   15
> And concluded the banquet by— —"   (1865)

Father William

A parody, this is much more famous than its original, Southey's *The Old Man's Comforts*, p. 301.

> "You are old, Father William," the young man said,
>   "And your hair has become very white,
> And yet you incessantly stand on your head—
>   Do you think, at your age, it is right?"
>
> "In my youth," Father William replied to his son,   5
>   "I feared it might injure the brain;
> But now that I'm perfectly sure I have none,
>   Why, I do it again and again."
>
> "You are old," said the youth, "as I mentioned before,
>   And have grown uncommonly fat;   10
> Yet you turned a back-somersault in at the door—
>   Pray, what is the reason of that?"
>
> "In my youth," said the sage, as he shook his gray locks,
>   "I kept all my limbs very supple

By the use of this ointment—one shilling the
    box— 15
    Allow me to sell you a couple."

"You are old," said the youth, "and your jaws
    are too weak
    For anything tougher than suet;
Yet you finished the goose, with the bones and
    the beak;
    Pray, how did you manage to do it?" 20

"In my youth," said his father, "I took to the
    law,
    And argued each case with my wife;
And the muscular strength which it gave to
    my jaw
    Has lasted the rest of my life."

"You are old," said the youth, "one would
    hardly suppose 25
    That your eye was as steady as ever;
Yet you balanced an eel on the end of your
    nose—
    What made you so awfully clever?"

"I have answered three questions, and that is
    enough,"
    Said his father; "don't give yourself airs! 30
Do you think I can listen all day to such
    stuff?
    Be off, or I'll kick you downstairs!" (1865)

The Mock Turtle's Song

"Will you walk a little faster?" said a whiting
    to a snail,
"There's a porpoise close behind us, and he's
    treading on my tail.
See how eagerly the lobsters and the turtles
    all advance!
They are waiting on the shingle—will you
    come and join the dance?
    Will you, won't you, will you, won't you,
    will you join the dance? 5
    Will you, won't you, will you, won't you,
    won't you join the dance?

"You can really have no notion how delight-
    ful it will be
When they take us up and throw us, with
    the lobsters, out to sea!"
But the snail replied, "Too far, too far!" and
    gave a look askance—
Said he thanked the whiting kindly, but he
    would not join the dance. 10
    Would not, could not, would not, could
    not, would not join the dance.
    Would not, could not, would not, could
    not, could not join the dance.

"What matters it how far we go?" his scaly
    friend replied,
"There is another shore, you know, upon the
    other side.
The further off from England the nearer is
    to France; 15
Then turn not pale, beloved snail, but come
    and join the dance.
    Will you, won't you, will you, won't you,
    will you join the dance?
    Will you, won't you, will you, won't you,
    won't you join the dance?" (1865)

Jabberwocky

'Twas brillig, and the slithy toves
    Did gyre and gimble in the wabe;
All mimsy were the borogoves,
    And the mome raths outgrabe.

"Beware the Jabberwock, my son! 5
    The jaws that bite, the claws that catch!
Beware the Jubjub bird, and shun
    The frumious Bandersnatch!"

He took his vorpal sword in hand;
    Long time the manxome foe he sought— 10
So rested he by the Tumtum tree,
    And stood awhile in thought.

And, as in uffish thought he stood,
    The Jabberwock, with eyes of flame,
Came whiffling through the tulgey wood, 15
    And burbled as it came!

One, two! One, two! And through and
    through
    The vorpal blade went snicker-snack!

He left it dead, and with its head
　　He went galumphing back.　　　　　20

"And hast thou slain the Jabberwock?
　　Come to my arms, my beamish boy!
O frabjous day! Callooh! Callay!"
　　He chortled in his joy.

'Twas brillig, and the slithy toves　　25
　　Did gyre and gimble in the wabe;
All mimsy were the borogoves,
　　And the mome raths outgrabe.　　(1872)

Glossary to *Jabberwocky*

The following glossary of the invented words in *Jabberwocky* is compiled from ingenious definitions given by Humpty Dumpty in Carroll's *Through the Looking-Glass;* the last definition is found in the *Preface* to *The Hunting of the Snark.*

Brillig. Four o'clock in the afternoon—the time when you begin *broiling* things for dinner.

Slithy. Lithe and slimy. *Lithe* is the same as *active.* It is like a portmanteau—there are two meanings packed up into one word.

Toves. Animals something like badgers—they're something like lizards—and they're something like corkscrews. They make their nests under sun-dials; also they live on cheese.

Gyre. To go round and round like a gyroscope.

Gimble. To make holes like a gimlet.

Wabe. A grass-plot round a sun-dial; so called because it goes a long way before it, a long way behind it, and a long way beyond it on each side.

Mimsy. Flimsy and miserable; another portmanteau word.

Borogove. A thin, shabby-looking bird with its feathers sticking out all round—something like a live mop.

Mome. Humpty says that he is not certain of the meaning of this word; but he thinks it's "short for *from home*—meaning that they'd lost their way."

Rath. A sort of green pig.

Outgrabe. Past tense of *outgribe,* meaning to make a noise like something between bellowing and whistling, with a kind of sneeze in the middle.

Frumious. Another portmanteau word meaning fuming and furious.

The Walrus and the Carpenter

The sun was shining on the sea,
　　Shining with all his might;
He did his very best to make
　　The billows smooth and bright—
And this was odd, because it was　　5
　　The middle of the night.

The moon was shining sulkily,
　　Because she thought the sun
Had got no business to be there
　　After the day was done—　　　　10
"It's very rude of him," she said,
　　"To come and spoil the fun!"

The sea was wet as wet could be,
　　The sands were dry as dry.
You could not see a cloud, because　　15
　　No cloud was in the sky;
No birds were flying overhead—
　　There were no birds to fly.

The Walrus and the Carpenter
　　Were walking close at hand;　　20
They wept like anything to see
　　Such quantities of sand.
"If this were only cleared away,"
　　They said, "it *would* be grand!"

"If seven maids with seven mops　　25
　　Swept it for half a year,
Do you suppose," the Walrus said,
　　"That they could get it clear?"
"I doubt it," said the Carpenter,
　　And shed a bitter tear.　　　　　30

"O Oysters, come and walk with us!"
　　The Walrus did beseech.
"A pleasant walk, a pleasant talk,
　　Along the briny beach;
We cannot do with more than four,　　35
　　To give a hand to each."

The eldest Oyster looked at him,
  But never a word he said;
The eldest Oyster winked his eye,
  And shook his heavy head—
Meaning to say he did not choose
  To leave the oyster-bed.

But four young Oysters hurried up,
  All eager for the treat;
Their coats were brushed, their faces washed,
  Their shoes were clean and neat—
And this was odd, because, you know,
  They hadn't any feet.

Four other Oysters followed them,
  And yet another four;
And thick and fast they came at last,
  And more, and more, and more—
All hopping through the frothy waves,
  And scrambling to the shore.

The Walrus and the Carpenter
  Walked on a mile or so,
And then they rested on a rock
  Conveniently low;
And all the little Oysters stood
  And waited in a row.

"The time has come," the Walrus said,
  "To talk of many things:
Of shoes—and ships—and sealing wax—
  Of cabbages—and kings—
And why the sea is boiling hot—
  And whether pigs have wings."

"But wait a bit," the Oysters cried,
  "Before we have our chat;
For some of us are out of breath,
  And all of us are fat!"
"No hurry!" said the Carpenter.
  They thanked him much for that.

"A loaf of bread," the Walrus said,
  "Is what we chiefly need;
Pepper and vinegar besides
  Are very good indeed—
Now, if you're ready, Oysters dear,
  We can begin to feed."

"But not on us!" the Oysters cried,
  Turning a little blue.
"After such kindness, that would be
  A dismal thing to do!"
"The night is fine," the Walrus said,
  "Do you admire the view?

"It was so kind of you to come!
  And you are very nice!"
The Carpenter said nothing but
  "Cut us another slice.
I wish you were not quite so deaf—
  I've had to ask you twice!"

"It seems a shame," the Walrus said,
  "To play them such a trick,
After we've brought them out so far,
  And made them trot so quick!"
The Carpenter said nothing but
  "The butter's spread too thick!"

"I weep for you," the Walrus said;
  "I deeply sympathize."
With sobs and tears he sorted out
  Those of the largest size,
Holding his pocket-handkerchief
  Before his streaming eyes.

"O Oysters," said the Carpenter,
  "You've had a pleasant run!
Shall we be trotting home again?"
  But answer came there none—
And this was scarcely odd, because
  They'd eaten every one.   (1872)

The White Knight's Ballad

A parody on Wordsworth's *Resolution and Independence*, p. 148, this should be compared with Lear's *Incidents in the Life of My Uncle Arly*, p. 826, another parody on the same poem.

I'll tell thee everything I can;
  There's little to relate.
I saw an aged, aged man,
  A-sitting on a gate.
"Who are you, aged man?" I said.
  "And how is it you live?"
And his answer trickled through my head
  Like water through a sieve.

He said "I look for butterflies
  That sleep among the wheat;

I make them into mutton-pies,
  And sell them in the street.
I sell them unto men," he said,
  "Who sail on stormy seas;
And that's the way I get my bread—
  A trifle, if you please."

But I was thinking of a plan
  To dye one's whiskers green,
And always use so large a fan
  That they could not be seen.
So, having no reply to give
  To what the old man said,
I cried, "Come, tell me how you live!"
  And thumped him on the head.

His accents mild took up the tale;
  He said, "I go my ways,
And when I find a mountain-rill,
  I set it in a blaze;
And thence they make a stuff they call
  Rowland's Macassar Oil—
Yet twopence-halfpenny is all
  They give me for my toil."

But I was thinking of a way
  To feed oneself on batter,
And so go on from day to day
  Getting a little fatter.
I shook him well from side to side,
  Until his face was blue;
"Come, tell me how you live," I cried
  "And what it is you do!"

He said, "I hunt for haddocks' eyes
  Among the heather bright,
And work them into waistcoat-buttons
  In the silent night.
And these I do not sell for gold
  Or coin of silvery shine,
But for a copper halfpenny,
  And that will purchase nine.

"I sometimes dig for buttered rolls,
  Or set limed twigs for crabs;
I sometimes search the grassy knolls
  For wheels of hansom-cabs.
And that's the way" (he gave a wink)
  "By which I get my wealth—
And very gladly will I drink
  Your Honor's noble health."

I heard him then, for I had just
  Completed my design
To keep the Menai bridge from rust
  By boiling it in wine.
I thanked him much for telling me
  The way he got his wealth,
But chiefly for his wish that he
  Might drink my noble health.

And now, if e'er by chance I put
  My fingers into glue,
Or madly squeeze a right-hand foot
  Into a left-hand shoe,
Or if I drop upon my toe
  A very heavy weight,
I weep, for it reminds me so
Of that old man I used to know—
Whose look was mild, whose speech was slow,
Whose hair was whiter than the snow,
Whose face was very like a crow,
With eyes, like cinders, all aglow,
Who seemed distracted with his woe,
Who rocked his body to and fro,
And muttered mumblingly and low,
As if his mouth were full of dough,
Who snorted like a buffalo—
That summer evening long ago
  A-sitting on a gate.   (1872)

The Baker's Tale

They roused him with muffins—they roused him with ice—
  They roused him with mustard and cress—
They roused him with jam and judicious advice—
  They set him conundrums to guess.

When at length he sat up and was able to speak,
  His sad story he offered to tell;
And the Bellman cried, "Silence! Not even a shriek!"
  And excitedly tingled his bell.

There was silence supreme! Not a shriek, not a scream,
  Scarcely even a howl or a groan,

---

1. **him**, the Baker, who had fainted when the Bellman, after mentioning the "unmistakable marks" of snarks, had said, "Some are Boojums."

As the man they called "Ho!" told his story
    of woe
  In an antediluvian tone.

"My father and mother were honest though
    poor—"
"Skip all that!" cried the Bellman in haste.
"If it once becomes dark, there's no chance of
    a Snark—   15
  We have hardly a minute to waste!"

"I skip forty years," said the Baker, in tears,
  "And proceed without further remark
To the day when you took me aboard of your
    ship
  To help you in hunting the Snark.   20

"A dear uncle of mine (after whom I was
    named)
  Remarked, when I bade him farewell—"
"Oh, skip your dear uncle!" the Bellman ex-
    claimed,
  As he angrily tingled his bell.

"He remarked to me then," said that mildest
    of men,   25
"'If your Snark be a Snark, that is right;
Fetch it home by all means—you may serve
    it with greens,
  And it's handy for striking a light.

"'You may seek it with thimbles—and seek
    it with care;
You may hunt it with forks and hope;   30
You may threaten its life with a railway-
    share;
  You may charm it with smiles and soap—'"

("That's exactly the method," the Bellman
    bold
  In a hasty parenthesis cried,
"That's exactly the way I have always been
    told   35
  That the capture of Snarks should be
    tried!")

"'But oh, beamish nephew, beware of the
    day,
  If your Snark be a Boojum! For then
You will softly and suddenly vanish away,
  And never be met with again!'   40

"It is this, it is this that oppresses my soul,
  When I think of my uncle's last words;
And my heart is like nothing so much as a
    bowl
  Brimming over with quivering curds!

"It is this, it is this—" "We have had that
    before!"   45
  The Bellman indignantly said.
And the Baker replied, "Let me say it once
    more.
  It is this, it is this that I dread!

"I engage with the Snark—every night after
    dark—
  In a dreamy, delirious fight;   50
I serve it with greens in those shadowy scenes,
  And I use it for striking a light;

"But if ever I meet with a Boojum, that day,
  In a moment (of this I am sure),
I shall softly and suddenly vanish away—   55
  And the notion I cannot endure!"   (1876)

William Schwenck Gilbert
1836-1911

The Yarn of the "Nancy Bell"

When offered to *Punch,* this poem was declined by the editor on the ground that it was too cannibalistic for his readers' tastes. It is a satire on conventional tales of shipwreck.

'Twas on the shores that round our coast
  From Deal to Ramsgate span,

2. **Deal, Ramsgate,** famous summer resorts about ten miles apart on the coast of Kent.

That I found alone on a piece of stone
  An elderly naval man.

His hair was weedy, his beard was long   5
  And weedy and long was he,
And I heard this wight on the shore recite
  In a singular minor key:

"Oh, I am a cook and a captain bold,
  And the mate of the *Nancy* brig,   10

And a bo'sun tight, and a midshipmite,
  And the crew of the captain's gig."

And he shook his fists, and he tore his hair,
  Till I really felt afraid,
For I couldn't help thinking the man had
    been drinking, 15
  And so I simply said:

"Oh, elderly man, it's little I know
  Of the duties of men of the sea,
And I'll eat my hand if I understand
  However you can be 20

"At once a cook, and a captain bold,
  And the mate of the *Nancy* brig,
And a bo'sun tight, and a midshipmite,
  And the crew of the captain's gig."

Then he gave a hitch to his trousers, which 25
  Is a trick all seamen larn,
And having got rid of a thumping quid,
  He spun this painful yarn:

" 'Twas in the good ship *Nancy Bell*
  That we sailed to the Indian Sea, 30
And there on a reef we come to grief,
  Which has often occurred to me.

"And pretty nigh all the crew was drowned
  (There was seventy-seven o' soul),
And only ten of the *Nancy's* men 35
  Said 'Here!' to the muster-roll.

"There was me and the cook and the captain
    bold,
  And the mate of the *Nancy* brig,
And the bo'sun tight, and a midshipmite,
  And the crew of the captain's gig. 40

"For a month we'd neither wittles nor drink,
  Till a-hungry we did feel,
So we drawed a lot, and, accordin' shot
  The captain for our meal.

"The next lot fell to the *Nancy's* mate, 45
  And a delicate dish he made;
Then our appetite with the midshipmite
  We seven survivors stayed.

"And then we murdered the bo'sun tight,
  And he much resembled pig; 50
Then we wittled free, did the cook and me,
  On the crew of the captain's gig.

"Then only the cook and me was left,
  And the delicate question, 'Which
Of us two goes to the kettle?' arose, 55
  And we argued it out as sich.

"For I loved that cook as a brother, I did,
  And the cook he worshiped me;
But we'd both be blowed if we'd either be
    stowed
  In the other chap's hold, you see. 60

" 'I'll be eat if you dines off me,' says Tom;
  'Yes, that,' says I, 'you'll be—'
'I'm boiled if I die, my friend,' quoth I;
  And 'Exactly so,' quoth he.

"Says he, 'Dear James, to murder me 65
  Were a foolish thing to do,
For don't you see that you can't cook *me*,
  While I can—and will—cook *you!*'

"So he boils the water, and takes the salt
  And the pepper in portions true 70
(Which he never forgot) and some chopped
    shalot,
  And some sage and parsley too.

" 'Come here,' says he, with a proper pride
  Which his smiling features tell,
' 'Twill soothing be if I let you see 75
  How extremely nice you'll smell.'

"And he stirred it round and round and
    round,
  And he sniffed at the foaming froth;
When I ups with his heels, and smothers his
    squeals
  In the scum of the boiling broth. 80

"And I eat that cook in a week or less,
  And—as I eating be
The last of his chops, why, I almost drops,
  For a wessel in sight I see!

---

11. **bo'sun**, boatswain, a junior officer having charge of the rigging.

71. **shalot**, a kind of onion.

"And I never larf, and I never smile, 85
  And I never lark nor play,
But sit and croak, and a single joke
  I have—which is to say:

"'Oh, I am a cook and captain bold,
  And the mate of the *Nancy* brig, 90
And a bo'sun tight, and a midshipmite,
  And the crew of the captain's gig!'" (1866)

The Aesthete

The Aesthete is a caricature of Oscar Wilde and his fellow aesthetes. It is sung in *Patience* by Bunthorne, a fleshly poet, in one of his melodramatic moods. See biographical sketch of Wilde, p. 951.

If you're anxious for to shine in the high aesthetic line as a man of culture rare,
You must get up all the germs of the transcendental terms, and plant them everywhere.
You must lie upon the daisies, and discourse in novel phrases of your complicated state of mind,
The meaning doesn't matter if it's only idle chatter of a transcendental kind.
  And everyone will say, 5
    As you walk your mystic way,
"If this young man expresses himself in terms too deep for *me*,
Why, what a very singularly deep young man this deep young man must be!"

Be eloquent in praise of the very dull old ways which have long since passed away,
And convince 'em, if you can, that the reign of good Queen Anne was Culture's palmiest day. 10
Of course you will pooh-pooh whatever's fresh and new, and declare it's crude and mean,
For Art stopped short in the cultivated court of the Empress Josephine.
  And everyone will say,
    As you walk your mystic way,
"If that's not good enough for him which is good enough for *me*, 15
Why, what a very cultivated kind of youth this kind of youth must be!"

Then a sentimental passion of a vegetable fashion must excite your languid spleen,
An attachment *à la* Plato for a bashful young potato, or a not-too-French French bean!
Though the Philistines may jostle, you will rank as an apostle in the high aesthetic band,
If you walk down Piccadilly with a poppy or a lily in your medieval hand. 20
  And everyone will say,
    As you walk your flowery way,
"If he's content with a vegetable love, which would certainly not suit *me*,
Why, what a most particularly pure young man this pure young man must be!"
(1881)

Said I to Myself, Said I

In *Iolanthe,* from which this song is taken, Phyllis, beloved by the half-fairy Strephon and by the entire House of Lords, is a Ward of Chancery, and so can marry only with the consent of the Lord Chancellor. He refuses to admit that Strephon may love Phyllis without the Court's permission, even though the "case bubbles over with poetic emotion." He says, "I have always kept my duty strictly before my eyes, and it is to this fact that I owe advancement to my present distinguished position." He then sings this song.

When I went to the Bar as a very young man
  (Said I to myself, said I),
I'll work on a new and original plan
  (Said I to myself, said I).
I'll never assume that a rogue or a thief 5
Is a gentleman worthy implicit belief

---

10. **reign . . . day.** The reign of Queen Anne (1702-1714) was an important period in the neo-classical movement in English literature; Gilbert finds its insistence on form tedious. See Vol. I, pp. 817 ff. 12. **Empress Josephine,** wife of Napoleon I and Empress of the French (1763-1814).

17. **vegetable fashion.** Wilde was a vegetarian. 18. **attachment *à la* Plato,** a Platonic love, which involved a purely spiritual comradeship. 19. **Philistines,** persons lacking liberal culture and refinement. See p. 538, note 82. 20. **Piccadilly,** a famous London street.

Because his attorney has sent me a brief
    (Said I to myself, said I).

I'll never throw dust in a juryman's eyes
    (Said I to myself, said I),   10
Or hoodwink a judge who is not over-wise
    (Said I to myself, said I),
Or assume that the witnesses summoned in force
In Exchequer, Queen's Bench, Common Pleas, or Divorce
Have perjured themselves as a matter of course   15
    (Said I to myself, said I).

Ere I go into court I will read my brief through
    (Said I to myself, said I),
And I'll never take work I'm unable to do
    (Said I to myself, said I),   20
My learned profession I'll never disgrace
By taking a fee with a grin on my face
When I haven't been there to attend to the case
    (Said I to myself, said I).

In other professions in which men engage   25
    (Said I to myself, said I),
The Army, the Navy, the Church, and the Stage
    (Said I to myself, said I),
Professional license, if carried too far,   29
Your chance of promotion will certainly mar;
And I fancy the rule might apply to the Bar
    (Said I to myself, said I).   (1882)

They'll None of 'Em Be Missed

This song is sung by Ko-Ko, the Lord High Executioner in *The Mikado*.

As some day it may happen that a victim must be found,
I've got a little list—I've got a little list
Of social offenders who might well be underground,
And who never would be missed—who never would be missed!
There's the pestilential nuisances who write for autographs—   5
All people who have flabby hands and irritating laughs—
All children who are up in dates, and floor you with 'em flat—
All persons who in shaking hands, shake hands with you like *that*—
And all third persons who on spoiling *tête-à-têtes* insist—
They'd none of 'em be missed—they'd none of 'em be missed!   10

Chorus

He's got 'em on the list—he's got 'em on the list;
And they'll none of 'em be missed—they'll none of 'em be missed!

There's a nigger serenader, and the others of his race,
And the piano-organist—I've got him on the list!
And the people who eat peppermint and puff it in your face,   15
They never would be missed—they never would be missed!
Then the idiot who praises, with enthusiastic tone,
All centuries but this, and every country but his own;
And the lady from the provinces who dresses like a guy,
And "who doesn't think she waltzes, but would rather like to try"!   20
And that singular anomaly, the lady novelist—
I don't think she'd be missed—I'm *sure* she'd not be missed!

Chorus

He's got her on the list—he's got her on the list;
And I don't think she'll be missed—I'm *sure* she'll not be missed!

---

7. **brief,** in English law, a condensed statement of the facts of a litigated case drawn up by an attorney for the use of a barrister in conducting proceedings in a court of justice. Only barristers are admitted to plead at the bar; attorneys, or solicitors, institute actions in behalf of their clients and furnish counsel (barristers) with necessary materials, facts, etc. 14. **Exchequer . . . Divorce,** branches of the High Court of Justice.

And that *Nisi Prius* nuisance, who just now is
    rather rife,   25
  The Judicial humorist—I've got *him* on the
    list!
All funny fellows, comic men, and clowns of
    private life—
  They'd none of 'em be missed—they'd none
    of 'em be missed!
And apologetic statesmen of a compromising
    kind,
Such as—What d'ye call him—Thing'em bob,
    and likewise Never Mind,   30
And 'St—'st—'st—and What's-his-name, and
    also You-know-who—
The task of filling up the blanks I'd rather
    leave to *you*.
But it really doesn't matter whom you put
    upon the list,
  For they'd none of 'em be missed—they'd
    none of 'em be missed!

            Chorus

You may put 'em on the list—you may put
  'em on the list;   35
And they'll none of 'em be missed—they'll
  none of 'em be missed!   (1885)

Let the Punishment Fit the Crime

  This song is sung by the Mikado after he
has been heralded by a procession and a
Chorus.

A more humane Mikado never
  Did in Japan exist,
    To nobody second,
    I'm certainly reckoned
  A true philanthropist.   5
It is my very humane endeavor
  To make, to some extent,
    Each evil liver
    A running river
  Of harmless merriment.   10

  My object all sublime
  I shall achieve in time—
To let the punishment fit the crime—
  The punishment fit the crime;

And make each prisoner pent   15
  Unwillingly represent
A source of innocent merriment,
  Of innocent merriment!

All prosy dull society sinners,
  Who chatter and bleat and bore,   20
    Are sent to hear sermons
    From mystical Germans
  Who preach from ten to four.
The amateur tenor, whose vocal villainies
  All desire to shirk,   25
    Shall, during off-hours,
    Exhibit his powers
  To Madame Tussaud's waxwork.

The lady who dyes a chemical yellow,
  Or stains her gray hair puce,   30
    Or pinches her figger,
    Is blacked like a nigger
  With permanent walnut juice.
The idiot who, in railway carriages,
  Scribbles on window panes,   35
    We only suffer
    To ride on a buffer
  In Parliamentary trains.

  My object all sublime, etc.

The advertising quack who wearies   40
  With tales of countless cures,
    His teeth, I've enacted,
    Shall all be extracted
  By terrified amateurs.
The music hall singer attends a series   45
  Of masses and fugues and "ops"
    By Bach, interwoven
    With Spohr and Beethoven,
  At classical Monday Pops.

25. *Nisi Prius*, literally *unless before*. This is a law term used of any cause involving issues of fact and appointed to be tried in the courts of Westminster unless before the day set the judges tried the cause in the county in which it arose.

28. **Madame . . . waxwork,** an exhibition of wax-portrait models of ancient and modern personages and historical tableaux, founded by Marie Tussaud (1760-1850) and located in Marylebone Road, London. 30. **puce,** dark brown. 38. **Parliamentary trains,** trains that each railway company is required to run daily each way over its system for the convenience of third-rate passengers at a fare of not over one penny a mile. 46. **masses . . . "ops."** A mass is the musical setting of certain portions of the service of the Sacrament of the Lord's Supper; a fugue is a musical composition developed from one or more given themes according to strict rules; "ops," from the Latin *opus,* are works. 47. **Bach . . . Beethoven,** Johann Sebastian Bach (1685-1750), a famous German composer and musician; Ludwig Spohr (1784-1859), a German composer; and Ludwig van Beethoven (1770-1827), a noted German composer. 49. **Monday Pops,** concerts of popular music given on Mondays. A singer of cheap music is punished by being made to listen to serious music.

The billiard sharp whom any one catches, 50
  His doom's extremely hard—
    He's made to dwell
    In a dungeon cell
  On a spot that's always barred.
And there he plays extravagant matches 55
  In fitless finger-stalls,
    On a cloth untrue
    With a twisted cue,
  And elliptical billiard balls!

My object all sublime, etc.   (1885)

Willow, Titwillow

Willow, Titwillow is a take-off on the so-called "willow songs," sung by persons about to die. This one, from *The Mikado*, is sung by Ko-Ko, the Lord High Executioner of the Town of Titipu, as he tries to convince the elderly lady Katisha that he will "perish on the spot" if she does not accept his love. She had protested that nobody had ever died of a broken heart.

On a tree by a river a little tom-tit
  Sang, "Willow, titwillow, titwillow!"
And I said to him, "Dicky-bird, why do you sit
  Singing, 'Willow, titwillow, titwillow'?
Is it weakness of intellect, birdie?" I cried, 5
  "Or a rather tough worm in your little inside?"
With a shake of his poor little head he replied,
  "Oh, willow, titwillow, titwillow!"

He slapped at his chest, as he sat on that bough,
  Singing, "Willow, titwillow, titwillow!" 10
And a cold perspiration bespangled his brow,
  Oh, willow, titwillow, titwillow!
He sobbed and he sighed, and a gurgle he gave,
Then he threw himself into the billowy wave,
And an echo arose from the suicide's grave—
  "Oh, willow, titwillow, titwillow!" 16

Now I feel just as sure as I'm sure that my name
  Isn't Willow, titwillow, titwillow,

56. **fitless finger-stalls**, ill-fitting coverings for the fingers.

That 'twas blighted affection that made him exclaim,
  "Oh, willow, titwillow, titwillow!" 20
And if you remain callous and obdurate, I
Shall perish as he did, and you will know why,
Though I probably shall not exclaim as I die,
  "Oh, willow, titwillow, titwillow!"   (1885)

James Kenneth Stephen
1859-1892

Of Lord B.

This is a satiric parody of Byron's digressive, consciously careless style in *Don Juan*. See *Don Juan*, I, ll. 1673 ff., p. 228.

A GRIEVANCE

Dear Mr. Editor: I wish to say—
  If you will not be angry at my writing it—
But I've been used, since childhood's happy day,
  When I have thought of something to inditing it—
I seldom think of things; and, by the way, 5
  Although this meter may not be exciting, it
Enables one to be extremely terse,
Which is not what one always is in verse.

I used to know a man—such things befall
  The observant wayfarer through Fate's domain. 10
He was a man, take him for all in all,
  We shall not look upon his like again—
I know that statement's not original;
  What statement is, since Shakespeare? or, since Cain,
What murder? I believe 'twas Shakespeare said it, or 15
Perhaps it may have been your Fighting Editor.

Though why an Editor should fight, or why
  A Fighter should abase himself to edit,
Are problems far too difficult and high

11. **He was a man**, etc., said by Hamlet of his father in *Hamlet*, I, ii, 187-188. 14. **Cain**, who slew his brother Abel, thus becoming the first murderer; cf. *Genesis*, 4.

For me to solve with any sort of credit; 20
Some greatly more accomplished man than I
  Must tackle them. Let's say then Shakespeare said it;
And, if he did not, Lewis Morris may
(Or even if he did). Some other day,

When I have nothing pressing to impart, 25
  I should not mind dilating on this matter;
I feel its import both in head and heart,
  And always did—especially the latter.
I could discuss it in the busy mart
  Or on the lonely housetop; hold! this chatter 30
Diverts me from my purpose. To the point:
The time, as Hamlet said, is out of joint,

And I perhaps was born to set it right,
  A fact I greet with perfect equanimity.
I do not put it down to "curséd spite"— 35
  I don't see any cause for cursing in it; I
Have always taken very great delight
  In such pursuits since first I read divinity—
Whoever will may write a nation's songs
As long as I'm allowed to right its wrongs. 40

What's Eton but a nursery of wrong-righters,
  A mighty mother of effective men,
A training-ground for amateur reciters,
  A sharpener of the sword as of the pen,
A factory of orators and fighters, 45
  A forcing-house of genius? Now and then,
The world at large shrinks back, abashed and beaten,
Unable to endure the glare of Eton.

_{23. **Lewis Morris**, a Welsh poet (1833-1907), author of *The Song of Two Worlds* and *The Epic of Hades*. 32. **as Hamlet said**, in *Hamlet*, I, v, 188. 39. **Whoever . . . wrongs**, a parody on the familiar proverb, "If I am permitted to make the songs of a nation, I care not who makes her laws." 41. **Eton**, one of the most famed of the English public schools, founded in 1440 by Henry VI. It is located in Buckinghamshire. It numbers among its graduates the really great men of England.}

I think I said I knew a man; what then?
  I don't suppose such knowledge is forbid; 50
We nearly all do, more or less, know men—
  Or think we do; nor will a man get rid
Of that delusion, while he wields a pen.
  But who this man was, what, if aught, he did,
Nor why I mentioned him, I do not know, 55
Nor what I "wished to say" a while ago.
              (1889)

A Sonnet

_{This sonnet parodies Wordsworth's *Thought of a Briton*, p. 162, and, in the final lines, his *The World Is Too Much with Us*, p. 159.}

Two voices are there: one is of the deep;
It learns the storm-cloud's thunderous melody,
Now roars, now murmurs with the changing sea,
Now bird-like pipes, now closes soft in sleep;
And one is of an old half-witted sheep 5
Which bleats articulate monotony,
And indicates that two and one are three,
That grass is green, lakes damp, and mountains steep:
And, Wordsworth, both are thine; at certain times,
Forth from the heart of thy melodious rimes 10
The form and pressure of high thoughts will burst;
At other times—good Lord! I'd rather be
Quite unacquainted with the A. B. C.
Than write such hopeless rubbish as thy worst.
              (1891)

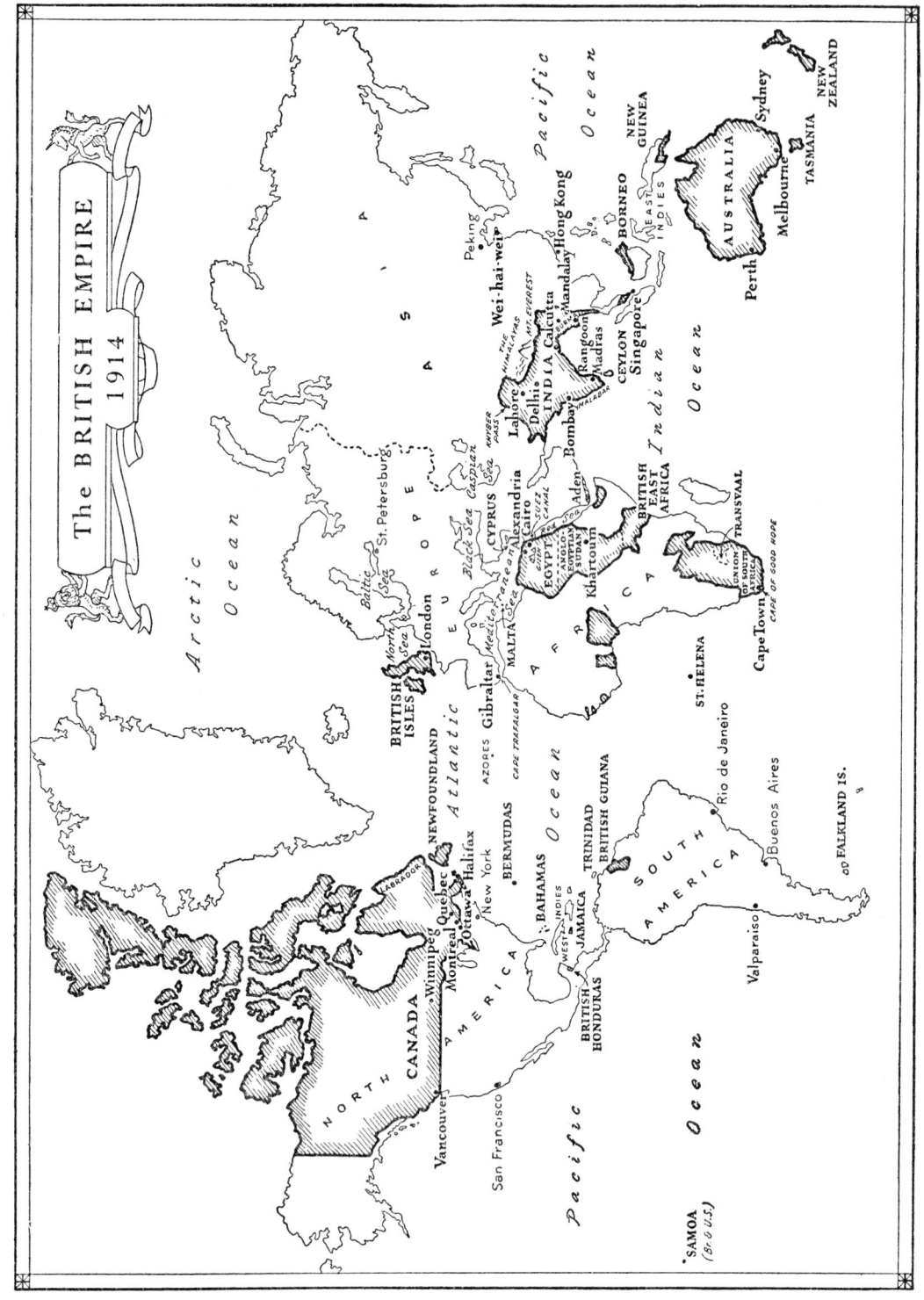

Chapter 8

The Break with Victorianism

Fading Traditions and New Patterns, 1880-1914

England Moves into the Twentieth Century

IN THE complex world that has been developing during the last three centuries no prevailing mold of thought and fashion can be expected to last more than fifty years. By 1880, for example, it is evident that many of the values in art and philosophy and literature which had been generally maintained during the heart of the Victorian period were becoming subtly altered. In spite of the fact that Queen Victoria was to reign for a score more years and that the effect of the way of life which she so clearly symbolized was to be felt for a long period thereafter, still the artist, the writer, and the thinking man of the 1880's deviated considerably from their fathers of the 1840's and 1850's. The changes wrought in this later day were not violent, dislocating changes; the curve and not the angle is the true figuration of an altering art. But the Englishman was advancing, however reluctantly and uncertainly, into a new age, which, although not fully divorced from its predecessor, is nevertheless more intelligible as a transitional age foreshadowing the hurly-burly which is the present. As one looks back upon this new age, the conclusion seems inevitable that it is an overture to a baffling kind of opera, the contemporary scene; and the final crashing, determining chords of this overture are the cataclysmic events

A transitional period

from August, 1914, to November, 1918, which are still spoken of, in grim realization of the present, as the first World War.

The growth of imperialism

From 1880 to 1914, in effect, England followed a course leading straight to a national crisis; and beyond this crisis the present volume does not go. The last two decades of the nineteenth century showed that England was committed to what some have called the besetting sin of an otherwise great century—the way of imperialism. Of course the British Empire had been in process of building for more than a century before; and the feeling for the greatness and inevitability of this empire, expressed rather blatantly by Rudyard Kipling (p. 885) and more sardonically by William Ernest Henley (p. 863)—to name but two latter-day prophets of this imperialism—had been recognized by Tennyson and even earlier writers. The political fact of the Empire had been long recognized. The economic side, however, did not come into the foreground much before the days of Cecil Rhodes of South Africa (1853-1902) or of Joseph Chamberlain (1836-1914), who as Colonial Secretary in 1896 proposed a commercial agreement binding together the many vast portions of the Empire and caring for them by the imposition of a strong protective tariff. The idea cut across the long established British tradition of free trade and was consequently met with great disfavor; but the conception was strongly prophetic of the concert of free dominions and colonies that is associated nowadays with the British Empire.

The spread of the British Empire in Africa

From the standpoint of the average Englishman, however, it was the acquisition of new lands for the British flag that was the important matter, for this acquisition meant more prestige for England, heightened the "noble responsibility" of the Anglo-Saxon race (a responsibility which Kipling referred to as "the white man's burden"), and increased the revenues of the British treasury. During the eighties Britain extended her colonial sway over the Egyptian Sudan, which was not definitely subdued, however, until 1898. In the meantime the dazzling dream of empire had been stimulated by the two Imperial Jubilees of 1887 and 1897, celebrating respectively the fiftieth and sixtieth anniversaries of Victoria's accession. The unparalleled greatness of the British rule "over palm and pine," symbolized most fittingly by the military pomp and pride on the one hand and the august, rock-ribbed respectability of the conventional-minded Victoria on the other, could have received no greater popular tribute. Yet the ambitions of the true imperialists were not gratified. Within a year after the Jubilee of 1897

A Late Victorian House

THE BREAK WITH VICTORIANISM

England had become seriously involved with the Transvaal Republic of Dutch émigrés in South Africa. As another chapter in the story of the expansion of Britain came the Boer War (1899-1902); it was, for the British government, an inefficiently conducted war which required the full resources of the entire Empire and troops from as far away as Canada and New Zealand. Eventually, however, the Transvaal was conquered and merged with the crown colony of Cape Town into another great British dominion, the Union of South Africa.

Germany in the ascendant

But before the Boer War was over, Queen Victoria had died, and with her went some small portion of the lives of millions of her subjects who had never known a time when she had not been the ruler of England. Her son and successor, Edward VII, had been during his long incumbency as Prince of Wales a notorious flaneur; but at the age of sixty he assumed the kingship and proved to be an unexpectedly able sovereign, whom many critics credit with having postponed the inevitable evil day of the first World War—inevitable because another great imperialism was rising to challenge the power of Britain. The expansive force of the German Empire since its establishment in 1871 had been enormous; it had grown under the remarkable leadership of Bismarck (1815-1898) to be the greatest power in Central Europe, and now under the hysterical megalomania of Emperor William II (1859-1941) was creating a great colonial empire and a great navy to defend it, and was threatening Britain's supremacy over the seas. The best insurance for Britain, an insurance ardently advocated by Edward VII, was to drop her insularity and splendid isolation and to work with other nations to achieve a "balance of power" in Europe. After many bickerings and progressions, which afford a fascinating chapter to the student of diplomatic history, Britain succeeded in establishing, with France and Russia, the Triple Entente (1907) to counterbalance the Triple Alliance of Germany, Austria-Hungary, and Italy, which had been set up during the 1880's. Europe, however, was already an armed camp only awaiting the overt act to set off the explosion. Four years after the death of Edward VII (1910) and the accession of his son George V (1865-1936), the explosion reverberated around the world.

Far less spectacular in the pages of history is England's domestic course during this same period. The nineteenth century viewed as a whole had been a prosperous century for the British upper- and middle-classes. But at the same time the poorer classes were very poor. The situation in Britain was, indeed, to be found all over the continent of Europe, and there had been numerous efforts to improve matters. But by 1880 these efforts had become more concerted and definite. The various British municipalities tried to better living conditions and to beautify themselves in some degree; there sprang up the public parks, recreation grounds, and museums which

A Late Victorian Interior

The movement for social reform

Sunday Visitors at Oxford

distinguish the British city today. There was slum-clearance and the founding of various settlement-houses, although these were nearly always the product of the enterprise of some private citizen or civic group. The Christian Mission (1865), which became in 1878 the Salvation Army led by the tireless General William Booth, was perhaps the first great social agency that accomplished results commensurate with its ambition; and Booth's *In Darkest England* (1890) became the *Uncle Tom's Cabin* of social work in the British Isles. Occasionally the reformers tried to group together for political action; here the attempts were likely to result in socialist parties like the Fabian Society, in which Shaw (p. 861) and Wells (p. 858) were at one time interested. Such socialistic groups were influenced vaguely by the writings of Karl Marx (1818-1883) but more directly by the works of Carlyle (p. 464), Ruskin (p. 501), Morris (p. 797), and lesser literary figures. Eventually, during the early years of the twentieth century and even before that, such matters as old-age pensions and unemployment insurance and housing projects were put into practice. Obviously the expense of doing all this had to be met somehow, and taxation seemed the best expedient in order to raise the money. The increased taxation was felt chiefly by the landed gentry; and the result was a violent reaction in the House of Lords. The trade-unions were not effective in coping with the problem from the working-man's point of view, and so the working-man was inclined to throw more and more of his weight into the Independent Labour Party, which therefore became one of the major parties in English politics, although its first real victory was not until 1924.

The Irish question

A particularly difficult social and political problem to vex England during these years was the perennial Irish question. Throughout the nineteenth century there had been agitation for home rule in Ireland. The names of Daniel O'Connell (1775-1847) and Charles Stewart Parnell (1846-1891) had led the list of those struggling to make Ireland free, or at least to give her the status of a Dominion of the British Crown. But neither O'Connell nor Parnell had succeeded; the first because he was probably too early, and the second largely for personal reasons. Unfortunately the religious issue had beclouded the whole political problem. Catholic southern Ireland insisted on a separate Irish Parliament; Protestant northern Ireland wished to continue direct allegiance to the British Crown. The House of Lords supported northern Ireland and blocked repeated efforts to pass a Home Rule bill. The agitation resulting from this *impasse* focussed attention on the House of Lords, the ultra-conservative and slightly obsolete house of Parliament, which had all too frequently adopted the attitude of the dog in the manger. A bill to remove the veto power of the House of Lords was ultimately passed in 1910; the event was of great historical importance in the chronicles of British government and brought Britain that much nearer true democracy.

The Hansom Cab "The Gondola of London"

The democratic aspects of the matter, however, were rather lost sight of in the popular outcry raised when a Home Rule bill was finally presented and passed; and for a time (1913-1914) it looked very much as if a civil war in Ireland were imminent. But the outbreak of the first World War postponed the issue. The resurgence of Ireland as a political power paralleled in a way her resurgence in literature (p. 852); and both phenomena are especially colorful events in the history of the present time.

General Aspects of English Literature, 1880-1914

FOR THE PRESENT DISCUSSION it is perhaps unnecessary to distinguish between the poetry and the prose of this period, because although there was some experimentation in verse, the really significant innovations in formal poetry do not weigh heavily until the years around 1915. Besides, as has already been implied, the important thing is not the external mold of this literature so much as the internal thought; and the determining factors in a study of this literature are the various cults and movements that had their day.

The first thing that must strike the observer of the literature of England from 1880 to 1914 is the fact that an enormous number of literary works of all kinds were produced. The sheer fecundity of this period has been amazing; and the same holds true in varying degrees of all the Western literatures. Not only has the actual quantity been huge; the scope and purpose of these works have varied in the most pronounced manner. All kinds of schools and cults and tendencies have appeared, some of them following similar paths, others in violent opposition. Consequently it is still difficult to appraise and classify these works, although the earliest of them are already a good lifetime away from the present. Yet the task is by no means so hopeless as some critics have thought.

The prolific quality of literature in this period

For example, one may consider for a moment the time-honored conflict in Victorian thought between a fundamentalistic religious belief and the findings of modern science. Not resolved during the mid-Victorian decades, this conflict seemed to fade into an intellectual stalemate referred to generally as "the Victorian compromise." Yet in the light of subsequent developments, it would seem that science gained the victory. At any rate, from about 1880 there is to be noted an increasingly scientific outlook in most literature, except among writers who ran away outright from science; and this utilizing of a scientific outlook led in turn to a critical examination of the bases on which this "strange disease of modern life," represented by science, was actually reposing. In short, there arose a new age of critical inquiry, much more factual—and much more profound—than that of the neo-classical age, yet with much of the same desire for reality.

The spirit of critical inquiry

Victorian Sports Costumes

The influence of foreign writers on the literature of the period

The next considerable factor in the shaping of this literature is the point that English letters were dependent as never before upon foreign and "international" writers. To be sure, every previous major period in English literature had been under some obligation to the foreign. The Old English period had a debt to Latin and Norse; the Middle English period had leaned upon the French; the Renaissance upon the Italian, Spanish, and classical languages as well as the French; the neo-classical age upon the Greek, Latin, and French; the romantic upon the French and German. Only the Puritan interlude of the seventeenth century had been particularly self-reliant; but it need not be repeated how much Milton owed to the Renaissance. The Victorians had enlarged their foreign horizon immeasurably beyond that of their predecessors. And after 1880 one can see in English letters the influence of the realism of the Frenchmen Balzac, Stendhal, Flaubert, and de Maupassant; the naturalism of the Frenchman Zola; the symbolism of the Frenchmen Baudelaire and Verlaine or of the Belgian Maeterlinck; the brilliant all-round achievements of the Russian novelists Tolstoi, Dostoevsky, Chekhov, and Turgenev; the German Nietzsche's idea of the superman asserting his will to save mankind; the Frenchman Bergson's philosophy of creative evolution; the Austrian Freud's emphasis upon the subconscious mind; the hedonistic philosophy of the Persian Omar Khayyàm; the American Mark Twain's pungent and often savage humor; the Norwegian Ibsen's or the Swedish Strindberg's severe indictments of conventional society. Moreover, in almost all of these influences there lie implicit and explicit revolts—revolts against authority and the established order of things. Even when it came to the fundamental facts of science, new discoveries such as the laws of relativity or the quantum theory might obtrude themselves and raise doubts whether two and two are four.

Ladies' Golf

Revolt against mid-Victorian standards

Above and beyond all this, the Englishman after 1880 was in his literature more and more conscious of social problems, as he was also in his politics. He was, indeed, better educated, if by education we mean the cultivated awareness of his environment and his responsibilities. It seems clear now that the Victorian compromise began to break down in the eighties and nineties. First came a severe disillusionment and dissatisfaction not only with the older beliefs but also with the new religion of science. Some, of course, followed in the glad gospel of Huxley (p. 561) and faced ahead. Others took refuge in a late romantic kind of aestheticism and revival of Greek and Roman paganism, which turned quickly into a jaded and artificial kind of decadence. Still others did as James Thomson (p. 760) and fell victims to a spiritual melancholia expressed in terms of absolute negation. All of these suffered from *le mal du siècle*, the disease of the century, or as the Germans put it, a *Weltschmerz*, a world-suffering. Some of the most striking figures in this period, none the less, are these same end-of-the-century romantic escapists like Oscar Wilde (p. 951), Aubrey Beardsley, or Ernest Dowson, who turn their backs on everything that the scientific spirit had brought upon art and literature as exemplified by the French realists and naturalists.

On the other hand, there were some rather violent optimists like Robert Louis Stevenson (p. 874), who took the pose of incurably healthy romanticists and covered up, not always successfully, a deep and an uneasy skepticism (as seen in *Pulvis et Umbra*, p. 929). But the majority of those who did not break and run fell in with the realistic upswing of literature and art, and we have the sober, honest, moving work of Thomas Hardy (p. 907) and George Gissing or the more precious manifestations of the same spirit in George Moore. Still, in all arts the old frontiers were broken down. The painters and sculptors, for example, indulged in various eccentricities of portraiture in which the individual was reacting to his environment; and so there appeared such forbidding technical differentiations as impressionism, post-impressionism, futurism, cubism, and surrealism, which it is not practical to discuss here. A musician like Claude Debussy (1862-1919) would emphasize a five-tone scale instead of the usual seven-tone scale; Richard Strauss (1864-1949), following in the steps of Wagner, opened up hitherto unexplored possibilities in modern orchestration. But in the final appraisal it is not so much the innovations in form or materials that are so important as the new freedom in subject-matter and treatment of topics heretofore considered unsuitable for general discussion. When playwrights like Henrik Ibsen (1828-1906) could discuss the disastrous effects of out-moded ideals and have their plays accepted, however grudgingly, by the public, it is a clear indication that tastes and standards had changed. And although there were always individuals who would preach the old-time gentility, such as Mrs. Humphrey Ward (1851-1920) or even the able Henry James (1843-1916), nevertheless they were obliged to recognize this growing atmosphere of liberalism—freedom from the more confining outlook of the mid-Victorian parlor.

A Man's Game

Realization of the limitations of modern culture

It is apparent after even a brief examination of the pages of the more important writers of this period that much of the complacency of the previous generation had begun to melt away. Tennyson's hero in *Locksley Hall* (p. 613), who had fancied himself as

> . . . the heir of all the ages, in the foremost files of time

had become the hero of Hardy's *God-Forgotten* (p. 909), who recognizes that he inhabits a "tainted ball,"

> . . . by pangs distraught
> And strife, and silent suffering.

The contrast could be illustrated almost indefinitely. The great material expansion and prosperity of the mid-century had not brought happiness to the people as a whole; and even that prosperity was limited, as the growing bread-lines indicated. Moreover, to some, science itself, the newest god, seemed to have feet of clay; its promise of solving all man's difficulties was fading, and man was the cog in the machine. In compensation for this distressing fact, the writers of the period hoped for a greater intensity, spontaneity, and imagination, whether their topics were revolutionary, imperialistic, or conventional; and whether or not their attitudes were idealistic, coldly scrutinizing, or assertive. In brief, the whole period before the first World War can significantly be called an age of restlessness and groping revolt; and if the student is bothered by this fact, he can take grim comfort in the thought that after the first World War this same restlessness and revolt became intensified until we come to a complete rupture with the older values. Indeed, the second World War is actually a revolution wrapped up in a war.

Realism and naturalism

Assuming, then, that there is always a certain amount of the literature of this period that can be called romantic—as there is in any major period of English literature—still the two forces that seem to be dominant in the majority of writers during these years are realism and naturalism. Few words in the language are more susceptible to abuse and overwork. In general it is proper to observe that both realism and naturalism apply to an artistic treatment of life. But there are several kinds of realism and indeed several kinds of naturalism as well; and it is often extremely difficult to tell where any one of these several kinds begins and where it leaves off or where the exact common limits of realism and naturalism may happen to be. For example, there are works of literature in which the characters appear to be human beings who live in commonplace surroundings; yet the events in which they find themselves may be unreal, even fantastic. Such a work is only superficially realistic—so it is with the usual moving picture and much popular drama and fiction. True realism takes into account not only the surface appearances but the basic realities of life as well, although the artist can step in, select and arrange his details to suit his particular purpose. Naturalism, on the other hand, aims at a completely objective, scientific exposition of life. With impartial, cool observation and an almost mechanical laboratory technique the naturalistic writer attempts to put down everything about his characters, however unconventional the material; he is inclined to make his creatures subjects for a clinical case-history, and to spare no details. That is his aim; but in actual practice the naturalist as well as his realist brother must make some degree of selection. The efforts of the naturalists and realists have both led to an emphasis upon what has been called the ugly in subject-matter,

The Old: Riding on Horseback

but only the incurably romantic mind could believe that such was actually the case. More important than taste or lack of taste in regard to details is the fundamental philosophy of realism and naturalism. Both trends in art are likely to view mankind as helpless before the overwhelming forces of nature. Since such an outlook is largely a matter of first principles, it has been the chief stumbling-block to the acceptance of realism in art. Yet it is quite unfair to think that either realism or naturalism is necessarily bound up with either the ugly or the pessimistic, unless one has to concede that all life is ugly and depressing. Realism and naturalism are merely methods of presenting a view of life, and they can be applied to any subject for any purpose.

In theory the attempt of the realists to represent life in its actuality was not new. William Wordsworth, a century before, had tried, he declared, not only "to choose incidents and situations from common life" but also "to relate or describe them throughout . . . in a selection of language really used by men" (p. 318). But nobody can possibly read Wordsworth's *Resolution and Independence* (p. 148) together with Henley's *In Hospital* (p. 864) or Kipling's *Tommy* (p. **887**) without perceiving at once that the true realism is in the work of the modern poets and not in that of Wordsworth. Henley and Kipling—to select two from a large group of modern realists—lived life energetically and did not theorize about it very much, whereas Wordsworth's world was one of reflection rather than action. Henley and Kipling made no remote search for poetic materials; they found them in the life that they knew and loved. They accepted life as it was, found it good, and neither doubted its wholesomeness nor debated about it, as the self-conscious hero of Tennyson's *Locksley Hall* did (p. 613). The vital force which these writers possessed was probably the principal element in their technique. They lived and advocated the "strenuous life"—as an American president of the same period and temperament called an existence of relentless, purposeful activity—and the characters in their stories and poems embody their own impulses and desires. Henley's method was developed under the influence of the French school of naturalists and under that of the American poet Walt Whitman (1819-1892). That he might be more realistic, Henley frequently wrote his poetry in unrimed rhythms. In much of his poetry, moreover, he avoided poetic diction and adopted a free, prose-like language reminiscent of that of Whitman. Kipling was the poet and story-teller of the British Empire—as already observed, he was the insistent and sometimes blaring trumpet of Imperialism. He was the journalist, the observer, and the reporter, and he drew his materials from his own experiences and seasoned them with his own physical energy and gusto. His writing came like a strong wind sweeping out of the east

The New: The Safety Bicycle

The Penny farthing

and blowing away the aesthetic fogs of the London drawing-rooms. He was essentially a man's writer, and his realism was direct, accurate, almost raw.

The new realism was not restricted, however, to the poetry of Henley and the verses and stories of Kipling. It runs throughout the fiction and drama of the period in many different phases, in the sordid novels of George Gissing (1857-1903), in the pessimistic stories of Thomas Hardy, in the tales of Arthur Morrison (1863-1945) and Thomas Burke (1887-1945), in Sir James Barrie's (1860-1937) sentimental Scottish sketches, in John Synge's (1871-1909) powerful little dramas of the Aran Islands, in the Irish plays of Lady Augusta Gregory (1852-1932), very notably in John Masefield's long narrative poems (p. 916), and indeed in so many literary forms that to copy life exactly and vividly was evidently one of the most frequent objectives of the authors in the post-Victorian period.

Journalistic tendencies

A blending of the romantic with the realistic—both in many different forms—is a rough characterization of the literature of this period. Since there was a great deal of writing about everyday events and matters of concern, which was given this romantic-realistic interpretation, it is not surprising to discover that much of this literature had a rather loud journalistic ring, which has militated somewhat against the chances of this literature for long survival. This journalism gives us reality, and even attempts to go beneath the surface reality; but its appeal is likely to be local, even parochial. On the other hand, the currents of realism and naturalism produced several effective writers whose appeal may prove to be lasting.

Impressionism and Symbolism

OF THE SUBLIMATIONS of the romantic alone, to be found in these years, the most important are impressionism and symbolism. Impressionism has been defined as the subjective presentation of a single aspect or point of view. The object of the impressionists in art and in life was to escape entirely from the commonplace details of living and to express themselves in moods that were to be given as few words and as much simplicity as possible. Poetry, they believed, should contain few ideas and little sentiment. Symbolism, on the other hand, attempts to invest its materials with a suggestion of some hidden spiritual or intellectual significance; it avoids direct expression whenever possible. The English writers of the time seem to have preferred the impressionistic to the symbolic, though much of their inspiration came from French poets of symbolism, and there were a few English symbolists.

Charles Baudelaire (1821-1867) was the founder of the French School; his *Fleurs du Mal* (1857) had charm in spite of its profound melancholy and morbid decadence. Paul Verlaine (1844-1896), author of *Poèmes*

A Tourist Party Abroad

Saturniens (1866) and *Jadis et Naguère* (1884), and his young protégé Jean Arthur Rimbaud (1854-1891) carried on the tradition in France and greatly influenced the poetry of the English impressionists. So also did Maurice Maeterlinck (1862-1949), the somber Belgian poet and dramatist, whose *Pelléas et Mélisande* (1892) and *L'Oiseau Bleu* (1909) were written in French. The French composer Claude Debussy, who wrote the music for the first of these plays, attempted with great success to do in music what the symbolists did in words.

Many of the English poets of the last two decades of the century who reacted against realism and who sought after the manner of the French symbolists to convey impressions by suggestion rather than by direct expression, belonged to the Rhymers' Club, which met in London at the Cheshire Cheese—Johnson's old meeting-place—to discuss poetic theories and to read their poems. To this club belonged among others John Davidson (1857-1900), Lionel Johnson (1867-1902), Ernest Dowson (1867-1900), Arthur Symons (1865-1945), John Todhunter (1839-1916), and W. B. Yeats (p. 1025). Others, like Oscar Wilde and the brilliant artists and writers Aubrey Beardsley (1872-1898) and Max Beerbohm (1872-1956), were associated with the members of the club at one time or another or were connected with the journal to which many of the symbolists contributed. This periodical was *The Yellow Book*, an illustrated quarterly that ran for thirteen numbers from 1894 to 1897. When Beardsley was discharged from its staff at the time of the Wilde trial, he and Arthur Symons founded *The Savoy*, a similar periodical that had, however, a much shorter existence.

To many of the impressionists and symbolists the step to Catholic mysticism was easy; and there is a rather considerable group of Catholic writers in this period, such as Gerard Manley Hopkins (p. 869), Alice Meynell (1847-1922), Francis Thompson (p. 881), Hilaire Belloc (1870-1953), and Gilbert Keith Chesterton (1874-1936), though none of them can be considered a major writer on the grounds of Catholicism alone.

The age more important than the men it produced

There is no doubt, then, that the age produced not only quantity but variety in its writings. As one looks at it from the safe distance of a full generation, however, it is not a period of great figures in literature. There were giants in the earlier nineteenth century, but there are none here. The literary historian is even inclined to hesitate in naming the best of the period. But undoubtedly certain authors have stuck their heads far enough above the crowd to deserve particular attention. Moreover, although the roster of names is not very impressive as to qualitative achievement, there is no question whatsoever that the period is both vital and interesting. It is, in fact, a refutation of Carlyle's theory that "history is the essence of innumerable biographies," for the biographies here are by no means so important as the history.

A Musicale

The Aesthetic Movement

THE VICTORIAN AGE produced its own rebels in the "pagan" poets Swinburne (p. 808) and Fitzgerald (p. 775) and in that famous group of sensuous mystics who took the name of the Pre-Raphaelite Brotherhood (p. 416). The Pre-Raphaelites sought through art an escape from the ugliness of Victorian life. Their objective was to create beauty out of the materials of a past age. The great apostle of beauty in art was Walter Pater (p. 580). Unlike the earlier Victorians he saw no social selfishness in living alone in the Ivory Tower of art. Such epicureanism was purely aesthetic, and its objective, though unsocial, was not ignoble. But he was followed in the eighties and nineties by a group of younger writers and artists who misunderstood or at least misapplied his doctrines. Although they claimed kinship with the Pre-Raphaelites and used as their motto the phrase "art for art's sake," they were at best decadent followers whose ecstasies were expressed in mannerisms, dress, and "intense" thrills over sunflowers, peacock-feathers, and objects of art. They were a velveteen-clad group of aesthetes, whose unconventionalities soon brought upon them satire and ridicule in the press and on the stage. The artist Whistler (1834-1903) belonged to this school, and the brilliant Irish poet, story writer, and dramatist, Oscar Wilde, was their leader, first at Oxford and later in the London drawing-rooms (p. 951). To the aesthetes art was detached from life and lived in a world of its own. Poetry, they believed, should have no function beyond creating an aesthetic thrill for its creator and its reader. It should have no definite intellectual content, no relationship to science, economics, politics, or philosophy. To produce verse that was beautiful in form and sparkling in color was enough. They discarded entirely Arnold's doctrine of high seriousness in literature (p. 527); their theory of art, if they can be said to have had one, was the negation of his. Their models were contemporary French writers. Victorian morality had no place in their poetry, and Tennyson they repudiated because he was Victorian and decorous. In spite of the attacks of *Punch* and of Gilbert and Sullivan's *Patience*, the aesthetes survived until the imprisonment of Wilde in 1895 brought the very name "aesthete" into disrepute.

The Irish Literary Renaissance

THE IRISH CONTRIBUTIONS to the stream of English literature have always been distinctive and original. Three of the best of the satirists, Swift, Wilde, and Shaw, and three of the most plaintive of the poets, Moore, Russell, and Yeats, were all born in Dublin, and they are but representative of a host of writers of Celtic blood and breeding who have enriched the literature of the British Isles. It is probably true, however, that in no previous era in English literature has the Irish contribution been so considerable or the number of Irish writers proportionately so numerous as in the modern period. This

Kate Greenaway Types

phenomenon was the result largely of a definite and conscious movement known as the Irish Literary Renaissance, which engaged at the end of the nineteenth century and the beginning of the twentieth the best genius of an unusual group of Irish writers. The founder and leader of the movement was William Butler Yeats (p. 1025). Associated with him was an earnest group of poets, dramatists, and essayists whose objective was to create unity of spirit and national consciousness among the Irish people by reviving their romantic past and interpreting their modern life and character. One of the most important phases of this renaissance was the so-called Irish Theater Movement, which resulted in the establishment of the Abbey Theater (1910) in Dublin and in the writing of numerous remarkable plays, which had a notable effect upon the development of the drama in both England and America. Among the miscellaneous writers who participated in the renaissance were—besides Yeats—G. W. Russell (Æ) (1867-1935), Edwin Martyn (1859-1924), George Moore (1852-1933), Lady Augusta Gregory (1852-1932), and John M. Synge (1871-1909; p. 985). In most of these writers the romance and mysticism of the Celtic past and the realism of modern Ireland were intermingled. Some, however, leaned more to one phase of the movement than to the other.

The general contributions of Irish literature

The most miscellaneous and, in some respects, the most Celtic of the group was Yeats himself. His writing was permeated with the characteristic melancholy and mysticism of the Celts, and to his native romanticism was added the tendency toward impressionism that made him an ardent admirer of the French symbolists and of the English poet William Blake (p. 111). In his later years Yeats turned in large measure to humanitarian and even proletarian considerations. Æ was a painter as well as a poet, and his scenes of the Donegal country have much of the haunting quality of his verse. Martyn wrote plays and reformed liturgical music; he is one of the central figures in George Moore's autobiographical *Hail and Farewell*. Lady Augusta Gregory published in 1902 a beautiful retelling of the Celtic legend of Cuchulain of Muirthemne; her one-act comedies, however, are playful but sympathetic interpretations of modern Irish life. Synge turned his pen while dying to the plaintive legend of Deirdre of the Sorrows, but most of his dramatic work is an interpretation of the bleak life of the Irish fisherman and peasant. With his mind disciplined and his spirit tempered by a prolonged study of Greek tragedy, he could not write ignobly, and in *The Shadow of the Glen* (1903) and *Riders to the Sea* (p. 986) his peasants have the stature of classical figures. His *Playboy of the Western World* (1907) aroused fierce resentment among the Irish when it was first played because of their objection to what they considered the author's maligning of the

The work of the leading writers in the Irish Renaissance

Kate Greenaway Types

Irish; it is now recognized as a powerful play; but it has not the artistic compression of his one-act tragic masterpieces. The one-act plays produced at the Abbey Theater established, in fact, a new dramatic type, and of these plays Synge's are unquestionably the best in the years before the first World War.

The Kailyard School

Scottish contributions to the literature of the period

WHILE THE IRISH were mingling romance and realism in the work of their literary renaissance, certain Scottish writers were attempting to interpret sympathetically the village life of modern Scotland. Unlike the Irish, they formed no "school," inaugurated no movement, and had no definite objective; the group, however, was dubbed by Henley, who knew Edinburgh almost as well as the Scotchmen themselves, the "Kailyard" (or Cabbage-patch) School. Among these interpreters in the vernacular of common life in Scotland belong Sir James M. Barrie, "Ian Maclaren," and S. R. Crockett. "Ian Maclaren" was the pseudonym of John Watson (1850-1907), a Scottish clergyman whose collection of stories *Beside the Bonnie Briar Bush* (1894) was widely popular for the simplicity with which it described rural Scottish life. S. R. Crockett (1860-1914) wrote in similar vein; perhaps the best of his numerous stories is *The Stickit Minister* (1893), the pathetic tale of an untrained (stickit) and sick preacher who struggles courageously on that he may educate a younger brother. Sir James Barrie (1860-1937), the best of the group, ranged quite beyond the "kailyard" and gave to English literature novels and plays of wider interest. To his early years belong his *Auld Licht Idylls* (1888), *A Window in Thrums* (1889), the immensely popular *The Little Minister* (novel 1891, drama, 1897), and *Sentimental Tommy* (1896). But in his later stories and dramas he turned to other themes and characters. In his play *Peter Pan, or the Boy Who Wouldn't Grow Up* (1904), he created a character almost as famous as Lewis Carroll's Alice and added a charming tale to the classics of the nursery. Among his most original dramas for adults are *Quality Street* (1901), *The Admirable Crichton* (1902), *Alice Sit-by-the-Fire* (1905), and *Dear Brutus* (1917). He is, finally, probably the only Scottish dramatist who has attained any distinction in the new realm of the one-act play. *The Twelve-Pound Look* (1910) is an admirable satire on the inflated egoist, and many of his short war plays are extremely effective. Barrie is deservedly the best known of Scottish writers since Stevenson.

Archery

The New Prose Fiction

REGARDING THE POETRY of the end of the nineteenth and the beginning of the twentieth centuries much has been said, along with the descriptions of the aesthetic, impressionistic, and Irish literary movements. Regarding the essay, comparatively little needs to be said, for in the period under review it was not a predominant form although copious in quantity. Indeed, the only essayist of first rank was the remarkable miscellaneous writer, Robert Louis Stevenson (p. 874), and his inclinations in this form of literature were rather back to Lamb and Hazlitt than forward to any new type or method. Max Beerbohm (1872-1956), Arnold Bennett (1867-1931), G. K. Chesterton (1874-1936), Hilaire Belloc (1870-1953), E. V. Lucas (1868-1938), Edmund Gosse (1849-1928), and many others of these miscellaneous writers have used the essay to express their personal reflections or their satirical and critical views of life and art, but it is not yet apparent that individually or as a group they have attained the distinction of the romantic essayists of the early nineteenth century, to say nothing of those of the Victorian age. In the modern period, indeed, the personal essay as such has faded into the background, and the "article" which has replaced it is too heterogeneous in content and too indeterminate in form to be sharply distinguished as a literary type. Of two types of prose writing, however, these statements cannot well be made. Both the novel and the drama have more than held their place in literature since 1880, and some extended comment on them must be made.

The essay in the period

In general the novel of the post-Victorian decades was shorter than that of the Victorian age. The early novel, which dragged its long way through successive numbers of the Victorian magazines and was published thereafter in the familiar three-volume set, was replaced by a shorter, quicker type. This reduction in length came partly from a quickening of the pace of living and partly from the influence of the compressed French fiction of Flaubert, de Maupassant, and others. In content and mood, too, there was a marked change. Some were swift-moving romances, considerably lighter and more flexible than Scott's novels and vastly more so than those of Bulwer-Lytton (p. 421). Some were cleverly satirical and witty. Many were realistic to the point of being sordid and depressing. Their didacticism, where they possessed any at all, was diffused rather than pointed. The post-Victorian author detached himself from his story instead of invading it as Thackeray and other Victorian novelists frequently did. Thus the characters in the later novels are more dramatic and less puppet-like, and the action seems to move along without any apparent intervention of a god-of-the-machine to control and direct it.

Characteristics of modern fiction

Of the romantic novelists the most distinguished is Robert Louis Stevenson (p. 874). His love of living, of travel, of action, of adventure on land and sea suffuses his stories. They are crowded with fascinating individuals—pirates, wreckers, cabin boys, highland warriors, and innumerable others—and the action is at times so brisk as to be breathless, with storms at sea, hunts for buried treasure, and plenty of good fighting. No novelist of his time provided so much lively escape into the realm of vicarious adventure unless, perhaps,

Romantic fiction writers: Stevenson and Doyle

Ladies' and Gentlemen's Doubles

it was another fascinating story-teller, born, like Stevenson, in Edinburgh. In 1887, just a year after two of Stevenson's best loved tales, *Kidnapped* and *Dr. Jekyll and Mr. Hyde*, appeared, Sir Arthur Conan Doyle (1859-1930) published the first of his Sherlock Holmes stories, *A Study in Scarlet*, and thereby added to English literature a character quite as famous as the composite personality of Jekyll and Hyde. *The Sign of the Four* followed in 1889, and *The Adventures of Sherlock Holmes*, a series of short stories, came two years later. Holmes was also the hero of a hair-raising tale called *The Hound of the Baskervilles* (1902), in many ways one of the finest of detective stories. The tales of Sherlock Holmes quite eclipsed Doyle's historical romances, but his *Micah Clarke* (1888), a tale of Monmouth's Rebellion in the reign of James II, and *The White Company* (1891), a stirring yarn of a free-lance company of mercenaries in England and France in the fourteenth century, are spirited and well written. It may be added of Stevenson and Doyle that they were among the first in the period to popularize the short story, a literary form that had a wide development in the post-Victorian era.

Samuel Butler

Yet the romance is not so typical of the post-Victorian novel as is the satirical tale, the realistic story, and the social study. Of the satirists the earliest and in some respects the most remarkable is Samuel Butler (1835-1902). Butler was a Nottingham man, who, after graduating from Cambridge and spending some years in New Zealand as a sheep-rancher, returned to England to settle down as a journalist and miscellaneous writer. He engaged in endless controversies over Darwinism, argued seriously that the creator of the Homeric epics was a woman, and published travel sketches after an extended visit to Italy. But he is best known by two satirical novels, *Erewhon* and *The Way of All Flesh*. *Erewhon* (an anagram for *nowhere*) was written in 1872; it is a Swiftian attack on contemporary England in which Butler assails not any one body of manners and morals but what he conceives to be the universal stagnation of thought that had settled like a blight on Victorian England. The history of *The Way of All Flesh* is unusual; Butler began it in 1872, set it aside in 1885, and never actually saw it in print, for it was not published until 1903, the year after his death. Probably it was too bitter for the decades in which it was written. It is a study of the idiosyncrasies and mishaps of several generations of the Pontifex family and belongs more definitely in the twentieth century than in the nineteenth. In this novel Butler was undeniably a generation ahead of his time.

The special influence of Zola and the experimental novel

The bitter realism and sharp satire in *The Way of All Flesh* gives it a kinship with the stories of a famous French novelist, who died in the same year as Butler and whose influence upon English writers of his time was profound. Emile Zola (1840-1902) was the leader of the naturalistic school of France, and his brilliantly accurate transfer to his novels of the rawness of life made him in his day notorious. Indeed, his first naturalistic novel,

Fashions

1889

1889

1890

1890

Thérèse Raquin (1867), created a wide protest. In his anticlerical novel cycle *Le Rougon-Macquart: histoire naturelle et sociale d'une famille sous le Second Empire* (1894-98) he presents in innumerable realistic—sometimes animalistic —details an immense panorama, salting his pictures of community and family life with sharp cynicism. In this series he does much of what Butler did in *The Way of All Flesh* and what Galsworthy accomplished in the *Forsyte Saga* and *A Modern Comedy* (p. 858).

One of the earliest of the English naturalists was George Robert Gissing (1857-1903). Unhappy and wretched in all that he undertook, he infused into his novels much of the pessimism that he acquired from his own experiences and from his study of the German philosopher Schopenhauer (1788-1860). He was like Zola in his fondness for depicting the lower depths of society and like Meredith (p. 768) in his power of analyzing states of mind. So he came to combine in his novels the outer world of realistic detail and the inner world of the mind of man. One of his earliest stories is *Workers of the Dawn* (1880); it was followed by *Demos* (1886) and *The Nether World* (1889), in which he is concerned with the industrial poor. He is better known, however, by his *New Grub Street* (1891) and *The Private Papers of Henry Ryecroft* (1903), a semi-autobiographical journal published in the last years of his life.

George Gissing

The novels of Henry James (1843-1916) would belong to the history of American literature, for he was born of American parents in New York City, if it were not for the fact that he lived in England for many years and became a British subject a year before his death. In Paris he made the acquaintance of Flaubert, de Maupassant, and Zola, and he belongs very clearly to the school of the naturalists. Unlike Gissing, however, he did not look for his materials in the lower depths of society; his novels deal for the most part with the socially élite. He was the brother of William James, the famous Harvard psychologist, and it is not difficult to understand, therefore, why he must be classified among the most subtle of the novelists of character. His subtlety, indeed, is sometimes so marked as to amount almost to obscurity. Among his numerous studies of human nature against a social background are *Daisy Miller* (1878), an account of the adventures of a young American girl traveling in Europe, *The Portrait of a Lady* (1881), another study of American types, and *The Ambassadors* (1903), which depicts the reactions of several Americans to the European scene. *The Turn of the Screw*, a long short-story, is one of the most subtly horrible ghost stories in English literature; but here as in his novels James is primarily the keen psychologist.

Henry James

The most stable, patrician, and deeply sympathetic novelist of the naturalistic school in England was John Galsworthy (1867-1933), equally distinguished in the field of drama. Like Zola he studied characters and their backgrounds in the minutest detail and carried his interpretations beyond

John Galsworthy

the individual and into the family group. He did not, however, draw from so many social divisions as did Zola; he preferred to analyze and to depict the propertied man of the late Victorian period and his own time. Thus are introduced into the *Forsyte Saga*, a novel-series, and its continuation *A Modern Comedy* (1906-1930), several generations of characters from the upper class against the background of the late Victorian, post-Victorian, and twentieth-century years.

Thomas Hardy (1840-1928; p. 907) is the greatest of the English realists during this period. He is also the most pessimistic, for his pessimism runs deeper than Zola's because its roots are not in any particular social group of characters, however bitter their lot, but in human life as a whole. His picture of men and women is more tragic than Galsworthy's, for he shows them as crushed by the forces of nature and social environment. Like Galsworthy he was distinguished as a poet and as a novelist. And since the spirit of the man emerges in his poetry as clearly as in his prose fiction, his novels are included in the comment on his verse that appears later (p. 907).

H. G. Wells

Herbert George Wells (1866-1946) is a versatile writer, but he can be classified among the novelists because he chose that literary form so frequently for the expression of his views and opinions. He is much less restrained and less patrician than Galsworthy, and his writings are so numerous and so varied as to give the impression that, like Francis Bacon, he held all knowledge to be his province. His earliest and perhaps his most original novels are fantastic romances like *The Time Machine* (1895) and *The War of the Worlds* (1898), in which he created imaginary worlds and then, playing God, studied human beings in them. That he could, however, make excellent individual and group analyses in a normal world he revealed in his justly popular *The History of Mr. Polly* (1910), the tale of a small shop-keeper in search of adventure, and *Tono-Bungay* (1909), in which he describes a new society in the process of displacing an older one. Wells is a scientist, a visionary, a socialist, a reformer, a propagandist, a critic, and a dozen other men in one, and his novels for that reason sometimes suggest that his reach exceeds his grasp.

Joseph Conrad

Joseph Conrad (1857-1924; p. 942), like Henry James, acquired a distinguished name for himself in the country of his adoption. That a man born in Poland and unacquainted with the English language until he was past twenty should nevertheless become a great English novelist is remarkable. From 1873 to 1895 Conrad was a sailor in the British mercantile marine; after the latter date he devoted himself to the writing of sea tales which he considered to be, like Stevenson's, romantic, but which are actually naturalistic. Perhaps of Conrad's contemporaries only John Masefield in some of his long narrative poems (p. 916) has depicted the sea in all its phases and the life of the deep-sea sailor as accurately, effectively, and understandingly as has this Polish immigrant. But like Masefield he was not interested solely in the

Motor Car, 1895

physical aspects of seafaring or in the stirring life of the sailor. That he was also a profound psychologist is shown in *Almayer's Folly* (1895), *The Nigger of the Narcissus* (1897), and—to mention only one other—*Lord Jim* (1900). His heroes are not just seamen; they are men with consciences, emotions, impulses, and these springs of action Conrad analyzed. Although the episodes in the sea tales give them a flavor of the Stevensonian romance, his relationship is more nearly with James, Galsworthy, and Masefield.

The most journalistic of the prominent novelists of the period and the most hard-headed about his profession was Arnold Bennett (1867-1931). He was an avowed follower of the realistic writers of the nineteenth century in France and Russia. An enormously productive writer, he often fell into mediocrity of a pot-boiling kind; but at his best, as in *The Old Wives' Tale* (1908), he has a remarkable fidelity to true detail and a bravura kind of reportorial genius. This is the story of two sisters, daughters of a small shopkeeper in a suburban town; and yet there are two fundamentally different temperaments—a realistic and a romantic—in their careers. This same combination of almost callous objectivity and a sort of plodding love of living is characteristic of all Bennett's typical work, particularly in those novels of the pottery section of Staffordshire and Lancashire (the Five Towns): the trilogy *Clayhanger* (1910), *Hilda Lessways* (1911), and *These Twain* (1916) and the feebler *Helen with the High Hand* (1910) and *Denry the Audacious* (1911). Bennett is an exceptionally readable author; but there is about him a certain hardness of spirit, with a particularly frank admission that his writing was his bread and butter and that he intended to follow as closely as possible the tried and true formulae for success with his public.

Arnold Bennett

The development of the short story was slower in England than in America, and the type did not become significant until toward the end of the nineteenth century. Then the brilliant and finished short stories of Stevenson and the stirring and exotic Indian tales of Kipling established it as a major form in English literature. Important writers of the short story in the first decades of the twentieth century include Thomas Hardy, H. G. Wells, G. K. Chesterton, Arthur Conan Doyle, W. W. Jacobs, Henry James, and, in Scotland, the members of the Kailyard School. But no one of these later writers equaled the romantic-realists who popularized the type at the end of the preceding century.

The short story

The New Drama

WHEN THE DRAMA is free to reflect life, as it was not in the Victorian period, it employs ordinarily the themes, moods, and objectives of other literary types. This is particularly true, of course, in dramas written by authors who

Motor Car, 1903

also write novels and poems. So it is that the characteristic mysticism of Yeats appears in both his poetry and his plays, and the social sympathies of Galsworthy are revealed in both his novels and his dramas. It is not surprising that the dramas of the post-Victorian period should have many of the characteristics of the other forms then current. Literary movements, moreover, find expression in drama, as well as in other forms, and the drama has, therefore, been considered in the discussion of the Irish Literary Renaissance and of the Kailyard School (pp. 852 and 854). What remains is a general consideration of post-Victorian drama and a more particular discussion of three or four of the most significant dramatists.

The influence of Ibsen

Just as the English impressionists derived their inspiration and technique from the French symbolists (p. 850), and the English naturalists derived theirs from Zola (p. 856), so in the realm of the drama a continental writer exercised upon English playwrights in the last two decades of the century a very profound effect. Henrik Ibsen (1828-1906), a Norwegian dramatist, dared to challenge the Mrs. Grundys of the Continent and of England by writing plays which dealt boldly with social problems and which in some instances even propounded unpopular and unconventional solutions. So in *A Doll's House* he represents the woman whose possessive and egoistic husband makes a doll of her as leaving him that she may recover her lost individuality. Ibsen's reply to those who protested that man and wife must remain inseparable was *Ghosts*, a drama in which hideous tragedy sprang from a wife's conventional and lying loyalty to a worthless husband. "Ibsenism," this frank treatment of social problems on the stage was called, and when Ibsen's plays and English ones like them appeared in London, they created a ferment of opposition. But the direct and frank treatment of human relationships in the home and in the social group was becoming common in the novels, and it was inevitable that the same themes and the same treatment should invade the theater. Before the end of the century they were accepted without much question.

Jones and Pinero

Two early dramatists who presented social problem plays to English audiences were Sir Henry Arthur Jones (1851-1929) and Sir Arthur Wing Pinero (1855-1934). These playwrights were the leading society dramatists in the two decades from 1890 to 1910. For the most part they dealt, like Ibsen, with social relationships and social problems. Jones's first important drama, in fact, *Breaking a Butterfly* (1885), was modeled after Ibsen's *A Doll's House*. Some of his most popular and significant plays in the decade following are *Saints and Sinners* (1891), *Michael and His Lost Angel* (1896), and *Mrs. Dane's Defense* (1900). The best known of Pinero's dramas are *The Second Mrs. Tanqueray* (1893), which answers in the negative and very pathetically the question whether a woman with a past can be admitted to polite society, *The Gay Lord Quex* (1899), and *Mid-Channel* (1909).

The comedies of Oscar Wilde (1854-1900; p. 951) were not affected by

Ladies' Hats

the breakdown of the old divisions into comedy and tragedy that appears in the plays of Jones, Pinero, and Galsworthy. With the possible exceptions of *Lady Windermere's Fan* (1892) and *A Woman of No Importance* (1895) Wilde's plays are not problem plays, for the author preferred to be sparkling rather than serious. In the first of these two, the old comedy of manners (Vol. I, pp. 824 ff.) was reborn, and the same social satire appears in *An Ideal Husband* (1895) and *The Importance of Being Earnest* (1895). These comedies are highly sophisticated, artificial, and witty; they scintillate with comic epigrams, inverted commonplaces, and flippant and pungent phrases.

Oscar Wilde

George Bernard Shaw (1856-1950) was born in the same year and the same city—Dublin—as Wilde. Although he does not restrict himself to the drama as the vehicle of his ideas and criticisms, he uses it more than any other form of literature and usually with great success. He has in full measure the Irish capacity for wit and satire. He is a perpetual protester against orthodoxies of all sorts. He supported the unconventional Ibsen when the Norwegian dramatist needed support, and he subscribed entirely to Ibsen's dramatic creed and method. His *Quintessence of Ibsenism* (1891) was followed within a year by his first play, *Widowers' Houses*, a presentation of the problem of slum landlordism; and since then a long succession of plays has poured from his pen. The best of these in the period of his activity down to 1914 are *Mrs. Warren's Profession* (1894), *Candida* (1894), *You Never Can Tell* (1896), *Man and Superman* (1903), *Major Barbara* (1905), *Fanny's First Play* (1911), *Androcles and the Lion* (1912), and *Pygmalion* (1912), but no selection can give a complete idea of the wealth of range and intellectual play in Shaw's dramas. Whimsical, witty, caustic, vigorous, unabashed, Shaw would probably reply to the accusation that he lives to glorify G. B. S. by asserting that on the contrary he lives to expose wrongs, attack shams, and destroy conventionality by ridiculing it.

George Bernard Shaw

It has already been observed that John Galsworthy (1867-1933) has won a distinguished place in the drama as well as in the novel. Certain qualities of the man and of his work have lifted his plays to a very high plane. Galsworthy was one of the aristocratic rebels of his time. He was a true patrician, with "quality" as his objective and with an unwillingness to stoop to vulgar literary tricks. The highest moral purpose of the drama is, he said, "to set before the public no cut-and-dried codes, but the phenomena of life and character, selected and combined, *but not distorted*, by the dramatist's outlook, set down without fear, favor, or prejudice, leaving the public to draw such poor moral as nature may afford." This detachment did not prevent him from exhibiting the sweet and balanced humanitarianism that is characteristic also of his novels. Finally, he developed further a new form of play which Jones and Pinero had popularized, neither comedy nor tragedy but serious drama in which all moods of life are mingled. In most of his plays he appears as a critic of contemporary social organization. In dealing

Galsworthy's plays

A La Mode

1910

with problems of society, and labor in particular, he shows high seriousness. He frequently presents ironically the tragedy of a human being crushed by a circumstance trivial in itself but powerful because of the importance which social organization attaches to it. Society, in the mass, he represents as impersonal, unfeeling, and often ruthless. It is obvious that his sympathies are with the weak or unlucky man who is ground between the meshed wheels of modern society and industry. Galsworthy wrote nearly a score of dramas in almost as many years. *The Silver Box* (1906), reminiscent in some ways of de Maupassant's bitterly ironic short story *A Piece of String*, was his first play. It was followed in rapid succession by *Joy* (1907), *Strife* (1909), *Justice* (1910), *The Little Dream* (1911), *The Pigeon* (1912), *The Eldest Son* (1912), and eight others which carried his career past the point at which the present comment must be terminated.

The Period in Review

Reaction against Victorianism

French influences

1912

The corrective spirit

THE CONFUSING VARIETY of forms, methods, moods, and movements that emerged out of the rebellion against Victorianism at the end of the nineteenth century and spread over into the first decades of the twentieth makes it difficult to bring the literature of the period into any clear unity, especially since it has not yet been thoroughly winnowed by time. Certain elements, however, seem to recur consistently. One is the spirit of reaction against Victorian restraint and conventionality. On the whole, the post-Victorian period is freer, more out-spoken, more "shocking"—in the Victorian sense of the word. Among the definite movements of the period are the manifestly decadent aestheticism of the end of the century, and the tendency toward impressionism after the manner of the French symbolists and realism after that of the French naturalists. The Irish writers created a revival of interest in Celtic legend and mysticism and in modern Irish life which expressed itself in much fine poetry and prose and especially in a remarkable series of one-act plays and full-length dramas. Romance continued well into the period, notably in the work of Stevenson. It is not, however, so prevalent an element as a new type of realism which manifested itself not only in Zolaesque invasions of the lower strata of society but also in brilliantly detached and unsentimental analyses of family and social groups and especially of individuals. These materials and methods are recurrent in the novels of the period and also in dramas that broke away from the emptiness and artificiality of Victorian plays and made successful interpretations of human life. The element of satire, finally, appears in a literature in which human problems are consciously and obviously balanced, weighed, and judged; for in much of the writing of these decades it is evident that the critical, corrective spirit is abroad. Just which of all these varied elements and which of the plays, poems, and novels which give them literary bodies will pass into the permanent stream of English literature only Time can tell.

POETRY

William Ernest Henley
1849-1903

Henley was born in Gloucester in 1849. He attended the Crypt Grammar School in his native city and was fortunate to come under the influence there of the Manx poet, T. E. Brown, who was headmaster. Brown not only inspired his young pupil and directed his reading but encouraged him at a time when he was most in need of encouragement. A tubercular disease necessitated the amputation of one of Henley's feet, and there was serious danger that he would lose the other foot. Fortunately, however, Dr. Joseph Lister, the great founder of modern antiseptic surgery, was practicing at that time in Edinburgh, and thither Henley went in 1873. For twenty months he was under treatment in the Edinburgh Infirmary, and the ravages of the disease were checked. The hospital experience was by no means unprofitable to him. During a good deal of the time he wrote verse, and many of his poems appeared in *The Cornhill Magazine* during the period of his sickness. Furthermore, Leslie Stephen, then editor of *The Cornhill,* took to Henley's bedside another young contributor to the magazine; and thus Henley developed with Robert Louis Stevenson a close friendship which lasted until broken by an unhappy misunderstanding years later. Some of the most vivid of Henley's poems are those which grew out of his experiences in the Edinburgh Infirmary, and which he collected in 1888 under the title *In Hospital*. His best known lyric, *Invictus* (written in 1875), was a defiant challenge to fate from his bed of pain.

Discharged from the hospital, he did hack-writing in Edinburgh for a short time and in 1877 went up to London to become editor of *London,* a short-lived magazine in which appeared Stevenson's *New Arabian Nights* and a series of poems modeled on old French verse forms by Henley himself. From 1882 to 1886 he was editor of *The Magazine of Art*. His most notable magazine connection was as editor of the *National Observer* in London. Under Henley's editorship this magazine became noted for its vigorous advocacy of British imperialism. True to its policy it published, along with other imperialistic items, Kipling's *Barrack-Room Ballads*. In 1888, in addition to publishing *In Hospital*, he also issued *A Book of Verse*. A sheaf of his reviews and criticisms appeared in 1890 under the title *Views and Reviews*. Two years later three plays which he had written in collaboration with Stevenson—*Beau Austin, Deacon Brodie,* and *Admiral Guinea*—appeared; these found their way to the stage but were not notably successful. His own play *Macaire*, published in 1895, was also a failure. In 1893 another volume of poetry, *The Song of the Sword*, came out; it was called later *London Voluntaries*. Five years afterwards a collection of his verses appeared under the simple title *Poems*, and in 1901 a second volume was published entitled *Hawthorn and Lavender*. He died two years later.

Henley's marked individuality and independence of spirit emerge in his poetry. He advocated all things new, and had no fear of facing novelty himself. He engaged in various metrical experiments and was fond of imitating the artificial forms of French verse like the *rondeau* and the *ballade* and of copying the lyrical devices of Heinrich Heine, the German romantic poet, who may perhaps have attracted Henley because he wrote verses while lying on a "mattress-grave." The individuality of Henley's poetry comes from both content and form. Much of it is vividly impressionistic as are, for example, the startlingly modern poems in his volume of hospital verse. He was a master of the pictorial phrase, and his concrete sketches of persons and places are unforgettable. He worshiped speed, and the tempo of some of his poems is breathless. Finally, in his use of unrimed rhythms—a form of verse which he employed very often—he is distinctly individual and modern. His poems without rimes have the rugged vigor of his boisterous personality; their technique is reminiscent of that of Walt Whitman, but though in them and in his other poems Henley often echoes other poets, he succeeds, nevertheless, in retaining his individuality.

from *In Hospital*

This is a series of poems based upon impressions of the Old Infirmary, Edinburgh, where Henley was a patient for twenty months, suffering from a tubercular disease.

ENTER PATIENT

The morning mists still haunt the stony street;
The northern summer air is shrill and cold;
And, lo, the hospital, gray, quiet, old,
Where Life and Death like friendly chafferers meet.
Through the loud spaciousness and drafty gloom 5
A small, strange child—so agéd yet so young!—
Her little arm besplinted and beslung,
Precedes me gravely to the waiting-room.
I limp behind, my confidence all gone.
The gray-haired soldier-porter waves me on,
And on I crawl, and still my spirits fail; 11
A tragic meanness seems so to environ
These corridors and stairs of stone and iron,
Cold, naked, clean—half-workhouse and half-jail.

WAITING

A square, squat room (a cellar on promotion),
Drab to the soul, drab to the very daylight;
Plasters astray in unnatural-looking tinware;
Scissors and lint and apothecary's jars.

Here, on a bench a skeleton would writhe from, 5
Angry and sore, I wait to be admitted;
Wait till my heart is lead upon my stomach,
While at their ease two dressers do their chores.

One has a probe—it feels to me a crowbar.
A small boy sniffs and shudders after bluestone. 10
A poor old tramp explains his poor old ulcers.
Life is (I think) a blunder and a shame.

BEFORE

Behold me waiting—waiting for the knife.
A little while, and at a leap I storm
The thick, sweet mystery of chloroform,
The drunken dark, the little death-in-life.
The gods are good to me—I have no wife, 5
No innocent child, to think of as I near
The fateful minute; nothing all-too dear
Unmans me for my bout of passive strife.
Yet I am tremulous and a trifle sick,
And, face to face with chance, I shrink a little; 10
My hopes are strong, my will is something weak.
Here comes the basket? Thank you. I am ready.
But, gentlemen my porters, life is brittle;
You carry Caesar and his fortunes—steady!

Waiting. 10. **bluestone,** cupric sulphate, or blue vitriol, used as an emetic.
Before. 14. **You . . . fortunes,** Julius Caesar's words, quoted by Plutarch in his *Life of Caesar.* They were addressed, during the war with Pompey, to a boatman who had Caesar as his passenger.

The poems of William Ernest Henley are reprinted from his *Poems* (1919) by permission of Charles Scribner's Sons, New York.

STAFF-NURSE: OLD STYLE

The great masters of the commonplace,
REMBRANDT and good SIR WALTER—only these
Could paint her all to you: experienced ease
And antique liveliness and ponderous grace;
The sweet old roses of her sunken face; 5
The depth and malice of her sly, gray eyes;
The broad Scots tongue that flatters, scolds, defies,
The thick Scots wit that fells you like a mace.
These thirty years has she been nursing here,
Some of them under SYME, her hero still. 10
Much is she worth, and even more is made of her.
Patients and students hold her very dear.
The doctors love her, tease her, use her skill.
They say "The Chief" himself is half-afraid of her.

STAFF-NURSE: NEW STYLE

Blue-eyed and bright of face but waning fast
Into the sear of virginal decay,
I view her as she enters, day by day,
As a sweet sunset almost overpast.
Kindly and calm, patrician to the last, 5
Superbly falls her gown of sober gray,
And on her chignon's elegant array
The plainest cap is somehow touched with caste.
She talks BEETHOVEN; frowns disapprobation
At BALZAC's name, sighs it at "poor GEORGE SAND's"; 10
Knows that she has exceeding pretty hands;
Speaks Latin with a right accentuation;
And gives at need (as one who understands)
Draft, counsel, diagnosis, exhortation.

MUSIC

Down the quiet eve,
Thro' my window with the sunset
Pipes to me a distant organ
Foolish ditties;

And, as when you change 5
Pictures in a magic lantern,
Books, beds, bottles, floors, and ceiling
Fade and vanish,

And I'm well once more . . .
August flares adust and torrid. 10
But my heart is full of April
Sap and sweetness.

In the quiet eve
I am loitering, longing, dreaming . . .
Dreaming, and a distant organ 15
Pipes me ditties.

I can see the shop,
I can smell the sprinkled pavement,
Where she serves—her chestnut chignon
Thrills my senses! 20

O, the sight and scent,
Wistful eve and perfumed pavement!
In the distance pipes an organ . . .
The sensation

Comes to me anew, 25
And my spirit for a moment
Thro' the music breathes the blessed
Airs of London.

APPARITION

This is an accurate sketch of Robert Louis Stevenson (p. 874), who visited Henley in the hospital in 1875 and became his close friend.

Thin-legged, thin-chested, slight unspeakably,
Neat-footed and weak-fingered; in his face—
Lean, large-boned, curved of beak, and touched with race,
Bold-lipped, rich-tinted, mutable as the sea,
The brown eyes radiant with vivacity— 5
There shines a brilliant and romantic grace,
A spirit intense and rare, with trace on trace
Of passion and impudence and energy.
Valiant in velvet, light in ragged luck,
Most vain, most generous, sternly critical, 10
Buffoon and poet, lover and sensualist;

Staff-Nurse: Old Style. 2. **Rembrandt,** a famous Dutch realistic painter (1606-1669). **Sir Walter,** Sir Walter Scott, p. 28, whose graphic word-paintings of Edinburgh characters, as in *The Heart of Midlothian,* were doubtless in Henley's mind. 10. **Syme,** James Syme (1799-1870), the greatest surgeon of his day. 14. "**The Chief,**" Dr. Joseph Lister, successor to Syme as chief surgeon at the Edinburgh Infirmary. See footnote p. 863.
Staff-Nurse: New Style. 7. **chignon,** a roll of hair worn on the back of the head. 9. **Beethoven,** Ludwig van Beethoven (1770-1827), the celebrated German musical composer; he was well established by 1872 as an old master. 10. **Balzac,** Honoré de Balzac (1799-1850), a French naturalistic writer of fiction. Conservative Englishwomen found his stories too frank. **George Sand,** the pseudonym of Mme Aurore Dudevant (1804-1876), a French novelist, celebrated for her romantic love affairs with the poet Musset, the composer Chopin, and others.

A deal of Ariel, just a streak of Puck,
Much Antony, of Hamlet most of all,
And something of the Shorter-Catechist.

DISCHARGED

Carry me out
Into the wind and the sunshine,
Into the beautiful world.
O the wonder, the spell of the streets!
The stature and strength of the horses, 5
The rustle and echo of footfalls,
The flat roar and rattle of wheels!
A swift tram floats huge on us . . .
It's a dream?
The smell of the mud in my nostrils 10
Blows brave—like a breath of the sea!

As of old,
Ambulant, undulant drapery,
Vaguely and strangely provocative,
Flutters and beckons. O yonder— 15
Is it?—the gleam of a stocking!
Sudden, a spire
Wedged in the mist! O the houses,
The long lines of lofty, gray houses,
Cross-hatched with shadow and light! 20
These are the streets . . .
Each is an avenue leading
Whither I will!

Free . . . !
Dizzy, hysterical, faint, 25
I sit, and the carriage rolls on with me
Into the wonderful world. (*1872-1875;* 1888)

Invictus

> The title means *Unconquered.* Cf. Swinburne's *Garden of Proserpine,* ll. 81-85, p. 815.

Out of the night that covers me,
  Black as the Pit from pole to pole,
I thank whatever gods may be
  For my unconquerable soul.

In the fell clutch of circumstance 5
  I have not winced nor cried aloud.
Under the bludgeonings of chance
  My head is bloody, but unbowed.

Beyond this place of wrath and tears
  Looms but the Horror of the shade, 10
And yet the menace of the years
  Finds, and shall find, me unafraid.

It matters not how strait the gate,
  How charged with punishments the scroll,
I am the master of my fate; 15
  I am the captain of my soul.
(*1875;* 1888)

I. M.
Margaritae Sorori

> Henley wrote this poem in memory of his wife's sister Margaret.

A late lark twitters from the quiet skies;
And from the west,
Where the sun, his day's work ended,
Lingers as in content,
There falls on the old, gray city 5
An influence luminous and serene,
A shining peace.

The smoke ascends
In a rosy-and-golden haze. The spires
Shine, and are changed. In the valley 10
Shadows rise. The lark sings on. The sun,
Closing his benediction,
Sinks, and the darkening air
Thrills with a sense of the triumphing night—
Night with her train of stars 15
And her great gift of sleep.

So be my passing!
My task accomplished and the long day done,
My wages taken, and in my heart
Some late lark singing, 20
Let me be gathered to the quiet west,
The sundown splendid and serene,
Death. (*1886;* 1888)

---

12. **Ariel,** the airy spirit that executes Prospero's bidding in Shakespeare's *Tempest.* **Puck,** the mischievous spirit of English folklore and of Shakespeare's *Midsummer-Night's Dream.* 13. **Antony,** Marcus Antonius (83-30 B.C.), the fiery orator in Shakespeare's *Julius Caesar;* a sensualist and lover in *Antony and Cleopatra.* Hamlet was melancholy. 14. **Shorter-Catechist,** an adherent to strict Calvinistic religious and ethical principles as embodied in the Shorter Catechism, compiled by the Westminster Assembly in 1646-1647.
Invictus. 2. **Pit,** hell.

On the Way to Kew

Kew, with its famous gardens, and Richmond are in the environs of London, a short distance up the Thames.

    On the way to Kew,
By the river old and gray,
Where in the Long Ago
We laughed and loitered so,
I met a ghost today,   5
A ghost that told of you—
A ghost of low replies
And sweet inscrutable eyes,
    Coming up from Richmond
As you used to do.   10

By the river old and gray,
The enchanted Long Ago
Murmured and smiled anew.
On the way to Kew,
March had the laugh of May,   15
The bare boughs looked aglow,
And old immortal words
Sang in my breast like birds,
    Coming up from Richmond
As I used with you.   20

With the life of Long Ago
Lived my thought of you.
By the river old and gray,
Flowing his appointed way,
As I watched I knew   25
What is so good to know—
Not in vain, not in vain,
Shall I look for you again,
    Coming up from Richmond
On the way to Kew.   (1888)

Ballade of a Toyokuni Color-Print

Utagawa Toyokuni (1769-1825) was a popular Japanese artist who painted many women, actors, and swordsmen.

Was I a Samurai renowned,
Two-sworded, fierce, immense of bow?
A histrion angular and profound?
A priest? a porter?—Child, although
I have forgotten clean, I know   5
That in the shade of Fujisan,
What time the cherry-orchards blow,
I loved you once in old Japan.

As here you loiter, flowing-gowned
And hugely sashed, with pins a-row   10
Your quaint head as with flamelets crowned,
Demure, inviting—even so,
When merry maids in Miyako
To feel the sweet o' the year began,
And green gardens to overflow,   15
I loved you once in old Japan.

Clear shine the hills; the rice fields round
Two cranes are circling; sleepy and slow,
A blue canal the lake's blue bound
Breaks at the bamboo bridge; and lo!   20
Touched with the sundown's spirit and glow,
I see you turn, with flirted fan,
Against the plum-tree's bloomy snow . . .
I loved you once in old Japan!

ENVOY

Dear, 'twas a dozen lives ago;   25
But that I was a lucky man
The Toyokuni here will show:
I loved you—once—in old Japan.   (1888)

What Is to Come

What is to come we know not. But we know
That what has been was good—was good to
    show,
Better to hide, and best of all to bear.
We are the masters of the days that were;
We have lived, we have loved, we have suffered . . . even so.   5

Shall we not take the ebb who had the flow?
Life was our friend. Now, if it be our foe—
Dear, though it spoil and break us!—need we
    care
        What is to come?

Ballade . . . Color-Print. 1. **Samurai**, a swordsman, a member of the ancient Japanese military aristocracy. 3. **histrion**, actor. 6. **Fujisan**, Fujiyama, the sacred mountain that forms a characteristic background for many Japanese prints. 7. **blow**, bloom. The flowering cherry is a tree common in Japan. 13. **Miyako**, a Japanese village on the island of Hondo.

Let the great winds their worst and wildest
    blow,   10
Or the gold weather round us mellow slow;
We have fulfilled ourselves, and we can dare
And we can conquer, though we may not
    share
In the rich quiet of the afterglow
    What is to come.   (1888)

Where Forlorn Sunsets Flare and Fade

Where forlorn sunsets flare and fade
  On desolate sea and lonely sand,
Out of the silence and the shade
  What is the voice of strange command
Calling you still, as friend calls friend   5
  With love that cannot brook delay,
To rise and follow the ways that wend
  Over the hills and far away?

Hark to the city, street on street
  A roaring reach of death and life,   10
Of vortices that clash and fleet
  And ruin in appointed strife,
Hark to it calling, calling clear,
  Calling until you cannot stay
From dearer things than your own most dear
  Over the hills and far away.   16

Out of the sound of the ebb-and-flow,
  Out of the sight of lamp and star,
It calls you where the good winds blow,
  And the unchanging meadows are—   20
From faded hopes and hopes agleam,
  It calls you, calls you night and day
Beyond the dark into the dream
  Over the hills and far away.   (1892)

Space and Dread and the Dark

Space and dread and the dark—
Over a livid stretch of sky
Cloud-monsters crawling, like a funeral train
Of huge, primeval presences
Stooping beneath the weight   5

---

8. **Over . . . away.** The refrain of a popular seventeenth-century song. See Gay's *Beggar's Opera* (Vol. I, p. 1107); also Stevenson's *A Song of the Road*, p. 876. 11. **fleet**, rush.

Of some enormous, rudimentary grief;
While in the haunting loneliness
The far sea waits and wanders with a sound
As of the trailing skirts of Destiny,
Passing unseen   10
To some immitigable end
With her gray henchman, Death.

What larve, what specter is this
Thrilling the wilderness to life
As with the bodily shape of Fear?   15
What but a desperate sense,
A strong foreboding of those dim
Interminable continents, forlorn
And many-silenced, in a dusk
Inviolable utterly, and dead   20
As the poor dead it huddles and swarms and
    styes
In hugger-mugger through eternity?

Life—life—let there be life!
Better a thousand times the roaring hours
When wave and wind,   25
Like the Arch-Murderer in flight
From the Avenger at his heel,
Storms through the desolate fastnesses
And wild waste places of the world!

Life—give me life until the end,   30
That at the very top of being,
The battle-spirit shouting in my blood,
Out of the reddest hell of the fight
I may be snatched and flung
Into the everlasting lull,   35
The immortal, incommunicable dream.
    (1892)

England, My England

Here is voiced a characteristic attitude toward British imperialism. An interesting comparison can be made between "England, My England" and Kipling's poems (pp. 887 ff.).

What have I done for you,
  England, my England?
What is there I would not do,
  England, my own?

---

13. **larve**, ghost.

With your glorious eyes austere,
As the Lord were walking near,
Whispering terrible things and dear
  As the Song on your bugles blown,
    England—
  Round the world on your bugles blown!

Where shall the watchful Sun,
  England, my England,
Match the master-work you've done,
  England, my own?
When shall he rejoice again
Such a breed of mighty men
As come forward, one to ten,
  To the Song on your bugles blown,
    England—
  Down the years on your bugles blown?

Ever the faith endures,
  England, my England—
"Take and break us; we are yours,
  England, my own!
Life is good, and joy runs high
Between English earth and sky;
Death is death; but we shall die
  To the Song on your bugles blown,
    England—
  To the stars on your bugles blown!"

They call you proud and hard,
  England, my England;
You with worlds to watch and ward,
  England, my own!
You whose mailed hand keeps the keys
Of such teeming destinies
You could know nor dread nor ease
  Were the Song on your bugles blown,
    England—
  Round the Pit on your bugles blown!

Mother of Ships whose might,
  England, my England,
Is the fierce old Sea's delight,
  England, my own
Chosen daughter of the Lord,
Spouse-in-Chief of the ancient Sword,
There's the menace of the Word
  In the Song on your bugles blown,
    England—
  Out of heaven on your bugles blown! (1892)

Gerard Manley Hopkins
1844-1889

Born in 1844, Hopkins received an early education intended to prepare him for the English Church, but in 1866 he came under the magnetic influence of John Henry Newman and was filled with religious enthusiasm that resulted in his becoming a Roman Catholic. The conversion, which came during his brilliant undergraduate days at Oxford, where he was popularly called the "Star of Balliol," created a sensation. When he was received into the Society of Jesus in 1868, he burned his early poems and abstained from writing for seven years. After serving as a missionary in the slums of Liverpool, where he was shocked by the vice and dirt of the city, he received a church in Oxford. In 1884 he was appointed to the staff of the revived Catholic University of Dublin, a post that he held until his death five years later.

Many of the poems of Father Hopkins are difficult to read and to understand. His bold poetic tricks and verbal eccentricities, his obscure imagery, and his subtle rhythms all obtrude between the reader and the poet's thought. Convinced that the startling innovations in the poetry of Hopkins, left in manuscript at the time of his death, would meet with indifference or ridicule if given too early to the literary world, Robert Bridges, his devoted friend, delayed publication until 1918, thirty or more years after the poems were written. The slender volume at once won extravagant praise from some of the post-war poets, who found in these tense and fervent poems an affinity with their own poetic manner; others called them purposely obscure.

Hopkins is more closely related to Milton, however, in his conception of the world without and within than he is to the post-Victorians. Both he and the great Puritan accepted the idea of a controlled universe but saw within it much conflict and division.

Painstaking care to understand the method by which Hopkins combined thought and feeling in words and the rhythmical pattern he followed will yield rich rewards. He tried to make utterance revivify experience, and to this end he uses word-clusters instead of conventional grammatical constructions; his passionate emotion explodes in a word instead of a phrase. Alliteration is a favorite device, as are also interior rimes and repetitions; but all three poetic instruments are used with surprising significance.

Some of the poems, says Hopkins, are written in what he calls "Sprung Rhythm," which is measured by feet of one to four syllables, with the stress always on the first syllable of the foot. He says too that this rhythm provides greater flexibility in the verse by allowing any one kind of foot to follow any other kind. "It is natural in Sprung Rhythm," he adds, "for the lines to be *rove over*, that is, for the scanning of each line immediately to take up that of the one before, so that if the first has one or more syllables at its end, the other must have so many the less at its beginning; and in fact the scanning runs on without break from the beginning, say, of a stanza to the end, and all the stanza is one long strain, though written in lines asunder." (Quoted by Bridges in the Preface to his edition of Hopkins's *Poems*, page 4.)

Heaven—Haven

(A NUN TAKES THE VEIL)

I have desired to go
    Where springs not fail,
To fields where flies no sharp and sided hail,
    And a few lilies blow.

And I have asked to be   5
    Where no storms come,
Where the green swell is in the haven dumb,
    And out of the swing of the sea.
                (*c. 1866;* 1918)

The Habit of Perfection

Elected Silence, sing to me
And beat upon my whorlèd ear;
Pipe me to pastures still and be
The music that I care to hear.

Shape nothing, lips; be lovely-dumb—   5
It is the shut, the curfew sent
From there where all surrenders come
Which only makes you eloquent.

Be shellèd, eyes, with double dark
And find the uncreated light;   10
This ruck and reel which you remark
Coils, keeps, and teases simple sight.

Palate, the hutch of tasty lust,
Desire not to be rinsed with wine;
The can must be so sweet, the crust   15
So fresh that come in fasts divine!

Nostrils, your careless breath that spend
Upon the stir and keep of pride,
What relish shall the censers send
Along the sanctuary side!   20

O feel-of-primrose hands, O feet
That want the yield of plushy sward,
But you shall walk the golden street
And you unhouse and house the Lord.

And, Poverty, be thou the bride   25
And now the marriage feast begun,
And lily-colored clothes provide
Your spouse not labored-at nor spun.
                    (*1866;* 1918)

The poems of Gerard Manley Hopkins are reprinted from his *Poems* (1918) by permission of the Hopkins family and The Oxford University Press.
The Habit of Perfection. 2. **whorlèd**, having whorls.

11. **ruck and reel**, crowding and confusion. 27. **lily-colored . . . spun.** Cf. *Matthew*, 6:28-29: "Consider the lilies of the field, how they grow; they toil not, neither do they spin. And yet I say unto you, That even Solomon in all his glory was not arrayed like one of these."

God's Grandeur

The world is charged with the grandeur of God.
   It will flame out, like shining from shook foil;
   It gathers to a greatness, like the ooze of oil
Crushed. Why do men then now not reck his rod?
Generations have trod, have trod, have trod;
   And all is seared with trade; bleared, smeared with toil;   6
   And wears man's smudge and shares man's smell: the soil
Is bare now, nor can foot feel, being shod.

And for all this, nature is never spent;
   There lives the dearest freshness deep down things;   10
And though the last lights off the black West went,
   Oh, morning, at the brown brink eastward, springs—
Because the Holy Ghost over the bent
   World broods with warm breast and with ah! bright wings.
                      (*1877; 1918*)

The Starlight Night

Look at the stars! look, look up at the skies!
   O look at all the fire-folk sitting in the air!
   The bright boroughs, the circle-citadels there!
Down in dim woods the diamond delves! the elves'-eyes!
The gray lawns cold where gold, where quick-gold lies!   5
   Wind-beat white-beam! airy abeles set on a flare!
   Flake-doves sent floating forth at a farm-yard scare!—
Ah well! it is all a purchase, all is a prize.
Buy then! bid then!—What?—Prayer, patience, alms, vows.
Look, look: a May-mess, like on orchard boughs!   10

Look! March-bloom, like on mealed-with-yellow sallows!
These are indeed the barn; within-doors house
The shocks. This piece-bright paling shuts the Spouse
Christ house, Christ and his mother and all his hallows.   (*1877; 1918*)

The Sea and the Skylark

On ear and ear two noises too old to end
   Trench—right, the tide that ramps against the shore;
   With a flood or a fall, low lull-off or all roar,
Frequenting there while moon shall wear and wend.

Left hand, off land, I hear the lark ascend,   5
   His rash-fresh re-winded new-skeinéd score
   In crisps of curl off wild winch whirl, and pour
And pelt music, till none's to spill nor spend.

How these two shame this shallow and frail town!
   How ring right out our sordid turbid time,
Being pure! We, life's pride and cared-for crown,   11

Have lost that cheer and charm of earth's past prime:
Our make and making break, are breaking, down
   To man's last dust, drain fast towards man's first slime.   (*1877; 1918*)

The Windhover

TO CHRIST OUR LORD

I caught this morning morning's minion, king-
   dom of daylight's dauphin, dapple-dawn-drawn Falcon, in his riding
   Of the rolling level underneath him steady air, and striding
High there, how he rung upon the rein of a wimpling wing

God's Grandeur. 3. **ooze . . . Crushed,** oil from crushed olives.
The Starlight Night. 5. **gold,** dewdrops. 6. **white-beam,** a small tree with leaves white on the underside. **abeles,** white poplars. 10. **May-mess,** medley, like blossoms in May.

11. **mealed-with-yellow sallows,** willows stained with yellow pollen. 13. **shocks,** leaves. 14. **hallows,** saints.
The Windhover. The windhover is a kestrel, or sparrow-hawk. Hopkins regarded this as his best poem. 4. **wimpling,** rippling.

In his ecstasy! then off, off forth on a swing,
  As a skate's heel sweeps smooth on a bow-
      bend—the hurl and gliding
Rebuffed the big wind. My heart in hiding
Stirred for a bird—the achieve of, the mastery
      of the thing!

Brute beauty and valor and act, oh, air, pride,
      plume, here
  Buckle! AND the fire that breaks from thee
      then, a billion   10
Times told lovelier, more dangerous, O my
      chevalier!

No wonder of it: shéer plód makes plow
      down sillion
Shine, and blue-bleak embers, ah, my dear,
  Fall, gall themselves, and gash gold-ver-
      milion.

                              (*1877;* 1918)

Pied Beauty

Glory be to God for dappled things—
  For skies of couple-color as a brinded cow;
    For rose-moles all in stipple upon trout
      that swim;
Fresh-firecoal chestnut-falls; finches' wings;
  Landscape plotted and pieced—fold, fallow,
      and plow;   5
    And all trades, their gear and tackle and
      trim.

All things counter, original, spare, strange;
  Whatever is fickle, freckled (who knows
      how?)
    With swift, slow; sweet, sour; adazzle,
      dim;
He fathers-forth whose beauty is past change:
      Praise him.

                              (*1877;* 1918)

Peace

When will you ever, Peace, wild wood-dove,
      shy wings shut,

12. **sillion,** the ridge between two furrows of plowed land. *Pied Beauty.* 3. **stipple,** a method in painting of applying colors in dots. 4. **chestnut-falls,** chestnuts newly stripped of their husks. 5. **plotted and pieced,** divided into fields. 6. **trim,** equipment. 7. **counter,** contrary to what is expected. **spare,** rare. 10. **whose . . . change.** Cf. *James,* 1:17: "Every good gift and every perfect gift is from above, and cometh down from the Father of lights, with whom is no variableness, neither shadow of turning."

Your round me roaming end, and under be
      my boughs?
When, when, Peace, will you, Peace? I'll not
      play hypocrite
To own my heart: I yield you do come
      sometimes; but
That piecemeal peace is poor peace. What
      pure peace allows   5
Alarms of wars, the daunting wars, the death
      of it?

O surely, reaving Peace, my Lord should
      leave in lieu
Some good! And so he does leave Patience
      exquisite,
That plumes to Peace thereafter. And when
      Peace here does house,
He comes with work to do. he does not come
      to coo,   10
  He comes to brood and sit.

                              (*1879;* 1918)

Felix Randal

Felix Randal the farrier, O he is dead then?
      my duty all ended,
Who have watched his mold of man, big-
      boned and hardy-handsome
Pining, pining, till time when season rambled
      in it and some
Fatal four disorders, fleshed there, all con-
      tended?

Sickness broke him. Impatient he cursed at
      first, but mended   5
Being anointed and all; though a heavenlier
      heart began some
Months earlier, since I had our sweet reprieve
      and ransom
Tendered to him. Ah, well, God rest him all
      road ever he offended!

This seeing the sick endears them to us, us too
      it endears.
My tongue had taught thee comfort, touch
      had quenched thy tears,   10
Thy tears that touched my heart, child, Felix,
      poor Felix Randal;

Peace. 4. **To own my heart,** to my own heart. 7. **reaving Peace,** when he takes peace away.

How far from then forethought of, all thy
    more boisterous years,
When thou at the random grim forge, power-
    ful amidst peers,
Didst fettle for the great gray drayhorse his
    bright and battering sandal!
                        (*1880;* 1918)

Spring and Fall
TO A YOUNG CHILD

Márgarét, are you gríeving
Over Goldengrove unleaving?
Leáves, líke the things of man, you
With your fresh thoughts care for, can you?
Áh! ás the heart grows older   5
It will come to such sights colder
By and by, nor spare a sigh
Though worlds of wanwood leafmeal lie;
And yet you wíll weep and know why.
Now no matter, child, the name: 10
Sórrow's spríngs áre the same,
Nor mouth had, no nor mind, expressed
What heart heard of, ghost guessed:
It ís the blight man was born for,
It is Margaret you mourn for.
                        (*1880;* 1918)

Inversnaid

This darksome burn, horseback brown,
His rollrock highroad roaring down,
In coop and in comb the fleece of his foam
Flutes and low to the lake falls home.

A windpuff-bonnet of fáwn-fróth   5
Turns and twindles over the broth
Of a pool so pitchblack, féll-frówning,
It rounds and rounds Despair to drowning.

Degged with dew, dappled with dew
Are the groins of the braes that the brook
    treads through,   10
Wiry heathpacks, flitches of fern,
And the beadbonny ash that sits over the
    burn.

Felix Randal. 14. **fettle,** make ready.
Spring and Fall. 8. **leafmeal,** powder covering the surface
of leaves.
Inversnaid. Inversnaid is a hamlet on the east shore of
Loch Lomond. Scotland. Cf. Wordsworth's *To a Highland
Girl* (p. 153). 1. **burn,** brook. 3. **coop,** hollow place between
ridges of waves (combs). 4. **Flutes,** forms streaks or channels.
6. **twindles,** twists. 9. **Degged,** dampened. 10. **braes,** hillsides.
11. **heathpacks,** clumps of heather. **flitches,** patches.

What would the world be, once bereft
Of wet and of wildness? Let them be
    left,
Oh, let them be left, wildness and wet;   15
Long live the weeds and the wilderness yet.
                        (*1881;* 1918)

Carrion Comfort

Not, I'll not, carrion comfort, Despair, not
    feast on thee;
Not untwist—slack they may be—these last
    strands of man
In me ór, most weary, cry *I can no more.* I
    can;
Can something, hope, wish day come, not
    choose not to be.
But ah, but O thou terrible, why wouldst
    thou rude on me   5
Thy wring-world right foot rock? lay a lion-
    limb against me? scan
With darksome devouring eyes my bruiséd
    bones? and fan,
O in turns of tempest, me heaped there; me
    frantic to avoid thee and flee?

Why? That my chaff might fly; my grain
    lie, sheer and clear.
Nay in all that toil, that coil, since (seems)
    I kissed the rod,   10
Hand rather, my heart lo! lapped strength,
    stole joy, would laugh, chéer.
Cheer whom though? the hero whose
    heaven-handling flung me, fóot tród
Me? or me that fought him? O which one?
    is it each one? That night, that year
Of now done darkness I wretch lay wrestling
    with (my God!) my God.
                        (*c. 1886;* 1918)

I Wake and Feel the Fell of Dark

I wake and feel the fell of dark, not day.
What hours, O what black hoürs we have
    spent
This night! what sights you, heart, saw;
    ways you went!
And more must, in yet longer light's delay.
    With witness I speak this. But where I
        say   5

Hours I mean years, mean life. And my lament
Is cries countless, cries like dead letters sent
To dearest him that lives alas! away.
  I am gall, I am heartburn. God's most deep decree
Bitter would have me taste: my taste was me;   10
Bones built in me, flesh filled, blood brimmed the curse.
  Selfyeast of spirit a dull dough sours. I see
The lost are like this, and their scourge to be
As I am mine, their sweating selves; but worse.

(*c. 1886;* 1918)

To R. B.

The fine delight that fathers thought; the strong
Spur, live and lancing like the blowpipe flame,
Breathes once and, quenchéd faster than it came,
Leaves yet the mind a mother of immortal song.
Nine months she then, nay years, nine years she long   5
Within her wears, bears, cares, and molds the same:
The widow of an insight lost she lives, with aim
Now known and hand at work now never wrong.
  Sweet fire the sire of muse, my soul needs this;
I want the one rapture of an inspiration.   10
O then if in my lagging lines you miss
The roll, the rise, the carol, the creation,
My winter world, that scarcely breathes that bliss
Now, yields you, with some sighs, our explanation.

(*1889;* 1918)

Robert Louis Stevenson

1850-1894

Robert Louis Stevenson, thin-legged, thin-chested, a mixture of Ariel, Puck, Antony, Hamlet, and the Calvinist preachers—so his friend Henley described him—was born in Edinburgh in 1850. From Edinburgh his natural adventurousness combined with his ill-health to drive him far afield until in 1894 his busy career as poet, essayist, and novelist ended high above the Pacific in the hills of Samoa.

Stevenson had a love of the sea which was born in his blood. Both his father and his grandfather were famous engineers and builders of lighthouses on the Scottish coast. Early in life he was marked out for the same career and for that purpose studied engineering at the University of Edinburgh. But his bad health and his restlessness turned him from this occupation to that of gay vagabond scribbler, and even the study of law could not interrupt his career as author. Few writers of the period took to their writing with such genuine enjoyment mingled with such seriousness. He wrote with gusto and abandon, but he never wrote carelessly. He read extensively and discriminatingly and "played the sedulous ape," as he said, to Hazlitt (see p. 361) and other finished writers whom he admired. The finish of style which he thus acquired was notable in his first volume of essays, *Virginibus Puerisque* (1881), and in two highly romantic short stories, *A Lodging for the Night* and *The Sire de Maletroit's Door*.

Stevenson's wanderings outside the British Isles began toward the end of the seventies when the disease that was already weakening him drove him to make a canoe trip in Belgium and France and a walking tour through the mountains of Southern France. He had early acquired a practice of recording his own experiences in romantic prose, and these journeys he treated imaginatively in *An Inland Voyage* (1878) and *Travels with a Donkey in the Cevennes* (1879). Both books, especially the second, are delightfully flavored with idyllic and picaresque moods. In his travels in France Stevenson met Mrs. Fanny Osbourne, an American; he conceived a romantic attachment for her, and in 1879 followed her to California. This journey he recorded in *The Amateur Emigrant*. Mrs. Osbourne nursed him through a dangerous illness, and they were married in 1880. Their experiences together at Calistoga, a crude California mining-town, he recorded in *The Silverado Squatters* (1883). Though half-dead with tuberculosis he continued to write courageously and indefatigably. *Familiar Studies of Men and Books* (1882) and *The New Arabian Nights* (1882), a series of fantastic tales, added to his reputation, and the appearance of *Treasure Island* in book form in 1883 made him definitely famous. Before this date he had returned to Scotland. He sought health later in the Swiss Alps, in Southern France, at Bournemouth on the English coast, and at Saranac Lake in the Adirondacks. During these trying years he wrote tirelessly. In the astonishing short-novel parable of *The Strange Case of Dr. Jekyll and Mr. Hyde* (1886) he struck a highly popular note of romance and pseudo-scientific mystery, and in *Kidnapped* (1886) he added to his tales of adventure. At Saranac Lake he wrote *The Master of Ballantrae*, another romantic story, and contributed twelve essays, one a month, to *Scribner's Magazine* for the year 1888. Among these is *Pulvis et Umbra*, which he characterized as "a Darwinian sermon," and which contains the expression of his philosophy of life. His two volumes of poetry, *A Child's Garden of Verses* (1885) and *Underwoods* (1887), had already appeared, as had also the first of the three dramas which he wrote in collaboration with W. E. Henley (see p. 863).

The last phase of the gypsy-author's life is the most fascinating of all. In 1888 he sailed from California in the schooner *Casco* for a long cruise among the islands of the Southern Pacific. His wanderings took him to Honolulu, and he visited the nearby leper colony at Molokai, where he gathered material for the spirited defense of Father Damien which an attack on the priest's memory led him to write a few months later. In Australia he was seriously sick again and very nearly died. At Samoa the year following he found at last a climate and an environment which suited his health and his romantic spirit; and here he spent in happiness and comparative good health the last four years of his life, writing in the quiet of his mountain home Vailima, directing the work about his plantation, acting as sort of chieftain to what he called "a kind of feudal clan of servants and retainers," and mixing benevolently in the political affairs of the Samoans, who loved him as Tusitala, the teller of tales. To this last period belong several romances, some written in collaboration with Lloyd Osbourne, his step-son. *The Wreckers, Catriona*, called in America *David Balfour* (the sequel to *Kidnapped*), the unfinished *Weir of Hermiston*, in some respects his best novel, all belong to the Samoan period; so also do his sparkling *Vailima Letters*, published by Sidney Colvin in 1895. He died literally, as he indicated in *Aes Triplex* he would like to die, with his pen in his hand, hard at work on his unfinished story *St. Ives*. He lies buried on the peak of Mt. Vaea, beneath a tomb which overlooks the Pacific.

Stevenson's attitude toward life shows a highly individual mixture of traits not often found in the same man. He had a moral earnestness in a high degree. Such stories as *Markheim* and *The Strange Case of Dr. Jekyll and Mr. Hyde* are parables;

in his most exciting romances there is no suggestion that the wicked are rewarded, and many of his essays are, as he says himself, lay sermons. Yet he upset many a theological apple-cart in his frank espousal of the worth of vital existence—as in the little poem called *The Celestial Surgeon*. And he threw over life the glow that romanticism gives.

To the late Victorians he demonstrated unmistakably that romance was not dead and that the thrill of stories of pirates, fighters, adventurers, romantic lovers, was still a thing to be desired. His fundamentally romantic quality as a teller of tales is not in the least impaired by the fact that from the realists he had learned the tricks of style that made the impossible seem the expected. Like Kipling he may be called a realist-romanticist.

Stevenson was, without much doubt, the foremost essayist of the last two decades of the century. In this form of composition his romantic spirit gave him a kinship with Lamb, Hazlitt, and the other romantic essayists of the early nineteenth century. His disposition and technique were, indeed, much like theirs. He had the same inclination to put himself into his writing, to base his ideas upon his own experiences, and to write essays of the narrative, confessional, personal type. He had, moreover, much of Lamb's charm, and his easy accounts of his boyhood experiences in Edinburgh, with their warm glow, resemble the essays that Lamb based on his early life. In his essays as in his stories and novels there is evidence of the master craftsman, for Stevenson was highly conscientious in all his work.

Stevenson's reputation rests on his prose fiction and essays rather than on his poetry. He is not, in fact, a great poet. Nevertheless, his poems have the grace and charm that are characteristic of his other writing. In *Underwoods* are many poems with a fine romantic flavor. His *A Child's Garden of Verses* is remarkable for its charm and simplicity. Very few poets can write good verses for children, for most adults find it impossible to enter into their world and to see life from their point of view. But Stevenson, like Lewis Carroll, had the happy ability to project himself into the child's mind and heart, with the result that his *A Child's Garden of Verses* is a nursery classic.

A Song of the Road

The gauger walked with willing foot,
And aye the gauger played the flute;
And what would Master Gauger play
But *Over the hills and far away*?

Whene'er I buckle on my pack 5
And foot it gayly in the track,
O pleasant gauger, long since dead,
I hear you fluting on ahead.

You go with me the selfsame way—
The selfsame air for me you play; 10
For I do think and so do you
It is the tune to travel to.

For who would gravely set his face
To go to this or t'other place?
There's nothing under heav'n so blue 15
That's fairly worth the traveling to.

On every hand the roads begin,
And people walk with zeal therein;
But whereso'er the highways tend,
Be sure there's nothing at the end. 20

Then follow you wherever hie
The traveling mountains of the sky,
Or let the streams of civil mode
Direct your choice upon the road;

For one and all, or high or low, 25
Will lead you where you wish to go;
And one and all go night and day
Over the hills and far away!

(1878)

The poems of Robert Louis Stevenson are reprinted from his *Complete Poems* (1928) by permission of Charles Scribner's Sons, New York.
1. **gauger**, a revenue officer who measures the contents of casks. 4. *Over . . . away*, the refrain of a popular seventeenth-century song. See Gay's *Beggar's Opera* (Vol. I, p. 1107); also Henley's *Where Forlorn Sunsets Flare and Fade*, p. 868.

A Camp

The bed was made, the room was fit,
By punctual eve the stars were lit;
The air was still, the water ran,
No need was there for maid or man,
When we put up, my ass and I,   5
At God's green caravanserai.   (1879)

In the States

Stevenson visited America in 1879-1880 and again in 1887-1888. This poem was written in San Francisco, where Stevenson had gone to marry Mrs. Osbourne.

With half a heart I wander here
  As from an age gone by,
A brother—yet though young in years,
  An elder brother, I.

You speak another tongue than mine,   5
  Though both were English born.
I toward the night of time decline;
  You mount into the morn.

Youth shall grow great and strong and free,
  But age must still decay;   10
Tomorrow for the States—for me,
  England and Yesterday.   (1880)

The Celestial Surgeon

If I have faltered more or less
In my great task of happiness;
If I have moved among my race
And shown no glorious morning face;
If beams from happy human eyes   5
Have moved me not; if morning skies,
Books, and my food, and summer rain
Knocked on my sullen heart in vain—
Lord, thy most pointed pleasure take
And stab my spirit broad awake;   10
Or, Lord, if too obdurate I,
Choose thou, before that spirit die,
A piercing pain, a killing sin,
And to my dead heart run them in!   (1882)

A Camp. From *Travels with a Donkey.* 6. **caravanserai,** a kind of inn in the East, where caravans stop at night.

To Alison Cunningham

FROM HER BOY

This is the dedicatory poem to *A Child's Garden of Verses,* from which the following lyrics through *The Cow,* p. 879, are taken. Alison Cunningham, or "Cummy," had been Stevenson's nurse during his sickly childhood.

For the long nights you lay awake
And watched for my unworthy sake;
For your most comfortable hand
That led me through the uneven land;
For all the story-books you read;   5
For all the pains you comforted;
For all you pitied, all you bore,
In sad and happy days of yore;
My second Mother, my first Wife,
The angel of my infant life—   10
From the sick child, now well and old,
Take, nurse, the little book you hold!

And grant it, Heaven, that all who read
May find as dear a nurse at need,
And every child who lists my rime,   15
In the bright, fireside, nursery clime,
May hear it in as kind a voice
As made my childish days rejoice!   (1885)

Bed in Summer

In winter I get up at night
And dress by yellow candle-light.
In summer, quite the other way,
I have to go to bed by day.

I have to go to bed and see   5
The birds still hopping on the tree,
Or hear the grown-up people's feet
Still going past me in the street.

And does it not seem hard to you,
When all the sky is clear and blue,   10
And I should like so much to play,
To have to go to bed by day?   (1881)

Pirate Story

Three of us afloat in the meadow by the swing,
  Three of us aboard in the basket on the lea.

Winds are in the air; they are blowing in the spring,
    And waves are on the meadow like the waves that are at sea.

Where shall we adventure, today that we're afloat,   5
    Wary of the weather and steering by a star?
Shall it be to Africa, a-steering of the boat,
    To Providence, or Babylon, or off to Malabar?

Hi! but here's a squadron a-rowing on the sea—
    Cattle on the meadow a-charging with a roar!   10
Quick, and we'll escape them, they're as mad as they can be,
    The wicket is the harbor, and the garden is the shore.   (1881)

Foreign Lands

Up into the cherry tree
Who should climb but little me?
I held the trunk with both my hands
And looked abroad on foreign lands.

I saw the next-door garden lie,   5
Adorned with flowers, before my eye,
And many pleasant places more
That I had never seen before.

I saw the dimpling river pass
And be the sky's blue looking-glass;   10
The dusty roads go up and down
With people tramping into town.

If I could find a higher tree
Farther and farther I should see,
To where the grown-up river slips   15
Into the sea among the ships,

To where the roads on either hand
Lead onward into fairyland,

8. **Providence**, an island in the Bahamas, West Indies. **Babylon**, the ancient capital of Assyria. **Malabar**, a district in West Madras, India. 12. **wicket**, a small gate.

Where all the children dine at five,
And all the playthings come alive. (1881)

Looking Forward

When I am grown to man's estate,
I shall be very proud and great,
And tell the other girls and boys
Not to meddle with my toys.   (1881)

The Land of Counterpane

When I was sick and lay a-bed,
I had two pillows at my head,
And all my toys beside me lay
To keep me happy all the day.

And sometimes for an hour or so   5
I watched my leaden soldiers go,
With different uniforms and drills,
Among the bedclothes, through the hills;

And sometimes sent my ships in fleets
All up and down among the sheets;   10
Or brought my trees and houses out,
And planted cities all about.

I was the giant great and still
That sits upon the pillow-hill,
And sees before him, dale and plain,   15
The pleasant Land of Counterpane. (1881)

System

Every night my prayers I say,
And get my dinner every day;
And every day that I've been good,
I get an orange after food.

The child that is not plain and neat,   5
With lots of toys and things to eat,
He is a naughty child, I'm sure—
Or else his dear papa is poor.   (1885)

Happy Thought

The world is so full of a number of things,
I'm sure we should all be as happy as kings.
    (1885)

The Cow

The friendly cow all red and white,
    I love with all my heart—
She gives me cream with all her might,
    To eat with apple-tart.

She wanders lowing here and there,
    And yet she cannot stray,
All in the pleasant open air,
    The pleasant light of day;

And blown by all the winds that pass
    And wet with all the showers,
She walks among the meadow grass
    And eats the meadow flowers. (1884)

A Mile an' a Bittock

A mile an' a bittock, a mile or twa,
Abüne the burn, ayont the law,
Davie an' Donal' an' Cherlie an' a',
    An' the müne was shinin' clearly!

Ane went hame wi' the ither, an' then
The ither went hame wi' the ither twa men,
An' baith wad return him the service again,
    An' the müne was shinin' clearly!

The clocks were chappin' in house an' ha',
Eleeven, twal, an' ane an' twa;
An' the guidman's face was turnt to the wa',
    An' the müne was shinin' clearly!

A wind got up frae affa the sea,
It blew the stars as clear's could be,
It blew in the een of a' o' the three,
    An' the müne was shinin' clearly!

Noo, Davie was first to get sleep in his head,
"The best o' frien's maun twine," he said;
"I'm weariet, an' here I'm awa' to my bed."
    An' the müne was shinin' clearly!

Twa o' them walkin' an' crackin' their lane,
The mornin' licht cam gray an' plain,
An' the birds they yammert on stick an' stane,
    An' the müne was shinin' clearly!

O years ayont, O years awa',
My lads, ye'll mind whate'er befa'—
My lads, ye'll mind on the bield o' the law,
    When the müne was shinin' clearly! (1884)

A Portrait

I am a kind of farthing dip,
    Unfriendly to the nose and eyes;
A blue-behinded ape, I slip
    Upon the trees of Paradise.

At mankind's feast, I take my place
    In solemn, sanctimonious state,
And have the air of saying grace
    While I defile the dinner plate.

I am "the smiler with the knife,"
    The battener upon garbage, I—
Dear Heaven, with such a rancid life,
    Were it not better far to die?

Yet still, about the human pale,
    I love to scamper, love to race,
To swing by my irreverent tail
    All over the most holy place;

And when at length, some golden day,
    The unfailing sportsman, aiming at,
Shall bag me—all the world shall say:
    Thank God, and there's an end of that! (1887)

I Will Make You Brooches

I will make you brooches and toys for your delight
Of bird-song at morning and star-shine at night.
I will make a palace fit for you and me
Of green days in forests and blue days at sea.
I will make my kitchen, and you shall keep your room,

---

23. **yammert**, chirruped. 27. **on . . . law**, in the shelter of the hill.
A Portrait. 1. **farthing dip**, a cheap candle. 9. "**the . . . knife**," a murderer who hides his intent behind smiles. The quotation is from Chaucer's *Knight's Tale*, l. 1141. 10. **battener**, one who feeds or grows fat upon.

A Mile an' a Bittock. A **bittock** is a little bit. 2. **Abüne the burn**, above the brook. **ayont the law**, beyond the hill. 9. **chappin'**, striking. 11. **guidman**, a householder. 13. **frae affa**, from over. 18. **maun twine**, must part. 21. **crackin' their lane**, chatting together.

Where white flows the river and bright blows
    the broom,
And you shall wash your linen and keep your
    body white
In rainfall at morning and dewfall at night.

And this shall be for music when no one else
    is near,
The fine song for singing, the rare song to
    hear!   10
That only I remember, that only you admire,
Of the broad road that stretches and the
    roadside fire.   (1895)

Mater Triumphans

Son of my woman's body, you go, to the drum
    and fife,
To taste the color of love and the other side of
    life—
From out of the dainty the rude, the strong
    from out of the frail,
Eternally through the ages from the female
    comes the male.

The ten fingers and toes, and the shell-like
    nail on each,   5
The eyes blind as gems and the tongue at-
    tempting speech;
Impotent hands in my bosom, and yet they
    shall wield the sword!
Drugged with slumber and milk, you wait
    the day of the Lord.

Infant bridegroom, uncrowned king, un-
    anointed priest,
Soldier, lover, explorer, I see you nozzle the
    breast.   10
You that grope in my bosom shall load the
    ladies with rings,
You, that came forth through doors, shall
    burst the doors of kings.   (1895)

My Wife

Trusty, dusky, vivid, true,
With eyes of gold and bramble-dew,
    Steel-true and blade-straight,
The great artificer
    Made my mate.   5

Honor, anger, valor, fire;
A love that life could never tire,
    Death quench or evil stir,
The mighty master
    Gave to her.   10

Teacher, tender, comrade, wife,
A fellow-farer true through life,
    Heart-whole and soul-free
The august father
    Gave to me.   (1895)

Bright Is the Ring of Words

Bright is the ring of words
    When the right man rings them,
Fair the fall of songs
    When the singer sings them.
Still they are caroled and said—   5
    On wings they are carried—
After the singer is dead
    And the maker buried.

Low as the singer lies
    In the field of heather,   10
Songs of his fashion bring
    The swains together.
And when the west is red
    With the sunset embers,
The lover lingers and sings,   15
    And the maid remembers.   (1895)

Sing Me a Song

Sing me a song of a lad that is gone,
    Say, could that lad be I?
Merry of soul he sailed on a day
    Over the sea to Skye.

Mull was astern, Rum on the port,   5
    Egg on the starboard bow;

---

6. **broom**, a shrub with stiff, green branches; it is very common in Scotland.
Mater Triumphans, Mother Triumphant.

Bright Is . . . Words. 8. **maker**, an old word for poet.
Sing Me a Song. 4-6. **Skye, Mull . . . Rum . . . Egg**, islands on the western coast of Scotland. The route from Mull to Skye is due north and passes, at the half-way point, between Rum on the left and Egg (Eigg) on the right; the distance is about forty miles. Stevenson made this trip in 1874 on board the schooner *Heron*.

Glory of youth glowed in his soul—
  Where is that glory now?

Sing me a song of a lad that is gone,
  Say, could that lad be I?   10
Merry of soul he sailed on a day
  Over the sea to Skye.

Give me again all that was there,
  Give me the sun that shone!
Give me the eyes, give me the soul, 15
  Give me the lad that's gone!

Sing me a song of a lad that is gone,
  Say, could that lad be I?
Merry of soul he sailed on a day
  Over the sea to Skye.   20

Billow and breeze, islands and seas,
  Mountains of rain and sun,
All that was good, all that was fair,
  All that was me is gone.   (1895)

Evensong

The embers of the day are red
Beyond the murky hill.
The kitchen smokes; the bed
In the darkling house is spread.
The great sky darkens overhead,   5
And the great woods are shrill.
So far have I been led,
Lord, by thy will;
So far I have followed, Lord, and wondered
  still.
The breeze from the embalmèd land   10
Blows sudden toward the shore,
And claps my cottage door.
I hear the signal, Lord—I understand.
The night at thy command
Comes. I will eat and sleep and will not
  question more.   (1895)

Requiem

The title means *Rest*. It is the first word of a Latin Mass for the dead, "Give eternal rest to them, O Lord." The last two lines of this poem are inscribed on Stevenson's monument in Samoa.

Under the wide and starry sky,
Dig the grave and let me lie.
Glad did I live and gladly die,
And I laid me down with a will.

This be the verse you grave for me: 5
Here he lies where he longed to be;
Home is the sailor, home from sea,
And the hunter home from the hill.
                                 (1884)

Evensong. 10. **embalmèd**, fragrant.

Francis Thompson
1859-1907

Near the end of the nineteenth century, in a decade made colorful by cultists, individualists, and numerous rebels against the restraint of the Victorians, there was in England a shy and childlike mystic who had more in common with the metaphysical poets of the seventeenth century (see Vol. I, p. 675) than with his contemporaries. This was the Catholic poet Francis Thompson. Had he been born in the Middle Ages, he might have expressed his visions of heavenly beauty in allegorical poems like those of the Pearl Poet (Vol. I, p. 165); but he lived in a practical world in which he found expression of his temperament difficult.

Francis Thompson was the son of a Lancashire doctor who had become converted to Roman Catholicism. He was educated at the Catholic college of Ushaw, near Durham, and later studied medicine at Owens College, Manchester. But he was the most impractical of men, and his interest lay only in the visions which his mind conjured up. He never took a degree in medicine, but withdrew from life and became friendless and solitary. Destitute and ill he went to London but failed to secure work because of his utter incapability of answering the practical and persistent demands of any sort of labor. Ultimately a few verses and an essay on *Paganism New and Old,* written on scraps of paper, came by good luck into the hands of the editor of *Merry England,* Wilfrid Meynell, a Catholic gentleman of the highest character. Meynell sought the writer, after some difficulty found him in sordid surroundings, and took him to his home. Here Thompson met the editor's wife, Alice Meynell—herself a poet—and life took on another color for him. The noble help which the Meynells gave to the friendless and destitute poet was much like that which the Unwins gave to Cowper (see p. 74). With their aid he overcame the habit of taking laudanum, which he had been using to deaden his misery; he moved into a good London lodging-house; above all he got friendship and encouragement. In 1893 he published his first volume of poems. This was the first of three volumes of verse; the second, *Sister Songs* (1895), was written for the daughters of his benefactors; the third, *New Poems* (1897), was written under the influence of Coventry Patmore, the aged friend of Ruskin and Tennyson. To these he added in 1905 a prose treatise entitled *Health and Holiness.* But much of the time Thompson was too ill to write. His sickness had developed into tuberculosis, and he died in London in 1907.

The Hound of Heaven

In his *Study of Francis Thompson's "Hound of Heaven"* (1912), Mr. J. F. O'Connor says: "As the hound follows the hare, never ceasing in its running, ever drawing nearer to the chase . . . so does God follow the fleeing soul by his Divine grace."

I fled Him, down the nights and down the days;
I fled Him, down the arches of the years;
I fled Him, down the labyrinthine ways
 Of my own mind; and in the mist of tears
I hid from Him, and under running laughter.
  Up vistaed hopes I sped; 6
  And shot, precipitated,
Adown Titanic glooms of chasméd fears,
 From those strong Feet that followed, followed after.
  But with unhurrying chase, 10
  And unperturbéd pace,
  Deliberate speed, majestic instancy,
  They beat—and a Voice beat
  More instant than the Feet—
 "All things betray thee, who betrayest Me." 15

  I pleaded, outlaw-wise,
By many a hearted casement, curtained red,
 Trellised with intertwining charities

(For, though I knew His love Who followed,
  Yet was I sore adread 20
Lest, having Him, I must have naught beside);
But, if one little casement parted wide,
 The gust of His approach would clash it to.
Fear wist not to evade, as Love wist to pursue.
Across the margent of the world I fled, 25
 And troubled the gold gateways of the stars,
  Smiting for shelter on their clangéd bars;
  Fretted to dulcet jars
And silvern chatter the pale ports o' the moon.
I said to dawn, Be sudden; to eve, Be soon; 30
 With thy young skyey blossoms heap me over
 From this tremendous Lover!
Float thy vague veil about me, lest He see!
 I tempted all His servitors, but to find
My own betrayal in their constancy, 35
In faith to Him their fickleness to me,
 Their traitorous trueness, and their loyal deceit.
To all swift things for swiftness did I sue;

The poems of Francis Thompson are reprinted from his *Complete Poetical Works* (1919) by permission of The Modern Library, Inc., New York.
8. **Titanic,** enormous, resembling the Titans, an ancient race of giants in Greek mythology. 12. **instancy,** insistency. 17. **hearted,** heart-shaped.

24. **wist,** knew. 25. **margent,** edge, boundary. 28. **Fretted . . . moon,** troubled the doors of the moon until they vibrated with sweet sounds.

Clung to the whistling mane of every wind.
  But whether they swept, smoothly fleet,
  The long savannahs of the blue; 41
  Or whether, Thunder-driven,
  They clanged his chariot 'thwart a heaven
Plashy with flying lightnings round the spurn o' their feet—
  Fear wist not to evade as Love wist to pursue. 45
    Still with unhurrying chase,
    And unperturbéd pace,
    Deliberate speed, majestic instancy,
      Came on the following Feet,
      And a Voice above their beat— 50
    "Naught shelters thee, who wilt not shelter Me."
I sought no more that after which I strayed
    In face of man or maid;
But still within the little children's eyes
    Seems something, something that replies;
They at least are for me, surely for me! 56
I turned me to them very wistfully;
But, just as their young eyes grew sudden fair
    With dawning answers there,
Their angel plucked them from me by the hair. 60
"Come then, ye other children, Nature's—share
With me" (said I) "your delicate fellowship;
    Let me greet you lip to lip,
    Let me twine with you caresses,
      Wantoning 65
    With our Lady-Mother's vagrant tresses,
      Banqueting
    With her in her wind-walled palace,
    Underneath her azured daïs,
    Quaffing, as your taintless way is, 70
      From a chalice
Lucent-weeping out of the dayspring."
    So it was done;
I in their delicate fellowship was one—
Drew the bolt of Nature's secrecies. 75
I knew all the swift importings
    On the willful face of skies;
    I knew how the clouds arise
    Spuméd of the wild sea-snortings;

All that's born or dies 80
  Rose and drooped with—made them shapers
Of mine own moods, or wailful or divine—
  With them joyed and was bereaven.
  I was heavy with the even,
  When she lit her glimmering tapers 85
  Round the day's dead sanctities.
  I laughed in the morning's eyes.
I triumphed and I saddened with all weather,
  Heaven and I wept together,
And its sweet tears were salt with mortal mine; 90
Against the red throb of its sunset-heart
  I laid my own to beat,
  And share commingling heat;
But not by that, by that, was eased my human smart.
In vain my tears were wet on Heaven's gray cheek. 95
For ah! we know not what each other says,
  These things and I; in sound *I* speak—
Their sound is but their stir, they speak by silences.
Nature, poor stepdame, cannot slake my drouth;
  Let her, if she would owe me, 100
Drop yon blue bosom-veil of sky, and show me
  The breasts o' her tenderness;
Never did any milk of hers once bless
  My thirsting mouth.
    Nigh and nigh draws the chase, 105
    With unperturbéd pace,
    Deliberate speed, majestic instancy;
      And past those noiséd Feet
      A voice comes yet more fleet—
    "Lo! naught contents thee, who content'st not Me." 110

Naked I wait Thy love's uplifted stroke!
My harness piece by piece Thou hast hewn from me,
  And smitten me to my knee;
  I am defenseless utterly.
  I slept, methinks, and woke, 115
And, slowly gazing, find me stripped in sleep.
In the rash lustihead of my young powers,

---

41. **savannahs,** open, level regions. 44. **Plashy,** speckled, sparkling. 66. **Lady-Mother,** Nature. 72. **Lucent-weeping,** dripping with luminous drops.

100. **owe,** own.

    I shook the pillaring hours
And pulled my life upon me; grimed with
        smears,   119
I stand amid the dust o' the mounded years—
My mangled youth lies dead beneath the heap.
My days have crackled and gone up in smoke,
Have puffed and burst as sun-starts on a
    stream.
    Yea, faileth now even dream
The dreamer, and the lute the lutanist;   125
Even the linked fantasies, in whose blossomy
    twist
I swung the earth a trinket at my wrist,
Are yielding; cords of all too weak account
For earth with heavy griefs so overplussed.
    Ah! is Thy love indeed   130
A weed, albeit an amaranthine weed,
Suffering no flowers except its own to mount?
    Ah! must—
    Designer infinite!—
Ah! must Thou char the wood ere Thou canst
    limn with it?   135
My freshness spent its wavering shower i' the
    dust;
And now my heart is as a broken fount,
Wherein tear-drippings stagnate, spilt down
    ever
    From the dank thoughts that shiver
Upon the sighful branches of my mind.   140
    Such is; what is to be?
The pulp so bitter, how shall taste the rind?
I dimly guess what Time in mists confounds;
Yet ever and anon a trumpet sounds
From the hid battlements of Eternity;   145
Those shaken mists a space unsettle, then
Round the half-glimpsèd turrets slowly wash
    again.
    But not ere him who summoneth
    I first have seen, enwound
With glooming robes purpureal, cypress-
    crowned;   150
His name I know, and what his trumpet saith.
Whether man's heart or life it be which yields
    Thee harvest, must Thy harvest fields
    Be dungèd with rotten death?

    Now of that long pursuit   155
    Comes on at hand the bruit;
That Voice is round me like a bursting
    sea:
    "And is thy earth so marred,
    Shattered in shard on shard?
Lo, all things fly thee, for thou fliest Me!
    Strange, piteous, futile thing,   161
Wherefore should any set thee love apart?
Seeing none but I makes much of naught"
    (He said),
"And human love needs human meriting,
    How hast thou merited—   165
Of all man's clotted clay the dingiest clot?
    Alack, thou knowest not
How little worthy of any love thou art!
Whom wilt thou find to love ignoble thee
    Save Me, save only Me?   170
All which I took from thee I did but take,
    Not for thy harms,
But just that thou might'st seek it in My arms.
    All which thy child's mistake
Fancies as lost, I have stored for thee at home;
    Rise, clasp My hand, and come!"   176

    Halts by me that footfall;
    Is my gloom, after all,
    Shade of His hand, outstretched caress-
    ingly?
    "Ah, fondest, blindest, weakest,   180
    I am He Whom thou seekest!
Thou dravest love from thee, who dravest
    Me."   (1891; 1893)

To a Snowflake

What heart could have thought you?—
Past our devisal
(O filigree petal!)
Fashioned so purely,
Fragilely, surely,   5
From what Paradisal
Imagineless metal,
Too costly for cost?
Who hammered you, wrought you,
From argentine vapor?—   10
"God was my shaper.
Passing surmisal,

---

118. **shook . . . me**, as Samson shook the pillars of the temple at Gaza and pulled down the roof on his head. See *Judges*, 16:29-30. 131. **amaranthine**, immortal, like the amaranth, which grows in the fields of Heaven. 135. **limn**, draw, as with charcoal. 150. **purpureal**, purple, as of royalty. **cypress-crowned**, as a symbol of sorrow and death.

156. **bruit**, noise, clamor. 159. **shard**, fragment. *To a Snowflake*. 10. **argentine**, silvery.

He hammered, He wrought me,
From curled silver vapor,
To lust of His mind— 15
Thou couldst not have thought me!
So purely, so palely,
Tinily, surely,
Mightily, frailly,
Insculped and embossed, 20
With His hammer of wind,
And His graver of frost."

Envoy

Go, songs, for ended is our brief, sweet play;
  Go, children of swift joy and tardy sorrow;
And some are sung, and that was yesterday,
  And some unsung, and that may be tomorrow.

Go forth; and if it be o'er stony way, 5
  Old joy can lend what newer grief must borrow;
And it was sweet, and that was yesterday,
  And sweet is sweet, though purchaséd with sorrow.

Go, songs, and come not back from your far way;
  And if men ask you why ye smile and sorrow, 10
Tell them ye grieve, for your hearts know Today,
  Tell them ye smile, for your eyes know Tomorrow. (1897)

Envoy. This poem was printed at the end of a volume of poems entitled *New Poems* (1897). 1. **Go, songs,** a common literary convention, used by Chaucer, Spenser, Southey, and others.

The Kingdom of God

"IN NO STRANGE LAND"

O world invisible, we view thee,
O world intangible, we touch thee,
O world unknowable, we know thee,
Inapprehensible, we clutch thee!

Does the fish soar to find the ocean, 5
The eagle plunge to find the air—
That we ask of the stars in motion
If they have rumor of thee there?

Not where the wheeling systems darken,
And our benumbed conceiving soars!— 10
The drift of pinions, would we hearken,
Beats at our own clay-shuttered doors.

The angels keep their ancient places—
Turn but a stone and start a wing!
'Tis ye, 'tis your estrangéd faces, 15
That miss the many-splendored thing.

But (when so sad thou canst not sadder)
Cry—and upon thy so sore loss
Shall shine the traffic of Jacob's ladder
Pitched betwixt Heaven and Charing Cross. 20

Yea, in the night, my Soul, my daughter,
Cry—clinging Heaven by the hems;
And lo, Christ walking on the water,
Not of Genesareth, but Thames! (1913)

The Kingdom of God. 19. **Jacob's ladder,** that on which Jacob dreamed he saw angels going up and down between earth and heaven (*Genesis*, 28:12). The idea of the words "in no strange land" was drawn from this passage. 20. **Charing Cross,** a locality near Trafalgar Square, in the heart of London. 24. **Genesareth,** the Sea of Galilee; the incident of Christ's walking on the sea is recorded in *Matthew*, 14:25-33.

Rudyard Kipling

1865-1936

Rudyard Kipling was throughout his literary career an outspoken imperialist, inveighing against "little Englanders," advocating vigorous national expansion, and claiming for the white man in general and for the Englishman in particular virtues not possessed by "the lesser breeds without the law." This attitude he came by naturally. He was born in Bombay, where his father was not only Professor of Architectural Sculpture in the British School of Art but a painter and verse writer as well. He was brought up by a native nurse and learned as a child to speak an East Indian dialect as well as English. When he was six, his parents took him to England, where he became later a student in the United Services College at Westward Ho in North Devon. Their plan was to have him trained for a government position in

India; his very bad eyesight, however, made such a program impossible for him, and he early turned to writing and began sending poems to the London journals. His school experiences he used later in his boys' story *Stalky & Co.* (1899), and his poor eyesight suggested the tragic tale of the painter who went blind in *The Light That Failed* (1890). At seventeen he was at Lahore serving as sub-editor on the *Civil and Military Gazette*. To this magazine he contributed a number of poems and stories that were collected under the titles, respectively, of *Departmental Ditties* (1886) and *Plain Tales from the Hills* (1887). Some of the best of his early stories were published about this time in Wheeler's Railway Library; among these were *Soldiers Three*, *The Phantom 'Rickshaw*, and *Wee Willie Winkie*. All of this work was done before he was twenty-four. An appointment to the editorial staff of the *Pioneer* at Allahabad in 1887 gave him an opportunity to journey all over India, and to see some actual fighting on the Afghanistan border. Two years later his faith in the soundness of the imperialistic doctrine was strengthened by a journey around the world which took him to South Africa, where he met Cecil Rhodes, to Australia, to America, to England, and so back to India. His *Barrack-Room Ballads* appeared in Henley's *Scots Observer* in 1892. In the same year he married Miss Caroline Starr Balestier, an American, and settled down for a fairly long residence near Brattleboro, Vermont. Here he wrote his famous animal stories for children, the two *Jungle Books* (1894 and 1895). The Kiplings were back in England in 1896, and after further traveling to South Africa and America he bought an estate in Sussex and settled down to the life of a country gentleman. With the exception of *Kim* (1901), that amazing tale of a boy's Odyssey through India, the best of Kipling's work was probably done before the turn of the century. His *Just So Stories*—illustrated by his father—he wrote for his own children in 1902. *Puck of Pook's Hill* came out in 1906. The following year Kipling was awarded the Nobel Prize for literature. This was the climax of his career, for although he continued to serve England with his pen during the First World War and lost his only son in the struggle, he never attained in the last three decades of his life to the literary heights which he scaled so easily in his early years in India.

Rudyard Kipling had all the elements of a popular writer. He had a keen sense for the dramatic, a remarkable power for observing characters and episodes, and a style with a strong and individual tang. He had the romantic love of deeds, of the out of the way and the stirring, and he revealed to English readers new worlds—India, the jungles, the seven seas, the far countries to which his British Tommies were sent. Moreover, in common with all writers of fiction at the end of the century, he had learned from the realists to value accuracy of detail and the revealing truth of phrase. It is not paradoxical to call him, as Stevenson might also be called, a romantic-realist. He could, if he chose, be mystic, as he was, for example, in *They* and *The Brushwood Boy*, but he did not often so choose. Furthermore he was in the main a man's author. There is in his work a boisterous and an expansive quality which is appropriate to the stuff of which his stories are composed. He is the interpreter of Imperial Britain, and the bringer of romance into the world of commerce, colonization, and steam engines.

Kipling's verse has the substance and the qualities of his stories. *Barrack-Room Ballads* and *The Seven Seas* possess an unrestrained gusto that is stirring and contagious. Like his stories they deal with heroes and fighters in a romantic and colorful environment. It is as the poet and story-teller of British India that he has made his place in English literature, and even though he has displeased some readers by his overexuberance, his material is fresh, and his technique is original and distinctive.

Tommy

Thomas, or Tommy Atkins, is the conventional nickname for a private British soldier. It was the hypothetical name used in instructing soldiers how to fill out blanks, reports, etc. Kipling's soldier poems are written in the dialect of the lower-class Londoner, who always omits the initial *h*.

I went into a public-'ouse to get a pint o' beer,
The publican 'e up an' sez, "We serve no red-coats here."
The girls be'ind the bar they laughed an' giggled fit to die,
I outs into the street again an' to myself sez I:

O it's Tommy this, an' Tommy that, an' "Tommy, go away"; 5
But it's "Thank you, Mister Atkins," when the band begins to play,
The band begins to play, my boys, the band begins to play—
O it's "Thank you, Mister Atkins," when the band begins to play.

I went into a theater as sober as could be,
They gave a drunk civilian room, but 'adn't none for me; 10
They sent me to the gallery or round the music-'alls,
But when it comes to fightin', Lord! they'll shove me in the stalls!

For it's Tommy this, an' Tommy that, an' "Tommy, wait outside";
But it's "Special train for Atkins" when the trooper's on the tide—
The troopship's on the tide, my boys, the troopship's on the tide, 15
O it's "Special train for Atkins" when the trooper's on the tide.

Yes, makin' mock o' uniforms that guard you while you sleep
Is cheaper than them uniforms, an' they're starvation cheap;
An' hustlin' drunken soldiers when they're goin' large a bit
Is five times better business than paradin' in full kit. 20
Then it's Tommy this, an' Tommy that, an' "Tommy, 'ow's yer soul?"
But it's "Thin red line of 'eroes" when the drums begin to roll—
The drums begin to roll, my boys, the drums begin to roll,
O it's "Thin red line of 'eroes" when the drums begin to roll.

We aren't no thin red 'eroes, nor we aren't no blackguards too, 25
But single men in barricks, most remarkable like you;
An' if sometimes our conduck isn't all your fancy paints,
Why, single men in barricks don't grow into plaster saints;
While it's Tommy this, an' Tommy that, an' "Tommy, fall be'ind,"
But it's "Please to walk in front, sir," when there's trouble in the wind— 30
There's trouble in the wind, my boys, there's trouble in the wind,
O it's "Please to walk in front, sir," when there's trouble in the wind.

You talk o' better food for us, an' schools, an' fires, an' all:
We'll wait for extry rations if you treat us rational.
Don't mess about the cook-room slops, but prove it to our face 35
The Widow's Uniform is not the soldier-man's disgrace.
For it's Tommy this, an' Tommy that, an' "Chuck him out, the brute!"
But it's "Savior of 'is country" when the guns begin to shoot;
An' it's Tommy this, an' Tommy that, an' anything you please;
An' Tommy ain't a bloomin' fool—you bet that Tommy sees! (1890)

Tommy, Danny Deever, "Fuzzy-Wuzzy," Gunga Din, and *Mandalay* from DEPARTMENTAL DITTIES AND BARRACK-ROOM BALLADS, by Rudyard Kipling, copyright 1892, 1920, reprinted by permission from Mrs. Kipling, Doubleday, Doran & Company, Inc., and The Macmillan Company of Canada Limited. **1. public-'ouse,** a house where intoxicating liquors are sold to be consumed on the premises. During the reign of Victoria British soldiers were not welcome in such places. **2. publican,** the owner of the house. **6. band . . . play,** i.e., when the soldiers are marching off to war to the music of the regimental band. **11. music-'alls,** public halls for vaudeville performances. **12. stalls,** front ranks; literally, orchestra seats.

22. "Thin . . . 'eroes," a phrase used by a war correspondent in describing a company of soldiers in action during the Crimean War. Cf. Tennyson's *Charge of the Light Brigade,* p. 637. **35. cook-room slops,** weak, unappetizing food. **36. Widow,** an affectionate nickname of Queen Victoria; Albert, the Prince Consort, died in 1861.

Danny Deever

"What are the bugles blowin' for?" said Files-on-Parade.
"To turn you out, to turn you out," the Color-Sergeant said.
"What makes you look so white, so white?" said Files-on-Parade.
"I'm dreadin' what I've got to watch," the Color-Sergeant said.
   For they're hangin' Danny Deever, you can hear the Dead March play,   5
   The regiment's in 'ollow square—they're hangin' him today;
   They've taken of his buttons off an' cut his stripes away,
   An' they're hangin' Danny Deever in the mornin'.

"What makes the rear-rank breathe so 'ard?" said Files-on-Parade.
"It's bitter cold, it's bitter cold," the Color-Sergeant said.   10
"What makes that front-rank man fall down?" said Files-on-Parade.
"A touch o' sun, a touch o' sun," the Color-Sergeant said.
   They are hangin' Danny Deever, they are marchin' of 'im round,
   They 'ave 'alted Danny Deever by 'is coffin on the ground;
   An' 'e'll swing in 'arf a minute for a sneakin' shootin' hound—   15
   O they're hangin' Danny Deever in the mornin'!

" 'Is cot was right-'and cot to mine," said Files-on-Parade.
" 'E's sleepin' out an' far tonight," the Color-Sergeant said.
"I've drunk 'is beer a score o' times," said Files-on-Parade.
" 'E's drinkin' bitter beer alone," the Color-Sergeant said.   20
   They are hangin' Danny Deever, you must mark 'im to 'is place,
   For 'e shot a comrade sleepin'—you must look 'im in the face;
   Nine 'undred of 'is county an' the Regiment's disgrace,
   While they're hangin' Danny Deever in the mornin'.

"What's that so black agin the sun?" said Files-on-Parade.   25
"It's Danny fightin' 'ard for life," the Color-Sergeant said.
"What's that that whimpers over'ead?" said Files-on-Parade.
"It's Danny's soul that's passin' now," the Color-Sergeant said.
   For they're done with Danny Deever, you can 'ear the quickstep play,
   The regiment's in column, an' they're marchin' us away;   30
   Ho! the young recruits are shakin', an' they'll want their beer today,
   After hangin' Danny Deever in the mornin'.
                                        (1890)

"Fuzzy-Wuzzy"
(SUDAN EXPEDITIONARY FORCE)

The "Fuzzy-Wuzzies," so called because of their long, frizzled hair, are natives of the Anglo-Egyptian Sudan, a country in northeast Africa. In 1884 a British army under General Graham was sent on an expedition against the Sudanese. Although British forces had conducted successful campaigns against the Paythans (Afghans) in the mountains on the Indian frontier, the Zulu natives of southeast Africa, and the natives of Burma—all exceedingly warlike tribes—they met new methods in the Sudan and were defeated in the engagement commemorated in the poem.

We've fought with many men acrost the seas,
   An' some of 'em was brave an' some was not:
The Paythan an' the Zulu an' Burmese;
   But the Fuzzy was the finest o' the lot.
We never got a ha'porth's change of 'im: 5
   'E squatted in the scrub an' 'ocked our 'orses,
'E cut our sentries up at Sua*k*im,
   An' 'e played the cat an' banjo with our forces.

Danny Deever. 1. **Files-on-Parade**, a term applied to a soldier assigned to close up the files or ranks. 2. **Color-Sergeant**, the non-commissioned officer who carried the regimental colors. 6. **regiment's . . . square.** The soldiers form the four sides of a square here facing inwards. This is the formation used on ceremonial occasions, or when a soldier is to be publicly executed. 7. **taken . . . away**, a custom applied to a disgraced soldier.

29. **quickstep**, a lively air played after the funeral march. *"Fuzzy-Wuzzy."* 5. **ha'porth's change**, half-penny's worth of change—i.e., we never got any advantage over him. 6. **'ocked our 'orses**, disabled our horses by cutting the tendons of the hock. 7. **Suakim**, a seaport on the Red Sea; headquarters of the British and Egyptian forces.

So 'ere's *to* you, Fuzzy-Wuzzy, at your
    'ome in the Sudan;
You're a pore benighted 'eathen but a
    first-class fightin' man;   10
We gives you your certificate, an' if you
    want it signed,
We'll come 'an 'ave a romp with you
    whenever you're inclined.

We took our chanst among the Kyber 'ills,
The Boers knocked us silly at a mile,
The Burman give us Irriwaddy chills,   15
    An' a Zulu *impi* dished us up in style:
But all we ever got from such as they
    Was pop to what the Fuzzy made us
    swaller;
We 'eld our bloomin' own, the papers say,
    But man for man the Fuzzy knocked us
    'oller.   20
    Then 'ere's *to* you, Fuzzy-Wuzzy, an' the
        missis and the kid;
    Our orders was to break you, an' of course
        we went an' did.
    We sloshed you with Martinis, an' it
        wasn't 'ardly fair;
    But for all the odds agin' you, Fuzzy-
        Wuz, you broke the square.

'E 'asn't got no papers of 'is own,   25
    'E 'asn't got no medals nor rewards,
So *we* must certify the skill 'e's shown
    In usin' of 'is long two-'anded swords:
When 'e's 'oppin' in an' out among the
    bush
With 'is coffin-'eaded shield an' shovel-spear,
An 'appy day with Fuzzy on the rush   31
    Will last an 'ealthy Tommy for a year.
    So 'ere's *to* you, Fuzzy-Wuzzy, an' your
        friends which are no more,
    If we 'adn't lost some messmates, we
        would 'elp you to deplore.
    But give an' take's the gospel, an' we'll
        call the bargain fair,   35

---

13. **Kyber 'ills**, the mountains between Afghanistan and British India, the home of the Paythans and the scene of much fighting. 14. **Boers**, Dutch settlers in South Africa, noted for their accuracy of gun-fire at long range. They defeated the British forces in the Battle of Majuba, 1881. 15. **Irriwaddy chills**. The Irrawaddy is the chief river of Burma. The malarial climate along the river made the Burmese campaign very difficult for the British. 16. **Zulu** *impi*, a body of the Zulu army, in southeastern Africa. In 1879 a Zulu force completely routed a British regiment. 23. **Martinis**, Martini-Henry rifles, used from 1876 to 1888, named after Frederick Martini (1832-1897), a Swiss inventor, and a Scottish gun-maker named Henry (d. 1894). 24. **the square**, the hollow square, a British defensive fighting formation; cf. p. 888, note 6.

    For if you 'ave lost more than us, you
        crumpled up the square!

'E rushes at the smoke when we let drive,
    An', before we know, 'e 's 'ackin' at our
        'ead;
'E's all 'ot sand an' ginger when alive,
    An' 'e 's generally shammin' when 'e 's
        dead.   40
'E's a daisy, 'e 's a ducky, 'e 's a lamb!
'E's a injia-rubber idiot on the spree,
'E's the on'y thing that doesn't give a damn
    For a Regiment o' British Infantree!
    So 'ere's *to* you, Fuzzy-Wuzzy, at your
        'ome in the Sudan;   45
    You're a poor benighted 'eathen but a
        first-class fightin' man;
    An' 'ere's *to* you, Fuzzy-Wuzzy, with
        your 'ayrick 'ead of 'air—
    You big black boundin' beggar—for you
        broke a British square!   (1890)

Gunga Din

You may talk o' gin and beer
When you're quartered safe out 'ere,
An' you're sent to penny-fights an' Aldershot
    it;
But when it comes to slaughter
You will do your work on water,   5
An' you'll lick the bloomin' boots of 'im that's
    got it.
Now in Injia's sunny clime,
Where I used to spend my time
A-servin' of 'Er Majesty the Queen,
Of all them black-faced crew   10
The finest man I knew
Was our regimental bhisti, Gunga Din.
    He was "Din! Din! Din!
    "You limpin' lump o' brick-dust, Gunga
        Din!
    "Hi! *Slippy hitherao!*   15
    "Water, get it! *Panee lao!*
    "You squidgy-nosed old idol, Gunga Din!"

The uniform 'e wore
Was nothin' much before,
An' rather less than 'arf o' that be'ind,   20

---

2. **out 'ere**, in India. 3. **Aldershot it**, live in Aldershot, a military camp in Hampshire. 9. **the Queen**, Victoria. 12. **bhisti**, water-carrier; literally, heavenly one. 15. *Slippy hitherao*, mock dialect for "slip here." 16. *Panee lao*, bring water quickly.

For a piece o' twisty rag
An' a goatskin water-bag
Was all the field-equipment 'e could find.
When the sweatin' troop-train lay
In a sidin' through the day,   25
Where the 'eat would make your bloomin'
    eyebrows crawl,
We shouted "Harry By!"
Till our throats were bricky-dry,
Then we wopped 'im 'cause 'e couldn't serve
    us all.
    It was "Din! Din! Din!   30
"You 'eathen, where the mischief 'ave you
    been?
"You put some *juldee* in it
"Or I'll *marrow* you this minute
"If you don't fill up my helmet, Gunga
    Din!"

'E would dot an' carry one   35
Till the longest day was done;
An' 'e didn't seem to know the use o' fear.
If we charged or broke or cut,
You could bet your bloomin' nut,
'E'd be waitin' fifty paces right flank rear.   40
With 'is mussick on 'is back,
'E would skip with our attack,
An' watch us till the bugles made "Retire,"
An' for all 'is dirty 'ide
'E was white, clear white, inside   45
When 'e went to tend the wounded under
    fire!
    It was "Din! Din! Din!"
With the bullets kickin' dust-spots on the
    green.
    When the cartridges ran out,
    You could 'ear the front-ranks shout,   50
"Hi! ammunition-mules an' Gunga Din!"

I sha'n't forgit the night
When I dropped be'ind the fight
With a bullet where my belt-plate should 'a'
    been.
I was chokin' mad with thirst,   55
An' the man that spied me first
Was our good old grinnin', gruntin' Gunga
    Din.
'E lifted up my 'ead,

An' 'e plugged me where I bled,
An' 'e guv me 'arf-a-pint o' water green.   60
It was crawlin' and it stunk,
But of all the drinks I've drunk,
I'm gratefullest to one from Gunga Din.
    It was "Din! Din! Din!
" 'Ere's a beggar with a bullet through 'is
    spleen;   65
" 'E's chawin' up the ground,
"An' 'e's kickin' all around:
"For Gawd's sake, git the water, Gunga
    Din!"

'E carried me away
To where a dooli lay,   70
An' a bullet come an' drilled the beggar clean.
'E put me safe inside,
An' just before 'e died,
"I 'ope you liked your drink," sez Gunga Din.
So I'll meet 'im later on   75
In the place where 'e is gone—
Where it's always double drill and no canteen.
'E'll be squattin' on the coals
Givin' drink to poor damned souls,
An' I'll get a swig in hell from Gunga Din!   80
    Yes, Din! Din! Din!
    You Lazarushian-leather Gunga Din!
    Though I've belted you an' flayed you,
    By the livin' God that made you,
    You're a better man than I am, Gunga Din!
                                        (1890)

Mandalay

Mandalay is one of the chief cities of Burma. A British force of occupation has been stationed there since 1885-1886, when the country was annexed.

By the old Moulmein Pagoda, lookin' east-
    ward to the sea,
There's a Burma girl a-settin', and I know she
    thinks o' me;
For the wind is in the palm-trees, and the
    temple bells they say:
"Come you back, you British soldier; come
    you back to Mandalay!"
    Come you back to Mandalay,   5

---

27. **"Harry By,"** O Brother. 29. **wopped**, hit. 32. ***juldee***, speed. 33. ***marrow***, hit. 41. **mussick**, leather water bag, made of goatskin.

70. **dooli**, stretcher. 82. **Lazarushian-leather**, army slang for dark-skinned.
Mandalay. 1. **Moulmein Pagoda**, a Buddhist temple in the city of Moulmein across the Gulf of Martaban from Rangoon, another chief city of Burma 375 miles south of Mandalay.

Where the old Flotilla lay:
Can't you 'ear their paddles chunkin'
    from Rangoon to Mandalay?
On the road to Mandalay,
Where the flyin'-fishes play,
An' the dawn comes up like thunder
    outer China 'crost the Bay!   10

'Er petticoat was yaller an' 'er little cap was
    green,
An' 'er name was Supi-yaw-lat—jes' the same
    as Theebaw's Queen,
An' I seed her first a-smokin' of a whackin'
    white cheroot,
An' a-wastin' Christian kisses on an 'eathen
    idol's foot:

    Bloomin' idol made o' mud—   15
    Wot they called the Great Gawd Budd—
    Plucky lot she cared for idols when I
        kissed 'er where she stud!
    On the road to Mandalay . . .

When the mist was on the rice-fields an' the
    sun was droppin' slow,
She'd git 'er little banjo an' she'd sing "Kulla-
    lo-lo!"   20
With 'er arm upon my shoulder an' 'er cheek
    agin my cheek
We useter watch the steamers an' the *hathis*
    pilin' teak.

    Elephints a-pilin' teak
    In the sludgy, squdgy creek,
    Where the silence 'ung that 'eavy you was
        'arf afraid to speak!   25
    On the road to Mandalay . . .

But that's all shove be'ind me—long ago an'
    fur away,
An' there ain't no 'busses runnin' from the
    Bank to Mandalay;
An' I'm learnin' 'ere in London what the
    ten-year soldier tells:
"If you've 'eard the East a-callin', you won't
    never 'eed naught else."   30

No! you won't 'eed nothin' else
But them spicy garlic smells,
An' the sunshine an' the palm-trees an'
    the tinkly temple bells;
On the road to Mandalay . . .

I am sick o' wastin' leather on these gritty
    pavin'-stones,   35
An' the blasted Henglish drizzle wakes the
    fever in my bones;
Tho' I walks with fifty 'ousemaids outer
    Chelsea to the Strand,
An' they talks a lot o' lovin', but wot do they
    understand?

    Beefy face an' grubby 'and—
    Law! wot do they understand?   40
    I've a neater, sweeter maiden in a cleaner,
        greener land!
    On the road to Mandalay . . .

Ship me somewheres east of Suez, where the
    best is like the worst,
Where there aren't no Ten Commandments
    an' a man can raise a thirst;
For the temple bells are callin', an' it's there
    that I would be—   45
By the old Moulmein Pagoda, looking lazy at
    the sea;

    On the road to Mandalay,
    Where the old Flotilla lay,
    With our sick beneath the awnings when
        we went to Mandalay!

    On the road to Mandalay!   50
    Where the flyin'-fishes play,
    An' the dawn comes up like thunder
        outer China 'crost the Bay!   (1890)

The King

"Farewell, Romance!" the Cave-men said;
    "With bone well carved he went away,
"Flint arms the ignoble arrowhead,
    "And jasper tips the spear today.

---

6. **old Flotilla**, steamers of the Flotilla Company plying between Rangoon and Mandalay on the Irrawaddy River. 10. **dawn comes up.** As observed by one on the road to Mandalay. 12. **Theebaw**, the last King of Burma (1876-1885). His wife, Supaiyah Lat, was notoriously cruel. 16. **Budd**, Buddha, worshiped by most Burmese. 22. **hathis**, elephants. **teak**, a valuable hard wood. 28. **Bank**, the Bank of England, where some London bus lines meet.

37. **Chelsea**, a district on the Thames River, London. **Strand**, a main thoroughfare in London.
The King from THE SEVEN SEAS, by Rudyard Kipling, copyright 1893, 1921, reprinted by permission from Mrs. Kipling, Doubleday, Doran & Company, Inc., and The Macmillan Company of Canada Limited.

"Changed are the Gods of Hunt and Dance, 5
"And he with these. Farewell, Romance!"

"Farewell, Romance!" the Lake-folk sighed;
  "We lift the weight of flatling years;
"The caverns of the mountain-side
  "Hold Him who scorns our hutted piers. 10
"Lost hills whereby we dare not dwell,
"Guard ye his rest. Romance, farewell!"

"Farewell, Romance!" the Soldier spoke;
  "By sleight of sword we may not win,
"But scuffle 'mid uncleanly smoke 15
  "Of arquebus and culverin.
"Honor is lost, and none may tell
"Who paid good blows. Romance, farewell!"

"Farewell, Romance!" the Traders cried;
  "Our keels have lain with every sea; 20
"The dull-returning wind and tide
  "Heave up the wharf where we would be;
"The known and noted breezes swell
  "Our trudging sail. Romance, farewell!"

"Good-by, Romance!" the Skipper said; 25
  "He vanished with the coal we burn.
"Our dial marks full-steam ahead,
  "Our speed is timed to half a turn.
"Sure as the ferried barge we ply
" 'Twixt port and port. Romance, good-by!" 30

"Romance!" the season-tickets mourn,
  "He never ran to catch his train,
"But passed with coach and guard and horn—
  "And left the local—late again!"
Confound Romance! . . . And all unseen 35
Romance brought up the nine-fifteen.

His hand was on the lever laid,
  His oil can soothed the worrying cranks,
His whistle waked the snowbound grade,
  His fog-horn cut the reeking Banks; 40
By dock and deep and mine and mill
The Boy-god reckless labored still!

Robed, crowned, and throned, He wove his spell,
  Where heart-blood beat or hearth-smoke curled,
With unconsidered miracle, 45
  Hedged in a backward-gazing world:
Then taught his chosen bard to say:
"Our King was with us—yesterday!"   (1894)

The "Mary Gloster"

The *Mary Gloster*, named after his wife, was the favorite freighter of the speaker of this dramatic monologue. As if his dilettante son were present, the old man, on his deathbed, gives instructions about his burial at sea where his wife was previously buried, and at the last moment envisions the sinking of the *Mary Gloster* with his body tied in the deck-cabin. The poem should be compared with Browning's famous dramatic monologue, *The Bishop Orders His Tomb at Saint Praxed's Church* (p. 670).

I've paid for your sickest fancies; I've humored
  your crackedest whim—
Dick, it's your daddy, dying; you've got to
  listen to him!
Good for a fortnight, am I? The doctor told
  you? He lied.
I shall go under by morning, and—Put that
  nurse outside.
'Never seen death yet, Dickie? Well, now is
  your time to learn, 5
And you'll wish you held my record before
  it comes to your turn.
Not counting the Line and the Foundry, the
  yards and the village, too,
I've made myself and a million; but I'm
  damned if I made you.
Master at two-and-twenty, and married at
  twenty-three—
Ten thousand men on the pay-roll, and forty
  freighters at sea! 10
Fifty years between 'em, and every year of it
  fight,
And now I'm Sir Anthony Gloster, dying, a
  baronite:
For I lunched with his Royal 'Ighness—what
  was it the papers had?
"Not least of our merchant-princes." Dickie,
  that's me, your dad!

---

7. **the Lake-folk,** prehistoric inhabitants of Switzerland who lived in villages built on piers or piles near the shores of the lakes. 16. **arquebus and culverin,** early kinds of firearms. 23. **known . . . breezes.** Records of prevailing winds were not kept before the nineteenth century. 40. **reeking Banks,** fog banks that the train runs through.

From THE SEVEN SEAS, by Rudyard Kipling, copyright 1893, 1933, reprinted by permission of Mrs. G. Bambridge, Doubleday & Company, Inc., and The Macmillan Co. of Canada, Ltd. 7. **the Line,** the freighters or merchant ships he owned and operated. **the Foundry,** the iron business of which he was half-owner. See ll. 41-42.

I didn't begin with askings. *I* took my job
    and I stuck;   15
I took the chances they wouldn't, an' now
    they're calling it luck.
Lord, what boats I've handled—rotten and
    leaky and old!
Ran 'em, or—opened the bilge-cock, precisely
    as I was told.
Grub that 'ud bind you crazy, and crews that
    'ud turn you gray,
And a big fat lump of insurance to cover the
    risk on the way.   20
The others they dursn't do it; they said they
    valued their life
(They've served me since as skippers). *I* went,
    and I took my wife.
Over the world I drove 'em, married at
    twenty-three,
And your mother saving the money and
    making a man of me.
I was content to be master, but she said there
    was better behind;   25
She took the chances I wouldn't, and I fol-
    lowed your mother blind.
She egged me to borrow the money, an' she
    helped me to clear the loan,
When we bought half-shares in a cheap 'un
    and hoisted a flag of our own.
Patching and coaling on credit, and living
    the Lord knew how,
We started the Red Ox freighters—we've
    eight-and-thirty now.   30
And those were the days of clippers, and the
    freights were clipper-freights,
And we knew we were making our fortune,
    but she died in Macassar Straits—
By the Little Paternosters, as you come to the
    Union Bank—
And we dropped her in fourteen fathom: I
    pricked it off where she sank.
Owners we were, full owners, and the boat
    was christened for her,   35
And she died in the *Mary Gloster*. My heart,
    how young we were!
So I went on a spree round Java and well-
    nigh ran her ashore,
But your mother came and warned me and
    I wouldn't liquor no more:
Strict I stuck to my business, afraid to stop
    or I'd think,
Saving the money (she warned me), and let-
    ting the other men drink.   40
And I met M'Cullough in London (I'd saved
    five 'undred then),
And 'tween us we started the Foundry—three
    forges and twenty men.
Cheap repairs for the cheap 'uns. It paid, and
    the business grew;
For I bought me a steam-lathe patent, and
    that was a gold mine too.
"Cheaper to build 'em than buy 'em," *I* said,
    but M'Cullough he shied,   45
And we wasted a year in talking before we
    moved to the Clyde.
And the Lines were all beginning, and we all
    of us started fair,
Building our engines like houses and staying
    the boilers square.
But M'Cullough 'e wanted cabins with marble
    and maple and all,
And Brussels an' Utrecht velvet, and baths
    and a Social Hall,   50
And pipes for closets all over, and cutting the
    frames too light,
But M'Cullough he died in the Sixties, and—
    Well, I'm dying tonight. . . .
I knew—*I* knew what was coming, when we
    bid on the *Byfleet's* keel—
They piddled and piffled with iron. I'd given
    my orders for steel!
Steel and the first expansions. It paid, I tell
    you, it paid,   55
When we came with our nine-knot freighters
    and collared the long-run trade!
And they asked me how I did it, and I gave
    'em the Scripture text,
"You keep your light so shining a little in
    front o' the next!"
They copied all they could follow, but they
    couldn't copy my mind,
And I left 'em sweating and stealing a year
    and a half behind.   60

---

18. **bilge-cock,** an opening in the bottom of the ship used for draining out water when the ship is in dry dock or, as here, for letting in water to sink the ship. 32. **Macassar Straits,** the channel separating the islands of Borneo and Celebes in the Malay Archipelago. 33. **Little Paternosters,** a group of islands in Macassar Strait. 34. **fathom,** a measure of about six feet. 41. **five 'undred,** five hundred pounds; between $2000 and $2500 in United States currency. 46. **Clyde,** a river in Scotland; the bay where it empties into the Atlantic Ocean above Glasgow is one of the leading shipbuilding centers of the world. 47. **Lines,** various shipping companies. 50. **Brussels,** a high-grade carpet named from Brussels, one of the great centers of Belgian industry. **Utrecht,** a city of Holland noted for the manufacture of textiles, lace, silk, etc.

Then came the armor-contracts, but that was M'Cullough's side;
He was always best in the Foundry, but better, perhaps, he died.
I went through his private papers; the notes was plainer than print;
And I'm no fool to finish if a man'll give me a hint.
(I remember his widow was angry.) So I saw what his drawings meant, 65
And I started the six-inch rollers, and it paid me sixty per cent.
Sixty per cent *with* failures, and more than twice we could do,
And a quarter-million to credit, and I saved it all for you!
I thought—it doesn't matter—you seemed to favor your ma,
But you're nearer forty than thirty, and I know the kind you are. 70
Harrer an' Trinity College! I ought to ha' sent you to sea—
But I stood you an education, an' what have you done for me?
The things I knew was proper you wouldn't thank me to give,
And the things I knew was rotten you said was the way to live.
For you muddled with books and pictures, an' china an' etchin's an' fans, 75
And your rooms at college was beastly—more like a whore's than a man's;
Till you married that thin-flanked woman, as white and as stale as a bone,
An' she gave you your social nonsense; but where's that kid o' your own?
I've seen your carriages blocking the half o' the Cromwell Road,
But never the doctor's brougham to help the missus unload. 80
(So there isn't even a grandchild, an' the Gloster family's done.)
Not like your mother, she isn't. *She* carried her freight each run.
But they died, the pore little beggars! At sea she had 'em—they died.
Only you, an' you stood it. You haven't stood much beside.
Weak, a liar, and idle, and mean as a collier's whelp 85
Nosing for scraps in the galley. No help—my son was no help!
So he gets three 'undred thousand, in trust and the interest paid.
I wouldn't give it you, Dickie—you see, I made it in trade.
You're saved from soiling your fingers, and if you have no child,
It all comes back to the business. 'Gad, won't your wife be wild! 90
'Calls and calls in her carriage, her 'andkerchief up to 'er eye:
"Daddy! dear daddy's dyin'!" and doing her best to cry.
Grateful? Oh, yes, I'm grateful, but keep her away from here.
Your mother 'ud never ha' stood 'er, and, anyhow, women are queer. . . .
There's women will say I've married a second time. Not quite! 95
But give pore Aggie a hundred, and tell her your lawyers'll fight.
She was the best o' the boiling—you'll meet her before it ends.
I'm in for a row with the mother—I'll leave you settle my friends.
For a man he must go with a woman, which women don't understand—
Or the sort that say they can see it they aren't the marrying brand. 100
But I wanted to speak o' your mother that's Lady Gloster still;
I'm going to up and see her, without its hurting the will.
Here! Take your hand off the bell-pull. Five thousand's waiting for you,
If you'll only listen a minute, and do as I bid you do.
They'll try to prove me crazy, and, if you bungle, they can; 105
And I've only you to trust to! (O God, why ain't it a man?)
There's some waste money on marbles, the same as M'Cullough tried—
Marbles and mausoleums—but I call that sinful pride.

---

66. **started . . . rollers**, started the rollers in the Foundry to roll out boiler plate for shipbuilding. 71. **Harrer**, Harrow, one of the famous preparatory English schools, located in Middlesex, eleven miles northwest of London. **Trinity College**, a college of Oxford University. 79. **Cromwell Road**, in earlier days a disreputable section of the city.

86. **galley**, the kitchen of a ship.

There's some ship bodies for burial—we've
    carried 'em, soldered and packed;
Down in their wills they wrote it, and nobody
    called *them* cracked. 110
But me—I've too much money, and people
    might . . . All my fault:
It come o' hoping for grandsons and buying
    that Wokin' vault. . . .
I'm sick o' the 'ole dam' business. I'm going
    back where I came.
Dick, you're the son o' my body, and you'll
    take charge o' the same!
I want to lie by your mother, ten thousand
    mile away, 115
And they'll want to send me to Woking; and
    that's where you'll earn your pay.
I've thought it out on the quiet, the same as
    it ought to be done—
Quiet, and decent, and proper—an' here's
    your orders, my son.
You know the Line? You don't, though. You
    write to the Board, and tell
Your father's death has upset you an' you're
    goin' to cruise for a spell, 120
An' you'd like the *Mary Gloster*—I've held
    her ready for this—
They'll put her in working order and you'll
    take her out as she is.
Yes, it was money idle when I patched her
    and laid her aside
(Thank God, I can pay for my fancies!)—the
    boat where your mother died,
By the Little Paternosters, as you come to the
    Union Bank, 125
We dropped her—I think I told you—and I
    pricked it off where she sank.
[Tiny she looked on the grating—that oily,
    treacly sea—]
'Hundred and Eighteen East, remember, and
    South just Three.
Easy bearings to carry—Three South—Three
    to the dot;
But I gave McAndrew a copy in case of dying
    —or not. 130
And so you'll write to McAndrew, he's Chief
    of the Maori Line;
They'll give him leave, if you ask 'em and say
    it's business o' mine.

I built three boats for the Maoris, an' very
    well pleased they were,
An' I've known Mac since the Fifties, and
    Mac knew me—and her.
After the first stroke warned me I sent him
    the money to keep 135
Against the time you'd claim it, committin'
    your dad to the deep;
For you are the son o' my body, and Mac was
    my oldest friend,
I've never asked 'im to dinner, but he'll see it
    out to the end.
Stiff-necked Glasgow beggar! I've heard he's
    prayed for my soul,
But he couldn't lie if you paid him, and he'd
    starve before he stole. 140
He'll take the *Mary* in ballast—you'll find her
    a lively ship;
And you'll take Sir Anthony Gloster, that
    goes on 'is wedding-trip,
Lashed in our old deck-cabin with all three
    port-holes wide,
The kick o' the screw beneath him and the
    round blue seas outside!
Sir Anthony Gloster's carriage—our 'ouse-flag
    flyin' free— 145
Ten thousand men on the pay-roll and forty
    freighters at sea!
He made himself and a million, but this
    world is a fleetin' show,
And he'll go to the wife of 'is bosom the same
    as he ought to go—
By the heel of the Paternosters—there isn't a
    chance to mistake—
And Mac'll pay you the money as soon as the
    bubbles break! 150
Five thousand for six weeks' cruising, the
    staunchest freighter afloat,
And Mac he'll give you your bonus the min-
    ute I'm out o' the boat!
He'll take you round to Macassar, and you'll
    come back alone;
He knows what I want o' the *Mary*. . . . I'll
    do what I please with my own.
Your mother 'ud call it wasteful, but I've
    seven-and-thirty more; 155
I'll come in my private carriage and bid it
    wait at the door. . . .

---

109. **packed**, made water-tight. 112. **Wokin' vault**, a vault in the extensive London Necropolis Cemetery near Woking, a town in Surrey. 128. **'Hundred . . . Three**, the nautical designation of the place where she was buried—118 degrees east longitude and three degrees south latitude.

141. **in ballast**, ready for the voyage. 147. **this . . . show**. Cf. poem by Thomas Moore beginning "This world is all a fleeting show, For man's illusion given." 153. **Macassar**, the capital of Celebes, situated at the southern point of the island.

For my son 'e was never a credit: 'e muddled
    with books and art,
And 'e lived on Sir Anthony's money and 'e
    broke Sir Anthony's heart.
There isn't even a grandchild, and the Gloster
    Family's done—
The only one you left me—O mother, the
    only one!   160
Harrer and Trinity College—me slavin' early
    an' late—
An' he thinks I'm dying crazy, and you're in
    Macassar Strait!
Flesh o' my flesh, my dearie, for ever an' ever
    amen,
That first stroke come for a warning. I ought
    to ha' gone to you then.
But—cheap repairs for a cheap 'un—the doc-
    tors said I'd do.   165
Mary, why didn't *you* warn me? I've allus
    heeded to you,
Excep'—I know—about women; but you are
    a spirit now;
An', wife, they was only women, and I was
    a man. That's how.
An' a man 'e must go with a woman, as you
    could not understand;
But I never talked 'em secrets. I paid 'em
    out o' hand.   170
Thank Gawd, I can pay for my fancies! Now
    what's five thousand to me,
For a berth off the Paternosters in the haven
    where I would be?
I believe in the Resurrection, if I read my
    Bible plain,
But I wouldn't trust 'em at Wokin'; we're
    safer at sea again.
For the heart it shall go with the treasure—
    go down to the sea in ships.   175
I'm sick of the hired women. I'll kiss my girl
    on her lips!
I'll be content with my fountain. I'll drink
    from my own well,
And the wife of my youth shall charm me
    —an' the rest can go to Hell!
(Dickie, *he* will, that's certain.) I'll lie in our
    standin'-bed,

An' Mac'll take her in ballast—an' she trims
    best by the head. . . .   180
Down by the head an' sinkin', her fires are
    drawn and cold,
And the water's splashin' hollow on the skin
    of the empty hold—
Churning an' choking and chuckling, quiet
    and scummy and dark—
Full to her lower hatches and risin' steady.
    Hark!
That was the after-bulkhead. . . . She's flooded
    from stem to stern. . . .   185
'Never seen death yet, Dickie? Well, now is
    your time to learn!   (1894)

Recessional

A recessional is a hymn sung as the choir leaves the church service. The poem was published in the *London Times* in July, 1897, near the close of the celebration, in London, of the sixtieth anniversary of the reign of Queen Victoria. High government officials and troops from all the colonies of the Empire, and nearly two hundred vessels of the Royal Navy, were assembled for the ceremonies. Thus it was an appropriate time for Kipling to sound a warning to the nation dazzled by the pomp and splendor of the occasion.

God of our fathers, known of old,
    Lord of our far-flung battle-line,
Beneath whose awful Hand we hold
    Dominion over palm and pine—
Lord God of Hosts, be with us yet,   5
Lest we forget—lest we forget!

The tumult and the shouting dies;
    The Captains and the Kings depart:
Still stands Thine ancient sacrifice,
    An humble and a contrite heart.   10
Lord God of Hosts, be with us yet,
Lest we forget—lest we forget!

---

170. **paid . . . hand**, paid them promptly. 175. **heart . . . treasure**. Cf. *Matthew*, 6:21: "For where your treasure is, there will your heart be also." **go . . . ships**, a Biblical phrase from *Psalms*, 107:23. 177-178. Cf. *Proverbs*, 5:15, 18: "Drink waters out of thine own cistern, and running waters out of thine own well . . . Let thy fountain be blessed; and rejoice with the wife of thy youth." 179. **standin'-bed**, a high bedstead.

180. **trims . . . head**, rides water most gracefully at the bow. *Recessional* and *The White Man's Burden* from THE FIVE NATIONS, by Rudyard Kipling, copyright 1903, 1931, reprinted by permission from Mrs. Kipling, Doubleday, Doran & Company, Inc., and The Macmillan Company of Canada Limited. 4. **palm and pine**. An indication of the extent of the British Empire. 5. **Lord . . . Hosts**, a very common phrase in the Bible. Cf. *Psalms*, 84:8—"O Lord God of hosts, hear my prayer." 6. **Lest we forget**. Cf. *Deuteronomy*, 6:12—"Then beware lest thou forget the Lord." 7. **tumult . . . dies**. Cf. *Job*, 39:25—"He smelleth the battle afar off, the thunder of the captains, and the shouting." 9. **sacrifice . . . heart**. Cf. *Psalms*, 51:17—"The sacrifices of God are a broken spirit: a broken and a contrite heart, O God, thou wilt not despise."

Far-called, our navies melt away;
   On dune and headland sinks the fire:
Lo, all our pomp of yesterday
   Is one with Nineveh and Tyre!
Judge of the Nations, spare us yet,
Lest we forget—lest we forget!

If, drunk with sight of power, we loose
   Wild tongues that have not Thee in awe,
Such boastings as the Gentiles use,
   Or lesser breeds without the Law—
Lord God of Hosts, be with us yet,
Lest we forget—lest we forget!

For heathen heart that puts her trust
   In reeking tube and iron shard,
All valiant dust that builds on dust,
   And guarding, calls not Thee to guard,
For frantic boast and foolish word—
Thy Mercy on Thy People, Lord!   (1897)

The White Man's Burden

   Published in *McClure's Magazine,* shortly after the conclusion of peace between the United States and Spain, December 10, 1898, this poem describes the duty, as Kipling saw it, of the United States toward Cuba and the Philippines. Both poem and title coincide with a definite attitude of Kipling and of conservative England toward imperialism.

Take up the White Man's burden—
   Send forth the best ye breed—
Go bind your sons to exile
   To serve your captives' need;
To wait in heavy harness,
   On fluttered folk and wild—
Your new-caught, sullen peoples,
   Half-devil and half-child.

Take up the White Man's burden—
   In patience to abide,
To veil the threat of terror
   And check the show of pride;
By open speech and simple,
   An hundred times made plain,
To seek another's profit,
   And work another's gain.

Take up the White Man's burden—
   The savage wars of peace—
Fill full the mouth of Famine
   And bid the sickness cease;
And when your goal is nearest
   The end for others sought,
Watch Sloth and heathen Folly
   Bring all your hope to nought.

Take up the White Man's burden—
   No tawdry rule of kings,
But toil of serf and sweeper—
   The tale of common things.
The ports ye shall not enter,
   The roads ye shall not tread,
Go make them with your living,
   And mark them with your dead.

Take up the White Man's burden—
   And reap his old reward:
The blame of those ye better,
   The hate of those ye guard—
The cry of hosts ye humor
   (Ah, slowly!) toward the light:—
"Why brought ye us from bondage,
   "Our loved Egyptian night?"

Take up the White Man's burden—
   Ye dare not stoop to less—
Nor call too loud on Freedom
   To cloak your weariness;
By all ye cry or whisper,
   By all ye leave or do,
The silent sullen peoples
   Shall weigh your Gods and you.

Take up the White Man's burden—
   Have done with childish days—
The lightly proffered laurel,
   The easy, ungrudged praise.
Comes now, to search your manhood
   Through all the thankless years,
Cold, edged with dear-bought wisdom,
   The judgment of your peers!   (1899)

---

16. **Nineveh and Tyre.** Nineveh was the ancient capital of Assyria; it is now buried under sand. Tyre, now an unimportant seaport, was once a great city of Phoenicia. 21. **Gentiles . . . Law.** Cf. *Romans,* 2:14—"For when the Gentiles which have not the law, do by nature the things contained in the law, these, having not the law, are a law unto themselves." A Gentile is here thought of by Kipling as anyone not English. 26. **shard,** fragment of shell.

39. **"Why . . . night?"** On their journey from Egypt the Israelites murmured against their leaders, Moses and Aaron, because they had no food. They exclaimed: "Would to God we had died by the hand of the Lord in the land of Egypt, where we sat by the flesh pots, and when we did eat bread to the full" (*Exodus,* 16:2-3).

A Smuggler's Song

Smuggling was long a profitable business on the coast of England, because of the high taxes on imports. Frequently, as indicated in this poem, clergymen allowed their churches to be used for storing smuggled goods, receiving in exchange gifts of brandy, lace, and tobacco, the chief articles brought in by the smugglers, called here "the Gentlemen" (l. 4).

If you wake at midnight, and hear a horse's feet,
Don't go drawing back the blind, or looking in the street,
Them that asks no questions isn't told a lie.
Watch the wall, my darling, while the Gentlemen go by!
    Five and twenty ponies,   5
    Trotting through the dark—
    Brandy for the Parson,
    'Baccy for the Clerk;
    Laces for a lady, letters for a spy,
And watch the wall, my darling, while the Gentlemen go by!   10

Running round the woodlump if you chance to find
Little barrels, roped and tarred, all full of brandy-wine,
Don't you shout to come and look, nor use 'em for your play.
Put the brishwood back again—and they'll be gone next day!

If you see the stable-door setting open wide;   15
If you see a tired horse lying down inside;
If your mother mends a coat cut about and tore;
If the lining's wet and warm—don't you ask no more!

If you meet King George's men, dressed in blue and red,
You be careful what you say, and mindful what is said.   20
If they call you "pretty maid," and chuck you 'neath the chin,
Don't you tell where no one is, nor yet where no one's been!

Knocks and footsteps round the house—whistles after dark—
You've no call for running out till the house-dogs bark.
Trusty's here, and *Pincher's* here, and see how dumb they lie—   25
They don't fret to follow when the Gentlemen go by!

If you do as you've been told, 'likely there's a chance,
You'll be give a dainty doll, all the way from France,
With a cap of Valenciennes, and a velvet hood—
A present from the Gentlemen, along o' being good!   30
    Five and twenty ponies,
    Trotting through the dark,
    Brandy for the Parson,
    'Baccy for the Clerk.
Them that asks no questions isn't told a lie—   35
Watch the wall, my darling, while the Gentlemen go by!   (1905)

A Smuggler's Song from PUCK OF POOK'S HILL, by Rudyard Kipling, copyright 1905, 1933, reprinted by permission from Mrs. Kipling, Doubleday, Doran & Company, Inc., and The Macmillan Company of Canada Limited.

19. **King George's men**, revenue officers and soldiers; the allusion to King George sets the time as the eighteenth or early nineteenth century. 29. **Valenciennes**, a kind of fine lace, formerly made at Valenciennes, a city of France.

Alfred Edward Housman
1859-1936

Alfred Edward Housman was born in Worcestershire, but he says that he had "a sentimental feeling for Shropshire because its hills were our western horizon." At Oxford, from 1877 to 1881, he attained success in classical studies, but his more ardent love of poetry probably accounted for his failure to pass the final examination, which cast a cloud over his subsequent career. In 1882 he went to London where for ten years he held a post in the Patent Office; during that period many long evenings were spent in reading Latin and Greek in the British Museum. Published studies in the minor Latin poets resulted in his appointment in 1892 to a professorship in Latin in University College, London, and to a similar position at Cambridge in 1911. Between 1886 and 1905 Housman lived in Highgate, London, and it was there that he wrote *A Shropshire Lad*. Most of the poems were composed in 1895, during a great burst of creative activity, just prior to publication. The title was suggested by a friend, A. W. Pollard, in place of the less attractive *Poems by Terence Hearsay* (see poem 8, line 3). In an autobiographical note, Housman says: "The Shropshire Lad is an imaginary figure, with something of my temper and view of life. Very little in the book is autobiographical." It was not until 1922 that Housman's next book, *Last Poems*, appeared. He died in 1936, and in the autumn of the same year his final work, *More Poems*, was issued by his brother Laurence.

Although Housman lists his chief sources as Shakespeare's songs, the Scottish Border ballads, and the German poet Heine, his verse shows distinctly the result of his saturation in the poetry of the Latin lyrists; there is about it a clean-limbed economy and directness with nothing of the unrestrained decoration of so much romantic verse. The quality of meagerness, in fact, suggests that the poet is speaking in silences rather than expressions. The mood is pagan and melancholy, not to say pessimistic. There is a classical element in the reiteration of the suggestion that youth and spring and all things lovely must come to dust and decay. But this Latin material is made to settle down securely on the English countryside in verse that is notably easy, felicitous, and poignant. Like Fitzgerald, Housman has attained high rank among English poets despite the meagerness of his output.

from *A Shropshire Lad*

2

Loveliest of trees, the cherry now
Is hung with bloom along the bough,
And stands about the woodland ride
Wearing white for Eastertide.

Now, of my threescore years and ten,
Twenty will not come again,
And take from seventy springs a score,
It only leaves me fifty more.

And since to look at things in bloom
Fifty springs are little room,
About the woodlands I will go
To see the cherry hung with snow.

4. REVEILLE

Wake! The silver dusk returning
  Up the beach of darkness brims,
And the ship of sunrise burning
  Strands upon the eastern rims.

Wake! The vaulted shadow shatters,
  Trampled to the floor it spanned,
And the tent of night in tatters
  Straws the sky-pavilioned land.

Up, lad, up! 'Tis late for lying.
  Hear the drums of morning play;
Hark, the empty highways crying,
  "Who'll beyond the hills away?"

Towns and countries woo together,
  Forelands beacon, belfries call;
Never lad that trod on leather
  Lived to feast his heart with all.

Up, lad; thews that lie and cumber
  Sunlit pallets never thrive;
Morns abed and daylight slumber
  Were not meant for man alive.

Clay lies still, but blood's a rover;
  Breath's a ware that will not keep.
Up, lad; when the journey's over
  There'll be time enough to sleep.

The poems from *A Shropshire Lad* are reprinted by consent of Henry Holt and Company, the authorized publishers.

Lyric 4. 8. **Straws,** is strewn across. 18. **pallets,** small beds.

5

Oh, see how thick the goldcup flowers
  Are lying in field and lane,
With dandelions to tell the hours
  That never are told again.
Oh, may I squire you round the meads
  And pick you posies gay?
—'Twill do no harm to take my arm.
  "You may, young man, you may."

Ah, spring was sent for lass and lad,
  'Tis now the blood runs gold,
And man and maid had best be glad
  Before the world is old.
What flowers today may flower tomorrow,
  But never as good as new.
—Suppose I wound my arm right round—
  "'Tis true, young man, 'tis true."

Some lads there are, 'tis shame to say,
  That only court to thieve,
And once they bear the bloom away
  'Tis little enough they leave.
Then keep your heart for men like me
  And safe from trustless chaps.
My love is true and all for you.
  "Perhaps, young man, perhaps."

Oh, look in my eyes then, can you doubt?
  —Why, 'tis a mile from town.
How green the grass is all about!
  We might as well sit down.
—Ah, life, what is it but a flower?
  Why must true lovers sigh?
Be kind, have pity, my own, my pretty—
  "Good-by, young man, good-by."

7

When smoke stood up from Ludlow,
  And mist blew off from Teme,
And blithe afield to plowing
  Against the morning beam
I strode beside my team,

The blackbird in the coppice
  Looked out to see me stride,
And hearkened as I whistled
  The trampling team beside,
And fluted and replied:

"Lie down, lie down, young yeoman;
  What use to rise and rise?
Rise man a thousand mornings
  Yet down at last he lies,
And then the man is wise."

I heard the tune he sang me,
  And spied his yellow bill;
I picked a stone and aimed it
  And threw it with a will.
Then the bird was still.

Then my soul within me
  Took up the blackbird's strain,
And still beside the horses
  Along the dewy lane
It sang the song again:

"Lie down, lie down, young yeoman;
  The sun moves always west;
The road one treads to labor
  Will lead one home to rest,
And that will be the best."

8

"Farewell to barn and stack and tree,
  Farewell to Severn shore.
Terence, look your last at me,
  For I come home no more.

"The sun burns on the half-mown hill,
  By now the blood is dried;
And Maurice amongst the hay lies still
  And my knife is in his side.

"My mother thinks us long away;
  'Tis time the field were mown.
She had two sons at rising day,
  Tonight she'll be alone.

"And here's a bloody hand to shake,
  And, oh, man, here's good-by;
We'll sweat no more on scythe and rake,
  My bloody hands and I.

Lyric 5. 1. **goldcup flowers**, marsh marigolds. 3. **dandelions . . . hours.** Children "tell time" by blowing the dandelion that has gone to seed and counting the seeds that fly away.
Lyric 7. 1. **Ludlow**, a town in Shropshire—on the Teme River. 6. **coppice**, thicket.

11. **yeoman**, a land-owning farmer.

"I wish you strength to bring you pride,
    And a love to keep you clean,
And I wish you luck, come Lammastide,
    At racing on the green.   20

"Long for me the rick will wait,
    And long will wait the fold,
And long will stand the empty plate,
    And dinner will be cold."

9

On moonlit heath and lonesome bank
    The sheep beside me graze,
And yon the gallows used to clank
    Fast by the four cross ways.

A careless shepherd once would keep   5
    The flocks by moonlight there,
And high amongst the glimmering sheep
    The dead man stood on air.

They hang us now in Shrewsbury jail;
    The whistles blow forlorn,   10
And trains all night groan on the rail
    To men that die at morn.

There sleeps in Shrewsbury jail tonight,
    Or wakes, as may betide,
A better lad, if things went right,   15
    Than most that sleep outside.

And naked to the hangman's noose
    The morning clocks will ring
A neck God made for other use
    Than strangling in a string.   20

And sharp the link of life will snap,
    And dead on air will stand
Heels that held up as straight a chap
    As treads upon the land.

So here I'll watch the night and wait   25
    To see the morning shine,
When he will hear the stroke of eight
    And not the stroke of nine;

    Lyric 8. 19. **Lammastide,** August first. 21. **rick,** a stack of grain, straw, or hay.
    Lyric 9. Compare Wilde's *The Ballad of Reading Gaol.* 9. **Shrewsbury,** the county seat of Shropshire; in its jail criminals sentenced to death were executed.

And wish my friend as sound a sleep
    As lads' I did not know,   30
That shepherded the moonlit sheep
    A hundred years ago.

13

When I was one-and-twenty
    I heard a wise man say,
"Give crowns and pounds and guineas,
    But not your heart, away;
Give pearls away and rubies,   5
    But keep your fancy free."
But I was one-and-twenty—
    No use to talk to me.

When I was one-and-twenty
    I heard him say again,   10
"The heart out of the bosom
    Was never given in vain;
'Tis paid with sighs a plenty
    And sold for endless rue."
And I am two-and-twenty,   15
    And oh, 'tis true, 'tis true.

18

Oh, when I was in love with you,
    Then I was clean and brave,
And miles around the wonder grew
    How well did I behave.

And now the fancy passes by,   5
    And nothing will remain,
And miles around they'll say that I
    Am quite myself again.

19. TO AN ATHLETE DYING YOUNG

The time you won your town the race
We chaired you through the market-place;
Man and boy stood cheering by,
And home we brought you shoulder-high.

Today, the road all runners come,   5
Shoulder-high we bring you home,
And set you at your threshold down,
Townsman of a stiller town.

    Lyric 13. 3. **crowns . . . guineas.** A crown is worth about $1.25, the other coins about $5.

Smart lad, to slip betimes away
From fields where glory does not stay   10
And early though the laurel grows
It withers quicker than the rose.

Eyes the shady night has shut
Cannot see the record cut,
And silence sounds no worse than cheers   15
After earth has stopped the ears.

Now you will not swell the rout
Of lads that wore their honors out,
Runners whom renown outran
And the name died before the man.   20

So set, before its echoes fade,
The fleet foot on the sill of shade,
And hold to the low lintel up
The still-defended challenge-cup.

And round that early-laureled head   25
Will flock to gaze the strengthless dead,
And find unwithered on its curls
The garland briefer than a girl's.

21. BREDON HILL

In summertime on Bredon
  The bells they sound so clear;
Round both the shires they ring them
  In steeples far and near,
  A happy noise to hear.   5

Here of a Sunday morning
  My love and I would lie,
And see the colored counties,
  And hear the larks so high
  About us in the sky.   10

The bells would ring to call her
  In valleys miles away:
"Come all to church, good people;
  Good people, come and pray."
  But here my love would stay.   15

And I would turn and answer
  Among the springing thyme,

Lyric 19. **11. laurel,** a tree or branch used as a symbol of triumph.
Lyric 21. **Bredon Hill,** a rounded elevation (960 ft. high), near the border between Worcestershire and Gloucestershire. **8. counties.** From Bredon Hill may be seen the variegated landscape of five shires—Worcester, Gloucester, Hereford, Warwick, and Oxford. **17. thyme,** a mint plant.

"Oh, peal upon our wedding,
  And we will hear the chime,
  And come to church in time."   20

But when the snows at Christmas
  On Bredon top were strown,
My love rose up so early
  And stole out unbeknown
  And went to church alone.   25

They tolled the one bell only,
  Groom there was none to see,
The mourners followed after,
  And so to church went she,
  And would not wait for me.   30

The bells they sound on Bredon,
  And still the steeples hum,
"Come to church, good people"—
  Oh, noisy bells, be dumb;
  I hear you; I will come.   35

26

Along the field as we came by
A year ago, my love and I,
The aspen over stile and stone
Was talking to itself alone.
"Oh, who are these that kiss and pass?   5
A country lover and his lass;
Two lovers looking to be wed;
And time shall put them both to bed,
But she shall lie with earth above,
And he beside another love."   10

And sure enough beneath the tree
There walks another love with me,
And overhead the aspen heaves
Its rainy-sounding silver leaves;
And I spell nothing in their stir,   15
But now perhaps they speak to her,
And plain for her to understand
They talk about a time at hand
When I shall sleep with clover clad,
And she beside another lad.   20

27

"Is my team plowing,
  That I was used to drive
And hear the harness jingle
  When I was man alive?"

Aye, the horses trample,
   The harness jingles now;
No change though you lie under
   The land you used to plow.

"Is football playing
   Along the river shore,
With lads to chase the leather,
   Now I stand up no more?"

Aye, the ball is flying,
   The lads play heart and soul;
The goal stands up, the keeper
   Stands up to keep the goal.

"Is my girl happy,
   That I thought hard to leave,
And has she tired of weeping
   As she lies down at eve?"

Aye, she lies down lightly,
   She lies not down to weep;
Your girl is well contented.
   Be still, my lad, and sleep.

"Is my friend hearty,
   Now I am thin and pine,
And has he found to sleep in
   A better bed than mine?"

Yes, lad, I lie easy,
   I lie as lads would choose;
I cheer a dead man's sweetheart—
   Never ask me whose.

40

Into my heart an air that kills
   From yon far country blows;
What are those blue remembered hills,
   What spires, what farms are those?

That is the land of lost content,
   I see it shining plain,
The happy highways where I went
   And cannot come again.

44

Shot? so quick, so clean an ending?
   Oh, that was right, lad, that was brave.
Yours was not an ill for mending;
   'Twas best to take it to the grave.

Oh, you had forethought, you could reason,
   And saw your road and where it led,
And early wise and brave in season
   Put the pistol to your head.

Oh, soon, and better so than later
   After long disgrace and scorn,
You shot dead the household traitor,
   The soul that should not have been born.

Right you guessed the rising morrow
   And scorned to tread the mire you must;
Dust's your wages, son of sorrow,
   But men may come to worse than dust.

Souls undone, undoing others—
   Long time since the tale began.
You would not live to wrong your brothers;
   Oh, lad, you died as fits a man.

Now to your grave shall friend and stranger
   With ruth and some with envy come;
Undishonored, clear of danger,
   Clean of guilt, pass hence and home.

Turn safe to rest, no dreams, no waking;
   And here, man, here's the wreath I've made.
'Tis not a gift that's worth the taking,
   But wear it, and it will not fade.

45

If it chance your eye offend you,
   Pluck it out, lad, and be sound;
'Twill hurt, but here are salves to friend you,
   And many a balsam grows on ground.

And if your hand or foot offend you,
   Cut it off, lad, and be whole;
But play the man, stand up and end you,
   When your sickness is your soul.

48

Be still, my soul, be still; the arms you bear
   are brittle,
   Earth and high heaven are fixed of old and
   founded strong.

Lyric 45. 1. **eye . . . sound.** From *Mark*, 9:47: "And if thine eye offend thee, pluck it out: it is better for thee to enter into the kingdom of God with one eye, than having two eyes, to be cast into hell fire." 5. **hand . . . off.** From *Mark*, 9:43-45: "And if thy hand offend thee, cut it off . . . And if thy foot offend thee cut it off . . ."

Think rather—call to thought, if now you
    grieve a little,
  The days when we had rest, O soul, for they
    were long.

Men loved unkindness then, but lightless in
    the quarry   5
  I slept and saw not; tears fell down, I did
    not mourn;
Sweat ran and blood sprang out and I was
    never sorry.
  Then it was well with me, in days ere I was
    born.

Now, and I muse for why and never find the
    reason,
  I pace the earth, and drink the air, and feel
    the sun.   10
Be still, be still, my soul; it is but for a season;
  Let us endure an hour and see injustice done.

Aye, look—high heaven and earth ail from
    the prime foundation;
  All thoughts to rive the heart are here, and
    all are vain:
Horror and scorn and hate and fear and
    indignation—   15
  Oh, why did I awake? when shall I sleep
    again?

49

Think no more, lad; laugh, be jolly.
  Why should men make haste to die?
Empty heads and tongues a-talking
Make the rough road easy walking,
And the feather pate of folly   5
  Bears the falling sky.

Oh, 'tis jesting, dancing, drinking
  Spins the heavy world around.
If young hearts were not so clever,
Oh, they would be young forever.   10
Think no more; 'tis only thinking
  Lays lads underground.

54

With rue my heart is laden
  For golden friends I had,
For many a rose-lipped maiden
  And many a lightfoot lad.

By brooks too broad for leaping   5
  The lightfoot boys are laid;
The rose-lipped girls are sleeping
  In fields where roses fade.

63

I hoed and trenched and weeded,
  And took the flowers to fair.
I brought them home unheeded;
  The hue was not the wear.

So up and down I sow them   5
  For lads like me to find,
When I shall lie below them,
  A dead man out of mind.

Some seed the birds devour,
  And some the season mars,   10
But here and there will flower
  The solitary stars,

And fields will yearly bear them
  As light-leaved spring comes on,
And luckless lads will wear them   15
  When I am dead and gone.   (1896)

from Last Poems

Although these poems were not published
until 1922, Housman said that most of them
were written between 1895 and 1910.

2

As I gird on for fighting
  My sword upon my thigh,
I think on old ill fortunes
  Of better men than I.

Think I, the round world over,   5
  What golden lads are low
With hurts not mine to mourn for
  And shames I shall not know.

What evil luck soever
  For me remains in store,   10
'Tis sure much finer fellows
  Have fared much worse before.

So here are things to think on
  That ought to make me brave,

Poems 2, 7, 10, 11, and 32 from *Last Poems* (1922) by
A. E. Housman are reprinted with the permission of Henry
Holt and Company, Inc.

As I strap on for fighting
  My sword that will not save.

7

In valleys green and still
  Where lovers wander maying,
They hear from over hill
  A music playing.

Behind the drum and fife,
  Past hawthornwood and hollow,
Through earth and out of life
  The soldiers follow.

The soldier's is the trade:
  In any wind or weather
He steals the heart of maid
  And man together.

The lover and his lass
  Beneath the hawthorn lying
Have heard the soldiers pass,
  And both are sighing.

And down the distance they
  With dying note and swelling
Walk the resounding way
  To the still dwelling.

10

Could man be drunk forever
  With liquor, love, or fights,
Lief should I rouse at morning
  And lief lie down of nights.

But men at whiles are sober
  And think by fits and starts,
And if they think, they fasten
  Their hands upon their hearts.

11

Yonder see the morning blink:
  The sun is up, and up must I,
To wash and dress and eat and drink
  And look at things and talk and think
And work, and God knows why.

Oh often have I washed and dressed
  And what's to show for all my pain?
Let me lie abed and rest:
Ten thousand times I've done my best
  And all's to do again.   *(1895)*

32

When I would muse in boyhood
  The wild green woods among,
And nurse resolves and fancies
  Because the world was young,
It was not foes to conquer,
  Nor sweethearts to be kind,
But it was friends to die for
  That I would seek and find.

I sought them far and found them,
  The sure, the straight, the brave,
The hearts I lost my own to,
  The souls I could not save.
They braced their belts about them,
  They crossed in ships the sea,
They sought and found six feet of ground.
  And there they died for me.   *(1922)*

from *More Poems*

The poems that make up this volume were published in 1936 from a manuscript left by Housman to his brother Laurence.

They say my verse is sad: no wonder;
  Its narrow measure spans
Tears of eternity, and sorrow,
  Not mine, but man's.

This is for all ill-treated fellows
  Unborn and unbegot,
For them to read when they're in trouble
  And I am not.

7

Stars, I have seen them fall,
  But when they drop and die
No star is lost at all
  From all the star-sown sky.
The toil of all that be
  Helps not the primal fault;
It rains into the sea
  And still the sea is salt.

"They say my verse is sad, etc.," and poems 7, 8, 9, 15, 22, 27, 37, and 38 from *More Poems* (Alfred A. Knopf, Inc., 1936) by A. E. Housman are reprinted with the permission of the Estate of A. E. Housman.
Stars, I have seen them fall. 6. **primal fault,** Adam's sin of disobedience in eating of the tree of the knowledge of good and evil, as a result of which Adam's descendants were compelled to toil for a living.

8

Give me a land of boughs in leaf,
    A land of trees that stand.
Where trees are fallen, there is grief;
    I love no leafless land.

Alas, the country whence I fare,
    It is where I would stay,
And where I would not, it is there
    That I shall be for aye.

And one remembers and forgets
    But 'tis not found again,
Not though they hale in crimsoned nets
    The sunset from the main.

9

When green buds hang in the elm like dust
    And sprinkle the lime like rain,
Forth I wander, forth I must,
    And drink of life again.

Forth I must by hedgerow bowers
    To look at the leaves uncurled,
And stand in fields where cuckoo flowers
    Are lying about the world.

15

Tarry, delight, so seldom met,
    So sure to perish, tarry still;
Forbear to cease or languish yet,
    Though soon you must and will.

By Sestos town, in Hero's tower,
    On Hero's heart Leander lies;
The signal torch has burned its hour
    And sputters as it dies.

Beneath him, in the nighted firth,
    Between two continents complain
The seas he swam from earth to earth
    And he must swim again.

22

Ho, everyone that thirsteth
    And hath the price to give,
Come to the stolen waters;
    Drink and your soul shall live.

Come to the stolen waters
    And leap the guarded pale,
And pull the flower in season
    Before desire shall fail.

It shall not last forever,
    No more than earth and skies;
But he that drinks in season
    Shall live before he dies.

June suns, you cannot store them
    To warm the winter's cold;
The lad that hopes for heaven
    Shall fill his mouth with mold.

27

To stand up straight and tread the turning mill,
To lie flat and know nothing and be still,
    Are the two trades of man; and which is worse
I know not, but I know that both are ill.

37

I did not lose my heart in summer's even
    When roses to the moonrise burst apart:
When plumes were under heel and lead was flying,
    In blood and smoke and flame I lost my heart.

I lost it to a soldier and a foeman,
    A chap that did not kill me, but he tried;
That took the saber straight and took it striking,
    And laughed and kissed his hand to me and died.

38

By shores and woods and steeples
    Rejoicing hearts receive
Poured on a hundred peoples
    The far-shed alms of eve.

Tarry, delight, so seldom met. 5. **Sestos . . . tower.** Hero was a priestess of Aphrodite (goddess of love) at Sestos, a town on the European side of the Hellespont; she was beloved by Leander, who swam nightly across the Hellespont from Abydos, Asia Minor, to meet her. During a storm Leander was drowned, and Hero in grief threw herself into the sea.

Ho, everyone that thirsteth. Cf. *Isaiah*, 55:1: "Ho, everyone that thirsteth, come ye to the waters, and he that hath no money; come ye, buy, and eat; yea, come, buy wine and milk without money and without price." Cf. also *Proverbs*, 9:17: "Stolen waters are sweet, and bread eaten in secret is pleasant." 6. **pale**, inclosure, barrier.

Her hands are filled with slumber
　For world-wide laborers worn;
Yet those are more in number
　That know her not from morn.

5 Now who sees night forever,
　He sees no happier sight:
Night and no moon and never
　A star upon the night.

(1936)

Thomas Hardy
1840-1928

Thomas Hardy was born in 1840 in Dorsetshire, the southern county that forms the principal background of his poetry and fiction. His father was a building constructor, and after attending the Dorchester schools, the boy was apprenticed at sixteen to John Hicks, a local architect and rebuilder of churches. Some of his spare time he put in at Latin and Greek; and he made the acquaintance of William Barnes, the Dorsetshire poet. Hardy, as Professor Carl Weber has pointed out to the editors, actively pursued the architect's profession as a junior assistant in the office of Mr. (later Sir) Arthur Blomfield in London, and became sufficiently skilled in the craft to win two prizes. He kept up a contact with art and literature by visiting galleries and museums, going to the theater, and writing much poetry. He also began his novel writing, and *Desperate Remedies* appeared in 1871, the first of a series that put Hardy in the front rank as a novelist. From the appearance of this novel until, nearly thirty years later, he could afford to be indifferent to financial returns from his writing, he published no poetry; then he again released verses.

Hardy divided his novels into three groups based upon their type and technique:

I. Novels of character and environment—*Under the Greenwood Tree* (1872); *Far from the Madding Crowd* (1874); *The Return of the Native* (1878); *The Mayor of Casterbridge* (1886); *The Woodlanders* (1887); *Tess of the D'Urbervilles* (1891); *Jude the Obscure* (1896).

II. Romances and fantasies—*A Pair of Blue Eyes* (1873); *The Trumpet-Major* (1880); *Two on a Tower* (1882); *The Well Beloved* (1897).

III. Novels of ingenuity (with emphasis on plot)—*Desperate Remedies* (1871); *The Hand of Ethelberta* (1876); *A Laodicean* (1882).

Hardy's novels of character and environment present the losing struggle of individuals against the pressures of nature and collective humanity which gradually strangle them to death. To Hardy chance was as malignant a force as the malevolent Nemesis of Greek drama, and his representation of its impersonal bludgeoning of its victims arouses in the reader much of the classical emotions of pity and fear. In many of the episodes of his novels there lurk melodramatic tendencies; but Hardy is essentially emotionless in the handling of his characters, and his sympathy with those who are in the fell clutch of circumstance he implies rather than expresses.

Hardy was a poet before he was a novelist, and only the impossibility of getting his early poems published forced him in 1870 into the field of prose fiction. He returned to poetry as soon as it was financially possible to do so. In 1898, while living in a house of his own designing in Dorsetshire, he published *Wessex Poems and Other Verses*, and in 1902 appeared *Poems of the Past and the Present*. The next year the first part of a gigantic poetical enterprise, *The Dynasts*, was published, and this vast epic-drama of the Napoleonic Wars continued to occupy his attention for five years, the second section appearing in 1906 and the third and last in 1908. *Time's Laughingstocks and Other Verses* was issued in 1909, and *Satires of Circumstance*, containing some of the most pungent of his poetry, in 1914. In 1923 his venture into drama—*The Queen of Cornwall*—was produced.

Hardy's poems have the same philosophy and tone as his novels and stories. They are exceedingly plain in style, stripped naked of the overdress of no small part of the Victorian lyrics. They have as a result a certain bleak, almost angular, quality. They have, too, an intense concentration and economy of expression. Many of them are barbed with satire. They reveal Hardy very adequately as a post-Victorian author who was a realist in technique and a pessimist in ideas, but who declared that his practical philosophy was distinctly meliorist in that he believed that the world was not hopelessly bad but could become better. His function in literature, he thought, was to bring about this change by assault on "man's inhumanity to man" and by dealing blows at the "robustious swaggering of optimism," which is "at bottom cowardly and insincere."

A Beauty's Soliloquy During Her Honeymoon

Too late, too late! I did not know my fairness
  Would catch the world's keen eyes so!
How the men look at me! My radiant rareness
  I deemed not they would prize so!

That I was a peach for any man's possession 5
  Why did not some one say
Before I leased myself in an hour's obsession
  To this dull mate for aye!

His days are mine. I am one who cannot steal her
  Ahead of his plodding pace— 10
As he is, so am I. One doomed to feel her
  A wasted form and face!

I was so blind! It did sometimes just strike me
  All girls were not as I,
But, dwelling much alone, how few were like me 15
  I could not well descry;

Till, at this Grand Hotel, all looks bend on me
  In homage as I pass
To take my seat at breakfast, dinner—con me
  As poorly spoused, alas! 20

I was too young. I dwelt too much on duty;
  If I had guessed my powers
Where might have sailed this cargo of choice beauty
  In its unanchored hours!

Well, husband, poor plain man; I've lost life's battle!— 25
  Come—let them look at me.
O damn, don't show in your looks that I'm your chattel
  Quite so emphatically! (*1892; 1922*)

Drummer Hodge

The background of this poem is the Boer War, waged in South Africa in 1899-1902 between the British and the Dutch settlers.

They throw in Drummer Hodge, to rest
  Uncoffined—just as found:
His landmark is a kopje-crest
  That breaks the veldt around;
And foreign constellations west 5
  Each night above his mound.

Young Hodge the Drummer never knew—
  Fresh from his Wessex home—
The meaning of the broad Karoo,
  The Bush, the dusty loam, 10
And why uprose to nightly view
  Strange stars amid the gloam.

Yet portion of that unknown plain
  Will Hodge forever be;
His homely Northern breast and brain 15
  Grow to some Southern tree,
And strange-eyed constellations reign
  His stars eternally. (*1899*)

The Darkling Thrush

I leant upon a coppice gate
  When Frost was specter-gray,

The poems of Thomas Hardy are reprinted from his *Collected Poems* (1928) by permission of The Macmillan Company, New York, Publishers.
  A Beauty's Soliloquy . . . Honeymoon. This monologue should be compared with Hardy's *Satires of Circumstance,* IV.

Drummer Hodge. 3. **kopje-crest,** the top of a small hill. 4. **veldt,** pronounced *felt,* a tract of grassland; cf. *field.* 9. **Karoo,** a dry, elevated region in Cape Colony. 10. **Bush,** vast area of scrub-covered country.
The Darkling Thrush. 1. **coppice gate,** gate leading to the thicket.

And Winter's dregs made desolate
  The weakening eye of day.
The tangled bine-stems scored the sky   5
  Like strings of broken lyres,
And all mankind that haunted nigh
  Had sought their household fires.

The land's sharp features seemed to be
  The Century's corpse outleant,   10
His crypt the cloudy canopy,
  The wind his death-lament.
The ancient pulse of germ and birth
  Was shrunken hard and dry,
And every spirit upon earth   15
  Seemed fervorless as I.

At once a voice arose among
  The bleak twigs overhead
In a full-hearted evensong
  Of joy illimited;   20
An aged thrush, frail, gaunt, and small,
  In blast-beruffled plume,
Had chosen thus to fling his soul
  Upon the growing gloom.

So little cause for carolings   25
  Of such ecstatic sound
Was written on terrestrial things
  Afar or nigh around,
That I could think there trembled through
  His happy good-night air   30
Some blessed Hope, whereof he knew
  And I was unaware.   (*1900;* 1900)

Autumn in King's Hintock Park

King's Hintock is a name invented by Hardy for Melbury Sampford, north of Dorchester in the county of Dorset.

  Here by the baring bough
    Raking up leaves,
  Often I ponder how
    Springtime deceives—
  I, an old woman now,   5
    Raking up leaves.

5. **bine,** a kind of climbing plant. 10. **Century's corpse,** the dead body of the nineteenth century; the poem was written in 1900.

  Here in the avenue
    Raking up leaves,
  Lords' ladies pass in view,
    Until one heaves   10
  Sighs at life's russet hue,
    Raking up leaves!

  Just as my shape you see
    Raking up leaves,
  I saw, when fresh and free,   15
    Those memory weaves
  Into gray ghosts by me,
    Raking up leaves.

  Yet, Dear, though one may sigh,
    Raking up leaves,   20
  New leaves will dance on high—
    Earth never grieves!—
  Will not, when missed am I
    Raking up leaves.   (*1901;* 1909)

God-Forgotten

I towered far, and lo! I stood within
  The presence of the Lord Most High,
Sent thither by the sons of Earth, to win
  Some answer to their cry.

—"The Earth, sayest thou? The Human
    race?   5
By Me created? Sad its lot?
Nay: I have no remembrance of such place:
  Such world I fashioned not."—

—"O Lord, forgive me when I say
Thou spakest the word and made it all."— 10
"The Earth of men—let me bethink me . . .
    Yea!
  I dimly do recall

"Some tiny sphere I built long back
(Mid millions of such shapes of mine)
So named . . . It perished, surely—not a
    wrack   15
  Remaining, or a sign?

"It lost my interest from the first,
My aims therefore succeeding ill;
Haply it died of doing as it durst?"—
  "Lord, it existeth still."—   20

"Dark, then, its life! For not a cry
Of aught it bears do I now hear;
Of its own act the threads were snapt whereby
    Its plaints had reached mine ear.

"It used to ask for gifts of good,   25
Till came its severance, self-entailed,
When sudden silence on that side ensued,
    And has till now prevailed.

"All other orbs have kept in touch;
Their voicings reach me speedily: 30
Thy people took upon them overmuch
    In sundering them from me!

"And it is strange—though sad enough—
Earth's race should think that one whose call
Frames, daily, shining spheres of flawless stuff   35
    Must heed their tainted ball! . . .

"But sayest it is by pangs distraught,
And strife, and silent suffering?—
Sore grieved am I that injury should be wrought
    Even on so poor a thing!   40

"Thou shouldst have learnt that *Not to Mend*
For Me could mean but *Not to Know:*
Hence, Messengers! and straightway put an end
    To what men undergo." . . .

Homing at dawn, I thought to see   45
One of the Messengers standing by.
—Oh, childish thought! . . . Yet often it comes to me
    When trouble hovers nigh.   (1902)

The To-Be-Forgotten

I heard a small sad sound,
And stood awhile among the tombs around.
"Wherefore, old friends," said I, "are you distrest,
    Now, screened from life's unrest?"

—"Oh, not at being here;   5
But that our future second death is near;
When, with the living, memory of us numbs,
    And blank oblivion comes!

"These, our sped ancestry,
Lie here embraced by deeper death than we;   10
Nor shape nor thought of theirs can you descry
    With keenest backward eye.

"They count as quite forgot;
They are as men who have existed not;
Theirs is a loss past loss of fitful breath;   15
    It is the second death.

"We here, as yet, each day
Are blest with dear recall; as yet, can say
We hold in some soul loved continuance
    Of shape and voice and glance.   20

"But what has been will be—
First memory, then oblivion's swallowing sea;
Like men foregone, shall we merge into those
    Whose story no one knows.

"For which of us could hope   25
To show in life that world-awakening scope
Granted the few whose memory none lets die,
    But all men magnify?

"We were but Fortune's sport;
Things true, things lovely, things of good report   30
We neither shunned nor sought . . . We see our bourne,
    And seeing it we mourn."   (1902)

---

45. **Homing . . . thought.** In this stanza, and, indeed, in the entire poem, the audacity of Hardy's irony is fully apparent; there is in man's dialogue with the Almighty a bleak hopelessness that would have shocked some of the earlier religious poets.

30. **Things . . . sought.** Cf. *Philippians*, 4:8: "Finally, brethren, whatsoever things are true, whatsoever things are honest, whatsoever things are just, whatsoever things are pure, whatsoever things are lovely, whatsoever things are of good report; if there be any virtue, and if there be any praise, think on these things."

At Casterbridge Fair

Casterbridge is Dorchester, chief city of the county of Dorset, in southern England. It was the scene of a weekly fair, or market, where gathered farmers who had produce to sell, ballad-singers who furnished entertainment, and people who came to make purchases or to amuse themselves.

1. THE BALLAD-SINGER

Sing, Ballad-singer, raise a hearty tune;
Make me forget that there was ever a one
I walked with in the meek light of the moon
    When the day's work was done.

Rime, Ballad-rimer, start a country song;   5
Make me forget that she whom I loved well
Swore she would love me dearly, love me long,
    Then—what I cannot tell!

Sing, Ballad-singer, from your little book;
Make me forget those heart-breaks, achings,
    fears;   10
Make me forget her name, her sweet sweet
    look—
Make me forget her tears.

2. FORMER BEAUTIES

These market-dames, mid-aged, with lips
    thin-drawn,
    And tissues sere,
Are they the ones we loved in years agone,
    And courted here?

Are these the muslined pink young things to
    whom   5
    We vowed and swore
In nooks on summer Sundays by the Froom,
    Or Budmouth shore?

Do they remember those gay tunes we trod
    Clasped on the green;   10
Aye; trod till moonlight set on the beaten sod
    A satin sheen?

They must forget, forget! They cannot know
    What once they were,
Or memory would transfigure them, and show
    Them always fair.   16

3. AFTER THE CLUB-DANCE

The Dorset Farmers' Club always holds a dance on the evenings of market-days.

Black'on frowns east on Maidon,
    And westward to the sea,
But on neither is his frown laden
    With scorn, as his frown on me!

At dawn my heart grew heavy,   5
    I could not sip the wine,
I left the jocund bevy
    And that young man o' mine.

The roadside elms pass by me—
    Why do I sink with shame   10
When the birds a-perch there eye me?
    They, too, have done the same!

4. THE MARKET-GIRL

Nobody took any notice of her as she stood
    on the causey curb,
All eager to sell her honey and apples and
    bunches of garden herb;
And if she had offered to give her wares and
    herself with them too that day,
I doubt if a soul would have cared to take a
    bargain so choice away.
But chancing to trace her sunburnt grace that
    morning as I passed nigh,   5
I went and I said, "Poor maidy dear!—and
    will none of the people buy?"
And so it began; and soon we knew what the
    end of it all must be,
And I found that though no others had bid,
    a prize had been won by me.

5. THE INQUIRY

And are ye one of Hermitage—
Of Hermitage, by Ivel Road,
And do ye know, in Hermitage

Former Beauties. 7. **Froom,** a river that flows through Dorchester. 8. **Budmouth,** Weymouth, a seaport and popular summer resort on the coast of Dorset. This is the chief part of the region that Hardy designates as Wessex in his novels. Anglo-Saxon Wessex (sixth century), the kingdom of the West Saxons, included what is now Dorset and the surrounding counties.

After the Club-Dance. 1. **Black'on,** Blackdown Hill, a high elevation near Dorchester. **Maidon,** Maiden Castle, on a neighboring hill, an ancient Celtic fort.
    The Market-Girl. 1. **causey,** the causeway, or bridge, across the river in Dorchester.
    The Inquiry. 1. **Hermitage,** a village near Dorchester on the road to Yeovil (Ivel).

A thatch-roofed house where sengreens grow?
And does John Waywood live there still— 5
He of the name that there abode
When father hurdled on the hill
    Some fifteen years ago?

Does he now speak o' Patty Beech,
The Patty Beech he used to—see, 10
Or ask at all if Patty Beech
Is known or heard of out this way?
—Ask if ever she's living yet,
And where her present home may be,
And how she bears life's fag and fret 15
    After so long a day?

In years agone at Hermitage
This faded face was counted fair,
None fairer; and at Hermitage
We swore to wed when he should thrive. 20
But never a chance had he or I,
And waiting made his wish outwear,
And Time, that dooms man's love to die,
    Preserves a maid's alive.

6. A WIFE WAITS

Will's at the dance in the Club-room below,
    Where the tall liquor-cups foam;
I on the pavement up here by the Bow,
    Wait, wait, to steady him home.

Will and his partner are treading a tune, 5
    Loving companions they be;
Willy, before we were married in June,
    Said he loved no one but me;

Said he would let his old pleasures all go
    Ever to live with his Dear. 10
Will's at the dance in the Club-room below;
    Shivering I wait for him here.

7. AFTER THE FAIR

The singers are gone from the Cornmarket-place
    With their broadsheets of rimes,

The street rings no longer in treble and bass
    With their skits on the times,
And the Cross, lately thronged, is a dim naked
    space 5
    That but echoes the stammering chimes.

From Clock-corner steps, as each quarter ding-dongs,
    Away the folk roam
By the "Hart" and Grey's Bridge into byways
    and "drongs,"
    Or across the ridged loam; 10
The younger ones shrilling the lately heard
    songs,
    The old saying, "Would we were home."

The shy-seeming maiden so mute in the fair
    Now rattles and talks,
And that one who looked the most swaggering there 15
    Grows sad as she walks,
And she who seemed eaten by cankering care
    In statuesque sturdiness stalks.

And midnight clears High Street of all but the
    ghosts
    Of its buried burghees, 20
From the latest far back to those old Roman
    hosts
    Whose remains one yet sees,
Who loved, laughed, and fought, hailed their
    friends, drank their toasts
    At their meeting-times here, just as these!
        (*1902;* 1909)

The Man He Killed

"Had he and I but met
    By some old ancient inn,
We should have sat us down to wet
    Right many a nipperkin!

---

4. **sengreens**, plants that grow on the walls of houses. 7. **hurdled**, made hurdles, i.e., frames used for fences, etc.
    A Wife Waits. 1. **Club-room**, the room used by the Farmers' Club. 3. **Bow**, a rounded corner at the intersection of the main streets of Dorchester.
    After the Fair. 1. **Cornmarket-place**, the central market-place in Dorchester. 2. **broadsheets of rimes**, ballads on current subjects printed on large sheets of paper.

5. **Cross.** A cross or a cross-shaped building is set up where a market is held. 6. **stammering chimes.** "The Chimes' will be listened for in vain here at midnight now, having been abolished some years ago."—Hardy. 7. **Clock-corner**, the corner of the market-place adjoining St. Peter's Church. 9. **"Hart,"** the White Hart, an inn on the London Road near the edge of Dorchester. **Grey's Bridge,** a stone bridge across the river near Dorchester. **"drongs,"** narrow lanes between walls (Dorset dialect). 19. **High Street,** the main street in Dorchester. 20. **burghees,** citizens. 21. **Roman hosts.** During the Roman occupation of Britain, Dorchester, known as Durnovaria, was a walled town; relics of Roman days are preserved in the museum in the city.
    The Man He Killed. 4. **nipperkin,** a half pint of ale.

"But ranged as infantry,
  And staring face to face,
I shot at him as he at me,
  And killed him in his place.

"I shot him dead because—
  Because he was my foe,
Just so—my foe of course he was;
  That's clear enough; although

"He thought he'd 'list, perhaps,
  Off-hand like—just as I—
Was out of work—had sold his traps—
  No other reason why.

"Yes; quaint and curious war is!
  You shoot a fellow down
You'd treat if met where any bar is,
  Or help to half-a-crown."   (1909)

The Curate's Kindness

A WORKHOUSE IRONY

I thought they'd be strangers aroun' me,
  But she's to be there!
Let me jump out o' wagon and go back and drown me
  At Pummery or Ten-Hatches Weir.

I thought: "Well, I've come to the Union—
  The workhouse at last—
After honest hard work all the week, and Communion
  O' Zundays, these fifty years past.

" 'Tis hard; but," I thought, "never mind it—
  There's gain in the end;
And when I get used to the place I shall find it
  A home, and may find there a friend.

"Life there will be better than t'other,
  For peace is assured.

13. 'list, enlist in the army. 20. half-a-crown, an English coin worth about 63 cents.
The Curate's Kindness. 4. Pummery, Poundbury, an ancient Celtic or Roman earthwork on a high elevation near Dorchester; it contains a small pond. Ten-Hatches Weir, a pond held back by a dam in the meadow near Dorchester. 5. Union, a poorhouse supported by a union of several adjoining parishes and directed by a board of several governors.

The men in one wing and their wives in another
  Is strictly the rule of the Board."

Just then one young Pa'son arriving
  Steps up out of breath
To the side o' the wagon wherein we were driving
  To Union; and calls out and saith:

"Old folks, that harsh order is altered,
  Be not sick of heart!
The Guardians they poohed and they pished and they paltered
  When urged not to keep you apart.

" 'It is wrong,' I maintained, 'to divide them,
  Near forty years wed.'
'Very well, sir. We promise, then, they shall abide them
  In one wing together,' they said."

Then I sank—knew 'twas quite a foredone thing
  That misery should be
To the end! . . . To get freed of her there was the one thing
  Had made the change welcome to me.

To go there was ending but badly;
  'Twas shame and 'twas pain;
"But anyhow," thought I, "thereby I shall gladly
  Get free of this forty years' chain."

I thought they'd be strangers aroun' me,
  But she's to be there!
Let me jump out o' wagon and go back and drown me
  At Pummery or Ten-Hatches Weir.   (1909)

from *Satires of Circumstance*

1. AT TEA

The kettle descants in a cozy drone,
  And the young wife looks in her husband's face,
And then at her guest's, and shows in her own

1. descants, sings.

Her sense that she fills an envied place;
And the visiting lady is all abloom, 5
And says there was never so sweet a room.

And the happy young housewife does not
    know
That the woman beside her was first his
    choice,
Till the fates ordained it could not be so . . .
Betraying nothing in look or voice 10
The guest sits smiling and sips her tea,
And he throws her a stray glance yearningly.

3. BY HER AUNT'S GRAVE

"Sixpence a week," says the girl to her lover,
"Aunt used to bring me, for she could confide
In me alone, she vowed. 'Twas to cover
The cost of her headstone when she died.
And that was a year ago last June; 5
I've not yet fixed it. But I must soon."

"And where is the money now, my dear?"
"Oh, snug in my purse . . . Aunt was so slow
In saving it—eighty weeks, or near." . . .
"Let's spend it," he hints. "For she won't
    know. 10
There's a dance tonight at the Load of Hay."
She passively nods. And they go that way.

9. AT THE ALTAR-RAIL

"My bride is not coming, alas!" says the
    groom,
And the telegram shakes in his hand. "I own
It was hurried! We met at a dancing-room
When I went to the Cattle-Show alone,
And then, next night, where the Fountain
    leaps, 5
And the Street of the Quarter-Circle sweeps.

"Aye, she won me to ask her to be my wife—
'Twas foolish perhaps!—to forsake the ways
Of the flaring town for a farmer's life.
She agreed. And we fixed it. Now she says:
'It's sweet of you, dear, to prepare me a nest, 11
But a swift, short, gay life suits me best.

By Her Aunt's Grave. 11. **Load of Hay**, a noted inn on Hampstead Road, London.
At the Altar-Rail. 4. **Cattle-Show**, a show held annually in Islington, London. 5. **Fountain**, the Eros fountain in Piccadilly Circus. 6. **Quarter-Circle**, a curved portion of Regent Street.

*What I really am you have never gleaned;
I had eaten the apple ere you were weaned.'"*
(1911)

"Ah, Are You Digging on My Grave?"

"Ah, are you digging on my grave
    My loved one?—planting rue?"
—"No; yesterday he went to wed
One of the brightest wealth has bred.
'It cannot hurt her now,' he said, 5
    'That I should not be true.'"

"Then who is digging on my grave?
    My nearest dearest kin?"
—"Ah, no; they sit and think, 'What use!
What good will planting flowers produce? 10
No tendance of her mound can loose
    Her spirit from Death's gin.'"

"But some one digs upon my grave?
    My enemy?—prodding sly?"
—"Nay; when she heard you had passed the
    Gate 15
That shuts on all flesh soon or late,
She thought you no more worth her hate,
    And cares not where you lie."

"Then, who is digging on my grave?
    Say—since I have not guessed!" 20
—"O it is I, my mistress dear,
Your little dog, who still lives near,
And much I hope my movements here
    Have not disturbed your rest?"

"Ah, yes! *You* dig upon my grave . . . 25
    Why flashed it not on me
That one true heart was left behind!
What feeling do we ever find
To equal among human kind
    A dog's fidelity!" 30

"Mistress, I dug upon your grave
    To bury a bone, in case
I should be hungry near this spot
When passing on my daily trot.

2. **rue**, an herb with bitter leaves; the symbol of sorrow.
12. **gin**, trap.

I am sorry, but I quite forgot   35
  It was your resting-place."   (1914)

In Time of "The Breaking of Nations"

Only a man harrowing clods
  In a slow silent walk,
With an old horse that stumbles and nods
  Half asleep as they stalk.

Only thin smoke without flame   5
  From the heaps of couch grass:
Yet this will go onward the same
  Though Dynasties pass.

Yonder a maid and her wight
  Come whispering by;   10
War's annals will fade into night
  Ere their story die.   (*1915;* 1915)

The Oxen

This poem crystallizes the wide-spread folk-belief that cattle fall on their knees at midnight of Christmas Eve, in the same way that the ox did in the stable of Bethlehem when Christ was born.

Christmas Eve, and twelve of the clock.
  "Now they are all on their knees,"
An elder said as we sat in a flock
  By the embers in hearthside ease.

We pictured the meek mild creatures where   5
  They dwelt in their strawy pen,
Nor did it occur to one of us there
  To doubt they were kneeling then.

So fair a fancy few would weave
  In these years! Yet, I feel,   10
If someone said on Christmas Eve,
  "Come; see the oxen kneel,

"In the lonely barton by yonder coomb
  Our childhood used to know,"
I should go with him in the gloom,   15
  Hoping it might be so.   (*1915;* 1917)

For Life I Had Never Cared Greatly

For Life I had never cared greatly,
  As worth a man's while;
Peradventures unsought,
Peradventures that finished in nought,
Had kept me from youth and through manhood till lately   5
  Unwon by its style.

In earliest years—why I know not—
  I viewed it askance;
Conditions of doubt,
Conditions that leaked slowly out,   10
May haply have bent me to stand and to show not
  Much zest for its dance.

With symphonies soft and sweet color
  It courted me then,
Till evasions seemed wrong,   15
Till evasions gave in to its song,
And I warmed, until living aloofly loomed duller
  Than life among men.

Anew I found nought to set eyes on,
  When, lifting its hand,   20
It uncloaked a star,
Uncloaked it from fog-damps afar,
And showed its beams burning from pole to horizon
  As bright as a brand.

And so, the rough highway forgetting,   25
  I pace hill and dale
Regarding the sky,
Regarding the vision on high,
And thus re-illumed have no humor for letting
  My pilgrimage fail.   (1917)

In Time of "The Breaking of Nations." Cf. *Jeremiah,* 51:20: "Thou art my battle ax and weapons of war: for with thee will I break in pieces the nations; and with thee will I destroy kingdoms." 6. **couch grass,** a kind of grass with long creeping root-stocks.

The Oxen. 13. **barton,** farmyard. **coomb,** a valley between steep hills.

John Masefield
1878-

John Masefield was a Herefordshire lad who at fourteen slipped into a ship to see the world, and for the next few years saw much of it, leading a vagabond life by sea and land and gathering a rich fund of knowledge and experience. The beginning of the century found him in America, acting as bartender's assistant in New York, working in a carpet factory in Yonkers, and doing other unpoetic jobs. He had already written some poetry (his *Saltwater Ballads* were published in 1902), and an enthusiastic reading of Chaucer increased his determination to be a poet. He had, he asserted later, an enthusiasm also for "Keats, then Milton, then Shelley." In 1903 he was a free-lance writer, scratching out an uncertain living with his pen and reading widely. With his *Ballads* (1903) and his volume of short stories called *A Mainsail Haul* (1905) his career as a writer was fairly launched. His first, and best-known play, *The Tragedy of Nan*, was published in 1909; *Multitude and Solitude*, a novel, appeared in the same year; and a collection of *Poems and Ballads* came out the year following.

Chaucer continued to influence him, and this influence probably accounted for his undertaking a series of long narrative poems. The first of these, *The Everlasting Mercy*, vivid, realistic, but serious and noble in tone, was published in 1911, and similar long poems appeared in rapid succession, *The Widow in the Bye Street* and *Dauber* in 1912, and *The Daffodil Fields* in 1913. It had been generally supposed that the vogue of the extended narrative poem was over, but Masefield proved that such long verse narratives, when essentially realistic and natural rather than romantic and imaginative, still have a legitimate place in literature. Masefield's record would not be complete without allusion to his *Reynard the Fox* (1919) and to his appointment as Poet Laureate in 1930.

One of the chief elements in Masefield's verse is his love of the sea. But this is not the only element in his poetry. His fondness for English landscape, and particularly for that of his native Herefordshire, is also marked. In his love for England he is not insular like Tennyson, or arrogant like Kipling. He has shown that he can be romantic on occasion, but most of his work is characterized by a vivid realism. And, finally, his poems have a suggestion of reserve power, as though they reflect his own quiet strength. The emotion in his poetry is never strained or convulsive, but it is sincere, deep, and profoundly affecting.

A Consecration

Not of the princes and prelates with peri-
    wigged charioteers
Riding triumphantly laureled to lap the fat
    of the years—
Rather the scorned—the rejected—the men
    hemmed in with the spears;

The men of the tattered battalion which
    fights till it dies,
Dazed with the dust of the battle, the din and
    the cries,   5
The men with the broken heads and the blood
    running into their eyes.

Not the be-medaled Commander, beloved of
    the throne,

The poems of John Masefield are reprinted from his *Poems* (complete edition, 1935) by permission of The Macmillan Company, New York, Publishers.
2. **laureled,** crowned with laurel; honored.

4. **The men.** Cf. Kipling's *Tommy*, p. 887.

Riding cock-horse to parade when the bugles are blown,
But the lads who carried the koppie and cannot be known.

Not the ruler for me, but the ranker, the tramp of the road,   10
The slave with the sack on his shoulders pricked on with the goad,
The man with too weighty a burden, too weary a load.

The sailor, the stoker of steamers, the man with the clout,
The chantyman bent at the halliards putting a tune to the shout,
The drowsy man at the wheel and the tired lookout.   15

Others may sing of the wine and the wealth and the mirth,
The portly presence of potentates goodly in girth;—
Mine be the dirt and the dross, the dust and scum of the earth!

Theirs be the music, the color, the glory, the gold;
Mine be a handful of ashes, a mouthful of mold.   20
Of the maimed, of the halt and the blind in the rain and the cold—
Of these shall my songs be fashioned, my tales be told.   AMEN.

(1902)

The Turn of the Tide

An' Bill can have my sea-boots, Nigger Jim can have my knife,
  You can divvy up the dungarees an' bed,
An' the ship can have my blessing, an' the Lord can have my life,
  An' sails an' fish my body when I'm dead.

An' dreaming down below there in the tangled greens an' blues,   5
  Where the sunlight shudders golden round about,
I shall hear the ships complainin' and the cursin' of the crews,
  An' be sorry when the watch is tumbled out.

I shall hear them hilly-hollying the weather crojick brace,   9
  And the sucking of the wash about the hull;
When they chanty up the topsail I'll be hauling in my place,
  For my soul will follow seawards like a gull.

I shall hear the blocks a-grunting in the bumpkins over-side,
  An' the slatting of the storm-sails on the stay,
An' the rippling of the catspaw at the making of the tide,   15
  An' the swirl and splash of porpoises at play.

An' Bill can have my sea-boots, Nigger Jim can have my knife,
  You can divvy up the whack I haven't scofft,
An' the ship can have my blessing, and the Lord can have my life,
  For it's time I quit the deck and went aloft. (1902)

Sea-Fever

I must go down to the seas again, to the lonely sea and the sky,
And all I ask is a tall ship and a star to steer her by,
And the wheel's kick and the wind's song and the white sail's shaking,
And a gray mist on the sea's face and a gray dawn breaking.

---

9. **carried the koppie**, captured the hill. 13. **clout**, cloth, rag, used in wiping engines. 14. **chantyman**, the leader of a song sung by sailors to lighten their work. 21. **maimed . . . blind.** Cf. *Luke*, 14:21: "Go out quickly into the streets and lanes of the city, and bring in hither the poor, and the maimed, and the halt and the blind."
  The Turn of the Tide. 2. **dungarees**, thin blue or brown overalls made from coconut fiber. 4. **sails . . . dead.** Dead sailors were wrapped in old sail-cloth when buried at sea.

9. **crojick brace**, the rope controlling the lower arm of the mizzenmast on which the crossjack (crojick), a square sail, is fastened. 11. **chanty up**, sing as they pull up. 13. **blocks**, pulleys through which the brace ropes travel. **bumpkins**, beams extending outward from the side of the ship; to them the pulleys are fastened. 14. **slatting . . . stay**, the flapping of the small heavy sails (set in stormy weather) against the strong ropes that support the mast. 18. **whack . . . scofft**, the share of food I haven't eaten.
  Sea-Fever. 2. **tall ship**, a fine vessel.

I must go down to the seas again, for the call
    of the running tide   5
Is a wild call and a clear call that may not be
    denied;
And all I ask is a windy day with the white
    clouds flying,
And the flung spray and the blown spume,
    and the sea-gulls crying.

I must go down to the seas again to the
    vagrant gypsy life,
To the gull's way and the whale's way where
    the wind's like a whetted knife;   10
And all I ask is a merry yarn from a laughing
    fellow-rover,
And quiet sleep and a sweet dream when the
    long trick's over.   (1902)

The West Wind

It's a warm wind, the west wind, full of birds'
    cries;
I never hear the west wind but tears are in
    my eyes.
For it comes from the west lands, the old
    brown hills,
And April's in the west wind, and daffodils.

It's a fine land, the west land, for hearts as
    tired as mine,   5
Apple orchards blossom there, and the air's
    like wine.
There is cool green grass there, where men
    may lie at rest,
And the thrushes are in song there, fluting
    from the nest.

"Will you not come home, brother? you have
    been long away,
It's April, and blossom time, and white is the
    spray;   10
And bright is the sun, brother, and warm is
    the rain—
Will you not come home, brother, home to us
    again?

The young corn is green, brother, where the
    rabbits run,
It's blue sky, and white clouds, and warm rain
    and sun.
It's song to a man's soul, brother, fire to a
    man's brain,   15
To hear the wild bees and see the merry
    spring again.

Larks are singing in the west, brother, above
    the green wheat,
So will ye not come home, brother, and rest
    your tired feet?
I've a balm for bruised hearts, brother, sleep
    for aching eyes,"
Says the warm wind, the west wind, full of
    birds' cries.   20

It's the white road westwards is the road I
    must tread
To the green grass, the cool grass, and rest for
    heart and head,
To the violets and the brown brooks and the
    thrushes' song,
In the fine land, the west land, the land where
    I belong.   (1902)

Cargoes

Quinquireme of Nineveh from distant Ophir,
Rowing home to haven in sunny Palestine,
With a cargo of ivory,
And apes and peacocks,
Sandalwood, cedarwood, and sweet white
    wine.   5

Stately Spanish galleon coming from the
    Isthmus,
Dipping through the Tropics by the palm-
    green shores,
With a cargo of diamonds,
Emeralds, amethysts,
Topazes, and cinnamon, and gold moidores. 10

---

8. **blown spume**, sea foam blown by the wind. 12. **trick**, a two-hour spell at the wheel or on the look-out; here the long trick is life.
    The West Wind. Cf. Shelley's *Ode to the West Wind*, p. 255. 3. **the old brown hills.** In the county of Hereford, where Masefield was born. See *London Town* and headnote, p. 919.

13. **corn**, grain, wheat.
    Cargoes. 1. **Quinquireme**, an ancient form of ship having five banks of oars. **Nineveh**, the ancient capital of the Assyrian Empire. **Ophir**, a region mentioned in the Old Testament as the source of gold (*1 Kings*, 10:11). 6. **Spanish galleon**, a sailing vessel having three or four decks, used by the Spaniards as treasure ships in their American commerce. **the Isthmus**, the Isthmus of Panama. 10. **moidores**, gold coins of Portugal and Brazil, worth about $3.25 each.

Dirty British coaster with a salt-caked smoke
    stack,
Butting through the Channel in the mad
    March days,
With a cargo of Tyne coal,
Road-rails, pig-lead,
Firewood, iron-ware, and cheap tin trays.   15
(1910)

London Town

Masefield was born in Herefordshire, and although he ran away to sea in early youth and has spent much of his life in cities, he has always retained an interest in his native hills and streams, and in the scenes of his boyhood. *London Town* is redolent with the local color of Hereford and the adjoining counties in western England.

Oh London Town's a fine town, and London
    sights are rare,
And London ale is right ale, and brisk's the
    London air,
And busily goes the world there, but crafty
    grows the mind,
And London Town of all towns I'm glad to
    leave behind.

Then hey for croft and hop-yard, and hill, and
    field, and pond,   5
With Bredon Hill before me and Malvern
    Hill beyond.
The hawthorn white i' the hedgerow, and all
    the spring's attire
In the comely land of Teme and Lugg, and
    Clent, and Clee, and Wyre.

Oh London girls are brave girls, in silk and
    cloth o' gold,
And London shops are rare shops where gallant things are sold,   10
And bonnily clinks the gold there, but drowsily blinks the eye,
And London Town of all towns I'm glad to
    hurry by.

Then, hey for covert and woodland, and ash
    and elm and oak,
Tewkesbury inns, and Malvern roofs, and
    Worcester chimney smoke.

13. **Tyne coal**, coal carried down the Tyne River, in Northumberland, England.
London Town. 5. **croft**, a small enclosed field.

The apple trees in the orchard, the cattle in
    the byre,   15
And all the land from Ludlow town to
    Bredon church's spire.

Oh London tunes are new tunes, and London
    books are wise,
And London plays are rare plays, and fine to
    country eyes,
But wretchedly fare the most there and merrily fare the few,
And London Town of all towns I'm glad to
    hurry through.   20

So hey for the road, the west road, by mill
    and forge and fold,
Scent of the fern and song of the lark by
    brook, and field, and wold,
To the comely folk at the hearth-stone and
    the talk beside the fire,
In the hearty land, where I was bred, my land
    of heart's desire.   (1910)

St. Mary's Bells

The setting of this poem is the Puerto de Santa Maria, a seaport in the province of Cadiz, Spain, on the Bay of Cadiz.

It's pleasant in Holy Mary
By San Marie lagoon,
The bells they chime and jingle
From dawn to afternoon.
They rime and chime and mingle,   5
They pulse and boom and beat,
And the laughing bells are gentle
And the mournful bells are sweet.

Oh, who are the men that ring them,
The bells of San Marie,   10
Oh, who but sonsie seamen
Come in from over sea,
And merrily in the belfries
They rock and sway and hale,
And send the bells a-jangle   15
And down the lusty ale.

It's pleasant in Holy Mary
To hear the beaten bells

15. **byre**, a cow house.
St. Mary's Bells. 11. **sonsie**, happy, lucky.

Come booming into music,
Which throbs, and clangs, and swells,   20
From sunset till the daybreak,
From dawn to afternoon.
In port of Holy Mary
On San Marie Lagoon.   (1910)

The Seekers

Friends and loves we have none, nor wealth
    nor blessed abode,
But the hope of the City of God at the other
    end of the road.

Not for us are content, and quiet, and peace
    of mind,
For we go seeking a city that we shall never
    find.

There is no solace on earth for us—for such
    as we—   5
Who search for a hidden city that we shall
    never see.

Only the road and the dawn, the sun, the
    wind, and the rain,
And the watch fire under stars, and sleep, and
    the road again.

We seek the City of God, and the haunt where
    beauty dwells,
And we find the noisy mart and the sound of
    burial bells.   10

Never the golden city, where radiant people
    meet,
But the dolorous town where mourners are
    going about the street.

We travel the dusty road till the light of the
    day is dim,
And sunset shows us spires away on the
    world's rim.

We travel from dawn to dusk, till the day is
    past and by,   15

---

12. **mourners . . . street.** Cf. *Ecclesiastes*, 12:5: ". . . man goeth to his long home, and the mourners go about the streets." See Vol. I, p. 608.

Seeking the Holy City beyond the rim of the
    sky.

Friends and loves we have none, nor wealth
    nor blest abode,
But the hope of the City of God at the other
    end of the road.   (1910)

Laugh and Be Merry

Laugh and be merry, remember, better the
    world with a song,
Better the world with a blow in the teeth of
    a wrong.
Laugh, for the time is brief, a thread the
    length of a span.
Laugh and be proud to belong to the old
    proud pageant of man.

Laugh and be merry: remember, in olden
    time   5
God made Heaven and Earth for joy He took
    in a rime,
Made them, and filled them full with the
    strong red wind of His mirth,
The splendid joy of the stars: the joy of the
    earth.

So we must laugh and drink from the deep
    blue cup of the sky,
Join the jubilant song of the great stars sweep-
    ing by,   10
Laugh, and battle, and work, and drink of
    the wine outpoured
In the dear green earth, the sign of the joy of
    the Lord.

Laugh and be merry together, like brothers
    akin,
Guesting awhile in the rooms of a beautiful
    inn,
Glad till the dancing stops, and the lilt of the
    music ends.   15
Laugh till the game is played; and be you
    merry, my friends.   (1910)

Roadways

One road leads to London,
    One road runs to Wales,
My road leads me seawards
    To the white dipping sails.

One road leads to the river,
   As it goes singing slow;
My road leads to shipping,
   Where the bronzed sailors go.

Leads me, lures me, calls me
   To salt green tossing sea;
A road without earth's road-dust
   Is the right road for me.

A wet road heaving, shining,
   And wild with seagull's cries,
A mad salt sea-wind blowing
   The salt spray in my eyes.

My road calls me, lures me
   West, east, south, and north;
Most roads lead men homewards,
   My road leads me forth

To add more miles to the tally
   Of gray miles left behind,
In quest of that one beauty
   God put me here to find.

(1910)

C. L. M.

C. L. M. is Masefield's mother, who died when the poet was still a young boy.

In the dark womb where I began
My mother's life made me a man.
Through all the months of human birth
Her beauty fed my common earth.
I cannot see, nor breathe, nor stir,
But through the death of some of her.

Down in the darkness of the grave
She cannot see the life she gave.
For all her love, she cannot tell
Whether I use it ill or well,
Nor knock at dusty doors to find
Her beauty dusty in the mind.

If the grave's gates could be undone,
She would not know her little son,
I am so grown. If we should meet
She would pass by me in the street,
Unless my soul's face let her see
My sense of what she did for me.

What have I done to keep in mind
My debt to her and womankind?
What woman's happier life repays
Her for those months of wretched days?
For all my mouthless body leeched
Ere Birth's releasing hell was reached?

What have I done, or tried, or said
In thanks to that dear woman dead?
Men triumph over women still,
Men trample women's rights at will,
And man's lust roves the world untamed.

   *   *   *   *   *

O grave, keep shut lest I be shamed.

(1910)

Sonnets

1

If I could come again to that dear place
Where once I came, where Beauty lived and
   moved,
Where, by the sea, I saw her face to face,
That soul alive by which the world has loved;
If, as I stood at gaze among the leaves,
She would appear again, as once before,
While the red herdsman gathered up his
   sheaves
And brimming waters trembled up the shore;
If, as I gazed, her Beauty that was dumb,
In that old time, before I learned to speak,
Would lean to me and revelation come,
Words to the lips and color to the cheek,
Joy with its searing-iron would burn me wise,
I should know all; all powers, all mysteries.

2

Roses are beauty, but I never see
Those blood drops from the burning heart of
   June
Glowing like thought upon the living tree,
Without a pity that they die so soon,
Die into petals, like those roses old,
Those women, who were summer in men's
   hearts
Before the smile upon the Sphinx was cold,
Or sand had hid the Syrian and his arts.

C.L.M. 23. **leeched**, sucked like a leech.

O myriad dust of beauty that lies thick
Under our feet that not a single grain   10
But stirred and moved in beauty and was
    quick
For one brief moon and died nor lived again;
But when the moon rose lay upon the grass
Pasture to living beauty, life that was.

3

I never see the red rose crown the year,
Nor feel the young grass underneath my tread,
Without the thought, "This living beauty here
Is earth's remembrance of a beauty dead.
Surely where all this glory is displayed   5
Love has been quick, like fire, to high ends,
Here, in this grass, an altar has been made
For some white joy, some sacrifice of friends;
Here, where I stand, some leap of human
    brains
Has touched immortal things and left its
    trace,   10
The earth is happy here, the gleam remains;
Beauty is here, the spirit of the place,
I touch the faith which nothing can destroy,
The earth, the living church of ancient joy."
                                    (1916)

On Growing Old

Be with me, Beauty, for the fire is dying,
My dog and I are old, too old for roving.
Man, whose young passion sets the spindrift
    flying
Is soon too lame to march, too cold for loving.
I take the book and gather to the fire,   5
Turning old yellow leaves; minute by minute,
The clock ticks to my heart; a withered wire
Moves a thin ghost of music in the spinet.
I cannot sail your seas, I cannot wander,
Your cornland, nor your hill-land nor your
    valleys,   10
Ever again, nor share the battle yonder
Where the young knight the broken squad-
    ron rallies.
Only stay quiet while my mind remembers
The beauty of fire from the beauty of embers.

Beauty, have pity, for the strong have power,
The rich their wealth, the beautiful their grace
Summer of man its sunlight and its flower,   17
Springtime of man all April in a face.
Only, as in the jostling in the Strand,
Where the mob thrusts or loiters or is loud,   20
The beggar with the saucer in his hand
Asks only a penny from the passing crowd,
So, from this glittering world with all its
    fashion
Its fire and play of men, its stir, its march,
Let me have wisdom, Beauty, wisdom and
    passion,   25
Bread to the soul, rain where the summers
    parch.
Give me but these, and though the darkness
    close
Even the night will blossom as the rose. (1922)

On Growing Old. Cf. Coleridge's *Youth and Age,* and note, p. 189. 3. **spindrift**, sea spray.

8. **spinet**, an obsolete form of harpsichord. 10. **cornland**, grainland. 19. **Strand**, a prominent street in London.

PROSE

Robert Louis Stevenson*

1850-1894

Aes Triplex

The title, meaning "Triple Bronze," is taken from Horace's *Odes* (1, 3, 9)—
    Ille robur et aes triplex
    Circa pectus erat qui fragilem truci
    Commisit pelago ratem
    Primus.
"Oak and triple brass encompassed the breast of him who first entrusted his frail craft to

The essays of Robert Louis Stevenson are reprinted by permission of Charles Scribner's Sons. New York.

*For a treatment of Stevenson's life and works see p. 874.

the wild sea." Stevenson uses the phrase as a symbol of courage. The essay appeared first in *The Cornhill Magazine* for April, 1878, and afterwards in *Virginibus Puerisque*.

THE changes wrought by death are in themselves so sharp and final, and so terrible and melancholy in their consequences, that the thing stands alone in man's experience, and has no parallel upon earth. It outdoes all other accidents because it is the last of them. Sometimes it leaps suddenly upon its victims, like a Thug; sometimes it lays a regular siege and creeps upon their citadel during a score of years. And when the business is done, there is sore havoc made in other people's lives, and a pin knocked out by which many subsidiary friendships hung together. There are empty chairs, solitary walks, and single beds at night. Again, in taking away our friends, death does not take them away utterly, but leaves behind a mocking tragical, and soon intolerable residue, which must be hurriedly concealed. Hence a whole chapter of sights and customs striking to the mind, from the pyramids of Egypt to the gibbets and dule trees of medieval Europe. The poorest persons have a bit of pageant going towards the tomb; memorial stones are set up over the least memorable; and, in order to preserve some show of respect for what remains of our old loves and friendships, we must accompany it with much grimly ludicrous ceremonial, and the hired undertaker parades before the door. All this, and much more of the same sort, accompanied by the eloquence of poets, has gone a great way to put humanity in error; nay, in many philosophies the error has been embodied and laid down with every circumstance of logic; although in real life the bustle and swiftness, in leaving people little time to think, have not left them time enough to go dangerously wrong in practice.

As a matter of fact, although few things are spoken of with more fearful whisperings than this prospect of death, few have less influence on conduct under healthy circumstances. We have all heard of cities in South America built upon the side of fiery mountains, and how, even in this tremendous neighborhood, the inhabitants are not a jot more impressed by the solemnity of mortal conditions than if they were delving gardens in the greenest corner of England. There are serenades and suppers and much gallantry among the myrtles overhead; and meanwhile the foundation shudders underfoot, the bowels of the mountain growl, and at any moment living ruin may leap sky-high into the moonlight, and tumble man and his merry-making in the dust. In the eyes of very young people, and very dull old ones, there is something indescribably reckless and desperate in such a picture. It seems not credible that respectable married people, with umbrellas, should find appetite for a bit of supper within quite a long distance of a fiery mountain; ordinary life begins to smell of high-handed debauch when it is carried on so close to a catastrophe; and even cheese and salad, it seems, could hardly be relished in such circumstances without something like a defiance of the Creator. It should be a place for nobody but hermits dwelling in prayer and maceration, or mere born-devils drowning care in a perpetual carouse.

And yet, when one comes to think upon it calmly, the situation of these South American citizens forms only a very pale figure for the state of ordinary mankind. This world itself, traveling blindly and swiftly in overcrowded space, among a million other worlds traveling blindly and swiftly in contrary directions, may very well come by a knock that would set it into explosion like a penny squib. And what, pathologically looked at, is the human body with all its organs, but a mere bagful of petards? The least of these is as dangerous to the whole economy as the ship's powder-magazine to the ship; and with every breath we breathe, and every meal we eat, we are putting one or more of them in peril. If we clung as devotedly as some philosophers pretend we do to the abstract idea of life, or were half as frightened as they make out we are, for the subversive accident that ends it

---

8. **Thug**, originally a member of a religious brotherhood of robbers and murderers in northern India. 21. **dule trees**, hanging-trees, gallows.
69. **maceration**, mortification of the flesh. 79. **penny squib**, a kind of cheap explosive or firecracker. 82. **petard**, a kind of bomb used to blow up besieged walls.

all, the trumpets might sound by the hour and no one would follow them into battle—the blue-peter might fly at the truck, but who would climb into a sea-going ship? Think (if these philosophers were right) with what a preparation of spirit we should affront the daily peril of the dinner-table: a deadlier spot than any battlefield in history, where the far greater proportion of our ancestors have miserably left their bones! What woman would ever be lured into marriage, so much more dangerous than the wildest sea? And what would it be to grow old? For, after certain distance, every step we take in life we find the ice growing thinner below our feet, and all around us and behind us we see our contemporaries going through. By the time a man gets well into the seventies, his continued existence is a mere miracle; and when he lays his old bones in bed for the night, there is an overwhelming probability that he will never see the day. Do the old men mind it, as a matter of fact? Why, no. They were never merrier; they have their grog at night, and tell the raciest stories; they hear of the death of people about their own age, or even younger, not as if it was a grisly warning, but with a simple childlike pleasure at having outlived some one else; and when a draught might puff them out like a guttering candle, or a bit of a stumble shatter them like so much glass, their old hearts keep sound and unaffrighted, and they go on, bubbling with laughter, through years of man's age compared to which the valley at Balaclava was as safe and peaceful as a village cricket-green on Sunday. It may fairly be questioned (if we look to the peril only) whether it was a much more daring feat for Curtius to plunge into the gulf, than for any old gentleman of ninety to doff his clothes and clamber into bed.

Indeed, it is a memorable subject for consideration, with what unconcern and gayety mankind pricks on along the Valley of the Shadow of Death. The whole is one wilderness of snares, and the end of it, for those who fear the last pinch, is irrevocable ruin. And yet we go spinning through it all, like a party for the Derby. Perhaps the reader remembers one of the humorous devices of the deified Caligula: how he encouraged a vast concourse of holiday-makers on to his bridge over the Baiae bay; and when they were in the height of their enjoyment, turned loose the Praetorian guards among the company, and had them tossed into the sea. This is no bad miniature of the dealings of nature with the transitory race of man. Only, what a chequered picnic we have of it, even while it lasts! and into what great waters, not to be crossed by any swimmer, God's pale Praetorian throws us over in the end!

We live the time that a match flickers; we pop the cork of a ginger-beer bottle, and the earthquake swallows us on the instant. Is it not odd, is it not incongruous, is it not, in the highest sense of human speech, incredible, that we should think so highly of the ginger-beer, and regard so little the devouring earthquake? The love of Life and the fear of Death are two famous phrases that grow harder to understand the more we think about them. It is a well-known fact that an immense proportion of boat accidents would never happen if people held the sheet in their hands instead of making it fast; and yet, unless it be some martinet of a professional mariner or some landsman with shattered nerves, every one of God's creatures makes it fast. A strange instance of man's unconcern and brazen boldness in the face of death!

We confound ourselves with metaphysical phrases, which we import into daily talk with noble inappropriateness. We have no idea of what death is, apart from its circumstances and some of its consequences to others; and although we have some experience of living there is not a man on earth who has flown so

---

3. **blue-peter,** a blue flag with a white square in the center; it is displayed as a signal when the vessel is ready to leave port. **truck,** a small wooden cap at the top of a mast or flagstaff, having holes for ropes. 35. **Balaclava.** See Tennyson's *Charge of the Light Brigade,* p. 637. 39. **Curtius,** Metius Curtius, a patriotic youth of Roman legend who sacrificed his life and saved the city by plunging into a gulf that in 362 B.C. suddenly opened in the Forum. A soothsayer had declared the act necessary to appease the wrath of the gods. 44. **Valley . . . Death.** A phrase in the *23d Psalm* (Vol. I, p. 605).

49. **the Derby,** a horse race at Epsom, England, established in 1780 by the Earl of Derby. 50. **deified Caligula,** the third emperor of Rome (37-41), who proclaimed himself a god. 53. **Baiae bay,** a fashionable seaside resort of the Romans near Naples. 54. **Praetorian guards,** the bodyguard of the Roman emperors, so called because originally they were the bodyguard of the praetor, a magistrate next to the consul. 75. **sheet,** the rope that controls the position of a sail. 77. **martinet,** a strict military disciplinarian.

high into abstraction as to have any practical guess at the meaning of the word *life*. All literature, from Job and Omar Khayyám to Thomas Carlyle or Walt Whitman, is but an attempt to look upon the human state with such largeness of view as shall enable us to rise from the consideration of living to the Definition of Life. And our sages give us about the best satisfaction in their power when they say that it is a vapor, or a show, or made out of the same stuff with dreams. Philosophy, in its more rigid sense, has been at the same work for ages; and after a myriad bald heads have wagged over the problem, and piles of words have been heaped one upon another into dry and cloudy volumes without end, philosophy has the honor of laying before us, with modest pride, her contribution towards the subject: that life is a Permanent Possibility of Sensation. Truly a fine result! A man may very well love beef, or hunting, or a woman; but surely, surely, not a Permanent Possibility of Sensation! He may be afraid of a precipice, or a dentist, or a large enemy with a club, or even an undertaker's man; but not certainly of abstract death. We may trick with the word life in its dozen senses until we are weary of tricking; we may argue in terms of all the philosophies on earth, but one fact remains true throughout—that we do not love life, in the sense that we are greatly preoccupied about its conservation; that we do not, properly speaking, love life at all, but living. Into the views of the least careful there will enter some degree of providence; no man's eyes are fixed entirely on the passing hour; but although we have some anticipation of good health, good weather, wine, active employment, love, and self-approval, the sum of these anticipations does not amount to anything like a general view of life's possibilities and issues; nor are those who cherish them most vividly, at all the most scrupulous of their personal safety. To be deeply interested in the accidents of our existence, to enjoy keenly the mixed texture of human experience, rather leads a man to disregard precautions, and risk his neck against a straw. For surely the love of living is stronger in an Alpine climber roping over a peril, or a hunter riding merrily at a stiff fence, than in a creature who lives upon a diet and walks a measured distance in the interest of his constitution.

There is a great deal of very vile nonsense talked upon both sides of the matter; tearing divines reducing life to the dimensions of a mere funeral procession, so short as to be hardly decent; and melancholy unbelievers yearning for the tomb as if it were a world too far away. Both sides must feel a little ashamed of their performances now and again when they draw in their chairs to dinner. Indeed, a good meal and a bottle of wine is an answer to most standard works upon the question. When a man's heart warms to his viands, he forgets a great deal of sophistry, and soars into a rosy zone of contemplation. Death may be knocking at the door, like the Commander's statue; we have something else in hand, thank God, and let him knock. Passing bells are ringing all the world over. All the world over, and every hour, some one is parting company with all his aches and ecstasies. For us also the trap is laid. But we are so fond of life that we have no leisure to entertain the terror of death. It is a honeymoon with us all through, and none of the longest. Small blame to us if we give our whole hearts to this glowing bride of ours, to the appetites, to honor, to the hungry curiosity of the mind, to the pleasure of the eyes in nature, and the pride of our own nimble bodies.

We all of us appreciate the sensations; but as for caring about the Permanence of the Possibility, a man's head is generally very bald, and his senses very dull, before he comes to that. Whether we regard life as a lane leading to a dead wall—a mere bag's end, as the French say—or whether we think of it

---

3. **Job**, the hero of one of the most poetical books in the Bible (Vol. I, p. 601). **Omar Khayyám.** See p. 776. 4. **Carlyle.** See p. 464. **Walt Whitman,** the American poet (1819-1892) noted for his individual themes and rhythms. 10. **vapor, or a show.** Cf. *Psalms*, 39:6: "Surely every man walketh in a vain shew." 11. **stuff with dreams.** Cf. *The Tempest*, IV, i, 156-158. 19. **Permanent . . . Sensation.** The definition of matter by John Stuart Mill (1806-1873), an English philosopher and political economist.

69. **the Commander's statue.** In the Spanish legend of Don Juan, Don Juan kills the governor of the city and then holds a banquet at his tomb. Invited to join the feast, the statue of the dead man appears and carries Don Juan to hell. 89. **a mere bag's end,** a translation of the French *cul de sac*, a blind alley.

as a vestibule or gymnasium where we wait our turn and prepare our faculties for some more noble destiny; whether we thunder in a pulpit, or pule in little atheistic poetry-books, about its vanity and brevity; whether we look justly for years of health and vigor, or are about to mount into a Bath-chair, as a step towards the hearse; in each and all of these views and situations there is but one conclusion possible: that a man should stop his ears against paralyzing terror, and run the race that is set before him with a single mind. No one surely could have recoiled with more heartache and terror from the thought of death than our respected lexicographer; and yet we know how little it affected his conduct, how wisely and boldly he walked, and in what a fresh and lively vein he spoke of life. Already an old man, he ventured on his Highland tour; and his heart, bound with triple brass, did not recoil before twenty-seven individual cups of tea. As courage and intelligence are the two qualities best worth a good man's cultivation, so it is the first part of intelligence to recognize our precarious estate in life, and the first part of courage to be not at all abashed before the fact. A frank and somewhat headlong carriage, not looking too anxiously before, not dallying in maudlin regret over the past, stamps the man who is well armored for this world.

And not only well armored for himself, but a good friend and a good citizen to boot. We do not go to cowards for tender dealing; there is nothing so cruel as panic; the man who has least fear for his own carcass, has most time to consider others. That eminent chemist who took his walks abroad in tin shoes, and subsisted wholly upon tepid milk, had all his work cut out for him in considerate dealings with his own digestion. So soon as prudence has begun to grow up in the brain, like a dismal fungus, it finds its first expression in a paralysis of generous acts. The victim begins to shrink spiritually; he develops a fancy for parlors with a regulated temperature, and takes his morality on the principle of tin shoes and tepid milk. The care of one important body or soul becomes so engrossing, that all the noises of the outer world begin to come thin and faint into the parlor with the regulated temperature; and the tin shoes go equably forward over blood and rain. To be otherwise is to ossify; and the scruple-monger ends by standing stock-still. Now the man who has his heart on his sleeve, and a good whirling weathercock of a brain, who reckons his life as a thing to be dashingly used and cheerfully hazarded, makes a very different acquaintance of the world, keeps all his pulses going true and fast, and gathers impetus as he runs, until, if he be running towards anything better than wildfire, he may shoot up and become a constellation in the end. Lord look after his health, Lord have a care of his soul, says he; and he has at the key of the position, and swashes through incongruity and peril towards his aim. Death is on all sides of him with pointed batteries, as he is on all sides of all of us; unfortunate surprises gird him round; mim-mouthed friends and relations hold up their hands in quite a little elegiacal synod about his path: and what cares he for all this? Being a true lover of living, a fellow with something pushing and spontaneous in his inside, he must, like any other soldier, in any other stirring, deadly warfare, push on at his best pace until he touch the goal. "A peerage or Westminster Abbey!" cried Nelson in his bright, boyish, heroic manner. These are great incentives; not for any of these, but for the plain satisfaction of living, of being about their business in some sort or other, do the brave, serviceable men of every nation tread down the nettle danger, and pass flyingly over all the stum-

---

7. **Bath-chair**, an invalid's chair on wheels, so called from the city of Bath, an English health resort where such chairs were common. 11. **run . . . mind.** Cf. *Hebrews*, 12:1: ". . . let us run with patience the race that is set before us." 15. **our . . . lexicographer**, Samuel Johnson (Vol. I, p. 1125), noted as a heavy tea-drinker; see l. 21. See the account of his fear of death as related by Boswell (Vol. I, p. 1162). 28. **looking . . . before.** Cf. Shelley's *To a Skylark*, l. 86, p. 260. 37. **eminent chemist**, Joseph Black (1728-1799), a Scottish chemist and physicist who discovered what is called "latent heat." He was in feeble health most of his life.

56. **heart on his sleeve.** Cf. *Othello*, I, i, 63-65—
'Tis not long after
But I will wear my heart upon my sleeve
For daws to peck at.

71. **mim-mouthed**, prudishly reticent, or affectedly proper in speech. 73. **elegiacal synod**, a glum group that pessimistically expects the worst. 80. **Nelson**, Lord Nelson (1758-1805), England's greatest naval commander; he made this remark just before the Battle of the Nile (1798). 85. **tread . . . danger.** From *1 Henry IV*, II, iii, 10.

bling-blocks of prudence. Think of the heroism of Johnson, think of that superb indifference to mortal limitation that set him upon his dictionary, and carried him through triumphantly until the end! Who, if he were wisely considerate of things at large, would ever embark upon any work much more considerable than a half-penny post card? Who would project a serial novel, after Thackeray and Dickens had each fallen in mid-course? Who would find heart enough to begin to live, if he dallied with the consideration of death?

And, after all, what sorry and pitiful quibbling all this is! To forego all the issues of living in a parlor with a regulated temperature—as if that were not to die a hundred times over, and for ten years at a stretch! As if it were not to die in one's own lifetime, and without even the sad immunities of death! As if it were not to die, and yet be the patient spectators of our own pitiable change! The Permanent Possibility is preserved, but the sensations carefully held at arm's length, as if one kept a photographic plate in a dark chamber. It is better to lose health like a spendthrift than to waste it like a miser. It is better to live and be done with it, than to die daily in the sickroom. By all means begin your folio; even if the doctor does not give you a year, even if he hesitates about a month, make one brave push and see what can be accomplished in a week. It is not only in finished undertakings that we ought to honor useful labor. A spirit goes out of the man who means execution, which outlives the most untimely ending. All who have meant good work with their whole hearts, have done good work, although they may die before they have the time to sign it. Every heart that has beat strong and cheerfully has left a hopeful impulse behind it in the world, and bettered the tradition of mankind. And even if death catch people, like an open pitfall, and in mid-career, laying out vast projects, and planning monstrous foundations, flushed with hope, and their mouths full of boastful language, they should be at once tripped up and silenced: is there not something brave and spirited in such a termination? and does not life go down with a better grace, foaming in full body over a precipice, than miserably straggling to an end in sandy deltas? When the Greeks made their fine saying that those whom the gods love die young, I cannot help believing they had this sort of death also in their eye. For surely, at whatever age it overtake the man, this is to die young. Death has not been suffered to take so much as an illusion from his heart. In the hot-fit of life, a-tiptoe on the highest point of being, he passes at a bound on to the other side. The noise of the mallet and chisel is scarcely quenched, the trumpets are hardly done blowing, when, trailing with him clouds of glory, this happy-starred, full-blooded spirit shoots into the spiritual land. (1878)

---

1. **heroism of Johnson.** He produced his dictionary under great difficulty (see Vol. I, pp. 1125 ff.) and began his greatest work, *Lives of the Poets*, at the age of sixty-seven. 9. **Thackeray and Dickens.** Both, like Stevenson, died with unfinished novels on their hands. 28. **By . . . folio.** Cf. Browning's *A Grammarian's Funeral*, ll. 85 ff., p. 683. 29. **doctor . . . year.** Stevenson did much of his literary work under the shadow of death.

36. **All who . . . work.** Cf. Browning's *Rabbi Ben Ezra*, ll. 133 ff., p. 700. 53. **whom . . . young.** A statement of the Greek poet Menander in *Dis Exapaton*, Fragment 4. It is quoted by Byron in *Don Juan*, IV, l. 89, p. 239. 63. **trailing . . . glory.** Cf. Wordsworth's *Ode on Immortality*, l. 64. p. 161.

Pan's Pipes

In classical mythology Pan is a woodland spirit and god of hills and woods, flocks, and herds. He is represented with horns and with the legs and feet of a goat, playing on his pipes and sometimes exciting sudden fear.

THE world in which we live has been variously said and sung by the most ingenious poets and philosophers: these reducing it to formulae and chemical ingredients, those striking the lyre in high-sounding measures for the handiwork of God. What experience supplies is of a mingled tissue, and the choosing mind has much to reject before it can get together the materials of a theory. Dew and thunder, destroying Attila and the

10. **Attila,** a famous King of the Huns (fifth century), surnamed "The Scourge of God" on account of the terrible destruction wrought by his armies.

Spring lambkins, belong to an order of contrasts which no repetition can assimilate. There is an uncouth, outlandish strain throughout the web of the world, as from a vexatious planet in the house of life. Things are not congruous and wear strange disguises: the consummate flower is fostered out of dung, and after nourishing itself awhile with heaven's delicate distillations, decays again into indistinguishable soil; and with Caesar's ashes, Hamlet tells us, the urchins make dirt pies and filthily besmear their countenance. Nay, the kindly shine of summer, when tracked home with the scientific spyglass, is found to issue from the most portentous nightmare of the universe—the great, conflagrant sun: a world of hell's squibs, tumultuary, roaring aloud, inimical to life. The sun itself is enough to disgust a human being of the scene which he inhabits; and you would not fancy there was a green or habitable spot in the universe thus awfully lighted up. And yet it is by the blaze of such a conflagration, to which the fire of Rome was but a spark, that we do all our fiddling, and hold domestic tea-parties at the arbor door.

The Greeks figured Pan, the god of Nature, now terribly stamping his foot, so that armies were dispersed; now by the woodside on a summer noon trolling on his pipe until he charmed the hearts of upland plowmen. And the Greeks, in so figuring, uttered the last word of human experience. To certain smoke-dried spirits matter and motion and elastic ethers, and the hypothesis of this or that other spectacled professor, tell a speaking story; but for youth and all ductile and congenial minds, Pan is not dead, but of all the classic hierarchy alone survives in triumph; goat-footed, with a gleeful and an angry look, the type of the shaggy world; and in every wood, if you go with a spirit properly prepared, you shall hear the note of his pipe.

For it is a shaggy world, and yet studded with gardens; where the salt and tumbling sea receives clear rivers running from among reeds and lilies; fruitful and austere; a rustic world; sunshiny, lewd, and cruel. What is it the birds sing among the trees in pairing-time? What means the sound of the rain falling far and wide upon the leafy forest? To what tune does the fisherman whistle, as he hauls in his net at morning, and the bright fish are heaped inside the boat? These are all airs upon Pan's pipe; he it was who gave them breath in the exultation of his heart, and gleefully modulated their outflow with his lips and fingers. The coarse mirth of herdsmen, shaking the dells with laughter and striking out high echoes from the rock; the tune of moving feet in the lamplit city, or on the smooth ballroom floor; the hooves of many horses, beating the wide pastures in alarm; the song of hurrying rivers; the color of clear skies; and smiles and the live touch of hands; and the voice of things, and their significant look, and the renovating influence they breathe forth—these are his joyful measures, to which the whole earth treads in choral harmony. To this music the young lambs bound as to a tabor, and the London shop-girl skips rudely in the dance. For it puts a spirit of gladness in all hearts; and to look on the happy side of nature is common, in their hours, to all created things. Some are vocal under a good influence, are pleasing whenever they are pleased, and hand on their happiness to others, as a child who, looking upon lovely things, looks lovely. Some leap to the strains with unapt foot, and make a halting figure in the universal dance. And some, like sour spectators at the play, receive the music into their hearts with an unmoved countenance, and walk like strangers through the general rejoicing. But let him feign never so carefully, there is not a man but has his pulses shaken when Pan trolls out a stave of ecstasy and sets the world a-singing.

Alas if that were all! But oftentimes the air is changed; and in the screech of the night wind, chasing navies, subverting the tall ships and the rooted cedar of the hills; in the random deadly levin or the fury of headlong

---

11. **Hamlet tells us.** *Hamlet*, V, i, 236-237—
Imperious Caesar, dead and turned to clay,
Might stop a hole to keep the wind away.
17. **hell's squib,** a kind of explosive or firecracker. 24. **fire . . . fiddling.** An allusion to the story of the emperor Nero's playing the fiddle while Rome burned (first century A.D.).

70. **young lambs . . . tabor.** From Wordsworth's *Ode on Immortality*, ll. 20-21, p. 160. 91. **subverting,** overturning. 93. **levin,** lightning.

floods, we recognize the "dread foundation" of life and the anger in Pan's heart. Earth wages open war against her children, and under her softest touch hides treacherous claws. The cool waters invite us in to drown; the domestic hearth burns up in the hour of sleep, and makes an end of all. Everything is good or bad, helpful or deadly, not in itself, but by its circumstances. For a few bright days in England the hurricane must break forth and the North Sea pay a toll of populous ships. And when the universal music has led lovers into the paths of dalliance, confident of Nature's sympathy, suddenly the air shifts into a minor, and death makes a clutch from his ambuscade below the bed of marriage. For death is given in a kiss; the dearest kindnesses are fatal; and into this life, where one thing preys upon another, the child too often makes its entrance from the mother's corpse. It is no wonder, with so traitorous a scheme of things, if the wise people who created for us the idea of Pan thought that of all fears the fear of him was the most terrible, since it embraces all. And still we preserve the phrase: a panic terror. To reckon dangers too curiously, to hearken too intently for the threat that runs through all the winning music of the world, to hold back the hand from the rose because of the thorn, and from life because of death: this it is to be afraid of Pan. Highly respectable citizens who flee life's pleasures and responsibilities and keep, with upright hat, upon the midway of custom, avoiding the right hand and the left, the ecstasies and the agonies, how surprised they would be if they could hear their attitude mythologically expressed, and knew themselves as tooth-chattering ones, who flee from Nature because they fear the hand of Nature's God! Shrilly sound Pan's pipes; and behold the banker instantly concealed in the bank parlor! For to distrust one's impulses is to be recreant to Pan.

There are moments when the mind refuses to be satisfied with evolution, and demands a ruddier presentation of the sum of man's experience. Sometimes the mood is brought about by laughter at the humorous side of life, as when, abstracting ourselves from earth, we imagine people plodding on foot, or seated in ships and speedy trains, with the planet all the while whirling in the opposite direction, so that, for all their hurry they travel back-foremost through the universe of space. Sometimes it comes by the spirit of delight, and sometimes by the spirit of terror. At least, there will always be hours when we refuse to be put off by the feint of explanation, nicknamed science; and demand instead some palpitating image of our estate, that shall represent the troubled and uncertain element in which we dwell, and satisfy reason by the means of art. Science writes of the world as if with the cold finger of a starfish; it is all true; but what is it when compared to the reality of which it discourses? where hearts beat high in April, and death strikes, and hills totter in the earthquake, and there is a glamour over all the objects of sight, and a thrill in all noises for the ear, and Romance herself has made her dwelling among men? So we come back to the old myth, and hear the goat-footed piper making the music which is itself the charm and terror of things; and when a glen invites our visiting footsteps, fancy that Pan leads us thither with a gracious tremolo; or when our hearts quail at the thunder of the cataract, tell ourselves that he has stamped his hoof in the nigh thicket.

26. **a panic terror,** fear that seizes people without obvious cause; the kind for which Pan was responsible.

46. **evolution.** In *Pulvis et Umbra* (1888), p. 932, Stevenson speaks of evolution as "a new doctrine, received with screams a little while ago by canting moralists, and still not properly worked into the body of our thoughts, lights us a step farther into the heart of this rough but noble universe." 71. **Romance.** Cf. Kipling's *The King*, p. 891.

Pulvis et Umbra

Stevenson took the title of this essay from one of Horace's *Odes* (4, 7): *"pulvis et umbra sumus"*—When we descend where father Aeneas, rich Tullus, and Ancus abide, we become *dust and a shade*.

In April, 1888, while at Saranac Lake, New York, for his health, Stevenson said in a letter to Miss Adelaide Boodle: "I wrote a paper the other day—*Pulvis et Umbra;*—I wrote it with great feeling and conviction; to me it seemed bracing and healthful; it is in such a world (so seen by me) that I am very glad to fight out my battle, and see some fine sunsets, and hear some excellent jests between whiles round the camp fire. . . . If my view be everything but the nonsense that it may be—to me it seems self-evident and blinding truth—surely of all things it makes this world holier. There is nothing in it but the moral side—but the great battle and the breathing times with their refreshments. I see no more and no less. And if you look again, it is not ugly, and it is filled with promise." The thought expressed in the essay should be compared with Pater's thought in the *Conclusion* to *Studies in the History of the Renaissance* (p. 583). The essay was first published in *Scribner's Magazine* for April, 1888 (see biographical sketch) and reprinted in *Across the Plains* (1892).

WE LOOK for some reward of our endeavors and are disappointed; not success, not happiness, not even peace of conscience, crowns our ineffectual efforts to do well. Our frailties are invincible, our virtues barren; the battle goes sore against us to the going down of the sun. The canting moralist tells us of right and wrong; and we look abroad, even on the face of our small earth, and find them change with every climate, and no country where some action is not honored for a virtue and none where it is not branded for a vice; and we look in our experience, and find no vital congruity in the wisest rules, but at the best a municipal fitness. It is not strange if we are tempted to despair of good. We ask too much. Our religions and moralities have been trimmed to flatter us, till they are all emasculate and sentimentalized, and only please and weaken. Truth is of a rougher strain. In the harsh face of life, faith can read a bracing gospel. The human race is a thing more ancient than the ten commandments; and the bones and revolutions of the Kosmos, in whose joints we are but moss and fungus, more ancient still.

I

Of the Kosmos in the last resort, science reports many doubtful things and all of them appalling. There seems no substance on this solid globe on which we stamp: nothing but symbols and ratios. Symbols and ratios carry us and bring us forth and beat us down; gravity that swings the incommensurable suns and worlds through space, is but a figment varying inversely as the squares of distances; and the suns and worlds themselves, imponderable figures of abstractions, NH_3 and H_2O. Consideration dares not dwell upon this view; that way madness lies; science carries us into zones of speculation, where there is no habitable city for the mind of man.

But take the Kosmos with a grosser faith, as our senses give it us. We behold space sown with rotary islands, suns and worlds and the shards and wrecks of systems: some, like the sun, still blazing; some rotting, like the earth; others, like the moon, stable in desolation. All of these we take to be made of something we call matter: a thing no analysis can help us to conceive; to whose incredible properties no familiarities can reconcile our minds. This stuff, when not purified by the lustration of fire, rots uncleanly into something we call life; seized through all its atoms with a pediculous malady; swelling in tumors that become independent, sometimes even (by an abhorrent prodigy) locomotory; one splitting into millions, millions cohering into one, as the malady proceeds through varying stages. This vital putrescence of the dust, used as we are to it, yet strikes us with occasional disgust, and the profusion of worms in a piece of ancient turf, or the air of a marsh darkened with insects, will sometimes check our breathing so that we aspire for cleaner places. But none is clean: the moving sand is infected with lice; the pure spring, where it bursts out of the mountain, is a mere issue of worms; even in the hard rock the crystal is forming.

6. **battle ... sun.** Cf. *1 Samuel*, 31:3: "And the battle went sore against Saul"; also the *Iliad*, XIX: "For no man fasting from food shall be able to fight with the foe all day till the going down of the sun." 15. **municipal**, pertaining to internal affairs. 24. **Kosmos**, the universe regarded as an orderly system.

37. NH_3 **and** H_2O, chemical formulas for ammonia and water respectively. 39. **that ... lies.** From *King Lear* III, iv, 21. King Lear, suffering in the storm, shuns the thought of his daughters' ingratitude by saying, "O, that way madness lies." 45. **shards**, fragments. 53. **lustration**, a ceremony of purification on entering a holy place. 55. **pediculous**, covered with lice. 57. **locomotory**, self-propelling.

In two main shapes this eruption covers the countenance of the earth: the animal and the vegetable: one in some degree the inversion of the other: the second rooted to the spot; the first coming detached out of its natal mud, and scurrying abroad with the myriad feet of insects or towering into the heavens on the wings of birds: a thing so inconceivable that, if it be well considered, the heart stops. To what passes with the anchored vermin, we have little clue: doubtless they have their joys and sorrows, their delights and killing agonies: it appears not how. But of the locomotory, to which we ourselves belong, we can tell more. These share with us a thousand miracles: the miracles of sight, of hearing, of the projection of sound, things that bridge space; the miracles of memory and reason, by which the present is conceived, and when it is gone, its image kept living in the brains of man and brute; the miracle of reproduction, with its imperious desires and staggering consequences. And to put the last touch upon this mountain mass of the revolting and the inconceivable, all these prey upon each other, lives tearing other lives in pieces, cramming them inside themselves, and by that summary process, growing fat: the vegetarian, the whale, perhaps the tree, not less than the lion of the desert; for the vegetarian is only the eater of the dumb.

Meanwhile our rotary island loaded with predatory life, and more drenched with blood, both animal and vegetable, than ever mutinied ship, scuds through space with unimaginable speed, and turns alternate cheeks to the reverberation of a blazing world, ninety million miles away.

2

What a monstrous specter is this man, the disease of agglutinated dust, lifting alternate feet or lying drugged with slumber; killing, feeding, growing, bringing forth small copies of himself; grown upon with hair like grass, fitted with eyes that move and glitter in his face; a thing to set children screaming;—and yet looked at nearlier, known as his fellows know him, how surprising are his attributes! Poor soul, here for so little, cast among so many hardships, filled with desires so incommensurate and so inconsistent, savagely surrounded, savagely descended, irremediably condemned to prey upon his fellow lives: who should have blamed him had he been of a piece with his destiny and a being merely barbarous? And we look and behold him instead filled with imperfect virtues: infinitely childish, often admirably valiant, often touchingly kind; sitting down, amidst his momentary life, to debate of right and wrong and the attributes of the deity; rising up to do battle for an egg or die for an idea; singling out his friends and his mate with cordial affection; bringing forth in pain, rearing with long-suffering solicitude, his young. To touch the heart of his mystery, we find in him one thought, strange to the point of lunacy: the thought of duty; the thought of something owing to himself, to his neighbor, to his God: an ideal of decency, to which he would rise if it were possible; a limit of shame, below which, if it be possible, he will not stoop. The design in most men is one of conformity; here and there, in picked natures, it transcends itself and soars on the other side, arming martyrs with independence; but in all, in their degrees, it is a bosom thought:—Not in man alone, for we trace it in dogs and cats whom we know fairly well, and doubtless some similar point of honor sways the elephant, the oyster, and the louse, of whom we know so little:—But in man, at least, it sways with so complete an empire that merely selfish things come second, even with the selfish: that appetites are starved, fears are conquered, pains supported; that almost the dullest shrinks from the reproof of a glance, although it were a child's; and all but the most cowardly stand amid the risks of war; and the more noble, having strongly conceived an act as due to their ideal, affront and embrace death. Strange enough if, with their singular origin and perverted practice, they think they are to be rewarded in some future life: stranger still, if they are persuaded of the

---

39. **What . . . man.** Cf. Hunt's *The Fish, the Man, and the Spirit*, ll. 15-28, p. 305.

65. **heart of his mystery.** Cf. *Hamlet*, III, ii, 382: "You would pluck out the heart of my mystery" (secret).

contrary, and think this blow, which they solicit, will strike them senseless for eternity. I shall be reminded what a tragedy of misconception and misconduct man at large presents: of organized injustice, cowardly violence, and treacherous crime; and of the damning imperfections of the best. They cannot be too darkly drawn. Man is indeed marked for failure in his efforts to do right. But where the best consistently miscarry, how tenfold more remarkable that all should continue to strive; and surely we should find it both touching and inspiring, that in a field from which success is banished, our race should not cease to labor.

If the first view of this creature, stalking in his rotatory isle, be a thing to shake the courage of the stoutest, on this nearer sight, he startles us with an admiring wonder. It matters not where we look, under what climate we observe him, in what stage of society, in what depth of ignorance, burthened with what erroneous morality; by camp fires in Assiniboia, the snow powdering his shoulders, the wind plucking his blanket, as he sits, passing ceremonial calumet and uttering his grave opinions like a Roman senator; in ships at sea, a man inured to hardship and vile pleasures, his brightest hope a fiddle in a tavern and a bedizened trull who sells herself to rob him, and he for all that simple, innocent, cheerful, kindly like a child, constant to toil, brave to drown, for others; in the slums of cities, moving among indifferent millions to mechanical employments, without hope of change in the future, with scarce a pleasure in the present, and yet true to his virtues, honest up to his lights, kind to his neighbors, tempted perhaps in vain by the bright gin-palace, perhaps long-suffering with the drunken wife that ruins him; in India (a woman this time) kneeling with broken cries and streaming tears, as she drowns her child in the sacred river; in the brothel, the discard of society, living mainly on strong drink, fed with affronts, a fool, a thief, the comrade of thieves, and even here keeping the point of honor and the touch of pity, often repaying the world's scorn with service, often standing firm upon a scruple, and at a certain cost, rejecting riches:—everywhere some virtue cherished or affected, everywhere some decency of thought and carriage, everywhere the ensign of man's ineffectual goodness:—ah! if I could show you this! if I could show you these men and women, all the world over, in every stage of history, under every abuse of error, under every circumstance of failure without hope, without help, without thanks, still obscurely fighting the lost fight of virtue, still clinging, in the brothel or on the scaffold, to some rag of honor, the poor jewel of their souls! They may seek to escape, and yet they cannot; it is not alone their privilege and glory, but their doom; they are condemned to some nobility; all their lives long, the desire of good is at their heels, the implacable hunter.

Of all earth's meteors, here at least is the most strange and consoling: That this ennobled lemur, this hair-crowned bubble of the dust, this inheritor of a few years and sorrows, should yet deny himself his rare delights, and add to his frequent pains, and live for an ideal, however misconceived. Nor can we stop with man. A new doctrine, received with screams a little while ago by canting moralists, and still not properly worked into the body of our thoughts, lights us a step farther into the heart of this rough but noble universe. For nowadays the pride of man denies in vain his kinship with the original dust. He stands no longer like a thing apart. Close at his heels we see the dog, prince of another genus: and in him too, we see dumbly testified the same cultus of an unattainable ideal, the same constancy in failure. Does it stop with the dog? We look at our feet where the ground is blackened with the swarming ant: a creature so small, so far from us in the hierarchy of brutes, that we can scarce trace and scarce

24. **Assiniboia,** a town in Saskatchewan, Canada. 26. **calumet,** the pipe of peace passed around by North American Indians when making treaties. 43. **drowns . . . river.** Before India came under British control, it was a common practice for children to be drowned in the Ganges, the sacred river, as sacrifices to appease an angry god.

47. **point of honor.** Cf. the old proverb, "There is honor amongst thieves." 48. **touch of pity.** Cf. *Richard III,* I, ii, 71—"No beast so fierce but knows some touch of pity." 62. **jewel . . . souls.** Cf. *Othello,* III, iii, 156—
  Good name in man and woman, dear my lord,
  Is the immediate jewel of their souls.
70. **lemur,** a nocturnal animal resembling a monkey. 75. **A new doctrine,** the doctrine of evolution. 85. **cultus,** worship; a favorite word with Stevenson.

comprehend his doings; and here also, in his ordered polities and rigorous justice, we see confessed the law of duty and the fact of individual sin. Does it stop, then, with the ant? Rather this desire of well-doing and this doom of frailty run through all the grades of life: rather is this earth, from the frosty top of Everest to the next margin of the internal fire, one stage of ineffectual virtues and one temple of pious tears and perseverance. The whole creation groaneth and travaileth together. It is the common and the god-like law of life. The browsers, the biters, the barkers, the hairy coats of field and forest, the squirrel in the oak, the thousand-footed creeper in the dust, as they share with us the gift of life, share with us the love of an ideal: strive like us—like us are tempted to grow weary of the struggle—to do well; like us receive at times unmerited refreshment, visitings of support, returns of courage; and are condemned like us to be crucified between that double law of the members and the will. Are they like us, I wonder, in the timid hope of some reward, some sugar with the drug? do they, too, stand aghast at unrewarded virtues, at the sufferings of those whom, in our partiality, we take to be just, and the prosperity of such as, in our blindness we call wicked? It may be, and yet God knows what they should look for. Even while they look, even while they repent, the foot of man treads them by thousands in the dust, the yelping hounds burst upon their trail, the bullet speeds, the knives are heating in the den of the vivisectionist; or the dew falls, and the generation of a day is blotted out. For these are creatures, compared with whom our weakness is strength, our ignorance wisdom, our brief span eternity.

And as we dwell, we living things, in our isle of terror and under the imminent hand of death, God forbid it should be man the erected, the reasoner, the wise in his own eyes —God forbid it should be man that wearies in well-doing, that despairs of unrewarded effort, or utters the language of complaint. Let it be enough for faith, that the whole creation groans in mortal frailty, strives with unconquerable constancy: surely not all in vain. (1888)

8. **Everest**, the highest mountain in the world (29,000 feet), in the Himalayas. 11. **whole . . . together.** Cf. *Romans*, 8:22: "For we know that the whole creation groaneth and travaileth in pain together until now." 22. **double law . . . will.** Cf. *Romans*, 7:23: "But I see another law in my members, warring against the law of my mind, and bringing me into captivity to the law of sin which is in my members."

35. **vivisectionist.** In his *Life of Robert Louis Stevenson* (11, 217) Graham Balfour says: "It must be laid to the credit of his reason and the firm balance of his judgment that although vivisection was a subject he could not endure even to have mentioned, yet, with all his imagination and sensibility, he never ranged himself among the opponents of this method of inquiry, provided, of course, it was limited, as in England, with the utmost rigor possible." 43. **wise . . . eyes.** Cf. *Isaiah*, 5:21: "Woe unto them that are wise in their own eyes, and prudent in their own sight!" 44. **wearies in well-doing.** Cf. *Galatians*, 6:9: "And let us not be weary in well-doing: for in due season we shall reap, if we faint not."

Rudyard Kipling*

1865-1936

The Man Who Was

This story was written originally for the *Civil and Military Gazette*, Lahore, when Kipling was sub-editor of that magazine in the very early days of his work as a journalist in India; it was published in 1887, together with other early stories, in *Plain Tales from the Hills*. Both the content and style are typical of Kipling's early work. Against a background of the military life of India is thrown the tragic tale of an officer and gentleman whose best years have been spent in convict exile, but who returns, like a lost soul, to his own regiment. Military ethics in a crack regiment, the superficial gayety of social life at an army post, the chronic suspicion and fear of Russia and the Russians that existed in India, all appear in a narrative that is full of dramatic contrasts and surprises. Kipling's technique here is characteristic of his early stories. He secures local color by a careful choice of details and words, and makes his crises more dramatic by suggesting rather than fully developing them.

*For the account of Kipling's life and works see p. 885.

LET IT BE clearly understood that the Russian is a delightful person till he tucks his shirt in. As an Oriental he is charming. It is only when he insists upon being treated as the most easterly of Western peoples, instead of the most westerly of Easterns, that he becomes a racial anomaly extremely difficult to handle. The host never knows which side of his nature is going to turn up next.

Dirkovitch was a Russian—a Russian of the Russians, as he said—who appeared to get his bread by serving the czar as an officer in a Cossack regiment, and corresponding for a Russian newspaper with a name that was never twice the same. He was a handsome young Oriental, with a taste for wandering through unexplored portions of the earth, and he arrived in India from nowhere in particular. At least no living man could ascertain whether it was by way of Balkh, Budukhsham, Chitral, Beloochistan, Nepaul, or anywhere else. The Indian government, being in an unusually affable mood, gave orders that he was to be civilly treated, and shown everything that was to be seen; so he drifted, talking bad English and worse French, from one city to another till he foregathered with her Majesty's White Hussars in the city of Peshawur, which stands at the mouth of that narrow sword-cut in the hills that men call the Khyber Pass. He was undoubtedly an officer, and he was decorated, after the manner of the Russians, with little enameled crosses, and he could talk and (though this has nothing to do with his merits) he had been given up as a hopeless task or case by the Black Tyrones, who, individually and collectively, with hot whisky and honey, mulled brandy and mixed spirits of all kinds, had striven in all hospitality to make him drunk. And when the Black Tyrones, who are exclusively Irish, fail to disturb the peace of head of a foreigner, that foreigner is certain to be a superior man. This was the argument of the Black Tyrones, but they were ever an unruly and self-opinionated regiment, and they allowed junior subalterns of four years' service to choose their wines. The spirits were always purchased by the colonel and a committee of majors. And a regiment that would so behave may be respected but cannot be loved.

The White Hussars were as conscientious in choosing their wine as in charging the enemy. There was a brandy that had been purchased by a cultured colonel a few years after the Battle of Waterloo. It has been maturing ever since, and it was a marvelous brandy at the purchasing. The memory of that liquor would cause men to weep as they lay dying in the teak forests of upper Burma or the slime of Irrawaddy. And there was a port which was notable; and there was a champagne of an obscure brand, which always came to mess without any labels, because the White Hussars wished none to know where the source of supply might be found. The officer on whose head the champagne-choosing lay, was forbidden the use of tobacco for six weeks previous to sampling.

This particularity of detail is necessary to emphasize the fact that that champagne, that port, and above all, that brandy—the green and yellow and white liqueurs did not count —was placed at the absolute disposition of Dirkovitch, and he enjoyed himself hugely —even more than among the Black Tyrones.

But he remained distressingly European through it all. The White Hussars were— "My dear true friends," "Fellow-soldiers glorious," and "Brothers inseparable." He would unburden himself by the hour on the glorious future that awaited the combined arms of England and Russia when their hearts and their territories should run side by side, and the great mission of civilizing Asia should

---

The Man Who Was, from LIFE'S HANDICAP, copyright, 1887; reprinted by permission of Mrs. George Bambridge, The Macmillan Co., Ltd., and The Macmillan Co. of Canada, Ltd.
2. till . . . shirt in, till he gives up customs or traits of his own country for those of another. When this story was written, the shirt of the Russian peasant was worn loosely over his other garments. 13. Cossack. The Cossacks were noted among Russian soldiers for their horsemanship. 20. Balkh . . . Nepaul, provinces through one of which persons must pass going from Russia to India. 28. her Majesty's White Hussars, a famous cavalry regiment of Great Britain. 36. Black Tyrones, an Irish regiment named from the county of Tyrone.

47. to choose their wines. A privilege usually reserved for the older officers. 56. Waterloo, the decisive battle of the Napoleonic Wars, won by the British under the Duke of Wellington (1815). Cf. Byron's *Childe Harold's Pilgrimage*, III, 181 ff., p. 215. 60. teak, a tall native Indian tree noted for the hardness of its wood. Burma, a province of British India. 61. Irrawaddy, the chief river of Burma, noted for its malarial climate. Cf. Kipling's "*Fuzzy-Wuzzy*," p. 889, note 15.

begin. That was unsatisfactory, because Asia is not going to be civilized after the methods of the West. There is too much Asia, and she is too old. You cannot reform a lady of many lovers, and Asia has been insatiable in her flirtations aforetime. She will never attend Sunday School, or learn to vote save with swords for tickets.

Dirkovitch knew this as well as anyone else, but it suited him to talk special-correspondently and to make himself as genial as he could. Now and then he volunteered a little, a very little, information about his own sotnia of Cossacks, left apparently to look after themselves somewhere at the back of beyond. He had done rough work in Central Asia, and had seen rather more help-yourself fighting than most men of his years. But he was careful never to betray his superiority, and more than careful to praise on all occasions the appearance, drill, uniform, and organization of her Majesty's White Hussars. And, indeed they were a regiment to be admired. When Mrs. Durgan, widow of the late Sir John Durgan, arrived in their station, and after a short time had been proposed to by every single man at mess, she put the public sentiment very neatly when she explained that they were all so nice that unless she could marry them all, including the colonel and some majors who were already married, she was not going to content herself with one of them. Wherefore she wedded a little man in a rifle regiment—being by nature contradictious—and the White Hussars were going to wear crape on their arms, but compromised by attending the wedding in full force, and lining the aisle with unutterable reproach. She had jilted them all—from Basset-Holmer, the senior captain, to Little Mildred, the last subaltern, and he could have given her four thousand a year and a title. He was a viscount, and on his arrival the mess had said he had better go into the Guards, because they were all sons of large grocers and small clothiers in the Hussars, but Mildred begged very hard to be allowed to stay, and behaved so prettily that he was forgiven, and became a man, which is much more important than being any sort of viscount.

The only persons who did not share the general regard for the White Hussars were a few thousand gentlemen of Jewish extraction who lived across the border, and answered to the name of Pathan. They had only met the regiment officially, and for something less than twenty minutes, but the interview, which was complicated with many casualties, had filled them with prejudice. They even called the White Hussars "children of the devil," and sons of persons whom it would be perfectly impossible to meet in decent society. Yet they were not above making their aversion fill their money belts. The regiment possessed carbines, beautiful Martini-Henry carbines, that would lob a bullet into an enemy's camp at one thousand yards, and were even handier than the long rifle. Therefore they were coveted all along the border, and since demand inevitably breeds supply, they were supplied at the risk of life and limb for exactly their weight in coined silver —seven and one-half pounds of rupees, or sixteen pounds and a few shillings each, reckoning the rupee at par. They were stolen at night by snaky-haired thieves that crawled on their stomachs under the nose of the sentries; they disappeared mysteriously from armracks; and in the hot weather when all the doors and windows were open, they vanished like puffs of their own smoke. The border people desired them first for their own family vendettas, and then for contingencies. But in the long, cold nights of the northern Indian winter they were stolen most extensively. The traffic of murder was liveliest among the hills at that season, and prices ruled high. The regimental guards were first doubled and then trebled. A trooper does not much care if he loses a weapon—government must make it good—but he deeply re-

---

10. **special-correspondently,** in the manner of a special newspaper correspondent. 14. **sotnia,** a cavalry squadron; literally, a hundred. 44. **the Guards,** a special group of soldiers assigned as a bodyguard of the sovereign. 55. **Pathan,** an Afghan tribe. Cf. Kipling's "*Fuzzy-Wuzzy,*" p. 888. 65. **Martini-Henry carbines,** rifles named after Frederic Martini (1832-1897), a Swiss inventor, and a Scotch gunmaker (d. 1894) named Henry; cf. p. 889, note 23. 66. **lob,** throw well into the air, as in a *lob* in cricket or tennis. 73. **rupee,** a silver coin worth about thirty-two cents.

sents the loss of his sleep. The regiment grew very angry, and one night-thief who managed to limp away, bears the visible marks of their anger upon him to this hour. That incident stopped the burglaries for a time, and the guards were reduced accordingly, and the regiment devoted itself to polo with unexpected results, for it beat by two goals to one that very terrible polo corps, the Lushkar Light Horse, though the latter had four ponies apiece for a short hour's fight, as well as a native officer who played like a lambent flame across the ground.

Then they gave a dinner to celebrate the event. The Lushkar team came, and Dirkovitch came, in the fullest full uniform of a Cossack officer, which is as full as a dressing-gown, and was introduced to the Lushkars, and opened his eyes as he regarded them. They were lighter men than the Hussars, and they carried themselves with the swing that is the peculiar right of the Punjab frontier force and all irregular horse. Like everything else in the service, it has to be learned; but, unlike many things, it is never forgotten, and remains on the body till death.

The great beam-roofed mess room of the White Hussars was a sight to be remembered. All the mess plate was on the long table— the same table that had served up the bodies of five dead officers in a forgotten fight long and long ago—the dingy, battered standards faced the door of entrance, clumps of winter roses lay between the silver candlesticks, the portraits of eminent officers deceased looked down on their successors from between the heads of sambar, nilgai, maikhor, and, pride of all the mess, two grinning snow-leopards that had cost Basset-Holmer four months' leave that he might have spent in England instead of on the road to Tibet, and the daily risk of his life on ledge, snowslide, and glassy grass slope.

The servants, in spotless white muslin and the crest of their regiments on the brow of their turbans, waited behind their masters, who were clad in the scarlet and gold of the White Hussars and the cream and silver of the Lushkar Light Horse. Dirkovitch's dull green uniform was the only dark spot at the board, but his big onyx eyes made up for it. He was fraternizing effusively with the captain of the Lushkar team, who was wondering how many of Dirkovitch's Cossacks his own long, lathy down-countrymen could account for in a fair charge. But one does not speak of these things openly.

The talk rose higher and higher, and the regimental band played between the courses, as is the immemorial custom, till all tongues ceased for a moment with the removal of the dinner slips and the First Toast of Obligation, when the colonel, rising, said, "Mr. Vice, the Queen," and Little Mildred from the bottom of the table answered, "The Queen, God bless her!" and the big spurs clanked as the big men heaved themselves up and drank the Queen, upon whose pay they were falsely supposed to pay their mess-bills. That sacrament of the mess never grows old, and never ceases to bring a lump into the throat of the listener wherever he be, by land or sea. Dirkovitch rose with his "brothers glorious," but he could not understand. No one but an officer can understand what the toast means; and the bulk have more sentiment than comprehension. It all comes to the same in the end, as the enemy said when he was wriggling on a lance point. Immediately after the little silence that follows on the ceremony there entered the native officer who had played for the Lushkar team. He could not of course eat with the alien, but he came in at dessert, all six feet of him, with the blue-and-silver turban atop, and the big black top-boots below. The mess rose joyously as he thrust forward the hilt of his saber, in token of fealty, for the colonel of the White Hussars to touch, and dropped into a vacant chair amid shouts of "*Rung ho!* Hira Singh!" (which being translated means "Go in and win!"). "Did I whack you over the knee, old man?" "Ressaldar Sahib, what the devil made you play

---

22. **Punjab,** a province of northwest British India. 37. **sambar . . . maikhor,** Asiatic game animals, resembling deer. 41. **Tibet,** a mountainous dependency of China.

63. **Mr. Vice,** the title bestowed upon Little Mildred, because he was acting as vice-chairman, one of the two presiding officers at a banquet. 92. **Ressaldar,** a native commander of a troop of cavalry. *Sahib* is equivalent to *honorable.*

that kicking pig of a pony in the last ten minutes?" "Shabash, Ressaldar Sahib!" Then the voice of the colonel, "The health of Ressaldar Hira Singh!"

After the shouting had died away, Hira Singh rose to reply, for he was the cadet of a royal house, the son of a king's son, and knew what was due on these occasions. Thus he spoke in the vernacular:

"Colonel Sahib and officers of this regiment, much honor have you done me. This will I remember. We came down from afar to play you; but we were beaten." ("No fault of yours, Ressaldar Sahib. Played on our own ground y'know. Your ponies were cramped from the railway. Don't apologize.") "Therefore perhaps we will come again if it be so ordained." ("Hear! Hear, hear, indeed! Bravo! Hsh!") "Then we will play you afresh" ("Happy to meet you"), "till there are left no feet upon our ponies. Thus far for sport." He dropped one hand on his sword-hilt and his eye wandered to Dirkovitch lolling back in his chair. "But if by the will of God there arises any other game which is not the polo game, then be assured, Colonel Sahib and officers, that we shall play it out side by side, though *they*"—again his eye sought Dirkovitch—"though *they*, I say, have fifty ponies to our one horse." And with a deep-mouthed *Rung ho!* that rang like a musket-butt on flagstones, he sat down amid shoutings.

Dirkovitch, who had devoted himself steadily to the brandy—the terrible brandy aforementioned—did not understand, nor did the expurgated translations offered to him at all convey the point. Decidedly the native officer's was the speech of the evening, and the clamor might have continued to the dawn had it not been broken by the noise of a shot without that sent every man feeling at his defenseless left side. It is notable that Dirkovitch "reached back," after the American fashion—a gesture that set the captain of the Lushkar team wondering how Cossack officers were armed at mess. Then there was a scuffle, and a yell of pain.

"Carbine stealing again!" said the adjutant, calmly sinking back in his chair. "This comes of reducing the guards. I hope the sentries have killed him."

The feet of armed men pounded on the veranda flags, and it sounded as though something was being dragged.

"Why don't they put him in the cells till morning?" said the colonel, testily. "See if they've damaged him, sergeant."

The mess-sergeant fled out into the darkness, and returned with two troopers and a corporal, all very much perplexed.

"Caught a man stealin' carbines, sir," said the corporal. "Leastways 'e was crawlin' towards the barricks, sir, past the main-road sentries; an' the sentry 'e says, sir—"

The limp heap of rags upheld by the three men groaned. Never was seen so destitute and demoralized an Afghan. He was turbanless, shoeless, caked with dirt, and all but dead with rough handling. Hira Singh started slightly at the sound of the man's pain. Dirkovitch took another liqueur glass of brandy.

"*What* does the sentry say?" said the colonel.

"Sez he speaks English, sir," said the corporal.

"So you brought him into mess instead of handing him over to the sergeant! If he spoke all the tongues of the Pentecost you've no business—"

Again the bundle groaned and muttered. Little Mildred had risen from his place to inspect. He jumped back as though he had been shot.

"Perhaps it would be better, sir, to send the men away," said he to the colonel, for he was a much-privileged subaltern. He put his arms round the rag-bound horror as he spoke, and dropped him into a chair. It may not have been explained that the littleness of Mildred lay in his being six feet four, and big in proportion. The corporal, seeing that an officer was disposed to look after the capture, and that the colonel's eye was beginning to blaze, promptly removed himself and his men. The

---

2. **Shabash**, bravo!

54. **flags**, flag-stones. 79. **all . . . Pentecost.** An allusion to the divers languages spoken by the apostles on the day of Pentecost as related in *Acts*, 2:1-12.

mess was left alone with the carbine thief, who laid his head on the table and wept bitterly, hopelessly, and inconsolably, as little children weep.

Hira Singh leaped to his feet with a long-drawn vernacular oath. "Colonel Sahib," said he, "that man is no Afghan, for they weep, '*Ai! Ai!*' Nor is he of Hindustan, for they weep '*Ow! Ho!*' He weeps after the fashion of the white men, who say '*Ow! Ow!*'"

"Now where the dickens did you get that knowledge, Hira Singh?" said the captain of the Lushkar team.

"Hear him!" said Hira Singh, simply, pointing at the crumpled figure, that wept as though it would never cease.

"He said, 'My God!'" said Little Mildred. "I heard him say it."

The colonel and the mess-room looked at the man in silence. It is a horrible thing to hear a man cry. A woman can sob from the top of her palate, or her lips, or anywhere else, but a man cries from his diaphragm, and it rends him to pieces. Also, the exhibition causes the throat of the onlooker to close at the top.

"Poor devil!" said the colonel, coughing tremendously.

"We ought to send him to hospital. He's been manhandled."

Now the adjutant loved his rifles. They were to him as his grandchildren—the men standing in the first place. He grunted rebelliously: "I can understand an Afghan stealing, because he's made that way. But I can't understand his crying. That makes it worse."

The brandy must have affected Dirkovitch, for he lay back in his chair and stared at the ceiling. There was nothing special in the ceiling beyond the shadow as of a huge black coffin. Owing to some peculiarity in the construction of the mess-room, this shadow was always thrown when the candles were lighted. It never disturbed the digestion of the White Hussars. They were, in fact, rather proud of it.

"Is he going to cry all night," said the colonel, "or are we supposed to sit with Little Mildred's guest until he feels better?"

The man in the chair threw up his head and stared at the mess. Outside, the wheels of the first of those bidden to the festivities crunched the roadway.

"Oh, my God!" said the man in the chair, and every soul in the mess rose to his feet. Then the Lushkar captain did a deed for which he ought to have been given the Victoria Cross[58]—distinguished gallantry in a fight against overwhelming curiosity. He picked up his team with his eyes, as the hostess picks up the ladies at the opportune moment, and pausing only by the Colonel's chair to say, "This isn't *our* affair, you know, sir," led the team into the veranda and the gardens. Hira Singh was the last, and he looked at Dirkovitch as he moved. But Dirkovitch had departed into a brandy paradise of his own. His lips moved without sound, and he was studying the coffin on the ceiling.

"White—white all over," said Basset-Holmer, the adjutant. "What a pernicious renegade he must be! I wonder where he came from?"

The colonel shook the man gently by the arm, and "Who are you?" said he.

There was no answer. The man stared round the mess-room and smiled in the colonel's face. Little Mildred, who was always more of a woman than a man till "Boot and Saddle" was sounded, repeated the question in a voice that would have drawn confidences from a geyser. The man only smiled. Dirkovitch, at the far end of the table, slid gently from his chair to the floor. No son of Adam, in this present imperfect world, can mix the Hussars' champagne with the Hussars' brandy by five and eight glasses of each without remembering the pit whence he has been digged and descending thither. The band began to play the tune with which the White Hussars, from the date of their formation, preface all their functions. They would sooner be disbanded than abandon that tune. It is a part of their system. The man straightened himself in his chair and drummed on the table with his fingers.

---

58. **Victoria Cross**, a bronze cross awarded to British soldiers or sailors for deeds of bravery.

"I don't see why we should entertain lunatics," said the colonel; "call a guard and send him off to the cells. We'll look into the business in the morning. Give him a glass of wine first, though."

Little Mildred filled a sherry glass with the brandy and thrust it over to the man. He drank, and the tune rose louder, and he straightened himself yet more. Then he put out his long-taloned hands to a piece of plate opposite and fingered it lovingly. There was a mystery connected with that piece of plate in the shape of a spring, which converted what was a seven-branched candlestick, three springs each side and one in the middle, into a sort of wheel-spoke candelabrum. He found the spring, pressed it, and laughed weakly. He rose from his chair and inspected a picture on the wall, then moved on to another picture, the mess watching him without a word. When he came to the mantelpiece, he shook his head and seemed distressed. A piece of plate representing a mounted hussar in full uniform caught his eye. He pointed to it, and then to the mantelpiece, with inquiry in his eyes.

"What is it—oh, what is it?" said Little Mildred. Then, as a mother might speak to a child, "That is a horse—yes, a horse."

Very slowly came the answer, in a thick, passionless guttural, "Yes, I—have seen. But —where is *the* horse?"

You could have heard the hearts of the mess beating, as the men drew back to give the stranger full room in his wanderings. There was no question of calling the guard.

Again he spoke, very slowly, "Where is *our* horse?"

There is no saying what happened after that. There is but one horse in the White Hussars, and his portrait hangs outside the door of the mess-room. He is the piebald drum-horse, the king of the regimental band, that served the regiment for seven-and-thirty years, and in the end was shot for old age. Half the mess tore the thing down from its place and thrust it into the man's hands. He placed it above the mantelpiece; it clattered on the ledge, as his poor hands dropped it, and he staggered toward the bottom of the table, falling into Mildred's chair. The band began to play the "River of Years" waltz, and the laughter from the gardens came into the tobacco-scented mess-room. But nobody, even the youngest, was thinking of waltzes. They all spoke to one another something after this fashion: "The drum-horse hasn't hung over the mantelpiece since '67." "How does he know?" "Mildred, go and speak to him again." "Colonel, what are you going to do?" "Oh, dry up, and give the poor devil a chance to pull himself together!" "It isn't possible, anyhow. The man's a lunatic."

Little Mildred stood at the colonel's side talking into his ear. "Will you be good enough to take your seats, please, gentlemen?" he said, and the mess dropped into the chairs.

Only Dirkovitch's seat, next to Little Mildred's, was blank, and Little Mildred himself had found Hira Singh's place. The wide-eyed mess-sergeant filled the glasses in dead silence. Once more the colonel rose, but his hand shook, and the port spilled on the table as he looked straight at the man in Little Mildred's chair and said, hoarsely, "Mr. Vice, the Queen." There was a little pause, but the man sprang to his feet and answered, without hesitation, "The Queen, God bless her!" and as he emptied the thin glass he snapped the shank between his fingers.

Long and long ago, when the Empress of India was a young woman, and there were no unclean ideals in the land, it was the custom in a few messes to drink the Queen's toast in broken glass, to the huge delight of the mess contractors. The custom is now dead, because there is nothing to break anything for, except now and again the word of a government, and that has been broken already.

"That settles it," said the colonel, with a gasp. "He's not a sergeant. What in the world is he?"

The entire mess echoed the word, and the volley of questions would have scared any man. Small wonder that the ragged, filthy invader could only smile and shake his head.

From under the table, calm and smiling urbanely, rose Dirkovitch, who had been aroused from healthful slumber by feet upon his body. By the side of the man he rose, and the man shrieked and groveled at his feet. It was a horrible sight, coming so swiftly upon the pride and glory of the toast that had brought the strayed wits together.

Dirkovitch made no offer to raise him, but Little Mildred heaved him up in an instant. It is not good that a gentleman who can answer to the Queen's toast should lie at the feet of a subaltern of Cossacks.

The hasty action tore the wretch's upper clothing nearly to the waist, and his body was seamed with dry black scars. There is only one weapon in the world that cuts in parallel lines, and it is neither the cane nor the cat. Dirkovitch saw the marks, and the pupils of his eyes dilated—also, his face changed. He said something that sounded like "Shto ve takete"; and the man, fawning, answered, "Chetyre."

"What's that?" said everybody together.

"His number. That is number four, you know." Dirkovitch spoke very quickly.

"What has a Queen's officer to do with a qualified number?" said the colonel, and there rose an unpleasant growl around the table.

"How can I tell?" said the affable Oriental, with a sweet smile. "He is a—how you have it?—escape—runaway, from over there."

He nodded toward the darkness of the night.

"Speak to him, if he'll answer you, and speak to him gently," said Little Mildred, settling the man in a chair. It seemed most improper to all present that Dirkovitch should sip brandy as he talked in purring, spitting Russian to the creature who answered so feebly and with such evident dread. But since Dirkovitch appeared to understand, no man said a word. They breathed heavily, leaning forward, in the long gaps of the conversation. The next time that they have no engagements on hand the White Hussars intend to go to St. Petersburg and learn Russian.

"He does not know how many years ago," said Dirkovitch, facing the mess, "but he says it was very long ago, in a war. I think that there was an accident. He says he was of this glorious and distinguished regiment in the war."

"The rolls! The rolls! Holmer, get the rolls!" said Little Mildred, and the adjutant dashed off bareheaded to the orderly-room, where the rolls of the regiment were kept. He returned just in time to hear Dirkovitch conclude, "Therefore I am most sorry to say there was an accident, which would have been reparable if he had apologized to that our colonel, which he had insulted."

Another growl, which the colonel tried to beat down. The mess was in no mood to weigh insults to Russian colonels just then.

"He does not remember, but I think that there was an accident, and so he was not exchanged among the prisoners, but he was sent to another place—how do you say?—the country. *So*, he says, he came here. He does not know how he came. Eh? He was at Chepany"—the man caught the word, nodded, and shivered—"at Zhigansk and Irkutsk. I cannot understand how he escaped. He says, too, that he was in the forests for many years, but how many years he has forgotten—that with many things. It was an accident; done because he did not apologize to that our colonel. Ah!"

Instead of echoing Dirkovitch's sigh of regret, it is sad to record that the White Hussars livelily exhibited unchristian delight and other emotions, hardly restrained by their sense of hospitality. Holmer flung the frayed and yellow regimental rolls on the table, and the men flung themselves atop of these.

"Steady! Fifty-six—fifty-five—fifty-four," said Holmer. "Here we are. 'Lieutenant Austin Limmason—*missing*.' That was before Sebastopol. What an infernal shame! Insulted one of their colonels, and was quietly shipped off. Thirty years of his life wiped out."

"But he never apologized. Said he'd see him ——first," chorused the mess.

"Poor devil! I suppose he never had the chance afterwards. How did he come here?" said the colonel.

---

16. **the cat,** the cat-o'-nine-tails, a whip with nine pieces of knotted cord. 19. **"Shto ve takete,"** who are you? 20. **"Chetyre,"** four.

67. **Chepany . . . Zhigansk . . . Irkutsk,** towns in Siberia, the place of exile for political prisoners in the days of the Russian monarchy. 86. **Sebastopol,** the siege of Sebastopol, a prominent Russian port, in the Crimean War (1854-1856).

The dingy heap in the chair could give no answer.

"Do you know who you are?"

It laughed weakly.

"Do you know that you are Limmason—Lieutenant Limmason, of the White Hussars?"

Swift as a shot came the answer, in a slightly surprised tone, "Yes, I'm Limmason, of course." The light died out in his eyes, and he collapsed afresh, watching every motion of Dirkovitch with terror. A flight from Siberia may fix a few elementary facts in the mind, but it does not lead to continuity of thought. The man could not explain how, like a homing pigeon, he had found his way to his own old mess again. Of what he had suffered or seen he knew nothing. He cringed before Dirkovitch as instinctively as he had pressed the spring of the candlestick, sought the picture of the drum-horse, and answered to the Queen's toast.

The rest was a blank that the dreaded Russian tongue could only in part remove. His head bowed on his breast, and he giggled and cowered alternately.

The devil that lived in the brandy prompted Dirkovitch at this extremely inopportune moment to make a speech. He rose, swaying slightly, gripped the table edge, while his eyes glowed like opals, and began:

"Fellow-soldiers, glorious—true friends and hospitables. It was an accident, and deplorable —most deplorable." Here he smiled sweetly all around the mess. "But you will think of this little, little thing. So little, is it not? The czar! Posh! I slap my fingers—I snap my fingers at him. Do I believe in him? No! But the Slav who has done nothing, *him* I believe. Seventy—how much?—millions that have done nothing—not one thing. Napoleon was an episode." He banged a hand on the table. "Hear you, old peoples, we have done nothing in the world—out here. All our work is to do; and it shall be done, old peoples. Get away!" He waved his hand imperiously, and pointed to the man. "You see him. He is not good to see. He was just one little—oh, so little—accident, that no one remembered. Now he is *That*. So will you be, brother-soldiers so brave—so will you be. But you will never come back. You will all go where he has gone, or"—he pointed to the great coffin shadow on the ceiling, and muttering, "Seventy millions—get away, you old people," fell asleep.

"Sweet, and to the point," said Little Mildred. "What's the use of getting wrath? Let's make the poor devil comfortable."

But that was a matter suddenly and swiftly taken from the loving hands of the White Hussars. The lieutenant had returned only to go away again three days later when the wail of the "Dead March" and the tramp of the squadrons told the wondering station, that saw no gap in the table, an officer of the regiment had resigned his new-found commission.

And Dirkovitch—bland, supple, and always genial—went away, too, by a night train. Little Mildred and another saw him off, for he was the guest of the mess, and even had he smitten the colonel with the open hand, the law of the mess allowed no relaxation of hospitality.

"Good-by, Dirkovitch, and a pleasant journey," said Little Mildred.

"*Au revoir*, my true friends," said the Russian.

"Indeed! But we thought you were going home?"

"Yes; but I will come again. My friends, is that road shut?" He pointed to where the north star burned over the Khyber Pass.

"By Jove! I forgot. Of course. Happy to meet you, old man, any time you like. Got everything you want—cheroots, ice, bedding? That's all right. Well, *au revoir*, Dirkovitch."

"Um," said the other man, as the tail-lights of the train grew small. "Of—all—the—unmitigated—"

Little Mildred answered nothing, but watched the north star, and hummed a selection from a recent burlesque that had much delighted the White Hussars. It ran:

> I'm sorry for Mister Bluebeard,
>   I'm sorry to cause him pain;
> But a terrible spree there's sure to be
>   When he comes back again. (1890)

Joseph Conrad

1857-1924

Although a Pole by birth, Joseph Conrad became not only a British citizen but also one of the great novelists in the English language and a master of English prose. He was born as Josef Teodor Konrad Korzeniowski near Kiev, then Russian Poland, December 3, 1857. He learned English after he was twenty years of age and became a British subject in 1886.

Following the death of his parents, both of whom as loyal Polish patriots suffered exile and privation at the hands of the Russians, Conrad was brought up under the guardianship of his maternal uncle, who sought in vain to curb the boy's natural feelings of patriotism. A youthful fondness for stories of adventure fed his yearning for complete freedom of mind and spirit. In 1873, while in Venice on a vacation trip with a private tutor, he got his first glimpse of the sea, and the next year he entered upon a new life in the service of the French Mercantile Marine. After three exciting years at Marseilles and in the West Indies, he transferred to a British ship, and in June, in his twenty-first year, and not knowing any English, he first set foot upon English soil.

During the next few years, Conrad spent all his spare moments on shipboard in learning the English language, largely by studying newspapers. His faithful work as a seaman won him promotion to the rank of master seaman in 1880. Then for fourteen years he served as one of the commanding officers of British merchant ships sailing to Australia, South Africa, South America, and the Orient. In 1890 he made a perilous journey to the Congo in the heart of Africa, where among other mishaps he contracted a devastating fever and was once nearly drowned. He never completely recovered from the ill effects of this expedition. During all these years, however, while on sea voyages, in various ports, and in Africa, Conrad stored up incidents, experiences, and impressions and observed characters, which he used later in his novels and stories.

Returning to England in January, 1891, Conrad spent several months in a hospital in London and suffered a long year of pain and depression. He made two short voyages in 1892-93, on one of which he came to know John Galsworthy (p. 857). Conrad read to him a few chapters of a novel that he had started several years before, and Galsworthy entreated him to continue writing. In January, 1894, he left the marine service and settled in London. By May he had finished his first novel, *Almayer's Folly*, which was published in 1895. Encouraged by the success of this book and by the praise of Galsworthy, H. G. Wells, Henry James, and other writers and critics, Conrad began a second book and settled down to a life of creative writing. After the publication of *Chance* in 1914, his position in English prose literature was secure. He died at his home near Canterbury in 1924.

As early as 1897, in the Preface to *The Nigger of the Narcissus*, Conrad set forth his literary and artistic creed, in part as follows: "Art itself may be defined as a single-minded attempt to render the highest kind of justice to the visible universe, by bringing to light the truth, manifold and one, underlying its every aspect. It is an attempt to find in its forms, in its colors, in its light, in its shadows, in the aspect of the matter, and in the facts of life what of each is fundamental, what is enduring and essential—their one illuminating and convincing quality—the very truth of their existence. . . . The artist . . . speaks to our capacity for delight and wonder, to the sense of mystery surrounding our lives; to our sense of pity, and beauty, and pain; to the latent feeling of fellowship with all creation—and to the subtle but invincible conviction of solidarity that knits together the loneliness of innumerable hearts, to the solidarity in dreams, in joy, in sorrow, in aspirations, in illusions, in hope, in fear, which binds men to each other, which binds together all humanity—the dead to the living and the living to the unborn. . . . Fiction—if it at all aspires to be art—appeals to temperament. And in truth it must be, like painting, like music, like all art, the appeal of one temperament to all the other innumerable temperaments whose subtle and resistless power endows passing events with their true meaning, and creates the moral, the emotional atmosphere of the place and time. . . . The artistic aim when expressing itself in words . . . must strenuously aspire to the plasticity of sculpture, to the color of painting, and to the magic suggestiveness of music—which is the art of arts. And it is only through complete, unswerving devotion to the perfect blending of form and substance; it is only through an unremitting never-discouraged core for the shape and ring of sentences that an approach can be made to plasticity, to color, and that the light of magic suggestiveness may be brought to play for an evanescent instant over the commonplace surface of words: of the old, old words, worn thin, defaced by ages of careless usage. The sincere endeavor to accomplish that creative task, to go as far on that road as his strength will carry him, to go undeterred by faltering, weariness, or reproach, is the only valid justification for the worker in prose. And if his conscience is clear, his answer to those who, in the fullness of a wisdom which looks for immediate profit, demand specifically to be edified, consoled, amused; who demand to be promptly improved, or encouraged, or frightened, or shocked, or charmed, must run thus: My task which I am trying to achieve is, by the power of the written word to make you hear, to make you feel—it is, before all, to make you see. That—and no more, and it is everything. If I succeed, you shall find there according to your deserts: encouragement, consolation, fear, charm—all you demanded—and, perhaps, also that glimpse of truth for which you have forgotten to ask. To snatch in a moment of courage, from the remorseless rush of time, a passing phase of life, is only the beginning of the task. The task approached in tenderness and faith is to hold up unquestioningly, without choice and without fear, the rescued fragment before all eyes in the light of a sincere mood. It is to show its vibration, its color, its form; and through its movement, its form, and its color, reveal the substance of its truth—disclose its inspiring secret: the stress and passion within the core of each convincing moment. In a single-minded attempt of that kind, if one be deserving and fortunate, one may perchance attain to such clearness of sincerity that at last the presented vision of regret or pity, of terror or mirth, shall awaken in the hearts of the beholders that feeling of unavoidable solidarity; of the solidarity in mysterious origin, in toil, in joy, in hope, in uncertain fate, which binds men to each other and all mankind to the visible world."*

To those aims and principles, Conrad held tenaciously all his life. They are at the base of all his writing, and they combine to give that writing its fine qualities of sincere workmanship, its artistic design, its authentic interpretation of man in his complex world.

Conrad's novels include *Almayer's Folly* (1895), *An Outcast of the Islands* (1896), *The Nigger of the Narcissus* (1897), *Lord Jim* (1900), *Nostromo* (1904), *The Secret Agent* (1908), *Under Western Eyes* (1911), *Chance* (1914), *Victory* (1915), *The Shadow Line* (1917), *The Arrow of Gold* (1918), *The Rescue* (1920), *The Rover* (1924), and *Suspense* (incomplete, 1925). Conrad achieved remarkable success as a writer of short stories published under various titles: *Tales of Unrest* (1898),

---

*From *The Nigger of the Narcissus* by Joseph Conrad, copyright 1897, 1914 by Doubleday & Company, Inc. Reprinted by permission of Messrs. William Heinemann and the trustees of the Conrad estate.

Typhoon (1903), *Youth* (1903), *A Set of Six* (1908), *'Twixt Land and Sea* (1912), *Within the Tides* (1915), and *Tales of Hearsay* (1925). "The Lagoon," printed below, is one of the best individual stories; others are "Heart of Darkness," "Typhoon," "The End of the Tether," "The Secret Sharer," "The Brute," "A Warrior's Soul," and "Prince Roman." Conrad published also two valuable autobiographical sketches: *The Mirror of the Sea* (1906) and *A Personal Record* (1912); and two volumes of essays: *Notes on Life and Letters* (1921) and *Last Essays* (1926).

*The Lagoon**

THE WHITE man, leaning with both arms over the roof of the little house in the stern of the boat, said to the steersman—

"We will pass the night in Arsat's clearing. It is late."

The Malay only grunted, and went on looking fixedly at the river. The white man rested his chin on his crossed arms and gazed at the wake of the boat. At the end of the straight avenue of forests cut by the intense glitter of the river, the sun appeared unclouded and dazzling, poised low over the water that shone smoothly like a band of metal. The forests, somber and dull, stood motionless and silent on each side of the broad stream. At the foot of big, towering trees, trunkless nipa palms rose from the mud of the bank, in bunches of leaves enormous and heavy, that hung unstirring over the brown swirl of eddies. In the stillness of the air every tree, every leaf, every bough, every tendril of creeper and every petal of minute blossoms seemed to have been bewitched into an immobility perfect and final. Nothing moved on the river but the eight paddles that rose flashing regularly, dipped together with a single splash; while the steersman swept right and left with a periodic and sudden flourish of his blade describing a glinting semicircle above his head. The churned-up water frothed alongside with a confused murmur. And the white man's canoe, advancing upstream in the short-lived disturbance of its own making, seemed to enter the portals of a land from which the very memory of motion had forever departed.

The white man, turning his back upon the setting sun, looked along the empty and broad expanse of the sea-reach. For the last three miles of its course the wandering, hesitating river, as if enticed irresistibly by the freedom of an open horizon, flows straight into the sea, flows straight to the east—to the east that harbors both light and darkness. Astern of the boat the repeated call of some bird, a cry discordant and feeble, skipped along over the smooth water and lost itself, before it could reach the other shore, in the breathless silence of the world.

The steersman dug his paddle into the stream, and held hard with stiffened arms, his body thrown forward. The water gurgled aloud; and suddenly the long straight reach seemed to pivot on its center, the forests swung in a semicircle, and the slanting beams of sunset touched the broadside of the canoe with a fiery glow, throwing the slender and distorted shadows of its crew upon the streaked glitter of the river. The white man turned to look ahead. The course of the boat had been altered at right-angles to the stream, and the carved dragon-head of its prow was pointing now at a gap in the fringing bushes of the bank. It glided through, brushing the overhanging twigs, and disappeared from the river like some slim and amphibious creature leaving the water for its lair in the forests.

The narrow creek was like a ditch: tortuous, fabulously deep; filled with gloom under the thin strip of pure and shining blue of the heaven. Immense trees soared up, invisible behind the festooned draperies of creepers. Here and there, near the glistening blackness of the water, a twisted root of some tall tree showed amongst the tracery of small ferns, black and dull, writhing and motionless, like an arrested snake. The short words of the

---

*From *Tales of Unrest*. Reprinted by permission of Doubleday and Company, Inc., publishers, Messrs. Ernest Benn, and the trustees of the Conrad estate.
16. **nipa palms**, East Indian palms of low stature.

paddlers reverberated loudly between the thick and somber walls of vegetation. Darkness oozed out from between the trees, through the tangled maze of the creepers, from behind the great fantastic and unstirring leaves; the darkness, mysterious and invincible; the darkness scented and poisonous of impenetrable forests.

The men poled in the shoaling water. The creek broadened, opening out into a wide sweep of a stagnant lagoon. The forests receded from the marshy bank, leaving a level strip of bright green, reedy grass to frame the reflected blueness of the sky. A fleecy pink cloud drifted high above, trailing the delicate coloring of its image under the floating leaves and the silvery blossoms of the lotus. A little house, perched on high piles, appeared black in the distance. Near it, two tall nibong palms, that seemed to have come out of the forests in the background, leaned slightly over the ragged roof, with a suggestion of sad tenderness and care in the droop of their leafy and soaring heads.

The steersman, pointing with his paddle, said, "Arsat is there. I see his canoe fast between the piles."

The polers ran along the sides of the boat glancing over their shoulders at the end of the day's journey. They would have preferred to spend the night somewhere else than on this lagoon of weird aspect and ghostly reputation. Moreover, they disliked Arsat, first as a stranger, and also because he who repairs a ruined house, and dwells in it, proclaims that he is not afraid to live amongst the spirits that haunt the places abandoned by mankind. Such a man can disturb the course of fate by glances or words; while his familiar ghosts are not easy to propitiate by casual wayfarers upon whom they long to wreak the malice of their human master. White men care not for such things, being unbelievers and in league with the Father of Evil, who leads them unharmed through the invisible dangers of this world. To the warnings of the righteous they oppose an offensive pretense of disbelief. What is there to be done?

19. **nibong palms**, Malay feather palms.

So they thought, throwing their weight on the end of their long poles. The big canoe glided on swiftly, noiselessly, and smoothly, towards Arsat's clearing, till, in a great rattling of poles thrown down, and the loud murmurs of "Allah be praised!" it came with a gentle knock against the crooked piles below the house.

The boatmen with uplifted faces shouted discordantly, "Arsat! O Arsat!" Nobody came. The white man began to climb the rude ladder giving access to the bamboo platform before the house. The juragan of the boat said sulkily, "We will cook in the sampan, and sleep on the water."

"Pass my blankets and the basket," said the white man, curtly.

He knelt on the edge of the platform to receive the bundle. Then the boat shoved off, and the white man, standing up, confronted Arsat, who had come out through the low door of his hut. He was a man young, powerful, with broad chest and muscular arms. He had nothing on but his sarong. His head was bare. His big, soft eyes stared eagerly at the white man, but his voice and demeanor were composed as he asked, without any words of greeting—

"Have you medicine, Tuan?"

"No," said the visitor in a startled tone. "No. Why? Is there sickness in the house?"

"Enter and see," replied Arsat, in the same calm manner, and turning short around, passed again through the small doorway. The white man, dropping his bundles, followed.

In the dim light of the dwelling he made out on a couch of bamboos a woman stretched on her back under a broad sheet of red cotton cloth. She lay still, as if dead; but her big eyes, wide open, glittered in the gloom, staring upwards at the slender rafters, motionless and unseeing. She was in a high fever, and evidently unconscious. Her cheeks were sunk slightly, her lips were partly open, and on the young face there was the ominous and

61. **juragan**, one of the rowers, whose seat is high in the stern of the boat. 62. **sampan**, a skiff used in river and harbor traffic in the Far East; sometimes it has a sail and usually a mat roofing over its cabin.

fixed expression—the absorbed, contemplating expression of the unconscious who are going to die. The two men stood looking down at her in silence.

"Has she been long ill?" asked the traveller.

"I have not slept for five nights," answered the Malay, in a deliberate tone. "At first she heard voices calling her from the water and struggled against me who held her. But since the sun of today rose she hears nothing—she hears not me. She sees nothing. She sees not me—me!"

He remained silent for a minute, then asked softly—

"Tuan, will she die?"

"I fear so," said the white man, sorrowfully. He had known Arsat years ago, in a far country in times of trouble and danger, when no friendship is to be despised. And since his Malay friend had come unexpectedly to dwell in the hut on the lagoon with a strange woman, he had slept many times there, in his journeys up and down the river. He liked the man who knew how to keep faith in council and how to fight without fear by the side of his white friend. He liked him —not so much perhaps as a man likes his favorite dog—but still he liked him well enough to help and ask no questions, to think sometimes vaguely and hazily in the midst of his own pursuits, about the lonely man and the long-haired woman with audacious face and triumphant eyes, who lived together hidden by the forests—alone and feared.

The white man came out of the hut in time to see the enormous conflagration of sunset put out by the swift and stealthy shadows that, rising like a black and impalpable vapor above the tree-tops, spread over the heaven, extinguishing the crimson glow of floating clouds and the red brilliance of departing daylight. In a few moments all the stars came out above the intense blackness of the earth and the great lagoon gleaming suddenly with reflected lights resembled an oval patch of night sky flung down into the hopeless and abysmal night of the wilderness. The white man had some supper out of the basket, then collecting a few sticks that lay about the platform, made up a small fire, not for warmth, but for the sake of the smoke, which would keep off the mosquitos. He wrapped himself in the blankets and sat with his back against the reed wall of the house, smoking thoughtfully.

Arsat came through the doorway with noiseless steps and squatted down by the fire. The white man moved his outstretched legs a little.

"She breathes," said Arsat in a low voice, anticipating the expected question. "She breathes and burns as if with a great fire. She speaks not; she hears not—and burns!"

He paused for a moment, then asked in a quiet, incurious tone—

"Tuan . . . will she die?"

The white man moved his shoulders uneasily and muttered in a hesitating manner—

"If such is her fate."

"No, Tuan," said Arsat, calmly. "If such is my fate. I hear, I see, I wait. I remember . . . Tuan, do you remember the old days? Do you remember my brother?"

"Yes," said the white man. The Malay rose suddenly and went in. The other, sitting still outside, could hear the voice in the hut. Arsat said: "Hear me! Speak!" His words were succeeded by a complete silence. "O Diamelen!" he cried, suddenly. After that cry there was a deep sigh. Arsat came out and sank down in his old place.

They sat in silence before the fire. There was no sound within the house, there was no sound near them; but far away on the lagoon they could hear the voices of the boatmen ringing fitful and distinct on the calm water. The fire in the bows of the sampan shone faintly in the distance with a hazy red glow. Then it died out. The voices ceased. The land and the water slept invisible, unstirring and mute. It was as though there had been nothing left in the world but the glitter of stars streaming, ceaseless and vain, through the black stillness of the night.

The white man gazed straight before him into the darkness with wide-open eyes. The fear and fascination, the inspiration and the wonder of death—of death near, unavoidable, and unseen, soothed the unrest of his race and stirred the most indistinct, the most intimate of his thoughts. The ever-ready suspicion of evil, the gnawing suspicion that lurks in our hearts, flowed out into the stillness round him —into the stillness profound and dumb, and made it appear untrustworthy and infamous, like the placid and impenetrable mask of an unjustifiable violence. In that fleeting and powerful disturbance of his being the earth enfolded in the starlight peace became a shadowy country of inhuman strife, a battlefield of phantoms terrible and charming, august or ignoble, struggling ardently for the possession of our helpless hearts. An unquiet and mysterious country of inextinguishable desires and fears.

A plaintive murmur rose in the night; a murmur saddening and startling, as if the great solitudes of surrounding woods had tried to whisper into his ear the wisdom of their immense and lofty indifference. Sounds hesitating and vague floated in the air round him, shaped themselves slowly into words; and at last flowed on gently in a murmuring stream of soft and monotonous sentences. He stirred like a man waking up and changed his position slightly. Arsat, motionless and shadowy, sitting with bowed head under the stars, was speaking in a low and dreamy tone—

". . . for where can we lay down the heaviness of our trouble but in a friend's heart? A man must speak of war and of love. You, Tuan, know what war is, and you have seen me in time of danger seek death as other men seek life! A writing may be lost; a lie may be written; but what the eye has seen is truth and remains in the mind!"

"I remember," said the white man, quietly. Arsat went on with mournful composure—

"Therefore I shall speak to you of love. Speak in the night. Speak before both night and love are gone—and the eye of day looks upon my sorrow and my shame; upon my blackened face; upon my burnt-up heart."

A sigh, short and faint, marked an almost imperceptible pause, and then his words flowed on, without a stir, without a gesture.

"After the time of trouble and war was over and you went away from my country in the pursuit of your desires, which we, men of the islands, cannot understand, I and my brother became again, as we had been before, the sword-bearers of the Ruler. You know we were men of family, belonging to a ruling race, and more fit than any to carry on our right shoulder the emblem of power. And in the time of prosperity Si Dendring showed us favor, as we, in time of sorrow, had showed to him the faithfulness of our courage. It was a time of peace. A time of deer-hunts and cock-fights; of idle talks and foolish squabbles between men whose bellies are full and weapons are rusty. But the sower watched the young rice-shoots grow up without fear, and the traders came and went, departed lean and returned fat into the river of peace. They brought news, too. Brought lies and truth mixed together, so that no man knew when to rejoice and when to be sorry. We heard from them about you also. They had seen you here and had seen you there. And I was glad to hear, for I remembered the stirring times, and I always remembered you, Tuan, till the time came when my eyes could see nothing in the past, because they had looked upon the one who is dying there—in the house."

He stopped to exclaim in an intense whisper, "O Mara bahia! O Calamity!" then went on speaking a little louder:

"There's no worse enemy and no better friend than a brother, Tuan, for one brother knows another, and in perfect knowledge is strength for good or evil. I loved my brother. I went to him and told him that I could see nothing but one face, hear nothing but one voice. He told me: 'Open your heart so that she can see what is in it—and wait. Patience is wisdom. Inchi Midah may die or our Ruler may throw off his fear of a woman!' . . . I waited! . . . You remember the lady with the veiled face, Tuan, and the fear of our Ruler before her cunning and temper. And if she wanted her servant, what could I do? But I fed the hunger of my heart on short glances and stealthy words. I loitered on the path to the bathhouses in the daytime, and when the sun had fallen behind the forest I crept along the jasmine hedges of the women's courtyard. Unseeing, we spoke to one another through the scent of flowers, through the veil of leaves, through the blades of long grass that stood still before our lips; so great was our prudence, so faint was the murmur of our great longing. The time passed swiftly ... and there were whispers amongst women—and our enemies watched—my brother was gloomy, and I began to think of killing and of a fierce death.... We are of a people who take what they want—like you whites. There is a time when a man should forget loyalty and respect. Might and authority are given to rulers, but to all men is given love and strength and courage. My brother said, 'You shall take her from their midst. We are two who are like one.' And I answered, 'Let it be soon, for I find no warmth in sunlight that does not shine upon her.' Our time came when the Ruler and all the great people went to the mouth of the river to fish by torchlight. There were hundreds of boats, and on the white sand, between the water and the forests, dwellings of leaves were built for the households of the Rajahs. The smoke of cooking-fires was like a blue mist of the evening, and many voices rang in it joyfully. While they were making the boats ready to beat up the fish, my brother came to me and said, 'Tonight!' I looked to my weapons, and when the time came our canoe took its place in the circle of boats carrying the torches. The lights blazed on the water, but behind the boats there was darkness. When the shouting began and the excitement made them like mad we dropped out. The water swallowed our fire, and we floated back to the shore that was dark with only here and there the glimmer of embers. We could hear the talk of slave-girls amongst the sheds. Then we found a place deserted and silent. We waited there. She came. She came running along the shore, rapid and leaving no trace, like a leaf driven by the wind into the sea. My brother said gloomily, 'Go and take her; carry her into our boat.' I lifted her in my arms. She panted. Her heart was beating against my breast. I said, 'I take you from those people. You came to the cry of my heart, but my arms take you into my boat against the will of the great!' 'It is right,' said my brother. 'We are men who take what we want and can hold it against many. We should have taken her in daylight.' I said, 'Let us be off'; for since she was in my boat I began to think of our Ruler's many men. 'Yes. Let us be off,' said my brother. 'We are cast out and this boat is our country now—and the sea is our refuge.' He lingered with his foot on the shore, and I entreated him to hasten for I remembered the strokes of her heart against my breast and thought that two men cannot withstand a hundred. We left, paddling down-stream close to the bank; and as we passed by the creek where they were fishing, the great shouting had ceased, but the murmur of voices was loud like the humming of insects flying at noonday. The boats floated, clustered together, in the red light of torches, under a black roof of smoke; and men talked of their sport. Men that boasted, and praised, and jeered—men that would have been our friends in the morning, but on that night were already our enemies. We paddled swiftly past. We had no more friends in the country of our birth. She sat in the middle of the canoe with covered face; silent as she is now; unseeing as she is now—and I had no regret at what I was leaving because I could hear her breathing close to me—as I can hear her now."

He paused, listened with his ear turned to the doorway, then shook his head and went on:

"My brother wanted to shout the cry of challenge—one cry only—to let the people know we were freeborn robbers who trusted our arms and the great sea. And again I begged him in the name of our love to be silent. Could I not hear her breathing close to me? I knew the pursuit would come quick enough. My brother loved me. He dipped his paddle without a splash. He only said, 'There is half a man in you now—the other half is in the woman. I can wait. When you are a whole man again, you will come back with me here to shout defiance. We are sons of the same mother.' I made no answer. All my strength and all my spirit were in my hands that held the paddle—for I longed to be with her in a safe place beyond the reach of men's anger and of women's spite. My love was so great, that I thought it could guide me to a country where death was unknown, if I could only escape from Inchi Midah's fury and from our Ruler's sword. We paddled with haste, breathing through our teeth. The blades bit deep into the smooth water. We passed out of the river; we flew in clear channels amongst the shallows. We skirted the black coast; we skirted the sand beaches where the sea speaks in whispers to the land; and the gleam of white sand flashed back past our boat, so swiftly she ran upon the water. We spoke not. Only once I said, 'Sleep, Diamelen, for soon you may want all your strength.' I heard the sweetness of her voice, but I never turned my head. The sun rose and still we went on. Water fell from my face like rain from a cloud. We flew in the light and heat. I never looked back, but I knew that my brother's eyes, behind me, were looking steadily ahead, for the boat went as straight as a bushman's dart, when it leaves the end of the sumpitan. There was no better paddler, no better steersman than my brother. Many times, together, we had won races in that canoe. But we never had put out our strength as we did then—then, when for the last time we paddled together! There was no braver or stronger man in our country than my brother. I could not spare the strength to turn my head and look at him, but every moment I heard the hiss of his breath getting louder behind me. Still he did not speak. The sun was high. The heat clung to my back like a flame of fire. My ribs were ready to burst, but I could no longer get enough air into my chest. And then I felt I must cry out with my last breath, 'Let us rest!' . . . 'Good!' he answered; and his voice was firm. He was strong. He was brave. He knew not fear and no fatigue . . . My brother!"

A murmur powerful and gentle, a murmur vast and faint; the murmur of trembling leaves, of stirring boughs, ran through the tangled depths of the forests, ran over the starry smoothness of the lagoon, and the water between the piles lapped the slimy timber once with a sudden splash. A breath of warm air touched the two men's faces and passed on with a mournful sound—a breath loud and short like an uneasy sigh of the dreaming earth.

Arsat went on in an even, low voice.

"We ran our canoe on the white beach of a little bay close to a long tongue of land that seemed to bar our road; a long wooded cape going far into the sea. My brother knew that place. Beyond the cape a river has its entrance, and through the jungle of that land there is a narrow path. We made a fire and cooked rice. Then we lay down to sleep on the soft sand in the shade of our canoe, while she watched. No sooner had I closed my eyes than I heard her cry of alarm. We leaped up. The sun was halfway down the sky already, and coming in sight in the opening of the bay we saw a prau manned by many paddlers. We knew it at once; it was one of our Rajah's praus. They were watching the shore, and saw us. They beat the gong, and turned the head of the prau into the bay. I felt my heart become weak within my breast. Diamelen sat on the sand and covered her face. There was no escape by sea. My brother laughed. He had the gun you had given him, Tuan, before you went away, but there was only a handful of powder. He spoke to me quickly: 'Run with her along the path. I shall keep them back, for they have no firearms, and landing in the face of a man with a gun is certain death for some. Run with her. On the other side of that wood there is a fisherman's house—and a canoe. When I have fired all the shots I will follow. I am a great runner, and before they can come up we shall be gone. I will hold out as long as I can, for she is but a woman—that can neither run nor fight, but she has your heart in her weak hands.' He dropped behind the canoe. The prau was coming. She and I ran, and as we rushed along the path I heard shots. My brother fired —once—twice—and the booming of the gong ceased. There was silence behind us. That

---

23. **sumpitan**, a kind of blowgun for discharging a dart (often poisoned), used by savages of Borneo and adjacent islands.

67. **prau**, a Malay boat propelled by oars or by sails.

neck of land is narrow. Before I heard my brother fire the third shot I saw the shelving shore, and I saw the water again; the mouth of a broad river. We crossed a grassy glade. We ran down to the water. I saw a low hut above the black mud, and a small canoe hauled up. I heard another shot behind me. I thought, 'That is his last charge.' We rushed down to the canoe; a man came running from the hut, but I leaped on him, and we rolled together in the mud. Then I got up, and he lay still at my feet. I didn't know whether I had killed him or not. I and Diamelen pushed the canoe afloat. I heard yells behind me, and I saw my brother run across the glade. Many men were bounding after him. I took her in my arms and threw her into the boat, then leaped in myself. When I looked back I saw that my brother had fallen. He fell and was up again, but the men were closing around him. He shouted, 'I am coming!' The men were close to him. I looked. Many men. Then I looked at her. Tuan, I pushed the canoe! I pushed it into deep water. She was kneeling forward looking at me, and I said, 'Take your paddle,' while I struck the water with mine. Tuan, I heard him cry. I heard him cry my name twice; and I heard voices shouting, 'Kill! Strike!' I never turned back. I heard him calling my name again with a great shriek, as when life is going out together with the voice—and I never turned my head. My own name! . . . My brother! Three times he called—but I was not afraid of life. Was she not there in that canoe? And could I not with her find a country where death is forgotten—where death is unknown!"

The white man sat up. Arsat rose and stood, an indistinct and silent figure above the dying embers of the fire. Over the lagoon a mist drifting and low had crept, erasing slowly the glittering images of the stars. And now a great expanse of white vapor covered the land; it flowed cold and gray in the darkness, eddied in noiseless whirls around the tree-trunks and about the platform of the house, which seemed to float upon a restless and impalpable illusion of a sea. Only far away the tops of the trees stood outlined on the twinkle of heaven, like a somber and forbidding shore—a coast deceptive, pitiless and black.

Arsat's voice vibrated loudly in the profound peace.

"I had her there! I had her! To get her I would have faced all mankind. But I had her—and—"

His words went out ringing into the empty distances. He paused, and seemed to listen to them dying away very far—beyond help and beyond recall. Then he said quietly—

"Tuan, I loved my brother."

A breath of wind made him shiver. High above his head, high above the silent sea of mist the drooping leaves of the palms rattled together with a mournful and expiring sound. The white man stretched his legs. His chin rested on his chest, and he murmured sadly without lifting his head—

"We all love our brothers."

Arsat burst out with an intense whispering violence—

"What did I care who died? I wanted peace in my own heart."

He seemed to hear a stir in the house—listened—then stepped in noiselessly. The white man stood up. A breeze was coming in fitful puffs. The stars shone paler as if they had retreated into the frozen depths of immense space. After a chill gust of wind there were a few seconds of perfect calm and absolute silence. Then from behind the black and wavy line of the forests a column of golden light shot up into the heavens and spread over the semicircle of the eastern horizon. The sun had risen. The mist lifted, broke into drifting patches, vanished into thin flying wreaths; and the unveiled lagoon lay, polished and black, in the heavy shadows at the foot of the wall of trees. A white eagle rose over it with a slanting and ponderous flight, reached the clear sunshine and appeared dazzlingly brilliant for a moment, then soaring higher, became a dark and motionless speck before it vanished into the blue as if it had left the earth forever. The white man, standing gazing upwards before the doorway, heard in the hut a confused and broken murmur of distracted words ending with a loud groan. Suddenly Arsat stumbled out with outstretched hands, shivered, and stood still for some time with fixed eyes. Then he said—

"She burns no more."

Before his face the sun showed its edge above the tree-tops rising steadily. The breeze freshened; a great brilliance burst upon the lagoon, sparkled on the rippling water. The forests came out of the clear shadows of the morning, became distinct, as if they had rushed nearer—to stop short in a great stir of leaves, of nodding boughs, of swaying branches. In the merciless sunshine the whisper of unconscious life grew louder, speaking in an incomprehensible voice round the dumb darkness of that human sorrow. Arsat's eyes wandered slowly, then stared at the rising sun.

"I can see nothing," he said half aloud to himself.

"There is nothing," said the white man, moving to the edge of the platform and waving his hand to his boat. A shout came faintly over the lagoon and the sampan began to glide towards the abode of the friend of ghosts.

"If you want to come with me, I will wait all the morning," said the white man, looking away upon the water.

"No, Tuan," said Arsat, softly. "I shall not eat or sleep in this house, but I must first see my road. Now I can see nothing—see nothing! There is no light and no peace in the world; but there is death—death for many. We are sons of the same mother—and I left him in the midst of enemies; but I am going back now."

He drew a long breath and went on in a dreamy tone:

"In a little while I shall see clear enough to strike—to strike. But she has died, and . . . now . . . darkness."

He flung his arms wide open, let them fall along his body, then stood still with unmoved face and stony eyes, staring at the sun. The white man got down into his canoe. The polers ran smartly along the sides of the boat, looking over their shoulders at the beginning of a weary journey. High in the stern, his head muffled up in white rags, the juragan sat moody, letting his paddle trail in the water. The white man, leaning with both arms over the grass roof of the little cabin, looked back at the shining ripple of the boat's wake. Before the sampan passed out of the lagoon into the creek he lifted his eyes. Arsat had not moved. He stood lonely in the searching sunshine; and he looked beyond the great light of a cloudless day into the darkness of a world of illusions.

(1898)

DRAMA

Oscar Wilde

1854-1900

Oscar Wilde was the son of Sir William Wilde, Irish surgeon, and Jane Francesca Elgee, who wrote lightly and gracefully under the name Speranza. Wilde was born in Dublin and educated in Trinity College there. In 1874 he went to Magdalen College, Oxford, where his brilliance gave him the Newdigate Prize for English Verse and a first class in *litterae humaniores*. In college he became an apostle of the new aesthetic movement, which the painter Whistler was just then making prominent. He advocated "art for art's sake," was very "intense" in his admiration of objects of art, and decorated his room with peacock plumes and blue china cups. He affected a languishing air, wore eccentric clothes and long hair, and carried lilies and sunflowers. The majority of his fellow students thought him effete and unmanly, and he was ducked for his creed in the Cherwell. Graduating from college he continued his affectations, declaring that he gave his genius to his life and only his talents to his writing. The "intense" movement of Wilde and the other aesthetes was ridiculed in cartoons in *Punch* and burlesqued in the Gilbert and Sullivan opera of *Patience* (1881), and the attacks did a good deal to drive the cult out of England. Wilde's aesthetic creed survived these early assaults, and he continued to be eccentric, paradoxical, and witty. The year after the production of *Patience* he made a lecture tour of the United States during which he attempted to overthrow the American taste for scroll work and other atrocities in domestic furniture, and was represented in cartoons as a soft and effeminate personage in outlandish clothes who waved a lily at his aesthetic audience. Two years later he married Constance Lloyd.

Wilde's first book was a selection of poems published in 1881. In 1888 he issued *The Happy Prince and Other Tales,* a collection of charmingly written fairy stories and allegories. Another collection of fairy stories, *A House of Pomegranates,* appeared in 1891. Wilde's famous novel, *The Picture of Dorian Gray,* appeared in 1891. This novel read like a moral allegory, but there were critics who believed that behind this screen of morality lurked the pointed ears and the leering mouth of a satyr. In the same year Wilde published *Intentions,* a collection of his reviews and criticisms. In 1892 his second volume of collected poems was issued.

Wilde's easy wit insured an immediate success for the brilliant series of dramas that he wrote in the early nineties. In 1892 *Lady Windermere's Fan* appeared at the St. James's Theatre and was at once popular. The same year Wilde also wrote *Salomé;* this the licenser of plays refused to license, but it was produced in Paris in French by Lugne-Poé at the Théâtre de L'Oeuvre. It was followed the next year by *A Woman of No Importance. An Ideal Husband* and *The Importance of Being Earnest,* both filled with wit and brilliant paradoxes, appeared in 1895. They were the last things that Oscar Wilde was to write, before the blow fell that wrecked his life.

Angered by aspersions on his character Wilde brought suit for libel against the Marquis of Queensbury. The suit was dismissed, and certain evidence presented at the trial led later to Wilde's conviction on a charge of sexual immorality. He was sentenced to two years' imprisonment with hard labor at Reading Gaol, and the eccentric dress of the apostle of the aesthetes was exchanged for the arrow-branded garb of the convict. Out of the bitterness of this experience was born one of the most realistic and moving of poems, *The Ballad of Reading Gaol.* It was written in 1898 in France where, under the name of Sebastian Melmoth, he was trying to forget his sorrows in drink. In Paris he also wrote *De Profundis*—the apologia for his life—which was published in 1905, five years after the broken exile had died.

Oscar Wilde's eccentricities were so marked, and his manner was so airy, that at times it was difficult to take his literary work seriously. Nevertheless, he was a brilliant writer. In a sense he was the heir of an earlier and prominent school of artists—the Pre-Raphaelites—and of an earlier and prominent critic—Walter Pater. Walter Pater's theory of art for art's sake and his epicurean philosophy (see p. 584) had a purely aesthetic basis, and he would certainly have disapproved of such warped interpretations of his ideas as Oscar Wilde made. Nevertheless, Wilde's artistic "intensity" was the logical offspring of Pater's aesthetic rapture.

The most important contributions to English literature that Wilde made before the great tragedy of his life are his plays. In their clever situations, quick wit, light persiflage, and sparkling dialogue they are the most original contributions to the drama of the period and are in some ways forerunners of the work of another Irish playwright, George Bernard Shaw. Of Wilde's poems the best—*The Ballad of Reading Gaol*—was born of his sorrow. It is a profound study of human defeat with details so real that they seem etched with acid. It is not without significance as to Wilde's state of mind in his last years that he signed the poem and *De Profundis* "Sebastian Melmoth"—for in that name he united the traditions of a martyr and of one who had, in the story of Charles R. Maturin (1782-1824), sold his soul to the devil.

The Importance of Being Earnest

Wilde's *Importance of Being Earnest* is probably the most clever and sparkling farce-comedy of the nineties. Although it has not the grotesqueness of a Gilbert and Sullivan opera, it has much of the same easy creation of utterly absurd situations, and the same rollicking raillery. It is a social satire, moreover, which pricks the bubbles of solemnly accepted and revered conventions. It presents a topsy-turvy world in which no character has the slightest sense of responsibility or can be counted upon to do the usual thing or even to say the expected. The flippancy of the farce is apparent in Wilde's designation of it as "a trivial comedy for serious people" and in his reported comment that "the first act is ingenious, the second beautiful, the third abominably clever."

CHARACTERS

JOHN WORTHING, J.P.
ALGERNON MONCRIEFF.
REV. CANON CHASUBLE, D.D.
MERRIMAN (Butler).
LANE (Manservant).
LADY BRACKNELL.
HON. GWENDOLEN FAIRFAX.
CECILY CARDEW.
MISS PRISM (Governess).

THE SCENES OF THE PLAY

ACT I. Algernon Moncrieff's Flat in Half-Moon Street, W.
ACT II. The Garden at the Manor House, Woolton.
ACT III. Drawing-Room of the Manor House, Woolton.
    Time—The Present.
    Place—London.

Characters. John Worthing, J. P., Justice of the Peace. Chasuble, a farcical tag-name; a chasuble is an ecclesiastical cloak. Act I. *Half-Moon Street, W.,* a short side street off Piccadilly in the West Section of London. Act II. *Woolton,* a town in Lancashire.

ACT I

SCENE.—*Morning-room in* ALGERNON'S *flat in Half-Moon Street. The room is luxuriously and artistically furnished. The sound of a piano is heard in the adjoining room.*

(LANE *is arranging afternoon tea on the table, and after the music has ceased,* ALGERNON *enters.*)

Algernon. Did you hear what I was playing, Lane?

Lane. I didn't think it polite to listen, sir.

Algernon. I'm sorry for that, for your sake. I don't play accurately—anyone can play accurately—but I play with wonderful expression. As far as the piano is concerned, sentiment is my forte. I keep science for Life.

Lane. Yes, sir.

Algernon. And, speaking of the science of Life, have you got the cucumber sandwiches cut for Lady Bracknell?

Lane. Yes, sir. (*Hands them on a salver.*)

Algernon (*inspects them, takes two, and sits down on the sofa*). Oh! . . . by the way,

Lane, I see from your book that on Thursday night, when Lord Shoreman and Mr. Worthing were dining with me, eight bottles of champagne are entered as having been consumed.

Lane. Yes, sir; eight bottles and a pint.

Algernon. Why is it that at a bachelor's establishment the servants invariably drink the champagne? I ask merely for information.

Lane. I attribute it to the superior quality of the wine, sir. I have often observed that in married households the champagne is rarely of a first-rate brand.

Algernon. Good Heavens! Is marriage so demoralizing as that?

Lane. I believe it *is* a very pleasant state, sir. I have had very little experience of it myself up to the present. I have only been married once. That was in consequence of a misunderstanding between myself and a young woman.

Algernon (languidly). I don't know that I am much interested in your family life, Lane.

Lane. No, sir; it is not a very interesting subject. I never think of it myself.

Algernon. Very natural, I am sure. That will do, Lane, thank you.

Lane. Thank you, sir. (LANE *goes out.*)

Algernon. Lane's views on marriage seem somewhat lax. Really, if the lower orders don't set us a good example, what on earth is the use of them? They seem, as a class, to have absolutely no sense of moral responsibility.

Enter LANE.

Lane. Mr. Ernest Worthing.

Enter JACK. LANE *goes out.*

Algernon. How are you, my dear Ernest? What brings you up to town?

Jack. Oh, pleasure, pleasure! What else should bring one anywhere? Eating as usual, I see, Algy!

Algernon (stiffly). I believe it is customary in good society to take some slight refreshment at five o'clock. Where have you been since last Thursday?

Jack (sitting down on the sofa). In the country.

Algernon. What on earth do you do there?

Jack (pulling off his gloves). When one is in town, one amuses oneself. When one is in the country, one amuses other people. It is excessively boring.

Algernon. And who are the people you amuse?

Jack (airily). Oh, neighbors, neighbors.

Algernon. Got nice neighbors in your part of Shropshire?

Jack. Perfectly horrid! Never speak to one of them.

Algernon. How immensely you must amuse them! (*Goes over and takes sandwich.*) By the way, Shropshire is your county, is it not?

Jack. Eh? Shropshire? Yes, of course. Hallo! Why all these cups? Why cucumber sandwiches? Why such reckless extravagance in one so young? Who is coming to tea?

Algernon. Oh! merely Aunt Augusta and Gwendolen.

Jack. How perfectly delightful!

Algernon. Yes, that is all very well; but I am afraid Aunt Augusta won't quite approve of your being here.

Jack. May I ask why?

Algernon. My dear fellow, the way you flirt with Gwendolen is perfectly disgraceful. It is almost as bad as the way Gwendolen flirts with you.

Jack. I am in love with Gwendolen. I have come up to town expressly to propose to her.

Algernon. I thought you had come up for pleasure? . . . I call that business.

Jack. How utterly unromantic you are!

Algernon. I really don't see anything romantic in proposing. It is very romantic to be in love. But there is nothing romantic about a definite proposal. Why, one may be accepted. One usually is, I believe. Then the excitement is all over. The very essence of romance is uncertainty. If ever I get married, I'll certainly try to forget the fact.

Jack. I have no doubt about that, dear Algy. The Divorce Court was specially invented for people whose memories are so curiously constituted.

Algernon. Oh! there is no use speculating

on that subject. Divorces are made in Heaven
——(JACK *puts out his hand to take a sandwich.* ALGERNON *at once interferes.*) Please don't touch the cucumber sandwiches. They are ordered specially for Aunt Augusta. (*Takes one and eats it.*)

Jack. Well, you have been eating them all the time.

Algernon. That is quite a different matter. She is my aunt. (*Takes plate from below.*) Have some bread and butter. The bread and butter is for Gwendolen. Gwendolen is devoted to bread and butter.

Jack (*advancing to table and helping himself*). And very good bread and butter it is, too.

Algernon. Well, my dear fellow, you need not eat as if you were going to eat it all. You behave as if you were married to her already. You are not married to her already, and I don't think you ever will be.

Jack. Why on earth do you say that?

Algernon. Well, in the first place girls never marry the men they flirt with. Girls don't think it right.

Jack. Oh, that is nonsense!

Algernon. It isn't. It is a great truth. It accounts for the extraordinary number of bachelors that one sees all over the place. In the second place, I don't give my consent.

Jack. Your consent!

Algernon. My dear fellow, Gwendolen is my first cousin. And before I allow you to marry her, you will have to clear up the whole question of Cecily. (*Rings bell.*)

Jack. Cecily! What on earth do you mean? What do you mean, Algy, by Cecily? I don't know anyone of the name of Cecily.

Enter LANE.

Algernon. Bring me that cigarette case Mr. Worthing left in the smoking-room the last time he dined here.

Lane. Yes, sir. (LANE *goes out.*)

Jack. Do you mean to say you have had my cigarette case all this time? I wish to goodness you had let me know. I have been writing frantic letters to Scotland Yard about it. I was very nearly offering a large reward.

Algernon. Well, I wish you would offer one. I happen to be more than usually hard up.

Jack. There is no good offering a large reward now that the thing is found.

Enter LANE *with the cigarette case on a salver.* ALGERNON *takes it at once.*

LANE *goes out.*

Algernon. I think that is rather mean of you, Ernest, I must say. (*Opens case and examines it.*) However, it makes no matter, for, now that I look at the inscription, I find that the thing isn't yours after all.

Jack. Of course it's mine. (*Moving to him.*) You have seen me with it a hundred times, and you have no right whatsoever to read what is written inside. It is a very ungentlemanly thing to read a private cigarette case.

Algernon. Oh! it is absurd to have a hard-and-fast rule about what one should read and what one shouldn't. More than half of modern culture depends on what one shouldn't read.

Jack. I am quite aware of the fact, and I don't propose to discuss modern culture. It isn't the sort of thing one should talk of in private. I simply want my cigarette case back.

Algernon. Yes; but this isn't your cigarette case. This cigarette case is a present from someone of the name of Cecily, and you said you didn't know anyone of that name.

Jack. Well, if you want to know, Cecily happens to be my aunt.

Algernon. Your aunt!

Jack. Yes. Charming old lady she is, too. Lives at Tunbridge Wells. Just give it back to me, Algy.

Algernon (*retreating to back of sofa*). But why does she call herself little Cecily if she is your aunt and lives at Tunbridge Wells? (*Reading.*) "From little Cecily with her fondest love."

Jack (*moving to sofa and kneeling upon it*). My dear fellow, what on earth is there in that? Some aunts are tall, some aunts are not tall. That is a matter that surely an aunt may be allowed to decide for herself. You seem to

---

1. **Divorces . . . Heaven.** The ironic opposite of the usual "Marriages are made in Heaven."

81. **Tunbridge Wells,** a city and popular resort in Kent noted for its mineral springs.

think that every aunt should be exactly like your aunt! That is absurd! For Heaven's sake give me back my cigarette case. (*Follows* ALGERNON *round the room.*)

Algernon. Yes. But why does your aunt call you her uncle? "From little Cecily, with her fondest love to her dear Uncle Jack." There is no objection, I admit, to an aunt being a small aunt, but why an aunt, no matter what her size may be, should call her own nephew her uncle, I can't quite make out. Besides, your name isn't Jack at all! it is Ernest.

Jack. It isn't Ernest; it's Jack.

Algernon. You have always told me it was Ernest. I have introduced you to everyone as Ernest. You answer to the name of Ernest. You look as if your name was Ernest. You are the most earnest looking person I ever saw in my life. It is perfectly absurd your saying that your name isn't Ernest. It's on your cards. Here is one of them. (*Taking it from case.*) "Mr. Ernest Worthing, B 4, The Albany." I'll keep this as a proof your name is Ernest if ever you attempt to deny it to me, or to Gwendolen, or to anyone else. (*Puts the card in his pocket.*)

Jack. Well, my name is Ernest in town and Jack in the country, and the cigarette case was given to me in the country.

Algernon. Yes, but that does not account for the fact that your small Aunt Cecily, who lives at Tunbridge Wells, calls you her dear uncle. Come, old boy, you had much better have the thing out at once.

Jack. My dear Algy, you talk exactly as if you were a dentist. It is very vulgar to talk like a dentist when one isn't a dentist. It produces a false impression.

Algernon. Well, that is exactly what dentists always do. Now, go on! Tell me the whole thing. I may mention that I have always suspected you of being a confirmed and secret Bunburyist; and I am quite sure of it now.

Jack. Bunburyist? What on earth do you mean by a Bunburyist?

Algernon. I'll reveal to you the meaning of that incomparable expression as soon as you are kind enough to inform me why you are Ernest in town and Jack in the country.

Jack. Well, produce my cigarette case first.

Algernon. Here it is. (*Hands cigarette case.*) Now produce your explanation, and pray make it improbable. (*Sits on sofa.*)

Jack. My dear fellow, there is nothing improbable about my explanation at all. In fact it's perfectly ordinary. Old Mr. Thomas Cardew, who adopted me when I was a little boy, made me in his will guardian to his granddaughter, Miss Cecily Cardew. Cecily, who addresses me as her uncle from motives of respect that you could not possibly appreciate, lives at my place in the country under the charge of her admirable governess, Miss Prism.

Algernon. Where is that place in the country, by the way?

Jack. That is nothing to you, dear boy. You are not going to be invited. . . . I may tell you candidly that the place is not in Shropshire.

Algernon. I suspected that, my dear fellow! I have Bunburyed all over Shropshire on two separate occasions. Now, go on. Why are you Ernest in town and Jack in the country?

Jack. My dear Algy, I don't know whether you will be able to understand my real motives. You are hardly serious enough. When one is placed in the position of guardian, one has to adopt a very high moral tone on all subjects. It's one's duty to do so. And as a high moral tone can hardly be said to conduce very much to either one's health or one's happiness, in order to get up to town I have always pretended to have a younger brother of the name of Ernest, who lives in the Albany, and gets into the most dreadful scrapes. That, my dear Algy, is the whole truth pure and simple.

Algernon. The truth is rarely pure and never simple. Modern life would be very tedious if it were either, and modern literature a complete impossibility!

Jack. That wouldn't be at all a bad thing.

Algernon. Literary criticism is not your forte, my dear fellow. Don't try it. You should leave that to people who haven't been at a University. They do it so well in the daily papers. What you really are is a Bunburyist. I was quite right in saying you were a Bunburyist. You are one of the most advanced Bunburyists I know.

Jack. What on earth do you mean?

Algernon. You have invented a very useful younger brother called Ernest, in order that you may be able to come up to town as often as you like. I have invented an invaluable permanent invalid called Bunbury, in order that I may be able to go down into the country whenever I choose. Bunbury is perfectly invaluable. If it wasn't for Bunbury's extraordinary bad health, for instance, I wouldn't be able to dine with you at Willis's tonight, for I have been really engaged to Aunt Augusta for more than a week.

Jack. I haven't asked you to dine with me anywhere tonight.

Algernon. I know. You are absolutely careless about sending out invitations. It is very foolish of you. Nothing annoys people so much as not receiving invitations.

Jack. You had much better dine with your Aunt Augusta.

Algernon. I haven't the smallest intention of doing anything of the kind. To begin with, I dined there on Monday, and once a week is quite enough to dine with one's own relatives. In the second place, whenever I do dine there I am always treated as a member of the family, and sent down with either no woman at all, or two. In the third place, I know perfectly well whom she will place me next to, tonight. She will place me next Mary Farquhar, who always flirts with her own husband across the dinner-table. That is not very pleasant. Indeed, it is not even decent . . . and that sort of thing is enormously on the increase. The amount of women in London who flirt with their own husbands is perfectly scandalous. It looks so bad. It is simply washing one's clean linen in public. Besides, now that I know you to be a confirmed Bunburyist I naturally want to talk to you about Bunburying. I want to tell you the rules.

Jack. I'm not a Bunburyist at all. If Gwendolen accepts me, I am going to kill my brother, indeed I think I'll kill him in any case. Cecily is a little too much interested in him. It is rather a bore. So I am going to get rid of Ernest. And I strongly advise you to do the same with Mr. . . . with your invalid friend who has the absurd name.

Algernon. Nothing will induce me to part with Bunbury, and if you ever get married, which seems to me extremely problematic, you will be very glad to know Bunbury. A man who marries without knowing Bunbury has a very tedious time of it.

Jack. That is nonsense. If I marry a charming girl like Gwendolen, and she is the only girl I ever saw in my life that I would marry, I certainly don't want to know Bunbury.

Algernon. Then your wife will. You don't seem to realize, that in married life three is company and two is none.

Jack (*sententiously*). That, my dear young friend, is the theory that the corrupt French drama has been propounding for the last fifty years.

Algernon. Yes; and that the happy English home has proved in half the time.

Jack. For heaven's sake, don't try to be cynical. It's perfectly easy to be cynical.

Algernon. My dear fellow, it isn't easy to be anything now-a-days. There's such a lot of beastly competition about. (*The sound of an electric bell is heard.*) Ah! that must be Aunt Augusta. Only relatives, or creditors, ever ring in that Wagnerian manner. Now, if I get her out of the way for ten minutes, so that you can have an opportunity for proposing to Gwendolen, may I dine with you tonight at Willis's?

Jack. I suppose so, if you want to.

Algernon. Yes, but you must be serious about it. I hate people who are not serious about meals. It is so shallow of them.

Enter LANE.

Lane. Lady Bracknell and Miss Fairfax. (ALGERNON *goes forward to meet them. Enter* LADY BRACKNELL *and* GWENDOLEN.)

Lady Bracknell. Good afternoon, dear Algernon, I hope you are behaving very well.

Algernon. I'm feeling very well, Aunt Augusta.

---

67. **corrupt French drama.** The "eternal triangle" mentioned by Algernon was a common situation in the French drama and novel during the second half of the nineteenth century. 79. **Wagnerian manner,** a stormy and startling manner, after the style of Richard Wagner (1813-1883), the noted German composer of opera and music drama.

Lady Bracknell. That's not quite the same thing. In fact the two things rarely go together. (*Sees* JACK *and bows to him with icy coldness.*)

Algernon (*to* GWENDOLEN). Dear me, you are smart!

Gwendolen. I am always smart! Aren't I, Mr. Worthing?

Jack. You're quite perfect, Miss Fairfax.

Gwendolen. Oh! I hope I am not that. It would leave no room for developments, and I intend to develop in *many directions*. (GWENDOLEN *and* JACK *sit down together in the corner.*)

Lady Bracknell. I'm sorry if we are a little late, Algernon, but I was obliged to call on dear Lady Harbury. I hadn't been there since her poor husband's death. I never saw a woman so altered; she looks quite twenty years younger. And now I'll have a cup of tea, and one of those nice cucumber sandwiches you promised me.

Algernon. Certainly, Aunt Augusta. (*Goes over to tea-table.*)

Lady Bracknell. Won't you come and sit here, Gwendolen?

Gwendolen. Thanks, mamma, I'm quite comfortable where I am.

Algernon (*picking up empty plate in horror*). Good heavens! Lane! Why are there no cucumber sandwiches? I ordered them specially.

Lane (*gravely*). There were no cucumbers in the market this morning, sir. I went down twice.

Algernon. No cucumbers!

Lane. No, sir. Not even for ready money.

Algernon. That will do, Lane, thank you.

Lane. Thank you, sir. (*Goes out.*)

Algernon. I am greatly distressed, Aunt Augusta, about there being no cucumbers, not even for ready money.

Lady Bracknell. It really makes no matter, Algernon. I had some crumpets with Lady Harbury, who seems to me to be living entirely for pleasure now.

Algernon. I hear her hair has turned quite gold from grief.

Lady Bracknell. It certainly has changed its color. From what cause I, of course, cannot say. (ALGERNON *crosses and hands tea.*) Thank you. I've quite a treat for you tonight, Algernon. I am going to send you down with Mary Farquhar. She is such a nice woman, and so attentive to her husband. It's delightful to watch them.

Algernon. I am afraid, Aunt Augusta, I shall have to give up the pleasure of dining with you tonight after all.

Lady Bracknell (*frowning*). I hope not, Algernon. It would put my table completely out. Your uncle would have to dine upstairs. Fortunately he is accustomed to that.

Algernon. It is a great bore, and, I need hardly say, a terrible disappointment to me, but the fact is I have just had a telegram to say that my poor friend Bunbury is very ill again. (*Exchanges glances with* JACK.) They seem to think I should be with him.

Lady Bracknell. It is very strange. This Mr. Bunbury seems to suffer from curiously bad health.

Algernon. Yes; poor Bunbury is a dreadful invalid.

Lady Bracknell. Well, I must say, Algernon, that I think it is high time that Mr. Bunbury made up his mind whether he was going to live or to die. This shilly-shallying with the question is absurd. Nor do I in any way approve of the modern sympathy with invalids. I consider it morbid. Illness of any kind is hardly a thing to be encouraged in others. Health is the primary duty of life. I am always telling that to your poor uncle, but he never seems to take much notice . . . as far as any improvement in his ailments goes. I should be much obliged if you would ask Mr. Bunbury, from me, to be kind enough not to have a relapse on Saturday, for I rely on you to arrange my music for me. It is my last reception and one wants something that will encourage conversation, particularly at the end of the season when everyone has practically said whatever they had to say, which, in most cases, was probably not much.

Algernon. I'll speak to Bunbury, Aunt Augusta, if he is still conscious, and I think I can promise you he'll be all right by Satur-

---

44. **crumpet,** a kind of cake cooked on a griddle.

day. You see, if one plays good music, people don't listen, and if one plays bad music, people don't talk. But I'll run over the program I've drawn out, if you will kindly come into the next room for a moment.

Lady Bracknell. Thank you, Algernon. It is very thoughtful of you. (*Rising, and following* ALGERNON.) I'm sure the program will be delightful, after a few expurgations. French songs I cannot possibly allow. People always seem to think that they are improper, and either look shocked, which is vulgar, or laugh, which is worse. But German sounds a thoroughly respectable language, and indeed, I believe it is so. Gwendolen, you will accompany me.

Gwendolen. Certainly, mamma. (LADY BRACKNELL *and* ALGERNON *go into the music-room,* GWENDOLEN *remains behind.*)

Jack. Charming day it has been, Miss Fairfax.

Gwendolen. Pray don't talk to me about the weather, Mr. Worthing. Whenever people talk to me about the weather, I always feel quite certain that they mean something else. And that makes me so nervous.

Jack. I do mean something else.

Gwendolen. I thought so. In fact, I am never wrong.

Jack. And I would like to be allowed to take advantage of Lady Bracknell's temporary absence . . .

Gwendolen. I would certainly advise you to do so. Mamma has a way of coming back suddenly into a room that I have often had to speak to her about.

Jack (*nervously*). Miss Fairfax, ever since I met you I have admired you more than any girl . . . I have ever met since . . . I met you.

Gwendolen. Yes, I am quite aware of the fact. And I often wish that in public, at any rate, you had been more demonstrative. For me you have always had an irresistible fascination. Even before I met you I was far from indifferent to you. (JACK *looks at her in amazement.*) We live, as I hope you know, Mr. Worthing, in an age of ideals. The fact is constantly mentioned in the more expensive monthly magazines, and has reached the provincial pulpits I am told: and my ideal has always been to love some one of the name of Ernest. There is something in that name that inspires absolute confidence. The moment Algernon first mentioned to me that he had a friend called Ernest, I knew I was destined to love you.

Jack. You really love me, Gwendolen?

Gwendolen. Passionately!

Jack. Darling! You don't know how happy you've made me.

Gwendolen. My own Ernest!

Jack. But you don't really mean to say that you couldn't love me if my name wasn't Ernest?

Gwendolen. But your name is Ernest.

Jack. Yes, I know it is. But supposing it was something else? Do you mean to say you couldn't love me then?

Gwendolen (*glibly*). Ah! that is clearly a metaphysical speculation, and like most metaphysical speculations has very little reference at all to the actual facts of real life, as we know them.

Jack. Personally, darling, to speak quite candidly, I don't much care about the name of Ernest . . . I don't think that name suits me at all.

Gwendolen. It suits you perfectly. It is a divine name. It has a music of its own. It produces vibrations.

Jack. Well, really, Gwendolen, I must say that I think there are lots of other much nicer names. I think, Jack, for instance, a charming name.

Gwendolen. Jack? . . . No, there is very little music in the name Jack, if any at all, indeed. It does not thrill. It produces absolutely no vibrations. . . . I have known several Jacks, and they all, without exception, were more than usually plain. Besides, Jack is a notorious domesticity for John! And I pity any woman who is married to a man called John. She would probably never be allowed to know the entrancing pleasure of a single moment's solitude. The only really safe name is Ernest.

Jack. Gwendolen, I must get christened at once—I mean we must get married at once. There is no time to be lost.

Gwendolen. Married, Mr. Worthing?

Jack (*astounded*). Well . . . surely. You know that I love you, and you led me to believe, Miss Fairfax, that you were not absolutely indifferent to me.

Gwendolen. I adore you. But you haven't proposed to me yet. Nothing has been said at all about marriage. The subject has not even been touched on.

Jack. Well . . . may I propose to you now?

Gwendolen. I think it would be an admirable opportunity. And to spare you any possible disappointment, Mr. Worthing, I think it only fair to tell you quite frankly beforehand that I am fully determined to accept you.

Jack. Gwendolen!

Gwendolen. Yes, Mr. Worthing, what have you got to say to me?

Jack. You know what I have got to say to you.

Gwendolen. Yes, but you don't say it.

Jack. Gwendolen, will you marry me? (*Goes on his knees.*)

Gwendolen. Of course I will, darling. How long you have been about it! I am afraid you have had very little experience in how to propose.

Jack. My own one, I have never loved anyone in the world but you.

Gwendolen. Yes, but men often propose for practice. I know my brother Gerald does. All my girl-friends tell me so. What wonderfully blue eyes you have, Ernest! They are quite, quite blue. I hope you will always look at me just like that, especially when there are other people present.

Enter Lady Bracknell.

Lady Bracknell. Mr. Worthing! Rise, sir, from this semi-recumbent posture. It is most indecorous.

Gwendolen. Mamma! (*He tries to rise; she restrains him.*) I must beg you to retire. This is no place for you. Besides, Mr. Worthing has not quite finished yet.

Lady Bracknell. Finished what, may I ask?

Gwendolen. I am engaged to Mr. Worthing, mamma. (*They rise together.*)

Lady Bracknell. Pardon me, you are not engaged to anyone. When you do become engaged to someone, I, or your father, should his health permit him, will inform you of the fact. An engagement should come on a young girl as a surprise, pleasant or unpleasant, as the case may be. It is hardly a matter that she could be allowed to arrange for herself. . . . And now I have a few questions to put to you, Mr. Worthing. While I am making these inquiries, you, Gwendolen, will wait for me below in the carriage.

Gwendolen (*reproachfully*). Mamma!

Lady Bracknell. In the carriage, Gwendolen! (Gwendolen *goes to the door. She and* Jack *blow kisses to each other behind* Lady Bracknell's *back.* Lady Bracknell *looks vaguely about as if she could not understand what the noise was. Finally turns round.*) Gwendolen, the carriage!

Gwendolen. Yes, mamma. (*Goes out, looking back at* Jack.)

Lady Bracknell (*sitting down*). You can take a seat, Mr. Worthing. (*Looks in her pocket for notebook and pencil.*)

Jack. Thank you, Lady Bracknell, I prefer standing.

Lady Bracknell (*pencil and notebook in hand*). I feel bound to tell you that you are not down on my list of eligible young men, although I have the same list as the dear Duchess of Bolton has. We work together, in fact. However, I am quite ready to enter your name, should your answers be what a really affectionate mother requires. Do you smoke?

Jack. Well, yes, I must admit I smoke.

Lady Bracknell. I am glad to hear it. A man should always have an occupation of some kind. There are far too many idle men in London as it is. How old are you?

Jack. Twenty-nine.

Lady Bracknell. A very good age to be married at. I have always been of opinion that a man who desires to get married should know either everything or nothing. Which do you know?

Jack (*after some hesitation*). I know nothing, Lady Bracknell.

Lady Bracknell. I am pleased to hear it. I do not approve of anything that tampers with natural ignorance. Ignorance is like a delicate exotic fruit; touch it and the bloom is gone. The whole theory of modern education is radically unsound. Fortunately in England, at any rate, education produces no effect whatsoever. If it did, it would prove a serious danger to the upper classes, and probably lead to acts of violence in Grosvenor Square. What is your income?

Jack. Between seven and eight thousand a year.

Lady Bracknell (*makes a note in her book*). In land, or in investments?

Jack. In investments, chiefly.

Lady Bracknell. That is satisfactory. What between the duties expected of one during one's lifetime, and the duties exacted from one after one's death, land has ceased to be either a profit or a pleasure. It gives one position, and prevents one from keeping it up. That's all that can be said about land.

Jack. I have a country house with some land, of course, attached to it, about fifteen hundred acres, I believe; but I don't depend on that for my real income. In fact, as far as I can make out, the poachers are the only people who make anything out of it.

Lady Bracknell. A country house! How many bedrooms? Well, that point can be cleared up afterwards. You have a town house, I hope? A girl with a simple, unspoiled nature, like Gwendolen, could hardly be expected to reside in the country.

Jack. Well, I own a house in Belgrave Square, but it is let by the year to Lady Bloxham. Of course, I can get it back whenever I like, at six months' notice.

Lady Bracknell. Lady Bloxham? I don't know her.

Jack. Oh, she goes about very little. She is a lady considerably advanced in years.

Lady Bracknell. Ah, now-a-days that is no guarantee of respectability of character. What number in Belgrave Square?

Jack. 149.

Lady Bracknell (*shaking her head*). The unfashionable side. I thought there was something. However, that could easily be altered.

Jack. Do you mean the fashion, or the side?

Lady Bracknell (*sternly*). Both, if necessary, I presume. What are your politics?

Jack. Well, I am afraid I really have none. I am a Liberal Unionist.

Lady Bracknell. Oh, they count as Tories. They dine with us. Or come in the evening, at any rate. Now to minor matters. Are your parents living?

Jack. I have lost both my parents.

Lady Bracknell. Both? . . . That seems like carelessness. Who was your father? He was evidently a man of some wealth. Was he born in what the Radical papers call the purple of commerce, or did he rise from the ranks of the aristocracy?

Jack. I am afraid I really don't know. The fact is, Lady Bracknell, I said I had lost my parents. It would be nearer the truth to say that my parents seem to have lost me . . . I don't actually know who I am by birth. I was . . . well, I was found.

Lady Bracknell. Found!

Jack. The late Mr. Thomas Cardew, an old gentleman of a very charitable and kindly disposition, found me, and gave me the name of Worthing, because he happened to have a first-class ticket for Worthing in his pocket at the time. Worthing is a place in Sussex. It is a seaside resort.

Lady Bracknell. Where did the charitable gentleman who had a first-class ticket for this seaside resort find you?

Jack (*gravely*). In a hand-bag.

Lady Bracknell. A hand-bag?

Jack (*very seriously*). Yes, Lady Bracknell. I was in a hand-bag—a somewhat large, black leather hand-bag, with handles to it—an ordinary hand-bag in fact.

Lady Bracknell. In what locality did this Mr. James, or Thomas, Cardew come across this ordinary hand-bag?

Jack. In the cloak-room at Victoria Station.

---

7. **Grosvenor Square,** a highly fashionable place of residence in London. 9. **seven . . . thousand,** seven thousand pounds, about $34,000. 15. **duties . . . death.** Wilde is playing on the word *duty*; in the second instance it means inheritance taxes. 25. **poachers,** those who steal game from a private estate. 33. **Belgrave Square,** a spacious square in London noted for its aristocratic mansions.

53. **Liberal Unionist,** a member of the Liberal party in England that in 1886 opposed Gladstone's policy of home rule for Ireland. After 1906, the members joined the Conservatives. 91. **Victoria Station,** the West End terminus of the Southern Railway.

It was given to him in mistake for his own.
Lady Bracknell. The cloak-room at Victoria Station?
Jack. Yes. The Brighton line.
Lady Bracknell. The line is immaterial. Mr. Worthing, I confess I feel somewhat bewildered by what you have just told me. To be born, or at any rate bred, in a hand-bag, whether it had handles or not, seems to me to display a contempt for the ordinary decencies of family life that remind one of the worst excesses of the French Revolution. And I presume you know what that unfortunate movement led to? As for the particular locality in which the hand-bag was found, a cloak-room at a railway station might serve to conceal a social indiscretion—has probably, indeed, been used for that purpose before now—but it could hardly be regarded as an assured basis for a recognized position in good society.
Jack. May I ask you then what you would advise me to do? I need hardly say I would do anything in the world to ensure Gwendolen's happiness.
Lady Bracknell. I would strongly advise you, Mr. Worthing, to try and acquire some relations as soon as possible, and to make a definite effort to produce at any rate one parent, of either sex, before the season is quite over.
Jack. Well, I don't see how I could possibly manage to do that. I can produce the handbag at any moment. It is in my dressing-room at home. I really think that should satisfy you, Lady Bracknell.
Lady Bracknell. Me, sir! What has it to do with me? You can hardly imagine that I and Lord Bracknell would dream of allowing our only daughter—a girl brought up with the utmost care—to marry into a cloak-room, and form an alliance with a parcel? Good morning, Mr. Worthing! (LADY BRACKNELL *sweeps out in majestic indignation.*)
Jack. Good morning! (ALGERNON, *from the other room, strikes up the Wedding March.* JACK *looks perfectly furious, and goes to the door.*) For goodness' sake don't play that ghastly tune, Algy! How idiotic you are!

(*The music stops, and* ALGERNON *enters cheerily.*)
Algernon. Didn't it go off all right, old boy? You don't mean to say Gwendolen refused you? I know it is a way she has. She is always refusing people. I think it is most ill-natured of her.
Jack. Oh, Gwendolen is as right as a trivet. As far as she is concerned, we are engaged. Her mother is perfectly unbearable. Never met such a Gorgon . . . I don't really know what a Gorgon is like, but I am quite sure that Lady Bracknell is one. In any case, she is a monster, without being a myth, which is rather unfair. . . . I beg your pardon, Algy, I suppose I shouldn't talk about your own aunt in that way before you.
Algernon. My dear boy, I love hearing my relations abused. It is the only thing that makes me put up with them at all. Relations are simply a tedious pack of people, who haven't got the remotest knowledge of how to live, nor the smallest instinct about when to die.
Jack. Oh, that is nonsense!
Algernon. It isn't!
Jack. Well, I won't argue about the matter. You always want to argue about things.
Algernon. That is exactly what things were originally made for.
Jack. Upon my word, if I thought that, I'd shoot myself . . . (*A pause.*) You don't think there is any chance of Gwendolen becoming like her mother in about a hundred and fifty years, do you, Algy?
Algernon. All women become like their mothers. That is their tragedy. No man does. That's his.
Jack. Is that clever?
Algernon. It is perfectly phrased! and quite as true as any observation in civilized life should be.
Jack. I am sick to death of cleverness. Everybody is clever now-a-days. You can't go anywhere without meeting clever people. The thing has become an absolute public nuisance. I wish to goodness we had a few fools left.
Algernon. We have.

---

4. **The Brighton line,** the railroad from London to Brighton, a seaport of Sussex, fifty miles south of London. 54. **trivet,** a three-legged stand. 57. **Gorgon,** in Greek myth one of three monstrous sisters with snaky hair; one of them, Medusa, turned to stone all who looked upon her face.

Jack. I should extremely like to meet them. What do they talk about?

Algernon. The fools? Oh! about the clever people, of course.

Jack. What fools!

Algernon. By the way, did you tell Gwendolen the truth about your being Ernest in town, and Jack in the country?

Jack (*in a very patronizing manner*). My dear fellow, the truth isn't quite the sort of thing one tells to a nice, sweet, refined girl. What extraordinary ideas you have about the way to behave to a woman!

Algernon. The only way to behave to a woman is to make love to her, if she is pretty, and to someone else if she is plain.

Jack. Oh, that is nonsense.

Algernon. What about your brother? What about the profligate Ernest?

Jack. Oh, before the end of the week I shall have got rid of him. I'll say he died in Paris of apoplexy. Lots of people die of apoplexy, quite suddenly, don't they?

Algernon. Yes, but it's hereditary, my dear fellow. It's a sort of thing that runs in families. You had much better say a severe chill.

Jack. You are sure a severe chill isn't hereditary, or anything of that kind?

Algernon. Of course it isn't!

Jack. Very well, then. My poor brother Ernest is carried off suddenly in Paris, by a severe chill. That gets rid of him.

Algernon. But I thought you said that . . . Miss Cardew was a little too much interested in your poor brother Ernest? Won't she feel his loss a good deal?

Jack. Oh, that is all right. Cecily is not a silly, romantic girl, I am glad to say. She has got a capital appetite, goes for long walks, and pays no attention at all to her lessons.

Algernon. I would rather like to see Cecily.

Jack. I will take very good care you never do. She is excessively pretty, and she is only just eighteen.

Algernon. Have you told Gwendolen yet that you have an excessively pretty ward who is only just eighteen?

Jack. Oh! one doesn't blurt these things out to people. Cecily and Gwendolen are perfectly certain to be extremely great friends. I'll bet you anything you like that half an hour after they have met, they will be calling each other sister.

Algernon. Women only do that when they have called each other a lot of other things first. Now, my dear boy, if we want to get a good table at Willis's, we really must go and dress. Do you know it is nearly seven?

Jack (*irritably*). Oh! it always is nearly seven.

Algernon. Well, I'm hungry.

Jack. I never knew you when you weren't.

. . .

Algernon. What shall we do after dinner? Go to a theater?

Jack. Oh, no! I loathe listening.

Algernon. Well, let us go to the Club?

Jack. Oh, no! I hate talking.

Algernon. Well, we might trot round to the Empire at ten?

Jack. Oh, no! I can't bear looking at things. It is so silly.

Algernon. Well, what shall we do?

Jack. Nothing!

Algernon. It is awfully hard work doing nothing. However, I don't mind hard work where there is no definite object of any kind.

Enter LANE.

Lane. Miss Fairfax.

Enter GWENDOLEN. LANE *goes out.*

Algernon. Gwendolen, upon my word!

Gwendolen. Algy, kindly turn your back. I have something very particular to say to Mr. Worthing.

Algernon. Really, Gwendolen, I don't think I can allow this at all.

Gwendolen. Algy, you always adopt a strictly immoral attitude toward life. You are not quite old enough to do that. (ALGERNON *retires to the fireplace.*)

Jack. My own darling!

Gwendolen. Ernest, we may never be married. From the expression on mamma's face I fear we never shall. Few parents now-a-days pay any regard to what their children say to them. The old-fashioned respect for the young is fast dying out. Whatever influence I ever had over mamma, I lost at the age of

---

69. **the Empire,** a popular amusement hall frequently mentioned in the literature of the nineties.

three. But although she may prevent us from becoming man and wife, and I may marry someone else, and marry often, nothing that she can possibly do can alter my eternal devotion to you.

Jack. Dear Gwendolen.

Gwendolen. The story of your romantic origin, as related to me by mamma, with unpleasing comments, has naturally stirred the deeper fibers of my nature. Your Christian name has an irresistible fascination. The simplicity of your character makes you exquisitely incomprehensible to me. Your town address at the Albany I have. What is your address in the country?

Jack. The Manor House, Woolton, Hertfordshire. (ALGERNON, *who has been carefully listening, smiles to himself, and writes the address on his shirt-cuff. Then picks up the Railway Guide.*)

Gwendolen. There is a good postal service, I suppose? It may be necessary to do something desperate. That, of course, will require serious consideration. I will communicate with you daily.

Jack. My own one!

Gwendolen. How long do you remain in town?

Jack. Till Monday.

Gwendolen. Good! Algy, you may turn round now.

Algernon. Thanks, I've turned round already.

Gwendolen. You may also ring the bell.

Jack. You will let me see you to your carriage, my own darling?

Gwendolen. Certainly.

Jack (*to* LANE, *who now enters*). I will see Miss Fairfax out.

Lane. Yes, sir. (JACK *and* GWENDOLEN *go off.* LANE *presents several letters on a salver to* ALGERNON. *It is to be surmised that they are bills, as* ALGERNON, *after looking at the envelopes, tears them up.*)

Algernon. A glass of sherry, Lane.

Lane. Yes, sir.

Algernon. Tomorrow, Lane, I am going Bunburying.

Lane. Yes, sir.

Algernon. I shall probably not be back till Monday. You can put up my dress clothes, my smoking jacket, and all the Bunbury suits . . .

Lane. Yes, sir. (*Handing sherry.*)

Algernon. I hope tomorrow will be a fine day, Lane.

Lane. It never is, sir.

Algernon. Lane, you're a perfect pessimist.

Lane. I do my best to give satisfaction, sir.

Enter JACK. LANE *goes off.*

Jack. There's a sensible, intellectual girl! the only girl I ever cared for in my life. (ALGERNON *is laughing immoderately.*) What on earth are you so amused at?

Algernon. Oh, I'm a little anxious about poor Bunbury, that's all.

Jack. If you don't take care, your friend Bunbury will get you into a serious scrape some day.

Algernon. I love scrapes. They are the only things that are never serious.

Jack. Oh, that's nonsense, Algy. You never talk anything but nonsense.

Algernon. Nobody ever does. (JACK *looks indignantly at him, and leaves the room.* ALGERNON *lights a cigarette, reads his shirt-cuff and smiles.*)

ACT II

SCENE.—*Garden at the Manor House. A flight of gray stone steps leads up to the house. The garden, an old-fashioned one, full of roses. Time of year, July. Basket chairs, and a table covered with books, are set under a large yew tree.*

(MISS PRISM *discovered seated at the table.* CECILY *is at the back watering flowers.*)

Miss Prism (*calling*). Cecily, Cecily! Surely such a utilitarian occupation as the watering of flowers is rather Moulton's duty than yours? Especially at a moment when intellectual pleasures await you. Your German grammar is on the table. Pray open it at page fifteen. We will repeat yesterday's lesson.

Cecily (*coming over very slowly*). But I don't like German. It isn't at all a becoming language. I know perfectly well that I look quite plain after my German lesson.

Miss Prism. Child, you know how anxious

your guardian is that you should improve yourself in every way. He laid particular stress on your German, as he was leaving for town yesterday. Indeed, he always lays stress on your German when he is leaving for town.

Cecily. Dear Uncle Jack is so very serious! Sometimes he is so serious that I think he cannot be quite well.

Miss Prism (*drawing herself up*). Your guardian enjoys the best of health, and his gravity of demeanor is especially to be commended in one so comparatively young as he is. I know no one who has a higher sense of duty and responsibility.

Cecily. I suppose that is why he often looks a little bored when we three are together.

Miss Prism. Cecily! I am surprised at you. Mr. Worthing has many troubles in his life. Idle merriment and triviality would be out of place in his conversation. You must remember his constant anxiety about that unfortunate young man, his brother.

Cecily. I wish Uncle Jack would allow that unfortunate young man, his brother, to come down here sometimes. We might have a good influence over him, Miss Prism. I am sure you certainly would. You know German, and geology, and things of that kind influence a man very much. (CECILY *begins to write in her diary.*)

Miss Prism (*shaking her head*). I do not think that even I could produce any effect on a character that, according to his own brother's admission, is irretrievably weak and vacillating. Indeed, I am not sure that I would desire to reclaim him. I am not in favor of this modern mania for turning bad people into good people at a moment's notice. As a man sows, so let him reap. You must put away your diary, Cecily. I really don't see why you should keep a diary at all.

Cecily. I keep a diary in order to enter the wonderful secrets of my life. If I didn't write them down I should probably forget all about them.

Miss Prism. Memory, my dear Cecily, is the diary that we all carry about with us.

Cecily. Yes, but it usually chronicles the things that have never happened, and couldn't possibly have happened. I believe that Memory is responsible for nearly all the three-volume novels that Mudie sends us.

Miss Prism. Do not speak slightingly of the three-volume novel, Cecily. I wrote one myself in earlier days.

Cecily. Did you really, Miss Prism? How wonderfully clever you are! I hope it did not end happily? I don't like novels that end happily. They depress me so much.

Miss Prism. The good ended happily, and the bad unhappily. That is what Fiction means.

Cecily. I suppose so. But it seems very unfair. And was your novel ever published?

Miss Prism. Alas! no. The manuscript unfortunately was abandoned. I use the word in the sense of lost or mislaid. To your work, child, these speculations are profitless.

Cecily (*smiling*). But I see dear Dr. Chasuble coming up through the garden.

Miss Prism (*rising and advancing*). Dr. Chasuble! This is indeed a pleasure.

Enter CANON CHASUBLE.

Chasuble. And how are we this morning? Miss Prism, you are, I trust, well?

Cecily. Miss Prism has just been complaining of a slight headache. I think it would do her so much good to have a short stroll with you in the park, Dr. Chasuble.

Miss Prism. Cecily, I have not mentioned anything about a headache.

Cecily. No, dear Miss Prism, I know that, but I felt instinctively that you had a headache. Indeed I was thinking about that, and not about my German lesson, when the Rector came in.

Chasuble. I hope, Cecily, you are not inattentive.

Cecily. Oh, I am afraid I am.

Chasuble. That is strange. Were I fortunate enough to be Miss Prism's pupil, I would hang upon her lips. (MISS PRISM *glares*). I spoke metaphorically.—My metaphor was drawn from bees. Ahem! Mr.

---

39. **As . . . reap.** Cf. *Galatians*, 6:7: "Be not deceived; God is not mocked: for whatsoever a man soweth, that shall he also reap."

52. **Mudie**, a well-established bookstore in London. It maintains a large circulating library. Many Victorian novels were published in three volumes; Wilde is making a sly allusion to their tiresome length.

Worthing, I suppose, has not returned from town yet?

Miss Prism. We do not expect him till Monday afternoon.

Chasuble. Ah, yes, he usually likes to spend his Sunday in London. He is not one of those whose sole aim is enjoyment, as, by all accounts, that unfortunate young man, his brother, seems to be. But I must not disturb Egeria and her pupil any longer.

Miss Prism. Egeria? My name is Laetitia, Doctor.

Chasuble (*bowing*). A classical allusion merely, drawn from the Pagan authors. I shall see you both no doubt at Evensong.

Miss Prism. I think, dear Doctor, I will have a stroll with you. I find I have a headache, after all, and a walk might do it good.

Chasuble. With pleasure, Miss Prism, with pleasure. We might go as far as the schools and back.

Miss Prism. That would be delightful. Cecily, you will read your Political Economy in my absence. The chapter on the Fall of the Rupee you may omit. It is somewhat too sensational. Even these metallic problems have their melodramatic side.

(*Goes down the garden with* Dr. Chasuble.)

Cecily (*picks up books and throws them back on table.*) Horrid Political Economy! Horrid Geography! Horrid, horrid German!

Enter Merriman *with a card on a salver.*

Merriman. Mr. Ernest Worthing has just driven over from the station. He has brought his luggage with him.

Cecily (*takes the card and reads it*). "Mr. Ernest Worthing, B 4 The Albany, W." Uncle Jack's brother! Did you tell him Mr. Worthing was in town?

Merriman. Yes, Miss. He seemed very much disappointed. I mentioned that you and Miss Prism were in the garden. He said he was anxious to speak to you privately for a moment.

Cecily. Ask Mr. Ernest Worthing to come here. I suppose you had better talk to the housekeeper about a room for him.

Merriman. Yes, Miss.

(Merriman *goes off.*)

Cecily. I have never met any really wicked person before. I feel rather frightened. I am so afraid he will look just like everyone else.

Enter Algernon, *very gay and debonair.*

He does!

Algernon (*raising his hat.*) You are my little cousin Cecily, I'm sure.

Cecily. You are under some strange mistake. I am not little. In fact, I am more than usually tall for my age. (Algernon *is rather taken aback.*) But I am your cousin Cecily. You, I see from your card, are Uncle Jack's brother, my cousin Ernest, my wicked cousin Ernest.

Algernon. Oh! I am not really wicked at all, cousin Cecily. You mustn't think that I am wicked.

Cecily. If you are not, then you have certainly been deceiving us all in a very inexcusable manner. I hope you have not been leading a double life, pretending to be wicked and being really good all the time. That would be hypocrisy.

Algernon (*looks at her in amazement*). Oh! of course I have been rather reckless.

Cecily. I am glad to hear it.

Algernon. In fact, now you mention the subject, I have been very bad in my own small way.

Cecily. I don't think you should be so proud of that, though I am sure it must have been very pleasant.

Algernon. It is much pleasanter being here with you.

Cecily. I can't understand how you are here at all. Uncle Jack won't be back till Monday afternoon.

Algernon. That is a great disappointment. I am obliged to go up by the first train on Monday morning. I have a business appointment that I am anxious . . . to miss.

Cecily. Couldn't you miss it anywhere but in London?

Algernon. No; the appointment is in London.

---

10. **Egeria,** in ancient myth, a nymph who was the wife and counselor of Numa Pompilius, the legendary second king of Rome; hence, any woman who acts as adviser to another person. 25. **Rupee,** an East Indian silver coin the value of which depends on time and place and the price of silver. Its normal worth is about thirty-two cents. 35. **W.,** Western London, a postal district.

Cecily. Well, I know, of course, how important it is not to keep a business engagement, if one wants to retain any sense of the beauty of life, but still I think you had better wait till Uncle Jack arrives. I know he wants to speak to you about your emigrating.

Algernon. About my what?

Cecily. Your emigrating. He has gone up to buy your outfit.

Algernon. I certainly wouldn't let Jack buy my outfit. He has no taste in neckties at all.

Cecily. I don't think you will require neckties. Uncle Jack is sending you to Australia.

Algernon. Australia! I'd sooner die.

Cecily. Well, he said at dinner on Wednesday night, that you would have to choose between this world, the next world, and Australia.

Algernon. Oh, well! The accounts I have received of Australia and the next world are not particularly encouraging. This world is good enough for me, cousin Cecily.

Cecily. Yes, but are you good enough for it?

Algernon. I'm afraid I'm not that. That is why I want you to reform me. You might make that your mission, if you don't mind, cousin Cecily.

Cecily. I'm afraid I've not time, this afternoon.

Algernon. Well, would you mind my reforming myself this afternoon?

Cecily. That is rather Quixotic of you. But I think you should try.

Algernon. I will. I feel better already.

Cecily. You are looking a little worse.

Algernon. That is because I am hungry.

Cecily. How thoughtless of me. I should have remembered that when one is going to lead an entirely new life, one requires regular and wholesome meals. Won't you come in?

Algernon. Thank you. Might I have a button-hole first? I never have any appetite unless I have a button-hole first.

Cecily. A Maréchal Niel? (*Picks up scissors.*)

Algernon. No, I'd sooner have a pink rose.

Cecily. Why? (*Cuts a flower.*)

Algernon. Because you are like a pink rose, cousin Cecily.

Cecily. I don't think it can be right for you to talk to me like that. Miss Prism never says such things to me.

Algernon. Then Miss Prism is a short-sighted old lady. (CECILY *puts the rose in his button-hole.*) You are the prettiest girl I ever saw.

Cecily. Miss Prism says that all good looks are a snare.

Algernon. They are a snare that every sensible man would like to be caught in.

Cecily. Oh! I don't think I would care to catch a sensible man. I shouldn't know what to talk to him about.

(*They pass into the house.* MISS PRISM *and* DR. CHASUBLE *return.*)

Miss Prism. You are too much alone, dear Dr. Chasuble. You should get married. A misanthrope I can understand — a womanthrope, never!

Chasuble (*with a scholar's shudder*). Believe me, I do not deserve so neologistic a phrase. The precept as well as the practice of the Primitive Church was distinctly against matrimony.

Miss Prism (*sententiously*). That is obviously the reason why the Primitive Church has not lasted up to the present day. And you do not seem to realize, dear Doctor, that by persistently remaining single, a man converts himself into a permanent public temptation. Men should be careful; this very celibacy leads weaker vessels astray.

Chasuble. But is a man not equally attractive when married?

Miss Prism. No married man is ever attractive except to his wife.

Chasuble. And often, I've been told, not even to her.

Miss Prism. That depends on the intellectual sympathies of the woman. Maturity can always be depended on. Ripeness can be trusted. Young women are green. (DR. CHASUBLE *starts.*) I spoke horticulturally. My metaphor was drawn from fruits. But where is Cecily?

---

44. **Maréchal Niel,** a beautiful yellow climbing rose, named after Adolphe Niel (1802-1869), the famous Marshal of France.

71. **Primitive Church,** the Christian believers of the first three centuries.

Chasuble. Perhaps she followed us to the schools.

Enter JACK *slowly from the back of the garden. He is dressed in the deepest mourning, with crape hatband and black gloves.*

Miss Prism. Mr. Worthing!

Chasuble. Mr. Worthing?

Miss Prism. This is indeed a surprise. We did not look for you till Monday afternoon.

Jack (*shakes* MISS PRISM's *hand in a tragic manner*). I have returned sooner than I expected. Dr. Chasuble, I hope you are well?

Chasuble. Dear Mr. Worthing, I trust this garb of woe does not betoken some terrible calamity?

Jack. My brother.

Miss Prism. More shameful debts and extravagance?

Chasuble. Still leading his life of pleasure?

Jack (*shaking his head*). Dead!

Chasuble. Your brother Ernest dead?

Jack. Quite dead.

Miss Prism. What a lesson for him! I trust he will profit by it.

Chasuble. Mr. Worthing, I offer you my sincere condolence. You have at least the consolation of knowing that you were always the most generous and forgiving of brothers.

Jack. Poor Ernest! He had many faults, but it is a sad, sad blow.

Chasuble. Very sad indeed. Were you with him at the end?

Jack. No. He died abroad; in Paris, in fact. I had a telegram last night from the manager of the Grand Hotel.

Chasuble. Was the cause of death mentioned?

Jack. A severe chill, it seems.

Miss Prism. As a man sows, so shall he reap.

Chasuble (*raising his hand*). Charity, dear Miss Prism, charity! None of us are perfect. I myself am peculiarly susceptible to draughts. Will the interment take place here?

Jack. No. He seems to have expressed a desire to be buried in Paris.

Chasuble. In Paris! (*Shakes his head.*) I fear that hardly points to any very serious state of mind at the last. You would no doubt wish me to make some slight allusion to this tragic domestic affliction next Sunday. (JACK *presses his hand convulsively.*) My sermon on the meaning of the manna in the wilderness can be adapted to almost any occasion, joyful, or, as in the present case, distressing. (*All sigh.*) I have preached it at harvest celebrations, christenings, confirmations, on days of humiliation and festal days. The last time I delivered it was in the Cathedral, as a charity sermon on behalf of the Society for the Prevention of Discontentment among the Upper Orders. The Bishop, who was present, was much struck by some of the analogies I drew.

Jack. Ah, that reminds me, you mentioned christenings I think, Dr. Chasuble? I suppose you know how to christen all right? (DR. CHASUBLE *looks astounded.*) I mean, of course, you are continually christening, aren't you?

Miss Prism. It is, I regret to say, one of the Rector's most constant duties in this parish. I have often spoken to the poorer classes on the subject. But they don't seem to know what thrift is.

Chasuble. But is there any particular infant in whom you are interested, Mr. Worthing? Your brother was, I believe, unmarried, was he not?

Jack. Oh, yes.

Miss Prism (*bitterly*). People who live entirely for pleasure usually are.

Jack. But it is not for any child, dear Doctor. I am very fond of children. No! the fact is, I would like to be christened myself, this afternoon, if you have nothing better to do.

Chasuble. But surely, Mr. Worthing, you have been christened already?

Jack. I don't remember anything about it.

Chasuble. But have you any grave doubts on the subject?

Jack. I certainly intend to have. Of course, I don't know if the thing would bother you in any way, or if you think I am a little too old now.

Chasuble. Not at all. The sprinkling, and, indeed, the immersion of adults is a perfectly canonical practice.

Jack. Immersion!

Chasuble. You need have no apprehensions. Sprinkling is all that is necessary, or indeed I think advisable. Our weather is so changeable. At what hour would you wish the ceremony performed?

Jack. Oh, I might trot around about five if that would suit you.

Chasuble. Perfectly, perfectly! In fact I have two similar ceremonies to perform at that time. A case of twins that occurred recently in one of the outlying cottages on your own estate. Poor Jenkins the carter, a most hard-working man.

Jack. Oh! I don't see much fun in being christened along with other babies. It would be childish. Would half-past five do?

Chasuble. Admirably! Admirably! (*Takes out watch.*) And now, dear Mr. Worthing, I will not intrude any longer into a house of sorrow. I would merely beg you not to be too much bowed down by grief. What seem to us bitter trials at the moment are often blessings in disguise.

Miss Prism. This seems to me a blessing of an extremely obvious kind.

Enter CECILY *from the house.*

Cecily. Uncle Jack! Oh, I am so pleased to see you back. But what horrid clothes you have on! Do go and change them.

Miss Prism. Cecily!

Chasuble. My child! my child! (CECILY *goes toward* JACK; *he kisses her brow in a melancholy manner.*)

Cecily. What is the matter, Uncle Jack? Do look happy! You look as if you had a toothache, and I have such a surprise for you. Who do you think is in the dining-room? Your brother!

Jack. Who?

Cecily. Your brother Ernest. He arrived about half an hour ago.

Jack. What nonsense! I haven't got a brother.

Cecily. Oh, don't say that. However badly he may have behaved to you in the past, he is still your brother. You couldn't be so heartless as to disown him. I'll tell him to come out. And you will shake hands with him, won't you, Uncle Jack? (*Runs back into the house.*)

Chasuble. These are very joyful tidings.

Miss Prism. After we had all been resigned to his loss, his sudden return seems to me peculiarly distressing.

Jack. My brother is in the dining-room? I don't know what it all means. I think it is perfectly absurd.

Enter ALGERNON *and* CECILY *hand in hand. They come slowly up to* JACK.

Jack. Good heavens! (*Motions* ALGERNON *away.*)

Algernon. Brother John, I have come down from town to tell you that I am very sorry for all the trouble I have given you, and that I intend to lead a better life in the future. (JACK *glares at him and does not take his hand.*)

Cecily. Uncle Jack, you are not going to refuse your own brother's hand?

Jack. Nothing will induce me to take his hand. I think his coming down here disgraceful. He knows perfectly well why.

Cecily. Uncle Jack, do be nice. There is some good in everyone. Ernest has just been telling me about his poor invalid friend, Mr. Bunbury, whom he goes to visit so often. And surely there must be much good in one who is kind to an invalid, and leaves the pleasures of London to sit by a bed of pain.

Jack. Oh, he has been talking about Bunbury, has he?

Cecily. Yes, he has told me all about poor Mr. Bunbury, and his terrible state of health.

Jack. Bunbury! Well, I won't have him talk to you about Bunbury or about anything else. It is enough to drive one perfectly frantic.

Algernon. Of course I admit that the faults were all on my side. But I must say that I think that Brother John's coldness to me is peculiarly painful. I expected a more enthusiastic welcome, especially considering it is the first time I have come here.

Cecily. Uncle Jack, if you don't shake hands with Ernest, I will never forgive you.

Jack. Never forgive me?

Cecily. Never, never, never!

Jack. Well, this is the last time I shall ever do it. (*Shakes hands with* ALGERNON *and glares.*)

Chasuble. It's pleasant, is it not, to see so perfect a reconciliation? I think we might leave the two brothers together.

Miss Prism. Cecily, you will come with us.

Cecily. Certainly, Miss Prism. My little task of reconciliation is over.

Chasuble. You have done a beautiful action today, dear child.

Miss Prism. We must not be premature in our judgments.

Cecily. I feel very happy. (*They all go off.*)

Jack. You young scoundrel, Algy, you must get out of this place as soon as possible. I don't allow any Bunburying here.

Enter MERRIMAN.

Merriman. I have put Mr. Ernest's things in the room next to yours, sir. I suppose that is all right?

Jack. What?

Merriman. Mr. Ernest's luggage, sir. I have unpacked it and put it in the room next to your own.

Jack. His luggage?

Merriman. Yes, sir. Three portmanteaus, a dressing-case, two hat-boxes, and a large luncheon-basket.

Algernon. I am afraid I can't stay more than a week this time.

Jack. Merriman, order the dog-cart at once. Mr. Ernest has been suddenly called back to town.

Merriman. Yes, sir. (*Goes back into the house.*)

Algernon. What a fearful liar you are, Jack. I have not been called back to town at all.

Jack. Yes, you have.

Algernon. I haven't heard anyone call me.

Jack. Your duty as a gentleman calls you back.

Algernon. My duty as a gentleman has never interfered with my pleasures in the smallest degree.

Jack. I can quite understand that.

Algernon. Well, Cecily is a darling.

Jack. You are not to talk of Miss Cardew like that. I don't like it.

Algernon. Well, I don't like your clothes. You look perfectly ridiculous in them. Why on earth don't you go up and change? It is perfectly childish to be in deep mourning for a man who is actually staying for a whole week with you in your house as a guest. I call it grotesque.

Jack. You are certainly not staying with me for a whole week as a guest or anything else. You have got to leave . . . by the four-five train.

Algernon. I certainly won't leave you so long as you are in mourning. It would be most unfriendly. If I were in mourning, you would stay with me, I suppose. I should think it very unkind if you didn't.

Jack. Well, will you go if I change my clothes?

Algernon. Yes, if you are not too long. I never saw anybody take so long to dress, and with such little result.

Jack. Well, at any rate, that is better than being always over-dressed as you are.

Algernon. If I am occasionally a little over-dressed, I make up for it by being always immensely over-educated.

Jack. Your vanity is ridiculous, your conduct an outrage, and your presence in my garden utterly absurd. However, you have got to catch the four-five, and I hope you will have a pleasant journey back to town. This Bunburying, as you call it, has not been a great success for you. (*Goes into the house.*)

Algernon. I think it has been a great success. I'm in love with Cecily, and that is everything. (*Enter* CECILY *at the back of the garden. She picks up the can and begins to water the flowers.*) But I must see her before I go, and make arrangements for another Bunbury. Ah, there she is.

Cecily. Oh, I merely came back to water the roses. I thought you were with Uncle Jack.

Algernon. He's gone to order the dog-cart for me.

Cecily. Oh, is he going to take you for a nice drive?

Algernon. He's going to send me away.

Cecily. Then have we got to part?

Algernon. I am afraid so. It's a very painful parting.

Cecily. It is always painful to part from people whom one has known for a very brief space of time. The absence of old friends one can endure with equanimity. But even a momentary separation from anyone to whom one has just been introduced is almost unbearable.

Algernon. Thank you.

Enter MERRIMAN.

Merriman. The dog-cart is at the door, sir. (ALGERNON *looks appealingly at* CECILY.)

Cecily. It can wait, Merriman . . . for . . . five minutes.

Merriman. Yes, miss.   [*Exit* MERRIMAN.

Algernon. I hope, Cecily, I shall not offend you if I state quite frankly and openly that you seem to me to be in every way the visible personification of absolute perfection.

Cecily. I think your frankness does you great credit, Ernest. If you will allow me I will copy your remarks into my diary. (*Goes over to table and begins writing in diary.*)

Algernon. Do you really keep a diary? I'd give anything to look at it. May I?

Cecily. Oh, no. (*Puts her hand over it.*) You see, it is simply a very young girl's record of her own thoughts and impressions, and consequently meant for publication. When it appears in volume form I hope you will order a copy. But pray, Ernest, don't stop. I delight in taking down from dictation. I have reached "absolute perfection." You can go on. I am quite ready for more.

Algernon (*somewhat taken aback*). Ahem! Ahem!

Cecily. Oh, don't cough, Ernest. When one is dictating, one should speak fluently and not cough. Besides, I don't know how to spell a cough. (*Writes as* ALGERNON *speaks.*)

Algernon (*speaking very rapidly*). Cecily, ever since I first looked upon your wonderful and incomparable beauty, I have dared to love you wildly, passionately, devotedly, hopelessly.

Cecily. I don't think that you should tell me that you love me wildly, passionately, devotedly, hopelessly. Hopelessly doesn't seem to make much sense, does it?

Algernon. Cecily!

Enter MERRIMAN.

Merriman. The dog-cart is waiting, sir.

Algernon. Tell it to come round next week, at the same hour.

Merriman (*looks at* CECILY, *who makes no sign*). Yes, sir.   [MERRIMAN *retires.*

Cecily. Uncle Jack would be very much annoyed if he knew you were staying on till next week, at the same hour.

Algernon. Oh, I don't care about Jack. I don't care for anybody in the whole world but you. I love you, Cecily. You will marry me, won't you?

Cecily. You silly you! Of course. Why, we have been engaged for the last three months.

Algernon. For the last three months?

Cecily. Yes, it will be exactly three months on Thursday.

Algernon. But how did we become engaged?

Cecily. Well, ever since dear Uncle Jack first confessed to us that he had a younger brother who was very wicked and bad, you of course have formed the chief topic of conversation between myself and Miss Prism. And of course a man who is much talked about is always very attractive. One feels there must be something in him after all. I daresay it was foolish of me, but I fell in love with you, Ernest.

Algernon. Darling! And when was the engagement actually settled?

Cecily. On the 4th of February last. Worn out by your entire ignorance of my existence, I determined to end the matter one way or the other, and after a long struggle with myself I accepted you under this dear old tree here. The next day I bought this little ring in your name, and this is the little bangle with the true lovers' knot I promised you always to wear.

Algernon. Did I give you this? It's very pretty, isn't it?

Cecily. Yes, you've wonderfully good taste, Ernest. It's the excuse I've always given for your leading such a bad life. And this is the box in which I keep all your dear letters. (*Kneels at table, opens box, and produces letters tied up with blue ribbon.*)

Algernon. My letters! But my own sweet Cecily, I have never written you any letters.

Cecily. You need hardly remind me of that, Ernest. I remember only too well that I was forced to write your letters for you. I wrote always three times a week, and sometimes oftener.

Algernon. Oh, do let me read them, Cecily?

Cecily. Oh, I couldn't possibly. They would make you far too conceited. (*Replaces box.*) The three you wrote me after I had broken off the engagement are so beautiful, and so badly spelled, that even now I can hardly read them without crying a little.

Algernon. But was our engagement ever broken off?

Cecily. Of course it was. On the 22nd of last March. You can see the entry if you like. (*Shows diary.*) "Today I broke off my engagement with Ernest. I feel it is better to do so. The weather still continues charming."

Algernon. But why on earth did you break it off? What had I done? I had done nothing at all. Cecily, I am very much hurt indeed to hear you broke it off. Particularly when the weather was so charming.

Cecily. It would hardly have been a really serious engagement if it hadn't been broken off at least once. But I forgave you before the week was out.

Algernon (*crossing to her, and kneeling*). What a perfect angel you are, Cecily.

Cecily. You dear romantic boy. (*He kisses her; she puts her fingers through his hair.*) I hope your hair curls naturally, does it?

Algernon. Yes, darling, with a little help from others.

Cecily. I am so glad.

Algernon. You'll never break off our engagement again, Cecily?

Cecily. I don't think I could break it off now that I have actually met you. Besides, of course, there is the question of your name.

Algernon. Yes, of course. (*Nervously.*)

Cecily. You must not laugh at me, darling, but it had always been a girlish dream of mine to love someone whose name was Ernest. (ALGERNON *rises,* CECILY *also.*) There is something in that name that seems to inspire absolute confidence. I pity any poor married woman whose husband is not called Ernest.

Algernon. But, my dear child, do you mean to say you could not love me if I had some other name?

Cecily. But what name?

Algernon. Oh, any name you like—Algernon, for instance. . . .

Cecily. But I don't like the name of Algernon.

Algernon. Well, my own dear, sweet, loving little darling, I really can't see why you should object to the name of Algernon. It is not at all a bad name. In fact, it is rather an aristocratic name. Half of the chaps who get into the Bankruptcy Court are called Algernon. But seriously, Cecily . . . (*Moving to her*) . . . if my name was Algy, couldn't you love me?

Cecily (*rising*). I might respect you, Ernest, I might admire your character, but I fear that I should not be able to give you my undivided attention.

Algernon. Ahem! Cecily! (*Picking up hat*). Your Rector here is, I suppose, thoroughly experienced in the practice of all the rites and ceremonials of the church?

Cecily. Oh, yes. Dr. Chasuble is a most learned man. He has never written a single book, so you can imagine how much he knows.

Algernon. I must see him at once on a most important christening—I mean on most important business.

Cecily. Oh!

Algernon. I shan't be away more than half an hour.

Cecily. Considering that we have been engaged since February the 14th, and that I only met you today for the first time, I think it is rather hard that you should leave me for so long a period as half an hour. Couldn't you make it twenty minutes?

Algernon. I'll be back in no time. (*Kisses her and rushes down the garden.*)

Cecily. What an impetuous boy he is. I like his hair so much. I must enter his proposal in my diary.

    Enter MERRIMAN.

Merriman. A Miss Fairfax has just called to see Mr. Worthing. On very important business, Miss Fairfax states.

Cecily. Isn't Mr. Worthing in his library?

Merriman. Mr. Worthing went over in the direction of the Rectory some time ago.

Cecily. Pray ask the lady to come out here; Mr. Worthing is sure to be back soon. And you can bring tea.

Merriman. Yes, miss. (*Goes out.*)

Cecily. Miss Fairfax! I suppose one of the many good elderly women who are associated with Uncle Jack in some of his philanthropic

work in London. I don't quite like women who are interested in philanthropic work. I think it is so forward of them.
              Enter MERRIMAN.
Merriman. Miss Fairfax.
              Enter GWENDOLEN.
                        [*Exit* MERRIMAN.
Cecily (*advancing to meet her*). Pray let me introduce myself to you. My name is Cecily Cardew.
Gwendolen. Cecily Cardew? (*Moving to her and shaking hands.*) What a very sweet name! Something tells me that we are going to be great friends. I like you already more than I can say. My first impressions of people are never wrong.
Cecily. How nice of you to like me so much after we have known each other such a comparatively short time. Pray sit down.
Gwendolen (*still standing up*). I may call you Cecily, may I not?
Cecily. With pleasure!
Gwendolen. And you will always call me Gwendolen, won't you?
Cecily. If you wish.
Gwendolen. Then that is all quite settled, is it not?
Cecily. I hope so (*A pause. They both sit down together.*)
Gwendolen. Perhaps this might be a favorable opportunity for my mentioning who I am. My father is Lord Bracknell. You have never heard of papa, I suppose?
Cecily. I don't think so.
Gwendolen. Outside the family circle, papa, I am glad to say, is entirely unknown. I think that is quite as it should be. The home seems to me to be the proper sphere for the man. And certainly once a man begins to neglect his domestic duties he becomes painfully effeminate, does he not? And I don't like that. It makes men so very attractive. Cecily, mamma, whose views on education are remarkably strict, has brought me up to be extremely short-sighted; it is part of her system; so do you mind my looking at you through my glasses?
Cecily. Oh, not at all, Gwendolen. I am very fond of being looked at.
Gwendolen (*after examining* CECILY *carefully through a lorgnette*). You are here on a short visit, I suppose.
Cecily. Oh, no, I live here.
Gwendolen (*severely*). Really? Your mother, no doubt, or some female relative of advanced years, resides here also?
Cecily. Oh, no. I have no mother, nor, in fact, any relations.
Gwendolen. Indeed?
Cecily. My dear guardian, with the assistance of Miss Prism, has the arduous task of looking after me.
Gwendolen. Your guardian?
Cecily. Yes, I am Mr. Worthing's ward.
Gwendolen. Oh! It is strange he never mentioned to me that he had a ward. How secretive of him! He grows more interesting hourly. I am not sure, however, that the news inspires me with feelings of unmixed delight. (*Rising and going to her.*) I am very fond of you Cecily; I have liked you ever since I met you. But I am bound to state that now that I know that you are Mr. Worthing's ward, I cannot help expressing a wish you were—well, just a little older than you seem to be—and not quite so very alluring in appearance. In fact, if I may speak candidly——
Cecily. Pray do! I think that whenever one has anything unpleasant to say, one should always be quite candid.
Gwendolen. Well, to speak with perfect candor, Cecily, I wish that you were fully forty-two, and more than usually plain for your age. Ernest has a strong upright nature. He is the very soul of truth and honor. Disloyalty would be as impossible to him as deception. But even men of the noblest possible moral character are extremely susceptible to the influence of the physical charms of others. Modern, no less than Ancient History, supplies us with many most painful examples of what I refer to. If it were not so, indeed, History would be quite unreadable.
Cecily. I beg your pardon, Gwendolen, did you say Ernest?
Gwendolen. Yes.
Cecily. Oh, but it is not Mr. Ernest Worthing who is my guardian. It is his brother—his elder brother.
Gwendolen (*sitting down again.*) Ernest

never mentioned to me that he had a brother.

Cecily. I am sorry to say they have not been on good terms for a long time.

Gwendolen. Ah! that accounts for it. And now that I think of it, I have never heard any man mention his brother. The subject seems distasteful to most men. Cecily, you have lifted a load from my mind. I was growing almost anxious. It would have been terrible if any cloud had come across a friendship like ours, would it not? Of course you are quite, quite sure that it is not Mr. Ernest Worthing who is your guardian?

Cecily. Quite sure. (*A pause.*) In fact, I am going to be his.

Gwendolen (*inquiringly*). I beg your pardon?

Cecily (*rather shy and confidingly*). Dearest Gwendolen, there is no reason why I should make a secret of it to you. Our little county newspaper is sure to chronicle the fact next week. Mr. Ernest Worthing and I are engaged to be married.

Gwendolen (*quite politely, rising*). My darling Cecily, I think there must be some slight error. Mr. Ernest Worthing is engaged to me. The announcement will appear in the *Morning Post* on Saturday at the latest.

Cecily (*very politely, rising*). I am afraid you must be under some misconception. Ernest proposed to me exactly ten minutes ago. (*Shows diary.*)

Gwendolen (*examines diary through her lorgnette carefully*). It is certainly very curious, for he asked me to be his wife yesterday afternoon at 5.30. If you would care to verify the incident, pray do so. (*Produces diary of her own.*) I never travel without my diary. One should always have something sensational to read in the train. I am so sorry, dear Cecily, if it is any disappointment to you, but I am afraid *I* have the prior claim.

Cecily. It would distress me more than I can tell you, dear Gwendolen, if it caused you any mental or physical anguish, but I feel bound to point out that since Ernest proposed to you he clearly has changed his mind.

Gwendolen (*meditatively*). If the poor fellow has been entrapped into any foolish promise I shall consider it my duty to rescue him at once, and with a firm hand.

Cecily (*thoughtfully and sadly*). Whatever unfortunate entanglement my dear boy may have got into, I will never reproach him with it after we are married.

Gwendolen. Do you allude to me, Miss Cardew, as an entanglement? You are presumptuous. On an occasion of this kind it becomes more than a moral duty to speak one's mind. It becomes a pleasure.

Cecily. Do you suggest, Miss Fairfax, that I entrapped Ernest into an engagement? How dare you? This is no time for wearing the shallow mask of manners. When I see a spade I call it a spade.

Gwendolen (*satirically*). I am glad to say that I have never seen a spade. It is obvious that our social spheres have been widely different.

Enter MERRIMAN, *followed by the footman. He carries a salver, tablecloth, and platestand.* CECILY *is about to retort. The presence of the servants exercises a restraining influence, under which both girls chafe.*

Merriman. Shall I lay tea here as usual, miss?

Cecily (*sternly, in a calm voice*). Yes, as usual. (MERRIMAN *begins to clear and lay cloth. A long pause.* CECILY *and* GWENDOLEN *glare at each other.*)

Gwendolen. Are there many interesting walks in the vicinity, Miss Cardew?

Cecily. Oh, yes, a great many. From the top of one of the hills quite close one can see five counties.

Gwendolen. Five counties! I don't think I should like that. I hate crowds.

Cecily (*sweetly*). I suppose that is why you live in town? (GWENDOLEN *bites her lip, and beats her foot nervously with her parasol.*)

Gwendolen (*looking round*). Quite a well-kept garden this is, Miss Cardew.

Cecily. So glad you like it, Miss Fairfax.

Gwendolen. I had no idea there were any flowers in the country.

Cecily. Oh, flowers are as common here, Miss Fairfax, as people are in London.

---

28. *Morning Post,* a well-known newspaper of London.

Gwendolen. Personally I cannot understand how anybody manages to exist in the country, if anybody who is anybody does. The country always bores me to death.

Cecily. Ah! This is what the newspapers call agricultural depression, is it not? I believe the aristocracy are suffering very much from it just at present. It is almost an epidemic amongst them, I have been told. May I offer you some tea, Miss Fairfax?

Gwendolen (*with elaborate politeness*). Thank you. (*Aside.*) Detestable girl! But I require tea!

Cecily (*sweetly*). Sugar?

Gwendolen (*superciliously*). No, thank you. Sugar is not fashionable any more. (CECILY *looks angrily at her, takes up the tongs and puts four lumps of sugar into the cup.*)

Cecily (*severely*). Cake or bread and butter?

Gwendolen (*in a bored manner*). Bread and butter, please. Cake is rarely seen at the best houses nowadays.

Cecily (*cuts a very large slice of cake, and puts it on the tray*). Hand that to Miss Fairfax. (MERRIMAN *does so, and goes out with footman.* GWENDOLEN *drinks the tea and makes a grimace. Puts down cup at once, reaches out her hand to the bread and butter, looks at it, and finds it is cake. Rises in indignation.*)

Gwendolen. You have filled my tea with lumps of sugar, and though I asked most distinctly for bread and butter, you have given me cake. I am known for the gentleness of my disposition, and the extraordinary sweetness of my nature, but I warn you, Miss Cardew, you may go too far.

Cecily (*rising*). To save my poor, innocent, trusting boy from the machinations of any other girl, there are no lengths to which I would not go.

Gwendolen. From the moment I saw you I distrusted you. I felt that you were false and deceitful. I am never deceived in such matters. My first impressions of people are invariably right.

Cecily. It seems to me, Miss Fairfax, that I am trespassing on your valuable time. No doubt you have many other calls of a similar character to make in the neighborhood.

Enter JACK.

Gwendolen (*catching sight of him*). Ernest! My own Ernest!

Jack. Gwendolen! Darling! (*Offers to kiss her.*)

Gwendolen (*drawing back*). A moment! May I ask if you are engaged to be married to this young lady? (*Points to* CECILY.)

Jack (*laughing*). To dear little Cecily! Of course not! What could have put such an idea into your pretty little head?

Gwendolen. Thank you. You may. (*Offers her cheek.*)

Cecily (*very sweetly*). I knew there must be some misunderstanding, Miss Fairfax. The gentleman whose arm is at present around your waist is my dear guardian, Mr. John Worthing.

Gwendolen. I beg your pardon?

Cecily. This is Uncle Jack.

Gwendolen (*receding*). Jack! Oh!

Enter ALGERNON.

Cecily. Here is Ernest.

Algernon (*goes straight over to* CECILY *without noticing anyone else.*) My own love! (*Offers to kiss her.*)

Cecily (*drawing back*). A moment, Ernest! May I ask you—are you engaged to be married to this young lady?

Algernon (*looking round*). To what young lady? Good heavens! Gwendolen!

Cecily. Yes, to good heavens, Gwendolen, I mean to Gwendolen.

Algernon (*laughing*). Of course not! What could have put such an idea into your pretty little head?

Cecily. Thank you. (*Presenting her cheek to be kissed.*) You may. (ALGERNON *kisses her.*)

Gwendolen. I felt there was some slight error, Miss Cardew. The gentleman who is now embracing you is my cousin, Mr. Algernon Moncrieff.

Cecily (*breaking away from* ALGERNON).

---

6. **agricultural depression.** About 1875 the farmers of England suffered an agricultural depression from which they had not yet recovered. The chief causes were the increasing competition from America and several bad crop-years at home.

Algernon Moncrieff! Oh! (*The two girls move toward each other and put their arms round each other's waists as if for protection.*)

Cecily. Are you called Algernon?

Algernon. I cannot deny it.

Cecily. Oh!

Gwendolen. Is your name really John?

Jack (*standing rather proudly*). I could deny it if I liked. I could deny anything if I liked. But my name certainly is John. It has been John for years.

Cecily (*to* Gwendolen). A gross deception has been practiced on both of us.

Gwendolen. My poor wounded Cecily!

Cecily. My sweet, wronged Gwendolen!

Gwendolen (*slowly and seriously*). You will call me sister, will you not? (*They embrace.* Jack *and* Algernon *groan and walk up and down.*)

Cecily (*rather brightly*). There is just one question I would like to be allowed to ask my guardian.

Gwendolen. An admirable idea! Mr. Worthing, there is just one question I would like to be permitted to put to you. Where is your brother Ernest? We are both engaged to be married to your brother Ernest, so it is a matter of some importance to us to know where your brother Ernest is at present.

Jack (*slowly and hesitatingly*). Gwendolen—Cecily—it is very painful for me to be forced to speak the truth. It is the first time in my life that I have ever been reduced to such a painful position, and I am really quite inexperienced in doing anything of the kind. However, I will tell you quite frankly that I have no brother Ernest. I have no brother at all. I never had a brother in my life, and I certainly have not the smallest intention of ever having one in the future.

Cecily (*surprised*). No brother at all?

Jack (*cheerily*). None!

Gwendolen (*severely*). Had you never a brother of any kind?

Jack (*pleasantly*). Never. Not even of any kind.

Gwendolen. I am afraid it is quite clear, Cecily, that neither of us is engaged to be married to anyone.

Cecily. It is not a very pleasant position for a young girl suddenly to find herself in. Is it?

Gwendolen. Let us go into the house. They will hardly venture to come after us there.

Cecily. No, men are so cowardly, aren't they? (*They retire into the house with scornful looks.*)

Jack. This ghastly state of things is what you call Bunburying, I suppose?

Algernon. Yes, and a perfectly wonderful Bunbury it is. The most wonderful Bunbury I have ever had in my life.

Jack. Well, you've no right whatsoever to Bunbury here.

Algernon. That is absurd. One has a right to Bunbury anywhere one chooses. Every serious Bunburyist knows that.

Jack. Serious Bunburyist! Good heavens!

Algernon. Well, one must be serious about something, if one wants to have any amusement in life. I happen to be serious about Bunburying. What on earth you are serious about I haven't got the remotest idea. About everything, I should fancy. You have such an absolutely trivial nature.

Jack. Well, the only small satisfaction I have in the whole of this wretched business is that your friend Bunbury is quite exploded. You won't be able to run down to the country quite so often as you used to do, dear Algy. And a very good thing, too.

Algernon. Your brother is a little off color, isn't he, dear Jack? You won't be able to disappear to London quite so frequently as your wicked custom was. And not a bad thing, either.

Jack. As for your conduct toward Miss Cardew, I must say that your taking in a sweet, simple, innocent girl like that is quite inexcusable. To say nothing of the fact that she is my ward.

Algernon. I can see no possible defense at all for your deceiving a brilliant, clever, thoroughly experienced young lady like Miss Fairfax. To say nothing of the fact that she is my cousin.

Jack. I wanted to be engaged to Gwendolen, that is all. I love her.

Algernon. Well, I simply wanted to be engaged to Cecily. I adore her.

Jack. There is certainly no chance of your

marrying Miss Cardew.

Algernon. I don't think there is much likelihood, Jack, of you and Miss Fairfax being united.

Jack. Well, that is no business of yours.

Algernon. If it was my business, I wouldn't talk about it. (*Begins to eat muffins.*) It is very vulgar to talk about one's business. Only people like stock-brokers do that, and then merely at dinner parties.

Jack. How you can sit there, calmly eating muffins, when we are in this horrible trouble, I can't make out. You seem to me to be perfectly heartless.

Algernon. Well, I can't eat muffins in an agitated manner. The butter would probably get on my cuffs. One should always eat muffins quite calmly. It is the only way to eat them.

Jack. I say it's perfectly heartless your eating muffins at all, under the circumstances.

Algernon. When I am in trouble, eating is the only thing that consoles me. Indeed, when I am in really great trouble, as anyone who knows me intimately will tell you, I refuse everything except food and drink. At the present moment I am eating muffins because I am unhappy. Besides, I am particularly fond of muffins. (*Rising.*)

Jack (*rising*). Well, that is no reason why you should eat them all in that greedy way. (*Takes muffins from* ALGERNON.)

Algernon (*offering tea-cake*). I wish you would have tea-cake instead. I don't like tea-cake.

Jack. Good heavens! I suppose a man may eat his own muffins in his own garden.

Algernon. But you have just said it was perfectly heartless to eat muffins.

Jack. I said it was perfectly heartless of you, under the circumstances. That is a very different thing.

Algernon. That may be. But the muffins are the same. (*He seizes the muffin-dish from* JACK.)

Jack. Algy, I wish to goodness you would go.

Algernon. You can't possibly ask me to go without having some dinner. It's absurd. I never go without my dinner. No one ever does, except vegetarians and people like that. Besides I have just made arrangements with Dr. Chasuble to be christened at a quarter to six under the name of Ernest.

Jack. My dear fellow, the sooner you give up that nonsense the better. I made arrangements this morning with Dr. Chasuble to be christened myself at 5.30, and I naturally will take the name of Ernest. Gwendolen would wish it. We can't both be christened Ernest. It's absurd. Besides, I have a perfect right to be christened if I like. There is no evidence at all that I ever have been christened by anybody. I should think it extremely probable I never was, and so does Dr. Chasuble. It is entirely different in your case. You have been christened already.

Algernon. Yes, but I have not been christened for years.

Jack. Yes, but you have been christened. That is the important thing.

Algernon. Quite so. So I know my constitution can stand it. If you are not quite sure about you ever having been christened, I must say I think it rather dangerous your venturing on it now. It might make you very unwell. You can hardly have forgotten that someone very closely connected with you was very nearly carried off this week in Paris by a severe chill.

Jack. Yes, but you said yourself that a severe chill was not hereditary.

Algernon. It usedn't to be, I know—but I daresay it is now. Science is always making wonderful improvements in things.

Jack (*picking up the muffin-dish*). Oh, that is nonsense; you are always talking nonsense.

Algernon. Jack, you are at the muffins again! I wish you wouldn't. There are only two left. (*Takes them.*) I told you I was particularly fond of muffins.

Jack. But I hate tea-cake.

Algernon. Why on earth then do you allow tea-cake to be served up for your guests? What ideas you have of hospitality!

Jack. Algernon! I have already told you to go. I don't want you here. Why don't you go?

Algernon. I haven't quite finished my tea

yet, and there is still one muffin left. (JACK *groans, and sinks into a chair.* ALGERNON *still continues eating.*)

ACT III

SCENE.—*Morning-room at the Manor House.* GWENDOLEN *and* CECILY *are at the window, looking out into the garden.*

Gwendolen. That fact that they did not follow us at once into the house, as anyone else would have done, seems to me to show that they have some sense of shame left.

Cecily. They have been eating muffins. That looks like repentance.

Gwendolen (*after a pause*). They don't seem to notice us at all. Couldn't you cough?

Gwendolen. They're looking at us. What effrontery!

Cecily. They're approaching. That's very forward of them.

Gwendolen. Let us preserve a dignified silence.

Cecily. Certainly. It's the only thing to do now.

Enter JACK, *followed by* ALGERNON. *They whistle some dreadful popular air from a British opera.*

Gwendolen. This dignified silence seems to produce an unpleasant effect.

Cecily. A most distasteful one.

Gwendolen. But we will not be the first to speak.

Cecily. Certainly not.

Gwendolen. Mr. Worthing, I have something very particular to ask you. Much depends on your reply.

Cecily. Gwendolen, your common sense is invaluable. Mr. Moncrieff, kindly answer me the following question. Why did you pretend to be my guardian's brother?

Algernon. In order that I might have an opportunity of meeting you.

Cecily (*to* GWENDOLEN). That certainly seems a satisfactory explanation, does it not?

Gwendolen. Yes, dear, if you can believe him.

Cecily. I don't. But that does not affect the wonderful beauty of his answer.

Gwendolen. True. In matters of grave importance, style, not sincerity, is the vital thing. Mr. Worthing, what explanation can you offer to me for pretending to have a brother? Was it in order that you might have an opportunity of coming up to town to see me as often as possible?

Jack. Can you doubt it, Miss Fairfax?

Gwendolen. I have the gravest doubts upon the subject. But I intend to crush them. This is not the moment for German skepticism. (*Moving to* CECILY.) Their explanations appear to be quite satisfactory, especially Mr. Worthing's. That seems to me to have the stamp of truth upon it.

Cecily. I am more than content with what Mr. Moncrieff said. His voice alone inspires one with absolute credulity.

Gwendolen. Then you think we should forgive them?

Cecily. Yes. I mean no.

Gwendolen. True! I had forgotten. There are principles at stake that one cannot surrender. Which of us should tell them? The task is not a pleasant one.

Cecily. Could we not both speak at the same time?

Gwendolen. An excellent idea! I nearly always speak at the same time as other people. Will you take the time from me?

Cecily. Certainly. (GWENDOLEN *beats time with uplifted finger.*)

Gwendolen and Cecily (*speaking together*). Your Christian names are still an insuperable barrier. That is all!

Jack and Algernon (*speaking together*). Our Christian names! Is that all? But we are going to be christened this afternoon.

Gwendolen (*to* JACK). For my sake you are prepared to do this terrible thing?

Jack. I am.

Cecily (*to* ALGERNON). To please me you are ready to face this fearful ordeal?

Algernon. I am!

Gwendolen. How absurd to talk of the equality of the sexes! Where questions of self-sacrifice are concerned, men are infinitely beyond us.

---

51. **German skepticism.** As here used, skepticism indicates merely an incredulous state of mind. The allusion is probably to Friedrich Wilhelm Nietzsche (1844-1900), German atheist, whose complete works were beginning to appear in 1895, the date of Wilde's comedy, or perhaps to the ideas promulgated by earlier German skeptics.

Jack. We are. (*Clasps hands with* ALGERNON.)

Cecily. They have moments of physical courage of which we women know absolutely nothing.

Gwendolen (*to* JACK). Darling!

Algernon (*to* CECILY). Darling! (*They fall into each other's arms.*)

Enter MERRIMAN. *When he enters, he coughs loudly, seeing the situation.*

Merriman. Ahem! Ahem! Lady Bracknell!

Jack. Good heavens!

Enter LADY BRACKNELL. *The couples separate in alarm. Exit* MERRIMAN.

Lady Bracknell. Gwendolen! What does this mean?

Gwendolen. Merely that I am engaged to be married to Mr. Worthing, Mamma.

Lady Bracknell. Come here. Sit down. Sit down immediately. Hesitation of any kind is a sign of mental decay in the young, of physical weakness in the old. (*Turns to* JACK.) Apprised, sir, of my daughter's sudden flight by her trusty maid, whose confidence I purchased by means of a small coin, I followed her at once by a luggage train. Her unhappy father is, I am glad to say, under the impression that she is attending a more than usually lengthy lecture by the University Extension Scheme on the Influence of a Permanent Income on Thought. I do not propose to undeceive him. Indeed I have never undeceived him on any question. I would consider it wrong. But of course, you will clearly understand that all communication between yourself and my daughter must cease immediately from this moment. On this point, as indeed on all points, I am firm.

Jack. I am engaged to be married to Gwendolen, Lady Bracknell!

Lady Bracknell. You are nothing of the kind, sir. And now, as regards Algernon! . . . Algernon!

Algernon. Yes, Aunt Augusta.

Lady Bracknell. May I ask if it is in this house that your invalid friend Mr. Bunbury resides?

Algernon (*stammering*). Oh, no! Bunbury doesn't live here. Bunbury is somewhere else at present. In fact, Bunbury is dead.

Lady Bracknell. Dead! When did Mr. Bunbury die? His death must have been extremely sudden.

Algernon (*airily*). Oh, I killed Bunbury this afternoon. I mean poor Bunbury died this afternoon.

Lady Bracknell. What did he die of?

Algernon. Bunbury? Oh, he was quite exploded.

Lady Bracknell. Exploded! Was he the victim of a revolutionary outrage? I was not aware that Mr. Bunbury was interested in social legislation. If so, he is well punished for his morbidity.

Algernon. My dear Aunt Augusta, I mean he was found out! The doctors found out that Bunbury could not live, that is what I mean—so Bunbury died.

Lady Bracknell. He seems to have had great confidence in the opinion of his physicians. I am glad, however, that he made up his mind at the last to some definite course of action, and acted under proper medical advice. And now that we have finally got rid of this Mr. Bunbury, may I ask, Mr. Worthing, who is that young person whose hand my nephew Algernon is now holding in what seems to me a peculiarly unnecessary manner?

Jack. That lady is Miss Cecily Cardew, my ward. (LADY BRACKNELL *bows coldly to* CECILY.)

Algernon. I am engaged to be married to Cecily, Aunt Augusta.

Lady Bracknell. I beg your pardon?

Cecily. Mr. Moncrieff and I are engaged to be married, Lady Bracknell.

Lady Bracknell (*with a shiver, crossing to the sofa and sitting down*). I do not know whether there is anything peculiarly exciting in the air of this particular part of Hertfordshire, but the number of engagements that go on seems to me considerably above the proper average that statistics have laid down for our guidance. I think some preliminary enquiry on my part would not be out of place. Mr. Worthing, is Miss Cardew at all connected with any of the larger railway stations in London? I merely desire information. Until yesterday I had no idea that there were any families or persons whose origin was a Terminus. (JACK *looks perfectly furious, but restrains himself.*)

Jack (*in a clear, cold voice*). Miss Cardew is the granddaughter of the late Mr. Thomas Cardew of 149, Belgrave Square, S.W.; Gervase Park, Dorking, Surrey; and the Sporran, Fifeshire, N.B.

Lady Bracknell. That sounds not unsatisfactory. Three addresses always inspire confidence, even in tradesmen. But what proof have I of their authenticity?

Jack. I have carefully preserved the Court Guide of the period. They are open to your inspection, Lady Bracknell.

Lady Bracknell (*grimly*). I have known strange errors in that publication.

Jack. Miss Cardew's family solicitors are Messrs. Markby, Markby, and Markby.

Lady Bracknell. Markby, Markby, and Markby? A firm of the very highest position in their profession. Indeed I am told that one of the Mr. Markbys is occasionally to be seen at dinner parties. So far I am satisfied.

Jack (*very irritably*). How extremely kind of you, Lady Bracknell! I have also in my possession, you will be pleased to hear, certificates of Miss Cardew's birth, baptism, whooping cough, registration, vaccination, confirmation, and the measles; both the German and the English variety.

Lady Bracknell. Ah! A life crowded with incident, I see; though perhaps somewhat too exciting for a young girl. I am not myself in favor of premature experiences. (*Rises, looks at her watch.*) Gwendolen! the time approaches for our departure. We have not a moment to lose. As a matter of form, Mr. Worthing, I had better ask you if Miss Cardew has any little fortune?

Jack. Oh, about a hundred and thirty thousand pounds in the Funds. That is all. Goodby, Lady Bracknell. So pleased to have seen you.

Lady Bracknell (*sitting down again.*) A moment, Mr. Worthing. A hundred and thirty thousand pounds! And in the Funds! Miss Cardew seems to me a most attractive young lady, now that I look at her. Few girls of the present day have any really solid qualities, any of the qualities that last, and improve with time. We live, I regret to say, in an age of surfaces. (*To* CECILY.) Come over here, dear. (CECILY *goes across.*) Pretty child! your dress is sadly simple, and your hair seems almost as Nature might have left it. But we can soon alter all that. A thoroughly experienced French maid produces a really marvelous result in a very brief space of time. I remember recommending one to young Lady Lancing, and after three months her own husband did not know her.

Jack (*aside*). And after six months nobody knew her.

Lady Bracknell (*glares at* JACK *for a few moments. Then bends, with a practiced smile, to* CECILY). Kindly turn round, sweet child. (CECILY *turns completely round.*) No, the side view is what I want. (CECILY *presents her profile.*) Yes, quite as I expected. There are distinct social possibilities in your profile. The two weak points in our age are its want of principle and its want of profile. The chin a little higher, dear. Style largely depends on the way the chin is worn. They are worn very high, just at present. Algernon!

Algernon. Yes, Aunt Augusta!

Lady Bracknell. There are distinct social possibilities in Miss Cardew's profile.

Algernon. Cecily is the sweetest, dearest, prettiest girl in the whole world. And I don't care twopence about social possibilities.

Lady Bracknell. Never speak disrespectfully of society, Algernon. Only people who can't get into it do that. (*To* CECILY). Dear child, of course you know that Algernon has nothing but his debts to depend upon. But I do not approve of mercenary marriages. When I married Lord Bracknell, I had no fortune of any kind. But I never dreamed for a moment of allowing that to stand in my way. Well, I suppose I must give my consent.

Algernon. Thank you, Aunt Augusta.

Lady Bracknell. Cecily, you may kiss me!

---

9. **Fifeshire, N. B.** Fifeshire is a county in Scotland, sometimes called North Britain. 14. **Court Guide,** a directory of the names and addresses of the nobility and gentry in a town. 43. **the Funds,** government bonds.

Cecily (*kisses her*). Thank you, Lady Bracknell.

Lady Bracknell. You may also address me as Aunt Augusta for the future.

Cecily. Thank you, Aunt Augusta.

Lady Bracknell. The marriage, I think, had better take place quite soon.

Algernon. Thank you, Aunt Augusta.

Cecily. Thank you, Aunt Augusta.

Lady Bracknell. To speak frankly, I am not in favor of long engagements. They give people the opportunity of finding out each other's character before marriage, which I think is never advisable.

Jack. I beg your pardon for interrupting you, Lady Bracknell, but this engagement is quite out of the question. I am Miss Cardew's guardian, and she cannot marry without my consent until she comes of age. That consent I absolutely decline to give.

Lady Bracknell. Upon what grounds, may I ask? Algernon is an extremely, I may almost say an ostentatiously, eligible young man. He has nothing, but he looks everything. What more can one desire?

Jack. It pains me very much to have to speak frankly to you, Lady Bracknell, about your nephew, but the fact is that I do not approve at all of his moral character. I suspect him of being untruthful. (ALGERNON *and* CECILY *look at him in indignant amazement.*)

Lady Bracknell. Untruthful! My nephew Algernon? Impossible! He is an Oxonian.

Jack. I fear there can be no possible doubt about the matter. This afternoon, during my temporary absence in London on an important question of romance, he obtained admission to my house by means of the false pretense of being my brother. Under an assumed name he drank, I've just been informed by my butler, an entire pint bottle of my Perrier-Jouet, Brut, '89; a wine I was specially reserving for myself. Continuing his disgraceful deception, he succeeded in the course of the afternoon in alienating the affections of my only ward. He subsequently stayed to tea, and devoured every single muffin. And what makes his conduct all the more heartless is that he was perfectly well aware from the first that I have no brother, that I never had a brother, and that I don't intend to have a brother, not even of any kind. I distinctly told him so myself yesterday afternoon.

Lady Bracknell. Ahem! Mr. Worthing, after careful consideration I have decided entirely to overlook my nephew's conduct to you.

Jack. That is very generous of you, Lady Bracknell. My own decision, however, is unalterable. I decline to give my consent.

Lady Bracknell (*to* CECILY). Come here, sweet child. (CECILY *goes over.*) How old are you, dear?

Cecily. Well, I am really only eighteen, but I always admit to twenty when I go to evening parties.

Lady Bracknell. You are perfectly right in making some slight alteration. Indeed, no woman should ever be quite accurate about her age. It looks so calculating. . . . (*In meditative manner.*) Eighteen, but admitting to twenty at evening parties. Well, it will not be very long before you are of age and free from the restraints of tutelage. So I don't think your guardian's consent is, after all, a matter of any importance.

Jack. Pray excuse me, Lady Bracknell, for interrupting you again, but it is only fair to tell you that according to the terms of her grandfather's will Miss Cardew does not come legally of age till she is thirty-five.

Lady Bracknell. That does not seem to me to be a grave objection. Thirty-five is a very attractive age. London society is full of women of the very highest birth who have, of their own free choice, remained thirty-five for years. Lady Dumbleton is an instance in point. To my own knowledge she has been thirty-five ever since she arrived at the age of forty, which was many years ago now. I see no reason why our dear Cecily should not be even still more attractive at the age you mention than she is at present. There will be a large accumulation of property.

Cecily. Algy, could you wait for me till I was thirty-five?

Algernon. Of course I could, Cecily. You know I could.

---

33. **Oxonian**, a student or a graduate of Oxford University.

Cecily. Yes, I felt it instinctively, but I couldn't wait all that time. I hate waiting even five minutes for anybody. It always makes me rather cross. I am not punctual myself, I know, but I do like punctuality in others, and waiting, even to be married, is quite out of the question.

Algernon. Then what is to be done, Cecily?

Cecily. I don't know, Mr. Moncrieff.

Lady Bracknell. My dear Mr. Worthing, as Miss Cardew states positively that she cannot wait till she is thirty-five—a remark which I am bound to say seems to me to show a somewhat impatient nature—I would beg of you to reconsider your decision.

Jack. But my dear Lady Bracknell, the matter is entirely in your own hands. The moment you consent to my marriage with Gwendolen, I will most gladly allow your nephew to form an alliance with my ward.

Lady Bracknell (*rising and drawing herself up*). You must be quite aware that what you propose is out of the question.

Jack. Then a passionate celibacy is all that any of us can look forward to.

Lady Bracknell. That is not the destiny I propose for Gwendolen. Algernon, of course, can choose for himself. (*Pulls out her watch.*) Come, dear (GWENDOLEN *rises*), we have already missed five, if not six, trains. To miss any more might expose us to comment on the platform.

Enter DR. CHASUBLE.

Chasuble. Everything is quite ready for the christenings.

Lady Bracknell. The christenings, sir! Is not that somewhat premature?

Chasuble (*looking rather puzzled, and pointing to* JACK *and* ALGERNON). Both these gentlemen have expressed a desire for immediate baptism.

Lady Bracknell. At their age? The idea is grotesque and irreligious! Algernon, I forbid you to be baptized. I will not hear of such excesses. Lord Bracknell would be highly displeased if he learned that that was the way in which you wasted your time and money.

Chasuble. Am I to understand then that there are to be no christenings at all this afternoon?

Jack. I don't think that, as things are now, it would be of much practical value to either of us, Dr. Chasuble.

Chasuble. I am grieved to hear such sentiments from you, Mr. Worthing. They savor of the heretical views of the Anabaptists, views that I have completely refuted in four of my unpublished sermons. However, as your present mood seems to be one peculiarly secular, I will return to the church at once. Indeed, I have just been informed by the pew-opener that for the last hour and a half Miss Prism has been waiting for me in the vestry.

Lady Bracknell (*starting*). Miss Prism! Did I hear you mention a Miss Prism?

Chasuble. Yes, Lady Bracknell. I am on my way to join her.

Lady Bracknell. Pray allow me to detain you for a moment. This matter may prove to be one of vital importance to Lord Bracknell and myself. Is this Miss Prism a female of repellent aspect, remotely connected with education?

Chasuble (*somewhat indignantly*). She is the most cultivated of ladies, and the very picture of respectability.

Lady Bracknell. It is obviously the same person. May I ask what position she holds in your household?

Chasuble (*severely*). I am a celibate, madam.

Jack (*interposing*). Miss Prism, Lady Bracknell, has been for the last three years Miss Cardew's esteemed governess and valued companion.

Lady Bracknell. In spite of what I hear of her, I must see her at once. Let her be sent for.

Chasuble (*looking off*). She approaches; she is nigh.

Enter MISS PRISM *hurriedly.*

Miss Prism. I was told you expected me in the vestry, dear Canon. I have been waiting for you there for an hour and three-quarters. (*Catches sight of* LADY BRACKNELL, *who has fixed her with a stony glare.* MISS PRISM *grows pale and quails. She looks anxiously round as if desirous to escape.*)

55. **Anabaptists,** members of a religious sect that arose in Germany in 1523. Among other doctrines they denied the efficacy of infant baptism; hence the name, which indicates one who baptizes again.

Lady Bracknell (in a severe, judicial voice). Prism! (MISS PRISM *bows her head in shame.*) Come here, Prism! (MISS PRISM *approaches in a humble manner.*) Prism! Where is that baby? (*General consternation. The Canon starts back in horror.* ALGERNON *and* JACK *pretend to be anxious to shield* CECILY *and* GWENDOLEN *from hearing the details of a terrible public scandal.*) Twenty-eight years ago, Prism, you left Lord Bracknell's house, Number 104, Upper Grosvenor Street, in charge of a perambulator that contained a baby, of the male sex. You never returned. A few weeks later, through the elaborate investigations of the Metropolitan police, the perambulator was discovered at midnight, standing by itself in a remote corner of Bayswater. It contained the manuscript of a three-volume novel of more than usually revolting sentimentality. (MISS PRISM *starts in involuntary indignation.*) But the baby was not there! (*Everyone looks at* MISS PRISM.) Prism, where is that baby? (*A pause.*)

Miss Prism. Lady Bracknell, I admit with shame that I do not know. I only wish I did. The plain facts of the case are these. On the morning of the day you mention, a day that is forever branded on my memory, I prepared as usual to take the baby out in its perambulator. I had also with me a somewhat old but capacious hand-bag in which I had intended to place the manuscript of a work of fiction that I had written during my few unoccupied hours. In a moment of mental abstraction, for which I never can forgive myself, I deposited the manuscript in the bassinette, and placed the baby in the hand-bag.

Jack (who has been listening attentively). But where did you deposit the hand-bag?

Miss Prism. Do not ask me, Mr. Worthing.

Jack. Miss Prism, this is a matter of no small importance to me. I insist on knowing where you deposited the hand-bag that contained that infant.

Miss Prism. I left it in the cloak-room of one of the larger railway stations in London.

Jack. What railway station?

Miss Prism (quite crushed). Victoria. The Brighton line. (*Sinks into a chair.*)

Jack. I must retire to my room for a moment. Gwendolen, wait here for me.

Gwendolen. If you are not too long, I will wait here for you all my life.

[*Exit* JACK *in great excitement.*

Chasuble. What do you think this means, Lady Bracknell?

Lady Bracknell. I dare not even suspect, Dr. Chasuble. I need hardly tell you that in families of high position strange coincidences are not supposed to occur. They are hardly considered the thing. (*Noises heard overhead as if someone was throwing trunks about. Everybody looks up.*)

Cecily. Uncle Jack seems strangely agitated.

Chasuble. Your guardian has a very emotional nature.

Lady Bracknell. This noise is extremely unpleasant. It sounds as if he was having an argument. I dislike arguments of any kind. They are always vulgar, and often convincing.

Chasuble (looking up). It has stopped now. (*The noise is redoubled.*)

Lady Bracknell. I wish he would arrive at some conclusion.

Gwendolen. This suspense is terrible. I hope it will last.

Enter JACK *with a hand-bag of black leather in his hand.*

Jack (rushing over to MISS PRISM.) Is this the hand-bag, Miss Prism? Examine it carefully before you speak. The happiness of more than one life depends on your answer.

Miss Prism (calmly). It seems to be mine. Yes, here is the injury it received through the upsetting of a Gower Street omnibus in younger and happier days. Here is the stain on the lining caused by the explosion of a temperance beverage, an incident that occurred at Leamington. And here, on the lock, are my initials. I had forgotten that in an extravagant mood I had had them placed there. The bag is undoubtedly mine. I am delighted to have it so unexpectedly restored

---

18. **Bayswater,** a section of London some distance from Grosvenor Street. 19. **three-volume novel.** See p. 965, l. 51.

87. **Leamington,** a city in Warwickshire; a fashionable summer resort.

to me. It has been a great inconvenience being without it all these years.

Jack (*in a pathetic voice*). Miss Prism, more is restored to you than this hand-bag. I was the baby you placed in it.

Miss Prism (*amazed*). You?

Jack (*embracing her*). Yes . . . mother!

Miss Prism (*recoiling in indignant astonishment*). Mr. Worthing! I am unmarried!

Jack. Unmarried! I do not deny that is a serious blow. But after all, who has the right to cast a stone against one who has suffered? Cannot repentance wipe out an act of folly? Why should there be one law for men and another for women? Mother, I forgive you. (*Tries to embrace her again.*)

Miss Prism (*still more indignant*). Mr. Worthing, there is some error. (*Pointing to* LADY BRACKNELL.) There is the lady who can tell you who you really are.

Jack (*after a pause*). Lady Bracknell, I hate to seem inquisitive, but would you kindly inform me who I am?

Lady Bracknell. I am afraid that the news I have to give you will not altogether please you. You are the son of my poor sister, Mrs. Moncrieff, and consequently Algernon's elder brother.

Jack. Algy's elder brother! Then I have a brother after all. I knew I had a brother! I always said I had a brother! Cecily—how could you have ever doubted that I had a brother? (*Seizes hold of* ALGERNON.) Dr. Chasuble, my unfortunate brother. Miss Prism, my unfortunate brother. Gwendolen, my unfortunate brother. Algy, you young scoundrel, you will have to treat me with more respect in the future. You have never behaved to me like a brother in all your life.

Algernon. Well, not till today, old boy, I admit. I did my best, however, though I was out of practice. (*Shakes hands.*)

Gwendolen (*to* JACK). My own! But what own are you? What is your Christian name, now that you have become someone else?

Jack. Good heavens! . . . I had quite forgotten that point. Your decision on the subject of my name is irrevocable, I suppose?

Gwendolen. I never change, except in my affections.

Cecily. What a noble nature you have, Gwendolen!

Jack. Then the question had better be cleared up at once. Aunt Augusta, a moment. At the time when Miss Prism left me in the hand-bag, had I been christened already?

Lady Bracknell. Every luxury that money could buy, including christening, had been lavished on you by your fond and doting parents.

Jack. Then I was christened! That is settled. Now, what name was I given? Let me know the worst.

Lady Bracknell. Being the eldest son you were naturally christened after your father.

Jack (*irritably*). Yes, but what was my father's Christian name?

Lady Bracknell (*meditatively*). I cannot at the present moment recall what the General's Christian name was. But I have no doubt he had one. He was eccentric, I admit. But only in later years. And that was the result of the Indian climate, and marriage, and indigestion, and other things of that kind.

Jack. Algy! Can't you recollect what our father's Christian name was?

Algernon. My dear boy, we were never even on speaking terms. He died before I was a year old.

Jack. His name would appear in the Army Lists of the period, I suppose, Aunt Augusta?

Lady Bracknell. The General was essentially a man of peace, except in his domestic life. But I have no doubt his name would appear in any military directory.

Jack. The Army Lists of the last forty years are here. These delightful records should have been my constant study. (*Rushes to bookcase and tears the books out.*) M. Generals . . . Mallam, Maxbohm, Magley, what ghastly names they have—Markby, Migsby, Mobbs, Moncrieff! Lieutenant 1840, Captain, Lieutenant-Colonel, Colonel, General 1869, Christian names, Ernest John. (*Puts book very quietly down and speaks quite calmly.*) I always told you, Gwendolen, my name was

---

12. **cast a stone.** Cf. *John*, 8:7. When the people were ready to stone the woman taken in adultery, Christ said to them, "He that is without sin among you, let him first cast a stone at her."

Ernest, didn't I? Well, it is Ernest after all. I mean it naturally is Ernest.

Lady Bracknell. Yes, I remember that the General was called Ernest. I knew I had some particular reason for disliking the name.

Gwendolen. Ernest! My own Ernest! I felt from the first that you could have no other name!

Jack. Gwendolen, it is a terrible thing for a man to find out suddenly that all his life he has been speaking nothing but the truth. Can you forgive me?

Gwendolen. I can. For I feel that you are sure to change.

Jack. My own one!

Chasuble (*to* Miss Prism). Laetitia! (*Embraces her.*)

Miss Prism (*enthusiastically*). Frederick! At last!

Algernon. Cecily! (*Embraces her.*) At last!

Jack. Gwendolen! (*Embraces her.*) At last!

Lady Bracknell. My nephew, you seem to be displaying signs of triviality.

Jack. On the contrary, Aunt Augusta, I've now realized for the first time in my life the vital Importance of Being Earnest.

(1895; 1899)

John Millington Synge
1871-1909

The Irish Literary Renaissance (p. 852) produced many gifted writers in the realms of lyric poetry, drama, prose narrative, and essay. There was William Butler Yeats (p. 1025), the greatest individual driving power and the most impressive lyric poet of the group; George Moore, the silken-smooth though somewhat decadent novelist; Lady Augusta Gregory; George Russell (Æ); and in a later day Lennox Robinson and Sean O'Casey. From the literary atmosphere of Dublin came also James Joyce, one of the most significant writers that the twentieth century has produced. But in the field of the drama, none of the school has qualified better for the title of *genius* than Synge.

Synge was born in a Dublin suburb on April 16, 1871. His father was a moderately successful lawyer of a well-established Irish Protestant family, which could trace its ancestry as far back as the days of King Henry VIII of England. The father died in Synge's infancy, and the mother, though in somewhat reduced circumstances, contrived to educate the boy, to say nothing of seven other children, as best she could. Synge received private instruction, and after due time matriculated at Trinity College, Dublin, where he graduated in 1893. In his college days, and even earlier, he had shown a threefold interest—in music, in languages, and in the great outdoors. Tramping about the country near Dublin was his great recreation, for he was a rather shy, retiring boy, who felt an almost Wordsworthian sensitivity to the beauties of nature. After his graduation he went through a period of indecision as to his future work; he studied music for a year in Germany and literature for several years in Paris, returning for a time each year to Ireland. He gradually drifted into miscellaneous journalistic writing in Paris and was well on his way to becoming one of the innumerable hack-writers of the Latin Quarter when he met William Butler Yeats.

The meeting with Yeats took place in 1898 and changed the entire course of Synge's life. Yeats told him to study his own country and absorb its beauty and culture. In compliance Synge spent several months on the bleak Aran Islands off the west coast of Ireland—an environment which impressed itself indelibly upon his thought and expression thenceforth. Some of his experiences he recounts in his travel-essay, *The Aran Islands* (1907). For the next few years he did miscellaneous writing for his living but spent most of his spare time roaming throughout Ireland and hobnobbing with the rising men and women of the Irish Renaissance. The eventual fruit of this relationship was a pair of one-act plays, *In the Shadow of the Glen* (1903) and *Riders to the Sea* (1904). These plays were produced by the Irish National Theater Society, an organization based upon the old Irish National Dramatic Company of the Fay brothers and the Irish Literary Theater sponsored by Lady Augusta Gregory, Yeats, George Moore, and Edwin Martyn; this organization was the forerunner of the later famous Abbey Theater of Dublin. With these two plays Synge's dramatic career was fairly begun.

In the Shadow of the Glen was a sardonic little play upon the loveless marriages of the Irish peasantry and was received in rather hostile fashion. But all conceded the grim magnificence of the tragic *Riders to the Sea*, which was based primarily on Synge's observation of the stark and primitive life on the barren, treeless Aran Islands. In December of 1904 Synge became a co-director of the new Abbey Theater. A two-act comedy, *The Tinker's Wedding* (not published until 1909), was neither so able an effort nor so successful a production as his first plays. Nor did his full-length miracle play, *The Well of the Saints* (1905), attract much attention. But *The Playboy of the Western World* (1907) was a sensation. It is a powerful satire upon the credulity, superstition, and brutality of the Irish peasantry; its theme is that of ignorant rustics who admire a weak and unimpressive stranger because they believe he has murdered his father. From the time when the play was first produced, it has caused disturbances from time to time whenever it has been given before an Irish audience. Yet in spite of such outbursts, it is safe to say that *The Playboy of the Western World* is Synge's most considerable achievement with a full-length drama. Not even his striking treatment of the often romanticized Irish legend of Deirdre, as he gives it to the world in *Deirdre of the Sorrows* (1910)—a play often bitter, often beautiful, often harshly realistic, and never pale—can quite match *The Playboy of the Western World*. It is good to think that these two plays mark the climax of Synge's career; he was unfortunately stricken with a cancer and died on March 24, 1909.

Riders to the Sea, given below, conveys superbly in one act the grim tragedy of men who fight for their living against nature, typified by a hostile ocean, and who fail. The drama unfolds with an austerity and an intensity worthy of a Sophocles. Simple, poignant, and massive in its effect, it demands consideration as the greatest one-act play in the entire range of English literature.

Riders to the Sea

DRAMATIS PERSONAE

MAURYA, *an old woman.*
BARTLEY, *her son.*
CATHLEEN, *her daughter.*
NORA, *a younger daughter.*
Men and Women.

SCENE.—*An Island off the west of Ireland*

Cottage kitchen, with nets, oil-skins, spinning-wheel, some new boards standing by the wall, etc. CATHLEEN, *a girl of about twenty, finishes kneading cake, and puts it down in the pot-oven by the fire; then wipes her hands, and begins to spin at the wheel.* NORA, *a young girl, puts her head in at the door.*

Nora (*in a low voice*). Where is she?
Cathleen. She's lying down, God help her, and may be sleeping, if she's able.

(NORA *comes in softly, and takes a bundle from under her shawl.*)

Riders to the Sea (1911) is reprinted by permission of Random House, Inc., New York.

Cathleen (spinning the wheel rapidly). What is it you have?

Nora. The young priest is after bringing them. It's a shirt and a plain stocking were got off a drowned man in Donegal.

(CATHLEEN *stops her wheel with a sudden movement, and leans out to listen.*)

Nora. We're to find out if it's Michael's they are, some time herself will be down looking by the sea.

Cathleen. How would they be Michael's, Nora? How would he go the length of that way to the far north?

Nora. The young priest says he's known the like of it. "If it's Michael's they are," says he, "you can tell herself he's got a clean burial by the grace of God, and if they're not his, let no one say a word about them, for she'll be getting her death," says he, "with crying and lamenting."

(*The door which* NORA *half closed is blown open by a gust of wind.*)

Cathleen (looking out anxiously). Did you ask him would he stop Bartley going this day with the horses to the Galway fair?

Nora. "I won't stop him," says he, "but let you not be afraid. Herself does be saying prayers half through the night, and the Almighty God won't leave her destitute," says he, "with no son living."

Cathleen. Is the sea bad by the white rocks, Nora?

Nora. Middling bad, God help us. There's a great roaring in the west, and it's worse it'll be getting when the tide's turned to the wind. (*She goes over to the table with the bundle.*) Shall I open it now?

Cathleen. Maybe she'd wake up on us, and come in before we'd done. (*Coming to the table.*) It's a long time we'll be, and the two of us crying.

Nora (goes to the inner door and listens). She's moving about on the bed. She'll be coming in a minute.

Cathleen. Give me the ladder, and I'll put them up in the turf-loft, the way she won't know of them at all, and maybe when the tide turns, she'll be going down to see would he be floating from the east.

(*They put the ladder against the gable of the chimney;* CATHLEEN *goes up a few steps and hides the bundle in the turf-loft.* MAURYA *comes from the inner room.*)

Maurya (looking up at CATHLEEN *and speaking querulously).* Isn't it turf enough you have for this day and evening?

Cathleen. There's a cake baking at the fire for a short space (*throwing down the turf*) and Bartley will want it when the tide turns if he goes to Connemara.

(NORA *picks up the turf and puts it round the pot-oven.*)

Maurya (sitting down on a stool at the fire). He won't go this day with the wind rising from the south and west. He won't go this day, for the young priest will stop him surely.

Nora. He'll not stop him, Mother, and I heard Eamon Simon and Stephen Pheety and Colum Shawn saying he would go.

Maurya. Where is he itself?

Nora. He went down to see would there be another boat sailing in the week, and I'm thinking it won't be long till he's here now, for the tide's turning at the green head, and the hooker's tacking from the east.

Cathleen. I hear some one passing the big stones.

Nora (looking out). He's coming now, and he in a hurry.

Bartley (comes in and looks round the room; speaking sadly and quietly). Where is the bit of new rope, Cathleen, was bought in Connemara?

Cathleen (coming down). Give it to him, Nora; it's on a nail by the white boards. I hung it up this morning, for the pig with the black feet was eating it.

Nora (giving him a rope). Is that it, Bartley?

Maurya. You'd do right to leave that rope, Bartley, hanging by the boards. (BARTLEY *takes the rope.*) It will be wanting in this place, I'm telling you, if Michael is washed

---

5. **Donegal,** a bay on the west coast of North Ireland; also the name of a city and a county. 7. **herself,** Maurya. 14. **clean burial,** burial with religious rites.

66. **hooker,** fishing boat.

up tomorrow morning, or the next morning, or any morning in the week, for it's a deep grave we'll make him by the grace of God.

Bartley (beginning to work with the rope). I've no halter the way I can ride down on the mare, and I must go now quickly. This is the one boat going for two weeks or beyond it, and the fair will be a good fair for horses, I heard them saying below.

Maurya. It's a hard thing they'll be saying below if the body is washed up and there's no man in it to make the coffin, and I after giving a big price for the finest white boards you'd find in Connemara.

(*She looks round at the boards.*)

Bartley. How would it be washed up, and we after looking each day for nine days, and a strong wind blowing a while back from the west and south?

Maurya. If it wasn't found itself, that wind is raising the sea, and there was a star up against the moon, and it rising in the night. If it was a hundred horses, or a thousand horses you had itself, what is the price of a thousand horses against a son where there is one son only?

Bartley (working at the halter, to CATHLEEN). Let you go down each day, and see the sheep aren't jumping in on the rye, and if the jobber comes, you can sell the pig with the black feet if there is a good price going.

Maurya. How would the like of her get a good price for a pig?

Bartley (to CATHLEEN). If the west wind holds with the last bit of the moon, let you and Nora get up weed enough for another cock for the kelp. It's hard set we'll be from this day with no one in it but one man to work.

Maurya. It's hard set we'll be surely the day you're drownd'd with the rest. What way will I live and the girls with me, and I an old woman looking for the grave?

(BARTLEY *lays down the halter, takes off his old coat, and puts on a newer one of the same flannel.*)

Bartley (to NORA). Is she coming to the pier?

36. **kelp**, dried seaweed for fertilizing and other farm purposes.

Nora (looking out). She's passing the green head and letting fall her sails.

Bartley (getting his purse and tobacco). I'll have half an hour to go down, and you'll see me coming again in two days, or in three days, or maybe in four days if the wind is bad.

Maurya (turning round to the fire, and putting her shawl over her head). Isn't it a hard and cruel man won't hear a word from an old woman, and she holding him from the sea?

Cathleen. It's the life of a young man to be going on the sea, and who would listen to an old woman with one thing and she saying it over?

Bartley (taking the halter). I must go now quickly. I'll ride down on the red mare, and the gray pony'll run behind me. . . . The blessing of God on you.

(*He goes out.*)

Maurya (crying out as he is in the door). He's gone now, God spare us, and we'll not see him again. He's gone now, and when the black night is falling, I'll have no son left me in the world.

Cathleen. Why wouldn't you give him your blessing and he looking round in the door? Isn't it sorrow enough is on every one in this house without your sending him out with an unlucky word behind him, and a hard word in his ear?

(MAURYA *takes up the tongs and begins raking the fire aimlessly without looking round.*)

Nora (turning toward her). You're taking away the turf from the cake.

Cathleen (crying out). The Son of God forgive us, Nora, we're after forgetting his bit of bread.

(*She comes over to the fire.*)

Nora. And it's destroyed he'll be going till dark night, and he after eating nothing since the sun went up.

Cathleen (turning the cake out of the oven). It's destroyed he'll be, surely. There's no sense left on any person in a house where an old woman will be talking forever.

(MAURYA *sways herself on her stool.*)

Cathleen (cutting off some of the bread and rolling it in a cloth; to MAURYA). Let you go down now to the spring well and give him this and he passing. You'll see him then and the dark word will be broken, and you can say "God speed you," the way he'll be easy in his mind.

Maurya (*taking the bread*). Will I be in it as soon as himself?

Cathleen. If you go now quickly.

Maurya (*standing up unsteadily*). It's hard set I am to walk.

Cathleen (*looking at her anxiously*). Give her the stick, Nora, or maybe she'll slip on the big stones.

Nora. What stick?

Cathleen. The stick Michael brought from Connemara.

Maurya (*taking a stick* Nora *gives her*). In the big world the old people do be leaving things after them for their sons and children, but in this place it is the young men do be leaving things behind for them that do be old.

(*She goes out slowly.* Nora *goes over to the ladder.*)

Cathleen. Wait, Nora, maybe she'd turn back quickly. She's that sorry, God help her, you wouldn't know the thing she'd do.

Nora. Is she gone round by the bush?

Cathleen (*looking out*). She's gone now. Throw it down quickly, for the Lord knows when she'll be out of it again.

Nora (*getting the bundle from the loft*). The young priest said he'd be passing tomorrow, and we might go down and speak to him below if it's Michael's they are surely.

Cathleen (*taking the bundle*). Did he say what way they were found?

Nora (*coming down*). "There were two men," says he, "and they rowing round with poteen before the cocks crowed, and the oar of one of them caught the body, and they passing the black cliffs of the north."

Cathleen (*trying to open the bundle*). Give me a knife, Nora; the string's perished with the salt water, and there's a black knot on it you wouldn't loosen in a week.

Nora (*giving her a knife*). I've heard tell it was a long way to Donegal.

Cathleen (*cutting the string*). It is surely. There was a man in here a while ago—the man sold us that knife—and he said if you set off walking from the rocks beyond, it would be seven days you'd be in Donegal.

Nora. And what time would a man take, and he floating?

(Cathleen *opens the bundle and takes out a bit of stocking. They look at them eagerly.*)

Cathleen (*in a low voice*). The Lord spare us, Nora! isn't it a queer hard thing to say if it's his they are surely?

Nora. I'll get his shirt off the hook the way we can put the one flannel on the other. (*She looks through some clothes hanging in the corner.*) It's not with them, Cathleen, and where will it be?

Cathleen. I'm thinking Bartley put it on him in the morning, for his own shirt was heavy with salt in it. (*Pointing to the corner.*) There's a bit of a sleeve was of the same stuff. Give me that and it will do.

(Nora *brings it to her and they compare the flannel.*)

Cathleen. It's the same stuff, Nora; but if it is itself, aren't there great rolls of it in the shops of Galway, and isn't it many another man may have a shirt of it as well as Michael himself?

Nora (*who has taken up the stocking and counted the stitches, crying out*). It's Michael, Cathleen, it's Michael; God spare his soul, and what will herself say when she hears this story, and Bartley on the sea?

Cathleen (*taking the stocking*). It's a plain stocking.

Nora. It's the second one of the third pair I knitted, and I put up threescore stitches, and I dropped four of them.

Cathleen (*counts the stitches*). It's that number in it. (*Crying out.*) Ah, Nora, isn't it a bitter thing to think of him floating that way to the far north, and no one to keen him but the black hags that do be flying on the sea?

Nora (*swinging herself round, and throwing out her arms on the clothes*). And isn't it a pitiful thing when there is nothing left of

---

36. **poteen**, moonshine whiskey being smuggled ashore. 67. **Galway**, a large city on the west coast of Ireland. 83. **keen**, lament with wailing. 84. **black hags**, sea-witches.

a man who was a great rower and fisher, but a bit of an old shirt and a plain stocking?

Cathleen (*after an instant*). Tell me is herself coming, Nora? I hear a little sound on the path.

Nora (*looking out*). She is, Cathleen. She's coming up to the door.

Cathleen. Put these things away before she'll come in. Maybe it's easier she'll be after giving her blessing to Bartley, and we won't let on we've heard anything the time he's on the sea.

Nora (*helping* CATHLEEN *to close the bundle*). We'll put them here in the corner.

(*They put them into a hole in the chimney corner.* CATHLEEN *goes back to the spinning-wheel.*)

Nora. Will she see it was crying I was?

Cathleen. Keep your back to the door the way the light'll not be on you.

(NORA *sits down at the chimney corner, with her back to the door.* MAURYA *comes in very slowly, without looking at the girls, and goes over to her stool at the other side of the fire. The cloth with the bread is still in her hand. The girls look at each other, and* NORA *points to the bundle of bread.*)

Cathleen (*after spinning for a moment*). You didn't give him his bit of bread?

(MAURYA *begins to keen softly, without turning round.*)

Cathleen. Did you see him riding down?

(MAURYA *goes on keening.*)

Cathleen (*a little impatiently*). God forgive you; isn't it a better thing to raise your voice and tell what you seen, than to be making lamentation for a thing that's done? Did you see Bartley, I'm saying to you?

Maurya (*with a weak voice*). My heart's broken from this day.

Cathleen (*as before*). Did you see Bartley?

Maurya. I seen the fearfulest thing.

Cathleen (*leaves her wheel and looks out*). God forgive you; he's riding the mare now over the green head, and the gray pony behind him.

Maurya (*starts, so that her shawl falls back from her head and shows her white tossed hair. With a frightened voice*). The gray pony behind him.

Cathleen (*coming to the fire*). What is it ails you, at all?

Maurya (*speaking very slowly*). I've seen the fearfulest thing any person has seen, since the day Bride Dara seen the dead man with a child in his arms.

Cathleen and *Nora.* Uah!

(*They crouch down in front of the old woman at the fire.*)

Nora. Tell us what it is you seen.

Maurya. I went down to the spring well, and I stood there saying a prayer to myself. Then Bartley came along, and he riding on the red mare with the gray pony behind him. (*She puts up her hands, as if to hide something from her eyes.*) The Son of God spare us, Nora!

Cathleen. What is it you seen?

Maurya. I seen Michael himself.

Cathleen (*speaking softly*). You did not, mother; it wasn't Michael you seen, for his body is after being found in the Far North, and he's got a clean burial by the grace of God.

Maurya (*a little defiantly*). I'm after seeing him this day, and he riding and galloping. Bartley came first on the red mare; and I tried to say, "God speed you!" but something choked the words in my throat. He went by quickly; and "the blessing of God on you," says he, and I could say nothing. I looked up then, and I crying, at the gray pony, and there was Michael upon it—with fine clothes on him, and new shoes on his feet.

Cathleen (*begins to keen*). It's destroyed we are from this day. It's destroyed, surely.

Nora. Didn't the young priest say the Almighty God wouldn't leave her destitute with no son living?

Maurya (*in a low voice, but clearly*). It's little the like of him knows of the sea . . . Bartley will be lost now, and let you call in Eamon and make me a good coffin out of the white boards, for I won't live after them. I've had a husband, and a husband's father, and six sons in this house—six fine men,

---

42. **Bride Dara . . . arms,** a probable allusion to a popular ghost story.

though it was a hard birth I had with every one of them and they coming to the world—and some of them were found and some of them were not found, but they're gone now with the lot of them . . . There were Stephen, and Shawn, were lost in the great wind, and found after in the Bay of Gregory of the Golden Mouth, and carried up the two of them on the one plank, and in by that door.

(*She pauses for a moment; the girls start as if they heard something through the door that is half open behind them.*)

Nora (*in a whisper*). Did you hear that, Cathleen? Did you hear a noise in the northeast?

Cathleen (*in a whisper*). There's some one after crying out by the seashore.

Maurya (*continues without hearing anything*). There was Sheamus and his father, and his own father again, were lost in a dark night, and not a stick or sign was seen of them when the sun went up. There was Patch after was drowned out of a curagh that turned over. I was sitting here with Bartley, and he a baby, lying on my two knees, and I seen two women, and three women, and four women coming in, and they crossing themselves, and not saying a word. I looked out then, and there were men coming after them, and they holding a thing in the half of a red sail, and water dripping out of it—it was a dry day, Nora—and leaving a track to the door.

(*She pauses again with her hand stretched out toward the door. It opens softly and old women begin to come in, crossing themselves on the threshold, and kneeling down in front of the stage with red petticoats over their heads.*)

Maurya (*half in a dream, to* CATHLEEN). Is it Patch, or Michael, or what is it at all?

Cathleen. Michael is after being found in the Far North, and when he is found there, how could he be here in this place?

Maurya. There does be a power of young men floating round in the sea, and what way would they know if it was Michael they had, or another man like him, for when a man is nine days in the sea, and the wind blowing, it's hard set his own mother would be to say what man was it.

Cathleen. It's Michael, God spare him, for they're after sending us a bit of his clothes from the Far North.

(*She reaches out and hands* MAURYA *the clothes that belonged to* MICHAEL. MAURYA *stands up slowly, and takes them in her hands.* NORA *looks out.*)

Nora. They're carrying a thing among them and there's water dripping out of it and leaving a track by the big stones.

Cathleen (*in a whisper to the women who have come in*). Is it Bartley it is?

One of the Women. It is surely, God rest his soul.

(*Two younger women come in and pull out the table. Then men carry in the body of* BARTLEY, *laid on a plank, with a bit of a sail over it, and lay it on the table.*)

Cathleen (*to the women, as they are doing so*). What way was he drowned?

One of the Women. The gray pony knocked him into the sea, and he was washed out where there is a great surf on the white rocks.

(MAURYA *has gone over and knelt down at the head of the table. The women are keening softly and swaying themselves with a slow movement.* CATHLEEN *and* NORA *kneel at the other end of the table. The men kneel near the door.*)

Maurya (*raising her head and speaking as if she did not see the people around her*). They're all gone now, and there isn't anything more the sea can do to me . . . I'll have no call now to be up crying and praying when the wind breaks from the south, and you can hear the surf is in the east, and the surf is in the west, making a great stir with the two noises, and they hitting one on the other. I'll have no call now to be going down and getting Holy Water in the dark nights after Samhain, and I won't care what

---

20. **curagh,** a small, frail boat, originally one made of twigs and wicker.

70. **Samhain,** a Gaelic term for All Souls' Day (November 2).

way the sea is when the other women will be keening. (*To* NORA.) Give me the Holy Water, Nora; there's a small cup still on the dresser. (NORA *gives it to her.*)

Maurya (*drops* MICHAEL's *clothes across* BARTLEY's *feet, and sprinkles the Holy Water over him*). It isn't that I haven't prayed for you, Bartley, to the Almighty God. It isn't that I haven't said prayers in the dark night till you wouldn't know what I'd be saying; but it's a great rest I'll have now, and it's time surely. It's a great rest I'll have now, and great sleeping in the long nights after Samhain, if it's only a bit of wet flour we do have to eat, and maybe a fish that would be stinking.

(*She kneels down again, crossing herself, and saying prayers under her breath.*)

Cathleen (*to an old man*). Maybe yourself and Eamon would make a coffin when the sun rises. We have fine white boards herself bought, God help her, thinking Michael would be found, and I have a new cake you can eat while you'll be working.

The Old Man (*looking at the boards*). Are there nails with them?

Cathleen. There are not, Colum; we didn't think of the nails.

Another Man. It's a great wonder she wouldn't think of the nails, and all the coffins she's seen made already.

Cathleen. It's getting old she is, and broken.

(MAURYA *stands up again very slowly, and spreads out the pieces of* MICHAEL's *clothes beside the body, sprinkling them with the last of the Holy Water.*)

Nora (*in a whisper to* CATHLEEN). She's quiet now and easy; but the day Michael was drowned you could hear her crying out from this to the spring well. It's fonder she was of Michael, and would anyone have thought that?

Cathleen (*slowly and clearly*). An old woman will be soon tired with anything she will do, and isn't it nine days herself is after crying and keening, and making great sorrow in the house?

Maurya (*puts the empty cup mouth downwards on the table, and lays her hands together on* BARTLEY's *feet*). They're all together this time, and the end is come. May the Almighty God have mercy on Bartley's soul, and on Michael's soul, and on the souls of Sheamus and Patch, and Stephen and Shawn (*bending her head*); and may He have mercy on my soul, Nora, and on the soul of every one is left living in the world.

(*She pauses, and the keen rises a little more loudly from the women, then sinks away.*)

Maurya (*continuing*). Michael has a clean burial in the Far North, by the grace of the Almighty God. Bartley will have a fine coffin out of the white boards, and a deep grave surely. What more can we want than that? No man at all can be living forever, and we must be satisfied.

(*She kneels down again and the curtain falls slowly.*) (1905)

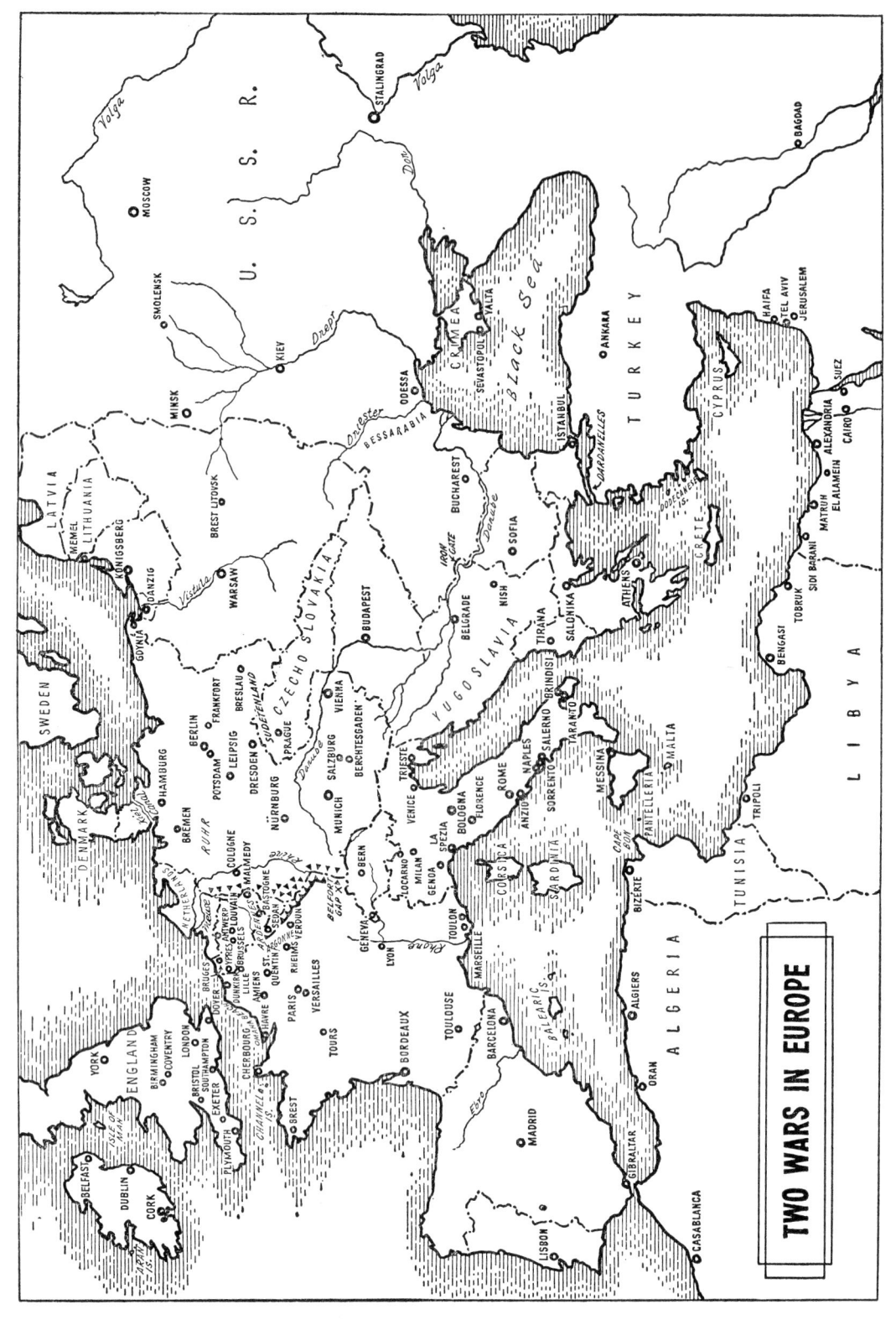

Chapter 9

The Struggle on the Darkling Plain

A Time of Conflict and Change, 1914-1957

Operation Crossroads

AT ELEVEN o'clock on the morning of November 11, 1918, the shooting stopped in the war "to make the world safe for democracy." "Everything for which America fought has been accomplished," read the official announcement from President Woodrow Wilson—one of the most dramatically ironic public statements in all history. For thinking men everywhere soon realized that the cessation of fighting established on that first Armistice Day was no more than an indefinite truce, if indeed it could be called even that—a truce which lasted only a little more than twenty years.

Moreover, in the generation between 1918 and 1939, minor wars—if any modern wars can be called minor—had visited all of the major quarters of the globe. Bolshevik Russia had become involved with her quondam allies and had invaded Poland; Bolivia and Paraguay had spilled blood in the Gran Chaco; the French had undertaken punitive expeditions in Morocco and in Syria; Spain had been bled in a disastrous civil war, which served as the immediate prelude to the Second World War; Ethiopia had been invaded by Italy; China had been pillaged by Japan. In short, scarcely a year in this critical twenty-one-year span had been free from either the rattling of the saber or outright bloodshed.

Wars between wars

We have every right, therefore, to consider the two World Wars, and all the violence that lay between them, as one struggle—a new Thirty Years'

Problems of peace

War of the twentieth century, a terrible human conflict of global proportions, the main issue of which was the vital question of the rights of ordinary men and women all over the world. In spite of the military victory of the antifascist forces in 1945, one must realize that the war is not over yet. Although glimmers of hope persist, the world is still very much in darkness. Now, however, the unleashing of the new, destructive forces of atomic energy has compelled men to recognize the absolute necessity for peaceful living; and so the United Nations, as a constructive unit, has probably a better chance to survive than had the League of Nations, formed after the First World War (1914-1918). The prognosis is nevertheless far from comforting. One would suppose that the more than four horrible years from July, 1914, to November, 1918, would have taught mankind something; yet a new generation had hardly become adult before there ensued six even more horrible years, from September 1, 1939, to September 2, 1945. One is impressed by the extent to which, ever since the beginning of the twentieth century, the world has come to depend upon force or the threat of force.

The causes of this critical state of the world's body are too complex for brief statement; but an outline of political tendencies in Europe between 1918 and 1939 may help to clarify the problem to some extent, if we bear in mind that political tendencies are bound up inextricably with sociological and economic considerations. The external aspects of the First World War were ostensibly resolved by the Treaty of Versailles (1919), which gave to Britain and France, as the countries which had suffered most in the war, the economic leadership of Europe, restoring Alsace and Lorraine to France, "rectifying" the Austro-Italian, Austro-Serbian, and German-Polish borders, creating the smaller nations of Czechoslovakia, Yugoslavia, Poland, Finland, Lithuania, Latvia, Esthonia, and Hungary, disposing of the German colonial empire, creating the League of Nations, and placing officially upon Germany the responsibility for having started the war. This treaty was bitterly resented by Germany, of course; the staggering reparations demanded were a bar to her recovery and to her re-establishment as the dominant economic power in central Europe, a goal to which her great industrial potential clearly entitled her. Furthermore, there cropped up inevitable inequities in the Treaty of Versailles as it was finally adopted—Italy, for example, who had left the old Triple Alliance (Germany, Austria-Hungary, and Italy) and had fought on the side of the Allies, was badly neglected, since the whole question of the Adriatic provinces was allowed to drift. In the United States, Woodrow Wilson's plea that the Treaty of Versailles be accepted was rejected by Congress because it meant that the nation would have to join the League of Nations; not until 1921 did Congress pass a resolution which proclaimed the end of the war. Yet there was general satisfaction and optimism in Britain and France by the end of 1919.

The Treaty of Versailles

Battleship and Aircraft Carrier

THE STRUGGLE ON THE DARKLING PLAIN

Russia

One great source of worry remained, however, for all the Allies. This was Russia, to England a traditional cause of perturbation. Russia had been forced out of the war, a loser, in the winter of 1917-1918. More important, in the chaos of defeat, she had undergone the greatest political and social revolution experienced anywhere during the last century. Very disturbing to western Europeans was the communist philosophy of her new regime, and quite revolting were the extremely authoritarian measures taken to implement at least part of that philosophy. In accord with communist philosophy, a dictatorship, alleged to represent the proletariat, abolished private ownership of the means of production. Beyond the limits of their theory, which sanctioned only temporary dictatorship, the leaders carried on a reign of terror against all conservative or moderate elements and gave no indication that the bureaucracy would ever suspend the control of the state over the individual. Although from 1921 until late in the twenties severe economic shortages required Lenin and the Communist Party to modify extreme state control over economic life, the Party never lost its grip on political power. On the death of Lenin in 1924, the top Communists engaged in a struggle for power which ended in 1929 with the rout of Trotsky and the emergence of Stalin as dictator. Stalin immediately launched the first of his five-year plans for gigantic industrialization and for complete state-ownership of all segments of the economy, including agriculture. As the dictatorship became increasingly oppressive, industrial and military might was achieved by the exploitation of the vast mass of peasants, hundreds of thousands of whom were killed or starved for their resistance to state regimentation. Although the great mass of British citizens were totally unsympathetic to communist theory and to Russian communist methods, Britain, because of her dependence upon foreign trade, early recognized the Soviet state. American recognition followed in the early thirties, but Russia remained in the eyes of the West an object of great uncertainty, awe, fear, and loathing.

The "have-nots"

Left as the focal points for a new infection of the peace of the world were Germany, Italy, and Japan. Germany, in resources the greatest power on the Continent after Russia (and much better organized than the Soviet state), had a vast industrial potential. This she eventually developed, unhampered by conservative Britain, France, and the United States, who were curiously indifferent as to what went on within her borders, so long as the letter of the Treaty of Versailles was observed. Italy was a sensitive nation with an inferiority complex, whose political aspirations had been overlooked in the peace negotiations; and Japan, the strongest of the Asiatic countries, had also been ignored in the deliberations and in addition was frustrated in her vast Asiatic ambitions by the presence in the Far East of colonial Britain, France, and the United States. These three focal points came to be called—and they welcomed the appellation—the "have-nots," as opposed to the "haves."

Artillery and Tanks

There was at least enough truth in this distinction to give the leaders of the have-nots the excuse they wanted. To change a nation from a have-not to a have, there must be efficient handling; and it was easy enough to persuade sufficient members of the people in Germany, Italy, and Japan—countries with little experience in democratic processes—to accept the rule of powerful oligarchies, the functions of which were embodied in a dictator who preached the complete subservience of the individual to the state in a system of government which came to be known as fascism.

Democracy versus totalitarianism

Leaving aside the many details of power-politics, the struggle for world-markets, "the place in the sun," all of which undoubtedly contributed mightily to the outbreak of the Second World War, the fact remains that this war was fought basically between the democratic and the totalitarian ways of life. Britain, France, and the United States, with their satellites, represented the democratic way; Germany, Italy, and Japan represented the totalitarian way. In the middle stood Russia, the subject of fierce debate but obviously far removed politically from the Anglo-Saxon traditions of individual liberties. It is one of the gross ironies of history that the Soviet should nevertheless—out of sheer self-defense as well as out of a real patriotism on the part of her people—have fought vigorously on the side of the democratic powers and have played an extremely important part in the defeat of the totalitarians.

The Second World War

It is not necessary to relate here the terrible details of the Second World War. France actually went under in 1940, and England, taking a terrible beating for a full year thereafter, barely managed to escape an invasion which would almost certainly have succeeded. The turning point came in 1941, with increasing financial and material contributions to the English from the United States, the inevitable attack by Germany against Russia, and finally the assault by the Japanese upon all the western powers in the Pacific, which forced the United States into open warfare and made available the unparalleled technical and natural resources of America, geared to a true war economy. Italy, a military jackal to the Nazi military tiger, was knocked out of effective action in 1943, although bitter fighting between the Germans and the Allies continued in that country until the end of the war; Germany surrendered on May 8, 1945; and the Japanese signed the papers of unconditional capitulation aboard the American battleship *Missouri* in Tokyo Bay on September 2, 1945.

Dissolution of wartime partnership

After victory, Russia and the western powers—the United States, England, and France—gradually exposed the disintegration of their wartime partnership. The growing division between East and West was sharply accentuated in 1947, when the American Marshall Plan for the economic recovery of Europe was announced. Russia was invited to join in a general European alliance to foster economic recovery but declined to do so. From this point until the death of Stalin in 1953, America based her security on the economic

Casualty 1941

and military recovery of Europe and on the policy of "containment"; whereas Russia based her security on strengthening her grasp upon her satellite nations and on a policy of creeping expansion. America's policy of containment led to the support of a separate West German Republic, the elimination of communist guerrillas in Greece, encouragement and aid to Yugoslavia in its successful break from Russian domination, and finally participation in the Korean War, which began on June 25, 1950. The invasion of South Korea by Russian-supported North Koreans and eventually by Chinese Communists came to an end, after protracted peace negotiations, in July, 1953. With the death of Stalin and an increasingly unstable and confused picture of leadership in Russia, Soviet policy became less rigid, and periods of cultural and diplomatic thaw tempered the usual policy of threat and bluster. By 1955 it was believed that a striking relaxation in international relations was taking place; this hope was climaxed by the Geneva meeting in July between the heads of Russia, the United States, Britain, and France. Although the atmosphere was congenial, it is hard to say that any concrete steps were taken to bring the East and the West closer to a permanent peace. In 1956 an aggressive Soviet policy in the Middle East following the Suez Canal crisis, and the brutal repression of a popular anti-communist revolt in Hungary during the same period, contributed greatly to a deterioration of what harmony had been established. However, mutual fear of nuclear warfare remained a strong impetus to peaceful negotiations.

In the turbulent postwar decade of 1946-1956, the conflict between the United States and Russia had shared importance with the struggle for national independence of formerly colonial peoples in Asia and Africa. Often there has been bitter strife. The decade has seen independence gained by the peoples of Indonesia, Indo-China (now partitioned into communist and western influenced halves), Tunisia, Morocco, and, in 1957, the British Gold Coast, renamed Ghana. And still the struggle for independence and the general native ferment continue in Africa. It seems likely that the world, overshadowed by the threat of atomic extinction, is in the process of some great revolution to bring about somehow a better society, more international in scope and more attentive to the needs of all peoples.

Colonial peoples' struggle for independence

English Chronicle, 1918-1957

WHEN PLACED beside the garish, kaleidoscopic sequence of events which passed before American eyes in the years after 1918, the history of Great Britain during that same period seems far less turbulent until the very end of the 1930's. Some of the social reforms wrought during that time in the United States, reforms which seemed to Americans so radical, had already

El Alamein 1942

been established in England. Yet England of the 1920's and 1930's had her scandals, private and public; her desperate attempts to regain equilibrium after the First World War; her problems, virtually insoluble, which were generated by the relaxation of traditional moral standards following the Armistice of 1918 and by maladjustments in the relations of capital and labor. There was never in England any of the false, "Coolidgean" prosperity of the 1920's that warped the outlook of the United States before the collapse of 1929. Though affected in painful manner by the great depression of the 1930's, Britain struck some sort of financial balance a little sooner than did the United States. After all, she is geographically a small unit, whose population, whatever its original ethnical background, has a reasonably homogeneous point of view; and behind her lie centuries of comparatively stable government.

Problems after the Armistice

The first few years after Armistice Day, 1918, were spent in a hopeful effort to pick up the fragments of the old way of life which the war had shattered once and for all. Britain had committed herself to the League of Nations, which seemed a portentous responsibility; but she had participated in the spoils of the victor, and she had exacted reparations from her defeated enemy. These considerations all appeared fair enough, for the nation had suffered greatly in the loss of human lives and property. Therefore the phrase "a land fit for heroes to live in" became her immediate slogan. The unemployment incidental to the return of hundreds of thousands of veterans to civil life was anticipated and relieved for a time by a dole of twenty-five shillings a week; but this measure proved to be only a stop-gap palliative. With a coalition government under David Lloyd George (1863-1945) in power, it was recognized that labor must be put back on its feet, for the dislocation of war-time prices following the Armistice had led to all kinds of labor troubles. After a series of strikes, an alliance of miners with railway and transport workers rode the Labour Party into power under the leadership of Ramsay MacDonald (1866-1937) in 1924.

The Irish Free State

If the domestic situation in the years between 1918 and 1923 was disturbed, the foreign situation was even worse. In Ireland the nationalist party, the Sinn Fein, had caused extreme worry to Britain during the First World War, especially in the famous Easter Rebellion of 1916; it was now agitating for an Irish Free State. The British Government, trying to suppress the agitation by force, sent a special Irish Constabulary Force, known popularly as the Black and Tans, which accomplished little but violence and needless bloodshed. The Irish Free State, comprising the Catholic counties of Ireland, was set up late in 1921; at first under the control of moderates and conservatives like Cosgrave, it was later taken over by the almost fanatical Eamon de Valera (1882-   ), whose every effort was to establish all Eire as an

The Queen Elizabeth

THE STRUGGLE ON THE DARKLING PLAIN

independent republic. Part of his goal was accomplished in 1947, although the Protestant northern counties remained outside the republic. Another political feat of de Valera was the keeping of Ireland as a neutral during the Second World War—an achievement which required great political skill.

Independence for India

Trouble arose also in India, which in both World Wars offered the Germans little real comfort, although the British had great difficulty in saving India from Japan during the dark months of 1942 and 1943. The problem, again, lay in the nationalistic aspirations of the people of India; but it was enormously complicated by the intransigent nature of this population, among whom religious differences meant a complete stratification of the people, so that an integrated political state seemed virtually impossible to achieve. The initially coercive policy of the English collided here with the man who was the leader of his people throughout the generation—Mohandas K. Gandhi (1869-1948), the Mahatma, one of the great figures of this century. The rock-bottom of ineptness was reached by the British in the Amritsar massacre of 1919. Gandhi's novel program of civil disobedience wrung concessions from reluctant Britain—she permitted first a national Indian Congress Party (1920), then Round Table conferences in London (1929 and 1930), then missions to India during the emergencies of 1940-1943; and finally she granted outright independence to India (1945-1947). Out of the great diversity of religious, ethnic, and linguistic groups in India, two new states were carved out roughly along religious lines and were proclaimed on August 15, 1947—India (for the Hindus) and Pakistan (for the Moslems).

Contrasting policies

Weakened by wars and economic problems and under the pressure of a world-wide desire of colonial peoples to assert their independence, the influence of the British Empire has been sorely tried in the last decade. In most instances, the British have acted with their traditional common sense and have guided native peoples toward self-government in an orderly fashion. In other cases, spurred by a wounded pride in the impending dissolution of their vast Empire, they have blindly resisted inevitable changes. The Near East has seen the sharpest and most dramatic fall of British influence, and unfortunately it has been in this vitally important area that British diplomacy has failed to react with mature and flexible wisdom.

Trouble in Palestine and Iran

Faced with a clearly forecast war between the Zionists and the Arabs in the old British mandate of Palestine, the British surrendered their mandate to the United Nations and withdrew their troops in May, 1948. Open and bitter fighting over the United Nation's proposed partition promptly followed. Meanwhile, in Iran, popular feeling against the domination of the country's economy by the Anglo-Iranian Oil Company was running high, whipped by the emotional Dr. Mossadegh (1880-   ), who nationalized the oil fields. The British were forced to evacuate the area in October, 1951.

Trams ~ Underground ~ Bus

Mossadegh was overthrown in August, 1953, and foreign interests were permitted to return; but the British rôle in the country's affairs was sharply reduced.

The Suez Canal crisis

The most decisive blow to British influence in the Near East came in 1956, when the British and French, acting ostensibly to protect the Suez Canal from the fighting that had erupted between the Israelis and the Egyptians, invaded the canal area. Under the pressure of adverse world opinion and the threat of force by the Russians, the British and French withdrew from Egypt after a few days without reaching their objectives, leaving Egypt's strong man, Colonel Nasser, in a stronger position than ever. After this, British influence in the Near East was virtually at an end, and the power vacuum this created was filled by the conflicting interests of the Soviet Union and the United States.

Colonial problems in Africa

In other parts of the world, notably in Africa, the British have handled their colonial problems reasonably well, especially in the Gold Coast, where they coöperated in guiding the natives to self-government and, in 1957, to the establishment of an independent nation. In Kenya, since a state of emergency was declared in September, 1952, to cope with the terrorist raids of the Mau-Mau, the British have had some measure of success by using a mixture of force and constitutional reform. The Kenya problem and many of Britain's other colonial problems still await final solution, but there is no doubt that the traditional colonial attitude of nineteenth-century Britain, immortalized in romantic fashion by Kipling (pp. 885 and 933), has been sadly discredited. However, if the British Empire is indeed being dissolved, the dissolution is only in keeping with the times, and there are those who argue that, through real statesmanship, out of it there will emerge a stronger Commonwealth.

The Labour Party and its problems

Although few of these problems cast grim shadows in 1923, one could not blame thoughtful British statesmen of that year for being pessimistic in the political murk surrounding them. The United States, chief of the creditor nations, was demanding payment of Britain's war-debts, which, incidentally, were never paid in cash. Germany, formerly the major economic power on the Continent, was about to go into a disastrous financial collapse. The advent of the British Labour Party to a position of dominance was unavoidable.

To the Conservatives the rise to power of Ramsay MacDonald seemed a calamity; it appeared possible to them that England was headed toward communism. As it happened, however, the Labour Party of 1924 was far from radical; MacDonald was not politically stable, and his position became more and more that of a liberal seduced by conservatives. The Labour Party was based upon a combination of socialism of the nineteenth-century brand (p. 580) and present-day trade-unionism; and its ascendancy did not succeed in preventing strikes. Moreover, it was unable to achieve a trade-compact with Soviet Russia because its victory over the Conservatives had not been sufficiently clear-cut. The Labour Party was in power less than a year, but during this year it had to contend with the collapse of a temporary industrial boom, caused by the French withdrawal from the Ruhr, which they had briefly seized, and with a general strike, called in May, 1926, in sympathy for striking miners. The country was paralyzed for ten days before the strike was broken.

The Conservatives returned to power at the end of 1924 under Stanley Baldwin (1867-1947) and managed to weather the public storm bred by the general strike. In spite of its colorless and reactionary nature, the Baldwin ministry was able to point to the granting of the vote to all adult women (1928). It was proud also of its part in the Locarno Pact (1925), which in the light of later developments appears to have been as quixotic as the Washington Disarmament Conference of a few years earlier, for the Locarno Pact attempted to guarantee the peace of Europe in general and the boundaries of France, Germany, Belgium, Poland, and Czechoslovakia in particular. When, in addition, the United States signed the Kellogg-Briand Pact (1928), which repudiated all military aggression, it seemed to many idealists that the road to the millennium was becoming discernible in the jungle of international animosities.

Return of the Conservatives

The Rumblings Before the Storm

THE FAILURE of British business to grow during the 1920's eventually brought Ramsay MacDonald back to power; but by this time he had lost touch with the leaders of the Labour Party and was more in political sympathy with the Liberals among the industrial class. The depression of 1929 led to a coalition government, for it meant, indeed, a war emergency of a new kind. Britain went off the gold standard in 1931 and resorted to various governmental subsidies. Britain had willy-nilly to pay attention to what was taking place on the Continent. Here Germany and Italy, self-proclaimed have-nots, were building up immense armaments and brandishing the sword and bayonet at every opportunity. The Japanese invaded Manchuria in 1931; the Italians marched into Ethiopia in 1935. The Germans, despite treaty obligations, in 1936 remilitarized their western border and launched upon their career of calculated Nazi aggression. Even so, Britain was incredibly slow to wake up to danger, and her endeavors to arm herself proved to be pathetically inadequate.

Depression and defense

As a matter of fact, Britain obviously did not understand, any more than did the United States, the true gravity of the state of the world; it was too pleasant to contemplate the present in terms of the past, without much

The Dole Queue

Death of George V: three monarchs in one year

thought of the future. The Jubilee of the twenty-fifth anniversary of the accession of George V (1935) brought sentimental comfort. The Empire seemed as strong as ever; the depression had, indeed, brought about a certain unity which had been lacking during the early 1920's. But after Stanley Baldwin had returned to power (1935), there came, in rapid succession, a series of disquieting events. George V died (January, 1936); his son, the popular Edward VIII, abdicated to marry an American divorcee (December, 1936). Edward's brother, the Duke of York, who succeeded as George VI, was admirably suited to the position of symbolic figurehead which the British Crown had come to be.

Leadership of Chamberlain

Stanley Baldwin, retiring in 1937, handed over the leadership of the Conservatives to Neville Chamberlain (1869-1940), son of Joseph Chamberlain of imperialistic fame (p. 842). The new prime minister was a man of personal integrity, a true representative of the Church of England, the landed gentry, the peers of the realm, all capitalists both of the middle class and of the aristocracy, and all who preferred to do that which promised temporary security. As it happened, it was most disastrous for Britain that her government should be in the hands of such a man and such a party at this particular time.

New wars and aggression

Germany and Italy had intervened in the new Spanish Civil War by sending aid to the fascistic Loyalists (Falangists) under Franco, while Russia had opposed them by giving aid and comfort to the Republicans. Neither England nor France, to say nothing of the United States, ventured to interfere in any official way. Meanwhile Hitler (1889-1945) annexed Austria (March, 1938); and when Czechoslovakia refused to give up her territory along the frontier with Germany, Hitler made the threat of a general European war so obvious and imminent that Chamberlain and Premier Daladier (1884-   ) of France closed their eyes to their obligation to defend Czechoslovakia (according to the Locarno Pact of 1925) and handed over that country, an unfortunate child of the Treaty of Versailles, to be devoured shortly thereafter by Nazi Germany. Such was the true significance of the incredible Munich Conference in September, 1938, when Chamberlain traveled to Germany and came back with an agreement which, he was certain, would bring "peace in our time."

Appeasement

And so a word in the English language came to have a new and pusillanimous significance. This was the word *appeasement,* which had now become synonymous with surrender. No longer was there any chance for Britain and France to make an alliance with Russia, chiefly because Russia, afraid of Germany, also realized that Britain and France were relatively helpless. Hitler, during the summer of 1939, renewed his now tried and true methods of pressure, this time on Poland; when Poland refused to appease, he invaded that country on September 1, and this time neither England nor France could afford to back down.

Dunkirk 1940

Britain and the Second World War

THE WAR ITSELF began slowly for the British people; it was not until April of 1940 that anything significant happened in western Europe. Hitler, who had immobilized the Russians by signing a remarkable non-aggression pact with the Soviets a week before he invaded Poland (a pact blown to bits, of course, in June of 1941), overwhelmed Poland in three weeks. In April and May Germany completed the occupation of Denmark and Norway; in the latter country, for the first time, the dreadful inadequacies of Allied preparation for the war and the hopeless fumbling of the Chamberlain ministry were pitilessly exposed. On May 10, 1940, the Germans in brilliant flanking movement by-passed the main defenses of the supposedly invincible Maginot line and invaded the Low Countries and Belgium. The power of their onslaught combined with the inadequate Allied defenses brought about the loss of the Low Countries to the Germans and imperiled the whole British Expeditionary Force. A skillful and heroic evacuation through Dunkirk saved most of the men, but not the armor. Shortly thereafter, on June 17, 1940, France was forced into ignominious capitulation.

Early German victories

England spent the summer of 1940 amid grim and desperate efforts to prepare for a German invasion of the island. And although that invasion never came, she was mercilessly pounded from the air for months, while the world marveled at her defensive fortitude. Now master of all continental Europe, Hitler even invaded northern Africa, with the objective of blocking the Suez Canal, cutting off Britain from the Mediterranean, and gaining the rich resources of the Near East.

When Hitler invaded Russia (June 22, 1941), it was clear that Britain had been granted a breathing spell. American aid now became more immediate; it became total when Japan struck at Pearl Harbor (December 7, 1941). Although the Germans reached almost to Moscow, and the Japanese overran all of the southwestern Pacific as far as the northern coast of Australia, the balance gradually shifted for the Allies from the defensive to the offensive. Slowly the Americans, ably assisted by the Australians and the New Zealanders, worked their way back through the Pacific—a rugged and brilliantly executed three-year campaign. The Allies, after clearing the Germans out of northern Africa (1942-1943), moved into Italy and defeated the weakest of their enemies (July 25, 1943), although they were obliged to maintain a costly holding campaign on the peninsula for the better part of two years thereafter. They performed the greatest feat of invasion ever recorded when they landed in France (June 6, 1944) and penetrated into Germany by September. When the Anglo-American forces and the revivified Russians met in central Germany, it was all over; the Germans capitulated on May 8, 1945. Just three months later, the Japanese, now under constant attack by American air and sea forces and realizing full well that a

Allies on the offensive

Victory for the Allies

Normandy 1944

complete invasion by American ground forces of their home islands was only a matter of months, if not of weeks, surrendered without reservations. Their collapse was unquestionably hastened by a frightful atomic-bomb attack on Hiroshima on August 6, 1945, which presaged an entire new era in technical science; and, to a lesser degree, by American naval assaults and the entry of Russia into the Pacific war. The final articles of surrender were signed exactly six years after Germany had invaded Poland.

Winston Churchill

Britain, however, was too preoccupied with the European and African theaters of war to take more than a nominal part in the overthrow of Japan. The great leader of her war effort, an ideal man for the position, was Winston Churchill (p. 1032), who assumed the prime ministership after the German breakthrough in the Low Countries (May, 1940). He was an inspired champion of the nation, especially when the going was roughest, a gifted orator of the traditional cast. But he represented, for all his inestimable services to the nation, an age which had passed. The complete victory of the Labour Party in the summer of 1945 was not unexpected, for the times were antithetic to a return of Conservative government of the old type, and no one wanted the coalition government which had ruled the nation during the war years to continue. The transition to a socialistic form of government proved to be easy and was accompanied with very little bitterness. The basic industries nationalized by the Labour Party had been under government control during the war; shareholders were compensated, and many of the old managers found positions side by side with union leaders on the new boards set up to control the industries.

1945 victory of Labour Party

St Bride's Church
1670-1684

The problem weighing more than anything else upon the Attlee ministry was the discouraging one of putting back on its feet a nation bled to the point of anemia by six devastating years of front-line warfare—a nation, moreover, which had not made a healthy recovery from the First World War. *Austerity,* a word made current by Sir Stafford Cripps while he was Chancellor of the Exchequer (1947-1950), was the keyword during the first six post-war years. Rationing continued and in many instances was more stringent than during the war years. Aggravating the severe economic situation was an especially hard winter in the first months of 1947, resulting in a coal shortage; then too, there was a lack of sufficient dollar credits, caused by the cessation of lend-lease and by British losses in the export trade and overseas investments. Britain was saved from what looked like financial ruin by increased American aid under the Marshall Plan. The British bore the rationing and the general austerity with cheerful good will, confident in their country's ability to meet and overcome the crisis.

Return of the Conservatives

In 1951 the Conservatives were returned to power by a narrow margin, and Winston Churchill again became the leader of his country. Except for denationalizing the steel and trucking industries, the Conservatives left

Labour legislation intact. Beginning in 1951, a recovery took place in Britain, although not necessarily as a result of the change in the political climate. The recovery was strengthened by a general West-European recovery that began a short time later. In 1952 King George VI died, and his daughter Elizabeth (1926-   ) was crowned Queen of England, June 2, 1953. Churchill, now Sir Winston, relinquished the prime ministership to Sir Anthony Eden (1897-   ) in April, 1955, and, in a general election held in the following month, the Conservatives increased their majority. Eden's term in office was rocky because of the international situation; and, at the height of the furor over the invasion of Egypt, he resigned from office (1956), citing ill-health as the reason. Harold Macmillan (1894-   ) became prime minister and received a slight majority in the following election.

Although Britain has regained a strong position in European industry, she is being seriously challenged by the astounding recovery of the West German Republic and to a lesser extent by the resurgence of Japan in the Far East. Prosperity for Britain in the future will depend largely on her ability to hold on to traditional trade outlets.

The Literature of the Age in General

St Brice's Church 1940

WE ARE ACCUSTOMED to designate as "contemporary literature" only the literature of the last thirty years or so, although there are some persons whose memories of the 1890's are still fresh. The fact is that we cannot blame the two World Wars for all the characteristics of contemporary literature, although the conflict of 1914-1918, in particular, gave an unmistakably new face to English and American letters. But it is still possible to treat the literature of the past forty years as a major unit of English literature.

Four periods

We cannot, of course, see this literature with the clarity possible when we survey an older period of literature. More than ever, since we are still so close in time to this literature, is it necessary for us to eschew rigid chronological divisions, but some are valid enough. The first of these would run, in point of time, from the outbreak of the First World War to about 1923. Here various cross-currents eddy about; but more powerful than the others is the desire of writers to hold on to the old, to preserve at least some of the traditional attitudes toward both form and substance that were to be found in the nineteenth century. A second period, between 1923 and 1929, is the famous "plateau of the 1920's," the fabulous Jazz Age, in which there was a general tendency to jettison, deny, and generally ridicule the older standards of spiritual values, morality, and faith. It represents the very extreme of anti-Victorianism. The years of the depression and of the prelude to the Second World War—from 1929 to 1939—make up a third period. Here the tendency is strongly toward the left in politics and toward collectivism in social outlooks; it does not think of man any longer as a hopeless individual wandering in a howling wilderness but rather as a worthy part of a mass, though that mass is greater than any one of its component parts. Finally there is the period of the Second World War, and its aftermath—1939 to the present—a period singularly unproductive of important literature but, because of its awesome potentialities for good or evil, worthy of respect and due recording. These four periods, however, are admittedly makeshift designations and overlap one another at best, for there are plenty of traditionalists writing throughout these forty-odd years, and there are those who preach the gospel of the Waste Land at any and all times.

Characteristics of contemporary literature

In view of the enormous output of contemporary writers and their multitudinous numbers and interests, to say nothing of the complex opportunities for outlet—books, magazines, newspapers, pamphlets, lectures, radio and television programs, the stage, the motion pictures, for example—it is impossible to express in a brief space a complete definition of contemporary literature. We must content ourselves with a consideration of only the important British literary characters on the scene. The literature between 1914 and 1957 is bold to the point of audacity in its treatment of preconceived standards of art and life. It is extremely self-conscious, often to a degree of obscurity and freakishness. It can be sentimental, although the age expresses an abhorrence for the sentimental. On the other hand, it seems to reflect the notion that this is more of a woman's world than it used to be. One is struck forcibly by the irreverent nature of contemporary literature, as compared with that of preceding ages, by its emphasis upon the scientific way of life, particularly where science and technology meet the human being and his environment, and by its preoccupation with sex. It cannot shake off the eternal verities, of course; but it can be absolutely arrogant in its contemplation of them and is prone to insist that the greatest of all eternal verities is change. It professes to know all the answers; but beneath this assumption of knowledge it is altogether unsure of itself. It subscribes to realism, though it is often romantic in an unhappy kind of way; it has courage but not much steadiness; it has energy without much direction; it knows a great deal, but it is also ignorant and lacking in essential wisdom.

Fumed Oak - 1911

Some Traditionalists

IN SPITE OF THE FACT that English literature since the romantic revival of the early nineteenth century has been given to complaint, one might suppose that the findings of science should at least have shown man his place, where he could resign himself to stay and submit to the order of things, as was preached in the eighteenth century by Pope in his *Essay on Man* (Vol. I, p. 1085). Such has never been the case, however; man of the twentieth century was not made to be content, and this is one of his positive virtues.

1920

Rolls-Royce 1935

Individual thinkers and writers, to be sure, have pointed out that man is of little importance as an individual and is entrapped by life in the mass. Such a conclusion will lead inevitably to a philosophy of negation. A great many writers of contemporary literature, some of whom will be mentioned later, adopted this pessimistic attitude. But there were many who still saw beauty in life; and in the worship of this beauty they recovered some of the glory which science had repudiated. All of these, in greater or less degree, were mystic; they felt that reason and a sense of fact were not enough, that memory might be as true as the commonplaces of ordinary existence, and that love was stronger than death.

Worshipers of beauty

The finest example of such a traditionalist is William Butler Yeats (p. 1025), who began as the presiding genius of the Irish Renaissance in the 1890's (p. 853) and developed during the twentieth century into one of the major poets of the age. The early phase of his poetry has already been touched upon; but it would be a manifest injustice to him if he were considered only as a Celtic romanticist, for with all his mysticism he was both humanist and humanitarian and a man with full awareness of realities. *Sailing to Byzantium* (p. 1031) is a beautiful expression of the often white-hot mystical experience that Yeats underwent in his attempts to fuse the romantic and idealistic with the stern exigencies of life. It is revealing to notice how often in his later poems, such as *The Second Coming* (p. 1030) and *Among School Children* (p. 1031)—and his later poems are coming to be regarded now as his best—Yeats presents first an actual scene or fact, then his subjective reaction to that scene, and then the mystic and symbolic interpretation of his reactions in terms of the purest imagination and felicity of phrase. He shows, therefore, that the mere process of living does not invalidate the "reality" of his dreams, for his intensely subjective poetry can still keep a firm hold upon actualities. It is true that he might well have kept away from spiritualism and theosophy; and he could also have spared us some of the obscure and strained imagery of his latest work. But what is really great about Yeats and his poetry, apart from his innate poetic genius, is that he was not static; he moved from one point to another in a positive development. He outgrew the Irish Renaissance, which he had helped to establish; when placed beside him, the other Celtic poets, with all their talents, seem either feeble romantics or parochial interpreters of life.

William Butler Yeats

Modern Interior

Weaker though he may be in poetic capabilities, Walter de la Mare (1873-1956) possesses an extremely delicate craftsmanship, a haunting, childlike imagination of melancholy cast, and a sensitive intuition. He is much more wistful than Yeats; his eyes are turned much more unavertedly toward the past. Yet though he may be rooted in romanticism, he is no Stevenson with a specious hope that all will be well. *The Listeners* (1912) presents in less than forty lines a traveler in a forest, a traveler seeking spiritual values, who comes to a lonely house and knocks on the door, but only phantom listeners

Walter de la Mare

hear him, and they can give him no answer. *The Last Coachload* (1921) paints a coach—the world—bearing its many passengers—mankind—to their inevitable destination—death. In another poem, the poet is happy enough for a moment; but "life is a dread thing, too, dark with horror and fear."

By and large, however, the English poets of the traditionalist group have neither the vitality nor the challenging power of their American contemporaries. In fact, the English writers of fiction and the drama outshine the poets, except for Yeats, though here again the great figures belong at least in part to the nineteenth century. Galsworthy and Shaw have already been mentioned (pp. 857-862). We might add that Shaw, a sublime egoist, never loses touch with reality; he is never effectively romantic and is always essentially satirical. Probably it would be more accurate to say that he is a law unto himself; but his liking for the honest man who tries to get somewhere even amid utter confusion, and his dislike of the pretentious, which is, after all, the true test of the satirist, are enough to keep him in the camp of the traditionalists, however much he must have winced at the label and however much he may have derided his being classified at all.

Shaw, satirist

As for Galsworthy, his fundamental sympathy for the beautiful in his characters, as in the instances of Old Jolyon and Fleur in *The Forsyte Saga,* did not blind him to the wrong-headedness of that throwback to nineteenth-century material acquisitiveness, Soames Forsyte. Galsworthy, the patrician in style, by no means averse to sentimentality, has often been accused by latter-day critics of a preference for viewing life from the upstairs parlor-window and of an unwillingness to get down into the street. In his plays, however, he chose themes which are universal and timeless—for example, *Strife* (1909), in its picture of the inconclusiveness of disputes between labor and capital, and *Loyalties* (1922), with its wide observation of petty adherence to cliques and shibboleths, as well as its frank facing of the anti-Semitic spirit, are as appropriate to the 1950's as to the time when they were written. And if it is still possible to complain that in Galsworthy the score of the game is too often nothing to nothing, one cannot well quarrel with his grasp of realities and his broad romantic humanitarianism.

Galsworthy, realist and humanitarian

The tradition of the Irish theater, first made resplendent by Yeats and Synge (p. 985), has been ably carried on by Sean O'Casey (1884-   ); but his talent is remarkably uneven. He is at his best dealing with the Irish revolutionary movement. *Juno and the Paycock* (1924) has superb characterization but violates almost every known principle of unity of action; still, the figures of old Boyle (the "Paycock") and of his wife are magnificent —the one because of his supreme typifying of the ne'er-do-well; the other because of her quiet courage in the face of the utter ruin of her family. In *The Plough and the Stars* (1926), a wife tries in vain—and quite disastrously —to keep her husband from taking part in the Easter Rebellion of 1916. But then in *The Silver Tassie* (1928), an anti-war play, O'Casey suddenly

Sean O'Casey

departs from his realistic manner and becomes allegorical; in *Within the Gates* (1933), he turns satirical of middle-class society and the Church and revives the old romantic motif of the joyous prostitute. His later plays, *The Star Turns Red* (1940) and *Purple Dust* (1941), are in the first instance Marxist propaganda and in the second instance caricature. Yet beside his power and the vital Irish dramatic tradition which he represents, the whimsical, light, sentimental, and dainty plays of Sir James Barrie (1860-1937) and the fantastic dream-creations of Lord Dunsany (1878-1957) seem to belong to an utterly vanished age.

On the whole, the fiction of the traditionalists has not weathered the storm in good condition, although many have tried to save the ship—too many, unfortunately, to be named here. Katherine Mansfield (p. 1069) achieved success in the short story; her delicately wrought tales are dedicated primarily to mood and atmosphere. Usually these moods are difficult to define exactly; but in many ways they remind us of those of Walter de la Mare and Anton Chekhov, for whom she revealed, in her journals and notebooks, warm admiration. Her characters tend to react with the thought that life is—something; but words fail them. The interested reader will derive as much satisfaction from her *Journal* as from her short tales and sketches, for here is told the fascinating and pathetic story of a gifted woman's decline, her mercurial mind alive and vital until but a short time before her death. Inconsecutive and fragmentary as the pages of the *Journal* may be, they represent the virtues as well as the limitations of their author's talents.

Katherine Mansfield

In the fields of historiography and biography—the latter, by the way, has been extremely popular and well handled in contemporary writing, except for an occasional overwhelming desire to debunk rather than to present a constructive picture of the subject—we find an arresting and typically satirical writer in Lytton Strachey (1880-1932). In his excellent *Queen Victoria* (1921), he paints his portrait with power and also with some romantic nostalgia in the dramatic moments. Even in his somewhat smug and condescending *Eminent Victorians* (1918), he shows much emotional drive. The same thing is true of such a work as the gripping *The Hundred Years* (1936) by Philip Guedalla (1889-1944).

History and biography

To be sure, the writers just discussed are those who have made themselves celebrated above the mass; there were many other historians and biographers who could be named in an exhaustive catalogue. Yet all of them, we can see now—whether writing in the fields just mentioned or in the broad creative fields of fiction, poetry, and drama—were trying their best to maintain some hope, however illusory, that human life had value. They had been formed by nineteenth-century thought, and it was not easy for science to tear them away from their mother. They could not believe that patriotism and honor and love could be anything but real. The rejected the mechanistic philosophy of life which a literal application of both biological and psychological science

imposed upon them. They thought well, even if they could not push their thinking to any logical conclusions. The question remains whether any human being can do so.

Wastelanders and Truth-Seekers of the Times

Impact of the new psychology

WE HAVE HEARD much about the impact of science upon the minds of the Victorian age, how this impact disillusioned some, cut the ground from under others, and forced every one to some sort of readjustment. In our age, the findings of psychology seem to have caused more of a spiritual upheaval than the doctrine of evolution did among the Victorians; the theory of behaviorism put forth by John B. Watson (1878-   ) or the analysis of the subconscious mind by Sigmund Freud (1856-1939) have produced conclusions more shocking to the older order than Darwin's were. When a person realizes that his reason may at any time be upset by the emotional reaction of his subconscious mind, he lays the knife against the very roots of the rational. If he thinks of himself as nothing but a set of conditioned reflexes and discovers that he and his fellow-men cannot accept truth simply because it is truth, or form opinions based upon reason, then he loses respect for men's intellect, his potentialities, and his spiritual essence.

Negativism and despair

To accept these completely revolutionary ideas is all very well, provided one understands that all such findings are tentative and that science is no more absolute than the humanities. As it happened, most intelligent men who thought about the matter at all found either that they must swallow whole the teachings and implications of the new science or else that they must accept them with sensible reservations, always remembering that the story was not and probably never could be complete. For there was no longer any likelihood that a thinking man could reject them altogether. The writers of contemporary literature, none of whom knew much about science although they all knew a great deal about living, were inclined to be too easily impressed by the negative implications of Freud, Watson, and others. The inference that man was a strange mixture of bone and tissue, mostly water, with sentient threads called nerves and some kind of quasi-electrical impulses called stimuli, a creature capable of being dissolved in the twinkling of an eye—to many this concept was so terrible that they abandoned hope. Unlike the brave whistling in the dark in which Stevenson indulged in his *Pulvis et Umbra* (p. 929)—and Stevenson represents a way out of the predicament which the traditionalists were inclined to seize upon—there arose the cries of voices in the wilderness among a large number of writers who are in many respects the most impressive writers of contemporary literature. Life was sterile, decadent, unrewarding to virtue as well as to vice; there was no Celestial City toward which man could strive, and no Inferno either; his

A Lyons Corner House

Heaven and his Hell were alike on this earth; in this life the end came with death, which meant annihilation and eternal oblivion.

All this was far from new; it was only that the twentieth century, with its hyperaccelerated urban culture, shows the "strange disease of modern life" in more aggravated form. We have seen melancholy and pessimism before in English literature; it reached a morbid stage in the graveyard verse of the supposedly rational eighteenth century. The twentieth century, however, with its skyscrapers and city battlements, its tumultuous means of transport and supply, and its enormous technological equipment, has given man more room, more places, and at the same time, ironically enough, more opportunity for claustrophobia to intensify his inherited miseries. The true paradox of the twentieth century is that we have far more abilities and opportunities for intellectual and artistic nourishment than other ages have had—abilities and opportunities that we are never tired of proclaiming—and yet we do relatively much less with them than did many a former and less rich age.

The paradox of the twentieth century

The Wastelander, essentially a romanticist, cannot actually feel more despair than a Shelley, let us say; and so, in order to achieve a like effect, he resorts to the hypodermic of exaggerated details. He is, naturally, extremely self-centered; in some instances he lives entirely in his own private world—the reduction to the absurd of the romanticist's subjective point of view—and builds up his own language, allowing his normal mental associations to race around until they produce a roaring stream of consciousness—his own consciousness, in general, not someone else's. Many Wastelanders are guilty of great obscurity, for the reasons just mentioned; yet so powerful is their impress upon the tastes and fashions of contemporary literature that obscurity becomes something of a fetish, a talisman to ward off the danger that the Wastelander might be too easily understood and his intellectual and emotional sterility exposed for what it is. Moreover, the Wastelander, like his romantic ancestor of the nineteenth century, is haunted often by the thought that other times were better. Hence his natural inclination toward a satirical consideration of the present. Then again, with a typical romantic inconsistency, the Wastelander strives for adventure, often of a grim and grisly type, while at the same time he wallows uneasily in the commonplace, which he can use to illustrate and point up his picture of arid desolation.

The two World Wars have added fuel to the Wastelander's furnace; to read the brooding, eloquent lines of the poetry of Wilfred Owen (p. 1033) is to understand the bitterness in the hearts of men cut down in their youth and denied the promise that should normally be theirs. "No Man's Land," wrote Owen, "under snow is like the face of the moon, chaotic, crater-ridden, uninhabitable, awful, the abode of madness." Quite properly, men like Owen could believe that they belonged to a lost generation; but whereas Owen died before the Armistice, others lived on, battening on their venomous dis-

Wilfred Owen

The Flying Scotsman

illusionment. Even when the writers were women, blessed with feminine insight and delicacy, they could still understand that the old order had changed and that, as for the new order, the world was wrong. The Jazz Age had come.

T. S. Eliot

In poetry, it is obvious that the most important spokesman for the Wastelanders is T. S. Eliot (p. 1078) in his earlier phase; this striking poet's *The Love Song of J. Alfred Prufrock* (p. 1085), *The Waste Land* (1922), *The Hollow Men* (1925), and other poems composed in the 1920's catch exactly the moods of vacillation, weakness, sordidness, and despair. Both as poet and critic, Eliot has long dominated the literary scene. He was born in the United States but lived abroad long enough to become first an internationalist and eventually a British subject. It is likely that the critics of the twenty-first century will consider Eliot and Yeats the most important English-speaking poets of the first half of the twentieth century. Like Yeats, Eliot has progressed remarkably from his earlier work—a sure sign of a significant writer—for his poetry in the 1930's and 1940's has taken on an increasingly religio-philosophical tone, culminating in such noble utterances as *Ash Wednesday* (p. 1087), *The Rock* (1934), and particularly *Four Quartets* (1943), which are powerful and moving, though extremely difficult, poetry.

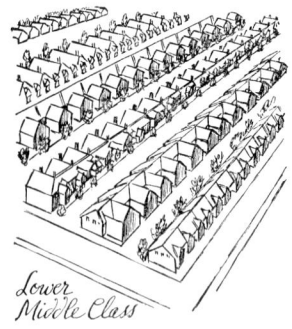

Lower Middle Class

Eliot's earlier work bristles with learned allusions and recondite imagery; much of it is derived from other poets, and many passages are tissues of quotations from or reminiscences of older writers. His affinity for the later Elizabethan and seventeenth-century periods, both as a poet and as critic, is most marked. Even in his latest poetry there is an undeniable bookishness. It is difficult to see the author of *The Waste Land* or *The Hollow Men* in the author of *Four Quartets;* but the polarity of the moods of despair and desolation on the one hand and the emotional stirrings of an orthodox, if rather unstable, faith (laboriously attained, to be sure) on the other is altogether typical of the age in which Eliot has been writing; and the very fact that he can attain both poles of the sphere makes him a greater writer in substance, let us say, than D. H. Lawrence or James Joyce (p. 1041).

Noel Coward

The best dramatist of the Waste Land is the one best fitted to demonstrate that the Wastelander has his lighter side. Noel Coward (p. 1117) has always had the theater for his chief passion; he has achieved success in comedy of manners, historical drama, domestic tragedy, operetta, and revue to such a marked degree that he remains one of the most versatile playwrights in the history of the English theater. Essentially an entertainer, he is in one way a twentieth-century Congreve, except that, in keeping with the spirit of his time, he dares to discuss and attack things that Congreve (1670-1729) would not have ventured to lay hands on. Coward is at his best when he is presenting the unconventional, particularly the unorthodox in domestic relations. The son in *The Vortex* (1923) castigates his lecherous mother; the nagged husband in *Fumed Oak* (1936) turns violently on his unpleasant little family; in *Private Lives* (1930) a divorced couple, each of whom has remarried, meet on their respective new honeymoons and forget about their new marriages. In *Design for Living* (1933) there is established a delightful *ménage à trois*, involving a woman and two men, in which triangle each member loves the other two and cannot choose between them. Something of the same insouciance about marital relationships is obvious in *Blithe Spirit* (1941). In *Hands Across the Sea* (1935) a farcical situation is developed with keen satire. On the other hand, *Bitter Sweet* (1929), a charming operetta for which he composed both words and music, is Coward's most successful venture in the field of musical entertainment, but it is essentially as lachrymose in its appeal as something out of the nineteenth century. Actually the revue *Conversation Piece* (1934) is a trifle more typical of its author. *Cavalcade* (p. 1118) is the panorama of an English family from the Boer War to the end of the First World War; it contains memorable scenes and true power; but again, its appeal to the English people to recover their greatness and dignity is revealing of Coward's sentimental and traditionalist streak, a streak clearly shown in *This Happy Breed* (1943), a play of middle-class London. A true successor to the Oscar Wilde tradition, Coward's taste may sometimes be enough to make a Victorian wince, but that is only to be expected from a writer of the twentieth-century Waste Land.

Upper Middle Class

Some of the best of the English Wastelanders have been novelists. Gallons of critical ink have been expended over such widely dissimilar individuals as W. Somerset Maugham, Aldous Huxley, D. H. Lawrence, and James Joyce. It is generally agreed that Maugham is an extremely gifted *littérateur*, a professional craftsman and entertainer in letters who is also a fine satirist; Huxley and Lawrence are basically preachers; Joyce is the subjective artist going his own way.

Novelists of the Waste Land

W. Somerset Maugham (1874-   ) has his literary roots deep in the Continental soil of the nineteenth century. The first of his many novels, *Liza of Lambeth* (1897), is a naturalistic novel (something uncommon in English letters), with the attitude toward life characteristic of a medical student, which Maugham once was. His masterpiece is clearly the distinguished novel written as a partial autobiography, *Of Human Bondage* (1915); but his many short stories and his plays, some of which have been based on his short stories, are notable. One of his specialties has been the South-Seas-plus-Hollywood-formula which presents white men and women breaking up morally under the spell of lands "east of Suez, where the best is like the worst." From Maugham's story *The Trembling of a Leaf* (1921) was adapted the once sensational play *Rain,* one of the great dramatic successes of the 1920's. *Rain* deals with the old romantic situation of a prostitute who unintentionally and ironically brings about the moral ruin of a supposedly upright man (in this case, a stiff-necked missionary) and at the same time manages to ennoble herself. In all of his work, Maugham reminds one somewhat of the French

W. Somerset Maugham

Efficiency Flats - 1933

fiction-writer Guy de Maupassant (1850-1893). He is original in his treatment of old themes, economical in his style, subtle in his overtones, adventurous in his plots, and always dramatic.

Aldous Huxley

It is indeed ironic that the grandson of Thomas Henry Huxley (p. 561) should be perhaps the most brilliant critic of the triumph of modern science over the human soul. Aldous Huxley (p. 1097) began his work as an author by shattering the illusions of the conventional reading public. Though scintillating, his first novels, beginning with *Crome Yellow* (1921), are iconoc'astic in the extreme; they proceed, explicitly and implicitly, to demolish Victorianism in all its various manifestations and then go on to lay man's whole life in intellectual and spiritual ruins. In speaking of his novel *Antic Hay* (1923), Huxley asserts that it "dramatizes with relentless logic the necessary implications, in terms of life, of the skepticism of Thomas Huxley —skepticism battening on the vitals of animal faith." His two best novels, *Point Counter Point* (1928) and *Brave New World* (1932), are corrosive studies of the modern scene. Here endocrine glands run wild, with plenty of resulting violence, lust, and perversion. Yet pervading all these novels is a certain brooding undertone, an unsatisfied "Why?" which can have no final answer. *After Many a Summer Dies the Swan* (1939) sends man in quest of immortality by way of science; and science turns up the answer that longevity can be attained through a diet of carp's intestines; but the horrible creatures which survive are worthy of comparison with Swift's Struldbrugs in *Gulliver's Travels*. *Time Must Have a Stop* (1944) reviews a man's life through his delirium attendant upon a fatal attack of coronary thrombosis.

Huxley, however, seems to have reached the ultimate in his study of man the animal; he finds it necessary to turn to man the thinker or, as in *Ends and Means* (1937), to "an inquiry into the nature of ideals and into the methods employed for their realization." For the change in this author is as remarkable as the change in T. S. Eliot, to which it is strikingly analogous. Out of the Waste Land, which is too stifling to sustain life for long, man must seek the mountains of idealism and religion, and although he may grope blindly when he reaches them, he is at least on higher ground. In point of fact, Huxley has come to repudiate the very intellect with which man has been endowed, the intellect which has given him his sharpest weapons. For he is too powerful an individual thinker to be satisfied with mere sensationalism or decadent wit, both of which he commands with prodigal hand.

In effect, it often becomes difficult to separate Huxley the novelist from Huxley the teacher and preacher—this in spite of the fact that, in his desire for cleverness, a temptation which he finds even yet hard to resist, he frequently lapses into sophomoric utterances. At best, he tends to regard man as a kind of test-tube specimen, to be viewed with detachment. His characters largely react in terms of their physical organisms; and their psychological entities are in consequence based on behaviorism.

Ballroom Dancing, 1920

THE STRUGGLE ON THE DARKLING PLAIN

There are many medical men who insist that the mood of the Wastelander is psychotic, just as the moods of Beddoes's *Death's Jest-Book* (p. 298) and Thomson's *The City of Dreadful Night* (p. 763) are psychotic. For that matter, *The City of Dreadful Night* presents the Waste Land as effectively as T. S. Eliot's poem *The Waste Land,* though in an altogether traditional manner; the poems are half a century apart, but they serve to illustrate how much the twentieth century, after all, owes to its predecessor. To call these two poems psychotic is altogether too simple a procedure, but no one can well argue that contemporary literature is not at least thoroughly neurotic. As it happens, one symptom of a neurotic disposition is a most disproportionate emphasis on sex. Contemporary literature certainly often seems obsessed with the subject; this manifestation is in part a revolt against the often foolish reticence of the Victorian writers, but it represents also a peculiar interest for its own sake, not to be explained entirely by the stress placed upon it by Freudianism. Perhaps the stress is due to the fact that the twentieth century in the western world is a highly feminized century, citified, sophisticated, but physically indolent.

Neurotic character of the Waste Land

The great high priest of sex in contemporary English literature, who often spoke as if this curious biological scheme of things had never been discovered by anyone else, was D. H. Lawrence (1885-1930). Here was a brilliant novelist who is now usually associated in the popular mind with pornography —most unfairly, it must be added, because all who knew him agree that he was a remarkably pure-minded and idealistic individual. Each of his three best novels, *Sons and Lovers* (1913), *The Plumed Serpent* (1926), and *Lady Chatterley's Lover* (1928), caused a sensation when it appeared. The first, *Sons and Lovers,* an autobiographical novel of a young boy living in a mining town and beset by emotional family harassments, is probably his masterpiece. *The Plumed Serpent* is an esoteric novel involving a white woman with the ancient pagan cults of Mexico; it questions the whole right of the decadent white race to survive. *Lady Chatterley's Lover,* a success of scandal, relates the passionate love-affair of an impoverished English noblewoman and the game-keeper of her invalid husband's estate. All three novels stress a new world unhampered by caste or family ties or notions of racial and religious superiority, and dedicated to Love. Few can deny the warmth and color of *Sons and Lovers* or *The Plumed Serpent;* in these the author established himself as a distinguished romanticist who somehow just barely fails to achieve his purpose. The trouble lies in an essential naïveté which leads Lawrence to misunderstand his reader; for instance, *Lady Chatterley's Lover* is potentially a great and moving love-story, but Lawrence's specious surface-realism, which prompted him to use blunt obscenities in the tender love passages, will either offend or move to laughter. There is no greater enemy of romance then a guffaw. Consequently, this ill-starred novel, which Lawrence himself characteristically insisted was his best, is only misapprehended

D. H. Lawrence

The Lambeth Walk, 1938

as a pornographical exhibit and is banned in unexpurgated form to the English-speaking peoples, while the expurgation robs the novel of its very fiber.

Lawrence's conflicts

Lawrence, a restless, tuberculosis-ridden creature, spent his life wandering over the earth; but his wanderings in the spiritual realm caused him the greater worriment, for he could never harmonize the physical and spiritual sides of his characters, although such a reconciliation was essential to his philosophy. He fumbled and groped; and his characters did the same, for they were tormented by social pressures and outworn moral scruples, against which they protested with passion. Perhaps the author had puritanical tendencies, as his friends say, although no casual reader will ever discern them. He impresses one instead as a decadent and impractical fighter of windmills and sheep, a gravely troubled man; and his inability to take sex for granted and go on from that point is a serious intellectual weakness. Although he is a skilled and sensitive craftsman, over all his significant work lowers a cloud of frustration and futility.

James Joyce

Notoriety akin to Lawrence's was also the portion of James Joyce (p. 1041); but the two men were in most respects the direct antithesis of one another. Since Joyce was born and educated in Ireland during the heyday of the Irish Renaissance, one would expect him to have shared in the efforts of that artistic movement; but he actually had little sympathy with it. His attack upon the Irish theater, the most valuable and at the same time the most sacrosanct institution of the Irish Renaissance, shows Joyce's particular individualism, an individualism which grew upon him to such an extent that he became an expatriate on the Continent and, what is more important, perhaps the greatest example in modern English literature of the subjective. *Dubliners* (1914), a collection of short stories, and his masterpiece, the novel *Ulysses* (p. 1042), exhibit his intimate knowledge of the Irish capital and of the Irish temperament; but in neither work is any nationalistic trend evident.

The real thing for Joyce is the study of mankind. He sees and comprehends and expresses the realities of man's existence on this earth—in other words, he is aware of man's physical existence; but he is also acutely sensitive to man's intellectual and spiritual existence and to his overweening pride and overwhelming futility. Joyce was always a learned individual with a peculiar interest in linguistics, which he cultivated in his later work to such an extent that it interfered seriously with his lines of communication to his readers. To his remarkable power of observation and his expressiveness he added erudition and an irrepressible love for the symbolic.

Ulysses takes three people through one day in their lives—Leopold Bloom, a Jewish advertising solicitor of Dublin; his wife, Molly; and young Stephen Dedalus, the protagonist of Joyce's earlier novel, *A Portrait of the Artist as a Young Man* (1916), who has now broken with his unloved family and is

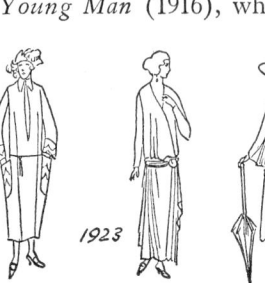

looking for some kind of spiritual father, a parallel with Telemachus's search for Ulysses. He finds the man in Bloom. In the meantime Bloom wanders all over Dublin; a great many other people appear in the pages of the novel, but they are all part of Bloom's experience. Each section of the novel corresponds to a section of the *Odyssey;* even the minor characters and the city streets are analogous in name or quality to figures and localities in the great Homeric epic. Bloom returns with Stephen late at night to find, not a chaste Penelope, but the adulterous Molly, whose uninhibited mental soliloquy at the end of the novel is a magnificent creation of feminine animality. And so *Ulysses* concludes on the affirmative C-major chord of Molly's life-giving vitality and yielding nature; yet the total effect of the novel is of almost unrelieved human sterility and desolation.

Joyce's last novel, *Finnegans Wake* (1939), is a fourth-dimensional work, for all time and space are telescoped into Ireland and Mr. Earwicker. The thesis seems to be that all life and all languages are one. Stylistically and linguistically *Finnegans Wake* is a freak. It is recognized by all of us that certain objects in our experience have associations peculiar to ourselves—sights, sounds, smells, tastes, and feelings. The pictures or moods which such associations conjure up for us are our own affair; they depend upon our inmost life (into which no one else can possibly reach), and it is difficult to convey them to others in ordinary language. But Joyce, in attempting to convey them, does not play fair with his reader. When an English word suggests to him a word, or set of words, not only in the same language but in other languages where they may have entirely different denotations and connotations, and when the author sees fit to play one word off against another so that, without a battery of notes to help him, the unfortunate reader cannot hope to follow, then we are justified in reproaching Joyce for indulging in a private game which only he himself, or his initiates, can be expected either to understand or to appreciate. And even when we understand, we are justified in asking whether it was worth the effort, whether the undeniable pyrotechnics and ingenious word-mongering were in any way useful to the reader. Nor is it any defense to say that communication can be restored by the mystical use of a secret key. Great literature needs no secret keys.

For all that, however, in his remarkable ability to portray the thought-processes of more than one character, Joyce has brought the writing of "stream of consciousness" literature to its highest peak in English letters. His influence upon many later writers has been immediate and direct. But another great contemporary influence at work on the writers of this age is Marcel Proust (1871-1922), whose multi-volume *Remembrance of Things Past* is a remarkable reconstruction of a human being's life (conscious as well as subconscious) and a display of man's associational powers. As a matter of fact,

Finnegans Wake

the strangely neglected Dorothy Richardson (1882-1957), in her multi-volumed *Pilgrimage* (1915-1938), was an earlier skilled practitioner of the type of writing to which she herself gave the name "interior monologue" in preference to "stream of consciousness writing." Yet this author's talent, when all is said and done, is far less striking than that of another woman born, as were both Dorothy Richardson and James Joyce, in the year of 1882.

Virginia Woolf

Virginia Woolf (p. 1061), who committed suicide in 1941 and so put an end to a career which was still in full flower, is by general consent the most important English woman writer of her generation. Her range of material interests and her grasp of reality, unusual though they are, never seem to concern her so much as the probing of psychological motives, reactions, and implications. One critic has put it well when he spoke of Virginia Woolf as a priestess of psychological minutiae. For her, time, measured in hours, minutes, and seconds, is important chiefly because a lifetime can be covered in the writer's imagination during those same hours, minutes, and seconds.

1925

On the other hand, Time, in the abstract, will continue long after the people affected by it have died; as in Proust's work, Time is the greatest of villains. In *The Years* (1937), one of Virginia Woolf's most moving novels, it is Time which is in reality the chief character. In *The Waves* (p. 1062), we have six characters whose lives are spread before us, not as a consecutive objective chronicle, but by the subtle device of studying the way in which each of these six characters reacts to the sea, which is a kind of symbol for Time. Time can triumph over persons and things, and even over sex, as in *Orlando* (1928); and yet there remains a curious residue of the permanent in the characters, as if Orlando, for example, were immortal, and all mankind were immortal, although subject to remorseless changes in which physical characteristics sink into nothingness. But we are never told this in so many words; Virginia Woolf is committed to a policy of indirection. In *To the Lighthouse* (1927), a boy is promised an excursion to a lighthouse; but by the time he actually visits this lighthouse, a whole generation has passed. And the boy, eager to reach the lighthouse in Part I, is both unimpressed and even bored by his final attainment of it as a man in Part III.

1923

The inner life, which is the preoccupation of Virginia Woolf, as of Joyce, is revealed to us with consummate craft and loving attention. It is not, however, the only life there is; and in that fact lies Virginia Woolf's great limitation. Matters like the invasion of Poland or the horrors of the concentration camp at Dachau, to her are embarrassingly physical. No argument and no subtlety can brush them aside.

Minor novelists

The number of gifted minor novelists in the contemporary period of English literature is legion; each one of them commands a sufficient following to make the task of the critic in labeling them either major or minor a most distasteful one. A solid but penetrating realist in the manner of George

Gissing (p. 857) is Frank Swinnerton (1884-   ), whose best work is probably *Nocturne* (1917). Of a different sort is the romanticist Hugh Walpole (1884-1941), with his Trollopian *The Cathedral* (1922) and Stevensonian *Herries Chronicles* (1930-1934). Much more incisive than either is E. M. Forster (1879-   ), whose *A Passage to India* (1924) is an ironic, almost cruel protest against material realism.

In this general field of the contemporary novel, the women have been out in force. May Sinclair (1865?-1946), whose first novel appeared before the end of the nineteenth century, turned the "stream of consciousness" technique to social comedy with good results in *A Cure of Souls* (1924) and *The Rector of Wyck* (1925); Ethel Lindesay Robertson (1870-1946), whose pen name was Henry Handel Richardson, illustrates impressively the tendency in modern fiction toward the broad panorama in her biographical trilogy, *The Fortunes of Richard Mahony* (1917-1930); Sheila Kaye-Smith (1888-1956) preaches the necessity of the self-dependence of modern woman in *Joanna Godden* (1921); Elizabeth Bowen (1899-   ) is a poetic champion of the lamb against bears, bulls, and wolves in *The House in Paris* (1935) and *The Death of the Heart* (1938). In *The Heat of the Day* (1949), her handling of the novel form is unchanged.

1935

Mention should also be made of the realist Séan O'Faoláin (1900-   ), who in *A Nest of Simple Folk* (1933), like O'Casey in the drama, gives us correctives to the over-romantic literary treatment of Ireland by the earlier Irish; of James Hanley (1901-   ), who in *Stoker Bush* (1935) presents a sailor's life in such a way as to make the sea-tales of John Masefield (p. 916) seem Victorian; and of Liam O'Flaherty (1896-   ), who in *The Informer* (1925) combines realism and melodrama with powerful results. Graham Green (1904-   ), Evelyn Waugh (1903-   ), and Wyndham Lewis (1884-   ) all made their reputations before the Second World War and they continue to produce interesting novels: Greene, *The End of the Affair* (1951) and *The Quiet American* (1955); Waugh, *Men at Arms* (1952), *Officers and Gentlemen* (1955), and *The Ordeal of Gilbert Pinfold* (1957); Lewis, *Self Condemned* (1954) and *Monstre Gai* and *Malign Fiesta* (1955). Alex Comfort, Patrick Leigh Fermor, and Hugo Charteris have made their reputations since the war.

1943

The poetry of the last thirty years is the product of the socially motivated '30's, the war-clouded '40's, and the uncertain and somewhat timid '50's. Two poets, W. H. Auden and Stephen Spender, perhaps more than any others, have best reflected the changing climate of these thirty years. W. H. Auden (p. 1145), a satirist of rather uncertain touch, was both irritated and disgusted by the decadence of the social order in Britain before the outbreak of the Second World War. In some little verse plays, written in collaboration with his friend Christopher Isherwood (1904-   ), and in such solid poetic

W. H. Auden

The Commonwealth on the March

efforts as *On This Island* (1937) and *Letter to Lord Byron* (1937), Auden does little more than express his awareness of this social decadence, touching up his comments with clever, penetrating, sometimes revolutionary discourse. The resemblance between Auden and Byron, as to satirical aspect, is enhanced by Auden's willingness to imitate on occasion the rambling, garrulous satire of the Byron of *Don Juan* or *Beppo*. But where Byron had a romantic dream and put this dream into action by going off to fight for the independence of Greece, Auden wanders about from England to Iceland to China to America, even during the years of the Second World War (although he drove an ambulance in Spain during the Civil War in that country), dabbling in communism, then turning to the refuge of the Catholic Church and later withdrawing from that refuge, becoming next a naturalized citizen of the United States. In his earlier work, at least, he brooded over the fact that he and other young men of his generation were suspended between two worlds—the outworn world of Europe and the unknown world that must somehow be born out of all this violence and chaos, if life is to have any meaning whatsoever. In *The Age of Anxiety* (p. 1158) he presents a conversation among four people of differing points of view, but the one who has the last word is he who goes about his daily business with as much common sense as can be mustered. Most of Auden's poetry, for all its occasional timeliness, has a curious kind of backward look. He sees the symbols of the old order receding but cannot catch a clear glimpse of what is coming to replace them. In two recent works, *Nones* (1951) and *The Shield of Achilles* (1955), his scorn is tempered by high spirits and wit. Especially in *The Shield of Achilles* he has put aside his intellectual misgivings, and the work, revealing his usual great metrical skill, is almost gay, though mixed with mockery.

This indeterminate opaqueness that appears in much of Auden's work is not so apparent in the poetry of the less gifted Stephen Spender (p. 1159). Spender's verse is most useful now for its statement of what has come over the point of view of the young revolutionary. In *World Within World* (1951), Spender, in a very sensitively written and sincerely self-critical autobiography, gives us a glimpse of the forming influences of this point of view. It is obvious that with Auden and Spender and others of their group all art must have social significance; indeed, these writers, by their implicit belief in this doctrine, represent ideally the preoccupation with sociological interests characteristic of the literature of the 1930's and 1940's. But the disillusionment, expressed by Spender in the following lines from "What I Expected" (p. 1162), is most revealing:

> What I expected was
> Thunder, fighting,

> Long struggles with men
> And climbing.
> After continual straining
> I should grow strong:
> Then the rocks would shake
> And I should rest long.
>
> What I had not foreseen
> Was the gradual day
> Weakening the will,
> Leaking the brightness away,
> The lack of good to touch
> The fading of body and soul
> Like smoke before wind
> Corrupt, unsubstantial.*

Army Nurse Corps

Scottish Canadian

Wren

Cyprian

Army Nurse

Gordon Highlander

Red Cross Nurse

Dog Patrol

We can find a similar disillusionment in American literature of the same period. Some of the poets since the Second World War, like Thomas Hardy a half century before, would prefer it to be otherwise and so call for a soul-searching on the part of present-day society, lest all be lost. Thus George Barker (p. 1162) pleads for a release from fear and sordidness. More violent and much more cynical, though equally willing to share responsibility for rebuilding the world, is the South African Roy Campbell (1901-1957). A tendency to escape into the world of Yeats and Lawrence is unmistakable in the rhapsodic poetry of Dylan Thomas. After Thomas's untimely death in 1953, critical interest in his poetry reached great proportions. It is difficult but thoroughly traditional in theme, if not in treatment. In addition to those poets of prewar reputation, like Edwin Muir (1887-   ), *Collected Poems, 1921-1951* (1952) and Dame Edith Sitwell (1887-   ), *Gardeners and Astronomers* (1953), who continue to produce good poetry, some of the young poets who bear watching are Andrew Young, Lawrence Durrell, Laurie Lee, and Robert Gittings.

The literature of England at mid-century is uncertain, even aimless. The loss of traditional values, of the social faith which animated many of the poets and novelists of the 1930's, the loss even of the conviction that the world of modern civilization is a Waste Land—all have contributed to a literary climate that is unclear and unsure. The momentous shadow of the atomic age, the titanic struggle between Russia and the United States, the upheaval of nationalities throughout the world, the very scope and power of objective events seem to have robbed British writers of their traditional vision.

The carefully integrated thought of the Middle Ages and the carelessly confident spirit of the Renaissance are alike impossible for the twentieth

---

*From *Poems* by Stephen Spender, copyright, 1934, by The Modern Library, Inc., and reprinted by permission of Random House, Inc., and Faber and Faber, Ltd.

The literature at mid-century

century to accept, let alone attain, for the world today does not have the unity of the one or the faith of the other. Nor is it desirable that we should merely emulate. Thus far it can hardly be said that we have succeeded in working out our salvation, as we must, but we still have nearly a half century left. The eighteenth-century deist might perhaps understand our achievements in material accomplishments and thought, but he would insist that in other ways of living we are still feeling out our path most uncertainly. The Middle Ages felt assured that its morality was the only one; but ever since that time mankind has been less and less sure as to what constitutes the true morality. On the whole, the twentieth century realizes that the clock cannot be turned back; but it still does not know what time it really is.

Yet contemporary literature is unafraid, and in its experimentation it is bold and venturesome. The enormous output of our age—fostered by the creative urges of individual authors and by the demands of widely disseminated mass media—takes all human experience as legitimate grist for its mill; and where expression is uninhibited, as it is generally among the English-speaking peoples, it is capable of great power and great imaginative flights. If it is arrogant to cover some of its weaknesses, then we must make the most of it. Besides, it is always well to give the Englishman credit for the sureness of his literary instincts. In all this generation of those who pry into matters that were once not supposed to be discussed at all, in all this playing and discarding of new cards, the English have held on steadfastly to their innate sense of artistic values. Even when they experiment, they seldom go to the extremes reached by some of their American contemporaries. The shining exception to this statement would probably be James Joyce, who is at the very least an internationalist; but if we ignore *Finnegans Wake* and the more esoteric sections of *Ulysses,* even he can be seen to have roots in the matchless English literary soil.

The British writers today may often lack the raw physical power of contemporary American authors; sometimes they are comparatively spinsterlike in their ordered little island. But one always gets the sense, in reading an important British writer, of correctness and ease of style, of plasticity and adaptability, of artistic finish and an appropriateness to artistic ends, of richness of vocabulary, vividness and mastery of phrase, strength and sinew and clarity of sentence structure, and above all control of the medium, whether it is natural or eccentric prose or verse. The Englishman knows that his language is his own and that he can always make it do his bidding. Where there is such a multiplicity of writers and writing as there is in the middle of the twentieth century, there will of course be much that is crude, flashy, tasteless, and ineffective. But English literature at its best is still, in this latter half of the twentieth century, the magnificent fruit of a plant nurtured with loving care for twelve hundred years and more.

William Butler Yeats
1865-1939

William Butler Yeats was born near Dublin of Anglo-Irish stock. His father was a distinguished portrait-painter and a member of the Royal Hibernian Academy. After attending schools in Hammersmith, London, and in Dublin, Yeats studied painting but soon gave up the brush for the pen. His first poems and articles went to the *Dublin University Review* and other Irish periodicals. In 1888, he went to London and was welcomed into the Rhymers' Club. The next year he published his first volume of verse, *The Wanderings of Oisin and Other Poems*. His interest in both the ancient culture and the contemporary political and social problems of his native country was always intense and expressed itself in many ways. He helped to organize Irish literary societies in London and in Dublin and, in collaboration with George Moore and others, established the Irish Literary Theater, which became in 1904 the famous Abbey Theater, home of the Irish Players.

In 1897, he published *The Secret Rose,* a group of Irish legends and tales in prose. Some of the best of his lyrics appeared in *Poems* (1895) and *The Wind among the Reeds* (1899). His greatest eminence is probably as a lyric poet, but his most notable contributions to the Irish literary movement are in the field of the drama. His plays are Gaelic in content and spirit and are usually in verse. His first one, *The Countess Kathleen,* was a romantic drama written in 1892; but his best-known one is a one-act play-poem entitled *The Land of Heart's Desire* (1894). Then, breaking with his early attachment to the symbolist movement and experimenting continuously, Yeats wrote numerous volumes of poetry and plays, among which were *The Green Helmet and Other Poems* (1910), *Poems Written in Discouragement* (1913), *Responsibilities: Poems and a Play* (1914), and *Reveries over Childhood and Youth* (1915). It was the 1920's, however, that saw Yeats's most mature blossoming, both in writing and in public affairs. In 1922 he was elected a senator in the new Irish Free State, and in 1923 he was awarded the Nobel Prize in literature. The pinnacle of his poetic achievement came in the collection *The Tower* (1928). In later years, he made a restless and almost frantic attempt to construct a philosophic justification for his beliefs in the reality of dreams and the life of the spirit. *A Vision,* published in 1925 as a private edition and revised in 1937, is a curious assortment of thoughts reflecting his interests in theosophy, magic, Swedenborgianism, and astrology. He had already given expression to some of these philosophic reflections in a series of essays called *Per Amica Silentia Lunae* (1918), in which he categorizes humanity under various phases of the moon in a polarity of subjective and objective types. Yeats died January 28, 1939, and was buried at Roquebrune, but his body was later brought back to Drumcliff Churchyard in Sligo.

Yeats represents the literary side of the new Irish national movement. He introduced into the stream of modern English literature a new romantic current, but he owed some of his inspiration to the Pre-Raphaelites, who influenced his father's painting, and some also to Shelley and to Maeterlinck. He owed even more to the French symbolists and to Blake, the mystic (see p. 111); but his work is, nevertheless, essentially his own. It has an elusive, elfin charm and much of the Celtic melancholy. It suggests rather than expresses sorrow, and has something of the plaintive quality of a far-off dirge. It is at once fragile, poignant, and simple. And whether Yeats wrote drama or poetry, his mood was thoroughly lyrical.

The Stolen Child

Where dips the rocky highland
Of Sleuth Wood in the lake,
There lies a leafy island
Where flapping herons wake
The drowsy water rats; 5
There we've hid our faery vats,
Full of berries,
And of reddest stolen cherries.
Come away, O human child!
To the waters and the wild 10
With a faery, hand in hand,
For the world's more full of weeping than
 you can understand.

Where the wave of moonlight glosses
The dim gray sands with light,
Far off by furthest Rosses 15
We foot it all the night,
Weaving olden dances,
Mingling hands and mingling glances
Till the moon has taken flight;
To and fro we leap 20
And chase the frothy bubbles,
While the world is full of troubles
And is anxious in its sleep.
Come away, O human child!
To the waters and the wild 25
With a faery, hand in hand,
For the world's more full of weeping than
 you can understand.

Where the wandering water gushes
From the hills above Glen-Car,
In pools among the rushes 30
That scarce could bathe a star,
We seek for slumbering trout
And whispering in their ears
Give them unquiet dreams;
Leaning softly out 35
From ferns that drop their tears
Over the young streams.
Come away, O human child!
To the waters and the wild
With a faery, hand in hand, 40
For the world's more full of weeping than
 you can understand.

Away with us he's going,
The solemn-eyed;
He'll hear no more the lowing
Of the calves on the warm hillside 45
Or the kettle on the hob
Sing peace into his breast,
Or see the brown mice bob
Round and round the oatmeal-chest.
For he comes, the human child, 50
To the waters and the wild
With a faery, hand in hand,
From a world more full of weeping than he
 can understand. (1889)

The White Birds

The white bird is a symbol of the soul.

I would that we were, my belovéd, white birds
 on the foam of the sea!
We tire of the flame of the meteor, before it
 can fade and flee;
And the flame of the blue star of twilight,
 hung low on the rim of the sky,
Has awaked in our hearts, my belovéd, a sadness that may not die.

A weariness comes from those dreamers, dew
 dabbled, the lily and rose; 5
Ah, dream not of them, my belovéd, the flame
 of the meteor that goes,
Or the flame of the blue star that lingers hung
 low in the fall of the dew:
For I would we were changed to white birds
 on the wandering foam: I and you!

I am haunted by numberless islands, and
 many a Danaän shore,
Where Time would surely forget us, and Sorrow come near us no more; 10
Soon far from the rose and the lily, and fret
 of the flames would we be,
Were we only white birds, my belovéd,
 buoyed out on the foam of the sea!
 (1892)

The poems of William Butler Yeats are reprinted from his *Collected Poems*, 1933, by permission of The Macmillan Company, New York, publishers, and Mrs. W. B. Yeats.
2. **Sleuth . . . lake.** The lake of Glen-Car, surrounded by wooded hills, is in the county of Sligo, in northwestern Ireland.
15. **Rosses**, stone headlands along the coast of Sligo. The vicinity was regarded as a favorite haunt of fairies.

9. **Danaän shore**, the land of eternal happiness, the fairy world of Irish tradition, inhabited by the ancient race of the Tuatha Dé Danaän.

The Rose of the World

The rose is here regarded as the traditional symbol of love. To Yeats the beauty of a woman sums up all other beauties in the world.

Who dreamed that beauty passes like a dream?
For these red lips, with all their mournful pride,
Mournful that no new wonder may betide,
Troy passed away in one high funeral gleam,
And Usna's children died.   5

We and the laboring world are passing by;
Amid men's souls, that waver and give place,
Like the pale waters in their wintry race,
Under the passing stars, foam of the sky,
Lives on this lonely face.   10

Bow down, archangels, in your dim abode.
Before you were, or any hearts to beat,
Weary and kind, one lingered by His seat;
He made the world to be a grassy road
Before her wandering feet.   (1893)

The Lake Isle of Innisfree

Innisfree is an island in Lough Gill, a lake in the county of Sligo, Ireland.

I will arise and go now, and go to Innisfree,
And a small cabin build there, of clay and wattles made;
Nine bean rows will I have there, a hive for the honey bee,
And live alone in the bee-loud glade.

And I shall have some peace there, for peace comes dropping slow,   5
Dropping from the veils of the morning to where the cricket sings;
There midnight's all a glimmer, and noon a purple glow,
And evening full of the linnet's wings.

I will arise and go now, for always night and day
I hear lake water lapping with low sounds by the shore;   10
While I stand on the roadway, or on the pavements gray,
I hear it in the deep heart's core.   (1893)

When You Are Old

When you are old and gray and full of sleep,
And nodding by the fire, take down this book,
And slowly read, and dream of the soft look
Your eyes had once, and of their shadows deep;

How many loved your moments of glad grace,   5
And loved your beauty with love false or true;
But one man loved the pilgrim soul in you,
And loved the sorrows of your changing face.

And bending down beside the glowing bars
Murmur, a little sadly, how love fled   10
And paced upon the mountains overhead
And hid his face amid a crowd of stars.   (1893)

Song

(from The Land of Heart's Desire)

The wind blows out of the gates of the day,
  The wind blows over the lonely of heart,
And the lonely of heart is withered away
  While the faeries dance in a place apart,
Shaking their milk-white feet in a ring,   5
  Tossing their milk-white arms in the air;
For they hear the wind laugh and murmur and sing
  Of a land where even the old are fair,
And even the wise are merry of tongue;
  But I heard a reed of Coolaney say,   10
"When the wind has laughed and murmured and sung,
  The lonely of heart is withered away."
          (1894)

The Rose of the World. 4. **Troy . . . gleam.** It was the beauty of Helen that occasioned the Trojan War and the burning of Troy, as related in Homer's *Iliad*. 5. **Usna's . . . died.** Naoise, a son of Usna, was in love with Deirdre, the heroine of Irish legends. King Conchobar of Ulster desired her for his wife, and Naoise and his two brothers carried her off to Scotland. Lured back by Conchobar, the brothers were treacherously slain, and Deirdre killed herself in sorrow. 14. **He**, God.
  The Lake Isle of Innisfree. 2. **wattles**, interwoven sticks and twigs. 3. **Nine bean rows.** The Irish shared the Pre-Raphaelite fondness for definite numbers. Cf. Rossetti's *Blessed Damozel*, l. 6, p. 784.

The Host of the Air

The "Host of the Air" is an especially malignant branch of the fairy race. Yeats says that the "poem is founded on an old Gaelic ballad that was sung and translated for me by a woman at Ballisodare, in County Sligo."

O'Driscoll drove with a song
The wild duck and the drake
From the tall and the tufted reeds
Of the drear Hart Lake.

And he saw how the reeds grew dark   5
At the coming of night tide,
And dreamed of the long dim hair
Of Bridget his bride.

He heard while he sang and dreamed
A piper piping away,   10
And never was piping so sad,
And never was piping so gay.

And he saw young men and young girls
Who danced on a level place
And Bridget his bride among them,   15
With a sad and a gay face.

The dancers crowded about him,
And many a sweet thing said,
And a young man brought him red wine
And a young girl white bread.   20

But Bridget drew him by the sleeve,
Away from the merry bands,
To old men playing at cards
With a twinkling of ancient hands.

The bread and the wine had a doom,   25
For these were the host of the air;
He sat and played in a dream
Of her long dim hair.

He played with the merry old men
And thought not of evil chance,   30
Until one bore Bridget his bride
Away from the merry dance.

He bore her away in his arms,
The handsomest young man there,
And his neck and his breast and his arms   35
Were drowned in her long dim hair.

O'Driscoll scattered the cards
And out of his dream awoke:
Old men and young men and young girls
Were gone like a drifting smoke;   40

But he heard high up in the air
A piper piping away,
And never was piping so sad,
And never was piping so gay.   (1899)

Into the Twilight

Out-worn heart, in a time out-worn,
Come clear of the nets of wrong and right;
Laugh, heart, again in the gray twilight,
Sigh, heart, again in the dew of the morn.

Your mother Eire is always young,   5
Dew ever shining and twilight gray;
Though hopes fall from you and love decay,
Burning in fires of a slanderous tongue.

Come, heart, where hill is heaped upon hill;
For there the mystical brotherhood   10
Of sun and moon and hollow and wood
And river and stream work out their will;

And God stands winding His lonely horn,
And time and the world are ever in flight;
And love is less kind than the gray twilight,   15
And hope is less dear than the dew of the morn.   (1899)

He Remembers Forgotten Beauty

When my arms wrap you round I press
My heart upon the loveliness
That has long faded from the world;
The jeweled crowns that kings have hurled
In shadowy pools, when armies fled;   5
The love tales wrought with silken thread
By dreaming ladies upon cloth
That has made fat the murderous moth;

The Host of the Air. 4. **Hart Lake,** a dreary pond bordered by trees, five miles south of Sligo. 25. **doom,** a curse.

Into the Twilight. 5. **Eire,** Ireland.

The roses that of old time were
Woven by ladies in their hair;   10
The dew-cold lilies ladies bore
Through many a sacred corridor
Where such gray clouds of incense rose
That only the gods' eyes did not close:
For that pale breast and lingering hand   15
Come from a more dream-heavy land,
A more dream-heavy hour than this;
And when you sigh from kiss to kiss
I hear white Beauty sighing, too,
For hours when all must fade like dew;   20
But flame on flame, deep under deep,
Throne over throne, where in half sleep
Their swords upon their iron knees
Brood her high lonely mysteries.   (1899)

The Song of Wandering Aengus

    Aengus is the Celtic god of love; his kisses changed to birds that constantly flew about his head.

I went out to the hazel wood,
Because a fire was in my head,
And cut and peeled a hazel wand,
And hooked a berry to a thread;
And when white moths were on the wing,   5
And moth-like stars were flickering out,
I dropped the berry in a stream
And caught a little silver trout.

When I had laid it on the floor,
I went to blow the fire a-flame,   10
But something rustled on the floor,
And some one called me by my name:
It had become a glimmering girl
With apple blossom in her hair
Who called me by my name and ran   15
And faded through the brightening air.

Though I am old with wandering
Through hollow lands and hilly lands,
I will find out where she has gone,
And kiss her lips and take her hands;   20
And walk among long dappled grass,

19. **Beauty sighing.** Cf. *The White Birds*, p. 1047. 21. **flame on flame, etc.** Everywhere, under all conditions, the high mysteries of Beauty brood in a half-sleep with their swords idle.

And pluck till time and times are done
The silver apples of the moon,
The golden apples of the sun.   (1899)

The Fiddler of Dooney

When I play on my fiddle in Dooney,
Folk dance like a wave of the sea;
My cousin is priest in Kilvarnet,
My brother in Moharabuiee.

I passed my brother and cousin: 5
They read in their books of prayer;
I read in my book of songs
I bought at the Sligo fair.

When we come at the end of time,
To Peter sitting in state,   10
He will smile on the three old spirits,
But call me first through the gate;

For the good are always the merry,
Save by an evil chance,
And the merry love the fiddle   15
And the merry love to dance:

And when the folk there spy me,
They will all come up to me,
With "Here is the fiddler of Dooney!"
And dance like a wave of the sea.   (1899)

An Irish Airman Foresees His Death

I know that I shall meet my fate
Somewhere among the clouds above;
Those that I fight I do not hate,
Those that I guard I do not love;
My country is Kiltartan Cross,   5
My countrymen Kiltartan's poor,
No likely end could bring them loss
Or leave them happier than before.
Nor law, nor duty bade me fight,
Nor public men, nor cheering crowds,   10
A lonely impulse of delight
Drove to this tumult in the clouds;

1. **Dooney.** Dooney and the other places named are hamlets on the west coast of Ireland. Sligo (l. 8) was Yeats's boyhood home. 2. **dance . . . sea.** Cf. Florizel's speech to Perdita in Shakespeare's *Winter's Tale*, IV, iv, 140-141—
    When you do dance, I wish you
  A wave o' the sea.

I balanced all, brought all to mind,
The years to come seemed waste of breath,
A waste of breath the years behind   15
In balance with this life, this death.   (1919)

The Second Coming

Various interpretations have been put upon the event designated as the second coming of Christ. Although the expression is not found in Scripture, synonyms of the event and allusions to it have been identified. One definition in the *Dictionary of the Bible* calls it "an Advent at the end of the age to judge the world, to destroy evil, to reward the saints, and to establish the Kingdom of Glory." Yeats here is prophesying disaster for our modern world; but he believes that even this disaster has its place in a divine pattern.

Turning and turning in the widening gyre
The falcon cannot hear the falconer;
Things fall apart: the center cannot hold;
Mere anarchy is loosed upon the world,
The blood-dimmed tide is loosed, and everywhere   5
The ceremony of innocence is drowned;
The best lack all conviction, while the worst
Are full of passionate intensity.

Surely some revelation is at hand;
Surely the Second Coming is at hand.   10
The Second Coming! Hardly are those words out
When a vast image out of *Spiritus Mundi*
Troubles my sight: somewhere in sands of the desert
A shape with lion body and the head of a man,
A gaze blank and pitiless as the sun,   15
Is moving its slow thighs, while all about it
Reel shadows of the indignant desert birds.
The darkness drops again; but now I know
That twenty centuries of stony sleep
Were vexed to nightmare by a rocking cradle,
And what rough beast, its hour come round at last,   21
Slouches towards Bethlehem to be born?
(1921)

12. *Spiritus Mundi*, the soul of the world, the organizing principle of the physical universe. Yeats uses the phrase also to mean the Great Memory.

Leda and the Swan

The union of mortals and immortals always had a strong symbolic value for Yeats. In classical mythology Leda, wife of the Spartan king Tyndareus, was beloved by Zeus, who visited her in the form of a swan. From their mating was born the beautiful Helen of Troy. The abduction of Helen from her husband, Menelaus, by Paris, who fled with her to Troy, was the cause of the legendary Trojan War. (According to another version Leda brought forth two eggs; from one sprang Helen and Pollux, and from the other Clytemnestra and Castor.) The poem appeared first in *A Vision* (1925) —an exposition of Yeats's symbolical interpretation of history and civilization—as the opening section of Book V, entitled "Dove or Swan." The conception of Helen may be regarded in Yeats's symbolism as the beginning of classical civilization, in much the same way as the incident of Mary and her dove may be said to mark the beginning of the Christian era.

A sudden blow: the great wings beating still
Above the staggering girl, her thighs caressed
By the dark webs, her nape caught in his bill,
He holds her helpless breast upon his breast.

How can those terrified vague fingers push   5
The feathered glory from her loosening thighs?
And how can body, laid in that white rush,
But feel the strange heart beating where it lies?

A shudder in the loins engenders there   9
The broken wall, the burning roof and tower
And Agamemnon dead.
                    Being so caught up,
So mastered by the brute blood of the air,
Did she put on his knowledge with his power
Before the indifferent beak could let her drop?
(1925)

10-11. **broken wall . . . dead**, well-known incidents in the Grecian attack upon Troy in the Trojan War. Agamemnon was the brother of Menelaus and the commander-in-chief of the allied Greek forces. While he was absent from home, his wife, Clytemnestra, another daughter of Leda and Zeus, fell in love with Aegisthus. Upon his return from Troy, Agamemnon was killed either by his wife or (according to Homer) by Aegisthus,

Sailing to Byzantium

Grown old and weary in his own country, an old man seeks repose for his soul in the more intellectual and ideal environment symbolized by Byzantium. In ancient geography Byzantium was a Greek city founded in the seventh century B.C. In 330 A.D. Constantine the Great made it the capital of the Roman Empire and changed the name to Constantinople. From 395 A.D. it was the famous capital of the Byzantine, or Eastern, Empire and was noted, Yeats says, for "an architecture that suggests the Sacred City in the Apocalypse of St. John." The present name of the city is Istanbul. In the poem the city is presented symbolically as the ideal journey's end for the old, since it was the one place in all the world in which the forces of body, mind, and spirit existed in proper balance. In *A Vision* Yeats expressed the belief that "in early Byzantium, maybe never before nor since in recorded history, religious, aesthetic, and practical life were one." The poem may be read as merely symbolical of the change from life to death.

That is no country for old men. The young
In one another's arms, birds in the trees
(Those dying generations) at their song,
The salmon-falls, the mackerel-crowded seas,
Fish, flesh, or fowl, commend all summer
  long   5
Whatever is begotten, born, and dies.
Caught in that sensual music, all neglect
Monuments of unaging intellect.

An aged man is but a paltry thing,
A tattered coat upon a stick, unless   10
Soul clap its hands and sing, and louder sing
For every tatter in its mortal dress;
Nor is there singing school but studying
Monuments of its own magnificence;
And therefore I have sailed the seas and come
To the holy city of Byzantium.   16

O sages, standing in God's holy fire
As in the gold mosaic of a wall,
Come from the holy fire, perne in a gyre,
And be the singing-masters of my soul.   20
Consume my heart away—sick with desire
And fastened to a dying animal
It knows not what it is—and gather me
Into the artifice of eternity.

Once out of nature I shall never take   25
My bodily form from any natural thing,
But such a form as Grecian goldsmiths make
Of hammered gold and gold enamelling
To keep a drowsy emperor awake;
Or set upon a golden bough to sing   30
To lords and ladies of Byzantium
Of what is past, or passing, or to come.

(1928)

4. **salmon-falls . . . seas,** a reference to the spawning period of salmon, which are noted for jumping up waterfalls at that time, and of mackerel, which crowd up streams.

19. **perne in a gyre,** spool in a circular or spiral motion. 30. **golden bough.** "I have read somewhere that in the Emperor's palace at Byzantium was a tree made of gold and silver, and artificial birds that sang."—Yeats.

Among School Children

Yeats was much interested in the educational system in Ireland. He wrote to a friend regarding a tour of inspection of the primary schools that he went "to study a very remarkable convent school." In this poem, he ponders the relation of the child to the adult, as represented by his own experience, and raises in his own mind certain questions —are the love and sacrifice necessary to raise children, however unrewarded, worth it all? Can the images which people hold in reverence be realized in actual life? The general conclusion reached is that, if the mind and body can be brought into harmony, the real and the ideal become the same thing—there can be no difference between the image and the actuality.

I walk through the long schoolroom
  questioning,
A kind old nun in a white hood replies;
The children learn to cipher and to sing,
To study reading-books and history,
To cut and sew, be neat in everything   5
In the best modern way—the children's
  eyes

In momentary wonder stare upon
A sixty year old smiling public man.

I dream of a Ledaean body, bent
Above a sinking fire, a tale that she   10
Told of a harsh reproof, or trivial event
That changed some childish day to tragedy—
Told, and it seemed that our two natures blent
Into a sphere from youthful sympathy,
Or else, to alter Plato's parable,   15
Into the yolk and white of the one shell.

And thinking of that fit of grief or rage
I look upon one child or t'other there
And wonder if she stood so at that age—
For even daughters of the swan can share   20
Something of every paddler's heritage—
And had that color upon cheek or hair;
And thereupon my heart is driven wild:
She stands before me as a living child.

Her present image floats into the mind—   25
Did quattrocento finger fashion it
Hollow of cheek as though it drank the wind
And took a mess of shadows for its meat?
And I though never of Ledaean kind
Had pretty plumage once—enough of that,   30
Better to smile on all that smile, and show
There is a comfortable kind of old scarecrow.

What youthful mother, a shape upon her lap
Honey of generation had betrayed,
And that must sleep, shriek, struggle to escape
As recollection or the drug decide,   35

Would think her son, did she but see that shape
With sixty or more winters on its head,
A compensation for the pang of his birth,
Or the uncertainty of his setting forth?   40

Plato thought nature but a spume that plays
Upon a ghostly paradigm of things;
Solider Aristotle played the taws
Upon the bottom of a king of kings;
World-famous golden-thighed Pythagoras   45
Fingered upon a fiddle stick or strings
What a star sang and careless Muses heard:
Old clothes upon old sticks to scare a bird.

Both nuns and mothers worship images,
But those the candles light are not as those   50
That animate a mother's reveries,
But keep a marble or a bronze repose.
And yet they too break hearts—O Presences
That passion, piety or affection knows,
And that all heavenly glory symbolize—   55
O self-born mockers of man's enterprise;

Labor is blossoming or dancing where
The body is not bruised to pleasure soul,
Nor beauty born out of its own despair,
Nor blear-eyed wisdom out of midnight oil.   60
O chestnut tree, great rooted blossomer,
Are you the leaf, the blossom or the bole?
O body swayed to music, O brightening glance,
How can we know the dancer from the dance?

(1928)

9. **Ledaean**, like Leda, whose graceful figure was a subject of medieval art. See *Leda and the Swan*, p. 1030. The poet is thinking of his beloved, Maud Gonne. 15. **Plato's parable.** Plato was a famous Greek philosopher of the fourth century B.C. This is probably a reference to the satirical discourse on the nature of man as related by Plato in the *Symposium*, 189 ff. As there presented, the sexes were three—male, female, and androgynous (union of the two). The last was a spherical creature, who because of an attack upon the gods was "cut in two as you might divide an egg with a hair." Plato frequently refers to the blending of mutually sympathetic natures. Such a union is symbolized by Yeats in the yolk and the white of an egg. 20. **daughters of the swan,** symbolical for children of high birth. 21. **paddler,** figurative for child of low birth. 26. **quattrocento,** of the supreme fifteenth-century period of Italian art.

41. **spume,** froth or foam. 42. **ghostly paradigm,** spiritual model or pattern. 43. **Aristotle,** the most celebrated and influential of the Greek philosophers (384-322 B.C.). He is more objective and realistic than the dreamer Plato. Whereas Plato is spiritual, Aristotle is pragmatical and earthy. **played the taws,** plied the whip. Aristotle was practical enough as a teacher of Alexander the Great (the King of Kings, 356-322 B.C.) to give the young prince the flogging that he needed. 45. **Pythagoras,** famous Greek philosopher and mathematician of the sixth century B.C., said to have had a golden thigh. He is credited with the invention of the lyre. He is the example of the mystic, with his creation of the theory concerning the music of the spheres. All of these philosophies—of Plato, of Aristotle, and of Pythagoras—are in contrast to the solid reality of birth and death, "old clothes upon old sticks to scare a bird." Cf. *Sailing to Byzantium*, ll. 9-10. 57. **Labor,** child-birth. 62. **bole,** tree trunk.

Sir Winston Churchill

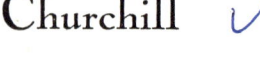

1874-

The inspired leader of Britain during the gloomy days of the Second World War, Winston Churchill has spent his entire life in military and public service. His mother was an American. He was educated first at the famous public school of Harrow and then at the military academy at Sandhurst, the "West Point" of Britain. He early assumed some of the characteristics of a military free-lance, for he served in the Spanish army and saw service against the Cuban insurrectionists in 1895, three years before the outbreak of the Spanish-American War. Later he became a correspondent to the *London Morning Post* in South Africa; and when the Boer War broke out in 1899, he took an active part in the fighting, and was captured but managed to escape. He entered Parliament as a member of the House of Commons in 1906. His activities, however, were never confined for long to any one field of service. He took part in the First World War as a matter of course, acting as First Lord of the Admiralty (until 1915) and as an officer of the famous Scots Fusiliers. But in public life he had already served as president of the Board of Trade (1908-1910), as Home Secretary (1910-1911), as Secretary of State for War and Air (1918-1921), as Secretary of State for the Colonies (1921-1922), and as Chancellor of the Exchequer (1924-1929). In an honorary capacity he had been named Lord Rector of Aberdeen University (1914-1918), of Edinburgh University (1929-1932), and Chancellor of Bristol University (1930).

With the outbreak of the Second World War, Churchill, who had always advocated stern measures against the rising powers of the totalitarian states, was temporarily shelved; but with the coincidence of the defeats in Norway and the explosion of German might on the Western Front in May, 1940, he was elevated to the premiership as the man best suited to the position; and he justified admirably the confidence which his nation had placed in him. He never lost his conservative imperialism, however; and with the winning of victory on the Continent in 1945, the achievement toward which Britain's force had been mainly directed, Churchill's usefulness to the nation appeared ended. He was turned out of office by a smashing victory for the Labour Party, headed by Clement Attlee, in July, 1945. With the return of the Conservatives to power in 1951, Churchill once again became Prime Minister and held this post until 1955, when he relinquished the prime ministership to Anthony Eden.

Churchill began his writings as a journalist in the South African War, and much of his literary work is in the field of political polemics. He has also written a valuable biography of his ancestor, the eighteenth-century Duke of Marlborough (1933-1938), and a thorough study of the First World War and contemporary European affairs in *The World Crisis* in five volumes (1923-1929). In 1948 he published *The Gathering Storm,* the first of the six volumes of his monumental memoirs, *The Second World War,* completed in 1953. He received the 1953 Nobel Prize for literature. In 1956 there appeared the first two volumes of his projected four-volume *A History of the English-Speaking Peoples.* As an orator and a spokesman of embattled Britain, however, he achieved his greatest fame—most deservedly, for he is a man of great force of personality, with a remarkable gift of phrase, and an astonishingly tough, tenacious spirit which seems to thrive under pressure. His many speeches in the House of Commons from 1938 to 1945 are masterly; not only are they able statements of Churchill's policies and official opinions, but they are also excellent examples of the immortal quality of the Anglo-Saxon tradition, which began in English literature with *Beowulf* and has never disappeared.

Prime Minister

On May 10, 1940, Germany invaded Holland and Belgium. Thereupon, at the appeal of King Leopold of Belgium, the British Army moved north into Belgium. On the same day,

Neville Chamberlain resigned the office of Prime Minister, and King George VI invited Winston Churchill to form a new administration. The following address was delivered in the House of Commons on May 13.

On Friday evening last I received His Majesty's Commission to form a new Administration. It was the evident wish and will of Parliament and the nation that this should be conceived on the broadest possible basis and that it should include all Parties, both those who supported the late Government and also the Parties of the Opposition. I have completed the most important part of this task. A War Cabinet has been formed of five Members, representing, with the Opposition Liberals, the unity of the nation. The three Party Leaders have agreed to serve, either in the War Cabinet or in high executive office. The three Fighting Services have been filled. It was necessary that this should be done in one single day, on account of the extreme urgency and rigor of events. A number of other key positions were filled yesterday, and I am submitting a further list to His Majesty tonight. I hope to complete the appointment of the principal Ministers during tomorrow. The appointment of the other Ministers usually takes a little longer, but I trust that, when Parliament meets again, this part of my task will be completed, and that the Administration will be complete in all respects.

I considered it in the public interest to suggest that the House should be summoned to meet today. Mr. Speaker agreed, and took the necessary steps, in accordance with the powers conferred upon him by the Resolution of the House. At the end of the proceedings today, the Adjournment of the House will be proposed until Tuesday, 21st May, with, of course, provision for earlier meeting if need be. The business to be considered during that week will be notified to Members at the earliest opportunity. I now invite the House, by the Resolution which stands in my name, to record its approval of the steps taken and to declare its confidence in the new Government.

From *Blood, Sweat, and Tears*, published by G. P. Putnam's Sons, 1941.

To form an Administration of this scale and complexity is a serious undertaking in itself, but it must be remembered that we are in the preliminary stage of one of the greatest battles in history, that we are in action at many points in Norway and in Holland, that we have to be prepared in the Mediterranean, that the air battle is continuous, and that many preparations have to be made here at home. In this crisis I hope I may be pardoned if I do not address the House at any length today. I hope that any of my friends and colleagues, or former colleagues, who are affected by the political reconstruction, will make all allowance for any lack of ceremony with which it has been necessary to act. I would say to the House, as I said to those who have joined this Government: "I have nothing to offer but blood, toil, tears, and sweat."

We have before us an ordeal of the most grievous kind. We have before us many, many long months of struggle and of suffering. You ask, What is our policy? I will say: "It is to wage war, by sea, land and air, with all our might and with all the strength that God can give us: to wage war against a monstrous tyranny, never surpassed in the dark, lamentable catalogue of human crime. That is our policy." You ask, What is our aim? I can answer in one word: Victory—victory at all costs, victory in spite of all terror, victory however long and hard the road may be; for without victory there is no survival. Let that be realized; no survival for the British Empire; no survival for all that the British Empire has stood for; no survival for the urge and impulse of the ages, that mankind will move forward towards its goal. But I take up my task with buoyancy and hope. I feel sure that our cause will not be suffered to fail among men. At this time I feel entitled to claim the aid of all, and I say, "Come, then, let us go forward together with our united strength." (1940)

Dunkirk

In May, 1940, the Germans forced the surrender of the Dutch Army and the Belgian Army, which left the British and the French forces in France and Belgium in a very precarious situation. After temporarily defending Dunkirk, on the coast of France, the British began on May 29 the most famous retreat in history. By June 1 four-fifths of the British Expeditionary Force on the Continent had been successfully evacuated; by June 4 the last Allied troops had left Dunkirk. The following speech was delivered by Mr. Churchill in the House of Commons on June 4.

FROM THE moment that the French defenses at Sedan and on the Meuse were broken at the end of the second week of May, only a rapid retreat to Amiens and the south could have saved the British and French Armies who had entered Belgium at the appeal of the Belgian King; but this strategic fact was not immediately realized. The French High Command hoped they would be able to close the gap, and the Armies of the north were under their orders. Moreover, a retirement of this kind would have involved almost certainly the destruction of the fine Belgian Army of over 20 divisions and the abandonment of the whole of Belgium. Therefore, when the force and scope of the German penetration were realized and when a new French Generalissimo, General Weygand, assumed command in place of General Gamelin, an effort was made by the French and British Armies in Belgium to keep on holding the right hand of the Belgians and to give their own right hand to a newly created French Army which was to have advanced across the Somme in great strength to grasp it.

However, the German eruption swept like a sharp scythe around the right and rear of the Armies of the north. Eight or nine armored divisions, each of about four hundred armored vehicles of different kinds, but carefully assorted to be complementary and divisible into small self-contained units, cut off all communications between us and the main French Armies. It severed our own communications for food and ammunition, which ran first to Amiens and afterwards through Abbeville, and it shore its way up the coast to Boulogne and Calais, and almost to Dunkirk. Behind this armored and mechanized onslaught came a number of German divisions in lorries, and behind them again there plodded comparatively slowly the dull brute mass of the ordinary German Army and German people, always so ready to be led to the trampling down in other lands of liberties and comforts which they have never known in their own.

I have said this armored scythe-stroke almost reached Dunkirk—almost but not quite. Boulogne and Calais were the scenes of desperate fighting. The Guards defended Boulogne for a while and were then withdrawn by orders from this country. The Rifle Brigade, the 60th Rifles, and the Queen Victoria's Rifles, with a battalion of British tanks and 1,000 Frenchmen, in all about four thousand strong, defended Calais to the last. The British Brigadier was given an hour to surrender. He spurned the offer, and four days of intense street fighting passed before silence reigned over Calais, which marked the end of a memorable resistance. Only 30 unwounded survivors were brought off by the Navy, and we do not know the fate of their comrades. Their sacrifice, however, was not in vain. At least two armored divisions, which otherwise would have been turned against the British Expeditionary Force, had to be sent to overcome them. They have added another page to the glories of the light divisions, and the time gained enabled the Graveline water

---

From *Blood, Sweat, and Tears*, published by G. P. Putnam's Sons, 1941.
2. **Sedan,** a city on the Meuse River in northeastern France, near the Belgian border. 4. **Amiens,** an important city on the Somme River, in northern France.

37. **Abbeville,** a commercial and manufacturing town between Amiens and the coast. **shore,** cut, sheared away. 38. **Boulogne,** a fortified seaport of France, on the English Channel. **Calais,** an important city in France, on the Strait of Dover. 41. **lorries,** low autotrucks for carrying heavy supplies. 71. **Graveline water lines.** Gravelines is a strongly fortified seaport town, 12 miles northeast of Calais; by means of sluices the whole adjacent country may be flooded.

lines to be flooded and to be held by the French troops.

Thus it was that the port of Dunkirk was kept open. When it was found impossible for the Armies of the north to reopen their communications to Amiens with the main French Armies, only one choice remained. It seemed, indeed, forlorn. The Belgian, British and French Armies were almost surrounded. Their sole line of retreat was to a single port and to its neighboring beaches. They were pressed on every side by heavy attacks and far outnumbered in the air.

When, a week ago today, I asked the House to fix this afternoon as the occasion for a statement, I feared it would be my hard lot to announce the greatest military disaster in our long history. I thought—and some good judges agreed with me—that perhaps 20,000 or 30,000 men might be re-embarked. But it certainly seemed that the whole of the French First Army and the whole of the British Expeditionary Force north of the Amiens-Abbeville gap would be broken up in the open field or else would have to capitulate for lack of food and ammunition. These were the hard and heavy tidings for which I called upon the House and the nation to prepare themselves a week ago. The whole root and core and brain of the British Army, on which and around which we were to build, and are to build, the great British Armies in the later years of the war, seemed about to perish upon the field or to be led into an ignominious and starving captivity.

That was the prospect a week ago. But another blow which might well have proved final was yet to fall upon us. The King of the Belgians had called upon us to come to his aid. Had not this Ruler and his Government severed themselves from the Allies, who rescued their country from extinction in the late war, and had they not sought refuge in what has proved to be a fatal neutrality, the French and British Armies might well at the outset have saved not only Belgium but perhaps even Poland. Yet at the last moment, when Belgium was already invaded, King Leopold called upon us to come to his aid, and even at the last moment we came. He and his brave, efficient Army, nearly half a million strong, guarded our left flank and thus kept open our only line of retreat to the sea. Suddenly, without prior consultation, with the least possible notice, without the advice of his Ministers and upon his own personal act, he sent a plenipotentiary to the German Command, surrendered his Army, and exposed our whole flank and means of retreat.

I asked the House a week ago to suspend its judgment because the facts were not clear, but I do not feel that any reason now exists why we should not form our own opinions upon this pitiful episode. The surrender of the Belgian Army compelled the British at the shortest notice to cover a flank to the sea more than 30 miles in length. Otherwise all would have been cut off, and all would have shared the fate to which King Leopold had condemned the finest Army his country had ever formed. So in doing this and in exposing this flank, as anyone who followed the operations on the map will see, contact was lost between the British and two out of the three corps forming the First French Army, who were still farther from the coast than we were, and it seemed impossible that any large number of Allied troops could reach the coast.

The enemy attacked on all sides with great strength and fierceness, and their main power, the power of their far more numerous Air Force, was thrown into the battle or else concentrated upon Dunkirk and the beaches. Pressing in upon the narrow exit, both from the east and from the west, the enemy began to fire with cannon upon the beaches by which alone the shipping could approach or depart. They sowed magnetic mines in the channels and seas; they sent repeated waves of hostile aircraft, sometimes more than a hundred strong in one formation, to cast their bombs upon the single pier that remained, and upon the sand dunes upon which the troops had their eyes for shelter. Their U-boats, one of which was sunk, and their motor launches took their toll of the vast traffic which now began. For four or five days an intense struggle reigned. All their armored divisions—or what was left of them—together with great masses of infantry and artillery, hurled themselves in vain upon the ever-narrowing, ever-contracting appendix within which the British and French Armies fought.

Meanwhile, the Royal Navy, with the willing help of countless merchant seamen, strained every nerve to embark the British and Allied troops; 220 light warships and 650 other vessels were engaged. They had to operate upon the difficult coast, often in adverse weather, under an almost ceaseless hail of bombs and an increasing concentration of artillery fire. Nor were the seas, as I have said, themselves free from mines and torpedoes. It was in conditions such as these that our men carried on, with little or no rest, for days and nights on end, making trip after trip across the dangerous waters, bringing with them always men whom they had rescued. The numbers they have brought back are the measure of their devotion and their courage. The hospital ships, which brought off many thousands of British and French wounded, being so plainly marked were a special target for Nazi bombs; but the men and women on board them never faltered in their duty.

Meanwhile, the Royal Air Force, which had already been intervening in the battle, so far as its range would allow, from home bases, now used part of its main metropolitan fighter strength, and struck at the German bombers and at the fighters which in large numbers protected them. This struggle was protracted and fierce. Suddenly the scene has cleared, the crash and thunder has for the moment—but only for the moment—died away. A miracle of deliverance, achieved by valor, by perseverance, by perfect discipline, by faultless service, by resource, by skill, by unconquerable fidelity, is manifest to us all. The enemy was hurled back by the retreating British and French troops. He was so roughly handled that he did not hurry their departure seriously. The Royal Air Force engaged the main strength of the German Air Force, and inflicted upon them losses of at least four to one; and the Navy, using nearly 1,000 ships of all kinds, carried over 335,000 men, French and British, out of the jaws of death and shame, to their native land and to the tasks which lie immediately ahead. We must be very careful not to assign to this deliverance the attributes of a victory. Wars are not won by evacuations. But there was a victory inside this deliverance, which should be noted. It was gained by the Air Force. Many of our soldiers coming back have not seen the Air Force at work; they saw only the bombers which escaped its protective attack. They underrate its achievements. I have heard much talk of this; that is why I go out of my way to say this. I will tell you about it.

This was a great trial of strength between the British and German Air Forces. Can you conceive a greater objective for the Germans in the air than to make evacuation from these beaches impossible, and to sink all these ships which were displayed, almost to the extent of thousands? Could there have been an objective of greater military importance and significance for the whole purpose of the war than this? They tried hard, and they were beaten back; they were frustrated in their task. We got the Army away; and they have paid fourfold for any losses which they have inflicted. Very large formations of German airplanes—and we know that they are a very brave race—have turned on several occasions from the attack of one-quarter of their number of the Royal Air Force, and have dispersed in different directions. Twelve airplanes have been hunted by two. One airplane was driven into the water and cast away by the mere charge of a British airplane, which had no more ammunition. All of our types—the Hurricane, the Spitfire and the new Defiant—and all our pilots have been vindicated as superior to what they have at present to face.

When we consider how much greater would be our advantage in defending the air above this Island against an overseas attack, I must say that I find in these facts a sure basis upon which practical and reassuring thoughts may rest. I will pay my tribute to these young airmen. The great French Army was very largely, for the time being, cast back and disturbed by the onrush of a few thousands of armored vehicles. May it not also be that the cause of civilization itself will be defended by the skill and devotion of a few thousand airmen? There never has been, I suppose, in all the world, in all the history of war, such an opportunity for youth. The Knights of the Round Table, the Crusaders, all fall back into the past—not only distant but prosaic; these young men, going forth every morn to guard their native land and all that we stand for, holding in their hands these instruments of colossal and shattering power, of whom it may be said that

"Every morn brought forth a noble chance
And every chance brought forth a noble knight,"

deserve our gratitude, as do all of the brave men who, in so many ways and on so many occasions, are ready, and continue ready, to give life and all for their native land.

I return to the Army. In the long series of very fierce battles, now on this front, now on that, fighting on three fronts at once, battles fought by two or three divisions against an equal or somewhat larger number of the enemy, and fought fiercely on some of the old grounds that so many of us knew so well—in these battles our losses in men have exceeded 30,000 killed, wounded and missing. I take occasion to express the sympathy of the House to all who have suffered bereavement or who are still anxious. The President of the Board of Trade is not here today. His son has been killed, and many in the House have felt the pangs of affliction in the sharpest form. But I will say this about the missing: We have had a large number of wounded come home safely to this country, but I would say about the missing that there may be very many reported missing who will come back home, some day, in one way or another. In the confusion of this fight it is inevitable that many have been left in positions where honor required no further resistance from them.

Against this loss of over 30,000 men, we can set a far heavier loss certainly inflicted upon the enemy. But our losses in material are enormous. We have perhaps lost one-third of the men we lost in the opening days of the battle of 21st March, 1918, but we have lost nearly as many guns—nearly one thousand—and all our transport, all the armored vehicles that were with the Army in the north. This loss will impose a further delay on the expansion of our military strength. That expansion had not been proceeding as fast as we had hoped. The best of all we had to give had gone to the British Expeditionary Force, and although they had not the numbers of tanks and some articles of equipment which were desirable, they were a very well and finely equipped Army. They had the first-fruits of all that our industry had to give, and that is gone. And now here is this further delay. How long it will be, how long it will last, depends upon the exertions which we make in this Island. An effort the like of which has never been seen in our records is now being made. Work is proceeding everywhere, night and day, Sundays and week days. Capital and Labor have cast aside their interests, rights, and customs and put them into the common stock. Already the flow of munitions has leaped forward. There is no reason why we should not in a few months overtake the sudden and serious loss that has come upon us, without retarding the development of our general program.

Nevertheless, our thankfulness at the escape of our Army and so many men, whose loved ones have passed through an agonizing week, must not blind us to the fact that what has happened in France and Belgium is a colossal military disaster. The French Army has been weakened, the Belgian Army has been lost, a large part of those fortified lines upon which so much faith had been reposed is gone, many valuable mining districts and factories have passed into the enemy's possession, the whole of the Channel ports are in his hands, with all the tragic consequences that follow from that,

---

6. **Knights . . . Table**, knights composing the legendary order established by King Arthur during the Middle Ages; the name was derived from the Round Table at which they sat. (See Vol. I, p. 277.) 7. **Crusaders**, heroes of several military expeditions undertaken by Christian powers in the 11th, 12th, and 13th centuries to recover the Holy Land from the Mohammedans. 14. "**Every . . . knight**," from Tennyson's *The Passing of Arthur*, 396-397:
> For now I see the true old times are dead,
> When every morning brought a noble chance,
> And every chance brought out a noble knight.

32. **President . . . Trade**, Sir Andrew Duncan, later Minister of Supply.

and we must expect another blow to be struck almost immediately at us or at France. We are told that Herr Hitler has a plan for invading the British Isles. This has often been thought of before. When Napoleon lay at Boulogne for a year with his flat-bottomed boats and his Grand Army, he was told by someone, "There are bitter weeds in England." There are certainly a great many more of them since the British Expeditionary Force returned.

The whole question of home defense against invasion is, of course, powerfully affected by the fact that we have for the time being in this Island incomparably more powerful military forces than we have ever had at any moment in this war or the last. But this will not continue. We shall not be content with a defensive war. We have our duty to our Ally. We have to reconstitute and build up the British Expeditionary Force once again, under its gallant Commander-in-Chief, Lord Gort. All this is in train; but in the interval we must put our defenses in this Island into such a high state of organization that the fewest possible numbers will be required to give effective security and that the largest possible potential of offensive effort may be realized. On this we are now engaged. It will be very convenient, if it be the desire of the House, to enter upon this subject in a secret Session. Not that the Government would necessarily be able to reveal in very great detail military secrets, but we like to have our discussions free, without the restraint imposed by the fact that they will be read the next day by the enemy; and the Government would benefit by views freely expressed in all parts of the House by Members with their knowledge of so many different parts of the country. I understand that some request is to be made upon this subject, which will be readily acceded to by His Majesty's Government.

We have found it necessary to take measures of increasing stringency, not only against enemy aliens and suspicious characters of other nationalities, but also against British subjects who may become a danger or a nuisance should the war be transported to the United Kingdom. I know there are a great many people affected by the orders which we have made who are the passionate enemies of Nazi Germany. I am very sorry for them, but we cannot, at the present time and under the present stress, draw all the distinctions which we should like to do. If parachute landings were attempted and fierce fighting attendant upon them followed, these unfortunate people would be far better out of the way, for their own sakes as well as for ours. There is, however, another class, for which I feel not the slightest sympathy. Parliament has given us the powers to put down Fifth Column activities with a strong hand, and we shall use those powers, subject to the supervision and correction of the House, without the slightest hesitation until we are satisfied, and more than satisfied, that this malignancy in our midst has been effectively stamped out.

Turning once again, and this time more generally, to the question of invasion, I would observe that there has never been a period in all these long centuries of which we boast when an absolute guarantee against invasion, still less against serious raids, could have been given to our people. In the days of Napoleon the same wind which would have carried his transports across the Channel might have driven away the blockading fleet. There was always the chance, and it is that chance which has excited and befooled the imaginations of many Continental tyrants. Many are the tales that are told. We are assured that novel methods will be adopted, and when we see the originality of malice, the ingenuity of aggression, which our enemy displays, we may certainly prepare ourselves for every kind of novel stratagem and every kind of brutal and treacherous maneuver. I think that no idea is so outlandish that it should not be considered and viewed with a searching, but at the same time, I hope, with a steady eye. We must

---

5. **Napoleon . . . year,** in 1805. 19. **our Ally,** France.

63. **Fifth Column activities,** activities of any minority group which from within gives aid to the enemy of the majority. The name is derived from an alleged remark of a Spanish general who attacked Madrid in 1939 and said that he had four columns attacking from the outside and one from the inside.

never forget the solid assurances of sea power and those which belong to air power if it can be locally exercised.

I have, myself, full confidence that if all do their duty, if nothing is neglected, and if the best arrangements are made, as they are being made, we shall prove ourselves once again able to defend our Island home, to ride out the storm of war, and to outlive the menace of tyranny, if necessary for years, if necessary alone. At any rate, that is what we are going to try to do. That is the resolve of His Majesty's Government—every man of them. That is the will of Parliament and the nation. The British Empire and the French Republic, linked together in their cause and in their need, will defend to the death their native soil, aiding each other like good comrades to the utmost of their strength. Even though large tracts of Europe and many old and famous States have fallen or may fall into the grip of the Gestapo and all the odious apparatus of Nazi rule, we shall not flag or fail. We shall go on to the end, we shall fight in France, we shall fight on the seas and oceans, we shall fight with growing confidence and growing strength in the air, we shall defend our Island, whatever the cost may be, we shall fight on the beaches, we shall fight on the landing grounds, we shall fight in the fields and in the streets, we shall fight in the hills; we shall never surrender, and even if, which I do not for a moment believe, this Island or a large part of it were subjugated and starving, then our Empire beyond the seas, armed and guarded by the British Fleet, would carry on the struggle, until, in God's good time, the New World, with all its power and might, steps forth to the rescue and the liberation of the old. (1940)

22. **Gestapo,** the Nazi secret police of Germany, assigned to discover and arrest persons opposed to the policies of the government.

Unconditional Surrender

Between May 1 and May 8, 1945, all the German armed forces surrendered to the Allies; the last unconditional surrender was signed in Berlin on May 8. On that memorable V-E Day, Mr. Churchill made the following speech on a world broadcast.

YESTERDAY morning at 2:41 a.m. at Headquarters, General Jodl, the representative of the German High Command, and Grand Admiral Doenitz, the designated head of the German State, signed the act of unconditional surrender of all German land, sea, and air forces in Europe to the Allied Expeditionary Force, and simultaneously to the Soviet High Command.

General Bedell Smith, Chief of Staff of the Allied Expeditionary Force, and General François Sevez signed the document on behalf of the Supreme Commander of the Allied Expeditionary Force, and General Susloparov signed on behalf of the Russian High Command.

Today this agreement will be ratified and confirmed at Berlin, where Air Chief Marshal Tedder, Deputy Supreme Commander of the Allied Expeditionary Force, and General de Lattre de Tassigny will sign on behalf of General Eisenhower. Marshal Zhukov will sign on behalf of the Soviet High Command. The German representatives will be Field-Marshal Keitel, Chief of the High Command, and the Commanders-in-Chief of the German Army, Navy, and Air Forces.

Hostilities will end officially at one minute after midnight tonight (Tuesday, May 8), but in the interests of saving lives the "Cease fire" began yesterday to be sounded all along the front, and our dear Channel Islands are also to be freed today.

The Germans are still in places resisting the Russian troops, but should they continue to do so after midnight they will, of course, deprive themselves of the protection of the laws of war, and will be attacked from all quarters by the Allied troops. It is not surprising that on such long fronts and in the existing disorder of the enemy the orders of the German High Command should not in every case be

From *Victory,* published by Little, Brown & Company, 1946.

obeyed immediately. This does not, in our opinion, with the best military advice at our disposal, constitute any reason for withholding from the nation the facts communicated to us by General Eisenhower of the unconditional surrender already signed at Rheims, nor should it prevent us from celebrating today and tomorrow (Wednesday) as Victory in Europe days.

Today, perhaps, we shall think mostly of ourselves. Tomorrow we shall pay a particular tribute to our Russian comrades, whose prowess in the field has been one of the grand contributions to the general victory.

The German war is therefore at an end. After years of intense preparation, Germany hurled herself on Poland at the beginning of September, 1939; and, in pursuance of our guarantee to Poland and in agreement with the French Republic, Great Britain, the British Empire and Commonwealth of Nations, declared war upon this foul aggression. After gallant France had been struck down we, from this Island and from our united Empire, maintained the struggle single-handed for a whole year until we were joined by the military might of Soviet Russia, and later by the overwhelming power and resources of the United States of America.

Finally almost the whole world was combined against the evildoers, who are now prostrate before us. Our gratitude to our splendid Allies goes forth from all our hearts in this Island and throughout the British Empire.

We may allow ourselves a brief period of rejoicing; but let us not forget for a moment the toil and efforts that lie ahead. Japan, with all her treachery and greed, remains unsubdued. The injury she has inflicted on Great Britain, the United States, and other countries, and her detestable cruelties, call for justice and retribution. We must now devote all our strength and resources to the completion of our task, both at home and abroad. Advance, Britannia. Long live the cause of freedom. God save the King.

(1945)

James Joyce
1882-1941

The eldest son of a large middle-class family, James Joyce was born in a suburb of Dublin, Ireland, February 2, 1882. Originally intended for the priesthood, Joyce was given the best education available; after attending the Jesuit Clongowes Wood College, in Clane, he went to Belvedere College, Dublin, and finally to the Royal University, from which he received his bachelor's degree in October, 1902.

During his years of study he showed marked originality and independence and displayed a special bent for creative writing and facility in a dozen or more languages. Joyce's first serious writing was a laudatory essay on Henrik Ibsen, published in 1900 in *The Fortnightly Review*. His interest in Ibsen and other non-Irish writers led Joyce to oppose the movement, begun in 1901, for the establishment of a national theater for Ireland.

In 1902 Joyce left Ireland on what proved to be a long self-imposed exile. He returned twice—in 1903, because of his mother's fatal illness, and in 1912, in the interest of publishing one of his books. In Paris in 1902, Joyce gave up the idea of studying medicine because he lacked the necessary fees, and also abandoned the notion of preparing for a career as a singer. In 1904, he served as a teacher in Clifton School, Dalkey, Ireland; then he taught in the Berlitz School in Trieste.

Joyce had done some writing of verse in the Elizabethan manner. After four London publishers had rejected the poems, the thin volume of lyrics, *Chamber Music,* was published in 1907. He had also left the manuscript for some short stories based upon Dublin life with a publisher in Dublin, who refused to risk publication, but he finally published the stories under the title *Dubliners* in 1914. These are masterly incidents, portraits, and dramatic episodes, and in many ways they foreshadow the longer and more individualistic prose works.

Joyce's first novel, *A Portrait of the Artist as a Young Man,* a thinly disguised account of the author's youthful years, first appeared serially in *The Egoist,* an English periodical, and was then published in book form in 1916, with the imprint "Dublin, 1904—Trieste, 1914." During the next few years Joyce suffered an eye ailment that frequently brought on nearly complete blindness. Nevertheless, he worked on a long sequel to *A Portrait*—his masterpiece, *Ulysses,* begun in Trieste in 1914 and finished in Paris in 1921. Expurgated portions were printed in *The Egoist,* and twenty-three installments appeared in the United States in *The Little Review* in 1918-1920. Three were confiscated by the United States Post Office, and the publishers were fined for sending allegedly immoral matter through the mails. In 1922 the novel was published in Paris. Five hundred copies were burned in New York by the United States Post Office, and a similar number were confiscated by the British Customs. These actions served only to stimulate the public interest in what was described by some as "an infamously obscene book" and by others as the "greatest fiction of the twentieth century." After the ban was removed by the United States Courts in 1933, the novel circulated freely.

Portions of Joyce's next novel, *Finnegans Wake,* appeared first in Paris in periodicals under the title of *Work in Progress.* This ponderous volume, published in 1939, which occupied Joyce for fifteen years or more, employs the same individualistic manner of writing—but in greatly increased complexity—as that used in *Ulysses.*

With his family Joyce left Paris in 1940 following the outbreak of the Second World War. After a brief stay in southern France, he managed to get to Zurich, Switzerland, where he died, January 13, 1941.

Joyce, a bold experimentalist, wrote with unabashed realism and frankness, and made use of a new form of narrative writing, a new prose style, and a rather startling vocabulary. His most conspicuous innovation, the so-called "stream of consciousness" technique, tries to approximate the operation of the human mind, in a fluid pre-communicative linguistic state, as it expresses a continuous flow of ideas, desires, or past experiences. It represents the subjectivity of the Waste Land carried to an extreme which occasionally exceeds the limits of taste and frequently makes communication between author and reader impossible. Critics have rightly spoken of Joyce, however, as a great creative artist, and the reader of modern fiction will note his marked influence upon many later writers.

from *Ulysses*

Ulysses is something of a prose epic in that it is vaguely patterned after the *Odyssey* of Homer. It consists of eighteen distinct episodes in a twenty-four-hour period in the lives of several persons in Dublin, who have parallels in the *Odyssey*. Leopold Bloom, a Jewish salesman, is Odysseus; Molly Bloom, his wife, is Penelope; Stephen Dedalus (Joyce himself in the author's earlier *Portrait of the Artist*) is Telemachus, son of Odysseus and Penelope. The incidents, the streets, the shops, and the resorts in Dublin are counterparts of what is found in the *Odyssey* and apparently are meant to represent the work of a twentieth-century Homer. Various attempts have been made—some long and elaborate—to supply a complete and itemized identity between the *Odyssey* and *Ulysses,* but the reader easily becomes lost in the intricate maze or wearied by the lengthy analysis.

Joyce's novel is written in various styles and employs numerous techniques and methods, including straight narrative, dramatic dialogue, question and answer, and a loosely punctuated monologue presenting some of the thoughts which drift on the surface of the "stream of consciousness." This last kind of writing is made up of sentences which are more than telegraphically compressed; snatches of popular songs; strings of words in rhyming or punning association; old memories mingled with fresh observations. It is intended to convey the complex, swiftly changing, and frequently only half-verbal content of man's mind. Through this combination of styles, the reader is confronted with a wealth—often a confusion—of detail by which he is made aware of not only the sights, sounds, and smells of Dublin but the desires, memories, emotions, and visceral sensations of the men and women who figure in each episode. Several of the episodes contain many separate scenes or divisions. Since each episode is a complete incident in itself, each may be read independently of the others. The excerpt printed below is the sixth episode of the novel, and may be regarded as fairly representative of Joyce's technique of writing. This episode has to do with the funeral of Paddy Dignam, who, we learn elsewhere, died of a stroke. The men in the carriage are on the way to the funeral. Martin Cunningham and Mr. Power are characters in Joyce's *Dubliners*, as are also Mr. Kernan and Hynes the reporter, who appear later. Mr. Dedalus, Stephen's father, is one of the chief persons in Joyce's *Portrait of the Artist as a Young Man*. The incident is related from the point of view of Mr. Bloom, and unless otherwise indicated the thoughts expressed in the "stream-of-consciousness" portions are his. The absence of quotation marks is characteristic of the novel as a whole. In its relationship to Homer's *Odyssey*, the funeral of Paddy Dignam corresponds to the descent to Hades, and Mr. Dignam to Elpenor. Other parallels are suggested in the footnotes.

MARTIN CUNNINGHAM, first, poked his silkhatted head into the creaking carriage and, entering deftly, seated himself. Mr Power stepped in after him, curving his height with care.

—Come on, Simon.

—After you, Mr Bloom said.

Mr Dedalus covered himself quickly and got in, saying:

—Yes, yes.

—Are we all here now? Martin Cunningham asked. Come along, Bloom.

Mr Bloom entered and sat in the vacant place. He pulled the door to after him and slammed it tight till it shut tight. He passed an arm through the armstrap and looked seriously from the open carriage window at the lowered blinds of the avenue. One dragged aside: an old woman peeping. Nose whiteflattened against the pane. Thanking her stars she was passed over. Extraordinary the interest they take in a corpse. Glad to see us go we give them such trouble coming. Job seems to suit them. Huggermugger in corners. Slop about in slipperslappers for fear he'd wake. Then getting it ready. Laying it out. Molly and Mrs Fleming making the bed. Pull it more to your side. Our windingsheet. Never know who will touch you dead. Wash and shampoo. I believe they clip the nails and the hair. Keep a bit in an envelope. Grow all the same after. Unclean job.

All waited. Nothing was said. Stowing in the wreaths probably. I am sitting on something hard. Ah, that soap in my hip pocket. Better shift it out of that. Wait for an opportunity.

All waited. Then wheels were heard from in front turning: then nearer: then horses' hoofs. A jolt. Their carriage began to move, creaking and swaying. Other hoofs and creaking wheels started behind. The blinds of the avenue passed and number nine with its craped knocker, door ajar. At walking pace.

They waited still, their knees jogging, till

Copyright, 1934, by Random House, Inc., New York. Reprinted by permission of Random House, Inc., and John Lane the Bodley Head, Ltd. 19. **an old woman.** The sight of the old woman peeping through the window turns Mr. Bloom's thoughts to the interest of old women in death; to the whole function of women in our civilization from birth to death; to the laying out of corpses, a typical "stream-of-consciousness" musing, which continues to the end of the paragraph.

they had turned and were passing along the tramtracks. Tritonville road. Quicker. The wheels rattled rolling over the cobbled causeway and the crazy glasses shook rattling in the doorframes.

—What way is he taking us? Mr Power asked through both windows.

—Irishtown, Martin Cunningham said. Ringsend. Brunswick street.

Mr Dedalus nodded, looking out.

—That's a fine old custom, he said. I am glad to see it has not died out.

All watched awhile through their windows caps and hats lifted by passers. Respect. The carriage swerved from the tramtrack to the smoother road past Watery lane. Mr Bloom at gaze saw a lithe young man, clad in mourning, a wide hat.

—There's a friend of yours gone by, Dedalus, he said.

—Who is that?

—Your son and heir.

—Where is he? Mr Dedalus said, stretching over, across.

The carriage, passing the open drains and mounds of ripped-up roadway before the tenement houses, lurched round the corner and, swerving back to the tramtrack, rolled on noisily with chattering wheels. Mr Dedalus fell back, saying:

—Was that Mulligan cad with him? His *fidus Achates?*

—No, Mr Bloom said. He was alone.

—Down with his aunt Sally, I suppose, Mr Dedalus said, the Goulding faction, the drunken little costdrawer and Crissie, papa's little lump of dung, the wise child that knows her own father.

Mr Bloom smiled joylessly on Ringsend road. Wallace Bros the bottleworks. Dodder bridge.

Richie Goulding and the legal bag. Goulding, Collis and Ward he calls the firm. His jokes are getting a bit damp. Great card he was. Waltzing in Stamer street with Ignatius Gallaher on a Sunday morning, the landlady's two hats pinned on his head. Out on the rampage allnight. Beginning to tell on him now: that backache of his, I fear. Wife ironing his back. Thinks he'll cure it with pills. All breadcrumbs they are. About six hundred per cent profit.

—He's in with a lowdown crowd, Mr Dedalus snarled. That Mulligan is a contaminated bloody doubledyed ruffian by all accounts. His name stinks all over Dublin. But with the help of God and His blessed mother I'll make it my business to write a letter one of those days to his mother or his aunt or whatever she is that will open her eyes as wide as a gate. I'll tickle his catastrophe, believe you me.

He cried above the clatter of the wheels.

—I won't have her bastard of a nephew ruin my son. A counterjumper's son. Selling tapes in my cousin, Peter Paul M'Swiney's. Not likely.

He ceased. Mr Bloom glanced from his angry moustache to Mr Power's mild face and Martin Cunningham's eyes and beard, gravely shaking. Noisy selfwilled man. Full of his son. He is right. Something to hand on. If little Rudy had lived. See him grow up. Hear his voice in the house. Walking beside Molly in an Eton suit. My son. Me in his eyes. Strange feeling it would be. From me. Just a chance. Must have been that morning in Raymond terrace she was at the window, watching the two dogs at it by the wall of the cease to do evil. And the sergeant grinning up. She had that cream gown on with the rip she never stitched. Give us a touch, Poldy. God, I'm dying for it. How life begins.

Got big then. Had to refuse the Greystones concert. My son inside her. I could have helped him on in life. I could. Make him independent. Learn German, too.

---

22. **Your . . . heir,** Stephen Dedalus. 32. *fidus Achates,* faithful Achates, in Virgil's *Aeneid* the constant companion of Aeneas. 34. **Sally . . . faction.** Simon Dedalus had married May Goulding, but obviously he is not fond of her family. 36. **costdrawer,** money-grubber. 40. **Dodder bridge,** over the River Dodder, one of four waterways in Dublin which here typify the four rivers of Hades.

61. **I'll . . . catastrophe,** from Shakespeare's *Henry IV,* Part 2, II, 1, 66. Falstaff, angry at the Hostess, shouts: "Away, you scullion! you rampallian! you fustilarian! I'll tickle your catastrophe." The last word is used in an indecent sense. 65. **counterjumper,** a store clerk. 71. **Full of his son.** The mention of the son of Mr. Dedalus recalls to Mr. Bloom the death of his own son Rudy in infancy and starts him on another "stream-of-consciousness" musing. 75. **Molly,** Mr. Bloom's wife. Milly (p. 1045) is their daughter Millicent, who is employed in a photographer's shop at Mullingar, West Meath, Ireland. When she wrote to her father, she called him *Dearest Papli.*

—Are we late? Mr Power asked.

—Ten minutes, Martin Cunningham said, looking at his watch.

Molly. Milly. Same thing watered down. Her tomboy oaths. O jumping Jupiter! Ye gods and little fishes! Still, she's a dear girl. Soon be a woman. Mullingar. Dearest Papli. Young student. Yes, yes: a woman too. Life. Life.

The carriage heeled over and back, their four trunks swaying.

—Corny might have given us a more commodious yoke, Mr Power said.

—He might, Mr Dedalus said, if he hadn't that squint troubling him. Do you follow me?

He closed his left eye. Martin Cunningham began to brush away crustcrumbs from under his thighs.

—What is this, he said, in the name of God? Crumbs?

—Someone seems to have been making a picnic party here lately, Mr Power said.

All raised their thighs, eyed with disfavor the mildewed buttonless leather of the seats. Mr Dedalus, twisting his nose, frowned downward and said:

—Unless I'm greatly mistaken. What do you think, Martin?

—It struck me too, Martin Cunningham said.

Mr Bloom set his thigh down. Glad I took that bath. Feel my feet quite clean. But I wish Mrs Fleming had darned these socks better.

Mr Dedalus sighed resignedly.

—After all, he said, it's the most natural thing in the world.

—Did Tom Kernan turn up. Martin Cunningham asked, twirling the peak of his beard gently.

—Yes, Mr Bloom answered. He's behind with Ned Lambert and Hynes.

—And Corny Kelleher himself? Mr Power asked.

—At the cemetery, Martin Cunningham said.

—I met M'Coy this morning, Mr Bloom said. He said he'd try to come.

The carriage halted short.

—What's wrong?

—We're stopped.

—Where are we?

Mr Bloom put his head out of the window.

—The grand canal, he said.

Gas works. Whooping cough they say it cures. Good job Milly never got it. Poor children! Doubles them up black and blue in convulsions. Shame really. Got off lightly with illness compared. Only measles. Flaxseed tea. Scarlatina influenza epidemics. Canvassing for death. Don't miss this chance. Dog's home over there. Poor old Athos! Be good to Athos, Leopold, is my last wish. Thy will be done. We obey them in the grave. A dying scrawl. He took it to heart, pined away. Quiet brute. Old men's dogs usually are.

A raindrop spat on his hat. He drew back and saw an instant of shower spray dots over the grey flags. Apart. Curious. Like through a colander. I thought it would. My boots were creaking I remember now.

—The weather is changing, he said quietly.

—A pity it did not keep up fine, Martin Cunningham said.

—Wanted for the country, Mr Power said. There's the sun again coming out.

Mr Dedalus peering through his glasses towards the veiled sun, hurled a mute curse at the sky.

—It's as uncertain as a child's bottom, he said.

—We're off again.

The carriage turned again its stiff wheels and their trunks swayed gently. Martin Cunningham twirled more quickly the peak of his beard.

—Tom Kernan was immense last night, he said. And Paddy Leonard taking him off to his face.

—O draw him out, Martin, Mr Power said eagerly. Wait till you hear him, Simon, on Ben Dollard's singing of *The Croppy Boy*.

—Immense, Martin Cunningham said pompously. *His singing of that simple ballad, Martin, is the most trenchant rendering I ever heard in the whole course of my experience.*

---

62. **Athos**, the name of his father's dog. 93. **Ben Dollard**, a former lover of Mrs. Bloom. 95-97. *His . . . experience.* Mr. Cunningham quotes from Kernan's critique of the singing.

—Trenchant, Mr Power said laughing. He's dead nuts on that. And the retrospective arrangement.

—Did you read Dan Dawson's speech? Martin Cunningham asked.

—I did not then, Mr Dedalus said. Where is it?

—In the paper this morning.

Mr Bloom took the paper from his inside pocket. That book I must change for her.

—No, no, Mr Dedalus said quickly. Later on, please.

Mr Bloom's glance travelled down the edge of the paper, scanning the deaths. Callan, Coleman, Dignam, Fawcett, Lowry, Naumann, Peake, what Peake is that? is it the chap was in Crosbie and Alleyne's? no, Sexton, Urbright. Inked characters fast fading on the frayed breaking paper. Thanks to the Little Flower. Sadly missed. To the inexpressible grief of his. Aged 88 after a long and tedious illness. Month's mind Quinlan. On whose soul Sweet Jesus have mercy.

It is now a month since dear Henry fled
To his home up above in the sky
While his family weeps and mourns his loss
Hoping some day to meet him on high.

I tore up the envelope? Yes. Where did I put her letter after I read it in the bath? He patted his waistcoat pocket. There all right. Dear Henry fled. Before my patience are exhausted.

National school. Meade's yard. The hazard. Only two there now. Nodding. Full as a tick. Too much bone in their skulls. The other trotting round with a fare. An hour ago I was passing there. The jarvies raised their hats.

A pointsman's back straightened itself upright suddenly against a tramway standard by Mr Bloom's window. Couldn't they invent something automatic so that the wheel itself much handier? Well but that fellow would lose his job then? Well but then another fellow would get a job making the new invention?

Antient concert rooms. Nothing on there. A man in a buff suit with a crape armlet. Not much grief there. Quarter mourning. People in law, perhaps.

They went past the bleak pulpit of Saint Mark's, under the railway bridge, past the Queen's theater: in silence. Hoardings. Eugene Stratton. Mrs Bandman Palmer. Could I go to see *Leah* tonight, I wonder. I said I. Or the *Lily of Killarney?* Elster Grimes Opera Company. Big powerful change. Wet bright bills for next week. *Fun on the Bristol.* Martin Cunningham could work a pass for the Gaiety. Have to stand a drink or two. As broad as it's long.

He's coming in the afternoon. Her songs.

Plasto's. Sir Philip Crampton's memorial fountain bust. Who was he?

—How do you do? Martin Cunningham said, raising his palm to his brow in salute.

—He doesn't see us, Mr Power said. Yes, he does. How do you do?

—Who? Mr Dedalus asked.

—Blazes Boylan, Mr Power said. There he is airing his quiff. Just that moment I was thinking.

Mr Dedalus bent across to salute. From the door of the Red Bank the white disc of a straw hat flashed reply: passed.

Mr Bloom reviewed the nails of his left hand, then those of his right hand. The nails, yes. Is there anything more in him that they she sees? Fascination. Worst man in Dublin. That keeps him alive. They sometimes feel what a person is. Instinct. But a type like that. My nails. I am just looking at them: well pared. And after: thinking alone. Body getting a bit softy. I would notice that from remembering. What causes that I suppose the skin can't contract quickly enough when the flesh falls off. But the shape is there. The shape is there still. Shoulders. Hips. Plump. Night of the dance dressing. Shift stuck between the cheeks behind.

20. **Little Flower,** a memorial society in the Catholic Church. 28. **I . . . envelope.** The printed notices make Mr. Bloom think of a letter he had received from Martha Clifford, a clandestine sweetheart to whom he is known as Henry Flower. She had called him Henry and had sent him a little flower. 37. **jarvies,** cab-drivers. 39. **pointsmen,** switchmen on the elevated railway. 53. **Hoardings,** billboards; they advertise names of actors and titles of plays or musical shows to be presented. 62. **He's . . . songs.** Blazes Boylan is that afternoon to bring some new songs to Mrs. Bloom, who has some ability as a singer. The love affair between her and Boylan plainly agitates Mr. Bloom. 63. **Sir Philip Crampton,** a famous Irish surgeon (1777-1858). 71. **quiff,** slang for oiled hair; perhaps a loose pronunciation of coif.

He clasped his hands between his knees and, satisfied, sent his vacant glance over their faces. Mr Power asked:

—How is the concert tour getting on, Bloom?

—O very well, Mr Bloom said. I hear great accounts of it. It's a good idea, you see . . .

—Are you going yourself?

—Well no, Mr Bloom said. In point of fact I have to go down to the county Clare on some private business. You see the idea is to tour the chief towns. What you lose on one you can make up on the other.

—Quite so, Martin Cunningham said. Mary Anderson is up there now.

—Have you good artists?

—Louis Werner is touring her, Mr Bloom said. O yes, we'll have all topnobbers. J. C. Doyle and John Mac Cormack, I hope and. The best, in fact.

—And *Madame*, Mr Power said, smiling. Last but not least.

Mr Bloom unclasped his hands in a gesture of soft politeness and clasped them. Smith O'Brien. Someone has laid a bunch of flowers there. Woman. Must be his deathday. For many happy returns. The carriage wheeling by Farrell's statue united noiselessly their unresisting knees.

Oot: a dullgarbed old man from the curbstone tendered his wares, his mouth opening: oot.

—Four bootlaces for a penny.

Wonder why he was struck off the rolls. Had his office in Hume street. Same house as Molly's namesake. Tweedy, crown solicitor for Waterford. Had that silk hat ever since. Relics of old decency. Mourning too. Terrible comedown, poor wretch! Kicked about like snuff at a wake. O'Callaghan on his last legs.

And *Madame*. Twenty past eleven. Up. Mrs Fleming is in to clean. Doing her hair, humming: *voglio e non vorrei*. No: *vorrei e non*. Looking at the tips of her hairs to see if they are split. *Mi trema un poco il*. Beautiful on that *tre* her voice is: weeping tone. A thrush. A throstle. There is a word throstle that expressed that.

His eyes passed lightly over Mr Power's goodlooking face. Greyish over the ears. *Madame:* smiling. I smiled back. A smile goes a long way. Only politeness perhaps. Nice fellow. Who knows is that true about the woman he keeps? Not pleasant for the wife. Yet they say, who was it told me, there is no carnal. You would imagine that would get played out pretty quick. Yes, it was Crofton met him one evening bringing her a pound of rumpsteak. What is this she was? Barmaid in Jury's. Or the Moira, was it?

They passed under the hugecloaked Liberator's form.

Martin Cunningham nudged Mr Power.

—Of the tribe of Reuben, he said.

A tall blackbearded figure, bent on a stick, stumping round the corner of Elvery's elephant house showed them a curved hand open on his spine.

—In all his pristine beauty, Mr Power said.

Mr Dedalus looked after the stumping figure and said mildly:

—The devil break the hasp of your back!

Mr Power, collapsing in laughter, shaded his face from the window as the carriage passed Gray's statue.

—We have all been there, Martin Cunningham said broadly.

His eyes met Mr Bloom's eyes. He caressed his beard adding:

—Well, nearly all of us.

Mr Bloom began to speak with sudden eagerness to his companion's faces.

—That's an awfully good one that's going the rounds about Reuben J. and the son.

—About the boatman? Mr Power asked.

—Yes. Isn't it awfully good?

---

14. **Mary Anderson,** a noted American actress (1859-1940), who played with great success in the United States and Great Britain. 19. **John Mac Cormack,** or McCormack (1885-1945), a well-known singer, born in Ireland. He became an American citizen in 1919. 24. **Smith O'Brien,** a memorial to William Smith O'Brien (1803-1864), Irish Nationalist. 34. **struck . . . rolls,** dismissed from office. 40. **O'Callaghan . . . legs,** a statue of John C. O'Callaghan (1805-1883), Irish historical writer. 44. ***voglio . . . vorrei . . . poco il,*** I would and yet I would not . . . my heart trembles a little; from the famous duet "La ci darem" in Mozart's opera *Don Giovanni.* 62. **Liberator's form,** the statue of Daniel O'Connell (1775-1847), famous Irish orator, patriot, and agitator. He was called the Liberator and the Uncrowned Monarch of Ireland. 65. **Reuben,** Reuben J. Dodd, a famous money-lender of Dublin. 67. **Elvery's elephant house,** a house of ill fame in Dublin in the early part of the century. 76. **Gray's statue,** the statue of Edmund Dwyer Gray (1845-1888), Irish journalist and a great supporter of the Parnell movement for Home Rule. 85. **Reuben . . . son,** a reference to the report that Dodd's son tried to commit suicide in the River Liffey and failed.

—What is that? Mr Dedalus asked. I didn't hear it.

—There was a girl in the case, Mr Bloom began, and he determined to send him to the isle of Man out of harm's way but when they were both. . . .

—What? Mr Dedalus asked. That confirmed bloody hobbledehoy is it?

—Yes, Mr Bloom said. They were both on the way to the boat and he tried to drown . . .

—Drown Barabbas! Mr Dedalus cried. I wish to Christ he did!

Mr Power sent a long laugh down his shaded nostrils.

—No, Mr Bloom said, the son himself . . .

Martin Cunningham thwarted his speech rudely.

—Reuben J. and the son were piking it down the quay next the river on their way to the isle of Man boat and the young chiseller suddenly got loose and over the wall with him into the Liffey.

—For God's sake! Mr Dedalus exclaimed in fright. Is he dead?

—Dead! Martin Cunningham cried. Not he! A boatman got a pole and fished him out by the slack of the breeches and he was landed up to the father on the quay. More dead than alive. Half the town was there.

—Yes, Mr Bloom said. But the funny part is . . .

—And Reuben J., Martin Cunningham said, gave the boatman a florin for saving his son's life.

A stifled sigh came from under Mr Power's hand.

—O, he did, Martin Cunningham affirmed. Like a hero. A silver florin.

—Isn't it awfully good? Mr Bloom said eagerly.

—One and eightpence too much, Mr Dedalus said drily.

Mr Power's choked laugh burst quietly in the carriage.

Nelson's pillar.

—Eight plums a penny! Eight for a penny!

—We had better look a little serious, Martin Cunningham said.

Mr Dedalus sighed.

—And then indeed, he said, poor little Paddy wouldn't grudge us a laugh. Many a good one he told himself.

—The Lord forgive me! Mr Power said, wiping his wet eyes with his fingers. Poor Paddy! I little thought a week ago when I saw him last and he was in his usual health that I'd be driving after him like this. He's gone from us.

—As decent a little man as ever wore a hat, Mr Dedalus said. He went very suddenly.

—Breakdown, Martin Cunningham said. Heart. He tapped his chest sadly.

Blazing face: redhot. Too much John Barleycorn. Cure for a red nose. Drink like the devil till it turns adelite. A lot of money he spent coloring it.

Mr Power gazed at the passing houses with rueful apprehension.

—He had a sudden death, poor fellow, he said.

—The best death, Mr Bloom said.

Their wide open eyes looked at him.

—No suffering, he said. A moment and all is over. Like dying in sleep. No-one spoke.

Dead side of the street this. Dull business by day, land agents, temperance hotel, Falconer's railway guide, civil service college, Gill's, catholic club, the industrious blind. Why? Some reason. Sun or wind. At night too. Chummies and slaveys. Under the patronage of the late Father Mathew. Foundation stone for Parnell. Breakdown. Heart.

White horses with white frontlet plumes came round the Rotunda corner, galloping. A tiny coffin flashed by. In a hurry to bury. A mourning coach. Unmarried. Black for the married. Piebald for bachelors. Dun for a nun.

—Sad, Martin Cunningham said. A child.

A dwarf's face mauve and wrinkled like little Rudy's was. Dwarf's body, weak as putty, in a whitelined deal box. Burial friendly

---

5. **isle of Man,** a large island in the Irish Sea, northeast of Dublin. 11. **Barabbas,** the prisoner whose release instead of that of Christ was demanded of Pilate by the Jews in observance of the custom at the Passover. See *Luke,* 23:19, and *John,* 18:40. 33. **florin,** an English silver coin worth two shillings, or forty-eight cents. 45. **Nelson's pillar,** the famous monument to Horatio, Lord Nelson (1758-1805).

65. **adelite,** a grayish-yellow mineral. 80. **chummies and slaveys,** chimney-sweepers and servants. 81. **Father Mathew,** Theobald Mathew (1790-1856), Irish apostle of temperance. During his centenary year, a marble statue of him was erected in O'Connell Street, Dublin. 82. **Parnell,** Charles Stewart Parnell (1846-1891), Irish statesman, most prominent leader of the Home Rule Party.

society pays. Penny a week for a sod of turf. Our. Little. Beggar. Baby. Meant nothing. Mistake of nature. If it's healthy it's from the mother. If not the man. Better luck next time.

—Poor little thing, Mr Dedalus said. It's well out of it.

The carriage climbed more slowly the hill of Rutland square. Rattle his bones. Over the stones. Only a pauper. Nobody owns.

—In the midst of life, Martin Cunningham said.

—But the worst of all, Mr Power said, is the man who takes his own life.

Martin Cunningham drew out his watch briskly, coughed and put it back.

—The greatest disgrace to have in the family, Mr Power added.

Temporary insanity, of course, Martin Cunningham said decisively. We must take a charitable view of it.

—They say a man who does it is a coward, Mr Dedalus said.

—It is not for us to judge, Martin Cunningham said.

Mr Bloom, about to speak, closed his lips again. Martin Cunningham's large eyes. Looking away now. Sympathetic human man he is. Intelligent. Like Shakespeare's face. Always a good word to say. They have no mercy on that here or infanticide. Refuse christian burial. They used to drive a stake of wood through his heart in the grave. As if it wasn't broken already. Yet sometimes they repent too late. Found in the riverbed clutching rushes. He looked at me. And that awful drunkard of a wife of his. Setting up house for her time after time and then pawning the furniture on him every Saturday almost. Leading him the life of the damned. Wear the heart out of a stone, that. Monday morning start afresh. Shoulder to the wheel. Lord, she must have looked a sight that night, Dedalus told me he was in there. Drunk about the place and capering with Martin's umbrella:

—*And they call me the jewel of Asia,*
 Of Asia,
 The geisha.

He looked away from me. He knows. Rattle his bones.

That afternoon of the inquest. The red-labelled bottle on the table. The room in the hotel with hunting pictures. Stuffy it was. Sunlight through the slats on the Venetian blinds. The coroner's ears, big and hairy. Boots giving evidence. Thought he was asleep first. Then saw like yellow streaks on his face. Had slipped down to the foot of the bed. Verdict: overdose. Death by misadventure. The letter. For my son Leopold.

No more pain. Wake no more. Nobody owns.

The carriage rattled swiftly along Blessington street. Over the stones.

—We are going the pace, I think, Martin Cunningham said.

—God grant he doesn't upset us on the road, Mr Power said.

—I hope not, Martin Cunningham said. That will be a great race tomorrow in Germany. The Gordon Bennett.

—Yes, by Jove, Mr Dedalus said. That will be worth seeing, faith.

As they turned into Berkeley street a streetorgan near the Basin sent over and after them a rollicking rattling song of the halls. Has anybody here seen Kelly? Kay ee double ell wy. Dead march from *Saul*. He's as bad as old Antonio. He left me on my ownio. Pirouette! The *Mater Misericordiae*. Eccles street. My house down there. Big place. Ward for incurables there. Very encouraging. Our Lady's Hospice for the dying. Dead house handy underneath. Where old Mrs Riordan died. They look terrible the women. Her feeding cup and rubbing her mouth with the spoon. Then the screen round her bed

---

9-10. **Rattle . . . owns,** quoted from the popular song *The Pauper's Drive,* by Thomas Noel and J. J. Hutchinson (1908). 11. **In . . . life.** "In the midst of life we are in death" is a sentence from the burial service in the Book of Common Prayer. 32. **stake . . . grave.** It was once the custom to drive a stake through the heart of a buried suicide in order to "lay" the demon it was thought to possess. Suicides were regarded as sinful, inspired by the devil; hence the refusal of Christian burial. 37-39. **drunkard . . . almost.** Martin Cunningham is the Joycean counterpart of Sisyphus, whose eternal task it was to roll a huge stone up a hill in Hades, only to have it tumble down again just as it was nearing the top. Cunningham's wife is his life-long burden.

47-49. **And . . . geisha.** This is one of many snatches of popular songs and ballads of the day found in *Ulysses*. The geisha is the professional singing and dancing girl of Japan. 52. **inquest,** held over the death of Mr. Bloom's father. See p. 1052, l. 35. 57. **Boots,** the conventional name given to the boy in a hotel or tavern who polishes the boots of the guests during the night. 72. **Gordon Bennett,** the name given to early automobile races in which the prize was a cup presented by James Gordon Bennett (1795-1872), American journalist and sportsman. He was born in Scotland.

for her to die. Nice young student that was dressed that bite the bee gave me. He's gone over to the lying-in hospital they told me. From one extreme to the other.

The carriage galloped round a corner: stopped.

—What's wrong now?

A divided drove of branded cattle passed the windows, lowing, slouching by on padded hoofs, whisking their tails slowly on their clotted bony croups. Outside them and through them ran raddled sheep bleating their fear.

—Emigrants, Mr Power said.

—Huuuh! the drover's voice cried, his switch sounding on their flanks. Huuuh! Out of that!

Thursday of course. Tomorrow is killing day. Springers. Cuffe sold them about twenty-seven quid each. For Liverpool probably. Roast beef for old England. They buy up all the juicy ones. And then the fifth quarter is lost: All that raw stuff, hide, hair, horns. Comes to a big thing in a year. Dead meat trade. Byproducts of the slaughterhouses for tanneries, soap, margarine. Wonder if that dodge works now getting dicky meat off the train at Clonsilla.

The carriage moved on through the drove.

—I can't make out why the corporation doesn't run a tramline from the parkgate to the quays, Mr Bloom said. All those animals could be taken in trucks down to the boats.

—Instead of blocking up the thoroughfare, Martin Cunningham said. Quite right. They ought to.

—Yes, Mr Bloom said, and another thing I often thought is to have municipal funeral trams like they have in Milan, you know. Run the line out to the cemetery gates and have special trams, hearse and carriage and all. Don't you see what I mean?

—O that be damned for a story, Mr Dedalus said. Pullman car and saloon diningroom.

—A poor lookout for Corny, Mr Power added.

—Why? Mr Bloom asked, turning to Mr Dedalus. Wouldn't it be more decent than galloping two abreast?

—Well, there's something in that, Mr Dedalus granted.

—And, Martin Cunningham said, we wouldn't have scenes like that when the hearse capsized round Dunphy's and upset the coffin on to the road.

—That was terrible, Mr Power's shocked face said, and the corpse fell about the road. Terrible!

—First round Dunphy's, Mr Dedalus said, nodding. Gordon Bennett cup.

—Praises be to God! Martin Cunningham said piously.

Bom! Upset. A coffin bumped out on to the road. Burst open. Paddy Dignam shot out and rolling over stiff in the dust in a brown habit too large for him. Red face: grey now. Mouth fallen open. Asking what's up now. Quite right to close it. Looks horrid open. Then the insides decompose quickly. Much better to close up all the orifices. Yes, also. With wax. The sphincter loose. Seal up all.

—Dunphy's, Mr Power announced as the carriage turned right.

Dunphy's corner. Mourning coaches drawn up drowning their grief. A pause by the wayside. Tiptop position for a pub. Expect we'll pull up there on the way back to drink his health. Pass round the consolation. Elixir of life.

But suppose now it did happen. Would he bleed if a nail say cut him in the knocking about? He would and he wouldn't, I suppose. Depends on where. The circulation stops. Still some might ooze out of an artery. It would be better to bury them in red: a dark red.

In silence they drove along Phibsborough road. An empty hearse trotted by, coming from the cemetery: looks relieved.

Crossguns bridge: the royal canal.

Water rushed roaring through the sluices. A man stood on his dropping barge between clamps of turf. On the towpath by the lock a slacktethered horse. Aboard of the *Bugabu*.

Their eyes watched him. On the slow weedy waterway he had floated on his raft coastward over Ireland drawn by a haulage

27. **dicky**, cheap, low grade. 28. **Clonsilla**, suburb of Dublin.

72. **sphincter**, a muscle controlling a body opening or passage.

rope past beds of reeds, over slime, mud-choked bottles, carrion dogs. Athlone, Mullingar, Moyvalley, I could make a walking tour to see Milly by the canal. Or cycle down. Hire some old crock, safety. Wren had one the other day at the auction but a lady's. Developing waterways. James M'Cann's hobby to row me o'er the ferry. Cheaper transit. By easy stages. Houseboats. Camping out. Also hearses. To heaven by water. Perhaps I will without writing. Come as a surprise, Leixlip, Clonsilla. Dropping down, lock by lock to Dublin. With turf from the midland bogs. Salute. He lifted his brown straw hat, saluting Paddy Dignam.

They drove on past Brian Boroimhe house. Near it now.

—I wonder how is our friend Fogarty getting on, Mr Power said.

—Better ask Tom Kernan, Mr Dedalus said.

—How is that? Martin Cunningham said. Left him weeping I suppose.

—Though lost to sight, Mr Dedalus said, to memory dear.

The carriage steered left for Finglas road.

The stonecutter's yard on the right. Last lap. Crowded on the spit of land silent shapes appeared, white, sorrowful, holding out calm hands, knelt in grief, pointing. Fragments of shapes, hewn. In white silence: appealing. The best obtainable. Thos. H. Dennany, monumental builder and sculptor.

Passed.

On the curbstone before Jimmy Geary the sexton's an old tramp sat, grumbling, emptying the dirt and stones out of his huge dustbrown yawning boot. After life's journey.

Gloomy gardens then went by, one by one: gloomy houses.

Mr Power pointed.

—That is where Childs was murdered, he said. The last house.

—So it is, Mr Dedalus said. A gruesome case, Seymour Bushe got him off. Murdered his brother. Or so they said.

—The crown had no evidence, Mr Power said.

—Only circumstantial, Martin Cunningham said. That's the maxim of the law. Better for ninety-nine guilty to escape than for one innocent person to be wrongfully condemned.

They looked. Murderer's ground. It passed darkly. Shuttered, tenantless, unweeded garden. Whole place gone to hell. Wrongfully condemned. Murder. The murderer's image in the eye of the murdered. They love reading about it. Man's head found in a garden. Her clothing consisted of. How she met her death. Recent outrage. The weapon used. Murderer is still at large. Clues. A shoelace. The body to be exhumed. Murder will out.

Cramped in this carriage. She mightn't like me to come that way without letting her know. Must be careful about women. Catch them once with their pants down. Never forgive you after. Fifteen.

The high railings of Prospects rippled past their gaze. Dark poplars, rare white forms. Forms more frequent, white shapes thronged amid the trees, white forms and fragments streaming by mutely, sustaining vain gestures on the air.

The felly harshed against the curbstone: stopped. Martin Cunningham put out his arm and, wrenching back the handle, shoved the door open with his knee. He stepped out. Mr Power and Mr Dedalus followed.

Change that soap now. Mr Bloom's hand unbuttoned his hip pocket swiftly and transferred the paperstuck soap to his inner handkerchief pocket. He stepped out of the carriage, replacing the newspaper his other hand still held.

Paltry funeral: coach and three carriages. It's all the same. Pallbearers, gold reins, requiem mass, firing a volley. Pomp of death. Beyond the hind carriage a hawker stood by his barrow of cakes and fruit. Simnel cakes those are, stuck together: cakes for the dead. Dogbiscuits. Who ate them? Mourners coming out.

He followed his companions. Mr Kernan and Ned Lambert followed, Hynes walking after them. Corny Kelleher stood by the opened hearse and took out the two wreaths. He handed one to the boy.

Where is that child's funeral disappeared to?

---

69. **Prospects,** Prospect Park. 75. **felly,** the rim of a wheel. 90. **Simnel cakes,** rich plum cakes with hard crust.

A team of horses passed from Finglas with toiling plodding tread, dragging through the funereal silence a creaking wagon on which lay a granite block. The waggoner marching at their head saluted.

Coffin now. Got here before us, dead as he is. Horse looking round at it with his plume skeowways. Dull eye: collar tight on his neck, pressing on a bloodvessel or something. Do they know what they cart out here every day? Must be twenty or thirty funerals every day. Then Mount Jerome for the protestants. Funerals all over the world everywhere every minute. Shoveling them under by the cartload doublequick. Thousands every hour. Too many in the world.

Mourners came out through the gates: woman and a girl. Leanjawed harpy, hard woman at a bargain, her bonnet awry. Girl's face stained with dirt and tears, holding the woman's arm looking up at her for a sign to cry. Fish's face, bloodless and livid.

The mutes shouldered the coffin and bore it in through the gates. So much dead weight. Felt heavier myself stepping out of that bath. First the stiff: then the friends of the stiff. Corny Kelleher and the boy followed with their wreaths. Who is that beside them? Ah, the brother-in-law.

All walked after.

Martin Cunningham whispered:

—I was in mortal agony with you talking of suicide before Bloom.

—What? Mr Power whispered. How so?

—His father poisoned himself, Martin Cunningham whispered. Had the Queen's hotel in Ennis. You heard him say he was going to Clare. Anniversary.

—O God! Mr Power whispered. First I heard of it. Poisoned himself!

He glanced behind him to where a face with dark thinking eyes followed towards the cardinal's mausoleum. Speaking.

—Was he insured? Mr Bloom asked.

—I believe so, Mr Kernan answered, but the policy was heavily mortgaged. Martin is trying to get the youngster into Artane.

—How many children did he leave?

—Five. Ned Lambert says he'll try to get one of the girls into Todd's.

—A sad case, Mr Bloom said gently. Five young children.

—A great blow to the poor wife, Mr Kernan added.

—Indeed yes, Mr Bloom agreed.

Has the laugh at him now.

He looked down at the boots he had blackened and polished. She had outlived him, lost her husband. More dead for her than for me. One must outlive the other. Wise men say. There are more women than men in the world. Condole with her. Your terrible loss. I hope you'll soon follow him. For Hindu widows only. She would marry another. Him? No. Yet who knows after? Widowhood not the thing since the old queen died. Drawn on a guncarriage. Victoria and Albert. Frogmore memorial mourning. But in the end she put a few violets in her bonnet. Vain in her heart of hearts. All for a shadow. Consort not even a king. Her son was the substance. Something new to hope for not like the past she wanted back, waiting. It never comes. One must go first: alone under the ground: and lie no more in her warm bed.

—How are you, Simon? Ned Lambert said softly, clasping hands. Haven't seen you for a month of Sundays.

—Never better. How are all in Cork's own town?

—I was down there for the Cork park races on Easter Monday, Ned Lambert said. Same old six and eightpence. Stopped with Dick Tivy.

—And how is Dick, the solid man?

—Nothing between himself and heaven, Ned Lambert answered.

—By the holy Paul! Mr Dedalus said in subdued wonder. Dick Tivy bald?

—Martin is going to get up a whip for the youngsters, Ned Lambert said, pointing ahead. A few bob a skull. Just to keep them going till the insurance is cleared up.

---

23. **mutes**, hired mourners. 47. **Artane**, a well-known private school for boys in Dublin; **Todd's** (l. 50) is a private school for girls. 63. **Hindu . . . only.** According to ancient practice a Hindu widow was supposed to cremate herself on her husband's funeral pyre. The British suppressed the practice. 66. **old queen**, Victoria, who died in 1901. Albert, her consort, died December 14, 1861, and was buried in a magnificent mausoleum at Frogmore, Windsor Castle, near London. 71. **Her son**, Edward VII, King of England 1901-1910. 90. **whip**, slang for contribution. 92. **bob**, a shilling.

—Yes, yes, Mr Dedalus said dubiously. Is that the eldest boy in front?

—Yes, Ned Lambert said, with the wife's brother. John Henry Menton is behind. He put down his name for a quid.

—I'll engage he did, Mr Dedalus said. I often told poor Paddy he ought to mind that job. John Henry is not the worst in the world.

—How did he lose it? Ned Lambert asked. Liquor, what?

—Many a good man's fault, Mr Dedalus said with a sigh.

They halted about the door of the mortuary chapel. Mr Bloom stood behind the boy with the wreath, looking down at his sleek combed hair and the slender furrowed neck inside his brandnew collar. Poor boy! Was he there when the father? Both unconscious. Lighten up at the last moment and recognize for the last time. All he might have done. I owe three shilling to O'Grady. Would he understand? The mutes bore the coffin into the chapel. Which end is his head?

After a moment he followed the others in, blinking in the screened light. The coffin lay on its bier before the chancel four tall yellow candles at its corners. Always in front of us. Corny Kelleher, laying a wreath at each fore corner, beckoned to the boy to kneel. The mourners knelt here and there in praying desks. Mr Bloom stood behind near the font and, when all had knelt dropped carefully his unfolded newspaper from his pocket and knelt his right knee upon it. He fitted his black hat gently on his left knee and, holding its brim, bent over piously.

A server, bearing a brass bucket with something in it, came out through a door. The whitesmocked priest came after him tidying his stole with one hand, balancing with the other a little book against his toad's belly. Who'll read the book? I, said the rook.

They halted by the bier and the priest began to read out of his book with a fluent croak.

Father Coffey. I knew his name was like a coffin. *Dominenamine.* Bully about the muzzle he looks. Bosses the show. Muscular christian. Woe betide anyone that looks crooked at him: priest. Thou art Peter. Burst sideways like a sheep in clover Dedalus says he will. With a belly on him like a poisoned pup. Most amusing expressions that man finds. Hhhn: burst sideways.

—*Non intres in judicium cum servo tuo, Domine.*

Makes them feel more important to be prayed over in Latin. Requiem mass. Crape weepers. Blackedged notepaper. Your name on the altarlist. Chilly place this. Want to feed well, sitting in there all the morning in the gloom kicking his heels waiting for the next please. Eyes of a toad too. What swells him up that way? Molly gets swelled after cabbage. Air of the place maybe. Looks full of bad gas. Must be an infernal lot of bad gas round the place. Butchers for instance: They get like raw beefsteaks. Who was telling me? Mervyn Brown. Down in the vaults of saint Werburgh's lovely old organ hundred and fifty they have to bore a hole in the coffins sometimes to let out the bad gas and burn it. Out it rushes: blue. One whiff of that and you're a goner.

My kneecap is hurting me. Ow. That's better.

The priest took a stick with a knob at the end of it out of the boy's bucket and shook it over the coffin. Then he walked to the other end and shook it again. Then he came back and put it back in the bucket. As you were before you rested. It's all written down: he has to do it.

—*Et ne nos inducas in tentationem.*

The server piped the answers in the treble. I often thought it would be better to have boy servants. Up to fifteen or so. After that of course . . .

Holy water that was, I expect. Shaking sleep out of it. He must be fed up with that job, shaking that thing over all the corpses they trot up. What harm if he could see what he was shaking it over. Every mortal day a fresh batch: middleaged men, old women, children, women dead in childbirth,

---

38. **A server**, etc. As his mental observations reveal, the details of the burial service are unfamiliar to Mr. Bloom, who is not a Catholic. 43. **Who'll . . . rook**, from the nursery rime "Who Killed Cock Robin?" 47. **Father Coffey.** The description of Father Coffey has identified him with Cerberus, the three-headed dog that guarded the approach to Hades.

56. **Non . . . Domine,** Enter not into judgment against thy servant, O Lord! 85. **Et . . . tentationem,** And lead us not into temptation.

men with beards, baldheaded business men, consumptive girls with little sparrow's breasts. All the year round he prayed the same thing over them all and shook water on top of them: sleep. On Dignam now.

—*In paradisum.*

Said he was going to paradise or is in paradise. Says that over everybody. Tiresome kind of a job. But he has to say something.

The priest closed his book and went off, followed by the server. Corny Kelleher opened the sidedoors and the gravediggers came in, hoisted the coffin again, carried it out and shoved it on their cart. Corny Kelleher gave one wreath to the boy and one to the brother-in-law. All followed them out of the sidedoors into the mild grey air. Mr Bloom came last, folding his paper again into his pocket. He gazed gravely at the ground till the coffincart wheeled off to the left. The metal wheels ground the gravel with a sharp grating cry and the pack of blunt boots followed the barrow along a lane of sepulchres.

The ree the ra the ree the ra the roo. Lord, I mustn't lilt here.

—The O'Connell circle, Mr Dedalus said about him.

Mr Power's soft eyes went up to the apex of the lofty cone.

—He's at rest, he said, in the middle of his people, old Dan O'. But his heart is buried in Rome. How many broken hearts are buried here, Simon!

—Her grave is over there, Jack, Mr Dedalus said. I'll soon be stretched beside her. Let Him take me whenever He likes.

Breaking down, he began to weep to himself quietly, stumbling a little in his walk. Mr Power took his arm.

—She's better where she is, he said kindly.

—I suppose so, Mr Dedalus said with a weak gasp. I suppose she is in heaven if there is a heaven.

Corny Kelleher stepped aside from his rank and allowed the mourners to plod by.

—Sad occasions, Mr Kernan began politely.

Mr Bloom closed his eyes and sadly twice bowed his head.

—The others are putting on their hats, Mr Kernan said. I suppose we can do so too. We are the last. This cemetery is a treacherous place.

They covered their heads.

—The reverend gentleman read the service too quickly, don't you think? Mr Kernan said with reproof.

Mr Bloom nodded gravely, looking in the quick bloodshot eyes. Secret eyes, secret searching eyes. Mason, I think: not sure. Beside him again. We are the last. In the same boat. Hope he'll say something else.

Mr Kernan added:

—The service of the Irish church, used in Mount Jerome, is simpler, more impressive, I must say.

Mr Bloom gave prudent assent. The language of course was another thing.

Mr Kernan said with solemnity:

—*I am the resurrection and the life.* That touches a man's inmost heart.

—It does, Mr Bloom said.

Your heart perhaps but what price the fellow in the six feet by two with his toes to the daisies. No touching that. Seat of the affections. Broken heart. A pump after all, pumping thousands of gallons of blood every day. One fine day it gets bunged up and there you are. Lots of them lying around here: lungs, hearts, livers. Old rusty pumps: damn the thing else. The resurrection and the life. Once you are dead you are dead. That last day idea. Knocking them all up out of their graves. Come forth, Lazarus. And he came fifth and lost the job. Get up! Last day! Then every fellow mousing around for his liver and his lights and the rest of his traps. Find damn all of himself that morning. Pennyweight of powder in a skull. Twelve grammes one pennyweight. Troy measure.

Corny Kelleher fell into step at their side.

—Everything went off A 1, he said. What?

He looked on them from his drawling eye. Policeman's shoulders. With your tooraloom tooraloom.

—As it should be, Mr Kernan said.

—What? Eh? Corny Kelleher said.

---

26. **O'Connell circle.** See p. 1047, l. 62 and note. 32. **Rome.** O'Connell died in Genoa, not Rome. He had gone to Italy to regain his health.

83. **Lazarus,** the brother of Mary and Martha. After his death he was resurrected by Jesus as he said, "Lazarus, come forth." See *John*, 11:43.

Mr Kernan assured him.

—Who is that chap behind with Tom Kernan? John Henry Menton asked. I know his face.

Ned Lambert glanced back.

—Bloom, he said, Madam Marion Tweedy that was, is, I mean, the soprano. She's his wife.

—O, to be sure, John Henry Menton said. I haven't seen her for some time. She was a finelooking woman. I danced with her, wait, fifteen seventeen golden years ago, at Mat Dillons, in Roundtown. And a good armful she was.

He looked behind through the others.

—What is he? he asked. What does he do? Wasn't he in the stationery line? I fell foul of him one evening, I remember, at bowls.

Ned Lambert smiled.

—Yes, he was, he said, in Wisdom Hely's. A traveller for blottingpaper.

—In God's name, John Henry Menton said, what did she marry a coon like that for? She had plenty of game in her then.

—Has still, Ned Lambert said. He does some canvassing for ads.

John Henry Menton's large eyes stared ahead.

The barrow turned into a side lane. A portly man, ambushed among the grasses, raised his hat in homage. The gravediggers touched their caps.

—John O'Connell, Mr Power said, pleased. He never forgets a friend.

Mr O'Connell shook all their hands in silence. Mr Dedalus said:

—I am come to pay you another visit.

—My dear Simon, the caretaker answered in a low voice. I don't want your custom at all.

Saluting Ned Lambert and John Henry Menton he walked on at Martin Cunningham's side, puzzling two keys at his back.

—Did you hear that one, he asked them, about Mulcahy from the Coombe?

—I did not, Martin Cunningham said.

They bent their silk hats in concert and Hynes inclined his ear. The caretaker hung his thumbs in the loops of his gold watch chain and spoke in a discreet tone to their vacant smiles.

—They tell the story, he said, that two drunks came out here one foggy evening to look for the grave of a friend of theirs. They asked for Mulcahy from the Coombe and were told where he was buried. After traipsing about in the fog they found the grave, sure enough. One of the drunks spelt out the name: Terence Mulcahy. The other drunk was blinking up at a statue of our Savior the widow had got put up.

The caretaker blinked up at one of the sepulchers they passed. He resumed:

—And, after blinking up at the sacred figure, *Not a bloody bit like the man*, says he. *That's not Mulcahy*, says he, *whoever done it*.

Rewarded by smiles he fell back and spoke with Corny Kelleher, accepting the dockets given him, turning them over and scanning them as he walked.

—That's all done with a purpose, Martin Cunningham explained to Hynes.

—I know, Hynes said, I know that.

—To cheer a fellow up, Martin Cunningham said. It's pure goodheartedness: damn the thing else.

Mr Bloom admired the caretaker's prosperous bulk. All want to be on good terms with him. Decent fellow, John O'Connell, real good sort. Keys: like Keyes's ad: no fear of anyone getting out, no passout checks. *Habeas corpus*. I must see about that ad after the funeral. Did I write Ballsbridge on the envelope I took to cover when she disturbed me writing to Martha? Hope it's not chucked in the dead letter office. Be the better of a shave. Grey spouting beard. That's the first sign when the hairs come out grey and temper getting cross. Silver threads among the grey. Fancy being his wife. Wonder how he had the gumption to propose to any girl. Come out and live in the graveyard. Dangle that before her. It might thrill her first. Courting death... Shades of night hovering here with

---

33. **John O'Connell**, the caretaker. He is regarded as the Homeric recall of Pluto, ruler of Hades, and his young wife as Proserpine. 43. **puzzling**, fumbling.

81. *Habeas corpus*, You have the body, the name given to a common-law writ with authority to bring the person in question before the court. 85. **Martha**. See p. 1046, l. 28 and note.

all the dead stretched about. The shadows of the tombs when churchyards yawn and Daniel O'Connell must be a descendant I suppose who is this used to say he was a queer breedy man great catholic all the same like a big giant in the dark. Will o' the wisp. Gas of graves. Want to keep her mind off it to conceive at all. Women especially are so touchy. Tell her a ghost story in bed to make her sleep. Have you ever seen a ghost? Well, I have. It was pitchdark night. The clock was on the stroke of twelve. Still they'd kiss all right if properly keyed up. Whores in Turkish graveyards. Learn anything if taken young. You might pick up a young widow here. Men like that. Love among the tombstones. Romeo. Spice of pleasure. In the midst of death we are in life. Both ends meet. Tantalizing for the poor dead. Smell of grilled beefsteaks to the starving gnawing their vitals. Desire to grig people. Molly wanting to do it at the window. Eight children he has anyway.

He has seen a fair share go under in his time, lying around him field after field. Holy fields. More room if they buried them standing. Sitting or kneeling you couldn't. Standing? His head might come up some day above ground in a landslip with his hand pointing. All honeycombed the ground must be: oblong cells. And very neat he keeps it too, trim grass and edgings. His garden Major Gamble calls Mount Jerome. Well so it is. Ought to be flowers of sleep. Chinese cemeteries with giant poppies growing produce the best opium Mastiansky told me. The Botanic Gardens are just over there. It's the blood sinking in the earth gives new life. Same idea those jews they said killed the christian boy. Every man his price. Well preserved fat corpse gentlemen, epicure, invaluable for fruit garden. A bargain. By carcass of William Wilkinson, auditor and accountant, lately deceased, three pounds thirteen and six. With thanks.

I daresay the soil would be quite fat with corpse manure, bones, flesh, nails, charnel-houses. Dreadful. Turning green and pink, decomposing. Rot quick in damp earth. The lean old ones tougher. Then a kind of a tallowy kind of a cheesy. Then begin to get black, treacle oozing out of them. Then dried up. Deadmoths. Of course the cells or whatever they are go on living. Changing about. Live for ever practically. Nothing to feed on feed on themselves.

But they must breed a devil of a lot of maggots. Soil must be simply swirling with them. Your head it simply swurls. Those pretty little seaside gurls. He looks cheerful enough over it. Gives him a sense of power seeing all the others go under first. Wonder how he looks at life. Cracking his jokes too: warms the cockles of his heart. The one about the bulletin. Spurgeon went to heaven 4 a.m. this morning. 11 p.m. (closing time). Not arrived yet. Peter. The dead themselves the men anyhow would like to hear an odd joke or the women to know what's in fashion. A juicy pear or ladies' punch, hot, strong and sweet. Keep out of the damp. You must laugh sometimes so better do it that way. Gravediggers in *Hamlet*. Shows the profound knowledge of the human heart. Daren't joke about the dead for two years at least. *De mortuis nil nisi prius*. Go out of mourning first. Hard to imagine his funeral. Seems a sort of a joke. Read your own obituary notice they say you live longer. Gives you second wind. New lease of life.

—How many have you for tomorrow? the caretaker asked.

—Two, Corny Kelleher said. Half ten and eleven.

The caretaker put the papers in his pocket. The barrow had ceased to trundle. The mourners split and moved to each side of the hole, stepping with care round the graves. The gravediggers bore the coffin and set its nose on the brink, looping the bands round it.

Burying him. We come to bury Caesar.

---

21. **grig**, tantalize. 39-40. **Same . . . boy.** Medieval literature records several legends of the murder of a Christian boy by Jews. Best known are the story of Hugh of Lincoln and Chaucer's *Prioress's Tale*. 59-60. **Your . . . gurls.** These two lines are from a popular song, snatches of which are quoted elsewhere in *Ulysses*. 75-76. **De . . . prius.** The word *nisi* in the Latin proverb *De mortuis nil nisi bonum* (say nothing but good about the dead) suggests to Mr. Bloom the legal phrase *nisi prius*, which means that a case in British law must be tried in the court of Westminster *unless* it has been *first* tried in the county where it originated. 91. **We . . . Caesar**, from Antony's oration over the body of Caesar. See Shakespeare's *Julius Caesar*, III, 2, 79.

His ides of March or June. He doesn't know who is here nor care.

Now who is that lankylooking galoot over there in the macintosh? Now who is he I'd like to know? Now, I'd give a trifle to know who he is. Always someone turns up you never dreamt of. A fellow could live on his lonesome all his life. Yes, he could. Still he'd have to get someone to sod him after he died though he could dig his own grave. We all do. Only man buries. No ants too. First thing strikes anybody. Bury the dead. Say Robinson Crusoe was true to life. Well then Friday buried him. Every Friday buries a Thursday if you come to look at it.

O, poor Robinson Crusoe,
How could you possibly do so?

Poor Dignam! His last lie on the earth in his box. When you think of them all it does seem a waste of wood. All gnawed through. They could invent a handsome bier with a kind of panel sliding let it down that way. Ay but they might object to be buried out of another fellow's. They're so particular. Lay me in my native earth. Bit of clay from the holy land. Only a mother and deadborn child ever buried in the one coffin. I see what it means, I see. To protect him as long as possible even in the earth. The Irishman's house is his coffin. Embalming in catacombs, mummies, the same idea.

Mr Bloom stood far back, his hat in his hand, counting the bared heads. Twelve. I'm thirteen. No. The chap in the macintosh is thirteen. Death's number. Where the deuce did he pop out of? He wasn't in the chapel, that I'll swear. Silly superstition that about thirteen.

Nice soft tweed Ned Lambert has in that suit. Tinge of purple. I had one like that when we lived in Lombard street west. Dressy fellow he was once. Used to change three suits in the day. Must get that grey suit of mine turned by Mesias. Hello. It's dyed. His wife I forgot he's not married or his landlady ought to have picked out those threads for him.

The coffin dived out of sight, eased down by the men straddled on the gravetrestles.

They struggle up and out: and all uncovered. Twenty.

Pause.

If we were all suddenly somebody else.

Far away a donkey brayed. Rain. No such ass. Never see a dead one, they say. Shame of death. They hide. Also poor papa went away.

Gentle sweet air blew round the bared heads in a whisper. Whisper. The boy by the gravehead held his wreath with both hands staring quietly in the black open space. Mr Bloom moved behind the portly kindly caretaker. Well cut frockcoat. Weighing them up perhaps to see which will go next. Well it is a long rest. Feel no more. It's the moment you feel. Must be damned unpleasant. Can't believe it at first. Mistake must be: someone else. Try the house opposite. Wait, I wanted to I haven't yet. Then darkened deathchamber. Light they want. Whispering around you. Would you like to see a priest? Then rambling and wandering. Delirium all you hid all your life. The death struggle. His sleep is not natural. Press his lower eyelid. Watching is his nose pointed is his jaw sinking are the soles of his feet yellow. Pull the pillow away and finish it off on the floor since he's doomed. Devil in that picture of sinner's death showing him a woman. Dying to embrace her in his shirt. Last act of *Lucia. Shall I nevermore behold thee?* Bam! expires. Gone at last. People talk about you a bit: forget you. Don't forget to pray for him. Remember him in your prayers. Even Parnell. Ivy day dying out. Then they follow: dropping into a hole one after the other.

We are praying now for the repose of his soul. Hoping you're well and not in hell. Nice change of air. Out of the fryingpan of life into the fire of purgatory.

Does he ever think of the hole waiting for himself? They say you do when you shiver in the sun. Someone walking over it. Call-

---

80. *Lucia, Lucia di Lammermoor,* a famous Italian romantic opera by Gaetano Donizetti (1797-1848). In the last act the hero, Edgardo, hearing that Lucia is dead, stabs himself. Before he dies he sings this beautiful aria, "Tu Che Spiegasti" ("Shall I never more behold thee?"). 85. **Ivy day.** October 9, the anniversary of Parnell's death, is observed by a memorial procession and a ceremony held in Glasnevin Cemetery, Dublin, the cemetery where Paddy Dignam is now being buried.

boy's warning. Near you. Mine over there towards Finglas, the plot I bought. Mamma poor mamma, and little Rudy.

The gravediggers took up their spades and flung heavy clods of clay in on the coffin. Mr Bloom turned his face. And if he was alive all the time? Whew! By Jingo, that would be awful! No, no: he is dead, of course. Of course he is dead. Monday he died. They ought to have some law to pierce the heart and make sure or an electric clock or a telephone in the coffin and some kind of a canvas airhole. Flag of distress. Three days. Rather long to keep them in summer. Just as well to get shut of them as soon as you are sure there's no.

The clay fell softer. Begin to be forgotten. Out of sight, out of mind.

The caretaker moved away a few paces and put on his hat. Had enough of it. The mourners took heart of grace, one by one, covering themselves without show. Mr Bloom put on his hat and saw the portly figure make its way deftly through the maze of graves. Quietly, sure of his ground, he traversed the dismal fields.

Hynes jotting down something in his notebook. Ah, the names. But he knows them all. No: coming to me.

—I am just taking the names, Hynes said below his breath. What is your christian name? I'm not sure.

—L, Mr Bloom said. Leopold. And you might put down M'Coy's name too. He asked me to.

—Charley, Hynes said writing. I know. He was on the *Freeman* once.

So he was before he got the job in the morgue under Louis Byrne. Good idea a postmortem for doctors. Find out what they imagine they know. He died on a Tuesday. Got the run. Levanted with the cash of a few ads. Charley, you're my darling. That was why he asked me to. O well, does no harm. I saw to that, M'Coy. Thanks, old chap: much obliged. Leave him under an obligation: costs nothing.

—And tell us, Hynes said, do you know that fellow in the, fellow was over there in the . . . He looked around.

—Macintosh. Yes, I saw him, Mr Bloom said. Where is he now?

—Macintosh, Hynes said, scribbling. I don't know who he is. Is that his name?

He moved away, looking about him.

—No, Mr Bloom began, turning and stopping. I say, Hynes!

Didn't hear. What? Where has he disappeared to? Not a sign. Well of all the. Has anybody here seen? Kay ee double ell. Become invisible. Good Lord, what became of him?

A seventh gravedigger came beside Mr Bloom to take up an idle spade.

—O, excuse me!

He stepped aside nimbly.

Clay, brown, damp, began to be seen in the hole. It rose. Nearly over. A mound of damp clods rose more, rose, and the gravediggers rested their spades. All uncovered again for a few instants. The boy propped his wreath against a corner: the brother-in-law his on a lump. The gravediggers put on their caps and carried their earthy spades towards the barrow. Then knocked the blades lightly on the turf: clean. One bent to pluck from the haft a long tuft of grass. One, leaving his mates, walked slowly on with shouldered weapon, its blade blueglancing. Silently at the gravehead another coiled the coffinband. His navelcord. The brother-in-law, turning away, placed something in his free hand. Thanks in silence. Sorry, sir: trouble. Headshake. I know that. For yourselves just.

The mourners moved away slowly, without aim, by devious paths, staying awhile to read a name on a tomb.

—Let us go round by the chief's grave, Hynes said. We have time.

—Let us, Mr Power said.

They turned to the right, following their slow thoughts. With awe Mr Power's blank voice spoke:

—Some say he is not in that grave at all.

---

42. **Levanted**, ran away.

81. **navelcord**. In *Ulysses* this is said to symbolize the link in the chain of lives and the reincarnation of life. 89. **chief's grave**, that of Parnell. See p. 1048, l. 82 and p. 1057 l. 85; and notes.

That the coffin was filled with stones. That one day he will come again.

Hynes shook his head.

—Parnell will never come again, he said. He's there, all that was mortal of him. Peace to his ashes.

Mr Bloom walked unheeded along his grove by saddened angels, crosses, broken pillars, family vaults, stone hopes praying with upcast eyes, old Ireland's hearts and hands. More sensible to spend the money on some charity for the living. Pray for the repose of the soul of. Does anybody really? Plant him and have done with him. Like down a coalshoot. Then lump them together to save time. All souls' day. Twenty-seventh I'll be at his grave. Ten shillings for the gardener. He keeps it free of weeds. Old man himself. Bent down double with his shears clipping. Near death's door. Who passed away. Who departed this life. As if they did it of their own accord. Got the shove, all of them. Who kicked the bucket. More interesting if they told you what they were. So and so, wheelwright. I travelled for cork lino. I paid five shillings in the pound. Or a woman's with her saucepan. I cooked good Irish stew. Eulogy in a country churchyard it ought to be that poem of whose is it Wordsworth or Thomas Campbell. Entered into rest the protestants put it. Old Dr Murren's. The great physician called him home. Well it's God's acre for them. Nice country residence. Newly plastered and painted. Ideal spot to have a quiet smoke and read the *Church Times*. Marriage ads they never try to beautify. Rusty wreaths hung on knobs, garlands of bronzefoil. Better value that for the money. Still, the flowers are more poetical. The other gets rather tiresome, never withering. Expresses nothing. Immortelles.

A bird sat tamely perched on a poplar branch. Like stuffed. Like the wedding present alderman Hooper gave us. Hu! Not a budge out of him. Knows there are no catapults to let fly at him. Dead animal even sadder. Silly-Milly burying the little dead bird in the kitchen matchbox, a daisychain and bits of broken chainies on the grave.

The Sacred Heart that is: showing it. Heart on his sleeve. Ought to be sideways and red it should be painted like a real heart. Ireland was dedicated to it or whatever that. Seems anything but pleased. Why this infliction? Would birds come then and peck like the boy with the basket of fruit but he said no because they ought to have been afraid of the boy. Apollo that was.

How many! All these here once walked round Dublin. Faithful departed. As you are now so once were we.

Besides how could you remember everybody? Eyes, walk, voice. Well, the voice, yes: gramophone. Have a gramophone in every grave or keep it in the house. After dinner on a Sunday. Put on poor old greatgrandfather Kraahraark! Hellohellohello amawfullyglad kraark awfullygladaseeragain hellohello amarawf kopthsth. Remind you of the voice like the photograph reminds you of the face. Otherwise you couldn't remember the face after fifteen years, say. For instance who? For instance some fellow that died when I was in Wisdom Hely's.

Rtststr! A rattle of pebbles. Wait. Stop.

He looked down intently into a stone crypt. Some animal. Wait. There he goes.

An obese grey rat toddled along the side of the crypt, moving the pebbles. An old stager: greatgrandfather: he knows the ropes. The grey alive crushed itself in under the plinth, wriggled itself in under it. Good hidingplace for treasure.

Who lives there? Are laid the remains of Robert Emery. Robert Emmet was buried here by torchlight, wasn't he? Making his rounds.

Tail gone now.

One of those chaps would make short work of a fellow. Pick the bones clean no matter who it was. Ordinary meat for them. A

---

16. **All souls' day,** November 2, a day in the Roman Catholic Church on which prayers are offered for all souls in Purgatory. 25. **cork lino,** linoleum. 27-28. **Eulogy . . . churchyard.** The *Elegy Written in a Country Churchyard* is by Thomas Gray (see p. 50), not Wordsworth (p. 118) or Campbell (p. 296).

82. **plinth,** the stone or block on which a column or pedestal stands. 85. **Robert Emmet,** Irish revolutionist (1778-1803), leader of the United Irishmen working for national independence.

corpse is meat gone bad. Well and what's cheese? Corpse of milk. I read in that *Voyages in China* that the Chinese say a white man smells like a corpse. Cremation better. Priests dead against it. Devilling for the other firm. Wholesale burners and Dutch oven dealers. Time of the plague. Quicklime fever pits to eat them. Lethal chamber. Ashes to ashes. Or bury at sea. Where is that Parsee tower of silence? Eaten by birds. Earth, fire, water. Drowning they say is the pleasantest. See your whole life in a flash. But being brought back to life no. Can't bury in the air however. Out of a flying machine. Wonder does the news go about whenever a fresh one is let down. Underground communication. We learned that from them. Wouldn't be surprised. Regular square feed for them. Flies come before he's well dead. Got wind of Dignam. They wouldn't care about the smell of it. Saltwhite crumbling mush of corpse: smell, taste like raw white turnips.

The gates glimmered in front: still open. Back to the world again. Enough of this place. Brings you a bit nearer every time. Last time I was here was Mrs. Sinico's funeral. Poor papa too. The love that kills. And even scraping up the earth at night with a lantern like that case I read of to get at fresh buried females or even putrefied with running gravesores. Give you the creeps after a bit. I will appear to you after death. You will see my ghost after death. My ghost will haunt you after death. There is another world after death named hell. I do not like that other world she wrote. No more do I. Plenty to see and hear and feel yet. Feel live warm beings near you. Let them sleep in their maggoty beds. They are not going to get me this innings. Warm beds: warm fullblooded life.

Martin Cunningham emerged from a sidepath, talking gravely.

Solicitor, I think. I know his face. Menton. John Henry, solicitor, commissioner for oaths and affidavits. Dignam used to be in his office. Mat Dillon's long ago. Jolly Mat convivial evenings. Cold fowl, cigars, the Tantalus glasses. Heart of gold really. Yes, Menton. Got his rag out that evening on the bowling green because I sailed inside him. Pure fluke of mine: the bias. Why he took such a rooted dislike to me. Hate at first sight. Molly and Floey Dillon linked under the lilactree, laughing. Fellow always like that, mortified if women are by.

Got a dinge in the side of his hat. Carriage probably.

—Excuse me, sir, Mr Bloom said beside them.

They stopped.

—Your hat is a little crushed, Mr Bloom said, pointing.

John Henry Menton stared at him for an instant without moving.

—There, Martin Cunningham helped, pointing also.

John Henry Menton took off his hat, bulged out the dinge and smoothed the nap with care on his coatsleeve. He clapped the hat on his head again.

—It's all right now, Martin Cunningham said.

John Henry Menton jerked his head down in acknowledgment.

—Thank you, he said shortly.

They walked on towards the gates. Mr Bloom, chapfallen, drew behind a few paces so as not to overhear. Martin laying down the law. Martin could wind a sappyhead like that round his little finger without his seeing it.

Oyster eyes. Never mind. Be sorry after perhaps when it dawns on him. Get the pull over him that way.

Thank you. How grand we are this morning. (1914-1921)

10. **Parsee . . . silence.** In Bombay, India, the large colony of Parsees (descended from the Fire-worshipers of Persia) placed their dead upon towers, where the flesh was devoured by birds of prey. 36-37. **I . . . world.** Mr. Bloom's thoughts paraphrase a sentence from Martha Clifford's letter, "I do not like that other world."

49. **Tantalus,** a kind of locked case or cellaret for wines and liquors; so called because its contents were visible but not obtainable without the key. The name is identical with that of the mythological king who for revealing the secrets of the gods was condemned to stand up to his chin in water under a loaded fruit tree, the fruit and the water retreating whenever he sought to satisfy his hunger or thirst. Cf. *tantalize.* 51. **Got . . . out,** became angry. 53. **the bias,** the weight inserted in the surface of the ball to make it roll in a curved line.

Virginia Woolf
1882-1941

Virginia Woolf, among all the many gifted British women writers of the twentieth century, was perhaps the most richly endowed in respect to fluid, delicate, yet vigorous style and poetic insight; she has taken her place next to James Joyce as a portrayer of the mercurial powers and the fitful restlessness of the twentieth-century mind. She was born in 1882; her father was the noted critic Sir Leslie Stephen (1832-1904), editor of *The Cornhill Magazine* and *The Dictionary of National Biography*. She began writing as a book reviewer for the *London Times Literary Supplement*. With her husband, Leonard Woolf, she established the Hogarth Press, which enabled them to gather together a group of intellectuals including the novelists E. M. Forster and V. Sackville-West; the poets and critics Edith, Osbert, and Sacheverell Sitwell; the biographer Lytton Strachey; and the economist John Maynard Keynes.

After she had written two relatively unimportant novels, *The Voyage Out* (1915) and *Night and Day* (1919), Virginia Woolf began to read James Joyce's *Ulysses* (p. 1042), then coming out in *The Little Review,* and a few years later she became acquainted with the work of the remarkable French psychological novelist, Marcel Proust (1871-1922). The effect of these two powerful creative minds upon her writing was, as she put it, "a memorable catastrophe," as is amply demonstrated by four unusual novels she wrote immediately afterwards—*Jacob's Room* (1922), *Mrs. Dalloway* (1925), *To the Lighthouse* (1927), and *The Waves* (1931)—to which might be added an earlier volume of short stories and sketches, *Monday or Tuesday* (1921).

We may term the four novels just mentioned "stream of consciousness" or "interior monologue" novels, although these phrases are too loose and too simplifying to afford an accurate definition. *Jacob's Room* is the world of a young man—his sojourn at Cambridge, his travels, his life in London, his studies abroad, his death in the First World War—all presented through the people about him, for whom the word *room* is symbolic. *Mrs. Dalloway,* covering a time span of only twelve temporal hours, compresses the lives of many persons into that short period, in a manner similar in objectives though not in methods to Joyce's *Ulysses*. The theory that emerges from this fascinating novel in particular is one of Virginia Woolf's favorites: everything that happened to Mrs. Dalloway and everything that she did in those twelve hours were shaped by what had happened to her and what she had done before. For Mrs. Dalloway, as for everybody and everything in twentieth-century British civilization about her, or, for that matter, in the whole world, time is all one piece —past, present, and future. In *To the Lighthouse,* a family vacationing in the Hebrides plans an excursion to a lighthouse which never takes place. Years later, after time has taken its usual toll, the little boy, once so disappointed, visits the lighthouse as a young man, only to be disillusioned. In this powerful and moving novel, Time, the real protagonist, has had its way with the lighthouse, with the home of the family, and with the young man himself. *The Waves* is a difficult, though characteristic, novel because Virginia Woolf, in her quest after the life of the human mentality, has cast aside all semblance of conventional structure. Six friends, at different points in their progress from birth to death, are caught and fixed by a series of soliloquies which imply rather than explain what has happened to them. The integrating element here is the sea (symbolic of Time) over which the sun (that is, the lives of the characters) plays in a series of beautiful lyrical intermezzi. The language throughout tends to be the author's, not the characters'. In fact, characterization, so essential to the conventional concept of a novel, has been subordinated to an interpretation of the universality of human spiritual experiences.

Farther into this intangible kingdom Virginia Woolf could not go, and her last two novels, *The Years* (1937) and *Between the Acts* (1941), are symptomatic of decline. Freakish but brilliant as a study of Time is her prose fantasy, *Orlando* (1928), in which the hero moves through English history and English literature from the time of Elizabeth I to the 1920's, changing sex on one occasion in order to bring into the picture the essential feminine elements in life. *Orlando* illustrates, moreover, a second favorite idea of Virginia Woolf's—namely, that there are many potential beings wrapped up in every individual human being. *Three Guineas* (1938) is notable for its passionate hatred of war, that inhuman institution which afflicts mankind, the awful being whose face is the face of death; in contrast, *Flush, a Biography* (1933) about Elizabeth Barrett Browning's pet spaniel, is a charming *tour de force*.

The almost mystic blending of time and personality in Virginia Woolf's novels should be coupled in the reader's mind with her love of life—an especially prominent trait—a gift at once beautiful, painful, and paradoxical; and with her faith in life, in which death, an ever-present fact, is only an incident. The life of the mind and the interplay of many human personalities, moving horizontally in a space-time relationship and vertically in a psychological projection in which the limitations of space and time no longer exist—these constitute Virginia Woolf's natural realm. It may take only a few seconds to wind a watch; but during those few seconds the mind can flash back and forth over a whole lifetime, summing up the lives of innumerable other human beings, considering indeed all eternity. Reality, as most people understand the term, becomes then far more than a materialistic fact. The lighthouse to which the young boy aspired was a beautiful, unattained figment; the lighthouse which the young man visited proved to be a mean, prosaic thing—yet both, as Virginia Woolf sees it, had true reality. Her blending of the tangible and intangible is marvelously delicate but, once understood, hauntingly impressive.

Unfortunately, Virginia Woolf cared little about the common middle-class problems of existence and survival, in which dreams are all too often rudely displaced by vulgar compromises. Hers was an aristocratic, poetic, essentially romantic intelligence which, because it regarded life as a "translucent envelope" which contains us all, found all her attempts to grip life in concrete terms uncertain and unsatisfying. For all Virginia Woolf's instinctive faith in life and in the integrity of the human personality, the cruel physical horrors of the Second World War were too much for her. On March 28, 1941, she committed suicide by drowning herself in a Sussex stream.

from *The Waves*

In the July 14, 1931, entry of *A Writer's Diary* (which contains excerpts from Virginia Woolf's twenty-six volume diary, compiled and published in 1953 by her husband) she gives this report of her work on *The Waves*: "But my *Waves* account runs, I think, as follows:—I began it, seriously, about September 10th 1929. I finished the first version on April 10th 1930. I began the second version on May 1st 1930. I finished the second version on February 7th 1931. I began to correct the second version on May 1st 1931, finished 22nd June 1931. I began to correct the typescript on 25th June 1931. Shall finish (I hope) 18th July 1931. Then remain only the proofs." February 7, 1931, the day she finished the second version, she has this entry: "What interests me in the last stage was the freedom and boldness with which my imagination picked up, used and tossed aside all the images, symbols which I had prepared. I am sure that this is the right way of using them—not in set pieces, as I had tried at first, coherently, but simply as images, never making them work out; only suggest. Thus I hope to have kept the sound of the sea and the birds, dawn and garden subconsciously present, doing their work under ground."

The novel is written in sections; each section is a series of monologues by the main characters. The course of the lives of these characters is indicated in a prose poem prefixed to each of the sections, in which the sun symbolizes their lives, and the pressing waves the inevitable passage of time, which will ultimately triumph over all. In the following section, therefore, it should be remembered that the characters are speaking from a time somewhat past the middle of their lives.

THE *sun no longer stood in the middle of the sky. Its light slanted, falling obliquely. Here it caught on the edge of a cloud and burnt it into a slice of light, a blazing island on which no foot could rest. Then another cloud was caught in the light and another and another, so that the waves beneath were arrow-struck with fiery feathered darts that shot erratically across the quivering blue.*

The topmost leaves of the tree were crisped in the sun. They rustled stiffly in the random breeze. The birds sat still save that they flicked their heads sharply from side to side. Now they paused in their song as if glutted with sound, as if the fullness of midday had gorged them. The dragon-fly poised motionless over a reed then shot its blue stitch further through the air. The far hum in the distance seemed made of the broken tremor of fine wings dancing up and down on the horizon. The river water held the reeds now fixed as if glass had hardened round them; and then the glass wavered and the reeds swept low. Pondering, sunken headed the cattle stood in the fields and cumbrously moved one foot and then another. In the bucket near the house the tap stopped dripping, as if the bucket were full, and then the tap dripped one, two, three separate drops in succession.

The windows showed erratically spots of burning fire, the elbow of one branch, and then some tranquil space of pure clarity. The blind hung red at the window's edge and within the room daggers of light fell upon chairs and tables making cracks across their lacquer and polish. The green pot bulged enormously, with its white window elongated in its side. Light driving darkness before it spilt itself profusely upon the corners and bosses; and yet heaped up darkness in mounds of unmoulded shape.

The waves massed themselves, curved their backs and crashed. Up spurted stones and shingle. They swept round the rocks, and the spray, leaping high, spattered the walls of a cave that had been dry before, and left pools inland, where some fish, stranded, lashed its tail as the wave drew back.

"I have signed my name," said Louis, "already twenty times. I, and again I, and again I. Clear, firm, unequivocal, there it stands, my name. Clear-cut and unequivocal am I too. Yet a vast inheritance of experience is packed in me. I have lived thousands of years. I am like a worm that has eaten its way through the wood of a very old oak beam. But now I am compact; now I am gathered together this fine morning.

"The sun shines from a clear sky. But twelve o'clock brings neither rain nor sunshine. It is the hour when Miss Johnson brings me my letters in a wire tray. Upon these white sheets I indent my name. The whisper of leaves, water running down gutters, green depths flecked with dahlias or zinnias; I, now a duke, now Plato, companion of Socrates; the tramp of dark men and yellow men migrating east, west, north and south; the eternal procession, women going with attaché cases down the Strand as they went once with pitchers to the Nile; all the furled and close-packed leaves of my many-folded life are now summed in my name; incised cleanly and barely on the sheet. Now a full-grown man; now upright standing in sun or rain, I must drop heavy as a hatchet and cut the oak with my sheer weight, for if I deviate, glancing this way, or that way, I shall fall like snow and be wasted.

The excerpt from *The Waves* by Virginia Woolf is reprinted by permission of Harcourt, Brace and Company and Leonard Woolf. Copyright, 1931, by the publishers.

"I am half in love with the typewriter and the telephone. With letters and cables and brief but courteous commands on the telephone to Paris, Berlin, New York I have fused my many lives into one; I have helped by my assiduity and decision to score those lines on the map there by which the different parts of the world are laced together. I love punctually at ten to come into my room; I love the purple glow of the dark mahogany; I love the table and its sharp edge; and the smooth-running drawers. I love the telephone with its lip stretched to my whisper, and the date on the wall; and the engagement book. Mr. Prentice at four; Mr. Eyres sharp at four-thirty.

"I like to be asked to come to Mr. Burchard's private room and report on our commitments to China. I hope to inherit an arm-chair and a Turkey carpet. My shoulder is to the wheel; I roll the dark before me, spreading commerce where there was chaos in the far parts of the world. If I press on, from chaos making order, I shall find myself where Chatham stood, and Pitt, Burke, and Sir Robert Peel. Thus I expunge certain stains, and erase old defilements; the woman who gave me a flag from the top of the Christmas tree; my accent; beatings and other tortures; the boasting boys; my father, a banker at Brisbane.

"I have read my poet in an eating-house, and, stirring my coffee, listened to the clerks making bets at the little tables, watched the women hesitating at the counter. I said that nothing should be irrelevant, like a piece of brown paper dropped casually on the floor. I said their journeys should have an end in view; they should earn their two pound ten a week at the command of an august master; some hand, some robe, should fold us about in the evening. When I have healed these fractures and comprehended these monstrosities so that they need neither excuse nor apology which both waste our strength, I shall give back to the street and the eating-shop what they lost when they fell on these hard times and broke on these stony beaches. I shall assemble a few words and forge round us a hammered ring of beaten steel.

"But now I have not a moment to spare. There is no respite here, no shadow made of quivering leaves, or alcove to which one can retreat from the sun, to sit, with a lover, in the cool of the evening. The weight of the world is on our shoulders; its vision is through our eyes; if we blink or look aside, or turn back to finger what Plato said or remember Napoleon and his conquests, we inflict on the world the injury of some obliquity. This is life; Mr. Prentice at four; Mr. Eyres at four-thirty. I like to hear the soft rush of the lift and the thud with which it stops on my landing and the heavy male tread of responsible feet down the corridors. So by dint of our united exertions we send ships to the remotest parts of the globe; replete with lavatories and gymnasiums. The weight of the world is on our shoulders. This is life. If I press on, I shall inherit a chair and a rug; a place in Surrey with glass houses, and some rare conifer, melon, or flowering tree which other merchants will envy.

"Yet I still keep my attic room. There I open the usual little book; there I watch the rain glisten on the tiles till they shine like a policeman's waterproof; there I see the broken windows in poor people's houses; the lean cats; some slattern squinting in a cracked looking-glass as she arranges her face for the street corner; there Rhoda sometimes comes. For we are lovers.

"Percival has died; (he died in Egypt; he died in Greece; all deaths are one death). Susan has children; Neville mounts rapidly to the conspicuous heights. Life passes. The clouds change perpetually over our houses. I do this, do that, and again do this and then that. Meeting and parting, we assemble different forms, make different patterns. But if I do not nail these impressions to the board and out of the many men in me make one;

---

25. **Chatham ... Pitt, Burke ... Peel.** William Pitt the Elder, first Earl of Chatham (1708-1778), and his son William Pitt the Younger (1759-1806) were both prime ministers of England. Edmund Burke (1729-1797) was the celebrated parliamentary orator and political friend of the American colonists in their struggle for independence (Vol. I, p. 1142). Sir Robert Peel (1788-1850) also was prime minister (in the 1830's); his reform of the police system as Home Secretary explains the nickname *bobby* for the London policeman.

exist here and now and not in streaks and patches, like scattered snow wreaths on far mountains; and ask Miss Johnson as I pass through the office about the movies and take my cup of tea and accept also my favourite biscuit, then I shall fall like snow and be wasted.

"Yet when six o'clock comes and I touch my hat to the commissionaire, being always too effusive in ceremony since I desire so much to be accepted; and struggle, leaning against the wind, buttoned up, with my jaws blue and my eyes running water, I wish that a little typist would cuddle on my knees; I think that my favourite dish is liver and bacon; and so am apt to wander to the river, to the narrow streets where there are frequent public-houses, and the shadows of ships passing at the end of the street, and women fighting. But I say to myself, recovering my sanity, Mr. Prentice at four; Mr. Eyres at four-thirty. The hatchet must fall on the block; the oak must be cleft to the centre. The weight of the world is on my shoulders. Here is the pen and the paper; on the letters in the wire basket I sign my name, I, I, and again I."

"Summer comes, and winter," said Susan. "The seasons pass. The pear fills itself and drops from the tree. The dead leaf rests on its edge. But steam has obscured the window. I sit by the fire watching the kettle boil. I see the pear tree through the streaked steam on the window-pane.

"Sleep, sleep, I croon, whether it is summer or winter, May or November. Sleep I sing—I, who am unmelodious and hear no music save rustic music when a dog barks, a bell tinkles, or wheels crunch upon the gravel. I sing my song by the fire like an old shell murmuring on the beach. Sleep, sleep, I say, warning off with my voice all who rattle milk-cans, fire at rooks, shoot rabbits, or in any way bring the shock of destruction near this wicker cradle, laden with soft limbs, curled under a pink coverlet.

"I have lost my indifference, my blank eyes, my pear-shaped eyes that saw to the root. I am no longer January, May or any other season, but am all spun to a fine thread round the cradle, wrapping in a cocoon made of my own blood the delicate limbs of my baby. Sleep, I say, and feel within me uprush some wilder, darker violence, so that I would fell down with one blow any intruder, any snatcher, who should break into this room and wake the sleeper.

"I pad about the house all day long in apron and slippers, like my mother who died of cancer. Whether it is summer, whether it is winter, I no longer know by the moor grass, and the heath flower; only by the steam on the window-pane, or the frost on the window-pane. When the lark peels high his ring of sound and it falls through the air like an apple paring, I stoop; I feed my baby. I, who used to walk through beech woods noting the jay's feather turning blue as it falls, past the shepherd and the tramp, who stared at the woman squatted beside a tilted cart in a ditch, go from room to room with a duster. Sleep, I say, desiring sleep to fall like a blanket of down and cover these weak limbs; demanding that life shall sheathe its claws and gird its lightning and pass by, making of my own body a hollow, a warm shelter for my child to sleep in. Sleep, I say, sleep. Or I go to the window, I look at the rook's high nest; and the pear tree. 'His eyes will see when mine are shut,' I think. 'I shall go mixed with them beyond my body and shall see India. He will come home, bringing me trophies to be laid at my feet. He will increase my possessions.'

"But I never rise at dawn and see the purple drops in the cabbage leaves; the red drops in the roses. I do not watch the setter nose in a circle, or lie at night watching the leaves hide the stars and the stars move and the leaves hang still. The butcher calls; the milk has to be stood under a shade lest it should sour.

"Sleep, I say, sleep, as the kettle boils and its breath comes thicker and thicker issuing in one jet from the spout. So life fills my veins. So life pours through my limbs. So I am driven forward, till I could cry, as I move from dawn to dusk opening and shutting, 'No more. I am glutted with natural happiness.' Yet more will come, more children;

more cradles, more baskets in the kitchen and hams ripening; and onions glistening; and more beds of lettuce and potatoes. I am blown like a leaf by the gale; now brushing the wet grass, now whirled up. I am glutted with natural happiness; and wish sometimes that the fullness would pass from me and the weight of the sleeping house rise, when we sit reading, and I stay the thread at the eye of my needle. The lamp kindles a fire in the dark pane. A fire burns in the heart of the ivy. I see a lit-up street in the evergreens. I hear traffic in the brush of the wind down the lane, and broken voices, and laughter, and Jinny who cries as the door opens, 'Come, Come!'

"But no sound breaks the silence of our house, where the fields sigh close to the door. The wind washes through the elm trees; a moth hits the lamp; a cow lows; a crack of sound starts in the rafter, and I push my thread through the needle and murmur, 'Sleep.'"

"Now is the moment," said Jinny. "Now we have met, and have come together. Now let us talk, let us tell stories. Who is he? Who is she? I am infinitely curious and do not know what is to come. If you, whom I meet for the first time, were to say to me, 'The coach starts at four from Piccadilly,' I would not stay to fling a few necessaries in a bandbox, but would come at once.

"Let us sit here under the cut flowers, on the sofa by the picture. Let us decorate our Christmas tree with facts and again with facts. People are so soon gone; let us catch them. That man there, by the cabinet; he lives, you say, surrounded by china pots. Break one and you shatter a thousand pounds. And he loved a girl in Rome and she left him. Hence the pots, old junk found in lodging-houses or dug from the desert sands. And since beauty must be broken daily to remain beautiful, and he is static, his life stagnates in a china sea. It is strange though; for once as a young man, he sat on damp ground and drank rum with soldiers.

"One must be quick and add facts deftly, like toys to a tree, fixing them with a twist of the fingers. He stoops, how he stoops, even over an azalea. He stoops over the old woman even, because she wears diamonds in her ears, and, bundling about her estate in a pony carriage, directs who is to be helped, what tree felled, and who turned out tomorrow. (I have lived my life I must tell you all these years and I am now past thirty, perilously, like a mountain goat leaping from crag to crag; I do not settle long anywhere; I do not attach myself to one person in particular; but you will find that if I raise my arm, some figure at once breaks off and will come.) And that man is a judge; and that man is a millionaire, and that man, with the eyeglass, shot his governess through the heart with an arrow when he was ten years old. Afterwards he rode through deserts with dispatches, took part in revolutions and now collects materials for a history of his mother's family, long settled in Norfolk. That little man with a blue chin has a right hand that is withered. But why? We do not know. That woman, you whisper discreetly, with the pearl pagodas hanging from her ears, was the pure flame who lit the life of one of our statesmen; now since his death she sees ghosts, tells fortunes, and has adopted a coffee-coloured youth whom she calls the Messiah. That man with the drooping moustache, like a cavalry officer, lived a life of the utmost debauchery (it is all in some memoir) until one day he met a stranger in a train who converted him between Edinburgh and Carlisle by reading the Bible.

"Thus, in a few seconds, deftly, adroitly, we decipher the hieroglyphs written on other people's faces. Here, in this room, are the abraded and battered shells cast on the shore. The door goes on opening. The room fills and fills with knowledge, anguish, many kinds of ambition, much indifference, some despair. Between us, you say, we could build cathedrals, dictate policies, condemn men to death, and administer the affairs of several public offices. The common fund of experience is very deep. We have between us scores of children of both sexes, whom we are educating, going to see at school with the measles, and bringing up to inherit our houses. In one way or another we make this day, this Friday, some by going to the Law Courts; others to the city; others to the nursery; others by marching and forming fours. A million hands stitch, raise hods with bricks. The activity is endless. And tomorrow it begins again; tomorrow we make Saturday. Some take train for France; others ship for India. Some will never come into this room again. One may die tonight. Another will beget a child. From us every sort of building, policy, venture, picture, poem, child, factory, will spring. Life comes; life goes; we make life. So you say.

"But we who live in the body see with the body's imagination things in outline. I see rocks in bright sunshine. I cannot take these facts into some cave and, shading my eyes, grade their yellows, blues, umbers into one substance. I cannot remain seated for long. I must jump up and go. The coach may start from Piccadilly. I drop all these facts— diamonds, withered hands, china pots and the rest of it, as a monkey drops nuts from its naked paws. I cannot tell you if life is this or that. I am going to push out into the heterogeneous crowd. I am going to be buffeted; to be flung up, and flung down, among men, like a ship on the sea.

"For now my body, my companion, which is always sending its signals, the rough black 'No,' the golden 'Come' in rapid running arrows of sensation, beckons. Some one moves. Did I raise my arm? Did I look? Did my yellow scarf with the strawberry spots float and signal? He has broken from the wall. He follows. I am pursued through the forest. All is rapt, all is nocturnal and the parrots go screaming through the branches. All my senses stand erect. Now I feel the roughness of the fibre of the curtain through which I push; now I feel the cold iron railing and its blistered paint beneath my palm. Now the cool tide of darkness breaks its waters over me. We are out of doors. Night opens; night traversed by wandering moths; night hiding lovers roaming to adventure. I smell roses; I smell violets; I see red and blue just hidden. Now gravel is under my shoes; now grass. Up reel the tall backs of houses guilty with lights. All London is uneasy with flashing lights. Now let us sing our love song— Come, come, come. Now my gold signal is like a dragon-fly flying taut. Jug, jug, jug, I sing like the nightingale whose melody is crowded in the too narrow passage of her throat. Now I hear crash and rending of boughs and the crack of antlers as if the beasts of the forest were all hunting, all rearing high and plunging down among the thorns. One has pierced me. One is driven deep within me. And velvet flowers and leaves whose coolness has been stood in water wash me round, and sheathe me, embalming me."

"Why, look," said Neville, "at the clock ticking on the mantelpiece? Time passes, yes. And we grow old. But to sit with you, alone with you, here in London, in this firelit room, you there, I here, is all. The world ransacked to its uttermost ends, and all its heights stripped and gathered of their flowers holds no more. Look at the firelight running up and down the gold thread in the curtain. The fruit it circles droops heavy. It falls on the toe of your boot, it gives your face a red rim—I think it is the firelight and not your face; I think those are books against the wall, and that a curtain, and that perhaps an armchair. But when you come everything changes. The cups and saucers changed when you came in this morning. There can be no doubt, I thought, pushing aside the newspaper, that our mean lives, unsightly as they are, put on splendour and have meaning only under the eyes of love.

"I rose. I had done my breakfast. There was the whole day before us, and as it was fine, tender, noncommittal, we walked through the Park to the Embankment, along the Strand to St. Paul's, then to the shop where I bought an umbrella, always talking, and now and then stopping to look. But can this last? I said to myself, by a lion in Trafalgar Square, by the lion seen once and for ever;—so I revisit my past life, scene by scene, there is an elm tree, and there lies Percival. For ever and ever, I swore. Then darted in the usual doubt. I clutched your hand. You left me. The descent into the Tube was like death. We were cut up, we were dissevered by all those faces and the hollow wind that seemed to roar down there over desert boulders. I sat staring in my own room. By five I knew that you were faithless. I snatched the telephone and the buzz, buzz, buzz of its stupid voice in your empty room battered my heart down, when the door opened and there you stood. That was the most perfect of our meetings. But these meetings, these partings, finally destroy us.

"Now this room seems to me central, something scooped out of the eternal night. Outside lines twist and intersect, but round us, wrapping us about. Here we are centred. Here we can be silent, or speak without raising our voices. Did you notice that and then that? we say. He said that, meaning . . . . She hesitated, and I believe suspected. Anyhow, I heard voices, a sob on the stair late at night. It is the end of their relationship. Thus we spin round us infinitely fine filaments and construct a system. Plato and Shakespeare are included, also quite obscure people, people of no importance whatsoever. I hate men who wear crucifixes on the left side of their waistcoats. I hate ceremonies and lamentations and the sad figure of Christ trembling beside another trembling and sad figure. Also the pomp and the indifference and the emphasis, always on the wrong place, of people holding forth under chandeliers in full evening dress, wearing stars and decorations. Some spray in a hedge, though, or a sunset over a flat winter field, or again the way some old woman sits, arms akimbo, in an omnibus with a basket—those we point at for the other to look at. It is so vast an alleviation to be able to point for another to look at. And then not to talk. To follow the dark paths of the mind and enter the past, to visit books, to brush aside their branches and break off some fruit. And you take it and marvel, as I take the careless movements of your body and marvel at its ease, its power— how you fling open windows and are dexterous with your hands. For alas! my mind is a little impeded, it soon tires; I fall damp, perhaps disgusting, at the goal.

"Alas! I could not ride about India in a sun-helmet and return to a bungalow. I cannot tumble, as you do, like half-naked boys on the deck of a ship, squirting each other with hose-pipes. I want this fire, I want this chair. I want some one to sit beside after the day's pursuit and all its anguish, after its listenings, and its waitings, and its suspicions. After quarrelling and reconciliation I need privacy—to be alone with you, to set this hubbub in order. For I am as neat as a cat in my habits. We must oppose the waste and deformity of the world, its crowds eddying round and round disgorged and trampling. One must slip paper-knives, even, exactly through the pages of novels, and tie up packets of letters neatly with green silk, and brush up the cinders with a hearth broom. Everything must be done to rebuke the horror of deformity. Let us read writers of Roman severity and virtue; let us seek perfection through the sand. Yes, but I love to slip the virtue and severity of the noble Romans under the grey light of your eyes, and dancing grasses and summer breezes and the laughter and shouts of boys at play—of naked cabin-boys squirting each other with hosepipes on the decks of ships. Hence I am not a disinterested seeker, like Louis, after perfection through the sand. Colours always stain the page; clouds pass over it. And the poem, I think, is only your voice speaking. Alcibiades, Ajax, Hector and Percival are also you. They loved riding, they risked their lives wantonly, they were not great readers either. But you are not Ajax or Percival. They did not wrinkle their noses and scratch their foreheads with your precise gesture. You are you. That is what consoles me for the lack of many things—I am ugly, I am weak— and the depravity of the world, and the flight of youth and Percival's death, and bitterness and rancour and envies innumerable.

"But if one day you do not come after breakfast, if one day I see you in some

---

81. **Alcibiades . . . Percival.** Alcibiades (450?-404 B.C.) was an Athenian statesman and general noted for his social charms and military prowess; Ajax was a Greek hero of the Trojan War famous for his great strength; Hector was the champion of the Trojans; Percival was the Welch Arthurian hero noted for his quest of the Holy Grail. But *Percival* is also the name of one of the characters in *The Waves* who recently has died and is referred to by Louis, Susan, and Neville. Indeed, Neville's association of the Arthurian hero and his deceased friend naturally produces the bitter reflection of the ensuing sentence.

looking-glass perhaps looking after another, if the telephone buzzes and buzzes in your empty room, I shall then, after unspeakable anguish, I shall then—for there is no end to the folly of the human heart—seek another, find another, you. Meanwhile, let us abolish the ticking of time's clock with one blow. Come closer." (1931)

Katherine Mansfield
1888-1923

"Katherine Mansfield" was the pseudonym of Kathleen Mansfield Beauchamp, who was born in Wellington, New Zealand, October 14, 1888. While still in school she showed signs of remarkable skill in writing. In 1903 she was sent to England to complete her education in Queen's College, London, where she served as editor of the college magazine and developed a special interest in music. She returned to New Zealand in 1906 but was back in London two years later on an allowance from her father of one hundred pounds a year.

By this time Miss Mansfield had chosen writing as a career, but her first efforts to get into print were not encouraging. Besides, her first marriage ended quickly and unhappily, and she had serious financial worries. For a brief period she turned to music, taking minor parts in a traveling opera company. This experience undermined her health, which she tried to recover by visiting Germany. While there she wrote her first important stories, which were published in *The New Age* in 1910-1911 and collected in book form, under the title *In a German Pension*, in 1911. Articles contributed to the same magazine and to *The Westminster Gazette* brought her small additional income. Through her writings she became acquainted with John Middleton Murry, the critic, with whom she edited a short-lived literary review called *Rhythm* (later *The Blue Review*), and with whom in 1912 she entered into a common-law marriage; this was legalized in 1918. Several of her stories which first appeared in *Rhythm* were later collected and published under the title *Something Childish and Other Stories* (in the United States, *The Little Girl*) in 1924.

With ill health continually besetting her, Miss Mansfield sought medical help in Paris early in 1914. She returned to her home in Buckinghamshire in the summer but never again found peace or comfort. During the remaining nine years of her life she hastened from one place to another in search of relief. After 1914 she labored ardently at her story-writing. A compelling incentive was the death of her brother, Leslie Beauchamp, who was killed in action in the autumn of 1915; she wrote stories as a "sacred debt" to him.

In November, 1915, she went to Bandol, in southern France, where she wrote *The Aloe*, eventually condensed and published as *Prelude* (1918). Upon her return to England in 1916 she wrote under the name of Matilda Berry for *Signature*, a literary review started by D. H. Lawrence. When she was found to be suffering from tuberculosis in 1917, she returned to Bandol, where she finished *Bliss and Other Stories*, her first genuine literary success, which was published in 1920. She returned to England in 1918 and contributed numerous reviews of current novels to the London *Athenaeum*, of which her husband had become editor; these reviews were later published as *Novels and Novelists* (1930). She spent most of the year 1920 in Switzerland, where she completed in a few months an outstanding group of stories published as *The Garden Party and Other Stories* (1922). But her health was rapidly failing. In desperation she became a follower of the Russian mystic Gurdjieff, and her last year was spent in Fontainebleau, near Paris, in the study and practice of his teachings. She died there on January 9, 1923.

Katherine Mansfield's work was incomplete, but it was always poignant and tender. Living in constant fear of death, Miss Mansfield cultivated in her writing the quality of sensitiveness. With a keen awareness of everything about her, she labored indefatigably to present minutely recorded details of everyday middle-class life. She called major literature "an initiation into truth." Her husband wrote of her: "She was natural and spontaneous as was no other human being I have ever met. She seemed to adjust herself to life as a flower adjusts itself to the earth and to the sun."

Other writings of Miss Mansfield, all published by her husband after her death, include *The Dove's Nest and Other Stories* (1923), *Journal* (1927), *Letters* (1928), *Selected Stories* (1929), *Poems* (1930), and *Scrapbook* (1939).

The Garden Party

AND after all the weather was ideal. They could not have had a more perfect day for a garden-party if they had ordered it. Windless, warm, the sky without a cloud. Only the blue was veiled with a haze of light gold, as it is sometimes in early summer. The gardener had been up since dawn, mowing the lawns and sweeping them, until the grass and the dark flat rosettes where the daisy plants had been seemed to shine. As for the roses, you could not help feeling they understood that roses are the only flowers that impress people at garden-parties; the only flowers that everybody is certain of knowing. Hundreds, yes, literally hundreds, had come out in a single night; the green bushes bowed down as though they had been visited by archangels.

Breakfast was not yet over before the men came to put up the marquee.

"Where do you want the marquee put, mother?"

"My dear child, it's no use asking me. I'm determined to leave everything to you children this year. Forget I am your mother. Treat me as an honored guest."

But Meg could not possibly go and supervise the men. She had washed her hair before breakfast, and she sat drinking her coffee in a green turban, with a dark wet curl stamped on each cheek. Jose, the butterfly, always came down in a silk petticoat and a kimono jacket.

"You'll have to go, Laura; you're the artistic one."

Away Laura flew, still holding her piece of bread-and-butter. It's so delicious to have an excuse for eating out of doors, and besides, she loved having to arrange things; she always felt she could do it so much better than anybody else.

Four men in their shirt-sleeves stood grouped together on the garden path. They carried staves covered with rolls of canvas, and they had big tool-bags slung on their backs. They looked impressive. Laura wished now that she had not got the bread-and-butter, but there was nowhere to put it, and she couldn't possibly throw it away. She blushed and tried to look severe and even a little bit short-sighted as she came up to them.

"Good morning," she said, copying her mother's voice. But that sounded so fearfully affected that she was ashamed, and stammered like a little girl, "Oh—er—have you come—is it about the marquee?"

"That's right, miss," said the tallest of the men, a lanky, freckled fellow, and he shifted his tool-bag, knocked back his straw hat and smiled down at her. "That's about it."

His smile was so easy, so friendly that Laura recovered. What nice eyes he had, small, but such a dark blue! And now she looked at the others, they were smiling too.

Reprinted from *The Garden Party* by Katherine Mansfield, by permission of Alfred A. Knopf, Inc., Mr. J. Middleton Murry, and The Society of Authors. Copyright 1922 by Alfred A. Knopf, Inc. 20. **marquee**, a large tent, such as used by a high-ranking officer, and common at outdoor entertainments.

"Cheer up, we won't bite," their smile seemed to say. How very nice workmen were! And what a beautiful morning! She mustn't mention the morning; she must be businesslike. The marquee.

"Well, what about the lily-lawn? Would that do?"

And she pointed to the lily-lawn with the hand that didn't hold the bread-and-butter. They turned, they stared in the direction. A little fat chap thrust out his under-lip, and the tall fellow frowned.

"I don't fancy it," said he. "Not conspicuous enough. You see, with a thing like a marquee," and he turned to Laura in his easy way, "you want to put it somewhere where it'll give you a bang slap in the eye, if you follow me."

Laura's upbringing made her wonder for a moment whether it was quite respectful of a workman to talk to her of bangs slap in the eye. But she did quite follow him.

"A corner of the tennis-court," she suggested. "But the band's going to be in one corner."

"H'm, going to have a band, are you?" said another of the workmen. He was pale. He had a haggard look as his dark eyes scanned the tennis-court. What was he thinking?

"Only a very small band," said Laura gently. Perhaps he wouldn't mind so much if the band was quite small. But the tall fellow interrupted.

"Look here, miss, that's the place. Against those trees. Over there. That'll do fine."

Against the karakas. Then the karaka-trees would be hidden. And they were so lovely, with their broad, gleaming leaves, and their clusters of yellow fruit. They were like trees you imagined growing on a desert island, proud, solitary, lifting their leaves and fruits to the sun in a kind of silent splendor. Must they be hidden by a marquee?

They must. Already the men had shouldered their staves and were making for the place. Only the tall fellow was left. He bent down, pinched a sprig of lavender, put his thumb and forefinger to his nose and snuffed up the smell. When Laura saw that gesture she forgot all about the karakas in her wonder at him caring for things like that—caring for the smell of lavender. How many men that she knew would have done such a thing? Oh, how extraordinarily nice workmen were, she thought. Why couldn't she have workmen for friends rather than the silly boys she danced with and who came to Sunday night supper? She would get on much better with men like these.

It's all the fault, she decided, as the tall fellow drew something on the back of an envelope, something that was to be looped up or left to hang, of these absurd class distinctions. Well, for her part, she didn't feel them. Not a bit, not an atom.... And now there came the chock-chock of wooden hammers. Some one whistled, some one sang out, "Are you right there, matey?" "Matey!" The friendliness of it, the—the—— Just to prove how happy she was, just to show the tall fellow how at home she felt, and how she despised stupid conventions, Laura took a big bite of her bread-and-butter as she stared at the little drawing. She felt just like a work-girl.

"Laura, Laura, where are you? Telephone, Laura!" a voice cried from the house.

"Coming!" Away she skimmed, over the lawn, up the path, up the steps, across the veranda, and into the porch. In the hall her father and Laurie were brushing their hats ready to go to the office.

"I say, Laura," said Laurie very fast, "you might just give a squiz at my coat before this afternoon. See if it wants pressing."

"I will," said she. Suddenly she couldn't stop herself. She ran at Laurie and gave him a small, quick squeeze. "Oh, I do love parties, don't you?" gasped Laura.

"Ra-ther," said Laurie's warm, boyish voice, and he squeezed his sister too, and gave her a gentle push. "Dash off to the telephone, old girl."

The telephone. "Yes, yes; oh yes. Kitty? Good morning, dear. Come to lunch? Do, dear. Delighted of course. It will only be a very scratch meal—just the sandwich crusts

---

37. karaka, a New Zealand tree.

and broken meringue-shells and what's left over. Yes, isn't it a perfect morning? Your white? Oh, I certainly should. One moment —hold the line. Mother's calling." And Laura sat back. "What, mother? Can't hear."

Mrs. Sheridan's voice floated down the stairs. "Tell her to wear that sweet hat she had on last Sunday."

"Mother says you're to wear that *sweet* hat you had on last Sunday. Good. One o'clock. Bye-bye."

Laura put back the receiver, flung her arms over her head, took a deep breath, stretched and let them fall. "Huh," she sighed, and the moment after the sigh she sat up quickly. She was still, listening. All the doors in the house seemed to be open. The house was alive with soft, quick steps and running voices. The green baize door that led to the kitchen regions swung open and shut with a muffled thud. And now there came a long, chuckling absurd sound. It was the heavy piano being moved on its stiff castors. But the air! If you stopped to notice, was the air always like this? Little faint winds were playing chase, in at the tops of the windows, out at the doors. And there were two tiny spots of sun, one on the inkpot, one on a silver photograph frame, playing too. Darling little spots. Especially the one on the inkpot lid. It was quite warm. A warm little silver star. She could have kissed it.

The front door bell pealed, and there sounded the rustle of Sadie's print skirt on the stairs. A man's voice murmured; Sadie answered, careless, "I'm sure I don't know. Wait. I'll ask Mrs. Sheridan."

"What is it, Sadie?" Laura came into the hall.

"It's the florist, Miss Laura."

It was, indeed. There, just inside the door, stood a wide, shallow tray full of pots of pink lilies. No other kind. Nothing but lilies— canna lilies, big pink flowers, wide open, radiant, almost frighteningly alive on bright crimson stems.

"O-oh, Sadie!" said Laura, and the sound was like a little moan. She crouched down as if to warm herself at that blaze of lilies; she felt they were in her fingers, on her lips, growing in her breast.

"It's some mistake," she said faintly. "Nobody ever ordered so many. Sadie, go and find mother."

But at that moment Mrs. Sheridan joined them.

"It's quite right," she said calmly. "Yes, I ordered them. Aren't they lovely?" She pressed Laura's arm. "I was passing the shop yesterday, and I saw them in the window. And I suddenly thought for once in my life I shall have enough canna lilies. The garden-party will be a good excuse."

"But I thought you said you didn't mean to interfere," said Laura. Sadie had gone. The florist's man was still outside at his van. She put her arm round her mother's neck and gently, very gently, she bit her mother's ear.

"My darling child, you wouldn't like a logical mother, would you? Don't do that. Here's the man."

He carried more lilies still, another whole tray.

"Bank them up, just inside the door, on both sides of the porch, please," said Mrs. Sheridan. "Don't you agree, Laura?"

"Oh, I *do*, mother."

In the drawing-room Meg, Jose and good little Hans had at last succeeded in moving the piano.

"Now, if we put this chesterfield against the wall and move everything out of the room except the chairs, don't you think?"

"Quite."

"Hans, move these tables into the smoking-room, and bring a sweeper to take these marks off the carpet and—one moment, Hans——" Jose loved giving orders to the servants, and they loved obeying her. She always made them feel they were taking part in some drama. "Tell mother and Miss Laura to come here at once."

"Very good, Miss Jose."

She turned to Meg. "I want to hear what the piano sounds like, just in case I'm asked to sing this afternoon. Let's try over 'This Life is Weary.'"

Pom! Ta-ta-ta *Tee*-ta! The piano burst out

---

19. **baize door,** a door covered with baize, a coarse woolen fabric.

81. **chesterfield,** a kind of large overstuffed sofa.

so passionately that Jose's face changed. She clasped her hands. She looked mournfully and enigmatically at her mother and Laura as they came in.

> This Life is *Wee*-ary,
> A Tear—a Sigh.
> A Love that *Chan*-ges,
> This Life is *Wee*-ary,
> A Tear—a Sigh.
> A Love that *Chan*-ges,
> And then ... Good-bye!

But at the word "Good-bye," and although the piano sounded more desperate than ever, her face broke into a brilliant, dreadfully unsympathetic smile.

"Aren't I in good voice, mummy?" she beamed.

> This Life is *Wee*-ary,
> Hope comes to Die.
> A Dream—a *Wa*-kening.

But now Sadie interrupted them. "What is it, Sadie?"

"If you please, m'm, cook says have you got the flags for the sandwiches?"

"The flags for the sandwiches, Sadie?" echoed Mrs. Sheridan dreamily. And the children knew by her face that she hadn't got them. "Let me see." And she said to Sadie firmly, "Tell cook I'll let her have them in ten minutes."

Sadie went.

"Now, Laura," said her mother quickly. "Come with me into the smoking-room. I've got the names somewhere on the back of an envelope. You'll have to write them out for me. Meg, go upstairs this minute and take that wet thing off your head. Jose, run and finish dressing this instant. Do you hear me, children, or shall I have to tell your father when he comes home to-night? And—and, Jose, pacify cook if you do go into the kitchen, will you? I'm terrified of her this morning."

The envelope was found at last behind the dining-room clock, though how it had got there Mrs. Sheridan could not imagine.

24. **flags,** markers for identifying kinds of sandwiches.

"One of you children must have stolen it out of my bag, because I remember vividly—cream cheese and lemon-curd. Have you done that?"

"Yes."

"Egg and——" Mrs. Sheridan held the envelope away from her. "It looks like mice. It can't be mice, can it?"

"Olive, pet," said Laura, looking over her shoulder.

"Yes, of course, olive. What a horrible combination it sounds. Egg and olive."

They were finished at last, and Laura took them off to the kitchen. She found Jose there pacifying the cook, who did not look at all terrifying.

"I have never seen such exquisite sandwiches," said Jose's rapturous voice. "How many kinds did you say there were, cook? Fifteen?"

"Fifteen, Miss Jose."

"Well, cook, I congratulate you."

Cook swept up crusts with the long sandwich knife, and smiled broadly.

"Godber's has come," announced Sadie, issuing out of the pantry. She had seen the man pass the window.

That meant the cream puffs had come. Godber's were famous for their cream puffs. Nobody ever thought of making them at home.

"Bring them in and put them on the table, my girl," ordered cook.

Sadie brought them in and went back to the door. Of course Laura and Jose were far too grown-up to really care about such things. All the same, they couldn't help agreeing that the puffs looked very attractive. Very. Cook began arranging them, shaking off the extra icing sugar.

"Don't they carry one back to all one's parties?" said Laura.

"I suppose they do," said practical Jose, who never liked to be carried back. "They look beautifully light and feathery, I must say."

"Have one each, my dears," said cook in her comfortable voice. "Yer ma won't know."

Oh, impossible. Fancy cream puffs so soon after breakfast. The very idea made one shudder. All the same, two minutes later Jose and Laura were licking their fingers with that absorbed inward look that only comes from whipped cream.

"Let's go into the garden, out by the back way," suggested Laura. "I want to see how the men are getting on with the marquee. They're such awfully nice men."

But the back door was blocked by cook, Sadie, Godber's man and Hans.

Something had happened.

"Tuk-tuk-tuk," clucked cook like an agitated hen. Sadie had her hand clapped to her cheek as though she had toothache. Hans's face was screwed up in the effort to understand. Only Godber's man seemed to be enjoying himself; it was his story.

"What's the matter? What's happened?"

"There's been a horrible accident," said Cook. "A man killed."

"A man killed! Where? How? When?"

But Godber's man wasn't going to have his story snatched from under his very nose.

"Know those little cottages just below here, miss?" Know them? Of course, she knew them. "Well, there's a young chap living there, name of Scott, a carter. His horse shied at a traction-engine, corner of Hawke Street this morning, and he was thrown out on the back of his head. Killed."

"Dead!" Laura stared at Godber's man.

"Dead when they picked him up," said Godber's man with relish. "They were taking the body home as I come up here." And he said to the cook, "He's left a wife and five little ones."

"Jose, come here." Laura caught hold of her sister's sleeve and dragged her through the kitchen to the other side of the green baize door. There she paused and leaned against it. "Jose!" she said, horrified, "however are we going to stop everything?"

"Stop everything, Laura!" cried Jose in astonishment. "What do you mean?"

"Stop the garden-party, of course." Why did Jose pretend?

But Jose was still more amazed. "Stop the garden-party? My dear Laura, don't be so absurd. Of course we can't do anything of the kind. Nobody expects us to. Don't be so extravagant."

"But we can't possibly have a garden-party with a man dead just outside the front gate."

That really was extravagant, for the little cottages were in a lane to themselves at the very bottom of a steep rise that led up to the house. A broad road ran between. True, they were far too near. They were the greatest possible eyesore, and they had no right to be in that neighborhood at all. They were little mean dwellings painted a chocolate brown. In the garden patches there was nothing but cabbage stalks, sick hens and tomato cans. The very smoke coming out of their chimneys was poverty-stricken. Little rags and shreds of smoke, so unlike the great silvery plumes that uncurled from the Sheridans' chimneys. Washerwomen lived in the lane and sweeps and a cobbler, and a man whose house-front was studded all over with minute bird-cages. Children swarmed. When the Sheridans were little they were forbidden to set foot there because of the revolting language and of what they might catch. But since they were grown up, Laura and Laurie on their prowls sometimes walked through. It was disgusting and sordid. They came out with a shudder. But still one must go everywhere; one must see everything. So through they went.

"And just think of what the band would sound like to that poor woman," said Laura.

"Oh, Laura!" Jose began to be seriously annoyed. "If you're going to stop a band playing every time some one has an accident, you'll lead a very strenuous life. I'm every bit as sorry about it as you. I feel just as sympathetic." Her eyes hardened. She looked at her sister just as she used to when they were little and fighting together. "You won't bring a drunken workman back to life by being sentimental," she said softly.

"Drunk! Who said he was drunk?" Laura turned furiously on Jose. She said, just as they had used to say on those occasions, "I'm going straight up to tell mother."

"Do, dear," cooed Jose.

"Mother, can I come into your room?" Laura turned the big glass door-knob.

"Of course, child. Why, what's the matter? What's given you such a color?" And Mrs. Sheridan turned round from her dressing-table. She was trying on a new hat.

"Mother, a man's been killed," began Laura.

"*Not* in the garden?" interrupted her mother.

"No, no!"

"Oh, what a fright you gave me!" Mrs. Sheridan sighed with relief, and took off the big hat and held it on her knees.

"But listen, mother," said Laura. Breathless, half-choking, she told the dreadful story. "Of course, we can't have our party, can we?" she pleaded. "The band and everybody arriving. They'd hear us, mother; they're nearly neighbors!"

To Laura's astonishment her mother behaved just like Jose; it was harder to bear because she seemed amused. She refused to take Laura seriously.

"But, my dear child, use your common sense. It's only by accident we've heard of it. If some one had died there normally—and I can't understand how they keep alive in those poky little holes—we should still be having our party, shouldn't we?"

Laura had to say "yes" to that, but she felt it was all wrong. She sat down on her mother's sofa and pinched the cushion frill.

"Mother, isn't it really terribly heartless of us?" she asked.

"Darling!" Mrs. Sheridan got up and came over to her, carrying the hat. Before Laura could stop her she had popped it on. "My child!" said her mother, "the hat is yours. It's made for you. It's much too young for me. I have never seen you look such a picture. Look at yourself!" And she held up her hand-mirror.

"But, mother," Laura began again. She couldn't look at herself; she turned aside.

This time Mrs. Sheridan lost patience just as Jose had done.

"You are being very absurd, Laura," she said coldly. "People like that don't expect sacrifices from us. And it's not very sympathetic to spoil everybody's enjoyment as you're doing now."

"I don't understand," said Laura, and she walked quickly out of the room into her own bedroom. There, quite by chance, the first thing she saw was this charming girl in the mirror, in her black hat trimmed with gold daisies, and a long black velvet ribbon. Never had she imagined she could look like that. Is mother right? she thought. And now she hoped her mother was right. Am I being extravagant? Perhaps it was extravagant. Just for a moment she had another glimpse of that poor woman and those little children, and the body being carried into the house. But it all seemed blurred, unreal, like a picture in the newspaper. I'll remember it again after the party's over, she decided. And somehow that seemed quite the best plan. . . .

Lunch was over by half-past one. By half-past two they were all ready for the fray. The green-coated band had arrived and was established in a corner of the tennis-court.

"My dear!" trilled Kitty Maitland, "aren't they too like frogs for words? You ought to have arranged them round the pond with the conductor in the middle on a leaf."

Laurie arrived and hailed them on his way to dress. At the sight of him Laura remembered the accident again. She wanted to tell him. If Laurie agreed with the others, then it was bound to be all right. And she followed him into the hall.

"Laurie!"

"Hallo!" He was half-way upstairs, but when he turned round and saw Laura he suddenly puffed out his cheeks and goggled his eyes at her. "My word, Laura! You do look stunning," said Laurie. "What an absolutely topping hat!"

Laura said faintly "Is it?" and smiled up at Laurie, and didn't tell him after all.

Soon after that people began coming in streams. The band struck up; the hired waiters ran from the house to the marquee. Wherever you looked there were couples strolling, bending to the flowers, greeting, moving on over the lawn. They were like bright birds that had alighted in the Sheridans' garden for this one afternoon, on their way to—where? Ah, what happiness it is to be with people who all are happy, to press hands, press cheeks, smile into eyes.

"Darling Laura, how well you look!"

"What a becoming hat, child!"

"Laura, you look quite Spanish. I've never seen you look so striking."

And Laura, glowing, answered softly, "Have you had tea? Won't you have an ice?

The passion-fruit ices really are rather special." She ran to her father and begged him. "Daddy darling, can't the band have something to drink?"

And the perfect afternoon slowly ripened, slowly faded, slowly its petals closed.

"Never a more delightful garden-party . . ." "The greatest success . . ." "Quite the most . . ."

Laura helped her mother with the good-byes. They stood side by side in the porch till it was all over.

"All over, all over, thank heaven," said Mrs. Sheridan. "Round up the others, Laura. Let's go and have some fresh coffee. I'm exhausted. Yes, it's been very successful. But oh, these parties, these parties! Why will you children insist on giving parties!" And they all of them sat down in the deserted marquee.

"Have a sandwich, daddy dear. I wrote the flag."

"Thanks." Mr. Sheridan took a bite and the sandwich was gone. He took another. "I suppose you didn't hear of a beastly accident that happened today?" he said.

"My dear," said Mrs. Sheridan, holding up her hand, "we did. It nearly ruined the party. Laura insisted we should put it off."

"Oh, mother!" Laura didn't want to be teased about it.

"It was a horrible affair all the same," said Mr. Sheridan. "The chap was married too. Lived just below in the lane, and leaves a wife and half a dozen kiddies, so they say."

An awkward little silence fell. Mrs. Sheridan fidgeted with her cup. Really, it was very tactless of father . . .

Suddenly she looked up. There on the table were all those sandwiches, cakes, puffs, all uneaten, all going to be wasted. She had one of her brilliant ideas.

"I know," she said. "Let's make up a basket. Let's send that poor creature some of this perfectly good food. At any rate, it will be the greatest treat for the children. Don't you agree? And she's sure to have neighbors calling in and so on. What a point to have it all ready prepared. Laura!" She jumped up. "Get me the big basket out of the stairs cupboard."

"But, mother, do you really think it's a good idea?" said Laura.

Again, how curious, she seemed to be different from them all. To take scraps from their party. Would the poor woman really like that?

"Of course! What's the matter with you today? An hour or two ago you were insisting on us being sympathetic, and now——"

Oh, well! Laura ran for the basket. It was filled, it was heaped by her mother.

"Take it yourself, darling," said she. "Run down just as you are. No, wait, take the arum lilies too. People of that class are so impressed by arum lilies."

"The stems will ruin her lace frock," said practical Jose.

So they would. Just in time. "Only the basket, then. And, Laura!"—her mother followed her out of the marquee—"don't on any account——"

"What, mother?"

No, better not put such ideas into the child's head! "Nothing! Run along."

It was just growing dusky as Laura shut their garden gates. A big dog ran by like a shadow. The road gleamed white, and down below in the hollow the little cottages were in deep shade. How quiet it seemed after the afternoon. Here she was going down the hill to somewhere where a man lay dead, and she couldn't realize it. Why couldn't she? She stopped a minute. And it seemed to her that kisses, voices, tinkling spoons, laughter, the smell of crushed grass were somehow inside her. She had no room for anything else. How strange! She looked up at the pale sky, and all she thought was, "Yes, it was the most successful party."

Now the broad road was crossed. The lane began, smoky and dark. Women in shawls and men's tweed caps hurried by. Men hung over the palings; the children played in the doorways. A low hum came from the mean little cottages. In some of them there was a flicker of light, and a shadow, crab-like,

---

1. **passion-fruit,** any edible fruit of a passion-flower, so named from a supposed resemblance of its parts to instruments of Christ's crucifixion.

63. **arum lilies,** calla lilies.

moved across the window. Laura bent her head and hurried on. She wished now she had put on a coat. How her frock shone! And the big hat with the velvet streamer—if only it was another hat! Were the people looking at her? They must be. It was a mistake to have come; she knew all along it was a mistake. Should she go back even now?

No, too late. This was the house. It must be. A dark knot of people stood outside. Beside the gate an old, old woman with a crutch sat in a chair, watching. She had her feet on a newspaper. The voices stopped as Laura drew near. The group parted. It was as though she was expected, as though they had known she was coming here.

Laura was terribly nervous. Tossing the velvet ribbon over her shoulder, she said to a woman standing by, "Is this Mrs. Scott's house?" and the woman, smiling queerly, said, "It is, my lass."

Oh, to be away from this! She actually said, "Help me, God," as she walked up the tiny path and knocked. To be away from those staring eyes, or to be covered up in anything, one of those women's shawls even. I'll just leave the basket and go, she decided. I shan't even wait for it to be emptied.

Then the door opened. A little woman in black showed in the gloom.

Laura said, "Are you Mrs. Scott?" But to her horror the woman answered, "Walk in please, miss," and she was shut in the passage.

"No," said Laura, "I don't want to come in. I only want to leave this basket. Mother sent——"

The little woman in the gloomy passage seemed not to have heard her. "Step this way, please, miss," she said in an oily voice, and Laura followed her.

She found herself in a wretched little low kitchen, lighted by a smoky lamp. There was a woman sitting before the fire.

"Em," said the little creature who had let her in. "Em! It's a young lady." She turned to Laura. She said meaningly, "I'm 'er sister, Miss. You'll excuse 'er, won't you?"

"Oh, but of course!" said Laura. "Please, please don't disturb her. I—I only want to leave——"

But at that moment the woman at the fire turned round. Her face, puffed up, red, with swollen eyes and swollen lips, looked terrible. She seemed as though she couldn't understand why Laura was there. What did it mean? Why was this stranger standing in the kitchen with a basket? What was it all about? And the poor face puckered up again.

"All right, my dear," said the other. "I'll thenk the young lady."

And again she began, "You'll excuse her, miss, I'm sure," and her face, swollen too, tried an oily smile.

Laura only wanted to get out, to get away. She was back in the passage. The door opened. She walked straight through into the bedroom, where the dead man was lying.

"You'd like a look at 'im, wouldn't you?" said Em's sister, and she brushed past Laura over to the bed. "Don't be afraid, my lass,—" and now her voice sounded fond and sly, and fondly she drew down the sheet—" 'e looks a picture. There's nothing to show. Come along, my dear."

Laura came.

There lay a young man, fast asleep—sleeping so soundly, so deeply, that he was far, far away from them both. Oh, so remote, so peaceful. He was dreaming. Never wake him up again. His head was sunk in the pillow, his eyes were closed; they were blind under the closed eyelids. He was given up to his dream. What did garden-parties and baskets and lace frocks matter to him? He was far from all those things. He was wonderful, beautiful. While they were laughing and while the band was playing, this marvel had come to the lane. Happy . . . happy. . . . All is well, said that sleeping face. This is just as it should be. I am content.

But all the same you had to cry, and she couldn't go out of the room without saying something to him. Laura gave a loud childish sob.

"Forgive my hat," she said.

And this time she didn't wait for Em's sister. She found her way out of the door, down the path, past all those dark people. At the corner of the lane she met Laurie.

He stepped out of the shadow. "Is that you, Laura?"

"Yes."

"Mother was getting anxious. Was it all right?"

"Yes, quite. Oh, Laurie!" She took his arm, she pressed up against him.

"I say, you're not crying, are you?" asked her brother.

Laura shook her head. She was.

Laurie put his arm round her shoulder. "Don't cry," he said in his warm, loving voice. "Was it awful?"

"No," sobbed Laura. "It was simply marvelous. But, Laurie——" She stopped, she looked at her brother. "Isn't life," she stammered, "isn't life——" But what life was she couldn't explain. No matter. He quite understood.

"Isn't it, darling?" said Laurie. (1922)

Thomas Stearns Eliot
1888-

T. S. Eliot was born in St. Louis, Missouri, of a branch of a distinguished Boston family. He lived in St. Louis until he was 18, and attended local schools; then, after a brief period at Milton Academy, near Boston, he matriculated at Harvard in 1906 and received the bachelor's degree in 1910 and the master's degree a year later. He continued his graduate work, first at the Sorbonne in Paris, then back at Harvard, and finally at Merton College, Oxford, eventually settling in England (1914). In 1915 he married Vivienne Haigh (d. 1947). In London he taught briefly at the Highgate School and then became a clerk in the famous Lloyds Bank. His interest in literature, particularly in poetry and criticism, had always been marked. By 1917 he had attracted enough attention among poets and lovers of poetry to be named an assistant editor of *The Egoist,* a periodical founded by Ezra Pound (1885-), who was a pioneer in the imagist school of contemporary poets. Pound's encouragement and poetic discernment did much for Eliot; in fact, Eliot's first volume of prose studies: *Ezra Pound, His Metric and Poetry* (1917) is a sincere tribute to a poet whom Eliot has always called, rather mistakenly, his master.

In 1917 appeared Eliot's first published poems of importance, *Prufrock and Other Observations.* The most famous of these today is "The Love Song of J. Alfred Prufrock," a classic conception of the twentieth-century version of Hamlet— timid, blasé, mediocre, and defeatist. Another collection, *Poems,* was issued in 1919. Two more volumes, one from 1925 and another from 1936, are cumulative collections including pieces from as far back as Eliot's Harvard days. *Three Critical Essays* (1919) and *The Sacred Wood* (1920) firmly established Eliot's position as a literary critic. In *The Sacred Wood* Eliot gave clear evidence that he was by taste and nature a classicist, anti-sentimental, anti-romantic, dedicated to finish in form and to balance and symmetry in expression. His impact on modern criticism has been exceeded only by his impact on modern poetry. His interest in seventeenth-century metaphysical poets did much to stimulate the popularity they enjoy today, as his distaste for many romantics and Victorians contributed to the low watermark of their current reputations. In authority in critical thought, he is the Dr. Johnson of our day, and his essays on individual authors are the most comprehensive and systematic study of English writers since *The Lives of English Poets.*

In 1922 he published *The Waste Land,* a poem which caught so aptly the spirit of disillusionment prevailing after the First World War that it gave its name to a whole tendency in the literature of the 1920's and early 1930's, and won for Eliot the Dial award. It is neither outright allegory nor plain narrative, but rather a difficult though fascinating mixture of associations, tags of quotations, bursts of conversation, descriptions, and fragmentary interior monologues, held together very loosely within the framework of the Grail legend and its primitive analogues. There were objections to its obscure language and allusion, to the long and learned footnotes, to the mythology and the psychoanalysis—but even the dissidents appreciated the fact that it was a landmark. Its subsequent influence, particularly upon Continental poets, has been great, although in England and America it has been somewhat overshadowed by Eliot's later work, cast in an entirely different, more nearly universal, mold.

Eliot founded his own magazine, *The Criterion,* in 1922. Until its discontinuation in 1939, it was not only an organ for Eliot's own views but also a bible for the rapidly growing Eliot cult. The poet's association with Faber and Faber, one of the best of British publishing-houses, put him in a still stronger position as an encourager and discourager of literary talent. In *The Criterion* appeared many of the essays later gathered together in various volumes.

Eliot became a naturalized British subject in 1927; and in the foreword to *For Lancelot Andrewes* (1928), he declared himself to be "an Anglo-Catholic in religion, a classicist in literature, and a royalist in politics." This statement, in strong contrast to the pessimism of *The Waste Land,* suggests one reason why Eliot is a major literary figure. He is dynamic, not static; a man driven, not satisfied. The change, moreover, has a logical development. To one of his intellectual background and training, classical taste, and attachment to tradition and authority, there was no farther distance to go down the road of pessimism and disillusionment. Eliot turned away, therefore, from the Lost Generation of the 1920's and looked to the mystical, as Ibsen and Strindberg—to take but two modern examples—had done before him. He had always been a classicist, and his leaning toward royalism stemmed naturally from these other two tendencies.

This new Eliot made his position very plain in nearly all of his important works written during the 1930's. In 1930 was published *Ash Wednesday,* a tortuous poem of conflict between his poetic intelligences and his desire to attain the grace of God. Much more assured are the fine Choruses from *The Rock* (1934), where the call for a return to Christian spiritual values is sounded unmistakably and brilliantly. His extremely absorbing drama on the story of Thomas à Becket, the Archbishop of Canterbury assassinated in 1170, entitled *Murder in the Cathedral* (1935), is further evidence that in Eliot the twentieth century had found a most articulate religious poet, though his spirit was still questing rather than attaining. Another play, *The Family Reunion* (1939), deals with the Holy Family but is far less incisive than *Murder in the Cathedral.*

Yet the ardent religious flame of the choruses from *The Rock* cooled somewhat during the later 1930's. Four moving poems—"East Coker" (1940), "Burnt Norton" (1941), "The Dry Salvages" (1941), and "Little Gidding" (1942)—published together in 1943 as *Four Quartets* are among Eliot's most beautiful and poignant expressions, but they are disturbing because they vacillate between his old desire for emotional security through religion and his still older defeatism. The same teetering is to be observed in his philosophical play, *The Cocktail Party* (1950), where a rather vapid group of society folk, who remind one of those in Eliot's earlier poetry, are influenced by a most spiritual psychiatrist; and one of them, at least, undergoes Christian sacrifice and martyrdom. *The Confidential Clerk* (1954), ostensibly a comedy in verse, actually leaves the reader with a sense of the isolation of a human being, the vanity of human wishes, and the importance of one's being able to live with things as they are rather than as they should be.

In 1948 Eliot received the Nobel prize for literature, and since 1947 he has occupied chairs of poetry at Harvard and Princeton and elsewhere. There is no doubt that he has come to represent, better than any other important poet of the twentieth century, the intellectual, social, and philosophical moods of the two decades between the First and Second World Wars. His conflicts between the intellectual and the emotional, between the sentimental and the anti-sentimental, between the romantic and the classical, bode well for his future, for such conflicts show the wideness of Eliot's scope. And in any event, his consummate skill in treating traditional forms is sufficient to promise him longevity as a poet and spokesman for his age.

from *The Sacred Wood*

TRADITION AND THE INDIVIDUAL TALENT

I

In English writing we seldom speak of tradition, though we occasionally apply its name in deploring its absence. We cannot refer to "the tradition" or to "a tradition"; at most, we employ the adjective in saying that the poetry of So-and-so is "traditional" or even "too traditional." Seldom, perhaps, does the word appear except in a phrase of censure. If otherwise, it is vaguely approbative, with the implication, as to the work approved, of some pleasing archaeological reconstruction. You can hardly make the word agreeable to English ears without this comfortable reference to the reassuring science of archaeology.

Certainly the word is not likely to appear in our appreciations of living or dead writers. Every nation, every race, has not only its own creative, but its own critical turn of mind; and is even more oblivious of the shortcomings and limitations of its critical habits than of those of its creative genius. We know, or think we know, from the enormous mass of critical writing that has appeared in the French language the critical method or habit of the French; we only conclude (we are such unconscious people) that the French are "more critical" than we, and sometimes even plume ourselves a little with the fact, as if the French were the less spontaneous. Perhaps they are; but we might remind ourselves that criticism is as inevitable as breathing, and that we should be none the worse for articulating what passes in our minds when we read a book and feel an emotion about it, for criticizing our own minds in their work of criticism. One of the facts that might come to light in this process is our tendency to insist, when we praise a poet, upon those aspects of his work in which he least resembles anyone else. In these aspects or parts of his work we pretend to find what is individual, what is the peculiar essence of the man. We dwell with satisfaction upon the poet's difference from his predecessors, especially his immediate predecessors; we endeavour to find something that can be isolated in order to be enjoyed. Whereas if we approach a poet without this prejudice we shall often find that not only the best, but the most individual parts of his work may be those in which the dead poets, his ancestors, assert their immortality most vigorously. And I do not mean the impressionable period of adolescence, but the period of full maturity.

Yet if the only form of tradition, of handing down, consisted in following the ways of the immediate generation before us in a blind or timid adherence to its successes, "tradition" should positively be discouraged. We have seen many such simple currents soon lost in the sand; and novelty is better than repetition. Tradition is a matter of much wider significance. It cannot be inherited, and if you want it you must obtain it by great labour. It involves, in the first place, the historical sense, which we may call nearly indispensable to anyone who would continue to be a poet beyond his twenty-fifth year; and the historical

---

From *Selected Essays 1917-1932* by T. S. Eliot, copyright, 1932, by Harcourt, Brace and Company, Inc., and reprinted with their permission. Canadian permission has been granted by Methuen & Co. Ltd., London.

sense involves a perception, not only of the pastness of the past, but of its presence; the historical sense compels a man to write not merely with his own generation in his bones, but with a feeling that the whole of the literature of Europe from Homer and within it the whole of the literature of his own country has a simultaneous existence and composes a simultaneous order. This historical sense, which is a sense of the timeless as well as of the temporal and of the timeless and of the temporal together, is what makes a writer traditional. And it is at the same time what makes a writer most acutely conscious of his place in time, of his contemporaneity.

No poet, no artist of any art, has his complete meaning alone. His significance, his appreciation is the appreciation of his relation to the dead poets and artists. You cannot value him alone; you must set him, for contrast and comparison, among the dead. I mean this as a principle of aesthetic, not merely historical, criticism. The necessity that he shall conform, that he shall cohere, is not one-sided; what happens when a new work of art is created is something that happens simultaneously to all the works of art which preceded it. The existing monuments form an ideal order among themselves, which is modified by the introduction of the new (the really new) work of art among them. The existing order is complete before the new work arrives; for order to persist after the supervention of novelty, the *whole* existing order must be, if ever so slightly, altered; and so the relations, proportions, values of each work of art toward the whole are readjusted; and this is conformity between the old and the new. Whoever has approved this idea of order, of the form of European, of English literature, will not find it preposterous that the past should be altered by the present as much as the present is directed by the past. And the poet who is aware of this will be aware of great difficulties and responsibilities.

In a peculiar sense he will be aware also that he must inevitably be judged by the standards of the past. I say judged, not amputated, by them; not judged to be as good as, or worse or better than, the dead; and certainly not judged by the canons of dead critics. It is a judgment, a comparison, in which two things are measured by each other. To conform merely would be for the new work not really to conform at all; it would not be new, and would therefore not be a work of art. And we do not quite say that the new is more valuable because it fits in; but its fitting in is a test of its value—a test, it is true, which can only be slowly and cautiously applied, for we are none of us infallible judges of conformity. We say: it appears to conform, and is perhaps individual, or it appears individual, and may conform; but we are hardly likely to find that it is one and not the other.

To proceed to a more intelligible exposition of the relation of the poet to the past: he can neither take the past as a lump, an indiscriminate bolus, nor can he form himself wholly on one or two private admirations, nor can he form himself wholly upon one preferred period. The first course is inadmissible, the second is an important experience of youth, and the third is a pleasant and highly desirable supplement. The poet must be very conscious of the main current, which does not at all flow invariably through the most distinguished reputations. He must be quite aware of the obvious fact that art never improves, but that the material of art is never quite the same. He must be aware that the mind of Europe—the mind of his own country—a mind which he learns in time to be much more important than his own private mind—is a mind which changes, and that this change is a development which abandons nothing *en route,* which does not superannuate either Shakespeare, or Homer, or the rock drawing of the Magdalenian draughtsmen. That this development, refinement perhaps, complication certainly, is not, from the point of view of the artist, any improvement. Perhaps not even an improvement from the point of view of the psychologist or not to the extent which we imagine; perhaps only in the end based upon a complication in economics and

---

89. **Magdalenian draughtsmen,** the men who drew in the Magdalenian Age. The name *Magdalenian* is applied to a stage of the Stone Age and is named from the archaeological remains found at La Madeleine in the Dordogne, France. The Magdalenian workmen used tools of horn and bone and reached a high quality of craftsmanship before the end of the period.

machinery. But the difference between the present and the past is that the conscious present is an awareness of the past in a way and to an extent which the past's awareness of itself cannot show.

Some one said: "The dead writers are remote from us because we *know* so much more than they did." Precisely, and they are that which we know.

I am alive to a usual objection to what is clearly part of my programme for the *métier* of poetry. The objection is that the doctrine requires a ridiculous amount of erudition (pedantry), a claim which can be rejected by appeal to the lives of poets in any pantheon. It will even be affirmed that much learning deadens or perverts poetic sensibility. While, however, we persist in believing that a poet ought to know as much as will not encroach upon his necessary receptivity and necessary laziness, it is not desirable to confine knowledge to whatever can be put into a useful shape for examinations, drawing-rooms, or the still more pretentious modes of publicity. Some can absorb knowledge, the more tardy must sweat for it. Shakespeare acquired more essential history from Plutarch than most men could from the whole British Museum. What is to be insisted upon is that the poet must develop or procure the consciousness of the past and that he should continue to develop this consciousness throughout his career.

What happens is a continual surrender of himself as he is at the moment to something which is more valuable. The progress of an artist is a continual self-sacrifice, a continual extinction of personality.

There remains to define this process of depersonalization and its relation to the sense of tradition. It is in this depersonalization that art may be said to approach the condition of science. I shall, therefore, invite you to consider, as a suggestive analogy, the action which takes place when a bit of finely filiated platinum is introduced into a chamber containing oxygen and sulphur dioxide.

II

Honest criticism and sensitive appreciation is directed not upon the poet but upon the poetry. If we attend to the confused cries of the newspaper critics and the susurrus of popular repetition that follows, we shall hear the names of poets in great numbers; if we seek not Blue-book knowledge but the enjoyment of poetry, and ask for a poem, we shall seldom find it. In the last article I tried to point out the importance of the relation of the poem to other poems by other authors, and suggested the conception of poetry as a living whole of all the poetry that has ever been written. The other aspect of this Impersonal theory of poetry is the relation of the poem to its author. And I hinted, by an analogy, that the mind of the mature poet differs from that of the immature one not precisely in any valuation of "personality," not being necessarily more interesting, or having "more to say," but rather by being a more finely perfected medium in which special, or very varied, feelings are at liberty to enter into new combinations.

The analogy was that of the catalyst. When the two gases previously mentioned are mixed in the presence of a filament of platinum, they form sulphurous acid. This combination takes place only if the platinum is present; nevertheless the newly formed acid contains no trace of platinum, and the platinum itself is apparently unaffected; has remained inert, neutral, and unchanged. The mind of the poet is the shred of platinum. It may partly or exclusively operate upon the experience of the man himself; but, the more perfect the artist, the more completely separate in him will be the man who suffers and the mind which creates; the more perfectly will the mind digest and transmute the passions which are its material.

The experience, you will notice, the elements which enter the presence of the transforming catalyst, are of two kinds: emotions and feelings. The effect of a work of art upon

---

27. Plutarch, the important Greek biographer (46?-120?). His major work is the *Parallel Lives* of twenty-three Greeks and twenty-three Romans. The work was translated into French during the Renaissance and from the French into English by Sir Thomas North (1579). North's translation was Shakespeare's main source of classical learning; it was from the *Lives* that he derived material for his *Julius Caesar, Coriolanus,* and *Antony and Cleopatra.*

51. susurrus, rustling whisper.

the person who enjoys it is an experience different in kind from any experience not of art. It may be formed out of one emotion, or may be a combination of several; and various feelings, inhering for the writer in particular words or phrases or images, may be added to compose the final result. Or great poetry may be made without the direct use of any emotion whatever: composed out of feelings solely. Canto XV of the *Inferno* (Brunetto Latini) is a working up of the emotion evident in the situation; but the effect, though single as that of any work of art, is obtained by considerable complexity of detail. The last quatrain gives an image, a feeling attaching to an image, which "came," which did not develop simply out of what precedes, but which was probably in suspension in the poet's mind until the proper combination arrived for it to add itself to. The poet's mind is in fact a receptacle for seizing and storing up numberless feelings, phrases, images, which remain there until all the particles which can unite to form a new compound are present together.

If you compare several representative passages of the greatest poetry you see how great is the variety of types of combination, and also how completely any semi-ethical criterion of "sublimity" misses the mark. For it is not the "greatness," the intensity, of the emotions, the components, but the intensity of the artistic process, the pressure, so to speak, under which the fusion takes place, that counts. The episode of Paolo and Francesca employs a definite emotion, but the intensity of the poetry is something quite different from whatever intensity in the supposed experience it may give the impression of. It is no more intense, furthermore, than Canto XXVI, the voyage of Ulysses, which has not the direct dependence upon an emotion. Great variety is possible in the process of transmutation of emotion: the murder of Agamemnon, or the agony of Othello, gives an artistic effect apparently closer to a possible original than the scenes from Dante. In the *Agamemnon,* the artistic emotion approximates to the emotion of an actual spectator; in *Othello* to the emotion of the protagonist himself. But the difference between art and the event is always absolute; the combination which is the murder of Agamemnon is probably as complex as that which is the voyage of Ulysses. In either case there has been a fusion of elements. The ode of Keats contains a number of feelings which have nothing particular to do with the nightingale, but which the nightingale, partly, perhaps, because of its attractive name, and partly because of its reputation, served to bring together.

The point of view which I am struggling to attack is perhaps related to the metaphysical theory of the substantial unity of the soul: for my meaning is, that the poet has, not a "personality" to express, but a particular medium, which is only a medium and not a personality, in which impressions and experiences combine in peculiar and unexpected ways. Impressions and experiences which are important for the man may take no place in the poetry, and those which become important in the poetry may play quite a negligible part in the man, the personality.

I will quote a passage which is unfamiliar enough to be regarded with fresh attention in the light—or darkness—of these observations:

And now methinks I could e'en chide myself
For doating on her beauty, though her death
Shall be revenged after no common action.
Does the silkworm expend her yellow labours
For thee? For thee does she undo herself?
Are lordships sold to maintain ladyships

---

11. **Brunetto Latini,** a great Florentine scholar (1210?-1294?), teacher of the Italian poet Dante Alighieri (1265-1321). Dante greatly admired Brunetto's learning but deplored his worldliness and vices and therefore depicts him in Canto XV of the *Inferno* among those who are being punished for violence against themselves, against art, against life, or against God and man. 35. **Paolo and Francesca.** The tragic story of these two lovers, ill-starred in life and condemned after death to whirl about in Hell on the ceaseless blasts of unsatisfied desire, is told with magnificent simplicity and great art by Dante in his *Inferno,* Canto V, 75 ff.

44. **Agamemnon,** a hero of the Greeks in the Trojan War. After the sack of Troy he returned to his home in Argos, where he was murdered by his faithless wife, Clytemnestra, and her lover, Aegisthus. Subsequently this murder was avenged by Agamemnon's son, Orestes. The tragic story was the subject of a play by Aeschylus (525-456 B.C.). 79 ff. **And now methinks,** etc., spoken by Vindici in the dark and dismal *The Revenger's Tragedy* (1607) by Cyril Tourneur (1575?-1626), III, v, 71-82.

> For the poor benefit of a bewildering minute?
> Why does yon fellow falsify highways,
> And put his life between the judge's lips,
> To refine such a thing—keeps horse and men
> To beat their valours for her? . . .

In this passage (as is evident if it is taken in its context) there is a combination of positive and negative emotions: an intensely strong attraction toward beauty and an equally intense fascination by the ugliness which is contrasted with it and which destroys it. This balance of contrasted emotion is in the dramatic situation to which the speech is pertinent, but that situation alone is inadequate to it. This is, so to speak, the structural emotion, provided by the drama. But the whole effect, the dominant tone, is due to the fact that a number of floating feelings, having an affinity to this emotion by no means superficially evident, have combined with it to give us a new art emotion.

It is not in his personal emotions, the emotions provoked by particular events in his life, that the poet is in any way remarkable or interesting. His particular emotions may be simple, or crude, or flat. The emotion in his poetry will be a very complex thing, but not with the complexity of the emotions of people who have very complex or unusual emotions in life. One error, in fact, of eccentricity in poetry is to seek for new human emotions to express; and in this search for novelty in the wrong place it discovers the perverse. The business of the poet is not to find new emotions, but to use the ordinary ones and, in working them up into poetry, to express feelings which are not in actual emotions at all. And emotions which he has never experienced will serve his turn as well as those familiar to him. Consequently, we must believe that "emotion recollected in tranquillity" is an inexact formula. For it is neither emotion, nor recollection, nor, without distortion of meaning, tranquillity. It is a concentration, and a new thing resulting from the concentration, of a very great number of experiences which to the practical and active person would not seem to be experiences at all; it is a concentration which does not happen consciously or of deliberation. These experiences are not "recollected," and they finally unite in an atmosphere which is "tranquil" only in that it is a passive attending upon the event. Of course this is not quite the whole story. There is a great deal, in the writing of poetry, which must be conscious and deliberate. In fact, the bad poet is usually unconscious where he ought to be conscious, and conscious where he ought to be unconscious. Both errors tend to make him "personal." Poetry is not a turning loose of emotion, but an escape from emotion; it is not the expression of personality, but an escape from personality. But, of course, only those who have personality and emotions know what it means to want to escape from these things.

III

ὁ δὲ νοῦς, ἴσως, θειότερόν τι καὶ ἀπαθές ἐστιν

This essay proposes to halt at the frontier of metaphysics or mysticism, and confine itself to such practical conclusions as can be applied by the responsible person interested in poetry. To divert interest from the poet to the poetry is a laudable aim: for it would conduce to a juster estimation of actual poetry, good and bad. There are many people who appreciate the expression of sincere emotion in verse, and there is a smaller number of people who can appreciate technical excellence. But very few know when there is expression of *significant* emotion, emotion which has its life in the poem and not in the history of the poet. The emotion of art is impersonal. And the poet cannot reach this impersonality without surrendering himself wholly to the work to be done. And he is not likely to know what is to be done unless he lives in what is not merely the present, but the present moment of the past, unless he is conscious, not of what is dead, but of what is already living. (1920)

---

42. **"emotion . . . tranquillity,"** Wordsworth's explanation of the poetic process. The passage describing this process is found in his *Preface* to the *Lyrical Ballads*, p. 326, ll. 30-46.

68. ὁ . . . ἐστιν. Possibly the mind is too divine, and is therefore unaffected—Aristotle's *On the Soul*, I, iv (translation by W. S. Hett).

THOMAS STEARNS ELIOT

The Love Song of J. Alfred Prufrock

J. Alfred Prufrock is the embodiment of the wealthy young man of modern times—blasé, intellectual, sensitive, but completely incapable of action or even decision. The poem is Prufrock's fragmentary soliloquy as he walks the streets in the evening, reluctant to come to a decision about love—or, for that matter, about anything. He imagines bits of conversation, typical drawing-room scenes; he thinks of death. And with death forever in his mind, love and intellectual inquiry become empty: life to him is an ironic picture, a meaningless pattern endlessly repeated. The epigraph indicates Eliot's view of life's futility, since death is inevitable. Since man no longer imagines he can conquer death, no longer believes he can bend the universe to his will, he is, for all his contemplation of death (as in the Lazarus symbol of l. 94) or of life, mediocre, and his actions and decisions are therefore inconsequential.

S'io credesse che mia risposta fosse
A persona che mai tornasse al mondo,
Questa fiamma staria senza piu scosse.
Ma perciocche giammai di questo fondo
Non torno vivo alcun, s'i'odo il vero,
Senza tema d'infamia ti rispondo.

Let us go then, you and I,
When the evening is spread out against the sky
Like a patient etherised upon a table;
Let us go, through certain half-deserted streets,
The muttering retreats   5
Of restless nights in one-night cheap hotels
And sawdust restaurants with oyster-shells:
Streets that follow like a tedious argument
Of insidious intent   9
To lead you to an overwhelming question . . .
Oh, do not ask, "What is it?"
Let us go and make our visit.

In the room the women come and go
Talking of Michelangelo.

The yellow fog that rubs its back upon the window-panes,   15
The yellow smoke that rubs its muzzle on the window-panes
Licked its tongue into the corners of the evening,
Lingered upon the pools that stand in drains,
Let fall upon its back the soot that falls from chimneys,   19
Slipped by the terrace, made a sudden leap,
And seeing that it was a soft October night,
Curled once about the house, and fell asleep.

And indeed there will be time
For the yellow smoke that slides along the street,
Rubbing its back upon the window-panes;   25
There will be time, there will be time
To prepare a face to meet the faces that you meet;
There will be time to murder and create,
And time for all the works and days of hands
That lift and drop a question on your plate;
Time for you and time for me,   31
And time yet for a hundred indecisions,
And for a hundred visions and revisions,
Before the taking of a toast and tea.

In the room the women come and go   35
Talking of Michelangelo.

And indeed there will be time
To wonder, "Do I dare?" and, "Do I dare?"
Time to turn back and descend the stair,
With a bald spot in the middle of my hair—   40
[They will say: "How his hair is growing thin!"]
My morning coat, my collar mounting firmly to the chin,
My necktie rich and modest, but asserted by a simple pin—
[They will say: "But how his arms and legs are thin!"]
Do I dare   45

The poetry of T. S. Eliot is reprinted from *Collected Poems 1909-1935* by T. S. Eliot, copyright, 1936, by Harcourt, Brace and Company, Inc. and reprinted with their permission. Canadian permission has been granted by Faber and Faber Limited, London. *S'io . . . rispondo,* if I could believe that my answer might be to a person who should ever return into the world, this flame would stand without more quiverings; but inasmuch as, if I hear the truth, never from this depth did any living man return, without fear of infamy I answer thee.—Dante's *Inferno,* Canto XXVII, ll. 61-66. 14. **Michelangelo,** the great Renaissance artist (1475-1564), here used as a symbol for a topic of conversation about art.

Disturb the universe?
In a minute there is time
For decisions and revisions which a minute
    will reverse.

For I have known them all already, known
    them all:—
Have known the evenings, mornings, after-
    noons, 50
I have measured out my life with coffee
    spoons;
I know the voices dying with a dying fall
Beneath the music from a farther room.
    So how should I presume?

And I have known the eyes already, known
    them all— 55
The eyes that fix you in a formulated phrase,
And when I am formulated, sprawling on a
    pin,
When I am pinned and wriggling on the
    wall,
Then how should I begin
To spit out all the butt-ends of my days and
    ways? 60
    And how should I presume?

And I have known the arms already, known
    them all—
Arms that are braceleted and white and bare
[But in the lamplight, downed with light
    brown hair!]
Is it perfume from a dress 65
That makes me so digress?
Arms that lie along a table, or wrap about a
    shawl.
    And should I then presume?
    And how should I begin?

. . . . .

Shall I say, I have gone at dusk through
    narrow streets 70
And watched the smoke that rises from the
    pipes
Of lonely men in shirt-sleeves, leaning out of
    windows? . . .

I should have been a pair of ragged claws
Scuttling across the floors of silent seas.

. . . . . .

And the afternoon, the evening, sleeps so
    peacefully! 75
Smoothed by long fingers,
Asleep . . . tired . . . or it malingers,
Stretched on the floor, here beside you and
    me.
Should I, after tea and cakes and ices,
Have the strength to force the moment to its
    crisis? 80
But though I have wept and fasted, wept and
    prayed,
Though I have seen my head [grown slightly
    bald] brought in upon a platter,
I am no prophet—and here's no great matter;
I have seen the moment of my greatness
    flicker,
And I have seen the eternal Footman hold
    my coat, and snicker, 85
And in short, I was afraid.

And would it have been worth it, after all,
After the cups, the marmalade, the tea,
Among the porcelain, among some talk of
    you and me,
Would it have been worth while, 90
To have bitten off the matter with a smile,
To have squeezed the universe into a ball
To roll it toward some overwhelming ques-
    tion,
To say: "I am Lazarus, come from the dead,
Come back to tell you all, I shall tell you
    all"— 95
If one, settling a pillow by her head,
    Should say: "That is not what I meant at
        all.
    That is not it, at all."

And would it have been worth it, after all,
Would it have been worth while, 100
After the sunsets and the dooryards and the
    sprinkled streets,
After the novels, after the teacups, after the
    skirts that trail along the floor—
And this, and so much more?—
It is impossible to say just what I mean!
But as if a magic lantern threw the nerves in
    patterns on a screen: 105

82. **my head . . . platter**, a reference to the execution of St. John the Baptist at the importuning of Salome. Cf. *Mark*, 6, especially verses 27 and 28. 94. **Lazarus**, the young man who was resurrected by Christ. Cf. *John*, 11:1-46.

Would it have been worth while
If one, settling a pillow or throwing off a
    shawl,
And turning toward the window, should say:
    "That is not it at all,
    That is not what I meant, at all."   110

    . . . . .

No! I am not Prince Hamlet, nor was meant
    to be;
Am an attendant lord, one that will do
To swell a progress, start a scene or two,
Advise the prince; no doubt, an easy tool,
Deferential, glad to be of use,   115
Politic, cautious, and meticulous;
Full of high sentence, but a bit obtuse;
At times, indeed, almost ridiculous—
Almost, at times, the Fool.

I grow old . . . I grow old . . .   120
I shall wear the bottoms of my trousers rolled.

Shall I part my hair behind? Do I dare to eat
    a peach?
I shall wear white flannel trousers, and walk
    upon the beach.
I have heard the mermaids singing, each to
    each.

I do not think that they will sing to me.   125

I have seen them riding seaward on the waves
Combing the white hair of the waves blown
    back
When the wind blows the water white and
    black.

We have lingered in the chambers of the sea
By sea-girls wreathed with seaweed red and
    brown   130
Till human voices wake us, and we drown.

    (1917)

111 ff. **Prince Hamlet**, etc., a conscious renunciation by the young man of any true resemblance between himself and the principal figure in a tragedy.

Ash Wednesday

    Ash Wednesday is Eliot's first long analytical and personal poem concerned with his own religious conversion. It is in part a study of the way a highly poetic and intellectual mind attempts to shed mundane considerations and earthly doubts in order that the spirit may obtain salvation. Apparently that is what Eliot has tried to do in his own case. But his honesty is so great that the poem is more a cry imploring grace, a plea for pardon and redemption through the church, showing also that neither the skeptical mind, which Eliot demonstrated in his earlier poems, nor his poetic sensitivity can be sloughed off as a snake sheds his skin.
    Eliot opens the poem with a statement of the change in his former attitude and of his decision not to return to the infirm glory of life; at the end of the first section he gives his prayer for mercy. He believes that his poetic flights are not what they once were; he is convinced of his unworthiness and of his need for repentance. The theme of the second section is "dust to dust"—the destruction of the body. The poet is willing to relinquish the human form if some greater sense of permanence can be reached. The third section deals with the ascent of three staircases, as one escapes the flesh. On the first stairs it is impossible to consider oneself except through human eyes and in human form; on the second stairs the image of old age makes it possible to leave behind the life of the flesh; and on the third stairs one abandons what is most dear—the sensual perceptions, the poet's delight in the image. The fourth section, much more mystical throughout, tells how the poet was led away from the images of earthly life, away from the pagan images of poetic delight, in order that he might, after dismissing the flesh, know once more the fertile, the replenishing, and the spiritual. The fifth section is a development of the opposing ideas of reality: 1. the Word of God, the word from which all others derive, and 2. the word of man unredeemed, who must seek the spiritual truth again, because he has walked in darkness and has denied the voice of truth and God. The poet is led to redemption by the veiled sister (ll. 168 and 177), the Madonna. He himself has found it difficult to lay aside his doubts; he himself has denied God between the rocks—the altars of primitive gods, now

empty of all sacrifice. The sixth section repeats, with a slight but important variation, the theme of the first. The poet sees the images of the white sails of poetic exploration; he remembers the poetic delight of the senses, and the smell of all that is earthly. He is now at the critical moment which calls for dying and for birth, in the spiritual sense. And so again, the image of life (the Virgin, the spirit of water or of all fertility) is the image evoked. He must be spiritually reborn or he is indeed dead, and so he prays for grace that he may be forgiven and saved.

The poem is, as a whole, a moving story of the struggle to relinquish the cherished weapon, a poetic intelligence of high order, to attain through the church (Anglo-Catholic) the grace of God. But it should be thought of throughout as a poem of conflict and repentance rather than of religious ecstasy.

I

Because I do not hope to turn again
Because I do not hope
Because I do not hope to turn
Desiring this man's gift and that man's scope
I no longer strive to strive towards such things   5
(Why should the agéd eagle stretch its wings?)
Why should I mourn
The vanished power of the usual reign?

Because I do not hope to know again
The infirm glory of the positive hour   10
Because I do not think
Because I know I shall not know
The one veritable transitory power
Because I cannot drink
There, where trees flower, and springs flow, for there is nothing again   15

Because I know that time is always time
And place is always and only place
And what is actual is actual only for one time
And only for one place
I rejoice that things are as they are and   20
I renounce the blessèd face
And renounce the voice
Because I cannot hope to turn again
Consequently I rejoice, having to construct something
Upon which to rejoice   25

And pray to God to have mercy upon us
And I pray that I may forget
These matters that with myself I too much discuss
Too much explain
Because I do not hope to turn again   30
Let these words answer
For what is done, not to be done again
May the judgement not be too heavy upon us

Because these wings are no longer wings to fly
But merely vans to beat the air   35
The air which is now thoroughly small and dry
Smaller and dryer than the will
Teach us to care and not to care
Teach us to sit still.

Pray for us sinners now and at the hour of our death   40
Pray for us now and at the hour of our death.

1 ff. **Because I . . . again**, etc. This is a direct translation of *"Perch'io non spero di tornar già mai,"* from the writings of the Florentine poet and philosopher Guido Cavalcanti (*c.* 1250-1300), a friend of Dante. But there is also some connection between the lines of Eliot and a sermon by the English divine Lancelot Andrewes (1555-1626), Bishop of Winchester: "Now at this time is the turning of the year. . . . Everything now turning that we also would make it our time to turn to God. . . . Upon this turning, *cardo vertitur,* the hinge turns, of our well and evil doing for ever. . . . Repentance itself is nothing but a kind of circling. . . . Which circle consists of two turnings. . . . First a turn wherein we look forward to God and with our whole heart resolve to turn to Him. Then a turn again wherein we look backward to our sins wherein we have turned from God. . . . The wheel turns apace, and if we turn not the rather these turnings may overtake us." 4. **Desiring . . . scope.** Cf. Shakespeare, *Sonnet* 29, line 7: "Desiring this man's art and that man's scope." 6. **Why should . . . wings?** The eagle here is reminiscent of the image in *L'Albatros* by the French poet Baudelaire (1821-1867), about whom Eliot has written an essay; but the image is certainly religious in purpose here. The Psalmist (*Psalms,* 103:5) says, "thy youth is renewed like the eagle's," and in the Middle Ages the eagle was always the symbol of baptismal grace. Connected with this is Dante's dream of the eagle, in *Purgatorio,* IX, and the legend in the medieval Bestiary that the aged eagle flies into a circle of fire where his feathers are burned away and he falls into a fountain of water, to emerge with his youth again restored. 10. **The infirm . . . hour.** It may be possible to oppose this to the last clause of the Lord's Prayer, "For thine is the kingdom, and the power, and the glory for ever and ever," or to associate it as a subconscious echo of "The uncertain glory of an April day," from Shakespeare's *The Two Gentlemen of Verona,* I, iii, 85.

35. **vans**, the fans of a winnowing-machine. 40. **Pray for us,** the Angelic Salutation in the Catholic Mass, "Ora pro nobis," best known in the *Ave Maria.*

II

Lady, three white leopards sat under a juniper-tree
In the cool of the day, having fed to satiety
On my legs my heart my liver and that which had been contained
In the hollow round of my skull. And God said   45
Shall these bones live? shall these
Bones live? And that which had been contained
In the bones (which were already dry) said chirping:
Because of the goodness of this Lady
And because of her loveliness, and because   50
She honours the Virgin in meditation,
We shine with brightness. And I who am here dissembled
Proffer my deeds to oblivion, and my love
To the posterity of the desert and the fruit of the gourd.
It is this which recovers   55
My guts the strings of my eyes and the indigestible portions
Which the leopards reject. The Lady is withdrawn
In a white gown, to contemplation, in a white gown.
Let the whiteness of bones atone to forgetfulness.
There is no life in them. As I am forgotten   60
And would be forgotten, so I would forget
Thus devoted, concentrated in purpose. And God said
Prophesy to the wind, to the wind only for only
The wind will listen. And the bones sang chirping   64
With the burden of the grasshopper, saying

Lady of silences
Calm and distressed
Torn and most whole
Rose of memory
Rose of forgetfulness   70
Exhausted and life-giving
Worried reposeful
The single Rose
Is now the Garden
Where all loves end   75
Terminate torment
Of love unsatisfied
The greater torment
Of love satisfied
End of the endless   80
Journey to no end
Conclusion of all that
Is inconclusible
Speech without word and
Word of no speech   85
Grace to the Mother
For the Garden
Where all love ends.

Under a juniper-tree the bones sang, scattered and shining
We are glad to be scattered, we did little good to each other,   90
Under a tree in the cool of the day, with the blessing of sand,

---

42. **Lady.** Cf. Eliot's essay on Dante: "In the Earthly Paradise Dante encounters a lady named Matilda, whose identity need not at first bother us." **three white leopards.** Again, cf. Eliot's essay on Dante: "I do not recommend, in first reading the first canto of the *Inferno*, worrying about the identity of the Leopard, the Lion, or the She-Wolf. It is really better, at the start, not to know or care what they do mean. What we should consider is not so much the meaning of the images, but the reverse process, that which led a man having an idea to express it in images. We have to consider the type of mind which by nature and *practice* tended to express itself in allegory; and for a competent poet, allegory means *clear visual images*." Actually, Dante's animals derive from *Jeremiah*, 5:6: "Wherefore a lion out of the forest shall slay them, and a wolf of the evenings shall spoil them, a leopard shall watch over their cities: every one that goeth out thence shall be torn in pieces: because their transgressions are many, and their backslidings are increased." But Eliot's leopards are obviously instruments of good, whereas Dante's beasts are sinister. **a juniper-tree.** The prophet Elijah "came and sat down under a juniper tree" in the wilderness (*I Kings*, 19:4). But Eliot may also be thinking of the Grimm's fairy tale, *The Juniper Tree*, in which Marlinchen buried a little boy's bones under a juniper tree. 45. **In the hollow . . . skull.** For the passages dealing with the destruction of the body, Eliot is indebted to Baudelaire's poem *Voyage à Cythère*. 46. **Shall . . . live?** Cf. *Ezekiel*, 37:3: "And he said unto me . . . can these bones live?" 54. **the fruit of the gourd.** Cf. *Jonah*, 4:10: "Thou hast had pity on the gourd."

63. **Prophesy to the wind.** Cf. *Ezekiel*, 37:9: "Prophesy unto the wind, prophesy, son of man." 65. **With . . . grasshopper.** Cf. *Ecclesiastes*, 12:5: "and the grasshopper shall be a burden, and desire shall fail." 69. **Rose of memory.** One of the titles of the Virgin Mary is *Rosa Mystica*, and in Dante's *Paradiso* (XXIII, ll. 73-74) she is "the Rose wherein the Word Divine made itself flesh." 73. **The single Rose,** Christ, who is the Rose of Sharon. Dante saw the whole company of saints in Paradise as the petals of one white rose. See also *Church-Rents and Schismes* (ll. 1-4) by the English metaphysical poet George Herbert (1593-1633):
   Brave rose, (alas!) where art thou? in the chair
   Where thou didst lately so triumph and shine
   A worm doth sit, whose many feet and hair
   Are the more foul, the more thou wert divine.
74. **Is . . . Garden.** No doubt this is a reference to the Garden of Gethsemane, where Christ prayed all through the night before His betrayal; cf. *Matthew*, 26:36-46. 81. **Journey . . . end.** Cf. the end of *Journey of the Magi* (p. 1092).

Forgetting themselves and each other, united
In the quiet of the desert. This is the land
    which ye
Shall divide by lot. And neither division nor
    unity
Matters. This is the land. We have our inher-
    itance.   95

III

At the first turning of the second stair
I turned and saw below
The same shape twisted on the banister
Under the vapour in the fetid air
Struggling with the devil of the stairs who
    wears   100
The deceitful face of hope and of despair.

At the second turning of the second stair
I left them twisting, turning below;
There were no more faces and the stair was
    dark,
Damp, jaggèd, like an old man's mouth
    driveling, beyond repair,   105
Or the toothed gullet of an agèd shark.

At the first turning of the third stair
Was a slotted window bellied like the fig's
    fruit
And beyond the hawthorn blossom and a
    pasture scene
The broadbacked figure drest in blue and
    green   110
Enchanted the maytime with an antique flute.
Blown hair is sweet, brown hair over the
    mouth blown,
Lilac and brown hair;
Distraction, music of the flute, stops and steps
    of the mind over the third stair,
Fading, fading; strength beyond hope and
    despair   115
Climbing the third stair.

Lord, I am not worthy
Lord, I am not worthy

    but speak the word only.

IV

Who walked between the violet and the
    violet   120
Who walked between
The various ranks of varied green
Going in white and blue, in Mary's colour,
Talking of trivial things
In ignorance and in knowledge of eternal
    dolour   125
Who moved among the others as they
    walked,
Who then made strong the fountains and
    made fresh the springs

Made cool the dry rock and made firm the
    sand
In blue of larkspur, blue of Mary's colour,
Sovegna vos   130

Here are the years that walk between, bearing
Away the fiddles and the flutes, restoring
One who moves in the time between sleep
    and waking, wearing

White light folded, sheathed about her,
    folded.
The new years walk, restoring   135
Through a bright cloud of tears, the years,
    restoring
With a new verse the ancient rhyme. Redeem
The time. Redeem
The unread vision in the higher dream
While jewelled unicorns draw by the gilded
    hearse.   140

93-94. **This . . . lot.** See *Ezekiel*, 48:29: "This is the land which ye shall divide by lot unto the tribes of Israel for inheritance, and these are their portions, saith the Lord God." 96. **the second stair.** The conception of the stairs in section III may have been suggested by Dante's *Purgatorio*, XXVI, 145-147:

> I pray you by that Goodness which doth deign
> To guide you to the summit of this stair
> Bethink you in due season of my pain.

But see also *The Song of Solomon*, 2:14: "O my dove, that art in the clefts of the rock, in the secret places of the stairs, let me see thy countenance."

117. **Lord . . . worthy.** See *Matthew*, 8:8: "The centurion answered and said, Lord, I am not worthy that thou shouldest come under my roof: but speak the word only, and my servant shall be healed." 123. **in Mary's colour,** suggested by the paintings of the Italians and of the English Pre-Raphaelites, who always depicted the Virgin Mary in white and blue. 130. **Sovegna vos,** "bethink you"; see quotation from Dante in note 96. 134. **White . . . sheathed.** Dante often uses the image of a figure swathed or sheathed (*fasciato*) in light or joy. 140. **jewelled unicorns.** These unicorns may derive from Guido Cavalcanti (see note 1) or from one of the Florentine engravings of the Triumphs of the Italian poet Petrarch (1304-1374), where the car in the Triumph of Chastity is drawn by unicorns. By tradition, the legendary unicorn could be captured only by a virgin and was therefore the symbol of chastity.

The silent sister veiled in white and blue
Between the yews, behind the garden god,
Whose flute is breathless, bent her head and
  signed but spoke no word

But the fountain sprang up and the bird sang
  down
Redeem the time, redeem the dream   145
The token of the word unheard, unspoken

Till the wind shake a thousand whispers
  from the yew

And after this our exile

V

If the lost word is lost, if the spent word is
  spent
If the unheard, unspoken   150
Word is unspoken, unheard;
Still is the unspoken word, the Word unheard,
The Word without a word, the Word within
The world and for the world;
And the light shone in darkness and   155
Against the Word the unstilled world still
  whirled
About the centre of the silent Word.

  O my people, what have I done unto
  thee.

Where shall the word be found, where will
  the word
Resound? Not here, there is not enough silence   160
Not on the sea or on the islands, not
On the mainland, in the desert or the rain
  land,

For those who walk in darkness
Both in the day time and in the night time
The right time and the right place are not
  here   165
No place of grace for those who avoid the
  face
No time to rejoice for those who walk among
  noise and deny the voice

Will the veiled sister pray for
Those who walk in darkness, who chose thee
  and oppose thee,
Those who are torn on the horn between
  season and season, time and time, between   170
Hour and hour, word and word, power and
  power, those who wait
In darkness? Will the veiled sister pray
For children at the gate
Who will not go away and cannot pray:
Pray for those who chose and oppose   175

  O my people, what have I done unto
  thee.

Will the veiled sister between the slender
Yew trees pray for those who offend her
And are terrified and cannot surrender
And affirm before the world and deny between
  the rocks   180
In the last desert between the last blue rocks
The desert in the garden the garden in the
  desert
Of drouth, spitting from the mouth the withered
  apple-seed.

  O my people.

---

142. **the yews.** The yew is by tradition the tree planted in English churchyards, being described an "an embleme of Resurrection from its perpetual verdure" by Sir Thomas Browne (1605-1682). 148. **And . . . exile,** from the prayer *Salve Regina,* which follows the celebration of the Catholic Mass: "To thee do we send up our sighs mourning and weeping in this valley of tears; turn, then, most gracious advocate, thine eyes of mercy towards us; and after this our exile, show unto us the blessed fruit of thy womb, Jesus." 149-154. **If the lost . . . for the world.** The whole of this passage is a variation on *John,* 1:1-14 and on "the word within a word, unable to speak a word," a phrase from "Lancelot Andrewes" in Eliot's essay *For Lancelot Andrewes* (see note 1). 158. **O my . . . thee.** See *Micah,* 6:3.

163. **those . . . darkness.** The Bible is full of allusions to those who walk in darkness: *Job,* 29:3; *Isaiah,* 9:2; *Psalms,* 82:5 and 91:6; *Ecclesiastes,* 2:14; *Isaiah,* 59:9; *John,* 8:12 and 12:35; *I John,* 1:6 and 2:11. 167. **deny thy voice,** probably an allusion to Peter's denial of Christ; see *Matthew,* 26:34-35. 169. **chose . . . thee.** See *Matthew,* 12:30: "He that is not with me is against me." 170. **torn on the horn,** as if by a bull. But perhaps the reference is to the horns of a dilemma, in which case those referred to are in the "agony of indecision." 180. **affirm . . . rocks,** probably a reference to "Madonna of the Rocks," by the Italian Renaissance painter Leonardo da Vinci (1452-1519), in which the artist affirmed in the painting of the rocks some of the geological theories he could not express in writing to the world, since it was heretical to oppose the Biblical and Aristotelian concepts of the Creation. 182. **The desert in the garden.** See *Isaiah,* 51:3: "he will make . . . her desert like the garden of the Lord." 183. **the withered apple-seed,** doubtless connected poetically with the fruit of the tree of knowledge of good and evil in the Garden of Eden, traditionally an apple.

VI

Although I do not hope to turn again   185
Although I do not hope
Although I do not hope to turn

Wavering between the profit and the loss
In this brief transit where the dreams cross
The dreamcrossed twilight between birth and
    dying   190
(Bless me father) though I do not wish to
    wish these things
From the wide window towards the granite
    shore
The white sails still fly seaward, seaward
    flying
Unbroken wings

And the lost heart stiffens and rejoices   195
In the lost lilac and the lost sea voices
And the weak spirit quickens to rebel
For the bent golden-rod and the lost sea smell
Quickens to recover
The cry of quail and the whirling plover   200
And the blind eye creates
The empty forms between the ivory gates
And smell renews the salt savour of the sandy
    earth

This is the time of tension between dying and
    birth
The place of solitude where three dreams
    cross   205
Between blue rocks
But when the voices shaken from the yew-
    tree drift away
Let the other yew be shaken and reply.

Blessèd sister, holy mother, spirit of the foun-
    tain, spirit of the garden,
Suffer us not to mock ourselves with false-
    hood   210
Teach us to care and not to care
Teach us to sit still
Even among these rocks,
Our peace in His will
And even among these rocks   215
Sister, mother
And spirit of the river, spirit of the sea,
Suffer me not to be separated

And let my cry come unto Thee.   (1930)

Journey of the Magi

"A cold coming we had of it,
Just the worst time of the year
For a journey, and such a long journey:
The ways deep and the weather sharp,
The very dead of winter."   5
And the camels galled, sore-footed, refractory,
Lying down in the melting snow.
There were times we regretted
The summer palaces on slopes, the terraces,
And the silken girls bringing sherbet.   10
Then the camel men cursing and grumbling
And running away, and wanting their liquor
    and women,
And the night-fires going out, and the lack of
    shelters,
And the cities hostile and the towns un-
    friendly
And the villages dirty and charging high
    prices: 15
A hard time we had of it.
At the end we preferred to travel all night,
Sleeping in snatches,
With the voices singing in our ears, saying
That this was all folly.   20

Then at dawn we came down to a temperate
    valley,
Wet, below the snow line, smelling of vege-
    tation;
With a running stream and a water-mill beat-
    ing the darkness,
And three trees on the low sky,
And an old white horse galloped away in the
    meadow.   25
Then we came to a tavern with vine-leaves
    over the lintel,
Six hands at an open door dicing for pieces
    of silver,

---

191. **Bless me father,** the opening formula of the confession. 193. **seaward,** suggested by Dante's *Paradiso*, III, ll. 85-87: "and his will is our peace; it is that sea to which all moves that it createth and that nature maketh." 200. **cry . . . plover.** See *Numbers,* 11:31. 214. **Our . . . will.** See note 193.

218. **Suffer . . . separated,** the ancient prayer *Anima Christi* (Suffer me not to be separated from Thee). 219. **And let . . . Thee.** See *Psalms,* 119:169: "Let my cry come near before thee, O Lord."

And feet kicking the empty wine-skins.
But there was no information, and so we continued
And arrived at evening, not a moment too soon 30
Finding the place; it was (you may say) satisfactory.

All this was a long time ago, I remember,
And I would do it again, but set down
This set down
This: were we led all that way for 35
Birth or Death? There was a Birth, certainly,
We had evidence and no doubt. I had seen birth and death,
But had thought they were different; this Birth was
Hard and bitter agony for us, like Death, our death.
We returned to our places, these Kingdoms,
But no longer at ease here, in the old dispensation, 41
With an alien people clutching their gods.
I should be glad of another death.   (1927)

Animula

"Issues from the hand of God, the simple soul"
To a flat world of changing lights and noise,
To light, dark, dry or damp, chilly or warm;
Moving between the legs of tables and of chairs,
Rising or falling, grasping at kisses and toys,
Advancing boldly, sudden to take alarm, 6
Retreating to the corner of arm and knee,
Eager to be reassured, taking pleasure
In the fragrant brilliance of the Christmas tree,
Pleasure in the wind, the sunlight and the sea; 10
Studies the sunlit pattern on the floor
And running stags around a silver tray;
Confounds the actual and the fanciful,
Content with playing-cards and kings and queens,
What the fairies do and what the servants say. 15
The heavy burden of the growing soul
Perplexes and offends more, day by day;
Week by week, offends and perplexes more
With the imperatives of "is and seems"
And may and may not, desire and control. 20
The pain of living and the drug of dreams
Curl up the small soul in the window seat
Behind the *Encyclopædia Britannica*.
Issues from the hand of time the simple soul
Irresolute and selfish, misshapen, lame, 25
Unable to fare forward or retreat,
Fearing the warm reality, the offered good,
Denying the importunity of the blood,
Shadow of its own shadows, spectre in its own gloom,
Leaving disordered papers in a dusty room; 30
Living first in the silence after the viaticum.

Pray for Guiterriez, avid of speed and power,
For Boudin, blown to pieces,
For this one who made a great fortune,
And that one who went his own way. 35
Pray for Floret, by the boarhound slain between the yew trees,
Pray for us now and at the hour of our birth.   (1929)

Animula. The title means *Little Life, Little Soul.* 32-36. **Pray for Guiterriez,** etc., pray for individuals I have known or heard of (noting their fates), for they were once little souls too. 37. **Pray . . . birth.** Note the inversion of the usual prayer, "pray for us now and at the hour of our death."

Wilfred Owen
1893-1918

One of the tragic losses in the First World War was Wilfred Owen, who was killed at the age of twenty-five while leading his men across the Sambre Canal, in France, on November 4, 1918. Owen was born in Oswestry, Shropshire, on March 18, 1893. His only formal education was secured at Birkenhead Institute, Liverpool.

Owen served in the war for two periods—first, in 1916-1917 until he was incapacitated and sent to a war hospital in Scotland; second, after his recovery, for the greater part of 1918. During this second period he was awarded the Military Cross, for gallantry under fire, a month before he was killed.

With an innate love for poetry, Owen had proved his worth as a poet a year or more before his untimely death. Many of his poems were written while he was recuperating in the hospital. While there, too, he became acquainted with Siegfried Sassoon, another young and vigorous poet, from whom he received much encouragement. Both wrote realistic and passionate poems condemning all the waste and horror of war, which they had seen at close range. It was Sassoon who collected and published the poems of Owen two years after his death. The volume contained a foreword written by Owen in which he said, "All a poet can do today is warn. That is why the true poet must be truthful."

Greater Love

Red lips are not so red
    As the stained stones kissed by the English dead.
Kindness of wooed and wooer
Seems shame to their love pure.
O Love, your eyes lose lure   5
    When I behold eyes blinded in my stead!

Your slender attitude
    Trembles not exquisite like limbs knife-skewed,
Rolling and rolling there
Where God seems not to care;   10
Till the fierce Love they bear
    Cramps them in death's extreme decrepitude.

Your voice sings not so soft,—
    Though even as wind murmuring through raftered loft,—
Your dear voice is not dear,   15
Gentle, and evening clear,
As theirs whom none now hear,
    Now earth has stopped their piteous mouths that coughed.

Heart, you were never hot,
    Nor large, nor full like hearts made great with shot;   20
And though your hand be pale,
Paler are all which trail
Your cross through flame and hail:
    Weep, you may weep, for you may touch them not.   (1920)

Apologia pro Poemate Meo

I, too, saw God through mud—
    The mud that cracked on cheeks when wretches smiled.
    War brought more glory to their eyes than blood,
    And gave their laughs more glee than shakes a child.

Merry it was to laugh there—   5
    Where death becomes absurd and life absurder.
    For power was on us as we slashed bones bare
    Not to feel sickness or remorse of murder.

I, too, have dropped off fear—
    Behind the barrage, dead as my platoon,   10
    And sailed my spirit surging, light and clear
    Past the entanglement where hopes lay strewn;

And witnessed exultation—
    Faces that used to curse me, scowl for scowl,

The poems of Owen are reprinted from *The Poems of Wilfred Owen*, edited by Edmund Blunden. By permission of The Viking Press, Inc.

Apologia pro Poemate Meo. The title means *Apology for My Poetry.*

Shine and lift up with passion of obla-
    tion,   15
Seraphic for an hour; though they were
    foul.

I have made fellowships—
    Untold of happy lovers in old song.
    For love is not the binding of fair lips
    With the soft silk of eyes that look and
        long,   20

By Joy, whose ribbon slips,—
    But wound with war's hard wire whose
        stakes are strong;
    Bound with the bandage of the arm that
        drips;
    Knit in the webbing of the rifle-thong.

I have perceived much beauty   25
    In the hoarse oaths that kept our courage
        straight;
    Heard music in the silentness of duty;
    Found peace where shell-storms spouted
        reddest spate.

Nevertheless, except you share
    With them in hell the sorrowful dark of
        hell,   30
    Whose world is but the trembling of a
        flare,
    And heaven but as the highway for a
        shell,

You shall not hear their mirth:
    You shall not come to think them well
        content
    By any jest of mine. These men are
        worth   35
    Your tears. You are not worth their mer-
        riment.   (1920)

Dulce et Decorum Est

Bent double, like old beggars under sacks,
Knock-kneed, coughing like hags, we cursed
    through sludge,
Till on the haunting flares we turned our
    backs,

15. **oblation**, sacrificial offering. 28. **spate**, outflow, small stream.
Dulce et Decorum Est. The title in its full form (see ll. 27-28) means *It is sweet and honorable to die for one's country.* It is quoted from Horace, *Odes,* III, 2, 13.

And towards our distant rest began to trudge.
Men marched asleep. Many had lost their
    boots,   5
But limped on, blood-shod. All went lame,
    all blind;
Drunk with fatigue; deaf even to the hoots
Of gas-shells dropping softly behind.

Gas! GAS! Quick, boys—An ecstasy of fum-
    bling,
Fitting the clumsy helmets just in time, 10
But someone still was yelling out and stum-
    bling
And floundering like a man in fire or lime.—
Dim through the misty panes and thick green
    light,
As under a green sea, I saw him drowning.

In all my dreams before my helpless sight 15
He plunges at me, guttering, choking, drown-
    ing.

If in some smothering dreams, you too could
    pace
Behind the wagon that we flung him in,
And watch the white eyes writhing in his face,
His hanging face, like a devil's sick of sin; 20
If you could hear, at every jolt, the blood
Come gargling from the froth-corrupted lungs,
Bitten as the cud
Of vile, incurable sores on innocent tongues,—
My friend, you would not tell with such high
    zest   25
To children ardent for some desperate glory,
The old Lie: Dulce et decorum est
Pro patria mori.   (1920)

Disabled

He sat in a wheeled chair, waiting for dark,
And shivered in his ghastly suit of gray,
Legless, sewn short at elbow. Through the park
Voices of boys rang saddening like a hymn,
Voices of play and pleasure after day,   5
Till gathering sleep had mothered them from
    him.
. . . .
About this time Town used to swing so gay
When glow-lamps budded in the light blue
    trees,

And girls glanced lovelier as the air grew dim,
In the old times, before he threw away his knees. 10
Now he will never feel again how slim
Girls' waists are, or how warm their subtle hands;
All of them touch him like some queer disease.

. . . .

There was an artist silly for his face,
For it was younger than his youth, last year.
Now, he is old; his back will never brace; 16
He's lost his color very far from here,
Poured it down shell-holes till the veins ran dry,
And half his lifetime lapsed in the hot race,
And leap of purple spurted from his thigh. 20

. . . .

One time he liked a blood-smear down his leg,
After the matches, carried shoulder-high.
It was after football, when he'd drunk a peg,
He thought he'd better join.—He wonders why.
Someone had said he'd look a god in kilts, 25
That's why; and may be, too, to please his Meg,
Aye, that was it, to please the giddy jilts
He asked to join. He didn't have to beg;
Smiling they wrote his lie; aged nineteen years.
Germans he scarcely thought of; all their guilt,
And Austria's, did not move him. And no fears
Of Fear came yet. He thought of jewelled hilts 31
For daggers in plaid socks; of smart salutes;
And care of arms; and leave; and pay arrears;
Esprit de corps; and hints for young recruits.
And soon he was drafted out with drums and cheers. 35

. . . .

Some cheered him home, but not as crowds cheer Goal.
Only a solemn man who brought him fruits,

Disabled. 23. **peg,** a drink of whiskey or brandy diluted with soda water.

Thanked him; and then inquired about his soul.

. . . .

Now, he will spend a few sick years in Institutes,
And do what things the rules consider wise,
And take whatever pity they may dole. 41
To-night he noticed how the women's eyes
Passed from him to the strong men that were whole.
How cold and late it is! Why don't they come
And put him into bed? Why don't they come?   (1920)

The End

After the blast of lightning from the East,
The flourish of loud clouds, the Chariot Throne;
After the drums of Time have rolled and ceased,
And by the bronze west long retreat is blown,

Shall life renew these bodies? Of a truth 5
All death will He annul, all tears assuage?—
Fill the void veins of life again with youth,
And wash, with an immortal water, Age?

When I do ask white Age, he saith not so:
"My head hangs weighed with snow." 10
And when I hearken to the Earth, she saith:
"My fiery heart shrinks aching. It is death.
Mine ancient scars shall not be glorified
Nor my titanic tears, the sea be dried."
(1920)

Anthem for Doomed Youth

What passing-bells for these who die as cattle?
  Only the monstrous anger of the guns.
  Only the stuttering rifle's rapid rattle
Can patter out their hasty orisons.
No mockeries for them from prayers or bells, 5
Nor any voice of mourning save the choirs,—
The shrill, demented choirs of wailing shells;
And bugles calling for them from sad shires.

The End. 2. **Chariot Throne,** the chariot used by Phoebus Apollo as he drew the sun across the heavens.

What candles may be held to speed them all?
Not in the hands of boys, but in their
    eyes   10
Shall shine the holy glimmers of good-byes.

The pallor of girls' brows shall be their pall;
Their flowers the tenderness of silent minds,
And each slow dusk a drawing-down of
    blinds.   (1920)

Aldous Huxley
1894-

On his father's side Aldous Huxley is the grandson of Thomas Huxley (p. 561); on his mother's he is the great-nephew of Matthew Arnold (p. 527). Huxley was born in Godalming, Surrey, July 26, 1894; in 1908 he entered Eton College with the intention of becoming a doctor, but gave up after he contracted an eye ailment. Two years later, with improved eyesight, he entered Balliol College, Oxford. Since a scientific career was out of the question because of his defective vision, he specialized in English literature and philology. In the meantime he had learned to read books and music in Braille and to write on the typewriter by the touch method.

After graduating in 1915, Huxley did odd jobs for the government during the last three years of the First World War. In 1919 he became a staff member of *The Athenaeum* and then of *The Westminster Gazette,* to both of which he contributed book reviews and critical essays on current art, drama, and music. His interest in poetry was given expression in an edited anthology of Oxford poetry (1916) and in several volumes of his own poems.

Most of the time between 1923 and 1930 Huxley lived in Italy, where he wrote and published some of his best novels, essays, and short stories. He spent the year 1925-1926 in India and the Dutch East Indies; then in 1930 he moved to southern France, which was his home for several years. In 1934 he visited Central America and the United States; he returned to this country in 1938, where he received treatment that gradually improved his eyesight. He now lives in southern California.

Huxley is best known for his prose writings, which are very numerous and which cover wide areas of serious thinking. (See p. 1016.) Among his collections of short stories are *Limbo* (1920), *Mortal Coils* (1922), *Little Mexican and Other Stories,* published in the United States as *Young Archimedes and Other Stories* (1924), *Two or Three Graces* (1926), and *Brief Candles* (1930). The novels, which created a much greater stir in the reading public, including *Crome Yellow* (1921), *Antic Hay* (1923), *Those Barren Leaves* (1925), *Point Counter Point* (1928), *Brave New World* (1932), *Time Must Have a Stop* (1944), *Ape and Essence* (1948), and *The Genius and the Goddess* (1955). His volumes of essays include *On the Margin* (1923), *Along the Road* (1925), *Jesting Pilate* (1926), *Essays New and Old* (1926), *Proper Studies* (1927), *Do What You Will* (1929), *The Holy Face and Other Essays* (1929), *Vulgarity in Literature* (1930), *Music at Night and Other Essays* (1931), *Texts and Pretexts,* an anthology of criticism (1932), *Beyond the Mexique Bay* (1934), *The Olive Tree and Other Essays* (1936), *An Encyclopaedia of Pacifism* (1937), and *Ends and Means* (1937). His other writings include a drama, *The World of Light* (1931); a biography of Father Joseph, Richelieu's secretary, *Grey Eminence* (1941); and several special studies: *The Art of Seeing* (1942), *The Perennial Philosophy* (1945), and *Science, Liberty and Peace* (1946). In addition he has edited the letters of D. H. Lawrence (1932).

Young Archimedes

"Young Archimedes" presents a dramatic episode in the tragedy of genius. Incidentally, it stresses the close relationship that exists between music and mathematics. In its romantic descriptions of nature, its realistic characterization, its flashes of humor, and its genuine pathos, it reveals Huxley in one of his more sympathetic moods. The brilliant intellect and technical skill of the hero align him with Archimedes, the celebrated philosopher and mathematician of the third century before Christ.

It was the view which finally made us take the place. True, the house had its disadvantages. It was a long way out of town and had no telephone. The rent was unduly high, the drainage system poor. On windy nights, when the ill-fitting panes were rattling so furiously in the window-frames that you could fancy yourself in an hotel omnibus, the electric light, for some mysterious reason, used invariably to go out and leave you in the noisy dark. There was a splendid bathroom; but the electric pump, which was supposed to send up water from the rain-water tanks in the terrace, did not work. Punctually every autumn the drinking well ran dry. And our landlady was a liar and a cheat.

But these are the little disadvantages of every hired house, all over the world. For Italy they were not really at all serious. I have seen plenty of houses which had them all and a hundred others, without possessing the compensating advantages of ours—the southward facing garden and terrace for the winter and spring, the large cool rooms against the midsummer heat, the hilltop air and freedom from mosquitoes, and finally the view.

And what a view it was! Or rather, what a succession of views. For it was different every day; and without stirring from the house one had the impression of an incessant change of scene: all the delights of travel without its fatigues. There were autumn days when all the valleys were filled with mist and the crests of the Apennines rose darkly out of a flat white lake. There were days when the mist invaded even our hilltop and we were enveloped in a soft vapor in which the mist-colored olive trees, that sloped away below our windows towards the valley, disappeared as though into their own spiritual essence; and the only firm and definite things in the small, dim world within which we found ourselves confined were the two tall black cypresses growing on a little projecting terrace a hundred feet down the hill. Black, sharp, and solid, they stood there, twin pillars of Hercules at the extremity of the known universe; and beyond them there was only pale cloud and round them only the cloudy olive trees.

These were the wintry days; but there were days of spring and autumn, days unchangingly cloudless, or—more lovely still—made various by the huge floating shapes of vapor that, snowy above the far-away snow-capped mountains, gradually unfolded, against the pale bright blue, enormous heroic gestures. And in the height of the sky the bellying draperies, the swans, the aerial marbles, hewed and left unfinished by gods grown tired of creation almost before they had begun, drifted sleeping along the wind, changing form as they moved. And the sun would come and go behind them; and now the town in the valley would fade and almost vanish in the shadow, and now, like an immense fretted jewel between the hills, it would glow as though by its own light. And looking across the nearer tributary valley that wound from below our crest down towards the Arno, looking over the low dark shoulder of hill on whose extreme promontory stood the towered church of San Miniato, one saw the huge dome airily

---

From *Young Archimedes and Other Stories* by Aldous Huxley. Copyright, 1924, by Aldous Huxley. Reprinted by permission of the publishers, Harper and Brothers, Chatto and Windus, and the Oxford University Press, Canadian branch. 35. **Apennines**, a mountain chain north of Florence, in central Italy. 47. **pillars of Hercules**, two promontories on the Strait of Gibraltar, fabled to have been set there by the mythological hero Hercules; they were supposed to mark the end of the known world. 71. **Arno**, a river in Tuscany which flows through the city of Florence. 74. **San Miniato**, a famous old church on a high elevation overlooking Florence; the elevation is known as the Piazzale Michelangelo. **huge dome**, of the massive Duomo, or Cathedral of Santa Maria del Fiore (St. Mary of the Flower). The dome is 350 feet high.

hanging on its ribs of masonry, the square campanile, the sharp spire of Santa Croce, and the canopied tower of the Signoria, rising above the intricate maze of houses, distinct and brilliant, like small treasures carved out of precious stones. For a moment only, and then their light would fade away once more, and the travelling beam would pick out, among the indigo hills beyond, a single golden crest.

There were days when the air was wet with passed or with approaching rain, and all the distances seemed miraculously near and clear. The olive trees detached themselves one from another on the distant slopes; the far-away villages were lovely and pathetic like the most exquisite small toys. There were days in summer-time, days of impending thunder when, bright and sunlit against huge bellying masses of black and purple, the hills and the white houses shone as it were precariously, in a dying splendor, on the brink of some fearful calamity.

How the hills changed and varied! Every day and every hour of the day, almost, they were different. There would be moments when, looking across the plain of Florence, one would see only a dark blue silhouette against the sky. The scene had no depth; there was only a hanging curtain painted flatly with the symbols of mountains. And then, suddenly almost, with the passing of a cloud, or when the sun had declined to a certain level in the sky, the flat scene transformed itself; and where there had been only a painted curtain, now there were ranges behind ranges of hills, graduated tone after tone from brown, or gray, or a green gold to faraway blue. Shapes that a moment before had been fused together indiscriminately into a single mass, now came apart into their constituents. Fiesole, which had seemed only a spur of Monte Morello, now revealed itself as the jutting headland of another system of hills, divided from the nearest bastions of its greater neighbor by a steep and shadowy valley.

At noon, during the heats of summer, the landscape became dim, powdery, vague, and almost colorless under the midday sun; the hills disappeared into the trembling fringes of the sky. But as the afternoon wore on the landscape emerged again, it dropped its anonymity, it climbed back out of nothingness into form and life. And its life, as the sun sank and slowly sank through the long afternoon, grew richer, grew more intense with every moment. The level light, with its attendant long, dark shadows, laid bare, so to speak, the anatomy of the land; the hills— each western escarpment shining, and each slope averted from the sunlight profoundly shadowed—became massive, jutty, and solid. Little folds and dimples in the seemingly even ground revealed themselves. Eastward from our hilltop, across the plain of the Ema, a great bluff cast its ever-increasing shadow; in the surrounding brightness of the valley a whole town lay eclipsed within it. And as the sun expired on the horizon, the further hills flushed in its warm light, till their illumined flanks were the color of tawny roses; but the valleys were already filled with the blue mist of evening. And it mounted, mounted; the fire went out of the western windows of the populous slopes; only the crests were still alight, and at last they too were all extinct. The mountains faded and fused together again into a flat painting of mountains against the pale evening sky. In a little while it was night; and if the moon were full, a ghost of the dead scene still haunted the horizons.

Changeful in its beauty, this wide landscape always preserved a quality of humanness and domestication which made it, to my mind at any rate, the best of all landscapes to live with. Day by day one travelled through its different beauties; but the journey, like our ancestors' Grand Tour, was always a journey through civilization. For all its mountains, its steep

---

2. **campanile**, the magnificent bell-tower of the Cathedral; it was designed by Giotto, famous Florentine architect of the early 14th century. **Santa Croce**, the oldest and finest church of the Franciscans. Because many of the famous men of Italy are buried in this shrine, it is called the Westminster Abbey of Florence. 3. **Signoria**, the fortress-like town-hall erected in the 14th century for the use of the city directors, who were members of a committee called Signoria. The structure is known also as the Palazzo of Vecchio. 42. **Fiesole**, a town three miles northeast of Florence.

45. **bastions**, literally, outward projections from the main enclosure of a fortification; here applied to hills. 61. **escarpment**, literally the very steep ground about a fortified place, cut to prevent hostile attack; here a steep, expansive slope. 89. **Grand Tour**, an extended tour on the continent of Europe, commonly taken by aristocratic young men as a part of their cultural education.

slopes and deep valleys, the Tuscan scene is dominated by its inhabitants. They have cultivated every rood of ground that can be cultivated; their houses are thickly scattered even over the hills, and the valleys are populous. Solitary on the hilltop, one is not alone in a wilderness. Man's traces are across the country, and already—one feels it with satisfaction as one looks out across it—for centuries, for thousands of years, it has been his, submissive, tamed, and humanized. The wide, blank moorlands, the sands, the forests of innumerable trees—these are places for occasional visitation, healthful to the spirit which submits itself to them for not too long. But fiendish influences as well as divine haunt these total solitudes. The vegetative life of plants and things is alien and hostile to the human. Men cannot live at ease except where they have mastered their surroundings and where their accumulated lives outnumber and outweigh the vegetative lives about them. Stripped of its dark woods, planted, terraced, and tilled almost to the mountains' tops, the Tuscan landscape is humanized and safe. Sometimes upon those who live in the midst of it there comes a longing for some place that is solitary, inhuman, lifeless, or peopled only with alien life. But the longing is soon satisfied, and one is glad to return to the civilized and submissive scene.

I found that house on the hilltop the ideal dwelling-place. For there, safe in the midst of a humanized landscape, one was yet alone; one could be as solitary as one liked. Neighbors whom one never sees at close quarters are the ideal and perfect neighbors.

Our nearest neighbors, in terms of physical proximity, lived very near. We had two sets of them, as a matter of fact, almost in the same house with us. One was the peasant family, who lived in a long, low building, part dwelling-house, part stables, storerooms and cowsheds, adjoining the villa. Our other neighbors—intermittent neighbors, however, for they only ventured out of town every now and then, during the most flawless weather—were the owners of the villa, who had reserved for themselves the smaller wing of the huge L-shaped house—a mere dozen rooms or so—leaving the remaining eighteen or twenty to us.

They were a curious couple, our proprietors. An old husband, gray, listless, tottering, seventy at least; and a signora of about forty, short, very plump, with tiny fat hands and feet and a pair of very large, very dark black eyes, which she used with all the skill of a born comedian. Her vitality, if you could have harnessed it and made it do some useful work, would have supplied a whole town with electric light. The physicists talk of deriving energy from the atom; they would be more profitably employed nearer home—in discovering some way of tapping those enormous stores of vital energy which accumulate in unemployed women of sanguine temperament and which, in the present imperfect state of social and scientific organization, vent themselves in ways that are generally so deplorable: in interfering with other people's affairs, in working up emotional scenes, in thinking about love and making it, and in bothering men till they cannot get on with their work.

Signora Bondi got rid of her superfluous energy, among other ways, by "doing in" her tenants. The old gentleman, who was a retired merchant with a reputation for the most perfect rectitude, was allowed to have no dealings with us. When we came to see the house, it was the wife who showed us round. It was she who, with a lavish display of charm, with irresistible rollings of the eyes, expatiated on the merits of the place, sang the praises of the electric pump, glorified the bathroom (considering which, she insisted, the rent was remarkably moderate), and when we suggested calling in a surveyor to look over the house, earnestly begged us, as though our well-being were her only consideration, not to waste our money unnecessarily in doing anything so superfluous. "After all," she said, "we are honest people. I wouldn't dream of letting you the house except in perfect condition. Have confidence." And she looked at me with an appealing, pained expression in her magnificent eyes, as though

77. **"doing in,"** slang for *cheating* or *taking in*.

begging me not to insult her by my coarse suspiciousness. And leaving us no time to pursue the subject of surveyors any further, she began assuring us that our little boy was the most beautiful angel she had ever seen. By the time our interview with Signora Bondi was at an end, we had definitely decided to take the house.

"Charming woman," I said, as we left the house. But I think that Elizabeth was not quite so certain of it as I.

Then the pump episode began.

On the evening of our arrival in the house we switched on the electricity. The pump made a very professional whirring noise; but no water came out of the taps in the bathroom. We looked at one another doubtfully.

"Charming woman?" Elizabeth raised her eyebrows.

We asked for interviews; but somehow the old gentleman could never see us, and the Signora was invariably out or indisposed. We left notes; they were never answered. In the end, we found that the only method of communicating with our landlords, who were living in the same house with us, was to go down into Florence and send a registered express letter to them. For this they had to sign two separate receipts and even, if we chose to pay forty centimes more, a third incriminating document, which was then returned to us. There could be no pretending, as there always was with ordinary letters or notes, that the communication had never been received. We began at last to get answers to our complaints. The Signora, who wrote all the letters, started by telling us that, naturally, the pump didn't work, as the cisterns were empty, owing to the long drought. I had to walk three miles to the post office in order to register my letter reminding her that there had been a violent thunderstorm only last Wednesday, and that the tanks were consequently more than half full. The answer came back: bath water had not been guaranteed in the contract; and if I wanted it, why hadn't I had the pump looked at before I took the house? Another walk into town to ask the Signora next door whether she remembered her adjurations to us to have confidence in her, and to inform her that the existence in a house of a bathroom was in itself an implicit guarantee of bath water. The reply to that was that the Signora couldn't continue to have communications with people who wrote so rudely to her. After that I put the matter into the hands of a lawyer. Two months later the pump was actually replaced. But we had to serve a writ on the lady before she gave in. And the costs were considerable.

One day, towards the end of the episode, I met the old gentleman in the road, taking his big maremman dog for a walk—or being taken, rather, for a walk by the dog. For where the dog pulled the old gentleman had perforce to follow. And when it stopped to smell, or scratch the ground, or leave against a gatepost its visiting-card or an offensive challenge, patiently, at his end of the leash, the old man had to wait. I passed him standing at the side of the road, a few hundred yards below our house. The dog was sniffing at the roots of one of the twin cypresses which grew one on either side of the entry to a farm; I heard the beast growling indignantly to itself, as though it scented an intolerable insult. Old Signor Bondi, leashed to his dog, was waiting. The knees inside the tubular gray trousers were slightly bent. Leaning on his cane, he stood gazing mournfully and vacantly at the view. The whites of his old eyes were discolored, like ancient billiard balls. In the gray, deeply wrinkled face, his nose was dyspeptically red. His white moustache, ragged and yellowing at the fringes, drooped in a melancholy curve. In his black tie he wore a very large diamond; perhaps that was what Signora Bondi had found so attractive about him.

I took off my hat as I approached. The old man stared at me absently, and it was only when I was already almost past him that he recollected who I was.

"Wait," he called after me, "wait!" And he hastened down the road in pursuit. Taken utterly by surprise and at a disadvantage—for it was engaged in retorting to the affront imprinted on the cypress roots—the dog per-

---

30. **centimes,** copper coins worth about one tenth of a cent each.

63. **maremman,** from Maremma, a low, marshy maritime country in Italy.

mitted itself to be jerked after him. Too much astonished to be anything but obedient, it followed its master. "Wait!"

I waited.

"My dear sir," said the old gentleman, catching me by the lapel of my coat and blowing most disagreeably in my face, "I want to apologize." He looked around him, as though afraid that even here he might be overheard. "I want to apologize," he went on, "about that wretched pump business. I assure you that, if it had been only my affair, I'd have put the thing right as soon as you asked. You were quite right: a bathroom is an implicit guarantee of bath water. I saw from the first that we should have no chance if it came to court. And besides, I think one ought to treat one's tenants as handsomely as one can afford to. But my wife"—he lowered his voice—"the fact is that she likes this sort of thing, even when she knows that she's in the wrong and must lose. And besides, she hoped, I dare say, that you'd get tired of asking and have the job done yourself. I told her from the first that we ought to give in; but she wouldn't listen. You see, she enjoys it. Still, now she sees that it must be done. In the course of the next two or three days you'll be having your bath water. But I thought I'd just like to tell you how . . ." But the Maremmano, which had recovered by this time from its surprise of a moment since, suddenly bounded, growling, up the road. The old gentleman tried to hold the beast, strained at the leash, tottered unsteadily, then gave way and allowed himself to be dragged off. ". . . how sorry I am," he went on, as he receded from me, "that this little misunderstanding . . ." But it was no use. "Good-bye." He smiled politely, made a little deprecating gesture, as though he had suddenly remembered a pressing engagement, and had no time to explain what it was. "Good-bye." He took off his hat and abandoned himself completely to the dog.

A week later the water really did begin to flow, and the day after our first bath Signora Bondi, dressed in dove-gray satin and wearing all her pearls, came to call.

"Is it peace now?" she asked, with a charming frankness, as she shook hands.

We assured her that, so far as we were concerned, it certainly was.

"But why *did* you write me such dreadfully rude letters?" she said, turning on me a reproachful glance that ought to have moved the most ruthless malefactor to contrition. "And then that writ. How could you? To a lady . . ."

I mumbled something about the pump and our wanting baths.

"But how could you expect me to listen to you while you were in that mood? Why didn't you set about it differently—politely, charmingly?" She smiled at me and dropped her fluttering eyelids.

I thought it best to change the conversation. It is disagreeable, when one is in the right, to be made to appear in the wrong.

A few weeks later we had a letter—duly registered and by express messenger—in which the Signora asked us whether we proposed to renew our lease (which was only for six months), and notifying us that, if we did, the rent would be raised 25 per cent, in consideration of the improvements which had been carried out. We thought ourselves lucky, at the end of much bargaining, to get the lease renewed for a whole year with an increase in the rent of only 15 per cent.

It was chiefly for the sake of the view that we put up with these intolerable extortions. But we had found other reasons, after a few days' residence, for liking the house. Of these, the most cogent was that, in the peasant's youngest child, we had discovered what seemed the perfect playfellow for our own small boy. Between little Guido—for that was his name—and the youngest of his brothers and sisters there was a gap of six or seven years. His two elder brothers worked with their father in the fields; since the time of the mother's death, two or three years before we knew them, the eldest sister had ruled the house, and the younger, who had just left school, helped her and in betweenwhiles kept an eye on Guido, who by this time, however, needed very little looking after; for he was between six and seven years old and as precocious, self-assured, and responsible as the children of the poor, left as they are to themselves almost from the time they can walk, generally are.

Though fully two and a half years older than little Robin—and at that age thirty months are crammed with a half a life-time's experience—Guido took no undue advantage of his superior intelligence and strength. I have never seen a child more patient, tolerant, and untyrannical. He never laughed at Robin for his clumsy efforts to imitate his own prodigious feats; he did not tease or bully, but helped his small companion when he was in difficulties and explained when he could not understand. In return, Robin adored him, regarded him as the model and perfect Big Boy, and slavishly imitated him in every way he could.

These attempts of Robin's to imitate his companion were often exceedingly ludicrous. For by an obscure psychological law, words and actions in themselves quite serious become comic as soon as they are copied; and the more accurately, if the imitation is a deliberate parody, the funnier—for an overloaded imitation of someone we know does not make us laugh so much as one that is almost indistinguishably like the original. The bad imitation is only ludicrous when it is a piece of sincere and earnest flattery which does not quite come off. Robin's imitations were mostly of this kind. His heroic and unsuccessful attempts to perform the feats of strength and skill, which Guido could do with ease, were exquisitely comic. And his careful, long-drawn imitations of Guido's habits and mannerisms were no less amusing. Most ludicrous of all, because most earnestly undertaken and most incongruous in the imitator, were Robin's impersonations of Guido in the pensive mood. Guido was a thoughtful child, given to brooding and sudden abstractions. One would find him sitting in a corner by himself, chin in hand, elbow on knee, plunged, to all appearances, in the profoundest meditation. And sometimes, even in the midst of his play, he would suddenly break off, to stand, his hands behind his back, frowning and staring at the ground. When this happened Robin became overawed and a little disquieted. In a puzzled silence he looked at his companion. "Guido," he would say softly, "Guido." But Guido was generally too much preoccupied to answer; and Robin, not venturing to insist, would creep near him, and throwing himself as nearly as possible into Guido's attitude—standing Napoleonically, his hands clasped behind him, or sitting in the posture of Michelangelo's Lorenzo the Magnificent—would try to meditate too. Every few seconds he would turn his bright blue eyes towards the elder child to see whether he was doing it quite right. But at the end of a minute he began to grow impatient; meditation wasn't his strong point. "Guido," he called again and, louder, "Guido!" And he would take him by the hand and try to pull him away. Sometimes Guido roused himself from his reverie and went back to the interrupted game. Sometimes he paid no attention. Melancholy, perplexed, Robin had to take himself off to play by himself. And Guido would go on sitting or standing there, quite still; and his eyes, if one looked into them, were beautiful in their grave and pensive calm.

They were large eyes, set far apart and, what was strange in a dark-haired Italian child, of a luminous pale blue-gray color. They were not always grave and calm, as in these pensive moments. When he was playing, when he talked or laughed, they lit up; and the surface of those clear, pale lakes of thought seemed, as it were, to be shaken into brilliant sun-flashing ripples. Above those eyes was a beautiful forehead, high and steep and domed in a curve that was like the subtle curve of a rose petal. The nose was straight, the chin small and rather pointed, the mouth drooped a little sadly at the corners.

I have a snapshot of the two children sitting together on the parapet of the terrace. Guido sits almost facing the camera, but looking a little to one side and downwards; his hands are crossed in his lap and his expression, his attitude are thoughtful, grave, and meditative. It is Guido in one of those moods of abstraction into which he would pass even at the height of laughter and play—quite suddenly

---

56. **Lorenzo.** Michelangelo's statue of Lorenzo de Medici (1449-1492), his great benefactor and patron, is part of a mausoleum. It shows Lorenzo seated, his right hand on his knee, his head resting on his left hand with his left elbow on the arm of the chair. 89. **parapet,** a railing for protection at the edge of a terrace.

and completely, as though he had all at once taken it into his head to go away and had left the silent and beautiful body behind, like an empty house, to wait for his return. And by his side sits little Robin, turning to look up at him, his face half averted from the camera, but the curve of his cheek showing that he is laughing; one little raised hand is caught at the top of a gesture, the other clutches at Guido's sleeve as though he were urging him to come away and play. And the legs dangling from the parapet have been seen by the blinking instrument in the midst of an impatient wriggle; he is on the point of slipping down and running off to play hide-and-seek in the garden. All the essential characteristics of both the children are in that little snapshot.

"If Robin were not Robin," Elizabeth used to say, "I could almost wish he were Guido."

And even at that time, when I took no particular interest in the child, I agreed with her. Guido seemed to me one of the most charming little boys I had ever seen.

We were not alone in admiring him. Signora Bondi when, in those cordial intervals between our quarrels, she came to call, was constantly speaking of him. "Such a beautiful, beautiful child!" she would exclaim with enthusiasm. "It's really a waste that he should belong to peasants who can't afford to dress him properly. If he were mine, I should put him into black velvet; or little white knickers and a white knitted silk jersey with a red line at the collar and cuffs! or perhaps a white sailor suit would be pretty. And in winter a little fur coat, with a squirrel skin cap, and possibly Russian boots . . ." Her imagination was running away with her. "And I'd let his hair grow, like a page's, and have it just curled up a little at the tips. And a straight fringe across his forehead. Everyone would turn round and stare after us if I took him out with me in Via Tornabuoni."

What you want, I should have liked to tell her, is not a child; it's a clock-work doll or a performing monkey. But I did not say so—partly because I could not think of the Italian for a clock-work doll and partly because I did

44. **Via Tornabuoni,** one of the principal streets of Florence.

not want to risk having the rent raised another 15 per cent.

"Ah, if only I had a little boy like that!" She sighed and modestly dropped her eyelids. "I adore children. I sometimes think of adopting one—that is, if my husband would allow it."

I thought of the poor old gentleman being dragged along at the heels of his big white dog and inwardly smiled.

"But I don't know if he would," the Signora was continuing, "I don't know if he would." She was silent for a moment, as though considering a new idea.

A few days later, when we were sitting in the garden after luncheon, drinking our coffee, Guido's father, instead of passing with a nod and the usual cheerful good-day, halted in front of us and began to talk. He was a fine handsome man, not very tall, but well-proportioned, quick and elastic in his movements, and full of life. He had a thin brown face, featured like a Roman's and lit by a pair of the most intelligent-looking gray eyes I ever saw. They exhibited almost too much intelligence when, as not infrequently happened, he was trying, with an assumption of perfect frankness and a childlike innocence, to take one in or get something out of one. Delighting in itself, the intelligence shone there mischievously. The face might be ingenuous, impassive, almost imbecile in its expression; but the eyes on these occasions gave him completely away. One knew, when they glittered like that, that one would have to be careful.

Today, however, there was no dangerous light in them. He wanted nothing out of us, nothing of any value—only advice, which is a commodity, he knew, that most people are only too happy to part with. But he wanted advice on what was, for us, rather a delicate subject: on Signora Bondi. Carlo had often complained to us about her. The old man is good, he told us, very good and kind indeed. Which meant, I dare say, among other things, that he could easily be swindled. But his wife . . . Well, the woman was a beast. And he would tell us stories of her insatiable rapacity: she was always claiming more than the half of the produce which, by the laws of the metayage system, was the proprietor's due. He complained of her suspiciousness: she was forever accusing him of sharp practices, of downright stealing—him, he struck his breast, the soul of honesty. He complained of her short-sighted avarice: she wouldn't spend enough on manure, wouldn't buy him another cow, wouldn't have electric light installed in the stables. And we had sympathized, but cautiously, without expressing too strong an opinion on the subject. The Italians are wonderfully non-committal in their speech; they will give nothing away to an interested person until they are quite certain that it is right and necessary and, above all, safe to do so. We had lived long enough among them to imitate their caution. What we said to Carlo would be sure, sooner or later, to get back to Signora Bondi. There was nothing to be gained by unnecessarily embittering our relations with the lady—only another 15 per cent, very likely, to be lost.

Today he wasn't so much complaining as feeling perplexed. The Signora had sent for him, it seemed, and asked him how he would like it if she were to make an offer—it was all very hypothetical in the cautious Italian style—to adopt little Guido. Carlo's first instinct had been to say that he wouldn't like it at all. But an answer like that would have been too coarsely committal. He had preferred to say that he would think about it. And now he was asking for our advice.

Do what you think best, was what in effect we replied. But we gave it distantly but distinctly to be understood that we didn't think that Signora Bondi would make a very good foster-mother for the child. And Carlo was inclined to agree. Besides, he was very fond of the boy.

"But the thing is," he concluded rather gloomily, "that if she has really set her heart on getting hold of the child, there's nothing she won't do to get him—nothing."

He too, I could see, would have liked the physicists to start on unemployed childless women of sanguine temperament before they tried to tackle the atom. Still, I reflected, as I watched him striding away along the terrace, singing powerfully from a brazen gullet as he went, there was force there, there was life enough in those elastic limbs, behind those bright gray eyes, to put up a good fight even against the accumulated vital energies of Signora Bondi.

It was a few days after this that my gramophone and two or three boxes of records arrived from England. They were a great comfort to us on the hilltop, providing as they did the only thing in which that spiritually fertile solitude — otherwise a perfect Swiss Family Robinson's island—was lacking: music. There is not much music to be heard nowadays in Florence. The times when Dr. Burney could tour through Italy, listening to an unending succession of new operas, symphonies, quartets, cantatas, are gone. Gone are the days when a learned musician, inferior only to the Reverend Father Martini of Bologna, could admire what the peasants sang and the strolling players thrummed and scraped on their instruments. I have travelled for weeks through the peninsula and hardly heard a note that was not "Salome" or the Fascists' song. Rich in nothing else that makes life agreeable or even supportable, the northern metropolises are rich in music. That is perhaps the only inducement that a reasonable man can find for living there. The other attractions — organized gaiety, people, miscellaneous conversation, the social pleasures — what are those, after all, but an expense of spirit that buys nothing in return? And then the cold, the darkness, the moldering dirt, the damp and squalor. . . . No, where there is no necessity that retains, music can be the only inducement. And that, thanks to the ingenious Edison, can now be taken about in a box and unpacked in whatever solitude one chooses to visit. One can live at Benin, or Nuneaton, or Tozeur in the Sahara, and still

---

2. **metayage**, a system of farming on shares. 46-47. **He . . . physicists.** See p. 1100, ll. 62 ff. 62. **Swiss . . . Robinson**, a romance of a family wrecked on a desert island, written by the Swiss author Johann Wyss (1781-1830). 65. **Dr. Burney**, Charles Burney (1726-1814), English music critic and historian. He toured the Continent in 1770 and in 1772 to gather material for his four-volume *History*. 70. **Martini**, Giambattista Martini (1706-1784), famous Italian musical composer, theorist, and teacher. He lived in Bologna, a prominent city in Northern Italy. 75. **"Salome,"** an opera by Richard Strauss (1864-1949), German composer and conductor, the opera is notable for the ecstatic love song by Salome, daughter of Herodias. See *Matthew*, 14:8. 91. **Benin**, a large town in Western Africa. 92. **Nuneaton**, a town in Warwickshire, England. 92. **Tozeur**, a town in Tunis, in northern Africa.

hear Mozart quartets, and selections from the Well-Tempered Clavichord, and the Fifth Symphony, and the Brahms clarinet quintet, and motets by Palestrina.

Carlo, who had gone down to the station with his mule and cart to fetch the packing-case, was vastly interested in the machine.

"One will hear some music again," he said, as he watched me unpacking the gramophone and the disks. "It is difficult to do much oneself."

Still, I reflected, he managed to do a good deal. On warm nights we used to hear him, where he sat at the door of his house, playing his guitar and softly singing; the eldest boy shrilled out the melody on the mandolin, and sometimes the whole family would join in, and the darkness would be filled with their passionate, throaty singing. Piedigrotta songs they mostly sang; and the voices drooped slurringly from note to note, lazily climbed or jerked themselves with sudden sobbing emphases from one tone to another. At a distance and under the stars the effect was not unpleasing.

"Before the war," he went on, "in normal times" (and Carlo had a hope, even a belief, that the normal times were coming back and that life would soon be as cheap and easy as it had been in the days before the flood), "I used to go and listen to the operas at the Politeama. Ah, they were magnificent. But it costs five lire now to get in."

"Too much," I agreed.

"Have you got *Trovatore*?" he asked.

I shook my head.

"*Rigoletto*?"

"I'm afraid not."

"*Bohème? Fanciulla del West? Pagliacci?*"

I had to go on disappointing him.

"Not even *Norma*? Or the *Barbiere*?"

I put on Battistini in "La ci darem" out of *Don Giovanni*. He agreed that the singing was good; but I could see that he didn't much like the music. Why not? He found it difficult to explain.

"It's not like *Pagliacci*," he said at last.

"Not palpitating?" I suggested, using a word with which I was sure he would be familiar; for it occurs in every Italian political speech and patriotic leading article.

"Not palpitating," he agreed.

And I reflected that it is precisely by the difference between *Pagliacci* and *Don Giovanni*, between the palpitating and the non-palpitating, that modern musical taste is separated from the old. The corruption of the best, I thought, is the worst. Beethoven taught music to palpitate with his intellectual and spiritual passion. It has gone on palpitating ever since, but with the passion of inferior men. Indirectly, I thought, Beethoven is responsible for *Parsifal*, *Pagliacci*, and the *Poem of Fire;* still more indirectly for *Samson and Delilah* and "Ivy, cling to me." Mozart's melodies may be brilliant, memorable, infectious; but they don't palpitate, don't catch you between wind and water, don't send the listener off into erotic ecstasies.

Carlo and his elder children found my gramophone, I am afraid, rather a disappointment. They were too polite, however, to say so openly; they merely ceased, after the first day or two, to take any interest in the machine and the music it played. They preferred the guitar and their own singing.

Guido, on the other hand, was immensely interested. And he liked, not the cheerful dance tunes, to whose sharp rhythms our little Robin loved to go stamping round and round the room, pretending that he was a whole reg-

1. **Mozart quartets**, a group of musical compositions for four stringed instruments by Wolfgang Mozart (1756-1791). 2. **Well-Tempered Clavichord**, a set of twenty-four pieces of music for the clavichord (the immediate ancestor of the piano) in all major and minor keys, by Johann Sebastian Bach (1665-1750). 2. **Fifth Symphony**, the best known of the nine symphonies composed by Ludwig van Beethoven (1770-1827). 3. **Brahms . . . quintet**, one of the last compositions of Johannes Brahms (1833-1897). 4. **motets by Palestrina**, ecclesiastical choral compositions by Giovanni da Palestrina (1525-1594), early Italian composer of church music. 19. **Piedigrotta songs**, popular songs of Naples. 33. **lire**, plural of *lira*, a silver Italian coin worth about twenty cents. 35. *Trovatore, Il Trovatore*, a famous Italian opera written by Giuseppe Verdi (1813-1901). 37. **Rigoletto**, an opera by Verdi. 39. **Bohème**, *La Bohème*, an opera by Giacomo Puccini (1858-1924). 39. **Fanciulla del West**, *The Girl of the Golden West*, an opera by Puccini, based upon a play of the same title by David Belasco (1859-1931), American dramatic manager and author. **Pagliacci**, an operatic setting of a simple Italian tale of everyday life, by Ruggiero Leoncavallo (1858-1919).

41. **Norma**, a popular Italian opera by Vincenzo Bellini (1801-1835). 41. **Barbiere**, *The Barber of Seville*, operatic masterpiece of Gioachino Rossini (1792-1868). 42. **Battistini**, Mattia Battistini (1857-1928), Italian dramatic baritone. 42. "**La ci darem.**" The full title is "La ci darem la mano," "Thy Little Hand, Love," a duet from *Don Giovanni*, perhaps the greatest of the operas by Mozart. 63. **Parsifal**, an opera by Richard Wagner (1813-1883), German originator of the music drama. 63. **Poem of Fire**, the same as *Prometheus*, an instrumental tone poem by the Russian pianist and composer, Alexander Scriabin (1872-1915). 64. **Samson and Delilah**, an opera by Charles Camille Saint-Saëns (1835-1921). 65. "**Ivy, cling to me,**" probably a popular London song. 67-68. **catch . . . water**, make you catch your breath. This is a nautical phrase used to indicate the point of danger, about at the water line of a ship.

iment of soldiers, but the genuine stuff. The first record he heard, I remember, was that of the slow movement of Bach's Concerto in D Minor for two violins. That was the disk I put on the turntable as soon as Carlo had left me. It seemed to me, so to speak, the most musical piece of music with which I could refresh my long-parched mind — the coolest and clearest of all draughts. The movement had just got under way and was beginning to unfold its pure and melancholy beauties in accordance with the laws of the most exacting intellectual logic, when the two children, Guido in front and little Robin breathlessly following, came clattering into the room from the loggia.

Guido came to a halt in front of the gramophone and stood there, motionless, listening. His pale blue-gray eyes opened themselves wide; making a little nervous gesture that I had often noticed in him before, he plucked at his lower lip with his thumb and forefinger. He must have taken a deep breath; for I noticed that, after listening for a few seconds, he sharply expired and drew in a fresh gulp of air. For an instant he looked at me—a questioning, astonished, rapturous look—gave a little laugh that ended in a kind of nervous shudder, and turned back towards the source of the incredible sounds. Slavishly imitating his elder comrade, Robin had also taken up his stand in front of the gramophone, and in exactly the same position, glancing at Guido from time to time to make sure that he was doing everything, down to plucking at his lip, in the correct way. But after a minute or so he became bored.

"Soldiers," he said, turning to me; "I want soldiers. Like in London." He remembered the rag-time and the jolly marches round and round the room.

I put my fingers to my lips. "Afterwards," I whispered.

Robin managed to remain silent and still for perhaps another twenty seconds. Then he seized Guido by the arm, shouting, "Vieni, Guido! Soldiers. Soldati. Vieni giuocare soldati."

It was then, for the first time, that I saw Guido impatient. "Vai!" he whispered angrily, slapped at Robin's clutching hand and pushed him roughly away. And he leaned a little closer to the instrument, as though to make up by yet intenser listening for what the interruption had caused him to miss.

Robin looked at him, astonished. Such a thing had never happened before. Then he burst out crying and came to me for consolation.

When the quarrel was made up—and Guido was sincerely repentant, was as nice as he knew how to be when the music had stopped and his mind was free to think of Robin once more—I asked him how he liked the music. He said he thought it was beautiful. But *bello* in Italian is too vague a word, too easily and frequently uttered, to mean very much.

"What did you like best?" I insisted. For he had seemed to enjoy it so much that I was curious to find out what had really impressed him.

He was silent for a moment, pensively frowning. "Well," he said at last, "I liked the bit that went like this." And he hummed a long phrase. "And then there's the other thing singing at the same time—but what are those things," he interrupted himself, "that sing like that?"

"They're called violins," I said.

"Violins." He nodded. "Well, the other violin goes like this." He hummed again. "Why can't one sing both at once? And what is in that box? What makes it make that noise?" The child poured out his questions.

I answered him as best I could, showing him the little spirals on the disk, the needle, the diaphragm. I told him to remember how the string of the guitar trembled when one plucked it; sound is a shaking in the air, I told him, and I tried to explain how those shakings get printed on the black disk. Guido listened to me very gravely, nodding from time to time. I had the impression that he understood perfectly well everything I was saying.

---

3. Bach's . . . Minor, said by Phillip Spitta (1841-1894), Bach's greatest biographer, to be the best of all Bach compositions. 47. "Vieni . . . soldati," come play soldiers.

50. "Vai!" "Go!" 66. *bello,* fine, beautiful; used freely in various expressions.

By this time, however, poor Robin was so dreadfully bored that in pity for him I had to send the two children out into the garden to play. Guido went obediently; but I could see that he would have preferred to stay indoors and listen to more music. A little while later, when I looked out, he was hiding in the dark recesses of the big bay tree, roaring like a lion, and Robin, laughing, but a little nervously, as though he were afraid that the horrible noise might possibly turn out, after all, to be the roaring of a real lion, was beating the bush with a stick, and shouting, "Come out, come out! I want to shoot you."

After lunch, when Robin had gone upstairs for his afternoon sleep, he reappeared. "May I listen to the music now?" he asked. And for an hour he sat there in front of the instrument, his head cocked slightly on one side, listening while I put on one disk after another.

Thenceforward he came every afternoon. Very soon he knew all my library of records, had his preferences and dislikes, and could ask for what he wanted by humming the principal theme.

"I don't like that one," he said of Strauss's "Till Eulenspiegel." "It's like what we sing in our house. Not really like, you know. But somehow rather like, all the same. You understand?" He looked at us perplexedly and appealingly, as though begging us to understand what he meant and so save him from going on explaining. We nodded. Guido went on. "And then," he said, "the end doesn't seem to come properly out of the beginning. It's not like the one you played the first time." He hummed a bar or two from the slow movement of Bach's D Minor Concerto.

"It isn't," I suggested, "like saying: All little boys like playing. Guido is a little boy. Therefore Guido likes playing."

He frowned. "Yes, perhaps that's it," he said at last. "The one you played first is more like that. But, you know," he added, with an excessive regard for truth, "I don't like playing as much as Robin does."

Wagner was among his dislikes; so was Debussy. When I played the record of one of Debussy's Arabesques, he said, "Why does he say the same thing over and over again? He ought to say something new, or go on, or make the thing grow. Can't he think of anything different?" But he was less censorious about the "Après-Midi d'un Faune." "The things have beautiful voices," he said.

Mozart overwhelmed him with delight. The duet from *Don Giovanni*, which his father had found insufficiently palpitating, enchanted Guido. But he preferred the quartets and the orchestral pieces.

"I like music," he said, "better than singing."

Most people, I reflected, like singing better than music; are more interested in the executant than in what he executes, and find the impersonal orchestra less moving than the soloist. The touch of the pianist is the human touch, and the soprano's high C is the personal note. It is for the sake of this touch, that note, that audiences fill the concert halls.

Guido, however, preferred music. True, he liked "La ci darem"; he liked "Deh vieni alla finestra"; he thought "Che soave zefiretto" so lovely that almost all our concerts had to begin with it. But he preferred the other things. The *Figaro* overture was one of his favorites. There is a passage not far from the beginning of the piece, where the first violins suddenly go rocketing up into the heights of loveliness; as the music approached that point, I used always to see a smile developing and gradually brightening on Guido's face, and when, punctually, the thing happened, he clapped his hands and laughed aloud with pleasure.

On the other side of the same disk, it happened, was recorded Beethoven's *Egmont* overture. He liked that almost better than *Figaro*.

---

28. **"Till Eulenspiegel,"** "Till Owlglass," a symphonic poem by Richard Strauss (1864-1949), based on the life and adventures of a famous rogue in medieval German folklore. Till, the hero, is finally sentenced and hanged as an adventurous prankster.
50. **Debussy,** Claude Debussy (1862-1918), French composer. His *Arabesques* belong to the Impressionistic School.
56. **"Après-Midi d'un Faune,"** "The Afternoon of a Faun," a well-known musical prelude by Debussy, based upon a poem of the same title by Stéphane Mallarmé (1842-1898), French symbolistic poet. 74. **"Deh . . . finestra,"** "Open Thy Window," a charming serenade from the opera *Don Giovanni*, by Mozart. 75. **"Che . . . zefiretto,"** "What a soft little Breeze," from *The Marriage of Figaro*, an opera by Mozart. 83. **Egmont overture,** from the incidental music which Beethoven wrote for Goethe's famous tragedy *Egmont*.

"It has more voices," he explained. And I was delighted by the acuteness of the criticism; for it is precisely in the richness of its orchestration that *Egmont* goes beyond *Figaro*.

But what stirred him almost more than anything was the *Coriolan* overture. The third movement of the Fifth Symphony, the second movement of the Seventh, the slow movement of the Emperor Concerto—all these things ran it pretty close. But none excited him so much as *Coriolan*. One day he made me play it three or four times in succession; then he put it away.

"I don't think I want to hear that any more," he said.

"Why not?"

"It's too . . . too . . ." he hesitated, "too big," he said at last. "I don't really understand it. Play me the one that goes like this." He hummed the phrase from the D Minor Concerto.

"Do you like that one better?" I asked.

He shook his head. "No, it's not that exactly. But it's easier."

"Easier?" It seemed to me rather a queer word to apply to Bach.

"I understand it better."

One afternoon, while we were in the middle of our concert, Signora Bondi was ushered in. She began at once to be overwhelmingly affectionate towards the child; kissed him, patted his head, paid him the most outrageous compliments on his appearance. Guido edged away from her.

"And do you like music?" she asked.

The child nodded.

"I think he has a gift," I said. "At any rate, he has a wonderful ear and a power of listening and criticizing such as I've never met with in a child of that age. We're thinking of hiring a piano for him to learn on."

A moment later I was cursing myself for my undue frankness in praising the boy. For Signora Bondi began immediately to protest that, if she could have the upbringing of the child, she would give him the best masters, bring out his talent, make an accomplished maestro of him—and, on the way, an infant prodigy. And at that moment, I am sure, she saw herself sitting maternally, in pearls and black satin, in the lee of the huge Steinway, while an angelic Guido, dressed like little Lord Fauntleroy, rattled out Liszt and Chopin, to the loud delight of a thronged auditorium. She saw the bouquets and all the elaborate floral tributes, heard the clapping and the few well-chosen words with which the veteran maestri, touched almost to tears, would hail the coming of the little genius. It became more than ever important for her to acquire the child.

"You've sent her away fairly ravening," said Elizabeth, when Signora Bondi had gone. "Better tell her next time that you made a mistake, and that the boy's got no musical talent whatever."

In due course, the piano arrived. After giving him the minimum of preliminary instruction, I let Guido loose on it. He began by picking out for himself the melodies he had heard, reconstructing the harmonies in which they were embedded. After a few lessons, he understood the rudiments of musical notation and could read a simple passage at sight, albeit very slowly. The whole process of reading was still strange to him; he had picked up his letters somehow, but nobody had yet taught him to read whole words and sentences.

I took occasion, next time I saw Signora Bondi, to assure her that Guido had disappointed me. There was nothing in his musical talent, really. She professed to be very sorry to hear it; but I could see that she didn't for a moment believe me. Probably she thought that we were after the child too, and wanted to bag the infant prodigy for ourselves, before she could get in her claim, thus depriving her of what she regarded almost

---

7. **Coriolan overture,** the Coriolanus Overture by Beethoven based upon a tragedy by Heinrich Joseph von Collin (1771-1811), Austrian poet and playwright. 9. **the Seventh,** by Beethoven, said to have been his favorite symphony. 10. **Emperor Concerto,** the last of Beethoven's five concertos for piano and orchestra. 52. **Steinway,** a famous make of piano, by Steinway and Sons, New York and Hamburg. 54. **Lord Fauntleroy,** title and child hero of a popular story by Frances Hodgson Burnett (1849-1924). His conventional dress consisted of velvet trousers and Eton waist with large collar and black tie. **Liszt,** Franz Liszt (1811-1886), Hungarian pianist and composer. **Chopin,** Frederic Chopin (1809-1849), French-Polish pianist and composer.

as her feudal right. For, after all, weren't they her peasants? If anyone was to profit by adopting the child it ought to be herself.

Tactfully, diplomatically, she renewed her negotiations with Carlo. The boy, she put it to him, had genius. It was the foreign gentleman who had told her so, and he was the sort of man, clearly, who knew about such things. If Carlo would let her adopt the child, she'd have him trained. He'd become a great maestro and get engagements in the Argentine and the United States, in Paris and London. He'd earn millions and millions. Think of Caruso, for example. Part of the millions, she explained, would of course come to Carlo. But before they began to roll in, those millions, the boy would have to be trained. But training was very expensive. In his own interest, as well as in that of his son, he ought to let her take charge of the child. Carlo said he would think it over, and again applied to us for advice. We suggested that it would be best in any case to wait a little and see what progress the boy made.

He made, in spite of my assertions to Signora Bondi, excellent progress. Every afternoon, while Robin was asleep, he came for his concert and his lesson. He was getting along famously with his reading; his small fingers were acquiring strength and agility. But what to me was more interesting was that he had begun to make up little pieces on his own account. A few of them I took down as he played them and I have them still. Most of them, strangely enough, as I thought then, are canons. He had a passion for canons. When I explained to him the principles of the form he was enchanted.

"It is beautiful," he said, with admiration. "Beautiful, beautiful. And so easy!"

Again the word surprised me. The canon is not, after all, so conspicuously simple. Thenceforward he spent most of his time at the piano in working out little canons for his own amusement. They were often remarkably ingenious. But in the invention of other kinds of music he did not show himself so fertile as I had hoped. He composed and harmonized one or two solemn little airs like hymn tunes, with a few sprightlier pieces in the spirit of the military march. They were extraordinary, of course, as being the inventions of a child. But a great many children can do extraordinary things; we are all geniuses up to the age of ten. But I had hoped that Guido was a child who was going to be a genius at forty; in which case what was extraordinary for an ordinary child was not extraordinary enough for him. "He's hardly a Mozart," we agreed, as we played his little pieces over. I felt, it must be confessed, almost aggrieved. Anything less than a Mozart, it seemed to me, was hardly worth thinking about.

He was not a Mozart. No. But he was somebody, as I was to find out, quite as extraordinary. It was one morning in the early summer that I made the discovery. I was sitting in the warm shade of our westward-facing balcony, working. Guido and Robin were playing in the little enclosed garden below. Absorbed in my work, it was only, I suppose, after the silence had prolonged itself a considerable time that I became aware that the children were making remarkably little noise. There was no shouting, no running about; only a quiet talking. Knowing by experience that when children are quiet it generally means that they are absorbed in some delicious mischief, I got up from my chair and looked over the balustrade to see what they were doing. I expected to catch them dabbing in water, making a bonfire, covering themselves with tar. But what I actually saw was Guido, with a burnt stick in his hand, demonstrating on the smooth paving-stones of the path, that the square on the hypotenuse of a right-angled triangle is equal to the sum of the squares on the other two sides.

Kneeling on the floor, he was drawing with the point of his blackened stick on the flagstones. And Robin, kneeling imitatively beside him, was growing, I could see, rather impatient with this very slow game.

"Guido," he said. But Guido paid no attention. Pensively frowning, he went on with

---

14. **Caruso,** Enrico Caruso (1873-1921), famous Italian operatic tenor. 36. **canon,** a composition in two or more voice parts; it uses the principle of imitation, somewhat like a round.

his diagram. "Guido!" The younger child bent down and then craned round his neck so as to look up into Guido's face. "Why don't you draw a train?"

"Afterwards," said Guido. "But I just want to show you this first. It's *so* beautiful," he added cajolingly.

"But I want a train," Robin persisted.

"In a moment. Do just wait a moment." The tone was almost imploring. Robin armed himself with renewed patience. A minute later Guido had finished both his diagrams.

"There!" he said triumphantly, and straightened himself up to look at them. "Now I'll explain."

And he proceeded to prove the theorem of Pythagoras—not in Euclid's way, but by the simpler and more satisfying method which was, in all probability, employed by Pythagoras himself. He had drawn a square and dissected it, by a pair of crossed perpendiculars, into two squares and two equal rectangles. The equal rectangles he divided up by their diagonals into four equal right-angled triangles. The two squares are then seen to be the squares on the two sides of any one of these triangles other than the hypotenuse. So much for the first diagram. In the next he took the four right-angled triangles into which the rectangles had been divided and rearranged them round the original square so that their right angles filled the corners of the square, the hypotenuses looked inwards and the greater and less sides of the triangles were in continuation along the sides of the square (which are each equal to the sum of these sides). In this way the original square is redissected into four right-angled triangles and the square on the hypotenuse. The four triangles are equal to the two rectangles of the original dissection. Therefore the square on the hypotenuse is equal to the sum of the two squares—the squares on the other two sides—into which, with the rectangles, the original square was first dissected.

In very untechnical language, but clearly and with a relentless logic, Guido expounded his proof. Robin listened, with an expression on his bright, freckled face of perfect incomprehension.

"Treno," he repeated from time to time. "Treno. Make a train."

"In a moment," Guido implored. "Wait a moment. But do just look at this. *Do*." He coaxed and cajoled. "It's so beautiful. It's so easy."

So easy. . . . The theorem of Pythagoras seemed to explain for me Guido's musical predilections. It was not an infant Mozart we had been cherishing; it was a little Archimedes with, like most of his kind, an incidental musical twist.

"Treno, treno!" shouted Robin, growing more and more restless as the exposition went on. And when Guido insisted on going on with his proof, he lost his temper. "Cattivo Guido," he shouted, and began to hit out at him with his fists.

"All right," said Guido resignedly. "I'll make a train." And with his stick of charcoal he began to scribble on the stones.

I looked on for a moment in silence. It was not a very good train. Guido might be able to invent for himself and prove the theorem of Pythagoras; but he was not much of a draughtsman.

"Guido!" I called. The two children turned up. "Who taught you to draw those squares?" It was conceivable, of course, that somebody might have taught him.

"Nobody." He shook his head. Then, rather anxiously, as though he were afraid there might be something wrong about drawing squares, he went on to apologize and explain. "You see," he said, "it seemed to me so beautiful. Because those squares"—he pointed at the two small squares in the first figure—"are just as big as this one." And, indicating the square on the hypotenuse in the second diagram, he looked up at me with a deprecating smile.

I nodded. "Yes, it's very beautiful," I said—"it's very beautiful indeed."

An expression of delighted relief appeared on his face; he laughed with pleasure. "You see, it's like this," he went on, eager to initiate

---

17. **Pythagoras**, a Greek philosopher and mathematician of the sixth century before Christ. **Euclid**, a Greek geometrician of the third century before Christ.

66. "**Cattivo Guido**," naughty Guido.

me into the glorious secret he had discovered. "You cut these two long squares"—he meant the rectangles—"into two slices. And then there are four slices, all just the same, because, because—oh, I ought to have said that before—because these long squares are the same, because those lines, you see . . ."

"But I want a train," protested Robin.

Leaning on the rail of the balcony, I watched the children below. I thought of the extraordinary thing I had just seen and of what it meant.

I thought of the vast differences between human beings. We classify men by the color of their eyes and hair, the shape of their skulls. Would it not be more sensible to divide them up into intellectual species? There would be even wider gulfs between the extreme mental types than between a Bushman and a Scandinavian. This child, I thought, when he grows up, will be to me, intellectually, what a man is to a dog. And there are other men and women who are, perhaps, almost as dogs to me.

Perhaps the men of genius are the only true men. In all the history of the race there have been only a few thousand real men. And the rest of us—what are we? Teachable animals. Without the help of the real men, we should have found out almost nothing at all. Almost all the ideas with which we are familiar could never have occurred to minds like ours. Plant the seeds there and they will grow; but our minds could never spontaneously have generated them.

There have been whole nations of dogs, I thought; whole epochs in which no Man was born. From the dull Egyptians the Greeks took crude experience and rules of thumb and made sciences. More than a thousand years passed before Archimedes had a comparable successor. There has been only one Buddha, one Jesus, only one Bach that we know of, one Michelangelo.

Is it by a mere chance, I wondered, that a Man is born from time to time? What causes a whole constellation of them to come contemporaneously into being and from out of a single people? Taine thought that Leonardo, Michelangelo, and Raphael were born when they were because the time was ripe for great painters and the Italian scene congenial. In the mouth of a rationalizing nineteenth-century Frenchman the doctrine is strangely mystical; it may be none the less true for that. But what of those born out of time? Blake, for example. What of those?

This child, I thought, has had the fortune to be born at a time when he will be able to make good use of his capacities. He will find the most elaborate analytical methods lying ready to his hand; he will have a prodigious experience behind him. Suppose him born while Stonehenge was building; he might have spent a lifetime discovering the rudiments, guessing darkly where now he might have had a chance of proving. Born at the time of the Norman Conquest, he would have had to wrestle with all the preliminary difficulties created by an inadequate symbolism; it would have taken him long years, for example, to learn the art of dividing MMMCCCCLXXXVIII by MCMXIX. In five years, nowadays, he will learn what it took generations of Men to discover.

And I thought of the fate of all the Men born so hopelessly out of time that they could achieve little or nothing of value. Beethoven born in Greece, I thought, would have had to be content to play thin melodies on the flute or lyre; in those intellectual surroundings it would hardly have been possible for him to imagine the nature of harmony.

From drawing trains, the children in the garden below had gone on to playing trains. They were trotting round and round; with blown round cheeks and pouting mouth, like the cherubic symbol of a wind, Robin puff-puffed, and Guido, holding the skirt of his smock, shuffled behind him, tooting. They ran forward, backed, stopped at imaginary stations, shunted, roared over bridges, crashed

---

19. **Bushman,** one of an aboriginal race of nomadic hunters of South Africa, of low cranial capacity. The Scandinavian ranks among the most literate races of the world. 42. **Buddha,** Indian philosopher of the fifth century before Christ. He was the founder of Buddhism.

49. **Taine,** Hippolyte Adolphe Taine (1828-1893), French historian and critic of literature who based his approach to literature on the overwhelming importance of race and environment. 56. **Blake,** William Blake (1757-1827), English poet and artist, whose creative work was far ahead of his generation. See p. 111.

through tunnels, met with occasional collisions and derailments. The young Archimedes seemed to be just as happy as the little tow-headed barbarian. A few minutes ago he had been busy with the theorem of Pythagoras. Now, tooting indefatigably along imaginary rails, he was perfectly content to shuffle backwards and forwards among the flower-beds, between the pillars of the loggia, in and out of the dark tunnels of the laurel tree. The fact that one is going to be Archimedes does not prevent one from being an ordinary cheerful child meanwhile. I thought of this strange talent distinct and separate from the rest of the mind, independent, almost, of experience. The typical child-prodigies are musical and mathematical; the other talents ripen slowly under the influence of emotional experience and growth. Till he was thirty Balzac gave proof of nothing but ineptitude; but at four the young Mozart was already a musician, and some of Pascal's most brilliant work was done before he was out of his teens.

In the weeks that followed, I alternated the daily piano lessons with lessons in mathematics. Hints rather than lessons they were; for I only made suggestions, indicated methods, and left the child himself to work out the ideas in detail. Thus I introduced him to algebra by showing him another proof of the theorem of Pythagoras. In this proof one drops a perpendicular from the right angle on to the hypotenuse, and arguing from the fact that the two triangles thus created are similar to one another and to the original triangle, and that the proportions which their corresponding sides bear to one another are therefore equal, one can show in algebraical form that c^2+d^2 (the squares on the other two sides) are equal to a^2+b^2 (the squares on the two segments of the hypotenuse) $+2ab$; which last, it is easy to show geometrically, is equal to $(a+b)^2$, or the square on the hypotenuse. Guido was as much enchanted by the rudiments of algebra as he would have been if I had given him an engine worked by steam, with a methylated spirit lamp to heat the boiler; more enchanted, perhaps—for the engine would have got broken, and remaining always itself, would in any case have lost its charm, while the rudiments of algebra continued to grow and blossom in his mind with an unfailing luxuriance. Every day he made the discovery of something which seemed to him exquisitely beautiful; the new toy was inexhaustible in its potentialities.

In the intervals of applying algebra to the second book of Euclid, we experimented with circles; we stuck bamboos into the parched earth, measured their shadows at different hours of the day, and drew exciting conclusions from our observations. Sometimes, for fun, we cut and folded sheets of paper so as to make cubes and pyramids. One afternoon Guido arrived carrying carefully between his small and rather grubby hands a flimsy dodecahedron.

"E tanto bello!" he said, as he showed us his paper crystal; and when I asked him how he managed to make it, he merely smiled and said it had been so easy. I looked at Elizabeth and laughed. But it would have been more symbolically to the point, I felt, if I had gone down on all fours, wagged the spiritual outgrowth of my os coccyx, and barked my astonished admiration.

It was an uncommonly hot summer. By the beginning of July our little Robin, unaccustomed to these high temperatures, began to look pale and tired; he was listless, had lost his appetite and energy. The doctor advised mountain air. We decided to spend the next ten or twelve weeks in Switzerland. My parting gift to Guido was the first six books of Euclid in Italian. He turned over the pages, looked ecstatically at the figures.

"If only I knew how to read properly," he said. "I'm so stupid. But now I shall really try to learn."

From our hotel near Grindelwald we sent the child, in Robin's name, various post cards of cows, Alp-horns, Swiss chalets, edelweiss,

---

9. **loggia,** an open gallery with a roof. 19. **Balzac,** Honoré de Balzac (1799-1850), famous French novelist. 22. **Pascal,** Blaise Pascal (1623-1662), French philosopher and mathematician. 47. **methylated . . . lamp,** a lamp that burns methyl alcohol. 66. **dodecahedron,** a box-shaped figure with twelve sides or faces. 68. "**E tanto bello.**" "It is so beautiful." 75. **os coccyx,** the end bone of the vertebral column. 90. **Grindelwald,** a village in the canton of Berne, Switzerland. 92. **Alp-horns,** carved wooden horns about three feet long with a cupped mouthpiece and a bell. **edelweiss,** famous flower of Switzerland, growing high in the Alps.

and the like. We received no answers to these cards; but then we did not expect answers. Guido could not write, and there was no reason why his father or his sisters should take the trouble to write for him. No news, we took it, was good news. And then one day, early in September, there arrived at the hotel a strange letter. The manager had it stuck up on the glass-fronted notice-board in the hall, so that all the guests might see it, and whoever conscientiously thought that it belonged to him might claim it. Passing the board on the way in to lunch, Elizabeth stopped to look at it.

"But it must be from Guido," she said.

I came and looked at the envelope over her shoulder. It was unstamped and black with postmarks. Traced out in pencil, the big uncertain capital letters sprawled across its face. In the first line was written: AL BABBO DI ROBIN, and there followed a travestied version of the name of the hotel and the place. Round the address bewildered postal officials had scrawled suggested emendations. The letter had wandered for a fortnight at least, back and forth across the face of Europe.

"Al Babbo di Robin. To Robin's father." I laughed. "Pretty smart of the postmen to have got it here at all." I went to the manager's office, set forth the justice of my claim to the letter, and, having paid the fifty-centime surcharge for the missing stamp, had the case unlocked and the letter given me. We went in to lunch.

"The writing's magnificent," we agreed, laughing, as we examined the address at close quarters. "Thanks to Euclid," I added. "That's what comes of pandering to the ruling passion."

But when I opened the envelope and looked at its contents I no longer laughed. The letter was brief and almost telegraphical in style. "SONO DALLA PADRONA," it ran, "NON MI PIACE HA RUBATO IL MIO LIBRO NON VOGLIO SUONARE PIU VOGLIO TORNARE A CASA VENGA SUBITO GUIDO."

"What is it?"

I handed Elizabeth the letter. "That blasted woman's got hold of him," I said.

Busts of men in Homburg hats, angels bathed in marble tears extinguishing torches, statues of little girls, cherubs, veiled figures, allegories and ruthless realisms—the strangest and most diverse idols beckoned and gesticulated as we passed. Printed indelibly on tin and embedded in the living rock, the brown photographs looked out, under glass, from the humbler crosses, headstones, and broken pillars. Dead ladies in the cubistic geometrical fashions of thirty years ago—two cones of black satin meeting point to point at the waist, and the arms: a sphere to the elbow, a polished cylinder below—smiled mournfully out of their marble frames; the smiling faces, the white hands, were the only recognizably human things that emerged from the solid geometry of their clothes. Men with black moustaches, men with white beards, young clean-shaven men, stared or averted their gaze to show a Roman profile. Children in their stiff best opened wide their eyes, smiled hopefully in anticipation of the little bird that was to issue from the camera's muzzle, smiled sceptically in the knowledge that it wouldn't, smiled laboriously and obediently because they had been told to. In spiky Gothic cottages of marble the richer dead privately reposed; through grilled doors one caught a glimpse of pale Inconsolables weeping, of distraught Geniuses guarding the secret of the tomb. The less prosperous sections of the majority slept in communities, close-crowded but elegantly housed under smooth continuous marble floors, whose every flagstone was the mouth of a separate grave.

These continental cemeteries, I thought, as Carlo and I made our way among the dead, are more frightful than ours, because these people pay more attention to their dead than we do. That primordial cult of corpses, that tender solicitude for their material well-being, which led the ancients to house their dead in stone, while they themselves lived between

---

31. **fifty-centime**, equal to about five cents. 43. **"SONO ... GUIDO,"** "I am at the Padrona's—I don't like it here—she has stolen my book—I don't want to play [the piano] any more—I want to go back home—come quickly—Guido."

49. **Homburg hat**, a man's soft felt hat with dented crown, first worn in Homburg, a town and fashionable watering-place of Prussia, noted for the manufacture of hats and machines.

wattles and under thatch, still lingers here; persists, I thought, more vigorously than with us. There are a hundred gesticulating statues here for every one in an English graveyard. There are more family vaults, more "luxuriously appointed" (as they say of liners and hotels) than one would find at home. And embedded in every tombstone there are photographs to remind the powdered bones within what form they will have to resume on the Day of Judgment; beside each are little hanging lamps to burn optimistically on All Souls' Day. To the Man who built the Pyramids they are nearer, I thought, than we.

"If I had known," Carlo kept repeating, "if only I had known." His voice came to me through my reflections as though from a distance. "At the time he didn't mind at all. How should I have known that he would take it so much to heart afterwards? And she deceived me, she lied to me."

I assured him yet once more that it wasn't his fault. Though, of course, it was, in part. It was mine too, in part; I ought to have thought of the possibility and somehow guarded against it. And he shouldn't have let the child go, even temporarily and on trial, even though the woman was bringing pressure to bear on him. And the pressure had been considerable. They had worked on the same holding for more than a hundred years, the men of Carlo's family; and now she had made the old man threaten to turn him out. It would be a dreadful thing to leave the place; and besides, another place wasn't so easy to find. It was made quite plain, however, that he could stay if he let her have the child. Only for a little to begin with; just to see how he got on. There would be no compulsion whatever on him to stay if he didn't like it. And it would be all to Guido's advantage; and to his father's, too, in the end. All that the Englishman had said about his not being such a good musician as he had thought at first was obviously untrue—mere jealousy and little-mindedness: the man wanted to take credit for Guido himself, that was all. And the boy, it was obvious, would learn nothing from him. What he needed was a real good professional master.

1. **wattles,** long, flexible stalks or rods.

All the energy that, if the physicists had known their business, would have been driving dynamos, went into this campaign. It began the moment we were out of the house, intensively. She would have more chance of success, the Signora doubtless thought, if we weren't there. And besides, it was essential to take the opportunity when it offered itself and get hold of the child before we could make our bid—for it was obvious to her that we wanted Guido just as much as she did.

Day after day she renewed the assault. At the end of a week she sent her husband to complain about the state of the vines: they were in a shocking condition; he had decided, or very nearly decided, to give Carlo notice. Meekly, shamefacedly, in obedience to higher orders, the old gentleman uttered his threats. Next day Signora Bondi returned to the attack. The padrone, she declared, had been in a towering passion; but she'd do her best, her very best, to mollify him. And after a significant pause she went on to talk about Guido.

In the end Carlo gave in. The woman was too persistent and she held too many trump cards. The child could go and stay with her for a month or two on trial. After that, if he really expressed a desire to remain with her, she could formally adopt him.

At the idea of going for a holiday to the seaside—and it was to the seaside, Signora Bondi told him, that they were going—Guido was pleased and excited. He had heard a lot about the sea from Robin. "Tanta acqua!" It had sounded almost too good to be true. And now he was actually to go and see this marvel. It was very cheerfully that he parted from his family.

But after the holiday by the sea was over, and Signora Bondi had brought him back to her town house in Florence, he began to be homesick. The Signora, it was true, treated him exceedingly kindly, bought him new clothes, took him out to tea in the Via Tornabuoni and filled him up with cakes, iced strawberryade, whipped cream, and chocolates. But she made him practice the piano more than he liked, and what was worse, she took away his Euclid, on the score that he

70. **padrone,** the landlord, her husband. 84. **"Tanta acqua!"** "So much water!"

wasted too much time with it. And when he said that he wanted to go home, she put him off with promises and excuses and downright lies. She told him that she couldn't take him at once, but that next week, if he were good and worked hard at his piano meanwhile, next week. . . . And when the time came she told him that his father didn't want him back. And she redoubled her petting, gave him expensive presents, and stuffed him with yet unhealthier foods. To no purpose. Guido didn't like his new life, didn't want to practice scales, pined for his book, and longed to be back with his brothers and sisters. Signora Bondi, meanwhile, continued to hope that time and chocolates would eventually make the child hers; and to keep his family at a distance, she wrote to Carlo every few days letters which still purported to come from the seaside (she took the trouble to send them to a friend, who posted them back again to Florence), and in which she painted the most charming picture of Guido's happiness.

It was then that Guido wrote his letter to me. Abandoned, as he supposed, by his family—for that they shouldn't take the trouble to come to see him when they were so near was only to be explained on the hypothesis that they really had given him up—he must have looked to me as his last and only hope. And the letter, with its fantastic address, had been nearly a fortnight on its way. A fortnight—it must have seemed hundreds of years; and as the centuries succeeded one another gradually, no doubt, the poor child became convinced that I too had abandoned him. There was no hope left.

"Here we are," said Carlo.

I looked up and found myself confronted by an enormous monument. In a kind of grotto hollowed in the flanks of a monolith of gray sandstone, Sacred Love, in bronze, was embracing a funerary urn. And in bronze letters riveted into the stone was a long legend to the effect that the inconsolable Ernesto Bondi had raised this monument to the memory of his beloved wife, Annunziata, as a token of his undying love for one whom, snatched from him by a premature death, he hoped very soon to join beneath this stone. The first Signora Bondi had died in 1912.

I thought of the old man leashed to his white dog; he must always, I reflected, have been a most uxorious husband.

"They buried him here."

We stood there for a long time in silence. I felt the tears coming into my eyes as I thought of the poor child lying there underground. I thought of those luminous grave eyes, and the curve of that beautiful forehead, the droop of the melancholy mouth, of the expression of delight which illumined his face when he learned of some new idea that pleased him, when he heard a piece of music that he liked. And this beautiful small being was dead; and the spirit that inhabited this form, the amazing spirit, that too had been destroyed almost before it had begun to exist.

And the unhappiness that must have preceded the final act, the child's despair, the conviction of his utter abandonment—those were terrible to think of, terrible.

"I think we had better come away now," I said at last, and touched Carlo on the arm. He was standing there like a blind man, his eyes shut, his face slightly lifted towards the light; from between his closed eyelids the tears welled out, hung for a moment, and trickled down his cheeks. His lips trembled and I could see that he was making an effort to keep them still. "Come away," I repeated.

The face which had been still in its sorrow, was suddenly convulsed; he opened his eyes, and through the tears they were bright with a violent anger. "I shall kill her," he said, "I shall kill her. When I think of him throwing himself out, falling through the air. . . ." With his two hands he made a violent gesture, bringing them down from over his head and arresting them with a sudden jerk when they were on a level with his breast. "And then crash." He shuddered. "She's as much responsible as though she had pushed him down herself. I shall kill her." He clenched his teeth.

To be angry is easier than to be sad, less painful. It is comforting to think of revenge. "Don't talk like that," I said. "It's no good. It's stupid. And what would be the point?" He had had those fits before, when grief became too painful and he had tried to escape from it. Anger had been the easiest way of escape. I had had, before this, to persuade him back into the harder path of grief. "It's stupid to talk like that," I repeated, and I led him away through the ghastly labyrinth of tombs, where death seemed more terrible even than it is.

By the time we had left the cemetery, and were walking down from San Miniato towards the Piazzale Michelangeio below, he had become calmer. His anger had subsided again into sorrow from which it had derived all its strength and its bitterness. In the Piazzale we halted for a moment to look down at the city in the valley below us. It was a day of floating clouds—great shapes, white, golden, and gray; and between them patches of a thin, transparent blue. Its lantern level, almost, with our eyes, the dome of the cathedral revealed itself in all its grandiose lightness, its vastness and aerial strength. On the innumerable brown and rosy roofs of the city the afternoon sunlight lay softly, sumptuously, and the towers were as though varnished and enamelled with an old gold. I thought of all the Men who had lived here and left the visible traces of their spirit and conceived extraordinary things, I thought of the head child. (1924)

8. San Miniato, cf. note 74, p. 1098.

Noel Coward

1899-

Noel Pierce Coward, the most versatile English dramatist of the 1920's and 1930's, was born at Teddington, Middlesex, a suburb of London, in 1899. His father was associated with a music publishing firm and later with a piano manufacturing concern; his family life was, therefore, one of "modest respectability only," as he himself has put it. His formal education was spasmodic, but he began early to attend a dramatic academy, and made his first public appearance on the stage in 1910, when he was eleven years old. From his youth he was passionately interested in all things theatrical. Incipient tuberculosis prevented him from entering military service during the First World War; he served in a Labor Corps, and later joined the Artists' Rifles, but was injured during training and spent most of the remainder of the war in a hospital.

Soon after his discharge from the service, Coward became interested in another aspect of the theater and at eighteen wrote his first full-length play, *The Rat Trap*, which never appeared on stage. Another play, *I'll Leave It to You*, was staged unsuccessfully in 1920. After several equally short-lived and light-hearted ventures, he produced in 1923 a serious work which finally brought him recognition as a dramatist. *The Vortex* is a powerful play about a young decadent of the 1920's and his equally decadent mother—a sort of twentieth-century Hamlet disillusioned by Gertrude and her immorality. Despite the seriousness of the theme, Coward made the most of his opportunity to display plenty of his characteristic wit, of much the same paradoxical and amorally cynical nature as that of Oscar Wilde and George Bernard Shaw. It was this same wittiness which he proceeded to develop to a high point of mastery in the excellent sophisticated drawing-room comedies which followed *The Vortex*. Among the better known of these, *Hay Fever* (1925) has long been a favorite of his, although it is one of the few plays he has written in which he has provided no suitable rôle for himself. In *Private Lives* (1930) he presents the unusual situation of a divorced couple's meeting on their respective second honeymoons and abandoning their new mates for each other—at least temporarily. *Design for Living* (1933) is a typically iconoclastic Coward comedy in which two men are so devoted to the same woman and to each other that they arrange an unorthodox *ménage à trois*. Not quite so strong is *Blithe Spirit* (1941), which depicts the nagging and haunting of a couple by the man's deceased first wife; all three are eventually united in death, with somewhat appalling prospects. *Present Laughter* (1943) is in some ways a satiric caricature of Coward himself, but here the brittle sophistication is already beginning to appear a little dated.

Coward has also had success with the operetta and musical comedy, of which *Bitter Sweet* (1929) and *Conversation Piece* (1934) are the best examples, combining as they do extremely able music (composed by Coward), clever staging (conceived by Coward), and entertaining dialogue (written by Coward). They are nostalgic and sentimental in an attractive rather than a mawkish manner, and they lend support to the theory that in his human point of view Coward is not far removed from the eighteenth-century combination of the realistic, the imaginative, the witty, the satirical, and the sentimental. In this last-named vein, with definitely tragic overtones, he wrote the arresting *Cavalcade* (1931) intended to offer a panorama of an English family of culture and prosperity during the first generation of the twentieth century—from the Boer War to the close of the First World War. The product is an understanding survey of great insight covering England through the Edwardian era; it is a moving, generally impressive, and often strangely powerful work which ends in a plea to England to recover her former dignity and greatness.

A film version of *Cavalcade* was even more effective and successful than the play; a number of Coward's plays have, with more or less success, been transplanted to the screen. In 1942, indeed, Coward wrote, directed, and starred in the sentimental but swift-moving motion picture, *In Which We Serve,* describing and lauding the spirit of the British Royal Navy and the British people in wartime. In *This Happy Breed* (1943; motion picture, 1944), the *Cavalcade* pattern is imposed upon the lives of a middle-class family from the end of the First to the beginning of the Second World War. Something of a summation of Coward's work and an excellent demonstration of his scope and breadth is *Tonight at 8:30* (1936), a collection of eight well-constructed one-act plays, now farcical, as in *Hands Across the Sea,* now brutally frank, as in *Fumed Oak,* now tender, now irreverent, but always exhibiting the craftsmanship which is one of Coward's finest assets.

Coward's autobiography, *Present Indicative* (1937), illustrates more than once the inevitable egocentricity of a brilliant man of the theater. Perhaps, he suggests, his importance in the world as a whole may be trivial; but his importance to himself is all in all. Naturally, therefore, he can be frivolous, tasteless, arrogant, offensive to certain individuals and groups, and exasperating in his sometimes blasé affectations. Of his sincerity and talent as a dramatic artist, however, there can be no dispute. His position is deservedly high in the annals of the present-day British theater. Thanks partly to his environment, thanks partly to his native abilities, he can do things which no dramatist in England during the 1890's could possibly have done.

Cavalcade

In his autobiography *Present Indicative,* Noel Coward tells of looking through stacks of books and copies of the *Illustrated London News* to get "a solid background" for his *Cavalcade.* He gives an exceptionally interesting account of his writing the play, the hours spent in planning its complicated staging and elaborate costuming, the long rehearsals, the first tense performance in Drury Lane Theatre, and the subsequent thrilling presentation before the Royal Family. "The emotional basis of *Cavalcade,*" he explains, "was undoubtedly music. The whole story was threaded on to a string of popular melodies . . . . [which]

probe the memory more swiftly than anything else, and *Cavalcade*, whatever else it did, certainly awakened many echoes." The play, he says, revealed "certainly [a] love of England . . . , a certain natural pride in some of our very typical characteristics, but primarily it was the story of thirty years in the life of a family." Jane Marryot, the main character, he describes as being "a bit of my own mother and millions of others, too; ordinary, kind, and unobtrusively brave; capable of deep suffering and incapable of cheap complaint."

SCENES

PART ONE

SCENE I: Sunday, December 31st, 1899 . . . . Drawing-room
SCENE II: Saturday, January 27th, 1900 . . . . Dockside
SCENE III: Friday, May 18th, 1900 . . . . Drawing-room
SCENE IV: Friday, May 18th, 1900 . . . . Theatre
SCENE V: Monday, January 21st, 1901 . . . . Kitchen
SCENE VI: Sunday, January 27th, 1901 . . . . Park
SCENE VII: Saturday, February 2nd, 1901 . . . . Drawing-room
SCENE VIII: Thursday, May 14th, 1903 . . . . Ballroom

PART TWO

SCENE I: Saturday, June 16th, 1906 . . . . Bar Parlour
SCENE II: Saturday, June 16th, 1906 . . . . Street
SCENE III: Wednesday, March 10th, 1909 . . . . Restaurant, Private Room
SCENE IV: Monday, July 25th, 1910 . . . . Seaside
SCENE V: Sunday, April 14th, 1912 . . . . Ship
SCENE VI: Tuesday, August 4th, 1914 . . . . Drawing-room
SCENE VII: 1914-1915-1916-1917-1918 . . . . Marching
SCENE VIII: Tuesday, October 22nd, 1918 . . . . Restaurant
SCENE IX: Tuesday, October 22nd, 1918 . . . . Railway Station
SCENE X: Monday, November 11th, 1918 . . . . Drawing-room
SCENE XI: Monday, November 11th, 1918 . . . . Trafalgar Square

PART THREE

SCENE I: Tuesday, December 31st, 1929 . . . . Drawing-room
SCENE II: Tuesday, 1930 . . . . CHAOS

PART ONE : SCENE I

PRINCIPALS—1899: JANE MARRYOT *(aged 31)*, ROBERT MARRYOT *(aged 35)*, ELLEN *(aged 25)*, BRIDGES *(aged 40)*.

SCENE: *The drawing-room of a London house. The room is charmingly furnished in the taste of the period. There are two windows at the back with a small balcony in front of each of them; apart from this structural necessity the decoration and furniture, etc., can be left to the discretion of the designer.*

TIME: *About 11:45 p.m. Sunday, December 31st, 1899.*

(*When the curtain rises,* ELLEN, *the parlour-maid, is discovered setting the table with a light supper consisting of sandwiches and cake. She is a pleasant-looking woman of twenty-five. Enter* BRIDGES, *the butler, with a bottle of champagne in a bucket of ice. He is older than* ELLEN, *about forty, with iron-grey hair.*)

Ellen. They won't need champagne if they've got 'ot punch, will they?

Bridges. You never know; best to be on the safe side.

Cavalcade by Noel Coward. Copyright 1931, 1932 by Noel Coward, reprinted by permission of Doubleday & Co., Inc.

Ellen. How was Cook when you come up?

Bridges. Running round that kitchen like a cat on a griddle; New Year's Eve's gone to 'er 'ead, and no mistake.

Ellen. She's been queer all day, she says she feels like as if it was the end of everything. So do I, for that matter.

Bridges. Don't start all that over again.

Ellen. Oh, Alfred!

Bridges. What?

Ellen. I can't bear to think what it's going to be like when you've gone.

Bridges. Well, don't.

Ellen. I can't 'elp it.

Bridges. It's no use upsetting yourself; think of the missus, think of all the other soldiers' wives. You're in the same boat as wot they are.

Ellen. You was never cut out for a soldier.

Bridges. Never mind what I was cut out for. I am one now.

Ellen. What's going to 'appen to me and Fanny if anything 'appens to you?

Bridges (putting his hands on ELLEN's *shoulders).* Look 'ere, old girl, you married me for better or for worse, didn't you?

Ellen. Yes, but——

Bridges. Well, if this turns out to be worse, so much the worse, see? And if it turns out to be better——

Ellen. So much the better—yes, a fat lot of comfort that is.

Bridges. Look at the missus, with a brother out there ever since the beginning, and now 'er 'usband going, and two growing boys to look after.

Ellen. What's the war for, anyhow? Nobody wanted to 'ave a war.

Bridges. We've got to 'ave wars every now and then to prove we're top-dog——

Ellen. This one don't seem to be proving much.

Bridges. 'Ow can you tell sitting at 'ome 'ere safe and sound? 'Ow can you tell what our brave boys are suffering out there in darkest Africa, giving their life's blood for their Queen and country?

Ellen. Africa looks very sunny and nice in the *Illustrated London News.*

Bridges. If this wasn't New Year's Eve, I'd lose my temper, and that's a fact.

Ellen. Well, it wouldn't be the first time. You'd better go and get the 'ot punch, they'll be in in a minute.

Bridges. You mark my words, Ellen, if we didn't go out and give them Boers wot for, they'd be over 'ere wreakin' 'avoc and carnage before you could say Jack Robinson.

Ellen. Oh, get along with you. (BRIDGES *goes out.* ELLEN *puts the finishing touches to the table and then, going to the windows, she pulls back the curtains.*)

Enter JANE MARRYOT. *She is a handsome woman of about thirty-one. She is wearing an evening gown and cloak. Enter* ROBERT, JANE's *husband, following her. He is older, about thirty-five, also in evening dress.*

Jane (throwing off her cloak). I thought we should never get here in time. I'm sure that cabby was tipsy, Robert. How nice the table looks, Ellen. Where did those flowers come from?

Ellen. They're from Bridges and me, ma'am, with our very best wishes, I'm sure.

Jane. Thank you, Ellen, very much indeed.

Robert. A charming thought, Ellen. Thank you both.

Ellen. Not at all, sir—it's—it's a pleasure indeed. (ELLEN *withdraws from the room covered with respectful embarrassment.* JANE *smiles at* ROBERT.)

Jane. Small things are so infinitely touching, aren't they? I feel I want to cry. Just a few gentle tears to usher in the new century.

Robert. Do, by all means, dearest: this evening was planned sentimentally.

Jane. Just the two of us saying, "Hail and Farewell."

Robert. Not farewell quite yet.

Jane. Soon—dreadfully soon.

Robert. You looked so beautiful at dinner.

Jane. Did I, Robert?

Robert. You look so beautiful now.

Jane. Do I, Robert?

Robert. I expect it's only that dress, really. Very deceiving.

Jane. Yes, Robert.

Robert. And that ornament in your hair.

Jane. Yes, Robert.

Robert. And the fact that I love you so dearly.

Jane. After so long. How can you?

Robert. Perhaps you're hideous and ill-dispositioned and tedious, really, and I never knew.

Jane. Perhaps.

Robert. Well, it's too late now. I'm set in the habit of loving you. I shall never know the truth.

Jane. I wonder if the boys are asleep.

Robert. Snoring, I expect.

Jane. Oh, no, Robert; not snoring. They both have perfect tonsils. Doctor Harrison said so.

Robert. Inherited from their mother, dear. You have the most exquisite tonsils in the world.

Jane. You're in a very facetious mood, Robert. It shocks me a little. This should be a solemn occasion. Your bow is crooked, too, and you look raffish.

Robert. Raffish?

Jane (suddenly running into his arms). Oh, my darling, my darling, why must you leave me? I shall miss you so.

Robert (smiling and holding her tenderly). The Bugle Call, dear, the Red, White and Blue——

    Britons never, never, never shall be slaves.

Jane. Don't tease me—not about that. What does it matter about the Boers—it can't matter, really.

Robert (seriously). It matters about Jim, doesn't it? He's out there.

Jane. Yes, I know, I know, but——

Robert. But what?

Jane (leaving his embrace). I'm sorry, dear. I was nearly behaving badly.

Robert. You couldn't behave badly.

Jane (lightly). Give him my love if you ever see him, if he's alive.

Robert. Of course he's alive. They're all alive. They're bound to be relieved soon.

Jane. Everyone has been saying that for weeks.

Robert. Baden-Powell's a fine man.

Jane. How long will it last, the war, I mean?

Robert. It can't last more than a few months.

Jane. Perhaps it will be over before you get there.

Robert. Perhaps.

Jane. I suppose you'd hate that. Wouldn't you?

Robert. Bitterly.

Jane. Thank Heaven for one thing. The boys are too young. They won't have to fight; Peace and Happiness for them. Oh, please God, Peace and Happiness for them, always. *(She leans against the window and looks out.)* Enter Bridges *with a bowl of punch, followed by* Ellen *entering, carrying a tray of punch glasses and almonds and raisins.*

Bridges. It's started, sir. Just twelve o'clock now.

Robert. Open the windows quick. (Robert *takes the punch from* Bridges *and fills two glasses.* Bridges *opens the windows wide. Outside can be heard the growing noise of sirens and chimes of bells.* Ellen *and* Bridges *are about to go.)*

Jane (suddenly). Stay and drink with us, won't you? Robert, two more glasses.

Bridges. Thank you very much, ma'am.

Ellen. Thank you, ma'am.

Robert (pouring them two glasses of punch). Here you are, Jane, Ellen, Bridges. 1900—1900.

Jane. 1900.

Ellen and Bridges (together). 1900. *(Suddenly* Jane *hears a sound upstairs. She puts down her glass hurriedly and runs out of the room.)*

Ellen. It sounded like Master Joe.

Robert (going to the door and calling after Jane*).* Dearest, bring them down here. Bring them both down. *(Coming slowly back into the room, smiling.)* How very impolite of the twentieth century to waken the children. *(The lights fade as the noise of chimes and sirens grows louder.)*

---

30. **Britons . . . slaves,** the refrain of "Rule, Britannia!" (1740), a famous patriotic song, by the British pre-romantic poet James Thomson (1700-1748).

48. **Baden-Powell's,** Sir Robert Baden-Powell (1857-1941), a British general in the Boer War, who probably is better known as the founder of the international organization of Boy Scouts.

(NOTE ON PART ONE: *In the interim of darkness between Scenes 1 and 2, 2 and 3, 3 and 4, newsboys are heard shouting latest news from the front.*)

PART ONE : SCENE II

PRINCIPALS: ROBERT, JANE, ELLEN, BRIDGES.
SCENE: *A Dockside.*
TIME: *About twelve noon, Saturday, January 27th, 1900.*

(*Before the stage becomes visible to the audience, down stage on the left* BRIDGES *and* ELLEN *appear in a pool of light.* BRIDGES *is wearing the uniform of a Private in the C.I.V.*[5] ELLEN *is gaily dressed, but weeping.*)

Bridges. Be brave, old woman.

Ellen. Oh, Alfred, Alfred, my 'eart's breaking.

Bridges. There, there—I'll soon be back—you see.

Ellen. I can't bear it.

Bridges. Think of the missus—you'll 'ave to look after 'er, you know.

Ellen. I can't think of anything but you going out among all them awful Boers and lying bleeding yer 'eart out on the battlefield.

Bridges. That's a cheerful outlook, I will say.

Ellen. And Fanny 'aving no father and me being widowed for life.

Bridges. You're getting morbid, you know. Fanny'll be all right, and so will you and so will I. She was right as rain when I kissed her good-bye. See her laugh, eh?

Ellen. She didn't mean to laugh; she's too young to understand.

Bridges. All the better, I say. I could do with a bit of a smile from you, now you mention it.

Ellen. All right——I'll try.

Bridges. That's a girl——(*He kisses her as the lights fade on them and a steamer siren sounds loudly. Down stage on the right* ROBERT *and* JANE *appear in a pool of light.* ROBERT *is in the uniform of a C.I.V. officer.* JANE *is quietly dressed.*)

Robert. I think I'd better be getting aboard.

---
5. C.I.V., the Colonial Imperial Volunteers.

Jane. It's come at last, hasn't it—this moment?

Robert. You'll be very brave, won't you?

Jane. Take care of yourself, my dearest.

Robert. I shall probably be seasick.

Jane. Lie down flat on every possible occasion.

Robert. I'll try to remember.

Jane. Bridges will look after you.

Robert. Perhaps he'll be lying down flat, too.

Jane. You mustn't worry about me being unhappy when you've gone. I'm going to keep myself very busy. Lady Brandon is organizing an enormous relief fund matinée in February. She asked me to help her, and there'll be lots of other things, too. I shan't give myself time to feel anything except just very proud.

Robert. I'll write and telegraph whenever it's possible. (*Pause.*)

Jane. This is horrid, isn't it?

Robert. I really must go.

Jane. Not just for a minute.

Robert. I'm going to kiss you once more now, and then I want you to turn away and go on talking, so that you won't see me actually leave you.

Jane (*in a stifled voice*). Very well, my darling. (ROBERT *kisses her lingeringly.*)

Jane (*turning away and talking rapidly*). Edward and Joe were terribly anxious to come, too, but I'm glad I didn't bring them really. Joe gets over-excited so easily, and he's had a very bad cold, anyhow. Edward could have come, I suppose, really, but that would have upset Joe so dreadfully, being left alone. Take care of yourself, my own dear—you're not here any more, so I can break down a little—I felt you go when I said about Joe being over-excited—Robert—Robert——

(ROBERT *has disappeared into the surrounding darkness. As she turns, the lights go up and* ROBERT *is seen threading his way through the crowd to the ship's gangway.* BRIDGES *is waiting for him, and they go aboard together.* JANE *walks over to* ELLEN, *who is sobbing bitterly, and puts her arms round her. The crowd is cheering wildly, although several mothers and sweethearts and wives are weep-*

ing. The steamer gives a short blast on its siren. A band strikes up "Soldiers of the Queen." The decks of the ship are lined with waving soldiers. The gangway is pulled away. Slowly the ship begins to move as the lights fade.)

PART ONE : SCENE III

PRINCIPALS: JANE MARRYOT, MARGARET HARRIS, EDITH HARRIS *(aged 10)*, EDWARD *(aged 12)*, JOE *(aged 8)*, ELLEN.
SCENE: *The same as Scene I.*
TIME: *About five o'clock on the afternoon of Friday, May 18th, 1900.*

(When the lights go up EDWARD *and* JOE MARRYOT *and* EDITH HARRIS *are discovered playing soldiers on the floor.* EDWARD *is aged twelve,* JOE *eight, and* EDITH HARRIS *about ten.)*

Joe (shooting off a cannon). Bang—bang, bang, bang.
Edith (giving a little squeak). Oh—oh, dear!
Edward. How many?
Edith. Seven.
Edward (curtly). Good! You'd better retreat.
Edith. I don't know how.
Joe. I'm going to shoot again.
Edith. I do wish you wouldn't. I've only got fourteen left.
Joe (yelling). Bang, bang, bang! Dirty old Kruger—dirty old Kruger——
Edward. Shut up! How dare you fire without orders.
Joe (saluting). I'm sorry, Bobs.
Edith. Edward.
Edward. What?
Edith. Need I always be the Boers?
Edward. Yes.
Edith. Why?
Joe. Because you're a girl—only a girl. Bang, bang, bang!

Edith (struggling with her cannon and ammunition). I'll teach you, you mean little pig! Bang, bang, bang! There! Bang—— *(The cannon sticks, so* EDITH *throws it at* JOE's *battalion, annihilating about fifty soldiers.)*
Joe (yelling). It's not fair.
Edward. Be quiet. Edith, that was cheating.
Edith (in tears). I'm sick of being the Boers—I'll never be the Boers again, never as long as I live!
The door opens. Enter JANE, *looking obviously worried and nervy. Enter* MARGARET HARRIS, *following* JANE. *She is a nicely dressed woman of about thirty.*
Jane. Children, why on earth are you making such an awful noise? I heard you right down in the hall. Edith, what's the matter? Joe, be quiet.
Edward. Edith doesn't like being the Boers—she's mutinied.
Jane. So I should think.
Joe. Bang, bang, bang! *(*JOE *throws* EDITH's *cannon back at her and hits her on the knee.* EDITH *screams.* JANE *slaps* JOE *sharply.)*
Jane. You're a naughty, wicked little boy. You go upstairs this minute. *(*MARGARET *rushes to* EDITH *and proceeds to comfort her.)*
Margaret. Edith, don't cry—it couldn't have hurt you so very much.
Jane. I can't bear it. Go away, all of you. Edward, take Joe away.
Edward. Sorry, mum.
Jane. Can't you play any other game but soldiers, soldiers—soldiers hurting each other —killing each other? Go away from me—go away—go away—go away—— *(*MARGARET, *seeing that* JANE *is in a bad state of nerves, bustles all three children out of the room.)*
Margaret. Go along, all of you. Edith, I'm ashamed of you, making such a fuss. It's only a tiny little scratch. Go upstairs and ask nurse to put some Pommade Devigne on it. Go along, now. *(Exeunt* EDITH, EDWARD *and* JOE. MARGARET *shuts the door after the children and comes back to* JANE. JANE *is wearily removing her hat in front of a mirror. A barrel organ in the street strikes up "Soldiers of the Queen.")*

---

3. **"Soldiers of the Queen,"** the most popular marching-song of the Boer War. 25. **Kruger,** Stephanus Johannes Paulus Kruger, better known as "Oom Paul" (Uncle Paul") Kruger (1825-1904), president of the South African Republic (the Boers) and leader of their fight against the British in South Africa. 28. **Bobs,** the nickname of Field Marshal Frederick Sleigh Roberts, Earl of Kandahar, Pretoria, and Waterford (1832-1914), the British hero in the Boer War.

Jane. There's no escape anywhere, is there?
Margaret. Shall I throw him something?
Jane. Make him go away. (MARGARET *goes to the window and out on to the balcony.*)
Margaret. Hi! Hi! (*The organ stops.*) Will you please go away further down the street? (*Throwing some money out and returning into the room.*) He's moving off. Do sit down, Jane dear, you've been standing up all the afternoon.
Jane (*sitting down*). Will these days never end? (*The barrel organ starts again, but much further off.*)
Margaret. News will come soon.
Jane. I don't believe I shall see either of them ever again.
Margaret. Don't give way to despair, Jane. It's foolish. You must have courage.
Jane. It's much easier to be brave when there's something to hear, something definite; this long suspense, these dragging, dragging weeks of waiting are horrible. The two people I love best in the world, so remote from me, beyond reach of my love, probably suffering—it's dreadful, dreadful——
Margaret. Mafeking is bound to be relieved within the next few days, all the papers say so.
Jane. They've been saying so for months—meanwhile Jim is dying there slowly, by inches, starvation and disease and horror. I can't bear to think of it and yet I can't stop thinking. I wake at night and see his face, as he was when he was a little boy. He was always awfully plucky, my little brother, and so very, very dear to me. (*She breaks down.*)
Enter ELLEN *with tea. She places it on the table and looks enquiringly at* MARGARET. MARGARET *shakes her head.*
Margaret. No news yet, Ellen. We've been standing outside the Mansion House for hours, and then we went to Fleet Street to the newspaper offices.

Ellen (to JANE). Have a nice cup of tea, ma'am, it'll make you feel better.
Jane. Thank you, Ellen.
Ellen. There ain't no cause to worry about the master, ma'am; he's all right. I feel it in me bones. You see, he's got my Alfred with 'im, and if anything 'appened to either of them we'd be bound to 'ear from one of them, if you know what I mean.
Jane. You must be fearfully worried, too, Ellen.
Ellen. Well, on and off, I am, but I say to myself—no news is good news, and what must be must be, and you'd never believe how it cheers me up. (ELLEN *goes out.*)
Margaret. Poor Ellen! (*A newsboy runs by, shouting.*)
Jane (*jumping up*). Quick! Quick! Give me a halfpenny. (JANE *rushes on to the balcony and leans over.*) What is it, Ellen—what is it? (ELLEN *apparently answers "nothing much," and* JANE *returns wearily.*)
Jane. Ellen's up those area steps like lightning every time a paper boy passes. No news is good news. What must be must be. Oh, God! (MARGARET *gets up with an air of determination.*)
Margaret. Now, look here, Jane. I'm going now, and I shall be back at a quarter to seven.
Jane. A quarter to seven—why?
Margaret. We're going out to dine at a restaurant and we're going to a theatre.
Jane. A restaurant! A theatre! I couldn't!
Margaret. You could and you will—it's senseless sitting at home all by yourself fretting and worrying, and it doesn't do any good. I'll get Ronnie James to take us, and if he can't, we'll go by ourselves, and I don't care what people say. We'll go to something gay—they say "Mirabelle" is very good.
Jane. I can't, Margaret—it's very sweet of you, but I really can't.
Margaret. I am now going home to have a bath and put on my new Redfern model, and I shall be back at a quarter to seven.
Jane. Margaret—no, really—I——
Margaret (*kissing* JANE). Don't argue—just do what you're told.
Jane. I haven't anything to wear.
Margaret. Nonsense! You have your blue

---

26. **Mafeking**, a town in the north-east of the Cape of Good Hope Colony of South Africa, and administrative seat of The British Protectorate of Bechuanaland For seven months it was besieged by the Boers; the British force which held out in the town was relieved in May 1900. The siege had caught the imagination of the British public to such an extent that when Mafeking was relieved, the celebration in London was the wildest of the entire Boer War For a long time thereafter, the slang term *maffick* or *Mafeking* meant "noisy and prolonged revelry." 41. **Mansion House**, the official residence of the Lord Mayor of London.

"Worth" and if that won't do, put on your presentation gown, feathers and all!

Jane. Margaret, don't be so silly.

Margaret. I mean it—it's a gesture. Robert and Jim would hate to think of you weeping and wailing. They're being gallant enough. We'd better try and be gallant, too. We'll dine at the Café Royal.

Jane. Margaret!

Margaret. Be ready at a quarter to seven.

(MARGARET *goes out.* JANE *makes a movement to call* MARGARET *back and then subsides into her chair. Suddenly directly under the window another barrel organ strikes up* "Soldiers of the Queen." JANE *jumps up and runs to the window.*)

Jane (on balcony). Go on, then—play louder—play louder! Soldiers of the Queen—wounded and dying and suffering for the Queen! Play louder, play louder! *(She comes back into the room laughing hysterically and proceeds to kick the children's toy soldiers all over the room; finally collapsing on to the sofa in a storm of tears as the lights fade.)*

PART ONE : SCENE IV

PRINCIPALS: JANE, MARGARET, MIRABELLE, ADA, EDGAR, TOM JOLLY, SIX C.I.V. GIRLS, CHORUS, STAGE MANAGER.

SCENE: *A theatre.*

TIME: *About 9 p.m. Friday, May 18th, 1900.*

(Before the lights go up, a spotlight illuminates JANE *and* MARGARET *in evening cloaks and gowns sitting in a stage box left. When the lights go up, it is seen that they are watching a typical musical comedy of the period. A Sextette of ample girls are singing a song called "The Girls of the C.I.V.," dressed rakishly in C.I.V. uniforms.)*

We're the girls of the C.I.V.
Form fours, get in line, one two three.
For our bravery is such
That the Boers won't like it much
When we chase them across the veldt and
    teach them double Dutch.

We're the girls of the C.I.V.
And we're out for a lark and a spree
In our uniforms so stunning
We shall soon have Kruger running
From the girls of the C.I.V.

(The SCENE *on the stage is excessively rural, with apple blossom predominating. When the girls have finished their number, they bounce off and the leading lady,* MIRABELLE, *enters. She is in reality a Princess, but has disguised herself as a farm girl in order that she might conceivably find a young man to love her for herself alone. Her costume is charming but slightly inappropriate for manual labour. She is met down stage by* LIEUT. EDGAR TYRELL, R. N., *a wooden young man with an excellent tenor voice.)*

Edgar (saluting). We meet again.

Mirabelle (curtseying). Yes, indeed.

Edgar. It seems a sin that beauty so rare should be hidden for ever in this small country village.

Mirabelle. Flatterer!

Edgar. No, no, I mean it.

Mirabelle. You are a sailor, sir, and I have been warned about sailors.

Edgar. What have they told you?

Mirabelle. That sailors are fickle, and that when they have loved a maid they sail away and leave her lonely.

Edgar. Do you believe that?

Mirabelle. I hardly know.

Edgar. Dearest, dearest Mirabelle—my heart is at your feet.

Mirabelle (gaily). Pick it up, sir, pick it up.

Edgar. Ah, do not tease me. Look into my eyes—can you not see the lovelight shining there?

Mirabelle. I know nothing of love.

Edgar. Let me teach you.

Mirabelle. I know nothing of life.

MIRABELLE WALTZ

Lover of My Dreams

She. A simple country maid am I,
    As innocent as any flower.
    The great big world has pass'd me
        by,

---

1. "Worth," then as now the name of a famous designer of women's fashions as well as of the creations of his establishment. 37. veldt, also veld, the name given by the Boers to the great stretches of grassland in South Africa (cf. the German *Feld* or the English *field*).

He. No lover comes my way to greet me
    shyly in my bower.
He. Oh, say not so!
    Such modesty enchants me:
    Could I but stay to while away with
    you a happy hour.
She. It must be Spring that fills my heart
    to over-flowing,
    Ah, whither am I going?
    What is the voice that seems to say:
    Be kind to love, don't let him call to
    you unknowing.
He. If true love comes to you, don't turn
    your face away.
She. Maybe 'tis something in the air;
    For Spring is made for lovers only.
He. Live for the moment and take care
    Lest love should fly and leave us
    lonely.
Both. Ah, if love should leave us lonely.

    Refrain

She. All my life I have been waiting
    Dreaming ages through;
    Until to-day I suddenly discover
    The form and face of he who is my
    lover.
    No more tears and hesitating;
    Fate has sent me you.
    Time and tide can never sever
    Those whom love has bound for ever,
    Dear lover of my Dreams come true.
He. All my life I have been waiting,
She. All my life I have been waiting,
He. Dreaming ages through;
She. Dreaming ages through;
He. Until to-day I suddenly discover
She. Until to-day I suddenly discover
He. The form and face of she who is my
    lover.
She. The form and face of he who is my
    lover.
He. No more tears and hesitating;
She. No more tears and hesitating;
He. Fate has sent me you—Time and tide
    can never sever,
She. Fate has sent me you—Time and tide
    can never sever,
He. Those whom love has bound for ever,
She. Those whom love has bound for ever,
He. Dear lover of my Dreams come true,
She. Dear lover of my Dreams come true,
Both. Dear lover of my
    Dreams come true,
    Dear lover of my Dreams come true,
    Dear lover of my Dreams come true.

Enter Tom Jolly, *comedian. He is dressed as a common sailor. Enter* Ada *with* Tom *(soubrette). She is dressed as a dairymaid.*

Tom. If I made a noise like a cow—would you kiss me?
Ada (laughing). Perhaps.
Tom. Moo—moo. (*He tries to kiss her.*)
Ada. No, no! I'm frightened of bulls.
Tom. If I made a noise like a sheep—then?
Ada. Who knows!
Tom. Baa, baa, baa——
Ada. No, no—no good at all.
Tom. I'll sing, then. Sailing, sailing, over the bounding main!
Ada. I'll kiss you now, I love donkeys!

    FUN OF THE FARM

    Verse

Ada. Tho' sailors are so brave and bold,
    It really must be dreadfully cold
    To sail across the sea.
Tom.   I quite agree,
        I quite agree,
    I'm sick of the ocean wild and free,
    Heigho, heigho, this is the place for
    me.
Ada. Now I am weary of the town
    And feel inclined to settle down
    A milk pail on my arm.
Tom.   I feel afraid,
        A London maid
    Would never know how the eggs
    are laid.
Ada. I'd find a cow
    And milk 'til the pail was full,
Tom. I'd shear the sow
    And probably milk the bull.
Both.   You must agree
        That it would be
    The height of true rusticity
    If you and I should settle on a farm.

    Refrain

Both. Oh, the Fun of the Farmyard,
    The roosters are crowing,
    The cattle are lowing,

The turkeys go gobbly gobbly goo;
This really is an alarm yard.
Ada. Like little Bo-Peep,
I lose my sheep,
And cannot find them anywhere.
Tom. I ought to be shot,
For I forgot
To coax the horse to meet the mare.
Both. Who left the canary
Locked up in the dairy?
Ada. Cheep, cheep, cheep, cheep,
Tom. Snort, snort, snort, snort,
Ada. Moo, moo, moo, moo,
Tom. Cock a doodle doodle do!
Both. Oh, dear, far from being a calm yard,
Quack, quack, quack, quack,
All the fun of the farm.

Tom. Tell me something, Ada.
Ada. What?
Tom. You're no dairymaid, are you?
Ada. Mr. Inquisitive.
Tom. What are you?
Ada (curtseying). Lady's maid to the Princess Mirabelle.

MIRABELLE *enters, unobserved, at the back.*

Tom. The Princess! Then he'll win his bet, after all.
Ada. Who? What bet?
Tom. Lieutenant Edgar. All the officers of the ship wagered him that he would not win the hand of the Princess Mirabelle. He said he'd marry her if she was ugly as sin; he needs the money.

EDGAR *enters.*

Edgar. What are you doing here, Tom?
Tom. Just farming! *(Laugh.)*
Mirabelle. Stop!
Enter full CHORUS.

FINALE

Chorus. What is—what is the matter here?
Mirabelle. Kind friends, you heard my call,
And so I thank you all
For while you chatter here
My heart has been betrayed.
Edgar. Ah, no—not so.
What foolish words you scatter here.
'Tis naught but your pride that's hurt
I am afraid.
Chorus. Who can he be,
'Tis plain to see,
He seems to know her well.
Who is this man
Who dares offend
The Princess Mirabelle?
Mirabelle. You've lied to me and cheated me.
Ada. Madame, don't let him see
Your poor heart breaking.
Edgar. Whate'er the future be,
True love you are mistaking.

WALTZ REFRAIN FINALE

All my life I have been dreaming,
Now my dreams must die.
Within my heart I felt a song awaken,
And now I find a melody forsaken.
All your vows were base and scheming,
All our Love's a lie.
Cruelly you would deceive me,
All I say to you is . . .

Enter STAGE MANAGER, *who raises his hand for silence.*

Stage Manager. Ladies and gentlemen—Mafeking has been relieved. (JANE *in her box utters a cry of relief. The players on the stage cheer wildly and the lights fade. The cheering is heard through the darkness; when the lights come up the audience is discovered cheering, waving hats and handkerchiefs, and programmes are fluttering from the crowded balconies; some of the audience join hands and sing "Auld Lang Syne." The lights fade.*)

PART ONE : SCENE V

PRINCIPALS: MRS. SNAPPER, COOK, ANNIE, ELLEN, BRIDGES, CABBY.
SCENE: *The kitchen of a London house. It is a typical basement kitchen. There is a door at the back opening on to the area steps, also two windows. Another door communicating with the upper parts of the house, and a small door leading into the scullery.*
TIME: *About 5 p.m. Monday, January 21st, 1901.*

(When the lights go up Cook *is making toast in front of the range.* Mrs. Snapper, [Ellen's *mother*] *is sitting on a chair beside a mail-cart in which reposes* [*mercifully invisible to the audience*] *the infant* Fanny. Annie, *a scullery-maid, stands about with her mouth open, obviously in a state of considerable excitement, occasionally putting ineffective finishing touches to the table.*)

Cook. 'Ere, Annie, 'old this fork a minute, or we'll have to call the Fire Brigade to put my face out. (Annie *takes the fork.* Cook *fans herself with her apron.*)

Mrs. S. I once knew a woman whose front 'air caught fire when she was making toast, and before you could count ten the 'ole room was ablaze. They'd never 'ave been able to recognize her remains if it 'adn't been for 'er cameo brooch.

Cook. They must 'ave known who she was. (*Coming over to the mail-cart.*) And 'ow's her ladyship—who's a lovely girl, eh? Don't burn that toast, Annie. (*She clicks her tongue at the infant* Fanny.) Yer dad's comin' 'ome, duck, safe and sound. (*She chants in order to entertain* Fanny.) Safe and sound, safe and sound.

Mrs. S. I only 'ope 'e is safe and sound, I'm sure.

Cook. The telegram said 'e was.

Mrs. S. Maybe it was a lie to spare Ellen's feelings.

Cook. You're a cheerful one, I must say.

Mrs. S. When I was a girl a friend of mine's 'usband come back unexpected from the Crimea with no legs at all. (*This is too much for* Annie, *who drops the toast and goes off into snuffles of laughter.*)

Cook. Stop it, Annie—now look what you've done—cut another piece, quick, they'll be 'ere in a minute.

Mrs. S. I do 'ope Ellen didn't cry at the station, it does make her nose so red.

Cook. Alfred will be so pleased to see 'er 'e won't mind if it's red or blue. Come on, Annie, 'urry.

Annie. 'Ere they are.

Cook. 'Ere, quick! The rosette for baby. (*She rushes to the dresser and snatches up a red, white and blue rosette.*) You pin it on 'er, Mrs. Snapper, while I tidy me 'air.

Annie (*at window*). They've come in a cab. Oo-er! (*There is a great air of tension and excitement in the kitchen, while* Ellen's *and* Bridges' *legs appear down the area steps. The* Cabby *follows with* Bridges' *kit-bag, which is dumped in the passage.*)

Bridges *enters first, looking very hale and hearty.*

Bridges (*entering*). You settle the cab, Ellen, I want to see my love-a-duck. 'Allo, Cook—'allo, Ma—where's my girl? (*He kisses* Cook *and* Mrs. Snapper, *and then puts his head inside the pram.*) 'Allo, Fanny. Coo, 'aven't you grown. Ma, you 'aven't 'arf bin feedin' 'er up. (*He makes delighted gurgling noises and prods the baby with his finger.*) See 'er laugh—she knows 'er dad. (*He puts his head inside again, apparently kissing her heartily.*)

Ellen *comes in flushed and happy.*

Ellen. I thought that train would never come—an whole hour I waited—an' all the people yellin' and screamin'. 'Ere, Alfred, take yer great 'ead out of that pram; you'll frighten 'er.

Bridges (*withdrawing*). She knows me, that's wot—she knows 'er old dad. Look at 'er rosette and all, smart as my eye. (*He turns and sees* Annie.) 'Ere, who's this? We 'aven't 'ad the pleasure.

Ellen. This is Annie.

Bridges. 'Ullo, Annie.

Annie (*giggling*). Welcome 'ome, Mr. Bridges. (Annie *and* Bridges *shake hands.*)

Bridges (*putting his arm round* Mrs. Snapper). Well, Ma, 'ow's everything?

Mrs. S. I mustn't grumble.

Bridges. So I should just think not. I got a surprise for you.

Mrs. S. What is it?

Bridges. Ellen knows; I told 'er in the cab. Tell 'er, Ellen.

Ellen. No, you. Go on.

Bridges. Well, you know I said in my letters about a lad called Smart—'Erbert Smart.

---

36. Crimea, the large peninsula of southern Russia projecting into the Black Sea, and the theater of the war (1853-1856) between the British and French on one side and the Russians on the other.

Cook. Yes, Ellen read your letters aloud.
Bridges. Not all of 'em, I 'ope.
Ellen. Get on with you, you never let yourself go further than a P.S. and a couple of crosses.
Bridges. Well, 'Erbert Smart's got a pub, see, and he's staying out in Africa, and I've bought it from 'im cheap, see? So much a year until it's paid off. We always wanted to 'ave somewhere of our own, and you can come and live with us, Ma—'ow's that suit?
Mrs. S. A pub—is it a respectable pub?
Bridges. All depends on 'ow you behave, Ma, you know what you are when you've 'ad a couple.
Mrs. S. (sniggering). Oh, Alfred, 'ow can you?
Bridges. Well, what d'you think about it?
Mrs. S. It sounds lovely—but 'ow about them upstairs?
Bridges. That's all right. I took the master into me confidence. He wished me luck.
Mrs. S. (breaking down). Oh, dear, I can 'ardly believe it, not 'aving to live alone any more—oh, dear!
Bridges. 'Ere, cheer up, Ma. Come on, 'ave a cup of tea. There ain't nothing to cry about. Let's all 'ave tea, for God's sake. Come on, Cook, me old girl—'ow'd you like to be a barmaid, eh? *(They all sit down to tea, a grand tea with eggs and shrimps. Everybody is talking at once. Suddenly the cry of a newsboy outside cuts through their conversation.)*
Bridges. What's 'e yelling about?
Cook (giving ANNIE *a halfpenny).* 'Ere, Annie, go and get one, quick. (ANNIE *runs out of the area steps. There is silence in the kitchen.)*
Bridges. What's up? What's the matter?
Ellen. It isn't anything to concern us.
Cook. Ellen, 'ow can you—it concerns the whole country.
ANNIE *comes clattering back with the paper.* BRIDGES *snatches paper from* ANNIE *and reads it.*
Bridges (reading). Whew! The Queen—it says she's sinking!

47. **The Queen . . . sinking.** Queen Victoria died the following day (January 22, 1901).

Mrs. S. There now—I told you so.
Cook (taking paper). Let's 'ave a look.
Annie. She's very old, ain't she?
Cook. Be quiet, Annie. What's that got to do with it?
Annie. Well, I never seen 'er.
Bridges. I 'ave—driving along Birdcage Walk once—years ago. Coo! England won't 'arf seem funny without the Queen! *(The lights fade out.)*

PART ONE : SCENE VI

PRINCIPALS: ROBERT, JANE, MARGARET, EDITH, EDWARD, JOE.
SCENE: *Kensington Gardens. There is a row of high railings down stage so that the audience can see through them the trees and shrubs and seats and people and dogs.*
TIME: *About noon, Sunday, January 27th, 1901.*

(During the course of this scene there should be no word spoken. Everyone is in black and they walk slowly as though perpetually conscious of the country's mourning. Even the children are in black and one WOMAN *leading a large brown dog has tied an enormous black crêpe bow on to his collar.* ROBERT *and* JANE *walk slowly from the left, followed by* EDWARD *and* JOE. MARGARET HARRIS *and* EDITH *come from right. They all meet and carry on a subdued conversation for a moment centre, and then part and go their different ways as the lights fade on the scene.)*

PART ONE : SCENE VII

PRINCIPALS: JANE, MARGARET, EDWARD, JOE, EDITH, ELLEN, BRIDGES, COOK, ANNIE.
SCENE: *Drawing-room of a London house.*
TIME: *About noon, Saturday, February 2nd, 1901.*

(When the lights go up, the children, EDWARD, JOE *and* EDITH, *all in black, are discovered out on the balcony.* MARGARET *and* JANE *are seated on the sofa. There is a small table beside* MARGARET *and* JANE *on which there is hot cocoa and cake.)*

Joe (on balcony). Mum, mum, there's a policeman on a lovely white horse!

Jane. Don't jump about, darling, and get hot and excited. Edward, keep Joe as quiet as possible.

Edward. All right, mum.

Jane. More cocoa, Margaret?

Margaret. No, thank you, dear.

Jane. I feel listless and sad, as though her death were a personal grief. Strange, isn't it?

Margaret. I think everyone feels that. *(She rises and goes to the window.)* All those crowds and crowds of people; they've been waiting for hours so patient and quiet. There's hardly a sound.

Joe (running in). Mum, could I ever be a policeman?

Jane. Perhaps, darling—if you're good.

Joe. Are all policemen good?

Jane. Yes, dear, as good as gold.

Joe. Why did Queen Victoria die, mum?

Jane. Because she was a very old lady, and very tired.

Joe. Could I have another piece of cake?

Jane. You won't be able to eat any luncheon.

Joe. I'd rather have the cake.

Jane (smiling). Very well, then—a small piece. Take some out to Edward and Edith.

Joe. Thanks, mum. *(Joe dashes out on to the balcony with the cake.)*

Margaret. How proud you must feel, Jane. All your troubles are over—Robert's home, Jim's home. Robert has a V.C.

Jane. Jim ought to have a V.C. too. All those dreadful months.

Edward (rushing in). They're coming! They're coming! Quick—quick!

Jane (rising). Run and fetch Ellen and Bridges and Cook. *(Edward tears out of the room.)*

Joe *rushes in.*

Joe. Mum, please come out. I dropped a bit of cake. I couldn't help it. Edward pushed me. *(Jane goes out and looks over. An intelligible voice is heard below.)*

Jane (leaning over). I'm very sorry, it was an accident. *(The voice mumbles something.)* He didn't throw it—he dropped it. It was an accident. *(She comes in again.)* Did you throw it, Joe, on purpose? *(Joe hangs his head.)* You're a very naughty little boy indeed, and I've a very good mind not to let you see the procession at all.

Edith *comes in. Following* Edith *are* Edward, Ellen, Bridges, Cook *and* Annie, *very smartened up.*

Edward. Mum, will father be riding in the beginning part or the end part?

Jane. The beginning, I think. Cook, you'd better come out here, Annie, too. Ellen, look after them, will you? Bridges, oughtn't you to be wearing a coat, it's very cold?

Bridges. I'm all right, thank you, ma'am. Warm as toast.

Edward (on balcony). Here they come—quickly, mum! *(Everybody crowds out on to the two balconies. There is dead silence and then far away the solemn music of the Dead March is heard. As it draws nearer the children jump about excitedly.)*

Joe (suddenly). Look, look—there's father—there's father!

Jane. Shhh! Joe, be quiet—keep still. *(The procession continues. Suddenly there is an outburst of cheering from the crowd which is instantly subdued.)* That's Lord Roberts. He held up his hand to stop them cheering.

Joe. Is that Bobs, mum—is that Bobs?

Edward. Look, look—one-armed Giffard. Oh, mother, look——

Jane. Shhh! Now then, Joe, Edward, stand absolutely still—to attention, like father showed you. *(The* Boys *stand rigid with their hands to their sides.* Bridges *stands rigid with his hands to his sides, on the other balcony. The music swells as the band passes directly underneath them. As it begins to die away* Cook *bursts into tears.)*

Jane. Five kings riding behind her.

Joe. Mum, she must have been a very little lady. *(The lights fade.)*

PART ONE : SCENE VIII

Principals: Robert, Jane, Duchess of Churt, Major Domo.

---

34. **V.C.**, The Victoria Cross, the chief military honor awarded to members of the British armed forces.

80. **Giffard**, Hardinge Stanley Giffard (1823-1921), Lord Chancellor under Prime Ministers Salisbury and Balfour.

SCENE: *The Grand Staircase of a London house. The head of the staircase is down stage. The stairs descending downwards and out of sight. Behind the well of the staircase can be seen, between columns, the beautifully decorated ballroom in which an orchestra is playing the popular waltzes of the day and people are dancing. The Ball is in full swing.*

TIME: *About 11 p.m. Thursday, May 14th, 1903.*

(When the lights go up, the full splendor of a typical Edwardian Ball should, if possible, burst upon the audience. On the right and left of the staircase a balustraded balcony leads to the ballroom at the entrance of which FOOTMEN *stand with programmes to hand to the guests. The* DUCHESS OF CHURT *stands near the head of the stairs. Near the* DUCHESS OF CHURT *stands the* MAJOR DOMO, *who announces each guest in stentorian tones. There is a steady babel of conversation and music, but above it all can be heard the names of guests as they are announced. One by one, or sometimes escorted, come the great beauties of the day. They are all received by the* DUCHESS *and then make their way towards the ballroom. Finally the* MAJOR DOMO *announces:* "SIR ROBERT *and* LADY MARRYOT" *and* ROBERT *and* JANE *appear,* ROBERT *with full decorations, and* JANE *in an elaborate ball gown. As they are received by their hostess the lights fade and the curtain falls.)*

PART TWO : SCENE I

PRINCIPALS: JANE, EDWARD *(aged 18)*, ELLEN, FANNY *(aged 7)*, MRS. SNAPPER, GEORGE, FLO, BRIDGES.

SCENE: *The Bar Parlour of a London pub.*

TIME: *About 5 p.m. Saturday, June 16th, 1906.*

(When the curtain rises High Tea is just over. Seated round the table are JANE, EDWARD, MRS. SNAPPER, FLO *and* GEORGE GRAINGER. FLO *and* GEORGE *are very smartly got up.* ELLEN *is seated at the piano with her back to the room.* FANNY, *aged 7, is dancing. When the dance is finished, everyone applauds.)*

Jane. She dances beautifully, Ellen. Come here, dear. (FANNY *goes to her.*) I knew you when you were a little tiny baby.

Flo. She's a born dancer, if you ask me—haighly talented, haighly.

Ellen (leaving the piano). She certainly does love it. On the go all day she is, jigging about.

Mrs. S. Can I press you to another cup, your ladyship?

Jane. No, thank you, we really must be going in a moment.

Flo (to EDWARD*).* 'Ow was Hoxford when you left it, Mr. Marryot?

Edward. Awfully nice.

Flo. I've never been there mayself, but George 'as, haven't you, George?

George. Oh, yes, nice place, Oxford. Very antique—if you know what I mean.

Ellen. I'm so glad to 'ear the master, Sir Robert, is well.

Jane. He was so sorry not to be able to come down, but as you know, he's a very busy man these days. He wished very specially to be remembered to you and your husband. He'll be sorry to hear that he's ill.

George. Ill! Alf ill! What's wrong with him? (MRS. SNAPPER *nudges* GEORGE *violently.* ELLEN *speaks hurriedly.)*

Ellen. Before you and Flo come, George, I was explaining to 'er ladyship about poor Alfred's bad leg.

George. Bad leg?

Mrs. S. (frowning at GEORGE*).* Yes, very bad—'e's been in 'orrible agony since Sunday.

George. Where is 'e?

Ellen. Upstairs in bed.

George. I'll pop up and see 'im.

Ellen. He's asleep now.

Flo. 'Ow did 'e come to 'ave the haccident?

Mrs. S. (firmly and with great emphasis). Cycling, Flo. He was cycling and 'e fell orf.

Flo. I didn't know 'e 'ad a cycle.

Mrs. S. 'E 'asn't any more.

Jane (rising). Well, you will tell him how

sorry we were not to have seen him, won't you? And I do hope he'll soon be quite well again. Come along, Edward. We really must go now.

Edward (rising). All right, Mother.

Ellen. It was so kind of you, ma'am, to come all this way to see us and to bring Fanny that lovely doll, and everything. Fanny, come and say good-bye to 'er ladyship. (FANNY *makes an abortive effort at a curtsey.* JANE *bends down and kisses* FANNY.)

Jane. Good-bye, Fanny. *(To* MRS. SNAPPER.) Good-bye, Mrs. Snapper. *(She shakes hands.)* Good-bye. *(She bows to* FLO *and* GEORGE.)

Flo. Pleased to 'ave made your acquaintance, I'm sure.

Jane (to ELLEN). Good-bye, Ellen, it's been delightful seeing you again, and to find you well and happy. Don't fail to remember me to Bridges; my husband and I miss you both still, it seems only yesterday that you were with us.

Ellen. We miss you, too, ma'am.

Jane. Time changes many things, but it can't change old friends, can it?

Ellen (emotionally). No ma'am. Oh, no, ma'am. (EDWARD, *who has been saying his good-bye to* MRS. SNAPPER *and* FLO *and* GEORGE, *joins* JANE.)

Edward. Good-bye, Ellen. Good luck.

Ellen. Good-bye, Master Edward. Thank you for coming——

JANE *and* EDWARD *are about to leave when the street door bursts open and* BRIDGES *staggers into the room. He looks unkempt and unshaven, and is obviously drunk. There is a moment of horrible silence.* BRIDGES *sees* JANE *and* EDWARD *and pulls up short.*

Ellen (in agonised tones). Oh, Alfred!

Bridges. Ow! So that's why you wash trying to get me out of the way——

Mrs. S. Alfred Bridges, be'ave yourself and take yer 'at orf.

Bridges (bowing low to JANE). Pleashed to see you again, milady, I'm shure—welcome to our 'ovel. *(He lurches toward* JANE. JANE *makes an instinctive movement away from* BRIDGES. BRIDGES *draws himself up unsteadily.)*

Bridges. Ow! I shee—proud and 'aughty, are we——

Ellen (wildly). Alfred, stop it! Stop it!

Jane (suddenly coming forward and taking both ELLEN's *hands in hers).* Ellen—dear Ellen—I'm so very, very sorry, and I quite understand. Please don't be upset and let me come and see you again soon. (JANE *goes out with* EDWARD. *Again there is silence.* ELLEN *bursts into hopeless sobbing.)*

Mrs. S. You drunken great brute!

Bridges. Shut yer mouth. You mind yours and I'll mind mine.

George. Look 'ere, 'ole man, you'd better come up and 'ave a lie down. *(He takes* BRIDGES' *arm.)*

Bridges (pushing GEORGE *away).* Leave me alone. Lot of shnobs—that's wot—lot of bloody shnobs. I'm not good enough to be 'ome when the quality comes. Ow, no—we'll see who'sh good enough.

Ellen (wailing). Oh, oh, oh! I'll never be able to raise me 'ead again—never—never——

Bridges. 'Oo give Fanny that doll? 'Er noble ladyship?

Mrs. S. (stepping forward). You let the child alone.

Bridges (pushing MRS. SNAPPER *so hard that she falls against the table).* I can buy me own child a doll, can't I? Don't want any bloody charity 'ere. *(He snatches the doll from* FANNY *and pitches it into the fire.* FANNY *screams.* FLO *makes a dart at the fireplace and finally gets the doll out.* FANNY *continues to scream.* ELLEN *goes for* BRIDGES. BRIDGES *hits* ELLEN. FLO *and* GEORGE *grab* BRIDGES *and push him out of the room.* ELLEN, *sobbing, takes* FANNY *in her arms.* MRS. SNAPPER *sinks into a chair.)*

Ellen. She was right——she was right. Time changes many things——*(The lights fade.)*

PART TWO : SCENE II

PRINCIPALS: FANNY, FLO.

SCENE: *A London street. The exterior of the public house—the bar parlour of which was the preceding scene—is down stage left. There is a street leading away into darkness up left, and another turning a corner* up right. A wedge of houses separates the two streets. There are people at most of the windows of the houses. Down stage right are more houses.

TIME: *About 10 p.m. Saturday, June 16th, 1906.*

(*The centre of the stage is crowded with people and barrows lit by naphtha flares. There is another pub up right from which comes the sound of a penny-in-the-slot piano and the sound of singing and laughter. Everyone is moving about and talking. Women with caps and shawls and string bags are shopping at the booths. Some sailors come out of the left pub with two flashily-dressed girls and roll across to the pub opposite, into which they disappear. A policeman walks through the crowd and goes off. A German band assembles down stage left and begins to play, effectively drowning the noise of three Coster youths playing mouth-organs. A few Costers in pearlies start dancing, a ring is made around them, and people applaud and yell from the windows. A Salvation Army band marches on right and proceeds to play and sing hymns, against the German band. A few people make a ring round them and begin singing.* FANNY *comes out of the pub left and begins to dance by herself. Some of the crowd laugh and those who are dancing stop and applaud her. A Coster darts forward and puts his pearly cap on* FANNY'S *head.* BRIDGES *comes reeling out of the pub——sees* FANNY, *and tries to grab hold of her. He is prevented by the crowd and* BRIDGES *is pushed off the stage up right. Suddenly from just where* BRIDGES *has gone there comes a shout and then an agonising scream. The policeman runs across in the direction of the noise. All the crowd, scenting a street accident, surge off, including the German band. Exeunt crowd and German band.* FLO *comes flying out of the pub and* FLO *disappears with the crowd.* FANNY *continues to dance in pool of light shed by a street lamp, to the rather dismal music of the Salvation Army.* FLO *comes rushing back and hammers on the door of the pub.*)

Flo. Ellen! Ellen! It's Alfred—'e's been run over—'e's dead. Ellen! Ellen! (*The lights fade.*)

PART TWO : SCENE III

PRINCIPALS: EDWARD (*aged 21*), JOE (*aged 17*), TIM BATEMAN, DOUGLAS FINN, LORD MARTLET (CHUBBY), MARION CHRISTIE, NETTA LAKE (*pianist*), ROSE DARLING (*Ada in "Mirabelle"*), CONNIE CRAWSHAY, DAISY DEVON.

SCENE: *Private room in a popular London restaurant. A supper table set for ten is on one side of the stage. There is a sofa up at the back and another down stage right, and an upright piano.*

TIME: *About 1 a.m. Wednesday, March 10th, 1909.*

(*Round the table are seated* EDWARD [*twenty-one*], TIM BATEMAN, DOUGLAS FINN, MARION CHRISTIE, NETTA LAKE *and* ROSE DARLING. *On the sofa up stage in a more or less amorous attitude are seated* LORD MARTLET [CHUBBY] *and* DAISY DEVON. *On the down stage sofa is seated* JOE [*aged seventeen*] *with* CONNIE CRAWSHAY, *a very fat blonde. Everyone is very gay. They are all in evening dress. The men in white ties and the women elaborately and slightly theatrically fashionable.* JOE *is obviously the youngest present and appears well on the way to being very drunk.*)

Rose (*rising, with a glass of champagne in her hand*). I want to propose a toast—to our host!

Everyone. Hear, hear! (*Etc.*)

Marion. A lovely little toastie to our lovely little hostie.

Rose. Health, wealth and happiness to our Eddie!

Everyone (*repeating*). Health, wealth and happiness! Eddie! (*Etc. They clink glasses.*)

Connie (*to* JOE). Here, sit up. They're drinking your brother's health.

Joe (*rising unsteadily*). Hear, hear—a thousand times hear, hear! (*They all sing "For*

---

15. **Coster youths.** "Coster," or costermonger, was the name given originally to street-vendors of fruits and vegetables, but tradition came to apply the name to street-entertainers; they cultivate a costume covered with buttons and sequins (cf. *pearlies* in line 16).

he's a jolly good fellow," which tails off into cries for "speech.")

Edward (rising). Ladies and gentlemen——

Joe (loudly). Hurray!

Edward. Shut up, Joe.

Joe. I won't shut up. Connie agrees with me, don't you, Connie?

Connie. Yes, dear, completely, dear. Shut up, dear.

Joe. Good old Connie. *(He subsides on* CONNIE's *lap.)*

Edward (continuing). First of all, in response to your charming toast, I want to apologise for the presence here to-night of my scrubby little brother Joe. *(Laughter.)*

Joe. Here—I say! (CONNIE *puts her hand over* JOE's *mouth.)*

Edward. He is a crawling, loathsome little creature, as you see, and he really ought not to be here at all, but in his little cot at Eton. I felt, however, that as his elder brother, it was my duty to show him how grown-up people behave. Bring him over here, Connie —he must be christened in Clicquot.

Connie. He's almost confirmed in it already. (CONNIE *drags* JOE *over to the table where, protesting loudly, he is anointed by* EDWARD *with champagne.)*

Joe. I must speak now. I want to speak.

Connie. Let him speak, dear, he's having a lovely time.

Joe. Ladies and gentlemen—I have always looked up to my elder brother Edward. He has always been my ideal of what a great big gas-bag should be, and I take this opportunity of asking Connie to marry me. *(Laughter.)*

Connie. Oh, isn't he sweet!

Rose. You can't have Connie, Joe, she's married already; you'd better choose me. I'm a widow. *(Everybody chants "The Merry Widow" waltz for a moment.)*

Joe. But I love Connie.

Connie. Very well, dear, come back to the sofa, dear. *(She leads* JOE *back.)*

Edward (to LORD MARTLET). Chubby, come out of that corner, you've been there long enough.

Daisy (coming down). Quite long enough. This takes me back to the old days of private hansoms. *(She fans herself.)* Give me a drink, somebody.

Marion (gloomily). I was once sick in a private hansom.

Rose. That must have been lovely, dear; tell us about it.

Marion. Well, it was the two hundredth performance of "Floradora."

Rose. By God, she's going to!

Marion. And they suddenly put me in the sextette without a rehearsal, and I suppose the excitement went to my stomach.

Rose. I was in "Mirabelle" then, with poor old Laura Marsden.

Edward. "Mirabelle"! I was taken to see that. Mother was there on Mafeking night. She took me a few weeks later to a matinée.

Marion. Taken to see it, were you! That dates us a bit.

Edward. I remember now. You were Ada——

Rose. Yes, I was Ada.

Marion. And Laura Marsden was Mirabelle, and Mikey Banks was Tom. What a cast that was!

Tim. What happened to Laura Marsden?

Rose. She died. *(She makes a significant drinking gesture.)*

Tim. Oh, I see.

Rose. Nine years ago. Give me another drink, or I shall get reminiscent like Marion. (NETTA *goes over to the piano and starts thumping the Mirabelle waltz.)* Oh, shut up!

Edward. Sing it, Rose.

Rose. I can't—haven't got any voice.

Everyone. Come on, Rose—sing it. Come on, you're among friends.

Rose. I can't sing it like Laura used to. *(She sings the refrain of the waltz, occasionally forgetting a word or two. Everybody applauds.)*

Marion. They do take you back, don't they, those old tunes. (NETTA *strikes up "Keep off the Grass." The girls sing it together. None of the men are really old enough to remember it.)*

---

41. **"The Merry Widow,"** the most celebrated and popular of the operettas by the Hungarian composer Franz Lehár (1870-1948).

58. **"Floradora,"** another highly successful and popular musical comedy (1899) by Owen Hall and Leslie Stuart.

Chubby. Play something we all know. (NETTA *starts "Mary" from "Miss Gibbs."* Everyone joins in. They all go into "The Merry Widow" waltz and sing it lustily as the lights fade.)

PART TWO : SCENE IV

PRINCIPALS: JANE, ROBERT, JOE, MARGARET, ELLEN, FANNY, MRS. SNAPPER, FLO, GEORGE, 1ST WOMAN, 2ND WOMAN, UNCLE GEORGE, UNCLE DICK.
SCENE: *The beach of a popular seaside resort.*
TIME: *About 6 p.m. Monday, July 25th, 1910.*

(*The Parade runs along the back about 10 feet above stage level. Down stage left a bandstand on the same level as the Parade juts out on to the beach. On the right the high supports of a swimming enclosure. There are bathing machines and huts and deck chairs—in fact, all the paraphernalia of a popular seaside town in July. The beach is crowded with people, some paddling, some playing games, and a lot clustered round an open-air stage, listening to* UNCLE GEORGE'S *concert party. The Concert Party consists of six men:* UNCLE DICK, UNCLE BOB, UNCLE HARRY, UNCLE JIM, UNCLE JACK *and* UNCLE GEORGE *himself. They are all dressed in straw hats, coloured blazers and rather grubby white flannel trousers. People are constantly passing to and fro along the Parade, and leaning on the railing, looking down on to the beach. When the curtain rises* UNCLE GEORGE *is singing "Put a little bit away for a rainy day." He finishes with a great flourish, then steps forward.*)

Uncle George. Ladies and gentlemen and kiddies—I am very happy to announce that the winner of this week's Song and Dance Competition is little Miss Fanny Bridges. (*Everyone applauds.*) And it gives me great pleasure to present her with this handsome prize as a souvenir of Uncle George and his merry men. Come on up, my dear. (ELLEN [*in black*] *hoists* FANNY *up from the front row.* FANNY *is hoisted up by* ELLEN. *She is wearing a white dress with a black sash.* UNCLE GEORGE *kisses* FANNY *and presents her with a box of chocolates. The audience clap and one little girl is led away yelling, apparently an unsuccessful competitor.*)

Uncle George. And now, to conclude this programme Uncle Dick will sing "Take me back to Yorkshire." (UNCLE DICK *rises and sings. All the rest join in the chorus, and then, after perfunctory applause, the crowd round the booth disperses.* UNCLE GEORGE *and his* MERRY MEN *pack up their props and disappear in due course up the steps on to the Parade. Exeunt* UNCLE GEORGE *and his* MERRY MEN. ELLEN *and* FANNY *walk across the beach with* MRS. SNAPPER, FLO *and* GEORGE. *They meet* MARGARET HARRIS, JANE *and* JOE.)

Jane. Why, it can't be—Ellen—what a surprise! (*They shake hands.*)
Ellen. Oh, ma'am—I'd no idea—fancy you being here!
Jane. Margaret, Joe, you remember Ellen, don't you?
Margaret (*shaking hands*). Of course! yes —how do you do, Ellen?
Joe. Hullo, Ellen.
Ellen. You remember mother—Mrs. Snapper—and Flo and George, my cousins by marriage?
Jane. Yes, indeed.
Mrs. S. Delighted, I'm sure. (*Everyone shakes hands and talks politely.*)
Ellen. Well, Master Joe, 'ow you 'ave grown. Quite the young man about town! How's Master Edward?
Joe. He's here. He and Edith have been to a concert on the pier. They'll be along soon.
Ellen (*to* JANE). I got your letter, ma'am, when my Alfred died; it was kind of you to write.
Jane. How is your business going?
Ellen. Oh, very well, really. I've managed to save quite a bit one way and another, and now I've closed the 'ole place for a month so as to give Fanny a holiday. She goes to dancing school now. She's going on the stage.
Margaret. Surely she's very young.
Mrs. S. She's set on it—plain set on it.
ROBERT *comes down on to the beach. He has grey hair now and looks very distinguished.*
Robert. Jane—there you are—Why, Ellen!

---
2. "Miss Gibbs," a musical comedy of 1900.

(He shakes hands. All the introductions start all over again. Two elderly women pass in front of them, talking.)

1st Woman. She went on board the ship dressed as a boy, and that's how the Captain recognized them.

2nd Woman. 'Er 'air probably come down under 'er cap.

1st Woman. I don't know 'ow she managed at meals. She couldn't wear 'er cap then.

2nd Woman. It's Mrs. Crippen that gets on my mind, poor dear, being all chopped up into little tiny pieces—— *(They pass on and up the steps. Meanwhile the* MARRYOTS *and* ELLEN *are parting company.)*

Ellen. It's been lovely seeing you again ma'am, and you, too, Mrs. Harris. I expect your Edith has grown into a great big girl by now. I remember her when she was ever so small. (To ROBERT.) Good-bye, sir—good-bye, Master Joe.

Robert. Good-bye, Ellen.

Joe. Good-bye.

Jane. You must come and see us one day—bring Fanny to tea.

Ellen. Thank you, ma'am—I'd like to see the 'ouse again. I was very 'appy there——

(The MARRYOTS *and* MARGARET *go off.* MRS. SNAPPER, ELLEN *and* FANNY *rejoin* FLO *and* GEORGE, *who have been standing waiting for them a little way off. The band, having assembled, breaks into a gay march. A man walks along with a tray of pink rock, yelling. All dialogue is drowned in the noise of the band. Several children dodge in and out, playing Tag. One child falls down and screams. Suddenly there is the noise of an aeroplane. Everyone screams and surges down to the beach, staring upwards. The band stops abruptly and cranes out of the bandstand. People half dressed rush out of bathing machines. Somebody starts cheering —then everyone takes it up. The aeroplane noise grows fainter. The band strikes up again. A troop of Boy Scouts with a very sour six-piece band march along the Parade. Suddenly there is a roll of thunder. Everyone looks up apprehensively, people on the beach begin to collect their children and belongings. It starts to rain, gently at first, then develops into a downpour. People put their coat collars up and run. Several umbrellas go up, then more, until the whole beach becomes a sea of umbrellas. Gradually everyone scurries off. The bandstand has by now let down its weather blinds. One fat old woman is left asleep in a deck chair. A tremendous roll of thunder wakes her abruptly and she struggles to get up, and falls back into the chair, which collapses.)*

PART TWO: SCENE V

PRINCIPALS: EDWARD, EDITH.

SCENE: *The deck of an Atlantic liner. This is quite a small inset scene. The rail of the Promenade Deck faces the audience. Behind it can be seen the lighted windows of the lounge. Above can be seen vaguely the Boat Deck, with ventilators and a funnel silhouetted against the stars.*

TIME: *About 7 p.m. Sunday, April 14th, 1912.*

*(*EDWARD *and* EDITH, *he in dinner-jacket, she in evening dress, are leaning on the rail.)*

Edith. It's too big, the Atlantic, isn't it?

Edward. Far too big.

Edith. And too deep.

Edward. Much, much too deep.

Edith. I don't care a bit, do you?

Edward. Not a scrap.

Edith. Wouldn't it be awful if a magician came to us and said: "Unless you count accurately every single fish in the Atlantic you die to-night?"

Edward. We should die to-night.

Edith. How much would you mind—dying, I mean?

Edward. I don't know really—a good deal, I expect.

Edith. I don't believe I should mind so very much now. You see, we could never in our whole lives be happier than we are now, could we?

---

11. **Mrs. Crippen . . . pieces.** The reference is to the most celebrated murder case in England in 1910. Early in the year, Dr. H. H. Crippen, an American-born dentist in London, murdered his wife by giving her poison and then buried her under the cement floor in their cellar. He then fled to Canada with his secretary but was apprehended when he landed; it was the first time that radio had been used to track a killer. His trial was a classic of British criminal jurisprudence; he was eventually found guilty and hanged.   38. **aeroplane.** The plane seen here is that which is carrying Louis Blériot (1872-1936) on the first flight across the English Channel.
42. **bathing machines,** movable bath-houses at the beach.

Edward. Darling, there *are* different sorts of happiness.

Edith. This is the best sort.

Edward (kissing her). Sweetheart!

Edith. Don't, darling, we don't want any more of the stewards to know we're on our honeymoon.

Edward. Why not? It gives them so much vicarious pleasure. Most of them have forgotten what it was like.

Edith. Are all honeymoons like this?

Edward (firmly). Exactly.

Edith. Oh, Edward—that's rather disheartening, isn't it? I do so want this to be unique.

Edward. It is, for us.

Edith. Did you ever think when we were children, going to the pantomime, and going to the zoo, and playing soldiers, that we should ever be married?

Edward. Of course I didn't.

Edith. Was I nice as a child?

Edward. Horrible!

Edith. So were you, and so was Joe—vile. You always used to take sides against me.

Edward. And yet we all liked one another really.

Edith. I think I liked Joe better than you, but then he was younger and easier to manage. Dear Joe, he was awfully funny at the wedding, wasn't he?

Edward. Ribald little beast!

Edith. He has no reverence, I'm afraid.

Edward. Absolutely none.

Edith. He's passing gallantly through the chorus-girl phase now, isn't he?

Edward. Gallantly but not quickly.

Edith. Well, darling, you took your time over it.

Edward. Now then, Edith——

Edith. You had several affairs before you married me, didn't you?

Edward. Light of my life, shut up!

Edith. You'd be awfully cross if *I* had, wouldn't you?

Edward. Had what?

Edith. Affairs—love affairs—before you.

Edward. Did you?

Edith. Hundreds.

Edward. Liar!

Edith. I rather wish I had, really. Perhaps I should have learnt some tricks to hold you with when you begin to get tired of me.

Edward. I never shall, tricks or no tricks.

Edith. Yes, you will one day. You're bound to; people always do. This complete loveliness that we feel together now will fade, so many years and the gilt wears off the gingerbread, and just the same as the stewards, we shall have forgotten what it was like.

Edward (seriously). Answer me one thing truly, dearest. Have you ever seen gingerbread with gilt on it?

Edith. Never!

Edward. Then the whole argument is disposed of. Anyhow, look at father and mother; they're perfectly happy and devoted, and they always have been.

Edith. They had a better chance at the beginning. Things weren't changing so swiftly; life wasn't so restless.

Edward. How long do you give us?

Edith. I don't know—and Edward—*(She turns to him.)* I don't care. This is our moment—complete and heavenly. I'm not afraid of anything. This is our own, for ever. (EDWARD *takes* EDITH *in his arms and kisses her.*)

Edward. Do you think a nice warming glass of sherry would make it any more heavenly?

Edith. You have no soul, darling, but I'm very attached to you. Come on—(EDITH *takes up her cloak which has been hanging over the rail, and they walk away. The cloak has been covering a life-belt, and when it is withdrawn the words "S. S. Titanic" can be seen in black letters on the white. The lights fade into complete darkness, but the letters remain glowing as the orchestra plays very softly and tragically "Nearer, My God, to Thee."*)

---

85. **"S. S. Titanic."** Shortly before midnight on the night of April 14, 1912, the White Star liner *Titanic*, at the time the largest ship in the world and supposedly "unsinkable," on its maiden voyage to New York rammed into an iceberg in mid-Atlantic while traveling (in spite of warnings) at full speed. A little less than three hours later it sank, carrying to their deaths more than fifteen hundred persons. It remains the greatest peace-time marine catastrophe in history. 89. **"Nearer . . . Thee."** Tradition has it that the ship's orchestra, which assembled on the main deck of the *Titanic* and played while such passengers as could be accommodated were being hustled into the too-few lifeboats, played the hymn "Nearer, My God, to Thee" at the end. The best authenticated reports have it that the melody played was "Autumn" by Sir Arthur Sullivan. The fact remains, however, that this melody is often used in England for a setting to the well-known hymn.

PART TWO : SCENE VI

PRINCIPALS: JANE, ROBERT, JOE, MARGARET.
SCENE: *The drawing-room of a London house. The room is dark; the blinds are down over the windows.*
TIME: *About 11:16 p.m. Tuesday, August 4th, 1914.*

(*There is the sound of voices outside. Enter* JANE *and* MARGARET, *both in travelling clothes.* JANE *turns on the lights and the room is seen to be enshrouded in dust-sheets.*)

Jane (*shuddering*). Why is it that a house that's been shut up for a little while feels so awful? (*She goes to the windows, pulls up the blinds, and opens the windows wide.*) There! That's better. It's stifling.

Margaret (*taking off her hat and coat*). That was definitely the most uncomfortable journey I've ever experienced.

JOE *rushes in.*
He still has his hat and coat on.

Joe. Mum, have you got any change? Father and I have both run out.

Margaret. I have—here—(*She fumbles in her bag.*) How much d'you want?

Joe. Four bob.

Margaret. There's half-a-crown and two shillings.

Joe. Thanks, Aunt Margaret. (JOE *goes out again.*)

Jane. Help me with these dust-sheets, Margaret. Put them anywhere. We'll get a char in to-morrow to clean up. (*They proceed to pull the dust-sheets off the furniture.*) I shall never go on a holiday again, ever. It's horrid when you're there, and much worse when you come back.

Margaret. Still it's better to be here in London if anything's going to happen.

Jane. It's going to happen all right. I'm afraid there's no doubt about it, now.

Margaret (*glancing out of the window*). There seem to be lots more people in the streets than usual—where on earth do they all come from?

JOE *comes in, this time without his hat and coat.*

19. **bob**, a shilling. 20. **half-a-crown**, two and a half shillings. 25. **char**, charwoman.

Joe. Well, that's that!
Jane. Where's father?
Joe. Groping about in the wine cellar like an angry old beetle. He says strong drink is essential in a crisis.
Jane. We must have something to eat, too. I wonder if there is anything.
Joe. There's a strong bit of cold tongue in the larder. I just put my head in and it sang the Marseillaise.
Jane. There must be some biscuits, or something. (JANE *goes out hurriedly.*)
Joe (*to* MARGARET). Cigarette? (*He offers her his case.*)
Margaret (*taking one*). Thank you, Joe.
Joe (*lighting them*). This is pretty thrilling, isn't it?
Margaret. Yes, I suppose so. I must really go and help Jane. (MARGARET *runs out, almost colliding with* ROBERT, *who is entering with two bottles and some glasses.*)
Robert. I could only find hock and port, and port's far too heavy at this time of night; so we'll have to drink to the downfall of Germany in their own damned wine.
Joe. I rather like Germans, don't you, Father?
Robert. Enormously. Move these things off the table, and help me open the bottles.
Joe (*doing so*). Got a corkscrew?
Robert. In my left pocket. (JOE *gropes for the corkscrew while* ROBERT *puts the bottles and glasses on the table.*)
Joe (*wrestling with a bottle*). If there is a war, how long do you think it will last?
Robert. Three months, at the outside.
Joe. I suppose we shall win, shan't we?
Robert. Yes—we shall win.
Joe (*hopefully*). Maybe it will last six months.
Robert. Leaving everything else aside, that would be economically quite impossible. Have you any idea of what a war costs, Joe, in actual money?
Joe. Hell of a lot, I should think.
Robert. You're quite right. And the Germans can afford it even less than we can. And then there's Russia.
Joe. Good old Russia!
Robert. And France and Italy and America.

Joe. And Japan and China and Finland—why, by God! we've got 'em licked before we start.

Robert. Don't be silly, Joe.

Joe. Are you glad you left the Army, Father, or sorry?

Robert. Absolutely delighted.

Joe. Will you go back again?

Robert. I expect so.

Joe. How will you feel about that?

Robert. Absolutely delighted.

Joe. I suppose I shall have to do something about it, too.

Robert. Do you want to?

Joe. Terribly.

Robert. Why?

Joe. I don't know. It's—it's sort of exciting, isn't it?

Robert. Yes, but don't set your hopes too high, Joey—it takes a lot of training to make a soldier. It will all be over before you get far.

Joe. I wish Edward hadn't been drowned, we could have started off together.

Robert (after a slight pause). Don't be too impulsive and patriotic and dashing, Joey. Think of your mother. Think of me, too, you're all we've got left. (ROBERT *abruptly puts down the bottle he is holding and goes out on to the balcony.* JOE *stands staring after* ROBERT *thoughtfully.*)

JANE *enters carrying a tray.* MARGARET *enters following* JANE, *with some plates.*

Jane. We found some potted meat and biscuits and Worcester Sauce; and the tongue doesn't look too bad.

Joe (taking the tray from JANE). It isn't its looks I object to, it's its personality. (JOE *puts the tray on the table. A newsboy runs by outside, shouting.* ROBERT *shouts from the balcony and goes hurriedly from the room.* JOE, JANE *and* MARGARET *stand stock still, waiting.*)

ROBERT *returns with the paper.*

Robert. We're at war, my dears.

Joe (grabbing the paper). Let me see—let me see——

Margaret. Listen—listen! (*From far away comes the sound of cheering.* MARGARET *runs out on the balcony for a moment, and then returns.* JANE *sinks down on a chair.*)

Jane. It's very hot, isn't it?

Joe. Don't look sad, mum. It won't last long; Father says it can't possibly; and it's terribly exciting.

Jane. I didn't mean to look sad; I feel rather tired.

Joe (handing JANE *a glass of wine).* Here, mum dear—have a nice sozzle. We ought all to get drunk really, and go roaring about the streets——

Jane. Edward missed this, anyhow. At least he died when he was happy, before the world broke over his head.

Robert. Don't take that view, dearest, it's foolish. We've had wars before without the world breaking.

Jane. My world isn't very big. (*A group of people pass along under the balcony laughing and cheering. Some of them start singing the "Marseillaise" and the others down them with "Rule Britannia."* JANE *gets up suddenly.*)

Jane. Drink to the war, then, if you want to. I'm not going to. I can't! Rule Britannia! Send us victorious, happy and glorious! Drink, Joey, you're only a baby, still, but you're old enough for war. Drink like the Germans are drinking, to Victory and Defeat, and stupid, tragic sorrow. But leave me out of it, please! (JANE *goes abruptly from the room. The lights fade.*)

PART TWO : SCENE VII

(*Above the proscenium* 1914 *glows in lights. It changes to* 1915-1916, 1917 *and* 1918. *Meanwhile, soldiers march uphill endlessly. Out of darkness into darkness. Sometimes they sing gay songs, sometimes they whistle, sometimes they march silently, but the sound of their tramping feet is unceasing. Below the vision of them brightly-dressed, energetic women appear in pools of light, singing stirring recruiting songs—"Sunday I walk out with a soldier," "We don't want to lose you," etc., etc. With* 1918 *they fade away, as also does the vision of the soldiers, although the soldiers can still be heard very far off, marching and singing their songs.*)

PART TWO : SCENE VIII

PRINCIPALS: JOE, FANNY.

Scene: *A restaurant.*
Time: *About 7:30 p.m. Tuesday, October 22nd, 1918.*

(Joe *and* Fanny *are seated at a table; they have just finished dinner.* Joe *is in officer's uniform.* Fanny *is in very charming day clothes. She is now nineteen and extremely attractive.*)

Joe (pouring some champagne into Fanny's *glass).* Have some more.

Fanny. Darling, I shall be tight. You don't want me to fall down during my first number, do you?

Joe. How much do you love me?

Fanny. Now, then, dear, we've had all this out before.

Joe. Will you send me a telegram to Dover?

Fanny. Of course I will. I promised, didn't I?

Joe. Once you get into the theatre, with all those changes, you might forget.

Fanny. I'll send Maggie out with it.

Joe. Dear old Maggie. Say good-bye to her for me, won't you?

Fanny. Aren't you coming down to talk to me while I make up?

Joe. No, I promised to go home. Mother's waiting for me.

Fanny. I shall have to give it to you now, then.

Joe. What?

Fanny. Just a little something I had made for you.

Joe. Oh, Fanny—what is it?

Fanny. Hold on a minute, dear. It's in my bag. *(She searches in her bag and produces a small packet.)* Here—with my love.

Joe (opening it). Oh, it's lovely.

Fanny. It's nothing really. Just a little souvenir of all the fun we've had.

Joe. You are a darling——

Fanny (grabbing it from Joe*).* Here, silly, you've missed the whole point. It opens— there. (Fanny *opens the little locket and discloses a minute photograph of herself.*)

Joe (taking it). It will be with me always, to the end of my days.

Fanny. You won't want it that long.

Joe. I almost wish I didn't love you quite so awfully. It makes going back much worse.

Fanny. I shall miss you dreadfully.

Joe. It has been fun, hasn't it?

Fanny. Lovely.

Joe. You don't regret it—any of it?

Fanny. Not a moment of it.

Joe. How wonderful you are. Do you really love me, I wonder, deep down inside, I mean?

Fanny. Yes, I think so.

Joe. Enough to marry me?

Fanny. Yes, but I wouldn't.

Joe. Why not?

Fanny. It would be too difficult. We shouldn't be happy married. Your mother wouldn't like it.

Joe. She'd be all right.

Fanny. Don't let's talk about it now. Let's wait until you come back.

Joe. Very well. *(There is silence for a moment.* Fanny *puts her hand on* Joe's *across the table.)*

Fanny. Listen, dear. I love you and you love me, and I've got to go now or I shall be late; and you've got to go, too, but I'm not going to say good-bye. We've had fun, grand fun, and I don't want you to forget me, that's why I gave you the locket. Please keep it close to you, Joey—darling Joey. (Fanny *goes as the lights fade.*)

PART TWO : SCENE IX

Principals: Jane, Joe.
Scene: *A railway station. The station is foggy and very dimly lit on account of air raids. The ticket barrier can be vaguely discerned and beyond it, the back of a train. Just above the barrier a lamp shines downwards partially illuminating a recruiting poster. On the right is an empty platform, but there are people moving about on it, and several Red Cross orderlies and nurses. There is a crowd of people, mostly women, clustered around the left barrier—occasionally a door in the train opens and a shaft of light falls on to the platform.*
Time: *About 11 p.m. Tuesday, October 22nd, 1918.*

(*A crowd of soldiers comes on from the left, wearing full equipment. They are greeted by some of the women. Presently a Sergeant enters, and after their good-byes have been said, the Sergeant gets them in line and marches them through on to the platform, where they can be seen getting into the train.* JANE *and* JOE *come on from the left.*)

JOE (*breathlessly*). Whew: I thought we were going to miss it, didn't you, mum?

JANE. Yes.

JOE. Not much time for long good-byes, darling.

JANE. I know. I'm glad, really—aren't you?

JOE. Yes. I never know what to say.

JANE. I'm almost hardened to it by now. This has happened so often.

JOE. Dearest mum, you are marvellous. You never make a fuss.

JANE. Don't be too sweet to me, Joey, I don't want to disgrace you, to behave badly.

JOE. You couldn't behave badly.

JANE. How funny! Do you know that Robert said that to me years and years ago. I must be very dull and unimaginative to be so reserved. It was the Boer War, then. This is very, very different. (*A whistle blows.* JOE *takes* JANE *in his arms.*)

JOE. Good-bye, darling.

JANE. Good-bye, darling—take care of yourself. (JOE *rushes through the barrier and jumps into the train just as it starts to move.* JANE *stands under the lamp looking after him. Two or three of the women at the barrier burst into loud sobbing, some soldiers in the train start singing. A big steaming locomotive comes slowly to a standstill at the right-hand platform. Almost immediately Red Cross orderlies begin to walk off the platform carrying wounded men on stretchers.* JANE *stands watching them; her face is quite expressionless. Then with a trembling hand she takes a cigarette out of her bag and lights it. The lights fade.*)

PART TWO : SCENE X

PRINCIPALS: JANE, ELLEN, GLADYS (*a parlourmaid*).

SCENE: *The drawing-room of a London house. The decoration of the room has changed slightly with the years, but not to any marked extent. It looks very much the same as it has always looked.*

TIME: *About 11 a.m. Monday, November 11th, 1918.*

(*As the lights go up on the scene, a* PARLOURMAID *shows* ELLEN *into the room.* ELLEN *has certainly changed with the years. She is very well dressed, almost smart.*)

GLADYS. Her ladyship will be down in a moment, madam.

ELLEN. Thanks. (GLADYS *goes out.* ELLEN *wanders about the room. There is a photograph of* EDWARD *on the table, and also one of* JOE. *She looks at them both and sighs.*)

JANE *enters.*
She is dressed in street clothes.

JANE. Ellen! Gladys said Mrs. Bridges, but I couldn't believe it was you.

ELLEN. I just thought I'd call. It's rather important, as a matter of fact.

JANE. Do sit down. I'm delighted to see you again.

ELLEN. Thanks. (*She sits down.*)

JANE. How's Fanny?

ELLEN. Oh, very well. She's in "Over the Moon," now, you know.

JANE. Yes. I went the other night. She was splendid. I felt very proud to know her.

ELLEN. It's about her I've come to see you, really.

JANE. Oh! Well?

ELLEN. It's—it's—er—rather difficult.

JANE. What is it? What on earth is the matter?

ELLEN. About her and Master—her and Joe.

JANE. Joe?

ELLEN. Yes. They've been—well—er—to put it frankly, if you know what I mean, they've been having an affair.

JANE. My Joe?

ELLEN. Yes—your Joe. His last two leaves he spent a lot of time with Fanny.

JANE (*slowly*). Oh, I see.

ELLEN. I wouldn't have come to see you about it at all, only I think Fanny's very upset about it, and now that the war's over—

or almost over, that is—and he'll be coming home—I thought——

Jane (*coldly*). What did you think?

Ellen. Well, I thought they ought to get married.

Jane. Does Fanny want to marry him?

Ellen. No—er—not exactly. That is—I haven't talked about it to her. She doesn't know I know.

Jane. How do you know?

Ellen. I found a letter from him——

Jane. And you read it?

Ellen. Yes—it's here. I've brought it with me. (*She fumbles in her bag.*)

Jane. I don't wish to see it, thank you.

Ellen. I only brought it because——

Jane (*cutting* ELLEN *short*). Is Fanny in any sort of trouble?

Ellen. Oh, no. Nothing like that.

Jane (*rising*). Then I think we'd better leave it until Joe comes home. Then he and Fanny can decide what they wish to do.

Ellen (*also rising*). I—I didn't mean to upset you.

Jane. I'm not in the least upset.

Ellen. It's been on my mind—it's been worrying me to death.

Jane. I think you should have spoken to Fanny before you came to me. I never interfere with my son's affairs.

Ellen. Well, I'm sure I'm very sorry.

Jane. Please don't let's discuss it any further. Good-bye, Ellen.

Ellen. I suppose you imagine my daughter isn't good enough to marry your son; if that's the case I can assure you you're very much mistaken. Fanny's received everywhere; she knows all the best people.

Jane. How nice for her; I wish I did.

Ellen. Things aren't what they used to be, you know—it's all changing.

Jane. Yes, I see it is.

Ellen. Fanny's at the top of the tree now; she's having the most wonderful offers.

Jane. Oh, Ellen!

Ellen. What is it?

Jane. I'm so very, very sorry.

Ellen. I don't know what you mean.

Jane. Yes, you do—inside, you must. Something seems to have gone out of all of us, and I'm not sure I like what's left. Good-bye, Ellen. (GLADYS *enters with a telegram.* JANE *takes telegram.*) Excuse me, will you. (*She opens it and reads it, and then says in a dead voice.*) There's no answer, Gladys.

Gladys (*excitedly*). It's all over, milady—it's eleven o'clock—the maroons are going off.

Jane. Thank you, Gladys, that will do.

Gladys. Yes, milady. (GLADYS *goes out.* JANE *stands holding the telegram. She sways slightly.*)

Ellen. What is it? What's happened? Oh, my God!

Jane. You needn't worry about Fanny and Joe any more, Ellen. He won't be able to come back after all because he's dead. (*She crumples up and falls to the ground. Maroons can be heard in the distance and people cheering. The lights fade.*)

PART TWO : SCENE XI

PRINCIPAL: JANE.
SCENE: *Trafalgar Square.*
TIME: *11 p.m. Monday, November 11th, 1918.*

(*Before the scene begins* JANE *appears far up stage in a pool of light. Her hat has been pushed on to one side, her clothes look dishevelled, and her handbag hangs on her arm wide open. Twined round her neck and over her hat are coloured paper streamers. She holds in her left hand a large painted wooden rattle, in her right hand a red, white and blue paper squeaker. Her face is dead white and quite devoid of expression. The lights go up.* JANE *can be seen threading her way like a sleep-walker through dense crowds of cheering, yelling people. They push her and jostle her. One man blows a long squeaking paper tongue into her face. There is a motor bus festooned with people and a Rolls Royce and one or two taxis and a hansom cab, all equally burdened with screaming humanity. They move at a snail's pace.* JANE *finally arrives down stage under a lamp-post in the centre. She stands there cheering wildly, with the tears rolling down her face. The lights dim*

---

57. **maroons**, huge firecrackers that simulate the report of a cannon; they are often used for signal purposes.

and the yelling crowds fade away. JANE *is left, still cheering and occasionally brandishing the rattle and blowing the squeaker. But she can't be heard at all because the full strength of the orchestra is playing "Land of Hope and Glory."*)

PART THREE : SCENE I

PRINCIPALS: ROBERT, JANE, MARGARET.
SCENE: *Drawing-room of a London house.*
TIME: *11:45 p.m. Tuesday, December 31st, 1929.*

(MARGARET *and* JANE, *both old women, are sitting by the fire.* MARGARET *is very made up, with dyed hair.* JANE'S *hair is white.* MARGARET *is wearing a coloured evening gown.* JANE *is in black.*)

Margaret. I assure you he's the most marvellous man I've ever met. I'd never go to another doctor in the world. He has the most wonderful touch—he's completely cured me, and anyhow the hotel is divine. It's really more a Hydro really, although, thank God, not in the English sense. You can eat what you like and do what you like——

Jane. And what do you like?

Margaret *(laughing).* Enjoying myself.

Jane. And you do.

Margaret. Certainly I do.

Jane. Good!

Margaret. Jane, dear, you really are hopeless.

Jane. I refuse to be jostled, Margaret. I'm perfectly comfortable where I am, without going gallivanting about the Continent taking cures for ailments I haven't got.

Margaret. How do you know you haven't got any ailments?

Jane. Because I'm sane and active, and as strong as a horse. So is Robert. We've both outstayed our welcome, that's the only thing that's wrong with us.

Margaret. I don't see any sense in sitting waiting for the grave.

---

5. **Land . . . Glory,** a British patriotic hymn whose musical setting is the middle section of the extremely popular Number 1 march of "Pomp and Circumstance" by Sir Edward Elgar (1857–1934). 17. **Hydro,** a resort where hydrotherapy is practiced, a spa. In British slang of the 1920's, however, it was applied to temperance hotels, where no alcoholic beverages were served; hence Margaret's remark in the next line.

Jane. I'm not waiting for anything. I have a perfectly good time. You're not the only one who enjoys yourself. I go to the Opera. I go to theatres, I go to the Zoo, and, I must say, so far I've found the Zoo infinitely the most entertaining.

Margaret. Dearest Jane—you really are amazing!

ROBERT *enters. His hair is also white, but he is otherwise hale and hearty.*

Robert. It's nearly time.

Margaret. Good heavens, I must fly. I wouldn't interfere with your little ritual for the world.

Jane. You wouldn't interfere—you're an old friend.

Margaret *(kissing* JANE*).* That's very sweet, Jane, but all the same I must go. I promised I'd be at the Embassy at eleven-thirty. Goodnight, dear. Good-night, Robert. No, don't see me down—the car's outside, isn't it?

Robert. Yes, it's been there for a long while.

Margaret. Happy New Year to you both. Remember you're both dining with me on Thursday.

Robert. Good-night, Margaret—same to you. (MARGARET *goes out.* ROBERT *goes over to* JANE.) Did Franklin bring the champagne up?

Jane. Yes, it's by the table.

Robert. Good!

Jane. Well, Robert—here we go again.

Robert. I believe you laugh at me inside—for my annual sentimental outburst.

Jane. No dear, I don't laugh at you.

Robert. One more year behind us.

Jane. One more year before us.

Robert. Do you mind?

Jane. Oh, no—everything passes—even time.

Robert. It seems incredible, doesn't it? Here we are in this same room!

Jane. Yes. I've hated it for years.

Robert. Do you want to move?

Jane. Of course not.

Robert. We might have some new curtains.

Jane. We have, dear.

Robert. Good God, so we have! I never noticed.

Jane. They've only been up a week.

Robert. They look very nice.

Jane. Dear Robert. *(She pats* ROBERT's *hand.)* What toast have you in mind for to-night—something gay and original, I hope?

Robert. Just our old friend—the future. The Future of England.

Jane. It's starting—the champagne, quick! (ROBERT *gets a champagne bottle out of the bucket and struggles with it.* JANE *opens the window.)*

Robert. I can't get the damned thing open.

Jane. Let me try.

Robert (doing it). There! (JANE *holds the glasses.* ROBERT *fills the glasses. Meanwhile the chimes and sirens are beginning outside.)*

Jane (holding up her glass). First of all, my dear, I drink to you. Loyal and loving always. *(She drinks.)* Now, then, let's couple the Future of England with the past of England. The glories and victories and triumphs that are over, and the sorrows that are over, too. Let's drink to our sons who made part of the pattern and to our hearts that died with them. Let's drink to the spirit of gallantry and courage that made a strange Heaven out of unbelievable Hell, and let's drink to the hope that one day this country of ours, which we love so much, will find dignity and greatness and peace again. *(They both lift their glasses and drink as the lights fade.)*

PART THREE : SCENE II

PRINCIPALS: ROBERT, JANE, FANNY, MARGARET, ELLEN, FULL COMPANY.
SCENE: *A Night Club.*
TIME: *Evening—1930.*

(This SCENE *begins with a night club in which* FANNY *is singing, seated on a piano. The decoration is angular and strange, and the song she is singing is oddly discordant.)*

TWENTIETH CENTURY BLUES

Verse
Why is it that civilised humanity
Must make the world so wrong?
In this hurly burly of insanity
Your dreams cannot last long.
We've reached a headline—
The Press headline—every sorrow,
Blues value is News value to-morrow.
Refrain
Blues, Twentieth Century Blues, are getting me down.
Who's escaped those weary Twentieth Century Blues?
Why, if there's a God in the sky, why shouldn't he grin?
High above this dreary Twentieth Century din,
In this strange illusion,
Chaos and confusion,
People seem to lose their way.
What is there to strive for,
Love or keep alive for? Say—
Hey, hey, call it a day.
Blues, nothing to win or to lose.
It's getting me down.
Blues, I've got those weary Twentieth Century Blues.

(When the song is finished, people rise from table and dance without apparently any particular enjoyment; it is the dull dancing of habit. The lights fade away from everything but the dancers, who appear to be rising in the air. They disappear and down stage left six "incurables" in blue hospital uniforms are sitting making baskets. They disappear and FANNY *is seen singing her song for a moment, then far away up stage a jazz band is seen playing wildly. Then down stage* JANE *and* ROBERT *standing with glasses of champagne held aloft, then* ELLEN *sitting in front of a Radio loud speaker; then* MARGARET *dancing with a young man. The visions are repeated quicker and quicker, while across the darkness runs a Riley light sign spelling out news. Noise grows louder and louder. Steam rivets, loud speakers, jazz bands, aeroplane propellers, etc., until the general effect is complete chaos. Suddenly it all fades into darkness and silence and away at the back a Union Jack glows through the blackness. The lights slowly come up and the whole stage is composed of massive tiers, upon which stand the entire Company. The Union Jack flies over their heads as they sing "God Save the King.")*   (1931)

Wystan Hugh Auden
1907-

One of the most significant and influential of the poets of his generation is Wystan Hugh Auden, born in York on February 21, 1907. Upon finishing his preparatory school course, Auden entered Christ Church, Oxford, in 1925. While there, he became interested in literature and in writing, and attracted some attention as a poet. After graduation he devoted five years to teaching in schools for boys, first in Scotland and then near Malvern, in Worcestershire. During 1935-1936 he was employed by the General Post Office in making documentary films.

In the meantime Auden had published several books: his first volume, *Poems*, in 1930; a critical analysis of contemporary life, *The Orators*, in 1932; a satirical drama, *The Dance of Death*, in 1933; and with Christopher Isherwood, English critic and novelist and a long-time personal friend, two satirical dramas—*The Dog Beneath the Skin*, in 1935, and *The Ascent of F 6*, in 1936; and a volume of miscellaneous verse, *Look, Stranger*, in 1936 (published in the United States as *On This Island*, 1937).

Always a wide reader and a keen observer of society, Auden found rich material for his varied creative purposes. His journey to Iceland in 1936 with Louis MacNeice resulted in a joint account of their experiences in *Letters from Iceland* (1937). A visit to China with Isherwood in 1938 furnished material for their *Journey to a War* (1939). Another satirical drama, *On the Frontier*, in collaboration with Isherwood, and *Selected Poems* appeared in 1938. In 1939 Auden came to the United States, where for two years he was a member of the staff of the New School for Social Research in New York. He is now a citizen of this country and in 1950 became a member of the English Department at the University of Michigan.

Other writings of Auden are *Another Time* (1940), *Some Poems* (1940), *The Double Man* (1941, published in England as *New Year Letter*), *For the Time Being* (1944), *Collected Poetry* (1945), *The Age of Anxiety* (1947), *Nones* (1952), and *The Shield of Achilles* (1955). He has edited several collections of poetry including *The Oxford Book of Light Verse* (1938).

Watch Any Day His Nonchalant Pauses

Watch any day his nonchalant pauses, see
His dextrous handling of a wrap as he
Steps after into cars, the beggar's envy.

"There is a free one," many say, but err.
He is not that returning conqueror,   5
Nor ever the poles' circumnavigator.

But poised between shocking falls on razor-
    edge
Has taught himself this balancing subterfuge
Of the accosting profile, the erect carriage.

The song, the varied action of the blood   10
Would drown the warning from the iron
    wood
Would cancel the inertia of the buried:

Travelling by daylight on from house to
    house
The longest way to the intrinsic peace,
With love's fidelity and with love's weak-
    ness.   (1930)

The first nine poems of Auden are reprinted by permission of Random House, Inc., New York, and Faber and Faber, Ltd., London. Copyright, 1945, by W. H. Auden.

There Are Some Birds in These Valleys

There are some birds in these valleys
Who flutter round the careless
With intimate appeal,
By seeming kindness trained to snaring,
They feel no falseness.   5

Under the spell completely
They circle can serenely,
And in the tricky light
The masked hill has a purer greenness.
Their flight looks fleeter.   10

But fowlers, O, like foxes,
Lie ambushed in the rushes.
Along the harmless tracks
The madman keeper crawls through brush-
    wood,
Axe under oxter.   15

Alas, the signal given,
Fingers on trigger tighten.
The real unlucky dove
Must smarting fall away from brightness   19
Its love from living.   (1932)

Epilogue

"O where are you going?" said reader to
    rider,
"That valley is fatal when furnaces burn,
Yonder's the midden whose odors will mad-
    den,
That gap is the grave where the tall return."

"O do you imagine," said fearer to farer,   5
"That dusk will delay on your path to the
    pass,
Your diligent looking discover the lacking
Your footsteps feel from granite to grass?"

"O what was that bird," said horror to hearer,
"Did you see that shape in the twisted
    trees?   10
Behind you swiftly the figure comes softly,
The spot on your skin is a shocking disease?"

"Out of this house"—said rider to reader
"Yours never will"—said farer to fearer
"They're looking for you"—said hearer to
    horror   15
As he left them there, as he left them there.
                                               (1932)

Doom Is Dark and Deeper Than Any Sea-Dingle

Doom is dark and deeper than any sea-dingle.
Upon what man it fall
In spring, day-wishing flowers appearing,
Avalanche sliding, white snow from rock-face,
That he should leave his house,   5
No cloud-soft hand can hold him, restraint
    by women;
But ever that man goes
Through place-keepers, through forest trees,
A stranger to strangers over undried sea,
Houses for fishes, suffocating water,   10
Or lonely on fell as chat,
By pot-holed becks
A bird stone-haunting, an unquiet bird.

There head falls forward, fatigued at evening,
And dreams of home,   15
Waving from window, spread of welcome,
Kissing of wife under single sheet;
But waking sees
Bird-flocks nameless to him, through doorway
    voices
Of new men making another love.   20

Save him from hostile capture,
From sudden tiger's spring at corner;
Protect his house,
His anxious house where days are counted
From thunderbolt protect,   25
From gradual ruin spreading like a stain;
Converting number from vague to certain,
Bring joy, bring day of his returning,
Lucky with day approaching, with leaning
    dawn.   (1934)

15. **oxter**, the armpit, or the arm.
Epilogue. This poem presents the age-old conflict between the instinct of self-preservation and the urge to risk adventure and danger. It resembles in structure an English folk-poem, "The Cutty Wren." (See *The Oxford Book of Light Verse*, p. 393.) 3. **midden**, heap of refuse.

Doom Is Dark. 1. **sea-dingle**, the hollow of water between the ridges of two giant waves. 11. **chat**, a kind of song sparrow.

from *On This Island*

[HERE ON THE CROPPED GRASS]

Here on the cropped grass of the narrow ridge
   I stand,
A fathom of earth, alive in air,
Aloof as an admiral on the old rocks,
   England below me:
Eastward across the Midland plains   5
An express is leaving for a sailor's country;
   Westward is Wales
Where on clear evenings the retired and rich
From the french windows of their sheltered
      mansions
See the Sugarloaf standing, an upright sen-
      tinel   10
   Over Abergavenny.

When last I stood here I was not alone;
      happy
Each thought the other, thinking of a crime,
And England to our meditations seemed
   The perfect setting: 15
But now it has no innocence at all;
It is the isolation and the fear,
   The mood itself;
It is the body of the absent lover,
An image to the would-be hero of the soul,   20
The little area we are willing to forgive
   Upon conditions.

For private reasons I must have the truth,
      remember
These years have seen a boom in sorrow;
The presses of idleness issued more despair   25
   And it was honored,
Gross Hunger took on more hands every
      month,
Erecting here and everywhere his vast
   Unnecessary workshops;
Europe grew anxious about her health,   30
Combines tottered, credits froze,
And business shivered in a banker's winter
   While we were kissing.

Today, no longer occupied like that, I give
The children at the open swimming pool   35
Lithe in their first and little beauty
   A closer look;
Follow the cramped clerk crooked at his desk,
The guide in shorts pursuing flowers
   In their careers;   40
A digit of the crowd, would like to know
Them better whom the shops and trams are
      full of,
The little men and their mothers, not plain but
   Dreadfully ugly.

Deaf to the Welsh wind now, I hear arising   45
From lanterned gardens sloping to the river
Where saxophones are moaning for a com-
      forter,
   From Gaumont theaters
Where fancy plays on hunger to produce
The noble robber, ideal of boys,   50
   And from cathedrals,
Luxury liners laden with souls,
Holding to the east their hulls of stone,
The high thin rare continuous worship
   Of the self-absorbed.   55

Here, which looked north before the Cam-
      brian alignment,
Like the cupped hand of the keen excavator
Busy with bones, the memory uncovers
   The hopes of time;
Of empires stiff in their brocaded glory,   60
The luscious lateral blossoming of woe
   Scented, profuse;
And of intercalary ages of disorder
When, as they prayed in antres, fell
Upon the noblest in the country night   65
   Angel assassins.

Small birds above me have the grace of those
      who founded
The civilization of the delicate olive,
Learning the laws of love and sailing
   On the calm Aegean;   70
The hawk is the symbol of the rule by thirst,

Here on the Cropped Grass. 10. **Sugarloaf**, a mountain in western England near Abergavenny, a small town in Monmouthshire. 23. **the truth**, the facts regarding present conditions in England. 48. **Gaumont**, Leon Gaumont (d. 1946), a well-known producer of motion pictures and owner of theaters in Britain and in France. 56. **Cambrian alignment**, the earliest division of the Paleozoic era in geology; so called from Cambria, or Wales, where the system was first differentiated. The Cambrian formations indicate a period of long duration. 63. **intercalary . . . disorder**, ages of disorder occurring among ages of order. 64. **antres**, caves. 66. **Angel assassins**, bombings from airplanes. 67-70. These lines refer to Greek civilization, which has perished. 71. **hawk . . . thirst** and ff., a warning of the possible doom of England's civilization.

The central state controlling the canals;
    And the blank sky
Of the womb's utter peace before
The cell, dividing, multiplied desire,   75
And raised instead of death the image
    Of the reconciler.

And over the Cotswolds now the thunder
    mutters:
"What little of the truth your seers saw
They dared not tell you plainly but combined
    Assertion and refuge   81
In the common language of collective lying,
In codes of a bureau, laboratory slang
    And diplomats' French.
The relations of your lovers were, alas, pictorial;   85
The treasure that you stole, you lost; bad luck
It brought you, but you cannot put it back
    Now with caresses.

"Already behind you your last evening hastens up
And all the customs your society has chosen   90
Harden themselves into the unbreakable
    Habits of death.
Has not your long affair with death
Of late become increasingly more serious;
    Do you not find   95
Him growing more attractive every day?
You shall go under and help him with the
    crops,
Be faithful to him, and to your friends
    Remain indifferent."

And out of the turf the bones of the war continue;   100
"Know then, cousin, the major cause of our
    collapse
Was a distortion in the human plastic by
    luxury produced,

Never higher than in our time were the vital
    advantages;
To matter entire, to the unbounded vigors of
    the instrument,
To all logical precision we were the rejoicing
    heirs.   105

But pompous, we assumed their power to be
    our own,
Believed machines to be our hearts' spontaneous fruit,
Taking our premises as shoppers take a tram.

While the disciplined love which alone could
    have employed these engines
Seemed far too difficult and dull, and when
    hatred promised   110
An immediate dividend, all of us hated.

Denying the liberty we knew quite well to be
    our destiny,
It dogged our steps with its accusing shadow
Until in every landscape we saw murder ambushed.

Unable to endure ourselves, we sought relief
In the insouciance of the soldier, the heroic
    sexual pose   116
Playing at fathers to impress the little ladies.

Call us not tragic; falseness made farcical our
    death:
Nor brave; ours was the will of the insane
    to suffer
By which since we could not live we gladly
    died: 120
And now we have gone for ever to our foolish
    graves."

The Priory clock chimes briefly and I recollect
I am expected to return alive
My will effective and my nerves in order
    To my situation.   125
"The poetry is in the pity," Wilfred said,
And Kathy in her journal, "To be rooted in
    life,
    That's what I want."
These moods give no permission to be idle,
For men are changed by what they do;   130
And through loss and anger the hands of the
    unlucky
    Love one another.

                                          (1936)

78. **Cotswolds**, vast hilly tracts in Gloucestershire, used for sheep raising. 115-117. These lines refer to the part played by capitalism in fostering war and low morals. *Insouciance* means *indifference*. 122. **Priory**, a monastic house. 126. **Wilfred**, Wilfred Owen, noted for his poems on war. See p. 1093. 127. **Kathy**, Katherine Mansfield. See p. 1069.

from *Letter to Lord Byron*
IV

In the *Letter to Lord Byron*, Auden has reproduced in a rather striking way both the facetious spirit and the ingenious method of Byron as displayed in his great satire *Don Juan* (pp. 224-246). Byron used an eight-line stanza, which was well suited to his mood and purposes. Auden achieved the same kind of effect in a seven-line stanza, which is like the Chaucerian stanza, or Rime Royal, in form. In three respects Auden is notably like Byron: he is an extreme individualist; he cannot endure strait-laced conventions of society; and he takes keen delight in shocking his complacent contemporaries. Auden's poems appeared first in *Letters from Iceland,* written by Auden and his friend MacNeice (p. 1022).

My passport says I'm five feet and eleven,
  With hazel eyes and fair (it's tow-like) hair,
That I was born in York in 1907,
  With no distinctive markings anywhere.
  Which isn't quite correct. Conspicuous there
On my right cheek appears a large brown mole,   6
I think I don't dislike it on the whole.

My name occurs in several of the sagas,
  Is common over Iceland still. Down under
Where Das Volk order sausages and lagers 10
  I ought to be the prize, the living wonder,
  The really pure from any Rassenschander,
In fact I am the great big white barbarian,
The Nordic type, the too too truly Aryan.

In games which mark for beauty out of twenty, 15
  I'm doing well if my friends give me eight
(When played historically you still score plenty);
  My head looks like an egg upon a plate;
  My nose is not too bad, but isn't straight;
I have no proper eyebrows, and my eyes 20
Are far too close together to look nice.

Beauty, we're told, is but a painted show,
  But still the public really likes that best;
Beauty of soul should be enough, I know,
  The golden ingot in the plain deal chest. 25
But mine's a rattle in a flannel vest;
I can't think what my It had on Its mind,
To give me flat feet and a big behind.

Apart from lyrics and poetic dramma,
  Which Ervine seems more angered by than sad at, 30
While Sparrow fails to understand their grammar,
  I have some harmless hobbies; I'm not bad at
  Reading the slower movements, and may add that
Out of my hours of strumming most of them
Pass playing hymn tunes out of A. and M. 35

Read character from taste. Who seem to me
  The great? I know that one as well as you.
"Why, Daunty, Gouty, Shopkeeper, the three
  Supreme Old Masters." You must ask me who
  Have written just as I'd have liked to do. 40
I stop to listen and the names I hear
Are those of Firbank, Potter, Carroll, Lear.

Then phantasies? My anima, poor thing,
  Must take the dreams my Alter Ego sends her,
And he's a marvelous diver, not a king. 45
  But when I'm sickening for influenza,

10-14. **Das Volk . . . Aryan**, a thrust at the German insistence on the superiority of the pure Aryan race. 17. **you**, Lord Byron. 22. **Beauty . . . show.** Cf. Shakespeare, *The Passionate Pilgrim*, st. 13: "Beauty is but a vain and doubtful good; A shining gloss that fadeth suddenly." 25. **deal**, pine or fir wood.

30. **Ervine**, St. John Greer Ervine (1883-), Irish playwright, critic, and novelist. He was associated with the Irish national theater. 31. **Sparrow**, John H. A. Sparrow (1906-), English critic. 35. **A. and M.** *Ancient and Modern Hymns,* a book used in the church service. 38. **Daunty, Gouty, Shopkeeper,** a playful substitution for Dante, Goethe, and Shakespeare. 42. **Firbank . . . Lear,** Ronald Firbank (1886-1926), English novelist, essayist, and dramatist, whose writings deal largely with eccentric characters; Paul Meredith Potter (1853-1921), English-born American dramatist and dramatizer of romantic novels, author of *The Ugly Duckling* (1890); "Lewis Carroll" (1832-1898), author of *Alice in Wonderland* and a book of parodies (see p. 825); Edward Lear (1812-1888), writer of nonsense verse and prose (see p. 824).

I play concertos with my own cadenza;
And as the fever rises find it properer
To sing the love duet from a grand opera.

My vices? I've no wish to go to prison. 50
  I am no Grouper, I will never share
With any prig who thinks he'd like to listen.
  At answering letters I am well aware
I'm very slack; I ought to take more care
Over my clothes; my promise always fails 55
To smoke much less, and not to bite my nails.

I hate pompositas and all authority;
  Its air of injured rightness also sends
Me shuddering from the cultured smug minority.
  "Perpetual revolution," left-wing friends 60
Tell me, "in counter-revolution ends.
Your fate will be to linger on outcast
A selfish pink old Liberal to the last."

"No, I am that I am, and those that level
  At my abuses reckon up their own. 65
I may be straight though they, themselves, are bevel."
  So Shakespeare said, but Shakespeare must have known.
I daren't say that except when I'm alone,
Must hear in silence till I turn my toes up,
"It's such a pity Wystan never grows up." 70

So I sit down this fine September morning
  To tell my story. I've another reason.
I've lately had a confidential warning
  That Isherwood is publishing next season
A book about us all. I call that treason. 75
I must be quick if I'm to get my oar in
Before his revelations bring the law in.

My father's forbears were all Midland yeomen
  Till royalties from coal mines did them good;
I think they must have been phlegmatic slow-men. 80

My mother's ancestors had Norman blood,
  From Somerset I've always understood;
My grandfathers on either side agree
In being clergymen and C. of E.

Father and Mother each was one of seven, 85
  Though one died young and one was not all there;
Their fathers both went suddenly to Heaven
  While they were still quite small and left them here
To work on earth with little cash to spare;
A nurse, a rising medico, at Bart's 90
Both felt the pangs of Cupid's naughty darts.

My home then was professional and "high."
  No gentler father ever lived, I'll lay
All Lombard Street against a shepherd's pie.
  We imitate our loves: well, neighbors say 95
I grow more like my mother every day.
I don't like business men. I know a Prot
Will never really kneel, but only squat.

In pleasures of the mind they both delighted;
  The library in the study was enough 100
To make a better boy than me short-sighted;
  Our old cook Ada surely knew her stuff;
My elder brothers did not treat me rough;
We lived at Solihull, a village then;
Those at the gasworks were my favorite men. 105

My earliest recollection to stay put
  Is of a white stone doorstep and a spot
Of pus where father lanced the terrier's foot;
  Next, stuffing shag into the coffee pot
Which nearly killed my mother, but did not; 110
Both psychoanalyst and Christian minister,
Will think these incidents extremely sinister.

With northern myths my little brain was laden,
  With deeds of Thor and Loki and such scenes;

---

47. **cadenza,** a flourish near the end of a solo musical selection. 51. **Grouper,** a member of the Oxford Group religious movement which flourished in the 1920's and 1930's, an important aspect of which was public confession of one's sins. 57. **pompositas,** exalted sense of importance. 64-66. **"No . . . bevel,"** from Shakespeare's Sonnet 121, 9-11. 70. **Wystan,** the poet himself. 74. **Isherwood,** Christopher Isherwood (1904-   ), an English realistic novelist, a long-time friend of Auden and collaborator in a book and several plays. See biographical sketch.

84. **C. of E.,** Church of England. 90. **Bart's,** Saint Bartholomew's Hospital, London. 92. **"high."** His parents belonged to the strict High Church as opposed to the more liberal Low Church. 97. **Prot,** Protestant. Members of the High Church always kneel. 104. **Solihull,** a place in the outskirts of Birmingham. 109. **shag,** a strong, coarse tobacco. 114. **Thor and Loki.** Loki, the Norse god of discord and mischief, was overcome by Thor, the Norse god of thunder.

My favorite tale was Andersen's *Ice Maiden;*
   But better far than any kings or queens 116
   I liked to see and know about machines:
And from my sixth until my sixteenth year
I thought myself a mining engineer.

The mine I always pictured was for lead, 120
   Though copper mines might, *faute de mieux,* be sound.
Today I like a weight upon my bed;
   I always travel by the Underground!
   For concentration I have always found
A small room best, the curtains drawn, the light on; 125
Then I can work from nine till tea-time, right on.

I must admit that I was most precocious
   (Precocious children rarely grow up good).
My aunts and uncles thought me quite atrocious
   For using words more adult than I should;
   My first remark at school did all it could 131
To shake a matron's monumental poise;
"I like to see the various types of boys."

The Great War had begun: but masters' scrutiny
   And fists of big boys were the war to us; 135
It was as harmless as the Indian Mutiny,
   A beating from the Head was dangerous.
   But once when half the form put down *Bellus,*
We were accused of that most deadly sin,
Wanting the Kaiser and the Huns to win. 140

The way in which we really were affected
   Was having such a varied lot to teach us.
The best were fighting, as the King expected,
   The remnant either elderly gray creatures,
   Or characters with most peculiar features.
Many were raggable, a few were waxy, 146
One had to leave abruptly in a taxi.

Surnames I must not write—O Reginald,
   You at least taught us that which fadeth not,
Our earliest visions of the great wide world; 150
   The beer and biscuits that your favorites got,
   Your tales revealing you a first-class shot,
Your riding breeks, your drama called *The Waves,*
A few of us will carry to our graves.

"Half a lunatic, half a knave." No doubt 155
   A holy terror to the staff at tea;
A good headmaster must have soon found out
   Your moral character was all at sea;
   I question if you'd got a pass degree:
But little children bless your kind that knocks
Away the edifying stumbling blocks. 161

How can I thank you? For it only shows
   (Let me ride just this once my hobby-horse),
There're things a good headmaster never knows.
   There must be sober schoolmasters, of course, 165
   But what a prep school really puts across
Is knowledge of the world we'll soon be lost in:
Today it's more like Dickens than Jane Austen.

I hate the modern trick, to tell the truth,
   Of straightening out the kinks in the young mind, 170
Our passion for the tender plant of youth,
   Our hatred for all weeds of any kind.
   Slogans are bad: the best that I can find
Is this: "Let each child have that's in our care
As much neurosis as the child can bear." 175

In this respect, at least, my bad old Adam is
   Pigheadedly against the general trend;
And has no use for all these new academies
   Where readers of the better weeklies send

---

115. **Andersen,** Hans Christian Andersen (1805-1875), Danish novelist and poet, best known as a writer of fairy tales and travels. 121. *faute de mieux,* for want of better. 136. **Indian Mutiny,** a futile revolt against British authority in India in 1857-1858. 137. **Head,** headmaster of the School. 138. **form,** grade or class in English schools. **Bellus,** Latin word meaning pleasant, delightful; the boys had used that word when they were supposed to use *bellum,* meaning war.

153. **breeks,** breeches, trousers. 168. **Dickens . . . Austen.** Dickens portrays a troubled world full of poverty and evil as opposed to the complacent, provincial world of Jane Austen. See pp. 26 and 424. 175. **neurosis,** nervous disorders.

The child they probably did not intend, 180
To paint a lampshade, marry, or keep pigeons,
Or make a study of the world religions.

Goddess of bossy underlings, Normality!
  What murders are committed in thy name!
Totalitarian is thy state Reality, 185
  Reeking of antiseptics and the shame
  Of faces that all look and feel the same.
Thy Muse is one unknown to classic histories,
The topping figure of the hockey mistress.

From thy dread Empire not a soul's ex-
    empted: 190
  More than the nursemaids pushing prams
    in parks,
By thee the intellectuals are tempted,
  O, to commit the treason of the clerks,
  Bewitched by thee to literary sharks.
But I must leave thee to thy office stool, 195
I must get on now to my public school.

Men had stopped throwing stones at one
    another,
  Butter and Father had come back again;
Gone were the holidays we spent with Mother
  In furnished rooms on mountain, moor,
    and fen; 200
  And gone those summer Sunday evenings,
    when
Along the seafronts fled a curious noise,
"Eternal Father," sung by three young boys.

Nation spoke Peace, or said she did, with
    nation;
  The sexes tried their best to look the same;
Morals lost value during the inflation, 205
  The great Victorians kindly took the blame;
  Visions of Dada to the Post-War came,
Sitting in cafés, nostrils stuffed with bread,
Above the recent and the straight-laced
    dead. 210

I've said my say on public schools elsewhere:
  Romantic friendship, prefects, bullying,
I shall not deal with, *c'est une autre affaire.*
  Those who expect them, will get no such
    thing,
  It is the strictly relevant I sing. 215
Why should they grumble? They've the
    Greek Anthology,
And all the spicier bits of Anthropology.

We all grow up the same way, more or less;
  Life is not known to give away her presents;
She only swops. The unself-consciousness 220
  That children share with animals and peas-
    ants
  Sinks in the "sturm und drang" of Ado-
    lescence.
Like other boys I lost my taste for sweets,
Discovered sunsets, passion, God, and Keats.

I shall recall a single incident 225
  No more. I spoke of mining engineering
As the career on which my mind was bent,
  But for some time my fancies had been
    veering;
  Mirages of the future kept appearing;
Crazes had come and gone in short, sharp
    gales, 230
For motor-bikes, photography, and whales.

But indecision broke off with a clean-cut end
  One afternoon in March at half-past three
When walking in a ploughed field with a
    friend;
  Kicking a little stone, he turned to me 235
  And said, "Tell me, do you write poetry?"
I never had, and said so, but I knew
That very moment what I wished to do.

Without a bridge passage this leads me
    straight
  Into the theme marked "Oxford" on my
    score 240
From pages twenty-five to twenty-eight.

---

184. **murders . . . name**, a parody of the words used by Madame Roland on the scaffold, November 8, 1793; "O liberty! liberty! how many crimes are committed in thy name!" 191. **prams**, baby carriages. 193. **treason of the clerks**, yielding to the temptation to write. 200. **fen**, damp meadows. 208. **Dada**, Dadaism, a fashion in art popular in France and Switzerland from 1917 to 1920, in some respects a forerunner of surrealism. The practitioners tried to show that incongruous objects could be grouped together with definite meaning.

212. **prefects**, student monitors in English schools. 213. **c'est . . . affaire**, that is something else. 216-217. **Greek . . . Anthropology**, probably a reference to obscene passages in classical texts. Byron complained that they had been expurgated from his school books. 222. **"sturm und drang,"** storm and stress, a phrase applied to a period of intellectual upheaval in Germany during the last part of the eighteenth century.

Aesthetic trills I'd never heard before
Rose from the strings, shrill poses from the
cor;
The woodwind chattered like a pre-war Russian,
"Art" boomed the brass, and "Life" thumped the percussion.   245

A raw provincial, my good taste was tardy,
    And Edward Thomas I as yet preferred;
I was still listening to Thomas Hardy
    Putting divinity about a bird;
But Eliot spoke the still unspoken word; 250
For gasworks and dried tubers I forsook
The clock at Grantchester, the English rook.

All youth's intolerant certainty was mine as
    I faced life in a double-breasted suit;
I bought and praised but did not read Aquinas,   255
    At the *Criterion's* verdict I was mute,
    Though Arnold's I was ready to refute;
And through the quads dogmatic words rang clear,
"Good poetry is classic and austere."

So much for Art. Of course Life had its passions too;   260
    The student's flesh like his imagination
Makes facts fit theories and has fashions too.
    We were the tail, a sort of poor relation
    To that debauched, eccentric generation
That grew up with their fathers at the War,   265
And made new glosses on the noun Amor.

Three years passed quickly while the Isis went
    Down to the sea for better or for worse;

Then to Berlin, not Carthage, I was sent
    With money from my parents in my purse,   270
And ceased to see the world in terms of verse.
I met a chap called Layard and he fed
New doctrines into my receptive head.

Part came from Lane, and part from D. H. Lawrence;
    Gide, though I didn't know it then, gave part.   275
They taught me to express my deep abhorrence
    If I caught anyone preferring Art
    To Life and Love and being Pure-in-Heart.
I lived with crooks but seldom was molested;
The Pure-in-Heart can never be arrested.   280

He's gay; no bludgeonings of chance can spoil it,
    The Pure-in-Heart loves all men on a par,
And has no trouble with his private toilet;
    The Pure-in-Heart is never ill; catarrh
    Would be the yellow streak, the brush of tar;
Determined to be loving and forgiving,   286
I came back home to try and earn my living.

The only thing you never turned your hand to
    Was teaching English in a boarding school.
Today it's a profession that seems grand to   290
    Those whose alternative's an office stool;
    For budding authors it's become the rule.
To many an unknown genius postmen bring
Typed notices from Rabbitarse and String.

The Head's M. A., a bishop is a patron,   295
    The assistant staff is highly qualified;
Health is the care of an experienced matron,
    The arts are taught by ladies from outside;
    The food is wholesome and the grounds are wide;

---

243. poses ... cor, blasts or coughs from the horn. 247. Edward Thomas, English essayist and nature poet (1878-1917). He was killed in the first World War. 249. divinity ... bird. See Hardy's *The Darkling Thrush,* p. 908. 250. Eliot, Thomas Stearns Eliot (1888-   ). See p. 1078. This line parodies a passage in his religious poem *Ash Wednesday* (see p. 1091, ll. 152 ff.). 251-252. gasworks ... rook, another thrust at Eliot, who refers to gasworks and dried tubers in his poem *The Waste Land.* Auden means that in his youth he followed the poetic tradition of Hardy rather than the modern imagery of an ugly civilization as used by Eliot. Grantchester is a village near Cambridge celebrated in verse by Rupert Brooke (1887-1915). 255. Aquinas, Saint Thomas Aquinas, celebrated thirteenth-century Italian philosopher. He exalted the Catholic doctrine above the classic Greek morality. 256. Criterion, a critical journal edited by T. S. Eliot. 257. Arnold, Matthew Arnold (1822-1888). See p. 527. 258. quads, college buildings enclosing a quadrangle. 266. Amor, Latin word for love. 267. Isis, local name for the River Thames.

269. Berlin, not Carthage. Berlin was the center of fascism; Carthage, the oldest seat of learning, where Byron was sent. 274. Lane, Edward William Lane (1801-1876), Arabic scholar, translator of *Arabian Nights*. D. H. Lawrence, a contemporary English writer who advocated the return to the primitive life and stressed love as the basis of true emotion (see p. 1017). 275. Gide, André Gide (1869-1951), French novelist, critic, and essayist, who writes chiefly about abnormalities in sex and revolutionary matters. 281. bludgeonings of chance, a phrase from Henley's *Invictus*, p. 866, line 7. 289. teaching ... school, a reference to Auden's teaching years, 1928-1933. 294. Rabbitarse and String, Gabbitas and Thring, an English school agency. 295. Head's M.A., the headmaster is a Master of Arts.

The aim is training character and poise, 300
With special coaching for the backward boys.

I found the pay good and had time to spend it,
   Though others may not have the good luck
      I did:
For you I'd hesitate to recommend it;
   Several have told me that they can't abide it.
   Still, if one tends to get a bit one-sided, 306
It's pleasant as it's easy to secure
The hero worship of the immature.

More, it's a job, and jobs today are rare:
   All the ideals in the world won't feed us 310
Although they give our crimes a certain air.
   So barons of the press who know their
      readers
   Employ to write their more appalling lead-
      ers,
Instead of Satan's horned and hideous min-
      ions,
Clever young men of liberal opinions. 315

Which brings me up to nineteen-thirty-five;
   Six months of film work is another story
I can't tell now. But, here I am, alive
   Knowing the true source of that sense of
      glory
   That still surrounds the England of the
      Tory, 320
Come only to the rather tame conclusion
That no man by himself has life's solution.

I know—the fact is really not unnerving—
   That what is done is done, that no past dies,
That what we see depends on who's observ-
      ing, 325
   And what we think on our activities.
   That envy warps the virgin as she dries
But "Post coitum, homo tristis" means
The lover must go carefully with the greens.

The boat has brought me to the landing-stage,
   Up the long estuary of mud and sedges; 331
   The line I travel has the English gauge;
      The engine's shadow vaults the little hedges;
      And summer's done. I sign the usual pledges

To be a better poet, better man; 335
I'll really do it this time if I can.

I'm home again, and goodness knows to what,
   To read the papers and to earn my bread;
I'm home to Europe where I may be shot;
   "I'm home again," as William Morris said,
   "And nobody I really care for's dead." 341
I've got a round of visits now to pay,
So I must finish this another day.   (1937)

from *In Time of War**

So from the years the gifts were showered;
    each
Ran off with his at once into his life:
Bee took the politics that make a hive,
Fish swam as fish, peach settled into peach.

And were successful at the first endeavor; 5
The hour of birth their only time at college,
They were content with their precocious
    knowledge,
And knew their station and were good for-
    ever.

Till finally there came a childish creature 9
On whom the years could model any feature,
And fake with ease a leopard or a dove;

Who by the lightest wind was changed and
    shaken,
And looked for truth and was continually
    mistaken,
And envied his few friends and chose his love.

II

They wondered why the fruit had been for-
    bidden;
It taught them nothing new. They hid their
    pride,
But did not listen much when they were chid-
    den;
They knew exactly what to do outside.

They left: immediately the memory faded 5
Of all they'd learnt; they could not under-
    stand

---

317. **six . . . work,** a reference to Auden's work with the General Post Office Film Unit in 1935-1936. 328. **"Post . . . tristis,"** "after cohabitation, man is sad."

In Time of War. This poem consists of a group of sonnets written when Auden was on a trip to China during the war. Reprinted here are sonnets I, II, IV, V, VI, VII, X, XVIII, and XXVII.

The dogs now who, before, had always aided;
The stream was dumb with whom they'd
    always planned.

They wept and quarreled: freedom was so wild.
In front, maturity, as he ascended,   10
Retired like a horizon from the child;

The dangers and the punishments grew
    greater:
And the way back by angels was defended
Against the poet and the legislator.

IV

He stayed: and was imprisoned in possession.
The seasons stood like guards about his ways,
The mountains chose the mother of his chil-
    dren,
And like a conscience the sun ruled his days.

Beyond him his young cousins in the city   5
Pursued their rapid and unnatural course,
Believed in nothing but were easy-going,
And treated strangers like a favorite horse.

And he changed little,
But took his color from the earth,   10
And grew in likeness to his sheep and cattle.

The townsman thought him miserly and
    simple,
The poet wept and saw in him the truth,
And the oppressor held him up as an example.

V

His generous bearing was a new invention:
For life was slow; earth needed to be careless;
With horse and sword he drew the girls' at-
    tention;
He was the Rich, the Bountiful, the Fearless.

And to the young he came as a salvation;   5
They needed him to free them from their
    mothers,
And grew sharp-witted in the long migration,
And round his camp fires learnt all men are
    brothers.

But suddenly the earth was full: he was not
    wanted.

And he became the shabby and demented,   10
And took to drink to screw his nerves to
    murder;

Or sat in offices and stole,
And spoke approvingly of Law and Order,
And hated life with all his soul.

VI

He watched the stars and noted birds in flight;
The rivers flooded or the Empire fell:
He made predictions and was sometimes right;
His lucky guesses were rewarded well.

And fell in love with Truth before he knew
    her,   5
And rode into imaginary lands,
With solitude and fasting hoped to woo her,
And mocked at those who served her with
    their hands.

But her he never wanted to despise,
But listened always for her voice; and when   10
She beckoned to him, he obeyed in meekness,

And followed her and looked into her eyes;
Saw there reflected every human weakness,
And saw himself as one of many men.

VII

He was their servant—some say he was blind—
And moved among their faces and their
    things;
Their feeling gathered in him like a wind
And sang: they cried—"It is a God that
    sings"—

And worshiped him and set him up apart,   5
And made him vain, till he mistook for song
The little tremors of his mind and heart
At each domestic wrong.

Songs came no more: he had to make them.
With what precision was each strophe
    planned,   10
He hugged his sorrow like a plot of land,

And walked like an assassin through the
    town,

---

10. **strophe**, a group of lines forming a metrical system in song or ode.

And looked at men and did not like them,
But trembled if one passed him with a frown.

X

As a young child the wisest could adore him;
He felt familiar to them like their wives:
The very poor saved up their pennies for him,
And martyrs brought him presents of their lives.

But who could sit and play with him all day?
Their other needs were pressing, work, and bed: 6
The beautiful stone courts were built where they
Could leave him to be worshiped and well fed.

But he escaped. They were too blind to tell
That it was he who came with them to labor,
And talked and grew up with them like a neighbor: 11

To fear and greed those courts became a center;
The poor saw there the tyrant's citadel,
And martyrs the lost face of the tormentor.

XVIII

Far from the heart of culture he was used:
Abandoned by his general and his lice,
Under a padded quilt he closed his eyes
And vanished. He will not be introduced

When this campaign is tidied into books: 5
No vital knowledge perished in his skull;
His jokes were stale; like wartime, he was dull;
His name is lost forever like his looks.

He neither knew nor chose the Good, but taught us,
And added meaning like a comma, when 10
He turned to dust in China that our daughters

Be fit to love the earth, and not again
Disgraced before the dogs; that, where are waters,
Mountains and houses, may be also men.

XXVII

Wandering lost upon the mountains of our choice,
Again and again we sigh for an ancient South,
For the warm nude ages of instinctive poise,
For the taste of joy in the innocent mouth.

Asleep in our huts, how we dream of a part 5
In the glorious balls of the future; each intricate maze
Has a plan, and the disciplined movements of the heart
Can follow forever and ever its harmless ways.

We envy streams and houses that are sure:
But we are articled to error; we 10
Were never nude and calm like a great door,

And never will be perfect like the fountains;
We live in freedom by necessity,
A mountain people dwelling among mountains. (1939)

Musée des Beaux Arts

About suffering they were never wrong,
The Old Masters: how well they understood
Its human position; how it takes place
While someone else is eating or opening a window or just walking dully along;
How, when the aged are reverently, passionately waiting 5
For the miraculous birth, there always must be
Children who did not specially want it to happen, skating
On a pond at the edge of the wood:
They never forgot
That even the dreadful martyrdom must run its course 10
Anyhow in a corner, some untidy spot
Where the dogs go on with their doggy life and the torturer's horse
Scratches its innocent behind on a tree.

In Brueghel's *Icarus*, for instance: how everything turns away

Musée des Beaux Arts. The title means *Museum of Fine Arts,* which is the name of the museum owning Brueghel's *Icarus.* 14. Brueghel, Pieter Brueghel (1520?-1569), famous Flemish painter. Icarus was an Athenian youth who tried to escape from Crete with his father by the use of artificial wings. He flew too near the sun; the wax of the wings melted and he fell into the sea and was drowned.

Quite leisurely from the disaster; the ploughman may 15
Have heard the splash, the forsaken cry,
But for him it was not an important failure; the sun shone
As it had to on the white legs disappearing into the green
Water; and the expensive delicate ship that must have seen
Something amazing, a boy falling out of the sky, 20
Had somewhere to get to and sailed calmly on.   (1940)

In Memory of W. B. Yeats

1

He disappeared in the dead of winter:
The brooks were frozen, the air-ports almost deserted,
And snow disfigured the public statues;
The mercury sank in the mouth of the dying day.
O all the instruments agree 5
The day of his death was a dark cold day.

Far from his illness
The wolves ran on through the evergreen forests,
The peasant river was untempted by the fashionable quays;
By mourning tongues 10
The death of the poet was kept from his poems.

But for him it was his last afternoon as himself,
An afternoon of nurses and rumors;
The provinces of his body revolted,
The squares of his mind were empty, 15
Silence invaded the suburbs,
The current of his feeling failed: he became his admirers.

Now he is scattered among a hundred cities
And wholly given over to unfamiliar affections;

In Memory of W. B. Yeats. For Yeats, see p. 1025. 1. He ... winter. Yeats died on January 28, 1939. 17. he ... admirers. Compare Shelley's *Adonais*, p. 268, line 370: "He is made one with Nature."

To find his happiness in another kind of wood 20
And be punished under a foreign code of conscience.
The words of a dead man
Are modified in the guts of the living.

But in the importance and noise of tomorrow
When the brokers are roaring like beasts on the floor of the Bourse, 25
And the poor have the sufferings to which they are fairly accustomed,
And each in the cell of himself is almost convinced of his freedom;
A few thousand will think of this day
As one thinks of a day when one did something slightly unusual.

O all the instruments agree 30
The day of his death was a dark cold day.

2

You were silly like us: your gift survived it all;
The parish of rich women, physical decay,
Yourself; mad Ireland hurt you into poetry.
Now Ireland has her madness and her weather still, 35
For poetry makes nothing happen: it survives
In the valley of its saying where executives
Would never want to tamper; it flows south
From ranches of isolation and the busy griefs,
Raw towns that we believe and die in; it survives, 40
A way of happening, a mouth.

3

Earth, receive an honored guest;
William Yeats is laid to rest:
Let the Irish vessel lie
Emptied of its poetry. 45

Time that is intolerant
Of the brave and innocent,
And indifferent in a week
To a beautiful physique,

Worships language and forgives 50
Everyone by whom it lives;
Pardons cowardice, conceit,
Lays its honors at their feet.

25. Bourse, the stock exchange.

Time that with this strange excuse
Pardoned Kipling and his views, 55
And will pardon Paul Claudel,
Pardons him for writing well.

In the nightmare of the dark
All the dogs of Europe bark,
And the living nations wait, 60
Each sequestered in its hate;

Intellectual disgrace
Stares from every human face,
And the seas of pity lie
Locked and frozen in each eye. 65

Follow, poet, follow right
To the bottom of the night,
With your unconstraining voice
Still persuade us to rejoice;

With the farming of a verse 70
Make a vineyard of the curse,
Sing of human unsuccess
In a rapture of distress;

In the deserts of the heart
Let the healing fountain start, 75
In the prison of his days
Teach the free man how to praise. (1940)

from *The Age of Anxiety*

In *The Age of Anxiety* Auden presents four modern sophisticates, three men and a woman, who meet in a bar and fall into conversation, which talk leads to a review of their respective lives, arranged in the customary seven ages of man. In the tense atmosphere of wartime, the psyches of these four people are close to the surface, and their drink stimulates all their perceptions and releases their spiritual inhibitions. Ultimately they proceed for a snack and nightcaps to the apartment of the woman, where Emble, the weakling of the men, is overcome and must remain to sleep off his intoxication. The other two men, Quant, the visionary, and Malin, who is throughout the leader of the conversation, depart on their separate ways; Malin concludes with the soliloquy given here.

PART VI, EPILOGUE

For the others, like me, there is only the
  flash 85
Of negative knowledge, the night when,
  drunk, one
Staggers to the bathroom and stares in
  the glass
To meet one's madness, when what
  mother said seems
Such darling rubbish and the decent
  advice
Of the liberal weeklies as lost an art 90
As peasant pottery, for plainly it is not
To the Cross or to Clarté or to Common
  Sense
Our passions pray but to primitive totems
As absurd as they are savage; science or
  no science,
It is Bacchus or the Great Boyg or Baal-
  Peor, 95
Fortune's Ferris-wheel or the physical
  sound
Of our own names which they actually
  adore as their
Ground and goal. Yet the grossest of our
  dreams is
No worse than our worship which for
  the most part
Is so much galimatias to get out of 100
Knowing our neighbor, all the needs and
  conceits of
The poor muddled maddened mundane
  animal
Who is hostess to us all, for each contrib-
  utes his
Personal panic, his predatory note
To her gregarious grunt as she gropes in
  the dark 105

55. *Pardoned . . . views.* Rudyard Kipling (p. 885) said some very sharp things about the English Conservatives of his time, and his views on politics in England probably prevented his being named poet laureate when Tennyson died in 1892 or again when Robert Bridges passed away in 1930. 56. **Paul Claudel**, a French poet, playwright, and diplomat (1868-1955), who has been termed by many the greatest contemporary poet. 71. **vineyard . . . curse**, a reference to the expulsion of Adam and Eve from the Garden of Eden. The metaphor represents the making of good out of bad.
  The excerpt from *The Age of Anxiety* by W. H. Auden is reprinted by permission of Random House, Inc. Copyright, 1947, by W. H. Auden.

92. **Clarté**, clarity, clearness, the "let-there-be-light" spirit, which was a watchword for the French Encyclopedists of the eighteenth century. 95. **Bacchus**, in classical mythology, the god of wine and regeneration. **Great Boyg**, Bog, the supreme god of the ancient Slavs. **Baal-Peor.** Baal was the god of the Canaanites in the Old Testament; he received various epithets according to the localities in which he was worshipped, and was therefore called Baal-Peor in the mountain sections of Moab. 100. **galimatias**, jumbled nonsense, gibberish.

For her lost lollypop. We belong to our kind,
Are judged as we judge, for all gestures of time
And all species of space respond in our own
Contradictory dialect, the double talk 109
Of ambiguous bodies, born like us to that
Natural neighborhood which denial itself
Like a friend confirms; they reflect our status,
Temporals pleading for eternal life with
The infinite impetus of anxious spirits,
Finite in fact yet refusing to be real, 115
Wanting our own way, unwilling to say Yes
To the Self-So which is the same at all times,
That Always-Opposite which is the whole subject
Of our not-knowing, yet from no necessity
Condescended to exist and to suffer death
And, scorned on a scaffold, ensconced in His life 121
The human household. In our anguish we struggle
To elude Him, to lie to Him, yet His love observes
His appalling promise; His predilection
As we wander and weep is with us to the end, 125
Minding our meanings, our least matter dear to Him,
His Good ingressant on our gross occasions
Envisages our advance, valuing for us
Though our bodies too blind or too bored to examine
What sorts excite them are slain interjecting 130
Their childish Ows and, in choosing how many
And how much they will love, our minds insist on
Their own disorder as their own punishment,
His Question disqualifies our quick senses,
His Truth makes our theories historical sins, 135
It is where we are wounded that is when He speaks
Our creaturely cry, concluding His children
In their mad unbelief to have mercy on them all
As they wait unawares for His World to come.

So thinking, he returned to duty, reclaimed by the actual world where time is real and in which, therefore, poetry can take no interest.

Facing another long day of servitude to wilful authority and blind accident, creation lay in pain and earnest, once more reprieved from self-destruction, its adoption, as usual, postponed. (1947)

140. **he**, Malin, the "moderator" of conversation.

Stephen Spender
1909-

The son of talented parents—his father, Edward H. Spender, was a novelist, journalist, and lecturer—Stephen Spender was born near London and attended University College, Oxford. While at the university, he served as one of the editors of the *Oxford Poetry* anthologies and published his first efforts at writing verse—*Nine Experiments* (1928) and *Twenty Poems* (1930). In a more significant volume, *Poems* (1933), he revealed genuine poetic gifts, shown both in technique and in purposefulness. He was, like many of the young poets of the 1930's, strongly stirred by left-wing ideas, as in *Vienna* (1934), a long didactic poem, and *Trial of a Judge* (1938). Since the Second World War, however, Spender has shown himself to be more and more of a romanticist; disillusioned by the harsh realities of modern power politics and social programs, he has turned to personal themes, as in *The Still Centre* (1939), *Selected Poems* (1940), *Ruins and Visions* (1941), and *Poems of Dedication* (1946). But he attracted much attention by a book of criticism, *The Destructive Element* (1935), and, along with other works in that field, has tried his hand at psychological fiction, political essays, and travel journals. Of late he has assumed the position of a miscellaneous writer and journalist. His autobiography *World Within World* was published in 1951.

Rolled Over on Europe

Rolled over on Europe: the sharp dew frozen
    to stars
Below us: above our heads the night
Frozen again to stars: the stars
In pools between our coats, and that charmed
    moon:
Ah, what supports? What cross draws out
    our arms,   5
Heaves up our bodies towards the wind
And hammers us between the mirrored
    lights?

Only my body is real: which wolves
Are free to oppress and gnaw. Only this rose
My friend laid on my breast, and these few
    lines   10
Written from home, are real.   (1933)

Your Body Is Stars

Your body is stars whose million glitter here:
I am lost amongst the branches of this sky
Here near my breast, here in my nostrils, here
Where our vast arms like streams of fire lie.

How can this end? My healing fills the
    night   5
And hangs its flags in worlds I cannot near.
Our movements range through miles, and
    when we kiss
The moment widens to enclose long years.

* * * * *

Beholders of the promised dawn of truth
The explorers of immense and simple lines,   10
Here is our goal, men cried, but it was lost

<small>The poems of Spender are reprinted by permission of Random House, Inc., New York, and Faber and Faber, Ltd., London. Copyright, 1934, by Random House, Inc.</small>

Amongst the mountain mists and mountain
    pines.

So with this face of love, whose breathings are
A mystery shadowed on the desert floor:
The promise hangs, this swarm of stars and
    flowers,   15
And then there comes the shutting of a door.
    (1933)

Without That Once Clear Aim

Without that once clear aim, the path of
    flight
To follow for a life-time through white air,
This century chokes me under roots of night
I suffer like history in Dark Ages, where
Truth lies in dungeons, from which drifts no
    whisper: 5
We hear of towers long broken off from sight
And tortures and war, in dark and smoky
    rumor,
But on men's buried lives there falls no light.
Watch me who walk through coiling streets
    where rain
And fog drown every cry: at corners of day   10
Road drills explore new areas of pain,
Nor summer nor light may reach down here
    to play.
The city builds its horror in my brain,
This writing is my only wings away.   (1933)

I Think Continually of Those

I think continually of those who were truly
    great.
Who, from the womb, remembered the soul's
    history
Through corridors of light where the hours
    are suns

Endless and singing. Whose lovely ambition
Was that their lips, still touched with fire,   5
Should tell of the Spirit clothed from head to
    foot in song.
And who hoarded from the Spring branches
The desires falling across their bodies like
    blossoms.

What is precious is never to forget
The essential delight of the blood drawn from
    ageless springs   10
Breaking through rocks in worlds before our
    earth.
Never to deny its pleasure in the morning
    simple light
Nor its grave evening demand for love.
Never to allow gradually the traffic to smother
With noise and fog the flowering of the
    spirit.   15

Near the snow, near the sun, in the highest
    fields
See how these names are feted by the waving
    grass
And by the streamers of white cloud
And whispers of wind in the listening sky.
The names of those who in their lives fought
    for life   20
Who wore at their hearts the fire's center.
Born of the sun they travelled a short while
    towards the sun,
And left the vivid air signed with their honor.
                      (1933)

The Pylons

The secret of these hills was stone, and cot-
    tages
Of that stone made,
And crumbling roads
That turned on sudden hidden villages.

Now over these small hills they have built
    the concrete   5
That trails black wire:
Pylons, those pillars
Bare like nude, giant girls that have no secret.

The Pylons. In aeronautics a pylon is a post, a tower, or the like marking a prescribed course of flight.

The valley with its gilt and evening look
And the green chestnut   10
Of customary root
Are mocked dry like the parched bed of a
    brook.

But far above and far as sight endures
Like whips of anger
With lightning's danger   15
There runs the quick perspective of the future.

This dwarfs our emerald country by its trek
So tall with prophecy:
Dreaming of cities
Where often clouds shall lean their swan-
    white neck.   (1933)

Not Palaces, an Era's Crown

Not palaces, an era's crown
Where the mind dwells, intrigues, rests;
The architectural gold-leaved flower
From people ordered like a single mind,
I build. This only what I tell;   5
It is too late for rare accumulation
For family pride, for beauty's filtered dusts;
I say, stamping the words with emphasis,
Drink from here energy and only energy,
As from the electric charge of a battery,   10
To will this Time's change.
Eye, gazelle, delicate wanderer,
Drinker of horizon's fluid line,
Ear that suspends on a chord
The spirit drinking timelessness;   15
Touch, love, all senses,
Leave your gardens, your singing feasts,
Your dreams of suns circling before our sun,
Of heaven after our world.
Instead, watch images of flashing brass   20
That strike the outward sense, the polished
    will,
Flag of our purpose which the wind engraves.
No spirit seek here rest. But this: No man
Shall hunger: Man shall spend equally.
Our goal which we compel: Man shall be
    man.   25

—That program of the antique Satan
Bristling with guns on the indented page
With battleship towering from hilly waves:

For what? Drive of a ruining purpose
Destroying all but its age-long exploiters.   30
Our program like this, yet opposite,
Death to the killers, bringing light to life.
(1933)

What I Expected

What I expected was
Thunder, fighting,
Long struggles with men
And climbing.
After continual straining   5
I should grow strong;
Then the rocks would shake
And I should rest long.

What I had not foreseen
Was the gradual day   10
Weakening the will
Leaking the brightness away,
The lack of good to touch
The fading of body and soul
Like smoke before wind   15
Corrupt, unsubstantial.

The wearing of Time,
And the watching of cripples pass
With limbs shaped like questions
In their odd twist,   20
The pulverous grief
Melting the bones with pity,
The sick falling from earth—
These, I could not foresee.

For I had expected always   25
Some brightness to hold in trust,
Some final innocence

What I Expected is from *Poems* by Stephen Spender. Reprinted by permission of Random House, Inc., New York, and Faber and Faber, Ltd., London. Copyright, 1934, by The Modern Library, Inc.

To save from dust;
That, hanging solid,
Would dangle through all   30
Like the created poem
Or the dazzling crystal.
(1933)

The Bombed Happiness

Children, who extend their smile of crystal,
And their leaping gold embrace,
And wear their happiness as a frank jewel,
Are forced in the mould of the groaning bull
And engraved with lines on the face.   5

Their harlequin-striped flesh,
Their blood twisted in rivers of song,
Their flashing, trustful emptiness,
Are trampled by an outer heart that pressed
From the sky right through the coral breast   10
And kissed the heart and burst.

This timed, exploding heart that breaks
The loved and little hearts, is also one
Splintered through the lungs and wombs
And fragments of squares in the sun,   15
And crushing the floating, sleeping babe
Into a deeper sleep.

Its victoried drumming enters
Above the limbs of bombed laughter
The body of an expanding State   20
And throbs there and makes it great,
But nothing nothing can recall
Gaiety buried under these dead years,
Sweet jester and young playing fool
Whose toy was human happiness.   25
(1939)

The Bombed Happiness. 6. harlequin-striped, bearing marks or stripes like those on the parti-colored suit worn by the Harlequin, a character in popular Italian comedy.

George Barker
1913-

It has been customary to think of George Barker as a disciple of W. H. Auden (p. 1145), but he is far too talented a poet and far too complex a satirist to be content as one dependent on anybody. He is actually a more romantic thinker than Auden, rich in his imagery and subtle in his language, though thoroughly Anglo-Saxon rather than Celtic in his use of word and phrase. He has a strong instinct for the historical, as well as a powerful religious spirit which leads him to an insistence upon the need for a thorough spiritual regeneration of our times.

Barker was born in England in 1913 and has been very much of a self-educated individual and a wide traveler. His first book to appear was a prose work, *Alanna Autumnal* (1933), but in the next two years he produced two volumes of poetry, which made it clear that it is as a poet that he should be considered. *Selected Poems* (1941), *Sacred and Secular Elegies* (1944), *Love Poems* (1947), *News of the World* (1950), and *A Vision of Beasts and Gods* (1954) complete the list. In these poems the dominant themes are those which attempt to reconcile a political liberalism with a personal religious emotion that cries out for the betterment of mankind. It is not surprising that he should be acutely aware of the need for avoiding war and economic depressions, for he had his literary initiation in the difficult days of the 1930's when the Great Depression was a reality and the threat of a world war was becoming a monstrous cloud over the whole of the western world. In fact, most of his best poems, which are narrative and expository rather than concentratedly lyrical, are those which deplore the betrayal of mankind by the graceless powers of avarice and materialism.

Vision of England '38

In the first section of this poem, the poet, looking back over the history of England and considering such revolutionaries as Wat Tyler, of the Peasants' Revolt of 1381, and Shelley (p. 248), reviews England's past and advises watching and patience. In the second section, mindful of England's rough path in the 1930's (p. 1003 ff.), he complains that the nation has remained purely commercial and Philistine and is consequently headed for spiritual and moral bankruptcy. In the third section the poet tours England from south to north and raises the question as to what legendary or historical leaders like King Arthur or Alfred the Great would think of the present situation. In the fourth section he concludes that the present generation is largely to blame, for, in the increasing pressures of fear, hate, and greed, the cardinal principle of love has been forgotten. In the final section he concentrates upon London, center of national avarice and materialism, and prays that there be less emphasis upon power and more emphasis upon humanity, particularly in reference to the submerged laboring classes.

I

I lay, not in Malvern or Alexandra Palace
From where the southern sorrow of the horizon is seen
Encompassing more of misery than a tear's whole circle,
But in Brighton I lay in bed, and behind my head
The tremendous panoply of England fell vertical, 5
The historical curtain exuding blood on my pillow;
Conspicuously suspended from diamonds of justice
Dredged from the depths of national despair.

Not sleeping not dreaming I saw the imperial procession
Flicker past my foot in postures of triumph or violence; 10
Some moved in shapes of gluttony or envy, others
Rode pride like lions, and some bore their own flowers.

Vision of England '38 is from George Barker's SELECTED POEMS. Copyright, 1941, by The Macmillan Company and used with their permission. 1. **Malvern**, an urban area in Worcestershire, England, the scene of the annual summer dramatic Malvern Festival. But it was in the hills about Malvern that Piers Plowman had his miraculous vision in another prophetic piece (Vol. I, p. 195). **Alexandra Palace**, in London; now the headquarters of the British Broadcasting Corporation (B.B.C.)'s television department. 4. **Brighton**, the celebrated English seaside resort on the south-eastern coast, popularized early in the nineteenth century by King George IV while he was still the Prince of Wales, and remarkable for its elaborate and intricate architecture.

I heard voices that whispered and voices that
    sang,
"Death is no glory," or "I shun not the fire."
Three women came screaming, wringing
    hands, flying,   15
With crowns on their brows, the last of them
    Victoria.

Behind them, randy as the angry beast who
    craves
Dominion for its ball and sceptre, loped the
    Disraelian lion.
The three queens with its scions in their loins
Flew forward screaming, hunting for their
    graves.   20

Nor could I halt this parade of historical
    character,
Not with a lifted hand and a cry, or an elec-
    tric candle;
Not with appeals or protests or references
    to authority:
The shuffling crowd streamed through in a
    bright dream.

O lamentable lips that ragged showed their
    burns,   25
As that beautiful youth with Saint Mary Red-
    cliffe in hand
Stepped forward and fell at my side and mur-
    mured:
"I warn you, not poison."

Who took my hand and left an orchid there,
With the mark of his lips that parted their
    shapes   30
To speak a word of hope: was it salacious
    Oscar
Or the lost Orphic who coughed blood at
    Naples?

"Remember me, remember me," cried the
    skull
That floated through with seaweed in its
    teeth.
"Drowned in a sudden squall I found him
    there,   35
Waiting under the wave, God ambushed me
    there."

Then I abandoned my attitude of ease on the
    bed
To touch the salt tear that the skull had shed:
And like a pearl it poised upon my hand,
    and I
Saw in its circle the temporal Harlequin
    dome.   40

Next the rhodomontade of the political opera
Shattered my gaze and daze as I saw enter
The onager, the serpent and the macaw,
Tussling together over the heart of man.

But what one tore or what all three ravaged,
Though the wounds bled, seemed to restore 46
Soon to its shape like a world after war,
And all that commemorates is the blood on
    the floor.

So I took Shelley's tear which like a single
    rain
Dropped into the blood that murmured at
    my feet: 50
And a ghost arose holding out its hands in
    pain,
Looking at me with eyes that supplicated fate.

"From tears and blood I spring in sorrow and
    anger,
The long anonymous inhabitant of dearth.
I'm Wat Tyler's wife and Robert Owen's
    lover,   55

---

15. **Three women,** presumably three English queens, Elizabeth, Anne, and Victoria, who reigned from 1558 to 1603, 1702 to 1714, and 1837 to 1901, respectively. 17. **randy,** lustful. 18. **Disraelian.** Benjamin Disraeli, Lord Beaconsfield (1804-1881), twice prime minister during the reign of Queen Victoria. He was an ardent imperialist; it was largely through his endeavors that Queen Victoria was proclaimed empress of India in 1876—a title held by British sovereigns until 1947. 26-28. **beautiful . . . poison.** Thomas Chatterton (1752-1770) was a gifted young English poet of pre-romantic persuasion (p. 7) who lived near the church St. Mary Redcliffe at Bristol. He was noted for his imitation of medieval verse. In the face of failure, as he saw it, he committed suicide by taking poison at the age of 17. 31. **Oscar,** Oscar Wilde (1854-1900). See p. 951. 32. **Orphic.** The lyre music of the legendary Greek poet, Orpheus, was supposed to have given him power over all creatures natural and supernatural. Barker here applies the word to the great English romantic poet John Keats (p. 273), who died (1821) of consumption in Naples.

33. **Skull,** the skull of the poet Shelley (p. 248), who was drowned (1822) in the Gulf of Spezia, Italy. 38-40. **touch . . . dome.** The poet sees in the tears from Shelley's skull an image of the temporal striped or many-colored dome of life. Cf. Shelley's *Adonais,* ll.462-463, p. 270:
  Life, like a dome of many-colored glass,
  Stains the white radiance of Eternity.
41. **rhodomontade,** inflated oratory, hurly-burly of noise and confusion. 43. **onager,** wild ass. The significance of these creatures as applied to politicians needs no further comment. 55. **Wat Tyler,** the English leader of the Peasants' Revolt of 1381, who was killed in the rebellion. Shelley's utopian dream of universal love as a solvent of all problems of life resembles the ideals of Tyler and Robert Owen, however far-fetched the reference to Tyler in this matter may be. **Robert Owen** (1771-1858), a noted British social reformer. As referred to here, the wife of Tyler and the mistress of Owen are anonymous and symbolic characters.

From whom you also came starving at birth.

"Remember me when the rose is too close,
Or when the triumphant dove coos sweetly
Filling the world with love, do not forget me.
I shall be here, the tenant of my woes." 60

"Wait," I said slowly. "Tell me why I,
Lying at night in my Brighton bed,
Receive the visitation of the conspicuously
    dead,
Terrifying me with their mad pageantry."

He lifted his head like a lover to me, 65
Smiling with a secret that no words revealed:
Then he said softly, "Mystery is no mystery
When Time divests it of its present mists.

"Therefore wait with patience: you will see
More than the theatrical zodiac of history. 70
Look closely enough and life will show her
    source
From higher than Chilterns and a grander
    course."

Then the rain tattooed the window. He was
    gone,
Leaving me alone in a room of time
So small that I filled it with a minute sigh, 75
For the host and the ghost were gone.

II

But I arose, with a star against my cheek
Roaring of winter with the tongues of Orion:
"The great winds rage in the mane of the lion,
But not great winds make the lion weak." 80

Near me the sea in nocturnal lamentation
Shrouded itself in hoods and wept a shower,
Retreating in sorrow from the lion's locks
Where he lies emaciated on capital rocks.

Cassiopeia wept. I felt her brilliant sym-
    pathy 85
Falling upon me as I walked by the waves;

I looked up at her outstretched arms in the
    sky
Too far to reach me and too near for a grave.

Then a saint walked up out of the sea,
Dragging his death behind him like a boat. 90
He had a rusty sword and he said to me:
"I killed an enormous monster, but the brute

"Still rules England with its scales of gold.
O my green girl given to the rape of the
    banker,
The careerist politician and the vague
    thinker, 95
Lie easy for one more night out in the cold."

He gave me his sword with a long look,
Then turned, and returned to his death.
I glanced down at the iron in my hand, and
    found
The blueblooded point that bleeds a book. 100

So I lay down against Saint George's green
    girl
To keep her warm an hour in my arms.
To see us lying by the waves' whirl
The dove also wept among the Great Dog's
    curls.

But Peace is dear and cannot be bought with
    sleep, 105
Any more than Birmingham can keep peace
    in steel:
So as I lay between a dream and a sleep
A tongue licked me, and I saw it was a sheep.

"This green," it said, "this pleasant place,
Not yet is fit for the foot of Christ. 110
How can your word or your sword sleep
While the Thames is the sweat of the people?

"I am Blake who broke my mind on God.
I tell you he does not touch this world
Till the disease is scoured from the sod 115

---

72. **Chilterns**, a range of chalk hills in south central England. 78. **Orion**, probably the most famous of the winter constellations visible in the northern hemisphere. Since it is a large and brilliant constellation, it may be assumed that it is used here as a symbol of power. 79. **great winds . . . lions**, storms of war over Britain. 85. **Cassiopeia**, a conspicuous constellation of the northern hemisphere almost opposite the Big Dipper (Ursa Major) across the Pole Star. Its W-shaped form suggests the image of *out-stretched arms* (l. 87). 89. **a saint**, evidently St. George, the patron saint of England. This particular saint was George of Cappadocia in Asia Minor, to whom were transferred the epic feats of Perseus, who in Greek legend slew the dragon, Medusa, and rescued the fair maid Andromeda. 106. **Birmingham**, the major center of Britain's iron and steel industry. 112. **Thames**. The river of London and most celebrated river in England has been referred to as "liquid history." 113. **Blake**, William Blake (p. 111), the romantic poet, who condemned the England of his day for its insincerity, hypocrisy, and greed.

By the blood of sin made fit for his hand."

The touch of the tongue as the Lamb kissed
Fired my spirit with the bliss of fate
When the spirit senses the great ultimate
To which it toils through mystery and
    mist.   120

Alone on the dark beach I stood.
The teeth of the seas tore the shore.
"O immensely sad land," I said, "where
Only the ghosts are good."

III

I ride my grief along the road   125
Leaving the littoral cities to their summer
    sins;
Brighton and Bournemouth with the pots of
    God
Brimming fire over the signs of the times.

But who could whistle or sing in the South
With its ramshackle witch-barns broken and
    ruined;   130
Where the disused thresher rusts among the
    lichens,
And the brood scuttles in the kitchens?

So I went northward to Salisbury on Friday.
But on the bridge I encountered a figure
Who crossed me with a look and shook his
    head: 135
"It's market day but even so we are dead.

"I'm William Longspee who lies in stone
In the north aisle of the Cathedral:
All the semblance of Salisbury's life is a pall
Covering the famous faces of the dead and
    gone.   140

"There's nothing here but the mere loveliness
Of the long lost Gothic ache to heaven:
Like the lily in which the dead dress,
Salisbury is a beautiful funeral."

And I saw the sweet alto of the spire sing
    upward   145
Like the long note of the God-mourning
    choir
Creating its tomb of music, or song's pyre
Over the bones of Salisbury in Wiltshire.

From the Bay of Swanage as I came down in
    Dorset
The shade of Alfred arose shaking a guilty
    hand;   150
He pointed westward to Weymouth and with
    a hoarse voice
Cried: "See what a fatal gift I gave England!"

Manoeuvring over the broad water like gnats
The naval seaplanes and the giant cruisers
Spread their shadows over the boats and
    bathers   155
Who played in Weymouth Bay among the
    shadows.

Then I saw that they floated in blood and
    blossoms,
The blood of the bathers, the blossoms of the
    boughs
That made the boats: under the dreadnought
    bosoms
Crushed and bruised under the huge bows. 160

Alfred arraigned. "O my people, what have
    I done
Unto thee, unto thee! O Arthur, Arthur!
Go, boy, over to Glastonbury and ask for
    Arthur,
Ask there for Arthur. Say England needs a
    father."

He struck the Georgian Memorial in the
    street with his hand   165

117. **Lamb**, reference to Blake, one of whose best-known poems in his *Songs of Innocence* is "The Lamb" (p. 114). It is not a coincidence, moreover, that Christ is also referred to as The Lamb. 126. **littoral**, pertaining to the sea-shore. 133. **Salisbury**, an important cathedral city in Wiltshire, England. The spire of its cathedral (l. 145) is notably high and pointed, and the entire structure has feminine rather than masculine lines. 137. **William Longspee**, William Longsword (Longespée), an illegitimate son of King Henry II of England, who was one of those to persuade his half-brother John, the King, to sign the Magna Charta in 1215. His tomb and effigy are in Salisbury Cathedral.

150. **Alfred**, Alfred the Great (848?-900?), the celebrated king of the West Saxons in Anglo-Saxon England (Vol. I, p. 6). His fatal gift (l. 152) was nationalism and the British naval tradition. 162. **Arthur**, King Arthur, a central figure in Celtic British legendry and the most famous sovereign of the chivalric tradition in medieval Europe, outshining even the historical Emperor Charlemagne. He is, therefore, used here as a traditional symbol of medieval unity and culture. 163. **Glastonbury**, a town in Somersetshire, England. In medieval legend it was the place in England to which the Biblical Joseph of Arimathea brought the Christian religion. It also was the alleged burial-place of both King Arthur and Queen Guinevere; it is the supposed site of Avalon, the Celtic abode of the blessed.

As I strike nettles, and left it in the gutter.
He sprang in the trough of a wave and floated away,
Went down muttering with his face in his hands.

And I heard the air full of the songs of swans.
So I went down westward to Abbotsbury, whose waters 170
Echo so many ends that here the swan's valediction
Dies in the morning and is never dead.

It is the native music of contemporary England
I reflected when wandering along the verge;
And awakens in me music I understand, 175
The note of the swan who bleeds for her purge.

And though the purge shall bleed her in revolution,
Dry up her unhappy heart whence song arises,
Rupture that loveliness with mechanical contortion,
If she achieves her perfect peace, it is the prize. 180

IV

North also to the broad vowels and the mountains,
Leaving the melancholy swans who mourn for the nation,
I went towards Mount Rydal where the exhausted fountain
Gaped dry and salty over Wordsworth's memorial.

Here the sun detonated among Cumberland cymbals, 185
Reminding me of time and my own shadow:
How soon I shall lie easy, evaded the shambles,
The tremendous pendulum of the stars and my own sorrow.

But then from the ground it arose, my shade,
Bearing the teeth that shook in my own jaw: 190
"I am you. Forget me. No more me. No more
Dallying with the Idalian in the glade."

He swung his arm to the east, and there
Down the mountain path came a young woman,
Wearing a tawdry blouse and careless hair, 195
Who hurried as though pursued by a rumour.

"He's behind me! He's behind me!" she cried, running.
Then I caught her hand and drew her from the road.
"Who?"—and the pulse of her hand, drumming,
Answered, "Fear is abroad! Fear is abroad!" 200

"I am the North," she said, "whom the South follows
Like bailiff or police who demand my money.
He caught me on the road and rifled my mine,
Took the gold from my teeth and left me hollow.

"Yes, the South in his bowler and morning jacket, 205
His leather satchel, and handkerchief in pocket,
He called me a whore, but when he'd had his worth
Not a penny he paid me for the child I bring forth."

She ran her hand through her hair. I saw
Jarrow on her third finger like a lead ring. 210
"Yes," she said, "he absconded after the war,
The husband for whom I wore flowers in the spring.

---

170. **Abbotsbury**, a village on the Dorsetshire coast, near the sea-port of Weymouth. 177. **revolution**. According to the poet, all changes in nature constitute revolution. 183. **Mount Rydal**, Rydal Mount in Westmorland, the home of Wordsworth (p. 118). It should be recalled that in his early life Wordsworth was a political as well as literary revolutionist.

192. **Idalian**. In Greek mythology Idalium was an ancient town on the island of Cyprus, a center for the worship of Aphrodite (the Roman Venus), goddess of love and beauty. The *Idalian* would therefore be Venus herself. 210. **Jarrow**, now a ship-building town in Durham, near Newcastle, known during the depression of the 1930's for its efforts to establish a revival of industry. In Anglo-Saxon times—and the contrast is most significant—it was the abode of the English historian, scholar, and miscellaneous writer, the Venerable Bede (Vol. I, p. 62). The imagery in these stanzas is rather violent, intended to represent the brutality that arises from the pursuit of "progress."

"Write it red in your lines, O write it red,
I starve with my children on the northern
 seaboard.
Warn well the pot-bellied and the over-
 fed,   215
I'll have their hearts to fill my echoing cupboard."

Then the December star sprang over a rock,
Filling the lines of her face with livid silver;
And a filigree of lace flittered over her shoul-
 der,
Making her anger a monument of silver. 220

"Nevertheless Venus is lovely," I said,
And heard Wordsworth turn over in his
 grave:
Windermere flashed in my face at the words,
Where it hung at her eye instead.

"Go down. Go down. The eagle's eyrie,   225
The angel's angle, the abandoned wife's
 hearth.
These are no places for the nose of the query.
Leave me to birth."

But beside Windermere I shall move at night
When the West Wind blows into my window   230
The tresses of Venus where they wave their
 light,
Even though I come from a dream of splendour.

Not less strong than the indomitable rock,
Not less lovely than the lake and the star,
The wife of England roves in the North, 235
Among the derelict cities and the memories
 of war.

                    v

Last in the Eastern Marshes I made a way
From town to town over the bog and slough,
Where the quartz cathedrals guide the stray
Like pillars in plains or pins in cloth: 240

With against my left ear the advancing sea
Gnawing the shore near Cromer, and water
Fallen around like glass, where tulips
 brought
A false sunrise, here I could see

The angel of stone in the attitude of song 245
Flicked with a tint of guilt above Norwich;
But its story only asked that the city be made
 rich,
More gilt and glory and less right and wrong.

And a fox over Cambridge and a fish over
 Yarmouth
Yapping and yawing for cash and credit: 250
Everywhere here I saw the larks of youth
Tethered to banks for a debit.

Then a sad yammering wormed along the air
Like underground mouths swarming in the
 sky, and I
Heard from the south arise like the rumour
 of despair,   255
The moan of the seven million in the capital
 city.

O London, magnificent monster in whose
 guts
The bishop lisps with notes and the poet
 writes
With penny words, whose hunger cannot
 glut
With glory or gluttony, on whom a world
 waits,   260

I saw you astride the South in coils
Of insatiable economic appetite:
Mauling the Sussex hills and the broad
Hampshire heath for a maudlin profit.

Where is the Cappadocian for that throat 265
To cut the health and wealth of England
 loose?
O Political Prince, from this rock release
The national man and woman, who groan!

---

221. **Venus**, here, the planet. The meaning of the line seems to be that, in spite of starvation and violence, love is still to be perceived and appreciated. 223. **Windermere**, the largest lake in England, running from Lancashire northward into Westmorland. It is indelibly associated with the life of Wordsworth (p. 118).

242. **Cromer**, a town on the north-east coast of Norfolk, England. 246. **Norwich**, the county city (seat) of Norfolk. 249. **Cambridge**. This city is famous not only because it has an outstanding university but also because it is the county city of Cambridgeshire. Barker in this stanza is saying that, whether they are in a university community or in a simple fishing-town (Yarmouth), youth today are being imprisoned. 265. **Cappadocian**. The reference is to St. George (see note 89).

I see him rise sweating from the North,
Up from the deep shaft or the steel yard— 270
He comes down not drummed or crowned or
  starred,

But nevertheless inheritor of the earth.

O equitable stars hasten that liberation!

(1941)

Dylan Marlais Thomas
1914-1953

Dylan Thomas was born in Wales in 1914 and was educated at Swansea Grammar School, where his father taught English. He published *18 Poems* in 1934 and *Twenty-Five Poems* in 1936, both volumes attracting less attention than they might have done if the star of Auden had not been at the time so definitely in the ascendant. *The Map of Love* and *The World I Breathe* both appeared in 1939, *New Poems* in 1943, and *Death and Entrances* in 1946. During the Second World War Thomas was a documentary film editor for the British Broadcasting Company. He came to America in 1950 for a short visit and returned in January, 1952 for an extended lecture tour. An extraordinary reader of poetry, he was enthusiastically received in dozens of American colleges and universities. He died on November 9, 1953 at St. Vincent's Hospital in New York.

In his first poems, Thomas showed an unquestionable affinity for the surrealistic, as well as a glut of imagery drawn from primitive Celtic rituals of rebirth and sacrifice; but in his later poems, without losing any of the typical Celtic "magic of words," he gained greater control of style and metaphor. Thomas, like Eliot, has been charged with willful obscurity; and if this is at times true, it is an obscurity that comes not from the use of far-fetched allusions to unfamiliar readings, but from a tremendous condensation of metaphor and syntax that sometimes seems impenetrable to rational analysis, a poetic density that creates a magic verbal world which is its own subject.

The death of Thomas at the age of 39 was accompanied by a spontaneous outburst of mourning and tribute unequalled for that of any other literary figure in our time. The spectacular character of the man, the undisputed excellence of some of his work, and the tragic untimeliness of his death has produced a veritable Thomas cult. At the present time it is difficult to assess how much of this extraordinary attention is due to peculiar circumstances and how much to the excellence of his work. The corpus of his work is quite small. There are only ninety-two poems in his *Collected Poems* (1953), all of them short lyrics. Two plays, *The Doctor and the Devils* (1953), a filmscript, and *Under Milk Wood* (1954), a verse play for broadcasting; three chapters of an uncompleted novel *Adventures in the Skin Trade* (1941); seven tales in prose, included in *The Map of Love* (1939); a thinly veiled autobiography *Portrait of the Artist as a Young Dog* (1940) comprehend the general scope of his creative output. There is no doubt, however, that at least a score of his short lyrics are among the finest that have been produced in this century. It remains for posterity to evaluate more fully whether he is entitled to the rank of a major poet. But few can remain unmoved by the richness of sound and metaphor, the startlingly fresh refurbishing of stale diction and syntax; many would agree with Sir Herbert Reed's judgment of Thomas's poetry—"the most absolute poetry that has been written in our time."

To-day, This Insect

Here, as in all of Thomas's poems, there is a reliance on words as the basis of images out of which an idea originates; the sound is even more important in generating this idea than the strict literal sense. In this poem Thomas is stating his creed that through the creation of poetry the poet can create also the magic of belief. No matter what the external symbols of disaster, Thomas insists that the poet should write of his "madman's love of man" and do what he can to bring this love to pass.

To-day, this insect, and the world I breathe,
Now that my symbols have outelbowed space,
Time at the city spectacles, and half
The dear, daft time I take to nudge the sentence,
In trust and tale have I divided sense,   5
Slapped down the guillotine, the blood-red double
Of head and tail made witnesses to this
Murder of Eden and green genesis.

The insect certain is the plague of fables.

This story's monster has a serpent caul,   10
Blind in the coil scrams round the blazing outline,
Measures his own length on the garden wall
And breaks his shell in the last shocked beginning;
A crocodile before the chrysalis,
Before the fall from love the flying heart-bone,   15
Winged like a sabbath ass this children's piece
Uncredited blows Jericho on Eden.

The insect fable is the certain promise.

Death: death of Hamlet and the nightmare madmen,
An air-drawn windmill on a wooden horse,   20
John's beast, Job's patience, and the fibs of vision,
Greek in the Irish sea the ageless voice:
"Adam I love, my madmen's love is endless,
No tell-tale lover has an end more certain,
All legends' sweethearts on a tree of stories,   25
My cross of tales behind the fabulous curtain."   (1936)

The Hand That Signed the Paper

The hand that signed the paper felled a city;
Five sovereign fingers taxed the breath,
Doubled the globe of dead and halved a country;
These five kings did a king to death.

The mighty hand leads to a sloping shoulder,
The finger joints are cramped with chalk;   6
A goose's quill has put an end to murder
That put an end to talk.

The hand that signed the treaty bred a fever,
And famine grew, and locusts came;   10
Great is the hand that holds dominion over
Man by a scribbled name.

The five kings count the dead but do not soften
The crusted wound nor stroke the brow;
A hand rules pity as a hand rules heaven;   15
Hands have no tears to flow.   (1936)

And Death Shall Have No Dominion

And death shall have no dominion.
Dead men naked they shall be one
With the man in the wind and the west moon;
When their bones are picked clean and the clean bones gone,
They shall have stars at elbow and foot;   5

To-day, This Insect; The Hand That Signed the Paper; And Death Shall Have No Dominion; When All My Five and Country Senses See; Among Those Killed in the Dawn Raid Was a Man Aged a Hundred; Holy Spring; Fern Hill are from THE COLLECTED POEMS OF DYLAN THOMAS. Copyright 1953 by Dylan Thomas, reprinted by permission of New Directions.
    To-day, This Insect, 8-21. **Murder of Eden . . . vision.** These lines contain a series of metaphors and allusions to illustrate how violence and evil break in upon the ideal peaceful condition of life typified by the Garden of Eden. This violence and evil is "the insect" of the poem. Jericho, the Old Testament city destroyed by Joshua (see the Biblical *Book of Joshua*), illustrates human destruction (l. 17); the windmill and the horse (l. 20), as well as the "fibs of vision" (l. 21) illustrate the dangers of impractical or false visions or ideals, as typified in Don Quixote's adventures. 21. **John's beast,** the Beast referred to in the *Book of Revelation*, the apocalyptic vision of St. John the Evangelist.

Though they go mad they shall be sane,
Though they sink through the sea they shall
  rise again;
Though lovers be lost love shall not;
And death shall have no dominion.

And death shall have no dominion. 10
Under the windings of the sea
They lying long shall not die windily;
Twisting on racks when sinews give way,
Strapped to a wheel, yet they shall not break;
Faith in their hands shall snap in two, 15
And the unicorn evils run them through;
Split all ends up they shan't crack;
And death shall have no dominion.

And death shall have no dominion.
No more may gulls cry at their ears 20
Or waves break loud on the seashores;
Where blew a flower may a flower no more
Lift its head to the blows of the rain;
Though they be mad and dead as nails,
Heads of the characters hammer through
  daisies; 25
Break in the sun till the sun breaks down,
And death shall have no dominion. (1936)

When All My Five and Country Senses See

This poem is a good example of Thomas's felicitous "word-madness." It is obviously an appeal for a return to the sensuous and sensual as the only way of creating and feeling.

When all my five and country senses see,
  The fingers will forget green thumbs and
    mark
How, through the halfmoon's vegetable eye,
Husk of young stars and handfull zodiac,
Love in the frost is pared and wintered by, 5
The whispering ears will watch love
  drummed away
Down breeze and shell to a discordant beach,
And, lashed to syllables, the lynx tongue cry
That her fond wounds are mended bit-
  terly. 9
My nostrils see her breath burn like a bush.

My one and noble heart has witnesses
In all love's countries, that will grope awake;
And when blind sleep drops on the spying
  senses,
The heart is sensual, though five eyes break.
  (1939)

Among Those Killed in the Dawn Raid Was a Man Aged a Hundred

When the morning was waking over the war
He put on his clothes and stepped out and he
  died,
The locks yawned loose and a blast blew
  them wide,
He dropped where he loved on the burst
  pavement stone
And the funeral grains of the slaughtered
  floor. 5
Tell his street on its back he stopped a sun
And the craters of his eyes grew springshoots
  and fire
When all the keys shot from the locks, and
  rang.
Dig no more for the chains of his grey-
  haired heart.
The heavenly ambulance drawn by a
  wound 10
Assembling waits for the spade's ring on the
  cage.
O keep his bones away from that common
  cart,
The morning is flying on the wings of his age
And a hundred storks perch on the sun's
  right hand. (1943)

Holy Spring

This is a spring song in time of war, which may well mean that it will be our last spring.

O

Out of a bed of love
When that immortal hospital made one more
  move to soothe
The cureless counted body,

When All My Five and Country Senses See. 14. five eyes, the five senses.
Among Those Killed in the Dawn Raid. Note that this poem is a sonnet in form. 6. sun, a symbol of life ever returning. 14. storks, symbols of life reborn as the ancient die.

And ruin and his causes
Over the barbed and shooting sea assumed an
    army   5
And swept into our wounds and
    houses,
I climb to greet the war in which I have no
    heart but only
That one dark I owe my light,
Call for confessor and wiser mirror but there
    is none   9
To glow after the god stoning night
And I am struck as lonely as a holy maker by
    the sun.

            No
Praise that the spring time is all
Gabriel and radiant shrubbery as the morning
    grows joyful
Out of the woebegone pyre
And the multitude's sultry tear turns cool on
    the weeping wall,   15
My arising prodigal
Sun the father his quiver full of the infants
    of pure fire,
But blessed be hail and upheaval
That uncalm still it is sure alone to stand
    and sing
Alone in the husk of man's home   20
And the mother and toppling house of the
    holy Spring,
If only for a last time.   (1946)

Fern Hill

This poem might well be compared with Wordsworth's Prelude *in intent, although it is radically different in style and philosophy. In both poems, however, there is the autobiographical account of the impression made by nature upon a youthful poet.*

Now as I was young and easy under the apple
    boughs
About the lilting house and happy as the
    grass was green,
    The night above the dingle starry,

Holy Spring. **8. That one ... light.** The poet, through this deliberately dark metaphor, explains that he does not have any real heart for war but is trying in a groping manner to discover its purpose.

        Time let me hail and climb
        Golden in the heydays of his eyes,   5
    And honoured among wagons I was prince
        of the apple towns
    And once below a time I lordly had the trees
        and leaves
        Trail with daisies and barley
    Down the rivers of the windfall light.

    And as I was green and carefree, famous
        among the barns   10
    About the happy yard and singing as the farm
        was home,
        In the sun that is young once only,
        Time let me play and be
        Golden in the mercy of his means,
    And green and golden I was huntsman and
        herdsman, the calves   15
    Sang to my horn, the foxes on the hills
        barked clear and cold,
        And the sabbath rang slowly
        In the pebbles of the holy streams.

    All the sun long it was running, it was
        lovely, the hay
    Fields high as the house, the tunes from the
        chimneys, it was air   20
        And playing, lovely and watery
        And fire green as grass.
    And nightly under the simple stars
    As I rode to sleep the owls were bearing the
        farm away,
    All the moon long I heard, blessed among
        stables, the nightjars   25
        Flying with the ricks, and the horses
        Flashing into the dark.

    And then to awake, and the farm, like a
        wanderer white
    With the dew, come back, the cock on his
        shoulder: it was all
        Shining, it was Adam and maiden,   30
        The sky gathered again
        And the sun grew round that very day.
    So it must have been after the birth of the
        simple light
    In the first, spinning place, the spellbound
        horses walking warm
        Out of the whinnying green stable   35
        On to the fields of praise.

And honoured among foxes and pheasants by the gay house
Under the new made clouds and happy as the heart was long,
    In the sun born over and over,
        I ran my heedless ways,   40
    My wishes raced through the house high hay
And nothing I cared, at my sky blue trades, that time allows
In all his tuneful turning so few and such morning songs
    Before the children green and golden
        Follow him out of grace,   45

Nothing I cared, in the lamb white days, that time would take me
Up to the swallow thronged loft by the shadow of my hand,
    In the moon that is always rising,
        Nor that riding to sleep   49
    I should hear him fly with the high fields
And wake to the farm forever fled from the childless land.
Oh as I was young and easy in the mercy of his means,
    Time held me green and dying
    Though I sang in my chains like the sea.

(1946)

General Index

The name of an author represented by selections appears in capitals and small capitals (BURNS, ROBERT); the number in boldface after the name is the page on which his biographical sketch or selections begin.

Selections that are reprinted in this book are listed in boldface italic; the number in boldface after the title is the page on which the piece begins; the other numbers are pages on which the selection is mentioned.

Abbey Theater, 853, 854, 986
Abou Ben Adhem and the Angel, **297**, 304
Adam Bede, 425
Addison, Joseph, 3, 19, 32, 428
Address to the Deil, **99**
Addressed to Haydon, **275**
Admirable Crichton, The, 854
Adonais, 16, 250, 251, **262**, 274
Advent, **751**
Adventures in the Skin Trade, 1169
Adventures of Sherlock Holmes, The, 856
Adventures of Ulysses, 338
Æ. See Russell, G. W.
Ae Fond Kiss, 9, **107**
Aes Triplex, **922**
Aesthete, The, **835**
Aesthetic movement, The, 852, 862
Aesthetics, and Morris, 420; and Pater, 580, 581, 852, 952; and Ruskin, 501; and Wilde, 835, 852, 951-952
After Many a Summer Dies the Swan, 1016
After the Club-Dance, **911**
After the Fair, **912**
Age of Anxiety, The, 1022, 1145, **1158**
"Ah, Are You Digging on My Grave?" **914**
Alanna Autumnal, 1163
Alice in Wonderland, 825
Alice Sit-by-the-Fire, 854
All Is Well, **726**
Allegory, of C. Rossetti, 749; of Shelley, 250; of Wilde, 952; romantic, 39
Almayer's Folly, 859, 942
Along the Road, 1097
Ambassadors, The, 857
American Revolution, 3
Among School Children, 1009, **1031**
Among Those Killed in the Dawn Raid, **1171**
And Death Shall Have No Dominion, **1170**
Andrea Del Sarto, **694**
Androcles and the Lion, 861
Angel, **716**
Animula, **1093**
Another on Fame, **283**
Another Time, 1145
Anthem for Doomed Youth, **1096**
Anti-Victorianism, 1007
Antic Hay, 1016, 1097
Ape and Essence, 1097
Apologia pro Poemate Meo, **1094**
Apologia pro Vita Sua, **407**, 445, 460, 715

Apology, An, **805**
Apparent Failure, **706**
Apparition, **865**
Apple Gathering, An, **751**
Aran Islands, The, 985
Aristocracies, **493**
ARNOLD, MATTHEW, 8, 90, 250, 406, 407, 408, 410, 411, 412, 414, 418, 419, 420, 426, **527-529**, 580, 721, 726, 768, 852, 1097; poetry of, 528-529; prose of, 528; romanticism of, 410
Arrow of Gold, The, 943
Art, 1, 2, 30, 410, 420; and late Victorian literature, 847; and Pater, 580, 581, 852; and Ruskin's criticism, 501, 502, 503, 524
Art of Seeing, The, 1097
Arthurian romance, 7, 57, 415, 646, 798, 809
Ascent of F 6, The, 1145
Ash Wednesday, 1014, 1079, **1087**
Asia, 256
Ask Me No More, **627**
At Casterbridge Fair, **911**
At the Fair, 912
At Tea, **913**
At the Altar-Rail, **914**
Atalanta in Calydon, 808, 810
Athenaeum, The, 1069, 1097
AUDEN, WYSTAN HUGH, 1021-1022, **1145**, 1162, 1169
Auguries of Innocence (Stanza from), **118**
Auld Lang Syne, 9, 84, **102**
Auld Licht Idylls, 854
Aurora Leigh, 710
Austen, Jane, 25, 26, 29, 422
Austerity of Poetry, **743**
Autobiographical writings, and essays, 418; and poems of Wordsworth, 12, 120, 125; in novels, 423; of Byron, 200, 224; of Cowper, 74; of Lamb, 337, 349; spiritual, of Carlyle, 464, 465, 466; spiritual, of Clough, 721; spiritual, of Coleridge, 165; spiritual, of Newman, 423, 445
Autumn Idleness, **796**
Autumn in King's Hintock Park, **909**
Autumn Song, **794**

Bab Ballads, 824, 825
Bacon, Francis, 19
Baker's Tale, The, **832**
Ballad, and Homer, 94; Burns's work with, 84; Coronach, 196; literary, of Campbell, 296; literary, of Coleridge, 11, 12, 164, 166; medieval, 7; of Keats, 16, 282; of Southey, 204, 296; of Wordsworth, 11; Percy

1175

collection, 7; popular, 282; Pre-Raphaelite, 787, 827; Scott's revival of, 13, 27, 190; Scott's translations of, 190; technique of Keats, 16; witch, 274
Ballad, 827
Ballad of Burdens, A, 812
Ballad of Dead Ladies, The, 792
Ballad of François Villon, A, 821
Ballad of Reading Gaol, The, 952, 953
Ballad-Singer, The, 911
Ballade of a Toyokuni Color-Print, 867
Barchester Towers, 422
Bard, The, 8, 47, 53, **55**
Barker, George, 1023, **1162-1163**
Barnaby Rudge, 422
Barrack-Room Ballads, 863, 886, **887**
Barrett, Elizabeth, 415, 656, **709-710**
Barrie, Sir James, 850, 854, 1011
Battle of Blenhiem, The, 296, **300**
Baudelaire, Charles, 850
Beauchamp's Career, 423
Beauty's Soliloquy During Her Honeymoon, A, 908
Bed in Summer, 877
Beddoes, Thomas Lovell, **298, 309,** 1017
Beerbohm, Max, 851, 855
Before, 864
Before the Beginning of Years, 811
Believe Me, If All Those Endearing Young Charms, 303
Belinda, 25
Belloc, Hilaire, 851, 855
Bells and Pomegranates, 656
Bennett, Arnold, 855, 859
Bentham, Jeremy, 22, 404
Beppo; A Venetian Story, 201
Beside the Bonnie Briar Bush, 854
Better Resurrection, A, 751
Between the Acts, 1062
Beyond the Mexique Bay, 1097
Biographia Literaria, 20, 165, 166, 318, **328**
Biography, by Carlyle, 464-465; by Macaulay, 428; by Swinburne, 809
Bishop Orders His Tomb at Saint Praxed's Church, The, 670
Bitter Sweet, 1015, 1118
Blackwood's Magazine, 18, 297, 409, 503; and De Quincey, 375, 390; and Keats, 274
Blair, Robert, 7, 9, 112
Blake, William, 9, 10, 74, **111-112,** 853; and Yeats, 1025; as engraver, 9, 111, 112; mysticism of, 9, 112, 113; Prophetic Books of, 111; symbolic poems of, 111, 112
Bleak House, 423
Blessed Damozel, The, 416, 783, **784**
Bliss and Other Stories, 1069
Blithe Spirit, 1015, 1118
Blot in the 'Scutcheon, A, 656
Boat Song, 196
Body's Beauty, 796
Bombed Happiness, The, 1162
Bonie Doon, 9, 105, **107**
Bonny Dundee, 198
Books, 134

Boot and Saddle, 659
Bothie of Tober-na-Vuolich, 721
Bothwell: a Tragedy, 809
Boucicault, Dion, 414
Bowen, Elizabeth, 1021
Brave New World, 1016, 1097
Break, Break, Break, 626
Bride of Abydos, The, 201
Bride of Lammermoor, The, 28
Bridge of Sighs, The, 298, **307**
Bridges, Robert, 869
Brief Candles, 1097
Bright Is the Ring of Words, 880
Bright Star! Would I Were Steadfast as Thou Art, 292
British Empire, expansion of, 400, 841-842; shrinking of, 1000-1002
Brontë, Anne, 716-717
Brontë, Charlotte, 409, 422, 716-717
Brontë, Emily, **716-717**
Browne, Thomas, 21, 374
Browning, Elizabeth Barrett, 415, 656, **709-710**
Browning, Robert, 119, 412, 414, 415, 418, 426, **655-657,** 709; dramas of, 413, 655; dramatic monologues of, 413, 655-657
Bulwer-Lytton, Edward, 413, 421-422
Bunyan, John, 197, 372
Buried Life, The, 731
Burke, Thomas, 850
Burney, Frances, 25, 365
Burning Cactus, The, 1160
Burns, Robert, 8, 9, 10, 13, 76, **83-85;** and Carlyle, 464; and his love of humanity, 9, 85, 90; as love poet, 8, 9, 84, 416; as patriot, 9, 84, 109; as revolutionist, 84, 89; dialect poems of, 9; realism of, 9; satire of, 9, 85
Butler, Samuel, 856, 857
By an Evolutionist, 654
By Her Aunt's Grave, 914
Byron, George Noel Gordon, Lord, 13, 14, 17, 22, 29, 31, 119, 120, 164, **200-202,** 249, 262, 273, 274, 296, 297, 299, 414, 418, 729, 809; and "Byronic hero," 14, 201, 212; and neo-classicism, 14, 200, 202, 273; and revolution, 14, 200-202; as romantic, 13, 14, 201, 202; break with older romantic poets, 13, 14; criticism of Wordsworth, 13, 119, 120; influence on Auden, 1022; letters of, 22; love of liberty, 14; narrative poetry of, 28, 191, 201; nature poetry of, 202; Oriental tales of, 191, 201; poetic dramas of, 201; satire of, 13, 14, 200, 202; world-wide influence of, 14, 200, 202

C. L. M., 921
Caleb Williams, 22, 26-27
Caliban upon Setebos, 701
Calverley, Charles Stuart, **824, 827**
Camp, A, 877
Campbell, Roy, 1023
Campbell, Thomas, 296
Candida, 861
Capitalism, 22, 403; and Carlyle, 486; novels dealing with, 423
Cargoes, 918

CARLYLE, THOMAS, 155, 298, 407, 408, 410, 411, 414, 419, 420, 426, 427, 428, 446, 460, **464-465**, 501, 502, 844, 851; and *laissez-faire*, 404, 465, 497; and Ruskin, 501, 502, 515; and utilitarian doctrine, 404, 501; style of, 465, 502-503
Carrion Comfort, 873
CARROLL, LEWIS, 825, **828**
Castaway, The, 82
Castle of Indolence, The, 6, 7, 32, 39, 72
Castle of Otranto, The, 23, 24
Castle Rackrent, 25
Cathedral, The, 1021
Cavalcade, 1015, **1118**
Cavalier Tunes, 658
Celestial Surgeon, The, 876, 877
Cenci, The, 17, 251, 300
Center of Indifference, 470
Chamber Music, 1041
Chance, 942
Chapter on Ears, A, 19
Character of the Happy Warrior, 158
Characteristics of Shakespeare's Dramas, 332
Characters of Shakespeare's Plays, 21
Charge of the Light Brigade, The, 637
Charteris, Hugo, 1021
Chartists, The, 404, 420
Chatterton, Thomas, 7, 149
Chaucer, Geoffrey, 297, 561, 916
Chekov, Anton, 1011
Chesterton, Gilbert K., 851, 855, 859
Child in the House, The, 580
Childe Harold's Pilgrimage, 14, 200-201, **212**
"*Childe Roland to the Dark Tower Came*," 684
Childhood and School-Time, 125
Child's Garden of Verses, A, 875, 876, **877**
Child's Laughter, A, 823
Chimney-Sweeper, The, **117**
Christabel, 12, 164, 165, 175
Christmas Eve and Easter Day, 656
Christ's Hospital Five-and-Thirty Years Ago, 164
CHURCHILL, SIR WINSTON, 1006, 1007, **1032**
Citation and Examination of William Shakespeare, 22, 299
City of Dreadful Night, The, 760-761, 763, 1017
Classes of Society, and the French Revolution, 3; aristocracy, 3, 5, 403; in Industrial Revolution, 5; new, of nineteenth century, 403; upper classes, 5; upper class and Galsworthy's novels, 858; and Meredith's novels, 423; and Thackeray, 424. See also Common People and Middle Class.
Classicism, 21; and Arnold, 527, 528, 726; and Eliot, 1078, 1079; and Gray, 47; and Housman, 910; and Landor, 21, 299, 300; and Macaulay, 439; and Pater, 439, 581, 585; and Swinburne, 417, 808; and Tennyson, 599; in Victorian literature, 426
Clayhanger, 859
Clod and the Pebble, The, **116**
Cloister and the Hearth, The, 422
Cloud, The, 15, 257
CLOUGH, ARTHUR HUGH, 418, **721**, 739, 742
Cobbet, William, 18, 22, 362
Cocktail Party, The, 1079

COLERIDGE, SAMUEL TAYLOR, 7, 10, 11, 12, 13, 16, 17, 20, 21, 22, 76, 118, 119, **163-166**, 190, 191, 201, 273, 296, 318, **328**, 337, 374, 414; and Kant, 12, 20, 165; and Wordsworth, 10, 20, 118-119, 125, 164-165, 166, 170; as a literary critic, 20, 21, 165; as a revolutionist, 164; satire of, 165; Shakespearean criticism of, 20, 165
Collected Poems (Thomas), 1169
Collected Poems, 1921-1951 (Muir), **1023**
Collected Poetry (Auden), 1145
COLLINS, WILLIAM, 6, 7, 50, **66-67**
Come Down, O Maid, 628
Come into the Garden, Maud, 638
Comedy, of Lady Augusta Gregory, 853; of Wilde, 861, 953; Restoration, 6; Victorian, 412
Comfort, Alex, 1021
Coming of Arthur, The, **646**
Common People, 3, 119; and Dickens, 424; and naturalistic novels, 857; and Scott, 28; and Victorian literature, 408; interest of Burns in, 9, 84; interest of romantic age in, 7; interest of Wordsworth in, 11
Composed by the Seaside, Near Calais, 151
Composed upon Westminster Bridge, 151
Confessions, 705
Confessions of an English Opium Eater, 20, 374, 375, 389
Confidential Clerk, The, 1079
Congreve, William, 1014
CONRAD, JOSEPH, 858, 859, **942-944**
Consecration, A, 916
Conversation Piece, 1015, **1118**
Cornhill Magazine, The, 409, 502, 863, 1061
Coronach, 196
Cotter's Saturday Night, The, 84, **95**
Countess Kathleen, The, 1025
Couplet, closed, 47; heroic, 7, 297; iambic pentameter, 297
Cow, The, 879
COWARD, NOEL, 1014-1015, **1117-1118**
COWPER, WILLIAM, 8, 73-74, 112
Crabbe, George, 7
Crabbed Age and Youth, 189
Cradle Song, A, 115
Cranford, 422
Criterion, The, 1079
Criticism, 18, 19, 20-22; and parodies, 823-825; Arnold's, 527, 528; artistic, 420-421, 502; by the essayists, 21; by the Pre-Raphaelites, 416, 417; Carlyle's, 465; Coleridge's, 20, 21, 165; De Quincey's, 20-21; economic, 502; Eliot's, 1078; Gilbert's, 825; Hazlitt's, 20, 21, 360-361; in Victorian period, 415, 419-420, 426; in Victorian verse, 415-416; Lamb's, 19, 21; Landor's, 22, 299, 300; literary, 18, 19, 20, 21, 22, 420-421, 527, 528; Macaulay's, 439; of *Endymion*, 274, 278; of life, 361, 424-425, 528, 845; of *Sartor Resartus*, 466; Pater's, 580, 581; Peacock's, 298; Ruskin's, 502-503; Shakespearean, 20, 21, 22, 165; Shelley's, 250; social, 4, 5, 22, 298, 420, 502, 862; stage, 825; stock phrases of, 528; Swinburne's, 808, 809; Thackeray's, 424-425
Crome Yellow, 1097
Crocodile, The, 828
Cromwell (Arnold), 527

Cromwell (Carlyle), 464
Cromwell, Oliver, 51
Crossing the Bar, 654
Crown of Wild Olive, The, 502
Cry of the Children, The, 415, 709, **710**
Culture, and Arnold, 527-528, 580; and Eliot, 425; Arnold's definition of, 420
Culture and Anarchy, 544
Curate's Kindness, The, 913
Cure of Souls, A, 1021

Daisy Miller, 857
Dance of Death, The, 1145
Danny Deever, 888
Darkling Thrush, The, 908
Darwin, Charles, 405, 562
David Copperfield, 345
Day Is Coming, The, 806
"De Gustibus . . .," 681
De la Mare, Walter, 1009-1010, 1011
De Maupassant, Guy, 1016
De Profundis, 952, 953
DE QUINCEY, THOMAS, 19, 20, 21, 31, **374-375**, 418, 761; as romanticist, 20, 375; classification of his works, 375; criticism of Shakespeare, 21; style of, 20, 375
Death and Entrances, 1169
Death-in-Love, 795
Death of the Heart, The, 1021
Death Song, A, 807
Death Stands Above Me, 315
Death's Jest-Book, or The Fool's Tragedy, 298, 1017
Debussy, Claude, 847, 851
Declaration of Rights, 315
Dedication (Byron), 225
Dedication to Poems and Ballads, 814
Defense of Guenevere, The, 798
Defense of Poetry, 22
Definition of a Gentleman, The, 458
Defoe, 27
Deirdre of the Sorrows, 986
Deism, 8; and Encyclopedists, 4; and Rousseau, 3
Dejection: an Ode, 187
Democracy, advance of, 400, 401, 403, 404; and Carlyle, 465, 482; and Chartists, 404; and Huxley, 419; and Macaulay, 419; and Trollope, 422; and Victorian novel, 409, 421; the new, 403-405
Demogorgon, 257
Departmental Ditties, 886, 887
Descent of Man, The, 406
Design for Living, 1015, 1117
Destruction of Sennacherib, The, 205
Destructive Element, The, 1160
Diana of the Crossways, 423
Dickens, Charles, 26, 408, 411, 421, 422, 423, 424-425, 426, 518, 927; and novels of reform, 423; mixture of realism and romanticism in, 424
Dictionary of National Biography, The, 1061
Didacticism, and Burns, 85; and Campbell, 296; and post-Victorian novel, 855; and Ruskin, 502; and Southey, 296; and Tennyson, 603; in poetry, 20, 85, 410; in satirical verse, 823-825; in Victorian literature, 410-411

Dipsychus, 721, **722**
Dirce, 312
Dirge (Beddoes), **309**
Dirge, A, 273
Dirge in Cymbeline, 68
Disabled, 1097
Discharged, 866
Dissertation upon Roast Pig, A, 338
Diverting History of John Gilpin, The, 74
Divine Image, The, 115
Do What You Will, 1097
Doctor and the Devils, The, 1169
DODGSON, CHARLES L., 825, **828**
Dog Beneath the Skin, The, 1145
Doll's House, A, 860
Don Juan, 13, 14, 201, 202, **224**, 838
Doom Is Dark and Deeper Than Any Sea-Dingle, 1146
Dostoevsky, Feodor, 846
Double Man, The, 1145
Dover Beach, 406, **744**
Dove's Nest, The, 1069
Doyle, Sir Arthur Conan, 855-856, 859
Drama, and Barrie, 854, 1011; and classical theory of unities, 434; and Gilbert, 414, 825; and Hazlitt's criticism, 361; and Ibsen, 846, 860; and Lamb, 337; chamber, of Browning, 413, 655-656; of Elizabethan age, 408; of Galsworthy, 860, 861-862, 1010; of Irish Renaissance, 860, 1010-1011; of Keats, 274; of manners, 2; of Shaw, 861, 1010; of Shelley, 17, 251; of Swinburne, 808, 809; of Tennyson, 413, 595; of the Waste Land, 1014-1015; of Wilde, 861, 952; of Yeats, 860, 1025; poetic, of Byron, 17, 201; poetic, of Shelley, 17, 270; post-Victorian, 859-862; realism in, 414; Restoration, 414; romantic, of Coleridge, 165; romantic, of Swinburne, 808, 809; social, of Galsworthy, 860, 861-862; social manners in, 414; Spanish, Fitzgerald's translations of, 776; tragedy, 251; Victorian, 412-414, 426
Dramatic monologue, of Browning, 413, 655, 656; of Newman, 715
Dramatis Personae, 656
Dream, A, 115
Dream-Children: A Reverie, 19, 338
Dream of Gerontius, The, 407, 446, **715**
Dream-Pedlary, 310
Drummer Hodge, 908
Dublin University Review, 1025
Dubliners, 1018, 1042, 1043
Duke of Gandia, The, 809
Dulce et Decorum Est, 1095
Duncan Gray, 108
Dunkirk, 1035
Dunsany, Lord, 1011
Durrell, Lawrence, 1023
Dynasts, The, 907

Eagle, The, 637
Earthly Paradise, The, 410, 805
Economics, 5, 18, 22, 30; and British Empire, 842; criticism of, 502; essays on, 485; problems of, 420, 423; Ruskin on, 502, 515, 524; theories of, 404, 405, 502
Edgeworth, Maria, 25

GENERAL INDEX 1179

Edinburgh Review, The, 18, 200, 408, 464
Education, and Arnold, 527, 528; and Huxley, 562; cultural, 528; in eighteenth century, 5; scientific method in, 528; university, 446
Edward VIII, 1004
Effect of the Sea After a Storm, 503
Egoist, The (Meredith), 423
Egoist, The (Pound), 1042, 1078
18 Poems, 1169
Elegiac Stanzas, 120, **157**
Elegy on the Death of John Keats, An, 262
Elegy Written in a Country Churchyard, 7, 8, 47, **50**
Eliot, George, 26, 402, 409, 411, 422, 423, 424, 425, 426
Eliot, T. S., 1014, **1078-1080,** 1169
Elizabeth, 21, 28, 408, 438
Elizabeth II, 1007
Elizabethan age, 28, 33; and Keats, 276; drama of, 298; influence on romanticism, 21, 22, 39; literature of, 21, 408; poetry of, 416
Elliott, Ebenezer, 298
Eminent Victorians, 1011
Emma, 26
Encyclopaedia Britannica, 428, 809
Encyclopaedia of Pacifism, An, 1097
Encyclopedists, The, influence of, 4
End, The, 1096
End of the Affair, The, 1021
Ends and Means, 1016, 1097
Endymion, 16, 247, 262, 274, **278**
England in 1819, 254
England, My England, 868
English, The, 486
English Bards and Scotch Reviewers, 13, 200, **203**
English Mail Coach, The, 375
Enoch Arden, 595-596
Enquiry Concerning Political Justice, 22, 118
Enter Patient, 864
Envoy, 885
Epicureanism, 420, 580, 852
Epilogue, 1146
Epilogue to *Asolando*, 708
Epistle to J. Lapraik, an Old Scottish Bard, 86
Epitaph, 190
Erewhon, 856
Escape, literature of, 30-31, 846-847
Essay, 2; Arnold's, 528; biographical, of Macaulay, 428; Carlyle's, 464, 465, 485, 502-503; De Quincey's, 19, 20, 21, 375; economic-social, 485, 502, 515; Hazlitt's, 19, 20, 21, 360-361; Huxley's, 562; Lamb's, 19, 20, 21; Macaulay's, 427-428; of post-Victorian era, 855; of romantic age, 17, 418; on art, 502-503; Pater's, 580, 581; personal, 19, 418, 876; political, 544; Ruskin's, 502, 515; Shakespearean criticism in, 20, 21; social, 544; Stevenson's, 855, 876
Essay on Comedy, 423
Essay Concerning Human Understanding, 2
Essays and Studies, 809
Essays of Elia, 19, **338**
Essays New and Old, 1097
Ethics and Evolution, 562
Evans, Mary Ann, 26, 402, 409, 411, 422, 423, 424, 425, 426

Eve of St. Agnes, The, 16, 274, **285**
Eve of Saint John, The, 190
Evelina, 25
Evensong, 881
Everlasting No, The, 466
Everlasting Yea, The, 476
Evolution, Stevenson on, 929; theory of, 405-406, 419, 562
Examiner, The, 18, 297
Excursion, The, 12, 74, 120, 125
Ezra Pound, His Metric and Poetry, 1078

Factory System, 5, 402-403; evils resulting from, 403; legislation on, 403-404; novels of, 423; women and children in, 403
Fall, Leaves, 719
Family Reunion, The, 1079
Fancy, 279
Far from the Madding Crowd, 907
Farce, in Victorian drama, 412; of Gilbert, 414
Fatal Sisters, The, 8, 47, **58**
Father William, 828
Felix Randal, 872
Fermor, Patrick Leigh, 1021
Fern Hill, 1172
Fiction, 23, 26, 409; and women, 409; historical, 27; in magazines, 18, 409; minor, of Victorian period, 421; of twentieth-century traditionalists, 1010-1011; of Waste Land, 1015-1021; revolutionary ideas in, 26; romantic, 23-29
Fiddler of Dooney, The, 1029
Fielding, Henry, 23, 25, 424
Final Chorus from *Hellas*, 271
Finnegans Wake, 1019, 1024, 1042
Fire That Filled My Heart of Old, The, 762
First World War, 995, 996, 1033, 1078
Fish, the Man, and the Spirit, The, 305
Fitzgerald, Edward, 417, 775-776, 852, 910
Flower, The, 641
Flower in the Crannied Wall, 646
Flush, a Biography, 1062
Fly, The, 112, **116**
Folklore, Celtic, 297, 853; classic, 274; of Ireland, 25, 297; of Scotland, 13, 190
Fool of Quality, The, 26
For I Must Sing of All I Feel and Know, 761
For Lancelot Andrewes, 1079
For Life I Had Never Cared Greatly, 915
For the Time Being, 1145
Foreign Lands, 878
Former Beauties, 911
Fors Clavigera, 502
Forsaken Garden, A, 819
Forsaken Merman, The, 410, **727**
Forster, E. M., 1021
Forsyte Saga, The, 857, 858, 1010
Fortnightly Review, The, 1041
Fortunes of Richard Mahony, The, 1021
Four Quartets, 1014, 1079
Fra Lippo Lippi, 688
France: an Ode, 164, **185**
Frankenstein, 24

Fraser's Magazine, 19, 409, 502; and *Sartor Resartus,* 466
French Revolution, The, 3, 30; and Carlyle, 465; and Wordsworth, 12, 118, 119
French Revolution, The, 464, 465, **482**
Freud, Sigmund, 846, 1012
Froude, Richard Hurrell, 407, 445, 715
Fumed Oak, 1015, 1118
Function of Criticism at the Present Time, The, 529
"Fuzzy-Wuzzy," 888

Galsworthy, John, 857-858, 942, 1010
Garden, The, 79
Garden by the Sea, A, 804
Garden of Love, The, 117
Garden of Proserpine, The, 813
Garden-Party, The, 1069, **1070**
Gardeners and Astronomers, 1023
Gaskell, Elizabeth Cleghorn, 26, 422, 423
Gathering Storm, The, 1033
Geist's Grave, 747
Genius and the Goddess, The, 1097
Genius in Beauty, 794
George III, 401, 405
George V, 1004
George VI, 1004, 1007
Germ, The, 416, 749, 783
Gertrude of Wyoming, 296
Ghosts, 860
Giaour, The, 201
Gifford, William, 18
Gilbert and Sullivan, 825, 852, 952
GILBERT, WILLIAM SCHWENCK, 414, 824, **825**, 833. See also Gilbert and Sullivan.
Gissing, George, 847, 857, 1021
Gittings, Robert, 1023
Give a Man a Horse He Can Ride, 762
Give a Rouse, 658
Gladstone, William, 404, 405
Glee for King Charles, 199
Glove, The, 667
Glove and the Lions, The, 297, **304**
Goblin Market, 752
God and the Bible, 528
God-Forgotten, 847, **909**
God's Grandeur, 871
Godwin, William, 15, 22, 26, 164, 494; and Wordsworth, 118; novels of, 26-27
Goethe, Johann Wolfgang von, 30, 165, 400, 581, 729; and Carlyle, 464, 479; and Pater, 581; and Tennyson, 629
Goldsmith, Oliver, 7, 296, 428
Gondoliers, The, 825
Gosse, Edmund, 855
Gothic romance, the, **23-25**; and Smollett, 23; and Walpole, 23-24
Grammarian's Funeral, A, **682**
Grand Style, The, 505
Grave, The, 7, 112; Blake's illustrations for, 9, 112
GRAY, THOMAS, 7, 8, **46-47**, 67, 580
Greater Love, 1094
Greek influence, Keats, 2, 16; Swinburne, 808, 810
Green Helmet and Other Poems, The, 1025

Greene, Graham, 1021
Gregory, Lady Augusta, 850, 853, 985
Grey Eminence, 1097
Guedalla, Philip, 1011
Gulliver's Travels, 1016
Gunga Din, 889
Guy Mannering, 28

Habit of Perfection, The, 870
Hail and Farewell, 853
Hallam, Arthur Henry, 594, 628, 630, 634, 641
Hand That Signed the Paper, The, **1170**
Hands Across the Sea, 1015, 1118
Hanley, James, 1021
Happy Prince and Other Tales, The, 952
Happy Thought, 878
Hard Times, 423, 518
HARDY, THOMAS, 847, 850, 858, **907-908**, 1023
Harp of the North, 194
Harp of the North, Farewell! 197
Harp That Once Through Tara's Halls, The, 303
Hawker, Robert Stephen, 298
Hay Fever, 1117
HAZLITT, WILLIAM, 19, 20, 21, 273, 338, **360-361**, 418; and Stevenson, 874, 876; romanticism of, 361; Shakespearean criticism of, 21, 361
He Remembers Forgotten Beauty, 1028
Heart Knoweth Its Own Bitterness, The, 750
Heart of Darkness, 944
Heart of Midlothian, The, 28, 29, 198
Heat of the Day, The, 1021
Heaven-Haven, 870
Hebraism and Hellenism, 544
Hellas (Songs from), 15, 27, 250, **270**
Hellenics, The, 300
HENLEY, WILLIAM ERNEST, 842, 849-850, **863-864**, 886
Henry Esmond, 421, 422, 425
Here on the Cropped Grass, 1147
Hereward the Wake, 422
Herries Chronicles, The, 1021
Hertha, 816
Higher Pantheism, The, 645, 821
Higher Pantheism in a Nutshell, The, 645, 821
Highland Mary, 108
History, 419, 427; and Carlyle, 465, 482, 493; Macaulay's conception of, 419, 427-428
History (Macaulay), **428**
History of England from the Accession of James II, 427
History of Frederick II of Prussia, Called Frederick the Great, 464, 465
History of Mr. Polly, The, 858
History of the English Speaking Peoples, A, 1033
H. M. S. Pinafore, 825
Hohenlinden, 296
Hollow Men, The, 1014
Holy Face and Other Essays, The, 1097
Holy Spring, 1171
Holy Thursday (Songs of Experience), 116
Holy Thursday (Songs of Innocence), 114
Holy Willie's Prayer, 9, 85, 88
Home They Brought Her Warrior Dead, 627
Home-Thoughts, from Abroad, 667

GENERAL INDEX

Home-Thoughts, from the Sea, 667
Homer, 275, 333, 421
HOOD, THOMAS, **297-298, 306**
Hope Evermore and Believe! 724
HOPKINS, GERARD MANLEY, 851, **869-870**
Host of the Air, The, 1025
Hound of Heaven, The, 882
Hound of the Baskervilles, The, 856
Hours of Idleness, 200, 203
House, 707
House in Paris, The, 1021
House of Life, The, 784, **794**
House of Pomegranates, A, 952
HOUSMAN, ALFRED EDWARD, **898-899**
"*How They Brought the Good News from Ghent to Aix,*" 657, **664**
Hugo, Victor, 808, 809
Humanitarianism, 5, 7, 8, 30, 843-844; and Blake, 10, 111; and Browning, 657; and E. B. Browning, 710; and Burns, 9, 84, 85; and Byron, 202; and Galsworthy, 861, 1010; and Hood and Elliott, 298; and industrial reform, 403; and Landor, 299; and Thomson, 32; and Victorian poetry, 415; and Wordsworth, 119; and Yeats, 853; in the romantic novel, 7, 25-27, 30, 31; in verse, 7, 298; in Victorian literature, 410
Hume, David, 372, 433
Humor, in Dickens, 424; in melodrama, 414; in verse, 297-298, 823-839; lack of, in Victorian prose writers, 420; of Austen, 25, 29; of Byron, 14; of Gilbert, 825; of Hood, 297; of Huxley, 419, 562; of Peacock, 297; of Scott, 29; Wordsworth's lack of, 12, 120
Hundred Years, The, 1011
HUNT, JAMES HENRY LEIGH, 18, 21, 282, **297, 304**, 360, 361; and Keats, 273-274, 275, 286
Hunting of the Snark, The, 825
Hunting Song, 194
HUXLEY, ALDOUS, 1015, 1016, **1097**
HUXLEY, THOMAS HENRY, 405, 406, 419, 420, 528, **561-562**, 580, 846, 1016, 1097; style of, 562
Hymn before Sunrise in the Vale of Chamouni, 165
Hymn to Artemis, 808
Hymn to Intellectual Beauty, 15, 250, **251**
Hymns, 8, 74, 75, 446; of Cowper, 8, 74; of Newman, 446; Wesleyan, 8
Hyperion, 16, 274, 278

I Know Not Whether I Am Proud, 313
I. M. Margaritae Sorori, 866
I Think Continually of Those, 1160
I Traveled Among Unknown Men, 124
I Wake and Feel the Fell of Dark, 873
I Wandered Lonely as a Cloud, 12, 120, 155
I Will Make You Brooches, 879
Ibsen, Henrik, 846, 847, 860, 1079
Idea of a University, The, 446
Ideal Husband, An, 952
Idealism, 1016
Idiot Boy, The, 120
Idylls of the King, The, 410, 594, 595, 646, 799
If Thou Indeed Derive Thy Light from Heaven, 120, **163**
I'll Leave It to You, 1117

Illustrated Journal of a Landscape Painter, 824
Illustrated London News, 1118
Imaginary Conversations, 21, 299
Imperialism, 842, 1000-1002; and Kipling, 842, 849, 885, 886; and nationalism, 400-402
Importance of Being Earnest, The, 861, 952, **953**
Impressionism, 850-851, 853, 862, 864
In a Drear-Nighted December, 277
In a German Pension, 1069
In a Gondola, 660
In a London Square, 725
In Harmony with Nature, 727
In Hospital, 849, 863, **864**
In Memoriam, 594, 628, 721
In Memory of W. B. Yeats, 1157
In the Shadow of the Glen, 853, 986
In the States, 877
In the Valley of Cauteretz, 641
In Time of "The Breaking of Nations," 915
In Time of War, 1154
In Which We Serve, 1118
Inchcape Rock, The, 301
Incidents in the Life of My Uncle Arly, 149, **826**
Indian Serenade, The, 250, **256**
Industrial Revolution, 4-5, 298, 402
Industrialism, 401, 402, 848; adjustments of, 402-403; and Carlyle, 465, 501; and Ruskin, 501, 502; and slavery, 403; growth and effects of, 402-403; *laissez-faire* doctrine in, 403, 404; legislative reform of, 403, 404; novels of, 423; of nineteenth century, 426; problems of, 426
Informer, The, 1021
Inquiry, The, 911
Intentions, 952
Interior monologue, 1020, 1061, 1079
Into the Twilight, 1028
Introduction: Songs of Innocence, 113
Introduction to Principles of Morals and Legislation, 404
Inversnaid, 873
Invictus, 863, 866
Iolanthe, 825, 835
Iphigeneia and Agamemnon, 313
Ireland, and Irish Literary Renaissance, 852-854, 985; and Maria Edgeworth, 25; and Moore, 297; and Yeats, 853, 1025; folklore of, 25, 297, 1025; literary revival in 1025; national movement in, 844, 1025; problems of, 25, 844
Irish Airman Foresees His Death, An, 1029
Irish Literary Renaissance, 852-854, 985-986, 1018. See also Ireland.
Is It Not Better, 313
Isherwood, Christopher, 1021, 1145
Isles of Greece, The, 235
Isolation. To Marguerite, 730
It Is a Beauteous Evening, Calm and Free, 151
Ite Domum Saturae, Venit Hesperus, 725
Ivanhoe, 28

Jabberwocky, 829
Jacobite's Farewell, A, 820
Jacob's Room, 1061
Jacobs, W. W., 859

1182 GENERAL INDEX

James, Henry, 847, 857, 859
Jane Eyre, 422, 716, 717
Jeffrey, Francis, 18, 191, 200
Jesting Pilate, 1097
Joanna Godden, 1021
John Anderson, My Jo, 84, **102**
John Halifax, Gentleman, 402
Jolly Beggars, The, 9, 85, **89**; Arnold's criticism of, 90
Jones, Sir Henry Arthur, 860
Jonson, Ben, 21, 276, 761, 809
Journal (Katherine Mansfield), 1011, 1070
Journalism, 5, 409; of Coleridge, 165; of Dickens, 425; of Hunt, 297; of Kipling, 850; of Meredith, 769; of Thackeray, 409; of Thomson, 760
Journey of the Magi, The, 1092
Journey to a War, 1145
Joyce, James, 985, 986, 1014, 1015, 1018-1020, 1024, **1041-1042**
Jude the Obscure, 907
Juggling Jerry, 769
Jungle Books, 886
Juno and the Paycock, 1010
Just So Stories, 886

Kailyard School, The, 854, 859, 860. See also Scotland.
Kant, Immanuel, 4, 12, 20, 165
Kaye-Smith, Sheila, 1021
Keats, John, 2, 13, 16, 17, 18, 30, 191, 247, 250, 251, 262, **273-275**, 299, 410, 414, 594, 655; and beauty, 16; Greek spirit of, 2, 16; odes, 16; opposition to neo-classicism, 16
Keble, John, 406, 445, 461, 463, 715
Kenilworth, 28, 29, 438
Kidnapped, 875
Kim, 886
King, The, 891
Kingdom of God, The, 885
Kingsley, Charles, 406, 408, 415, 422, 423, 716; and Newman, 445, 460
Kipling, Rudyard, 842, 849-850, 876, **885-886**, 933, 1002
Knowledge Its Own End, 447
Kubla Khan, 12, 164, 165, 184

La Belle Dame sans Merci, 16, 274, 282
La Gioconda, 581
Labor, 5; and Carlyle, 420, 465, 481, 486; and Galsworthy, 862, 1010; and inventions, 402; novels of, 423; women and children in, 5, 403
Labor, 491
Laboratory, The, 663
Lady Chatterley's Lover, 1017
Lady Geraldine's Courtship, 709
Lady of Lyons, The, 413
Lady of Shalott, The, 596, 597, 646
Lady of the Lake, The, 13, 27, 190, **194**
Lady, Was It Fair of Thee? 309
Lady Windermere's Fan, 861, 952
Lagoon, The, 944
Laissez-faire, 403, 404, 497; and Carlyle, 404, 465, 497
Lake Isle of Innisfree, The, **1027**
Lamb, Charles, 19, 20, 21, 22, 164, 165, 273, 337-338, 374, 418, 855; and Stevenson, 855, 876; poetry and drama of, 337; romanticism of, 19; Shakespearean criticism of, 21, 298
Lamb, Mary, 21, 337, 338
Lamb, The, 112, **114**
Lament, A, 262
Lamia, 274
Land of Counterpane, The, 878
Land of Heart's Desire, The, 1025
Landor, Walter Savage, 21-22, **299-300**, **311**; and romanticism, 299
Laodamia, 120, 278
Lark Ascending, The, 769, **772**
Last Coachload, The, 1010
Last Days of Pompeii, The, 421
Last Essays on Church and Religion, 528
Last Poems, 904
Last Word, The, 744
Latest Decalogue, The, 724
Laugh and Be Merry, 920
Lawrence, David Herbert, 1014, 1015, 1017-1018, 1069
Lay of the Last Minstrel, The, 13, 190, **192**, 203, 440
Lay Sermons, Addresses, and Reviews, 406, 562
Lays of Ancient Rome, The, 427
Lead, Kindly Light, 407, **715**
League of Nations, 996
Lear, Edward, 149, **824, 826**
Leaves Are Falling; So Am I, The, 313
Lectures on Universities, 446
Leda and the Swan, 1030
Lee, Laurie, 1023
Leech-Gatherer, The, 148
Legend, Arthurian, 7, 57, 646, 798; Celtic, 7, 47; Danish, 727; Don Juan, 224; Greek, 417, 599, 808; Irish, 980, 1025; medieval, 410; Norse, 47; Scottish, 13; Spanish, 224; Welsh, 8. See also Folklore.
Leonardo da Vinci, 581
Let My Voice Ring Out and Over the Earth, 763
Let the Punishment Fit the Crime, 837
Letter to Charles Brown, 295
Letter to Charles Cowden Clarke, 358
Letter to Dr. Wharton, 64
Letter to His Mother, 59, 61
Letter to Horace Walpole, 62
Letter to James Augustus Hessey, 294
Letter to John Hamilton Reynolds, 292, 294
Letter to Lord Byron: IV, 1022, 1149
Letter to Mr. Stonhewer, 63
Letter to Richard West, 60
Letter to Samuel Taylor Coleridge, 357
Letter to Thomas Manning, 359
Letter to William Wordsworth, 358
Letters (Thomas Gray), 59
Letters (John Keats), 292
Letters (Charles Lamb), 357
Letters from Iceland, 1145
Levana and Our Ladies of Sorrow, 390
Lewis, Matthew, 24
Lewis, Wyndham, 1021
Liber Amoris, 361
Light That Failed, The, 886
Limbo, 1097

Lines (When the lamp is shattered), 272
Lines Composed a Few Miles Above Tintern Abbey, 11, 12, 119, 120, **121**
Lines on the Mermaid Tavern, 276
Lines Written in Early Spring, 121
Lines (Written in Kensington Gardens), 732
Listeners, The, 1009
Literary Remains of Richard Hurrell Froude, The, 407
Literature and Dogma, 528
Literature of Knowledge and Literature of Power, 21, 394
Little Black Boy, The, 114
Little Boy Lost, A, 117
Little Mexican and Other Stories, 1097
Little Minister, The, 854
Little Review, The, 1042, 1061
Little While, A, 719
Lives of the English Poets, The, 237, 530, 1078
Liza of Lambeth, 1015
Lochinvar, 193
Locke, John, 2, 20
Locksley Hall, **613**, 632, 847
Locksley Hall Sixty Years After, 595, 613, **618**
Lodging for the Night, A, 874
London, 117
London, 1802, 152
London Magazine, The, 19, 409
London Morning Post, 1033
London Times Literary Supplement, 1061
London Town, 919
Longsword, 27
Look, Stranger, 1145
Looking Forward, 878
Lord Jim, 859, 943
Lord Ullin's Daughter, 296
Loss and Gain, 423, 446
Lost Days, 796
Lost Leader, The, 119, **666**
Lotos-Eaters, The, 278, 596, **608**
Love Poems, 1163
Love Song of J. Alfred Prufrock, The, 1014, **1085**
Loyalties, 1010
Lucas, E. V., 855
Lucifer in Starlight, 773
Luther, Martin, 542
Lyra Apostolica, 407, 446, 461, 715
Lyric, Cavalier, 297; in *The Princess,* 595, 596, 626; of Beddoes, 298; of Blake, 112; of Burns, 85; of Hardy, 908; of Housman, 899; of Landor, 299; of Moore, 297; of Peacock, 298; of C. Rossetti, 749; of D. Rossetti, 416, 783-784; of Shelley, 15, 250, 270; of Swinburne, 808, 809; of Tennyson, 595, 596; of Thomas, 1169; of Wesley, 8; of Yeats, 1025
Lyrical Ballads, 10-11, 17, 20, 119, 120, 164, **318**
Lyrics from Maud, 638
Lyrics to Ianthe, 311

MACAULAY, THOMAS BABINGTON, 419-420, **427-428**, 580
"Maclaren, Ian" (John Watson), 854
MacNeice, Louis, 1145
Macpherson, James, 7
Maeterlinck, Maurice, 846, 851

Magazines, and Thackeray, 409; and the Victorian novel, 421; development of modern, 18-19; in Victorian era, 408-409, 421; miscellaneous contents of, 409; monthly, 408; quarterly, 408, 851; weekly, 409
Maid of Athens, Ere We Part, 205
Malign Fiesta, 1021
Malory, Sir Thomas, 410, 646
Malthus, Thomas, 22
Man and Superman, 861
Man He Killed, The, 912
Man Who Was, The, 933
Mandalay, 890
Manfred, 17, 201, 212
Manning, Cardinal, 445
Man's a Man for A' That, A, 84, **110**
Man's Place in Nature, 406, 562
MANSFIELD, KATHERINE, 1011, **1069**
Mansfield Park, 26
Map of Love, The, 1169
Marching Along, 658
Market-Girl, The, 911
Marmion, 13, 190, 192
"Mary Gloster," The, 892
Mary Morison, 85
Mary Stuart, 809
Marx, Karl, 404, 844
MASEFIELD, JOHN, 850, 858, **916**, 1021
Masks and Faces, 413
Match, A, 811
Mater Triumphans, 880
Materialism, and Arnold, 527; and Barker, 1163; and Carlyle, 465, 501; in Victorian period, 407, 419, 420
Maturin, Charles, 24
Maud, 595, **638**
Maugham, W. Somerset, 1015-1016
Mayor of Casterbridge, The, 907
Mazeppa, 201
Medievalism, and Keats, 16, 285; and Morris, 798; and Swinburne, 417, 808; in novel, 23, 27; in Victorian era, 410; influence of, on Gothic romance, 23; influence of, on romanticism, 7, 10, 23, 55; of D. G. Rossetti, 416, 784; romance of, 7, 27, 33, 164
Meditation under Stars, 774
Meeting at Night, 666
Meeting with Coleridge, 367
Melancholy, 50; and Thomson, 761; Celtic, of Yeats, 853, 1025; of Arnold, 406, 528; of Byron, 200; of Collins, 6, 67; of Gray, 8; mood of romantic mind, **1**, 7
Melmoth the Wanderer, 24
Melodrama, in Gothic novel, 24; in Hardy's novels, 907; in Scott's poems, 190; in Victorian drama, 412; of Boucicault, 414; of Bulwer-Lytton, 413, 421-422; of Byron, 200; of Dickens, 424, 425
Memorabilia, 682
Memorial Verses, 729
Men and Women, 656
Men at Arms, 1021
MEREDITH, GEORGE, 423, 426, **768-769**, 857; essays of, 423; novels of, 423, 768; poetry of, 769
Methodism, 8
Meynell, Alice, 851, 882
Michael, 119, **142**

Middle Ages, and Rossetti, 784; and Ruskin, 502; and Swinburne, 808; influence on Browning, 415; influence on romantic mind, 7, 23, 407; influence on Victorians, 410
Middle Class, 5; and Arnold, 527-528, 538; and Dickens, 424; and Thackeray, 424; in Victorian era, 405, 411, 412, 420
Middlemarch, 425
Mikado, The, 825, 836
Mile an' a Bittock, A, 879
Mill, John Stuart, 404, 465, 467, 925
Mill on the Floss, The, 425
Milton (Arnold), **558**
Milton (Blake), **111**
Milton, John, 7, 50, 99, 262, 428, 870, 916; resemblance of Wordsworth to, 12, 121, 126
Minor Romantic Poets, **296-300**
Minstrel Boy, The, 303
Minstrelsy of the Scottish Border, The, 13, 190
Mock Turtle's Song, The, 829
Modern Comedy, A, 857, 858
Modern Love, 769, 771
Modern Painters, 501, 502, **503**
Monday or Tuesday, 1061
Monna Innominata, 760
Monstre Gai, 1021
Moore, George, 847, 852, 853, 985, 1025
Moore, Thomas, 224, 247, **297**, **302**, 439; friendship with Byron, 224
Morality, 411; and George Eliot, 422; and Ruskin, 502; and Tennyson, 595; and Thackeray, 424-425; and Wilde, 952; in Tennyson's *Idylls*, 646, 799; in Victorian literature, 410, 411-412, 426; in Victorian poetry, 416, 825; revolt against Victorian, 852, 862
Morality, 733
More Poems, 905
Morris, William, 410, 415, 416, 420, 426, 580, **797-798**, 809, 844
Morrison, Arthur, 850
Mortal Coils, 1097
Morte D'arthur, 594, 646
Morte Darthur, 646, 799
Most Sweet It Is with Unuplifted Eyes, 163
Mrs. Dalloway, 1061
Mrs. Dane's Defense, 860
Mrs. Warren's Profession, 861
Muir, Edwin, 1023
Murder in the Cathedral, 1079
Murry, John Middleton, 1069
Musée des Beaux Arts, 1156
Music, 865
Music, and romantic expression, 30
Music at Night and Other Essays, 1097
Mutability (The flower that smiles today), **261**
Mutability (We are as clouds that veil the midnight moon), **251**
My First Acquaintance with Poets, 367
My Heart Leaps Up, 12, 148
My Last Duchess, 659
My Silks and Fine Array, 112
My Sister's Sleep, 783, 786

My Star, 681
My Wife, 880
Mysteries of Udolpho, The, 24, 319
Mysticism, and Blake, 9, 111, 112; and Kipling, 886; and Macaulay, 427; and Newman, 407, 446; and Pre-Raphaelites, 417; and C. Rossetti, 749; and D. G. Rossetti, 784; and Yeats, 1009; Celtic, 853, 862; in romanticism, 8, 9

Napoleon, 5, 119, 399
Naturalism, and Conrad, 858; and realism, 848-849; French influence on, 846, 856-857, 862; of Boucicault, 414
Nature, 1, 6, 10, 30; and Blake, 9, 112; and Burns, 83; and Byron, 202; and Collins, 6, 67, 69; and Gray, 8, 47; and melancholy, 6-7; and Pre-Raphaelites, 416-417; and romanticism, 1; and Rousseau, 4; and Ruskin, 503; and Shelley, 15, 251, 262; and Thomson, 6, 32, 33; and Wordsworth, 11, 12, 119, 120, 121, 148-149; Coleridge's feeling for, 164; in Victorian literature, 406, 410; poetry, 6, 12, 17, 47, 76
Negation, of twentieth century, 1009, 1012
Neo-classicism, 1, 2, 10, 11, 20, 29, 30, 33, 47, 48, 50, 67, 85, 119, 299, 845; age of 2, 3, 6, 224; and Jane Austen, 25; and Byron, 14, 200, 202, 273; and Crabbe, 7; and Gray, 8, 47; and Keats, 16, 278; and periodical literature, 18, 19; and the Gothic romance, 23, 25; and the novel, 23, 25; *clichés* of, 6; conventions of, 6, 32; decline of, 6, 29; literature of, 2; of Burns, 9, 85; standards of, 6, 52; style of, 10, 35, 52
Nephelidia, 822
Nest of Simple Folk, A, 1021
Neuroticism, and Waste Land, 1017
New Arabian Nights, The, 863, 875
New Grub Street, 857
New Poems (Thomas), 1169
New Year Letter, 1145
Newman, John Henry, 407-408, 411, 420, 423, **445-446**, 527, 528, 715, 721, 869
News of the World, 1163
Newspapers, 18, 164
Nicholas Nickleby, 423
Nigger of the Narcissus, The, 859, 942
Night and Day, 1061
Night Is Darkening, The, 719
Night Thoughts, 7
Nightmare Abbey, 298
Nine Experiments, 1159
No Coward Soul Is Mine, 720
Nocturne, 1021
Nones, 1022, 1145
North and South, 423
Northanger Abbey, 26
Northern Farmer, New Style, 595, **643**
Northern Farmer, Old Style, 595, **641**
Nostromo, 943
Not Palaces, an Era's Crown, 1161
Novel, 2, 4, 7, 23-29, 426; and Landor, 299; and problems of human relationship, 422-423, 425, 856; and women, 409, 1021; detective, 27, 856; Gothic, 23-25, 27, 46, 165, 190; historical, 23, 27-29, 191, 421-422,

856; medievalism in, 23; melodramatic, 422; naturalistic school of, 856-858; of Hardy, 907; of manners, 23, 25-26, 413, 421, 422; of Masefield, 858, 927; of Newman, 446; of purpose, 23, 26-27, 422-423, 424; of Rousseau, 4, 26; of Scott, 13, 27-29, 190-191; of the Brontës, 716-717; of the Waste Land, 1015; Oriental, 24; picaresque, 23, 25, 424; post-Victorian, 854-859; problem, 422, 423; propagandistic, 26-27, 423; psychological, 423, 425, 857; romantic, 23-29, 855-856; satiric, 855; sensational, 421; sentimental, 23, 26; serial method of writing, 409, 421; social, 421, 422, 857-858; social-political, 425; social revolutionary, 26; supernatural, 24, 421; Victorian, 408, 409, 411, 412, 421-425, 426, 855; Waverley, 28
Now Sleeps the Crimson Petal, 628
Nuns Fret Not at Their Convent's Narrow Room, 159, 378

O That 'Twere Possible, 639
O, Wert Thou in the Cauld Blast, **110**
Obscurity, of the Wastelanders, 1013
O'Casey, Sean, 1010-1011, 1021
Ode, 47, 52, 160, 255; of Collins, 67; of Keats, 16, 274, 281; Pindaric, 2, 52
Ode (Keats), 280
Ode, 1746 (How sleep the brave), 67, **68**
Ode on a Distant Prospect of Eton College, 47, **48**
Ode on a Grecian Urn, 2, 16, 278, **281**
Ode on Intimations or Immortality, 12, 120, **160**
Ode on Melancholy, 16, 251, **280**
Ode on Popular Superstitions, 7, 67
Ode on the Death of a Favorite Cat, 47, **49**
Ode on the Death of Mr. Thomson, 72
Ode on the Death of the Duke of Wellington, 595
Ode to a Nightingale, 16, 184, 265, **284**
Ode to Duty, 120, **155**
Ode to Evening, 6, 67, **69**
Ode to Psyche, 283
Ode to Simplicity, 67, **68**
Ode to Spring, 8, 47
Ode to the West Wind, 251, **255**
Odyssey, 1019, 1042
Oenone, 599
Of A' the Airts, 9, **102**
Of Human Bondage, 1015
Of Lord B., 838
Of Old Sat Freedom on the Heights, 611
Officers and Gentlemen, 1021
Often Rebuked, Yet Always Back Returning, 720
O'Faolain, Sean, 1021
O'Flaherty, Liam, 1021
Oh, Breathe Not His Name! 302
Oh, Let the Solid Ground, 640
Old China, 19, 338
Old English Baron, The, 27
Old Man's Comforts, The, 296, **301**, 828
Old Mortality, 28, 29, 437
Old Stoic, The, 720
Old Wives' Tale, The, 859
Olive Tree and Other Essays, The, 1097
Oliver Twist, 423

Olney Hymns, 8, 74, **75**
On Fame, 282
On Familiar Style, 21
On First Looking into Chapman's Homer, 275, 278
On Going a Journey, 20, **361**
On Growing Old, 922
On Heroes, 464
On His Seventy-Fifth Birthday, 315
On History, 429, 493
On Reading New Books, 20
On Seeing the Elgin Marbles, 275
On the Advisableness of Improving Natural Knowledge, 562
On the Danger of War, 774
On the Extinction of the Venetian Republic, 151
On the Fear of Death, 20
On the Feeling of Immortality in Youth, 20
On the Frontier, 1145
On the Knocking at the Gate in Macbeth, 21, 387
On the Loss of the Royal George, 75
On the Margin, 1097
On the Poetical Character, 67
On the Receipt of My Mother's Picture, 74, 79
On the Sea, 276
On the Way to Kew, 867
On This Day I Complete My Thirty-Sixth Year, 247
On This Island, 1022, 1145, **1147**
Once in a Saintly Passion, 761
One Year Ago, 312
Opera, comic, of Gilbert, 414, 824, 825
Orators, The, 1145
Ordeal of Gilbert Pinfold, The, 1021
Ordeal of Richard Feverel, The, 423
Orientalism, in Landor's poetry, 299; in Moore's poetry, 297; in novel, 24
Origin of Species, 405, 406, 632
Orlando, 1020, 1062
Ossian, 7
Owen, Wilfred, 1013-1014, **1093-1094**
Owl and the Pussy-Cat, The, 824, **826**
Oxen, The, 915
Oxford, 406-408, 445. *See also* Oxford Movement.
Oxford Book of Light Verse, The, 1145
Oxford Movement, 406-408, 445, 463, 527, 715
Oxford Poetry, 1159
Ozymandias, 253

Palace of Art, The, 580, **603**
Pamela, 23
Pan's Pipes, 927
Pantheism, of Shelley, 262; of Tennyson, 645; of Wordsworth, 416
Pantisocracy, 12, 164, 237, 296
Paracelsus, 655
Parliament, development of, in Victorian era, 403-404; Long, 435
Parody, 149, 417; and criticism, 824; of Peacock and Hood, 297
Parting at Morning, 667
Passage to India, A, 1021

Passions, The, 70
Past and Present, 410, 464, **485**
PATER, WALTER, 420, 439, **580-581;** and Wilde, 852, 952
Pathetic Fallacy, The, 507
Patience, 825, 835, 852, 952
Patriotism, of Burns, 9, 84; of Byron, 202; of Scott, 27; of Tennyson, 595, 637
Patronage, neo-classical, 33
Pauline, 655
Peace, 872
Peacock, Thomas Love, 297-298, 769
Percy, Bishop Thomas, 7, 13
Per Amica Silentia Lunae, 1025
Perennial Philosophy, The, 1097
Pericles and Aspasia, 21, 299
Periodical literature, 18-19, 21, 408-409, 416, 851, and literary criticism, 18, 21. See also Magazines.
Persuasion, 26
Peter Bell, 120
Peter Pan, or the Boy Who Wouldn't Grow Up, 854
Philomela, 40, **733**
Philosophy, and doctrine of utility, 404; and Pater, 580-581, 952; Browning's, 657; Carlyle's, 465; epicurean, 952; German, 464; Hardy's, 907-908; hedonistic, 580; of evolution, 405-406; political, 404; social, 405-406, 413, 465; stoic school of, 479, 720, 726; Tennyson's, 599, 603; Victorian, 420, 595
Physical Basis of Life, The, 562
Pickwick Papers, 421
Picture of Dorian Gray, The, 952
Pied Beauty, 872
Pied Piper of Hamelin, The, 657
Pigeon, The, 862
Pilgrimage, 1020
Pillar of the Cloud, The, 715
Pinero, Sir Arthur Wing, 860
Pippa Passes, 656, **657**
Pirate Story, 877
Pirates of Penzance, The, 825
Pis-Aller, 744
Plain Tales from the Hills, 886, 933
Plato, 160, 331, 549; and Pater, 581; and Shelley, 15, 22; and Wordsworth, 12; Platonic doctrine of recollection, 160; Platonic idea of eternal beauty, 251; Platonic system of beauty, 15
Plato and Platonism, 580
Playboy of the Western World, 853, 986
Plays, heroic, of Boucicault, 414; Irish, 853-854, 985-986; of Barrie, 854; of Beddoes, 298; of Browning, 655; of Galsworthy, 861-862; of Henley and Stevenson, 863; of Robertson, 414; of Wilde, 952; one-act, 853, 854; poetical, of Gilbert, 414; social, 860, 861, 862; Victorian, 412-414. See also Drama.
Plough and the Stars, The, 1010
Plumed Serpent, The, 1017
Poe, Edgar Allan, 24, 761
Poems (Auden), 1145
Poems (Eliot), 1078
Poems (Spender), 1159
Poems (Yeats), 1025
Poems and Ballads (Masefield), 916

Poems and Ballads (Swinburne), 808
Poems by Currer, Ellis, and Acton Bell, 717
Poems by Two Brothers, 593
Poems of Dedication, 1160
Poems Written in Discouragement, 1025
Poet, The, 596
Poet Laureate, Southey, 13, 119, 224, 296, 434; Tennyson, 400, 412, 593, 594; Wordsworth, 119, 593, 594
Poetical Sketches, 111, **112**
Poetry, and Arnold's theories, 552; and Macaulay, 427; and *Preface to Lyrical Ballads,* 11; and Ruskin, 509; and women, 409; and Wordsworth, 10, 11, 118-119; classical, 554; critical, 824; didacticism in, 410; dramatic, 17; dramatic monologue, 413, 655, 656, 715; graveyard, 7, 8, 1013; in the periodicals, 409, 851; influence of Coleridge and Wordsworth on, 11-12; love, 8, 9, 84, 710; lyrical, 3, 9, 15, 250, 251, 256, 299, 408, 808, 809, 1025; Milton's definition of, 332; morality in, 412; narrative, 13, 27, 190-191, 201, 274, 296, 850, 858, 916; nature, 6, 8, 10, 11, 15, 16, 32, 33, 47, 74, 76, 84, 119, 120, 121, 148, 164, 251, 262; neo-classical, 8, 10, 33; of aesthetic movement, 852; of friendship, 8, 9; of Galsworthy, 858; of Hardy, 858, 907-908; of impressionists, 850-851; of post-Victorian era, 595, 850, 853, 862; of romanticism, 6-17, 27, 33, 55, 67, 69; of twentieth-century traditionalists, 1009-1010; of Waste Land, 1014, 1021; Old English battle, 56; pastoral, 262, 739; patriotic, 9; religious, 8, 74, 446, 715, 869-870; romantic, 594; satirical, 200, 201, 202, 224, 417, 823; social, 710; supernatural, in, 10, 11, 165; symbolic, of Blake, 111; transitional, 8-10; twentieth century, 655; Victorian, 409, 412, 414-418, 426, 595-596
Poetry of Pope, The, 21, **394**
Point Counter Point, 1016, 1097
Poison Tree, A, 117
Political Register, The, 18
Politics, and Macaulay, 427; and magazines, 408; and Tennyson, 594; conservatism of English in, 5; of De Quincey, 375; of romantic age, 3, 5, 29-30; of Rousseau, 3-4
Poor Old Pilgrim Misery, 309
Poor Relations, 19, **345**
Pope, Alexander, 3, 6, 11, 14, 47, 203; Byron's admiration for, 200, 203
Porter, Jane, 27
Portrait, A, 879
Portrait of a Lady, The, 857
Portrait of the Artist as a Young Dog, 1169
Portrait of the Artist as a Young Man, A, 1018, 1042
Praeterita, 501
Praise for the Fountain Opened, 75
Praise of Chimney-Sweepers, *The,* **341**
Preface to Lyrical Ballads, 11, 22, 120, **318,** 328, 330, 596
Preliminary Confessions, 375
Prelude, 1069
Prelude, The, 12, 74, 120, **125**
Pre-Raphaelite Brotherhood, The, 416-417, 418, 749, 783, 784, 808-809, 827, 852; and Ruskin, 416, 502; and Wilde, 952; and Yeats, 1025
Present Indicative, 1118

Present Laughter, 1118
Pride and Prejudice, 25-26
Pride of Youth, 795
Prime Minister, 1033
Princess, The, 401, 415, 594, 595, **626**
Prisoner of Chillon, The, 201, 207
Private Lives, 1015, 1117
Private Papers of Henry Ryecroft, The, 857
Pro Rege Nostro (England, My England), 868
Proem from Endymion, 278
Proem to The Ring and the Book, 707
Progress of Poesy, The, 47, 52, 363
Prometheus Bound, 250, 709
Prometheus Unbound (Songs from), 15, 27, 250, 251, **256**
Proper Studies, 1097
"Prophetic Books" (Blake), 111
Prose, neo-classical, 2; of Arnold, 528; of Landor, 299; of Macaulay, 428; of the Brontës, 716; romance, of Morris, 798; romantic, 17-29, 875; Victorian, 409, 410, 411, 414, 418-421, 426; Wordsworth's definition of, 321
Prospice, 706
Proud Maisie, 198
Proust, Marcel, 1019
Prufrock and Other Observations, 1078
Psychology, impact of, on literature, 1012
Pulvis et Umbra, 847, 875, **929**, 1012
Punch, 409, 417, 418, 852, 952
Purple Dust, 1011
Pusey, Edward Vouverie, 407, 488, 548
Pygmalion, 861
Pylons, The, 1161

Qua Cursum Ventus, 721
Quarterly Review, 18, 191, 361, 408; and Keats, 247, 262, 274
Queen Mab, 249, 250
Queen Mary, 595
Queen Victoria, 1011
Quentin Durward, 28
Qui Laborat, Orat, 721, **723**
Quiet American, The, 1021
Quiet Work, 726

Rabbi Ben Ezra, 491, **698**
Radcliffe, Mrs. Anne, 24, 319
Radicalism, of Godwin, 15, 22; of Hazlitt, 361; of Thomson, 760
Rain, 1015
Rat Trap, The, 1117
Reade, Charles, 413, 422
Realism, 1, 4, 10; and Balzac, 587; and Butler, 856; and Dickens, 424; and Eliot, 1087; and Hardy, 858, 908; and Kipling, 887; and Masefield, 916; and romance, 409-411; and romanticism, 10, 31; in drama, 414; in literature and art, 1; in post-Victorian novel, 855-859; in twentieth-century literature, 1008; in Victorian novel, 422; in Victorian poetry, 410, 418; of Browning, 657; of Burns, 9; of Galsworthy, 857; of modern Ireland, 853; of Pre-Raphaelites, 416; of Scott, 29; of the post-Victorian era, 845, 847-850, 855, 856-857, 858, 862; of Trollope, 422; of Wilde, 952; of Woolf, 1062; of Wordsworth, 119; Victorian, 410, 426, 784
Recessional, 896
Recluse, The, 120, 125
Rector of Wyck, The, 1021
Red, Red Rose, A, 109
Reeve, Clara, 27
Reform, and Carlyle, 465; and Dickens, 423; and Ruskin, 515; and Victorian reformers, 420; industrial, 465; political, 399, 403-404, 497; religious, 406-407, 445; social, 4, 22, 76, 399, 843-844
Reform Bills, 400, 403-404, 427, 594; and Tennyson, 611
Relation of Art to Morals, The, 319, **524**
Religion, and Barker, 1163; and Clough, 721; and Eliot, 1014, 1079, 1087; and Hopkins, 869-870; and Newman, 406-408, 420, 445, 446; and Oxford Movement, 406-408, 445, 446; and poetry, 8, 74, 446; and C. Rossetti, 749; and science, 402, 405-406, 562, 594, 845; and Southey, 296; and Swinburne, 809; Arnold's definition of, 528; cycles of, 407; evangelical, 8; neo-classical, 8; of Rousseau, 3-4; of Wordsworth, 119-120; radical developments in, 164; romantic movement in, 407-408
Reliques of Ancient English Poetry, 7
Remembrance (Brontë), **717**
Remembrance (Shelley), **272**
Remembrance of Things Past, 1019
Remorse, 165
Renaissance, 30, 31, 273, 274, 447, 576; and Browning, 655, 670; and D. G. Rossetti, 784; architecture, 502; art, 502
Requiem, 881
Requiescat, 734
Resolution and Independence, 120, **148**, 826, 849
Respectability, 681
Responsibilities: Poems and a Play, 1025
Return of the Native, The, 907
Reveries over Childhood and Youth, 1025
Revolt Against Classicism, The, 439
Revolt of Islam, The, 27, 250, 380
Revolution, 3, 4, 5, 118, 399, 405-406, 848; Age of, 4, 5; and Burns, 84, 89; and Byron, 14; and Carlyle, 465, 482; and fiction, 26; and Keats, 274; and Landor, 299; and Rousseau, 3-4; and Shelley, 15, 249, 250, 251; and Wordsworth, 12, 118, 119; artistic, 3; Industrial, 3, 4-5, 30, 298, 402; in literature, 6; intellectual forces behind, 4; literature of, 273; philosophical, 4; political, 3, 4, 30, 399; social, 3, 4, 399
Richardson, Dorothy, 1020
Richardson, Henry Handel (Henrietta), 1021
Richardson, Samuel, 23
Richelieu, 413
Riders to the Sea, 853, **986**
Rime of the Ancient Mariner, The, 11, 12, 164, **166**
Ring and the Book, The, 656-657, 707
Roadways, 920
Rob Roy, 28
Robertson, Ethel Lindesay, 1021
Robertson, Thomas William, 414
Robin Hood, 276
Rock, The, 1014, 1079
Rolled Over on Europe, 1160

Romance, and realism, 409-411; Arthurian, 7, 288; burlesque, of Peacock, 297; Gothic, 23, 25, 46, 190, 319; in Victorian period, 421, 422; in Victorian poetry, 410; literary, 28; medieval, 7, 23, 33, 164, 212; metrical, 190; of E. B. Browning, 710; of post-Victorian period, 855; of Stevenson, 422, 855, 875, 876; of Tennyson, 415, 594; philosophical, of Carlyle, 466; philosophical, of Pater, 580; poetical, of Tennyson, 638; satirical, 297-298. See also Novel.
Romanticism, 1-31, 47, 48, 119, 202, 296, 543, 591; and beauty, 1, 16; and Dickens, 424; and Gautier, 586; and Heine, 586; and Kipling, 897; and Macaulay, 427, 439; and nature, 1, 6, 10; and Pater, 439, 581; and primitive, 10; and religion, 407-408; and D. G. Rossetti, 783, 784; and Stendhal, 587; and Stevenson, 862, 876; approach to, 6-10; as medium for English expression, 2; essay of, 418; "graveyard" school, 7; growth of, 6; humanitarian element of, 7, 8, 298; ideals of, 165; in art and literature, 1; in twentieth century, 1008, 1009; in verse, 10; in Victorian literature, 426; in Victorian poetry, 418; influence of, on the Waste Land, 1013; influence of medieval on, 7, 10, 23, 55, 410; influence of past on, 7, 10; literature of, 30-31, 273; melancholy element in, 1, 6, 7, 8, 31; minor poets of, 17, 296-300; novel of, 23-29; novelist of, 400; of De la Mare, 1009; of impressionists, 850, 853; of Pre-Raphaelites, 416; of Swinburne, 417, 809; of Victorian poets, 417; of Victorian prose writers, 426; of Yeats, 1009; poetry of, 10-17, 48; prose of, 17-29; summary of, 29-31; supernatural in, 7, 10; writers of, 6, 10
Romanticism, 585
Romola, 411, 422, 425
Rondeau, 305
Roots of Honor, The, 515
Rosabelle, 192
Rose Aylmer, 311
Rose of the World, The, 1027
Rossetti, Christina, 416, 748-749, 783
Rossetti, Dante Gabriel, 416-417, 426, 748, **783-784**, 827; and Swinburne, 808
Rossetti, William Michael, 416
Rousseau, Jean Jacques, 3-4, 26, 31, 164, 365, 368, 482, 494, 498, 589; and Byron, 14; and nature, 4; and Wordsworth, 118; novels of, 4, 26
Rubáiyát of Omar Khayyám, The, 417, 775, **776**
Ruddigore, 825
Rugby Chapel, 528, **745**
Ruins and Visions, 1160
Rule, Britannia! 32, 39
Ruskin, John, 319, 407, 408, 410, 411, 416, 419, 420, 467, **501-503**, 580, 783, 784, 844; and Carlyle, 501, 502, 515
Russell, G. W., 852, 853, 985
Ruth, 306

Sacred and Secular Elegies, 1163
Sacred Wood, The, 1078, **1080**
Said I to Myself, Said I, 835
Sailing to Byzantium, 1009, **1031**
St. Leon, 26
St. Mary's Bells, 919

St. Paul and Protestantism, 528
Sainte-Beuve, Charles, 543, 553
Saintsbury, George Edward Bateman, 298
Salomé, 952
Saltwater Ballads, 916
Sanford and Merton, 26
Sartor Resartus, 464, **465**, 491
Sassoon, Siegfried, 1094
Satire, 2; in Landor's poetry, 299-300; in post-Victorian essay, 855; in post-Victorian novel, 855, 856; in the novel, 25; in verse, 417-418, 823-824, 825; Irish, 852; of Jane Austen, 25, 26; of Burns, 9, 85; of Butler, 856; of Byron, 13, 14, 29, 200-202, 224; of Clough, 722; of Coleridge, 165; of Gilbert, 414, 825, 833; of Hardy, 918-919; of Hazlitt, 19; of O'Casey, 1011; of Peacock, 298; of post-Victorian period, 856, 862; of Shaw, 861, 1010; of Shelley, 251; of Tennyson, 415, 594; of Thackeray, 424; of Victorian period, 417-418; of Waste Land, 1013; social, of Wilde, 953
Satires of Circumstance, 907, **913**
Saul, 672
Say Not the Struggle Naught Availeth, 721, **723**
Schiller, Friedrich, 464
Scholar-Gypsy, The, 410, 528, **734**
Science, 402-403, 845; and Arnold, 406; and contemporary literature, 1008, 1012; and Aldous Huxley, 1016; and T. H. Huxley, 405-406, 419-420, 561-562; and inventions, 402; and labor, 402; and novel, 858; and religion, 402, 405-406, 552; and society, 402-403; and theology, 405-406; and Victorian age, 405-406; in Tennyson's poetry, 594; natural, 4; theory of evolution and, 405-406
Science and Culture, 324, **571**
Science, Liberty, and Peace, 1097
Scorn Not the Sonnet, 163
Scotland, and Burns, 9, 83, 84, 85; and Sir Walter Scott, 13, 27, 28, 29; and the Kailyard School, 854, 860; ballads of, 13, 190; folklore of, 13, 190; history of, 190; legendary past of, 13, 190; novels of, 28; songs of, 13
Scots, Wha Hae, 84, **109**
Scott, Sir Walter, 13, 18, 26, 27-29, **190-191**, 296, 400, 421, 428, 855; appraisal of, 29, 191; as a poet, 13, 27, 190; as antiquarian, 13, 191; historical novels of, 28; novels of, 13, 28-29, 190-191; position among the romantic writers, 13, 28-29
Scottish Chiefs, The, 27
Sea and the Skylark, The, 871
Sea-Fever, 917
Sea-Limits, The, 787
Seasons, The, 6, 32, 33, 39
Second Coming, The, 1009, **1030**
Second Mrs. Tanqueray, The, 860
Second World War, 995, 1005-1006, 1033
Second World War, The, 1033
Secret Rose, The, 1025
Secret Sharer, The, 944
Seekers, The, 920
Selected Poems (Auden), 1145
Selected Poems (Barker), 1163
Selected Poems (Spender), 1160
Self Condemned, 1021

Self-Dependence, 731
Sense and Sensibility, 26
Sensitive Plant, The, 15, 250
Sentimentalism, 7; and Barrie, 850; and Browning, 657; and E. B. Browning, 710; and Wastelander, 1008; of Burns, 9, 84; of Dickens, 424-425; of Lamb, 19, 337; of Shelley, 250; of Tennyson, 595-596; of Wordsworth, 149; in novel, 26, 424; in novel of purpose, 26; lack of, in Jane Austen, 25, 26
Sesame and Lilies, 502
Seven Lamps of Architecture, 502
Seven Seas, The, 886
Shakespeare, William, 20, 68, 165, 580; criticism of, 20, 21, 22, 299, 332, 809; revival of criticism of, 20, 21, 22
Shakespeare, 726
Shameful Death, 804
Shaughraun, The, 414
Shaw, George Bernard, 844, 852, 861, 952, 1010
She Dwelt Among the Untrodden Ways, 124
She Walks in Beauty, 205
She Was a Phantom of Delight, 155
Shelley, Mary Godwin, 24, 249; influence on Shelley's poetry, 249
SHELLEY, PERCY BYSSHE, 13, 15, 16, 17, 22, 27, 31, 165, 191, 201, 202, 248-251, 273, 274, 299, 300, **315**, 414, 629, 761, 916; and Barker, 1163; and Browning, 655; and nature, 15; and revolution, 15, 249, 250; and Swinburne, 808; and Yeats, 1025; attachment for Byron, 15, 250; influence of Mary Godwin on, 249; influence of Italy on, 250; literary criticism of, 22; love of humanity, 15; moral peculiarities of, 248; poetic drama of, 251, 270, 300; prose of, 251; quality of poetry of, 15, 250; satire of, 251
Shield of Achilles, The, 1022, 1145
Shropshire Lad, A, 899
Sign of the Cross, The, 715
Sign of the Four, The, 856
Silas Marner, 402, 425
Silence, 306
Silent Noon, 794
Silver Box, The, 862
Silver Tassie, The, 1010
Silverado Squatters, The, 875
Sinclair, May, 1021
Sing Me a Song, 880
Sing-Song, 749, 759
Sire de Maletroit's Door, The, 874
Sister Helen, 787
Sitwell, Dame Edith, 1023
Six Dramas of Calderon, 776
Skepticism, and scientific investigation, 406; and Tennyson, 594
Sketch of His Own Character, 59
Slumber Did My Spirit Seal, A, 125
Smith, Adam, 22
Smith, Sidney, 18
Smollett, Tobias, 23, 25; and Dickens, 424
Smuggler's Song, A, 898
So We'll Go No More A-Roving, 224
Social Conditions, 4, 5, 501; and Arnold, 527-528; and E. B. Browning, 710; and factory system, 4-5, 402-403; and Hood, 298; and Industrial Revolution, 4, 5, 402; and novels of Dickens, 423; and problems of Victorian England, 410, 411, 419; and Ruskin, 501, 502; and Shelley, 325; and social relationships, 860; and Victorian literature, 410, 415, 784; change in, 402-403, 843-844; criticism of, 4, 5, 22, 298, 415, 419-420, 502, 861-862; legislation on, 403-404, 465; problems of, 5, 411, 426; reform in, 22
Social consciousness, and poetry, 1021-1022
Social Contract, The, 4
Socialism, of Morris, 797-798
Society, abuses of, 4-5; and late Victorian literature, 845; Burns's indictment of, 85; capitalistic system of, 22; criticism of, 4, 5, 22, 823-825; problems of, 401-402, 843, 860
Sofa, The, 74, 76
Sohrab and Rustum, 410, 528
Soldier, Rest! Thy Warfare O'er, 195
Soldier's Song, 197
Solitary Reaper, The, 12, 120, 154
Some Poems, 1145
Something Childish and Other Stories, 1069
Song (Beddoes), 309
Song (Beddoes), 310
Song (Brontë), 718
Song (C. Rossetti), 749
Song (Shelley), 260
Song (Yeats), 1027
Song in the Songless, 775
Song of the Bower, The, 791
Song of the Brook, The, 637
Song of the Road, A, 876
Song of the Shirt, The, 298, 306
Song of Wandering Aengus, The, 1029
Song to the Men of England, 254
Songs Before Sunrise, 809
Songs from Pippa Passes, 657
Songs from The Princess, 626
Songs of Experience, 9, 111, **116**
Songs of Innocence, 9, 111, **113**
Sonnet, of E. B. Browning, 710; of Keats, 273, 274; of C. Rossetti, 760; of D. G. Rossetti, 784; of Wordsworth, 12, 119, 120, 121, 159
Sonnet, A (Stephen), 839
Sonnet, The (D. G. Rossetti), 794
Sonnet on Chillon, 207
Sonnet: On the Death of Richard West, 49, 321
Sonnet to Mrs. Unwin, 82
Sonnets (John Masefield), 921
Sonnets from the Portuguese, 710, **713**
Sons and Lovers, 1017
Sophocles, 69, 776; and Arnold, 528, 726
Sordello, 656, 657
Soul, 716
Soul's Beauty, 796
SOUTHEY, ROBERT, 12, 13, 18, 119, 201, 247, **296, 300,** 824, 828; and Coleridge, 12, 164, 165
Space and Dread and the Dark, 868
Specimens of English Dramatic Poets, 21
SPENDER, STEPHEN, 1021, 1022-1023, **1159-1160**
Spenser, Edmund, 6, 273; and Keats, 16, 274; imitations of, 6, 32, 39
Spirit of the Age, The, 361

Splendor Falls on Castle Walls, The, 627
Spring, 32, 33
Spring and Fall, 873
Staff-Nurse: New Style, 865
Staff-Nurse: Old Style, 865
Stage, 412-413; government regulations of, 412; introduction of social manners on, 414; popular, 413
Stalky & Co., 897
Stanzas for Music (There be none of Beauty's daughters), **207**
Stanzas for Music (There's not a joy the world can give like that it takes away), **206**
Stanzas Written in Dejection, Near Naples, 253, 313
Stanzas Written on the Road Between Florence and Pisa, 247
Star Turns Red, The, 1011
Starlight Night, The, 871
STEPHEN, JAMES KENNETH, **825, 838**
Sterne, Laurence, 23, 26, 362, 364
STEVENSON, ROBERT LOUIS, 13, 24, 361, 408, 422, 847, 855-856, 858, 859, 863, **874-876**, 886, 1009, 1012; and Henley, 863-865, 874; and vivisection, 933
Stickit Minister, The, 854
Still Centre, The, 1160
Stillborn Love, 795
Stoker Bush, 1021
Stolen Child, The, 1026
Stones of Venice, The, 502, 503, 524, 670
Story, adventure, of Stevenson, 875; animal, of Kipling, 886; detective, of Doyle, 856; fairy, of Wilde, 952; ghost, of James, 857; mystery, of Stevenson, 875; sea, of Conrad, 858-859; short, 856, 859; short, of Stevenson, 859, 875. See also Novel.
Strachey, Lytton, 1011
Strafford, 413, 655
Strange Case of Dr. Jekyll and Mr. Hyde, The, 875
Strange Fits of Passion Have I Known, 123
Strauss, Richard, 847
Strawberry Hill, 23
"Stream of consciousness," 1019, 1061
Strife, 862, 1010
Studies in the History of the Renaissance, 580, 581, 583, 930
Study in Scarlet, A, 856
Study of Poetry, The, 90, **552**
Sullivan, Arthur, 825
Summer, 32, 33
Sunday at Hempstead, 761
Sunday up the River, 761
Superannuated Man, The, 337, **349**
Supernaturalism, in novel, 7, 23, 24, 421; in romantic poetry, 7, 10; in verse, 164, 165; of Pre-Raphaelites, 416
Suspiria de Profundis, 20, 375, **389**
Sweet Afton, 9, 84, **102**
Sweet and Low, 626
Swift, Jonathan, 6, 852, 1016
SWINBURNE, ALGERNON, 250, 414, 417, 418, 426, 639, 776, **808-810**, 852
Swinnerton, Frank, 1021
Symbolism, 846, 850-851, 862, 1025

Symons, Arthur, 851
Sympathy, 718
SYNGE, JOHN MILLINGTON, 850, 853-854, **985-986**, 1010
System, 878

Table Talk, 21, 165
Tale of Two Cities, A, 422
Tales from Shakespeare, 21, 338
Tales of Unrest, 944
Tam o' Shanter, 104
Task, The, 8, 74, **76**
Tate, Nahum, 8
Taylor, Jeremy, 21, 331
Taylor, Tom, 413
Tears, Idle Tears, 627
Technique, in contemporary literature, 1024
TENNYSON, ALFRED, LORD, 17, 250, 278, 319, 400, 401, 406, 410, 412, 413, 414, 415, 416, 426, 529, 543, 580, **593-596**, 655, 657, 710, 716, 721, 809, 842, 847, 852; and Keats, 274; and Longfellow, 412; dramas of, 413
Tess of the D'Urbervilles, 907
Texts and Pretexts, 1097
Thackeray, William Makepeace, 26, 408, 409, 421, 422, 424-425, 426, 543, 855, 927
Thaddeus of Warsaw, 27
Theater, 412. See also Stage.
Thel's Motto, 118
Theology, and Newman, 445, 446; and Oxford movement, 406-407; and science, 405-406; and Stevenson, 876. See also Religion.
There Are Some Birds in These Valleys, 1146
"There Is No God," the Wicked Saith, 722
Thérèse Raquin, 856-857
They'll None of 'Em Be Missed, 836
This Happy Breed, 1015, 1118
This World Is Very Odd We See, 722
THOMAS, DYLAN, 1023, **1169**
THOMPSON, FRANCIS, 851, **892-893**
THOMSON, JAMES (1700-1748), 6, 7, 10, **32-34**, 47, 67, 72, 369
THOMSON, JAMES (1834-1882), **760-761**, 846, 1017
Those Barren Leaves, 1097
Thought of a Briton on the Subjugation of Switzerland, 162, 839
Three Critical Essays, 1078
Three Enemies, The, 749
Three Guineas, 1062
Three Shadows, 797
Three Years She Grew in Sun and Shower, 124
Through the Looking-Glass, 825
Thyrsis, 528, 629, 721, **739**
Ticket-of-Leave Man, The, 413
Tiger, The, 112, **116**
Time, 261
Time Long Past, 260
Time Machine, The, 858
Time Must Have a Stop, 1097
Time-Piece, The, 78
'Tis the Last Rose of Summer, 303
To—(Music, when soft voices die), **261**
To—(One word is too often profaned), 250, **272**

GENERAL INDEX

To a Friend, 726
To a Highland Girl, 120, **153**
To a Louse, **101**
To a Mountain Daisy, 84, **100**
To a Mouse, 84, **98**
To a Skylark (Shelley), 15, 156, **258**
To a Skylark (Wordsworth), **156**, 258
To a Snowflake, **884**
To Age, 315
To Alison Cunningham, **877**
To Autumn, 16, **291**
To-Be-Forgotten, The, **910**
To Davie, 85
To-day, This Insect, **1170**
To Imagination, **718**
To Jeanie, 84
To Marguerite—Continued, **730**
To Mary, 81
To Mary in Heaven, **103**, 108
To My Ninth Decade, 315
To Night, 15, 250, **261**
To One Who Has Been Long in City Pent, **275**
To R. B., **874**
To Sea, To Sea! **309**
To the Cuckoo, **154**
To the Daisy (Bright Flower! whose home is everywhere), **153**
To the Daisy (With little here to do or see), 120, **152**
To the Evening Star, **112**
To the Lighthouse, 1020, 1061
To Thomas Moore, **224**
To Youth, 314
Toccata of Galuppi's, A, **679**
Tolstoi, Leo, 846
Tommy, 849, **887**
Tonight at 8:30, 1118
Tono-Bungay, 858
Tory, and Carlyle, 420; in literature, 18; magazines, 18, 408
Tower, The, 1025
Tractarianism, 406, 548; and Arnold, 528. See also Oxford Movement.
Tracts for the Times, 406, 407, 445, 488
Trade Unions, 404-405, 844
Tradition and the Individual Talent, **1080**
Traditionalists, 1008-1012
Tragedy, Browning's translations from Greek, 657; of Beddoes, 298; of Landor, 299; of Tennyson, 595; Victorian, 412
Tragedy of Nan, The, 916
Translations, 420-421; Browning's, 657; Calverley's, 824; Carlyle's, 464; Fitzgerald's, 776; Scott's, 190, 319
Travels with a Donkey in the Cevennes, 875
Treasure Island, 875
Trembling of a Leaf, The, 1015
Trial by Jury, 414, 825
Trial of a Judge, 1159
Tristram of Lyonesse, 809
Trollope, Anthony, 422, 1021
Troy Town, **792**
Turgenev, Ivan, 846

Turn of the Screw, The, 857
Turn of the Tide, The, 917
Turner, J. M. W., 501, 502, 503
Twelve-Pound Look, The, 854
Twenty Poems, 1159
Twenty-Five Poems, 1169
Two or Three Graces, 1097
Two Races of Men, The, 19, **353**
Two Sonnets (Thomson), **762**
Typhoon, 944

Ulysses (Joyce), 1018-1019, **1042**, 1061
Ulysses (Tennyson), 415, 594, 596, **611**
Unconditional Surrender, 1040
Under Milk Wood, 1169
Under the Greenwood Tree, 907
United Nations, 996
Unto This Last, 502, **515**
Unwin, Mary, 74, 76, 77, 81
Uphill, 752
Utilitarianism, 22, 404, 407, 455; and Carlyle, 404, 420, 488, 501; and Ruskin, 501; society of, 404

Valentine's Day, 19
Vanity Fair, 425
Vathek, 24
Verse, and aesthetic movement, 852; and parodies, 149, 297, 417; blank, 11, 32, 33, 74, 299, 864; for children, 876; forms, 864; humanitarian, 7, 298; humorous, 297-298, 823-839; Latin, 299; laughing critics in, 823-839; libertarian, 10, 11, 12; "light-horse," 190; metaphysical, 8; narrative, 13, 27; neo-classical, 6, 33; nonsense, 417, 824-825; of friendship, 8; of the Brontës, 716-717; religious, 446, 749; satirical, 251, 417, 824-825; social, 298; Victorian, 414-418
Versification, 52; assonance, 67; ballade, 864; experiments in meter, 416; hexameter, of Clough, 721; iambic pentameter, 297, 776, 799; in *Christabel,* 175; of Hopkins, 870; onomatopoeia, 67; quatrains of Fitzgerald, 417, 776; rondeau, 864; "society-verse," 47; Spenserian stanza, 33, 262; *terza rima,* 799; verse-forms, 33, 40, 47
Victoria, 119, 399, 400, 404, 405, 412, 593, 841; and Gladstone, 404
Victorian Age, 17, 21, 299, 399-426, 427, 593, 862; Carlyle's contribution to, 465; conventions of, 411, 824; decline of, 841; didacticism of, 411; drama of, 412-414, 859; essay of, 855; humanitarianism of, 404, 415, 423; interest in lectures, 408; literature of, 400, 402, 418, 426; magazines in, 408-409; materialism of, 407, 419, 420; medievalism in, 410; morality in, 400, 411-412; novel of, 408, 411, 421-422; opposition to ideals of, 501; philosophies of, 595; poetry of, 410, 412, 414-418, 426; popular character of literature in, 408; prose of, 408, 411, 414, 418-421, 426; Puritan elements, 411; reaction against, 400, 411, 841, 846-847, 862; religion of, 405-408, 845; romance and realism in, 409-411; romanticism of, 410; science in, 402-403, 405-406; social and industrial adjustment in, 401-403; social critics of, 420, 843-844; social influence of on

literature, 408-409; social problems of, 410-411, 415; social standards of, 411; theaters of, 412-413; theology of, 405-408
Victory, 943
Vienna, 1159
Vinci, Leonardo da, 581
Virginibus Puerisque, 874
Vision, A, 1025
Vision of Beasts and Gods, A, 1163
Vision of England '38, 1163
Vision of Judgment, The, 201
Visit to Italy, 460
Voice of the Lobster, The, 828
Vortex, The, 1014, 1117
Voyage Out, The, 1061
Vulgarity in Literature, 1097

Wages, 645
Wagner, Richard, 847
Waiting, 864
Walking with God, 75
Walpole, Horace, 23, 24, 46, 48, 49, 52, 59, 383
Walpole, Hugh, 1021
Walrus and the Carpenter, The, 830
Wanderings of Oisin and Other Poems, The, 1025
Ward, Mrs. Humphrey, 847
Waste Land, The, 1014, 1078, 1079
Waste Land, 1008, 1012, 1078; and romanticism, 1013; drama of, 1014-1015; novelists of, 1015, 1021; poetry of, 1014-1021
Watch Any Day His Nonchalant Pauses, 1145
Water Babies, The, 406
Watson, John B., 1012
Waugh, Evelyn, 1021
Waverley, 28, 29, 191
Waves, The, 1020, 1061, 1062
Way of All Flesh, The, 856
Wealth of Nations, 22
Wells, Herbert George, 844, 858, 859, 942
Wesley, Charles, 8
Wesley, John, 8
Wessex Poems and Other Verses, 907
West, Richard, 46, 48
West Wind, The, 918
Westminster Gazette, The, 1097
Westminster Review, 409
Westward Ho! 422
What I Expected, 1022-1023, 1162
What Is to Come, 867
"What Went Ye Out for to See?" 723
When a Man Hath No Freedom, 247
When All My Five and Country Senses See, 1171
When I Have Fears That I May Cease to Be, 276
When the Hounds of Spring, 810
When We Two Parted, 202
When You Are Old, 1027
Where Forlorn Sunsets Flare and Fade, 868
Where Shall the Lover Rest, 192
Whiff of Grapeshot, The, 482
White Birds, The, 1026
White Knight's Ballad, The, 149, 831

White Man's Burden, The, 897
Who Killed John Keats? 247, 265
Why I Am a Liberal, 708
Wife Waits, A, 912
Wilberforce, Bishop, 405, 406, 594
WILDE, OSCAR, 835, 847, 851, 861, **951-953**, 1015
Willie Brew'd a Peck o' Maut, 103
Willow, Titwillow, 838
Wilson, John, 18
Wind among the Reeds, The, 1025
Windhover, The, 871
Window in Thrums, A, 854
Winter, 32, 33
Witch of Atlas, The, 15, 250
Within the Gates, 1011
Without Her, 795
Without That Once Clear Aim, 1160
Wollstonecraft, Mary, 22, 371
Woman of No Importance, A, 861, 952
Women, and Tennyson, 594; as writers of novels of manners, 25-26, 422; in Victorian writing, 409, 422, 425; novelists of the Waste Land, 1021; position in eighteenth century, 5; under factory system, 403
WOOLF, VIRGINIA, 1020, **1061-1062**
Wordsworth, Dorothy, 118, 119, 148
WORDSWORTH, WILLIAM, 9, 10-12, 13, 16, 18, 20, 22, 31, 76, **118-121**, 166, 201, 202, 273, 278, **318**, 374, 414, 502, 528, 552, 593, 596, 729, 732, 769, 826, 839, 849; and Coleridge, 10, 11, 12, 20, 118-119, 164-165, 166, 170; as poet of humanity, 12, 119; as poet of nature, 11, 12, 17, 119, 120, 121, 148, 410; as revolutionist, 12, 118-119, autobiographical poems of, 12, 74, 120, 125; influence of, 121; lack of humor of, 12, 121; literary criticism of, 22; "Lucy poems" of, 119, 123; sonnets of, 12, 119, 120, 121, 159
Work in Progress, 1042
Work Without Hope, 189
World Crisis, The, 1033
World I Breathe, The, 1169
World Is a Bundle of Hay, The, 247, 487
World Is Too Much with Us, The, 159
World of Light, The, 1097
World Wars. See First World War, Second World War.
World Within World, 1022, 1160
Worlds on Worlds Are Rolling Ever, 270
Wuthering Heights, 717

Yarn of the "Nancy Bell," The, 833
Years, The, 1020, 1062
YEATS, WILLIAM BUTLER, 851, 852, 853, 985, 986, 1009, 1014, **1025**
Yeoman of the Guard, The, 825
Yes, I Write Verses Now and Then, 313
You Ask Me, Why, Though Ill at Ease, 611
Young, Andrew, 1023
Young Archimedes and Other Stories, 1097
Young, Edward, 7
Your Body Is Stars, 1160
Youth and Age, 165, 189, 314
Youth in Age, 775

Zola, Emile, 846, 856-857, 860

Index of First Lines

A cold coming we had of it 1092
A late lark twitters from the quiet skies . . . 866
A little black thing among the snow 117
A little while, a little while 719
A mile an' a bittock, a mile or twa 879
A more humane Mikado never 837
A slumber did my spirit seal 125
A sonnet is a moment's monument 794
A square, squat room (a cellar on promotion) . . 864
A sudden blow: the great wings beating still . 1030
A thing of beauty is a joy forever 278
Abou Ben Adhem (may his tribe increase) . . . 304
About suffering they were never wrong . . . 1156
Across the sea, along the shore 723
Ae fond kiss, and then we sever 107
After the blast of lightning from the east . . . 1096
Again at Christmas did we weave 633
Ah, are you digging on my grave 914
Ah, did you once see Shelley plain 682
Ah, what avails the sceptered race 311
All along the valley, stream that flashest white . 641
All Nature seems at work. Slugs leave their lair . 189
All service ranks the same with God 657
All that I know 681
All the bells of heaven may ring 823
Along the fields as we came by 902
Am I failing? For no longer can I cast . . . 771
An old, mad, blind, despised, and dying king . . 254
An' Bill can have my sea-boots, Nigger Jim can have my knife 917
And are ye one of Hermitage 911
And death shall have no dominion 1170
Anear the center of that northern crest . . . 767
As I gird on for fighting 904
As ships, becalmed at eve, that lay 721
As some day it may happen that a victim must be found 836
Ask me no more—the moon may draw the sea . 627
At the midnight in the silence of the sleep-time . 708
Auld Neebor, I'm three times doubly o'er your debtor 85
Avert, High Wisdom, never vainly wooed . . 774
Awake, Aeolian lyre, awake 53
Away my verse; and never fear 311

Bards of Passion and of Mirth 280
Be still, my soul, be still; the arms you bear are brittle 903
Be with me, Beauty, for the fire is dying . . . 922
Beauty like hers is genius. Not the call . . . 794
Because I do not hope to turn again 1088
Before the beginning of years 811
Behold her, single in the field 154
Behold! in various throngs the scribbling crew . 203
Behold me waiting—waiting for the knife . . 864
Believe me, if all those endearing young charms . 303
Bent double, like old beggars under sacks . . 1095
Bird of the bitter bright gray golden morn . . 821
Black'on frowns east on Maidon 911
Blue-eyed and bright of face but waning fast . . 865
Boats sail on the rivers 759
Bob Southey! You're a poet—Poet-laureate . . 225
Boot, saddle, to horse, and away 659
Break, break, break 626

Bright Flower! whose home is everywhere . . 153
Bright is the ring of words 880
Bright star! would I were steadfast as thou art . 292
Bring the bowl which you boast 199
But do not let us quarrel any more 694
But, knowing now that they would have her speak 799
By night we lingered on the lawn 634
By shores and woods and steeples 906
By the old Moulmein Pagoda 890
By this he knew she wept with waking eyes . . 771

Calm is the morn without a sound 629
Carry me out 866
Children, who extend their smile of crystal . . 1162
Christmas Eve, and twelve of the clock . . . 915
Cold in the earth—and the deep snow piled above thee 717
Coldly, sadly descends 745
Come, dear children, let us away 727
Come down, O maid, from yonder mountain height 628
Come hither, lads, and harken 806
Come into the garden, Maud 638
Comrades, leave me here a little, while as yet 'tis early morn 613
Consider the sea's listless chime 787
Could man be drunk forever 905
"Courage!" he said, and pointed toward the land . 608
Creep into thy narrow bed 744

Dear, had the world in its caprice 681
Dear Mr. Editor: I wish to say 838
Death stands above me, whispering low . . . 315
Do ye hear the children weeping, O my brothers . 710
Does the eagle know what is in the pit . . . 118
Does the road wind uphill all the way 752
Doom is dark and deeper than any sea-dingle . 1146
Dosn't thou 'ear my 'erse's legs, as they canters awaäy 643
Dost thou look back on what hath been . . . 632
Down the quiet eve 865
Duncan Gray came here to woo 108

Earth has not anything to show more fair . . 151
Elected Silence, sing to me 870
Eternal Spirit of the chainless Mind 207
Even as a child, of sorrow that we give . . . 795
Ever let the Fancy roam 279
Every night my prayers I say 878

Fair Star of evening, Splendor of the West . . 151
Fall, leaves, fall; die, flowers, away 719
Fame, like a wayward girl, will still be coy . . 283
"Farewell, Romance!" the Cave-men said . . 891
Farewell to barn and stack and tree 900
Fear death?—to feel the fog in my throat . . 706
Felix Randal the farrier, O he is dead then . . 872
Five years have past; five summers, with the length 121
Flow gently, sweet Afton, among thy green braes 102
Flower in the crannied wall 646
Fly away, fly away over the sea 759
For I have loved the rural walk through lanes . 76
For I must sing of all I feel and know 761
For Life I had never cared greatly 915

INDEX OF FIRST LINES

For the long nights you lay awake 877
For the others, like me, there is only the flash . 1158
Four years!—and didst thou stay above . . . 747
Friends and loves we have none 920
From the depth of the dreamy decline of the dawn 822

Give a man a horse he can ride 762
Give me a land of boughs in leaf 906
Glory be to God for dappled things 872
Glory of warrior, glory of orator, glory of song . 645
Go, for they call you, shepherd, from the hill . . 734
Go, songs, for ended is our brief, sweet play . . 885
God of our fathers, known of old 896
Goethe in Weimar sleeps, and Greece 729
Great spirits now on earth are sojourning . . . 275
Grow old along with me 698

Ha! wh'are ye gaun, ye crowlin ferlie . . . 101
Had he and I but met 912
Hail to the Chief who in triumph advances . . 196
Hail to thee, blithe Spirit 258
Half a league, half a league 637
Hark! ah the nightingale 733
Harp of the North, farewell! The hills grow dark 197
Harp of the North! that moldering long hast hung 194
He clasps the crag with crooked hands . . . 637
He disappeared in the dead of winter 1157
He is gone on the mountain 196
He rises and begins to round 772
He sat in a wheeled chair, waiting for dark . . 1095
He stood alone within the spacious square . . 764
Heavenborn Helen, Sparta's queen 792
"Heigho," yawned one day King Francis . . . 667
Here by the baring bough 909
Here on the cropped grass of the narrow ridge I
  stand 1147
Here, where the world is quiet 813
Ho, everyone that thirsteth 906
Home they brought her warrior dead 627
Hope evermore and believe, O man 724
How changed is here each spot man makes or fills 739
How do I love thee? Let me count the ways . . 714
How doth the little crocodile 828
How fevered is the man, who cannot look . . 282
How many times do I love thee, dear 309
How sleep the brave who sink to rest 68

I am a kind of farthing dip 879
I am poor brother Lippo, by your leave . . . 688
I am that which began 816
I arise from dreams of Thee 256
I bring fresh showers for the thirsting flowers . 257
I built my soul a lordly pleasure-house . . . 603
I caught this morning morning's minion, king- . 871
I come from haunts of coot and hern 637
I did not lose my heart in summer's even . . 906
I envy not in any moods 630
I fled Him, down the nights and down the days 882
I have desired to go 870
I have no wit, no words, no tears 751
I heard a small sad sound 910
I heard a thousand blended notes 121
I held it truth, with him who sings 629
I hoed and trenched and weeded 904
I know a little garden close 804
I know not whether I am proud 313
I know that I shall meet my fate 1029
I lay, not in Malvern or Alexandra Palace . . 1163

I leant upon a coppice gate 908
I lived with visions for my company 714
I looked and saw your eyes 797
I met a traveler from an antique land 253
I must go down to the seas again 917
I never see the red rose crown the year . . . 922
I passed beside the reverend walls 633
I plucked pink blossoms from mine apple-tree . 751
I send my heart up to thee, all my heart . . . 660
I sprang to the stirrup, and Joris, and he . . . 664
I strove with none; for none was worth my strife . 315
I thank all who have loved me in their hearts . 714
I think continually of those who were truly great 1160
I thought once how Theocritus had sung . . . 713
I thought they'd be strangers aroun' me . . . 913
I, too, saw God through mud 1094
I towered far, and lo! I stood within 909
I traveled among unknown men 124
I wake and feel the fell of dark, not day . . . 873
I walk through the long schoolroom questioning . 1031
I wander through each chartered street . . . 117
I wandered lonely as a cloud 155
I was a stricken deer that left the herd . . . 79
I was angry with my friend 117
I was thy neighbor once, thou rugged Pile . . 157
I weep for Adonais—he is dead 262
I went into a public-'ouse to get a pint o' beer . 887
I went out to the hazel wood 1029
I went to the Garden of Love 117
I will arise and go now, and go to Innisfree . . 1027
I will make you brooches and toys for your delight 879
I would that we were, my belovèd, white birds on
  the foam of the sea 1026
If aught of oaten stop, or pastoral song . . . 69
If from the public way you turn your steps . . 142
If I could come again to that dear place . . . 921
If I have faltered more or less 877
If I leave all for thee, wilt thou exchange . . . 714
If I were a queen 759
If it chance your eye offend you 903
If love were what the rose is 811
If there were dreams to sell 310
If thou indeed derive thy light from Heaven . . 163
If thou must love me, let it be for naught . . 714
If thou wilt ease thine heart 309
If you wake at midnight and hear a horse's feet . 898
If you're anxious for to shine in the high aesthetic
  line as a man of culture rare 835
I'll tell thee everything I can 831
In a coign of the cliff between lowland and high-
  land 819
In a drear-nighted December 277
"In harmony with Nature?" Restless fool . . . 727
In our old shipwrecked days there was an hour . 771
In summertime on Bredon 902
In the dark womb where I began 921
In this lone, open glade I lie 732
In vain to me the smiling mornings shine . . . 49
In valleys green and still 905
In winter I get up at night 877
In Xanadu did Kubla Khan 184
In yonder grave a druid lies 72
Into my heart an air that kills 903
Iphigeneia, when she heard her doom 313
Is it not better at an early hour 313
Is my team plowing 902
Is there, for honest poverty 110
Is this a holy thing to see 116

INDEX OF FIRST LINES

Is thy face like thy mother's, my fair child	212
"Issues from the hand of God, the simple soul"	1093
It is a beauteous evening, calm and free	151
It is an ancient Mariner	166
It keeps eternal whisperings around	276
It little profits that an idle king	612
It was a summer evening	300
It's a warm wind, the west wind, full of birds' cries	918
It's pleasant in Holy Mary	919
I've paid for your sickest fancies; I've humored your crackedest whim	892
Jenny kissed me when we met	305
John Anderson, my jo, John	102
Just for a handful of silver he left us	666
Kentish Sir Byng stood for his King	658
King Charles, and who'll do him right now	658
King Francis was a hearty king	304
Know'st thou not at the fall of the leaf	794
Lady, was it fair of thee	309
Large glooms were gathered in the mighty fane	766
Late, my grandson! half the morning have I paced these sandy tracts	618
Laugh and be merry, remember, better the world with a song	920
Lead, Kindly Light, amid the encircling gloom	715
Leodogran, the king of Cameliard	646
Let my voice ring out and over the earth	763
Let us begin and carry up this corpse	682
Let us go then, you and I	1085
Light flows our war of mocking words, and yet	731
Like the ghost of a dear friend dead	260
Little Fly	116
Little Lamb, who made thee	114
Look at the stars! look, look up at the skies	871
Love is and was my lord and king	636
Love seeketh not itself to please	116
Loveliest of trees, the cherry now	899
Maid of Athens, ere we part	205
Man is blind because of sin	744
Many in aftertimes will say of you	760
Márgarét, are you grieving	873
Mary! I want a lyre with other strings	82
Men of England, wherefore plow	254
Milton! thou shouldst be living at this hour	152
Morning and evening	753
Most sweet it is with unuplifted eyes	163
Mother shake the cherry-tree	759
Much have I traveled in the realms of gold	275
Music, when soft voices die	261
My boat is on the shore	224
"My bride is not coming, alas!" says the groom	914
My first thought was, he lied in every word	684
My hair is gray, but not with years	207
My heart aches, and a drowsy numbness pains	284
My heart leaps up when I behold	148
My lov'd, my honor'd, much respected friend!	95
My mother bore me in the southern wild	114
My passport says I'm five feet and eleven	1149
My silks and fine array	112
My soul is an enchanted boat	256
My spirit is too weak—mortality	275
No coward soul is mine	720
No, for I'll save it! Seven years since	706
No, no! go not to Lethe, neither twist	280
No stir in the air, no stir in the sea	301
No! those days are gone away	276
Nobly, nobly Cape Saint Vincent to the northwest died away	667
Nobody took any notice of her as she stood on the causey curb	911
Not, I'll not, carrion comfort, Despair, not feast on thee	873
Not of the princes and prelates with periwigged charioteers	916
Not palaces, an era's crown	1161
Nought loves another as itself	117
Now as I was young and easy under the apple boughs	1172
Now let the golden prison ope its gates	716
Now sleeps the crimson petal, now the white	628
Now that I, tying thy glass mask tightly	663
Now the storm begins to lower	58
Nuns fret not at their convent's narrow room	159
O Blithe Newcomer! I have heard	154
O Galuppi, Baldassare, this is very sad to find	679
O Goddess! hear these tuneless numbers, wrung	283
O listen, listen, ladies gay	192
O living will that shalt endure	636
O lyric Love, half angel and half bird	707
O Mary, at thy window be	85
O Mortal man! who livest here by toil	39
O my agéd Uncle Arly	826
O, my luve is like a red, red rose	109
O only Source of all our light and life	723
O that 'twere possible	639
O thou, by Nature taught	68
O Thou, wha in the Heavens dost dwell	88
O thou! whatever title suit thee	99
O, wert thou in the cauld blast	110
O what can ail thee, knight-at-arms	282
"O where are you going?" said reader to rider	1146
O wild West Wind, thou breath of Autumn's being	255
O, Willie brew'd a peck o' maut	103
O world invisible, we view thee	885
O world! O life! O time!	262
O yet we trust that somehow good	631
Obscurest night involved the sky	82
O'Driscoll drove with a song	1028
Of Adam's first wife, Lilith, it is told	796
Of a' the airts the wind can blaw	102
Of Heaven or Hell I have no power to sing	805
Of old sat Freedom on the heights	611
Often rebuked, yet always back returning	720
Oh, breathe not his name! let it sleep in the shade	302
Oh! for a closer walk with God	75
Oh, for a lodge in some vast wilderness	78
Oh, let the solid ground	640
Oh London Town's a fine town	919
Oh, see how thick the goldcup flowers	900
Oh, talk not to me of a name great in story	247
Oh, that those lips had language! Life has passed	79
Oh, there is blessing in this gentle breeze	125
Oh, to be in England	667
Oh, when I was in love with you	901
Oh! young Lochinvar is come out of the west	193
Old Adam, the carrion crow	310
On a starred night Prince Lucifer uprose	773
On a tree by a river a little tom-tit	838
On ear and ear two noises too old to end	871
On either side the river lie	597
On moonlit heath and lonesome bank	901

First Line	Page
On the way to Kew	867
Once a dream did weave a shade	115
Once did she hold the gorgeous east in fee	152
Once I was part of the music I heard	775
Once in a golden hour	641
Once in a saintly passion	761
One lesson, Nature, let me learn of thee	726
One more Unfortunate	307
One road leads to London	920
One, who is not, we see; but one, whom we see not, is	821
One word is too often profaned	272
One year ago my path was green	312
Only a man harrowing clods	915
Others abide our question. Thou art free	726
Our vicar still preaches that Peter and Poule	197
Out of a bed of love	1171
Out of the night that covers me	866
Out-worn heart, in a time out-worn	1028
Overhead the tree-tops meet	658
Piping down the valleys wild	113
Pitch here the tent, while the old horse grazes	769
Poor old pilgrim Misery	309
Proud Maisie is in the wood	198
Put forth thy leaf, thou lofty plane	725
Quinquireme of Nineveh from distant Ophir	918
Rarely, rarely, commest thou	260
Red lips are not so red	1094
Riches I hold in light esteem	720
Ring out, wild bells, to the wild sky	635
Rolled over on Europe: the sharp dew frozen to stars	1160
Roses are beauty, but I never see	921
Rough wind, that moanest loud	273
Round the cape of a sudden came the sea	667
Ruin seize thee, ruthless King	55
Said Abner, "At last thou art come! Ere I tell, ere thou speak	672
Say, is it day, is it dusk in thy bower	791
Say not the struggle naught availeth	723
Scorn not the Sonnet; Critic, you have frowned	163
Scots, wha hae wi' Wallace bled	109
Season of mists and mellow fruitfulness	291
See, winter comes to rule the varied year	33
Shall I sonnet-sing you about myself	707
She dwelt among the untrodden ways	124
She fell asleep on Christmas Eve	786
She stood breast-high amid the corn	306
She walks in beauty, like the night	205
She was a phantom of delight	155
Shot? so quick, so clean an ending	903
Should auld acquaintance be forgot	102
Sing, Ballad-singer, raise a hearty tune	911
Sing me a song of a lad that is gone	880
"Sixpence a week," says the girl to her lover	914
"So careful of the type?" but no	632
So from the years the gifts were showered; each	1154
So many worlds, so much to do	633
So we'll go no more a-roving	224
Soldier, rest! thy warfare o'er	195
Son of my woman's body, you go, to the drum and fife	880
Souls of Poets dead and gone	276
Space and dread and the dark	868
St. Agnes' Eve—Ah, bitter chill it was	286
Stand close around, ye Stygian set	312
Stars, I have seen them fall	905
Stern Daughter of the Voice of God	155
Stop, Christian passer-by!—Stop, child of God	190
Strange fits of passion have I known	123
Strew on her roses, roses	734
Striving to sing glad songs, I but attain	762
Strong Son of God, immortal love	629
Sunset and evening star	654
Sweet and low, sweet and low	626
Sweet dreams, form a shade	115
Sweet Highland Girl, a very shower	153
"Sweet, thou art pale"	749
"Sweet, thou art young"	750
Swifter far than summer's flight	272
Swiftly walk o'er the western wave	261
Take me away, and in the lowest deep	716
Take up the White Man's burden	897
Tarry, delight, so seldom met	906
Tears, idle tears, I know not what they mean	627
Tell me now in what hidden way is	792
That is no country for old men. The young	1031
That son of Italy who tried to blow	743
That's my last Duchess painted on the wall	659
The Assyrian came down like the wolf on the fold	205
The auld wife sat at her ivied door	827
The awful shadow of some unseen Power	251
The bed was made, the room was fit	877
The blessed damozel leaned out	784
The burden of fair women. Vain delight	812
The City is of Night; perchance of Death	763
The curfew tolls the knell of parting day	50
The Danube to the Severn gave	630
The embers of the day are red	881
The face of all the world is changed, I think	713
The fine delight that fathers thought; the strong	874
The fire that filled my heart of old	762
The flower that smiles today	261
The friendly cow all red and white	879
The gauger walked with willing foot	876
The gray sea and the long black land	666
The great masters of the commonplace	865
The hand that signed the paper felled a city	1170
The harp that once through Tara's halls	303
The hour which might have been yet might not be	795
The kettle descants in a cozy drone	913
The leaves are falling; so am I	313
The linnet in the rocky dells	718
The Lord let the house of a brute to the soul of a man	654
The lost days of my life until today	796
The Minstrel boy to the war is gone	303
The morning mists still haunt the stony street	864
The night is darkening round me	719
The Owl and the Pussy-Cat went to sea	826
The poet in a golden clime was born	596
The sea gives her shells to the shingle	814
The sea is calm tonight	744
The secret of these hills was stone, and cottages	1161
The singers are gone from the Cornmarket-place	912
The skies have sunk, and hid the upper snow	725
The splendor falls on castle walls	627
The sun is warm, the sky is clear	253
The sun, the moon, the stars, the seas, the hills, and the plains	645
The sun was shining on the sea	830

INDEX OF FIRST LINES

The time draws near the birth of Christ . . . 630
The time draws near the birth of Christ . . . 635
The time you won your town the race 901
The twentieth year is well-nigh past 81
The wind blows out of the gates of the day . . 1027
The wind has such a rainy sound 759
The wish, that of the living whole 631
The world is a bundle of hay 247
The world is charged with the grandeur of God . 871
The world is so full of a number of things . . 878
The world is too much with us; late and soon . 159
The world's great age begins anew 271
The year's at the spring 657
Their sense is with their senses all mixed in . . 772
There are some birds in these valleys 1146
There be none of Beauty's daughters 207
There came an image in Life's retinue 795
There is a fountain filled with blood 75
There is a silence where hath been no sound . . 306
"There is no God," the wicked saith 722
There lies a vale in Ida, lovelier 599
There should be no despair for you 718
There was a roaring in the wind all night . . . 149
There was a time when meadow, grove, and stream 160
There were four of us about that bed 804
There's nae mair lands to tyne, my dear . . . 820
There's not a joy the world can give 206
These market-dames, mid-aged, with lips thin-
 drawn 911
They have no song, the sedges dry 775
They roused him with muffins 832
They say my verse is sad: no wonder 905
They throw in Drummer Hodge, to rest . . . 908
Thin-legged, thin-chested, slight unspeakably . . 865
Think no more, lad; laugh, be jolly 904
This Advent moon shines cold and clear . . . 751
This darksome burn, horseback brown 873
This is the day, which down the void abysm . . 257
This sunlight shames November where he grieves . 796
This world is very odd we see 722
"Thou drinkest deep" 750
Thou fair-haired angel of the evening 112
Thou ling'ring star, with less'ning ray 104
Thou shalt have one God only; who 724
Thou still unravished bride of quietness . . . 281
Three of us afloat in the meadow by the swing . 877
Three years she grew in sun and shower . . . 124
Thus piteously Love closed what he begat . . . 772
Thy voice is on the rolling air 636
Tiger! Tiger! burning bright 116
'Tis the last rose of summer 303
'Tis the middle of night by the castle clock . . 176
'Tis the voice of the Lobster: I heard him declare 828
'Tis time this heart should be unmoved . . . 247
To-day, this insect, and the world I breathe . . 1170
To fair Fidele's grassy tomb 68
To Mercy, Pity, Peace, and Love 115
To my ninth decade I have tottered on . . . 315
To one who has been long in city pent . . . 275
To sea, to sea! The calm is o'er 309
To see a World in a grain of sand 118
To stand up straight and tread the turning mill . 906
To the Lords of Convention 'twas Claver'se who
 spoke 198
Toll for the brave 75
Tonight the winds begin to rise 630
Tonight ungathered let us leave 635
Too late, too late! I did not know my fairness . 908

Too poor for a bribe, and too proud to importune . 59
Trusty, dusky, vivid, true 880
Turning and turning in the widening gyre . . 1030
'Twas brillig, and the slithy toves 829
'Twas on a Holy Thursday 114
'Twas on a lofty vase's side 49
'Twas on the shores that round our coast . . . 833
Two voices are there: one is of the deep . . . 839
Two voices are there; one is of the sea 162

Under the arch of Life, where love and death . 796
Under the wide starry sky 881
Unfathomable Sea! whose waves are years . . 261
Unlike are we, unlike, O princely Heart . . . 713
Up into the cherry tree 878
Up with me! up with me into the clouds . . . 156

Vanity, saith the preacher, vanity 670
Verse, a breeze amid blossoms straying 189

Wake! For the Sun, who scattered into flight . 776
Wake! The silver dusk returning 899
Waken, lords and ladies gay 194
Was I a Samurai renowned 867
Watch any day his nonchalant pauses, see . . . 1145
We are as clouds that veil the midnight moon . 251
We cannot kindle when we will 733
We saw the swallows gathering in the sky . . . 771
We were apart; yet, day by day 730
Weary of myself, and sick of asking 731
Wee, modest, crimson-tipéd flow'r 100
Wee, sleekit, cowrin, tim'rous beastie 98
Weep yet awhile 750
Welcome, old friend! These many years . . . 315
Well! If the Bard was weather-wise, who made . 187
We've fought with many men acrost the seas . 888
"What are the bugles blowin' for?" 888
What can I give thee back, O liberal 713
What cometh here from west to east a-wending . 807
What have I done for you 868
What heart could have thought you 884
What I expected was 1162
What is he buzzing in my ears 705
What is to come, we know not. But we know . 867
What links are ours with orbs that are . . . 774
What of her glass without her? The blank gray . 795
What passing-bells for those who die as cattle . 1096
Whate'er you dream, with doubt possessed . . 726
Wheer 'asta beän saw long and meä liggin' 'ere
 loän 641
When a man hath no freedom to fight for at home 247
When all my five and country senses see . . . 1171
When Britain first, at Heaven's command . . . 39
When chapman billies leave the street 104
When Contemplation, like the night-calm felt . 134
When green buds hang in the elm like dust . . 906
When I am dead, my dearest 749
When I am grown to man's estate 878
When I have fears that I may cease to be . . . 276
When I play on my fiddle in Dooney 1029
When I was one-and-twenty 901
When I was sick and lay a-bed 878
When I went to the Bar as a very young man . 835
When I would muse in boyhood 905
When lyart leaves bestrow the yird 90
When Music, heavenly maid, was young . . . 70
When my arms wrap you round I press . . . 1028
When smoke stood up from Ludlow 900

When the hounds of spring are on winter's traces .	810
When the lamp is shattered	272
When the morning was waking over the war . .	1171
When we two parted	202
When weary with the long day's care	718
When will you ever, Peace, wild wood-dove, shy wings shut	872
When you are old and gray and full of sleep . .	1027
Whene'er across this sinful flesh of mine . . .	715
Where art thou gone, light-ankled Youth . . .	314
Where dips the rocky Highland	1026
Where forlorn sunsets flare and fade	868
Where shall the lover rest	192
While briers an' woodbines budding green . . .	86
Who dreamed that beauty passes like a dream .	1029
Who has seen the wind	759
Who is the happy Warrior? Who is he . . .	158
Who killed John Keats	247
Who prop, thou ask'st, in these bad days, my mind	726
Why are your songs all wild and bitter sad . .	762
"Why?" Because all I haply can and do . . .	708
Why did you melt your waxen man	787
'Will sprawl, now that the heat of day is best .	701
"Will you walk a little faster?" said a whiting to a snail	829
Will's at the dance in the Club-room below . .	912
With fingers weary and worn	306
With half a heart I wander here	877
With little here to do or see	152
With rue my heart is laden	904
With trembling fingers did we weave . . .	631
Without that once clear aim, the path of flight	1160
Worlds on worlds are rolling ever	270
Ye banks, and braes, and streams around . . .	108
Ye Clouds! that far above me float and pause .	185
Ye distant spires, ye antique towers	48
Ye flowery banks o' bonie Doon	107
Yes; I write verses now and then	313
Yes! in the sea of life enisled	730
Yonder see the morning blink	905
"You are old, Father William," the young man cried	301
"You are old, Father William," the young man said	828
You ask me, why, though ill at ease . . .	611
You may talk o' gin and beer	889
You say, but with no touch of scorn . . .	635
You strange, astonished-looking, angle-faced . .	305
Your body is stars whose million glitter here .	1160
Your ghost will walk, you lover of trees . . .	681
Your hands lie open in the long, fresh grass . .	794

Index
to The Literature of England maps
VOLUME TWO

THIS INDEX includes the names which appear on the front end-sheet map and the four chapter maps (with the exception of London proper on the Chapter 7 map). The letter and figure after a name (F4) indicate the location of that place on the front end-sheet map.

A
Abbotsford, 6
Aberdeen, county, F4; town, 6
Aden, 8
Afton River, 6
Ailsa Craig, 6
Aldershot, G10
Alexandria, 8, 9
Algeria, 9
Algiers, 9
Alloway, 6
Ambleside, 6 inset
Amiens, 9
Anglesey, E8
Anglo-Egyptian Sudan, 8
Ankara, 9
Annan, F6
Antrim, D7
Antwerp, 9
Anzio, 9
Aran Islands, A8; 9
Ardennes, 9
Argonne, 9
Argyll, D5
Armagh, C7
Ascot, G10
A[t]ens, 9

B
Brussels, 9
Bucharest, 9
Buckingham, G10; 7 inset
Budapest, 9
Burma, 8
Bury St. Edmunds, H9
Bute, D6
Buttermere, 6 inset
Buxton, G8

C
Cairo, 8
Caithness, E3
Calcutta, 8
Cambridge, county, H9; town, H9; 6
Canada, 8
Canterbury, I10, 6
Cape Bon, 9
Cape of Good Hope, 8
Cape Town, 8
Cape Trafalgar, 8
Cardigan, E9
Carnarvon, E8
Casablanca, 9
Cavan, C8
Ceylon, 8
Channel Islands, 8
Cherbourg, 9
Cheshire, F8

Dorking, G10
Dorset, F11
Dover, I11; 6, 9
Down, D7
Dresden, 9
Dromore, 6
Dublin, county, C8; town, C8; 6, 9
Dulwich, 7 inset
Dumbarton, county, E5; town, 6
Dumfries, county, E6; town, 6
Dundee, 9
Dunkirk, 9
Dunmail Raise, 6 inset
Durham, county, G7; town, G7, 6

E
Ealing, 7 inset
Easedale, 6 inset
East Indies, 8
Ebro River, 9
Ecclefechan, F6
Edgeworthstown, 6
Edinburgh, county, F6; town, F6, 6
Edmonton, 7 inset
Egypt, 8
Eigg Island, D5
El Alamein, 9
Elgin, E4
Ellisland, 6
Enfield, 7 inset
England, F8; 6
English Channel, G11; 6
Ennerdale Water, 6 inset
Epping Forest, 7 inset
Epsom, H10
Essex, H10; 7 inset
Esthwaite Water, 6 inset
Eton, 7 inset
Ettrick, 6
Exeter, E11; 6, 9
Exmoor Forest, 6

F
Falmouth, D12
Farringford, G11
Felpham, 6
Fife, F5
Fin[ch]ley, 7 inset

I
Inchcape Rock (Bell Rock), 6
India, 8
Inverness, county, E4; town, 6
Invernaid, 6
Ireland, B8; 6, 9
Irish Sea, E8; 6
Irvine, 6
Isle of Dogs, 7 inset
Isle of Man, E7; 6, 9
Isle of Portland, F11
Isle of Skye, D4
Isle of Wight, G11; 6
Istanbul, 9

J
Jamaica, 8
Jerusalem, 9

K
Kenilworth, G9
Kent, H10; 7 inset
Keswick, 6 inset
Kew, 7 inset
Khartoum, 8
Khyber Pass, 8
Kiel Canal, 9
Kiev, 9
Kildare, C8
Killiecrankie Pass, 6
Kilmarnock, 6
Kingston, 7 inset
Kinross, F5
Kirriemuir (Thrums), F5
Konigsberg, 9

L
Labrador, 8
Lahore, 8
Lake Country, 6
Lake Windermere, 6 inset
Laleham, 7 inset
Lammermuir Hills, 6
Lancashire, F8
Lancaster, 6
Langdale Pikes, 6 inset
La Spezia, 9
Latvia, 9
Leamington, G9
Leicester, G9
Leinster, C8
Leipsig, 9
Libya, 9
Li[ch]field, G9

N
Nairn, E4
Naples, 9
Nether Stowey, 6
Netherlands, 9
New Zealand, 8
Newbury, 6
Newcastle, G6; 6
Newfoundland, 8
Newhaven, H11
Newmarket, H9
Nish, 9
Nith River, 6
Norfolk, H9
North Sea, H5; 6, 8
Northampton, G9
Northumberland, F6
Nottingham, county, G8; town, G9
Nürnburg, 9

O
Odessa, 9
Olney, 6
Omaha Beach, 9
Oran, 9
Orkney Islands, F2; 6
Ottery St. Mary, 6
Ouse River, 6
Oxford, county, G10; town, G10, 6

P
Paisley, 6
Pallas, 6
Pantelleria, 9
Paris, 9
Peebles, F6
Pembroke, E10
Penrith, 6 inset
Pentland Hills, 6
Perth, county, E5; town, 8
Plinlimnon, 6
Plymouth, 9
Porlock, 6
Portsmouth, G11
Potsdam, 9
Prague, 9
Preston, F8
Putney, 7 inset

R
Racedown, 6
Radnor, F10
Ramsgate, I10

Somerset, F11
Sorrento, 9
Southampton, G11; 6, 9
Spey River, 6
Spithead, 6
Stafford, county, F9; town, F9
Stalingrad, 9
Stirling, county, E6; town, 6
Stockton, G7
Stoke, 6
Stoke Poges, 7 inset
Stonehenge, 6
Stratford-on-Avon, G9
Strawberry Hill, 7 inset
Streatham, 7 inset
Sudetenland, 9
Suez, 9
Suez Canal, 8
Suffolk, H9
Surrey, G10; 7 inset
Sussex, H11
Sweden, 9

T
Tara, 6
Taranto, 9
Tasmania, 8
Teignmouth, E11
Tel Aviv, 9
Teme River, F9
Teviot River, 6
Tewkesbury, F10
Thames River, H10; 6, 7
Thirlmere, 6 inset
Thornaby, G7
Tintagel, D11
Tintern Abbey, 6
Tipperary, B9
Tirana, 9
Titchfield, G11
Tobruk, 9
Toulon, 9
Toulouse, 9
Tours, 9
Transvaal, 8
Trent River, G8
Trieste, 9
Tripoli, 9
Tunbridge Wells, H11
Tunisia, 9
Turkey, 9
Tweed River, 6
Twickenham, 7 inset
Tyne River, G6